Australia

Paul Smitz, Susie Ashworth, Carolyn Bain, Neal Bedford, Verity Campbell, Pete Cruttenden, Susannah Farfor, Sarah Johnston, Jill Kirby, Lisa Mitchell, Sally O'Brien, Josephine Quintero, Jane Rawson, Nina Rousseau, Andrew Stone, Eddie Butler-Bowdon, Matthew Evans, Tim Flannery & David Millar

Contents

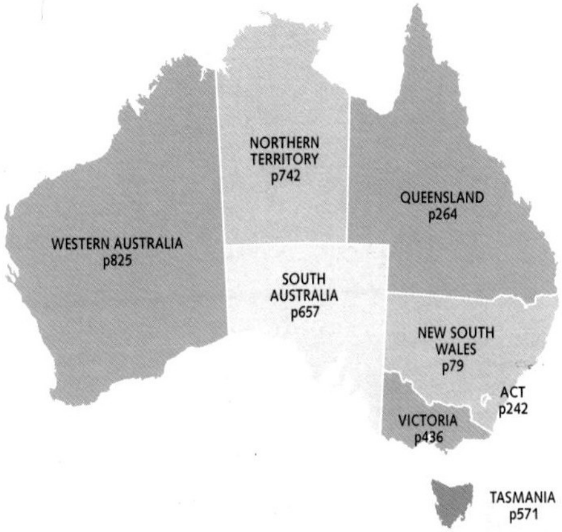

NORTHERN TERRITORY p742
QUEENSLAND p264
WESTERN AUSTRALIA p825
SOUTH AUSTRALIA p657
NEW SOUTH WALES p79
ACT p242
VICTORIA p436
TASMANIA p571

Lonely Planet books provide independent advice. Lonely Planet does not accept advertising in guidebooks, nor do we accept payment in exchange for listing or endorsing any place or business. Lonely Planet writers do not accept discounts or payments in exchange for positive coverage of any sort.

Destination: Australia

Australia is an intriguing enigma not only to people elsewhere in the world, who look at a map and see this curiously chunky bit of terra firma floating way down in the southern hemisphere, but also to the locals, who can spend years making leisurely explorations and still feel they've only begun to comprehend the full nature of their own mammoth back yard. It's not just Australia's size that defies the exhaustion of travel possibilities – Australia also has a sublime, time-bending quality that can't be overruled by any itinerary.

In a city, you'll experience an urban blur of fashion-festooned boutiques, plate-clattering restaurants and vivacious humankind, but suddenly be mesmerised in a gallery or lose yourself in one long fluid moment inside a wine glass. In the interior, you might be surrounded by noise in a beer-washed pub or hear the thump of rocks under your 4WD, only to be transfixed by a slow, silent swirl of outback dust or an outrageously beautiful sunset. Some roads are so long and straight that no matter how fast you go, it's as if you're barely moving. Around the coast, you'll be tasting the foam of ocean surf or pedalling furiously down a mountain, then end up diving down into a coral garden, taking an endless breath in the depths of a rainforest, or slowly realising you have an entire beach to yourself.

Only one thing is consistent: every traveller in Australia faces the same wondrous dilemma – where to begin...

OLIVER STREWE

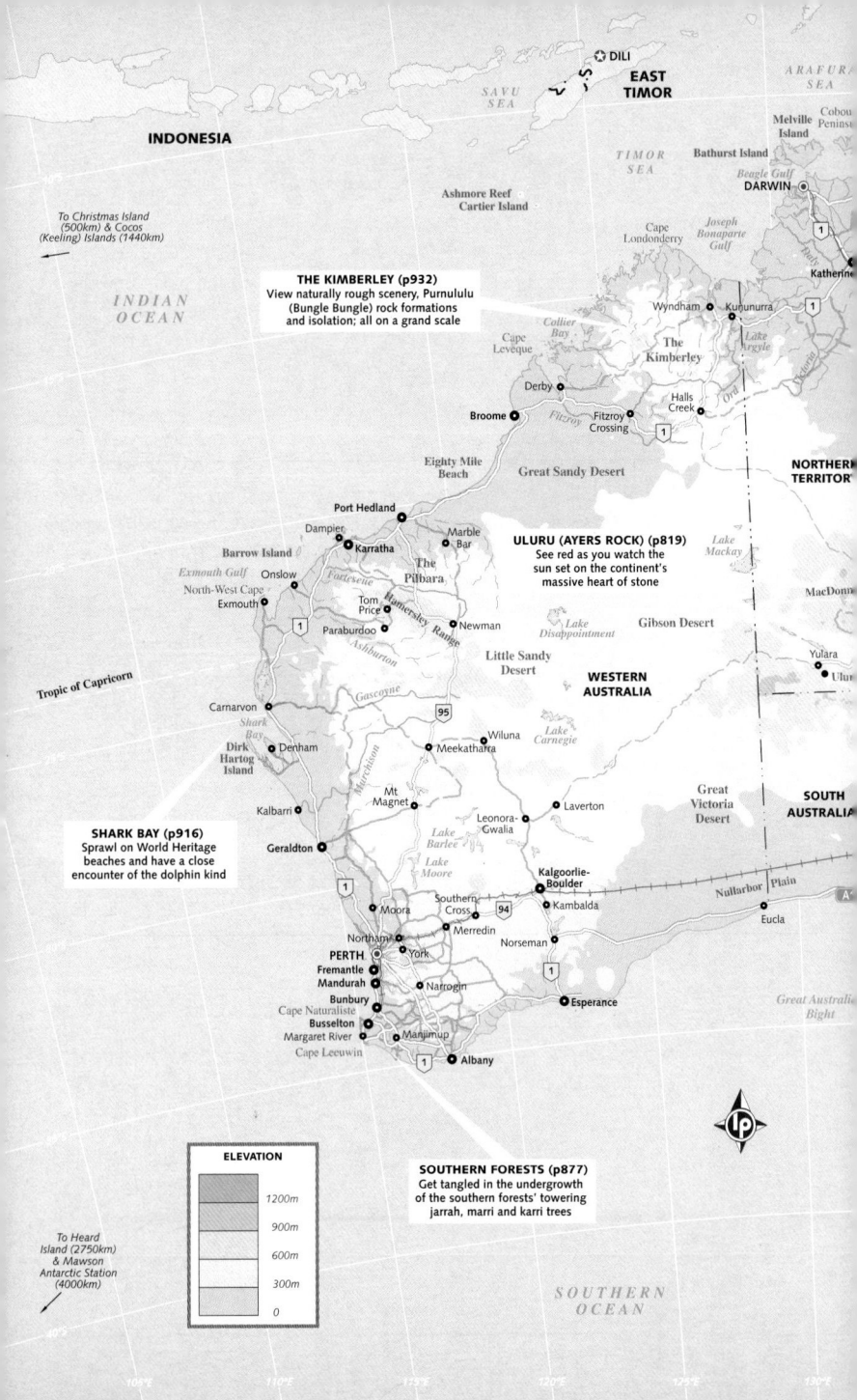

INDONESIA

DILI

EAST TIMOR

SAVU SEA

ARAFURA SEA

TIMOR SEA

Melville Island
Cobou Penins
Bathurst Island

Beagle Gulf
DARWIN

To Christmas Island
(500km) & Cocos
(Keeling) Islands (1440km)

INDIAN OCEAN

Ashmore Reef
Cartier Island

Cape Londonderry

Joseph Bonaparte Gulf

Katherine

THE KIMBERLEY (p932)
View naturally rough scenery, Purnululu
(Bungle Bungle) rock formations
and isolation; all on a grand scale

Collier Bay

Cape Leveque

Wyndham   Kununurra

The Kimberley

Lake Argyle

Ord

Derby

Fitzroy

Fitzroy Crossing

Halls Creek

NORTHERN TERRITORY

Broome

Eighty Mile Beach

Great Sandy Desert

Port Hedland

Dampier   Marble Bar
Karratha

Barrow Island

Exmouth Gulf   Onslow

North-West Cape
Exmouth

The Pilbara

Fortescue

Tom Price
Hamersley Range

Paraburdoo

Newman

ULURU (AYERS ROCK) (p819)
See red as you watch the
sun set on the continent's
massive heart of stone

Lake Mackay

MacDonne

Ashburton

Little Sandy Desert

Gibson Desert

Lake Disappointment

WESTERN AUSTRALIA

Yulara
Ulur

Tropic of Capricorn

Carnarvon

Shark Bay

Gascoyne

Murchison

Denham

Dirk Hartog Island

95

Wiluna

Lake Carnegie

Meekatharra

Kalbarri

Mt Magnet

Leonora-
Gwalia

Laverton

Great Victoria Desert

SOUTH AUSTRALIA

Geraldton

Lake Barlee

Lake Moore

Kalgoorlie-
Boulder

Nullarbor Plain

A

SHARK BAY (p916)
Sprawl on World Heritage
beaches and have a close
encounter of the dolphin kind

Moora

Southern Cross
94
Merredin

Kambalda

Eucla

Northam
PERTH
Fremantle
Mandurah

York

Norseman

Bunbury
Cape Naturaliste
Busselton
Margaret River
Cape Leeuwin

Narrogin

Manjimup

Esperance

Great Australic
Bight

1   Albany

LP

ELEVATION

1200m
900m
600m
300m
0

To Heard
Island (2750km)
& Mawson
Antarctic Station
(4000km)

SOUTHERN FORESTS (p877)
Get tangled in the undergrowth
of the southern forests' towering
jarrah, marri and karri trees

SOUTHERN OCEAN

100°E   110°E   115°E   120°E   125°E   130°E

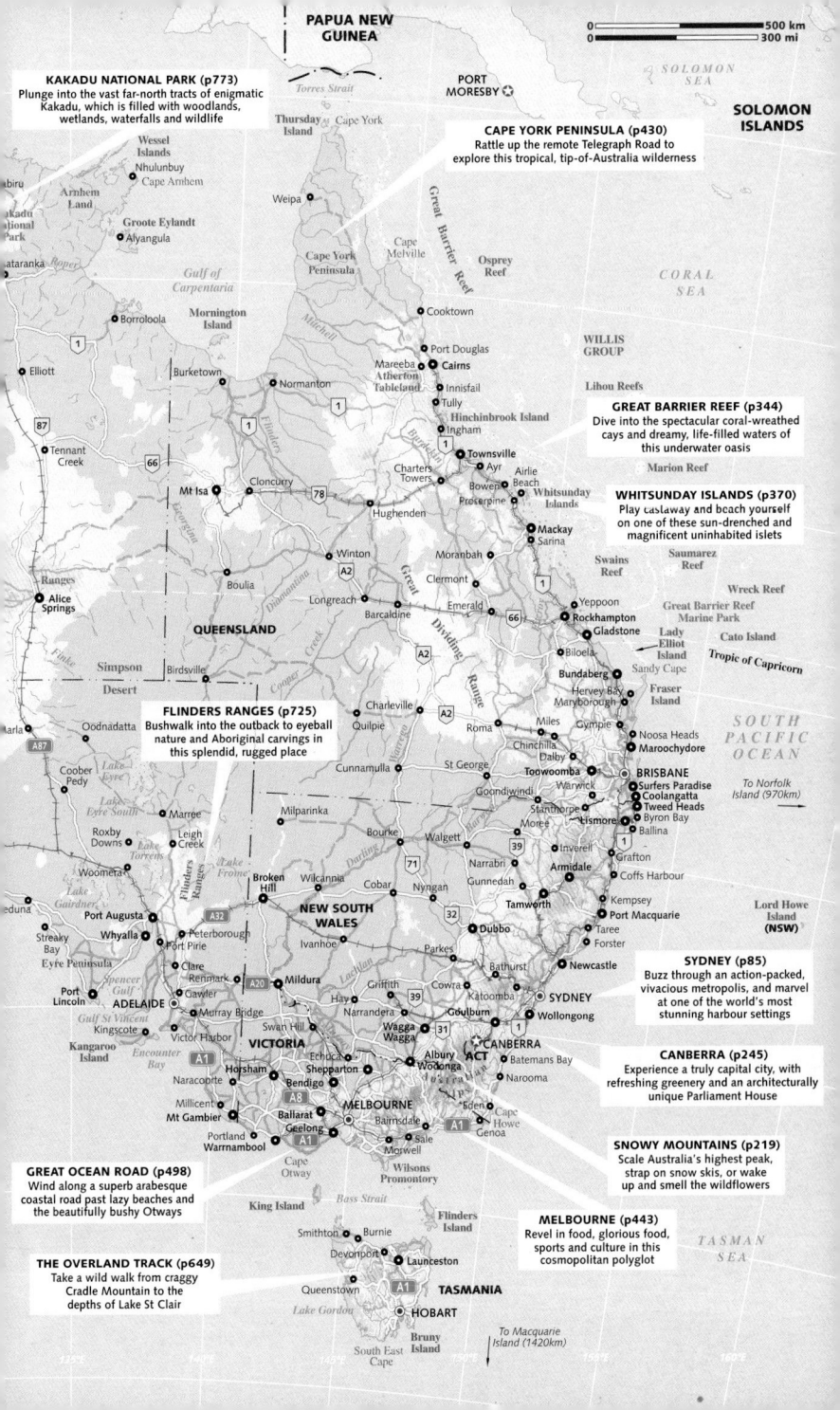

Australia's wealth of environmental diversity and open-air beauty is exemplified in over 500 wilderness-protected parks. As well as experiencing the highlights pictured here, you certainly shouldn't miss getting misty-eyed in the tropical rainforests of the **Daintree National Park** (p426) in Queensland, marvelling at the parched expanse of the **Simpson Desert National Park** (p359), taking the white-water ride of your life through Tasmania's **Franklin-Gordon Wild Rivers National Park** (p648), and seeing the sandstone splendour of **Purnululu (Bungle Bungle) National Park** (p947) in the Kimberley, Western Australia. For an encore of beauty, sink into the colourful coral embrace of the **Great Barrier Reef Marine Park** (p344).

Bushwalk across the length of Tasmania's spectacular **Cradle Mountain-Lake St Clair National Park** (p649)

ROB BLAKERS

RICHARD I'ANSON

Take a plunge at the base of Jim Jim Falls in **Kakadu National Park** (p773)

RICHARD I'AN

Check out the towering limestone cliffs of **Port Campbell National Park** (p505)

RICHARD I'ANSON

Rock your world by visiting the arid **Uluru-Kata Tjuta National Park** (p817)

GRANT DIXON

Climb to the top of the continent in
Kosciuszko National Park (p221)

Take a breathtaking trek through the
Blue Mountains National Park (p144)

GLENN BEANLAND

Feel free to make a leisurely escape from the Australian mainland to a sea-locked paradise, or just plant your beach-bum on some of the most sublime sun-bleached sand in the world. Not all worthy locales got their pictures on these pages. There's also **Port Douglas** (p418) in Queensland's north, which has resorted to upmarket exclusivity, and **Byron Bay** (p180) in NSW, which can't decide if it's hip or hippy. Meanwhile, on the southernmost tip of WA, **Albany** (p884) specialises in rugged coves, while surfers usually have a swell time at Victoria's **Bells Beach** (p500).

BERNARD NAPTHINE

Discover great beaches around the next bend on the **Great Ocean Road** (p498)

Take in an exquisite sunset with a camel ride on **Cable Beach** (p935)

MICHAEL LAAR

RICHARD I'ANSON

Make your own footprints in the sand at **Fraser Island** (p327)

GILLIANNE TEDDER

Surf the magic waves at Sydney's **Bondi Beach** (p102)

Revel in the untrammelled coastline of **Bruny Island** (p599)

GRANT DIXON

CHRISTOPHER GROENHOUT

Be part of the dazzling glam of **Surfers Paradise** (p300)

Relax on the pristine **Whitsunday Islands** (p370)

JOHN BANAGAN

The sheer variety of outdoor activities that can be actively pursued Down Under is made possible by this enormous country's challenging natural splendour. Do-it-yourself highlights not illustrated here include stepping under the tall-canopied grandeur of Western Australia's **southern forests** (p877), getting your hands dirty fossicking for opals at **Coober Pedy** (p735) in the dusty outback of SA, and admiring pods of humpback whales (or is it the other way around?) at **Hervey Bay** (p323) in Queensland. Try your feet at bushwalking in the adventurous wilds of **Cape York Peninsula** (p430) and riding the awesome surf at **Marrawah** (p640) on Tasmania's unsympathetic northwest coast.

Observe, up close, the dolphins at **Monkey Mia** (p918)

DENNIS JONES

Rock-climb along the gloriously rough ramparts of the **Flinders Ranges** (p725)

ANDREW MARSHALL & LEANNE WA[...]

BOB CHARLTON

Snorkel down the eastern coral-garden path off **Lady Elliot Island** (p334)

GRANT DIXON

Trek from the heights of Cradle Mountain to the depths of Lake St Clair on the awesome **Overland Track** (p649)

Ski down the crisp white slopes of the Snowy Mountains at **Thredbo** (p224)

JOHN BANAGAN

Dive through the underwater paradise of the **Great Barrier Reef** (p344)

LEONARD DOUGLAS ZELL

When you need a break from the great outdoors, head for the great indoors. Beyond the city highlights photographed here you'll find **Canberra** (p245), an urban garden ideal for those with a keen eye for art and modern architecture; the Georgian serenity and enthusiastic youthful modernity of **Hobart** (p581); and the graciously old-fashioned yet highly festive atmosphere of **Adelaide** (p665). On the other side of the country there's maritime **Fremantle** (p850), an arts-and-crafty place with a penchant for laid-back entertainment.

Catch a race or two in **Melbourne** (p443)

JULIET COOMBE

Check out the cosmopolitan vibe of **Brisbane** (p273)

DAWN DELANEY

Take in the high-energy distractions and wonderful harbourside panorama of **Sydney** (p85)

CHRISTOPHER GROE

Getting Started

Australia is on the whole a traveller-friendly, tourism-conscious country that provides options for travellers on all budgets. Time is of the essence here, as travel times between points in remote areas or for cross-country trips can be as vast as the landscape. So decide what you want to see and how you're going to get there, and then make sure you don't underestimate how long you'll need for your visit.

WHEN TO GO

Truth be told, any time is a good time to be *somewhere* in Australia. Weather-wise, when it's cold down south, it's magnificent in the north and the Centre; when it's too hot and sweaty up north, the southern states are at their natural finest. There's also the fact that festivals and other public spectacles are on show every month, from the numerous summertime food-and-wine banquets and large-scale jazz or rock gigs that mark the start of the year, through mid-year arts celebrations and whimsical beer-can regattas to end-of-year footy finals, horse races and yachting contests.

The seasons in Australia are the antithesis of those in Europe and North America. It is summer from December to February, when the weather and longer daylight hours are tailor-made for swimming and outdoor activities across much of the country; no prizes for guessing that this is Australia's tourism high season. The period June through August is the winter season, with temperatures dropping the further south you travel – it's officially designated the tourism low season but it's also the time when travellers head north, where the humidity of the wet season has subsided and the temperature is highly agreeable (the Dry roughly lasts from April to September, and the Wet from October to March, with the heaviest rain falling from January onwards). Autumn (March to May) and spring (September to November) both enjoy a lack of climatic extremes.

See Climate (p959) in the Directory for more information.

Unless you want to be competing with hordes of grimly determined local holiday-makers in 'Are we there yet?' mode for road space, seats on all forms of transport, hotel rooms and camp sites, restaurant tables

DON'T LEAVE HOME WITHOUT...

- Double-checking the visa situation (p977)
- Suncream, sunglasses and a hat to deflect ultra-fierce UV rays (p1019)
- Knowing what your embassy/consulate in Australia can and can't do to help you if you're in trouble (p965)
- A travel insurance policy specifically covering you for any planned high-risk activites (p968)
- A vaccination against the bad 1980s music 'hits' that plague supermarkets and many pubs
- Extra-strength insect repellent to fend off merciless flies and mosquitoes (p962)
- A willingness to call absolutely everyone 'mate', whether you know or like them or not
- Taking yourself less seriously, for the inevitable times when locals 'take the piss' out of you
- A ready supply of toothpaste to smear on your head before bushwalking, so that when snarling dropbears land on you they slide right off

and the better vantage points for every major attraction, you should to avoid Australia's prime destinations during school and public holidays. See Holidays (p968) for more information. During these times, you're also likely to encounter mysterious, spontaneous rises in the price of everything from accommodation to petrol.

COSTS

The often malnourished Australian dollar has made the country a fairly economical destination. Manufactured goods tend to be relatively expensive, but daily living costs such as food and accommodation are relatively cheap. The biggest cost in any trip to Australia will be transport, simply because it's such an expansive country.

How much you should budget for depends on what kind of traveller you are and how you'll be occupying yourself. If you regard sightseeing and having a good time as integral parts of the travel experience, prefer to stay in at least mid-range hotels, motels or B&Bs, and have a stomach that demands regular restaurant visits, then $80 to $100 (per person travelling as a couple) should do it. Travellers with a demanding brood in tow will find there are many ways to keep kids inexpensively satisfied, including beach and park visits, camping grounds and motels equipped with pools and games rooms, junior-sized restaurant meals and youth/family concessions for attractions. For more information on travelling with children see p959.

At the low-cost end, if you camp or stay in hostels, cook your own meals, restrain your urge for entertainment and sightseeing, and travel around by bus (or in your own vehicle), you could probably eke out an existence on $45 per day; for a budget that realistically enables you to have a good time, raise the stakes to $60 per day.

TRAVEL LITERATURE

Considering Australia's enormity and its social extremes – from cityscapes to isolation, yuppies to nomads – it's perhaps surprising that relatively little in the way of travel literature has appeared on this continental subject. That said, some inspiring, thought-provoking and just plain entertaining books have been written about this country.

Robyn Davidson's *Tracks* (1980) details her courageous and at the same time willfully lunatic trek across 2700km of the outback from Alice Springs to the West Australian coast, equipped only with humour, determination and a handful of wild camels. Another raw experience is captured in Bruce Chatwin's *Songlines* (1998), in which the famously self-indulgent but outwardly perceptive author writes about (and sometimes unwittingly embodies) the cultural collision between central Australian Aborigines and 'modern' society.

In *Christmas Island, Indian Ocean* (2003), journalist Julietta Jameson relates how a mind's-eye fascination with this remote Australian territory during the *Tampa* refugee crisis evolved into a three-month exploration of the island's natural and multicultural history. (For details of the *Tampa* incident see p43.)

Back on the mainland, the affable Tim Bowden drives his beloved 4WD ('Penelope') across the Kimberley, Pilbara and Nullarbor, and writes in knowledgeable, enthusiastic and occasionally twee style about his ensuing meditations on history and Aboriginal art in *Penelope: Bungles to Broome* (2002). A different kind of road trip is described in Tony Horwitz's entertaining *One for the Road* (1999), a high-speed account of life on and along the highway during a round-Oz hitchhiking trip.

LONELY PLANET INDEX

Litre of petrol (city price)
A$0.80 to A$1

Litre of bottled water
A$2 to A$3

Glass of beer (VB)
A$2.50

Souvenir T-shirt
A$20

Street snack (meat pie)
A$2 to A$2.50

TOP TENS
MUST-SEE MOVIES

One of the best places to do your essential trip preparation (ie daydreaming) is in a comfy lounge with a bowl of popcorn in one hand, a remote in the other and your eyeballs pleasurably glued to a small screen. Head down to your local video store to pick up these Australian flicks, which range from the intelligent and thrilling to the uber-cheesy. See p65 for some reviews.

- *Lantana* (2001)
  Director: Ray Lawrence
- *Picnic at Hanging Rock* (1975)
  Director: Peter Weir
- *Mad Max II: The Road Warrior* (1981)
  Director: George Miller
- *Rabbit-Proof Fence* (2002)
  Director: Phillip Noyce
- *Breaker Morant* (1980)
  Director: Bruce Beresford

- *Moulin Rouge* (2001)
  Director: Baz Luhrmann
- *Shine* (1996)
  Director: Scott Hicks
- *Bliss* (1985)
  Director: Ray Lawrence
- *Muriel's Wedding* (1994)
  Director: PJ Hogan
- *The Castle* (1997)
  Director: Rob Sitch

TOP READS

When it comes to a good novel, even the most imaginative and unreal story will speak of truths that exist beyond the page. These page-turners have won critical acclaim in Australia and abroad, not least because they have something to reveal to the reader about contemporary Australian issues, culture and relationships. See Literature (p66) for reviews of some of these and other books.

- *True History of the Kelly Gang* (2000)
  Peter Carey
- *Dirt Music* (2003)
  Tim Winton
- *A Child's Book of True Crime* (2002)
  Chloe Hooper
- *Gould's Book of Fish* (2003)
  Richard Flanagan
- *Dark Palace* (2000)
  Frank Moorhouse

- *The Service of Clouds* (1997)
  Delia Falconer
- *Eucalyptus* (1999)
  Murray Bail
- *The Hunter* (1999)
  Julia Leigh
- *Drylands* (1997)
  Thea Astley
- *Remembering Babylon* (1993)
  David Malouf

OUR FAVOURITE FESTIVALS & EVENTS

Australians will seize on just about any excuse for a celebration, which is due as much to good-humoured exuberance, an enjoyment of the arts and an (often highly vocal) appreciation of sport as it is to the eagerly consumed output of many fine vineyards and breweries. These are our top 10 reasons to get festive – other events are listed on p966 and throughout this book.

- Sydney to Hobart Yacht Race
  (Tasmania) December to January (p966)
- Hobart Summer Festival
  (Tasmania) December to January (p590)
- Tamworth Country Music Festival
  (NSW) January (p192)
- Sydney Gay & Lesbian Mardis Gras
  (NSW) February (p109)
- Adelaide Festival of Arts
  (SA) March (p675)

- Melbourne International Comedy Festival
  (Victoria) March to April (p463)
- Outback Muster
  (Queensland) May (p355)
- Beer Can Regatta
  (NT) August (p759)
- Stompen Ground
  (WA) September/October (p938)
- Melbourne Festival
  (Victoria) October (p463)

For comfortably predictable reading, pick up a copy of Bill Bryson's *Down Under* (2001), in which the mass-market humourist takes his usual well-rehearsed potshots at a large target. And though it contains fewer than 100 pages on Australia, Paul Theroux's *The Happy Isles of Oceania* (1993) is worth reading just to catch the writer at his bombastic best when he dismisses the country as 'fly-blown', then writes, 'The Australian Book of Etiquette is a very slim volume, but its outrageous Book of Rudeness is a hefty tome'.

INTERNET RESOURCES

Aussie Index (www.aussie.com.au) Exhaustive online directory of Australian businesses.

Australian Government (www.gov.au) Gateway to all federal, state, territory and local government sites.

Australian Newspapers Online (www.nla.gov.au/npapers) National Library–maintained listing of Australian newspaper websites.

Australian Tourist Commission (www.australia.com) Official, federal government-run tourism site with nationwide info for visitors.

Guide to Australia (www.csu.edu.au/australia) Links to sundry domestic sites focusing on attractions, culture, the environment, transport etc.

Lonely Planet (www.lonelyplanet.com) Get started with summaries on Australia, links to Australia-related sites and travellers trading information on the Thorn Tree.

Itineraries

CLASSIC ROUTES

EAST COAST RUN

1 month / Sydney to Cairns
(5 days estimated minimum travel time)

Australia's lush and sun-loving east coast is where hordes of travellers choose to stay on the beaten track, following a beach-sprinkled route from the highlife of Sydney to the tropical tourism hub of Cairns.

After shedding the big-city trappings of **Sydney** (p85), the Pacific Hwy meanders through central and northern New South Wales (NSW) towns that include idyllic locales by the beach. Along the way, drag your feet in the sheltered serenity of **Port Stephens** (p165), the watersports-mad **Myall Lakes National Park** (p167) and the magnificent plateau-top rainforests of **Dorrigo National Park** (p195). After investigating the lifestyles of the feral and famous in bemusing **Byron Bay** (p180), head north over the Queensland border into the brown-skinned state capital, **Brisbane** (p273) via **Surfers Paradise** (p300), where avid consumers will be distracted by the area's shopping, nightlife and unrepentant kitsch.

North of Brisbane the Bruce Hwy takes over, wending its way along the coast into Queensland's far north. Nature lovers should head up to the peaceful whale-watching haven of **Hervey Bay** (p323). Further north is the sandy bliss of the **Whitsunday Islands** (p370), the coral charms of the **Great Barrier Reef** (p344) and the at-your-service town of **Cairns** (p396).

Most travellers fly into Sydney and head north along the coast by bus, train, car, Kombi or thumb, but there's no reason why you can't tackle the route from the other end and work your way down. See Getting There & Away under Sydney (p135), Brisbane (p292) and Cairns (p406) for information on transport to and from each city, or browse Getting Around (p985) for more details.

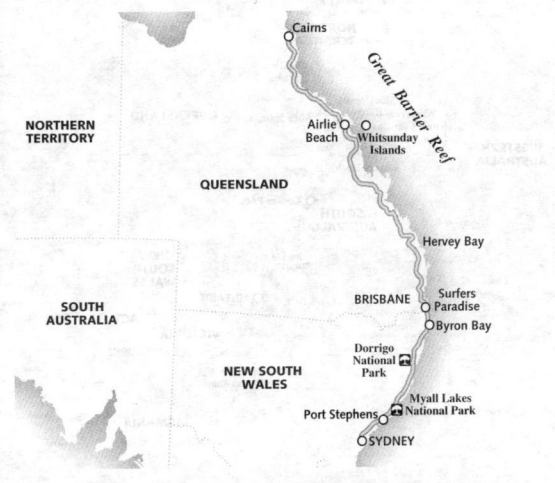

The East Coast Run is jammed with holidaymaking hurly-burly, all 2864 beach-combing, wave-riding, tree-hugging, late-rising kilometres of it. You could do the run in a matter of days, but why would you? Take a month or two and really chill out.

INTO THE OUTBACK

2 months / Melbourne to Darwin
(1 week estimated minimum travel time)

The Stuart Hwy is a must-do route for anyone longing for an outback experience. Locally understated as 'the Track', this hot, dusty piece of bitumen bisects the awesome central deserts as it stretches from the South Australian (SA) crossroads town of Port Augusta to the Top End city of Darwin in the Northern Territory (NT).

Begin this outback odyssey in **Melbourne** (p433), where you can stock up on superb food and be an inner-city barfly before riding the Princes Hwy west and diverting onto the magical contours of the **Great Ocean Road** (p498). After rejoining the highway, head across to **Adelaide** (p665), SA's mellow but artistically vibrant capital. The going gets sparser after you pass Port Augusta, with the empty terrain and soporific silence eventually broken by the opal-tinted dugout town of **Coober Pedy** (p735).

Once you've paid your respects to **Uluru (Ayers Rock)** (p819) and visited the spectacular, vertigo-inducing **Watarrka (Kings Canyon) National Park** (p815), make for the desert oasis of **Alice Springs** (p794) in the heart of the steep-sided **MacDonnell Ranges** (p808). Between 'the Alice' and the laid-back NT capital, **Darwin** (p750), you'll gawk at the bizarre **Devil's Marbles** (p794), down a beer (or three) at the **Daly Waters Pub** (p791) and marvel at the landscapes, wildlife and Aboriginal rock art of World Heritage–listed **Kakadu National Park** (p773).

You can, of course, do this route from top to bottom. See the individual Getting There & Away sections under Melbourne (p483), Adelaide (p663) and Darwin (p765) for information on transport to and from each city, or browse Getting Around (p985) for general details, and Outback Travel (p993) for specific tips on how to make this journey memorable but safe.

Don your sunnies, practise swatting flies and launch into this long, sweaty and utterly unique 5018km journey through the middle of the continent. Don't rush from coast to coast in a fortnight: give yourself two horizon-stretching months instead.

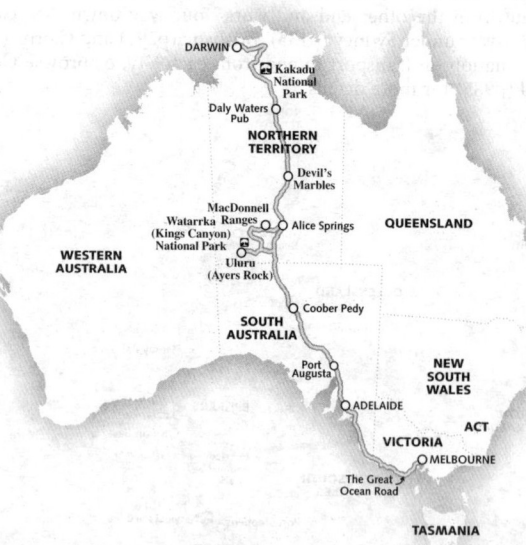

THE GIANT LOOP

6 months / Sydney to Sydney
(6 weeks estimated minimum travel time)

After bidding *au revoir* to **Sydney** (p85) and following your sun-tanned nose up along the east coast into Queensland (see the East Coast Run on p17), veer west from **Townsville** (p374) towards the tunnel-threaded Queensland mining town of **Mt Isa** (p350). Leave a vigorous trail of footprints (via **Tennant Creek**; p792) in the red centre, where you can take in **Alice Springs** (p794) and the awesome splendour of **Uluru (Ayers Rock)** (p819) before dog-legging it to **Darwin** (p750). Cross into Western Australia (WA) for a pitstop at pretty **Kununurra** (p948), then negotiate the Great Northern Hwy to the cosmopolitan getaway of **Broome** (p934).

Take a peninsular sidetrack to the marine brilliance of **Ningaloo Reef** (p921) and the snorkel-friendly **Cape Range National Park** (p926), followed by a date with a bottle-nosed dolphin at **Monkey Mia** (p918). Continue south to the 'life is a beach' city of **Perth** (p833) and the latte-flavoured enclave of **Fremantle** (p850), then wine away the hours at **Margaret River** (p874) until you're ready to tackle the flat immensity of the **Nullarbor Plain** (p899).

In SA bushwalkers trudge towards the challenging **Flinders Ranges** (p725), while tipplers refuel their palates in the **Barossa Valley** (p698). Beyond **Adelaide** (p665) it's a shortish trek into Victoria to check out surfboard-strewn **Torquay** (p499) and cultured **Melbourne** (p443), from where there's a high-speed ferry to the unmissable island highlights of **Tasmania** (p571). Further along the Victorian coast you can enjoy the secluded wilderness of **Wilsons Promontory National Park** (p559), lead an inactive life at **Ninety Mile Beach** (p563), cruise around **Narooma** (p217) on the southern NSW coast, and bask in idyllic **Jervis Bay** (p215). After you've detoured to the national capital, **Canberra** (p245), return to the bright lights of Sydney.

Experiencing the farthest reaches of the land can mean tallying over 14,000km of highway, not counting sidetrips to beaches, forests, mountains, reefs, towns... Where you start and finish is up to your imagination, but allow for around six months of discovery.

ROADS LESS TRAVELLED

INLAND EAST COAST
1 month / Sydney to Cairns
(5 days estimated minimum travel time)

This is a trip that parallels the immensely popular east-coast route, but avoids the almost perpetual traffic, and it also exposes you to introspective old settlements and some singular Australian back-country.

If you're starting in **Sydney** (p85), breathe in the gorgeous indigenous scenery of the **Blue Mountains** (p143) and throw in a light-headed detour to the wineries of the **Lower Hunter Valley** (p159) before linking up with the New England Hwy to reach the nation's self-titled 'horse capital', **Scone** (p163).

A visit to the boot scootin', stretch-denim nexus of the country music scene, **Tamworth** (p191), is followed by stops in the cool, well-educated environs of **Armidale** (p193) and quaint **Tenterfield** (p197), which claims to be the cradle of Australian Federation.

Over the Queensland border is the **Granite Belt** (p319), an elevated plateau of the Great Dividing Range that's renowned for its boutique wineries. Just up the road are the view-blessed historic buildings of **Toowoomba** (p320), while a triad of sunburnt roads (Burnett, Dawson and Gregory Hwys) take you past the sandstone splendour of **Carnarvon Gorge** (p347). Then it's a long and dusty drive to the gold-rush town of **Charters Towers** (p384) and an equally long trek to the formidable lava tubes of **Undara Volcanic National Park** (p393) before you arch east to **Cairns** (p396).

See the Getting There & Away sections under Sydney (p135) and Cairns (p406) for transport information on each city, or browse Getting Around (p985) in the Transport chapter for details on popular travel options, be it by air, bike, bus or train.

This route takes you away from the east-coast tourist clutter and through 2811km of variegated rural life, pioneering towns, vineyards and remote gorges. Suppress any need for speed and take a month to have a good, long look around.

ACROSS THE CONTINENT

1–2 months / Cairns to Perth
(2.5 weeks estimated minimum travel time)

Those who prefer solitude and travelling rough will love the Australian outback, which is criss-crossed with innumerable roads and tracks, some sealed and others little more than a pair of dirty ruts. There are many potential hazards in heading off the beaten track, so wherever you go, make sure you're well informed and fully prepared – see Outback Travel (p993) for more information.

The following is a long, difficult route from the tropics to the Indian Ocean. Start in **Cairns** (p396), gateway to the arduous Peninsula Development Rd that (in case you're interested) snakes towards the tip of **Cape York** (p430). Head west to **Normanton** (p394), the biggest town in the Gulf of Carpentaria region, then south down the jauntily named Matilda Hwy to the mining roughhouse of **Mt Isa** (p350).

To the southwest is the frontier outback town of Urandangi, after which you run into the **Plenty Hwy** (p996), a monotonous (or gloriously desolate) road with plenty of bone-jolting challenges (4WD recommended). Over 500km later you'll hit the Stuart Hwy and then the dead-centre city of **Alice Springs** (p794). The Lasseter Hwy turn-off takes you to weighty **Uluru (Ayers Rock)** (p819) and the captivating **Kata Tjuta (the Olgas)** (p820) rock formations, beyond which is the beginning of the **Great Central Road** (p995). This lonely trail, suitable for well-prepared 2WDs and lined with saltbush, spinifex and desert oaks, stretches 750km to the tiny gold-mining town of **Laverton** (p898), from where it's another almost 400km to the blunt gold-mining concern of **Kalgoorlie-Boulder** (p893). Finally, the ocean beckons from behind the beaches of Scarborough and Cottesloe in **Perth** (p833).

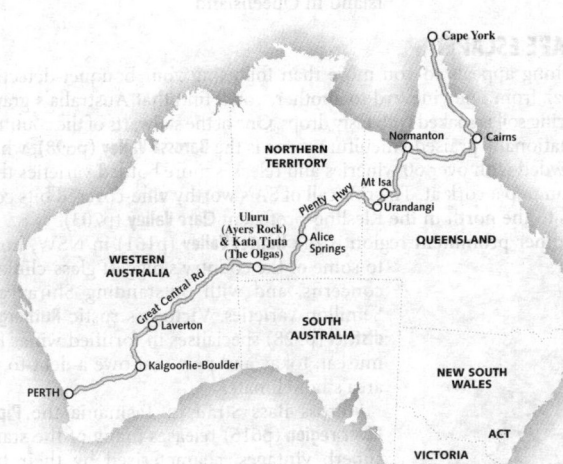

Few roads are less travelled than this monster 4560km trail from the tidal rivers of the Gulf Savannah to the pounding surf at the bottom of Western Australia, with undulating desertscapes in between. Conditions can be unpredictable, so plan on up to two months.

TAILORED TRIPS

WALK ON THE WILD SIDE

Appreciate Australia's stunning natural beauty from the inside by taking unhurried walks through its pristine national parks. Within Tasmania's wonderfully tangled interior is the 80.5km **Overland Track** (p649), a famous trail traversing the Cradle Mountain-Lake St Clair National Park and treating its followers to volcano-blasted peaks, crystal-clear tarns and wild moorlands. Tasmania is also the setting for the **South Coast Track** (p652), which tip-toes around the edge of the sublime Southwest National Park.

Jutting out from the Victorian coast is **Wilsons Promontory National Park** (p559), with over 130km of walking tracks and some grand beaches to sprawl along, while the **Heysen Trail** (p661) runs a massive 1200km across

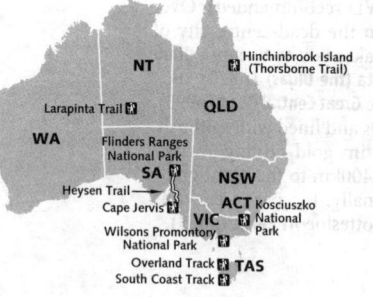

SA from Cape Jervis on the tip of Fleurieu Peninsula to the rocky gorges and sawtooth ridges of the **Flinders Ranges National Park** (p729). For another rough encounter, step out along the 220km **Larapinta Trail** (p811) that follows the backbone of the West MacDonnell Ranges.

There's less strenuous walking on the rolling alpine plains of the Main Range in **Kosciuszko National Park** (p221), home to the country's highest peaks. And for unadulterated beauty, don't miss being surrounded by granite mountains, tropical forests and thick mangroves while navigating the 32km-long **Thorsborne Trail** (p388) across Hinchinbrook Island in Queensland.

A GRAPE ESCAPE

If nothing appeals to you more than following your bouquet-detecting schnozz from one vineyard to another, you'll find that Australia's grape-nurturing soil is soaked with tasty drops. One of the stalwarts of the country's internationally praised viticulture scene is the **Barossa Valley** (p698), which is crowded with over 60 wineries and releases more bottled varieties than you can pop a cork at. The roll-call of SA's worthy vine-covered bits continues to the north in the Riesling-proficient **Clare Valley** (p703).

Another prominent region is the **Hunter Valley** (p161) in NSW, home

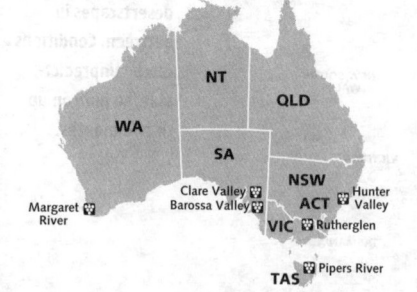

to some of the country's biggest glass-clinking concerns, and with outstanding Shiraz and Semillon varieties. Victoria's rustic **Rutherglen district** (p528) specialises in fortified wines like muscat, tokay and port that owe a debt to the area's hot climate.

Across Bass Strait in Tasmania the **Pipers River region** (p616) releases many of the state's superb vintages, characterised by their full, fruity flavour. Western Australia is a huge state contributing only a small percentage of the national wine output; nevertheless, the **Margaret River region** (p874) in the state's southwest has dozens of big and little cellar doors for you to knock on.

CHILDISH DELIGHTS

There's a plethora of manmade and natural Australian sights and activities to capture the attention of the shrillest, most discerning child. For irresistible, top-of-the-Richter-scale distractions, head for the **Gold Coast** (p298), where you'll find the feisty rides of several big-budget theme parks. There's more stage-managed fun at period places like **Swan Hill Pioneer Settlement** (p525), with seats up for grabs on a paddle steamer, vintage cars and horse-drawn wagons. Kids will probably enjoy the larger-than-life cheesiness of the country's 'big' things, like Nambour's **Big Pineapple** (p318), Ballina's **Big Prawn** (p178) and the **Big Rocking Horse** (p685) in the Adelaide Hills. See also Making it Big (p24) and the index under 'big' for a listing of where to find other 'big' things in this book.

The **West Coast Wilderness Railway** (p645) is an unforgettable ride though some of west-coast Tasmania's most exhilarating terrain, between Queenstown and Strahan. Melbourne's spirited **Moomba celebration** (p463), staged in early March, includes carnivals, fireworks and Dragon Boat events, and is just one example of the calendar-filling festivals held around the country.

With its conspicuous natural assets, Australia is a great place to sit and watch wildlife go by, as in when southern right whales spout their way past King George Sound near **Albany** (p884) between July and October. A refreshing ocean dip must be near or at the top of the outdoor activities list, with beaches like those at **Merimbula** (p218), in NSW, perfect for the occasion.

FOLLOW THE FANS

Local sports can prompt passionate appreciation from genuine contest-lovers and ludicrously overblown emotions from those who confuse their team's fortunes with their own. So to see Aussies at their best and worst, just buy a ticket to a big sporting event. The year's first grand-slam tennis tournament, the **Australian Open** (p63), attracts ball-watchers to Melbourne in January, while in March the same city echoes with the unrelenting roar of the **Australian Formula One Grand Prix** (p63). Over Easter, surfing dudes/dudettes make to Torquay for the **Bells Beach Surf Classic** (p500).

The heartland of **Australian rules football** (p479) is Melbourne, where stadiums get packed with one-eyed fans between March and September; simultaneously, Sydney and Brisbane are ruled by **rugby league** (p132). September also sees jogging crews attempt to race bottomless boats down a dry riverbed in Alice Springs during the light-hearted **Henley-on-Todd Regatta** (p801). Thousands flock to remote **Birdsville** (p359) for some boozy, dusty horse races.

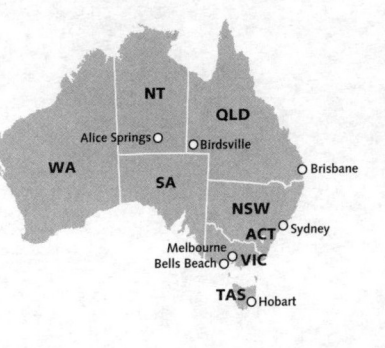

People who love to wager a bet on the **Melbourne Cup** (p63) horse race temporarily freeze beside a radio on the first Tuesday of November each year, while December's **Sydney to Hobart Yacht Race** (p63) sees large crowds assemble at either end to indulge in dockside festivities, though few care about what happens in between.

MAKING IT BIG

Australia has a bizarre obsession with cheesy 'big things'. You can't miss them if you pass them on the highway, but if you decide to do a 'big' crawl here are a few of our favourites.

The one that started it all is the **Big Banana** (Coffs Harbour, NSW, p174), built in 1968 and still going strong after appearing in 325,000 tourist photos. The **Big Golden Guitar** (Tamworth, NSW, p191) is one of the more 'functional' biggies, a permanent monument and tribute to country music.

On the NSW coastline, you'll find the **Big Oyster** (Manning Valley, NSW, p168), which some locals cherish as a quirky monument to the oyster beds of the Manning River, while others label it a ridiculous waste of space. More

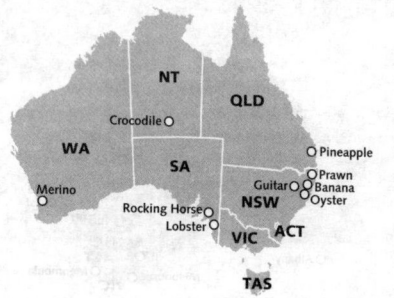

popular is the spectacular **Big Prawn** (Ballina, NSW, p178), which some devotees liken to the Sphinx. In Queensland, there's the permanently sundrenched **Big Pineapple** (Nambour, Queensland, p318); and nestled in the Adelaide Hills among vineyards, there's the garish **Big Rocking Horse** (Gumeracha, SA, p685). Not far from here is the brilliant orange **Larry the Big Lobster** (Kingston SE, SA, p708), which off-loads lobster sandwiches from the tuckshop underneath. Only obvious from the air, the **Big Crocodile** (Alice Springs, NT, p768) celebrates one of the country's most famous (and dangerous) critters, while the **Big Merino** (Wagin, WA, p902) pays homage to one of Australia's most profitable imports.

The Authors

PAUL SMITZ   Coordinating Author & Australian Capital Territory

Paul is Australian but prefers not to try and define what that means – such a generalisation is pointless considering the diverse communities, social subtleties and personal differences within this country. However, he's quite happy to admit that he loves exploring Australia, be it the deceptive homogeneity of Canberra (where he was born and which he revisited for this guide), the urban attractiveness of Melbourne (where he now lives), the ancient outback dunes of Lake Mungo (where he'd rather not live if he can help it) or the Tasmanian wilderness (which wouldn't have him, even if he wanted to live there).

The Coordinating Author's Favourite Trip

A long time ago I left on a round-Australia odyssey, so carefully thought-out that I ran out of fuel in Melbourne. I later continued the journey due west (with a tad more petrol money), to be confronted by the ocean-shadowing drop of the Great Australian Bight (p724) and the spectacular emptiness of the Nullarbor Plain (p899) – I envy anybody their first glimpses of these places. A southwestern jaunt took in the Stirling Range (p884), the dizzying Gloucester Tree (p878) and Perth (p833), before I headed north via the excellent Kalbarri gorges (p913) to Shark Bay (p916), where a bob in the ocean gave me an unforgettable face-to-face with local dolphins.

SUSIE ASHWORTH   Western Australia

A childhood of holidays spent in a family caravan and long weekend drives gave Susie a yearning for the Australian highway that never quite left her. In 1997 she succumbed and left Sydney in an old Holden towing a camper trailer to explore outback, coast and country towns for six months. Updating the stunning southern WA section of the country enabled her to indulge her love of long dusty drives, spectacular beaches and forests, and fine food and wine. Susie lives in Melbourne where she works as a freelance editor and as an occasional author for Lonely Planet.

CAROLYN BAIN   Tasmania

Melbourne-born Carolyn covered Tasmania for this book. Some of her fondest childhood memories are of family holidays exploring various coastal areas of Australia, and after years spent studying, travelling and then researching guidebooks in far-flung corners of the world, she was thrilled to cover such a first-class destination so close to home. This trip gave her the perfect excuse to cross Bass Strait and explore Tassie's scenic coastline, national parks, quaint villages, and – most importantly – excellent tearooms and wineries.

NEAL BEDFORD   Queensland

Having observed Australia and its inhabitants for most of his life from across the Tasman, Neal believes he is well suited to comment on the country's highlights and lowlights. His love-hate relationship with Australia started early – watching it win far too many trans-Tasman fixtures was hard to take – but if the place was so bad, why were so many of his relatives living there? Biting the bullet, he made his first trip to the Gold Coast and Brisbane at the age of 16. Since then, he has managed to chill out or party hard (depending how the mood takes him) up and down the coast umpteen times over the ensuing years.

VERITY CAMPBELL   Victoria & The Culture

A Melbourne-based writer, Verity jumped at the chance to revisit and delve into all corners of her beloved home-town, armed with tomes of experience in the travel-writing trade. Covering day-trips in the Around Melbourne section was an added bonus. Among other titles, she has researched, written and coordinated Lonely Planet's *East Coast Australia* guide.

PETE CRUTTENDEN   Western Australia

West Australian-born, Pete lived in Port Hedland and Geraldton as a young child before settling with his family 'over East'. Even though he'd visited WA many times over the years, he'd never seen much of the area north of Perth, so was more than happy to check it out for this guide, especially as he'd driven through the Western Australian deserts for Lonely Planet's *Outback Australia* guide a couple of years before. And no complaints either – this is one of Australia's most beautiful regions and is well worth a visit.

SUSANNAH FARFOR   Northern Territory

After growing up in Melbourne, Susannah set off to see if the world really was round. Five-and-a-half years later, she wound up back where she started, surmising that the theory was solid. A frequent visitor to the Territory, she has driven, flown, paddled, hiked and biked in the region, worked on a cattle station, hooked the occasional barramundi and camped out under the stars. Susannah has worked as an editor at Lonely Planet's Melbourne and Oakland offices, and researched and wrote the Northern Territory chapter for this book, in addition to Lonely Planet's comprehensive *Northern Territory* guide.

SARAH JOHNSTON   Queensland

Although based in London for the past decade, journalist Sarah Johnstone hasn't really strayed that far from her Queensland roots. Homesickness, or work, has kept her returning to the land of her birth every year, and updating the Sunshine–Capricorn Coast section of this book took her into territory she's known since childhood holidays and weekends. In London, freelancer Sarah has previously worked for Reuters and as a features/deputy editor on several travel magazines – among many other jobs. Her writing has also appeared in national newspapers, including the *Times* and the *Independent on Sunday*.

JILL KIRBY   South Australia

After leaving England to travel the world, Jill eventually made Australia her home in 1995, exploring the country both as a backpacker and as a journalist/TV producer. She was bowled over by SA's lifestyle and ended up in Adelaide, happily involved in producing TV programmes covering local entertainment, history, business and industry. Sidelines included researching and writing about SA for an Internet travel guide and a TV travel programme, and also covering local stories for the British media. Her love of Australian beaches, wine and wildlife (not necessarily in that order) keeps her exploring this vast continent.

LISA MITCHELL   Queensland

Lisa's earliest travel memories are of hitting the road at dawn and heading north with her family of six. Holidays were spent exploring the country roads, coastal towns and national parks of Queensland, NSW and Victoria. She reckons there's no better place to unwind than the laid-back villages of Mission Beach, Magnetic Island and Cape Tribulation; or drifting around the Whitsundays on a sloop. She'd just as soon climb Queensland's highest peak, Mt Bartle Frere, and trek the Thorsborne Trail on Hinchinbrook Island, if only it weren't for those endless horizons and starry skies in the Gulf Savannah…

SALLY O'BRIEN   New South Wales

Sally has flitted back and forth between Sydney and other cities from a young age. One memorable stint in the harbour city lasted 25 years and saw her living in the eastern suburbs, southeastern suburbs and inner-west (never the North Shore). Despite attending schools near Coogee, Bronte and Bondi, she didn't cut class, only learned to surf when she moved to Victoria and never appreciated beer gardens until she realised Melbourne's weather conspired against them. Sally made up for lost time while crafting her Sydney chapter, absconding to beaches and beer gardens frequently, all in the name of 'research'.

JOSEPHINE QUINTERO   Victoria

Born in England, Josephine backpacked with a guitar in the late '60s (didn't everyone?) and spent a year in an Israeli kibbutz. She graduated from UC Berkeley, California, and worked for Bay Area newspapers and magazines. In Kuwait she edited the *Kuwaiti Digest* and made side trips to Yemen and India. Held hostage during the Iraq invasion of Kuwait, she moved to the relaxed shores of Andalucía (Spain) shortly thereafter. Since then she has contributed to numerous guidebooks and writes regularly for in-flight magazines, including *Highlife* (British Airways) and *Red Hot* (Virgin Airways). This was Josephine's first encounter with 'the friendliest people in the world', updating regional Victoria.

JANE RAWSON   New South Wales

One of a mere handful of Australians who didn't grow up on the coast, Jane was born in the inland enclave of Canberra, where she pretended to believe salt water lowers the intelligence. Writing North Coast NSW gave her a chance to test the theory: she may be dumber now, but she had a lot of fun. Exploring the farms and rural cities of New England and the Central West was familiar territory – paddocks and slender nightlife options are in the blood of every Canberran. In the northwest, Jane finally beat a family record, set in WA in 1981, of counting 41 dead kangaroos per kilometre.

NINA ROUSSEAU   Queensland

Nina Rousseau updated the Far North Queensland section of this book. She eats Vegemite on toast for breakfast, won't say no to a cuppa in the arvo and has a rubber elbow when it comes to a XXXX beer with her mates. With a pair of new thongs and a 'she'll be right' attitude Nina headed up north and returned to 'God's country' – one of her favourite parts of Australia. Research for this book included watching an entire series of *The Crocodile Hunter* (for which she was paid extra).

ANDREW STONE   New South Wales

Andrew, a Brit, discovered Australia only relatively recently but he became an instant fan. His first visit lasted six months during which he bludged off friends in Sydney and took their ancient Landcruiser out on extended road trips to explore the 'back of beyond' bits of NSW while they went to work. He jumped at the chance to return and carry on doing the same for this edition of *Australia*, much to their annoyance.

CONTRIBUTING AUTHORS

Julian Burnside QC wrote the boxed text 'Asylum Seekers & Mandatory Detention' (p58). Julian is a Melbourne-based Queen's Counsel and human rights advocate. Julian acted as counsel for Liberty Victoria for the *Tampa* asylum seekers and for the Woomera escapees. Julian and his wife, Kate Durham, established the Spare Rooms for Refugees campaign (www.sparoomsforrefugees.com), designed to encourage practical support for refugees within the Australian community.

Eddie Butler-Bowdon wrote the History chapter (p32). Eddie has lived and studied in Adelaide, Sydney and Melbourne, and holds a Bachelor of Arts and a Master of Arts in History. In 1991 he began his career in museums at the Powerhouse Museum, Sydney. He is now senior curator of the Australian Society and Technology Department at Melbourne Museum. Currently on display at Melbourne Museum (p452) are three 'Eddie' exhibitions: Neighbours & Suburban Melbourne (the long-running TV series *Neighbours* screens in 55 countries); the Streets of Melbourne; and Phar Lap: A True Legend (the taxidermied race-horse Phar Lap is Australia's most popular museum artefact). Eddie is published on a variety of social history topics.

Matthew Evans wrote the Food & Drink chapter (p71). Matthew was a chef before he crossed to the 'dark side' as food writer and restaurant critic. He is currently chief restaurant reviewer for the *Sydney Morning Herald*, co-editor of the *Sydney Morning Herald Good Food Guide*, and has a recipe column read by four million people. Matthew is the award-winning author of four food books, including Lonely Planet's *World Food Italy*, and there is little that he wouldn't eat (that isn't endangered), as long as he lives to tell the story.

Tim Flannery wrote the Environment chapter (p45). Tim's a naturalist, explorer and writer. He is the author of a number of award-winning books, including *The Future Eaters* and *Throwim Way Leg* (an account of his adventures as a biologist working in New Guinea) and the landmark ecological history of North America, *The Eternal Frontier*. Tim lives in Adelaide where he is director of the South Australian Museum (p667) and a professor at the University of Adelaide.

David Millar wrote the Health chapter (p1017). David is a travel-medicine specialist, diving doctor and lecturer in wilderness medicine who graduated in Hobart, Tasmania. He has worked in all states of Australia (except the Northern Territory) and as an expedition doctor with the Maritime Museum of Western Australia, accompanying a variety of expeditions around Australia, including the *Pandora* wreck in Far North Queensland and Rowley Shoals off the northwest coast. David is currently a medical director with the Travel Doctor in Auckland.

Gary Presland wrote the boxed text 'Aboriginal Australians' (p34). After an early career at sea, Gary studied history and archaeology at university. He has written extensively on Aboriginal history and is the author of *Aboriginal Melbourne: The Lost Land of the Kulin People*.

Tony Wilson wrote the boxed text 'Sporting Australia' (p62). Tony received his break into the media in 1998 as the winner of the ABC TV travel-documentary show *Race Around the World*, for which he visited 10 countries in 100 days, recording a four-minute story from each one. He has written regular features for Melbourne's *Age* newspaper on major sporting events, as well as authoring two children's books, *The Minister for Traffic Lights* and *Grannysaurus Rex*. Tony is now based in Melbourne, and is a breakfast radio presenter on that city's iconic alternative music station 3RRR.

Snapshot

International affairs have dominated the collective Australian mindset recently, with the biggest issue being the Iraq war in early 2003. Despite opinion polls showing widespread public opposition to any military action not sanctioned by the United Nations, Prime Minister John Howard 'pre-deployed' troops to the Middle East while simultaneously insisting he hadn't yet committed Australia to war, a claim contradicted by US President George W Bush who quickly declared Australia part of his 'coalition of the willing'. Throughout the invasion of Iraq, Australians remained deeply divided over their country's participation. This divide was widened by the failure of the invading force (in the first few months of occupation) to find the weapons of mass destruction that were cited to justify the war in the first place. For more information on Australia's involvement in the Iraq war see p39.

The terrorist bombings in Kuta in October 2002 that killed over 190 people, including 89 Australians, prompted local soul-searching over what was later confirmed as the deliberate targeting of Australians (see p44 for more on the Bali bombings). In response to the attacks, the government poured money into a domestic campaign to 'protect our way of life from a possible terrorist threat'. But some controversial raids on the homes of Indonesians living in Australia and vague initiatives like a National Security Hotline for reporting all 'suspicious' activities were criticised for doing little more than fuelling a climate of fear.

In the midst of these events, the focus on asylum seekers was much less than during the *Tampa* and 'children overboard' vortex of late 2001 (for details see the boxed text 'Asylum Seekers & Mandatory Detention'; p58), though media attention is still given to the conditions refugees face under mandatory detention, and to outbreaks of violence by detainees, such as the $8.5 million fire damage to five detention centres in January 2003. Issues affecting Australian Aborigines (see the boxed text 'Aboriginal Australians'; p34) have received scant coverage recently, with land rights rarely mentioned and the public debate over whether to say 'sorry' now hushed.

In politics, the opposition Australian Labor Party (ALP) has lost ground to the conservative policies of the ruling Liberal and National coalition, which claimed victory in the 2001 federal elections by maintaining a hardline attitude towards asylum seekers and which has maintained its support base in opinion polls throughout the 2003 Iraq war. The ALP's performance has not been helped by leadership struggles. Ditto the Democrats, who lost supporters after a bitter and implosive leadership dispute. In both cases, party leadership came under fire after poor performances in state elections and a public perception that the parties were in internal disagreement over key issues. Disenfranchised voters from both the ALP and the Democrats reacted by swinging far left to the now newsworthy, oft-quoted Greens. See p42 for more general information on the nature of politics in Australia.

Australia's economy has remained relatively stable over the last year or two, even while the economies of other advanced countries have felt the worse for wear. This has mainly been due to a strong commercial and residential construction sector, which has helped the country cope with a drought-impacted agricultural sector and a tourist industry that felt the pinch in 2003 because of the SARS virus outbreak. That said, business confidence has been eroded by the collapse of several large insurance companies, massive payouts to some departing executives and enormous hikes in public liability insurance (p954) that forced the closure of numerous small businesses and community events.

Australia's environment has suffered from a long-term drought, enduring significant water shortages and agricultural losses (see p47 for details on the effects of drought in Australia). Headlines were also captured by some of the worst bushfires in the country's history, including the 2001 'Black Christmas' fires around Sydney and southern New South Wales, and the January 2003 bushfires that encircled Canberra (see the boxed text 'Bushfires'; p245) and ran wild across the country's southeast – in Kosciuszko National Park alone, 60% of the terrain was blackened and grave fears were held for local endangered species (see the boxed text 'High-Country Firestorms', p223, for details).

The profound realm of popular film or music culture (p64) is always a hot topic, with every mass-market periodical carrying updates on harassed celebrity-folk like Nicole Kidman and Russell Crowe. Locally produced television shows or big-rating US programmes also provoke tongue-wagging, but nothing is bigger than sport (see the boxed text 'Sporting Australia'; p62). Commercial networks willingly delay reports on international crises in favour of 'exclusives' on Australian sporting successes or controversies.

History by Eddie Butler-Bowdon

Eddie Butler-Bowdon has lived and studied in Adelaide, Sydney and Melbourne. In 1991 he began his career in museums at the Powerhouse Museum (p93), Sydney. He is now senior curator of the Australian Society and Technology Department at Melbourne Museum (p452). Eddie is published on a variety of social history topics.

Australia's human history began about 45,000 years ago with the arrival of the people now known as Aborigines across the straits from what is known today as Indonesia and Papua New Guinea. For more information see the boxed text 'Aboriginal Australians' (p34).

HISTORY FROM 1788
Convicts & Settlement

In 1797 an observer claimed that London, with a population of less than one million, had 10,000 thieves and 50,000 whores. These figures were disputed but nevertheless suggest a very large criminal underclass. In 1819, when the convicts aboard a ship headed 'to the bay' were asked to name their trade, three-quarters of them simply answered 'thief'. Questioned further they might have offered a more elaborate description of their calling – Henry Mayhew, the 19th-century observer of London street culture, recorded the following argot: 'Drag Sneaks' stole baggage and goods from carts or carriages; 'Star-Glazers' cut the panes out of shop windows; 'Skinners' were women who made off with men's clothes after enticing them to undress. The list went on.

It is from such a place and culture that the convicts came. It is to Australia that they were sent – the only continent colonised by Europeans as a gaol. James Cook had claimed the country for the King at Possession Island in 1770. And 17 years later, in 1787, after Captain James Cook visited and charted Australia's east coast, a fleet now referred to as the 'First Fleet' was despatched there on the basis of Cook's accounts.

The 11 ships of this first fleet were loaded with seed, live animals, other supplies, soldiers, and 548 male and 188 female convicted criminals. These were the first among a total of 160,000 convicts transported to an open gaol; or, as art critic Robert Hughes puts it in *The Fatal Shore* (1987), his epic on the convict experiment, a gaol with 'a wall 14,000 miles thick'.

The fact that Australia was already inhabited was not regarded as an impediment to what Aboriginal people viewed from the first as an invasion. At Sydney Cove, surrounded by today's Opera House, Circular Quay and the commercialised historic area known as The Rocks (p89), the colony began. The first years were particularly tough, starvation rations applying equally to soldiers and convicts (the threat of starvation hung over the colony for at least 16 years). Food acted as the chains that bound them to the system. Gradually, the colony became more self-sufficient. Crops were sown and animals were raised and the colony became less dependent on Britain for food. Critically, an innovative wool industry developed; the expression 'Australia rides on the sheep's back' held currency until the 1960s. For the first 30 years, however, whaling and sealing proved a greater boon to the economy than farming.

Convict society was tightly controlled and stratified. Depending upon their skills, some convicts were assigned to private employers while other convicts were harnessed onto public works. Hyde Park Barracks (p97) in

TIMELINE

60,000–35,000 BC	8000 BC
The exact date is debatable, but Aborigines settle in Australia sometime between 60,000 and 35,000 BC	Tasmania's Aborigines are separated from the mainland when sea levels rise

Sydney, now a heritage site, was built in 1819 to house the latter. When convicts had served out their sentence they became free citizens and were entitled to the same 20-hectare grant of land as ordinary soldiers and the gradually increasing number of free settlers. These small selectors would build their own wattle-and-daub huts and raise crops and a few animals.

Some historians have argued that convict literacy and work skills were above average for their backgrounds and suggest it was their entrepreneurship that got them into strife. For some, being transported was a good move. For example, the businesswoman Mary Reiby (now on the A\$20 note) was transported for horse stealing and ended up with interests in property, trade, retailing and sealing in NSW and Van Diemen's Land (now Tasmania).

Even so, it remains difficult to see the convict as an economic migrant. The entire system was backed by physical force. Up to 500 lashes were given for transgressions. But the worst horror was the ever-present threat of being sent to special convict gaols such as Port Arthur (p605), east of Hobart. There, 'incorrigibles' were dealt a range of cruel and unusual punishments, often by sadistic gaolers. Apart from floggings and beatings, one of the most feared practices was lengthy solitary confinement in the 'black cells'. Ultimately there was execution, and 100 convicts were hanged in Van Diemen's Land in 1824. The transportation of convicts ceased in 1852, except in Western Australia, which took 7000 in the 1860s.

Maritime trade, together with strategic imperatives and, in some cases, penal requirements, drove expansion from Sydney: to Norfolk Island (p206) in 1788; Newcastle in 1804; Van Dieman's Land in 1804 (Launceston and Hobart); Moreton Bay (Brisbane) in 1825; Fremantle (Perth) in 1829 (though its isolation permitted only very slow growth); Melbourne in 1835; and the convict-free Adelaide in 1836.

Overland exploration also provided new scope for European expansion. In 1813 the Blue Mountains were crossed, the land beyond them a pastoral vista of economic bounty (the western plains were reached by the explorers Gregory Blaxland, William Lawson and William Wentworth). In 1829 the great river systems of the southeast, the Murrumbidgee, the Darling and the Murray, were first identified and settlement followed. In northern Queensland, the west and the north were progressively explored about mid-century. Aboriginal people participated in these explorations, often showing Europeans the best course to take. And in the wake of explorers, came 'squatters', driving sheep and cattle. Once again, local Aborigines pointed out the best land and the location of water. This Aboriginal involvement with the pastoral industry continues, particularly on the large cattle stations of the Northern Territory.

Gold & Land

In 1851 gold was discovered near the town of Bathurst, west of the Blue Mountains, and the discovery was made public. Within the year large quantities of gold were found in creek beds and old watercourses in central Victoria at Clunes, Ballarat, Castlemaine and Bendigo. The finds were big news around the world, the image of Australia as a penal colony

Sydney's Aboriginal Past by V Attenbrow is a detailed study of a regional Aboriginal history. More importantly, it is also an excellent introduction to the way in which such studies are done.

Port Arthur –
www.portarthur.org.au

Port Arthur is often described as the most powerful historic site in Australia, and this website gives a good idea why that is so. It also provides all the important practical details you need to know.

1642	1768
Abel Tasman discovers Tasmania and names it Van Diemen's Land after a Dutch governor	James Cook begins his search for the Great South Land and lands on the southeastern tip of the continent

ABORIGINAL AUSTRALIANS by Gary Presland

Recent estimates of Australia's Aboriginal population at the time of European invasion suggest there were perhaps one million people across the continent.

The precise time of arrival in Australia of ancestral Aborigines will likely never be known. What is currently conjectured is that the initial landfall occurred perhaps about 46,000 years ago, at a time of lower sea levels, during the Ice Age. These people came via the region of southeast Asia, and in order to reach continental Australia had to cross water passages at least 70km wide. From the point of arrival (now long since inundated by rising sea level) people spread through all of Australia's environmental zones, within a comparatively short period. Archaeological sites close to Melbourne in the southeast and on the Swan River near Perth in the southwest have been dated to about 40,000 years ago. Two human burials at Lake Mungo (p240) in western NSW have recently been re-dated to a similar figure.

Australia was a continent consisting of hunter-gatherers. With regional variations, in all of the country's diverse ecological zone, people made their living by focusing on the available natural resources. But this was not a purely passive exercise. There are many instances of Aborigines acting to maximise the returns of their hunting and foraging strategies. In western Victoria elaborate systems were devised for trapping eels; in the northern wetland environments it was common practice to replant tubers to promote future growth. And in every part of the continent fire was used as a tool in the clearing of vegetation, to aid movement and to promote new growth. In many regions this 'firestick farming' maintained a grassland environment.

Across the continent cultural elements were maintained and transmitted in oral forms. Of particular importance was the use of songs to convey the stories regarding the creative activities of ancestor figures during the 'Dreaming'. Short songs containing powerful information might relate to specific localities or, when a series is strung together, a dreaming track. In this latter case, such series are sometimes called songlines and can refer to tracks extending over considerable distances. A detailed knowledge of such songs was held to be a sign of great power in an individual. See the boxed text 'Aboriginal Spirituality' (p60) for more information about traditional Aboriginal religion.

There were about 250 languages spoken within Australia and Tasmania, divided into approximately 700 dialects. The most important social group was the clan, as the group that identified with specific tracts of land. Because of their close identification with land and their day-to-day hunting and foraging strategies, clans were essentially localised in their operations. There was regular movement but Aborigines were not nomadic; rather, they moved within their estates according to a range of determinants, including seasonal variation and the need to be at specific places for ritual and totemic purposes. In many parts of the country early observers commented on the permanent 'villages' of local people.

Many clans were linked as part of exchange networks that saw the movement of objects and ideas over long distances. In this way, pearl objects and baler shells from the Gulf of Carpentaria in the north found their way to Spencer Gulf, 3000km to the south.

Permanent European settlement in Australia began in Sydney in January 1788, but Aboriginal people had already had occasional contact with other people for hundreds of years prior to this. From the 15th century onwards European ships periodically sighted Australian shores, and Dutch and English ships touched briefly on Australia's northwest coast in the 17th-century. From the mid-18th century Southeast Asian fishermen regularly fished in coastal waters for *trepang* (sea cucumber). They also traded

1788 — The First Fleet arrives at Sydney Harbour with its cargo of convicts.

1801–03 — Mathew Flinders circumnavigates Australia with his faithful companion, Trim the cat.

with local Aborigines and took a number of men back to Indonesia.

Following the settlement of Sydney, occupation of Aboriginal land occurred progressively across Australia. This invasion took place from a number of directions and was resisted by local Aboriginal groups. Frontier violence was not uncommon but there were also many instances of cooperation for mutual benefit. In the more-populated eastern colonies the impacts on the indigenous populations were dramatic and sudden, including death through introduced diseases and a dramatic decline in birth rate. The dispossession of their land was a major factor in the rapid demise of most elements of traditional Aboriginal culture.

Through more than 40,000 years Aboriginal Australians had successfully adapted their way of life to many challenges. The European invasion brought rapid and massive changes but Aboriginal culture survived and continues in a wide variety of contemporary forms.

Since the late 1960s, use of the term 'Koori' (or Koorie) to refer to Aborigines has become widespread. The word means 'people' in a number of languages from southeastern Australia and is one of a number of such terms used to distinguish the indigenous people of specific regions. A Koori is an indigenous person from NSW or Victoria, just as a Murri is from Queensland, a Nunga is from South Australia and a Nyungar from Western Australia.

At the time of first occupation of Aboriginal land, beginning in 1788, the Australian continent had been regarded as terra nullius, land that was owned by nobody. This fiction went largely unchallenged until the mid- to late-20th century. In 1968 a group of Gurundji stockmen on Wave Hill cattle station in the Northern Territory instigated the first Aboriginal land claim. Although this claim failed, it set in motion a still-continuing movement by Aboriginal people to reclaim their land.

In 1982 a small group of Torres Strait Islanders from Mer (Murray Island) headed by Koiki (Eddie) Mabo began legal proceedings in the Queensland Supreme Court to establish their traditional ownership of their land. The case eventually progressed to the High Court of Australia which, in 1992, upheld their claim. This landmark judgement refuted the legal fiction of *terra nullius* and established that Aborigines had the right to claim title to traditional lands.

In the following years the federal Labor government enacted legislation to make the Mabo decision law. However, the legislation excluded pastoral leases, which lead to confusion within the pastoral industry and a lack of confidence within the mining and resource industries. There was also widespread scare-mongering regarding the rights of Aboriginal people to make claims on land, particularly fuelled by prominent individuals such as Pauline Hanson.

A conservative federal government lead by John Howard was elected in 1996. Soon after, in another watershed case, brought by the Wik people of northern Queensland, the High Court ruled that pastoral leases and native title could coexist. Fearful of a deluge of Aboriginal land-rights claims, the Howard government moved quickly to diminish the rights of Aborigines in this respect. A 10-point plan was devised, which effectively eliminated many of the reforms of the previous Labor government and reduced the range of allowable claims. Under the plan, Aborigines have access to pastoral land for the purposes of visiting sacred sites and holding ceremonies, and to gather resources such as food and water. Native title was abolished on pastoral leases when it would interfere with the rights of the pastoralist.

Gary Presland has written extensively on Aboriginal history and is the author of Aboriginal Melbourne: The Lost Land of the Kulin People.

making way for that of the new El Dorado. By 1852, 1800 hopefuls were disembarking weekly at Melbourne. Most came from England, Scotland or Ireland, but other Europeans and Americans were also among the first to arrive. Later, about 40,000 people came from China.

Within the colonies, the excitement verged on hysteria. Tradesmen downed tools, policemen abandoned their posts, prostitutes followed the money. Catherine Spence, a journalist and social reformer, visited Melbourne during the height of the gold fever. Her comments reflected the concerns that many old colonists felt about the impact of gold on social stability: 'This convulsion has unfixed everything. Religion is neglected, education despised...everyone is engrossed by the simple object of making money in a very short time.'

As a social type, the individual gold digger was unheard of before the mid-19th century. What made California and the Australian colonies different was capitalism. In California, where the international rush began in 1849, the right of 'finders keepers' was written into the US Constitution, while in Australia it was given more grudgingly, under pressure and for the cost of a licence. The licence was expensive and did not entitle political representation. This situation led to a rebellion at the Eureka Stockade at Ballarat in 1854 where authorities shot over 30 diggers and gaoled others. The Eureka flag, featuring the Southern Cross, became a symbol of resistance and can still be viewed at Ballarat's sound-and-light show 'Blood on the Southern Cross' (p532).

Gold hit the Australian colonies like a thunderbolt. The non-Aboriginal population rose from 437,665 in 1851 to 1,151,947 in 1861 (Aborigines were officially made invisible by the statistician). By 1881 the population had doubled again. GDP increased five-fold in the 1850s and trebled again by 1888. Victoria's finds were the richest; in other areas the gold tended to last only a few years. It was Queensland's turn from the 1860s where it was found at places such as Gympie, Charters Towers and Palmer River, and Western Australia's from the 1880s at places such as Halls Creek, Kalgoorlie and Coolgardie. Gold was also found in 1872 south of Darwin by workers laying the Overland Telegraph from Adelaide.

Every find was soon followed by hordes hoping to extricate a 'Welcome Stranger' – the record-breaking 72kg nugget found in 1869 near Dunolly in Victoria (estimated to be worth $4 million today). During the economic depression of the 1890s, many hopefuls from the eastern colonies went to WA. Coolgardie grew from nothing in 1893 to a booming town consisting of 15,000 people, 23 hotels, six banks and two stock exchanges in just 10 years. Few struck it lucky, however, and the death toll from disease was high.

Nevertheless, many stayed in WA and found a life for themselves in other sectors. This was the real legacy of the gold rushes. Financial and human capital was parlayed into developing the cities and the country, pushing the European frontier further and further inland. For many, the dream of finding gold mutated into the more attainable goal of gaining a grant of land to farm.

Often these parcels of land were too small to be viable; in other areas the issue was water. In South Australia in 1865, the southern edge of

Victorian Goldfields –
www.goldfields.org.au

Heritage, food, wine, events – this site offers a comprehensive guide to touring the central goldfields region of Victoria. Just click, print, and get in the car.

Northern Territory History –
www.northern exposure.com.au/ history.html

This site gives an insight into European history in the Northern Territory; it is less thorough on Aboriginal history.

1860	1901
John Stuart makes the first south–north crossing of the country (along the route that is today the Stuart Hwy)	Sir Edmund Barton becomes the first prime minister of Australia

the saltbush country was identified by a government surveyor George Goyder. Goyder's Line basically ran east-west across SA south of the Flinders Ranges. North of the line, Goyder claimed, agriculture would be too susceptible to drought; the land was only fit for grazing. However, several seasons of good rainfall initially led to the government and new selectors ignoring the line. Then drought struck and ruined farmers had to retreat south. The ruins of their desiccated dreams still glow golden in the late afternoon.

In Victoria, scratching a living from a small selection proved so difficult that dissent fomented, particularly among the Irish. It often seemed that local police and magistrates were more interested in using the law to oppress than enforce justice. Ned Kelly (1855–80), a bushranger whose gang killed three policemen, came from such a setting. Kelly presented to the authorities a hot-headed passion until his capture in Glenrowan, and then a menacing equanimity until his execution in Melbourne (he was hanged at the Old Melbourne Gaol). Kelly is Australia's most persistent folk hero. His trademark metal helmet with an eye-slit featured in the Opening Ceremony of the Sydney 2000 Olympic Games (the original metal helmet is in Melbourne). The Old Melbourne Gaol (p452) displays the grisly Kelly 'death mask'; for more on Ned Kelly see the boxed text 'Kelly Country' (p557).

The Workingman's Paradise

During the 1890s, calls for the separate colonies to federate became increasingly strident. Supporters argued that it would improve the economy and the position of workers by enabling the abolition of inter-colony tariffs and protection against competing foreign labour.

Each colony was determined, however, that its interests should not be overshadowed by those of the other colonies. For this reason, the constitution that was finally adopted gave only very specific powers to the Commonwealth, leaving all residual powers with the states. It also gave each state representation in the upper house of parliament (the Senate), regardless of size or population. Today Tasmania, with a population of less than half a million, has as many senators in federal parliament as NSW, with a population of around six million. As the Senate is able to reject legislation passed by the lower house, this legacy of Australia's colonial past has had a profound effect on its politics, entrenching state division and ensuring that the smaller states have remained powerful forces in the government of the nation.

In the absence of a separate national capital – federal parliament didn't move to Canberra until 1927 – the Federation ceremony was held in Sydney, 1 January 1901, when Australia became a nation. The Earl of Hopetoun, as Queen Victoria's representative, was sworn in as the Governor-General. Now, over a century later, the British monarch remains Australia's head of state. Those who argued in the 1890s that Australia should become a republic as part of the Federation process would still be waiting today.

Whereas the right to representation was often tied to property in the colonies, the federal parliament was to operate on the one-person-one-vote system. Initially this included Aborigines but their right to a federal

Stuart Macintyre's *A Concise History of Australia* was commissioned with international and local readers in mind. Professor Stuart Macintyre, one of Australia's leading historians, manages to bind new insights and conventional scholarship into this highly readable account of the national past. A very direct sense of connection between the past and today pervades the text and has given it a name as the best single-volume history of Australia available.

vote was effectively removed in 1902 and was not restored until 1962. Australia became the second country in the world where women could vote, after New Zealand. Both women and the labour movement, which melded trade unionism with strands of socialism, had argued for a place in an egalitarian society. At Barcaldine in central Queensland, shearers and other rural workers formed the Australian Labor Party. By 1914 Labor had held power in every parliament in the country. From the 1890s Australian parliaments brought some internationally innovative social reforms: fair wages backed by arbitration, a limited age pension, the right to unionism and so on.

The protection of Australian industry through tariffs and the control over labour supply was critical to this pact between the left and right sides of politics. Immigration, necessarily, was a key part of the equation. But Australia's credo of control and exclusion extended beyond the economic and into ethnicity and race. Other English-speaking nations took a similar approach – the US, Britain, Canada – but only Australia clearly articulated its vision as clearly, leading to the Immigration Restriction Act, or White Australia Policy, which was designed to prevent the immigration of Asians and Pacific Islanders. For more information, see Immigration & Cultural Identity (p40).

Cities & Suburbanisation

When people think of Australia they commonly think of the outback; of koalas, kangaroos and 'fair dinkum' frontier types. But *Neighbours*, a TV soapie made in suburban Melbourne and screened in over 50 countries, is closer to the mark. Indeed, Australia has long been the most suburban of nations. In 1900, two-thirds of the population lived in towns or cities with a population of at least 1000.

The wealth from the mining, pastoral and agricultural sectors found its most lasting expression in the cities. Within a single decade, from 1891 to 1901, the population of Perth quadrupled to 44,000. Brisbane was also transformed from a town into a city in the same decade. During the 1880s, the population of Melbourne doubled to over half a million, thereby briefly eclipsing Sydney's. In 1889 'Marvellous Melbourne' had the world's tallest building – briefly.

The boom collapsed in the 1890s, but in 1895 visitor Mark Twain was struck by how Melbourne was 'a stately city architecturally as well as in magnitude'. Twain's reference to magnitude can be applied to any of Australia's cities. Rows of terrace housing and semi-detached housing were built in the suburbs immediately ringing the city centres, but beyond them was fully detached housing on blocks as large as a quarter-acre.

Historian Graeme Davison has argued that Australia deserves the title 'first suburban nation'. If life as a small selector proved too difficult in the bush, a diluted version was more attainable in the suburbs. Here, the going tended to be smoother financially, yet the yearning for privacy, fresh air and a sense of nature could be partially fulfilled. Suburbs also satisfied the class-conscious desire for neighbourhoods that had some distance from the terrace housing where the poor mostly lived and paid rent. In short, the privately owned detached house on a decent block became the Australian dream.

1967	1971
Aborigines are finally given the status of citizens	The Aboriginal flag is first displayed on National Aborigines' Day

War

Nearly every country town in Australia has a war memorial, often these are located in the main street. Usually constructed of stone, the memorials record the names of the local young men who died in WWI and WWII. In Canberra, the prime site and sheer size of the Australian War Memorial (p249) illustrates the importance of war in the national consciousness. Set some distance away from Lake Burley Griffin and on a gentle rise, it directly eyeballs the national parliament across the other side of the lake.

Don Bradman - Australia's cricketing legend.

KATE NOLAN

The Australian War Memorial acknowledges and records a wider military commitment – 140 years of participating in wars and campaigns fought almost exclusively overseas: the Maori Wars of New Zealand in the 1860s; Sudan (1885); Boxer Rebellion (1900–01); Boer War (1899–1902); WWI (1914–18); WWII (1939–45); Korea (1950–53); Malaya (1948–63); Vietnam (1962–73); Gulf War (1991); Afghanistan (2001); and Iraq (2003). Regional peacekeeping operations have included East Timor (1998) and the Solomon Islands (2003).

Over this same period, no enemy soldier has set foot on Australian soil, although in 1942 and 1943 Darwin and the northwest coast of Australia were bombed from the air, killing about three people, and in 1942 Japanese minisubmarines entered Sydney Harbour, resulting in the deaths of 21 people.

WWI is the conflict by which all others are measured in Australia. The conscription issue split the country; Irish Catholics especially voted against compulsory service in two referenda. Then there was the death toll: from a population of five million, Australia lost 58,000, making its sacrifice proportionally second only to New Zealand's among the Allies. One in six of those who left Australian shores to assist in the conflict did not return. Those who did return often suffered from poorly diagnosed trauma. Mud, barbed wire, mustard gas and dead bodies made sweet dreams difficult. For their part, mothers and wives remained at the emotional frontline for decades.

See p65 for a review of the Australian film Gallipoli.

Gallipoli (in Turkey) and the Somme, Ypres or Passchendaele (in Belgium and France) – Australians quickly learnt these foreign names. Following a bungled landing on 25 April 1915, Australian and New Zealand troops had tried but failed to win the Gallipoli Peninsula. Over eight months, 8104 died and 18,000 were wounded. It is central to national lore that at Gallipoli, rather than in 1901, Australia came of age – Gallipoli became the new nation's most sacred piece of turf, and remains so now more than ever. For information about Australians' reverence to the Anzacs, see p57.

Phar Lap – www.museum.vic.gov .au/pharlap/

Why is one of Australia's key national legends about a long-dead race-horse? This site provides the answers.

Perhaps as a backlash to this horror, between the two world wars the two popular heroes were sports figures: Don Bradman, the unsurpassed cricketer, and Phar Lap, the champion racehorse. Both were made available to fans through new media, radio and 'talkie' newsreels. Phar Lap especially helped divert people's minds from the hardships of the economic depression of the 1930s. He stands proud – taxidermied and showcased – at the Melbourne Museum (p452).

WWII is probably the only time when military conflict appeared vital to Australia's existence. In 1942 Singapore fell to Japanese forces and Britain

1972	1974
Gough Whitlam leads the Australian Labor Party to its first federal parliamentary victory in 23 years	Cyclone Tracy hits Darwin on Christmas Eve, killing 65 people

made it clear that Australia would have to fend for itself (while simultaneously calling for more troops!). In response, Australia for once showed a rare streak of independent – though rather predictable – thinking. It grafted its traditional loyalty to the British Empire onto another largely white, English-speaking nation: at Australia's request, the USA sent troops to fight, and ultimately defeat, the Japanese.

Thus began a relationship with the USA that has seen Australia respond with military assistance in several wars, notably Korea, Vietnam and, most recently, Iraq. From the US perspective, the importance of the Australian involvement in these wars has been mostly political rather than military. Indeed, to many outsiders it seemed bizarre that Australia should wish to send troops to Iraq, which is nowhere near the Asia-Pacific region.

But to Australians who know their history it was simply the latest instalment in a 140-year-long history of seeking identity and security in the world by fighting for greater powers in far-flung places. It is hardly surprising then that despite a series of overtures in recent decades to Asian nations for a greater role in the region's affairs, Australia remains on the outer.

Immigration & Cultural Identity

While colonial society was riven with ethnic and religious snobberies, the gold rushes brought a new intensity to cultural diversity. In 1861, 64% of the Australian population was foreign-born; about 15% of these were not from the British Isles. The Chinese, the largest group, consistently suffered official and non-official prejudice. In northern Queensland especially, there were several outbreaks of violence at the goldfields. However, by the 1880s the Chinese were more accepted. Indeed, around the 1880s Australia had become a relatively tolerant society of immigrants from diverse backgrounds.

In the 1880s the heavyweight Peter Jackson was one of Australia's best boxers. In the 1890s he left for the US, to seek greater challenges; he carried the hopes of a large number of sporting fans with him. But as a black former West Indian, Jackson found racist attitudes in the US much harder to deal with than anything he had experienced in Australia. Eventually he returned to Australia and died in Roma, Queensland, his headstone reading, 'Here Lies A Man'. Conversely, another black boxer Clarence Reeves – the Alabama Kid – arrived in Australia from the US in 1938. For the next 10 years he fought in stadiums and in the tent boxing troupes that toured Australia. He married an Adelaide woman and had two children. No matter – the Australian government split the family and deported him. He was black, regretted the Labor minister, and there was no bending the rules.

Just as Peter Jackson caught the tail end of a more tolerant era in Australian racial attitudes, the Alabama Kid caught the end of its most intolerant era. In 1901 Australia stood at the crossroads as to the society it wanted. That it chose a 'White Australia' policy as part of the Federation package was by no means inevitable. In Queensland, for instance, an element of local support resisted efforts to repatriate some of the Pacific Islanders who had come to work in the sugar industry. Though some of

Australian War Memorial – www.awm.gov.au/
The War Memorial is just one of several national institutions located in Canberra.

1976	1977
The Aboriginal Land Rights Act is passed in the Northern Territory	The 1st edition of *Australia* rolls out of Lonely Planet's Melbourne warehouse

A STORY FROM THE STOLEN GENERATION

Between 1918 and 1970, Australian governments forcibly removed almost 100,000 Aboriginal children (most of them under the age of five) from their parents and relocated them miles away, either in institutions or with (white) foster parents. Contact with the family was actively discouraged: relocations were always over a far-enough distance, often interstate, to ensure that few made it home when they tried to escape. Many children were told their parents had died, and parents were rarely told where their children had been sent.

In institutional care the children received only minimal education; living conditions were rough and food often scarce. Many experienced sexual or other abuse. The survivors of this relocation are now known as the 'stolen generation', and are a hot political topic in Australia. One of them, Lorraine Mafi-Williams, wrote the following account for Lonely Planet:

I was 12 years old when we were stolen from our parents. Brother John was 14, Bell 16, Lucy was nine, Elaine seven and Cid, the baby, three. There was no warning. The white welfare officer came in his truck with two white policemen. It was early in the morning. Dad had gone to work... The last time I saw my mum she was crying. I never saw mum cry like this before, only at funerals. Her whole body heaved with sobs. I remember saying, 'It's alright mum, we're only going down town'. I thought we'd be back soon enough. I was wrong.

I was put onto the open-air back of a truck with my brothers and sisters. By the time we got to Armidale (New South Wales), we were caked in red dirt from the road and looked truly neglected. By this time I was in a state of confusion. Cid and John were taken straight to Kinchella Boys Home. Bell was taken to work at a cattle station 100 miles away. Elaine, Lucy and I were taken to the Armidale Children's Orphanage. I was there for about a year and during that time I was very rebellious. My young mind didn't register that I was confined to an institution, separated from my parents. And why? Because I was an Aboriginal child... What made these people do such things? I was lost and lonely and tried everything to escape – even suicide – but that came later.

My little sister Lucy was a sickly child and she wet the bed nearly every night. When the orphanage matron found out, she began beating Lucy with a strap every morning. I would tell Lucy to wake me up in the night so I could swap her bed sheets with my dry ones and put my dry nightdress on her. When the matron inspected the beds in the morning she would find mine wet, so I took the beatings instead.

Several months later I was sent away to Cootamundra Girls Home to be trained as a domestic servant. I'd wash filthy clothes, scrub dirty floors and wipe shitty babies' bums. I worked from dawn to dark in return for a bed and three feeds a day. I was 13 years old.

When I was 18, I finally made it to freedom. I was released from Cootamundra Girls Home and I got a job in Sydney. I would ask other Kooris if they knew my mum and dad. One day a tall, well-built, handsome black man approached me and said, 'You're Lorraine Turnball?... I'm your cousin Darcy'. He told me where mum and dad were living.

It didn't take me long to pack and board the train for Taree, where my parents were living on Purfleet Mission – the place I was born. That early morning meeting with my parents will stay in my heart forever. Mum and Dad were on the station when I got off the train. I was now a woman, no longer the child they knew. The three of us clung together and cried. I was 19 and I was the last to make it home.

The late Lorraine Mafi-Williams, a Bundjakung-Dainggati woman, became a successful film-maker and writer and a leading Aboriginal activist (despite the emotional scars left by her childhood). She wrote these words for Lonely Planet's Aboriginal Australia & the Torres Strait Islands (2001).

1983	1986
Ash Wednesday bushfires in Victoria and South Australia kill 76 people and devastate homes	Uluru (Ayers Rock) is handed back to the traditional owners and leased to the Australian government

Continent of Hunter-Gatherers: New Perspectives in Australian Prehistory by H Lourandos is an interesting survey of significant pre-European Aboriginal sites, set within the range of environmental zones across the continent.

the Kanakas (see p268 for more information about this group of people) had forcibly been recruited, many now had families here and some had married Europeans or Aborigines. Indeed, at a community level, social mobility, intermarriage and ideals of fair play often overrode any perceived notion of an official pecking order regarding race and ethnicity.

From 1901 to the late 1940s a limited number of Greeks and Italians were admitted but otherwise the door was closed to non-British. However, Australia's sense of vulnerability following WWII gave new resonance to the cry, 'populate or perish'. A new policy aimed to increase the 1947 population of 7.6 million by 2% annually: 1% through natural increase and 1% through immigration. British immigration was much preferred, and more generously assisted, but the immigration net increasingly took in continental Europeans. Between 1947 and 1967, 800,000 non-British migrants arrived in Australia. Subsequently, migrants came from a range of places – geographical and cultural – that are too numerous to mention here.

The postwar immigration program has been an enormously successful social experiment, despite some resistance. By 1981 the population was 15.1 million; it is now 20 million. The emphasis today is on skilled migrants (51%), family reunion programs (38%) and refugees (11%). About 27% of Australians now consider that their background is other than Anglo-Celtic. But in a sense, that distinction becomes more meaningless every year. Indeed, many families are discovering a more complex background than they had previously known about – or were prepared to acknowledge.

Recent Times

By the 1960s, postwar prosperity saw Australia settle into a more comfortable age. Eighty-five percent of the population lived in a suburban setting, most on the eastern seaboard of the country. Some could not bear the mainstream and went overseas, mostly to Britain – the cultural commentator Clive James, artiste Barry Humphries, feminist and writer Germaine Greer, and art critic Robert Hughes each developed stellar careers outside Australia. Others stayed and continued to cringe about brick veneer houses, Holden cars, beer, football, a weekly lottery and the lawn mower. They complained that this tableau of clichés was what the resilience of the convict, the guts of the pioneer, the derring-do of the gold seeker and the courage of the population during wartime, had come to.

Such cultural despair has not been justified. If the first half of the 20th century involved plenty of pulling together as a nation, the second half saw courage and fortitude expressed by groups that previously had little or no voice. Women, together with youths, blacks and gays, occupy a fundamentally different societal 'space' compared with 40 years ago. Whether in sport, the workplace or under the law, all have won ground but each group considers it has yet more to win. In the case of Aborigines, many athletes still face discrimination on and off the field; internationally acclaimed artists are paid little for their work; and despite the promise of the Mabo and Wik High Court decisions of the early 1990s, many subsequent Native Title claims have come to nothing.

1988	1992
The Bicentennial celebration: there are so many yachts on Sydney Harbour that you can almost walk across it	The High Court rejects the concept of *terra nullius* (land belonging to no-one) in the Mabo decision

---

SORRY DAY

On 26 May 1997, a Royal Commission handed down its findings on the Stolen Generation – Aboriginal and Torres Strait Islander children who had been forcibly removed from their families during the government's policy of assimilation.

The report, *Bringing Them Home*, condemned the policy and made many recommendations at a state and community level, suggesting that a national Sorry Day be held to recognise the past sufferings and to move towards reconciliation. On 26 May the following year the first Sorry Day was celebrated with community activities and the signing of 'sorry books' across Australia. The federal government's response to the report was to offer a $63 million assistance package, but the formal apology sought by the indigenous community has so far been refused. Prime Minister John Howard believes that his government should not be held accountable for the actions of a past government and there is clearly a fear that compensation claims will result from any admission of responsibility. Despite this, popular support for reconciliation is at an all-time high. Reconciliation Week is held each year from 27 May to 3 June.

Despite this, Australia has not only stayed in touch with the parallel social developments elsewhere in the world but frequently set the pace. The federal system, with so many parliaments, has unwittingly assisted these changes. For example, in the 1970s former SA premier Don Dunstan was a trailblazer for other states: reforms included legalised homosexuality; the return of Aboriginal land; equal opportunity legislation; and more assistance to the arts, including to a resurgent film industry. In Canberra, the Whitlam government also made major social reforms.

But the forces of conservatism have also had their say. Most infamously, the Gough Whitlam Labor government was sacked by the then governor-general, Sir John Kerr, in 1975. This event created a constitutional crisis which reinforced that Australia's head of state was the representative of the British monarch and that the position was more than ceremonial. Many thought that the crisis would lead to Australia becoming a republic. However, this was not to be – as recently as 1999 a referendum to enable a republic (one not supported by the incumbent Prime Minister John Howard) was defeated.

In the early 1990s, former Labor prime minister Paul Keating's initiatives to remake the nation and attain the republican dream – stronger integration with Asia and reconciliation with Aboriginal people based on the legal recognition of prior occupancy – were dodged, white-anted or comprehensively sunk as Australia approached the centenary of Federation. These roads remain open but Australia has retreated from the intersection.

Indeed, the difference between the two main political parties – Liberal and Labor – on these big issues can be difficult to discern. The conservatives (Liberal) are driven by convictions that can be carbon-dated to the 1950s, Labor by concern that any other stance will lose votes. Their respective responses to the *Tampa* incident of August 2001 demonstrated this when several hundred asylum seekers aboard a sinking boat were rescued just offshore by a Norwegian vessel – the *Tampa* – and then denied sanctuary in Australia.

1999	2001
The majority of Australians (55%) vote to remain a constitutional monarchy; peacekeeping forces are sent to Timor	The Australian government rejects asylum seekers from the *Tampa* vessel

In the midst of the national hysteria that followed (an overwhelming majority of Australians supported the government's action), the asylum seekers were accused of trying to throw their children overboard and were therefore unfit to become Australian citizens. This accusation was subsequently proved false but not before the government won a huge majority at the November 2001 federal election. For more information, see the boxed text 'Asylum Seekers & Mandatory Detention' (p58).

Many of the *Tampa* refugees had originated from Afghanistan or Iraq, although their claims to hardship and refugee status were fiercely challenged at the time. However, the Australian government saw no contradiction in committing troops to fight the regimes of both countries, claiming that a major justification for the action was to free Afghanis and Iraqis from oppression. The Australian people were particularly ambivalent toward involvement with the US and Britain in Iraq, and, to their credit it must be said, resisted attempts by government hawks to somehow link Iraq with the bombing in October 2002 in Bali by Islamic extremists in which 89 Australians died.

Environment by Tim Flannery

Australia's plants and animals are just about the closest things to alien life you are likely to encounter on Earth. That's because Australia has been isolated from the other continents for a very long time – at least 45 million years. The other habitable continents have been able to exchange various species at different times because they've been linked by land bridges. Just 15,000 years ago it was possible to walk from the southern tip of Africa right through Asia and the Americas to Terra del Fuego. Not Australia, however. Its birds, mammals, reptiles and plants have taken their own separate and very different evolutionary journey, and the result today is the world's most distinct – and one of its most diverse – natural realms.

The first naturalists to investigate Australia were astonished by what they found. Here the swans were black – to Europeans this was a metaphor for the impossible – while mammals such as the platypus and echidna were discovered to lay eggs. It really was an upside-down world, where many of the larger animals hopped, where each year the trees shed their bark rather than their leaves, and where the 'pears' were made of wood (see p55).

If you are visiting Australia for a short time, you might need to go out of your way to experience some of the richness of the environment. That's because Australia is a subtle place, and some of the natural environment – especially around the cities – has been damaged or replaced by trees and creatures from Europe. Places like Sydney, however, have preserved extraordinary fragments of their original environment that are relatively easy to access. Before you enjoy them though, it's worthwhile understanding the basics about how nature operates in Australia. This is important because there's nowhere like Australia, and once you have an insight into its origins and natural rhythms, you will appreciate the place so much more.

Tim Flannery is a naturalist, explorer and writer. He is the author of a number of award-winning books including *The Future Eaters* and *Throwim Way Leg* (an account of his adventures as a biologist working in New Guinea), and the landmark ecological history of North America, *The Eternal Frontier*. Tim Flannery lives in Adelaide where he is director of the South Australian Museum (see p667) and a professor at the University of Adelaide.

The splendid isolation of Trephina Gorge Nature Park (p809), Northern Territory.

PAUL SINCLAIR

A UNIQUE ENVIRONMENT

There are two really big factors that go a long way towards explaining nature in Australia: its soils and its climate. Both are unique. Australian soils are the more subtle and difficult to notice of the two, but they have been fundamental in shaping life here. On the other continents, in recent geological times processes such as volcanism, mountain building and glacial activity have been busy creating new soil. Just think of the glacial-derived soils of North America, north Asia and Europe. They feed the world today, and were made by glaciers grinding up rock of differing chemical composition over the last two million years. The rich soils of India and parts of South America were made by rivers eroding mountains, while Java in Indonesia owes its extraordinary richness to volcanoes.

All of these soil-forming processes have been almost absent from Australia in more recent times. Only volcanoes have made a contribution, and they cover less than 2% of the continent's land area. In fact, for the last 90 million years, beginning deep in the age of dinosaurs, Australia has been geologically comatose. It was too flat, warm and dry to attract glaciers, its crust too ancient and thick to be punctured by volcanoes or folded into mountains. Look at Uluru (p819) and Kata Tjuta (the Olgas; p820). They are the stumps of mountains that 350 million years ago were the height of the Andes. Yet for hundreds of millions of years they've been nothing but nubbins.

Under such conditions no new soil is created and the old soil is leached of all its goodness, and is blown and washed away. The leaching is done by rain. Even if just 30cm of it falls each year, that adds up to a column of water 30 million km high passing through the soil over 100 million years, and that can do a great deal of leaching! Almost all of Australia's mountain ranges are more than 90 million years old, so you will see a lot of sand here, and a lot of country where the rocky 'bones' of the land are sticking up through the soil. It is an old, infertile landscape, and life in Australia has been adapting to these conditions for aeons.

B Beale and P Fray's *The Vanishing Continent* gives an excellent overview of soil erosion across Australia. Fine colour photographs make the issue more graphic.

Left facing page:

Plants that have evolved to withstand drought, bushfire and flood, such as this native grass tree, dominate the landscape.
DAVID CURL

An aerial view of Kata Tjuta (The Olgas; p820), Northern Territory.
CHRISTOPHER GROENHOUT

The Salinity Crisis by Q Beresford et al reveals everything you ever wanted to know about one of Australia's greatest environmental challenges, Western Australia's salinity crisis. A chronicle of unbelievable ignorance, greed and destruction.

Australia's misfortune in respect to soils is echoed in its climate. In most parts of the world outside the wet tropics, life responds to the rhythm of the seasons – summer to winter, or wet to dry. Most of Australia experiences seasons – sometimes very severe ones – yet life does not respond solely to them. This can clearly be seen by the fact that although there's plenty of snow and cold country in Australia, there are almost no trees that shed their leaves in winter, nor do any Australian animals hibernate. Instead there is a far more potent climatic force that Australian life must obey: El Niño.

The cycle of flood and drought that El Niño brings to Australia is profound. Our rivers – even the mighty Murray River, the nation's largest, which runs through the southeast – can be miles wide one year, while you can literally step over its flow the next. This is the power of El Niño, and its effect, when combined with Australia's poor soils, manifests itself compellingly. As you might expect from this, relatively few of Australia's birds are seasonal breeders, and few migrate. Instead, they breed when the rain comes, and a large percentage are nomads, following the rain across the breadth of the continent.

So challenging are conditions in Australia that its birds have developed some extraordinary habits. The kookaburras, magpies and blue wrens you are likely to see – to name just a few – have developed a breeding system called 'helpers at the nest'. The helpers are the young adult birds of previous breedings, which stay with their parents to help bring up the new chicks. Just why they should do this was a mystery until it was realised that conditions in Australia can be so harsh that more than two adult birds are needed to feed the nestlings. This pattern of breeding is very rare in places like Asia, Europe and North America, but it is common in a wide array of Australian birds.

Australia is, of course, famous as being the home of the kangaroo and other marsupials. Unless you visit a wildlife park, such creatures are not easy to see as most are nocturnal. Their lifestyles, however, are exquisitely attuned to Australia's harsh conditions. Have you ever wondered why kangaroos, alone among the world's larger mammals, hop? It turns out that hopping is the most efficient way of getting about at medium speeds.

Left to right:

One of the most familiar small birds of southeastern Australia is the fairy-wren, often known as the 'blue wren'.

ROB DRUMMOND

The kookaburra possesses the most identifiable Australian birdcall.

GRAHAM BELL

The very native koala in a very familiar surroundings at Healesville Sanctuary (p492), Victoria.

JOHN BANAGAN

This is because the energy of the bounce is stored in the tendons of the legs – much like in a pogo-stick – while the intestines bounce up and down like a piston, emptying and filling the lungs without needing to activate the chest muscles. When you travel long distances to find meagre feed, such efficiency is a must.

Marsupials are so efficient that they need to eat a fifth less food than equivalent-sized placental mammals (everything from bats to rats, whales and ourselves). But some marsupials have taken energy efficiency much further. If you get to visit a wildlife park or zoo you might notice that far-away look in a koala's eyes. It seems as if nobody is home – and this in fact is near the truth. Several years ago biologists announced that koalas are the only living creatures that have brains that don't fit their skulls. Instead they have a shrivelled walnut of a brain that rattles around in a fluid-filled cranium. Other researchers have contested this finding, however, pointing out that the brains of the koalas examined for the study may have shrunk because these organs are so soft. Whether soft-brained or empty-headed, there is no doubt that the koala is not the Einstein of the animal world, and we now believe that it has sacrificed its brain to energy efficiency. Brains cost a lot to run – our brains typically weigh 2% of our bodyweight, but use 20% of the energy we consume. Koalas eat gum leaves, which are so toxic that they use 20% of their energy just detoxifying this food. This leaves little energy for the brain, and living in the treetops where there are so few predators means that they can get by with few wits at all.

The peculiar constraints of the Australian environment have not made everything dumb. The koala's nearest relative, the wombat (of which there are three species), have large brains for a marsupial. These creatures live in complex burrows and can weigh up to 35kg, making them the largest herbivorous burrowers on Earth. Because their burrows are effectively air-conditioned, they have the neat trick of turning down their metabolic activity when they are in residence. One physiologist who studied their thyroid hormones found that biological activity ceased to such an extent in sleeping wombats that, from a hormonal point of view, they appeared to be dead! Wombats can remain underground for a week at a time, and can get by on just a third of the food needed by a sheep of equivalent size. One day perhaps, efficiency-minded farmers will keep

DID YOU KNOW?

Despite anything an Australian tells you about koalas (aka dropbears), there is no risk of one falling onto your head (deliberately or not) as you walk beneath the trees.

Pizzey and Knight's *Field Guide to Birds of Australia* is an indispensable guide for bird-watchers, and anyone else even peripherally interested in Australia's feathered tribes. Knight's illustrations are both beautiful and helpful in identification.

The solitary common wombat emerges from its burrow after dark to graze on grasses, herbs and tree roots.

MITCH REARDON

DID YOU KNOW?

Of Australia's 155 species of land snakes, 93 are venomous. Australia is home to something like 10 of the world's 15 most venomous snakes.

wombats instead of sheep. At the moment, however, that isn't possible, for the largest of the wombat species, the northern hairy-nose, is one of the world's rarest creatures, with only around 100 surviving in a remote nature reserve in central Queensland.

One of the more common marsupials you might catch a glimpse of in the national parks around Australia's major cities are the species of antechinus. These nocturnal, rat-sized creatures lead an extraordinary life. The males live for just 11 months, the first 10 of which consist of a concentrated burst of eating and growing. And like teenage males, the day comes when their minds turn to sex, and in the antechinus this becomes an obsession. As they embark on their quest for females they forget to eat and sleep. Instead they gather in logs and woo passing females by serenading them with squeaks. By the end of August – just two weeks after they reach 'puberty' – every single male is dead, exhausted by sex and burdened with carrying around swollen testes. This extraordinary life history may also have evolved in response to Australia's trying environmental conditions. It seems likely that if the males survived mating, they would compete with the females as they tried to find enough food to feed their growing young. Basically, antechinus dads are disposable. They do better for antechinus posterity if they go down in a testosterone-fuelled blaze of glory.

One thing you will see lots of in Australia are reptiles. Snakes are abundant, and they include some of the most venomous species known. Where the opportunities to feed are few and far between, it's best not to give your prey a second chance, hence the potent venom. Around Sydney and other parts of Australia, however, you are far more likely to encounter a harmless python that a dangerously venomous species. Snakes will usually leave you alone if you don't fool with them. Observe, back quietly away and don't panic, and most of the time you'll be OK.

A must see for wildlife watchers is the frilled (or frill-necked) lizard.

GARY STEER

There are about 60 species of banksias in Australia.

DAWN DELANEY

Some visitors mistake lizards for snakes, and indeed some Australian lizards look bizarre. One of the more abundant is the sleepy lizard. These creatures, which are found throughout the southern arid region, look like animated pine cones. They are the Australian equivalent of tortoises, and are harmless. Other lizards are much larger. Unless you visit the Indonesian island of Komodo you will not see a larger lizard than the desert-dwelling perentie. These beautiful creatures with their leopard-like blotches can grow to more than 2m long, and are efficient predators of introduced rabbits, feral cats and the like.

Australia's plants can be irresistibly fascinating. If you happen to be in the Perth area in spring it's well worth taking a wildflower tour. The best flowers grow on the arid and monotonous sand plains, and the blaze of colour produced by the kangaroo paws, banksias and similar native plants can be dizzying. The sheer variety of flowers is amazing, with 4000 species crowded into the southwestern corner of the continent. This diversity of prolific flowering plants has long puzzled botanists. Again, Australia's poor soils seem to be the cause. The sand plain is about the poorest soil in Australia – almost pure quartz. This prevents any one fast-growing species from dominating. Instead, thousands of specialist plant species have learned to find a narrow niche, and so coexist. Some live at the foot of the metre-high sand dunes, some on top, some on an east-facing slope, some on the west and so on. Their flowers need to be striking in order to attract pollinators, for nutrients are so lacking in this sandy world that even insects like bees are rare.

If you do get to walk the wildflower regions of the southwest, keep your eyes open for the sundews. Australia is the centre of diversity for these beautiful, carnivorous plants. They've given up on the soil supplying their nutritional needs and have turned instead to trapping insects with the sweet globs of moisture on their leaves, and digesting them to obtain nitrogen and phosphorus.

If you are very lucky, you might see a honey possum. This tiny marsupial is an enigma. Somehow it gets all of its dietary requirements from nectar and pollen, and in the southwest there are always enough flowers around for it to survive. No-one, though, knows why the males need sperm larger even than those of the blue whale, or why their testes are so massive. Were humans as well endowed, men would be walking around with the equivalent of a 4kg bag of potatoes between their legs!

H Cogger's *Reptiles and Amphibians of Australia* is a bible to those interested in Australia's reptiles, including its goodly assortment of venomous snakes, and useful protection for those who are definitely not. This large volume will allow you to identify the species, and you can wield it as a defensive weapon if necessary.

NATIONAL & STATE PARKS

Australia has more than 500 national parks – nonurban protected wilderness areas of environmental or natural importance. Each state defines and runs its own national parks, but the principle is the same throughout Australia. National parks include rainforests, vast tracts of empty outback, strips of coastal dune land and rugged mountain ranges.

Public access is encouraged as long as safety and conservation regulations are observed. In all parks you're asked to do nothing to damage or alter the natural environment. Camping grounds (often with toilets and showers), walking tracks and information centres are often provided for visitors. In most national parks there are restrictions on bringing in pets.

Some national parks are so isolated, rugged or uninviting that you wouldn't want to go there unless you were an experienced bushwalker or 4WD traveller. Other parks, however, are among Australia's major attractions.

State parks and state forests are other forms of nature reserves, owned by state governments and with fewer regulations than national parks. Although state forests can be logged, they are often recreational areas

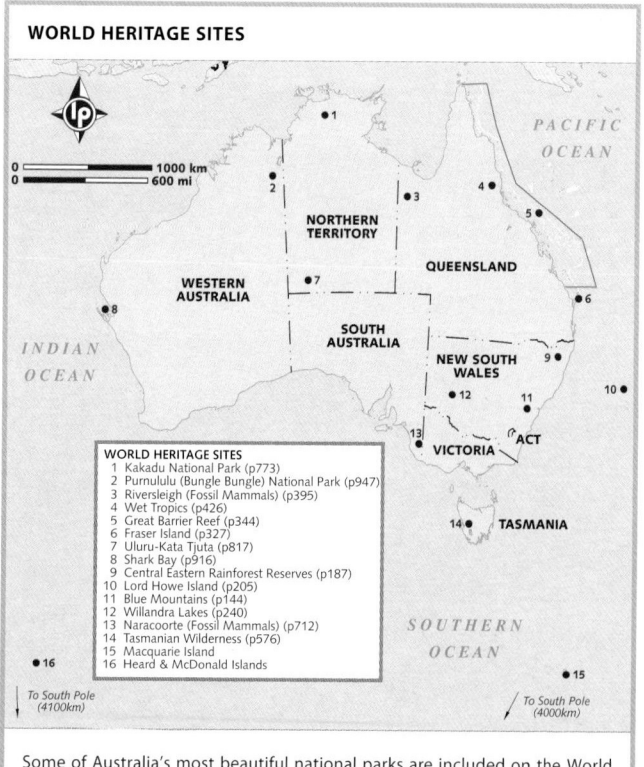

WORLD HERITAGE SITES

PACIFIC OCEAN

0 — 1000 km
0 — 600 mi

NORTHERN TERRITORY

WESTERN AUSTRALIA

QUEENSLAND

SOUTH AUSTRALIA

NEW SOUTH WALES

INDIAN OCEAN

ACT

VICTORIA

TASMANIA

WORLD HERITAGE SITES
1 Kakadu National Park (p773)
2 Purnululu (Bungle Bungle) National Park (p947)
3 Riversleigh (Fossil Mammals) (p395)
4 Wet Tropics (p426)
5 Great Barrier Reef (p344)
6 Fraser Island (p327)
7 Uluru-Kata Tjuta (p817)
8 Shark Bay (p916)
9 Central Eastern Rainforest Reserves (p187)
10 Lord Howe Island (p205)
11 Blue Mountains (p144)
12 Willandra Lakes (p240)
13 Naracoorte (Fossil Mammals) (p712)
14 Tasmanian Wilderness (p576)
15 Macquarie Island
16 Heard & McDonald Islands

SOUTHERN OCEAN

To South Pole (4100km)

To South Pole (4000km)

Right facing page:

Kakadu National Park (p773) is only one of Australia's World Heritage Sites.

TOM BOYDEN

Some of Australia's most beautiful national parks are included on the World Heritage Register (a United Nations register of natural and cultural places of world significance). See http://whc.unesco.org/heritage.htm for more information about these sites.

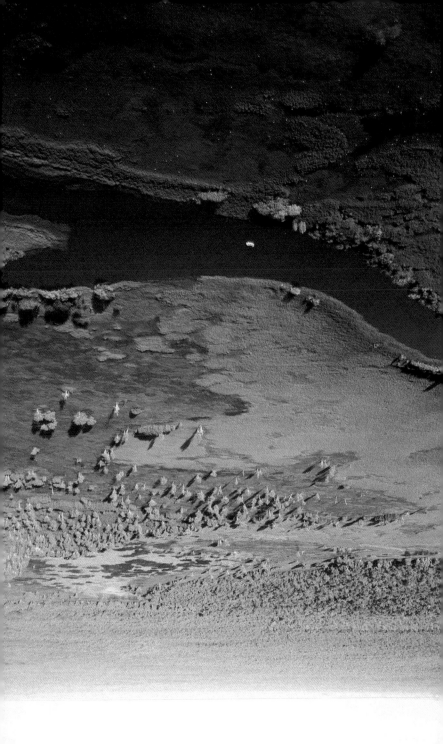

R Strahan's *The Mammals of Australia* is a complete survey of Australia's somewhat cryptic mammals. Every species is illustrated, and almost everything known about them is covered in the individual species accounts, which have been written by the nation's experts.

with camping grounds, walking trails and signposted forest drives. Some permit horses and dogs.

For the addresses of national and state park authorities, see the National Parks section in each state and territory chapter.

WATCHING WILDLIFE

Some regions of Australia offer unique opportunities to see wildlife. One of the most fruitful places is Tasmania. The island is jam-packed with wallabies, wombats and possums, principally because foxes, which have decimated marsupial populations on the mainland, are yet to reach there. It is also home to the Tasmanian devil – our Australian hyena but less than a third the size of its African ecological counterpart. They're common on the island. In some national parks you can watch them tear apart road-killed wombats. Their squabbling as they do so is fearsome, the shrieks ear-splitting. It's the nearest thing Australia can offer

The Tasmanian devil is a nocturnal marsupial.

MITCH REARDON

to experiencing a lion kill on the Masai Mara.

For those intrigued by the diversity of tropical rainforests, Queensland's world heritage is well worth visiting. Birds of paradise, cassowaries and a variety of other birds can be seen by day, while at night you can search for tree-kangaroos (yes, some kinds of kangaroos do live in the treetops). In your nocturnal wanderings you are highly likely to see curious possums, some of which look like skunks, and other marsupials that today are restricted to a small area of northeast Queensland. Fossils from as far afield as western Queensland and southern Victoria indicate that such creatures were once widespread.

Australia's deserts are a real hit-and-miss affair as far as wildlife is concerned. If visiting in a drought year, all you might see are dusty plains, the odd mob of kangaroos and emus, and a few struggling trees. Return after big rains, however, and you'll encounter something close to a Garden of Eden. Fields of white and gold daisies stretch endlessly into the distance, perfuming the air. The salt lakes fill with fresh water, and

Emu running through the Pinnacles Desert (p862), Western Australia.

CHRISTOPHER GROENHOUT

Birdlife along a waterway within Kakadu National Park (p773), Northern Territory.
MITCH REARDON

millions of water birds – pelicans, stilts, shags and gulls – can be seen feeding on the superabundant fish and insect life of the waters. It all seems like a mirage, and like a mirage it will vanish as the land dries out, only to spring to life again in a few years or a decade's time. For a more reliable bird spectacular, Kakadu (p773) is well worth a look, especially towards the end of the dry season around November.

The largest creatures found in the Australian region are marine mammals such as whales and seals, and there is no better place to see them than South Australia. In springtime southern right whales crowd into the head of the Great Australian Bight. You can observe them near the remote Aboriginal community of Yatala as they mate, frolic and suckle their young. Kangaroo Island (p692), south of Adelaide, is a fantastic place to see seals and sea lions. There are well-developed visitors centres to facilitate the viewing of wildlife, and nightly penguin parades occur at some places where the adult blue penguins make their nest burrows. Indeed, Kangaroo Island's beaches are magic places, where you're able to stroll among fabulous shells, whale bones and even jewel-like leafy sea dragons amid the sea wrack.

The fantastic diversity of Queensland's Great Barrier Reef is legendary, and a boat trip out to the reef from Cairns or Port Douglas is unforgettable. Just as extraordinary but less well-known is the diversity of Australia's southern waters, for the Great Australian Bight is home to more kinds of marine creatures than anywhere else on earth. A stroll along any of the beaches from Cape Leeuwin at the tip of Western Australia to Tasmania is likely to reveal glimpses of that diversity in the shape of creatures washed up from the depths. The exquisite shells of the paper nautilus are occasionally found on the more remote beaches, where you can walk the white sand for kilometres without seeing another person.

If your visit extends only as far as Sydney, however, don't give up on seeing Australian nature, for the Sydney sandstone – which extends approximately 150km around the city – is one of the most diverse and spectacular regions in Australia. In springtime, spectacular red waratahs abound in the region's parks, while the woody pear (a relative of the waratah) that so confounded the early colonists can also be seen, alongside more than 1500 other species of flowering plants. Even in a Sydney backyard you're likely to see more reptile species (mostly skinks) than can be found in all of Great Britain – so keep an eye out!

T Flannery's *The Future Eaters* is a 'big picture' overview of evolution in Australasia, covering the last 120 million years of history, with thoughts on how the environment has shaped Australasia's human cultures.

ENVIRONMENTAL CHALLENGES

The European colonisation of Australia, commencing in 1788, heralded a period of catastrophic environmental upheaval, with the result that Australians today are struggling with some of the most severe environmental problems to be found anywhere. It may seem strange that a population of just 20 million, living in a continent the size of the USA minus Alaska, could inflict such damage on its environment, but Australia's long isolation, its fragile soils and difficult climate have made it particularly vulnerable to human-induced change.

Damage to Australia's environment has been inflicted in several ways, the most important being the introduction of pest species, destruction of forests, overstocking rangelands, inappropriate agriculture and interference with water flows. Beginning with the escape of domestic cats into the Australian bush shortly after 1788, a plethora of vermin, from foxes to wild camels and cane toads, have run wild in Australia, causing extinctions in the native fauna. One out of every 10 native mammals living in Australia prior to European colonisation is now extinct, and many more are highly endangered. Extinctions have also affected native plants, birds and amphibians.

The destruction of forests has also had a profound effect. Most of Australia's rainforests have suffered clearing, while conservationists fight with loggers over the fate of the last unprotected stands of 'old growth'. Many Australian rangelands have been chronically overstocked for more than a century, the result being extreme vulnerability of both soils and rural economies to Australia's drought and flood cycle, as well as extinction of many native species. The development of agriculture has involved land clearance and the provision of irrigation, and here again the effect has been profound. Clearing of the diverse and spectacular plant communities of the Western Australian wheatbelt began just a century ago, yet today up to one-third of that country is degraded by salination of the soils. Between 70kg and 120kg of salt lies below every square metre of the region, and clearing of native vegetation has allowed water to penetrate deep into the soil, dissolving the salt crystals and carrying brine towards the surface.

In terms of financial value, just 1.5% of Australia's land surface provides over 95% of agricultural yield, and much of this land lies in the irrigated regions of the Murray-Darling Basin. This is Australia's agricultural heartland, yet it too is under severe threat from salting of soils and rivers. Irrigation water penetrates into the sediments laid down in an ancient sea, carrying salt into the catchments and fields. If nothing is done, the lower Murray River will become too salty to drink in a decade or two, threatening the water supply of Adelaide, a city of over a million people.

Despite the enormity of the biological crisis engulfing Australia, governments and the community have been slow to respond. It was in the 1980s that coordinated action began to take place, but not until the '90s that major steps were taken. The establishment of Landcare (an organisation enabling people to effectively address local environmental issues; www.landcareaustralia.com.au) and the expenditure of $2.5 billion through the National Heritage Trust Fund have been important national initiatives. Yet so difficult are some of the issues the nation faces that, as yet, little has been achieved in terms of halting the destructive processes. Individuals are also banding together to help. Groups like the Australian Bush Heritage Fund (www.bushheritage.asn.au) and the Australian Wildlife Conservancy (AWC; www.australianwildlife.org) allow people to donate funds and time to the conservation of native species. Some such groups have been spectacularly successful; the AWC, for example, already manages many endangered species over its 1.3 million acre holdings.

So severe are Australia's problems that it will take a revolution before they can be overcome, for sustainable practices need to be implemented in every arena of life – from farms to suburbs and city centres. Renewable energy, sustainable agriculture and water use lie at the heart of these changes, and Australians are only now developing the road-map to sustainability that they so desperately need if they are to have a long-term future on the continent.

Under threat – the Murray River.
JOHN HAY

The Culture by Verity Campbell

NATIONAL PSYCHE
Colonisation & Myth-Making

Australia's national identity is rooted in its past. The seminal times of the colony were characterised by extreme hardship, resentment at being sent so far with so little, and an incalculable sense of loss of loved ones and homes left behind. To cope with this struggle against nature and tyranny, Australians forged a culture based on the principles of a 'fair go' and back-slaps for challenges to authority, and told stories of the Aussie 'battler' that were passed down through generations.

The Eureka Stockade (1854), one of Australia's first anti-authoritarian struggles, saw miners, or 'diggers', rising up against what they saw as unjust gold-mining licences. Ultimately the miners won out, but not before great loss of life. Some chose to see this battle as an age-old clash between the poor Irish Catholics and the ruling English Protestants, this time on foreign soil where the Irish had come to start life afresh and had no intention of returning to the status quo of old Britain.

The next major challenge to the Brits came with Gallipoli, fought on Turkish soil during WWI. The Australian and New Zealander contingent, the Anzacs', lost their bloodied conflict, and blamed the Brits for sending them to fight an unwinnable battle. The Anzacs were revered as heroic battlers, remembered as those who showed the British and Europeans that Australians weren't just parochial colonials, but tough Aussies, fighting with courage, honour and tenacity.

Ned Kelly is another of Australia's beloved heroes. He's become a rich subject for artistic exploration of Australian identity through literature (p67), cinema (the so-so *Ned Kelly*, 2003, is only one of a number of screen adaptations; see p65) and painting (p69). Was Ned a thief and murderer, or a poor Irish hero, railing against a society diseased with injustice and poverty? Most Australians prefer to believe the latter account, of Ned as a true-blue Aussie battler, striving for equality and justice – and handsome to boot.

The colonial battle with the parched land has been relived through tales of valour and misfortune. The much-told story of Burke and Wills' infamous crossing of the continent ended in failure. The ironic twist was an illuminating illustration of the colonialists lack of connection with the Australian landscape: they died of starvation surrounded by 'bush' food. For more information about Burke and Wills, see p741. Since then there have been various stories of tamings of the bush: the films *Crocodile Dundee* and the *Crocodile Hunter*, for example, both depict dinky-di Aussies mud-wrestling crocodiles in the 'wilds' of the bush. These stereotypes celebrate a nostalgia and romanticism for the 'heroism' of the early white settlers.

Reality Check

Immigration has had a huge effect on Australian culture, as migrants have brought their own stories, cultures and myths to meld with those of the colonial 'battler'. Many migrants have come with a huge sense of hope and expectancy, to start life afresh. Colonial history has been revisited through art, literature and cinema, and as a result, the iconic 'battler' has become less relevant. And there's a long-overdue acknowledgment that the original inhabitants of this country are fundamental to a true definition of Australian culture today.

Melbourne-based writer Verity Campbell wrote this Culture chapter. Verity is an avid cinema-goer, reads copious amounts of contemporary fiction – much of it Australian – and is an amateur collector of contemporary visual art – all of it Australian. The lists of great Australian books, bands and films occasioned many rowdy dinner parties, and Verity thanks all those people who contributed their personal 'best ofs' – though she's not sure if she used any of them.

ASYLUM SEEKERS & MANDATORY DETENTION *by Julian Burnside*

The issue of asylum seekers and refugees has dominated media headlines in Australia in recent years. Despite the fact that these people are the most powerless people on the face of the earth, the tiny number of refugees reaching Australia has become a prominent issue in Australian politics. This is because refugee-bashing seems – shockingly – to win votes.

Asylum seekers who arrive without papers are kept in detention, without charge, until they are either given a visa or deported. This process may take many months, or even years. Whilst it proceeds, these already traumatised, isolated people languish behind razor wire (literally) in extremely harsh conditions.

Australia is the only country in the world to pursue a policy of mandatory, automatic and indefinite detention without real access to court challenge.

History

Modern Australia was founded by immigration in 1788. Only Aborigines, 1% of the country's population, can trace their Australian antecedents further than 215 years. Despite this, Australia's history regarding refugees and immigration is not a noble one.

Australia's 'White Australia' policy (p40) of 1901 (not fully removed until 1973) was based on the expectation that Australia's indigenous population would 'naturally' die out, and involved the introduction of a dictation test for potential immigrants that effectively blocked the immigration of non-Europeans.

In 1938 Australian participation in the Evian conference called by Franklin Roosevelt to discuss the fate of Jewish refugees ended when Australia's representative walked out, saying 'We have no racial problems in Australia and no desire to import any.'

In 1993 the (Labor) government introduced a system of mandatory detention for 'informal arrivals'. 'Boat people' (as they became known) – people principally from Vietnam who had hitherto been received with compassion – were now to be locked up, without trial, until their claims for asylum could be determined.

The 1996 election of John Howard's Liberal coalition, in which race featured strongly because of the extreme right-wing One Nation party, led to a marked increase in the stridency of utterances about refugee policy.

Mandatory Detention

Refugees are the only people in Australia who can be imprisoned indefinitely regardless of the fact that they have not committed any offence. Unlike convicted criminals, who know when their sentences will end, refugees are given no sentence. A refugee's life in detention is characterised by the desperate uncertainty and hopelessness of not knowing how long they will be held there.

Manipulating Public Opinion

The government seeks to reduce opposition to its policy of indefinite detention by holding the majority of asylum seekers in the most remote and inhospitable parts of the country. In this way the chance of refugees being noticed, and identified as human beings in distress, is greatly reduced. In addition, the media is banned from entering detention centres (on the dubious grounds of upholding the inmates' 'privacy'). Members of the public who contradict the government's views are branded elitists, traitors or fools.

The government sought to manipulate public opinion on asylum seekers during the election campaign of November 2001, particularly with the so-called *Tampa* and 'children overboard' affairs (p43). After the *Tampa* incident the government instigated the 'Pacific Solution', in which refugees are packed off to detention in Nauru and Papua New Guinea.

The government demonises asylum seekers by dubbing them 'illegals', thus suggesting they are criminals. In fact, people who arrive in Australia informally are not 'illegal'. They have a right under international conventions to seek asylum in any place they can reach.

Asylum seekers commit no offence by arriving without papers, without an invitation, to seek Australia's protection. Significantly, informal arrivals are not charged with an offence by arriving as they do: they are simply placed in detention.

The government also seeks to alarm the public about the numbers of refugees seeking asylum in Australia. In fact, it is extremely difficult (and dangerous) to reach Australia in a small, leaking boat, and only a tiny number of asylum seekers has managed it. By contrast, countries adjacent to the world's trouble spots have hundreds of thousands of refugees coming across their borders – and yet they cope. To put this in context, consider that Africa has a total of 5½ million refugees, and Asia has about 8½ million. At the time of the *Tampa* incident (August 2001), the largest number of informal asylum seekers reaching Australia in any one year was 4100: and most of them were people fleeing the Taliban or Saddam Hussein.

The Process

When a person arrives in Australia and seeks asylum, they tell their story to an officer of the Department of Immigration & Multicultural & Indigenous Affairs (DIMIA). That officer decides whether to believe the story and, if so, whether the story constitutes a valid claim for refugee status. If applicants are knocked back, they can appeal to a member of the Refugee Review Tribunal (RRT).

While asylum seekers try to overturn rulings of the RRT, they remain in detention. It is difficult to imagine the sense of injustice they suffer during the months or years it takes to challenge the RRT. These are generally people who have fled the worst regimes in the world: places where injustice and oppression and arbitrary detention are normal. After a few months of tangling with the Australian system, many asylum seekers come to the view that our regime is as bad as the one they escaped.

Informal arrivals to Australia, if successful in their claim for asylum, receive a three-year Temporary Protection Visa (TPV) rather than a Permanent Protection Visa. TPV holders are treated by the government in such a way as to render Australia less attractive to people seeking to enter illegally and claim asylum in the country. They are ineligible for most government programs, including federally funded employment programs and services such as English-language tuition. They cannot leave the country and re-enter it, even if their family is held elsewhere (eg in Australian detention in Nauru or Papua New Guinea). And if the department considers that circumstances at home are such that the fear of persecution has been reduced to an acceptable level, the TPV holder will be sent home.

The Situation Today

At the time of writing the number of asylum seekers held in detention was around 800, including 139 children. Hundreds of these refugees have been held for more than 12 months. Those who cannot be returned to their homelands due to a lack of diplomatic arrangements have been held for three or even four years. Another 500, approximately, are held in Nauru. Of those in Nauru there are 80 who for many months have been acknowledged as refugees but who remain locked up on one of the remotest islands on the planet. Like the prisoners held in Guantanamo by the USA following the Afghanistan war, these people are incarcerated without trial and isolated from any legal help; unlike those in Guantanamo, they are not suspected of any offence at all.

From Nothing to Zero

From Nothing to Zero was published by Lonely Planet in May 2003. The book presents extracts from letters written by refugees held in Australia's detention centres, and is the outcome of a letter-writing campaign that involved thousands of ordinary Australians nationwide. The book provides first-person descriptions of the horrendous journeys undertaken by refugees in order to escape persecution at home. It describes the refugees' treatment on arrival in Australia, the impressions of children held in detention and of asylum seekers held on islands as part of the 'Pacific Solution'. The book also details day to day life in detention and reveals the refugees' thoughts about Australia and its government.

From Nothing to Zero reveals the human consequences of Australia's policy of mandatory detention. These letters show powerfully the one thing the government wants us to forget: that the people behind the razor wire are human beings.

All profits from the sale of *From Nothing to Zero* go to the Refugee & Immigration Legal Centre and the Asylum Seeker Resource Centre, Footscray, in Melbourne.

Julian Burnside is a Melbourne-based Queen's Counsel and human rights advocate. Julian acted as counsel for Liberty Victoria for the Tampa asylum seekers and for the Woomera escapees. Julian and his wife, Kate Durham, established the Spare Rooms for Refugees campaign (www.spareroomsforrefugees.com), designed to encourage practical support for refugees within the Australian community.

The immense prosperity the landscape has given has forged the title 'lucky country', the land of opportunity, and for most Australians this rings true. Australians enjoy a sophisticated, modern society with immense variety, a global focus, if not a regional one, and a sense of optimism, if tempered by world events.

Although there is some truth in the worn stereotypes that Australians are open-minded, down-to-earth, big-hearted, laconic, larrikin-minded, egalitarian and honest, these definitions are largely one-dimensional, often derived from colonial times. Australian culture is much richer for its indigenous heritage and its multicultural mix. So while on your travels in Australia you may hear 'g'day' from an Akubra-wearing, laconic, whiskery-chinned bush larrikin, his voice will be but one among many. This exciting time of redefinition for multicultural Australia will throw up unexpected people and experiences in your path. It's a young culture melding with the oldest culture in the world; and the incredibly rich opportunities are only starting to be realised.

LIFESTYLE

Australians have been sold to the world as outdoorsy, sporty, big-drinking, croc-wrestling, thigh-slapping country folk, but despite the stereotypes, you could count the number of Australians that wrestle crocodiles on one hand, most Australians can barely swim a lap and many wouldn't be seen dead in an Akubra hat. Peek into the Australian lounge room and you may be surprised with what you find.

ABORIGINAL SPIRITUALITY

Early European settlers and explorers usually dismissed all Aborigines as 'savages' and 'barbarians'. It was some time before the Aboriginal people's deep, spiritual bond with the land, and their relationship to it, began to be understood by white Australians.

Traditional Aboriginal religious beliefs centre on the continuing existence of spirit beings that lived on earth during creation time (or Dreamtime), which occurred before the arrival of humans. These beings created all the features of the natural world and were the ancestors of all living things. They took different forms but behaved as people do, and as they travelled about they left signs to show where they had passed.

Despite being supernatural, the ancestors were subject to ageing and eventually returned to the sleep from which they'd awoken at the dawn of time. Here their spirits remain as eternal forces that breathe life into the newborn and influence natural events. Each ancestor's spiritual energy flows along the path it travelled during the Dreamtime and is strongest at the points where it left physical evidence of its activities, such as a tree, hill or claypan. These features are called 'sacred sites'. These days the importance of sacred sites is more widely recognised among the non-Aboriginal community, and most state governments have legislated to give these sites a measure of protection.

Every person, animal and plant is believed to have two souls – one mortal and one immortal. The latter is part of a particular ancestral spirit and returns to the sacred sites of that ancestor after death, while the mortal soul simply fades into oblivion. Each person is spiritually bound to the sacred sites that mark the land associated with his or her spirit ancestor. It is the individual's obligation to help care for these sites by performing the necessary rituals and singing the songs that tell of the ancestor's deeds. By doing this, the order created by that ancestor is maintained.

The links between the people and their spirit ancestors are totems, each person having their own totem, or Dreaming. These totems take many forms, such as trees, caterpillars, snakes, fish and magpies. Songs explain how the landscape contains these powerful creator ancestors, who can exert either a benign or a malevolent influence. They also have a practical meaning: telling of the best places and the best times to hunt, and where to find water in drought years. They can also specify kinship relations and identify correct marriage partners.

SIX O'CLOCK CLOSING *by Eddie Butler-Bowdon*

During WWI hotels were forced to close at 6pm; the law stayed in place until the post-war era. Over the last hour of trading the tempo would reach fever pitch. Men would 'shout' (buy) their 'school' (drinking mates) a 'round' (a beer each) and virtually 'skull' (drink very fast). As the hands on the pub clock drew to a single vertical line, the barman or barmaid called for 'Last drinks', soon followed by 'Time gentlemen, time' – it was time to swallow what was left and stumble home to 'the trouble and strife' (wife) where a 'blue' (fight) sometimes ensued.

The 'Australian Dream' has long been to own an overgrown house on a quarter-acre block, so sprawling suburbia is endemic in Australian towns and cities. Inside the average middle-class suburban home, you'll probably find a married heterosexual couple, though it is becoming increasingly likely they will be defacto, or in their second marriage. Gay marriage is not sanctioned by law in Australia, but most Australians are open-minded about homosexuality, especially in the Gay mecca, Sydney – see Gay & Lesbian Travellers (p967) for more information.

Our 'Dad and Mum' couple will have an average of 1.4 children, probably called Joshua and Chloe, Australia's names of the moment (and yes, Kylie is still popular). The average gross wage of either parent is probably around $A899 per week (compared to the UK's average of A$1160).

Our typical family, like most Australians, probably loves the sun. Australians have the highest rate of skin cancer in the world, with one in two people affected. Our family drags a caravan off to the beach every holiday, and on weekends they probably watch sport, go to the movies or head to the shops. However, don't get the idea that they're particularly active! Despite their love of the outdoors, recent studies show Australians are couch potatoes, with up to 60% of the population obese or overweight (figures just behind the US, world leaders in failing the pinch test). For more detail on Australians and their obsession with watching sports, see the boxed text 'Sporting Australia' (p62).

Our family not only travels domestically, they also love to travel overseas. It's probably fair to say that Australia has produced some of the most successful travel businesses in the world: Flight Centre, Intrepid and Lonely Planet, to name just a few. And our couple like a few quiet ones up the pub, though despite the long-held reputation that Australians are boozers, recent figures show they drink less than Brits and are way behind the world's leaders, Luxembourgers. Today wine is the number one drink of choice. For more on Australia's drinking habits in the old days, see the boxed text 'Six O'Clock Closing' (above).

'At the last Census (2001) some 23% of the population were foreign-born'

POPULATION & DEMOGRAPHICS

Australia has been strongly influenced by immigration, and its multicultural mix is among the most diverse in the world. At the last Census (2001) some 23% of the population were foreign-born, compared with an estimated 11.5% in the US. Many foreign-born Australians came from Italy and Greece after WWII, but recent immigrants have mostly come from New Zealand and the UK, and from China, Vietnam, Africa and India, among many other places. Some 2.2% of the population identify as being of Aboriginal origin; most of them living in the Northern Territory, which has, not coincidentally, the lowest life expectancy rates in the country. Australia's other indigenous people, Torres Strait Islanders, are primarily a Melanesian people, living in north Queensland and on the islands of the Torres Strait between Cape York and Papua New Guinea.

SPORTING AUSTRALIA *by Tony Wilson*

Not every Australian loves sport. For a while we even had a prime minister who didn't. Paul Keating loved polished furniture, Mahler and 17th-century French clocks. Nevertheless, as a politician, he knew which way the numbers fell. It was a joy to watch Keating watch sport. Smile chiselled in place. Turning up when he had to. Cheering just after everyone else.

Other prime ministers have been more at one with the national obsession. Most famously of all, former prime minister Bob Hawke, on the morning in 1983 when *Australia II* finally won the America's Cup, wafted his champagne glass to a waking public and declared that 'any boss who sacks anyone for not coming to work today is a bum.'

In 2001 Saul Eslake, an economist, warned that Australia 'is obsessed by sport and almost completely indifferent to success in any other field. Including, in particular, success in business.'

Eslake has a point. When the British 'Barmy Army' recently came to these shores for an Ashes cricket tour, they sang a song 'Three dollars to the pound', as though Australians would suddenly turn away from 15 years of glorious on-field domination to think about the FTSE. Rightly or wrongly, Australian national pride is tied up in sporting success. Politicians know this, which explains why, as a percentage of GDP, Australia splashes more money on elite sports funding than just about any other country on Earth.

Strangely, for all this national pride, the number one most-watched sport in Australia is a local one. **Australian Rules football** (p480) is like tribal warfare. Around Melbourne you can quickly pass through Carlton, Collingwood, Hawthorn, North Melbourne, Footscray, Essendon, Richmond and St Kilda – all of which have a team in the elite Australian Football League (AFL; www.afl.com.au). Once this league was exclusively Victorian, but since 1982 it has expanded nationally. It will pain most Victorians to admit it, but between 1992 and 2002, interstate teams won the premiership six times. Interestingly, on each of these occasions, the interstate coach wore a moustache.

The most spectacular aspects of the game are the long kicking, the high marking, and the brutal collisions (shirtfronts) that nobody likes to see ('blah blah, safety of the players blah blah'), but that nevertheless get replayed 10 times on the evening news. One champion player, Leigh Matthews (now Brisbane's coach), once stunned an opponent by cupping his hand under his bloodied nose before drinking his own blood.

There are some people (in New South Wales and Queensland, generally) who will argue that **rugby league** is the national football code. The best way to deal with these types is to quietly tell them that they're wrong. Sometimes they'll be stocky types with forearms like Christmas hams, in which event I'd ask that you not cite me as your source.

If, however, very large men laying very large tackles is your thing, a National Rugby League (NRL) game (www.nrl.com.au) will deliver (see p132 for more information). Unlike AFL, players represent their states (NSW or Qld) in the annual State of Origin series. To see one of these games is to acquire a terrifying appreciation of Newton's laws of motion: a force travelling in one direction can only be stopped with the application of an equal and opposite force. Ouch. There are also international games, although they might as well be called 'Australia versus North England', or 'Australia versus New Zealanders who can't play union'.

Historically, **rugby union** was an amateur sport played by 'our sort of people, old chap' and its century-long rivalry with professional rugby league was the closest thing sport had to a clash of ideologies. In 1995, however, rugby turned professional and after years of 'defections' to league, the trend reversed with league stars such as Wendall Sailor and Lote Tuqiri crossing the fence to union.

The Wallabies is the national team. Apart from the World Cup, Bledisloe Cup matches against New Zealand are the most anticipated fixtures (it's great watching the Australians determinedly not watching the All Blacks' *haka*) and form part of a Tri-Nations tournament that also includes South Africa. Australia also has three teams in the Super 12s: the Waratahs (Sydney), the Reds (Brisbane) and the Brumbies (ACT). See www.rugby.com.au for match schedules.

Australia is a nation of swimmers. Whereas any of you could be taken by a shark at any moment, we parry them away with skill and finesse. OK, that might be a bit of a stretch, but girt by sea and public pools, and with **swimming** on school curriculums, Australians can swim.

Swim stars are our cereal-box celebrities, and currently Ian Thorpe and Grant Hackett are the best. Both have won Olympic gold medals and both have broken world records. In post-race interviews they are rarely as out of breath as an average person laden with heavy shopping.

The English (or possibly the French) invented **cricket**, and it's beautiful *(c'est magnifique)*. For a newcomer to the sport, perhaps the best advice is not to expect too much action. Like baseball, cricket is about accumulation. It can build to soaring crescendos, but sometimes it doesn't – so bring a good book. Until the 1930s, Test matches could last up to nine days with no result, but through the Geneva Convention, they were cut back to a maximum of five. Today, there is huge interest in a form of the game called one-day cricket, which appears at first glance to be more entertaining. It is also at these games that spectators are more likely to throw food.

At the time of writing, Australian teams are the best in the world at both Test and one-day cricket. The men have not lost the Ashes to England since 1987. If you're English and wish to avoid talking about this uncomfortable fact, it's recommended you consider travelling around Australia as a mute.

Come January, somebody usually fries an egg on court at Melbourne Park, just to show that you can. The Australian Open (www.ausopen.com.au) is one of **tennis'** four Grand Slams. Up to half a million people watch day and night matches, and the Rod Laver Arena (named after the only man to win two Grand Slams – 1962 and 1969) was the first stadium in the world to develop a retractable roof.

Lleyton Hewitt is now the great hope, having won both Wimbledon and the US Open. His relentless shouting of quotes from *Rocky* movies, however, does bring him detractors, and many locals reminisce fondly about Patrick Rafter, a dual major winner. Both Hewitt and Rafter have tasted success in the Davis Cup. At the time of writing, Australia has 28 titles, second after the USA on 31.

Australian **soccer** still has to cope with *that day* in 1997, when in the dying stages we conceded two goals to Iran to squander a spot at the World Cup finals in France. The Socceroos have only qualified once, in 1974 (when England didn't!), but for a few weeks in 2003 FIFA allocated the Oceania region a full spot in the 2006 World Cup. It looked like we'd only have to get over traditional soccer powers like the Cook Islands and American Samoa to get to Germany. Eventually, though, the FIFA vote was ruled offside, and Australian soccer supporters got back to being miserable.

Locally, the National Soccer League (www.socceraustralia.com.au) is improving, although the best players (like Harry Kewell) are destined to chase the better competition, contracts and mineral water on offer in Europe.

On the first Tuesday in November, the nation stops for a **horse race**, the Melbourne Cup (www.racingvictoria.net.au). It is a handicap run over 3200m, and in Melbourne, Cup Day is a public holiday (strange but true). Our most famous Cup winner was called Phar Lap, who won in 1930, before dying of a mystery illness in America. Phar Lap is now stuffed (even more so than he was after carrying 10 stone over two miles), and is a prize exhibit at the Melbourne Museum (p452).

There are 1.2 million netballers in the country, which makes **netball** Australia's most popular participation sport (www.netball.asn.au). Internationally, Australia has been dominant, winning World Championships a plenty (although not the most recent one). And now socially, mixed netball is growing in popularity, one theory being that if you're going to do your knee, you might as well do it while meeting members of the opposite sex.

The list of sports could go on. From **hockey** (www.hockey.org.au) to the Bells Beach **Surf Classic** (www.surfingaustralia.com) to the spectacular Sydney to Hobart **yacht race**, beginning on Boxing Day in Sydney Harbour (http://rolexsydneyhobart.com). From the **Formula One** Grand Prix (www.grandprix.com.au) to **basketball** (www.nbl.com.au; www.wnbl.com.au) to **greyhound racing** and its failed flirtation with monkey jockeys in the 1930s (this is true, the monkeys used their tails as whips!). There is something for every sporting taste in Australia. Paul Keating will tell you that there is also something here for fans of 17th-century French clocks, and there is. Even if the TV coverage isn't quite as extensive.

Tony, a freelance writer based in Melbourne, has worked in print, radio and TV as well as playing in the Hawthorn FC (Australian rules) reserves.

Internal migration is a major factor too, with Queensland experiencing the highest growth of any state or territory as Australians follow the sun. Australians love to travel overseas, too, and many don't come home; at last count 900,000 Aussies were setting up home abroad – that's a huge number when you consider the total population.

The most recent Census (2001) counted some 18,970,000 people in Australia, with a whopping 64% living in the cities. Population density is the lowest in the world, with an average of 2.5 people per square kilometre – no-one's within cooee in the outback. Most people live along the eastern seaboard, between Melbourne and Brisbane, with a smaller concentration on the coastal region in and around Perth. Despite the extraordinarily low population density, population policy is fiercely debated in Australia. Opponents of increased immigration argue the dry Australian landscape can't sustain more people (just one of their arguments); others say population growth is an economic imperative, particularly considering Australia's declining birthrates.

'at last count 900,000 Aussies were setting up home abroad'

RELIGION

Some 16% of Australians described themselves as having no religion in the 2001 Census. The largest religious affiliations in the country were Catholic (27%), Anglican (21%), other Christian denominations (21%), with non-Christian religions including Buddhism (2%) and Islam (1.5%) making up 5% of Australians. Buddhism is Australia's fastest growing religion, up 79% since the last Census (1996). The largest Buddhist temple in the southern hemisphere is in Wollongong. See the boxed text 'Aboriginal Spirituality' (p60) for information on traditional Aboriginal spiritual beliefs.

ARTS

Australians are known for having a love affair with sport and little more than a fleeting attraction to the arts, but statistics tell otherwise. Australia Council for the Arts figures show Australians love the arts, with attendance figures for galleries or performing arts almost double that for all codes of football (though of course seasonal factors and television coverage of sport has an effect on attendance figures). Cinema is the top pursuit, with 67% of the population lining up for flicks and popcorn annually. Bookworms all over Australia fork out about $1 billion on books each year, around 25% of Australians attend a music concert annually, and some 21% of Australians gallery-hop. All in all Australia has a thriving arts scene.

Cinema

Most people need little introduction to Australia's vibrant movie industry, one of the first established in the world and playground for screen greats Errol Flynn, 'our' Nicole (Kidman) and come-hither-eyed Russell Crowe (born in New Zealand, but who's trifling over details?).

The industry really kicked off when social upheaval and cultural re-examination in the '60s and '70s led to the establishment of the Australian Film Commission, a cinematic forum for Australians to thrash out issues of identity. *Walkabout*, in the early '70s, was one of the first films to explore indigenous Australia. Other films focused on revisiting colonisation, war and the country's relationship to England, such as *Gallipoli* and *Breaker Morant*, which mythologised the gung-ho Aussie male as pawn to the British Empire. *Mad Max* and *Mad Max II* were genre-busters, and box-office hits that did well overseas – to everyone's surprise.

A CELEBRATION OF AUSTRALIAN FILM

Aussie Kitsch

Muriel's Wedding (1994, director PJ Hogan) From bouquet bitch-fight to phoney marriage, the bumpy ride towards self-discovery for ABBA-devotee, Muriel, is utterly hilarious one minute and despairingly bleak the next. A timeless celebration of kitsch.

The Castle (1997, director Rob Sitch) 'Darryl vs Goliath': this feel-good comedy pits a lovable, larrikin Dad (Darryl) against greedy developers. All-Australian stereotypes are poked fun at here through icons and vernacular – non-Aussies may find some parts a bit hard to follow.

Box-Office Hits

Mad Max II (1981, director George Miller) Don't miss this awesome best film of the cult-classic *Mad Max* trilogy, one of the best action movies ever produced. This timeless classic has ouch after ouch of mind-blowing stunts in a convincing futuristic waste land. *Mad Max* (1979) is equally good, if you can excuse the appalling soundtrack. *Mad Max III* (1985) is, ahem, well anyway, stay tuned for *Mad Max IV*.

Crocodile Dundee (1986, director Peter Faiman) Box-office blitzer ticks every cliche in the book during this budding romance between the New York glamour-puss (wearing a G-string in the outback, if you don't mind) and the backward bush larrikin (yawn).

Crocodile Hunter: Collision Course (2002, director John Stainton) Much better than Crocodile Dundee and relies on fewer cultural and gender stereotypes. The sincere wide-eyed enthusiasm of Steve Irwin is infectious – crikey!

Indigenous Stories

The Tracker (2002, director Rolf de Heer) Beautiful cinematography segues paintings with the haunting voice of indigenous musician Archie Roach. Racism and paternalism in Australia's brutal colonial history are explored in this layered fugitive-finding story. Excellent.

Beneath Clouds (2001, director Ivan Sen) Brutally honest look at contemporary indigenous life, through the eyes of monosyllabic teens on a road journey. Even-handed, mature and intelligent – an inspiring debut by its indigenous director.

Walkabout (1971, director Nicholas Roeg) Poetic meditation on white and indigenous kinship to their land, city or outback, and each other, with quirky cinematographic features and an underlying sensuality.

This mesmerising, if wandering and sometimes plodding film is a cult classic.

Rabbit-Proof Fence (2002, director Phillip Noyce) This true story follows three sisters on their remarkable 2400 kilometre journey home along the rabbit-proof fence. An important history lesson and addition to the Stolen Generations discourse.

Human Dimensions

Bliss (1985, director Ray Lawrence) Kooky, sexual romp through the life of Harry Joy, advertising exec and spineless twot, and his appalling family.

Bad Boy Bubby (1994, director Rolf de Heer) Sick mother, twisted son, this cult classic will have you squirming in your seat.

Lantana (2001, director Ray Lawrence) Warts-and-all analysis of love, trust and betrayal in relationships, so well conceived and believable it could be happening right next door. An excellent example of the Australian drama genre that offers mature analysis of the human condition.

Head On (2001, director Ana Kokkinos) Young, gay, dealing with his strict Greek upbringing, and way off the rails, this 24-hour glimpse into Ari's life is bleak, relentless but compelling.

Myth or Reality

Few could deny that messages portrayed in films can inform the sense of identity of a nation; films reach wide markets and the messages are often easily digested. For an understanding of the seminal moments in the development of Australia's national psyche, watch these important Australian films:

Breaker Morant (1980, director Bruce Beresford) War crimes and justice are examined in this Beresford masterpiece, set during the late stages of the Boer War. It's based on the story of Lieutenant Harry Morant, hero or scapegoat of the British Empire, depending on your take.

Ned Kelly (2003, director Gregor Jordan) Pure eye candy with the exquisite landscapes, but you can't help feel a bit disappointed with this tepid interpretation of the Kelly story: the predictable romance (yawn), the unconvincing character portraits (especially Fitzpatrick) – and why does Heath Ledger look constipated? Watchable, but no cigar.

Gallipoli (1982, director Peter Weir, screenplay David Williamson) The ultimate Aussie mateship movie, exploring naivety, social pressure to enlist and ultimately the utter futility and human waste of this campaign. Intelligent, understated delivery brings the message home.

Government tax incentives in the early '80s introduced investor-clout, spurring a handful of hopefuls desperate to secure the international success of the *Mad Max* movies. Examples include the appalling *Mad Max III,* and *Crocodile Dundee* – movies that did nothing to hose down stereotypes of stubbled Aussie blokes.

In the late '80s and '90s the spotlight was turned home to the suburban quarter-acre block where the larrikin Aussie battler fought for a 'fair go' in side-splitting satirical celebrations of Australian myths and stereotypes. The best of these were *Muriel's Wedding* and *The Castle*. At the same time delightfully quirky films, such as *Bad Boy Bubby* and the screen adaptation of Peter Carey's *Bliss*, showed Australians could do more than take the piss out of themselves.

The building of Fox Studios Australia (Sydney) and Warner Roadshow Studios on the Gold Coast (Queensland) in the past few years has attracted big-budget US productions such as *Mission Impossible II* and *Moulin Rouge* to the country. While the economic benefits are many, the local industry can only dream of the 80% box-office share that US releases claim in Australia.

In the last few years most films made for an Australian audience have abandoned the worn-out ocker stereotypes and started to explore the country's diversity. Indigenous stories have found a mainstream voice on the big-screen, with films such as *The Tracker, Beneath Clouds* and *Rabbit Proof Fence*, illustrations of a nation starting to come to terms with its racist past and present. Cultural and gender stereotypes continue to erode in a genre of intimate dramas exploring the human dimension, such as *Lantana,* and *Head On,* the latter featuring a gay Greek-Australian as the lead character. By staying relevant to contemporary Australians, the industry continues to survive and thrive.

Literature

Through story and ballads, early postcolonisation literature mythologised the hardships of pioneers and unjust governments. Nationalism was a driving force, especially in the late 1800s with the celebration of the country's centenary (1888) and Federation in 1901. AB 'Banjo' Paterson was *the* bush poet of the time, famous for his poems *The Man from Snowy River, Clancy of the Overflow* and *Waltzing Matilda,* the country's on-again-off-again national anthem. Henry Lawson, a contemporary of Paterson, wrote short stories evoking the era; one of his best, *The Drover's Wife,* is a moving tale of the woman's lot in the settling life. Jeannie Gunn's *We of the Never Never* (1908) explored relations between early pioneers and Aborigines through patronising eyes. All these stories set in stone the desert as 'heart' of a nation, the hardworking Aussie 'battler' as soldier against adversity.

In the postwar era, Australian writers began to re-evaluate their colonial past. Patrick White, arguably Australia's finest novelist and the country's only Nobel Prize winner for Literature to date, helped turn the tables on the earlier writer's fascination with romanticism with *Voss* (see the boxed text 'Essential Australian Holiday Reads'; opposite) and his deeply despair-inducing *The Tree of Man* (1955). Later novelists, such as the Booker-prize winner Thomas Keneally, keenly felt the devastation and rage of the Aborigines, as depicted in his excellent novel *The Chant of Jimmy Blacksmith* (1972), also made into a film.

Australia's literary scene, long dominated by writers of British and Irish descent, has evolved in the last few decades to better reflect the country's multicultural makeup. Indigenous writers tend to focus on coming to terms with identity in often intensely personal autobiographies. Sally

'Waltzing Matilda, the country's on-again-off-again national anthem'

ESSENTIAL AUSTRALIAN HOLIDAY READS

Voss (Patrick White, 1957) By no means a light read, this richly metaphoric, superbly written novel explores the megalomania-fuelled era of exploration, which is contrasted with the starchy English-styled urban life. This honest insight into the colonial exploration era is a masterpiece, and a must for literature devotees.

Remembering Babylon (David Malouf, 1993) A white man lives for 16 years with Aborigines, and when reunited with early colonial Australia begins a search for identity in a society filled with fear. Compelling insight into the social dynamics of early colonial Australia.

True History of the Kelly Gang (Peter Carey, 2000) This Booker-prize winning interpretation of Ned Kelly's trials brings him to life in language and spirit, with Carey's take depicting him as ultimate victim of an unjust system. Beautifully told and paced – you won't be able to put it down.

My Place (Sally Morgan, 1988) The simple prose warms the reader to this moving autobiographical journey of the author's discovery of her Aboriginal heritage. This exploration of the Stolen Generation is good background in a heartfelt package.

Benang (Kim Scott, 2000) Through anecdote and documentation, the racist treatment of the narrator and Aboriginal people in general is explored in this complex, moving, but sometimes frustrating work. It shared the Miles Franklin Award with *Drylands* (see below) in 2000.

Cloud Street (Tim Winton, 1991) Tim Winton's books aren't complicated; his gift is his ability to write earthy text superbly evoking a sense of place. *Cloud Street*, arguably his best novel, is a must for visitors to Perth – and a great read for any road trip.

Drylands (Thea Astley, 1999) Explores the self-destruction of a rural community through Astley's unadorned writing style, with her typical critique of contemporary society through the characters often forgotten.

Morgan's *My Place* (see the boxed text 'Essential Australian Holiday Reads'; above) is one of the most popular books ever written by an indigenous Australian, along with Ruby Langford's *Don't Take Your Love to Town* (1988), a moving autobiography of courage against adversity. Kim Scott's excellent *Benang* (see the boxed text 'Essential Australian Holiday Reads'; above) is a challenging but rewarding read. Malaysian-born Australian Hsu-Ming Teo's *Love and Vertigo* took out the *Australian/Vogel* literary award in 1999, while Hong-Kong born Brian Castro shared the award in 1982; his novels, especially *Birds of Passage*, often explore coming to terms with diversity and identity.

Other contemporary authors, such as Peter Carey and David Malouf, often focus on fictitious reinterpretations of Australian history as a means of exploring personal and national identity. Carey, Australia's best-known novelist and twice winner of the prestigious Booker Prize, writes knock-out books; his finest are *Oscar & Lucinda* and *True History of the Kelly Gang*. Thea Astley and Tim Winton, winners of Australia's most prestigious literary award, the Miles Franklin, usually focus on human relations, but with a strong sense of place in the Australian landscape. See the boxed text 'Essential Australian Holiday Reads' (above) for examples of their work.

Australian children's literature is popular worldwide. Classics like May Gibbs' *Complete Adventures of Snugglepot and Cuddlepie* (1946) and Norman Lindsay's *The Magic Pudding* (1918) captivated imaginations by bringing the Australian bush to life. More recently, there are belly laughs aplenty in books by John Marsden (written for young teens), Morris Gleitzman and Paul Jennings. Andy Griffiths' *Just* series are popular with under 12s, especially *The Day My Bum Went Psycho* – say no more.

For the aeroplane, Australia's best-selling author, Bryce Courtenay, pumps out brick-sized historical blockbusters, such as *Matthew Flinders' Cat* and *The Potato Factory*.

Music

Australian popular music really kicked off in the '70s, fed by a thriving pub-rock scene and the huge success of *Countdown*, a music TV show that exposed local bands. Eff-off rock legends AC/DC started out in the early '70s; their 1980 album *Back in Black* blitzed some 10 million sales in the US alone. Cold Chisel also started out around that time, their stubbled Aussie blokedom and earnest rock was an instant success; *Cold Chisel* and *East* are their best albums. Paul Kelly's first forays in the music scene were in the '70s, too, though his solo album *Post* (1985) put his passionate folk ballad blend on the map. Midnight Oil's politico-pop reached a head at the time of *Diesel and Dust* (1987); while the Divinyls, with lead siren Chrissy Amphlett, are best remembered for raunch single 'I Touch Myself'. Nick Cave is one of a number of indie performers who came to prominence in the late '70s and left for overseas in a diaspora of Aussie talent in the '80s.

By the late '80s, notably around the time *Countdown* was wound down (1987), Australian rock music began to be dominated by the lucrative ditty-pop market. Enter Kylie, one-time fluffy-haired nymphet from *Neighbours*, whose bum first hit the stage with *Locomotion* in 1987, and, as they say, the rest is history. John Farnham released *Whispering Jack* in 1986 and it became the biggest-selling album in Australian history (there's no accounting for taste).

Feeding on the pub-rock legacy of the '70s, live music continues to find an audience, with local bands like Powderfinger, The Avalanches, Grinspoon, The Whitlams, Gerling and Spiderbait working hard on the local scene, but not competing internationally with the big-name Oz exports Kylie, Natalie Imbruglia, Silverchair and this week's soapie cross-over sensation. Kasey Chambers, who is a country music queen, sweetly sticks

---

SPOTLIGHT ON DAVID WILLIAMSON

David Williamson is Australia's best-known playwright; his widely performed work has won international acclaim, with Madonna recently performing in his play *Up for Grabs* in London. His topical satirical comedies tend to focus on Australia's middle class, but here he tells us more:

LP: What is the future of Australian theatre?
DW: *Healthy. Theatre reflects its immediate society in a very direct way. It doesn't have to wait four years for the funding to be raised as does film. There's a hunger for a reflection of the issues a particular society faces and theatre caters for that hunger.*
LP: Can you describe the traits of Australian actors and how they differ to UK or US actors?
DW: *I think Australian actors bring a special honesty to their craft. There's a directness and lack of pretension.*
LP: Your favourite Australian film?
DW: *Unashamedly* Gallipoli, *which I wrote. It was a great privilege to be working with Peter Weir at the peak of his form on the interpretation of a seminal Australian moment.*
LP: Your favourite Australian play?
DW: *Unashamedly* The Club, *which I also wrote about the internal politics in a football club. I think I got everything right and in balance in this play. Only time will tell if I'm right.*
LP: How would you describe Australians today? How may you write about them in five years' time?
DW: *Australians today? I'm not especially enamoured about the mass hysteria exhibited over the boat people. These were persecuted people fleeing some of the worst regimes on earth, and they deserved better treatment than being treated as pariahs. In five years time I hope we've grown a little more compassionate.*

hers up the music industry by singing she's 'Not Pretty Enough' to be star material – and goes to number one. Very Australian.

Contemporary Indigenous music is thriving, and the annual 'The Deadlys' awards are a good place to find out who's setting the pace (www.vibe.com.au). Jimmy Little, the country-folk stalwart, began his career in the '50s, but it was in the '90s that indigenous music hit mainstream, thanks largely to the immense popularity of Yothu Yindi and the single 'Treaty', lifted from their excellent album, *Tribal Voice* (1991). Archie Roach's spine-tingling voice set the soundtrack scene for the film *The Tracker* (p65), but he's best known for albums such as *Sensual Being*, his latest, and *Charcoal Lane* (1991), arguably his best. With fellow singer/songwriter and partner Ruby Hunter, Archie has toured the US and UK – both artists are well worth checking out. Compelling singer/storyteller Kev Carmody and the multi-talented Christine Anu are also both worth looking out for, as are the up-and-coming folksy harmonies of the Sydney-based trio the Stiff Gins. Indigenous Australia also has its very own Kylie-styled pop babe duo, Shakaya, picked up by Sony Australia.

Local radio stations have a 'content quota' to play at least 15% Australian music, but for a 100% dose, tune into the national radio station Triple J (www.triplej.net.au/listen/) for 'Home and Hosed', 9pm to 11pm weeknights. Also check out Message Stick, www.abc.net.au/message, for 100% indigenous arts and music information. See Festivals & Events in individual state and territory chapters for information about Australia's many fabulous live music festivals.

Visual Arts

Paintings in the early days of colonial Australia depicted the landscape through European eyes. It wasn't until the 1880s, in tune with the growing nationalist movement, that the unique qualities of the landscape and light were captured by a group of artists known as the Heidelberg School. In the 1940s another influential group, the Angry Penguins, threw romantic Impressionist convention out and introduced a period of cultural re-evaluation; Arthur Boyd and Sir Sidney Nolan, with his famous *Ned Kelly* series, are two famous protagonists. More recent artists explored Australia's suburbia (Jeffrey Smart), Sydney and the human condition (Brett Whiteley), and the imagery and vibrant colours of the landscape (Fred Williams). Patricia Piccinini is the latest Australian art darling; her work represented the country in the 2003 Venice Biennale.

Indigenous culture has brought huge benefits to Australia's art. Visual imagery is a fundamental part of indigenous life, a connection between past and present, the supernatural and the earthly, and the people and the land. The early forms of indigenous artistic expression were rock carvings (petroglyphs), body painting and ground designs.

Arnhem Land, in Australia's tropical Top End, is an area of rich artistic heritage. Some of the rock art galleries in the huge sandstone Arnhem Land plateau are at least 18,000 years old, and range from hand-prints to paintings of animals, people, mythological beings and European ships. Two of the finest sites are accessible to visitors, the Ubirr and Nourlangie in Kakadu National Park. The art of the Kimberley is perhaps best known for its images of the Wandjina, a group of ancestral beings who came from the sky and sea and were associated with fertility. The superb Quinkan galleries at Laura on the Cape York Peninsula, in North Queensland, are also among the finest in the country. Among the many creatures depicted on the walls are the Quinkan spirits.

Great Southern Land (2003, Festival Mushroom Records) – Finely tuned to the backpacker market, this best-of album selects 19 Oz classics from Cold Chisel's 'Khe Sanh', The Angels' 'Am I Ever Gonna See Your Face Again' (response: no way, get fucked, fuck off!) to Men at Work's 'Down Under' – it's the perfect accompaniment to full-volume singalongs.

Painting in central Australia has flourished to such a degree that it is now an important source of income for communities. It has also been an important educational tool for children, through which they can learn different aspects of religious and ceremonial knowledge. Western Desert painting, also known as 'dot' painting, partly evolved from 'ground paintings', which formed the centrepiece of dances and songs. These 'paintings' were made from pulped plant material and the designs were made on the ground using dots of this mush. Dot paintings depict Dreaming stories. (The Dreaming is a complex concept that forms the basis of Aboriginal spirituality, incorporating the creation of the world and the spiritual energies operating around us. A story is a tale from the Dreaming that taps into the concepts of legend, myth, tradition and the law.) Bark painting is an integral part of the cultural heritage of Arnhem Land indigenous people, and one of their main features is the use of rarrk designs (cross-hatching). These designs identify the particular clans, and are based on body paintings handed down through generations.

Food & Drink by Matthew Evans

Born in convict poverty and raised on a diet heavily influenced by Great Britain, Australian cuisine has come a long way. This is now one of the most dynamic places in the world to have a feed, thanks to immigration and a dining public willing to give anything new, and better, a go. Sydney and Melbourne can claim to be dining destinations worthy of touring gourmands from New York to Paris. More importantly real people, including travellers, will feel the effects of a blossoming food culture across the country.

This, however, has only been because of recent history. Australia, despite its world-class dining opportunities, doesn't live to eat. As a nation we're new to the world of good food, of being mesmerised by the latest TV chef, devouring cookbooks and subscribing to foodie magazines in the hundreds of thousands. The eating in Australia has never been better, and it's improving by the day.

Yet, despite our fascination with tucker, at heart we're still mostly a nation of simple eaters, with the majority of Australians still novices in anything beyond meat and three veg. This is changing, though, as the influx of immigrants (and their cuisine) has found locals trying (and liking) everything from lassi to laksa. This passionate minority has led to a rise in dining standards, better availability of produce and a frenetic buzz about food in general. It's no wonder Australian chefs, cookbooks and foodwriters are so sought after overseas.

We've coined our own phrase, Modern Australian, to describe our cuisine. If it's a melange of east and west, it's Modern Australian. If it's not authentically French, or Italian, it's Modern Australian – our attempt to classify the unclassifiable. Cuisine doesn't really alter from one region to another, but some influences are obvious, such as the Italian migration to Melbourne and the southeast Asian migration to Darwin.

Dishes aren't usually too fussy, the flavours often bold and interesting. Spicing ranges from gentle to extreme, coffee is great (though it still reaches its greatest heights in the cities), and the meats are tender, full flavoured and usually bargain priced.

The truth may be that most Australians would rather a nice dip in the sea, followed by a bowl of potato wedges with sour cream than the world-class fine dining that our cities boast, but at least now, for residents and travellers alike, there's the option of great dining if we want it.

STAPLES & SPECIALITIES

Australia's best food comes from the sea. Nothing compares to this continent's seafood, harnessed from some of the purest waters you'll find anywhere, and usually cooked with care.

Connoisseurs prize Sydney rock oysters (a species living along the New South Wales coast). There are sea scallops from Queensland, and estuary scallops from Tasmania and South Australia. Rock lobsters are fantastic and fantastically expensive, and mud crabs, despite the name, are a sweet delicacy. Another odd sounding delicacy are 'bugs' – like shovel-nosed lobsters without a lobster's price tag; try the Balmain and Moreton Bay varieties. Marron are prehistoric-looking freshwater crayfish from Western Australia, while their smaller cousins, yabbies, can be found throughout the southeast. Prawns are incredible, particularly sweet school prawns or the eastern king (Yamba) prawns found along northern NSW.

Matthew Evans was a chef before he crossed to the 'dark side' as food writer and restaurant critic. He is currently chief restaurant reviewer for the *Sydney Morning Herald,* co-editor of the *Sydney Morning Herald Good Food Guide,* and has a recipe column read by four million people. Matthew is the award-winning author of four food books, including Lonely Planet's *World Food Italy.*

DID YOU KNOW?

We eat kangaroos (and emus) – not many countries consume their coat of arms.

Add to that countless wild fish species and we've got one of the greatest bounties on earth. In fact, the Sydney Fish Market (p97) trades in several hundred species of seafood every day, second only to Tokyo.

Despite their greatness, not many actual dishes can truly lay claim to being uniquely Australian. Even the humble 'pav' (Pavlova), the meringue dessert with cream and passionfruit, may be from New Zealand. Ditto for lamingtons, large cubes of cake dipped in chocolate and rolled in desiccated coconut.

Anything another country does, Australia does, too. Vietnamese, Indian, Fijian, Italian – doesn't matter where it's from, there's an expat community and interested locals desperate to cook and eat it. Dig deep enough, and you'll find Jamaicans using scotch bonnet peppers and Tunisians making tagine. And you'll usually find their houses are the favourite haunts of their locally raised friends.

Almost everything we eat from the land (as opposed to the sea) was introduced. Even super-expensive black truffles are now being harvested in Tasmania. The fact that the country is huge (similar in size to continental USA) and varies so much in climate, from the tropical north to the temperate south, means that there's an enormous variety of produce on offer.

In summer, mangoes are so plentiful that Queenslanders actually get sick of them. Tasmania's cold climate means its strawberries and stonefruit are sublime. Lamb from Victoria's lush Gippsland is highly prized, the veal of White Rocks in WA is legendary, while the tomatoes of SA are the nation's best.

There's a small but brilliant farmhouse cheese movement, hampered by the fact that all the milk must be pasteurised (unlike in Italy and France, the home of the world's best cheeses). Despite that, the results can be great. Keep an eye out for the goat's cheese from Gympie, Kytren and Kervella, the cheddar from Pyengana (p615), sheep's milk cheese from Mount Emu Creek, Milawa's washed rind, and anything from Heidi Farm, among others.

Australians' taste for the unusual usually kicks in at dinner only. Most people still eat cereal for breakfast, or perhaps eggs and bacon on weekends.

'the Sydney Fish Market trades in several hundred species of seafood every day, second only to Tokyo'

TRAVEL YOUR TASTEBUDS

Some unusual foods you may spy on your travels include wild mushrooms, such as bright orange pine mushrooms, and slippery jacks, so-called because they can get quite slimy after rain. Much of the most interesting (if not always the most delicious) produce is native. There's kangaroo, a deep, purpley-red meat, which is quite sweet. Fillets are so tender and lean they have to be served rare. The tail is often braised in the same way oxtail is cooked. In the north, you may encounter crocodile, a white meat not dissimilar to fish with a texture closer to chicken. In the outback you may be encouraged to try witchetty grubs, which look like giant maggots and taste nutty, but with a squishy texture. In the tropics you may find green ants. The way to eat them is to pick them up and bite off their lightly acidic bottoms. Sugar ant abdomens are full of sweet sap, so again just bite off the tail end.

Much of the native flora has evolved to contain unpalatable chemicals. Despite this, you may enjoy fiery bush pepper, sweetly aromatic lemon myrtle, aniseed myrtle, coffee-like flecks of wattle seed, vibrant purple rosella flowers, super sour davidson plums, lightly acidic bush tomato (akudjura), and, of course, the Hawaii-appropriated macadamia nut.

The wildest food of all is Vegemite, a dangerously salty yeast-extract spread with iconic status. Most commonly used on toast, it's also not bad on cheese sandwiches. It's often carried overseas for homesick expats, or licked from fingers by freckle-faced youngsters. Outsiders tend to find the flavour coarse, vulgar and completely overwhelming. But what would they know?

They devour sandwiches for lunch with nearly the same verve as they do in the UK, and then eat anything and everything in the evening. Yum cha (the classic southern Chinese dumpling feast), however, has found huge popularity with urban locals in recent years, particularly on weekends. Some non-Chinese even have it with the traditional Chinese, first thing in the morning.

DRINKS

You're in the right country if you're after a drink. Once a nation of tea and beer swillers, Oz is now turning its attention to coffee and wine. In fact, if you're in the country's southern climes, you're probably not far from a wine region right now.

Purists will rave about Cabernet Sauvignon from Coonawarra, Riesling from Tassie or the Clare Valley, Chardonnay from Margaret River and Shiraz from the Barossa Valley. But there are many more regions that produce fine wine.

The closest region to Sydney, the Hunter Valley, first had vines in the 1830s, and does a lively unwooded Semillon that is best aged. Further inland, there's Canberra, Cowra, Orange and Mudgee. Just out of Melbourne are the Mornington and Bellarine Peninsulas, Mount Macedon and the Yarra Valley. There's even a wine region in Queensland, though not all of it is good.

SA is Australia's vinous heartland (visit the National Wine Centre in Adelaide, p671). Most wineries have small cellar doors where you can taste for free or a minimal fee. If you like the wine, you're generally expected to buy.

Plenty of good wine comes from big producers with economies of scale on their side, but the most interesting wines are usually made by small vignerons where you pay a premium, but the gamble means the payoff in terms of flavour is often greater. Much of the cost of wine (nearly 42%) is due to a high taxing program courtesy of the Australian government.

Beer, for years, has been of the bland, chilled-so-you-can-barely-taste-it variety. Now microbrewers and boutique breweries are filtering through. Keep an eye out for WA's Little Creatures (a fragrant drop sometimes called the Sauvignon Blanc of beer; see p855), James Squire amber ale from Sydney, Hazards from Hobart and Mountain Goat from Melbourne. More widespread is the robust, full-figured Cooper's from Adelaide. Most beers have an alcohol content between 3.5% and 5%. That's less than many European beers but stronger than most of the stuff in North America. Light beers come in under 3% alcohol and are finding favour with people observing the super stringent drink-driving laws.

The terms for ordering beer vary with the state. In NSW you ask for a 'schooner' (425mL) if you're thirsty and a 'middy' (285mL) if you're not quite so dry. In Melbourne and Tassie it's a 'pot' (285mL), and in most of the country you can ask for a glass of beer and just see what turns up. Pints (425mL or 568mL, depending on where you are) aren't common, though Irish pubs and European-style ale houses tend to offer pints for homesick Poms.

In terms of coffee, Australia is leaping ahead, with Italian-style espresso machines in virtually every café, boutique roasters all the rage and, in urban areas, the qualified barista (coffee maker) virtually the norm. Expect the best coffee in Melbourne, decent stuff in most other cities, and a chance of good coffee in many rural areas. Melbourne's café scene rivals the most vibrant in the world – the best way to immerse yourself is by wandering the city centre's café-lined lanes.

DID YOU KNOW?
Australian wine is drunk by connoisseurs around the globe.

DID YOU KNOW?
Australia's first espresso cafés opened in the 1950s – the Coluzzi Bar (p127), in Sydney, and Pellegrini's (p469), in Melbourne, are still in business.
EDDIE BUTLER-BOWDON

CELEBRATIONS

Celebrating in the Australian manner often includes equal amounts of food and alcohol. A birthday could well be a barbecue (barbie) of steak (or prawns), washed down with a beverage or two. Weddings are usually a big slap-up dinner, though the food is often far from memorable. Christenings are more sober, mostly offering home-baked biscuits and a cup of tea.

Many regions and cities are now holding food festivals. Melbourne, for instance, has its own month-long food and wine festival in March (p463). There are harvest festivals in wine regions, and various communities, such as the town of Orange (under the FOOD – Food Of Orange District – banner), hold annual events.

For many an event, especially in the warmer months, Australians fill the car with an Esky (an ice-chest, to keep everything cool), tables, chairs, a cricket set or a footy, and head off for a barbie by the lake/river/beach. If there's a total fire ban (which occurs increasingly each summer), the food is precooked and the barbie becomes more of a picnic, but the essence remains the same.

Christmas in Australia often finds the more traditional (in a European sense) baked dinner being replaced by a barbecue, full of seafood and quality steak. It's a response to the warm weather. Prawn prices skyrocket, chicken may be eaten with champagne at breakfast, and the meal is usually in the afternoon, after a swim, and before a really good, long siesta.

Various ethnic minorities have their own celebrations. The Tongans love an *umu* or *hangi*, where fish and vegetables are buried in an earthen pit and covered with coals; Greeks may hold a spit barbecue; and the Chinese go off during their annual Spring Festival (Chinese New Year) every January or February (it changes with the lunar calendar).

WHERE TO EAT & DRINK

The best value food in most cities is lurking in Chinatown. Melbourne's Little Bourke St (p469) and the lanes nearby boast lots of little joints selling roast duck or wonton soups.

Typically, a restaurant meal in Australia is a relaxed affair. It may take 15 minutes to order, another 15 before the first course arrives, and maybe half an hour between entrées and mains. The upside of this is that any table you've booked in a restaurant is yours for the night, unless you're told otherwise. So sit, linger and live life in the slow lane.

A competitively priced place to eat is in a club or pub that offers a counter meal. This is where you order at the kitchen, usually staples such as a fisherman's basket, steak, mixed grills, chicken cordon bleu or Vienna schnitzel, take a number and wait until it's called out over the counter or intercom. You pick up the meal yourself, saving the restaurant money on staff and you on your total bill.

www.australiangourmet
pages.com.au

A website devoted to wine, food, restaurants and more in Australia run by a *Vogue Entertaining + Travel* contributor. Subscribe (for free) and you'll receive several weekly updates on subjects as diverse as food labelling, food stores and stories found overseas. Even better, there's no advertising.

TALKING STRINE

The opening dish in a three-course meal is called the entrée, the second course (the North American entrée) is called the main course and the sweet bit at the end is called dessert, sweets, afters or pud. In lesser restaurants, of course, it's called desert.

When an Australian invites you over for a baked dinner it might mean a roast lunch. Use the time as a guide – dinner is normally served after 6pm. By 'tea' they could be talking dinner or they could be talking tea. A coffee definitely means coffee, unless it's after a hot date when you're invited up to a prospect's flat.

TOP EATING AROUND AUSTRALIA

Berardo's on the Beach (p315; ☎ 07-5448 0888; 8/49 Hastings St, Noosa Beach; dishes $10-25) Great beach, great food, great dreaming you never have to go home again.

Café Di Stasio (p474; ☎ 03-9525 3999; 31 Fitzroy St, St Kilda; mains $24-35) The Italian ristorante you never found in Italy.

Star of Greece (p688; ☎ 08-8557 7420; The Esplanade, Port Willunga; mains $20-30) A cliff-top café on the edge of the McLaren Vale wine region, with stunning views and great seafood.

Solitary (p149; ☎ 02-4782 1164; 90 Cliff Drive, Leura Falls; mains $24-32) Graceful service, honest, regionally biased food, and views of the Jamison Valley.

Fins (p185; ☎ 02-6685 5029; The Beach Hotel, Byron Bay; mains $28-35) The freshest seafood, boldly spiced, in an iconic hotel.

Solo diners find that cafés and noodle bars are welcoming, good fine-dining restaurants often treat you like a star, but sadly, some mid-range places may still make you feel a little ill at ease.

One of the most interesting features of the dining scene is the Bring Your Own (BYO), a restaurant that allows you to bring your own alcohol. If the restaurant also sells alcohol, the BYO bit is usually limited to bottled wine only (no beer, no casks) and a corkage charge is added to your bill. The cost is either per person, or per bottle, and ranges from nothing to $15 per bottle in fancy places. Be warned, however, that BYO is a dying custom, and many if not most licensed restaurants don't like you bringing your own wine, so ask when you book.

Most restaurants open around noon for lunch and from 6pm or 7pm for dinner. Australians usually eat lunch shortly after noon, and dinner bookings are usually made for 7.30pm or 8pm, though in major cities some restaurants stay open past 10pm. Regularly updated, independent reviews can be found in local restaurant guides, or online at www.australiangourmet pages.com.au or through www.citysearch.com.au.

Quick Eats

There's not a huge culture of street vending in Australia, though you may find a pie or coffee cart in some places. Most quick eats traditionally come from a milk bar, which serves old-fashioned hamburgers (with bacon, egg, pineapple and beetroot if you want) and other takeaway foods. Fish and chips is still hugely popular, most often a form of shark (often called flake; don't worry, it can be delicious) dipped in heavy batter, and eaten at the beach on a Friday night.

American-style fast food has taken over in recent times, though many Aussies still love a meat pie, often from a milk bar, but also from bakeries, kiosks and some cafés. If you're at an Aussie Rules football match, a beer, a meat pie and a bag of hot chips are as compulsory as wearing your team's colours to the game.

Pizza has become one of the most popular fast foods; most pizzas that are home-delivered are of the American style (thick and with lots of toppings) rather than Italian style. That said, more and more woodfired, thin Neapolitan-style *pizze* can be found, even in country towns. In the city, Roman-style *pizze* (buy it by the slice) is becoming more popular, but you can't usually buy the other pizza in anything but whole rounds.

There are some really dodgy mass-produced takeaway foods, bought mostly by famished teenage boys, including the dim sim (a bastardisation of the dim sum dumplings from China) and the Chiko Roll (for translations, see p78).

DID YOU KNOW?

We love pie floaters (p78) – a typically South Australian treat.

VEGETARIANS & VEGANS

You're in luck. Most cities have substantial numbers of local vegetarians, which means you're well catered for. Cafés seem to always have vegetarian options, and even our best restaurants may have complete vegetarian menus. Take care with risotto and soups, though, as meat stock is often used.

Vegans will find the going much tougher, but local Hare Krishna restaurants or Buddhist temples often provide relief, and there are usually dishes that are vegan-adaptable at restaurants.

The Australian Vegetarian Society has a useful website (www.veg-soc.org), which lists a number of vegetarian and vegetarian-friendly places to eat.

'Just don't leave before it's your turn to buy!'

WHINING & DINING

Dining with children in Australia is relatively easy. Avoid the flashiest places and children are generally welcomed, particularly at Chinese, Greek or Italian restaurants. Kids are usually more than welcome at cafés; you'll find bistros and clubs often see families dining early. Many fine-dining restaurants don't welcome small children (assuming they're all ill-behaved).

Most places that do welcome children don't have separate kids' menus, and those that do usually offer everything straight from the deep fryer – crumbed chicken and chips, that kind of thing. Better to find something on the menu (say a pasta or salad) and have the kitchen adapt it slightly to your children's needs.

The best news for travelling families, weather permitting, is that there are plenty of free or coin-operated barbecues in parks. Beware of weekends and public holidays when fierce battles can erupt over who is next in line for the barbecue.

HABITS & CUSTOMS

At the table, it's good manners to use British knife and fork skills, keeping the fork in the left hand, tines down, and the knife in the right, though Americans may be forgiven for using their fork like a shovel. Talking with your mouth full is considered uncouth, and fingers should only be used for food that can't be tackled another way.

If you're lucky enough to be invited over for dinner at someone's house, always take a gift. You may offer to bring something for the meal, but even if the host downright refuses – insisting you just bring your scintillating conversation – still take a bottle of wine. Flowers or a box of chocolates are also acceptable.

'Shouting' is a revered custom where people rotate paying for a round of drinks. Just don't leave before it's your turn to buy! At a toast, everyone should touch glasses.

Australians like to linger a bit over coffee. They like to linger a really long time while drinking beer. And they tend to take quite a bit of time if they're out to dinner (as opposed to having takeaway).

BILLS & TIPPING

The total at the bottom of a restaurant bill is all you really need to pay. It should include GST (as should menu prices) and there is no 'optional' service charge added. Waiters are paid a reasonable salary, so they don't rely on tips to survive. Often, though, especially in urban Australia, people tip a few coins in a café, while the tip for excellent service can go as high as 15% in whiz-bang establishments. The incidence of add-ons (bread, water, surcharges on weekends etc) is rising.

DOS & DON'TS

Do...

- Do show up for restaurant dinner reservations on time. Not only may your table be given to someone else, staggered bookings are designed to make the experience more seamless.
- Do take a small gift, and/or a bottle of wine to dinner parties.
- Do offer to wash up or help clear the table after a meal at a friend's house.
- Do ring or send a note (even an email) the day or so after a dinner party, unless the friends are so close you feel it unnecessary. Even then, thank them the very next time you speak.
- Do offer to take meat and/or a salad to a barbecue. At the traditional Aussie barbie for a big group, each family is expected to bring part or all of their own tucker.
- Do shout drinks to a group on arrival at the pub.
- Do tip (up to 15%) for good service, when in a big group, or if your kids have gone crazy and trashed the dining room.

Don't...

- Don't freak out when the waiter in a restaurant attempts to 'lap' your serviette (napkin) by laying it over your crotch. It's considered to be the height of service. If you don't want them doing this, place your serviette on your lap before they get a chance.
- Don't ever accept a shout unless you intend to make your shout soon after.
- Don't expect a date to pay for you. It's quite common among younger people for a woman to pay her own way.
- Don't expect servile or obsequious service. Professional waiters are intelligent, caring equals whose disdain can perfectly match any diner's attempt at contempt.
- Don't ever tip bad service.

Smoking is banned in most eateries in the nation, so sit outside if you love to puff. And never smoke in someone's house unless you ask first. Even then it's usual to smoke outside. See the boxed text 'Dos & Don'ts' (above) for other tips on general food-and-drink etiquette.

COOKING COURSES

Many good cooking classes are run by food stores such as **Simon Johnson** (☎ 02-9319 6122) in Sydney, the **Essential Ingredient** (☎ 03-9827 9047) in Melbourne, and **Black Pearl Epicure** (☎ 07-3257 2144) in Brisbane. Others are run by markets, such as the **Sydney Seafood School** (☎ 02-9004 1111) at the Sydney Fish Markets or the **Queen Victoria Market Cooking School** (☎ 03-9320 5835) at the Queen Victoria Market in Melbourne. The following, however, run longer courses for the inspired.

www.campionand
curtis.com

Run by two food writers who trained as chefs, this website has information on cooking schools, restaurants, cook books plus plenty of their own modern Australian recipes. They'll email a monthly newsletter, too.

Howqua Dale Gourmet Retreat (☎ 03-5777 3503; Gippsland, Victoria) Highly regarded weekend cooking schools and tours are run by amazing chef Marieke Brugman.
Elise Pascoe Cooking School (☎ 02-4236 1666; www.cookingschool.com.au; South Coast, NSW) Food writer and remarkable cook Elise Pascoe runs mostly weekend cooking classes in a stunning setting just south of Sydney.
Sunnybrae (☎ 03-5236 2276; near the Great Ocean Rd, Victoria) Chef George Byron takes his kitchen garden straight to the stove at this legendary school a couple of hours outside Melbourne.
Le Cordon Bleu (☎ 1 800 064 802; Sydney, NSW) The original must-do French course is available thanks to a joint venture down under. Courses from 10 weeks to five years (part-time).

EAT YOUR WORDS

For a bit more insight into Australian cuisine, stick your nose into one or more of these books.

Australian Regional Food Guide by Sally Hammond. A great guide to where to buy good food at the source as you travel around.

Good Food Guide The *Age* and the *Sydney Morning Herald* newspapers both put out annual restaurant guides that rate over 400 restaurants in each state.

Secret Men's BBQ Business by Alan Campion. An insight into the way men and barbies come together in modern society.

Australian Fare by Stephen Downes. Subtitled 'How Australian Cooking became the World's Best', this is one man's one-eyed view, with interesting historical context going back to the 1956 Olympics.

Australian Seafood Handbook edited by GK Yearsley, PR Last and RD Ward. Don't know what fish that is? This tells you the real name, the local name and plenty more besides.

Penguin's Good Australian Wine Guide by Huon Hooke and Ralph Kyte-Powell. Annual publication with lots of useful information on many readily available wines.

James Halliday's Wine Atlas by James Halliday. Complete with CD-Rom, all about the wine regions and what to expect when you get there.

The Cook's Companion by Stephanie Alexander. Australia's single-volume answer to Delia Smith. If it's in here, most Australians have probably seen it or eaten it.

Chalk and Cheese by Will Studd. Everything you ever wanted to know about Australia's blossoming boutique cheese and its makers.

Glossary

Australians love to shorten everything, including peoples' names, so expect many other words to be abbreviated. Some words you might hear:

barbie – a barbecue, where (traditionally) smoke and overcooked meat are matched with lashings of coleslaw, potato salad and beer

Chiko Roll – a fascinating large, spring roll-like pastry for sale in takeaway shops. Best used as an item of self-defence rather than eaten

Esky – an insulated ice chest to hold your tinnies, before you hold them in your tinny holder. May be carried onto your tinny, too

middy – a mid-sized glass of beer (NSW)

pav – pavlova, the meringue dessert topped with cream, passionfruit and kiwifruit or other fresh fruit

pie floater – a meat pie served floating in thick pea soup (SA)

pot – a medium glass of beer (Vic, Tas)

rat coffin – a meat pie; the traditional ones are made with minced beef. Compulsory eating (with White Crow tomato sauce) at footy matches

sanger/sando – a sandwich

schooner – a big glass of beer (NSW); but not as big as a pint

snags – (aka surprise bags) sausages

snot block – a vanilla slice

Tim Tam – a commercial chocolate biscuit that lies close to the heart of most Australians. Best consumed as a Tim Tam Shooter, where the two diagonally opposite corners of the rectangular biscuit are nibbled off, and a hot drink (tea is the true aficionado's favourite) is sucked through the fast-melting biscuit like a straw. Ugly but good

tinny – usually refers to a can of beer, but could also be the small boat you go fishing for mud crabs in (and you'd take a few tinnies in your tinny, in that case)

tinny holder – insulating material that you use to keep the tinny ice cold, and nothing to do with a boat

New South Wales

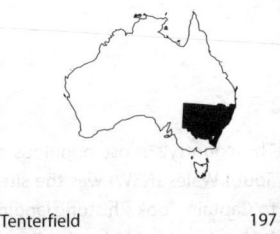

CONTENTS

The country's most populous state and home to its largest, most spectacular city, New South Wales (NSW) was the site of Australia's first permanent European settlement, thanks to Captain Cook's historic landing in 1770. If you're expecting NSW to act as little more than Sydney's hinterland or backyard, then you're in for a pleasant surprise. The state is rich in history – both Aboriginal and European. Some of it is tainted with the startling brutality of its status as a penal settlement and gulag for the United Kingdom's undesirables, but there's also a palpable sense of its gold-rush era excitement and the pioneering exploration and expansion westward from Sydney. NSW is also the country's most diverse state. Where else can you experience true Australian outback landscapes, ski in Alpine country, explore verdant rainforests, surf along an almost unbroken line of beaches, and savour every cultural delight of one of the world's most vibrant, multicultural and cosmopolitan cities?

NSW is the popular gateway for most visitors to Australia, and the road, rail and air networks allow for greater freedom of movement than in some other Australian states. If you arrive in Sydney, the choice is yours. North to the resort towns and golden beaches and eventually the Great Dividing Range? West to the Blue Mountains or a host of other rugged National Parks? South to the scenic but less developed coastal towns that still support a fishing industry? East to the Pacific Ocean – the state's swimming pool? It's a wonderful area to find all the 'typically Australian' things you've been looking for, and a few that you didn't know existed.

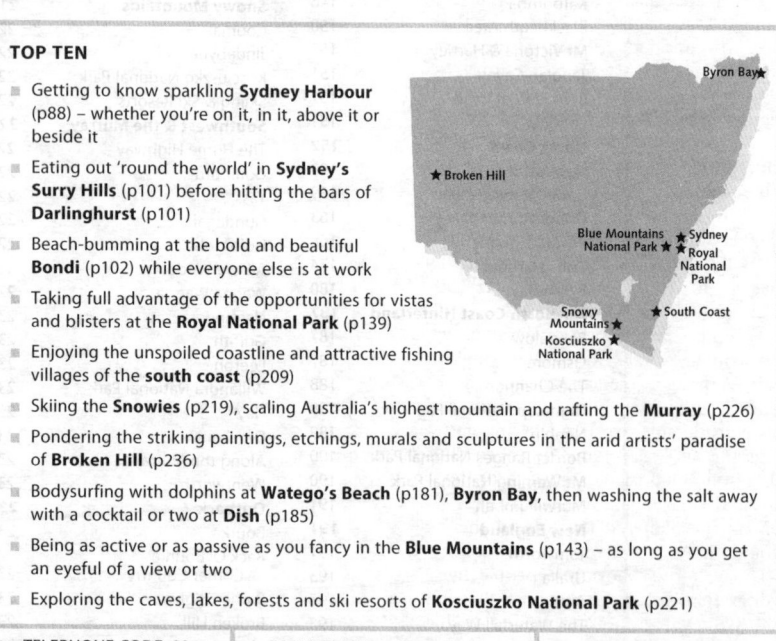

TOP TEN

- Getting to know sparkling **Sydney Harbour** (p88) – whether you're on it, in it, above it or beside it
- Eating out 'round the world' in **Sydney's Surry Hills** (p101) before hitting the bars of **Darlinghurst** (p101)
- Beach-bumming at the bold and beautiful **Bondi** (p102) while everyone else is at work
- Taking full advantage of the opportunities for vistas and blisters at the **Royal National Park** (p139)
- Enjoying the unspoiled coastline and attractive fishing villages of the **south coast** (p209)
- Skiing the **Snowies** (p219), scaling Australia's highest mountain and rafting the **Murray** (p226)
- Pondering the striking paintings, etchings, murals and sculptures in the arid artists' paradise of **Broken Hill** (p236)
- Bodysurfing with dolphins at **Watego's Beach** (p181), **Byron Bay**, then washing the salt away with a cocktail or two at **Dish** (p185)
- Being as active or as passive as you fancy in the **Blue Mountains** (p143) – as long as you get an eyeful of a view or two
- Exploring the caves, lakes, forests and ski resorts of **Kosciuszko National Park** (p221)

| ■ TELEPHONE CODE: 02 | ■ POPULATION: 6,609,300 | ■ AREA: 802,000 SQ KM |

HISTORY

The north and west coasts of Australia had been charted in the 1640s by Abel Tasman, who named the continent New Holland. In 1770, Captain James Cook sailed up the east coast, landing at Botany Bay and naming the area New South Wales. With a need for an alternative to the prison colonies in North America, Joseph Banks (the botanist on Cook's 1770 expedition) put forth the idea of using NSW, as it was considered 'uninhabited'. In January 1788, the First Fleet sailed into Botany Bay under the command of Captain Arthur Phillip. Disappointed by what he saw, he headed north and found 'the finest harbour in the world'.

The early settlers did it hard, with famine threatening the population in 1790. Eventually the colony expanded and grew less reliant on Great Britain. By the 1830s, the general layout of NSW was understood, and the Blue Mountains had been penetrated. In addition the Lachlan, Macquarie, Murrumbidgee and Darling Rivers had been explored.

The discovery of gold in the 1850s brought about significant changes in the social and economic structure of the colony. By the turn of the twentieth century, Sydney was a vigorous city of almost 500,000 people and it had a great port.

Aboriginal People

When the British first arrived at Sydney Cove there were somewhere between 500,000 and one million Aborigines in Australia, and more than 250 regional languages – many as distinct from each other as English is from Chinese.

Around what is now Sydney, there were approximately 3000 Aborigines using three main languages encompassing several dialects and subgroups. Although there was considerable overlap, Ku-ring-gai was generally spoken on the northern shore; Dharawal along the coast south of Botany Bay; and Dharug and its dialects were spoken on the plains at the foot of the Blue Mountains.

Today, more Aboriginal people live in Sydney than in any other Australian city. The Sydney region is estimated to have over 30,000 indigenous inhabitants, most of whom are descended from migratory inland tribes. This figure includes a small number of Torres Strait Islanders, a people native to the group of islands just off the Australian coast, near Papua New Guinea. The suburbs of Redfern and Waterloo have a large and vital Koori population (many Aborigines in southeastern Australia describe themselves as Kooris).

GEOGRAPHY & CLIMATE

The state divides neatly into four regions. The narrow coastal strip runs between Queensland and Victoria and has many beaches, national parks, inlets and coastal lakes. The Great Dividing Range also runs the length of the state, about 100km inland from the coast, and includes the New England tablelands north of Sydney, the spectacular Blue Mountains west of Sydney, and, in the south of the state, the Snowy Mountains, which offer winter skiing and summer bushwalking.

West of the Great Dividing Range is the farming country of the western slopes and the dry western plains, which cover two-thirds of the state. The plains fade into the barren outback in the far west, where summer temperatures can soar to well over 40°C.

The major rivers are the Murray and the Darling, which meander westward across the plains. As a general rule, it gets hotter the further north you go and drier the further west. In winter, the Snowy Mountains are, not surprisingly, covered with snow.

Sydney is blessed with a temperate climate. The temperature rarely falls below 10°C (except overnight in winter) and, although summer temperatures can hit 40°C, the average summer maximum is a pleasant 25°C. The average monthly rainfall ranges from 75mm to 130mm.

INFORMATION

Tourism New South Wales (☎ 02-9931 1111; www .tourism.nsw.gov.au) is the state government's main tool for marketing NSW. The main tourist information centre is in Sydney, but most towns have their own tourist offices.

NSW National Parks & Wildlife Service (NPWS; Map pp94-6; ☎ 02-9253 4600; www.nationalparks .nsw.gov.au; 102 George St, The Rocks; ☺ 9am-5pm Mon-Fri, 9.30am-4.30pm Sat & Sun) controls the state's many national parks. Information about

NEW SOUTH WALES

NEW SOUTH WALES

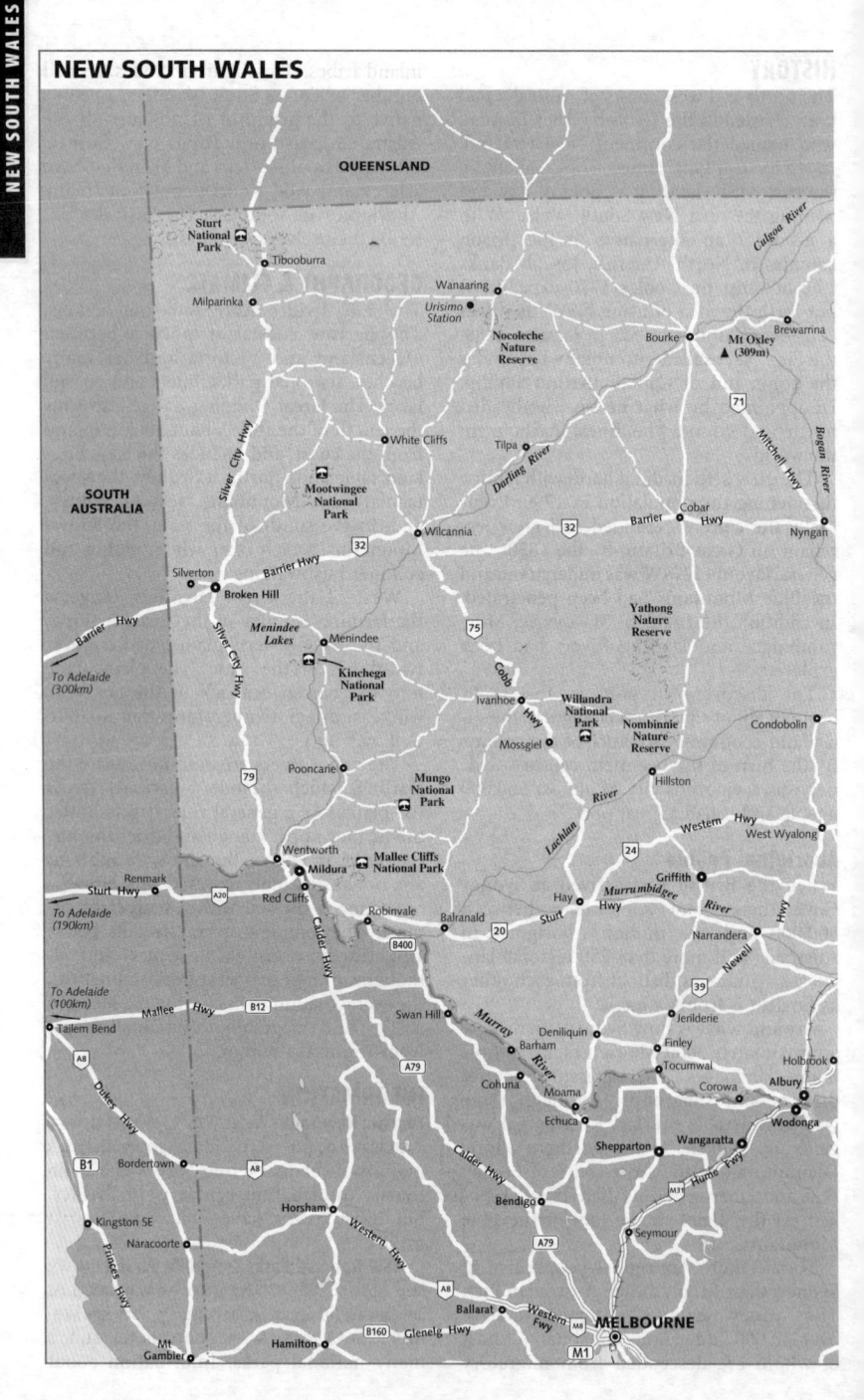

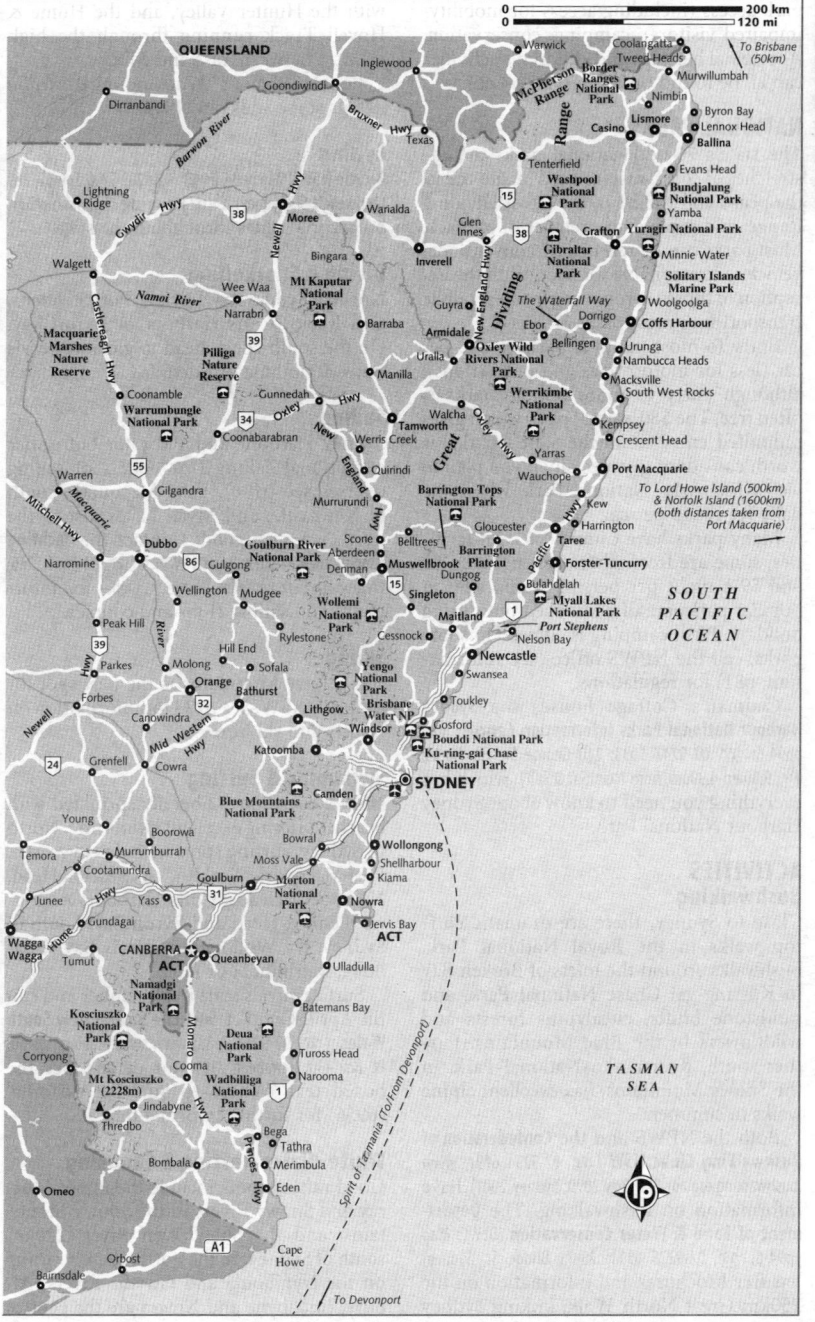

0   200 km
0   120 mi

QUEENSLAND
Warwick
Inglewood   Coolangatta
Goondiwindi   Tweed Heads   To Brisbane
Dirranbandi   Border   (50km)
                     Bruxner   McPherson Ranges
                          Hwy   Range   National
                     Texas   Park
                                   Murwillumbah
                              Casino   Nimbin
Lightning   Gwydir Hwy   Tenterfield   Byron Bay
Ridge   Lennox Head
           Warialda   Washpool   Lismore   Ballina
Walgett   Moree   38   National
           Newell   Glen   Park   Evans Head
      Macquarie   Innes   15   Bundjalung
Wee Waa Bingara   Inverell   38   National Park
   Narrabri   Guyra   Grafton   Yamba
Namoi River Mt Kaputar   Gibraltar Yuragir National Park
         National   Armidale National
Macquarie Park   Barraba   Park   Minnie Water
Marshes   Ebor
Nature   Pilliga   Manilla Uralla The Waterfall Way Solitary Islands
Reserve Nature   Oxley Wild   Marine Park
      Reserve   Gunnedah   Rivers National Dorrigo Coffs Harbour
Coonamble   Park   Bellingen Urunga
Warrumbungle   Walcha   Werrikimbe Nambucca Heads
National Park Oxley Hwy   National   Macksville
   Coonabarabran   Tamworth Park   South West Rocks
Warren   Werris Creek   Kempsey
      New   Gilgandra   Quirindi   Crescent Head
Mitchell Macquarie   Murrurundi   Barrington Tops Port Macquarie
Hwy River   National Park   Kew
Narromine   Dubbo   Scone Belltrees Gloucester
         Gulgong   Aberdeen   Barrington Harrington
Wellington 86   Mudgee Denman Plateau   Taree
Peak Hill   Goulburn River Muswellbrook Dungog Forster-Tuncurry
39   National Park   15 Singleton Bulahdelah SOUTH
Parkes Molong Rylestone Wollemi Maitland Myall Lakes PACIFIC
   Orange   Hill End National Cessnock National Park OCEAN
Forbes   Sofala   Park   Port Stephens
      Bathurst   Yengo   Nelson Bay
Canowindra   Lithgow National Newcastle
Grenfell Mid Western Park Brisbane Swansea
24 Cowra Hwy Katoomba Water NP Toukley
                 Windsor Gosford
Young   Blue Mountains Camden Bouddi National Park
   Boorowa   National Park   Ku-ring-gai Chase
Temora Murrumburrah   National Park
Cootamundra   Bowral SYDNEY
Junee Yass Moss Vale Wollongong
   Gundagai Goulburn Morton Shellharbour
Wagga Home 31 National Kiama
Wagga Tumut   Park Nowra
   CANBERRA   Queanbeyan Jervis Bay
   ACT   Namadgi   ACT
      National
Kosciuszko Park   Ulladulla
National   Deua
Park   Cooma National Batemans Bay
Corryong   Park
   Mt Kosciuszko Wadhilliga Tuross Head
   (2228m)   National Narooma TASMAN
      Thredbo Jindabyne Park   SEA
         Bega
Bombala   Tathra
   Merimbula
Omeo   Eden
         Cape
Orbost   Howe
Bairnsdale   To Devonport

To Lord Howe Island (500km)
& Norfolk Island (1600km)
(both distances taken from
Port Macquarie)

Spirit of Tasmania (To/from Devonport)

LP

park access (including access for mobility-impaired visitors), camping, conservation, Aboriginal heritage and children's activities can all be found on the service's website.

NATIONAL PARKS

The state's 70-odd national parks include stretches of coast, vast forested inland tracts, the peaks and valleys of the Great Dividing Range, and some epic stretches of outback. Most parks can be reached by conventional vehicles in reasonable weather. With the exception of those surrounding Sydney, public transport into most parks is scarce.

Entry to most national parks is $10 per car (less for motorcycles and pedestrians), although entry to more remote parks is often free. The $80 annual pass, which gives unlimited entry to all the state's parks, is worth considering, especially if you plan to visit Kosciuszko National Park, where the daily fee is $15 per car.

Many parks have camp sites with facilities; some are free, others cost between $3 and $9 a night per person. Camp sites at popular parks are often booked out during holidays. Bush camping is allowed in some parks; call the NPWS office (see Information; p81) for regulations.

Cadman's Cottage houses the **Sydney Harbour National Parks Information Centre** (Map pp94-6; ☎ 02-9247 5033; 110 George St, The Rocks; ☾ 9.30am-4.30pm, from 10am Sat & Sun), which has everything you need to know about Sydney Harbour National Park.

ACTIVITIES
Bushwalking

Close to Sydney, there are dramatic cliff-top walks in the Royal National Park, bushwalks around the inlets of Broken Bay in Ku-ring-gai Chase National Park, and sandstone bluffs, eucalyptus forests and wildflowers in the Blue Mountains. Further south, Kosciuszko National Park, in the Snowy Mountains, has excellent alpine walks in summer.

Both the NPWS and the **Confederation of Bushwalking Clubs NSW** (☎ 02-9294 6797; www .bushwalking.org.au; GPO Box 2090, Sydney 2001) have information on bushwalking. The **Department of Land & Water Conservation** (DLWC; Map pp94-6; ☎ 02-9228 6111; 23-33 Bridge St, Sydney) has free brochures and information on the 250km Great North Walk, linking Sydney

with the Hunter Valley, and the Hume & Hovell Track running through the high country between Yass and Albury.

Lonely Planet's *Walking in Australia* details some walks in NSW.

Cycling

Bicycle NSW (Map pp94-6; ☎ 02-9283 5200; Level 2, 209 Castlereagh St, Sydney) can provide information on cycling routes throughout the state.

Diving & Snorkelling

North of Sydney, try Terrigal, Port Stephens, Seal Rocks, Coffs Harbour or Byron Bay. On the south coast, head to glorious Jervis Bay, Merimbula or Eden.

Sailing

Sydney Harbour and Pittwater both offer exceptional sailing (for details of sailing courses see p106). Lake Macquarie south of Newcastle, and Myall Lakes just to the north, are also good. Contact the **Yachting Association of New South Wales** (☎ 02-9660 1266; Wentworth Park Complex, Wattle St, Glebe) for information on sailing clubs and courses.

Skiing

The Snowy Mountains is the best spot for skiing in NSW. See p223 for information on resorts and ski hire.

Swimming & Surfing

NSW's coastline is liberally sprinkled with beaches offering excellent swimming. North of Sydney, surfing spots include Newcastle, Port Macquarie, Seal Rocks, Crescent Head, Nambucca Heads, Coffs Harbour, Angourie, Lennox Head and Byron Bay. South of Sydney, try Wollongong, Jervis Bay, Ulladulla, Merimbula or Eden.

Surf carnivals start in December and run till April. Contact **Surf Life Saving New South Wales** (☎ 02-9984 7188; www.surflifesaving.com.au; PO Box 430, Narrabeen 2101) for details. See the boxed text 'Where to Surf in Australia' (p956) for further information.

White-Water Rafting & Canoeing

Good rafting spots include the upper Murray and Snowy Rivers in the Snowy Mountains, and the Shoalhaven River, 220km south of Sydney. In the north, there's rafting on the Nymboida and Gwydir Rivers. Albury, Jindabyne and Nowra are the centres for the southern rivers; Coffs Harbour and Nambucca Heads for the northern.

There's an abundance of canoeing spots in NSW, but in particular you might like to try Port Macquarie, Barrington Tops (for white-water canoeing), Myall Lakes, Jervis Bay and the Murrumbidgee River near Canberra. **New South Wales Canoeing Incorporated** (☎ 02-9660 4597; www.nswcanoe.org.au; Wentworth Park Complex, Wattle St, Glebe) can provide information, and publishes *The Canoeing Guide to NSW* ($32.95).

TOURS

Various companies operate tours to destinations such as the Blue Mountains (p148) and the Hunter Valley (p161). You can tailor your trip to include areas that interest you, such as wineries, skiing, bushwalking and surfing.

GETTING THERE & AWAY

NSW, the home of Sydney, is the most obvious arrival choice for most international visitors to Australia, with a number of airports, including Sydney's Kingsford Smith Airport. There are also hundreds of train and bus connections throughout the state and the rest of Australia. You can even arrive via boat, with the odd cruise ship docking in Sydney Harbour at the Overseas Passenger Terminal. By car and motorcycle, you'll probably reach NSW via the Hume Hwy if you're coming from the south, or via the Pacific Hwy if you're coming from the north. The Princes Hwy heads south from the capital along the state's charming southern coast.

GETTING AROUND

For transport around Sydney see p135.

Air

Smaller airlines like **Regional Express** (Rex; ☎ 13 17 13; www.regionalexpress.com.au) and **Eastern Australia Airlines** (☎ 13 12 23) operate comprehensive networks within the state, and other airlines serve particular regions.

Bus

Buses are often quicker and cheaper than trains, but not always. If you want to make stops on the way to your ultimate destination, look for cheap stopover deals rather than buying separate tickets. Once you have

reached your destination, there are usually local bus lines, although services may not be frequent. In remote areas, school buses may be the only option. The drivers will usually pick you up, but they're not obliged to do so.

Train

CountryLink (Map pp94-6; ☎ 13 22 32; www .countrylink.info) has the most comprehensive state rail service in Australia and will, in conjunction with connecting buses, take you to most sizable towns in NSW. All CountryLink services must be booked in advance; you can do this either by phone, online or in person at Central Station or one of the CountryLink Travel Centres at Circular Quay (Wharf 6), Wynyard Station or Town Hall Station. Passage for bicycles and surfboards must also be reserved in advance.

The frequency of services and their value for money are variable, so compare options with private bus services. CountryLink offers 1st- and economy-class tickets, as well as a quota of discount tickets; return fares are double the single fare. Australian students travel for half the economy fare.

The Backpacker Discovery Pass offers unlimited travel on the train and coach network in NSW (including trips to Brisbane, Surfers Paradise and Melbourne) for international travellers with a foreign passport. It costs from $165 (14 days) to $330 (six months). There's also the East Coast Discovery Pass, which can cover you from Melbourne to Cairns.

SYDNEY

☎ 02 / pop 4,041,400

Australia's oldest and largest European settlement is a vibrant city built around one of the most spectacular harbours in the world. Instantly recognisable thanks to its Opera House, harbour and bridge, Sydney also boasts lesser-known attractions like the historic Rocks, Victorian-era Paddington, heavenly beaches such as Bondi and Manly, and two superb coastal national parks on the city fringe.

An array of ethnic groups contribute to the city's social life – the dynamism of the Chinese community in particular has played an important role in altering the city's Anglo-Mediterranean fabric, and in preparing it to become a key player in Asia. The success of the 2000 Olympic Games only served to bolster Sydneysiders' pride in their waterside playground. It's just the place to combine relaxed hedonism, brash industriousness and look-at-me antics.

HISTORY

It was at Sydney Cove, where the ferries run from Circular Quay today, that the first European settlement was established in 1788, so it's not surprising that Sydney has a strong sense of history. But that doesn't stop the city from being far brasher and livelier than many of its younger Australian counterparts.

The city is built on land once occupied by the Eora tribe, whose presence lingers in the place names of some suburbs and whose artistic legacy can be seen at many Aboriginal engraving sites around the city. Many ascribe Sydney's raffish spirit to the fact that the military were essentially in charge of things in the late 18th century and early 19th century. Paying for labour and local products in rum (hence their name, the Rum Corps), the soldiers upset, defied and outmanoeuvred three of the colony's early governors, including one William Bligh, of *Bounty* mutiny fame.

ORIENTATION

The harbour divides Sydney into northern and southern halves, with the Sydney Harbour Bridge and the Harbour Tunnel joining the two shores. The city centre and most places of interest are south of the harbour. The central area is long and narrow, stretching from The Rocks and Circular Quay in the north to Central Station in the south. It is bounded by Darling Harbour to the west and a string of pleasant parks to the east.

SYDNEY IN...

Two Days

Start your day in Sydney with a walk around the historic Rocks area and Sydney Cove before heading to the **Sydney Opera House** (p92) and the **Royal Botanic Gardens** (p98). Walk to the **Art Gallery of New South Wales** (p98) before scooting off to **Bondi** (p102), enjoying lunch in a breezy restaurant or café, then enjoying a dip in Sydney's most famous beach. That night, catch a performance at the Opera House, before or after dining at one of Sydney's city restaurants.

Your next day should start with a ferry or JetCat trip to **Manly** (p104), where a cruisey open-air breakfast awaits, followed by a swim or long walk along the Manly Scenic Walkway. That night, head out to either **Darlinghurst** (p101) or **Surry Hills** (p101) for dinner and drinks.

Four Days

By the third day, you'll be itching to scale the **Sydney Harbour Bridge** (p89), so join a Bridgeclimb tour and see the harbour from high up. You'll need some serious sustenance after that, so lunch (preferably yum cha) in **Chinatown** (p93) is looking good. That night, take in the bright lights and trashy good times available at **Kings Cross** (p99).

On the fourth day, get out of town by taking the train to the majestic **Blue Mountains** (p143), and join in the sighing as you gaze upon the **Three Sisters** (p146). Have lunch in **Katoomba** (p146) before heading back to Sydney or staying the night in one of the mountain villages.

One Week

All of the above beckon, plus a trip to the 'insular peninsula' known as the **Northern Beaches** (p105), where you can frolic amongst the linen-wearing, pinot-sipping moneyed sets of **Palm Beach** (p105). If that doesn't appeal, a trip to the **Hunter Valley** (p159) will make you an expert on fine red wine in no time. The next day take a tour of one of **Sydney Harbour National Park's** (p88) attractions, before a ferry ride to **Watson's Bay** (p101) transports you to beer-garden heaven at the Watson's Bay Hotel.

Shop till you drop on your last day in Sydney, loading up on fashion in Sydney's **Paddington** (p101) and then goodies for the folks back home in **The Rocks** (p89) or at one of Sydney's many markets. Dinner with a view is a must on your final night.

East of the city centre are the inner-city suburbs of Darlinghurst, Kings Cross and Paddington. Further east again are exclusive suburbs like Double Bay and Vaucluse. To the southeast of these are the ocean-beach suburbs of Bondi and Coogee. Sydney's Kingsford Smith Airport is in Mascot, 10km south of the city centre, jutting into Botany Bay.

West of the centre are the previously working-class but now gentrified suburbs of Pyrmont, Glebe and Balmain. The inner west includes Newtown and Leichhardt.

Suburbs stretch a good 20km north and south of the centre, their extent limited by national parks. The suburbs north of the bridge are known collectively as the North Shore. The western suburbs sprawl for 50km to the foothills of the Blue Mountains, encompassing the once separate settlements of Parramatta and Penrith.

Maps

Just about every brochure you pick up includes a map of the city centre, but Lonely Planet's *Sydney City Map* ($7.80) has good coverage of the city centre and also covers the Blue Mountains. If you're intending to drive around the city, the *Sydney* UBD street directory ($35) is invaluable. For topographic maps, visit the **Department of Land and Water Conservation** (DLWC; Map pp94-6; ☎ 9228 6111; 23-33 Bridge St, City).

INFORMATION
Bookshops

Ariel (Map pp94-6; ☎ 9332 4581; 42 Oxford St, Paddington) Good for art and design titles.

Dymocks Books (Map pp94-6; ☎ 9235 0155; 424-430 George St, City) In excess of 250,000 titles spread over three floors.

Gleebooks (Map pp90-1; ☎ 9660 2333; 49 Glebe Point Rd, Glebe) Frequent winner of 'bookshop of the year' awards.

Lesley McKay's (Map pp90-1; ☎ 9327 1354; 346 New South Head Rd, Double Bay) Extremely helpful, well-informed staff/readers.

Travel Bookshop (Map pp94-6; ☎ 9261 8200; 175 Liverpool St, City) Crammed with, you guessed it, travel books.

Emergency

Lifeline (☎ 13 11 14) Over-the-phone counselling services, including suicide prevention.

NRMA (Map pp94-6; ☎ 13 21 32; 388 George St, City) For auto insurance and roadside service.

Police Stations (Map pp94-6; ☎ 000; 132 George St, The Rocks; 570 George St, City)

Rape Crisis Centre (☎ 1800 424 017, 9819 6565)

Wayside Chapel (Map p100; ☎ 9358 6577; 29 Hughes St, Potts Point) 24-hour crisis centre in the heart of Kings Cross.

Internet Access

Internet cafés are found throughout Sydney, especially around Kings Cross, Bondi and Glebe. Some stay open 24 hours. Rates are around $5 an hour. Plenty of hostels and hotels offer Internet access to their guests, as do public libraries (you'll need to book though).

Global Gossip (Map p100; ☎ 9326 9777; 111 Darlinghurst Rd, Kings Cross; ☷ 8am-midnight) Also in Bondi, near Central Station and in the city.

Travellers Contact Point (Map pp94-6; ☎ 9221 8744; Level 7, 428 George St, City) Free for first 30 minutes, though it's email only.

Left Luggage

Luggage lockers at Central Station (small/medium/large for 24hr $4/6/8; ☷ 6.30am-9.30pm)

Travellers Contact Point (Map pp94-6; ☎ 9221 8744; Level 7, 428 George St, City) Stores luggage for $20 per piece per month.

Medical Services

Kings Cross Travellers Clinic (Map p100; ☎ 9358 3066; 13 Springfield Ave, Kings Cross; ☷ 10am-1pm & 2-6pm Mon-Fri, 10am-noon Sat) Bookings advised for morning-after pill scripts and dive medicals.

Sydney Hospital (Map pp94-6; ☎ 9382 7111; 8 Macquarie St, City) This central city hospital has a 24-hour emergency ward.

Travellers Medical & Vaccination Centre (Map pp94-6; ☎ 9221 7133; Level 7, 428 George St, City; ☷ 9am-5.30pm Mon, Wed & Fri, 8am-5.30pm Tue, 9am-7.30pm Thu, 9am-1pm Sat) The best place to get your shots and medical advice related to travel.

Money

Airport bureaux de change (☷ 5.15am-10.30pm)

American Express (Map pp94-6; ☎ 1300 139 060; 105 Pitt St, City; ☷ 8.30am-5pm Mon-Fri) This branch can help with travel arrangements; there are other branches throughout town. There's also an exchange booth inside the Travel Bookshop.

Travelex (Map pp94-6; ☎ 9231 2877; 175 Pitt St, City; ☷ 9am-5pm Mon-Fri, 10am-2pm Sat) Other branches throughout Sydney and in HSBC bank branches.

There are plenty of banks and ATMs throughout Sydney. Seven-day change bureaus include the one in the coach terminal at Central Station (open 8am to 8pm), another opposite Wharf 6 at Circular Quay (open 8am to 10pm) and one at the pedestrian juncture of Springfield Ave and Darlinghurst Rd, Kings Cross (open 8am to midnight).

Post

The original **general post office** (GPO; Map pp94–6; 1 Martin Place, City; ☾ 8.15am-5.30pm Mon-Fri, 10am-2pm Sat) is central, and there's another **post office** (Map pp94–6; 130 Pitt St, City) with counter service. The **poste restante service** (Map pp94–6; 310 George St, City; ☾ 8.15am-5.30pm Mon-Fri, 10am-2pm Sat) has computer terminals that enable you to check if mail is waiting for you. You'll need identification.

Publications

The 'Metro' lift-out in Friday's *Sydney Morning Herald* provides a comprehensive listing of what's on in the city over the coming week. Free music and entertainment papers include *Drum Media, Revolver, 3D World* and *Sydney Star Observer* (the last one is gay).

There are plenty of guidebooks that cover Sydney. Lonely Planet's *Sydney* and *New South Wales* are general guides and there's also the handy-sized *Best of Sydney* guide.

Telephone

Global Gossip (Map p100; ☎ 9326 9777; 111 Darling-hurst Rd, Kings Cross; ☾ 8am-midnight) Offers discount long-distance and international calls.

Telephone Booths Can be found all over the city.

Telstra Phone Centre (Map pp94–6; 231 Elizabeth St, City; ☾ 7am-11pm Mon-Fri, 7am-7pm Sat & Sun) Has telephones galore and phone-card machines for international calls.

Tourist Information

City Host Information Kiosks (Map pp94–6; ☾ 9am-5pm winter, 10am-6pm summer) Circular Quay (cnr Pitt & Alfred Sts); Martin Place (between Elizabeth & Castlereagh Sts); Town Hall (cnr Druitt & George Sts)

Sydney Coach Terminal (Map pp94–6; ☎ 9281 9366; Eddy Ave, Central Station; ☾ 6am-10.30pm) Bus and hotel bookings, plus luggage storage.

Sydney Visitors Centre (☎ 9667 6050; Sydney International Airport; ☾ 6am-midnight) It can book discounted hotel rooms, tours and entertainment tickets.

Sydney Visitors Centre (Map pp94–6; ☎ 9240 8786; 106 George St, The Rocks; ☾ 9am-6pm)

Visitors Centre (Map pp94–6; ☎ 9281 0788; Darling Harbour; ☾ 10am-6pm) Next to the Imax Theatre.

Travel Agencies

Backpackers World (Map p100; ☎ 9380 2700; 212 Victoria St, Kings Cross)

YHA Membership & Travel Centre (Map pp94–6; ☎ 9261 1111; 422 Kent St; ☾ 9am-5pm Mon-Fri, 9am-2pm Sat) YHA bookings worldwide – also try the travel agent in the Sydney Central YHA.

Other Services

Travellers Aid Society (Map pp94–6; ☎ 9211 2469; Platform 1, Central Station; ☾ 8am-2.30pm Mon-Fri) Provides general information, travel assistance, phone recharge and hot showers.

SIGHTS
Sydney Harbour

Sydney's stunning harbour (**Port Jackson**) is both a major port and the city's playground. It stretches some 20km inland to join the mouth of the Parramatta River. The headlands at the entrance are known as North Head and South Head. The most scenic part of the harbour is between the Heads and the Harbour Bridge, 8km inland. **Middle Harbour** is a large inlet that heads northwest a couple of kilometres inside the Heads.

Sydney's **harbour beaches** are generally sheltered, calm coves with little of the frenetic activity of the ocean beaches. On the south shore, they include Lady Bay (nude), Camp Cove and Nielsen Park. On the North Shore there are harbour beaches at Manly Cove, Reef Beach, Clontarf, China-man's Beach and Balmoral.

SYDNEY HARBOUR NATIONAL PARK

This park protects the scattered pockets of bushland around the harbour and includes several small islands. It offers some great walking tracks, scenic lookouts, Aboriginal carvings and a handful of historic sites. On the south shore it incorporates South Head and Nielsen Park; on the North Shore it includes North Head, Dobroyd Head, Middle Head and Ashton Park. Fort Denison, Goat, Clarke, Rodd and Shark Islands are also part of the park. Pick up information at **Sydney Harbour National Parks Information Centre** (Map pp94–6; ☎ 9247 5033; 110 George St, The Rocks; ☾ 9.30am-4.30pm Mon-Fri, 10am-4.30pm Sat & Sun), which is housed inside historic Cadman's Cottage.

Previously known as Pinchgut, **Fort Denison** is a small, fortified island off Mrs Macquaries Point, originally used to isolate troublesome convicts. The fort was built during the Crimean War amid fears of a Russian invasion (seriously!). **Tours** of Fort Denison can be booked at, and depart from, Cadman's Cottage. Take your pick of the heritage tour (adult/child/family $22/18/75) or the brunch tour (adult/child $50/45).

There are tours of **Goat Island**, just west of the Harbour Bridge, which has been a shipyard, quarantine station and gunpowder depot. Take a heritage tour (adult/child/family $20/16/65) or a Gruesome Tales tour ($25). Tours are booked at, and depart from, Cadman's Cottage.

The Rocks   Map pp94–6

Sydney's first European settlement was established on the rocky spur of land on the western side of Sydney Cove, from which the Harbour Bridge now crosses to the North Shore. It was a squalid, raucous and notoriously dangerous place full of convicts, whalers, prostitutes and street gangs, though in the 1820s the nouveaux riches built three-storey houses on the ridges overlooking the slums, starting the city's obsession with prime real estate, which continues today.

It later became an area of warehouses and maritime commerce and then slumped into decline as modern shipping and storage facilities moved away from Circular Quay. An outbreak of bubonic plague in the early 20th century led to whole streets being razed, and then the construction of the Harbour Bridge resulted in further demolition.

Since the 1970s redevelopment has turned much of The Rocks into a sanitised, historical tourist precinct, full of narrow cobbled lanes, fine colonial buildings, converted warehouses, tearooms and Australiana. If you ignore the kitsch, it's a delightful place to stroll around, especially in the poky backstreets and in the less-developed, tight-knit community of Millers Point.

Cadman's Cottage (☎ 9247 5033; 110 George St, The Rocks; ☼ 9.30am-4.30pm Mon-Fri, 10am-4.30pm Sat & Sun) is the oldest house in Sydney (1816) and the former home of the last government coxswain, John Cadman; it's now home to the Sydney Harbour National Parks Information Centre.

Despite the entire helpful tourist infrastructure, the beauty of The Rocks is that it's as much fun to wander around aimlessly as it is to visit particular attractions. Soak up the atmosphere, sample the frequent entertainment in The Rocks Square on Playfair St, browse the stores for gifts, grab a beer at one of the pubs, admire the views of Circular Quay and Campbells Cove, and join the melee at the weekend **Rocks Market** (George St).

A short walk west along Argyle Street, through the awe-inspiring **Argyle Cut** (excavated by convicts) takes you to the other side of the peninsula and **Millers Point**, a delightful district of early colonial homes with a quintessentially English village green. Nearby is the 1848 **Garrison Church** and the more secular delights of the Lord Nelson Hotel and the Hero of Waterloo Hotel, which tussle over the title of Sydney's oldest pub.

Sydney Observatory (☎ 9217 0485; Watson Rd, Observatory Hill; admission free; ☼ 10am-5pm) has a commanding, copper dome–bedecked position atop Observatory Park overlooking Millers Point and the harbour. Nightly sky-watching visits (adult/child/family $10/5/25) are possible, but must be booked in advance. In the old military hospital building close by, the **SH Ervin Gallery** (☎ 9258 0123; Watson Rd, Observatory Hill; adult/child $6/4; ☼ 11am-5pm Tue-Fri, noon-5pm Sat & Sun), in the National Trust Centre, has temporary exhibitions on Australian art that invariably prove popular. It's also the home of the annual Salon des Refuses show, for rejected Archibald Prize contenders.

At Dawes Point, on Walsh Bay, just west of the Harbour Bridge, are several renovated wharves. **Pier One** now houses a luxury hotel; **Pier Four** is beautifully utilised as the home of the prestigious Sydney Theatre, Bangarra Dance Theatre, Sydney Dance Company and Australian Theatre for Young People (ATYP). Others appear to be getting the 'luxury waterfront apartments' treatment.

Sydney Harbour Bridge

The much-loved, imposing 'old coat hanger' crosses the harbour at one of its narrowest points, linking the southern and northern shores and joining central Sydney with the satellite business district in North Sydney. The bridge was completed in 1932 at a cost of $20 million and has always been a favourite icon, partly because of its sheer size,

SYDNEY HARBOUR & INNER SUBURBS

INFORMATION	
German Consulate	1 E6
Netherlands Consulate	2 F6

SIGHTS & ACTIVITIES	pp88-107
Admiralty House	3 C3
Brett Whiteley Studio	4 C6
Centennial Park	5 E6
EastSail Sailing School	6 E5
Fox Studios Australia	7 D6
Hordern Pavilion	(see 7)
Inner City Cycles	8 B6
Kirribilli House	9 D3
Moore Park	10 D6
North Sydney Olympic Pool	11 C3
Sydney Flying Squadron	12 C3
Taronga Zoo	13 E3
Total Skate	14 E6
Vaucluse House	15 G3

SLEEPING	pp110-19
Alishan International Guest House	16 B6
Doyles Palace Hotel	17 H2
Glebe Point YHA	18 A5
Glenferrie Lodge	19 C3
Haven Inn	20 A5
Kangaroo Bakpack	21 C6
Kirribilli Court Private Hotel	22 D3
Metro Inn	23 E5
Savoy Hotel	24 E5
Tricketts Bed & Breakfast	25 A5
Wattle House	26 A5

EATING	pp119-27
Aqua Dining	(see 11)
Badde Manors	27 B6
Bistro Lulu	28 D6
Café Niki	29 C6
Iku Wholefoods	(see 27)

Il Baretto	30 C6
Jones the Grocer	31 E6
Maya da Dhaba	32 C6
Ripples	33 C3
Spanish Tapas	34 B6
Tanjore	(see 34)

DRINKING	pp127-9
Lansdowne Hotel	35 B6
London Hotel	36 A4
Lord Dudley Hotel	37 E6
Paddington Inn Hotel	38 D6
Strawberry Hills Hotel	39 C6

ENTERTAINMENT	pp129-32
Belvoir St Theatre	40 C6
Chauvel Cinema	41 D6
Lyric Theatre	42 B5
Star City	(see 42)

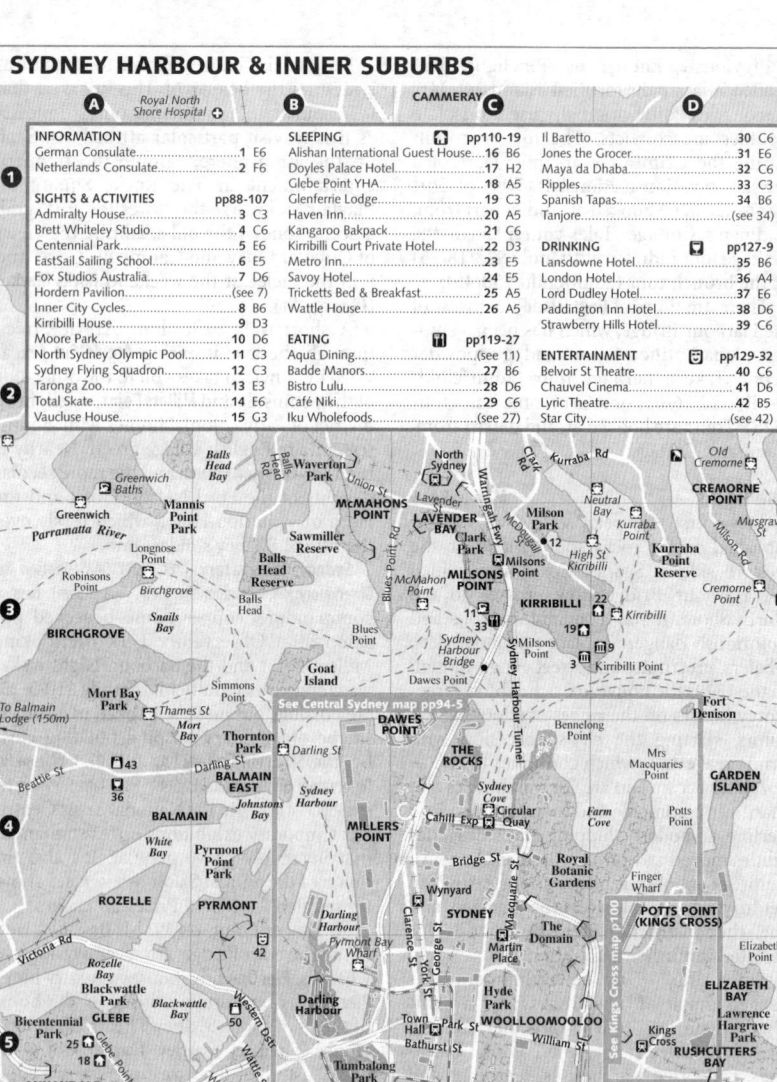

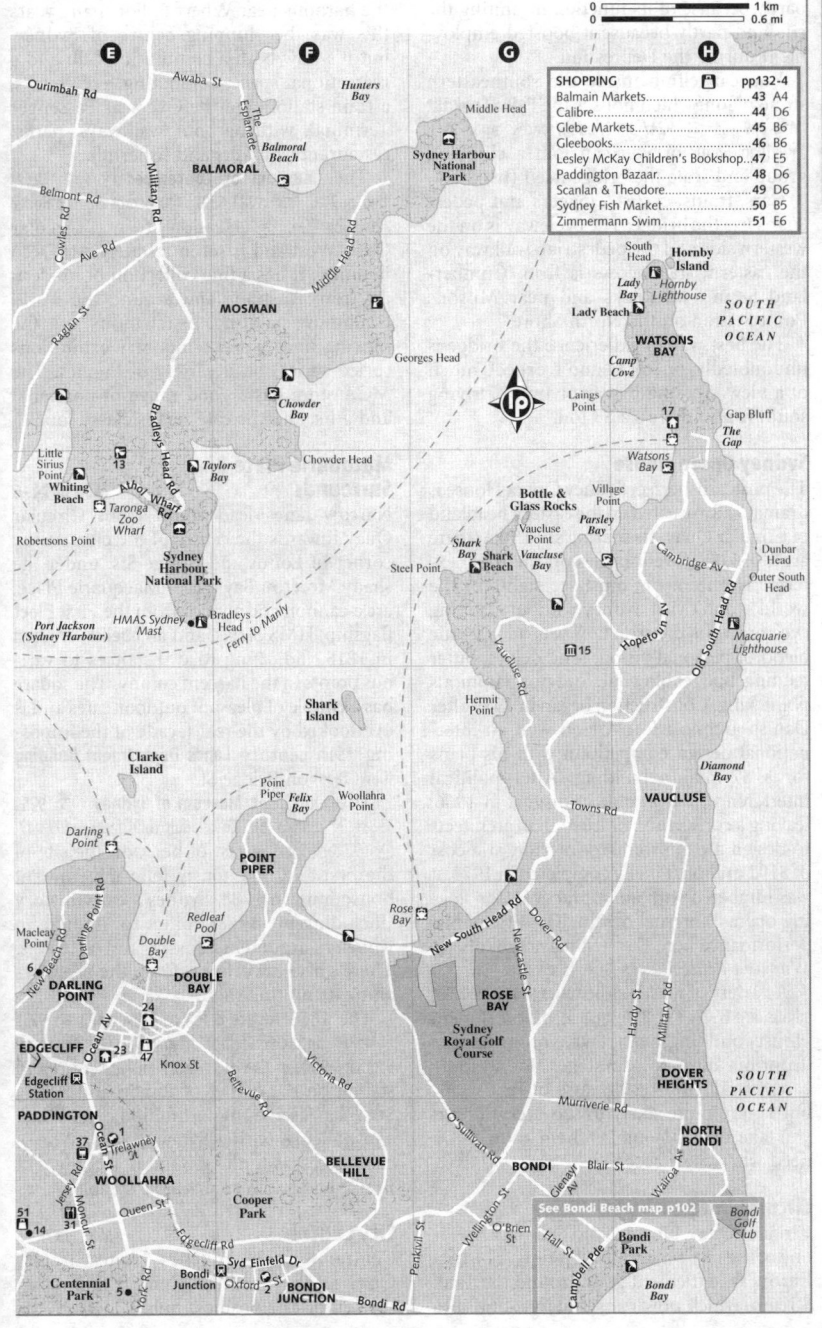

See Bondi Beach map p102

partly because of its function in uniting the city and partly because it boosted employment during the Depression.

You can climb inside the southeastern stone pylon, which houses the **Pylon Lookout** (Map pp94-6; ☎ 9247 3408; adult/concession $8.50/3; ☼ 10am-5pm), or you can join a climbing group and scale the bridge itself (p108).

Cars, trains, cyclists, joggers and pedestrians use the bridge. The cycleway is on the western side and the pedestrian walkway on the eastern; stair access is from Cumberland St in The Rocks and near Milsons Point Station on the North Shore.

The best way to experience the bridge is undoubtedly on foot; don't expect much of a view crossing by car or train. Driving south (only) there's a $3 toll.

Sydney Opera House

The postcard-perfect Sydney Opera House is dramatically situated on the eastern headland of Circular Quay. Its soaring shell-like (there are 1,056,000 Swedish tiles on the roof) exterior is one of *the* must-see sights in the world – don't visit Sydney without clapping eyes on it. Its construction was an operatic blend of personal vision, long delays, bitter feuding, budget blowouts and pusillanimous politicking. Construction began in 1959 after Danish architect Jorn Utzon won an international design competition with his plans for a $7-million building. After political interference, Utzon quit in disgust in 1966, leaving a consortium of Australian architects to design a compromised interior, at a cost of $102 million. Finally completed in 1973, it was lumbered with an impractical (for staging operas) internal design. The first public performance here was, tellingly, Prokofiev's *War and Peace*.

A variety of worthwhile **tours** (☎ 9250 7250; admission $17-28; ☼ 8.30am-5pm) of the Opera House buildings can take you from the 'front of house' to backstage. Not all tours can visit all theatres because of rehearsals, but you're more likely to see everything if you take an early tour. Let them know if you need wheelchair access.

Circular Quay

Circular Quay, built around Sydney Cove, is one of the city's major focal points. The first European settlement grew around the Tank Stream, which now runs underground into the harbour near Wharf 6. For many years this was the shipping centre of Sydney, but it's now both a commuting hub and a recreational space, combining ferry quays, a train station and the Overseas Passenger Terminal, with harbour walkways, parks, restaurants, buskers and fisherfolk.

The **Museum of Contemporary Art** (MCA; Map pp94-6; ☎ 9241 5892; 140 George St, The Rocks; admission free; ☼ 10am-5pm) fronts Circular Quay West and is set in a stately Art Deco building. It has a fine collection of modern art from Australia and around the world (sculpture, painting, installations and the moving image) and temporary exhibitions (price varies) on a variety of themes. The MCA store has a good range of postcards and gifts, and the café serves classy food.

Macquarie Place & Surrounds   Map pp94–6

Narrow lanes lead south from Circular Quay towards the centre of the city. At the corner of Loftus and Bridge Sts, under the shady Moreton Bay figs in Macquarie Place, are a cannon and anchor from the First Fleet flagship, HMS *Sirius*, and an **obelisk**, erected in 1818, indicating road distances to various points in the nascent colony. The square has a couple of pleasant outdoor cafés and is overlooked by the rear façade of the imposing 19th-century **Lands Department Building** (DLWC Bldg) on Bridge St.

The excellent **Museum of Sydney** (☎ 9251 5988; 37 Phillip St, City; adult/child/family $7/3/17; ☼ 9.30am-5pm) is east of here, on the site of the first and infamously fetid government house built in 1788. Sydney's early history (including pre-1788) comes to life here in whisper, argument, gossip and artefacts. There's also a worthy café on the premises and a damn fine shop.

The 1856 **Justice & Police Museum** (☎ 9252 1144; 8 Phillip St, City; adult/child/family $7/3/17; ☼ 10am-5pm Sat & Sun), in the old water-police court and station on the corner of Phillip and Albert Sts, has fascinating exhibitions on crime and policing, with a Sydney focus. Wheelchair access is to the ground floor only, but Braille and audio guides are available.

City Centre   Map pp94–6

Central Sydney stretches from Circular Quay in the north to Central Station in the south. The business hub is towards the northern end, but most redevelopment is occurring at the southern end and this is gradually shifting the focus of the city.

Sydney lacks a true civic centre, but **Martin Place** lays claim to the honour, if only by default. This grand, revamped pedestrian mall extends from Macquarie St to George St and is impressively lined by the monumental buildings of financial institutions and the colonnaded Victorian post office at No 1. There's plenty of public seating, a cenotaph commemorating Australia's war dead and an amphitheatre where lunchtime entertainment is sometimes staged.

The **Sydney Town Hall**, a few blocks south of here on the corner of George and Druitt Sts, was built in 1874. The elaborate chamber room and concert hall inside matches its outrageously ornate exterior. Next door, the Anglican **St Andrew's Cathedral**, built around the same time, is the oldest cathedral in Australia.

The city's most sumptuous shopping complex, the Byzantine-style **Queen Victoria Building** (QVB), is next to the town hall and takes up an entire city block bordered by George, Druitt, York and Market Sts. Another lovingly restored shopping centre is the **Strand Arcade**, on Pitt St Mall and George St.

There are 45-minute tours of the splendidly over-the-top **State Theatre** (☎ 9373 6652; 49 Market St; adult/child $12/8; ☺ 11.30am-3pm Mon-Fri), which was built in 1929.

To the southwest are the **Spanish Quarter** and **Chinatown**, dynamic areas spreading and breathing life into the city's lacklustre southeastern zone, where Central Station lies isolated on the southern periphery.

Darling Harbour   Map pp94–6

This huge waterfront leisure park on the city centre's western edge, once a thriving dockland area, was reinvigorated in the 1980s by a combination of vision, politicking and big money. The supposed centrepiece is the **Harbourside centre**, which has struggled to shrug off its 'white elephant' tag ever since it was built, despite extensive refurbishment in the last few years. It houses shops and restaurants. The real attractions are the stunning aquarium, excellent museums and Chinese Garden.

Until recently, the emphasis here was on tacky tourist 'entertainment', but the snazzy

new wining and dining precincts of **Cockle Bay Wharf**, built opposite Harbourside, and **King St Wharf** have lent the area a bit more kudos with Sydneysiders and visitors alike. The monorail and metrail link Darling Harbour to the city centre.

Ferries leave from Circular Quay's Wharf 5 and stop at Darling Harbour's Aquarium and Pyrmont Bay wharves ($4.30). The Sydney Explorer bus (p108) stops at four points around Darling Harbour every 20 minutes.

The main pedestrian approaches are across footbridges from Market and Liverpool Sts. The one from Market St leads to **Pyrmont Bridge**, now a pedestrian-and-monorail-only route, but once famous as the world's first electrically operated swingspan bridge.

The **Visitors Centre** (☎ 9281 0788; ☺ 10am-6pm) is under the highway, next to Imax.

SYDNEY AQUARIUM

Near the eastern end of Pyrmont Bridge, this magnificent **aquarium** (Map pp94-6; ☎ 9262 2300; Aquarium Pier, Darling Harbour; adult/child/family $23/11/50; ☺ 9am-10pm) displays the richness of Australian marine life. Three 'oceanariums' are moored in the harbour with sharks, rays and big fish in one, and Sydney Harbour marine life and seals in the others. There are also informative and well-presented exhibits of freshwater fish and coral gardens. The transparent underwater tunnels are eerily spectacular.

AUSTRALIAN NATIONAL MARITIME MUSEUM

This wonderful thematic **museum** (Map pp94-6; ☎ 9298 3777; 2 Murray St, City; adult/concession/family $10/6/25; ☺ 9.30am-5pm) tells the story of Australia's relationship with the sea, from Aboriginal canoes and the First Fleet to surf culture and the America's Cup. Even the building, with its sail-like roof and wave-like lines, harkens to the sea. The museum is near the western end of Pyrmont Bridge, and has good disabled access. Regular guided tours are available, too.

POWERHOUSE MUSEUM

Sydney's hippest **museum** (Map pp94-6; ☎ 9217 0100; 500 Harris St, Ultimo; adult/concession/family $10/3/23; ☺ 10am-5pm) covers the decorative arts, social history, and science and technology, with eclectic exhibitions

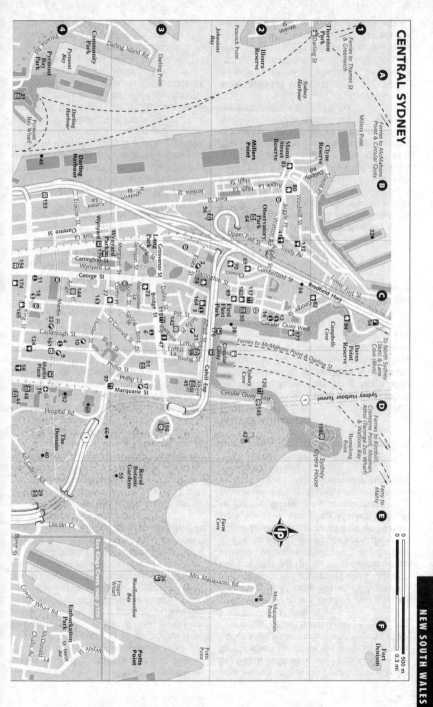

CENTRAL SYDNEY

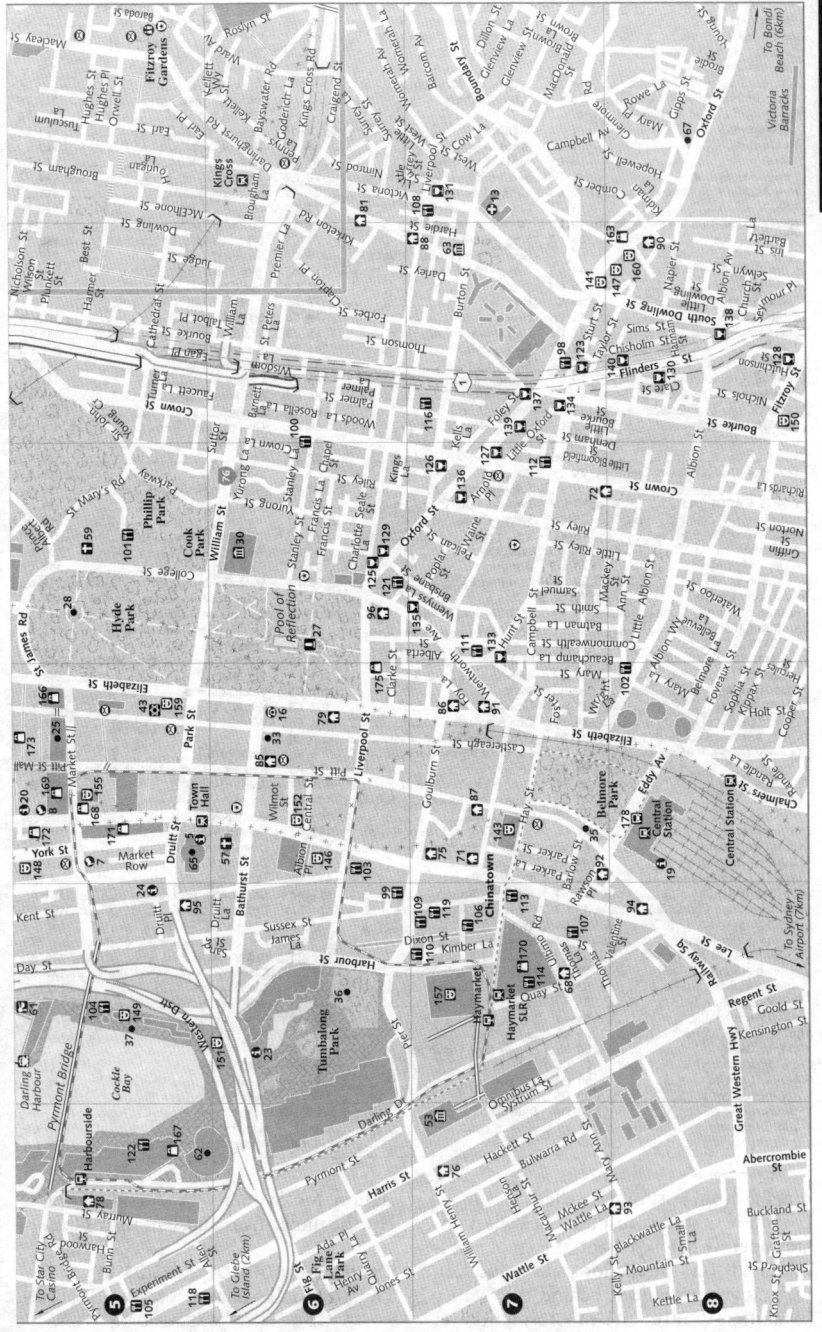

ranging from costume jewellery and modern music to space capsules. The collections are superbly displayed and the emphasis is on hands-on interaction and education via enjoyment. Find it behind the Sydney Exhibition Centre – it's in a former power station for Sydney's now-defunct trams. For the under-fives and seniors it's free.

CHINESE GARDEN OF FRIENDSHIP
The tranquil **Chinese Garden** (Map pp94-6; ☎ 9281 6863; adult/child/family $4.50/2/10;

9.30am-5.30pm), in the southeastern corner of Darling Harbour, was designed by landscape architects from Guangdong, and is an oasis of lush serenity. Enter through the Courtyard of Welcoming Fragrance, circle the Lake of Brightness and finish with tea and cake in the **Chinese teahouse** (10am-4.30pm), or by having your photo taken in a Chinese opera costume (hey, Liv Tyler did).

STAR CITY

Looking for subdued good taste and muted colour schemes? Dream on, at the mammoth temple of mammon that is **Star City** (Map pp90-1; ☎ 9777 9000; 80 Pyrmont St, Pyrmont; 24hr), which is on the northwestern headland of Darling Harbour. Star City includes a **casino**, two **theatres**, and a lurid volcano, as well as the inevitable try-hard nightclub, flash hotel and retail outlets (if you have any money left over). There's a metrail and monorail stop here, and bus No 888 also sweeps through.

SYDNEY FISH MARKET

With over 15 million kilograms of seafood sold here annually, this enormous **fish market** (Map pp90-1; ☎ 9004 1100; cnr Pyrmont Bridge Rd & Bank St, Pyrmont; 7am-4pm) is the place to get on first-name terms with a bewildering array of still-thrashing piscatorial pals. You can see fish auctions (early mornings), eat sushi, attend seafood cooking classes (call for details) and wonder if you'll ever get the stink out of your nostrils. It's west of Darling Harbour, on Blackwattle Bay. The metrail (the stop's called Fish Market) is the best way to get here.

Macquarie Street   Map pp94–6

Sydney's greatest concentration of early public buildings grace Macquarie St, which runs along the eastern edge of the city from Hyde Park to the Opera House. Many of the buildings were commissioned by Lachlan Macquarie, the first governor to have a vision of the city beyond being a convict colony. He enlisted convict forger Francis Greenway as an architect to realise his plans.

Two Greenway gems on Queens Square, at the northern end of Hyde Park, are **St James Church** (1819–24) and the 1819 Georgian-style **Hyde Park Barracks Museum**

(☎ 9223 8922; Queens Square, Macquarie St, City; adult/child/family $7/3/17; 9.30am-5pm). The barracks were built originally as convict quarters, then became an immigration depot, and later a court. The museum details the history of the building and provides an interesting perspective on Sydney's social history, with the best use of rats (see for yourself) we've ever seen in a display. Next door is the lovely **Mint Building** (☎ 9217 0311; Macquarie St, City), which was originally the southern wing of the infamous Rum Hospital built by two Sydney merchants in 1816 in return for a monopoly on the rum trade. It became a branch of the Royal Mint in 1854. There's a café on the premises, but nothing else is open to the public.

The Mint's twin is **Parliament House** (☎ 9230 2047; Macquarie St, City; admission free; 9.30am-4pm Mon-Fri), which was originally the northern wing of the Rum Hospital. This simple, proud building has been home to the NSW Parliament since 1829. The public gallery is open on days when parliament is sitting. Wheelchair access is excellent.

Next to Parliament House is the **State Library of NSW** (☎ 9273 1414; Macquarie St, City; 9am-5pm Mon-Fri, 11am-5pm Sat & Sun), which is more of a cultural centre than a traditional library. It holds over five million tomes, the smallest being a tablet-sized Lord's Prayer, and hosts innovative temporary exhibitions in its **galleries** (9am-5pm Mon-Fri, 10am-5pm Sat & Sun). The library's modern wing (easy to spot) also has a great bookshop, filled with Australian titles. Disabled access is excellent.

The **Sydney Conservatorium of Music** (☎ 9351 1222; Macquarie St, City) was built by Greenway as the stables and servants' quarters of Macquarie's planned government house. Macquarie was replaced as governor before the house could be finished, partly because of the project's extravagance. See p131 for more information about the music recitals held here.

Built between 1837 and 1845, **Government House** (☎ 9931 5222; Macquarie St, City; admission free; grounds 10am-4pm daily, house 10am-3pm Fri-Sun) dominates the western headland of Farm Cove and, until early 1996, was the official residence of the governor of NSW. It's a marvellous example of the Gothic Revival style. Tours of the house depart every half-hour from 10.30am.

Art Gallery of NSW

The **art gallery** (AGNSW; Map pp94-6; ☎ 9225 1744; Art Gallery Rd, City; admission free; ☺ 10am-5pm) has an excellent permanent display of 19th- and 20th-century Australian art, Aboriginal and Torres Strait Islander art, 15th- to 19th-century European and Asian art, and some inspired temporary exhibits. It's in the Domain, east of Macquarie St. Free guided tours are held at 1pm. There's a free Aboriginal dance performance at noon Tuesday to Saturday. There's usually a charge for some temporary exhibitions. The frequently controversial, much-discussed Archibald Prize exhibition is held here annually, with portraits of the famous and not-so-famous bringing out the art critic in almost every Sydneysider. Wheelchair access is good.

Australian Museum

This natural history **museum** (Map pp94-6; ☎ 9320 6000; www.amonline.net.au; 6 College St, City; adult/child/family $8/3/19; ☺ 9.30am-5pm) has an excellent Australian wildlife collection and a gallery tracing Aboriginal history and the Dreamtime. It's on the eastern flank of Hyde Park, on the corner of College and William Sts. There's an indigenous performance at noon and 2pm every Sunday, and a range of kids' activities in the holidays. It's also wheelchair accessible.

Royal Botanic Gardens

The city's favourite picnic spot, jogging route and place to stroll is the enchanting **Royal Botanic Gardens** (Map pp94-6; ☎ 9231 8111; Mrs Macquaries Rd, City; admission free; ☺ 7am-sunset, visitors centre 9.30am-5pm) which borders Farm Cove, east of the Opera House. The gardens were established in 1816 and feature plant life from the South Pacific. They include the site of the colony's first paltry vegetable patch, which has been preserved as the First Farm exhibit.

There's a fabulous **Sydney Tropical Centre** (Map pp94-6; adult/child $2.20/1.10; ☺ 10am-4pm) housed in the interconnecting Arc and Pyramid glasshouses. It's a great place to visit on a cool, grey day. The multistorey Arc has a collection of rampant climbers and trailers from the world's rainforests, while the Pyramid houses the Australian collection, including monsoonal, woodland and tropical rainforest plants. Other attractions in the gardens include the Fernery, the Succulent Garden and the Rose Garden.

Free guided **tours** depart at 10.30am daily from the information booth at the Gardens Shop. As far as wildlife goes, you can't fail to notice the gardens' resident colony of grey-headed flying foxes (*Pteropus poliocephalus*), who spend their days hanging around (literally) and their nights in flight. The park's paths are for the most part wheelchair accessible, although there are some flights of stairs scattered about.

Other Parks & Gardens

The **Domain** (Map pp94-6) is a pleasant grassy area east of Macquarie St that was set aside by Governor Phillip for public recreation. Today it's used by city workers as a place to escape the city hubbub, and on Sunday afternoon it's the gathering place for soap-box speakers who do their best to engage or enrage their listeners.

On the eastern edge of the city centre is the formal **Hyde Park** (Map pp94-6), once the colony's first racetrack and cricket pitch. It has a grand avenue of trees, delightful fountains, and a giant public chessboard. It contains the dignified **Anzac Memorial** (Map pp94-6) which has a free exhibition on the ground floor covering the 10 overseas conflicts in which Australians have fought. **St Mary's Cathedral** (Map pp94-6; ☎ 9220 0400; cnr College St & St Mary's Rd, City; ☺ 6.30am-6pm) overlooks the park from the east (with its new copper spires) and the 1878 **Great Synagogue** (Map pp94-6; ☎ 9267 2477; 187a Elizabeth St) from the west. Free tours of the synagogue take place at noon Tuesday and Thursday (entry at 166 Castlereagh St).

Sydney's biggest park is **Centennial Park** (Map pp90-1), which has running, cycling, skating and horse-riding tracks, duck ponds, barbecue sites and sports pitches. It's 5km from the centre, just southeast of Paddington.

Moore Park (Map pp90-1) abuts the western flank of Centennial Park and contains sports pitches, a golf course, an equestrian centre, the Fox film studio and entertainment complex, the Aussie Stadium and the Sydney Cricket Ground (SCG). **Sportspace Tours** (☎ 9380 0383; adult/child/family $20/13/52; ☺ 10am & 1pm Mon-Fri) offers behind-the-scenes guided tours (1½ hours) of the SCG and Aussie Stadium.

BEST VIEWS IN TOWN...

Sydney is an ostentatious city that offers visitors a dramatic spectacle. You can see the complete panorama by whooshing to the top of **Sydney Tower** (Map pp94-6; ☎ 9223 0933; www.sydney skytour.com.au; cnr Market & Castlereagh Sts; adult/child/conc/family $22/13.20/15.85/55; ⏰ 9am-10.30pm, until 11.30pm Sat), a needle-like column with an observation deck and revolving restaurants set 250m above the ground. The views extend west to the Blue Mountains and east to the ocean, as well as to the streets of inner Sydney below. Skytour is a virtual reality ride through Australia's history and landscape, and is included in the admission price. To get to the tower, enter Centrepoint from Market St and take the lift to the podium level where you buy your ticket.

The **Harbour Bridge** is another obvious vantage point: try the **Pylon Lookout** (Map pp94-6) or a **Bridgeclimb** tour (p108).

There are impressive ground-level views of the city and harbour from **Mrs Macquaries Point**, and from **Observatory Hill** in Millers Point. **Blues Point Reserve** and **Bradleys Head** are the best vantage points on the North Shore.

The most enjoyable and atmospheric way to view Sydney is by boat. If you can't persuade someone to take you sailing, jump aboard a ferry at Circular Quay. The Manly ferry offers an unforgettable cruise down the length of the harbour east of the bridge for a mere $5.40.

If you're in the vicinity of Kings Cross, the northern end of Victoria St in **Potts Point** is an excellent vantage point to take in the cityscape and its best-known icons, especially at night.

Kings Cross

The Cross is a cocktail of strip joints, prostitution, crime, and drugs shaken and stirred; with a handful of great restaurants, smart cafés, upmarket hotels and backpacker hostels. It attracts an odd mix of highlife, lowlife, sailors, tourists and suburbanites looking for a big night out.

The Cross has always been lovably raffish, from its early days as a centre of bohemianism to the Vietnam War era, when it became the vice centre of Australia. It appeals to the larrikin spirit, which always enjoys a bit of devil-may-care and 24-hour drinking. Many travellers begin and end their Australian adventures in the Cross, and it's a good place to swap information, meet up with friends, find work, browse notice boards and buy/sell a car.

Darlinghurst Rd is the trashy main drag. This doglegs into Macleay St, which continues into salubrious Potts Point. Most hostels are on Victoria St, which diverges from Darlinghurst Rd just north of William St, near the iconic Coca Cola sign. The thistlelike **El Alamein Fountain** (Map p100), in the Fitzroy Gardens, has a market here every Sunday.

In the dip between the Cross and the city is **Woolloomooloo**, one of Sydney's oldest areas, and an interesting place to stroll around. The **Finger Wharf** houses apartments, restaurants and a hotel. **Harry's Café**

de Wheels (Map p100), next to the wharf, must be one of the few pie carts in the world to be a tourist attraction. It opened in 1945, stays open 18 hours a day and is the place to go for a late-night fill-up.

The easiest way to get to the Cross from the city is by train ($2.20). It's the first stop outside the city loop on the line to Bondi Junction. Bus Nos 324, 325 and 327 from Circular Quay pass through the Cross. You can stroll from Hyde Park along William St in 15 minutes. A longer, more interesting route involves crossing the Domain, traversing the pedestrian bridge behind the Art Gallery of NSW, walking past Woolloomooloo's wharf and climbing McElhone Stairs from Cowper Wharf Rd, ending up at the northern end of Victoria St.

Inner East

The backbone of Darlinghurst, Surry Hills and Paddington, **Oxford St** is one of the more happening places for late-night action. It's a strip of shops, cafés, bars and nightclubs whose flamboyance and spirit can be largely attributed to the vibrant and vocal gay community. The route of the Sydney Gay & Lesbian Mardi Gras parade passes this way.

The main drag of Oxford St runs from the southeastern corner of Hyde Park to the northwestern corner of Centennial Park, though it continues in name to Bondi

KINGS CROSS

0 — 200 m
0 — 0.1 mi

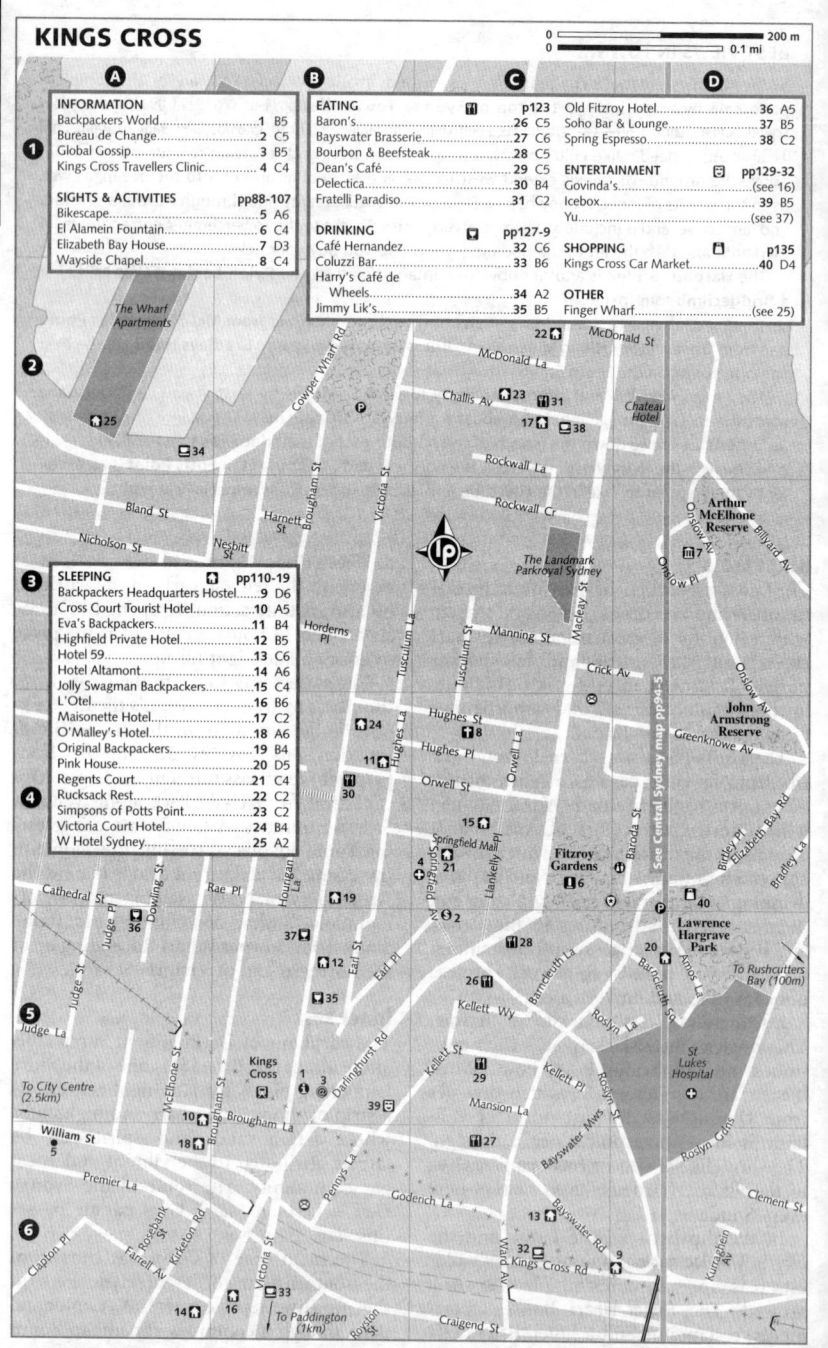

INFORMATION
Backpackers World	1 B5
Bureau de Change	2 C5
Global Gossip	3 B5
Kings Cross Travellers Clinic	4 C4

SIGHTS & ACTIVITIES pp88-107
Bikescape	5 A6
El Alamein Fountain	6 C4
Elizabeth Bay House	7 D3
Wayside Chapel	8 C4

EATING p123
Baron's	26 C5
Bayswater Brasserie	27 C6
Bourbon & Beefsteak	28 C5
Dean's Café	29 C5
Delectica	30 B4
Fratelli Paradiso	31 C2

DRINKING pp127-9
Café Hernandez	32 C6
Coluzzi Bar	33 B6
Harry's Café de Wheels	34 A2
Jimmy Lik's	35 B5

Old Fitzroy Hotel	36 A5
Soho Bar & Lounge	37 B5
Spring Espresso	38 C2

ENTERTAINMENT pp129-32
Govinda's	(see 16)
Icebox	39 B5
Yu	(see 37)

SHOPPING p135
Kings Cross Car Market	40 D4

OTHER
Finger Wharf	(see 25)

SLEEPING pp110-19
Backpackers Headquarters Hostel	9 D6
Cross Court Tourist Hotel	10 A5
Eva's Backpackers	11 B4
Highfield Private Hotel	12 B5
Hotel 59	13 C6
Hotel Altamont	14 A6
Jolly Swagman Backpackers	15 C4
L'Otel	16 B6
Maisonette Hotel	17 C2
O'Malley's Hotel	18 A6
Original Backpackers	19 B4
Pink House	20 D5
Regents Court	21 C4
Rucksack Rest	22 C2
Simpsons of Potts Point	23 C2
Victoria Court Hotel	24 B4
W Hotel Sydney	25 A2

Junction. Taylor Square is the main hub. (An orientation warning: Oxford St's street numbers restart on the Darlinghurst-Paddington border, west of the junction with South Dowling and Victoria Sts.) Bus Nos 380 and 382 from Circular Quay, and No 378 from Railway Square, run the length of the street.

DARLINGHURST

Darlinghurst is a vital area of urban cool full of bright young things. There's no better way to soak up its studied ambience than to loiter in a few outdoor cafés and do as the others do. Darlinghurst is wedged between Oxford and William Sts, and encompasses the vibrant 'Little Italy' of Stanley St in East Sydney. The **Sydney Jewish Museum** (Map pp94-6; ☎ 9360 7999; 148 Darlinghurst Rd; adult/child/family $10/6/22; ✆ 10am-4pm Sun-Thur, 10am-2pm Fri, closed Jewish holidays), on the corner of Darlinghurst Rd and Burton St, has evocative and powerful exhibits on Australian Jewish history and the Holocaust.

SURRY HILLS

South of Darlinghurst is Surry Hills, home to a mishmash of inner-city residents and a swag of good pubs. Once the undisputed centre of Sydney's rag trade and print media, many of its warehouses have been converted to flash apartments. A cute **market** is held on the first Saturday of the month in Shannon Reserve, on the corner of Crown and Foveaux Sts. The **Brett Whiteley Studio** (Map pp90-1; ☎ 9225 1744; 2 Raper St; adult/concession $7/5; ✆ 10am-4pm Sat & Sun) is in the artist's old studio. You'll be able to identify it by the two large matches (one burnt, one intact) at the door. Surry Hills is a short (uphill) walk east of Central Station or south from Oxford St. Catch bus No 301, 302 or 303 from Circular Quay.

PADDINGTON

Next door to Surry Hills, Paddington is an attractive residential area of leafy streets, tightly packed Victorian terrace houses and numerous small art galleries. It was built for aspiring artisans, but during the lemming-like rush to the outer suburbs after WWII the area became a slum. A renewed interest in Victorian architecture and the pleasures of inner-city life led to its restoration

during the 1960s and today many terraces swap hands for a million dollars.

Most facilities, shops, cafés and bars are on Oxford St but the suburb doesn't really have a geographic centre. Most of its streets cascade northwards down the hill towards Edgecliff and Double Bay. It's always a lovely place to wander around, but the best time to visit is on Saturday when the **Paddington Bazaar** (p134) is in full swing.

At **Moore Park**, much of the former RAS Showgrounds has been converted into **Fox Studios** (Map pp90-1; ☎ 9383 4333; Lang Rd; ✆ 10am-midnight) film and entertainment complex. As well as the film studio, the complex includes cinemas, a bowling alley and a shopping/dining precinct.

Eastern Suburbs

A short walk northeast of the Cross is the harbourside suburb of **Elizabeth Bay**. **Elizabeth Bay House** (Map p100; ☎ 9356 3022; 7 Onslow Ave; adult/child/family $7/3/17; ✆ 10am-4.30pm Tue-Sun), by architect John Verge, is one of Sydney's finest colonial homes and dates from 1839.

Beautiful **Rushcutters Bay** is the next bay east. Its handsome harbourside park is just a five-minute walk from the Cross and a great spot for cooped-up travellers to stretch their legs.

Further east is the ritzy suburb of **Double Bay**, which is well endowed with old-fashioned cafés and exclusive stores. The views from the harbour-hugging New South Head Rd as it leaves Double Bay, passes **Rose Bay** and climbs east towards wealthy **Vaucluse** are stupendous. **Vaucluse House** (Map pp90-1; ☎ 9388 7922; Wentworth Rd, Vaucluse; adult/child/family $7/3/17; ✆ 10am-4.30pm Tue-Sun), in Vaucluse Park, is a beautifully preserved colonial mansion dating from 1827. The Bondi Explorer bus (p108) stops here.

At the entrance to the harbour is **Watsons Bay**, a snug community with restored fisherman's cottages, a palm-lined park and a couple of nautical churches. If you want to forget you're in the middle of a large city, it's handy. Nearby **Camp Cove** is one of Sydney's best harbour beaches, and there's a nude beach (mostly male) near South Head at **Lady Bay**. South Head has great views across the harbour entrance to North Head and Middle Head. **The Gap** is a dramatic cliff-top lookout on the ocean side, which has a reputation for suicides.

Bus Nos 324 and 325 from Circular Quay service the eastern suburbs via Kings Cross. Sit on the left side heading east to make the most of the views.

Southern Beaches

Bondi lords it over every other beach in the city, despite not being the best one for a swim, surf or, damn it, a place to park. The suburb itself has a unique atmosphere due to its mix of old Jewish and other European communities, dyed-in-the-wool Aussies, New Zealanders who never went home, working travellers and the *seriously* good-looking.

Bondi has shed much of its previously seedy façade – a lick of paint, some landscaping and flash cafés set it up to be 'rediscovered' by the world and his wife in the early 1990s, and it hasn't quietened down since.

The ocean road is Campbell Pde, home to most of the commerce. There are **Aboriginal rock engravings** on the golf course in North Bondi.

Catch bus No 380, 382, L82 or 389 from the city to get to the beach or, if you're in a hurry, catch a train to Bondi Junction and pick up one of these buses as they pass through the Bondi Junction bus station.

Just south of Bondi is **Tamarama**, a lovely cove with strong rips. Get off the bus as it kinks off Bondi Rd onto Fletcher St, just before it reaches Bondi Beach. Tamarama is a five-minute walk down the hill.

There's a superb beach hemmed in by a bowl-shaped park and sandstone headlands at **Bronte**, south of Tamarama. The cafés with outdoor tables on the edge of the park make it a great chill-out destination. Catch bus No 378 from Railway Square or catch a train to Bondi Junction and pick the bus up there; sit on the left side for a breathtaking view as the bus descends Macpherson St. You can walk to Bronte along the wonderful cliff-top footpath from Bondi Beach or from Coogee via Gordon's Bay, Clovelly and the sun-bleached Waverley Cemetery.

Clovelly Bay is a narrow scooped-out beach to the south. As well as the saltwater baths

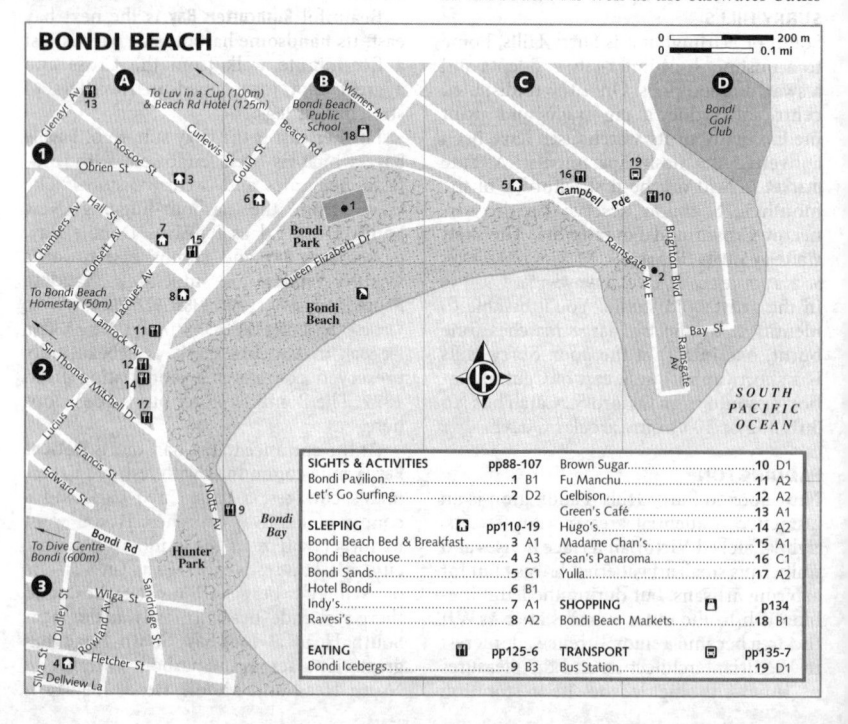

BONDI BEACH

0 — 200 m
0 — 0.1 mi

SIGHTS & ACTIVITIES	pp88-107
Bondi Pavilion	1 B1
Let's Go Surfing	2 D2

SLEEPING	pp110-19
Bondi Beach Bed & Breakfast	3 A1
Bondi Beachouse	4 A3
Bondi Sands	5 C1
Hotel Bondi	6 B1
Indy's	7 A1
Ravesi's	8 A2

EATING	pp125-6
Bondi Icebergs	9 B3

Brown Sugar	10 D1
Fu Manchu	11 A2
Gelbison	12 A2
Green's Café	13 A1
Hugo's	14 A2
Madame Chan's	15 A1
Sean's Panorama	16 C1
Yulla	17 A2

SHOPPING	p134
Bondi Beach Markets	18 B1

TRANSPORT	pp135-7
Bus Station	19 D1

here, there's a wheelchair-access boardwalk so the chairbound can take a sea dip.

Something of a poor cousin to Bondi, **Coogee** has spruced itself up in recent years. It has a relaxed air, a good sweep of sand and a couple of established hostels and hotels. You can reach Coogee by catching bus No 372 from Railway Square or No 373 from Circular Quay. Alternatively, take a train to Bondi Junction and pick up bus No 314 or 315 from there.

EASTERN BEACHES ESCAPE

Bondi too busy? Coogee too crazy? Head a little further south to Maroubra and you'll certainly get the feeling that this beach hasn't been overtaken by outsiders. In fact, it's avowedly local – punch-ups have been known to occur when visitors 'drop in' on waves earmarked for locals, and it sometimes seems that *every* wave is earmarked for a local. There's a dearth of groovy businesses here, which is one reason why you may end up loving the place – plus the beach is bigger than either Bondi or Coogee.

Inner West

West of the centre is the higgledy-piggledy peninsula suburb of **Balmain**. It was once a notoriously rough neighbourhood of dockyard workers but has been transformed into an arty, middle-class area of restored Victoriana flush with pubs and cafés. It's a great place for a stroll. Catch a ferry from Circular Quay or bus No 442 from the QVB.

Cosy, bohemian **Glebe** is southwest of the centre, bordering the northern edge of the University of Sydney. It has a large student population, a cruisy café-lined main street, a tranquil Buddhist temple, aromatherapy and crystals galore, and several decent places to stay. A market is held at Glebe Public School, on Glebe Point Rd, on Saturday. It's a 10-minute walk from Central Station along smoggy Broadway or you can walk from the city centre across Darling Harbour's Pyrmont Bridge and along Pyrmont Bridge Rd (20 minutes). Bus Nos 431 to 434 from Millers Point run via George St along Glebe Point Rd. The Metro Light Rail also travels through Glebe.

Bordering the southern flank of the university is **Newtown**, a melting pot of social and sexual subcultures, students and home renovators. King St, its relentlessly urban main drag, is full of funky clothes stores, bookshops and cafés. While it's definitely moving upmarket, Newtown comes with a healthy dose of grunge, and harbours a decent live-music scene. The best way to get there is by train, but bus Nos 422, 423, 426 and 428 from the city all run along King St.

Predominantly Italian **Leichhardt**, southwest of Glebe, is becoming increasingly popular with students, lesbians and young professionals. Its Italian eateries on Norton St have a citywide reputation. Bus Nos 436 to 440 run from the city to Leichhardt.

North Shore   Map pp90–1

On the northern side of the Harbour Bridge is **North Sydney**, a high-rise office centre with little to tempt the traveller.

McMahons Point is a lovely, forgotten suburb wedged between the two business districts, on the western side of the bridge. There's a line of pleasant alfresco cafés on Blues Point Rd, which runs down to Blues Point Reserve on the western headland of Lavender Bay. The reserve has fine city views.

Luna Park, on the eastern shore of Lavender Bay, is closed, but the big mouth is a highly visible landmark. At the end of Kirribilli Point, just east of the bridge, stand **Admiralty House** and **Kirribilli House**, the Sydney residences of the governor general and the prime minister respectively (Admiralty House is the one nearer the bridge).

East of here are the upmarket suburbs of **Neutral Bay**, **Cremorne** and **Mosman**, all with pleasant coves and harbourside parks perfect for picnics. Ferries go to all these suburbs from Circular Quay.

On the northern side of Mosman is the pretty beach suburb of **Balmoral**, which faces Manly across Middle Harbour. There are picnic areas, a promenade and three beaches.

TARONGA ZOO

In a superb harbourside setting, **Taronga Zoo** (Map pp90–1; ☎ 9969 2777; Bradleys Head Rd, Mosman; adult/child/family $23/13/57; ⏲ 9am-5pm) has more than 2000 critters (from seals to tigers, koalas to giraffes, gorillas to platypuses) all (thankfully) well cared for. Ferries to the zoo depart from Circular Quay's Wharf 2, half-hourly from 7.15am on weekdays, 8.45am Saturday and 9am Sunday. The zoo is on a steep hillside and it makes sense to work your way down if you plan to depart by ferry. If you can't be bothered to climb to the top entrance, take the bus or the Sky Safari cable car. A **ZooPass** (adult/child $29/15), sold at Circular Quay and elsewhere, includes return ferry rides, the Sky Safari and zoo admission.

Manly   Map below

The jewel of the North Shore, Manly is on a narrow peninsula that ends at the dramatic cliffs of North Head. It boasts harbour and ocean beaches, a ferry wharf, all the trappings of a full-scale holiday resort and a great sense of community. It's a sun-soaked place not afraid to show a bit of tack and brashness to attract visitors, and makes a refreshing change from the prim upper-middle-class harbour enclaves nearby.

The **Manly Visitors Centre** (☎ 9977 1088; Manly Wharf; ⌚ 9am-5pm Mon-Fri, 10am-4pm Sat & Sun), just outside the ferry wharf, has free pamphlets on the 10km Manly Scenic Walkway and bus information. Ferries and JetCat catamarans operate between Circular Quay and Manly. JetCats seem to traverse the harbour before you get a chance to blink, while the ferries do the trip in a cool 30 minutes and offer fantastic views.

The ferry wharf is on the Manly Cove foreshore. A short walk along Manly's pedestrian mall, The Corso, brings you to the ocean beach lined by towering Norfolk pines. North and South Steyne are the roads running along the foreshore. A footpath follows the shoreline from South Steyne around the small headland to tiny **Fairy Bower Beach** and the picturesque cove of **Shelly Beach**.

The **Manly Art Gallery & Museum** (☎ 9949 2435; West Esplanade Reserve; adult/child/concession $3.50/free/1.10; ⌚ 10am-5pm Tue-Sun), on the Manly Cove foreshore, focuses on the suburb's special relationship with the beach.

Oceanworld (☎ 9949 2644; West Esplanade; adult/child/family $16/8/25; ⌚ 10am-5.30pm) is next door. The big drawcards are the sharks and

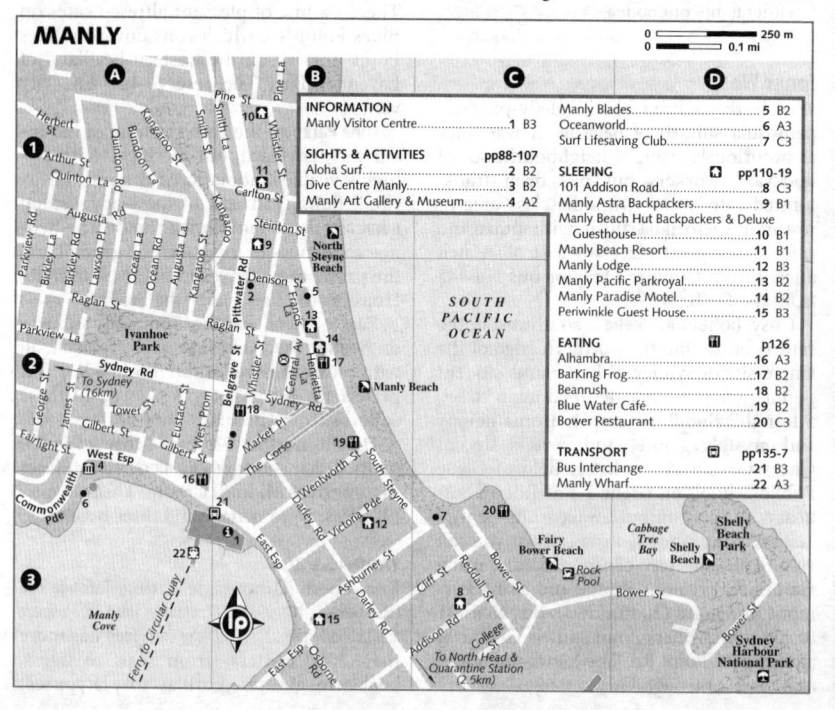

stingrays. Check to see what times you can view divers feeding the sharks. An underwater perspex tunnel offers dramatic (but dry) close encounters with the fish, plus there's some wheelchair and pram access. Behind the gallery is the wonderful 9km-long **Manly Scenic Walkway**. The walkway also has a 2km-long wheelchair accessible path.

North Head, at the entrance to Sydney Harbour, is about 3km south of Manly. Most of the dramatic headland is in Sydney Harbour National Park. The **Quarantine Station** represents an interesting slice of Sydney's social history; it housed suspected disease carriers from 1832 right up until 1984. To visit the station, book a guided tour (☎ 9247 5033), held daily at 1.15pm except Tuesday and Thursday (adult/child $11/7.70). The station is reputedly haunted and there are spooky three-hour ghost tours (adults only) at night from Friday to Sunday ($22 to $28).

Northern Beaches

A string of ocean-front suburbs sweeps 30km north along the coast from Manly, ending at beautiful, well-heeled **Palm Beach** and the spectacular Barrenjoey Heads at the entrance to Broken Bay. Beaches along the way include **Freshwater**, **Curl Curl**, **Dee Why**, **Collaroy** and **Narrabeen**. The most spectacular are **Whale Beach** and **Bilgola** (near Palm Beach), both with dramatic, steep headlands. Several of the northernmost beach suburbs also back onto **Pittwater**, a lovely inlet off Broken Bay and a favoured sailing spot.

Bus Nos 136 and 139 run from Manly to Curl Curl and Freshwater respectively. Bus No L90 from Wynyard Park bus interchange in the city runs to Newport and then north to Palm Beach.

ACTIVITIES
Canoeing & Kayaking

The obvious choice for a kayaking experience in Sydney is Sydney Harbour – although you might want to bear in mind that the harbour is both big and busy, especially if you're a novice. Contact the **New South Wales Canoeing Association** (☎ 9660 4597; www.nswcanoe.org.au; Wentworth Park Complex, Wattle St, Ultimo) for information on canoe courses and hire.

Natural Wanders (☎ 9899 1001; www.kayaksydney .com) has exhilarating kayak tours of the har-

bour which pass under the bridge and stop in secluded bays ($90 for a half-day tour).

Cycling

Sydney's geography, humidity and drivers can all lead to frustration for the cyclist – the best spot to get some spoke action is Centennial Park. **Bicycle NSW** (Map pp94-6; ☎ 9283 5200; www.bicyclensw.org.au; Level 2, 209 Castlereagh St, City) publishes a handy book *Cycling Around Sydney*, which details routes and cycle paths.

CYCLE HIRE

Many cycle-hire shops require a hefty deposit (about $500) or a credit card.

Cheeky Monkey (Map pp94-6; ☎ 9212 4460; 456 Pitt St, City; ☾ 8.30am-6.30pm Mon-Sat; per day/week $25/100) Very cheap – but extras will cost you.

Inner City Cycles (Map pp90-1; ☎ 9660 6605; 151 Glebe Point Rd, Glebe; ☾ 9.30am-6pm Mon-Wed & Fri, to 8pm Thu, to 4pm Sat, 11am-3pm Sun; per day/week $33/90)

Wooly's Wheels (Map pp94-6; ☎ 9331 2671; 82 Oxford St, Paddington; ☾ 9am-6pm Mon-Wed & Fri, to 8pm Thu, to 4pm Sat, 11am-4pm Sun; per day/week $33/180) Across from the Victoria Barracks and very handy to Centennial Park.

Diving

The best shore dives in Sydney are at the Gordons Bay Underwater Nature Trail, north of Coogee; Shark Point, Clovelly; and Ship Rock, Cronulla. Popular boat dive sites are Wedding Cake Island, off Coogee; around the Sydney Heads; and off the Royal National Park.

Dive Centre Bondi (☎ 9369 3855; 192 Bondi Rd, Bondi) **Dive Centre Manly** (Map p104; ☎ 9977 4355; 10 Belgrave St, Manly) The two branches of this dive outfit have courses starting from $350 and a good reputation.

In-line Skating

The beach promenades at Bondi and Manly and the paths of Centennial Park are the most favoured spots for skating.

Manly Blades (Map p104; ☎ 9976 3833; 49 North Steyne, Manly) Hires blades (from $12), scooters (from $7) and baby joggers (from $12) from their handily located premises, which will let you whizz around Manly in no time.

Total Skate (Map pp90-1; ☎ 9380 6356; 36 Oxford St, Woollahra; first hour $10, per hour thereafter $5) Perfectly positioned near Centennial Park and includes protective gear such as helmets and kneepads in the in-line skate hire fee.

Sailing

There are plenty of sailing schools in Sydney and even if you're not serious about learning the ropes, an introductory lesson can be a fun way of getting out on the harbour.

EastSail Sailing School (Map pp90-1; ☎ 9327 1166; www.eastsail.com.au; d'Albora Marina, New Beach Rd, Rushcutters Bay) A sociable outfit with a lot of boats. They run a range of courses from introductory ($470) to racing level.

Sydney by Sail (Map pp94-6; ☎ 9280 1110; www.sydneybysail.com) Departs daily from the Australian National Maritime Museum in Darling Harbour and offers a comprehensive introductory sailing course ($450) that takes place over a whole weekend. A wide range of other sailing packages are also available.

Scenic Flights

Viewing the harbour from the heavens is a memorable experience (especially on a sunny day). It ain't cheap, but it is spectacular.

Sydney by Seaplane (☎ 9974 1455; www.sydney byseaplane.com) offers glorious tours of Sydney's harbour, the Northern Beaches and the coastline, plus areas further afield, like the Hawkesbury River and Ku-ring-gai National Park. Flights start from around $95 for 15 minutes.

Surfing

South of the Heads, the best spots are Bondi, Tamarama, Coogee and Maroubra. Cronulla, south of Botany Bay, is also a serious surfing spot. On the North Shore, there are a dozen surf beaches between Manly and Palm Beach; the best are Manly, Curl Curl, Dee Why, North Narrabeen, Mona Vale, Newport Reef, North Avalon and Palm Beach itself.

Aloha Surf (Map p104; ☎ 9977 3777, 44 Pittwater Rd, Manly; half/full day board hire $25/50) Hire surfing equipment and try your luck on Manly Beach.

Learn to Surf (☎ 1800 851 101; www.wavessurfschool .com.au; from $65) Positive feedback and trips to the Royal National Park (p139) and Byron Bay (p180).

Let's Go Surfing (Map p102; ☎ 9365 1800; www.lets gosurfing.com.au; 128a Ramsgate Ave, Bondi; from $55) You can learn to surf on Bondi Beach with this outfit.

Swimming

Sydney's harbour beaches offer sheltered swimming spots. But if you just want to frolic, nothing beats being knocked around in the waves that pound the ocean beaches, where swimming is safe if you follow instructions and swim within the flagged areas patrolled by lifeguards. There are some notorious but clearly signposted rips, even at Sydney's most popular beaches, so don't underestimate the surf just because it looks safe.

Outdoor pools in the city:

Andrew 'Boy' Charlton Pool (Map pp94-6; ☎ 9358 6686; Mrs Macquaries Rd, The Domain; 6.30am-8pm; adult/child $4.50/3.50) Saltwater, smack bang on the harbour and popular with gays, this is Sydney's best pool. It's more for serious lap-swimmers

PUBERTY BLUES

Essential reading for every teenaged Aussie girl in the 1970s and 1980s (and scarily relevant today), the cult novel *Puberty Blues* (by Kathy Lette and Gabrielle Carey) details the ups and downs of Debbie and Sue, two thirteen-year-old girls desperate for acceptance by the tough Greenhills Gang of Cronulla Beach. Enduring hunger (chicks were not allowed to be seen eating in public), heavy smoking (legal and otherwise), boredom (their main duties were to watch the boys surf and then fetch them a Chiko Roll), disappointing, even brutal, deflowerings at the hands of Neanderthals in the backs of panel vans (embellished with stickers that proclaimed 'To all you virgins, thanks for nothin'!' or 'Don't laugh – your daughter might be in here') and relentless peer pressure (the rules regarding Levis or Amco jeans are mind-boggling), Debbie and Sue are eventually accepted by the gang, only for that acceptance to become a cultural prison. The film of the same name (1981), directed by Bruce Beresford, was a well-received social document, and a fascinating meditation on the sexist nature of 1970s beach culture and the descent into (hard) drug abuse that often followed the flower-power-meets-endless-summer era's supposedly harmless flirtations with smoking pot. The climax of the film shows Debbie and Sue taking matters into their own hands and learning to surf, much to the disgust of the gang. Thankfully, the (still) male-dominated world of surfing is steadily changing, as more and more young women discover the joys of hanging ten. Keep an ear out while you're in Sydney for fragments of the hilarious dialogue used in both the film and the book, which can sometimes be heard in many of Sydney's beachside suburbs today. Deadset, ya slack moll.

than those wishing to splash around, but the five-star change rooms will soon psych you into it.

North Sydney Olympic Pool (Map pp90-1; ☎ 9955 2309; Alfred St South, Milsons Point; ⌚ 5.30am-9pm Mon-Fri, 7am-7pm Sat & Sun; adult/child $4.20/2) Just near the entrance to Luna Park, this is a nice outdoor pool (there's an undercover 25m one too) on the North Shore.

Sydney Aquatic Centre (☎ 9752 3699; Olympic Blvd, Sydney Olympic Park, Homebush Bay; ⌚ 5am-8.45pm Mon-Fri, 6am-6.45pm Sat & Sun) State-of-the-art facilities as used in the Sydney 2000 Olympic Games, where many world records were smashed, thus proving its reputation as a 'fast pool'.

WALKING TOUR

Setting out on foot is a good way to explore Australia's largest city; most of the best sights are conveniently located near the Harbour.

> **WALKING TOUR**
>
> Distance: 5km
> Duration: 1.5 hours

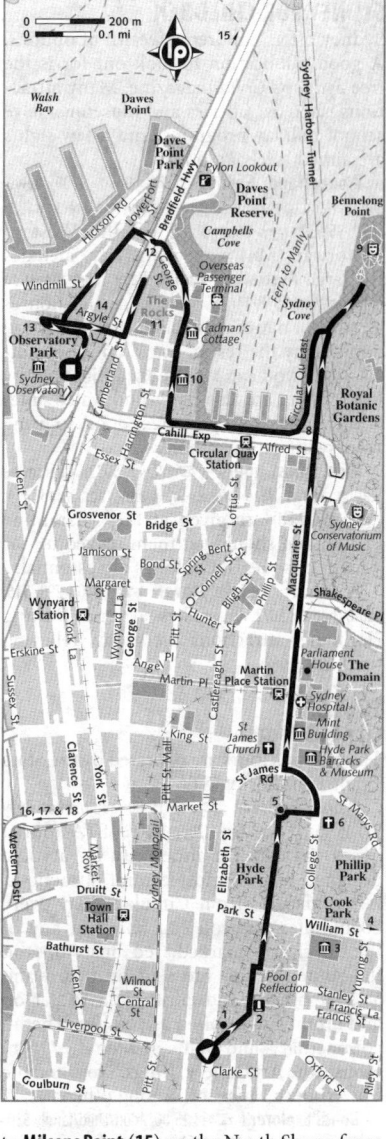

Start in **Hyde Park** (**1**; p98) at Museum Station's Liverpool St exit. Walk northeast through the park past the **Anzac Memorial** (**2**; p98). On the right, on College St, is the **Australian Museum** (**3**; p98). From here, William St (the eastward extension of Park St) heads east to **Kings Cross** (**4**; p99). Across Park St, at the end of the avenue of trees, is the wonderful **Archibald Fountain** (**5**). To the east, on College St, is the impressive **St Mary's Cathedral** (**6**; p98).

Keep going north to reach **Macquarie St** (**7**; p97) with its collection of early colonial buildings and, after a few blocks, **Circular Quay** (**8**; p92) and the spectacular **Sydney Opera House** (**9**; p92). On the west side of Circular Quay, behind the **Museum of Contemporary Art** (**10**; p92), George St runs through **The Rocks** (**11**; p89).

Walk north on George St, which curves around under the **Harbour Bridge** (**12**, p89) into Lower Fort St. Turn right (north) for the waterfront or left to climb **Observatory Hill** (**13**; p89). From here Argyle St heads east, through the **Argyle Cut** (**14**; p89) and back to The Rocks.

Nearby, on Cumberland St, you can climb stairs to the Harbour Bridge and walk across

to **Milsons Point** (**15**) on the North Shore; from here you can take a train back to the city.

West of Hyde Park you can walk along Market St, which leads to Pyrmont Bridge (for pedestrians and the monorail only) and **Darling Harbour** (p93). Pyrmont Bridge Rd crosses Darling Harbour and leads to **Anzac Bridge** and the **Sydney Fish Markets** (p97).

SYDNEY FOR CHILDREN

Sydney offers children a wealth of options. A good publication to look out for is the free *Sydney's Child* magazine. Many attractions, such as galleries and museums, have school-holiday programs, and a few sights are aimed solely at kids.

Wonderland Sydney (☎ 9830 9100; www .wonderland.com.au; Wallgrove Rd, Eastern Creek; adult/ child $50/32; ❁ 10am-5pm), off the Western Motorway (M4) west of the city, includes the large **Australian Wildlife Park** (park admission only adult/child $18/11; ❁ 9am-5pm), which houses all sorts of native Australian animals. If you don't fancy the rest of the Wonderland attractions, you can visit the wildlife park by itself. There are also pools and water slides at the amusement park next door, so bring your swimsuit in summer.

Kids' ghost tours (☎ 9247 5033; Quarantine Station, North Head Scenic Dr, Manly; admission $14; ❁ 5.45pm Fri) are given at the Quarantine Station and should get them revved up for a night of squeals. Bookings are essential.

A dinky **People Mover** (☎ 0408-290 515; adult/child $3.50/2.50) snakes around Darling Harbour's attractions every day, relieving tired little legs.

TOURS
City Bus Tours

The best bus tours are operated by the State Transit Authority (STA).

Sydney Explorer (☎ 13 15 00; adult/child/family $30/15/75; ❁ 8.40am-5.20pm) Red STA tourist buses navigate the inner city on a route designed to pass most central attractions. A bus departs from Circular Quay every 20 minutes but you can board at any of the 26 clearly marked, red bus stops on the route. Tickets are sold on board and at STA offices, and entitle you to get on and off the bus as often as you like. There's commentary, and sights include the Opera House, the Art Gallery, Kings Cross and the Powerhouse Museum, among others.

Bondi Explorer (☎ 13 15 00; adult/child/family $30/ 15/75; ❁ 8.45am-4.15pm) Operates along similar lines, running a much larger circuit from Circular Quay to Kings Cross, Double Bay, Rose Bay, Vaucluse, Watsons Bay, the Gap, Bondi Beach and Coogee, returning to the city along Oxford St. Just riding around the circuit takes two hours, so if you want to get off at many of the 19 places of interest along the way, start early. Buses depart every 30 minutes or so, and tickets can be purchased on board or at STA offices.

Harbour Cruises

There's a wide range of cruises on the harbour, from ferry boats and cruisers to paddle-steamers and sailing ships.

Harboursights Cruises (☎ 13 15 00; adult/child/ family from $15/7.50/38) Run by the STA, these excellent short cruises allow you to take in the sights, sounds and, sometimes, smells of the harbour. Take your pick from the Morning Cruise (one hour), the Afternoon Cruise (2½ hours) or the Evening Harbour Lights Cruise (1½ hours). Tickets can be bought at ferry ticket offices in Circular Quay.

Magistic Cruises (☎ 8296 7222; www.magisticcruises .com.au; King St Wharf 5, Darling Harbour or Wharf 6, Circular Quay; adult/child/family $20/15/55) With regular departures daily and all the Sydney Harbour icons on the itinerary, the fancy boats of Magistic are a good way to see the sights (with a free beer) in an hour.

Matilda Rocket Express (☎ 9264 7377; www .matilda.com.au; Aquarium Wharf, Pier 26, Darling Harbour; adult/child/family $21/11/50) A good option for those wanting to savour it quickly, these cruises will take you to Darling Harbour, Watson's Bay, Sydney Aquarium, Taronga Zoo, The Rocks, the Opera House and the Royal Botanic Gardens. The best bit is that you can start your cruise at one of five locations. Commentary, tea, coffee and biscuits all provided.

Walking Tours

Bridgeclimb (Map pp94-6; ☎ 8274 7777; www .bridgeclimb.com; 5 Cumberland St, The Rocks; adult $145-175, child $100-125) Once, it was only daredevils and bridge painters who scaled the heights and saw the breathtaking views from the Harbour Bridge. Now everyone (who's not afraid of heights) can do it. The 3½-hour tour (day or night), for which you're thoroughly well prepared by enthusiastic staff, is worth every uphill step. Go to the toilet *before* you start the climb.

Maureen Fry (☎ 9660 7157; www.ozemail.com.au /~mpfry; 15 Arcadia Rd, Glebe) Maureen caters mainly for groups, but she can take individuals or perhaps fit you in with a group. A two-hour guided walk costs $16 per person, with a minimum of 10 people. Options include Sydney and its suburbs, or lesser-known destinations within a few hours' reach of Sydney.

Sydney Aboriginal Discoveries (☎ 9599 1693; www.abtrade.com.au/salt_plains.htm; $90-180) Offers a variety of interesting tours that are focused on indigenous culture and history. Options include a harbour cruise, an enjoyable walkabout tour, a feast of native Australian foods, and a Dreamtime cruise. We've had good feedback about these tours.

Sydney Architecture Walks (☎ 0403-888 390; Level 4, Customs House, 31 Alfred St, Circular Quay; adult/child $20/15) These enthusiastic building buffs will open your eyes to Sydney's architecture, both old and new. Those into the Opera House will love the Utzon walk. Strolls last two hours, and depart from Customs House in Alfred St, Sydney.

FESTIVALS & EVENTS

Sydney has plenty of festivals and special goings-on year-round. Visitors centres can advise you what's on when you're in town.

JANUARY
Sydney Festival This massive event floods the city with art in January, including free outdoor concerts in the Domain.
Australia Day (26 January) Australia's birthday is celebrated with BBQs, picnics and fireworks on the harbour.

FEBRUARY
Chinese New Year Celebrated in Chinatown with fireworks in late January or early February.
Tropfest This home-grown short-film festival ensures its flicks are fresh with the inclusion of compulsory props (announced just before the competition). Big-name stars are often the judges (eg Keanu Reeves, Nicole Kidman, Russell Crowe).
Sydney Gay & Lesbian Mardi Gras The highlight of this world-famous festival is the colourful, sequined parade along Oxford St, culminating in a bacchanalian party at the Fox Studios, in Moore Park, in late February.

MARCH/APRIL
Royal Easter Show This 12-day event is an agricultural show and funfair held at Homebush Bay. Bring the kids and pet the baby animals.

MAY
Sydney Writers' Festival Celebrates the literary in Sydney, with guest authors, talks and forums.

JUNE
Sydney Film Festival A 14-day orgy of cinema held at the State Theatre and other cinemas.
Sydney Biennale An international art festival held in even-numbered years at the Art Gallery of NSW, the Powerhouse Museum and other venues.

JULY
Yulefest Christmas comes early, and is as close to white as Australia gets in this popular Blue Mountains celebration.

AUGUST
City to Surf Run This 14km-long fun run takes place on the second Sunday in August and attracts a mighty 40,000 entrants who run from Hyde Park to Bondi Beach.

SEPTEMBER
Carnivale There's plenty of colour at this multicultural arts festival held in early spring.
Royal Botanic Gardens Spring Festival Spring into spring, with concerts, colourful flower displays and plenty of pollen.

OCTOBER
Rugby League Grand Final The two best teams left standing in the National Rugby League (NRL) meet to decide who's best.
Manly Jazz Festival Held over the Labour Day long weekend in early October and featuring lots of jazz performances, mostly free.
Kings Cross Carnival Taking place in late October or early November, this street fair includes a bed race.

NOVEMBER
Sculpture by the Sea Held in mid-November, the Bondi-to-Bronte walk is transformed into an outdoor sculpture gallery.

DECEMBER
Christmas Day (25 December) Thousands of backpackers descend on Bondi Beach on Christmas Day, much to the consternation of the civil authorities and the overworked lifesavers.
Boxing Day (26 December) Sydney Harbour is a sight to behold as hundreds of boats crowd its waters to farewell the yachts competing in the gruelling Sydney to Hobart Yacht Race.
New Year's Eve (31 December) The Rocks, Kings Cross and Bondi Beach are traditional gathering places for alcohol-sodden celebrations on New Year's Eve, although alcohol-free zones and a massive police presence are aimed to quell the rowdier elements.

OUTDOOR CINEMA
Summer lends itself to getting outdoors in Sydney, and watching the movies under the stars has become a popular summer tradition. **Moonlight Cinema** (☎ 1900 933 899; Centennial Park Amphitheatre; adult/child $14/9.50) shows flicks with a populist/art-house bent in Centennial Park from early December to late February. **OpenAir Cinema** (☎ 1300 366 649; Mrs Macquaries Point, The Domain; adult/child $18/16) is the same sort of thing, running from early January to mid-February, but you'll catch the sea breezes coming off Sydney Harbour. Tickets for both venues sell out quickly, especially for the weekend sessions.

GAY & LESBIAN SYDNEY

In Sydney, one could be forgiven for thinking that gay is the new straight… Gay and lesbian culture forms a vocal, vital, well-organised and colourful part of Sydney's social fabric. In 2002 Sydney played host to the best-dressed Olympics ever – the Gay Games.

The colourful Sydney Gay & Lesbian Mardi Gras is Australia's biggest annual tourist event, and the joyful-hedonism-meets-political-protest Oxford St parade is watched by over half-a-million people. The Sleaze Ball (a Mardi Gras fundraiser) takes place in October, with leather taking the place of Lycra. The parties for both events are held in Moore Park. Tickets are restricted to Mardi Gras members. Gay and lesbian international visitors wishing to attend the parties should contact the **Mardi Gras office** (☎ 9549 2100; www.mardigras.org.au) well in advance – tickets sell fast.

The Taylor Square region of Oxford St is the hub of gay life in Sydney, although there are 'pockets' in suburbs such as Paddington, Newtown, Alexandria and Leichhardt. Gay beach life is focussed on Lady Bay (nude) and Tamarama (also known as Glamarama). You may also want to check out Red Leaf Pool, on New South Head Rd, just past Double Bay or Andrew 'Boy' Charlton pool (p106). For men, tans and heavy pecs are a 'classic' look. The scene for women is a bit more inclusive.

However, there's still a homophobic side to some 'true blue' Aussies, and violence against homosexuals isn't unheard-of, particularly during school holidays. For the record, in New South Wales (NSW) the age of consent for homosexual sex is 16 for both men and women.

The Sydney Gay & Lesbian Mardi Gras has established an online travel service, Mardi Gras Travel (www.mardigras.org.au/international), to assist gay and lesbian travellers coming to Australia. The free gay press includes the *Sydney Star Observer* and *Lesbians on the Loose*. These can be found in shops and cafés in the inner east and west. They all have excellent listings of gay and lesbian organisations, services and events. **Gay & Lesbian Tourism Australia** (GALTA; www.galta.com.au; PO Box 208, Darlinghurst NSW 2010) can provide a wealth of information about gay and lesbian travel in Oz.

If you're keen to take part in Sydney's gay nightlife scene you can find plenty of listings in the local gay press. The following represent a mix of old favourites and newer club nights that cover both low-key and 'out there' bases.

ARQ (Map pp94-6; ☎ 9380 8700; 16 Flinders St, Darlinghurst) This excellent, large club has a 24-hour licence and very flattering lighting, which should be compulsory in more places. Good DJs are often heard here, and it's a popular place to 'recover' on Sundays.

SLEEPING

As Australia's largest city, Sydney has a huge variety of accommodation, from a large selection of travellers' hostels, many of which offer discounts for longer stays and for memberships in various programs (such as YHA, VIP etc), to deluxe hotels with harbour views and a high staff-to-guest ratio. In between, there are cosy B&Bs, comfortable motels, and authentic Aussie pubs. The city proper has a wide range of options. The largest concentration of hostels is in Kings Cross, but there are clusters (some might say ghettoes) in other areas, including Glebe, Manly, Bondi and Coogee. In these suburbs you'll also find stylish boutique hotels. Glebe is a good option for those wanting to stay close to the city without being in the thick of traveller-world. The North Shore has less in the way of sleeping (apart from Manly), but rewards its guests with a tad more serenity.

For long-stay accommodation, peruse the 'flats to let' and 'share accommodation' ads in the *Sydney Morning Herald* on Wednesday and Saturday. Hostel notice boards are also good sources of information.

Budget

Facilities vary from small dorms with a bathroom, TV, fridge and cooking facilities to just a plain room with a couple of bunks. Some hostels have set hours for checking in and out, although all have 24-hour access once you've paid.

Things to consider when you're shopping around include whether a key deposit is required; whether alcohol is permitted; phone, Internet and satellite-TV access; whether free pickup is available; if visitors are allowed; and the standard of security on the premises.

Sydney also has some fine budget hotels and guesthouses, which work out to be only

Colombian (Map pp94–6; ☎ 9360 2151; cnr Oxford & Crown Sts, Darlinghurst) The newest kid on the gay block and kitted out like an interior decorator's dream. It's a good mix of handlebar moustaches, good music, ventilation, buff bods, plenty of space and quite a few women.

Exchange Hotel (Map pp94–6; ☎ 9331 1936; 34 Oxford St, Darlinghurst) This long-running temple of drinking and dancing has quite a few gay entertainment options, from the Lizard Lounge (popular with lesbians and friends) and Phoenix (predominantly men).

Flinders Hotel (Map pp94–6; ☎ 9360 4929; 63 Flinders St, Darlinghurst) The laneway behind this pub is *the* place to spend the morning after Mardi Gras and Sleaze. You can also go in anytime and just have a beer and a boogie.

Imperial Hotel (☎ 9519 9899; 35 Erskineville Rd, Erskineville) The film *Priscilla – Queen of the Desert* was inspired by the nightly drag here, and it's world-class. For the ladies – there's Go Girl on Thursday.

Lansdowne Hotel (Map pp90–1; ☎ 9211 2325; 2 City Rd, Chippendale) Upstairs at the Lansdowne Hotel there's a brilliant Saturday nighter called Red Room. It's mostly for lesbians, but the atmosphere is pretty inclusive.

Midnight Shift (Map pp94–6; ☎ 9360 4463; 85 Oxford St, Darlinghurst) It's hard to believe that a gay scene existed before this place (also nicknamed the Midnight Shirtlift). The ground floor is quite pubby, but upstairs it's a licence to booze and cruise with less conversation. We like the fact that you can find a range of men here – not all of them clones.

Newtown Hotel (☎ 9557 1329; 174 King St, Newtown) In Sydney's other gay enclave, the Newtown does a roaring trade with gay folk who just want to go to the local and have a good time. The drag acts are pretty good too.

Oxford Hotel (Map pp94–6; ☎ 9331 3467; 134 Oxford St, Darlinghurst) With an industrial hardcore theme going on at ground level and the luxe ambience of Gilligans and Gingers cocktail bars upstairs, this place covers the bases on Taylor Square.

Stonewall (Map pp94–6; ☎ 9360 1963; 175 Oxford St, Darlinghurst) Nicknamed 'Stonehenge' by those who find it too ancient for their liking, this place is usually pumping and pumped-up. In recent times, the ceiling has collapsed here, causing one DJ to proclaim 'I finally brought the house down!'.

Taxi Club (Map pp94–6; ☎ 9331 4256; 40-42 Flinders St, Darlinghurst) Chances are, if you can't remember the end of last night you finished it off at the Taxi Club. Refreshingly seedy after all these years, this place is a national treasure that no tourist brochure's going to tout. Mind the stairs.

fractionally more expensive than hostels if you're travelling with friends. A refundable key deposit is often required.

GUESTHOUSES & BUDGET HOTELS
City Centre

Y on the Park (Map pp94–6; ☎ 9264 2451; www .ywca-sydney.com.au; 5-11 Wentworth Ave; s $70-120, d & tw $100-140; ❋) This child-friendly YWCA (that takes young and not-so-young men, too) has an enviable position, with Hyde Park across the road and the city centre and Oxford St a short walk away. The standard is high, with simple but spotless well-furnished rooms, some well-appointed business rooms and some very comfortable, secure dorm beds ($32 per person per night).

Kings Cross Area

Maisonette Hotel (Map p100; ☎ 9357 3878; maisonettehotel@bigpond.com; 31 Challis Ave; s & d $90, tr $115) Brand-spanking new when we popped

in (you could still smell the new carpet and paint), this friendly place represents excellent value, with small, bright rooms and spotless bathrooms. There are also single rooms with share bathrooms, and good weekly rates for longer stays.

Royal Sovereign Hotel (Map pp94–6; ☎ 9331 3672; royalsov@solotel.com.au; cnr Liverpool St & Darlinghurst Rd; d from $80) Located directly above one of our favourite drinking dens, the small but nifty rooms here put you in the thick of it at a bargain price. The communal bathrooms are immaculate, and some of the rooms have air-conditioning (although you'll have to bring your own earplugs if you're a light sleeper).

Highfield Private Hotel (Map p100; ☎ 9326 9539; www.highfieldhotel.com; 166 Victoria St; s/d $55/ 70) A clean and welcoming hotel owned by a Swedish family (and therefore popular with Swedish guests), this place has good security, simple rooms (shared bathrooms) and 24-hour access.

Balmain

Balmain Lodge (☎ 9810 3700, fax 9810 1500; 415 Darling St; s/d $65/80; P) Located on Balmain's backbone, Darling St, this is a handy place with capable management and spartan, clean rooms. Wheelchair access is available, as is parking, making this a convenient option for less mobile travellers, or those keen on this delightful suburb's village atmosphere. Bathrooms are shared.

Coogee

Grand Pacific Private Hotel (☎ 9665 6301; cnr Beach & Carr Sts; s/d $35/45) In *no* way grand, but charming in a dilapidated, down-at-heel way, and the beachside location is great. Grab that person you're having a dirty affair with (having bumped off their spouse) and hole up for a seedy seaside weekend straight from a true crime novel.

North Shore

Glenferrie Lodge (Map pp90-1; ☎ 9955 1685; www.glenferrielodge.com; 12a Carabella St, Kirribilli; s $60, d & tw $75; ▯) This hotel is in a large, beautiful old house with a ridiculous sculpture out the front (you can't miss it). It has clean rooms with fridge, and helpful, friendly management. Bathrooms are shared, but they're kept in damn good nick. Prices for simpler rooms are cheaper, and there are also a few dorm beds available, with reductions for longer stays on all rooms. Both these places are accessible from Milsons Point train station or Kirribilli wharf by ferry.

Also recommended:
Manly Astra Backpackers (Map p104; ☎ /fax 9977 2092; 68 Pittwater Rd, Manly; d $60)
Kirribilli Court Private Hotel (Map pp90-1; ☎ 9955 4344; 45 Carabella St, Kirribilli; s/tw/d $40/45/55)

HOSTELS
City Centre

Sydney Central YHA (Map pp94-6; ☎ 9281 9111; sydcentral@yhansw.org.au; 11 Rawson Pl; dm $25-30, d/tw $75/85; P ▯) This huge heritage-listed, renovated building on the corner of Pitt St and Rawson Pl is very close to Central Station. It has wonderful kitchens, wheelchair access, a barbecue, sauna, 24-hour security access, a **travel desk** (☎ 9281 9444) that can organise tours to anywhere in Australia, and its own bar and small supermarket. Some twin

rooms are set up for disabled travellers, but these should be booked in advance. Despite its size (over 500 beds), it's advisable to call ahead and reserve your place.

Wanderers on Kent (Map pp94-6; ☎ 9267 7718; www.wanderersonkent.com.au; 477 Kent St; dm $24-33; s & d $85; ▧ ▯) This has good, wheelchair-accessible rooms and great access to central Sydney. Security is a strong point, and there are electronic lockers, plus a solarium, so you can get that sun-damaged look that's so popular in Oz.

Kings Cross Area

Original Backpackers (Map p100; ☎ 9356 3232; www.originalbackpackers.com.au; 160-162 Victoria St; dm/s/d $22/45/65) A hostel for over 20 years, this really is the original backpackers in the area. A big 176-bed place in two historic houses, it has friendly staff, good security, safety and facilities (laundry, kitchen etc), plus Blinky the dog. It's open 24 hours and all rooms have fridge and TV. The TV series *Crash Palace* is filmed here, in case you're interested.

Eva's Backpackers (Map p100; ☎ 9358 2185; www.evasbackpackers.com.au; 6-8 Orwell St; dm $24, d & tw $60) Eva's is a perennial favourite with many travellers, particularly Germans. It's family owned and operated, and is clean (the carpet still feels pretty springy!) and well managed. There's a good rooftop barbecue area and a sociable kitchen/dining room. It's often full, so it's best to book ahead.

Jolly Swagman Backpackers (Map p100; ☎ 9358 6400; www.jollyswagman.com.au; 27 Orwell St; dm $23, d & tw $60) This 134-bed hostel has 24-hour security and a social life that gets the thumbs up from more than a few travellers. The rooms are modern and have lockers, fridges, reading lamps, fans and TV (no TV in dorms). Safety standards are high, and the staff is friendly and helpful with information about getting work and getting around.

Also recommended:
Backpackers Headquarters Hostel (Map p100; ☎ 9331 6180; headquartershostel@mail.com; 79 Bayswater Rd, Rushcutters Bay; dm $24)
Pink House (Map p100; ☎ 9358 1689; www.qd.com .au/~theglobe/pinkhouse_main.html; 6-8 Barncleuth Sq, Kings Cross; dm $24)
Rucksack Rest (Map p100; ☎ /fax 9358 2348; 9 McDonald St, Potts Point; dm $24, d & tw $50)
Kangaroo Bakpak (Map pp90-1; ☎ 9319 5915; 665 South Dowling St, Surry Hills; dm $24)

Glebe

Glebe Point YHA (Map pp90-1; ☎ 9692 8418; glebe@yhansw.org.au; 262-264 Glebe Point Rd; dm $23-27, d & tw per person $32; 💻) This large, friendly hostel offers good facilities – a kitchen, TV lounge, laundry and clean linen. The rooms are simple but clean, as are the bathrooms, and credit-card reservations are accepted. The busy front desk can also help with plenty of local info.

Bondi

Bondi Beachouse (Map p102; ☎ 9365 2088; bondi@intercoast.com.au; 63 Fletcher St; dm $26, s $60, d & tw $70; 🏿 💻) The staff here are as clued-up as you'd expect from a YHA joint, and there are excellent communal areas to be enjoyed, plus some delightful rooftop views from the spa over Tamarama Beach. Catch bus No 380 from the city or Bondi Junction and alight at the Fletcher St stop.

Indy's (Map p102; ☎ 9365 4900; fax 9365 4994; 35a Hall St; dm $30) With a relaxed, easy-going vibe, this hostel is a socially gregarious backpacking option. Facilities are well-used but OK, and it's security conscious. There's a kitchen, courtyard and Internet access, and the staff have good connections if you're looking for work.

Coogee

Coogee Beachside Accommodation (☎ 9315 8511; www.sydneybeachside.com.au; 178 Coogee Bay Rd; d & tw $75) A good option for budget travellers looking for simple but clean double and twin rooms in a converted house with kitchen facilities

and tidy shared bathrooms. A few family rooms are also available, at $95 per night.

Wizard of Oz Backpackers (☎ 9315 7876; www.wizardofoz.com.au; 172 Coogee Bay Rd; dm $27) Smack bang on Coogee Bay Rd in a refurbished California bungalow (which was actually this author's 5th-grade teacher's home in a former life!), this place is laid-back and casual and run by the same people from Coogee Beachside Accommodation (free airport pick-up available for both). Dorms sleep from four to 14 people, and communal rooms are in good working order. Both of these places open their offices between about 8am and noon and from 5pm to 8pm.

Manly

Manly Beach Hut Backpackers (Map p104; ☎ 9977 8777; www.manlybeachhut.com.au; 77 Whistler St; dm $25, d & tw $55, tr $80; 💻) This place has extremely good dorms, doubles, twins and triples. Standards are high, with cleanliness, atmosphere and 'extras' all first-rate, plus it's wheelchair accessible.

North Shore

Sydney Beachhouse YHA (☎ 9981 1177; mail@sydney beachouse.com.au; 4 Collaroy St, Collaroy; dm $20-25, d & tw $60, f $105) This clean, airy place gets some great reviews from travellers (it's wheelchair and child friendly) and is close to some of Sydney's best beaches. If you really want to feel like an extra from *Home & Away*, then this is probably your best bet. To get here, catch bus Nos L90 or L88 from Railway Square, Town Hall or Wynyard train stations.

HALLS OF RESIDENCE

Many colleges at the **University of Sydney** (☎ 9351 2222) and the **University of NSW** (☎ 8300 4253) are eager for casual guests during holidays. Most quote B&B or full-board rates but it's often possible to negotiate a lower rate if you're only after a bed.

University of Sydney

This is southwest of the city centre, close to Glebe and Newtown.

St Andrews College (☎ 9557 1133; fax 9261 1969; 19 Carillion Ave, Newtown; d & tw $50-55) This college is known as Sydney Summer YHA between early December and early February. You can also contact the **YHA** (☎ 9261 1111; 422 Kent St, City) for details.

University of NSW

This university is only a short bus ride from the southern ocean beaches and Oxford St.

Kensington Colleges (☎ 9315 0000; kenso-colleges@unsw.edu.au; Gate 6, High St, Randwick; s $33, d & tw $60) The three Kensington Colleges – Basser, Baxter and Goldstein – offer YHA accommodation in the summer holidays, with breakfast included.

PUBS
Kings Cross
O'Malley's Hotel (Map p100; ☎ 9357 2211; www.oma lleyshotel.com.au; 228 William St; s/d/tr $70/80/90) This is a friendly Irish pub that has traditionally decorated, well-furnished rooms with bathrooms at great prices. It's also surprisingly quiet, given its location, although there is a lot of Irish music played here for those allergic to jigs.

CAMPING
Sydney's caravan parks, most of which also have sites for tents, are a fair way out of town. The following are up to 26km from the city centre.

Lane Cove River Caravan Park (☎ 9888 9133; www.lanecoveriver.com; Plassey Rd, North Ryde; camp/caravan site $23/26) This cheery place is 14km north of the city and has good facilities (including over 150 caravan sites, plus cabins). You can cool off in the pool too, when temperatures swelter in this part of the city.

Lakeside Caravan Park (☎ 9913 7845; info@sydney lakeside.com.au; Lake Park Rd, Narrabeen; camp/caravan site $25/32) This camping area is 26km north of Sydney, in the prime real estate area of the northern beaches. If caravanning doesn't appeal, there are good cabins and lakeside 'villas'.

Grand Pines Caravan Park (☎ 9529 7329; www .thegrandpines.com.au; 289 The Grand Pde, Sans Souci; camp/caravan site $35/45) This is a friendly, good-quality caravan park 17km south of Sydney on beautiful Botany Bay, where you can take your pick from sites, vans and cabins. High standards are maintained, and feedback is positive.

Mid-Range
BED & BREAKFASTS
Bondi
Bondi Beach Homestay (☎ 9300 0800; 10 Forest Knoll Ave; bondibnb@bigpond.net.au; s/d $80/125; **P**) In a charmingly decorated home with friendly owners, this is one of Bondi's hidden gems. Bathrooms are shared, but they're so scrupulously clean you could probably eat off the floors. Breakfast on the terrace is a must in summer.

Bondi Beach Bed & Breakfast (Map p102; ☎ 9365 6522; info@bondibeach-bnb.com.au; 110 Roscoe St; s $100, d & tw $150, tr $190; **P**) Nadia and Michael go all out to make this place feel like your own home (only cleaner). You're close to all the good stuff in Bondi, but you can also find a park. It's a small place, so be sure to make reservations, and ask about discounts for the low season.

Glebe & Balmain
Alishan International Guest House (Map pp90–1; ☎ 9566 4048; kevin@alishan.com.au; 100 Glebe Point Rd, Glebe; s/d $100/115) In a big old house in the centre of Glebe, the Alishan is clean, quiet and well run (multilingual staff), with good communal areas and a room that can accommodate disabled travellers. There are also a few dorm beds ($27 to $33) available, but it's certainly not a party hostel.

Manly
Manly Beach Hut Deluxe Guesthouse (Map p104; ☎ 9977 8777; www.manlybeachhut.com.au; 7 Pine St; d $100) This guesthouse is particularly good for those wishing to stay in a quiet, Federation-style house in Manly. The standards are high, and the quality, cleanliness and atmosphere are all first-rate (in high season there's a minimum stay of one week). There are some rooms without bathroom and good discounts in the low season.

101 Addison Road (Map p104; ☎ 9977 6216, fax 9976 6352; 101 Addison Rd; s/d $100/140) A sweet-looking four-star B&B with lovely rooms and very cosy communal areas. If you fancy tickling the ivories of a grand piano, Jill the owner is happy to oblige. There are only a couple of rooms, so book ahead to take advantage of the peace and quiet that this part of Manly affords.

Periwinkle Guest House (Map p104; ☎ 9977 4668; periwinkle.manly@bigpond.com; 18-19 East Esplanade; s/d $135/165; **P**) This is a beautifully restored Victorian house facing the harbour beach at Manly Cove. Rooms are elegant and well appointed, and there's a stylish but cosy kitchen. Laundry facilities are available, and so are some cheaper rooms with share bathrooms.

MOTELS
City Centre & The Rocks
Pentura Hotel (Map pp94-6; ☎ 9283 8088; 300 Pitt St; d & tw $140; **P**) We get a few letters recommending this place and with good reason. Its location is close to both the north of the city and the area around Chinatown and Central Station, plus the rooms are in very good condition. Staff are helpful, too.

Quality Hotel SC Sydney (Map pp94-6; ☎ 9282 0987; www.qualitysydney.com.au; 111 Goulburn St; d $145; P ☒) This was once known as the Southern Cross, and after a thorough refurbishment, it certainly deserves its new moniker. Rooms are very comfortable and well appointed (wheelchair friendly), especially for the price. It's handy to both the CBD and Darling Harbour, too.

Hyde Park Inn (Map pp94-6; ☎ 9264 6001; www.hydeparkinn.com.au; 271 Elizabeth St; s $145, d & tw $160, tr $180; P ☒) Nothing much to look at from the outside, it's easy to miss this well-situated hotel, which has some great views over Hyde Park and perfectly suitable 'standard' rooms with kitchenette (deluxe ones cost around $15 more). The Hyde Park Inn also has some good two-room apartments for families or larger groups.

RG Hotel (Map pp94-6; ☎ 9281 6999; www .rghotel.com.au; 431 Pitt St; d $125-145; P ☒ 💻) Handily located near Sydney's Capitol Theatre, Chinatown, Darling Harbour and Central Station, the courteous RG has serviceable rooms and a handy business centre, plus a rooftop pool if you feel like escaping the city's bustle.

George Street Private Hotel (Map pp94-6; ☎ /fax 9211 1800; 700a George St; d $85) Despite its location amid the adult book exchanges and grotty bars of this part of town, this is a decent choice. Rooms are sparsely furnished, clean and there are cooking and laundry facilities. Cheaper rooms without bathrooms are also available.

Sydney Central Private Hotel (Map pp94-6; ☎ 9212 1005; scph@bigpond.com.au; 75 Wentworth Ave; s $90, d & tw $110; ☒) The rooms in this long-standing 160-room hotel vary in age, and the newer ones (with bathrooms and air-conditioning) represent better value in terms of comfort and facilities. The cheap rooms are cheap, in every respect. The traffic (road and train) can be noisy, but you're close to Central, should you need to catch an early train.

Chinatown & Darling Harbour

Vulcan Hotel (Map pp90-1; ☎ 9211 3283; vulcan ho@ozemail.com.au; 500 Wattle St, Ultimo; d & tw from $100; P ☒ 💻) Another good option that keeps you close to the city centre is the Vulcan, a newish place with very appealing rooms in a charming heritage-listed building. The rooms at Vulcan have all the mod cons and décor touches usually found in the top-end places.

Aaron's Hotel (Map pp94-6; ☎ 9281 5555; res@ aaronshotel.com.au; 37 Ultimo Rd, Haymarket; d from $100; ☒) Right in the heart of Chinatown and very close to Darling Harbour, this hotel has plainly decorated, clean, light-filled rooms with sparkling bathrooms. It's popular with group bookings.

Hotel Ibis (Map pp94-6; ☎ 9563 0888; www .accorhotels.com.au; 70 Murray St, Pyrmont; d $160; P ☒ 💻) This is one of those places that sprouted up around Darling Harbour in the development-mad 1990s – staffed by the young and enthusiastic, perfectly acceptable and containing not one whit of soul or character. Still, some of the views of Darling Harbour are appealing.

Capitol Square Hotel (Map pp94-6; ☎ 9211 8633; www.goldspear.com.au; cnr George & Campbell Sts; d $165; P ☒) A very convenient place to stay near Chinatown and Darling Harbour, especially given that extremely good deals are often available. Rooms go for a 'plush' feel in an effort to remind guests that they're in a four-star joint. Wheelchair access is available, too.

Wake Up! (Map pp94-6; ☎ 9288 7888; www .wakeup.com.au; 509 Pitt St; d & tw $90) This is a newish place that has plenty of dorm beds, but also very presentable double and twin rooms with bathrooms. This place is just on Railway Square, making public transport a breeze, and is enthusiastically run (and recommended).

Kings Cross

Victoria Court Hotel (Map p100; ☎ 9357 3200; info@ victoriacourt.com.au; 122 Victoria St; d $135-165; P) This is a quiet, sweetly run hotel with old-fashioned service and comfortable rooms in a lovely pair of sensitively renovated Victorian houses. There's security parking, and a pleasant courtyard. One budget room without a private bathroom is also available for $95.

Hotel 59 (Map p100; ☎ 9360 5900; hotel59@ enternet.com.au; 59 Bayswater Rd; s/d from $100/125) This small, friendly hotel in the quiet stretch of Bayswater Rd has charming rooms and friendly staff who go out of their way to make your stay a happy one. There's also a small café, which turns out great cooked breakfasts. Reservations are a good idea.

Cross Court Tourist Hotel (Map p100; ☎ 9368 1822; www.crosscourthotel.com.au; 203 Brougham St; s/d/tr $75/85/95) A friendly, well-run place with 20 rooms and some great views (a deluxe room with private bathroom costs $105), this is one of the better small, simple hotels in the area.

Bernly Private Hotel (Map p100; ☎ 9358 3122; www.bernlyprivatehotel.com.au; 15 Springfield Ave; s/d/t $85/95/135) This polite, larger-than-it-looks hotel has simple rooms with fairly old décor, reliable and courteous 24-hour reception and a rooftop garden. There are also numerous rooms without private bathrooms and some dorms. Its backstreet location may make some nervous late at night, although the greatest risk probably comes from dodging dog poo.

Darlinghurst & Surry Hills
Hotel Altamont (Map p100; ☎ 9360 6000; hotel altamont@yahoo.com; 207 Darlinghurst Rd; d $130; 🖫) This is quite a find in Darlinghurst, featuring smart-looking rooms with private bathrooms, and a lovely dog, aptly named Slick. Communal areas are welcoming (especially the terrace) and its mighty handy for the Cross and the area surrounding it. There are also dorm beds available and discounts for longer stays.

L'Otel (Map p100; ☎ 9360 6868; hotel@lotel.com.au; 114 Darlinghurst Rd; d from $150; 🖫) This hip, stylish 16-room place is friendly and very well appointed, thanks to designers *du jour* Burley Katon Halliday, who've gone for a blindingly white look for the most part. Rooms have phone, fax and dataport connections and a general air of subdued smartness.

City Crown Motel (Map pp94-6; ☎ 9331 2433; www.citycrownmotel.com.au; 289 Crown St; d $85; 🖫 🖳) With clean, simple rooms (none of them particularly spacious), this is a popular place during Mardi Gras, when prices increase by 50%. Still, you're a stone's throw from Oxford St and the city.

Paddington
Sullivans Hotel (Map pp094-6; ☎ 9361 0211; sydney@sullivans.com.au; 21 Oxford St; d $130-145; 🅿 🖫) Situated in an area often referred to as 'Paddinghurst', this well-managed 64-room motel has simple but smart rooms and a charming courtyard area. It's popular with gay travellers, making booking essential during Mardi Gras.

Edgecliff to Watson's Bay
Doyles Palace Hotel (Map pp90-1; ☎ 9337 5444; www.doyles.com.au; Military Rd, Watsons Bay; d $145-370; 🅿 🖫) Freshly tarted-up and in one of the most beautiful spots in all Sydney, this is really a top-end hotel, but there are some delightful mid-range rooms (with park views) available. The renovations were skilfully done, and reservations are strongly advised. Drinking and dining within the Doyles' empire is a bit of a rite of passage in Sydney, so it's no surprise that they have added sleeping to the list.

Savoy Hotel (Map pp90-1; ☎ 9326 1411; www .savoyhotel.com.au; 41 Knox St, Double Bay; d $120-150; 🅿 🖫) This lies smack bang in Double Bay's coffee-lounge belt, which is just off busy New South Head Rd, and has nicely decorated rooms and a few suites that cost a little more than mid-range would allow. It's a quiet spot, popular with those who like their social life classy, but relaxed.

Metro Inn (Map pp90-1; ☎ 9328 7977; www .metroinns.com.au; 230 New South Head Rd, Edgecliff; d $160; 🖫) Like many creatures of a certain age in this neighbourhood, the Metro Inn has been getting some work done over the years. Some rooms (all neat and shiny) have great views of the harbour, and it's close to Edgecliff train station. Service is courteous too, and if you book on the Internet, there are some fearsome discounts.

Bondi
Like most beachside suburbs, Bondi's hotels are prone to summer price rises.

Bondi Sands (Map p102; ☎ 1800 026 634; www .bondisands.com; 252 Campbell Pde; d & tw $90-120) Managed by the charming Ilana, whose five-star background is evident in her diligence and dedication, the Bondi Sands caters for those after double and twin rooms. They're simple, clean affairs, with shared bathrooms, but a few (ask for No 7, 8, 17 or 18) have stunning views. If you miss out on those, there's always the wonderful rooftop area. Low-season reductions are both generous and negotiable.

Beach Road Hotel (☎ 9130 7247; 71 Beach Rd; s/d $75/90; 🖫) This chipper hotel is a large, boxlike pub two blocks back from the beach. Heavy on the beach-themed décor, it has several bars, a couple of eateries and a nightclub. Rooms are clean and bright and come with TV and decent bathrooms. The whole feel of the place is very low-key and casual, which is nice.

Coogee
Dive Hotel (☎ 9665 5538; www.divehotel.com.au; 234 Arden St; d & tw $150-165) This delightful, small boutique hotel has been beautifully decorated in a modern style that retains interesting original tilework and a sense of beachhouse space. There are more expensive rooms with views available, and each room has a kitchenette and groovy bathroom.

Glebe
Haven Inn (Map pp90-1; ☎ 9660 6655; bookings@haveninnsydney.com.au; 196 Glebe Point Rd; d $150-195; P ⌘) When we popped into this helpful inn on the corner of Wigram Rd, renovations were in progress, and things were looking good. Rooms are comfortable and well appointed, plus there's a heated swimming pool and secure parking. Avoid the overpriced continental breakfasts though, and head down Glebe Point Rd instead.

Wattle House (Map pp90-1; ☎ 9552 4997; stay@wattlehouse.com.au; 44 Hereford St; d $80) A lovely Victorian house accommodating 26 people (some dorm accommodation is available for $27 per person per night), this place is excellent – super-tidy, friendly and efficient. It's nonsmoking, alcohol-free and reservations are advised. It has a minimum stay of three nights, although this can be negotiated. All bathrooms are shared.

Newtown
Billabong Gardens (☎ 9550 3236; book@billabonggardens.com.au; 5-11 Egan St; d $90; P) This quality long-standing motel/hostel is clean and quiet and has good word-of-mouth reviews from many travellers. There's a small solar-heated pool and good kitchen. There are also budget rooms without private bathrooms, and some dorm rooms with bathrooms. Guests can be picked up at the airport by arrangement. From Railway Square, catch bus No 422, 423, 426 or 428 up Newtown's King St, and get off at Missenden Rd. By train, go to Newtown Station and turn right; Egan St is about four blocks along, on the left.

Manly
Manly Lodge (Map p104; ☎ 9977 8655; enquiries@manlylodge.com.au; 22 Victoria Pde; d & tw $145-160; ⌘) This is a quaint guesthouse with a holiday atmosphere and a vaguely Spanish appearance. Rooms have bathroom, TV, video and fridge; some have spas. There's also a communal sauna, spa and gym, and a pleasant outdoor area, plus larger suites and family rooms. Rates are lower in spring, autumn and winter.

Manly Paradise Motel (Map p104; ☎ 9977 5799; www.manlyparadise.com.au; 54 North Steyne; d $110-165; P ⌘) Catering to family holiday makers and business travellers for many years, this efficient and thoughtful place can provide children's cots if required, plus there's an elevator and rooftop pool. Rooms are very 1980s, but spacious and well cared for. There are some more expensive rooms available (to $190), which will give you sea views.

Manly Beach Resort (Map p104; ☎ 9977 4188; manlybch@ozemail.com.au; 6 Carlton St; s $115, d & tw $140, tr $150; P) This is a reasonable 1970s-era motel (breakfast included) with good security and car parking. There are also family rooms available and one studio, plus a separate backpackers' section. The sign says 'affordable and friendly', but it's really only affordable as far as we can tell.

Airport
Hotel Ibis Sydney Airport (☎ 8339 8500; res@ibis-sydneyairport.com.au; 205 O'Riordan St, Mascot; s & d $100; P ⌘ ⌨) Hey, you know the drill, and this airport hotel follows it to the letter. Good facilities, free airport shuttle and efficient service – but no one stays in these 'could be anywhere' places for kicks – they do so because the flight's leaving early, or they missed it altogether.

PUBS
City Centre & The Rocks
Grand Hotel (Map pp94-6; ☎ 9232 3755; 30 Hunter St; s/d/t $80/100/110) The heritage-listed Grand Hotel has a pretty good inner-city pub. Rooms are quite modest (bathrooms are shared), sizes vary and all have TV, fridge and tea- and coffee-making facilities. But the real selling point remains the location, which puts you within spitting-distance of the harbour.

Lord Nelson Brewery Hotel (Map pp94-6; ☎ 9251 4044; www.lordnelson.com.au; 19 Kent St; d $120; ⌘) This swish boutique pub has its own brewery and is in a historic sandstone building in the less-obviously touristy part of The Rocks. All rooms (with lovely dormer windows) have fax machines and dataport facilities, although the ones with bathrooms cost $180.

Australian Hotel (Map pp94-6; ☎ 9247 2229; info@australianheritagehotel.com; 100 Cumberland St; d $125) Despite the fact that it has shared bathrooms, we like this place for the pub downstairs and the extremely cosy communal rooms. Bedrooms are just as attractive, and the terrace area allows you to inhale Sydney Harbour.

Mercantile Hotel (Map pp94-6; ☎ 9247 3570; merc@tpg.com.au; 25 George St; d $140) This green-tiled hotel is a restored pub with a strong Irish connection. It's right near the bridge and the rooms are good. Breakfast is included in the price and there are some rooms without private bathrooms for $110. Be warned, St Patrick's Day is a madhouse at this pub.

Palisade Hotel (Map pp94-6; ☎ 9247 2272; www.palisadehotel.com; 35 Bettington St; d/tw $115/125) Standing sentinel-like at Millers Point, the Palisade Hotel has nine solidly furnished rooms, some with breathtaking views of the harbour and its fine bridge. It's a lovely old heritage building (although the share bathrooms reflect its age), and it's in a part of The Rocks that has thankfully avoided (at the time of research) that twee, 'ye olde worlde' tourist-trap feel. It's also a decent spot for a beer.

Darling Harbour
Glasgow Arms Hotel (Map pp94-6; ☎ 9211 2354; admin@glasgowarmshotel.com.au; 527 Harris St, Ultimo; s/ d $110/125; ✗) Just across the road from the excellent Powerhouse Museum, this award-winning hotel has traditionally decorated rooms and access to many of Chinatown's and Darling Harbour's attractions, plus a verdant courtyard.

Bondi
Hotel Bondi (Map p102; ☎ 9130 3271; hotelbondi@ ozemail.com.au; 178 Campbell Pde; s $75, d & tw $110, tr $130) Hotel Bondi is the peach-coloured layer-cake on the beachfront. The rooms are small and tidy, but be warned – the Bondi Hotel below is a very popular nightspot with people who can only be classified as noisy drunks. Still, if you have a view of the beach you'll be laughing.

Coogee
Coogee Bay Boutique Hotel (☎ 9665 0000; 9 Vicar St; d $100; P ✗) Right in the centre of Coogee, this heritage hotel with a casual feel has rooms available in its original Coogee Bay Hotel building as well as in the newer, fancier and quieter wing (these are top-end prices though). Enter from Vicar St, parallel to Arden St. Rooms have fridge, TV and telephone – and you can hear many of the bands playing downstairs if you're trying to sleep in the pub rooms.

Top End
Hotels and serviced apartments charging from $165 a double abound in Sydney, but since many cater to business people their rates may be lower on weekends. Serviced apartments sometimes sleep more than two people and, with lower weekly rates, they can be an inexpensive option if shared by a group.

Establishment Hotel (Map pp94-6; ☎ 9240 3100; info@establishmenthotel.com; 5 Bridge Lane, City; d from $290; ✗) Slicker than grease and smooth as silk, this 31-room hotel plays host to the likes of low-key moguls and secretive stars. Every (stylish) mod-con is provided and eating and drinking options are literally at your feet in the same building.

Four Seasons (Map pp94-6; ☎ 9238 0000; www .fourseasons.com; 199 George St, City; d from $360; P ✗ 💻) Easily one of the main contenders for the title of 'best hotel in Sydney', the Four Seasons features luxurious rooms, extraordinarily professional staff and knockout views (city, Opera House, or harbour – take your pick) from over half its rooms. Packages are available and no request is too tricky – particularly for business travellers. Wheelchair friendly.

Tricketts Bed & Breakfast (Map pp90-1; ☎ 9552 1141; trickettsbandb@hotmail.com.au; 270 Glebe Point Rd, Glebe; s $150, d $180-200; P 💻) The lovely Liz Trickett has lovingly restored this magnificent 19th-century mansion, and her attention to detail is evident throughout. Rooms are downright sumptuous, and all have bathrooms. Reservations are advised, as this place tends to attract a great deal of repeat business.

Simpsons of Potts Point (Map p100; ☎ 9356 2199; www.simpsonspottspoint.com.au; 8 Challis Ave, Potts Point; s/d from $145/165; P ✗) The former grand residence of a member of parliament, this charming B&B offers extremely comfortable rooms and plush communal areas, including a delightful conservatory for breakfast. It's a popular honeymoon choice.

Regents Court (Map p100; ☎ 9358 1533; regcourt@iname.com; 18 Springfield Ave, Potts Point; d $220-255; P ✗ 🖳) One of Potts Point's smartest options, this is a swanky, modernist haven of discretion, with natty black and white bathrooms, well-equipped kitchenettes for each room and a wonderful rooftop garden.

W Hotel Sydney (Map p100; ☎ 9331 9000; www.whotels.com; 6 Cowper Wharf Rdwy, Woolloomooloo; d from $400; P ✗ 🖳) This is a lavish interpretation of minimalist chic, with some splendid views available and the great temptation of the Water Bar on the premises. Business travellers will be mighty pleased with the slick technology available in the rooms, and the lofts are full of spacious freedom.

Park Hyatt (Map pp94-6; ☎ 9241 1234; www.sydney.hyatt.com; 7 Hickson Rd, The Rocks; d from $700; P ✗ 🖳) The super-luxurious Park Hyatt has one of the best locations in Sydney – snaking along the waterfront at the edge of Campbells Cove, almost at the Harbour Bridge and facing the Opera House. Watch out for reduced-price weekend packages that can offer substantial discounts. If you need a 24-hour butler service, then this is the hotel for you.

Bed & Breakfast Sydney Harbour (Map pp94-6; ☎ 9247 1130; 142 Cumberland St, The Rocks; s/d from $215/230; ✗) This charming B&B gets rave reviews from guests and has a marvellous location. We love the fact that it captures an authentically Australian flavour without succumbing to Australiana overload. A few small rooms with share bathrooms are also available at mid-range rates.

Russell (Map pp94-6; ☎ 9241 3543; www.therussell.com.au; 143a George St, City; s/d from $220/235; ✗) This superbly located hotel is small and friendly, with rooms straight out of a Laura Ashley catalogue, pleasant lounge areas and a sunny roof garden. A smattering of cheaper rooms with share bathrooms are also available. Mind the perilously steep stairs though!

Medusa (Map pp94-6; ☎ 9331 1000; www.medusa.com.au; 267 Darlinghurst Rd, Darlinghurst; d from $270; P ✗ 🖳) This 18-room hotel is pure Sydney – glamorous, well-situated, a little bit flashy, a lot sexy, professional and decadent.

You could lose yourself (or any number of people) in the beds here, and when you suss out the luxury gadgets, gizmos and features of each room, you'll never want to leave. It's popular with affluent gay travellers and design buffs.

Manly Pacific Parkroyal (Map p104; ☎ 9977 7666; www.parkroyal.com.au; 55 North Steyne, Manly; d from $250; P ✗ 🖳) This big hotel has full-frontal views of the beach and is easily Manly's fanciest place to stay. There's a gym, heated rooftop pool, spa, sauna and undercover parking, plus a real sense of seaside swank.

Ravesi's (Map p102; ☎ 9365 4422; www.ravesis.com.au; cnr Campbell Pde & Hall St, Bondi; d $120-275, ste $245-450; ✗) With only 16 rooms, Ravesi's is popular and it's easy to see why. Rooms were being renovated when we visited, with the minimalist look that Sydney loves so much right now. It's right on the beach and the views are straight from heaven. A popular drinking spot attached to the hotel is your entrance.

EATING

With great local produce, innovative chefs and BYO licensing laws, it's no surprise that eating out is one of the great delights of a visit to Sydney.

City Centre

There's no shortage of places for a snack or meal in the city, especially on weekdays. They are clustered around the train stations, in shopping arcades and tucked away in the food courts to be found in just about every office building more than 20 storeys high. The 'Spanish Quarter' consists of a cluster of seven or eight Spanish restaurants and bars on Liverpool St between George and Sussex Sts, and represents a great spot to nibble on tapas and imbibe sangria.

Apartment (Map pp94-6; ☎ 9241 1488; 155 Macquarie St; mains $8.50-14) Apartment looks like no apartment we've ever seen, but hey, it's in a Renzo Piano–designed building and that makes us want to move in and call it home. Grab a coffee, a well-executed salad Nicoise ($13.50) and enjoy the light-filled, whiter than white space, filled with appreciative suits.

Bodhi (Map pp94-6; ☎ 9360 2523; Cook & Phillip Park; yum cha $4-9) The animal lovers at Bodhi offer tasty, healthy vegetarian yum cha in flash-looking surrounds. It's got a nice (albeit sometimes windy) outdoor seating area and fast service. Avoid the 'mock meat' delicacies and dive right into the straight-up vegie fare.

Obelisk Café (Map pp94-6; ☎ 9241 2141; 7 Macquarie Pl; mains $7.50-12) Situated – surprise, surprise – near an obelisk, this place has outdoor tables and good sandwiches, soups and coffee. It's not big, but it does the trick.

Mint Café (Map pp94-6; ☎ 9233 3337; 10 Macquarie St; mains $4.50-16) It may well be situated in Sydney's old mint, but it won't cost a mint to sit on the charming balcony here (or at the internal communal table) and enjoy a tasty pizza or some banana bread. An excellent place to start a jaunt down elegant Macquarie St.

Casa Asturiana (Map pp94-6; ☎ 9264 1010; 77 Liverpool St; tapas $4-10) This restaurant specialises in northern Spanish (hence the name Asturiana) cooking, and reputedly has the best tapas in Sydney. It's an ideal spot for a quick lunch or a dinner that's big on grazing, chatting, drinking and grinning.

Chinatown

Chinatown has expanded well beyond the confines of the officially designated pedestrian mall on Dixon St. You can spend a small fortune at some outstanding Chinese restaurants or eat well for next to nothing in a food court.

BBQ King (Map pp94-6; ☎ 9267 2586; 18-20 Goulburn St; mains $10-30) As the name suggests, you come here for barbecued food, and a lot of people would agree that this place is king. It's an old-school Chinese eatery, with bustling service, huge pots of tea and a scant regard for the niceties of fancy décor. There may be a queue, but it won't last long, and the great roast duck and pork are worth the wait. It's popular as a post-cinema haunt, as it stays open till about 2.30am.

Marigold Citymark (Map pp94-6; ☎ 9281 3388; Levels 4 & 5, 683-689 George St, Haymarket; yum cha $7) This 800-seat yum cha palace serves lunchtime yum cha daily and has an extensive menu of other dishes. Join the hordes – it's especially boisterous and interesting if you catch sight of a mammoth wedding banquet in full force.

Golden Century Seafood Restaurant (Map pp94-6; ☎ 9212 3901; 393-399 Sussex St, Haymarket; ☾ noon to 4am daily) With lots of fish tanks displaying your nervous-looking dinner, this place is a favourite late-night eating spot for many of Sydney's chefs and hotel workers. The flavours are exotic and engaging, the service fast and slick.

Emperor's Garden BBQ & Noodles (Map pp94-6; ☎ 9281 9899; 213-215 Thomas St; mains $4-10) A popular café-style Chinese eatery specialising in meat and poultry dishes (marinated duck tongue $9), with a great little takeaway section where you can pick your goodies, all whilst ogling the crimson-hued barbecued offerings hanging in the window.

Chinese Noodle Restaurant (Map pp94-6; ☎ 9281 9051; Shop 7, Prince Centre, 8 Quay St; mains $5-9) At this intimate, busy eatery decorated with grapes and Persian rugs, the noodles are handmade in the traditional northern Chinese style by the expert Cin – and the crowds are glad of it. Small, sweet and the perfect quick noodle fix for lunch or dinner.

Darling Harbour & Pyrmont

The Harbourside Shopping Centre, Cockle Bay and King St Wharves have dining options as far as the eye can see – some hit, many miss. Pyrmont is a good option for those wanting to eat close to the action, without battling hordes (especially on weekends).

Zaaffran (Map pp94-6; ☎ 9211 8900; Level 2, 345 Harbourside, Darling Harbour; mains $17-26) In a city with a million cheap Indian joints, this place stands out. The food is expertly cooked and it makes good use of its location in Darling Harbour (generally populated

---

BEST EATS IN SYDNEY
by Matthew Evans

Sailor's Thai (p121; ☎ 9251 2466; 106 George St, The Rocks; mains $15.50-26) Sydney's best Thai food.

Fratelli Paradiso (p123; ☎ 9357 1744; 12 Challis Ave, Potts Point; mains $11-20) The best breakfast in town.

Bécasse (p122; ☎ 9280 3202; 48 Albion St, Surry Hills; mains $28) Best classical cuisine.

Chinese Noodle Restaurant (opposite; ☎ 9281 9051; Shop 7, Prince Centre, 8 Quay St, Chinatown; mains $5-9) Best dumplings.

Bondi Iceberg's (p125; ☎ 91303120; 1 Notts Av, Bondi; mains $32-46) Coolest venue.

FILLING UP AT A FOOD COURT

One quick, easy and wallet-conscious way to stop your tummy rumbling as you pound the pavements of Darling Harbour and Chinatown is the ubiquitous food court. Packed with small kitchens offering a variety of Asian dishes, they're something of a Chinatown institution, and worth dipping your chopsticks into (if you can find room during lunchtime!). Generally, they open until about 10pm daily.

Harbour Plaza Food Court (Map pp94–6; cnr Dixon & Goulburn Sts, Haymarket) The pagoda-style Harbour Plaza has a wide range of cheap Asian meals.

Market City Shopping Centre (Map pp94–6; ☎ 9212 1388; Level 3, 2-13 Quay St, City) This mammoth place has a fresh produce market on the first level, a factory outlet on the second level and more food from more places than you can imagine on the third level. You'll find Paddy's Markets here, too (p134).

Sussex Centre (Map pp94–6; ☎ 9281 6388; 401 Sussex St, City) The food court here has a range of cheap, tasty dishes, making it a sensible choice for those who *want* to eat and run.

Dixon House Food Court (Map pp94–6; cnr Little Hay & Dixon Sts, Haymarket) This food court offers a selection of about 20 vendors, with low, low prices.

by quite ordinary restaurants). Its take on beef vindaloo ($25) reminds you that well-known dishes need not be ordinary or bland. And vegetarians will thanks their lucky stars for the choices on offer.

Sayori (Map pp94–6; ☎ 9566 2866; cnr Allen & Harris Sts, Pyrmont; mains $13-16) This place offers good-value no-frills Japanese food for takeaways or sit-down meals. The bento boxes are great value, or go for the sushi mains ($13.80). The number of real live Japanese people dining here is always a good sign.

Chinta Ria...Temple of Love (Map pp94–6; ☎ 9264 3211; Level 2, Cockle Bay Wharf, 201 Sussex St; mains $15-26) Perched on a leafy rooftop at the northern end of Cockle Bay Wharf, this Malaysian-hawker food-inspired temple serves tasty, reasonably priced meals in colourful style – the enormous Buddha will put you in a jolly mood from the moment you enter. Its laksa ($14.80) is definitely worth getting excited about.

Concrete (Map pp94–6; ☎ 9518 9523; 224 Harris St, Pyrmont; mains $14-17) True to its name, there's quite a bit of minimalist concrete going on here – but it's also chock-full of noise, laughter and cheer as people get down to the business of gorging on breakfast and lunch offerings. And they don't get stingy with the plump prawns when it comes to a linguine hit.

The Rocks & Circular Quay

Some restaurants and cafés in The Rocks are overtly aimed at tourists, however there are plenty of options for diners seeking something different from the standard 'locals never come here' joints.

Rockpool (Map pp94–6; ☎ 9252 1888; 107 George St, The Rocks; mains $49-60) This place is always featured in the 'best of' lists, and with good reason – it's one of the most famous and most highly regarded restaurants in Sydney, and its influence is considerable. Chef Neil Perry churns out some of the most beautiful (in all senses) dishes in Sydney – and it's a particularly good place to sample Sydney's best seafood. Go for the southern rock lobster tajine with roast apricots and couscous for two and thank them (and us) profusely.

Sailor's Thai (Map pp94–6; ☎ 9251 2466; 106 George St; mains $15.50-26) Sit at the long, communal stainless steel table and feast on some of the best Thai eating this side of Bangkok. A power crowd of arts bureaucrats and politicians mingles with the young and lively, all to good effect. Save superlatives for the food though.

MCA Café (Map pp94–6; ☎ 9241 4253; 140 George St, The Rocks; mains $10-29) At the slick Museum of Contemporary Art's Café, the outside tables have eye-catching views of the Quay and Opera House. The chilli corn cakes with bacon, rocket and tomato salsa ($10) is good museum-viewing fuel, or a pasta dish should see you right. The service is also praiseworthy, although popular dishes become unavailable with frightening speed on weekends.

There are several average cafés and kiosks amid the ferry wharves, notable mainly for being open 24 hours.

Sydney Cove Oyster Bar (Map pp94-6; ☎ 9247 2937; Circular Quay East; mains $27-34) In a sunny spot close to the Opera House, on the eastern side of Circular Quay, this place offers Australian produce and wine, with oysters served in a variety of ways ($14.50 to $29) for a quintessential Sydney experience. Sadly, they won't be the best oysters you'll have in Sydney, but what the hell, the view's charming!

Darlinghurst & East Sydney

Victoria St is the main café and restaurant strip in Darlinghurst. There's a second cluster of (mostly Italian) restaurants in Stanley St, East Sydney, just south of William St, between Crown and Riley Sts.

Pizza Mario (Map pp94-6; ☎ 9332 3633; 50 Burton St; mains $12-22) The best pizza you'll find in Sydney is also the most authentic. In fact, Pizza Mario is a certified Neapolitan pizzeria, and the wafer-thin crusts, spare but tasty toppings and 'no variations' rule on the menu will make you swear you're in Naples. Get in early and beat the hordes, as this place really is special. To find it, go to the 'piazza' area that's part of the Republic apartment complex (Palmer St).

Fu Manchu (Map pp94-6; ☎ 9360 9424; 249 Victoria St; mains $8-18) The original Fu, and some of the best Asian eating in Darlinghurst. The vibe is 21st-century Hong Kong slick chic, with chopsticks and elbows getting a thorough work-out. The steamed barbecue pork or vegetarian buns ($6 for two) are plump little parcels from paradise.

Bill & Toni's (Map pp94-6; ☎ 9360 4702; 74 Stanley St; mains $14) No one comes here for fine dining, they come here because it's a tradition, a stalwart of the cheap and cheerful, and in our opinion, a national treasure. The service is lightning-fast, you get your orange cordial for free and everyone leaves with a smile. The cuisine? Basic Italian – spag bol, veal parmigiana etc.

Balkan (Map pp94-6; ☎ 9360 4970; 209 Oxford St; mains $18-34) The Balkan (of long standing and a recent interior face-lift) is a continental restaurant specialising in meat, meat and more meat. The traditional raznjici and cevapcici ($20.90) are worth getting your tongue around.

Surry Hills

Crown St is the main thoroughfare through Surry Hills, but it's a long street and the restaurants occur in fits and starts. It's worth a wander along, though, as it has interesting shops and eateries. Parking here is rather scarce.

Longrain (Map pp94-6; ☎ 9280 2888; 85 Commonwealth St; mains $25-38) There are no reservations here, and it seems that all of Sydney's beautiful set are as keen to graze on the superb Asian-inspired offerings as you are. Good thing there's an excellent bar on the beautifully kitted-out premises, with cocktails so fine that even a hypoglycaemic can stand the wait. Any of the fish dishes deserve their own church.

Uchi Lounge (Map pp94-6; ☎ 9261 3524; 15 Brisbane St; mains $13.50-16.50) Patronised (and staffed) by creative types who aren't about to let a wallet crisis get in the way of dressing to impress, Uchi Lounge resembles a final-year art school exhibition, where the blissful Japanese food takes centre stage. The wasabi mussels ($9) accompanied by an ice-cold Asahi beer made us want to move in. The groovy little ground-floor bar is the perfect place to wait for a table (and wait you will – no reservations).

Il Baretto (Map pp94-6; ☎ 9361 6163; 496 Bourke St; mains $15-18) Packed to the rafters when we visited and dishing up some of the most heavenly pasta we had in Sydney. There's a numbering system that still seems to need fine-tuning, but basically, it's best to get your number and wait in the pub across the road and they will come and get you. Our *spaghetti alle vongole* ($16) was to die for.

Maltese Café (Map pp94-6; ☎ 9361 6942; 310 Crown St, Surry Hills; mains $6-7) For pasta on the cheap, visit this cheap and cheerful café near the intersection of Crown and Oxford Sts. The pastizzi ($0.70) are delicious and make handy, cheap snacks – in fact, they're a bit of a compulsory group-catering staple.

Bécasse (Map pp94-6; ☎ 9280 3202; 48 Albion St; mains $28) There's nothing flashy or garish about Bécasse, but it will stand out as one of the most memorable dining experiences of your trip. The muted, elegant décor is the perfect complement to the superbly created dishes. The Degustation Menu ($70) is seven courses of gustatory heaven, with salmon, venison, barramundi, suckling lamb and some delightful sweet morsel competing for the title of our favourite dish. Reservations essential.

Café Niki (Map pp90-1; ☎ 9319 7517; 544 Bourke St; mains $15-18) This great little corner café has all sorts of tempting goodies to eat and some seriously powerful coffee. It's the perfect spot to discuss the artworks of Brett Whiteley after a trip to his studio/gallery (p101).

There are half-a-dozen nondescript but good-value Lebanese eateries around the corner of Cleveland and Elizabeth Sts, at the southern end of Surry Hills, where most dishes are between $5 and $10, plus some Indian and Turkish places spice up Cleveland St between Crown and Bourke Sts.

Maya Da Dhaba (Map pp90-1; ☎ 8399 3785; 431 Cleveland St; mains $7.90-15) Serving better-than-average Indian fare in natty surrounds covered in wall hangings, the popular Maya Da Dhaba also offers good value. The andrakhi lamb chops ($12) arrive sizzling and juicy, so tuck in.

Kings Cross & Around

The Cross has a mixture of fast-food joints serving greasy fare designed mainly to soak up beer, tiny cafés servicing locals and travellers, and some swanky eateries that are among the city's best.

Fratelli Paradiso (Map p100; ☎ 9357 1744; 12 Challis Ave, Potts Point; mains $11-20) You can have lunch here, and it's great, but what keeps us getting out of bed in the morning is the idea of breakfast here. The eggs are magnificent, the rice pudding superb, the coffee from God. Service is friendly, sometimes cheeky, and always brisk – just like in Italy.

Delectica (Map p100; ☎ 9380 1390; 130 Victoria St, Potts Point; mains $11-14) This lovely place is modern and airy and has truly charming service. You might be amid backpacker chaos, but you won't notice. And the food (breakfast and lunch) is lovely, too.

Bayswater Brasserie (Map p100; ☎ 9357 2177; 32 Bayswater Rd; mains $19-30) This is a classy but casual restaurant with excellent service, where you can also pop in for a drink at the back-room bar if you want to relax before dining. One of our faves is the confit duck leg and pork belly with beetroot relish and witlof salad ($28).

Bourbon & Beefsteak (Map p100; ☎ 9358 1144; 24 Darlinghurst Rd; mains $23-30) With its splendidly tacky and eclectic disco-meets-brothel décor, this place has long been a haunt for sailors, tourists, night owls and steak lovers

alike. It serves food (and alcohol) 24 hours a day, and was under new management when we visited – hopefully, none of the seedy charm of the place will be sacrificed to the gods of good taste.

Dean's Café (Map p100; ☎ 9368 0953; 5 Kellett St; mains $8-15) The cosily bohemian, slightly grotty Dean's Café serves irresistible and 'monstrous' nachos and a good selection of drinks. It's a great place to satisfy the munchies or unwind after a big night out, as it's open late.

Paddington & Woollahra

Bistro Lulu (Map pp90-1; ☎ 9380 6888; 257 Oxford St; mains $26) The subdued lighting, dark wood, smart service and wonderful bistro food will make you swear you're in Paris. Vegetarians are actually given a choice of dishes that invites debate, and for the carnivores, it's hard to beat the steak with fritts (chips!), thanks to chef Joe Pavlovich. A small but functional wine list makes for a very enjoyable experience.

Buzo (☎ 9328 1600; 152 Jersey Rd, Woollahra; mains $19-25) Buzo is an intimate, charming restaurant that feels like a neighbourhood secret. Homely Italian and French dishes (dinner only) pepper the straightforward menu (with a smattering of good wines) – we had a great Sicilian roast leg of lamb ($25). Nab a window seat if you can and admire the red-and-white checked tablecloths, hanging garlic and honest victuals.

And the Dish Ran Away with the Spoon (☎ 9361 6131; 226 Glenmore Rd, Paddington; mains $5-10) It's hard to believe that the 'skinny burger' ($8) is low-fat, as it tastes too good to be true. In this charming little place, locals pack in to lunch on great pasta and hormone-free organic chooks. It's a very good spot to pick up picnic fixings or takeaway lunches and dinners.

Jones the Grocer (Map pp90-1; ☎ 9362 1222; 68 Moncur St, Woollahra; mains $8-16) With the lovely food on display it's easy to see why this is one of Sydney's favourite places to stock up on fancy deli goods. The mixed platter at lunchtime is a good refuelling option. But it's also nice for the old coffee-and-cake break.

Glebe

Glebe Point Rd was Sydney's original 'eat street' but what it lacks in cutting-edge dining experiences it retains in laid-back, unfaddish atmosphere, good-value food and convivial service.

Tanjore (Map pp90-1; ☎ 9660 6332; 34 Glebe Point Rd; mains $11-17) A pioneer of South Indian food in Australia, Tanjore attracts a range of locals, Indian-food lovers and celebrities. Everything is cooked to order and the tandoori dishes are so good you'll need to make reservations as earth tones and earthy appetites collide.

Iku Wholefoods (Map pp90-1; ☎ 9692 8720; 25a Glebe Point Rd; mains $2.50-9) This stalwart of healthy eating offers wonderful vegan and vegetarian food in a relaxed, small setting (takeaway is a good idea) at bargain prices. It's a handy spot for either dinner or lunch, and while other branches are scattered throughout the city, this one remains a favourite of ours.

Spanish Tapas (Map pp90-1; ☎ 9571 9005; 28 Glebe Point Rd; tapas $7.50-14) There's quite a party vibe here, with average to great tapas dishes, low lights, music and a convivial bunch of diners. Grab a jug of sangria ($16) and throw yourself into the festive spirit.

Badde Manors (Map pp90-1; ☎ 9660 3797; 37 Francis St; mains $11.50) This is a long-established local haunt and something of a must-visit after a trip to the Glebe markets. It can be pretty hectic here, so don't take offence if the staff are a tad brusque – it's called Badde Manors for a reason. The cakes and tarts are excellent.

Newtown

A swag of funky cafés and restaurants lining King St offer an interesting introduction to the suburb's community life.

Rosalina's (☎ 9516 1429; 30 King St; mains $14-16) Cuter than cute, Rosalina's is like a clichéd 'little Italian place' from central casting, complete with dodgy mural. Charming service, home-made vino and great pasta make it very popular on weekends, so book ahead. Those hankering for a classic steak Dianne ($16) will be in heaven.

Green Gourmet (☎ 9519 5330; 115 King St; mains $13-15) Spotlessly clean and kind to animals, Green Gourmet offers great Chinese-Malaysian vegetarian lunch and dinner at good prices. On weekends, grab a few morsels of cruelty-free yum cha and wash it all down with one of the excellent teas on offer. There's no smoking, of course, and no drinking either.

Linda's Backstage Restaurant (☎ 9550 6015; Newtown Hotel, 174 King St; mains $16-19) The pub is a popular gay haunt with drag shows and the added bonus of a great little restaurant out the back. Chef Linda Robertson uses the freshest ingredients and Southeast Asian and European influences to make her diners happy. The champagne jelly with poached stonefruits ($9.50) is a very civilised way to finish a meal.

Bacigalupo (☎ 9565 5238; 284 King St; mains $9-15) If traipsing along King St has caused your tummy to rumble, Bacigalupo's mammoth blackboard full of good pasta dishes and hearty specials will ease the pain. It's a cheery, high-ceilinged place, with egg-yolk yellow walls and lots of loud conversation.

Singapore Gourmet (☎ 9550 6453; 520 King St; mains $4-9) The basic décor and rock-bottom prices here haven't changed in years, and that makes for good eating for the budget-conscious, with big servings of mee goreng ($7) and seafood laksa ($9) raising smiles all round.

Old Fish Shop Café (☎ 9519 4295; 249a King St; mains $9-10) Yep, it used to be a fish shop. Now it's a cute corner café with garlic hanging from the ceilings, paint peeling off the walls, open windows to catch King St's fumes and rumblings, and simple, yummy sandwiches and pizzas.

Leichhardt

You can still get a cheap spag bol in Norton St, but the classic bistros are now rubbing shoulders with the classy restaurants, plus a few Greek, Chinese and Thai interlopers.

Grappa (☎ 9560 6090; Shop 1, 267-277 Norton St; mains $28-36) You'll enter Grappa via a less-than-attractive garage, and ascend to a spacious eatery with an open kitchen, snazzy bar and elegant décor – perfect for a swanky yet relaxed dining experience. There's a good range of dishes (the grilled seafood plate is a gem; $29), and an impressive list of grappa, hence the name.

Bar Italia (☎ 9560 9981; 169-171 Norton St; mains $8.50-16) This enormously popular restaurant, café and gelateria offers pasta mains and bar snacks, but one of its biggest drawcards is its famous gelato, which is a must-have accessory for any Norton St passegiata (stroll). The outdoor courtyard, good honest food and a little red wine makes for a very enjoyable meal. Don't expect much in the way of Italian design from your surroundings – all the pleasure is in the eating.

Grind (☎ 9568 5535; 151 Norton St; mains $8.50-15) This is a small, modern and popular place, which occupies a prime position on Norton St, and there's a balcony too, so enjoy the good pasta dishes and big breakfasts while you watch 'il mondo' go by.

Elio (☎ 9560 9129; 159 Norton St; mains $18-28) With personal, attentive and informed service, Elio offers high-quality pasta dishes in stylish surrounds – think red feature wall, blond wood and good-looking guys and girls. In winter, the rabbit and olive pie with roast parsnips and green peas ($24.50) will warm you right up.

Bondi

The burger joints and greasy spoons are still in plentiful supply along Campbell Pde between Hall St and Beach Rd, but on other streets, they're being squeezed out by cafés, bistros and a slew of serious foodie joints. You'll generally have to forgo a sea view if you're seriously pinching the pennies, but of course you can always do as the locals do and take a steaming paper package or a pizza down to the beach.

Sean's Panaroma (Map p102; ☎ 9365 4924; 2/270 Campbell Pde; mains $24-35) Sean and his team have never let us down when we're looking for excellent food in intimate surrounds. It attracts a good-looking crowd, but don't let that put you off – the food is straight from heaven. For starters, grab someone special and share an Oxheart tomato salad ($18) before delving into more substantial territory and a judicious wine list. Easily one of Sydney's more romantic dinner spots.

Brown Sugar (Map p102; ☎ 9365 6262; 100 Brighton Blvd; mains $7.50-13) This cramped space really churns out brekky to the smooth set on weekends – and one bite of their black-stone eggs ($9.50) will tell you why. It's much less frantic on weekdays, and the lunch dishes and salads are truly tasty.

Yulla (Map p102; ☎ 9365 1788; Level 1, 38 Campbell Pde; mains $21-26) When you combine the Middle Eastern/Israeli food, the beach views and the more-than-reasonable prices, this place deserves repeat visits. The hummus we've enjoyed here is perhaps the best we've found. It's also a good breakfast choice on weekends.

Green's Café (Map p102; ☎ 9130 6181; 140 Glenayr Ave; mains $3.50-14) A green-hued, laid-back brekky or lunch experience awaits those coming to Green's. We enjoyed the relaxing, unhurried air as we devoured salad packed with green goodness and delicately boosted by a tangy dressing. Very satisfying.

Luv in a Cup (106 Glenayr Ave; mains $7.50-15) This place is as cute and cramped as a bug's ear and the staff may well be the sweetest in Sydney. The menu is limited, but once you're tried the fantastic 'Luv eggs' you'll be too in luv to notice. It's mostly a breakfast and lunch place, but they were starting to open up for Friday and Saturday nights when we visited.

Madame Chan's (Map p102; ☎ 9365 7288; 86 Gould St; mains $13) Our favourite Madame has Asian décor touches scattered throughout (you can't miss the dragon mural) and tasty stir-fry noodle dishes for those needing fast sustenance. You can specify the sort of noodles, sauces and ingredients in your meal, or just go with what's suggested on the blackboard.

Hugo's (Map p102; ☎ 9300 0900; 70 Campbell Pde; mains $30-38) Hugo's is well known among Bondi dwellers as a good place to have a better-than-average-meal in swish 'look at me' surrounds. It can seem a bit sceney, but once you've tried some of the food and had one of the daiquiris, you won't care. Staff are disconcertingly attractive, so if this makes you nervous, put on some glad rags.

Fu Manchu (Map p102; ☎ 9300 0416; Level 1, 80 Campbell Pde; mains $12.50-28) For really good Chinese-Malaysian food, Fu Manchu is hard to beat. Try the heavenly steamed buns for starters and then move onto the delicious curries, stir-fries and rice dishes. Yum cha is available on weekends between 11.30am and 3.30pm.

Gelbison (Map p102; ☎ 9130 4042; 10 Lamrock Ave; mains $9.50-19) An old favourite with many beach bums, film industry types (including Mel Gibson) and assorted gluttons looking for great Italian staples, Gelbison never seems to change, and in Bondi that's a rare thing. The pizza and pasta inspire such devotion that a local band took the step of naming themselves after the beloved joint.

Bondi Icebergs (Map p102; ☎ 9130 3120; 1 Notts Ave; mains $32-46) So damn hot we get scorch marks just walking past, this new venture dares to charge a cancellation fee to errant diners. Why anyone would fail to show (reservations essential, and hard to come by) we've no idea – the décor is 21st-century cool-meets-warm, the views over Bondi to die for, the food fantastic. One bite of the warm salad of Moreton Bay Bugs with kipfler potatoes, tarragon and fresh peas will make you glad you came.

Coogee

There are a number of cheap takeaways on Coogee Bay Rd, but you're better off hitting the cafés in the streets running off it, which have healthier food, sunnier interiors and outdoor tables.

A Fish Called Coogee (☎ 9664 7700; 229 Coogee Bay Rd; mains $8-16) This great little fishmonger sells fresh fish and seafood cooked many different ways. Grab some takeaway fish and chips ($8) and sit on the beach – because the tables here are often full, and anyway, it's more Australian that way.

Rice (☎ 1300 887 423; 100 Beach St; mains $11-17) Perhaps the flashest-looking noodle joint in Sydney, this stunning place serves noodles to your specifications and also curries, salads, stir fries and meat dishes. It's a nice spot for lunch or dinner, away from the madding crowds of Coogee Bay Rd.

Jack & Jill's Fish Café (☎ 9665 8429; 98 Beach St; mains $12-17) This homy, simple place serves good seafood dishes at reasonable prices. Next door to Rice, it's away from the crowds, but close to the northern end of Coogee Beach. We recommend the Cajun-spiced barramundi with rice ($16.50).

Erciyes 2 (☎ 9664 1913; 240 Coogee Bay Rd; mains $8.50-10) This spic-and-span offshoot of Erciyes in Surry Hills offers great Turkish pizza and a range of dips and kebabs. It's BYO, does takeaway food and also has belly dancing on Friday and Saturday. Definitely worth a visit if you feel like something quick, simple and scrummy.

Barzura (☎ 9665 5546; 62 Carr St; mains $20-22) A welcoming café with outdoor seating that lets you breathe in the fresh sea air, Barzura is deservedly popular with locals and day-trippers alike. The food's good, too, so it's best to book a table on weekends.

Manly

The ocean end of The Corso is jam-packed with takeaway places and outside tables. Manly Wharf and South Steyne have plenty of airy eateries that catch the sea breeze and seem bustling even on wet weekdays – so be prepared for crowds on sunny weekends!

Blue Water Café (Map p104; ☎ 9976 2051; 28 South Steyne; mains $14-25) With huge portions, an entree should be enough for most at this bustling, popular café in a prime position. The whopping great chicken burger with all the trimmings ($13.50) will really satisfy a post-surf hunger, although all the boards on the wall will make you keen to get back out there into the foam.

BarKing Frog (Map p104; ☎ 9977 6307; 48 North Steyne; mains $12-17) Popping into BarKing Frog and watching the world go by should be compulsory. It's nice-looking, does healthy lunchtime fare and invites dawdling over a coffee and the paper.

Bower Restaurant (Map p104; ☎ 9977 5451; 7 Marine Pde; mains $23-29) Follow the foreshore path east from the main ocean beach to reach this small restaurant, within spray's-breath of tiny Fairy Bower beach. It has wonderful breakfasts, delicious main courses and it's BYO, too. Heaven!

Alhambra (Map p104; ☎ 9976 2975; 54a The Esplanade; mains $23) We love coming to Manly, because it means we can be distracted by the heavenly smells wafting from Alhambra, and then we decide it's time to make sure they've maintained their standards. The Spanish-inspired dishes are excellent, and are nicely matched by the Moorish décor. Grab some mates, a few beers and graze on tapas to your heart's (and belly's) content.

Beanrush (Map p104; ☎ 9977 2236; 7 Whistler St; mains $2.20-9.50) A small hole-in-the-wall café with truly great coffee and sweet staff. Definitely worth a visit if your engine needs revving. The snacks are mighty fine, too.

North Shore

Aqua Dining (Map pp90-1; ☎ 9964 9998; cnr Paul & Northcliff Sts, Milsons Point; mains $33-36) The fit-out was accomplished by Soma design, and while its muted mushroom tones and clean lines are admirable, it never really competes with the view of the Bridge and the harbour. Service here is sterling – that rare mix of courteous, knowledgeable (the wine list beggars belief) and amiable. Put your hand up for the saddle of lamb ($35) and don't even think about a post-prandial swim in the Olympic swimming pool that you're overlooking!

Ripples (Map pp90-1; ☎ 9929 7722; Olympic Dr, Milson's Point; mains $20-25) Ripples was a new arrival when we popped in, and was being touted by all and sundry. Go for breakfast or lunch and be rewarded with fine food, tasty views and the smug sense of being in the thick of Sydney's most attractive geography. It is located diagonally across from Aqua Dining at North Sydney's Olympic Pool.

DRINKING
Bars
CITY CENTRE
Tank Stream Bar (Map pp94-6; ☎ 9240 3109; 1 Tank Stream Way) Tucked away behind the swanky Establishment, this convivial bar, capably run by the charming Sonia, is a great place to unwind after the hard working day. It's subtly decorated with an interesting blend of original features and new flourishes, with plenty of ventilation, and nary a TV screen in sight.

Establishment (Map pp94-6; ☎ 9240 3000; 252 George St) Cashed-up and convinced it's still the '80s, the smartly suited crowd here appreciates the fine art of a smart cocktail after a hard day's stockbroking, and so do the designer-dudded types who love 'em. Noise levels approach a dull roar, what with all that marble going on.

Bar Europa (Map pp94-6; ☎ 9232 3377; Basement, 82 Elizabeth St) The basement location, flattering lighting and sexy screens separating Bar Europa's three rooms all combine to create a charming drinking den for legal eagles and those who've just shopped till they dropped.

KINGS CROSS & DARLINGHURST
Jimmy Lik's (Map p100; ☎ 8354 1400; 186 Victoria St, Potts Point) Long on bench space and its cocktail list, Jimmy Lik's also serves excellent Thai food. Generally, there's a bit of a wait for restaurant seating, and with heavenly bar snacks (try the smoked trout in betel leaf) beckoning, who's in a hurry to score a table?

Chicane (Map pp94-6; ☎ 9380 2121; 1a Burton St, Darlinghurst) You'll feel all grown up once you step into Chicane's world of up-to-the-minute design, comfortable seating, good wines and luscious cocktails, low ceilings, a fireplace and smooth service. Even the bathrooms are groovy.

Soho Bar & Lounge (Map p100; ☎ 9358 6511; 171 Victoria St, Potts Point) In an old Art Deco pub, the revamped ground floor bar has played host to numerous Sydneysiders' social lives. It's a cosy, relaxed drinking lounge, with a cruisy cocktail menu and cigars available.

Kinselas (Map pp94-6; ☎ 9331 3299; 383 Bourke St, Darlinghurst) In what used to be a funeral parlour, this place has come back from the dead more times than we can recall. The downstairs part is poker machines and bad carpet, but the bar upstairs is stylish, modern and incredibly popular with the bright young things. The cocktails are very good too. On hot summer nights, hanging on the miniscule balcony is *de rigueur*.

Baron's (Map p100; ☎ 9358 6131; Level 1, 5 Roslyn St, Kings Cross) God bless Baron's! Everything looks like it's in a state of decay here – sticky carpet, shabby chairs, yellowing walls – but where else are you going to find a quiet, really late-night drink and a game of backgammon?

SURRY HILLS
Mars Lounge (Map pp94-6; ☎ 9267 6440; 16 Wentworth Ave) A handful of futuristic-looking booths serve as the perfect spot to sip a cocktail and marvel at the fact that the staff here all look as though they're auditioning to be Michael Jackson's backing dancers.

Cafés
Coluzzi Bar (Map p100; ☎ 9380 5420; 322 Victoria St, Darlinghurst) You come here for coffee, not food, and it's almost a meal in itself, so robust is the flavour. Coluzzi has achieved legendary status, and if you have to have coffee in Darlinghurst, this is the place.

Spring Espresso (Map p100; ☎ 9331 0190; 65 Macleay St, Potts Point; mains $7.50-12) For life-changing coffee and good snacks, try this diminutive and bustling café; entry is via Challis Ave and you may have a bit of a wait on your hands during the morning rush, when it seems that half of Potts Point needs a heart-starter.

Café Hernandez (Map p100; ☎ 9331 2343; 69 Kings Cross Rd, Kings Cross; snacks $5-9) With a delightful old-world atmosphere and some of the best coffee in Sydney, Hernandez has been attracting everyone from taxi drivers to arty students for years. At times you'll think you're in Madrid, especially when it's 3am and this joint's jumping (open 24 hours). Be warned though, there's no bathroom.

Pubs

There are *plenty* of pubs in Sydney, in every
suburb. Sadly, pokie machines seem to be
a feature of almost every one of them now.
Generally, big nights on the turps take place
in The Rocks and around Kings Cross –
where you'll hear and smell the action
pretty quickly. Attractive, more low-key
places can be found in inner-city suburbs
such as Surry Hills and Darlinghurst, and
big breezy barns make for a great drinking
session by the ocean beaches.

THE ROCKS

Lord Nelson Brewery Hotel (Map pp94-6; ☎ 9251
4044; 19 Kent St, The Rocks) The Lord Nelson is
an atmospheric old (1842) pub that claims
to be the 'oldest pub' in town (although
others do, too!) and brews its own beers
(Quayle Ale, Trafalgar Pale Ale, Victory
Bitter, Three Sheets, Old Admiral, Nelsons
Blood and The Lord's Water). It might not
be wise to sample them all in one sitting.

Hero of Waterloo (Map pp94-6; ☎ 9252 4553;
81 Lower Fort St, Millers Point) On the corner of
Windmill St, the Hero of Waterloo has
music on weekends, including traditional
Irish music. It also has its original dungeon,
where drinkers would sleep off a heavy
night before a stint on the high seas.

Australian Hotel (Map pp94-6; ☎ 9247 2229;
100 Cumberland St, The Rocks) On the corner of
Gloucester and Cumberland Sts, this laid-
back, friendly hotel has renowned local
brews on tap, and it's also a nice sleeping
option (p118).

KINGS CROSS, WOOLLOOMOOLOO & DARLINGHURST

Old Fitzroy Hotel (Map p100; ☎ 9356 6848; 129 Dowling St, Woolloomooloo) Is it a pub? A theatre? A
bistro? Actually it's all three. Grab a bowl
of laksa, see the acting stars of tomorrow
and wash it all down with a beer, for about
$30. The little balcony is unbeatable on a
hot, steamy night.

Bourbon & Beefsteak (Map p100; ☎ 9358 1144;
24 Darlinghurst Rd, Kings Cross) On the dogleg of
Darlinghurst Rd, this institution is still
going strong after many years of 24-hour
boozing. Garish, ritzy and slightly seedy,
it's also a pretty good spot to pick up a
beer-soaking steak.

Green Park Hotel (Map pp94-6; ☎ 9380 5311;
360 Victoria St, Darlinghurst) The good old Green

Park has tiled walls and a bar; it's a popular
local watering hole and a cool hang-out for
pool-shooters. The last dose of renovations
provided much-needed drinking space and
better toilets. Punters go back and forth
between this place and the Darlo Bar with
great regularity.

Darlo Bar (Map pp94-6; ☎ 9331 3672; cnr Liverpool
St & Darlinghurst Rd, Darlinghurst) Occupying its
own tiny block, this is surely the narrowest
pub in Sydney. It's pretty much a neighbourhood pub, but it's a very interesting
neighbourhood. The service is friendly and
the furniture is retro mix 'n' match, with a
boisterous scene on weekend evenings.

Burdekin Hotel (Map pp94-6; ☎ 9331 2066;
2 Oxford St, Darlinghurst) This is one of a number
of busy drinking options along Oxford St.
It has a wonderfully stylish cocktail bar
called the **Dug Out**, which you'll find at the
back entrance, down a short flight of stairs.
Grab a lethal martini and chill out with the
good-looking crowd.

SURRY HILLS

Hollywood Hotel (Map pp94-6; ☎ 9281 2765; 2 Foster
St) This Art Deco pub looks nondescript
from the outside, but the inside reveals
one of Sydney's most appealing Friday
night drinking dens. A mixed (dare we say,
bohemian) crowd crams in and gets down
to the business of starting the weekend
with gusto.

Palace Hotel (Map pp94-6; ☎ 9361 5170; 122
Flinders St) On the junction with South Dowling St, this is a handy, low-key pub good
for socialising. There are pool tables, a nice
Art Deco ambience, good beer, and things
to eat should you feel peckish.

Cricketers Arms (Map pp94-6; ☎ 9331 3301; 106
Fitzroy St) A cruisy, cosy vibe fills this Art
Nouveau pub with arty locals and those
appreciative of good DJ skills displayed
from Thursday to Sunday. There are open
fireplaces, too.

PADDINGTON

Paddington Inn Hotel (Map pp90-1; ☎ 9380 5277;
338 Oxford St) This sociable pub is very popular
on weekend nights and during the day on
Saturday, but it's pretty large and there's
room for everyone if you practice your
elbow work. The exterior makes good use
of peeling paint – the interior is surprisingly swanky.

Lord Dudley Hotel (Map pp90-1; ☎ 9327 5399; 236 Jersey Rd, Woollahra) The Lord Dudley is as close as Sydney really gets to an English pub atmosphere, with dark walls and wood and good beer in pint glasses. It's the sort of place that gets packed with Rugby Union types and their shoulders.

BALMAIN & GLEBE
London Hotel (Map pp90-1; ☎ 9555 1377, fax 9810 4188; 234 Darling St, Balmain) This is a good place for a cleansing ale, especially after a trawl through the nearby Saturday market at St Andrew's.

Riverview Hotel (☎ 9555 8337; 29 Birchgrove Rd, Balmain) This avowedly local pub was once owned by Australian swimming legend Dawn Fraser (a Balmain icon if ever there was one). It's quiet, low-key and a bit of a treasure.

At the unique bric-a-brac-filled **Friend in Hand Hotel** (☎ 9660 2326; 58 Cowper St, Glebe), you can enjoy trivia nights on Tuesday, crab racing on Wednesday, or just beer any day.

BONDI
Bondi Icebergs (Map p102; ☎ 9130 3120; 1 Notts Ave) Getting its name from the members' habit of swimming in winter with blocks of ice in the pool, this is one of Sydney's best-located drinking spots. If you're not into winter swimming, go for a beer in the newly renovated 'Bergs (live bands play frequently during January and February). There's also one of Sydney's most 'it' restaurants on the premises (p125).

Beach Road Hotel (☎ 9130 7247; 71 Beach Rd, Nth Bondi) Weekends here resemble a boisterous multilevel alcoholiday, with Bondi types (think bronzed, buff and brooding) and jolly out-of-towners playing pool, drinking beer and dancing to the regular bands and DJs.

WATSON'S BAY
Watson's Bay Hotel (Map pp90-1; ☎ 9337 4299; 10 Marine Pde) Surrounded by overpriced seafood restaurants (both called Doyles) and home to a lovely boutique pubstay (called Doyles), you'll be pleased to know that you can have the Doyles experience simply by buying a jug of beer, sitting down in the beer garden and enjoying the superlative view of Sydney Harbour. A time-honoured tradition, but avoid weekends, when it's packed to the gills.

ENTERTAINMENT
The *Sydney Morning Herald* 'Metro' liftout is published on Friday and lists events in town for the coming week. Free newspapers, such as *Drum Media*, *Revolver* and *3D World* also have useful listings and are available from bookshops, bars, cafés and record stores.

Ticketek (Map p94-6; ☎ 9266 4800; www .ticketek.com.au; 195 Elizabeth St; ✆ 9am-7pm Mon-Fri, 9am-4pm Sat) is the city's main booking agency for theatre, concerts, sports and other events. Phone bookings can be made and it also has agencies around town.

Halftix (Map pp94-6; ☎ 9279 0855; www .halftix.com.au; 91 York St, City; ✆ daily except Sun) also has a booth at the upper end of Martin Place and sells half-price seats for shows. Tickets are only available for shows that night, and they can't tell you where you'll be sitting.

Cinemas
Generally, cinema tickets cost between $12 and $15 for adults. Populist theatre chains such as Hoyts, Village and Greater Union also have numerous suburban theatres. Movie listings can be found in Sydney's daily newspapers.

George Street Cinemas (Map pp94-6; ☎ 9273 7431; 505 George St, City) This monster-sized movie palace combines the Hoyts, Village and Greater Union chains in an orgy of popcorn-fuelled mainstream entertainment. They've got more screens than you've had hot dinners.

Dendy (Map pp94-6; ☎ 9252 8879; Shop 9, 2 Circular Quay East) Right near the Opera House, this is a lavish new cinema with a great bar. The **original branch** (☎ 9233 8166; 19 Martin Pl, City) also has a good bar and well-chosen first-run art-house movies.

Chauvel Cinema (Map pp90-1; ☎ 9361 5398; cnr Oxford St & Oatley Rd, Paddington) This cinema, with its association with the Australian Film Institute (AFI), plays quality releases new and old (with a liberal dose of the quirky and out-there), and also has themed festivals (Jewish, Queer etc).

Verona Cinema (Map pp94-6; ☎ 9360 6099; Level 1, 17 Oxford St, Paddington) This cinema also has a café and bar, so you can discuss the good (invariably nonmainstream) flick you've just seen. Just down the street is **Academy Twin Cinema** (Map pp94-6; ☎ 9361 4453; 3a Oxford St, Paddington), a smaller cinema that was fitted out in the 1970s, with art-house and independent offerings.

IMAX (Map pp94-6; ☎ 9281 3300; Southern Promenade, Cockle Bay; adult/child $17/12) This is the world's biggest movie screen. If you're into being wowed by massive images, some in 3D, then the IMAX is for you. Movies shown tend to be either thrill-fests or nature docos.

Govinda's (Map p100; ☎ 9380 5155; 112 Darlinghurst Rd; dinner & movie $16; ☻ 6-10.30pm) The Hare-Krishna Govinda's is an all-you-can-gobble vegetarian smorgasbord, which also gives you admission to the cinema upstairs.

Nightclubs

Sydney's dance club scene is alive and kicking, with local and international DJs making thousands of people wave their hands in the air every weekend. Some places have strict door policies and a lot of attitude, others are great places to catch up with all sorts of people.

Home (Map pp94-6; ☎ 9266 0600; Cockle Bay Wharf, 101 Wheat Rd, Darling Harbour; cover charge $25) A monster-sized pleasure dome sprawling over three levels, this club has a sound system that makes other clubs sound like they're plugged in to transistor radios. Even with a capacity of 2000 people, this place gets packed, especially for club night Sublime (Friday). Some gay nights happen here, too.

Slip Inn (Map pp94-6; ☎ 9299 4777; 111 Sussex St, City; cover charge $15-20) Warrenlike and full of different rooms for different moods, this place is full of cool kids and those who love a bit of turntablist-inspired dancing – with funk, techno and housey breaks on the menu.

Yu (Map p100; ☎ 9358 6511; 171 Victoria St, Potts Point; cover charge $10-20) Yu wants you to get down to the best of house and funk, played by some of Sydney's most venerable DJs. We love After Ours, which solves the dilemma of what to do on a Sunday night. The club itself is slick-looking and full of slick-looking clubbers.

Icebox (Map p100; ☎ 9331 0058; 2 Kellett St, Kings Cross; cover charge $5-15) If you're hankering for those 'Summer of Love' sounds of the late '80s and early '90s, Icebox has Stun on Wednesday nights. Progressive and hard house can be heard Thursday to Sunday,

for those who like to party hard until the wee hours.

Q Bar (Map pp94-6; ☎ 9360 1375; Level 2, 44 Oxford St; Fri & Sat cover charge $20) With more reincarnations than Cleopatra over the years, this stayer has DJs playing every night of the week. We like Thursday night's Prom Night, when there's an 'anything goes' musical vibe in the air. On weekends, it might seem that this place should be named Queue Bar.

GoodBar (Map pp94-6; ☎ 9360 6759; 11a Oxford St, Paddington; cover charge $5-10) This hanky-sized club is still attracting gorgeous young fly-girls and B-boys who get past the face control at the door. Its Thursday night groove-fest, Step Forward, is easily its best night, with reggae, funk and hip hop on the musical menu.

Live Music

Sydney doesn't have as dynamic a music scene as Melbourne, but you can still find live music most nights of the week. For detailed listings of venues and acts, see the listings in the papers mentioned in the Entertainment introduction (p129).

CLASSICAL

Sydney Opera House (Map pp94-6; ☎ 9250 7777; www.sydneyoperahouse.com; Bennelong Point, Circular Quay East) This is the ground zero for performance in Australia, and its Concert Hall and Opera Hall (holding 2500 and 1500 people respectively) are a must for anyone wishing to really experience the nun's scrum (an Opera House nickname). Everything is performed here – theatre, comedy, music, dance and opera – but it's this last art form that really should be sampled while you're here. The box office opens from 9am to 8.30pm Monday to Saturday and 2½ hours before a Sunday performance.

City Recital Hall (Map pp94-6; ☎ 8256 2222; www.cityrecitalhall.com; 2 Angel Pl, City) This is a purpose-built 1200-seat venue with wonderful acoustics that hosts live music performances. Its architecture is based on the 19th-century European blueprint, and it's an excellent place to hear the Australian Brandenburg Orchestra, among others.

Eugene Goosens Hall (☎ 9333 1500; 700 Harris St, Ultimo) The ABC's intimate Eugene Goosens Hall often has good classical recitals that are broadcast live. Don't even think about attending one if you've got a cough!

Sydney Conservatorium of Music (Map pp94-6; ☎ 9351 1222; www.usyd.edu.au/su/conmusic; Macquarie St, City) A few years and $145 million later, this historic music venue is back in the business of showcasing the talents of its students and their teachers. Choral, jazz, operatic and chamber recitals are held here from March to July, plus a range of free lunch-time recitals and lectures. Visit the website for more info.

JAZZ & BLUES
Sydney has a healthy and innovative jazz and blues circuit, with quite a few venues worth a swing.

Basement (Map pp94-6; ☎ 9251 2797; 29 Reiby Pl, Circular Quay) This place has decent food, good music (plus the odd spoken word and comedy gig) and some big international names dropping by to spread the jazz and blues gospel.

Empire Hotel (☎ 9557 1701; cnr Parramatta Rd & Johnston St, Annandale) Blues buffs should look no further than the well-run Empire for live acts (aided and abetted by a very good sound system) Tuesday to Sunday nights.

Soup Plus (Map pp94-6; ☎ 9299 7728; 383 George St, City) Soup Plus has live jazz at lunch and dinner time, as well as cheap food and a casual atmosphere. It's the mainstream end of jazz for the most part, so don't expect any radical tonal experimentation.

Strawberry Hills Hotel (Map pp90-1; ☎ 9698 2997; 453 Elizabeth St, Surry Hills) This refurbished pub features live jazz in the forms of the Eclipse Alley Five from 4pm to 7pm on Saturday, and Bill Dudley & the New Orleanians from 5pm to 8pm on Sunday.

Wine Banc (Map pp94-6; ☎ 9233 5399; 53 Martin Pl, City) Hands down, this is the sexiest place to hear live jazz in Sydney. The whole place looks like it was carved out of an architect's bunker dreams, and the table service is flawless. A brilliant wine list only adds to the appeal.

ROCK & POP
There's sometimes no charge to see young local bands, while between $5 and $20 is charged for well-known local acts, and at least $60 for international performers. There are a number of venues worth considering.

Annandale Hotel (☎ 9550 1078; 17 Parramatta Rd, Annandale) Thankfully, this place was rescued from the live-music graveyard a few years

ago, and it's back to doing what it does best – playing host to a sometimes eclectic assortment of local and international alternative music acts.

Cat & Fiddle (☎ 9810 7931; 456 Darling St, Balmain) In an heroic move, the Cat & Fiddle ripped out its pokies and brought back nightly live music. There's even a small theatre on the premises (about 30 seats).

Enmore Theatre (☎ 9550 3666; 130 Enmore Rd, Newtown) The Enmore hosts major Australian and overseas acts. The Rolling Stones played a brilliant 'intimate' concert here in early 2003.

Hordern Pavilion (Map pp90-1; ☎ 9383 4000; Driver Ave, Moore Park) Not in use as much as it once was, but the Hordern often hosts international acts, such as Moby.

Metro Theatre (Map pp94-6; ☎ 9287 2000; 624 George St, City) This is easily the best place to see well-chosen local and alternative international acts (plus the odd DJ) in well-ventilated comfort.

Selina's (☎ 9665 0000; Coogee Bay Hotel, cnr Coogee Bay Rd & Arden St, Coogee) Selina's, a veritable 'rawk' institution, often has top Australian and international rock bands, resulting in much sticky carpet and tinnitus.

Hopetoun Hotel (Map pp94-6; ☎ 9361 5257; 416 Bourke St, Surry Hills) This great little venue offers flexibility for artists and patrons alike and features an array of modern musical styles – from folk to rap to DJs and local bands getting their first taste of life on the road.

Sandringham Hotel (☎ 9557 1254; 387 King St, Newtown) We were nervous that renovations at the Sando would mean the end of live music here, but thankfully, you can still pay a minimal amount of money (say, $5) and get your earwax blasted out from Thursday to Sunday. Quieter acts will merely coax it out.

Sydney Entertainment Centre (Map pp94-6; ☎ 9266 4800; Harbour St, Haymarket) This big concrete box is for the Elton Johns and Kylie Minogues of this world. It seats just over 12,000, and despite being purpose-built for these bigger gigs, the sound quality is only adequate at best.

Sport
Spend a day or two in Sydney and you'll notice a little something about its inhabitants. They're shiny, they're hard, they're psyched – and they get (and stay) this way

NEW SOUTH WALES

RUGBY LEAGUE

Sydney is one of rugby league's world capitals, and catching a game while you're in town is an important part of understanding Sydney's tribal mind. With its origins in working-class culture, in recent times rugby league has been something of a pitched battle between dyed-in-the-wool supporters and business interests from the big end of town who want to meddle with the game in the hope of making big bucks. Humph! The decision to axe one of Sydney's oldest clubs, the South Sydney Rabbitohs, saw thousands of green-and-red bedecked protesters take to Sydney's streets. Needless to say, local (and vocal) passion won the day. Other Sydney-based teams include the Sydney Roosters, the Parramatta Eels, the Penrith Panthers, Wests Tigers and the St George Illawarra Dragons.

National Rugby League (NRL; www.nrl.com.au) games are played from March to October at a variety of venues, including Aussie Stadium in Moore Park and Telstra Stadium in Homebush Bay, culminating in the Grand Final. If you can't decide on a team to follow, but want to see a real grudge match, the State of Origin series features plenty of beef and biff. Three matches a year are held between New South Wales (the Blues) and Queensland (the Maroons), with at least one match played in Sydney. Tickets to this are scarce, but TV coverage is plentiful.

through exercise. Sydney's sunshine, parks, beaches and love of showing off all conspire to make this a delightful city for staying fit or watching sport. If you like to watch, have a credit card handy and book tickets to a variety of sporting events, big and small. If you're the one being sporty, it can be as simple as putting your feet in some jogging shoes or putting in some laps at a beachside pool, or as tricky as getting a golf game on a sunny weekend.

The **Sydney Cricket Ground** (SCG), Moore Park, is the venue for sparsely attended state cricket matches, well-attended five-day Test matches and sell-out one-day World Series cricket matches. Moore Park also has a **golf course.**

The (sometimes) high-flying Sydney Swans, NSW's contribution to the **Australian Football League** (AFL) play matches between March and September. Their home ground is the SCG (for more information on AFL, see the boxed text 'Winners, Losers & the Rules of the Game'; p480).

Sydney's oldest and largest 18-footer yacht club is the **Sydney Flying Squadron** (Map pp90-1; ☎ 9955 8350; 76 McDougall St, Milsons Point). You can catch a ferry from there to watch skiff racing from 2pm to 4pm on Saturdays between October and April (adult/child $14/10).

Theatre & Comedy

Wharf Theatre (Map pp94-6; ☎ 9250 1700; Pier 4, Hickson Rd, Walsh Bay) The Sydney Theatre Company (STC), the city's top theatre company,

has its own venue here. It's also the home of the Australian Theatre for Young People (ATYP), Bangarra Dance Theatre, Sydney Philharmonia Choirs and the Sydney Dance Company. A restaurant on the premises (called The Wharf) delivers much better than average pre- and post-show fare.

Capitol Theatre (Map pp94-6; ☎ 9320 5000; 17 Campbell St, Haymarket) Lavishly restored after being saved from demolition, this big theatre is home to big-name concerts and long-running musicals.

Lyric Theatre (Map pp90-1; ☎ 9657 9657; Star City, Darling Harbour) The large Lyric Theatre stages flashy musical extravaganzas and has good acoustics. We suspect the theatre owes its existence as a placatory gesture to those who didn't want a mother-lovin' big casino in town.

Belvoir St Theatre (Map pp90-1; ☎ 9699 3444; 25 Belvoir St, Surry Hills) Something of a home for original and often experimental Australian theatre, its excellent resident production company is known as Company B, which gets actors like Geoffrey Rush to say 'no' to Hollywood in return for a meaty stage role.

Sydney Comedy Store (Map pp90-1; ☎ 9357 1419; www.comedystore.com.au; Fox Studios, Moore Park; tickets $15-27.50) In its purpose-built home in the Fox Studios, this comedy venue has improv, stand-up and open-mike nights.

SHOPPING

The hub of city shopping is **Pitt St Mall**, with department stores, shopping centres and numerous shops all within arm's reach.

It's much more relaxing to shop for fashion on popular inner-city strips such as Oxford St, Paddington; for furnishings and antiques on Queen St, Woollahra; for music and DJing needs around Crown St, Surry Hills; for outdoor gear around the corner of Kent and Bathurst Sts in town; or at Sydney's popular markets. The Rocks is where you'll generally find what's known as 'Australiana' (ie souvenirs).

Late-night shopping is on Thursday night, when most stores stay open until 9pm.

Aboriginal Art

Aboriginal & Tribal Art Centre (Map pp94–6; ☎ 9247 9625; 117 George St, The Rocks) Opposite the MCA, this gallery has a broad art and artefact range for sale, plus exhibitions. Overseas packing and shipping can also be arranged, with UPS.

Gavala Aboriginal Art (Map pp90–1; ☎ 9212 7232; Harbourside Shopping Centre, Darling Harbour) Proudly proclaiming itself as Sydney's only Aboriginal-owned retail centre and gallery, this is a great place to source everything from a T-shirt to a bark painting, or an Aboriginal flag. Check out the giant boomerang hanging from the ceiling.

Aboriginal Shop (☎ 9247 4344; Sydney Opera House) Shoppers make some truly tragic efforts on the didgeridoo here – but the sales assistant doesn't wince. She deserves a medal for patience. Tea towels, didges, paintings and whatever else takes your fancy can be shipped worldwide.

Walkabout Gallery (☎ 9550 9964; 70 Norton St, Leichhardt) This friendly gallery is part of the World Vision Indigenous Programs, which means you can be sure that Aboriginal artists are getting properly paid, and that the Aboriginal community Australia-wide is benefiting from the sales here.

Australiana

RM Williams (Map pp94–6; ☎ 9262 2228; 389 George St, City) This is a long-established manufacturer and distributor of Aussie outdoor gear, such as Driza-Bones (oilskin riding coats), the classic elastic-sided riding boot beloved by almost every Aussie and moleskin trousers.

Australian Wine Centre (Map pp94–6; ☎ 9247 2755; Goldfields House, 1 Alfred St, Circular Quay) Downstairs in this building, behind Circular Quay, this centre has wines from every Australian wine-growing region. It will package and send wine overseas, and of course you're welcome to sample a few drops.

Strand Hatters (☎ 9231 6884; Shop 8, Strand Arcade, Pitt St Mall) Wearing a hat to protect oneself from the sun is a good idea in this country – wearing an authentic rabbit-felt Akubra from this place will ensure you'll never look anything but local – maybe.

Gowings (Map pp94–6; ☎ 9264 6321; cnr George & Market Sts, City) 'Walk Through, No-one Asked to Buy' proclaims the sign. Five floors of staples for every type of Australian (though it mostly deals in men's gear). Get your thongs (that's flip-flops for you Americans), your flannelette shirt and a damn cheap haircut to boot.

Flame Opals (Map pp94–6; ☎ 9247 3446; 119 George St, The Rocks) If you've been seduced by the colourful opal, this is a good place to pick one up. Prices range from about $20 to 'if you have to ask, you can't afford it', and the staff are more than happy to help with any questions. It's also tax-free for overseas customers.

Clothing

Scanlan & Theodore (Map pp90–1; ☎ 9361 6722; 433 Oxford St, Paddington) Regularly topping the lists of the favourite designers of with-it gals, Scanlan & Theodore excel in beautifully made pieces for the evening or for the office, with fabrics you just can't help but fondle.

Calibre (Map pp90–1; ☎ 9380 5993; 416 Oxford St, Paddington) Smart suiting and hip weekend wardrobe supplies for men are the speciality here. Even if you're a complete fashion misfit, the staff here will sort you out, with tact and diplomacy.

Zimmerman Swim (Map pp90–1; ☎ 9360 5769; 24 Oxford St, Woollahra) Half the boobs and bums on Bondi are covered by this wonderful swimwear label, because the Zimmerman sisters understand that Sydneysiders spend a lot of time in their cossies, while still wanting to look sexy.

Country Road (Map pp94–6; ☎ 9394 1823; 142 Pitt St, City) At the more conservative end of Australian fashion, but plenty popular for their comfy jumpers, pants, dresses and suits. It seems that almost everyone (male *and* female) has had a Country Road–something in the wardrobe at some point.

NEW SOUTH WALES

Markets

Paddington Bazaar (Map pp90-1; ☎ 9331 2646; St John's Church, 395 Oxford St, Paddington; ☼ Sat) One of Sydney's most popular markets, it offers everything from vintage clothing and funky designer fashions, to jewellery, food, massage and holistic treatments. More unusual wares include temporary henna tattoos, butterflies under glass, and hammocks. Don't even think about finding a place to park – this is one for public transport.

Paddy's Markets (Map pp94-6; ☎ 1300 361 589; cnr Hay & Thomas Sts, Haymarket; ☼ Sat & Sun) There are two Paddy's Markets. The one on the corner of Hay and Thomas Sts in Haymarket, in the heart of Chinatown, is a Sydney institution where you'll find the usual market fare at rock-bottom prices alongside less predictable wares such as wigs, board games, cheap cosmetics, mobile phones and live budgies. There's also a good selection of fresh fruit, vegetables and seafood. Paddy's Market in Flemington, on Parramatta Rd near Sydney Olympic Park, operates (along with a huge fruit and vegetable market) on Friday and Sunday.

Rocks Market (☎ 9255 1717; George St, The Rocks; ☼ Sat & Sun) Held at the top end of George St, under the bridge, this market is closed to traffic. It's a little on the touristy 'Australiana' side, but is still good for a browse – wares include jewellery, antiques, souvenirs, fossils, gems, crystals, retro postcards, musical instruments and a good selection of juggling paraphernalia.

Balmain Markets (Map pp90-1; ☎ 0418-765 736; St Andrew's Church, 223 Darling St, Balmain; ☼ Sat) This is a really good local market, with lots of crafty stuff like handmade candles, kids' clothing and essential oils. It's also a great spot to hunt down fashion accessories and tasty snacks in the church hall itself.

Glebe Markets (Map pp90-1; ☎ 4237 7499; Glebe Public School, cnr Glebe Point Rd & Derby Pl; ☼ Sat) This market has an assortment of books, clothing, ceramics, glassware, leather goods, herbal teas, oddities and curios. The crowds can be pretty heavy.

Bondi Beach Markets (Map p102; ☎ 9315 8988; Bondi Beach Public School, cnr Campbell Pde & Warners Ave; ☼ Sun) At the northern end of Campbell Pde, this market is good for hip clothing, swimwear, jewellery, furniture, knick-knacks and beautiful-people watching.

Shopping Centres & Department Stores

Queen Victoria Building (QVB; Map pp94-6; ☎ 9264 1955; 455 George St, City) The magnificent QVB takes up a whole block with its late 19th-century Romanesque grandeur, and has almost 200 shops on four levels. It's the city's most beautiful shopping centre, bar none. You'll find plenty of nice fashion outlets, and plenty of places to buy gifts for those not familiar with Australian knick-knacks. The lower level, which connects to Town Hall Station, also has food bars, shoe repair shops, dry-cleaners and newsagents to service the rushing commuters.

Skygarden Arcade (Map pp94-6; ☎ 9231 1811; 77 Castlereagh St, City) This large, modern complex has a range of fashion shops and some food outlets, plus a monster-sized branch of Borders for books and music.

Strand Arcade (Map pp94-6; ☎ 9232 4199; Pitt St Mall, City) Several leading Australian fashion designers and craftspeople have shops at the thoughtfully restored Strand Arcade, between Pitt St Mall and George St. Designer boutiques nestle amid old-fashioned coffee shops, artisans and hairdressing salons.

Market City (Map pp94-6; ☎ 9212 1388; Quay St, Haymarket) This mammoth shopping centre houses Paddy's Markets, a slew of restaurants, cinemas and heaps of retail outlets (mostly the end-of-season variety).

Centrepoint (Map pp94-6; ☎ 9231 1000; cnr Pitt & Market Sts, City) This shopping centre, situated beside the Imperial Arcade and beneath Sydney Tower, has four storeys of fashion and jewellery shops. You can cut through Pitt St to Castlereagh St through here, and there are also connecting above-ground walkways with David Jones and Grace Bros.

David Jones (Map pp94-6; ☎ 9266 5544; cnr Elizabeth & Market Sts, City) Considered the city's premier department store, with two locations on Market St, it's a good place to look for top-quality goods. The interior itself, which harkens back to Sydney's golden age of city shopping, is worth a visit even if you don't want to buy anything.

Grace Bros (Map pp94-6; ☎ 9238 9111, 436 George St) The seven-level Grace Bros is one of Sydney's largest stores; it's had extensive refurbishments in the last few years. You'll find everything from cafés to cosmetics and everything in between.

GETTING THERE & AWAY

Sydney's Kingsford Smith Airport is Australia's busiest, so don't be surprised if there are delays. It's only 10km south of the city centre making access easy, but this also means that flights cease between 11pm and 5am due to noise regulations.

You can fly into Sydney from all the usual international points and from all over Australia. Both **Qantas** (☎ 13 13 13) and **Virgin** (☎ 13 67 89) have frequent flights to other capital cities – for standard one-way fares see the Australian Air Fares map (p986). Smaller airlines, linked to Qantas, fly within NSW.

The private bus operators are competitive and service is efficient. Make sure you shop around for discounts if you hold a VIP or YHA card. Always compare private operator prices to the government's **CountryLink** (Map pp94-6; ☎ 13 22 32; www.countrylink.info) network of trains and buses, which has discounts of up to 40% on economy fares. The state's rail network is an extensive one, with train travel comfortable for the most part.

The government's CountryLink rail network is complemented by coaches. Major operators include **McCafferty's/Greyhound** (☎ 9212 3433; www.mccaffertys.com.au) and **Murrays** (☎ 13 22 51). All interstate and principal regional train and bus services operate to and from Central Station. Tickets for these services must be booked in advance.

The **Sydney coach terminal** (☎ 9281 9366; cnr Eddy Ave & Pitt St, City) deals with all the companies and can advise you on the best prices. It's on the corner of Pitt St and Eddy Ave, outside Central Station. Coach operators have offices either in the terminal or nearby. Most buses stop in the suburbs on the way in and out of cities.

There is now a new ferry service operating between Sydney and Devonport (Tasmania). **TT Lines** (☎ 13 20 10; www.spiritof tasmania.com.au) runs the *Spirit of Tasmania III* (from $230 per person, 20½ hours) departing from Sydney 3pm Tuesday, Friday and Sunday, arriving around 11.30am the next day.

GETTING AROUND

For information on buses, ferries and trains, phone ☎ 13 15 00 between 6am and 10pm daily.

To/From the Airport

Sydney airport is 10km south of the city centre. The international and domestic terminals are a 4km bus trip apart on either side of the runway.

Airport Link (☎ 13 15 00; www.airportlink.com.au) is a train line that runs from city train stations to the airport terminals (domestic and international) and vice versa. Trains run from approximately 5am to 12.45am daily. A one-way fare from Central Station costs adult/child $10/7.

Airport Express (☎ 13 15 00; www.sta.nsw.gov.au) is a State Transit Authority (STA) yellow-and-green bus (No 300) that travels between the city, Kings Cross and the airport, with its own bus stops. The one-way fare is adult/child/family $7/3.50/17.50. The trip from the airport to Circular Quay takes about 35 minutes. The service runs about every 10 to 20 minutes from 6.30am to around 7.30pm Monday to Friday.

A taxi from the airport to Circular Quay should cost between $20 and $30.

Bus

Sydney's bus network extends to most suburbs. Fares depend upon the number of 'sections' you pass through. As a rough guide, short jaunts cost $1.50, and most other fares in the inner suburbs are $2.60. Regular buses run between 5am and midnight, when Nightrider buses take over.

The major starting points for bus routes are Circular Quay, Argyle St in Millers Point, Wynyard Park and the Queen Victoria Building on York St, and Railway Square. Most buses head out of the city on George or Castlereagh Sts, and take George or Elizabeth Sts coming in. Pay the driver as you enter, or dunk your prepaid ticket in the green ticket machines by the door.

The bus information kiosk on the corner of Alfred and Pitt Sts at Circular Quay is open daily. There are other information offices on Carrington St and in the Queen Victoria Building on York St.

Car & Motorcycle
BUYING/SELLING A CAR

Sydney is the capital of car sales for most travellers. Parramatta Rd is lined with used-car lots. The **Kings Cross Car Market** (Map p100; ☎ 1800 808 188; www.carmarket.com.au; cnr Ward Ave & Elizabeth Bay Rd, Kings Cross) gets mixed reports, but it seems popular with travellers. Always read the fine print on anything you sign with regards to buying or selling a car. Several dealers will sell you a car with an undertaking to buy it back at an agreed price – do not accept any verbal guarantees – get it in writing. The *Trading Post*, a weekly rag available from all newsagents, is also a good place to look for second-hand vehicles.

Before you buy any vehicle, regardless of the seller, we strongly recommend that you have it thoroughly checked by a competent mechanic. The **NRMA** (Map pp94-6; ☎ 13 21 32; www.nrma.com.au; 74 King St, City; ☺ 9am-5pm Mon-Fri) can organise this. We've heard some real horror stories from readers who've failed to get their vehicles checked.

The **Register of Encumbered Vehicles** (REVS; ☎ 9633 6333) is a government organisation that can check to ensure the car you're buying is fully paid-up and owned by the seller.

RENTAL

Avis (☎ 13 63 33), **Budget** (☎ 13 27 27), **Delta Europcar** (☎ 1300 131 390), **Hertz** (☎ 13 30 90) and **Thrifty** (☎ 1300 367 227) all have desks at the airport. Their rates sometimes include insurance and unlimited kilometres. Some require you to be over 25 years old. Avis and Hertz also provide hand-controlled cars for disabled travellers. The Yellow Pages lists many other car-hire companies, some specialising in renting near-wrecks at rock-bottom prices – always read the fine print on your rental agreement carefully if you decide on this option.

Bikescape (Map p100; ☎ 9356 2453; www.bike scape.com.au; 191 William St, East Sydney; per day from $95) is a thoroughly trustworthy source of motorcycles for hire – think well-serviced, low mileage and well-informed staff, who can also organise excellent tours.

TOLL ROADS

The **Harbour Tunnel** shoulders some of the Harbour Bridge's workload. It begins about half-a-kilometre south of the Opera House, crosses under the harbour just to the east of the bridge, and rejoins the highway on the northern side. There's a southbound (only) toll of $3 for both. If you're heading from the North Shore to the eastern suburbs, it's much easier to use the tunnel. The Eastern Distributor imposes a northbound toll (from $3.50 to $7.50).

Fare Deals

The SydneyPass offers three, five or seven days unlimited travel over a seven-day period on all STA buses and ferries as well as the red TravelPass zone (inner suburbs) of the rail network. The passes cover the Airport Express, the Explorers, the JetCats, RiverCats and three STA-operated harbour cruises. They cost adult/child/family $90/45/225 (three days), $120/60/300 (five days) and $140/70/350 (seven days). Passes are available from STA offices, train stations, and from Airport Express and Explorer bus drivers.

TravelPasses are designed for commuters and offer cheap weekly travel. There are various colour-coded grades offering combinations of distance and service. A Red TravelPass (Rail, Bus & Ferry) costs $30. TravelPasses are sold at train stations, STA offices and major newsagents.

If you're just catching buses, get a Travel-Ten ticket, which gives a big discount on 10 bus trips. There are various colour codes for distances so check which is the most appropriate for you. A red TravelTen (available from newsagents and STA offices) costs $23.50 and can be used to reach most places mentioned in the Sydney section.

Ferry Ten tickets are similar and cost from $26.50 for 10 inner-harbour (ie short) ferry trips, or $39.30 including the Manly ferry. They can be purchased at the Circular Quay ferry ticket office.

Several transport-plus-entry tickets are available, which work out cheaper than catching a ferry and paying entry separately. They include the ZooPass and the AquariumPass.

Ferry

Sydney's ferries provide the most enjoyable way to get around. Many people use ferries to commute so there are frequent connecting bus services. Some ferries operate between 6am and midnight, although ferries servicing tourist attractions operate much shorter hours. Popular places accessible by ferry include Darling Harbour, Balmain, Hunters Hill and Parramatta to the west; McMahons Point, Kirribilli, Neutral Bay, Cremorne, Mosman, Taronga Zoo and Manly on the North Shore; and Double Bay, Rose Bay and Watsons Bay in the eastern suburbs.

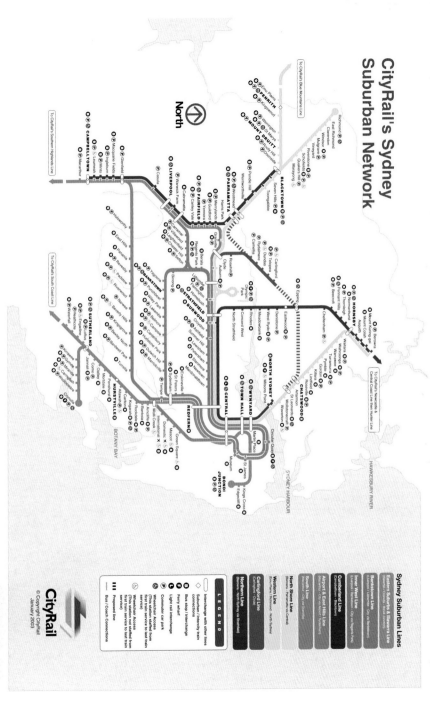

CityRail's Sydney Suburban Network

SYDNEY TRAIN NETWORK

Sydney Suburban Lines

- Eastern Suburbs & Illawarra Line
- Bankstown Line
- Inner West Line
- Airport & East Hills Line
- South Line
- North Shore Line
- Western Line
- Carlingford Line
- Northern Line

LEGEND

- Interchange with other lines
- Suburban / Intercity train connections
- Bus stop / Interchange
- Ferry wharf
- Light rail interchange
- Commuter car park
- Wheelchair Access
- Wheelchair Access (This station not staffed from first train service to last train service)
- Proposed line
- Bus / Coach Connections

CityRail
© Copyright CityRail
January 2003

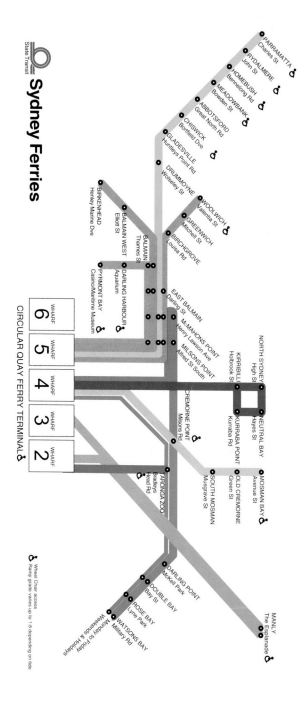

Sydney Ferries

State Transit

CIRCULAR QUAY FERRY TERMINALS &

| WHARF 6 | WHARF 5 | WHARF 4 | WHARF 3 | WHARF 2 |

& Wheel Chair access
& Ramp grade varies up to 1:8 depending on tide

PARRAMATTA
Charles St
RYDALMERE
John St
HOMEBUSH
Bennelong Rd
MEADOWBANK
Bowden St
ABBOTSFORD
Great North Rd
CHISWICK
Bortfield Dve
GLADESVILLE
Huntleys Point Rd
DRUMMOYNE
Wolseley St
WOOLWICH
Valentia St
GREENWICH
Mitchell St
BIRCHGROVE
Louisa Rd

BIRKENHEAD
Henley Marine Dve
BALMAIN WEST
Elliott St
BALMAIN
Thames St
PYRMONT BAY
Casino/Maritime Museum
DARLING HARBOUR
Aquarium
EAST BALMAIN
Darling St
McMAHONS POINT
Henry Lawson Ave
MILSONS POINT
Alfred St South

NORTH SYDNEY
High St
KIRRIBILLI
Holbrook St
KURRABA POINT
Kurraba Rd
NEUTRAL BAY
Hayes St
OLD CREMORNE
Green St
SOUTH MOSMAN
Musgrave St
MOSMAN BAY
Avenue St &

CREMORNE POINT
Milsons Rd

TARONGA ZOO
Bradleys
Head Rd

DARLING POINT
McKell Park
DOUBLE BAY
Bay St
ROSE BAY
Lyne Park
WATSONS BAY
Military Rd
Monday to Friday
Weekends & Holidays

MANLY
The Esplanade &

There are three kinds of ferry: regular STA ferries, fast JetCats that go to Manly ($6.30, no concession fares) and River-Cats that traverse the Parramatta River to Parramatta ($6.10/3 per adult/child). All ferries depart from Circular Quay. At Wharf 4 you'll find the **ferry information office** (☎ 9207 3170; ⏱ 7am-5.45pm Mon-Sat, 8am-5.45pm Sun) next to the ticket booths. Most regular harbour ferries cost $4.30, although the longer trip to Manly costs $5.40.

On weekdays at lunchtime, you can catch Doyle's own water taxi to Watsons Bay from the Harbourmaster's Steps on the western side of Circular Quay. The taxi costs $10 per person return, and services run daily between 11.15am and 3.45pm.

Metro Light Rail & Monorail

The **Monorail** and **Metro Light Rail** (MLR; ☎ 8584 5288, www.metrolightrail.com.au) are of limited use for Sydney residents but are a little more useful for tourists. The MLR operates 24 hours a day between Central Station and Pyrmont via Darling Harbour and China-town. The service runs to Lilyfield via the Fish Market, Wentworth Park, Glebe, Jubilee Park and Rozelle Bay from 6am to 11pm Sunday to Thursday (to midnight Friday and Saturday). Tickets cost $2.60 to $4.90 per adult, $1.40 to $3.60 per concession fare and adult/concession/family $8/6/20 for a day pass. Tickets can be purchased on board.

The Monorail circles Darling Harbour and links it to the city centre. There's a monorail every three to five minutes, and the full loop takes about 14 minutes. A single trip costs adult/concession $4/2.20, but with the day pass ($8) or family pass ($20) you can ride as often as you like for a full day. The monorail operates from 7am to 10pm Monday to Thursday, to midnight on Friday and Saturday and from 8am to 10pm Sunday.

Taxi

There are heaps of taxis in Sydney. Flag fall is $2.55, and the metered fair is $1.45 per kilometre or 62.2c per minute waiting time. There are extra charges for fares between 10pm and 6am, for heavy luggage (optional), Harbour Bridge and Tunnel tolls, and a radio booking fee. The four big taxi companies offer a reliable service:

Legion (☎ 13 14 51)
Premier Cabs (☎ 13 10 17)
RSL Cabs (☎ 13 22 11)
Taxis Combined (☎ 8332 8888)

Train

Sydney has a vast suburban rail network and frequent services, making trains much quicker than buses. The underground City Circle comprises seven city-centre stations. Lines radiate from the City Circle, but do not extend to the northern and southern beaches, Balmain or Glebe. All suburban trains stop at Central Station, and usually one or more of the other City Circle stations as well (a ticket to the city will take you to any station on the City Circle). Trains run from around 5am to midnight.

After 9am on weekdays and at any time on weekends, you can buy an off-peak return ticket for not much more than a standard one-way fare.

Staffed ticket booths are supplemented by automatic ticket machines at stations. If you have to change trains, it's cheaper to buy a ticket to your ultimate destination – but don't depart from an intermediary station en route to your destination or your ticket will be invalid.

For train information, ask at any station or drop by the rail information booth near the ferry ticket office at Circular Quay.

AROUND SYDNEY

There are superb national parks to the north and south of Sydney, and historic small towns to the west, established in the early days of European settlement and surviving today as pockets engulfed by urban sprawl.

BOTANY BAY

It's a common misconception that Sydney is built around Botany Bay. Sydney Harbour is actually Port Jackson and Botany Bay is 10km to 15km south on the city's fringe. This area is a major industrial centre so don't expect too many unspoilt vistas. Despite this, the bay has pretty stretches and holds a special place in Australian history. This was Captain Cook's first landing point in Australia, and it was named by Joseph Banks, the expedition's naturalist, for the many botanical specimens he found here.

AROUND SYDNEY

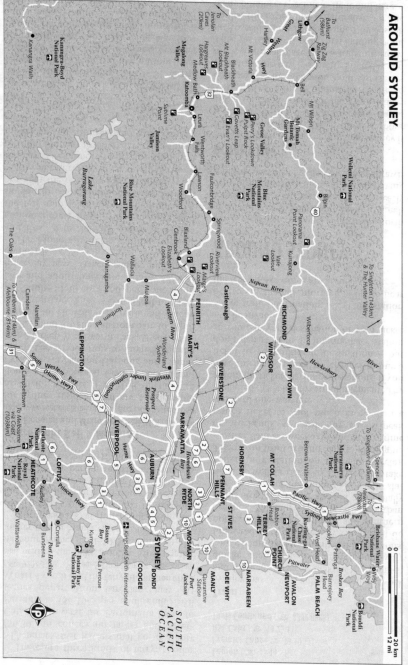

0   20 km
0   12 mi

SOUTH PACIFIC OCEAN

The **Botany Bay National Park** (www.nationalpar ks.nsw.gov.au) encompasses both headlands of the bay. At Kurnell, on the southern headland, monuments mark Cook's landing place. The 436-hectare park has bushland and coastal walking tracks, picnic areas and an 8km cycle track. The park's **Discovery Centre** (☎ 02-9668 9111; ☽ 10am-3pm) describes the impact of European arrival, and has information on the surrounding wetlands. The park is open from 7am to 7.30pm daily. Entry costs $6 per car but pedestrians are not charged and, since the monuments and most walking tracks are close to the entrance, you may as well park outside. From Cronulla train station (10km away), catch **Kurnell Bus Company's** (☎ 02-9523 4047) No 987 bus ($5.50 return).

La Perouse, on the northern headland, is named after the French explorer who arrived in 1788, just six days after the arrival of the First Fleet. Although the First Fleet soon sailed to Sydney Harbour, La Perouse camped at Botany Bay for six weeks before sailing off into the Pacific and disappearing. The fabulous **Laperouse Museum & Visitors Centre** (☎ 02-9311 3379; adult/child/family $5.50/ 3.50/13.20; ☽ 10am-4pm Wed-Sun), in the old (1882) cable station, charts the history of La Perouse's fateful expedition; there's also an excellent Aboriginal gallery with exhibits on local indigenous history.

Just offshore is **Bare Island** (☎ 02-9247 5033; adult/concession/family $7.70/5.50/22), a decaying concrete fort built in 1885 to discourage a feared Russian invasion. Entry is by guided tour only, on the hour between 12.30pm and 3.30pm on Saturday and Sunday.

There's no entry fee to this northern segment of the national park. Catch bus No 394 from Circular Quay or No 393 from Railway Sq.

ROYAL NATIONAL PARK

This coastal park of dramatic cliffs, secluded beaches, scrub and lush rainforest is the oldest gazetted national park in the world. It begins at Port Hacking, just 30km south of Sydney, and stretches 20km further south. A road runs through the park with detours to the small township of Bundeena on Port Hacking, to the beautiful beach at Wattamolla, and to windswept Garie Beach. The spectacular two-day, 26km coastal walking trail running the

length of the park is highly recommended. Garie, Era and Burning Palms are popular surfing spots; swimming can be delightful at Wattamolla. A walking and cycling trail follows the Port Hacking River south from Audley, and other walking tracks pass tranquil freshwater swimming holes. You can swim in Kangaroo Creek but not the Port Hacking River. To do the coastal walks you'll need a permit, but they're granted for free when you phone the visitors centre.

There's a friendly **visitors centre** (☎ 02-9542 0648; ☽ 8.30am-4.30pm) at the top of the hill at the park's main entrance, off the Princes Hwy near Audley. Staff can help you with camping permits, maps and bushwalking details.

You can hire exercise accoutrements at the **Audley Boat Shed** (☎ 02-9545 4967; Farnell Rd), where rowboats, canoes and kayaks cost $16/30 per hour/day, aqua bikes $12 per 30 minutes, and bicycles $14/30 per hour/day.

Entry to the park costs $10 per car, but is free for pedestrians and cyclists. The road through the park and the offshoot to Bundeena are always open, but the detours to the beaches are closed at sunset.

The **Bundeena-Maianbar Heritage Walk** was still awaiting completion when we visited, but stage one should be ready by the time you read this. The walk promises good coastal views and some Aboriginal sites of interest.

Sleeping

Cronulla Beachouse YHA (☎ 02-9527 7772; enquir ies@cronullabeachyha.com; Level 1, 40 Kingsway, Cronulla; s $25-27, d & tw $60-66; **P**) This is one of the friendliest hostels we've ever visited, run by two gregarious brothers who know 'the Shire' inside out. Facilities are comfy and well maintained, with a cheery vibe from staff and travellers alike. You can also get the key for the Garie Beach YHA (see below), and it's a great place to join others doing the 26km coastal walk or get your surfing skills up. Catch the train to Cronulla Station, and keep walking left until you reach Kingsway. Wheelchair accessible.

Garie Beach YHA (☎ 02-9261 1111; Garie Beach, Royal National Park; dm $10) This small (12-bed), basic (no electricity or phone, bring food) and secluded hostel is close to one of the best surf beaches in NSW. You need to book, collect a key and get detailed directions from the **YHA Membership & Travel Centre** (Map pp94-6; ☎ 02-9261 1111; 422 Kent St, City) or from Cronulla's YHA. The nearest food store is 10km away.

Beachhaven Bed & Breakfast (☎ 02-9544 1333; www.beachhavenbnb.com.au; 13 Bundeena Dr, Bundeena; d from $175) Offering a choice of 'Tudor Suite' or 'Beachhouse' (ie your own little house), this quirky, kinda lavish place receives positive feedback and is right on heavenly Horderns Beach.

The only **camp site** (adult/child $7.50/4) accessible by car is at Bonnie Vale, near Bundeena. Free bush camping is allowed in several areas – one of the best places is **Providential Head**, after the coastal walk – but you must obtain a permit ($3) beforehand from the visitors centre.

Getting There & Away

You can reach the park from Sydney by taking the Princes Hwy and turning off south of Loftus. From Wollongong, the coast road north is a spectacular drive and there are fantastic views of the Illawarra Escarpment and the coast from Bald Hill Lookout, just north of Stanwell Park, on the southern boundary of the Royal National Park.

The Sydney–Wollongong railway forms the western boundary of the park. The closest station is at Loftus, 4km from the park entrance and another 2km from the visitors centre. Bringing a bike on the train is a good idea. Engadine, Heathcote, Waterfall and Otford are on the park boundary and have walking trails leading into the park.

A scenic route is to take a train from Sydney to the suburb of Cronulla (changing at Sutherland on the way; $4.40), then a **Cronulla National Park Ferries** (☎ 02-9523 2990) boat to Bundeena in the northeastern corner of the park (adult/child $3.30/1.60). Ferries depart from Cronulla Wharf, just below the train station. Cronulla National Park Ferries also offers daily Hacking River cruises in summer (a reduced timetable in winter) for $15/10/40 per adult/child/family.

PARRAMATTA

Parramatta (an Aboriginal word meaning 'where the eels lie down'), 24km west of Sydney, was the second European settlement in Australia and contains a number of historic buildings dating from early colonial days. When Sydney proved to be a poor area for farming, Parramatta was selected in 1788 for the first farm. Now consumed by Sydney's westward sprawl, Parramatta is a thriving commercial centre, with some architectural gems (*always* from another era) nestled amongst the modern developments, which are, for the most part, forgettable.

The incredibly helpful and knowledgeable **Parramatta visitors centre** (☎ 02-9630 3703; 346 Church St; ⏱ 10am-5pm Mon-Fri, 10am-4pm Sat & Sun) is the best place to get acquainted with the area. It has *lots* of brochures and leaflets, plenty of info on access for visitors with impaired mobility, and it's close to public transport.

On the western edge of the city, **Parramatta Park** was the site of the area's first farm and contains a number of relics. The elegant **Old Government House** (☎ 02-9635 8149; adult/concession/family $7/5/17; ⏱ 10am-4pm Mon-Fri, 10.30am-4pm Sat & Sun) sits atop a rise overlooking the Parramatta River. Built from 1799 as a country retreat for the early governors of NSW, it's the oldest remaining public building in Australia and now houses a museum.

St John's Cathedral (☎ 02-9635 5904; O'Connell St; ⏱ 10am-3pm Tue-Fri) and the **Parramatta Town Hall** (Church St Mall) form a pleasant civic centre near the junction of Church and Macquarie Sts. **St John's Cemetery** (☎ 02-9686 6861; O'Connell St; ⏱ daylight hrs), between the cathedral and the park, contains the graves of many of the first settlers.

There are more historic buildings east of the city centre. **Elizabeth Farm** (☎ 02-9635 9488; 70 Alice St, Rosehill; adult/child/family $7/3/17; ⏱ 10am-5pm) is the oldest surviving home in the country. The founders of Australia's wool industry,

---

EELS ALIVE

The name 'Parramatta' came from an Aboriginal word meaning 'where the eels lie down', so it comes as no surprise that Parramatta's rugby league team is known as the Parramatta Eels. *The* glamour team in the 1980s, the mighty Eels won the Premiership in 1981, 1982 and 1983, were runners-up in 1984 and won again in 1986. Perhaps after that effort, they felt the need for a lie down – the team hasn't scaled those heights for some time, although things are picking up in the 21st century.

John and Elizabeth Macarthur built it in 1793 and its deep veranda and simple lines became the prototype for early Australian homesteads. There's wheelchair access to every part of the house except the kitchen.

The exquisite **Experiment Farm Cottage** (☎ 02-9635 8149; 9 Ruse St, Harris Park; adult/concession/family $5.50/4/14; ⏰ 10.30am-3.30pm Tue-Thu, 11am-3.30pm Sat & Sun) is a beautiful colonial bungalow built on the site of the first land grant issued in Australia.

Getting There & Around

The most scenic way to reach Parramatta is by RiverCat from Circular Quay ($6.40, 50 minutes) – otherwise catch a train from Central Station ($3.80). By car, exit the city via Parramatta Rd and detour onto the Western Motorway tollway ($2.20) at Strathfield. A good way to take in Parramatta's sights is to hop on the Parramatta Explorer bus at the RiverCat terminal. Eleven sights are on the loop, and tickets cost $10/5 per adult/child.

PENRITH

Penrith, on the calm Nepean River, is at the base of the forested foothills of the Blue Mountains. Despite being 50km west of the city centre, it's virtually an outer suburb of Sydney. The **Penrith visitors centre** (☎ 02-4732 7671; ⏰ 9am-4.30pm) is in the car park of the huge Panthers World of Entertainment complex on Mulgoa Rd.

The **Museum of Fire** (☎ 02-4731 3000, Castlereagh Rd; adult/child/family $5/3/12.50; ⏰ 10am-3pm, closes 5pm Sun) is the best thing to see in the area, with equipment and memorabilia related to fire and fire fighting, which is all too relevant to the area.

You can reach Penrith by train from Central Station ($6.60) or by driving west along Parramatta Rd and taking the Western Motorway tollway at Strathfield ($2.20).

CAMDEN AREA

Camden is promoted as the 'birthplace of the nation's wealth' because it was here that John and Elizabeth Macarthur conducted the sheep-breeding experiments that laid the foundation for Australia's wool industry. Camden is on the urban fringe, 50km southwest of the city centre, off the Hume Hwy. **John Oxley Cottage** (☎ 02-4658 1370; Camden Valley Way, Elderslie; ⏰ 10am-3pm), an historic house

on the town's northern outskirts, hosts the Camden visitors centre, with plenty of information on the area's attractions.

The 400-hectare **Mount Annan Botanic Garden** (☎ 02-4648 2477; Mt Annan Dr, Mt Annan; adult/child/family $4.40/2.20/8.80; ⏰ 10am-6pm Oct-Mar, 10am-4pm Apr-Sep) is the native plant garden of Sydney's Royal Botanic Gardens and is midway between Camden and Campbelltown, to the east. Take a train to Campbelltown Station ($6) and a Busways bus No 895 or 896 from there. By car, take tourist drive 18, off the F5 Fwy.

South of Camden is the small town of **Picton**. A number of historic buildings still stand, including the train station and the 1839 **George IV Inn** (☎ 02-4677 1415; 180 Old Hume Hwy/Argyle St). The Inn brews great Bavarian-style beer in its own brewery and provides modest accommodation. Menangle St West is listed by the National Trust and worth a wander.

KU-RING-GAI CHASE NATIONAL PARK

This 15,000 hectare national park, 24km north of the city centre, borders the southern edge of Broken Bay and the western shore of Pittwater. It has that classic Sydney mixture of sandstone, bushland and water vistas, plus walking tracks, horse-riding trails, picnic areas, Aboriginal rock engravings and spectacular views of Broken Bay, particularly from West Head at the park's northeastern tip. There are several roads through the park and four entrances. Entry is $10 per car.

The **Kalkari visitors centre** (☎ 02-9457 9853; Ku-ring-gai Chase Rd; ⏰ 9am-5pm) is about 2.5km into the park from the Mt Colah entrance on Ku-ring-gai Chase Rd; it's staffed by friendly volunteers. The road descends from the visitors centre to the picnic area at **Bobbin Head** on Cowan Creek. **Halvorsen** (☎ 02-9457 9011; Bobbin Head) rents rowboats for $25/60 per hour/day and eight-seater motorboats for $60/130.

Recommended walks include the America Bay Trail and the Gibberagong and Sphinx tracks. The best places to see **Aboriginal engravings** are on the Basin Trail and the Garigal Aboriginal Heritage Walk at West Head. There's a mangrove boardwalk at Bobbin Head. It's unwise to swim in Broken Bay because of sharks, but there are netted swimming areas at Illawong Bay and the Basin.

Sleeping

Basin campsites (☎ 02-9974 1011; adult/child $9/4.50)
Camping is permitted at the Basin (bookings essential) on the western side of Pittwater. Getting there takes a walk of about 2.5km from West Head Rd, or a ferry or water-taxi ride from Palm Beach (below).

Pittwater YHA (☎ 02-9999 5748; pittwater@hansw .org .au; Ku-ring-gai National Park, via Church Point; dm $22, d & tw $60) This idyllic, beautifully situated hostel, a couple of kilometres south of the Basin, is noted for its friendly wildlife and considerate management. You should book ahead and bring food. To get here, take bus No 156 from Manly Wharf to Church Point, then the ferry from Church Point to Halls Wharf – after all that, you're in for a 10-minute uphill walk but it's definitely worth the effort.

Getting There & Away

There are four road entrances to the park: Mt Colah, on the Pacific Hwy; Turramurra, in the southwest; and Terrey Hills and Church Point, in the southeast. **Shorelink Buses** (☎ 02-9457 8888) runs bus No 577 every 30 minutes from Turramurra Station to the park entrance ($3.10) on weekdays; one bus enters the park as far as Bobbin Head. The schedule changes on weekends with fewer buses going to the entrance but more to Bobbin Head.

The **Palm Beach Ferry Service** (☎ 02-9918 2747) runs to the Basin hourly from 9am to 5pm Monday to Thursday, 9am to 8pm Friday and 9am to 6pm Saturday, Sunday and public holidays ($8/4 for adult/concession). You can also use **Church Point Water Taxis** (☎ 0428-238 190) for the trip between Church Point and Palm Beach ($38.50 for up to six people).

To get to the Pittwater YHA Hostel take the **Church Point Ferry Service** (☎ 02-9999 3492) from Church Point to Halls Wharf ($7 return); the hostel is a 10-minute uphill walk from here. Bus No 156 runs from Manly to Church Point. From the city centre, bus No E86 is a direct peak-hour service to Church Point, or catch bus No L88, L90 or 190 from Wynyard Park as far as Warringah Mall and transfer to No 156 from there.

HAWKESBURY RIVER

The mighty Hawkesbury River enters the sea 30km north of Sydney at Broken Bay. It's dotted with coves, beaches and picnic spots, making it one of Australia's most attractive rivers. Before reaching the ocean, the river expands into bays and inlets like Berowra Creek, Cowan Creek and Pittwater on the southern side, and Brisbane Water on the northern. The river flows between a succession of national parks – Marramarra and Ku-ring-gai Chase to the south; and Dharug, Brisbane Water and Bouddi to the north. Windsor (see Windsor & Richmond for details; p143) is about 120km upstream.

A great way to get a feel for the river is to catch the **Riverboat Postman** (☎ 02-9985 7566; Brooklyn Wharf, Brooklyn; adult/child/family $35/20/80). This mail boat does a 40km round trip Monday to Friday, running upstream as far as Marlow, near Spencer. It leaves Brooklyn at 9.30am and returns at 1.15pm. There are also coffee cruises and all-day cruises (booking recommended). The 8.16am train from Sydney's Central Station ($5.20) gets you to Brooklyn's Hawkesbury River Station in time to meet the morning Riverboat Postman.

You can hire houseboats in Brooklyn, Berowra Waters and Bobbin Head. These aren't cheap but renting midweek during the low season is affordable for a group. **Ripples** (☎ 02-9985 5555; www.ripples.com.au; 87 Brooklyn Rd, Brooklyn) has a good fleet of comfortable houseboats, with admirable reductions during quiet times and midweek. The cost for six people for a weekend is around $1050.

The settlements along the river have their own distinct character. Life in **Brooklyn** revolves totally around boats and the river. The town is on the Sydney–Newcastle railway line, just east of the Pacific Hwy. **Berowra Waters** is a quaint community further upstream, clustered around a free 24-hour winch ferry that crosses Berowra Creek. There are a couple of cafés overlooking the water and a marina, where you can hire an outboard boat for about $55 for a half-day. Berowra Waters is 5km west of the Pacific Hwy; there's a train station at Berowra, but it's a 6km hike down to the ferry.

Wisemans Ferry is a tranquil settlement overlooking the Hawkesbury River roughly halfway between Windsor and the mouth of the river. Free 24-hour winch ferries are the only means of crossing the river here.

Wisemans Ferry Inn (☎ 02-4566 4301; Old Northern Rd, Wisemans Ferry; d & tw $60, f $72) is an historic inn with decent (if a little cramped) rooms. There's often a lot going on in the pub, from singers to lingerie waitresses, if that's your thing. All rooms have their own bathroom.

Standards are high at the **Del Rio Riverside Resort** (☎ 02-4566 4330; visit@delrioresort.com.au; Chaseling Rd, Webbs Creek, Wisemans Ferry; camp/caravan site per night $21/24), just 3km southwest of the village centre. There are also attractive cabins available, with tranquil water views. Take the Webbs Creek winch ferry and then follow the signs.

Yengo National Park, a rugged sandstone area covering the foothills of the Blue Mountains, stretches from Wisemans Ferry to the Hunter Valley. It's a wilderness area with no facilities and limited road access. North of the river, a scenic road leads east from Wisemans Ferry to the Central Coast, following the river before veering north through bushland and orange groves. An early convict-built road leads north from Wisemans Ferry to tiny, delightful **St Albans**. **Settlers Arms Inn** (☎ 02-4568 2111; settlersarms@hotmail.com; 1 Wharf St, St Albans; d $110) is a charming inn that dates from 1836, and the public bar is worth having a beer or a meal in. It has a few pleasant rooms and there's good food available.

WINDSOR & RICHMOND

Windsor, Richmond, Wilberforce, Castlereagh and Pitt Town are the five 'Macquarie Towns' established on rich agricultural land on the upper Hawkesbury River in the early 19th century by Governor Lachlan Macquarie. You can visit them on the way to or from the Blue Mountains if you cross the range on the Bells Line of Rd – an interesting alternative to the Great Western Hwy.

The **Hawkesbury visitors centre** (☎ 02-4588 5895; Bicentennial Park, Ham Common, Windsor Rd, Clarendon; ☽ 9am-1pm & 1.30-5pm Mon-Fri, 10am-3pm Sat & Sun) is across from the Richmond Royal Australian Air Force (RAAF) base. It's the main information centre for the upper Hawkesbury area and is immensely helpful.

Windsor has some fine old buildings, notably those around the picturesque Thompson Square on the banks of the Hawkesbury River. The **Hawkesbury Museum & Tourist Centre** (☎ 02-4577 2310; 7 Thompson Sq, Windsor; adult/child $3/1; ☽ 10am-4pm) is in a building that dates from the 1820s, and was used as the Daniel O'Connell Inn during the 1840s. There are a variety of displays in the museum.

The 1815 **Macquarie Arms Hotel** has a nice veranda fronting the square and is reckoned to be the oldest pub in Australia, but there are quite a few 'oldest pubs' in NSW. Other old buildings include the convict-built **St Matthew's Church of England**, completed in 1822 and designed, like the **courthouse**, by the convict architect Francis Greenway.

You can reach Windsor by train from Sydney's Central Station ($6), but public transport to other Macquarie Towns (apart from Richmond) is scarce. By car, exit the city on Parramatta Rd and head northwest on the Windsor Rd from Parramatta.

The next largest of the Macquarie Towns is **Richmond**, which has its share of colonial buildings and a pleasant village-green-like park. It's 6km west of Windsor, at the end of the metropolitan railway line and at the start of the Bells Line of Rd across the Blue Mountains.

The office of the **National Parks & Wildlife Service** (NPWS; ☎ 02-4588 5247; Bowmans Cottage, 370 George St, Richmond; ☽ 9am-12.30pm & 1.30-5pm Mon-Fri) can give you information about national parks facilities in the region.

The pretty **Ebenezer Church** (1809), 5km north of Wilberforce, is the oldest church in Australia still used as a place of worship.

Wilberforce is the starting point for the Putty Rd, a 160km isolated back road that runs north to Singleton in the Hunter Valley. The **Colo River**, 15km north along this road, is a picturesque spot popular for swimming, canoeing and picnicking.

BLUE MOUNTAINS

This excellent natural habitat has been Sydney's wilderness getaway for years. It has magnificent scenery, excellent bushwalks, gum trees, gorges, outdoor activities, great eating and enough tourism infrastructure to keep you as comfy or as rugged as you like.

History

The Blue Mountains, part of the Great Dividing Range, were initially an impenetrable barrier to white expansion from Sydney. Despite many attempts to find a route through the mountains – and a bizarre belief among many convicts that China, and freedom, was just on the other side – it took 25 years before a successful crossing was made by Europeans. A road was built soon afterwards which opened the western plains to settlement.

The first whites to venture into the mountains found evidence of Aboriginal occupation but few Aboriginal people. It seems likely that European diseases had travelled from Sydney long before the explorers and wiped out most of the indigenous people.

The Blue Mountains National Park has some truly fantastic scenery, excellent bushwalks and all the gorges, gum trees and cliffs you could ask for. The foothills begin 65km inland from Sydney and the mountains rise up to 1100m.

For the past century, the area has been a popular getaway for Sydneysiders seeking to escape the summer heat. Despite the intensive tourist development, much of the area is so precipitous that it's still only open to bushwalkers.

Climate

Be prepared for the climatic difference between the Blue Mountains and the coast – you can swelter in Sydney but shiver in Katoomba. It usually snows sometime between June and August, when the region has a Yuletide Festival, complete with Christmas decorations and dinners.

Bushfires are a constant menace in the summer months, with access frequently denied to certain parts of the mountains. Pick up information from visitors centres.

Orientation

The Great Western Hwy from Sydney follows a ridge running east–west through the Blue Mountains. Along this less-than-beautiful road, the Blue Mountains towns merge into each other – Glenbrook, Springwood, Woodford, Lawson, Wentworth Falls, Leura, Katoomba, Medlow Bath, Blackheath, Mt Victoria and Hartley. On the western fringe of the mountains is Lithgow (p151).

To the south and north of the highway's ridge, the country drops away into precipitous valleys, including the Grose Valley to the north, and the Jamison Valley south of Katoomba.

The Bells Line of Rd is a much more scenic and less congested alternative to the Great Western Hwy. It's the more northerly

of the two crossings, beginning in Richmond (see Windsor & Richmond; p143) and running north of the Grose Valley to emerge in Lithgow, although you can cut across from Bell to join the Great Western Hwy at Mt Victoria.

National Parks

The **Blue Mountains National Park** protects large areas to the north and south of the Great Western Hwy. It's the most popular and accessible of the three national parks in the area, and offers great bushwalking, scenic lookouts, breathtaking waterfalls and the chance to see Aboriginal stencils.

Wollemi National Park, north of the Bells Line of Rd, is the state's largest forested wilderness area and stretches all the way to Denman in the Hunter Valley. It has limited access and the park's centre is so isolated that a new species of tree, named the Wollemi pine, was only discovered in 1994.

Kanangra-Boyd National Park is southwest of the southern section of the Blue Mountains National Park. It has bushwalking opportunities, limestone caves and grand scenery, and includes the spectacular Kanangra Walls Plateau, which is surrounded by sheer cliffs and can be reached by unsealed road from Oberon or from Jenolan Caves.

Entry to these national parks is free, unless you enter the Blue Mountains National Park at Bruce Rd, Glenbrook, where it costs $6 per car; walkers are not charged.

Sleeping

Accommodation ranges from camping grounds and hostels to guesthouses and luxury hotels. Katoomba is the main centre. Prices are fairly stable throughout the year, but most places charge more on weekends, public holidays and during Yulefest (July). Prices listed in the following sections are peak rates. If you intend to camp in the national parks, check with the NPWS first.

Getting There & Away

Katoomba is 109km from Sydney's city centre, but it's still almost a satellite suburb. Trains run approximately hourly from Central Station. The trip takes two hours ($11.40) and there are stops at plenty of Blue Mountains townships on the way.

By car, leave the city via Parramatta Rd and detour onto the Western Motorway tollway (M4; $2.20) at Strathfield. The motorway becomes the Great Western Hwy west of Penrith.

To reach the Bells Line of Rd, head out on Parramatta Rd and from Parramatta drive northwest on the Windsor Rd to Windsor. The Richmond Rd from Windsor becomes the Bells Line of Rd west of Richmond.

HAZY DAYS

The blue haze, which gave the Blue Mountains their name, is a result of the ultrafine oily mist given off by eucalyptuses.

Getting Around

Mountainlink (☎ 02-4782 3333) runs buses between Katoomba, Medlow Bath, Blackheath and (infrequently) Mt Victoria, with some services running down Hat Hill Rd (to Perrys Lookdown) and Govetts Leap Rd (to Govetts Leap). The buses take you to within about 1km of Govetts Leap, but for Perrys Lookdown you have to walk a further 6km. Services are less frequent on weekends. In Katoomba, buses leave from the top of Katoomba St, opposite the Carrington Hotel.

The **Blue Mountains Bus Company** (☎ 02-4782 4213) runs between Katoomba, Leura, Wentworth Falls, and east as far as Woodford, and to the Scenic Railway, Skyway and Scenisender. There's roughly one service an hour from Katoomba train station.

There are train stations in Blue Mountains towns along the Great Western Hwy. Trains run roughly hourly between stations east of Katoomba and roughly two-hourly between stations to the west.

GLENBROOK TO LEURA
Bookshops

To find books and guides on walking in the area, try **Megalong Books** (☎ 02-4784 1302; 183 The Mall, Leura). There are plenty of books on the Blue Mountains. *The Blue Mountains on Foot* by Bruce Williams and Reece Scannell is a useful book, and Lonely Planet's *Walking in Australia* details the Blue Gum Forest Walk. Cyclists will do well to check out Robert Sloss' *Bushwalking-Hiking-Cycling in the Blue Mountains*. Books, maps and walking-track guides are sold at visitors centres.

Sights & Activities

From Marge's and Elizabeth's Lookouts, just north of Glenbrook, there are good views east to Sydney. The section of the Blue Mountains National Park, south of Glenbrook, contains **Red Hand Cave**, an old Aboriginal shelter with hand stencils on the walls. It's an easy 7km return walk, southwest of the NPWS visitors centre.

The famous artist and author Norman Lindsay (1879–1969) lived in Springwood from 1912 until his death. His home is now the **Norman Lindsay Gallery & Museum** (☎ 02-4751 1067; 14 Norman Lindsay Cres, Faulconbridge; adult/child $8/4; ☒ 10am-4pm). It houses many of his risqué paintings, cartoons, illustrations and sculptures. The grounds are well worth a wander.

Just south of the town of Wentworth Falls, there are great views of the Jamison Valley. You can see the spectacular 300m **Wentworth Falls** from Falls Reserve, which is the starting point for a network of walking tracks.

Leura is a quaint tree-lined town full of country stores and cafés. **Leuralla** (☎ 02-4784 1169; 36 Olympian Pde; museum/house & garden adult/child $8/4, garden only $5/2; ☒ 10am-5pm) is an Art Deco mansion, which houses a fine collection of 19th-century Australian art, as well as a toy and model-railway museum. The historic house, set in five hectares of lovely gardens, is a memorial to HV 'Doc' Evatt, a former Labor Party leader and first president of the United Nations. There's also a nice lookout across the road, with two statues and an amphitheatre.

Sublime Point, south of Leura, is a great cliff-top lookout. Nearby, **Gordon Falls Reserve** is a popular picnic spot, and from here you can take the cliff-top path or Cliff Drive 4km west past Leura Cascades to Katoomba's Echo Point.

Sleeping & Eating

There are NPWS **camping areas** accessible by road at Euroka Clearing near Glenbrook, Murphys Glen near Woodford, Ingar near Wentworth Falls and at Perrys Lookdown near Blackheath. To camp at Euroka Clearing, you need a permit (adult/child $5/3 per day) from the **Richmond NPWS** (☎ 02-4588 5247; Bowmans Cottage, 370 George St, Richmond), and your own drinking water. The tracks to Ingar and Murphys Glen may be closed after heavy rain.

Hawkesbury Heights YHA (☎ /fax 02-4754 5621; 836 Hawkesbury Rd, Hawkesbury Heights; dm $17) This purpose-built hostel is surrounded by bush. It's an ecofriendly property with solar power, a 'green' toilet and a wood stove. Reservations are essential, but worth it.

Hana (☎ 02-4784 1345; 121 The Mall, Leura; set menus $12-15) The authentic Japanese food on offer here includes some excellent set-menu options and great sushi and sashimi for dinner. Service is sweet, the space is inviting and there's parking.

Leura Gourmet (☎ 02-4784 1438; 159 The Mall, Leura; mains $3.50-15.50) A deli and a café, the Leura Gourmet has lovely views towards Katoomba and is a nice place to unwind with coffee while you ogle a selection of foodstuffs for a picnic lunch. Breakfasts are filling and fab.

Artisan Bakery (☎ 02-4784 3121; 179 The Mall, Leura) This bakery serves the best bread in town, and a great range of tasty, affordable snacks too. Come in for breakfast and stock up on caffeine and carbs before you head out on a hike.

KATOOMBA

☎ 02 / pop 17,900

Katoomba and the adjacent centres of Wentworth Falls and Leura form the tourist centre of the Blue Mountains. Despite the number of visitors and its proximity to Sydney, Katoomba retains an otherworldly ambience, an atmosphere accentuated by its Art Deco guesthouses and cafés, its thick mists and occasional snowfalls. A New Age scene has also developed, mixing peaceably with a strong born-again Christian presence.

Orientation

Steep Katoomba St is the main drag. The major scenic attraction is **Echo Point**, near the southern end of Katoomba St. From here are some of the best views of the Jamison Valley and the magnificent **Three Sisters** rock formation. Katoomba's train station is at the top of Katoomba St.

Information

INTERNET ACCESS

Try the **Katoomba Adventure Centre** (☎ 1800 624 226; 1 Katoomba St) which has two (slow) computer terminals and charges from $2 for 20 minutes.

MEDICAL SERVICES

The **Blue Mountains District Hospital** (☎ 4784 6500; Great Western Hwy, Katoomba) has a casualty ward for medical emergencies.

MONEY

There are numerous banks with ATMs located in Katoomba and other mountain towns.

POST & TELEPHONE

The post office is tucked in behind the shopping centre, one street back from Katoomba St as you head downhill towards Waratah St. There are telephone booths all over Katoomba, and every town in the Blue Mountains will have at least one.

TOURIST INFORMATION

There are Blue Mountains information centres open daily on the highway at **Glenbrook** (☎ 1300 653 408; Great Western Hwy; ☻ 9am-5pm Mon-Fri, 8.30am-4.30pm Sat & Sun) and at the spruced-up **Echo Point** (☎ 1300 653 408; ☻ 9am-5pm) in Katoomba, which has wheelchair access. The **Blue Mountains Heritage Centre** (☎ 4787 8877; Govetts Leap Rd, Blackheath; ☻ 9am-4.30pm) is about 3km off the Great Western Hwy. The website you'll want is www.bluemountains tourism.org.au.

Sights

The most popular (for a reason) sight in the Blue Mountains is at Echo Point, where views of the **Three Sisters** draw gasps and launch a thousand photographs. They look particularly attractive when floodlit at night.

To the west of Echo Point, at the junction of Cliff Dr and Violet St, are the **Scenic Railway**, **Scenic Skyway** and **Scenisender** (☎ 4782 2699; ☻ 9am-5pm). The railway runs to the bottom of the Jamison Valley (adult/child $12/6 return), where the popular six-hour walk to the **Ruined Castle** rock formation begins. The railway was built in the 1880s to transport coal-miners and its 45-degree incline is one of the steepest to be found in the world.

The Scenic Skyway is a cable car that traverses Katoomba Falls gorge 200m above the valley floor (adult/child $10/5 one way). Finally, there's the Scenisender, an enclosed wheelchair-accessible cable car (adult/child $12/6 return).

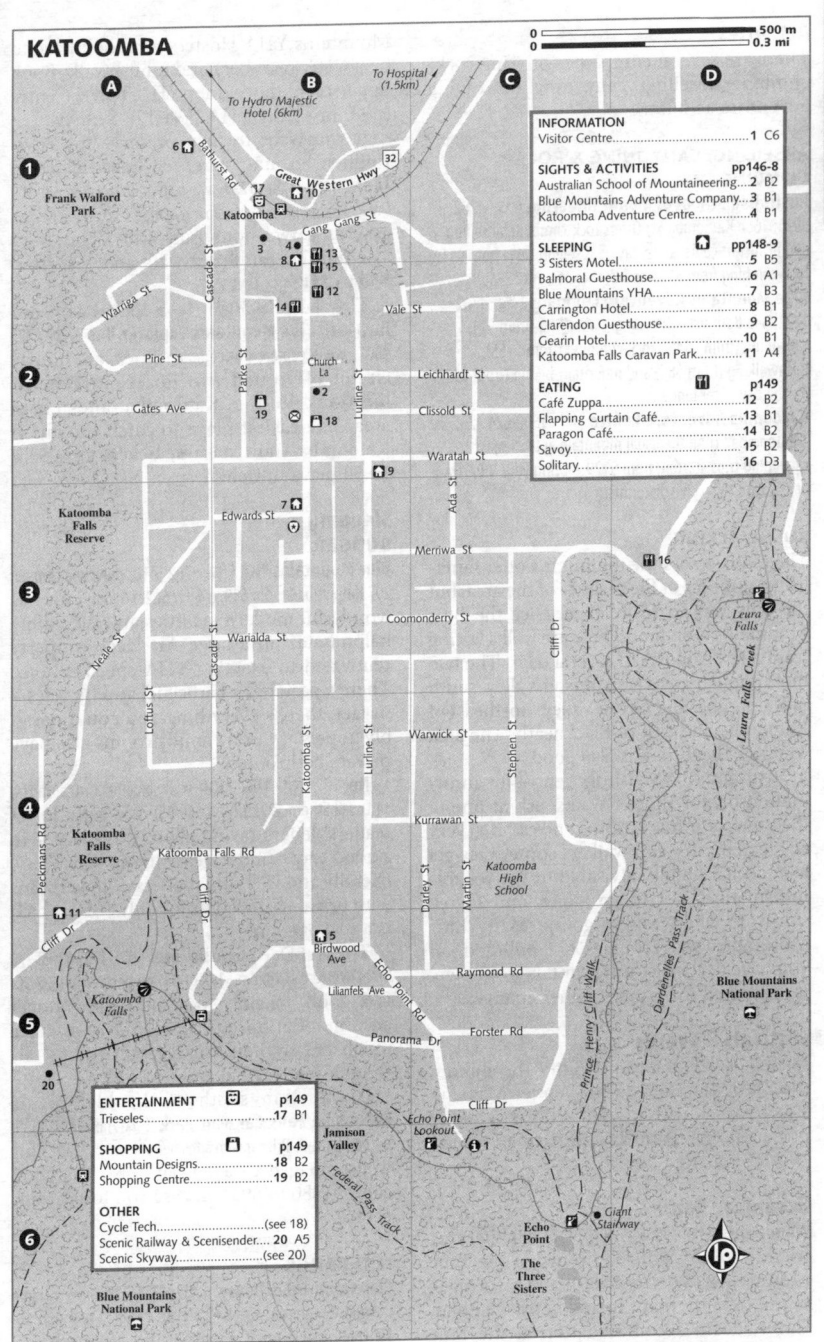

KATOOMBA

| 0 | 500 m |
| 0 | 0.3 mi |

To Hydro Majestic
Hotel (6km)

To Hospital
(1.5km)

Frank Walford
Park

Bathurst Rd

Great Western Hwy

Katoomba

Gang Gang St

Cascade St

Waratga St

Parke St

Pine St

Vale St

Gates Ave

Church La

Lurline St

Leichhardt St

Clissold St

Waratah St

Ada St

Katoomba
Falls
Reserve

Edwards St

Merriwa St

Coomonderry St

Neale St

Warialda St

Cascade St

Loftus St

Katoomba St

Lurline St

Warwick St

Stephen St

Cliff Dr

Leura Falls Creek

Leura
Falls

Kurrawan St

Katoomba
High
School

Katoomba
Falls
Reserve

Peckmans Rd

Katoomba Falls Rd

Cliff Dr

Darley St

Martin St

Raymond Rd

Birdwood
Ave

Echo Point Rd

Lilianfels Ave

Forster Rd

Panorama Dr

Katoomba
Falls

Cliff Dr

Blue Mountains
National Park

Prince Henry Cliff Walk

Dardenelles Pass Track

Echo Point
lookout

Jamison
Valley

Echo
Point

Giant
Stairway

Federal Pass Track

The
Three
Sisters

Blue Mountains
National Park

Activities

There are several companies offering rock-climbing, abseiling, canyoning and caving adventure activities.

ABSEILING, CANYONING & ROCK-CLIMBING

Australian School of Mountaineering (☎ 4782 2014; 166b Katoomba St) Offers rock-climbing, abseiling and bushcraft courses – a day of abseiling costs from $119, rock-climbing from $135 and bushcraft from $275.

Blue Mountains Adventure Company (☎ 4782 1271; 84a Bathurst Rd) Arranges abseiling (from $119), canyoning (from $145), rock-climbing (from $155), bushwalking (from $85) and mountain-biking (from $95) for the day or for longer.

Katoomba Adventure Centre (☎ 1800 624 226; 1 Katoomba St) All the usual mountain activities, with canyoning trips starting from $129 – bring your VIP/YHA or ISIC card to receive discounts.

BUSHWALKING

The roads across the mountains offer tantalising glimpses of the majesty of the area, but the only way to really experience the Blue Mountains is on foot. There are walks lasting from a few minutes to several days. The two most popular areas are Jamison Valley, south of Katoomba, and Grose Valley, northeast of Katoomba and east of Blackheath. The area south of Glenbrook is also good.

Visit an NPWS visitors centre for information or, for shorter walks, ask at one of the tourist information centres. It's very rugged country and walkers sometimes get lost, so it's highly advisable to get reliable information, not to go alone, and to tell someone where you're going. Many Blue Mountains watercourses are polluted, so you have to sterilise water or take your own. Be prepared for rapid weather changes.

Festivals & Events

Yulefest is celebrated in winter throughout the Blue Mountains, with Winter Magic (a street parade with market stalls etc) taking place on the Saturday nearest to June's Winter Solstice.

Organised Tours

Wonderbus (☎ 9555 9800) is a backpacker-friendly outfit with day tours of the Blue Mountains ($70 to $100) and overnight trips ($215) that include the Jenolan Caves, dorm accommodation at the Blue

Mountains YHA Hostel (you don't have to be a YHA member) and a bushwalk. Book in person at the Sydney YHA Travel Centre (p88) or at any YHA hostel in Sydney.

If you want to help preserve the environment around here, try **Tread Lightly Eco Tours** (☎ 4788 1229; www.treadlightly.com.au; 100 Great Western Hwy, Medlow Bath). Tours are as easy as a two-hour bushwalk or as hard as a full-day rainforest walk and cost from $30 to $165.

The daily (9.30am to 5.30pm) hop-on/hop-off **Blue Mountains Explorer Bus** (☎ 4782 4807; www.explorerbus.com.au) does an hourly circuit of around two dozen attractions/locations in the Katoomba and Leura area. The easiest place to catch the bus is Katoomba train station; tickets cost $25/12.50 per adult/child.

Sleeping

BUDGET

Blue Mountains YHA (☎ 4782 1416; www.yha.com.au; 207 Katoomba St; dm $19, d & tw $62, f $100) This has wonderful modern facilities and incredibly helpful staff in a large Art Deco property renovated to exacting YHA specifications. There's parking, a barbecue, and bicycles – in fact, there's everything you could possibly hope for. Comfy family rooms also have private bathrooms.

No 14 (☎ 4782 7104; www.bluemts.com.au/no14; 14 Lovell St; dm $22, d & tw $59-65) We get a lot of readers' letters raving about this place – in a good way – and it's easy to see why. Cosy, friendly and well run, it offers double rooms with private bathrooms for only $65 – which is a real bargain.

The Art Deco **Gearin Hotel** (☎ 4782 4395; 273 Great Western Hwy; dm $16.50, d & tw per person $27.50) is a good, friendly local pub with budget accommodation. Some of the rooms are much better than average pub rooms, although mattresses can be squeaky.

About 2km south of the highway is **Katoomba Falls Caravan Park** (☎ /fax 4782 1835; Katoomba Falls Rd; caravan sites per person $15.85) This well-managed caravan park also has good cabins ($80 to $93), in case you forget your caravan.

MID-RANGE

Clarendon Guesthouse (☎ 4782 1322; www.clarendonguesthouse.com.au; 68 Lurline St; d $88) This guesthouse, corner of Lurline and Waratah Sts, has both old-fashioned and motel-style rooms and is quite atmospheric, with log fires, a cocktail bar and a swimming pool. It's also a popular venue for cabaret acts, which you can have included in a weekend accommodation package. Breakfast is included.

3 Sisters Motel (☎ 4782 2911; 348 Katoomba St; d $110) Ten minutes' walk from town at the bottom end of Katoomba St and close to the Three Sisters, this motel reduces the price of its doubles (all with bathrooms) to $80 midweek. Rooms are clean, and while not spectacular, they are comfortable.

Balmoral Guesthouse (☎ 4782 2264; www.balmoralhouse.com.au; 196 Bathurst Rd; d $125-140) This historic guesthouse (1876) has attractive period details in abundance and charming rooms with bathrooms (there are also some cheaper rooms without). In winter, it's kept cosy with a log fire, and you can even indulge in a game of *boules*.

TOP END

Hydro Majestic Hotel (☎ 4788 1002; www.hydromajestic.com.au; Great Western Hwy, Medlow Bath; s $280-360) This lovingly restored hotel is at the top of the hotel scale. A massive relic of an earlier era (complete with the croquet lawn that narrowly escaped destruction in the 2002–03 bushfires), it's a few kilometres west of Katoomba at Medlow Bath. The more expensive suites ($860 to $1060) have incredible views of the valley.

Carrington Hotel (☎ 4782 1111; www.thecarrington.com.au; 15-47 Katoomba St; d $170-445) The grand Carrington Hotel is another gorgeous old place that has been refurbished to within an inch of its life – very lavish. Check to see if specials are available, and tuck into the good breakfasts (all included). The veranda near reception is a charming spot to unwind with a drink or a pot of tea.

Eating

Solitary (☎ 4782 1164; 90 Cliff Dr, Leura Falls; mains $24-31.50) Achingly romantic, this is our favourite restaurant in the area. Try the North African tajine of kid with couscous, fresh dates and harissa ($28.50), washed down with something from the very good wine list. Service is charming, and the dessert list sexy. Reservations essential on weekends.

Flapping Curtain Café (☎ 4782 1622; 10 Katoomba St; mains $3.50-10.50) The sign says 'helpful, friendly food served by simple,

tasty people'. The Welsh Rarebit ($5.50) is indeed helpful and friendly. It's open for breakfast and lunch – and they're so nice they accept the Seniors Card!

Savoy (☎ 4782 5050; 26-28 Katoomba St; mains $17.50-24.50) The pleasantly quirky, pastel-hued, leopard-printed, Art Deco Savoy has an interesting menu with snacks and more substantial dishes. All the kids dining here when we visited looked mighty happy, and so did their parents.

Café Zuppa (☎ 4782 9247; 36 Katoomba St; mains $12.50-18.80) This café has a good atmosphere, Art Deco fittings and a good range of straightforward dishes, some in kids' portions. Open for breakfast, lunch and dinner.

Paragon Café (☎ 4782 2928; 65 Katoomba St; mains $14.95-21.95) The Paragon is Katoomba's undisputed Art Deco masterpiece (it's heritage listed), and a stroll along Katoomba St demands that you pop in and at least have a coffee while writing a love letter in Golden Age of Cinema surrounds. The chocolates and old-fashioned lollies are a source of great joy too. It doesn't do dinner though.

Entertainment

The **Clarendon** (☎ 4782 1322; www.clarendonguesthouse.com.au; 68 Lurline St) is known for its good cabaret acts. None of the pubs in Katoomba are particularly salubrious, but they have beer. For live music, try **Trieseles** (☎ 4782 4026; 287 Bathurst Rd), which has live acts, predominantly rock.

Shopping

Mountain Designs (☎ 4782 5999; 190 Katoomba St) stocks a good range of camping and outdoor paraphernalia (including maps).

Getting Around

BICYCLE

You can hire bicycles from **Cycle Tech** (☎ 4782 2800; 182 Katoomba St; half/full day $27.50/49.50), where prices include a spares kit and helmet.

BUS

Blue Mountains Bus Company (☎ 4782 4213; Highland St, Leura) runs a service between Katoomba train station, the 3 Sisters Motel (five minutes' walk from Echo Point), and the Scenic Railway and Scenic Skyway. There's a bus roughly every 45 minutes.

Mountainlink (☎ 4751 1077; www.mountainlink.com.au) runs a service (among other services in the Blue Mountains) between Echo Point and Gordon Falls via Katoomba St and Leura Mall. There are regular trips from Monday to Saturday, none on Sunday.

CAR
Redicar (☎ 4784 3443; 80 Megalong St, Leura) is a budget option for those looking to hire a car, ute, van or 4WD.

BLACKHEATH AREA
The little town of Blackheath is a good base for visiting the Grose and Megalong Valleys. There are superb lookouts a few kilometres east of the town, such as **Govetts Leap** and **Evans Lookout**. To the northeast, via Hat Hill Rd, are **Pulpit Rock**, **Perrys Lookdown** and **Anvil Rock**.

A cliff-top track leads from Govetts Leap to Pulpit Rock, and there are several walks from Govetts Leap down into the Grose Valley. Get details on the walks from the **NPWS visitors centre** (☎ 02-4787 8877; Govetts Leap Rd, Blackheath; ☻ 9am-4.30pm). Perrys Lookdown is the beginning of the shortest route (four hours return) to the beautiful **Blue Gum Forest** in the base of the valley.

The **Megalong Valley**, south of Blackheath, is largely cleared farmland but it's still a beautiful place, with awesome sandstone escarpments. The road down from Blackheath passes through pockets of rainforest and you can walk the beautiful 600m **Coachwood Glen Nature Trail**. A couple of kilometres further on is the small valley settlement of Werribee, where there are several horseriding outfits. **Werriberri Trail Rides** (☎ 02-4787 9171; Megalong Rd, Megalong Valley; rides from $28) can show you the area on horseback and best of all, the horses are well looked after.

Blackheath is a short drive along the Great Western Hwy from Katoomba. It's also on the railway line from Sydney – two stops past Katoomba. From Blackheath, it's a 15-minute winding drive into the Megalong Valley via Shipley and Megalong Rds.

Sleeping
There's rudimentary backpack **camping** at Acacia Flat, in the Grose Valley near the Blue Gum Forest. It's a walk down from Govetts Leap or Perrys Lookdown. You can also camp at **Perrys Lookdown**, which has a car park and is a convenient base for walks into the Grose Valley, although

you'll need to bring your own water. Bear in mind that you can only stay for one night though.

Blackheath Caravan Park (☎ 02-4787 8101; Prince Edward St; camp/caravan sites per person $8.80/12.10, per family $22/28.20) This friendly caravan park is off Govetts Leap Rd, about 600m from the highway. It also has caravans available, and some disabled facilities.

Gardners Inn (☎ 02-4787 8347; 255 Great Western Hwy; s/d $45/80) This cosy and friendly inn is the oldest hotel (1832) in the Blue Mountains. Rooms are reasonable (bathrooms are shared), the breakfasts come with great jams and Denise's pies are justifiably famous.

MT VICTORIA & HARTLEY
Mt Victoria, the highest point in the mountains, is a small village with a semirural atmosphere 16km northwest of Katoomba on the Great Western Hwy.

Everything is an easy walk from the train station, where there's the **Mt Victoria Museum** (☎ 02-4787 1190; Mt Victoria Railway Station; ☻ 2-5pm Sat & Sun, plus hols), which has an interesting collection of Australiana. Interesting buildings include the **Tollkeeper's Cottage** (1849) and the 1870s **church**.

The charming **Mt Vic Flicks** (☎ 02-4787 1577; Harley Ave; adult/child $8/6) is a cinema of the old school, with a small candy bar, real cups of tea and the occasional piano player. Surprisingly well-picked flicks are shown from Thursday to Sunday.

About 11km past Mt Victoria, on the western slopes of the range, is the tiny, sandstone 'ghost' town of **Hartley**, which flourished from the 1830s but declined when it was bypassed by the railway in 1887. There are several buildings of historic interest, including the 1837 courthouse.

The **NPWS visitors centre** (☎ 02-6355 2117; ☻ 10am-1pm & 2-4.30pm) is in the Farmer's Inn (1845). You can wander around the village for free, but to enter the **courthouse** (adult $4.40; ☻ tours hourly 10am-3pm) you must book a tour.

Sleeping & Eating
Hotel Imperial (☎ 02-4787 1878; www.bluemts.com.au /hotelimperial; 1 Station St, Mt Victoria; d $189-209) This fine old hotel has arguably the best backpackers' rooms in the region, although there are only four beds in the dorm. The hotel faces the highway and quieter Station

St, and the public bar is pretty good for a beer. It also has dorm beds for $25, and cheaper doubles ($125 to $155) with shared bathrooms.

Victoria & Albert Guesthouse (☎ 02-4787 1241; 19 Station St, Mt Victoria; d $140) This lovely and comfortable guesthouse (1914) is in the grand old style (there are also some cheaper rooms without private bathrooms available). There's a café and a good restaurant, and according to a sign 'breast-feeding is welcome', so we presume it's child-friendly.

THE AUTHOR'S CHOICE

Collits' Inn (☎ 02-6355 2072; www.collitsinn .com.au; Hartley Vale Rd, Hartley Vale; d from $180) In a beautifully renovated 1823 inn, you'll find elegant rooms and magnificent French-influenced food. It's worth it just for dinner alone. Reservations are essential, and cottages are also available. Follow the signs off the Great Western Hwy, along a rough unpaved road (you'll need your own transport).

JENOLAN CAVES

Southwest of Katoomba on the western fringe of Kanangra Boyd National Park, the **Jenolan Caves** (☎ 02-6359 3311) are the best-known limestone caves in Australia. One cave has been open to the public since 1867, although parts of the system are still unexplored. There are nine caves you can visit by guided tour. There are about 11 tours between 10am and 4.30pm weekdays, between 9.30am and 5pm weekends, and a 'ghost tour' at 7.30pm Saturday; tours last one to two hours and prices start at $15/11 for an adult/child. It's advisable to arrive early during holiday periods, as the best caves can be 'sold out' by 10am.

Sleeping

Jenolan Caves Resort (☎ 02-6359 3322; www.jenolan caves.com; Gatehouse $90-120, Mountain Lodge Units $210-480, Caves House $165-490) There's a range of accommodation here – from the cheaper Gatehouse (sleeping up to six people), to the lavish, old-fashioned Caves House. 'Low season' here means weeknights, two-night weekends and three-night long weekends; 'high season' means Saturday

night only and two-night public holiday weekends. It's an atmospheric place to bed down; no matter what choice you make.

Getting There & Away

The caves are on plenty of tour itineraries from Sydney and Katoomba. By car, turn off the Great Western Hwy at Hartley and they're a 45-minute drive along Jenolan Caves Rd. The Six Foot Track from Katoomba to Jenolan Caves is a fairly easy three-day walk, but make sure you get information from an NPWS visitors centre.

BELLS LINE OF ROAD

This back road between Richmond and Lithgow is the most scenic route across the Blue Mountains. It's highly recommended if you have your own transport. There are fine views towards the coast from Kurrajong Heights on the eastern slopes of the range, there are orchards around Bilpin, and there's sandstone cliff and bush scenery all the way to Lithgow.

Midway between Bilpin and Bell, the delightful **Mt Tomah Botanic Garden** (☎ 02-4567 2154; adult/child/family $4.40/2.20/8.80; ☽ 10am-4pm May-Sep, 10am-5pm Oct-Apr) is a cool-climate annexe of Sydney's Royal Botanic Gardens. As well as native plants there are displays of exotic species, including some magnificent rhododendrons. Parts of the park are wheelchair accessible.

North of the Bells Line of Rd, at the little town of **Mt Wilson**, are formal gardens and a nearby remnant of rainforest known as the **Cathedral of Ferns**.

LITHGOW

☎ 02 / pop 20,000

Nestled in the western foothills of the Blue Mountains, Lithgow is an industrial town that straddles the border with NSW's Central West. It didn't really get going until the 1870s, when the Zig Zag Railway brought supply trains across the mountains, after which it promptly became a coal-mining centre.

Inside old Bowenfels railway station, at 1 Cooerwull Rd at the edge of town, the **Lithgow visitors centre** (☎ 6353 1859; www .tourism.lithgow.com; 1 Cooerwull Rd; ☽ 9am-5pm) is well stocked with brochures covering the entire region. Super-helpful staff advises on walking and driving routes and can point you towards the local attractions and a range of activities.

The highest scenic lookout in the Blue Mountains is at **Hassan Walls**, 4km south of town.

The **Zig Zag Railway** (☎ 6353 1795; Chifley Rd; adult/child/family return $17/8.50/45) is at **Clarence**, about 11km east of Lithgow. It was built in 1869 and was quite an engineering wonder in its day. Trains descended from the Blue Mountains by this route until 1910. A section has been restored, and steam trains run the 12km trip daily. One-way tickets are available for hikers wishing to walk the Zig Zag Walking Track. Trains depart Clarence station at 11am, 1pm and 3pm. Special steam trains operate only on Wednesday, Saturday and Sunday and holidays.

Sleeping

Down a side road behind the tourist office, there's **Lithgow Caravan Park** (☎ 6351 4350; Cooerwull Rd; camp/caravan site $14/17.50). It's well managed and has some decent cabins available (from $59). Linen is not supplied though.

Several pubs also have accommodation, including **Grand Central** (☎ 6351 3050; cnr Main & Eskbank Sts; per person $23) Standard rooms with shared bathrooms are available, all with breakfast.

Lithgow Valley Motel (☎ 6351 2334; 45 Cooerwull Rd; s $65, d & tw $72) is off the highway and has good rooms that are clean and serviceable, with a Japanese restaurant on the premises.

Getting There & Away

There are frequent CityRail trains between Lithgow and Sydney ($17). Regular trains between Lithgow and Katoomba cost $6.

NORTH COAST

When secretaries in damp London bedsits yearn for sunny Australia, it's the north coast they imagine. When Australian families think 'summer holidays', they think 'north coast'. When surfers wax their boards, when country-town teens pine for a place they can be free, when Sydneysiders need a 'short break', the north coast is the place they're thinking of.

Head north out of Sydney and through the central coast, and you hit the north coast. It's a fantastic stretch of white-sand beaches, great surf breaks, national parks, dolphins, adventure sports and alternative lifestyles. Parts of it are overdeveloped and overpopulated, particularly during summer school holidays, and other parts are bland resorts aimed at families who come back year after year after year. But take a few random right-hand turns off the Pacific Hwy as you head north, and you're bound to find gorgeous, deserted beaches; tiny, sleepy towns; and stretches of beautiful forest.

SYDNEY TO NEWCASTLE

The Central Coast, between Broken Bay and Newcastle, is a strange combination of the beautiful and the awful – superb lakes, surf beaches and magnificent national parks cut by swathes of rampant suburban housing.

Leave the Sydney–Newcastle freeway at **Brooklyn** to take a cruise on Australia's last **riverboat postal ferry** (☎ 02-9985 7566; $15; departs 1.30pm) or visit historic **Dangar Island**, with bird-watching and bushwalks. **CityRail** (☎ 13 15 00; www.cityrail.nsw.gov.au) runs trains from Sydney ($6, 1 hour) and Newcastle ($11.40, 1 hour 40 minutes) to Brooklyn's Hawkesbury River station.

The largest town in the area is **Gosford** (population 55,000). There are frequent **CityRail** (☎ 13 15 00; www.cityrail.nsw.gov.au) trains to Sydney ($8) and Newcastle ($9.80). From Gosford station, on Mann St, **Busways** (☎ 02-4368 2277; www.busways.com.au) services radiate frequently to nearby towns and the coast. The **visitors centre** (☎ 02-4385 4074; www.cctourism.com.au; 200 Mann St; 9.30am-4pm Mon-Fri, 10am-2pm Sat) covers all of the Central Coast. The 1926 **Hotel Gosford** (☎ 02-4324 1634; 179 Mann St; s/d from $45/65) has clean, refurbished rooms and a great old elevator.

Southwest of Gosford, trails ramble through the rugged sandstone and between the wildflowers of **Brisbane Water National Park**. **Bulgandry Aboriginal Engraving Site** is 6km along Woy Woy Rd from Kariong. CityRail trains stop at Wondabyne train station inside the park upon request. Southeast of Gosford, **Bouddi National Park** extends north along the coast from the mouth of Brisbane Water and has excellent coastal bushwalking and camping. Both parks are managed by the **NPWS** (☎ 02-4324 4911; central.coast@npws.nsw.gov.au; 207 Albany Street North, Gosford; 8.30am-4.30pm Mon-Fri).

GET OFF THE BUS!

Just because you bought an east-coast coach pass, doesn't mean you have to get on in Sydney then get off in Byron Bay. There are lots of side-trips you can take along the way. It'll only cost you a few extra bucks, and you'll see a side of Australia that so many overseas visitors miss: national parks, the classic cattle stations and goldfields of New England, tiny north-coast towns and the wineries of the Hunter Valley.

Consider hopping off the bus at these places:

- Newcastle for buses to Anna Bay ($10), trains to Barrington Tops Guesthouse ($11) or Hunter Valley tours
- Port Macquarie for buses to beautiful Bellingen ($28) and on to Dorrigo National Park ($31)
- Kempsey for laid-back South West Rocks ($11)
- Byron Bay for escapes into the far north coast hinterland or Lennox Head ($5)
- Murwillumbah for treks to Mt Warning with the YHA

Alternatively, take the less-travelled New England Hwy between Sydney and Brisbane. Long-distance buses along this route stop at Gosford and Newcastle; Muswellbrook and Scone in the Upper Hunter; Tamworth, Australia's country music capital; Armidale (gateway to the Waterfall Way, beautiful national parks and the cute towns of Uralla and Nundle); and rural Tenterfield, where you'll see some authentic Australia. Another option is the Melbourne to Byron Bay bus route, which travels through fascinating Bendigo, Victoria; various out-of-the-way port towns along the NSW Riverina; Dubbo, home to Western Plains Zoo, the gateway to unique Lightning Ridge; and entirely Australian outback towns along the Newell Hwy, including Coonabarabran near Warrumbungles National Park and the artesian baths at Moree. These buses end up in Queensland before heading back down the coast to Byron Bay via Tweed Heads.

The National Trust–classified township of **Pearl Beach**, on the eastern edge of Brisbane Water National Park, is a quiet enclave with a lovely beach set in bushland as well as a couple of restaurants. For holiday rentals, contact **Pearl Beach Real Estate** (☎ 02-4341 7555; www.pearlbeachrealestate.com.au; 1 Pearl Pde; houses from $110).

Terrigal

The beachside hamlet of Terrigal grooves to an ocean beat. Surfers carry their boards past breezy cafés on the main street, which stretches alongside a truly stunning beach.

Near the beach, chilled-out **Terrigal Beach Lodge YHA** (☎ 02-4385 3330; 12 Campbell Cres; yha@terrigalbeachlodge.com.au; dm/s/d $20/40/50; ☐) is often full, despite the nothing-special standard of rooms and facilities. Boards are free. Modest **Terrigal Beach House Motel** (☎ 02-4384 1423; www.accommodationterrigal.com; 7 Painters Lane; d $50-90) has a hostel feel and some great ocean views. Two-bedroom apartments start from $350 per week.

Sun-drenched **Patcinos** (☎ 02-4385 1960; cnr Church St & Campbell Cres; mains $6-12) catches the ocean breeze. Enjoy toasted banana bread or vegetarian and deli-style meals. Serving provincial Thai, **Al-Oi Thai** (☎ 02-4385 6611; 3 Kurrawyba Ave; mains $9-19) has lots of unusual – and unusually tasty – dishes.

From Gosford, **Busways** (☎ 02-4368 2277; www.busways.com.au) services run to Terrigal ($4) at least hourly.

NEWCASTLE

☎ 02 / pop 133,690

Newcastle has to be one of Australia's most livable cities. There may not be much to see here, but that makes it even better: you can spend every day on the beach and every night searching out Newcastle's next big band, and not feel guilty about it. If it's good enough for the locals, it's good enough for you.

Australians who haven't kept up with the news might tell you Newcastle is a horrible, polluted industrial town. Don't listen to them. Since BHP closed its steel plant in 1987, a successful urban renewal programme has turned Newcastle into a downright pretty, cosmopolitan little city where you can get a good coffee, catch a superb wave and hear some fine rock. It's also a great base for visiting the Hunter Valley's vineyards.

Orientation

The central business district (CBD) sits on a peninsula bordered by the Hunter River and the sea, tapering down to the long sand spit out to **Nobby's Head**.

The train station, post office, banks and some fine historic buildings – an area known as the East End – stand at the CBD's north-eastern edge. The shopping centre is Hunter St, which is a pedestrian mall between New-comen and Perkins Sts. The lively suburb of Hamilton is adjacent to Newcastle West; Cooks Hill is south of Hunter St.

Queens Wharf Tower on the waterfront and the obelisk above King Edward Park have great views of the city and the water.

Across the river – minutes by ferry – is Stockton, a modest settlement with strik-ing views back to Newcastle and exposed shipwrecks lurking in its waters.

Information
BOOKSHOPS

Angus & Robertson (☎ 4929 4601; 147 Hunter St Mall)

Cook's Hill Books & Records (☎ 4929 5079; 72 Darby St) Huge, eccentrically organised selection of mostly second-hand books and records.

Pepperina Books, Music & Coffee (☎ 4925 2939; 37 Bolton St) A smattering of CDs and a café – the book selection is eclectic, but not comprehensive.

INTERNET ACCESS

The **Newcastle Region Library** (☎ 4974 5300; Laman St) has Internet access. You can also log on at the hostels (Nomads is cheapest), or for free at the Regional Museum if you buy something from its café.

MEDICAL SERVICES

John Hunter Hospital (☎ 4921 3000; Lookout Rd, New Lambton) Head out to the university if you need emergency care.

Royal Newcastle Hospital (☎ 4923 6000; Pacific St) Right by the YHA, the Royal has no emergency department.

MONEY

Banks are in Hunter St Mall. Most have for-eign exchange: Westpac will change Amex travellers cheques for free.

TOURIST INFORMATION

The Newcastle **visitors centre** (☎ 1800 654 558, 4974 2999; www.newcastletourism.com; 363 Hunter St; ☷ 9am-5pm Mon-Fri, 10am-3.30pm Sat & Sun) books accommodation and tours, and has exten-sive Hunter Valley information.

Dangers & Annoyances

Newcastle seems to have an unusually large number of car break-ins. Don't leave any-thing even slightly valuable in your car.

Sights & Activities
SWIMMING & SURFING

Right by the East End, **Newcastle Beach** is great for both surfers and swimmers. If you're paranoid about sharks, the 1922 **ocean baths** are just the ticket (there's a shallow pool for toddlers). Newcastle Beach has a kiosk (nothing beats a potato scallop with sauce after a few hours in the waves) and changing sheds. Surfers should check out **Nobby's Beach**, just north of the baths: the fast left-hander known as the **Wedge** is at its north end.

South of Newcastle Beach, below King Edward Park, is Australia's oldest ocean bath, the convict-carved **Bogey Hole**. If your swimsuit is chafing you, scramble around the rocks and under the headland to the (unofficial) nude beach, **Susan Gilmour Beach**.

The most popular surfing break is at **Bar Beach**, 1km south. Nearby **Merewether Beach** has two huge saltwater pools. Frequent local buses from the CBD run as far south as Bar Beach, but only No 207 continues to Merewether.

You'll find plenty of surfers on the beach who can let you in on the best spots. **Avago Sports** (☎ 0404-278 072; avagosports@hunterlink.net .au; Newcastle Beach; ☷ 7am-7pm) will deliver a surfboard or body-board pack, includ-ing wetsuit, rash shirt and maps, tips and charts, to wherever you're staying ($39).

SEA KAYAKING

Blue Water Sea Kayaking (☎ 0409-408 618; www.sea kayaking.com.au; Newcastle Cruising Yacht Club Marina, Har-nell St, Wickham) leads tours of Newcastle Har-bour ($40) and the Hunter River estuaries ($90). Rent a kayak for $15 an hour.

FLIGHTS

Air Sports (☎ 0412-607 815; www.air-sports.com.au; King Edward Park) will take you on a tandem flight starting from $165. It also runs courses.

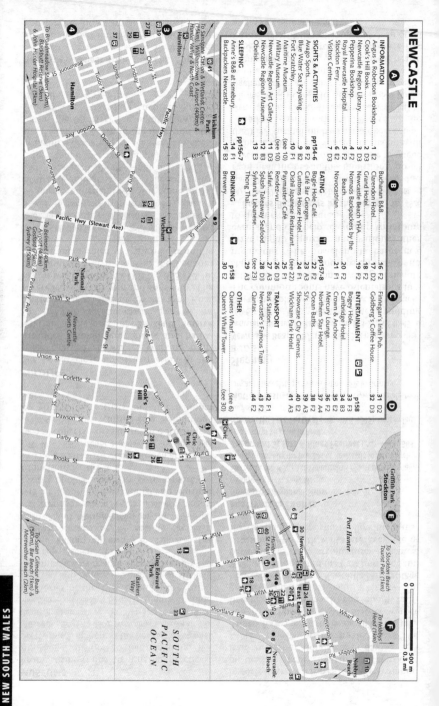

NEW SOUTH WALES

MUSEUMS

From steam trains to nursing practices, Aboriginal history to hang gliding, it's pretty much all here at the **Newcastle Regional Museum** (☎ 4974 1400; www.nrmuseum.com.au; 787 Hunter St; admission free; ☷ 10am-5pm Tue-Sun, 10am-5pm Mon school holidays; ▣). Highlights include memories of the 1989 earthquake written by local kids, and an exhibition of stickers accumulated by coal miners. Kids enjoy the interactive science exhibits.

The **Military Museum** (☎ 4929 3066; Fort Scratchley; admission free; ☷ noon-4pm Sat, Sun & holidays) and **Maritime Museum** (☎ 4929 2588; Fort Scratchley; admission free; ☷ noon-4pm Tue-Sun) will let you in on the colonial and wartime history of Newcastle. Pay $1 to explore the tunnels under the fort.

The excellent **Newcastle Region Art Gallery** (☎ 4974 5100; Laman St; admission free; ☷ 10am-5pm Tue-Sun) collects works by revered Australian artists and hosts cutting-edge exhibitions by young local artists and international stars.

WILDLIFE

See koalas close up at a fraction of the price charged elsewhere! Walking trails meander through grey gums and native wildlife enclosures at **Blackbutt Reserve** (☎ 4952 1449; www.ncc.nsw.gov.au; Carnley Ave, New Lambton Heights; admission free; ☷ 9am-5pm). Koalas are fed between 2pm and 3pm daily. The fastest bus from the CBD is No 363 ($2.40, 35 minutes), but it stops at the Lookout Rd entrance, which is a fair hike from the creatures.

The **Wetlands Centre** (☎ 4951 6466; www.wetlands.org.au; Sandgate Rd, Shortland; adult/concession $4.50/3; ☷ 9am-3pm Mon-Fri, 9am-5pm Sat & Sun) is a swampy wonderland which is home to 200 bird and animal species. Take a sensory walk, designed for the sight impaired, or hire a canoe ($7 for 2 hours). Call about twilight walks and kids' canoe days. Take the Pacific Hwy toward Maitland and turn left at the cemetery (signs say 'Newcastle Fruit & Veg Market'), or catch Bus No 106 from the railway station.

Tours

Newcastle's Famous Tram (☎ 4963 7954; www.huntertourism.com/tram; adult/child $10/6) toodles around the East End for 45 minutes, giving you the low-down on all sites that are of historic interest. It leaves the railway station on the hour between 10am and 2pm (last tram at 1.45pm Monday to Friday).

Newcastle has two self-guided walks. The **Bathers Way** is a coastal walk that will take you from Nobby's Beach to Merewether Beach. Signposts teach you about indigenous, convict and natural history in between swims. The **Newcastle East Heritage Walk** wanders around the East End for 3km, between the city's architectural treasures. Brochures for both walks are available at the visitors centre, or just follow the signs.

Festivals & Events

Newcastle Regional Show This show (it's like a country fair) is in early March.
Surfest (☎ 4982 1264) Australia's oldest professional competition; hits the beaches of Newcastle in late March.
Beaumont St Jazz & Blues Festival (☎ 4974 2883) This festival kicks off in April.
Newcastle Jazz Festival (☎ 4963 1515) Jams in late August.
Mattara Festival (☎ 4928 4093; www.mattarafestival.org.au) This celebrates Newcastle and is in October.

Sleeping
BUDGET

Newcastle Beach YHA (☎ 4925 3544; yhanewcastle@hunterlink.net.au; 30 Pacific St; dm $23-27, s $40-45, d $60-65; ▣) This heritage-listed building sits a stumble away from Newcastle Beach. The common rooms have ostentatious furniture, and the bedrooms are huge. Friendly staff can give you good tips on bands and nightclubs. The hostel hosts barbecues, pizza nights, quizzes and various other events, and can help set you up with tours to the surrounding area.

Nomads Backpackers by the Beach (☎ 4926 3472; www.backpackersbythebeach.com.au; 34 Hunter St; dm/d $20/50; ▣) Bright, clean, modern and right near the beach, this multistorey hostel is very relaxed and you won't have to queue to use the Internet. Nomads teams up with the YHA for full-on backpacker barbecues.

Backpackers Newcastle (☎ 1800 333 436; backpackers45@hotmail.com; 42-44 Denison St, Hamilton; dm $20, d from $50; ▣) Close to Beaumont St, Backpackers Newcastle has pleasant gardens, a pool and a table tennis. The managers are keen surfers and will drive you to the beach, lend you a surfboard and give you a free lesson. They'll also pick up and drop off at any Newcastle train station.

Stockton Beach Tourist Park (☎ 4928 1393; Pitt St, Stockton; camp sites from $16, cabins $50-90) Beside the beach off King St, this time-worn caravan park is handy for the Stockton–Newcastle ferry.

MID-RANGE

Buchanan B&B (☎ 4926 5828; www.buchanan-bb.com.au; 20 Church St; s $75-95; d $120-145; 🖳) There's real attention to detail at Buchanan, with fresh flowers, fruit and Berocca in every room, beautiful high French beds and a delicious homemade breakfast.

Anne's B&B at Ismebury (☎ 4929 5376; www.users.hunterlink.net.au; 3 Stevenson Pl; d $125-180, tw $170-190; ste $275-300) In a quiet little street near the beach, Anne's B&B offers any number of combinations of rooms, some with spa and kitchenette.

Clarendon Hotel (☎ 4927 0966; www.clarendon hotel.com.au; 347 Hunter St; d $121-132, ste $143-154; 🐾) You'd never mistake this boutique place for a chain – every room has its own colour scheme, with luxurious linens, up-to-the-minute furniture and vividly painted walls. Packages with dinner, breakfast and champagne and strawberries are $110 per person.

Also recommended are the **Grand Hotel** (☎ 4929 3489; 32 Church St; s/d $45/65), where comfortable, quiet doubles are better value than dingy singles, and the **Novocastrian** (☎ 4926 3688; fax 4929 5795; 21 Parnell Pl; d $110-185, f $165; 🐾) a motel right above Nobby's Beach with recently renovated rooms.

Eating

Newcastle has a great selection of restaurants, from cheap 'here's a picture of your noodles' Asian to classy Mod Oz cafés. Darby St is your best bet for coffee and cake, the East End has the pricier options and the water views, while Beaumont St is all about ethnic eclecticism.

EAST END

Bogie Hole Café (☎ 4926 1790; cnr Hunter & Pacific Sts; mains $10-20) There's a reason (or four) this place is always packed: it's metres from the beach, the dishes are huge, the prices are reasonable, and it has cold beer. The masses of sidewalk tables make it five. Bogie Hole does all the standards – pastas, salads, burgers, steaks and chicken – and it does them well.

Oishii Japanese Restaurant (☎ 4926 1105; 35 Hunter St; sushi $9-17, mains $15-23) Not your quick-snack-of-sushi kind of place (though it has some sushi), Oishii's menu is *teri-* and *teppan-yaki* heavy, specialising in all kinds of grilled, barbecued and fried seafood.

Paymaster's Café (☎ 4925 2600; 18 Bond St; mains $15-27; 🕑 closed Mon & Tue) Consider dressing in cream linen for your visit to the Paymaster's. The wicker chairs, sea breezes and heritage surrounds may provoke you to cry, 'fetch me another G&T, major; I've come over all malarial'. The Asian-influenced menu is full of delicious surprises such as red curry duck omelette.

Customs House Hotel (☎ 4925 2585; 1 Bond St; mains $11-26) Once HQ for confiscating contraband, this lovely old building is now part pub, part classy bistro. Take your dinner – the fusion/comfort-focused menu includes gourmet burgers, Atlantic salmon and confit of duck – out to the patio and get an eyeful of fountains and foreshore.

BEAUMONT ST

Thong Thai (☎ 4969 5655; 74 Beaumont St; mains $10-15; 🕑 dinner only, closed Tue) Clean, simple and spicy, this laminated-table eatery serves up all the classics to Novocastrian families wanting a quick, cheap feed.

Sylvana's Lebanese (☎ 4961 2899; Shop 4, 79 Beaumont St; dishes $4-12) Up a small laneway, Sylvana's won't disappoint if all you want is a falafel and some *baba ganoush*. But why stop there? Sylvana's has expanded into Polish food (who doesn't want a little tabbouleh with their pirozhki?) and has an extensive Turkish delight list, as well as the slightly terrifying 'vodka hearts' dessert.

Café-Bar Georges (☎ 4969 6886; 79 Beaumont St; mains $6-25) Newcastle loves Georges, where simple dishes, such as roast pork or steamed vegetables, are cooked with care and flair. The big windows and chrome-and-black décor make the place feel relaxed and modern.

Safari (☎ 4969 3833; 50 Beaumont St; mains $12-22; 🕑 closed Mon) If Asian, Italian and Middle Eastern just don't crank your dial anymore, get a plateful of African at Safari. Mainly South African – with treats such as monkey gland steak (no monkeys involved) and Dutch beef Bredie (beef and green bean stew) – Safari also serves North African tajines and East African chicken. Surprisingly, there are plenty of vegetarian options. Unsurprisingly, you can get South African beer.

DARBY ST

Rendez-vu (☎ 4929 2244; 115 Darby St; mains $10-25; ☾ 24hr Fri & Sat) They may not be able to spell, but they can cook. Gigantic, delicious sandwiches, super-fresh produce and a deliriously tropical cocktail list draw big crowds to Rendez-vu's sidewalk tables.

Splash Takeaway Seafood (☎ 4929 4394; 126 Darby St; boxes $7-14) Sick of the beach? Pick up a book at Cook's Hill Books, grab a feed of fish from Splash, and pull up some lawn in the Civic Park for a perfect afternoon. From battered flake to marinated mussels, Splash has seafood combos for all tastes and budgets.

Drinking

The **Brewery** (☎ 4929 6333; 150 Wharf Rd) Right on the harbour, show up for happy hour (5pm to 7pm) and you'll share the jetty with Novocastrian office workers and uni students. There are DJs or bands on the weekend. For more foreshore atmosphere, have a beer at the **Customs House Hotel** (☎ 4925 2585; 1 Bond St).

Finnegan's Irish Pub (☎ 4926 4777; 21-23 Darby St) Novocastrians have taken this reasonably new, comfy establishment to their hearts and livers, and if you like your schooners disguised as pints, you will, too.

Goldberg's Coffee House (☎ 4929 3122; 137 Darby St; meals $6-20; ☾ open until midnight) If Sartre were reincarnated as a surfie, this is where he'd get his short blacks. Goldberg's dim European atmosphere encourages lengthy stays, while the patio out the back is a welcome respite from Darby St traffic.

Entertainment

CINEMA

Showcase City Cinemas (☎ 4929 5019; 31 Wolf St; admission $10) Hollywood new releases alternate with foreign and independent movies.

LIVE MUSIC

For all the money poured into attracting high-tech business, cleaning up the air and greening the foreshore, the one thing that really gave Newcastle's reputation a boost was the super-successful band, Silverchair. Newcastle is *the* place for live music on the north coast. The popularity of different venues waxes and wanes, so get the latest from hostel staff, music store employees

or Thursday's paper. Most pubs only have shows Wednesday to Sunday.

Cambridge Hotel (☎ 4962 2459; 789 Hunter St) This is the archetypal Newcastle band pub. While it's eased off a bit since launching Silverchair, touring national bands and local acts still play here.

Northern Star Hotel (☎ 4961 1087; cnr Beaumont & James Sts) This hotel on Beaumont St (cunningly disguised as Finn McCools – go into the back room for gigs) is your best bet for up-and-coming or alternative bands, while **SJ's** (☎ 4961 2537; cnr Beaumont & Hudson Sts; ☾ bands Fri & Sat) bright lights, hard chairs and stricter-than-usual dress code suggest you'll have an uncomfortable, but fashionable, night out.

Wickham Park Hotel (☎ 4962 3501; 61 Maitland Rd) Off Beaumont but still in Hamilton, this gay-friendly venue has a great welcoming, neighbourhood pub feel. All kinds show up for Thursday's amateur night, and some of them are even good. On Sunday afternoon there is an acoustic show in the beer garden.

NIGHTCLUBS

Mercury Lounge (☎ 4926 1119; 23 Watt St) TVs screen cult cartoons and the dimly lit bar serves great cocktails (though most of the crowd here are drinking water). Dancing starts around 11pm. There's dancing at the **Crown & Anchor Hotel** (☎ 4929 1027; cnr Hunter & Perkins Sts) on the weekends, popular with under 21s.

Getting There & Away

AIR

Qantas (☎ 13 13 13; www.qantas.com.au; 79 Hunter St; ☾ 9am-5pm Mon-Fri, 8.45am-12.15pm Sat) flies to Belmont, about 25 minutes' drive south of Newcastle, or Williamtown, the same distance north. Sydney to Belmont fares start around $100; Melbourne to Williamtown is around $180.

BUS

Nearly all long-distance buses stop behind Newcastle station.

Port Stephens Coaches (☎ 4982 2940; www.psbuses .nelsonbay.com; 17a Port Stephens Dr, Anna Bay) Goes from Nelson Bay via Anna Bay and Williamtown airport to Newcastle ($10, 1¼hr, 13 times daily) and from Newcastle to Sydney ($20, 2hr 10min, once daily).

Rover Coaches (☎ 4990 1699; www.rovercoaches .com.au; 231-233 Vincent St, Cessnock) Travels to Cessnock ($10.60, 1¼hr, 5 times daily).

Sid Fogg's Coaches (☎ 4928 1088; www.sidfoggs
.com.au; RMB 2324 Main Rd, Fullerton Cove) Travels to
Canberra ($52, 7½hr, once daily).

CAR
ARA (☎ 1800 243 122, 4962 2488; www.ararental.com.au;
86 Belford St, Broadmeadow) rents cars from $29 a
day. You'll find the big rental agencies
along Tudor St in Hamilton.

TRAIN
CityRail (☎ 13 15 00; www.cityrail.nsw.gov.au) trains
travel frequently to Sydney ($17, 3 hours).

Getting Around
TO/FROM THE AIRPORT
Port Stephens Coaches (☎ 4982 2940; www.psbuses.nel
sonbay.com; 17a Port Stephens Dr, Anna Bay) goes to
and from Williamtown airport frequently
($5.10, 35 minutes) en route to Nelson Bay.
Local bus Nos 310, 311, 322 and 363 go to
Belmont from Newcastle train station ($2.50,
1½ hours). A **taxi** (☎ 4979 3000) costs $42 to
either airport.

BUS
Most **local buses** (☎ 13 15 00; www.newcastle.sta.nsw
.gov.au) operate every half-hour on weekdays,
less frequently on weekends. Fares are time-
based, with one-hour ($2.50), four-hour
($4.90) and all day ($7.60) passes available.
The main depot is near the train station.

FERRY
From Queens Wharf, the Stockton ferry
($1.80) runs every half hour from 5.15am
until midnight on Friday and Saturday,
stopping at 11pm Monday to Thursday
and 10pm on Sunday.

LOWER HUNTER VALLEY
☎ 02
There's only one reason to come to the
Lower Hunter: wine. If you're not interested in wine, tasting wine, drinking wine
or being drunk on wine, you may get bored
very quickly (though it's true that you can
now – unlike a few years ago – get a beer in
the Hunter). If you like wine, then you'll be
like a pig in the unmentionable.

Before you hit the Hunter, try to figure
out what kind of a visit you want to have.
If you don't care much about wine, think
about taking a tour from Newcastle; the
hostels or the visitors centre (154) can

STAYING UNDER .05
Do whatever you can to avoid driving while
you're in the Hunter. If you have to have a
car, remember it's illegal to drive with a
blood alcohol level over 0.05% (it's also
theoretically illegal to ride a bike if you're
over the limit). Wine tastes come in 20mL
doses. Five of these in an hour will put the
average woman close to being over the
limit. A big guy can usually have about
twice as much. Rather than tasting the full
range at every vineyard, ask for what's best,
and just try that. Start with dry whites earlier in the day, and finish up with heavy reds
or dessert wines when you're almost done.

help you out. If you know you like wine,
but you're not sure where to start with
this whole tasting business, visit some of
the bigger vineyards: they're friendly and
relaxed, and have a huge range of wines to
choose from. If this is your first visit to the
Hunter, drop by some of the smaller vineyards mentioned here to taste the area's
specialities. Whatever your plan is, grab a
copy of the *Hunter Valley Wine Country
Visitors Guide* (available at visitors centres
all over NSW): it has summaries of all the
vineyards, and an excellent map. Really,
there are so many wineries to choose from,
you can't go wrong, and it's all free.

Orientation
Most of the Lower Hunter's attractions lie
in an area bordered to the north by the
New England Hwy and to the south by the
Wollombi/Maitland Rd. The main town
serving the area is Cessnock, close to the
southern edge of the vineyards. Most of
the action happens along Broke Rd (possibly the worst-paved road in the state). The
'town' of Pokolbin – really just a collection
of restaurants and stores – is at the intersection of Broke and McDonald Rds. The map
that comes with the free *Hunter Valley Wine
Country Visitors Guide* is very useful.

Information
INTERNET ACCESS
Check your emails at **Cessnock library** (☎ 4993
4399; www.cessnock.nsw.gov.au; 65-67 Vincent St, Cessnock; ☯ 9am-5pm Mon & Wed, 9am-5pm & 6.30-8pm
Tue, Thu & Fri, 9am-noon Sat).

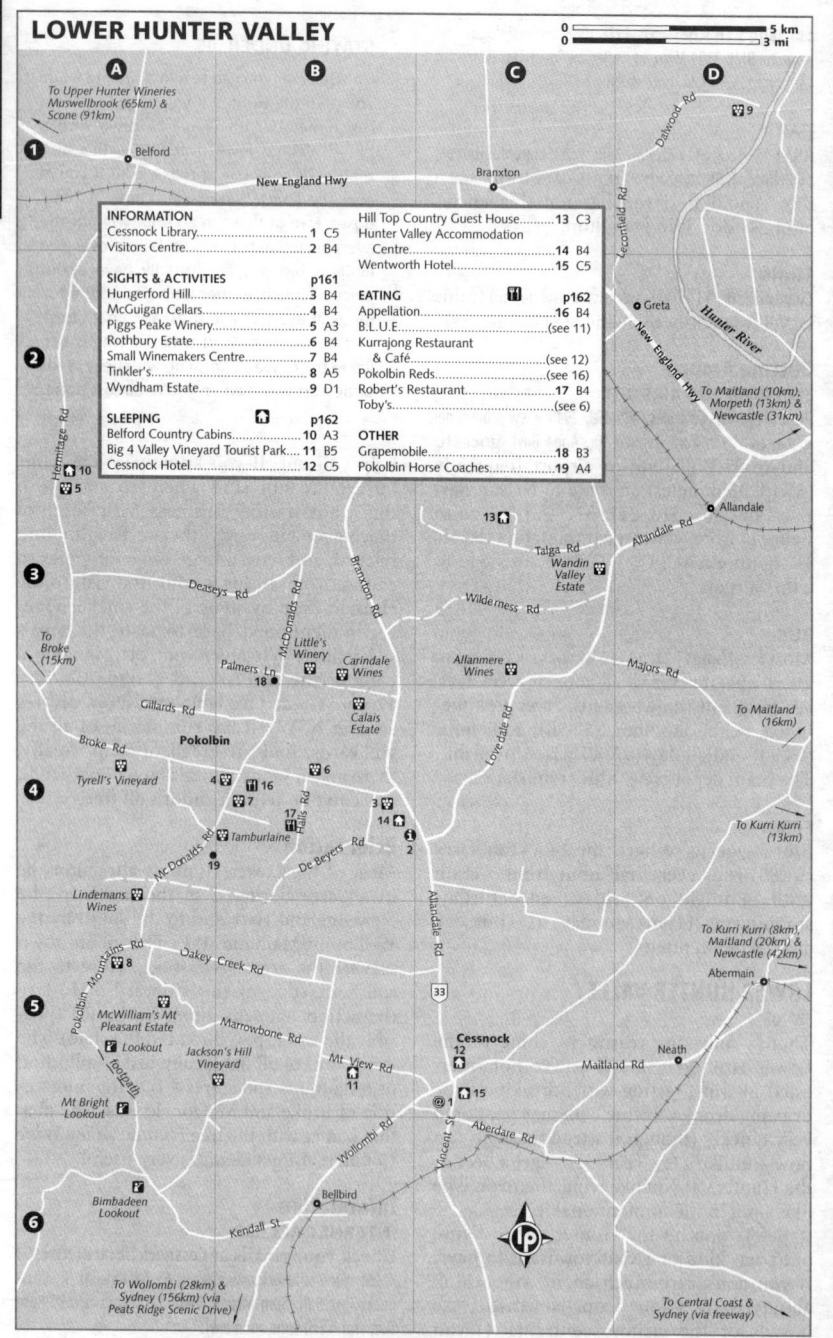

LOWER HUNTER VALLEY

| 0 | | | 5 km |
| 0 | | | 3 mi |

To Upper Hunter Wineries
Muswellbrook (65km) &
Scone (91km)

Belford

New England Hwy

Branxton

INFORMATION
Cessnock Library................................1 C5
Visitors Centre.................................2 B4

SIGHTS & ACTIVITIES p161
Hungerford Hill.................................3 B4
McGuigan Cellars..............................4 B4
Piggs Peake Winery...........................5 A3
Rothbury Estate.................................6 B4
Small Winemakers Centre..................7 B4
Tinkler's..8 A5
Wyndham Estate................................9 D1

SLEEPING 🏠 p162
Belford Country Cabins.....................10 A3
Big 4 Valley Vineyard Tourist Park....11 B5
Cessnock Hotel..................................12 C5

Hill Top Country Guest House...........13 C3
Hunter Valley Accommodation
  Centre...14 B4
Wentworth Hotel..............................15 C5

EATING 🍴 p162
Appellation.......................................16 B4
B.L.U.E..(see 11)
Kurrajong Restaurant
  & Café......................................(see 12)
Pokolbin Reds..............................(see 16)
Robert's Restaurant...........................17 B4
Toby's..(see 6)

OTHER
Grapemobile.....................................18 B3
Pokolbin Horse Coaches....................19 A4

Greta

Hunter River

To Maitland (10km),
Morpeth (13km) &
Newcastle (31km)

Allandale

Wandin
Valley
Estate

Talga Rd

Deaseys Rd

Branxton Rd

Wilderness Rd

To Broke
(15km)

Little's
Winery

Carindale
Wines

Allanmere
Wines

Majors Rd

Palmers Ln

Gillards Rd

Calais
Estate

To Maitland
(16km)

Broke Rd

Pokolbin

Tyrell's Vineyard

Lovedale Rd

To Kurri Kurri
(13km)

Tamburlaine

De Beyers Rd

To Kurri Kurri (8km),
Maitland (20km) &
Newcastle (42km)

Lindemans
Wines

Oakey Creek Rd

Abermain

McWilliam's Mt
Pleasant Estate

Marrowbone Rd

Mt View Rd

Cessnock

Neath

Maitland Rd

Lookout

Jackson's Hill
Vineyard

Mt Bright
Lookout

Bimbadeen
Lookout

Kendall St

Wollombi Rd

Vincent St

Aberdare Rd

Bellbird

To Wollombi (28km) &
Sydney (156km) (via
Peats Ridge Scenic Drive)

To Central Coast &
Sydney (via freeway)

NEW SOUTH WALES

TOURIST INFORMATION

Hunter Valley visitors centre (☎ 4990 4477; www.winecountry.com.au; Allandale Rd; ⏰ 9am-5pm Mon-Sat, 9am-4pm Sun) Huge and well-organised with very helpful staff who are excellent at finding accommodation. Info also posted outside if you arrive out of hours.

Maitland visitors centre (☎ 4931 2800; www.mait landtourism.nsw.gov.au; cnr New England Hwy & High St; ⏰ 9am-5pm)

Sights

WINERIES

Most cellar doors are open from 10am to 4.30pm at least.

Family-friendly, easy-going and affordable **McGuigan Cellars** (☎ 4998 7402; www.mcguigan wines.com.au; McDonalds Rd; tour $2, 11am, noon & 2pm Sat & Sun; ⏰ 9.30am-5pm) is a great place to start your wine-tasting career. There's a cheese factory on the premises (that's what that smell is).

Attitude-free **Wyndham Estate** (☎ 4938 3444; wyndhamestate.com.au; 700 Dalwood Rd; free tour 11am; ⏰ 10am-4.30pm) is off the New England Hwy. Wyndhams has festivals, music and a restaurant (try the tasting platter that matches foods and wines).

Also among the megawineries, friendly, informative **Rothbury Estate** (☎ 4998 7363; Broke Rd; free tour 10.30am; ⏰ 9.30am-4.30pm) has frequent music events. It draws its grapes from vineyards all over the country so you can taste their Hunter wines and compare them with wines from elsewhere. Their café, **Toby's**, has good sandwiches ($10).

Family-run **Tinkler's** (☎ 4998 7435; Pokolbin Mountains Rd; ⏰ 9am-5pm) has been kicking around for five generations, though only the last of the family turned their talents from farming to wine-making. The Shiraz and the nonconfrontational Volcanic Ash dessert wine are definitely worth a taste. The Tinkler ancestors rest happy in their graves: avocados, eating grapes, honey and all kinds of fruit are also for sale.

At **Hungerford Hill** (☎ 4998 7666; www.hunger fordhill.com.au; 1 Broke Rd; ⏰ 9am-5pm Mon-Fri, 10am-5pm Sat & Sun) try one of their heart-warming fortified wines. It's not cheating to enjoy the Hilltops Shiraz, grown in Young, in the south of the state.

Relaxed and chatty, **Piggs Peake Winery** (☎ 1800 676 312, 6574 7000; 697 Hermitage Rd; ⏰ 10am-4pm Mon-Sat, 10am-3pm Sun) makes a range of 'contemporary' wines like tempra-

nillo and marsanne. Even more boutique, the **Small Winemakers Centre** (☎ 4998 7668; www .smallwinemakerscentre.com.au; McDonalds Rd; ⏰ 10am-5pm) acts as a cellar door for 10 wine makers who don't have their own vineyards.

MAITLAND

The former coal-mining centre of Maitland is the northern gateway into the Hunter. Established as a convict settlement in 1818, Maitland has hung on to a lot of its old Georgian and Victorian buildings, its churches in particular. Many of Maitland's streets are one-way, and none of them seem to meet at right angles, so driving around here is a real laugh-riot. If you have a car, park it (though you may never find it again), walk around and soak up the atmosphere. Maitland seems to have an unusually high number of op-shops, so this may be your chance to pick up that Maitland High School sweater or 'I'm barking mad for the Maitland Kennel Club' badge you've always wanted. Failing that, get a bit of culture at the **Maitland City Art Gallery** (☎ 4933 1657; Church St; admission free; ⏰ 1-4pm).

Tours

Visitors centres and many places to stay in Sydney and Newcastle can help you organise a tour of the Lower Hunter.

Take a wine- and cheese-tasting outing with **Hunter Valley Day Tours** (☎ 4938 5031; www.huntertourism.com/daytours; ⏰ 8am-9pm) and they'll pick you up from Cessnock, Maitland or anywhere in the valley ($80), or Newcastle ($95).

Grapemobile (☎ 0500 804 039; www.grapemobile .com.au; cnr McDonalds Rd & Palmers Lane) organises bike rides through the vineyards, including a support bus and meals.

Pokolbin Horse Coaches (☎ 4998 7305; www .hunterweb.com.au/pokolbinhorsecoaches; McDonalds Rd) runs day tours in an open-air carriage that will knock you back $69.

Enough of ground-level grapes! You need to see these vineyards from a long way up in the air, preferably at sunrise! **Balloon Aloft** (☎ 1800 028 568, 1938 1955; www .balloonaloft.com; Lot 1 Main Rd, North Rothbury; flights $225-250) can help you.

Tumbleweed Trike Tours (☎ 4938 1245; scottocon nell@optusnet.com.au) will motor you around the Hunter on customised motorbikes that have one seat up the front, two at the back.

Festivals & Events

For up-to-date information, see www.wine country.com.au or pick up the free *Hunter Valley Wine Country Visitors Guide* from visitors centres.

The **Harvest Festival** runs from February to May. During May's **Lovedale Long Lunch**, seven wineries and chefs gang up to produce gut-bursting lunches, served with music and art. Cessnock has its turn in September, when it celebrates **Budfest** (nothing to do with toking bongs, apparently), while October is for listening, with **Jazz in the Vines** (jazzinthevines.com.au) going head-to-head with **Opera in the Vineyards** (www.4-d.com.au).

Sleeping

Staff at the visitors centre are expert at matching accommodation to your budget and standards. Cessnock is a perfectly acceptable alternative to staying in the vineyards. Prices are higher on weekends, and there is usually a minimum two-night stay.

VINEYARDS

Belford Country Cabins (☎ 6574 7100; www.belford cabins.com.au; 659 Hermitage Rd; midweek d $100, extra person $20; ⚡) In bushland at the top end of Hermitage Rd, out among the kangaroos and possums, these comfortable, homy, self-contained cabins have at least two bedrooms; one cabin sleeps 12. There's a pool, barbecues and a games room.

Hill Top Country Guest House (☎ 4930 7111; www.hilltopguesthouse.com.au; 81 Talga Rd; midweek d $90-240) Off Lovedale Rd, this guesthouse has great views, horse riding, in-house massage, canoeing, a pool and a billiard room.

Hunter Valley Accommodation Centre (☎ 4991 4222; www.huntervalleyaccommodation.com; 210 Allandale Rd; midweek dm/s/d $25/60/70) It doesn't look like much, but it's affordable and well located, right by the visitors centre. Motel rooms have bathrooms; dorm rooms have a bathroom for $10 more. There's a pool.

CESSNOCK

Cessnock Hotel (☎ 4990 1002; 234 Wollombi Rd; s/d from $35/65) This restored pub has very cute, cottagey rooms – a real cut above the usual pub accommodation.

Wentworth Hotel (☎ 4990 1364; 36 Vincent St; s/d from $50/70) This pub has taken some care with its furnishings, and will give you breakfast with your room.

Big 4 Valley Vineyard Tourist Park (☎ 4990 2573; Mt View Rd; camp sites/caravan sites/deluxe cabins $20/40/80) This well-run park has a pool and an onsite Thai restaurant. De luxe cabins come with air-con, linen, bathroom and kitchen. It's just 1km to town or the nearest winery.

Prices at motels adjust to whatever the market will bear, with doubles starting at $65 mid-week. The **Cessnock Motel** (☎ 4990 2699; 13 Allandale Rd) and **Hunter Valley Motel** (☎ 4990 1722; 30 Allandale Rd) are outside town on the road to the vineyards.

MAITLAND

Imperial Hotel (☎ 4933 6566; www.shenanigans.com .au; 458 High St; s/d $50/65) A fair way from the vineyards, but very central within Maitland. Comfy rooms come with breakfast.

Eating

VINEYARDS

Many wineries have picnic tables and barbecues.

Pokolbin Reds (☎ 4998 7977; Pokolbin Village, Broke Rd; mains $24-30) Top-notch food, friendly service and a great wine list: a place this good should take on airs, but Pokolbin Reds manages to keep its feet on the ground. Anywhere that'll whip up a curry when someone says, 'I don't know what I want; do you have a curry?' deserves a gold star on its forehead.

Robert's Restaurant (☎ 4998 7330; Halls Rd; mains $32) Book ahead, as Robert's has quite a reputation. Award-winning chef Robert Molines also gives cooking classes.

Appellation (☎ 4998 7945; Pokolbin Village, Broke Rd; mains $8-15) Pull up a nouveau stool in the funky black-and-primary décor of Appellation and enjoy affordability. A café, bar and restaurant, it also does takeaway. Tuesday is $10 pasta night and on Sunday you can get a roast dinner with dessert for $20.

CESSNOCK

Kurrajong Restaurant & Café (☎ 4991 4414; 234 Wollombi Rd; mains $10-20; ☺ lunch Tue-Sun, dinner Tue-Sat) In the Cessnock Hotel, the Kurrajong serves updated steak sandwiches and nouveau bangers and mash in pleasant Victorian surroundings.

B.L.U.E (☎ 4991 7444; Big 4 Valley Vineyard Tourist Park, Mt View Rd; mains $10-15) In the caravan park, B.L.U.E has all the Thai classics and a good vegetarian selection.

Getting There & Around

There is almost no public transport around the vineyards. It may be easiest to hire a car in Sydney or Newcastle, or join an organised tour (see Tours; p161).

From Sydney, **Kean's** (☎ 1800 043 339, 6543 1322) buses run to Cessnock ($27, 2 hours 20 minutes). From Newcastle, **Rover Coaches** (☎ 4990 1699; www.rovercoaches.com.au) has buses to Cessnock ($10.60, 1¼ hours) and **Sid Fogg's** (☎ 1800 045 952) runs up the valley to Dubbo ($54, 6 hours) via Maitland.

CityRail (☎ 13 15 00; www.cityrail.nsw.gov.au) trains from Newcastle ($4.40, 30 minutes) and **CountryLink** (☎ 13 22 32; www.countrylink.nsw.gov.au) trains from Sydney ($30, 3 hours) stop in Maitland.

Grapemobile (☎ 0500 804 039; www.grapemobile.com.au; cnr McDonalds Rd & Palmers Lane) hires bikes from their vineyard location ($12/hr, $22/half day, $30/day).

Vineyard Shuttle Service (☎ 4998 7779; www.vineyardshuttle.com.au) will take you from your accommodation to anywhere in the valley and back for $10, which is great if you don't want to stint on wine with dinner.

UPPER HUNTER VALLEY

☎ 02

The Upper Hunter's classic vineyard landscapes, loomed over by rugged granite outcrops, rival those of Napa or Bordeaux. Local wine makers are never too busy to share their intimate knowledge of the vines, so allow time to explore, especially since the area is far more spread out than the lower valley.

The nearest town to the wineries is Denman, a sleepy little place 25km southwest of Muswellbrook. A great route into the Upper Hunter from Sydney follows the very winding Putty Rd from Windsor to Singleton, passing through some of the most breathtakingly scenic parts of Wollemi and Yengo National Parks.

Information

The Muswellbrook **visitors centre** (☎ 6541 4050; www.muswellbrook.org.au; 87 Hill St; ◷ 9am-5pm), at the north end of town, is in the same premises as the **Upper Hunter Wine Centre** (☎ 6541 4211; www.hunterwine.com.au; ◷ 10am-5pm), where you can taste wine from all over the area.

Scone **visitors centre** (☎ 6545 1526; cnr Kelly & Susan Sts; ◷ 9am-5pm; 🖳) has information about Scone's frequent race meets.

Sights

WINERIES

Rosemount Estate (☎ 6549 6400; www.rosemountestates.com.au; Rosemount Rd; ◷ 10am-4pm), around 8km from Denman, is one of Australia's biggest exporters – if you're American, this is one Australian winery you may well be familiar with.

The quintessential small independent wine maker, **James Estate** (☎ 6547 5168; www.jamesestatewines.com.au; 951 Rylstone Rd, Sandy Hollow; ◷ 10am-4.30pm), lies in a beautiful valley 18km west of Denman. Its medal-winning Reserve Shiraz has been rated among the world's top 100 wines.

There are other smaller wineries out at Wybong. Ask at the Upper Hunter Wine Centre for details (see Information).

GOULBURN RIVER NATIONAL PARK

At the southwestern edge of the Hunter Valley, this national park follows the Goulburn River as it cuts through sandstone gorges. The route was used by Aboriginal people travelling from the western plains to the sea – the area is rich in cave art. Emus may steal your sandwiches and if you're around early in the morning or late in the afternoon, you might spot a platypus or a cute red-necked wallaby (watch out for them on the roads).

There are short bushwalks to various lookouts, and basic **camp sites** (☎ 6372 7199; admission free) with no facilities or drinking water. The Mudgee **NPWS office** (☎ 6372 7199) and Mudgee visitors centre (p199) have more information. The only partly sealed approach road is from Merriwa, 35km west of Sandy Hollow on the Denman road, but the unsealed portions are pretty decent.

HORSE STUD FARMS

Welcome to *My Friend Flicka* land, the answer to the dreams of the little girl in all of us. With over 40 horse stud farms in the area, Scone dubs itself 'the horse capital of Australia', quite within its rights.

BURNING MOUNTAIN

Off the highway, 20km north of Scone, is an underground coal seam that has been smoking for over 5000 years. A steep 3.5km-return walking track leads up through the nature reserve to puffing vents. Don't expect volcanic displays; do expect fart jokes.

Festivals

The town comes alive in May for 12 days during the **Horse Festival** (☎ 6545 3688) with racing carnivals, open studs, stock-horse shows and working events.

Tours

Upper Hunter Tours (☎ 6547 2442; www.upperhunter tours.com.au; 87 Hill St, Muswellbrook) runs day tours of some of the bigger studs ($11 to $260 per person, depending on number of studs visited and number of people; call Craig for details).

Sleeping & Eating

VINEYARD

Morna May Cottage (☎ 6547 2088; www.mornamay .com.au; 310 Rosemount Rd; s/d $80/ 120) This is one of the few places where you can lie in a claw-footed bathtub and look out over vineyards with almost no chance of seeing anyone. Both spacious cottages are self-contained; one has two bedrooms.

DENMAN

Royal Hotel (☎ 6547 2226; www.upper-hunter.com /Denman/Royal; Ogilvie St; s/d $25/35) Drop by this hotel for a real taste of country life, and a bar full of blokes in Stubbies and Chesty Bonds singlets. Accommodation at the Royal is simple but decent, and popular with grape-pickers. Its **Renaissance Restaurant** (mains $16-20) has fancy, big-city dishes like lemon ricotta chicken and Mediterranean lamb.

MUSWELLBROOK

There are a few motels around the visitors centre.

Noah's in the Valley (☎ 6543 2833; www.noahs inthevalley.com.au; 91 Bridge St; s/d $70/85) This slightly worn motor inn pretends to be a resort but is really just a serviceable motel with a pool.

Old Manse (☎ 6543 3965; www.anoldmanse .com.au;106 Hill St; s/d $70/90; ⚓) Built in 1877 and decorated in the famed 'Swedish sauna' style, the Old Manse is relaxed and central. There's a pool, rooms have a bathroom and kitchen, and breakfast is included.

Palatino's in the Hunter (☎ 6541 2211; 142 Bridge St; mains $12-20; ⊙ 9am-late) Every wine on the extensive list here is available by the glass, the food is better than you'd expect for a country town, and the atmosphere

is very casual. You can dine at candle-lit courtyard tables or inside the historic (and haunted) Loxton House.

SCONE

Scone YHA (☎ 6545 2072; yhascone@hunterlink.net.au; 1151 Segenhoe Rd; dm/d $18/45) You know you're out in the country at this wonderfully laid-back hostel, which is a renovated schoolhouse. Hammocks hang from towering lemon gums and there are paddocks full of horses. The manager has worked hard on the hostel's garden, which means you get fresh herbs and tomatoes, plus eggs. Inside, everything is as neat as a new pin. A taxi from Scone train station will cost you about $5.

Belmore Hotel (☎ 6545 2078; 98 Kelly St; s/d $15/ 30) The rooms here are basic, a bit grubby, but bearable. By the time you read this, however, renovations may have been completed. There's a beer garden and tavern grill out the back.

Segenhoe B&B (☎ 6543 7382; users.hunterlink .net.au/~mbfsr/; 56 Main Rd, Aberdeen; d $110-150; ⚓) In the Scots-obsessed hamlet of Aberdeen, Segenhoe B&B is as olde worlde as all gette outte. This big sandstone house, built in 1834, sits in a pretty Italianesque garden. Rooms are laden with frills and bows, and the kind owners offer not just breakfast, but port and whisky as well (though maybe not with breakfast).

Asser House Café (☎ 6545 3571; 202 Kelly St; mains $4-10; ⊙ 10am-5pm Mon-Fri, 10am-3pm Sat) Choose from all kinds of sandwiches and some sizeable and yummy cakes. The coffee's good and the atmosphere is sturdily old-fashioned.

Entertainment

Scone Civic Theatre (☎ 6545 1569; 144 Kelly St) This cinema shows mostly mainstream new releases in an Art Deco cinema.

Getting There & Around

Kean's (☎ 1800 043 339, 6543 1322) operates bus services that run from Sydney to Muswellbrook ($35, 3½ hours) and Scone ($42, 3 hours, 50 minutes) and from Port Macquarie to Scone ($75, 11 hours). **Country-Link** (☎ 13 22 32; www.countrylink.nsw.gov.au) trains travel from Sydney to Scone ($47.30, 1 hour 18 minutes) and Muswellbrook ($41.80, 4 hours).

NEWCASTLE TO PORT MACQUARIE
Port Stephens

About an hour's drive north of Newcastle, this huge sheltered bay stretches more than 20km inland and takes in the 'dolphin capital of Australia', **Nelson Bay** (population 7000), all kinds of adventure activities, and several near-deserted beaches fringed by bungalows.

INFORMATION

The point-and-pick menu of activity options at the Nelson Bay **visitors centre** (☎ 1800 808 900, 02-4981 1579; www.portstephens .org.au; Victoria Pde; ☼ 9am-5pm) is a masterpiece of organisation.

SIGHTS

At the mouth of the Myall River, opposite Nelson Bay, are the small towns of **Tea Gardens**, on the river, and **Hawks Nest**, on the beach. **Jimmy's Beach** at Hawks Nest fronts a glass-like stretch of water, while **Bennett's Beach** has great views of Broughton Island.

On the southern side of the Tomaree Peninsula, **One Mile Beach** is usually deserted except for surfers. Further south you can hang loose at the surfside village of **Anna Bay**, backed by the incredible **Stockton Bight**, the longest barrier sand dune in Australia, which stretches 35km to Newcastle. At the far west end of the beach the wreck of the *Sygna* founders in the water.

About a half hour by boat from Nelson Bay, **Broughton Island** is human-free but home to muttonbirds, little penguins, and tons of species of fish. The diving is great and the beaches are incredibly secluded.

Look out for the **Rock** (not one of Australia's 'big things', as it's actually smaller than the genuine article – Uluru) at the Pacific Hwy turnoff to Tea Gardens.

ACTIVITIES

You can hire gear from **Dive Nelson Bay** (☎ 02-4981 2491; divenelsonbay@ozemail.com.au; Shop 5, 35 Stockton St; introductory course $180) or take dive classes in the bay and at Broughton Island.

Also hiring gear, **Hawks Nest Dive Centre** (☎ 02-4997 0442; www.hawksnestdive.com.au; 87a Marine Dr, Tea Gardens; dive courses from $90) provides many kinds of dive courses, from beginners ($90) to comprehensive Open Water Certification ($500). The centre also runs

LOWER NORTH COAST

0 — 20 km
0 — 12 mi

snorkelling tours ($40) and Broughton Island walking tours ($70).

Even if you've never been on a horse before, **Horse Paradise** (☎ 02-4965 1877; users.bigpond .com/horseparadise; Nelson Bay Rd, Williamtown; tours from $35), will take you on a little ride through the dunes or the Port Stephens bushland.

Other activities available through the visitors centre include fishing, helicopter rides and tours of Barrington Tops National Park, Hunter Valley wineries and Maitland architecture.

TOURS

Imagine (☎ 02-4984 9000; www.portstephens.org.au /imagine; 123 Stockton St; cruises from $20) Ride a sailboat run by Frenchmen and look for dolphins (Imagine claims a 99% success rate spotting them). Eco-accredited by the Nature and Ecotourism Accreditation Program (NEAP), Imagine also has snorkelling tours.

Moonshadow (☎ 02-4984 9388; www.moonshadow .com.au; Shop 3, 35 Stockton St; cruises from $18) Moonshadow's cruises start with the basic dolphin watch, and run to seven-hour visits to Broughton Island. Eco-accredited by NEAP, Moonshadow's big catamarans include a bar and underwater cameras.

Port Stephens 4WD Eco-Tours (☎ 02-4982 7277; tours from $20) Drive around Stockton sand dunes, visit the Sygna and go sand-boarding (you'll be cleaning out the crannies for days afterwards).

Sand Safaris (☎ 02-4965 0215; www.sandsafaris.com .au; 173 Nelson Bay Rd, Williamtown; tours from $110) Sand Safaris gives you your very own quad bike (a superstable motorbike that looks embarrassingly like a lawnmower) and takes you out on the dunes for some full-on – yet ecologically sensitive – hooning around.

SLEEPING

In Nelson Bay, Government St between Stockton and Church Sts is lined with motels and hotels, as is Ocean Beach in Hawkes Nest. Shoal Bay, virtually a suburb of Nelson Bay, mixes accommodation with stores and restaurants. Anna Bay is the closest hamlet to One Mile Beach.

Nelson Bay B&B (☎ 02-4984 3655; www.nelsonbay bandb.nelsonbay.com; 81 Stockton St, Nelson Bay; d $80-180) More like a tiny boutique hotel, this gay-friendly, modern guesthouse is secluded among tall trees off a semiprivate drive. One room has its own spa bath.

Shoal Bay Holiday Park (☎ 1800 600 200, 02-4981 1427; www.beachsideholidays.com.au; Shoal Bay Rd, Shoal Bay; camp sites/d from $19/39; 🖳 🏕) Cabins at this top-notch caravan park range from

faux-African tents-on-platforms to the Outrigger Villa, with two bedrooms, bathroom, kitchen, TV, VCR, cable and air-con (d from $80). There are daily activities for kids.

Melaleuca Surfside Backpackers (☎ 02-4981 9422; www.myportstephens.com/melaleuca; 33 Eucalyptus Dr, One Mile Beach; camp sites/dm/d $13/25/70) These wooden cabins, set amid peaceful scrub right across from the beach, were custom-built from red cedar.

Samurai Beach Bungalows (☎ 02-4982 1921; www.portstephens.org.au/samurai; cnr Frost Rd & Robert Connell Cl, Anna Bay; dm/d $20/55) Rustically furnished wooden-floored cabins are separated by bushland and lawns; it's very pleasant. There's an outdoor camp kitchen, surfboards and bikes.

O'Carrollyn's (☎ 02-4982 2801; www.ocarrollyns .com.au; 36 Eucalyptus Dr, One Mile Beach; d $90-160) These cabins are all wheelchair accessible, with custom-built bathrooms and wheelchair access to a beautiful, near-deserted beach. All are self-contained, and include TV and VCR. The cabins are surrounded by landscaped gardens, and there's a high chance you'll see koalas from your front step.

Other recommendations:

Shoal Bay Resort & Spa (☎ 1800 181 810, 02-4981 1555; www.shoalbayresort.com; Beachfront Rd, Shoal Bay; d $90-300; 🏊) On-site health club and day spa and multiple swimming pools. In low season, self-contained Zenith apartments (d $90) are great value.

Tea Gardens Hotel/Motel (☎ 02-4997 0203; Marine Dr, Tea Gardens; s/d from $44/60) Cute pink-and-blue rooms front the pub's grassy beer garden and pool.

Shoal Bay Backpackers & Motel (☎ 02-4981 0982; www.portstephens.org.au/shoalbaymotel-yha; 59-61 Beachfront Rd, Shoal Bay; dm/d $19/60; 🏊) Right on the beach, but a little worn.

One Mile Beach Holiday Park (☎ 02-4982 1112; www.onemilebeach.com; 260 Gan Gan Rd, One Mile Beach; camp sites/d cabins from $22/55) On the beach, with a swimming pool, sauna, game room and tennis courts. Beach house cabins (from d $135) have three bedrooms, air-con, TV, VCR, stereo, bathroom, full kitchen and laundry.

EATING

Nelson Bay marina has several places to eat, suitable for most budgets and tastes.

Chez Jules (☎ 02-4981 4500; Cinema Mall, Stockton St, Nelson Bay; mains $22-26) Your grandma would love the award-winning European food and posh atmosphere. Jules does dinner-and-a-movie deals with the nearby cinema.

Rob's on the Boardwalk (☎ 02-4984 4444; D'Albora Marina, Nelson Bay; mains $12-27) The standout from several seafood restaurants along the waterfront, Rob's has great oysters, a good wine list and a big, relaxed outdoor eating area.

Incredible Edibles (☎ 02-4981 4511; cnr Donaldson & Stockton Sts, Nelson Bay; sandwiches from $5) This great deli is the perfect place to get a sandwich to take on your dolphin-spotting tour.

Lazy Dayz Café & Tea Shoppe (☎ 02-4997 1889; 71 Marine Dr, Tea Gardens; mains $5-18) Cheerful staff serve startlingly fresh fish, burgers of all kinds, salads and steaks in this hybrid beach takeaway/country café.

GETTING THERE & AROUND
To drive from Nelson Bay to Tea Gardens, you have to backtrack to Raymond Terrace.

Port Stephens Coaches (☎ 02-4982 2940; www.ps buses.nelsonbay.com; 17a Port Stephens Dr, Anna Bay) goes from Nelson Bay via Anna Bay to Newcastle ($10, 1¼ hours, 13 times daily). The 9am bus from Nelson Bay continues to Sydney ($25, 3½ hours).

Port Stephens Ferry Service (☎ 0412-682 117, 02-4982 2958; www.portstephens-multimedia.com.au; Nelson Bay Public Jetty) chugs from Nelson Bay to Tea Gardens and back three times a day ($17 return, 1 hour).

Barrington Tops National Park
This **World Heritage wilderness** lies on the rugged Barrington Plateau, which rises to almost 1600m. Northern rainforest butts into southern sclerophyll here, creating one of Australia's most diverse ecosystems. Even hedonists who care naught for biodiversity will get a kick out of giant strangler figs, mossy Antarctic beech forests, limpid rainforest swimming holes and pocket-sized pademelons (note: it is illegal to put pademelons in your pocket).

There are walking trails and lookouts near Gloucester Tops, Careys Peak, Williams River (wheelchair accessible) and Jerusalem Creek. Be prepared for cold snaps, and even snow, at any time. All drinking water must be boiled.

Day tours to Barrington Tops can be organised through Nelson Bay **visitors centre** (☎ 1800 808 900, 02-4981 1579; www.portstephens.org .au; Victoria Pde; 9am-5pm). **Barrington Canoe Adventures** (☎ 02-6558 4316; www.canoebarrington.com .au; 774 Barrington East Rd) runs white-water trips out of its riverside lodge, 14km from Gloucester. Weekend packages including accommodation and guide cost $290. Rent a kayak from $55 a day.

From Newcastle, the road through Morpeth and Paterson to Dungog is dreamy, passing by rolling green fields, historic towns, frolicking horses and stands of silver birch and ghost gums.

There's camping at **Devil's Hole** (free), **Junction Pools** (per person $3) and **Gloucester River** (per person $5). Contact Gloucester **NPWS office** (☎ 02-6538 5300) for more information.

CountryLink (☎ 13 22 32; www.countrylink.nsw .gov.au) train/coach combos run from Newcastle to Dungog ($11, 1½ hours).

Myall Lakes National Park
Boaters, fishers, sailboarders and canoeists love Myall, a patchwork of coastal lakes, islands, forest and beaches. There are bushwalks through coastal rainforest

---

THE AUTHOR'S CHOICE

Barrington Guest House (☎ 02-4995 3212; www.barrington-g-house.com.au; Salisbury; d with/without bathroom $105/70) Words cannot do justice to the trapped-in-a-time-warp atmosphere of this guesthouse on the southern fringe of Barrington Tops National Park. Book a room and you don't just get a place to sleep; you also get full board. Meals (nice and bland, to keep the oldies happy) are served on the dot of 8am, noon and 6pm. You'll be summoned to the dining room by a dinner bell, and seated in groups to facilitate conversation about the old days and the weather. Need more? Expect cordial and Nice biscuits for morning tea, and chocolate crackles for supper.

Opened in the 1930s (many of the guests seem to have been visiting regularly since then), Barrington also features a player piano, hordes of live-in possums, a kangaroo that likes to sleep in guests' beds, a river swimming hole, daily guided bushwalks and quiz nights. The park itself is one of Australia's most biologically diverse – alpine forest butts up against subtropical rainforest, producing a profusion of species. The ones you'll most likely see are tiny pademelons, hordes of grey kangaroos and rosellas, possums and the occasional glider.

and past beach dunes at **Mungo Brush** in the south, perfect for spotting wildflowers and dingoes. The best beaches and surf are in the north around **Seal Rocks**, where humpback whales sometimes visit.

Buladelah **visitors centre** (☎ 02-4997 4981; fax 4997 4210; cnr Crawford St & Pacific Hwy; ☺ 9am-5pm) has guides for hikers and information about camp grounds and **houseboat hire**. Canoes, sailboards and runabouts can be hired here.

Well-outfitted **Myall Shores Ecotourism Resort** (☎ 02-4997 4495; www.myallshores.com.au; Lake Rd, Bombah Pt; camp sites/d from $17/35), right on the water and in dense bushland, has cabins, a restaurant and bar, petrol, gas and basic groceries. The road from Bulahdelah is unsealed and lined with salmon gums and dairy farms.

Seal Rocks Camping Reserve (☎ 1800 112 234, 02-4977 6164; Kinka Rd, Seal Rocks; camp sites from $13, d from $43) is beside an excellent beach with onsite vans and cabins (d from $50); call ahead if you want one. There's a store-takeaway at Seal Rocks. The road from Bungwahl is largely unsealed. A **bunkhouse** (☎ 02-4997 6016; 2619 Lakes Way, Bungwahl) may have opened at the Seal Rocks turn-off by the time you read this.

Buhladelah has several motels. You can drive from Tea Gardens to Bulahdelah via the Bombah Point ferry ($3/0.60 per car/pedestrian) which crosses on the half-hour, 8am to 6pm.

The Lakes Way is a beautiful twisting road between Bulahdelah and Forster-Tuncurry with great views of lakes and forest. **Great Lakes Coaches** (☎ 1800 043 263) services this route, charging $47 from Sydney or $30 from Newcastle.

Forster-Tuncurry
☎ 02 / pop 17,996

Forster-Tuncurry are twin towns on either side of the sea entrance to Wallis Lake. Forster (pronounced Foster), the more-visited of the two, has all the charm of a mini–Gold Coast – high rises everywhere, and more development planned – but its beaches are pretty, there's an ocean bath and it's a good place to mingle with Aussie holiday makers. The **visitors centre** (☎ 6554 8799; www.greatlakes.org.au; Little St; ☺ 9am-5pm) is on the lake side of town.

Dolphin Lodge YHA (☎ 6555 8155; dolphin_lodge@hotmail.com; 43 Head St; dm/s/d $21/34/50; 🖳) has small common areas, but the staff are

very helpful, all rooms have bathrooms and the beach is right out the back. **Great Lakes Motor Inn** (☎ 6554 6955; glmotorinn@tsn.cc; 24 Head St; s/d from $50/70) is a comfortable motel between the beach and the shops. Suites with kitchen start at $90.

Overlooking the estuary, tiny **Rock Pearl** (☎ 0421-312 302; Pacific Arcade, Wharf St; mains $17) has modern, fusion interpretations of standard seafood dishes. **Jullienne's Coffee Café** (☎ 6557 5123; cnr Beach & Wharf Sts; mains $5-14) is good for breakfast. Slam tequila shots at **El Barracho** (☎ 6554 5573; 12 Wharf St; mains $16-22) with a mucho festivo crowd of Forsterians.

CountryLink (☎ 13 22 32; www.countrylink.nsw.gov.au) operates a bus-train combination to Sydney ($47, 5½ hours). Long-distance **King Bros** (☎ 6562 4724; www.kingbrosbus.com.au), **Great Lakes** (☎ 1800 043 263) and **McCafferty's/Greyhound** (☎ 13 14 99; www.mccaffertys.com.au) coaches stop in Forster between Sydney and Brisbane.

Manning Valley

From Forster-Tuncurry, the Pacific Hwy swings inland to riverside **Taree**, a large town serving the farms of the fertile Manning Valley. The **visitors centre** (☎ 1800 182 733, 6652 1900; Pacific Hwy; ☺ 9am-5pm) is down the street from the **Big Oyster**. The Oyster just didn't draw the crowds its backers hoped for, and eventually an adult education centre muscled in and began using the shellfish as offices. These days it's the crowning glory of a car yard.

Further west up the valley **Wingham Brush**, a patch of rainforest near the timber town of Wingham, is home to giant Moreton Bay figs and flying foxes. Its boardwalks are a thoroughfare from the town to the **Manning River** (why not take a dip?).

On the coast near Taree, the cute resort town of **Old Bar** has long, quiet beaches. **Badgers Beachouse** (☎ 6557 4224; badgersbeachouse@hotmail.com; David St; dm/d $30/50; 🖳) has a great 1970s-style living room and feels like the group house you always wished you lived in: a little grotty, but immensely cheerful.

PORT MACQUARIE
☎ 02 / pop 33,700

Port Macquarie rides on the koala's back. Surrounded by koala habitat, the town's best attractions are all related to this immoderately popular marsupial: there must

CHRIS MELLOR

Cruise at leisure the sparkling waters of **Sydney Harbour** (p88)

Travel the harbour in style
on a **ferry** (p136)

GILLIANNE TEDDER

CHRIS MELLOR

Spot the distinctive **Sydney Opera House** (p92)

MANFRED GOTTS

Feast your eyes on magnificent vistas in the **Royal National Park** (p139)

JOHN BORTHWICK

Be exhilarated by the surf at
Watego's Beach (p181)

Explore the south coast's old whaling-port
town of **Eden** (p218)

MANFRED GOTTS

Beach-bum with the bold and the beautiful at **Bondi** (p102)

ROSS BARNETT

be more taxidermied koalas per head of population here than anywhere else on the coast.

The town was founded in 1821 as a penal settlement for convicts who found life in Sydney Cove too easy. Port still has a bit of that edgy frontier atmosphere – maybe it's the ghosts of all those recalcitrants. This is a great spot for adventure activities; prices are lower than they are further north.

Information

The **visitors centre** (☎ 1800 025 935, 6659 4400; www.portmacquarieinfo.com.au; Clarence St; ☼ 8.30am-5pm Mon-Fri, 9am-4pm Sat & Sun) has lots of info on tours and adventure activities. The **NPWS office** (☎ 6586 8300; 152 Horton St; ☼ 9am-4.30pm Mon-Fri) can help with national park info.

Port Surf Hub (☎ 6584 4744; 57 Clarence St; ☼ 10am-7pm) has Internet access, as do hostels.

Sights
MUSEUMS & HISTORIC BUILDINGS

Viewing Port's colonial past is as easy as standing in the town centre, where you'll find the 1835 **garrison** (cnr Clarence & Hay Sts) and the 1869 **courthouse** (☎ 6584 1818; www.portmacquarieinfo.com.au/historiccourthouse; cnr Clarence & Hay Sts; admission $2; ☼ 10am-3.45pm Mon-Fri).

Visit **Roto House** (☎ 6584 2180; Lord St; admission by donation; ☼ 10am-4pm Mon-Fri, 9am-1pm Sat & Sun), built in 1890, to see how the landed middle classes used to live. The curator can tell you all the juicy details of the former owners' family history.

Port Macquarie Historical Society Museum (☎ 6583 1108; www.midcoast.com.au/~pmmuseum.htm; 22 Clarence St; admission $5; ☼ 9.30am-4.30pm Mon-Sat, 1-4.30pm Sun) is worth a visit if only for the terrifying baby dolls. They also have some great commemorative china, and an award-winning collection of Victorian frocks. With a whole room dedicated to the life of Matthew Flinders' cat Trim, the **Maritime Museum** (☎ 6583 1866; 6 William St; admission $4; ☼ 11am-3pm Tue-Sun) has its fair share of charm.

WILDLIFE

The **Koala Hospital** (☎ 6584 1522; www.midcoast.com.au/users/koalahos/; Lord St; admission by donation; ☼ 24hr) cares for sick and injured koalas picked up around Port Macquarie. You can wander through the outdoor enclosures or watch feedings (7.30am and 3pm). If you just have to get your hands on one of these cuddly little critters, visit **Billabong Koala Park** (☎ 6585 1060; 61 Billabong Dr, west of Pacific Hwy Interchange; adult/child $9.50/6; ☼ 9am-5pm), which breeds marsupials for zoos and private parks. Come for the pattings (10.30am, 1.30pm and 3.30pm) as the rest of the park is filler.

About 3km south of town, **Sea Acres Rainforest Centre** (☎ 6582 3355; Pacific Dr; adult/child $10/5.50; ☼ 9am-4.30pm) protects a 72-hectare pocket of coastal rainforest. There's an ecology centre and a café, and you can spot brush turkeys and lace monitors from the wheelchair-accessible boardwalk. There are access points to **Kooloonbung Creek Nature Reserve**, which has boardwalks and bushwalking trails, around the town centre.

Activities

There's great swimming and surfing at several beaches, starting at Town Beach and running south. Cruise operators line the waterfront near Town Wharf. The visitors centre can help with houseboat hire.

Boasting the biggest walls between Sydney and Coolangatta, **Centre of Gravity** (☎ 6581 3899; www.centre-of-gravity.com; 52 Jindalee Rd; ☼ noon-5pm Tue-Sat, till 9pm Tue & Thu) is an indoor rock climbing centre which also runs climbing courses. Entry is $15; hire of all the gear you'll need is $15.

Coastal Skydivers (☎ 6584 3655; www.coastalskydivers.com; Port Macquarie Airport; tandem skydive $290) also runs two-day free-fall courses.

Hastings River Boat Hire (☎ 6583 8811; Port Marina, Park St; ☼ 8am-4pm) have canoes from $12, ski bikes from $30.

High Adventure (☎ 1800 063 648, 6556 5265; www.highadventure.com.au; Pacific Hwy, John's River) runs courses rather than one-off tandem flights. Most of these run for several days and start at around $500.

Call **Port Macquarie Camel Safaris** (☎ 1800 501 879, 5538 4300; www.nnsw.worldtourism.com.au/pm-camelsafaris; Lighthouse Beach, Matthew Flinders Dr) for info on more extensive tours; $12 gets you a 20-minute ride along Lighthouse Beach and a little talk on the history and behaviour of the camel.

Party boats leave from **Settlement Point Boatshed** (☎ 6583 6300; Settlement Point Rd; ☼ 6am-7pm) and cost from $40 for two hours; runabouts from $25 for two hours.

NEW SOUTH WALES

PORT MACQUARIE

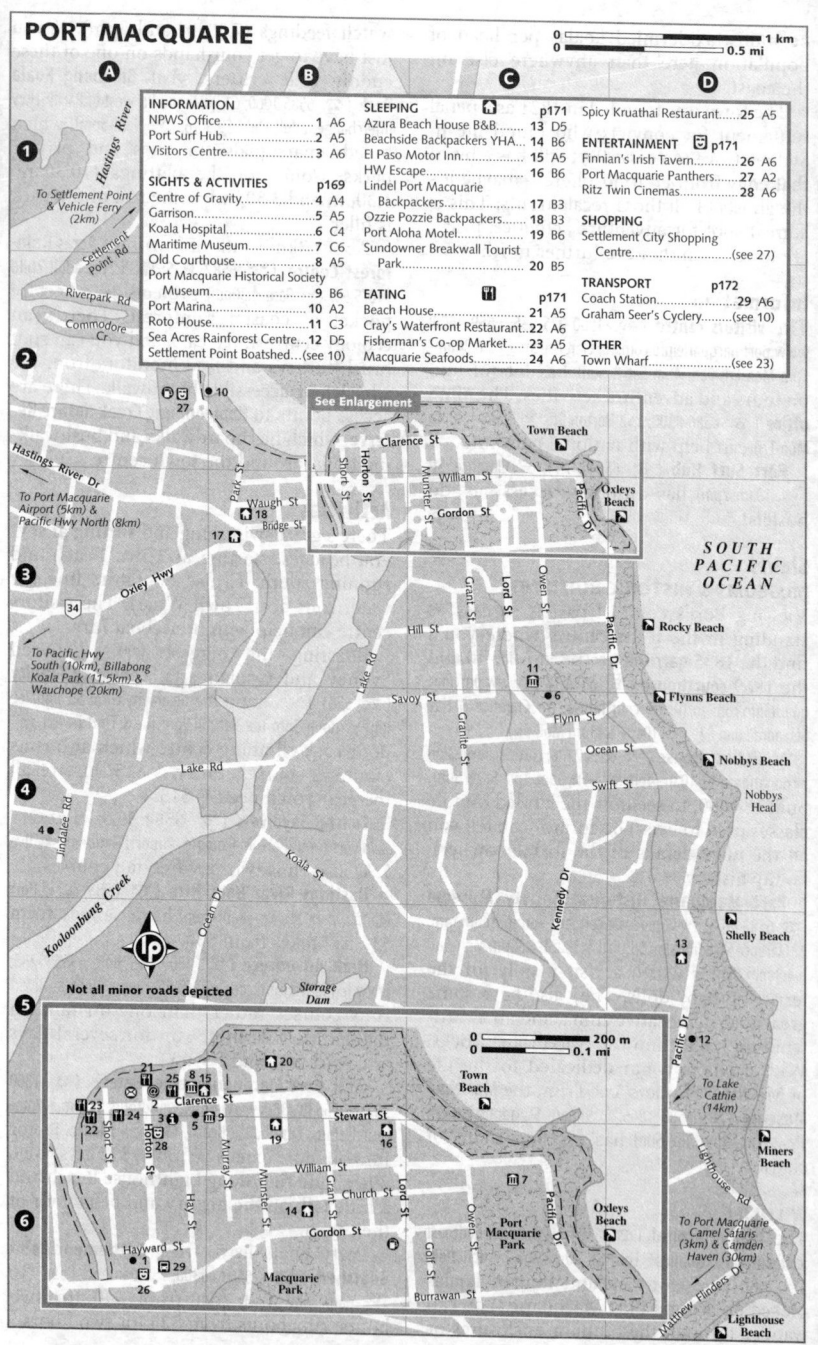

0 — 1 km
0 — 0.5 mi

INFORMATION
NPWS Office................................1 A6
Port Surf Hub..............................2 A5
Visitors Centre...........................3 A6

SIGHTS & ACTIVITIES p169
Centre of Gravity........................4 A4
Garrison.....................................5 A5
Koala Hospital............................6 C4
Maritime Museum.......................7 C6
Old Courthouse..........................8 A5
Port Macquarie Historical Society
  Museum...................................9 B6
Port Marina...............................10 A2
Roto House................................11 C3
Sea Acres Rainforest Centre........12 D5
Settlement Point Boatshed.....(see 10)

SLEEPING p171
Azura Beach House B&B..........13 D5
Beachside Backpackers YHA....14 B6
El Paso Motor Inn....................15 A5
HW Escape..............................16 B6
Lindel Port Macquarie
  Backpackers..........................17 B3
Ozzie Pozzie Backpackers.......18 B3
Port Aloha Motel....................19 B6
Sundowner Breakwall Tourist
  Park.....................................20 B5

EATING p171
Beach House...........................21 A5
Cray's Waterfront Restaurant...22 A6
Fisherman's Co-op Market........23 A5
Macquarie Seafoods...............24 A6

Spicy Kruathai Restaurant......25 A5

ENTERTAINMENT p171
Finnian's Irish Tavern.............26 A6
Port Macquarie Panthers.......27 A2
Ritz Twin Cinemas.................28 A6

SHOPPING
Settlement City Shopping
  Centre...........................(see 27)

TRANSPORT p172
Coach Station......................29 A6
Graham Seer's Cyclery........(see 10)

OTHER
Town Wharf......................(see 23)

Tours

Port Macquarie Cruise Adventures (☎ 1300 555 890; www.cruiseadventures.com.au; Town Wharf) Five different cruises exploring inland waterways with dolphin-spotting in glass-sided boats ($20 to $55). Enjoy or endure a mandatory visit to Oyster World.

Seaplane Scenic Flights (☎ 0412-507 698; Town Wharf; from $60) Standard 15-minute flight takes in beach, town and Innes Ruins views.

Sleeping

BUDGET

Ozzie Pozzie Backpackers (☎ 6583 8133; ozzie pozzie@bigpond.com; 36 Waugh St; dm/d $26/60; 💻) The managers have done a lot to make this suburban hostel a nice place to hang out, even adding wheelchair ramps. They also offer free pick-ups, bikes, fishing and surfing gear and backpacker barbecue nights.

Lindel Port Macquarie Backpackers (☎ 1800 688 882, 6583 1791; lindel@ midcoast.com.au; 2 Hastings River Dr; dm/d from $26/60; 💻) This backpackers is in one of Port's oldest houses – it's got plenty of atmosphere, but it's a bit dim inside. The pool is surrounded by palms and you can rent bikes and fishing gear.

Beachside Backpackers YHA (☎ 6583 5512; port macqyha@hotmail.com; 40 Church St; dm/d $20/50) Not really by the side of the beach, but closer than the other hostels, it has free use of bikes and surfboards, as well as surfing lessons and barbecue nights. Phone for pick-ups.

Sundowner Breakwall Tourist Park (☎ 1800 636 452, 6583 2755; www.sundowner.net.au; 1 Munster St; camp sites/cabins from $19/55; 💻) This well-run caravan park is right near Town Beach. Some cabins have spa baths.

MID-RANGE

There are more than 30 motels scattered around town. Cheaper places are on Hastings River Dr; apartments and pricier options are on Pacific Dr. Many Port motels don't do single rates.

Port Aloha Motel (☎ 6583 1455; www.portaloha .com.au; 3 School St; d from $70; ❄) Cheaper rooms in this pleasant motel are on the bottom floor; on the top floor you'll pay $90 in low-season, but you get a balcony, a lot more sunshine and a self-contained kitchen.

El Paso Motor Inn (☎ 1800 027 965, 6583 1944; www.port-macquarie.net/elpaso; 29 Clarence St; d from $100; ❄) El Paso was once quite the resort, and its prices reflect that. You still get a pool and in-house movies, and the motel is

very convenient to restaurants. Get a back room, as the in-town location also means in-town noise.

Azura Beach House B&B (☎ 6582 2700; www .azura.com.au; 109 Pacific Dr; s $100-125, d $115-145) Azura is slick, modern and very comfortable. With pool, outdoor spa, leafy courtyard, rainforest views and Shelly Beach right across the road, it's good value.

TOP END

HW Escape (☎ 6583 1200; www.hwescape.com.au; 1 Stewart St; d $150-235; ❄) The lovely rooms in this boutique hotel are very carefully furnished, there's a nice pool, and some of the rooms overlook the ocean, but the prices are still a little steep for what you get.

Eating

Fisherman's Co-op market (☎ 6583 1604; Town Wharf, Clarence St) If you've got access to a barbecue, drop by the co-op for fresh, cheap seafood straight off the boats. **Macquarie Seafoods** (☎ 6583 8476; 68 Clarence St; fish from $1.50) can sell you the fried, battered or grilled version, with chips.

Spicy Kruathai (☎ 6583 9043; cnr Clarence & Hay Sts; main $9-17) Extra-fresh seafood makes an authentic Southeast Asian menu even more satisfying. It's popular, so book ahead.

Cray's Waterfront Restaurant (☎ 6583 7885; 74 Clarence St; mains $19-29) Overlooking the wharf, this upmarket seafood restaurant serves meals that taste as good as they look.

Beach House (☎ 6584 5692; Horton St; mains $12-22) Crowds throng to the terraces of the Beach House, in the Royal Hotel. Overlooking the esplanade, it's a great spot for a beer and a burger, or oysters and a glass of chardonnay. There are also gourmet pizzas.

Entertainment

Port Macquarie Panthers (☎ 6580 2300; Settlement City, Bay St) This huge complex at Settlement City has restaurants, bars, a coffee shop and a casino. Bands play regularly.

Finnian's Irish Tavern (☎ 6583 4646; 97 Gordon St) A pub that also serves food, this cheery, popular spot has bands (mostly covers), or you can join other patrons as they sit around watching the dog races.

Ritz Twin Cinemas (☎ 6583 8400; cnr Clarence & Horton Sts; admission $9) The cinema shows mainstream releases. Tickets are cheaper on Wednesday, Friday and Sunday.

Getting There & Away

Qantas (☎ 13 13 13; www.qantas.com.au) flies to Sydney (from $200, 1 hour).

McCafferty's/Greyhound (☎ 13 14 99; www .mccaffertys.com.au) runs buses to Sydney ($48, 7 hours), Brisbane ($48, 6½ hours), Byron Bay ($48, 6 hours) and Coffs Harbour ($25, 2 hours); they all stop at the coach station on Horton St. Destinations with **Kean's** (☎ 1800 043 339, 6543 1322) include Bellingen ($28), Dorrigo ($31), Armidale ($45.50), Tamworth ($54.50) and Scone ($75).

CountryLink (☎ 13 22 32; www.countrylink.nsw .gov.au) train/coach combo to Sydney costs $71.50.

The Oxley Hwy west to Wauchope and onto the New England tablelands near Walcha is a spectacular drive.

A 24-hour vehicle **ferry** ($2.50) operates from Settlement Point, accessing minor coastal roads further north.

Getting Around

There are local **buses** (☎ 6583 2161) all around town.

At Port Marina, **Graham Seer's Cyclery** (☎ 6583 2333; Park St; ☒ 9am-5pm Mon-Fri, 9am-2pm Sat) rents bikes by the hour ($7), day ($22) and week ($55).

PORT MACQUARIE TO COFFS HARBOUR

Want to see an Australian magic trick? In **Kempsey**, home of the Akubra, the **visitors centre** (☎ 1800 642 480, 02-6563 1555; kempsey.midcoast.com.au; Pacific Hwy; ☒ 9am-5pm Mon-Fri, 10am-4pm Sat & Sun) shows how a rabbit can be turned into a hat. Next door, the **Macleay River Historical Museum** (☎ 02-6562 7572; admission $3.30; ☒ 10am-4pm) documents the history of this farming area.

Crescent Head (population 1100), on the coast 18km southeast of Kempsey, is the surf long-boarding capital of Australia (there's also good short-board riding off Plummer Rd). **David Wilcox Real Estate** (☎ 1800 352 272, 02-6566 0306; www.davidwilcoxre.com.au; 12 Main St) has vacation rentals from $180 per week and can help with visitor information. **Crescent Head Holiday Park** (☎ 1800 006 600, 02-6566 0251; Pacific St; camp sites/cabins from $15/50; ☐) is right on the beach. **Bush & Beach Retreat** (☎ 02-6566 0235; 353 Loftus Rd; dm/d/f $20/80/110), a rambling, friendly homestead with a pool, is about 4km outside Crescent Head and right near the beach.

Tucked beneath the headlands of **Hat Head National Park**, the quiet township of **Hat Head**, with its paperbark-lined main street, has a beautiful sheltered beach, great fishing, a few shops and a caravan park. There's basic camping on the northern side of town near **Smoky Cape Lighthouse**.

Purists and pedants alike will hate the **Pub with No Beer** (☎ 02-6564 2101; pubnobeer@midcoast. com.au; Taylors Arm Road, Taylors Arm), made famous by Slim Dusty's gold-record song. The place is shameless enough to trumpet its 'Icy Cold Beer'. It's 25km off the highway at Macksville, serves lunch and has hotel and camping accommodation.

South West Rocks

☎ 02 / pop 3500

Uncrowded beaches, native forests, **cave diving**, some novel eating options and a very laid-back atmosphere make South West Rocks a great place to spend a few days. The entertainingly unhelpful **visitors centre** (☎ 6566 7099; 1 Ocean Dr; ☒ 10am-4pm) has, luckily, plenty of brochures.

A kind of Dickensian version of Alcatraz, the ace 19th-century **Trial Bay Gaol** (☎ 6566 6168; Quarry Rd, Arakoon; admission $4.50; ☒ 9am-4.30pm, last entry 4.15pm) was once home to a (failed) humanitarian penal experiment. The ruins of the great grey walls and still-intact cells loom over the choppy seas below.

Rent boats, kayaks, sailboards and surf skis from **Trial Bay Watersports** (☎ 0429-041 312; Trial Bay Beach); it also runs sailboarding lessons and kayak tours (from $30). **South West Rocks Dive Centre** (☎ 6566 6959; www.southwestrock sdive.com.au; 98 Gregory St) runs dive tours to Fish Rock, allegedly Australia's best cave dive.

SLEEPING & EATING

Smoky Cape Lighthouse Keepers Cottages (☎ 6566 6301; www.smokycapelighthouse.com; Lighthouse Rd, Arakoon; B&B; s/d from $110/165) Not for the vertiginous, these cottages perch high above the ocean on a bracingly breezy cape; the view at breakfast is incredible. Choose from B&B or self-contained cottages that sleep six (from $350 for two nights).

Trial Bay Tourist Park (☎ 6566 6142; www .trialbay.com.au; 161-171 Phillip Dr; camp sites/cottages from $15/75) This is so well-run it has fresh flowers in the toilet blocks. The on-site **takeaway** makes 'dirty burgers' (as if egg, bacon and pineapple weren't enough, it

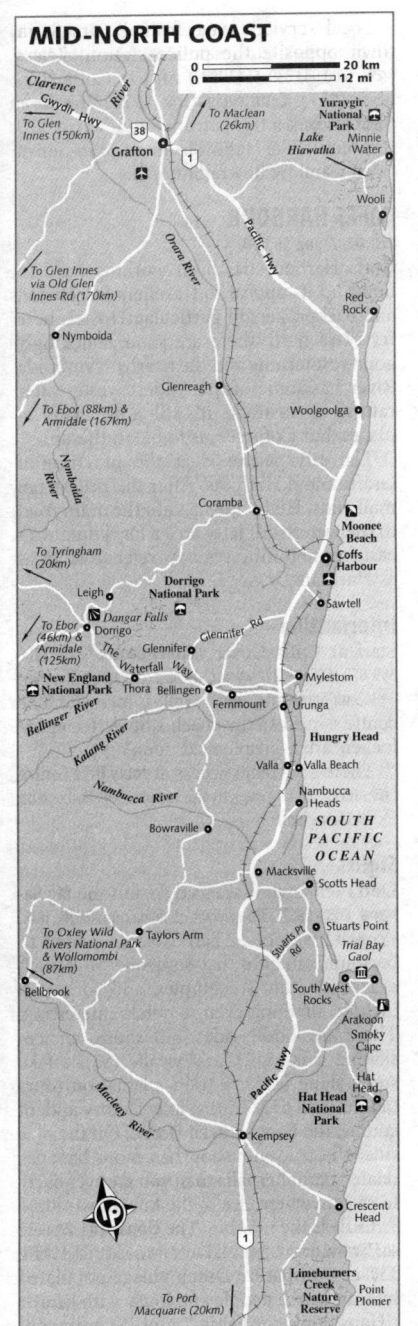

MID-NORTH COAST

also includes chips and gravy *in the bun*) and deep-fried Mars bars.

Other recommendations:

Grass Trees Escape (☎ 9905 7415; www.takeabreak .com.au; Fern Tree Close, Arakoon; d from $160) Self-contained cabins with huge windows set in bushland.

The Bay Motel (☎ 6566 6909; Livingstone St; s/d from $55/70) Ocean view rooms (d from $90) are good value. The pub downstairs overlooks the beach and serves meals.

Horseshoe Bay Beach Park (☎ 6566 6370; Livingstone St; camp sites/cabins from $20/60) Right in town, and on sheltered Town Beach.

LJ Hooker Holiday Accommodation (☎ 6566 6313; southwestrocks@ljh.com.au; 2 Gregory St) Handles long-term holiday rentals.

Geppy's (☎ 6566 6196; cnr Livingstone & Memorial Sts; mains $15-28; ☯ dinner only) This award-winner specialises in local seafood and game. There's live jazz on Wednesday. At the other end of the scale, **Paragon Pizza** (☎ 6566 7711; Paragon Ave; pizzas from $10.50) doesn't try to hide the fact it makes a pizza with prawns, bacon, banana, avocado and pineapple.

GETTING THERE & AWAY
Local buses leave from Belgrave Street in Kempsey. **King Bros** (☎ 6562 4724; www.kingbros bus.com.au) goes to Crescent Head ($6.50) Monday to Saturday and South West Rocks ($6.50) on weekdays.

Nambucca Heads
☎ 02 / pop 6000
Quiet Nambucca Heads, at the mouth of the Nambucca ('Many Bends' in Gumbaing-gir) River, attracts holiday makers who like to fish, swim and laze around.

The **visitors centre** (☎ 1800 646 587, 6568 6954; www.nambucca-web.com; 4 Pacific Hwy; ☯ 9am-5pm) is beside the turn-off on the Pacific Hwy. The **Mosaic Wall** (Bowra St), a 30m-long crockery extravaganza, was inspired by either the ocean or a strong aversion to doing the washing up. Look for Elvis.

Off Bowra St, Wellington Dr leads downhill to the waterfront and the Vee Wall breakwall with gentle graffiti by locals and travellers: the messages are like those in pub toilets, but in prettier colours. Ridge St forks left onto Liston St to **Main Beach** and the **Headland Historical Museum** (☎ 6568 6380; Liston St; admission $1; ☯ 2-4pm Wed, Sat & Sun) or right along Parkes St to North Head for stunning views from **Captain Cook Lookout**.

Boatshed Boathire (☎ 6568 5550; 1 Wellington Dr) rents boats, canoes and fishing gear.

SLEEPING

Nambucca Backpackers Hostel (☎ 6568 6360; Newman St; dm/s $21/30; 🖳) About 1km from the beach and a bit of a hike from town, the hostel has friendly owners but facilities are a bit run down.

B&B Beilby's Beach House (☎ 6568 6466; www .midcoast.com.au/~beilbys; 1 Ocean St; d $55-70; 🖳) It seems like everyone who stays at Beilby's just loves it. Built above the sea, this guesthouse is just a quick walk through bush to the beach, and has a pool and all-you-can-eat breakfast. Children are welcome.

Scott's B&B Guesthouse (☎ 6568 6386; 4 Wellington Dr; d $95) More casual and relaxed than your average B&B, this stylish old weatherboard guesthouse has spacious rooms overlooking the river. The new owners have given the place a real facelift.

White Albatross Holiday Resort (☎ 6568 6468; www.white-albatross.com.au; Wellington Dr; camp sites/ cabins from $20/50) This award winning caravan park is close to the lagoon and Main Beach. A de luxe waterfront villa is $105.

EATING

Bookshop Café (☎ 6568 5855; Bowra St; sandwiches from $6.50; 🖳) Second-hand bookshop, Internet café and sandwich joint all squished into one, this is a good place to down a smoothie and a toasted focaccia.

Starfish Café (☎ 6569 4422; 5 Main St; mains $13-27) There's a great view from the back veranda, and a modern menu that takes in oysters, green curry and carpetbag steak. Live music Thursday.

Boatshead Seafood Brasserie (☎ 6568 9292; 1 Wellington Dr; 3-course set menu $27) Whether it's fried calamari and chips for takeaway or sumptuous barramundi fillets, this is the place.

Bluewater Brasserie at the V-Wall Tavern (☎ 6568 6394; Wellington Dr; mains $14-25) Out of keeping with the rough-and-tumble pub it lives in, this brasserie is slightly fancy and has Mod Oz aspirations.

GETTING THERE & AWAY

Long-distance coaches stop on the Pacific Hwy in front of the shopping plaza, just south of the visitors centre. Buses to Sydney cost $50; Byron Bay $43.

Local services leave from Bowra St in town opposite the police station. **Kean's** (☎ 1800 043 339, 6543 1322) runs to Coffs Harbour ($17). **CountryLink** (☎ 13 22 32; www.coun trylink.nsw.gov.au) trains from Sydney cost $79 (8 hours). The station is about 3km out of town – follow Bowra St north.

COFFS HARBOUR

☎ 02 / pop 60,000

Coffs Harbour has been working hard to build up its appeal to travellers in general, and backpackers in particular. Hostels here try extra hard, there are some shockingly good restaurants and the nearby Nymboida River has some of the wildest white-water rafting in Australia. It's still a bit grotty in places, but Coffs seems to be on the up.

The city centre is at the junction of Grafton and High Sts. After the pedestrian mall ends, High St turns into the main road to the waterfront jetty area a few kilometres east (some businesses now refer to High St as Harbour Dr).

Information

Staff at Coffs Coast **visitors centre** (☎ 1300 369 070, 6652 1522; www.coffscoast.com.au; Pacific Hwy; ⏱ 9am-5pm) are very well informed. The centre is next to the coach stop; left-luggage lockers are available next door.

There's Internet access at **Jetty Dive Centre** (☎ 6651 1611; www.jettydive.com.au; 398 Harbour Dr; ⏱ 8.30am-5pm).

Sights

Don't tell anyone we said so, but the **Big Banana** (☎ 6652 4355; www.bigbanana.com; Pacific Hwy; ⏱ 8am-5pm) sucks. There is some delight to be found: mainly that someone built such a massive tourist complex and forgot to include anything even remotely interesting. There are kiddie rides, gift shops, an ice-skating rink ($12), a 'skywalk' ($5), a fake snow slope ($15), a train, plantation tours (adult/child $12/7.50), a lolly factory and, of course, the Banana itself (free!). On the plus side, the souvenir shop has more banana-related paraphernalia than you are ever likely to see anywhere else in the known world.

Little is the new big. The **Clog Barn** (☎ 6652 4633; www.clogbiz.com; 215 Pacific Hwy; adult/child $4.50/ 3.50) is a miniature Dutch village populated by tiny Dutch people and lousy with lizards ('Hans, look out behind you! It's a dragon!

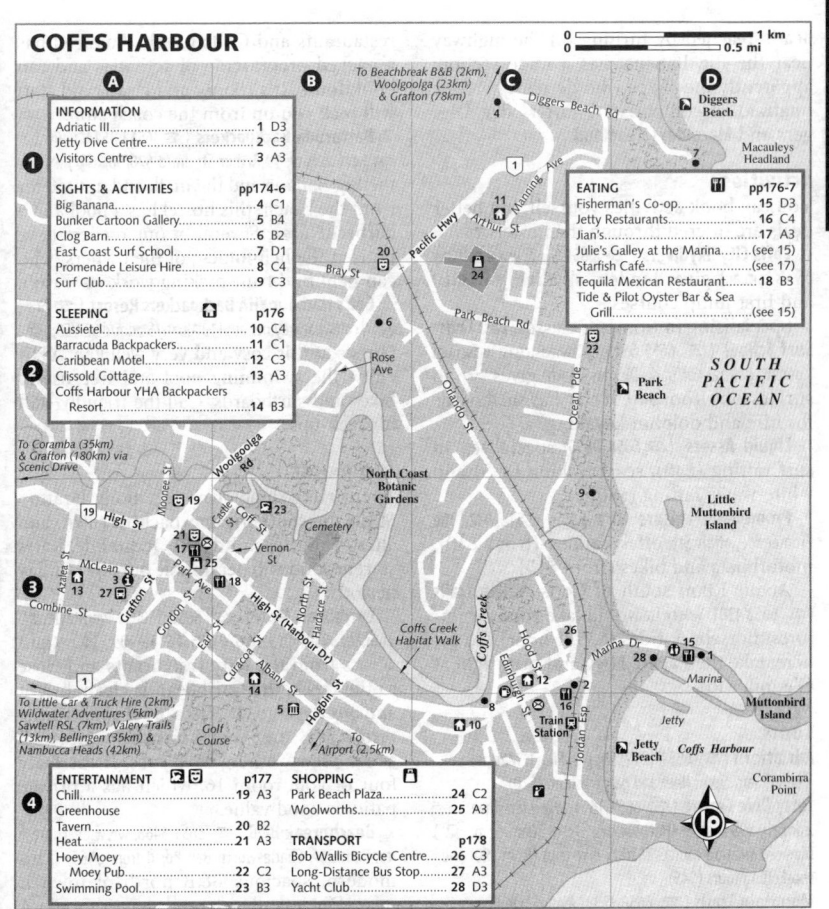

Arrrrgh!'). The PA pipes incessant polka music for your enjoyment. The manager (he's that guy in the wooden shoes) hosts free clog-making demonstrations at 11am and 4pm.

Out near the airport, **Bunker Cartoon Gallery** (☎ 6651 7343; City Hill Dr; admission $2; ⏱ 10am-4pm) is a great little gallery of original cartoon art in an old WWII bunker.

The **North Coast Botanic Gardens** (☎ 6648 4188; Hardacre St; admission by donation; ⏱ 9am-5pm) is huge, and harbours many endangered species and examples of the region's rainforest types. It's a great spot to lie on the grass, surrounded by towering eucalypts full of kookaburras. The 6km **Coffs Creek Habitat Walk** passes by, starting from

opposite the council chambers on Coff St and finishing near the sea.

The harbour's northern breakwall runs out to **Muttonbird Island**, named for the more than 12,000 pairs of birds who migrate here annually. It's the southern boundary of the **Solitary Islands Marine Park**, where warm tropical currents meet temperate southern currents, and attract unusual varieties of fish and divers (look out for extremely rough conditions).

BEACHES
The main beach is **Park Beach**, which has a picnic ground and is patrolled at weekends and during school holidays: be careful of rips. **Jetty Beach** is more sheltered. **Diggers**

NEW SOUTH WALES

Beach, reached by turning off the highway near the Big Banana, has a nude section; apparently the chaps who de-pant here are unafraid of comparison. Surfers like Diggers and **Macauleys Headland**.

Activities

You can book activities yourself, but better deals are offered through the hostels.

Coffs City Skydivers (☎ 6651 1167; www.coffssky divers.com.au) gives tandem skydiving ($310) and first-jump courses.

Specialising in women's classes, **East Coast Surf School** (☎ 6651 5515; www.eastcoastsurfschool .com.au; Central Car park, Diggers Beach) gives group surf lessons from $40. It also has surfboards for hire and dolphin kayaking.

Liquid Assets (☎ 6658 0850) specialises in surf rafting ($40), sea kayaking ($35) and white-water rafting ($80).

Promenade Leisure Hire (☎ 6651 1032; The Promenade, High St) offer canoes (from $10), motorboats and bikes (from $15).

About 13km south of Coffs, **Valery Trails** (☎ 6653 4301; Valery Trails) will take you on rainforest horseback rides ($35, 1 hour). To get here, take the Pacific Hwy and turn right at Glennifer Rd.

Tours

Adriatic III (☎ 6651 1277; Shop 5, Pier 1, Marina; 🕑 7.30am-5pm) Reef and game fishing ($70).

Jetty Dive Centre (☎ 6651 1611; www.jettydive .com.au; 398 High St (Harbour Dr); 🕑 8.30am-5pm; 🖳) Dive certification courses ($200), dive trips (from $90) and snorkelling tours ($45).

Mountain Trails (☎ 6658 3333) Award-winning eco-friendly 4WD rainforest, waterfall and bush tucker tours ($55 to $85).

Wildwater Adventures (☎ 6653 3500; 754 Pacific Hwy at South Boambee Rd) White-water rafting day trips on the Nymboida River (from $155) and Gwydir River ($360 for 2 days).

WOW rafting (☎ 1800 640 330, 6654 4066; www .wowrafting.com.au; 1448 Coramba Rd, Coramba; 🕑 8.30am-7.30pm) One- and two-day trips ($155-325) on the Nymboida River.

Sleeping

Prices rise sharply during holidays, and it can be hard to find a bed.

BUDGET

Aussietel (☎ 6651 1871; fun@aussietel.com; 312 High St; dm/d $26/65; 🖳) Situated right near Jetty

restaurants and Coffs Creek, Aussietel has a packed programme of activities and can book tours. It's roomy and clean, and staff will pick you up from the coach stop.

Barracuda Backpackers (☎ 6651 3514; www.bac kpackers.coffs.tv; 19 Arthur St; dm/d $20/50; 🖳) Near the Big Banana and the mall, and not too far from the beach, this hostel has a pool and a barbecue area. Several of our readers have praised the helpfulness of the owners, who can help find fruit-picking work in season.

Coffs Harbour YHA Backpackers Resort (☎ 6652 6462; coffsyha@key.net.au; 110 Albany St; dm/d $22/55; 🖳) Guests at this cosy and very well kept YHA enjoy the swimming pool and free use of bikes and surfboards. Call the friendly staff for pick-ups.

MID-RANGE

There are strings of motels along Grafton St on the southern approach to town, and along Park Beach Rd and Ocean Pde. Rates start around $60 per double outside holiday periods.

Caribbean Motel (☎ 6652 1500; www.stayincoffs .com.au; 353 High St; d $70-185, f $115-205; 🔡) Right across from the Jetty restaurants and close to the creek, the Caribbean is clean, bright and pretty cute. It has a pool and a little restaurant; some rooms have balconies with ocean views, others have spas. If there are four of you, room 16, which has a private patio, is good value.

Beachbreak B&B (☎ 6651 6468; www.beachbreak .com.au; 25A Charlesworth Bay Rd; d from $165) This modern, spacious B&B north of town is near Diggers Beach and has a pool. A couple of resorts nearby have restaurants.

Clissold Cottage (☎ 6651 2715; 4 Azalea Ave; d from $85) A little cottage in the grounds of a Federation-era house, Clissold is very private. Furnished in flowery country style, the cottage also has a big, deep claw-foot bath.

Eating

If you're near Coffs around dinner time, stop. You won't get food this good anywhere else on the coast between Newcastle and Byron Bay.

JETTY

The Jetty is the main restaurant strip and there's really no point eating elsewhere; most of the CBD closes down around 6pm. As well as the listings here, you'll find budget Italian, Vietnamese, Thai, Indian, and fish and chips. Kitchens start closing around 8.30pm, so come early and make a reservation if you have your heart set on a particular place.

Foreshores Café (☎ 6652 3127; 394 High St, or Harbour Dr; mains $6-18; ☉ breakfast & lunch) Quick and friendly service, huge breakfasts (including good vegie options) and ocean breezes on the terrace make this a great spot to start the day.

Passion Fish Brasserie (☎ 6652 1423; 384a High St; mains $17-29; ☉ from 6pm Tue-Sun) Known nationwide, Passion Fish gets raves from the critics. Mainly featuring seafood, the menu is heavily Asian influenced.

Il Mercato (☎ 6651 4944; 390 High St; mains $14-25) Bright red walls and abstract photography make this modern Italian restaurant a cheery place to have a coffee or a meal. Pastas and risottos have a Middle Eastern twist, but the desserts are typically Italo-delicious.

MARINA
Fisherman's Co-op (☎ 6652 2811; 69 Marina Dr; ☉ 9am-6pm) Fresh fish right off the boats; between 11am and early evening you can get cooked fish (fish and chips are $7.50), or pick up a super-fresh sushi lunchbox for $6.

Tide & Pilot Oyster Bar & Sea Grill (☎ 6651 6888; Marina Dr; mains $22-27) Right on the ocean (if you're lucky, you might spot a whale), this swanky seafood joint has truly great food. Try the barramundi with macadamia crust. The downstairs **bistro** (mains $12.50-16.50; ☉ 7am-late) has views of the car park (you'd have to be really lucky to spot a whale). It's popular and relaxed.

Julie's Galley at the Marina (☎ 6650 0188; Marina Dr; burgers $4-7; ☉ 8am-6.30pm) Have your breakfast egg-and-bacon roll with the blokes off the boats. All kinds of burgers (several vegie options) are served by the cheery chef.

CBD
The downtown area is good for lunch, or for coffee all day, but most places are closed in the evening. The pedestrian area opposite Palm Mall has lots of sidewalk cafés.

Starfish Café (☎ 6651 5005; City Centre Mall; mains $5-12; ☉ 8am-4pm Mon-Fri, 8am-noon Sat) Coffee, sandwiches, salads and cakes please the shopping crowds and it makes a darn tasty BLT.

Jian's (☎ 6658 0202; High St; mains $6-15; ☉ 9am-5pm Mon-Fri, 9am-2pm Sat) This is a great place for a quick feed of sushi or Japanese noodle soup.

Tequila Mexican Restaurant (☎ 6652 1279; 224 High Street; mains $13-17; ☉ dinner) One of the few places downtown that's open for dinner, you can sink into comfortable wooden booths and enjoy tapas platters, vegie fajitas and, of course, tequila.

Entertainment
See Thursday's edition of the *Coffs Harbour Advocate* for listings.

CLUBBING
Heat (☎ 6652 6426; 15 City Centre Mall) It can get a little feisty on the Coffs club circuit, and Heat is no exception. Some come for the dancing, others come on a serious mission to score. Things get hotter, in both respects, later in the evening.

Chill (☎ 6658 0877; 76 Grafton St) Chill has taken over the premises of the venerable Saloon Club. Still in its infancy, anything could happen.

LIVE MUSIC
Hoey Moey Pub (☎ 6852 3833; Ocean Pde) Your best bet for local acts and AC/DC (rock) cover bands, this party pub caters to the demanding backpacker market. It also has pool comps and trivia nights.

Sawtell RSL Club (☎ 6653 1577; 1st Ave, Sawtell) Big-name touring bands play here in suburban Sawtell, about 5km south of town. The hostels usually organise transport, or call **Sawtell Coaches** (☎ 6653 3344) for bus schedules.

Greenhouse Tavern (☎ 6651 5488; Bray St) This pub complex has bands, several bars and a pleasant conservatory-themed beer garden.

Getting There & Away
Qantas (☎ 13 13 13; www.qantas.com.au) flies to Sydney (from $230) and Brisbane (from $300).

The long-distance bus stop is beside the visitors centre. **McCafferty's/Greyhound** (☎ 13 14 99; www.mccaffertys.com.au) runs buses to Sydney ($55, 7 hours) Brisbane ($39, 6 hours), Byron Bay ($37, 4 hours) and Port Macquarie ($25, 2 hours).

CountryLink trains (☎ 13 22 32; www.countrylink .nsw.gov.au) run to Sydney ($79, 8 hours), Byron Bay ($42, 4½ hours) and Brisbane ($72, 5½ hours). The station is near the jetty.

Coffs is a good place to pick up a ride along the coast on a yacht or cruiser. Ask around or put a notice in the yacht club at the harbour.

Getting Around

Kings Bros (☎ 6652 2877; www.kingsbrosbus.com.au) runs several routes around town. The useful No 365 loop runs along High St and Ocean Pde to Park Beach Plaza.

Bob Wallis Bicycle Centre (☎ 6652 5102; 13 Orlando St; ☺ 8.30am-5.30pm Mon-Fri, 8.30am-1pm Sat) hires bikes for $17 per day.

A Little Car & Truck Hire (☎ 6651 3004; carhire@ ozemail.com.au; 32 Alison St) rents cars from $29 per day. It also has 4WDs.

COFFS HARBOUR TO BYRON BAY

Sure, **Woolgoolga** (or Woopi) has surf beaches, but it also has the **Raj Mahal**, a real slice of the subcontinent. Giant elephants loom out the front of the decrepit concrete extravagance, on the north side of town. Its origins are something of a mystery, but it's possible that it was once a temple. Knee-length weeds doubtless hide whole families of snakes, and no one really knows if the rows of shuttered snack and sari shops will ever open again, but if you're a fan of the eccentric and un-expected, have a look. **Guru Nanak Gurdwara**, a still-active 1970s temple south of town, is where the town's Sikh population worships. **Bluebottles Brasserie** (☎ 02-6654 1962; 53 Wharf St; mains $13-20) serves imaginative seafood.

Yuraygir National Park covers the 60km stretch of coast north from **Red Rock**, a sleepy village with a beautiful inlet, to Angourie Point, just south of Yamba. The park has fine beaches and bushwalks in the coastal heath. There are great camping grounds along the coast, including the Illa-roo Rest Area near **Minnie Water**, signposted off the highway 10km south of Grafton.

Grafton (population 17,300), with its wide streets, big verandas and spectacular jacarandas, feels like the border post for the subtropics. Fitzroy St is lined with historic houses, including the **Grafton Regional Art Gallery** (☎ 02-6642 3177; 158 Fitzroy St; admission by donation; ☺ 10am-4pm Tue-Sun) and **Clarence River Historical Society** (☎ 02-6652 5212; 190 Fitzroy St;

admission $3; ☺ 1-4pm Tue-Thu & Sun). **McCafferty's/ Greyhound** (☎ 13 14 99; www.mccaffertys.com.au) runs buses to Sydney ($55, 10 hours) and Coffs Harbour ($20, 1 hour).

At the river mouth, east of the highway through cane fields and sprawling channels, the fishing town of **Yamba** (population 4000) is a thriving resort with good beaches. Just south, **Angourie Point** is one of the coast's top spots for experienced surfers and has a spring-water quarry pool. The **Pacific Hotel** (☎ 02-6646 2466; 1 Pilot St; d from $45) is on a hill above Yamba beach.

King Bros (☎ 02-6646 2019; www.kingbrosbus .com.au; 70 Skinner St, Grafton) travels between Grafton and Yamba ($8, 1½ hours) and on to Angourie Point. There are four daily ferries per day ($4.20) from Yamba to **Iluka**.

World Heritage listed Iluka Rainforest is a short detour off the highway. This is the southern end of **Bundjalung National Park**, with excellent surf beaches and wildlife. There's a busy **camping ground** (☎ 02-6646 6134; camp sites/cabins from $11/70) at Woody Head; you must book in advance.

Ballina

☎ 02 / pop 16,500
Ballina feels like an inland country town that just happens to have a beach. The **visitors centre** (☎ 6686 3484; balinfo@balshire.org.au; Las Balsas Plaza; ☺ 9am-5pm Mon-Fri, 9am-4pm Sat & Sun) is at the eastern end. Staff book river cruises, including day-trips to Lismore on the classic **MV Bennelong** (☎ 0414-664 552; Fawcett St Wharf; adult/child $70/35).

Around the corner is the **Naval & Maritime Museum** (☎ 6681 1002; Regatta Ave; admission by donation; ☺ 9am-4pm) which displays the 1973 Las Balsas expedition raft that floated here from Ecuador – it's worth a visit to read about this lunatic undertaking. Ballina is also home to the **Big Prawn** (☎ 6686 0086; Pacific Hwy; ☺ 24hr), a classic 'big', with a 24-hour restaurant and plenty of prawn-related knick-knacks for the kitsch-loving masses. It looks its finest lit up at night.

Shelly Beach is the closest patrolled beach to town; it's east of the CBD.

SLEEPING & EATING

Ballina Lakeside Holiday Park (☎ 1800 888 268, 6686 3953; www.ballinalakeside.com.au; Fenwick Dr; camp sites/cabins/luxury villas $16.50/45/100) This award-winning caravan park near Shaws Bay

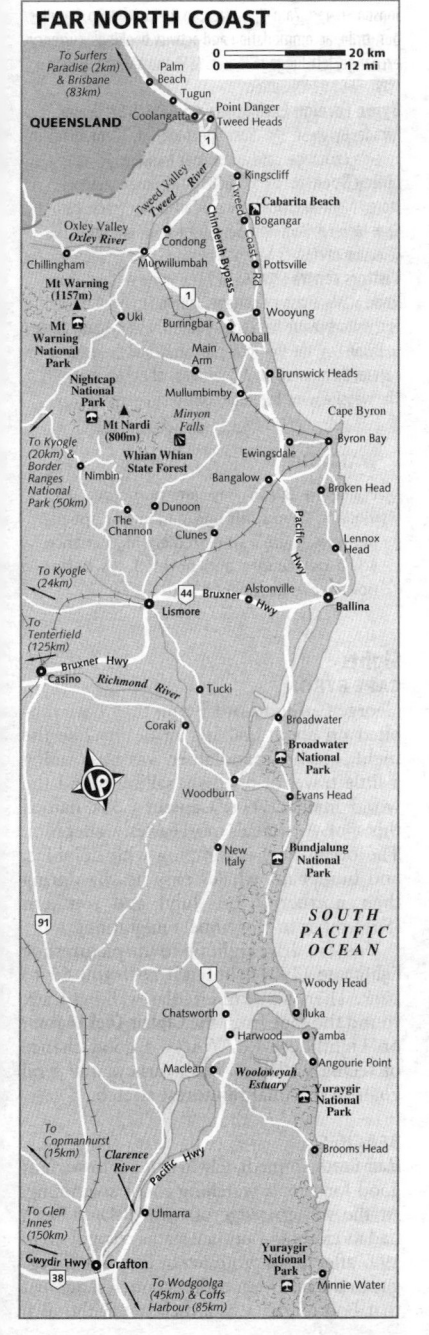

FAR NORTH COAST

To Surfers Paradise (2km) & Brisbane (83km)

0 —————— 20 km
0 —————— 12 mi

QUEENSLAND

Palm Beach
Tugun
Point Danger
Coolangatta
Tweed Heads

Kingscliff

Cabarita Beach
Bogangar

Oxley Valley
Oxley River
Condong
Pottsville

Chillingham
Murwillumbah

Mt Warning
(1157m)

Uki
Burringbar
Mooball
Wooyung

Mt Warning National Park
Main Arm

Nightcap National Park
Mullumbimby
Brunswick Heads

Mt Nardi (800m)
Minyon Falls
Cape Byron

Whian Whian State Forest
Ewingsdale
Byron Bay

To Kyogle (20km) & Border Ranges National Park (50km)
Nimbin
Bangalow
Broken Head

The Channon
Dunoon

Clunes
Lennox Head

To Kyogle (24km)

Bruxner Hwy
Alstonville
Lismore
Bruxner Hwy
Ballina

To Tenterfield (125km)

Bruxner Hwy
Casino
Richmond River
Tucki

Coraki
Broadwater

Broadwater National Park

Woodburn
Evans Head

New Italy
Bundjalung National Park

SOUTH PACIFIC OCEAN

Woody Head

Chatsworth
Iluka

Harwood
Yamba

Maclean
Angourie Point
Woolooweyah Estuary
Yuraygir National Park

To Copmanhurst (15km)
Clarence River
Brooms Head

To Glen Innes (150km)
Ulmarra

Gwydir Hwy
Grafton
Yuraygir National Park

To Wodgoolga (45km) & Coffs Harbour (85km)
Minnie Water

Lagoon has a swimming pool, mini-golf course, gym and camp kitchen.

Flat Rock Camping Park (☎ 6686 4848; Flat Rock; camp sites $14) This terrific little beachside camping ground is 5km north of Ballina on the coastal road to Lennox Head. Birdlife abounds.

Ballina Travellers Lodge YHA (☎ 6686 6737; lenballina@ozemail.com.au; 36 Tamar St; dm $21, d $50-60) Choose between motel rooms, hostel-style doubles or dorms. There's no garden, but there's a pool and kitchen. You can hire bikes and fishing gear.

Brundah (☎ 6686 8166; www.babs.com.au/brundah; 37 Norton St; s/d from $115/135) This magnificent Federation-era homestead has impeccable rooms overlooking lush gardens and a huge acacia.

Shelly's on the Beach (☎ 6686 9844; Shelley Beach Rd; mains $8-17; ☺ breakfast & lunch) Enjoy big breakfasts, lots of fresh ingredients and tables overlooking the beach (there's a serious risk of seeing dolphins).

Australian Hotel (☎ 6686 2015; 103 River St; mains $9-17) Embrace Ballina at the Aussie. Classic pub meals – chicken parma anyone? – are served in the family bistro and beer garden. The Aussie Battler lunch (fish and chips and a schooner of beer for $6.50) is great value. If the family-friendly atmosphere gets too much, try the front bar Friday lunchtimes, when they have lingerie girls from the Gold Coast.

GETTING THERE & AWAY

Long-distance buses stop at the Big Prawn.

From Tamar St, **Blanch's** (☎ 6686 2144; www .tropicalnsw.com.au/blanchs) has several buses to Byron Bay ($7.50, 1 hour) via Lennox Head or Bangalow. **Kirklands** (☎ 6622 1499; www.kirk lands.com.au) runs to Lismore ($11, 40 minutes). **McCafferty's/Greyhound** (☎ 13 14 19; www.mccaf fertys.com.au) also travels to Lismore ($15, 40 minutes).

Lennox Head
☎ 02 / pop 4500

If you've spent a couple of days in Byron Bay, Lennox Head, 11km north of Ballina and 18km south of Byron, feels like the quietest, calmest place on earth. Even without a trip to Byron, Lennox is a lovely, small beachside town.

Lennox has some of the best surf on the coast, including long right-hander breaks, especially in winter. **Lake Ainsworth**, a lagoon just back from the beach, has water that's softened – and made icky brown – by tannins from the tea trees that grow on its banks (it makes your skin feel great). It's also popular for sailing and sailboarding, and has a sandy, shady little beach.

Lennox Head Beach House YHA (☎ 6687 7636; lennoxbacpac@hotmail.com; 3 Ross St; dm/d $26/ 60) is one of the better hostels on the coast, cheery and clean. The owners rustle up chocolate cakes, teach guests sailboarding, and hand out free massages on Thursdays (you can pay for reflexology week-round). **Randall's on Ross** (☎ 6687 7922; www.tropicalnsw.com.au /randalls; 9 Ross St; d $120-130), with its white-tiled floors, spa baths, minimalist décor and big, comfy Japanese-styled beds, is the diametric opposite of your average country B&B. **Lake Ainsworth Caravan Park** (☎ 6687 7249; lakeains@balshire.org.au; Ross St; camp sites $16-22, cabins $38-70; 🖳) has a lot of rules, which is probably why it's so quiet and calm.

Café de Mer (☎ 6687 7132; 70 Ballina St; mains $8.50-21) is very popular and has a Mod Oz menu. **Red Rock** (☎ 6687 4744; Ballina St; mains $6-14; 🕑 breakfast & lunch; 🖳), just up the street, is a bit more casual. **Mi Thai** (☎ 6687 5820; 76 Ballina St; mains $11-17) does all the usual Thai dishes, plus some excellent and innovative desserts.

Blanch's (☎ 6686 2144; www.tropicalnsw.com.au /blanchs) has several buses to Byron Bay ($5, 30 minutes).

BYRON BAY
☎ 02 / pop 5400

The beaches are superb. The restaurants, cafés and nightlife are excellent. You can have your chakras aligned or kayak with dolphins. It's no wonder Byron is incredibly packed with tourists to the point where it's almost impossible to walk along the footpath; or that many refer to it as North Bondi. Byron is exciting, exhausting, frustrating and gorgeous.

Information
Accommodation booking office (☎ 6680 8666; www.byronbayaccom.net) This office is hugely helpful if you want to book accommodation before you arrive.
Backpackers World (☎ 6685 8858; www.backpacker sworld.com.au; Shop 6, Byron St; 🕑 9am-7pm Mon-Sat, 11am-6pm Sun; 🖳) Primarily a travel agent.
Byron Bus & Backpacker Centre (☎ 6685 5517; 84

Jonson St; 🕑 7am-7pm) Next to the coach stop, handles bus, train, accommodation and activity bookings, currency exchange, left-luggage lockers ($5) and a Global Gossip (☎ 6680 9140) outlet.
Byron Foreign Exchange (☎ 6685 7787; Central Arcade, Byron St; 🕑 9am-8pm Mon-Sat, 10am-4pm Sun) Foreign exchange, cash and money transfers.
Linley Bookstore (☎ 6685 5015; linleyjonesbook store@bigpond.com.au; Shop 2 Carlyle St; 🕑 8.30am-5pm Mon-Fri, 9am-4pm Sat, 10am-4pm Sun) Great selection of classics and local authors.
Visitors centre (☎ 6680 9279; www.visitbyronbay .com; Stationmaster's Cottage, Jonson St; 🕑 9am-5pm) The visitors centre has copies of the Disabled Access Guide to Byron Bay, the free local paper *Echo* and the guide to natural therapists *Body & Soul*. Maps of the town are $1. The website www.byron-bay.com is also very useful.

WARNING

Police in Byron Bay are numerous and vigilant. If you infringe parking or speeding laws, there's an extremely high chance you'll get caught and ticketed. It's better not to take the chance.

Sights
CAPE BYRON
George Gordon Lord Byron may have rabbited on about walking in beauty like the night, but his grandfather was busy doing a little travel of his own, sailing round the world in the 1760s. Captain Cook named this spot, Australia's most easterly, after him. The ocean here is jumping with dolphins, and humpback whales pass nearby during their northern (June-July) and southern (September to November) migrations.

You can drive right up to the picturesque **lighthouse** (1901), but it'll cost you $5 to park. There's a 4km circular walking track round the cape from the **Captain Cook Lookout** on Lighthouse Rd. You've a good chance of seeing wallabies, bush turkeys and feral goats in the final rainforest stretch.

BEACHES
Main Beach, immediately in front of town, is as good for people watching as for swimming. At the western edge of town **Belongil Beach** had its clothing-optional status recognised in 1997 after locals protested by listening to reggae in the buff – an earlier council statement that Bob Marley was a dick was withdrawn

once confused councillors worked out what the protestors really wanted.

Clarks Beach, at the eastern end of Main Beach, can have good surf but the best surf is at the next few beaches: **The Pass**, **Watego's** and **Little Watego's**.

South of Cape Byron, **Tallow Beach** extends 7km down to a rockier stretch around **Broken Head**, where a succession of small beaches dot the coast before opening onto **Seven Mile Beach**, which goes all the way to Lennox Head. The suburb of **Suffolk Park** (with more good surf, particularly in winter) starts 5km south of town.

Activities

Adventure sports abound in Byron Bay and most operators offer a free pick-up service from local accommodation. It's cheapest to book through hostels.

Big Top fiends will love the two-hour circus classes ($40) at **Flying Trapeze & Circus Adventure** (☎ 0417-073 668; Byron Bay Beach Club, Bayshore Dr). **Rockhoppers** (☎ 0500 881 881; www.rockhoppers.com.au; 87 Jonson St) leads adrenalin-charged rainforest mountain bike adventures ($80) and Mt Warning treks ($55).

ALTERNATIVE THERAPIES

The *Body & Soul* guide, available from the visitors centre, is a handy guide to all the alternative therapies Byron has to offer. It's a great read.

Ambaji (☎ 6685 6620; www.ambaji.com.au; 6 Marvell St; ☺ 9am-5pm Mon-Sat) Unashamedly new age, with blueprint healing, craniosacral balancing, crystal singing bowls and life coaching. Sceptics will love the hour-long massage ($60) with Byron gossip thrown in.

Pure Byron Day Spa (☎ 6685 5988; 5 Jonson St; ☺ 9.30am-5.30pm daily) Swedish massage, reiki, facials and a vibrating sauna ($30).

Relax Haven (☎ 6685 8304; Belongil Beachouse, Childe St; ☺ 10am-8pm daily) Probably Byron's cheapest float and massage deal ($50).

Yoga Arts (☎ 6680 8684; www.yogaarts.com.au; 6 Byron St; 9am-12.30pm & 2-5pm Mon, Tue, Thu & Fri) Drop-in yoga classes taught in various styles ($12).

BOATING

You can paddle with dolphins with **Dolphin Kayaking** (☎ 6685 8044; www.dolphinkayaking.com.au; half-day tour $40). **Cape Byron Marine Charters** (☎ 6685 8323; 4/75 Jonson St) arranges deep-sea fishing, snorkelling and whale-watching trips.

DIVING

About 3km off-shore, **Julian Rocks Marine Reserve** is a meeting point for cold southerly and warm northerly currents, attracting a profusion of marine species and divers alike.

Byron Bay Dive Centre (☎ 1800 243 483, 6685 8333; www.byronbaydivecentre.com.au; 9 Marvell St) Introductory courses $130, Open Water Certification $350.

Sundive (☎ 6685 7755; www.sundive.com.au; 8 Middleton St) Charges the same rates.

FLYING

Byron Gliding Club (☎ 6684 7627; www.byrongliding.com; Tyagarah Airport) does joy rides in gliders from $80. **Byron Airwaves** (☎ 6629 0354, 0427-615 950; www.byronair.cjb.net) has tandem hanggliding ($110) and courses (from $1050).

Byron Bay Skydivers (☎ 6684 1323; www.skydivebyronbay.com; Tyagarah Airport) has tandem dives for $275, or $370 if you want to do Australia's longest freefall (and who doesn't?).

SURFING

Byron Bay waves are often quite mellow. Most hostels provide free boards to guests or you can rent equipment.

Aussie Surf Adventures (☎ 1800 113 044, 4396 1797; www.surfadventures.com.au) This outfit gets rave reviews for its five-day surfing tours ($590) which run from Sydney to Byron. Rates include all meals.

Byron Bay Surf School (☎ 1800 707 274; www.byronbaysurfschool.com; Byron Bay Dive Centre, 9 Marvell St) Beginners classes start at $45.

Surfaris (☎ 1800 634 951; www.surfaris.com) The old hand in the surf tour market, Surfaris runs five-day Sydney to Byron tours for $500.

Festivals & Events

The **East Coast Blues and Roots Festival** (☎ 9266 4800; www.bluesfest.com.au; tickets from $80), at Easter, is a highlight on the Australian music calendar. The **Byron Bay Writers Festival** (☎ 6685 5115; www.byronbaywritersfestival.com.au) is in July.

For details of Byron Bay and area markets, see the boxed text 'Markets' in the Far North Coast Hinterland (p187).

Sleeping

BUDGET

Book ahead for Byron accommodation. It's more expensive, but standards are higher: there's a lot of competition here for the backpacker dollar.

BYRON BAY

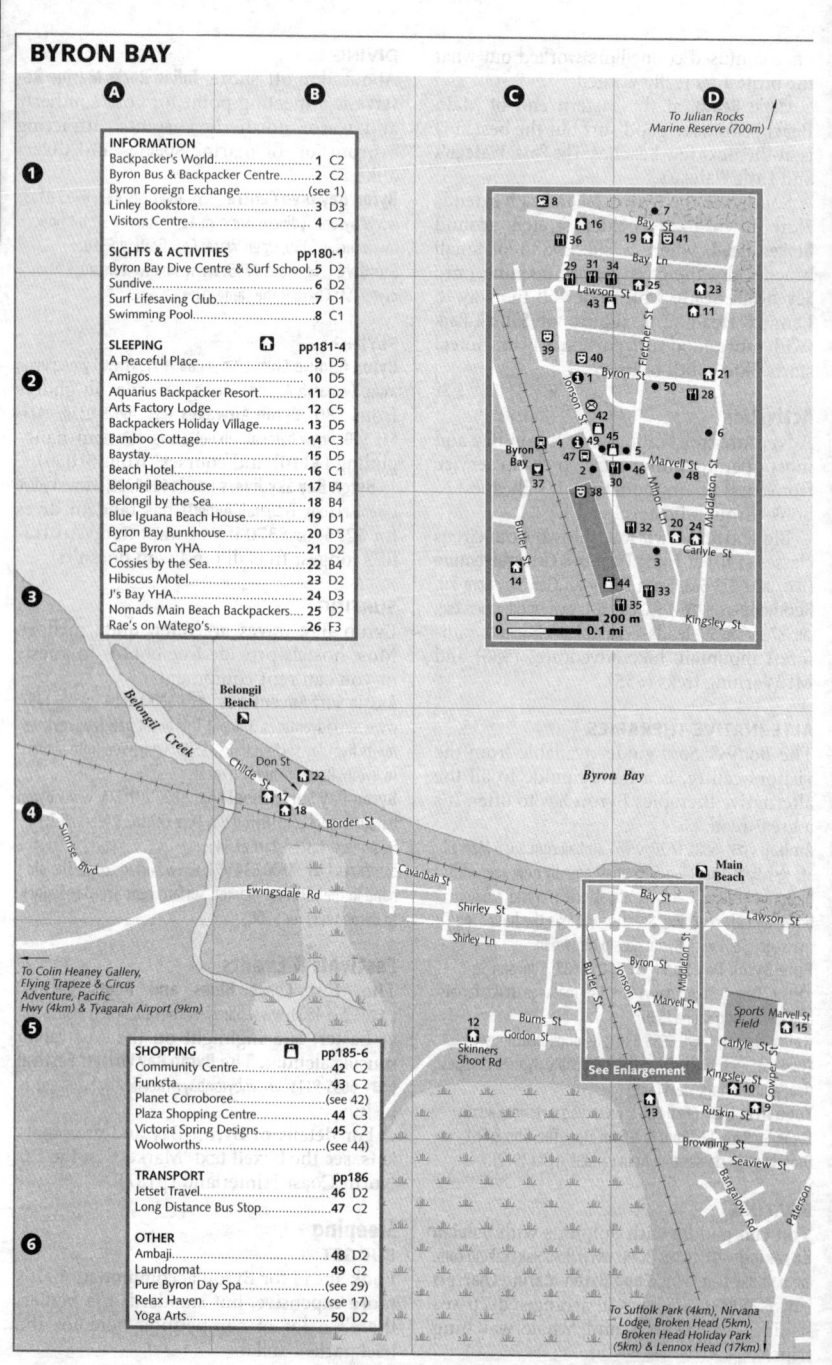

INFORMATION
Backpacker's World	**1** C2
Byron Bus & Backpacker Centre	**2** C2
Byron Foreign Exchange	(see 1)
Linley Bookstore	**3** D3
Visitors Centre	**4** C2

SIGHTS & ACTIVITIES pp180-1
Byron Bay Dive Centre & Surf School	**5** D2
Sundive	**6** D2
Surf Lifesaving Club	**7** D1
Swimming Pool	**8** C1

SLEEPING pp181-4
A Peaceful Place	**9** D5
Amigos	**10** D5
Aquarius Backpacker Resort	**11** D2
Arts Factory Lodge	**12** C5
Backpackers Holiday Village	**13** D5
Bamboo Cottage	**14** C3
Baystay	**15** D5
Beach Hotel	**16** C1
Belongil Beachouse	**17** B4
Belongil by the Sea	**18** B4
Blue Iguana Beach House	**19** D1
Byron Bay Bunkhouse	**20** D3
Cape Byron YHA	**21** D2
Cossies by the Sea	**22** B4
Hibiscus Motel	**23** D2
J's Bay YHA	**24** D3
Nomads Main Beach Backpackers	**25** D2
Rae's on Watego's	**26** F3

SHOPPING pp185-6
Community Centre	**42** C2
Funksta	**43** C2
Planet Corroboree	(see 42)
Plaza Shopping Centre	**44** C3
Victoria Spring Designs	**45** C2
Woolworths	(see 44)

TRANSPORT pp186
Jetset Travel	**46** D2
Long Distance Bus Stop	**47** C2

OTHER
Ambaji	**48** D2
Laundromat	**49** C2
Pure Byron Day Spa	(see 29)
Relax Haven	(see 17)
Yoga Arts	**50** D2

To Julian Rocks
Marine Reserve (700m)

Byron Bay

Belongil
Beach

Belongil Creek

Don St
Childe St

Border St

Cavanbah St

Sunrise Blvd

Ewingsdale Rd

Shirley St

Shirley Ln

To Colin Heaney Gallery,
Flying Trapeze & Circus
Adventure, Pacific
Hwy (4km) & Tyagarah Airport (9km)

Burns St

Gordon St

Skinners
Shoot Rd

Main
Beach

Bay St

Byron St

Marvell St

Lawson St

Sports Marvell St
Field

Carlyle St

Kingsley St

Ruskin St

Browning St

Seaview St

Bangalow Rd

Paterson

See Enlargement

To Suffolk Park (4km), Nirvana
Lodge, Broken Head (5km),
Broken Head Holiday Park
(5km) & Lennox Head (17km)

0   200 m
0   0.1 mi

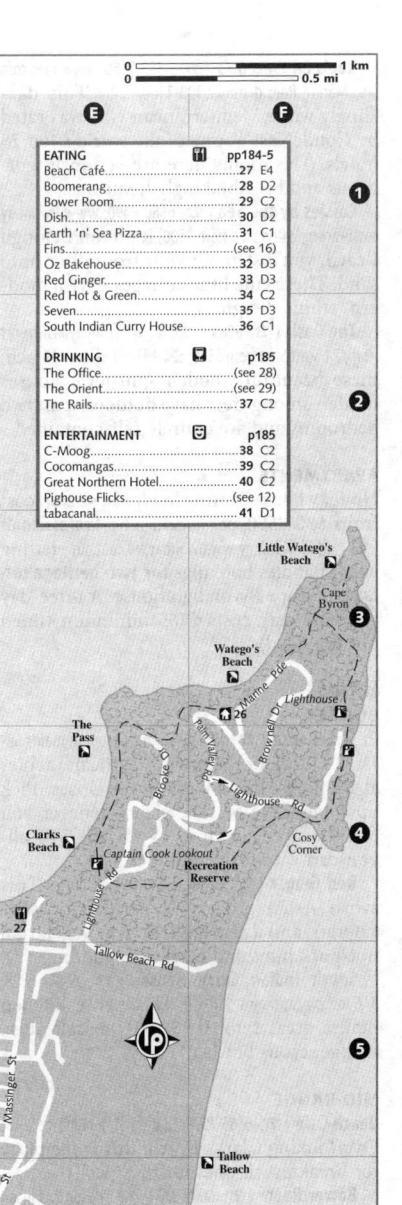

Belongil Beachouse (☎ 6685 7868; www.belongil beachouse.com; Childe St; dm $25-28, d $60-70; apt $80-120, self-contained cottages $140-195; 💻) Across from Belongil Beach, this is a fantastic place to stay, and great value for money. Polished floorboards, stained glass in the dorm doors and mosaics add to the atmosphere. Rest Haven spa is on the premises.

Arts Factory Lodge (☎ 6685 7709; www.arts factory.com.au; Skinners Shoot Rd; camp sites/dm/d from $11/22/55; 💻) If you dig the alternative lifestyle, this is the place for you. Get a load of the permaculture gardens, teepees, didgeridoo lessons, DJs, yoga classes and atmospheric Piggery Café and Pighouse Flicks (see Entertainment; p185). There are free minibuses around town.

Backpackers Holiday Village (☎ 1800 350 388, 6685 8888; 116 Jonson St; dm $22-25, d $50-60; 💻) Lively common areas, clean dorms, and a travel desk where you can book flights are all a bonus, but the real winner is the self-contained two-bedroom apartments ($53 to $63).

Cape Byron YHA (☎ 1800 652 627, 6685 8788; www.nrg.com.au/byronyha; cnr Middleton & Byron Sts; dm $22-28, d $30-40, with bathroom $70-110) This outstanding complex is situated close to the town centre and has its own shops and heated pool. It's very clean and orderly, and also has a travel agent and dive shop on site.

Other recommendations:

Aquarius Backpacker Resort (☎ 1800 229 955, 6685 7663; www.byron-bay.com/aquarius; 16 Lawson St; dm from $25, d $60-160; 💻) Close to Main Beach. Has a bar, café, pool and garden. Dorms have bathroom, TV and fridge.

J's Bay YHA (☎ 1800 678 195, 6685 8853; www.byron -bay.com/jsbay; 7 Carlyle St; dm $20-27, d $60-100; 💻) Very clean. Bikes and boards for hire and facilities for disabled travellers.

Byron Bay Bunkhouse (☎ 1800 241 600, 6685 8311; www.byronbay-bunkhouse.com.au; 1 Carlyle St; dm $20-25, d $50; 💻) Pancake breakfast included, noisy and cheerful, big veranda.

Blue Iguana Beach House (☎ 6685 5298; 14 Bay St; dm $25, d $55-65) Tiny, friendly and right by the beach, you need to book ahead.

Nomads Main Beach Backpackers (☎ 1800 150 233, 6685 8695; 19-23 Lawson St; dm $18-25, d $45-100) The four-bed dorms are the best value for money.

Broken Head Holiday Park (☎ 6685 3245; Beach Rd, Broken Head; camp sites/cabins from $18/55) The best of Byron's caravan parks, at the southern end of Tallow Beach.

CROWDED HOUSE *by Meg Worby*

Beware the growing trend of 'B&Bs' that are 'just on the market', who ask for upfront payment into a private account. Some of Byron's locals are cashing in when the town is full to overflowing, offering up their houses at not-so-friendly rates and then staying at a mate's for the weekend. Problem is, when you turn up you'll find a house full of other people, similarly jipped (think cold showers, no loo paper and plumbing problems). It's better to book as early as possible, especially if there's a festival on.

MID-RANGE

Bamboo Cottage (☎ 6685 5509; www.byron-bay.com /bamboocottage; 76 Butler St; d from $80) Great value, the bedrooms in this pretty 1930s house are sumptuous and brightly – perhaps *too* brightly – coloured. French, English, sign language and some Japanese are spoken.

Amigos (☎ 6680 8622; www.amigosbb.com; 32 Kingsley St; s $45-65, d $70-120) A cute blue and green house with hammocks in the garden and spotless rooms decorated with Mexican rugs. The cottage in the backyard is great.

A Peaceful Place (☎ 6685 6560; www.byron -bay.com/apeacefulplace; 41 Ruskin St; s/d from $45/75) Run by a friendly couple, this B&B is quiet, clean and free of TVs. Stan has a glass studio out the front and sometimes gives classes to guests.

Other recommendations:

Baystay (☎ 6685 7509, 0419-618 401; www.byron-bay .com/baystay; 30 Marvell St; d from $90) Comfortable B&B with a private sauna and tropical continental breakfast.

Belongil by the Sea (☎ 6685 8111; www.belongil beach.com; 33-35 Childe St; d from $70, cabins $95-220) Has seen better days, but has palm trees, a large swimming pool and the beach is just across the road.

Hibiscus Motel (☎ 6685 6195; www.byronbayresorts .com/hibiscus; 33 Lawson St; d $135-295; 🐾) Excellent location, right in town and right near Main Beach. Clean and functional rooms.

TOP END

Beach Hotel (☎ 6685 6402; www.beachhotel.com.au; cnr Jonson & Bay Sts; d from $220, spa rooms $275-385; 🐾) Nothing is more central than this beachfront hotel. Ground floor rooms open onto lush gardens and a heated pool; upper-storey rooms have ocean views. Babysitting services are available.

Rae's on Watego's (☎ 6685 5366; www.raes.com .au; Marine Pde; d from $300-1100; 🐾) This dazzlingly white Mediterranean villa was rated by CondeNast as one of the world's top 25 hotels. The rooms here are seriously gorgeous and breathtakingly luxurious.

Cossies by the Sea (☎ 6680 8490; www.byronbay cossies.com; 2 Don St; d from $300) Right on Belongil Beach, you'll step out your front door onto sand. These cute little cottages have a modern, ethnic design.

The Oasis (☎ 6685 7390; www.byronbayoasisresort .com; 24 Scott St; d from $360; 🐾) By Tallow Beach, these beautiful wooden split-level houses hidden among trees have outdoor spas, two bedrooms and are entirely self-contained.

APARTMENTS

Holiday houses during low/peak season cost from $300/550 per week. The **Professionals** (☎ 6685 6552; www.byronbaypro.com.au) letting agent handles bookings for two **heritage cottages** at Cape Byron lighthouse. A three-day weekend stay costs $465 minimum (linen not provided).

Eating
BUDGET

Oz Bakehouse (☎ 6685 7717; 20 Jonson St; mains $8-12; 🖳) Ideal for those who get the munchies at all times, this bakery never closes. Pick up a pie, cake or sandwich whenever you feel the need, or drop by for the $10 all-you-can-eat Mexican dinner.

Red Ginger (☎ 6680 9779; 109 Jonson St) This swish Asian grocery is perfect for self-caterers, and it also has takeaway vegetarian not-pork buns and black rice pudding.

South Indian Curry House (☎ 6685 6828; 5/2 Jonson St; mains $10-19) This petite kitchen makes great sambal ($2.50), masala dosa and generous bowls of curry.

MID-RANGE

Beach Café (☎ 6685 7598; Lawson St; breakfast $9-15) Overlooking Clarks Beach, this is *the* place for breakfast (it does lunch as well).

Bower Room (☎ 6685 7771; cnr Lawson & Jonson Sts; mains $14-28) Pull up a chair on the veranda overlooking the Byron Bay hubbub. The modern Italian menu includes appetizer-sized portions, perfect with something cold from the cocktail list ($6 to $12).

Red Hot & Green (☎ 6685 5363; 17 Lawson St; mains $14-20) Walk down the alleyway and dig into award-winning noodles or sip tea from all across Asia. The colonial tea-room ambience, all rattan and marble, is somewhat tempered by the house music.

Earth 'n' Sea Pizza (☎ 6685 6029; 11 Lawson St; pizzas $14-30) Some travellers swear this is the best pizza they've ever had; others disagree violently.

Seven (☎ 6685 7478; Shop 13 The Plaza, Jonson St; mains $8-22) Making the most of its strip mall location with cunning use of obscure soul music and palm trees, Seven makes truly great breakfasts – and Middle Eastern and Asian-influenced lunches.

Dish (☎ 6685 7320; cnr Jonson & Marvell Sts; mains $27-30) This opulent place has a modern Australian menu and impressive wine list. Hit the adjoining Dish Raw Bar – with super-stylish black-and-white leather furnishings – for a half-dozen oysters, a cocktail and a superb dessert.

TOP END
Rae's on Watego's (☎ 6685 5366; Marine Pde; mains $30-60) Famous chefs dream up divine Thai combinations, such as mud crabs in Malaysian satay sauce, or crispy suckling pig with bean curd and chilli sauce. Call ahead and Rae's will tailor dishes to your needs.

Boomerang (☎ 6685 5707; 4/4 Middleton St; mains $30-35; ☽ dinner only, closed Sun) The Mod Oz menu takes advantage of fresh produce and game from the local area, with dishes like sumac roasted rabbit with eggplant puree.

Fins (☎ 6685 5029; The Beach Hotel; ☽ 6-10pm; mains $28-35) Byron's most central hotel offers superb, fresh seafood in this excellent little restaurant.

Drinking
Beach Hotel (cnr Jonson & Bay Sts) This enormous beachfront beer garden draws everyone from pensioners on bus tours to fire twirlers on acid. All of Byron is happening around you.

The Rails (☎ 6685 7662; Jonson St) A great place to get loaded and embarrass yourself – it's so easy to hop on a train and bail to Queensland. What's more, the kitchen here makes great tofu burgers and the atmosphere keeps it utterly real.

The Office (☎ 6685 5707; 4/4 Middleton St) Part of Boomerang (see Eating; above), The Office tempts corporate types with its wine, whisky and cigar bar.

Bower Room (☎ 6685 7771; cnr Lawson & Jonson Sts) If it's a cocktail you're craving the Bower Room can help you. There's nothing can't be cured by a warm evening, a veranda and a mojito. Take your cocktails with sushi and a healthy helping of hip at **Dish Raw Bar** (☎ 6685 7320; cnr Jonson & Marvell Sts).

Entertainment
Byron Bay's nightlife has something over all the other towns on the north coast. Check the gig guide in Thursday's *Byron Shire News* or tune into Bay 91.3 FM.

CINEMA
Pighouse Flicks (☎ 6685 7709; Skinners Shoot Rd; admission $11) lounge cinema at the Arts Factory Lodge (see Sleeping; p183) offers 'dinner and a movie' deals nightly. The seats are covered in faux fur.

CLUBBING
tabacanal (☎ 6680 8010; Shop 4, 9 Fletcher St) From 4pm to 10pm this place is a laid-back loungebar and restaurant; after 10pm the DJs start spinning.

Cocomangas (☎ 6685 8493; 32 Jonson St) You can dance the night away at this nightclub, open until 3am (closed Sunday) with special retro, funk and techno nights.

C-Moog (☎ 6680 7022; The Plaza, Jonson St) Another late-night club, C-Moog spins funk and beats.

LIVE MUSIC
Great Northern Hotel (☎ 6685 6454; Jonson St) This enormous, boisterous pub has live music almost every night.

The Rails (☎ 6685 7662; Jonson St) There's live music just about every night and things really get kicking on the weekends.

Shopping
Planet Corroboree (☎ 6685 8866; Shop 2/7-9 Byron St) In the community centre, Corroborree stocks all kinds of Aboriginal arts – modern and traditional – from bark paintings to CDs of contemporary musicians.

Victoria Spring Designs (☎ 6680 7399; 1 Marvell St) Sumptuous Victorian-styled homewares (the queen, not the state), lingerie, jewellery and silk saris.

Funksta (☎ 6680 7370; 8/6 Lawson St) Super-hip men's and women's wear made from torn-apart vintage treasures.

Pure Byron Day Spa (☎ 6685 5988; The Orient, Jonson St) If it's smelly, Pure Byron sells it: massage oils, soaps, moisturisers and all kinds of aromatherapy cures.

Getting There & Away

AIR

The closest airport is at Ballina ($244 from Melbourne, $125 from Sydney) but most people use the larger Coolangatta airport on the Gold Coast (p298).

BUS

Long-distance buses stop on Jonson St. They go to Surfers Paradise ($28, 2 hours), Brisbane ($33, 3 hours), Coffs Harbour ($37, 4 hours) and Sydney ($65, 12 to 14 hours).

Kirklands (☎ 6622 1499; www.kirklands.com.au) goes to Lismore ($13.20, 1 hour 10 minutes), Murwillumbah ($11.90, 2 hours) and Coolangatta Airport ($23, 2 hours 10 minutes).

Blanch's (☎ 6686 2144; www.tropicalnsw.com.au /blanchs) goes to Ballina ($7.50, 55 minutes), Lennox Head ($5, 30 minutes), Bangalow ($5.70, 25 minutes) and Mullumbimby ($4.60, 30 minutes).

McCafferty's/Greyhound (☎ 13 14 19; www .mccaffertys.com.au) travels to Byron Bay ($16, 1 hour).

TRAIN

The quickest **CountryLink** (☎ 13 22 32; www.coun trylink.nsw.gov.au) train from Sydney ($104) is the 7.15am XPT, which reaches Byron around 8pm.

Getting Around

Byron Bay Bicycles (☎ 6685 6067; 93 Jonson St) hires mountain bikes for $22 per day.

Earth Car Rentals (☎ 6685 7472; www.byron -bay.com/earthcar; 14 Middleton St) hires older cars from $38 a day. **Jetset Travel** (☎ 6685 6554; Old Bakery Complex, Marvell St) rents newer, small cars from $49.

BYRON BAY TO TWEED HEADS

The Pacific Hwy continues north past the **Big Avocado** (at Tropical Fruit World off the Tweed Heads–Murwillumbah road, and not worth the detour) to the Queensland border at Tweed Heads.

The pretty Coolamon Scenic Drive leaves the highway just south of Brunswick Heads, passing through **Mullumbimby** (population 2700). Mullum was once legendary for its

marijuana; these days it's just a quiet farming town. A couple of average motels and pubs offer accommodation. Join locals for a bite at popular **Lu Lu's** (☎ 02-6684 2415; 100 Dalley St; mains $5-15) which has great coffee and unusual snacks. **Café Mazah** (☎ 02-6684 2348; 47 Burringbar St; mains $6.50-13) cooks betelnut chicken and other Middle Eastern fare. Newcomer **Café al Dente** (☎ 02-6684 3676; Stuart St; mains $7-16; ☯ breakfast & lunch) is wowing Mullum with dishes like chargrilled spatchcock with rosemary.

Blanch's (☎ 02-6686 2144; www.tropicalnsw.com.au /blanchs) runs from Mullumbimby to Byron ($4.60, 30 minutes). The **CountryLink** (☎ 13 22 32; www.countrylink.nsw.gov.au) train to Sydney is $98 (13 hours).

In **Main Arm**, about 12km west of Mullumbimby (head out of town on Burringbar St, then follow Main Arm Rd and the blue 'camping' signs), is **Maca's Camping Ground** (☎ 02-6684 5211; Main Arm Rd; camp sites $16-20, on-site vans $25-40), on a macadamia-nut plantation. It has a communal kitchen, hot showers, laundry and a dam to swim in.

Take the Chinderah Bypass to the legendary **Moo Moo Café** (☎ 02-6677 1730; Ampol Service Station; ☯ until 5pm), in the town of Mooball. It collects bovine kitsch and farm memorabilia, and humungous burgers with the works cost only $9.

Along the coastal Tweed Coast road, **Bogangar (Cabarita Beach)** and **Kingscliff** are the main resorts. The **Emu Park Lodge** (☎ 02-6676 1190; www.tropicalnsw.com.au/accommodation/emu parklodge; 77 Coast Rd; dm/d $21/45) is across from Cabarita Beach. Staff at this tidy hostel organise outings to Mt Warning (around $85) and bikes, boards and fishing rods are free. Ring for a free pick-up from Kingscliff or Tweed Heads.

Tweed Heads marks the southern end of the Gold Coast strip. At Point Danger (named by Captain Cook to warn others of the treacherous rocks and shoals), the towering **Captain Cook Memorial** straddles the state border. Tweed Heads accommodation spills over into Coolangatta and up the Gold Coast (p303), where there's more choice.

Surfside (☎ 13 12 30; www.surfside.com.au) has buses from Tweed to Murwillumbah ($4.80, 50 minutes), to Kingscliff ($3.10, 20 minutes), and Cabarita Beach ($4.50, 30 minutes), stopping on Bay St near Tweed Mall.

FAR NORTH COAST HINTERLAND

Stretching inland from the Pacific Hwy, the far north hinterland of NSW is green, rolling and lush, punctuated by dramatic mountains. Big with alternative lifestylers since the Aquarius Festival hit Nimbin in 1973, this area is sometimes known as 'Rainbow Country'. The area's three national parks – Border Ranges, Mt Warning and Nightcap – are all World Heritage rainforest.

BANGALOW

☎ 02 / pop 900

The very picture of gentrification, Bangalow (10 minutes west of Byron) has a charming country pub, fine eateries, antique shops and heritage buildings. Pop into the **CWA Handicrafts Store** (31 Byron St), which has all your crocheted tea cosy needs covered.

Bangalow Hotel (☎ 6687 1314; 1 Byron St; s/d $45/65) is a quaint place with only a few rooms, so book ahead. The restaurant here, **Country Fresh** (mains $8 to $20), has a menu of hearty, modern food, and it's darn pleasant

---

MARKETS

The Hinterland's weekend markets are great for music, trinkets and some of the country's best people watching. The biggest market is at The Channon.

Bangalow (☎ 6687 1911) 4th Sunday, Showground
Byron Bay (☎ 6687 7181) 1st Sunday, Butler St Reserve
The Channon (☎ 6688 6433) 2nd Sunday, Coronation Park
Lennox Head (☎ 6672 2874) 2nd & 5th Sunday, Lake Ainsworth foreshore
Lismore (☎ 6628 7333) 1st & 3rd Sunday, Lismore Shopping Sq
Mullumbimby (☎ 6684 3370) 3rd Saturday, Stuart St
Murwillumbah (☎ 6679 1489) 2nd Sunday, Sunnyside Plaza; (☎ 6672 2874) 4th Sunday, Showground
Nimbin Aquarius Fair (☎ 6689 1183) 3rd Sunday, Community Centre, Cullen St
Uki (☎ 6679 5369) 3rd Sunday, Old Buttery

---

taking a meal on the back veranda. There are regular live bands. Gorgeous **Riverview Guest House** (☎ 6687 1317; 99 Byron St; d $165-185) is right on the creek (where platypi play every night) and has beautifully furnished rooms and delicious breakfasts.

Near the bottom of the hill, locals meet at **The Urban** (☎ 6687 7678; 39 Byron St; mains $10-14; ☺ 8am-5pm) for leisurely coffee, late breakfasts and Bangalow gossip. At **Wild About Food** (☎ 6687 2555; 33 Byron St; mains $17-24; ☺ dinner Tue-Sat), Mod Oz dishes are eaten in an elegant setting of wall-to-wall Bakelite green.

LISMORE

☎ 02 / pop 43,000

A great base for visiting the hinterland, or even Byron, Lismore is close to rainforest, beaches and the river, has some interesting cafés and places to stay and has a thriving arts scene. Sometimes known as the Wok, Lismore is hot as hell in summer.

The **visitors centre** (☎ 6622 0122; Ballina St; ☺ 9.30am-4pm Mon-Fri, 10am-3pm Sat & Sun) has a rainforest display ($1). Have a seat and read the compelling oral history record *Memories of the '60s and '70s*. Little kids dig the **Heritage Park** playground, next to the centre, with its skate park and **train rides** ($1.50; ☺ 10am-2pm Thu, 10am-4pm Sat & Sun).

There are no fusty McCubbins at the **Lismore Regional Art Gallery** (☎ 6622 2209; www .lismore.nsw.gov.au/gallery; 131 Molesworth St; admission by donation; ☺ 10am-4pm Tue-Fri, 10.30am-2.30pm Sat & Sun). Expect contemporary artists expressing local concerns in novel ways.

It's quiet, cool and leafy in the pocket of oxymoronic dry rainforest in **Rotary Park** (☎ 6622 0122; Uralba St, off Rotary Dr). **Tucki Tucki Nature Reserve** (☎ 6628 1177; Wyrallah Rd, 16km south of town) protects koala habitat. Initiation ceremonies were once held at the Aboriginal **bora ring** nearby.

See Ballina (p178) for information on **river cruises** from Lismore.

Sleeping

Lismore Backpackers (☎ 6621 6118; currendi@nor .com.au; 14 Ewing St; dm $20, s/d from $30/45) With its quiet, calm atmosphere, this drug-and-alcohol-free hostel attracts a more grown-up crowd.

Winsome Hotel (☎ 6621 2283; www.winsome -hotel.com; 11 Bridge St; s/d $35/50) This pub is special, from the Hammond organ in the common room to the eclectically furnished rooms (Nos 17, 21 and 24 are particularly good) – you may feel like you're staying in an art installation. Shared bathrooms are among the prettiest in the state.

Tulloona House (☎ 6624 2897; 106 Ballina Rd, Goonellabah; s/d $80/100 with breakfast) 'Never throw anything away' might be the motto of Tulloona's owners. This National Trust–classified Victorian mansion is packed to bursting with antique bric-a-brac. It's 5km towards Ballina; pick-ups can be arranged.

Lismore Palms Caravan Park (☎ 6621 7067; 42-48 Brunswick St; camp sites/cabins from $14/50) The best of Lismore's three caravan parks, this one has pleasant staff and atmosphere. It's right on the river and has self-contained cabins and a pool.

Eating

Mecca Café (☎ 6621 3901; 80 Magellan St; meals $3.50-11; ☒ breakfast & lunch Mon-Sat) Cunningly combining trendy with comfortable, Mecca's old-fashioned, high-ceilinged, black-and-cream décor and great music make it an ideal place to read the paper over breakfast.

Au Peche Mignon (☎ 6621 5643, 36 Carrington St; pastries from $2; ☒ 8am-5pm Mon-Fri, 8am-12.30pm Sat) This great little French patisserie, near Magellan St, has rich coffee, croissants and cakes.

Georgio's Vegetarian Italia (☎ 6622 3177; 73 Magellan St Arcade; mains $8-12.50; ☒ 8.30am-3pm Mon-Sat, 6-9pm Wed-Sat) Not just vegetarian, also 'fresh, hand-picked and chemical-free'. Have a double helping of the guilt-free tofu cacciatore.

The Left Bank Café (☎ 6622 2338; 133 Molesworth St; mains $8-16) Like all gallery cafés worth their sea-salt, the Left Bank – which is on the left bank by the Transit Centre – is delightfully pretentious and makes a very good cup of coffee.

20,000 Cows Café (☎ 6622 2517; 58 Bridge St; mains $6-10; ☒ dinner Wed-Sun) Over the river towards Nimbin, this vegan café with comfily cobbled-together ethnic décor dishes up Indian and Middle Eastern delights.

Drinking

Mecca Café (☎ 6621 3901; 80 Magellan St) On Friday and Saturday nights they close the kitchen at this splendid café and open the bar. Cosy booths make it a pleasant place for a drink or three.

Northern Rivers Hotel (☎ 6621 5797; Bridge St) What a socially conscious place this pub is – while you're meeting the Lismore locals over a schooner, the in-house crèche (Thursday to Saturday nights) will mind your kids.

Entertainment

Powerhouse Niteclub (☎ 6622 4736; 77 Molesworth St) Inside the Canberra Hotel, the Powerhouse claims to be the 'only true nightspot in Lismore', whatever that means. They have live bands Thursday to Saturday.

Winsome Hotel (☎ 6621 2283; 11 Bridge St) Enjoy live bands, DJs, pool competitions and all kinds of other entertainment under the benevolent eye of the Big Regina (one of Australia's least-known 'big things': a huge portrait of HM Queen Elizabeth II).

Getting There & Away

Rex (☎ 13 17 13; www.regionalexpress.com.au) has flights to Sydney ($95, 1 hour 15 minutes).

McCafferty's/Greyhound (☎ 13 14 19; www.mccaffertys.com.au) travels to Byron Bay ($16, 1 hour), Ballina ($15, 40 minutes), Murwillumbah ($18, 3 hours) and Brisbane ($27, 4 hours 20 minutes).

Kirklands (☎ 6622 1499; www.kirklands.com.au) runs to Ballina ($11, 40 minutes) and to Byron Bay ($13.20, 1 hour 10 minutes). **Marsh's** (☎ 6689 1220) school bus runs to Murwillumbah ($7).

The **CountryLink** (☎ 13 22 32; www.countrylink.nsw.gov.au) train to Sydney costs $98 (12 hours).

THE CHANNON

One of the tinier towns in the area, The Channon (off the Nimbin–Lismore road) swells to bursting on the second Sunday of each month, when it hosts the biggest of the region's markets.

The Channon Teahouse Eatery & Gallery (☎ 02-6688 6276; Mills St; mains $4-12; ☒ 10am-5pm, dinner Sat; ☐) makes light meals, sells handicrafts and second-hand goods, and operates a booking service for local B&Bs.

A basic **camping ground** (☎ 02-6688 6321; Channon Rd; camp sites from $5) near the fairgrounds opens on market weekends.

NIGHTCAP NATIONAL PARK

The 800m-plus Nightcap Range, originally a flank of the huge Mt Warning volcano, dominates this World Heritage wilderness.

The eastern region is accessed via The Channon. A beautiful 700m walk leads through rainforest to Protestors Falls, named after a 1979 campaign against logging. There is camping at Terania Creek (one night only) with no fires or swimming – it can muck up the fragile environment here.

The 12km sealed road to **Mt Nardi** (800m) rises steeply northeast of Nimbin. There are several walking trails that lead from the summit, including the beautiful Pholis Walk to Mt Matheson.

Terania Caravan Park (☎ 02-6688 6121; 390 Terania Creek Rd; camp sites/cabins from $7/70) is on the road between The Channon and the park.

NIMBIN
☎ 02 / pop 1300

Since the Aquarius Festival of 1973, Nimbin, 30km north of Lismore, has been synonymous with hippies. If you're genuinely interested in an alternative lifestyle, you'll get a lot out of Nimbin; if you just want to check out the weirdos, take a day-tour from Byron (see Tours; opposite). You'll probably get offered pot on the street. If you don't like that kind of thing, you might find the persistent dealers annoying.

Despite the size of its reputation, Nimbin is a tiny village. The helpful **Nimbin Connexion** (☎ 6689 1764; www.nimbinaustralia.com; 80 Cullen St; ☻ 10am-6pm; ☲) on the northern side of town handles transport and accommodation bookings, foreign exchange and Willing Workers on Organic Farms (Wwoof) memberships – there are over 90 participating farms in the region.

Nimbin Museum (☎ 6689 1123; 62 Cullen St; admission $2; ☻ 9am-5pm) is interpretive and expressionistic, more a work of art than of history. Across the street, the **Hemp Embassy** (☎ 6689 1842; www.hempembassy.net; 51 Cullen St; ☻ 'whenever') raises consciousness about marijuana legalisation, as well as providing all the tools and fashion items you'll need to get high. The embassy leads the **Mardi Grass** festival each May. Smokers are welcome at the coffee shop next door.

Djanbung Gardens (☎ 6689 1755; www.earthwise .org.au; 74 Cecil St) is a permaculture education centre, café and bookshop. If you want to visit, call ahead to make an appointment, or see opposite for tours. The town's biggest employer is the **Rainbow Power Company**

(☎ 6689 1430; 1 Alternative Way), designers of home-energy systems using sun, wind and water. Again, if you want to visit it's best to join a tour.

Nimbin Rocks is an Aboriginal sacred site (not open to visitors) clearly visible from the Lismore road a few kilometres south of town. Hanging Rock Creek has waterfalls and a good swimming hole. To get there, go to the end of Stony Shute Rd (about 14km), turn right, then left and left again.

Tours
Jim's Alternative Tours (☎ 6685 7720; www.byron -bay.com/jimstours) is a long-running Byron outfit with a definite party bent. It runs day-trips from Byron ($30).

Nimbin Shuttle (☎ 6680 9189) travels from Byron to the monthly Aquarius Fair ($20), or will drive you to and from Nimbin any day of the week for $22.

Nimbin Connexion (☎ 6689 1764; 80 Cullen St; ☻ 10am-6pm) runs bus tours of Djangbung Gardens and **Rainbow Power Company** (admission $3; ☻ 1-2pm Mon-Fri).

Sleeping
Nimbin Rox Hostel (☎ 6689 0022; nimbinroxhostel .com; 74 Thornburn St; camp sites/dm/d $10/20/40) Rox has hammocks, permaculture gardens, craft workshops, live bands, Thai massage and a pool. Everything is clean and new and the atmosphere is relaxed and friendly.

Garden Retreat Bed & Breakfast (☎ 6689 1145; Tuntable Falls Rd; s/d $40/60) The friendly, interesting owners have been here since the Aquarius Festival, and the comfortable, cheery house, 10 minutes drive from town, is decorated accordingly. The garden is beautiful, and there can't be a prettier outdoor toilet in the Hinterland.

Rainbow Retreat Backpackers (☎ 6689 1262; 75 Thorburn St; camp sites/dm/d $8/15/40) Very basic, but totally in the age-of-Aquarius spirit, you'll feel like you've fallen through a timewarp at Rainbow Retreat. Relax, chill out, play the didgeridoo or camp out in the gypsy vans. There's a free courtesy bus from Byron Bay.

Other recommendations:
Nimbin Backpackers at Granny's Farm (☎ 6689 1333; www.nimbinbackpackers.com; 110 Cullen St; dm/d $20/50) Two pools and train-carriage accommodation: get in early to get one of the single compartments.
Nimbin Hotel (☎ 6689 1246; Cullen St; dm $15) Pretty basic and grungy, but right in town.

Grey Gum Lodge (☎ 6689 1713; www.nimbinaus tralia.com/greygumlodge; 2 High St; s/d/f $32/50/60) All rooms in this weatherboard house have bathroom, TV and fridge, and the family room sleeps four adults.

Nimbin Tourist Caravan Park (☎ 6689 1402; Sibley St; camp sites from $19) Next to the local swimming pool, down Cullen St past the Hotel.

Eating

Rainbow Café (☎ 6689 1997; 64A Cullen St; mains $3-7) The original Nimbin institution makes delicious cakes, breakfast and vegetarian fare and has a big backyard.

Ellora Cave (☎ 6689 1616; 81 Cullen St; mains around $6) Underneath the school, this restaurant is run by an old Indian couple and serves vegan cuisine. Get an entrée, main, dessert and a drink for $14. They also run Indian vegan cooking classes on weekends.

Nimbin Trattoria & Pizzeria (☎ 6689 1427; 70 Cullen St; mains $7-16, pizzas $4-23; ☻ dinner) Pizzas, pastas, salads and some damn fine desserts.

Getting There & Away

The **Nimbin Shuttle** (☎ 6680 9189) operates to and from Byron Bay ($12 one way, except Sunday).

BORDER RANGES NATIONAL PARK

This enormous World Heritage wilderness area (31,500 hectares) covers the NSW side of the McPherson Range along the Queensland border. More than a quarter of Australia's native bird species can be found within the park. The eastern section, with escarpments of the massive Mt Warning caldera, is the most easily accessible. The **Tweed Range Scenic Drive** (gravel but useable in all weather) loops for 100km through the park from Lillian Rock, midway between Uki and Kyogle, to Wiangaree, north of Kyogle on the Woodenbong road. It has some breathtaking lookouts over the Tweed Valley to Mt Warning and the coast. There are rainforest walks from the picnic area at **Brindle Creek**.

There are a couple of basic **camping grounds** ($3) on the Tweed Range Scenic Drive, at Forest Tops and Sheep Station Creek. Bring water. For bookings call Kyogle **NPWS** (☎ 02-6632 1473; kyogle@npws.nsw.gov.au).

MT WARNING NATIONAL PARK

The dramatic peak of Mt Warning (1157m) dominates the entire district. Captain Cook, with true Yorkshire pragmatism, named the

mountain after using it as a landmark to avoid Point Danger (named by guess who).

Local Aborigines call the mountain Wol-lumbin, or 'Fighting Chief of the Mountains'. It began life 20 million years ago as the central magma chamber of a 4000 sq km volcano, stretching from Coraki in the south to Beenleigh (Queensland) in the north, and from Kyogle to an eastern rim now buried beneath the sea. Erosion has since carved out the deep Tweed and Oxley valleys around Mt Warning, but sections of the flanks survive in the Nightcap Range to the south and parts of the Border Ranges to the north. These days the crater around Mt Warning is known as a centre of spiritual energy.

Off the Murwillumbah–Uki road, a 6km access road runs to the car park at the base of the mountain. Much of the 4.5km **summit walk** rises through rainforest. Allow five hours for the return trip and take water. The trail is well marked, but you'll need a torch for pre-dawn climbing.

Sleeping & Eating

No camping is allowed within the park.

Mt Warning Caravan Park (☎ 02-6679 5120; Mt Warning Rd; camp sites/cabins from $16/50) About 2km down the road that approaches Mt Warning, this caravan park has kitchen facilities, a well-stocked kiosk and plenty of wild critters.

Mt Warning Forest Hideaway (☎ 02-6679 7277; www.foresthideaway.com.au; Byrrill Creek Rd; d from $60, f $120) Choose from self-contained multi-bedroom apartments or kitchenette studios at this little dog-friendly creekside resort in bushland 12km southwest of Uki.

Uki Dreaming (☎ 02-6679 5777; 1451 Kyogle Rd; s/d $40/80) This simple guesthouse is in the tiny township of Uki, on the park border. It's friendly and clean, and has a pool table. There's also a licensed **café** (☎ 02-6679 5351; mains $6-15) serving vegetarian pizza, pastas, breakfasts and lunches, and a **healing centre** (☎ 02-6679 4235) with a world-renowned psychic.

Healing by the schooner is offered at the **Mount Warning Hotel** (☎ 6679 5111; Main St), where the veranda offers a great view of the mountain.

Getting There & Away

Marsh's (☎ 02-6689 1220) school bus leaves Knox Park in Murwillumbah at 7.10am and can drop you off at the Mt Warning approach

NEW SOUTH WALES

road. It continues to Uki, Nimbin and Lismore, then back again in the afternoon.

The hostels at Murwillumbah and Bogangar (Cabarita Beach; p186), on the Tweed Coast, organise trips to the mountain.

MURWILLUMBAH
☎ 02 / pop 9000

Mount Warning looms over the sugar cane fields around Murwillumbah, a quiet town on the banks of the Tweed River. It's a very relaxing place to spend a few days.

On the Pacific Hwy near the train station, the **visitors centre** (☎ 6672 1340; info@tactic.nsw.gov .au; 9am-4.30pm) incorporates an NPWS office and books accommodation.

The excellent **Tweed River Regional Art Gallery** (☎ 6672 0409; 5 Tumbulgum Rd; admission free; 10am-5pm Wed-Sun) is up the road from the hostel. Home to the Australian Portrait Collection, it administers the world's richest daubing competition, the Doug Moran National Portrait Prize, worth $100,000 to the winning painter.

Off the main street near the Imperial Hotel, the **Tweed River Historical Society Museum** (☎ 6672 1865; Queensland Rd; admission $2; 11am-4pm Wed & Fri, 10am-3pm every 4th Sun) has an awesome collection of antique hi-fi and radio equipment.

Sleeping & Eating
Brightly painted and relaxing, **Riverside YHA Backpackers** (☎ 6672 3763, www.nnsw.worldtourism .com.au/RiversideBackpackers; 1 Tumbulgum Rd; dm/d $23/ 50;) is beside the Tweed River, on your right after crossing the bridge into town. Float on an inner tube or take a canoeing or cycling trip. Stay two nights for a free trip to Mt Warning.

On the main street, the jaw-droppingly pink **Imperial Hotel** (☎ 6672 1036; 115 Main St; s/d $25/40) has clean and comfortable rooms ($50 with bathroom), a bistro and a nightclub.

At **Al & Rosie's Eatery** (☎ 6672 2831; 7 Wharf St; mains $12-18) Rosie dishes up Filipino food, augmented by Aussie burgers and steaks.

Getting There & Away
Most long-distance buses between Sydney ($65, 14 hours) and Brisbane ($16, 1½ hours) drop off passengers near the train station. **McCafferty's/Greyhound** (☎ 13 14 19; www.mccaf fertys.com.au) travels to Lismore ($18, 3 hours). **Surfside** (☎ 13 12 30; www.surfside.com.au) runs to

Tweed Heads ($4.80, 50 minutes). **Marsh's** (☎ 6689 1220) school bus runs to Uki ($2), Nimbin ($5) and Lismore ($7). **CountryLink** (☎ 13 22 32; www.countrylink.nsw.gov.au) trains from Sydney ($105, 13¾ hours) connect with buses to Queensland.

NEW ENGLAND

Atop the Great Dividing Range, vast tablelands of sheep and cattle-grazing country dotted with rainforest tumble over the eastern escarpment onto coastal plains below. Unlike much of Australia, New England – which has a strangely Scottish flavour – has four distinct seasons. If you're travelling along the eastern seaboard, it's well worth diverting inland to visit some of the area's little towns and get a glimpse of the Australian lifestyle away from the coast.

The New England Hwy, which runs from Hexham (northwest of Newcastle) to Brisbane, has far less traffic than the coastal roads and is an inland alternative to the Pacific Hwy.

TAMWORTH
☎ 02 / pop 35,330

Tamworth's claim to fame is the massive Country Music Festival: its sweaty, true-blue glow pervades every other attraction in this country music capital. Guitar-shaped structures are all the rage, starting with the **visitors centre** (☎ 6755 4300; www.tamworthdirect .com.au; cnr Peel & Murray Sts; 9am-5pm).

Off the New England Hwy in South Tamworth, the **Big Golden Guitar** stands in front of the **Gallery of Stars** (☎ 6765 2688; The Ringers; admission $8; 9am-5pm). Unless you really love waxworks or ersatz country musicians, it's not worth the entry price. More interesting is the **Truck Drivers' Memorial**, about 100m south.

If you really do love country music, spend your money at the excellent **Australian Country Music Foundation Museum** (☎ 6766 9696; 93 Brisbane St; admission $5.50; 10am-2pm Mon-Sat), not far from the train station. Its Golden Guitar display has photos and lists of winners from every awards ceremony; the Hall of Fame features Slim Dusty and Buddy Williams among others, and may be your only chance to see the *Adventures of Smoky Dawson* comic.

There are recording studios, such as **Nashgrill** (☎ 6762 1652; 75 Denison St) and **Big Wheel Recording** (☎ 6765 5677; 24 Wilburtree St), that are open to the public by arrangement; one day's notice is usually enough.

Festivals & Events

Tamworth's population doubles during the **Country Music Festival**, held over the Australia Day long weekend in late January. Over 800 acts perform at more than 2000 events (75% of them free), all culminating with the Australian country music awards, the Golden Guitars.

Sleeping

Unless you book years in advance, you'll be lucky to find a bed or camp site anywhere during the festival, when prices skyrocket. Most of the **pubs** in town have accommodation, and there are tons of **motels** on the highways out of town. The visitors centre can help book **B&Bs**.

The managers of the clean, safe **Tamworth YHA (Country Backpackers)** (☎ 6761 2600; tamyha@yahoo.com; 169 Marius St; dm/d $20/50; 🖳), opposite the train station, are real pros and do a great job organising farmstays, jackaroo courses and casual work. Rates include breakfast.

City Sider Motor Inn (☎ 6766 4777; www.citysidermotorinn.com.au; 237 Marius St; s/d $75/90; 🐾) Notable for its in-town location, City Sider is clean and comfortable and has a pool and laundry.

Ashby House (☎ 1800 027 947, 6762 0033; www.ashbyhousemotorinn.com.au; 83-85 Ebsworth St; d from $107; 🐾) This boutique motor inn has lovely wide verandas and a pool.

Eating

Tamworth Hotel (☎ 6766 2923; 147 Marius St; mains $13-20) The Art Deco front bar is gorgeous and the food is above average. Dress standards are also higher than usual, and you may be frowned at if you turn up in grubby travelling duds.

Inland Café (☎ 6761 2882; 407 Peel St; mains $11-27; 🕑 breakfast & lunch, dinner Thu & Sat) Perhaps the only place in Tamworth where you'll overhear conversations about Pilates, the Inland is very Darlinghurst from the menu to the fittings.

Stetson's Steakhouse & Saloon BBQ (☎ 6762 2238; Craigends Lane; mains $15-20; 🕑 dinner only)

Near the Golden Guitar, this award-winning cowboy-theme restaurant has massive steak dinners for under $25.

Ashby House (☎ 6762 0033; 83-85 Ebsworth St; mains $18-27; 🕑 dinner only) The romantic restaurant at Ashby House serves seasonal game, local steaks and farm-fresh produce with an air of sophistication.

Entertainment

Tamworth always has live country music in its pubs: check Thursday's *Northern Daily Leader* (the visitors centre keeps a copy all week). Dress codes are stricter in Tamworth than elsewhere in the region, so scrub up before you go out.

Venues rotate, but good bets are the **City Tavern** (☎ 6766 2442; 211 Peel St), **Imperial Hotel** (☎ 6766 2613; cnr Brisbane & Marius Sts) and **Good Companions** (☎ 6766 2850; 9 Brisbane St). West of downtown, the **Pub** (☎ 6765 5655; Gunnedah Rd) is probably the best venue in town.

Getting There & Away

Qantas (☎ 13 13 13; www.qantas.com.au) has flights to Sydney ($165, 1 hour).

Most long-distance buses stop beside the visitors centre; typically Sydney is $50 (8 hours). **Kean's** (☎ 1800 043 339, 6543 1322) buses go to Scone ($17, 2 hours), Armidale ($22, 3 hours), Bellingen ($49, 6 hours), Coffs Harbour ($51, 6½ hours) and Nambucca Heads ($54.50, 7½ hours). **McCafferty's/Greyhound** (☎ 13 14 19; www.mccaffertys.com.au) buses go to Armidale ($28, 2½ hours).

CountryLink (☎ 13 22 32; www.countrylink.nsw.gov.au) trains coming from Sydney ($71.50, 6 hours) continue on north to Armidale ($16.50, 2 hours).

AROUND TAMWORTH

Highly recommended jackaroo/jillaroo courses are run by **Leconfield station** (☎ 02-6769 4328; www.leconfield.com; 'Bimboda', Kootingal) They cost $440 for five days and include sheep shearing, lassoing, milking and swimming the horses. The station owners will pick you up from Tamworth YHA. The **Dag Inn** (☎ 02-6769 3234; www.thedag.com.au; Crawney Rd), a 20,000 acre sheep and cattle station, has three-day jackaroo/jillaroo courses ($373). The Dag also has a multitude of farmstay and other options: check its website for details. Telephone for free pick-ups from Tamworth.

Australia's national paragliding champion-ships are held in February and March at Ma-nilla, 44km north of Tamworth along the New England Hwy. Godfrey Wenness, record-holder for the world's longest paragliding flight (335km), found that inland thermals here make for excellent, long cloud-hopping flights. Contact **Manilla Paragliding** (☎ 02-6785 6545; skygodfrey@aol.com; tandem flights $120).

About 45km to the southeast of Tam-worth, **Nundle** is one of the most unexpect-edly charming towns you could stumble across. The friendly folks at the **Underground Gold Museum** (☎ 02-6769 3372; exhibition admission $2, mine tour admission $6; ☺ 9am-6pm) brew an awesome cup of tea, although their museum is overpriced. **Nundle Woolen Mill** (☎ 02-6769 3330; exhibition admission $3; ☺ 10am-4pm Wed-Sun) is a real live yarn factory which also sells unique designer knitwear. **Happy Valley Books & Bounty**, next to the pub, has big-city-style second-hand delights without the big-city price tags. Give in to Nundle's allure and stay the night at **Jenkins Street Guest House** (☎ 02-6769 3239; Jenkins St; s/d $90/140); its restaur-ant is famous for its local produce.

URALLA
☎ 02

It seems like there's a surprise around every corner in Uralla. If you have a car and plan to spend some time in Armidale or Tamworth, consider making this lively little town your base: you'll see a much more interesting side of New England. Bushranger **Captain Thunder-bolt** – whose six-year career included several episodes of holding up Uralla publicans then spending the proceeds on beer – was killed here in 1870. The **visitors centre** (☺ 6778 4496; visituralla.com.au; New England Hwy; ☎ 9.30am-4.30pm) is next to the **Thunderbolt statue**.

Sights
McCrossin's Mill Museum (☎ 6778 3022; Salisbury St; admission $4; ☺ noon-5pm) has panache and hu-mour to burn. You'll have already got your $4 worth reading the captions on the 'Death of Thunderbolt' paintings, but head upstairs for the top-notch 'history of the cricket bat' and the moving display about one Uralla boy's experience of WWI. The **Brass & Iron Lace Foundry** (☎ 6778 5065; 6 East St; admission $3; ☺ 9am-5pm) has been churning out metal things since 1872. Get the owner to show you around the antique machinery and ask

him about the glass eyes. South along the highway to Tamworth, **Thunderbolt's Rock** is where the captain used to wait for likely victims. Uralla also has one of Australia's best antiquarian bookstores, **Australian Book Collector** (☎ 6778 4682; 100 Bridge St).

An interesting loop goes southeast from Uralla to **Gostwyck**, an Australian sheep station that looks like an English country squire's hamlet, complete with photogenic vine-covered chapel. From there go via **Dangar Falls** up to Armidale.

Sleeping & Eating
Also known as the Coachwood & Cedar, the **Top Pub** (☎ 6778 4110; Bridge St; s/d $30/55) has nice motel-style rooms, with a shear-ing shed motif in the bathrooms. Pub meals are served and the **Funk Lush lounge** here has regular bands and the odd big name. The gay-friendly **Chesterfields B&B** (☎ 6778 3113; Bridge St; s/d from $40/55), run by the local hair stylist, also has a café on the premises. The rooms are adorable, and every bed comes with a well-worn antique soft toy.

Getting There & Away
Kean's (☎ 1800 043 339) goes from Uralla to Coffs Harbour ($30) and Armidale ($11.50), but only three times a week.

ARMIDALE
☎ 02 / pop 22,300

The New England regional centre of Armi-dale is famous for its spectacular autumn foliage and heritage buildings – even Video Ezy is in a Federation house. The 1000m al-titude means it's pleasantly cool in summer and frosty (but often sunny) in winter.

The **visitors centre** (☎ 1800 627 736, 6772 4655; www.new-england.org/armidale; 82 Marsh St; ☺ 9am-5pm Mon-Fri, 9am-4pm Sat, 10am-4pm Sun) at the bus station runs free heritage tours of the city; buses depart at 10am.

Fast Track Computers (☎ 6771 1287; 209 Beardy St; ☺ 9am-5pm Mon-Fri, 9am-noon Sat) has Internet access.

Sights
There are some elegant old buildings around the town centre: **Hanna's Arcade** has particu-larly nice fittings and a good lolly shop. On the corner of Faulkner and Rusden Sts is the well-presented **Armidale Folk Museum** (☎ 6770 3536; admission by donation; ☺ 1-4pm).

At the southern edge of town, the **New England Regional Art Museum** (☎ 6772 5255; Kentucky St; admission by donation; ♥ 10.30am-5pm), has a sizable permanent collection and good contemporary exhibitions. Downstairs, the **Museum of Printing** ($3.50; ♥ 11am-4pm Thu-Sun) has printing machines from all eras, historic prints and kitsch 20th century labels from local products. Next door, the **Aboriginal Cultural Centre & Keeping Place** (☎ 6771 1249; Kentucky St; admission $3; ♥ 9.30am-4pm weekdays) hosts changing exhibitions.

Tours
University of New England (☎ 1800 818 865) runs weekly campus tours.
Wilderness Rides (☎ 6778 2172; 'Bora', Enmore) Unforgettable horse treks through the Blue Mountain Gorge. $110 per person per day includes all food and camping.
Waterfall Way Tours (☎ 6772 2018; www.waterfall way.com.au) Natural history tours of World Heritage listed national parks between Armidale and Coffs Harbour ($55 to $110) in small groups.

Sleeping
There are motels around the visitors centre and on Barney St. Head out of town on the Glen Innes Rd to find doubles under $60.

Smith House (☎ 6772 0652; www.smithhouse.com .au; 100 Barney St; s/d $35/50) Partly student accommodation, this is one of the best places to stay in Armidale. Large, comfortable motel-style rooms share bathrooms; one sprawling room sleeps six and has its own bathroom.

Creekside Cottages (☎ 6772 2018; www.waterfall way.com.au/creekside; 5 Canambe St; s/d from $80/95) Self-contained cottages have log fires, and you can get eggs and vegies from the organic garden. Kids are welcome, and there's a cubby house, tennis court and trampoline.

Comeytrowe B&B (☎ 6772 5869; www.aussie vacations.com/bb/39Comeytrowe.html; 184 Marsh St; s/d $80/110; ✖) Four poster beds, antique furnishings in the bathrooms, shady verandas and an old-fashioned cottage garden make this a very romantic place to stay.

Other recommendations:
Pembroke Tourist & Leisure Park (☎ 6772 6470; www.pembroke.com.au; 39 Waterfall Way; camp sites/ dm/cabins $15/20/50; ⌨) East of town (2km) on Waterfall Way (Grafton Rd). YHA-affiliated, clean kitchen, pool and masseur.
Tattersalls Hotel (☎ 6772 2247; 174 Beardy St; s/d from $27/50) Basic but clean and neat and central. Pub meals ($8 to $15) are traditional and tasty.

Eating
Café Midalé (☎ 6772 8166; 173 Beardy St; mains $6-10; ♥ breakfast & lunch) Midalé has a huge range of sandwiches, bagels and croissants and an equally extravagant coffee list. Next door, **Filling Groovy** (☎ 6772 3343, 171 Beardy St; sandwiches $4-8) specialises in sandwiches and smoothies.

Jean Pierre's (☎ 6722 2201; 118 Beardy St; mains $12-20; ♥ lunch Thu & Fri, dinner Mon-Sat) This is an odd yet successful combination of a country town café and French bistro, with pastas thrown in for good measure.

Caz Minio's Pasta (☎ 6771 4555; 201A Brown St; mains $6-11; ♥ 9am-9pm Mon-Sat) This great little restaurant (it only has two tables) makes delicious pan-fried pasta sauces, heavenly tiramisu and very filling Italian-style toasted sandwiches. They have pre-made meals to go, and the deli shelves are packed full with oils, spices and all kinds of goodies.

Drinking
The **Wicklow** (☎ 6772 2421; 85-87 Marsh St) This complex of indoor and outdoor bars is very trendy and packed with students. The Wicklow also serves food.

New England Hotel (☎ 6772 7622; Beardy St Mall) At the other end of the scale, the Newie is your classic country pub. The patrons are far more likely to be wearing Stubbies than low-rider jeans.

Getting There & Away
Qantas (☎ 13 13 13; www.qantas.com.au) flies to Sydney ($170, 1¼ hours) and Brisbane ($265, 1 hour 10 minutes).

McCafferty's/Greyhound (☎ 13 14 19; www.mc caffertys.com.au) goes to Sydney ($52, 10 hours), Brisbane ($48, 7 hours), Tamworth ($28, 2½ hours) and Scone ($27, 4 hours). **Keans** runs to Tamworth ($22, 3 hours) and east along the Waterfall Way to Dorrigo ($18.50), Bellingen ($26), Coffs Harbour ($26.50) and Port Macquarie ($45.50).

CountryLink (☎ 13 22 32; www.countrylink.nsw .gov.au) buses run to Glen Innes ($13, 1¼ hours) and Tenterfield ($31, 2½ hours). Trains go to Tamworth ($16.50, 2 hours) and Sydney ($79.50, 8 hours).

Getting Around
Armidale Bicycle Centre (☎ 6772 3718; 244 Beardy St) rents bikes by the hour ($5.50), day ($22)

and week ($55); it delivers the bikes to wherever you're staying.

THE WATERFALL WAY

A spectacular set of World Heritage–listed national parks line the Waterfall Way from Armidale to Dorrigo and Bellingen, near Coffs Harbour. The entire area is full of magnificent gorges and waterfalls; in summer the road is lined with yellow paper daisies. You can easily drive the distance in a day, but as this is one of the loveliest parts of NSW, why not take a few?

From Armidale, the road heads east 40km to **Wollomombi Falls**, one of Australia's highest. Tame paths lead to nearby lookouts and more strenuous multi-day tracks head down into the wilderness gorges of **Oxley Wild Rivers National Park**. At the southern edge of the park is **Apsley Falls**.

New England National Park, 11km off the Waterfall Way on a good gravel road, is home to platypi, glider possums, grey kangaroos and *Peripatus*, the missing link between worms and insects (you'll really have to keep your eyes peeled to spot one of these). Over 20km of bushwalking trails mostly begin from wheelchair-accessible **Point Lookout**, where there are views that actually might take your breath away (one bushwalker, arriving at the point, was heard to exclaim, 'Australia *rocks!*'). Nearby **cabins** cost $40 to $70 per night, while sites at **Thungutti Camping Area** cost $3/2 per adult/child. Bookings are handled by the Dorrigo **NPWS office** (☎ 02-6657 2309).

Boulderers will get a kick out of the gigantic granite formations at **Cathedral Rock National Park**; wetland swamps here are perfect for bird-watching. Camping ($3/2) is also available. Near Ebor township, **Ebor Falls** are a spectacular part of **Guy Fawkes River National Park**, deep in gorge country that's popular for canoeing and bushwalking. Access is from Hernani, 15km northeast of Ebor, then it's another 30km to Chaelundi Rest Area for camping and trailheads. There are great views from Ebor Falls rest area, or stop to have a look at the little old **graveyard** nearby.

Dorrigo
☎ 02 / pop 1190

Dorrigo is tiny and pleasant, and the atmospheric **pub** is a great place to stop, revive and survive with one small beer (light, of course). The **visitors centre** (☎ 6657 2486; 36 Hickory St; ☼ 10am-4pm) is opposite **Dorrigo Computer Services** (☎ 6657 2982; 59 Hickory St; ☐).

Smeared all over the top of the Dorrigo plateau, **Dorrigo National Park's** magnificent rainforest is the most accessible of Australia's World Heritage wilderness areas. The entire plateau was formed by the Ebor volcano some 18 million years ago. Its enriched soil has given rise to a plethora of flora and fauna species.

The turn-off to the park is about 2km east of town on the Waterfall Way. The **Rainforest Centre** (☎ 6657 2309; Dome Rd; ☼ 9am-5pm) has museum-quality educational displays and a stuffed potoroo. Helpful staff can advise on bushwalks and camping (illegal inside the park). The **skywalk**, a boardwalk floating above the canopy, has heavenly views out to sea. An easy 6km walking trail ducks down under the canopy, past the bird bridge and several waterfalls. Longer bushwalks begin at Never Never picnic area, 10km down Dome Rd (mostly unsealed).

Just north of the Dome Rd turn-off, **Dorrigo Mountain Resort** (☎ 6657 2564; www.dorrigo mountainresort.com.au; Waterfall Way; camp sites/ cabins from $17.50/50) has basic, self-contained wooden cabins and birds-eye views. The National Trust registered **Dorrigo Hotel-Motel** (☎ 6657 2016; cnr Cudgery & Hickory Sts; d from $45) has a good bistro. Rooms in the pub are cheaper; in the motel you'll pay $56, or $85 with a spa bath.

At **Art Place Gallery** (☎ 6657 2622; 18-20 Cudgery St; mains $6-10; ☼ breakfast & lunch) eat your breakfast surrounded by local paintings and ceramics. **Misty's** (☎ 6657 2855; www.dorrigo.com /mistys; 33 Hickory St; mains $22-26; ☼ dinner Thu-Sun, brunch Sun) has a state-wide reputation. Its menu is tiny but the dishes are ambitious. There's a self-contained **cottage** (d with breakfast from $85) in the back garden.

Kean's (☎ 1800 043 339, 6543 1322) goes to Dorrigo from Port Macquarie via Bellingen ($11.50). Buses also run to Armidale ($18.50) and Tamworth ($41).

Bellingen
☎ 02 / pop 2600

It's a spectacular drive along the Waterfall Way from Dorrigo to Bellingen. The road drops 1000m through dense rainforest, with occasional breaks in the canopy offering great views down the Bellinger Valley to the coast. If you're the type who vomits from car sickness, you have a 98% chance of doing it on this road.

Bellingen itself is just downright lovely. There's no reason to ever leave (those of you with jobs will lose them, while others with children may not see them grow up, but Bellingen is worth it). Bellingen has everything necessary for a fulfilling life – great food and coffee, river swimming, rainforest walks and comfy beds.

Get up late, wander to the closest café, have a long, slow breakfast, read the paper, go for a swim in the river, buy a pair of shoes, wander down to **Fernmouth** and watch the cows as they're herded home for milking (3pm), take a nap, go **canoeing** in the moonlight, have dinner (wearing your new shoes), go to the pub, go to bed. Repeat as necessary. Add a long walk now and again.

SIGHTS & ACTIVITIES
A few kilometres east of town in Fernmount, **Bellingen Canoe Adventures** (☎ 6655 9955; www.bellingen.com/canoe; 4 Tyson St) rents out canoes (from $11) and organises eco-friendly river tours ($45 to $90). The sunset tour is a corker.

A huge colony of flying foxes (grey-headed fruit bats) lives on **Bellingen Island**, right in town, from December to March. It's an impressive sight when thousands head off at dusk to feed (best seen while standing on the bridge).

There are rope swings into the river near the YHA hostel, and some great swimming holes around the **Never Never River** near Glennifer, about 10km north of town. The **Syndicate Track** to the Dorrigo Plateau rainforest (15km) follows an old tramline once used by timber cutters. To find the start of the track, take the Gordonville Rd to Glennifer and turn into Adams Rd just after you cross the Never Never River.

FESTIVALS & EVENTS
The **Bello Market** (☎ 6655 2151), held every third Saturday at Bellingen Park on Church St, has 250 stalls and plenty of live entertainment. Folks come from all over the region.

The **Bellingen Jazz Festival** (☎ 6655 9345; www .bellingenjazz.com.au) is held in August, the **Global Carnival** (www.globalcarnival.com), a performing arts festival, is in October, and **Stamping Ground** (☎ 6655 2472; www.userland.com.au/stamping), a festi-

val of international dance performances and workshops, is in early January.

SLEEPING
Bellingen YHA Backpackers (☎ 6655 1116; www.bell ingen.com/belloyha; 2 Short St; camp sites/dm/d $14/18/45; 💻) Right on the river at the end of Church St, comfortable and friendly, this hostel not only has hammocks, a piano and bike hire ($5 per day), it also has a 'nude wall'. Staff organise canoe trips, tours to Dorrigo National Park and days at the nude beach. They'll also pick you up from Urunga by arrangement.

Koompartoo Retreat (☎ 6655 2326; cnr Rawson & Dudley Sts; d $135) Totally self-contained, these timber chalets with private balconies are set in bushland at the southern edge of town. Take advantage of the discounts for longer stays: you owe it to yourself to stay a week.

Rivendell Guest House (☎ 6655 0060; www.mid coast.com.au/~rivendell; 10-12 Hyde St; s $85-130, d $95-130) All the rooms in this Federation house, in town, have French doors to the veranda. There's a pool, a log fire, an extensive library ('but Jerry, we can't leave till I finish reading *Jane Eyre…*') and breakfast, port and chocolates.

There's a pretty **caravan park** (☎ 6655 1338; Dowle St; camp sites/on-site vans from $16/55) across the bridge down by Bellingen Island. The bats can be a bit noisy.

EATING
Cool Creek Café (☎ 6655 1886; 5 Church St; mains $6.50-21.50) Great food, fun management, live music on the weekends. The Cleopatra salad – a variation on the patriarchal Caesar – will fill you to the brim with goodness. Desserts are sublime.

Lodge 241 Gallery Café (☎ 6655 2470; Hyde St; mains $7-13; 🕑 8am-5pm, dinner Fri & Sat) Why have breakfast anywhere else? The ricotta hotcakes are downright awesome, there are tons of vegetarian options, the produce is organic and the coffee is good enough that you may overdose. Try the stuffed baby trout at lunchtime.

Café Bare Nature (☎ 6655 1551; 111 Hyde St; pizzas from $12) For the 'real pizza mind', this place cooks up healthy and imaginative pizzas, pastas, crepes and salads.

SHOPPING
Lonely Palate (☎ 6655 1714; 7 Church St) Find out what lime or banana wine taste like, with

this fruit winery's free tastings. They also do a sideline in organic and international groceries.

Kakadu Clothing (☎ 6655 2204; Hyde St) In the beautiful, historic Hammond & Wheatley Emporium, Kakadu has out-of-the-ordinary mens and womens clothing, ethnic-style homewares and some nifty luggage.

The Old Butter Factory (☎ 6655 9599; 1 Doepel Lane) Several craft workshops, a gallery, a café and a masseur make their homes in this historic complex.

GETTING THERE & AWAY

Kean's (☎ 1800 043 339, 6543 1322) travels from Dorrigo ($11.50), Tamworth ($49), Armidale ($26) and Port Macquarie ($28).

NORTH OF ARMIDALE

Glen Innes (population 6250), is obsessed with Scotland and beards. The **visitors centre** (☎ 02-6732 2397; www.gleninnestourism.com; ☼ 9am-5pm Mon-Fri, 9am-3pm Sat & Sun) is in the bus station. Overlooking the town off the eastern end of the Gwydir Hwy, the **Standing Stones**, erected in 1990 to commemorate the town's Celtic roots, look strangely powerful even among the gum trees. The town centre is full of **heritage buildings**. The **Land of the Beardies Museum** (☎ 02-6732 1035; cnr West Ave & Ferguson St; admission $4; ☼ 10am-noon & 2-5pm Mon-Fri, 2-5pm Sat & Sun) fills an old hospital to bursting with artifacts of old Glen Innes (the nativity scene in a disused toilet is particularly charming). If you're around on a weekend, take a **pub crawl on horseback** (☎ 02-6732 1599; www.pubcrawlsonhorseback.com.au; Bullock Mtn Homestead; tour $265).

The **Australian Celtic Festival** is the first weekend in May. The **Land of the Beardies Bush Festival** is celebrated in November with music, dancing and a long beard competition.

There are several **motels** along the highway. Try authentic bush tucker like witchetty grub salads ($8) and 'roo burgers ($5) at **Koori Cuisine Restaurant** (☎ 02-6732 5960; New England Hwy; mains $4-9) inside Cooramah Aboriginal Culture Centre, south of town.

Dramatic, forested and wild, **Gibraltar Range & Washpool National Parks** lie south and north of the Gwydir Hwy, about 70km east of Glen Innes on the road to Grafton. CountryLink buses can drop you at the Gibraltar Ranges visitors centre or the entrance to Washpool.

Walking tracks lead to camping areas. Washpool has some beautiful swimming holes amid the cool, quiet rainforest.

TENTERFIELD

☎ 02 / pop 3500

At the junction of the New England and Bruxner Hwys, Tenterfield is the birthplace of both Federation (thanks to a speech given in town by 19th-century NSW Premier Henry Parkes) and of the flamboyant 'boy from Oz', Peter Allen. The **visitors centre** (☎ 6736 1082; cnr Rouse & Miles Sts; ☼ 9.30am-5pm Mon-Fri, 9.30am-4pm Sat, 9.30am-3.30pm Sun) has bushwalking guides and can book tours to nearby national parks.

The **saddle shop** (High St) celebrated by Peter Allen in his song 'Tenterfield Saddler' is still open for business. About 11km outside town lies **Thunderbolt's Hideout**, where bushranger Captain Thunderbolt did just that. On your way there check out the **Tenterfield Weather Rock** near the baths.

Bald Rock National Park is 35km northeast of Tenterfield. You can hike to the top of the huge granite monolith (which looks like a stripey little Uluru) and **camp** ($5) near the base.

Several **pubs** offer accommodation. **Motels** line Rous St leading south out of town. **Peter Allen Motor Inn** (☎ 6736 2499; 177 Rouse St; s/d from $55/65; ☒) has up-to-date furnishings, and you are given an apple when you check in. **Tenterfield Lodge** (☎ 6736 1477; 2 Manners St; camp sites/cabins from $13/40, dm $20) is a ramshackle 1870s farmhouse in a caravan park. The helpful owner has lots of contacts to organise work.

Buses between Sydney and Brisbane along the New England Hwy stop in Tenterfield. **Kirklands** (☎ 6622 1499) buses to Lismore ($30, 2 hours 50 minutes, weekdays only) stop at Tabulam and Casino.

TENTERFIELD TO CASINO

The exceedingly twisted road to Casino leads through the quietly beautiful Upper Clarence cattle country: there are plenty of chances to wave hello to dinner. **Forgotten Country Ecotours** (☎ 02-6687 7845; www.nnsw.worldtourism.com.au /ForgottenCountryEcotours; 2/23 Castle Dr, Lennox Head) runs two-day trips from Byron for $335.

Clarence River Wilderness Lodge (☎ 02-6665 1337; www.clarenceriver.com; Paddy's Flat Rd; camp sites $8, cabins from $36) A long way from anywhere up a rough but scenic road, this lodge is in a beautiful river gorge with great swimming. There's also bushwalking, bird-watching, canoe expeditions and gold fossicking. Turn onto Paddy's Flat Rd, 3km west of Tabulam, and drive 30km (follow the signs).

The Gorge Station (☎ 02-6665 1285; Gorge Creek Rd; camp sites/dm/s/cabins $15/18/45/70) This classic cattle station offers fishing and rainforest walks, and has access to Richmond Range National Park. Take the Bonalbo turn-off (look for the carvings) from the Bruxner Hwy and drive 19km.

Australia's Beef Capital, **Casino** (population 11,900) celebrates its beef festival in late May and early June. The **visitors centre** (☎ 02-6662 3566; Centre St; � 9am-4pm Mon-Fri, 9am-12.30pm Sat) is on the highway near the Richmond River. There's a **miniature railway** (cnr West St & Queensland Rd; admission $3; � 10am-4pm Sun) north of town, and frill-necked lizards in the riverside parks.

CENTRAL WEST

Stretching 400km inland from the Blue Mountains, NSW Central West gradually shifts from rolling agricultural heartland into vast plains and finally the harsher outback soil of the Far West. The vast area has some of the earliest inland towns in Australia, steeped in bushranger and gold-rush era history.

The Newell Hwy, the most direct route between Melbourne and Brisbane, passes through the Central West. Dubbo is the main transit hub for the region. An alternative Sydney-Melbourne route, the Olympic Way, runs from Albury on the Murray River through Wagga Wagga to Cowra.

BATHURST
☎ 02 / pop 30,050
Laid out on a grand scale, Bathurst is Australia's oldest inland settlement. It's one of the more atmospheric of NSW inland towns: The broad streets, gas lamps, formidable Victorian buildings and leafy, manicured parks all reek of days gone by.

The **visitors centre** (☎ 1800 681 000, 6332 1444; www.bathurst.nsw.gov.au; 28 William St; � 9am-5pm) has a pioneer-era Cobb & Co coach (no, you can't play on it). **Intercept Café** (☎ 6334 3300; 133 George St) has Internet access and bands.

The **historical museum** (☎ 6332 4755; Russell St; admission $2; � 10am-4pm Tue, Wed, Sat & Sun) lives in the majestic courthouse building. A few blocks away, the **Regional Art Gallery** (☎ 6331 6066; 70-78 Keppel St; admission free; � 10am-5pm Tue-Sat, 11am-2pm Sun) focuses on artists from and images of the local area, with a particular interest in Hill End. The **Chifley Home** (☎ 6332 1444; 10 Busby St; admission $4; � 11am-3pm Sat-Mon) is the sweet, simple suburban home Ben Chifley lived in while he was Prime Minister (1946–49). Bathurst is no Kirribilli.

Rev-heads will be in heaven at the **National Motor Racing Museum** (☎ 6332 1872; Pit Straight; admission $7; � 9am-4.30pm) – Bathurst's **Mt Panorama** has been Australia's street-car racing centre since 1917 and many of the winners (including a kick-arse '76 Torana, an inexplicable '65 Cortina and Peter Brock's '84 Commodore) are on display. The graffiti in the ladies' is well worth a look. You can drive the curvy circuit yourself, though there's a heart-breaking 60km/h speed limit – if you get everyone else in the car to speak and move in slow motion it'll feel faster. When you cross the finish line, it's OK to punch the air.

Sleeping
Park Hotel/Motel (☎ 6331 3399; 201 George St; s/d $50/70) This nice old pub at the corner of Keppel St is perfectly comfortable, but can get a bit rowdy on weekends.

Abercrombie Motel (☎ 6331 1077; 362 Stewart St; s/d from $55/65) It lacks the luxuries, but the Abercrombie is perfectly serviceable and clean in an old-fashioned way.

A Winter-Rose Cottage (☎ 6332 2661; www.winter-rose.com.au; 79 Morrissett St; d $90-110) This cosy B&B has a really nice garden, with its own vegetables. If you're staying awhile, ask for rooms in the self-contained garden cottage.

Eating
There's an upscale café culture downtown.

Crowded House Café (☎ 6334 2300; 1 Ribbon Gang Lane; mains $14.50-27) Crowded House's polished floorboards, big windows, directors chairs and sweeping wooden bar create a warm and expectant atmosphere. The food lives up to it – roast pork loin with pumpkin and apple and port jus, served with green olive and parsley salad ($24.50) is the kind of thing you'll get. The cheaper café menu includes pastas and fish and chips.

Ziegler's Café (☎ 6332 1565; 52 Keppel St; mains $10-20) You could sit for hours in the leafy courtyard at Ziegler's: it's the perfect place for coffee and a book, though you could also order one of the tasty modern Australian dishes.

Benjarong Thai Restaurant (☎ 6331 3627; 129 George St; mains $12-16; ☯ closed Mon) More authentic than the typical country-town Asian café, Benjarong's house specialties include prawns and spicy Thai salads.

Getting There & Away

Selwood's (☎ 6362 7963; www.selwoods.com.au) links Bathurst with Orange ($7.80, 45 minutes) and Sydney ($28, 3½ hours).

The quickest **CountryLink** (☎ 13 22 32; www.countrylink.nsw.gov.au) trains from Sydney ($37.50, 3½ hours) operate during rush hours; CountryLink coaches go to Orange ($10, 45 minutes) and Dubbo ($33, 2½ hours). CountryLink coach/train combinations also run to Melbourne ($98, 9¾ hours).

AROUND BATHURST

About 70km south of Bathurst along awesomely windy roads are the famous **Abercrombie Caves** (☎ 02-6368 8603; www.jenolancaves .org.au; self-guided; admission $12; ☯ 10am-4pm). The complex has one of the world's largest natural tunnels, The Grand Arch. There's **camping** near the cave ($6.50).

Australia's oldest surviving gold town, **Sofala**, is a good-looking little place with some unusually well-preserved timber buildings. Peter Weir shot his 1974 film *The Cars that Ate Paris* here. Grab an Evans Shire tea while you're in town. Thirty-five kilometres down an unsealed road, the ghost town of **Hill End** was the scene of an 1870s gold rush. The **NPWS visitors centre** (☎ 02-6337 8206; Hospital Lane; admission $2.20; ☯ 9.30am-12.30pm & 1.30-4.30pm), inside the old hospital, includes a fascinating **museum** ($2.50). Book here for the three **NPWS camping grounds** (adult/child $5/3). There are a few residents hanging on, and many of them can be found at the dusty **Royal Hotel** (☎ 02-6337 8261; Beyers Ave; s/d/f $33/55/90), the only pub remaining of an original 28.

Further northeast towards Mudgee, the village of **Rylstone** has pretty sandstone buildings, good coffee and cheesecake at **Bizzy Birds** (☎ 02-6379 1189; cnr Louee & Cudgeegong Sts) and access to **Wollemi National Park**.

MUDGEE

☎ 02 / pop 8200

A really good-quality old country town, Mudgee (an Aboriginal word meaning 'Nest in the Hills') has a lively spirit while still hanging on to its heritage. What's more, it's surrounded by fine vineyards that make big, fat, flavoursome red wines.

The **visitors centre** (☎ 1800 816 304, 6372 1020; mudgee-gulgong.org; 84 Market St; ☯ 9am-5pm Mon-Fri, 9am-3.30pm Sat, 9.30am-2pm Sun) is near the post office. If you're going wine tasting, grab a copy of the Mudgee-Gulgong visitors guide.

Wineries

Most of the 20 or so wineries here are locally-owned ventures and the vineyards are clustered together, making the region ideal for cycling. There's a wine festival every September.

Huntington Estate (☎ 6373 3825; huntwine@ hwy.com.au; Cassilis Rd; ☯ 9am-5pm Mon-Fri, 10am-5pm Sat, 10am-3pm Sun) Host of the immensely popular Chamber Music Festival in December (email if you want to be put on the waiting list for tickets), Huntington also makes a jaw-droppingly good shiraz.

Poet's Corner (☎ 6372 2208; Craigmoor Rd, 2.5km off Henry Lawson Rd; ☯ 10am-4.30pm Mon-Sat, 10am-4pm Sun) Formerly Craigmoor, this friendly vineyard has produced a vintage annually since 1858, making it one of Australia's oldest (these days it's owned by the Pernod company). Try the Henry Lawson shiraz.

Pieter Ven Gent (☎ 6373 3807; Black Springs Rd; ☯ 9am-5pm Mon-Sat, 11am-5pm Sun) Get some old-fashioned winery atmosphere at this vineyard, where tastings can be taken in old choir stalls and where the dim tasting room is lined with oak barrels.

Sleeping & Eating

Lawson Park Hotel (☎ 6372 2183; cnr Church & Short Sts; s/d from $40/55) This beautiful, historic hotel has very comfortable rooms, most with direct access to the veranda. The **Red Heifer Grill** (mains $11-18) will sell you a big, spiced-up steak you can slap on their central grill, or try a trout wrapped in foil. Match it with a local wine from the bar.

Lauralla Guesthouse (☎ 6372 4480; www.lauralla .com.au; cnr Lewis & Mortimer Sts; s/d from $85/125) This old-fashioned mansion has open fires and canopied beds and some rooms have spas, but the price is a little steep for what you get. The in-house restaurant, **The Grapevine**, serves degustation dinners ($60) featuring regional produce and lasting around two hours. They'll pick you up if you're staying elsewhere.

Mudgee Riverside Caravan & Tourist Park (☎ 6372 2531; 22 Short St; camp sites/cabins from $14/50) In a leafy setting, this relaxed caravan park has a camp kitchen, offers multiple-night discounts and hires bicycles ($5 per hour).

Paragon Hotel (☎ 6372 1313; cnr Gladstone & Perry Sts; s/d $25/50) Clean, comfortable rooms in this fairly quiet pub come with a big breakfast. Ask for one of the recently renovated upstairs rooms.

Tramp Café (☎ 6372 6665; 61 Market St; mains $5-18; ☷ breakfast & lunch) Enter this quiet courtyard café through an archway near the corner of Church St.

Getting There & Away

CountryLink (☎ 13 22 32; www.countrylink.nsw.gov .au) buses to Lithgow are timed to meet Sydney trains ($45.50, 5 hours 20 minutes).

GULGONG
☎ 02 / pop 2100

There was a time during the gold-rush when Gulgong was so packed, dogs in the main street had to wave their tails up and down rather than side to side (or so they say). Things are much quieter these days (though the town does seem trapped in time), but staff at the **visitors centre** (☎ 6374 1202; 109 Herbert St; ☷ 8am-4.30pm Mon-Fri, 9am-3pm Sat, 9.30am-2pm Sun) can tell you all about the good old days, when Anthony Trollope, Elizabeth Jessie Hickman (Australia's only lady bushranger) and Cranky Sam Poo (an irritable Chinese bushranger) hung around these parts. Walk up on the hill behind the centre to see where **gold** was discovered.

The huge **Gulgong Pioneer Museum** (☎ 6374 1513; 73 Herbert St; admission $5; ☷ 9am-5pm) has more stuff in it than any other country-town museum in the state. Originally built from bark, the **opera house** (☎ 6374 1162; 99-101 Mayne St) has been running longer than any other in Australia. Poet Henry Lawson lived in Gulgong as a kid – find out about him at the **Henry Lawson Centre** (☎ 6374 2049; 147 Mayne St; admission $4; ☷ 10am-3.30pm Wed-Sat, 10am-1pm Sun-Tue).

Rooms at the **Centennial Hotel** (☎ 6374 1241; 141-143 Mayne St; s/d $45/55) are comfortable enough, and you get a bathroom and breakfast for your tariff. Touristy but cute, the **Saint & Sinner** (☎ 6374 1343; 111 Mayne St; mains $4-12) makes a great egg sandwich (and even serves it on a green and yellow plate) and also serves pizzas. There are interesting 'Aussie Icon' paintings on the wall.

CountryLink (☎ 13 22 32; www.countrylink.nsw .gov.au) runs two buses to Mudgee ($5.50, 30 minutes).

ORANGE
☎ 02 / pop 36,000

The local fruit growers and town council need to get together and come to an agreement: while pears, apples and stone fruits are grown here in profusion, you will find nary an orange. The town is actually named after – of course – William of Orange. Banjo Paterson (he wrote the lyrics to Waltzing Matilda) was born here, and the town is renowned for its autumn colours (some of which are orange).

The **visitors centre** (☎ 1800 069 466, 6393 8226; www.orange.nsw.gov.au; Civic Square, Byng St; ☷ 9am-5pm daily) sits beside **Orange Regional Gallery** (☎ 6393 8136; open 10am-5pm Tues-Sat, 1-4pm Sun), which collects Brett Whiteley and sculptural ceramics.

Cook Park (Clinton & Summer Sts) is very manicured and is a great place to see the autumn colours. **Orange Botanic Gardens** (☎ 6393 8226; Kearneys Dr; free; ☷ 7.30am-dusk) is on Clover Hill, 2km north of the city centre. The bush church and Bible garden are very cute.

Many award-winning vineyards lie southwest of town towards **Mt Canabolas** (1395m), an extinct volcano. You can drive to the top or there are a couple of steep walking tracks. The Orange Region Wines brochure is available from the tourist office, and the local taxi company (☎ 6362 1333) will take you on a tour.

Australia's first real gold rush took place at **Ophir**, 27km north of Orange along mostly unsealed roads. The area is now a nature reserve of sorts, and it's still popular with fossickers.

Sleeping & Eating

Because Orange attracts a lot of fruit pickers, budget accommodation is scarce and expensive.

Metropolitan Hotel (☎ 6362 1353; 107 Byng St; s/d $40/55) This friendly, comfortable pub also has a good **veranda restaurant** (mains $15-20) upstairs. The affiliated **Town Square Motel** (☎ 6369 1444; 246 Anson St; s/d $97/110; ♿) has one wheelchair accessible room, and all rooms have VCRs and Austar.

Curran's Inn (☎ 6361 0346; RMB 13 Mitchell Hwy; d from $135, f from $145) About 4km out of town on the way to Bathurst, Curran's is in an 1845 farmhouse (there are still sheep and cows milling about). With large bathrooms and private living rooms, these B&B rooms are really good value. There's also a tennis court.

Lolli Redini (☎ 6361 7748; 48 Sale St; mains $10-28) If you want to hang out with Orange's beautiful people, you've come to the right place. The Italian-Australian menu has a deliciously long dessert list. Next door, **Hawkes General Store** (☎ 6362 5851; 46 Sale St) serves good coffee on a nice patio. They also sell kitchen implements and body care products, and they have a great Boston terrier.

Getting There & Away
McCafferty's/Greyhound (☎ 13 14 99; www.mccaffertys.com.au) has daily services to Dubbo ($27.50, 1 hour 45 minutes), while **Selwood's** (☎ 6362 7963; www.selwoods.com.au) has services that depart for Sydney ($33, 4 hours 15 minutes) and Bathurst ($7.80, 45 minutes) from the railway station.

CountryLink (☎ 13 22 32; www.countrylink.nsw.gov.au) trains go to Sydney ($45, 5 hours) and Dubbo ($22, 1 hour 45 minutes).

COWRA
☎ 02 / pop 9400
Ever since August 1944, when 1000 Japanese prisoners broke out of a POW camp here (231 of them died, along with four Australians), Cowra has aligned itself with Japan and with the cause of furthering world peace.

You must go to the **visitors centre** (☎ 6342 4333; www.cowratourism.com.au; Olympic Park, Mid Western Hwy; ⏲ 9am-5pm) and watch the hologram film about the breakout – it's gorgeous and strange, a tiny work of art.

The Australian and Japanese **war cemeteries** are 5km south of town – the ages of some of the interred might surprise you. A nearby **memorial** marks the site of the break-out, and you can still see the camp

foundations. The superb **Japanese Garden** (☎ 6341 2233; Binni Creek Rd; $7.70; ⏲ 8.30am-5pm) on Bellevue Hill has beautifully maintained, traditional gardens which smoothly incorporate local gum trees. There's a **sakura** (cherry blossom festival) around the second weekend in October. Give the **peace bell** (Civic Sq, Darling St) a bash; it might make you feel better.

The darkest place for star-gazing in all of Australia is **Darby Falls Observatory** (☎ 6345 1900; Mt McDonald Rd; admission $8; ⏲ 7-10pm nightly, 8.30-11pm during daylight savings). From town, follow Wyangala Dam Rd for 22km and turn onto Mt McDonald Rd, then follow the signs. Turn off your headlights as soon as you see the red fairy lights leading up to the observatory.

The Mill (☎ 6341 4141; 6 Vaux St; ⏲ 10am-6pm) is Cowra's oldest building, and a winery to boot. Taste some of the region's famous chardonnay with a platter of local produce ($22 for two people).

Tours
Ideal Tours (☎ 6341 3350; www.australianacorner.com; 1 Kendal St) run tours of wineries.

Sleeping & Eating
There are some beautiful old hotels on Kendal St, perfect for cheap counter meals. Accommodation, however, tends to be seedy.

Imperial Hotel (☎ 6341 2588; 16 Kendal St; s $30-50, d $50-65) This is the best of Cowra's pubs. Rooms are comfortable, modern and motel-like. Some have bathrooms and all prices include breakfast.

THE AUTHOR'S CHOICE

Neila (☎ 6341 2188; 5 Kendal St; mains $26; ⏲ dinner Thu-Sat) This is what Australia does best – fresh produce, innovative menus and a complete lack of pretension. The menu is brief but every dish is exquisitely prepared – take your pick, it's bound to be good. Drop this stylish, modern Mediterranean menu featuring Asian fusion techniques into a small country town, and enjoy the results: the locals are unbowed by the fine cuisine and stylish presentation, and still have conversations with one another from opposite sides of the room. Enjoy this great combination of relaxation and truly good food.

NEW SOUTH WALES

Cowra Motor Inn (☎ 6342 2011; 3 Macquarie St; s/d $50/60; 🕮) Well located, down a quiet side street but right in town, Cowra Motor Inn is affordable and comfortable.

Breakout Brasserie (☎ 6342 4555; Macquarie St; mains $5-10) Coffees, cakes and toasted sandwiches are served at shady outdoor tables.

Getting There & Away

CountryLink (☎ 13 22 32; www.countrylink.nsw.gov.au) runs a coach/train combination to Brisbane ($129, 24 hours), Melbourne ($86, 7½ hours) and Sydney ($52, 5½ hours) and coaches to Canberra ($27, 6 hours) and Bathurst ($16.50, 1 hour 50 minutes).

AROUND COWRA

Backpackers Farmstay Riverslea Historic Homestead (☎ 02-6385 8433; www.backpackers-farmstay.com.au; Darby's Fall Rd, Woodstock; camp sites/dm from $10/20, d $75; 🖳) Only 18km from Cowra, this award-winning ranch offers romance, seclusion and riverside activities, including horseback riding, fishing and outings to Darby Falls Observatory.

The small town of **Canowindra** lies between Cowra and Forbes. The whole of its dogleg main street, Gaskill St, is heritage listed. The **Age of Fishes Museum** (☎ 02-6344 1008; cnr Gaskill & Ferguson Sts; admission $7.70; 🕑 10am-4pm) is very proud of its display of unique fossil fishes found nearby. To join real palaeontologists as they work in the area, call **Gondwana Dreaming** (☎ 02-6285 1872) for details of upcoming tours. **Rendell Coaches** (☎ 1800 023 328, 02-6884 4199) go to Dubbo ($33), Orange ($27.50) and Canberra ($33), but only in school holidays.

FORBES

☎ 02 / pop 8500

You may recognise Forbes from the Australian independent film *The Dish* (although the film took place in nearby **Parkes**, a lot of it was filmed here). The **visitors centre** (☎ 6852 4155; cnr Newell Hwy & Union St; 🕑 9am-5pm) is inside the old train station.

Forbes' wide streets are lined with grand 19th-century gold-rush-funded buildings. **Ben Hall**, a landowner who became Australia's first official bushranger, was betrayed and shot near Forbes. He's buried in the town's cemetery: people still miss him, if the notes on his grave are anything to go by. The **historical museum** (☎ 6852 3856;

9 Cross St; admission $2; 🕑 2-4pm June-Sept, 3-5pm Oct-May) houses Ben Hall relics and other memorabilia.

The **Bushrangers Hall of Fame** (☎ 6851 1881; 135 Lachlan St; admission $5; 10am-6pm) has guided tours of old underground tunnels used to transfer gold from banks into waiting coaches. Above ground, inside the **Albion Hotel** (☎ 6851 1881; 135 Lachlan St; d $50), you can get a room and a feed in pleasant surroundings.

If you want to see The Dish itself, head north to **Parkes Radio Telescope** (☎ 6861 1777; www.parkes.atnf.csiro.au/visitors_centre/; Newell Hwy; 🕑 8.30am-4.15pm). See sets from the film and find out more about Parkes' role in broadcasting the first moon landing.

DUBBO

☎ 02 / pop 37,400

Surrounded by sheep and cattle country, this large agricultural town stands at the regional crossroads of the Mitchell and Newell Hwys.

Robo's Cybernet (☎ 6881 6880; 100 Talbragar St; 🕑 8.30am-5pm Mon-Fri, 8.30am-noon Sat) has super-speedy Internet and is sometimes open till late at night (if the local policemen are playing computer games). The **visitors centre** (☎ 1800 674 443, 6884 1422; www.dubbo.com.au; Macquarie St; 🕑 9am-5pm) isn't particularly useful.

Sights

The animatronic characters at the **Old Dubbo Gaol** (☎ 6882 8122; off Macquarie St; admission $7; 🕑 9am-4.30pm) probably scare the pants off little kids – some of them are downright creepy, as are parts of the well-preserved gaol. The **Dubbo Regional Gallery** (☎ 6881 4342; 165 Darling St; admission by donation; 🕑 11am-4.30pm Tue-Sun) is unusually cutting-edge and quite thought provoking for a country gallery.

Dubbo's star attraction is the **Western Plains Zoo** (☎ 6882 5888; www.zoo.nsw.gov.au; Obley Rd; adult/child $23/12.50 two-day pass; 🕑 9am-5pm, last entry 3.30pm), 5km southwest of town. It's the largest open-range zoo in Australia. Seeing the cute tongues of the rare black rhinoceroses is enough to justify the admission price; patting the albino wallaby is gravy. You can walk the 6km circuit or join the crawling line of cars, but for way cool fun, fang around the zoo on a hired bike ($11). You can also hire a golf cart for $44. Guided morning zoo walks start at 6.45am ($3 plus admission).

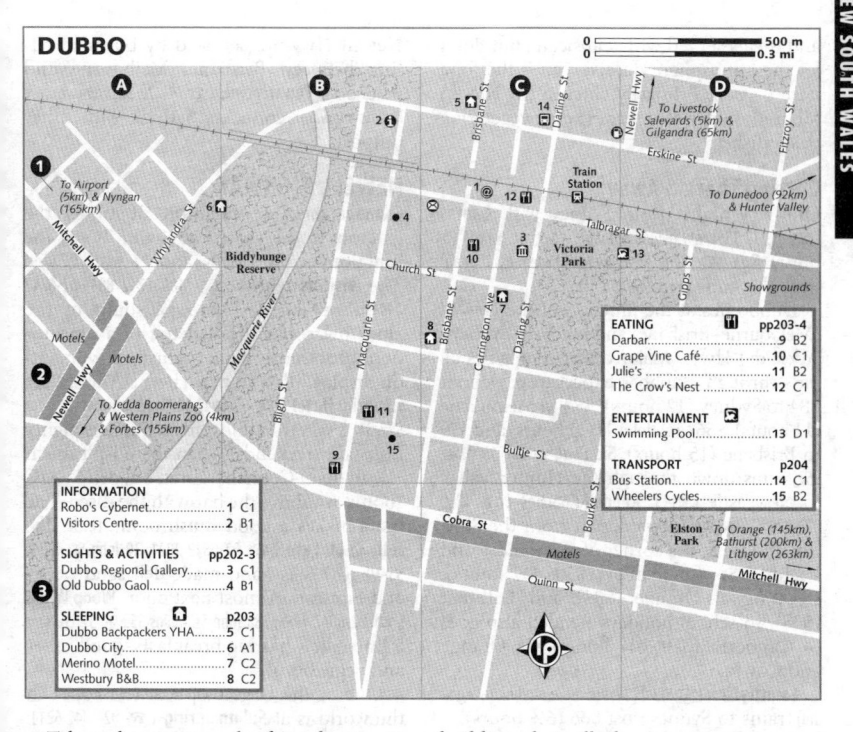

DUBBO

0 — 500 m
0 — 0.3 mi

To Airport (5km) & Nyngan (165km)

Biddybunge Reserve

To Jedda Boomerangs & Western Plains Zoo (4km) & Forbes (155km)

Train Station

To Livestock Saleyards (5km) & Gilgandra (65km)

To Dunedoo (92km) & Hunter Valley

Erskine St

Talbragar St

Victoria Park

Showgrounds

Motels

Motels

Cobra St

Quinn St

Elston Park

To Orange (145km), Bathurst (200km) & Lithgow (263km)

Mitchell Hwy

EATING	pp203-4
Darbar	9 B2
Grape Vine Café	10 C1
Julie's	11 B2
The Crow's Nest	12 C1

| ENTERTAINMENT | |
| Swimming Pool | 13 D1 |

TRANSPORT	p204
Bus Station	14 C1
Wheelers Cycles	15 B2

INFORMATION	
Robo's Cybernet	1 C1
Visitors Centre	2 B1

SIGHTS & ACTIVITIES	pp202-3
Dubbo Regional Gallery	3 C1
Old Dubbo Gaol	4 B1

SLEEPING	p203
Dubbo Backpackers YHA	5 C1
Dubbo City	6 A1
Merino Motel	7 C2
Westbury B&B	8 C2

Take a boomerang-chucking lesson or decorate your own boomerang at **Jedda Boomerangs** (☎ 6882 3110; Minore Rd; admission $7; ☺ 10am-4pm) before the zoo turnoff from the highway. Find out what the country really smells like at the **Livestock Saleyards** (☎ 6882 2155; http://dubbo.saleyards.info//; Newell Hwy), north of town. Sale days are Monday and Thursday.

Sleeping

Dubbo Backpackers YHA (☎ 6882 0922; yhadubbo@hwy.net.au; 87 Brisbane St; camp sites from $8, dm/d $17/45; ☐) The owner is more than helpful, handling discount zoo tickets and bike hire ($8), the rooms are cosy and homey, and the kitchen is clean.

Merino Motel (☎ 6882 4133; Church St; s/d $50/60; ☒) Very central, the charming Merino is set around geranium-edged lawns. Rooms are basic but comfortable.

Westbury B&B (☎ 6884 9445; westburydubbo@bigpond.com; cnr Brisbane & Wingewarra Sts; s & d $80-110; ☒) More a boutique hotel than a B&B, good-value Westbury is decorated in an old-fashioned style to match the heritage

building, but all the trappings are very modern.

Dubbo City (☎ 6882 4820; Whylandra St; camp sites/cabins from $14/45) This pleasant caravan park on the riverbank has a pool and is a 20-minute walk from town.

Eating

The Crows Nest (☎ 6882 3333; Talbragar St; mains $7-12) Upstairs in the Pastoral Hotel, the Nest has pastas on Tuesday for $6.95 and the intriguing Indo-Fijian night on Thursday ($9.95).

Darbar (☎ 6884 4338; 215 Macquarie St; mains $7-17.50; ☺ dinner) The food at this licensed Indian restaurant (with a very pleasant courtyard) is great, but you may starve to death waiting for it to be served.

Grape Vine Café (☎ 6884 7354; 144 Brisbane St; mains $5-10; ☐) Snacks, cakes and light meals are served in a dim coffeehouse atmosphere, or take your great cup of coffee to the leafy courtyard.

Julie's (☎ 6882 0177; 248 Macquarie St; mains $13-20) You, with your big city ways, may scoff at a menu featuring 'from the chookyard' and meals served with 'capsican', but don't let the atmosphere deceive you – the food here is *good*. Primarily chicken (or chook) focused, Julie's also makes some vegetarian pasta dishes.

Getting There & Away
One-way flights from Sydney with **Qantas** (☎ 13 13 13; www.qantas.com.au) start at $160 (1 hour). **Rex** (☎ 13 17 13; www.regionalexpress.com.au) does the same trip for $130.

Dubbo lies at the junction of the Newell (Melbourne–Brisbane) and Mitchell (Sydney–Adelaide) Hwys. Major coach companies all pass through Dubbo – expect to pay about $84 to Sydney (12 hours), $83 to Melbourne (11 hours), $56 to Adelaide (11 hours) and $79 to Brisbane (15 hours). **Sid Fogg's** (☎ 1800 045 952) runs down through the Hunter Valley to Newcastle ($54). **Rendell Coaches** (☎ 1800 023 328; Dubbo Bus Station) depart from the Shell Roadhouse at the corner of Whylandra and Victoria Sts for Sydney ($50, 6½ hours), stopping at Orange ($33) and Bathurst ($38). In school holidays Rendell also goes to Canberra ($50, 6¼ hours) via Orange and Cowra.

CountryLink (☎ 13 22 32; www.countrylink.nsw.gov.au) trains to Sydney cost $66 (6½ hours).

Getting Around
Wheelers (☎ 6882 9899; 25 Bultje St; ☽ closed Sun) rents mountain bikes for $15 per day.

NORTHWEST

From Dubbo, roads radiate to far-flung parts of the state. The Newell Hwy is the quickest route between Melbourne and Brisbane, briefly joining the Oxley Hwy from Tamworth at Coonabarabran. The Castlereagh Hwy forks off the Newell at Gilgandra, running north into rugged opal country towards the Queensland border (its surfaced section ends soon after Lightning Ridge). The Mitchell Hwy also heads northwest into Queensland via Nyngan, where the Barrier Hwy breaks off west to Broken Hill.

Getting There & Away
Qantas (☎ 13 13 13; www.qantas.com.au) and **Rex** (☎ 13 17 13; www.regionalexpress.com.au) fly to several of the main towns. Those on the

Newell Hwy are serviced by buses travelling between Brisbane, Melbourne and Adelaide. **CountryLink** (☎ 13 22 32; www.countrylink.nsw.gov.au) connects Sydney with other outposts.

NEWELL HIGHWAY
Coonabarabran (population 3000) is the gateway to the Warrumbungles. It's at the junction of the Oxley and Newell Hwys. The **visitors centre** (☎ 1800 242 881, 02-6842 1441; Newell Hwy; ☽ 9am-5pm), south of the clocktower, has the skeleton of a diprotodon (or seriously giant prehistoric wombat) on display. It's a ripper. The YHA-associate **Imperial Hotel** (☎ 02-6842 1023; 70 John St; s/d from $22/31) has retro atmosphere, but gets plenty noisy on weekends, when there isn't much else to do in Coonabarabran but drink. A/C rooms are above the bar with the disco. The **bistro** makes a good mushroom steak. **The Jolly Cauli Café** (☎ 02-6842 2021; 30 John St; mains $5-10; 🖳) sells hand-made deli sandwiches and espresso. Almost next door, **Woop Woop** (☎ 02-6842 4755; 38a John St; mains $5.50-13), down a little alley, has big breakfasts, good cakes and vegie burgers.

One of the largest optical telescopes in the world is at **Siding Spring** (☎ 02-6842 6211; www.sidingspringexploratory.com.au; National Park Rd; ☽ 9.30am-4pm). Its visitors centre ($5.50) has some good educational displays, including one which reveals the weight of a tinnie on Venus.

To look through a telescope yourself, visit tiny **Observatory & Astro Mini-Golf** (☎ 02-6842 3303; Timor Rd), 2km west of Coonabarabran. Times vary for nightly star-gazing shows ($12.50), while the exhibition centre and mini golf course ($8 each) are open from 2pm to 5pm.

Almost everyone is awed by the spectacular granite domes and spires of **Warrumbungle National Park**, 33km west of Coonabarabran. The park has over 30km of bushwalking trails (including some good short walks) and explosive wildflower displays during spring, as well as challenging rock climbing routes (permit required). Park entrance fees of $6 per car are payable at the NPWS **visitors centre** (☎ 02-6825 4364; ☽ 9am-4pm) in the park, which also handles camp site registration ($3 to $7.50). Even in summer, temperatures get frosty quickly after dark or on the peaks.

Tibuc Cabins (☎ 6842 1740; www.coonabarabran .com/tibuc/; National Park Rd; cabins from $72) Basic cabins (only one has power) with a pioneering, back-to-the-bush feel are on the edge of the national park. Swim in a spring-fed pool or cook yourself a barbecue. Bring your own linen and blankets.

Narrabri (population 7300), the cotton-growing centre, is near the **Australia Telescope**, an enormous complex of six radio telescopes, each 22m wide. The CSIRO **visitors centre** (☎ 6861 1777; Yarrie Lake Rd; admission free, 20-minute film $4; ☷ 8.30am-4.15pm Mon-Fri) is 25km west of town. In town, the new **Cotton Centre** (☎ 6792 6443; www.australiancottoncentre.com .au; Newell Hwy; ☷ 8.30am-4.30pm) has some great interactive displays. It's partly sponsored by genetic engineers Monsanto.

The most accessible and popular part of **Mt Kaputar National Park** is **Sawn Rocks**, a pipe organ formation about 40km northeast of Narrabri (20km unsealed). The southern part of the park has dramatic lookouts, climbing, bushwalking and camping.

Moree (population 20,000), a large town on the Gwydir River, has therapeutic **artesian bore baths** (☎ 6752 7480; cnr Anne & Gosport Sts; admission $4; ☷ 6am-8.30pm Mon-Fri, 7am-7pm Sat & Sun). The **Moree Plains Gallery** (☎ 6757 3320; admission free; ☷ 10am-5pm Tue-Fri, 10am-2pm Sat) specialises in Aboriginal art.

CASTLEREAGH HIGHWAY

Just north of the pretty town of **Gilgandra**, pull off the highway at the spot where, in 1818, John Oxley probably proclaimed 'Oh, bugger it!'. Expecting to find a giant inland sea, he instead discovered that the Macquarie River petered out into a boggy marsh. West of here, the **Macquarie Marshes'** prolific birdlife is best seen during breeding season (usually spring, but varying with water levels). Drive along the unsealed Gibson Way between Carinda and Coonamble, passing by Quambone. From there sealed roads go south to Warren.

Lightning Ridge

Near the Queensland border, this fiercely independent and strikingly imaginative mining community (the world's only source of black opals) has real frontier spirit. It remains a place where hundreds of battlers dream of striking it rich, and now and again some of them even do (though the pokies

are as rich a resource as the opal fields). The town itself is a fairly prosperous settlement (they have wasabi and fresh basil at the supermarket, and a **wave pool** built by volunteers) with a strong community spirit; it's only when you get out onto the fields that the strangeness of the place hits you.

The fossicking season kicks off on the Easter long weekend, celebrated with horse and goat races. Several **underground mines** and **opal showrooms** are open to the public and there's a **gem festival** every July.

Head 2km out of town along Pandora St to the soothing **artesian bore baths** (admission free; ☷ 24hr). Clothing is optional after midnight.

Black Opal Tours (☎ 02-6829 0368; half-day tours $35; 9.30am) are a good way to see the fields, do a bit of fossicking, hear mining stories and visit oddities like the **ironstone castle**.

There are a few **motels** and **caravan parks** in town. The **Tram-o-Tel** (☎ 02-6829 0448; 2 Morilla St; d from $27.50) has self-contained accommodation in tram cars. After dark you can do some serious drinking with miners and other eccentric local folk at the **Diggers Rest Hotel** (☎ 02-6829 0404; Opal Street) or the **Bowling Club** (☎ 02-6829 0408; Morilla St), which has a decent **bistro**, shows movies on Monday nights (watching *Gosford Park* here was quite an experience) and has a meat raffle and bands on Fridays.

CountryLink (☎ 13 22 32; www.countrylink.nsw.gov .au) buses to Dubbo ($56, 4½ hours) stop on Lightning Ridge's main road, **Morilla St. Kynoch Coaches** (☎ 07-4639 1639) go to Toowoomba in Queensland ($81, 8½hr) twice weekly.

LORD HOWE ISLAND

☎ 02 / pop 300

Beautiful Lord Howe is a tiny subtropical island 550km east of Port Macquarie and 770km northeast of Sydney. Seven million years ago it belonged to the same ancient shield volcano as **Ball's Pyramid**, a spectacular spire rising from the ocean 23km to the southeast. Listed on the World Heritage Register for its rare bird and plant life, the island is an eco-tourist's dream.

Lord Howe is not a budget destination, although prices fall considerably in winter. Unless you have a boat you'll have to fly here, and both food and accommodation are expensive.

Orientation & Information

Boomerang-shaped Lord Howe is about 11km long by 3km wide, with most people living in the flat area north of the airport. Island time is GMT+10.30 hours, a half-hour ahead of Sydney (except in summer).

The **visitors centre** (☎ 1800 240 937, 6563 2114; www.lordhoweisland.info; cnr Lagoon & Middle Beach Rds; ✆ 9am-5pm Sun-Fri) screens a worthwhile 20-minute audiovisual presentation.

Nearby on Ned's Beach Rd you'll find the post office, Thompson's general store and Westpac Bank (no ATM).

Sights & Activities

Visit between September and April and you'll be amazed by the huge number of seabirds nesting in this tiny oasis.

One of the pleasures of Lord Howe is **bushwalking** in the low hills and rainforests. The southern end is dominated by the towering twins, Mt Lidgbird (777m) and Mt Gower (875m). You can climb Mt Gower in about eight hours return (a licensed guide is required).

The daily **fish-feeding** frenzy takes place in late afternoon at Ned's Beach, where **sea kayaking** is popular. There's good **surf** at Blinky Beach, and off the island's western shore lies the world's southernmost **coral reef**, sheltered by a wide lagoon. You can inspect the brilliantly coloured sea life from glass-bottom boats or rent snorkelling and diving equipment from outfitters at Lagoon Beach.

Tours

Thompson's store handles bookings for **Ron's Ramble** ($15), an interesting three-hour walk covering the island's history, geology, flora and fauna.

Sleeping

Camping is prohibited and all accommodation must be booked in advance. There are plenty of lodges and self-contained apartments, some of which cut rates or close in winter.

Ocean View Apartments (☎ 6563 2041; Lagoon Rd; d from $83; f units from $124) In truth, these self-contained apartments afford no ocean views, but they do have tennis courts and the island's only swimming pool.

Arajilla Retreat (☎ 1800 063 928, 6563 2002; www.lordhowe.com.au; Lagoon Rd; B&B d ste $416-660) Recently rebranded and refurbished, the plush apartments at this appealing, upmarket resort-style place have modern facilities. Each suite has its own deck overlooking kentia palm forest.

Eating

Eating out is expensive and bookings are essential. **Pinetrees** (☎ 6563 2177) serves three-course set meals ($40) and has a fish fry ($25) on Monday evening. **Arajilla Restaurant** (☎ 1800 063 928, 6563 2002; Lagoon Rd; mains $27) serves tempting modern Australian cuisine, such as grilled scallop tart with ginger and sweet potato purée. **Blue Peters** (Lagoon Beach), its sister restaurant, serves simpler fare.

Getting There & Away

Flight and accommodation packages are usually the only way to get a decent deal. Prices start from around $1029 in winter.

Try **Fastbook Pacific Holidays** (☎ 1300 261 153, 9212 5977; reservations@fastbook.com.au) in Sydney or **Oxley Travel** (☎ 1800 671 546; www.oxleytravel.com.au) in Port Macquarie.

Qantas (☎ 13 13 13) has six flights a week from Sydney ($730 return), and a weekly flight from Brisbane (around $870 return) on Sunday.

Getting Around

You can hire bicycles, motorcycles and cars on the island, but a bicycle is all you need. There is a 25km/h speed limit throughout the island. Since there are no streetlights after dark, bring a torch.

NORFOLK ISLAND

☎ 6723 / pop 1800

Norfolk Island is a green speck in the vast South Pacific Ocean, 1600km northeast of Sydney and 1000km northwest of Auckland. It's the largest of a cluster of three islands emerging from the Norfolk Ridge, which stretches from New Zealand to New Caledonia, the closest landfall, almost 700km north.

Norfolk is particularly popular with older Australians and New Zealanders on package holidays. Tourism accounts for more than 90% of the local economy but it is not a cheap destination. Airfares are expensive and there is no budget accommodation available. There are a few millionaires living on the island, enjoying its status as a tax-free haven.

History

Little is known about the island's history prior to it being sighted by James Cook on 10 October 1774. Fifteen convicts were among the first settlers who arrived on 6 March 1788, only weeks after the First Fleet arrived at Port Jackson. As a result of food shortages, shipwrecks and native timber that proved too brittle for building, many gave up and moved to New Norfolk, Tasmania.

Norfolk Island was abandoned for 11 years before colonial authorities decided to try again in 1825. Governor Darling planned this second penal settlement as 'a place of the extremest punishment short of death'. Under such notorious sadists as commandant John Giles Price, Norfolk became known as 'hell in the Pacific'.

The second penal colony lasted until 1855, when the prisoners were shipped off to Van Diemen's Land (Tasmania) and the island was handed over by Queen Victoria to the descendants of the mutineers from the HMS *Bounty*, who had outgrown their adopted Pitcairn Island. About a third of the present population is descended from the 194 Pitcairners who arrived on 8 June 1856.

Orientation & Information

The island measures only 8km by 5km, with vertical cliffs surrounding much of the coastline, apart from a small plain (formerly swamp) around the historic settlement of Kingston. The service town of Burnt Pine is at the centre of the island, near the airport.

The **visitors centre** (☎ 22 147; www.norfolkisland .com.au; Taylors Rd; ☉ 8.30am-5pm Mon-Fri, 8.30am-3pm Sat & Sun) is next to the post office in Burnt Pine. **Westpac Bank** (☎ 22 120) and the **Commonwealth Bank** (☎ 22 144) have branches nearby, the latter with an ATM. Most shops have Eftpos.

The **Communications Centre** (Norfolk Telecom; ☎ 22 244) on New Cascade Rd has telephone, fax and internet facilities, and you can also access the Internet at **Norfolk Island Data Services** (☎ 22 427; Village Pl; $3.50/hr).

TALKING NORFOLK

Visiting Norfolk Island can seem like you're stepping back in time, and hearing the islanders engage in the curious native language only enhances this effect. Brought by the Pitcairners in 1856 and still spoken among the descendants of the *Bounty* mutineers, the dialect is a mix of English and Polynesian, with a touch of Scottish thrown in (*ucklun*, meaning 'us', is derived from 'our clan').

Many of the words and phrases are easily recognisable as being a simplified, or pidgin, English, but when a local launches into Norfolk at full pace, you can forget about following it! Most of the time you'll hear plain English spoken, but phrases you might hear include: *watawieh you?* (how are you?); *kushu* (fine); *webout you gwen?* (where are you going?); *wha* (I beg your pardon); and *dars gude* (that's good).

VISAS

The island is a self-governing external territory of Australia. Travelling to Norfolk Island from Australia (or New Zealand) means you will get an exit stamp in your passport and board an international flight. Upon arrival on Norfolk you automatically get a 30-day entry visa. You will need a re-entry visa or valid national passport upon return.

Kingston

Kingston, built by convicts of the second penal colony, is Norfolk's star attraction. Many historic buildings have been restored and the finest of these along Quality Row still house the island's administrators, as well as four small **museums** (☎ 23 088; www.museums.gov.nf; single/combined tickets $6/18; ☉ 11am-3pm). Near the sea, the **convict cemetery** has some poignant epitaphs, hinting at the island's difficult past.

Sights & Activities

You could easily spend an hour poking around the **Bounty Folk Museum** (☎ 22 592; Middlegate Rd; admission $7.50; ☉ 10am-4pm), crammed with motley souvenirs from the convict era and *Bounty* mutineers.

West of Burnt Pine, magnificent **St Barnabas Chapel** (Douglas Dr; tours adult/child $12/6) was built by the (Anglican) Melanesian Mission,

NEW SOUTH WALES

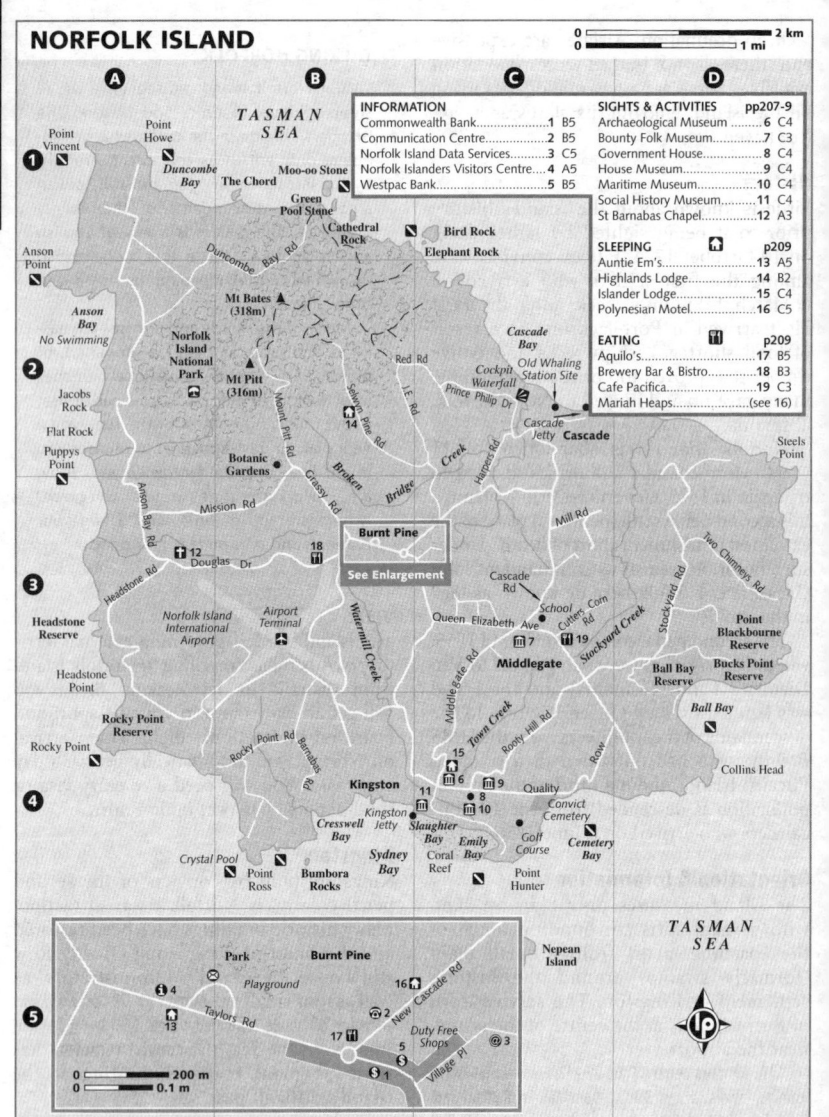

NORFOLK ISLAND

0 ———— 2 km
0 ———— 1 mi

INFORMATION
Commonwealth Bank..................1 B5
Communication Centre................2 B5
Norfolk Island Data Services........3 C5
Norfolk Islanders Visitors Centre....4 A5
Westpac Bank..........................5 B5

SIGHTS & ACTIVITIES pp207-9
Archaeological Museum 6 C4
Bounty Folk Museum..............7 C3
Government House..................8 C4
House Museum......................9 C4
Maritime Museum.................10 C4
Social History Museum..........11 C4
St Barnabas Chapel...............12 A3

SLEEPING
Auntie Em's...........................13 A5
Highlands Lodge.....................14 B2
Islander Lodge.......................15 C4
Polynesian Motel.....................16 C5

EATING
Aquilo's................................17 B5
Brewery Bar & Bistro..............18 B3
Cafe Pacifica........................19 C3
Mariah Heaps.....................(see 16)

TASMAN SEA

Point Vincent
Point Howe
Duncombe Bay
The Chord
Moo-oo Stone
Green Pool Stone
Cathedral Rock
Bird Rock
Elephant Rock
Anson Point
Duncombe Bay Rd
Mt Bates (318m)
Norfolk Island National Park
Red Rd
Cascade Bay
Old Whaling Station Site
Cockpit Waterfall
Prince Philip Dr
Cascade Jetty
Cascade
Anson Bay
No Swimming
Mt Pitt (316m)
Selwyn Pine Rd
Mt Pitt Rd
Jacobs Rock
Flat Rock
Puppys Point
Botanic Gardens
Broken Bridge
Grassy Rd
Creek
Harpers Rd
Steels Point
Mission Rd
Anson Bay Rd
Mill Rd
Burnt Pine
Headstone Rd
Douglas Dr
See Enlargement
Cascade Rd
Two Chimneys Rd
Stockyard Rd
Point Blackbourne Reserve
Headstone Reserve
Norfolk Island International Airport
Airport Terminal
Watermill Creek
School
Queen Elizabeth Ave
Cutters Corn Rd
Stockyard Creek
Ball Bay Reserve
Bucks Point Reserve
Headstone Point
Middlegate
Ball Bay
Rocky Point Reserve
Rocky Point
Rocky Point Rd
Barnabas Rd
Middlegate Rd
Town Creek
Rooty Hill Rd
Row
Collins Head
Kingston
Kingston Jetty
Cresswell Bay
Slaughter Bay
Sydney Bay
Bumbora Rocks
Emily Bay
Coral Reef
Quality Row
Golf Course
Point Hunter
Convict Cemetery
Cemetery Bay
Crystal Pool
Point Ross

TASMAN SEA
Nepean Island

Burnt Pine
Park
Playground
Taylors Rd
New Cascade Rd
Duty Free Shops
Village Pl

0 ———— 200 m
0 ———— 0.1 m

---

which was based on the island from 1866 to 1920. It's never really closed; visitors are supposed to close the door behind them.

Nature lovers will enjoy the island's lush vegetation and rugged coastline. The enriched volcanic soil and mild, subtropical climate provide perfect growing conditions for the 40-odd plant species unique to the

island, including the ubiquitous Norfolk Island pine. Covering the northern part of the island, **Norfolk Island National Park** offers various bushwalking tracks, with excellent views afforded from Mt Pitt (316m) and Mt Bates (318m).

There's a sheltered beach with pristine waters at **Emily Bay** in the south, from where glass-bottom boats depart to view the coral reef. Several companies can arrange snorkelling, diving and fishing trips. **Bounty Divers** (☎ 22 751; www.bountydivers.nf) takes people out to the wreck of the HMS *Sirius*.

Sleeping

Accommodation is expensive and must be booked in advance. Most visitors come on package deals, starting from around $990 for seven nights in winter and around $1450 in summer, sometimes including car hire and breakfast.

Polynesian Motel (☎ 22 309, fax 23 040; New Cascade Rd; d from $85) This is one of a few cheaper, 1970s motel-style resorts.

Auntie Em's (☎ 22 373, fax 22 827; Taylors Rd; d from $110) This family-run guesthouse, centrally located in Burnt Pine, has plenty of old-style charm.

Islander Lodge (☎ 22 114, fax 23 014; Middlegate Rd; d from $155) Perched on a hillside, these self-contained apartments enjoy fantastic views of Kingston and various bays.

Highlands Lodge (☎ 22 741, fax 22 045; Selwyn Pine Rd; d $162-222) This comfortable guesthouse, nestled on the hillside below the national park, has bright, airy rooms with pleasing bush views.

Eating

Interesting 'progressive' dinners ($40) at local residents' homes and the island fish fry ($25) – a sunset fish dinner held at Puppy's Point – can be booked through tour operators.

There are cheap meals at various pubs and clubs. The **Brewery Bar & Bistro** (☎ 23 515; Douglas Dr), opposite the airport, serves cheap counter meals ($6.50) and brews its own beer. There are tours ($10) every Thursday.

Cafe Pacifica (☎ 23 210; Cutters Corn Rd) Set inside a plant nursery near the Bounty Folk Museum, this upscale café serves delightful lunches, brunch and teas.

Look out also for **Mariah Heaps** (☎ /fax 22 255; New Cascade Rd; mains $20) and **Aquillo's** (☎ 22 459; New Cascade Rd; mains from $15).

Getting There & Away

Most flights are booked as part of a package deal. There's a departure tax of $35 if you're Australia bound and $22 if you're heading to New Zealand, payable at the airport.

Alliance (☎ 1300 130 092) flies on Saturday and Sunday between Norfolk and Brisbane ($700 return) and Sydney (from $600). **Norfolk Jet Express** (☎ 13 737, in Australia ☎ 1800 816 947) flies from Melbourne via Sydney (from $659) on Wednesday, Saturday and Sunday, and from Brisbane (return from around $600) on Friday and Saturday. **Air New Zealand** (☎ 22 195, in NZ ☎ 0800 737 000) flies from Auckland.

At the time of writing there were no flights between Lord Howe and Norfolk Islands.

Getting Around

Car hire can be organised at the airport for as little as $30 a day. The speed limit around most of the island is 50km/h. Cows have right of way on the island's roads, and there's a $300 fine for hitting one. Bicycle hire can be arranged through the visitors centre.

SOUTH COAST

Beautiful scenery, excellent beaches, good surfing and diving, attractive fishing towns, historic settlements, and spectacular forests and national parks line the coast between Sydney and the Victorian border. It's far less developed and busy than the coast north of Sydney – great if you crave space and serenity, less so for party animals who won't find any equivalents to destinations such as Byron Bay. Although it's quiet most of the year, this coast is fairly thick with Australian families during holiday periods.

There are thousands of guesthouses, hotels, resorts and camping grounds in the area between Sydney and the Victorian border, as well as activities as diverse as scuba diving, hang-gliding, skydiving, horse riding, fishing, caving and bushwalking. There's also scenic flights and island visits, with whale- and dolphin-watching in season.

Getting There & Away

A car is the best way to really make the most of the south coast, giving freedom of access to the inland and to off-the-beaten-track treasures of the region. The Princes Hwy runs along the coast from Sydney to the Victorian border. Although a longer and slower route to Melbourne than the Hume Hwy, it's much more interesting. The Snowy

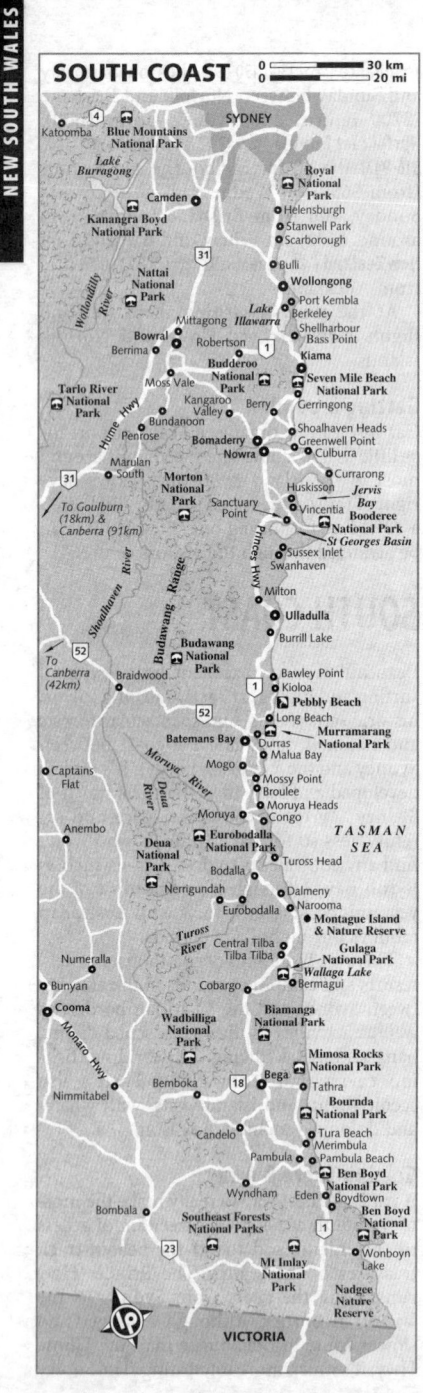

SOUTH COAST

0 — 30 km
0 — 20 mi

Mountains, 150km from Sydney, can also be reached via the south coast.

Rex (☎ 13 17 13) flies from Sydney to Merimbula (one way from $177) and Moruya (one way from $146), and from Melbourne to Merimbula (one way $180).

Premier Motor Service (☎ 13 34 10), a Nowra-based company, runs buses daily between Eden and Sydney ($57) and Eden and Melbourne ($46), stopping at several points along the way, including Bega (from Sydney) and Narooma (from Melbourne). For short hops between coastal towns it's much cheaper than the big lines.

Sapphire Coast Express (☎ 1800 812 135, 03-9763 4473) runs between Ulladulla/Batemans Bay and Melbourne ($85) twice a week. **CountryLink** (☎ 13 22 42; www.countrylink.info) serves Bega on its daily Eden–Canberra run ($42).

Priors (☎ 1800 816 234) runs between Parramatta and Narooma once a day Monday to Friday and between Sydney and Batemans Bay on Sunday, stopping at most major coastal destinations along the way.

Murrays (☎ 13 22 51) has daily buses from Canberra to Batemans Bay ($24) and south along the coast to Narooma ($36 from Canberra, $16 from Batemans Bay).

The train from Sydney goes as far south as Bomaderry and costs from $15 one way.

WOLLONGONG
☎ 02 / pop 228,800

Only 80km south of Sydney, Wollongong is the state's third-largest city. Although a sprawling industrial centre that includes the biggest steelworks in Australia at nearby Port Kembla, Wollongong has some good surf beaches and beautiful hinterland. The city centre and beaches are pleasantly low-rise and low-key and a large resident student population makes the town centre a lively place.

The name Illawarra, which is often applied to Wollongong and its surrounds, refers specifically to the hills behind the city (the Illawarra Escarpment) and the coastal Lake Illawarra to the south. The hills provide a fine backdrop to the city and great views over the coast.

Orientation
Crown St is the main commercial street, and a large two-block pedestrian mall lies between Keira and Kembla Sts. Keira St is

part of the Princes Hwy. Through-traffic bypasses the city on the Southern Fwy.

Information

Wollongong **visitors centre** (☎ 1800 240 737, 4227 5545; www.tourismwollongong.com; cnr Crown & Kembla Sts; ☺ 9am-5pm Mon-Fri, 9am-4pm Sat, 10am-4pm Sun) is efficient and well stocked, with good information on the town and region.

Plugged In (☎ 4227 1279; 74 Crown St) offers fast Internet access. Alternatively, visitors can log on for free at the city **library** (Stewart St).

Sights & Activities

The shore is definitely the place to explore, offering empty expanses of sand and a pretty harbour. The fishing fleet is based in the southern part of the harbour, **Belmore Basin**. It was cut from solid rock in 1868, and there are two handsome late 19th century lighthouses on the foreshore. **North Beach** generally has better surf than the Wollongong City Beach and is also great for secluded strolls.

The **City Gallery** (☎ 4228 7500; cnr Kembla & Burelli Sts; admission free; ☺ 10am-5pm Tue-Fri, noon-4pm Sat & Sun) houses an extensive permanent collection of local 20th-century painting, some interesting Aboriginal art and a rather more mixed bag of contemporary art and installations.

The enormous **Nan Tien Buddhist Temple** (☎ 4272 0600; Berkeley Rd, Berkeley; admission free; ☺ 9am-5pm Tue-Sun), a few kilometres south of the city, is a peaceful place standing in stark but welcome contrast to the surrounding industrial sprawl. It's also the biggest Buddhist temple in the southern hemisphere. Visit the Japanese gardens, pagoda, vegetarian restaurant and various temple buildings.

Sleeping

There's plenty of accommodation in and around the city, including five-star hotels, but you have to go a little way out before you can camp.

Quality Hotel City Pacific (☎ 4229 7444; www.citypacifichotel.com.au; 112 Burelli St; budget s/d $65/85, standard/deluxe d from $130/175; ☒) It's a fair way from the beach, but this place has bright, modern standard/deluxe rooms and older, good-value budget rooms.

Harp Hotel (☎ 4229 1333; 124 Corrimal St; d $70; ☒) In contrast to the rather dingy pub beneath them, the rooms here are well equipped, modern and pleasant, if a little on the small side. Given the central location it's not bad value.

Downtown Motel (☎ 4229 8344; www.downtownmotel.com; 76 Crown St; d from $79) For the location and price you won't do better, though the rooms are small.

Keiraleagh House (☎ 4228 6765; fax 4228 6216; 60 Kembla St; dm/s/d $18/30/45) North of Market St, this large hostel – the only one in the city – looks shabby but is friendly and has comfortable single rooms and garden space.

There are a number of council-run caravan parks, all charging similar prices that rise slightly during school and Christmas holidays.

Novotel Northbeach (☎ 4226 3555; www.novotelnorthbeach.com; 2-14 Cliff Rd; d $230-450; ☒) The place to spoil yourself in town, this Novotel's rooms (some with balconies) offer wonderful beach and mountain views. The facilities, including gym, pool and a sumptuous buffet breakfast, are good although there are better places for lunch and dinner.

Windang Beach Tourist Park (☎ 4297 3166; windangtp@wollongong.nsw.gov.au; Fern St, Windang; camp/caravan sites from $19/24, cabins from $49) With beach and lake frontage, this park is 15km south of Wollongong.

Eating

Cafés and restaurants abound in the city centre and along the beachfront. Keira St has the greatest concentration of restaurants, with an especially good selection of Vietnamese, Chinese and Japanese places.

Santana Coffee Shop (☎ 4227 6603; 53 Crown St; breakfast & light lunch $12) One of few places open early in the city centre on Sunday, Santana serves hearty breakfasts and gourmet sandwiches, and there are magazines and books to browse through.

Elementary Organics (☎ 4226 6300; 47 Crown St; breakfast $7) This little place serves fresh juices and a small but tasty selection of fresh, home-made organic and vegie breakfasts and lunches.

Food World Gourmet Café (☎ 4225 9655; 148 Keira St; mains $8) The menu and the decor are pretty standard issue for a Chinese restaurant but the food in this bustling canteen is a cut above the usual – wontons freshly made in a clear yummy broth, for example.

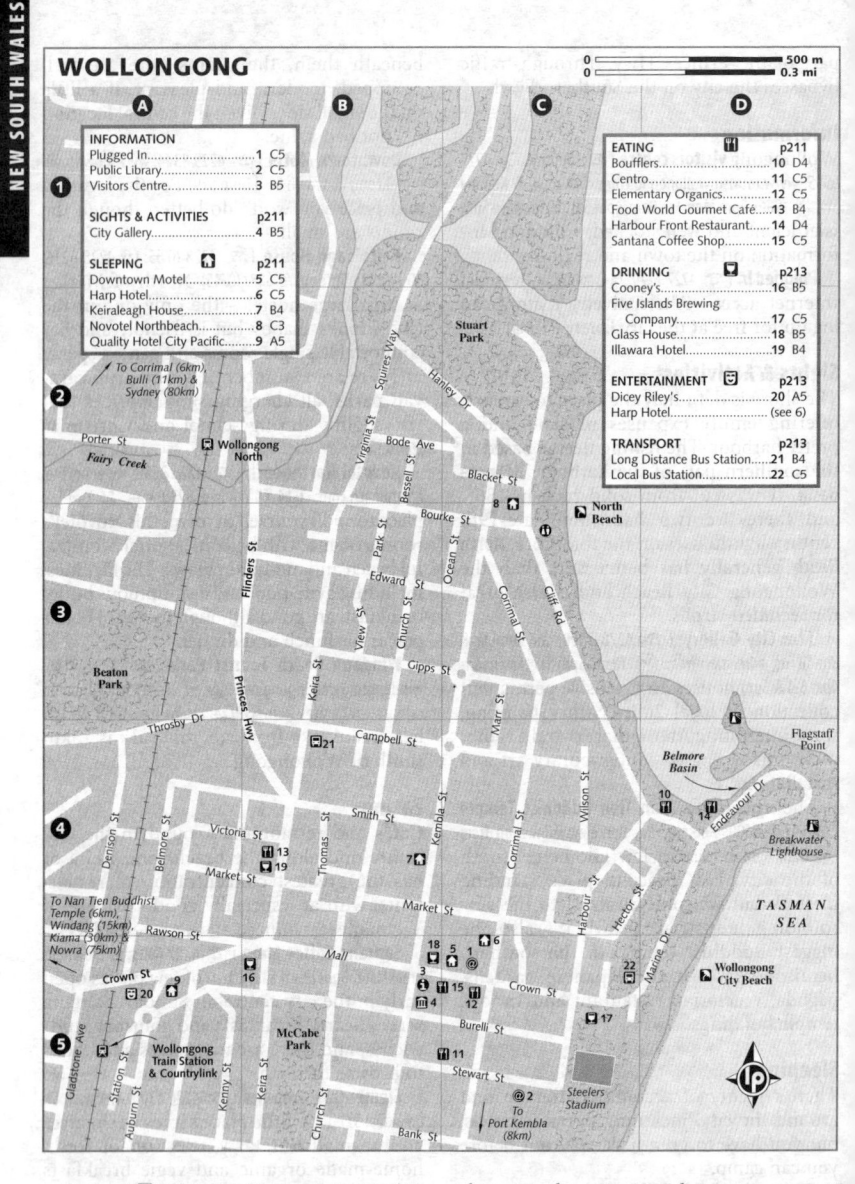

WOLLONGONG

0 ————— 500 m
0 ————— 0.3 mi

INFORMATION
Plugged In.........................1 C5
Public Library....................2 C5
Visitors Centre..................3 B5

SIGHTS & ACTIVITIES p211
City Gallery.......................4 B5

SLEEPING p211
Downtown Motel..............5 C5
Harp Hotel........................6 C5
Keiraleagh House..............7 B4
Novotel Northbeach.........8 C3
Quality Hotel City Pacific....9 A5

EATING p211
Boufflers.........................10 D4
Centro.............................11 C5
Elementary Organics........12 C5
Food World Gourmet Café....13 B4
Harbour Front Restaurant......14 D4
Santana Coffee Shop........15 C5

DRINKING p213
Cooney's..........................16 B5
Five Islands Brewing
 Company........................17 C5
Glass House.....................18 B5
Illawara Hotel...................19 B4

ENTERTAINMENT p213
Dicey Riley's....................20 A5
Harp Hotel................(see 6)

TRANSPORT p213
Long Distance Bus Station....21 B4
Local Bus Station..............22 C5

Centro (☎ 4227 1797; 28 Stewart St; pasta $12, mains $18) Serving fine Italian food in funky, modern surroundings, Centro is a favourite with local business folk.

Several places overlook the water around Belmore Basin, including these two:

Boufflers (☎ 4227 2989; Belmore Basin; fish & chips from $6) Generous portions of fresh fish and chips are the attraction here; you can eat outside while taking in the harbour view.

Harbour Front Restaurant (☎ 4227 2999; 2 Endeavour Dr; mains $30) Decidedly upmarket, this is a great place for lunch or dinner. Seafood, unsurprisingly, is the strong point. We found the home-made gnocchi with blue swimmer crab to be excellent, if a little oily.

Drinking

There are a few decent bars and clubs in town, the survival of many ensured by Wollongong's student population. It's often lively in town even during the week.

Five Islands Brewing Company (☎ 4220 2854; WIN Entertainment Centre) A spacious, sleek, modern place with tall plate-glass windows and its own micro-brewery. The atmosphere is laid-back, the home brew excellent and there's some good bistro-style food and bar snacks.

Glass House (90 Crown St) A smart café by day, by night Glass House turns into a febrile drinking, dancing and pick-up joint for local students (and the odd predatory young Sydneysider). It's fun, but if you're older than 25 you'll probably feel ancient here.

Other good pubs in town:

Cooney's (☎ 4229 1911; 234 Keira St)
Illawarra Hotel (☎ 4229 5411; cnr Market & Keira Sts)

Entertainment

Information on performing arts, sporting facilities and indoor activities can be found in *Recreation Wollongong*, a brochure available at the visitors centre. Several clubs and pubs host live entertainment.

Harp Hotel (☎ 4229 1333; 124 Corrimal St) Sports fans after large-screen action will be happy most days, and live-music devotees can listen to local bands play during weekends. Not the place for a quiet beer though, and the fug of stale, beer-soaked carpet is inescapable.

Dicey Riley's (☎ 4229 1952; 333 Crown St) Bands here play mostly Irish music from Thursday to Saturday night.

Getting There & Away

BUS

The **bus station** (☎ 4226 1022) is on the corner of Keira and Campbell Sts. **Premier Motor Services** (☎ 13 34 10) runs several daily services to Sydney ($13 one way) and regular services to Bega ($48), Eden ($55) and Melbourne ($69).

TRAIN

City Rail (☎ 13 15 00) runs several daily trains to/from Sydney (one way/day-return $8.80/ 10.40, 1½ hours). Some continue south to Kiama, Gerringong and Bomaderry (Nowra).

Getting Around

Several local bus companies serve the area, including **Dions** (☎ 4228 9855), **Premier** (☎ 4271 1322) and **Greens** (☎ 4267 3884). The main bus station is at the bend where Crown St becomes Marine Dr, near the beach. You can reach most beaches by rail, and trains are fairly frequent.

AROUND WOLLONGONG

Rising dramatically behind Wollongong, the **Illawarra Escarpment** is a great place to enjoy woodland walks and grand coastal views. There are **walking tracks** on Mt Kembla and Mt Keira, less than 10km from the city centre, but you'll need your own transport to get there. Enjoy spectacular views over the town and coast from the **Bulli Scenic Lookout** (pronounced bull-eye), north off the Princes Hwy. The visitors centre or the local **NPWS office** (☎ 02-4225 1455; 4/55 Market St ⊙ 8.30am-4.30pm Mon-Fri) should have copies of the useful, free NPWS leaflet guide to the escarpment.

Several excellent surf beaches lie north of Wollongong, including **Sandon Point**, **Austinmer**, **Headlands** (only for experienced surfers) and **Sharkies**. The pubs at Clifton and Scarborough have meals, accommodation and great sea views.

On the road to Otford and Royal National Park, the views from **Lawrence Hargrave Lookout**, at Bald Hill above Stanwell Park, are superb. Hargrave, a pioneer aviator, made his first flying attempts in the area in the early 20th century; today **Stanwell Park** is used for hang-gliding. **Sydney Hang Gliding Centre** (☎ 02-4294 4294; www.hanggliding.com.au; tandem flights from $165) operates from here. An even more dramatic way to see the area is to skydive above it at 250km/h with **Skydive the Beach** (☎ 02-4225 8444; www.skydivethebeach.com; tandem dives $270-320).

South of Wollongong, **Lake Illawarra** is popular for water sports.

WOLLONGONG TO NOWRA

South of Lake Illawarra, **Shellharbour**, a popular holiday resort, is one of the oldest towns along the coast. There are decent stretches of relatively empty beach on **Windang Peninsula** north of town and scuba diving off **Bass Point** to the south.

Kiama is a pretty seaside town famous for its blowhole, which can spout up to

TOP FIVE NATIONAL PARKS OF THE NSW SOUTH COAST

The south coast has a stunning range of national parks. All have driving and bushwalking tracks and offer diverse experiences, including fishing, surfing, exploring human history and bird-watching. Park use and camping fees apply at most parks.

Booderee

On the southern peninsula of Jervis Bay, this beautiful park is bounded by the ocean: rugged cliffs and angry seas on one side and gentle lapping waves on the other. Attractions include cliffs, beaches, temperate rainforest, heathland, dune lakes and the lovely botanic gardens. There's also a good range of beachfront camping (p216).

Eurobodalla

A bird-watcher's paradise, Eurobodalla occupies a coastal strip between Tilba Tilba and Moruya. The varied coastal, estuarine and freshwater habitats attract many migratory species and protect a number of endangered ones. Old Aboriginal sites and unique geology are other attractions.

Mimosa Rocks

Between Tathra and Bermagui, this park's attractions include its remoteness, some well-designed camp sites set in handsome forest and its combination of lagoon and ocean beaches.

Bournda

Long beaches, bays, lagoons, eucalypt forest, sedgelands and large freshwater lakes provide breathtaking scenic variety. It's also an important wilderness for several bird species, including the osprey.

Ben Boyd

South of Eden, this extensive park is replete with interesting nooks and crannies. There's an impressive lighthouse, whale-watching and numerous whale-industry and Aboriginal heritage sites. Keen hikers can tackle the bracing 30km 'Light to Light' track, which takes three to four days (p219).

60m. Kiama **visitors centre** (☎ 02-4232 3322) is nearby. Kiama also boasts surf beaches including a small enclosed one right near the town centre. Trains run regularly from Sydney (2 hours), as do buses. Be warned that Premier Motor Services does not normally drive down the hill into Kiama, but drops off on the highway, a steep and busy couple of kilometres away.

There are several places to stay in Kiama, including **Blowhole Point Holiday Park** (☎ 02-4232 2707; blowhole@kiama.net; camp/caravan sites from $22/25, vans with bathroom from $76), which is almost entirely surrounded by sea. This virtual island is a great place to stay when it's not too windy, but the sites are rather close and regimented.

Kiama Backpackers Hostel (☎ 02-4233 1881; 31 Bong Bong St; dm/d $20/49; 🖳) is only 25m from the station and a couple of minutes from the beach. It looks better inside than out.

Figtrees of Kiama (☎ 02-4232 4219; www.kiama .com.au/figtrees; 90 Barney St; d $150) is high on a hill at the edge of town. Most rooms at this pleasant guesthouse have good sea views and verandas.

Bird-watchers will want to visit **Barren Grounds Bird Observatory** (☎ 02-4236 0195; admission free) at Jamberoo, 10km east of the highway. This nature reserve offers free **camp sites**, and has a range of activities.

Kiama Coachlines (☎ 02-4232 1531; 154 Shoalhaven St) runs Monday to Friday from Kiama to the **Minnamurra Rainforest** in Budderoo National Park. You have about three hours to explore before returning ($10).

Gerringong, 10km south of Kiama, has fine sweeping beaches and surf. Stay at either the council-run **Holiday Park** (☎ 02-4234 1285 werri@kiama.net; Werri Beach; camp sites from $25; cabins from $90) at the surfy northern end of the beach, or at the small **YHA hostel** (☎ 02-4234

1249; Nestor House; dm/f $20/54) behind the Uniting Church on Fern St, a few hundred metres from the beach.

The small, pretty town of **Berry** was an early settlement. Today it has a number of National Trust classified buildings, a **museum** and many antique, craft and coffee **shops**. Unsurprisingly, it's popular and packed every weekend. The **Hotel Berry** (☎ 02-4464 1011; 120 Queen St; lunch & dinner $11-19) has a decent bistro menu and a cosy half-enclosed veranda. The **Great Southern** (☎ 02-4464 1009; 95 Queen St) is a fun pub/motel where you can drink atop saddle seats while you take in the memorabilia, including a torpedo hanging from the ceiling and a motorcycle on the bar.

There are several great cafés and delis on the main road (Queen St), including **Berry Jetz** (☎ 02-4464 3320; breakfast $5-9), good for fresh juices, and the pricey but superb **Emporium Food Co** (☎ 02-4464 3291; lunch from $10), which has excellent coffee and custard tarts.

Berry has a great choice of mid-range and slightly more upmarket accommodation options. The **Bunyip Inn** (☎ 02-4464 2064; 122 Queen St; s/d from $77/120) is a smart guesthouse in a period building, which also has one wheelchair-accessible room.

Berry Village Boutique Motel (☎ 02-4464 3570; www.berrymotel.com.au; 72-76 Queen St; d from $105; 🔁) is modern and appealing, with large rooms and huge beds.

Berry Hotel (☎ 02-4464 1011; berrypub@shoal.net .au; 120 Queen St; B&B s/d mid-week from $35/55) is a large, comfortable place. The rooms here are old-fashioned but excellent value.

Some upmarket, self-catering houses are available for rent in the area through **South Coast Accommodation Services** (☎ 02-4464 2477; www.accommodationservices.com.au; per night $120-650).

There are scenic roads from Berry to pretty **Kangaroo Valley**, and you can canoe and swim on the Shoalhaven and Kangaroo Rivers. **Mild to Wild** (☎ 02-4464 2211; www .m2w.com.au; 84 Queen St, Berry; ☼ 9am-6pm) runs outdoor activities in the area, including canoeing, canyoning and mountain biking.

The coast near Berry boasts the glorious **Seven Mile Beach**, a huge, empty stretch of sand, backed by attractive forest. **Seven Mile Beach Holiday Park** (☎ 02-4234 1340; www .kiama.net/holiday/sevenmile; Gerroa Rd, Gerroa; camp sites/beach huts/cabins from $20/90/120) is a tad crowded but has a wide range of accommodation options and is close to the beach.

Seahaven Cafe (☎ 02-4234 3796; 19 Riverleigh Ave, Gerroa; mains $10) looks out along the sweep of the beach and serves tasty home-made breakfasts and lunches.

Just west of Shoalhaven Heads, **Coolangatta** (no, not the Queensland Coolangatta, this was the original) has buildings that were constructed by convicts in 1822. They now form part of the **Coolangatta Estate** (☎ 02-4448 7131; 1335 Bolong Rd, Shoalhaven Heads; admission free; ☼ 9am-5pm), where you can wander around the old buildings and visit the winery. There's also a decent restaurant.

SHOALHAVEN
☎ 02 / pop 2738
The coastal strip south of Gerringong to Durras Lake, just north of Batemans Bay, is a popular holiday destination known as Shoalhaven. On the Shoalhaven River, the sprawling and busy twin towns of **Nowra** and **Bomaderry** form the main population centre. The region is popular for water sports, and white-water rafting is available inland on the higher reaches of Shoalhaven. The Shoalhaven **visitors centre** (☎ 1800 024 261, 4421 0778; ☼ 9am-4.30pm) is on the corner of Princes Hwy and Pleasant Way. The free *Visit Shoalhaven* booklet contains lots of self-drive touring information. The **NPWS** (☎ 4423 2170; 55 Graham St; ☼ 9am-4.30pm Mon-Fri) has an office in town.

Accommodation options in Shoalhaven include **M&M's Guesthouse** (☎ 4422 8006; www .nowrabackpackers.com; 1A Scenic Dr; dm/d with light breakfast $25/60), which is near the bridge on the Nowra side of the river, opposite the Olympic pool. Clean and friendly, this is a well-run guesthouse and hostel.

White House (☎ 4421 2084; www.whitehouseguest house.com; 30 Junction St, Shoalhaven; B&B dm/s/d $25/50/ 70; 🖳) is a pleasant, if old-fashioned, family-run guesthouse with wide verandas. The dorm rooms are a bit poky.

Five kilometres east of Nowra on the northern bank of the Shoalhaven River is **Nowra Animal Park** (☎ 4421 3949; Rockhill Rd; admission $8; ☼ 9am-5pm). It's a pleasant place to meet some of Australia's native animals and you can **camp** (from $10) in bushland here.

There are some beautiful escarpment walks inland at **Morton National Park**. The Fitzroy Falls **visitors centre** (☎ 4887 7270; ☼ 9am-5pm) is located just north of Kangaroo Valley.

South of Nowra, **Jervis Bay** is a serenely beautiful stretch of coastline with white sandy beaches, bush and forest. **Huskisson**, one of the oldest towns on the bay, is an attractive centre handy for water sports and whale- and dolphin-watching. There's a boardwalk and museum near the **Lady Denman Heritage Complex** (☎ 4441 5675; Cnr Woollamia Rd & Dent St; maritime museum; admission $8; ☽ 10am-4pm), on the Nowra side of Huskisson, which boasts historic buildings, artefacts, Aboriginal crafts, and boats, including a large old paddle-steamer that's currently under restoration.

Booderee National Park takes up the southeastern spit of land on the bay and it's quite lovely. Booderee is an Aboriginal word meaning 'bay of plenty', and so it is. Those with cars will pay a parking fee ($10 per car for 24 hours); book camping on the attractive, beachfront sites (from $8.70) through the NPWS **visitors centre** (☎ 4443 0977; Jervis Bay Rd; ☽ 9am-4pm). **Booderee Botanic Gardens** (☎ 4442 1122; www.booderee.np.gov.au; Caves Beach Rd; admission free; ☽ 8am-4pm Mon-Fri, 10am-5pm Sat & Sun), also in the national park, offers some picturesque, gentle walks around different habitats.

Jervis Bay is perfectly formed to explore at leisure by kayak. Hire kayaks (around $33 for three hours) or book guided trips through **Jervis Bay Kayaks** (☎ 4441 7157). A few different operators offer dolphin- and whale-watching tours from Huskisson, including **Dolphin Explorer Cruises** (☎ 4441 5455; adult/child $20/10), which offers three cruises daily.

Places to stay and eat in Jervis Bay include **Beach 'n' Bush Backpackers** (☎ 4441 6880; www.beachnbush.com.au; 57 St Georges Ave, Vincentia; B&B dm from $22; ☐), a small, comfortable backpackers offering a light breakfast and tour bookings.

Jervis Bay Guesthouse (☎ 4441 7658; gdaymate@ ozemail.com.au; 1 Beach St, Huskisson; d $120-220) is a pretty, historic house offering attractive, light and airy rooms with bathroom and a veranda overlooking the bay.

Hyams Beach General Store (☎ 4443 3874; 76-78 Cyrus St, Hyams Beach; breakfast/lunch $9/10) is a bustling place that makes a great food stop on the way to or from the beach, serving freshly made breakfasts and lunches every day and dinners Tuesday to Saturday.

Seagrass (☎ 4441 6124; 13 Currambene St, Huskisson; mains $24), an upmarket place, has contemporary décor and modern Australian food.

Ulladulla is an area of beautiful lakes, lagoons and beaches. There's swimming and surfing; try **Mollymook** beach, just north of town. Accommodation options include **South Coast Backpackers** (☎ 4454 0500; 63 Princes Hwy; dm/d $22/45), which is near the top of the hill north of the shopping centre and has spacious five-bed dorms.

If you're peckish, **Harbourside** (☎ 4455 3377; 84 Princes Hwy; mains $25) is a great lunch or dinner stop for views and excellent and inventive seafood, such as crab, leek and coriander ravioli.

Pebbly Beach (day pass $5) is about 10km off the highway, in Murramarang National Park. There's no public transport available, but its charms include wild kangaroos and lorikeets that will eat from your hand (although there are many signs telling you why this is a bad idea). If you want to stay overnight, try **Pebbly Beach Holiday Cottages** (☎ 4478 6023; camp sites/ cabins from $5/77). **Pigeon House Mountain** (719m) offers a relatively challenging three-hour return walk; there are wonderful views at the top. There are many motels in Ulladulla.

Premier Motor Services runs from Ulladulla to Sydney ($27), Nowra ($14), Batemans Bay ($11) and Eden ($36).

BATEMANS BAY & AROUND

The fishing port of Batemans Bay (pop 10,200) is one of the south coast's largest holiday centres. The Batemans Bay **visitors centre** (☎ 02-4472 6900, reservations 1800 802 528; Princes Hwy; ☽ 9am-5pm) is near the town centre.

Batemans Bay is packed with accommodation options to suit all budgets. The town itself doesn't hold many attractions, but it's a handy base if you have no transport. To make the most of the hinterland, however, you really do need access to a car.

Accommodation options include **Country Comfort** (☎ 02-4472 6333; www.countrycomfort.com .au; cnr Princes Hwy & Canberra Rd; courtyard/river-facing d $85/97; ☒), which is just over the bridge from town and commands views over the bay and forest. It's probably the nicest motel-style place to stay.

Shady Willows Holiday Park & YHA (☎ 02-4472 4972; www.yha.com.au; Old Princes Hwy; camp sites/dm/d from $15/18/40, cabins with bathroom from $56) is pleasant enough, although the cabins are tightly packed. The managers can arrange local tours and activities, including kayaking and trips to Pebbly Beach.

Unwind with gorgeous views of the **Blue Mountains** (p143)

SIMON RICHMOND

Ponder the striking sculptures in the arid artists' paradise of **Broken Hill** (p236)

ANDREW MARSHALL & LEANNE WALKER

CHRIS BELL

Immerse yourself in Grose Valley's **Blue Gum Forest** (p150)

GRANT

Climb to the top of **Mt Kosciuszko** (p223)

Play on the snowy slopes of **Thredbo** (p224)

JOHN BAB

PAUL SINCLAIR

Find clear and tranquil waters in the lakes of **Kosciuszko National Park** (p221)

Take a summer walk among the wild-flowers of the **Snowy Mountains** (p219)

ROB BLAKERS

The promenade area on Clyde Rd is the best place to find food. The **Starfish Deli** (☎ 02-4472 4880; Promenade Plaza; mains $11-20) is a modern place with an outdoor dining area. Alternatively, watch still-twitching seafood being unloaded from the boat as you eat incredibly fresh fish and chips at the **Boatshed** (lunch $7) next door. **Aussie Pancakes** (☎ 02-4472 5727; Promenade Plaza; breakfast $8) serves cheap breakfasts, snack and fresh juices.

An attractive alternative base in the area, about 30km south of town off the Princes Hwy, is the **Oaks Ranch** (☎ 02-4471 7403; 238 Old Mossy Point Rd; d $120), a great family place offering appealing rooms close to some lovely beaches. It's set in 300-acre grounds and there's horse riding, golf, tennis, swimming, bird-watching and bush walks.

About 60km inland from Batemans Bay, on the scenic road to Canberra, is **Braidwood**, home to many old buildings and a thriving arts and crafts community. There's fairly unspoiled coast down the side roads south of **Moruya**, including **Eurobodalla National Park**, a rich and ecologically important network of coast, estuary and fresh water habitats.

Unsurprisingly this area is a bird-watcher's paradise where an abundance of exotically named migratory species hang out, such as the Bar-Tailed Godwit and the endangered Long-Nosed Potoroo. There are simple camping facilities at Eurobadalla and scope for surfing, bushwalking and even canoeing and boating if you bring your own equipment.

For further information contact the Narooma **NPWS office** (☎ 02-4476 2888; ☺ 8.30am-5.30pm Mon-Fri).

NAROOMA & AROUND

Perhaps the loveliest holiday town on this coast, Narooma (pop 3400) boasts serene, forest-edged inlets and lakes, emerald green waters and some rugged coastline. It's especially popular for serious sport fishing. The **visitors centre** (☎ 02-4476 2881; www.naturecoast-tourism.com.au; Princes Hwy; ☺ 9am-5pm) is close to the town centre. The **NPWS office** (☎ 02-4476 2888; cnr Field St & Princes Hwy; ☺ 9am-4pm Mon-Fri) stocks brochures for all nearby parks.

About 10km off the Narooma coast is **Montague Island**, a nature reserve with an historic lighthouse and resident seals and penguins. It's only accessible by boat with an NPWS-accredited guide. **Tours** (adult/child $69/50) depart

morning and evening (weather and tides permitting) and go for around four hours, with a minimum of eight passengers. The clear waters around the island are popular with divers, especially from February to June, and there is whale-watching in October through to November.

Accommodation in Narooma includes **Amooran Court** (☎ 02-4476 2198; www.amoorancourt .com.au; 30 Montague St; d midweek from $80; ☒), which has attractive, recently refurbished rooms (including one wheelchair-accessible room) overlooking the sea.

Bluewater Lodge – Narooma YHA (☎ 02-4476 4440; www.yha.com.au; 8 Princes Hwy; dm/s/d/f $23/30/42/50; ☐) is a terrific hostel set in a pretty garden.

Two excellent self-catering options in the area are **Clark Bay Cottages** (☎ 02-4476 1640; clark bayfarm@mail.com; 463 Riverview Dr; d 2 nights min $110; ☒), which has quirky Nissen-hut style units on a great spot overlooking the inlet and offers award-winning facilities for disabled guests; and **Mystery Bay Cottages** (☎ 02-4473 7431; www .mysterybaycottages.com.au; 121 Mystery Bay Rd; d from $104), which has attractive cottages set on appealing, spacious grounds a short walk from a deserted beach, 10km south of Narooma.

Casey's Cafe (☎ 02-4476 1241; Cnr Canty & Wagonga Sts; breakfast $6; ☐) in Narooma, opposite the Westpac bank, has great coffee, fresh juices and good vegetarian choices on the menu.

Simply Seafood (☎ 02-4476 2403; 31 Riverside Dr; mains $26; ☺ closed Sun night & Mon) serves wonderful seafood on a deck in the marina. The seared tuna on noodles in a miso broth, with Asian greens and pickled seaweed, is light and lovely.

Off the highway 15km south of Narooma, and perched on the side of **Mt Dromedary** (806m), is the delightful 19th-century gold-mining boom town of **Central Tilba**. Heritage-listed, it is a pretty centre for arts and crafts. From the nearby town of **Tilba Tilba** you can walk to the top of Mt Dromedary (also called Gulaga). The return walk (11km) takes about five hours. Slake your thirst and grab some lunch at **Tilba Valley Wineries** (☎ 02-4473 7308; 947 Old Hwy; lunches around $9).

South of the beautiful bird-filled **Wallaga Lake** and off the Princes Hwy, **Bermagui** (population 2000) is a pretty fishing port made famous when American cowboy-novelist Zane Grey visited in 1936. There are great walks nearby and it's a handy base for visits to both **Gulaga/Wallaga Lake and Mimosa Rocks National Parks**, and for **Wadbilliga National Park**, inland in the ranges. Bermagui's **visitors centre** (☎ 02-6493 3054; Lamont St; ☼ 10am-4pm) is just beyond the marina.

Stay at **Blue Pacific** (☎ 1800 244 921, 02-6493 4921; 73 Murrah St; dm/s/f $25/50/70), a motel-style place with small but comfortable and well-equipped rooms ideal for self-catering. Eat at **Saltwater** (☎ 02-6493 4328; mains $20), a bright, modern place on the harbour.

More interesting than the inland highway, the largely unsealed Sapphire Coast Dr between Bermagui and Tathra runs alongside the Mimosa Rocks National Park. On the Princes Hwy is **Cobargo**, another unspoilt old town. The main 2WD access to rugged Wadbilliga National Park is near here.

SOUTH TO THE VICTORIAN BORDER

The coast here is quite undeveloped, and there are many good beaches and some awe-inspiring forests full of wildlife. Choose between the faster Princes Hwy and the slower – but more scenic – Sapphire Coast Dr. This links Pambula with Bega via Tathra and continues north, where some sections remain unsealed.

It's no surprise that there are some gorgeous national parks along this largely unspoiled bit of coast. Just north of Tathra beautiful, thickly-wooded **Mimosa Rocks National Park** hugs 20km of coastline ranging from dramatic weather-pounded volcanic rock to lagoons and beaches. There are several **camping grounds** if you want to stay over. The park lies a few kilometres north of Tathra and is well worth a visit.

South of Tathra, **Bournda National Park**, offers more wooded seclusion along with vast stretches of beach. Inland there's some great and varied hiking country taking in lakes, heathland, wetland and forest. There's also scope for canoeing and swimming in Bournda Lagoon's warm waters. There's a well-organised camping ground in the park. For more information contact the **Merimbula NPWS office** (☎ 02-6495 5001).

Merimbula

☎ 02 / pop 4900

Merimbula is a big and busy holiday resort and retirement town, with an impressive 'lake' (actually a large inlet) and beaches. Despite being well developed, the setting remains beautiful, and nearby **Pambula Beach** is quiet, in a suburban kind of way.

The **visitors centre** (☎ 6497 2548; bookings 1800 150 457; www.sapphirecoast.com.au; Beach St; ☼ 9am-5pm Mon-Sat, 9am-4pm Sun) is on the waterfront at the bottom of Market St. At the wharf at the eastern point is the small **Merimbula Aquarium** (☎ 6495 3227; Lake St; adult/child $8.80/4.40; ☼ aquarium 10am-5pm, restaurant 11.30am-3pm & 6-8.30pm) which holds shoals of tropical fish and sharks in large tanks. Feeding time is at 11.30am on Mondays, Wednesdays and Fridays or on weekdays during school holidays. The appealing restaurant/café attached has great views across the water.

Some of the better sleeping options in Merimbula include **Wandarrah YHA Lodge** (☎ 6495 3503; www.yha.com.au; 8 Marine Pde; dm/d from $22/46; ▯), near the surf beach just south of the bridge. This is a spacious, modern hostel which runs tours to Eden and nearby national parks.

Merimbula Divers Lodge (☎ 1800 651 861, 6495 3611; www.merimbuladiverslodge.com.au; 15 Park St; dm/d/f $22/60/100), just off Main St, has accommodation in clean and bright two-bedroom, self-contained units. An accredited PADI centre, the lodge offers dive courses and local diving, with whale-watching in October and November.

Bella Vista (☎ 6495 1373; 16 Main St; B&B d $150) is a large, beautifully decorated guesthouse close to town, and has big, comfortable rooms and a deck overlooking the inlet.

Eating options aren't varied or great in town. **Waterfront** (☎ 6495 2211; 1 Market St; breakfast $8), overlooking the water, is a good café but only a fair to middling restaurant.

Eden

☎ 02 / pop 3200

South of Eden, the road turns away from the coast and runs through beautiful forests. Forty kilometres later it enters Victoria. Inland is the gorgeous **South East Forests National Park**. Eden, on Twofold Bay, is an old whaling port and a place of great charm. It's much less touristy than towns further up the coast.

The staff at Eden **visitors centre** (☎ 6496 1953; Imlay St; ☼ 9am-5pm Mon-Fri, 9am-noon Sat & Sun) is welcoming and helpful.

The intriguing **Killer Whale Museum** (☎ 6496 2094; 94 Imlay St; adult/child $5/2; ☼ 9.15am-3.45pm Mon-Sat, 11.15am-3.45pm Sun) is a place

EDEN'S KILLER ATTRACTION

The coast of Eden, Twofold Bay in particular, is a prime spot for watching migrating humpback and southern right whales resting and feeding before their migration to Antarctic waters. In the 19th century this made it a prime spot for whale fishers, who raced out in open whaling boats to kill them and harvest their lucrative blubber.

What made Eden's whale industry unique was the strange alliance formed between the whale hunters and killer whales (orcas), who helped the whale fishers find, trap and kill their migrating cousins by herding them into the bay and preventing them from diving to escape. In return for their efforts the orcas would feed on the tongues and lips of the dead whales. It's the only known instance of orcas and humans hunting together. The most deadly orca was called Old Tom and his skeleton, along with the details of his fascinating story, rest in Eden's excellent Killer Whale Museum (p218). Don't miss it.

packed with wonderfully improbable, but seemingly well-documented, nautical tales. Read about a modern-day Jonah, a heroic porpoise and perhaps most extraordinarily read about Old Tom the killer whale (see the boxed text 'Eden's Killer Attraction'; above). If you don't believe the more incredible parts of the story on the museum walls, look at Old Tom's skeleton and have a close look at his teeth. In October and November you can book **whale-watching cruises** at the visitors centre. **CatBalou Cruises** (☎ 6496 2027; adult/child $55/40) has won several tourism awards.

Crown & Anchor (☎ 6496 1017; www.crown andanchoreden.com.au; 239 Imlay St; B&B d from $150) is a wonderfully romantic old colonial-era guesthouse, with great bay views and stylishly decorated rooms. A three-course breakfast is thrown in.

Budget travellers can stay at **Australasia Hotel** (☎ 6496 1600; fax 6496 1462; 160 Imlay St; dm/s/d from $17/22/28), which offers basic but clean and good-value older-style rooms.

Eden is a fishing port and the region's oysters are famous. **Oyster Bar Cafe** (☎ 6496 1304; Eden Wharf; mains $17; ☻ Tue-Sun) offers terrific food along with impressively sour-faced service (don't take it personally). The Asian-style calamari salad is delicious and filling, and the desserts are superb, too. For simply prepared and very fresh seafood try the **Wheelhouse Restaurant** (☎ 6496 3392; 253 Imlay St; mains $18) just around the corner on the wharf.

Ben Boyd National Park & Around

To the north and south of Eden is Ben Boyd National Park. Edrom Rd is the main access road to the north of the park. Wonboyn Rd is 4km south of Edrom Rd, and gives access to **Nadgee Nature Reserve** and to **Wonboyn**, a small settlement on Wonboyn Lake at the northern end of the reserve. Many roads in the parks have unsealed sections that can be slippery after rain.

Wonboyn Lake Resort (☎ 02-6496 9162; fax 6496 9100; Wonboyn Lake; cabins from $82), reached via Edrom and Green Cape Rds, is an absolutely beautiful small resort with lake frontage.

Wonboyn Cabins & Caravan Park (☎ 02-6496 9131; www.wonboyncabins.com.au; Wonboyn Lake; camp sites/cabins from $16/45), accessed via Wonboyn Rd, is a laid-back spot on the lake, among a community of 200 people. The birdsong is deafening and there's a small licensed store.

Groups may be interested in staying at Green Cape Lightstation's **heritage cottages** (☎ 02-6495 5000), an old lighthouse in a breathtaking position at the southern tip of Ben Boyd National Park.

SNOWY MOUNTAINS

The Snowy Mountains, affectionately called the Snowies, form part of the Great Dividing Range where it straddles the NSW–Victorian border. Mt Kosciuszko (pronounced 'kozzee-osko' and named after a Polish hero of the American War of Independence), in NSW, is Australia's highest mainland summit (2228m). Much of the Snowies are contained within Kosciuszko National Park, an area of year-round interest, with skiing in winter (see Skiing & Ski Resorts; p223), and bushwalking and vivid wildflowers in summer.

The upper waters of the Murray River form both the state and national-park boundaries in the southwest. The Snowy River, made famous by Banjo Paterson's poem *The Man from Snowy River* and the film based on it, rises just below the summit of Mt Kosciuszko. The Murrumbidgee River also rises in the national park.

You can take white-water rafting trips on the Murray River in summer when the water is high enough, and fishing and horse riding are also popular.

Getting There & Away

Cooma is the eastern gateway to the Snowy Mountains: see the Cooma section following for public transport details.

The most spectacular mountain views can be enjoyed from the Alpine Way (sometimes closed in winter), running between Khancoban, on the western side of the national park, and Jindabyne. You'll need a car to use this road. There are restrictions on car parking in the national park, particularly during the ski season – check with the NPWS or visitors centres at Cooma or Jindabyne before entering.

COOMA

☎ 02 / pop 6900

Cooma was the construction centre for the Snowy Mountains hydro-electric scheme, built by workers from all over the world. The **Avenue of Flags**, in Centennial Park, flies the flags of the 28 nationalities involved. It's next to the Cooma **visitors centre** (☎ 1800 636 525, 6450 1742; www.visitcooma.com.au; 119 Sharp St; ☼ 9am-5pm; ☐).

The **Snowy Mountains hydro-electric scheme Information Centre** (☎ 1800 623 776, 6453 2004; www.snowyhydro.com.au; ☼ 8am-5pm Mon-Fri, 8am-1pm Sat & Sun), on the Princes Hwy 2km north of town, has high-tech interactive exhibits and videos of this amazing project, which took 25 years and more than 100,000 people to build. It's also a good place to find out about visits to the three power stations in the area.

The heritage walk around town is good way to take in the sights and historical buildings and to get a flavour for Cooma's late 19th century history. Maps are available from the visitors centre, where you can also arrange to tour **Cooma Gaol**. The **Southern Cloud Memorial** incorporates some

of the wreckage of the *Southern Cloud*, an aircraft that crashed in the Snowies in 1931 and wasn't found until 1958.

Sleeping & Eating

Prices are lower here than in Jindabyne or the ski resorts, but in winter it still pays to book well ahead – preferably in the summer.

White Manor (☎ 6456 1152; www.whitemanor.com; 252 Sharp St; s/d low season $63/68; ☒) Behind a cheerful riot of pot plants, the rooms here are spic, and indeed, span.

Bunkhouse Motel (☎ 6452 2983; www.bunkhouse motel.com.au; 28 Soho St; dm/s/d/f low season from $20/35/50/65) Each dorm in this friendly place has its own kitchen and bath, the doubles are comfortable and there's a quiet, vine-covered courtyard.

Decent places to eat include **Organic Vibes** (☎ 6452 6566; 82a Sharp St; lunch around $9) for fresh juices, **Sharp Food** (☎ 6452 7333; 122 Sharp St; lunch $10; ☼ closed Sun) for pleasant courtyard lounging, and the **Lott** (☎ 6452 1414; 178-180 Sharp St; breakfast $6, lunch & dinner $7-11; ☐) for a cosy atmosphere, hearty meals and good coffee.

Many migrant workers from the Snowy Mountains hydro-electric scheme went on to settle in Cooma. For a small country town it has an amazing array of authentic **ethnic restaurants**, including Thai, Malaysian, Chinese, Italian, Lebanese and Vietnamese.

Getting There & Away

Qantas (☎ 13 13 13) flies from Sydney to Cooma Airport, about 15km from Cooma (one way $155).

All buses except the V/Line service (which stops near Centennial Park) stop at the Snowstop Village, on Sharp St, a few blocks east of the visitors centre. **Harvey World Travel** (☎ 6452 4677) handles bus bookings.

All bus access is via Canberra ($37/30, 1½ hours). From Canberra, **CountryLink** (☎ 13 22 32) runs to Cooma daily. **V/Line** (☎ 13 61 96) runs from Canberra via Cooma to Melbourne on Tuesday, Friday and Sunday and returns from Melbourne on Monday, Thursday and Saturday. Some services continue on to the ski resorts in the high season. Services are frequent in winter, but less so at other times.

Summit Coaches (☎ 6297 2588) runs return trips from Cooma to Jindabyne and Thredbo on Monday, Wednesday, Friday and Sunday. The **Oz Experience** (☎ 1300 300 028) runs from Canberra to Cooma on Tuesday and Friday, and returns to Canberra on Thursday and Sunday.

Thrifty Car Rental (☎ 6452 5300) has an office in town and **Hertz Airport Rentals** (☎ 6452 6255) has an office at the airport.

For more information on getting to and from the Snowy Mountains see p220.

JINDABYNE
☎ 02 / pop 4400

Occupying a pretty lakeside location, and an excellent base for summer and winter outdoor activities in the nearby mountains, Jindabyne is a modern town on the shore of the artificial Lake Jindabyne. Winter brings the skiing crowds, the rest of the year (temperatures permitting) you can take your pick from horse riding, mountain biking, swimming, sailing and wakeboarding. You can even scuba dive down to the houses of the old town swallowed by the lake. Apparently there's an old jalopy still in its garage down there. The NPWS-operated Snowy Region **visitors centre** (☎ 6450 5600; ☜ 8.30am-5pm) is in the centre of town on Kosciuszko Rd.

Local adventure companies offer a great range of activities in the area. **Jindabyne Adventure Booking** (☎ 1800 815 588; nkbenterprises@bigpond.com) runs activities including fishing, sailing, wakeboarding, lake cruises and a good range of mountain-biking tours. **Paddy Pallin** (☎ 6456 2922; www.snowy.net.au/~paljin) organises guided walks and adventure activities all year. It also sells and rents outdoor equipment of all sorts. It's opposite the Thredbo turn-off just out of town. **Man From Snowy River Adventures** (☎ 6456 5033; www.snowyriverhorsebackadventure.com.au), based near Jindabyne, runs horse treks ranging from one day to several days.

Sleeping
Winter sees a huge influx of visitors; prices soar, many places are booked out months ahead and overnight accommodation all but disappears. Prices also rise on Friday and Saturday nights throughout the year.

Banjo Patterson Inn (☎ 1800 046 275, 6456 2372; 1 Kosciuszko Rd; s/d/f from $50/70/110) A large, modern, comfortable place, rooms here have balconies and good facilities and there's a decent bar downstairs. Lake view rooms cost about $20 more.

Snowy Mountains Backpackers (☎ 1800 333 468, 6456 1500; www.snowybackpackers.com.au; 7 Gippsland St; dm/d low season $20/50, high season $35/80; ☐) This place has clean, bright rooms, full wheelchair access and a laundry.

Snowline Caravan Park (☎ 1800 248 148, 6456 2099; fax 6456 2180; dm/camp sites/cabins low season from $16/17/47) Rates rise dramatically during the high season at this pleasant lakeside place.

Some out of town options include **Bimblegumbie** (☎ 6456 2185; www.bimblegumbie.com.au; Alpine Way; B&B d low/high season $59/79), a friendly place with a range of comfortable cabins and B&B rooms. The upmarket **Crackenback Farm** (☎ 6456 2198; www.crackenback.com.au; Alpine Way; B&B d low/high season $75/140) just up the road from Bimblegumbie offers stylish rooms, a decent restaurant and a pampering day spa. **Kosciuszko Mountain Retreat** (☎ 6456 2224; camp sites low/high season $15/23, cabins low season from $60), in a beautiful spot just below the snow line near Sawpit Creek in the national park, can be crowded and pricey in the high season.

Eating
Dining options in Jindabyne are slowly improving.

Il Lago (☎ 6456 1171; 19 Nugget's Crossing; mains $18; ☜ from 5pm Tue-Sat low season; lunch in the high season) There's a good-value Italian menu here that includes local trout dishes and gourmet pizzas.

Brumby Bistro (☎ 6456 2526; Kosciuszko Rd; mains $17) The steaks are huge and tasty, although the veg, perspiring in steel trays under hot lamps, is more English carvery than fancy French bistro.

Other lunch and dinner alternatives include **Cafe Darya** (☎ 6457 1867; 9 Snowy Mountain Plaza, old Town Centre; dinner $24), a newish, unlicensed Persian place; **Mitzi's Retreat** (☎ 6457 2888; Upstairs, Central Park Shops, 1 Snowy River Ave; mains $21), which offers a European menu; and **Crackenback Cottage** (☎ 6456 2198; Alpine Way; lunch $10-15, mains $20-30; ☜ lunch daily & dinner Wed-Sun), an upmarket café.

KOSCIUSZKO NATIONAL PARK
The state's largest national park (6900 sq km) includes caves, lakes, forest, ski resorts and Mt Kosciuszko. The busiest time is winter, but it's also popular in summer when there are excellent bushwalks and

NEW SOUTH WALES

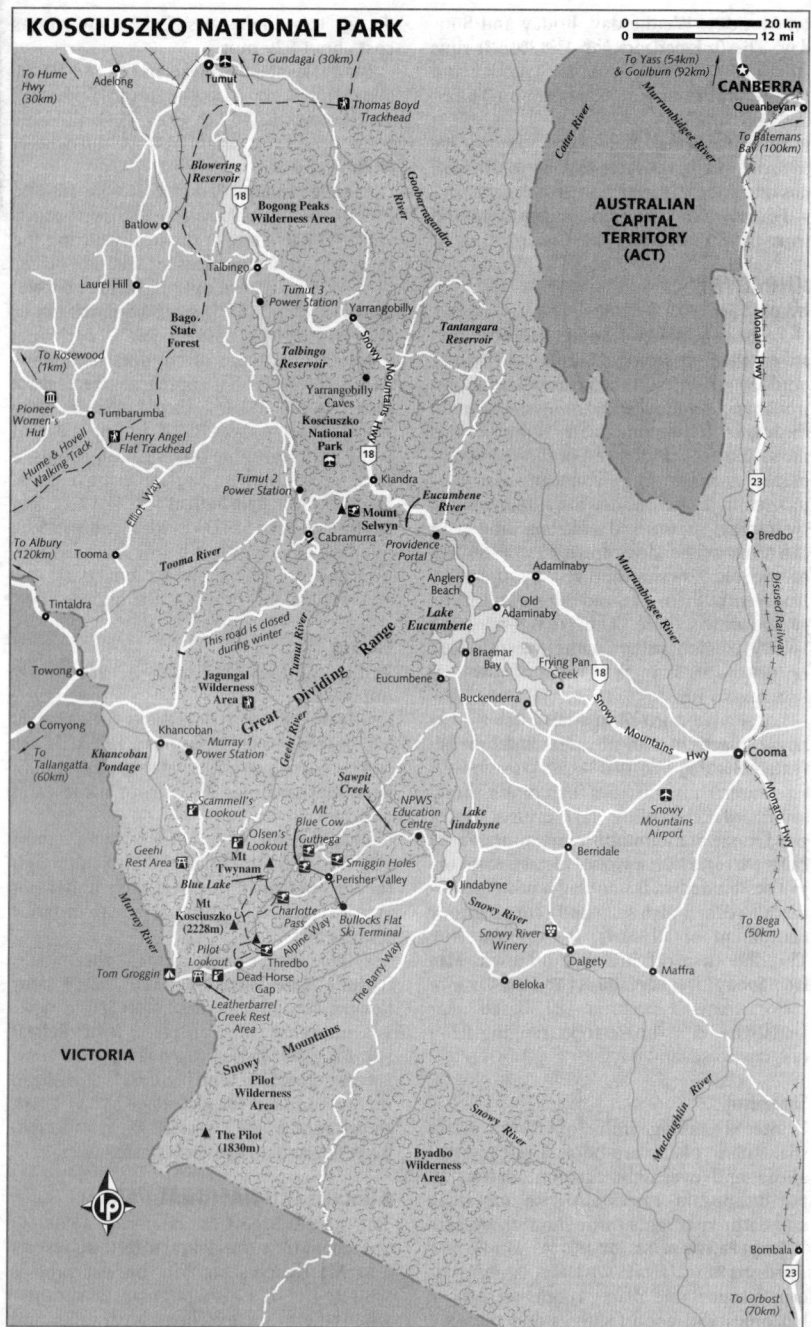

KOSCIUSZKO NATIONAL PARK

0 _____ 20 km
0 _____ 12 mi

To Hume Hwy (30km)
Adelong
To Gundagai (30km)
Tumut
Thomas Boyd Trackhead
To Yass (54km) & Goulburn (92km)
CANBERRA
Queanbeyan
To Batemans Bay (100km)

Cotter River
Murrumbidgee River

Blowering Reservoir
Bogong Peaks Wilderness Area
18
Batlow

AUSTRALIAN CAPITAL TERRITORY (ACT)

Talbingo
Laurel Hill
Tumut 3 Power Station
Yarrangobilly
Goobragandra River

Bago State Forest
Talbingo Reservoir
Tantangara Reservoir

To Rosewood (1km)
Yarrangobilly Caves
Kosciuszko National Park
18

Pioneer Women's Hut
Tumbarumba
Henry Angel Flat Trackhead
Tumut 2 Power Station
Kiandra
Eucumbene River

Monaro Hwy
23

Hume & Hovell Walking Track
Mount Selwyn
Cabramurra
Providence Portal

To Albury (120km)
Tooma
Tooma River
Anglers Beach
Adaminaby
Bredbo

Murrumbidgee River

Tintaldra
This road is closed during winter
Lake Eucumbene
Old Adaminaby

Great Dividing Range
Disused Railway

Towong
Jagungal Wilderness Area
Braemar Bay
Frying Pan Creek
18

Geehi River
Tooma River
Eucumbene
Buckenderra

Corryong
Khancoban
Murray 1 Power Station
Scammell's Lookout
Sawpit Creek
NPWS Education Centre
Lake Jindabyne
Snowy Mountains Hwy
Cooma

To Tallangatta (60km)
Khancoban Pondage

Geehi Rest Area
Mt Blue Cow
Guthega
Smiggin Holes
Perisher Valley
Snowy Mountains Airport

Olsen's Lookout
Mt Twynam
Berridale

Blue Lake
Mt Kosciuszko (2228m)
Charlotte Pass
Bullocks Flat Ski Terminal
Jindabyne

Pilot Lookout
Alpine Way
Thredbo
Snowy River
Snowy River Winery
To Bega (50km)

Murray River
Tom Groggin
Dead Horse Gap
Dalgety
Maffra

Leatherbarrel Creek Rest Area
Beloka

VICTORIA
Mountains
The Barry Way

Snowy Pilot Wilderness Area

The Pilot (1830m)
Snowy River

Byadbo Wilderness Area

Maclaughlin River

LP

Bombala
23

To Orbost (70km)

marvellous alpine wildflowers in January. There are NPWS offices in Khancoban (p225) and Tumut (p225) and the main visitors centre is in Jindabyne (p221).

Mt Kosciuszko and the main ski resorts are in the south of the park. Charlotte Pass (40km) is the highest resort village in Australia. It's less than 8km from the top of Mt Kosciuszko, and there's an 18km round-trip walking track to the summit. There are several other walking tracks from Charlotte Pass, including the 20km walk, which includes Blue, Albina and Club Lakes.

From Jindabyne, Kosciuszko Rd leads through Sawpit Creek (15km) to Perisher Valley (33km) and on to Charlotte Pass (40km). The spectacular Alpine Way runs from Jindabyne to Thredbo (33km) and around to Khancoban (116km) on the southwestern side of the mountains. Accessibility on all roads is subject to snow conditions.

Entry to the national park, including the ski resorts, costs $15 per car, per day. This makes the $80 annual pass a worthwhile investment.

Take adequate clothing and be prepared for all conditions; even in summer there is sometimes snow on the ground. At the resorts, the summer/low season runs from the October long weekend to the June long weekend; winter/high season (and therefore higher prices) starts after that.

Sleeping

Bush camping is permitted in most of the park and there's plenty of accommodation at the ski resorts. There's a YHA hostel at Thredbo – see p224. **Stillwell Lodge** (☎ 02-6457 5073; www.stillwell-lodge.com.au; Perisher Valley; B&B d low season from $99) is a good base for Kosciuszko's summit walking trails.

Getting There & Away

Canberra is the jumping-off point for the park. From there, CountryLink and V/Line buses run to Cooma.

Summit Coaches (☎ 02-6297 2588) runs to Thredbo from Canberra via Jindabyne and Cooma several times a week. Jindabyne to Thredbo costs $24 and takes one hour. Shuttles will take you from Cooma or Jindabyne to the ski resorts in winter.

In winter you can normally drive as far as Perisher Valley, but snow chains must be carried (even if there's no snow) and fitted

HIGH-COUNTRY FIRESTORMS

Massive and catastrophic fires, the worst for many decades, raged through as much as two-thirds of the park in early 2003. They threatened the survival of a range of park flora and fauna, including the incredibly rare corroboree frog, the mountain pigmy possum and the brown falcon. It's too early to tell the long-term extent of the damage to wildlife and the fragile alpine soil, but it's certain that some areas of the park will be closed for years to allow them to recover and to keep walkers safe from the hazard of fire-damaged trees falling. Hiking is still possible and many popular trails are back in use, but make sure you take local advice before planning any hiking.

to your wheels when directed – there are heavy penalties if you don't have them.

The simplest and safest way to get to Perisher/Smiggins in winter is to take the **Skitube** (☎ 02-6456 2010; same-day return trip adult/child $27/$16), a tunnel railway up to Perisher Valley and Mt Blue Cow from below the snow line at Bullocks Flat, on the Alpine Way. You can hire skis and equipment at Bullocks Flat, and luggage lockers and overnight parking are also available. The Skitube runs a reduced timetable in summer.

SKIING & SKI RESORTS

Whether you're after downhill skiing, snowboarding or Nordic skiing, the Snowies are a fantastic winter playground during the season which runs from early June to early October. Most years, snow is guaranteed in July, August and September and all the resorts now have snow-making equipment. The open slopes of the Australian Alps are a ski-tourer's paradise and Nordic (cross-country) skiing is very popular. The national park includes some famous several-day trails. There's cross country racing (classic or skating) in Perisher Valley. On the steep slopes of the Main Range near Twynam and Carruthers, the cross-country downhill (XCD) fanatics get their adrenaline rushes. In winter, the cliffs near Blue Lake become a practice ground for alpine climbers. Snowboard hire and lessons are widely available, and the major resorts have developed purpose-built runs and bowls.

One of the cheapest (and most fun) ways to get out on the slopes is to gather a bunch of friends and rent a lodge or apartment. Bring food and drink, as supplies at the resorts are expensive. Jindabyne and Cooma, both some distance below the snow line, offer cheaper accommodation (buses shuttle between towns and slopes).

Information

Extensive and invaluable information about the resorts, accommodation and ski packages may be found online at www.ski.com.au. For general snow and road reports, ring the various visitors centres. Most radio stations between Sydney and Melbourne also broadcast hourly reports.

Costs

Lift pass and lesson charges vary – for details see the following information on the various resorts. Equipment hire costs from $50 a day at the resorts, less off-mountain, although problems and adjustments are harder to fix. Towns en route to the snow, and many garages, hire ski equipment and snow chains. **Ski Kaos** (☎ 02-9976-5555; www.skikaos.com), a Sydney-based operator running mainly coach-based ski trips into the Snowies, is worth a look for budget packages. It offers weekend deals including transport from Sydney and around the ski fields and resorts, accommodation and lift passes (together with discounts on equipment hire) from around $300 and full week packages from $600.

Thredbo

☎ 02 / pop 2900

Thredbo has the longest run – 3km through 670m of vertical drop – in the country and some of Australia's best skiing. As well as the long runs, the absence of T-bar lifts makes Thredbo popular with snowboarders. The introduction of new turbo-charged snow-making machines should also improve the ride.

The cost for adult lift-only tickets is $80 a day or $340 for a five-day pass. Beginner/experienced skier lift and lesson packages cost from $213/160 for two days and from $434/340 for five days (two-hour group lessons). There is a purpose built beginners' area, Friday Flat, with its own slow-speed quad chairlift ($43) and a 'magic carpet' for kids to move up the slope.

The chairlift to the top of Mt Crackenback runs right through the summer ($22 return). From the top of the chairlift it's a 2km walk to a lookout point with good views of Mt Kosciuszko, or 7km to the top of the mountain itself.

Known for its wildflowers, Thredbo is also a good place to visit in summer, with many scenic bushwalking tracks and plenty of activities, including mountain biking, bobsledding, fly-fishing, platypus spotting and even, improbably enough, golf. **Thredbo Resort Centre** (☎ 1800 020 589, 6459 4294; www.thredbo.com.au; Friday Dr) is well-stocked with visitor information. The free *Summer Walks Map & Activities Guide* is worth picking up. Ask at the resort centre about guided wildflower walks.

SLEEPING & EATING

Although prices do drop in summer, there are no spectacular bargains. Most commercial lodges offer B&B accommodation during the summer, from about $70 for a single.

Alpenhorn (☎ 6457 6223; www.ski.com.au/alpenhorn; Buckwong Pl; d/f low season $90/130, high season $370/520) A friendly, comfortable and recently refurbished lodge with en-suite bathrooms and good mountain views.

Thredbo YHA Lodge (☎ 6457 6376; thredbo@yhansw.org.au; 8 Jack Adams Pathway; dm/d low season $21/26) During the high season this is members-only accommodation, and prices range from $46 to $112 per person for two nights. There is a ballot for winter places (during July and August – the ballot closes in April). The **YHA Travel Centre** (☎ 9261 1111) in Sydney is the best place to start making inquiries.

Credo (☎ 6457 6844; Riverside Cabins; mains $26) A restaurant with a pricey but tempting menu, for example: white fish on sauté potato with lemon oil and salsa verde.

Perisher Blue

☎ 02 / elevation 1680m

Perisher Blue (☎ 6459 4495, 1300 655 811; www.perisherblue.com.au), which includes Perisher Valley, Smiggin Holes, Mt Blue Cow and Guthega, has 50 lifts accessible with one ticket. New snow cannons and faster lifts should improve the skiing here.

You'll find there are a variety of alpine and cross-country runs, valley and bowl skiing, snowboarding areas and night-boarding sessions on the downhill runs and plenty of the right terrain for beginner and intermediate skiers. There are purpose-designed snowboarding areas and nightboarding sessions on the downhill runs.

An adult one-/five-day lift ticket costs $80/340; other passes are also available. A combined lesson and lift pass costs $80/295 (for beginners) and $108/433 (for the more experienced).

There's a lot of accommodation in Perisher Valley and Smiggin Holes (more than 4000 beds), but it can be very expensive; check the website for current vacancies and prices. One of the more reasonable places is the **The Lodge** (☎ 6457 5341; www.ski.com.au/thelodge; db & b per person around $200, high season), at Smiggin Holes. Perisher Blue is quiet in the off season and most facilities close.

Charlotte Pass
☎ 02 / elevation 1780m

At the base of Mt Kosciuszko, **Charlotte Pass** (☎ 6457 5458; www.charlottepass.com.au) is the highest and one of the oldest and most isolated resorts in Australia. In winter you have to snowcat the last 8km from Perisher Valley ($30 each way, book ahead). Five lifts serve rather short but uncrowded runs and this is good ski-touring country. Daily lift passes cost $85. Transport pick-up is from the Charlotte Pass Village information desk at the Perisher Skitube terminal.

Mt Selwyn
☎ 02 / elevation 1492m

Halfway between Tumut and Cooma, **Mt Selwyn** (☎ 1800 641 064, 6454 9488), in the north of the park, is a day-resort only. There is no access during the summer. It has 12 lifts, is ideal for beginners and families and is also the cheapest resort; adult/child lift tickets cost $58/29, lift/lesson packages $78/52 and equipment hire costs $30/20. There are several caravan parks in and near Adaminaby, home of – don't all rush now – the **Big Trout**.

Snow Goose Hotel/Motel (☎ 6454 2202; fax 6454 2608; Baker St; B&B s/d high season $65/105, low season $55/85) The small rooms are fairly pricey but the setting is pretty.

Adaminaby Bus Service (☎ 6454 2318) runs between the township and Mt Selwyn in winter; bookings are essential.

The Alpine Way

From **Khancoban** on the western side of the ranges, this spectacular route runs through dense forest around the southern end of Kosciuszko National Park to Thredbo and Jindabyne. Two of the best mountain views are from **Olsen's Lookout**, 10km off the Alpine Way on the Geehi Dam dirt road, and **Scammell's Lookout**, just off the Alpine Way at a good picnic spot.

There's an **NPWS office** (☎ 02-6076 9373; Scott St; ⏱ 8.30am-noon & 1-4pm) in Khancoban, where you can pick up the self-drive *Alpine Way Guide* and buy park-use tickets.

There are several accommodation options at Khancoban, including **Khancoban Backpackers & Fisherman's Lodge** (☎ 02-6076 9471; www.alpineinn.com.au; Alpine Way; s/d $19/28). This is a very basic place; you need to supply your own bedding and cooking utensils. Booking and check-in for the lodge is at the nearby **Khancoban Alpine Inn** (☎ 02-6076 9471; www.alpineinn.com.au; Alpine Way; small s/d $55/65, good-sized s/d $77/89). There's a pool, pleasant garden and **bistro** (mains $7.50), where home-cooked daily specials are on offer.

Tumut Area
☎ 02

The pretty town of Tumut (pop 6200) is on the Snowy Mountains Hwy outside the northwestern side of the park. Tumut **visitors centre** (☎ 6947 7025; www.tumut.nsw.gov.au; Gocup & Adelong Rds intersection; ⏱ 8am-6pm Dec-Apr, 8am-5pm May-Nov) has information on the national park and a guide to the Snowy Mountains hydro-electric scheme.

Visit **Yarrangobilly Caves** ($3 per vehicle), 70km south of Tumut. Guided tours at 11am, 1pm and 3pm cost $11 per person; or self-guided tours, possible from 9.30am to 4.30pm, are $8.80 per person. You can fish and bushwalk in this lovely place, and there's a thermal pool – at a constant and pleasant 27°C – beside the river. The **NPWS office** (☎ 6454 9579) is open from 9.30am to 4.30pm.

In the fruit-growing area south of Tumut is **Batlow**, where fruit-picking work is often available. Near the town is **Hume & Hovell's Lookout**, where the two explorers did just that in 1824. **Paddy's River Dam**, about 12km southeast, off the road to Tumbarumba, was built by Chinese gold-miners in the 1850s, and there's a trail to the nearby **waterfalls**.

Continuing south you will reach **Tumbarumba**, site of the early exploits of the bushranger Mad Dog Morgan. About 8km west of Tumbarumba, the **Pioneer Women's Hut** (☎ 6948 2635; King St; 🕙 11am-4pm Wed, 10am-4.15pm Sat & Sun) is a low-key and interesting community museum.

SOUTHWEST & THE MURRAY

This is wide, endlessly rolling country with some of the state's best farming areas and most interesting history. The Murray River forms the boundary between NSW and Victoria – most of the larger towns are on the Victorian side. Part of this area is known as the Riverina because of the Murray and Murrumbidgee Rivers and their tributaries.

Getting There & Away

The region is served by a number of airlines, including **Rex** (☎ 13 17 13).

Several roads run through the southwest – the Hume Hwy being the major one. There are quieter routes like Olympic Way, which runs through Cowra, Wagga Wagga and Albury. Routes to Adelaide include the Sturt Hwy through Hay and Wentworth. You'll also pass through the southwest if travelling between Brisbane and Melbourne on the Newell Hwy.

Major bus routes cross the region, running from Sydney and Brisbane to both Melbourne and Adelaide. Melbourne to Sydney bus services run on the Hume Hwy and trains run close to it. **Fearnes Coaches** (☎ 1800 029 918) runs daily trips between Sydney and Wagga ($48), Gundagai ($48), Yass ($42), Goulburn ($30) and Mittagong ($24). **CountryLink** (☎ 13 22 42, 13 22 32) reaches most other towns in the area.

THE HUME HIGHWAY

The Hume is the main road between Melbourne and Sydney, Australia's two largest cities. It's the fastest and shortest route and, although it's not the most interesting, there are worthwhile diversions along the way.

One of the simplest diversions is at the Sydney end: take the coastal Princes Hwy past Royal National Park to Wollongong.

Just after Wollongong take the Illawarra Hwy up the picturesque Macquarie Pass to meet the Hume near Moss Vale. Further south you can leave the Hume to visit Canberra or continue beyond Canberra through the Snowy Mountains on the Alpine Way, rejoining the Hume near Albury.

The Hume is a divided freeway most of the way from Sydney to the Victorian border, with a few stretches of narrow, two-lane road carrying a lot of traffic.

SYDNEY TO GOULBURN

The large towns of **Mittagong** and **Bowral** adjoin each other along the Hume Hwy. The Southern Highlands **visitors centre** (☎ 02-4871 2888; http://southern-highlands.com.au; 62-70 Main St, Mittagong; 🕙 8am-5.30pm) is well stocked with information and maps covering the local area including Morton National Park. The **Tulip Time Festival**, held in the area from the end of September to early October, is a brilliant show of spring colour and many private gardens are open to visitors.

Four kilometres south of town, a winding 65km road leads west to the **Wombeyan Caves** (☎ 02-4843 5976; www.jenolancaves.org.au; adult/child/family $21/11/49; 🕙 8.30am-5pm for self-guided tour), with their spectacular limestone formations. The drive up is through superb mountain scenery and there are pretty camping ground and cabins at the caves.

Bowral is where the late great cricketer Sir Donald Bradman, undoubtedly Australia's greatest sporting hero and game's supreme batsman, spent his boyhood. There's a cricket ground here and the **Bradman Museum** (☎ 02-4862 1247; www.bradman.org.au; St Jude St; adult/child $7.50/3.50; 🕙 10am-5pm; wheelchair access), which explores the history of the game downstairs while upstairs is dedicated to the career of 'the Don' himself.

A little further south along the Hume is tiny **Berrima**, founded in 1829 and remarkably little changed since then. It claims to have the oldest continuously licensed pub in Australia (the Surveyor General), and is full of art galleries, interesting antique and curio shops, and more teashops than you can shake a buttered scone at. The **White Horse Inn** (☎ 02-4877 1204; www.whitehorseinn.com.au; Market Pl; s/d from $70/80) has some reasonable guestrooms. A great upmarket place to eat just south of Berrima is **Eling Forest Winery** (☎ 02-4878 9499; Hume Hwy, Sutton Forest; mains $26;

lunch & dinner Wed-Sat, lunch Sun). The largely Italian and rather florid menu boasts of things such as 'seared swordfish fillet rolled in *deutscher* caviar on fava bean salad with cold-press olive oil dressing'.

South of Berrima is the small, appealing town of **Bundanoon**, one of the gateways to **Morton National Park**, with the deep gorges and high sandstone plateaus of the **Budawang Range**. The park visitor centre is at Fitzroy Falls, the other gateway to the park, on the road between Moss Vale and Nowra – see the Shoalhaven section (p215). The wonderful **Bundanoon YHA Hostel** (☎ 02-4883 6010; bundyha@hinet.net.au; Railway Ave; s/d $20/48, camp sites per person $10) occupies an old Edwardian guesthouse in ample, shaded gardens.

Bundanoon is on the railway line between Sydney ($15) and Canberra via Goulburn ($14). Going to/from Canberra it's much cheaper to take CountryLink to Goulburn, then City Rail from Goulburn to Canberra. CountryLink buses run to Wollongong daily.

GOULBURN
☎ 02 / pop 20,900
Founded in 1833, Goulburn is at the heart of a prosperous sheep-grazing district famous for its fine merino wool, hence the rather stern looking three-storey-high **Big Merino** (affectionately known as Rambo) towering over the Old Hume Hwy in town (the new highway bypasses the town). The shop attached will cater for all your tacky fridge magnet and sheep-based souvenir needs. You'll also be invited to scale Rambo's innards, which are packed with information about the wool trade. At the top you can gaze through his eyes at, appropriately enough, the giant woolsheds on the horizon.

Goulburn **visitors centre** (☎ 1800 353 646, 4823 4492; www.igoulburn.com; 201 Sloane St; 9am-5pm) has a good self-guided walking tour brochure taking in some of the town's handsome historic buildings, including the impressive **courthouse**, still in use. The **Old Goulburn Brewery** (☎ 4821 6071; 23 Bungonia Rd; 9am-5pm), Australia's oldest brewery, was designed in 1836 by convict and architect Francis Greenway, who also designed the Hyde Park Barracks in Sydney. There's still a modest brewery making decent English-style ale here, which you can tour, and you can stay in the characterful (if dark, ancient and

cramped) **mews-style rooms** (B&B per person $40) out back. Beyond these attractions, there's not much else to hold a traveller in town.

YASS
☎ 02 / pop 4900
Another wool town, Yass is closely connected with the early explorer Hamilton Hume, after whom the highway is named. The **visitors centre** (☎ 6226 2557; http://yass.nsw.gov.au; Comur St on Coronation Park; 9am-4.30pm Mon-Fri, 9am-4pm Sat & Sun) is helpful. Next door is the **Hamilton Hume Museum** (☎ 6226 2557; Comur St; admission $2), which has exhibits relating to Hume. The museum is run by volunteers, so check opening times at the visitors centre. Sections of the **Hume and Hovell Walking Track**, which offer half-day and longer walks, begin here. The National Trust–listed **Cooma Cottage** (☎ 6226 1470; adult/child $4.40/2.20; 10am-4pm Thu-Mon) was Hume's home from 1839 to 1873; the cottage is 4km out of town on the Yass Valley Way.

About 20km southeast of Yass, at **Wee Jasper**, are the limestone **Carey's Caves** (☎ 6227 9622; adult/child $9.90/4.95; tours noon & 1.30pm Fri-Mon). You can also join the Hume and Hovell Walking Track here.

Just east of Yass, the Barton Hwy branches off the Hume for Canberra. **Transborder Express** (☎ 6241 0033) has several daily buses ($13, 50 minutes).

GUNDAGAI
☎ 02 / pop 2000
Gundagai, 386km from Sydney, is one of the more interesting small towns encountered along the Hume. The **visitors centre** (☎ 6944 0250; www.gundagaishire.nsw.gov.au; 249 Sheridan St; 8am-5pm Mon-Fri, 9am-noon & 1-5pm Sat & Sun) houses **Rusconi's Marble Masterpiece**, a 21,000-piece cathedral model. For the $2 entry fee you get to hear a snatch of the tune *Along the Road to Gundagai*, which you will then probably hum mindlessly for the next few days. Rusconi also made the **Dog on the Tuckerbox** memorial, which you can see at the service station 8km south of town on the Hume Hwy.

The long, rickety **Prince Alfred Bridge** (closed to traffic, but you can walk across it) spans the flood plain of the Murrumbidgee River. In 1852 Gundagai suffered Australia's worst flood disaster and 78 deaths were recorded. Gold rushes and bushrangers were part of the town's colourful early history. The notorious bushranger Captain Moonlight was tried in Gundagai's 1859 **courthouse** and is now buried in the town.

Other places of interest include **Gundagai Historical Museum** (☎ 6944 1995; Homer St; admission $3; ☻ 9am-noon Mon-Fri, 9am-2pm Sat, 11am-3pm Sun, or by appointment) and the **Gabriel Gallery** (☎ 6944 1722; Sheridan St; admission free), which has a great display of historic photos. The latter is in an unlikely setting above the Mitre 10 hardware shop, and is open during store hours.

There are several motels in town, offering ordinary rooms from about $55. One of the better places is the **Sovereign Inn** (☎ 6944 1655; www.sovereigninn.com.au; 26-28 West St; budget/ queen d $69/89; ☒), which has well-equipped rooms, one with wheelchair access.

Eat at the **Niagara Cafe** (☎ 6944 1109; 142 Sheridan St; mains $12), a place of character, frozen in about 1930. As you eat you can admire the photos of former prime ministers dining here.

HOLBROOK
☎ 02 / pop 1300
The halfway point between Sydney and Melbourne, Holbrook was known as Germanton until WWI, during which it was renamed after a British war hero; in Holbrook Park there's a replica of the submarine in which the brave deeds that earned him the Victoria Cross took place.

The large **Woolpack Inn Museum** (☎ 6036 2131; 83 Albury St; adult/child $4/1) has tourist information; ring to check opening times.

ALBURY WODONGA
☎ 02 / pop 42,100
Divided by the Murray River just below the Hume Weir, the towns of Albury (in NSW) and Wodonga (in Victoria) have merged. With several decent restaurants, some lively bars (generally well supported by the local student population) and a few places of interest, the Albury side is probably the most attractive part of this new urban entity. It's a good base for trips to the snowfields and high country of both Victoria and NSW, the vineyards around Rutherglen (Victoria), and the tempestuous upper Murray River (the river becomes languid below Albury). It's also a pleasant spot to break the journey between Sydney and Melbourne.

Information
The large Albury Wodonga **visitors centre** (☎ 1300 796 222; gateway@alburywodongatourism.biz; Hume Hwy; ☻ 9am-5pm), offering information on both NSW and Victoria, is just over the bridge on the Wodonga side.

There's Internet access at **Cyber Heaven** (☎ 6023 4320; 505b Kiewa St; ☻ 10am-6pm Mon-Fri, 10am-2pm Sat).

Sights & Activities
In summer you can swim in the Murray River in **Noreuil Park**. From September to April (water levels permitting) you can take a **river cruise** (☎ 6041 5558, 0408-200 531) on the paddle-steamer *Cumberoona*. Cruises start at $13 and schedules change, so ring ahead to check.

The **Botanic Gardens** are at the end of Dean St. A worthwhile walk from the gardens, particularly at dawn or dusk, takes you up the small hill where the handsome, white tower of the war memorial commands some pleasing views over the area.

Albury Regional Museum (☎ 6021 4550; Wodonga Pl; admission free; ☻ 10.30am-4.30pm), in Noreuil Park, contains some interesting but rather slim displays on Aboriginal culture, the local ecosystem and 20th-century migration into the area. See the tree marked by explorer William Hovell on his 1824 expedition with Hume from Sydney to Port Phillip. Charles Sturt departed for his 1838 exploration of the Murray from here.

In town, the **Albury Regional Art Gallery** (☎ 6023 8187; 546 Dean St; admission free; ☻ 10.30am-5pm Mon-Fri, 10.30am-4pm Sat & Sun) has a small, permanent collection including contemporary Australian photography.

In November the annual **Ngangirra Festival**, which features Aboriginal art, music, dance and language, is held at Mungabareena Reserve.

Albury Backpackers (see the following Sleeping section) runs half-day to seven-day canoeing trips on the Murray and you don't have to stay at the hostel to join one. It's worth asking about bike hire here; there are good cycling tracks around town and the visitors centre has a bike-track brochure.

Oz E Wildlife (☎ 6040 3677; Ettamogah; admission $7; ☻ 9am-late), 11km north on the Hume Hwy, has a collection of Aussie animals. Most of the animals arrive sick or injured, so this is a sanctuary. There are facilities here for disabled visitors. A few kilometres north again, the grotesque **Ettamogah Pub** (☎ 6026 2366; Burma Rd; ☒ 10am-late) looms up near the highway – it's a real-life version of a famous Aussie cartoon pub that brews its own beer.

The interesting **Jindera Pioneer Museum** (☎ 6026 3622; Urana St; admission $5; ☒ 10am-3pm Mon-Sat) is 16km northwest of Albury, in Jindera. This township is in an area known as Morgan Country because of its association with bushranger Mad Dog Morgan.

Sleeping

New Albury (☎ 6021 3599; 491 Kiewa St; s/d $48/60; ☒) This large pub and hotel nestled among restaurants and pubs offers basic but goodvalue rooms and was in the midst of an extensive renovation at the time of writing.

Albury Regent (☎ 6021 8355; 666 Dean St; s/d/f $70/77/99; ☒) This place is centrally located but on a quiet end of the road. The rooms have self-contained kitchenettes, TVs and direct-dial phones. There's a disabled unit available.

Albury Backpackers (☎ 6041 1822; 0417-691 339; www.alburybackpackers.com.au; 452 David St; dm/d $17/40) This scruffy but friendly place is popular with budget travellers. It runs some terrific canoeing trips on the Murray, can organise skiing in winter and is an excellent place to arrange bike rental. Staff can also help guests find farm work and fruit-picking jobs.

Eating

Dean St has a surprisingly large number of decent restaurants, especially around the junction with David St; and quite a café culture has sprung up.

Zen X (☎ 6023 6455; 467 Dean St; sushi $3-7, mains $15; ☒ lunch & dinner) A great Japanese restaurant serving delicious sushi.

Electra Cafe (cnr Dean & Macauley Sts; mains $19) An eclectic menu of European, Middle Eastern and Asian dishes, plus some imaginative desserts (plum-curd tart, for example) make this an appealing place for dinner.

Canteen Cuisine (☎ 6041 4242; 479 Dean St; mains $12) Great for breakfasts, and serving generous lunch and dinner portions, this place opens early and closes late every day.

Two tasty Thai options are **Thai Lotus Flower** (☎ 6041 3330; 610 Dean St; mains $10-15; ☒ lunch Wed-Fri, dinner daily) and the modern, popular **Thai Puka** (☎ 6021 2504; 652 Dean St; mains $10-15; ☒ lunch Wed-Fri, dinner daily).

Entertainment

Hotel Termo (☒ 6041 3544; 417 Dean St) is a laidback but vibrant place with a youngish crowd and a showcase of often surprisingly decent live music and local DJing.

Getting There & Away

Qantas (☎ 13 13 13) flies between Albury and Sydney at least once daily (from $200). **Rex** (☎ 13 17 13) flies from Albury to Melbourne daily (from $120).

CountryLink (☎ 6041 9555, 13 22 32) at the train station books bus and train tickets. McCafferty's/Greyhound, running between Sydney (8 hours) and Melbourne (4 hours), stops at Viennaworld (a service station/ diner), on the highway across from Noreuil Park, and will stop at the Caltex service station on the northern highway on request. CountryLink buses run to Echuca (4 hours) on Tuesday, Thursday and Saturday. **V/Line** (☎ 13 61 96) runs to Canberra (5 hours) and to Mildura (10 hours) along the Murray.

The nightly **XPT train service** (☎ 6041 9555) between Sydney and Melbourne stops in Albury. If you're travelling between the two capital cities it's much cheaper to stop over in Albury on a through ticket than to buy two separate tickets.

WAGGA WAGGA
☎ 02 / pop 44,500

Wagga Wagga, on the Murrumbidgee River, is the state's largest inland city. Despite its size, the city retains a relaxed country-town feel. The name means 'place of many crows' in the local Wiradjuri people's language and is usually abbreviated to one word, pronounced 'wogga'.

Orientation & Information

The long main street, Baylis St, which runs north from the train station, becomes Fitzmaurice St at the northern end. The **visitors centre** (☎ 6926 9621; www.tourismwaggawagga.com .au; Tarcutta St; ☒ 9am-5pm) is close to the river.

There's Internet access at **Civic Video** (☎ 6921 8866; 21 Forsyth St; ☒ 10am-10pm). Alternatively, try the cheaper service at the impressive public **library** (Morrow St), next door to the art gallery.

Sights & Activities

The excellent **Botanic Gardens** (☎ 6925 2934; Baden Powell Dr; ☒ 10am-5pm Tue-Sat, noon-4pm Sun) are about 1.5km south of the train station.

The interpretive centre is open 11am to 3pm Thursday to Sunday; there's a small zoo with an aviary of native birds; and a kid-size model railway operating twice monthly. Check the train schedule at the visitors centre.

There are two wineries nearby. **Wagga Wagga Winery** (☎ 6922 1221; Oura Rd; ☺ 11am-late) also has a restaurant. The **Charles Sturt University Winery and Cheese Factory** (☎ 6933 2435; Coolamon Rd; ☺ 11am-5pm Mon-Fri, 11am-4pm Sat & Sun) is part of the wine science school at the university.

The **Regional Art Gallery** (☎ 6926 9660; admission free; ☺ 10am-5pm Mon-Sat, noon-4pm Sun) houses the National Art Glass Gallery, well worth a visit.

The **Wiradjuri Walking Track**, which includes some lookouts, begins at the visitors centre (pick up a map here) and eventually returns here after a 30km tour of the area. There's a shorter 10km loop past Wollundry Lagoon. From the **beach** near the Wagga Wagga Caravan Park you can go swimming and fishing. **River cruises** (☺ Wed-Mon) operate weather and river levels permitting; ask at the visitors centre. Wagga's flat, wide spaces make it suitable for cycling; pick up the bike-track brochure. Military buffs will be interested in Wagga's long association with the armed forces; there's a self-guided drive brochure of **military sites** and **museums**.

Sleeping

There's plenty of accommodation, mostly motel style, to choose from.

Manor (☎ 6921 5962; www.themanor.com.au; 38 Morrow St; B&B s/d $60/98; ⊠) This small, well-restored guesthouse has some comfortable old-fashioned rooms (with shared bathroom) and a fine-dining restaurant.

Central Point Motel (☎ 6821 7272; fax 6921 3446; 164-166 Tarcutta St; s/d/f $74/88/128; ⊠) A central location opposite the visitors centre, smart rooms and a profusion of pot plants make this an appealing motel.

Victoria Hotel (☎ 6921 5233; www.vichotel.net; Baylis St; s/d $22/33) This is a convenient, central, budget option.

Wagga Wagga Guest House (☎ 6931 8702; fax 6931 8712; 149 Gurwood St; dm/d $20/38; ⊡) The first hostel-type accommodation in town, this small, chaotic and friendly place welcomes longer-stay travellers looking for fruit-picking work. It also has access for disabled guests.

Eating

Baylis/Fitzmaurice St has a surprisingly diverse range of places to eat, including several Italian restaurants, good coffee shops and bakeries.

Three Chefs (☎ 6921 5897; Townhouse International, 70 Morgan St; mains $14-22) This elegant, modern place serves Mediterranean food with some quirky touches, such as grilled asparagus and haloumi cheese with poached quail eggs and truffle oil.

Saigon Restaurant (☎ 6921 2212; 89 Morgan St; dishes $10) A Vietnamese place popular for takeaways and good-value restaurant meals.

If you crave Mexican, try **Montezuma's** (☎ 6921 4428; 85 Baylis St; mains around $15), or if you're after a curry, consider the **Indian Tavern Tandoori** (☎ 6921 3121; 14-16 Pall Mall; mains $10-20).

Getting There & Away

Qantas (☎ 13 13 13) flies daily to Sydney (from $160) and **Rex** (☎ 13 17 13) flies daily to Melbourne (from $130).

CountryLink buses leave from the train station (☎ 13 22 32, 6939 5488), where you can make bookings. Wagga is on the railway line between Sydney (6¼ hours) and Melbourne (4¼); the one-way fare to both cities is $75 and there are daily services. **McCafferty's/Greyhound** (☎ 13 14 99) and **Fearnes** (☎ 6921 2316) run daily to Sydney (7 hours) and Brisbane (18 hours).

NARRANDERA

☎ 02 / pop 4100

Near the junction of the Newell and Sturt Hwys, Narrandera is in the Murrumbidgee Irrigation Area (MIA). The **visitors centre** (☎ 1800 672 392, 6959 1766; www.narrandera.nsw.gov. au; Cadell St, Narrandera Park; ☺ 9am-5pm) hands out a walking-tour map of the town and **Lake Talbot** – partly a long, artificial lake, partly a big swimming complex. Bush (including a koala regeneration area) surrounds the lake and a series of walking trails make up the **Bundidgerry Walking Track**.

South of Narrandera, about 80km down the Newell Hwy, is **Jerilderie**, immortalised by the bushranger Ned Kelly, who held up the whole town for three days in 1879. Kelly relics can be seen in the **Jerilderie Museum** (☎ 5886 1511; Powell St; entry by donation; ☺ 9.30am-4pm). Next door, the **Willows**, a house dating from 1878, is a combination of museum, souvenir shop and café.

Sleeping & Eating

There's a range of accommodation in town.

Historic Star Lodge (☎ 6959 1768; www.historic starlodge.com.au; 64 Whitton St; s/d $60/90, with bathroom $68/110) An elegant old hotel offering comfortable if old-fashioned B&B and a fine-dining (and award-winning) restaurant.

Royal Mail Hotel (☎ 6959 2007; 137 East St; s/d/f $15/30/40) This pub has big, clean and good-value rooms (bathroom is shared).

There are several restaurants on East St, including **Classique Cafe Restaurant** (☎ 6959 1411; 124 East St; lunch $10), serving really good coffee, home-made cakes and fresh sandwiches.

Getting There & Away

McCafferty's/Greyhound (☎ 13 14 99) goes to Sydney ($55, 10 hours) and Adelaide ($124, 12 hours), stopping at the Mobil roadhouse on the Stuart Hwy.

GRIFFITH

☎ 02 / pop 16,000

Griffith was planned by Walter Burley Griffin, the American architect who designed Canberra, and it's the main town of the MIA. You'll find Griffith **visitors centre** (☎ 6962 4145; www.griffith.nsw.gov.au; cnr Banna & Jondaryan Sts; ☼ 9am-5pm) underneath the life-size WWII fighter plane. There's information about local wine trails here.

The **NPWS office** (☎ 6966 8100; www.npws.nsw .gov.au; 200 Yambil St; ☼ 8.30am-4.30pm Mon-Fri) gives information about Cocoparra, Willandra and Oolambeyan National Parks.

Fast Internet access is available at **Bits and Bytes** (☎ 6964 7822; 41 Yambil St; ☼ 9am-6pm Sun-Fri, 9am-1pm Sat).

Sights & Activities

On a hill northeast of the town centre, **Pioneer Park Museum** (☎ 6962 4196; Remembrance Dr; admission $7; ☼ 9am-4.30pm) is a re-creation of an early Riverina village and is worth seeing.

Descendants of the Italian farmers who helped to develop this area make up a large percentage of the population. You can visit eight **wineries** locally – the visitors centre has opening times and a map.

Cocoparra National Park, just east of Griffith, isn't a large park, but its hills and gullies provide some contrasts and there's a fair presence of wildlife including Turquoise Parrots. August to October is usually the time to see spring flowers and birdlife.

Sleeping

Summit International Hostel (☎ 6964 4236; www .griffithinternational.com.au; 112 Binya St; dm members/nonmembers $15/17; ☐) Across the road from the Anglican cathedral, this place helps international visitors find fruit-picking work and has Internet access.

Hotel Victoria (☎ 6962 1299; fax 6962 1081; 232 Banna Ave; s/d $75/90; ☒) This modernised hotel right in the centre of town offers basic but very smart new rooms.

Yambil Inn Motel (☎ 6964 1233; fax 6964 1355; 155-157 Yambil St; s/d $84/89; ☒) A pleasant motel in a quiet street near the main shops and restaurants.

There is a camping ground on Woolshed Flat in the north of **Cocoparra National Park**, not far from Woolshed Falls. Bring your own water. Free bush camping is permitted away from the roads.

Eating

Italian is the region's dominant cuisine and there are plenty of Italian places to choose from.

Il Corso (☎ 6964 4500; 232 Banna Ave; mains $15) One of several decent, family-run Italian restaurants in town, this is a no frills kind of place but serves popular home-made pasta and tasty traditional pizza.

Cafe Deli (☎ 6964 5559; Shop 15, Griffin Plaza; lunch from $7) One of the better places in town for a daytime coffee, snack, sandwich or juice.

L'Oasis (☎ 6964 5588; 150 Yambil St; mains $15; ☼ lunch & dinner Tue-Sat) Diverse flavours, fresh produce and a wide selection of local wines make this place, tucked away from the main street, worth snuffling out. The desserts are great, too.

Michelin (☎ 6964 9006; 72 Banna Ave; mains $20) This is probably the swankiest place in town, all plate glass and minimal modernity. The wine list is extensive and the food is mostly fresh, simple French fare.

Getting There & Away

Rex (☎ 6922 0176) flies between Griffith and Sydney (one way from $159).

All buses, except CountryLink (which stops at the train station), stop at the **Griffith Travel & Transit Centre** (☎ 6962 7199; 121 Banna Ave) at the Mobil service station opposite the visitors centre. You can book McCafferty's/Greyhound, V/Line and CountryLink tickets here, with connections to regional coach lines. Daily services include Sydney ($61), Melbourne (from $46), Adelaide (from $87), Canberra (from $36), Brisbane (from $88) and Wagga ($24).

LEETON

☎ 02 / pop 6900

Leeton is the MIA's oldest town (1913) and, like Griffith, was designed by Walter Burley Griffin. It remains close to the architect's original vision and is developing into a thriving commercial centre.

The Leeton **visitors centre** (☎ 6953 6481; tourism@leeton.nsw.gov.au; 10 Yanco Ave; ◷ 9am-5pm Mon-Fri, 9.30am-12.30pm Sat & Sun) is on the main road into town from Narrandera. Ask here about presentations at the **SunRice centre**, which may answer all those nagging rice questions you've been saving up.

Lillypilly Estate (☎ 6953 4069; ◷ tastings 9am-5pm Mon-Sat, tours 4pm Mon-Fri) and **Toorak Wines** (☎ 6953 2333; ◷ tastings 10am-5.30pm Mon-Sat, tours 11.30am Mon-Fri) are two wineries on either side of Leeton.

WILLANDRA NATIONAL PARK

This World Heritage–listed national park, on the plains 160km northwest of Griffith as the crow flies, has been carved from a huge sheep station on a system of usually dry lakes. Its 19,400 hectares represent less than 10% of the area covered by Big Willandra station in its 1870s heyday. There are several short walking tracks in the park and the Merton Motor Trail loops around the eastern half.

Park entry costs $6 per car. There's a camping ground near the homestead, and with permission you can bush camp. There is also shared self-catering accommodation (bring supplies as there's no shop) in the former 'men's quarters', for four people in bunk rooms. A cottage sleeping eight costs $40 for four people, plus $10 for each additional person. If you want to enjoy this wilderness in style and comfort, try the lovingly restored and rather stylish historic homestead. Contact the **NPWS** (☎ 02-6966 8100; www.npws.nsw.gov.au) in Griffith for more details.

The main access is off the Hillston to Mossgiel road, around 40km west of Hillston. The NPWS in Griffith has park brochures. It takes very little rain to close roads here and winter rain from June to August often does. Phone the **park manager**

(☎ 02-6967 8159) or NPWS in Griffith to check conditions.

It may also be worth asking the NPWS about **Oolambeyan National Park**, a new national park being developed at another former station in the area to protect the Plains Wanderer, an endangered native bird.

HAY

☎ 02 / pop 2700

In flat, treeless country, Hay is a substantial and attractive outback town on the junction of the Sturt and Cobb Hwys. The **visitors centre** (☎ 6993 4045; www.hay.nsw.gov.au; 407 Moppett St; ◷ 9am-5pm Mon-Fri, 10am-noon Sat & Sun) is off Lachlan St.

There are some fine swimming spots along the Murrumbidgee River, and interesting old buildings like the **Old Hay Gaol** (Church St; adult/child $1/0.50; ◷ 9am-5pm) and **Bishops Lodge** (☎ 6993 4444; Roset St; admission $4.50; ◷ 10am-noon, 2-4.30pm Mon-Fri), a corrugated-iron mansion built in 1889. **Dreamtime Interpretations Gallery** (☎ 6993 1730; 84 Lachlan St; open by appointment) is a good place to look at and buy Aboriginal art.

It may sound unlikely, but **Shearoutback – The Australian Shearer's Hall of Fame** (☎ 6993 4000; www.shearoutback.com.au; Sturt Hwy; adult/child $15/10; ◷ 9am-5pm, shearing demonstrations 10.30am, 1 & 3.30pm) is an impressive (if perhaps overpriced) tribute to the sheep-shearing trade, a central profession here in the heart of merino country. This place captures the sights, feel and even smells of a sheep-shearing shed and does a great job of evoking the tough lives of shearers who endure this physically punishing trade. The live shearing demonstrations by a local champ are worth timing your visit for. There is access for disabled visitors here.

Hay was the location of three internment camps during WWII, and the **Hay Internment & POW Camps Interpretive Centre** (☎ 6993 2112; admission $2; ◷ 9am-5pm Mon-Fri), inside railway carriages at the **old railway station**, gives an insight into that period. The old railway station is now being managed as a community initiative; you can check email there in the **Hay Telecentre** (◷ 8.30am-5pm Mon-Fri).

The most charming place to stay in Hay is the **Bank B&B** (☎ 6993 1730; www.users.tpg.com.au /users/tssk; 86 Lachlan St; B&B s/d $70/90; ⊠), which is right in the centre of town and in a building with heaps of character.

New Crown Hotel (☎ 6993 1600; 117 Lachlan St; dm/s/d $20/44/55; ☒) has decent rooms (including bathroom and TV) and is a friendly place for a drink.

Eat at the **Jolly Jumbuck** (☎ 6993 4718; 184 Lachlan St; mains $13; ⊙ lunch & dinner), which has the most interesting menu in town.

DENILIQUIN
☎ 02 / pop 7800

Deniliquin is an attractive, bustling country town on a wide bend of the Edward River.

The Deniliquin **visitors centre** (☎ 1800 650 712, 5881 2878; www.deniliquin.info; cnr Napier & George Sts; ⊙ 9am-4pm Mon-Fri, 10am-3pm Sat & Sun) is inside the **Peppin Heritage Centre**, which has the same opening times. The heritage centre has displays on irrigation, and the history of wool-growing in the area. There's Internet access at **Purtills Service Station** (162 Hardinge St; ⊙ 7am-9pm).

Island Sanctuary, on the riverbank in town, has pleasant walks among the river red gums and lots of animals, including flocks of boisterous white cockatoos.

Don't forget the annual **Ute Festival**, when boys – and some girls – from the bush (about 3000 of them) get together for a weekend of talk and action in their 'utility vehicles'. It takes place on the long weekend in October. If that's not macho enough for you there's also the **Deniliquin Stampede**, a two-day rodeo over Easter. Contact the visitors centre for details.

Sleeping & Eating

There are several caravan parks and plenty of motels, but as trucks roll through town all night, choose one off the highway.

Riverview Motel (☎ 5881 2311; 1 Butler St; s/d $60/69) This is a pretty, quiet spot with big verandas overlooking the river.

McLean Beach Caravan Park (☎ 5881 2448; Butler St; camp sites/vans/cabins $18/30/60) At the northwestern end of Butler St, by a nice river beach and set in pleasant woodlands.

Crossing (☎ 5881 7827; Heritage Centre; mains $12-15; ⊙ 9am-5pm & dinner Thu-Sat) This place serves fine breakfasts, tempting sandwiches and fresh juices by day and gourmet pizzas during the evening.

Getting There & Away

Long-distance buses stop at the Bus Stop Cafe on Whitelock St. **CountryLink** (☎ 13 22 42) runs to Wagga ($45) on Wednesday, Friday and Sunday (from where trains run to Sydney and Melbourne), and to Albury ($23) on Tuesday, Thursday and Saturday. **V/Line** (☎ 13 61 96) also runs daily to Melbourne ($32). **Deniliquin Travel Centre** (Cressy St) is the ticket agent.

ALONG THE MURRAY

Most of the major river towns are on the Victorian side (see the Victoria chapter, p436), but it's easy to hop back and forth across the river. You can cross the border at the twin towns of Moama (NSW) and Echuca (Victoria). The **visitors centre** (☎ 1800 804 446, 03-5480 7555; www.echucamoama .com; 2 Heygarth St; ⊙ 9am-5pm) serves both towns and is located in Echuca beside the bridge that crosses into NSW. Ask about trips on the paddle-steamers that ply these waters, reminders of when the Murray and Darling Rivers were main highways of communication and trade.

The largest NSW town on the river is Albury (p228). Downstream from here is **Corowa**, a wine-producing centre; the Lindemans winery has been here since 1860. **Tocumwal**, on the Newell Hwy, is a quiet riverside town with sandy beaches and a giant fibreglass Murray Cod in the town square. The Lime Spider deli nearby on the main road is a good place to stop for a coffee, juice or snack.

WENTWORTH
☎ 03 / pop 1400

The old river port of **Wentworth** lies at the impressive confluence of the Murray and Darling Rivers, 30km northwest of Mildura. Enormous river red gums shade the banks, and there are numerous lookouts and walking tracks. The **visitors centre** (☎ 5027 3624; www.wentworth.nsw.gov.au; 28 Darling St; ⊙ 9.30am-4pm Mon-Fri, 10am-2pm Sat & Sun) is on the main road.

The riverboat MV *Loyalty* runs **cruises** (☎ 5027 3302; 2-hr cruise adult/child $14/6; ⊙ 1.45pm Mon-Thu & 10.45am Sat) leaving from the Wentworth & District Services Memorial Club.

The **Perry Dunes** are impressive orange sand dunes 6km north of town, off the road to Broken Hill.

Harry Nanya Tours, based in town, runs day and half-day tours with Aboriginal guides into Mungo National Park (p240).

Wentworth Central Motor Inn (☎ 5027 3777; www.fringeofthedesert.com.au; 41 Adams St; s/d $50/55; ✷) is a clean, modern, comfortable motel that can arrange tours in the local area.

OUTBACK

You don't have to travel to central Australia to experience red-soil country, limitless horizons and vast blue skies. The far west of NSW is rough, rugged and sparsely populated. It also produces a fair proportion of the state's wealth, particularly from the mines of Broken Hill. Look out for the touring brochure *The Living Outback*, available at most outback visitors centres.

Seek local advice before travelling on secondary roads west of the Mitchell Hwy. Carry plenty of water, and if you break down stay with your vehicle. Many dirt roads are OK for 2WDs, but they can be very corrugated, and sandy or dusty in patches. Much of the country is flat and featureless as far as the eye can see, but there are plenty of birds, mobs of emus, and kangaroos along the roadside to watch – and to watch out! – for.

BOURKE
☎ 02 / pop 2600

The relaxed town of Bourke, about 800km northwest of Sydney, is on the edge of the outback; the Australian expression 'back of Bourke' describes anywhere that's remote. On the Darling River, it was once a major river port and in the 1880s it was possible for wool leaving here to be in London in just six weeks – somewhat quicker than a sea-mail parcel today!

The **visitors centre** (☎ 6872 1222/2800; tourinfo@lisp.com.au; Anson St; ☼ 9am-5pm daily from Easter to Oct, Mon-Fri at other times) is a mine of information. Half-day tours run from here depending on numbers of people, or pick up the useful *Mud Map Tours* brochure. The historical and agricultural **Mateship Country Tour** ($22) lasts 3½ hours. You can book paddle-steamer tours (unless the river's in flood or drought). Visit the **NPWS office** (☎ 6872 2744; 51 Oxley St; ☼ 8.30am-4.30pm Mon-Fri) if you plan to go to the Aboriginal art sites at **Mt Gunderbooka**.

Brewarrina (or Bree) is 95km east of Bourke. You can see **The Fisheries** – stone fish traps in

the Darling River that the Ngemba Aboriginal people used. 'Brewarrina' means 'good fishing'.

Places to Stay & Eat
Bourke YHA (☎ 6870 1017; www.yha.com.au; 17 Oxley St; dm/s/d $21/33/47) In the handsome old bank building, this place is likely to be undergoing renovations for some time to come, but it's still a good budget option and the owners can arrange station tours and camel treks.

Bourke Riverside Motel (☎ 6872 2539; fax 6872 1471; 3 Mitchell St; s/d $50/83) This wonderfully eccentric building, in a waterside setting, features stylish décor dating from 1875.

Kidman's Camp (☎ 6872 1612; fax 6872 3107; camp sites $14, cabins s/d $36/44) This quiet camping ground is on the riverbank 8km north of town.

Several stations in the Bourke area (a very large area!) offer accommodation. The visitors centre has details.

The Gecko Cafe serves light lunches but is closed on weekends.

Getting There & Away
Rex (☎ 13 17 13) flies between Sydney and Bourke ($193). **Air Link** (☎ 13 17 13) has five flights a week from Dubbo to Bourke ($220 one way). **CountryLink** (☎ 13 22 32) buses run to Dubbo ($56) four times a week and connect with trains to Sydney ($66). **Bourke Courier Service** (☎ 6872 2092; cnr Oxley & Richard Sts) sells bus and plane tickets (opening hours depend on flight times).

Bus company **Travel West** (☎ 07-4655 2222; travelwest@growzone.com.au) runs a weekly service between Cunnamulla (Queensland) and Bourke.

BACK O' BOURKE – CORNER COUNTRY

There's no sealed road west of Bourke in NSW. The 713km from Bourke to Broken Hill via Wanaaring and Tibooburra are lonely, unsealed roads. The far western corner of the state is a semidesert of red plains, heat, dust and flies, and running along the border with Queensland is the Dog Fence, patrolled every day by boundary riders who each look after a 40km section.

Tiny **Tibooburra**, the hottest place in the state, is in the northwestern corner and has a number of 19th-century stone buildings. Pick up the informal *Tibooburra: A Guide* *of Sorts* from anywhere in town; it's locally written, with a mud map and lots of information.

Sturt National Park starts right on the northern edge of town; the **NPWS office** (☎ 08-8091 3308; 🕑 8.30am-4.30pm Mon-Fri) is on Briscoe St.

There are a few accommodation options, including **Granites Motel & Caravan Park** (☎ 08-8091 3305; fax 08-8091 3340; camp sites/cabins from $12/46, s/d motel units $52/66), which is on the edge of town and waiting for the shade trees to grow.

Family Hotel (☎ 08-8091 3314; fax 08-8091 3430; Briscoe St; hotel s/d $25/50, motel $60/70) is a fine sandstone building, constructed in the 1880s, as is the nearby Two Storey hotel.

Dead Horse Gully (camping $5) is a basic NPWS camping ground 2km north of town; you'll need to bring drinking water.

You can normally reach Tibooburra – driving slowly and carefully – from Bourke or Broken Hill in a conventional vehicle, except after rain (which is pretty rare!). The road from Broken Hill is part-sealed.

South of Tibooburra, **Milparinka**, once a gold town, now consists of little more than a solitary hotel and some old sandstone buildings. In 1845 members of Charles Sturt's expedition were forced to camp near here for six months. About 14km northwest of the settlement at **Depot Glen** is the grave of James Poole, Sturt's second-in-command, who died of scurvy.

Sturt National Park

Sturt National Park occupies the very northwestern corner of the state, bordering both SA and Queensland. It's a wilderness containing flood plains, rocky gorges, flat-topped mesas rising 150m above the red plains and, further west, the sand hills of the Strzelecki Desert. It has 300km of driveable tracks, camping areas and walks around the **Jump Up Loop Rd** and **Gorge Loop Rd**. The NPWS at Tibooburra has brochures for each. Park use and camping fees will have been introduced by the time this book is published.

At **Cameron Corner**, 140km northwest of Tibooburra, there's a post to mark the place where Queensland, SA and NSW meet. It's a favourite goal for visitors and a 4WD is not always necessary to get there. Staff at **Cameron Corner Store** (☎ 08-8091 3872) can advise on road conditions, and there's fuel and basic **accommodation** (s/d $40/58) here.

BARRIER HIGHWAY

The Barrier Hwy is the main sealed route in the state's west, heading from Nyngan 594km to Broken Hill. It's an alternative route to Adelaide and it's the most direct route between Sydney and Western Australia.

Cobar still has a productive copper mine, and earlier mining history is revealed in old buildings like the Great Western Hotel, with its stretch of iron lacework ornamenting the veranda.

Pick up touring mud maps from the visitors centre in the **Great Cobar Heritage Centre** (☎ 02-6836 2448; Barrier Hwy; information centre entry free, heritage centre $5.50; 🕑 8.30am-5pm Mon-Fri, 9am-5pm Sat & Sun). There is Internet access at the **public library** (☎ 02-6836 2744). Accommodation options include **Cross Roads Motel** (☎ 02-6836 2711; cnr Bourke & Louth Rds; s/d $65/72; 🗶), a quiet motel off the main road. **Town and Country Motor Inn** (☎ 02-6836 1244; fax 6836 1383; 52 Marshall St; s/d $77/88; 🗶) has wheelchair access and the restaurant, Giovanni's, serves Italian food.

Wilcannia, on the Darling River, was a busy, prosperous port in the days of paddle-steamers. When river transport diminished, its wealth dried up and the town fell into decline. Today it's trying hard to outlive a reputation for being a rough, boozy place, and it's certainly a poor and ragged town. Many of the historic buildings are in a sad state of dilapidation, but it's safe enough, although the pubs can be a little feral. By contrast, the **Wilcannia Motel** (☎ 08-8091 5802; wilcanniamotel@bigpond.com.au; 68-74 Hood St; s/d/f $68/77/101; 🗶 🖵) is smart and welcoming and makes a good geographic base for exploring the area, as it lies conveniently between the national parks of **Mutawintji** and **Kinchega**, in addition to the soon-to-be created **Peery National Park**. If you're planning on refuelling in Wilcannia, be aware that the petrol stations close at 8.30pm.

About 91km northwest of Wilcannia is **White Cliffs**, an opal-mining settlement. For a taste of life in a small outback community it's worth the drive out here, although you should book accommodation ahead during school holidays. You can fossick for opals around the old diggings (watch out for unfenced shafts) and there are underground homes and motels – 'dug-outs' – to look at. The general store has a mud map of the area. Emus often graze by the high-tech dishes of the **White Cliffs Experimental Solar Power Station** (☎ 08-8091 6633; admission by donation to Royal Flying Doctor Service; ◷ on request).

It's worth seeing if you can find **Jock's Place** (☎ 08-8091 6753). Jock is a local character who'll give you an entertaining tour of a dug-out home and mine. There's some exquisite jewellery on show and for sale at **Barbara & Doug's Outback Treasures** (☎ 08-8091 6634; Smith's Hill).

Accommodation includes **PJ's Underground** (☎ 08-8091 6626; pjsunderground@bigpond.com; Turley's Hill; B&B d $90-115), an old opal mine converted into a surprisingly bright and cosy guesthouse. This place has bags of character, can provide meals for guests and has an interesting section of the old mine that has been left untouched.

White Cliffs Opal Pioneer Reserve (☎ /fax 08-8091 6688; camp sites from $11) is a small, hot, camping ground.

Mutawintji National Park

This beautiful park in the sandstone Byn-guano Range, 131km north of Broken Hill, has fairly reliable water holes and is therefore a focus for wildlife. It is well worth the two-hour drive from Broken Hill or White Cliffs on an isolated dirt road, but not after rain.

The Mutawintji National Park is Aboriginal land and contains ancient rock engravings and cave paintings. The major art site is off-limits to visitors, except when taken on guided **tours** (◷ Wed-Sat from Apr-Oct) run by the Mutawintji Aboriginal community. Check details with the **NPWS office** (☎ 08-8080 3200) in Broken Hill. Self-guided walking trails are provided, and rock paintings can be seen in some areas. The **Homestead Creek** (camp sites per adult/child $5/3) camping ground has bore water and vehicle entry to the park is free.

BROKEN HILL

☎ 08 / pop 19,800

Out in the far west, Broken Hill is an oasis in the semi-arid wilderness. A mining town, it's fascinating not only for its comfortable existence in a rugged environment, but also for its mining trade-union history. It has also become a major centre for Australian art and artists, who are drawn to the area's austere beauty and the intensity and reliability of the light here. A walk around town will probably take in numerous wall murals, sculptures and several art galleries.

History

The Broken Hill Proprietary Company Ltd (BHP) was formed in 1885 after Charles Rasp, a boundary rider, discovered a silver lode. Early conditions in the mine were appalling. Hundreds of miners died, and many more suffered from lead poisoning and lung disease. This gave rise to the other great force in Broken Hill: the unions. Many miners were immigrants, but all were united in their efforts to improve conditions.

The Big Strike of 1919 and 1920 lasted for over 18 months. The miners won a 35-hour week and the end of dry drilling, responsible for the dust that afflicted so many of them. The concept of 'one big union', which had helped to win the strike, was formalised in 1923 with the formation of the Barrier Industrial Council.

Today the world's richest deposits of silver, lead and zinc are still being worked, though zinc is of greatest importance to 'Silver City', as Broken Hill is known.

The ore-body is diminishing and modern technology has greatly reduced the number of jobs, and while mining has declined, art has thrived.

Orientation & Information

In many ways Broken Hill is more a part of SA than NSW. It's 1170km from Sydney but only 509km from Adelaide; its clocks are set on Adelaide (central) time, half an hour behind Sydney (eastern) time; and the telephone area code (☎ 08) is the same as that for SA.

The city is laid out in a grid and the central area is easy to get around on foot. Argent St is the main street.

The **visitors centre** (☎ 8087 6077; www.murra youtback.org.au; cnr Blende & Bromide Sts; ◷ 8.30am-5pm) hands out some useful information. Pick up the excellent free booklet *Broken Hill, The Accessible Outback* for a mass of helpful regional information. There's also a handy guide to the art around town. The visitors centre is also where buses arrive (book through the town's travel agents) and there's a car-rental desk on the premises.

The **NPWS office** (☎ 8080 3200; 183 Argent St; ◷ 8.30am-4.30pm Mon-Fri) can help with local national-park inquiries and bookings.

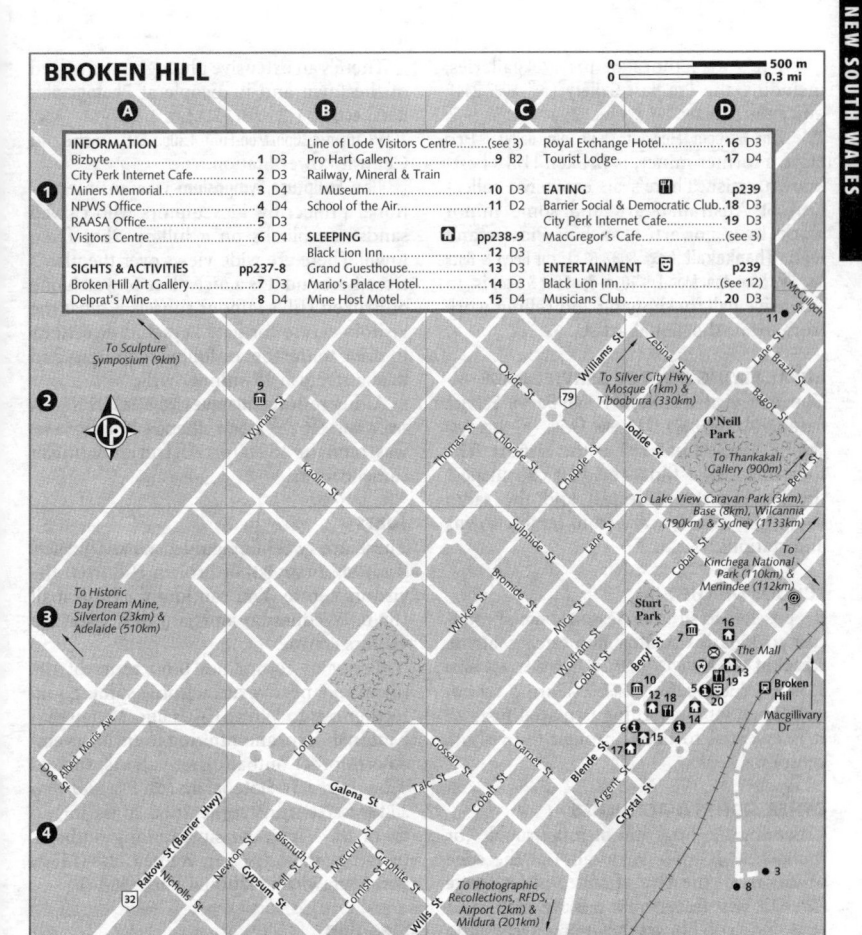

BROKEN HILL

0 ____ 500 m
0 ____ 0.3 mi

INFORMATION	
Bizbyte	1 D3
City Perk Internet Cafe	2 D3
Miners Memorial	3 D4
NPWS Office	4 D4
RAASA Office	5 D3
Visitors Centre	6 D4

SIGHTS & ACTIVITIES	pp237-8
Broken Hill Art Gallery	7 D3
Delprat's Mine	8 D4

Line of Lode Visitors Centre	(see 3)
Pro Hart Gallery	9 B2
Railway, Mineral & Train Museum	10 D3
School of the Air	11 D2

SLEEPING	pp238-9
Black Lion Inn	12 D3
Grand Guesthouse	13 D3
Mario's Palace Hotel	14 D3
Mine Host Motel	15 D4

Royal Exchange Hotel	16 D3
Tourist Lodge	17 D4

EATING	p239
Barrier Social & Democratic Club	18 D3
City Perk Internet Cafe	19 D3
MacGregor's Cafe	(see 3)

ENTERTAINMENT	p239
Black Lion Inn	(see 12)
Musicians Club	20 D3

The **Royal Automobile Association of South Australia** (RAASA; ☎ 8088 4999; 261 Argent St; 🕑 8.30am-5pm Mon-Fri & 8.30-11.30am Sat) provides reciprocal service to other autoclub members.

Internet access is available at **Bizbyte** (☎ 8087 7352; 435 Argent St; 🕑 9am-5.50pm Mon-Fri) and **City Perk Internet Cafe** (☎ 8088 1443; Argent St; 🕑 8.30am-5pm).

Sights
MINES

There's an excellent underground tour at **Delprat's Mine** (☎ 8088 1604; 2-hr tour adult/child $30/26; 🕑 tours 10.30am Mon-Fri, 2pm Sat), where you don miners gear and descend 130m. Children under six years are not allowed.

Delprat's is up Iodide St, across the railway tracks, and then follow the signs; it's a five-minute drive on a gated dirt track.

The **Historic Day Dream Mine** (☎ 8088 5682; 1-hr tour adult/child $13/5.50; 🕑 10am-3.30pm), begun in 1881, is 20km from Broken Hill, off Silverton Rd. All ages are allowed, and sturdy footwear is essential. Tours leave regularly.

ART GALLERIES

Broken Hill's red earth and harsh light has inspired many artists, and the **Broken Hill Regional Art Gallery** (☎ 8088 5491; cnr Chloride & Blende Sts; admission $2; 🕑 10am-5pm Mon-Fri, 1-5pm Sat & Sun) is a great place to see some really striking work depicting the area.

There's a plethora of private galleries, including the **Pro Hart Gallery** (☎ 8087 2441; www.prohart.com.au; 108 Wyman St; adult/child $4/2; 🕙 9am-12.30pm Mon-Sat, 1.30-5pm daily). Pro Hart, a former miner, is Broken Hill's best-known artist. There's an extensive collection of Australian art, and some minor works by major artists such as Picasso and Dali. **Thankakali** (☎ 8087 6111; cnr Beryl & Buck Sts; 🕙 9am-4pm Mon-Fri, 10am-3pm Sat & Sun) is an extensive gallery showing and selling work from local Aboriginal artists.

ROYAL FLYING DOCTOR SERVICE BASE
You can visit the **Royal Flying Doctor Service Base** (RFDS; ☎ 8080 1777; tour $5.50; 🕙 9am-5pm Mon-Fri, 11am-4pm Sat & Sun) at the airport. The tour includes a film, and you can inspect the headquarters, aircraft and the radio room that handles calls from remote towns and stations.

SCHOOL OF THE AIR
It's possible to sit in on lessons being broadcast to kids in isolated homesteads at the **School of the Air** (☎ 8087 6077; Lane St; admission $3.50; 🕙 8.30am-9.30am Mon-Fri). During school holidays a tape-recording is played instead. It is essential to book through the visitors centre.

OTHER SIGHTS & ACTIVITIES
Crowning the huge hill of mine rubble (or mullock as it's known locally) at the edge of town is the **Line of Lode Visitors Centre** (☎ 8088 6000; Federation Hill; memorial admission $2; 🕙 9am-10pm). It houses the impressively stark, rusting-steel memorial to all the miners who have died since Broken Hill first became a mining town. Inside the monument, a sobering series of plaques for each year itemise an appalling litany of gruesome deaths. The visitors centre makes an excellent vantage point over Broken Hill and is a great spot to enjoy sunrise or sunset. There's a good café/restaurant attached (see Eating; p238).

A trainspotter's dream, the **Railway, Mineral & Train Museum** (cnr Bromide & Blende Sts; adult/child $2.50/2; 🕙 10am-3pm) is in the Silverton Tramway Company's old station. The tramway was a private railway running between Cockburn (SA) and Broken Hill via Silverton until 1970. There's an impressive array of locomotives and rolling stock to clamber on and around.

There's an extensive photographic record of the town and its people at **Photographic Recollections** (☎ 8087 9322; Eyre St; adult/child $4.50/2; 🕙 10am-4.30pm Mon-Fri, 1-4.30pm Sat), in the old Central Power Station.

The **Sculpture Symposium** was an international project by 12 sculptors who carved sandstone blocks on a hilltop 9km from town. There are wide views over the plains from here and it is a nice place to watch one of Broken Hill's famous sunsets. Call at the visitors centre for gate keys and directions to drive to the top, or follow road signs and take a steepish 15-minute walk.

A tiny restored **mosque** (☎ 8088 1713; cnr Buck and William Sts; 🕙 Sunday afternoons by arrangement) was built in 1891 for Afghan and Indian camel drivers.

Tours
There are two-hour guided **walks** (🕙 10am Mon, Wed & Fri Mar-Oct) of Broken Hill from the visitors centre. You can join the bush mail run on Wednesday and Saturday; ask at the visitors centre.

Plenty of companies offer tours of the town and nearby attractions, some going further out to White Cliffs and Mutawintji National Park, and offering tours of several days to other outback destinations, such as Tibooburra. **Tri State Safaris** (☎ 8088 2389; www.tristate.com.au) runs some good tours for up to 11 days into the surrounding outback, including day trips into White Cliffs ($152) and Mutawintji National Park ($140).

Sleeping
High ceilings, wide corridors and huge verandas are standard when it comes to pubs in this hot city. There are also several **self-contained cottages** (per night from $60) in town; the visitors centre keeps a list.

BUDGET
Tourist Lodge YHA (☎ 8088 2086; mcrae@pcpro.net.au; 100 Argent St; dm/s/d members $19/29/46, nonmembers $23/34/52; 🗪) This is a justifiably popular and central YHA hostel with a pool.

Black Lion Inn (☎ 8087 4801; fax 8087 8356; 34 Bromide St; s/d $24/31) This congenial pub has some pleasant, good-value rooms (share bathroom) in an adjoining building.

Mario's Palace Hotel (☎ 8088 5944; mariospalace@bigpond.com; cnr Argent & Sulphide Sts; s/d $32/45, with bathroom $48/67) This impressive old pub

(1888) is covered inside with murals and has a fantastic veranda, although the fittings are showing their age, including asthmatic and ineffective air-conditioning in some rooms. The pub was featured in the movie *Priscilla, Queen of the Desert,* and the wonderfully eccentric five-bed Priscilla Suite (complete with carpeted walls) can be had from $85 a night.

Lake View Caravan Park (☎ /fax 8088 2250; 1 Mann St; camp sites from $16, on-site vans/cabins $35/46) Three kilometres northeast of town, this park enjoys a quiet, prime location on the edge of the bush, and a pool.

MID-RANGE
Grand Guesthouse (☎ 8087 5305; www.angelfire.com /pe/kww; 317 Argent St; B&B s/d/f $55/65/91; s/d with bathroom $65/75; ✿) Recently renovated, this guesthouse is in one of the huge old buildings in the town centre.

Mine Host Motel (☎ 8088 4044; fax 8088 1313; 120 Argent St; s/d $75/85; ✿) Rooms at this central hotel are reasonable value, though the pool area and courtyard are hot and bare.

Base (☎ 8087 7770; Barrier Hwy; s/d $35/55) Eight kilometres east of the post office, this place was, until 1996, the Royal Flying Doctor Service base until it moved to the airport. It has large rooms, a convivial common room and a garden in a pleasant bush setting.

TOP END
Royal Exchange Hotel (☎ 8087 2308; www.royal exchangehotel.com; 320 Argent St; standard/superior/ deluxe $100/150/195; ✿) This is certainly the pick of places to stay in Broken Hill. Plush rooms with superb facilities are housed in this elegant, newly renovated Art Deco building right in the centre of town. There's also a comfortable lounge and bar.

Eating
Broken Hill is a pub and club town and most of them have reasonably priced and filling meals. Don't expect fine dining, however, and even simple, fresh food that hasn't come out of a frier can be hard to find. There's a cluster of cafés and restaurants at the eastern end of Argent St.

MacGregor's Cafe (☎ 8087 1345; Line of Lode Visitors Centre, Federation Way; mains $15-20; ✿ 9am-10pm) The food is good enough, although not outstanding, but the setting, especially at sunset, is really special.

City Perk Internet Cafe (☎ 8088 1443; 305 Argent St) A funkily decorated place serving decent coffee and fresh juices and offering fast Internet access.

Barrier Social & Democratic Club (The Demo; ☎ 8088 4477; 218 Argent St; mains $8; ✿ 7-9am, noon-2pm, 6.30-8.30pm) The meals here are good value and filling.

Entertainment
Broken Hill stays up late, especially on Thursday, Friday and Saturday.

Barrier Social & Democratic Club (The Demo; ☎ 8088 4477; 218 Argent St) The Demo runs a nightclub on Saturday and often has live country-type bands.

Black Lion Inn (☎ 8087 4801; 34 Bromide St) This is a party pub and good for a drink. There is a three-page cocktail list, and happy hours on some nights.

Musicians Club (☎ 8088 1777; 276 Crystal St) You can eat here before playing a traditional Australian game of Two-Up (gambling on the fall of two coins) on Friday and Saturday nights from 10pm, and of course on Anzac Day (25 April). There's often live music, too.

Getting There & Away
AIR
Rex (☎ 13 17 13) has flights to Broken Hill from Sydney and Adelaide (both flights cost $265).

BUS
McCafferty's/Greyhound (☎ 13 20 30) runs daily to Adelaide (from $58) and Sydney (from $89). Most buses depart from the visitors centre. Book tickets at the local travel agents.

There is no public service north to Tibooburra, but ask at the visitors centre about freight contractors who may give lifts to travellers (although their fears of a public liability claim are making this a rarity).

TRAIN
Broken Hill is on the Sydney to Perth railway line, and the *Indian Pacific* passes through on Tuesday and Friday (departing 6.30pm central standard time) bound for Sydney, and on Thursday and Sunday (departing 8.20am) heading for Perth. For timetables and fares, contact the **Great Southern Railway** (☎ 13 21 47; www.trainways.com.au).

There's a direct CountryLink service on Tuesday (departing 7.30am, around 14 hours) direct to Sydney ($117). The **CountryLink** (☎ 8087 1400; ☣ 8am-5pm Mon-Fri) booking office is at the train station.

AROUND BROKEN HILL
Silverton
☎ 08

Silverton, 25km northwest of Broken Hill, is an old silver-mining town that reached its peak in 1885, when it had a population of 3000 and public buildings designed to last for centuries. In 1889 the mines closed and the population (and many of the houses) moved to Broken Hill. Today it's an interesting little ghost town, used as a setting in the movies *Mad Max II* and *A Town Like Alice*. A number of buildings still stand, including the **old gaol** (adult/student $2.50/1.50; ☣ usually daily), now the museum, and the **Silverton Hotel** (☎ 8088 5313; ☣ 9am-9pm). The hotel has a display of photographs taken on the film sets and you mustn't leave without taking the infamous 'Silverton test'. Ask at the bar. We mean it! There are also several **art galleries**.

Bill Cannard runs a variety of **camel tours** (☎ 8088 5316; Silverton Rd, PO Box 751 BH 2880; 15-min/1-hr tours $5/20, 2-hr sunset ride $50) from Silverton. One- to three-day safaris are available April to September.

Silverton Hotel (☎ 8088 5313; s/d $33/44) offers some basic 'graveyard accommodation' (overlooking the burial ground) in rather meagre prefabricated cabins. **Penrose Park** (☎ 8088 5307; camp sites $4, 8-bed bunkhouse with/without kitchen $30/25) is a less morbid option.

The road beyond Silverton becomes bleak and lonely almost immediately. The **Mundi Mundi Plains** lookout, 5km north of town, gives an idea of just how desolate it gets. Further along, the **Umberumberka Reservoir**, 13km north of Silverton, is a popular picnic spot.

Menindee Lakes
The lakes are part of a water storage development on the Darling River, 112km southeast of Broken Hill. **Menindee** is the closest town to the area. There are a couple of motels and camping grounds. Burke and Wills stayed at **Maidens Hotel** (☎ 08-8091 4208; Yartla St; s/d $28/40) on their ill-fated trip north in 1860. The hotel has recently been renovated; the oldest part of the building burnt down in 1999, but the front section is still

classic early 20th century. **Menindee Lakes Caravan Park** (☎ 08-8091 4315) is a low-key camping ground on the edge of the water, where you can swim and fish. It's out of town, on the Broken Hill road.

Kinchega National Park is close to town, and the lakes are a haven for birdlife. The visitors centre is at the site of the old Kinchega woolshed, about 16km from the park entrance. There are three well-marked driving trails through the park, and accommodation at the shearers' quarters (book at the Broken Hill NPWS office) and plenty of good camp sites along the river.

Scotia Sanctuary
One of several privately run 'Earth Sanctuaries' in Australia, Scotia is 163km south of Broken Hill, and 30km off the highway. An arid-zone conservation area, it has recently successfully re-introduced several endangered animals, including the bilby. There are some excellent nocturnal tours and a range of **accommodation** (☎ 03-5027 1200; scotia@ruralnet.net.au), including comfortable rooms in the homestead, and camping.

MUNGO NATIONAL PARK
Southeast of Menindee and northeast of Mildura is **Lake Mungo**, part of the World Heritage–listed Willandra Lakes Region. Mungo is a dry lake that is the site of the oldest archaeological finds in Australia – human skeletons and artefacts date back 46,000 years or possibly more. A 25km semicircle ('lunette') of huge sand dunes has been created by the unceasing westerly wind, which continually exposes fabulously ancient remains. These shimmering white dunes are known as the **Walls of China**.

Mungo is 110km from Mildura and 150km from Balranald on good, unsealed roads that, however, become instantly impassable after rain. These towns are the closest places selling fuel.

Award-winning **Harry Nanya Tours** (☎ 1800 630 864, 03-5027 2076; carnma@ruralnet.net.au) runs tours to Lake Mungo daily from Mildura and Wentworth, and employs Aboriginal guides who give cultural information. Be aware, however, that the last time we tried to go on a tour it was cancelled just a couple of hours after we had booked and just before it was due to start, owing to insufficient numbers. Check ahead, especially if you're travelling into Wentworth. Several Mildura-based companies also offer tours; check at the Mildura visitors centre (see Mildura; p522).

Information

The **NPWS office** (☎ 03-5021 8900; ✆ 8.30am-4.30pm Mon-Fri), on the corner of the Sturt Hwy at Buronga, near Mildura, has park information. There's a visitors centre (not always staffed) in the park, by the old Mungo woolshed. Pay your day-use fee of $6 per car on an honesty system here. A road leads across the dry lake bed to the Walls of China, and you can drive a complete 70km loop of the dunes when it's dry. There's a self-guided drive brochure at the visitors centre.

Sleeping

Accommodation fills up during school holidays; book camp sites through the NPWS office in Buronga.

Mungo Lodge (☎ 03-5029 7297; mungoldg@rur alnet.net.au; s/d $78/88) On the Mildura road, about 4km from the visitors centre, this is a comfortable quiet spot with a restaurant (book ahead).

Main Camp (camp sites per person $3) is 2km from the visitors centre, and **Belah Camp** (camp sites per person $3) is on the eastern side of the dunes. To pay your camp fees, simply put money in an envelope at the visitors centre. The **Shearers' Quarters** (adult/child $17/5.50) bunkhouses are next to the visitors centre.

Australian Capital Territory

CONTENTS

The Australian Capital Territory (ACT) occupies a bushy inland plot totalling 2366 sq km, with rugged, blue grey ranges to the south and to the west. Within these smallish territorial boundaries are the spread-out environs of the national capital, Canberra, a spaciously clean metropolis with a serious aesthetic (but don't be fooled, it's dancing on the inside). Only a few gear shifts from the city are some relaxing old towns and an abundance of camera-friendly natural sights. The splendid ridges and rivers of Namadgi National Park cover 40% of the territory. Bushwalkers and birdwatchers, cyclists and journalists will all find plenty to occupy them here.

When Australia's separate colonies were federated in 1901 and became states, a decision to build a national capital was written into the constitution. In 1908 the site was selected, diplomatically situated between arch-rival cities of Sydney and Melbourne, and in 1911 the Commonwealth government bought land for the Australian Capital Territory.

TOP TEN

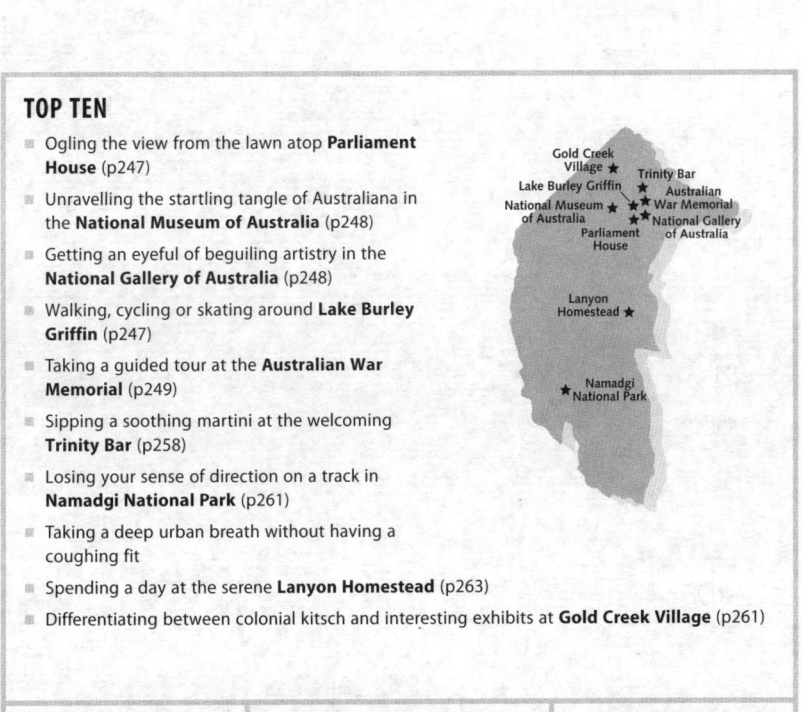

- Ogling the view from the lawn atop **Parliament House** (p247)
- Unravelling the startling tangle of Australiana in the **National Museum of Australia** (p248)
- Getting an eyeful of beguiling artistry in the **National Gallery of Australia** (p248)
- Walking, cycling or skating around **Lake Burley Griffin** (p247)
- Taking a guided tour at the **Australian War Memorial** (p249)
- Sipping a soothing martini at the welcoming **Trinity Bar** (p258)
- Losing your sense of direction on a track in **Namadgi National Park** (p261)
- Taking a deep urban breath without having a coughing fit
- Spending a day at the serene **Lanyon Homestead** (p263)
- Differentiating between colonial kitsch and interesting exhibits at **Gold Creek Village** (p261)

■ TELEPHONE CODE: 02	■ POPULATION: 321,700	■ AREA: 2366 SQ KM

AUSTRALIAN CAPITAL TERRITORY

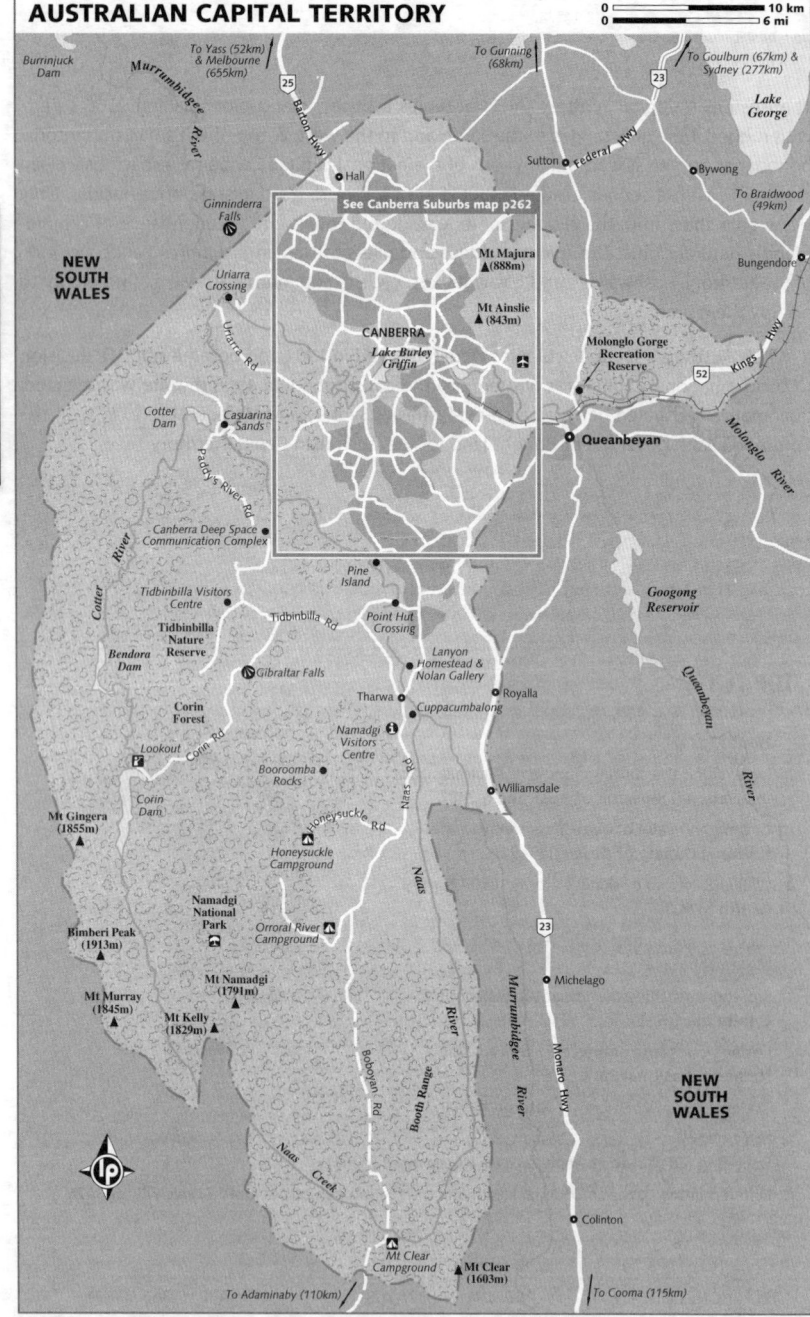

0 _____ 10 km
0 _____ 6 mi

To Yass (52km)
& Melbourne
(655km)

To Gunning
(68km)

To Goulburn (67km) &
Sydney (277km)

Burrinjuck
Dam

Murrumbidgee River

25

23

Lake
George

Barton Hwy

Hall

Sutton

Federal Hwy

Bywong

To Braidwood
(49km)

Ginninderra
Falls

See Canberra Suburbs map p262

NEW
SOUTH
WALES

Uriarra
Crossing

Mt Majura
▲(888m)

Bungendore

Uriarra Rd

CANBERRA
Lake Burley
Griffin

Mt Ainslie
▲ (843m)

Molonglo Gorge
Recreation
Reserve

Kings Hwy

52

Cotter
Dam

Casuarina
Sands

Paddy's River Rd

Queanbeyan

Molonglo River

Cotter River

Canberra Deep Space
Communication Complex

Pine
Island

Googong
Reservoir

Tidbinbilla Visitors
Centre

Tidbinbilla Rd

Point Hut
Crossing

Tidbinbilla
Nature
Reserve

Bendora
Dam

Gibraltar Falls

Tharwa

Lanyon
Homestead &
Nolan Gallery

Royalla

Queanbeyan River

Corin
Forest

Conn Rd

Cuppacumbalong

Lookout

Namadgi
Visitors
Centre

Corin
Dam

Booroomba
Rocks

Williamsdale

Mt Gingera
(1855m)
▲

Honeysuckle Rd

Naas Rd

Honeysuckle
Campground

Namadgi
National
Park

Bimberi Peak
(1913m)
▲

Orroral River
Campground

Mt Murray
(1845m)
▲

Mt Namadgi
(1791m)
▲

Naas River

23

Michelago

Mt Kelly
(1829m) ▲

Murrumbidgee River

Monaro Hwy

NEW
SOUTH
WALES

Bobeyan Rd

Booth Range

Naas Creek

Colinton

Mt Clear
Campground

Mt Clear
(1603m) ▲

To Adaminaby (110km)

To Cooma (115km)

CANBERRA

☎ 02 / pop 309,800

Canberra is a city that thrives outdoors, amid lakeside parks, green hills and patches of naturally ragged bushland that lie in and around the suburbs. When the inhabitants aren't admiring the autumnal dressage of millions of trees, the crisp and often clear-skied days of winter (when the city experiences an average of six sunny hours each day), the blooming colours of spring or the depths of a waterhole during a hot summer's day, they can take a cultural dip in Canberra's bewildering array of museums or work on an appetite in one of the many healthily competitive restaurants and cafés. This is also one of the few Australian cities in which kangaroos do occasionally jump into view.

The relative serenity and orderliness of the Australian capital isn't to everybody's taste, especially the unapologetically homogenous suburbia. But the days when Canberra was an incubator for a uniform public service are long gone, with more than half the workforce now employed in the private sector. And the thriving arts scene means that theatres and galleries are full of thoughtful, provocative and nicely designed fare.

Exploring Canberra will expose you to intriguing modern architecture, a highly visible collective of distraction-seeking university students, the political enclave on and around Capital Hill, and a growing barfly scene. So pack an open mind and investigate the possibilities.

HISTORY

When Australia's separate colonies were federated in 1901 and became states, a decision to build a national capital was written into the constitution. In 1908 the site was selected, diplomatically situated between arch-rivals Sydney and Melbourne, and in 1911 the Commonwealth government bought land for the ACT. American architect Walter Burley Griffin then beat 136 other entries to win an international competition to design the city. On 12 March 1913, when the foundation stones of the new capital were being laid, the city was officially baptised 'Canberra', believed to be an Aboriginal term for 'meeting place'.

Canberra took over from Melbourne as the seat of national government in 1927, but the city's expansion only got under way after WWII. In 1960 the ACT's population was 50,000 and by 1967 had topped 100,000; today it's over 305,000.

ORIENTATION

The city is arranged around Lake Burley Griffin. From the north side the main arterial road, Northbourne Ave, intersects compact Canberra City (aka Civic). The pedestrian malls to the east comprise Canberra's main shopping areas.

AUSTRALIAN CAPITAL TERRITORY

BUSHFIRES

In mid-January 2003, several massive bushfires combined to strike the western and southern outskirts of Canberra. Over a single weekend, the fires claimed four lives, 530 homes, 30 farms and the historic Mt Stromlo Observatory, and decimated large swathes of Namadgi National Park. Almost all of the 5500 hectares of the Tidbinbilla Nature Reserve, including most of the wildlife, was destroyed – the sole survivor of the reserve's 20 koalas was christened 'Lucky' and had a public recuperation at the city's zoo. Looking out from the observation deck of Telstra Tower after the blaze had passed, you could clearly see the expanses of burnt-out land, including a black arc that had been extinguished almost at the foot of Black Mountain.

The aftermath of the fires heard an impassioned public debate over the competency of emergency services and the need for the 'bush capital' to address the natural kindling overgrowing some residential areas. Meanwhile, in the national park, an amazing process of regeneration was taking place, with greenery beginning to sprout from blackened tree trunks and the charred earth, and the surviving wildlife starting to reappear. It wasn't clear how long it would take for the Australian bush and its inhabitants to re-establish themselves, or how much flora would now be allowed to run wild in proximity to the suburbs, but the display of nature's resilience was a welcome sign of ongoing life.

CANBERRA IN...

Two Days

Have breakfast in a **Kingston** or **Manuka** café (p257), then disappear into the parliamentary triangle, the slice of **Parkes** that includes **Parliament House** (p247), the once-busy corridors of **Old Parliament House** (p247) and the well-hung **National Gallery** (p248). After a breather on the foreshore of **Lake Burley Griffin** (p247) head into the city to grab a table in **Garema Place** (p256) followed by a home-brew at **Wig & Pen** (p258). After a sleep at **University House** (p255) dive into the iconic chaos of the **National Museum** (p248) and stroll through the **Botanic Gardens** (p249). In the evening, have a feast at **Dickson Asian Noodle House** (p257) and a martini at **Trinity** (p258).

Four Days

Follow as above, then start the third day with a munch at **Tilley's** (p259) and spend the rest of it at the **zoo** (p249) and getting a sombre history lesson at the **War Memorial** (p249). Celebrate with a meal at **Green Herring** (p258) or **Aubergine** (p258), then chill at **Toast** (p259). Put aside at least one leisurely day to have a **picnic**, a **walk** and perhaps a **swim** somewhere around Canberra.

South of the city, Northbourne Ave becomes Commonwealth Ave and spans Lake Burley Griffin to Capital Circle. This road encircles Parliament House on Capital Hill, the apex of Walter Burley Griffin's parliamentary triangle. Located within and near the parliamentary triangle are a number of important buildings, including the High Court of Australia, the National Gallery of Australia and Old Parliament House.

The rest of the city is made up of suburban clusters, each with their own 'town centres'.

Maps

The **NRMA** (Map pp250-1; ☎ 13 21 32; 92 Northbourne Ave, Braddon) has a *Canberra & Southeast New South Wales* map ($7), good for tours of the countryside. The Canberra visitors centre (p247) stocks city maps and cartography for lookouts and bushwalks.

INFORMATION
Airline Offices

Brindabella Airlines (☎ 6248 8711; www.brinda bella-airlines.com.au) Flights to/from Albury Wodonga and Newcastle.
Qantas (Map pp250-1; ☎ 13 13 13; www.qantas .com.au; Jolimont Centre, Northbourne Ave, Civic)
Regional Express (Rex; ☎ 13 17 13; www.regional express.com.au)
Virgin Blue (☎ 13 67 89; www.virginblue.com.au)

Bookshops

Electric Shadows Bookshop (Map pp250-1; ☎ 6248 8352; City Walk, Civic) Specialises in books on theatre and film, plus arthouse videos.

Gilbert's (Map pp250-1; ☎ 6247 2032; Center Cinema Bldg, Bunda St, Civic) Eclectic second-hand books.
Map World (Map pp250-1; ☎ 6230 4097; Jolimont Centre, 65 Northbourne Ave, Civic) Stocks numerous maps and travel guides.
National Library Bookshop (Map pp250-1; ☎ 6262 1424; Parkes Pl, Parkes) Superb Australian fiction selection.
Paperchain Bookstore (Map pp250-1; ☎ 6295 6723; 2/14 Furneaux St, Manuka) All-purpose booklist.
Smiths Alternative Bookshop (Map pp250-1; ☎ 6247 4459; 76 Alinga St, Civic) New Age 'science' to gay and lesbian literature.

Cultural Centres

Alliance Française (Map p262; ☎ 6247 5027; 66 McCaughey St, Turner)
Das Zentrum (Map pp250-1; ☎ 6230 0441; Griffin Centre, Bunda St, Civic)
Spanish-Australia Club (Map p262; ☎ 6295 6506; Jerrabomberra Ave, Narrabundah)

Emergency

Ambulance (☎ 000, TTY 106)
Canberra Rape Crisis Centre (☎ 6247 2525, TTY 6247 1657) 24-hour help.
Fire (☎ 000, TTY 106)
Lifeline (☎ 13 11 14) 24-hour crisis counselling.
Police (☎ 000, TTY 106)

Internet Access

Public libraries, several hostels and the Jolimont Centre have public Internet access. **Café Cactus** (Map pp250-1; ☎ 6248 0449; Center Cinema Bldg, Bunda St, Civic; ☼ 8am-7pm Mon-Fri, 9.30am-9pm Sat, 10.30am-6pm Sun) is an upbeat, friendly Internet café.

Medical Services

Canberra Hospital (Map p262; ☎ 6244 2222, emergency dept ☎ 6244 2611; Yamba Dr, Garran)
Capital Chemist (Map p262; ☎ 6248 7050; Sargood St, O'Connor; ⏰ 9am-11pm)
Travellers' Medical & Vaccination Centre (Map pp250-1; ☎ 6257 7156; 5th fl, 8-10 Hobart Pl, Civic; ⏰ 8.30am-4.30pm Mon-Fri, 8.30am-7pm Thu) Appointment essential.

Money

American Express (Map pp250-1; ☎ 6247 2333; 1st fl, Centrepoint, City Walk, Civic)
Thomas Cook (Map pp250-1; ☎ 6247 9984; Canberra Centre, Bunda St, Civic)

Post

Pick up poste restante at the **GPO** (Map pp250-1; ☎ 13 13 18; 53-73 Alinga St, Civic). Mail can be addressed: poste restante Canberra GPO, Canberra City, ACT 2601.

Tourist Information

Canberra visitors centre (Map p262; ☎ 1300 554 114, 6205 0044; www.canberratourism.com.au; 330 Northbourne Ave, Dickson; ⏰ 9am-5.30pm Mon-Fri, 9am-4pm Sat & Sun)
Community Information & Referral Service (Map pp250-1; ☎ 6248 7988; www.cirsact.org.au; Griffin Centre, 19 Bunda St; ⏰ 10am-4pm Mon-Fri,10am-1pm Wed)

SIGHTS

Canberra's many significant buildings, museums and galleries are splayed out on either side of Lake Burley Griffin, while most appealing natural features lie in the territory's west and southwest. Wheelchair-bound visitors will find most sights are fully accessible. Note that nearly all attractions close on Christmas day.

Bus No 34 from the city interchange is handy for many of the following sights. For more information on bus services see p261.

Lookouts

Black Mountain (812m) is topped by the 195m-high **Telstra Tower** (Map p262; ☎ 1800 806 718; Black Mountain Dr; adult/child $3.30/1.10; ⏰ 9am-10pm), which has a spectacularly unappealing concrete exterior but the best windblown vista around. **Mt Ainslie** (Map p262), northeast of the city, stands 843m and has fine views day and night; walking tracks to the mountain start behind the War Memorial and end at the 888m **Mt Majura** (Map p262).

Lake Burley Griffin

Named after Canberra's architect, **Lake Burley Griffin** (Map pp250-1) was filled by damming the Molonglo River in 1963. Around its 35km shore are many places of interest.

Built in 1970 for the bicentenary of Cook's landfall, the **Captain Cook Memorial Water Jet** (Map pp250-1; admission free; ⏰ 10am-noon & 2-4pm, also 7-9pm during daylight-saving) flings a six-tonne column of water up to 147m into the air. At nearby **Regatta Point** is a skeleton globe on which Cook's three great voyages are traced; also close is the **National Capital Exhibition** (Map pp250-1; ☎ 6257 1068; www.nationalcapital.gov.au /exhibition/index.htm; admission free; ⏰ 9am-5pm), displaying the city's history. Further east is the stone-and-slab **Blundells' Cottage** (Map pp250-1; ☎ 6257 1068; adult/child/family $2/1/5; ⏰ 11am-4pm), built in 1860 to house workers on the estate.

On Aspen Island is the 50m-high **National Carillon** (Map pp250-1; ☎ 6257 1068; recitals 12.45-1.35pm Tue & Thu, 2.45-3.35pm Sat & Sun), gifted from Britain on Canberra's 50th anniversary in 1963. The tower's 53 bronze bells weigh from 7kg to six tonnes. Bookings are required for Carillon **tours** (adult/child/family $8/4/20; ⏰ 12.45pm Mon, Wed & Fri).

Parliament House

The striking **Parliament House** (Map pp250-1; ☎ 6277 5399; www.aph.gov.au; admission free; ⏰ 9am-5pm) is worth a few hours' exploration (see the boxed text 'Design for a Nation'; p248). There are free 45-minute **guided tours** on nonsitting days and 20-minute tours on sitting days (every half-hour from 9am to 4pm daily), but you're welcome to self-navigate and watch parliamentary proceedings from the public galleries. Tickets for question time (2pm sitting days) in the **House of Representatives** are free but must be booked through the Sergeant at Arms (☎ 6277 4889); tickets aren't required for the **Senate Chamber**.

Old Parliament House

Get a whiff of bygone parliamentary activity in **Old Parliament House** (Map pp250-1; ☎ 6270 8222; www.oph.gov.au; King George Tce, Parkes; adult/concession/family $2/1/5; ⏰ 9am-5pm), seat of government from 1927 to 1988, by wandering through the prime minister's suite or silently addressing the House of Representatives. There's a free **guided tour** (40 min; 9.30, 10.15, 11 & 11.45am, 12.45, 1.30, 2.30 & 3.15pm).

AUSTRALIAN CAPITAL TERRITORY

DESIGN FOR A NATION

Opened in 1988, Parliament House cost $1.1 billion, took eight years to build and replaced Old Parliament House, which had served for 61 years. It was designed by Romaldo Giurgola of Mitchell, Giurgola & Thorp architects, winners of a design competition that attracted 329 entries from 28 countries.

The structure was built into the hillside and covered by grass to preserve the site's original landscape. Its splendid interior incorporates different combinations of Australian timbers in each main section and more than 3000 original artworks.

The main axis of Parliament House runs northeast–southwest in a direct line with Old Parliament House, the Australian War Memorial and Mt Ainslie. Two high, granite-faced walls curve out from the axis to the corners of the building; the House of Representatives (east of the walls) and the Senate (to the west) are linked to the centre by covered walkways.

Enter the building across the 90,000-piece **forecourt mosaic** by Michael Nelson Tjakamarra, the theme of which is 'a meeting place' and which represents possum and wallaby Dreaming, and through the white marble **Great Verandah** at the northeastern end of the main axis. In the **foyer**, the grey-green marble columns symbolise a forest, and marquetry wall panels are inlaid with designs of Australian flora.

The first floor overlooks the **Great Hall** and its 20m-long **tapestry**, inspired by the original Arthur Boyd painting of eucalypt forest hanging outside the hall, while in the public gallery above the Great Hall is the 16m-long **embroidery** created by more than 500 members of the Embroiders Guild of Australia.

The Great Hall is the centre of the building, with the flagpole above it and passages to chambers on each side. One of only four known copies of the 1297 **Magna Carta** is on display here.

On the building's grassy rooftop are 360-degree views and a 81m-high flagpole carrying a flag the size of a double-decker bus.

The building incorporates the **National Portrait Gallery** (☎ 6270 8236; www.portrait.gov.au), which exhibits painting, photography and new media portraiture. The gallery has a lakeside annex at **Commonwealth Place** (Map pp250-1).

Opposite the main entrance is the culturally significant **Aboriginal Tent Embassy**, established in 1972 in response to governmental refusal to recognise land rights. It's where the Aboriginal flag gained prominence.

National Gallery of Australia

The stunning **National Gallery** (Map pp250-1; ☎ 6240 6502; www.nga.gov.au; Parkes Pl, Parkes; permanent collection free; ⊗ 10am-5pm) has an Australian collection ranging from traditional Aboriginal art to 20th-century works by Arthur Boyd and Albert Tucker, plus art from the early decades of European settlement. Sharing gallery space with paintings are sculptures (visit the Sculpture Garden), photographs, furniture, ceramics, fashion and silverware. In addition to regular all-inclusive **guided tours** (11am & 2pm), there's also a **tour** (11am Thu & Sun) focussing on Aboriginal and Torres Strait Islander art.

High Court of Australia

The rarefied heights of the foyer and main courtroom of the grandiose **High Court** (Map pp250-1; ☎ 6270 6811; www.hcourt.gov.au; Parkes Pl, Parkes; admission free; ⊗ 9.45am-4.30pm Mon-Fri, closed public holidays) are in keeping with the building's name, while its mishmash of thick concrete blocks, pillars and beams possibly represents the full weight of the law. Have a chat to a knowledgeable attendant about judicial life. High Court sittings, which usually occur for two weeks each month (except January and July), are open to the public; call for times.

National Museum of Australia

This wonderfully engaging **museum** (Map pp250-1; ☎ 1800 026 132, 6208 5000; www.nma.gov.au; Lawson Cres, Acton Peninsula; admission free; ⊗ 9am-5pm) is one big abstract Australian storybook. Using creativity, controversy, humour and fearless self-contradiction, the museum dismantles national identity and provokes visitors to come up with ideas of their own. From the Garden of Australian Dreams to the use of interactive technology, it's a collision of aesthetics, and all the more inspiring for it. Don't miss the introductory Circa show.

RICHARD NEBESKY

View Parliament House from memorial-lined **Anzac Parade** (p254)

Engage your senses at the excellent
National Museum of Australia (p248)

ROSS BARNETT

CHRIS MELLOR

Add to the field of poppies at
the Wall of Remembrance at the
Australian War Memorial (p249)

Walk through a 'forest' of marble columns at **Parliament House** (p247)

JOHN BANAGAN

RICHARD NEBESKY

Stroll among the indigenous plants in the **Australian National Botanic Gardens** (p249)

Enjoy an early-morning row across misty **Lake Burley Griffin** (p247)

DENNIS

Bus No 34 runs here. There's also a free bus on weekends and public holidays, departing regularly from 10.30am from platform 7 in the city bus interchange.

Australian National Botanic Gardens

Spread over 90 hectares on Black Mountain's lower slopes are these beautiful **gardens** (Map pp250-1; ☎ 6250 9450; www.anbg.gov.au/anbg; Clunies Ross St, Acton; admission free; ☽ 9am-5pm, 9am-8pm summer), devoted to Australian floral diversity. The **Aboriginal Plant Use Walk** (1km, 45 minutes) passes through the cool **Rainforest Gully** and has signs explaining how Aborigines related to indigenous plants. The **Eucalypt Lawn** is peppered with 600 species of this ubiquitous tree.

The **visitors centre** (☽ 9.30am-4.30pm) is the departure point for free **guided walks** (11am & 2pm, also 10am summer). Nearby is **Hudsons in the Gardens** (☎ 6248 9680; ☽ 8.30am-4.30pm; mains $8-12), a pleasant café popular with stroller-pushing parents.

National Zoo & Aquarium

This engaging **zoo and aquarium** (Map p262; ☎ 6287 8400; www.zooquarium.com.au; Lady Denman Dr, Yarralumla; adult/child/concession/family $19/10.50/16/55; ☽ 9am-5pm) has a roll-call of fascinating animals, including capuchins, newly hatched sharks, diminutive sun (Malay) bears, alpine dingoes and creatures in the lobster tank that resemble living hacky-sacks. Also competing for attention are otters, a tigon (the unnatural result of breeding tiger-lion crosses in captivity) and a disconcerting snow leopard lair.

Australian War Memorial

The massive **war memorial** (Map pp250-1; ☎ 6243 4211; www.awm.gov.au; Treloar Cres, Campbell; admission free; ☽ 10am-5pm) houses pictures, dioramas, relics and exhibitions detailing the events, weapons and human toll of wartime; most of the heavy machinery is arrayed within **ANZAC Hall**. Entombed among the Hall of Memory's mosaics is the **Unknown Australian Soldier**, whose remains were returned from a WWI battlefield in 1993 and who symbolises all Australian war casualties.

There are free **guided tours** (90 min; 10am, 10.30am, 11am, 1pm, 1.30pm & 2pm daily) and a *Self-guided Tour* leaflet ($3).

Along **Anzac Parade**, Canberra's broad commemorative way, are 11 memorials to various campaigns.

Questacon

The **National Science and Technology Centre** (Map pp250-1; ☎ 1800 020 603, 6270 2800; www .questacon.edu.au; adult/child/concession/family $11/6/7/32; ☽ 9am-5pm) is a child magnet, with its lively and educational interactive exhibits on the merits of everyday science and technology. Kids can learn indigenous bushcraft from the Burarra people, explore the physics of fun parks and cause tsunamis. There are also science shows; tickets cost a few dollars extra.

Canberra Museum & Gallery

This stylish **museum and gallery** (Map pp250-1; ☎ 6207 3968; www.museumandgalleries.act.gov.au /museum/index.asp; Civic Sq, London Circuit, Civic; admission free; ☽ 10am-5pm Tue-Thu, 10am-7pm Fri, noon-5pm Sat & Sun) is devoted to Canberra's social history and visual arts. The interesting permanent exhibition, 'Reflecting Canberra', includes a charred dishwasher salvaged from a house destroyed in the January 2003 bushfires. Visiting collections have run the aesthetic gamut from traditional Palestinian crafts to Korean sculptors.

ScreenSound Australia

The **National Screen and Sound Archive** (Map pp250-1; ☎ 6248 2000; www.screensound.gov.au; McCoy Circuit, Acton; admission free; ☽ 9am-5pm Mon-Fri, 10am-5pm Sat & Sun) preserves Australian moving picture and sound recordings for posterity. Highlights of the permanent exhibition include Norman Gunston's priceless interview with a vapid Zsa Zsa Gabor, and the 1943 Oscar awarded to high-voltage propaganda flick *Kokoda Front Line*. Temporary exhibitions usually have an admission fee.

National Library of Australia

This enormously symmetrical **library** (Map pp250-1; ☎ 6262 1111; www.nla.gov.au; Parkes Pl, Parkes; admission free; ☽ main reading room 9am-9pm Mon-Thu, 9am-5pm Fri & Sat, 1.30-5pm Sun) has accumulated over six million items, most of which can be accessed in one of eight reading rooms. Bookings are required for the free one-hour **guided tour** (☎ 6262 1271). The **exhibition gallery** (admission free; ☽ 9am-5pm) has offered visual treats like Augustus Pugin's famous antipodean Gothic designs.

National Archives of Australia

Canberra's original post office now houses the **National Archives** (Map pp250-1; ☎ 6212 3600;

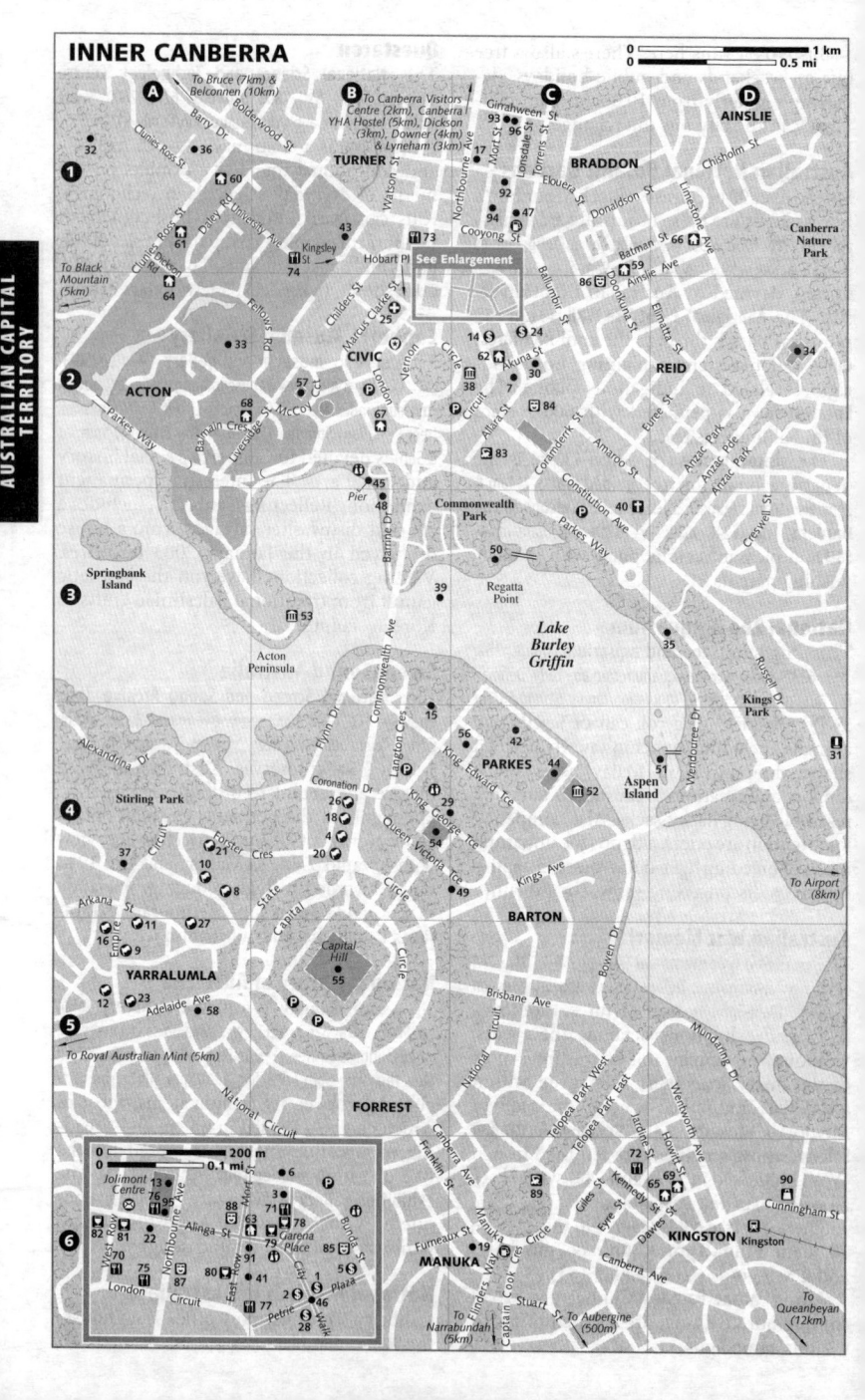

AUSTRALIAN CAPITAL TERRITORY

INNER CANBERRA

0 _____ 1 km
0 _____ 0.5 mi

To Bruce (7km) & Belconnen (10km)

To Canberra Visitors Centre (2km), Canberra YHA Hostel (5km), Dickson (3km), Downer (4km) & Lyneham (3km)

Girrahween St

AINSLIE

BRADDON

Canberra Nature Park

TURNER

See Enlargement

REID

CIVIC

ACTON

To Black Mountain (5km)

Commonwealth Park

Springbank Island

Regatta Point

Lake Burley Griffin

Acton Peninsula

Kings Park

Stirling Park

PARKES

Aspen Island

To Airport (8km)

BARTON

Capital Hill

YARRALUMLA

To Royal Australian Mint (5km)

FORREST

KINGSTON

Kingston

MANUKA

To Narrabundah (5km)

To Aubergine (500m)

To Queanbeyan (12km)

Jolimont Centre

Garema Place

0 _____ 200 m
0 _____ 0.1 mi

AUSTRALIAN CAPITAL TERRITORY

www.naa.gov.au; Queen Victoria Tce, Parkes; admission free; 9am-5pm), a repository for Commonwealth government records in the form of personal papers, photographs, films, maps and paintings. The centrepiece **Federation Gallery** holds original charters, including Australia's 1900 Constitution Act and the 1967 amendment ending constitutional discrimination against Aboriginal people. Public research facilities include a **reading room**.

Royal Australian Mint

At the wealthy **Mint** (Map p262; ☎ 6202 6891; www.ramint.gov.au; Denison St, Deakin; admission free; 9am-4pm Mon-Fri, 10am-4pm Sat & Sun) is a gallery showcasing the history of Australian coinage, including the 'holey dollar' and the 'dump'. You can view the production of proof (collectible) coins and circulating coins; note that production ceases over the weekend. For a souvenir, mint your own brand-new $1 coin; to prove you're in the cradle of capitalism, it costs you $2.

Australian National University (ANU)

The attractive grounds of the **ANU** (Map pp250-1; ☎ 6125 5111; www.anu.edu.au) have lain between Civic and Black Mountain since 1946 and make for a pleasant wander. Drop into the **Drill Hall Gallery** (Map pp250-1; ☎ 6125 5832; Kingsley St; admission free; noon-5pm Wed-Sun) to see special exhibitions and paintings from the university's art collection; a permanent fixture is the near-phosphorescent hue of Sidney Nolan's *Riverbend*. Collect the ANU *Sculpture Walk* brochure to get a fine-arts appreciation of the university grounds.

Australian Institute of Sport (AIS)

The country's elite and aspiring-elite athletes hone their sporting prowess at the **AIS** (Map p262; ☎ 6214 1444; www.aisport.com.au; Leverrier Cres, Bruce). Tours (adult/child/concession/family $12/6/9/33 at 10am, 11.30am, 1pm & 2.30pm), led by resident athletes, include information on training routines and diets, displays on Australian champions and the

Sydney Olympics, and interactive exhibits where you can humble yourself at basketball, rowing and skiing.

Other Attractions

You can only peek through the gates of the prime minister's official residence, the **Lodge** (Map pp250-1; Adelaide Ave, Deakin), and the governor general's official residence, **Government House** (Map p262; Dunrossil Dr, Yarralumla). **Scrivener Dam lookout** gives a good view of both.

Canberra's 80-odd diplomatic missions are mostly nondescript suburban houses in Yarralumla, but some are architecturally worthwhile and periodically open to the public. The **Thai embassy** (Map pp250-1; Empire Circuit, Yarralumla), with its pointy orange-tiled roof, is reminiscent of Bangkok temples. The **Papua New Guinea high commission** (Map pp250-1; ☎ 6273 3322; Forster Cres, Yarralumla) resembles a *haus tamberan* (spirit house) from the Sepik region and has a **cultural display** (☼ 9am-1pm & 2-4pm Mon-Fri).

The 79m-tall **Australian-American Memorial** (Map pp250-1; Kings Ave, Russell), a pillar topped by an eagle that, from a distance, looks like Bugs Bunny's ears, recognises US support for Australia during WWII.

The **Church of St John the Baptist** (Map pp250-1; Constitution Ave, Reid) was finished in 1845, its stained-glass windows donated by pioneer families. The adjoining **St John's Schoolhouse Museum** (Map pp250-1; ☎ 6249 6839; Constitution Ave, Reid; admission $2.20; ☼ 10am-noon Wed, 2-4pm Sat & Sun) houses memorabilia from Canberra's first school.

The enterprising **Canberra Tradesmen's Union Club** (Tradies; Map p262; ☎ 6248 0999; 2 Badham St, Dickson; ☼ 8am-5am) has garnished its endless rows of poker machines with a **Bicycle Museum** (admission free), which includes the aptly named Boneshaker Tricycle. The Tradies also operates the Downer Club, where you can make planetary observations at the **Canberra Space Dome & Observatory** (Map p262; ☎ 6248 5333; www.ctuc.asn.au/planetarium; 72 Hawdon Pl, Dickson; adult/child/family $8.50/6/24; ☼ observatory 7.30, 8.30 & 9.30pm Tue-Sat, planetarium 7 & 8.30pm Tue-Sat); bookings essential.

ACTIVITIES

Canberra partakes in plenty of vitalising activities. Bushwalking is plentiful, swimming in river-fed waterholes is a must, and you can hire bikes and skates to roam the city.

Boating

Lake Burley Griffin Boat Hire (Map pp250-1; ☎ 6249 6861; Acton Jetty, Civic) has canoe, kayak, surf ski and paddleboat hire (from $12 per hour); swimming in the lake, however, isn't recommended.

Bushwalking

Tidbinbilla Nature Reserve (p261) has marked tracks. Another great area for walking is **Namadgi National Park** (p261), which is one end of the difficult, 655km-long Australian Alps Walking Track.

Local bushwalking maps are available at **Mountain Designs** (Map pp250-1; ☎ 6247 7488; 6 Lonsdale St, Braddon). The *Namadgi National Park* map ($4.40), available from the Canberra and Namadgi visitors centres, details 23 walks.

Cycling

Canberra has an extensive cycle path network. One popular track circles the lake, while others shadow the Murrumbidgee River. The visitors centre sells the *Canberra Cycleways* map ($6.50) and *Cycle Canberra* ($15), the latter published by **Pedal Power ACT** (www.pedalpower.org.au).

Mr Spokes Bike Hire (Map pp250-1; ☎ 6257 1188; Barrine Dr, Civic; ☼ 9am-5pm Wed-Sun, daily during school holidays) is near the Acton Park ferry terminal. Bikes per hour/half-day/day cost $12/30/40. **Canberra YHA Hostel** (p255), **Canberra City Accommodation** (p255) and **Victor Lodge** (p256) also rent bikes. **Row'n'Ride** (☎ 6254 7838, 0410-547 838) delivers bikes (hired per day/week $39/90) to your door.

In-line Skating

Mr Spokes Bike Hire (Map pp250-1; ☎ 6257 1188; Barrine Dr, Civic) has skating for $11 for the first hour, then $5.50 for each subsequent hour. It also rents skates, as does **Adrenalin Sports** (Map pp250-1; ☎ 6257 7233; Shop 7, 38 Akuna St, Civic), which costs $17 per 2 hours.

Swimming

Canberra's swimming pools include the **Canberra Olympic Pool** (Map pp250-1; ☎ 6248 0132; Allara St, Civic) and the heritage-listed **Manuka Swimming Pool** (Map pp250-1; ☎ 6295 1349; Manuka Circle, Manuka).

See Around Canberra (p261) for information on some inviting waterholes around the city.

WALKING TOUR

The focus of the parliamentary triangle (defined by Lake Burley Griffin, Commonwealth Ave and Kings Ave) is **Parliament House** (1; p247) on Capital Hill. Head north along Commonwealth Ave towards the lake, passing the Canadian, New Zealand and UK **high commissions** on your left. Turn right (east) at Coronation Dr to King George Tce and **Old Parliament House** (2; p247); opposite the main entrance is the **Aboriginal Tent Embassy** (3; p248).

Crossing diagonally (northwest) across the Old Parliament House lawn to King Edward Tce, you arrive at the **National Library of Australia** (4; p249). Beside it is **Questacon** (5; p249), Canberra's interactive science

WALKING TOUR

Distance: 12km
Duration: 3 hours

museum. Towards Kings Ave along King Edward Tce is the **High Court of Australia** (6; p248), while across Parkes Pl is the wonderful **National Gallery of Australia** (7; p248).

Follow King Edward Tce to Kings Ave, turn left (northeast) and follow the avenue across the lake. You'll see the **National Carillon** (8; p247), on Aspen Island to your left. Before reaching the **Australian-American Memorial** (9; p252), at the end of Kings Ave, turn left (northwest) at the roundabout onto Parkes

AUSTRALIAN CAPITAL TERRITORY

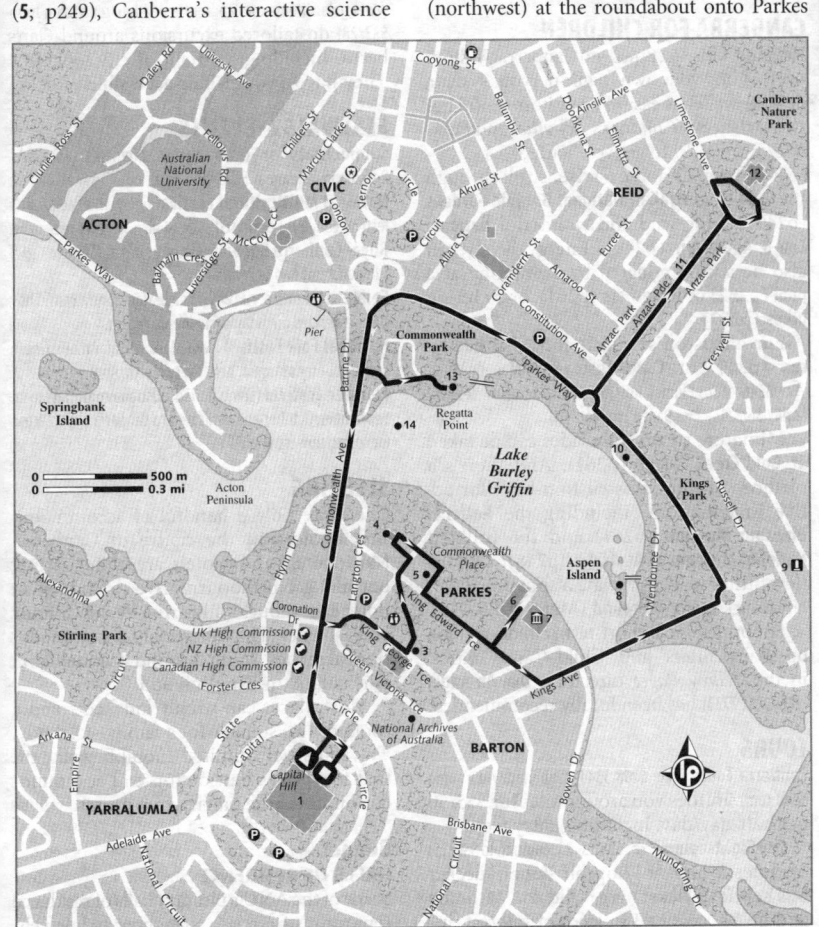

Way, which follows the lake's northern shore. After 1km turn left (south) off Parkes Way to the historic **Blundells' Cottage** (**10**; p247).

Continue along Parkes Way to the next roundabout. **Anzac Parade** (**11**), leading northeast from here, is lined with memorials and ends at the largest, the **Australian War Memorial** (**12**; p249). Return to Parkes Way and follow it to Commonwealth Ave. Turn left (south) and, after 500m, turn left (east) again onto Albert St and follow the path to the **National Capital Exhibition** (**13**; p247) at Regatta Point. Gaze at the **Captain Cook Memorial Water Jet** (**14**; p247) on the lake.

Continue south along Commonwealth Ave to eventually return to Parliament House.

CANBERRA FOR CHILDREN

Keeping kids occupied in Canberra without overloading your own fragile nervous system, or your wallet, is easy. The visitors centre has two factsheets (*Children's Activities* and *Parks & Playgrounds*) to get you started.

For fresh air and exercise, stroll through the lovely **Australian National Botanic Gardens** (p249) or the wild and wonderful **National Zoo & Aquarium** (p249). Energy levels can also be accommodated by swimming at a **pool** (p252) or **waterhole** (p261), or by hiring **bikes** (p252).

For hands-on scientific fun, visit **Questacon** (p249) or **CSIRO Discovery** (Map pp250-1; ☎ 6246 4646; Clunies Ross St, Acton; adult/concession/family $6/3/15; ☼ 9am-5pm Mon-Fri).

Miniature steam train rides can be taken at **Gold Creek Village** (p261). And there's a plethora of museums custom-built for active imaginations, including the **National Dinosaur Museum** (p261) and the brilliant **National Museum of Australia** (p248). The littlest littlies will appreciate a spin on Civic's landmark **merry-go-round** (Map pp250-1).

For professional short-term childcare, look up 'Baby Sitters' and 'Child Care Centres' in the *Yellow Pages* directory. **Dial An Angel** (☎ 6282 7733) has been locally recommended.

TOURS

Canberra Tours (☎ 6298 3344; canberradaytours@bigpond.com) shuttles you around sites for $35/50 per half-day/day, including entry fees.

City Sightseeing (☎ 6257 3423; adult/child $30/15) operates a hop-on, hop-off double-decker bus service. Tickets are valid for 24 hours and give access to 14 places of interest, in-cluding Parliament House and Questacon. The first departure is at 9am from the block south of the Jolimont Centre; services run every 40 minutes after that, up to and including 5pm.

SS Maid Marion (☎ 0418-828 357; adult/child $10/5) operates one-hour cruises that pick-up/drop-off at lakeside locales such as Acton Park ferry terminal and the National Library. There are up to five cruises daily.

For aerial views, take a one-hour ride with **Balloon Aloft** (☎ 6285 1540; tours per adult/child from $180/120) or a noisier flight with **Venture Helicopters** (☎ 6257 0777; Canberra Airport; tours from $80).

The reputable **Go Bush Tours** (☎ 6231 3023; www.gobushtours.com.au; tours per adult/concession from $33/28) do tailored excursions around Canberra, including a circuit of city lookouts. They have a wheelchair-accessible vehicle.

FESTIVALS & EVENTS

Summernats Car Festival (www.summernats.com.au) Revs up in January at Exhibition Park.

National Multicultural Festival (www.multicultural festival.com.au) Celebrated over 10 days in February.

Royal Canberra Show (www.rncas.org.au/Show /default.htm) End of February.

Celebrate Canberra (www.celebratecanberra.com) The city's extended birthday party in mid-March.

National Folk Festival (www.folkfestival.asn.au). One of the country's largest, held every March/April.

Floriade festival (www.floriadeaustralia.com) Held in September/October and dedicated to Canberra's spectacular spring flowers.

SLEEPING

There are only a handful of accommodation choices in the centre of Canberra. Most hotels and motels are either strung out along Northbourne Ave or hidden in northern suburbs like Ainslie, O'Connor and Downer. The other main accommodation area lies south around Capital Hill, particularly in Kingston and Barton.

Most places can supply kids' cots and a room or two suitable for a family-sized stay. Travellers with limited mobility will find that few places outside top-end accommodation have true barrier-free rooms.

Budget
HALLS OF RESIDENCE
Some of the ANU's pleasant halls of residence rent rooms from late November to late Feb-

ruary during university holidays. Most offer similar facilities and room prices start from around $50 (up to $15 more for B&B).

Bruce Hall (Map pp250-1; ☎ 6267 4000) and **Burton & Garran Hall** (Map pp250-1; ☎ 6267 4333) are at the northern end of Daley Rd. The affiliated **Ursula College** (Map pp250-1; ☎ 6279 4303) and **John XXIII College** (Map pp250-1; ☎ 6279 4905) lie to the south, opposite Sullivans Creek.

HOSTELS
Canberra City Accommodation (Map pp250-1; ☎ 6257 3999; www.canberrabackpackers.net.au; 7 Akuna St, Civic; dm $24-26, s/d $55/70; 🖳) This bright, well-managed hostel has an impressive list of services, including a pool, 24-hour reception, a bar, cable TV, continental breakfasts ($4.50) and bicycle hire ($16 per day). It remains fond of backpackers, but has all the facilities to attract other individuals and families.

Canberra YHA Hostel (Map p262; ☎ 6248 9155; canberra@yhansw.org.au; 191 Dryandra St, O'Connor; dm/d/f from $19/55/85; 🅿 🖳) This excellent, purpose-built hostel is in a peace-inducing clump of bushland 6km northwest of the centre, where you'll find bicycles for hire, well-equipped kitchen space and lots of places to just sit. Bus No 35 takes you there.

City Walk Hotel (Map pp250-1; ☎ 1800 600 124, 6257 0124; 2 Mort St, Civic; dm $22-24, s $45-70, d $60-80) This budget hotel is smack in the middle of Civic and is in pretty good shape besides a slight mustiness. The climate is assisted by the fact that you can't smoke or drink alcohol inside.

CAMPING & CARAVAN PARKS
Canberra Motor Village (Map p262; ☎ 6247 5466; canmotorvillage@ozemail.com.au; Kunzea St, O'Connor; camp site $15-21, caravan site $28, d $60-125; 🅿) Dozing in a peaceful bush setting 6km northwest of Civic, this place has an abundance of amenities, motel rooms and self-contained cabins in various sizes, and a laidback ignore-your-watch feel.

Eaglehawk Holiday Park (☎ 6241 6411; www.eaglehawk.contact.com.au; Federal Hwy, Sutton; camp/caravan site $17/22, s & d $70-125, f $90-145; 🅿) This friendly highwayside complex is 12km north of the centre, just over the New South Wales border. It has plenty of sheltered accommodation (campers get the edge of a field) and meals are available at the sometimes noisy pub next door.

Mid-Range
Slightly cheaper motel accommodation can be found in Queanbeyan, 12km southeast of Canberra.

University House (Map pp250-1; ☎ 6125 5211; www.anu.edu.au/unihouse; 1 Balmain Cres, Acton; s $70-130, d $115-180; 🅿) This 1950s building, with furniture to match, is soothingly positioned in the midst of the rambling university grounds. The spacious rooms have small balconies, and there's a pleasant courtyard where you can let your thoughts wander, plus a good wine selection in the cellar bottle shop.

Eagle Hawk Rydges Resort (☎ 6241 6033; www.rydges.com.au; Federal Hwy, Sutton; s & d from $100, f $145; 🅿 🐾) It's well outside the centre on its own expansive block of land, but that's exactly what attracts families to this recreational facility-laden resort. Users of good-standard motels will already be familiar with the rooms.

Motel Monaro (Map pp250-1; ☎ 6295 2111; www.bestwestern.com.au/motelmonaro; 27 Dawes St, Kingston; s/d $90/100; 🅿 🐾) This well-maintained motel, on a quiet street near the coffee-scented Kingston shopping centre, is run by the same convivial folk who manage Victor Lodge next door (see the Author's Choice boxed text; p256). It has a couple of large, multi-bed rooms that are ideal for groups. Book ahead when parliament is sitting.

Tall Trees Motel (Map p262; ☎ 6247 9200; www.bestwestern.com.au/talltrees; 21 Stephen St, Ainslie; d $120-160; 🅿 🐾) The green, fountain-decorated grounds of this accommodating motel and its location in leafy Ainslie lend it a relaxed air. It's a good place to base yourself if you want to be relatively near the centre but outside any hubbub.

Acacia Motor Lodge (Map pp250-1; ☎ 6249 6955; www.acaciamotorlodge.com; 65 Ainslie Ave, Braddon; s/d $75/85; 🅿 🐾) The friendly Acacia is less than 500m from the city centre, making it a pretty good deal despite the small rooms and ramshackle aura; quirky architecture buffs will like the floor-to-ceiling doors. Prices include a light breakfast.

Motel-style **Miranda Lodge** (Map p262; ☎ 6249 8038; book@parkviewcanberra.com.au; 534 Northbourne Ave, Downer; s/d $100/120; 🅿 🐾) has clean-cut rooms in a variety of sizes (some with spa) and puts a full cooked breakfast under your bleary morning eyes. The owners also run the nearby, equally priced

AUSTRALIAN CAPITAL TERRITORY

Parkview Lodge (Map p262; 526 Northbourne Ave, Downer; P 🐾); direct all inquiries to Miranda Lodge.

The pillared facade of **Blue & White Lodge** (Map p262; ☎ 6248 0498; blueandwhitelodge@bigpond .com; 524 Northbourne Ave, Downer; s $80-85, d $90-95, f $110-130; P 🐾) does a good impression of a Masonic temple, though the exterior colour scheme is pure Mediterranean. The prim and comfortable rooms come with cooked breakfasts. The owners also manage the similarly styled **Canberran Lodge** (Map p262; 528 Northbourne Ave, Downer; P 🐾).

The adobe-washed bricks of **Northbourne Lodge** (Map p262; ☎ 6257 2599; 522 Northbourne Ave, Downer; s/d $65/80; P 🐾) aren't altogether convincing, but it has a stylish interior and does breakfast for an extra $10. All rooms have bathrooms.

Top End

Old Stone House (☎ 6238 1888; stnhsebb@tpg.com.au; 41 Molonglo St, Bungendore; s/d $125/180; P 🐾) For a bit of well-catered country living, wander out to Bungendore, 35km east of Canberra. Minding its own private business here is a charismatic 1867 stone house offering B&B in four antique-furnished rooms. There's also a nice garden and you can arrange set dinners ($40–50 per person).

Novotel (Map pp250-1; ☎ 1300 656 565, 6245 5000; www.novotel.com.au; 65 Northbourne Ave, Civic; s & d $160-210; P 🐾 🖳) The 200-room Novotel occupies prime central real estate, adjacent to the Jolimont Centre and just a few minutes' stroll from a satisfying selection of restaurants and shops. Four-star mod-cons include in-room data points, a business centre and a pool.

Olims Canberra Hotel (Map pp250-1; ☎ 1800 020 016, 6248 5511; www.olimshotel.com; cnr Ainslie & Limestone Aves, Braddon; s & d $105-145; P 🐾) This 1927 National Trust heritage–listed build-ing and its later refurbishments surround a terraced courtyard garden. The facade's concrete stubble looks a little worn from close up, but the rooms are well appointed and the facilities are very good.

Pacific International Apartments – Capital Tower (Map pp250-1; ☎ 1800 224 584, 6276 3444; www.pacificinthotels.com.au; 2 Marcus Clarke St, Civic; apt from $195; P 🐾) Rooms on the southern side of this apartment complex's curving facade face Lake Burley Griffin's soporific waters; alternatively, fix your gaze on the courtyard pool. The three-bedroom apartments can fit up to six people.

EATING

Canberra's diverse eateries include some lip-smacking long-stayers. Some places open in a blaze of publicity and die of customer starvation, but even this adds to the local scene's dynamism. Most eateries are in Civic, which has raised its menu standards to compete with upmarket selections in Kingston, Manuka and Griffith. There's also a fantastic Asian strip in Dickson and many other possibilities scattered throughout the suburbs.

Civic

Garema Pl has changed a lot since the days when it served as a nocturnal skateboarding rink and is now replete with eateries and outdoor seating. West Row restaurants are lively at lunchtime.

Caffe della Piazza (Map pp250-1; ☎ 6248 9711; 19 Garema Pl; mains $14-20) It's stretching credibility to compare Garema Pl to a full-on piazza, but it's no exaggeration to say that this decade-old restaurant offers excellent, hearty Italian fare, prime outdoor seating and a heady wine list. Plunge your fork into a mound of *pappardelle con salmone*.

Lemon Grass (Map pp250-1; ☎ 6247 2779; 65 London Circuit; mains $8-16) A favourite of local Thai connoisseurs, this informal place cooks a long list of tasty vegetarian, stir-fry and seafood dishes. If you're a fan of king prawns and garlic, order the *goong gratiam*.

Fringe Benefits Avec Jean-Pierre (Map pp250-1; ☎ 6247 4042; 54 Marcus Clarke St; mains $30) Sample lambs brains, barramundi and other meat-dominated mains in this elegantly simple, award-winning restaurant, where the chef gets top billing. Desserts include *bavarois mandarine* (honey-mandarin mousse with chocolate sauce and lemon tuille).

THE AUTHOR'S CHOICE

Victor Lodge (Map pp250-1; ☎ 6295 7777; www.victorlodge.com.au; 29 Dawes St, Kingston; dm/s/d $25/50/65; P 🖳) This highly welcoming place is a terrific budget option, providing linen, a commercial kitchen (cleaned by the staff), a BBQ area, filling breakfasts and bicycle hire ($15). They'll pick up from Jolimont or the train station; otherwise catch bus No 38, 39 or 80.

Gods Café & Bar (Map pp250-1; ☎ 6248 5538; Arts Centre, University Ave, Acton; mains $8-15) Though yet to open a Mt Olympus branch, this café in the neighbouring university district of Acton makes a refreshing pitstop after wandering the university campus. Offerings range from toasted focaccias to grilled veal kidney. Eat in the main low-lit den or the light-filled sidehall.

Asian Café (Map pp250-1; ☎ 6262 6233; 32 West Row; mains $9-19) Chinese and Malaysian standards like roast duck and laksa are dished out in this brightly coloured café, along with non-Asian stowaways like King Island black-pepper steak. Takeaway is available.

Tosolini's (Map pp250-1; ☎ 6247 4317; cnr London Circuit & East Row; mains $13-20) Fancy pork and veal terrine or three-cheese lasagne? Tosolini's has predominantly rich meaty meals, though there are also some good meatless salads. The roadside tables are less appealing when the traffic cranks up.

Little Saigon (Map pp250-1; ☎ 6230 5003; Alinga St; mains $9-15) There are plenty of Vietnamese meals to clamp your teeth on in this simple eatery. Early afternoon sees a roaring trade in 'lunch boxes': takeaway chicken, beef, pork or vegetarian ($5) accompanied by rice or noodles.

Fast food is on the menu at the Canberra Centre's **food hall** (Bunda St; meals $5-12), including sushi, kebabs, burgers, laksa, gourmet rolls and smoothies.

Manuka
Southeast of Capital Hill is the well-groomed café culture of Manuka shopping centre, which considers itself an upmarket hub for diplomats and businesspeople.

Alanya (Map pp250-1; ☎ 6295 9678; Style Arcade, Franklin St; mains $16-21) This long-standing, authentic Turkish restaurant has plenty of banquet options (including vegetarian) and stand-alone mains like the excellent *hünkâr beğendi* (eggplant, cream and diced lamb).

Atlantic (Map pp250-1; ☎ 6232 7888; 20 Palmerston La; mains $25-30) Loitering discreetly in a small laneway, this is the place to dine formally on a select seafood menu of snapper, kingfish and Western Australian lobster. The rooftop terrace is for sunny liaisons.

My Café (Map pp250-1; ☎ 6295 6632; Franklin St; mains $8-15) This self-possessed café has cheerful meringue walls and sidewalk tables that are inevitably claimed at lunchtime. It's popular for its breakfasts and gourmet bagels and focaccias; try the 'Kakadu' version for a taste of kangaroo.

Legends (Map pp250-1; ☎ 6295 3966; Franklin St; mains $20) Legends serves dependable Spanish food, including house specialities like paella and *bacalao* (salted cod), and there are lots of delicious tapas dishes ($7 to $8.50) to nibble.

Kingston
Kingston has enough gleaming cafés and outdoor seating to give Manuka a run for its latte.

Silo (Map pp250-1; ☎ 6260 6060; 36 Giles St; lunches $10-13) This accomplished bakery can be soothingly subdued outside the breakfast and lunch rushes. Besides breakfast standards like eggs Florentine, it offers unexpected fare like potato, anchovy and chilli jam pizzas. And just try walking out without a passionfruit and mascarpone tartlet.

Santa Lucia (Map pp250-1; ☎ 6295 1813; 21 Kennedy St; mains $12-20) Canberra's first Italian restaurant is three decades old and still going strong. The patent red-and-white-checked tablecloths get smeared with pizza, pasta and meat dishes, and the rustic Italian music is played with gusto.

First Floor (Map pp250-1; ☎ 6260 6311; Green Sq; mains $18-25) Sitting above Green Sq is this fine-dining, minimalist-decor establishment, where the seasonal menus have included lime and chilli-marinated spatchcock and Morocco-spiced eggplant. Sip wines from around Australia.

Dickson
Dickson's consumer precinct is an Asian smorgasbord, where Chinese, Thai, Laotian, Vietnamese, Korean, Japanese, Turkish and Malaysian restaurants compete with other gastronomic treats like Granny's Bakery.

Dickson Asian Noodle House (Map p262; ☎ 6247 6380; 29 Woolley St; mains $9-14) This perennially popular Laotian and Thai café is booked up towards the end of the week, though thankfully there's always takeaway. Within minutes of ordering, eat your fill of wok-fried, Hokkien-style or soup-laden noodles. Pick of the menu is the addictive combination laksa.

Âu Lac (Map pp250-1; ☎ 6262 8922; 39 Woolley St; mains $8-10) This simple Vietnamese vegetarian restaurant employs soybean as a culinary chameleon, making it pretend to be a beef curry, fried fish or honey-roast chicken. The meals are tasty and the service quick. Also recommended:

Green Herring Restaurant (Map p262; ☎ 6230 2657; Ginninderra Village, O'Hanlon Pl, Nicholls; mains $23-26)

Bernadette's Café & Restaurant (Map p262; ☎ 6248 5018; Wakefield Gardens, Ainslie; mains $8-17)

Kingsland Vegetarian Restaurant (Map p262; ☎ 6262 9350; Shop 5, Dickson Plaza, off Woolley St, Dickson; mains $7.50-13)

Aubergine (☎ 6260 8666; 18 Barker St, Griffith; mains $30, degustation with/without wine $110/80)

DRINKING

Canberra's liberal licensing laws have nourished a vigorous drinking scene, with pubs and bars concentrated in Civic but some good establishments also setting themselves up in northern suburbs like Dickson and O'Connor, and southwards in Kingston.

Phoenix (Map pp250-1; ☎ 6247 1606; 21 East Row, Civic) Walking into the cosy Phoenix is like walking into a mellow share-house party, albeit one with a penchant for incense sticks and antique decorations like old jugs. It's a great place for slurred conversation and is unpretentious enough to get away with playing Led Zeppelin on a Friday night.

Toast (Map pp250-1; ☎ 6230 0003; City Walk, Civic) Upstairs behind the Electric Shadows cinema (p259), this great little bar is decked out with pool tables, antique computer games and a relaxed young crowd who come here to lift their spirits (literally) and watch the odd gig (see Live Music; p259).

Hippo (Map pp250-1; ☎ 6257 9090; 17 Garema Pl, Civic) Chilled-out Hippo is indeed hip and, appropriately for a lounge-bar, its dimensions are small. The polished floorboards and red poufs are accosted by a young crowd of cocktail slurpers, who also file in for Wednesday night jazz ($5).

Wig & Pen (Map pp250-1; ☎ 6248 0171; cnr Alinga St & West Row, Civic) This jovial brewery pub is frequented by a down-to-earth crowd. It produces real English ale, served without gas and at a higher temperature than Australian beers. Popular brews include Bulldog Best Bitter and the delicious Pass Porter dark ale.

All Bar Nun (Map pp250-1; ☎ 6257 9191; MacPherson St, O'Connor) This popular suburban bar has a diminutive interior tailor-made for crowded carousing, and tables appealingly

---

THE AUTHOR'S CHOICE

Trinity Bar (Map pp250-1; ☎ 6262 5010; 28 Challis St, Dickson) Sleek, DJ-equipped Trinity has fine vodkas, martinis and cocktails to sample, plus beer pulled from ceiling-hung taps. Start the evening standing at the space-engulfing bar, then marvel at how quickly you slouch on a bar stool and end up slumped incoherently on a couch.

---

sprawled on the sidewalk. Despite its name, it would undoubtedly serve a nun if one ventured in.

King O'Malley's (Map pp250-1; ☎ 6257 0111; 131 City Walk, Civic) More Irish theme park than pub, this derivative liver-disposal centre is notable for its labyrinthine interior, a boisterous end-of-week crowd of office escapees, and the fact that its name literally takes the piss out of the teetotalling bureaucrat who kept Canberra 'dry' until 1928.

For a bit more of the same, head across Northbourne Ave to **P.J. O'Reilly's** (Map pp250-1; ☎ 6230 4752; cnr Alinga St & West Row, Civic), locally referred to as Plastic McPaddy's.

The **Durham Castle Arms** (Map pp250-1; ☎ 6295 1769; Green Sq, Kingston) is known in pint-size shorthand as The Durham. This cosy village pub wannabe might seem anachronistic in the middle of café-filled Kingston, but those who prefer Guinness to an espresso don't mind. Next door is **Filthy McFadden's** (Map pp250-1; ☎ 6239 5303; 62 Jardine St, Kingston), another of Canberra's whisky-drenched Irish dens.

ENTERTAINMENT

Canberra's Friday night wind-down is the week's biggest social event. Mainstream music is as big here as anywhere else, but the city is curiously good at nurturing alternative-music malcontents, and they pop up around town. For entertainment listings, see the 'Times Out' section of Thursday's *Canberra Times* and the free monthly street mag *bma*. For arts news, try the free monthly magazine *Muse*.

Casino

At **Casino Canberra** (Map pp250-1; ☎ 6257 7074; www.casinocanberra.com.au; 21 Binara St, Civic; ☼ noon-6am) you can 'play to win', though there's no money-back guarantee if you lose. The only dress requirement is that you look 'neat and tidy'.

Cinemas

Multiplex cinemas are on Mort St, Civic, and in various suburban shopping malls.

Center Cinema (Map pp250-1; ☎ 6249 7979; Bunda St, Civic; adult/child/concession $14/7/8.50) This downstairs art-house cinema is where you'll see the likes of *Bowling for Columbine* and foreign-language film festivals; matinee sessions (pre-5pm) cost adults $8.50 and all Wednesday sessions are $7.

Electric Shadows (Map pp250-1; ☎ 6247 5060; City Walk, Civic; adult/child/concession $14/7/8.50) Another cinema that prefers the artful approach to a blockbuster rampage. It offers similar matinee and Wednesday discounts to the Center Cinema.

Live Music

Many pubs have free live music.

ANU Union Bar (Map pp250-1; ☎ 6125 2446; www.anuunion.com.au; Union Court, Acton; admission $5-15; ☽ gigs usually 8pm) The Uni Bar is the mainstay of Canberra's live-music scene, with bands up to three times a week during semester. Big touring acts often play in the high-ceilinged Refectory.

Tilley's Devine Cafe Gallery (Map p262; ☎ 6249 1543; cnr Wattle & Brigalow Sts, Lyneham; usually $30) People of all ages breeze in and out of Tilley's cool interior, with its scuffed furniture, dark booths and eclectic menu of musicians and comedians. It also does poetry nights, writers sessions and great cooked breakfasts.

Toast (Map pp250-1; ☎ 6230 0003; City Walk, Civic; admission $2-5; ☽ gigs Fri & Sat) This highly likeable bar has live music (solo acoustic, bands, CD launches) at week's end. It also likes going retro; think Dead Kennedys and Sex Pistols, not ABBA.

Nightclubs

In Blue (Map pp250-1; ☎ 6248 7405; cnr Mort & Alinga Sts, Civic; disco $5 on Sat; ☽ disco Thu-Sat from 7pm) The decibel-ignorant In Blue has a downstairs space that's more sports bar than nightclub, and an upstairs disco that goes for glam over groove – come here if you feel like raucous, centrally located predictability.

icbm & Insomnia (Map pp250-1; ☎ 6248 0102; 50 Northbourne Ave, Civic; Insomnia $5 on Sat; ☽ icbm 7pm-late, Insomnia 9pm-late Wed-Sat) Young drink-

ing crowds similar to those at In Blue also attend this clubbing complex, with the music-blasted bar icbm downstairs and the dancehall Insomnia upstairs, but it arguably plays better clubbing music and diversifies with weekly comedy nights.

Club Mombasa (Map pp250-1; ☎ 0419 609 106; www.clubmombasa.com.au; 128 Bunda St, Civic; events $5-7; ☽ 8pm-late Wed-Sun) The energetic patrons of Club Mombasa spend their long evenings counting the beat to African and Latin rhythms, reggae, hip-hop, funk and drum'n'bass.

Performing Arts

Canberra Theatre Centre (Map pp250-1; ☎ box office 1800 802 025, 6275 2700; www.canberratheatre.org.au; Civic Sq, London Circuit, Civic; ☽ box office 9am-5.30pm Mon-Sat) There are many dramatic goings-on within this highly cultured centre, from Shakespeare to David Williamson plays and indigenous dance troupes. Information and tickets are supplied by Canberra Ticketing, in the adjacent North Building (Eftpos is not available).

Gorman House Arts Centre (Map pp250-1; ☎ 6249 7377; Ainslie Ave, Braddon) Gorman House hosts various theatre and dance companies that stage their own productions, including the innovative moves of the **Australian Choreographic Centre** (☎ 6247 3103).

SHOPPING

The Australian capital is a crafty city, and a good place for picking up creative gifts and souvenirs from galleries, museum shops or markets.

Canberra Centre (Map pp250-1; ☎ 6247 5611; Bunda St, Civic) The city's best shopping centre admits customers to dozens of speciality stores, including fashion boutiques, food emporiums and jewellery shops. The ground-floor information desk can help with wheelchair and stroller hire.

Craft ACT (Map pp250-1; ☎ 6262 9333; www.craftact.org.au; 1st fl, North Bldg, Civic Sq, Civic) There are wonderful exhibitions of contemporary work here, with cutting-edge designs in the shape of bags, bowls, pendants and prints. It's worth visiting just to see the latest imaginative efforts of local and interstate artists.

Old Bus Depot Markets (Map pp250-1; ☎ 6292 8391; Wentworth Ave, Kingston; ☽ 10am-4pm Sun) This popular indoor market specialises in hand-crafted goods and regional edibles, including the output of the Canberra district's 20-plus wineries.

Gold Creek Village (see the Around Canberra section; p261) has numerous shops selling good-quality leatherwork, woodwork, jewellery and other crafts. Visit **Aboriginal Dreamings Gallery** (Map p262; ☎ 6230 2922; 19 O'Hanlon Pl, Nicholls) for an excellent selection of authentic Aboriginal products.

GETTING THERE & AWAY
Air
Canberra airport (☎ 6275 2236) is serviced by Qantas, Virgin Blue and Regional Express (see the Airline Offices section, p246), with flights to Sydney (from $75 one way, 45 minutes) and Melbourne (from $90 one-way, 1 hour). There are also direct flights to Adelaide (from $160 one way) and Brisbane (from $140 one way).

Brindabella Airlines (☎ 6248 8711; www.brinda bella-airlines.com.au) flies between Albury Wodonga, Canberra and Newcastle.

Bus
The interstate bus terminal is at the **Jolimont Centre** (Map pp250-1; Northbourne Ave, Civic), which has left-luggage lockers, showers, public Internet access and free phone lines to the visitors centre and some budget accommodation. Inside, the **Travellers Booking Centre** (☎ 1300 733 323, 6249 6006; ⏰ 6am-11.45pm) and **CountryLink travel centre** (☎ 13 22 32, 6257 1576; ⏰ 7.15am-5pm Mon-Fri) book seats on most services.

McCafferty's/Greyhound (☎ 13 14 99; www .mccaffertys.com.au) has frequent services to Sydney (adult/concession $35/24, 4 to 5 hours) and also runs to and from Adelaide (adult/concession $130/105, 20 hours) and Melbourne (adult/concession $60/50, 9 hours). There are regular services to Cooma (adult/concession $37/30, 1½ hours) and Thredbo (adult/concession $54/43, 3 hours) in winter.

Murrays (☎ 13 22 51; ⏰ counter 7am-7pm) has daily express services to Sydney (adult/concession $35/24, 3¼ hours) and also runs to Batemans Bay (adult/concession $24/22, 2½ hours), Narooma (adult/concession $36/32, 4½ hours) and Wollongong (adult/concession $31/24, 3½ hours).

Transborder Express (☎ 6241 0033) runs daily to Yass (adult/concession $13/9, 50 minutes),

while **Summit Coaches** (☎ 6297 2588) runs to Thredbo (adult/concession $51/45, 3 hours) via Jindabyne on Monday, Wednesday, Friday and Saturday.

Car & Motorcycle
The Hume Hwy connects Sydney and Melbourne, passing about 50km north of Canberra. The Federal Hwy runs north to connect with the Hume near Goulburn and the Barton Hwy meets the Hume near Yass. To the south, the Monaro Hwy connects Canberra with Cooma.

Rental car prices start at around $45 a day. Major companies with Canberra city offices (and desks at the airport):

Avis (Map pp250-1; ☎ 13 63 33, 6249 6088; 17 Lonsdale St, Braddon)

Budget (Map pp250-1; ☎ 1300 362 848, 6257 2200; cnr Mort & Girrahween Sts, Braddon)

Hertz (Map pp250-1; ☎ 13 30 39, 6257 4877; 32 Mort St, Braddon)

Thrifty (Map pp250-1; ☎ 13 61 39, 6247 7422; 29 Lonsdale St, Braddon)

Another option is **Rumbles** (Map p262; ☎ 6280 7444; 11 Paragon Mall, Gladstone St, Fyshwick).

Train
Kingston train station (Map pp250-1; Wentworth Ave) is the city's rail terminus. You can book trains and connecting buses inside the station at the **CountryLink travel centre** (☎ 13 22 32, 6295 1198; ⏰ 6.15am-5.30pm Mon-Sat, 10.30am-5.30pm Sun).

CountryLink trains run to/from Sydney (adult/child $50/24, 4 hours, 3 daily). There's no direct train to Melbourne, but a CountryLink coach to Cootamundra links with the train to Melbourne ($90, 9 hours, 1 daily); the service leaves Jolimont at 10am. A daily V/Line Canberra Link service involves a train between Melbourne and Albury Wodonga, then a connecting bus to Canberra ($58, 8½ hours, 1 daily). A longer but more scenic bus/train service to Melbourne is the V/Line Capital Link ($58, 10½ hours) running every Tuesday and Friday via Cooma and the East Gippsland forests to Sale, where you board the Melbourne-bound train.

GETTING AROUND
To/From the Airport
Canberra airport is 7km southeast of the city. Taxi fares to the city average $18.

AROUND CANBERRA •• Picnic, Swimming & Walking Areas **261**

Deane's Buslines (☎ 6299 3722) operates the AirLiner bus ($5, 20 minutes, 11 times daily Mon-Fri) which runs between the airport and the city interchange (bay 6).

Bus

Canberra's public transport provider is the **ACT Internal Omnibus Network** (Action; ☎ 13 17 10, 6207 7611; www.action.act.gov.au). The main city interchange is along Alinga St, East Row and Mort St in Civic. Visit the **information kiosk** (Map pp250-1; East Row, Civic; ☼ 7.15am-4pm Mon-Fri) for free route maps and timetables, or buy the all-routes *Canberra Bus Map* ($2) from newsagents.

You can purchase single-trip tickets (adult/concession $2.40/1.30), but a better bet for most visitors is a daily ticket (adult/concession $6/3). Pre-purchase tickets from Action agents (including the visitors centre and some newsagents) or buy them from the driver.

For details on the **City Sightseeing** (☎ 6257 3423; adult/child $30/15) hop-on, hop-off double-decker bus service see p254.

Car & Motorcycle

Canberra has an annoyingly circuitous road system, but there are no one-way inner-city streets to further tax your sense of direction, and the wide, relatively uncluttered main roads make driving easy, even at so-called 'peak hour' times.

There's plenty of well-signposted parking in Civic. The visitors centre has a *Motorbike Parking in Canberra* pamphlet.

Taxi

Call **Canberra Cabs** (☎ 13 22 27).

AROUND CANBERRA

For information and maps on attractions around Canberra, ransack the visitors centre.

PICNIC, SWIMMING & WALKING AREAS

Picnic and barbecue spots are scattered throughout the ACT, though they're rarely accessible by public transport. **Black Mountain** is handy for picnics, and swimming spots lie along the **Murrumbidgee** and **Cotter Rivers**. Other popular riverside areas

include **Uriarra Crossing**, **Casuarina Sands**, **Kambah Pool Reserve**, **Cotter Dam** and **Pine Island**.

Across the NSW border in the northwest is **Ginninderra Falls** (☎ 02-6278 4222; Parkwood Rd; adult/child/family $4.50/2.50/10; ☼ 10am-6pm summer, 10am-4pm winter). Swim to it in the fantastic Upper Gorge Pool.

Tidbinbilla Nature Reserve (☎ 02-6205 1233; off Paddy's River Rd), 45km southwest of the city, is threaded with bushwalking tracks, though recovery from the January 2003 fires will take a long time. The facilities at **Corin Forest** (☎ 6235 7333; www.corin.com.au; Corin Rd), which included a flying fox and an alpine slide, were destroyed in the 2003 fires, but were being rebuilt at the time of research; check the website for updates.

Namadgi National Park (camp sites $2.60-3.40 per person) has eight peaks higher than 1700m and offers bushwalking and camping. For further information visit the Namadgi **visitors centre** (☎ 02-6207 2900; Naas Rd; ☼ 9am-4pm Mon-Fri, 9am-4.30pm Sat & Sun), 2km south of Tharwa.

CANBERRA SPACE CENTRE

Within the Canberra Deep Space Communication Complex, 40km southwest of the city, is the **Canberra Space Centre** (☎ 02-6201 7800; www.cdscc.nasa.gov; off Paddy's River Rd; admission free; ☼ 9am-5pm), where there are interesting displays of spacecraft and deep-space tracking technology, plus a piece of lunar basalt scooped up by Apollo XI in 1969.

GOLD CREEK VILLAGE

The attractions at **Gold Creek Village** (Map p262; ☎ 6253 9780; Gold Creek Rd, Barton Hwy, Nicholls; admission free; ☼ 10am-5pm) are a neat combination of colonial kitsch and interesting exhibits.

Giant bones and fossil workshops await at the attention-getting **National Dinosaur Museum** (☎ 02-6230 2655; www.nationaldinosaurmuseum.com.au; adult/child/concession/family $9.50/6.50/7.50/30; ☼ 10am-5pm), while the **Australian Reptile Centre** (☎ 02-6253 8533; adult/child/concession/family $7.50/5/6/26; ☼ 10am-5pm) showcases reptilian life, from tree skinks and scrub pythons to the world's three deadliest (yet surprisingly nonaggressive) land snakes.

Ginninderra Village (admission free; ☼ 10am-5pm) has a couple of worthwhile galleries and an appealing 1860s schoolhouse. Nearby is

AUSTRALIAN CAPITAL TERRITORY

CANBERRA SUBURBS

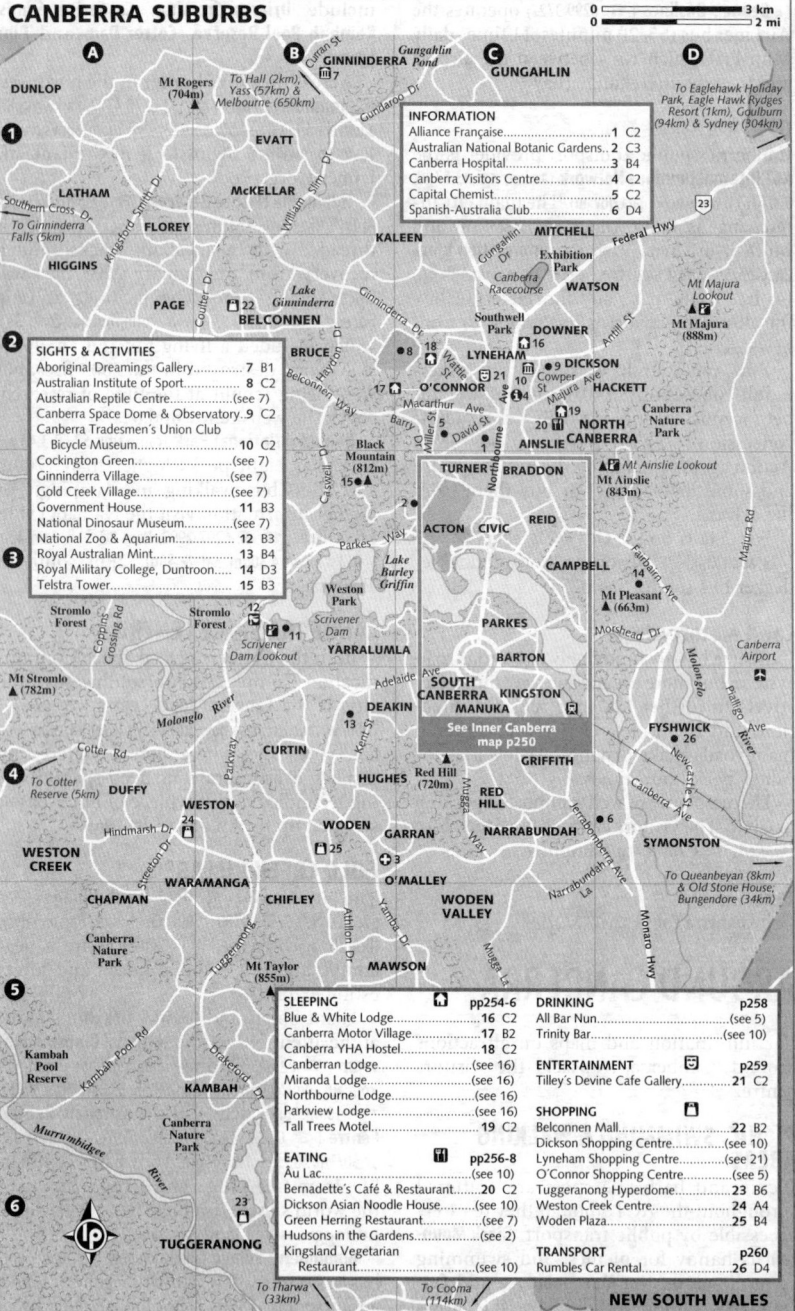

0	3 km
0	2 mi

INFORMATION
Alliance Française..........................**1** C2
Australian National Botanic Gardens..**2** C3
Canberra Hospital..........................**3** B4
Canberra Visitors Centre................**4** C2
Capital Chemist.............................**5** C2
Spanish-Australia Club...................**6** D4

SIGHTS & ACTIVITIES
Aboriginal Dreamings Gallery...........**7** B1
Australian Institute of Sport............**8** C2
Australian Reptile Centre................(see 7)
Canberra Space Dome & Observatory...**9** C2
Canberra Tradesmen's Union Club
  Bicycle Museum............................**10** C2
Cockington Green.........................(see 7)
Ginninderra Village........................(see 7)
Gold Creek Village.........................(see 7)
Government House..........................**11** B3
National Dinosaur Museum...............(see 7)
National Zoo & Aquarium.................**12** B3
Royal Australian Mint.....................**13** B4
Royal Military College, Duntroon......**14** D3
Telstra Tower...............................**15** B3

SLEEPING	pp254-6
Blue & White Lodge........................**16** C2	
Canberra Motor Village...................**17** B2	
Canberra YHA Hostel.....................**18** C2	
Canberran Lodge............................(see 16)	
Miranda Lodge..............................(see 16)	
Northbourne Lodge.........................(see 16)	
Parkview Lodge.............................(see 16)	
Tall Trees Motel............................**19** C2	

EATING   pp256-8
Au Lac.......................................(see 10)
Bernadette's Café & Restaurant.......**20** C2
Dickson Asian Noodle House...........(see 10)
Green Herring Restaurant................(see 7)
Hudsons in the Gardens..................(see 2)
Kingsland Vegetarian
  Restaurant.................................(see 10)

DRINKING   p258
All Bar Nun..................................(see 10)
Trinity Bar...................................(see 10)

ENTERTAINMENT   p259
Tilley's Devine Cafe Gallery............**21** C2

SHOPPING
Belconnen Mall.............................**22** B2
Dickson Shopping Centre.................(see 10)
Lyneham Shopping Centre................(see 21)
O'Connor Shopping Centre...............(see 5)
Tuggeranong Hyperdome..................**23** B6
Weston Creek Centre......................**24** A4
Woden Plaza................................**25** B4

TRANSPORT   p260
Rumbles Car Rental.......................**26** D4

NEW SOUTH WALES

Cockington Green (☎ 02-6230 2273; www.cockington green.com.au; adult/child/concession/family $12/6/9/33; ✆ 9.30am-5pm), an immaculately manicured, too-quaint miniature English village.

OTHER ATTRACTIONS

Beside the Murrumbidgee, 20km south of Canberra, is the beautiful National Trust property **Lanyon Homestead** (☎ 02-6237 5136; Tharwa Dr; adult/concession/family $7/4/15; ✆ 10am-4pm Tue-Sun), explorable via a guided tour. On-site, but in a separate building, is the **Nolan**

Gallery (☎ 02-6237 5192; adult/concession/family $3/2/6; ✆ 10am-4pm Tue-Sun), containing paintings by celebrated Australian artist Sidney Nolan, including famous Ned Kelly art and spray-canned caricatures. You can buy a combined ticket to both homestead and gallery (adult/ concession/family/ $8/5/18.50).

Near Tharwa, **Cuppacumbalong** (☎ 02-6237 5116; Naas Rd; ✆ 11am-5pm Wed-Sun & public holidays) is a 1922 homestead and heritage garden, now a quality Australian craftware studio and gallery.

Queensland

CONTENTS

Queensland is known as the sunshine state, and for good reason. Visitors centres will have you believe that the state receives 300 days of sunshine a year, and while that's hard to believe, the place definitely does have more than its fair share of sunny days. Whether you prefer walking through one of Queensland's excellent national parks, kicking back on sandy, sun-drenched beaches, diving on the incredible Great Barrier Reef, or roaming through the vast expanse of the outback, you're certain to find something to suit your taste.

Brisbane, the state capital, is a lively and cosmopolitan cultural centre, and far and away the largest city. In the north, Cairns is a busy travellers' centre and a base for a whole range of side trips and activities. Between Brisbane and Cairns there are strings of towns and islands offering virtually every pastime you can imagine connected with the sea. Inland, several spectacular national parks are scattered over the ranges.

North of Cairns the Cape York Peninsula remains a wilderness against which people still test themselves. Just inland from Cairns is the lush Atherton Tableland, with countless beautiful waterfalls and scenic spots. Further inland, on the main route across Queensland to the Northern Territory (NT), is the vast outback, a place of big, open skies and dusty roads.

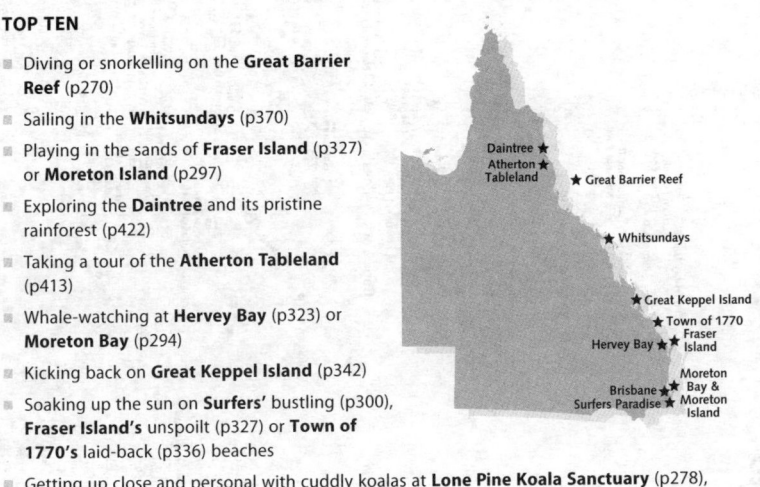

TOP TEN

- Diving or snorkelling on the **Great Barrier Reef** (p270)
- Sailing in the **Whitsundays** (p370)
- Playing in the sands of **Fraser Island** (p327) or **Moreton Island** (p297)
- Exploring the **Daintree** and its pristine rainforest (p422)
- Taking a tour of the **Atherton Tableland** (p413)
- Whale-watching at **Hervey Bay** (p323) or **Moreton Bay** (p294)
- Kicking back on **Great Keppel Island** (p342)
- Soaking up the sun on **Surfers'** bustling (p300), **Fraser Island's** unspoilt (p327) or **Town of 1770's** laid-back (p336) beaches
- Getting up close and personal with cuddly koalas at **Lone Pine Koala Sanctuary** (p278), and not so cuddly crocodiles at **Australia Zoo** (p310)
- Partying like there's no tomorrow in **Fortitude Valley** (p291), Brisbane, or **Surfers Paradise** (p306)

Map labels: Daintree, Atherton Tableland, Great Barrier Reef, Whitsundays, Great Keppel Island, Town of 1770, Hervey Bay, Fraser Island, Brisbane, Moreton Bay & Moreton Island, Surfers Paradise

QUEENSLAND

- TELEPHONE CODE: 07   - POPULATION: 3,635,100   - AREA: 1,727,000 SQ KM

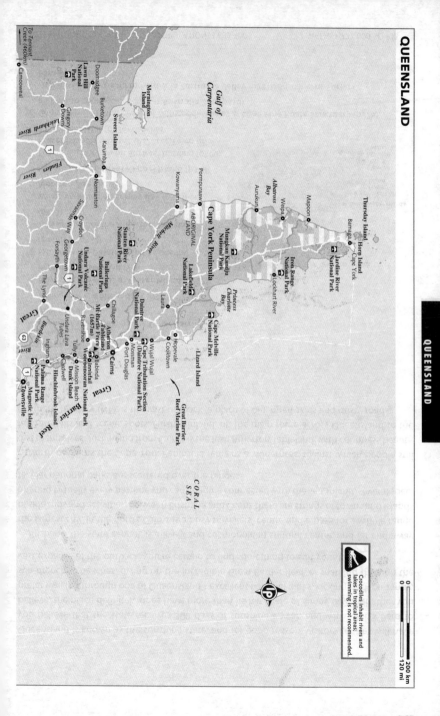

QUEENSLAND

Gulf of
Carpentaria

Cape York Peninsula

ABORIGINAL
LAND

Mornington
Island

Swers Island

Karumba

Normanton

Croydon

Georgetown

The Lynd

Forsayth

Savannah Way

Flinders River

Leichhardt River

Gregory
Downs

Burketown

Doomadgee

Lawn Hill
National
Park

Camooweal

To Tennant
Creek (460km)

Pompuraaw

Kowanyama

Aurukun

Weipa

Mapoon

Albatross
Bay

Iron Range
National Park

Lockhart River

Princess
Charlotte
Bay

Thursday Island
Horn Island
Bamaga
Cape York

Jardine River
National Park

Mungkan Kandju
National Park

Mitchell River

Lakefield
National
Park

Laura

Staaten River
National Park

Undara Volcanic
National Park

Bulleringa
National Park

Chillagoe

Mt Bartle Frere
(1657m)

Ravenshoe

Atherton
Tableland

Mareeba

Cooktown

Hopevale

Cape Melville
National Park

Lizard Island

Wujal Wujal
Cape Tribulation Section
(Daintree National Park)

Daintree
National Park

Mossman

Port Douglas

Cairns

Undara Lava
Tubes

Tully

Innisfail

Mission Beach

Wooroonooran
National Park

Dunk Island

Cardwell

Hinchinbrook Island

Ingham

Paluma Range
National Park

Magnetic Island

Townsville

Great Barrier
Reef Marine Park

Great Barrier Reef

Brisbane
River

Great
Dividing
Range

CORAL
SEA

266 QUEENSLAND

Crocodiles inhabit rivers and
lakes in tropical areas;
swimming is not recommended.

0   200 km
0   120 mi

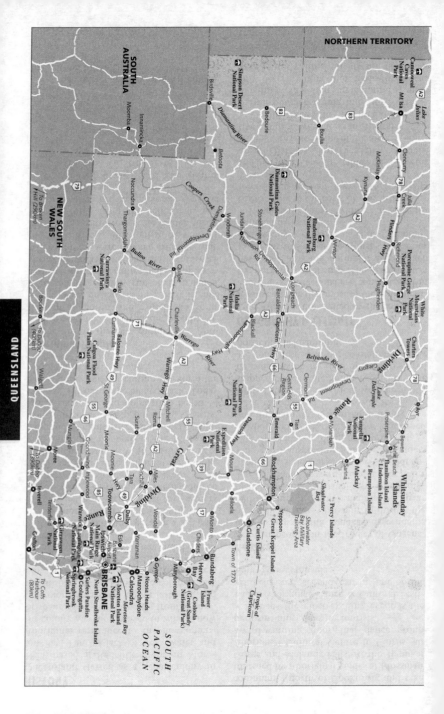

HISTORY

Queensland started as a penal colony in 1824, based at Redcliffe Point on Moreton Bay. Due to lack of fresh water and Aboriginal resistance to the newcomers, the colony was soon moved to what is now Brisbane. Considered too far from Sydney, the colony there also didn't last long and was disbanded in 1839. The colonies did, however, provide a base for free settlers who soon moved in and began exploring the area around Moreton Bay and the Brisbane hinterland.

By 1859 Queensland became a separate colony independent of New South Wales. Wholesale land acquisition by settlers (Queensland's early white settlers indulged in one of the greatest land grabs of all time) met with fierce, but ultimately futile, Aboriginal resistance. With the discovery of gold and other minerals in the 1860s and '70s, and a highly successful experimentation with sugar-cane production, Queensland's economy and population began to explode – it has never looked back. Today both mining and agriculture still form the backbone of the economy.

Aboriginal People

By the turn of the 19th century, the Aborigines who had survived the bloody settlement of Queensland, which saw some of the worst massacres in Australia, had been comprehensively run off their lands, and the white authorities had set up evershrinking reserves to contain the survivors. A few of these were run according to wellmeaning, if misguided, missionary ideals, but the majority were strife-ridden places where people from different areas and cultures were thrown unhappily together as virtual prisoners.

It wasn't until the 1980s that control of the reserves was transferred to their residents and the reserves became known as 'communities'. However, these freehold grants, known as Deeds of Grant in Trust, are subject to a right of access for prospecting, exploration or mining.

Visitor interest has created opportunities for some contact with Aboriginal culture. In addition to the fantastic rock-art sites at various locations, you can encounter living Aboriginal culture at the Yarrabah community south of Cairns and the Hopevale community north of Cooktown, and take tours led by Aboriginal guides at Mossman Gorge and Malanda Falls. At the Tjapukai Aboriginal Cultural Centre in Cairns, an award-winning Aboriginal dance group performs most days for tourists.

Perhaps the most exciting event is the Laura Aboriginal Dance & Cultural Festival, held every second year in June on the Cape York Peninsula.

Kanakas

Another people on the fringes of Queensland society are the Kanakas, descendants of Pacific islanders brought in during the 19th century to work, mainly on sugar plantations, under virtual slave conditions. The first Kanakas were brought over in the 1860s, and soon a brisk business in kidnapping and transporting South Sea islanders (known as blackbirding) had sprung up.

About 60,000 Kanakas were kidnapped and brought to Queensland before the trade was banned by the 1901 Pacific Islands Labourers Act. Most were promptly shipped back to the South Pacific, but the descendants of the 1600 or so who stayed are concentrated in the coastal area to the north of Rockhampton.

GEOGRAPHY & CLIMATE

Queensland is dominated by the coast, and it's no surprise that most of the settlements and tourist attractions are concentrated in the narrow coastal strip. This narrow strip has some amazing natural features such as the Great Barrier Reef, lush rainforests, endless fields of sugar cane and stunning national parks.

Inland is the Great Dividing Range, which comes close to the coast of Queensland before slicing its way down into NSW and Victoria.

Then there are the tablelands – fertile areas of flat agricultural land that run to the west – which are some of the most productive grain-growing areas in Australia.

Finally, there's the vast inland area, the barren outback fading into the Northern Territory (NT). Rain can temporarily make this desert bloom, but basically it's an area of dusty, lonely roads and one-horse towns.

In the far northern Gulf Country and Cape York Peninsula there are huge empty regions cut by countless dry riverbeds, which can become swollen torrents in the wet season. During this time, the whole area becomes a network of waterways, sometimes bringing road transport to a complete halt.

Queensland seasons are more a case of hot and wet or cool and dry than of summer and winter. November/December to April/ May is the wetter, hotter half of the year, while the real Wet, particularly affecting northern coastal areas, is January to March. Cairns usually gets about 1300mm of rain in these three months, with daily temperatures in the 30s (°C). This is also the season for cyclones and, if one hits, the Bruce Hwy can be blocked by the ensuing floods.

In the south, Brisbane and Rockhampton get about 450mm of rain from January to March, and temperatures in Brisbane rarely drop below 20°C. Queensland doesn't really experience 'cold weather', except inland or upland at night from about May to September. Inland, of course, there's also a lot less rain than near the coast (see When to Go p13).

INFORMATION

Queensland has none of the state-run visitors centres that you find in some other states. Instead, there are tourism offices, often privately run, that act as booking agencies for the various hotels, tour companies and so on that sponsor them. As a result, you may not always get full, unbiased or straightforward answers to your questions.

The **Queensland Tourist & Travel Corporation** (☎ 13 88 33; www.tq.com.au) is the government-run body responsible for promoting Queensland interstate and overseas. Its offices act primarily as promotional and booking agencies, not visitors centres, but they are worth contacting when you're planning a trip to Queensland. It also runs the website www.accessiblequeensland.com, which is a good source of information for disabled visitors to the state. The **head office** (Map pp284-6; ☎ 07-3535 4557; qtcbrisbane@tq.com.au; 30 Makerston St; 🕑 8.30am-5pm Mon-Fri, 9am-1pm Sat) is in Brisbane.

Queensland's recent push to increase tourism has resulted in the $110 million **Queensland Heritage Trails Network** (☎ 1800 638 250, 07-3224 4665; www.heritagetrails.qld.gov.au). The Trails Network consists of five trails, some new, some upgraded, that crisscross the sunshine state and pass through 43 major historical attractions. The five trails:

Matilda Hwy NSW border to the Gulf of Carpentaria through the outback.
Overlander's Way Townsville to Mt Isa.
Pacific Coast Hwy Maryborough to Cairns along the coast.
Southeast Queensland Country & Warrego Hwy Brisbane to Charleville.
Tropical North Queensland A collection of trails through Cape York Peninsula.

For more information, see the appropriate sections in this chapter.

The **Royal Automobile Club of Queensland** (RACQ; ☎ 13 19 05; www.racq.com.au) has a series of excellent, detailed road maps covering the state, region by region. RACQ offices are a very helpful source of information about road and weather conditions, and they can also book accommodation and tours.

Adults travelling with children can check out www.families.qld.gov.au for details of child-care centres statewide, or call the **Child Care Information Service** (Map pp284-6; ☎ 1800 637 711, 07-3224 4225; 111 George St, Brisbane). The website www.police.qld.gov.au/toursafe has safety tips for travelling in Queensland.

For comprehensive information on the state you could try Lonely Planet's *Queensland* guidebook.

NATIONAL PARKS

Queensland has about 220 national parks and state forests, and while some comprise only a single hill or lake, others are major wilderness areas. Many islands and stretches of coast are national parks.

Inland three of the most spectacular national parks are **Lamington**, on the forested rim of an ancient volcano on the NSW border; **Carnarvon**, with its 30km gorge southwest of Rockhampton; and, near Mackay, rainforested **Eungella**, swarming with wildlife.

Many parks have camping grounds with toilets and showers, and there are often privately run camping grounds, motels and lodges on the park fringes. Big parks usually have a network of walking tracks.

You can get information directly from park rangers, or from the Queensland Parks & Wildlife Service (QPWS) agencies in most major towns. The QPWS is part of the Environmental Protection Agency (EPA), which has a useful website, www.epa.qld.gov.au.

The main visitors centres:

Central Region Office (☎ 07-4936 0511; cnr Yeppoon & Norman Sts, North Rockhampton)

Naturally Queensland Information Centre (Map pp284-6; ☎ 07-3227 8185; nqic@epa.qld.gov.au; 160 Ann St, Brisbane)

Northern Region Office (☎ 07-4046 6601; Level 1, 2-4 McLeod St, Cairns)

Southern Region Office (☎ 07-3202 0200; 55 Priors Pocket Rd, Moggill)

To camp in a national park (whether in a fixed camping ground or in the bush) you need a permit, available in advance either by calling ☎ 13 13 04, or by booking through the EPA website. Camping in national parks and state forests costs $4 per person per night, or $16 per family. Some camping grounds fill up at holiday times, so you may need to book well ahead. A list of camping grounds is available from QPWS/EPA offices.

The handy *Camping in Queensland* booklet ($7.95) lists camping grounds and facilities at all the national parks and state forests throughout Queensland.

ACTIVITIES
Adrenaline-Charged Activities
Queensland has its fair share of activities to satisfy adrenaline junkies. Bungee jumping and similar thrill rides can be found at major tourist stops, such as Surfers Paradise, Airlie Beach and Cairns. If you need something a tad more heart-stopping, tandem skydiving and parachuting are also easy to find here.

Bushwalking
This is a popular activity year-round. There are excellent bushwalking possibilities in many parts of the state, including several of the larger coastal islands such as Fraser and Hinchinbrook. National parks and state forests often have marked walking trails. Bushwalking favourites among the mainland national parks include Lamington in the southern Border Ranges, Main Range in the Great Divide, Cooloola (Great Sandy National Park) just north of the Sunshine Coast, and Wooroonooran south of Cairns, which contains Queensland's highest peak, Mt Bartle Frere (1657m).

You can get full information from national park and state forest offices. There are bushwalking clubs around the state and several useful guidebooks, including

Bushwalks of the Great South East ($24.95), a QPWS publication with graded walks between Fraser Island and the NSW border. Lonely Planet's *Walking in Australia* includes three walks in Queensland, which range between two and five days in length.

A recent initiative of the state government is the creation of the Great Walks of Queensland. The six walking tracks, set to be completed by mid-2006, are the Whitsundays, Sunshine Coast hinterland, Mackay highlands, Fraser Island, Gold Coast hinterland and the Wet Tropics (tropical North Queensland). The Whitsundays and Fraser Island walks should be up and running by mid-2004. The walks are designed to allow walkers to experience rainforests and bushlands without disturbing the ecosystem. For more information, see the EPA website, www.epa.qld.gov.au.

There are numerous state forests that are open to the public for leisure activities like bushwalking, camping and picnicking. The Forestry Services section of the **Department of Primary Industry** (Map pp284-6; ☎ 07-3234 0111; 160 Mary St, Brisbane) has lots of information on the facilities available at the different state forests in Queensland.

Diving & Snorkelling
The Great Barrier Reef provides some of the world's best diving, and there are dozens of operators vying to teach you how to scuba dive or provide you with the ultimate dive safari. The Queensland coast is one of the world's cheapest places to take your scuba-diving certification – multiple-day diving courses cost anywhere between $250 and $650 – and you almost always do a good part of your learning in the warm waters of the Barrier Reef itself.

Every major town along the coast has one or more diving schools – the three most popular places are Airlie Beach, Cairns and Townsville – but standards vary from place to place and course to course. Diving professionals are notoriously fickle and good instructors move around from company to company – ask around to see which company is currently well regarded.

When choosing a course, look at how much of your open-water experience will be out on the reef. Many budget courses only offer shore dives, which are frequently less interesting than diving on the reef. Normally you have to show you can tread water for 10 minutes and swim 200m before you can start a course. Most schools require a medical, which usually costs extra (around $50).

While school standards are generally high, each year a number of newly certified divers are stricken with 'the bends' and end up in the decompression chamber in Townsville. This potentially fatal condition is caused by bubbles of nitrogen that form in the blood when divers ascend too quickly to the surface – always ascend slowly and, on dives over 9m in depth, take a rest stop en route to the surface.

For divers, trips and equipment hire are available just about everywhere. You'll need evidence of your qualifications, and some places may also ask to see your diving log book. You can snorkel just about everywhere, too. There are coral reefs off some mainland beaches and around several of the islands, and many day trips out to the Great Barrier Reef provide snorkelling gear free.

During the Wet (usually January to March), floods can wash a lot of mud out into the ocean, and visibility for divers and snorkellers is sometimes affected.

Lonely Planet's *Diving & Snorkeling Australia's Great Barrier Reef* is an excellent guide to all the dives available on the reef.

Sailing & Fishing
Sailing enthusiasts will find many places with boats and/or sailboards for hire, both along the coast and inland. Manly (near Brisbane), Airlie Beach and the Whitsunday Islands are possibly the biggest centres and you can indulge in almost any type of boating or sailing. The Whitsundays, with their plentiful bays and relatively calm waters, are particularly popular for sailing; day trips start at $80 and multiple-day trips from $350. Bareboat charters (sailing yourself) are also possible – see 'Sailing the Whitsunday Islands' p372.

Fishing is one of Queensland's most popular sports and you can hire fishing gear and/or boats in many places. Karumba, Cooktown and North Stradbroke Island are some of the more frequented spots.

Surfing
The southeastern coast of Queensland has some magnificent breaks, most notably at Coolangatta, Burleigh Heads, Surfers Paradise, Noosa and Town of 1770. Various surf shops offer board hire, or you can cheaply

---

> **WARNING**
>
> From around October to April, avoid swimming at unprotected beaches north of Rockhampton, where deadly box jellyfish may lurk. If in any doubt, check with locals. If you're still not sure, don't swim; a sting from a box jellyfish has been known to kill in a matter of minutes. Great Keppel Island is usually safe, but during the box-jellyfish season, anywhere further north should be considered risky.
>
> Also in northern waters, saltwater crocodiles are a hazard. They may be found close to the shore in the open sea, or near creeks and rivers – especially tidal ones – sometimes at surprising distances inland.

---

buy second-hand. Surfing lessons are a good idea before you hit the big surf; Surfers and Noosa are good places to learn.

Swimming
North of Fraser Island the beaches are sheltered by the Great Barrier Reef, so they're great for swimming but not good for surfing. The clear, sheltered waters of the reef hardly need to be mentioned. There are also innumerable good freshwater swimming spots around the state.

White-Water Rafting & Canoeing
The Tully and North Johnstone Rivers between Townsville and Cairns are the big ones for white-water rafting. You can do day trips for between $85 and $150, or longer expeditions starting at around $450. See the Cairns section (p400) for details.

Sea-kayaking is also a popular activity, with various trips running from Cairns, Mission Beach, Cape Tribulation, Noosa and Maroochydore.

Coastal Queensland is full of waterways and lakes, so there's no shortage of canoeing territory. You can rent canoes or join canoe tours in several places – among them Noosa, North Stradbroke Island, Townsville and Cairns.

TOURS
There are a multitude of tour operators across the length and breadth of Queensland, offering anything from a 1½-hour trip around Surfers Paradise in a boat on

wheels to a week-long outback adventure. Choosing one can often be a hit-and-miss affair, but you'll find some of the best the state has to offer are mentioned throughout the chapter. Tourism Queensland's website, www.tq.com.au, is another good source of information on tour operators.

GETTING THERE & AROUND

Most travellers will arrive in Queensland from New South Wales, and while your car or bus can legally be inspected crossing the border, it hardly ever happens. You probably won't even notice that you've passed from one state to the other. Brisbane is the main port of call for inbound flights into Queensland. For more information, see the Transport chapter (p981).

Air

Qantas Airways (☎ 13 13 13; www.qantas.com.au) and **Virgin Blue** (☎ 13 67 89; www.virginblue.com.au) fly to Queensland's major cities, connecting them to the southern states and to the NT. There is also a multitude of smaller airlines operating up and down the coast, across the Cape York Peninsula and into the outback. Air may be the only way to reach the Gulf of Carpentaria or the Cape York Peninsula during the Wet. Smaller operators include **Alliance Airlines** (☎ 1300 130 092; www.flightwest.com.au) and **Sunshine Express** (☎ 13 13 13; www.sunshineexpress.com.au), a Qantas affiliate. **Macair** (☎ 13 13 13; www.macair.com.au) is the major outback carrier.

Boat

It's possible, with difficulty, to make your way along the coast or even over to Papua New Guinea or Darwin by crewing on the numerous yachts and cruisers that sail Queensland waters. Ask at harbours, marinas or sailing clubs. Manly (near Brisbane), Airlie Beach, Townsville and Cairns are good places to try. You'll normally have to contribute some money for your passage. For information regarding crewing, see also the boxed text 'Sailing the Whitsunday Islands' (p372).

Bus

McCafferty's/Greyhound (☎ 13 20 30, 13 14 99; www.mccaffertys.com.au), the largest bus company in Australia, offers comprehensive coverage of Queensland and all the major tourist destinations, as well as excellent interstate connections.

The busiest route is up the coast on the Bruce Hwy from Brisbane to Cairns – there are various passes that cover this route, allowing multiple stops along all or part of the coast. YHA/VIP members and International Student Identity Card (ISIC) holders receive a discount on all passes and standard express fares.

McCafferty's/Greyhound offers passes that give you three, six or 12 months to cover a set route. The main limitation is that you can't backtrack, except on 'dead-end' short sectors such as Darwin to Kakadu, Townsville to Cairns and from the Stuart Hwy to Uluru. Rates range from $310 for a one-month unlimited-stop tour from Sydney to Cairns, to $1080 for the Aussie Reef & Rock pass, which covers the east coast from Sydney to Cairns, Darwin, Uluru and Alice Springs.

The more flexible Aussie Kilometre Pass gives you a specified amount of travel to be completed within 12 months, the shortest being 2000km ($320), which is enough for the Brisbane to Cairns run. Allow about 4000km ($530) for the whole east coast.

The other major bus routes are the inland routes going from Brisbane to Mt Isa (continuing into the NT); from Townsville to Mt Isa; and from Rockhampton to Longreach.

Premier Motor Service (☎ 13 34 10; www.premierms.com.au), a small bus operator, runs a limited service from Brisbane to Sydney and Cairns.

Car

Most locals enjoy the luxury of getting around Queensland by car; therefore, roads are generally in good condition, in particular along the coast and main thoroughfares in the hinterland and outback. However, they can often turn into badly maintained sealed roads or dirt tracks in the more remote areas of the state. And it seems quite a few drivers aren't much into speeding – in fact, things are slow paced and they sometimes don't make the speed limit.

Car hire information is scattered throughout the chapter.

Train

The main railway line is the Brisbane to Cairns run. There are also inland services from Brisbane to Charleville, from Rockhampton to Longreach, and from Townsville to Mt Isa. Local services include the *Gulflander* and the *Savannahlander* – see Gulf Savannah on p392 for details. The *Tilt Train* service from Brisbane to Cairns is the world's fastest narrow-gauge railway service, with a top speed of 170km/h. For a list of train services departing Brisbane (and sample fares), see p293.

The Sunshine Rail Pass gives you unlimited travel on all rail services in Queensland for 14 days (economy/1st class $300/430), 21 days ($340/530) or 30 days ($430/640). Another option is the East Coast Discovery, which allows unlimited travel for a period of six months ($205 per person) between Brisbane and Cairns in one direction.

For bookings and information, phone **Queensland Rail's booking service** (☎ 13 22 32; www.traveltrain.qr.com.au; ☷ 6am-8.30pm). If you plan to travel on long-distance trains in Queensland, book as far ahead as you can.

BRISBANE

☎ 07 / pop 1.5 million

Brisbane (known locally as BrisVegas) is the third-largest city in Australia and is fast becoming one of the most desirable places to live. With a prosperous, cosmopolitan atmosphere, a great street-café scene, beautiful riverside parks, a busy cultural calendar and above-average nightlife, it's not hard to see why. As well as having a fantastic climate, Brisbane is the arts capital of Queensland, with dozens of theatres, cinemas, concert halls, galleries and museums. The city is also surrounded by some of the state's major tourist destinations, including the Gold and Sunshine Coasts and the islands of Moreton Bay. Brisbane attracts over five-million visitors each year.

The first settlement here was established at Redcliffe on Moreton Bay in 1824 – a penal colony for difficult convicts from the Botany Bay colony in NSW. After struggling with inadequate water supplies and hostile Aborigines, the colony was relocated to safer territory on the banks of the Brisbane River, before the whole colony idea was abandoned in 1839.

Moreton Bay was thrown open to free settlers in 1842, an action which marked the beginning of Brisbane's rise to prominence and the beginning of the end for the region's Aborigines.

ORIENTATION

The central business district (CBD) of Brisbane is bound by a U-shaped loop of the Brisbane River, about 25km upstream from the river mouth. The action is centred on the

QUEENSLAND

BRISBANE IN...

Two Days

Start with breakfast at one of the casual cafés on **Brunswick St Mall** (p289), Fortitude Valley. From here catch a bus to the CBD and take a stroll down **Queen St Mall**, the heart of Brisbane. Learn about the history of the city at the new **Museum of Brisbane** (p276), then cross the river and meander through the **South Bank Parklands** (p277). Stop in at the **Queensland Museum** (p276) and at the **Queensland Art Gallery** (p277) before heading to the **West End** (p289) for dinner. If you still have some energy left, head to **Fortitude Valley** (p290) for a drink or two, or a night out clubbing.

Day two, take a river ferry to **Lone Pine Koala Sanctuary** (p278), then a bus to the top of **Mt Coot-tha** (p277) for far-reaching views. Back in the city, dine at **Chinatown** (p289) in Fortitude Valley. If you feel like living it up, spend both nights at the glorious **Conrad Treasury** hotel (p288).

Four Days

After exhausting all the possibilities of the two-day itinerary, either catch an early train to Cleveland, from where you can take a ferry to **North Stradbroke Island** (p296) and its superb beaches, or hire a bicycle and avail yourself of Brisbane's **500km of bike tracks**. On the fourth day take it easy and board a river ferry for Bretts Wharf and lunch at the **Breakfast Creek Hotel** (p290). Spend the afternoon digesting the huge steak while wandering back to the CBD along the river, then take in the **City Botanic Gardens** (p276) and the arty **QUT Art Museum** (p276).

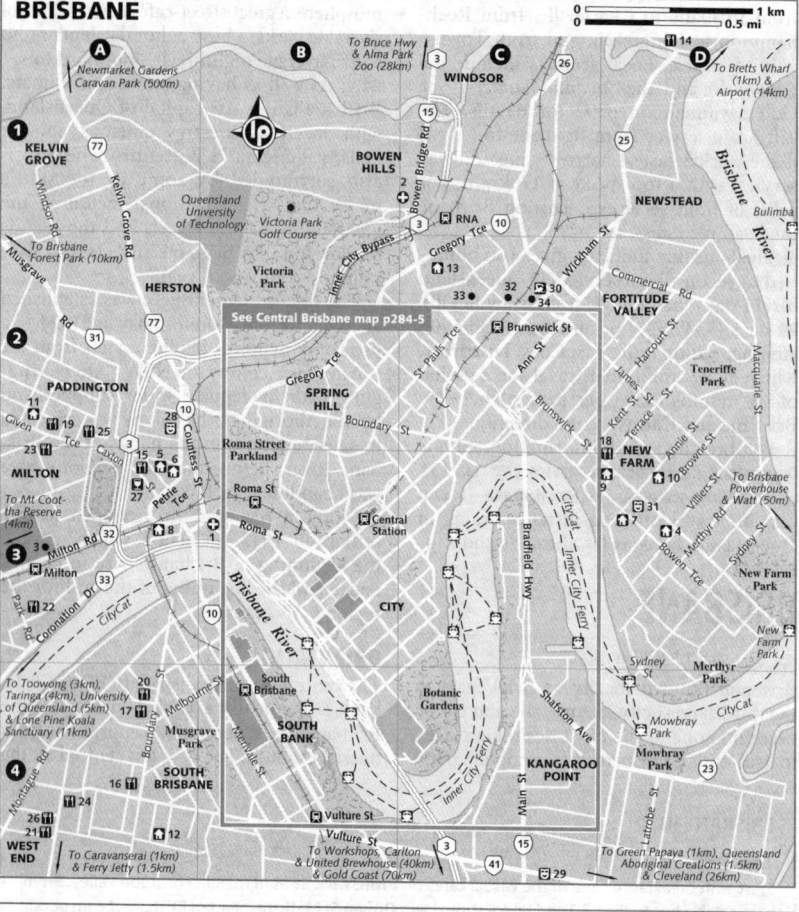

BRISBANE

To Bruce Hwy & Alma Park Zoo (28km)

To Brett's Wharf (1km) & Airport (14km)

Newmarket Gardens Caravan Park (500m)

WINDSOR

KELVIN GROVE

BOWEN HILLS

NEWSTEAD

Queensland University of Technology

Victoria Park Golf Course

RNA

HERSTON

To Brisbane Forest Park (10km)

Victoria Park

FORTITUDE VALLEY

PADDINGTON

See Central Brisbane map p284-5

Brunswick St

SPRING HILL

Teneriffe Park

MILTON

Roma Street Parkland

NEW FARM

To Mt Coot-tha Reserve (4km)

Roma St

Central Station

To Brisbane Powerhouse & Watt (50m)

Milton

CITY

New Farm Park

To Toowong (3km), Taringa (4km), University of Queensland (5km) & Lone Pine Koala Sanctuary (11km)

South Brisbane

Botanic Gardens

New Farm Park

Merthyr Park

Musgrave Park

SOUTH BANK

Mowbray Park

SOUTH BRISBANE

KANGAROO POINT

Mowbray Park

WEST END

Vulture St

To Caravanserai (1km) & Ferry Jetty (1.5km)

Vulture St

To Workshops, Carlton & United Brewhouse (40km) & Gold Coast (70km)

To Green Papaya (1km), Queensland Aboriginal Creations (1.5km) & Cleveland (26km)

QUEENSLAND

pedestrianised Queen St Mall, which runs down to the Treasury Casino and Victoria Bridge to South Bank. The Roma St Transit Centre, where you'll arrive if you're coming by bus, train or airport shuttle, is on Roma St, about 500m west of the city centre.

South across Victoria Bridge is South Brisbane, with the Queensland Museum &

Art Gallery and the South Bank Parklands; further south is the hip West End.

River transport provides a fast and easy way of getting around the city. CityCats (fast catamarans) and Inner City Ferries run from the University of Queensland in the west to Bretts Wharf in the east – pick up a copy of the *Brisbane River Experience* guide from the visitors centre.

Maps
Visitors centres hand out free maps with detail of the CBD, but not much else. Otherwise, try *Brisbane and Region* by Hema Maps ($5.95) or *Suburban Brisbane* by Gregory's ($5.95).

INFORMATION
Bookshops
Archives Fine Books (Map pp284-6; ☎ 3221 0491; 40 Charlotte St) A fantastic range of second-hand titles.
Borders Bookstore (Map pp284-6; ☎ 3210 1220; cnr Albert & Elizabeth Sts) Largest bookstore in Brisbane.
World Wide Maps & Guides (☎ 3221 4330; Anzac Square, 267 Edwards St) Biggest range of travel guides and maps to be found in Brisbane.

Emergency
Ambulance (☎ 000, 3364 1246)
Brisbane Rape Crisis Centre (☎ 3844 4008)
Fire (☎ 000, 3247 5539)
Lifeline (☎ 131 114)
Police (☎ 000, 3364 6464)
RACQ Queen St (Map pp284-6; ☎ 131 905; Queen St); St Pauls Tce (Map pp284-6; ☎ 131 905; 300 St Pauls Tce) Roadside service.

Internet Access
The southwestern end of Adelaide St is peppered with Internet cafés. Most of Brisbane's backpacker hostels offer Internet access.
Central City Library (Map pp284-6; ☎ 3403 4166; City Plaza Complex) Free Internet access for half an hour per day, but it must be booked in advance.
Global Gossip (Map pp284-6; ☎ 3229 4033; 288 Edward St; ☽ 8am-midnight)
State Library of Queensland (Map pp284-6; ☎ 3840 7666; South Bank) Free Internet access, but advanced booking is essential.

Left Luggage
Central Station (Map pp284-6; ☎ 3235 2222; Ann St) Lockers $4 for 24hr.
Roma St Transit Centre (Map pp284-6; ☎ 3235 2222; Roma St) Lockers $6 for 24hr.

BRISBANE FOR DISABLED VISITORS
Disabled visitors can obtain some useful maps and brochures – check out *Access Brisbane, Accessible Brisbane Parks, Brisbane Mobility Map* and *Brisbane Braille Trail* – about disabled access in Brisbane from **BCC Customer Services Centre** (☎ 3403 8888; City Plaza Complex), behind the City Hall; from city libraries; or by contacting the **Disability Information Awareness Line** (☎ 1800 177 120; dial@families.qld.gov.au).

Medical Services
Brisbane Sexual Health Clinic (Map p274; ☎ 3227 8666; 270 Roma St)
Dentist (☎ 3221 0677; 138 Albert St; ☽ 24hr)
Pharmacy (☎ 3221 4585; 141 Queen St; ☽ 24hr)
Royal Brisbane Hospital (Map p274; ☎ 3253 8111; Hertson Rd, Hertson; ☽ 24hr casualty ward)
Travellers' Medical Service (Map pp284-6; ☎ 3211 3611; 1st fl, 245 Albert St; ☽ 24hr)
Travellers' Medical & Vaccination Centre (TMVC; Map pp284-6; ☎ 3221 9066; 5th fl, 247 Adelaide St) Vaccinations and medical advice for travellers.

Money
Exchange bureaus are open at Brisbane airport for all arriving flights. Most banks have exchange bureaus as well as ATMs.
American Express (Amex; Map pp284-6; ☎ 1300 139 060; 131 Elizabeth St)
Thomas Cook Queen St Mall (☎ 3210 6325; Myer Centre, street level, Queen St Mall); Edward St (☎ 3221 9422; 276 Edward St)
Travelex (☎ 3229 8610; Lennon Plaza, Queen St Mall)

Post
General Post Office (Map pp284-6; ☎ 3221 6378; Queen St) Imposing Victorian building between Edward and Creek Sts; has a poste-restante counter.

Tourist Information
Brisbane Tourism visitors centre (Map pp284-6; ☎ 3006 6200; www.ourbrisbane.com; ☽ 9am-6pm Mon-Thu, 9am-8pm Fri, 9am-5pm Sat, 9.30am-4.30pm Sun) Conveniently located in the middle of the Queen St Mall, this is the best place to find out about sights and activities in the city. It can book almost anything for you.
South Bank visitors centre (Map pp284-6; ☎ 3867 2051; Stanley St Plaza; ☽ 9am-6pm, closes 9pm Fri) A useful information point in the South Bank Parklands.

Travel Agencies

STA Travel (Map pp284-6; ☎ 3221 3722; 111 Adelaide St)

Trailfinders (Map pp284-6; ☎ 3229 0887; 91 Elizabeth St)

YHA Membership & Travel office (Map pp284-6; ☎ 3236 1680; 154 Roma St) Can arrange travel, YHA membership and YHA hostel bookings.

SIGHTS

Most of Brisbane's major sights can be found in the CBD or within easy walking distance of it. The freebie brochure *Brisbane's Living Heritage* (www.brisbane livingheritage.com), available from the visitors centres, highlights many of the sights Brisbane has on offer.

City Centre   Map pp284–6

Brisbane City Hall (☎ 3403 4048; btwn Ann & Adelaide Sts; admission free, viewing tower adult/child $2/1; ☑ lift & viewing tower 10am-3pm Mon-Fri, 10am-2pm Sat) is a historic sandstone edifice overlooking the sculptures and fountains of King George Square. It's surrounded by modern skyscrapers, but the observation platform up in the bell tower still provides one of the best views across the city. On the ground floor is the new **Museum of Brisbane** (☎ 3403 4048; admission free; ☑ 10am-5pm), showcasing the city's past, present and future through static and interactive displays and a 30-minute film on Brisbane's humble beginnings. The museum also incorporates the **Brisbane City Gallery**, which features a mixture of local and international artists.

There are many attractive historical buildings dotted around the city centre. Probably the most grand is the old **Treasury Building** (☎ 3306 8888; 21 Queen St), near the Victoria Bridge, which is now Brisbane's 24-hour casino. Just to the south is another building of note, the **Commissariat Stores Building** (☎ 3221 4198; 115 William St; adult/child $4/2; ☑ 10am-4pm Tue-Sun), built in 1829 and recently reopened as a convict and colonial museum. The **Old Windmill & Observatory** (Wickham Tce), which is closed to the public, was built in 1828 and pips the Stores at the post as Brisbane's oldest surviving building. It can be found just northeast of the Roma St Transit Centre.

Further south of the Stores along George St is **Parliament House** (☎ 3406 7111; cnr Alice & George Sts; admission free; ☑ 9am-5pm Mon-Fri), where you're free to watch the lawmakers in action from the public balcony on sitting days. Free tours leave on demand each weekday (only two tours daily when parliament is sitting). The structure dates from 1868, with a roof clad in Mt Isa copper.

Continuing south on George St you'll hit the **QUT Art Museum** (☎ 3864 2797; 2 George St; admission free; ☑ 10am-4pm Tue-Fri, noon-4pm Sat & Sun), in the Queensland University of Technology (QUT) campus. This challenging museum features contemporary art from around the world but focuses mainly on home-grown works, including pieces from QUT students. Exhibits change constantly and guided tours are available, but must be booked.

Next door is **Old Government House** (☎ 3864 8005; George St; admission free; ☑ 10am-4pm Mon-Fri), the original home of the Governors of Brisbane, built in 1862. Some of the rooms have been restored to their original state, but there's not a huge amount to see.

Brisbane's **City Botanic Gardens** (☎ 3403 0666; Albert St; ☑ 24hr, free guided tours 11am & 1pm Mon-Sat) is a pleasant respite from the busy city and a firm favourite of lunching office workers. The gardens are dominated by lots of open, grassy walking areas and are popular with strollers, joggers, picnickers, cyclists and in-line skaters. The park is partly lit up at night and you stand a good chance of seeing tame possums here. There's a pleasant café inside the former curator's cottage at the southern end.

Another garden offering quiet respite close to the centre is the new **Roma St Parkland** (☎ 3006 4545; Albert St; admission free; ☑ dawndusk, free guided tours 10am & 2pm Thu-Sun Sep-May, 11am & 2pm Thu-Sun Jun-Aug), where you'll find subtropical gardens (the world's largest in a city centre), kid's playgrounds and a small outdoor theatre.

Queensland Cultural Centre

In South Bank, just over the Victoria Bridge from the CBD, is the extensive Queensland Cultural Centre.

At the back of the complex, the **Queensland Museum** (Map pp284-6; ☎ 3840 7555; enter on Grey St; admission free; ☑ 9.30am-5pm) has an eclectic collection of exhibits relating to the history of Queensland, from a skeleton of Queensland's own dinosaur *Muttaburrasaurus* to the Avian Cirrus, the tiny plane in which

Queensland's Bert Hinkler made the first England to Australia solo flight in 1928. There's also a section entitled *Discover Queensland*, which focuses mainly on the diversity of the state's wildlife, but also includes a fantastic selection of Melanesian artefacts and a captured German tank from WWI. Be sure to check out the museum's **Sciencentre** (www.sciencentre.qld.gov.au), a hands-on science exhibit with interactive displays, optical illusions, a perception tunnel and regular film shows.

The **Queensland Art Gallery** (Map pp284-6; ☎ 3840 7303; www.qag.qld.gov.au; enter on Melbourne St; admission free; ☼ 10am-5pm Mon-Fri, from 9am Sat & Sun, free guided tours 11am, 1pm & 2pm Mon-Fri, 11am, 1pm & 3pm Sat & Sun) has an impressive permanent collection of works by European and Australian artists, and also features visiting exhibitions. If you have kids in tow over the school holiday period, this is a perfect place to bring them; the gallery organises all manner of activities to keep them entertained.

South Bank Parklands
Map pp284–6

These impressive **parklands** (admission free; ☼ dawn-dusk) owe their existence to Expo '88, but unlike most relics from international shows, South Bank has been extensively redeveloped over the years to keep things fresh and interesting.

The most distinctive feature here is **Pauls Breaka Beach**, an unusual artificial swimming beach designed to resemble a tropical lagoon. Behind the beach is **Stanley St Plaza**, a renovated section of historic Stanley St, with shops, cafés and a visitors centre.

Running inland from the plaza is Ernest St, where you'll find the IMAX Theatre (see Cinemas in the Entertainment section on p291).

The parklands are within easy walking distance of the city centre, but you can also get here by CityCat or Inner City Ferry (there are three jetties along the riverbank), or by bus or train from Roma St or Central stations.

Maritime Museum
At the western end of the South Bank promenade, the **Maritime Museum** (Map pp284-6; ☎ 3844 5361; Sidon St, South Brisbane; adult/child $6/3, tug-boat trips $50/30; ☼ 9.30am-4.30pm) has a wide range of maritime displays, including

artefacts recovered from wrecks along the Queensland coast, ship models and the HMAS *Diamantina*, a restored 1945 naval frigate that you can clamber around to indulge your naval-battle fantasies. For more nautical pleasure, tug-boat trips from the museum to the mouth of the Brisbane River and back again take place on Sunday (and occasionally Saturday) from April to mid-June. Trips include morning and afternoon tea, and lunch; bookings are essential.

Naval Stores
Originally built in the mid-1880s to house munitions and weapons, the **Naval Stores** (Map pp284-6; ☎ 3403 888; riverside, Kangaroo Point; admission free; ☼ 10am-4pm Sat-Mon) now plays a more peaceful role in Brisbane. Inside you'll find displays on the history of Brisbane's naval defences, the Brisbane River and Kangaroo Point. Best of all is the interactive map, which shows the development of Brisbane from its humble beginnings in 1824 to the present day.

Mt Coot-tha Reserve
A short bus ride or drive west of the city centre, **Mt Coot-tha Reserve** is a huge bush and parkland that has an excellent botanic garden and a great lookout over the city, with impressive views; on a clear day you can see all the way to Moreton Bay and the bay islands. There's a café serving snacks, plus the posh **Summit Restaurant** (☎ 3369 9922; mains around $30), which serves great food, though you pay more because of the location.

Just north of the road to the lookout, on Sir Samuel Griffith Dr, is the turn-off to **JC Slaughter Falls**, reached by a short walking track. Also here is a 1.8km **Aboriginal Art Trail**, which takes you past eight art sites with works by local Aboriginal artists.

The very beautiful **Brisbane Botanic Gardens** (☎ 3403 8888; admission free; ☼ 8.30am-5.30pm, free guided walks 11am & 1pm Mon-Sat), at the foot of the mountain, cover 52 hectares and include an enclosed tropical dome, an arid zone, rainforests and a Japanese garden, plus a restaurant.

Within the gardens is the **Sir Thomas Brisbane Planetarium** (Cosmic Skydome; ☎ 3403 2578; adult/child $10.50/6.50), the largest planetarium in Australia. There are 45-minute shows at 3.30pm Wednesday to Friday; 1.30pm, 3.30pm and 7.30pm Saturday; and 1.30pm

QUEENSLAND

and 3.30pm Sunday. The shows are not recommended for young children.

Take bus No 471 to Mt Coot-tha; it departs about once every hour from Adelaide St, opposite King George Square. The same bus passes the Brisbane Botanic Gardens on its way back down, so you can either walk or ride down to the gardens and get a later bus back to town. The last trip to the city leaves at around 4pm Monday to Friday, and 5pm weekends.

Brisbane Forest Park

This 28,500-hectare natural bushland reserve in the D'Aguilar Range is a hugely popular recreation area for city dwellers, and starts around 10km from the city centre. At the park entrance the Brisbane Forest Park **visitors centre** (☎ 3300 4855; 60 Mt Nebo Rd; ☽ 8.30am-4.30pm Mon-Fri, from 9am Sat & Sun) has information about bush **camping** (per person/family $4/16) in the park and maps of walking trails. Guided walks are also available. Although there is public transport to the visitors centre (bus No 385 from the corner of Albert and Adelaide Sts), there is none to the actual walks, which are a fair distance from the centre. If you are planning on attacking the park walks, it's best to have your own transport.

Beside the visitors centre is **Walk-About Creek** (adult/child/family $3.50/2/10; ☽ 9am-4.30pm), a freshwater study centre where you can see a resident platypus up close, as well as fish, lizards, pythons and turtles.

Workshops

A trainspotter's dream come true, **Workshops** (☎ 3432 5100; www.theworkshops.qm.qld.gov.au; North St, Ipswich; adult/child/family $12.50/6.50/36, tours $5/3/13; ☽ 9.30am-5pm) is located in the oldest working railway yard in Australia. The museum is devoted solely to rail, and even if trains bore you to tears you'll definitely find

something of interest. There are a plethora of engines to climb on and explore, plenty of hands-on activities and displays, and a massive model railway for kids of all ages. Guided tours depart throughout the day.

The museum is about 40km southwest of the city centre. To get here, take a CityTrain to Ipswich train station, then hop on bus No 4 or 5.

Wildlife Sanctuaries
LONE PINE KOALA SANCTUARY

Just a 35-minute bus ride south of the city centre, **Lone Pine Koala Sanctuary** (☎ 3378 1366; adult/child $15/10, VIP & YHA cardholder $12; ☽ 8.30am-5pm) is the largest of its kind in the world. Set in attractive parklands beside the river, it's home to 130 or so koalas, as well as kangaroos, possums and wombats. The koalas are undeniably cute and most visitors readily cough up the $15 to have their picture taken hugging one. You can get here on the hourly No 430 express bus ($3.40), which leaves from the Queen St Mall bus station (under the Myer Centre).

Alternatively, the **MV Mirimar** (☎ 3221 0300) cruises to the sanctuary along the Brisbane River from North Quay, next to Victoria Bridge. It departs daily at 10am, returning from Lone Pine at 1.30pm (adult/child $16/10 one way, $25/15 return).

ALMA PARK ZOO

Twenty-eight kilometres north of the city centre off Bruce Hwy (exit Boundary Rd), the **Alma Park Zoo** (☎ 3204 6566; Alma Rd, Dakabin; adult/child/family $20/10/50; ☽ 9am-5pm, last entry 4pm) has a large collection of Australian native birds and mammals, including koalas, kangaroos, emus and dingoes, as well as exotic species such as Malaysian sun bears, leopards and monkeys. You can touch and feed many of the animals – feeding times are between 11am and 2.30pm. A special

---

BRIGHTENING UP THE CITY

What do you do with a dull grey box that sticks out like a sore thumb? Why, turn it into a piece of art of course. Tired of unimaginative traffic signal boxes (TSBs) scattered across the city, the city council formed a project to recruit volunteer artists to paint the TSBs. The idea was to create a street-side art gallery to avail the senses, and it has worked – most, if not all, of the 700 or so TSBs have been lovingly, colourfully and artfully painted. Some blend in well with their surroundings, while others still stick out like sore thumbs (but well-dressed sore thumbs). And it's a credit to the Brisbane population that these works of art have yet to be vandalised.

zoo train runs every day on the Caboolture line from Roma St Transit Centre at 9am, connecting with the zoo bus at Dakabin.

ACTIVITIES

Brisbane is not only about sightseeing, it also has its fair share of activities. And being a relatively flat city, cycling and in-line skating are among the most popular free-time activities for locals and visitors alike.

Climbing

The **Cliffs rock-climbing area** (Map pp284–6), on the southern banks of the Brisbane River at Kangaroo Point, is a decent venue that is floodlit every evening. Several operators offer climbing and abseiling instruction here, including **Jane Clarkson's Outdoor Adventures** (☎ 3870 3223; 200 Moggill Rd, Taringa; climbing $15; ♈ 9.30am-5.30pm Mon-Fri, 9am-4pm Sat, 10am-3pm Sun). You can join its rock-climbing club meets any Wednesday night at 6pm; just make your way to the base of the cliffs.

Cycling

Brisbane has some excellent bike tracks, particularly along the Brisbane River. Pick up a copy of the city council's *Brisbane Bicycle Experience Guide* booklet from visitors centres, which highlights 500km of cycleways around the city.

A good way to spend a day is to ride the riverside bicycle track from the city Botanic Gardens out to the University of Queensland. It's about 7km one way and you can stop for a beer at the Regatta pub in Toowong.

Brisbane Bicycle Sales (Map pp284-6; ☎ 3229 2433; 87 Albert St; bike hire per hr/day $12/25; ♈ 8.30am-5pm Mon-Sat, from 10am Sun) hires out mountain bikes, as does **Valet Cycle Hire** (☎ 0408-003 198; Holt St, Eagle Farm). The latter also offers afternoon guided tours ($38).

Bicycles are allowed on CityTrains, except on weekdays during peak hours. You can also take bikes on CityCats and ferries for free.

In-line Skating

For something a little different, take an in-line skate tour of Brisbane with **Planet Inline** (☎ 3255 0033; www.planetinline.com; tours $15-20), which take place every Sunday, weather permitting. Lessons are also available if you're not comfortable on eight wheels. In-line skates can be hired from **Skatebiz** (Map pp284-6; ☎ 3220 0157; 101 Albert St; ♈ 9am-5.30pm Mon-Thu, 9am-9pm Fri, 9am-4pm Sat, 10am-4pm Sun).

Swimming

There are several good swimming pools in Brisbane, generally open from 6am or 7am until 7pm daily and costing around $5/3 for adults/children.

Splash Leisure Pool (Map pp284-6; ☎ 3831 7665; 400 Gregory Tce, Spring Hill) One of the biggest in Brisbane.

Valley Swimming Pool (Map p274; ☎ 3852 1231; 432 Wickham St, Fortitude Valley)

Pauls Breaka Beach (Map pp284-6; South Bank Parklands)

Other Activities

Take to the skies over Brisbane from $230 with any of the following places.

Brisbane Skydiving Centre (☎ 1800 061 555; www.brisbaneskydive.com.au)

Fly Me to the Moon (☎ 3423 0400; www.flymetothemoon.com.au)

Balloon Aloft (☎ 5578 2244; www.balloonaloft.net; 13 Lake Dr, Carrara)

WALKING TOUR

With its downtown parks, riverside paths, historic buildings and gentle landscape, Brisbane is a great place to explore on foot. *Heritage Experience Guides*, free walking-trail booklets produced by the city council, make great walking companions. To date, three are available: *Impressions on the Landscape*, *Shadows of the Past* and *Reflections on the River*. The following walk, which covers about 5km and takes anything between a couple of hours to a full day, dips into all three.

> **WALKING TOUR**
>
> Distance: 5.3km
> Duration: 1.5–2 hours

The logical starting point for a walking tour of the centre is the imposing classical-style **Brisbane City Hall** (1; p276), where you should take the lift up to the top of the bell tower for the view over the CBD, and read up on the history of the city at the Museum of Brisbane.

QUEENSLAND

From City Hall, turn southeast and head along Albert St until you hit the **Queen St Mall** (**2**). This busy pedestrian mall is the commercial centre of Brisbane, and is lined with fine façades dating back to Australia's federation, including the glorious frontage of the old **Hoyts Regent Theatre** (**3**), a short detour east.

Turn right onto Queen St Mall and follow it until you hit George St. Diagonally opposite you'll see the unmistakable Italian-Renaissance **Former Treasury Building** (**4**; p276). Turn left onto George St and you'll pass another spectacular Italian-Renaissance building, the **Land Administration Building** (**5**; now the Conrad Treasury Hotel). Take the small alley just south of the hotel (Stephens Lane) onto William St and head

right, passing the historic **Commissariat Stores Building** (**6**; p276).

Cross the Victoria Bridge to **South Bank Parklands** (**7**). The modern complex on the right contains the excellent **Queensland Museum** (**8**; p276) and **Queensland Art Gallery** (**8**; p277), while to the left is the **Performing Arts Centre** (**9**), the state's leading venue for concerts and theatre. Spreading southeast of the Performing Arts Complex is a relaxing riverfront park.

Follow the modernist walkway southeast through the parkland. Just beyond the Performing Arts Centre, on the left-hand side and tucked away among the trees, is an ornate wooden **Nepalese Pagoda** (**10**), from the '88 Expo. Further south you'll pass the curi-

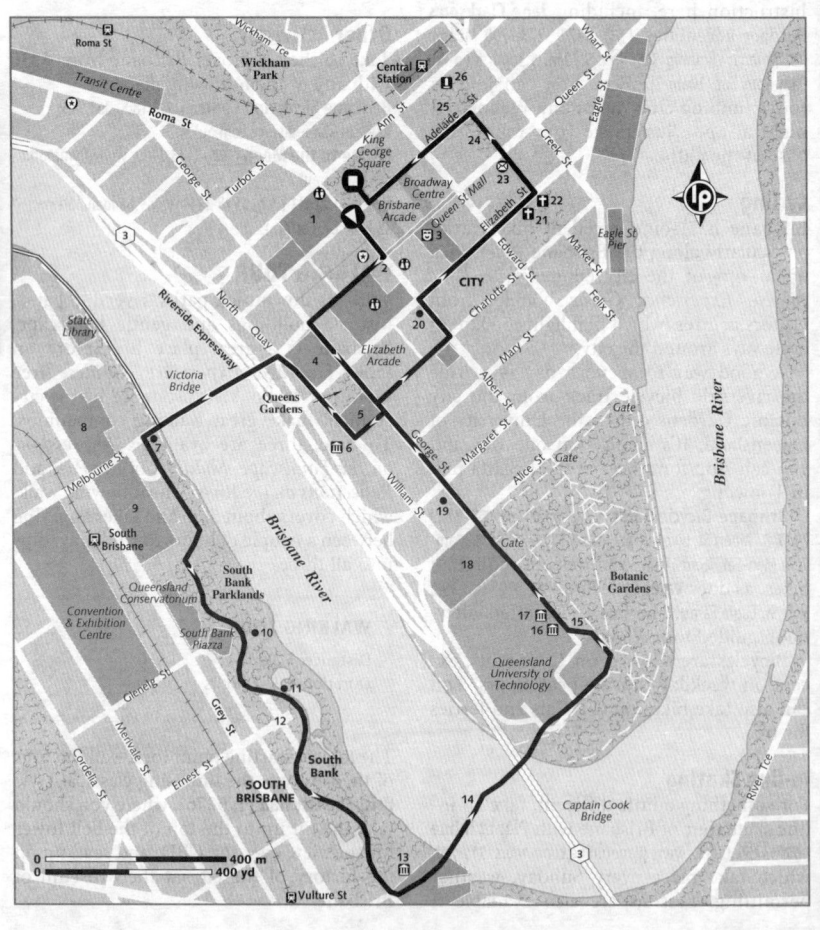

ous **Pauls Breaka Beach** (11), a hugely popular artificial beach and swimming lagoon named after a Queensland milkshake, and **Stanley St Plaza** (12), a showy tourist arcade.

Keep to the walkway until you hit the **Maritime Museum** (13; p277) and the start of the newly constructed **Goodwill Bridge** (14), which leads back across the river to the CBD. Across the bridge you'll find yourself at the southern end of the **Botanic Gardens** (15; p276). Stroll through the quiet avenues of trees and enter the Queensland University of Technology campus (QUT); check out the columned foyer of the **Old Government House** (16; p276), built in 1860, and the **QUT Art Museum** (17; p276).

Heading northwest past the QUT on your left, Queensland's regal copper-topped **Parliament House** (18; p276) will soon come into view. Continuing northwest back on George St, you'll come across the **Mansions** (19), an ornate terrace from 1890. Follow George St northwest for another couple of blocks before turning right down Charlotte St, and then take a left turn onto Albert St. Look up for the Art Deco frontage of the defunct **Greater Union Cinema Building** (20) as you head northwest towards the Queen St Mall.

Hang a right at Elizabeth St and head northeast. Once you've crossed over Edward St you can't miss the 1874 **St Stephen's Cathedral** (21) and the 1850 **St Stephen's Chapel** (22), Brisbane's oldest church, on the right-hand side.

Across from St Stephen's, an alley leads northwest to the historic **Post Office** (23) building on Queen St. Cross the road and cut through **Post Office Square** (24) – still heading northwest – to Adelaide St. On the far side is **Anzac Square** (25), which is usually full of wild ibis. At the northwestern end of the park is the Greek Revivalist **cenotaph** (26), where an eternal flame burns in remembrance of Australian soldiers who died in WWI. A short walk southwest along Adelaide St will take you to King George Square.

BRISBANE FOR CHILDREN

Brisbane is tops for kids and families. Two of the better attractions for children are the **Queensland Cultural Centre** (p276) and the **Workshops** (p278) – both have events and hands-on activities throughout the year for children. The river is a big plus; many children will enjoy a **river-boat trip**, especially if it's

to the **Lone Pine Koala Sanctuary** (p278), where they can cuddle up to one of the lovable creatures. Imaginative **playgrounds** in the city centre include **Roma St Parkland** (p276) and the **South Bank Parklands** (p277); the latter has a well-designed **swimming pool** for children.

The free monthly booklet *Brisbane's Child* (www.brisbaneschild.com.au) and *MumMe* (www.mum me.com.au; $3), a monthly magazine, have information about Brisbane for parents.

Daycare or babysitting options include **Anytime Babysitting** (☎ 3882 3455), **Dial an Angel** (☎ 3878 1077) and **Starfish Events Childcare** (☎ 3373 6511).

TOURS
Brewery Tours

There are hugely popular guided tours (probably because of the number of free samples at the end) of the **Castlemaine-Perkins XXXX brewery** (Map p274; ☎ 3361 7400; Milton Rd; $8.50; ☑ tours 11am, 1.30pm & 4pm Mon-Thu). Most hostels organise trips or you can call and book yourself onto a tour. And in the finest Aussie tradition, there's a barbecue tour on Wednesday night for $18.50 (bookings essential). The brewery is a 20-minute walk west of Roma St Transit Centre or you can take the CityTrain to Milton station.

There's another brewery tour at the **Carlton & United Brewhouse** (☎ 3826 5858; cnr Darlington Dr & Pacific Hwy; admission $15; ☑ tours 10am, noon & 2pm Mon-Fri), south of the city centre. There is no public transport to it, but a special bus runs there from the Roma St Transit Centre, at 11am Tuesday and Thursday ($30 return, book with the brewery).

City Tours

The hop-on, hop-off **City Sights bus tour** (day tickets adult/child $20/15) shuttles around 19 of the city's major landmarks, departing every 45 minutes between 9am and 3.45pm from Post Office Square on Queen St. Day tickets can be bought on the bus and allow you to get off and on whenever and wherever you want. The same ticket covers you for unlimited use of conventional city bus and ferry services. Its **City Nights tour** (adult/child $20/15; ☑ 6pm Mar-Oct & 6.30pm Nov-Feb), departing from the City Hall, goes a little further afield and includes Mt Coot-tha Lookout and a cruise on a CityCat.

Several different companies offer interesting walking tours of Brisbane, including

Brian Ogden's Historical Tours (☎ 3217 3673; www.ogdenswalkingtours.com.au; adult/child $11/5.50), which is strong on convict history; and **Artours** (☎ 3899 0661; www.artours.coaus.com; from $45, incl lunch), which focuses on Brisbane's art galleries. **Ghost Tours** (☎ 3844 6606; www .ghost-tours.com.au; adult/child from $22/13) offers something a little different: guided tours of Brisbane's haunted heritage, murder scenes, cemeteries and the infamous Boggo Rd Gaol. If that's not enough for you, you can overnight (per person $65) in one of the gaol's cells, amongst the resident ghosts.

River Cruises

River Queen (☎ 3221 1300) offers cruises of the Brisbane River in the restored wooden paddle-steamers *Kookaburra Queen* and *Kookaburra Queen II*. They leave daily from the Eagle St Pier at 11.45am and cost $60/40/24 with a seafood lunch/buffet lunch/tea and bickies. A dinner cruise is at 7pm from Monday to Thursday and 6pm Sunday (seafood/buffet $70/55). The Friday-evening cruise is at 6.45pm (seafood/buffet $70/60).

Other Tours

Rob's Rainforest Tours (☎ 0409-496 607; www .powerup.com.au/~frogbus7/) offers a range of **day trips** ($55 incl lunch & snacks) that take in the rain-forests at Mt Glorious and Kondalilla Falls, the Glass House Mountains and Lamington National Park. Several readers have written with high praise for the tours.

Bushwacker Ecotours (☎ 5520 7238; www.bush wacker-ecotours.com.au), an eco-friendly tour group, has quite an extensive array of both day and overnight trips into the Gold Coast hinterland. Prices start at around $35 for a half-day trip and top out at $800 for a four-night excursion, which includes transportation, accommodation and meals.

Araucaria Ecotours (☎ 5544 1283; ecotoura@eis .net.au) is based at Running Creek Rd, 18km east of Rathdowney in the Gold Coast hinterland. It offers three-day wilderness **tours** (self-catering/with meals $210/300) in the Mt Barney National Park area, leaving Brisbane on Wednesday morning, including a detour to the Daisy Hill Koala Information Centre and the Karawatha Wetlands. The cost includes accommodation at the Mt Barney Lodge.

FESTIVALS & EVENTS

Information on festivals and events in Brisbane can be found at the visitors centres or at www.ourbrisbane.com/ourbrisevents. Major happenings:

Cockroach Races This bizarre ritual takes place at the Story Bridge Hotel on Australia Day, 26 January.

GAY & LESBIAN BRISBANE

With a name like Queensland, you'd think the sunshine state would be *the* place to head for the best of Australia's gay and lesbian scene. Unfortunately this isn't the case, and while Brisbane can't compete with Sydney or Melbourne, what you'll find here is quality rather than quantity.

The small but lively scene, centred in Fortitude Valley, is covered by the fortnightly *Q News* (www.qnews.com.au). *Queensland Pride*, another gay publication, takes in the whole of the state. *Dykes on Mykes* (www.queerradio.org), a radio show on Wednesday from 9pm to 11pm on FM102.1, is another source of information on the city. Major events on the year's calendar include the **Queer Film Festival** held in late March, which showcases gay, lesbian, bisexual and transgender films and videos, and **Brisbane Pride Festival** in June. Pride attracts up to 25,000 people every year, and peaks during the parade held mid-festival. For more information, call ☎ 0418-152 801.

Popular gay and lesbian venues:

Sportsman's Hotel (Map pp284–6; ☎ 3831 2892; 130 Leichhardt St) This is a fantastically popular gay venue, with a different theme or show for each night of the week.

Options Nightclub (Map pp284–6; ☎ 3839 1000; 18 Little Edward St) Options is another good gay and lesbian choice.

Wickham Hotel (Map pp284–6; ☎ 3852 1301; cnr Wickham & Alden Sts) Wickham is a classic old Victorian pub with good dance music, drag shows and dancers.

GPO (see Drinking p290) and **Family** (see Entertainment p291) are both mixed venues.

The friendly B&B **Carringtons** (Map pp284–6; ☎ 3315 2630; www.carringtons.com.au; Gregory Tce, Spring Hill; s/ste $75/135), set in a restored colonial home, is one of the better gay accommodation options in the city.

Chinese New Year Always a popular event in the Valley in February.

Brisbane Festival of Music Held in July on odd-numbered years.

International Film Festival Ten days of quality films in July.

Valley Fiesta Food and music festival held in Chinatown and Brunswick St Mall in mid-July.

`Ekka' Royal National Agricultural Show The country comes to town in early August.

Livid Annual one-day alternative rock festival in October.

Woodford Folk Festival Over New Year's Eve, 78km north of Brisbane in Woodford.

SLEEPING

Brisbane, like any large city, has an excellent selection of accommodation options that will suit any type of budget. Most, however, are outside the CBD, but more often than not are within walking distance or have good public-transport connections.

The inner suburbs have their own distinct flavour. Petrie Tce and Paddington, just west of the city centre, combine trendy restaurants and rowdy bars, while Fortitude Valley (or the Valley, as it's locally known), northeast of the city, is an alternative neighbourhood with a small Chinatown and a lively café and night-life scene. New Farm, southeast beyond the Valley, is a mix of quiet suburbia and upwardly mobile. Spring Hill, just north of the CBD, is also quiet and within easy striking distance of downtown and the Valley. West End, south of the river, has a decidedly chilled-out atmosphere and some great cafés and restaurants.

The main motel drags are Wickham St and Gregory Tce, on the northern edge of the city, and Main St in Kangaroo Point, which is also the link road to the southern Gold Coast Hwy.

The **Brisbane Visitors Accommodation Service** (Map pp284-6; ☎ 3236 2020; 3rd fl, Roma St Transit Centre) has a free booking service, and brochures and information on hostels and other budget options in Brisbane and up and down the coast.

Budget
HOSTELS

Brisbane's hostels are generally of a high standard and will almost always have laundry facilities, a TV lounge and plenty of information on sights, activities and hostels up and down the coast.

THE AUTHOR'S CHOICE

Tourist Guest House (Map p274; ☎ 1800 800 589, 3252 4171; www.touristguesthouse.com.au; 555 Gregory Tce; s $45-55, d $55-65; P ⊠) This beautifully restored Queenslander is one of the best accommodation options in Brisbane. The colonial theme is present in every room and the attention to detail is evident throughout. Rooms are spacious, bright, homely and, some say, have that little bit extra – a ghostly matron that tucks you in at night! Other bonuses include a relaxing sundeck out back, free breakfast and pick-up from the Transit Centre, wheelchair access and a kitchen and laundry for guests.

City Centre   Map pp284-6
Tinbilly (☎ 1800 446 646, 3238 5888; 462 George St; www.tinbilly.com; dm $20-24, tw & d $75; ⊠ ▯) This modern, new hostel may not have the character of some hostels, but it sure has the facilities to match anything you've seen. Each room (dorm rooms included) has air-con, a bathroom and individual lockers. The hostel has wheelchair-accessible rooms, well-equipped kitchens, a job centre, travel agency and its very own bar.

Palace Backpackers (☎ 1800 676 340, 3211 2433; www.palacebackpackers.com.au; cnr Ann & Edward Sts; dm $20-23, s/d $36/50; ▯) The popular Palace occupies four floors of the lovely old colonial People's Palace, and facilities include a huge kitchen, a tour-information desk, a job club and a great rooftop sundeck. The rooms are a little cramped and it can sometimes get rather rowdy as its popular backpackers' bar, the Down Under Bar & Grill (see Drinking p290), is in the basement.

Petrie Terrace
& Paddington   Map p274
Brisbane City Backpackers' (☎ 1800 062 572, 3211 3221; www.citybackpackers.com; 380 Upper Roma St; dm $17-21, s $45, d $55-65; P ⊠ ▯) Backpackers are well catered for at this hostel; there's a job centre, a hostel bar, a swimming pool, a terrace with views of the Brisbane River, a lift and wheelchair-accessible rooms. It does, however, lack a bit of personal touch.

Banana Benders Backpackers (☎ 1800 241 157, 3367 1157; bbender@bigpond.net.au; 118 Petrie Tce; dm $20-22, tw & d $50; ▯) Painted yellow and blue on the outside, this is another good choice;

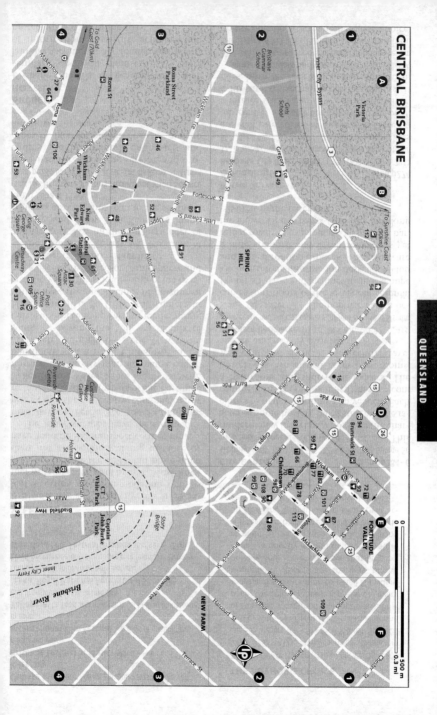

CENTRAL BRISBANE

QUEENSLAND

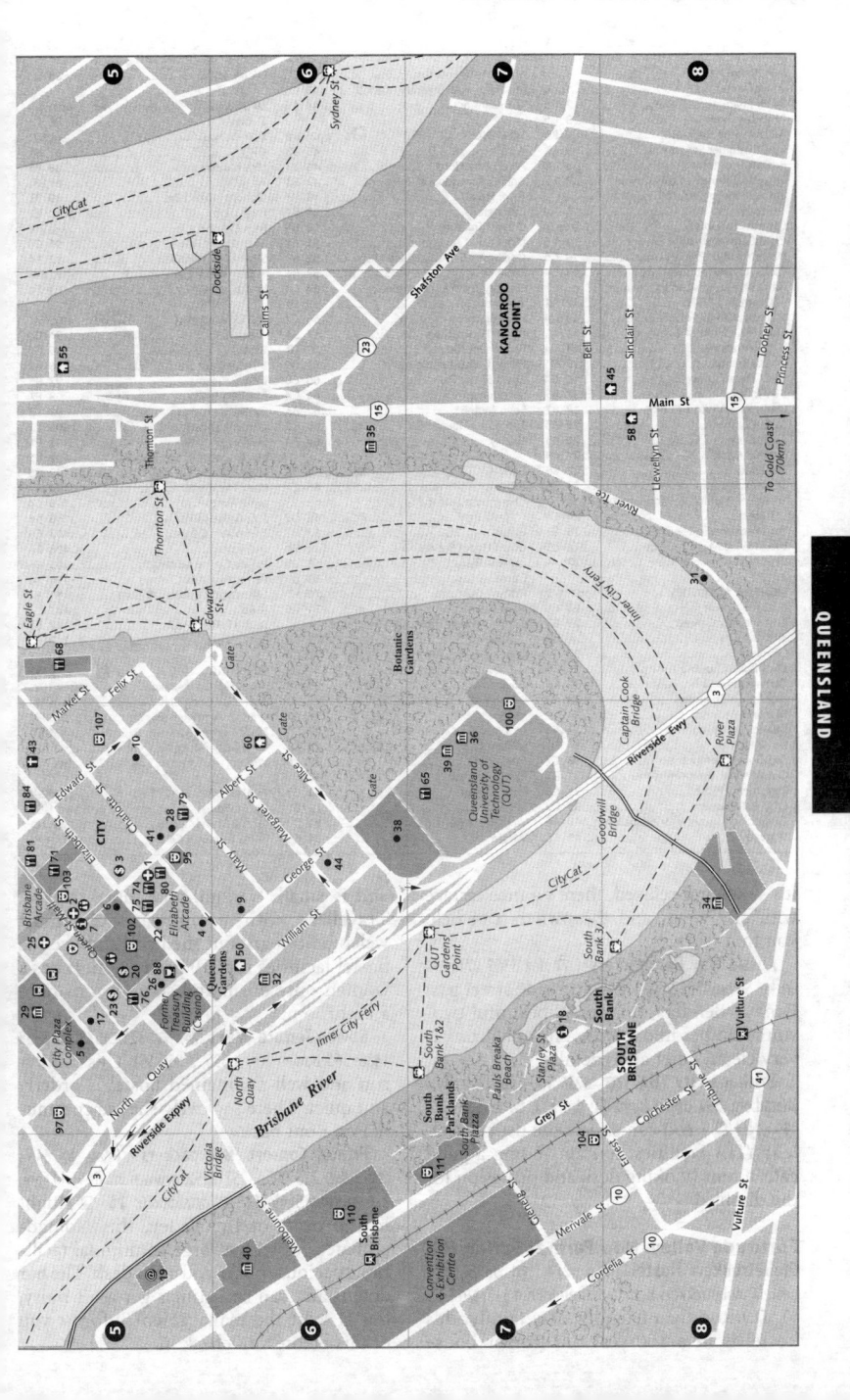

QUEENSLAND

INFORMATION
24 Hr Dentist.....................................1 C5
24 Hr Pharmacy.................................2 C5
American Express..............................3 C5
Archives Fine Books..........................4 B5
BCC Customer Services.....................5 B5
Borders Bookstore.............................6 C5
Brisbane Tourism Visitors Centre.......7 B5
Brisbane Visitors Accommodation
  Service..8 A4
Central City Library.....................(see 5)
Child Care Information Service...........9 C6
Department of Primary Industry.......10 C5
Global Gossip Internet Café.............11 C4
Naturally Queensland Information
  Centre..12 B4
Queensland Rail Travel Centre.........13 C4
Queensland Tourist & Travel
  Corporation...................................14 A4
RACQ Branch...................................15 D1
RACQ Head Office............................16 C4
STA Travel.......................................17 B5
South Bank Visitors Centre...............18 B7
State Library....................................19 A5
Thomas Cook...................................20 B5
Thomas Cook...................................21 C4
Trailfinders......................................22 B5
Travelex..23 B5
Travellers' Medical & Vaccination
  Centre..24 C4
Travellers' Medical Service...............25 B5
World Wide Maps & Guides..............26 B5
YHA Membership & Travel Office......27 A4

SIGHTS & ACTIVITIES pp276-9
Brisbane Bicycle Sales 28 C5
Brisbane City Gallery........................29 B5
Brisbane City Hall......................(see 29)
Cenotaph...30 C4
Cliffs Rock-Climbing Area.................31 D8
Commissariat Stores Building............32 B6
MacArthur Chambers........................33 C4
Maritime Museum............................34 C8
Museum of Brisbane...................(see 29)
Naval Stores....................................35 E6
Old Government House.....................36 C7
Old Windmill & Observatory.............37 B4
Parliament House.............................38 C6
QUT Art Museum.............................39 C7
Queensland Museum & Art Gallery.....40 A6
Skatebiz..41 C5

St John's Cathedral..........................42 D3
St Stephen's Cathedral.....................43 C5
The Mansions..................................44 C6

SLEEPING pp283-8
A1 Motel..45 E8
Albert Park Hotel.............................46 B3
Annie's Shandon Inn........................47 B3
Astor Hotel......................................48 B3
Carringtons......................................49 B2
Conrad Treasury..............................50 B6
Dahrl Court Apartments....................51 C2
Dorchester Self-Contained Units.......52 B3
Explorer's Inn...................................53 B4
Gregory Terrace Motor Inn................54 C1
Il Mondo..55 E5
Kookaburra Inn................................56 C2
Palace Backpackers..........................57 B4
Paramount Motel..............................58 E8
Prince Consort Backpackers..............59 D1
Royal on the Park.............................60 C6
Sheraton Brisbane............................61 C4
Soho Motel......................................62 B3
Thornbury House B&B.......................63 C2
Tinbilly..64 A4

EATING pp288-90
Artisans on the Yard.........................65 C7
Chinahouse Seafood
  Restaurant....................................66 D2
Circa..67 D3
Down Under Bar & Grill...............(see 57)
Eagle St Pier....................................68 D5
E'cco...69 D3
Fatboys Cafe....................................70 E2
Food Court.......................................71 C5
Garuma Hidden Tranquility Restaurant
  & Bar..72 E1
Gilhooley's Downtown......................73 C4
Gilhooley's.......................................74 C5
Govinda's...75 C5
Il Centro.....................................(see 68)
Malone's..76 B5
McWhirters Marketplace...................77 D1
Mellino's..78 C2
Metro Cafe.......................................79 C5
Pané e Vino......................................80 C5
Pig n' Whistle...................................81 C5
Veg Out...82 E1
Vietnamese Restaurant.....................83 D2
Woolworths......................................84 C5

Woolworths......................................85 D3

DRINKING pp290-1
Dooley's...86 E2
Down Under Bar.........................(see 57)
GPO...87 E1
Irish Murphy's..................................88 B5
Jorge...(see 88)
Options Nightclub.............................89 B3
Press Club..90 E2
Ric's Cafe Bar.............................(see 70)
Sportsman's Hotel............................91 C3
Story Bridge Hotel............................92 E4
Tinbilly Bar & Cafe.....................(see 64)
Wickham Hotel.................................93 E1

ENTERTAINMENT pp291-2
Arena...94 D1
Brisbane Festival Hall.......................95 C5
Brisbane Jazz Club...........................96 E4
Dendy Cinema..................................97 B5
Empire...98 E2
Family..99 E2
Gardens Theatre.............................100 C7
Healer..101 E1
Hoyts Cinemas...............................102 B5
Hoyts Regent Theatre.....................103 C5
Imax Theatre..................................104 A7
Indie Temple..................................105 C4
Jazz & Blues Bar.............................106 B4
Metro Arts Centre...........................107 C5
Monastery......................................108 E2
Palace Centro Cinema.....................109 F1
Performing Arts Centre...................110 A6
Queensland Conservatorium............111 A7
R-Bar...(see 50)
Splash Leisure Pool.........................112 B1
Zoo..113 E2

SHOPPING p292
Australian Geographic..................(see 102)
Australian Geographic...................(see 71)
Crafts Village Market....................(see 18)
Myer Centre.................................(see 102)
Southbank Aboriginal Centre.........(see 18)
Wintergarden Centre.....................(see 71)

TRANSPORT pp292-4
Bus Station..................................(see 102)
Qantas Travel Centre.....................(see 24)
Roma St Transit Centre....................(see 8)

it's small and relaxed, there's a nice terrace with city views and the owners can help you find work.

Aussie Way Backpackers (☎ /fax 3369 0711; 34 Cricket St; dm/d $22/50) Down the side street past Banana Benders, this small, beautiful two-storey timber house with a front balcony is very clean, quiet and friendly.

Brisbane City YHA (☎ 3236 1004; brisbanecity@ yhaqld.org; 392 Upper Roma St; dm $23, tw & d $55-70; P ✗ ▢) You can expect the usual excellent YHA facilities here, including a good café, a tour booking desk and provision for the disabled.

Fortitude Valley, New Farm & Spring Hill
Globetrekkers Hostel (Map p274; ☎ 3358 1251; hostel@globetrekkers.net; 35 Balfour St; dm $17, s/d $33/40; ▢) Run by a friendly, arty family, this hostel is in a 100-year-old timber house

and is small, tranquil and super relaxed. Travellers with campervans are most welcome to park out the back and use the hostel facilities for $10 per person. It has a women-only dorm and some rooms have a bathroom.

Bowen Terrace (Map p274; ☎ 3254 1575; fax 3358 1488; 365 Bowen Tce; s $35, d $50-55) This family-run and well-maintained hostel is orderly and quiet. There's a lovely shaded communal area out back.

Prince Consort Backpackers (Map pp284-6; ☎ 1800 225 005, 3257 2252; www.nomadsworld.com; 230 Wickham St; dm $15-19, d/tr $50/70; ✗ ▢) Right in the heart of the Valley, this Nomad-affiliated hostel has large communal facilities, spacious rooms and a job desk. The bar downstairs can sometimes get a bit noisy, but at least the management informs you of this before you check in.

Homestead (Map p274; ☎ 1800 658 344, 3358 3538; fax 3354 1609; 57 Annie St; dm $16-19, d & tw $45) This is a large, lively place with reasonable facilities, including a small pool and a games room. There's a job club, and courtesy buses to the city.

Kookaburra Inn (Map pp284-6; ☎ 3832 1303; www .kookaburra-inn.com.au; 41 Phillips St; s/d $35/55) Housed in an old Queenslander on a quiet, leafy street in Spring Hill, this relaxed, clean hostel is the place to come for a good night's sleep.

West End
Somewhere to Stay (Map p274; ☎ 1800 812 398, 3846 2858; www.somewheretostay.com.au; 45 Brighton Rd; dm $18-25, s/d from $32/45; P 💻) This big, rambling Queenslander has cool balconies and a small pool with an attractive shaded deck. It's set in a decent garden and has a nice, relaxed atmosphere.

CAMPING
Newmarket Gardens Caravan Park (☎ 3356 1458; fax 3352 7273; 199 Ashgrove Ave, Ashgrove; camp/caravan sites from $16/19, on-site vans/cabins from $31/55; 🐕) This clean, quiet site is just 4km north of the city centre, and is connected to town by several bus routes and the CityTrain (Newmarket station).

Alternatively, **Globetrekkers Hostel** (see p286) will allow travellers to camp in their vehicles in the backyard.

Mid-Range
APARTMENTS
Dahrl Court Apartments (Map pp284-6; ☎ 3832 3400; www.dahrlcourt.com.au; 45 Phillips St; r per night/week $90/550; P 🐕) Tucked away on a quiet residential street, but still close to the CBD, the bright, roomy apartments here have a separate kitchen, small breakfast room, phone, TV and a full-sized bath. There's also a small pool and gym.

Allender Apartments (Map p274; ☎ 3358 5832; www.allenderapartments.com.au; 3 Moreton St; studio/ste $85/100; P 🐕) In a two-storey yellow-brick block, these good-value units are large, well furnished and quiet, despite being on a busy road.

Dorchester Self-Contained Units (Map pp284-6; ☎ 3831 2967; dorchesterinn@bigpond.com; 484 Upper Edward St; s/d/tr $70/80/90; P 🐕) This is a two-storey block of renovated one-bedroom units, each with a kitchenette, phone and TV. There are also laundry facilities.

GUESTHOUSES & B&BS
Thornbury House B&B (Map pp284-6; ☎ 3832 5985; thornburyhouse@primus.com.au; 1 Thornbury St; s/d $85/100) This charming B&B tucked away on a quiet suburban street in Spring Hill is housed in a renovated two-storey Queenslander. The rooms are bright and airy.

Paddington B&B (Map p274; ☎ 3369 8973; fax 3876 6655; 5 Latrobe Tce; s/d $85/110, self-contained units per week $425) About 2km west of the city centre, this two-storey Queenslander has rooms overlooking a peaceful garden.

Annie's Shandon Inn (Map pp284-6; ☎ 3831 8684; anniesshandoninn@hotmail.com; 405 Upper Edward St; s $50-60, d $60-70) Stepping into this quaint B&B is like stepping back 40 years – it's filled to the brim with an eclectic collection of knick-knacks from the past. The rooms are well kept and some have a bathroom.

HOTELS
Explorer's Inn (Map pp284-6; ☎ 1800 623 288, 3211 3488; explorer@powerup.com.au; 63 Turbot St; r from $80; 🐕) This modern hotel is right in the CBD and has a restaurant, bar and immaculate, well-equipped rooms (with bathroom).

Albert Park Hotel (Map pp284-6; ☎ 3831 3111; www.albertparkhotel.com.au; 551 Wickham Tce; r/ste from $95/125; P 🐕) Overlooking Roma St Parkland, this hotel has extremely comfortable and well-furnished rooms.

Il Mondo (Map pp284-6; ☎ 3392 0111; www .ilmondo.com.au; 25 Rotherham St; d from $80; P 🐕) This quirky, postmodern building has lots of metalwork and angles, and a range of well-appointed rooms. There's also a pool, a restaurant, and one room is equipped for disabled visitors.

Astor Hotel (Map pp284-6; ☎ 3144 4000; www .astorhotel.com.au; 193 Wickham Tce; r/ste from $100/115; 🐕) Close to the city, near the junction with Upper Edward St, this modern and friendly place offers a variety of tasteful suites and rooms. It often has specials, so call ahead.

MOTELS
Paramount Motel (Map pp284-6; ☎ 3393 1444; www .paramountmotel.com.au; 649 Main St; s/d $70/85; P 🐕) This immaculately kept motel has modern, spacious units along with self-contained apartments. The staff are very friendly and there's a pool and laundry facilities.

Soho Motel (Map pp284-6; ☎ 1800 188 889, 3831 7722; www.sohomotel.com.au; 333 Wickham Tce; s/d $70/85; P 🐕) This is one of the better motels in the centre and it's only a short walk uphill from Roma St Transit Centre. Rooms are comfortable and frequently booked out – reserve early.

Gregory Terrace Motor Inn (Map pp284-6; ☎ 1800 801 772, 3832 1769; fax 3832 2640; 397 Gregory Tce; r from $110; P 🔀) This four-star establishment overlooks Victoria Park and is just across from the Centenary Pool.

A1 Motel (Map pp284-6; ☎ 3391 6222; fax 3891 0720; 646 Main St; units from $75; 🔀) A1, at Kangaroo Point, is a friendly place with tidy, renovated rooms.

Top End

Conrad Treasury (Map pp284-6; ☎ 1800 506 889, 3306 8888; www.conradtreasury.com.au; 130 William St; r from $320; P 🔀) Perhaps the grandest hotel in town, the Conrad is housed in the beautifully restored former Land Administration Building. The hotel has 97 rooms and suites (no two of which are the same) with either a city or park view. Avoid the Cabinet Room at night – it's supposedly haunted.

Royal on the Park (Map pp284-6; ☎ 1800 773 337, 3221 3411; www.royalonthepark.com.au; cnr Alice & Albert Sts; r from $125; P 🔀) This very attractive four-star hotel is just across from the Botanic Gardens and offers 153 rooms, a pool, spa, gym and two restaurants.

Sheraton Brisbane (Map pp284-6; ☎ 3835 3535; www.sheraton.com/brisbane; 249 Turbot St; r from $200; P 🔀) Dominating the northern side of town, this luxurious hotel has over 400 rooms. There are a number of rooms for the disabled, a pool and frequent specials.

EATING

Like Brisbane's accommodation options, many of the city's best restaurants and cafés are in the neighbourhoods of Fortitude Valley, New Farm, West End, Petrie Tce and Paddington. The CBD also has its fair share of eateries.

City Centre

The best cheap options are the food courts in the big shopping centres on Queen St Mall. The **Wintergarden Centre** (Map pp284–6) and **Myer Centre** (Map pp284–6) have hugely popular sushi bars and kiosks selling noodles, curries, kebabs and standard Aussie fare. You can eat well for under $8 in any of these places. The Charlotte St end of the **Elizabeth Arcade** also has some excellent fast-food establishments specialising in Asian cuisine.

Metro Cafe (Map pp284-6; ☎ 3221 3181; cnr Albert & Mary Sts; breakfast around $7, sandwiches $4-6; 🕒 6.30am-4.30pm Mon-Fri) Sandwiches made fresh to go are the order of the day at this extremely popular sandwich shop. Fuller meals are also available.

Artisans on the Yard (Map pp284-6; George St, QUT campus; lunch $6-10) This relaxed student hangout has an eclectic selection of meals, ranging from panini to fish and chips. There's plenty of courtyard seating.

Govinda's (Map pp284-6; ☎ 3210 0255; upstairs, 99 Elizabeth St; Sun feast $4, all you can eat $8; 🕒 lunch Mon-Sat, Sun feast from 5pm) This Hare Krishna–run place does tasty, vegetarian meals.

Pané e Vino (Map pp284-6; ☎ 3220 0044; cnr Albert & Charlotte Sts; mains $15-20) If you're after modern Italian try this very popular place. Its street-side seating is usually packed with city workers for lunch and dinner.

Pig 'n' Whistle (Map pp284-6; ☎ 3229 9999; Queen St Mall; mains around $15; 🕒 24hr) and **Malone's** (Map pp284-6; ☎ 3210 0305; Queen St Mall; mains around $15; 🕒 24hr) are two open-air restaurants at opposite ends of the mall. Both serve good food and cold beers around the clock.

Down Under Bar & Grill (Map pp284-6; ☎ 3211 9277; cnr Ann & Edward Sts; dishes around $8) This place is located under the Palace Backpackers and offers reasonable pub meals, though it soon turns over to its primary purpose as a bar (see Drinking p290).

E'cco (Map pp284-6; ☎ 3831 8344; 100 Boundary St; mains around $30; 🕒 lunch Tue-Fri, dinner Tue-Sat) Up there with the best Queensland has to offer, E'cco is a must for any culinary aficionado. The menu includes treats like quail, duck and seared scallops, and the desserts are legendary. Everyone in town knows this, of course, so you'll need to book well in advance.

Another feted brasserie is **Circa** (Map pp284-6; ☎ 3832 4722; 483 Adelaide St; mains around $30; 🕒 lunch Tue-Fri, dinner Mon-Sat), which, at the time of writing, is viewed in some circles as Brisbane's number one restaurant. Its broad menu of game and seafood is a delight to the taste buds and the service is impeccable.

There are also plush city-centre restaurants in the Riverside Centre and Eagle St Pier. One that stands out from the crowd is **Il Centro** (Map pp284-6; ☎ 3221 6090; Eagle St Pier; mains around $30; ☻ lunch Sun-Fri, dinner daily), winner of Brisbane's best restaurant for 2002, and Queensland's best for 2001, with its modern Italian menu. Views of the river from its dining area and bar are another plus.

Self-caterers should head for the nearest **Woolworths** supermarket; there is one at the corner of Edward and Elizabeth Sts, and another at the corner of Boundary and Wickham Sts in Spring Hill.

It's also worth checking out **Gilhooley's** Albert St (Map pp284-6; ☎ 3229 0672; 124 Albert St); Elizabeth St (Map pp284-6; ☎ 3221 8566; 283 Elizabeth St; dishes $13-20), with two locations downtown that serve very good basic fare like stews, beef and Guinness pie, and steaks.

Fortitude Valley & New Farm

The Valley is one of the best eating areas to explore, especially on Friday evenings and Saturday, when it's bustling with people.

Fatboys Cafe (Map pp284-6; ☎ 3252 3789; 323 Brunswick St; dishes around $15; ☻ 6am-midnight Mon-Wed, 24hr Thu-Sun) This modern café, next to Ric's Cafe Bar, is extremely popular with a youngish crowd. It's a great place for when you want to just sip a coffee and watch the Saturday-market crowds.

Mellino's (Map pp284-6; ☎ 3252 3551; 330 Brunswick St Mall; pizza & pasta around $10, mains around $16; ☻ 24hr) Opposite Fatboys, this café is one of the cheapest on the mall, and the food is above average.

Veg Out (Map pp284-6; ☎ 3852 2668; cnr Brunswick & Wickham Sts, McWhirters Arcade; dishes $8-14) This wholesome vegetarian and organic café is right on the mall and serves good, cheap vegie burgers and hot, canteen-style meals.

Vietnamese Restaurant (Map pp284-6; ☎ 3252 4112; 194 Wickham St; mains around $10) This licensed and BYO restaurant offers good Vietnamese food at very reasonable prices. It gets pretty busy most evenings.

Chinahouse Seafood Restaurant (Map pp284-6; ☎ 3216 0570; 173 Wickham St; yum cha $3.50, mains around $11) This Chinese restaurant has a wide selection of seafood dishes, but best of all is its yum cha (dim sum), which is only available at lunch.

Garuva Hidden Tranquility Restaurant & Bar (Map pp284-6; ☎ 3216 0124; 324 Wickham St; dishes around $20) Garuva is quite a special place –

not many restaurants can testify to having a rainforest under their roof. It comes highly recommended and offers stylish dining in private, screened compartments. It's very popular, so you need to book.

Himalayan Cafe (Map p274; ☎ 3358 4015; 640 Brunswick St; dishes $10-18; ☻ closed Mon) This vividly colourful Nepalese and Tibetan restaurant is decked out with thousands of prayer flags and is very popular. You can sample Tibetan dishes such as *momos* (steamed dumplings) and *thukpa* (vegetable and noodle soup).

Watt (☎ 3358 5464; 119 Lamington St; dishes around $20; ☻ closed Mon) At the southeastern end of New Farm, this chic waterfront eatery and bar is part of the Brisbane Powerhouse theatre and arts centre, and serves up good, modern Australian cuisine.

For fresh fruit and vegies there's a great produce market inside **McWhirters Marketplace** (Map pp284-6; cnr Brunswick & Wickham Sts) in the Valley.

West End

Like the Valley, West End has a cosmopolitan range of cafés, including quite a few budget places.

Three Monkeys Coffee House (Map p274; ☎ 3844 6045; 58 Mollison St; dishes $10-18) Next door to the Jazzy Cat is the Three Monkeys, another relaxed café. This place has pseudo-Moroccan décor, good coffee and cakes, and a wide range of food.

Expressahead (Map p274; 171 Boundary St; breakfast $7, mains $8) This seriously chilled-out café is quite often packed, testifying to its top-notch Italian dishes and yummy, filling breakfasts.

THE AUTHOR'S CHOICE

The **Jazzy Cat Cafe** (Map p274; ☎ 3864 2544; 56 Mollison St; mains around $16) There's not much more you can ask of this great little café. Situated in a beautifully restored Queenslander, the Jazzy Cat has a distinct bohemian feel, relaxing music, tons of mags and papers to read, a covered veranda out back and plenty of character. The food (international cuisine) is lovingly prepared and presented and tasty to boot. It's a perfect place for an evening meal or a coffee on a lazy afternoon.

QUEENSLAND

Tongue & Groove (Map p274; ☎ 3846 0334; 63 Hardgrave Rd; mains $13-20) It's a bit hard to pin down the Tongue & Groove. One minute it's a hip café and bar, the next a popular restaurant, and then a live-music venue. However you find it, the international cuisine stays the same – excellent.

Green Papaya (☎ 3217 3599; 898 Stanley St, East Brisbane; mains $16-22) This wonderful Vietnamese restaurant is a Brisbane institution for two reasons: its exceptionally good food and its owner, Lien Yeomans, who has gained celeb status in the city. Be sure to book ahead.

Kim Thanh (Map p274; ☎ 3844 4954; 93 Hardgrave Rd; mains around $13) Simple but stylish surroundings complement the fine Vietnamese food at this local favourite.

Other eateries worth a mention:

Gunshop Cafe (Map p274; 53 Mollison St; dishes around $10) Child-friendly café.

Sol Breads (Map p274; ☎ 3255 1225; 27 Vulture St; breads & cakes $2-4) Organic bakery with lots of scrummy cakes and snacks.

Caravanserai (☎ 3217 2617; 1-3 Dornoch Tce; mains $10-18) Lovely Turkish restaurant with an open kitchen in the centre.

Petrie Terrace, Paddington & Milton   Map p274

Caxton St and its western extension, Given Tce, are the best hunting grounds.

Caxton Thai (☎ 3367 0300; 47 Caxton St; dishes $12-17) This friendly little BYO has good food, no pretensions and a take-away service.

Sultan's Kitchen (☎ 3368 2194; 163 Given Tce; dishes $15-20) It's worth making the trek uphill for the great food at this excellent BYO Indian restaurant. It's friendly and popular and set in a pleasant garden; book on weekends.

Jakarta Indonesian Restaurant (☎ 3368 1842; 215 Given Tce; dishes $10-16; ☒ closed Mon) This reasonably priced restaurant serves rice, noodle, seafood, meat and vegetarian dishes, and has evocative bamboo décor.

Paddo Tavern (☎ 3369 0044; 186 Given Tce; dishes from $8) Right in the heart of Paddington, this big, local pub has a good, cheap bistro and an inviting patio out front.

La Dolce Vita (☎ 3368 1191; 20 Park Rd; pizzas & pastas around $16) The tacky décor of this restaurant – Italian statues and fountains beneath a giant model of the Eiffel Tower – can be forgiven due to its fine food. The menu is pure Italian.

Breakfast Creek

Breakfast Creek Hotel (Map p274; ☎ 3262 5988; 2 Kingsford Smith Dr; dishes $13-17, steaks $20-25) On the northern side of a bend in the Brisbane River is this famous hotel. It's in a great rambling building dating from 1889, and is a Brisbane institution. Forget about any of the mains here, go straight for the steaks; its selection peaks with the mighty 450g rump. To get here take bus No 322 or 300 from the corner of Adelaide and Edward Sts in the city, or take the CityCat to Bretts Wharf and walk back along the river for about 1km.

DRINKING

The drinking establishments of Brisbane are generally situated around the CBD, the Valley, and Petrie Tce. The CBD, however, is often dead on weekends, when most punters head for the more lively inner suburbs.

Press Club (Map pp284-6; ☎ 3852 4000; 339 Brunswick St) With a mixture of mystic and space-age décor, comfy couches, plenty of dark corners and groovy music, it's not surprising this bar attracts a regular crowd from all ages. There's live music Wednesday and Sunday.

Ric's Cafe Bar (Map pp284-6; ☎ 3854 1772; 321 Brunswick St) Over in the Brunswick St Mall, this place has live bands downstairs, DJs in the lounge bar upstairs and even space for a bit of quiet conversation on the tables in the street.

Dooley's (Map pp284-6; ☎ 3252 4344; 394 Brunswick St) This big, unpretentious Irish pub has loads of pool tables and is a pleasant spot to sip a beer, except on Saturday when it's positively heaving.

GPO (Map pp284-6; ☎ 3252 1322; 740 Ann St) The old post office in the Valley is the location of this funky bar. Downstairs you'll find a stylish bar filled with young trendies, while upstairs offers chilled tunes and the occasional live band.

Jorge (Map pp284-6; ☎ 3012 9121; 183 George St) This modern bar is great for wine, cocktails and quality DJs.

Irish Murphy's (Map pp284-6; ☎ 3221 4377; cnr George & Elizabeth Sts) This big, old-fashioned public house is a popular choice for an after-work drink and is refreshingly down to earth compared to most city pubs.

Story Bridge Hotel (Map pp284-6; ☎ 3391 2266; 196 Main St) This beautiful old pub beneath the bridge at Kangaroo Point is a perfect place for a pint after a long day sightseeing.

Caxton Hotel (Map p274; ☎ 3369 5544; 38 Caxton St) On Friday and Saturday nights this flashy hotel is full to almost bursting with young things out on the town looking to pick up. Expect mainstream dance anthems.

Backpacker bars are popular with both travellers and locals.

Down Under Bar & Grill (Map pp284-6; ☎ 3211 9277; cnr Ann & Edward Sts) Tucked beneath the Palace Backpackers, this bar is packed seven nights a week. It's a good place to go if you like it loud, beery and laddish.

Fiddler's Elbow (Map p274; ☎ 1800 062 572, 3211 3221; 380 Upper Roma St) At the back of Brisbane City Backpackers, this pseudo-Irish bar has live music twice a week and is generally only open to residents of the hostel.

Tinbilly Bar & Cafe (Map pp284-6; ☎ 1800 446 646, 3238 5888; 462 George St) At the bottom of Tinbilly hostel, this modern bar has huge TV screens.

Elephant & Wheelbarrow (Map pp284-6; ☎ 1800 225 005, 3257 2252; www.nomadsworld.com; 230 Wickham St) While not strictly a backpackers' bar, it is heavily frequented by travellers staying at the Prince Consort Backpackers above it.

ENTERTAINMENT

Brisbane's entertainment scene has picked up dramatically over the last few years; international bands frequently play, clubs have become nationally renowned, there's plenty of theatre, and the gay and lesbian scene is expanding. Pick up copies of the free entertainment papers *Time Off* (www .timeoff.com.au), *Rave* (www.ravemag.com .au) and *Scene* (www.sceneonline.com.au) from any café in the Valley. Another good source of information is the website www.brisbane247.com.

Cinemas

There are mainstream cinemas along the Queen St Mall.

Hoyts Cinemas (Map pp284-6; ☎ 3027 9999; Level A, Myer Centre, Queen St) Screens blockbusters and other mainstream fare nightly in its dingy multiscreen in the basement of the Myer Centre.

Hoyts Regent Theatre (Map pp284-6; ☎ 3027 9999; 107 Queen St Mall) A lovely old cinema worth visiting for the building alone.

Arthouse cinemas in Brisbane:

Dendy Cinema (Map pp284-6; ☎ 3211 3244; 346 George St)

Palace Centro (Map pp284-6; ☎ 3852 4488; 39 James St)

Village Twin (Map pp284-6; ☎ 3358 2021; 701 Brunswick St)

IMAX Theatre (Map pp284-6; ☎ 3844 4222; cnr Ernest & Grey Sts) Pay to see movies by the dimension: 2D/3D movies are $15/17.

Live Music

Brisbane is a good place to catch some live music, and rightly so considering its history. Groups such as the influential '70s punk band The Saints, and more recently Powderfinger and Regurgitator, all hail from Brisbane. The Bee Gees even spent some of their formative years here. Cover charges start at around $6 for local acts and go up from there.

Zoo (Map pp284-6; ☎ 3854 1381; 711 Ann St) More than one band has rated this place as the best small venue in Australia. There are DJs on nonband nights.

Tongue & Groove (Map p274; ☎ 3846 0334; 63 Hardgrave Rd) This great little venue has varied live music from Thursday to Sunday (also see Eating p290).

Brisbane Festival Hall (Map pp284-6; ☎ 3229 7788; 65 Charlotte St) and **Arena** (Map pp284-6; ☎ 3252 5690; 210 Brunswick St) are popular venues for touring rock bands.

Jazz & Blues Bar (Map pp284-6; ☎ 3238 2222; ground fl, Holiday Inn, Roma St) The city's major venue for jazz and blues, this bar features good local and international acts live on stage Wednesday to Saturday.

Brisbane Jazz Club (Map pp284-6; ☎ 3391 2006; 1 Annie St) Jazz purists head here on Saturday and Sunday nights.

Healer (Map pp284-6; ☎ 3852 2575; 27 Warner St) For smooth R&B, visit this small venue in a converted church.

Nightclubs

Even though Brisbane's clubbing scene can rival most places in Australia, it's still a bit behind the times when it comes to dress code. Many clubs will turn away those not wearing a collared shirt or dressy shoes, and will demand ID. Of course, you won't find this everywhere, but it's better to be safe than sorry. Entrance fees are around $5 to $10.

Family (Map pp284-6; ☎ 3852 5000; 8 McLachlan St) Voted Australia's number one club in 2002, Family is the city's premier party location. There are four levels, two dance floors, four bars, four funky themed booths and a top-notch sound system.

QUEENSLAND

Empire (Map pp284-6; ☎ 3852 1216; 339 Brunswick St) This huge, converted hotel has several rooms featuring different types of music. Generally it's drum and base upstairs at the Moon Bar and house downstairs at the Corner Bar.

Monastery (Map pp284-6; ☎ 3257 7081; 621 Ann St) Expect house, techno and break beat at this modern nightclub in the Valley. Friday night is generally heaving.

R-Bar (Map pp284-6; ☎ 3220 1477; 235 Edward St) This café-bar-club opens late Wednesday to Saturday and plays a variety of dance music.

Indie Temple (Map pp284-6; ☎ 3220 1477; 235 Edward St) This central, alternative club at Rosie's Tavern is popular at weekends, and pulls in a younger crowd of students and rock fans.

Sport

You can see interstate cricket matches and international test cricket at the **Brisbane Cricket Ground** (Gabba; Map p274; ☎ 3008 6166; www.thegabba.org.au) in Woolloongabba, just south of Kangaroo Point. The cricket season runs from October to March.

During the other half of the year, rugby league is the big spectator sport. The Brisbane Broncos plays its home games at the ANZ/Queen Elizabeth II Stadium in Nathan. Brisbane also has an Australian Football League (AFL) club, the Brisbane Lions, based at the Gabba.

Theatre & Opera

The Queensland Cultural Centre has a dedicated phone line that handles bookings for all of the South Bank theatres; call ☎ 13 62 46.

Performing Arts Centre (Map pp284-6; ☎ 3840 7444; www.qpat.com.au; Queensland Cultural Centre, Stanley St, South Bank) The centre features concerts, plays, dance performances and film screenings in its three venues.

Queensland Conservatorium (Map pp284-6; ☎ 3875 6375; 16 Russell St) South of the Performing Arts Centre, this is Brisbane's big opera venue, and plays host to plenty of international names.

Brisbane Powerhouse (☎ 3358 8600; 119 Lamington St) Housed in a stylish, modernised brick building, this progressive little theatre puts on an ambitious programme of plays, music and dance.

Other theatres:

Metro Arts Centre (Map pp284-6; ☎ 3221 1527; 109 Edward St)

Gardens Theatre (Map pp284-6; ☎ 3864 4455; QUT, George St)

Brisbane Arts Theatre (Map pp284-6; ☎ 3369 2344; 210 Petrie Tce)

SHOPPING

Brisbane has six outdoor megastores in a row along Wickham St in Fortitude Valley, just south of the intersection with Gipps St. It's possible to hire camping gear from a couple of the stores.

Around the intersection of Ann and Brunswick Sts are dozens of trendy fashion boutiques with names like BrotherSista, Tarmac and Honor Lulu, selling club-wear and young designers' gear.

The **Australian Geographic** Wintergarden Centre (Map pp284-6; ☎ 3003 0355; Queen St Mall); Myer Centre (Map pp284-6; ☎ 3220 0341; Myer Centre, Queen St Mall) stores stock everything from books and calendars on Australian flora and fauna to glow-in-the-dark dinosaurs.

Aboriginal art can be found at **Queensland Aboriginal Creations** (☎ 3224 5730; Little Stanley St) and the **Southbank Aboriginal Centre** (Map pp284-6; ☎ 3844 0255; Stanley St Plaza).

Markets

On weekends the funky **Valley Market**, with a diverse collection of crafts, clothes and junk, is held in the Brunswick St Mall. The **Crafts Village Market** (Map pp284-6; Stanley St Plaza) at South Bank has a great range of clothing, arts and crafts from Friday to Sunday.

Every Sunday from 8am to 4pm, the carnival-style **Riverside Centre Market** and **Eagle St Pier Market** host over 150 craft stalls, including glassware, weaving and leatherwork. There are also children's activities.

GETTING THERE & AWAY
Air

The **Qantas travel centre** (Map pp284-6; ☎ 13 13 13; 247 Adelaide St; ☯ 8.30am-5pm Mon-Fri, 9am-1pm Sat) has frequent flights to the southern capitals and to the main Queensland centres. Standard one-way fares from Brisbane with Qantas include Sydney ($100), Melbourne and Adelaide ($180), and Perth ($500). Within Queensland, one-way fares include Townsville ($130), Rockhampton ($85), Mackay ($145) and Cairns ($170).

Virgin Blue (☎ 13 67 89; www.virginblue.com.au) flies to all the same destinations and its fares are generally a couple of dollars cheaper.

Macair (☎ 13 13 13; www.macair.com.au) flies to many destinations in the Queensland outback; see p348 for details. **Alliance Airlines** (☎ 1300 130 092; www.flightwest.com.au) flies from Brisbane to Townsville ($100), while **Sunshine Express** (☎ 13 13 13; www.sunshineexpress.com .au) connects Brisbane with Hervey Bay and Maryborough ($165).

Bus

Brisbane's **Roma St Transit Centre** (Map pp284-6; Roma St), about 500m west of the city centre, is the main terminus and booking office for all long-distance buses and trains. The centre has shops, food outlets, ATMs, an accommodation booking service and a backpackers' employment service.

The bus companies have booking desks on the 3rd level of the centre. **McCafferty's/ Greyhound** (☎ 13 20 30, 13 14 99; www.mccaffertys.com .au) is the main company on the Sydney–Brisbane run ($90, 16 hours). **Premier Motor Service** (☎ 13 34 10; www.premierms.com.au) often has cheaper deals on this route. Buses also head to Melbourne ($185, 24 hours), Adelaide (from $235, 30 hours), and Darwin ($375, 47 hours) via Longreach ($110, 16 hours) and Mt Isa ($145, 25 hours).

McCafferty's/Greyhound runs daily services north to Cairns ($185, 28½ hours), stopping at Noosa Heads ($28, 3 hours), Hervey Bay ($45, 5 hours), Rockhampton ($85, 11 hours), Mackay ($130, 16 hours) and Townsville ($160, 23 hours).

Car

The big rental firms have offices in Brisbane, and there are a number of smaller operators:

Integra Car Rentals (Map p274; ☎ 3252 5752; www.integracar.com.au; 398 St Pauls Tce; ☽ 7.30am-5.30pm Mon-Fri, 8am-4pm Sat, 8am-3pm Sun)

Car-azy Rentals (Map p274; ☎ 3257 1104; carazy@bigpond.net.au; 86 Bridge St; ☽ 8am-5pm Mon-Fri, 8am-1pm Sat, 9am-noon Sun)

National (Map p274; ☎ 3854 1499; www.nationalcarre ntal.com.au; 12 Brooke St, Bowen Hills; ☽ 8am-5pm)

If you have a car, beware of the two-hour parking limit in the city and inner suburbs – parking inspectors are merciless.

Train

New South Wales' **CountryLink** (☎ 13 22 32; www .countrylink.nsw.gov.au) has a daily XPT (express passenger train) service between Brisbane and Sydney. The northbound service runs overnight, and the southbound service runs during the day (economy/1st class/sleeper $110/155/235, 15 hours).

Services within Queensland:

Spirit of the Outback (seat/economy sleeper/1st-class sleeper $175/210/315, 24 hours) Brisbane–Longreach via Rockhampton twice weekly.

Spirit of the Tropics ($155/200/300, 24 hours) Brisbane–Townsville twice a week via Mackay.

Sunlander ($187/235/352, 32 hours) Departs Tuesday, Thursday and Saturday for Cairns via Townsville.

Tilt Train (economy $280, 25 hours) Brisbane–Cairns train leaves Brisbane at 6.25pm Monday, Wednesday and Friday, returning from Cairns at 8.15am Sunday, Wednesday and Friday.

Westlander ($85/130/200, 16½ hours) Brisbane–Charleville via Roma twice a week.

Concessions are available to children under 16 years, students with a valid ISIC card, and senior citizens. For details contact **Queensland Rail's booking service** (☎ 13 22 32; www.traveltrain.qr.com.au; ☽ 6am-8.30pm).

GETTING AROUND

For all city bus, train and ferry information, ring the **Trans-Info Service** (☎ 13 12 30; www.trans info.qld.gov.au; ☽ 6am-10pm). Bus and ferry information is also available at the **Brisbane Tourism visitors centre** (Map pp284-6; ☎ 3006 6200; Queen St Mall; ☽ 9am-6pm Mon-Thu, 9am-8pm Fri, 9am-5pm Sat, 9.30am-4.30pm Sun), the **bus station information centre** (Map pp284-6; ☽ 8.30am-5.30pm Mon-Thu, 8.30am-8pm Fri, 9am-4pm Sat, 10am-4pm Sun) under the Queen St Mall, and the **Queensland Rail Travel Centre** (Map pp284-6; Central Station, Ann St; ☽ 7am-5pm Mon-Fri, 9am-12.30pm Sat).

If you're going to be using public transport a lot on any single day, it's worth getting an unlimited Day Rover ticket (adult/child $8.40/4.20) for buses, ferries and CityCats. Alternatively, an Off-Peak Saver ($4.60/ 2.30) is valid from 9am to 3.30pm and after 7pm Monday to Friday, and all day Saturday and Sunday (not valid on ferries and CityCats on weekends). A Ten Trip Saver (Zone 1 $14/6.90) gives you 10 trips for the price of eight. A South East Explorer ticket ($8.60, serves the metropolitan area) covers CityTrain services as well.

To/From the Airport

Brisbane's airport is about 15km northeast of the city. Probably the easiest way to get to and from the airport is with the **Airtrain** (☎ 3215 5000; www.airtrain.com.au; tickets $9; ☯ services 5am-8pm), which runs every 15 minutes from the Roma St and Central train stations. There are also half-hourly services ($18) from Gold Coast CityTrain stops to the airport.

Coachtrans runs the half-hourly **Skytrans** (☎ 3236 1000; tickets $9, $11 with drop-off at hotel; ☯ services 5.45am-10pm) shuttle bus between the Roma St Transit Centre and the airport, and the **Airporter** (☎ 5506 9777; www.coachtrans.com.au; one way/return $35/65) bus between Brisbane airport and the Gold Coast.

Suncoast Pacific (☎ 3236 1901; www.suncoastpacific .com.au) has a direct service to the Sunshine Coast for $35 return.

A taxi into the centre from the airport will cost around $30.

Boat

Brisbane has a fast and efficient ferry service along and across the Brisbane River in the form of the nippy blue CityCat catamarans. The cats run every 20 to 30 minutes, between 5.50am and 10.30pm, from the University of Queensland in the west to Bretts Wharf in the east, and back – see the Brisbane (p274) and Central Brisbane (pp284–6) maps for the exact route. Many of its stops are wheelchair-accessible.

Also useful are the Inner City Ferries, which zigzag across the river between North Quay, near Victoria Bridge, and Mowbray Park. Services run till about 9pm from Sunday to Thursday and until about 11.30pm on Friday and Saturday. There are also several cross-river ferries; most useful is the Eagle St Pier to Kangaroo Point service. Fares range from $1.80 for cross-river trips to $3.80 for the length of the route. Off-Peak, Day Rover and South East Explorer cards are valid on CityCats and Inner City Ferries.

Bus

The Loop, a free bus that circles the city area, stopping at QUT, Queen St Mall, City Hall, Central Station and Riverside, runs every 10 minutes on weekdays between 7am and 6pm.

The main stop for local buses is in the underground bus station in the Myer Centre, where there's an information centre.

You can also pick up many buses from the colour-coded stops along Adelaide St, between George and Edward Sts.

Routes are priced by the sector. Most of the inner suburbs fall into Zone 1 (adult/child $1.80/0.90) and Zone 2 ($2.60/1.30).

Buses run every 10 to 20 minutes Monday to Friday, from 5am till about 6pm, and with the same frequency on Saturday morning (starting at 6am). Services are less frequent at other times, and cease at 7pm Sunday, and midnight on other days.

Taxi

You can usually hail a taxi with ease in most parts of downtown Brisbane and its neighbouring districts. Two of the main operators in Brisbane are **Black & White** (☎ 13 10 08) and **Yellow Cab Co** (☎ 13 19 24).

Train

The fast CityTrain network has seven lines, which run as far as Gympie North in the north (for the Sunshine Coast) and Nerang and Robina in the south (for the Gold Coast). All trains go through Roma St, Central and Brunswick St stations. A journey in the central area is $1.80.

MORETON BAY

Moreton Bay, at the mouth of the Brisbane River, is reckoned to have some 365 islands. Most people head for North Stradbroke, for its great beaches and surfing, and Moreton Island, to participate in the dolphin feeding at Tangalooma. Of the coastal suburbs lining the bay, Manly, with its large marina and pleasant cafés, is the most inviting.

Tours

Humpbacks are a regular sight in the bay between June and November. **Moreton Bay Whalewatching** (☎ 07-3880 0477; www.whalewatching .net) offers day trips leaving from the Redcliffe jetty, while **Brisbane Day Tours** (☎ 07-3236 1240) organises everything from the Roma St Transit Centre. Trips generally go for around $100/60 per adult/child.

THE BAYSIDE

Redcliffe, the first white settlement in Queensland, is 35km north of Brisbane. The local Aboriginal people called it Humpybong

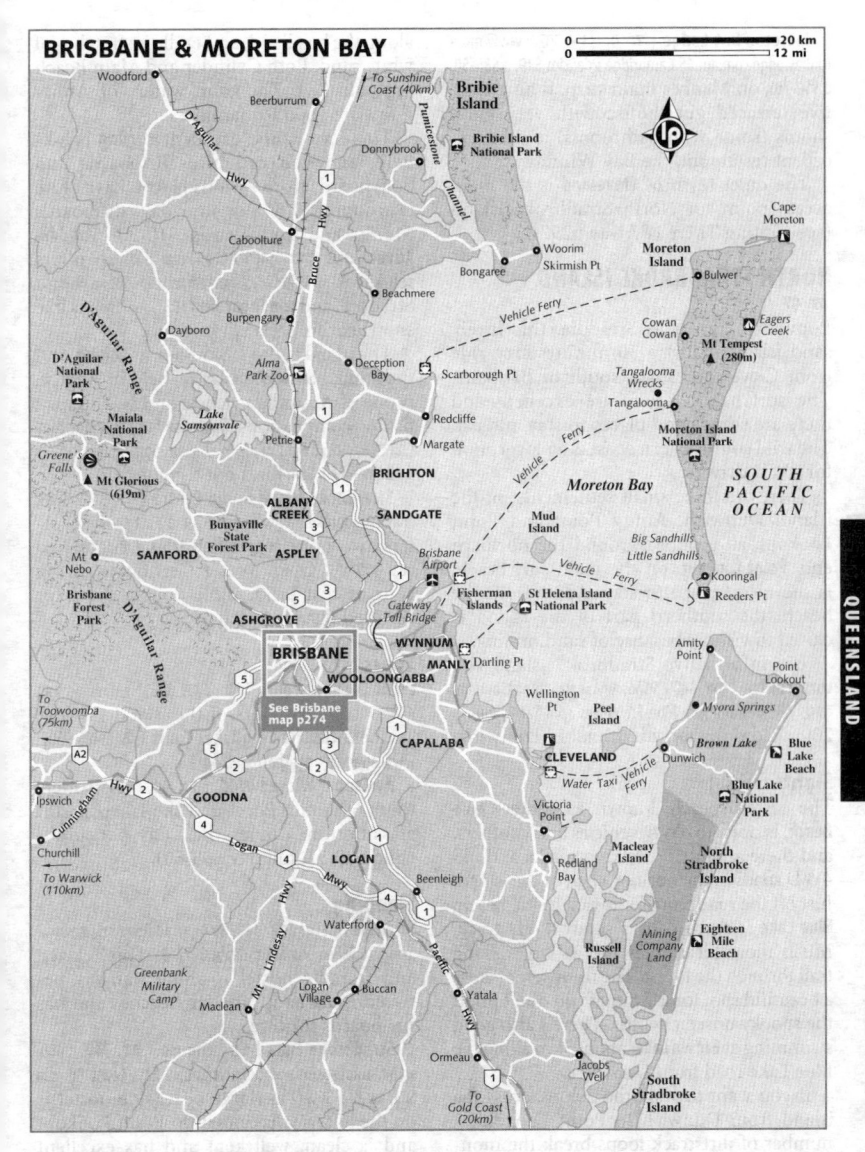

BRISBANE & MORETON BAY

0 ————— 20 km
0 ————— 12 mi

Woodford
D'Aguilar Hwy
Beerburrum
To Sunshine Coast (40km)
Pumicestone Channel
Bribie Island
Bribie Island National Park
Donnybrook
Caboolture
Bruce Hwy
Woorim
Skirmish Pt
Bongaree
Beachmere
Cape Moreton
Moreton Island
Bulwer
Cowan Cowan
Eagers Creek
Mt Tempest (280m)
Tangalooma Wrecks
Tangalooma
Moreton Island National Park

D'Aguilar Range
Dayboro
Burpengary
D'Aguilar National Park
Alma Park Zoo
Deception Bay
Scarborough Pt
Maiala National Park
Lake Samsonvale
Petrie
Redcliffe
Margate
Greene's Falls
Mt Glorious (619m)
ALBANY CREEK
BRIGHTON
SANDGATE
Bunyaville State Forest Park
Mt Nebo
SAMFORD
ASPLEY
Brisbane Airport
Mud Island
SOUTH PACIFIC OCEAN
Moreton Bay
Big Sandhills
Little Sandhills
Kooringal
Reeders Pt
Brisbane Forest Park
ASHGROVE
Gateway Toll Bridge
Fisherman Islands
St Helena Island National Park
WYNNUM
BRISBANE
MANLY
Darling Pt
See Brisbane map p274
WOOLOONGABBA
Amity Point
Point Lookout
Wellington Pt
Peel Island
Myora Springs
To Toowoomba (75km)
A2
CAPALABA
CLEVELAND
Dunwich
Brown Lake
Blue Lake Beach
Blue Lake National Park
Ipswich
Cunningham Hwy
GOODNA
Churchill
To Warwick (110km)
Logan Mwy
LOGAN
Beenleigh
Victoria Point
Macleay Island
North Stradbroke Island
Redland Bay
Waterford
Greenbank Military Camp
Mt Lindesay Hwy
Logan Village
Buccan
Maclean
Yatala
Pacific Hwy
Russell Island
Mining Company Land
Eighteen Mile Beach
Ormeau
Jacobs Well
South Stradbroke Island
To Gold Coast (20km)

QUEENSLAND

(Dead Houses), and the name is still applied to the peninsula. Vehicle ferries to Bulwer on Moreton Island leave from **Scarborough**, at the northern tip of the headland.

There are several interesting coastal towns south of the Brisbane River mouth. **Manly** is an attractive seaside suburb with the largest marina in the southern hemisphere after Fre-

mantle in Western Australia. Every Wednesday there are yacht races out in the bay, and many of the captains are happy to take guests on board free of charge. Inquire at one of the yacht clubs along the waterfront. The **visitors centre** (☎ 07-3348 3514; www.wynnum-manly.net; 43 Cambridge Pde; ☿ 9am-5pm Mon-Fri, 10am-3pm Sat & Sun) is on the main street.

Moreton Bay Lodge (☎ 07-3396 3020; www.more
tonbaylodge.com.au; 45 Cambridge Pde; dm $19, s $35-50,
d $50-70), on Manly's main strip, is an attrac-
tive terraced guesthouse with very good
rooms (some with bathrooms) and an excellent restaurant, the Bay Window.

The quiet town of **Cleveland** is the main
access point for North Stradbroke Island
(see Getting There & Away p297).

NORTH STRADBROKE ISLAND
☎ 07

Popularly known as Straddie, this lovely
sand island is just a 30-minute ferry ride
from Cleveland, 30km south of Brisbane.
The surf beaches here are excellent and
there are some good places to stay and eat.
The wild southeastern coast is a playground
for 4WD drivers.

There are three small settlements on the
island: Dunwich, Amity Point and Point
Lookout, all grouped around the northern
end. **Point Lookout**, on the main surf beach,
is the nicest place to stay. Apart from the
beach, the southern part of the island is
closed to visitors because of sand mining.

The informative Stradbroke Island **visitors centre** (☎ 3409 9555; www.stradbroketourism.
com; ☯ 8.30am-5pm Mon-Fri, closes 3pm Sat & Sun) is
200m from the ferry terminal in Dunwich.

Sights
The eastern beach, known as **Eighteen Mile
Beach**, is open to 4WD vehicles and campers,
and there are lots of walking tracks and old
4WD roads in the northern half of the island.
Just off the road from Dunwich to the beach,
Blue Lake is reached by a sandy 4WD track.
Much more pleasant is the 2.7km walking
trail through the forest. The freshwater lake is
a beautiful spot for a swim, if you don't mind
the spooky unseen depths. There's also good
swimming at **Brown Lake**, about 3km along the
Blue Lake road from Dunwich.

If you want to walk the 20km across the
island from Dunwich to Point Lookout, a
number of dirt-track loops break the monotony of bitumen road. A pleasant diversion
near the coast, about 4km north of Dunwich,
is **Myora Springs**, which is surrounded by lush
vegetation and walking tracks.

Activities
Straddie's best **beaches** are around Point Lookout, where there's a series of points and bays

along the headland, and endless stretches of
white sand. Both Cylinder and Main Beach
are patrolled. The calm waters of Amity
Point are good for families.

There are some excellent **surfing** breaks
here, and you can hire surfboards and
bodyboards from various places; kayak hire
is around $20/50 per hour/day, surfboards
$15/40 and bodyboards $10/30. **Straddie
Adventures** (☎ 3409 8414; Point Lookout) offers
sea-kayaking trips (incl snorkelling stops $35) around
Straddie, and **sandboarding** ($25), which is like
snowboarding, except on sand.

The island is also famous for its **fishing**, and
the annual Straddie Classic, held in August,
is one of Australia's richest and best-known
fishing competitions. **Dunwich Sports & Hobbies**
(☎ 3409 9252; Bingle Rd; ☯ 7.30am-5pm Mon-Fri, closes
4pm Sat & 3pm Sun) hires out fishing gear.

Stradbroke Island Scuba Centre (☎ 3409 8888;
www.stradbrokeislandscuba.com.au; 1 East Coast Rd) offers two-hour **snorkelling trips** (adult/child incl
gear $60/40). Open Water Certificate diving
courses cost $350, while double dives for
certified divers start at $95.

Tours
Point Lookout Tours (☎ 3409 8051) runs good
4WD half-day tours of the island for $30,
as does **Straddie Kingfisher Tours** (☎ 3409 9502;
www.straddiekingfishertours.com.au).

Awesome Wicked Wild (☎ 3409 8045) offers
tours of Amity Point and the lakes in 20ft
glass-bottom canoes (half day per adult/
child $25/35, full day $35/50).

Sleeping
Straddie Hostel (☎ 3409 8979; straddiehostel@hotmail
.com; 76 Mooloomba Rd; dm/d $17/40) This relaxed
and friendly hostel is about halfway between Main and Cylinder Beaches and has
surfboards for hire.

Stradbroke Island Guesthouse (☎ 3409 8888;
www.stradbrokeislandscuba.com.au; 1 East Coast Rd; dm
$22, tw & d $50) This large beachside hostel is
on the left as you come into Point Lookout
and is clean, well kept and has excellent
facilities, including a dive school right on
its doorstep (see Stradbroke Island Scuba
Centre above). Guests can hire bikes for
$10/15 for a half/full day.

Whalewatch Ocean Beach Resort (☎ 3409
8555; www.whalewatchresort.com.au; Samarinda Dr, Point
Lookout; apt for 2 nights from $300; ☒) If you're
looking for something a lot more upmarket,

this is the place. The apartments here are fully self-contained, have three rooms, two bathrooms, large lounges and superb views of the ocean. There's also a swimming pool, gym and spa for guests. Prices skyrocket in the high season.

If you're thinking of staying a while, a holiday flat or house can be good value, especially outside the holiday seasons; prices start at around $350 per week for one- or two-bedroom apartments. There are numerous real estate agents on the island, including **Ray White** (☎ 3409 8255; www.raywhite straddie.com.au; Mintee St).

There are eight council-run **camping grounds** (camp/caravan sites per person $6/9.50, extra persons $4/5.80, foreshore camping $3.80) on the island, but the most attractive are the places grouped around Point Lookout. The Adder Rock Camping Area and Thankful Rest Camping Area both overlook lovely Home Beach, while the Cylinder Beach Camping Area sits right on Cylinder Beach, one of the most popular beaches on the island. Sites should be booked (well in advance!) through the visitors centre.

Eating

There are a couple of general stores selling groceries in Point Lookout, but it's worth bringing basic supplies. Note that few places to eat are open later than 8pm.

Point Lookout Bowls Club (☎ 3409 8182; East Coast Rd; meals $5-15) Next door to the Masonic Club, the bowls club has some of the cheapest meals on the island.

Stonefish Cafe (☎ 3409 8549; cnr Mooloomba Rd & Mintee St; mains $15-20; ☷ breakfast & lunch) The Stonefish is a relaxed café with a small deli next door.

La Focaccia (☎ 3409 8778; Meegera Pl; pizza & pasta around $15, mains $19) This popular Italian place close to Cylinder beach has great salads, sandwiches and more substantial meals.

Getting There & Away

The gateway to North Stradbroke Island is the seaside town of Cleveland. The best way to get there from Brisbane is by CityTrain; services leave every 30 minutes from 5am to 12.50am ($7.30, 1 hour), and buses meet the trains at Cleveland station ($0.90).

Stradbroke Ferries (☎ 3286 2666; www.stradbroke ferries.com.au) runs a water taxi to Dunwich almost every hour from about 6am to 6pm

($13 return, 45 minutes). Stradbroke Ferries also operate a slightly less frequent vehicle ferry from 5.30am to 4.30pm weekdays (passenger/vehicle $10/90), and until later on weekends.

The **Stradbroke Flyer** (☎ 3826 1964; www.flyer .com.au) runs an almost-hourly fast catamaran service ($12) to One Mile Jetty, 1.5km north of central Dunwich.

Getting Around

Local buses (☎ 3409 7151) meet the ferries at Dunwich and One Mile Jetty, and run across to Point Lookout ($9). The last bus to Dunwich leaves Point Lookout at about 6pm. If you miss it, there's the **Stradbroke Cab Service** (☎ 3409 9800).

MORETON ISLAND
☎ 07

North of Stradbroke, Moreton Island comes a close second to Fraser Island for excellent sand-driving and wilderness, and sees far fewer visitors. Apart from a few rocky headlands, it's all sand, with **Mt Tempest** towering to 280m, the highest coastal sandhill in the world. The island's birdlife is prolific, and at its northern tip is a **lighthouse**, built in 1857. Sand-mining leases on the island have been cancelled and 90% of the island is now a national park. Off the west coast are a number of artificial shipwrecks, the **Tangalooma Wrecks**, which provide good **snorkelling** and **diving**.

Moreton Island has no paved roads, but 4WD vehicles can travel along beaches and a few cross-island tracks – seek local advice about tides and creek crossings. The EPA publishes a map of the island, which you can get from the vehicle ferry offices or the **rangers** (☎ 3408 2710) at False Patch Wrecks near the Tangalooma Wild Dolphin Resort. Vehicle permits for the island cost $30 and are available through the ferry operators or from EPA offices.

Tangalooma, halfway down the western side of the island, is a popular tourist resort sited at an old whaling station. The main attraction is the **wild-dolphin feeding**, which takes place each evening at around sunset. Usually about eight or nine dolphins swim in from the ocean and take fish from the hands of volunteer feeders, but you need to be a guest of the resort to be involved.

The only other settlements, all on the west coast, are **Bulwer** near the northwestern tip, **Cowan Cowan** between Bulwer and Tangalooma, and **Kooringal** near the southern tip. The shops at Kooringal and Bulwer are expensive, so bring what you can from the mainland.

Without your own vehicle, walking is the only way to get around the island, and you'll need several days to explore it. Fortunately, there are loads of good walking trails and decommissioned 4WD roads. It's worth making the strenuous trek to the summit of Mt Tempest, about 3km inland from Eagers Creek.

About 3km south and inland from Tangalooma is an area of bare sand known as the **Desert**, while the **Big Sandhills** and the **Little Sandhills** are towards the narrow southern end of the island. The biggest lakes and some swamps are in the northeast.

Tours

Sunrover Expeditions (☎ 1800 353 717, 3880 0719; www.sunrover.com.au; adult/child $120/90) is a friendly and reliable 4WD tour operator with good day tours. Tours depart Roma St Transit Centre in Brisbane at 6.45am on Friday, Sunday and Monday. There's also a three-day safari for $300/200.

Gibren Expeditions (☎ 1300 559 355; www.gibren expeditions.com.au; 2-/3-day tours from $210/250) offers tours of the island with heaps of activities thrown in, including snorkelling, sandboarding, sea-kayaking and scuba diving.

Sleeping

There are a few holiday flats and houses for rent at Kooringal, Cowan Cowan and Bulwer.

Bulwer Cabins (☎ 3203 6399; www.moreton-island .com; cabins from $90) These accommodating self-contained units, 200m from the beach at Bulwer, sleep up to six.

Tangalooma Wild Dolphin Resort (☎ 1300 652 250, 3268 6333; www.tangalooma.com; packages $180-330) If price is no obstacle, this is the most desirable locale. It has plush rooms, nice beaches and tame dolphins. Rates include transfers, overnight accommodation and dolphin feeding.

There are five EPA **camping grounds** (per person/family $4/16), all with water, toilets and cold showers. For information and camping permits, contact the **EPA** (☎ 3227 8185; 160 Ann St, Brisbane) or the **ranger** (☎ 3408 2710) at False Patch Wrecks.

Getting There & Around

The **Tangalooma Flyer** (day/overnight trip $38/64), a fast catamaran operated by the Tangalooma Wild Dolphin Resort, sails to Moreton daily at 10am from a dock at Holt St, off Kingsford-Smith Dr (in Eagle Farm, just south of the airport); a courtesy bus departs the Roma St Transit Centre in Brisbane at 9am. Book in advance.

The **Moreton Venture** (☎ 3895 1000) is a vehicle ferry that runs daily except Tuesday from Howard-Smith Dr, Lyton, at the Port of Brisbane, to Tangalooma. The return fare is $155 for a 4WD (including up to three passengers); pedestrians are charged $25/15 return per adult/child.

The **Combie Trader** (☎ 3203 6399; www.moreton -island.com) runs at least once daily except Tuesday, sailing between Scarborough and Bulwer. The return fare is $27/16 per adult/child for foot passengers and $155 per vehicle with up to four passengers.

You can hire 4WDs to explore the island from **Moreton Island 4WD Hire** (☎ 3410 1338) in Bulwer for $115 per day.

ST HELENA ISLAND

This little island, only 6km from the mouth of the Brisbane River, was until 1932 a high-security prison and is now a national park. The remains of several prison buildings, plus parts of Brisbane's first tramway, built in 1884, now form part of a prison island tour.

AB Sea Cruises (☎ 3396 3994; www.sthelenaisland .com.au; trips 9.15am Mon-Fri, 11am & 7pm Sat & Sun) runs day trips to St Helena from Manly Harbour, including a tramway ride and a 'dramatised tour' of the prison (adult/child $65/35), complete with floggings if you so desire. Its night tour ($75/40) leaves on weekends only.

You can reach Manly from central Brisbane in about 35 minutes by train on the Cleveland line.

GOLD COAST

☎ 07 / pop 376,500

Love it or loathe it, the Gold Coast is hard to ignore. This 35km stretch of beach between Southport and the NSW border is home to some of the most intensive tourist development in Australia, a continuous landfill of ultra-expensive high-rise holiday apartments and cheap motels, punctuated by airport-sized shopping centres and clusters of restaurants and convenience stores.

Yet a mere 50 years ago none of this was here. The incredible transformation of the Gold Coast from a string of sleepy seaside towns to the modern multiplex was fuelled by some savvy manipulation of the Asian holiday market in the 1950s and 1960s. These days more than two-million visitors descend on the strip every year, drawn by the sand, sea and surf, plus a whole host of theme parks and other glitzy artificial attractions.

The Gold Coast is tourism on a grand scale, and the relentless commercialism isn't to everyone's taste. Fortunately, the Gold Coast has a little-visited but beautiful hinterland less than 30km from the beach, with some excellent national parks, including Lamington and Springbrook, two of Queensland's best.

ORIENTATION

The undisputed capital of the Gold Coast is Surfers Paradise, and it's here that you'll find most of the tourist attractions and accommodation, and the best nightlife. However, if it's surf you're after, many of the best breaks can be found further south at places like Burleigh Heads and Kirra Beach The twin towns of Tweed Heads and Coolangatta mark the southern end of the Gold Coast, as well as the border with NSW, while Southport, just north of Surfers, is the most northerly of the high-rise developments.

The Gold Coast Hwy runs right along the coastal strip, leaving the Pacific Hwy just north of Coolangatta and rejoining it inland from Southport. The Gold Coast airport is at Coolangatta.

INFORMATION
Disabled Visitors

Freedom Wheels (☎ 5554 5132; www.freedomwheels rentals.com; 18 Cessnock Close) is a good place to try for specially designed vehicles for the disabled.

Internet Access

There are surprisingly few Internet cafés on the Gold Coast, but most backpackers' hostels have emailing facilities. Try the following Internet cafés:

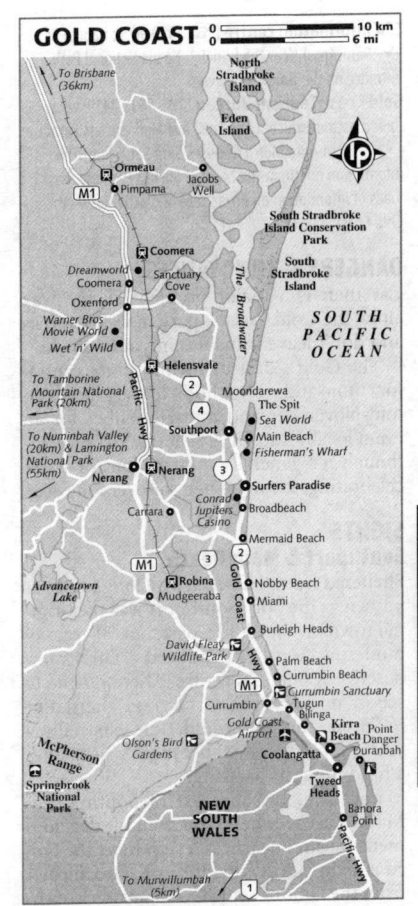

Email Centre (☎ 5538 7500; Orchid Ave, Surfers Paradise)
PB's OZ Internet Cafe Coolangatta (☎ 5599 4536; 152 Griffith St, Coolangatta); Burleigh Heads (☎ 5520 0007; 66 Goodwin Tce, Burleigh Heads)

Money

American Express (Amex; ☎ 1300 139 060; Pacific Fair Shopping Centre, Hooker Blvd, Broadbeach)
Thomas Cook (☎ 5531 7770; Cavill Ave Mall, Surfers Paradise)
Travelex (☎ 5531 7917; Cavill Ave Mall, Surfers Paradise)

Tourist Information

Coolangatta visitors centre (☎ 5536 7765; cnr Griffith & Warner Sts; ☒ 8am-5pm Mon-Fri, 8am-4pm Sat, 9am-1pm Sun) At the southern end of the Gold Coast strip, this visitors centre is another good source of information.

EPA information centre (☎ 5520 9603; Kabool Rd; ⏱ 9am-4pm) Near the Burleigh Heads National Park entrance on the Gold Coast Hwy.

Gold Coast Tourism Bureau (☎ 5538 4419; www .goldcoasttourism.com.au; Cavill Ave Mall, Surfers Paradise; ⏱ 8.30am-6pm Mon-Fri, closes 5pm Sat & Sun) This information booth, in the heart of Surfers Paradise, has loads of information on attractions and activities on the Gold Coast.

DANGERS & ANNOYANCES

Car theft is a major problem all the way along the Gold Coast – park in well-lit areas and don't leave valuables in your vehicle.

The Gold Coast turns into party central for thousands of school leavers between mid-November and mid-December for an event locally known as Schoolie's Week. Although it's generally a lot of fun for those celebrating, it can be hell for everyone else.

SIGHTS
Southport & Main Beach

Sheltered from the ocean by a long sand bar known as the Spit, Southport was the original town on the Gold Coast, but 50 years of modernisation has produced a fairly non-descript residential centre. There is little to see or do here, but it's a good alternative to Surfers for accommodation, especially if you're looking for a quiet night's sleep after a hard night of partying.

Immediately southeast of Southport is Main Beach, where the tourist developments begin in earnest. From here, the Spit runs 3km north, dividing the Broadwater from the South Pacific Ocean. At the southern end of the strip there are several malls and the Sea World theme park (see the boxed text 'Gold Coast Theme Parks' p302). The **Marina Mirage**, an upmarket shopping and dining complex, is the departure point for cruises. On the ocean side, the beaches and surf are excellent, under-used and backed by a peaceful area of parkland.

Surfers Paradise

In 1965 a local entrepreneur named Bernie Elsey had the brainwave of employing meter maids in skimpy gold lamé bikinis to feed the parking meters on the main strip, and Surfers Paradise has never looked back. If you love party nights and lazy days, you're almost guaranteed to have a good time here.

The place has come a long way since 1936, when there was just the brand-new Surfers Paradise Hotel, a tiny beachfront hideaway for those who found Southport too racy.

Some clever marketing in Asia in the 1960s started the boom, which turned a little surf town into a beachfront urban jungle. The popularity of Surfers these days rests not so much on the sand and surf but on the shopping and nightlife, and the town's proximity to attractions such as the Gold Coast theme parks.

Cavill Ave, with a pedestrian mall at its beach end, is the main thoroughfare, while Orchid Ave, one block in from the Esplanade, is the nightclub and bar strip.

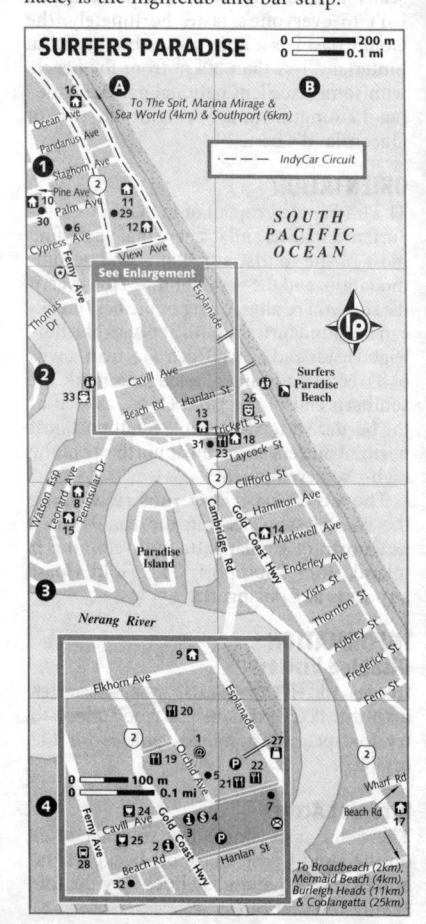

Southern Gold Coast

Just south of Surfers Paradise is Broad-beach, home to **Conrad Jupiters Casino**, Queensland's first legal casino (see Entertainment p306). The **Burleigh Heads National Park**, on the northern side of the mouth of Tallebudgera Creek, is a small but diverse forest reserve with walking trails around and through the rocky headland, as well as a lookout and picnic area. On the northern side is one of Australia's most famous surfing point breaks, which attracts plenty of pro-surfers and plenty of attitude.

There are three wildlife sanctuaries in the vicinity of Burleigh Heads. **Currumbin Wildlife Sanctuary** (☎ 5534 1266; www.currumbin-sanctuary.org.au; Gold Coast Hwy, Currumbin; adult/child $22/14; ☑ 8am-5pm), run by the National Trust, is an excellent bushland park mobbed by technicoloured lorikeets and other birds, with tree kangaroos, koalas, emus and lots more Australian fauna. There are 'behind the scene tours' for an extra $5/2.50, and night tours that include transfers from Gold Coast hotels for $46/29. Get off at Surfside bus stop No 20 for the sanctuary.

David Fleay Wildlife Park (☎ 5576 2411; West Burleigh Rd; adult/child/family $13/6.50/33; ☑ 9am-5pm) is run with the help of the QPWS and has a fine collection of native wildlife and 4km of walking tracks through mangroves and rainforest. To get here, take the Tallebudgera–Burleigh exit from the Gold Coast Hwy.

Olson's Bird Gardens (☎ 5533 0208; 746 Currumbin Creek Rd; adult/child/family $10/5/28; ☑ 9am-5pm) is an attractive subtropical garden with over 100 aviaries housing exotic birds, walking tracks, informative bush talks and a hedge maze. The sanctuary also offers basic accommo-dation in exchange for work in the gardens, which includes feeding the birds and taking care of the gardens. To get here, turn off the Bruce Hwy south of Currumbin Creek.

At the southern tip of the Gold Coast are the twin towns of **Coolangatta** and **Tweed Heads**. There are some great surf breaks here and none of the attitude of Burleigh Heads. Two beaches regularly used for both national and international competitions because of their top-notch waves are Kirra and Duranbah. Kirra is known for its heavy, quick waves and Durunbah, locally known as D-Bah, has a fast-breaking wave and often has surf when it's flat elsewhere. Both are suited to experienced surfers.

Plenty of places offer boards for hire, and the local op-shops are full of second-hand boards.

ACTIVITIES
Bungee Jumping

In Surfers a former car park on Cypress Ave is home to **Banzai Bungey** (☎ 5526 7611; jumps from $80). This place has been upstaged a bit by the nearby **Sling Shot** (☎ 5570 2700; per person $30) – basically a giant catapult in which you are the projectile – and the **Flycoaster** (☎ 5539 0474; per person $39), in which you swing like a pendulum after being released from a hoist 20m up. Photos and video of your facial distortions are available.

Horse Riding

Numinbah Valley Adventure Trails (☎ 5533 4137; www.numinbahtrails.com.au) has three-hour horse-riding treks through beautiful rainforest and river scenery in the Numinbah Valley, 30km south of Nerang, for $60/50 per adult/child, or $70/60 with pick-ups from the coast.

Gum Nuts Horse Riding Resort (☎ 5543 0191), on the Nerang–Broadbeach road in Carrara, has half-day riding for $55/33 per adult/child ($60/38 in the afternoon) or a full day with lunch for $95/60. Prices include Gold Coast pick-ups.

Water Sports & Surfing
You'd be downright silly not to get wet on the Gold Coast. The surf here is some of the best around, and even though it can get rather crowded at times, it's a good place to try your hand, so to speak, at surfing. Learn to surf with any of the following, for between $40 and $45 a lesson.

Cheyne Horan School of Surf (☎ 1800 227 873, 0403-080 484) Cheyne Horan has won both Australian and World surf titles.

Surfers Beach Hut Beach Hire (☎ 1800 787 337, 5526 7077; beach end of Cavill Ave Mall, Surfers Paradise; ☻ 8am-5pm) Also hires short boards and bodyboards for $10/30 per hour/day and long boards for $15/40.

Nancy Emerson School of Surf (☎ 0413-380 933; www.surfclinics.com)

Brad Holmes Surf Coaching (☎ 0418-757 539; www.bradholmessurfcoaching.com)

Godfathers of the Ocean (☎ 5593 5661; www.godfathersoftheocean.com)

Ex Screeme (☎ 1800 678 263)

For gear hire:

Retro Groove (☎ 5599 3952; 3 McLean St, Coolangatta; ☻ 9am-5pm Mon-Sat) Surfboard hire for $25/40 per half/full day.

Nicks Watersports Hire (☎ 0412-243 111) Rents out all types of surfboards ($30), as well as other gear like sea-kayaks, sailboards, catamarans, jet skis and in-line skates. Boards are delivered (free of charge) up and down the Gold Coast.

A few companies have diving courses and set dives (from $90) on the coast.

Buddyline Dive Tours & Aqua Sports & Dive (☎ 1800 814 222; www.aquasports.com.au; 32 Strat haird Rd, Bundall)

Queensland Scuba Diving Company (☎ 5526 7722; Mariners Cove Marina, Main Beach)

Other Activities
Seaworld Helicopters (☎ 5588 2224) At the Sea World theme park; prices start at $50 for five-minute flights over South Stradbroke Island.

Dreamworld Helicopters (☎ 5588 1111) Rides from $40.

Balloon Down Under (☎ 5530 3631) Thirty-minute rides for $175, one hour for $230 over hinterland, includes champagne picnic.

Tandem Skydiving (☎ 5599 1920) 10,000ft jump for $275.

GOLD COAST THEME PARKS

Immediately northwest of Surfers Paradise is a string of big, American-style theme parks, all competing for the most thrilling ride or the most entertaining show. Discount tickets are sold in most of the tourist offices on the Gold Coast; the 3 Park Super Pass (adult/child $147/94), available at Sea World, Movie World and Wet 'n' Wild, covers entry to all three parks.

Dreamworld (☎ 5588 1111; www.dreamworld.com.au; Pacific Hwy, Coomera; adult/child $60/36; ☻ 9.30am-5pm), on the Pacific Hwy 17km north of Surfers, is thrill-ride central, with such delights as the Giant Drop, a terminal-velocity machine where you free fall from 38 storeys. There are also plenty of attractions to keep the kids entertained, including the new Nickelodeon Park and a bunch of wildlife shows, the highlight of which is the interactive tiger show, one of only two in the world.

Sea World (☎ 5588 2222, 5588 2205 for show times; www.seaworld.com.au; Sea World Dr, Main Beach; adult/child $60/36; ☻ 10am-5pm), a huge aquatic theme park, has loads of animal performances, including twice-daily dolphin shows (10.45am and 3pm) and sea-lion shows (11.30am and 2.15pm), and shark-feeding; there are also waterslides and rollercoasters, and a zoo with some famous polar bears.

Warner Bros Movie World (☎ 5573 8485; www.movieworld.com.au; Pacific Hwy, Oxenford; adult/child $60/36; ☻ 9.30am-5pm), otherwise known as `Hollywood on the Gold Coast', claims to be Australia's number-one tourist attraction. Warner Bros cartoon characters wander around keeping the kids happy, and there are stunt shows, movie sets and some good thrill rides, including the Scooby-Doo Spooky Coaster.

Wet 'n' Wild (☎ 5573 2255; www.wetnwild.com.au; Pacific Hwy, Oxenford; adult/child $35/22; ☻ 10am-5pm winter, closes 9pm summer) is one of Australia's best water-sports parks and has an incredible variety of ways to get wet – great raft slides, a twister (in which you pelt down a water-sprayed, tightly spiralled tube), a 70km/h speed slide, and Mammoth Falls (a white-water rapids ride on a giant rubber ring). If all that sounds too energetic, you can always just float around on a big rubber ring.

Skate Biz (☎ 5527 0066; Southport Mall, Marine Pde; ⏰ 9am-5.30pm Mon-Thu, 9am-9pm Fri, 9am-4pm Sat, 10am-4pm Sun) Hires out in-line skates with pads and all the gear (2hr/overnight/24hr $13/17/20).

TOURS
Hinterland Trips
Mountain Trek Adventures (☎ 0500 844 100) offers full-day tours, which include Lamington National Park and Tamborine Mountain for $125/75 per adult/child. **Southern Cross 4WD Tours** (☎ 1800 067 367, 5547 7120) has similar tours for around the same price.

There are several big commercial companies operating out of Surfers that are slightly cheaper. **Australian Day Tours** (☎ 1300 363 436) charges $65/36 for its Springbrook day tour and $65/35 to Lamington National Park. **Grayline Tours** (☎ 1300 360 776) has similar rates.

Cruises
During summer months, various cruise companies operate from the Marina Mirage centre on the Spit, or from the Tiki Village Wharf at the river end of Cavill Ave. Most of the cruises include lunch and drinks, and a meander around the harbour and canals (adult/child around $34/20), or they head to South Stradbroke Island (from $45/26, including lunch). Check with the **Gold Coast Tourism Bureau** (☎ 5538 4419; Cavill Ave Mall, Surfers Paradise) for operators, or take a wander around the departure points.

A couple of companies offer the curious experience of exploring Surfers by road and river in a boat on wheels. The **Aquabus** (☎ 5539 0222; www.aquabus.com.au) makes a 75-minute trip from Orchid Ave up Main Beach and the Spit, and then sails back on the Broadwater ($27/21 per adult/child). **Aqua Duck** (☎ 5538 3825; www.aquaduck.com.au) has a similar itinerary for the same price and leaves from the same location.

FESTIVALS & EVENTS
Quicksilver Pro-Surfing Competition Mid-March sees some of the world's best surfers out on the waves.
Surf Lifesaving Championships Also in mid-March, expect to see some stupidly fit people running about in not much.
Gold Coast International Marathon Run in July.
IndyCar – see the boxed text 'Indy Car' above.
Schoolies' Week Not just a week, but a month-long party by school-leavers from mid-November to mid-

INDYCAR
Since 1991 Surfers Paradise has been host to what has been dubbed Queensland's biggest party – the Australian leg of the IndyCar series (the US equivalent of Formula One motor racing). Each October, the main streets of central Surfers are transformed into a temporary race circuit, around which hurtle some of the world's fastest cars – their drivers push them up to speeds of more than 300km/h.

On a good year around a quarter of a million spectators descend on Surfers for the race and the three-day carnival that precedes it. Surfers is fairly over the top at the best of times, but IndyCar gives the town a chance to *really* let its hair down. It's a great time to be there, or a great time to be anywhere else, depending on how you feel about the place.

General-admission charges to the races range from $33 to $75 per day at the gate, cheaper if you prebook. Four-day grandstand seating is between $200 and $520. For more information, call ☎ 1800 300 055 or check www.indy.com.au.

December. Generally involves lots of alcohol and a few organised events in the first week.

SLEEPING
Backpacker hostels aside, all accommodation rates are seasonal; tariffs given here rise by as much as 50% during the school holidays and 100% at Christmas time.

Budget motels line the Gold Coast Hwy and advertise cheap deals on flashing neon signs. Holiday apartments can be excellent value, especially for a group of three or four, or if you stay more than two nights. Many of the apartments have a two-night minimum stay, increasing to seven nights during the peak holiday seasons.

Budget
HOSTELS
Backpacker hostels are scattered from one end of the Gold Coast to the other. Many that aren't located in and around the centre of Surfers offer free pick-up from the **Surfers Paradise Transit Centre** (cnr Beach & Cambridge Rds), and put on free shuttle buses to clubs (generally Wednesday and Saturday) and beaches.

Some will also find work for you on the coast. The helpful **In Transit** (☎ 5592 2911) backpackers-accommodation booking desk at the Transit Centre makes bookings for free.

Trekkers (☎ 1800 100 004, 5591 5616; www.tmvweb design.com.au/trekkers; 22 White St, Southport; dm $22, tw & d $55) This old Queenslander has been expertly renovated and furnished, and there's a lovely garden with a pool. It's big, friendly and some dorms have a bathroom.

Aquarius Backpackers (☎ 1800 229 955, 5527 1300; 44 Queen St, Southport; dm from $15, tw & d $45; P) Bright, clean rooms, a large pool, good communal facilities and a licensed bar, make this purpose-built hostel a great choice on the coast.

Surfers Paradise Backpackers Resort (☎ 1800 282 800, 5592 4677; www.surfersparadisebackpackers.com.au; Gold Coast Hwy, Surfers Paradise; dm/d/tr $22/55/80;) About 1km south of the centre, this place offers great facilities, including a pool, small gym and sauna, pool room and bar, tennis court and bright, spacious rooms (triples have a kitchen).

Cheers Backpackers (☎ 1800 636 539, 5531 6539; cheersbackpackers@hotmail.com; 8 Pine Ave, Surfers Paradise; dm/d $19/50;) This big, party hostel is well set up, with a decent pool, an excellent bar area and a large courtyard. It's within staggering distance of most of the clubs, and there are regular events such as video nights and karaoke evenings.

Surf & Sun Backpackers (☎ 1800 678 194, 5592 2363; www.surfnsun-goldcoast.com; 3323 Gold Coast Hwy, Surfers Paradise; dm/d $22/55) Another party place just north of the Surfers centre, this converted motel earns points for being 100m from the beach and right on the route of the IndyCar race. There's a nice pool, and surfboards for hire.

Backpackers in Paradise (☎ 5538 4344; fax 5538 2222; 40 Peninsular Dr; dm $15-20, d $55) This backpackers is close to the clubs and has a bar as well as nightclub vouchers.

Sleeping Inn Surfers (☎ 1800 817 832, 5592 4455; www.sleepinginn.com.au; 26 Peninsular Dr; dm $21, d/tr from $55/80;) A clever conversion of two apartment buildings, this clean and modern hostel is close to the centre for those who want to party, but it still offers privacy, as well as peace and quiet for those who don't.

Coolangatta YHA (☎ 5536 7644; booking@coolangatta yha.com; 230 Coolangatta Rd, Bilinga; dm/d $23/50; P) On the far side of the Gold Coast Hwy, just north of the airport, this big hostel is well equipped but it's a long way from the action. As compensation, breakfast is included and there's a courtesy bus to Kirra Beach and Duranbah; you can also hire bikes.

CAMPING & CARAVAN PARKS

There are caravan-camping parks all the way along the Gold Coast from Main Beach to Coolangatta. Most of the foreshore parks are run by the local council and are of a high standard.

Burleigh Beach Tourist Park (☎ 5581 7755; burly@gctp.com.au; Goodwin Tce; camp/caravan sites $19/21, cabins $85) This good council-run place is set back from the road near the beach. Try for a site at the back of the camping ground, away from the thousands of squawking birds at dawn and dusk.

Mid-Range
APARTMENTS

Trickett Gardens Holiday Inn (☎ 5539 0988; www.trickettgardens.com.au; 24-30 Trickett St, Surfers Paradise; d/f $100/150; P) This friendly low-rise apartment block is great for families, with its central location, heated pool and well-equipped, self-contained units.

Paradise Towers (☎ 5592 3337; www.paradise towers.com; 3049 Gold Coast Hwy, Surfers Paradise; apt from $55; P) Considering its location and facilities, this high-rise apartment building is fantastic value. Most rooms come complete with kitchen, and all have a balcony and great views. There's a pool on the 1st floor, and this place is gay-and-lesbian friendly.

Olympus (☎ 5538 7288; bookings@olympusapartments.com.au; 62 The Esplanade, Surfers Paradise; d from $120; P) Just 200m north of Elkhorn Ave and opposite the beach, this high-rise block has well-kept, spacious apartments with one or two bedrooms.

International Beach Resort (☎ 1800 657 471, 5539 0099; www.internationalresort.com.au; 84 The Esplanade, Surfers Paradise; r from $80, with sea view $100; P) Another seafront high-rise, this place is just across from the beach and has good one- and two-bedroom units.

Chateau Beachside (☎ 5538 1022; chateau@strand.com.au; cnr The Esplanade & Elkhorn Ave, Surfers Paradise; r from $130; P) Right in the heart of Surfers, this seafront apartment block has good-sized rooms, some with a kitchen. There's a pool if you need a change from the salty water, a spa and sauna and a cheap restaurant (see Eating opposite).

For other apartments and flats, try the **Gold Coast Accommodation Service** (☎ 5592 0067; www.goldcoastaccommodationservice.com.au; 1 Beach Rd).

HOTELS & MOTELS

Silver Sands Motel (☎ 5538 6041; www.silversands motel.com.au; 2985 Gold Coast Hwy, Surfers Paradise; r from $70; 🗷) One of the cheapest options in the centre, the rooms here are well cared for.

Shipwreck Motel (☎ 5536 3599; cnr Musgrave & Winston Sts, Kirra Beach; units $60-70; P 🗷) With less-developed Kirra Beach right on its doorstep and very tidy one- and two-bedroom units, the Shipwreck Motel is a top choice in the southern part of the Gold Coast.

On the Beach Holiday Units (☎ /fax 5536 3624; www.onthebeachmotel.com.au; 118 Marine Pde, Coolangatta; units $60-70; 🗷) This complex of old but spacious units is just across from the beach and great value considering its location.

There are quite a few cheap motels just south of Surfers Paradise along the highway at Mermaid Beach, including the **Mermaid Beach Motel** (☎ 5575 1577; www.mermaidbeachmotel .com.au; 2395 Gold Coast Hwy; units $55-65; 🗷), where the rates are excellent for the Gold Coast and the units are basic but clean.

Top End

There are several plush resorts if you really want to splash out.

Palazzo Versace (☎ 1800 098 000, 5509 8000; www.palazzoversace.com; Sea World Dr, Main Beach; d from $375; P 🗷) Those who *can*, come to this outrageously glamorous resort owned by Donatella Versace. You can see the hand of Versace in everything from the staff uniforms to the curtains in the sumptuous rooms, and this is reflected in the price tag. Rooms top out at a mere $3000 a night.

Hillhaven Holiday Apartments (☎ 5535 1055; www.hillhaven.com.au; 2 Goodwin Tce, Burleigh Heads; units from $230; P 🗷) High on the headland overlooking Burleigh Heads, this 10-storey apartment building has oldish but comfortable two- and three-bedroom units with spectacular views. Ask for the top-floor apartments, which have recently been refurbished.

EATING

The most pleasant places to eat on the beachfront right up and down the coast are the **surf lifesaving clubs**. All are located right on the beach, have large balconies overlooking the ocean and offer a good selection of steaks, roasts, pasta, and fish and chips for around $10 to $20. Clubs include **Southport Beach** (☎ 5591 5083), **Burleigh Beach** (☎ 5520 2972), **Coolangatta Beach** (☎ 5536 4648), **Greenmount Beach** (☎ 5536 1506) and **Rainbow Bay** (☎ 5536 6736). The last two are near Coolangatta.

With a large number of Asian visitors, the coast has plenty of cheap, authentic Japanese, Korean and Malaysian fare available.

Golden Star (☎ 5592 2484; Raptis Plaza, Cavill Ave, Surfers Paradise; meals $9) This all-you-can-eat Chinese place is one of several in the plaza and has a pretty good selection of Chinese standards.

New Seoul (☎ 5538 6177; Shop 9, Centre Arcade, Surfers Paradise; dishes $14-18) One of a number of great Asian restaurants in Centre Arcade, New Seoul has authentic Korean dishes and cheap lunch specials.

Arirang (☎ 5539 8008; Shop 8, Centre Arcade, Surfers Paradise; mains $9-16) This unpretentious Korean restaurant has a large range of rice and noodle dishes at the right price.

Seafood Village (☎ 5592 6789; Shop 28, Centre Arcade, Surfers Paradise; dishes $10-18) Try this popular place for cheap Chinese and Malay lunches.

Tandoori Place (☎ 5592 1004; cnr Gold Coast Hwy & Trickett St, Surfers Paradise; mains $15-20) For fine Indian cuisine, with a decent selection of vegetarian and clay-oven Tandoori dishes, head to this friendly restaurant.

Costa Dora (☎ 5538 5203; 27 Orchid Ave, Surfers Paradise; dishes around $20) On the pavement on Orchid Ave, this good, cheap Italian place serves up the usual pasta favourites.

Chateau Beachside (☎ 5538 1022; cnr The Esplanade & Elkhorn Ave, Surfers Paradise; breakfast $5-10, dishes around $10) Right on the seafront, the restaurant at this hotel (see Sleeping opposite) is another cheap option, with large breakfasts and burgers, pizzas, pastas and seafood.

Raptis Plaza food court (off Cavill Ave Mall, Surfers Paradise) There are plenty of choices here, including a carvery, Italian food, a burger joint, Thai and an excellent Japanese place, Sumo, which does cheap takeaways.

Pantry (☎ 5576 2818; 15 Connor St, Burleigh Heads; dishes $8-12) An upbeat and friendly café, the Pantry has salads, focaccias and all-day breakfasts.

Oskars (☎ 5576 3722; 43 Goodwin Tce, Burleigh Heads; mains around $25) One of the Gold Coast's top restaurants, this posh place on the seafront has a menu that's loaded with fish dishes.

Griffith St, one block back from the beach in Coolangatta, has plenty of chilled-out cafés, perfect for a quick bite to eat, or a bit of people-watching.

Other fine eating establishments:

Daniele (☎ 5535 0822; 43 Goodwin Tce, Burleigh Heads; mains around $20) Italian cuisine and ocean views.

Saks (☎ 5527 1472; Marina Mirage, Main Beach; mains $24) Marina views and international dishes.

DRINKING

Surfers easily wins first prize as party central on the Gold Coast. During the summer months it doesn't really matter which night you head out on the town, as you'll find bars and clubs packed. More often than not there's no cover charge for bars.

Melbas (☎ 5538 7411; 46 Cavill Ave) Melbas is a modern bar that attracts a well-dressed, trendy crowd that heaves most nights.

Gilhooley's (☎ 5538 9122; cnr Gold Coast Hwy & Cavill Ave) This pseudo-Irish pub has live music and a small terrace.

Quest (☎ 5526 9000; cnr Victoria Ave & Surf Pde, Broadbeach) The Egyptian styling and striking colours make this upmarket bar a popular venue for many locals with a bit of cash to spend.

Mermaids on the Beach (☎ 5520 1177; Goodwin Tce; Burleigh Heads) For a quiet drink with wonderful views of Surfers in the distance, head here, where, as the name suggests, you'll be right on the beach.

ENTERTAINMENT
Casinos

On the inland side of the highway, **Conrad Jupiters Casino** (☎ 5592 8100; Gold Coast Hwy, Broadbeach; admission free; ☢ 24hr) was Queensland's first legal casino and is a Gold Coast landmark. As you'd expect, it's totally over the top, with more than 100 gaming tables. Also here is **Jupiters Theatre** (☎ 1800 074 144), with live music and glamorous stage shows.

Cinemas

Cinema options on the Gold Coast:

Broadbeach: Mermaid 5 Cinemas (☎ 5572 6977; Pacific Fair shopping centre, 2514 Gold Coast Hwy)

Pacific Square 12 Cinemas (☎ 5572 2666; Pacific Fair shopping centre, cnr Hooker Blvd & Gold Coast Hwy)

Coolangatta 6 Cinema Centre (☎ 5536 8900; Level 2, Showcase on the Beach Centre, Griffith St)

Clubs & Live Music

Most of the clubs in Surfers Paradise are clustered together in the Mark complex on Orchid Ave, and offer vouchers for backpackers, which give free admission and cheap drinks and food. Wednesday and Saturday are generally the big party nights for backpackers, although some clubs only open Thursday to Sunday. The cover charge is usually somewhere between the $5 and $10 mark.

Fever (☎ 5592 6222; 26 Orchid Ave) One of the top clubs on the Gold Coast, Fever plays host to plenty of international DJs.

Berlin Bar (☎ 5592 2127; Orchid Ave) This very funky club has cool written all over it, from the music to the furniture.

Cocktails & Dreams (☎ 5592 1955; Orchid Ave) This backpacker-frequented club puts on regular theme nights. It's an 'anything goes' kind of place, but the bouncers aren't shy about evicting punters who go too far. Also here is the **Party** (☎ 5538 2848), linked to Cocktails by an internal stairway.

Shooters (☎ 5592 1144; 15 Orchid Ave) Shooters is about the most popular backpackers bar on the coast; expect it to be packed to almost bursting on weekends.

Troccadero (☎ 5536 4200; 9 Trickett St) This is the premier venue for big-name bands.

SHOPPING

If you're looking for souvenirs, presents, knick-knacks and such, Surfers has a plethora of shops to choose from, though it's not the cheapest place around. Two markets worth checking out:

Craft Market (The Esplanade, Surfers Paradise; ☢ 5.30-10pm Fri) Anything from concrete ornaments to sparkly shoes.

Carrara Market (cnr Nerang–Broadbeach road & Market St, Carrara; 6am-5pm Sat & Sun) Expect to find almost anything here.

GETTING THERE & AWAY
Air

Qantas Airways (☎ 13 13 13; www.qantas.com.au) and **Virgin Blue** (☎ 13 67 89; www.virginblue.com.au) fly direct to the Gold Coast airport from Sydney (from $110) and Melbourne (from $165).

Freedom Air (☎ 1800 122 000; www.freedomair.com) flies from the Gold Coast to Auckland, Hamilton, Christchurch and Dunedin in New Zealand.

Bus

Long-distance buses stop at the bus stations in Southport, Surfers Paradise and Coolangatta. **McCafferty's/Greyhound** (☎ 13 20 30, 13 14 99) and **Premier Motor Service** (☎ 13 34 10) will usually let you make a free stop on the Gold Coast if you've a through ticket from Brisbane. The **Surfers Paradise Transit Centre** (cnr Beach & Cambridge Rds) is where you'll arrive if you are coming by bus. Inside are various bus-company booking desks, a cafeteria and left-luggage lockers ($4 per 12 hours).

McCafferty's/Greyhound and **Coachtrans** (☎ 5506 9777) have frequent services to Brisbane ($16, 1½ hours), Byron Bay ($28, 2 hours) and Sydney ($88, 16 hours).

Car, Moped & Bicycle

There are dozens of car-rental firms around, with fliers in every hostel, motel and hotel. A few of the cheaper ones, and a contact for bicycle and moped hire:

Costless (☎ 5592 4499; 3269 Gold Coast Hwy; 🕑 8am-5.30pm Mon-Fri, closes 5pm Sat & Sun)

Moped City (☎ 5592 5878; 102 Ferny Ave; 🕑 8.30am-5pm) Rents bicycles/mopeds from $10/25 per hour or $15/50 per day.

Red Back Rentals (☎ 5592 1655; www.redback rentals.com.au; Surfers Paradise Transit Centre; 🕑 7.30am-5pm Mon-Fri, from 8am Sat & Sun)

Red Rocket (☎ 1800 673 682, 5538 9074; Mark Complex, Orchid Ave; 🕑 8am-5pm)

Train

The Gold Coast is served by train stations at Nerang and Robina, which have CityTrain links to Brisbane's CBD. The stations aren't particularly close to any of the main Gold Coast centres, but **Surfside Buslines** (☎ 13 12 30, 5571 6555) runs shuttles from Nerang and Robina to Surfers ($4, 15 minutes) and beyond, as well as the theme parks. From Brisbane to the Gold Coast costs $9 (one hour).

GETTING AROUND
To/From the Airport

Gold Coast Tourist Shuttle (☎ 5574 5111) makes transfers (one way/return $14/24) from the Gold Coast airport to points up and down the coast.

Coachtrans (☎ 5506 9777) operates the Airporter bus between Brisbane airport and the Gold Coast ($35/65).

Otherwise, hop on bus No 1 or 1A for downtown Surfers ($4.50/9).

Bus

Surfside Buslines (☎ 13 12 30, 5571 6555) runs a frequent service up and down the Gold Coast Hwy to Southport, Tweed Heads and beyond (bus No 1 and 1A), 24 hours a day. You can buy individual fares, get an Ezy Pass for a day's unlimited travel ($10), or a weekly one ($43).

GOLD COAST HINTERLAND

Inland from Coolangatta the mountains of the McPherson Range stretch back 60km to the NSW border. The national parks here are a paradise for walkers, and this unspoilt environment is easily accessible by car – a perfect antidote to the noise and clamour of the coast. For those without transport, there are plenty of tours from the seaside resorts, which will give you a taste of the hinterland (see Tours p303, or visit the Tamborine Mountain visitors centre). Expect a lot of rain in the mountains from December to March, and in winter the nights can be cold.

TAMBORINE MOUNTAIN

Just 45km northwest of the Gold Coast, this 600m-high plateau is on a northern spur of the McPherson Range. Patches of the area's original forests remain in nine small national parks. There are gorges, spectacular cascades like **Witches Falls**, **Cameron Falls** and **Cedar Creek Falls** near North Tamborine, and walking tracks to various lookouts with great views over the coast. Most settlements in the area are cutesy heritage communities set up for the benefit of tour groups.

The **visitors centre** (☎ 07-5545 3200; Doughty Park; 🕑 10.30am-3.30pm Sun-Fri, from 9.30am Sat) at North Tamborine has plenty of brochures, a small display on the area's ecology, and information on the well-established wineries scattered around the mountain. To get to Tamborine Mountain, turn off the Pacific Hwy at Oxenford or Nerang.

SPRINGBROOK NATIONAL PARK

This national park is perched atop a 900m-high plateau, which, like the rest of the McPherson Range, is a remnant of the huge volcano that once centred on Mt Warning in NSW.

QUEENSLAND

The national park is in three sections: **Springbrook**, **Mt Cougal** and **Natural Bridge**. The vegetation is cool-temperate rainforest and eucalypt forest, with gorges, cliffs, forests, waterfalls, an extensive network of walking tracks and several picnic areas.

The village of Springbrook is balanced right on the edge of the plateau, with numerous waterfalls (when there's enough rain) that tumble more than 100m down to the coastal plain below. There are several places where you can get the giddy thrill of leaning right out over the edge, including **Purling Brook Falls**, near the Gwongorella Picnic Area on Springbrook Rd, and **Best of All Lookout**, which is reached via Lyrebird Ridge Rd.

Just south of Gwongorella is the national park **visitors centre** (☎ 07-5533 5147; ☺ 8am-4pm), where you can pick up leaflets on walking tracks for all three sections and register for the **camping ground** (per person/family $4/16) next to Gwongorella.

The **Natural Bridge section**, off the Nerang–Murwillumbah road, has a 1km walking circuit leading to a rock arch spanning a water-formed cave, which is home to a huge colony of glow-worms.

Sleeping

Three kilometres off the Springbrook Rd, and the highest place on the plateau (960m), is **Springbrook Mountain Lodge** (☎ 07-5533 5366; springbrookelodge@ion.tm; 317 Repeater Station Rd; dm/s/d $32/50/65). This place comprises a chalet-style lodge with a large kitchen, recreation areas, great views and several self-contained cabins. Pick-ups from the Gold Coast cost $20 on a two-night stay.

LAMINGTON NATIONAL PARK

West of Springbrook, this 200-sq-km park covers much of the McPherson Range and adjoins the Border Ranges National Park in NSW. The park includes most of the spectacular Lamington Plateau, which reaches 1100m in places, as well as densely forested valleys below.

Much of the vegetation is subtropical rainforest. There are beautiful gorges, caves, waterfalls and lots of wildlife. Commonly spotted animals include satin and regent bowerbirds, and pademelons (a type of small wallaby) in the late afternoon. Somewhat incongruously, the park was named after Lord Lamington, then governor of Queensland,

who visited once, just after the park was founded, to shoot koalas.

The two most popular and accessible sections of the park are **Binna Burra** and **Green Mountains**, both reached via paved roads from Canungra. Binna Burra can also be reached from Nerang. The park has 160km of walking tracks, ranging from an excellent tree-top canopy walk along a series of rope-and-plank suspension bridges at Green Mountains, to the 24km Border Trail that links the two sections of the park.

Walking-trail guides are available from the **ranger stations** Binna Burra (☎ 07-5533 3584; Binna Burra; ☺ 1.30-3.30pm Mon-Fri, from 9am Sat & Sun); Green Mountains (☎ 07-5544 0634; Green Mountains; ☺ 9-11am Mon & Wed-Fri, 1-3.30pm Tue & Fri).

Sleeping & Eating

Surrounded by forest is the excellent **Binna Burra Mountain Lodge** (☎ 1800 074 260, 07-5533 3622; www.binnaburralodge.com.au; log cabins per person $160, with bathroom $190, camp/caravan sites $10/13.50, on-site safari tents from $40). This mountain retreat offers rustic log cabins and camp sites clustered around a central restaurant (meals from $13), all with good views over the national park. The tariff includes all meals, walking and climbing gear, and activities such as guided walks, bus trips and abseiling.

O'Reilly's Guesthouse (☎ 1800 688 722, 07-5544 0644; www.oreillys.com.au; Lamington National Park Rd; guesthouse s/d $125/200, units s/d $160/330), the famous guesthouse at Green Mountains, is still run by the O'Reilly family and has been very stylishly redeveloped over the years. Tariffs include activities such as bushwalks, spotlighting walks and 4WD bus trips. There's also a good restaurant and a cheaper bistro.

There is a national park **camping ground** (per person/family $4/16) close to O'Reilly's, and bush camping is permitted in several areas in the park; limited numbers of camping permits are available from the ranger at Green Mountains.

MT LINDESAY HIGHWAY

This highway runs south from Brisbane, across the Great Dividing Range west of Lamington and into NSW at Woodenbong.

Beaudesert, in cattle country 66km from Brisbane and 20km southwest of Tamborine Mountain, has a pioneer museum, a visitors centre on Jane St and several pubs and motels.

West of Beaudesert is the stretch of the Great Dividing Range known as the **Scenic Rim**. Further south, **Mt Barney National Park** is undeveloped but popular with bushwalkers and climbers. It's in the Great Dividing Range, just north of the state border. You reach it from the Rathdowney–Boonah road. There's a **visitors centre** (☎ 07-5544 1222; ☼ varying hours) on the highway at **Rathdowney**.

GETTING THERE & AWAY

The cheapest way to get from the Gold Coast to Tamborine Mountain is with the **school bus** (☎ 07-5545 1298). It only runs Monday to Friday during the school term (one way/return $7.20/14.40).

The **Binna Burra bus service** (☎ 1800 074 260, 07-5533 3622) operates daily between Surfers Paradise and Binna Burra ($22/44, 1 hour) via the Nerang train station and Gold Coast airport, departing from Surfers Paradise at 1.15pm and from Binna Burra at 10.30am; book ahead.

Allstate Scenic Tours (☎ 07-3285 1777) runs a bus service between Brisbane and O'Reilly's Guesthouse from Sunday to Friday, leaving the Brisbane Transit Centre at 9.30am (day trip $28/44).

Mountain Coach Company (☎ 07-5524 4249) has a daily service from the Gold Coast to Green Mountains via Tamborine Mountain ($25/50).

SUNSHINE COAST

Another weekend getaway from the Queensland capital, the coast north of Brisbane has traditionally been sleepier and less developed than the Gold Coast to the south. That's changing, though, as concrete high-rises spread from trendy Mooloolaba, an hour and a half from Brisbane, to Alexandra Headlands and Maroochydore.

North of Maroochydore, there's a patch of still unspoilt coastline at Coolum and Peregian Beach. After this you arrive in Noosa, an exclusive, staunchly low-rise and leafy resort that sometimes feels like an antipodean answer to France's Nice.

Lining the highway from Brisbane to the hinterland town of Nambour you will find some forgettable theme parks and special-interest museums. For many visitors, the sole unmissable attraction here is

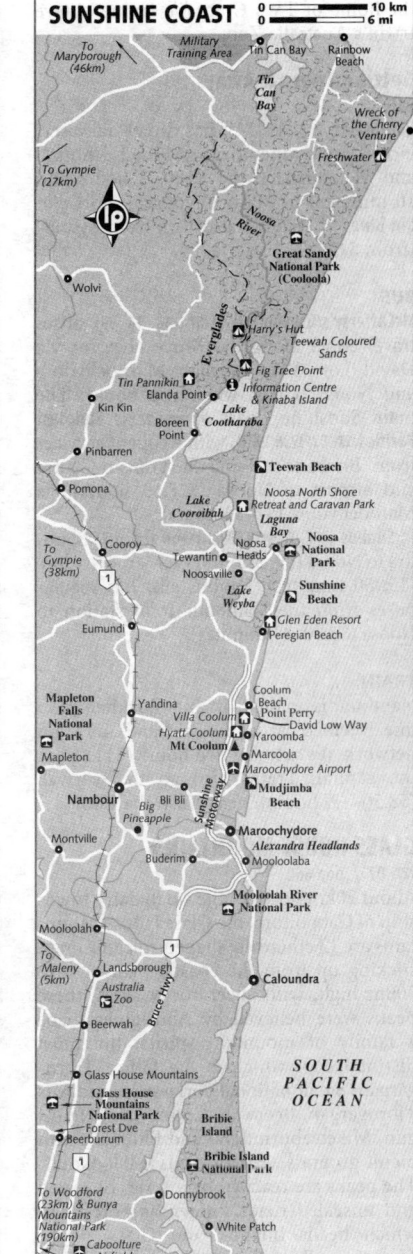

SUNSHINE COAST

the home of TV's *Crocodile Hunter*, Steve Irwin's Australia Zoo.

Getting There & Away

AIR

QantasLink (☎ 13 13 13) has direct daily services from Sydney (from $140, 1½ hours) and Melbourne (from $180, 2 hours and 10 minutes) to Maroochydore airport. **Virgin Blue** (☎ 13 67 89) also flies from Sydney (from $120).

BUS

McCafferty's/Greyhound (☎ 13 14 99) buses travel either along the Bruce Hwy, or via David Low Way through Maroochydore and Noosa (check when you book). The main Sunshine Coast operator is **Suncoast Pacific** (☎ 07-3236 1901), with frequent services from Brisbane's Roma St Transit Centre and airport to Noosa ($28, 3 hours) via Maroochydore ($24, 2 hours).

Sunbus (☎ 07-5450 7888) runs from Caloundra to Noosa ($9, 2 hours) via Maroochydore ($5, 50 minutes). Sunbus also has regular buses from the Nambour train station to Noosa ($7.50, 40 minutes).

TRAIN

Nambour is on the Brisbane–Rockhampton line. Deemed part of the Brisbane CityTrain network, it's actually two hours ($11) from the capital. Trains also go to Beerwah ($8.50, 1½ hours), near Australia Zoo.

GLASS HOUSE MOUNTAINS

☎ 07 / pop 660

About 20km north of the small dairy township of Caboolture, the Glass House Mountains are 13 ethereally shaped volcanic crags sticking up from the coastal plain. Up to 300m high, with sheer rocky sides, these peaks were believed by Aborigines to be a family of mountain spirits, the most distinctive of which is the father Tibrogargan. Small national parks surround Mts Tibrogargan, Beerwah, Coonowrin, Ngungun, Miketeeburnulgrai and Elimbah, with picnic grounds, walking trails and lookouts. The peaks are reached by a series of sealed and unsealed roads known as Forest Dr, which heads inland from Glass House Mountains Rd.

There are walking trails (really low-grade mountain climbs) on Tibrogargan, Beer-

wah and Ngungun. The **District Forest Office** (☎ 5496 0166; Beerburrum) has more information. **Wind Dancer** (☎ 5438 7003) does balloon flights ($220 to $240) past the mountains at sunrise. It's a spectacular flight, but you need to book one or two months ahead.

Nearby is – crikey! – **Australia Zoo** (☎ 5494 1134; www.crocodilehunter.com; Glasshouse Mountains Rd, Beerwah; adult/child/family $21/13/60; ☺ 8.30am-4pm). From a tiny reptile park in the 1980s, this has become huge, as owner Steve 'Crocodile Hunter' Irwin has proved to possess a mesmerising hold over crocs and international TV viewers alike. You won't catch yer man himself here often. However, with such a reputation to uphold, this animal Disneyworld doesn't disappoint. There are regular crocodile, snake, otter etc shows. Phone about free transfers from Noosa or Beerwah train stations.

CALOUNDRA

☎ 07 / pop 50,150

At the southern end of the Sunshine Coast, Caloundra is a quiet little family resort with good fishing and pleasant surf beaches – with only a mild case of Gold Coast syndrome. Of its seven lovely beaches, **Bulcock Beach**, good for windsurfing, is near the main street.

Information

Caloundra visitors centre (☎ 5491 0202; Caloundra Rd; ☺ 9am-5pm) About 2km west of the centre.

Sleeping

Caloundra City Backpackers (☎ 5499 7655; www .caloundracitybackpackers.com.au; 84 Omrah Ave; dm/s/d $17/30/40) Built in 2001, this much-lauded motel-style hostel is spotless and friendly, even if the rooms are not huge. Singles/doubles are also available with bathroom $45/50.

Anchorage Motor Inn (☎ 5491 1499; fax 5491 7279; 18 Bowman Rd; d/tr/f 80/90/100; ⌘) Well-appointed modern rooms lead off a covered, plant-lined walkway opposite the hotel's pool, spa and tennis court. Look for the *faux* Polynesian thatch roof.

La Promenade (☎ 5499 7133; www.lapromenade .com.au; 4 Tay Ave; d/f from $120/160; ⌘) These upmarket units near Bulcock Beach have terracotta-tiled floors, stylish furniture and spa baths. There's a trendy café and a communal rooftop area. Rates are lower for longer stays.

Other recommendations:

Caloundra Motel (☎ 5491 1411; fax 5492 7411; 30 Bowman Rd; s/d/tr $50/60/70) Cheerful colours, basic but clean.

Hibiscus Holiday Park (☎ 5491 1564; fax 5492 6938; cnr Bowman & Landsborough Park Rds; camp/caravan sites $19/21, on-site vans for 2 people $40) Wonderfully lush waterfront gardens.

Eating

The **Caloundra RSL** (☎ 5491 1544; 19 West Tce; $6.50-20) has won several minor dining awards, but its interior is pure Las Vegas. For somewhere less gaudy, head for the Thai restaurant, **Blue Orchid** (☎ 5491 9433; 22 Bulcock St; mains $12-20; ☽ dinner).

MAROOCHY

☎ 07 / pop 44,100

The line of high-rise apartments, the music blaring from the cars, the heaving crowds along the indisputably lovely beach – yep, you could be forgiven for mistaking parts of Maroochy for the southern Gold Coast. Maroochy is made up of Mooloolaba – the most developed suburb here – Alexandra Headlands and Maroochydore, which are catching up fast. Some people prefer Mooloolaba to Noosa, saying it's less pretentious, but to see it at its best, arrive in low season and during the week.

Information

Information booths Mooloolaba (Brisbane Rd; ☽ 9am-5pm); Maroochydore airport (☽ 8.45am-4.30pm, depending on flight arrivals)

Maroochy visitors centre (☎ 5479 1566, 1800 882 032; cnr Sixth Ave & Melrose St, Maroochydore; ☽ 9am-5pm Mon-Fri, 9am-4pm Sat & Sun)

Sights & Activities

Underwater World (☎ 5444 8488; adult/child $23/13; ☽ 9am-6pm) is the southern hemisphere's largest oceanarium, featuring an impressive shark tunnel, plus seal shows. It's in the **Wharf** tourist complex.

Scuba World (☎ 5444 8596; the Wharf) arranges dives with the Underwater World sharks (certified/uncertified divers $95/125). The company also takes certified divers on coral dives off the coast ($55).

Brothers Neilsen (☎ 5444 3545; cnr The Esplanade & Venning St, Mooloolaba) has surfboards for $40 a day and bodyboards for $20 a day (rates drop in winter).

Sleeping

Cotton Tree Beachouse (☎ 5443 1755; www.cottontree backpackers.com; 15 The Esplanade, Cotton Tree; dm/s/d $21/35/42; ☐) With its leafy front garden and relaxing waterfront location, this Queenslander is strong on charm, but more homey than luxurious. That could alter, though, when promised renovations are completed.

Palace Backpackers Mooloolaba (☎ 5444 3399; fax 5477 6455; 75-77 Brisbane Rd; dm $21, d & tw $50; ☐) Central, with the most modern and comfortable amenities of any hostel in town. This place is noisy when one of the big, party-style bus tours pulls in.

Mooloolaba Riverfront B&B (☎ 5452 5400, 0418-989 099; pm@rpdata.com.au; 7 Bindaree Cres; s/d $95/125; ☒) This small riverfront residence is tucked away from the main drag, but is still within walking distance of the CBD. Breakfast included.

Twin Pines Motel (☎ 5444 2522; twinpines@optus net.com.au; 36 Brisbane Rd, Mooloolaba; s/d $70/85; ☒) A decent mid-range option, this motel's chief advantage is its central location.

Other recommendations:

Mooloolaba Motel (☎ 5444 2988; fax 5444 8386; 45-56 Brisbane Rd, Maroochydore; s & d $110; ☒) Very comfortable and centrally located.

Maroochydore YHA Backpackers (☎ 5443 3151; fax 5479 3156; 24 Schirmann Dr, Maroochydore; dm/d $19/40; ☐) Pleasant collection of older brick buildings, away from the centre.

Pincushion Beach Park (☎ 5443 7917; fax 5443 9876; cnr Cotton Tree & Alexandra Pdes; camp/caravan sites for 2 people $18/21) Popular waterfront caravan park.

Eating

Raw Energy (☎ 5446 1444; Shop 3, The Esplanade, Mooloolaba; dishes $9-13) Paninis, pasta, fruit juices and the inevitable wheatgrass will fire you up in this colourful, funky juice bar.

Augello's (☎ 5478 3199; cnr the Esplanade & Brisbane Rd, Mooloolaba; dishes $11-20) Concoctions like Moroccan chicken pizza, with sun-dried tomatoes and lime yoghurt dressing, have helped make this one of Australia's top spots for pizza, but if all you crave is a margherita, that's fine, too.

Casablanca (☎ 5478 3633; The Esplanade, Mooloolaba; dishes $9-26) Vaguely North African (in decoration only), Casablanca sells everything from sandwiches and salads to bouillabaisse, mussels and barramundi fillets. Duck and sweet potato won tons? This could be the start of something beautiful.

For cheap eating, try the all-you-can-eat deals at the vegie Indian **Krishna's** (2/7 First Ave, Maroochydore; lunch $7, dinner $8; ⊗ lunch Mon-Fri, dinner Fri & Sun) or the **Sunshine Plaza food court** (Horton Pde, Maroochydore; meals from $8).

Getting There & Away

Long-distance buses stop at the **Suncoast Pacific bus terminal** (☎ 5443 1011; First Ave, Maroochydore), just off Aerodrome Rd.

AROUND MAROOCHY

With your own transport, you can easily base yourself in the less crowded, up-and-coming **Coolum** and **Peregian Beaches**, neighbouring Maroochy or Noosa. The area is good for surfing, but also offers wonderful coastal views from **Point Perry** or the chance to climb **Mt Coolum**. Beside the surf lifesaving club, **the tourist information booth** (David Low Way; ⊗ 9am-5pm) has brochures on B&Bs, caravan parks and other accommodation.

Other recommendations:

Villa Coolum (☎ 07-5446 1286; www.villacoolum.com; 102 Coolum Tce, Coolum Beach; d/f $80/90) Rustic Queenslander-style units with leafy verandas.

Glen Eden Resort (☎ 07-5448 1955; www.gleneden resort.com.au; 388 David Low Way, Peregian Beach; d/f $115/135) Lovely self-contained apartments right near the beach.

Hyatt Regency Coolum (☎ 07-5446 1234; www .coolum.regency.hyatt.com; Warran Rd, Coolum Beach; s & d from $220; ⊗) Five-star golf and spa resort.

NOOSA

☎ 07 / pop 36,400

There can't be too many towns that could so starkly lend a name to a recipe collection as this place did with *Noosa: The Cookbook*, but what began as a surfing haven in the 1960s became one of Australia's most exclusive resorts and a major foodies' mecca from the 1990s onwards. Media stars, glammed-up fashionistas, the moneyed and well heeled now intermingle with board-shorted surfers among the restaurants and shops of Noosa Heads' Hastings St.

Refreshingly low-rise, Noosa's *coup de grace* is to have developed its trendy café latte landscape without losing sight of simple seaside pleasures. From the eastern 'Paris end' of bustling Hastings St, it's only a short walk to the beachfront Noosa National Park. Noosaville, to the west, and Sunshine Beach, south, retain a laid-back ambience, while the Sunshine Coast hinterland and the wilderness of the Cooloola coast (Great Sandy National Park) are within easy reach.

Orientation

The name Noosa covers a group of communities around the mouth of the Noosa River. Most action focuses on Noosa Heads, but there are places to stay and eat west along the Noosa River in Noosaville and Tewantin – the departure point for the Noosa River Ferry.

Uphill from Noosa Heads is Noosa Junction. Over on the east coast of the Noosa headland is the peaceful resort of Sunshine Beach, with one of the best surf breaks in the area.

Information
BOOKSHOPS

Dwyer's (☎ 5474 9989; Shop 5, Laguna on Hastings, Hastings St) Opposite Aroma's café.

SURFING NOOSA

With a string of fine breaks around an unspoilt national park, Noosa is a fine place to catch a wave. The best year-round break is probably Sunshine Corner, at the northern end of Sunshine Beach, though it has a brutal beach dump. The point breaks around the headland only perform during the summer, but when they do, expect wild conditions and good walls at Boiling Point and Tea Tree, on the northern coast of the headland.

There are also gentler breaks on Noosa Spit at the far end of Hastings St, where most of the surf schools do their training. Options include **Wavesense** (☎ 5474 9076, 1800 249 076; www.wavesense .com.au), **Noosing Surf Lessons** (☎ 0412-330 850) and **Merrick's Learn to Surf** (☎ 0418-787 577; www.learntosurf.com.au). Two-hour group lessons on longboards cost from $35.

If you just want to rent equipment, **Noosa Longboards** (www.noosalongboards.com; ☎ 5447 2828, 64 Hastings St; ☎ 5474 2722, 187 Gympie Tce) has longboards for $45 per day, shortboards for $30 and bodyboards for $20.

INTERNET ACCESS
Internet cafés are clustered around Noosa Junction. Access costs $6-8 per hour.
Adventure Travel Bugs (☎ 5474 8530; 9 Sunshine Beach Rd)
Internet Arcadia (☎ 5474 8988; Arcadia St)

TOURIST INFORMATION
Noosa visitors centre Noosa Harbour (☎ 5447 4988; Hastings St; ⏰ 9am-5pm); Tewantin (☎ 5474 3700; Lake St; ⏰ 9am-5pm)

Sights
NOOSA NATIONAL PARK
This small but lovely national park extends for about 2km southwest from the headland that marks the end of the Sunshine Coast. It has fine walks, great coastal scenery and a string of popular bays for surfing on the northern side. **Alexandria Bay** on the eastern side has the best sands and is also an informal nudist beach.

The main entrance at the end of Park Rd (the eastern continuation of Hastings St) has a car park, picnic areas and the **EPA centre** (☎ 5447 3243; ⏰ 9am-3pm), where you can obtain a walking track map.

For a panoramic view, you can walk or drive up to the **Laguna Lookout** from Viewland Dr in Noosa Junction. From Sunshine Beach, access to the park is via McAnally Dr or Parkedge Rd.

Activities
Surfing lessons are big business in Noosa; see 'Surfing Noosa' (opposite) for details. The town is also a mecca for kite-surfing, where riders slot their feet into a wakeboard and harness themselves to a giant kite to surf and jump over waves. For lessons, call **Noosa Adventures & Kite-Surfing** (☎ 0438-788 573), which offers courses from $95 (two hours) to $350 (eight hours). Conditions at the river mouth and Lake Weyba are best between October and January.

Kayaking is an enduringly popular pastime. **Noosa Ocean Kayak Tours** (☎ 0418-787 577) offers two-hour kayaking tours around Noosa National Park or up the Noosa River for $50. You can also hire kayaks for $40/50 a day for one/two people.

Tours
Boats run from the wharf at Tewantin up the Noosa River into the 'Everglades' area of the Great Sandy National Park. Companies include:
The Everglades Water Bus Co (☎ 5447 1838; adult/child $55/40 for 4-hr cruise)
Noosa River Cruises (☎ 5449 7362; adult/child $65/45 for 6-hr cruise)
Beyond Noosa (☎ 5449 9177; adult/child $70/45 for 8-hr cruise)

See the boxed text 'Notes from a Small Island: Exploring Fraser' (p328) for trips to Fraser Island.

Sleeping
BUDGET
Cash-conscious travellers might also want to check accommodation listings under Cooloola Coast (p317).

YHA Halse Lodge (☎ 5447 3377, 1800 242 567; www.halselodge.com.au; 2 Halse Lane, Noosa Heads; dm/d $25/65; 🖳) This 100-year-old Queenslander wins on charm, friendliness and location (on a leafy hill, a few minutes from Hastings St), but its rooms are a bit cramped. Despite that, it's still Noosa's best hostel, and travellers will suffer if a threatened closure proceeds.

Koala Beach Resort (☎ 5447 3355; www.koala-backpackers.com; 44 Noosa Dr, Noosa Junction; dm $22, tw & d $55; 🖳) The Noosa branch is imbued with the typical characteristics of the Koala brand: popular bar, eternal party atmosphere, central location and adequate accommodation. In fact, the rooms here are quite large.

Costa Bella (☎ 5447 3663; 7 Selene St, Sunrise Beach; dm $20, tw & d $45-50) An array of beachfront options is available, from individually booked beds in a twin room in the older Melaluka Units, to en suite doubles ($60) in the flash new Wistari units.

Other recommendations:
Noosa River Caravan Park (☎ 5449 7050; fax 5474 3024; Munna Point; camp sites from $18, caravan sites $22 for 2 people) Popular riverside park; book ahead.
Sandy Court (☎ 5449 7225; fax 5473 0397; 30 James St, Noosaville; dm/d $20/55) Charming budget motel.

MID-RANGE
Prices in this bracket can rise by 50% at busy times and by 100% from December to January. For private units to rent, call **Accom Noosa** (☎ 5447 3444; www.accomnoosa.com.au; 41 Hastings St). There's often a three-night minimum stay for these.

QUEENSLAND

NOOSA

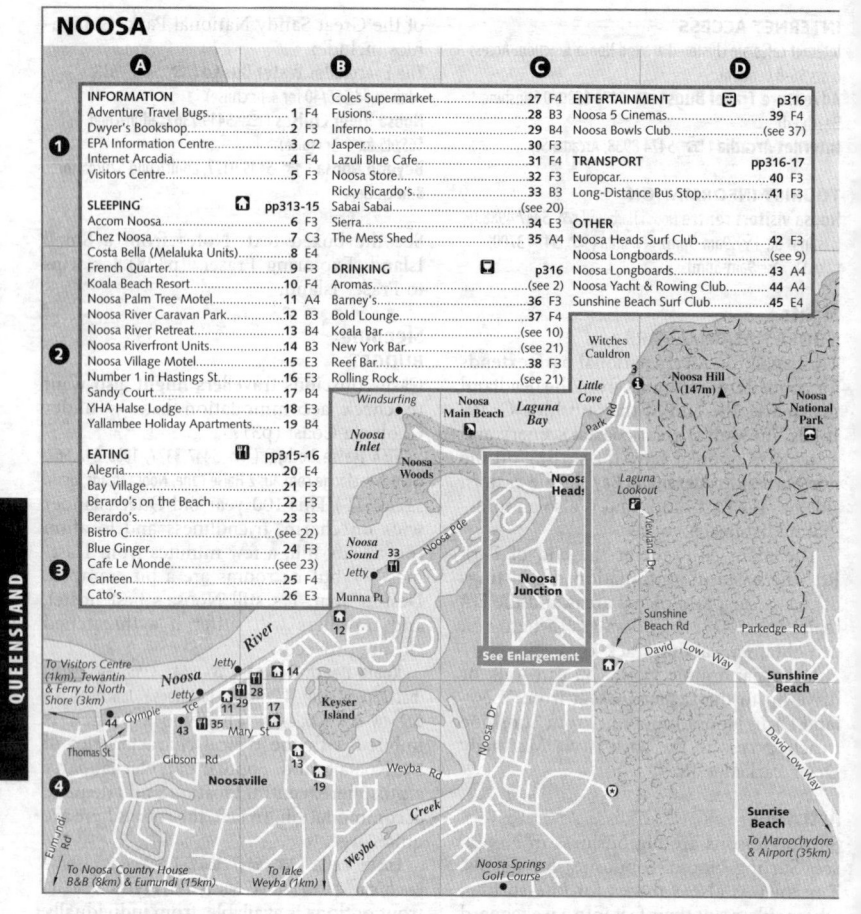

INFORMATION	
Adventure Travel Bugs	1 F4
Dwyer's Bookshop	2 F3
EPA Information Centre	3 C2
Internet Arcadia	4 F4
Visitors Centre	5 F3

SLEEPING	pp313-15
Accom Noosa	6 F3
Chez Noosa	7 C3
Costa Bella (Melaluka Units)	8 E4
French Quarter	9 F3
Koala Beach Resort	10 F4
Noosa Palm Tree Motel	11 A4
Noosa River Caravan Park	12 B3
Noosa River Retreat	13 B4
Noosa Riverfront Units	14 B3
Noosa Village Motel	15 E3
Number 1 in Hastings St	16 F3
Sandy Court	17 B4
YHA Halse Lodge	18 F3
Yallambee Holiday Apartments	19 B4

EATING	pp315-16
Alegria	20 E4
Bay Village	21 F3
Berardo's on the Beach	22 F3
Berardo's	23 F3
Bistro C	(see 22)
Blue Ginger	24 F3
Cafe Le Monde	(see 23)
Canteen	25 F4
Cato's	26 E3

Coles Supermarket	27 F4
Fusions	28 B3
Inferno	29 B4
Jasper	30 F3
Lazuli Blue Cafe	31 F4
Noosa Store	32 F3
Ricky Ricardo's	33 B3
Sabai Sabai	(see 20)
Sierra	34 E3
The Mess Shed	35 A4

DRINKING	p316
Aromas	(see 2)
Barney's	36 F3
Bold Lounge	37 F4
Koala Bar	(see 10)
New York Bar	(see 21)
Reef Bar	38 F3
Rolling Rock	(see 21)

ENTERTAINMENT	p316
Noosa 5 Cinemas	39 F4
Noosa Bowls Club	(see 37)

TRANSPORT	pp316-17
Europcar	40 F3
Long-Distance Bus Stop	41 F3

OTHER	
Noosa Heads Surf Club	42 F3
Noosa Longboards	(see 9)
Noosa Longboards	43 A4
Noosa Yacht & Rowing Club	44 A4
Sunshine Beach Surf Club	45 E4

Noosa Village Motel (☎ 5447 5800; noosavillage@bigpond.com.au; 10 Hastings St, Noosa Heads; d/tr from $110/145) A lick of bright blue paint, good furnishings and tender loving care have kept this motel looking fresh. One of the few downtown, it does get some noise.

Noosa Palm Tree Motel (☎ 5449 7311; fax 5474 3246; 233 Gympie Tce, Noosaville; d/units $70/80; ☒) Another cheerfully painted, decent option, the Palm Tree offers motel rooms, or units with their own kitchen.

Noosa River Retreat (☎ 5474 2811; fax 5474 2844; cnr Weyba Rd & Reef St, Noosaville; d/f from $75/145; ☒) Self-contained one- and two-bed units are set around a pool and garden in this pleasant, modern resort. All units have kitchens; those on the upper floor feature spa baths.

Noosa Country House B&B (☎ 5471 0121; www.babs.com.au/noosacountry; 93 Duke Rd, Noosa Valley; d $125-140) This Queenslander home, with its spa deck, wood fire and preponderance of wildlife makes a comfortable kids-free retreat. It's 10 minutes from Noosa, heading towards Eumundi.

Chez Noosa (☎ 5447 2027; fax 5447 2195; 236 David Low Way, Sunshine Beach; d $70-80; ☒) Although the highway is close, the tropical garden absorbs some of the noise. These modern self-contained units are good value.

Other recommendations:

Yallambee Holiday Apartments (☎ 5449 8632; fax 5474 2844; 219 Weyba Rd, Noosaville; d $75-120, f $145-200) Relaxed, red-brick block with units decorated in different styles.

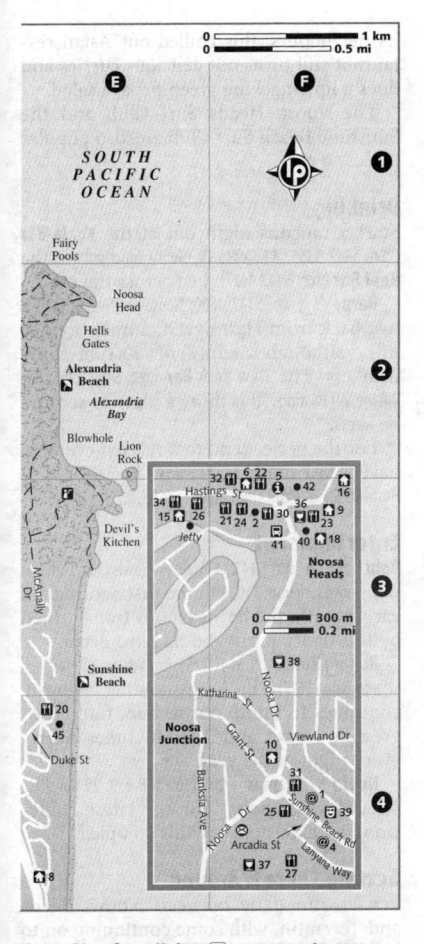

the national park, and reached by a funky sloping lift, this exclusive complex has great views over Laguna Bay. Minimum two-night stay applies.

Eating
HASTINGS STREET

Sierra (☎ 5447 4800; 10 Hastings St; dishes $12-22) Having trouble deciding whether to have the banana or blueberry pancakes for breakfast? Have them both, and then come back for a helping of grilled Atlantic salmon at dinner. Memo to self: return for lunch tomorrow.

Jasper (☎ 5474 9600; 42 Hastings St; dishes $10-28) Matching calm, white décor with delicately flavoured food, this popular restaurant is also notable for its pleasant staff. Sand-crab linguine and seafood laksa are among many good menu choices.

Blue Ginger (☎ 5447 3211; 30 Hastings St; mains $20-25; ☽ dinner) The food compensates for the sterile atmosphere in this Asian restaurant.

THE AUTHOR'S CHOICE

Overseas visitors should not miss **Berardo's on the Beach** (☎ 5448 0888; 49 Hastings St; dishes $10-25) where you can enjoy typically superlative Mod Oz cuisine in a beachfront setting, in one of Australia's premier resorts (it serves a breakfast worth jumping out of bed for – especially the eggs). This busy casual bistro does lunch, dinner and cocktails as well.

Noosa Riverfront Units (☎ 5449 7595; fax 5449 8997; 277 Gympie Tce, Noosaville; d/tr/f $65/75/80) Old-fashioned but somehow charming holiday units.

TOP END

Well-known names like Sheraton and Sebel are also in town.

French Quarter (☎ 5430 7100; www.frenchquarter .com.au; 62 Hastings St, Noosa Heads; 1-/2-bed unit $230/270; ☒) With spa baths and charming breakfast bars, these elegant units are an excellent place to put your feet up after a shopathon along Hastings St and before a walk in the nearby national park.

Number 1 in Hastings St (☎ 5449 2211; fax 5449 2001; cnr Hastings St & Morwong Dr, Noosa Heads; 2-/3-bed unit $300/310; ☒) On the hillside beside

Cafe Le Monde (☎ 5449 2366; 52 Hastings St; dishes $7-28) This all-day place is popular for its prices and quantities rather than for the quality of its food. With lashings of fish and chips, veg Asian stir-fries, tapas, souvlaki and more, just about every palate is catered for.

You can eat well for around $8 at the **food court** (Bay Village shopping centre). Self-caterers may find the **Noosa Store** (33 Hastings St; ☽ 6am-10pm) useful.

NOOSA JUNCTION

Lazuli Blue Cafe (☎ 5448 0055; 9 Sunshine Beach Rd; snacks & meals $6-13; ☽ 7am-4pm Mon-Sat, 8am-noon Sun) This bright and breezy little café serves healthy juices and smoothies, sandwiches and pastas, plus $5 all-day breakfasts.

QUEENSLAND

Canteen (☎ 5447 5400; 4-6 Sunshine Beach Rd; dishes $7-20) Dimly lit with milk-bar booths, this all-day café and restaurant would suit Melbourne. It's a tad overpriced (more than $9 for a sandwich), but still a pleasant place to mooch around, drinking coffee and reading its newspapers and magazines.

Self-caterers should try **Coles supermarket** (Noosa Fair shopping centre).

NOOSAVILLE

The Mess Shed (☎ 5449 8602; 14 Thomas St, Noosaville; meals $7-10; ☯ dinner Tue-Sun) It promises no frills, but this timber-and-corrugated-iron canteen offers plenty of fun as diners cram in together along bench seats. Take the BYO alcohol option or choose the free orange cordial to accompany your spag bol, veg pasta, pizza or veal.

Inferno (☎ 5449 0961; 251 Gympie Tce; meals $15-25; ☯ dinner daily) Near the corner of Edward St, Inferno constantly pleases with its gourmet pizzas and tasty pastas; the risotto gets mixed reviews.

Fusions (☎ 5474 1699; 271 Gympie Tce; dishes $12-27) Pasta and wood-fired gourmet pizzas join focaccia and sandwiches on the menu of this Mediterranean-inspired bistro.

SUNSHINE BEACH

There's a cluster of restaurants in Duke St, surrounded by **take-away places**.

Alegria (☎ 5474 5533; 56 Duke St; tapas $8-11, other dishes $15-25) An elegant hangout for trendy young things, Alegria serves very tasty tapas, gourmet pizzas and other Mediterranean-inspired food. Great wines.

Sabai Sabai (☎ 5473 5177; 46 Duke St; mains $19-25) Maybe not as new or popular as some of its neighbours, this chilled-out Asian restaurant still turns out delicious curries and does a lip-smacking green papaya salad.

The Noosa Heads Surf Club and the Sunshine Beach Surf Club are also popular places to eat.

Drinking

Start a raucous night out at the **Koala Bar** (☎ 5447 3355; 44 Noosa Dr, Noosa Junction) or the **Reef Bar** (☎ 5447 4477), just across the road.

Barney's (☎ 5447 4800; Noosa Dr, Noosa Heads), just back from Hastings St, attracts a huge mix, although mainly of 20-something drinkers. The **New York Bar** (☎ 5447 2255; Bay Village, off Hastings St) is more a place to see and be seen.

For the perfect end to a relaxed evening, have a last tipple at **Aromas** (☎ 5474 9788; 32 Hastings St) a Parisian-style café.

Entertainment

Bold Lounge (☎ 5447 3433; Noosa Bowls Club, Lanyana Way, Noosa Junction; $10) On the first Saturday of each month, the bowls club is transformed by this dance party and its retro décor.

Rolling Rock (☎ 5447 2255; Bay Village, off Hastings St; admission $6-7) This long-standing favourite continues to pump out techno, funk, progressive house and Top 40 tunes nearly every night of the year.

Noosa 5 Cinemas (☎ 1300 366 339; 29 Sunshine Beach Rd; Noosa Junction) For the latest Hollywood blockbusters, try this complex.

Getting There & Around

Ferries run daily between Noosa Heads and Tewantin, with some continuing on to Noosa North Shore. The services operate

---

GO ON: SPLURGE

It's hard to pick a bad restaurant in Noosa, but these are among its more renowned.

Berardo's (☎ 5447 5666; 50 Hastings St; mains $29-35) A newer star in the local culinary firmament, Berardo's has won a fistful of awards, with dishes including duck entrées, rack of lamb, plentiful seafood and a good after-dinner cheese platter.

Ricky Ricardo's (☎ 5447 2455; Noosa Wharf, Quamby Pl, Noosa Sound; mains $18-35) This casually elegant Mediterranean-influenced restaurant is another high-achieving newcomer, and enjoys a waterfront location.

Bistro C (☎ 5447 2855; On the Beach Arcade, Hastings St; breakfast $6-14, lunch $12-15, dinner $17-28) As famous for its quirky people sculptures as its fried egg calamari, this yuppie bistro enjoys a wonderful location overlooking the beach. Bit noisy, though.

Cato's (☎ 5449 4888; 14-16 Hastings St; dishes $16-30) Part of the Sheraton complex, this high-ceilinged, airy café offers European-inspired seafood and modern Australian dishes.

between 8.30am and 6pm (later on week-ends) and fares are $5 to $8.50 one way or $10 to $12.50 for an all-day pass. Catch the **Riverlight Ferry** (☎ 5449 8442) if you'd like an onboard commentary while still being able to jump on and off, or the cheaper **Purple People Mover** (☎ 5474 2444), which also goes to Noosa North Shore. Tickets are available onboard.

With no bus terminal in Noosa, long-distance buses stop at the corner of Noosa Dr and Noosa Pde, just back from Hastings St.

Sunbus (☎ 5450 7888) runs frequent daily services up and down the coast between Noosa and Maroochydore, and has local services linking Noosa Heads, Noosaville and Noosa Junction etc. Some buses from Noosa Heads to Nambour train station stop at Eumundi ($5.50).

Henry's Airport Buses (☎ 5474 0199) runs frequent services to Brisbane airport ($38) and, on request, to Maroochydore airport ($15).

Europcar (☎ 5447 3777; 13 Noosa Dr, Noosa Junction) hires cars from $45 per day and 4WD vehicles from $165 for trips to the Great Sandy National Park. (Driving them to Fraser Island is prohibited.)

Koala Bike Hire (☎ 5474 2733) delivers mountain bikes to your door for $17 to $24 per day.

COOLOOLA COAST

Stretching north from Noosa to Rainbow Beach, the Cooloola Coast is a 50km strip of long sandy beaches, backed by the Cooloola section of the Great Sandy National Park. Remote, undeveloped and a good place for spotting kangaroos, it nevertheless attracts crowds at peak times.

With a 4WD you can drive up the beach at low tide to Rainbow Beach, passing the Teewah Coloured Sands and the wreck of the Cherry Venture, swept ashore in 1973.

Lake Cooroibah

About 2km north of Tewantin, the Noosa River widens out into Lake Cooroibah. Catch the **Noosa River Ferry** (☎ 07-544/ 1321; cars $4.50; ⏰ 6am-10.30pm, until 12.30am Fri & Sat) from the end of Moorindil St in Tewantin; each crossing takes about five minutes. You can drive in a conventional vehicle to the lake's eastern shore or the beaches of Laguna Bay.

Those keen to see wildlife, go canoeing or revel in relaxed bush living should stay at **Noosa North Shore Retreat** (☎ 07-5447 1225; www.noosaretreat.com.au; dm/d $20/50). It's difficult to get from the resort into late-night Noosa without your own transport, but there's a restaurant and pub on site. Cabins ($110 a night) have a two-night minimum stay.

Noosa North Shore Caravan Park (☎ 07-5447 1706; camp sites from $14, caravan sites $20 for 2 people) is nearby.

Lake Cootharaba

North of Lake Cooroibah is Lake Cootharaba, reached by driving northwest of Tewantin. **Boreen Point**, on Cootharaba's western shore, is the starting point for kayaking trips into the Cooloola section of the Great Sandy National Park.

From Boreen Point, a partially unsealed road leads up to **Elanda Point**, where there's a **ranger's station** (☎ 07-5449 7364) and the **Elanda Point Canoe Company** (☎ 07-5485 3165), which charges $35 per day for canoes and kayaks; a river taxi to the national park **camping ground** (per person/family $4/16) costs $10 each way.

Set in wonderful bushland, the **Tin Pannikin** (☎ 07-5485 3055; www.tinpannikin.com; 41 Kildeys Rd, Boreen Point; d $100) is a B&B that has a couple of tame kangaroos. It offers packages, with bush tucker and bands (listed online), as well as bed-only specials.

A much-loved Aussie pub, the **Apollonian Hotel** (☎ 07-5485 3100; Laguna St, Boreen Point) is popular for Sunday lunch, although more for the atmosphere than the food.

Great Sandy National Park (Cooloola)

East and north of the lakes is the Great Sandy National Park. This 54,000-hectare varied wilderness of mangroves, forest and heathland is traversed by the Noosa River. With a 4WD (available in Noosa), you can drive through the park all the way to Rainbow Beach, but kayaking from Boreen Point is a more relaxing way to sightsee. You can also hire tinnies (powered boats) from several places on Gympie Tce in Noosaville, or take an organised cruise – see Tours p313. There's an **EPA visitors centre** (☎ 07-5449 7364) at Kinaba Island.

The park contains about 10 camping grounds, including **Fig Tree Point** (per person/family $4/16), at Lake Cootharaba's northern edge, **Harry's Hut** (per person/family $4/16),

4km further up the river, and **Freshwater** (per person/family $4/16), about 6km south of Double Island Point on the beach. Contact the rangers at Elanda Point or Kinaba for bookings.

SUNSHINE COAST HINTERLAND

There are organised tours of this region, but with your own transport you can better explore the appealing landscape between towns and villages.

The main tourist attraction, 6km south of the commercial town of **Nambour**, is the **Big Pineapple** (☎ 07-5442 1333; Nambour Connection Rd; admission free; ☾ 9am-5pm). One of Australia's numerous kitsch 'big things', this 15m-high fibreglass fruit sits beside a pineapple plantation, a macadamia orchard and an extensive souvenir shop. A small train chugs through the plantation.

About 7km north of the Big Pineapple on the Bruce Hwy, you'll arrive at **Yandina**, where it's worth booking a meal at the renowned Asian restaurant, **Spirit House** (☎ 07-5446 8994; 4 Ninderry Rd; meals from $25; ☾ lunch daily, dinner Wed-Sat). If travelling with children, also stop at the **Yandina Ginger Factory** (☎ 07-5446 7096; 50 Pioneer Rd; admission free; ☾ 9am-5pm).

Further north both locals and visitors flock to the **Eumundi markets** (☾ 8am-2pm Wed, 6am-2pm Sat), which sell local produce and lots of alternative New Age stuff. The local bus between Noosa Heads and Nambour stops here, or there are direct bus transfers for $12 return.

Inland from Nambour, the Blackall Range creates a scenic hinterland with appealing national parks and rather chintzy rustic villages. The scenic Mapleton to Maleny road runs along the ridge of the range, past rainforests at **Mapleton Falls National Park**, 4km west of Mapleton, and **Kondalilla National Park**, 3km north of Montville. Both Mapleton and Kondalilla **waterfalls** plunge more than 80m, and their lookouts offer wonderful forest views.

Midway between Mapleton and Maleny is **Montville**, with potteries, dinky craft shops and restaurants. Ask the **visitors centre** (☎ 07-5478 5544; 202 Main St; ☾ 10am-4pm) about nearby B&Bs.

The **Woodford Folk Festival**, held annually during the five days leading up to New Year's Eve, is the closest Australia has to Woodstock. Woodford is near Maleny.

SOUTH BURNETT REGION

Further inland again, the South Burnett region includes Australia's leading peanut-growing area. The main attraction is the **Bunya Mountains National Park**, more than 1000m above sea level and accessible by sealed road from Dalby or Kingaroy. There are three **camping grounds** (per person/family $4/16), plus walking tracks to waterfalls and lookouts. The **ranger** (☎ 07-4668 3127) is at Dandabah, by the park entrance.

DARLING DOWNS

West of the Great Dividing Range in southern Queensland stretch the rolling plains of the Darling Downs. With some of Australia's most fertile land, this was the first part of Queensland to be settled, and it enjoys a rich history. Warwick, Roma and Goondiwindi are typical country towns, but leafy Toowoomba and wine-growing Stanthorpe have a more 'New England' feel.

Getting There & Away

AIR

QantasLink (☎ 13 13 13) flies Brisbane to Roma (from $180, 70 minutes).

BUS

McCafferty's/Greyhound (☎ 13 14 99) has several major bus services passing through the Darling Downs. The Brisbane–Longreach service runs along the Warrego Hwy via Toowoomba ($21, 2 hours), Dalby ($34, 4 hours), Miles ($40, 5½ hours) and Roma ($55, 8 hours). Its inland Brisbane–Adelaide and Brisbane–Melbourne services pass through Warwick ($34, 3 hours) and Stanthorpe ($45, 4½ hours), or Goondiwindi ($50, 5 hours), depending on the route.

McCafferty's/Greyhound also has buses between Toowoomba and the Gold Coast ($45), and between Brisbane and Rockhampton via Toowoomba and Miles.

TRAIN

The *Westlander* runs twice a week (Tuesday and Thursday) from Brisbane to Charleville via Ipswich, Toowoomba and Roma. One-way fares are $65 for an economy seat and $114 for an economy sleeper. There are connecting bus services from Charleville to Quilpie and Cunnamulla. For details, get in touch with **Queensland Rail's booking service** (☎ 13 22 32; www.traveltrain.qr.com.au).

IPSWICH TO WARWICK

Almost an outer suburb of Brisbane, Ipswich was a convict settlement as early as 1827 and a pioneering Queensland town. The Ipswich City Heritage Trails leaflets from the **visitors centre** (☎ 07-3281 0555; Queen's Park, Queen Victoria Pde; 🕑 9am-5pm Mon-Sat, 10am-4pm Sun) list some interesting buildings.

Southwest of Ipswich the Cunningham Hwy to Warwick crosses the Great Dividing Range at **Cunningham's Gap** (named after a botanist from London's Kew Gardens). Here the road winds rather treacherously through the 1100m-high mountains of **Main Range National Park**, with dense rainforest and numerous walking trails and lookouts. The **ranger station** (☎ 07-4666 1133) is west of Cunningham's Gap on the southern side of the highway, and there's a small camping ground opposite.

WARWICK

☎ 07 / pop 12,000

Warwick, 162km southwest of Brisbane, is a good place to heed the adage about stopping to smell the roses. Its Leslie Park and Jubilee Rose Gardens are perfumed with many varieties, including the red City of Warwick (*Arofuto*) genus. Once home to champion sheep-shearer Jackie Howe, the fastest man with a pair of old-fashioned blades, today the town focuses on rodeo, with a major event every October.

The **visitors centre** (☎ 4661 3122; 49 Albion St; 🕑 8.30am-5pm) stocks material on Warwick's historic buildings, as well as those of the neighbouring Southern Downs.

If you don't mind smallish bedrooms, stay at the atmospheric **Abbey of the Roses** (☎ 4661 9777; cnr Locke & Dragon St; s & d $90), a converted convent. Otherwise, there are several motels and caravan parks. Don't miss the charming, domed **Bramble Patch Cafe** (☎ 4661 9022; 8 Albion St; meals $8.50-13 🕑 8.30am-4pm), a popular place for breakfast and lunch and home to all things berry.

STANTHORPE & THE GRANITE BELT

South of Warwick is the Granite Belt, an elevated plateau of the Great Dividing Range. This 'high country' is renowned for its fruit, vegetables and 30 to 40 boutique wineries.

Stanthorpe is the largest town, and the coldest place in Queensland (there's a Brass Monkey festival each July). During winter in particular, it's a chichi weekend getaway for those who love to sip wine around the log fire of their cosy cottage. From October to mid-June (provided there's been plenty of rainfall in the year) Stanthorpe's fruit-picking opportunities are a major attraction for working backpackers.

Information

Visitors can get information on the town and surrounding area from **Stanthorpe visitors centre** (☎ 07-4681 2057, 1800 060 877; Leslie St; 🕑 8.30am-5pm).

Sights & Activities

About 26km south of Stanthorpe, a sealed road turns off the highway, leading 9km east to the **Girraween National Park** (visitors centre ☎ 07-4684 5157), which features towering granite boulders surrounded by pristine forests. Wildlife abounds, and the park adjoins Bald Rock National Park over the border in New South Wales. There are two good **camping grounds** (per person/family $4/16) in Girraween, plus numerous walking trails.

Grape Escape (☎ 1300 361 150) operates winery tours ($60), tours of Girraween ($45) and more.

Sleeping

Backpackers of Queensland (☎ 0429-810 998; www.backpackersofqueensland.com.au; 80 High St, Stanthorpe; dm nightly/weekly $25/125; 🖳 🐾) During the fruit-picking season, this modern hostel, with stone cabins and good facilities, caters only to working backpackers staying weekly. During winter, overnight stays are possible.

Vines Motel (☎ 07-4681 3844; www.thevinesmotel.com.au; 2 Wallangara Rd, Stanthorpe; s/d/f $70/75/85; 🐾) This immaculately kept motel has one room with wheelchair access, plus self-contained cottages for couples or groups ($100 to $150).

Das Helwig Haus (☎ 07-4683 4227; www.webstation.com.au/accom/helwig; Mt Stirling Rd, Glen Aplin; s $80, d $110-160) Named the best B&B in Queensland by Brisbane's *Sunday Mail*, this homestead 9km from Stanthorpe is surrounded by a poppy garden and self-contained apartments. Rates include a German buffet breakfast.

QUEENSLAND

Other recommendations:
Country Style Tourist Park (☎ 07-4683 4358; New England Hwy, Glen Aplin; camp sites with camp kitchen $16, caravan sites $14, cabins for 2 people $65) For working backpackers and tourists alike.
Boulevard Motel (☎ 07-4681 1777; fax 07-4683 3218; 76 Maryland St, Stanthorpe; s/d/f $52/58/72) Good cheapie motel.

Eating
O'Mara Hotel (☎ 07-4681 1044; 45 Maryland St, Stanthorpe; meals $5.50-$17; ⌚ lunch & dinner Mon-Sat) Lead-lights and early 20th-century pictures make this atmospheric pub somewhere you might almost expect to see WWI diggers (soldiers).
Anna's (☎ 07-4681 1265; cnr Wallangara Rd & O'Mara Tce; meals $15-$20; ⌚ dinner Mon-Sat) Mamma mia! This Italian restaurant, with its passed-down family recipes and outstanding Queenslander home, has won so many awards, its walls are covered in them. Friday and Saturday buffets ($23 and $28) are legendary.

GOONDIWINDI
☎ 07 / pop 5500
West of Warwick on the NSW border, Goondiwindi (gun-doo-*win*-dy) is something of a one-horse town, the horse in question being Gunsynd, a remarkably successful racehorse. There's a statue of the 'Goondiwindi Grey' in MacIntyre St. Visitors can also take a tour of the **MacIntyre Cotton Gin** (☎ 4671 2277; ⌚ Apr-Jul), 4km east of town; call for appointments.
The **visitors centre** (☎ 4671 2653; 4 McLean St; ⌚ 9am-5pm) is housed in the Goondiwindi-Waggamba Library complex.
For reasonably priced accommodation, try **Binalong Motel** (☎ 4671 1777; fax 4671 1617; 30 Maclean St; s/d $55/65).

TOOWOOMBA
☎ 07 / pop 89,400
Perched on the edge of the Great Dividing Range, with breathtaking views of the Lockyer Valley 700m below, Toowoomba enjoys a more temperate climate than much of surrounding southeast Queensland. During the late 19th century middle-class Brisbanites started to make the 130km trek inland for weekend 'constitutionals', and Toowoomba's healthy mountain air was canned and sold as a souvenir. This renowned garden city has another claim to fame, as the birthplace of that archetypal Aussie sweet, the lamington – a confection of sponge cake, chocolate icing and desiccated coconut.

Information
Toowoomba visitors centre 86 James St (☎ 4639 3797; ⌚ 9am-5pm); 476 Ruthven St (☎ 4638 7555; ⌚ 10am-1pm & 2-4pm Mon-Fri)

Sights & Activities
The inspiring **Cobb & Co Museum** (☎ 4639 1971; 27 Lindsay St; adult/child $5/3; ⌚ 10am-4pm) is more than a collection of carriages and traps from the horse-drawn age; it's also a showcase for Toowoomba's Aboriginal and multicultural communities, and includes a children's play area. **Queen's Park** (cnr Lindsay & Campbell Sts) houses the botanic gardens, although some might prefer the **Ju Raku En Japanese Garden** (West St).
Picnic Point, on the eastern edge of town just south of the Warrego Hwy, is the most accessible of the town's several 'escarpment parks', which all enjoy wonderful views. The annual **Carnival of Flowers** is held in September.

Sleeping & Eating
Jeffrey's Rainforest Motel (☎ 4635 5999; fax 4639 9823; 864 Ruthven St; s from $50, d & tw from $55) There are also a few caravan sites ($15) at this modest motel on the town outskirts.
Downs Motel (☎ 4639 3811; fax 4639 3806; 669 Ruthven St; s/d $55/60, deluxe s/d $70/75) Inside a dusky rose-brown exterior you'll find budget units and very pleasant deluxe rooms.
Vacy Hall (☎ 4639 2055; fax 4632 0160; 135 Russell St; s & d $105-190) Larger than most Australian B&Bs, this atmospheric heritage residence offers 12 period rooms with parquetry floors, rugs and fireplaces.
Bon Amici (☎ 4632 4533; 191 Margaret St; snacks $4-10) Come to this cosy, atmospheric café for delectable cakes, sandwiches and breakfasts.
Oxygen (☎ 4613 1131; 517 Ruthven St; dishes $8.50-20; ⌚ 10am-5pm Mon-Wed, closes 9pm Thu-Sat, closes 4pm Sun) The Asian-influenced organic food in this noodle bar–cum–trendy café is fresh and absolutely delicious.
Weis Restaurant (☎ 4632 7666; 2 Margaret St; lunch $40, dinner $50) This award-winning Toowoomba institution still reels in the crowds with a daily gourmet seafood smorgasbord.

TOOWOOMBA TO ROMA

At Jondaryan, 45km west of Toowoomba, is the historic **Jondaryan Woolshed** (☎ 07-4692 2229; Evanslea Rd; adult/child $13/6; ☼ 9am-4pm). This large complex has rustic old buildings, antique farm and industrial machinery, period displays, and daily blacksmithing and shearing demonstrations. Stay in the shearers quarters for $28 per room, or camp from $9.

A further 167km west the **Miles Historical Village** (☎ 07-4627 1492; Murilla St; adult/child/family $10/3/20; ☼ 8am-5pm) is one of the best of its kind, and also houses a visitors centre. You can stay at the **Hotel Australia** (☎ 07-4627 1106; 55 Murilla St; s/d $17/29), or there are several caravan parks and motels.

ROMA

☎ 07 / pop 5900

It would be too easy to make fun of Roma's self-description as the 'modern face of gas'. That's nothing to do with its extensive sheep and cattle industries, but all to do with its natural gas and oil deposits, which still supply Brisbane through a 450km pipeline.

The major landmark is the **Big Rig Complex** (☎ 4622 4355; McDowell St; adult/child $10/7, with night show $16/11; ☼ 9am-5pm, night show at 6pm), a museum based around an old steam-operated oil rig at the eastern edge of town. There's a visitors centre in the complex, which can help with accommodation if you're stopping en route to the Carnarvon Gorge (p347).

FRASER COAST

Most visitors to this stretch of coast make a beeline for the majestic Fraser Island. The world's largest sand island was created over millennia by longshore drift, or sand washing off Australia's east coast. Touristy Hervey Bay is the major access point for the island, but it's also possible to catch a ferry from scenic Rainbow Beach.

By the time you reach Bundaberg further north, you've entered a region of sugar cane, rum and coral. Fruit-picking jobs also bring working travellers to this town.

Getting There & Away

AIR

QantasLink (☎ 13 13 13) flies to Bundaberg from Brisbane several times a day ($230, 50 minutes).

BUS

McCafferty's/Greyhound (☎ 13 1499) has a coastal service that runs from Brisbane along the Bruce Hwy, detouring to Bundaberg ($60, 7 hours) and Hervey Bay ($45, 5 hours). **Premier Motor Services** (☎ 07-3236 4444, 13 34 10) and **Suncoast Pacific** (☎ 07-3236 1901) also pass by on the Brisbane to Rockhampton route. Smaller local companies connect Gympie to Rainbow Beach and Tin Can Bay.

TRAIN

The main coastal railway line from Brisbane to Rockhampton and Cairns passes through Gympie ($36, 2½ hours), Maryborough West ($50, 3½ hours) and Bundaberg ($60, 4¼ hours). There is a Trainlink bus from Maryborough West to Hervey Bay ($5.50, 40 to 50 minutes).

GYMPIE

☎ 07 / pop 10,600

Gympie likes to promote itself as 'the town that saved Queensland' with its once-rich gold deposits. Most mining stopped in the 1920s, and the principal reminders of its illustrious past are the rather hotchpotch **Gold Mining & Historical Museum** (☎ 5482 3995; 215 Brisbane Rd; adult/child $6.60/1.10; ☼ 9am-4.30pm), which is visible from the Bruce Hwy on the southern outskirts of town, and a week-long **Gold Rush Festival** every October.

Just north of Gympie lies a well-curated **Woodworks Forestry & Timber Museum** (☎ 5483 7691; Fraser Rd; adult/student $4/2; ☼ 9am-4pm Mon-Fri, 1-4pm Sun). One highlight is the cross-section of a huge bunya pine that lived through the Middle Ages, Columbus' discovery of America and the industrial revolution, only to be felled in the early 20th century.

There's a **visitors centre** (☎ 5482 5444; ☼ 8.30am-3.30pm) on the Bruce Hwy, just south of the Gold Mining Museum.

Gympie has several motels and caravan parks, and it's on the main bus and train routes north from Brisbane.

TIN CAN BAY

☎ 07 / pop 2000

This small community's main allure has been its tame dolphins and dolphin-feeding excursions. Sadly, at the time of writing all but one of the resident animals had died, so check with the visitors centres in Rainbow Beach or Hervey Bay before setting out.

QUEENSLAND

RAINBOW BEACH
☎ 07 / pop 1050

Its name derives from its coloured sand cliffs, but unspoilt Rainbow Beach feels more like the pot of gold at the end of a weary traveller's rainbow. Its pandanus tree-lined beaches and red-hued cliffs arc round Wide Bay, offering a sweeping panorama from the lighthouse at Double Island Point in the south to Fraser Island in the north. Its proximity to that island (15 minutes by ferry from Inskip Point, 13km north) makes it an idyllic jumping-off point. And the view from the Carlo Sandblow, a 120m-high dune on the hill overlooking this tiny town, has been known to make the most cynical sightseer gasp.

Information
INTERNET ACCESS
Cooloolo Home Video (☎ 5486 3135; Shop 5, 8 Rainbow Beach Rd; $4 per hour)

TOURIST INFORMATION
EPA Office (☎ 5486 3160; www.smartservice.qld.gov.au; Rainbow Beach Rd; ☺ 7am-4pm) On the way into town.
Rainbow Beach visitors centre (☎ 5486 3227; 8 Rainbow Beach Rd; ☺ 7am-6pm) Privately run centre, offering free maps to the area.

Activities
For those not wishing to hire a 4WD (see Getting There & Around below), **Surf & Sand Safaris** (☎ 5486 3131; $55/28 adult/child) runs twice-daily, four-hour trips south along the beach, taking in the coloured sands that rise steeply above the beach and the lighthouse. They then continue beyond the point to the wreck of the **Cherry Venture** – a freighter that ran aground here in 1973.

Paragliding above the Carlo Sandblow, where the national championships are held every January, is an unforgettable experience. **Rainbow Paragliding** (☎ 5486 3048, 0418-754 157) offers tandem glides for $130.

Surfing is popular, as is scuba diving at Wolf Rock off Double Island Point, where you'll find gropers, turtles, manta rays and harmless grey nurse sharks. Contact **Wolf Rock Dive Centre** (☎ 5486 8004, 0438-740 811).

Sleeping & Eating
Fraser's on Rainbow (☎ 5486 8885, 1800 100 170; www.frasersonrainbow.com; 18 Spectrum Ave; dm $18-22, d with bathroom $60) This converted motel has very reasonable dorms and doubles, with a huge (and sometimes noisy) TV room and bar, and friendly staff.

Rocks Backpacker Resort (☎ 5486 3711; rocks backpackers@bigpond.com; 3 Spectrum Ave; dm/d $18/40) Another converted motel, quite similar to Fraser's on Rainbow, this place has two types of room. The more modern of these are flashier, but have slightly less character, than their rival's.

Rainbow Sands (☎ 5486 3400, 1800 633 516; sam .rainbow@bigpond.com; 42-46 Rainbow Beach Rd; d $70) A fairly standard motel, with clean, modern rooms and leafy back garden, this is the best mid-range option in town.

Rainbow Shores Resort (☎ 5486 3999, 1800 801 789; www.rainbowshores.com.au; Inskip Ave; d $115, villas & beach houses from $135) These open-plan, modern, architect-designed villas, snuggled in bushland only metres from the beach, provide a perfect getaway or romantic retreat (minimum two-night stay). The resort, 1km north of town towards Inskip Point, also has luxury apartments and beach houses.

Rainbow Beach Holiday Village & Caravan Park (☎ 5486 3222; fax 5486 3401; Rainbow Beach Rd; camp sites $18-20, caravan sites $23, cabins from $80 for 2 people) Right by the main beach, with units transported from Sydney's Olympic Village, this park offers a civilised camping experience.

To play castaway, get a permit from the **EPA** (☎ 5486 3160) and set up camp in one of the paradisiacal grounds along Inskip Point – Sarawak, Beagle, Natone or Dorrigo.

Archie's (☎ 5486 3277; 12 Rainbow Beach Rd; mains $5.50-15) This popular café perfectly encapsulates Rainbow's laid-back surfer chic, serving delicious smoothies, vegie burgers, nachos and more.

Getting There & Around
McCafferty's/Greyhound (☎ 13 14 99) has daily services from Brisbane ($31, 5½ hours). **Polley's Coaches** (☎ 5482 2700; 27 Duke St, Gympie) also has twice-daily return services between Gympie and Rainbow Beach every weekday ($13, 1¼ hours).

With a 4WD it's possible to drive south along the beach and through the Cooloola section of the Great Sandy National Park to Noosa, as well as head for Fraser Island. Ask the Rainbow Beach EPA (above) for a permit if you wish to camp.

Aussie Adventure (☎ 5486 3599; 4/54 Rainbow Beach Rd) and **Safari 4x4** (☎ 4124 4244, 1800 689 819; 27 Goondi St) offer 4WD vehicle hire for

$110 to $150 per day. For ferry details, see Getting There & Away (p331).

MARYBOROUGH
☎ 07 / pop 21,200

Junk-shop browsers will love the National Trust–classified **Brennan & Geraghty's Store** (☎ 4121 2250; 64 Lennox St; adult/child $3.30/1.10; ☼ 10am-3pm daily), Maryborough's best tourist attraction. This historic general store opened for business in 1871 and has been preserved as a museum, with its original stock, shelving, trading records and other remnants. There's a privately run **visitors centre** (☎ 4121 4111; 30 Ferry St; ☼ 10am-2pm Mon-Fri) about 1km south of Kent St on the Bruce Hwy.

There are several motels and caravan parks in the town, plus budget accommodation in some of the old hotels.

HERVEY BAY
☎ 07 / pop 36,100

You need to see its long expanse of beaches for yourself to appreciate why Hervey Bay is such a popular pensioners' paradise and holiday destination for Queensland families. Heaven knows, the procession of shopping centres and superstores as you enter town via Boat Harbour Dr is pretty uninviting, and the line of motels with their *Wayne's World*–style dichotomy of 'No Vacancy/Yes Vacancy' signs cluttering the waterfront Esplanade is scarcely better. However, the 10km of sand stretching from the picturesque suburb of Point Vernon to the congested areas of Pialba, Scarness, Torquay and Urangan offers plenty of op-portunity for swimming, fishing and gazing at Fraser Island across the water.

Hervey Bay is not the only gateway to the island (see the boxed text 'Notes from a Small Island: Exploring Fraser' p328), but it does have the most developed tourist infrastructure for ferrying people across. You can also fly to Lady Elliot Island from here, or go whale-watching in winter and autumn. The town's many caravan parks make it a favourite among travellers with campervans.

Information
INTERNET ACCESS
Internet cafés abound along the Esplanade, with prices around $6-8 per hour.
Adventure Travel Centre (see Tourist Information next) A central, well-equipped option.

TOURIST INFORMATION
Adventure Travel Centre (☎ 4125 9288, 1800 554 400; 410 The Esplanade; ☼ 7am-10pm)
Fraser Island Backpackers Booking Office (☎ 4124 8444; 363 The Esplanade; ☼ 8.30am-7pm)
Hervey Bay Tourism & Development Bureau (☎ 4124 2912, 1800 811 728; cnr Urraween & Maryborough Rds; ☼ 8.30am-5pm Mon-Fri, 10am-4pm Sat & Sun) On the town outskirts.

Sights
Vic Hislop's Great White Shark Expo (☎ 4128 9137; cnr The Esplanade & Elizabeth St, Urangan; adult/child $12/5; ☼ 8.30am-6pm) wins hands down as Queensland's most hilariously tacky museum. Step right up! The Great White is steadfastly presented as deadly, but with the species now endangered, this sideshow

---

A WHALE OF A TIME

Viewed in the flesh, humpback whales certainly surpass anything watched in a nature documentary. Up to 15m in length and 40 tonnes in weight, they're majestic and awe-inspiring – and seen regularly around the waters of Hervey Bay.

Up to 3000 humpbacks (*Megaptera novaeangliae*) enter the bay between the last week of July and the end of October, on the return leg of their annual migration between Antarctica and the warmer waters off northeastern Australia. Having mated and given birth in the north, they arrive in Hervey Bay in groups of about a dozen (known as pulses), before splitting into smaller groups of two or three (pods).

No-one is quite sure why the whales make the diversion en route back to Antarctica. The prevailing theory is that it offers the adults a chance to enjoy a bit of R&R and gives the new calves more time to develop the layers of blubber necessary for survival in icy southern waters. Whatever the reason, the whales have come to feel increasingly at home in Hervey Bay over the years. Some even roll up beside the numerous whale-watching boats with one eye clear of the water, making those on board wonder who's actually watching whom.

QUEENSLAND

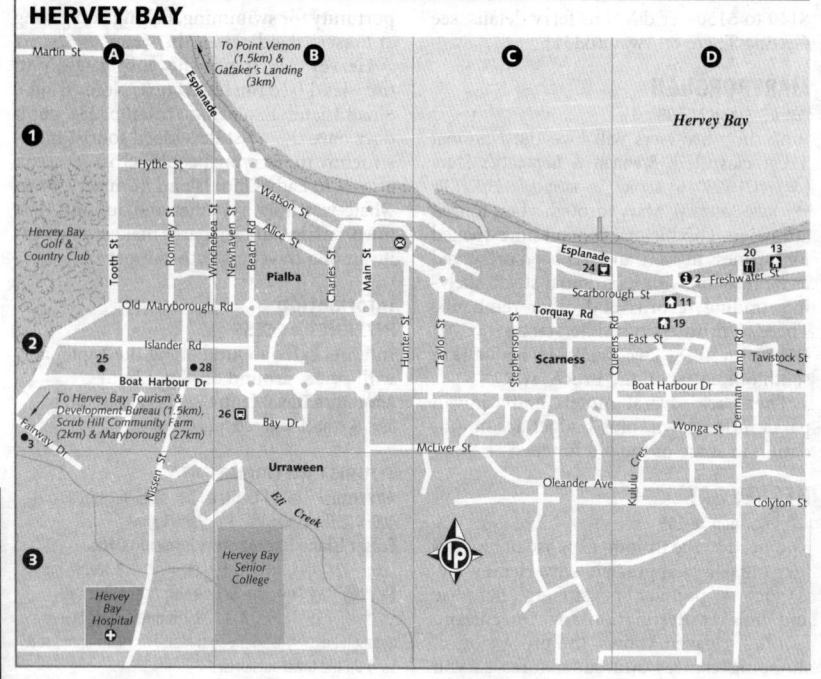

HERVEY BAY

of films, sensationalist newspaper cuttings and toothy taxidermied sharks is perhaps best viewed like the 1970s film *Jaws* – as highly entertaining trash.

Reef World (☎ 4128 9828; Pulgul St, Urangan; adult/child $14/8, shark dives $55; ⏰ 9.30am-5pm) offers a more considered, touchy-feely shark experience, with a chance for visitors to swim with lemon, whaler and other non-predatory sharks. This revamped aquarium also has fish, coral and touch tanks where you can pet turtles and stingrays.

Aboriginal bush tucker excursions offered by **Tom's Tours** (☎ 4128 1005, after hours 4128 7968; adult/child $25/15) are excellent, even though they include a visit to the rather faded **Natureworld** (☎ 4124 1733). Tom gives you the chance, for a small surcharge, to paint your own boomerang. **Scrub Hill Community Farm** (☎ 4124 6908; adult/child $16.50/5.50) also offers bush tucker tours.

Activities
SEA-KAYAKING
Fraser Coast Sea Kayaking (☎ 4124 8208; paddle line@hotmail.com) will take you paddling by

twilight in the bay, through the waterways of Fraser Island and more.

SCENIC FLIGHTS
Tiger Fly (☎ 4124 9313) charges $75 for a half-hour ride in a restored 1931 Tiger Moth over the bay and Fraser Island.

WHALE- AND DOLPHIN-WATCHING
Between mid-July and late October, whale-watching tours operate out of Hervey Bay daily (weather permitting). Sightings are guaranteed from 1 August to 1 November, when you get a free subsequent trip if the whales don't show. At other times of the year, many boats offer dolphin-spotting tours, with the same guarantee. The boats cruise from Urangan Harbour to Platypus Bay and then travel from pod to pod to find the most active whales. Some inquisitive animals come right up to the boats, surfacing only metres away. Most skippers also drop a hydrophone (microphone) into the water to pick up the whales' haunting songs.

When choosing a boat, consider whether you have the sea legs to enjoy a voyage on

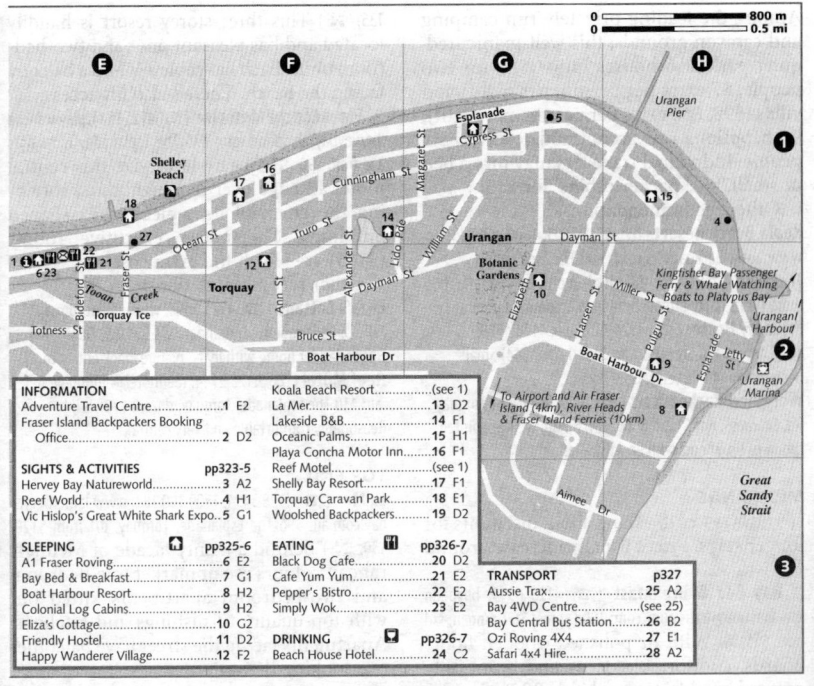

INFORMATION	
Adventure Travel Centre	1 E2
Fraser Island Backpackers Booking	
Office	2 D2

SIGHTS & ACTIVITIES	pp323-5
Hervey Bay Natureworld	3 A2
Reef World	4 H1
Vic Hislop's Great White Shark Expo	5 G1

SLEEPING	pp325-6
A1 Fraser Roving	6 E2
Bay Bed & Breakfast	7 G1
Boat Harbour Resort	8 H2
Colonial Log Cabins	9 H2
Eliza's Cottage	10 G2
Friendly Hostel	11 D2
Happy Wanderer Village	12 F2

Koala Beach Resort	(see 1)
La Mer	13 D2
Lakeside B&B	14 F1
Oceanic Palms	15 H1
Playa Concha Motor Inn	16 F1
Reef Motel	(see 1)
Shelly Bay Resort	17 F1
Torquay Caravan Park	18 E1
Woolshed Backpackers	19 D2

EATING	pp326-7
Black Dog Cafe	20 D2
Cafe Yum Yum	21 G1
Pepper's Bistro	22 E2
Simply Wok	23 E2

DRINKING	pp326-7
Beach House Hotel	24 C2

TRANSPORT	p327
Aussie Trax	25 A2
Bay 4WD Centre	(see 25)
Bay Central Bus Station	26 B2
Ozi Roving 4X4	27 E1
Safari 4x4 Hire	28 A2

a small boat and how large a crowd you wish to be with. Prices for half-day tours are about $65 for adults, $40 for children or $195 for a family. Full-day tours cost only marginally more, if you wish to spend eight hours on the water.

On a full-day tour, **Princess II** (☎ 4124 0400) is a 32-passenger craft with a good track record of close encounters.

Boats operating half-day tours:

Quick Cat (☎ 4128 9611, 1800 671 977) A small, stable vehicle run by an award-winning company.

Seaspray (☎ 4125 3586, 1800 066 404) Carrying a maximum of 47 passengers.

Whalesong (☎ 4125 6222, 1800 689 610) Larger award-winning vessel with underwater viewing windows and kids' corner.

Spirit of Hervey Bay (☎ 4125 5131, 1800 642 544) Another comfortable larger boat with underwater viewing.

Sleeping
BUDGET
Most of the vast number of Hervey Bay hostels do pick-ups from the main bus stop, and organise trips to Fraser Island and other activities.

A1 Fraser Roving (☎ 4125 6386, 1800 989 811; www.fraserroving.com.au; 412 The Esplanade, Torquay, dm $18, d & tw 40; 🖳) The rooms are sparsely furnished, but spacious and refreshingly clean; the staff are friendly and helpful. All of which – when added to its central location, free breakfast, sturdy lockers and excellent amenities – make this large, modern hostel one of the best in town.

Colonial Log Cabins (☎ 4125 1844, 1800 818 280; www.coloniallogcabins.com; cnr Boat Harbour Dr & Pulgul St, Urangan; dm $20, d & tw from $48, cabins from $58; 🖳) Set in bushland near the marina, where possums and parrots visit regularly, this award-winning, YHA-associated resort offers a wide range of accommodation. The convivial bar, restaurant and pool area, plus amenable staff, give it a welcoming vibe.

Torquay Caravan Park (☎ 4125 1578; fax 4125 6706; The Esplanade; camp sites $18, caravan sites $23 for 2 people) The most easterly of three council-run beach-front tourist parks, this has playgrounds, boat ramps and mini-golf facilities.

Happy Wanderer Village (☎ 4125 1103; hwanderer@hervey.com.au; 105 Truro St, Torquay; camp sites from $18, caravan sites $29, cabins from $44 for 2 people)

Among the leading privately run camping and caravan grounds, this well-manicured, quiet park also houses units ($80 for two people, $7 extra per person, per night) and villas ($90, $10 extra per person, per night); both options can accommodate up to six people. Individual travellers may hire a bed in small 'backpacker cabins' for $15.

Other recommendations:

Koala Beach Resort (☎ 4125 3601, 1800 354 535; www.koala-backpackers.com ; 408 The Esplanade, Torquay; dm/d $19/45; 🖳) High-profile and popular, but more for its party atmosphere than accommodation.

Friendly Hostel (☎ 4124 4107; fax 4124 4619; 182 Torquay Rd, Scarness; dm $19, d & tw $44) Small hostel in an old Queenslander home.

Woolshed Backpackers (☎ 4124 0677; 181 Torquay Rd, Scarness; dm $17, d & tw $44) Small, well-appointed group of tin 'sheds' with an Australiana theme.

MID-RANGE

It's always worth asking about discounts for longer stays. Prices usually increase around Christmas.

Bay Bed & Breakfast (☎ 4125 6919; baybedn breakfast@australis.aunz.com; 180 Cypress St, Urangan; s/d from $55/80) With its polished wooden floorboards, comfortable décor and beautifully arrayed breakfast spread, this B&B provides an immaculate home away from home.

Oceanic Palms (☎ 4128 9562; 50 King St, Urangan; s/d from $50/85) Down the lush, tropical garden path, crossing the small bridge over the pond, you arrive at a series of decent ground-floor bedrooms off a central living room. This B&B's guests have use of the outside dining area and barbeque.

Lakeside B&B (☎ 4128 9448; 27 Lido Pde, Urangan; d/tr/f $105/120/140) The suburban street of brick houses isn't massively appealing, but that's more than offset by this B&B's goodhumoured owners, the clean self-contained units and the chance to spot turtles and birds on the lake.

Boat Harbour Resort (☎ 4125 5079; boathar bourrs@aol.com; 650 The Esplanade, Urangan; d/t/f $100/110/120) If you feel too decadent relaxing on the veranda of your rustic, wooden cabin or lounging around your comfy room, you can always be proud that your accommodation here follows an eco-friendly design. The resort is just minutes inland from the Urangan marina.

Shelly Bay Resort (☎ 4125 4533; www.shellybay resort.com.au; 466 The Esplanade, Torquay; d/f from $95/ 135; 🔀) This three-storey resort is handily located and has pleasant one- and two-bedroom units. Each has cable TV and a balcony facing the beach. There's also lift access.

Playa Concha Motor Inn (☎ 4125 1544; playaconcha .herveybay@bigpond.com; 475 The Esplanade, Torquay; s & d from $90; 🔀) Leafy trees give this central motel an edge over its neighbours, softening the effect of its typically box-shaped buildings. The newer executive rooms ($105) are worth the extra cost.

Other recommendations:

Eliza's Cottage (☎ 4125 2594; www.jenjai.com.au /elizas; 84 Elizabeth St, Urangan; s/d $55/65) Quaint old Queenslander home with leafy, picture-book entrance.

Reef Motel (☎ 4125 2744; reefmotel@dingoblue.net .au; 410 The Esplanade, Torquay; d from $70; 🖳) Reasonably comfortable and very central.

TOP END

La Mer (☎ 4128 3494, 1800 100 181; www.lamerhervey bay.com.au; 396 The Esplanade, Torquay; d/f from $120/ 150; 🔀) Behind a jaunty facade of Mediterranean colours are upmarket one-bedroom and two-bedroom apartments kitted out with top-quality furnishings and kitchens. Apartments facing the street have balconies overlooking the water.

Eating & Drinking

Cafe Yum Yum (☎ 4125 4107; cnr Bideford & Truro Sts; dishes $5-8.50; ⏱ 7.30am-4.30pm Mon-Fri, 8.30am-1pm Sat) Possibly the closest Hervey Bay has to a funky, alternative café, Yum Yum displays its owners' cosmopolitan backgrounds – with lavish rolls and lamb kofta on the menu, Turkish music regularly in the background, and German books on the shelves.

Simply Wok (☎ 4125 2077; 417 The Esplanade; breakfast $5.50-11, lunch $8-12, dinner $11-20) Whether tucking into a fabulously fresh breakfast, lunching or dining on delicious fusion cuisine or partaking of coffee and cake, it's always fun to have a scribble on this restaurant's paper tablecloths (felt-tip pens provided).

Pepper's Bistro (☎ 4125 2266; 421 The Esplanade, Torquay; dishes $13-20) The Torquay Hotel's popular eatery serves up generous portions of superior-quality pub grub. Dishes include Asian noodles and Caesar salad, plus steaks and seafood.

Black Dog Cafe (☎ 4124 3177, 381 The Esplanade; dishes $10-22; ⏱ lunch Thu-Sun, dinner daily) This trendy modern café offers treats like *yakitori*

(Japanese satay) and sushi, as well as steaks and more conventional grills. Discounts for YHA/VIP cardholders.

Gataker's Landing (☎ 4124 2470; 353 The Esplanade, Point Vernon; dishes $10-28; ⊙ lunch daily, dinner Wed-Sun) Wonderfully located (just out of town), through a garden centre and overlooking some unspoilt waterfront, this ornately decorated, inventive modern Australian restaurant and bar is where locals come for a treat.

Beach House Hotel (☎ 4128 1233; The Esplanade) is one of the best central places to sink a cold beer.

Getting There & Away

Sunshine Express (☎ 5450 6222, 5450 6233) is based at the Sunshine Coast airport and has daily flights between Brisbane and Hervey Bay ($165). Hervey Bay airport is off Booral Rd, Urangan.

The **Queensland Rail** (☎ 132232; 132235) *Tilt Train* stops at Maryborough West ($50 economy, 3½ hours), where a Trainlink bus ($5.50) transfers to Hervey Bay.

Hervey Bay is on a main bus route between Brisbane ($45, 5 hours) and Rockhampton ($75, 5½ hours). **Wide Bay Transit** (☎ 4121 3719) has nine services every weekday, and three services every Saturday, between Maryborough and Hervey Bay marina ($5.25, 1½ hours).

For details on the Fraser Island ferry, see Getting There & Away (p331).

Getting Around

Most places to stay will pick you up from the bus station if you call ahead. Wide Bay Transit buses pass infrequently along the coastal strip, and aren't much use for local transport.

Rayz Bike Hire (☎ 0417-644 814; half/full day $10/14) has outlets along the Esplanade or will deliver to your door.

Hiring a 4WD is discussed in the boxed text 'Notes from a Small Island: Exploring Fraser' (p328).

FRASER ISLAND

Seen from the coast, Fraser Island appears too lush and green to be the world's biggest sand island, but its ecology is one of the many wonders of the place. Rainforests and some 200 freshwater lakes dot a landscape that, considering its 120km by 15km

surface area and enormous depth, contains more sand than the Sahara desert – reputedly.

Despite first impressions – usually of its thousands of trees – once on the island, sand makes its presence more intimately felt: getting in your eyes, your shoes and your swimming costume. Dunes, known locally

NOTES FROM A SMALL ISLAND: EXPLORING FRASER

There's a sci-fi other-worldliness to Fraser Island, as Landrovers, sport utility vehicles (SUVs) and buses with towering wheel bases and fat, chunky tyres all pull in to refuel against an idyllic beach backdrop of white sand and waving palm trees. The surfeit of sand and the lack of paved roads mean that only these 4WD vehicles can negotiate the island. If you're a committed hiker, you can cover some attractions, perhaps with the help of the fairly expensive **Fraser Island Taxi Service** (☎ 07-4125 5511), but most other travellers are presented with the three choices described following. (Please bear in mind, when choosing a mode of transport, that the greater the number of individual vehicles driving on the island, the greater the environmental damage.)

Tours

One-, two- or three-day package tours leave from Hervey Bay, Rainbow Beach and Noosa on the Sunshine Coast. They take in a selection of sites, typically a stretch of rainforest, the fast-moving Eli Creek, a couple of lakes, the coloured Pinnacles and the *Maheno* shipwreck.

Advantages: this is the easiest option, providing informed commentary. Last-minute bookings are generally available with larger companies, and there is the chance to leave from Hervey Bay and return to Rainbow Beach or Noosa, or vice versa.

Disadvantages: some travellers won't enjoy the formal itinerary or the large number (sometimes 40 to 80) of passengers – this is much less of a drawback on smaller tours, but those generally require earlier bookings.

There are plenty of tour operators to choose from.

Fraser Island Company (☎ 07-4125 3933, 1800 063 933; www.fraserislandco.com.au; Hervey Bay; 1/2/3 days from $100/185/320) Tours of 16-24 people, with two- or three-day versions staying at the Fraser Island Wilderness Retreat or Cathedral Beach.

Trailblazer Tours (☎ 07-5449 8151, 1800 626 673; Noosaville; 3-day safari $275) Highly-recommended, thrice-weekly trip with maximum 17 people, also covering the coast from Noosa to Rainbow Beach. Choose either from the company's own beach house or a night under the stars.

Sand Island Safaris (☎ 07-4124 6911, 1800 246 911; Hervey Bay; 3 days $290) Well-regarded small group tours, spending nights at Eurong.

FraserExperience (☎ 07-41244244, 1800606422; www.safari4wdhire.com.au; Hervey Bay; 2/3 days $170/265) Smaller groups, promising that travellers have a say in how long they stay at attractions.

Kingfisher Bay Tours (☎ 07-4120 3333, 1800 072 555; www.kingfisherbay.com; Fraser Island; 1/2/3 days from $105/270/$350 twin share) Ranger-guided tours accommodated at Kingfisher Bay Resort.

Fraser Venture (☎ 07-4125 4444, 1800 249 122; www.fraser-is.com; Hervey Bay; 1/2/3 days $100/210/340 twin share) Huge, cheerful herd-'em-on-the-bus tours, staying at Eurong. Daily pick-ups from Hervey Bay, Noosa and Rainbow Beach.

Self-drive Backpacker Tours

Hostels in Hervey Bay organise guests into groups of about nine per vehicle to drive their own convoy to the island and camp out, usually for two nights, three days. Some instruction about driving 4WD vehicles is given and drivers nominated.

as 'sandblows', stand up to 224m tall before you, while your 4WD moves slowly along the soft tracks. It's an amazing environment, but as 350,000 people arrive annually to delight in the outdoor pursuits of camping, walking and off-road driving, Fraser also feels like a giant sandpit for adults and children alike.

Coming here, there are certain essentials to know: 4WDs are necessary (see the boxed text 'Notes from a Small Island: Exploring Fraser' above). The lakes are lovely to swim in, but the sea's lethal: undertows and man-eating sharks make it a definite no-go. And feeding the island's dingoes has made them increasingly aggressive in recent years (see the boxed text 'Deadly Dingoes' p331).

Yet none of this detracts from the enjoyment of a location unlike any other on earth. If the dunes, the forests, the lakes, the birds and mammals aren't enough, gaze up at the night sky. With little light behind you, the Milky Way blazes bright.

Advantages: probably the cheapest way to see the island, this option provides an opportunity to enjoy the adventure of a lifetime, but with the safety net of a group.

Disadvantages: there's a chance your group won't get along, as well as the risk of getting bogged in sand because of driver inexperience (although some say that's part of the fun). There have been complaints about inadequately stocked first-aid kits, dangerous cooking stoves and keys that snap in the ignition lock. Those weren't with the hostels listed below, but it's always good to ask around and check equipment before you leave.

Unless stated, prices exclude food and fuel (usually $30 to $40).

A1 Fraser Roving (☎ 07-4125 6386, 1800 989 811; www.fraserroving.com.au; $130) As one of the newest hostels, has modern vehicles and equipment.

Smuggler's Rest (☎ 07-4128 2122, 1800 502 115; $170) Boasts no hidden extras, uses modern equipment and adds Frisbee, soccer and a treasure hunt.

Koala Beach Resort (☎ 07-4125 3601, 1800 354 535; www.koala-backpackers.com; $135) Reasonably well-regarded tours in late-model Landrovers.

Colonial Log Cabins (☎ 07-4125 1844, 1800 818 280; www.coloniallogcabins.com; $135) Fairly standard, decent example of these sorts of tours.

4WD Vehicle Hire

Hire companies lease out 4WD vehicles in Hervey Bay, Rainbow Beach and on the island itself. They require a $500 to $2500 bond (usually a credit-card imprint), which you will lose if you drive in saltwater – so don't run the waves. There's also an excess of $2000 to $4000, but for around $25 to $40 per day this can be reduced to $500. An instruction video will usually be shown, but when planning your trip, reckon on covering 20km an hour on the inland tracks and 50km an hour on the eastern beach. Fraser has had some nasty accidents, often due to speeding. Most companies will help arrange ferries, and permits (p330), and hire camping gear.

Advantages: complete freedom to roam the island, and to therefore escape the crowds.

Disadvantages: having to drive in conditions where even experienced 4WDers often have difficulties, and being responsible for any vehicle damage.

Rates for multiple-day rentals are about $120 for a Suzuki Sierra to $180 for a Landcruiser.

Ozi Roving 4X4 (☎ 07-4125 6355; 10 Fraser St, Torquay, Hervey Bay) With its own panel-beating shop, doesn't overcharge for damage.

Aussie Trax (☎ 07-4124 4433, 1800 062 275; 56 Boat Harbour Dr, Hervey Bay) Large fleet from older Sierras and ex-army Landrovers to newer, costlier Defender wagons.

Safari 4X4 Hire (☎ 07-4124 4244, 1800 689 819; 102 Boat Harbour Dr, Hervey Bay) Can also arrange vehicles for you to pick up in Rainbow Beach.

Bay 4WD Centre (☎ 07-4128 2981, 1800 687 178; 54 Boat Harbour Dr, Hervey Bay) Mixed reports about this company's vehicles.

Air Fraser Island (☎ 07-4125 3600; Hervey Bay) Slightly more expensive, charging $145 to $195 per day. Fly-drive packages available.

Kingfisher Bay 4WD Hire (☎ 07-4120 3366; Fraser Island) Medium-sized fleet, from Suzuki Sierras to Landcruisers; all $195 per day.

History

Known to local Butchulla Aborigines as K'gari (Paradise), the island takes its European name from James and Eliza Fraser. The captain of the *Stirling Castle* and his wife were shipwrecked on the island's northwest coast in 1836. He died here, and she probably would have followed without the help of the Aborigines.

As European settlers awoke to the value of Fraser's timber, that same tribe of Aborigines was unfortunately displaced (although not without a fight) and tracts of rainforest were cleared in the search for turpentine (satinay), a waterproof wood prized by shipbuilders. The island was also mined for its mineral sand for many years.

In the late 20th century the focus shifted from exploitation to protection. Sand mining ceased in 1975, after residents took legal action. Logging stopped in 1991, after the island was brought under the auspices of the

QPWS, as part of the Great Sandy National Park. In 1993 native title was recognised and the island listed as a World Heritage area.

Information

FUEL, SUPPLIES & TELEPHONES

Cathedral Beach, Eurong, Kingfisher Bay, Happy Valley & Orchid Beach.

PERMITS

If travelling independently, you'll need a permit to take a vehicle onto the island and to camp. Pick one up at **QPWS kiosk** (☎ 07-4125 8473) at the River Heads ferry terminal. Vehicle permits cost $31, and camping ones the standard $4 per person per night for any Queensland national park. If you forget to buy a vehicle permit on the mainland, it costs $41 (cash) on the island, but you could also face a $50 fine.

Permits are also available online at www .smartservice.qld.gov.au or from EPA offices – including the **Naturally Queensland Information Centre** (Map pp284-6; ☎ 07-3227 8815; nqic@epa.qld.gov.au; 160 Ann St) in Brisbane, and from Rainbow Beach (p322).

RANGER STATIONS

Stations offer information leaflets, tidetimes, free firewood (one armful per camp) and drinking water. Eurong is the main station; others close outside high season (usually school holidays, Christmas and Easter).

Eurong (☎ 07-4127 9128; ⏱ 10.30am-4pm Mon, 7am-4pm Tue-Thu, 7am-3pm Fri, 2-4pm Sat & Sun)

Central Station (☎ 07-4127 9191; ⏱ 10am-noon)

Dundubara (☎ 07-4127 9138; ⏱ 8-9am & 3-4pm)

Waddy Point (☎ 07-4127 9190; ⏱ 7-8am & 4-4.30pm)

Sights & Activities

From the island's southern tip, vehicles should use the old mining track between Hook Point and **Dilli Village**, rather than the beach. From here on, the eastern beach is the main thoroughfare. A short drive north of Dilli will take you to the resort at **Eurong**, the start of the inland track across to Central Station and Wanggoolba Creek (for the ferry to River Heads).

In the middle of the island is **Central Station**, starting point for numerous walking trails. From signposted tracks head to the beautiful **Lakes McKenzie**, **Jennings**, **Birrabeen** and **Boomanjin**. Like many of Fraser's lakes, these

are 'perched', formed by water accumulating on top of a thin impermeable layer of decaying twigs and leaves. They also join Iceland's famous Blue Lagoon as open-air beauty salons, where you can exfoliate your skin with the mineral sand and soften your hair in the clear water. Lake McKenzie is possibly the most spectacular, but Lake Birrabeen is also amazing, and usually less crowded.

About 4km north of Eurong along the beach is a signposted walking trail to **Lake Wabby**. An easier route is from the lookout on the inland track. Wabby is surrounded on three sides by eucalypt forest, while the fourth side is a massive sandblow, which is encroaching on the lake at a rate of about 3m a year. The lake is deceptively shallow and diving is dangerous – in recent years, several people have been paralysed by doing so. You can often find turtles and huge catfish in the eastern corner of the lake under the trees.

Driving north along the beach you'll pass **Happy Valley**, with many places to stay, and **Eli Creek**, a fast-moving, crystal-clear waterway that will carry you effortlessly downstream. About 2km from Eli Creek is the wreck of the *Maheno*, a passenger liner that was blown ashore by a cyclone in 1935 while being towed to a Japanese scrapyard.

Roughly 5km north of the *Maheno* you'll find the **Pinnacles** – a section of coloured sand cliffs – and about 10km beyond, **Dundubara**. Then there's a 20km stretch of beach before you come to the rock outcrop of **Indian Head**, the best vantage point on the island. Sharks, manta rays, dolphins and (during the migration season) whales can often be spotted from the top of the headland.

From Indian Head the trail branches inland, passing the **Champagne Pools**, the only safe spot on the island for saltwater swimming. This inland road leads back to **Waddy Point** and **Orchid Beach**, the last settlement on the island. Many tracks north of this are closed, for environmental protection. The 30km of beach up to **Sandy Cape**, the northern tip, with its lighthouse, is off-limits to hire vehicles. The beach from Sandy Cape to Rooney Point is closed to all vehicles, as is the road from Orchid Beach to Platypus Bay.

Sleeping & Eating

The QPWS runs **camping grounds** (per person/ family $4/16) with coin-operated hot showers, toilets and barbecues at Central Station,

Dundubara and Waddy Point. Its camping grounds at Lake McKenzie, Lake Boomanjin and Wathumba have cold showers; there are none at the Lake Allom grounds. You can also camp on designated stretches of the eastern beach. To camp in any of these public areas you need a permit. (At the time of writing, Dilli Village was being run as a camping ground by the QPWS, but its status was under review.)

In privately run accommodation, prices drop considerably in the low season (ie not school holidays, Christmas and Easter).

Cathedral Beach Resort & Camping Park (☎ 07-4127 9177; fax 07-4127 9234; Cathedral Beach; camp sites $27 for 2 people, cabins $120-140) This family-orientated, privately run park, about 34km north of Eurong, has a comfortable tent village and more. Cabins are reduced to $100 for subsequent nights, but can only be rented weekly during school holidays ($620).

Fraser Island Beachhouses (☎ 07-4127 9205, 1800 626 230; www.fraserislandbeachhouses.com.au; Eurong Second Valley; d/f $165/240) These idyllically located beach houses are luxurious, but still in tune with the island's relaxed, outdoorsy feel. Two-night minimum stay applies.

Kingfisher Bay Resort (☎ 07-4120 3333, 1800 072 555; www.kingfisherbay.com; Kingfisher Bay; s & d from $260, 2-bedroom villas from $280) Sophisticated motel rooms and wonderful, raised wooden villas combine in this luxury place on the west coast. There are restaurants, bars and shops, plus a communal wilderness lodge for those on Kingfisher's adventure tours.

Eurong Beach Resort (☎ 07-4127 9122; www .fraser-is.com; d from $100, cottages for 2 people $100, 2-bedroom units for 4 people $210) The main resort on

the east coast has accommodation – from slightly worn to newly luxurious – to suit diverse budgets. The food, however, has been woeful – a situation hopefully changing under the new owners, Kingfisher Bay Resort. It's $6 for each extra person in double rooms, units and cottages. For those travelling alone, bunk beds in four-bed cabins ($17) are sometimes available.

Other recommendations:

Fraser Island Wilderness Retreat (☎ 07-4127 9144; retreat@fraserislandco.com.au; Happy Valley; d & tr $155, f $190) Timber lodges, plus bar, bistro and shop.

Sailfish on Fraser (☎ 07-4127 9494; fax 07-4127 9499; Happy Valley; d $220, $10 each for next 4 people) Modern luxury apartments.

Self-caterers should come well equipped, as supplies on the island are limited and pricey.

Getting There & Away

Access to Fraser is generally by ferry. The most commonly used services are the vehicle ferries from River Heads, about 10km south of Hervey Bay, which land on the island's west coast either at Wanggoolba Creek or Kingfisher Bay. However, there's a fast catamaran service for pedestrians from Hervey Bay's Urangan marina to Kingfisher Bay, while yet more vehicle ferries operate from Inskip Point (near Rainbow Beach) to Hook Point on the island's south.

Fraser Venture (☎ 07-4125 4444) makes the 30-minute crossing from River Heads to Wanggoolba Creek. It departs daily from River Heads at 9am, 10.15am and 3.30pm, returning from the island at 9.30am, 2.30pm

---

DEADLY DINGOES

It's hard not to feel sorry for Lindy Chamberlain. If Australia had known in 1980 what it does now, perhaps her cry that 'A dingo's got my baby' would have been taken seriously and the Mt Isa mother (played by Meryl Streep in *A Cry in the Dark,* and the subject of a 2002 opera) might not have been wrongfully convicted in Darwin for murder. Tragically, it took another death, of a nine-year-old Brisbane boy on Fraser Island in 2001, before the debate over whether Australia's native dogs are dangerous to humans was settled conclusively.

That fatal mauling at Waddy Point was the worst in an increasing number of attacks on Fraser in the preceding years. Although 30 of the island's estimated 160 dingoes were culled soon afterwards – much to the disgust of Aboriginal and environmental groups – most of the blame for the dingoes' growing aggressiveness must lie with tourists who fed or harassed them over the years.

Consequently, there's now a minimum $225 fine for feeding dingoes or leaving food where it may attract them to camping grounds. The QPWS provides a leaflet on being 'Dingo Smart' in its Fraser Island information pack.

and 4pm. On Saturday there is also a 7am service from River Heads, returning at 7.30am from the island. The return fare for vehicle and the first four occupants is $110, plus $6 for each extra passenger. Walk-on passengers pay $17 return.

The **Kingfisher Bay Resort** (☎ 07-4120 3333, toll free 1800 072 555) operates two boats. Its vehicle ferry does the 45-minute crossing from River Heads to Kingfisher Bay daily, for $110 per vehicle and the first four occupants. Departures from River Heads are at 7.15am, 11am and 2.30pm, and from the island at 8.30am, 1.30pm and 4pm. Its fast catamaran passenger ferry crosses between the Urangan marina and Kingfisher Bay every few hours from 8.45am to 8pm (later Friday and Saturday). The fare is $38/19 per adult/child.

Near Rainbow Beach, the **Fraser Island Ferry Service** (☎ 07-5486 3120) has regular ferries making the 15-minute trip from Inskip Point to Hook Point on the island's south, from 7am to 5.30pm daily (sometimes later in peak season). It's $60 return for a vehicle and occupants, $10 for walk-on passengers.

Air Fraser Island (☎ 07-4125 3600) flies out of Hervey Bay airport and lands on the island's eastern beach.

Getting Around
See the boxed text 'Notes from a Small Island: Exploring Fraser' (p328) for information on getting around Fraser Island.

CHILDERS
☎ 07 / pop 1500
This pretty heritage town still attracts budget travellers with its year-round fruit-picking opportunities, despite an increasing realisation of just how back-breaking this work can be, and despite the Palace Hostel fire in 2000 that killed 15 of their number. There's now a moving **Childers Backpackers Memorial** upstairs in the renovated – albeit sadly too late – Palace building. The **visitors centre** (☎ 4126 3886; 🕙 9am-4pm Mon-Fri, 9am-3pm Sat & Sun) is downstairs. Even if you're merely passing through, it's worth stopping at **Mammino** (☎ 4126 2880; 115 Lucketts Rd), whose macadamia-nut and other confectionery will leave you muttering a Homer Simpson-esque 'Mmmm, ice cream'. The company is just outside Childers; as you head along the Bruce Hwy to Bundaberg, turn left towards Woodgate.

Sugarbowl Caravan Park (☎ 4126 1521; Churchill St; sites per night/week from $18/105) On the highway north of the centre, with good amenities, this really is the most convenient caravan park for workers, despite complaints about the attitude of the staff.

Other recommendations:
Childers Tourist Park & Camp (☎ 4126 1371; 111 Stockyard Rd; sites per night/week from $16/100) Quiet, convivial site, about 7km from town.
Federal Hotel (☎ 4126 1438; fax 4126 2407; 71 Churchill St; dm per night/week $19 /90) Old but friendly and central pub-cum-hostel.

BUNDABERG
☎ 07 / pop 44,550
From 'the hummock', the only hill in this flat landscape, the eye sees fields of waving sugarcane from Bundaberg to the coral-fringed coast. That's the source of the famous Bundy rum, and the income for some, but not all, local 'cockies' (farmers).

It's copped some bad press in recent years, with the murder of British backpacker Caroline Stuttle, but this otherwise fairly typical Australian country town still attracts travellers looking for work picking anything from avocados to zucchinis. Others come here to see turtles at nearby Mon Repos or snorkel off Lady Musgrave Island in the southern Great Barrier Reef.

Information
INTERNET ACCESS
Bundaberg Email Centre (☎ 4154 3549; 200 Bourbong St; $5 an hour)

TOURIST INFORMATION
Bundaberg visitors centre 271 Bourbong St (☎ 4153 8888, 1800 308 888; 🕙 9am-5pm); 186 Bourbong St (☎ 4153 9289; 🕙 8.30am-4.45pm Mon-Fri, 10am-1pm Sat & Sun)

Sights
You can see the vats and other inner workings of the celebrated **Bundaberg Rum Distillery** (☎ 4131 2900; Avenue St; adult/child/concession $7.70/5.50/2.20), provided you relinquish your mobile phone and all other electronic or flammable items, and wear fully enclosed shoes (or hire a pair for $12). The distillery is about 2km east of the town centre, and tours are hourly from 10am to 3pm Monday to Friday and 10am to 2pm on weekends. They finish with a tot of rum and the chance to buy sou-

venirs decorated with the laddish polar bear from Bundaberg Rum's high-profile ads.

The best museums in the attractive **Botanic Gardens** (Gin Gin Rd) are: the **Fairymead House Sugar Museum** (☎ 4153 6786; adult/child $4/1; ☯ 10am-4pm), with everything from explanatory videos to artefacts by Polynesian 'Kanaka' sugar workers and a colourful collection of 1950s anodised-aluminium sugar containers; and the **Hinkler House Museum** (☎ 4152 0222; adult/child $4/1; ☯ 10am-4pm), onetime home to Bert Hinkler, in 1928 the first solo flier between England and Australia. The gardens are 2km north of town across the Burnett River.

Activities

The **Bundy Belle** (☎ 0427-099 009; adult/child $15/10) is an old-fashioned ferry that chugs down the Burnett River twice a day for 2½-hour trips.

If you wish to snorkel among coral off one of the magnificent Southern Reef Islands (p334), **Lady Musgrave Barrier Reef Cruises** (☎ 4159 4519, 1800 072 110; www.lmcruises.com.au; adult/child $140/75, local transfers $9) has trips to Lady Musgrave Island. Its vessels *Lady Musgrave* or *Spirit of Musgrave* depart for the approximately 10-hour journey from Port Bundaberg, 17km northeast of town. Trips leave at 8.30am daily, except Wednesday and Friday. Transfers to camp on the island cost

---

TALKING TURTLE

You almost expect to hear the hushed commentary of wildlife programme-maker David Attenborough during the egg-laying and hatching at Mon Repos, Australia's most accessible turtle rookery. But on this beach 15km northeast of Bundaberg it's no disappointment to be accompanied instead by the knowledgeable staff from the **EPA visitors centre** (☎ 4159 1562; ☯ 7.30am-4pm Mon-Fri). From November to March, when loggerhead and other marine turtles drag themselves up the beach to lay their eggs, and young then emerge, the office organises nightly **viewings** (adult/child/family $5/2.50/12.50; ☯ 7pm-6am). It's best to arrive as early as 5.30pm to queue. After 7pm you'll be allocated to a group and led on to the beach in turns. Take warm clothing, rain protection and insect repellent – and be prepared to amuse the kids during the wait.

$275. From mid-August to mid-October the company also offers whale-watching trips ($85, plus $9 for transfers).

Salty's (☎ 4151 6422; 208 Bourbong St) offers very cheap four-day PADI Open Water diving courses for around $170, diving off the shore near Bargara (see Around Bundaberg p334).

Sleeping

Bundaberg Backpackers & Travellers Lodge (☎ 4152 2080; fax 4151 3355; cnr Targo & Crofton Sts; dm $21) Opposite the bus terminal, this is by far the cleanest and most modern of the central hostels. It's largely full of working travellers, for whom it will help find harvesting jobs.

Bundaberg B&B (☎ 4153 5503; 328 Bourbong St; s/d $65/80) As unpretentious and down-to-earth as its name, this 1920s Queenslander offers comfortable lodgings with a young family about 2km west of the CBD. The owners do transfers from the train and bus stations.

Chalet Motor Inn (☎ 4152 9922; 242 Bourbong St; s & d from $65) In the tight cluster of motels just west of the train station, this well-kept establishment offers reasonable comfort at a good price.

Waterview Estate (☎ 4151 3344; 2 Gavin St; s/d from $65/85) With dark, polished floorboards, chandeliers, ruched curtains and a glass-fronted veranda overlooking some of the 12 acres of grounds, this heritage B&B promises the subtropical good life.

Other recommendations:

Ingelbrae (☎ 4154 4003; ingelbrae@interworx.com.au; 17 Branyan St; tw $70, d $90) Another fabulous Aussie heritage B&B.

City Centre Backpackers (☎ 4151 3501; ccback packers@hotmail.com; 216 Bourbong St; dm per night/ week $19/118, d per night/week $40/125) Not luxurious, but friendly.

Eating

Restaurants tend to open for lunch and dinner Monday to Friday (sometimes excluding Monday), and dinner only on Saturday and Sunday.

Talking Point Cafe (☎ 4152 1811; 79 Bourbong St; dishes $4-7; ☯ Mon-Fri 8am-4pm, Sat 8am-1.30pm) Wash down a tasty fresh sarnie, panini or focaccia with a strong cappuccino or soy latte. Yeast-free, gluten-free and vegetarian options are available.

Il Gambero (☎ 4152 5342; 57 Targo St; lunch $6.50-10.50, dinner $9-25) Its low-rent, shiny red tablecloths over white plastic sheeting, country

QUEENSLAND

kitchen–style chairs, spangly curtain and corner stage make you feel you've stepped into a pasta-pizza joint in a Baz Luhrmann movie. More *Strictly Ballroom* than *Moulin Rouge*, mind.

Spices Plus (☎ 4154 3320; cnr Quay & Targo Sts; dishes $8-14) Generally, Indian cuisine is one of the few culinary areas where Australia doesn't score. But in this large, high-ceilinged room, you'll be served food authentic enough to put you in mind of the restaurants of Delhi or along London's Brick Lane. It's worth the probable wait.

Numero Uno (☎ 4151 3666; 163 Bourbong St; meals $13-20) This popular licensed Italian bistro serves everything from gourmet pizzas and risotto to, err, bangers and mash.

For a gourmet treat, head to **Hugo's** (see Around Bundaberg below).

Entertainment
Moncrieff Theatre (☎ 4153 1985; 177 Bourbong St; admission $5.50) This big, old, one-screen cinema shows several films daily.

Getting There & Away
QantasLink (☎ 13 13 13) flies to Bundaberg several times a day from Brisbane (from $230, 50 minutes).

The main bus stop is **Stewart's coach terminal** (☎ 4153 2646; 66 Targo St). One-way bus fares from Bundaberg include Brisbane ($60), Hervey Bay ($26), Rockhampton ($55) and Gladstone ($45).

Bundaberg is also a stop for trains between Brisbane and Rockhampton or Cairns. There are daily trains heading both north and south. The one-way fare to Brisbane (4¼ hours) is $60 economy.

AROUND BUNDABERG
In many people's eyes, the beach hamlets around Bundaberg are more attractive than the town itself. Some 10km north is **Moore Park**, with wide, flat beaches. Some 16km east lies **Bargara**, which particularly is developing its own little scene. Families find Bargara attractive for both the turtle-shaped playground on its main foreshore and for the sheltered swimming areas for kids at Kellys Beach. Foodies love it for the refined modern Australian restaurant and café **Hugo's** (☎ 07-4159 0990; cnr The Esplanade & Bauer St; dishes $6-26; 🕑 7am-late, closes 5pm Mon) and for the more relaxed **Bargara Beach Hotel** (☎ 07-4159

2232; cnr See & Bauer Sts; meals $11-22). Snorkellers and divers come here for the coral near to shore around Barolin Rocks and in the Woongarra Marine Park. Call the **Bargara Beach Dive Centre** (☎ 07-4159 2663; 4/16 See St; 🕑 9am-5pm) for equipment hire or lessons.

The visitors centres in Bundaberg can help you find motels or caravan parks in the area.

Recommended places:
Dunhelm House (☎ 07-4159 0909; 540 Bargara Rd; s/d $55/80) An old Queenslander housing a chintzy, English-style B&B near Mon Repos Turtle Rookery.
Iluka Forest Retreat (☎ 07-4159 3230; iluka@eco travellercentral.info; 127 Logan Rd, Innes Park; dm/d $20/40) Very basic, but delightfully located, hippie hideaway.

CAPRICORN COAST

Don't pass through the central coast of Queensland, which straddles the tropic of Capricorn, without going snorkelling or diving. The Southern Reef Islands are among the most beautiful coral cays of the Great Barrier Reef, while Great Keppel Island, reached via the unashamedly Aussie town of Rockhampton and scenic seaside village of Yeppoon, has good fringing coral. Chill out in the tucked-away townships of Agnes Water and Town of 1770, but remember they also provide access to the reef.

SOUTHERN REEF ISLANDS
The southernmost, 'Capricornia' section of the Great Barrier Reef begins 80km northeast of Bundaberg around Lady Elliot Island and continues 140km northwards to Tryon Island, east of Rockhampton. The cays here are fairly expensive to reach, but you'll be rewarded with a Robinson Crusoe–style quiet, plus excellent snorkelling and diving among relatively untouched coral. Access is mainly from Bundaberg, Gladstone, Hervey Bay or the Town of 1770.

Lady Elliot Island
This 40-hectare vegetated coral island is possibly the region's most beautiful, with superb diving straight off the beach, as well as numerous shipwrecks, coral gardens, bommies (submerged rock) and blowholes to explore. It's perfect for those who suffer seasickness (but not for nervous fliers) as it's reached by light plane.

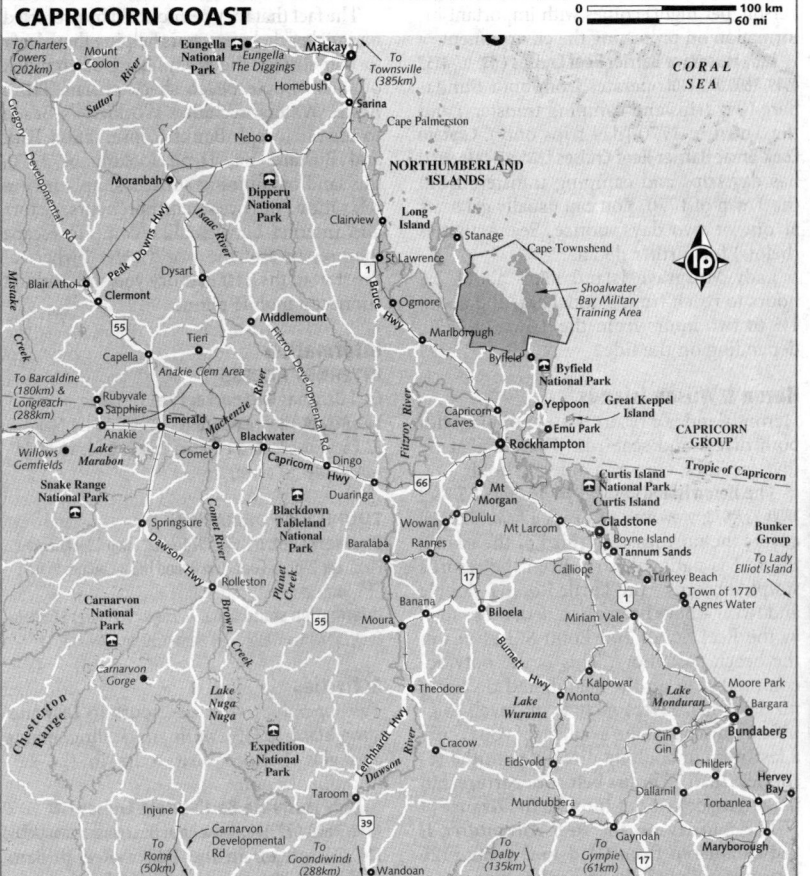

CAPRICORN COAST

Lady Elliot Island Resort (07-5536 3644, 1800 072 200; www.ladyelliot.com.au; s/d tents $220/290; s/d rooms from $250/390) In this low-key resort, you're paying for the underwater scenery more than the rather basic accommodation. Prices include breakfast, dinner and activities.

Seair flies from Bundaberg and Hervey Bay for $175 return, and on request from Maroochydore, Brisbane and Coolangatta. Day trips from Bundaberg or Hervey Bay cost $250, from Maroochydore, Brisbane and Coolangatta $650. Book through the resort.

Lady Musgrave Island

This 15-hectare cay and its surrounding aqua-blue lagoon provide a popular destination for coral-spotting day-trippers, and a desert-island camp for those on diving and snorkelling retreats. The island was once mined for guano (which is the dried excrement of fish-eating birds) and still smells of it, but today it's an uninhabited national park with dedicated fans who hold their nose and come every year. As well as coral, there's a chance of spotting turtles.

A **camping ground** (per person/family $4/16) lies on the island's west side, with bush toilets and little else. Campers need a permit and to be totally self-sufficient, even bringing their own water. Numbers are limited to 40 at a time, so apply well ahead for a permit at the Gladstone **EPA office** (07-4971 6500; www.smart service.qld.gov.au; 136 Goondoon St). You can book 11 months beforehand. Your permit ($4 per person, per night) comes with important information on protecting the environment.

Lady Musgrave Barrier Reef Cruises (☎ 07-4159 4519, 1800 072 110) operates from both Bundaberg (day trips and camping transfers) and the Town of 1770 (day trips only). **Captain Cook Great Barrier Reef Cruises** (☎ 07-4974 9077) has day trips and camping transfers from the Town of 1770. You can usually get seats at one or two days' notice. See Activities (below) for further details.

Lady Musgrave Island takes about 2½ hours to reach from Bundaberg, and about 1½ to two hours from the Town of 1770, depending on the tide.

Heron & Wilson Islands

Heron Island is a resort island popular with both divers and seabirds. There are many dive facilities, trips and a dive school.

The **Heron Island Resort** (☎ 07-4972 9055, P & O 1800 737 678; www.poresorts.com; s/d from $310/420) covers the northeastern third of the island; the rest is national park. Even the resort's simplest rooms – the Turtle Rooms (double and twin) – have been upgraded; those such as the Reef Suites and Point Suites nearer the beach cost more. This is the only accommodation on the island, and there are no day trips. Prices include all meals. Significant discounts are available if you secure a last-minute booking directly with the resort less than 72 hours before departure, but it's often booked out months in advance

The journey on the *Reef Adventurer II* fast catamaran from Gladstone costs $126 return standby ($176 with a booking).

Wilson Island has been reinvented as an expensive designer retreat. **P & O** (☎ 1800 737 678) sells five-night combined Heron and Wilson Island packages from $2300/3400 for a single/double.

AGNES WATER & TOWN OF 1770
☎ 07
'The new Noosa', 'the next Byron Bay' – Agnes Water and the Town of 1770 rank among Australia's most talked-up, and bought-up, real estate. A few years ago these sleepy villages, with some of the east coast's prettiest beachfront, could have been described as the ones that got away. Today access roads from Miriam Vale and Bundaberg have been improved and big-fish developers have moved in.

The fact that they're encircled by protected national park, however, is helping these leafy former surfers' hideaways hang on to much of their simple beach-shack charm. From Agnes Waters' secluded Workman's Beach to the Sir Joseph Banks Conservation Park and Bustard Bay Head lookout at 1770, this land of stunning sunsets simply invites relaxation. Surfwear entrepreneurs, actors and Internet bigwigs alike come to escape the pressures of the world here – where at the start of the 21st century you still couldn't connect a mobile phone.

Information
INTERNET ACCESS
Cool Bananas Backpackers (see Sleeping opposite)
Yok Attack Thai restaurant (☎ 4974 7454; Shop 22, Endeavour Plaza, cnr Captain Cook Dr & Round Hill Rd, Agnes Water; $7 per hr)

TOURIST INFORMATION
Discovery Centre (☎ 4974 7002; Shop 12, Endeavour Plaza, cnr Captain Cook Dr & Round Hill Rd, Agnes Water; ☼ 9am-5pm)
Information stand (Rural Transaction Centre, 3 Captain Cook Dr, Agnes Water; ☼ 9am-4.30pm Mon-Fri)

Activities
Two operators offer day tours to **Lady Musgrave Island** (p335), with snorkelling, diving and glass-bottom boat tours in the surrounding lagoon.

Lady Musgrave Barrier Reef Cruises (☎ 4159 4519, 1800 072 110; www.lmcruises.com.au; adult/child $140/75) sets off in the *DiscoveReef* at 8am, excluding Monday and Thursday.

WHAT'S IN A NAME?

The Town of 1770 derives its unusual moniker from being the place where Captain James Cook first came ashore in 1770 in what is now the state of Queensland. While his famous botanist Joseph Banks explored the wildlife, the good captain claimed this land for England. However, it wasn't until Australia's Bicentennary of European settlement in 1988 that the small collection of buildings around this wonderful bay was granted the status of a town and formally named. By the same logic, New York could be called the City of 1609 and Cape Town rebadged the Town of 1652.

Captain Cook Great Barrier Reef Cruises (☎ 4974 9077, 1300 666 631; www.1770reefcruises.com; adult/child $130/70) takes the *Spirit of 1770* out at 8am every day except Monday and Friday (daily during school holidays). This vessel does camping transfers for $225 per person ($245 return during school holidays).

If you really need to get away from it all, try the even less trafficked and unspoilt **Fitzroy Reef Lagoon**, a coral outcrop visited only by **1770 Holidays** (☎ 4974 9422, 1800 177 011; www .1770holidays.com; adult/child $125/65), which zips off in its *Reef Jet* at 8.15am on Tuesday, Thursday and Sunday. The same company also runs enjoyable day tours in its *LARCs* (large amphibious vehicles); these day trips take in Middle Island, Bustard Head and Eurimbula National Park, and operate on Monday, Wednesday and Saturday, and cost $95/55 per adult/child.

Agnes Waters' main beach is Queensland's northernmost surfing beach. Check at tourist information counters about other activities.

Sleeping

Cool Bananas Backpackers (☎ 4974 7660, 1800 227 660; www.coolbananas.biz.com; 2 Springs Rd, Agnes Water; dm $22; 🖳) Something of a backpackers' Shangri-La, these new, expensively built premises are run by mega-enthusiastic former surfer dudes who really look after guests. Tours, campfires, videos and pick-ups arranged? Ab-so-lutely!

Beach Shacks (☎ 4974 9463; beachshack@1770.net; 578 Captain Cook Dr, Town of 1770; d from $140) The higher up you go in these four magnificent Balinese-style bungalows – with bamboo, old-fashioned ceiling fans and mosquito nets – the better the views of the nearby water. Corrugated iron–walled showers add an Australian touch.

Bustard Bay Lodge (☎ 4974 9639; info@stayat 1770.com; 19 Endeavour St, Town of 1770; s/f $55/140) Sit on the veranda of this clean, family-run B&B high on the headland and watch the sun sink, flaming into the sea.

Hideaway (☎ 4979 9144; hoban@bigpond.com; 2510 Round Hill Round, Agnes Water; s/d $100/120) An ideal rural retreat for those looking for Australian wildlife, fine dining and a kid-free environment. Breakfast included, dinner $35 extra per person.

There's beachfront camping, albeit often cheek-by-jowl, at **Agnes Water Caravan Park** (☎ 4974 9193; 51 Jeffrey Ct) and **Town of 1770 Camping Ground** (☎ 4974 9286; Captain Cook Dr). The more adventurous might like to investigate **houseboat hire** (☎ 4974 9643).

Getting There & Away

McCafferty's/Greyhound (☎ 13 14 99) has a feeder service ($17) from Agnes Water and 1770 to Fingerboard Rd, by the Bruce Hwy. From here, you can connect to main coastal routes.

GLADSTONE

☎ 07 / pop 276,600

There *are* patches of beauty between the towering chimneys of the power station, aluminium smelter, cement plant and the nascent oil project, but as one Greenpeace document puts it, Gladstone's waterfront industries are 'a prime example of why the Great Barrier Reef is dying'. Most visitors find themselves here on business or in transit to Heron Island.

The **Gladstone visitors centre** (☎ 4972 9000; Bryan Jordan Dr; ☼ 8.30am-5pm Mon-Fri, 9am-5pm Sat & Sun) is located at the marina, the departure point for boats to Heron Island. The **EPA office** (☎ 4971 6500; www.smartservice.qld.gov.au; 136 Goon doon St; ☼ 8.30am-5pm Mon-Fri) has information on the Southern Reef Islands. The **Gladstone City Library** (☎ 4970 1232; 144 Goondoon St; ☼ 9.30am-5.45pm Mon-Fri, 9am-4.30pm Sat) offers free Internet access.

For a nice picnic or kiosk lunch, head for the **Tondoon Botanic Gardens** (☎ 4979 3326; Glenlyon Rd; admission free; ☼ 9am-6pm Oct-Mar, 8.30am-5.30pm Apr-Sep), an area of entirely native plants 7km south of the CBD. Alternatively, make for the beach at **Tannum Sands**, 20km south of Gladstone.

Auckland Hill B&B (☎ 4972 7300; www .ahbb.com.au; 15 Yarroon St; s/d from $95/110) This magnificent Queenslander is a generous labyrinth of differently styled, elegant rooms, including one with wheelchair access. Breakfast $15.

Gladstone Backpackers (☎ 4972 5744; 12 Rollo St; dm from $22, d $50) is bit shabby, but relatively friendly, and also recommended.

Most coast buses stop at Gladstone ($45 one way from Brisbane), and it's on the Brisbane to Rockhampton rail route ($75 one way from Brisbane). You can also fly there with QantasLink ($123 from Brisbane).

QUEENSLAND

STINGERS

It mightn't look or feel pretty, but unless you stay out of the water a 'stinger suit' is your only protection against Queensland's lethal box jellyfish. Also known as the sea wasp or stinger, the jellyfish is found in coastal waters north of Rockhampton during the summer months. The danger period is generally from around November to April, although it varies.

If someone has been stung, douse the stings with vinegar (available on many beaches or from nearby houses) and call an ambulance (artificial respiration may be required). Some coastal resorts erect stinger nets that provide small areas for safe swimming; otherwise stay out of the sea when the sea wasps are around. Or, if you simply must snorkel, visit a sports store for a clingy, Lycra all-body stinger suit.

ROCKHAMPTON

☎ 07 / pop 59,500

Larger-than-life figurines of cattle greet the visitor at nearly every turn in the beef capital of Australia, but there's no bull about Rockhampton. From its inception as a Fitzroy River port in 1853 to its transformation into a centre of the cattle industry, it's retained a straight-talking, true-blue Aussie streak. It's not only a place to hop off the train or bus and head for Yeppoon and Great Keppel Island, but also somewhere to experience the real, unburnished Australia.

An administrative and educational centre, 'Rocky' sits astride the tropic of Capricorn, marking the start of the tropical north. And on humid summer's nights, graduating students and other merry-makers really do go troppo, stealing the testicles from the concrete and fibreglass bulls. Rumour even has it that one poor council worker regularly patrols Rockhampton with spares.

Information

INTERNET ACCESS

Rockhampton library (☎ 4936 8265; 69 William St; ⌚ 9.15am-5.30pm Mon-Sat, except 1-8pm Wed)
Sumatras (☎ 4921 4900; cnr East & William St; ⌚ 10am-4pm Mon-Thu, 7pm-late Wed-Sun)

TOURIST INFORMATION

Capricorn visitors centre (☎ 4927 2055; Gladstone Rd; ⌚ 8am-5pm) About 3km south of town, by the tropic of Capricorn marker.
Rockhampton visitors centre (☎ 4922 5339; Customs House, 208 Quay St; ⌚ 8.30am-4.30pm Mon-Fri, 9am-4pm Sat & Sun)

Sights

There are some fine old buildings, particularly on Quay St. Leaflets from the visitors centres map out walking trails.

For a regional centre, the **Rockhampton City Art Gallery** (☎ 4936 8248; 62 Victoria Pde; admission free; ⌚ 10am-4pm Mon-Fri, 11am-4pm Sat & Sun) is a revelation, with works by leading Australian artists like Charles Blackman, Sir Russell Drysdale, Sir Sidney Nolan, Clifton Pugh and Albert Namatjira. The huge permanent collection, with works rotated in and out of storage, is supplemented by innovative temporary exhibitions, for which there are varying admission charges.

Rockhampton's **Botanic Gardens** (☎ 4922 1654; Spencer St; admission free; ⌚ 6am-6pm), in the city's south, really are memorable, with flaming bougainvilleas, bunya pines, and a small but interesting zoo.

Dreamtime Cultural Centre (☎ 4936 1655; Bruce Hwy; adult/child $13/5.50; ⌚ 10am-3.30pm Mon-Fri) is one of the largest Queensland displays of Aboriginal and Torres Strait Islander culture. There's so much to learn and explore that staff recommend you take a tour, at 10.30am and 1pm.

Activities

For a taste of authentic Orstraylia, **Reef 'n' Beef Adventures** (☎ 0427-159 655, 1800 753 786) offers very highly recommended day tours to Koorana Crocodile Farm (p341), Capricorn Caves (p340) and a cattle farm ($65), two-day trips to an atmospheric ghost town and the Styx River ($88), and longer four-day tours ($220).

Sleeping

BUDGET

Most hostels in town offer pick-ups from the train or bus station, and cheap packages to Great Keppel Island.

Above the Oxford Hotel, bordering a pedestrian mall, **Downtown Backpackers** (☎ 4922 1837; fax 4922 1050; 91 East St; dm/tw $19/38;

) offers good, clean budget accommodation in a handy location.

North of the river, **Rockhampton City YHA** (☎ 4927 5288; www.yha.com.au; 60 MacFarlane St; dm $23, d & tw $50;) has clean but slightly cramped dorms.

MID-RANGE

Criterion Hotel (☎ 4922 1225; criterion@cyberinternet .com.au; 150 Quay St; s/d from $30/40, s/d/tr/f ste $50/55/65/75;) Designed for the city's elite, with Italian tiles and Javanese cedar, the Criterion is more elegant than many heritage hotels. Today it offers only slightly faded, atmospheric rooms by the Fitzroy River, the best of which are the renovated corner suites.

Motel 98 (☎ 4927 5322; www.motel98.com.au; 98 Victoria Pde; s/d $85/95;) Whether because of the quality furnishings, the lovely poolside area or the excellent restaurant, this family-run motel is a cosy place to turn in for the evening.

Dreamtime Lodge Motel (☎ 4936 4600; dream lodge@rocknet.net.au; Bruce Hwy; s/d $90/95, f from $100;) Beside the Dreamtime Cultural Centre and with indigenous owners, this attractive resort and sometime convention centre has modern rooms and apartments organised around a leafy pool and outdoor eating area. Facilities are provided for travellers with disabilities.

O'Dowd's Irish Pub (☎ 4927 0344; www.odowds .com.au; 100 William St; s/d/f $30/45/65, motel s/d from $70/80;) At the front is a beautifully renovated hotel with a strong Irish theme and upstairs pub accommodation. Behind that, there's a motel with less quaint but more comfortable rooms.

Eating

Sumatras (☎ 4921 4900; cnr East & William St; meals $5-22; 10am-4pm Mon-Thu, 7pm-late Wed-Sun) The emphasis is on good, filling tucker in this roomy, air-conditioned oasis. It serves huge all-day breakfasts ($18), attracts crowds of office workers with its $5 lunches, and on Thursday evening there's a $13 all-you-can-eat Indian buffet.

Ascot Hotel (☎ 4922 4719; 117 Musgrave St; mains $20-30) Also a backpackers, the Ascot is most noteworthy for its delicious stone-grilled

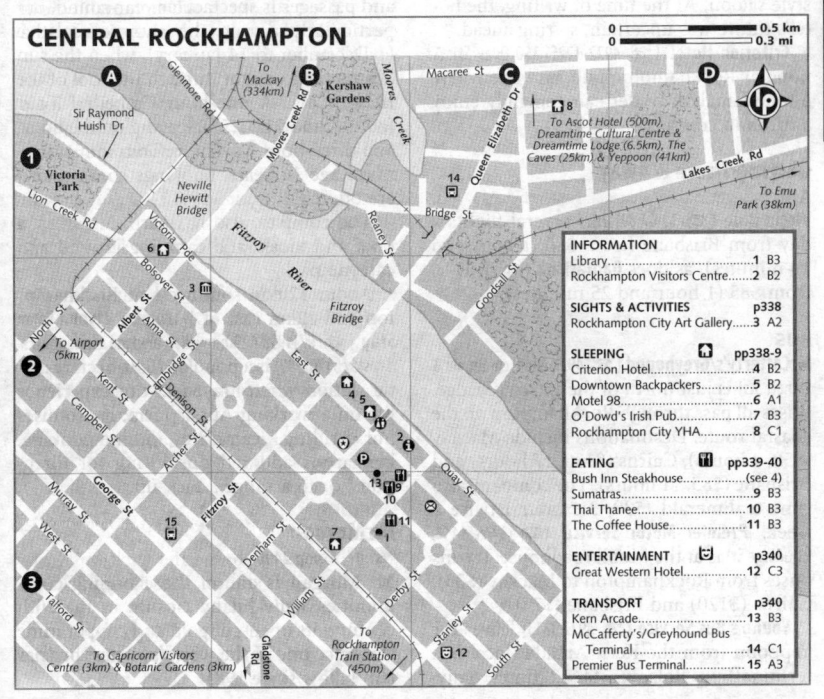

CENTRAL ROCKHAMPTON

INFORMATION	
Library	1 B3
Rockhampton Visitors Centre	2 B2

SIGHTS & ACTIVITIES	p338
Rockhampton City Art Gallery	3 A2

SLEEPING	pp338-9
Criterion Hotel	4 B2
Downtown Backpackers	5 B2
Motel 98	6 A1
O'Dowd's Irish Pub	7 B3
Rockhampton City YHA	8 C1

EATING	pp339-40
Bush Inn Steakhouse	(see 4)
Sumatras	9 B3
Thai Thanee	10 B3
The Coffee House	11 B3

ENTERTAINMENT	p340
Great Western Hotel	12 C3

TRANSPORT	p340
Kern Arcade	13 B3
McCafferty's/Greyhound Bus Terminal	14 C1
Premier Bus Terminal	15 A3

QUEENSLAND

steaks. Try crocodile or kangaroo, or tuck into beef, chicken or seafood.

Thai Tanee (☎ 4922 1255; cnr William & Bolsover Sts; mains $12-18; ❤ dinner) This popular restaurant serves tasty Thai cuisine, untainted by MSG.

Bush Inn Steakhouse (☎ 4922 1225; 150 Quay St; meals $10-18) This popular place serves decent pub food including steak, chicken, fish, Asian stir-fry and pizza.

Coffee House (☎ 4927 5722; cnr William & Bolsover Sts; mains $19-29, tapas $6-8) Don't be fooled by the low-fi name; this upmarket, all-day establishment serves the sort of delicious modern Australian cuisine you might expect in a state capital city. From Great Keppel prawns and Roma tomatoes to Tey's Bros beef and Jindi brie, it makes a virtue of local produce.

Entertainment

Great Western Hotel (☎ 4922 1862; 39 Stanley St; admission adult $8) Over the years it's been a Rockhampton ritual for surburban cowboys to test their bull-riding skills every Friday in the rodeo ring behind this pub's Western-style saloon. At the time of writing, the hotel's future was uncertain, so ring ahead.

Criterion Hotel (☎ 4922 1225; 150 Quay St) A popular Rockhampton pub, and one where a lone female traveller can generally enjoy a drink in comfort.

Getting There & Away

AIR

Virgin Blue (☎ 13 67 89) has several flights a day from Brisbane (from $80, 1 hour and 10 minutes), as does **QantasLink** (☎ 13 13 13) from $85 (1 hour and 25 minutes).

BUS

McCafferty's/Greyhound (☎ 4927 2844; cnr Brown & Linnett Sts) is just north of the Fitzroy Bridge. Buses all pass through Rockhampton on the coastal route. Destinations include Mackay ($50, 4 hours), Cairns ($130, 17 hours) and Brisbane ($85, 11 hours). The company also runs to Emerald ($39, 3½ hours) twice a week. **Premier Motor Service** (☎ 3236 4444; 91 George St) is at the Mobil roadhouse. It runs buses from Rockhampton to Mackay ($33), Cairns ($120) and Brisbane ($75).

Young's Bus Service (☎ 4922 3813) leaves for Yeppoon from the Kern Arcade (local bus terminal) in Bolsover St 12 times daily.

Rothery's Coaches (☎ 4922 4320) travels twice daily between Rockhampton airport and Rosslyn Bay ($15) – the marina for Great Keppel Island.

TRAIN

Queensland Rail runs the high-speed *Tilt Train* services daily between Brisbane and Rockhampton (economy $95, 7 hours). The Tilt Train continues to Cairns, business class only ($220). It leaves Rockhampton at 2.15am so that you travel through the most beautiful part of the countryside in daylight and arrives at 7.20pm the same day. The slower Rockhampton–Cairns *Sunlander* (economy seat/economy sleeper $145/$195, 20 hours) leaves at 8.15pm.

The slow *Spirit of the Outback* runs twice-weekly between Brisbane, Rockhampton, Emerald and Longreach.

AROUND ROCKHAMPTON

In the Berserker Range, which is 23km north of Rockhampton, are the **Capricorn Caves** (☎ 07-4934 2883; www.capricorncaves.com.au; Caves Rd; ❤ 9am-4pm). This series of limestone caves and passages is spectacular year-round, but particularly during the summer solstice (1 December to 14 January), when the sun beams vertical light through the roof of the Belfry Cave. A one-hour Cathedral Tour (adult/child $15/7.50), leaving on the hour, and three-hour Adventure Tour ($60, minimum age 16 years, bookings compulsory) are offered.

The complex also has barbecue areas, a pool and kiosk, and camping ground and caravan park.

About 120km southwest of Rockhampton and 22km east of Baralaba, **Myella Farm Stay** (☎ 07-4998 1290; myella@bigpond.com.au; 2-/3-day stay $170/240) is a popular 1040-hectare cattle station where travellers can experience life on a working Aussie farm; it promises horse-riding, campfires, home-cooking, kangaroos and red dust. Ring for directions, or to arrange a pick-up.

Mt Morgan

☎ 07 / pop 2400

Mt Morgan is one of those mining communities sadly hit by closure in the 20th century; its open-cut gold and copper mine was once one of the world's richest but has lain fallow since 1981.

There's an excellent half-hour **historic train ride** from the attractive old Mt Morgan train station to Cattle Creek and back; ask the **visitors centre** (☎ 07-4938 2312; Railway Pde; 🕓 9am-4pm) in the station about this and the local **heritage trail**.

The highlight of the joke-riddled, two-hour **Mount Morgan Mine Tours** (☎ 07-4938 1081; 38 Central St; adult/child/family $20/12/50) is a cave with dinosaur footprints on its ceiling. Tours depart at 9.30am and 1.30pm, but the company also makes pick-ups from Rockhampton.

There are several caravan parks, pubs and motels, including **Miners' Rest Motel Units** (☎ 07-4938 2350; 44 Coronation Dr; s/d $50/60).

Young's Bus Service (☎ 07-4922 3813) has return services between Rockhampton and Mt Morgan Monday to Saturday ($7.50 one way). **McCafferty's/Greyhound** (☎ 13 14 99) also passes through on its inland Rockhampton to Brisbane run.

YEPPOON

☎ 07 / pop 10,780

The Gateway to Great Keppel Island, Yeppoon is an attractive seaside village in its own right. Its pleasant beaches give way in the north to rainforest around Byfield. Travelling south, you pass Rosslyn Bay, the departure point for Great Keppel, before wending your way along scenic coastline. The ocean breeze gives Yeppoon much milder summers.

Information

INTERNET ACCESS

Dreamers Coffee Club (☎ 4939 5797; 4 James St)

TOURIST INFORMATION

Capricorn Coast visitors centre (☎ 4939 4888, 1800 675 785; Ross Creek Roundabout; 🕓 9am-5pm) At the town entrance.

Sleeping

Seaspray Holiday Units (☎ 4939 1421; seasprayunits@bigpond.com; 45 Wattle St, Cooee Bay; s/d/tr $70/80/90) In your relaxed beachcomber unit, you can open the top half of the old-fashioned, horizontally split door and lean out to chat to the neighbours or gaze at the palms and frangipani trees. At night, the sea lulls you to sleep.

While Away (☎ 49395719; whileaway@bigpond.com; 44 Todd Ave; s $85, d from $95; 🐕) This immaculate, upmarket B&B has played host to international stars and thousands of ordinary European and Australian travellers. It's wheelchair accessible and 50m from a quiet stretch of beach.

Tropical Nites (☎ 4939 1914; 34 Anzac Pde; s/d/tr/f from $65/75/90/100; 🐕) On a main thoroughfare, this tidy motel faces the beach.

Yeppoon Backpackers (☎ 4939 4702; fax 4939 8080; 30 Queen St; dm/d $20/45; 🖵) In an attractive old timber house on the hill overlooking the town and beach, this friendly hostel has a big backyard, pool and reasonable facilities. Free pick-ups from and drop-offs to Rockhampton are made twice daily.

Ask the visitors centre for details on Yeppoon's many caravan parks, including **Beachside Caravan Park** (☎ 4939 3738; Farnborough Rd; camp sites from $14, caravan sites $16 for 2 people).

Getting There & Away

Young's Bus Service (☎ 4922 3813) operates a loop service from Rockhampton to Yeppoon, Rosslyn Bay, Emu Park and back ($7.50 one way) 12 times a day, Monday to Friday, and six times a day on Saturday and Sunday.

AROUND YEPPOON

About 5km south of Yeppoon lies **Rosslyn Bay Boat Harbour**, the departure point for ferries to Great Keppel Island. If you're driving your own vehicle, there's a free day car park at the harbour. Next door, the **Rosslyn Bay Inn Resort** (☎ 07-4933 6333; $8 per day) is the closest lock-up car park.

Continuing southwards for 13km, you pass three headlands with fine views – **Bluff Point**, **Double Head**, and **Pinnacle Point** – before arriving in **Emu Park**. This is the home to the 'Singing Ship' memorial to Captain Cook, a sculpture with drilled tubes and pipes that whistle or moan dolefully in the wind. Some 15km south of Emu Park is the turnoff to the **Koorana Crocodile Farm** (☎ 07-4934 4749; Coowonga Rd; adult/child $14/7; 🕓 10am-3pm). This is nowhere near as flash as Australia Zoo, owned by Steve 'Crocodile Hunter' Irwin (p310), but a good, educational experience, all the same. The animals here are farmed for handbags and shoes.

Alternatively, drive 40km north from Yeppoon to the state forests of **Byfield**, where you can camp (self-registration permits at various sites) or hunker down in **The Waterpark Cabins** (☎ 07-4935 1241; Yaxely's Rd; cabins $90-130), four 19th century–style (apart from the

QUEENSLAND

spa baths) timber cabins. Hiking, canoeing and exploring local potteries are just some of the possible activities. Ask the Yeppoon visitors centre for details.

GREAT KEPPEL ISLAND

'Queensland: beautiful one day, perfect the next' – visitors familiar with that crusty old tourism slogan could find it coming back to haunt them on Great Keppel. With a network of bush tracks emerging onto secluded coral beaches, this continental outcrop offers several options to while away the time. The fact that it's only semi-developed, gorgeous and cheap makes Great Keppel seem flawless to many travellers, but the overwhelming quiet can get to

some. So, as when heading to any paradise on earth, pack a good book.

Sights & Activities

The tips of air-tubes bobbing above the surrounding waters are testament to the popularity of **snorkelling**. Visitors usually start out investigating **Shelving Beach**, becoming progressively more adventurous as they hike to **Monkey Point** and **Clam Bay**. The coral here is OK (although you will see marine life), but better around **Middle** and **Halfway Islands** (See Other Keppel Bay Islands, p346).

Snorkelling at the more remote beaches involves a bushwalk, anyhow, but you can cut out the snorkelling part and simply walk, too. The longest bush track leads to

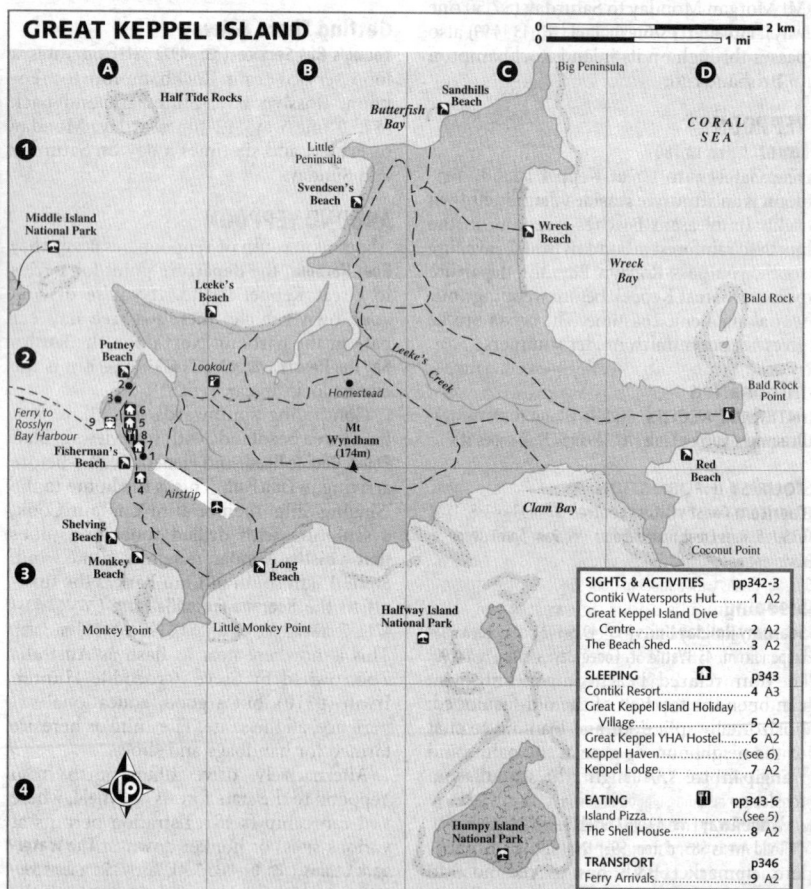

GREAT KEPPEL ISLAND

the lighthouse near **Bald Rock Point** on the island's far side, but it's quite hard going (more than three hours return). The **Mt Wyndham** circuit walk (2½ hours) takes in the homestead and shearing shed.

With 18km of white-sand beaches, you don't need to go far for a swim. **Fisherman's Beach**, where the ferries come in, rarely gets crowded, and it's even quieter just round the corner at **Putney Beach**.

For watersports, the **Beach Shed** (Putney Beach) and **Contiki Watersports Hut** (Fisherman's Beach) both hire out sailboards, catamarans, motorboats and snorkelling gear, and can take you water-skiing, parasailing or camel-riding.

Prodive (☎ 07-4939 5044, ext 4556) at the Contiki Resort, and the **Great Keppel Island Dive Centre** (☎ 07-4939 5022) on Putney Beach offer introductory dives with gear supplied for around $100, or two qualified dives for $140 to $160.

Tours

Freedom Fast Cats (☎ 07-4933 6244, 1800 336 244) offers daily coral cruises (adult/senior/child/family $50/27/40/125), leaving Rosslyn Bay at 9am. It also has lunch cruises (Tuesday and Sunday), boomnet cruises (Sunday), where you ride on a net trailed behind the boat, and more.

Keppel Tourist Services (☎ 07-4933 6744) operates morning and afternoon coral cruises, departing at 9.15am and 2pm respectively, and which visit the **Middle Island Underwater Observatory** (adult/senior/child/family $50/40/25/125).

Sleeping

BUDGET

Great Keppel Island Holiday Village (☎ 07-4939 8655; www.gkiholidayvillage.com.au; dm $24, s/d tent $35/50, cabins with bathroom from $100) Some guests lie in hammocks under fig trees, while others barbeque steak or get down to a game of Scrabble in this relaxed, friendly place. The dorms and showers are pretty shabby, but the safari tents are charming (if rather warm after sunrise), and snorkelling gear is loaned for free.

Great Keppel YHA Hostel (☎ 07-4933 6416; yhagreatkeppelisland@bigpond.com.au; s/d tent $28/40, d & tw cabin $80, tr/f cabin $90/120) Affiliated with the YHA, but owned by and located within the perimeters of Keppel Haven (see following), this hostel has nice staff and pleasant en

suite cabins. However, its permanent tents, made of sweltering green vinyl, are not quite so attractive.

MID-RANGE

Keppel Haven (☎ 07-4933 6744; fax 4933 6429; s/d tent $28/40, d & tw bunkhouses $80, cabins from $120) The bunkhouses here are outstanding, and there are cabins and tents. Unfortunately, the size of the place makes it a bit impersonal.

Keppel Lodge (☎ 07-4939 4251; fax 07-4939 8251; s/d/tr/f $85/110/150/190) With its four bedrooms arranged round a large central living room, Keppel Lodge is ideal for group bookings. Solo travellers can rent rooms as individual motel-type suites. You might want to check that the other three rooms aren't rented out to people who know each other, as you may feel left out.

TOP END

Contiki Resort (☎ 07-4939 5044, 1300 305 005; s/d/tr from $230/320/380; ▯ ▧) The idea, sometimes bandied around, that this is Ibiza come to Queensland will only wash with those who've never been to Ibiza. Although this upmarket place does exhibit an 18 to 35 party ethos, with organised activities for buff guests wearing music festival–style passes and fraternising around the pool, it's just a little too isolated and quiet for that Balearic comparison. Rates are all-inclusive, but a minimum three-night stay applies.

Eating

Island Pizza (☎ 07-4939 4699; lunch $5.50-28; dinner $15-28; ☺ dinner Tue-Sun, lunch Sat & Sun during school holidays) Keppel is not generally a gourmet paradise, but this restaurant's thick-crust pizzas, with innovative and generous toppings, taste as good as the tempting aroma suggests. Hot dogs and pastas are also sold.

Shell House (Devonshire teas $6-8) Conch and other souvenirs from the sea make this a lovely grotto in which to sit back and enjoy afternoon tea.

Keppel Haven Bar Bistro (☎ 07-4933 6744; dishes $7-22) Given the quantity churned out for day-trippers and overnight guests, the cuisine here stands up to scrutiny reasonably well. There's an outdoor veranda overlooking lawn and waving palm trees.

Contiki Resort's **Reef Burger Bar** (snacks $8.50-10.50, pizzas $17-23), open from mid-morning to late, is convenient and functional.

THE GREAT BARRIER REEF

Larger than the Great Wall of China and the only living thing visible from space, the Great Barrier Reef is one of the seven wonders of the natural world. The conglomeration of colourful coral that stretches along the Queensland seaboard is the planet's biggest reef system, where in fact 2600 separate reefs form an outer ribbon parallel to the coast and lie dotted around the lagoon between this and the mainland.

Scientists lovingly nickname this phenomenon the GBR, while NASA astronauts have eulogised it as a 'white scar on the face of the Pacific Ocean'. One BBC TV programme rated it second only to the Grand Canyon on a list of 50 Places To See Before You Die. Did we mention this reef is pretty ace?

At a Glance

Length: 2000km, from north of Bundaberg to Torres Strait
Width: 80km at its broadest
Distance from shore: 300km in the south, 30km in the north
Age: estimated between 600,000 and 18 million years old (contentious)

From Little Polyps, Mighty Reefs Grow

An industrious family of tiny animal, the coral polyp is responsible for creating the GBR and other reefs. All corals are primitive hollow sacs with tentacles on the top, but it's the hard, as opposed to soft, corals that are the architects and builders. These excrete a small amount of limestone as an outer skeleton to protect and support their soft bodies. As polyps die and new ones grow on top, their billions of skeletons cement together into an ever-growing natural bulwark.

Different polyps form varying structures, from staghorn and brain patterns to flat plate or table corals. However, they all need sunlight, so few grow deeper than 30m below the surface. The coral's skeletons are white, while the reef's kaleidoscopic colours come from the living polyps.

One of the most spectacular sights on the Great Barrier Reef occurs for a few nights after a full moon in late spring or early summer,

when vast numbers of corals spawn. With tiny bundles of sperm and eggs visible to the naked eye, the event resembles a gigantic underwater snowstorm.

Did You Know?

Marine environments, including coral reefs, demonstrate the greatest biodiversity of any ecosystems on earth – much more so than rainforests. The Great Barrier Reef is home to marine mammals such as whales, dolphins and dugongs (sea cows). With new varieties still being discovered, its flora and fauna also includes:

- 1500 species of fish
- 400 types of coral
- 4000 breeds of clams and other molluscs
- 800 echinoderms, including sea cucumbers
- 500 varieties of seaweed
- 200 bird species
- 1500 different sponges

…and six types of turtle.

Sorting the Reef from the Cays

Reefs fall into three categories: barrier or ribbon reefs, platform reefs and fringing reefs.

The barrier reef proper lies on the outer, seaward edge of the reef system, lining the edge of the continental shelf in an often-unbroken formation.

Platform reefs grow on the land side of these barrier reefs and often support coral cay islands. These occur when the reef grows to be above sea level, even at high tide; dead coral is ground down by water action to form sand, and sometimes vegetation takes root. Many famous Great Barrier Reef islands – such as Green Island near Cairns, the Low Isles near Port Douglas, Heron Island off Gladstone and Lady Musgrave Island north of Bundaberg – are coral cays.

Closer to shore you'll find fringing reefs surrounding the hillier, continental islands. Great Keppel, most of the Whitsundays, Hinchinbrook and Dunk, for example, were once the peaks of mainland coastal ranges, but rising sea levels submerged most of these mountains, leaving only the tips exposed. Today these are good places to spot coral close to the beach. Fringing reefs also border the mainland in places, such as near Bundaberg.

Taking the Temperature of the Barrier Reef

I hear the Great Barrier Reef has been under threat lately. What's the story? Coral polyps need a water temperature of 17.5 to 28°C to grow and cannot tolerate too much sediment. Global warming and El Niño conditions are occasionally overheating sections of the world's oceans, leading to bleaching – as the brightly coloured living polyps die, leaving only the white skeleton. Pollution has also poisoned some coral, plus some questions persist about the long-term effects of the crown-of-thorns starfish. All in all, some pessimists predict there will be no reefs left anywhere in the world in 40 years' time.

What's being done? The **Great Barrier Reef Marine Park Authority** (☎ 07-4750 0700; Reef HQ bldg, Townsville) looks after the welfare of most of the reef. It is monitoring bleaching problems and working on increasing the percentage of reef 'no-take' zones where it is forbidden to remove animal or plant life (eg no fishing). Environmental campaigners are pushing plans to cut mainland pollutants from farms and industry entering the water.

Is there any way I can help? Sure. Take all litter with you, even biodegradable material like apple cores. Admire, but don't touch or harass, marine animals and be aware that if you touch or walk on coral you'll damage it (it can also create some very nasty cuts).

Speaking of which, what's the best way to get to see some coral anyway? Obviously, snorkelling and diving will get you up close and personal. However, you can also view fish and coral from a glass-bottomed boat, a semi-submersible boat or an 'underwater observatory'. Tour operators are listed throughout this book. You can also ask the Marine Park Authority for advice, or visit its Reef HQ aquarium to see a living coral reef without leaving dry land.

I keep hearing about 'bommies'. What are those? 'Bommie' is a diminutive of *bombora*, an Aboriginal word for submerged rock. It's a term used for large coral outcrops that rise up towards the surface.

And what wildlife can I realistically hope to see? Apart from all the psychedelically patterned tropical fish, there's the the chance to swim with manta rays, squid, turtles and more.

Any creatures to beware of? There's nothing to be too alarmed about, but make sure you know to avoid scorpion fish, stonefish and jellyfish (see the boxed text 'Stingers' p338). No reef shark has ever attacked a diver, and while sea snakes are venomous, the position of their fangs at the back of their mouths makes them of little threat to humans.

Well, that's reassuring and it all sounds quite wonderful, so where do I go? It's said you could dive here every day of your life and still not see the entire Great Barrier Reef. Individual areas vary from time to time, depending on the weather or any recent damage, but places to start include:

- Cairns – the commonest choice, so rather over-trafficked (p396)
- Port Douglas – gateway to the Low Isles and the Agincourt Reefs (p418)
- Lizard Island – superb diving at the Cod Hole (p429)
- *Yongala* shipwreck – one of Australia's best, off Townsville (p377)
- Heron Island – popular diving resort where it's wise to book ahead (p336)
- Lady Elliot Island – shipwrecks and gorgeous coral (p334)
- Fitzroy Reef Lagoon – untouched for years, tourist numbers are still limited (p337)

For more information, see Lonely Planet's *Diving & Snorkeling Australia's Great Barrier Reef*.

The kiosks at Keppel Haven and Great Keppel Island Holiday Village have a few essentials, but if you want to cook bring your own supplies.

Drinking

The low-key Contiki Resort Splash pub-bar (see Sleeping earlier) is open day and night, with pool tables, arcade games and indoor seating. The modern, concrete-interiored club **Salt** (admission $5) is open six nights, except Sunday.

Getting There & Away

Transfers between Rockhampton airport and Great Keppel Island run several times a day for $150 per person return. Contact the Contiki resort or **Horizon Airways** (☎ 07-4921 1855).

Two companies run ferries to Great Keppel from Rosslyn Bay Harbour. However, unless you're happy to carry your luggage over sand, check with your accommodation beforehand that they meet the boat you've chosen.

Freedom Fast Cats (☎ 07-4933 6244, 1800 336 244) departs the Keppel Bay Marina in Rosslyn Bay at 9am, noon and 3pm, and leaves Great Keppel at 10am, 2pm and 4pm (adult/child/family $31/16/80 return). This company is known locally for being pretty punctual.

Keppel Tourist Services (☎ 07-4933 6744) operates services leaving Rosslyn Bay at 7.30am, 9.15am, 11.30am and 3.30pm, returning at 8.15am, 2pm and 4.30pm (adult/child/family $30/15/70 return).

As well as **Young's Bus Service** (see Getting There & Away p341), **Rothery's Coaches** (☎ 07-4922 4320) runs services to Rosslyn Bay, this time twice-daily from Rockhampton airport ($15).

OTHER KEPPEL BAY ISLANDS

While you can make day trips to the fringing coral reefs of **Middle** or **Halfway Islands** from Great Keppel Island (ask your accommodation or at Keppel Holiday Village), you can also **camp** (per person/family $4/16) on several national park islands, including **Middle, North Keppel** and **Miall Islands**. You'll need all your own supplies, including water. Get information and permits from the **EPA** (☎ 07-4933 6608; www.smartservice.qld.gov.au) in Rosslyn Bay.

Tiny, privately owned **Pumpkin Island** (☎ 07-4939 2431), just south of North Keppel, has five simple, cosy cabins with water, solar power, kitchen and bathroom; bring food and linen. The cabins cost $155 for four people ($25 for each extra person), or you can camp ($15).

The catamaran **Funtastic** (☎ 0438-909 582) will take you across. Sample prices to Pumpkin are $175 return for one person, $245 for three and $315 for five.

CAPRICORN HINTERLAND

According to the official road-numbering system, the Capricorn Hwy running inland from Rockhampton is Australia's very own Route 66, so get your kicks by heading for the Blackdown Tableland National Park or the even more spectacular Carnarvon National Park. Alternatively, at Emerald some 270km west of the coast, you'll find yourself on the doorstep of central Queensland's gemfields. It's best to visit in the cooler months between April and November.

Blackdown Tableland National Park

The Blackdown Tableland is a spectacular 600m sandstone plateau that rises suddenly out of the flat plains of central Queensland. This impressive national park features stunning panoramas, waterfalls, great bushwalks, Aboriginal rock art, plus some unique wildlife and plant species.

The picturesque **South Mimosa Creek camping ground** (dingo rangers ☎ 07-4986 1964; per person/family $4/16) is a self-registration camping area about 6km on from Horseshoe Lookout. It has pit toilets and fireplaces – you'll need water, firewood and/or a fuel stove. Bookings are advised.

The turn-off to the Blackdown Tableland is 11km west of Dingo and 35km east of the coal-mining centre of Blackwater. The gravel road, which begins at the base of the tableland, isn't suitable for caravans and can be unsafe in wet weather – the first 8km stretch is steep, winding and often slippery. Bushfires from September to January can lead to park closures.

Gemfields

The lure of the gemfields is like the lady-luck pull of Queensland's ubiquitous pokies (poker machines). So, although you won't find the trademark Australian stone of opal on the fields west of **Emerald**, you will hear numerous tales of fossickers unearthing sapphires, rubies or zircons worth squillions, just minutes after drifting into town. Many of these stories are even true, as the gemfields around Anakie, Sapphire, Rubyvale and Willows are the world's largest of their kind and renowned for large, rare sapphires.

To join the ranks of the serious rockhounds, you'll need a fossicking licence (adult/couple $5.30/7.50) from the Emerald courthouse or one of the general stores on the gemfields. If you just wish to dabble, you can buy a bucket of 'wash' (mine dirt in water) from one of the fossicking parks and hand-sieve and wash it.

In **Anakie**, 42km west of Emerald, the **visitors centre** (☎ 07-4985 4525; 1 Anakie Rd; ☼ 8am-6pm) has maps of the fields and fossicking licences. It also offers tag-along tours, where you follow professional miners for $75, and digging tours for $120.

In **Sapphire**, 10km further north, **Pat's Gems** (☎ 07-4985 4544; ☼ 8.30am-5pm) offers $6 buckets of wash and, for kids of all ages, $10 'lucky bags' spiked with gem chips.

Another 8km on lies **Rubyvale**, the main town on the fields, and 2km further than that is the excellent **Miners Heritage Walk-in Mine** (☎ 07-4985 4444; Heritage Rd, Rubyvale; adult/child $6.60/2.75; ☼ 9am-5pm), where you can tour the underground passages of a working sapphire mine. If the quiet enthusiasm of the guides here (and their knowledge of sapphires) doesn't infect you with the fossicking bug, nothing will.

Replete with camp sites, rustic cabins and budget cabins, **Sunrise Cabins & Camping** (☎ 07-4985 4281; 57 Sunrise Rd, Sapphire; camp sites $11-15 for 2 people, cabin s/d $32/36) is very pleasant. It also supplies information, licences and maps, and hires fossicking gear.

Rubyvale Hotel (☎ 07-4985 4754; fax 07-4985 4463; 2 Keilambete Rd; s & d from $85), formerly the New Royal Hotel, has four cosy log cabins set in lush, landscaped gardens out back. Cabins will sleep eight ($160), and include open fires. Good pub lunches and dinners are served daily ($7 to $14).

There are caravan-camping parks at Anakie, Rubyvale and Willows Gemfields.

Springsure

☎ 07 / pop 770

Springsure, 66km south of Emerald on the way to Carnarvon Gorge, has a most attractive backdrop of granite mountains and sunflower fields. The **Virgin Rock**, an outcrop

of Mt Zamia on the northern outskirts, was named after early settlers claimed to have seen the image of the Virgin Mary in the rock face.

Springsure has a motel, a couple of pubs and a caravan park.

Carnarvon National Park

Carved out over millions of years by a creek running through sandstone, **Carnarvon Gorge** is an amazing oasis, with river oaks, flooded gums, cabbage palms and moss gardens, plus caves full of Aboriginal art, deep pools and platypuses in the creek. Standing on the valley floor, the sheer 200m rock walls towering above can give you what leading Australian novelist Tim Winton would call 'that big church feeling'.

For most people, Carnarvon Gorge *is* the Carnarvon National Park, because the other sections – including Mt Moffatt, Ka Ka Mundi and Salvator Rosa – are pretty inaccessible. Coming from Emerald, the turn-off to the gorge is 60km south of Rolleston; coming from Roma it's 110km north of Injune. After the turn-off, there's 23km of sealed road, followed by an unsealed 21km. After rain, the dirt sections are impassable.

The road leads to a **visitors centre** (☎ 4984 4505; ☼ 8am-5pm) and scenic picnic ground. The main walking track starts from here, following Carnarvon Creek through the gorge, with detours to various points of interest. These include the **Moss Garden** (3.6km from the picnic area), **Ward's Canyon** (4.8km), and the **Art Gallery** (5.6km) and **Cathedral Cave** (9.3km) – the last two of which are decorated with Aboriginal stencils and hand paintings. You should allow at least a few days for a visit here, and bring lunch and water as no shops exist.

You cannot drive from Carnarvon Gorge to other sections of the park, although you can reach beautiful Mt Moffatt via an unsealed road from Injune (4WD necessary). For further information, contact the **Injune Information Centre** (☎ 4626 1053).

SLEEPING

It's best to book several months ahead, especially from April to October.

Carnarvon Gorge Wilderness Lodge (☎ 4984 4503, 1800 644 150; info@carnarvon_gorge.com.au; Wyseby Rd; s/d from $130/260) This upmarket accommodation near the park entrance offers cosy safari cabins nestled in bush, plus a restaurant, bar and pool. Rates drop for longer stays, and in low season. Full board costs $165 per person, per night, twin share.

Takarakka Bush Resort (☎ 4984 4535; takarakka@takarakka.com.au; Wyseby Rd; camp sites adult/child $9/5, caravan sites $24 for 2 people, cabins $70) Following the sign, turn right 4km before you reach the picnic ground to arrive at this picturesque bush oasis. Simply furnished, elevated canvas cabins with private verandas surround a camping area.

Big Bend (☎ 4984 4505; fax 4984 4915; camp sites per person, per night $4) One for the real bush-lover, this permit-only, limited-numbers camping ground is a 10km walk up the gorge. There are toilets but no showers, and fires are forbidden.

Getting There & Away

McCafferty's/Greyhound (☎ 13 14 99) has a twice-weekly (Tuesday and Thursday) coach service from Rockhampton to Emerald ($39, 3½ hours). **Emerald Coaches** (☎ 4982 4444) has an Emerald–Longreach service ($55, 5 hours) every Friday night, returning on Sunday.

The twice-weekly (Wednesday and Sunday) *Spirit of the Outback* train also runs from Rockhampton to Emerald ($50 economy, 5 hours) and Longreach ($110 economy, 13½ hours).

OUTBACK

Heading west from the Queensland coast across the Great Dividing Range, the land becomes drier, and the towns smaller and further apart.

The outback, although sparsely settled, is well serviced by major roads, namely the Overlander's Way (Flinders and Barkly Hwys) and the Matilda Hwy (Landsborough Hwy and Burke Developmental Rd), both part of the Queensland Heritage Network.

The Flinders Hwy runs east-west across northern Queensland from Townsville to Cloncurry, where it becomes the Barkly Hwy, continuing through Mt Isa and into the NT. West of Mt Isa the road deteriorates in places to a narrow, poorly maintained strip of bitumen. The Capricorn Hwy runs along the tropic of Capricorn from Rockhampton to Barcaldine, and the Landsbor-

ough and Mitchell Hwys run from the NSW border south of Cunnamulla via Longreach to Cloncurry.

Once you turn off these major arteries, road conditions deteriorate rapidly, services are remote and you need to be fully self-sufficient, carrying spare parts, fuel and water. Some sights and accommodation options (in particular the outback stations) close from November to March, the hottest time in the outback.

Getting There & Away
AIR
Qantas affiliate **Macair** (☎ 13 13 13; www.macair.com.au) connects the rest of Queensland to many of the larger outback towns, including Townsville to Mt Isa (one way $400) and Longreach ($330), Cairns to Mt Isa ($680), and Brisbane to Charleville ($310).

BUS
McCafferty's/Greyhound (www.mccaffertys.com.au) operates three major bus routes through the outback: from Townsville to Mt Isa ($115, 12 hours) and on to the NT, from Rockhampton to Longreach ($60, 7 hours), and from Brisbane to Mt Isa ($150) via Longreach.

TRAIN
Queensland Rail (☎ 3235 1331; www.traveltrain.qr.com.au) has three train services heading inland from the coast: the *Spirit of the Outback* from Brisbane to Longreach (economy/1st class $210/315) via Rockhampton, and with connecting buses to Winton; the *Westlander* from Brisbane to Charleville ($130/200), with connecting buses to Cunnamulla and Quilpie; and the *Inlander* from Townsville to Mt Isa ($159/237). All run twice weekly.

CHARTERS TOWERS TO CLONCURRY
The Flinders Hwy is probably the most boring route in Queensland, as scenic drives go. There are, however, a few points of interest along the way to break the monotony. The highway was originally a Cobb & Co coach run, and along its length are small towns established as coach stopovers. **Pentland**, 105km west of Charters Towers, and **Torrens Creek**, 50km further on, both have pubs, fuel and camping grounds. At **Prairie**, 200km west of Charters Towers, is the friendly, historic and supposedly haunted

Prairie Hotel (☎ /fax 07-4741 5121; Flinders Hwy; s/d from $22/39; 🔊).

Hughenden, a busy commercial centre on the banks of the Flinders River, bills itself as 'the home of beauty and the beast'. The beast, imprisoned in the **Flinders Discovery Centre** (☎ 07-4741 1021; 37 Gray St; adult/child $2/free; 🕑 9am-5pm), is a replica skeleton of *Muttaburrasaurus*, one of the largest and most complete dinosaur skeletons found in Australia. The museum has displays on the town's history and doubles as a visitors centre.

The beauty is the **Porcupine Gorge National Park** (☎ 07-4741 1113), an oasis in the dry country north of Hughenden. The park's **Pyramid Lookout** is about 70km along the mostly unsealed, often-corrugated Kennedy Developmental Rd. You can camp here and it's an easy 30-minute walk down into the gorge, with its fine rock formations and a permanent creek. Few people come to the park, and there's a fair bit of wildlife.

Royal Hotel-Motel (☎ 07-4741 1183; royal100@tpg.com.au; 21 Moran St; s/d $60/75; 🔊) One of Hughenden's better motels; choose between large, spotless, older-style units and smaller, newer ones.

There's also a **caravan park** (☎ 07-4741 1190; camp sites $10, cabins from $40) opposite the train station, and the **Grand Hotel** (☎ /fax 07-4741 1588; 25 Gray St; s/d $25/35) has decent budget accommodation.

Watch for wild emus and brolgas on the Hughenden–Cloncurry stretch. **Richmond**, 112km from Hughenden, and **Julia Creek**, 149km further on, are both small towns with motels and camping parks with caravan sites. Richmond has an impressive marine fossil museum and visitors centre: **Kronosaurus Korner** (☎ 4741 3429; 91 Goldring St; adult/child/family $10/5/22; 🕑 8.30am-4.45pm). The museum has over 200 exhibits, including Australia's best vertebrate fossil, the Richmond *Pliosaur*.

From Julia Creek, the bitumen Wills Developmental Rd heads north to Normanton (432km), Karumba (494km) and Burketown (467km). See the Gulf Savannah (p392) for more information on these towns.

CLONCURRY
☎ 07 / pop 2748

The centre for a copper boom in the 19th century, the Curry was the largest copper producer in the British Empire in 1916. Today it's a pastoral centre, and the town's major claim to fame is as the birthplace of the Royal Flying Doctor Service (RFDS). Australia's highest recorded temperature in the shade, a cool 53.1°C, was measured here in 1889.

The **Cloncurry library** (☎ 4742 1588; 19 Scarr St) provides Internet access.

Cloncurry's **Mary Kathleen Park & Museum** (☎ 4742 1361; www.cloncurry.qld.gov.au; McIlwraith St; adult/child $7/3; 🕑 8am-4.30pm Mon-Fri), on the eastern side of town, acts as a visitors centre. It's partly housed in buildings transported from the former uranium-mining town of Mary Kathleen and includes relics of the Burke and Wills expedition, and a big array of local rocks and minerals.

John Flynn Place (☎ 4742 1251; Daintree St; adult/child $8.50/4; 🕑 8am-4.30pm Mon-Fri, 9am-3pm Sat & Sun Apr-Oct) houses an interesting, easy-to-follow exhibition that commemorates Flynn's work in setting up the invaluable RFDS, as well as the new **Discovery Centre**, which delves into the history of the town.

The Burke Developmental Rd, north from Cloncurry, is sealed all the way to Normanton (376km) and Karumba (449km).

Sleeping

Gidgee Inn (☎ 4742 1599; www.gidgeeinn.com.au; Matilda Hwy; r from $95) This attractive upmarket motel is built from rammed red earth and trimmed with corrugated iron. The rooms are modern and spotless, and the place has a highly recommended bar and grill (mains from $18 to $24).

Gilbert Park Tourist Village (☎ 4742 2300; gilpark@topend.com.au; 2 McIlwraith St; camp sites from $15, units $65) Gilbert Park is clean and neat, set amid desert vegetation and hillocks of red rock. The units are modern and self-contained.

CLONCURRY TO MT ISA
This 121km stretch of the Barkly Hwy has several interesting stops. At **Corella River**, 44km west of Cloncurry, there's a memorial cairn to the Burke and Wills expedition, which passed here in 1861. Another 1km down the road is the **Kalkadoon & Mitakoodi Memorial**, which marks an old Aboriginal tribal boundary.

The turn-off to **Lake Julius**, Mt Isa's reserve water supply, is 100km west of Cloncurry. From the turn-off, it's 90km of unsealed, bumpy road north to the lake, which is a popular spot for fishing, canoeing, sailing and other water sports.

Lake Julius Recreation Camp (☎ 4742 5998; fax 4742 5110; Lake Julius Rd; camp sites/dm/4-person units $2.85/7.30/36) is a good place to head for if you're craving peace and quiet. There are bushwalks along the river, and canoes ($15 per day) and motor boats ($55) to explore the lake. The units have air-con and sleep up to eight people. Use of the camp's kitchen is an extra $12 per day.

Battle Mountain, not far north of Lake Julius, was the scene of the last stand of the Kalkadoon people in 1884. One of the last tribes to resist white settlement, the Kalkadoons were all but wiped out in a bloody massacre that marked the end of Aboriginal resistance in the region.

About 30km northeast of the lake is the tiny township of **Kajabbi**, where the historic **Kalkadoon Hotel** (☎ /fax 4742 5979; kalkahtl@ bigpond.com; Stanfield St; s/d from $30/40) has Saturday night barbecues, budget accommodation and an annual yabbie race (April).

MT ISA
☎ 07 / pop 20,525

Mt Isa is a town of striking beauty, with stark red ridges and olive-green clumps of spinifex. It owes its prosperity to the behemoth mine that squats to the west of town, belching smoke from its 270m lead-smelter stack. The mine is rich in copper, silver, lead and zinc, and job opportunities have attracted people from about 50 different ethnic groups, most of whom are men (there are supposedly three males to every female!). Prospector John Campbell Miles, who discovered the first ore deposits in 1923, gave Mt Isa its name – a corruption of Mt Ida, a Western Australian goldfield. Since the ore deposits were large and low-grade, working them required an investment only a company could afford. **Mt Isa Mines** (☎ 4744 2011; www.mim.com.au; Railway Ave) was founded in 1924 but it was during and after WWII that Mt Isa flourished. Today the mine is among the world's top three producers of silver and top 10 of copper and zinc.

The Isa also lays its claim to fame as the birthplace of Pat Rafter, the former US Open tennis champion, and the airport has a Pat Rafter Court coffee shop.

There's a strong community feel in this rough-and-ready town. Locals stroll across pedestrian crossings with absolute certainty that cars will stop for them, and honking horns are usually from drivers waving hello.

If you're after the authentic outback experience, then the Isa, as it's known locally, shouldn't be missed.

Orientation & Information
Barkly Hwy, which becomes Marian St, is the main entry road. The city centre is in the area between Grace and Isa Sts, and West and Simpson Sts.

Outback at Isa (☎ 4749 1555; www.riversleigh.qld .gov.au; 19 Marian St; ☺ 9am-5pm) Isa's massive new multimillion dollar tourist project, completed in August 2003, is your first stop, where you'll find the helpful visitors centre.

The best Net access is at **Mt Isa Library** (☎ 4744 4267; library@mountisa.qld.gov.au; West St), which also offers temporary membership ($120 deposit) allowing you to borrow two books. **Mt Isa Newsagency** (☎ /fax 4743 9105; 25b Miles St) also has Net access.

Sights & Activities
Outback at Isa (☎ 4749 1555; www.riversleigh.qld .gov.au; 19 Marian St; ☺ 9am-5pm), featuring the Hard Times mine, set up as a 'working mine', is a prime tourist attraction, where you'll don a hard hat and be guided through the underground mine shaft. The complex also features the Sir James Foot building, and exhibition space, focusing on indigenous people, settlement, mining and the region's flora and fauna; there's also a theatrette with footage of the early days, an amphitheatre and an Outback Park. The **Riversleigh Fossils Centre**, housed in the Outback at Isa complex, has a comprehensive collection of fossils (one of the world's best) spanning 25 million years. In the attached laboratory, you can observe Isa's resident palaeontologist separate fossils from their casings.

Mt Isa puts on a mean sunset, and the **City Lookout**, off Hilary St, has spectacular views of the mine and town. At the eastern end of Pamela St is another excellent **lookout**.

John Middlin Mining Display & Visitor Centre (☎ 4749 1429; fax 4749 1559; 1 Church St; adult/child $3/1; ☺ 9am-4pm Mon-Fri) has a simulated underground experience, and **Frank Aston Museum** (☎ 4743 0610; www.mountisa.qld.gov.au /tourism/attractions/underground.html; Shackleton St; adult/child $6/1; ☺ 9am-4pm) exhibits flying-

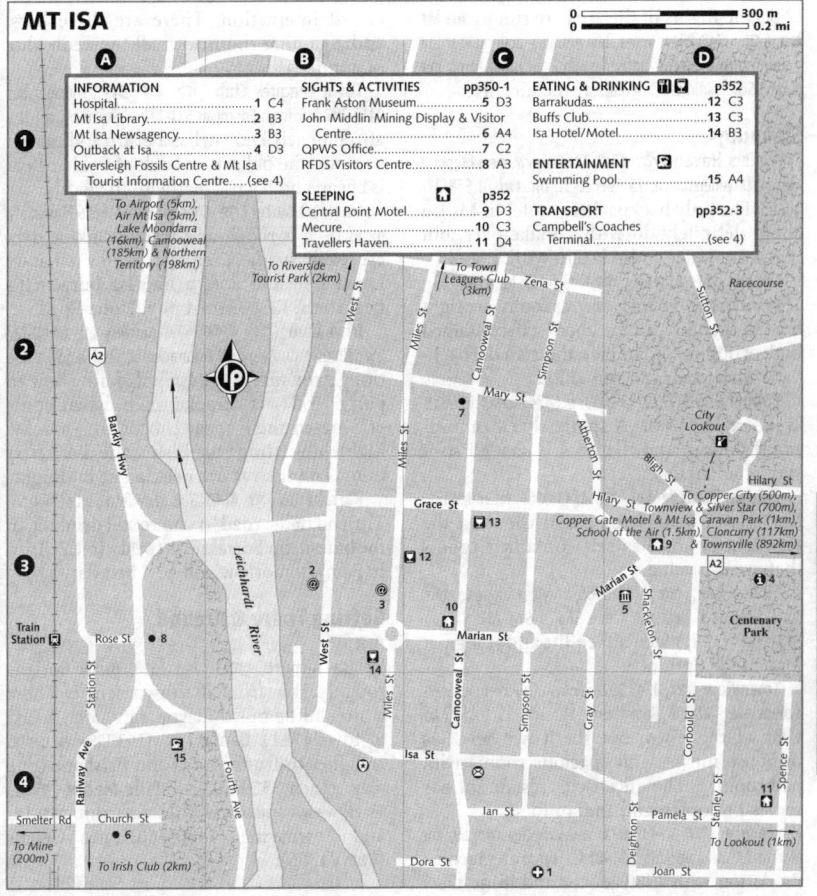

MT ISA

| 0 | | 300 m |
| 0 | | 0.2 mi |

INFORMATION
Hospital..............................**1** C4
Mt Isa Library.....................**2** B3
Mt Isa Newsagency.............**3** B3
Outback at Isa....................**4** D3
Riversleigh Fossils Centre & Mt Isa
  Tourist Information Centre.....(see 4)

To Airport (5km);
Air Mt Isa (5km);
Lake Moondarra
(16km), Camooweal
(185km) & Northern
Territory (198km)

SIGHTS & ACTIVITIES   pp350-1
Frank Aston Museum...............**5** D3
John Middlin Mining Display & Visitor
  Centre............................**6** A4
QPWS Office..........................**7** C2
RFDS Visitors Centre................**8** A3

SLEEPING   p352
Central Point Motel................**9** D3
Mecure.............................**10** C3
Travellers Haven...................**11** D4

EATING & DRINKING   p352
Barrakudas............................**12** C3
Buffs Club............................**13** C3
Isa Hotel/Motel.......................**14** B3

ENTERTAINMENT
Swimming Pool......................**15** A4

TRANSPORT   pp352-3
Campbell's Coaches
  Terminal.............................(see 4)

To Riverside
Tourist Park (2km)

To Town
Leagues Club
(3km)

Racecourse

City
Lookout

To Copper City (500m),
Townview & Silver Star (700m),
Copper Gate Motel & Mt Isa Caravan Park (1km),
School of the Air (1.5km), Cloncurry (117km)
& Townsville (892km)

Centenary
Park

Train
Station

To Mine
(200m)

To Irish Club (2km)

To Lookout (1km)

QUEENSLAND

---

doctor radios and gemstones, and has Aboriginal cultural displays.

The **Royal Flying Doctor Service Visitors Centre** (☎ 4743 2800; Barkly Hwy; ☻ 9am-5pm Mon-Fri) and **School of the Air** (☎ 4744 9100; www.mtisasde.qld.edu.au; Kalkadoon High School, Abel Smith Pde; admission $2 donation; ☻ tours 9am & 10am Mon-Fri during school term) show how these services are accessed by remote communities.

Lake Moondarra, 16km north of town, is a popular recreational area.

Mt Isa's annual **rodeo** is in the second weekend in August.

Tours

Check with the Mt Isa Tourist Information Centre for the most up-to-date information.

Campbell's Tours and Travel (☎ 4743 2006, 1800 242 329; www.campbellstravel.com.au; 19 Marian St; ☻ 6-7.45am Mon-Fri, 6-9.30am & 5.30-7.45pm Sat & Sun) Campbell's runs fascinating two-hour surface tours of the mine (adult $22) at 9am and 1pm Monday to Friday and 11am Saturday (these are well worth taking). It also runs camping safaris (adult $550) to Lawn Hill National Park, Adels Grove and the Riversleigh fossil sites from April to October.

Jabiru Adventure Tours (☎ 4749 5950; 130-138 Old Mica Creek Rd; www.jabiruadventuretours.com; adult $85; ☻ departs 8am & 2pm) runs half-day tours – an indigenous guide takes you to the underground hospital, tent house, sunrock, cascades and Lake Moondarra, culminating in a smorgasbord meal.

Scenic flights of the area are run by **Air Mt Isa** (☎ 4743 2844; www.flexi.net.au/~actiong/matilda _country/html_pages/mount_isa/mtisaairmtisa.html; per person $61, minimum 3 people) at the airport.

Sleeping

Travellers Haven (☎ 4743 0313; www.users.bigpond .net.au/travellershaven; 75 Spence St; dm/tw/s/d $18/21/ 30/42) The only backpackers' hotel in Mt Isa could definitely do with a make-over, but it's clean, quiet and relaxed, with a pool.

Copper Gate Motel (☎ 4743 3233; fax 4749 1157; 97-99 Marian St; s/d $55/65) Noisy, as rooms are right on the highway, but a good self-contained budget option for families; there's a big backyard where kids can run amok.

Copper City (☎ 4743 2033; fax 4743 2290; 105 Butler St; s $68-72, d $78-82) A spotlessly clean midrange option, and the pool is shaded so it stays cool all day.

Central Point Motel (☎ 4743 0666; centralpoint@ bigpond.com; 6 Marian St; s/d $73/83) Close to the city centre, and has self-contained rooms that are top value.

Silver Star (☎ 4743 3466; rtaylos@bigpond.com; cnr Marian St & Doughan Tce; s $65, d $74-78) Silver Star has been given a face-lift and is a great mid-range option.

Townview (☎ 4743 3328; www1.tpgi.com.au/users /townview; 112-116 Kookaburra St; s/d $95/108) No view of the town, but the Townview has in-house movies and spacious rooms with bathrooms. The licensed restaurant-bar serves Ethiopian and Indian food.

Mecure (☎ 4743 3024; www.mecure.com.au; cnr Marian & Camooweal Sts; r $190) Corporate accommodation with 1980s décor and mine-view rooms.

Two shady caravan parks are **Mt Isa Caravan Park** (☎ 4743 3252; mtcvpark@austarnet.com.au; 112 Marian St; camp/powered sites $15/18, cabins $45-60) and **Riverside Tourist Park** (☎ 4743 3904; fax 4743 9417; 195 West St; camp/powered sites $16/20, cabins $67).

Eating & Drinking

There are no trendy eateries in the Isa, and eating consists mainly of multinational fast-food chains. All the pubs and clubs do meals (your best bet for food), and run free courtesy buses that pick you up from your accommodation – ingenious!

Buffs Club (☎ 4743 2365; courtesy bus 0413-126 666; www.buffs.com.au; cnr Camooweal & Grace Sts; meals $12-30) An absolute hoot! The Buffs is terrific fun and has live acts with lots of crowd interaction. There are three bars, and a gaming room with all the neon glitz of a minicasino.

Town Leagues Club (☎ 4749 5455, courtesy bus 0412-795 455; Ryan Rd; meals $11-17) Townies, as it's affectionately known, has a bistro and garden bar, plus the obligatory bank of Pokies. Beer is cheap and it's popular with the locals.

Isa Hotel-Motel (☎ 4743 2611; cnr Miles & Marian Sts; meals $5-19) A rough-and-ready drinking den, especially in the evening, but it's a handy lunch spot and does a fine Isa burger. It's next to the fiesty Murri pub, Hotel Boyd.

Irish Club (☎ 4743 2577, courtesy bus 0411-427 256; Nineteenth Ave; Rish & karaoke admission $5) One thing's for sure – the Isa kids know how to party. Friday is karaoke night, when punters stretch their vocal chords in a smoky, nightclub setting ; the Rish is the disco next door. The Irish starts peaking at midnight.

Barrakudas (☎ 4749 0388; 26 Miles St; admission $5) The end of the road. If you're still drinking in the blue-neon Barrakudas (peak time 2.30am to 5am), tomorrow will be a bad day.

Getting There & Around

AIR

Mt Isa Airport (☎ 4743 4598; Barkly Hwy) is roughly 5km from the town centre. There is no shuttle bus, but you can catch a taxi to town ($11). **Qantas** (☎ 13 13 13; www.qantas .com) flies to/from Mt Isa and Brisbane (one way/return $520/1032), while **Macair** (☎ 13 13 13; www.macair.com.au) flies to/from Mt Isa and Townsville ($400/760) and Cairns ($680/1366).

BUS

Campbell's Coaches (☎ 4743 2006; www.campbells travel.com.au; 19 Marian St; ⊙ 6am-7.30pm) terminal is at Outback at Isa, and is the main McCafferty's/Greyhound depot. Daily services run between Mt Isa and Townsville (one way $115, 12 hours), continuing all the way on to Tennant Creek ($102, 7 hours), Darwin ($240, 21 hours), Alice Springs ($210, 14 hours) or Brisbane ($150, 25 hours).

CAR

You can rent cars and 4WDs. The following companies all have offices at the airport:

Avis (☎ 4743 3733)
Budget (☎ 4749 1828)
Hertz (☎ 4743 4142)
Thrifty (☎ 4743 2911; ⊙ 8am-5pm)

TRAIN

The air-conditioned **Inlander** (http://qroti.com
/longdistance/inlander) runs between Mt Isa and
Townsville (one-way economy seat/1st-class
sleeper $110/237, 20 hours) and Brisbane
($273/552, 46 hours). The train station is on
Station St, over the Leichardt River towards
the mine.

MT ISA TO THREE WAYS

Established in 1884 as a service centre for the
vast cattle stations of the Barkly Tablelands,
Camooweal now consists of a couple of historic buildings – **Freckleton's General Store**, in
particular, is worth a visit – as well as a pub,
hostel and a few roadhouses (with extremely
expensive fuel). The town is 185km from Mt
Isa and 13km east of the NT border.

From Camooweal you can head north on
an unsealed road to the **Lawn Hill (Boodjamulla)
National Park** (☎ 07-4748 5572), where there are a
few camp sites, and Burketown; see p395 for
details. Eight kilometres south of town is the
Camooweal Caves National Park (☎ 07-4744 7888),
with a network of unusual caves with sinkhole openings. These have few of the usual
limestone features because of the constant
flooding. There are no facilities here, and the
caves are for experienced cavers only.

There's nothing much along the whole
460km from Camooweal to the Three Ways
junction in the NT. The first petrol station
from Camooweal appears after 260km. You
can camp or stay nearby in motel-style rooms
at **Barkly Homestead** (☎ 08 8964 4549; fax 8964 4543;
Barkly Hwy; camp/caravan sites $7/22, s/d $80/90).

MT ISA TO LONGREACH

The shortest route to Longreach from Mt
Isa means heading east along the Barkly
Hwy to the Landsborough Hwy, 14km
east of Cloncurry. Here the Landsborough
heads southeast, passing through McKinlay
(91km), Kynuna (168km), Winton (339km)
and eventually hitting Longreach (516km).

McKinlay is a tiny settlement that probably would have been doomed to eternal
insignificance had it not been used as a
location in the amazingly successful movie
Crocodile Dundee.

Walkabout Creek Hotel (☎ 07-4746 8424; walkabout
creekhotel@bigpond.com; Landsborough Hwy; camp sites
$6, s/d $42/55; 🔅), which featured in the film,
is cluttered with photos and other *Crocodile
Dundee* memorabilia, although renovations

have detracted from its knockabout charm.
You can camp out the back, or the small
motel-style rooms are a block west of the
pub.

A further 74km southeast, and not much
bigger than McKinlay, is **Kynuna**. It's home
to **Magoffin's Matilda Expo** (☎ 07-4746 8401;
Landsborough Hwy; admission variable; 🕑 8am-5pm), a
contemporaneously gaudy and ramshackle
'museum' that claims to have the real story
behind *Waltzing Matilda*. The museum's
colourful owner, Richard Magoffin, does
renditions of the song, two-hour live shows
at 7.30pm from April to October, and promises a peek at what he says is the original
handwritten manuscript penned by Banjo
Patterson in 1895. Whether you believe it or
not, Magoffin's is well worth a visit (there's
a variable 'exit fee' depending on season
and how much you want to pay), and it's a
stark contrast to the flashy Waltzing Matilda
Centre at Winton.

There's a lot to like about the historic
little **Blue Heeler Hotel** (☎ 07-4746 8650; www
.blueheelerpub.com; Landsborough Hwy, Kynuna; camp/
caravan sites $3.30/14, r & units $33-55; 🔅), from its
walls covered with scrawled messages and
signatures, to its unquestionably essential
surf life-saving club. The nearest beach
may be almost 1000km away, but the pub
hosts a surf life-saving carnival every April,
complete with surfboard relays, a tug-of-
war and a beach party at night. The Blue
Heeler is a friendly place with good meals,
pub rooms, spotless motel units and camp
sites in the adjacent Jolly Swag-Van Park.

The turn-off to the **Combo Waterhole**,
which Banjo Patterson is said to have visited in 1895 before he wrote *Waltzing Matilda*, is signposted off the highway about
12km east of Kynuna.

Winton
☎ 07 / pop 1321

Winton is a cattle- and sheep-raising centre, and the railhead for transporting cattle
brought from the Channel Country by road
train. The town is a friendly, laid-back place
with two major claims to fame: the region-
ally inspired verse of Banjo Paterson, and
the founding of Qantas airlines in 1920
(see the boxed text 'The Origins of Qantas'
p356).

The **town library** (☎ 4657 1188; 75 Vindex St)
has Internet access.

The town's biggest attraction is the **Waltzing Matilda Centre** (☎ 4657 1466; www.matilda centre.com.au; 50 Elderslie St; adult/child/family $14/12/30; ⏰ 8.30am-5pm), which doubles as the visitors centre. Here you can also pick up the Shin Plaster pass, which covers entry to the town's attractions, for $15 per person. There's a surprising number of exhibits here for a museum devoted to a song, including an indoor billabong complete with a squatter, troopers and a jolly swagman, a hologram display oozing cringe-inducing nationalism, and the **Jolly Swagman statue** – a tribute to the unknown swagmen who lie in unmarked graves in the area. There are plenty of interactive displays to keep the little ones entertained as well. The centre also houses the **Qantilda Pioneer Place**, which has a huge range of fascinating artefacts (tools, clothes, documents), and displays on the founding of Qantas.

The **Royal Theatre**, out the back of the **Gift & Gem Centre** (☎ 4657 1296; 73 Elderslie St), is a wonderful open-air theatre with canvas-slung chairs, corrugated tin walls and a star-studded ceiling. A replica opal mine, known as the 'opal walk', leads from the gem centre to a small museum (admission $2), which is basically the projection room of the theatre. Nostalgia night ($6) screenings take place at 8pm on Wednesday from April to October.

Arno's Wall (Vindex St) is Winton's quirkiest attraction – a 70m-long work-in-progress, featuring a huge range of household items ensnared in the mortar, from televisions to motorcycles. The wall can be found behind the North Gregory Hotel.

Winton's major festival is the five-day **Outback Festival**, held every odd year during the September school holidays.

SLEEPING & EATING
North Gregory Hotel (☎ 1800 801 611, 4657 1375; northgregoryhotel@hotmail.com; 67 Elderslie St; s/d $44/55; ✖) If you're looking for the epitome of the big, friendly country pub, this is the place. It has dozens of comfortable, old-fashioned rooms upstairs, with spotless shared facilities. There's also an excellent bistro (mains $10 to $18).

Matilda Country Tourist Park (☎ 1800 001 383, 4657 1607; 43 Chirnside St; camp sites/cabins $17/60) This camping ground, at the northern end of town, has lawn sites and good barbecue fa-cilities, and puts on regular campfire meals, complete with bush poetry and yarns.

GETTING THERE & AWAY
Winton is on the **McCafferty's/Greyhound** (www.mccaffertys.com.au) Brisbane to Mt Isa bus route ($125, 18½ hours). There are also connecting bus services between Winton and Longreach ($30) that meet the twice-weekly *Spirit of the Outback* train (for more information on this train see p348).

South of Winton
Eighty-five kilometres southwest of Winton, the friendly **Carisbrooke Station** (☎ 4657 3984; carisbrooke@bigpond.com; Cork Mail Rd; camp sites/self-contained units $5/33) has a wildlife sanctuary, Aboriginal paintings and bora rings (circular ceremonial grounds). Day tours of the station (available with advance notice) leave from Winton or the homestead for $110 per person (minimum of two people).

At **Lark Quarry Environmental Park** (☎ 4657 1812; adult/child $9/5), 110km southwest of Winton, there is what is thought to be the world's best-preserved evidence of a dinosaur stampede. It takes about 90 (worthwhile) minutes to drive from Winton to Lark Quarry in a conventional vehicle, but the mostly dirt road is impassable in wet weather. Contact the Waltzing Matilda Centre in Winton for more information. Alternatively, **Diamantina Outback Tours** (☎ 4657 1514; www.dotours.com.au; $85 per person, minimum of 4) runs day trips from Winton to Lark Quarry.

LONGREACH
☎ 07 / pop 3673
This prosperous outback town was the home of Qantas early last century (see the boxed text 'The Origins of Qantas' p356), but these days it's equally famous for the Australian Stockman's Hall of Fame & Outback Heritage Centre, one of outback Queensland's biggest attractions.

Longreach's human population is vastly outnumbered by more than a million sheep, and there are a fair few cattle too.

The **visitors centre** (☎ 4658 3555; www.longreach .qld.gov.au; Qantas Park, Eagle St; ⏰ 9am-5pm Mon-Fri Nov-Mar, 9am-5pm Mon-Fri, 9am-noon Sat & Sun Apr-Oct) is in the heart of town. The **Longreach library** (☎ 4658 4104; 96a Eagle St), opposite the visitors centre, has free Internet access.

CAPTAIN STARLIGHT

Longreach was the starting point for one of Queensland's most colourful early crimes when, in 1870, Harry Redford and two accomplices stole 1000 head of cattle and walked them 2400km to South Australia, where they were sold. Redford's exploit opened up a new stock route south, and when he was finally brought to justice in 1873, he was found not guilty by an adoring public. Ralph Boldrewood's classic Australian novel *Robbery Under Arms* later immortalised Redford as Captain Starlight.

In May Longreach plays host to the **Outback Muster**, an unusual three-day festival featuring a variety of events related to droving.

Sights

AUSTRALIAN STOCKMAN'S HALL OF FAME & OUTBACK HERITAGE CENTRE

This beautifully conceived **centre** (☎ 4658 2166; Landsborough Hwy; adult/child/family $20/9/44, valid 2 days; ☷ 9am-5pm), 2km east of town towards Barcaldine, has recently undergone a multimillion-dollar face-lift. The excellent displays are divided into periods ranging from the first white settlement through to today, and cover all aspects of the pioneering pastoral life. The Hall was built as a tribute to the early explorers and stockmen, and also commemorates the crucial roles played by pioneer women and Aboriginal stockmen. Much of the redevelopment has focused on upgrading the Aboriginal section of the museum.

Allow at least half a day to visit the Hall of Fame, as it gives a fascinating insight into the development of outback Australia.

OTHER ATTRACTIONS

The town's other big attraction is the newly renovated **Qantas Founders Outback Museum** (☎ 4658 3737; Landsborough Hwy; adult/child/family $15/8/30; ☷ 9am-5pm). The complex houses a life-size replica of an Avro 504K, the first aircraft owned by the fledgling airline, along with interactive multimedia displays including a theatrette and working displays showing the pioneering history of Qantas. Next door is the original Qantas hangar, where six DH-50 biplanes were assembled

in 1926. It now contains a mint-condition DH-61, which is dwarfed by the massive 747 parked outside.

Another attraction is **Banjo's Outback Theatre & Pioneer Shearing Shed** (☎ 4658 2360; Stork Rd; adult/child $15/9, with meal $28/16). It's a ramshackle place with two-hour shows most Saturday evenings, and Tuesday and Thursday mornings. The shows include bush poems, songs, yarns and skits, as well as demonstrations of shearing, and wool classing and spinning.

The **Powerhouse Museum** (☎ 4658 3933; 12 Swan St; adult/child $5/free; ☷ 2-5pm Apr-Oct, varying days & hr Nov-Mar) contains the huge old diesel and gas-vacuum engines used until 1985, when a new power station opened on the edge of town.

Tours

The **Outback Travel Centre** (☎ 4658 1776; 115a Eagle St) has a variety of tours, including a full-day tour on Tuesday and Friday that takes in the town's major sites and ends with a dinner cruise on the Thomson River (adult/child $120/100), or you can just take the dinner cruise ($44/25). **Billabong Boat Cruises** (☎ 4658 1776; 115a Eagle St) also offers dinner cruises for $35/25.

Outback Aussie Tours (☎ 1300 787 890; www .outbackaussietours.com.au; 124b Eagle St) takes a combined Winton day tour that includes Carisbrooke Station and Lark Quarry ($145/90).

Sleeping

Old Time Cottage (☎ 4658 1550; 158 Crane St; d $80, extra person $10; ☷) This quaint little place is a good choice for a group or family as it sleeps up to six. Set in an attractive garden, the self-contained old-style timber cottage is fully furnished, with a polished-wood floor.

Aussie Betta Cabins (☎ 4658 3811; 63 Sir Hudson Fysh Dr; s/d $65/75; ☷) There are six self-contained cabins in this tidy, palm-lined complex near the hall of fame. Each of the cabins has two bedrooms and sleeps up to five.

Albert Park Motel (☎ 1800 812 811, 4658 2411; apmi@tpg.com.au; Sir Hudson Fysh Dr; s/d $90/100) The upmarket Albert Park Motel, east of the centre, has 56 large, modern and well-appointed rooms, as well as a pool, spa and a licensed restaurant.

QUEENSLAND

THE ORIGINS OF QANTAS

Qantas, the Queensland & Northern Territory Aerial Service, had humble beginnings as a joy-flight and air-taxi service in Queensland's outback – and at times it has seemed like every second outback town has claimed to be the birthplace of Australia's major airline.

The idea to establish the airline came about when two former Flying Corps airmen, Hudson Fysh and Paul McGuinness, travelled through outback Queensland to prepare the route for the famous London to Melbourne Air Race. Together they saw the potential for an air service to link the remote outback centres and, with the financial backing of local pastoralists, they established an airline.

The fledgling company was registered for business at Winton on 16 November 1920, and soon after it moved to Longreach, opening an office in Duck St. Qantas' first regular air service began on 22 November 1922, between Cloncurry and Charleville. Longreach remained the airline's head-quarters until it moved to Brisbane in 1930.

Qantas' first overseas passenger flight occurred on 17 April 1935, between Brisbane and Singapore. It took four days. The airline moved to Sydney in 1938, and by 1958 the flying kangaroo symbol was a familiar sight at airports in 23 countries. The acquisition of Boeing 707s in 1959, then 747s in 1971 saw the airline expand further.

Today Qantas operates 187 aircraft, flies to 32 countries and transports 19 million passengers a year. It has a proud safety record, although there have been some well-publicised hiccups, most notably the September 1999 accident at Bangkok airport, when a London-bound Qantas Boeing 747 slid off the end of the runway.

Longreach Caravan Park (☎ 4658 1770; fax 4658 0775; 180 Ibis St; camp/caravan sites $15/17, on-site vans/self-contained cabins $30/55) This neat, unassuming little place has pleasant, shady camp sites, a well-kept toilet and shower block, and a good barbecue area.

Eating

There are several cafés and takeaways, and a bakery, on Eagle St in the centre of town. The pubs offer the usual suspects.

Bush Verandah Restaurant (☎ 4658 2448; 120 Galah St; mains around $18; ☺ dinner Wed-Sat) This is a small, licensed eatery with rustic décor and a country-style à la carte menu featuring beef, poultry and seafood dishes. The slightly run-down exterior goes with the bush theme, supposedly.

Longreach Club (☎ 4658 1016; 31 Duck St; meals $10-15) The relaxed Longreach Club is recommended for its range of cheap specials and smorgasbord. The à la carte menu is also worth a try.

Getting There & Away

McCafferty's/Greyhound (☎ 4927 2844; www.mccaffertys.com.au) buses stop at the rear of the **Outback Travel Centre** (☎ 4658 1776; www.lotc.com.au; 115a Eagle St). There are daily services to Winton ($30, 2½ hours), Mt Isa ($80, 8½ hours) and Brisbane ($110, 16 hours), and three a week to Rockhampton ($60, 7 hours).

The *Spirit of the Outback* train runs twice a week between Longreach and Rockhampton (economy $100, 14 hours).

LONGREACH TO WINDORAH

The Thomson Developmental Rd is the most direct route towards Birdsville from Longreach.

The first 215km of the trip is a narrow sealed road that passes by **Stonehenge**, a tiny settlement in a dry, rocky landscape with half-a-dozen tin houses and a pub. The **Stonehenge Hotel** (☎ 07-4658 5944; fax 07-4658 5927; Stafford St; s/d $30/40) has rooms with shared facilities and daily meals, and sells fuel.

Jundah, 65km south of Stonehenge, is an administrative centre with a cheap caravan park, a pub and a general store. The second part of the route, from Jundah to Windorah, is mostly over unsealed roads of dirt, gravel and sand.

LONGREACH TO CHARLEVILLE
Ilfracombe

☎ 07 / pop 160

This small town, 28km east of Longreach, modestly calls itself the Hub of the West and boasts a train station, general store, swimming pool, golf course, a pub and the new **Wellshot Centre** (3 McMaster Dr) that depicts the development of the pastoral industry in the area. Along the highway you'll see the **Ilfracombe Machinery & Heritage Museum** (Landsborough Hwy; admission free; open permanently), a scattered collection of historic buildings and brightly painted farming equipment, carts and buggies.

The hospitable **Wellshot Hotel** (☎ 4658 2106; fax 4658 3926; Landsborough Hwy; camp/caravan sites $5/10, s/d $20/40) is a charming little historic hotel with an eclectic assortment of memorabilia, clean, simple rooms out the back and a camping ground next door. The hotel also serves good country-style meals.

Barcaldine
☎ 07 / pop 1496

Barcaldine (bar-*call*-din), at the junction of the Landsborough and Capricorn Hwys 107km east of Longreach, gained a place in Australian history in 1891 when it became the headquarters of a major shearers' strike. The confrontation led to the formation of the Australian Workers' Party, now the Australian Labor Party (ALP). The **Tree of Knowledge**, a ghost gum near the train station, was the organisers' meeting place and stands as a monument to workers and their rights. The **visitors centre** (☎ 4651 1724; www .barcaldine.qld.gov.au; Oak St; ⏰ 8.15am-4.30pm) is beside the train station, and Internet access is available at the **library** (☎ 4651 1170; 71 Ash St).

Barcaldine's **Australian Workers Heritage Centre** (☎ 4651 2422; Ash St; adult/child/family $11/6.50/28; ⏰ 9am-5pm Mon-Sat, from 10am Sun) is one of the outback's most impressive attractions, and was built to commemorate the role of workers in forming Australian social, political and industrial movements. Set in landscaped gardens, the centre's excellent displays include a circular theatre-tent, an old one-teacher schoolhouse and a replica of Queensland's Legislative Assembly. Its newest exhibition, 'Women in Australia's Working History', is dedicated to the normally unsung heroes of working life.

Mad Mick's Funny Farm (☎ 4651 1172; 84 Pine St; adult/child $10/6; ⏰ most mornings Apr-Oct) is a ramshackle farmlet with historic buildings, a fauna park, art studios, a doll collection, and billy tea and damper. The admission price includes smoko.

SLEEPING & EATING
Shakespeare Hotel (☎ 4651 1610; shakehtl@ tpg.com.au; 95 Oak St; s/d $18/35) Polished boards, tidy, bright rooms and good hosts make this among the best choices of accommodation in town.

Homestead Caravan Park (☎ /fax 4651 1308; 24 Box St; camp/caravan sites $10/17, cabins from $40) Behind the Ampol petrol station, this neat, friendly camping ground puts on free billy tea and damper, in the late afternoon, for guests. Cabins are equipped with air-con, TV and fridge.

Barcaldine also has several decent motels and B&Bs.

Witch's Kitchen (☎ 4651 2269; 61 Oak St; meals $6-18) This pleasant, imaginatively titled little bistro at the Union Hotel serves tasty, generous-portion dishes straight from the cauldron.

Blackall
☎ 07 / pop 1404

South of Barcaldine is Blackall, supposedly the site of the mythical black stump (the imaginary marker of the extent of civilisation). Information on the town and the surrounding area is available from the **visitors centre** (☎ 4657 4637; www.blackall.qld.gov.au; Short St; ⏰ 9am-5pm). The **Blackall Woolscour** (☎ 4657 4637; Evora Rd; adult/child $9.90/5.50; ⏰ 8am-4pm May-Nov, by appointment only Dec-Apr), 4km northeast, is the only steam-driven scour (wool cleaner) left in Queensland. Built in 1908, the scour operated until 1978, and has now been fully restored to do what it does best – get rid of sheep dags. Steam-engine train rides are available from May to September.

In the centre of town on Shamrock St, the **Jackie Howe Memorial Statue** is a tribute to the legendary shearer from Warwick.

CHARLEVILLE
☎ 07 / pop 3519

As far as this part of the outback is concerned, Charleville is a veritable city, and has been since its settlement. The town was an important centre for early explorers, Cobb & Co had their largest coach-making factory based here and Qantas' first paying passenger flight took to the skies from Charleville, bound for Cloncurry. Being on the Warrego River, Charleville is something of an oasis.

There's a **visitors centre** (☎ 4654 3057; www.murweh.qld.gov.au; Sturt St; ⏰ 8.30am-5pm Apr-Oct, 9am-5pm Mon-Fri Nov-Mar) on the southern edge of town. The **Charleville library** (☎ 4654 1296; 69 Edward St) has Internet access.

At the Meteorological Bureau, 4km south of the visitors centre, is the newly renovated **Cosmos Centre** (☎ 4654 3057; www.cosmoscentre.com; off Airport Dr; adult/child/family $15/12/35; ⊙ 10am-6pm, observation show-times vary). Here you can tour the sky with an expert guide as you look through high-powered telescopes, including a telescope aboard the Hubble satellite. There's also a bunch of interactive space exhibits for young and old.

Southeast of the visitors centre, the **QPWS office** (☎ 4654 1255; Park St; ⊙ 8.30am-4.30pm Mon-Fri) operates a small **captive-breeding program** where you can see several endangered species, including the yellow-footed rock wallaby and the bilby.

SLEEPING & EATING

There are a couple of caravan parks and motels scattered around town.

Hotel Corones (☎ 4654 1022; bigpub@growzone .com.au; 33 Wills St; s/tw $25/50; s/tw motel units $59/69; ⊠) One of Queensland's grand old country pubs, Corones has a charmingly preserved interior and dozens of comfortable pub rooms upstairs, only the cheapest of which don't have air-con.

Poppa's Coffee Shop (dishes around $8) In the Hotel Corones bar, this place is reminiscent of a good city street-café, with cheap lunches and dinners, and open doors spilling a lively atmosphere out into the night.

THE CHANNEL COUNTRY

The remote and sparsely populated southwestern corner of Queensland, bordering the NT, South Australia (SA) and NSW, takes its name from the myriad channels that crisscross it. The summer heat is unbearable, so a visit is best made in winter (May to September).

In this inhospitable region it hardly ever rains, but water from the monsoon further north pours into the Channel Country along the Georgina, Hamilton and Diamantina Rivers and Cooper Creek. The mass of water floods towards the great depression of Lake Eyre in SA, eventually drying up in water holes or saltpans en route. Only rarely (the early 1970s, 1989, 1995, 2000 and again in 2001) does the water reach Lake Eyre and fill it.

For a short period after each wet season, the Channel Country becomes fertile, and cattle are grazed here.

GETTING THERE & AROUND

Some roads from the east and north to the fringes of the Channel Country are sealed, but during the October to May wet season even these can be cut off, while dirt roads become quagmires. Visiting this area requires a sturdy vehicle (4WD if you want to get off the beaten track) and some outback driving experience. Always carry plenty of drinking water and petrol, and if you're heading off the main roads notify the police.

The main road through this area is the **Diamantina Developmental Rd**. It runs south from Mt Isa through Boulia to Bedourie, then east through Windorah and Quilpie to Charleville. It's a long and lonely 1340km, about two-thirds of which is sealed.

Mt Isa to Birdsville

It's 295km of sealed road from Mt Isa south to Boulia, and the only facilities along the route are at **Dajarra**, which has a pub and a roadhouse.

Boulia

☎ 07 / pop 290

Boulia is the 'capital' of the Channel Country, and home to a mysterious supernatural phenomenon known as the **Min Min Light**, an 'earthbound UFO' resembling car headlights that hovers a metre or so above the ground before vanishing and reappearing elsewhere.

The **Min Min Encounter complex** (☎ 4746 3386; bouliamin@bigpond.com; Herbert St; adult/child/family $12/7.70/28; ⊙ 8.30am-5pm Mon-Fri, from 9am Sat & Sun) has an hourly show that attempts to convert nonbelievers with sophisticated robotics, imaginative sets and eerie lighting and effects. It's well worth a visit. The complex is also the town's visitors centre.

The Boulia **Camel Races**, held mid-July, is among Australia's largest. Free camp sites are provided for the festival.

The modern, spacious **Desert Sands Motel** (☎ 4746 3000; fax 4746 3040; Herbert St; s/d $80/90; ⊠) is the town's more indulgent accommodation option. The units come with tea- and coffee-making facilities.

There's also a pub with decent rooms and food.

The sealed Kennedy Developmental Rd runs east from Boulia, 369km to Winton. The **Middleton Hotel** (☎ /fax 4657 3980; Kennedy Developmental Rd; s/d $30/45), 168km before Winton, is the only fuel stop en route. The hotel serves meals daily and rents out simple dongas with shared facilities.

Bedourie
☎ 07 / pop 120

From Boulia it's 200km of mainly unsealed road south to Bedourie, the administrative centre for the huge Diamantina Shire Council.

Royal Hotel (☎ 4746 1201; fax 4746 1101; Herbert St; s/d $55/65; ❸) Built in 1880, the charming Royal Hotel is an adobe brick building with two stone-built motel-style units out the back, which are clean, tidy and comfy.

There's also a caravan park and fairly expensive motel units at the friendly **Simpson Desert Oasis** (☎ 4746 1291; simpsondesertoasis@big pond.com.au; Herbert St; camp/caravan sites $2/16, units $90-95; ❸), which incorporates a fuel stop, supermarket and restaurant.

Birdsville
☎ 07 / pop 120

This tiny settlement is the most remote place in Queensland, and therefore one of the most remote in Australia, and possesses one of the country's most famous pubs: the Birdsville Hotel. Only 12km from the SA border, Birdsville is at the northern end of the 517km **Birdsville Track**, which leads to Marree in SA. In the late 19th century, Birdsville was quite a busy place as the customs collection point for cattle driven south across the border via the Birdsville Track. A customs charge was levied for each head of cattle leaving Queensland through the town. With Federation, the charge was abolished and Birdsville became a near ghost town. In recent years a thriving cattle industry and growing tourism profile have revitalised the town. Its big event is the annual **Birdsville Races** on the first weekend in September, which attracts up to 6500 racing and boozing enthusiasts.

Birdsville gets its water from a 1219m-deep artesian well, which delivers the water at over 100°C.

Tourist information is available from the **Wirrarri Centre** (☎ 4656 3300; www.diamantina .qld.gov.au; Billabong Blvd; ☽ 8.30am-6pm Mar-Oct, 8.30am-4.30pm Mon-Fri Nov-Feb). The centre also provides Internet access.

Don't miss the **Birdsville Working Museum** (☎ 4656 3259; Macdonald St; adult/child/family $7/5/20; ☽ 8am-5pm Mar-Oct, tours 9am, 11am & 3pm). Inside this big tin shed is one of the most impressive private museums in Australia, with a fascinating collection of drover's gear, shearing equipment, wool presses and much more.

There are banking and postal facilities at **Birdsville Fuel Service** (☎ 4656 3236; Adelaide St; ☽ 7am-6pm), and the town also has another roadhouse, a hospital and a caravan park.

Dating back to 1884, the famous **Birdsville Hotel** (☎ 4656 3244; birdsvillehotel@bigpond.com.au; Adelaide St; s/d $80/100; ❸) faces resolutely into the Simpson Desert, having survived fire and cyclone. Tastefully renovated, it has modern motel-style units out the back, and serves lunch and dinner in its licensed restaurant. Busiest night at the hotel is Friday, when locals crowd the bar for happy hour and the weekly 'chook raffle'.

Birdsville Track
To the south, the Birdsville Track passes between the **Simpson Desert** to the west and **Sturt's Stony Desert** to the east. The first stretch from Birdsville has two routes, but only the longer, more easterly Outside Track is open these days. It crosses sandy country at the edge of the desert. Contact Birdsville's **Wirrarri Centre** (☎ 07-4656 3300) for road conditions, and keep friends and relatives informed of your movements.

Simpson Desert National Park
About 80km west of Birdsville, the waterless Simpson Desert National Park is Queensland's biggest national park at 10,000 sq km. Conventional cars can tackle the Birdsville Track quite easily, but the Simpson requires a 4WD and far more preparation. Official advice is that crossings should only be tackled by parties of at least two 4WD vehicles, and that you should have a radio to call for help if necessary. Alternatively, you can hire a satellite phone from **Birdsville police** (☎ 07-4656 3220) for $23 a day, which can be returned to Oodnadatta police in SA. Permits are required to traverse the park, and are available from the Birdsville **QPWS office** (☎ 07-4656 3272/3249; cnr Billabong Blvd & Jardine St), or from the town's petrol stations. For more information, contact the QPWS in Birdsville or Longreach (☎ 07-4652 7333). For the park's SA sections, you need a separate permit, available through the **South Australian National Parks & Wildlife Service** (☎ 1800 816 078).

Birdsville to Charleville

The Birdsville Developmental Rd heads east from Birdsville, meeting the Diamantina Developmental Rd after 268km of rough gravel and sand – watch out for cattle grids and sudden dips at the many dry creek crossings. **Betoota**, the sole 'town' between Birdsville and Windorah, closed in late 1997, meaning motorists have to carry enough fuel to cover the 395km distance.

Windorah is either very dry or very wet. The town's general store sells fuel and groceries. The pub offers motel units, self-contained cabins and a small camping ground. **Quilpie** is an opal-mining town and the railhead from which cattle are transported to the coast. It has a good range of facilities, including a **visitors centre** (☎ 07-4656 2166; Brolga St; ☷ 8am-5pm Mon-Fri, 9am-3.30pm Sat, 10am-4.30pm Sun mid-Apr–Oct, 8am-5pm Mon-Fri Nov–mid-Apr), two pubs, a motel, a caravan park and several petrol stations. From here it's another 210km to Charleville.

South of Quilpie and west of Cunnamulla are the remote **Yowah Opal Fields** and the town of **Eulo**, which co-hosts the World Lizard Racing Championships with Cunnamulla in late August. **Thargomindah**, 130km west of Eulo, has a couple of motels and a guest house. From Thargomindah camel trains used to cross to Bourke in NSW. **Noccundra**, another 140km further west, was once a busy little community. It now has only a hotel and a population of eight. If you have a 4WD you can continue west to Innamincka, in SA, on the Strzelecki Track, via the site of the famous **Dig Tree**, where Burke and Wills camped in their ill-fated 1860–61 expedition (see p741 for more information).

WHITSUNDAY COAST

It's time to get wet. Whether you're lazing on a yacht or skimming shallow reefs with mask and snorkel, you'll still wish you had aqualungs and a lifetime to explore the exotic Great Barrier Reef Marine Park beneath these irresistible waters. The Whitsunday Coast is Queensland's water-sports playground and Airlie Beach, its capital. If only it weren't for those life-threatening jellyfish; damn 'stingers'. Get used to the idea of wearing a stinger safety suit from

October to May; it's better protection than Factor 30 sunscreen.

There are tremendous opportunities for bush camping and rainforest walks, but luxuriating in the Whitsunday Island resorts is always a respectable alternative.

MACKAY

☎ 07 / pop 74,000

Pretty Mackay has a vibrant café and bar scene among its lush, palm-lined streets. At sunset squillions of rainbow lorikeets chatter madly in the town's trees; it's the best live entertainment around. The Mackay area offers some terrific Aussie back-to-bush experiences, scenery and walks, but you'll need a car to make the most of them. It's the access point for Pioneer Valley and Eungella National Park west of the town, Cape Hillsborough National Park to the north, Brampton and Carlisle Islands, as well as the Great Barrier Reef. Port Mackay boasts the world's largest sugar-loading terminal.

Orientation

The blue Pioneer River wends its way through Mackay with the town settled on its southern side. Victoria St is the main strip, on which restaurants, cafés and bars cluster. The long-distance bus station is fairly central, on the corner of Victoria and Macalister Sts, while the train station and airport are about 6km south of the city centre, signposted from the Bruce Hwy.

Information

Paper Chain (☎ 4953 1331; 8a Sydney St) Huge, musty, second-hand bookshop.
Internet Cafe (☎ 4953 3188; Bazaar Arcade, 128 Victoria St)
Mackay visitors centre (☎ 4952 2677; www .mackayregion.com; 320 Nebo Rd; ☷ 8.30am-5pm Mon-Fri, 9am-4pm Sat & Sun) Head 3km south of the city.
QPWS (☎ 4944 7800; www.epa.qld.gov.au; cnr Wood & River Sts) Has plans to relocate; ask at either visitors centre.
RACQ (☎ 4957 2918; 214 Victoria St)
Town Hall visitors centre (☎ 4951 4803; 63 Sydney St; ☷ 8.30am-5pm Mon-Fri, 9am-4pm Sat & Sun)

Sights

If you have a few days and transport, some top sights and adventures are one to two hours away; see p364 for details.

Mackay Marina, on Harbour Rd, is becoming a groovy spot to dine and hang out. You

Charter a boat and sail the Whitsunday Islands via the glorious gateway of **Airlie Beach** (p372)

RICHARD I'ANSON

Bushwalk the **Thorsborne Trail** (p388)

JOHN BANAGAN

BOB CHARLTON

Watch the turtles do their thing at **Mon Repos** (p333)

Dive among the spectacular coral of the **Great Barrier Reef** (p344)

LEONARD DOUGLAS ZELL

WAYNE W

Laze some days away on the iridescent white sand of Fitzroy Island's **Nudey Beach** (p407)

BOB CHARLTON

Watch for majestic humpback whales around **Hervey Bay** (p323)

Take a scenic flight over the indigo gardens around the **Whitsunday Islands** (p370)

JOHN BA

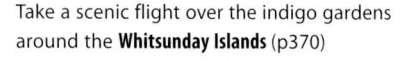

WAYNE WALTON

Chill out on the palm-fringed sands of **Mission Beach** (p389)

can picnic here or walk along the break water for a surreal view of the sugar-loading terminal. **Harbour Beach**, next to it, is the best swimming close to town, but further north is **Bucasia Beach**, a glorious stretch for swimming and long walks, and there's a caravan park for holiday-makers. Also up here, between **Blacks Beach** and **Dolphin Heads**, is the **Eimeo Hotel** (☎ 4954 6106; Mango Ave; 🕑 lunch noon-2pm, dinner 6-8pm), a hilltop pub with brilliant Coral Sea views that's perfect for relaxed drinks, although counter meals are average. Mackay Transit Coaches putters up here.

Illawong Fauna Sanctuary (☎ 4959 1777; illawong sanctuary@bigpond.com; Eungella Rd, Mirani; adult/child $13/7, half-day tour $60; 🕑 9am-6.30pm) is a relaxed place for families and overseas visitors to check out native animals. Because it's a sanctuary for sick critters, many of them are given names and some 'perform' for their carers; check out the barking owl! Feeding times are best (crocodiles 2.15pm, koalas 3pm). It's about 43km west of Mackay, but half-day tours include transfers.

Tours

Farleigh Sugar Mill (☎ 4963 2700; Armstrong St, Farleigh; adult/child/family $16/9/38; 🕑 1-3pm Mon-Fri Jun-Dec) It's worth seeing how much sweat and grind goes into satisfying your sweet tooth. These tours explore the process from harvest to cane train. It's extremely hot and noisy in the mill, with lots of stairs to climb, and visitors must wear enclosed shoes, long-sleeved shirts and pants. Farleigh Mill is 10km northwest of Mackay. Tours begin from the car park.

Beyond Mackay's sugar cane sea are superb rainforest experiences and platypus spotting. **Reeforest Adventure Tours** (☎ 4959 8360, 1800 500 353; www.reeforest.com; day trip adult/children/YHA $115/65/95) runs several 'eco' day trips, including tremendous 'Forest Flying' (p364), and does camping drop-offs to Eungella and Cape Hillsborough National Parks and Finch Hatton Gorge. **Jungle Johno Tours** (☎ 4951 3728; larrikin@mackay.net.au; day trip per adult from $80) offers day trips to Eungella. Other recommendations:

Pro Dive (☎ 4951 1150; www.prodivemackay.com; 44 Evans Ave; courses from $195) Explore the 125-year-old Llewellyn shipwreck.

Mackay Water Taxis (☎ 4942 7372; Mackay Marina) Deep-sea fishing ($155) or snorkelling ($135).

Seaquest Luxury Sailing Holidays (☎ 4946 6038; www.seaquest.com.au; day trips $180) Swanky sailing on a $2 million yacht; includes snorkelling.

Sleeping
BUDGET

Weary budget motels line the 3km southern approach to the city centre on Nebo Rd, but tongues are wagging about new backpacker accommodation coming to town (ask at the visitors centre).

MidCity Motor Inn (☎ 4951 1666; midcitymotorinn mackay@bigpond.com; 2 Macalister St; d from $85; 🐾) There's a lovely palm-fringed outdoor pool area at this tidy little Inn located in a quiet spot by the river. It's a short walk to the town centre and the rooms have bright, welcoming décor. The best backpackers in town is **YHA Larrikin Lodge** (☎ 4951 3728; www.yha.com.au; 32 Peel St; dm/d $17/40). There's nothing 'larrikin' about these modern rooms or the large, shady outdoor area. Jungle Johno Tours (see above) is based here.

A little out of the action are **Beach Tourist Park** (☎ 4957 4021; 8 Petrie St, Illawong Beach; camp/ caravan sites $16/22, cabins from $60) on the bus No 1 line and **Central Tourist Park** (☎ 4957 6141; 15 Malcomson St, North Mackay; camp/caravan sites $13/ 16, cabins from $28), accessible by bus No 5/6.

MID-RANGE

There's a bunch of unique accommodation options around Mackay (see also p364).

Whitsunday Waters Resort (☎ 4954 9666, 1800 075 088; www.whitsundaywaters.com.au; Beach Rd, Dolphin Heads; d from $95; 🐾 🖵) This relaxed resort's carefree mood makes these motel-style units appealing – request ocean views to complete the experience. Munch on the wild side at the candlelit restaurant where specialities include crocodile salad and grilled kangaroo.

Illawong Beach Resort (☎ 4957 8427; www .illawong-beach.com.au; 73 Illawong Dr, Illawong Beach; self-contained units $120; 🐾) It's more casual here and grounds are neat as a pin rather than lush tropical. Moody Muddies Restaurant is a classy end to your breezy beach days, and prices include a hot/cold buffet breakfast. The resort does airport pick-ups, or take Bus No 1 to Petrie St.

Shakespeare International Motel (☎ 4969 0200, 1800 075 057; fax 4957 3826; 309 Shakespeare St; d $112; 🐾) About 10 minutes' walk into town, enjoy the queen-size beds and tasty restaurant meals here.

QUEENSLAND

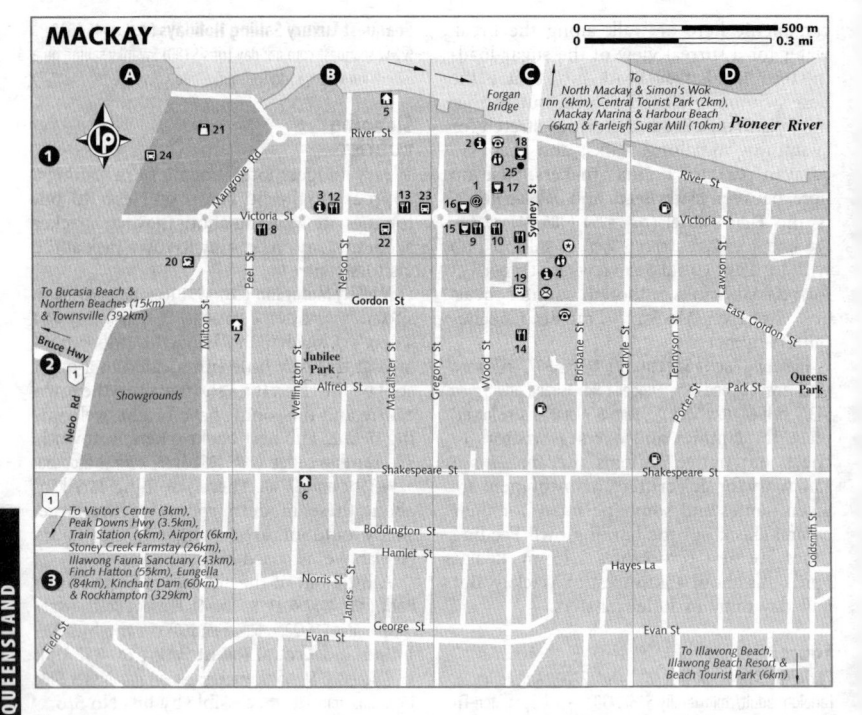

MACKAY

Eating

Kevin's Place (☎ 4953 5835; cnr Victoria & Wood Sts; mains $18-23; ☼ closed Sun) The colonnaded balcony of Kevin's Place oozes *Gone with the Wind* charm. This heritage-listed building with its ornate, classical revival architecture tops off a fabulous Singapore- or Malay-style meal. Locals rave about the $35 banquet or try the five spices calamari and prawns. Lunch is great value at $7. Bookings are advised.

Simon's Wok Inn (☎ 4942 0601; Mt Pleasant Plaza, Nth Mackay; mains $17-25; ☼ dinner only, closed Sun & Mon) Healthy, stir-fried meals are deliciously flavoured with fresh herbs and spices and served piping hot with excellent sticky rice. It's BYO, but there's a bottle shop next door. Alfresco dining is odd – on the edge of the plaza car park. Alternatively, eat in. Bookings advised.

Sorbello's Italian Restaurant (☎ 4957 8300; 166b Victoria St; mains $8-19) You'll enjoy the excellent wine and beer list here, not to mention creamy $5 cocktails. Sorbello's has relaxed, friendly service, and besides the usual Italian fare, the wood-fired piz-

zas are especially yum, with thin crusts and quality toppings. Pity the tables are pygmy size. Bookings advised.

Sedgies Gourmet Coffee House (☎ 4957 4845; cnr Nelson & Victoria Sts; meals $8-14) Sedgies does excellent sandwiches on speciality breads, plus salads, hot spuds, cakes and breakfast, too. You've got to try the coffee and tea – with over 40 varieties – served in a special mug and hot till the last drop.

There are plenty of cafés in town, although their menus and décor offer few points of difference. Other recommendations:

Coco's Bar & Grill (☎ 4951 3288; Austral Hotel, cnr Peel & Victoria Sts; dishes $14-22) Locals say, 'best steaks in town'.

Low Fat Cafe Pure & Natural (☎ 4957 6136; Sydney St; dishes $5-9) Tempting, low-fat – eat twice as much!

Kebab House (☎ 4944 0393; cnr Victoria & Wood Sts; dishes $5-8; ☼ 11am-5am Fri-Sun) Fast and cheap.

Supermarket (☎ 4957 6569; 78 Sydney St)

Drinking & Entertainment

Platinum Lounge (☎ 4957 2220; cnr Victoria & Wood Sts) Platinum Lounge is upstairs in an Art Deco–style building with an equally attractive interior and whiff of sophistication. Balconies overlooking the street are just made for early evening drinks; think Havana, Cuba. Depending on the night in question, Platinum is the place for pool, live music, DJs or karaoke.

Molloys Irish Bar (☎ 4957 7737; 148 Victoria St) Of course it's cosy with a cheerful atmosphere, it's an Irish pub! But it's more authentic than most, and quite large, with comforting snack food and live music most nights. There's great memorabilia for the culturally inclined Guinness drinker.

Gordi's Cafe & Bar (☎ 4951 2611; 85 Victoria St) Gordi's is an easy-going backpacker hangout. It has a beer-swilling, jungle-bar kind of atmosphere that cruises during the day and gets bouncy by night. Live music, loud patrons and karaoke nights are staples here, and there's a nightclub upstairs.

Other recommendations:

Main Street (☎ 4957 7737; 148 Victoria St; admission $5; ☯ closed Mon-Wed) Above Molloys, R&B, retro, dance.

McGuire's Hotel (☎ 4957 7464; 17 Wood St) Live music.

Spotted Dick (☎ 4957 2368; 2 Sydney St) Live music.
BC Cinemas (☎ 4942 4066; 30 Gordon St)

Getting There & Away
Travelworld (☎ 4944 2144, 1800 633 241; bookings@ mkytworld.com.au; cnr Victoria & Macalister Sts) handles all transport arrangements and is located at the bus station where a 24-hour café also sells bus tickets.

AIR
Qantas (☎ 13 13 13) flights can be booked at Travelworld. One week advance-purchase fares (prices quoted here are for adult one-way fares) from Mackay cost: $145 to Brisbane, $295 to Townsville, $345 to Cairns and $133 to Rockhampton.

Hamilton Island Aviation (☎ 4946 8249) has return flights to Hamilton Island for $240. **Island Air Taxis** (☎ 4946 9933) also flies to Hamilton Island ($120).

BUS
McCafferty's/Greyhound (☎ 13 20 30; www.mccaffertys.com.au) and **Premier Motor Service** (☎ 13 34 10; www.premierms.com.au) can shuttle you from Mackay to Cairns (McCafferty's/Premier $100/95 per adult, 12 hours), Townsville ($70/59, 6 hours), Airlie Beach ($35/19, 2 hours) and Brisbane ($130/109, 16 hours). Both leave from the **bus station** (☎ 4944 2144; cnr Victoria & Macalister Sts; ☯ 24hr).

TRAIN
The **Sunlander** (☎ 4952 7418) runs from Brisbane to Cairns via Mackay. An economy/1st-class sleeper to/from Brisbane costs $175/260 per adult (18 hours); a seat to/from Cairns costs $105 (14 hours). The train station is at Paget, 5km south of the city centre.

Getting Around
Rental-car companies **Budget** (☎ 4951 1400), **Avis** (☎ 4951 1266) and **Hertz** (☎ 4951 4685) have counters at the airport. Car hire costs from $70 per day.

Mackay Transit Coaches (☎ 4957 3330) operates local bus services from two bus stops in town: at the back of Canelands Shopping Centre, and from the corner of Victoria and Gregory Sts, outside Centrelink. The visitors centre has timetables.

Mackay Taxis (☎ 131 008) from the city centre to the airport, marina or train station cost about $12.

QUEENSLAND

AROUND MACKAY
Pioneer Valley

You're missing a great country Queensland experience if you don't spend a couple of days enjoying the sights west of Mackay.

The Eungella Rd takes you through fertile **Pioneer Valley** to Marian, where you can turn off to **Kinchant Dam** and the **Kinchant Waters Leisure Resort** (☎ 07-4954 1453; Kinchant Dam Rd, Mirani; camp/caravan sites $10/24, self-contained units $75), which is about 60km west of Mackay. This super-casual resort has oodles of space to play and is ideal for families. You can hire canoes and aqua bikes or watch the fun from the so-laid-back-it's-falling-over outdoor café.

Head out of Mackay 10km on the Peak Downs Hwy to the Eungella Rd turn-off. Drive 29km along the Eungella Rd to Marian, take the Eton turn-off, driving 10km to North Eton. Turn right at Kinchant Dam Rd by the large chimney. It's 8km to the dam.

THE AUTHOR'S CHOICE

Readers rave about **Stoney Creek Farmstay** (☎ 07-4954 1177; www.stoneycreek.webcentral .com.au; Peak Downs Hwy; dm $20, cottage $120) and it's no wonder with these hospitable owners. The farm offers a rare bush experience of horse riding ($60), cattle mustering ($65), and billy tea and damper 'smokos'. A beautifully crafted cedar cottage for two has a quaint veranda and intriguing inside toilet. Shower in the open air or stroll to your private swimming hole. The backpacker bunkhouse is basic, but a good-value three-day package ($240) includes meals and activities. A bus from **Shell City Cabs petrol station** (☎ 07-4944 4922; cnr Victoria & Tennyson Sts, Mackay; $12) heads 28km southwest of Mackay to the pick-up point.

Alternatively, from Marian continue along the Eungella Rd to Mirani and visit the **Illawong Fauna Sanctuary** (p361). Further along, park at the **Pinnacle Hotel** (☎ 07-4958 5207; Mackay-Eungella Rd, Pinnacle) and chomp down a genuine Australian meat pie – all 220g of it.

Next stop, **Finch Hatton Gorge**. The gorge turn-off is 1.5km before the township of Finch Hatton. It's 9km into the gorge and the last 3km are on good, unsealed roads,

but after heavy rain creek crossings make access difficult or impossible.

At the gorge you can go **Forest Flying** (☎ 07-4958 3359; www.forestflying.com; Finch Hatton; $45). You want to do this. Yes, you do. Flyers whizz around the rainforest canopy sitting in a harness attached to a 340m-long cable. Keep your eyes peeled for rainforest critters as you brush through palm leaves and swing by the fruit bat colony (seasonal August to May). Definitely book ahead.

More tranquil pursuits at the gorge include a 1.6km rainforest walk to a fantastic swimming hole beneath **Araluen Falls**, or a 2.6km walking trail to the **Wheel of Fire Falls**, and picnics at the car park. You can stay at **Finch Hatton Gorge Cabins** (☎ 07-4958 3281; camp sites $6, dm/d $19/80), set in enchanting subtropical surrounds, or there's the bush basic-but-fun-loving **Platypus Bushcamp** (☎ 07-4958 3204; www.bushcamp.net; camp sites $8, huts s/d $20/60) with its own swimming hole and platypus viewing.

Back on the road to Eungella, Finch Hatton is a teensy township, but the **Criterion Hotel** (☎ 07-4958 3252; s/d $20/30) has country pub character, or try **Finch Hatton Caravan Park** (☎ 07-4958 3222; finchparkau@yahoo.com.au; camp/ caravan sites $15/36).

A further 20km and you reach beautiful **Eungella National Park** (*young*-gulla), meaning 'Land of Clouds'. Eungella has the oldest and longest stretch of subtropical rainforest in Australia and has been cut off from other rainforest areas for roughly 30,000 years. It breeds weird beasties that exist nowhere else, such as the Eungella gastric brooding frog, which incubates its eggs in its stomach and gives birth by spitting out the tadpoles! Charming.

There are excellent rainforest walks signposted on the 5km road between Eungella township and Broken River, but it's the shy platypus you'll hope to see. They live at pretty **Broken River**. You can be fairly sure of seeing platypuses most days from the viewing platform near the bridge. The best times are immediately after dawn and at dusk, but you must be patient, still and silent. Rangers lead night walks that reveal the park's party animals.

Sleeping and eating options are limited. **Broken River Mountain Retreat** (☎ 074958 4528; www.brokenrivermr.com.au; cabins from $70) has modern cabins and an attractive, wood-finished lounge and restaurant. The retreat is set in manicured lawns, near the platypus-viewing platform. Or there's the lovely QPWS **Fern Flat Campground** (☎ 07-4958 4552; Broken River; per person/family $4/16), run on a first-come, first-served basis, near the **ranger's office** (☎ 07-4958 4552; ☽ 8am-4pm) and kiosk.

Back at Eungella township, **Eungella Chalet** (☎ 07-4958 4509; d $55-80) is a tired, old guesthouse with a dining room and bar, but it has arresting views of Pioneer Valley. **Hideaway Cafe** (☎ 07-4958 4533; ☽ 8am-4pm) has scrumptious home-made food and the eccentric but utterly enchanting **Suzanne's Magical Garden**. **Eungella General Store** (☎ 07-4958 4520; ☽ 8am-6.30pm) has tasty café meals, groceries and fuel.

GETTING THERE & AWAY
Buses don't cover Finch Hatton or Eungella, but some organised tours do camping drop-offs (see p361 for more information). Otherwise, hire a car; you won't be sorry.

Cape Hillsborough National Park
All cliffs, dunes, scrub, rainforest and secluded woodland, there's little to do here but relax and hang out with kangaroos on the beach or spot turtles. This small coastal park, 54km north of Mackay, takes in 300m-high Cape Hillsborough and nearby Andrews Point and Wedge Island, which are joined by a causeway at low tide. There are three short walking tracks and a rangers' office on the foreshore next to a lovely picnic area. Visitors can get information from the Cape Hillsborough Nature Resort (see following) or the Mackay **QPWS** (☎ 4944 7800).

Cape Hillsborough Nature Resort (☎ 4959 0152; www.capehillsboroughresort.com.au; camp sites/cabins/d $13/80/85) is very low-key, with friendly owners, wandering wildlife and a small restaurant. Bush meets ocean at the grassy, QPWS **Smalleys Beach Campground** (☎ 4959 0410; Smalleys Beach; per person/family $4/16). Register on-site.

The Cumberland Islands
Brampton and Carlisle are the most popular island destinations of this group, 32km northeast of Mackay. Both are mountainous national parks, joined by a sandbank, which you can wade across when its low tide (about 20m). The islands have forested slopes, sandy beaches, OK walks and fringing coral reefs with great snorkelling.

Brampton Island Resort (☎ 4951 4499, 1800 737 678; www.poresorts.com/brampton; s/d $325/430) Brampton is popular with couples and honeymooners, but children are not particularly catered for. Marine Helicopters runs a 15-minute transfer service from Mackay (adult $188 return), or there's a daily launch service from Mackay ($92 return). Contact the resort to organise transfers.

Carlisle Island is uninhabited, but there is a QPWS **camping ground** at Southern Bay, directly across from the Brampton Island Resort. You must be self-sufficient and bring your own water, but there is a free gas barbecue, toilet and picnic shelter here. Campers can take the Brampton ferry, but it costs another $15 by dinghy to Carlisle if the tide is too high to wade across.

If you want real Robinson Crusoe, self-sufficient–style camping, ask the **QPWS** (☎ 4944 7800; www.epa.qld.gov.au) about Scawfell and Goldsmith Islands. Permits can be purchased at the website www.smartservice.qld .gov.au/AQ/ or by calling ☎ 13 13 04.

AIRLIE BEACH
☎ 07 / pop 3030
Airlie is a jumping resort town and gateway to the Whitsunday Islands. While backpackers arrive in busloads with plans for a lazy Whitsunday sail or fish-in-your-face dive, yachties and local holiday-makers are also lured by its bounteous pleasure-boating. There's an excellent range of accommodation, loads of good eateries and a loud, lively nightlife.

Nearly everything of importance lies along Shute Harbour Rd, the town's main artery, and although Airlie doesn't have any great beaches, a glorious artificial lagoon, right on the foreshore, more than makes up for it. It's free, and open 24 hours. Whether you plan to sail, dive, snorkel or day-trip to the islands, there's a bamboozling number of options so be prepared to wade through them. Most boats to the islands leave from Shute Harbour, 21km east of Airlie Beach, or from the Abel Point Marina, which is 1.5km southwest. Whale-watching boat trips between July and September are another attraction.

Information
Airlie Beach visitors centre (☎ 4946 6665, 1800 819 366; abtic@whitsunday.net.au; 277 Shute Harbour Rd; ☽ 7.30am-8pm) Opposite Beaches Backpackers.

Airlie Waterfront Travel (☎ 4948 1302, 1800 464 000; 6 The Esplanade; ⏰ 6.45am-8pm) For Internet access.

QPWS (☎ 4946 7022; www.epa.qld.gov.au; cnr Shute Harbour & Mandalay Rds; ⏰ 9am-5pm Mon-Fri, 9am-1pm Sat) 6km past Airlie towards Shute Harbour.

Tourism Whitsundays visitors centre (☎ 4945 3711, 1800 801 252; www.whitsundaytourism.com; ⏰ 9am-5pm Mon-Sat, 10am-5pm Sun) On the Bruce Hwy at Proserpine.

Activities

Sailing opportunities are plenty (see the boxed text 'Sailing the Whitsunday Islands'; p372 for details).

Straddle a quad bike (a four-wheeled motorcycle) and go mental at top speed (if you dare) on over 10km of purpose-built adventure track with **Quad Bike Bush Adventures** (☎ 4946 1020; www.bushadventures.com.au; 385 Sugarloaf Rd, Sugarloaf; from $70). The company also runs outdoor laser skirmish combat games in the jungle ($55). It's the same as paintball but without the bruises. You can do both for $155, which includes transfers.

Salty Dog Sea Kayaking (☎ 4946 1388; www.salty dog.com.au; half-/full-day tours $50/$90) runs sea-kayaking tours from Shute Harbour with a swim and snorkel thrown in. Or you can skim the glorious green marine on your own in a rental kayak, from $40. Otherwise, Salty Dog and **Aussie Sea Kayak Company** (☎ 0407-049 747) both operate extended sea-kayaking tours that include camping on

AIRLIE BEACH

INFORMATION	
Airlie Beach Visitors Centre	1 B2
Airlie Waterfront Travel	2 C2

SIGHTS & ACTIVITIES	
Newsagent	3 B2
Oceania Dive	4 A2
Pro Dive	5 A2

SLEEPING	⌂ pp367-8
Airlie Beach Hotel	6 C2
Airlie Beach Motor Lodge	7 A2
Airlie Waterfront B&B	8 A1
Backpackers by the Bay	9 D3
Boathaven Spa Resort	10 D3
Club Habitat YHA	11 C2
Magnum's Backpackers	12 B2
Sunlit Waters	13 A2
Water's Edge Luxury Apartments	14 C3
Whitsunday Moorings B&B	15 A1
Whitsunday Terraces Resort	16 C3

EATING	⌂ pp368-9
Airlie Thai	17 C2
Armada Lounge Bar & Restaurant	18 B2
Cafe Gourmet	19 B2
Chatz Bar 'n' Brasserie	20 C2
Harry's Corner	21 B2
Mangrove Jack's	22 C2
Shipwrecked Bar & Grill	23 C2
Sidewalk Cantina	24 C2
Supermarket	25 B2
Sushi Hi!	26 C2
The Juice Bar	(see 18)
Village Deli	27 B2

DRINKING	⌂ p369
Beaches	28 B2
Legends Bar 'n' Grill	29 C2
Mama Africa's	30 B2
Morocco's	31 A2
Paddy Shenanigans	32 B2

ENTERTAINMENT	⌂ p369
M@ss	(see 12)
Whitsunday Sailing Club	33 D1

TRANSPORT	pp369-70
Long Distance Bus Stop	34 D2
Whitsunday Transit Bus Stop	35 C2
Whitsunday Transit Bus Stop	36 A2

OTHER	
Maritime Safety Queensland	37 C2
UTAG Travel	38 C2
Where?What?How? Travel	39 B2

the Whitsunday Islands, all meals and gear provided, all fishy questions answered.

You could get high with **Whitsunday Parasail** (☎ 4948 0000; from $50), or there's the sensory-overload option – tandem sky diving with **Skydive Airlie Beach** (☎ 4946 9115; $250). See p369 for information on joy flights over the Whitsunday Islands and the Great Barrier Reef.

DIVING

Airlie is a hot spot for dive instruction and you'll find the options mind boggling, so clarify arrangements to avoid disappointment. Many of the day-trip or overnight sailing tours offer diving at extra cost. Some of these boats have a full-time dive instructor on board, others may transfer you to another boat for the dive. Ask how many dives the tour offers and whether they dive on the fringing reefs that surround the Whitsunday Islands or travel further to the Great Barrier Reef. Be wary of extremely cheap dive options; we have had reader reports of unstable diving equipment.

There are a number of scuba dive schools in town. Dive companies are only as good as their instructors, however, and the staff turnover is pretty high throughout the industry. Note that some courses may spend most of the time in the pool or classroom. It's worth talking to the tourist office and other backpackers to get a feel for which companies currently offer the best service.

Two large, dive-specific companies in-Airlie Beach are **Oceania Dive** (☎ 4946 6032, 1800 075 035; www.whitsundaysonline.com/oceaniadive.php; 257 Shute Harbour Rd) and **Pro Dive** (☎ 4948 1888; www.prodive.com.au; 344 Shute Harbour Rd), offering five-day open-water courses for beginners and three-day courses for certified divers on the Great Barrier Reef for between $480 and $540.

Festivals & Events

Each November, Airlie Beach parties around the **Whitsunday Wine & Food Festival** and the **Whitsunday Reef Festival** with street parades, competitions, fireworks and family activities.

Sleeping

There are plenty of backpackers along the main strip, but some need more than a lick of paint.

BUDGET

Sunlit Waters Studio Apartments (☎ 4946 6352; 20 Airlie Cres; s $70, d $70-90; 🞉) This place at the top end of town offers excellent value. Sunlit's bright, fresh studios have dazzling harbour views and one spacious studio sleeps up to five. There's a relaxed and friendly vibe around the small, azure-tiled pool and communal balcony. It's not exactly a secret either, so book ahead.

Backpackers by the Bay (☎ 4946 7267, 1800 646 994; www.backpackersbythebay.com; 12 Hermitage Dr; dm/d $20/48). It's only a five-minute walk from the centre of town to this small, relaxed and friendly hostel. It certainly has the best views of the lot with a pool overlooking Boathaven Bay, and rooms draw inspiration from serene Coral Sea tones. The kitchen is also well equipped.

Bush Village Backpackers' Resort (☎ 4946 6177, 1800 809 256; fax 4946 7227; 2 St Martin's Rd, Cannonvale; dm $25, d $50-70; 🞉 🖳) Bush Village, 2km west of Airlie, has a cosy stretch of top-notch cabins with cooking facilities, fridge, en suite and TV. There's a bar, pool and pleasant garden, and rates include breakfast, linen and towels. It's out of the action, but a courtesy bus runs into town until 11.30pm.

Other recommendations:
Club Habitat YHA (☎ 4946 6312, 1800 247 251; 394 Shute Harbour Rd; dm/d $22/54; 🞉) Central, yet quiet.
Magnum's Backpackers (☎ 4946 6266; www .magnums.com.au; Shute Harbour Rd; dm $12-15, d $37) Central, noisy, but loads of fun (see also its entry under Drinking & Entertainment; p369).
Flametree Tourist Village (☎ 4946 9388, 1800 069 388; www.flametreevillage.com.au; Shute Harbour Rd; camp/caravan sites $18/22, on-site vans $40) Bird-filled gardens, 11km east of Airlie.

MID-RANGE

Airlie Waterfront B&B (☎ 4946 7631; www.airlie waterfrontbnb.com.au; cnr Broadwater & Mazlin Sts; d from $145; 🞉) Style and attention to detail set this B&B far apart from the rest. Airlie Waterfront offers a modern approach to French Provincial charm with its lead-light windows, sandstone floors, quality linen and antique-style furniture. Fresh flowers scent each room and continental tropical breakfasts are served on your patio with views over Airlie's boat-speckled bay. There is a studio or one- and two-bedroom apartments, perfectly located within sauntering distance to the lagoon and cafés.

QUEENSLAND

Whitsunday Moorings B&B (☎ 4946 4692; www.whitsundaymooringsbb.com.au; 37 Airlie Cres; s/d $115/135; ✹) These generously sized rooms with cool, earthy interiors are set in a lush and intimate garden. Enjoy ocean views from a pool built for two or the sunset seat for lovers. Damask linen and fine china accompany a breakfast served in style.

Cane Cutters Cottage (☎ 4946 7400; www.yacht charters.com.au/cottage.htm; 4b Braithwaite Ct, Cannonvalley; d $120) About 14km out of town, this secluded historic cottage is restored with modern flair: corrugated iron, painted timber and antique features blend beautifully and it's well appointed for self-catering. Your shaded veranda overlooks tropical gardens alive with animal and bird life. There's a minimum two-night stay and bookings are required.

Whitsunday Terraces Resort (☎ 4946 6788, 1800 075 062; www.whitsundayterraces.com.au; Golden Orchid Dr, Airlie Beach; d $130; ✹) Well located, just back from Shute Harbour Rd, this casual resort has top views from each room and a cruisy restaurant and pool area, but the quality of furnishings varies. Ask to see rooms first.

Other recommendations:

Airlie Beach Hotel (☎ 4964 1999, 1800 466 233; www.airliebeachhotel.com.au; cnr The Esplanade & Coconut Grove; s/d $95/105; ✹) Slick, more corporate than holiday ambience, disabled facilities.

Airlie Beach Motor Lodge (☎ 4946 6418, 1800 810 925; www.airliebeachmotorlodge.com.au; 6 Lamond St; s/d $95/105)

Club Crocodile (☎ 4946 7155, 1800 075 151; www .clubcroc.com.au; Shute Harbour Rd, Cannonvale; d $120; ✹ ▯) Nightly entertainment.

Coral Point Lodge (☎ 4946 9500; fax 4946 9469; 54 Harbour Ave, Shute Harbour; s/d $70/85; ✹) Pleasant views of busy Shute Harbour.

TOP END

Water's Edge Luxury Apartments (☎ 4948 2655; http://watersedge.whitsunday.net.au; 4 Golden Orchid Dr; d from $170; ✹) Water's Edge cultivates a carefree, luxurious attitude in these suites with large lounge areas and a rich décor that exudes warmth. Outside, slip from one of three edgeless pools into the shade of an island-style thatched shelter. The location is excellent.

Coral Sea Resort (☎ 4946 6458; www.coralsea resort.com; 25 Ocean View Ave; d from $220; ✹ ▯) At the end of a low headland overlooking the water, the Coral Sea Suite ($300) with dreamy views, Balinese influences, double hammock and sultry outdoor spa tantalises the senses to romance, and beyond!

Boathaven Spa Resort (☎ 4948 4948; www.boat havenresort.com; 440 Shute Harbour Rd; d $150-180; ✹ ▯) Contemporary comforts at quite reasonable prices and a quiet location close to town appeal here. Rooms offer earthy, hushed hues, upmarket furnishings and glorious Boathaven Bay views from your private balcony spa.

Eating

Most of the eateries are on or just off Shute Harbour Rd. If you're preparing your own food, there's a small supermarket opposite Magnum's and a larger one in Cannonvale.

THE AUTHOR'S CHOICE

Armada Lounge Bar & Restaurant (☎ 4948 1600; 350 Shute Harbour Rd; mains $13-28; ✹ lunch & dinner) Dine upstairs and outdoors under a rippling canopy at smooth, classy Armada. Sultry and stylish, Armada's attractive mix of Japanese and Balinese décor and dim lighting set an amorous mood. The food presentation is inspired – prawn skewer skyscrapers! – but follows up with tantalizing flavours. Inside, Armada aims for sophisticated, velour lounge chic: it's the place to sip slowly over good conversation. The beer and wine lists are excellent, but it's the chocolate-covered martini ($12) and extraordinary other cocktails that will stoke your fire.

Sushi Hi! (☎ 4948 0400; 390 Shute Harbour Rd; mains $6-8; ✹ closes around 9pm) Healthy, light, cleansing Japanese food is welcome any time on a hot day or night. Sushi Hi! is a zero-frills place with a huge menu from sushi rolls and stir-fries to tempura.

Sidewalk Cantina (☎ 4946 6425; The Esplanade; mains $14-25; ✹ closed Tue & Wed) Set one street back from streaming Shute Harbour, Sidewalk is a fairly ordinary café for breakfast or lunch, but converts to a moody, candlelit, streetside cantina by night with a full complement of Mexican dishes.

Chatz Bar 'n' Brasserie (☎ 4946 7223; 390 Shute Harbour Rd; mains $12-16) The delectable Chatz Tower Burger. Say no more. Except for, say, the generous Chatz chicken and vegetarian burgers, and assorted yummy vegetarian dishes. Mmmm.

Village Deli (☎ 4964 1121; Whitsunday Village Resort, opposite Australia Post; mains $7-14) The Village is a casual, hip café-style deli with a huge menu of tasty meals for breakfast, lunch and dinner. Sip a well-made coffee, or wine from the well-chosen wine list.

Other recommendations:

Airlie Thai (☎ 4964 4683; 1st fl, Beach Plaza, The Esplanade; mains $14-26)

Harry's Corner (☎ 4946 7459; 273 Shute Harbour Rd; breakfast $5-7) Lagoon-side, good-value breakfast for early birds.

Shipwrecked Bar & Grill (☎ 4946 6713; cnr Shute Harbour Rd & The Esplanade; lunch $12-17, dinner $20-30) Upmarket but family-friendly.

Mangrove Jack's (☎ 4946 6233; 297 Shute Harbour Rd; mains $15 -23) For wood-fired oven pizza.

Cafe Gourmet (☎ 4946 6172; 289 Shute Harbour Rd; $4-10; ☺ 7am-4.30pm) Dedicated to the quick, humble, lunchtime sandwich.

Drinking & Entertainment

Magnum's (☎ 4946 6266; Shute Harbour Rd) Slouched at sturdy wooden tables with jugs of beer, a spirited crowd joins in the regular afternoon party games here. Buck the electronic bull, surf the artificial wave or enjoy an aimless afternoon listening to live music. By night, Magnum's M@ss nightclub plays crowd-pleasers and has foam party nights. It's loud, lively and always a laugh.

Mama Africa's (☎ 4948 0438; 263 Shute Harbour Rd; ☺ 10pm-5am) It's a shame this club, next to Panache on the Beach restaurant, doesn't open regularly; it's such a cool spot to hang out. With its zebra-striped floor, tribal motifs, kick-back lounge chairs and a vibe that taps straight into your pulse, it's no wonder Mama's rocks. Music meets your command.

The **Juice Bar** (☎ 4946 6465; 354 Shute Harbour Rd; ☺ 10pm-5am) Next door to Armada, Juice has a distinctly city edge to its minimalist décor: polished concrete floor, a chill area with frothing, aerated watertanks and a small dance floor to pack the crowd tight. It mixes the music up a little, with R&B, dance and top 40.

The backpacker party shuffles between **Morocco's** (☎ 4946 6001), up at the top end of Shute Harbour Rd, and Magnum's and **Beaches** (☎ 4946 6244), which is in the middle of the strip.

Other recommendations:

Paddy Shenanigans (☎ 4946 5055; 352 Shute Harbour Rd)

Legends Bar 'n' Grill (☎ 4946 6250; cnr Shute Harbour Rd & Coconut Grove) Spins retro music.

Whitsunday Sailing Club (☎ 4946 6138; end of Coconut Grove; ☺ Thu & Sat) Outdoor cinema; bring a chair.

Getting There & Away

AIR

The closest major airports are at Proserpine and on Hamilton Island. The small Whitsunday airport, about 11km past Airlie Beach towards Shute Harbour, is home to several carriers. **Island Air Taxis** (☎ 4946 9933; www.avta.com.au/whitsundays.html) flies to Hamilton Island (one way $60 per adult) and Lindeman Island (one way $80). **Aviation Adventures** (☎ 4946 9988; www.whitsundayunlimited .com.au) offers transfers (one way from $70) to Daydream, South Molle and Long Islands.

Helireef (☎ 4946 9102), **Air Whitsunday Seaplanes** (☎ 4946 9111), Island Air Taxis and Aviation Adventures offer joy flights over the Whitsunday Islands and the Great Barrier Reef.

BOAT

See the boxed text 'Sailing the Whitsunday Islands' (p372) for information on getting around the islands by boat.

BUS

Most **McCafferty's/Greyhound** (☎ 13 20 30; www .mccaffertys.com.au) and **Premier Motor Service** (☎ 13 34 10; www.premierms.com.au) coaches make the detour from the highway to Airlie Beach (prices quoted are for one-way adult fares): Brisbane (McCafferty's/Premier $144/123, 18 hours), Townsville ($49/43, 4 hours), Mackay ($35, 2 hours) and Cairns ($83/76, 11 hours). The bus stop is near the end of the Esplanade. Shute Harbour Rd travel agents take bookings.

Local bus company **Whitsunday Transit** (☎ 1300 655 449) connects Proserpine, Cannonvale, Abel Point, Airlie Beach and Shute Harbour. Buses operate daily from 6am to 10.30pm and stop outside Mangrove Jack's or just up from Pro Dive. Grab a schedule from any travel agency.

Getting Around

The car rental companies are along Shute Harbour Rd.

QUEENSLAND

Airlie Beach Budget Autos (☎ 4948 0300) Opposite McDonald's.
Avis (☎ 4946 6318) Next to Magnum's.
Thrifty (☎ 4946 7727) Next to Sushi Hi!.
Whitsunday Taxis (☎ 13 10 08)

CONWAY NATIONAL PARK & STATE FOREST

A new walkers' paradise is in the making. By June 2004, QPWS expects to finish its 36km **Whitsundays Great Walk**, transversing the rugged ranges and rainforest valleys, coastal woodlands and mangroves of this area. You'll need to be reasonably fit and have three days to fill. Adventurers seeking altitude should hike the 2.4km up **Mt Rooper Lookout** in the national park for top views of the Whitsunday Passage and islands.

Or there's the beautiful **Cedar Creek Falls** trail in the state forest. The turn-off is on your right, 18km from Airlie Beach on the Proserpine–Airlie road. **Fawlty's 4WD Tropical Tours** (☎ 07-4946 6665; adult/child $42/25) runs good-value, full-day rainforest tours to the falls.

Contact **QPWS** (☎ 4946 7022) in Airlie for more park and forest information.

WHITSUNDAY ISLANDS

Just about every outdoor-loving Australian dreams of soaking up the rays and reef on a yacht in the Whitsundays. The blue-green waterways surrounding these islands are Marine Park and fall within the Great Barrier Reef World Heritage Area that stretches from Cape York in the north to Bundaberg in the south. We're all responsible for preserving this natural wonderland for generations to enjoy, so you may kiss the fish if you can catch them, but don't feed them, and please, don't pet the coral.

The Whitsunday Islands fall into five groups – the Whitsunday, Molle, Lindeman, Repulse and Gloucester Islands – scattered along both sides of the Whitsunday Passage, and all within a day's journey (50km) of Shute Harbour. The Great Barrier Reef is at least 60km from the mainland. There are more than 90 islands, mostly uninhabited and mostly continental (the tips of underwater mountains), and many have colourful fringing coral reefs.

Here is also the chance for some idyllic camping and walking. All but four of the Whitsundays are predominantly or completely national park (the exceptions are Dent Island and the resort islands of Hamilton, Daydream and Hayman). The other main resorts are on South Molle, Lindeman, Long and Hook Islands. People staying in the resorts are generally on cheap package holidays booked in advance, but some resorts offer affordable standby rates that may include meals. Ask Airlie Beach travel agencies or try **UTAG Travel** (☎ 07-4946 6255; cnr The Esplanade & Shute Harbour Rd, Airlie Beach).

CAMPING

You can pitch your tent at QPWS camping grounds on 17 of the islands, but you must haul along your own gear, food, drinking water, fuel stoves and nature-loving attitude (leave only footprints). Camping grounds are occasionally closed to alternate traffic between them and minimise the impact on the environment.

To organise your trip, visit the excellent **QPWS office** (☎ 07-4946 7022; www.epa.qld.gov.au; cnr Mandalay & Shute Harbour Rds), which provides permits (per person/family $4/16) and enthusiastic advice on highlights. It's 5km past Airlie Beach, on the local bus line. You can also purchase permits at www.smartservice.qld.gov.au/AQ, or by calling ☎ 13 13 04.

Camping Connections (☎ 07-4946 5255; Where?What?How? Travel, Shop 1, 283 Shute Harbour Rd), opposite McDonald's, runs a direct boat service to camping grounds for between $50 and $150 return.

Or, relax on a hosted camp. Several companies have been granted permits to run cushy camping tours to most of the islands, and the guides have good local knowledge. Just bring your swimming costume.
Aussie Sea Kayak Company (☎ 0407-049 747) Choose from nine trip options.
Derwent Yacht Charter (☎ 07-4946 4195) Transfers on a 72ft ketch and camping, $295.
Salty Dog Sea Kayaking (☎ 07-4946 1388) Three-day ($385) or six-day ($1020) kayak tours and camping.
Sea Kayaking Whitsundays (☎ 07-4948 9711) Seasonal kayak tours and camping; ask about the full-moon tour.
Whitsunday Sightseeing (☎ 07-4946 6611) Three-day, two-night safaris, $280.

GETTING THERE & AROUND

Hamilton and Lindeman islands are the only islands with airports. **Island Air Taxis** (☎ 4946 9933; Shute Harbour Rd; ☻ 7.45am-5.30pm)

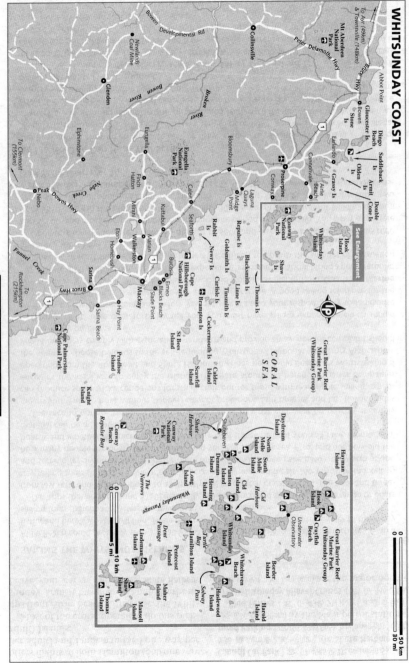

WHITSUNDAY COAST

offers flights to both Hamilton ($60 one way per adult) and Lindeman ($80 one way per adult) Islands.

Most of the cruise operators do bus pick-ups from Airlie Beach. Otherwise, the Whitsunday Transit bus goes to Shute Harbour. Leave your car at either the **Shute Harbour**

Council Car Park (☎ 07-4946 9557; overnight $8; 6.30-10.30am & 2.30-6.30pm) or **Shute Harbour Secured Parking** (☎ 07-4946 9666; day/overnight $6/12; 6.30am-6.30pm) by the Shell petrol station.

Blue Ferries (☎ 07-4946 5111; 6.30am-6pm) and **Whitsunday Allover Cruises** (☎ 07-946 6900, 1300 366 494; 7am-6pm) are the major opera-

---

SAILING THE WHITSUNDAY ISLANDS

Airlie Beach could probably save a small forest if it recycled its glossy boat-trip brochures. Grab a fistful and here's what you'll find. There are roughly three types of sailing trips: one- to three-day sailing tours, bareboat charters or crewing on a private yacht.

Day trips (between $80 and $150) generally include lunch and snorkelling, on a range of boats from fast rafts and island-hoppers to a leisurely sail on a ketch or catamaran. The two- and three-day sailing tours (from $350) include yacht accommodation and meals. Most include snorkelling and some offer diving as an option (for more information on diving see p367). It's worth asking how many people the boat takes and how long you will spend at sea. Also, find out how old the boat is and whether the picture on the brochure is of the *same* boat you will take. Promotional material can be misleading.

The second option, 'bareboat' charter, doesn't refer to what you wear on board – it simply means you rent the boat without skipper, crew or provisions. Stiff breezes and fast-flowing tides can produce some tricky conditions for small craft but for those with reasonable sailing experience, it's the ideal way to enjoy the islands. There are around 12 bareboat charter companies operating from the Abel Point and Shute Harbour marinas near Airlie Beach. It's worth asking if the one you choose belongs to the self-regulating Whitsunday Bareboat Operators Association. WBOA members comply with association standards and provide an avenue for complaint should you have any problems.

Despite what some operators may tell you, you *must* have sailing experience which *should* be tested by the charter company before you set sail. It's also your responsibility to familiarise yourself with the islands' passages and safe anchoring practice. A good sailing reference for the Whitsundays is the book, *100 Magic Miles*, by David Colfelt, available from **Quadrant Marine** (☎ 07-4946 4033) at Abel Point Marina. If your experience is rusty, think about hiring a guide (around $200 a day) at least for the first day; even then it's difficult to absorb the amount of instruction given in a short time.

Operators usually require a booking deposit of $600 and a security bond of between $1000 and $2000, and most companies have a minimum hire period of seven days. You'll pay anywhere from $350 a day in the high season for a Catalina 30, sleeping two, to around $800 a day for a Seawind 1200 multi-hulled Catamaran, sleeping up to eight. Based at Abel Point Marina, two WBOA members are: **Cumberland Charter Yachts** (☎ 07-4946 7500; www.ccy.com.au) and **Queensland Yacht Charters** (☎ 07-4946 7400; www.yachtcharters.com.au).

At Sea No One Can Hear You Scream

The final option, crewing on a private boat, is risky. Readers have sent in hair-raising accounts of 'illegal charters' that range from sexual harassment to poor safety and inexperienced crew. Illegal charters are most often advertised on photocopied leaflets that read: 'Crew Wanted: Share an adventurous sailing experience and expenses'. While there are, no doubt, many legitimate private owners who wish to share the beauty of the Whitsundays with you, it's important to research any offer *before* you sail into the sunset.

Visit the Maritime Safety officer at **Maritime Safety Queensland** (☎ 07-4946 2200; www .transport.qld.gov.au/maritime; Level 1, 384 cnr Waterson Way & Shute Harbour Rd) in Airlie Beach. Officers can tell you the right questions to ask and if the vessel has current commercial registration and is crewed by professionals. You could save yourself from an upsetting – or potentially dangerous – experience. Wise words aside, happy sailing!

tors for transfers to resorts on South Molle, Daydream, Long, Lindeman and Hamilton Islands. They operate from Shute Harbour.

Camping Connections does drop-offs to island camping grounds; see p370 for more information.

Long Island

There's good rainforest here – it's nearly all national park – with 13km of walking tracks and some fine lookouts. The island is skinny (2km wide) but long enough (9km) to house three resorts and a QPWS **camping ground** (per person/family $4/16) in seclusion.

Peppers Palm Bay (☎ 07-4946 9233, 1800 095 025; www.palmbay.com.au; d from $380) Thai-style cabins snuggle on the shore of idyllic Palm Bay at this boutique retreat. Here is a place that insists on the ultimate indulgence – relaxation – by the azure blue pool, around the airy lounge with massive stone fireplace and bar, or on the veranda of your tastefully furnished room, lazing in a double hammock. Rates include a sumptuous breakfast hamper. Check standby rates and treat yourself.

Otherwise, there's the secluded, solar-powered **Whitsunday Wilderness Lodge** (☎ 07-4946 9777; www.southlongisland.com; 5 nights $2990), or worn-out **Club Crocodile** (☎ 07-4946 9400, 1800 075 125; www.clubcroc.com.au; d $380), which needs more than its planned soft refurbishing to offer value for money.

South Molle Island

South Molle is the largest of the Molle group at 4 sq km and is virtually joined to Mid Molle and North Molle islands. It has long stretches of beach and is crisscrossed by 15km of wonderful walking tracks. The highest point is Mt Jeffreys (198m), but the climb up Spion Kop is also worthwhile. South Molle is mainly national park, but there's a QPWS camping ground and the resort in the north, where the boats come in.

South Molle Island Resort (☎ 4946 9433, 1800 075 080; www.southmolleisland.com.au; d $174-282) A popular resort with families, the views are great, but the communal areas and most rooms are merely adequate, and rates don't include meals. There is nightly entertainment though.

Hook Island

The second largest of the Whitsundays at 53 sq km, Hook Island is mainly national park

and blessed with great beaches and camping grounds. There's impressive snorkelling around the northern camping grounds, and Crayfish Beach is an awesome spot. You can make your own way here with Camping Connections, or ring the commercial operators for tour/camping options (p370).

Hook Island Wilderness Resort (☎ 07-4946 9380; camp sites/dm/d $15/24/90) For years this was the only island resort within the reach of tight budgets, but it also became very rundown. The resort was up for sale at the time of research. Let's hope new owners revitalise the place. Ask travel agents for an update.

Whitsunday Island

Whitsunday Island is food for the soul. The largest of the Whitsundays, this island covers 109 sq km and rises to 438m at Whitsunday Peak. On its southeast coast, 6km-long Whitehaven Beach is the longest and finest beach in the group (some say in the country), with good snorkelling off its southern end. *Everyone* day-trips to Whitehaven Beach, but it's magic to linger overnight.

Perhaps the most celebrated view of all the Whitsundays comes from here – looking up from Hill Inlet on Tongue Point down towards pristine Whitehaven Beach.

There's plenty of **camping** (per person/family $4/16), but no resort here; see p370 for camping options.

Daydream Island

Tiny Daydream Island, about 1km long and 500m wide, is the nearest island resort to Shute Harbour.

Daydream Island Resort & Spa (☎ 07-4948 8488, 1800 075 040; www.daydream.net.au; d from $326) From the funky, bubbly reception area and friendly staff to fresh, colourfully furnished rooms, Daydream's attitude would improve any mood. It is a mainly couple-oriented resort, but also family- and wheelchair-friendly, and it has a day spa that rejuvenates sun-battered bodies. The southern end of the island displays signs of a weary theme park with its ailing man-made reef and bizarre mini-golf course.

Hamilton Island

Hamilton Island (☎ 07-4946 9999, 1800 075 110; www.hamiltonisland.com.au; d $245-505) You'll either love or loathe Hamilton Island, the most heavily

QUEENSLAND

developed island in the Whitsundays. Hamilton is more like a town than a resort, with its own airport, a 200-boat marina, shops, 11 restaurants, bars and accommodation for more than 2000 people, a few high-rise buildings and five types of accommodation. Self-catering is an option here and children are well catered for. There are water sports aplenty and rangers available to guide guests through walks and wildlife.

Hamilton's an appealing day trip from Shute Harbour, and you can use some of the resort's facilities. Call **Blue Ferries** (☎ 07-4946 5111).

Island Air Taxis (☎ 07-4946 9933) connects Hamilton with Shute Harbour or Proserpine ($60 one way per adult), Lindeman Island ($80) and Mackay ($120). **Hamilton Island Aviation** (☎ 07-4946 8249) flies return from Mackay to Hamilton Island for $240.

Lindeman Island
It's a bit of a hike to southerly Lindeman (mostly national park), but the rewards are lots of secluded bays and 20km of impressive walking trails. Tremendous numbers of grass trees make striking photographs and the view from Mt Oldfield (210m) is grand.

Day-tripping is an option, but it's a *very* long day; call **Whitsunday Allover Cruises** (☎ 07-4946 6900; adult/child $120/60) for details on day trips.

Club Med Resort (☎ 07-4946 9333, 1800 258 263; www.clubmed.com.au; d $320-470) The internationally famous Club Med style, with its usual emphasis on fun, flourishes here.

There's a QPWS **camping ground** (per person/family $4/16), or go with a commercial tour operator (see p370 for tour details).

Island Air Taxis (☎ 07-4946 9933; one way per adult $80) flies to Lindeman.

BOWEN
☎ 07 / pop 13,200
In answer to your question, it's a mango, that huge orange blob outside the visitors centre. It's there to welcome you to Bowen, which is a thriving fruit and vegetable centre in spite of its seemingly wide, empty streets. Most travellers come here for seasonal picking work (April to August), but there are some lovely beaches and holiday accommodation just north of town at popular Horseshoe and Rose Bays.

Check the **visitors centre** (☎ 4786 4222; Bruce Hwy; ✆ 8.30am-5pm), 5km south of Bowen, for more accommodation options. Once you hit town, keep an eye out for some terrific **murals** that depict the town's history, then head on to a kick-back piece of paradise 5km away at Rose Bay.

Sleeping & Eating
Rose Bay Resort (☎ 4786 1064; www.rosebayresortvillas.com; Pandanus St; d $125) sits on an intimate cove-front of willowy casuarina and swishing palm trees. These top-end apartments at mid-range prices deliver tastes of Mexico with their terracotta and mustard hues and tranquil bay views framed by bald granite boulders. You can stay four nights on a very reasonable weekly rate. **Beachside Holiday Units** (☎ 4786 2561; beachside@boweninternet.com.au; 38 Horseshoe Bay Rd; d $72; ✿) fronts an abundant tropical garden by peaceful Horseshoe Bay, 6km north of town.

Bowen's backpackers specialise in housing fruit-pickers. It's a competitive scene, so ring around to find out what deals are available. For starters, try **Bowen Backpackers** (☎ 4786 3433; bowenbacpackers@bigpond.com; beach end Herbert St; dm/d $20/24; ✆ closed Dec-early Mar) and **Barnacles Backpackers** (☎ 4786 4400; barnaclebackpackers@bigpond.com.au; 16 Gordon St; dm/d $17/19).

There are a couple of modern pubs and cafés in town, but cosy **Horseshoe Bay Cafe** (☎ 4786 3280, Horseshoe Bay; ✆ 10am-3pm, 6-9pm Tue-Sun) produces far from ordinary hot dogs and burgers, and restaurant-style dinners.

Getting There & Away
The long-distance bus stop is outside **Bowen Travel** (☎ 4786 2835; William St), where you can purchase bus tickets (prices quoted are one-way adult fares) to Rockhampton ($94, 8 hours), Airlie Beach ($26, 11½ hours) and Townsville ($36, 3 hours). The *Sunlander* (☎ 4952 7418) train (from Brisbane, economy sleeper $199) stops at Bootooloo Siding, 3km south of the city centre.

NORTH COAST

TOWNSVILLE
☎ 07 / pop 150,000
The outback meets the tropics in attractive, energetic Townsville. The main highway scoots west across to the NT from here and

the Great Barrier Reef lies east, two hours away. It's the 'big smoke' for Queensland's gigantic inland agricultural and mining regions, and home to thousands of resident army boys and university students. From its lively esplanade and excellent museums to its thriving nightlife, Townsville strives for big-city sophistication. Make sure there's time to visit gorgeous Magnetic Island; it's only a 20-minute boat trip away.

Orientation

Red rock Castle Hill (290m) presides over Townsville. Ross Creek winds about its city centre, which lies on the north side of the creek over the Dean St Bridge or Victoria Bridge (pedestrians only). The centre is easy to get around on foot.

Flinders St Mall, the shopping precinct, stretches to the left from the northern side of Dean Bridge, towards the train station. To the right of the bridge is Flinders St East, lined with many of the town's oldest buildings, plus eateries, nightclubs and the Sunferries terminal for Magnetic Island departures (there's another terminal on Sir Leslie Thiess Drive on the breakwater).

The Townsville Transit Centre, the arrival and departure point for long-distance buses, is on café-lined Palmer St, just south of Ross Creek. This is not to be confused with the Transit Mall on Stokes St, between Sturt St and Flinders St Mall, which is the departure point for local buses and taxis.

Information

Australia Post (Post Office Plaza, entrance Sturt St)
Flinders Mall visitors centre (☎ 4721 3660; ☽ 9am-5pm Mon-Fri, 9am-1pm Sat & Sun) Between Stokes and Denham Sts, in same booth as police.
Internet Den (☎ 4721 4500; 265 Flinders Mall) Internet access.
Jim's Book Exchange (☎ 4771 6020; Post Office Plaza, Flinders Mall)
Reef & National Parks visitors centre (☎ 4721 2399; Northtown Shopping Centre, Flinders Mall; ☽ 9am-5pm Mon-Fri, 10am-4pm Sat & Sun)
RACQ (☎ 4775 3999; 202 Ross River Rd, Aitkenvale) Aitkenvale is about 7km south of the city centre.
Townsville City Library (☎ 4727 9666) Next to The Brewery, Internet access.
Townsville Enterprise Limited visitors centre (☎ 4778 3555; www.townsvilleonline.com.au; Bruce Hwy; ☽ 9am-5pm) Well-organised, private tourism organisation, 8km south of the city centre.

Sights

Reef HQ (☎ 4750 0800; www.reefhq.org.au; 2-68 Flinders St East; adult/child $20/9.50; ☽ 9am-5pm) is a must-see for anyone not planning to dive or snorkel on the Great Barrier Reef. Its aquarium is a living coral reef, swimming with marine beasties and beauties. A wave machine simulates the ebb and flow of the ocean. There are hands-on reef displays and tours scheduled throughout the day. Plunge deeper still into the **IMAX cinema** (☎ 4721 1481; adult/child $12/7; ☽ 10.30am-4.30pm), next door.

The **Strand**, northwest of town, is a vibrant beachfront esplanade with a marina, cafés, parks and stinger enclosure. At its top end is the enormous artificial **Coral Memorial Rockpool** on the edge of the ocean, open 24 hours, and it's free.

If you're feeling energetic, the panoramic views from the top of **Castle Hill** are worth the 2km scramble to the summit; the path to the top begins at the end of Victoria St.

Cotter's Market (Flinders St Mall; ☽ 8.30am-1pm Sun) has about 200 craft and food stalls, as well as live entertainment, and wheelchair access is fine.

SANCTUARIES & PARKS

Billabong Sanctuary (☎ 4778 8344; www.billabongsanctuary.com.au; Bruce Hwy; adult/child $23/12; ☽ 8am-5pm), 17km south of Townsville, is a 10-hectare wildlife park where many animals roam free. You can cuddle a koala, wombat or python, and feed a crocodile or eagle at shows scheduled throughout the day. See p377 for more information on tours to this sanctuary.

If you fancy a lazy picnic, Townsville is spoiled for pretty parks and gardens. The visitors centre has a complete list. The **Palmetum** (☎ 4727 8330; University Rd, Douglas; ☽ daylight hrs), about 15km southwest of the city centre off University Rd, is a lush, 17-hectare botanic garden devoted to native palms that are arranged in natural environments, from desert to rainforest. There's a fine old Queenslander tearoom, in case you forgot your picnic.

About 35km southeast of Townsville on the Bruce Hwy is the turn-off to the **Australian Institute of Marine Science** (AIMS; ☎ 4753 4444; www.aims.gov.au; ☽ 8am-3pm Mon-Fri, tours 10am-noon Fri Mar-Nov), a fascinating marine-research facility on Cape Ferguson that conducts free, two-hour tours.

TOWNSVILLE

QUEENSLAND

MUSEUMS
You could spend a few days visiting Townsville's well-run museums and art gallery. The visitors centre has a full list.

The eerie focus of the **Museum of Tropical Queensland** (☎ 4726 0600; www.mtq.qld.gov.au; adult/child $9/5; ⏰ 9am-5pm) is the ill-fated *Pandora*, probably Australia's most famous shipwreck. The tropical science centre has intriguing (promise) interactive exhibits, an extensive natural history collection, and an Aboriginal and Torres Strait Islander exhibition.

If you plan to dive to the *Yongala* shipwreck, visit the **Maritime Museum** (☎ 4721 5251; 42-68 Palmer St; adult/concession/family $5/4/12; ⏰ 10am-4pm Mon-Fri, 1-4pm Sat & Sun). The *Yongala* was overcome by a cyclone in 1911. The wreck has since transformed into a coral reef teeming with marine life that seems to guard this underwater cemetery. The museum has relics, historic newspaper articles and a video of the first archaeological survey of the wreck.

Activities
The task of regaining your land legs after a marine holiday is made all the more challenging with the prospect of abseiling, mustering, rafting and airborne adventures to be had around Townsville.

Woodstock Trail Rides (☎ 4778 8888; www.woodstocktrailrides.com.au; Flinders Hwy) runs a terrific outback experience on its cattle station. For $120, including transfers, a day visit includes billy tea and damper, cattle mustering, calf branding and whip cracking, as well as a camp oven lunch and ice-cold beer at day's end. Trail rides and an overnight bush camp are also available.

Right Training (☎ 4725 4571, 0427-802 428; info@paci.com.au) would like to plunge you into vertical adventure. A three-hour abseil and rock climb on Mt Stewart costs $90 and a 100m abseil off Castle Hill costs $100. Experienced climbers can hire guides and gear.

For the adrenalin junkies, there's seriously scary rafting with **R 'n' R White Water Rafting** (☎ 1800 079 977; www.raft.com.au) on the Tully River ($155), or else **Coral Sea Skydivers** (☎ 4772 4889) will dump you into the sky, either in tandem ($290) or on your own after a two-day free-fall course (from $535).

DIVING & SNORKELLING
Apart from the Great Barrier Reef snorkel and dive, the big attraction for divers is the stunning and spooky *Yongala* shipwreck (this page). There are half a dozen dive companies, all offering *Yongala* options, but you need to have an open-water certificate to see it. Dive companies are only as good as their staff, who change frequently in this business. Ask other travellers for current recommendations.

Diving Dreams Australia (☎ 4721 2500; www.divingdreams.com; 252 Walker St; ⏰ 9am-6pm Mon-Fri, 9am-3pm Sat) Five-day certificate course with nine dives, from $475.

Gladiator Boat Charters (☎ 4771 6150, 1800 776 150; www.tropicaldiving.com.au; 14 Palmer St; ⏰ 9am-5pm Mon-Sat)

Pro Dive (☎ 4721 1760, 1300 131 760; www.prodivetownsville.com.au; 14 Plume St; ⏰ 9am-5pm Mon-Fri, 10am-4pm Sat, noon-4pm Sun) Five-day certificate courses with nine dives, $585.

Reef & Island Tours (☎ 4721 3555; opposite visitors centre in Flinders St Mall; adult/child/concession $143/72/99; ⏰ 9am-5pm Mon-Fri, 9am-2pm Sat, 9am-1pm Sun) Glass-bottom boat day trips include snorkelling.

Tours
If superb rainforest, a beautifully restored mining town or Australia's longest waterfall tempt you, **Townsville Tropical Tours** (☎ 4721 6489; www.townsvilletropicaltours.com.au) has good-value day trips (from $120) that take in the Paluma Range National Park, Hidden Valley, Charters Towers or Wallaman Falls. It also tours the Billabong Sanctuary (adult/concession/family $34/32/85).

Sleeping
BUDGET
All these places are within a 10-minute walk of town. Those on the south side of Ross Creek are handy to the Townsville Transit Centre and Palmer St restaurants.

Coral Lodge B&B Inn (☎ 4771 5512, 1800 614 613; urwelcum@ultra.net.au; 32 Hale St; s/d $60/70; 🖳) An old Queenslander with loads of character, this quiet, well-run, friendly place has pretty rooms and good kitchen facilities. One quaint double includes loft-style bunks, and there's a lovely garden and barbecue area. It's the pick of the bunch in the town centre. The price includes a continental breakfast.

Civic Guest House (☎ 4771 5381, 1800 646 619; civichouse@austarnet.com.au; 262 Walker St; dm/s/d $20/43/48; 🖳) Tiny rooms are brightly decorated and there's a fresh and friendly feel to this well-run hostel. Its courtesy bus does

QUEENSLAND

pick-ups and the free Friday night barbecue is a good way to meet people.

Globetrotters Hostel (☎ 4771 3242; globetrotters@ austarnet.com.au; 45 Palmer St; dm/s/d $20/40/44) There's an airy feel to this quiet, old hostel on the Palmer St restaurant strip. The rooms are small but clean, air-con is available in some and the beds are back-friendly.

Cosy **Reef Lodge** (☎ 4721 1112; reeflodgetowns ville@bigpond.com; 4 Wickham St; dm $18-22, d $42; 🔀) is next to the nightlife, while big, bright (like a kid's playground) **Townsville Transit Centre Backpackers** (☎ 4721 2322, 1800 628 836; www.tcbackpacker.com.au; cnr Palmer & Plume Sts; dm/d $17/50; 🖵 🔀) is at the bus station.

MID-RANGE

Rocks (☎ 4771 5700; www.therocksguesthouse.com; 20 Cleveland Tce; s/d $90/110; 🔀) Wow. This beautifully restored historic home, replete with period furnishings and a veranda with superb bay views, is to be treasured. High ceilings, old cabinets brimming with memorabilia, sherries at six and plenty of space to lounge – it's another world at the Rocks. Disabled facilities are good, and breakfast is provided.

Ocean Breeze by the Strand (☎ 4729 8100; www .accomtownsville.com.au/properties/ocean_breeze.htm; 81 Mitchell St, North Ward; d $90; 🔀) It's the simple blue and white décor that gives these new, self-contained apartments their fresh and breezy feel. The motel-style 'studios' are large, but you could rollerblade around the one-bedroom apartments ($110 per night). Apartments closest to the Strand have the best views from balconies.

Yongala Lodge (☎ 4772 4633; www.historic yongala.com.au; 11 Fryer St; d from $85; 🔀) Close to the Strand, the lodge has a terrific colonial veranda for evening drinks. It's an eclectic combination of historic home, Greek restaurant and motel rooms out back that almost recapture the charm with their imitation antique furnishings.

City Oasis Inn (☎ 4771 6048, 1800 809 515; www .cityoasis.com.au; 143 Wills St; d $100, executive d $125; 🔀) Neat as a pin, in a good central city location, the highlight is the oasis-style pool with waterfall. Executive suites are stately and have balconies, but all rooms have satellite TV.

Other recommendations:

Strand Park Hotel (☎ 4750 7888; thestrandpark@ hotmail.com; 59-60 The Strand; d from $120; 🔀) Rooms crowded by rococo-style furnishings; wheelchair access.

Beach House Motel (☎ 4721 1333; fax 4771 6893; 66 The Strand; d from $85) Basic but Strand-side.

Ridgemont Executive Motel (☎ 4771 2164, 1800 804 168; www.ridgemont.com.au; 15-19 Victoria St; d $105; 🔀) Steep walk but welcoming views from restaurant.

TOP END

Mariners North Luxury Holiday Apartments (☎ 4722 0777; www.marinersnorth.com.au; 7 Mariners Dr; f from $150; 🔀) If views are your ultimate indulgence, you won't beat these. Mariners North's two-bedroom apartments capture wondrous vistas of the Strand and Magnetic Island. While living areas and balconies are huge and the kitchen excellent, the furnishings are spare and bland. A minimum two-night stay applies and a deposit is required.

Eating

C Bar (☎ 4724 0333; The Strand; mains $6-17) C Bar is the best breakfast spot in town, right on the foreshore with magic views of Magnetic Island from its outdoor deck. The food is exceptional and servings are generous; no wonder it's always packed. They do lunch and dinner too, outside or in.

Benny's Hot Wok Cafe & Bar (☎ 4724 3243; 17-21 Palmer St; mains $15-20) Groovy. You've got to love the shiny black floors, bamboo and stone features, ancient oriental sculptures and mood lighting. Benny's exudes funky Asian ambience and a good selection of Thai, Malaysian and Japanese meals, well prepared and presented.

Will & Lucy's Na Kula Cafe (☎ 4721 6060; cnr Sturt & Stanley Sts; lunch $4-10) Pink and green walls and corrugated iron features splash a happy mood around this city lunch spot. The home-made pies and sausage rolls, vegetarian focaccias, and the selection of speciality breads and gourmet fillings, are excellent. Yum. Plenty of magazines to read, too.

Naked Fish (☎ 4724 4623; 60 The Strand; mains $15-21; 🕑 closed Sun) It's like dining on the bottom of the sea in this cool blue-green interior with a starry ceiling. Apart from seafood, they also serve Cajun and Moroccan dishes, tempura and risotto. The food is top notch and beautifully presented.

C'est Si Bon (☎ 4772 5828; Shop 2, 48 Gregory St; lunch from $6) It looks a little sterile, but this gourmet deli with long lunch tables does delicious home-made pies, bagels, baguettes and salads. A glass of wine with lunch? Certainly.

Cactus Jack's Bar & Grill (☎ 4721 1478; 21 Palmer St; mains $13-23) Lively, licensed and Mexican: you'll need to book on weekends to squeeze into this festive cantina serving comfort food. Margaritas? Naturally, you must sip several.

Scirocco (☎ 4724 4508; 61 Palmer St; mains $15-25; ☽ closed Mon) Something a little more refined, Scirocco presents understated elegance with its high ceilings and delicate motif-painted walls. The menu is highly imaginative. How about pickled beetroot and goat's cheese risotto, or for dessert, a lime and pineapple tart with coconut ice cream? It's not at all snooty either.

Other recommendations:

Tim's Surf 'n' Turf (☎ 4721 4861; Ogden St; mains $10-16) Basic, dinosaur-size meals.

Sandwich Express (Northtown Shopping Centre, Flinders Mall; sandwiches $4-7) Speedy sandwiches.

Flynn's Irish Bar (☎ 4721 1655; Flinders St East; dishes $7-13; ☽ closed Sun) Beef-and-Guiness pies.

Drinking

The Brewery (☎ 4724 9999; 242 Flinders St) It's the focal point of downtown. This imposing old building turned boutique brewery makes six terrific beers on-site and attracts a lively crowd every day. Reasonable light meals are available and the outdoor tables are great for people watching (see also this entry under Entertainment; above).

Embassy (☎ 4724 5000; 13 Sturt St) Subdued orange and blue lighting coupled with modern, blocky Japanese design make this a sleek inner sanctum. Tantalising meals are available, but you'll linger for the ambience and DJ who spins real vinyl into funk and house music. Sophistication is the vibe, dress is smart casual.

Heritage Cafe 'n' Bar (☎ 4771 2799; 137 Flinders St East) A café-bar loaded with style, the Heritage attracts a 25-plus crowd with its food, wine and beer theme nights and is the place to enjoy more tempered indulgence. Dress is smart casual.

Portraits Wine Bar (☎ 4771 3335; 151 Flinders St East) A dark, close interior invites you inside Portraits, the quiet nook of the rowdy Exchange Hotel. It's all about close encounters, high spirits and fat glasses of wine, although the wine list isn't exceptional.

Other recommendations:

Blue Bottle Cafe & Gallery (☎ 4771 2121; Shop 2-4 Gregory St) Quieter lounge-bar with occasional acoustic music.

Exchange Hotel (☎ 4771 3335; 151 Flinders St East) Beer, bourbon & barn atmosphere (see also this entry under Entertainment; below).

Mad Cow Tavern (☎ 4771 5727; 129 Flinders St East) Loud and lively.

Entertainment

Bank Niteclub (☎ 4771 6148; 169 Flinders St East; admission $5; ☽ closed Sun) Definitely the sleekest club in town, Bank is a superbly restored old bank building with a marble bar, padded chill zone and slinky *Basic Instinct* ambience. The bartenders impress with showy bottle tossing. The beat is house and dance. The dress? Whatever's *in*! Admission may not apply after 11pm.

Millenium Club (☎ 4772 4429; 450 Flinders St West; admission $10; ☽ 8pm-5am Wed-Sat) Four levels to amuse you at this unpretentious club: a lounge bar with live music, a pool table den, a downstairs that goes off with top 40 hits, and an upstairs event venue for top DJs and pure dance. Admission only applies upstairs.

Playpen (☎ 4721 5555; cnr Flinders St West & Knapp St; admission $6 after 10pm) Playpen runs loads of promotions to entice a crowd seeing that it's located 1.5km from town. The gothic-inspired Factory Bar downstairs is all dance, the Lion Bar is a pool-player nook, or there's relaxed O'Leary's Jazz & Wine Bar upstairs.

Other recommendations:

Brewery (☎ 4724 2999; 242 Flinders St) Free nightclub upstairs, Friday and Saturday.

Exchange Hotel (☎ 4771 3335; 151 Flinders St East) Live music.

BC Cinemas (☎ 4771 4101; cnr Sturt & Blackwood Sts) Mainstream films.

Jupiters Casino (☎ 4722 2333; Sir Leslie Thiess Dr) Basics: pokies, roulette, blackjack.

Getting There & Away

AIR

Qantas (☎ 4753 3311, 13 13 13; 345 Flinders St Mall) has daily flights between Townsville and all the major cities, including Cairns ($130 one way per adult) and Brisbane ($130), and regular flights to Mackay ($295), Alice Springs ($460) and Mt Isa ($470).

BUS

McCafferty's/Greyhound (☎ 4772 5100, 13 20 30; Townsville Transit Centre, cnr Palmer & Plume Sts) Frequent services to Brisbane ($160 one way per adult, 23 hours),

QUEENSLAND

Rockhampton ($103, 11 hours), Mackay ($67, 7 hours), Airlie Beach ($49, 4 hours), Mission Beach ($48, 4 hours) and Cairns ($50, 6 hours). Daily services inland to Mt Isa ($115, 12 hours) via Charters Towers ($27, 1¾ hours), continuing on to the NT.

Townsville Transit Centre (☎ 4721 3082; transittsv@ bigpond.com.au; 21 Plume St) Long-distance bus station.

Transit Centre Backpackers (☎ 4721 2322; Townsville Transit Centre) Premier Motor Service agent.

CAR

Hertz (☎ 4775 5950; airport)

Thrifty (☎ 4725 4600, 1800 658 959; airport)

Townsville Car Rentals (☎ 4772 1093; 12 Palmer St) For small cars, scooters and bicycles.

TRAIN

The Brisbane–Cairns *Sunlander* train travels through Townsville four times a week. Prices quoted here are for one-way adult fares. From Brisbane to Townsville takes 24 hours (economy seat/sleeper $163/211, 1st-class sleeper $315). Proserpine is four hours from Townsville (economy seat $51), Rockhampton 11 hours (economy seat $108) and Cairns 7½ hours (economy seat $57). The more luxurious Queenslander class, which includes a sleeper and meals, is available on two services a week.

The *Inlander* train heads from Townsville on Wednesday and Sunday to Mt Isa (economy seat/sleeper $110/159, 1st-class sleeper $237, 20 hours) via Charters Towers (economy seat $23, 3 hours).

Bookings can be made for both train journeys through the **Queensland Rail Travel Centre** (☎ 4772 8358; www.traveltrain.qr.com.au; 502 Flinders St; ☼ 9am-5pm Mon-Fri, 1-4.30pm Sat, 8.30am-4.15pm Sun, closed for lunch).

Getting Around
TO/FROM THE AIRPORT

Townsville airport is 5km northwest of the city at Garbutt. A taxi to the centre costs $15, or else **Airport Transfers** (☎ 4775 5544; one way/return $7/11) runs transfers from the Townsville Transit Centre and most accommodation near the city centre.

BUS

Sunbus (☎ 4725 8482; www.sunbus.com.au) runs local bus services around Townsville. Route maps and timetables are available at the visitors centre in Flinders Mall and at the newsagent in the Transit Mall.

TAXI

Taxis congregate outside the Transit Mall, or call **Townsville Taxis** (☎ 4778 9555, 13 10 08).

MAGNETIC ISLAND
☎ 07 / pop 2500

Not long after stepping onto lovely Magnetic Island, you'll slip into its easy-going attitude and lazier pace of life. The four tiny beach villages here offer few distractions, but there are some excellent bushwalks, and with a little effort you can have a tropical beach all to yourself.

It's certainly an attractive getaway. Giant granite boulders, hoop pines and eucalypts cover the island, which is half national park and a haven for rock wallabies, bats and brushtail possums. The surrounding waters are also part of the precious Great Barrier Reef World Heritage Area. Captain Cook named Magnetic island in 1770 when his ship's compass went peculiar as he sailed by; if only he knew what he was missing.

Orientation & Information

Magnetic Island is easy and cheap to get to, only 8km from Townsville. It's roughly triangular in shape. A sealed road follows the east coast for 10km from Picnic Bay, on the island's southern point, to Horseshoe Bay in the north. A local bus ploughs the route regularly. There's a rough 8km track along the west coast leading from Picnic Bay to a wonderfully secluded beach at West Point.

A visitors centre is planned for Nelly Bay, but until then, pop into Townsville's **visitors centre** (☎ 4721 3660; Flinders Mall; ☼ 9am-5pm Mon-Fri, 9am-1pm Sat & Sun). There's a **QPWS** (☎ 4778 5378; Hurst St; ☼ 7.30am-4pm) at Picnic Bay.

Some backpacker operators offer Internet access.

Picnic Bay

Perhaps it's the twinkling night views of Townsville that draw families and couples to Picnic Bay. The Mall along the waterfront has a good handful of eateries and is a favourite hang-out for that elegant, curious bird, the curlew. There's a stinger-free enclosure here and you can hire snorkelling gear from the mall.

To the west of town is **Cockle Bay**, with the wreck of *HMS City of Adelaide*, and secluded **West Point**. Heading east round the coast is **Rocky Bay**, where there's a short, steep walk

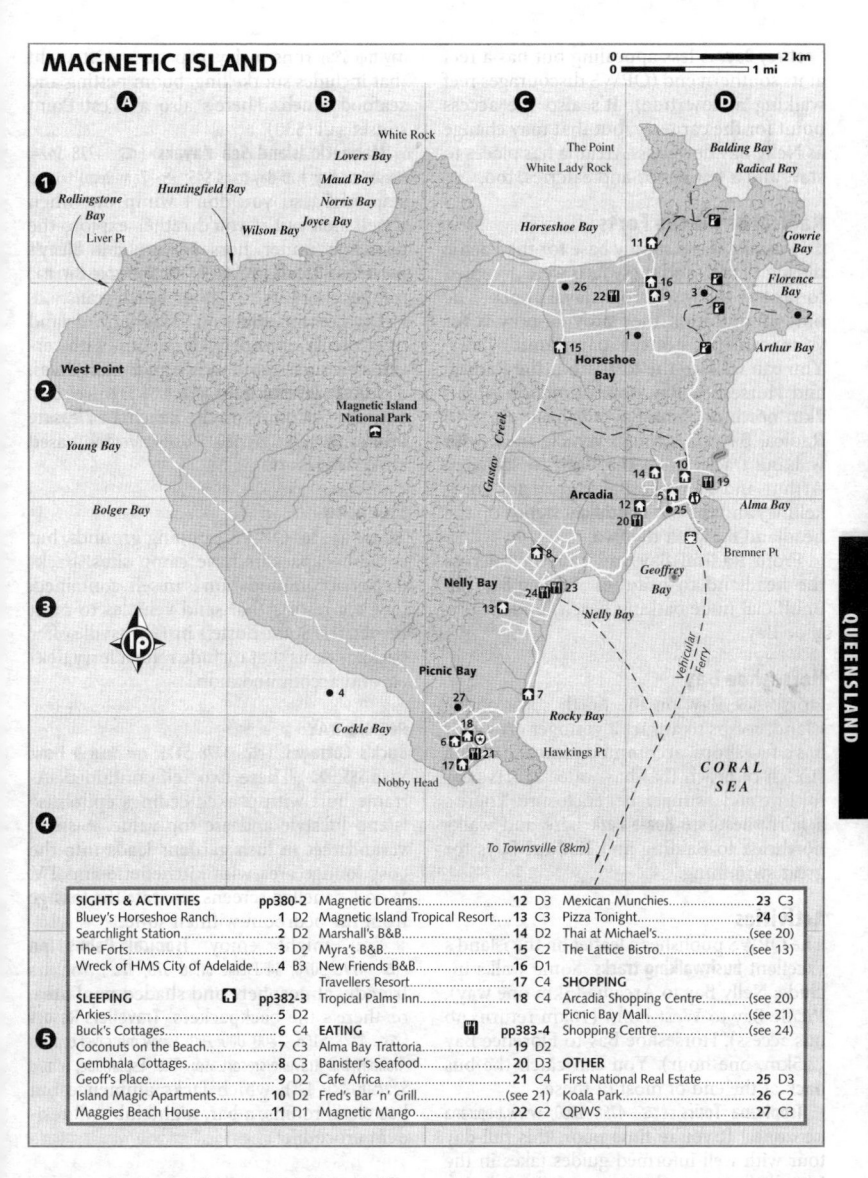

MAGNETIC ISLAND

0 ————— 2 km
0 ————— 1 mi

White Rock
Lovers Bay
Maud Bay
The Point
White Lady Rock
Balding Bay
Radical Bay

Rollingstone Bay
Huntingfield Bay
Norris Bay
Joyce Bay
Horseshoe Bay
Gowrie Bay

Liver Pt
Wilson Bay

Florence Bay

West Point
Horseshoe Bay
Arthur Bay

Magnetic Island National Park

Young Bay

Gustav Creek

Bolger Bay
Arcadia
Alma Bay

Nelly Bay
Bremner Pt

Geoffrey Bay

Nelly Bay

Vehicular ferry

Picnic Bay

Cockle Bay
Rocky Bay

Hawkings Pt

Nobby Head
CORAL SEA

To Townsville (8km)

QUEENSLAND

SIGHTS & ACTIVITIES	pp380-2	Magnetic Dreams	12 D3	Mexican Munchies	23 C3
Bluey's Horseshoe Ranch	1 D2	Magnetic Island Tropical Resort	13 C3	Pizza Tonight	24 C3
Searchlight Station	2 D2	Marshall's B&B	14 D2	Thai at Michael's	(see 20)
The Forts	3 D2	Myra's B&B	15 C2	The Lattice Bistro	(see 13)
Wreck of HMS City of Adelaide	4 B3	New Friends B&B	16 D1		
		Travellers Resort	17 C4	SHOPPING	
SLEEPING	pp382-3	Tropical Palms Inn	18 C4	Arcadia Shopping Centre	(see 20)
Arkies	5 D2			Picnic Bay Mall	(see 21)
Buck's Cottages	6 C4	EATING	pp383-4	Shopping Centre	(see 24)
Coconuts on the Beach	7 C3	Alma Bay Trattoria	19 D2		
Gembhala Cottages	8 C3	Banister's Seafood	20 D3	OTHER	
Geoff's Place	9 D2	Cafe Africa	21 C4	First National Real Estate	25 D3
Island Magic Apartments	10 D2	Fred's Bar 'n' Grill	(see 21)	Koala Park	26 C2
Maggies Beach House	11 D1	Magnetic Mango	22 C2	QPWS	27 C3

down to its beautiful beach. The popular **Picnic Bay Golf Course** is open to the public.

Nelly Bay

Nelly Bay has recently become the island's main ferry port (it used to be Picnic Bay). At the time of writing, a three-year waterfront development that includes a marina,

accommodation and dining was underway, conspiring to make Nelly Bay the island's happening hub – hopefully a low-key one.

Arcadia

Arcadia village has the lovely **Alma Bay** cove. There's plenty of shade, picnic tables and a kids' playground here. The main beach,

Geoffrey Bay, is less appealing but has a reef at its southern end (QPWS discourages reef walking at low tide). It's also the access point for the car ferry, but that may change as Nelly Bay develops. Arcadia has places to stay, and a few shops and eateries, too.

Radical Bay & the Forts

Townsville was a supply base for the Pacific during WWII, and these **forts** were designed to protect the town from naval attack. The only ammunition they provide now is for your camera – great panoramic views. You can walk to the forts from the Radical and Horseshoe Bay Roads junction, about 2km north of Alma Bay. Or head north to Radical Bay via a rough vehicle track with walking tracks off it that lead to secluded Arthur and Florence Bays (great for snorkelling) and the old **searchlight station** on the headland between the two.

From Radical Bay you can walk across the headland to beautiful **Balding Bay** (an unofficial nude bathing beach) and Horseshoe Bay.

Horseshoe Bay

Horseshoe Bay, on the north coast of the island, seems to attract a younger crowd. It has a few shops, accommodation and a long stretch of beach that has water-sports gear for hire and a stinger-net enclosure. There's a fairly desolate **Koala Park** here and walks northeast to Balding and Radical Bays for great swimming.

Activities

The QPWS publishes a leaflet on the island's excellent **bushwalking tracks**. Some walks include: Nelly Bay to Arcadia (5km one way), Picnic Bay to West Point (16km return; no bus access), Horseshoe Bay to Florence Bay (2.5km, one hour). You can catch the bus back at the end of most of these.

Tropicana Tours (☎ 4758 1800; www.tropicanatours.com.au) If you're time poor, this full-day tour with well-informed guides takes in the island's best spots in its stretch jeep. Enjoy close encounters with wildlife, nibbles and wine at sunset on West Point and chummy karaoke on the way home. The tour costs $125 and includes transfers. Thumbs up!

If you missed the Whitsundays, you can still indulge in a day's sailing here. **Jazza Sailing Tours** (☎ 0427-373 011, 4758 1887;

day trip $80) runs a day trip on a 42ft yacht that includes snorkelling, boom netting and seafood lunch. There's also a West Point sunset sail ($30).

Magnetic Island Sea Kayaks (☎ 4778 5424; Horseshoe Bay; half-day tours $45; ☷ 7am-9pm) tours start early, so you don't wimp out when it gets hot, but if you'd rather explore the coastline under horsepower, call **Bluey's Horseshoe Ranch** (☎ 4778 5109; Horseshoe Bay; trail rides $65) about its two-hour beach trails.

Dive companies on Magnetic Island offer plenty of underwater action with certificate courses, and wreck and night dives. Try **Ocean Dive Australia** (☎ 4758 1391; Nelly Bay), based at Coconuts on the Beach, or **Pleasure Divers** (☎ 4778 5788, 1800 797 797; Arcadia), based at Arkies resort.

Sleeping

There are no QPWS camping grounds, but some backpackers have camp sites. Backpacker accommodation is in self-contained, low-key resorts that send vehicles to meet the ferries. Some hostels in Townsville offer package deals that include return ferry tickets and accommodation.

PICNIC BAY

Buck's Cottages (☎ 4778 5115; cnr Yule & Picnic Sts; d $55; ☷) These two self-contained, A-frame huts with peaked ceilings epitomise island lifestyle and are top value. A small veranda set in lush gardens leads into the cosy lounge area with kitchenette and TV. Wood-panelled screens separate the lounge from the bedroom with en suite.

You might enjoy **Tropical Palms Inn** (☎ 4778 5076; 34 Picnic St; d $75; ☷) for its friendly atmosphere and shaded pool area, or there's the backpackers' **Travellers Resort** (☎ 4778 5166, 1800 000 290; www.mbtravel.com.au /holiday/ma_travellersresort.asp; The Esplanade; dm/d $20/50; ☷ ☐), which lacks ambience but has clean rooms, a bar, nightclub and resident crocodile!

NELLY BAY

Gembhala Cottages (☎ 4778 5435; 28 Mango Parkway; d from $85; ☷) The pathway to your Balinese-inspired cottage meanders through a flourishing, lantern-lit tropical garden. Inside, louvre windows filter the light, and carved-wood features and open-air bathrooms complete the unique design. There's a pool and comfy outdoor area and the bus stops right out front. The owners do ferry drop-offs.

Coconuts on the Beach (☎ 4778 5777, 1800 065 696; www.bakpakgroup.com; camp sites/dm/d $8/12/60; 🖳) So laid-back-it's-falling-over; that's Coconuts. This is the best backpacker island experience, with fantastic bay views from its pool and outdoor area. Come sunset, it's time to party. It's a fair walk to the shops, but there's a bar and cheap café with a limited menu.

Magnetic Island Tropical Resort (☎ 4778 5955; fax 4778 5601; 56 Yates St; dm/d $20/80; 🕃) A-frame cabins with en suites encircle large bird-filled gardens here. The bright, 'tropical double' rooms are best. There's a pool, lawn tennis court, alluring restaurant and bar, but the communal kitchen needs work.

ARCADIA

First National Real Estate (☎ 4778 5077; 21 Marine Pde; www.magneticislandfn.com.au) manages some very comfortable two-bedroom apartments, costing from $85 per night, including **Island Magic Apartments** (22 Armand Way; 2-bedroom apt $110; 🕃), across the road from gorgeous Alma Bay, and **Magnetic Dreams** (56 Hayles Ave, $100; 🕃) – contemporary apartments with city-living flair and a shaded pool.

On a budget, **Arkies** (☎ 4778 5177, 1800 663 666; www.arkiesonmagnetic.com; 7 Marine Pde; dm from $15, d $50; 🕃 🖳) is short on charm but big on party vibe with two pools and loads of entertainment, including toad racing. The rooms are big, with daggy décor, but some dorms have tranquil views.

Otherwise, **Marshall's B&Bs** (☎ 4778 5112; 3 Endeavour Rd; s/d $45/65) friendly hosts offer basic rooms in their modest home.

HORSESHOE BAY

Myra's B&B (☎ 4758 1277, 1800 001 094; myras@ bigpond.com; 101 Swensen St; s/d $50/70; 🕃) Myra has two pretty rooms and a delightful cabin out back in this rambling bush-meets-tropics setting alive with creatures. It's out of the way, but great value. Bicycles are free and they'll drive you to and from local eateries and the ferry.

New Friends B&B (☎ 4758 1220; 48B Horseshoe Bay Rd; s/d $65/80; 🕃) There's less privacy at this well-kept B&B, with rooms inside the main home, but the pool and large shaded terrace surrounding the house are great and it's 200m from the beachfront shops.

Maggies Beach House (☎ 4778 5144; www.maggies beachhouse.com.au; Pacific Dr; dm $21, d from $52; 🕃 🖳) Maggies has the best spot on the beachfront and dorms with balconies and great views. The TV lounge area is cramped, but the café (meals $8 to $16) and bar beside the pool is the place to chill, if you can, in the tropics.

Geoff's Place (☎ 4778 5577, 1800 285 577; www .geoffsplace.com.au; 40 Horseshoe Bay Rd; camp sites $10, dm $18-20, d $58; 🖳) There's plenty of shady camping in these grounds and Geoff's is close to everything. It's a very relaxed and friendly atmosphere around the bar and pool. Beds are in the island's trademark A-frame cedar cabins; some have en suites.

Eating

The island's dress code is a shorts and thongs affair. Opening hours are goofy during quiet periods (late January to March).

PICNIC BAY

There's a small supermarket here on the waterfront mall.

Fred's Bar 'n' Grill (☎ 4778 5911; Picnic Bay Mall; mains $15-20) Friendly service in unpretentious surrounds overlooking Picnic Bay make Fred's the choice place to munch. Dishes are well cooked with contemporary flavours, and daily specials are particularly good value. Otherwise, **Cafe Africa's** (☎ 4758 1119; Picnic Arcade; lunch $5-9) specialities include breakfast all day, sweet or savoury crepes and damn fine coffee.

NELLY BAY

There's a small supermarket, bakery and café on the main road next to Pizza Tonight.

Pizza Tonight (☎ 4758 1400; 53 Sooning St; dishes $10-20) Next to the supermarket, this unassuming pizza place also does good lasagne and burgers with salad and chips. Eat outdoors only, or take away, at good prices.

The Lattice Bistro (☎ 4778 5955; 56 Yates St; dishes $15-25) For something more upmarket, this large, airy restaurant on a latticed veranda overlooks gardens bursting with birdlife. The menu doesn't offer any surprises, but the setting is romantic.

Mexican Munchies (☎ 4778 5658; 37 Warboy St; mains $15-20; 🕑 closed Wed) It's the usual line-up – enchiladas, burritos and sangria – at this ultra-casual restaurant. It's looking a little tattered, or should that be, relaxed?

ARCADIA

In the small Arcadia shopping centre, the bakery (open early) is good for breakfast.

Alma Bay Trattoria (☎ 4778 5757; 11 Olympus St; mains $16-20; ☺ closed Mon & Tue) It's not easy to find such an eclectic and tempting menu as this on the island. Seating is inside or on a patio overlooking the bay. To get here, cross the little bridge below the surf life-saving club, and go early!

You can eat at tables outside or take away from these two. **Thai at Michael's** (☎ 4778 5217; Bright Ave; mains $12-17) has a simple menu that covers all the favourite Thai curries and pad thai, while **Banister's Seafood** (☎ 4778 5700; 22 McCabe Cres; mains $5-22) does, you guessed it, good fish and chips.

HORSESHOE BAY

There are a few OK eateries and a pub on the beachfront.

Magnetic Mango (☎ 4778 5018; Apjohn St; lunch $9-17, dinner $20-27; ☺ 10am-5pm Tue-Wed, 10am-10pm Sat-Mon, closed Thu & Fri) Everything here is home-made and you're guaranteed to have trouble choosing between yummy dishes. The menu is huge, desserts are scrumptious and mangoes feature heavily, of course. Even better, dining is alfresco in a leafy mango orchard lit with fairy lights by night.

Getting There & Away

Sunferries (☎ 4771 3855; Flinders St East; ☺ 6.45am-7pm Mon-Fri, 7am-5.30pm Sat & Sun) operates a frequent passenger ferry daily between Townsville and Magnetic Island (return $17, 20 minutes). Ferries leave from the terminal on Flinders St East, also stopping at the breakwater terminal on Sir Leslie Thiess Drive. There's a free car park at the breakwater terminal. If it's full, try the $4 per day car park across the road.

Magnetic Island Car & Passenger Ferry (☎ 4772 5422; Ross St; ☺ 7.15am-5.30pm, closes 3.45pm Sat) does the crossing many times each day from the southern end of Ross Creek. Return fares are: car $123, motorcycle $40, passengers $17, bicycles free. The car ferry arrives at Arcadia, but this may change. Be sure to ask when you book.

Getting Around

BICYCLE

Magnetic Island is ideal for cycling. You can rent mountain bikes (about $14 a day) from the booth by the jetty on the Espla-

nade in Picnic Bay, or from the waterfront on Horseshoe Bay.

BUS

Magnetic Island Bus Service (☎ 4778 5130; fares $2-4.50) ploughs between Picnic Bay and Horseshoe Bay at least 14 times a day, meeting all ferries and stopping at, or near, all accommodation.

MOKE & SCOOTER

Moke Hire (☎ 4778 5491; Horseshoe Bay)

Moke Magnetic (☎ 4778 5377; Picnic Bay Mall) Mokes from $65 a day.

Roadrunner Scooter Hire (☎ 4778 5222; Picnic Bay Mall) Scooters from $28 a day.

Tropical Topless Car Rentals (☎ 4758 1111; Picnic Bay)

NORTH COAST HINTERLAND

Just a couple of days' drive and you can swelter in Australia's famed outback. The Flinders Hwy heads 800km due west from Townsville to Cloncurry.

Ravenswood

☎ 07 / pop 350

At Mingela, 88km from Townsville, think about making the 40km detour to Ravens-wood. It's a tiny mining town among scattered red-earth hills that dates back to gold-rush days. There is little to see, but that's the point. You come here to experience the solitude of mining life. Hop on a stool at the pubs and chat over a beer; most miners are happy to welcome a fresh face. Then visit the old post office and the restored courthouse turned **museum** (☎ 4770 2047; adult/child $2/1; ☺ 10am-3pm, closed Tue), staffed by the gregarious Woody, and you're done.

You can sleep over at the **Imperial Hotel** (☎ 4770 2131; Macrossan St; s/d $45/60) or the **Railway Hotel** (☎ 4770 2144; Barton St; s/d $22/44), a couple of 1870s gems, but book ahead. The council **camping ground** (camp site $6) is a sun-battered football field.

Charters Towers

☎ 07 / pop 9400

The gold rush is over, but the locals don't seem to know it. Charters Towers thrives in isolation 130km inland from Townsville. Its main industries are cattle and mining, followed closely, it seems, by gardening and religion, given the glorious parks and diverse denominations. There has even been a gold revival since the 1980s as modern processes allow companies to rework old deposits. This place was fabulously rich during the gold rush and still has a remarkable number of fine, 19th-century homes and restored public buildings.

The gleam of gold was first spotted in 1871 in a creek bed at the foot of Towers Hill by an Aboriginal boy, Jupiter Mosman. Within a few years the surrounding area was peppered with diggings and a large town had grown. In its heyday around the end of the 19th century, Charters Towers was known as 'The World' for its wealth and diversity. It had almost 100 mines, a population of 30,000, a stock exchange and 25 pubs.

It's possible to make a day trip from Townsville, but much better to stay over and enjoy this friendly, industrious community.

INFORMATION
Charters Towers Computers (☎ 4787 2988; 59 Gill St) For Internet access; otherwise, try the library on Gill St.
Charters Towers visitors centre (☎ 4752 0314; www.charterstowers.qld.gov.au; Mosman St; ☼ 9am-5pm) At the top of Gill St.
World Theatre cinema (☎ 4787 4344; Mosman St)

SIGHTS & ACTIVITIES
If you want to glimpse the tough outback life, stay at a cattle station. **Bluff Downs** with its pretty, historic homestead and **Plain Creek** is about two hours' drive from town.

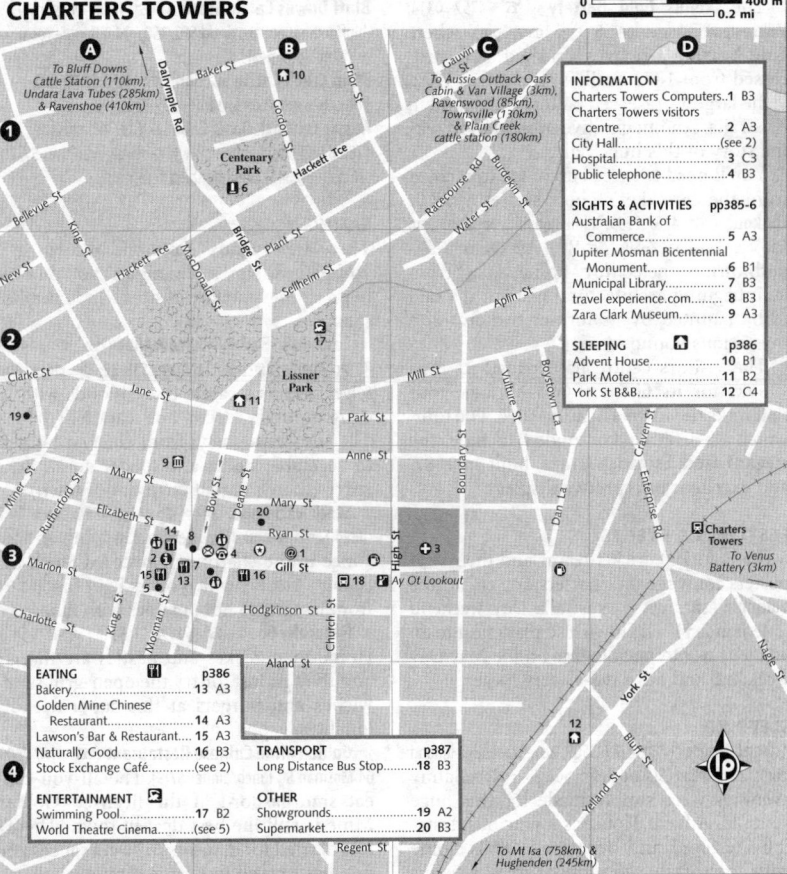

CHARTERS TOWERS

0 ——— 400 m
0 ——— 0.2 mi

To Bluff Downs Cattle Station (110km), Undara Lava Tubes (285km) & Ravenshoe (410km)

To Aussie Outback Oasis Cabin & Van Village (3km), Ravenswood (85km), Townsville (130km) & Plain Creek cattle station (180km)

Centenary Park 🛈6

Lissner Park

To Charters Towers
To Venus Battery (3km)

INFORMATION	
Charters Towers Computers	1 B3
Charters Towers visitors centre	2 A3
City Hall	(see 2)
Hospital	3 C3
Public telephone	4 B3

SIGHTS & ACTIVITIES	pp385-6
Australian Bank of Commerce	5 A3
Jupiter Mosman Bicentennial Monument	6 B1
Municipal Library	7 B3
travel experience.com	8 B3
Zara Clark Museum	9 A3

SLEEPING	p386
Advent House	10 B1
Park Motel	11 B2
York St B&B	12 C4

EATING	p386
Bakery	13 A3
Golden Mine Chinese Restaurant	14 A3
Lawson's Bar & Restaurant	15 A3
Naturally Good	16 B3
Stock Exchange Café	(see 2)

ENTERTAINMENT	
Swimming Pool	17 B2
World Theatre Cinema	(see 5)

TRANSPORT	p387
Long Distance Bus Stop	18 B3

OTHER	
Showgrounds	19 A2
Supermarket	20 B3

Ay Ot Lookout

To Mt Isa (758km) & Hughenden (245km)

QUEENSLAND

There's plenty of activity going on such as cattle branding and ear marking, but you'll spend more time watching than participating. See below for other details.

Gold City Bush Safaris (☎ 4787 2118; ☼ 8am-6pm) is run by a fourth-generation Charters Towers local. Geoff Phillips has more than 100 years of stories to tell on his $20 two-hour orientation or Venus Battery tours. They're tailored to suit your interests and his chatty character; you may never get home.

A wonderful place to escape in time is the **Zara Clark Museum** (☎ 4787 4661; Mosman St; adult/child $4.40/2.20; ☼ 10am-3pm). The clutter of memorabilia, from bakery carts to the original 'one-arm bandits' (poker machines), antique clothing and an extensive military collection, is fascinating.

The **Venus Gold Battery** (☎ 4752 0314; Millchester Rd; admission $6; ☼ 10am-5pm), where gold-bearing ore was crushed and processed from 1872 until as recently as 1972, is the largest preserved battery of its kind in Australia. An imaginative presentation tells the story of this huge relic.

You'll need the free cup of tea to recover from the caretaker's ghost stories at **Ay Ot Lookout** (☎ 4787 2799; admission $3; ☼ 8am-3pm Apr-Sep, closed Sat & Sun, Oct-Mar). Ay Ot is a superb turn of the century home. Apart from its intriguing architectural history, it's said to be haunted by its former owner and a mysterious young woman.

The visitors centre has created its own spooks for its **Ghosts of Gold** heritage tour that links the town's historic sites. The tour, which is self-guided or guided, includes the elegant **Stock Exchange Arcade**, built in 1887, and excellent interpretive displays.

FESTIVALS & EVENTS
More than 100 cricket teams and their supporters converge on Charters Towers for the **Goldfield Ashes** every Australia Day weekend (late January). The town also plays host to an amateur **country music festival** on the May Day weekend, and has a **rodeo** every Easter.

SLEEPING
Advent House (☎ 4787 3508; adventhouse@bigpond .com; 29 Gordon St; s/d from $60/80; ☒) Balmy evenings were simply made for this huge veranda. Advent House is a gracious, tastefully restored and decorated 1880s home with comfortable communal areas, a swim-

ming pool and gregarious hosts who make it an excellent sleepover.

York St B&B (☎ 4787 1028; 58 York St; dm/s/d $17/65/80; ☒) Less formal, with bright and cheerful décor, this renovated 1880s timber house has a good communal country kitchen, disabled facilities, a wide veranda and pool, but is 1.5km from town. The unattractive, basic backpacker rooms are separate to the house.

Park Motel (☎ 4787 1022; fax 4787 4268; cnr Mosman & Deane Sts; d $60-80; ☒) The guest rooms upstairs are the gem of this attractive old hotel/motel. Ask for the humble honeymoon suite with its high ceilings and double-base bed. Downstairs is a cosy, deep-pink bar and quaint restaurant. Otherwise, motel units are available, and it's a stroll to town.

Other recommendations:

Bluff Downs Cattle Station (☎ 4770 4084; www .bluffdowns.com.au; dm/d $22/150; ☒) Double room price includes meals.

Plain Creek Cattle Station (☎ 4983 5228; reid .robyn@bigpond.com; d from $95; ☒)

Aussie Outback Oasis Cabin & Van Village (☎ /fax 4787 8722; 61-77 Flinders Hwy; camp/caravan sites $7/18, cabins from $45) Good disabled access.

EATING
There aren't loads of options in town so if you plan to stay a few nights, you'd better like a simple pub fare of steaks and crumbed sausages.

Lawson's Bar & Restaurant (☎ 4787 4333; 82 Mosman St; lunch $8-11, mains $16-22; ☼ closed Mon & Tue) Lawson's caters to all moods with its contemporary décor and candlelit tables. The meals are tasty, from chicken burgers to vegetable stacks and tender goat's meat curry (there's a goat farm out of town).

Stock Exchange Cafe (☎ 4787 7954; lunch $6-9; closed Sun, Dec-Apr) It's pleasant sipping an iced coffee in the charmingly restored Stock Exchange Arcade, which offers light lunch fare from lasagne to hot potatoes with fillings.

Naturally Good (☎ 4787 4211; 58 Gill St; lunch $4-6) Home-made cakes and pasties are the go, and they go fast, or try the open-grill sandwiches and burgers at this super-friendly lunchtime spot.

Golden Mine Chinese Restaurant (☎ 4787 7609; 64 Mosman St; lunch/dinner $7/9) The all-you-can-eat smorgasbord at the licensed Golden Mine is still the best deal in town. There's lots of fried food, meats in sweet sauces and noodles, served in a large dining room.

GETTING THERE & AWAY
McCafferty's/Greyhound (☎ 13 20 30) has daily services from Townsville to Charters Towers ($27 one way per adult, 1¾ hours), continuing to Mt Isa on selected days ($106, 10¼ hours). Buses arrive and depart outside the Catholic church on Gill St.

The train station is on Enterprise Rd, 1.5km east of the centre. The twice-weekly *Inlander* runs from Townsville to Charters Towers (economy seat $23, 3 hours) and on to Mt Isa (economy/1st-class sleeper $148/221, 17 hours). Ask about fare discounts.

Travel Experience.com (☎ 4787 2622; 13 Gill St) handles travel tickets.

TOWNSVILLE TO MISSION BEACH
Paluma Range National Park

Don't miss the beautiful Mt Spec–Big Crystal Creek section of this national park. It straddles the 1000m-plus Paluma Range west of the Bruce Hwy and has Australia's most southerly pocket of tropical rainforest, with wonderful coastal views. It's about 62km north of Townsville (47km south of Ingham).

There are two access routes from the Bruce Hwy. Travelling north, take the turn-off left after Rollingstone, then left onto the signposted ring road up to Paluma Range. The uphill road is narrow and spectacular, and winds along the southern edge of the park, passing **Little Crystal Creek** (with a waterfall and good swimming beside a stone bridge) and **McClelland's Lookout** (with three good walking trails) on the way to the mountain village of Paluma (18km from the ring road).

Travelling south, turn right at Mutarnee to access the ring road, just after the Frosty Mango café. Take the turn-off to **Big Crystal Creek**, which has good swimming, a barbecue area and a self-registration **camping ground** (per person/family $4/16). To complete the drive, get back onto the ring road and take the right turn-off to Paluma.

The **Jourama Falls** area of the park is 6km along good unsealed road off the highway. The signpost is 91km north of Townsville (24km south of Ingham). Waterview Creek, walking distance from the falls (600m) has good swimming holes with loads of cute turtles, lookouts, a picnic area and a self-registration **camping ground** (per person/family $4/16) with barbecues. Check availability with the **ranger** (☎ 07-4777 3112) in peak season.

Townsville Tropical Tours (☎ 07-4721 6489) runs day trips to the park, or accommodation is available at **Paluma Rainforest Cottages** (☎ 07-4770 8520; d $90). Make sure you stop at **Frosty Mango** (☎ 07-4770 8184; light meals $5-10) at Mutarnee. It's a roadside restaurant serving everything mango-ish.

For more information, contact Ingham's **QPWS** or **visitors centre** (see below), or the Townsville **visitors centre** (☎ 07-4778 3555).

Ingham & Around

Ingham is a major sugar-producing town and you'll want to stop here for directions to spectacular **Wallaman Falls**. Otherwise, the accommodation and eating options are few and disappointing.

The falls, within Lumholtz National Park 50km west of town, have the longest single drop of any in Australia at 278m. It's a powerful sight in wet season. There's a self-registration QPWS **camping ground** (per person/family $4/16) with a swimming hole nearby. Pop into the Ingham **visitors centre** (☎ 07-4776 5211; cnr Lannercost St & Townsville Rd; ☼ 9am-5pm Mon-Fri, 9am-2pm Sat & Sun) or the **QPWS** (☎ 07-4777 2808; 49 Cassidy St) for information.

Between Ingham and Cardwell, the Bruce Hwy briefly climbs high above the coast with tremendous views over the winding, mangrove-lined waterways known as the Everglades, which separate Hinchinbrook Island from the coast. The best view of them is from **Casual Cassowary Tea House** (☎ 07-4777 7046; ☼ 10am-5pm Mon, 9am-5pm Tue-Sat), 19km north of Ingham, which has self-contained cottages (singles/doubles $66 per night). The Devonshire teas here are magnificent, with 32 fine quality teas to choose from.

Lucinda, a port town 24km from Ingham, is the access point for the southern end of Hinchinbrook Island. It's worth coming down here just to see the 6km-long jetty used for shipping sugar.

Cardwell
☎ 07 / pop 1420

Quiet Cardwell is one of north Queensland's earliest towns, yet there's surprisingly little to it. The Port Hinchinbrook marina development, 2km south of town, is the departure point for Hinchinbrook Island and may awaken this beachside stretch in years to come. For travellers with wheels, there are a bunch of great forest drives, picnic spots and walks with swimming holes in the area, including the **Cardwell Forest Drive**, a 26km round trip.

The QPWS **Reef & Rainforest Centre** (☎ 4066 8115; www.epa.qld.gov.au; ☉ 8am-4.30pm), beside the main jetty, has a great rainforest interpretive display and information on Hinchinbrook Island and the drives.

SLEEPING

Mudbrick Manor (☎ 4066 2299; Stoney Creek Rd; www .mudbrickmanor.com.au; d $95-$120; ☒) Amazing! This sprawling, adobe-style home, furnished with casual country flair is a *heavenly* retreat. You'll spend lazy days on the veranda by an enchanting courtyard, soaking up this sociable, super-casual atmosphere. The indoor lounge is huge, yet cosy, with activities galore to occupy you, and there's a lovely pool. Breakfast is included, but ask your hosts about their three-course dinners. You'll stay another night.

Port Hinchinbrook Resort (☎ 4066 2000; www .porthinchinbrook.com.au; d from $155; ☒) As a resort, this marina development has big plans but a long way to go. There's a nice marina-front café and some comfortable, modern cabins, but it feels empty. Try for standby rates on arrival.

On the main strip, the **Hinchinbrook Hop** (☎ 4066 8671; 186 Victoria St; camp sites $12, dm $14) has small, bright dorms and a good roadside café; the **Kookaburra Holiday Park** (☎ 4066 8648; www.kookaburraholidaypark.com.au; 175 Bruce Hwy; dm $18) includes a YHA hostel.

Cardwell Central Backpackers was busy laying bricks for its new backpacker hostel when we were in town. It should be open by the time you read this. The hostel will be 100m from the transit centre and will have an Internet café. Call Mudbrick Manor (☎ 4066 2299) for bookings.

GETTING THERE & AWAY

All buses between Townsville and Cairns stop at Cardwell: Townsville ($33), Cairns ($27). Cardwell is also on the Brisbane to Cairns railway line. Contact the **Queensland Rail's booking service** (☎ 13 22 32; www.traveltrain.qr .com.au; ☉ 6am-8.30pm) for more information.

Hinchinbrook Island National Park

Lucky you, if you have time to explore this stunning and unspoiled wilderness. Hinchinbrook's granite mountains rise dramatically from the sea. The mainland side is thick with lush tropical forest, while long, sandy beaches and tangled mangroves curve round its eastern shores. All 399 sq km of the island is national park, and rugged Mt Bowen (1121m) is its highest peak. There's plenty of wildlife, especially pretty-faced wallabies and the iridescent-blue Ulysses butterfly. It's definitely worth a day trip.

Hinchinbrook is well known to bushwalkers and naturalists. Walking opportunities here are excellent; however, some trails may close between November and March due to adverse weather. The highlight is the **Thorsborne Trail** (also known as the East Coast Trail), a 32km track from Ramsay Bay to Zoe Bay (with its stunning waterfall), and on to George Point at the southern tip. It's a three- to five-day walk, although you can walk shorter sections if you don't have that much time. This is the real bush experience, however. You'll need to draw water from creeks as you go (all water should be chemically purified or boiled before drinking), keep your food out of reach of the native bush rats, and keep an eye out for estuarine crocodiles in the mangroves. Take plenty of insect repellent.

Hinchinbrook Island Resort (☎ 07-4066 8585, 1800 777 021; www.hinchinbrookresort.com.au; d from $673, cabins $150), on the northern peninsula, at Cape Richards, has treehouse-style rooms for 50 people. It's very low-key and eco-friendly, and prices include meals. Its self-contained beach cabins are the budget option.

There are six QPWS **camping grounds** (per person/family $4/16) along the Thorsborne Trail, plus others at Macushla and Scraggy Point in the north. There is a limit of 45 people allowed on the main trail at any one time, so it's necessary to book ahead (up to one year for school holiday periods). Pick up the informative Thorsborne Trail and Hinchinbrook leaflets from the QPWS **Reef & Rainforest Centre** (☎ 07-4066 8601) in Cardwell. To purchase your permits ($4 per night), call ☎ 13 13 04 or pay online at www.smartservice.qld.gov.au/AQ.

GETTING THERE & AWAY

Hinchinbrook Island Ferries (☎ 07-4066 8270; www .hinchinbrookferries.com.au) runs a daily ferry from April to October and three services a week from November to March, from Port Hinchinbrook Marina. Services are suspended in February during the wet season. A day trip costs $85 and a one-way transfer for walkers costs $60. Walkers usually catch another ferry at the southern end of the island to Lucinda, back on the mainland, with **Hinchinbrook Wilderness Safaris** (☎ 07-4777 8307). It's $57 one way, and the price includes transport from Lucinda to Cardwell after the ferry ride.

Tully

☎ 07 / pop 2700

The big excitement in tiny Tully is spending five frothy hours white-water rafting its wild river. It's supposedly the wettest place in Australia with an average annual rainfall of over 4000mm. Walkers also have good reason to stop, with 150km of new tracks, while other travellers come to pick bananas. Even so, nearby Mission Beach has more appealing creature comforts.

Day trips with **Raging Thunder Adventures** (☎ 4030 7990; www.ragingthunder.com.au) or **R 'n' R White Water Rafting** (☎ 4051 7777, 1800 079 039; www.raft.com.au) cost about $135 and include barbecue lunch and transfers from Mission Beach, Cairns or Port Douglas.

The new **Misty Mountain** and **Kennedy Trails** cover existing logging roads that wind through the lush Tully Valley and, in part, retrace the steps of explorer Edmund Kennedy. Alternatively, Aboriginal guides will share their rainforest survival skills along the old trading route, **Echo Creek Walking Trail**. You can book tours through **El Rancho Del Rey** (☎ 4066 7770; www.elrancho.com.au; Ranch Rd via Davidson Rd, Tully; dm/s $66/135), which has homestead or bunk accommodation that includes meals. For more information on heritage walking trails, ask at the **visitors centre** (☎ 4068 2288; ⏱ 8.30am-4.45pm Mon-Fri, 9am-2.30pm Sat & Sun) on the highway or check Tourism Tropical North Queensland's website www.tropicalaustralia.com.au.

Tully's limited accommodation is geared towards fruit-pickers. There's the loud and high-density **Banana Barracks** (☎ 4068 0455; bananabarracks@comnorth.com.au; 50 Butler St; dm $18) or the quieter, old-fashioned **Savoy** (☎ 4068 2400; 4 Plumb St; dm $17).

MISSION BEACH

☎ 07 / pop 1090

It's no wonder Mission Beach is a favourite spot to chill on the backpacker circuit with its cosy village atmosphere and the dreami-est stretch of palm-fringed sand along the northeast coast. It's also kayaking distance to tranquil Dunk Island and the hub for a 14km string of coastal settlements that include Wongaling Beach, South Mission Beach, Bingil Bay and Garners Beach.

The town was named after an Aboriginal mission founded in 1914 and destroyed by a cyclone in 1918. There's a memorial commemorating explorer Edmund Kennedy at Tam O'Shanter Point, which was the starting point for Kennedy's overland expedition to Cape York in 1848. All but three of the party of 13 died, including Kennedy, who was killed by Aborigines.

Information

Mission Beach visitors centre (☎ 4068 7099; Porter Promenade; ⏱ 9am-5pm)
Wet Tropics Centre (Porter Promenade; ⏱ 10am-5pm)

Sights & Activities

Mission Beach has all those near-death experiences you've been longing to try. You can **skydive** from here, **raft** the Tully River rapids (see this page), learn to **dive** or go **crocodile spotting** in the mangroves at night.

Sea kayaking is a fantastic way to learn about the Great Barrier Reef Marine Park with guides who really know and love the area. **Coral Sea Kayaking** (☎ 4068 9154; www.coralseakayaking.com) offers a half-day ($55) and one-day trip ($89) around Mission Beach and Dunk Island, and three-, five- and seven-day trips as far as Hinchinbrook Island. **Sunbird Adventures** (☎ 4068 8229) has morning sea-kayaking and snorkelling trips for $48, and a full-day paddle to Dunk Island for $80.

Day trips to pretty Dunk Island (p391) are popular. **MV Lawrence Kavanagh** (☎ 4068 7211) and **Quick Cat Cruises** (☎ 4068 7289) compete heavily for business at the Clump Point Jetty, offering good-value Great Barrier Reef and Dunk and Bedarra Island trips between them.

Rainforest walks around Mission Beach can get exciting if you meet a southern cassowary. This large, flightless, blue bird is an endangered species that needs protection, even though it can disembowel you with its toenail. Don't feed cassowaries or run over them with cars. Mission Beach was their precious habitat before people shuffled along and built brick nests on their turf.

QUEENSLAND

Sleeping

BUDGET

Sanctuary (☎ 4088 6064; 1800 777 012; www.sanctuary atmission.com; Holt Rd, Bingil Bay; s/d $55/60; 🖳) A hut with floor-to-ceiling mesh is all that separates you from boisterous rainforest critters at this unique treetop sanctuary about 11km north of Mission Beach. The gleaming communal treehouse has an excellent café, or you can self-cater. More modern cabins are available for $135. Note, the terrain here is incredibly steep! Sanctuary doesn't accommodate kids under 11, and transfers are available.

Beach Shack (☎ 4068 7783, 1800 333 115; www .missionbeachshack.com; 86 Porter Promenade; dm/d $18/ 40; ⚡ 🖳) Staying here is like staying at a friend's large, colourful, comfy home. Beach Shack has a great attitude, $5 barbecues several nights a week and free bicycles and pool table. It won't take long to ease into this hassle-free zone. They also book good-value trips to the Great Barrier Reef.

Treehouse (☎ 4068 7137; treehouse.yha@znet.net .au; Frizzel Rd; camp sites $13, dm/d $24/56) This impressive timber stilt treehouse with lush rainforest views and pool has seen better days, but it's looking for new owners. It's out of Mission Beach, but there's a courtesy bus into town. YHA cards are accepted.

Other recommendations:

Scotty's Beach House (☎ 4068 8676, 1800 665 567; www.scottysbeachhouse.com.au; 167 Reid Rd, Wongaling Beach; dm/d $21/50; ⚡ 🖳) Friendly atmosphere, café & party bar.

Mission Beach Retreat (☎ 4088 6229, 1800 001 056; www.missionbeachretreat.com.au; 49 Porter Promenade; dm/d $18/39; ⚡) Central.

Hideaway Holiday Village (☎ 4068 7104; hideaway@austarnet.com.au; 58-60 Porter Promenade; camp/caravan sites $20/23, cabins from $54) Central and tidier than you are.

There are two caravan parks in Mission Beach and another at South Mission Beach. If you plan to stay a while, call ahead to **Mission Beach Holidays & Rentals** (☎ 4088 6611; www.missionbeachholidays.com.au; 8 Porter Promenade) about holiday home rental.

MID-RANGE & TOP END

Perrier Walk Guest House (☎ 4068 7141; www.perrier walk.nq.nu; d $150; ⚡) Sublime. Think 'contemporary Mexican villa' as you conjure up this exquisite guesthouse drenched in vibrant colours of indigo, orange, jade and sunflower. Private gardens brim with exotic plants, and water features will surpass your imagination if the outdoor-style bathrooms don't! Ask to see the room with the sea-green bath. This place is the tantalising experience we all deserve once in a while, and the price includes a wonderful breakfast.

DragonHeart B&B (☎ 4068 7813; www.dragon heartbnb.com; 350 Bingil Bay Rd; d $95-$130) These surprising Balinese-style cottages are eclectic in their design and colourful decoration. Ask for the gorgeous 'Bathhouse' cottage with Asian screens separating shower and loo from you, and there's a dinky, sunken bath. Dinners are catered for but cost extra, or there's an excellent kitchen. You'll need a car to get here.

Mackays Mission Beach (☎ 40687212; www.mackays missionbeach.com; 7 Porter Promenade; d $85-105) The best things about clean, fresh Mackays are its granite inlaid pool surrounded by tropical plants and its location – a stroll to the shops and beach. The deluxe doubles have it all; and ask about good-value packages.

Licuala Lodge B&B (☎ 4068 8194; www.licuala lodge.com.au; s/d $100/120; ⚡) You're separate from the main home in a tidy timber pole house with compact, brightly furnished rooms. The 'jungle' pool and gardens are a special treat and there's complimentary alcohol. It is 3.5km from town.

Sejala on the Beach (☎ 4088 6611; 1 Pacific St, Mission Beach; s/d $165/185; ⚡) You've got to love the tropics-inspired semi-outdoor bathrooms here. These huts are surrounded by secluded, landscaped gardens and the design is contemporary with a twist. Ask to see the hut right by the beach.

Eating

Blarneys (☎ 4068 8472; 10 Wongaling Beach Rd; mains $17-25; 🕑 closed Sun dinner & Mon) The service is polished, yet the atmosphere relaxed, in this lattice-screened restaurant with bamboo-thatched ceilings. It's cosy, candle-lit and the à la carte menu offers a good selection of rich, mostly meat dishes such as beef Wellington, and steak and kidney pie. The entrée portions are generous and the garlic bread is especially yummy. It's 5km away in Wongaling Beach.

Toba Restaurant & Bar (☎ 4068 7582; Porter Promenade; mains $15-25) Just by the Village Green shopping mall, Toba has an Asian menu featuring the usual suspects: beef rendang, tofu and vegie Thai curry, and nori rolls. While meals are presented with flair, the portions are not generous. The décor will inspire, however, with its sultry fusion of warm colours, and there's a Balinese hut with seating on cushions for small parties.

Piccolo Paradiso (☎ 4068 7008; Village Green; mains $9-16; ☺ closed Mon) It's predominantly pizza and pasta here, but a small selection of other mains, such as tiger prawn coconut curry or barramundi with tomato and caper dressing, are tasty, well-presented, big meals. Dining is in a casual courtyard by candlelight, and it's always busy.

Cafe Coconutz (☎ 4068 7397; Porter Promenade; mains $16-20) Coconutz has a large menu for lunch or dinner with Asian influences and plenty more to please. Dining is mostly outside. Next door is the bar, the place to hang out for cool drinks or coffee and cake. The vibe is more upbeat for drinks after dark.

Shrubbery Taverna (☎ 4068 7803; mains $17-19) Set beside the beach amid rustling palms and waves washing upon the shore, Shrubbery is a friendly outdoor taverna serving up OK Greek meals. It also has a happy hour-and-a-half from 4.30pm to 6pm.

Port o' Call Cafe (☎ 4068 7390; Shop 6, Porter Promenade; breakfast $4-9) The tiny Port o' Call, beside the bus stop, does early breakfasts, basic lunch fare and good, strong coffee in stupid cups with too-small handles.

Getting There & Around
McCafferty's/Greyhound (☎ 13 20 30; www.mccaffertys.com.au) buses stop at the Port o' Call Cafe in Mission Beach, while **Premier Motor Service** (☎ 13 34 10; www.premierms.com.au) stops at the Mission Beach Resort in Wongaling Beach. Average one-way fares per adult are Cairns ($16) and Townsville ($48).

The Mission Beach Bus Service runs regularly from Bingil Bay to South Mission Beach.

DUNK ISLAND
Dunk Island is an easy day trip from Mission Beach. It's just 4.5km off the coast and blessed with nearly 150 species of birdlife and exotic butterflies in season.

Rainforest walks here revive the spirit. From the top of Mt Kootaloo (271m; 5.6km), entrances to the Hinchinbrook Channel fan before you, or there's the rewarding but difficult island circuit (9.2km) that passes

by secluded beaches. You can also check out the alternative lifestyle of **Bruce Arthur's Artists Colony** (admission $4; ☺ 10am-1pm Mon & Thu).

Unfortunately, the resort on Dunk now charges a day pass (adult/child $28/14), but that includes complimentary lunch and a swim in the beachside butterfly pool. You can test your jet or water ski skills, snorkel or tube ride at the jetty (for a price of course), where there's a snack bar serving pizza, pies and light meals ($5 to $16).

The **Dunk Island Resort** (☎ 07-4068 8199, 1800 737 678; www.poresorts.com.au/dunk; d from $456) on palm-fringed Brammo Bay had a good refurbishment in 2003. Rooms are spacious and contemporary in design, which means lots of wicker furniture, and the breezy guest complex feels indulgent. Tariffs include breakfast and dinner.

The QPWS **camping ground** (☎ 07-4068 8199; per person/family $4/16) has nine shaded sites with good amenities by the resort's water-sports office; call for bookings.

Getting There & Away
A transfer to Dunk Island costs about $22 per adult, but some operators offer package trips that include lunch and other island stops.
Dunk Island Express Water Taxis (☎ 07-4068 8310)
Macair (☎ 13 13 13) Flights from Cairns cost $180.
MV Lawrence Kavanagh (☎ 07-4068 7211)
Quick Cat Cruises (☎ 07-4068 7289)

MISSION BEACH TO CAIRNS
The scenery from Mission Beach to Cairns is wonderfully fertile. North of El Arish, you can leave the Bruce Hwy and take an alternative route to Innisfail via quaint Silkwood and Mena Creek, buried in sugar cane about 20km southwest of Innisfail.

At Mena Creek, **Paronella Park** (☎ 07-4065 3225; www.paronellapark.com.au; adult/concession $17/15; ☺ 9am-5pm) is a rambling, tropical garden with the enchanting ruins of a Spanish castle built in the 1930s. Floods, fire and the moist tropics have rendered these mossy remains almost medieval. The story behind Paronella is of one man's quest to bring a whimsical entertainment centre to the area's hard-working folk. Tours run regularly and there's a caravan park next door.

If you want to know more about sugar processing, steam trains and the slave-labour heritage of the industry, pop by the

Australian Sugar Museum (☎ 07-4063 2656; adult/child $5/3; ☷ 9am-5pm Mon-Sat, 9am-3pm Sun May-Oct, 9am-5pm Mon-Fri, 9am-3pm Sat, 9am-noon Sun Nov-Apr) at Mourilyan, 7km south of Innisfail.

Innisfail
☎ 07 / pop 8530

The traffic is always at a standstill around Innisfail's pedestrian-friendly streets, but you won't mind, it's such a pretty place to stop by. This prosperous sugar city suffered a devastating cyclone in 1918, but its reconstruction came at the height of the sleek 1920s and '30s Art Deco movement. Innisfail's residents are proudly restoring buildings in keeping with the glamorous era.

The **visitors centre** (☎ 4061 7422; Bruce Hwy; ☷ 9am-5pm Mon-Fri, 10am-3pm Sat & Sun), about 3.5km south of town, has a **town walk** brochure.

Johnstone River Crocodile Farm (☎ 4061 1121; Flying Fish Point Rd; adult/child $16/8; ☷ 8.30am-4.30pm) breeds thousands of crocodiles so we can enjoy them as handbags and steak. But your skin will crawl at the sight of 300 crocs slam-dancing over a pile of raw chicken heads for dinner (feeding times 11am and 3pm). You can pet a freshwater croc and watch the guides *sit* on one-tonne Gregory, their fattest reptile. Tours run continuously.

Just off the Bruce Hwy about 3.5km south of town, tidy **Mango Tree Van Park** (☎ 4061 1656; mangotreepark@bigpond.com; 6 Couche St; camp sites $15, cabins $65; ☷) has two great cottage-style cabins, or there's the ordinary **Barrier Reef Motel** (☎ 4061 4988; barrierreefmotel@bigpond.com; s/d $70/82; ☷) with small rooms and free satellite TV, next to the visitors centre.

Hostels cater to the banana plantation workers. The homey atmosphere at **Codge Lodge** (☎ 4061 8055; 63 Rankin St; dm/d $20/40) makes it the best choice, or there's **Backpackers Paradise** (☎ 4061 2284; 73 Rankin St; dm $15).

From Innisfail the Palmerston Hwy winds west up to the magical Atherton Tableland, passing through the rainforest of **Palmerston (Wooroonooran National Park)**, which has creeks, waterfalls, scenic walking tracks and a self-registration **camping ground** (per person/family $4/16) at Henrietta Creek, just off the road.

Innisfail to Cairns

Australia's ancient landscape may be a pile of rubble in geological terms, but Queensland's highest peak, **Mt Bartle Frere** (1622m), is still a

challenging climb. It falls within the dramatic Bellenden Ker range, which skirts the Bruce Hwy between Innisfail and Cairns.

Experienced, fit walkers can begin the two-day, 15km walk up the mountain from **Josephine Falls**, which is 8km from the highway and about 22km north of Innisfail. This is a tranquil picnic spot with excellent swimming holes and natural water slides, but the slippery rocks are dangerous. The Innisfail and Cairns visitors centres have brochures describing the hike, or try the **park ranger** (☎ 07-4067 6304).

About 2km north of the Josephine Falls turn-off is the **Bramston Beach** turn-off. It's about 17km to this lazy coastal getaway. There's just one general store, the cheery **Bramston Beach Holiday Motel** (☎ 07-4067 4139; 1 Dawson St; d $69) and a large, palm-treed caravan park, **Bramston Beach Plantation Resort** (☎ 07-4067 4133; 1 Evans Rd; cabins $60), which has plans to build new cabins.

From Gordonvale, 33km north of Babinda, the winding Gillies Hwy leads up onto the Atherton Tableland. Otherwise, another 4km north is the turn-off to the **Yarrabah Aboriginal Community** (37km) where you can visit the **Menmuny Museum** (☎ 07-4056 9154, 0405 281 011; adult/concession $13/5; ☷ 8am-4pm Mon-Fri). The museum has an interpretive boardwalk as well as spear- and boomerang-throwing demonstrations and art and craft exhibits. A tribal elder may also be available to answer questions on community life, so call ahead to let them know you're coming.

GULF SAVANNAH

The Gulf Savannah is the very vision of outback Australia and you know what that means – horizons so wide they tickle the moon and the sun. A huge number of tidal creeks and rivers cut through this tough country, feeding into the impressive Gulf of Carpentaria. Most travellers come to experience a peace of mind among the vast tracts of bush, saltpans, savannah grasslands and mystical night skies that endures long after they return home. Expect a warm welcome at these tiny historic towns, propped up by a few locals and relics of gold-mining days.

Out here, there are more cattle and crocodiles than people, and your best friend is a broad-brimmed hat.

Explore the wild and remote **Cape York Peninsula** (p430)

Avoid getting *too* close and personal with crocodiles at **Australia Zoo** (p310)

Marvel at the strangler fig trees and dense rainforest of the **Daintree National Park** (p426)

Hug the cuddly koalas at the **Lone Pine Koala Sanctuary** (p278)

MITCH RE

Wonder at the wild, red expanses of cattle stations in the **outback** (p348)

Refresh yourself at a stunning waterfall in the picturesque **Atherton Tableland** (p413)

RICHARD I'ANSON

LAWRIE WILLIAMS

Spot water dragons on a cruise of **Lake Barrine** (p417)

RICHARD I'

Party all night in cosmopolitan **Brisbane** (p291)

34 words

There are just two seasons: the Wet (December to March) and the Dry. Driving is the best way to see the region, but during the Wet, dirt roads turn to muck and sealed roads can be flooded.

Information
In Cairns, **Gulf Savannah Development** (☎ 07-4031 1631, 1800 630 119; www.gulf-savannah.com.au; 74 Abbott St, Cairns; ◷ 9am-5pm Mon-Fri) visitors centre offers a most comprehensive information service.

Getting There & Around
At the time of writing, bus companies were no longer offering inland services, but discussions were underway. Check with Gulf Savannah Development.

AIR
Macair (☎ 13 13 13) flies a few times a week from Cairns to Normanton ($325), Karumba ($375) and Burketown ($431), or try **SkyTrans** (☎ 07-4046 2462) for Karumba flights ($345).

BUS
Coral Reef Coaches (☎ 07-4098 2600; www.coralcoaches.citysearch.com.au) runs a service between Cairns and Karumba three times a week, stopping at Undara, Mt Surprise, Croydon and Normanton. From Karumba, the service continues on to Mt Isa twice a week.

CAR & MOTORCYCLE
There are two main roads into the Gulf region. The Savannah Way, which recently changed its name from the Gulf Developmental Rd, takes you from the Kennedy Hwy, south of the Atherton Tableland, across to Normanton on 450km of sealed road. The Burke Developmental Rd (Matilda Hwy) runs north from Cloncurry to Normanton (378km sealed) via the Burke & Wills Roadhouse, but it's mostly single-lane traffic and driving requires good concentration.

Other roads through the region are unsealed so before driving on any of them, make sure you seek advice on road conditions, fuel stops and what to carry with you (carry plenty of water). The **RACQ** (☎ 07-4033 6433; www.racq.com.au; 520 Mulgrave St, Earlville) in Cairns has an excellent brochure on how to handle the Gulf Savannah's challenging road conditions.

TRAIN
QR Traveltrain (☎ 07-4036 9429, 13 22 32; tnqres@qr.com.au) runs the *Savannahlander* weekly, running through Cairns, Almaden, Forsayth and Mt Surprise ($100 one way per adult). The train leaves Cairns every Wednesday and returns from Mt Surprise every Saturday. QR Traveltrain has a range of four-day packages (from $130 to $200) that offer side trips from Mt Surprise to the Undara Lava Tubes, Cobbold Gorge and Chillagoe.

The *Gulflander* vintage train travels the 153km between Croydon and Normanton (one-way $46, 4 hours), leaving Normanton every Wednesday and returning from Croydon on Thursday.

THE SAVANNAH WAY
Undara Volcanic National Park
Bring along a lively imagination or Undara's huge lava tubes might inspire you as much as a mountain train tunnel. They're the biggest attraction in this area, however, and the largest system of its kind in the world. The tubes formed around 190,000 years ago after the eruption of a volcano. Massive lava flows drained towards the sea, forming a surface crust as they cooled. Meanwhile, molten lava continued to flow through the centre of the tubes, eventually leaving hollow basalt chambers.

You may only visit the tubes with **Savannah Guides** (☎ 07-4058 0952; www.savannah-guides.com.au) who run full-day tours ($93, including lunch), half-day tours ($63) and two-hour introductory tours ($33) from the lodge.

The facilities for campers are excellent at **Undara Lava Lodge** (☎ 07-4097 1411, 1800 990 992; www.great-barrier-reef.com/undara; camp sites $6, dm $24, railway carriage s/d $75/150), but the railway carriages are a beautifully restored treat (ask about the meal packages). Bush breakfasts are outdoors with billy tea and birdsong. The bistro serves lunch and dinner, but self-caterers must bring all supplies. In the evenings there are free campfire activities and a slide show.

Undara Lava Lodge is 275km west of Cairns on sealed road (Palmerston Hwy, which becomes Kennedy Hwy), except for the last 7km. The turn-off to Undara is just after Forty Mile Scrub National Park, on the road to Mt Surprise – follow the signs.

Undara to Croydon

The side trips to tiny towns are what make this stretch so memorable. At Mt Surprise, you'll find the region's oldest building, a **post office** built in 1870 that brims with bush memorabilia. It's also a centre for gem **fossicking**, and local businesses can give you tips, tools and a licence to dig for the semi-precious stones. Accommodation options include two caravan parks and the **Mt Surprise Hotel** (☎ 07-4062 3118; s/d $25/50).

Tallaroo Hot Springs (☎ 07-4062 1221; tallaroo@bigpond.com; admission $9; camp sites $6), 50km west of Mt Surprise, is not exactly the place to cool off with springs that range in temperature from 52° to 74°C. There's a camping ground here and kiosk offering light meals. Call to ensure it's open.

From Mt Surprise, you can take the 150km **Explorers' Loop** southwest to the old gold-mining townships of Einasleigh and Forsayth. QR Traveltrain has tour packages that include Forsayth; see p393 for details. Spectacular **Cobbold Gorge** is 45km south of Forsayth, but can only be explored on a guided tour (April to October). **Savannah Guides** (☎ 07-4058 0952; www.savannah-guides.com.au) has a bunch to choose from, including a gorge boat cruise ($32) and a full-day tour (June to August only) that covers the gorge, fossicking, croc spotting, 4WD driving, swimming and lunch ($110). **Cobbold Camping Village** (☎ 407 062 5470; www.cobboldgorge.com.au; camp/caravan sites $6/20, cabins s/d $50/80; 🞧) handles tour bookings and its kiosk does yummy home-cooked curries and roasts ($12).

The loop finishes at Georgetown (population 300), back on the Savannah Way. There are several places to stay, a good bakery, fuel, mechanical and tyre repairs, and Internet access at the **TerrEstrial visitors centre** (☎ 07-4062 1485; St George St; ☽ 8.30am-4.30pm Mon-Fri, closed noon-1pm), which also has information on Mt Surprise, Einasleigh and Forsayth.

Croydon

☎ 07 / pop 220

For a while there in the 1880s, everything you touched turned to gold in Croydon. Once the 'Vegas' of the Gulf Savannah, it was crammed with bars and budding millionaires, many with more muscle than cents, but the riches ran dry towards the end of WWI and the town became a

skeleton of its former self. There are well-preserved **historic buildings** worth seeing, especially the **general store**, still in business, and precious **Lake Belmore**. **Savannah Guides** (☎ 4058 0952; www.savannah-guides.com.au) does **walking tours** from the **visitors centre** (☎ 4745 6125; www.croydonshire.com.au; ☽ 8am-5pm Mon-Fri mid-Apr–mid-Oct, 8am-5pm daily mid-Oct–mid-Apr).

You can sleep on the veranda at the **Club Hotel** (☎ 4745 6184; cnr Brown & Sircom Sts; dm $16, motel s/d $37/47). It's a corrugated iron pub with heaps of character, basic rooms and meals and, bless them, a pool!

Normanton

☎ 07 / pop 1450

You've hit the 'big smoke' at Normanton, a bustling centre with a handful of **historic buildings**, including the *Gulflander*'s classic Victorian-era train station. The town was established on Norman River as a port for the Cloncurry copper fields before becoming Croydon's gold-rush port. June is an excellent time to stop and enjoy the area's biggest social event, the Normanton **Rodeo & Outback Show**. Otherwise, **croc spotting**, **barramundi fishing** and a beer at the 'Purple Pub' are big pastimes. Check with **Carpentaria Shire Council** (☎ 4745 1268; council@carpentaria.qld.gov.au; ☽ 8.30am-5pm Mon-Fri) for information on Normanton and Karumba.

Accommodation includes the recently overhauled **Normanton Caravan Park** (☎ 4745 1121; Brown St; camp/caravan sites $14/20, dm from $25, units from $65; 🞧), the well-kept **Gulfland Motel & Caravan Park** (☎ 4745 1290; www.gulflandmotel.com.au; 11 Landsborough St; camp/caravan sites $7/18, s/d $80/90; 🞧) and the **Albion Hotel** (☎ 4745 1218; fax 4745 1675; Haig St; s/d $50/60; 🞧), which has motel-style units.

Karumba

☎ 07 / pop 1350

Karumba may be a remote fishing village, but more and more travellers are arriving to watch dreamy sunsets melt into the Arafura Sea over seafood platters. It's on the Gulf of Carpentaria, 79km from Normanton by a good, sealed, dual road. The Gulf offers brilliant fishing, and the surrounding wetlands and mangroves are packed with birdlife and saltwater crocodiles. Adventurers can take the weekly barge north to Weipa on the Cape York Peninsula with **Gulf Freight Services** (☎ 08-8946 9400, 1800 640 079).

There's a great bakery in town and a mobile grocery truck does the rounds for self-caterers, but you'll end up at the legendary **Sunset Tavern** (☎ 4745 9183; Karumba Point; mains $15-25), which serves excellent meals outdoors.

For accommodation, try **Ash's Holiday Units** (☎ 4745 9132; www.ashsholidayunits.com; Karumba Point; d $73), **Karumba Lodge Hotel** (☎ 4745 9121; karumbalodge@bigpond.com; s/d $72/83) or the **Gulf Country Caravan Park** (☎ /fax 4745 9148; cnr Yappar St & Massey Dr; camp/caravan sites $18/20, cabins $61).

NORMANTON TO CLONCURRY

You'll enjoy this beautiful stretch of savannahland and red-rock country on the Matilda Hwy. Everyone stops at the **Burke & Wills Roadhouse** (☎ 07-4742 5909; fax 4742 5958; camp/caravan sites $5/17, dongas s/d $39/50; 🕑 7am-8pm; 🔀), halfway to Cloncurry, for tucker and fuel, and then pops into the **Quamby Hotel** (☎ 07-4742 5952, singles $10), further on, for a cleansing beer. The hotel has one room with air-con (no extra charge), and meals are served if weary travellers scream loudly enough.

At Cloncurry you'll find the upmarket **Gidgee Inn** (☎ 07-4742 1599; www.gidgeeinn.com.au; s/d $95/105; 🔀) built from rammed red earth, or there's the tidy **Gilbert Park Tourist Village** (☎ 07-4742 2300; camp/caravan sites $16/19, cabins $70).

NORMANTON TO NORTHERN TERRITORY

While driving the unsealed, isolated, dusty stretch from Normanton to the NT, keep in mind that mad, ill-equipped explorers such as the doomed Burke and Wills *walked* twice these distances in summer. You can visit **Camp 119**, the northernmost camp of their wretched 1861 expedition. It's signposted 37km west of Normanton.

If you make it to **Burketown**, give yourself a clap. European settlers were no match for this feisty place and died in droves; check out the cemetery. These days, it's a favourite hangout for cattle and travellers who have read Nevil Shute's *A Town Like Alice*, part of which is set here. From September to November you can see the extraordinary natural phenomenon known as 'Morning Glory' – incredible tubular cloud formations extending the full length of the horizon that roll in from the Gulf of Carpentaria early morning.

Locals at the 130-year-old **Burketown Pub** (☎ 07-4745 5104; fax 07-4745 5146; Beames St; pub s $44, motel s/d $72/92; 🔀) like a fresh face and a chat.

The **Doomadgee Aboriginal Community** (☎ 07-4745 8188), 93km west of Burketown, has a retail area and welcomes visitors, but village access is at the discretion of the community council. Further along is Hell's Gate, the last outpost of police protection for settlers heading north to Katherine in pioneer times. It was the scene of many ambushes as Aboriginal people tried to stop their lands being overrun. All weary road warriors stop at the **Hell's Gate Roadhouse** (☎ 07-4745 8258; hellsgategulf country@bigpond.com; on-site tent $35, motel d $70) for a square meal before crossing the border.

BURKETOWN TO CAMOOWEAL

You may not have planned a stop at Gregory Downs, but chances are you'll find the pristine **Gregory River**, its banks covered in luxuriant, ancient rainforest, too beautiful to pass by. It's 117km south of Burketown on the sealed Wills Developmental Rd, which becomes the Gregory Downs Camooweal Rd. Lawn Hill National Park is a two-hour drive inland from here on a mostly well-graded, unsealed road.

The **Gregory Downs Hotel** (☎ 07-4748 5566; gregorydownshotel@bigpond.com; d $75; 🔀), a friendly pub at the main turn-off to Lawn Hill National Park, has motel-style units and fuel. It's possible to camp free on the riverbank, but there are no amenities. **Billy Hanger's General Store** (☎ 07-4748 5540; donga s/d $28/38; 🔀), opposite the pub, is crammed with goodies and offers guided canoe trips downriver and to a quiet waterhole.

Lawn Hill National Park

Flesh-eating kangaroos, ancient rainforest and crystal-clear green waters; Lawn Hill is Australia's version of *Jurassic Park*. In arid country 100km west of Gregory Downs, this national park is an oasis of gorges, creeks, ponds and tropical vegetation that Aborigines have enjoyed for perhaps 30,000 years. Remains of their paintings and camp sites are everywhere, and you can visit two rock-art sites.

Lawn Hill Creek is home to the smaller, freshwater crocodiles – the carnivorous kangaroos are fossilised in the World Heritage-listed **Riversleigh Fossil Field** at the southern end of the park. It's one of the world's pre-eminent fossil sites with fossils up to 25 million years old! You can do a half-day tour of the field ($45) from Adel's Grove or else visit the **Riversleigh Fossils Centre** (☎ 07-4749 1555; www.riversleigh.qld.gov.au; 19 Marian St; ☯ 9am-5pm) in Mt Isa.

Lawn Hill has 20km of walking tracks and an excellent **camping ground** (☎ 07-4748 5572; fax 07-4748 5549; camp sites $6) that must be booked well in advance (April to September) with the park rangers. Paddling up the creek gives a wondrous perspective of the gorge and swimming near the waterfalls is heavenly. Hire canoes from Adel's Grove.

Adel's Grove (☎ 07-4748 5501; adelsgrove@bigpond .com; camp sites $8, on-site tents $140) camping ground is 10km east of the park entrance, set in lush surrounds by Lawn Hill Creek. Fuel and basic groceries are available and there's a restaurant and bar. On-site tent prices include dinner and breakfast for two. There is access for the disabled.

Bowthorn Homestead (☎ 07-4745 8132; www .ozemail.com.au/~bowthorn; d $80) is about 100km north of Lawn Hill. This is a great opportunity to stay on a working cattle station. The price includes all meals, a guided day trip and laundry service. Now that's top value. Bookings are essential.

GETTING THERE & AWAY
A 4WD vehicle is recommended, but it's not always necessary in the dry season. From Mt Isa – after you leave the Barkly Hwy – the last 230km or so are mostly unsealed and often impassable after rain. All roads in this area can be dangerous in the wet season – check with local authorities before venturing out. **Campbell's Tours & Travel** (☎ 07-4743 2006; www.campbellstours.com.au; per person from $550) in Mt Isa do a three-day safari out to Lawn Hill and Riversleigh from April to October on Tuesday and Friday, with accommodation and meals provided at Adel's Grove.

FAR NORTH QUEENSLAND

Tropical, wild and rugged, Queensland's Far North is a stunning destination and tourist mecca. Though geographically small, the region contains the richest pocket of biodiversity in Australia, if not the world. The Great Barrier Reef Marine Park offers spectacular reefs, and the Wet Tropics World Heritage Area contains ancient rainforest and pristine white-sand beaches. Inland is the picturesque Atherton Tableland, teeming with waterfalls, and beyond historic Cooktown lies the dusty isolation of Cape York and the very tip of Australia, Cape York Peninsula.

Locals speak reverently about their region and will look at you with undisguised pity if you're from 'down south', which could mean only as far as Townsville. Many conform to the stereotype of the 'real' Australian: a singlet-wearing tough guy in an Akubra hat, whose idea of dressing up is to change into a newer pair of thongs.

As a community, Far North Queenslanders are welcoming, helpful and will often talk your ear off. Mentioning the weather will spark lengthy discussions of cyclones (past or present), fronts, and the yearly rainfall in millimetres (most people seem to have knowledge of this dating back at least five years!).

Far North Queensland is a fascinating region with unlimited opportunities for exploration and fun.

CAIRNS
☎ 07 / pop 98,981

Tourists flock to Cairns like migratory birds in mating season and the city is positively booming. Its status as an international and domestic player in both tourism and business is firmly entrenched. In 2003 Cairns' foreshore was nipped, tucked and given enough cosmetic surgery to rival the population of Hollywood. Cairns Port Authority and Cairns City Council created a 'New Cairns' with a project costing over $45 million. With the Pier Marketplace at its heart, the surrounding mudflats were replaced with a glorious swimming lagoon, thick grassy parkland and a boardwalk that, at the time of writing, was still under construction. The port's marinas were substantially upgraded and the schmick Reef Fleet terminal is now the main departure point for tours to the Reef and islands off Cairns. There's also a five-year plan (and around $100 million funding) to upgrade Cairns' airport to an international standard. Groaning under the weight of tourism, Cairns now has the infrastructure to support the industry.

An adrenalin-junky's playground, Cairns is a fabulous base for exploring the Reef, Atherton Tableland, Port Douglas and beyond, and a popular place to hook up with fellow travellers. It has an irrepressible energy and a lush tropical setting.

Cairns appeared among the mangroves in 1876 as an intended port for the Hodgkinson River goldfield. Subsequently, Cairns was chosen as the starting point for the railway line to the Atherton Tableland during the 1880 tin rush. Cairns marks the end of the Bruce Hwy and the railway line from Brisbane.

Orientation

Cairns' CBD is in the area between the Esplanade and McLeod St and Wharf and Aplin Sts. Reef Fleet terminal is the main departure points for reef trips. Further south is Trinity Wharf and the transit centre, where long-distance buses arrive and depart. Cairns train station is hidden inside Cairns Central Shopping Centre on McLeod St. Local buses (Sunbus) leave from the Lake St Transit Centre.

Information

BOOKSHOPS

Absells Chart & Map Centre (☎ 4041 2699; Andrejic Arcade, 55-59 Lake St) Absells' owners could chart the Far North blindfolded, so extensive is their knowledge of the region. Sells a broad range of topographic, nautical and area maps, and has provided maps for *Survivor Down Under*.

Angus & Robertson (☎ 4041 0591; Shop 141, McLeod St, Cairns Central Shopping Centre)

Australian Geographic (☎ 4041 6211; Shop 3, Ground Level, Pier Marketplace) Stocks specialist titles on Australia's natural landscape.

Exchange Bookshop (☎ 4051 1443; www.exchange bookshop.com; 78 Grafton St) Wide range of contemporary titles, both new and second-hand books.

FILM & PHOTOGRAPHY

For your photography needs visit **Garricks Camera House** (☎ 4031 8466; cairns@garricks.com.au; Cairns Central Shopping Centre) or **Smiths Camera & Video** (☎ 4051 2125; smiths@cairns.net.au; 86 Lake St).

GAY & LESBIAN TRAVELLERS

Some excellent resources:

Gay Australia Travel (☎ 4053 6255; www.gayaus traliatravel.com; 5/120 Collins Ave, Edge Hill; ☼ 9am-5.30pm Mon-Fri, closes 11.30pm Sat)

Gay Cairns Travel (☎ 4053 6244; www.gaycairns.com) Same office as Gay Australia Travel.

Gay & Lesbian Recorded Information Service (☎ 4041 6146)

Check out www.gayconcierge.com.au for a listing of party highlights during the week of Sydney's Gay & Lesbian Mardi Gras in February (p109).

INTERNET ACCESS

Internet cafés are clustered at Abbott St, between Shields and Aplin Sts. Prices per hour range from $2 to $5.

Call Station (☎ 4052 1572; fax 4052 1576; 123 Abbott St)

Global Gossip (☎ 4041 6411; www.globalgossip.com; 125 Abbott St)

Inbox Café (☎ 4041 4677; www.inboxcafe.com.au; 119 Abbott St)

MEDICAL SERVICES

Cairns City 24 Hour Medical Centre (☎ 4052 1119; admin@rightroundtheworld.com; cnr Florence & Grafton Sts)

Cairns Base Hospital (☎ 4050 6333; The Esplanade)

Cairns Travel Clinic (☎ 4041 1699; ctlmed@iig .com.au; 15 Lake St)

MONEY

All of the major banks have branches, with ATMs, throughout central Cairns, and most have foreign-exchange sections. There's also **Thomas Cook** (☎ 4031 3040; 13 Spence St) and **American Express Travel** (☎ 4051 8811; Orchid Plaza, Abbott St).

POST

The **main post office** (☎ 13 1318; www.auspost.com; 13 Grafton St) handles poste restante, and there are postal branches in Orchid Plaza and Cairns Central.

TOURIST INFORMATION

If you can't find tourist information in Cairns, then you'll never find porn on the Internet either.

There are dozens of privately run 'information centres' (basically tour-booking agencies), but government-run **Tourism Tropical North Queensland** (☎ 4031 7676; www.tnq.org.au; 51 The Esplanade; ☼ 8.30am-5.30pm) will offer unbiased opinion.

Gulf Savannah Tourist Organisation (☎ 4051 4658; www.gulf-savannah.com.au; 74 Abbott St; ☼ 8.45am-5pm) has information about the Gulf and what's on offer in this diverse region.

TRAVEL AGENCIES

STA Travel (☎ 4031 8398; www.statravel.com.au; Cairns Central Shopping Centre, McLeod St)

STA Travel (☎ 4031 4199; Shop 9, Shields St)

QUEENSLAND

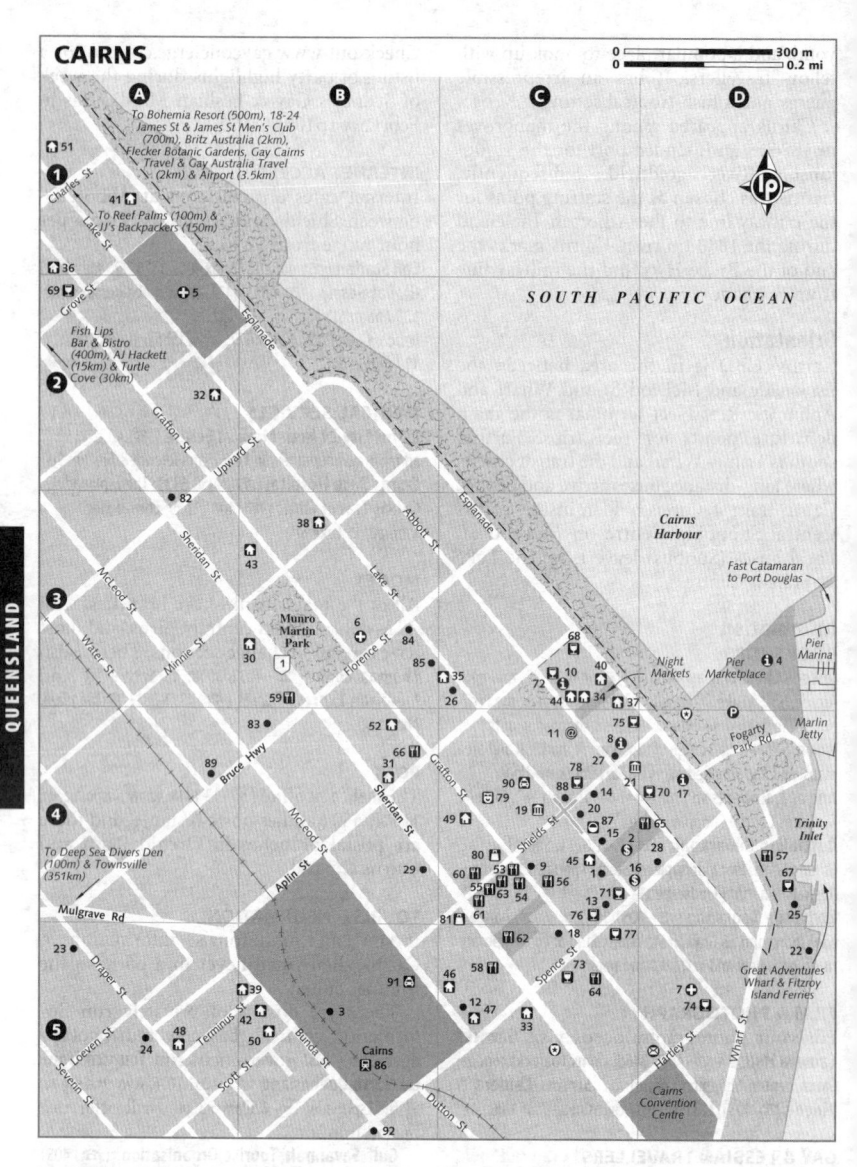

CAIRNS

0 _____ 300 m
0 _____ 0.2 mi

To Bohemia Resort (500m), 18-24
James St & James St Men's Club
(700m), Britz Australia (2km),
Flecker Botanic Gardens, Gay Cairns
Travel & Gay Australia Travel
(2km) & Airport (3.5km)

To Reef Palms (100m) &
JJ's Backpackers (150m)

Fish Lips
Bar & Bistro
(400m), AJ Hackett
(15km) & Turtle
Cove (30km)

Munro
Martin
Park

SOUTH PACIFIC OCEAN

Cairns
Harbour

Fast Catamaran
to Port Douglas

Night
Markets

Pier
Marketplace

Pier
Marina

Marlin
Jetty

Trinity
Inlet

Great Adventures
Wharf & Fitzroy
Island Ferries

Cairns
Convention
Centre

To Deep Sea Divers Den
(100m) & Townsville
(351km)

Rendez-Vous Futé (☎ 4031 3533; www.australie-voy
ages.com, French only; 28 Spence St). French-speaking agency.
Navi Tour (☎ 4031 6776, 1300 558 800; 1st Fl, Orchid
Plaza, 58 Lake St) Caters for Japanese tourists.

USEFUL ORGANISATIONS
Community Information Service (☎ 4051 4953;
www.cisci.org.au)

QPWS (☎ 4046 6602; www.env.qld.gov.au; 2-4 McLeod
St) Camping permits and walking trail information.
RACQ (☎ 4033 6711; www.racq.com.au; 520 Mulgrave
Rd, Earlville) Maps and information on Cape York road
conditions; 24-hour recorded road-report service
(☎ 1300 130 595).
Wilderness Society (☎ 4041 6666; www.wilderness
.org.au /local/cairns/index.html; 130 Grafton St)

Dangers & Annoyances

Locals recommend that you avoid walking through Munro Martin Park at night.

Sights

Cairns' prime geographical position is reinforced by its fascinating sights. Some of the most interesting ones are out of the CBD, but definitely worth the trip.

Flecker Botanic Gardens (☎ 4044 3398; Collins Ave, Edge Hill; ☻ 7.30am-5.30pm Mon-Fri, 8.30am-5.30pm Sat & Sun) specialises in cycads, heliconias, gingers and palms, and has a stunning collection of natives and exotics. Informative tours are held at 1pm Monday to Friday (adult/child $5/free) and there are self-guided walking trails (eg, the Gondawan Evolution Trail). **Botanic Gardens Licensed Café** (meals $7-14) is a serene breakfast setting.

Opposite the gardens a rainforest boardwalk leads to **Saltwater Creek** and **Centenary Lakes**. For more serious walkers, trails through **Mt Whitfield Conservation Park** have several lookouts offering views of Cairns and Trinity Inlet.

Owned and run by Aborigines, the **Tjapukai Cultural Park** (☎ 4042 9999; www.tjapukai .com.au; Kamerunga Rd, Carevonica; adult/child $28/14, with transfers $73/37; ☻ 9am-5pm) is a thoroughly enjoyable experience. It features the Creation legend, told using giant holograms; a corroboree; and boomerang- and spear-throwing demonstrations. The retail gallery sells authentic didgeridoos.

Cairns Regional Gallery (☎ 4031 6865; www .cairnsregionalgallery.com.au; cnr Abbott & Shields Sts; adult/ child under 10 $4/free; ☻ 10am-5pm Mon-Sat, opens 1pm Sun), in a gorgeous heritage building, is worth a wander. Exhibitions reflect the consciousness of the region, with an emphasis on indigenous art. You may see installations like reinforced umbrellas covered in a thick layer of grass, or a cork echidna made from recycled metal forks.

Cairns Foreshore Promenade is just that – a place to promenade. Backpackers preen around the 4000-sq-m saltwater **swimming lagoon**, which, upon opening, attracted media interest regarding the issue of topless bathing (the unofficial rule now seems to be no running while topless). Fitness enthusiasts blade, cycle and work up a sweat along the **Esplanade Walking Trail**, and locals and travellers spill from the CBD and restaurants along the Esplanade to wander around the area at night.

Undersea World (☎ 4041 1777; www.iig.com.au /underseaworld; Pier Marketplace, adult/child/family $13/ 7/25; ☺ 8am-8pm) is a great family activity. Watch sharks being hand-fed at 10am, noon, 1.30pm and 3pm by courageous divers.

Cairns Museum (☎ 4051 5582; www.cairns museum.org.au; cnr Lake & Shields Sts; adult/child $5/2; ☺ 9.30am-4.30pm Mon-Sat) has some interesting historic displays on the Far North.

Cascade Falls, 22km from Cairns, has a series of beautiful swimming holes. There is a terrific **mangrove boardwalk** on Airport Ave, 200m before the airport.

For markets, see Shopping (p406) and Eating (p403).

Activities
DIVING & SNORKELLING
Cairns is the scuba-diving capital of the Barrier Reef and a popular place to gain PADI open-water certification. There's a plethora of dive courses starting from no-frills four-day courses that combine pool training and reef dives (around $300) to four-day open-water courses ($430 to $580). Five-day courses ($540 to $650) include two days' pool theory and three days' living aboard a boat. These live-aboard courses are far more rewarding and often have higher safety standards. Find out whether prices include a medical check (around $45), daily reef tax ($5) and passport photos (around $8). Advanced courses are also available for certified divers.

A selection of reputable dive schools in Cairns:

Down Under Dive (☎ 1800 079 099; www.downunder dive.com.au; 287 Draper St; ☺ 7am-7pm)

Deep Sea Divers Den (☎ 4031 2223; www.divers-den .com; 319 Draper St; ☺ 6am-6pm)

Pro-Dive (☎ 4031 5255; www.prodive-cairns.com.au; cnr Abbott & Shields Sts; ☺ 9am-9pm)

Cairns Reef Dive (☎ 4052 1811, 1800 222 252; www.cairnsreefdive.com.au; Shop 2, Global Palace, 86 Lake St; ☺ 7am-5pm)

More comprehensive reef trips last one to 11 days and cost roughly $200 to $3600. Live-aboard trips explore the outer and northern reefs, including Cod Hole, Homes Reef and Osprey Reef.

Operators specialising in trips for certified divers:

Coral Sea Diving Company (☎ 4041 2024; www.coral seadiving.com.au; ☺ 9am-5pm) Visibility usually 40m or more. Shark feeding offered.

Explorer Ventures/Nimrod (☎ 4031 5566; www .explorerventures.com; 206 Draper St; ☺ 9am-5pm Mon-Fri) Extended itineraries for far northern reefs in November.

Mike Ball Dive Expeditions (☎ 4031 5484; www.mikeball.com; 143 Lake St; ☺ 8am-6pm)

For more information about diving at Lizard Island check out:

Australian Museum Online (www.austmus.gov.au)

Diving Cairns (www.divingcairns.com.au)

Lizard Island Charters (www.lizardislandcharters.com .au/diving-snorkelling.htm)

An excellent way to learn about the reef is at **Reef Teach** (☎ 4031 7794; www.reefteach.com.au; 14 Spence St; admission $13; ☺ 10am-9pm Mon-Sat, lectures 6.15pm & 8.30pm Mon-Sat). The madcap lecturer is like an ocean-obsessed Ace Ventura – this guy talks FAST. You'll learn basic fish and coral identification, and how to treat the Reef respectfully, as well as more obscure facts, such as which creature breathes through its anus.

WHITE-WATER RAFTING
There's exciting white-water rafting down the Barron, Tully, Russell and North Johnstone Rivers.

Tours are graded according to the degree of difficulty, from armchair rafting (Grade 1) to heart palpitations (Grade 5). Approximate prices for tours (leaving from Cairns) are full-day Tully $150, half-day Barron $85, two-/four-day North Johnstone $650/ 1500, and full-day Russell $130; check whether wetsuit hire (around $10) and national park fees ($6) are included.

The major rafting companies in Cairns:

Raging Thunder (☎ 4030 7990; www.ragingthunder .com.au) Wide range of adrenalin-inducing tours.

RnR (☎ 4051 4055; www.raft.com.au; ☺ 8.30am-5.30pm) Adventure rafting and family tours.

Foaming Fury (☎ 4031 3460, 1800 801 540; www.foamingfury.com.au) Sedate, family rafting.

OTHER ACTIVITIES
Once again, the range is enormous (operators will be running Extreme Ironing tours soon). Some of the more popular sports are skydiving and bungee jumping:

Skydive Cairns (☎ 4031 5466, 1800 444 568; www.skydive.net.au; 56 Sheridan St; solo dive $470; ☺ 7am-5pm)
Springmount Station (☎ 4093 4493; www.spring mountstation.com; half/full day $90/110, child half-price) Horse-riding, camp-outs and farmstays.
AJ Hackett (☎ 4057 7188, 1800 622 888; www.ajhackett.com.au; end McGregor Rd; bungee $110-140, s/tw/tr minjin swing per person $80/59/39, bungee & minjin swing combo $140; ☺ 10am-5pm) Courtesy bus runs 9.15am, noon and 3pm.

It's also possible to go ballooning, parasailing and on scenic helicopter flights – check with your tour operator.

Cairns for Children
Central childcare facilities that offer daycare:
Child's Play (☎ 4031 1095; Anderson St; child over-/under-3 per day $39/43)
Juniors Child Care Centre (☎ 4032 1390; 160-162 Hoare St; child over-/under-2 per day $38/40)

Opposite Caravella Backpackers 149, at the Esplanade Walking Trail, there's playground equipment and a skate bowl.

Tours
There's a bewildering variety of tours on offer in Cairns, but the market's so tight that they're generally good value and have seasoned and entertaining guides.

CAIRNS
Cairns Discovery Tours (☎ 4053 5259; www.cairns holiday.com/scenic/cairns-discovery.htm; adult/child $50/25; ☺ depart/return 12.45/5.45pm) is guided by horticulturalists, and takes in Cairns, Flecker Botanic Gardens, the Royal Flying Doctor base and Palm Cove.

ATHERTON TABLELAND
On the Wallaby (☎ 4050 0650; www.onthewallaby .com; day/overnight/2-night, 3-day tours $80/150/170; ☺ depart/return 8am/7pm) Based in Yungaburra. Fun package tours, night canoeing and wildlife spotting.
Uncle Brian's Tours (☎ 4050 0615; www.visitcairns .com.au/the_atherton_tablelands.htm; adult/child $80/60; ☺ depart/return 8.30am/8.30pm Mon, Wed, Fri & Sat) Babinda–Josephine Falls–Lake Eacham.
Wooroonooran Safaris (☎ 4031 0800; www .wooroonooran-safaris.com.au; adult/child $135/110; ☺ depart/return 8am/6pm) Wooroonooran National Park and Goldfield Trail.

Bandicoot Bicycles (☎ 4041 0100; bandicoot01@ hotmail.com; 159 Sheridan St; day tour $110; ☺ depart/ return 8am/5.45pm Mon-Fri) Sensational bike tours.

DAINTREE RIVER & CAPE TRIBULATION
Cape Tribulation is one of the most popular day-trip destinations from Cairns. Tour operators push the 'safari' angle, but the road is sealed (suitable for a conventional vehicle) until just before the Cape Tribulation Beach House.

Jungle Tours (☎ 1800 817 234; www.adventure tours.com.au; day trip adult/child $130; ☺ depart/return 7.30am/6.45pm) has excellent readers' reports and **Billy Tea Bush Safaris** (☎ 4032 0077; www .billytea.com.au; day trip adult/child $130/90; ☺ depart/ return 7.10am/6.30pm) runs eco tours.

COOKTOWN & CAPE YORK
Wilderness Challenge (☎ 4035 4488; www.wilderness -challenge.com.au; adult/child two-day tour $360/330; Mon, Wed & Fri) runs interesting tours to Cooktown and Cape York.

GREAT BARRIER REEF & ISLANDS
Reef tours usually include lunch, snorkelling gear (with dives an optional extra) and pick-up from your accommodation. Tours generally cost between $60 and $150. Major tour operators:
Great Adventures (☎ 1800 079 080; www.great adven tures.com.au) Trips to Norman Reef, Moore Reef, Fitzroy Island or Green Island. Over 300. Has a semi-submersible and a glass-bottomed boat.
Sunlover (☎ 4031 1055, 1800 810 512; www.sunlover .com.au) Sails to Arlington Reef. Maximum 250. Semi-submersible and glass-bottom boat tour.
Compass (☎ 4050 0666, 1800 815 811; www.reeftrip.com; 100 Abbott St) Hastings Reef and Breaking Patches. Maximum 100. Boom netting.
Noah's Ark Cruises (☎ 4041 0036) Hastings Reef and Michaelmas Cay. Maximum 32. Popular with backpackers. Lots of snorkelling.
Falla (☎ 4031 3488; www.thefalla.com) Upolu Cay. Maximum 35. Old converted pearl lugger. Deep- and shallow-water sites.
Passions of Paradise (☎ 4050 0676; www.passions.com.au) Upolu Cay and Paradise Reef. Maximum 65. Catamaran. Party reputation.

UNDARA LAVA TUBES
For an inland adventure, **Undara Experience** (☎ 4097 1411; www.undara.com.au; two-day tours adult/child $350/175; ☺ depart/return 8am/7.30pm) has coach trips to the Undara Lava Tubes.

Sleeping

Accommodation options in Cairns are as plentiful as its cane toads, and the amount of choice can be overwhelming. Competition is cut-throat and prices fluctuate dramatically. During the low and shoulder seasons (1 November to 31 May) cheap standby rates are available, but in the high season (1 June to 31 October) prices shoot up; lower weekly rates apply throughout the year. Prices quoted here are for the high season.

Accommodation agencies are a useful contact point as they can match accommodation according to your budget and have access to any sleeping options that have recently opened. The **Accommodation Centre** (☎ 4051 4066, 1800 807 730; www.accomcentre.com.au; 36 Aplin St) is an extremely helpful centre with wheelchair access and tourist information; it's also a contact point for working holidays in Japan. **Accom Cairns** (☎ 4051 3200; www.accommcairns.com.au; 127 Sheridan St) mainly gives advice on mid-range and top-end options, but it also has listings for short-term rental (with a minimum of four weeks) studio apartments.

BUDGET

The main backpacker strip is at the Esplanade, between Aplin and Shields Sts. To entice guests, these hostels rely on waterfront position and proximity to the frenetic Esplanade party scene, rather than clean rooms, well-maintained facilities and comfortable beds. Hostels and guesthouses north of the railway line are quieter, well run and better value. Some of the best hostels:

Global Palace (☎ 4031 7921, 1800 819 024; www.globalpalace.com.au; City Place, cnr Lake & Shields Sts; dm $23, tw & d $50; 🛜) There are three-, four- and five-bed rooms with no bunks. Global Palace is well run and has a stylish interior, breezy timber veranda overlooking City Place, a small rooftop pool and comprehensive tour desk.

Calypso Inn (☎ 4031 0910, 1800 815 628; www.calypsobackpackers.com; 5-9 Digger St; dm/s & d $18/40) If you're working the party circuit, then you've arrived at HQ. Laze poolside and party hard at Zanzibar (all-you-can-eat dinner $6), which is the cheapest bar in town.

Gecko's Backpackers (☎ 4031 1344, 1800 011 344; www.geckosbackpackers.com.au; 187 Bunda St; dm/s $18/25, d $40-45) In a converted Queenslander,

Gecko's is a welcoming, relaxed backpackers, and its breezy communal area is an excellent place to chill. Rooms are comfortable, with polished floorboards and painted furniture, and there's a big, clean kitchen. Disabled facilities available.

Cairns Girls Hostel (☎ 4051 2767, 1800 011 950; www.cairnsgirlshostel.com.au; 147 Lake St; dm $16, s/tw $20/18) This is one of the cheapest and cleanest hostels in the heart of town (sorry guys!). It's spacious, with two communal areas, and has well-maintained older rooms. Not strictly gay but it's extremely popular with lesbians. Super-cheap weekly rates.

Esplanade Beach Hostel (☎ 4031 6884, 1800 061 712; h89@jimmys.com.au; 89 The Esplanade; dm/s/d $20/40/48) Formerly Hostel 89, this is the pick of the bunch on the Esplanade. It's well run, clean and attracts a mature crowd. Excellent tour desk.

Also recommended:

McLeod St Youth Hostel (☎ 4051 0772; www.yha.com.au; 20-24 McLeod St; dm $21, tw & d $46-50; 🛜 🖳)

Billabong Central Backpackers (☎ 4051 6946; 69 Spence St; dm/d $19/38)

JJ's Backpackers (☎ 4051 7642, 1800 666 336; fax 4051 7223; 11 Charles St; dm $15-17, tw & d $38)

Caravella Backpackers 77 (☎ 4051 2159; info@caravella.com.au ; 77 The Esplanade; dm/s/d $21/32/47)

Budget guesthouses and self-contained places:

Ryan's Rest (☎ 4051 4734; ryansrest@hotmail.com; 18 Terminus St; d $45-48) Ryan's Rest is a charming, quiet guesthouse with breezy verandas and upstairs double rooms with character.

Dreamtime Travellers Rest (☎ 4031 6753; www.dreamtimetravel.com.au; 4 Terminus St; dm/d $20/45) Dreamtime is in a brightly renovated timber Queenslander, and has super-friendly staff and a lovely atmosphere.

Travellers Oasis (☎ 4052 1377, 1800 621 353; www.travoasis.com.au; 8 Scott St; dm/s/d $20/30/44; 🛜 🖳) Close to the train station, this hostel comprises two renovated Queenslanders and is quiet, clean and relaxed.

MID-RANGE

Self-contained apartments (often better value than motel rooms) are springing up around town. There are some excellent self-contained apartment and motel options.

Shooting Star Apartments (☎ 4047 7200; www.shootingstarapartments.com.au; 117 Grafton St; apt $90; 🛜 🖳) This bright-blue complex is great value, especially if you're staying for a week, when the nightly rate drops to $52. Spacious rooms are spic and span, with a small kitchen and cable TV, and there's a terrific pool and barbeque area.

Mid City (☎ 4051 5050; www.midcity.com.au; 6 McLeod St; apt $140; ✗ ☐) Opposite Myer, Mid City has a shady balcony and a view of tropical bush from the bedroom. Modern rooms with a full kitchen make these two-bedroom apartments popular. Advisable to book ahead.

Reef Palms (☎ 4051 2599, 1800 815 421; www.reef palms.com.au; 41-47 Digger St; apt $82-115; ✗) Surrounded by a lush garden, Reef Palms is just out of the city centre, but only a couple of blocks back from the Esplanade, and the self-contained apartments are affordable and great value.

Cascade Garden Apartments (☎ 4051 8000; cascadegardens@harveyworld.com.au; 175 Lake St; apt $120-138; ✗ ☐) Has modern, one-bedroom apartments in a tropical-garden setting close to Cairns' CBD.

Balinese (☎ 4051 9922; www.balinese.com.au; 215 Lake St; s/d $85/95; ✗ ☐) Cave-like rooms with Indonesian-style furnishings offer a cool retreat. Airport pick-up available from 7am to 7pm.

Tropical Queenslander (☎ 4031 1666; www.tropical queenslander.com.au; s/d//f $90, child over 14 $14 extra; ✗) This is in no way a traditional Queenslander; rather, it's a Flag Inn with excellent-value family rooms.

Floriana Guesthouse (☎ 4051 7886; flori@cairns info.com; 183 The Esplanade; r $45-90) Oodles of charm and character, and you'll hear birds cheeping outside your window. Personalised rooms, with some overlooking the Esplanade, are self-contained but may have only a sink and a microwave. Flat 1 is a treat.

TOP END

Self-contained accommodation is swamping the market, and most top-end places are apartments with laundry facilities in the rooms. Some excellent options:

Getaway Apartments (☎ 4041 7800, 1800 079 031; 157-159 Grafton St; apt $130-170; ✗ ☐) Minimum three nights' stay. Enormous brand-new two-bedroom, two-bathroom apartments with a full kitchen (marble benchtops and stainless steel appliances), laundry facilities, luxurious swimming pool and private balcony.

Inn Cairns (☎ 4041 2350; www.inncairns.com.au; 71 Lake St; apt $135-160) A spacious boutique hotel in the heart of the city. Inn Cairns has 4½-star apartments with cable TV, a gorgeous saltwater pool with a barbeque gazebo area, plus a rooftop sitting area.

Break Free Royal Harbour (☎ 4080 8888; 73-75 The Esplanade; apt $160-190; ✗ ☐) In a great position. All rooms have ocean views, spa bath, TV, video and stereo.

Il Palazzo (☎ 4041 2155, 1800 813 222; www.il palazzo.com.au; 62 Abbott St; apt $200; ✗ ☐) An excellent choice. This stylish boutique hotel is in a central spot and offers relaxed luxury.

Villa Vaucluse (☎ 4051 8566, 1800 623 263; www.villa vaucluse.com.au; 141-143 Grafton St; apt $150; ✗ ☐) Brand new apartments in central Grafton St.

For gay and lesbian options in and around Cairns:

18-24 James (☎ 4051 4644, 1800 621 824; www .18-24james.com.au; 18-24 James St; r $154) Exclusively gay and lesbian. Rooms are clean and stylish, with free airport transfer and a complimentary poolside breakfast. Package deals, linked with Turtle Cove, are available.

Turtle Cove (☎ 4059 1800; www.turtlecove.com.au; Captain Cook Hwy; s/d $120/140) An exclusively gay and lesbian resort promising a 'slice of gay heaven'. There's a swanky restaurant (mains from $9 to $27), cocktail bar, 16-man jacuzzi and a private beach where clothing is optional. Turtle Cove also runs tours: 'a gay day away' to the Reef ($130) and Daintree ($150). Turtle Cove is between Ellis Beach and Wangetti, 3.4km after Rex lookout.

Eating

Don't be alarmed if you suddenly think you're in Texas – meals in the Far North are enormous, fit for steer rustling rather than swanning about on the Esplanade. Cairns, with its Aussie tucker and hotpot of international cuisines, can adapt to any appetite.

Restaurants, cafés and pubs cluster along Shields St (the major eat street) and the Esplanade, (for a late-night pit stop and tourist-oriented restaurants). Also, many pubs and clubs serve counter meals (see Drinking, p405).

CAFÉS & QUICK EATS

Lunchtime food courts can be found upstairs at **Orchid Plaza** (Abbott St) and at the **Night Markets** (The Esplanade), where you can snack on Aussie-Chinese.

Lillipad (☎ 4051 9565; 72 Grafton St; breakfast & lunch $4-8; ⏲ Mon-Sat) There's love in the food at Lillipad. Breakfasts are excellent value: the Full Monty is a mammoth fry-up with sausages, bacon, eggs, tomatoes and mushrooms on toast. For something less artery-hardening, muesli with fresh tropical fruit is delicious. Be sure to read the table 'numbers', which are an eclectic mix of celebrity photos. Breakfast and lunch available until 3pm; cake and coffee until 4pm.

Tiny's Juice Bar (☎ 4031 4331; 45 Grafton St; meals $4-8) It may be tiny but it packs a mighty punch. Delicious rolls and wraps give you an instant vitamin infusion, and Tiny's spicy peanut sauce, with fresh ginger, works excellently with a warm tofu pattie. Drinks are equally fresh and zesty – try the energy booster or boysenberry smoothie.

Beethoven Café (☎ 4051 0292; 105 Grafton St; meals $3.60-7) Busy, popular and relaxed, Beethoven is a café with no pretensions. Appease hunger pains with generous fresh salad sandwiches and be tempted by sticky chocolate éclairs and pastries.

Sushi lovers should check out **Sushi Express** (☎ 4041 4388; upstairs Orchid Plaza; sushi plates $2-4) and **Sushi Zipang** (☎ 4051 3328; 39 Shields St; sushi plates $2-5, meals $7.50-19).

RESTAURANTS

Some of the best restaurants for fancier dining:

Red Ochre Grill (☎ 4051 0100; 43 Shields St; mains $23-50; ⏲ lunch & dinner) Here you can devour native fauna – roo, emu and crocodile – and feast on the famous Australian bush – lemon myrtle, quandong (native peach) and wattle seed. Local produce is stylishly interpreted and the result is an innovative menu. Splash out and try the Australian game platter; the hot Turkish donuts with a lemon-myrtle ice-cream tower doused in wild-lime syrup are enough to make you move to Cairns. One of the best fine-dining restaurants in Cairns.

Perrotta's at the Gallery (☎ 4031 5899; 38 Abbott St; mains around $25; ⏲ breakfast, lunch & dinner) Adjoining the art gallery, Perrotta's is a breezy and stylish café-restaurant with city charm and excellent Genovese coffee (shipped in from Melbourne, way down south). Perrotta's menu, a sensational blend of fresh local produce and sinfully rich gourmet treats, is definitely worth a splurge. Feast on an entrée

of Tableland-fig, prosciutto and gorgonzola bruschetta, followed by a carpaccio of yellow fin tuna, and finish with a sublime roast nectarine and marscapone tart (are you salivating yet?).

Yanni's Greek Taverna (☎ 4041 1500; cnr Aplin & Grafton Sts; mains $21-28) Unleash your inner plate-smasher at Yanni's. Every Friday and Saturday night, from around 9pm, diners are treated to a bellydance performance and given plates to smash. Yanni's has a great reputation around Cairns and dishes up a tasty range of chargrills and seafood.

Fish Lips Bar & Bistro (☎ 4041 1700; 228 Sheridan St; meals $10.50-32) A seafood extravaganza, Fish Lips is not only a great name but also a lip-smacking experience. Away from the main drag, Fish Lips is worth the trip. It's a convivial restaurant with professional service and quality meals. Be sure to book during high season.

Mondo (☎ 4052 6780; Wharf St; mains $9-30) Location, dahlings, location! Attached to the Hilton, Mondo is green and shady with prime waterfront views. Erratic service is Mondo's only downside, but you can feast on fine mod-Oz cuisine.

Also recommended:

Tandoori Oven (☎ 4031 0043; 62b Shields St; meals $15-22) Authentic, steaming North Indian curries.

La Fettuccina (☎ 4031 5959; 43 Shields St; mains $22-27) Romantic Italian restaurant. Home-made pasta.

Piranha Bar & Café (☎ 4051 9459; Shields St; mains $9-18) Big Mexican meals, a menu for the 'non-amigo' and portions for kids.

SELF-CATERING

Self-caterers be warned: the council has a bizarre rule that makes it illegal for supermarkets to open later than 5.30pm Saturday and 6pm Sunday. There's a Woolworths on Sheridan St, between Shields and Spence Sts, but the wonderful **Rusty's Bazaar** (Grafton St, between Shields & Aplin Sts; ⏲ Fri & Sat) is where many locals do their weekly shop. Rusty's sells fresh fruit and veg, Asian herbs, seafood and honey. Niche self-catering options:

Patrice's Delicatessen (☎ 4051 3888; 43 Sheridan St; sandwiches $5-10) Gourmet deli items and sandwiches. Dutch liquorice, Belgian chocolate etc.

Asian Foods Australia (☎ 4052 1510; 101-105 Grafton St) Asian foodstore. Dry goods.

Neil's Organics (☎ 4051 5688; 21 Sheridan St) Organic produce, fruit and veg.

Drinking

You're won't die of thirst in Cairns – there are pubs on every corner. Street-press magazine *Barfly* covers music gigs, movies, pubs and clubs. Nightclub-goers take note: clubs refuse entry after 3am, and while you can keep drinking if you're in a club already, once you leave you won't be allowed back in. Cairns' bouncers are vigilant, so take your ID. Popular Cairns venues:

Courthouse Hotel (☎ 4031 4166; 38 Abbott St; meals $8-20) It feels weird drinking in this former government building (kind of like swearing in church), but at night it comes alive and fills up with a crowd of young funksters.

Cock & Bull (☎ 4031 1160; 6 Grove St; meals $5-12) Ye olde English meets tropical north. This is a top spot for a drink and, if you fancy a spot of darts, there's a board out the back. Counter meals and tasty grills.

Cairns Yacht Club (☎ 4031 2750; 4 Wharf St; mains $10-17) Drinks here are ridiculously cheap, and tasty meals are served from the Galley Bistro. Its customers look brown and nautical.

Fox & Firkin (☎ 4031 5305; cnr Lake & Spence Sts; meals $13-22) 'For a firkin good time' is the not-so-subtle slogan of the Fox, a fine drinking establishment with a wide timber veranda overlooking Lake St. It's a busy place and often full of travellers drinking lager and comparing reef trips. Live music from Tuesday to Sunday.

Johno's Nightclub & Bar (☎ 4051 8770; cnr Abbott & Aplin Sts; meals $7-9) Old-school musicians play great blues and rock every night (free entry before 9pm). Johno's is huge: a hang-glider is suspended from the roof. The World-Famous Gong Show is free every Sunday, and chipper bar staff call you 'darlin' and 'bloke'. Packed most nights.

Shenanigans (☎ 4051 2490; 48 Spence St; meals $8-15) An Irish-style pub decorated in dark timber with a huge beer garden and outside bistro; inside there is arctic air-con, a front bar and a dance floor, with video clips screening. There's a Eureka Gaming Lounge (where the luck may have run out for many) and karaoke on Monday nights. It's a place where you can indeed get up to some shenanigans.

Rattle 'n' Hum (☎ 4031 3011; 67 The Esplanade; meals $15-30) A cavernous, dark-wood bar that pumps meals from its pizzeria and grill, and

mainstream music from the stereo. It has a frat-house feel, and jug after jug of beer is consumed by punters who create a rowdy, lively atmosphere.

Wool Shed Chargrill & Saloon (☎ 4031 6304; 24 Shields St; meals $10-15) This is a phenomenally popular get-pissed-quick bar that's legendary with locals and backpackers. It has party games and backpacker theme nights, and really, really drunk people dancing on tables.

Chapel Café (☎ 4041 4222; Level 1, 91 The Esplanade; meals $18-30) Low-watt globes hang low over the green booths. Large groups dine on tempura prawns and soy roasted duck on the veranda with esplanade views. It's a stylish bar and a relaxed place for a drink. Live acoustic music some nights.

Sports Bar (☎ 4041 2533; 33 Spence St; admission $6) A huge barn-like venue with an eatery. DJs and live music play most nights, and the place is packed with people dancing and drinking in earnest.

Tropos (☎ 4031 2530; cnr Spence & Lake Sts; admission $6) Wear something short, tight and white! This young high-energy dance crowd drinks frappés with names like 'attitude improvement' on Tropos' enormous veranda furnished with pool tables.

Playpen International (☎ 4051 8211; cnr Lake & Hartley Sts; admission $6) Oh, and how! This young crowd plays till dawn. Energetic dancers give pole-dancing a go, and roving spotlights cut through dry-ice steam. Playpen attracts big-name bands and its dance club, the Millennium Bar, is open late till 5am.

Fitzroy Island Resort (☎ 4051 9588) runs 'party nights' ($10) from May to January on the Raging Thunder Beach Bar on the island. It departs from the new Reef Fleet terminal at 7pm and returns at midnight, making for a concentrated drinking session!

GAY & LESBIAN VENUES

Nu Trix (☎ 4051 8223; 53 Spence St; admission $6) A happening gay and lesbian nightclub that opens late and parties hard.

James St Men's Club (☎ 4051 4644; 18-24 James St; admission $10; ☺ noon-midnight) Has a pool, sauna, spa etc, and is a relaxed place for gay men to hang out.

Turtle Cove (p403) and Liberty Resort (p413) also have bars which stay open till the wee hours.

Entertainment

Cairns City Cinemas (☎ 4031 1077; 108 Grafton St; adult/child $13/9) and **Central Cinemas** (☎ 4052 1166; Cairns Central; adult/child $13/9) show mainstream, new-release flicks.

Shopping

Shopping is an airport-lounge experience with every second shop selling opals, Coogi, Ken Done and 'authentic' made-in-Korea didgeridoos and boomerangs.

For an authentic termite-made didge you'll need stamina to trawl through the didgeridoo shops in Cairns' CBD. Tjapukai Cultural Park (p399) is the best place to buy authentic Aboriginal items.

Head to the **Night Markets** (The Esplanade; ☼ 4.30pm-midnight) and **Mud Markets** (Pier Marketplace; ☼ Sat morning) if your supply of 'Cairns – Australia' T-shirts is running low or you need your name on a grain of rice.

City Place Disposals (☎ 4051 6040; cnr Grafton & Shields Sts) and **Northern Disposals** (☎ 4051 7099; 47-49 Sheridan St) have cheap camping and outdoor gear.

Getting There & Away

AIR

Qantas (☎ 4050 4033; www.qantas.com.au; cnr Lake & Shields Sts) and **Virgin Blue** (☎ 13 67 89; www.virginblue.com.au) have daily flights between Cairns and Brisbane ($170), Sydney ($390), Melbourne ($450), Darwin ($450, via Alice Springs $930), Townsville ($130) and Mt Isa ($680). Flights to Thursday Island cost $420/830 one way/return.

Macair (☎ 13 13 13; www.macair.com.au) flies to Lizard Island (one way/return $300/600) and Dunk Island (one way/return $180/360). Rates can drop by as much as 15% to 30% when you purchase your ticket three days in advance.

Regular flights leave Cairns airport for a Auckland (Air New Zealand); Kuala Lumpur (Malaysian Airlines, Air Niugini); Hong Kong (Cathay Pacific); Port Moresby, Singapore and Manila (Air Niugini); and Tokyo (Japan Airlines).

BOAT

Quicksilver (☎ 4031 4299; www.quicksilver-cruises.com; one way/return Cairns–Palm Cove–Port Douglas $24/36) departs from the Pier Marina in Cairns at 8am, and from Port Douglas at 5.15pm; the journey takes 1½ hours.

BUS

McCafferty's/Greyhound (☎ 13 14 99; www.mccaffertys.com.au) and **Coral Reef Coaches** (☎ 4098 2600; www.coralcoaches.citysearch.com.au) operate from the transit centre at Trinity Wharf.

McCafferty's/Greyhound has daily bus services between Cairns and Brisbane ($185, 28½ hours), Rockhampton ($130, 17 hours), Mackay ($100, 12 hours) and Townsville ($50, 6 hours), which offer free stopovers, of no more than six nights, along the way.

Coral Reef Coaches runs regular services between Cairns and Port Douglas, Mossman, Daintree Village, Cape Tribulation and Cooktown, via either the inland road or the coastal road. It also runs a service to Karumba, and will drop passengers at the turn-off to Undara Lava Tubes – you'll have to arrange a pick-up from there.

White Car Coaches (☎ 4091 1855; whitecars@top.net.au), running to Kuranda and the Atherton Tableland, depart from 48 Spence St (outside Shenannigans). There's a timetable there and you buy your ticket from the driver.

CAR & MOTORCYCLE

Hiring a car or motorcycle is the best way to travel around Far North Queensland. Most companies prohibit you from taking vehicles to Cooktown or Chillagoe as the road is unsealed and rough in parts. There is a glut of car-rental companies on Lake St, between Aplin and Florence Sts. The following recommended companies hire cars, 4WDs, campervans or motorcycles:

Budget Rent a Car (☎ 4051 9222; 1800 020 304; www.budget.com.au; 153 Lake St; ☼ 7.30am-5.30pm)

Sheridan Rent a Car (☎ 4051 3942; owers@top.net.au; 36 Water St; ☼ 8am-5pm)

4WD Hire Service (☎ 4031 3094, 1800 077 353; www.4wdhire.com.au; 440 Sheridan St; ☼ 8am-5pm Mon-Fri) 4WD hire for Cape York.

Motor Easy Rider Cycles (☎ 4052 1188; www.easyridermotorcyclehire.com.au; 144 Sheridan St; ☼ 7.30am-6pm)

Travellers Auto Barn (☎ 4041 3722, 1800 674 374; www.travellers-autobarn.com.au; 123 Bunda St; ☼ 9am-6pm Mon-Sat, 10.30am-3pm Sun) Campervans.

Britz Australia (☎ 4032 2611; www.blue-travel.net/britz/au01.htm; 411 Sheridan St; ☼ 9am-5pm) Campervans.

TRAIN

Queensland Rail (☎ 1800 620 324; http://qroti.bit.net.au/traveltrain/; McLeod St, Cairns Central; ☼ 8am-5pm Mon-Fri, 7am-1pm Sat) has two trains that run between Cairns and Brisbane: the *Queenslander* (one way $180, 32 hours), which departs 8.35am Tuesday; and the *Sunlander* (one way $235, 32 hours) departing 8.35am Monday, Thursday and Saturday.

The scenic *Savannahlander* (one way $100, 4 days) leaves 6.30am Wednesday, and runs between Cairns and Forsayth, stopping at Almaden, Lappa Junction and Mt Surprise on the way. You can add on bus tours to Chillagoe, Undara Lava Tubes and Cobbold Gorge.

See Getting There & Away (p413) for information on travelling to Kuranda.

Getting Around
TO/FROM THE AIRPORT
The airport is about 7km from central Cairns. **Australia Coach** (☎ 4048 8355; australiacoach@blackandwhitetaxis.com.au; adult/child $7.50/3.50) meets all incoming flights and runs a shuttle bus to the CBD. **Black & White Taxis** (☎ 4048 8333, 13 10 08) charges about $14.

BICYCLE
Hire bikes from **Bandicoot Bicycles** (☎ 4041 0100; bandicoot01@hotmail.com; 153 Sheridan St; full-day hire $17; ⏰ 8am-5pm Mon-Fri, 8am-noon Sat). **Bike Man** (☎ 4041 5566; www.bikeman.com.au; 30 Florence St; minimum weekly hire $40, 4 weeks $50; ⏰ 8.30am-5.30pm Mon-Fri, 8.30am-2pm Sat, 10am-2pm Sun) has excellent weekly rates.

BUS
Sunbus (☎ 4057 7411; www.sunbus.com.au) runs regular services in and around Cairns that leave from the Lake St Transit Centre at City Place, Lake St. Schedules for most routes are posted at City Place. Buses run from early morning to late evening. Destinations include Edge Hill (bus Nos 6, 6A and 7), Flecker Botanic Gardens (No 7), Machans Beach (No 7), Holloways Beach (Nos 1C and 1H), Yorkeys Knob (Nos 1C, 1D and 1H), Trinity Beach (Nos 1, 1A and 2X), Clifton Beach (Nos 1 and 1B), and Palm Cove (Nos 1, 1B and 2X). All are served by the (almost) round-the-clock night service (N) on Friday and Saturday. Heading south, bus No 1 goes as far as Gordonvale.

TAXI
Black & White Taxis (☎ 4048 8333, 13 10 08) has a rank on the corner of Lake and Shields Sts and one outside Cairns Central.

ISLANDS OFF CAIRNS
Green Island, Fitzroy Island and Frankland Islands National Park are popular day trips. All the islands are great for snorkelling. Ferries depart from the Reef Fleet terminal.

Green Island
☎ 07
A luxury resort dominates Green Island, a small coral cay with a beautiful beach, 27km east of Cairns. The resort has a separate section for day-trippers, and facilities include a pool, bar and several eateries. From the shore, you can spot reef sharks, turtles and schools of tiny fish.

Activities involve swimming at the idyllic beach, or you can sip champagne and eat strawberries poolside. The gentle rainforest walk is 350m and well signposted with information.

Marineland Melanesia (☎ 4051 4032; adult/child $10/5) has an aquarium with fish, turtles, stingrays and crocodiles, and a collection of Melanesian artefacts.

Reef suites at the **Green Island Resort** (☎ 4031 3300, 1800 673 366; www.greenislandresort.com.au; ste $470-560) are split-level and have their own private balcony. The island suites sleep up to four people. Rooms are luxurious and stylish.

Great Adventures (☎ 4051 0455; www.greatadventures.com.au; 1 Wharf St, Cairns) has regular services to Green Island by fast catamaran (return $50), departing Cairns at 8.30am, 10.30am and 1pm, returning noon, 2.30pm and 4.30pm, as well as package tours. **Big Cat** (☎ 4051 0444; www.bigcat-cruises.com.au) also runs fun tours (adult/child $56/32), which depart from Cairns at 9am and 1.15pm, and return 1pm and 5pm.

Fitzroy Island National Park
☎ 07
A steep mountain top peeping from the sea, Fitzroy Island has coral-littered beaches and a quaint resort. Day-trippers can use the resort's facilities, and hire water-sports equipment and fishing rods. Diving courses and sea-kayak tours are run by the resort, and the most popular snorkelling spot is around the rocks at **Nudey Beach** (1.2km from the resort).

There are a number of walks, which vary in difficulty, for those who can leave the poolside. The 20-minute **Secret Garden Walk**, with major skinks basking on rocks, is a

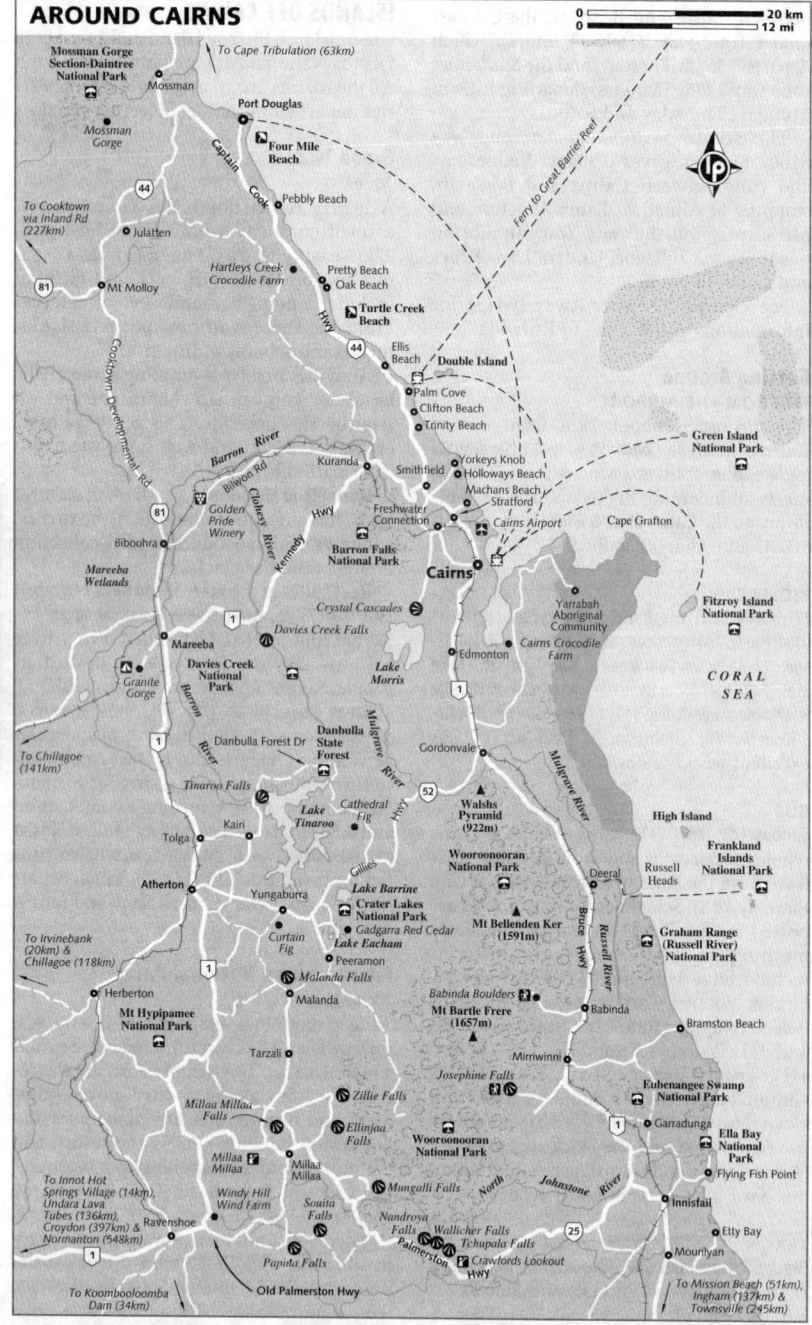

leisurely stroll, whereas the **Lighthouse & Summit Trail** is a steep, two-hour climb.

Fitzroy Island Resort (☎ 4051 9588; fax 4052 1335; dm $31, bungalows $120-300) has a bar-kiosk selling light snacks ($5 to $14) and a waterfront restaurant (meals from $9 to $23). All rooms, except villa units, share facilities.

Raging Thunder (☎ 4030 7907) has ferries (adult/child $36/18 return) that leave three times each day from Trinity Wharf. From Cairns, it's a 35km boat trip that takes about one hour.

Frankland Islands National Park

☎ 07

A group of five islands surrounded by coral, the Frankland Islands have gorgeous, sandy **beaches** and offer a beautiful day's **snorkelling**. Camping is allowed in the national park, and permits are available from Cairns **QPWS** (☎ 4046 6602; www.env.qld.gov.au; 2-4 McLeod St), but you'll need to be self-sufficient as there's no drinking water.

Frankland Islands Cruise & Dive (☎ 4031 6300; 1800 079 039; adult/child $139/72) operates excellent day trips to the island, which include a cruise down the idyllic Mulgrave River. Drop-offs are available for campers ($144 per person).

CAIRNS' NORTHERN BEACHES

☎ 07 / pop 17,190

You realise where all the locals live when you see Cairns' relaxed northern beaches, a string of coastal communities linked by the Captain Cook Hwy.

The following beaches, listed in order from Cairns, all have stinger nets in summer (except Machans, which has no swimming beach). Turn-offs from the highway are well signposted if you're travelling by car, and **Sunbus** (☎ 4057 7411; www.sunbus.com.au) runs regular services that leave from the Lake St Transit Centre terminal at Lake St.

Machans Beach

☎ 07

Cane fields flank Machans Beach Rd, the turn-off from the highway. Machans Beach has somehow managed to escape the tentacles of property developers, and small weatherboard homes line the esplanade.

There's nowhere to stay, but there are two eating options:

Wok Wild (☎ 4055 0398; O'Shea Esplanade; mains $9-14; ☽ lunch Tue-Sun, dinner Wed-Sun) is a chilled-out café-restaurant and gallery that cooks delicious breakfasts and offers a selection of noodle dishes.

Little Italy (☎ 4055 9967; Machan St; mains $13-26) is a cosy Italian eatery serving old favourites like veal, chicken and pasta dishes.

Holloways Beach

☎ 07

Holloways Beach is a picturesque spot with a grassy area between its esplanade and the beach, and some funky cafés and bars.

Pacific Sands (☎ 4055 0277; www.pacificsandscairns.com; 1-19 Poinciana St; apt $95) has spacious two-bedroom apartments two blocks from the beach, and a saltwater pool with BBQ area.

Strait on the Beach (☎ 4055 9616; Oleander St; meals $4-12) is a small shop and beachfront café sporting unique wooden furniture. It's perfect for breakfast or a light lunch, and the sound of the wind chime is peaceful.

Next door, **Coolum's on the Beach** (☎ 4055 9200; cnr Hibiscus & Oleander Sts; mains $15-28; ☽ dinner daily, breakfast & lunch Sun) serves oysters in seven different ways. Its outdoor decking is perfect for a cocktail – Hollowasted or Cranberry Crunch, anyone? Coolum's also has a lively Sunday session (2pm to 4pm) with Latino-salsa jazz.

Yorkeys Knob

☎ 07

Yorkeys is a sprawling but low-key place with a long white-sand beach and the impressive **Yorkey's Knob Boat Club & Marina** (☎ 4055 7711; 25 Buckley St; ☽ 10am-late) around the headland. If you're driving, take a spin to the top of the knob, where the views are spectacular.

Beach Place (☎ 4055 7139; thebeachplace79@hotmail.com; 79 Sims Esplanade; apt $200) is sensational for families – there's lots of room. Large two-bedroom, two-bathroom units with a spacious balcony and beachfront views are a home away from home. The Beach Place also runs a café–takeaway and newsagent. Minimum three nights' stay.

Yorkey's Beach Bures (☎ 4055 7755; Wattle St; d $90) is a terrific Fijian-style lodge with open-air timber cabins in a leafy setting. Minimum three nights' stay.

York Beachfront Apartments (☎ 4055 8733; www.yorkapartments.com.au; 61-63 Sims Esplanade; apt $130-140) is a great mid-range option, and weekly stays include free Sunday breakfast at the boat club.

QUEENSLAND

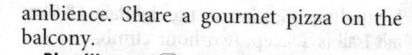

CAIRNS' NORTHERN BEACHES

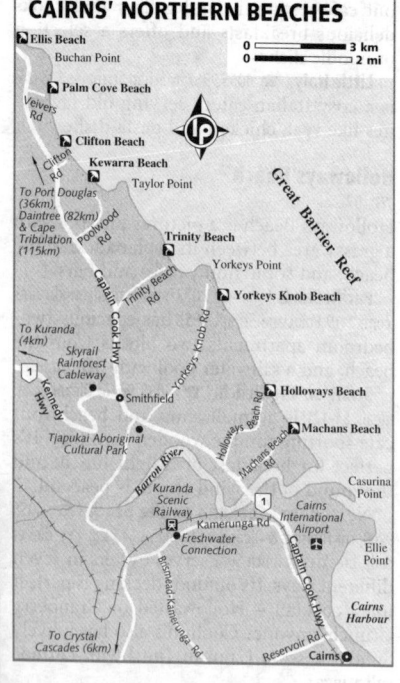

For beachfront camping head to the compact **Yorkeys Knob Beachfront Caravan Park** (☎ 4055 7201; Sims Esplanade; camp/caravan sites $18/22, cabins $70).

Blue Moon Grill (☎ 4055 8333; 25 Buckley St; meals around $15) at the boat club serves grills, pastas and burgers, and has water views, and yachts moored at the marina.

Trinity Beach
☎ 07

Take the Trinity Beach Rd turn-off to thriving Trinity Beach, one of Cairns' prettiest beaches. High-rise developments have long since destroyed its castaway ambience, but it's still a restful place.

Roydon (☎ 4057 6512; www.roydon.com.au; 83-87 Vasey Esplanade; r $162) is superb value. It offers huge two-bedroom, two-bathroom apartments with a spacious balcony, living area and full kitchen.

One block back from the beach, **Tropic Sun** (☎ 4057 8888; fax 4057 6577; 46 Moore St; d $95) has fully self-contained units.

L'Unico Trattoria (☎ 4057 8855; 75 Vasey St; meals $15-30) serves excellent food in stylish

ambience. Share a gourmet pizza on the balcony.

Blue Waters (☎ 4055 6194; 77 Vasey Esplanade; meals $4.50-11; ▯) is a cheaper takeaway–café. It also sells groceries.

Trinity Beach Hotel (☎ 4057 6106; Moore St; meals $8-16) is an old pub perched high on a hill with fabulous views. Meals are basic pub grub, but it's the cold beers that people really come for.

Clifton Beach
☎ 07

Relaxed and residential, Clifton Beach is a popular spot in high season. Clifton Beach has a broad range of accommodation and it's a great place for groups and families.

Clifton Palms Holiday Units (☎ 4055 3839; www .cliftonpalms.com.au; 35-41 Upolu Esplanade; cabins $64, r $108-205; ✿) has spacious self-contained cabins and apartments with lots of natural light.

Clifton Sands Holiday Units (☎ 4055 3355; www .oztays.com/3154; 81 Guide St; d $70; ✿) has one-bedroom, self-contained units.

Agincourt Beachfront Apartments (☎ 4055 3500; www.agincourt.com.au; 69 Arlington Esplanade; r $100-120; ✿ ▯) are luxury one-bedroom apartments that overlook the beach. Minimum two nights' stay.

Clifton Capers Bar & Grill (☎ 4055 3355; Guide St; mains $17-22) is a pleasant and informal place with a large à la carte menu.

Palm Cove
☎ 07

Palm Cove is an idyllic setting that encourages indulgence, laziness and pampering. Waves lapping the shore, palm trees rustling gently and the sticky, humid air make for a sultry destination. Funnily enough, about 100 property developers feel the same way and the once-sleepy cove, already packed with boutique hotels and expensive eateries, is experiencing a fresh wave of holiday-unit mania, with massive complexes sprouting like mushrooms. Palm Cove is popular with European tourists, especially Germans, and is a honeymooners' paradise.

ORIENTATION & INFORMATION

From the Captain Cook Hwy, turn off at Veivers Rd and follow it to Williams Esplanade, which extends the length of the beach as far as the jetty (Quicksilver and Sunlover pick up here for reef trips).

The **visitors centre** (☎ 4055 3433; www
.accomcentre.com.au; Shop 9, Williams Esplanade; ☺ 8am-
6pm) has maps. At Paradise Village Shopping
Centre, there's Internet access, a post office,
newsagent and money exchange.

SIGHTS & ACTIVITIES
Beachside strolls and leisurely swims will be
your chief activities, but if you need more
stimuli head to **Wild World** (☎ 4055 3669; www
.wildworld-aus.com.au/night.html). The **Night Zoo** is a
terrific kids' activity.

SLEEPING
You don't worry about money at Palm Cove,
and most accommodation is top end.

Paradise on the Beach (☎ 4055 3300, 1800 444
577; www.paradiseonthebeach.com; Williams Esplanade; r
$160-255; ❄ ▯) It is just that. Freshly reno-
vated modern rooms have wooden louvres
and a deep spa. There's a private bar, handy
for afternoon G&Ts.

Palm Cove Accommodation (☎ 4055 3797; palm
coveaccom@optusnet.com.au; 19 Vievers Rd; r $75) This
is a fantastic budget option. Rooms are airy
and bright.

Silvesters Palms (☎ 4055 3831; www.silvesterpalms
.com; 32 Vievers Rd; $110-185) Up the hill, Silves-
ters offers cosy self-contained units. The
owners speak German.

Palm Cove Cairns City Council Camping Grounds
(☎ 4055 3824; hunter_irene@hotmail.com; camp/caravan
sites $12/17) An incredibly popular spot that's
packed during high season (bookings essential for powered sites). Next to the jetty,
it's perfect for early-morning fishing.

Sebel Reef House (☎ 4055 3633; www.reefhouse
.com.au; 99 Williams Esplanade; r $275-480, ste $480-595)
Part of the Sebel group, Reef House has
adapted the 'Queenslander experience'
(outdoor living) to a luxurious boutique
resort. Rooms have a crisp white interior
with wicker furniture, mosquito netting
draped romantically over the bed and
discreet splashes of colour. The Sebel's restaurant (mains $32) is equally extravagant –
be sure to book ahead.

Angsana (☎ 4055 3000; www.angsana.com;
1 Vievers Rd; r $360-1000) Very *King & I* – it's
a magnificent regal white building with
walkways flanked by tall imposing palms,
and Indonesian interior design. There are
three pools, or you can indulge yourself
with an aromatherapy massage (treatments
from $110).

EATING & DRINKING
Far Horizons (☎ 4055 3000; Angsana, Vievers Rd; mains
$9-26) The setting and design is pure tropics.
Service is professional, the mod-Oz cuisine
innovative, the wine list incredibly tempting and far-horizon views wonderful.

Cocky's at the Cove (☎ 4059 1691; Vievers Rd;
$3.90-9.50) Unpretentious and relaxed eat-
ery serving cheap sandwiches and all-day
brekky.

CSLC (☎ 4059 1244; Vievers Rd; meals $9-20) A
locals' haunt serving pub grub in its fabulous garden bar. CSLC has a strict dress
code: 'thongs or shoes must be worn at
all times'.

Il Fornio (☎ 4059 1666; Paradise Village; pizzas $15-
17) This pizzeria will transport you to Italy
with its tasty 'authentic Roman pizzas'.

Apres Bar & Grill (☎ 4059 2000; 119-120 Williams
Esplanade; meals $16-30) A dark-wood drinking
den with bar staff in loud yellow-print
hibiscus shirts.

Palm Cove Tavern (☎ 4059 1339; Vievers Rd; mains
$11-22) has a lively Sunday session.

Ellis Beach
☎ 07
Round the headland past Palm Cove, Ellis
Beach has a beautiful sheltered white-sand
beach.

Ellis Beach Oceanfront Bungalows (☎ 4055
3538, 1800 637 036; www.ellisbeachbungalows.com.au;
Captain Cook Hwy; camp/caravan sites $26/32, cabins $68,
bungalows $129-155) is a well-tended place, con-
veniently located right on the beach. Cabins
have a private balcony.

Across the road **Ellis Beach Bar & Grill**
(☎ 4055 3534; Captain Cook Hwy; meals $5-22) pumps
out tasty burgers and salad, and has live
music every Sunday. Don't miss **Ellis Beach
Surf Life Saving Club** (☎ 4055 3695; Captain Cook
Hwy) for a quiet ale.

Soon after Ellis Beach is **Hartleys Creek Crocodile Farm** (☎ 4055 3576; www.hartleyscreek.com;
adult/child $24/12; ☺ 8am-5pm Mon-Fri, free tour
11am, feeding 3pm). Make sure you're there at
crocodile-feeding time!

KURANDA
☎ 07 / pop 1456
From 10am to 3pm Kuranda is a seething
mass of camera-toting tourists with more
bumbags than you can poke a didgeridoo
at. After 3pm, when the Skyrail and Scenic
Rail depart, you can experience the 'real'

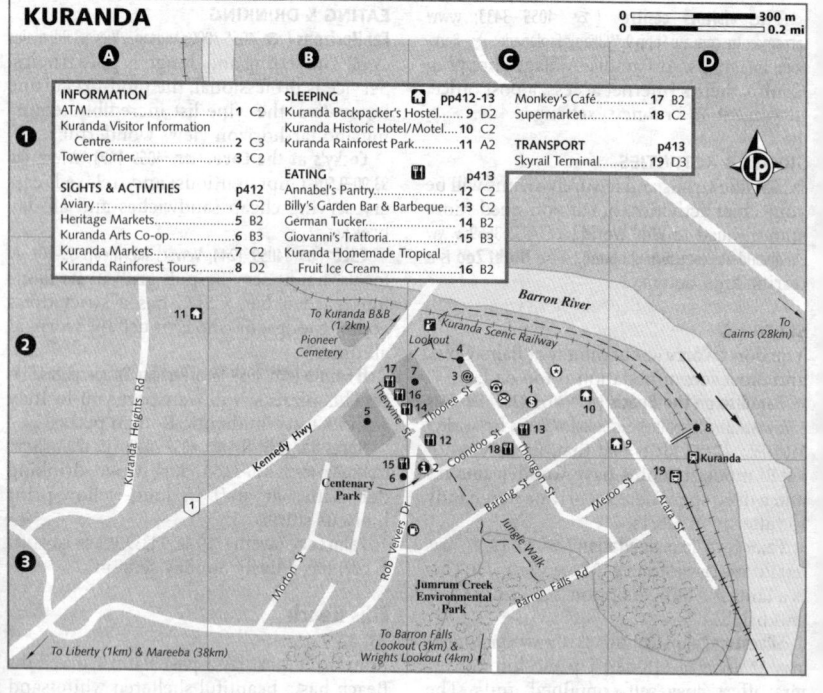

KURANDA

0 — 300 m
0 — 0.2 mi

A | **B** | **C** | **D**

INFORMATION
ATM...1 C2
Kuranda Visitor Information
Centre.......................................2 C3
Tower Corner.............................3 C2

SIGHTS & ACTIVITIES p412
Aviary...4 C2
Heritage Markets.......................5 B2
Kuranda Arts Co-op...................6 B3
Kuranda Markets.......................7 C2
Kuranda Rainforest Tours..........8 D2

SLEEPING pp412-13
Kuranda Backpacker's Hostel.......9 D2
Kuranda Historic Hotel/Motel....10 C2
Kuranda Rainforest Park...........11 A2

EATING p413
Annabel's Pantry......................12 C2
Billy's Garden Bar & Barbeque..13 C2
German Tucker........................14 B2
Giovanni's Trattoria.................15 B3
Kuranda Homemade Tropical
Fruit Ice Cream....................16 B2

Monkey's Café..........................17 B2
Supermarket............................18 C2

TRANSPORT p413
Skyrail Terminal.......................19 D3

To Kuranda B&B (1.2km)
Pioneer Cemetery
Kuranda Scenic Railway
Barron River
Lookout
To Cairns (28km)
Kuranda Heights Rd
Kennedy Hwy
Therwine St
Thooree St
Coondoo St
Thongon St
Barang St
Jungle Walk
Centenary Park
Rob Vievers Dr
Morton St
Jumrum Creek Environmental Park
Barron Falls Rd
Mcloo St
Arara St
Kuranda
To Liberty (1km) & Mareeba (38km)
To Barron Falls Lookout (3km) & Wrights Lookout (4km)

Kuranda, a mellow mountain town set in stunning rainforest.

The **Kuranda visitors centre** (☎ 4093 9311; www .ozemail.com.au/~krts; Centenary Park; 🕐 10am-4pm) has maps and a helpful website. **Tower Corner** (☎ /fax 4093 7400; 14 Thongon St) has Net access (30 minutes for $4).

Sights & Activities

Kuranda's famous markets, which now heavily target the tourist dollar, are still the village's prime attractions. The markets are split into two sections: **Kuranda Markets** (☎ 4093 8772; 7 Therwine St; 🕐 9am-3pm Wed-Fri & Sun) is where you'll find food and food products (eg emu oil), and **Kuranda Heritage Markets** (☎ 4093 8060; www.kurandaline.com.au/market/; Rob Vievers Dr; 🕐 9am-3pm) sells tourist-oriented arts and crafts.

Kuranda Arts Co-op (☎ /fax 4093 9026; www .artskuranda.asn.au; Kuranda Settlement Village, 12 Rob Veivers Dr; 🕐 10am-4pm) is the best place for genuine arts and crafts.

Over the footbridge behind the train station, **Kuranda Rainforest Tours** (☎ 4093 7476; www.kurandarainforesttours.com; adult/child/family

$12/6/30; 🕐 hourly 10.30am-2.30pm) runs sedate 45-minute cruises along the Barron River. Check opening times during the wet season (October to March).

There are several signed walks in the markets, and a short walking track through **Jumrum Creek Environmental Park**, off Barron Falls Rd. The park has a big population of fruit bats.

Further down, Barron Falls Rd divides: the left fork takes you to a **lookout** (wheelchair access) over the falls, while further along the right fork brings you to **Wrights Lookout**, which looks down at Barron Gorge National Park.

The **Aviary** (☎ 4093 7411; www.theaviarykuranda .com; 8 Thongon St; adult/child $12/6; 🕐 10am-3pm) has Australian birds and parrots.

Sleeping

Kuranda Rainforest Park (☎ 4093 7316; www.kuran datouristpark.com; Kuranda Heights Rd; camp/caravan sites $11/17, s/d $25/40, cabins $66-95) Amid a gorgeous rainforest setting, you'll hear birds trilling at dawn. Budget rooms share a kitchen and bathroom, and there are self-contained cabins with poolside or garden views. The park is roughly 10 minutes' walk from town, off the road directly opposite the Kuranda turn-off on the Kennedy Hwy.

Kuranda B&B (☎ 4093 7151; www4.tpg.com.au /users/ausavsup; 28 Black Mountain Rd; r $120; ⊠) Retreat to this excellent B&B, 20 minutes' walk from town, on Ripple Creek. Two huge rooms are immaculate, and prices include continental breakfast.

Kuranda Backpacker's Hostel (☎ 4093 7355; www .kurandabackpackershostel.com; 6 Arara St; dm/s/d $17/ 35/40) Excellent value, this rambling timber hostel is clean with a huge garden and plenty of places to relax. The friendly owners have a wealth of information about the area.

Kuranda Historic Hotel-Motel (☎ 4093 7206; www.gdapyubs.com.au/kurandahotelmotel/; cnr Coondoo & Arara Sts; s/d $45/60) Basic motel rooms. Its Garden Bar & Grill serves good pub grub (dishes $7 to $13).

Liberty (☎ 4093 7556, 1300 650 464; www.liberty resort.com.au; 3 Green Hills Rd; dm $45, r $205-300; ⊠ 🖳) A luxurious gay and lesbian resort (heteros welcome). Villas are secluded and stylish, and the Barracks has fancy dorm accommodation. Liberty has a sensational pool, gym, bar-restaurant and cosy cinema (adult movies screened after 10.30pm), and a sexy, languid atmosphere.

Eating & Drinking

Annabel's Pantry (☎ 4093 9271; Therwine St; pies $3.50-4.50) Makes gourmet Australiana pastries, such as the 'Matilda' roo pie.

German Tucker (☎ 4057 9688; Coondoo St; meals $5-8) The place for fat kransky.

Veg Out Café (☎ 4093 8483; Shop 5, 24 Condoo St; meals $5-10) A Hare Krishna café in Red House that prepares vegan, wheat- and sugar-free food. Eat Rama's rice combo while Hare chants play softly in the background. A place to de-stimulate.

Billy's Garden Bar & Barbeque (☎ 4093 7203; Coondoo St; mains $10-22) Colourful garden bar with BBQs, and wooden decking built around a majestic native fig tree. Food at Billy's is scrumptious – try the tasty curries on the specials board.

Kuranda Homemade Tropical Fruit Ice Cream (☎ 0419 644 933; www.kuranda-icecream.com.au; ice cream $2.80-4.80) Sells home-made ice-cream flavours like black sapote and chocolate-pudding fruit in the red ice-cream van next to the markets.

Monkey's Café (☎ 4093 7451; 1 Therwine St; meals $9.50-16; ⊠ lunch) Specialises in fresh gourmet sandwiches.

Peppers Famous Foods (☎ 4093 8733; Kuranda Settlement Village, 12 Rob Vievers Dr; meals around $15) Fresh bread baked on the premises, mod-Oz fare and (it's rumoured) 'vegetarian pizzas to die for'. There's laid-back music Wednesday and Sunday nights.

Getting There & Away

White Car Coaches (☎ 4091 1855; whitecars@top.net .au) travels between Kuranda and Cairns eight times daily (one way/return $1/2). It departs Cairns from 8.30am to 5.30pm Monday to Friday, and 8.30am to 1pm Saturday and Sunday. Buses leave from either the Lake St Transit Centre or 48 Spence St (outside Shennanigans) in Cairns. Buses leave Kuranda from the bus terminal at Therwine St, near the visitors centre.

John's Bus also runs a $1 bus service between Kuranda and Cairns, departing from Cairns Lake St Transit Centre and the White Car Coach terminal at Spence St.

See Getting There & Away (p406) for car-rental details.

Kuranda Scenic Railway (☎ 4036 9288; one way/ return $31/44) takes 1¾ hours to wind its way through 34km of picturesque mountains and 15 tunnels. It leaves Cairns at 8.30am and 9.30am Sunday to Friday (8.30am on Saturday), returning from Kuranda Freshwater Connection station at 2pm and 3.30pm Sunday to Friday (3.30pm Saturday).

Skyrail Rainforest Cableway (☎ 4038 1555; www.skyrail.com.au; cnr Kamerunga Rd & Cook Hwy; one way/return $32/46 ⊠ 8am-5pm, last departure from Cairns & Kuranda 3.30pm), at 7.5km, is one of the world's longest gondola cableways. It offers bird's-eye rainforest views and has two stops en route. Only day-packs can be carried on board.

ATHERTON TABLELAND

Inland from the coast between Innisfail and Cairns, the lush Atherton Tableland is a region of beautiful scenery, with lakes and waterfalls, national parks and state forests, small villages and busy rural centres. The Tableland's altitude is more than 1000m in places. One or two days in the Tableland are thoroughly enjoyable.

Nonindigenous Australians and other migrants came to the Tableland in the 1870s searching for gold and (later) tin. Roads and railways were built, and logging and farming became the primary industries. The region's traditional owners, the Ngadjonji tribe of the wider Djirbal-language group, met the intrusion with violent resistance, but were themselves violently overcome.

GETTING THERE & AROUND

Hire car is the ideal way to get around as there are so many stops over short distances, but **White Car Coaches** (www.atherton-tableland.com/Whitecar%20Coaches.htm) also has regular bus services connecting Cairns with the Tableland. See Getting There & Away (p406) for more details.

Mareeba

☎ 07 / pop 6900

Mareeba, the rough diamond of the Tableland, is where the rainforest meets the outback. It's a great place to pick up seasonal work, and it has a few attractions. If you're around in July, be sure to see the **Mareeba Rodeo**.

First stop is the incredibly helpful **Mareeba Heritage Museum & Tourist Information Centre** (☎ 4092 5674; www.mareebaheritagecentre.com.au; Centenary Park, 345 Byrnes St; 8am-4pm).

Mareeba Wetlands (☎ 4093 2514; www.mareebawetlands.com; adult/child $8/5; 10am-4pm Apr-Dec) is a bird-lovers' extravaganza. Six-thousand acres of savannah woodland are home to over 180 species of birds, and the reserve is a haven for mammals and reptiles. Canoe tours cost $6/11 for a half-/one-hour trip. To reach the Wetlands, take the Pickford Rd turn-off from Biboohra, 7km north of Mareeba.

Granite Gorge (admission $2) offers waterfalls, walking trails round huge granite formations, rock-wallaby feeding and a camping ground. To reach it, follow Chewco Rd out of Mareeba for 7km; there's a turn-off to your right from there.

Coffee aficionados will love **Coffeeworks** (☎ 4092 4101, 1800 355 526; www.arabicas.com.au; 136 Mason St; coffee $2.50-3.30, tours adult/under-12s $5/free), and you can taste mango wine at **Golden Pride Winery** (☎ 4093 2524; www.goldendrop.com; Bilwon Rd; half-bottle/bottle $16/25; 8am-5pm). Head north on the road to Mount Molloy for 11km and turn right at Bilwon Rd. It's another 2km to the winery.

Aviation and military buffs should definitely check out **Beck Museum** (☎ 4092 3979; www.holidaynq.com.au/AthertonTabs/BeckCollection/beck-collection.html; Kennedy Hwy; adult/child $13/7; 10am-4pm).

SLEEPING & EATING

Accommodation choices in Mareeba are slim:

Jackaroo Motel (☎ 4092 2677; www.jackaroomotel.com; 340 Byrnes St; s/d $66/77;) Without doubt the best accommodation in town. It has clean rooms, wheelchair facilities and a cool saltwater swimming pool.

Arriga Farmstay (☎ 4093 2114; www.bnbnq.com.au/arriga; 1720 Dimbula Rd; r $65, full board available) A working cane farm. Rooms are in a colonial homestead and all produce is organically grown.

Riverside Caravan Park (☎ 4092 2309; 13 Egan St; camp/caravan sites $11/14, caravans $25-35) On the Barron River, with beautiful views.

Natasi's (10 Byrnes St; meals $3-6.50;) Serves burgers and sandwiches.

Chillagoe

☎ 07

Chillagoe's population is small, unless you count the number of termites that inhabit the rich ochre mounds dotting its arid landscape. Chillagoe lives up to any romantic notions you may have of the outback. Around town are impressive limestone caves, rock pinnacles, Aboriginal rock art and ruins of early 20th-century smelters. Chillagoe is 140km west of Mareeba and close enough to make a day trip from Cairns, but an overnight stay is preferable.

The **Hub** (☎ 4094 7111; jimevans@bigpond.com.au; Queen St; 8am-5pm Mon-Fri, closes 3.30pm Sat & Sun) is the visitors centre, and where you book QPWS **cave tours** ($11-14) of the stunning Donna (9am), Trezkinn (11am) and Royal Arch (1.30pm) limestone caves.

SLEEPING & EATING

Chillagoe Cabins (☎ 4094 7206; www.chillagoe.com; Queen St; s/d $78/98;) Modelled on old miners' huts, the self-contained cabins are the best accommodation in Chillagoe. The friendly owners are animal carers and you may be able to pat a convalescing kangaroo. Chillagoe Cabins also offers package tours, with pick-up from Cairns and Mareeba.

Chillagoe Bush Camp & Eco-Lodge (☎ 4094 7155; bushlodge@bigpond.com; Hospital Ave; s/tw $28/50, d $55-70;) Another excellent option.

There's a range of cabins to suit all types of budgets, and a communal area with meals.

Chillagoe Caves Lodge (☎ 4094 7106; caveslodge chillagoe@bigpond.com; 7 King St; powered sites per person $7, budget s/d with shared facilities $40/45, motel s/d $60/65; ☒) Offers basic motel rooms with super-clean, spacious bathrooms, and free in-house movies. Budget rooms with shared facilities are available, and there's a restaurant.

Chillagoe Tourist Village (☎ 4094 7177; raewin@ bigpond.com; Queen St; camp/caravan sites per person $6/8, cabins s/d $35/45, units s/d $50/60; ☒) Guinea fowls cluck and peck around the great-value cabins and swimming pool.

Post Office Hotel (☎ 4094 7119; pohotel@bigpond .com.au; 37 Queen St; meals $10-16) Graffiti scrawls cover the walls from skirting board to ceiling, and the solid marble bar is a tangible piece of history. Meals are enormous: a piece of rump covers the plate. The Post Office is the last bastion for punters seeking solace in a quiet beer.

GETTING THERE & AWAY
To reach Chillagoe, take a White Car Coach to Mareeba. The **Chillagoe Bus Service** (☎ 4094 7155), run by Eco-Lodge, departs from Chillagoe post office (in the Hub) at 7.30am Monday to Friday and returns from Mareeba train station at 1pm Monday, Tuesday, Thursday and Friday and at 11.30am on Wednesday. It costs $33/66 one way/return.

If you're travelling by car, be careful driving from Mareeba to Cairns as there are no fences and the Brahmin cattle certainly don't expect to move out of your way. All but the last 25km of the route is sealed and shouldn't present a problem for conventional vehicles during the dry season.

Atherton
☎ 07 / pop 5889
'Capital' of the Tableland, Atherton is a prosperous town and a handy place to regroup. **Atherton Tableland Information Centre** (☎ 4091 4222; www.athertonsc.qld.gov.au; cnr Robert & Herberton Rds; ☒ 9am-5pm) has useful information, and **Washouse Internet café** (☎ 4091 2619; www.freedom4life.com/internetaccess; 1 Robert St; 30 min $3) has Net access.

As you approach Atherton from Herberton in the southwest, **Hou Wang Temple & Chinatown** (☎ 4091 6945; athchinatn@austarmetro.com.au; Herberton

Rd; interpretive museum & tour adult/child/ family $7/2/16; ☒ 10am-4pm) is a 100-year-old Chinese temple on the site of Atherton's original Chinatown (from the 1800s to the mid-1900s).

The best attraction in town is **Crystal Caves** (☎ 4091 2365; www.crystalcaves.com.au; 69 Main St; adult/child/family $11/6/33; ☒ 8.30am-5pm Mon-Fri, 8.30am-4pm Sat, 10am-4pm Sun), a mineralogical museum in an artificial cave that winds for a block underground. You must wear a hard hat, and the last 'miners' need to be there one hour before closing. There is wheelchair access.

Lake Tinaroo
☎ 07
From Atherton or nearby Tolga it's a short drive to this lake created for the Barron River hydroelectric power scheme. A fisherman's haven, Lake Tinaroo is open year-round for barramundi fishing. **Tinaroo Falls**, at the northwestern corner of the lake, is the main settlement.

Clean and modern with lake views, **Tinaroo Terraces** (☎ 4095 8555; www.laketinaroo terraces.com.au; r $59-99) is fantastic chilled-out accommodation that is superb value. Redclaw equipment can be hired.

Lake Tinaroo Holiday Park (☎ 4095 8232; fax 4095 8808; Dam Rd; camp/caravan sites $15/20, cabins $48-60) is a pleasant camping ground by the lake that also has boat hire (half/full day $70/80). BYO linen.

The brightly painted **Pensini's Café & Restaurant** (☎ 4095 8242; Lake Tinaroo Lookout; meals $7-28) is a modern bar and bistro with a vista of Tinaroo Dam.

From the dam, the unsealed 4WD-only **Danbulla Forest Drive** winds through the **Danbulla State Forest** beside the lake, finally emerging on the Gillies Hwy 4km northeast of Lake Barrine. The road passes several spectacular self-registration lakeside **camping grounds** (per person/family $4/16), run by the **QPWS** (☎ 4095 8459) in Lake Tinaroo.

There's a volcanic crater at **Mobo Creek**, and 6km from the Gillies Hwy a short walk takes you down to the **Cathedral Fig**, a gigantic strangler fig tree.

Yungaburra
☎ 07 / pop 1007
Yungaburra is the archetypal picturesque village: quaint, heritage-listed and full of 19th-century architecture. It's a romantic

getaway and the perfect base from which to explore the Atherton Tableland.

Yungaburra Markets (☎ 4095 2111; Gillies Hwy; ☼ 7am–noon) is held on the fourth Saturday of every month when the town is besieged by avid shoppers.

The magnificent **Curtain Fig** tree is a must-see attraction. There's wheelchair access. Spindly aerial roots hang in a feathery curtain and it's like a *Lord of the Rings* prop.

SLEEPING

Kookaburra Lodge (☎/fax 4095 3222; www.kookaburra-lodge.com; cnr Oak St & Eacham Rd; s/d $75/80; 🐾). High on the hill, small and stylish, its rooms are bright and modern and each one has its own veranda.

On the Wallaby (☎ 4095 2031; www.onthewallaby.com; 34 Eacham Rd; dm/d $20/45) A legendary and popular hostel that runs excellent tours (see Cairns Tours p401).

Eden House (☎ 4095 3355; www.edenhouse.com.au/cottages.html; 20 Gillies Hwy; r $145-165) Pamper yourself and luxuriate in a double spa. Elegant, luxurious, individually themed rooms in a historic 1912 homestead. Rates include a country breakfast hamper.

> **THE AUTHOR'S CHOICE**
>
> **Gables** (☎/fax 4095 2373; 5 Eacham Rd; r $75) is in a 1920s Queenslander, and you'll feel like you're in your own home at this excellent-value B&B. Guests are given a beautiful platter of tropical fruit and their choice of bread and milk on arrival. Two self-contained rooms are available: one has a sumptuous bathroom with a double spa, and the other has more space and a separate shower and toilet.

EATING

Nick's Swiss-Italian Restaurant (☎ 4095 3330; www.nicksrestaurant.com.au; Gillies Hwy; meals $9-27; ☼ lunch Wed-Sun, dinner Tue-Sun) Nick is a Yungaburra personality (especially when he gets fired up on the piano accordion) and his fun family restaurant serves easy-pleaser pastas, rösti and schnitzels.

Burra Inn (☎ 4095 3657; 1 Cedar St; mains $21-24; ☼ dinner, closed Tue) Intimate, cosy bistro that serves mod-Oz cuisine. If you order before 6pm, the early-bird special promises free dessert.

> **THE AUTHOR'S CHOICE**
>
> **Eden House Heritage Restaurant** (☎ 4095 3355; www.edenhouse.com.au/restaurant.html; 20 Gillies Hwy; mains around $20-29) Fine-dining that's swish and elegant. Eden's restaurant has a beautiful setting under a huge tree. Try duckling braised with verjuice and thyme, with grilled pear, figs and baked polenta. The wine list is a comprehensive tome.

Lake Eacham Hotel (☎ 4095 3515; lakeeachamhotel@ledanet.com.au; 6 Kehoe Pl; s/d $51/62) A historic country pub with counter meals and accommodation.

Crater Lakes National Park & Around

Part of the Wet Tropics World Heritage Area, the two mirror-like volcanic lakes of Lake Eacham and Lake Barrine, off the Gillies Hwy east of Yungaburra, are beautiful swimming and picnicking spots encircled by **rainforest walking tracks**. Both lakes are national parks, but camping is not allowed.

Accessible from either lake, and 12km from Yungaburra, the native **Gadgarra Red Cedar** is more than 500 years old. On the drive there you may encounter an indignant gaggle of geese.

LAKE EACHAM

A secluded lake with whip birds cracking in lush rainforest, Lake Eacham is a sensational spot for a picnic on the green grassy slope. An excellent information source is the ranger's station, where you may get to hold the native Australian python that lives there.

Bird lovers flock to **Chambers Wildlife Rainforest Lodge** (☎ 07-4095 3754; http://rainforest-australia.com; Eacham Close; r $120), a lodge with self-contained units and mad-keen bird-watching owners.

Lake Eacham Caravan Park (☎ 07-4095 3730; www.lakeeachamtouristpark.com; 71 Lakes Dr; camp/caravan sites $13/19, cabins s/d/tr $60/69/160), less than 2km down the Malanda road from Lake Eacham, has a pretty camping ground.

Surrounded by rainforest, **Crater Lakes Rainforest Cottages** (☎ 07-4095 2322, 1800 992 322; www.craterlakes.com.au; Lot 1, Eacham Close; r $190) has self-contained timber cottages that are a beautiful place to stay. Each room has an individual touch, and each day you receive a breakfast hamper (which you may have to share with curious feathered friends), port and chocolates.

LAKE BARRINE
Spoil yourself with a Devonshire Tea at **Lake Barrine Rainforest Cruise & Tea House** (☎ 07-4095 3847; fax 07-4095 3260; Gillies Hwy; adult/child/family $10/6/23; ❧ 9am-5pm) and spot water dragons and tortoises on the 45-minute cruise (five daily).

Malanda
☎ 07 / pop 1022
Part of the waterfall circuit, Malanda is about 15km south of Lake Eacham. **Malanda Falls Environmental Centre** (☎ 4096 6957; http://atherton-tableland.com/Malanda%20Falls%20Environmental%20Centre.htm; Atherton Rd; ❧ 10am-4pm) has an interpretive display and arranges fascinating 1½-hour **guided rainforest walks** (adult/child/family $5/1/12; ❧ departs 10am & 1pm Thu-Sun) led by a Ngadjonji tribal elder.

On the Atherton road on the outskirts of town are **Malanda Falls**.

SLEEPING & EATING
On the Millaa Millaa Rd, 10km from Malanda, is the tiny village Tarzali, offering some accommodation options.

Fur 'n' Feathers (☎ 4096 5364; www.rainforesttreehouses.com.au; Hogan Rd, Tarzali via Malanda; d $155-230) This stunning group of all-timber pole houses sits amid a patch of pristine old-growth rainforest. The riverfront treehouses are self-contained, private and perfect for bird-watching and spotting wildlife (a male cassowary and his chicks live here). This is one of the best B&Bs in Far North Queensland.

Malanda Falls Caravan Park (☎ 4096 5314; www.ppawd.com/malandafallsvanpark/; 38 Park Ave; camp/caravan sites $15/18, bunkhouse $35, cabins $49-69) You'll probably see more wildlife in the spacious grounds here than you will around Cape Trib! The park is next to Malanda Falls.

Tree Kangaroo Café (☎ 4096 6658; Atherton Rd; meals $6-10) Right next door to the Environmental Centre if you're in need of refreshments.

Millaa Millaa & the Waterfall Circuit
☎ 07
The 16km 'waterfall circuit' near this small town, 24km south of Malanda, passes some of the most picturesque falls on the Tableland. You enter the circuit by taking Theresa

Creek Rd, 1km east of Millaa Millaa on the Palmerston Hwy. **Millaa Millaa Falls**, the largest of the falls, are a perfect sheet of water dropping over a fern-fringed escarpment. These are the most spectacular and have the best swimming hole. Continuing round the circuit, you reach **Zillie Falls** and then **Ellinjaa Falls**, before returning to the Palmerston Hwy just 2.5km out of Millaa Millaa. A further 5.5km down the Palmerston Hwy there's a turn-off to **Mungalli Falls**, 5km off the highway.

There you'll find **Mungalli Falls Rainforest Village** (☎ 4097 2358; www.mungallifalls.com; Junction Rd; dm $25, cabins $50-80), catering to large groups with accommodation for up to 600 people. There's a kiosk (meals from $10 to $25), and horse-riding ($65 for 3½ hours) is available.

Mungalli Creek Dairy (☎ 4097 2232; www.millaa.com/Mungalli/mungalli.htm; 254 Brooks Rd; ❧ 10am-4pm) is a biodynamic dairy farm where you can taste cheese such as kaffir lime quark, and sinfully rich cheesecake.

Millaa Millaa Tourist Park (☎ 4097 2290; www.millaapark.com; cnr Malanda Rd & Lodge Ave; camp/caravan sites $15/18, bunkhouse $12, cabin s $28, cabins d $45-85, villa $85) Set on 2.8 hectares rich in wildlife, the park has a range of accommodation options, including a four-star villa, and is 1.5km from Millaa Millaa Falls.

Lunch at the charming **Falls Teahouse** (☎ 4097 2237; www.fallssteahouse.com.au; Palmerston Hwy; meals $8-14, s $65-95, d $95-140; ❧ 10am-5pm), overlooking the rolling Tableland hills, is delicious (scrumptious home-made bread!). Rooms are furnished individually with period furniture, and B&B accommodation is available. It is just out of the township, on the turn-off to Millaa Millaa Falls.

Mt Hypipamee National Park
Between Atherton and Ravenshoe, the Kennedy Hwy passes the eerie Mt Hypipamee crater, which could be a scene from a science fiction film and is well worth stopping for. It's a scenic 800m (return) walk from the picnic area, past **Dinner Falls**, to this narrow, 138m-deep crater with its moody-looking lake far below.

Herberton
☎ 07 / pop 946
A sleepy Tableland town on Wild River, Herberton is a historic tin-mining town that was booming in the early 1900s. Many of its buildings are still intact.

As you enter the town from Atherton, you'll pass **Herberton Historical Village** (☎ 4096 2271; 6 Broadway; adult/child $10/5; ☼ 10am-4pm), with a private collection of 28 original buildings.

SLEEPING & EATING
Green Springs Holiday Farm (☎ 4096 2292; www .greensprings.com.au; off Wieland Rd, Wondecla; d/f $88/ $99, cottage $110) In a 1930s homestead with a huge veranda, Green Springs specialises in family accommodation farmstays. Kids can feed the animals, spot wildlife and go for donkey rides.

Wild River Caravan Park (☎ 4096 2121; 23 Holdcroft Dr; camp/caravan sites $9/17, caravans $28, units $39) Has self-contained units and a pretty aspect.

Risley's (☎ 4096 2111; 55 Grace St; mains $22-27; ☼ 6pm Wed-Sun, lunch Sat & Sun) Incorporating Risley's art collection, this is a high-quality cosmopolitan restaurant in the middle of meat-and-three-veg land.

Ravenshoe
☎ 07 / pop 830
With an altitude of 904m, Ravenshoe is the highest town in Queensland. Once a timber town, Ravenshoe is now the 'wind capital of Australia'.

Ravenshoe Visitor Centre (☎ 4097 7700; top town@ledanet.com.au; 24 Moore St; ☼ 9am-4pm) has maps and the Nganyaji Interpretive Centre.

WindyHill Wind Farm is Australia's largest wind farm, with 20 wind turbines producing a clean green energy supply. Public viewing access is 24 hours, with views of the quiet energy source. Windy Hill can be reached either from the Kennedy Hwy from Ravenshoe or from Millaa Millaa, along the scenic Old Palmerston Hwy.

Little Millstream Falls are 2km south of Ravenshoe on the Tully Gorge Rd, and **Tully Falls** are 24km south. About 6km past Ravenshoe and 1km off the road are the 13m-high **Millstream Falls** (no swimming), said to be the widest in Australia.

Kennedy Highway
About 32km west of Ravenshoe is the small township of **Innot Hot Springs**, where a hot spring heats up the cool waters of the town's creek. You can 'take the waters' at **Innot Hot Springs Village** (☎ 4097 0136; www.users.bigpond.com /jkm72/about.html; camp/caravan sites $17/19, budget s/d $35/45, cabins s/d $67/77), a park that has seven pools and a creek running beside it. Guests have free use of the thermal pools (nonguest adult/child $6/4).

PORT DOUGLAS
☎ 07 / pop 5867
Port Douglas is a beautiful holiday destination – Four Mile Beach, backed by palm trees, stretches languorously along the Coral Sea, and there are stunning views from Flagstaff Hill Lookout.

Though Port has wooed the lucrative tourist market with boutique accommodation, stylish eating options and organised tours, the down-to-earth locals have managed to keep its relaxed village feel.

Locals in Port are a friendly bunch who are obsessed with all things nautical. If you hear wolf whistles, don't be surprised to see a magnificent yacht rather than a human form. There are some excellent sailing and fishing tours available, and you can make trips to the Low Isles, Great Barrier Reef, Mossman Gorge, Atherton Tableland and Cape Tribulation from Port Douglas.

Port was a rival for Cairns in the early days of Far North Queensland's development, before Cairns got the upper hand. In the mid-1980s Christopher Skase, the late Australian entrepreneur, backed the development of the Sheraton Mirage complex, the huge resort that dominates Four Mile Beach. Although the resort became a huge money-making machine, Skase himself fled to Majorca, where he died in 2001 still owing his creditors over $1 billion.

Orientation & Information
From the Captain Cook Hwy it's 6km along a low spit of land to Port Douglas. Davidson St, the main entry road, ends at a T-intersection with Macrossan St; the shopping strip is to the left, and to the right is the Esplanade and Four Mile Beach. Though Port is compact, some of the mid-range and cheaper accommodations are just out of the town centre.

Port Douglas **visitors centre** (☎ 4099 5599; www .reefandrainforest.com.au; 23 Macrossan St; ☼ 8am-6.30pm) has maps, and there's Net access at **Uptown** (☎ 4099 5568; www.uptown.com.au; 48 Macrossan St), costing $5 for 30 minutes.

Sights & Activities
Informative, educational and interesting **Rainforest Habitat** (☎ 4099 3235; www.rainforest habitat.com.au; Port Douglas Rd; adult/child $24/12; ☼ 8am-

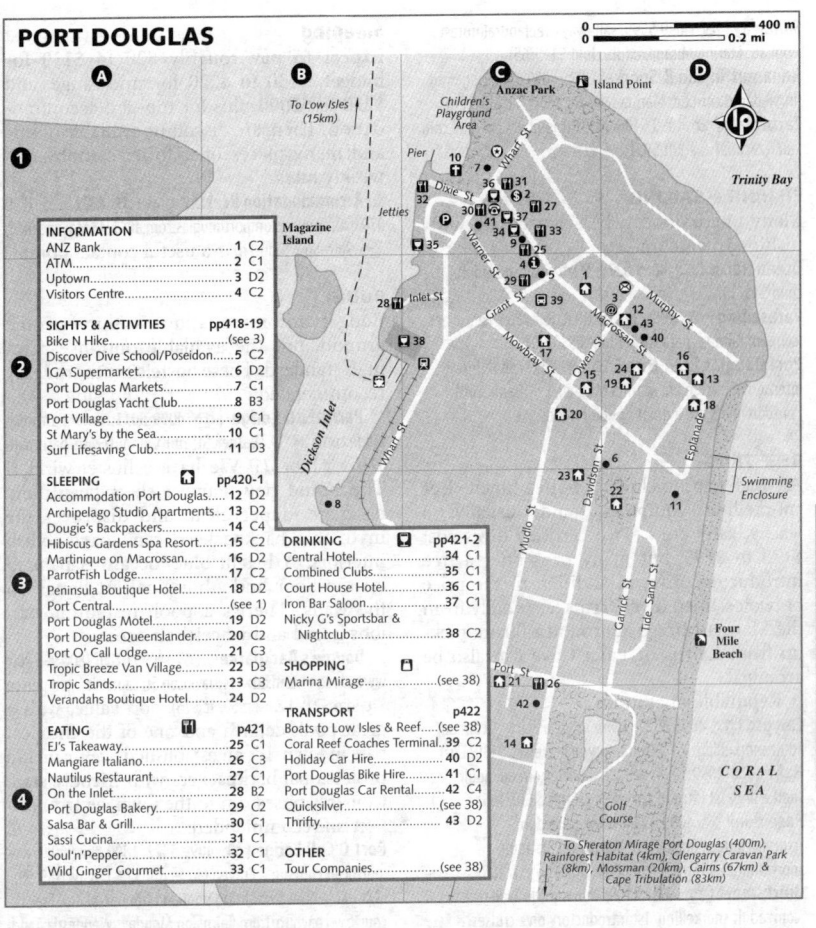

PORT DOUGLAS

INFORMATION	
ANZ Bank	1 C2
ATM	2 C1
Uptown	3 D2
Visitors Centre	4 C2

SIGHTS & ACTIVITIES	pp418-19
Bike N Hike	(see 3)
Discover Dive School/Poseidon	5 C2
IGA Supermarket	6 D2
Port Douglas Markets	7 C1
Port Douglas Yacht Club	8 B3
Port Village	9 C1
St Mary's by the Sea	10 C1
Surf Lifesaving Club	11 D3

SLEEPING	pp420-1
Accommodation Port Douglas	12 D2
Archipelago Studio Apartments	13 D2
Dougie's Backpackers	14 C4
Hibiscus Gardens Spa Resort	15 C2
Martinique on Macrossan	16 D2
ParrotFish Lodge	17 C2
Peninsula Boutique Hotel	18 D2
Port Central	(see 1)
Port Douglas Motel	19 D2
Port Douglas Queenslander	20 C2
Port O' Call Lodge	21 C3
Tropic Breeze Van Village	22 D3
Tropic Sands	23 C3
Verandahs Boutique Hotel	24 D2

EATING	p421
EJ's Takeaway	25 C1
Mangiare Italiano	26 C3
Nautilus Restaurant	27 C1
On the Inlet	28 B2
Port Douglas Bakery	29 C2
Salsa Bar & Grill	30 C1
Sassi Cucina	31 C1
Soul'n'Pepper	32 C1
Wild Ginger Gourmet	33 C1

DRINKING	pp421-2
Central Hotel	34 C1
Combined Clubs	35 C1
Court House Hotel	36 C1
Iron Bar Saloon	37 C1
Nicky G's Sportsbar & Nightclub	38 C2

SHOPPING	
Marina Mirage	(see 38)

TRANSPORT	p422
Boats to Low Isles & Reef	(see 38)
Coral Reef Coaches Terminal	39 C2
Holiday Car Hire	40 D2
Port Douglas Bike Hire	41 C1
Port Douglas Car Rental	42 C4
Quicksilver	(see 38)
Thrifty	43 D2

OTHER	
Tour Companies	(see 38)

5.30pm, 5pm-10pm Jul-Oct) is an excellent tourist activity (suits ages zero to 100) and well worth the admission fee. The *Bird & Animal Spotter's Guide* ($2) is invaluable, and you'll see iridescent parrots, wading birds, fruit bats and prehistoric-looking cassowaries.

Port Douglas Markets (Anzac Park, bottom Macrossan St; 8.30am-1.30pm Sun) make for a leisurely Sunday morning wander along the grassy banks of Anzac Park. Port's markets have been here long before the tourists. Pick up fruit and veg and local arts and crafts.

St Mary's by the Sea (Anzac Park) is a tiny non-denominational white-timber chapel that was built in 1911.

Several companies offer PADI Open Water certification as well as advanced dive certificates. The long-running and well-respected **Discover Dive School/Poseidon** (4099 5544; www.discoverdiveschool.com; Shop 6, Grant St) offers small classes (a maximum of six people), and **Quicksilver Dive School** (4055 3255; www.quicksilverdive.com.au; Novotel, Palm Cove) both have four-day Learn to Dive courses, which include two days' pool and theory in Palm Cove and two days' open water on the Quicksmart boat from Port Douglas.

Tours
LOW ISLES TRIPS
There are several cruises to the Low Isles, a small coral cay surrounded by a lagoon and topped by a lighthouse.

QUEENSLAND

Sailaway (☎ 4099 5599; sailaway@reefandrainforest .com.au; Marina Mirage; adult/child $115/65)

Ragamuffin Sail & Snorkel (☎ 4099 5922; ragamuf fin@ledanet.com.au; Marina Mirage; adult & child $110)

Zachariah (☎ 4098 5405; http://members.ozemail.com .au/~zacariah/; adult $95)

FISHING & SAILING

Many operators can be accessed via www .fishingcairns.com.

Ocean Racer (☎ 4099 6277; Marina Mirage; adult/ child $45/30)

Parasailing (☎ 4099 3175; xtraactionwater@optusnet .com.au; tandem parasail/jet bikes $50/90)

Port Douglas Boat Hire (☎ 4099 6277; boathire@ internetnorth.com.au; Marina Mirage; ⏰ 8am-8pm) Pontoon boats are a great option for kids.

REEF TRIPS

All reef trips include a buffet lunch, free snorkelling equipment and, usually, a wacky, zany crew. Two certified dives cost $175 to $195, but many trips offer a free introductory dive, in addition to the price of two certified dives. Trips leave daily from the Marina Mirage at around 8.30am; pick-up from Cairns or Palm Cove can also be arranged.

Reputable operators:

Calypso (☎ 4099 3377; www.calypsocharters.com.au; adult snorkelling/1st introductory dive cruises $130/170)

Haba (☎ 4099 5254; www.habadive.com.au; adult snorkelling/1st introductory dive cruises $130/185)

Poseidon (☎ 4099 4134; www.poseidon -cruises.com.au; Shop 2, 32 Macrossan St; adult snorkelling/1st introductory dive cruises $135/185)

Quicksmart (☎ 4087 2100; www.quicksilver-cruises .com; adult snorkelling/1st introductory dive cruises $125/185)

Aristocat (☎ 4099 4727; www.aristocat.com.au; Marina Mirage, Shop 18, Wharf St; adult snorkelling/1st introductory dive cruises $135/free)

OTHER TOURS

There are numerous operators offering day trips to Cape Tribulation, some via Moss-man Gorge. Many of the tours out of Cairns also do pick-ups from Port Douglas.

Bike 'n' Hike (☎ 4099 4000; www.bikenhike.com.au; 42 Macrossan St) These guys are sick for moun-tain bikes and adventure sports.

Reef & Rainforest Connections (☎ 4099 5599; www.reefandrainforest.com.au; tours $79-195) covers most of the Far North. It has a combination of day tours, including to Cooktown.

Sleeping

Expect to pay roughly $20 to $130 for budget, $130 to $220 for mid-range, and $220 to $2000-plus for top-end accommo-dation. There are discounts available online and many places offer lower standby and weekly rates.

Accommodation Port Douglas (☎ 4099 5355, 1800 079 030; www.accomportdouglas.com.au; 1/48 Macrossan St; ⏰ 9am-5pm Mon-Fri) is a useful contact point.

BUDGET

Budget accommodation is thin on the ground, but the available options are of high standard. These hostels are thoroughly recommended:

ParrotFish Lodge (☎ 4099 5011; www.parrotfish lodge.com; 37/39 Warner St; dm without/with bathroom $23/26, d & tw $75) We have a hostel winner! The brand new ParrotFish is beautifully designed, super clean and disproves the myth that backpackers' can't have stylish interiors. A bright-blue 'ocean' is painted on the floor and Aboriginal art hangs on the walls. There's a pool, restaurant-bar, jobs board and wheelchair access.

Dougie's Backpackers (☎ 4099 6200, 1800 996 200; www.dougies.com.au; 111 Davidson St; camp sites per person $10, dm $21, d & tw $60, tr $75) Top value, with a great poolside area and one of the cheapest bars in town. It's an established, well-run and professional backpackers with friendly staff. Courtesy buses run to the town centre.

Also recommended:

Port O'Call Lodge (☎ 4099 5422, 1800 892 800; www .portocall.com.au; 7 Craven Close; dm $23, d & tw $89-99; ✳ 🖥) YHA. Swimming pool and fun bar-bistro. Free courtesy coach to/from Cairns on Monday, Wednesday and Saturday.

Port Central (☎ 4051 6722; www.portcentral.com.au; 36 Macrossan St; s/d $69/76; ✳) No reception, just a telephone.

Tropic Breeze Van Village (☎ /fax 4099 5299; 24 Davidson St; camp/caravan sites $19/22, cabins $71)

MID-RANGE

Archipelago Studio Apartments (☎ 4099 5387; www.archipelago.com.au; 72 Macrossan St; r $118-199; ✳ 🖥) Archipelago is close to the Espla-nade (ocean views available) and Macrossan St, and offers well-maintained units with kitchenettes, and a saltwater pool. German-speaking owners.

Tropic Sands (☎ 4099 4533; www.tropicsands.com .au; 21 Davidson St; r $160; ✳) Fully self-contained,

THE AUTHOR'S CHOICE

Verandahs Boutique Hotel (☎ 4099 6650; www.verandahsportdouglas.com.au; 7 Davidson St; self-contained units $225; ✷ ▣) Sensational value, Verandahs' incredibly spacious two-bedroom apartments are loaded with style. Fully self-contained, with a modern kitchen, the wooden floorboards and clean simple lines create a peaceful space, while the verandas form a natural extension of the open-plan living space.

open-plan apartments with a private balcony and an excellent, modern kitchen. There's a small pool. Minimum two nights' stay.

Port Douglas Motel (☎ 4099 5248; www.port douglasmotel.com; 9 Davidson St; r $88-95, studios $105-115; ✷) Studio rooms are spacious, with a bathroom. Old rooms, but it's close to both the beach and shops.

Also recommended:

Martinique on Macrossan (☎ 4099 6222; www .martinique.com.au; 66 Macrossan St; r $162; ✷ ▣) Central one-bedroom units.

Port Douglas Queenslander (☎ 4099 5199; www .queenslander.com.au; 8-10 Mudlo St; self-contained units $124-188; ✷ ▣) Central, with a view of bushland.

Hibiscus Gardens Spa Resort (☎ 4099 5315; www .hibiscusportdouglas.com.au; 22 Owens St; apt $140-445; ✷ ▣)

TOP END

Peninsula Boutique Hotel (☎ 4099 9100; www .peninsulahotel.com.au; 9-13 The Esplanade; ste $320-420) Designer chic. The Peninsula's key features are its prime waterfront position on Four Mile Beach and its luxurious split-level pool with mosaic stripes. Rooms are small, but the bathroom is luxurious, with a double spa. Peninsula also has Hi Tide, its fine-dining restaurant-bar.

Sheraton Mirage Port Douglas (☎ 4099 5888, 1800 073 535; www.sheraton.com/mirageportdouglas; Davidson St; r $619-830, ste $2895) In a league of its own, the Mirage is steeped in '80s opulence.

Eating

Port has lively eating and drinking venues, serving everything from gourmet food to the humble deep-fried spud.

Wild Ginger Gourmet (☎ 4099 5972; 22 Macrossan St; meals $2-10) Gourmet sandwiches are bursting with so much goodness that you'll want

to race up Flagstaff Hill Lookout. Try the lavash wrap with fresh, crispy salad. Smoothies and juices are fresh and delicious.

Soul 'n' Pepper (☎ 4099 4499; 2 Dixie St; meals $4.50-10.50) Opposite the pier, this laid-back outdoor café plays soul. The owner is extraordinarily jaunty and has a wealth of information about Port Douglas. Hire bait and tackle supplies from its shop next door.

EJ's Takeaway (☎ 4099 4128; 23 Macrossan St; meals $6.50-15.50) Look no further, you have found the perfect fish and chipper.

Mangiare Italiano (☎ 4099 4664; cnr Davidson & Port Sts; pizzas $13.50-19.50) Call here for steaming pizzas.

Salsa Bar & Grill (☎ 4099 4922; 26 Wharf St; mains $24.50-29) Lots of atmosphere and a crisp colour scheme of lime-green, red and white. Excellent food, with an emphasis on local produce (revenge is exacted with crocodile tortellini).

Sassi Cucina (☎ 4099 6100; cnr Wharf & Macrossan Sts; mains $25-35) A slick and stylish Italian restaurant with a considered menu, comprehensive wine list and impeccable service. A culinary experience where you'll want more than one meal from the menu.

On the Inlet (☎ 4099 5255; 3 Inlet St; mains $17-50) Excellent seafood and water views. A bucket of prawns/oysters with beer/wine for $15 is an unbeatable late-afternoon special. Music on Sunday from 3pm to 6pm.

Nautilus Restaurant (☎ 4099 5330; 17 Murphy St; mains $33-75) Arguably Port's finest restaurant, and counts Bill Clinton and Jerry Seinfeld among its past customers. Service is impeccable and the menu sublime. You'll definitely need to book.

Drinking

All pubs and clubs serve counter meals.

Iron Bar Saloon (☎ 4099 4776; 5 Macrossan St; mains $20-40) Stuffed full of Australiana, this is the last of the great outback woolsheds. Cane toads hop to the finish line on Tuesday, Thursday and Sunday. Live music plays Wednesday to Sunday, and the Iron Bar heats up after midnight. Meals are a meat-fest of native beasts (roo etc).

Court House Hotel (☎ 4099 5181; cnr Macrossan & Wharf Sts; meals $13-20) Has an outdoor garden bistro serving thumping counter meals. Live cover bands perform at weekends.

Combined Clubs (☎ 4099 5553; Ashford St; meals $7.50-14) You won't go bankrupt at Combined

QUEENSLAND

Clubs. A popular locals' watering hole, this is a comfortable, friendly club with a family atmosphere, right on the marina. Pots are a ludicrous $1.90 and there's Playstation and computer games for the kids.

Central Hotel (☎ 4099 5271; 9 Macrossan St; meals $10-16) A rambling hotel with counter meals and live music on the veranda bar.

Last stop is **Nicky G's Sportsbar & Nightclub** (☎ 4099 5200; Marina Mirage; ☾ 10pm-5am).

Getting There & Away

For information on getting to Cairns see p406.

Coral Reef Coaches (☎ 4098 2600; www.coral coaches.citysearch.com.au) runs daily bus services between Port Douglas and Cairns, Daintree Village, Cape Tribulation and Cooktown. Contact the head office in Mossman (on the number provided above) to arrange a pick-up.

Quicksilver (☎ 4031 4299; www.quicksilver-cruises .com; one way/return Cairns–Palm Cove–Port Douglas $24/ 36) departs for Cairns from Marina Mirage in Port Douglas at 5.15pm; the journey takes 1½ hours.

Getting Around

TO/FROM THE AIRPORT

Airport Connections (☎ 4099 5950; www.tnqshuttle .com) runs a shuttle bus service to/from Cairns airport (one way/return $23/46; ☾ 3.30am-4.30pm), as does **Coral Reef Coaches** (☎ 4098 2600; www.coralcoaches.citysearch.com.au). **Port Douglas Local Shuttle** (☎ 4099 5351) does a continuous loop from the Rainforest Habitat to the Marina Mirage (one way between $1.50 and $3.90). Flag the driver at the marked bus stops.

BICYCLE

Pedalling around compact Port is a sensible transport method. Hire bikes from **Bike 'n' Hike** (☎ 4099 4000; www.bikenhike.com.au; 42 Macrossan St; bike hire half/full day $11/16.50; ☾ 8.30am-6.30pm Apr-Jan, 9am-5pm Feb & Mar) and **Port Douglas Bike Hire** (☎ 4099 5799; braden@top.net.au; cnr Wharf & Warner Sts; half-day/24-hr hire $10/14; ☾ 9am-5pm).

CAR

Port Douglas is one of the last places before Cooktown where you can hire a 4WD.

Port Douglas Car Rental (☎ 4099 4988; www.port carrental.com.au; 81 Davidson St; ☾ 6.30am-8.30pm Mon-Fri, 6.30am-1.30pm Sat & Sun)

Holiday Car Hire (☎ 4099 4999; 54 Macrossan St; ☾ 8am-5.30pm Mon-Fri, 8am-noon Sat & Sun)

Thrifty (☎ 4099 5555; www.thrifty.com; 50 Macrossan St; ☾ 9am-4pm Mon-Fri, 9am-noon Sat & Sun)

TAXI

Port Douglas Taxis (☎ 4099 5345; 45 Warner St) offers 24-hour service.

MOSSMAN

☎ 07 / pop 1941

Shadowed by Mt Demi, Mossman is fringed by cane fields in constant stages of cultivation. The Kuku Yalanji people are the traditional owners of the stunning **Mossman Gorge**. There are some crystal-clear swimming holes, which can be treacherous after heavy rain, and a 2.4km **walking trail** that loops through superb lowland forest.

Mossman QPWS (☎ 4098 2188; www.epa.qld.gov.au; Demi View Plaza, 1 Front St; ☾ 9am-5pm Mon-Fri), near the main turn-off to the gorge, has maps and information.

Excellent walks led by Aboriginal guides are run by **Kuku-Yalanji Dreamtime Walks** (☎ 4098 2595; www.yalanji.com.au; adult/concession $17/8.50; ☾ 9am-4pm Mon-Fri, walks depart 10am, noon & 2pm Mon-Fri).

Mossman Gorge B&B (☎ 4098 2497; www.bnbnq .com.au/mossgorge/; Lot 15, Gorge View Cres; s $65-95, d $85-110; ☒) is a gorgeous timber B&B with stunning views of the gorge. Rates include breakfast, which is locally baked croissants and muffins, and fresh fruit salad.

White Cockatoo (☎ 4098 2222; www.thewhite cockatoo.com; 9 Alchera Dr; r $79-99; ☒) has spacious, self-contained rooms that can sleep up to six people. Part of the property operates as a nudist resort from 1 October to 1 May.

For wholesome, home-made meals, visit **Goodies Café** (☎ 4098 1118; 33 Front St; meals $10).

Getting There & Around

Coral Reef Coaches (☎ 4098 2600; www.coralcoaches .citysearch.com.au; 37 Front St) runs daily services between Port Douglas and Cairns.

DAINTREE VILLAGE

☎ 07

The Captain Cook Hwy continues 36km beyond Mossman to Daintree Village. The turn-off to the Daintree River cable ferry is 24km from Mossman.

Daintree Village was originally established as a logging town in the 1870s. The area's red cedars attracted timber cutters because of their strength, versatility and beauty, and the logs were floated down the Daintree River for further transportation. The river is now more commonly used for cruises, with frequent crocodile sightings the big selling point. While neither Daintree Village nor the surrounding countryside is part of the Wet Tropics World Heritage Area, there are still pockets of untouched rainforest.

Daintree Village has a number of small tour operators:

Electric Boat Cruises (☎ 1800 686 103; Daintree Rd; adult $18-59, child $9-29; ☽ 8am-5pm)

Chris Dahlberg's Specialised River Tours (☎ 4098 6169; Daintree Village Jetty; $40; ☽ departs summer 6am, winter 6.30am)

Peter Cooper's Mangrove Ecosystem Tours (☎ 4098 2066; Public Wharf; adult/child $20/10; ☽ departs hourly)

Sleeping & Eating

Red Mill House (☎ 4098 6233; www.redmillhouse.com.au; Stewart St; s $40-60, d $66-88) This excellent B&B, in the centre of town, has comfortable rooms and a lovely spacious garden.

River Home Cottages (☎ /fax 4098 6225; Upper Daintree Rd; d $120) This cattle property is a fine place to experience bush hospitality. The cottages are self-contained with sweeping views. Rates include breakfast.

Kenadon Homestead Cabins (☎ /fax 4098 6142; kenadon@austanet.com.au; Dagmar St; s/d $70/80) The self-contained cabins are fairly basic.

Daintree Eco Lodge and Spa (☎ 4098 6100; www.daintree-ecolodge.com.au; 20 Daintree Rd; s $440-500, d 480-540) A sumptuous luxury experience with timber cabins set deep in the rainforest. Aromatherapy and massages available.

There are a couple of eateries in the village centre, including the casual **Jacanas Restaurant** (meals $5 to $18).

Daintree Tea House Restaurant (☎ /fax 4098 6161; Daintree Rd; meals from $13) About 3km south of Daintree, the Tea House specialises in wild barramundi and light meals.

Baaru House (☎ 4098 6100; meals $9-21) Part of the Daintree Eco Lodge & Spa, the restaurant is open to nonguests and is reasonably priced, so make the most of it! The chef uses native produce.

CAPE TRIBULATION AREA

About 11km before Daintree Village is the turn-off to the Daintree River ferry that takes you into the Cape Tribulation area. After crossing the river it's another 34km by sealed road to Cape Tribulation. The indigenous Kuku Yalanji people called the area Kulki, but the name Cape Tribulation was given by Captain Cook after his ship ran aground on Endeavour Reef.

Part of the Wet Tropics World Heritage Area, the region from the Daintree River north to Cape Tribulation is extraordinarily beautiful and famed for its ancient rainforest, sandy beaches and the rugged mountains of **Thornton Peak** (1375m) and **Mt Sorrow** (770m). It's one of the few places in the world where the tropical rainforest meets the sea.

Electricity is powered by generators in this section; few places have air-con and not everywhere has 24-hour power. Cape Trib is one of the most popular day trips from Port Douglas and Cairns, and accommodation is booked solid in peak periods.

You can get fuel and supplies at **Cow Bay Service Station & General Store** (☎ 07-4098 9127; Buchanan Creek Rd) and **Mason's Store** (☎ 07-4098 0070), just past Myall Creek.

Daintree River cable ferry (cars/motorcycles/bicycles & pedestrians one way $16/8/3; ☽ 6am-midnight every 15 min) takes two minutes to cross the river.

Coral Reef Coaches runs daily bus services from Cairns to Cape Tribulation. For information on organised trips to the area, see Cairns (p401), and Port Douglas (p419) Tours.

The following sections chart a route from the Daintree River to Cape Tribulation.

Cape Kimberly
☎ 07

Cape Kimberley Rd, 3km beyond the Daintree River crossing, leads to **Cape Kimberley Beach**, a beautiful quiet beach backed with tropical bush that offers some shade.

At the beach is **Club Daintree** (☎ 4090 7500; www.koala-backpackers.com; Cape Kimberley Beach; camp/caravan sites $20/26, dm $22, cabins $99), a huge camping ground with small cabins and bunkbeds, a lively bar, restaurant, tour office and pool.

Snapper Island
☎ 07

Just offshore from Cape Kimberley, Snapper Island is a national park with a QPWS **camping ground** (per person/family $4/16). You'll

CAPE TRIBULATION AREA

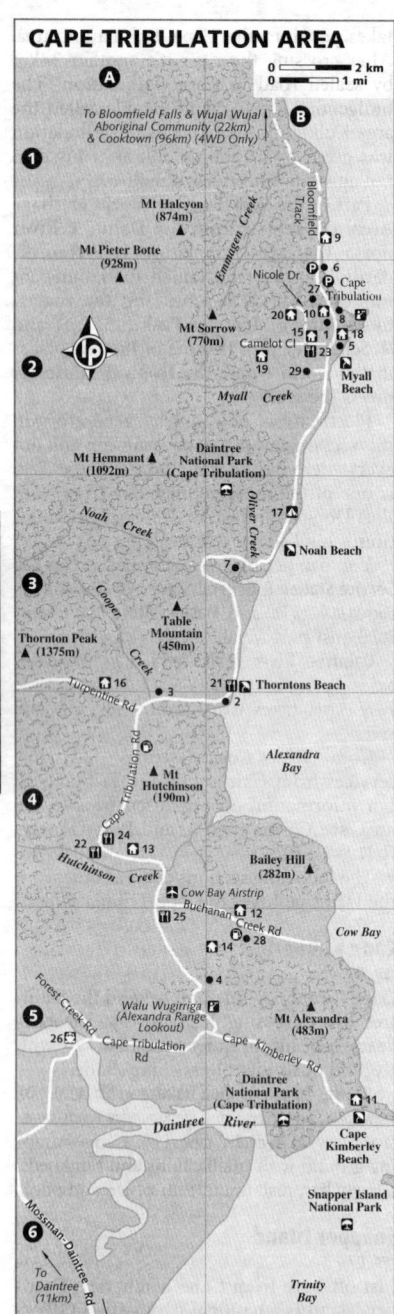

need a permit from **Mossman QPWS** (☎ 4098 2188; www.epa.qld.gov.au). Crocodylus Village (see Cow Bay p425) runs **sea-kayaking tours** to the island.

Cow Bay
☎ 07

Cow Bay is simply beautiful. Trees provide beach shade, and you can fish or just lie down and chill out– it doesn't get more relaxing than this.

Before the turn-off to the Jindalba Boardwalk is the **Walu Wugirriga (Alexandra Range) lookout**, with an information board and marvellous views over the **Alexandra Range**.

Daintree Rainforest Environmental Centre (☎ 4098 9171; www.daintree-rec.com.au; adult/child $12/6; ☼ 9am-5pm) has a 25m-high tower that starts at the rainforest floor and reaches high into the canopy. Jindalba Boardwalk snakes through the rainforest behind the centre.

SLEEPING & EATING
Epiphyte B&B (☎ 4098 9039; www.rainforestbb.com; 22 Silkwood Rd; s/d/tr $45/65/80) One of the best accommodation options on this stretch of road, Epiphyte is a welcoming B&B with

two rooms, and a veranda looking onto Thornton's Peak.

Crocodylus Village (☎ 4098 9166; Buchanan Creek Rd; dm $20, tents $75) A tent city in thick rainforest, this is a budget resort. It has a big communal pool area, small shop and open-air café-bar, and hires bikes and runs kayak tours.

Daintree Wilderness Lodge (☎ 4098 9021; www .daintreewildernesslodge.com.au; 83 Cape Tribulation Rd; s & d $250, tr/quads $290/330) Seven well-spaced timber cabins are set in magnificent rainforest, connected by an elevated boardwalk. Wildlife is abundant and there's a natural springwater 'jungle jacuzzi'. With an excellent restaurant (meals $22 to $38), this is a perfect couples' retreat.

Fan Palm Boardwalk Café (☎ 4098 9119; 80 Cape Tribulation Rd; meals $6-15) A mellow café serving deliciously healthy wraps and sandwiches, as well as more substantial meals like fish and chips, and rib-eye steak. Desserts such as lime and mango cheesecake look and taste divine. The wheelchair-access boardwalk to see giant palms (noncustomers $2) is a leisurely activity.

Daintree Icecream Company (☎ 4098 9114; Cape Tribulation Rd; ice cream/mango juice $4/3; ☼ noon-5pm) YUM! Four delectable flavours in one cup: wattleseed, blueberry, hazelnut and mango.

Le Bistrot/Floravilla (☎ 4098 9016; Cape Tribulation Rd; meals $19-30) South Pacific thatched huts (very aloha), and serves emu prosciutto and crocodile carpaccio. There's a tiny gallery.

Cooper Creek
☎ 07

Cooper Creek Wilderness Cruises (☎ 4098 9052; www.ccwild.com/tours.htm; adult $26) offers day and night guided interpretive rainforest walks.

Heritage Lodge (☎ 4098 9138; www.users.bigpond .com/david_louisebradley/index.html; Turpentine Rd; s & d $187; ☒) Has comfortable accommodation with 24-hour power. Ye olde timber cabins (two per block) have wooden slats, and there's a pool and wonderful swimming hole near the lodge in Cooper Creek.

Thorntons Beach
☎ 07

A short walk from Thorntons Beach is the neo-hippy, open-air licensed **Café on Sea** (☎ 4098 9718; Thorntons Beach; meals $10-15) with excellent healthy food, including delicious fish burgers.

Noah Beach
☎ 07

Marrdja Botanical Walk is a beautiful interpretive boardwalk that follows the creek through the rainforest and mangroves to a lookout over Noah Creek.

Noah Beach Camping Area (☎ 4098 0052; Noah Beach; per person/family $4/16) is a QPWS self-registration camping ground set 100m back from the beach. Big red-trunked trees provide shade for 16 sites.

CAPE TRIBULATION
☎ 07

Mason's Store (☎ 4098 0070; www.masonstours.com.au; ☼ 7am-7pm) is a one-stop supply shop that sells take-away food and runs tours.

At the **Bat House** (☎ 4053 4467; www.austrop.org .au/bat_house.html; minimum donation $2; ☼ 10.30am-2.30pm Tue-Fri & Sun) there are environmental displays and a fruit bat called Eggie, whose owner is passionate about bats.

Taste seasonally available tropical fruits at **Cape Trib Exotic Fruit Farm** (☎ 4098 0057; www .capetrib.com.au; tastings $10; ☼ 4pm). Try to miss the durian season at this pungent fruit farm.

Book at PK's Jungle Village (p426) for fun and informative night walks and wildlife spotting with **Jungle Adventures** (night walks $30; ☼ depart 7.30pm).

Sleeping & Eating
Gorgeous B&B retreats are the best mid-range options in Cape Trib. Basic cabins, with no additional features, are more expensive, but place you in the heart of the rainforest.

Rainforest Hideaway B&B (☎ 4098 0108; www .rainforesthideaway.com; 19 Camelot Close; s $60-70, d $90) Unique timber-lined rooms with hand-crafted furniture are surrounded by rainforest. Breakfast of fresh tropical fruit and free-range eggs is included.

Tropical Paradise B&B (☎ 4098 0072; 23 Nicole Dr; d $120) Private accommodation with views of the Coral Sea and Mt Sorrow. Tropical Paradise runs excellent sea-kayak tours.

Cape Trib Farmstay (☎ 4098 0042; www.capetrib farmstay.com; Cape Tribulation Rd; cabins $90) A working tropical-fruit orchard with private timber cabins. There's a communal kitchen, and the views of Mt Sorrow are great value.

Cape Trib Beach House (☎ 4098 0030; www .capetribbeach.com.au; Cape Tribulation Rd; dm $25, cabins $70-125) Rooms with flyscreens are set deep in the rainforest, and the complex is right

WORLD HERITAGE LISTING – WHAT DOES IT GUARANTEE?

Far North Queensland's Wet Tropics areas are amazing pockets of biodiversity. They cover only 0.01% of Australia's surface area but have 36% of the mammal species, 50% of the bird species, around 60% of the butterfly species and 65% of the fern species. The Wet Tropics' 3000km boundary includes diverse swamp and mangrove forest habitats, eucalypt woodlands and tropical rainforest.

Among travellers, and even Australians, there's a widespread misconception that `the Daintree', the accessible coastal lowland rainforest between the Daintree River and Cape Tribulation, is the limit of the region's Wet Tropics World Heritage Area. In fact, the listed area stretches from Townsville to Cooktown and covers 894,420 hectares of coastal zones and hinterland. The greater Daintree rainforest reaches as far as the Bloomfield River and is protected as part of Daintree National Park.

The Daintree area is well known for good reason. In 1983 the controversial Bloomfield Track was bulldozed through coastal lowland rainforest from Cape Tribulation to the Bloomfield River, attracting international attention to the fight to save the lowland Daintree rainforests. The conservationists lost that battle, but the publicity generated by the blockade indirectly led to the federal government's moves in 1987 to nominate Queensland's wet tropical rainforests for World Heritage listing. Despite strenuous resistance by the Queensland timber industry and state government, the area was inscribed on the World Heritage List in 1988, and one of the key outcomes was a total ban on commercial logging in the area.

That may not be enough, however. The Cow Bay area that most travellers visit, an area of unique and threatened plant species, is a 1000-block real estate subdivision on freehold private land – look around and you'll see `for sale' signs aplenty. World Heritage listing, unfortunately, doesn't affect land ownership rights or control.

Established in 1994, the Daintree Rescue Program, a buy-back scheme, has attempted to consolidate and increase public land ownership in the area, lowering the threat of land clearing and associated species extinction. Check out www.austrop.org.au for more information.

at the beach. There's a friendly open-air bar and small communal kitchen. The Beach House also runs sea-kayak trips to Myall beach.

PK's Jungle Village (☎ 4098 0082, 1800 232 333; www.pksjunglevillage.com; Cape Tribulation Rd; camp sites $24, dm $25-30, cabins d $70-80) PK's has a pool, volleyball facilities, bar area and vibrant party scene. Rooms are spartan and have no flyscreens, so prepare to be eaten alive unless you have a mosquito net.

Ferntree Resort (☎ 4098 0000; www.voyages.com .au; Camelot Close; villas $250-350) Plush accommodation in the form of villas with upstairs lofts, polished floorboards and handmade wooden furniture. There's a restaurant (mains $20 to $35), and the pool is open to nonguests.

Dragonfly Café (☎ 4098 0121; www.dragonflycape trib.com; Camelot Close; meals $10-15; ▣) A beautiful timber-pole licensed café that showcases local art. It's very chilled out.

CAPE TRIBULATION TO COOKTOWN

North of Cape Tribulation, the spectacular **Bloomfield Track** is unsealed (4WD only) and continues through the forest to the Wujal Wujal Aboriginal Community, on the far

side of the Bloomfield River crossing. Some steep sections of the Bloomfield Track may be impassable after heavy rain; check road conditions at **Mason's Store** (☎ 07-4098 0070), just past Myall Creek in Cape Tribulation, before heading off.

A must-see along the way is **Bloomfield Falls** (after crossing the Bloomfield River turn left; the car park is 1km from here). North from Wujal Wujal the track heads for 46km through the tiny settlements of **Bloomfield**, **Rossville** and **Helenvale** to meet the sealed Cooktown Developmental Rd, 28km south of Cooktown.

The **Lion's Den Hotel** (☎ 07-4060 3911; fax 07-4060 3958; Helenvale; camp sites $7; meals around $10) is a colourful 1875 bush pub. With its corrugated, graffiti-covered tin walls and slab-timber bar it attracts a steady stream of travellers and local characters.

COOKTOWN
☎ 07 / pop 1638

Sitting at the mouth of the croc-infested Endeavour River, Cooktown has a reckless, outpost ambience. It's a hard-drinking town and many people seem cast adrift here.

Locals go by the relaxed pace of 'Cooktown time' and they *live* to fish. Fishermen will regale you with stories of oversized red emperors and mangrove jacks (none of which ever get away).

Cooktown can claim to be Australia's first nonindigenous settlement, however transient. From June to August 1770, Captain Cook beached his barque *Endeavour* here, during which time the expedition's chief naturalist, Joseph Banks, collected 186 species of Australian plants from the banks of the Endeavour River and wrote the first European description of a kangaroo.

While Cook had amicable contact with the local Aboriginal people, race relations in the area turned sour a century later when Cooktown was founded as the unruly port for the Palmer River gold rush (1873–83). Battle Camp, about 60km inland from Cooktown, was the site of a major battle between Europeans and Aborigines.

In 1874, Cooktown was the second-largest town in Queensland, with 94 pubs and a population over 30,000. As many as half of the inhabitants were Chinese, who were mercilessly persecuted before being driven from the country in the 1880s.

The Peninsula Development Rd, due for completion in 2005, is still unsealed in sections and a 4WD is necessary from Cape Tribulation. The trek to Cooktown is rewarded, not only by its welcoming community and frontier atmosphere, but also by some fascinating reminders of the area's past.

Information

Cooktown QPWS (☎ 4069 5777; ian.king@epa .qld.gov.au; Webber Esplanade; ☯ 8am-3.30pm Mon-Thu, closes 3pm Fri) Permits and information. Ranger often around in the afternoon.

Cooktown Travel Centre (☎ 4069 5446; cooktown travel@bigpond.com; Charlotte St; ☯ 8.30am-5pm Mon-Fri, closes noon Sat) Tourist information.

Lure Shop (☎ 4069 5396; Charlotte St) Net access.

Cooktown Library (☎ 4069 5009; Helen St) Net access.

Sights

Cooktown hibernates during the wet season (locals call it the dead season), and reduced hours or closure may apply to attractions and tours; call beforehand to check.

Nature's Powerhouse (☎ 4069 6004; www .naturespowerhouse.info; both galleries adult/child $2/free;

☯ 9am-5pm) is an environment interpretive centre in Cooktown's **botanic gardens**. The Powerhouse has two excellent galleries: **Charlie Tanner Gallery** (Charlie was Cooktown's 'snake man') has fantastic displays about snakes, termite mounds, crocodiles, 'only on the Cape' wildlife (the bare-backed fruit bat will give you nightmares) and inspirational stories from Taipan-bite survivors; the **Vera Scarth-Johnson Gallery** displays a collection of intricate and beautiful botanical illustrations of the region's native plants. There are **walking trails** that lead from the gardens to the **beaches** at Cherry Tree and Finch Bays.

Housed in the imposing 1880s St Mary's Convent, the **James Cook Museum** (☎ 4069 5386; jcmuseum@tpg.com.au; cnr Furneaux & Helen Sts; adult/child $7/2; ☯ 9.30am-4pm) explores Cooktown's intriguing past.

Grassy Hill lookout (162m) has spectacular 360-degree views, and it's a 1½-hour walk to the summit of **Mt Cook** (431m), with even better views. The trail starts by the Mt Cook National Park sign on Melaleuca St, beyond the swimming pool.

Charlotte St and Bicentennial Park have a number of interesting **monuments**, including the much-photographed bronze **Captain Cook statue**.

Tours

Tours can be booked directly with the tour comapnies or at the tourist office. The following are rates for one person, but group bookings are much cheaper.

Cooktown Tours (☎ 4069 5125; www.cooktowntours .com; tours $20-120) runs guided coach and 4WD tours around Cooktown to: Black Mountain and the Lion's Den Hotel; Coloured Sands, Elim Beach and Hopevale Aboriginal Community; and Split Rock galleries and Lakefield National Park.

Bart's Bush Adventures (☎ 4069 6229; bart bush@ tpg.com.au; 1 Hutchinson St; ☯ 8am-5pm year-round) offer a 4WD Miner's Adventure (adult/child $145/75) and Bloomfield Falls Adventure (adult/child $125/65) with accredited Savannah guides.

Fishing is a major pastime in Cooktown; to find out about the best fishing spots check out www.cooktowns.com/gettingaround /see_do/fishing/fishing.htm. Tours go up the Endeavour, Annan and McIvor Rivers and to the Reef.

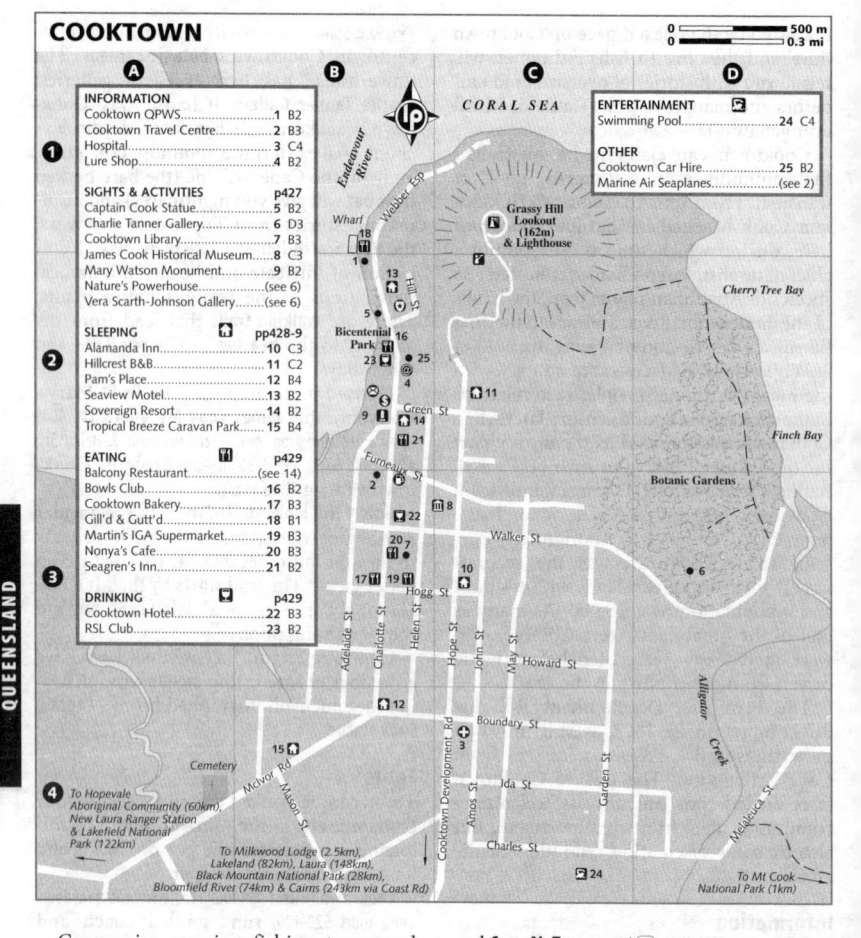

COOKTOWN

0 — 500 m
0 — 0.3 mi

CORAL SEA

Endeavour River

Webber Esp

Wharf

Grassy Hill Lookout (162m) & Lighthouse

Cherry Tree Bay

Bicentennial Park

Green St

Finch Bay

Furneaux St

Botanic Gardens

Walker St

Hogg St

Adelaide St • Charlotte St • Helen St • Hope St • John St • May St

Howard St

Alligator Creek

Boundary St

Garden St

Melaleuca St

McIvor Rd • Mason St

Cooktown Development Rd

Ida St

Amos St

Cemetery

Charles St

To Hopevale
Aboriginal Community (60km),
New Laura Ranger Station
& Lakefield National
Park (122km)

To Milkwood Lodge (2.5km),
Lakeland (82km), Laura (148km),
Black Mountain National Park (28km),
Bloomfield River (74km) & Cairns (243km via Coast Rd)

To Mt Cook
National Park (1km)

INFORMATION
Cooktown QPWS................1 B2
Cooktown Travel Centre......2 B3
Hospital............................3 C4
Lure Shop.........................4 B2

SIGHTS & ACTIVITIES   p427
Captain Cook Statue..........5 B2
Charlie Tanner Gallery........6 D3
Cooktown Library...............7 B3
James Cook Historical Museum...8 C3
Mary Watson Monument.....9 B2
Nature's Powerhouse........(see 6)
Vera Scarth-Johnson Gallery......(see 6)

SLEEPING   pp428-9
Alamanda Inn...................10 C3
Hillcrest B&B....................11 C2
Pam's Place.....................12 B4
Seaview Motel.................13 B2
Sovereign Resort..............14 B2
Tropical Breeze Caravan Park....15 B4

EATING   p429
Balcony Restaurant........(see 14)
Bowls Club......................16 B2
Cooktown Bakery..............17 B3
Gill'd & Gutt'd..................18 B1
Martin's IGA Supermarket...19 B3
Nonya's Cafe...................20 B3
Seagren's Inn..................21 B2

DRINKING   p429
Cooktown Hotel................22 B3
RSL Club.........................23 B2

ENTERTAINMENT
Swimming Pool.................24 C4

OTHER
Cooktown Car Hire.............25 B2
Marine Air Seaplanes.......(see 2)

Companies running fishing tours and charters:

Reel River Sportfishing (☎ 4069 5346; reelriver@hot mail.com; half-/full-day tour $135/260) Longest running.
Gone Fishing (☎ 4069 5980; www.cooktown.com /gone_fishing/; half-/full-day tour $ 135/260) Reef and river fishing. Croc-spotting $55, from 6pm to 8pm. Children welcome.

Cooktown Cruises (☎ 4069 5712; ashtyn@tpg.com.au; adult/child $25/13; ◌ 1pm Easter-Dec) runs a sedate two-hour cruise to the head of the Endeavour River.

Tours to Lizard Island are run by **Marine Air Seaplanes** (☎ 4069 5915, 0407-638 973; www .marineair.com.au; eco-tour $310, scenic reef flights $115-305, camping drop-off $550; ◌ 10.30am-5.30pm year-round)

and **Cape Air Transport** (☎ 4069 5007; www.milkwood -lodge.com; tours $310; ◌ 10am-4pm Apr-Nov).

Sleeping

Seaview Motel (☎ 4069 5377; seaviewm@tpg.com.au; Webber Esplanade; s/d $65/79; ◌) A rambling motel with prime water frontage and spectacular views of Cook's landing site. Clean motel rooms.

Hillcrest B&B (☎ 4069 5305; fax 4069 5893; 130 Hope St; r from $60; ◌) Hillcrest is a charming timber B&B. Guesthouse rooms are imbued with an old-fashioned character and air-con units are available. There's a lovely communal area, and Hillcrest is close to town. Rates include breakfast, plus there's a pool and restaurant.

Milkwood Lodge (☎ 4069 5007; www.milkwood -lodge.com; Annan Rd; cabins s/d $90/110) About 2.5km out of town, the airy self-contained timber-pole cabins are in a lush bushland setting with views from the private balcony. A relaxing and peaceful retreat where you can hear geckos calling at night.

Sovereign Resort (☎ 4069 5400; www.sovereign -resort.com.au; cnr Charlotte & Green Sts; r $150-160, apt $180; ⊠ ▢) Luxury, top-end accommodation right in the heart of town, Sovereign is a colonial-style resort with modern, well-appointed rooms and a superb pool area (you'll never want to get out!). Its **Balcony Restaurant** (mains $19-32) is excellent.

Budget accommodation:

Alamanda Inn (☎ 4069 5203; www.cooktowns.com /gettingaround/where_stay/Alamanda_Inn; Hope St; s $28-56, d $40-75; ⊠)

Pam's Place (☎ 4069 5166; www.cooktownhostel.com; cnr Charlotte & Boundary Sts; dm $19-20, s/d $36/46) Hostel.

Tropical Breeze Caravan Park (☎ 4069 5417; McIvor Rd; camp sites $16, cabins s/d $60/65, cabins with fan/air-con $60/65, units with fan $55-65, units with air-con $60-76; ⊠) Book ahead for the high season.

Eating & Drinking

Grab supplies from **Martin's IGA supermarket** (☎ 4069 5633; cnr Helen & Hogg Sts) and **Cooktown Bakery** (☎ 4069 5612; Charlotte St).

Gill'd 'n' Gutt'd (☎ 4069 5863; Webber Esplanade; meals $6-12) Sensational fish-and-chip shop with super-fresh Spanish mackerel and barramundi.

Nonya's Café (☎ 4069 5723; Charlotte St; meals $8-17) A welcome change from the counter-meal circuit, serving fresh salads, tapas, tasty Malay curries with rice, and chicken satay, plus the usual take-away menu.

Seagren's Inn (☎ 4069 5357; Charlotte St; mains $16-30) More upmarket, serving mod-Oz cuisine in a heritage timber building.

Drinking is one of the more popular Cooktown activities, and there are some great old pubs and clubs along Charlotte St that all serve meals.

Cooktown Hotel (☎ 4069 5308; cnr Charlotte & Walker Sts; meals around $12) Known as the Top Pub, this friendly hotel has heaps of character and is generally full *of* characters.

Bowls Club (☎ 4069 6173; Charlotte St; meals around $14) Set up in the 1970s by avid bowlers, the Bowls Club is a relaxing place for a beer, and is popular with families. Meals are deli-

cious – they do excellent spicy Thai green chicken curry and grilled reef fish.

RSL Club (☎ 4069 5780; Charlotte St; meals $8-14) Another top spot for a decent feed and a refreshing ale.

Getting There & Around

Coral Reef Coaches (☎ 4098 2600; www.coralcoaches .citysearch.com.au) travels between Cooktown and Cairns (for details, see Cairns Getting There & Away p406). It also has services to Hopevale ($20 one way) on Monday and Thursday.

Cooktown Car Hire (☎ 4069 5007, 0407-730 646; www.milkwood-lodge.com; Milkwood Lodge, Annan Rd), at Milkwood Lodge, rents 4WDs from $99 to $150 (bond $2200) per day.

For a taxi, call ☎ 4069 5387.

LIZARD ISLAND

☎ 07 / pop 1007

Lizard Island, the furthest north of the Great Barrier Reef resort islands, is about 100km from Cooktown. The continental island has a dry, rocky and mountainous terrain, with superb beaches that are excellent for snorkelling and diving, and bushwalks to **Cook's Look** (368m).

Captain Cook and his crew were the first nonindigenous people to visit the island. Having patched up the Endeavour in Cooktown, they sailed north and stopped on Lizard Island, where Cook and Joseph Banks climbed to the top of Cook's Look to search for a way through the Great Barrier Reef. Banks named the island after its large lizards, which are from the same family as Indonesia's komodo dragons. Jigurru (Lizard Island) has long been a sacred place for the Dingaal Aboriginal people.

Worlds collided in 1881, when a group of Dingaal people attacked Mary Watson, wife of a man who ran a bêche-de-mer operation on the island. A Chinese worker was killed, and Mary fled the island in a bêche-de-mer boiling pot with her child and another worker. The three eventually died of thirst on a barren island to the north; Mary left a diary of their last days.

Accommodation options are extreme on Lizard Island – camping or five-star luxury.

QPWS **camping ground** (per person/family $4/16) is at the northern end of Watson's Bay; contact the **Cooktown QPWS** (☎ 4069 5446; www.env.qld.gov.au) or go online for permits.

Campers must be totally self-sufficient, but there are toilets, gas barbecues and tables. Fresh water is available from a pump 250m from the site.

Expect isolation and an enviable location at **Lizard Island Resort** (☎ 4060 3999; fax 4060 3991; Anchor Bay; s/d $800/1200). Rates include all meals.

Getting There & Away
See Cairns Getting There & Away (p406) and Cooktown Tours (p427) for information.

CAIRNS TO COOKTOWN – THE INLAND ROAD
The 341km Peninsula Development Rd loops north from Cairns through Kuranda, Mareeba, Mt Molloy, Mt Carbine and Palmer River to Lakeland, where it splits off to Cape York Peninsula. From Lakeland the road to Helenvale is unsealed, but suitable for a conventional vehicle.

Mt Molloy's claim to fame is that the Swedish and Danish version of the TV show *Survivor* was filmed at **Camp Molloy**, the town's camping ground. Five kilometres away is the **National Hotel** (☎ 07-4094 1133; Main St; s/d $25/50), a country pub serving counter meals ($6 to $15).

The Palmer River gold rush (1873–83) occurred about 70km to the west, throwing up boomtowns Palmerville and Maytown; little of either remain today. At the Palmer River crossing, **Palmer River roadhouse** (☎ 07-4060 2020; camp/caravan sites $7/13; ☒ 7am-late) is a solitary place with horrendously expensive fuel.

South of Cooktown the road passes through the sinister-looking rock piles of **Black Mountain National Park** – a range of hills formed 260 million years ago and made up of thousands of granite boulders. Aborigines call it Kalcajagga, or 'place of the spears', and it's home to unique species of frog, skink and gecko.

CAPE YORK PENINSULA

Cape York Peninsula is one of the wildest and least populated areas of Australia. Clouds of red dust signal approaching 4WDs and you'll drive many kilometres on corrugated roads to reach the next 'town', usually an isolated roadhouse. The Cape is hot, dry work and it's no surprise that road signs list 'Ice Cold Beer' ahead of petrol or food.

Reaching the Tip, the Australian mainland's northernmost point, is still one of the great road adventures. Beyond the Tip lie the Torres Strait Islands. There are also a huge range of organised tours (see below) that cover the Cape and Thursday Island.

If you're driving to the top, you'll need preparation and a 4WD. Don't be fooled into thinking you can make it in a conventional vehicle (see Getting There & Away p432). The ideal set-up is companion vehicles: two 4WDs travelling together so one can haul the other out of trouble if necessary.

The HEMA map *Cape York & Lakefield National Park*, and the RACQ maps *Cairns/Townsville and Cape York Peninsula* are the best (see also Absells Chart & Map Centre p397). Of the numerous books about the Peninsula, Ron and Viv Moon's *Cape York – An Adventurer's Guide* is the most comprehensive. Lonely Planet's *Outback Australia* and *Queensland* guides also have extensive information for travellers to Cape York.

Information & Permits
The RACQ and QPWS offices in Cairns (p398) and Cooktown (p427) have a wealth of information and are recommended starting points for planning and to obtain permits. You don't need a permit to visit Aboriginal or Torres Strait Islander communities, but you do to camp on Aboriginal land (which is effectively most of the land north of the Dulhunty River in northern Cape York). You can organise this at the Injinoo-run Jardine River Ferry & Roadhouse, about 40km south of Bamaga. Designated camping grounds are provided in a number of areas, including Seisia, Pajinka, Loyalty Beach and Punsand Bay. Apart from Bamaga, most of the mainland Aboriginal communities are well off the main track north, and rarely have facilities or accommodation for travellers.

Tours
There are countless tour operators who run trips to the Cape. Tours are around six to 14 days and take around four to 12 passengers. Cairns is the main starting point for tours, but see also Tours under Cooktown (p427). Tours generally run between April and December, but these dates may be affected by an early or late wet season.

Most tours visit Laura, Split Rock galleries, Lakefield National Park, Coen, Weipa,

CAPE YORK PENINSULA

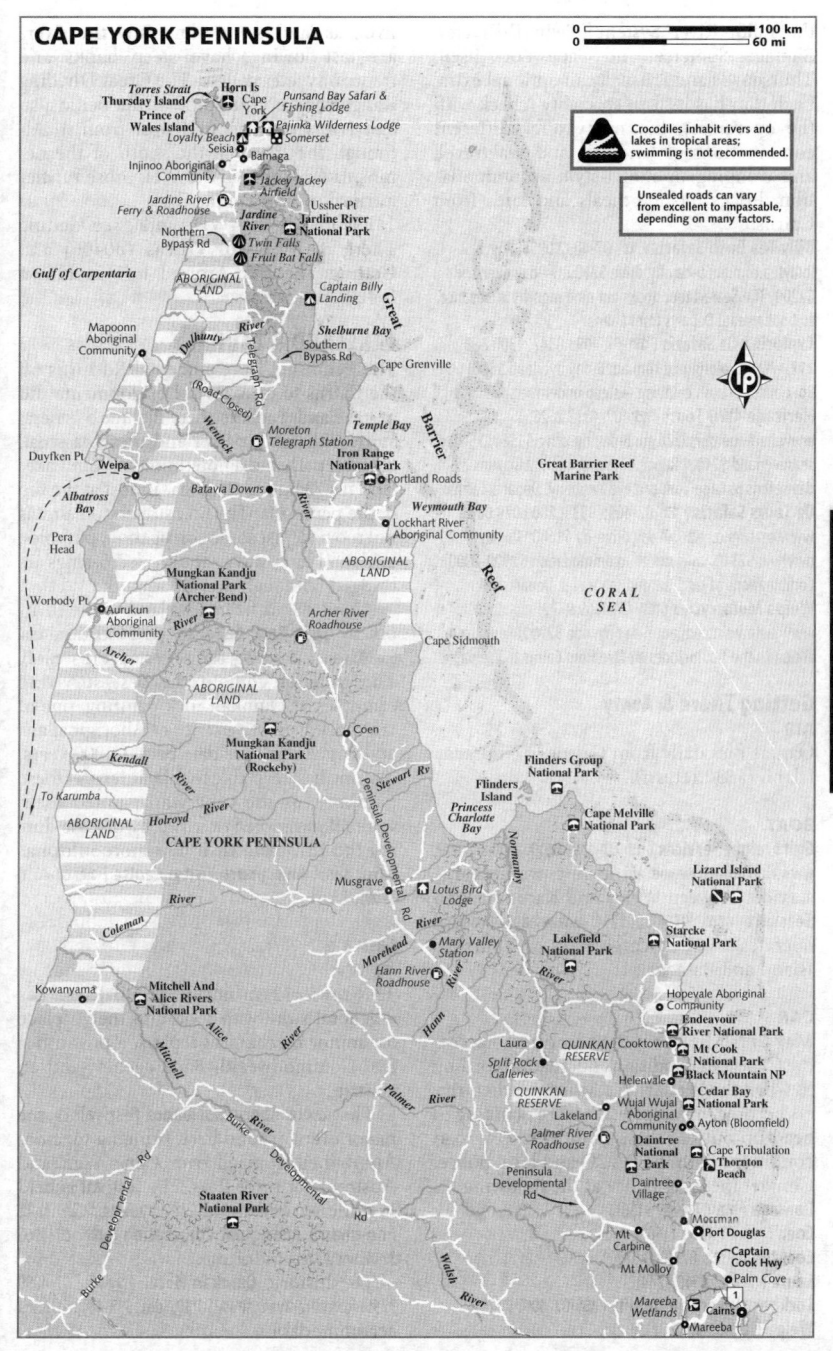

0 ⊏⊏⊏⊐ 100 km
0 ⊏⊏⊏⊐ 60 mi

Crocodiles inhabit rivers and lakes in tropical areas; swimming is not recommended.

Unsealed roads can vary from excellent to impassable, depending on many factors.

Torres Strait
Thursday Island
Prince of
Wales Island
Horn Is
Cape York
Punsand Bay Safari & Fishing Lodge
Pajinka Wilderness Lodge
Loyalty Beach
Somerset
Seisia
Bamaga
Injinoo Aboriginal Community
Jackey Jackey Airfield
Jardine River Ferry & Roadhouse
Jardine River
Ussher Pt
Jardine River National Park
Northern Bypass Rd
Twin Falls
Fruit Bat Falls

Gulf of Carpentaria
ABORIGINAL LAND
River
Captain Billy Landing

Mapoonn Aboriginal Community
Dulhunty
Telegraph Rd
(Road Closed)
Shelburne Bay
Southern Bypass Rd
Cape Grenville

Duyfken Pt
Weipa
Wenlock
River
Moreton Telegraph Station
Iron Range National Park
Portland Roads
Temple Bay

Great Barrier Reef Marine Park

Albatross Bay
Batavia Downs
Weymouth Bay
Lockhart River Aboriginal Community

Pera Head

Worbody Pt
Aurukun Aboriginal Community
Mungkan Kandju National Park (Archer Bend)
River
Archer
Archer River Roadhouse
Cape Sidmouth

ABORIGINAL LAND

CORAL SEA

Kendall
River
ABORIGINAL LAND
Mungkan Kandju National Park (Rokeby)
Coen
Stewart Ry
Flinders Group National Park
Flinders Island
Princess Charlotte Bay
Cape Melville National Park

To Karumba
River
Holroyd
CAPE YORK PENINSULA
Peninsula Developmental Rd

Lizard Island National Park

Coleman
River
Musgrave
Lotus Bird Lodge
Lakefield National Park
Starcke National Park

Mary Valley Station
Morehead
Hann River Roadhouse
River

Kowanyama
Mitchell And Alice Rivers National Park
Alice
River
Hann

Hopevale Aboriginal Community
Endeavour River National Park
Laura
Split Rock Galleries
QUINKAN RESERVE
Cooktown
Mt Cook National Park
Black Mountain NP
Helenvale

Mitchell
Palmer
River
QUINKAN RESERVE
Lakeland
Wujal Wujal Aboriginal Community
Cedar Bay National Park
Ayton (Bloomfield)

Burke
Developmental
Palmer River Roadhouse
Daintree National Park
Cape Tribulation
Thornton Beach

Staaten River National Park
Peninsula Developmental Rd
Daintree Village

Mossman
Mt Carbine
Port Douglas
Captain Cook Hwy
Mt Molloy
Palm Cove

Walsh
River
Mareeba Wetlands
Cairns
Mareeba

QUEENSLAND

the Elliot River System (Twin Falls etc), Bamaga, Somerset and Cape York itself; Thursday Island is usually an optional extra. Each tour has its own speciality (check with the operators), but many offer different combinations of land, air and sea travel, and camping or motel-style accommodation. Prices include meals and fares from Cairns.

Billy Tea Bush Safaris (☎ 07-4032 0055; www .billytea.com.au; 9-day fly-drive $2100, 14-day overland $2200) The Seafari tour books out nine months in advance, so book ahead! Departs from Cairns.

Exploring Oz Safaris (☎ 07-4093 8347, 1300 888 112; www.exploring-oz.com.au; 6-day overland $800) Specialises in bush camping – sleep under the stars.

Heritage 4WD Tours (☎ 07-4038 2628; www.heritagetours.com.au; 6-day fly-drive $1580, 15-day sea/overland $2400) Range of tour options. Also runs 25-day safaris to Cape York and the Kimberly. Departs Cairns.

Oz Tours Safaris (☎ 07-4055 9535, 1800 079 006; www.oztours.com.au; 7-day drive-fly $1680, 15-day overland $2340, with motel accommodation $2500-2800) Combinations of land, air and sea travel. Departs Cairns.

Weipa Motorcycles (☎ 07-4069 9712; www.eatmydirt.com.au; 7-day fly-ride $2900) Tours from Weipa to the Tip. Includes air fare from Cairns to Weipa.

Getting There & Away
AIR
Qantas flies daily from Cairns to Thursday Island ($830 return).

BOAT
Gulf Freight Services (☎ 07-4069 8619, 1800 640 079; www.riversidemarine.com.au) operates weekly barge services between Weipa and Karumba, and **Seaswift** (☎ 07-4035 1234; www.seaswift.com.au) operates a weekly cargo ferry to Thursday Island and Bamaga.

CAR
May to November is the best time to access the Cape, but conditions fluctuate according to when the Wet arrives, which is when rivers become impassable. If you're planning to head up outside these months, check road conditions with the RACQ and local police. Contact the local police at the following:

Bamaga (☎ 07-4069 3156)
Coen (☎ 07-4060 1150)
Cooktown (☎ 07-4069 5320)
Laura (☎ 07-4060 3244)
Lockhart River Community (☎ 07-4060 7120)
Weipa (☎ 07-4069 9119)

Even as late as June and July the rivers are fast-flowing, have steep banks and frequently alter course. The Great Dividing Range runs up the spine of the peninsula, and rivers run east and west from it. Although the rivers in the south of the peninsula flow only in the Wet, those further north flow year-round.

For details on 4WD rental, see Getting There & Away for Cairns (p0406) and Getting There & Around for Cooktown (p429).

LAKELAND & LAURA
The Peninsula Developmental Rd turns off the Cairns to Cooktown Developmental Rd at Lakeland. Facilities here include a general store with food, petrol and diesel, a small caravan park and a hotel-motel. From Lakeland it's 734km to Bamaga, almost at the top of the peninsula. The first stretch to Laura is not too bad, just some corrugation, potholes, grids and causeways – the creek crossings are bridged (although they flood in the Wet).

About 48km from Lakeland is the turn-off to **Split Rock Galleries** (Split Rock/entire trail $5/10, paid into honesty box, no photography allowed). The galleries contain the best surviving examples of Quinkan rock painting, one of the most distinctive styles of Aboriginal art, and depictions here date back 14,000 years. No-one has been able to fully interpret these paintings, as the tribe who painted them were all massacred or killed by disease during the 1873 gold rush. For more information, visit **Ang-gnarra Visitor Centre** (☎ 07-4090 3200), Laura.

Laura
☎ 07
This town, 12km north of Split Rock, has a general store with food and fuel, a place for minor mechanical repairs, a post office and Commonwealth Bank agency, and an airstrip.

The **Laura Aboriginal Dance Festival** is the major event around here, bringing together Aborigines from all over Cape York and Australia for three days. The festival is held in June of odd-numbered years. Contact **Ang-gnarra Aboriginal Corporation** (☎ 07-4060 3214; www.laura-festival.com).

The historic **Quinkan Hotel** (☎ /fax 07-4060 3255; camp/caravan sites $6/10, dm $15-40) offers accommodation.

Lakefield National Park

☎ 07

The main turn-off to Lakefield National Park is just past Laura, about a 45-minute drive.

Lakefield is the second-largest national park in Queensland, and the most accessible on Cape York Peninsula. It's best known for its **wetlands** and prolific **birdlife**. The extensive river system drains into Princess Charlotte Bay on its northern perimeter. This is the only national park on the peninsula where fishing is permitted.

There's a good **camping ground** (per person/family $4/16) with showers and toilets at Kalpowar Crossing. See the rangers at the ranger bases at **New Laura** (☎ 4060 3260) or **Lakefield** (☎ 4060 3271), further north in the park, to arrange camping permits.

About 26km before Musgrave is the resort **Lotus Bird Lodge** (☎ 4059 0773, 1800 674 974; www.cairns.aust.com/lotusbird; r with meals & tours $200).

Princess Charlotte Bay, which includes the coastal section of Lakefield National Park, is the site of some of Australia's biggest **rock-art galleries**. Unfortunately, the bay is extremely hard to reach except from the sea.

LAURA TO ARCHER RIVER ROADHOUSE

North from Laura, the roads deteriorate further. At the 75km mark, there's the Hann River crossing and **Hann River Roadhouse** (☎ 07-4060 3242; fax 07-4060 3394; Peninsula Development Rd; camp/caravan sites $14, r $65; meals from $7; ☷ 7am-10pm), a pit stop selling food, petrol and, of course, cold beers.

Twenty kilometres from the roadhouse, there's a turn-off for the 6km drive east to **Mary Valley Station** (☎ 07-4060 3254; camp sites $12, s/d $30/45). Book ahead for breakfast, lunch and dinner.

Another 62km on is **Musgrave**, with its historic Musgrave Telegraph Station, built in 1887, and **Musgrave Roadhouse** (☎ /fax 07-4060 3229; Peninsula Development Rd; camp sites $14, s/d $32/50; ☷ 7.30am-10pm).

Coen, 108km north of Musgrave, has a pub, two general stores, hospital, school and police station; you can get mechanical repairs done here. Coen has an airstrip and a racecourse, where picnic races are held in August.

Homestead Guest House (☎ 07-4060 1157; fax 07-4060 1158; s/tw $40/60) has simple, clean rooms; **Exchange Hotel** (☎ 07-4060 1133; fax 07-4060 1180; s $40-60, d $52-68) serves breakfast and dinner.

The Archer River crossing, 65km north of Coen, used to be a real terror, but now, with its concrete causeway, is quite easy. **Archer River Roadhouse** (☎ /fax 4060 3266; camp sites $14, s/d $45/60; ☷ 7am-10pm), on the banks of the Archer River, is a good place to make a stop.

Northern National Parks

Three national parks can be reached from the main track north of Coen. To stay at any of them you must be totally self-sufficient.

Only about 3km north of Coen, before the Archer River Roadhouse, you can turn west to the remote **Mungkan Kandju National Park**. The **ranger station** (☎ 07-4060 3256) is in Rockeby, about 75km off the main track. Contact the **Coen QPWS** (☎ 07-4060 1137) for more information.

Roughly 21km north of the Archer River Roadhouse, a turn-off leads 135km through the **Iron Range National Park** to the tiny coastal settlement of Portland Roads (no camping). Although still pretty rough, this track has been improved. Register with the **ranger** (☎ 07-4060 7170) on arrival; camping is permitted at designated sites. The national park has Australia's largest area of lowland rainforest, with some animals that are found no further south in Australia.

The **Jardine River National Park** includes the headwaters of the Jardine and Escape Rivers, where the explorer Edmund Kennedy was killed by Aborigines in 1848.

WEIPA

☎ 07 / pop 2502

Weipa is 135km from the main track. The turn-off is 47km north of the Archer River crossing. This modern mining town works the world's largest deposits of bauxite (the ore from which aluminium is processed). The mining company Comalco runs regular tours of its operations from May through to December.

Weipa Camping Ground (☎ 4069 7871; www.fishingcairns.com.au/page13-7c.html; camp/caravan sites $18/20, cabins $64-105, cabins from $50) operates as the town's informal visitors centre, and can book mining and fishing tours, and also provides permits for nearby camping grounds. Its shady park is right next to the shopping centre, with a private beach and a saltwater pool. Best to book ahead for stays in peak time.

QUEENSLAND

NORTH TO THE JARDINE

Back on the main track, after Batavia Downs, there is almost 200km of rough road and numerous river crossings (the Dulhunty being the major one) before you reach the **Jardine River Ferry & Roadhouse** (☎ 07-4069 1369; ⏰ 8am-5pm). From the Wenlock River there are two possible routes to the Jardine ferry: the more direct but rougher old route (Telegraph Rd, 155km), and the longer but quicker Bypass roads (193km), which branch off the old route about 40km north of the Wenlock River. Don't miss **Twin Falls**, one of the most popular camping and swimming spots on the Cape; there's a signpost off the main road about 90km before the roadhouse.

The river crossing is run by the Injinoo Community Council and operates during the Dry only ($88 return, plus $11 for trailers). The fee includes a permit, which allows you to bush camp in designated areas north of the river.

Stretching east to the coast from the main track is the **Jardine River National Park**. The Jardine River spills more fresh water into the sea than any other river in Australia. It's impenetrable country.

THE TIP

☎ 07

The first settlement north of the Jardine River is **Bamaga**, home to the Cape York Peninsula's largest Torres Strait Islander community. The town has a post office (and Commonwealth Bank agency), hospital, supermarket, bakery, mechanic and few places to stay.

Resort Bamaga (☎ 4069 3050; www.resortbamaga.com.au; r $160-180, mains $20-30; ✖ ▢) is the only four-star accommodation on the Cape. If you need some luxury, then this is the place. 4WD hire available.

Seisia, on the coast 5km northwest, has the central **Seisia Resort & Camping Ground** (☎ 4069 3243, 1800 653 243; www.fishingcairns.com.au /page13-7d.html; camp sites $22, s/d $90/115).

Northeast of Bamaga, off the Cape York track and about 11km southeast of Cape York, is **Somerset**, which was established in 1863 as a haven for shipwrecked sailors and a signal to the rest of the world that this was British territory. It was hoped that it might become a major trading centre, but its trading functions were moved to Thursday Island in 1879, and there's nothing much left now, though there are lovely views.

On the western side of the Tip is the scenic **Punsand Bay Safari & Fishing Lodge** (☎ 4069 1722; fax 4069 1403; camp sites $22, tents $120, cabins with meals $170). This place is very well set up and it runs 4WD tours.

THURSDAY ISLAND & TORRES STRAIT ISLANDS

☎ 07

Torres Strait Islands have been a part of Queensland since 1879, the best known of them being Thursday Island (or TI as it's locally known). The 70 other islands are sprinkled from Cape York in the south to almost Papua New Guinea in the north.

Torres Strait Islanders came from Melanesia and Polynesia about 2000 years ago, bringing with them a more material culture than that of the mainland Aboriginal people.

It was a claim by a Torres Strait Islander, Eddie Mabo, to traditional ownership of Murray Island that eventually led to the High Court handing down its groundbreaking Mabo ruling. The court's decision in turn became the basis for the Federal government's 1993 Native Title legislation. See the boxed text 'Aboriginal Australians' (p34) for more information. Thursday Island is hilly and just over 3 sq km in area. At one time it was a major pearling centre, and the cemeteries tell the hard tale of what a dangerous occupation it was. Some pearls are still produced here from seeded 'culture farms'. Thursday Island is a friendly, easygoing place, and its main appeal is its cultural mix – Asians, Europeans and Pacific Islanders have all contributed to its history.

Peddells Ferry Island Tourist Bureau (☎ 4069 1551; www.peddellsferry.com.au; Engineers Wharf; ⏰ 8.30am-5pm, until noon Sat) will tell you everything you need to know.

Sights & Activities

There are some fascinating reminders of Thursday Island's rich history around town. The **All Souls Quetta Memorial Church** was built in 1893 in memory of the shipwreck of the *Quetta*, which struck an unchartered reef in the Adolphus Channel in 1890, with 133 lives lost.

The Japanese section of the town's cemetery is crowded with hundreds of graves of pearl divers who died from decompression sickness. The **Japanese Pearl Memorial** here is dedicated to them. **Green Hill Fort**, on the western side of town, was built in 1893, when there were fears of a Russian invasion.

Torres Strait Heritage Museum & Art Gallery (☎ 4069 2222; adult/child $5.50/3) is within the Gateway Torres Strait Resort on Horn Island.

Sleeping & Eating

Jardine Motel (☎ 4069 1555; www.jardinemotel.com.au; Victoria Pde; s/d $130/150) has four-star deluxe accommodation, and the budget **Jardine Lodge** ($70-90), with full use of the motel facilities. Self-contained flats are available.

Other options:

Grand (☎ 4069 1557; 6 Victoria Pde; r from $110) Ocean and mountain views.

Federal Hotel (☎ 4069 1569; Victoria Pde; pub d from $60, motel s/d $95/135) Classic Queenslander, with motel and pub rooms, harbour views and counter meals.

Rainbow Motel (☎ 4069 2460; fax 4069 2714; Douglas St; s/d $70/100) Clean, and the best burger bar in town.

Getting There & Around

Qantas flies daily from Cairns to Thursday Island ($830 return). The airport is on Horn Island. The air fare includes a shuttle across the harbour between Horn and Thursday Islands. Several smaller airlines operate flights around the other islands in the strait.

There are regular ferry services between Seisia and Thursday Island (one way/return $40/75, 1 hour) run by **Peddells Ferry Service** (☎ 4069 1551; www.peddellsferry.com.au; Engineers Wharf). In the dry season it also has a service between Punsand Bay, Panjinka and Thursday Island (one way/return $40/75).

Horn Island Ferry Service (☎ 4069 1011) operates hourly between Thursday Island and Horn Island. The ferries run roughly hourly between 6am and 6pm ($6 one way, 15 minutes).

There are plenty of taxis (and water taxis) on Thursday Island.

Victoria

CONTENTS

VICTORIA

For people needing a break from the tourist trails of NSW and Queensland, Victoria offers an opportunity to stray off the beaten coastal track. Victoria is the smallest mainland state, though that still means it's roughly as big as Great Britain. Lovers of landscape will be awestruck by Gippsland's ancient wilderness areas, the rugged shoreline of the Great Ocean Road, and the eerie snowgums of the high country. And wildlife? Devotees can't get enough of the penguins at Phillip Island, and the kangaroos, koalas and chatty lyrebirds at home in the state's many national parks. Food and wine lovers can eat and drink their merry way around the wineries and fresh-produce hubs, while history buffs can relive the gold-rush era in the goldfield towns or explore the string of townships along the Murray River that evoke the days of the paddle-steamer. Activities abound – skiing, surfing, rock-climbing, hiking, sailing – alongside ample opportunities to take it down a notch. Pamper yourself at Daylesford's hot springs or stroll an endless beach, which you'll probably have all to yourself.

And, of course, there's good old Melbourne, Australia's cultural and sporting capital. This city of Victorian-era buildings, parks and leafy boulevards is a vibrant, multicultural centre, where you can join the rowdy masses at the Melbourne Cup or the Aussie rules Grand Final and then spend the evening at the theatre, the opera, or a trendy little bar.

TOP TEN

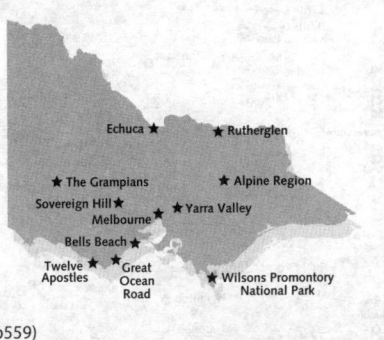

- It's got legs! Learning the subtleties of fine wines, by touring (and tasting) at the wineries around **Rutherglen** (p528) and the **Yarra Valley** (p491)
- Doing the dinky-di with a pie and dead horse (sauce) at a night footy match at Melbourne's **MCG** (p479)
- Dining, wining or rocking till you drop in Melbourne; time your visit for one of the fantastic **festivals** (p463 and p469)
- Watching wombats in the beautiful bush around **Wilsons Promontory National Park** (p559)
- Getting active in the **Alpine region** (p546). It's all available here, from cross-country skiing to getting doused in white water on a raft
- Taking a trip along the spectacular coastal route of the **Great Ocean Road** (p498) – but let someone else do the driving while you 'wow' at the views
- Experiencing bygone days by visiting **Sovereign Hill** (p532), Ballarat's re-creation of an 1860s mining township
- Kicking back on a Murray River paddle-steamer at **Echuca** (p525)
- Impressing the folks back home with the ultimate holiday shot of the **Twelve Apostles** at **Port Campbell National Park** (p505)
- Surfing **Bells Beach** (p500), home to the bronzed body beautiful, and awesome swells (especially in autumn)

VICTORIA

| ■ TELEPHONE CODE: 03 | ■ POPULATION: 4,822,700 | ■ AREA: 227,420 SQ KM |

VICTORIA

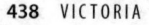

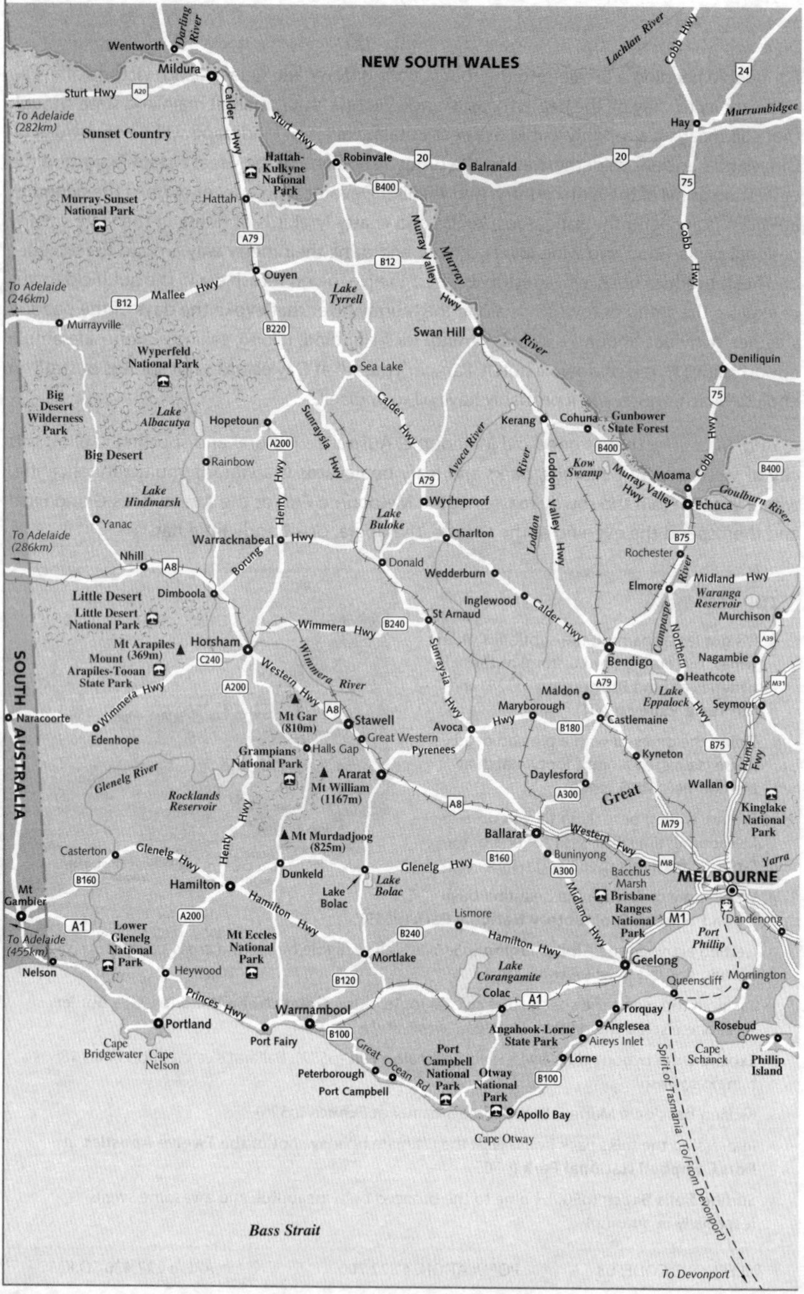
NEW SOUTH WALES
SOUTH AUSTRALIA
Bass Strait
Wentworth
Darling River
Mildura
Sturt Hwy
A20
To Adelaide (282km)
Sunset Country
Calder Hwy
Sturt Hwy
Hattah-Kulkyne National Park
Robinvale
20
Balranald
Lachlan River
Cobb Hwy
24
Hay
Murrumbidgee
75
Cobb Hwy
Murray-Sunset National Park
Hattah
B400
A79
B12
Ouyen
Murray Valley Hwy
Murray River
To Adelaide (246km)
Mallee Hwy
B12
Lake Tyrrell
Murrayville
B220
Swan Hill
Wyperfeld National Park
Sea Lake
Deniliquin
Big Desert Wilderness Park
Lake Albacutya
Hopetoun
Sunraysia Hwy
Calder Hwy
Avoca River
Kerang
Cohuna
Gunbower State Forest
A200
B400
Big Desert
Rainbow
Henty Hwy
River
Loddon Valley Hwy
Kow Swamp
Murray Valley Hwy
Moama
Cobb Hwy
B400
A79
Lake Hindmarsh
Wycheproof
Echuca
Goulburn River
Yanac
Lake Buloke
Charlton
Loddon
To Adelaide (286km)
Warracknabeal
Hwy
B75
Rochester
Nhill
A8
Borung
Donald
Wedderburn
Elmore
Midland Hwy
Little Desert
Dimboola
Inglewood
Waranga Reservoir
Little Desert National Park
St Arnaud
Calder Hwy
Murchison
Wimmera Hwy
B240
Mt Arapiles
Horsham
Wimmera River
Sunraysia Hwy
Campaspe River
Northern Hwy
A39
Mount Arapiles-Tooan State Park
(369m)
C240
Western Hwy
Bendigo
Nagambie
A200
Heathcote
M31
Wimmera Hwy
Mt Gar (810m)
A8
Maldon
A79
Lake Eppalock
Seymour
Naracoorte
Stawell
Maryborough
Hwy
Edenhope
Great Western
Avoca
B180
Castlemaine
Grampians National Park
Halls Gap
Pyrenees
B75
Kyneton
Ararat
Hume Fwy
Glenelg River
Mt William (1167m)
Daylesford
Wallan
Rocklands Reservoir
A300
Great
Kinglake National Park
A8
M79
Mt Murdadjoog (825m)
Ballarat
Western Fwy
Casterton
Glenelg Hwy
Henty Hwy
Dunkeld
Buninyong
B160
Glenelg Hwy
Bacchus Marsh
M8
Yarra
B160
Hamilton
Lake Bolac
Lake Bolac
A300
MELBOURNE
Mt Gambier
Hamilton Hwy
Lismore
Brisbane Ranges National Park
Midland Hwy
Dandenong
A1
A200
Lower Glenelg National Park
Mt Eccles National Park
B240
Hamilton Hwy
M1
Port Phillip
To Adelaide (455km)
Mortlake
Geelong
Nelson
Heywood
B120
Lake Corangamite
Queenscliff
Mornington
Colac
A1
Princes Hwy
Warrnambool
Torquay
Portland
Anglesea
Rosebud
Port Fairy
B100
Angahook-Lorne State Park
Cowes
Cape Bridgewater
Cape Nelson
Great Ocean Rd
Port Campbell National Park
Aireys Inlet
Cape Schanck
Phillip Island
Lorne
Peterborough
Otway National Park
B100
Port Campbell
Apollo Bay
Cape Otway
Spirit of Tasmania (To/From Devonport)
To Devonport

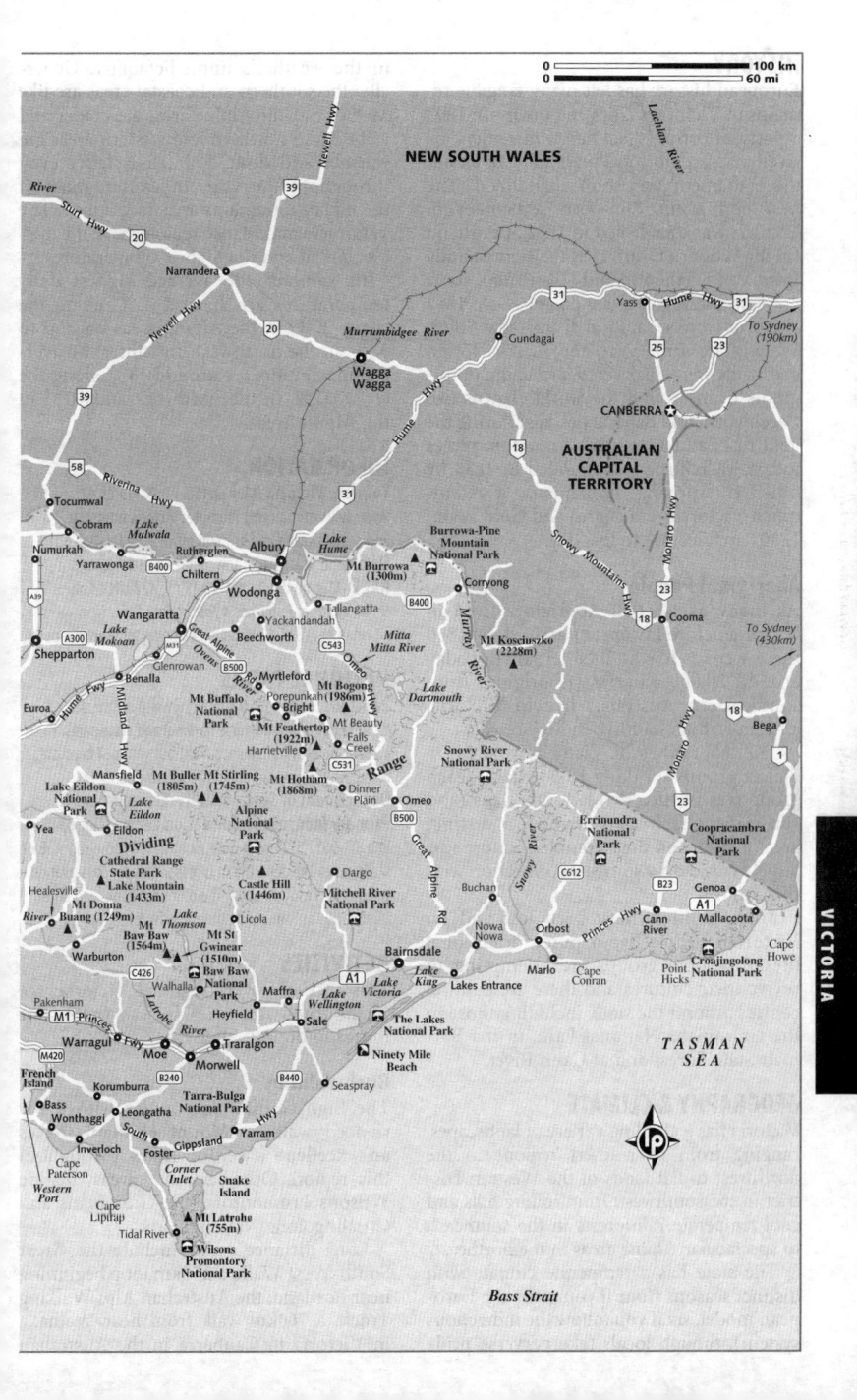

HISTORY

European history has left many tangible remains in Victoria's cities and towns. In 1803 a party of convicts, soldiers and settlers arrived at Sorrento (on Port Phillip Bay), but the settlement was soon abandoned. The first permanent European settlement in Victoria was established in 1834 at Portland (in the Western District) by the Henty family from Van Diemen's Land (Tasmania), some 46 years after Sydney was colonised. In 1851 Victoria won separation from New South Wales. The same year, the rich Victorian goldfields were discovered, attracting immigrants from around the world. Towns like Beechworth and Ballarat boomed during the gold rush, and are veritable museum pieces today. Melbourne was founded in 1835 by other enterprising Tasmanians; it retains much Victorian-era charm and Gold Boom 1880s architecture to this day.

Aboriginal People

As many as 100,000 Aborigines lived in Victoria before Europeans arrived; by 1860 there were as few as 2000 left alive. Today around 20,000 Koories (Aborigines from southeastern Australia) live in Victoria, and more than half live in Melbourne.

The Aborigines of Victoria lived in 38 dialect groups speaking 10 languages; each group was in turn divided into clans (and sub-clans). Each clan 'owned' a distinct area of land, and their complex culture was largely based on a spiritual connection with that land.

Many cultures have been lost and no Victorian people live a purely traditional lifestyle. Some groups are attempting to revive their cultures and there are cultural centres around the state, including those in the Grampians National Park, in the Barmah State Forest and at Cann River.

GEOGRAPHY & CLIMATE

Victoria has a startling variety of landscapes, ranging from near-desert regions in the northwest to flat lands of the Western District in the southwest; from rolling hills and cool-temperate rainforests in the southeast, to spectacular Alpine areas in the northeast.

The state has a temperate climate with distinct seasons (four if you go by the European model, six if you follow the indigenous system), though locals take perverse pride in the weather's unpredictability. Generally, the southern and coastal areas are like Melbourne; the Alpine areas are colder and wetter; and northern and western areas are warmer and drier. Rainfall is fairly even throughout the year. In winter, most of the higher mountains are snowcapped. The Wimmera and Mallee regions have the lowest rainfall and the highest temperatures.

In summer the average highest daily temperatures are around 25°C along the coast, 20°C in the Alpine areas and up to 35°C in the northwest. In winter the average maximums are around 13°C along the coast, 17°C in the northwest and 10°C in the Alpine areas.

INFORMATION

Tourism Victoria (Map pp450-1; ☎ 13 28 42; www.visitvictoria.com) Promotes Victoria interstate and overseas, and has its main office at Federation Sq in Melbourne. Most larger towns have visitors centres.
RACV (Map pp450-1; ☎ 13 19 55; 422 Little Collins St, Melbourne) Publishes a *Tourist Park Guide* (members/nonmembers $14/8.50) listing camping and caravan parks.

NATIONAL PARKS

Parks Victoria (☎ 13 19 63; www.parks.vic.gov.au) Victoria has over 81 diverse national and state parks. Parks Victoria doesn't have a shop front but will mail brochures. Alternatively, you can download information.
Department of Sustainability, Environment & Primary Industries Information Centre (Map pp450-1; ☎ 03-9637 8325; www.dse.vic.gov.au; 8 Nicholson St, East Melbourne) The department is responsible for conservation policies for Victoria's parks. The office has books and other information on parks and outdoor activities.

ACTIVITIES

This section covers regional Victoria; see Melbourne's Activities section (p459) for things to do in that city.

Bushwalking

The high country is popular with experienced walkers. Mount Hotham makes an excellent base for hikes throughout this region. Other popular areas include Wilsons Promontory, the Grampians and Croajingolong National Park.

Long-distance walks include the Great South-West Walk, a 250km loop beginning near Portland; the Australian Alps Walking Track, a 760km walk from near Walhalla in Victoria to Canberra in the Australian

Capital Territory (ACT); and the Victorian section of the Bicentennial National Trail through the high country.

There are more than 30 bushwalking clubs. Contact the **Federation of Victorian Walking Clubs** (☎ 03-9455 1876; http://home.vicnet.net .au/~vicwalk/; 332 Banyule Rd, Viewbank) or have a look in the *Yellow Pages* under Clubs – Bushwalking.

The **Department of Sustainability, Environment & Primary Industries Information Centre** (Map pp450-1; ☎ 03-9637 8325; www.dse.vic.gov.au; 8 Nicholson St, East Melbourne) sells walking guides, including *120 Walks in Victoria* by Tyrone T Thomas ($33) and *Melbourne's Mountains – Exploring the Great Divide* by John Siseman ($22). Lonely Planet's own *Walking in Australia* ($33) covers 19 walks in Victoria.

Canoeing & Kayaking

Trips can be as short as a couple of hours, or extended adventures. The Glenelg River in the southwest has riverside camp sites for canoeists.

Rivers are graded according to their degree of difficulty. Grade one (such as parts of the Yarra River) are easy-flowing rivers; grade five (such as the Indi River and parts of the Murray) are long stretches of rapids, only suitable for very experienced canoeists.

Sea-kayaking offers opportunities to see wildlife such as sea lions, gannets, penguins and dolphins.

For more information, contact the **Victorian Board of Canoe Education** (☎ 03-9459 4251; 332 Banyule Rd, Viewbank).

Cycling

Wine regions such as Rutherglen and the Pyrenees Ranges are popular for cycling tours, and the high country is favoured by mountain bikers. Mountain bikes can be hired here from **Viking Lodge** (☎ 03-5758 3247) in Falls Creek.

Bicycle Victoria (☎ 03-9328 3000; www.bv.com.au; Level 10, 446 Collins St, Melbourne) is a mine of information, and holds events such as the Great Victorian Bike Ride (November) and Easter Bike Ride (April). Cycle tourists can drop into Melbourne Bicycle Touring Club meetings (8pm Wednesday). Meetings are held at the Trades Hall Building, 54 Victoria St, Carlton.

Fiona Colquhoun's book *Railtrails of Victoria* ($25) details car-free country rides,

and Lonely Planet's *Cycling Australia* ($33) has a very good Victoria section.

Many Melbourne bike shops rent bikes. A hybrid bike with panniers from touring specialists **Christie Cycles** (☎ 03-9818 4011; 80 Burwood Rd, Hawthorn) costs around $20 a day or $75 a week, including both weekends. Mountain bikes from **St Kilda Cycles** (☎ 03-9534 3074; 11 Carlisle St, St Kilda) cost around $20 a day, with helmet and lock.

Diving

Some of Victoria's diving is world class. It can get a little chilly, and 7mm wetsuits or even drysuits are needed.

Port Phillip Bay has some excellent sites. The Bellarine Peninsula is popular, with Queenscliff a good base. Other areas include Torquay, Anglesea, Lorne, Apollo Bay, Port Campbell and Portland (all on the Great Ocean Road); Flinders, Sorrento and Portsea (on the Mornington Peninsula); and Kilcunda, Wilsons Promontory and Mallacoota (on the east coast).

Hang-Gliding & Paragliding

Hang-gliding and paragliding schools include the **Eagle School of Hang-Gliding** (☎ 03-5750 1174; www.eagleschool.com.au) and **Tandem Paragliding** (☎ 03-5755 1753; www.alpineparagliding .com) near Bright, and **Wingsports Flight Academy** (☎ 0419-378 616; www.wingsports.com.au) in Apollo Bay.

Most operators offer tandem flights in powered hang-gliders, as well as tandem paragliding or hang-gliding.

Horse Riding & Trekking

There are dozens of horse-riding ranches with rides from one hour to a full day.

Treks – anything from overnight rides to week-long expeditions – are also available. Operators include **Bogong Horseback Adventures** (☎ 03-5754 4849; www.bogonghorse.com.au) at Mt Beauty; **Grampians Horse Riding Centre** (☎ 03-5383 9255) and **Watson's Country Rides** (☎ 03-5777 3552; www.watsonstrailrides.com.au) and **McCormack's Mountain Valley Trail Rides** (☎ 03-5775 2886). Grampians is in the Halls Gap area and the latter two are near Mansfield.

Rock-Climbing

Mt Arapiles, in the Western District, is famous for its huge variety of climbs. Rock-climbing is becoming increasingly popular

VICTORIA

in the Grampians National Park, and there are good granite climbs at Mt Buffalo.

There are plenty of other sites. The outdoor and adventure shops on Hardware Lane in Melbourne city are good sources of information. The **Victorian Climbing Club** (GPO Box 1725P, Melbourne 3001) publishes the *Rock-climbers Handbooks* series, and meets at 8pm on the last Thursday of most months at the **Australian Gemmological Association** (380-382 Spencer St, Melbourne).

Several operators in the Grampians and Natimuk do lessons and tours.

Sailing

There is a whole flotilla of yacht clubs based around Melbourne's Port Phillip Bay, and plenty of schools where you can learn to sail – see Sailing in the Melbourne section (p460). Other popular sailing areas include the Gippsland Lakes and Lake Eildon. You can sometimes hire yachts, which can work out to be quite economical when shared between a few people. There are also schools where you can learn to sail.

Skiing

Skiing in Victoria began in the 1860s when Norwegian goldminers introduced the sport in the high country around Harrietville. The season officially commences on the first weekend of June. Skiable snow usually arrives later in the month, and often stays until the end of September. For more information, visit www.visitvictoria.com/ski.

Surfing

With its exposure to the Southern Ocean swell, Victoria's coastline provides quality surf. The three most popular surfing areas are Phillip Island, the Mornington Peninsula and the Great Ocean Road's coastline – all less than two hours' drive from Melbourne.

Along the Great Ocean Road you can take lessons with **Go Ride a Wave** (☎ 03-5263 2111; www.graw.com.au), which holds lessons in Torquay, Anglesea, Ocean Grove and Lorne; the **Westcoast Surf School** (☎ 03-5261 2241) operates in Torquay. On Phillip Island try **Island Surf School** (☎ 03-5952 2578).

Telephone **surf reports** (statewide ☎ 1900 931 996, Mornington Peninsula ☎ 1900 983 268) are updated daily. *Surfinder Vic* ($20) is a useful guide, available from surf and sports shops.

White-Water Rafting

Guided white-water rafting trips are run on various high country rivers. The best times are during the snow melts from around August to December.

Operators include **Peregrine Adventures** (☎ 03-9662 2700), **Australian Adventures Experience** (☎ 03-0500 599 499; www.ausadventures.com) and **Snowy River Expeditions** (☎ 03-5155 0220). **Paddle Sports** (☎ 03-9478 3310), based in Preston in Melbourne, is another company offering guided rafting trips.

TOURS

Various companies operate bus tours to destinations such as Sovereign Hill, Healesville Sanctuary, the Great Ocean Road and Phillip Island. Recommended operators include:

Go West (☎ 03-9828 2008; www.gowest.com.au) Runs day tours of the Great Ocean Road and Phillip Island.
Culture Link (☎ 03-8810 4106; www.culturelink .com.au) Offers tours like Go West's and more.
Autopia Tours (☎ 03-9326 5536; www.autopiatours .com.au) Popular with backpackers.

There's a wide range of activity-based tours:

Echidna Walkabout (☎ 03-9646 8249; www.adven tures.com.au) Runs bushwalking day trips to the west of Melbourne where you're likely to see kangaroos and koalas ($145).
Eco Adventure Tours (☎ 03-5962 5115; www.hotkey .net.au/~ecoadven) Offers fabulous night bush walks in the Yarra Valley.
Bunyip Bushwalking Tours (☎ 03-9531 0840; www.bunyiptours.com) Eco-accredited, it specialises in bushwalking tours of Phillip Island, Wilsons Promontory and the Grampians.

GETTING THERE & AROUND

For getting around Melbourne, see that section (p483).

Air

Regional Express (Rex; ☎ 13 17 13; www.regional express.com.au) flies between Melbourne and Mildura ($120 one-way), Portland ($140), and Albury ($120). The unlimited travel backpacker fares are a good deal. **QantasLink** (☎ 13 13 13; www.qantas.com) also flies between Melbourne and Mildura ($125). Fully flexible fares between Melbourne and Sydney on **Virgin Blue** (☎ 13 67 89; www.virginblue.com.au) cost $200, though you can pay less than half these rates if you check the website for last-minute deals. Other interstate flights include Melbourne to Merimbula with Rex ($180) and Melbourne to Devonport with Qantas ($180).

Bus & Train

Bus and train services within country Victoria are operated by **V/Line** (☎ 13 61 96; www.vline.vic.gov.au). You can buy tickets over the phone or in Melbourne at Spencer St and Flinders St train stations, major suburban stations and most travel agents.

We quote one-way economy full fares, but there are various special deals when travelling off-peak.

Most services do not require a reservation, although you do need one to travel on an interstate train (the *Overland*, the *Ghan* or the XPT) to a destination within Victoria.

ALTERNATIVE BUSES

If you fast-track down the highways between Melbourne and either Sydney or Adelaide, you'll miss seeing some great places.

Wild-Life Tours (☎ 03-9534 8868; www.wildlifetours .com.au) Has trips between Melbourne and Adelaide via the Great Ocean Rd and the Grampians (from $150), and between Melbourne and Sydney via Canberra (from $150). You can stop over, anywhere along the way.

Oz Experience (☎ 02-9213 1766; www.ozexperience .com) Offers a similar hop-on hop-off service countrywide.

Wayward Bus (☎ 1800 882 823; www.waywardbus .com.au) Runs through southeastern Australia, connecting Melbourne with Adelaide. Also offers a good 3½-day trip from Melbourne to Adelaide (from $310), which takes in the Great Ocean Rd, the coast of southeast South Australia and the Coorong.

V/LINE SERVICES

The following information is some of the main rail routes, bus routes and fares from Melbourne.

Southwest to Geelong Trains run to Geelong ($10); some trains continue on the inland route to Warrnambool ($40). A daily bus service runs along the Great Ocean Rd from Geelong through Lorne ($26) to Apollo Bay ($32); it continues through to Warrnambool on Friday (also on Monday during summer).

Northwest to Ballarat Trains run to Ballarat ($17), Stawell ($37), Horsham ($50) and on to Adelaide; buses run from Stawell to Halls Gap in the Grampians.

North through Bendigo Trains run to Bendigo ($25), and to Swan Hill ($51); buses continue from Bendigo to Echuca ($32).

North to Albury Wodonga Trains run to Albury Wodonga ($46) and continue to Sydney; buses run from Wangaratta ($35) to Beechworth ($40) and Bright ($46).

East through Moe Trains run to Moe ($18) and then to Sale ($32); buses connect from Sale to Bairnsdale ($40), Lakes Entrance ($50), Cann River ($58) and Merimbula ($59.20).

OTHER BUS SERVICES

McCafferty's/Greyhound (☎ 13 14 99; www.mccaf fertys.com.au; ☎ 13 20 30; www.greyhound.com.au) Runs between Melbourne and Adelaide (via Ballarat and Horsham), and between Melbourne and Sydney (via the Hume Hwy). A variety of travel passes are available.

Firefly (☎ 02-9211 6556, ☎ 1300 730 740; www.fire flyexpress.com.au) Runs between Melbourne and Sydney, and Melbourne and Adelaide.

Premier Motor Service (☎ 13 34 10; www.premierms .com.au) Travels the coast between Cairns and Melbourne, via Sydney.

MELBOURNE

☎ 03 / pop 3,160,171

Australia's second-largest city is a vibrant, cosmopolitan, multicultural mix, renowned for its obsession with the arts, sport and the thriving café, bar and restaurant scene. If you miss Melbourne, you'll have missed out on some of Australia's richest cultural offerings.

In the last 10 years, the city has undergone a renaissance. Once deserted after dark, the business district now has a village-like feel. Lying in the shadows of the glass towers, innumerable hip boutiques, restaurants and bars line alleys and Victorian-era arcades off the main streets. Melbourne's riverside and bayside location has also been rediscovered – with exciting developments in new precincts such as Southgate, NewQuay and Docklands, and, of course, imposing and adventuresome Federation Square. And still there are the perennial favourites, such as bayside St Kilda and funky Fitzroy, only a short tram ride away.

HISTORY

In May 1835 John Batman 'bought' around 240,000 hectares of land from the indigenous owners, the Aborigines of the Kulin clan. The concept of buying or selling land was unknown to the Aborigines, and in exchange for their land they received some tools, flour and clothing.

VICTORIA

MELBOURNE IN...

Two Days

Start your day with breakfast in Fitzroy's cosmopolitan **Brunswick St** (p471), then get your bearings on Melbourne's beloved trams – loop the city on the **free city-circle tram** (p486). Visit the **Queen Victoria Market** (p451) and the **Immigration Museum** (p452), followed by a stroll through the Australian art gallery at **Federation Square** (p448), and the stunning **Royal Botanic Gardens** (p454). Reward your efforts with a late lunch at **Southgate** (p471), overlooking the river and hubbub of the city. Wine and dine the evening away at your pick of Melbourne's fine city eateries, then head to the theatre, or cap off the night at one the city's funky little bars.

Spoil yourself at Acland Street's cake shops, and dip your toes in the sea – a visit to **St Kilda** (p457) is a must on your second day. If it's the weekend you should also catch the ferry over to **Williamstown** (p459). Head back into the city to explore its many hidden Victorian-era arcades (the **Walking Tour**, p460, is a great way to do this) and the **Melbourne Gaol** (p452), and finish off with a jaunt through **Chinatown** (p449).

Four Days

Follow the itinerary for two days, then on your third day add a trip to the **Melbourne Zoo** (p455), stopping for lunch in Melbourne's Italian quarter, **Carlton** (p471). You may then want to kick back or hire canoes at **Yarra Bend Park** (p455). On your fourth day reward yourself with one of Melbourne's favourite pastimes, **shopping** (p481), or head out of town for a day trip: the **Dandenongs** (p492) and **Phillip Island** (p495) are excellent choices.

John Pascoe Fawkner arrived soon after and was a driving force behind the new settlement. By the time he died in 1869, Melbourne was flourishing and he was known as the grand old man of Victoria; Batman, however, had died soon after his 'deal' with the Aborigines, a victim of his own excesses.

By 1840 there were more than 10,000 Europeans living in the Melbourne area. The wealth from the goldfields built a city that was known as 'Marvellous Melbourne' and this period of prosperity lasted until the depression at the end of the 1880s. But by then, in its streets, parks and buildings, Melbourne had acquired its Victorian-era character.

ORIENTATION

Melbourne's suburbs sprawl around Port Phillip Bay, with the city centre on the north bank of the Yarra River, about 5km inland from the bay. The Yarra winds through Melbourne and divides the city in half, both geographically and socio-economically. The northern and western suburbs have always been working-class areas, the southern and eastern suburbs the more affluent areas.

Most places of interest to travellers are either within the inner-suburban area or beyond the urban fringe (p486).

Visitors centres have free maps that cover the city and inner suburbs. Street directories are produced by Melway, UBD and Gregory's; Lonely Planet's *Melbourne City Map* ($7.80) gives good coverage of the city and environs.

If you're driving in from the airport, the freeway whisks you past the impressive but controversial Gateway to Melbourne, a gargantuan structure composed of leaning yellow and red beams symbolic (so we're told) of a technologically advanced city.

City Centre

Melbourne's city centre is bordered by the Yarra to the south, the Fitzroy Gardens to the east, Victoria St to the north and Spencer St to the west. However, the huge Docklands project is considerably extending the western border, Federation Square is changing the southeastern border and Southgate has taken the city across the river.

The city centre is laid out in a grid one mile (1.61km) long and 0.5 mile (805m) wide, once known as the Golden Mile. The main streets running east–west are Collins and Bourke Sts, crossed by Swanston and Elizabeth Sts. The heart of the city is the Bourke St Mall, between Swanston and Elizabeth Sts.

Long-distance buses and the airport bus arrive at either the Spencer St coach terminal (V/Line, Skybus, Firefly) or the Melbourne Transit Centre on Franklin St (McCafferty's/Greyhound).

On the corner of Swanston and Flinders Sts, Flinders St train station is the main station for suburban trains. 'Under the clocks' at the station is a popular meeting place. The other major station, for country and interstate trains, is Spencer St train station. (Note that Melbourne Central is just a station on the underground rail loop – it takes its name from the shopping centre above it.)

The revitalised inner suburbs circling the city centre are East Melbourne, North Melbourne, Carlton, Fitzroy, Collingwood, Richmond, South Yarra and South Melbourne. Suburbs on the bay include St Kilda, which has long been Melbourne's most diverse and permissive area, and Williamstown, southwest of the city at the mouth of the Yarra, which has a country-town, maritime flavour.

INFORMATION
Bookshops
Borders South Yarra (Map p457; Jam Factory, 500 Chapel St, South Yarra); Carlton (Map pp446-8; 380 Lygon St, Carlton) Mega-bookstore chain with great selection of CDs.
City Basement Books (Map pp450-1; 28 Elizabeth St, City) Monster second-hand bookshop.
Dymocks (Map pp450-1; 234 Collins St, City)
Hares & Hyenas (Map p457; 135 Commercial Rd, South Yarra) Gay and lesbian bookshop.
Little Bookroom (Map pp450-1; 185 Elizabeth St, City) Specialises in kids' books.
Map Land (Map pp450-1; 372 Little Bourke St, City) Excellent selection with a great range of topographical maps.
McGills (Map pp450-1; 187 Elizabeth St, City) Interstate and foreign newspapers and magazines.
Readings (Map pp446-8; 309 Lygon St, Carlton) Melbourne institution offering good service.
Syber's Books (Map p458; 19a Carlisle, St Kilda; ☺ noon-5pm Fri-Mon) Second-hand bookshop.

Emergency
Ambulance (☎ 000)
Fire (☎ 000)
Lifeline (☎ 13 11 14) 24-hour, seven-day over-the-phone counselling service in six languages.
Police Flinders Lane (Map pp450-1; ☎ 9650 7077; 226 Flinders Lane, City); Flinders St (Map pp450-1; ☎ 9247 6491; 637 Flinders St, near Spencer St, City) Both are 24-hour police stations.

RACV Emergency Roadside Service (☎ 13 11 11) Provides 24-hour, 7-day car breakdown assistance.

Internet Access
Prices are around $4 per hour.
e:fifty five (Map pp450-1; 55 Elizabeth St, City) Half-price Internet with a drink.
Global Gossip (Map p450-1; ☎ 9663 0511; 440 Elizabeth St, City)
Netcity (Map p458; 63 Fitzroy St, St Kilda)
World Wide Wash (Map pp446-8; 361 Brunswick St, Fitzroy) Laundrette and Internet café.

Medical Services
Alfred Hospital (Map p457; ☎ 9276 2000; Commercial Rd, Prahran)
Melbourne Sexual Health Centre (Map pp446-8; ☎ 9347 0244; 580 Swanston St, Carlton) Provides free checkups and other medical services. Appointments are preferred.
Royal Children's Hospital (Map pp446-8; ☎ 9345 5522; Flemington Rd, Parkville)
Royal Melbourne Hospital (Map pp446-8; ☎ 9342 7000; Grattan St, Parkville)
Royal Women's Hospital (Map pp446-8; ☎ 9344 2000; 132 Grattan St, Carlton)
St Vincent's Hospital (Map pp446-8; ☎ 9288 2211; 41 Victoria Pde, Fitzroy)
Travellers' Medical and Vaccination Centre (TMVC; Map pp450-1; ☎ 9602 5788; Level 2, 393 Little Bourke St, City) Appointments are necessary.

Money
There are foreign-exchange booths (which open for all flights) at Melbourne's international airport, and exchange offices such as **Thomas Cook** (☎ 9654 4222; 261 Bourke St, City; ☺ 9am-5pm Mon-Fri, 10am-5pm Sat, 11am-4pm Sun) in the city centre. Your other option is the banks – see Money (p970) for more information.

Post
GPO (General Post Office; Map pp450-1; ☎ 13 13 18; 250 Elizabeth St, City)
Poste restante (380 Bourke St; ☺ 6am-5.30pm Mon-Fri) Mail can be collected from the GPO Private Box Room. Mail is held for a month – bring your passport.

Tourist Information
Consult Lonely Planet's *Melbourne* guidebook for in-depth information about the city, and for other useful information.
Melbourne Visitor Centre (Map pp450-1; ☎ 9658 9658; www.thatsmelbourne.com.au; Federation Sq, cnr Swanston & Flinders Sts, City; ☺ 9am-6pm) Melbourne and Victoria's main visitors centre. Excellent service

VICTORIA

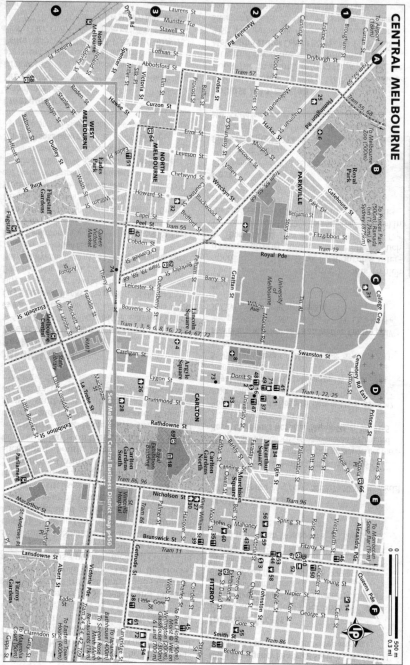

CENTRAL MELBOURNE

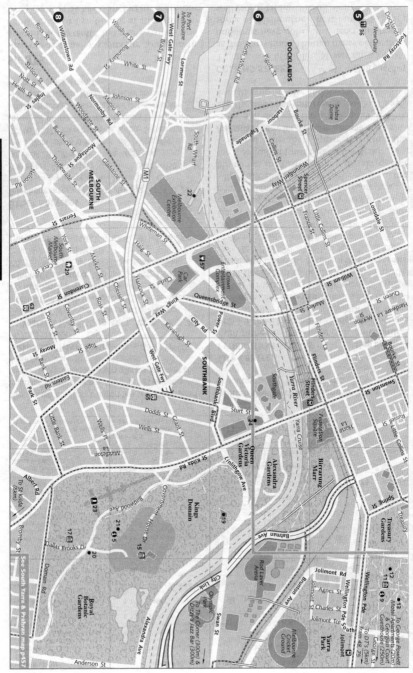

VICTORIA

To Port Melbourne

West Gate Fwy

DOCKLANDS

NewQuay

Docklands Dr

Footscray Rd

8

7

6

5 🏨 36

Ross St

Evans St

Woodruff St

Lorimer St

Brady St

North Wharf Rd

Harbour

Esplanade

Bourke St

Telstra Dome

Williamstown Rd

Tarleton St

White St

Johnson St

Munro St

South Wharf Rd

Collins St

Wurundjeri Way

Spencer Street 🚉

Stallion St

Nott St

Heath St

Ingles St

Normanby Rd

Woodgate St

Buckhurst St

Montague St

Gladstone St

SOUTH MELBOURNE

Melbourne Exhibition Centre

●22

Little Collins St

Francis St

Lonsdale St

Stead Rd

Thistlewaite St

York St

Cecil St

Ferrars St

Whiteman St

Haig St

Crown Entertainment Complex

Car Park

🏨57

Queen St

William St

Hardware La

Market St

Little Collins St

Market St

Coventry St

South Melbourne Market

🍴29

Clarendon St

Dorcas St

Chessell St

Ross St

Kings Way

Queensbridge St

Power St

City Rd

Kavanagh St

Flinders La

Queen St

Flinders St

Bourke St

Swanston St

Little Collins St

SOUTHBANK

West Gate Fwy

Southbank Blvd

Sturt St

●24

Southgate

Yarra River

Yarra Cruise

Federation Square

Flinders Street 🚉

Horse La

Little Collins St

Russell St

Eastern Rd

Topp St

Moray St

Park St

Bank St

Wells St

Dodds St

Grant St

Wells St

Little Bank St

Wells Pl

Middleton

St Kilda Rd

Linlithgow Ave

Queen Victoria Gardens

Alexandra Gardens

Birrarung Marr

Batman Ave

Birdwood Ave

Government House Dr

Kings Domain

●19

Spring St

Treasury Gardens

Albert Rd

To St Kilda (6km)

🏨23

21●

●5

17 🏛

●20

Dallas Brooks Dr

Bromby St

Domain Rd

15 🏛

Royal Botanic Gardens

Alexandra Ave

City Link

Olympic Park

To The Corner (300m) & Dizzy's Jazz Bar (300m)

Rod Laver Arena

Jolimont Rd

Wellington Pde

Agnes St

Charles St

Jolimont Tce

Jolimont

Bunton Ave

Swan St

Yarra Park

Melbourne Cricket Ground

●12

11 🏛

●9

●13 To George Powlett Motel Apartments (20m) & Georgian Court Guesthouse (20m)

To DT's (5km); George St

To DT's (5km); Tram 48, 75

Anderson St

See South Yarra & Prahran map p457

INFORMATION		King Boutique Accommodation...........27 E3	Bar Open..53 F2
Borders...1 D2		Medley Hall..28 D3	Gay Trade Bar...54 F3
Commonwealth Bank...............................2 D2		Nomads Market Inn................................29 C8	Lambsgo Bar...55 F2
Commonwealth Bank...............................3 F2		Nunnery...30 E3	Laundry..56 E2
Melbourne Sexual Health Centre.............4 D3		Ormond College.......................................31 C1	Mercury Lounge.....................................57 C7
Royal Botanic Gardens Visitors Centre....5 E7		Queensberry Hill YHA Hostel...................32 B3	Night Cat...58 F2
Royal Children's Hospital.........................6 B1		Travel Inn...33 D2	Old Bar..59 E2
Royal Melbourne Hospital.......................7 C2			Standard Hotel..60 E2
Royal Women's Hospital..........................8 D2		EATING 🍴 pp469-75	Yelza...61 F3
Visitors Information..................................9 F5		Abla's...34 E2	
World Wide Wash...................................10 F2		Bangla Sweets & Curry Café....................35 E2	ENTERTAINMENT 🎭 pp476-81
		Bhoj...36 A5	Arthouse..62 C3
SIGHTS & ACTIVITIES pp448-60		Brunetti's...37 D2	Butterfly Club..63 C8
Captain Cook's Cottage...........................11 F5		Builders Arms Hotel.................................38 F3	Cinema Nova...................................(see 1)
Conservatory...12 F5		De Los Santos..39 E3	Comedy Club....................................(see 1)
Fairies' Tree...13 F5		Gluttony, It's a Sin..................................40 F2	Comic's Lounge.......................................64 B3
Fitzroy Swimming Pool...........................14 F1		Jimmy Watson's.......................................41 D2	CUB Malthouse Theatre..........................65 D7
Government House...................................15 E7		La Porchetta..42 C3	Dan O'Connell Hotel...............................66 E1
La Mama Theatre.....................................16 D2		Mao's...43 E2	Evelyn Hotel..67 F2
La Trobe's Cottage...................................17 E8		Mario's...44 F2	Festival Hall...68 A4
Melbourne Museum.................................18 E3		Mecca Bah.......................................(see 36)	IMAX Cinema..69 D3
Myer Music Bowl.....................................19 E6		Old Kingdom Restaurant.........................45 F3	Rainbow Hotel...70 F2
National Herbarium.................................20 E8		Pavilion Café....................................(see 13)	
Old Melbourne Observatory....................21 E7		Retro..46 F1	SHOPPING 🛍 pp481-3
Polly Woodside Maritime Museum.........22 B7		Shakahari...47 D2	Readings..71 D2
Shrine of Remembrance...........................23 E8		Thresherman's Bakehouse.......................48 D2	Recycled Recreation................................72 F3
Theatres Building......................................24 D6		Tiamo...49 D2	
Tudor Village....................................(see 13)		Vegie Bar..50 F1	TRANSPORT pp483-6
		Warung Agus..51 B3	Borsari Cycles..73 D2
SLEEPING 🛏 pp464-9			
Chapman Gardens YHA Hostel.............25 A1		DRINKING 🍸 pp475-6	OTHER
Downtowner on Lygon............................26 D3		Babka Bakery Cafe...................................52 F2	Victoria Market Tours.............................74 C3

offering everything from transport timetables and Internet to accommodation bookings. Also organises Melbourne Greeter Service, where volunteers offer personal tours of the city – book at least three days ahead.

Backpackers Travel Centre (Map pp450-1; ☎ 9654 8477; 1/250 Flinders St, City)

Backpackers World (Map pp450-1; ☎ 9639 9686; 450 Elizabeth St, City) Backpacker-oriented travel agency.

Information booth (Map pp450-1; Bourke St Mall, City; ☼ 9am-5pm Mon-Fri, 10am-5pm Sat & Sun)

Information Victoria (Map pp450-1; ☎ 1300 366 356; 356 Collins St, City) Stocks publications and maps about Melbourne and Victoria.

YHA Travel (Map pp450-1; ☎ 9670 9611; 83 Hardware Lane, City)

Other Services

Telephone Interpreting Service (☎ 13 14 50) 24-hour, seven-day service, in over 100 languages.

Travellers' Aid Society Swanston St (Map pp450-1; ☎ 9654 2600; 2nd fl, 169 Swanston St, City; ☼ 8.30am-5pm Mon-Fri); Spencer St (Map pp450-1; ☎ 9670 2873; lower concourse, Spencer St train station, City; ☼ 7.30am-7.30pm Mon-Fri, closes 11.30am Sat & Sun) Offers advice, showers, luggage storage and more to stranded travellers. Wheelchair recharging and other services for disabled travellers.

SIGHTS

Melbourne's major sights are found in or around the **city centre**, but many visitors find another day or two to take in attractions in lively seaside **St Kilda**, in Fitzroy's cosmo-politan **Brunswick Street**, and in the villagey seaside port of **Williamstown**.

City Centre

FEDERATION SQUARE Map pp450-1

Built to be the city's new civic and cultural hub for the 21st century, Federation Square was completed in late 2002. With its sharp geometry and skewwhiff angles, the controversial structure has its fair share of critics, but it does seem to be drawing the crowds. Inside you'll find the excellent **Ian Potter Centre** (☎ 8662 1555; ☼ 10am-5pm Mon-Thu, 10am-9pm Fri, 10am-6pm Sat & Sun; admission to permanent/special collections free/$12), showcasing the National Gallery's collection of Australian art, with everything from indigenous works to prominent contemporary artists. You can pick up a brochure that leads you to the works of the big names in Australian art, or take one of the free guided tours (ask at the desk).

Also at Federation Square you'll find the **Australian Centre for the Moving Image**, with cinemas and state-of-the-art facilities (p476), and the **Melbourne visitor centre** (p445). There's a smattering of cafés and restaurants.

COLLINS STREET Map pp450-1

The top end of Collins St was once known as the 'Paris End'. Though many of the finer buildings have gone, this street still boasts some of Melbourne's best buildings – it's well worth taking a stroll along.

Facing each other on the corners of Russell and Collins Sts are two historic churches, **St Michael's Church** (1866) and the **Scots Church** (1873). Next door to Scots, **Kay Craddock's Antiquarian Bookseller** (☎ 9654 8506; 156 Collins St), the place for bibliophiles, is at home in the basement of the lovely Neo-Gothic **Assembly Hall** (1914) – don't miss the foyer. The **Athenaeum Theatre** (188 Collins St) dates back to 1886; you may be able to peek into the musty auditorium if it's open. Across the road is the magnificent **Regent Theatre**, built in 1929 and now only opened for blockbuster stage shows.

The **Block Arcade**, running between Collins and Elizabeth Sts, is a stunning late-19th-century shopping arcade, complete with mosaic floor. Step back in time by taking tea in the old-fashioned **Hopetoun Tearooms**.

Melbourne's financial sector begins west of Elizabeth St. The interior of the **Common-wealth Bank of Australia** (CBA; 333 Collins St) and ANZ's **Gothic Revival Bank** (386-388 Collins St) are must-sees. The **Bank of New Zealand** (477 Collins St) and the former **Bank of Australasia** (394 Collins St), now part of the Sebel hotel chain, are also worth a look.

The Gothic façade of the three **Olderfleet buildings** (471-477 Collins St) has been preserved, and at **Le Meridien at Rialto** (495 Collins St) an imaginative five-star hotel hides behind the façades of two Venetian Gothic buildings. Cross the road to get the best views.

The **Rialto Towers Observation Deck** (☎ 9629 8222; 525 Collins St, City; adult/child $12/6.80; ☺ 10am-10pm Sun-Thu, 10am-11pm Fri & Sat) on the 55th floor of Melbourne's tallest building (the Rialto Towers) offers spectacular 360-degree views, and free telescope use. If you're on a tight budget, you can also visit the **Sofitel Melbourne** for good, free views (p461).

SWANSTON STREET
Map pp450-1

It may be the ugly duckling of the city centre, but Swanston St boasts some fantastic architecture, including the stunning Art Deco 1932 **Manchester Unity Building** (cnr Swanston & Collins Sts), and the 1920s **Capitol Theatre** (109-117 Swanston St) with its honeycombed ceiling. The **Melbourne Town Hall** (cnr Swanston & Collins Sts) was built in 1869 with the portico added during the gold-boom highs and showing Parisian influences of the 1880s.

The **Melbourne City Baths** (420 Swanston St) was built in 1903 in the Edwardian style

and continues to be a great place to swim a few laps (p460).

Built in stages from 1854, the classical-styled **State Library** (cnr Swanston & La Trobe Sts) has an impressive domed Reading Room.

BOURKE STREET
Map pp450-1

The section of Bourke St between Elizabeth and Swanston Sts is a pedestrian walkway (shared with trams), and is the city's main shopping and meeting place.

The north side of the mall is dominated by the Myer and David Jones department stores, and the old GPO building, on the corner of Bourke and Elizabeth streets. On the south side, **Royal Arcade**, built in 1869, is Melbourne's oldest arcade and is lined with an assortment of interesting shops. The eastern end of Bourke St, beyond the mall and the seedy Russell St corner, has some excellent cafés and restaurants, interesting book and music shops, and mainstream cinemas.

SPRING STREET
Map pp450-1

At the top end of Collins St, the **Old Treasury Building** was built in 1858 with basement vaults to store much of the £200 million worth of gold mined from the Victorian goldfields. It functions as the **Gold Treasury Museum** (☎ 9651 2233; adult/child $7/3.50; ☺ 9am-5pm Mon-Fri, 10am-4pm Sat & Sun), housing permanent exhibitions detailing the history of the city (in a more conventional way than the Melbourne Museum does). It's well worth visiting. In the basement is an audio exploration of gold's effect on the city's development.

Between Bourke and Little Collins Sts, the **Windsor hotel** (see this entry also on p468, for a Sleeping review; and p470 for Eating) is a marvellous reminder of 19th-century gold-boom Melbourne.

The **State Houses of Parliament** are open on weekdays. There are regular free **tours** (☎ 9651 8568) when parliament isn't sitting; when it is sitting, you can watch from the public galleries.

CHINATOWN
Map pp450-1

Since the days of the gold rush, Little Bourke St has been a centre for Chinese people in Melbourne.

The interesting **Museum of Chinese Australian History** (☎ 9662 2888; 22 Cohen Pl; adult/child $6.50/4.50; ☺ 9am-5pm) documents the long history of Chinese people in Australia. Two

VICTORIA

MELBOURNE CENTRAL BUSINESS DISTRICT

VICTORIA

of the highlights are the dragons: the retired Dai Loong (Great Dragon), and the new dragon that comes out to party on Chinese New Year. The museum also conducts two-hour walking tours ($15/10) around Chinatown; bookings are essential.

There are many old buildings and warehouses on Little Bourke St and the lanes that run off it. One of the best examples is the ostentatious one-time headquarters of the **Sun Kum Lee Trading Company** (112-114 Little Bourke St), now the Shanghai Village Restaurant. Go for Sunday morning yum cha (dishes $4.50 to $5.50) – it's the liveliest time to visit.

QUEEN VICTORIA MARKET   Map pp450–1
Chaotic, friendly, odorous – Melbourne's favourite **market** (☎ 9320 5822; cnr Elizabeth & Victoria Sts; ☼ 6am-2pm Tue & Thu, 6am-6pm Fri, 6am-3pm Sat, 9am-4pm Sun) must be on your list. Although officially designated as the market in 1878, the land had been put to varying uses beforehand, from cattle yards to part of Melbourne's first cemetery – an estimated 9000 bodies still remain under the car park!

Pick your way through the throng, avoiding the odd jabbing elbow and squashed fruit underfoot, to find everything from gooey Brie to next season's fashion. If you're visiting between late November and mid-February, time your visit for the bustling **night market** (☼ 5.30-10pm Wed). Throughout the year, eating a bratwurst on Saturday morning while listening to the thigh-slapping musicians outside the deli is a Melbourne must.

The market offers a variety of walks – the very popular two-hour **Foodies Dream tour** ($22; ☼ 10am Tue & Thu-Sat) leads you on a great taste-hopping exploration of the market. There are also occasional **cooking classes** (from $65) where you can learn how to sear 'roo Oz-style (on a BBQ, of course). There are classes for kids, too, during school holidays. Bookings are necessary for all tours and classes.

OLD MELBOURNE GAOL

This gruesome **gaol and museum** (Map pp450-1); ☎ 9663 7228; Russell St; adult/child/family $13/7.50/34; ☼ 9am-5pm), built from bluestone in 1841, is a dark, dank and spooky place. Over 100 people were hanged here, including local outlaw-cum-hero Ned Kelly. The gaol is also known for its death masks, a testimony to the 'science' of phrenology. There are fun, if hair-raising 1½-hour 'theatrical' **night tours** (adult/child/family $20/13/50; 7.30pm & 8.30pm Wed & Fri-Sun), but they're not recommended for children under 12 – book well in advance through **Ticketek** (☎ 13 28 49).

IMMIGRATION MUSEUM

The **museum** (Map pp450-1; ☎ 9927 2700; 400 Flinders St; adult/child $6/free; ☼ 10am-5pm) in the old Customs House offers a sensitive and moving historical account that mixes display and audio in a mesmerising way – it's well worth visiting to help you discover what makes Australians tick. The building alone is worth a visit, with the stunning Long Room, a magnificent piece of Renaissance Revival architecture.

MELBOURNE MUSEUM

Melbourne's **museum** (Map pp446-8; ☎ 13 11 02; Carlton Gardens; adult/child $6/free; ☼ 10am-5pm) opened amid controversy due to its siting (in a park), design (see for yourself), and apparent aims (theme park–styled kid-focused education with hands-on gismos galore). There's everything here from Bunjilaka, the Aboriginal Centre, and a living forest gallery to the kitchen sink of 26 Ramsay St (from *Neighbours*, if you're

not one of the 120 million who watch it daily!). There's an Australian gallery, with a room dedicated to that great Aussie icon – no, not Kylie – Phar Lap, the legendary racehorse. Bring the kids and allow two to three hours.

Southbank

Across the river from the city centre you'll find the **arts precinct**; the **Southgate** (Map pp450–1) development with riverside walks and three levels of restaurants, cafés and bars, all of which enjoy a view of the city skyline and river; and further west along the Yarra the **Crown Entertainment Complex.**

ARTS PRECINCT   Map pp450–1

This area to the east of Southbank, on St Kilda Rd, is the heart of Melbourne's high culture.

The **National Gallery of Victoria** (180 St Kilda Rd) was closed for a complete refurbishment at the time of research, but was scheduled to re-open early in 2004. Its Australian collection is located at the **Ian Potter Centre** in Federation Square (p448).

The **Victorian Arts Centre** (☎ 9281 8000; 100 St Kilda Rd) is made up of two buildings: the Melbourne Concert Hall and the Theatres Building. The interiors of both buildings are stunning. The **Melbourne Concert Hall** (☼ 1½hr before performances), the circular building closest to the Yarra, is the main venue for major artists and companies, and the home of the Melbourne Symphony Orchestra. Most of the hall is below ground. The **Theatres Building** (☼ 9am-11pm Mon-Sat, 10am-5pm Sun) is topped by a spire, which is lit up at night. Underneath it are the State Theatre, the Playhouse and the George Fairfax Studio. Two free galleries in the Theatres Building exhibit stock held by the **Performing Arts Museum** on all aspects of the performing arts.

There are one-hour tours of the concert and theatre complex at noon and 2.30pm ($10/7.50 per adult/child) from Monday to Saturday. On Sunday you can visit the backstage areas at 12.15pm ($14). As backstage tours are not always available, call ahead for details (☎ 9281 8000); children under 12 are not allowed backstage.

For tickets to events, visit the box office in the Theatres Buildings, or you can book at **Ticketmaster** (☎ 13 61 00) or **Ticketek** (☎ 13 28 49).

CROWN ENTERTAINMENT COMPLEX

This place could be labelled with many an adjective, but subtlety most certainly wouldn't be one of them. The sprawling **complex** (Map pp446-8) includes the luxury Crown Towers Hotel, a giant cinema complex, nightclubs, restaurants, high-end boutiques, the obligatory Planet Hollywood...oh yes, and a casino, clad in gold-leaf and glitzy décor, promising your ticket to Broadway will be popping out of the machine at any moment, if only you'll just keep trying. A visit to Crown feels like spending time in an international airport when where you really want to be is on the connecting flight home.

MELBOURNE EXHIBITION CENTRE

Across Clarendon St from the casino is the **Melbourne Exhibition Centre** (Map pp446-8; 2 Clarendon St, Southbank). This huge exhibition space is cloaked with very '90s thrusting blades, straight lines and sharp angles. The building hosts trade exhibitions.

POLLY WOODSIDE MELBOURNE MARITIME MUSEUM

This low-key **museum** (Map pp446-8; ☎ 9699 9760; Lorimer St East; adult/child/family $9/6/25; ☼ 10am-4pm) is on the riverfront, close to the Melbourne Exhibition Centre. An old iron-hulled sailing ship dating from 1885, the *Polly Woodside* has been lovingly restored by volunteers and is now the museum's centrepiece.

MELBOURNE AQUARIUM

On the north side of the river opposite Crown, the highlights of the Melbourne Aquarium (Map pp450-1; ☎ 9620 0999; cnr Queenswharf Rd & King St; adult/child/family $22/12/55; ☼ 9.30am-6pm) are the 360-degree fish bowl viewing area, the jellyfish tanks and the coral atoll – and kids will love the rides. Not so impressive are the exorbitant entrance fees and overall feel of the place, which fails to convey the beauty and mystery of the deep, and seems more focussed on advertising the corporate sponsors. Sydney's aquarium is much better.

Docklands

Near the rear of Spencer St train station, the Docklands was originally a wetland and lagoon area used by Koories as a hunting ground; more recently it was the city's main industrial and docking area until the mid-1970s. With its proximity to the city centre, the area has become the focus of Melbourne's next big development boom – most of it due to be completed before the Commonwealth Games hits the city in 2006. Among the proposed developments are a $40 million giant Ferris wheel and cinema studios.

You can't miss the state-of-the-art **Telstra Dome**, the sporting and entertainment venue. You can also visit one of the first residential and commercial developments off the drawing board, **NewQuay**, with restaurants and bars (p471). Many Melburnians haven't made up their minds about the area yet; some see it as a sterile glamour-zone, more at home in Sydney than in Melbourne; others see it as a good use of the bayside location Melbourne had long turned its back on. To keep abreast of the developments visit www.docklands.com.au.

You can either get there by the free city-circle tram or by the ferry service that runs every 1½ hours between Federation Square and NewQuay ($7 one way), with various stops along the way, including Southgate and Crown Casino.

Scienceworks Museum & Melbourne Planetarium

Under the shadow of the West Gate Bridge, the fabulous **museum and planetarium** (☎ 9392 4800; 2 Booker St, Spotswood; adult/child $6/free, including Planetarium show $12/4; ☼ 10am-4.30pm) offers hands-on educative gizmos and gadgets – they're popular with kids, if they can elbow out the dads. The planetarium is a must-see journey through the night sky illustrated on a 15m domed ceiling; shows start at noon, 1pm, 2pm and 3pm. The museum is only a 15-minute walk from Spotswood train station down Hudsons Rd.

Parks & Gardens

Victoria has dubbed itself the 'Garden State', so it's only fitting that Melbourne has a wonderful array of public parks and gardens.

KINGS DOMAIN

Beside St Kilda Rd, which runs past the huge Kings Domain, stands the massive **Shrine of Remembrance** (☼ 10am-5pm), built as a memorial to Victorians killed in WWI. It's worth climbing to the balcony for fine views.

VICTORIA

Near the shrine is **La Trobe's Cottage** (Map pp446-8; ☎ 9654 5528; admission $2.20; ⊙ 11am-4pm Mon, Wed, Sat & Sun), the original Victorian government house, sent out from the 'mother country' in prefabricated form in 1839.

On the other side of Birdwood Ave from the Shrine of Remembrance are the **Old Melbourne Observatory** and the Royal Botanic Gardens' **visitors centre**. The **National Herbarium**, close by, is near Gate F of the Royal Botanic Gardens.

Imposing **Government House** (Map pp446-8; ☎ 9654 5528; Government House Dr; adult/child/family $11/5.50/20; guided tours Mon & Wed) is a copy of Queen Victoria's palace on England's Isle of Wight. Book at least three days in advance for tours.

At the city end of the park is the **Sidney Myer Music Bowl** (Map pp446-8), an outdoor performance area.

The Royal Botanic Gardens form a corner of the Kings Domain.

ROYAL BOTANIC GARDENS

A visit to the acres of greenery at Australia's finest **botanic gardens** (Map pp446-8; Birdwood Ave, South Yarra; admission free; ⊙ 7.30am-8.30pm Nov-March, till 5.30pm or 6pm Apr-Oct), also among the finest in the world, is a must. Pick up guide-yourself leaflets at one of the several entrances. The **visitors centre** (☎ 9252 2429; ⊙ 9am-5pm Mon-Fri, 10am-5.30pm Sat & Sun) is by the Old Melbourne Observatory on Birdwood Ave. There's a café by the visitors centre and a café/kiosk beside the lake.

Gardens discovery tours (adult/child $4.50/3.50), **Aboriginal heritage walks** ($16/11) and more are offered by the park. Book at the visitors centre.

There's a surprising amount of wildlife, and if you peer over one of the small bridges, you'll probably see some eels. Up to 10,000 grey-headed flying foxes live in the gardens year-round (mainly in the fern gully), but they are unfortunately placing a lot of stress on the trees. An alternative site has been set up for them in the suburb of Ivanhoe, and at the time of research the park staff were using visual and noise deterrents to encourage the bats to head to their new abode.

The gardens are encircled by a horse-exercising track known as the **Tan**, now a 4km running track that is Melbourne's favourite jogging venue.

FITZROY & TREASURY GARDENS   Map pp446-8

The Fitzroy Gardens, dividing the city centre from East Melbourne, are known for their stunning elm-lined avenues, spongy lawns – perfect for picnics – and, after dark, bold possums hoping for a feed. They also have a handful of sites, worth a couple of hours of your time. Drop in to the **visitors centre** (☎ 9417 6204; ⊙ 10am-3pm) to pick up a self-guided walking tour brochure.

Captain Cook's Cottage (☎ 9419 4677; adult/child $3.70/1.80; ⊙ 9am-5pm), believed to be the former Yorkshire home of Cook's parents, was presented to Victoria for its centenary in 1934. Although dismantled into some 253 trunks for the journey, the cosy home was carefully rebuilt and is furnished as it would have been circa 1750. (The high bedheads were built to support upright sleeping, which supposedly promoted growth in children!) The garden here is worth strolling through, too; you'll find some of the plants that famously allowed Captain Cook's crews to avoid scurvy: cabbage and citrus.

Nearby, the **Conservatory** (⊙ 9am-5pm; admission free) bursts with five floral displays every year.

If you've got time and/or you have children with you, you may want to visit the miniature **Tudor Village**, unfortunately looking a bit the worse for wear, and the **Fairies' Tree**, carved in the 1930s in one of the original red gums of the park. The shaded terrace of the **Pavilion Café**, a few steps away, is the perfect place to take five over a cuppa.

You'll probably meet some possums after dark in the Fitzroy and Treasury Gardens. As cute as the little darlings are, too many possums in too small an area has caused serious damage to some trees in the parks – look out for the sheet metal collars preventing the possums from climbing threatened trees. The rangers recommend you don't feed the possums.

OTHER PARKS & GARDENS

The pleasant **Flagstaff Gardens** once provided good views of the bay and in 1840 a flagstaff (hence the name) was erected to signal the arrival of ships bringing much-anticipated supplies to the colony. This hill, with much of the area now covered by the car park of the Queen Victoria Market, situated just to the northeast, was also the site of Melbourne's first cemetery. A memorial to the pioneers buried here can be found in the gardens; beside it are three small plaques reminding visitors of the Aboriginal fatalities of the pioneer era.

The **Carlton Gardens** surround the historic **Royal Exhibition Building**, built for the Great Exhibition of 1880.

Along the Yarra River

The Yarra is a surprisingly pleasant river. Despite being known as 'the river that flows upside down', it's just muddy, not particularly polluted.

Boat cruises along the Yarra depart from the Southgate promenade. Bike paths start from the city and follow the river to various destinations. For more information and bike-hire outlets, see p441.

YARRA BEND PARK

Northeast of the city centre, the Yarra is bordered by the Yarra Bend parklands, large areas of bushland that feel so remote it's hard to believe the city's all around you.

The **Studley Park Boathouse** (☎ 9853 1972; Boathouse Rd, Kew; ☯ 9am-5pm) has a café, and rowboats and canoes for hire ($22 per hour for two people); bring photo ID. Kanes footbridge takes you across to the other side of the river, from where it's about a 20-minute walk to **Dights Falls** at the confluence of the Yarra River and Merri Creek. You can also walk to the falls along the southern bank. Bus Nos 200, 201 or 207 from Lonsdale St in the city will drop you a short walk from the boathouse.

Further upriver, Fairfield Park is the site of the **Fairfield Park Boathouse** (☎ 9486 1501; Fairfield Park Dr, Fairfield; ☯ 9am-5pm), an overly restored boathouse with a garden restaurant in superb surrounds. Some of the meals aren't worth writing home about, so consider sticking to drinks. You can also hire canoes and rowboats here ($24 per hour for two people). Bus No 546 from the Victoria Market drops you a few minutes' walk from the boathouse, but there's no service on weekends.

Yarra Park

Yarra Park roughly describes the large expanse of parkland to the southeast of the city centre, containing the Birrarung Marr parklands, the Melbourne Cricket Ground (usually called the MCG), the Melbourne

Park National Tennis Centre, Olympic Park and several other sports ovals.

MELBOURNE CRICKET GROUND

The **Melbourne Cricket Ground** (MCG, familiarly known as 'the G') is one of the world's great sporting venues. The first game of Australian rules football was played near here in 1858, and in 1877 the first test-cricket match between Australia and England was played here. The MCG was the central stadium for the 1956 Melbourne Olympics, and it will be used in the 2006 Commonwealth Games, hosted by Melbourne.

The MCG is undergoing a total facelift for the Commonwealth Games, but the **tours** (☎ 9657 8879; adult/child/family $16/10/40; ☯ 10am-3pm on non-event days) of the ground will continue running.

Carlton & Parkville

This cosmopolitan old area blends the intellectual (Melbourne University, established in 1853), the gastronomic (Lygon Street, home to Italian food), and the Australian landscape (Royal Park). And a visit to the zoo is a must. Combine all four by visiting the zoo, and after your visit strolling through parklands and the university to a meal at bustling Lygon St.

ROYAL PARK

The once-mammoth reservation of Royal Park, established in the 1870s, has been eroded over the years by sports ovals, stadiums, a public golf course and the Melbourne Zoo. Nevertheless it's a lovely place to get away from it all.

MELBOURNE ZOO

Melbourne's **zoo** (☎ 9285 9300; www.zoo.org.au; Elliott Ave, Parkville; adult/child/family $16/7.80/45; ☯ 9am-5pm) is Australia's oldest (1862) – it's a great place to visit. Don't miss 'Bugs & Butterflies', a walk-through tropical enclosure aflutter with native butterflies, right by the bug collection, where you can get up close to giant burrowing cockroaches or infamous redback spiders. The collection of more typical Australian animals is fabulous, too, the long-flight aviary's a definite plus, and the zoo's elephants now have a long-awaited new enclosure. Love zoos or hate them, few could deny Melbourne's has some of the most sympathetic enclosures in

VICTORIA

the world, and a progressive take on animal welfare. Plan to spend at least two hours.

If you're visiting over summer see if you can time your visit for the fabulous **Zoo Twilights Festival** – see p472 for details. You could even bed down for the night – see 'The Author's Choice' boxed text (p467).

From the city, take tram No 55 from William St (Monday to Saturday), No 68 from Elizabeth St (Sunday), or the Upfield-line train to Royal Park train station.

LYGON STREET   Map pp446–8

Carlton is Melbourne's Italian quarter, and Lygon St is its backbone. Lygon St was also one of Melbourne's first bohemian streets, and while it no longer has much offbeat appeal, not all the hangouts have gone. Places like **Tiamo** and **Jimmy Watson's** have resisted change; and **La Mama** (p481), a tiny experimental theatre, is still going strong on Faraday St.

Every November, the Lygon St Festa is a frolicking food-and-fun street party.

Fitzroy & Collingwood

Fitzroy is where Melbourne's bohemian subculture moved when the lights got too bright in Carlton.

Brunswick St, especially around Johnston St, is one of Melbourne's most lively and vibrant streets, and you'll find a good selection of young-designer and retro-clothes shops, bookshops, and cafés, bars and restaurants at every turn. An interesting cross-section of people frequent Brunswick St, so don't be surprised to overhear conversations covering everything from the price of real estate to the pain involved in foreskin piercing. **Johnston St** is the centre of Melbourne's Spanish-speaking community. It hosts the **Hispanic Festival** in November. Lovers of contemporary art should head to **Gertrude St** to gallery-hop the cluster of tiny galleries and boutiques exhibiting some of the products of Melbourne's busy art scene.

Smith St forms the border between Fitzroy and Collingwood, and the grungy streetscape is a reminder of how Brunswick St used to be. Here you'll find seedy characters, seamy bars and an all-round glamour-free vibe, with a vibrant mix of Asian and vegetarian stores and eateries, cutting-edge designer boutiques and a great range of 'op shops' (second-hand shops).

East Melbourne   Map pp450–1

East Melbourne is a residential pocket with elegant Victorian houses. **Tasma Terrace**, behind Parliament House, is a magnificent row of terraces built in 1878–9. It houses the **National Trust**; wander in for a glimpse of restored glory in the hallway and shop. The grandiose, Neo Gothic **St Patrick's Cathedral** is behind Parliament House.

Richmond

There is still evidence of Richmond's Greek-Australian past on **Swan St**, but the Vietnamese community has totally transformed the stretch of Victoria St between Church and Hoddle Sts into an exciting strip known as 'Little Saigon' (p473).

The **Bridge Rd** area has a sprinkling of cafés and restaurants, but the focus on the city end is clothes shopping (p482), with good eateries up the other end.

South Yarra & Toorak

Welcome to the 'right' side of the river, to the wealthy playgrounds of the bronzed and beautiful. Toorak is the poshest suburb in Melbourne, with an exclusive cluster of shops known as **Toorak Village** along Toorak Rd. The South Yarra end of Toorak Rd is an eclectic mix of shops focussed squarely on the grooming industry, from laundries and top range designer gear (for 40+ shoppers), to spray-on tan salons. Turn the corner to the South Yarra end of **Chapel St**, between Toorak Rd and Commercial Rd, where it all happens darlings. This is ground zero for mainstream style-conscious diehards – it's virtually wall-to-wall clothing boutiques (with a healthy sprinkling of bars and cafés for latte lovers) – and a great place for people-watching. It's worth taking a wander if you have the time.

Como House (Map p457; ☎ 9827 2500; cnr Williams Rd & Lechlade Ave, South Yarra; adult/child/family $10/5.50/28; ⏰ 10am-5pm) is well worth a visit for anyone who's interested in seeing how some of Melbourne's early colonialists lived. There are frequent and excellent obligatory one-hour guided tours of the house. To get there, catch tram No 8 from Swanston St and get off at stop 34.

Prahran

Prahran's sector of **Chapel St** stretches from Commercial Rd down to Dandenong Rd, becoming grungier with each step away

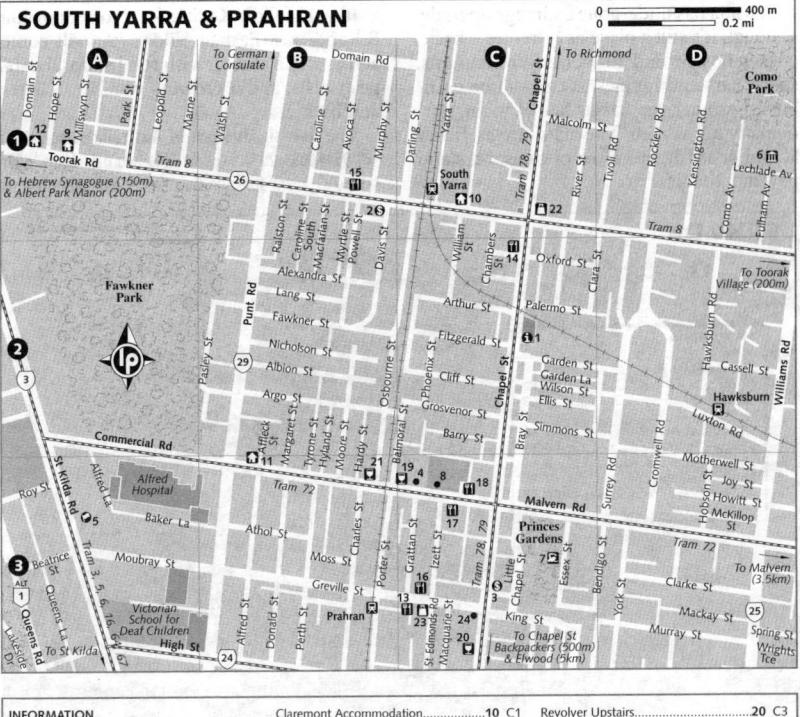

SOUTH YARRA & PRAHRAN

0 —— 400 m
0 —— 0.2 mi

from groomed South Yarra. Prahran has a delightful mix of influences, with a range of ethnic and economic backgrounds all vying for a piece of the action – all behind lovely, if oft-neglected, Art Deco and Victorian shopfronts.

Prahran Market (Map above) is just around the corner from Chapel St on Commercial Rd. **Commercial Rd** is something of a hub for Melbourne's gay and lesbian community, and has a diverse collection of nightclubs, bars, bookshops and cafés. See the boxed text 'Hello There Gorgeous! Out in Queer Melbourne' (p478) for some of the entertainment options along this strip.

Running off Chapel St beside the Prahran Town Hall, **Greville St** is the area's shopping alternative, with a fabulous collection of retro, grunge and designer clothing shops, bookshops, and some good bars and cafés.

St Kilda

St Kilda is one of Melbourne's liveliest and most cosmopolitan areas.

In Melbourne's early days, St Kilda was a fashionable seaside resort. The suburb entered a gradual decline, and by the 1960s it was downright seedy. Its cheap rents and faded glory attracted immigrants and refugees, bohemians and down-and-outers.

St Kilda has undergone an image upgrade, although it's still a place of extremes – backpacker hostels and fine-dining restaurants, sports cars and junkies. It can still be perilous to wander the streets late at night, particularly for women. The main streets, **Fitzroy St** and **Acland St**, are a sea of cafés, bars and pavement tables.

If you follow **Carlisle St** across St Kilda Rd and into East St Kilda, you will come across some great Jewish food shops, European delis, and a growing number of cafés and bars.

The **Jewish Museum of Australia** (Map below; ☎ 9534 0083; 26 Alma Rd, St Kilda; adult/child/family $7/4/16; ⏱ 10am-4pm Tue-Thu, 11am-5pm Sun) covers

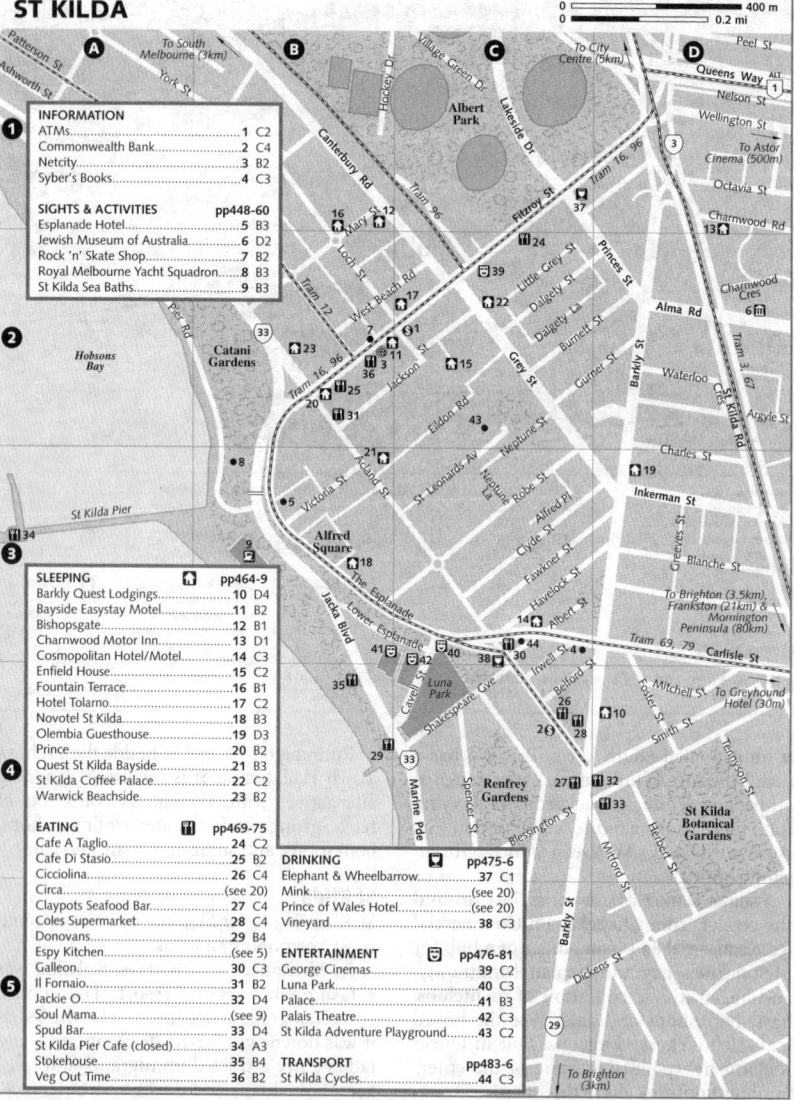

ST KILDA

0 ———— 400 m
0 ———— 0.2 mi

INFORMATION
ATMs......................................1 C2
Commonwealth Bank................2 C4
Netcity...................................3 B2
Syber's Books.........................4 C3

SIGHTS & ACTIVITIES pp448-60
Esplanade Hotel......................5 B3
Jewish Museum of Australia......6 D2
Rock 'n' Skate Shop.................7 B2
Royal Melbourne Yacht Squadron......8 B3
St Kilda Sea Baths...................9 B3

SLEEPING pp464-9
Barkly Quest Lodgings.............10 D4
Bayside Easystay Motel............11 B2
Bishopsgate............................12 B1
Charnwood Motor Inn..............13 D1
Cosmopolitan Hotel/Motel.......14 C3
Enfield House..........................15 C2
Fountain Terrace.....................16 B1
Hotel Tolarno.........................17 C2
Novotel St Kilda......................18 B3
Olembia Guesthouse................19 D3
Prince....................................20 B2
Quest St Kilda Bayside.............21 B3
St Kilda Coffee Palace.............22 C2
Warwick Beachside.................23 B2

EATING pp469-75
Cafe A Taglio.........................24 C2
Cafe Di Stasio........................25 B2
Cicciolina..............................26 C4
Circa.................................(see 20)
Claypots Seafood Bar..............27 C4
Coles Supermarket..................28 C4
Donovans..............................29 B4
Espy Kitchen......................(see 5)
Galleon.................................30 C3
Il Fornaio..............................31 B2
Jackie O................................32 D4
Soul Mama..........................(see 9)
Spud Bar...............................33 D4
St Kilda Pier Cafe (closed).......34 A3
Stokehouse............................35 B4
Veg Out Time........................36 B2

DRINKING pp475-6
Elephant & Wheelbarrow...........37 C1
Mink.................................(see 20)
Prince of Wales Hotel...........(see 20)
Vineyard...............................38 C3

ENTERTAINMENT pp476-81
George Cinemas......................39 C2
Luna Park..............................40 C3
Palace...................................41 B3
Palais Theatre........................42 C3
St Kilda Adventure Playground...43 C2

TRANSPORT pp483-6
St Kilda Cycles.......................44 C3

the religious, historical, cultural and artistic aspects of Jewish life.

The **St Kilda Festival** in February is a showcase for local artists, musicians and writers, and features street parties, parades, concerts and lots more.

SEASIDE   Map p458

The **St Kilda Pier** is a favourite for strollers and a perfect spot to soak up the city and bay views. Both little penguins and native water rats call the breakwater home, and you can take a boat cruise with **Penguin Waters Cruises** (☎ 0412-311 922) to see the penguins. The two-hour sunset cruises (adult/child $55/30), including a barbecue and drinks, run from Southgate.

The laughing face of **Luna Park** (☎ 1902 240 112; Lower Esplanade; ☾ 7-11pm Fri, 11am-11pm Sat, 11am-6pm Sun, daily on public holidays) has been a symbol of St Kilda since 1912. Even with the multi million dollar refurbishment, much of Luna Park's old-world charm is still in evidence, and the heritage-listed rollercoaster ride is a must for thrill-seekers. Single rides cost $6.50/5 per adult/child.

Built in 1880 on the Esplanade, the **Esplanade Hotel** (☎ 9534 0211; 11 The Esplanade), is the musical and artistic heart and soul of St Kilda. The actress Sarah Bernhardt stayed here back in 1891. Today the 'Espy' has bands (often free; see p478 for details), comedy nights (p476), great food (p474) and a uniquely grungy atmosphere; also see Drinking on p475.

Williamstown

Back in 1837, Williamstown was designated the main seaport on Port Phillip Bay. When the Yarra River was deepened and the Port of Melbourne developed in the 1880s, Williamstown became a secondary port. After being bypassed and forgotten for years, Williamstown was rediscovered. It's now a popular weekend destination. Day-trippers by the ferryload come to enjoy the history and seaside atmosphere – and the fabulous bay and city views. A visit to Williamstown – preferably arriving by ferry – is a must.

Nelson Place follows the foreshore and is lined with historic buildings. The **visitors centre** (☎ 9397 3791; cnr Syme St & Nelson Pl; ☾ 9am-5pm) sells a great *Heritage Walks* booklet ($6).

Forty-five-minute **cruises** on the steam tug **Wattle** (☎ 9328 2739) leave from **Gem Pier** between noon and 5pm on Sundays ($5). The **Enterprize** (☎ 9397 3477; Gem Pier; adult/child/family $18/7.50/45) is a timber replica of the ship that carried founding father John Pascoe Fawkner to the settlement. It usually runs one-hour sails on weekends; it is recommended that you ring ahead for times and availability. **HMAS Castlemaine** (☎ 9397 2363; Gem Pier; adult/child $5/2.50; ☾ noon-5pm Sat & Sun) is now a maritime museum exhibiting nautical memorabilia.

Opposite the visitors centre, the **Customs Wharf Gallery** (☎ 9399 9726; 126 Nelson Pl; admission $2; ☾ 11am-5.30pm) is a good place to pick up presents, with plenty of Australia- and Melbourne-themed art and crafts.

Williamstown Beach, on the south side of the peninsula, is pleasant for a swim. From Nelson Place head to the end of Cole St and turn right.

The **Railway Museum** (☎ 9397 7412; Champion Rd, North Williamstown; adult/child $6/3; ☾ noon-5pm Sat & Sun, noon-4pm Wed school holidays) is a great spot for rail enthusiasts and the kids, with row upon row of old steam trains and locomotives. 'Heavy Harry', a mere 260 tons, is a highlight. It's right by the North Williamstown train station.

GETTING THERE & AWAY

From the city, Williamstown is about a 10-minute drive across the West Gate Bridge, or a short train ride (you may need to change at Newport). But the nicest way to get there is by ferry – see p484 for more information.

Hobsons Bay Coastal Trail follows the foreshore from Skeleton Creek (near Altona), via Williamstown to the West Gate Bridge, passing the Scienceworks Museum. Pedestrians and cyclists can take the **punt ferry** (☎ 0419-999 458) across the river from under the West Gate Bridge. It operates between 10.15am and 5pm on weekends and during school holidays (one way/return $4/5).

ACTIVITIES
Bushwalking

Pick up a copy of *Daywalks Around Melbourne* by Glenn Tempest ($32); **Parks Victoria** (☎ 13 19 63; www.parks.vic.gov.au) has brief (and free) park notes you can download. The Dandenongs (p492) offer some of the best hiking opportunities close to Melbourne.

In-Line Skating

The best and most popular tracks follow the shoreline from Port Melbourne to Brighton. You can hire from places like **Rock 'n' Skate Shop** (Map p458; ☎ 9525 3434; 22 Fitzroy St, St Kilda) for $8 for the first hour, less for subsequent hours.

Sailing

There are about 20 yacht clubs around the bay and races are held most weekends (some clubs race on Wednesday as well). Some clubs welcome visitors as crew on racing boats. These are some of the biggest clubs:
Hobsons Bay Yacht Club (☎ 9397 6393; 268 Nelson Pl, Williamstown)
Royal Brighton Yacht Club (☎ 9592 3092; www.rbyc .org.au; 253 St Kilda St, Brighton Marina) Has a useful website.
Royal Melbourne Yacht Squadron (☎ 9534 0227; Pier Rd, St Kilda West)

Learn to sail at the **Melbourne Sailing School** (☎ 9587 8517; 46 Balmoral Dr, Parkdale), which offers three-hour intro lessons for $80 and the Competent Crew certificate (handy if you plan to hitch a ride on a yacht) for $390.

Swimming

The bay beaches are popular during summer. St Kilda beach gets busy at the first ray of sunlight, but they all get packed bum-to-bum on scorching days. The Bellarine (p489) and Mornington Peninsulas (p493) have fabulous ocean beaches. Melbourne's beaches are generally clean, and during the summer months, pollution levels on the beaches are tested by the **Environmental Protection Agency** (www.epa.vic.gov.au) and published daily in the *Age* and on the EPA's website. Pools near the city:
Fitzroy Swimming Pool (Map pp446-8; ☎ 9417 6493; cnr Alexandra Pde & Young St) Swim $3.60.
Melbourne City Baths (Map pp450-1; ☎ 9663 5888; 420 Swanston St, City) Swim $3.80.
Melbourne Sports and Aquatic Centre (☎ 9926 1555; Aughtie Dr, Albert Park Lake) Swim adult/child $5.30/4.
Prahran Aquatic Centre (Map p457; ☎ 8290 7140; Essex St, Prahran) Swim $3.50.
St Kilda Sea Baths (Map p458; ☎ 9525 3011; 10-18 Jacka Blvd, St Kilda) A whopping $11/5 per adult/child in the saltwater indoor heated pool.

Windsurfing & Kiteboarding

Elwood and Middle Park beaches are designated windsurfing areas. **Repeat Performance**

Sailboards (Map p458; ☎ 9525 6475; 87 Ormond Rd, Elwood) offers 1½-hour beginners' windsurfing lessons for $55, one-hour kiteboarding lessons for $75, and also hires out equipment.

WALKING TOUR

The following walking tour introduces you to some of Melbourne's hidden corners. It takes you through historic arcades, up gracious boulevards, and past some of the city's loveliest buildings.

WALKING TOUR

Distance: 2.2km
Duration: 1½ to 2 hours

The walk begins on the corner of Flinders and Swanston Sts outside **Young & Jackson** (1), one of the city's oldest hotels (1853) and home to a late-19th-century nude painting, Chloe, upstairs in the dining hall. Chloe was apparently too risqué for the National Gallery and found her way to this pub in 1909 – she's now something of a Melbourne icon. Opposite is the city's public transport icon **Flinders St train station** (2). Head west up Flinders St, turning right onto Degraves St, with its trendy cafés and tiny shops. It's always easy to get waylaid at **Degraves Espresso Bar** (3), which oozes charm and brews arguably the best coffee in the city. Look north along Degraves St for the beautiful **Majorca Building** (4), one of Melbourne's most sought-after addresses. Follow **Centre Way** (5) arcade through to leafy Collins St. This section of the famous street has retained much of its former glory thanks to Art Deco classics like **Newspaper House** (6) – note the stunning glass mosaic on the façade – and **Howey House** (7).

Cross over into the **Australia on Collins** (8) shopping mall, taking the escalator to the 1st floor to exit onto Little Collins St. Pop into the **Royal Arcade** (9) opposite – built in 1869, the Royal is Melbourne's oldest arcade. Head back towards Collins St by strolling through lovely, café-lined **Block Place** (10), a few steps to the right. You'll soon reach the **Block Arcade** (11). Built in the 1890s it's the city's grandest and most beautiful arcade, with its mosaic floors, glassed ceiling and detailed plasterwork miraculously still intact. Just before you turn left onto Collins St, pop into the shop (Chelsea) on the eastern corner to have

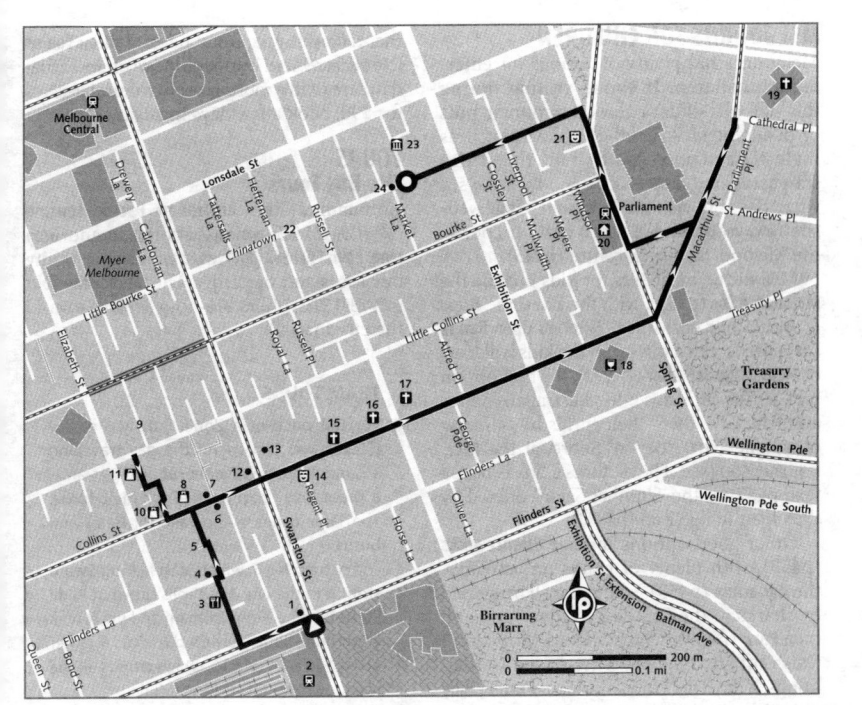

a look at its frescoed ceiling, a reminder of the Block Arcade's glory days.

Follow Collins St up to Swanston St, passing some fine boutiques and the glorious **Manchester Unity Building (12)**, a 1930s Art Deco marvel, built to inspire Melburnians when the end of the Great Depression was nigh. Walk through the arcade and take one of the panelled lifts upstairs (any floor) to appreciate how many original features remain. The **Town Hall (13)** opposite is a classic example of gold boom ostentation, and was the model for many a suburban town hall. The **Regent Theatre (14)** is just past the gargantuan Westin hotel. Hidden behind the white classical façade of the **Baptist Church (15)**, opposite, is an 1845 structure, making the building the oldest Baptist church in Victoria. The Russell St corner is watched over by **Scots (16)** and **St Michael's (17)** churches, textbook examples of High Victorian architecture designed by the prolific Joseph Reed (who, with Frederick Barnes, appears to have built just about every 1860s–70s building in the city).

The last section of Collins St was once known as the 'Paris end' of the city, but today only the plane trees and the exclusive boutiques are at all reminiscent of the City of Light. Take the lift up to the 35th floor of the **Sofitel Melbourne (18)** for a bird's-eye view of the city. You can peer through the café, eat lunch (see the boxed text 'Something Different'; p470), or even just visit the toilets for great views. After you've finished at the Sofitel, cross over to Macarthur St, passing Parliament's back garden, and walk along to **St Patrick's Cathedral (19)**, a Gothic Revival masterpiece. Backtrack to the small park on the corner with Spring St, where you'll see a bluestone fountain carved by Stanford, a one-time horse thief who spent some years in the Old Melbourne Gaol. Continue past the lovely 1883 **Windsor hotel (20)**, designed by the same architect who built the Royal Arcade; you could stop for lunch in the dining room (see the boxed text 'Something Different'; p470). Close by, the **Princess Theatre (21)** was built a few years later. Next, turn down Little Bourke St for **Chinatown (22)**. End the walk with a visit to the **Museum of Chinese Australian History (23)** and some well-earned yum cha at the 1880s **Sun Kum Lee Trading Company (24)**.

MELBOURNE FOR CHILDREN

Melbourne has plenty of options for entertaining children. If you're visiting during the school holidays the city council puts on loads of kid-friendly activities, such as night-time nature spotting in the parks, stargazing and concerts. A good way to see what's on is to visit the **Melbourne's Child** website (www.melbournechild.com.au) and, of course, the Melbourne visitor centre (p445).

Melbourne must-sees for kids include the **Melbourne Zoo** (p455), with the awesome Bugs & Butterflies enclosure, **Victoria's Open Range Zoo** (p486), with a bus safari the kids will love, or **Healesville Sanctuary** (p492), the best option for getting up close to Australian native animals. Give them their thrills by camping overnight with 'Roar 'n' Snore' at the Melbourne Zoo (see 'The Authors Choice' boxed text; p467) or the 'Slumber Safari' offered by the Open Range Zoo (p486).

Other good options include **Scienceworks** (p453), with plenty of hands-on activities, the **Aquarium** (p453), where they'll be circled by sharks in the 360-degree aquarium, and **Luna Park** (p459), which should (hopefully) finish off any hyperactivity. At the Dandenongs, a day trip away, a ride on **Puffing Billy** (p493) is always a hit.

There are also a couple of places to hire canoes and rowboats to paddle with the ducks along the Yarra – see **Yarra Bend Park** (p455) for options. Another good choice is **Collingwood Children's Farm** (☎ 9417 5806; St Helliers St, Abbotsford; adult/child/family $8/4/16; ☻ 9am-5pm), with farm animals and cow milking usually at 10am, by a gorgeous Yarra setting – there's no food available, so bring a picnic. There's also a small **Farmers Market** here on the second Saturday of every month (☎ 0429-146 627; admission $2; ☻ 8am-1pm).

One of the best playgrounds in town is the **St Kilda Adventure Playground** (☎ 9209 6348; Neptune St; admission free; ☻ 3.30-6pm Mon-Fri, 10am-5.30pm Sat & Sun), with tea and coffee for parents. While you're in St Kilda, you may want to check out the **pony rides** (☎ 9598 4128; ☻ 10am-5pm Sat & Sun, weather permitting; ride $4) in the Catani Gardens on the St Kilda foreshore. Finally, for free thrills, take a ride on the free city-circle tram that rattles a loop around the city (p486).

If you want to play sans ankle biters, ask for recommendations at your hotel's reception or look up 'Child Care Centres' in the *Yellow Pages* phone book. **Kids on Collins** (☎ 9629 4099; Level 3, 600 Collins St, City) offers casual day care (with 'rooftop play') for under-sixes for $90; book a few days in advance.

TOURS
City Bus Tours

Companies like **Australian Pacific Touring** (☎ 1300 655 965; www.aptouring.com.au) and **Gray Line** (☎ 1300 858 687; www.grayline.com) run city bus tours and day trips. The **Melbourne Tour** (☎ 8361 9988) offers 3¼-hour whirls around the city for $40.

> **TRAM TOURS**
>
> For the price of a Zone 1 daily Metcard ($5.20), you can spend the day travelling around the city and inner suburbs by tram – a great way to get a feel for Melbourne. The same ticket is also valid for trains and buses.
>
> Try tram No 8, which starts along Swanston St in the city, then rolls down St Kilda Rd beside the Kings Domain and up Toorak Rd through South Yarra and Toorak. Another good ride is the No 16, which cruises all the way down St Kilda Rd to St Kilda.
>
> And don't forget the free city-circle tram – see the boxed text 'Free City-Circle Tram' (p486) for more information.

The **Melbourne Tour** (☎ 9376 6900) sells 24-hour passes onboard for $30/20 per adult/child. This bus does a circuit around the city and another around South Melbourne, between 9am and 4pm (later on weekends), with stops at major attractions. There's a ticket booth by the city square, which is the first stop. Discounts for ticket holders are valid at various attractions, and you can hop on and off all day.

River Cruises

Melbourne River Cruises (Map pp450-1; ☎ 9629 7233; adult/child from $16.50/8.80) offers a choice of hourly cruises running up or down the Yarra, or a combination of both. It also runs 45-minute steamboat cruises on the weekends ($20 per person). There's a kiosk by the clocks of Flinders St train station.

You can also cruise to Williamstown (p459) and to the penguin colony at St Kilda Pier (p459).

Walking Tours

Melbourne's Golden Mile Heritage Trail is a 4km self-guided tour starting at the Immigration Museum on Flinders St and ending at the Melbourne Museum. The walk takes about two hours and is an excellent introduction to historical Melbourne. A booklet costs $4 and can save you up to $30 in admission fees along the way. Buy yours at the Melbourne visitor centre (p445).

The Royal Botanic Gardens (p454) offer various walking tours including an Aboriginal heritage walk. The Museum of Chinese Australian History (p449) offers walks of Chinatown, and the Queen Victoria Market (p451) has a fabulous Foodies Dream tour, among others. **White Hat Tours** (☎ 0500 500 655; www.whitehat.com.au; per person $20) offers a range of unique strolls from the 'Murder & Mystery' tour to 'Melbourne by Lamplight'.

FESTIVALS & SPECIAL EVENTS

Melburnians like any excuse for a knees-up. 'What's on' lists are available from the Melbourne visitor centre and its website www.thatsmelbourne.com.au. (See p476 for ticketing information.)

JANUARY
International Jazz Festival This event attracts a wealth of local and overseas performers.
Australia Day (26 January) Celebrated with everything from an Aussie BBQ to fireworks at Federation Square.
Big Day Out (26 January; www.bigdayout.com) Nearly 40,000 revellers go off to over 40 alternative international and Australian rock bands. Don't miss out.
Australian Open (www.ausopen.com.au) The two-week Grand Slam tennis championship attracts over 500,000 spectators. Some matches get beamed live to the giant video screen at Federation Square – BYO beanbag.

FEBRUARY
Midsumma Gay & Lesbian Festival (www.midsumma .org.au) Features the Red Raw rave and Pride March, and plenty of fun and games.
Chinatown Comes to life with the celebration of Chinese New Year.
International Music & Blues Festival (www.musicmelbourne.com) Jumps, bops and hops for three days by the Yarra; pulls in big names such as Dylan and Ray Charles.
St Kilda Festival Imagine 350,000 people in less than 1 sq km and you've got the biggest free music festival in Australia, a manic one-day riot of music, arts, nosh and beer.

MARCH
Melbourne Moomba Festival A four-day lively family event – and it's free.
Australian Formula One Grand Prix (www.grandprix .com.au) Held at the Albert Park circuit.
Melbourne Queer Film Festival (www.melbourne queerfilm.com.au) The 10-day festival showcases gay artists, with everything from full-length features to experimental works.
Melbourne Food & Wine Festival (www.melbfood winefest.com.au) Enjoy lunch with 999 other diners at one of the festival's highlights, the 'World's Longest Lunch' (followed by the world's longest diet).
Australian Football League (www.afl.com.au) Football fever hits Melbourne for the start of the AFL footy season.

APRIL
Melbourne International Comedy Festival (www .comedyfestival.com.au) Laughs take over the town when the local jokesters are joined by a wealth of international acts.
Anzac Day (25 April) Commemorating those who died in war. The day begins with a dawn service at the Shrine of Remembrance, followed by a march along St Kilda Rd to the city.

MAY
St Kilda Film Festival Showcases contemporary Australian short films with the healthy cash prize drawing competitors from all genres.

JULY
Melbourne International Film Festival (www .melbournefilmfestival.com.au) Film junkies can get their fill – get yourself a festival 'passport' ticket and enjoy.

SEPTEMBER
Royal Melbourne Show (www.royalshow.com.au) Animals, rides and showbags by the dozen – it's a good one for the kids.
Melbourne Fringe Festival (www.melbournefringe. com.au) Celebrates left-of-centre arts – those events not likely to make it to October's Melbourne Festival.
Grand Final (www.afl.com.au) The climax of the AFL footy season is played on the last Saturday in September – and it's also Melbourne's biggest day for barbecues.

OCTOBER
Melbourne Festival (www.melbournefestival.com.au) Combines big-name Australian and international performing and visual artists.
Lygon St Festa Food stalls and bands aplenty at this Italian street party in Carlton. The entertainment also includes the manic waiters' race.

VICTORIA

NOVEMBER
Melbourne Cup (www.vrc.net.au) This famous horse race is run on the first Tuesday. Melburnians don silly hats and get plastered, and virtually the whole country grinds to a standstill.

DECEMBER
Shakespeare in the Park Keep an eye out for the outdoor evening performances in the Royal Botanic Gardens such as *A Midsummer Night's Dream* and *Romeo and Juliet*.
Test Match Cricket Head for the MCG on Boxing Day, when tens of thousands turn up for the first day of the international cricket.
New Year's Eve This public party attracts revellers by the thousands to Southgate and includes massive fireworks.

SLEEPING
See the 'Where to Stay' boxed text (below) for options. If you decide to stay longer, look in the *Age* classifieds on Wednesday and Saturday under 'Share Accommodation'. You can also try the noticeboard at Readings bookshop (p445). During major events and festivals, accommodation in Melbourne is very scarce, and you'll need to book well in advance.

WHERE TO STAY

If you want to be right in the heart of the action, stay in the **city** centre, within staggering distance of some of Melbourne's best bars and restaurants, and within walking distance of most of the top sights. **East Melbourne** is an excellent second choice – it's a quiet, leafy, well-to-do residential district, and a pleasant walk through gorgeous parks from the city centre. Shabbychic **St Kilda** is the perfect choice for sea breezes, pubs and café culture. **Fitzroy** is another great choice for Melbourne's arty scene, with cafés, restaurants and more very-Melbourne pubs than you can down a pot at. All in all, any inner-city suburb will be a good choice – the action is only a tram ride away!

Budget
HOTELS & HOSTELS
Melbourne has many budget options, but we've only listed our top picks in what we consider the best areas to stay. The YHA hostels have the same prices all year, but at the others you can expect to pay a little less in winter and a little more in summer. Most offer cheaper weekly rates.

Colleges can be a good alternative for longer-term stays, especially during student vacations. Expect to pay around $60 per double. Check the housing website of **RMIT** (☎ 9925 2000; www.rmit.edu.au/housing), beautiful **Medley Hall** (Map pp446-8; ☎ 9663 5847; www.medleyhall.unimelb.edu.au; 48 Drummond St, Carlton), which has a top location, or **Ormond College** (Map pp446-8; ☎ 9348 1688; College Cres, Melbourne University).

City Centre & Around
Greenhouse Backpackers (Map pp450-1; ☎ 9639 6400, 1800 249 207; www.friendlygroup.com.au; 228 Flinders Lane; dm/s/d $26/55/70; 🖳) Brilliantly located right in the thick of things, the Greenhouse is a colourful, friendly and well-run operation with excellent facilities – plus there's a rooftop garden. Rooms are bare, but very clean. Book ahead.

The Friendly Backpacker (Map pp450-1; ☎ 9670 1111; www.friendlygroup.com.au; 197 King St; dm $24; 🖳) Run by the same outfit as Greenhouse, no prizes for guessing this place is also well run and welcoming. Here you'll get small dorm rooms (with lockers), immaculate bathrooms, free Internet, hot drinks and breakfast, but it's not quite as good a locale.

Exford Hotel Backpackers (Map pp450-1; ☎ 9663 2697; www.exfordhotel.com.au; cnr Russell & Little Bourke Sts; dm $20-24, d $60; 🅿 🖳) This good option is right by buzzing Chinatown. There's a jam-packed bar that parties hard until 7am, but at least you won't have too far to crawl to the rooms in the upper section, which are no-frills but OK. Book ahead.

Toad Hall (Map pp450-1; ☎ 9600 9010; www.toadhall-hotel.com.au; 441-451 Elizabeth St; dm/s/d $25/60/70, d with bathroom $90; 🅿) Labyrinthine Toad Hall is a quiet option with clean rooms, if a tad old-fashioned and pokey. There's a pleasant shaded courtyard out the back.

Stork Hotel (Map pp450-1; ☎ 9663 6237; www.storkhotel.com; 504 Elizabeth St; s/d/tr $45/60/75) Don't mind the few cracks here and there – the rooms are clean and cosy, and the shared bathrooms are well-tended. The pub downstairs means you won't have to look too far for a beer, a hit of pool or a cheap feed.

Hotel Bakpak (Map pp450-1; ☎ 9329 7525; 1800 645 200; www.bakpak.com/franklin; 167 Franklin St; dm $19-25, s/d $50/60) This massive hotel has a basement 'roo' bar, free brekky, a rooftop 'garden', a zillion activities organised daily and no-frills, if ward-like, rooms. There's free pick-up from the airport (but ring first to find out times).

Nomads Market Inn (Map pp446-8; ☎ 9690 2220; www.marketinn.com.au; 115 Cecil St, South Melbourne; dm $19-23, d $58; 💻) Within walking distance of Southgate and close to public transport. You must book ahead.

North Melbourne   Map pp446-8
Both of Melbourne's YHA hostels are in North Melbourne, 15 minutes' walk northwest of the city centre. Rates listed are for nonmembers.

Queensberry Hill Hostel (☎ 9329 8599; www.yha .com.au; 78 Howard St; dm $27-28, s/d $65/75, with bathroom $75/88; P 💻) This huge hostel is the YHA's squeaky-clean showpiece. The facilities are top-notch, with pool table, rooftop gardens and much more, but few would call it homely.

Chapman Gardens Hostel (☎ 9328 3595; www .yha.com.au; 76 Chapman St; dm/d $28/65; P 💻) This option is smaller and older, so it's a bit more intimate than Queensberry Hill (though that's not saying too much). It's friendly, though, and well run.

Fitzroy   Map pp446-8
Nunnery (☎ 9419 8637; www.bakpak.com/nunnery; 116 Nicholson St; dm $23-27, s $55-65, d $70-85; 💻) Set in stately Victorian buildings, the Nunnery is part hostel, part guesthouse, with charm, heaps of facilities, and an enviable city fringe position. The guesthouse accommodation is particularly good, sharing a lovely courtyard and kitchen. Book well ahead. From Bourke St, catch tram No 96 to stop 13.

South Yarra & Around   Map p457
Claremont Accommodation (☎ 9826 8000; www.hotel claremont.com; 189 Toorak Rd; dm/s/d $25/65/75; P 💻) This well-run, lovely Victorian guesthouse boasts rooms that are spotless and have polished floorboards, but are a little small and characterless. The communal bathrooms are clean, too, and as all rates include breakfast, it's a good deal. Public transport stops almost at the door. There's no safe, so bring your own lock for the lockers.

Chapel St Backpackers (☎ 9533 6855; www.csback packers.com.au; 22 Chapel St, Windsor; dm $20-26, d $75 with bathroom; 💻) This place is within walking distance of both South Yarra and St Kilda.

Some dorms have bathrooms, and breakfast is free. Take the Sandringham-line train to Windsor station.

Richmond
Richmond Hill Hotel (☎ 9428 6501; www.richmond hillhotel.com.au; 353 Church St; dm $24, s $45-75, d $55-85; P) This well-tended, grandiose Victorian-era terrace is an excellent option. The mixed bag of rooms range from OK, if drab, dorms to very-good-value economy rooms; they all have good shared bathrooms. In the latter category the best rooms are Nos 53, 54, 56 and 57, which all have private balconies. Book well ahead! Get there by tram No 75 from Flinders St, and change to tram No 78 or 79, which run along Church St; get off at stop 58.

St Kilda & Around   Map p458
From Swanston St in the city, tram No 16 takes you down St Kilda Rd to Fitzroy and Acland Sts. There's also the faster light-rail service (No 96 via Spencer and Bourke Sts) to the old St Kilda train station and along Fitzroy and Acland Sts.

Enfield House (☎ 9525 4433, 1800 302 121; www .bakpak.com; 2 Enfield St; dm $22-24, d $65; P 💻) This gracious Victorian-era hostel offers plenty of organised activities, some female-only dorms and a courtyard – it's not spotless, but it's busy, messy and friendly. The rooms are OK and rates include breakfast.

Olembia Guesthouse (☎ 9537 1412; www.olembia .com.au; 96 Barkly St; dm/s/d $24/50/75; P) An excellent and quiet option that's more boutique hotel than hostel – it's a couples' kind of place. The rooms are quite small but well kept and comfy, and there's a good kitchen and plenty of spots to curl up with a book. Book well ahead.

St Kilda Coffee Palace (☎ 9534 5283, 1800 654 098; 24 Grey St; dm $19-24, d $60; 💻) This labyrinthine and crusty backpacker has its fair share of detractors and devotees. If you're here to party you'll love it – there's always a pub-crawl or something happening. The rooftop is a bonus, too. Breakfast is included and pick-ups provided.

Cosmopolitan Hotel/Motel (☎ 9534 0781; www .cosmopolitanhotel.com.au; 2-8 Carlisle St; d $100; P) Offers dorm beds for $90 a week, in a self-contained house.

Charnwood Motor Inn (☎ 9525 4199; www.charn woodmotorinn.com; 3 Charnwood Rd; s/d $85/90; P 🐾)

VICTORIA

Ultra daggy and a bit tired, but in a quiet, leafy street and with generous-sized rooms.

CAMPING & CARAVAN PARKS

There are a few caravan/camping parks in the metropolitan area, but these are the best two options, both about 10km from the city.

Ashley Gardens Holiday Village (☎ 9318 6866; www.ashleygardens.com.au; 129 Ashley St, Braybrook; camp sites for 2 people $25, cabins from $65; P) A well-kept and well-equipped park with a kids' play area and regular bus transport (No 220) to the city.

Melbourne Holiday Park (☎ 9354 3533; www.big 4melb.com; 265 Elizabeth St, Coburg East; camp sites for 2 people $24, cabins from $65; P) A good runner-up, but it's not very convenient for public transport.

Mid-Range

APARTMENTS

East Melbourne

Eastern Town House (☎ 9418 6666; www.eastern townhouse.com.au; 90 Albert St; studios $125; P X) Hardly a townhouse, but modern and cheerful enough, the Eastern offers good-value and airy studio rooms with a fully equipped kitchen and good-sized bathroom – they're better than the standard rooms (which cost slightly more). It's opposite parklands.

George Powlett Motel Apartments (☎ 9419 9488; www.georgepowlett.com.au; cnr George & Powlett Sts; s/d $103/110; P X) If the Eastern is full, this an OK runner-up, offering service with a smile and rooms with a small kitchenette.

St Kilda   Map p458
Quest St Kilda Bayside (☎ 9593 9500; www.quest apartments.com.au; 1 Eildon Rd; apt for 2 people $132, for 4 $190; P X) These apartments share a quiet, leafy location, and yet are only a stone's throw from Fitzroy St. The roomy apartments are well-equipped, with good bathroom, kitchen and laundry, if a little uninspiring. Book well ahead, as these are excellent value.

Barkly Quest Lodgings (☎ 9525 5000; www.questapartments.com.au; 180 Barkly St; apt for 2 people $135; P X) These clean, if slightly dreary, apartments are up near Acland Street. It's not quite as good a location as the Bayside, but it's surprisingly quiet considering it's on busy Barkly Street. Extra people cost $17.

Williamstown

Quest Williamstown (☎ 9393 5300; www.questapar tments.com.au; 1 Syme St; 1-bedroom apt $195; P X) It doesn't get much better than this: Gem Pier on the doorstep, a terrific spot opposite parklands and the restaurant strip a short walk away. Most of the modern and spotless fully self-contained apartments here have bay views as well. It's excellent value for money, and you can catch the ferry into town for sightseeing.

B&BS & GUESTHOUSES

Breakfast is included in the rates listed in this section.

Fitzroy   Map pp446–8
King Boutique Accommodation (☎ 9417 1113; www .kingaccomm.com.au; 122 Nicholson St, Fitzroy; s $120-165, d $150-195; P) This absolutely gorgeous 1860s building is all pomp and ceremony on the outside and understated charm and elegance on the inside. It's right opposite Carlton Gardens and a short walk to the city centre.

East Melbourne

Georgian Court Guesthouse (☎ 9419 6353; www .georgiancourt.aunz.com; 21-25 George St; s $80-105, d $100-120; P X ▣) This lovely old house has a fabulous setting in a quiet, leafy street. It's a shame then, that the interior is fairly characterless, though the rooms are well-equipped and clean.

Magnolia Court (☎ 9419 4222; www.magnolia -court.com.au; 101 Powlett St; r $140-230; P X) Most of the rooms are a bit small and bland for the price, but the drawcards are the lovely Victorian-era building itself, the lush small garden and the sun-drenched terrace out front – oh, and it's a short walk to the city.

Williamstown

Bed & Breakfast at Stephanie's (☎ 9397 5587; www.bandbatstephanies.com.au; 154-160 Ferguson St; s & d from $135; P X) Although Stephanie's is a bit out of the action (it's 10 minutes' walk from Nelson Place), it makes up for it by offering a range of luxurious older-style rooms in a polished Edwardian mansion. It's a friendly spot.

Captains Retreat (☎ 9397 0352; captainsretreat@ ozemail.com.au; 2 Ferguson St; s/d from $100/120) A few steps from the bay, in a charming 1882 double-storey weatherboard.

St Kilda
Map p458

Bishopsgate (☎ 9525 4512; www.bishopsgate.com.au; 57 Mary St; s $145-175, d $165-195, apt for 2 people $195; P ☒) This homely and charming terrace house has three immaculate light-filled rooms and a pretty garden at the front that's the perfect spot to debrief over an afternoon beer. There's a slick fully self-contained apartment on Fitzroy St, too.

Fountain Terrace (☎ 9593 8123; www.fountain errace.com.au; 28 Mary St; s $135-195, d $165-235; P ☒) Just up the road from Bishopsgate, Fountain Terrace is bigger, though equally welcoming, and has Dennis the dog, and rooms a little more on the floral side. The Melba suite is magnificent, overlooking the leafy street, and has its own private balcony. There's also a wheelchair-friendly room.

South Yarra
Map p457

Tilba (☎ 9867 8844; www.thetilba.com.au; cnr Domain St & Toorak Rd West; r $155-215; P ☒) This elegant Edwardian has been lovingly restored into a B&B with a variety of utterly charming rooms – and it's right opposite parklands. Book well ahead.

HOTELS & MOTELS
City Centre
Map pp450-1

Hotel Y (☎ 9329 5188; www.ywca.net; 489 Elizabeth St; s $80-100, d $100-120, tr $115; P ☒ ☐) Run by the YWCA, Hotel Y is an excellent option right near the Queen Victoria Market. There's a great range of facilities (a café, communal kitchen and laundry), it's wheelchair accessible and there's the added bonus of free use of the pool and gym at the City Baths. Book ahead.

City Limits Motel (☎ 9662 2544; www.citylimits .com.au; 20-22 Little Bourke St; s & d $145; P ☒) Great location, great hotel. This friendly, small option has excellent-value rooms with clean, bright décor and small kitchenettes. Floors seven and eight also offer lovely low-rise city views. Book ahead, because good things get snapped up quickly.

Oakford Gordon Place (☎ 9663 2888; sales.ogp@ oakford.com; 24 Little Bourke St; studio s & d $105, 1-/2-bedroom apt $125/145; P ☒) Ignore the piped music and the plastic plants – these over-sights in taste can't detract from the lovely courtyards in this unique three-storey National Trust–listed oasis. The rooms at the Oakford Gordon are good, too, if a little worn in parts. Book ahead.

THE AUTHOR'S CHOICE

Roar 'n' Snore (☎ 9285 9355; Elliott Ave, Parkville; adult/child $100/90) at the Melbourne Zoo offers an overnight camping experience with guided night tour, dinner and breakfast included – it's guaranteed to delight adults and children alike. Children must be over four years; it's offered on Friday and Saturday nights only and you must book well in advance.

Victoria Hotel (☎ 9653 0441; www.victoriahotel.com .au; 215 Little Collins St; s/d $60/80, with bathroom $95/140; P) Once one of Melbourne's oldest hotels, the Victoria has been revitalised and has grown to oversized proportions. The location is brilliant and service comes with a warm smile, so you can forgive the plain (but spotless) rooms and deadly dull corridors.

Hotel Enterprize (☎ 9629 6991; www.hotelenterpr ize.com.au; 44 Spencer St; r $100-130; P ☐) Rooms here are set around a deep potted-plant courtyard. The budget rooms are a bit dark, but roomy enough – they're good for the price and location.

Other recommendations:

Explorer Inn (☎ 9621 3333; 16 Spencer St; r $140; P ☒) Small but squeaky-clean rooms.

City Square Motel (☎ 9654 7011; 67 Swanston St; s/d $80/105; P ☒) Awesome position, shame about the soul-less rooms.

Richmond

Richmond Hill Hotel (☎ 9428 6501; www.richmond hillhotel.com.au; 353 Church St; s/d $105/120; P) This terrific option is a grandiose Victorian-era terrace with a garden at the front and an assortment of rooms. Cosy room No 52 at the front is possibly the best room in the house with its own private balcony; rooms Nos 32 to 34 out the back offer leafy views and will be quieter. Rates include breakfast. Book well ahead.

Carlton & Parkville
Map pp446-8

Downtowner on Lygon (☎ 9663 5555; www.down towner.com.au; 66 Lygon St; rooms $150; P ☒) This cheery hotel has a good location and airy, contemporary rooms with far more style than you'd expect for the price. The added bonus is that guests can use the facilities at the City Baths for free. Kick back for just $10 more in a spa room.

VICTORIA

Travel Inn (☎ 9347 7922; www.the-travel-inn.com.au; cnr Grattan & Drummond Sts; r $120-145; P ⊠) Ugly salmon pink on the outside, but very friendly and comfy inside. There's a small pool, too.

Ramada Inn (☎ 9380 8131; 539 Royal Pde; s/d $105/110; P ⊠). Basic 1950s-style inn.

South Yarra
Map p457

Hotel Saville (☎ 9867 2755; www.saville.com.au; 5 Commercial Rd; s/d from $120/130; P ⊠ 🖳) Ignore the outside of this octagonal high-rise monstrosity if you can, because inside the rooms are light, comfortable and roomy. Each room has a small balcony – book room Nos 606 or 607 for the best views of the city. Tram No 72 from Swanston St (in the city) runs past the front.

Albany Motor Inn (☎ 9866 4485; www.albanymotel.com.au; cnr Toorak Rd & Millswyn St; s $95-130, d $100-140; P ⊠) The friendly Albany offers a mixed bag of rooms from standard, slightly drab rooms, to roomy older-style options in the mansion annexe (overlooking Fawkner Park) – room six is best here. There are also small but ultramodern and spotless rooms with king-sized beds, unfortunately overlooking the car park. It's a good choice and well located.

Albert Park Manor (☎ 9821 4486; www.albertparkmanor.com.au; 405 St Kilda Rd; r $85-145; P ⊠) This place offers pleasant, if frilly, rooms. It's on a busy intersection, but it's friendly and quiet inside.

St Kilda
Map p458

Hotel Tolarno (☎ 9537 0200; www.hoteltolarno.com.au; 42 Fitzroy St; r $115-165; P ⊠) Arguably the most quintessential St Kilda option around, this friendly and character-filled choice embraces local art and colour. The balcony suite ($145) has great views over Fitzroy St – the perfect vantage point from which to enjoy St Kilda's always interesting goings-on. The standard rooms are good value, too, if a tad worn.

Warwick Beachside (☎ 9525 4800; www.warwickbeachside.com.au; 363 Beaconsfield Pde; d $70-95, 1-bedroom unit $90-105, weekly rates cheaper; P) It's too good to be true: this large complex of 1950s-style holiday flats is right opposite St Kilda beach and a short stagger from Fitzroy Street – and just look at the rates! The rooms themselves are tidy, if faded, but the proprietors are thinking of putting the

property on the market, so this bargain of the century may be shortlived.

Bayside Easystay Motel (☎ 9525 3833; www.easystay.com.au; 63 Fitzroy St; r $90-130; P ⊠) Right in the heart of the action, this motel has pleasant-enough, well-appointed rooms with kitchenettes.

Cosmopolitan Hotel/Motel (☎ 9534 0781; www.cosmopolitanhotel.com.au; 2-8 Carlisle St; d $100, apt $145; P) An eyesore with ugly but functional rooms – the apartments are slightly overpriced, but the doubles are decent.

Top End
Most of Melbourne's top hotels offer weekend packages, so have a good look around if you're after a bit of creature comfort.

Adelphi Hotel (Map pp450-1; ☎ 9650 7555; www.adelphi.com.au; 187 Flinders Lane, City; r $300-540; P ⊠) The intimate and mega-slick Adelphi has a great rooftop bar with city views, the superb Ezard at Adelphi restaurant in the basement (p470) and the famous glass-bottomed lap pool, which extends over the street no less. The rooms are modern, spare and extremely well appointed.

Windsor (Map pp450-1; ☎ 9633 6000; www.thewindsor.com.au; 103-115 Spring St, City; d from $230; P ⊠) Built in 1883–84 and refurbished in the 1990s, the Windsor is the epitome of old-world elegance from the ostentatious Victorian-era façade, right down to the floral bedspreads. It has all the comforts and facilities expected of a five-star hotel; breakfast included.

Grand Hotel (Map pp450-1; ☎ 9611 4567; www.grandhotelsofitel.com.au; 33 Spencer St, City; studios $210; P ⊠) The top floors of this stately 1880s building have been refurbished into this fabulous hotel. The cheapest and possibly best value options are the roomy studios offering full kitchen facilities, king-sized beds and fantastic views from your private balcony. There's a pool, too. Enjoy.

The Prince (Map p458; ☎ 9536 1111; www.theprince.com.au; 2 Acland St, St Kilda; r $200-520; P ⊠) The ultimate in unadorned sophistication, polish and quality – right down to the *Aesop* toiletries. These near-perfect rooms are complemented by the Aurora Spa Retreat, for ultimate indulgence, only footsteps away.

Novotel St Kilda (Map p458; ☎ 9525 5522; www.novotelstkilda.com; 14-16 The Esplanade, St Kilda; d $170; P ⊠) It's anything but in keeping with the feel of the suburb, but you'll be won over by the position, the warm service, the first-rate facilities and the knock-out bay views (double rooms overlooking the bay cost $195).

EATING

Melbourne's reputation as the cuisine capital of Australia is hotly debated. The European (especially Italian) influence remains as strong as ever in the vibrant café scene that dominates the city and inner suburbs — you'll also find everything from Vietnamese to Moroccan. If you only have a few days in Melbourne, spend one night eating in St Kilda, another in the city centre, and a third in either Fitzroy or Carlton.

City

BOURKE STREET AREA & CHINATOWN   Map pp450–1

The area in and around Chinatown, which follows Little Bourke St from Spring St to Swanston St, offers a diverse range of eating options with everything from Chinese and Japanese to Italian and Greek. Many of the city's restaurants are only open for lunch and dinner, and close on Sunday; check in advance.

Pellegrini's (☎ 9662 1885; 66 Bourke St; pasta $11-13) This 1950s-style espresso bar hasn't changed for years. Pull up a stool, pick from mamma's favourite pasta, pizza and risotto, and enjoy your nosh shoulder-to-shoulder with other Pellegrini's devotees. We love this place, and it's not just because we get called 'bella'.

Yamato (☎ 9663 1706; 28 Corrs Lane; dishes $6-16) It's a tight squeeze in this very popular, no-frills Japanese restaurant. Expect good-value and crunchy-fresh eats, which can be somewhat let down by the appalling tinny background music. Groups can book the shoes-off tatami room.

Supper Inn (☎ 9663 4759; 15-17 Celestial Ave; dishes $7-23; ☼ 5.30pm-2.30am) This buzzing restaurant packs in a mixed crowd, despite the décor, so come early or expect to queue for this long-standing favourite, dishing up reasonable Cantonese dishes. It's a great last stop for an early morning belly-lining feed on your way home.

LONELY PLANET STAFF FAVOURITES

Melbourne is Lonely Planet's town, and has been for almost 30 years now. It's not surprising then that we have some pretty firm ideas about eating out in this city. Below are some Lonely Planet opinions on the best of eating out in Melbourne:

Best Value

I vote for the **Moroccan Soup Bar** (Map pp446-8; ☎ 9482 4240; 183 St Georges Rd, North Fitzroy; dishes $6-15), because there's no menu, no prices, you're hard pushed to spend $20 a head, the service is sassy and in your face, and the food is just the most delicious this side of Essaouira. Try the chickpea and yogurt with burnt butter and pinenuts. *(Simon Westcott – global publisher)*

Best Unpretentious Café

For a welcome reminder that St Kilda is more than just beautiful people and chrome-and-wasabi bars, check out the **Galleon Cafe** (Map p458; ☎ 9534 8934; 9 Carlisle St, St Kilda; dishes $7.50-11). Scrummy fruit crumble, chicken and leek pie and rice pudding are among the comfort-food offerings that have made this humble café into an institution. The coffee is good, the staff are friendly, and you may even spot the odd unshaven rockstar keepin' it real. *(Janet Brunckhorst – computer guru)*

Best Wine List

The wine menu is as thick as the telephone book at **Syracuse** (Map pp446-8; ☎ 9670 1777; 23 Bank Pl, City; tapas $4-10, mains $19-27), and the decadent old-world feel is divine. Syracuse exudes bucket-loads of charm, thanks to the gracious waiters, some dazzling wine, and elegant but unpretentious food. In one word: wonderful.

(Anastasia Safioleas – editor)

Best Vegetarian

Melbourne's premier vegetarian café, **Vegie Bar** (Map pp446-8; ☎ 9417 6935; 380 Brunswick St, Fitzroy; dishes $3-10) not only serves excellent all-vegie food but is a great spot to go to get into Fitzroy/Brunswick St culture.

(Tashi Wheeler – readers' letters)

VICTORIA

Becco (☎ 9663 3000; 11-25 Crossley St; mains $22-29; ☒ Mon-Sat) One of the city's best eateries, cool and classic Becco attracts diners for its superb takes on old Italian favourites combined with faultless service.

Flower Drum (☎ 9662 3655; 17 Market Lane; mains $30-50) Indulge yourself at this mega-plush Melbourne institution, offering some of the best Chinese cuisine ever likely to tantalise your tongue, complemented by supreme service. Lunch time is a good (and cheaper) option, but you must book ahead at any time.

Nudel Bar (☎ 9662 9100; 76 Bourke St; mains $14-19) Also consider the buzzing Nudel Bar – the green tea noodles are best.

OTHER CITY CENTRE
AREAS   Map pp450-1

Basso (☎ 9650 0077; 195 Little Collins St; pizza slice $4.90-5.50; mains $15-20; ☒ 11.30am-11pm Mon-Fri) Head down to the concrete-bunker-like Basso with clean-cut style, friendly service and up to 20 different slabs of delectable pizza. From the leek and gorgonzola to the minimalist fuss but maxi taste of the tomato-dolloped pancetta, there's something for everyone. Eat your slice in, or on the run.

Degraves Espresso Bar (☎ 9654 1245; 23 Degraves St; dishes $7-13) Degraves Street is a pedestrian thoroughfare between Flinders St and Flinders Lane, packed with tables and chairs spilling out from the cafés lining the sides. Beloved shoebox-sized Degraves is the best of the bunch, an atmospheric and refreshingly suit-free zone with warm, inviting service and to-die-for coffee.

Kimchi House (☎ 9663 5919; 70 Little La Trobe St; mains $12-14; ☒ Mon-Sat) This hidden gem looks like a workaday factory from the outside, but inside it's a simple yet intimate and contemporary space. Excellent Korean food is dished up here to those in the know – do-it-yourself on the charcoal barbecues.

Ezard at Adelphi (☎ 9639 6811; 187 Flinders Lane; mains $33-36; ☒ Mon-Sat) One of Melbourne's finest restaurants, Ezard merges Asian and European flavours to create an inspired 'mod Oz' dining experience par excellence! Book ahead.

Sushi Deli (☎ 9670 6688; 395 Little Bourke St; sushi & meals $1.50-9) We love the hole-in-the-wall Sushi Deli for its bubbly staff and flavour-packed food. Get here early to bag one of the seats, or take away like the regulars do.

Stalactites (☎ 9663 3316; cnr Lonsdale & Russell Sts; dishes $3.50-20) The type of place you stagger in to at three in the morning, when the décor (bizarre stalactite ceilings) will really mess with your mind. This enduring Melbourne icon serves Greek eats and great souvlakis for lining the stomach, and it's open 24 hours.

Other recommendations:

Mo Mo (☎ 9650 0660; basement, 115 Collins St; dishes $29-35; ☒ Mon-Sat) Middle East–inspired eats in an inviting, classic eatery.

Syracuse (☎ 9670 1777; 23 Bank Pl; tapas $4-10, mains $19-27; ☒ Mon-Fri) Delicious tapas and European ambience.

Lounge (☎ 9663 2916; 1st fl, 243 Swanston St; dishes $9-16) A good-vibe spot with a great balcony.

Don Don Japanese Cafe (☎ 9662 3377; 321 Swanston St; dishes $4-8) Great for a bento box or noodles on the run.

Crossways (☎ 9650 2939; 123 Swanston St; all-you-can-eat $5.50; ☒ 11.30am-2.30pm Mon-Sat) Vegetarian food – the chanting and literature are free.

SOMETHING DIFFERENT

Need a change? Try either of these options:

Cafe La (Map pp450-1; ☎ 9653 7744; Level 35, Sofitel Melbourne; 25 Collins St, City; lunch $25, dinner $18.50-32) Dine with the skyscrapers at this unadorned café, 35 floors up. The weekday buffet lunch is particularly good value: $25 fixes you with a wine at hand and a great assortment of dishes. The restaurant next door, **Le Restaurant** (Map pp450-1; ☎ 9653 7744; Level 35, Sofitel Melbourne; 25 Collins St, City; mains $37-45), is among the city's best.

111 Spring Street (Map pp450-1; ☎ 9633 6000; Windsor hotel, 103-115 Spring St, City) Melbourne's exquisite 19th-century Windsor, thanks to its National Trust protection, has retained its Victorian-era opulence. Afternoon tea ($30), darlings, or three-course lunch with wine ($35) is served in the restaurant – the rhythmic chopping of the ceiling fans accentuates the la-di-da Empire ambience of this elegant room. If you're here on Sunday, a brunch buffet meal ($50) is served in the Windsor's *pièce de résistance*, the Grand Dining Ballroom, decorated in 24-carat gold leaf no less.

North Melbourne

Map pp446–8

Warung Agus (☎ 9329 1737; 305 Victoria St; mains $14-18; ☼ 6-10pm Tue-Sun) If you can forgive the grass-green carpet, this popular and welcoming restaurant has a great range of Balinese food, and all meals are usually good.

La Porchetta (☎ 9326 9884; 308 Victoria St; pizza & pasta $5-10) This booming Australian pizza chain offers no-frills, value-for-money eats.

Southgate & Crown Entertainment Complex

Map pp450–1

Southgate has plenty of bars, cafés and restaurants to choose from, most of which have outdoor terraces and balconies from where you can enjoy riverside views and the city skyline.

Mecca (☎ 9682 2999; Mid-level, Southgate; mains $26-30) We love stylish Mecca for its service (perfect), wine list (extensive) and its imaginative North African–inspired dishes (superb). Anything it does with a tajine is divine, but save yourself for the beloved scent of rose in a swoon-worthy strawberry and rose petal pavlova. Go.

Blue Train Cafe (☎ 9696 0440, Mid-level, Southgate; dishes $6-17) Manic Blue Train has sussed out a winning formula that keeps the punters returning: great-looking staff, city views, finger-clickingly efficient service and a never-ending menu. Stick to the pasta and wood-fired pizzas here; other meals can go off the rails (sorry) when they're packed on the weekends – and watch you don't get mown over by the staff.

Further along the Yarra from Southgate, the restaurant precinct in **Crown Entertainment Complex** has something for all budgets.

NewQuay

Map pp446–8

A handful of restaurants at the new Docklands development, NewQuay, boast fabulous waterside spots – come here for sunset.

Mecca Bah (☎ 9642 1300; 55a NewQuay Promenade; mains $10-18) Mecca Bah rides on the coat-tails of its much better cousin, Mecca in Southgate (see above). We weren't overly impressed with our long-awaited mains and lack of elbowroom, though the mezze gets the thumbs up – sit outside.

Bhoj (☎ 9600 0884; Rakaia Way; mains $8-16) This is the best option at NewQuay, lauded by many in the know as offering the best Indian in inner Melbourne. We agree, but if you like your curries hot, say so.

Carlton

Map pp446–8

Tram No 1 or 22, running along Swanston St, gets you here from the city centre, or you can stroll north up Russell St.

Abla's (☎ 9347 0006; 109 Elgin St; dishes $16-18; ☼ 6-11pm Mon-Sat, noon-3pm Thu-Fri) An old-time favourite and arguably the best Lebanese in Melbourne, Abla won't let you leave until you're patting your tummy contentedly. This is hospitality at its best.

Jimmy Watson's Wine Bar (☎ 9347 3985; 333 Lygon St; mains $16-22) Legendary among wine lovers, elegant Jimmy's boasts an extensive wine list complemented by excellent European-style food. The leafy courtyard is a winner; or enjoy a session of sidewalk people-watching, armed with a glassful of Jimmy's very own chardonnay.

Brunetti (☎ 9347 2801, 194-204 Faraday St) Shoebox-sized Brunetti was recently renovated into a place so big we joked they'd never fill the airy spaces, but try get a seat if you can. Brusque service, hectic pace and pricey to boot, but still they come. The authentic Italian, Brunetti has the best gelati in Melbourne, delicious pasticceria (the vanilla *canoli*, a custard-filled pastry, is a must) and coffee so strong you might not sleep for days.

Tiamo (☎ 9347 5759; 303 Lygon St; dishes $10.50-16) Popular with pre-movie diners, this mood-lit Italian bistro oozes character with poster-plastered walls. Mountains of food combined with ultra-quick service are a winning combination that has had Melburnians coming back for decades.

Other recommendations:
Shakahari (☎ 9347 3848; 201-203 Faraday St; dishes $14-17) For inspired vegetarian meals.
Thresherman's Bakehouse (☎ 9349 2319; 221 Faraday St) Barn-like, with excellent-value $6 lunch deals – enough to feed an army.

Fitzroy & Collingwood

BRUNSWICK STREET & AROUND

With so much to choose from it can be difficult to see the wood from the trees, but this selection should help you see things a little more clearly. Tram No 11 or 112, running along Collins St, takes you up along Brunswick St.

Mao's (Map pp446-8; ☎ 9419 1919; 263 Brunswick St; mains $12.50-22; ☼ Tue-Sun) Mao's is a favourite for its casual vibe, super-friendly staff, offbeat but stylish fit-out and, most importantly, its modern, delicious twist on the

VICTORIA

classic Chinese menu. The Hunan hotpot here is delicious, so enjoy the sinfully fatty chunks. Book the cosy booth if there's a few of you.

Moroccan Soup Bar (☎ 9482 4240; 183 St Georges Rd; dishes $6-15; ⏰ 6-10pm Tue-Sun) Although it's a bit out of the way, every step will be rewarded once you taste the smoky hummus at this much-loved and very popular eatery. While there are often hair-pullingly long waits for so-so service, and the lack of an alcohol licence and menu may annoy, any gripes will be quashed when you pick up your bill: $15 per person for a gigantic set menu? We'll be back.

Babka Bakery Cafe (Map pp446-8; ☎ 9416 0091; 358 Brunswick St; dishes $4-14) Who said pies had to be claggy and gristled? Babka's put all dinky-di pies to shame – try the lamb and dried apricot, served with crunchy-fresh greens, a dollop of tangy relish, and as much of the freshly baked bread as you want ($9.50). Babka's other dishes mostly have Eastern European inspiration. Lunch time is best here.

De Los Santos (Map pp446-8; ☎ 9417 1567; 175 Brunswick St; tapas $7-15) This cosy and intimate modern Spanish eatery is a great place to come with a group. Spread your table with tapas (the hot fried cheese puffs have to be tasted to be believed); order with your eyes; worry about your stomach later.

Vegie Bar (Map pp446-8; ☎ 9417 6935; 380 Brunswick St; dishes $3-10) A Brunswick St stalwart, the sprawling, buzzing Vegie Bar is perennially packed with a mixed bag of customers, here for the sometimes fabulous, sometimes average all-vegie eats. The burgers are a sure-fire winner any time; avoid the *tempeh* (fermented soy-bean cake) unless greasy cardboard appeals. Come hungry, as the servings are huge.

Mario's (Map pp446-8; ☎ 9417 3343; 303 Brunswick St; dishes $5-18) Snubbing the easy-come, easy-go wannabe cafés on the strip, this sceney café is one of the originals, and doesn't it know it. Come for the great coffee, kick-start breakfasts and a selection of good pasta dishes.

Bangla Sweets & Curry Café (Map pp446-8; ☎ 9417 1877; 199 Brunswick St; mains $7-14) Low-key Bangla's gets full points for the sweets cabinet, bursting at the seams with a colourful array of Punjabi and Bengali treats.

MELBOURNE'S BEST BREAKFASTS...

Melburnians put their favourite pastime (eating) first on their weekend 'to do' list. Cafés fill up from a respectful 10am onwards and many serve breakfast until at least 3pm, if not all day. Ease a belt hole at the following hand-picked favourites.

Gluttony, It's a Sin (☎ 9416 0336; 278 Smith St, Collingwood; breakfasts $5-13) It's a sin, and we don't care. This cosy, retro café embraces its name with a vengeance, serving veritable mountains of food – the 'gluttony' breakfast is always a good choice. Come hungry, leave waddling.

Cafe Segovia (Map pp450-1; ☎ 9650 2373; 33 Block Pl, City; dishes $6-19) One of the first cafés to jam Block Place, Segovia is still one of the best. Breakfast here is a real treat with Parisian-like ambience and some truly generous and delicious serves – without the crush of devotees who flock here at lunch. Block Place is one of the most atmospheric eat-streets in the city – park yourself at a lane-way table and enjoy.

Galleon Cafe (Map p458; ☎ 9534 8934; 9 Carlisle St, St Kilda; dishes $7.50-11) It's well worth visiting the beloved Galleon, an enduring kid- and dog-friendly hangout for St Kilda's alternative community. From sardines on toast to porridge or Coco Pops for breakfast, this character-filled and very welcoming spot is testimony that food doesn't have to be 'upsized', gourmet or complicated to appeal. Long live the Galleon.

Retro (Map pp446-8; ☎ 9419 9103; 413 Brunswick St, Fitzroy; breakfasts $4.50-13) This welcoming favourite is a celebration of 1950s kitsch, with comfy couches, laminate tables and no-two-the-same chairs. The biggish breakfasts pull in the crowds, and kids are welcome – the water feature wall is always a hit with greasy breakfast-covered mitts. Come for the famous retro or vego breakfast with the works.

Red Emperor (Map pp450-1; ☎ 9699 4170; Upper Level, Southgate; yum cha $4-9; ⏰ yum cha: noon-3pm Mon-Sat, 11am-4pm Sun) Great city and river views, excellent service and possibly the best yum cha in Melbourne. Join the throng and enjoy.

MELBOURNE TRAIN NETWORK

metlink

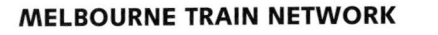

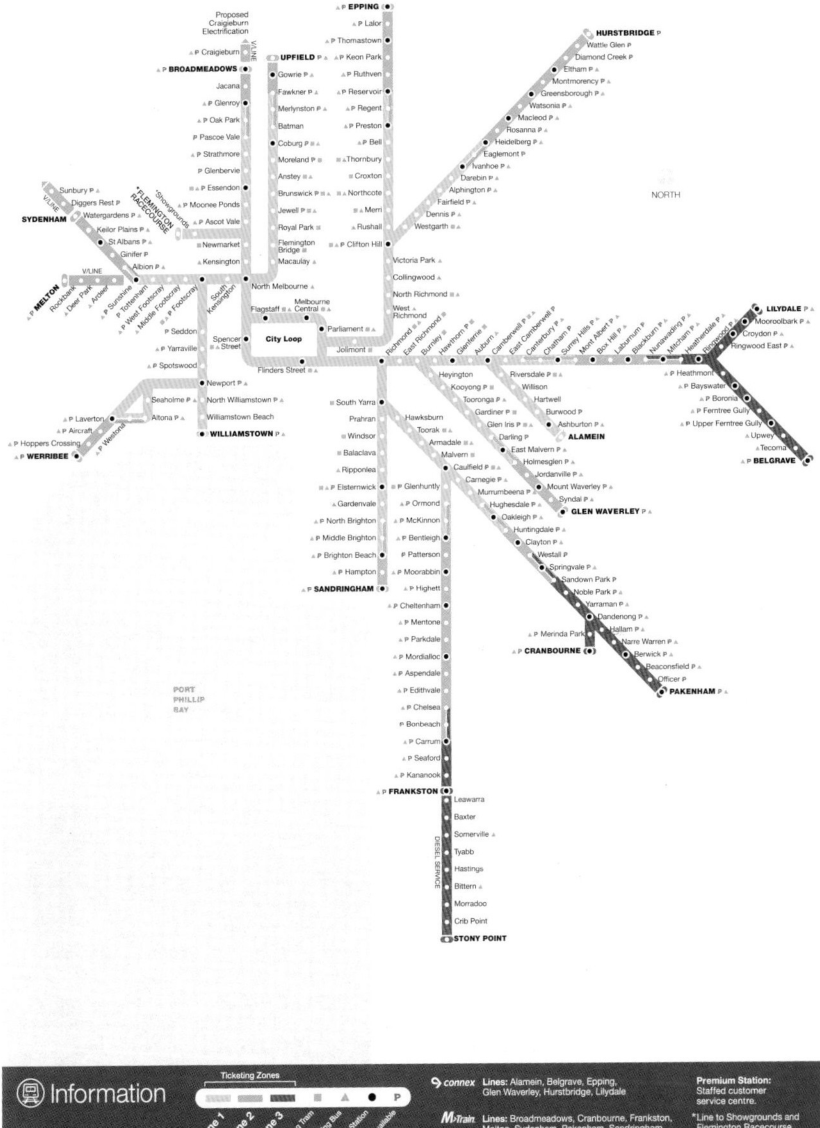

Information

Ticketing Zones

Zone 1 | Zone 2 | Zone 3 | Connecting Train | Connecting Bus | Premium Station | Parking Available

connex Lines: Alamein, Belgrave, Epping, Glen Waverley, Hurstbridge, Lilydale

M>Train Lines: Broadmeadows, Cranbourne, Frankston, Melton, Sydenham, Pakenham, Sandringham, Upfield, Werribee, Williamstown

Premium Station: Staffed customer service centre.

*Line to Showgrounds and Flemington Racecourse, only open for special events.

MELBOURNE TRAM NETWORK

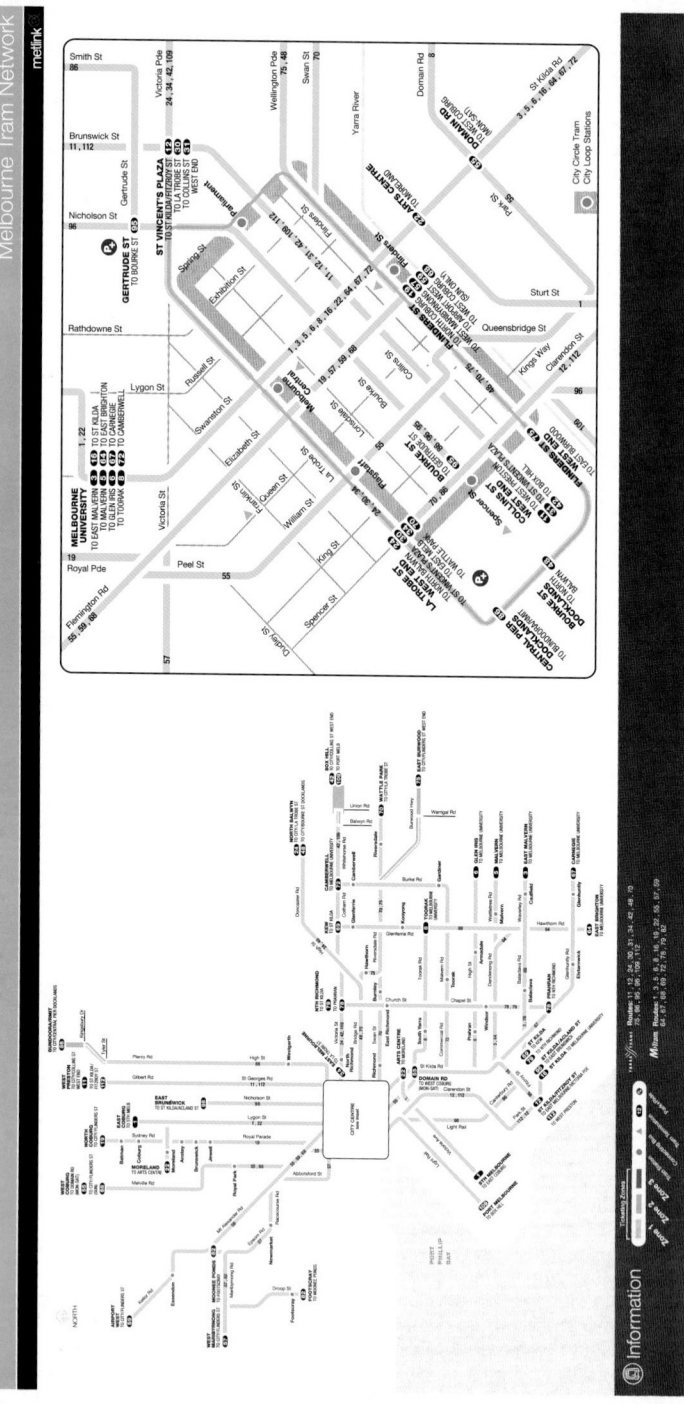

SMITH STREET

Old Kingdom (☎ 9417 2438; 197 Smith St; mains $8-14) We keep coming back for Old Kingdom's speciality, the exquisite Peking duck, one of Melbourne's finest. The expert table-side slicing is a treat in itself, but it wouldn't be so entertaining without the no-fuss charisma of Simon, the head waiter. Order at least a day ahead; one duck ($40) is enough for three.

Richmond
VICTORIA STREET

The stretch of Victoria St between Hoddle and Church Sts is wall-to-wall Asian supermarkets and dirt-cheap Vietnamese restaurants. Tram No 42 or 109 from Collins St gets you there. The food is fresh and authentic, and you can have a huge bowl of soup that's a meal in itself for around $7; main courses generally cost between $8 and $15.

Saigon Rose (Map pp446-8; ☎ 9429 8328; 86 Victoria St; mains $8-15) The Rose is one of a new breed of jazzed-up restaurants in this strip with the fashion of the day: clean-cut décor and natural hues. Sure, it looks good, but don't come hoping to whisper sweet nothings – your partner won't be able to hear, as the acoustics are appalling. The house speciality, crunchy herb-salted prawns, is excellent.

Minh Minh (Map pp446-8; ☎ 9427 7891; 94 Victoria St; mains $6-15) A long-time favourite, with good Thai, Chinese and Vietnamese dishes.

BRIDGE ROAD

This strip has slowly but surely made its presence felt on the culinary map. The restaurants at the city end are tucked between the many fashion boutiques – they make a good spot to take a break from the sound of the cash register 'cha-chinging'. Take tram No 48 or 75 from Flinders St.

Richmond Hill Cafe & Larder (☎ 9421 2808; 48-50 Bridge Rd; lunch $11-24, dinner $26-28) With roomy, understated style, the Cafe & Larder offers friendly but formal service for a well-heeled crowd who flock here for the wonderful breakfast, lunch and dinner menu. Attached is the produce store, featuring a chilly cheese-room lined with rounds from Australia and beyond – cheese lovers, your search is over.

Tofu Shop International (☎ 9429 6204; 78 Bridge Rd; bowls $6-13) Pull up a stool at this enduringly popular, cosy vegetarian café to enjoy the hearty range of dishes. Anything with tofu is good, and one lick of the rose-water ice cream and you'll be hooked.

Further along Bridge Rd are other good eateries:

Djakarta (☎ 9428 7086; 338 Bridge Rd; mains $11-19) Excellent Indonesian cuisine in a charming kitsch setting.

Kanzaman (☎ 9429 3402; 458 Bridge Rd; mains $17-25) Great falafel.

South Yarra & Prahran
TOORAK ROAD & CHAPEL STREET   Map p457

These two streets have a zillion eateries for all budgets. While there are a couple of excellent options (listed below), most are fairly unremarkable, set to catch the passing trade, not the locals (ie repeat visits). Tram No 8 from Swanston St in the city takes you along Toorak Rd.

Da Noi (☎ 9866 5975; 95 Toorak Rd; mains $26-35) Blink and you'll miss wee little Da Noi, with its cosy Parisian café feel. The added bonus to the relaxed ambience here is the Sardinian-inspired food and the anxiety-provoking, but very rewarding menu-less experience – the choices depend on the mood and market buys of the chef. A visit is a must if you're in the area.

Caffe e Cucina (☎ 9827 4139; 581 Chapel St; mains $15-25; ☷ Mon-Sat) You know you're in Chapel St when the style police size you up on the way into this dark, sceney den. Everything from the excellent Italian food and wine to the décor is nearing perfection here, and the coffee is second to none.

COMMERCIAL ROAD   Map p457

The border between South Yarra and Prahran is marked by Commercial Rd, a centre for Melbourne's gay and lesbian community; it has a handful of bars, restaurants and cafés.

Prahran Market (177 Commercial Rd) Pop in here for the market's impressive 'food and wine emporium' (p457).

Sweet Basil (☎ 9827 3390; 209 Commercial Rd; dishes $12-18; ☷ Tue-Sun) This sparsely decorated restaurant serves up delicious twists on Thai dishes with a decent range for vegetarians. You should book ahead.

Red Orange (☎ 9510 3654; 194 Commercial Rd; dishes $14-27) Another good option, offering a mix of tasty dishes inspired by the French and Vietnamese – and everyone in between.

VICTORIA

GREVILLE STREET   Map p457

Greville St runs off Chapel St beside the Prahran Town Hall.

Greville Bar (☎ 9529 4800; 143 Greville St; dishes $20-21) Punters continue to flock here for the sophisticated and timeless wood-panelled interior, the intimate setting, and the extensive and interesting Italian-inspired dinner menu. It's also a great spot for an afternoon tipple, so sit at a window spot and enjoy.

Blakes Cafeteria (☎ 9510 3900; 132 Greville St; dishes $14-19) Snubbing the overdesigned *Vogue Living* interiors common to many of the A-list eateries, Blakes is popular, busy and refreshingly simple, from the no-fuss menu right down to the naked light bulbs. It's an excellent spot to mellow out over a coffee and the papers.

St Kilda

ACLAND STREET   Map p458

The southeast section of Acland St is lined with decent eating and drinking options to suit all budgets – don't miss the cake shops, though you won't of course. The following list includes some of our favourites:

Claypots Seafood Bar (☎ 9534 1282; 213 Barkly St; dishes $10-17) It might not look much from the outside, but the spicy seafood claypots here are delicious and the attentive service and uncluttered style brings punters back again and again. There's a courtyard here, too.

Galleon Cafe (☎ 9534 8934; 9 Carlisle St; dishes $7.50-11) See the boxed text 'Melbourne's Best Breakfasts' (p472) for a full review. Lunch and dinner here are good, too.

Cicciolina (☎ 9525 3333; 130 Acland St; lunch $7.50-15, dinner $18-27) Intimate and dimly lit, this fine Italian eatery is the perfect place to come on a romantic soiree. There's a bar at the back you can enjoy while you wait, which you invariably will – this gem is popular, but doesn't take bookings.

Spud Bar (☎ 9534 8888; 43 Blessington St; potatoes $6-6.50) One in a row of tiny and very cute St Kilda shops. Here you can stuff your spud with as many goodies as you want. It's the perfect meal to take to the beach.

FITZROY STREET   Map p458

Fitzroy St has more iffy takeaways than you can poke a stick at, abutting some of Melbourne's best dining options. Contrast is the name of the game in St Kilda.

Il Fornaio (☎ 9534 2922; 2 Acland St; dishes $8-16) This concrete car park shell retained its edgy industrial feel when it was transformed into this buzzy Italian bakery/café/restaurant. Everything here, from the breads and breakfasts to lunches and dinners, is excellent. And don't get us started on the cakes. Eat outside on balmy summer evenings.

Cafe di Stasio (☎ 9525 3999; 31 Fitzroy St; mains $24-35) Di Stasio has simple has-been '80s décor, but with Italian food this good, dammit, why should it change? Come hungry, so you don't forgo dessert. You may also want to ring ahead to find out if their two-course $20 lunch deals are on offer.

Circa (☎ 9536 1122; 2 Acland St; mains $30-35) Superb and sophisticated, and one of Melbourne's best eateries.

There are some standout cheap eateries along this strip:

Veg Out Time (☎ 9534 0077; 63A Fitzroy St; dishes $7-13) A tiny Asian-inspired vegetarian café.

Cafe A Taglio (☎ 9534 1344; 157 Fitzroy St; pizza slices $4.50-5.50, mains $10-18) The best eat-in or takeaway pizza in St Kilda, served by the slice.

SEASIDE   Map p458

Soul Mama (☎ 9525 3338; St Kilda Baths Complex, Jacka Blvd; bowls $9.90 or $12) Boasting prime real estate, vegetarian Soul Mama resists what lesser (probably meat-eating) mortals would succumb to: inflated prices. Point and choose what you want and they'll serve it up in a bowl. Thanks to the location, it's a winning recipe, even if you might wait eons for a table.

Stokehouse (☎ 9525 5555; 30 Jacka Blvd; downstairs mains $10-20) Great foreshore location with a packed downstairs bar/bistro with outdoor seating (good for people watching) and good fish and chips, and wood-fired pizza. Upstairs, there's fine dining.

Donovans (☎ 9534 8221; 40 Jacka Blvd; mains $24-35) Wonderful and, like the Stokehouse, boasts bay views – it's one of Melbourne's favourites.

Espy Kitchen (☎ 9534 0211; 11 The Esplanade; dishes $10-16) The Esplanade Hotel's kitchen is always busy, with dishes ranging from burgers to lamb vindaloo. Play a game of pool or catch a band after you've eaten.

Williamstown

Williamstown's eating strip, Nelson Pl, is wall-to-wall restaurants, chockers with

VICTORIA

weekend tourists. Most serve adequate cuisine whipped up for tourists (yawn), but there are a few stand-outs.

Breizoz French Creperie (☎ 9397 2300; 139 Nelson Pl; crepes $6-12) Sweet-tooths and savoury lovers should follow their nose to Breizoz, an atmospheric, lofty old bank-cum-crepery. You'll find it near the tourist office.

Sam's Boatshed (☎ 9399 9959; Syme St; mains $14-24) This is notable for the boat-bow bar, the great gourmet pizzas and the live jazz-swing on busy weekend afternoons.

Anchorage (☎ 9397 7799; 34a The Strand; mains $27-29) A recommended seaside option, specialising in seafood and boasting possibly the best bay views in Melbourne.

DRINKING
City Centre   Map pp450–1
Melbourne's thriving bar and pub scene is an important part of the city's cultural landscape. Here are just a few of the central city's better bars:

Robot (☎ 9620 3646; 12 Bligh Pl) Set among humming high rises, cute little Robot is a favourite for all things Japanese: beers, sake and nori rolls for munchy-attacks – even Astro Boy makes an appearance in the décor. Cosy café by day, packed at night.

Phoenix (☎ 9650 4976; 82 Flinders St) This multi-floor hotspot has safari-themed décor and plenty of hidden corners – ready-made dens for gossip. There's something for everyone here thanks to the great vibe and welcoming staff.

e:fiftyfive (☎ 9620 3899; Basement, 55 Elizabeth St) Atmospheric, seductive lighting, comfy couches – 55's very popular and comfy Internet lounge/bar is a great spot to have a beer – or three. It's a travellers' hangout and busy most of the time.

Meyers Place (☎ 9650 8609; 20 Meyers Pl) Cosy and intimate, this hip cubby-hole attracts a 30-something crowd of faithfuls most nights.

Scubar (☎ 9670 2400; 389 Lonsdale St; ☽ Wed-Sat) Retro lovers eat your hearts out – this bunker feels like it's been renovated by a mad collector of retro junk. Attracts a mixed crowd and is a good place for a funk/drum 'n' bass shake of your booty.

Other city centre bars:

Tony Starr's Kitten Club (☎ 9650 2448; 1st fl, 267 Little Collins St) Where you can prop your gorgeous self at the bar for the signature cocktails.

Double Happiness (☎ 9650 4488; 21 Liverpool St; ☽ Mon-Sat) Hip doses of Mao propaganda.
Rue Bebelons (☎ 9663 1700; 267 Little Lonsdale St) An intimate café/bar that's busy by day or night.

Fitzroy   Map pp446–8
Bar Open (☎ 9415 9601; 317 Brunswick St) Usually the last stop of the night, this multi level bar is a haven to all kinds, who are often found lolling or dribbling in the dark corners of this well-worn and very popular spot. Upstairs, bands kick on to all hours.

Standard Hotel (☎ 9419 4793; 293 Fitzroy St) Very Fitzroy, and one of its original pubs, this laid-back locals' drinking hole has occasional live music, good food and a leafy courtyard.

Lambsgo Bar (☎ 8415 0511; 135 Greeves St) Nearly everyone knows each other here, and if they don't, they will by the end of the night – intimate and friendly, this bar is propped by regular barflies. The owner hails from Holland, hence the Dutch groupies and the enviable selection of imported ales.

Night Cat (☎ 9417 0090; 141 Johnston St; cover charge around $8; ☽ Thu-Sun) The Night Cat has a great atmosphere, innumerable retro suspended lamps, cosy corners, and a dance floor so big you can swing several cats. Expect live jazz, soul, blues and funk.

Laundry (☎ 9419 7111; 50 Johnston St; admission free-$6) Nightly DJs and regular live bands play these two funky floors with everything from electro lounge to karaoke, if you dare. Sunday arvo leans towards jazz.

Other recommendations:

Yelza (☎ 9416 2689; 245 Gertrude St; ☽ Wed-Sun) For baroque-overload.
The Old Bar (☎ 9417 4155; 74 Johnston St) A packed and friendly generation-X hangout with the Clash et al spinning nightly.

St Kilda   Map p458
Esplanade Hotel (☎ 9534 0211; 11 The Esplanade) Watch your bags, and mind you don't get stuck to the festering carpets. This atmospheric dive ROCKS, and endures a love-hate relationship with the thousands of Melburnians who have staggered through the doors over decades. Bands play nightly (p478). If you leave Melbourne and haven't been to the Espy, you'll never hear the end of it.

Prince of Wales Hotel (☎ 9536 1111; 29 Fitzroy St) A long-standing institution, this hotel survived a renovation that threatened to

VICTORIA

extinguish its tantalising mix of St Kilda locals, seedy lowlife, a touch of camp, and plenty of rough and tumble. Jam the sidewalks with picnic tables and let the drinking (and ogling) begin. Very St Kilda! See p478 for information about live-music bands.

Other recommendations:

Mink (☎ 9536 1199; 2B Acland St)

Vineyard (☎ 9534 1942; 71A Acland St) 'Who-cares?' service, but an excellent choice for a drink while you watch the sun setting over Luna Park.

Elephant & Wheelbarrow (☎ 9534 7888; 169 Fitzroy St) This backpacker-hangout has *Neighbours* trivia nights on Monday.

ENTERTAINMENT

The best source of 'what's on' information is the *EG (Entertainment Guide)*, which comes with the Friday *Age* newspaper. *Beat* (www.beat.com.au) and *Inpress* are free music and entertainment magazines available from pubs, cafés and venues.

Ticketmaster (☎ 13 61 00; www.ticketmaster .com.au) One of the main booking agencies. Ticketmaster has outlets in Myer stores, major theatres and shopping centres.

Ticketek (☎ 13 28 49; www.ticketek.com) Also handles sporting and theatre events.

Half-Tix (Map pp450-1; ☎ 9650 9420; Town Hall, City; ✆ 10am-2pm Mon & Sat, 11am-6pm Tue-Thu, 11am-6.30pm Fri) Sells half-price tickets on the day of the performance. Make sure you know where you'll be sitting – it rarely sells the best seats at half-price. Cash payments only.

Cinemas

The main chains are Village, Hoyts and Greater Union. The main group of city cinemas is around the intersection of Bourke and Russell Sts. Tickets cost around $13.50/10.50/9.50 per adult/student/child.

OPEN-AIR CINEMA

During the summer months, the wonderful open-air **Moonlight Cinema** (☎ 1900 933 899; www.moonlight.com.au) in the Royal Botanic Gardens screens classic, art house and cult films at sundown. Tickets cost $14/9.50 per adult/child. Bookings are handled by **Ticketek** (☎ 13 28 49), and tickets can be bought at the gate from 7pm onwards. Entry is through Gate D on Birdwood Ave. BYO rug, picnic and wine!

Australian Centre for the Moving Image (ACMI; Map pp450-1; ☎ 8663 2200; Federation Sq, City) It's hard to capture exactly what goes on here, but everything to do with films, video and digital media is explored in the galleries, while the cinema shows experimental, offbeat, genre- and theme-based screenings.

Astor (Map p458; ☎ 9510 1414; cnr Chapel St & Dandenong Rd, East St Kilda) The place for Art Deco nostalgia, cult-classic double bills and brilliant chock-top ice creams.

IMAX Theatre (Map pp450-1; ☎ 9663 5454; Carlton Gardens; 3D adult/child $17/12) Part of the museum complex, you can expect an eye-popping spectacle of specially made 2- and 3-D movies for these giant screens. Great for the kids.

There are many other independent and art house cinemas:

Kino Dendy (Map pp450-1; ☎ 9650 2100; Collins Place, 45 Collins St, city) Cheap tickets Monday: $8.50.

Lumiere (Map pp450-1; ☎ 9639 1055; 108 Lonsdale St, City) 'Bargain Mondays': $5 before 5pm, $7 after 5pm.

Cinema Nova (Map pp446-8; ☎ 9347 5331; 380 Lygon St, Carlton) Cheap tickets Monday: $5 before 4pm, $7.50 after 4pm.

George Cinemas (Map p458; ☎ 9534 6922; 135 Fitzroy St, St Kilda)

Cinema Europa (Map p457; ☎ 1300 555 400; Jam Factory, 500 Chapel St, South Yarra) Tuesday cheap tickets ($9).

Comedy

During the international **Comedy Festival** (www.comedyfestival.com.au) in April, local comedians join international acts to perform in pubs, clubs, theatres and streets.

Comedy Club (Map pp446-8; ☎ 9650 1977; 1/380 Lygon St, Carlton; tickets $28; ✆ from 8.30pm Fri & Sat) This place is Melbourne's main venue for comedy, showcasing international and big-name home-grown talent.

Butterfly Club (Map pp446-8; ☎ 9690 2000; 204 Bank St, South Melbourne; tickets $20; ✆ from 8.30pm Thu-Sun) This terrace house is bursting at the seams with wacky collectables – feast your eyes over a cocktail or three before the show starts at 9.30pm. The eccentric cabaret performances are usually hilarious – just don't sit up the front. Tram No 12 or 112 from Collins St will take you there.

Other recommendations:

Esplanade Hotel (Map p458; ☎ 9534 0211; 11 The Esplanade, St Kilda; tickets $10; ✆ 5pm Sun) A great place to see comedians fall flat on their face. (For more information on the 'Espy' see p459.)

Comic's Lounge (Map pp446-8; ☎ 9348 9488; 26 Errol St, North Melbourne; tickets $10-20; ⏰ from 8.30pm)

Live Music

Melbourne's main music venues are the Rod Laver Arena, the Concert Hall at the **Victorian Arts Centre** (Map p450-1; ☎ 1300 136 166; 100 St Kilda Rd, City), **Festival Hall** (Map pp446-8; ☎ 9329 9699; 300 Dudley St, West Melbourne), the **Forum** (Map pp450-1) and the **Palais Theatre** (Map p458; ☎ 9534 0651; Lower Esplanade, St Kilda). The city's pubs have been the proving ground for many of Australia's best outfits: here acts like AC/DC, INXS and Nick Cave & the Bad Seeds took their first tentative steps towards becoming part of rock's rich tapestry.

To find out who's playing where, look in the *EG*, *Beat* or *Inpress*, or listen to the gig guides on FM radio stations like 3RRR (102.7) or 3PBS (106.7).

Hi-Fi Bar & Ballroom (Map pp446-8; ☎ 9654 7617; www.thehifi.com.au; 125 Swanston St, City; admission $5-18) This is a popular city venue where more-successful home-grown acts perform, as do irregular international shows. Anything goes at the Hi-Fi, from metal, rock, blues and roots to the occasional tribute night.

Arthouse (Map pp446-8; ☎ 9347 3917; cnr Elizabeth & Queensberry Sts, City; admission usually free) A long-time supporter of alternative Oz live music, this venue is ground zero for death metal, thrash, ska... It features everything from Vaginal Carnage to the Nihilists – you get the picture.

Evelyn Hotel (Map pp446-8; ☎ 9419 5500; 351 Brunswick St, Fitzroy; admission free to $15) Perennially popular live-music venue, attracting international and local indie bands and often the first point of call for up-and-coming local acts.

BUSH DOOF by David Burnett

Warbling magpies, crusty camper-vans pottering down dusty bush tracks, blue Australian skies arching overhead...and 120 decibels of thumping electronic bass, throbbing through the gum trees.

This superficially odd amalgamation of urban music and rural escape is at the heart of every 'bush doof' – Melbourne's particular contribution to the world of electronic dance music.

In recent years Melbourne has become the centre of Australia's thriving electronic music scene, most of the action focused on the city's many techno bars and mainstream dance clubs. But, largely unnoticed by the sweaty hordes doing the Melbourne Stomp in giant downtown venues, a parallel scene with a world audience has emerged to make south-eastern Australia one of a handful of 'must visit' destinations for underground DJs from Goa to Tel Aviv.

The bush doof evolved from the outdoor 'raves' of the early 90s – the key ingredients being dance music, a huge sound-system, a few hundred 'ferals' stomping away on a dusty dirt dance floor, trippy lighting (and, as one might expect, the appropriate recreational chemicals). Small hit-and-run dance parties, intended to slip under the radar of the local constabulary, have lately become large, well-organised, multi-stage festivals, often featuring major international acts and two or three days of round-the-clock beats.

Hundreds of visitors from dance-crazy countries like Israel, Japan, Sweden and the UK descend on the doofs of south-eastern Australia during the warmer months, and it can be hard at times to find an Aussie accent among the punters, each sporting an unnaturally wide grin. The summer of 2002–03 alone saw major international psy-trance acts such as Matt Boom, Talamasca and Astral Projection play to dance floors perhaps a tenth the size of their typical European audiences, in beautiful bush settings a few hours' drive from Melbourne.

Earthcore (www.earthcore.com) the largest regular outdoor event near Melbourne, which attracts as many as 10,000 people each November – held its 10th anniversary party in 2003. The **Rainbow Serpent Festival** (www.doofcentral.com), usually held on the Australia Day long weekend in January, is another very popular shindig.

If you're in Melbourne between November and April, keep an eye on the street press for details of upcoming doofs – event organisers often arrange buses or car-pools for those without transport. Tickets range from $15 for a small party to $100 or more for the larger, multiday festivals. Byron Bay (p000), north of Sydney, is another hub for the outdoor dance scene.

Oh, and why 'doof'? 'Cause that's what it sounds like (doof, doof, doof, doof...).

VICTORIA

Other recommendations:

The Corner (☎ 9427 7300; 57 Swan St, Richmond; admission free-$31) Biggish-name international and local acts.

Esplanade Hotel (Map p458; ☎ 9534 0211; 11 Upper Esplanade, St Kilda) Live music nightly and on Sunday after-noons. They're often free, so you can't complain about quality! (For more information on the famous 'Espy' see p459).

Prince of Wales Hotel (Map p458; ☎ 9536 1166; 29 Fitzroy St, St Kilda; admission $12-38) A long-standing institution, offering a good range.

HELLO THERE GORGEOUS! OUT IN QUEER MELBOURNE   *by Justine Dalla Riva*

The Melbourne queer scene is just that, queer! In contrast to Sydney, Melbourne enjoys a more relaxed, less sceney atmosphere. Melbourne is also the queer co-habiting couples capital of Australia. Distances between clusters of venues around the city ensure tight cycle-butts and toned calves remain the fashion, unless of course you're a taxi catcher.

Market Hotel (Map p457; ☎ 9826 0933; 143 Commercial Rd, South Yarra; admission $10-15) Hot, sweaty and semi sophisticated, this club is where the 'grinders' end up, usually on the dance floor until morning.

Peel Hotel (☎ 9419 4762; cnr Peel & Wellington Sts, Collingwood; admission Fri & Sat $10 after 10pm) An infamous institution, where once an enormous phallus used to hang over the main bar, now the Peel lets the 'average' guy do his own thing on the dance floor.

Prince of Wales (Map p458; ☎ 9536 1177; www.theprince.com.au; 29 Fitzroy St, St Kilda; girl bar $15) This notorious den of inequity houses one of the hottest 'girl bar' nights in Melbourne (upstairs one Friday a month, check the website for dates) and a downstairs back bar with a mixed male crowd throughout the week.

Glasshouse Hotel (☎ 9419 4748; 51 Gipps St, Collingwood; admission free-$10) Like some of the girls propped up at the bar, this venue is the mainstay of the fickle lesbian scene. Pick-ups and pool cues are all the rage.

Xchange Hotel (Map p457; ☎ 9867 5144; 119 Commercial Rd, South Yarra; admission $5-8) Boy-band dropout meets senior sleaze in this popular pub/Internet/video/TV/pole-dancing venue. Something for everyone makes the Xchange worth a visit.

DT's (☎ 9428 5724; 164 Church St, Richmond; admission free) From the outside DT's looks deserted, but inside it's a Shangri-la. The industrial strength airconditioner comes in handy on the rather hot Sunday 'spin and win' drinks nights.

Builders Arms Hotel (Map pp446-8; ☎ 9419 0818; cnr Gertrude & Gore Sts, Fitzroy; admission free) Every Thursday, Q+A night becomes one long queue, as young gay things wait patiently to mingle for an hour or three. Be early, but not too early!

Greyhound Hotel (Map p458; ☎ 9534 4189; 1 Brighton Rd, St Kilda; admission $5-7 Sat & Sun) Kylie Minogue eat your heart out, the Drag Queens here have to be seen to be believed! Saturdays are great nights to cut your teeth on many a thirty-something bicep.

Gay Trade Bar (☎ 9417 6700; 9 Peel St, Collingwood; admission free) Relax at this all-week venue, with themed cheap-drinks nights like 'toss the boss' and expensive professional bar dancers.

Laird (☎ 9417 2832; 149 Gipps St, Abbotsford; admission free) This men-only 'spit and polish' leather bar runs throughout the week with a variety of DJs on offer.

Jackie O (Map p458; ☎ 9537 0377; 204 Barkly St, St Kilda; mains $11-20) If sipping, sucking, and licking are your thing, then you can't go past the 'first lady of Acland St' for an aperitif, accommodating staff and a relaxed dining atmosphere. No, this is not a sauna.

The **ALSO Foundation** (www.also.org.au) organises some of the hottest dance parties, including **Red Raw** and **WinterDaze**. ALSO is responsible for **Moist @ Wet on Wellington** (☎ 9827 4999; 162 Wellington St, Collingwood), the first women-only pool party and sauna night; check the website. See Festivals & Special Events (p463) for more information on gay and lesbian events.

To stay up to date with what's on, listen to **JOY FM** (www.joy.org.au), Melbourne's gay and lesbian radio station at 94.9 FM, or pick up one of the local street-press publications: **Melbourne Community Voice** (www.mcv.net.au) and **Bnews** (www.bnews.net.au). Drop into **Hares & Hyenas bookshop** (Map p457; ☎ 9824 0110; 135 Commercial Rd, South Yarra) for all your literary needs.

Justine is a self-confessed cable-addicted, pool-playing, sensitive lesbian bar-hopper.

FOLK, SOUL, JAZZ & BLUES

From January to March the Melbourne Zoo (p455) has a **Zoo Twilights Festival**, open-air sessions with jazz, Latin, swing – you name it. Admission is included in zoo entry, so you can make a day and a night of it. Performances run from 6.30pm to 9.30pm Thursday to Sunday all January, and from Friday to Sunday from February to 9 March.

Rainbow Hotel (Map pp446-8; ☎ 9419 4193; 27 St David St, Fitzroy; admission free-$6) A laid-back, backstreet pub, which fires up to a steamy dance-pit with everything from jazz, blues and Cajun to funk and soul. Attracts a 30- to 40-something crowd. Lots of fun.

Bennetts Lane Jazz Club (Map p450-1; ☎ 9663 2856; 25 Bennetts Lane, City; admission $10-15) A quintessentially dim stalwart on the Melbourne jazz scene.

Dizzy's Jazz Bar (☎ 9428 1233; 90 Swan St, Richmond; ☼ Wed-Sat; admission free-$15) Large and spacious with a good bar, this smoke-free venue is a great spot to blow your horn.

Dan O'Connell Hotel (Map pp446-8; ☎ 9347 1502; 225 Canning St, Carlton) An Irish pub with folk/blues bands most nights. It's home to the mother of all St Patrick's Day parties.

Nightclubs

Melbourne's diverse club scene is a mixed bag. What's here today might be gone tomorrow.

ALTERNATIVE CLUBS

Melbourne has a vibrant alternative club scene.

Honkytonks (Map pp450-1; ☎ 9662 4555; Duckboard Pl, City; admission free-$10; ☼ Wed-Sun) If you manage to find the place, you'll be rewarded with ace views over Flinders St, an eclectic interior, a never-ending cocktail list and some of the best DJs in the business. It's boisterous and fun, so go find out what all the fuss is about.

Lounge (Map pp450-1; ☎ 9663 2916; 1st fl, 243 Swanston St, City; admission free-$6) Bar, café (p470) and art space that's been host to the alternative scene for well over a decade, and more than a few boozy boy-meets-girl rendezvous. There are pool tables here, too.

Laundry (Map pp450-1; ☎ 9419 7111; 50 Johnston St, Fitzroy; admission free-$6) Nightly DJs play everything from electro lounge to the latest techno beats. Attracts an early-20s crowd (also see p475).

Revolver Upstairs (Map p457; ☎ 9521 5985; 229 Chapel St, Prahran; admission $6-12) Highly popular cavernous venue with a 20-something crowd, art-covered walls (refreshingly grungy for Chapel St) and an action-packed program featuring DJs, bands, performances and film nights. There's food here, too – you'll need the sustenance if you plan to make the most of the 24-hour opening hours on weekends.

Club UK (Map pp450-1; ☎ 9663 2075; 169 Exhibition St; admission free-$5) and **Elephant & Wheelbarrow** (Map pp450-1; ☎ 9534 7888; 94-96 Bourke St, City), close by, both cater to homesick lovers of all things British. There are oodles of drink deals guaranteed to get you sloshed, so don't be surprised to find a drunkard's hand on your bottom.

MAINSTREAM CLUBS

Metro Nightclub (Map pp450-1; ☎ 9663 4288; 20-30 Bourke St, City; admission $8-10; ☼ Thu-Sat) This ginormous club has eight bars and two dance floors over three levels pumped with retro '80s, funky '70s and doofing '90s music. Goo (alternative, supposedly) on Thursday and Pop (Top 40) on Saturday are the busiest nights.

Mercury Lounge (Map pp446-8; ☎ 9292 5480; Level 3, Crown Entertainment Complex, Southbank; admission around $10) With DJs every night and a host of live local and international acts, there's all the razzamatazz and beautiful people you'd expect from Crown.

Palace (Map p458; ☎ 9534 0655; Lower Esplanade, St Kilda; admission around $10) Huge complex with everything from retro sounds to commercial dance beats. Twister on Saturday is the best night by far, and you can party on to greet the birds at 7am.

Sport

AUSTRALIAN RULES

Australian Football League (AFL; www.afl.com.au) runs Aussie rules football – otherwise known as 'the footy'. It's incredibly popular, with games at the **MCG** (p455) regularly pulling crowds of 50,000 to 80,000; the Grand Final on the last Saturday in September fills the ground with more than 90,000 fans. The sheer energy of the barracking at a big game is exhilarating, and despite the fervour, crowd violence is almost unknown – especially now that there are alcohol-free areas at the grounds.

WINNERS, LOSERS & THE RULES OF THE GAME *by John Ryan & David McClymont*

It's virtually impossible to say a bad word about the **Australian Football League (AFL)** Grand Final, the highlight of Melbourne's sporting calendar. Trying to tell a Melburnian you're not interested in the footy is like trying to tell a lemming not to throw itself off a cliff. If you find yourself in the city on the last weekend in September, the most important day of the year, just give in to the mayhem. Pick a team, buy a scarf, wave a flag, have a beer, watch the match on TV, celebrate with the winners and commiserate with the losers. Come Sunday, the madness will be over for another year.

To the novice, the term 'rules' might seem to be stretching the truth. One could easily be excused for thinking that the sight of 36 men hurling themselves after the oval-shaped ball is an unsophisticated free-for-all. But to the initiated, every move, play and umpiring decision carries enormous weight and even ritual: Aussie rules isn't described as Melbourne's main religion for nothing.

The rules are a mishmash of rugby, Gaelic football and total insanity. Players can kick or punch the ball (handpass), but not throw it. They can run with the ball, as long as they bounce it every 15 metres. They can tackle, bump and 'shirtfront' (an especially-popular manoeuvre involving the near-removal of an opponent's head), but they mustn't push.

If a player catches the ball after it's been kicked (a 'mark'), they can stop play and the ball is then played from the point where the mark occurred. A tackled player must attempt to get rid of the ball (if someone gets tackled, just scream 'baaaallll!!!!' – don't worry why). All of these – and a hundred other little regulations – combine to create one of the most athletic, fast and physical sports in existence. If you're lucky enough to catch a blockbuster at the 'G, you'll be a convert quicker than you can scream 'You £%@* maggot!'

To find out more about Aussie rules and the AFL, check out www.afl.com.au.

Being the shrine of Aussie rules, the MCG is the best place to see a match, although the new Telstra Dome has poached its fair share of games. Tickets can be bought at the ground for most games for around $17.60/2.20 per adult/child. Seats can be booked (this might be necessary at big games) through Ticketmaster for about $29.80/5.30. Note: you can't use an umbrella at the MCG.

CRICKET

In summer, an international **test match**, **one-day internationals**, the national cricket competition and local district matches are played at the MCG. General admission to international one-day matches is around $28.50; reserved seats start around $38. Finals cost more. Head for the MCG on Boxing Day, when tens of thousands turn up for the first day of the international cricket test match.

HORSE RACING

Melbourne's horse races are held at Flemington, Caulfield, Moonee Valley and Sandown racecourses.

The **Melbourne Cup** (www.vrc.net.au), one of the world's great horse races, is the feature event of Melbourne's Spring Racing Carnival, which runs through October and climaxes with the Melbourne Cup Carnival on the first Tuesday in November. The cup brings the whole country to a standstill. Entry costs $35, or book reserved seats through Ticketmaster from $105. The Thursday after the Cup, Oaks Day, once a 'ladies'-only event, is now almost as popular – with both sexes – as the Cup. Entry costs $30.

MOTOR SPORTS

Fans of blokes (and the odd 'sheila') driving in circles very fast will be pleased to know that the **Australian Formula One Grand Prix** (www.grandprix.com.au) is held at Albert Park in March. The **Australian Motorcycle Grand Prix** (www.grandprix.com.au/bikes) runs at Phillip Island in October.

RUGBY

Rugby Union has been slow to catch on in Melbourne, but despite this the MCG and Telstra Dome attract huge crowds to international matches. **Rugby League**, on the other hand, has made some impact on Melbourne's sport-mad public. **Melbourne Storm** (www.melbournestorm.com.au), the only Melbourne side in the national league, won the Grand Final in 1999 after competing in the league for only a couple of years, heralding wild celebrations that were evidence of the game's rise in popularity.

April to September is the season for both codes. Melbourne Storm's home matches are played at Olympic Park.

SOCCER

Soccer has a fairly strong following in Melbourne with two teams competing in the national competition. The **Victorian Soccer Federation** (www.soccervictoria.org.au) gives details on venues and matches.

TENNIS

For two weeks every January the Melbourne Park Tennis Centre on Batman Ave hosts the **Australian Open** (www.ausopen.com.au), with top players from around the world competing in the year's first grand slam tournament. Tickets for the Open range from around $30 for early rounds to $100 for finals.

Theatre

The excellent **Melbourne's Online Theatre Magazine** (www.stageleft.com.au) has reviews of what's on in the city. In summer watch out for open-air productions in the Royal Botanic Gardens (p454).

Victorian Arts Centre (Map pp450-1; ☎ 9281 8000; 100 St Kilda Rd, City) Melbourne's major venue for the performing arts (p452).

La Mama (Map pp446-8; ☎ 9347 6142; 205 Faraday St, Carlton) An intimate forum for experimental, innovative theatre – and a long-standing Carlton institution.

CUB Malthouse (Map pp446-8; ☎ 9685 5111; 113 Sturt St, Southbank) Established Aussie playwrights are featured by the Playbox theatre company, resident at the Malthouse.

Princess Theatre (Map pp450-1; ☎ 9299 9800; 163 Spring St, City) This beautifully renovated landmark theatre is the venue for superslick musicals.

Regent Theatre (Map pp450-1; ☎ 9299 9500; 191 Collins St, City) Another gorgeous venue for musicals.

SHOPPING

Shopping in Melbourne is a highlight for many visitors, with the city and inner suburbs of Fitzroy, Richmond, Prahran and South Yarra shopping hot spots par excellence. Charge up your cards and go.

Standing side by side, **Myer** (Map pp450-1; ☎ 9661 1111; 314 Bourke St, City) and **David Jones** (Map pp450-1; ☎ 9643 2222; 310 Bourke St, City) are the city's main department stores, dominating much of the Bourke St Mall.

Aboriginal Art

Melbourne has a handful of quality Aboriginal art galleries, with artwork from all over the country.

Aboriginal Gallery of Dreamings (Map pp450-1; ☎ 9650 7291; 73-75 Bourke St, City) A good selection of traditional works and well-versed staff to fill in the stories behind each painting; you'll be able to get something decent with $500.

Kimberley Art Gallery (Map pp450-1; ☎ 9654 5890; 76 Flinders Lane, City) The art is less conventional, but this gallery has a good selection of up-and-coming younger artists.

Koorie Heritage Trust (Map pp450-1; ☎ 9639 6555; 234-236 Flinders Lane, City) Promotes Koori culture in the local region and has a fine collection of art for sale.

PAMPER YOURSELF

Travelling can take it out of you, and even if it doesn't, you may still need to treat yourself.

Japanese Bathhouse (☎ 9419 0268; www.japanesebathhouse.com; 59 Cromwell St, Collingwood; adult/child $24/11; ☻ noon-9pm Tue-Fri, noon-6pm Sat & Sun) Take your weary bones to this very authentic bathhouse for the ultimate in tranquil relaxation. You don't need to bring anything, but you should allow at least two hours and you must book ahead. A half-hour shiatsu session and bath costs $65 per adult. Take tram No 42 or 109 from Collins St and get off at stop 17.

Clothing

Big name labels and fashion clobber are best found in the **City** along Collins St (between Swanston St & Elizabeth Sts), in **Australia on Collins** (Map pp450-1; 121-260 Collins St, City), a largish shopping centre, and in the Bourke St Mall. If you're after something unique, say, something by an Australian designer, then head to Little Collins St (the part between Swanston and Russell Sts), Howey Pl, Centre Way or the Block Arcade. Greville St in **Prahran** (Map p457) is the place for hip

---

TO MARKET, TO MARKET

Melburnians love a good bargain, and what better way to catch one than at the many colourful markets?

Queen Victoria Market (Map pp450-1; ☎ 9320 5822; cnr Elizabeth & Victoria Sts, City; ☽ 6am-2pm Tue & Thu, 6am-6pm Fri, 6am-3pm Sat, 9am-4pm Sun) The mother of all Melbourne markets with souvenir stalls, cheap clothing, shoes and even pet supplies – if you can't find it here it doesn't exist. (See p451 for a full review of this icon.)

Camberwell Market (Station St, Camberwell; ☽ dawn-noon Sun) A dirt-cheap and very popular trash and treasure market. Just $3 for a good pair of heels? Yes please. Get there early for the bargains. It's three minutes' walk from the Camberwell train station.

Esplanade Art & Craft Market (The Esplanade, St Kilda; ☽ 10am-4pm Sun) A popular art and craft market where sometimes there's no accounting for taste!

South Melbourne Market (Map pp446-8; ☎ 9209 6295, cnr Cecil & Coventry Sts, South Melbourne; ☽ 8am-2pm Wed, 8am-6pm Fri, 8am-4pm Sat & Sun) A popular suburban market selling everything from fruit to clothing, knick-knacks and homewares.

Prahran Market (Map p457; ☎ 8290 8220; 177 Commercial Rd, Prahan; ☽ dawn-5pm Tue & Sat, dawn-6pm Thu & Fri) Quality fruit and vegetables and a very good deli section.

If supermarkets are more your style try **Coles Express** (2 Elizabeth St, City; ☽ 24hr) and **IGA Xpress Supermarket** (90 Spencer St, City; ☽ 5am-1am). These are great for night owls with the munchies and city dwellers alike.

---

young designer stores, second-hand vintage and retro gear, and a couple of designer outlets (up the train station end). Brunswick St, **Fitzroy** (Map pp446-8), offers a similar range of hip designer, retro and street wear and some club gear as well. Johnston, Gertrude and Smith Sts have some up-and-coming designer shops.

Bridge Rd, **Richmond**, between Punt Rd and Church St, is a teeming girl-zone from dusk till dawn, chock-a-block with the latest mainstream fashion at budget prices. Sharpen your elbows and dive in. The Queen Victoria Market in the city is another good choice for cheap clothing.

Chapel St in **South Yarra** (Map p457) has long had a reputation as Melbourne's premier style strip, and the street continues to be one of the most popular fashion hangouts for beautiful people. Expect top labels and top prices, though there are a few cheap places, too.

Fashion junkies may want to consider the pink bus **Shopping Spree tours** (☎ 9596 6600) – $65 for all the outlets your credit card can handle.

Duty-Free

Duty-free shops abound in the city centre. Remember that a duty-free item may not have had much duty on it anyway and could be cheaper in an ordinary shop.

Film & Photography

There's a cluster of camera shops along Elizabeth St between Bourke and Lonsdale Sts.

Michael's Camera, Video, Digital (Map pp450-1; ☎ 9672 2224; cnr Elizabeth & Lonsdale Sts, City) Helpful staff; it stocks a huge range of accessories, new and second-hand cameras (SLR and digital), video-cams, binoculars and more.

Vintech Camera Service Centre (Map pp450-1; ☎ 9602 1820; 5th floor, 358 Lonsdale St, City) Vintech has a good reputation.

Music

JB Hi-Fi (Map pp450-1; ☎ 9670 3611; 289 Elizabeth St, City) Super-busy store that caters to all tastes and is Melbourne's discount CD mecca.

Borders South Yarra (Map p457; ☎ 9824 2299; 500 Chapel St, South Yarra); Carlton (Map pp446-8; ☎ 9348 0222; 380 Lygon St, Carlton) The only selection that matches JB Hi-Fi.

Missing Link (Map pp450-1; ☎ 9654 5507; 262 Flinders Lane, City) An indie evergreen.

Au Go Go (Map pp450-1; ☎ 9670 0677; 2 Somerset Pl, City) Another staple of the indie scene, with plenty of pre-loved stuff, too.

Gaslight (Map pp450-1; ☎ 9650 9009; 85 Bourke St, City) Boasts a wider and more mainstream selection.

Basement Discs (Map pp450-1; ☎ 9654 1110; 24 Block Pl, City) The best selection of jazz, blues and world music, and free concerts some lunch times (from 12.45pm to 1.15pm).

Discurio (Map pp450-1; ☎ 9600 1488; 113 Hardware Lane, City) A close runner-up to Basement Discs, it also stocks classical.

Greville Records (Map p457; ☎ 9510 3012; 152 Greville St, Prahran) Gets the nod for vinyl and imports.

Outdoor Gear

Ground zero for quality outdoor gear in Melbourne is along Little Bourke St between Elizabeth St and Hardware Lane. Here you'll find at least half a dozen stores, including **Bogong Equipment** (Map pp450-1; ☎ 9600 0599; 374 Little Bourke St, City) and the ever-popular **Kathmandu** (Map pp450-1; ☎ 9642 1942; 360 Bourke St, City), both good options, selling trekking and camping gear. Along Hardware Lane you'll find **Auski** (Map pp450-1; ☎ 9670 1412; 9 Hardware Lane, City), which stocks a good range of ski wear and equipment, and **Rider+** (Map pp450-1; ☎ 9670 5450; 17 Hardware Lane, City), with not as much ski gear, but surf and skate gear, too. You can hire snow gear at both these places. A little further afield in Collingwood, it's worth mentioning **Recycled Recreation** (Map pp446-8; ☎ 9416 4066; 110 Smith St). It has a large range of boots, tents, outdoor wear and backpacks, new and used.

Sam Bear (Map pp450-1; ☎ 9663 2191; 225 Russell St, City), a Melbourne institution since the 1950s, is a great place to go for tough, durable work clothing and footwear, offering brands such as Blundstone, King Gee and Hard Yakka. It's also good for camping and walking gear.

Australia produces some of the world's best surfing equipment and surf/streetwear. Check out **Surf Dive 'N' Ski** (Map pp450-1; ☎ 9650 1039; 209-215 Bourke St, City) to see some of the best of what's on offer.

GETTING THERE & AWAY

International and interstate flights operate out of Melbourne airport, long-distance trains run from **Spencer St station** (Map pp450-1), and there are two long-distance bus terminals – the Spencer St coach terminal for V/Line and Firefly services, and the **Melbourne Transit Centre** (Map pp450-1) for McCafferty's/Greyhound services on Franklin St.

The *Spirit of Tasmania* ferry run by **TT Lines** (☎ 13 20 10; www.spiritoftasmania.com.au) departs from Port Melbourne's Station Pier each night at 9pm bound for Devonport,

Tasmania (10 hours). One-way adult fares range from $105 to $257. There are discounts for children, seniors and students. The cost for vehicles depends on the size of the vehicle and the season. The fare for a standard car (5m or less in length) or a campervan is $55 in peak season, and is free for the rest of the year.

GETTING AROUND
To/From the Airport

Melbourne airport is at Tullamarine, 22km northwest, or roughly half an hour from the city centre. A taxi between the airport and city centre costs about $40.

Skybus (☎ 9670 7992) operates a 24-hour shuttle service between the airport and Spencer St coach terminal in the city centre (adult/child $13/6 one way). Buses depart every 15 minutes from 7am to 6.30pm, half-hourly until 12.30am, hourly from 1am until 5am, and half-hourly until 7am. Buy tickets from the driver; bookings are not usually necessary. If there's room, you can take your bicycle, as long as the front wheel's been removed. The **Peninsula Airport Bus** (☎ 9783 1199; adult/child one way $16/13) runs between St Kilda and the airport.

Public transport between the city and the airport is limited. You could take tram No 59 from Elizabeth St to Moonee Ponds Junction – from there **Tullamarine Bus Lines** (☎ 9338 3817) runs bus Nos 478 and 479 to the airport twice daily; bus No 500 runs to the airport from Broadmeadows train station. You can do either trip on a Zone 1 and 2 Metcard. If you make the connections, you could do it on a two-hour ticket ($4.60). If not, you will need an all-day ticket ($8.50), which doesn't cost much less than the Skybus fare and is lots more hassle.

Bicycle

Melbourne's a great city for cycling. Bike paths run around Port Phillip Bay from Port Melbourne to Mordialloc, and up the Yarra for more than 20km – there are also plenty of others. The Melbourne visitor centre provides information and maps on city paths, and the *Melway* street directory is also useful. You may also want to pick up a copy of *Bike Rides Around Melbourne* ($32).

Bicycles can be taken on suburban trains (free) during off-peak times.

Tram tracks are a major hazard: your wheel can get stuck in them and they're slippery, so take care.

Quite a few places have bicycles for hire, including helmet and lock. Try these:

St Kilda Cycles (Map p458; ☎ 9534 3074; 11 Carlisle St, St Kilda) $20 per day.

Hire a Bicycle (Map pp450-1; ☎ 0412-616 633; Alexandra Gardens, near Princes Bridge, City) $17 for two hours.

Borsari Cycles (Map p446-8; ☎ 9347 4100; 193 Lygon St, Carlton) $30 per day.

Car

CAR & TRAM

Treat trams with caution. You can only overtake a tram on the left and must always stop behind a tram when it halts to drop or collect passengers (except where there are central 'islands' for passengers).

Melbourne has a notoriously confusing road rule, known as the 'hook turn'. To turn right at many major intersections in the city centre, you have to pull to the left, wait until the light of the street you're turning into changes from red to green, then complete the turn. Look for the black-and-white hook-turn sign hanging from overhead cables.

Car Rental

Avis (☎ 13 63 33; www.avis.com.au), **Budget** (☎ 1300 362 848; www.budget.com.au; 398 Elizabeth St, City), **Hertz** (☎ 13 30 39; www.hertz.com.au) and **Thrifty** (☎ 1300 367 227; www.thrifty.com.au; 390 Elizabeth St, City) have desks at Melbourne airport, and you can find plenty of other outlets in the city. For disabled travellers, Avis and Hertz provide hand-controlled vehicles.

The *Yellow Pages* lists car-rental firms, including local operators who rent newer cars but don't have the nationwide network (and overheads) of the big operators. Try **Atlas** (☎ 9663 6233; www.atlasrent.com.au).

Rent-a-wreck-style operators rent older vehicles at much lower rates. Their costs and conditions vary widely and some companies only allow you to travel within a certain distance of the city, typically 100km. You might try **Rent-a-Bomb** (☎ 9428 0088; www.rentabomb.com.au; 507 Bridge Rd, Richmond) and **Ugly Duckling** (☎ 9525 4010; 108 St Kilda Rd, St Kilda).

CITY LINK

Melbourne's **City Link** (☎ 13 26 29) tollway system has two main links. The southern link runs from the South Eastern Fwy at Toorak Rd, and branches to the southeastern edge of the city centre at Exhibition St, or to Kings Way. The western link runs from the Calder Fwy intersection with the Tullamarine Fwy to the West Gate Fwy, on the western edge of the city centre.

The most annoying thing about City Link isn't the cost but the inconvenience. Tolls are 'collected' from a transponder in the car (an e-tag), which you obtain after opening a City Link account. Motorists are allowed up to 12 day passes per 12 months; these are the best option for visitors. You can buy a day pass ($9.10) at a post office or by telephoning City Link – if you go through the toll without a pass, you must ring within 24 hours or you'll cop a hefty fine. Car-rental companies have various options to cover toll charges.

PARKING

If you're lucky enough to find a parking space in the city centre, you'll pay about $2 an hour. Watch out for clearway zones that operate during peak hours; parking in one means big fines and having your car towed away. Inner residential areas often have 'resident only' parking zones, or parking restrictions that run until midnight, rather than 5pm or 6pm as elsewhere. This makes parking near nightlife areas in Fitzroy or St Kilda nigh impossible – take a tram or a taxi.

Note that a sign telling you you're allowed to park for, say, two hours, reads 2P.

There are more than 70 car parks in the city. Rates vary but you'll pay around $7 an hour, $24 a day during the week – less on weekends. You'll pay around $8.50 flat rate for parking after 6pm (usually until midnight).

Ferry

Williamstown Ferries (☎ 9682 9555; www.williamstownferries.com.au) Operates ferries between the city and Gem Pier in Williamstown, with regular departures from Southgate (berth 7) between 10.30am and 5pm daily. The return fare for adults/children is $18/9. You can ask to be dropped at the *Polly Woodside* (p453) and Scienceworks (p453). On weekends there's a ferry between St Kilda Pier and Williamstown, departing from St Kilda hourly between 11.30am and 4.30pm, and departing from Williamstown hourly from 11am to 5pm. The fare is $10/5.

Melbourne River Cruises (☎ 9629 7233) Also runs at least three times a day between Federation Square and Gem Pier, Williamstown ($24.20/13.20 return).

Public Transport

The public transport system of buses, trains and trams is privatised. For timetable and fare information, contact the **Met Information Centre** (☎ 13 16 38; www.victrip.com.au). The **Met Shop** (Town Hall, Swanston St, City; ⏱ 8.30am-5pm Mon-Fri, 9am-3pm Sat) has information and sells souvenirs and tickets. Staffed train stations also have some information.

After the trams, buses and trains stop running (around midnight), NightRider buses depart from the **City Square** (Map pp450–1) in Swanston St for many suburban destinations. The fare is a flat $6.

BUS

Generally, buses continue from where the trains finish, or go to places such as hospitals, universities, suburban shopping centres and the outer suburbs, not reached by other services.

BUYING A TICKET

Small businesses, such as newspaper kiosks and milk bars, sell most tickets but not Short Trip tickets. Machines on trams sell Short Trip, two-hour and all-day tickets, and only take coins. Machines at train stations sell many types of tickets but not Short Trip tickets. Large machines at train stations take coins, some notes and some bank cash cards; small machines at stations take coins only. Some stations have booking offices that sell most tickets. On buses you can buy Short Trip, two-hour and all-day tickets from the driver.

DISABLED TRAVELLERS

A *Mobility Map* is available from the visitor centre at Federation Square, or check the **Access Melbourne website** (www.accessmelbourne .vic.gov.au). **Travellers' Aid Disability Access Centre** (☎ 9654 7690; 2nd fl, 169 Swanston St, City; ⏱ 9am-5pm Mon-Fri, 11am-4pm Sat & Sun) offers assistance, including wheelchair recharging.

TAXI

The main taxi ranks in the city are outside the major hotels, outside Flinders St and Spencer St train stations, on the corner of William and Bourke Sts, and on Lonsdale St outside Myer. Finding an empty taxi in the city on Friday or Saturday night can be extremely difficult.

There are several taxi companies, but all taxis are painted yellow. Major companies include **Embassy** (☎ 13 17 55) and **Silver Top** (☎ 13 10 08). All companies charge the same fares. Accessible taxis for disabled travellers are plentiful, but you'll need to book ahead.

TICKETS & ZONES

There's an array of tickets and an unpopular automated ticketing system. Once you've bought the ticket, it must be validated for each trip. Roving customer service officers are likely to fine you if you haven't managed to buy and validate a ticket.

The metropolitan area is divided into three zones. Zone 1 covers the city and inner suburbs (including St Kilda), and most visitors won't need to venture beyond that unless they're going right out of town.

Zone 1 tickets cost $2.70 for two hours, $5.20 for all day and $23 for a week (longer periods are available). You can break your journey and change between trams, buses and trains with these tickets.

Short Trip tickets ($1.80) allow you to travel two sections on buses or trams in Zone 1, or you can buy a Short Trip 10 Card ($15), which gives you 10 short trips. You can't break your journey on a Short Trip ticket.

TRAIN

Suburban trains are faster than trams or buses, but they don't go to many inner suburbs. Flinders St train station is the main terminal.

During the week, most trains start running at 5am and finish at midnight, and should run every three to eight minutes during peak hour, every 15 to 20 minutes at other times and every 40 minutes after 7pm. On Saturday they run every half-hour from 5am to midnight, while on Sunday it's every 40 minutes from 8am to 11pm.

The city service includes an underground City Loop, which is a quick way to get from one side of town to the other.

TRAM

Tram routes cover the city and inner suburbs. Tram stops are numbered out from the city centre. There are also 'light-rail' services

VICTORIA

FREE CITY-CIRCLE TRAM

Every 12 minutes or so between 10am and 6pm, free city-circle trams (painted burgundy and gold) travel a loop along Flinders, Spring and La Trobe Sts to Footscray Rd (near NewQuay), and then back along Flinders St.

to some suburbs, including St Kilda, running along disused rail lines.

In theory, trams run along most routes every six to eight minutes during peak hour and every 12 minutes at other times. Services are less frequent on weekends and late at night.

Be extremely careful getting on and off a tram: by law, cars are supposed to stop when a tram stops to pick up and drop off passengers, but that doesn't always happen.

AROUND MELBOURNE

There are some excellent excursions within an hour or so of the city. If you seek forested ranges, head east to the Dandenongs or the Yarra Valley, or northwest to picnic at Mt Macedon and Hanging Rock. Animal lovers will enjoy Phillip Island's famous penguins, though Healesville Sanctuary and Victoria's Open Range Zoo are also worth seeing. While tipplers indulge at the Yarra Valley wineries, sun lovers can bask at the rugged ocean beaches of the Mornington and Bellarine Peninsulas.

MELBOURNE TO GEELONG

It's a one-hour drive southwest down the Princes Fwy (M1) to Geelong. If you can, leave Melbourne over the soaring West Gate Bridge – the views over the city are simply exhilarating.

The fabulous **Victoria's Open Range Zoo** (☎ 03-9731 9600; www.zoo.org.au; K Rd, Werribee; adult/child $16/7.80; ☼ 9am-5pm) is about 30 minutes from Melbourne. A 50-minute safari-bus tour takes you to see the animals, many of them endangered but successfully bred in captivity here. If you don't want to go home, go bush with a camping 'Slumber Safari' ($175/160 per adult/child), and wake overlooking African animals grazing on the grassy plains below.

Adjacent to the zoo is the **Werribee Park Mansion** (☎ 13 19 63; adult/child $10.50/5.40; ☼ 10am-4.30pm), an overgrown 1870s mansion surrounded by formal gardens. Don't miss the 'Bachelor's Wing' billiard room complete with hippo-head stool, and the macabre art in the garden Grotto. Follow your nose to the **Victorian Rose Garden** (admission free) close by, well worth strolling through. A joint ticket to the zoo and mansion costs $24/12 per adult/child.

Several trains daily run from the city to Werribee train station. Around eight trains a day are met by bus No 439 (none on Sunday), which runs the 5km to the turnoff for both the zoo and the mansion, though some services will take you right in. Alternatively, the **Werribee Park Shuttle** (☎ 03-9748 5094; adult/child $15/7.50 return) runs a daily service between Flinders St station and the zoo and mansion. You must book ahead.

The **You Yangs** are a fist of granite peaks some 10km off the freeway, and worth visiting if you have the time. Climbing up **Flinders Peak** (40 minutes return) gives fine views, or look out for the Aboriginal rock wells (cut for storing water) at **Big Rock**. You'll need your own transport to visit the park.

GEELONG
☎ 03 / pop 130,194

Geelong boomed during the gold rush, as it was a major gateway to the goldfields. After the gold rush the city became the country's wool centre and a major port. For most Victorians, the word 'Geelong' conjures up AFL football and Ford: the city is the home of the Geelong Cats and the Ford car factory. Sprawling Geelong is not the sort of town in which you'd want to spend a honeymoon, but the central part has plenty of historic buildings, and some fine views of the lovely, yet industrial, port – the city has similarities to Newcastle, north of Sydney.

It's worth spending a few hours here visiting the Wool Museum, the Art Gallery and the waterfront, and if you're into nightlife, you'll probably give Geelong's the thumbs up.

Information

If you're driving in from the north, take the scenic foreshore route instead of the highway – even if you're just passing through.

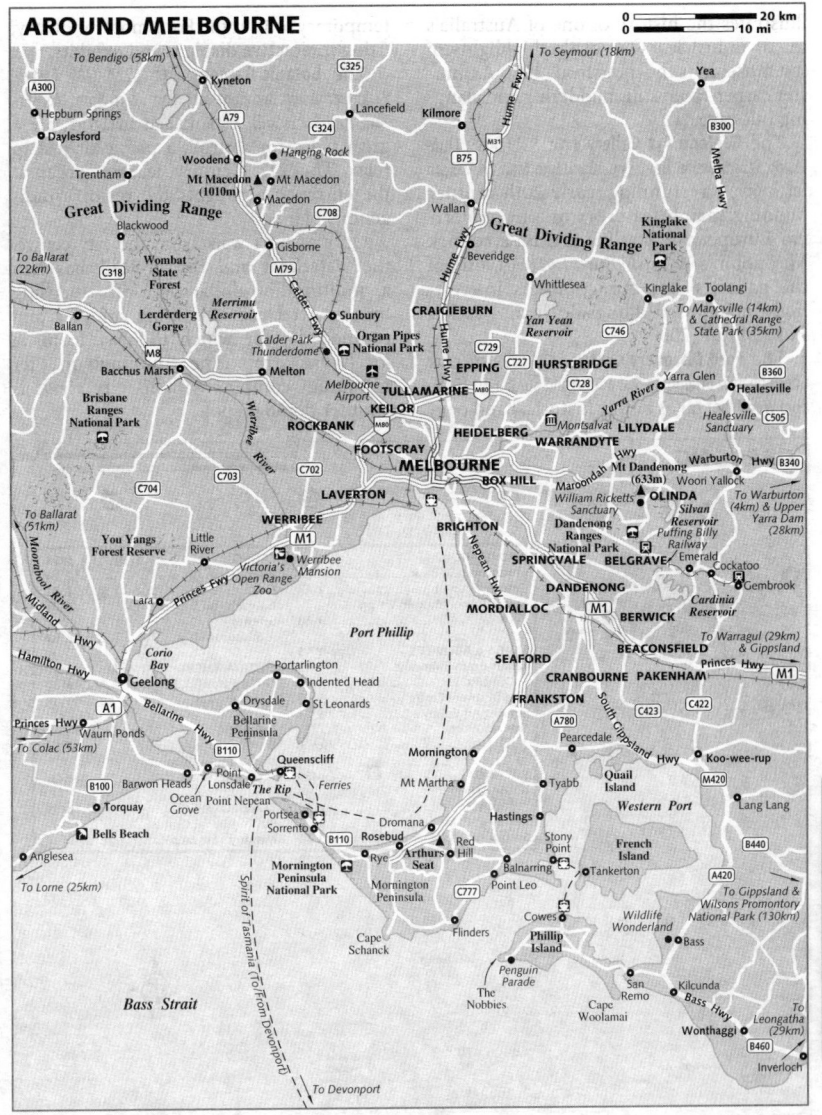

AROUND MELBOURNE

VICTORIA

Turn left into Bell Pde (about 2km after the Ford factory) and follow the Esplanade along the foreshore.

Geelong & Great Ocean Road visitors centre (☎ 5275 5797; www.greatoceanroad.org/geelong; cnr Princes Hwy & St Georges Rd; ☼ 9am-5pm) About 7km north of the city centre, it's on the left as you come in from Melbourne.

National Wool Museum visitors centre (☎ 5222 2900; ☼ 9am-5pm)

Sights

The **National Wool Museum** (☎ 5227 0701; 26 Moorabool St; adult/child $7.30/3.65; ☼ 9.30am-5pm) is housed in the 1872 bluestone wool store. This interesting museum beautifully illustrates the history of one of Australia's major industries. One of the highlights of the museum is the monstrous 1910 Axminster carpet-loom still shuddering and clanging out carpets.

The **Geelong Art Gallery** (☎ 5229 3645; Little Malop St; admission free; 🕙 10am-5pm Mon-Fri, 1-5pm Sat & Sun), a stunning early-20th-century building, mainly features works by pioneer-era European-Australian artists. Frederick McCubbin's *A Bush Burial (1890)*, one of the gallery's star attractions, is interestingly juxtaposed alongside Juan Davila's *Bush Burial (2000)*.

The **Ford Discovery Centre** (☎ 5227 8700; cnr Gheringhap & Brougham Sts; adult/child $6/3; 🕙 10am-5pm Wed-Mon) takes both a historical and con-temporary look at the Ford motor industry, using interactive displays and exhibits.

The **Botanic Gardens** (☎ 5227 0387, Eastern Park; admission by donation; 🕙 7am-5pm Mon-Fri, 7am-7pm Sat & Sun), established in 1851, are a great place for a stroll, a picnic or just to relax. The '21st Century' feature garden at the entrance highlights the region's indigenous plants.

Only a short walk from the city centre, the **Waterfront** and **Eastern Beach** has had a multimillion-dollar face-lift, focusing on the Art Deco swimming complex and promenade, for which the bay forms a lovely backdrop. The Cunningham Pier restaurant complex with its city views is another popular spot.

GEELONG

INFORMATION	
Commonwealth Bank	1 B4
Geelong Hospital	2 C4
National Wool Museum Visitors Centre	3 B3

SIGHTS & ACTIVITIES	pp487-9
Eastern Beach Swimming Complex	4 C4
Ford Discovery Centre	5 B3
Geelong Art Gallery	6 B4
National Wool Museum	(see 3)

SLEEPING	p489
National Hotel Backpackers	7 B4
Pevensey House	8 C4
Sundowner Motor Inn	9 A2

EATING	p489
Beach House	10 C4
Cats	11 B4
Gilligan's Fish & Chips	12 B3
Safeway Supermarket	13 B4

ENTERTAINMENT	p489
Geelong Hotel	14 B4
Lyric Nightclub	15 B4

SHOPPING	
Bay City Shopping Centre	16 B4
Market Square Shopping Centre	(see 13)

TRANSPORT	p489
Bus Port Transit Centre	17 B3
McHarry's Bus Stop	18 B4

More than 100 of Geelong's historic buildings are classified by the National Trust. Several are open to the public, including the **Heights** and the neo-Gothic **Barwon Grange**. Ask at the visitors centre for details.

Sleeping

National Hotel Backpackers (☎ 5229 1211; www.n ationalhotel.com.au; 191 Moorabool St; dm/s/d $19/22/45) The only backpacker accommodation in central Geelong, this old pub has a quirky bar; it dishes up great noodles, and has plenty happening most nights.

Sundowner Motor Inn (☎ 5244 7700; www.sun downermotorinns.com.au; 13 The Esplanade; d $109-145; P) This is one of Geelong's best options since it overlooks Corio Bay, and is only a pleasant shoreside stroll from the city centre. Some rooms have bay views.

Pevensey House (☎ 5224 2810; www.pevensey -house.com.au; 17 Pevensey Cres; d $155-175; P) This excellent heritage-listed B&B is a stone's throw from the Botanic Gardens.

City Southside Caravan Park (☎ 5243 3788; 87 Barrabool Rd, Belmont; camp sites $19, d cabins from $55; P) On the banks of the Barwon River.

Eating

There are plenty of greasy/cheap-eating choices along Moorabool St. The area around Little Malop St west of the mall, however, is where you'll find a clutch of retro Melbourne-style bars/cafés with better offerings.

Cats (☎ 5229 3077; 90 Little Malop St; dishes $8-19) This large, laid-back café/bar is a notable option. Its $10 lunch deal is particularly good value and includes a generous glass of wine (hiccup).

Other good options are by the shore.

Gilligan's Fish & Chips (☎ 5222 3200; 100 Western Beach; meal deals from $6; ☯ 11.30am-8pm) You can't miss this marine-themed spot, and the fresh-off-the-boat fish and chips here are truly wonderful, hence the crowds.

Beach House (☎ 5221 8322; Eastern Beach Reserve; dishes $7.50-18) Originally a bathing pavilion, this offers fine dining upstairs (nice views) and quick-eats by the pool.

Entertainment

Geelong has a surprisingly busy nightlife thanks to the many students and workers hankering for nights out. Many city pubs have bands, especially on weekends. Check Friday's *Geelong Advertiser* or the freebie *Forte* magazine for gig guides.

Geelong Hotel (☎ 5221 5699; cnr Moorabool & Myers Sts) Barn-sized venue with uni nights Thursday and dance-mixing DJs and live bands on other nights. Happy hours often start here at 10pm so expect a big one.

Lyric Nightclub (☎ 5221 1414; cnr Gheringhap & Little Ryrie Sts) An old bluestone church building that's part nightclub. This is another good option.

On winter Saturdays check to see if the mighty Cats are playing a home game at Kardinia Park, just south of the city centre on Moorabool St.

Getting There & Around

Frequent **V/Line** (☎ 13 61 96) trains make the one-hour trip between Melbourne and Geelong ($10). At least twice-daily V/Line buses run from Geelong along the Great Ocean Road to Apollo Bay ($21) via Torquay ($5.20) and Lorne ($13). On Friday (and Monday in summer), a bus goes on to Port Campbell and Warrnambool.

McHarry's Bus Lines (☎ 5223 2111; www.mcharrys .com.au) runs frequent buses from the train station and Bus Port Transit Centre (corner Gheringhap and Brougham Sts) around the Bellarine Peninsula.

BELLARINE PENINSULA

The Bellarine Peninsula forms the western side of the entrance to Port Phillip. It has a laid-back vibe, compared with the hip Mornington Peninsula on the eastern side, and is a lot less developed – though this is changing. There are quaint towns, like Port-arlington, farmlands that are mostly flat and some lovely stretches of dune-backed surf beaches. If you're short on time, head for trendy Queenscliff.

Accommodation prices soar between Christmas and the end of January, and many caravan parks have a weekly minimum stay requirement at this time.

GETTING THERE & AWAY

McHarry's Bus Lines (☎ 03-5223 2111; www.mcharrys .com.au) operates the Bellarine Transit service, with frequent buses from the train station and Bus Port transit centre in Geelong to most places on the peninsula, including Barwon Heads and Ocean Grove (both cost

VICTORIA

$4.10), and Queenscliff and Point Lonsdale (both $6.40).

Car and passenger ferries sail daily between Queenscliff and Sorrento and Portsea; see Ferry (p493) under Mornington Peninsula for details.

Queenscliff
☎ 03 / pop 3743

Queenscliff was established as a base for the pilots who steered ships through the treacherous Port Phillip Heads. This is one of the most dangerous seaways in the world and is known as 'the Rip'. The pilots weren't always successful – the coast is littered with over 200 shipwrecks.

In the 19th century, wealthy Melburnians and the squattocracy of the Western District flocked to the town on holiday, and some of the extravagant hotels and guesthouses built during that time are operating again today. Lovely Queenscliff has definitely been 'rediscovered', and it's well worth stopping for a visit.

INFORMATION
Visitors Centre (☎ 5258 4843; www.queenscliffe.vic.gov.au; 55 Hesse St; ☼ 9am-5pm) is in the library, right in the heart of town on the main drag.

SIGHTS & ACTIVITIES
The most impressive old buildings line Gellibrand St, which runs parallel to Hesse St, overlooking parklands and Port Phillip Bay. You can't miss the **Ozone Hotel** and the **Queenscliff Hotel**. Lathamstowe (44 Gellibrand St), now a B&B, and a row of old **pilots' cottages** (66-68 Gellibrand St) are here, too. **Fort Queenscliff** (☎ 5258 1488; adult/child $5/3) was built in the 19th century to protect Melbourne from a feared Russian invasion. There are one-hour guided tours on weekends and public holidays at 1pm and 3pm, and also at 11am during September, December and January.

The **Bellarine Peninsula Railway** (☎ 5258 2069; adult/child one way $8/4) runs steam trains every Sunday, plus Tuesday and Thursday during school holidays, and at least five days a week from late December to late January. You can **hire bikes** (☎ 5258 3403) near the pier. Take the steam train to Drysdale and cycle the 16km back – it's downhill all the way.

The **Marine Discovery Centre** (☎ 5258 3344; www.nre.vic.gov.au/mafri/discovery; Weeroona Pde) holds excellent programmes during school holidays. Everything is on offer here: from **snorkelling** and **canoeing** to a trip that takes you out to tackle the infamous Rip. The peninsula is also popular for **diving**.

Sea All Dolphin Swims (☎ 5258 3889; adult/child $95/85, sightseers $50/40) runs 'snorkelling with the dolphins' trips from September to April. You'll also see seals. Book ahead.

The **Queenscliffe Maritime Museum** (☎ 5258 3440; Weeroona Pde; adult/child $5/2; ☼ 10.30am-4.30pm Mon-Fri, 1.30-4.30pm Sat & Sun) is an interesting spot as the home of the last lifeboat to serve the Rip, and a quaint boat shed lined with paintings.

SLEEPING
Queenscliff Inn YHA & Guesthouse (☎ 5258 4600; queenscliff@yhavic.org.au; 59 Hesse St; dm/d $22/55, guesthouse d $95-110) Too good to be true, this friendly spot oozes old-world charm, and tender loving care, right down to the perfectly puffed pillows. Book rooms 27 or 28 for sea views. All bathrooms are shared and rates in the guesthouse include a scrumptious breakfast. It's in the heart of town, right next door to the visitors centre.

Queenscliff boasts some truly superb late-1800s Victorian-era hotels – even if you don't stay, it's worthwhile poking your head in or coming for a meal in the lavish dining rooms.

Queenscliff Hotel (☎ 5258 1066; www.queenscliffhotel.com.au; 16 Gellibrand St; B&B d $190-290) This is hands-down the best of the Victorian-era hotels: it retains its stunning period features, without being overly renovated or stuffy. Rooms 2 and 3 have sea views. Most rooms have shared bathrooms.

Queenscliff Recreation Reserve (☎ 5258 1765, fax 5258 1750; 138 Hesse St; camp sites $20-26) This is the closest caravan park to the town centre (10 minutes' walk). It needs more trees, but it's right by the beach.

EATING
While you're in Queenscliff, you should dine at one of the splendid Victorian-era hotels.

Vue Grand Hotel (☎ 5258 1544; 46 Hesse St; dinner mains $27, lunch $25) Few dining rooms could beat the ostentatious hoo-ha of this hotel's Grand Dining Room. Walk through the stunning tiled entrance to the lovely conservatory and courtyard. Lunch specials in the courtyard include two courses and wine for $25 – a bargain for food of this quality.

Queenscliff Hotel (mains $26-29; ☾ noon-2pm daily, 7pm-midnight Wed-Sat) Another fine option, more low-key than Vue Grand's dining room, but with food that's just as good.

Cafe Cliffe (☎ 5258 1066; 25 Hesse St; mains $9-12; ☾ 10am-4pm) Less formal but still sleek, Cafe Cliffe has a large, leafy courtyard and a good, tasty selection of Italian-inspired eats.

Point Lonsdale

☎ 03

Five kilometres southwest of Queenscliff (it's a pleasant walk along the beach between the two towns), Point Lonsdale is a laid-back little town with a cluster of fine cafés. It's well worth walking to the **lighthouse** (1902), from where you can watch ships navigate 'the Rip', the treacherous entrance to the bay. Below the lighthouse is fenced-off **Buckley's Cave**, where escaped convict William Buckley apparently spent some time. The 'wild white man' lived with the local Aborigines during his 32 years on the run.

Port Lonsdale Guesthouse (☎ 5258 1142; www .pointlonsdaleguesthouse.com.au; 31 Pt Lonsdale Rd; rooms from $66) has comfortable, if a little twee, older-style or modern rooms. **Royal Park Caravan Park** (☎ 5258 1765, fax 5258 1750; Pt Lonsdale Rd; camp sites $20-26, cabins $65; ☾ Dec to Easter) is a leafy, compact park overlooking Lonsdale Bay.

Barwon Heads

☎ 03

Pretty Barwon Heads was made famous by the popular Aussie TV series *Sea Change*. It has sheltered river beaches, good for families. There are also short walks around the headland, the **Bluff** (nice views), and good scuba diving on the rocky ledges below. Further out, there are wrecks that failed to navigate the tricky entrance to the bay. **Thirteenth Beach**, 2km or so west, has excellent surf. Just 4km east is Ocean Grove.

Barwon Heads Park (☎ 5254 1115; www.barwon coast.com.au; Ewing Blyth Dr; camp sites from $18, cottages from $85-150; ☾) features lovely, first-class cottages, and some have great views – better value than some of the guesthouses around. Book ahead.

You can't miss **At the Heads** (☎ 5254 1277; mains $12-20), a relaxing restaurant with a fabulous spot jutting out into the Barwon River. It's a family-friendly favourite for meals (the fish burger is delicious), and for

the whopping cakes ($6), which taste as good as they look.

CALDER HIGHWAY

The Calder Hwy runs northwest from Melbourne to Bendigo. A handful of sights, just off the highway, make a pleasant day trip from Melbourne.

It's only worth stopping by sprawling **Sunbury** if you want to see grand **Rupertswood** (☎ 03-9740 5020; www.rupertswood.com; r from $160), in the centre of town (1.3km from the train station). It's the birthplace of the **Ashes**, the Holy Grail of English and Australian cricket. If you don't stay overnight, you'll have to make do with admiring it from the outside.

Just north of Gisborne it's worth taking the turn off the Calder Hwy for **Mt Macedon** (1013m). The route up Mt Macedon Rd takes you past mansions with beautiful gardens. At the top of the mountain take the summit road to a memorial cross via the **Camel's Hump** (a 10-minute walk each way) for good views. Beyond the summit turn-off, the road heads to quaint Woodend, or take the signed road on the right to Hanging Rock – well worth visiting for the views from the summit.

Hanging Rock was made famous by Joan Lindsay's novel – and the subsequent film – *Picnic at Hanging Rock*, about the disappearance of a group of schoolgirls on a hot summer's day. It's a sacred site of the Wurundjeri Aborigines, and was a refuge for bushrangers. The reserve is popular for picnics, and there's a café and walking track to the top (40 minutes return). You may see koalas. **Picnic race meetings** and other events are a feature here; see the website below for details.

Hanging Rock Reserve (☎ 1800 244 711; www .hangingrock.info; car/pedestrian $8/4 ☾ 8am-6pm) is some 80km (an hour's drive) from Melbourne and 6km northeast of Woodend. There are daily trains from Melbourne to Woodend ($10, 1 hour). From there, a taxi (☎ 5427 2641) to the rock costs about $15 one way (book at least a day ahead), or it's a pleasant bicycle ride.

THE YARRA VALLEY

The Yarra Valley, not far beyond the northeastern outskirts of Melbourne, is a good area for cycling and bushwalking. There are dozens of wineries, plus the famous Healesville Sanctuary, well worth visiting.

Yarra Valley visitors centre (☎ 03-5962 2600; www.yarravalleytourism.asn.au; Harker St; ☉ 9am-5pm) is off the highway in Healesville. There's also one in the Upper Yarra Valley, on the highway at Warburton. There's a **Parks Victoria office** (☎ 03-5954 4044) at Woori Yallock.

There are quite a few state and national parks in the area, most with walking trails and some with camping, including **Warrandyte State Park**, **Yarra Ranges National Park** and **Kinglake National Park**. The various visitors centres and the Parks Victoria office have information. Alternatively, drop into **Information Victoria** (Map pp450-1; ☎ 1300 366 356; 356 Collins St, City) in Melbourne before you leave.

The **Centenary Trail** follows a disused railway line between Warburton and Lilydale. At 38km, it's a good, steady bike ride.

There are some great scenic drives. The Warburton, Healesville and Marysville triangle (via the Acheron Way) takes you through some stunning countryside; between Healesville and the lovely small town of **Marysville** you'll drive through spectacular mountain ash forest. It's a short drive from Warburton up to the lookout at **Mt Donna Buang**, with the closest (but unskiable) snow to Melbourne in winter.

Healesville Sanctuary

Healesville Sanctuary (☎ 03-5957 2800; www.zoo .org.au; Badger Creek Rd, Healesville; adult/student/child $16/12/7.80; ☉ 9am-5pm), some 4km out of Healesville, is one of the best places in Australia to see Australian fauna. At the renowned Platypus House, you'll see these amazing creatures going about their business underwater. Around 15 platypuses live in Badger Creek, which runs through the grounds of the sanctuary itself. The staff give regular demonstrations, such as snake shows, but the best is the amazing Birds of Prey presentation, where raptors swoop above your head. It's held at noon, 2.30pm and 3.30pm (weather permitting).

The **Badger Weir Picnic Area**, a kilometre or so past the sanctuary, is a gorgeous spot for a picnic and has short rainforest walks – listen out for lyrebirds.

Tours

Yarra Valley Winery Tours (☎ 03-5962 3870; www .yarravalleywinerytours.com.au) Runs daily bus tours of the wineries starting at $90 per person (minimum two), including lunch.

Eco Adventure Tours (☎ 03-5962 5115; www.hotkey .net.au/~ecoadven) Offers eco-tourism accredited two-hour nocturnal walks (adult/child $23/17, minimum four) through the national parks – you may spot wombats, greater gliders and even tawny frogmouths.

Getting There & Away

Suburban trains go as far as Lilydale. **McKenzie's Bus Lines** (☎ 03-5962 5088; www.victrip.com.au) has daily services from Lilydale train station to Healesville and on to the Healesville Sanctuary (Zone 3 Metcard). Around one service a day leaves from the Spencer St coach terminal in Melbourne and travels to Healesville (Zone 1, 2 and 3 Metcard).

Martyrs Bus Service (☎ 5966 2035; www.martyrs .com.au) runs from Lilydale train station to Yarra Junction and Warburton at least four times daily.

THE DANDENONGS

On a clear day, the Dandenong Ranges can be seen from the centre of Melbourne, which is 35km to their west. Mt Dandenong is the highest point (633m). The landscape is a patchwork of exotic trees, national parks with a lush understorey of tree ferns, and urban sprawl. The Dandenongs are a popular getaway spot and one of the most accessible options for bushwalking close to Melbourne.

Dandenong Ranges & Knox visitors centre (☎ 03-9758 7522; www.yarrarangestourism.com; 1211 Burwood Hwy, Upper Ferntree Gully; ☉ 9am-5pm) is near the Upper Ferntree Gully train station. Ring **Parks Victoria** (☎ 13 19 63) for maps of the park walks, and for information on the region's superb gardens, such as the **National Rhododendron Gardens** (best visited in spring and autumn).

Dandenong Ranges National Park, a combination of five parks, offers walks ranging from short strolls to four-hour trails. One of its most accessible parks is **Sherbrooke Forest**, which has a towering cover of mountain ash trees. You can reach the start of its eastern loop walk (10km; 3 hours), just 1km or so from Belgrave station, by walking to the end of Old Monbulk Rd past Puffing Billy's station. Combining this walk with a ride on Puffing Billy makes a great day out. The walks at **Ferntree Gully National Park**, home to large numbers of lyrebirds and the infamous '1000' steps, are 10-minutes' walk from the Upper Ferntree Gully train station.

William Ricketts Sanctuary (13 19 63; Mt Dandenong Tourist Rd; adult/child $5.40/2.10; 10am-4.30) features Ricketts' sculptures blended beautifully with damp fern gardens – his work was inspired by nature and the years he spent living with Aboriginal people. It's well worth a look. Bus 688 runs here from Croydon train station.

Puffing Billy

Puffing Billy (03-9754 6800; www.puffingbilly.com.au; Old Monbulk Rd, Belgrave; Belgrave-Gembrook return adult/child/family $38/17/77) is one of the Dandenongs' main attractions. The restored steam train puffs its way through the forested hills and fern gullies between Belgrave and Gembrook Station. Kids love hanging their legs out the windows.

Puffing Billy operates at least three times a day, departing from the Belgrave Puffing Billy station, a short walk from Belgrave station.

Sleeping

The Dandenongs has plenty of accommodation options, though not many in the budget or mid-range categories!

Emerald Backpackers (03-5968 4086; www.emeraldbackpackers.com.au; 2 Lakeview Ct, Emerald; dm/d $17/40;) This basic hostel is geared towards travellers working in the area's plant nurseries, so you'll have to book well ahead.

Observatory Cottages (03-9751 2436; www.observatorycottages.com.au; 10 Observatory Rd, Mt Dandenong; r $150-260) Right near the peak of Mt Dandenong, these sumptuous cottages are one of the best value accommodation options in the area.

Getting There & Away

At least one train per hour runs from Flinders St train station directly to Belgrave on the Belgrave line.

MORNINGTON PENINSULA

The Mornington Peninsula, separating Port Phillip and Western Port, is a little over an hour's drive from the city centre. It's been a summer resort since the 1870s, and it still makes a perfect day trip on a steamy day.

INFORMATION

Peninsula visitors centre (03-5987 3078; www.visitmorningtonpeninsula.org; Nepean Hwy, Dromana; 9am-5pm)

GETTING THERE & AWAY
Bus & Train

At least one train per hour makes the one-hour run from Flinders St train station to Frankston. From Frankston at least six trains per day continue on to Stony Point, on the Western Port side of the peninsula.

From Frankston train station, **Portsea Passenger Services** (03-5986 5666), bus No 788, runs at least six times daily along the peninsula, via Sorrento and Portsea ($8), to stop right outside Point Nepean (in the Mornington Peninsula National Park).

Ferry

Peninsula Searoad Transport (03-5258 3244; www.searoad.com.au) runs a daily car and passenger ferry between Sorrento and Queenscliff on the Bellarine Peninsula. The crossing takes 40 minutes, departing from Queenscliff and Sorrento on the hour, every hour from 7am to 6pm. One-way tickets cost around $48 per car (including two adult passengers); adult foot passengers are charged $8.

The **Portsea to Queenscliff Passenger Ferry** (03-5984 1602) also runs ferries, but you'll need to ring ahead to find out the schedule.

Mornington to Sorrento

The attractive residential suburbs of **Mornington** and **Mt Martha** have excellent bay beaches. Turn off the Nepean Hwy at Mornington and take the slower but much more scenic route around the coast, which rejoins the highway at **Dromana**. Just inland is the **Arthurs Seat State Park**, the scenic drive winding its way up to the summit lookout. The park has a maze and a handful of short walking tracks; the chairlift here has closed indefinitely.

Sorrento
 03

The oldest town on the peninsula, very hip Sorrento has a pleasant seaside atmosphere ('frenetic' would be the word in summer) and some fine 19th-century buildings. Although Sorrento back beach (ie the ocean beach) isn't recommended for swimming, the tidal rock pool (especially at low tide) is a great spot for both adults and children to swim and snorkel in safety. Dolphin-watching cruises in the bay are popular.

The purpose-built **Sorrento YHA** (5984 4323; sorrento@yhavic.org.au; 3 Miranda St; dm $20; P) has good facilities. The friendly staff organise three-day trips from Melbourne including swimming with dolphins, accommodation and transport for $229. To get here under your own steam, take bus No 788 to stop 18.

Oceanic Whitehall Guesthouse & Motel (☎ 5984 4166; whitehal@cdi.com.au; 231 Ocean Beach Rd; s/d from $90/105; **P**) is a grand old limestone guesthouse (1903) offering homely rooms only a short walk from Ocean Beach and the town centre. Breakfast included.

Portsea
☎ 03

Portsea is also a popular getaway for Melbourne's well-to-do and has some great beaches. The back beach has good surf but can be dangerous, so head for the life-saving club and swim between the flags. The front (ie bay) beaches are safer for swimming, and if things get too hot, you can wander up to the Portsea Hotel for a drink in the beer garden that overlooks the pier.

Diving enthusiasts should try **Dive Victoria** (☎ 5984 3155; www.divevictoria.com.au; 3752 Point Nepean Rd), which offers a dive package for $115 including gear, and snorkelling trips for $60 including gear.

Portsea Hotel (☎ 5984 2213; www.portseahotel .com.au; 3746 Point Nepean Rd; s/d $60/130, d with bathroom $160-195) is not glamorous, but it's well priced and well positioned. The top-end rooms have views. Rates include breakfast.

Mornington Peninsula National Park

The stunning **Point Nepean** section of the Mornington Peninsula National Park is on the tip of the peninsula – it's well worth a visit. The **visitors centre** (☎ 03-5984 4276; ❤ 9am-5pm, longer in summer) is near the entrance to Point Nepean. Cars are not allowed in the park, so you'll need to take the regular bus service (the loop takes 2 hours), or walk (around 7km). Park admission costs $13/7.50 per adult/child including the bus service, or $7/3.50 if you walk. See p493 for public transport information.

The other sections of the park include the beautiful and rugged ocean beaches of Blairgowrie, Rye, St Andrews, Gunnamatta, and Cape Schanck, where you'll find the lighthouse, as well as Green Bush and a beach strip near Flinders. There are several good walks around the peninsula, some quite long, and you can find yourself all alone on those wild surf beaches. Swimming is dangerous, but there are patrolled areas at Gunnamatta and Portsea during summer.

Cape Schanck Lighthouse (☎ 03-5988 6154; adult/child $4/2; ❤ 10am-5pm) is an operational lighthouse with a kiosk, museum and visitors centre. Guided tours are held half-hourly in summer and cost $7/5 per adult/child. Take the boardwalk down the cliff-face coastal walk for stunning ocean views, or stay overnight in the **lighthouse keeper's cottages** (☎ 9568 6411; d from $150).

French Island

Off the coast in Western Port, French Island was once partly a prison farm. Today the prison is a guesthouse, two-thirds of the island is national park, and with few vehicles on the island it has retained a wonderful sense of remoteness. The other attractions are the many bushwalks, bike rides (best in summer), a huge variety of birdlife, and koalas aplenty. Not surprisingly, this tranquil eco-friendly island is becoming popular with travellers.

French Island Eco Tours (☎ 03-9770 1822; www .frenchislandecotours.com.au) conducts a variety of different tours, including a half-day tour ($60) focusing on the island's heritage and wildlife.

McLeod Eco Farm (☎ 03-5678 0155; dm $35, d $116) is a historic property (formerly the island's prison), with kitchen facilities, lounge, organic farm and beautiful gardens. It's 21km from the ferry, but pick-ups are included in the price. Rooms are very basic.

French Island Farm (☎ 03-5980 1278; french _island_farm@yahoo.com.au; s/d $60/120) This spotless option offers 360-degree views from a sunny hill-top, kitchen, lounge, en suite bathrooms and free pick-ups. Rates include a cooked breakfast with the works.

Another good option is the **Tankerton General Store** (☎ 03-5980 1209; www.frenchislandbandb .com.au; s/d $55/110), with a simple, but comfy cottage out the back. Breakfast included.

French Island State Park Camping (☎ 03-5980 1294) is on the western shore, about 4km walk from the ferry. The lovely beachside spot has pit toilets and drinking water (you must treat it). You aren't allowed to light fires, so bring a fuel stove. Tankerton General Store (about 6km away) sells limited supplies. Camping is free but bookings are essential.

Tortoise Head Guest House (☎ 03-5980 1234; s/d $70/140), a short walk from the ferry, has knockout views, but is a little worn in parts for the price. The cabins are the best value. Breakfast included.

Inter Island Ferries (☎ 03-9585 5730; www.inter islandferries.com.au) runs between Stony Point on the Mornington Peninsula and Phillip Island (adult/child $8.50/4 one way), via French Island. There are at least two trips daily year-round. At least six trains a day run between Melbourne and Stony Point (☎ 13 16 38; www.victrip.com.au).

You can hire bikes ($11/6 adult/child per day) from the kiosk at the jetty on summer weekends and public holidays, or from the **Tankerton General Store** (☎ 03-5980 1209) on weekdays.

PHILLIP ISLAND

Most tourists to Victoria make a beeline to this holiday isle, just 125km southeast of Melbourne by road, for its much-hyped penguin parade. There are other things to see, too, including Seal Rocks and the Nobbies, some lovely walks and the world-renowned surf beaches.

The island is connected to the mainland by a bridge at San Remo. The main town is Cowes, on the north coast.

Information

Visitors centre (☎ 1300 366 422; piinfo@waterfront.net .au; Phillip Island Tourist Rd; ☽ 9am-5pm) The centre is located 1km beyond the bridge.

Sights & Activities
PENGUIN PARADE

Little penguins (called fairy penguins by Melburnians) are the smallest penguin species in the world, and have to catch a whopping 14 times their weight in food for their offspring during the feeding season (November to January). Every evening at Summerland Beach, the penguins emerge from the sea, just after dusk, and toddle up the beach to their nests. They're a delightful sight, but as this is Victoria's biggest tourist attraction, expect crowds, especially on weekends and holidays. You should also book ahead ($14/7/35 per adult/child/family) at the island's visitors centre, or at the **visitors centre** (☎ 5951 2800; ☽ from 10am) at Summerland Beach. And make sure you bring plenty of warm gear.

You can also have a buffet breakfast as the penguins head off to sea – if you can manage to get out of bed by sunrise, that is. Book ahead by calling ☎ 1300 366 422; the cost is $50/35 per adult/child.

SEAL ROCKS & THE NOBBIES

Off Point Grant, the extreme southwest tip of the island, a group of rocks called the Nobbies rises from the sea, offering spectacular views. Beyond these are Seal Rocks, home to Australia's largest colony of fur seals. The rocks are most crowded from October to December.

The **Seal Rocks Sea Life Centre** had closed down at the time of research, but the kiosk and gift shop were still functioning.

BEACHES

The ocean beaches are on the south side and there's a life-saving club at Woolamai – this beach is notorious for its rips and currents, so swim only between the flags. Good surf breaks for beginners can be found at Shelly and Smiths beaches; leave Flynn's Reef for the pros. If you're not a good swimmer, head for the bay beaches around Cowes or quieter ocean beaches such as Smiths (which is patrolled during summer holidays).

A number of surf shops on the island rent equipment. **Island Surfboards** (☎ 03-5952 2578; 147 Thompson Ave, Cowes) offers two-hour surfing lessons, including equipment, for $40 per person.

KOALAS & OTHER WILDLIFE

The **Koala Conservation Centre** (☎ 03-5951 2800; Phillip Island Tourist Rd; adult/child/family $5.60/2.60/14; ☽ 10am-4.30pm) has treetop boardwalks where you can view the koalas up close. The centre is run by the self-funded Phillip Island Nature Park, so the money goes into research and conservation.

Phillip Island Wildlife Park, about 1km south of Cowes, has native animals you can handfeed, but when we visited it was looking fairly neglected and the aggressive emus were positively frightening. For a few dollars more, you're better off going to **Wildlife Wonderland** (☎ 03-5678 2222; Bass Hwy; family/adult/child $33.90/11.90/6.90; ☽ 10am-6pm daily, last entry 5pm), off the island, on the highway about 10km from San Remo. Here you can also get up close and personal with Aussie wildlife – without risking your fingers!

VICTORIA

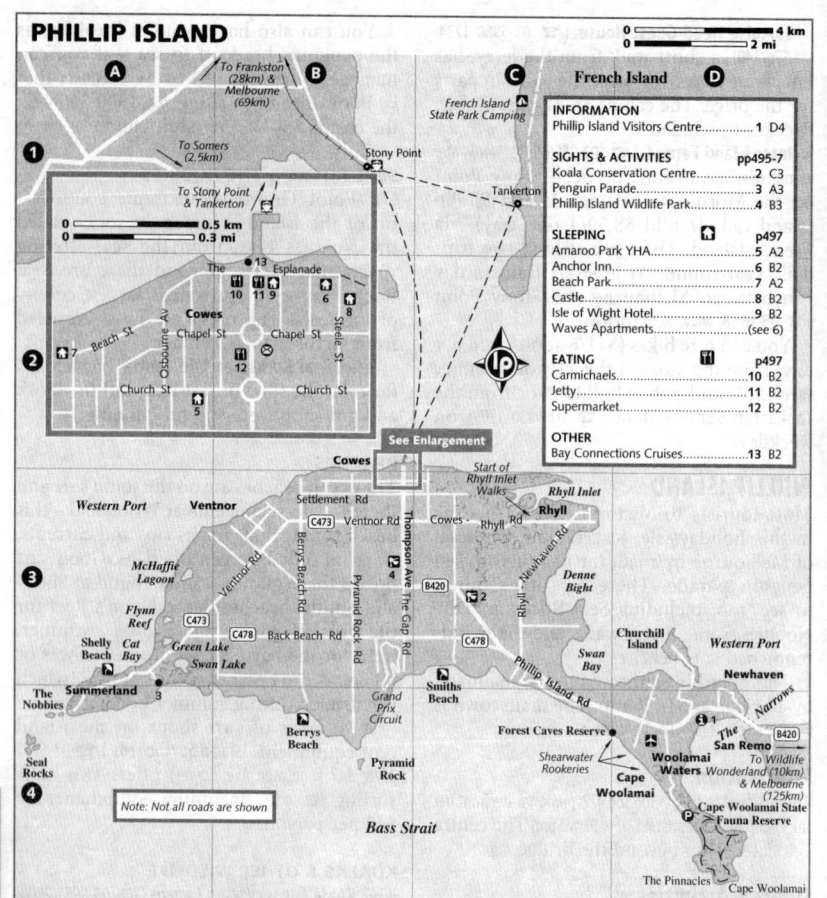

PHILLIP ISLAND

INFORMATION	
Phillip Island Visitors Centre..............	**1** D4

SIGHTS & ACTIVITIES	pp495-7
Koala Conservation Centre.................	**2** C3
Penguin Parade................................	**3** A3
Phillip Island Wildlife Park................	**4** B3

SLEEPING	🏠	p497
Amaroo Park YHA.............................	**5** A2	
Anchor Inn.....................................	**6** B2	
Beach Park.....................................	**7** A2	
Castle...	**8** B2	
Isle of Wight Hotel...........................	**9** B2	
Waves Apartments............................	(see 6)	

EATING	🍴	p497
Carmichaels...................................	**10** B2	
Jetty..	**11** B2	
Supermarket...................................	**12** B2	

OTHER	
Bay Connections Cruises.....................	**13** B2

The island's birdlife includes colonies of **mutton birds** (short-tailed shearwaters), found particularly in the sand dunes around Cape Woolamai. These migratory birds arrive for breeding almost on the same day each year – 24 September – and stay on the island until late April before undertaking a journey of a mere 15,000km (!) to the Arctic region. Your best chance of seeing these uber-travellers is at the penguin parade, as they fly in at dusk during spring and summer, or at the Forest Caves Reserve near Cape Woolamai.

OTHER ATTRACTIONS

The island has some lovely walking tracks. Rugged, windswept **Cape Woolamai** has a range of options from a two-hour walk to

the stunning granite Pinnacles, to a complete loop of the cape (8km, 4 hours return). For something more tranquil, take a stroll around the bird-lovers' paradise of **Rhyll Inlet**, where there's a wonderful ½-hour (return) stroll to the inlet through mangroves alive with crabs. There are also longer explorations available.

Small **Churchill Island** (adult/child/family $7.70/3.70/19) has a National Trust–listed homestead (1872) and beautiful cottage gardens – it's worth visiting if you have time. The island is connected to Phillip Island by a bridge and the turn-off is signposted about 1km out of Newhaven.

The **Grand Prix Circuit** pays homage to the role motor sport has played on Phillip

Island. The visitors centre at the track has a **museum** (☎ 03-5952 9400; adult/child/family $11/5.50/28; ☺ 10am-5pm).

Tours

Island Scenic Tours (☎ 03-5952 1042) Runs trips most nights from Cowes to the penguin parade (adult/child $30/15, including entry) and also offers a three-hour island tour ($30/15).

Duck Truck Tours (☎ 03-5952 2548; phillipisland@yhavic.org.au) Operated by the Amaroo Park YHA; offers day trips to the island from Melbourne, which include the Penguin Parade and Koala Conservation Centre, for $70 per person. It also offers daily tours of the island ($25).

Bay Connections Cruises (☎ 03-5952 3501) Runs boat trips to French Island (adult/child $65/45).

Sleeping

There is a plethora of accommodation options, but vacancies can be scarce during school holidays, so book ahead. The visitors centre has an accommodation booking service and the website www.phillipisland .net.au is a good place to start. The places listed here are all in Cowes.

Amaroo Park YHA (☎ 03-5952 2548; phillipisland@yhavic.org.au; 97 Church St; camping for 2 people $25, dm/s/d $20/33/50, cabins with bathroom from $80; ☐) This well-run hostel has leafy grounds, a pool, and a charming old homestead. The 10-bed dorms are clean, if a little cramped. V/Line bus drivers drop you some 300m from the door, or ring the hostel about the $15 shuttle service to and from Melbourne. The hostel also runs Duck Truck 'Penguins Plus!' packages, with three nights' dorm accommodation, a picnic lunch, entry to the penguin parade, an island tour, bike hire and transport to/from Melbourne – all for $136.

Isle of Wight Hotel (☎ 03-5952 2301; The Esplanade; s/d $65/85; ⊠) Few would call the poo-brown motel-like rooms appealing, but they're clean, right in the swing of things and a thong's throw from the beach. Also check out this entry under Eating & Drinking.

Anchor Inn & Waves Apartments (☎ 03-5952 1351; www.thewaves.com.au; 1 The Esplanade; s/d $100/115, apartments $180; ⊠) These beachside, snazzy four-star apartments have a balcony, spa and kitchenette. The motel rooms are good, too – for $20 more you'll get a balcony overlooking the beach. Breakfast included.

Castle (☎ 03-5952 1228; www.thecastle.com.au; 7-9 Steele St; s/d Sun-Thu from $115/155) The ultimate luxury B&B designed to spoil you rotten.

The restaurant here is fabulous, too (set menus from $48).

There are a dozen or so caravan parks; most of them are in Cowes. Generally, sites range seasonally from $17 to $30, and on-site vans and cabins cost from $38 to $90. **Beach Park** (☎ 03-5952 2113; 2 McKenzie Rd) has a leafy beach-side spot; book ahead. Note that you aren't allowed to camp or even sleep in your car in any public area on the island.

Eating & Drinking

There are several quick-eat options with tacky décor to pull in the crowds along Thompson Ave, Cowes' main drag, but the best eating in Cowes is along the waterfront on the Esplanade.

Carmichaels (☎ 03-5952 1300; 17 The Esplanade; mains $15-32) One of the island's best eateries, Carmichaels offers sea views from its sun-drenched terrace, casual but on-the-ball service, and superb eats. Breakfast ($5 to $13) is excellent value, but the to-die-for calamari and the generous and well-selected wine by the glass make a long lunch here a must.

Jetty (☎ 03-5952 2060; cnr Thompson Ave & The Esplanade; dishes $17-21) Modern and relaxed, the Jetty packs in families and tour-groups for its so-so mix of mod-Oz cuisine. The desserts ($8), however, are excellent (sticky date pudding, yum) and the kids' meals ($5) here are good value – the mountain of chips will keep them occupied for hours.

Isle of Wight Hotel (☎ 03-5952 2301; The Esplanade; mains $8-18) Head upstairs to the bistro for the 'gourmet' take on chicken parmigiana – ignore the shabby surrounds, because the views are first class. The bar fires up on weekend nights, with three burly bouncers circling the 20-something crowds.

Getting There & Around

V/Line (☎ 13 61 96; www.vline.vic.gov.au) has at least one bus/train service daily between Melbourne and Cowes ($17, 3¼ hours). Amaroo Park YHA (see above) offers tour packages and a daily bus service between Melbourne and the hostel (where you must be a guest) for $15 per person. You must book ahead.

Inter Island Ferries (☎ 03-9585 5730; www.interislandferries.com.au) runs between Stony Point on the Mornington Peninsula and Phillip Island

VICTORIA

(adult/child $8.50/4 one way), via French Island. There are at least two trips each day year-round. At least six trains a day run between Melbourne and Stony Point (for details contact ☎ 13 16 38; www.victrip .com.au).

There is no public transport on the island; see p497 for information on bus tours to and around the island. You can hire bikes from Amaroo Park YHA for $15 per day (nonguests welcome).

GREAT OCEAN ROAD

The Great Ocean Road (B100) is one of the world's most spectacular coastal drives, especially between Anglesea and Apollo Bay. Contrasting the fabulous surfer-style beaches is the lush green of the Otway Ranges, stretching from Aireys Inlet to Cape Otway and offering great bushwalking. Most of the coastal section of the Otways is part of the Angahook-Lorne State Park.

There are **visitors centres** (www.greatoceanrd .org.au) in Torquay, Lorne, Apollo Bay, Port Campbell, Warrnambool, Port Fairy and Portland, all open daily.

Accommodation is scarce during the summer school holidays (end of December to the end of January) and Easter, and prices are inflated.

Tours

Autopia Tours (☎ 1800 000 507, 03-9326 5536; www .autopiatours.com.au) has tours down the Great Ocean Road through to the Grampians and Adelaide. **Let's Go Bush Tours** (☎ 03-9640 0826) runs two-day tours to the Twelve Apostles and back to Melbourne ($125 including accommodation, breakfast and dinner).

A relaxed way to see the region is on the **Wayward Bus** (☎ 1800 882 823, 08-8410 8833; www.waywardbus.com.au), which follows the coast on its 3½-day amble between Melbourne and Adelaide. **Groovy Grape** (☎ 1800 661 177; www.groovygrape.com.au) has a similar deal, specifically catering to backpackers. **Great Ocean Road Adventure Tours** (☎ /fax 03-5289 6841) offers a range of tours, including bushwalking and cycling, through the Angahook-Lorne State Park and the Otway Ranges.

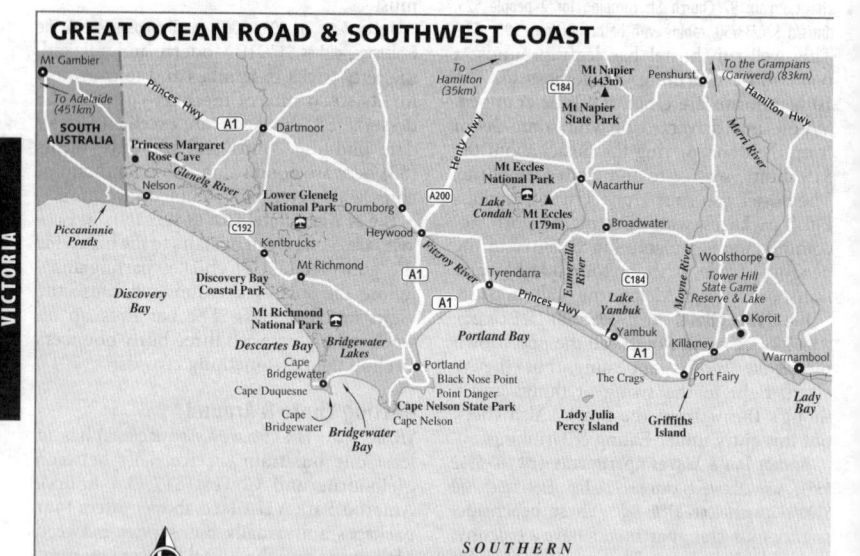

GREAT OCEAN ROAD & SOUTHWEST COAST

Getting There & Away

V/Line (☎ 13 61 96; www.vlinepassenger.com.au) runs a train from Melbourne to Geelong ($10), from where a coach runs along the coast to Anglesea ($8), Lorne ($13), and Apollo Bay ($21) at least twice daily. On Friday there is an additional V/Line service continuing on from Apollo Bay to Port Campbell and Warrnambool ($40).

McHarry's Bus Lines (☎ 03-5223 2111) runs between Geelong and Torquay ($5.20).

TORQUAY

☎ 03 / pop 8000

Torquay is a popular holiday town, especially with the surfing set. If you are not into riding waves, you may feel out of it. There are entire commercial centres, like Surf City Plaza, devoted to the surfing industry.

The **visitors centre** (☎ 5261 4219; www.visit surfcoast.com; Surf City Plaza, Beach Rd; 🕑 9am-5pm; 💻) is right in the thick of things.

Sights & Activities

The excellent **Surfworld Australia Surfing Museum** (☎ 5261 4606; www.surfworld.org.au; Surf City Plaza, Beach Rd; adult/child/family $7.50/4.90/18; 🕑 9am-5pm) is next to the visitors centre and a must for those with any interest in waves.

Sheltered **Fisherman's Beach** is popular with families, and the **Back Beach** is patrolled by lifeguards during summer. About 3km southwest of Torquay, **Jan Juc** has good surf.

Kids of all ages will enjoy the loony, fun things at the **Tiger Moth World Adventure Park** (☎ 5261 5100; Blackgate Rd; admission $9; children under 4 years free; 🕑 10am-5pm), which offers canoeing, air shows and flights in vintage Tiger Moths.

Surfing gear can be hired at several shops in Bell St, or buy your own at the second-hand surf shops in Baines Court.

Go Ride a Wave (☎ 1300 132 441; www.graw.com .au; 15 Bell St), with shops also in Anglesea, Ocean Grove and Lorne, has two-hour surf lessons for $40 and hires out boards and wet suits. The same owners run **Go Paddling** (☎ 1300 132 441), which hires out kayaks (2 hours from $32) and organises coastal kayak trips.

Surfing lessons are available at **Westcoast Surf School** (☎ /fax 5261 2241; 🕑 daily in summer

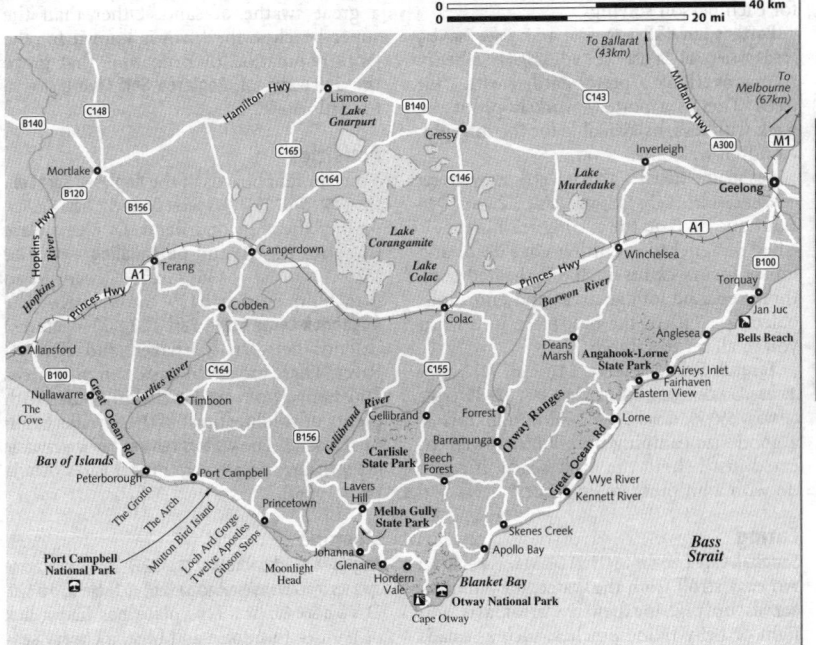

holidays, weekends rest of year); phone to make arrangements.

The **Surf Coast Walk** follows the coastline from Jan Juc to Moggs Creek, west of Aireys Inlet. The full walk takes about 11 hours.

About 7km from Torquay is the turn-off to the **Bells Beach Recreation Reserve**. The powerful point break at Bells is the site of a world-championship surfing contest every Easter.

Sleeping

Bells Beach Lodge (☎ 5261 7070; www.bellsbeachlodge .com.au; 51-53 Surfcoast Hwy; dm $20-23, d $45-55; 🖳) A bustling, friendly hostel with lived-in appeal; not for those who fold their socks. The owners are able to book tours and accommodation, and hire out mountain bikes, cars and surfboards.

Bundanoon Beach Houses (☎ 5261 2226; bund anoonbh@iprimus.com.au; cnr Pride & Price Sts; 40 Bristol Rd; r $100-230; 🏵) A frisbee throw from the beach, these self-contained cottages are nothing flashy, but fabrics are bright and there's lots of shiny wood; the master bedroom has a spa you can toss a coin for. The cottages sleep up to six; the cost goes down for each person staying.

Potter's Inn B&B (☎ 5261 4131; pottersinn@big pond.com.au; 40 Bristol Rd; s/d $85/95) Cheery rooms overlook a pretty garden with fruit trees. There's a pottery workshop out the back with lessons available for the intrepid. Children welcome.

Seabourne House (☎ 5261 2916; www.seabour nehouse.com.au; 11 The Esplanade; d/ste $220/300; 🏵) Boutique B&B on the surfing seashore: polished designer tiles, cutting-edge décor and lots of luxury extras, including heated pool, three separate lounge areas and enormous balconies. This is the best place in town if you're all set to splurge.

Torquay Public Reserve (☎ 5261 7070; www .torquayforeshore.com; Bell St; camp sites $19-35, onsite caravans $50-90, cabins $45-55) Although this is a good-size camping park and it's well located just behind the back beach, it could do with a bit more green space.

Eating

Sandbah Cafe (☎ 5261 6414; 21 Gilbert St; dishes $6-12) An easy stroll from the water, the Sandbah serves up big, inexpensive breakfasts and light or belly-filling lunches, such as salads or quiches and overflowing plates of pasta.

THE AUTHOR'S CHOICE

Imperial Rhino (☎ 5261 6780; 3 Bell St; dishes $6-10) This place has quickly become the grooviest eatery in town (for good reason), so get here early or be prepared to loiter in the doorway. You can pick up BYO from right across the road. Suitably Zen, with diners sharing long wooden tables in minimalist surroundings. Nothing minimalist about the oodles of noodles though; choose from vermicelli, hokkein, rice stick or just plain flat, tossed with such tasty treats as Asian vegies and tofu. The Thai-red curry is eye-wateringly authentic.

Tapas (☎ 5261 2854; 9 Gilbert St; dishes $8-12) This licensed restaurant does just about everything – except traditional Spanish tapas. No-one's complaining; the price is right and the menu includes focaccias, ciabattas, burgers, all-day breakfast and hot daily specials.

ANGLESEA
☎ 03 / pop 2200

Anglesea is an attractive family resort with a great swathe of sand. Other than the super beaches, the town is known for the large population of kangaroos that graze the fairways of **Anglesea Golf Club** (Noble St) towards dusk.

Activities

You can rent boards at the **Anglesea Surf Centre** (☎ 5263 1530; 111 Great Ocean Rd; from $25/hr), or buy them second-hand. **Go Ride a Wave** (☎ 1300 132 441) and **Go Paddling** (☎ 1300 132 441) are at 1436 Great Ocean Road (see both entries p499 for details). The **Angahook-Lorne State Park** (22,000 hectares) extends between Fairhaven and Kennett River. There are seven basic camping areas and some great camera-clicking walks with plenty of wildlife; most of these walks begin near Lorne. The **visitors centres** (www.greatocean rd.org.au) have details, or contact **Parks Victoria** (☎ 13 19 63).

Sleeping

Anglesea Backpackers (☎ 5263 2664; www.home .iprimus.com.au/angleseabackpacker/; 40 Noble St; dm $20-23, s & d $60-80; 🖳) This place has had a lick of paint – turquoise and blue, a cheery sea-breeze choice – and offers sparkling clean accommodation and facilities. The owner wants to sell up though, so be ready for some changes.

Rivergums (☎ 5263 3066; 10 Bingley Pde; s/d $110/130; 🖳) Best thing about this homey B&B is the private riverfront location. It's quiet and secluded, with a separate entrance and patio but, if you run out of milk, it's only a short-cut walk to the shops via the adjacent church footpath.

Anglesea Motor Inn (☎ 5263 3888; www.anglesea oz.com; 109 Great Ocean Rd; s/d $100/220; 🖳) All the creature comforts are available at this sleek, modern motel. The only drawback could be the busy road, so go for a room at the back.

Anglesea Family Holiday Park (☎ 5263 1583, fax 5263 3055; Cameron Rd; camp sites $22, cabins $70-120) Well-placed for beach bums, within earshot of the sea. The cabins vary from basic to seriously deluxe with spa bath and the works.

AIREYS INLET
☎ 03 / pop 1000

Aireys Inlet is less commercial than some other towns and has great beaches and a good vibe.

There are decent walking tracks near **Split Point Lighthouse**, nicknamed the White Lady.

About 2km inland, **Blazing Saddles** (☎ 5289 7322; Bimbadeen Dr) has beach and bush **horse rides** from $60 for 2¼ hours to $100 for a full day with lunch. There are pony rides for children.

GORATS (☎ 5289 6841; 63 Pearse Rd; tours from $35/hr) rents out **mountain bikes**.

Sleeping
Surf Coast Backpackers (☎ 5289 6886, 0419-351 149; 5 Cowen Ave; dm $22-25) Surf Coast is up there with the best; rooms are light and airy and have bathrooms, and there's a cosy kitchen and living room with a piano. The location is ace: 1.5km out of Aireys, close to Fairhaven Beach and en route to Lorne. The agreeable owner will book horse rides on the beach and other activities.

Lightkeeper's Inn (☎ 5289 6666; lki@bigpond.com .au; 64 Great Ocean Rd; d $105-135; 🖳) Not your average motel, the buildings are made of rammed earth, which means they are super quiet. The pretty gardens also help make this motel stand out from the anonymous, Legoland norm.

Aireys Inlet Holiday Park (☎ 5289 6230, fax 5289 7399; 19-25 Great Ocean Rd; tent/caravan sites $21/33, cabins $65-80; 🖳) The new owners have plenty of ambitious plans for the park, including backpackers' cabin-accommodation at cut-price rates.

LORNE
☎ 03 / pop 1200

Lorne is the most fashionable town on the Great Ocean Road. It has a tidy landscaped look, with some excellent beaches and hip places to eat, drink, shop and hang out. The **visitors centre** (☎ 5289 1152; lornevic@iprimus.com.au; 144 Mountjoy Pde; 🕙 9am-5pm) offers an accommodation referral service and, after hours, posts vacancies in the window.

Sights & Activities
If you don't want to bushwalk, at least take a scenic drive through the hills behind town. Head up to the magnificent **Teddy Lookout**, follow the Deans Marsh–Lorne road into the Otways or take Erskine Falls Rd inland to the **Erskine Falls**.

The **Lorne Historical Society** (☎ 5289 2972; 10 Mountjoy Pde; adult/child $2/0.50; 🕙 1-4pm Sun) has interesting photographic and archival material. It shares premises with the **Lorne Fig Tree Community House** (🕙 10am-4pm Mon-Fri & 11am-2pm Sat), which has Internet access.

Qdos (☎ 5289 1989; www.qdosarts.com; 35 Allenvale Rd; 🕙 10am-6pm Thu-Tue) is a mellow, eco-friendly art gallery, sculpture garden and café in a bushland setting that's well worth a visit. There's lots going on, including art classes for adults and children, plus regular music gigs and occasional live theatre; the food's pretty good, as well.

Perfect your stroke with **Paddle with the Platypus** (☎ 5236 6345; platycat@bigpond.com.au; adult/child $75/50), which offers half-day canoeing trips starting at dawn to lovely Lake Elizabeth in the Otways, 40km north west of Lorne, where you are likely to see platypuses.

Events
New Year's Eve is a razzle-dazzle time in Lorne, usually featuring the **Fall's Festival** (www.fallsfestival.com), a big-time concert out at Erskine Falls. During the first week of January, several thousand swimmers splash their way across Loutit Bay in the **Pier to Pub** (www.lornesurfclub.com.au) swim.

VICTORIA

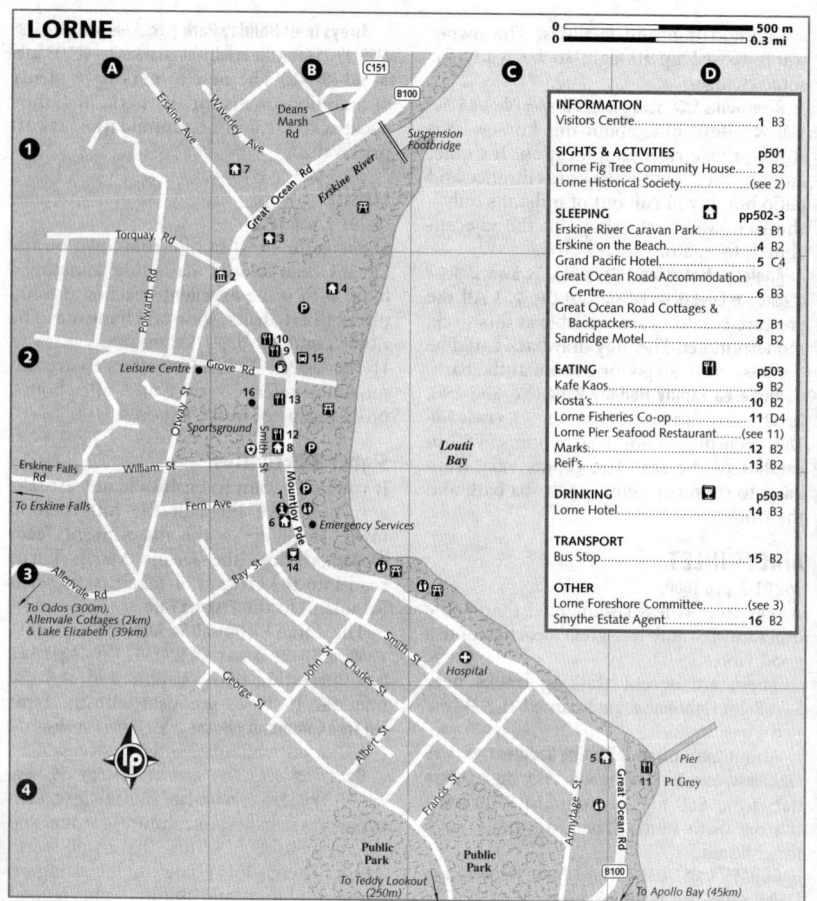

LORNE

0 ——————————— 500 m
0 ——————————— 0.3 mi

Sleeping

Lorne is a popular place for the hols, and there are plenty of accommodation options. **Smyth Estate Agent** (☎ 5289 1278; www.smythestate agent.com.au; 96 Mountjoy Pde) and **Great Ocean Road Accommodation Centre** (☎ 5289 1800; www.lorne realestate.com.au; 136 Mountjoy Pde) can book houses and apartments from $90 per night.

BUDGET

Great Ocean Road Cottages & Backpackers (☎ 5289 1809; lorne@yhavic.org.au; 10 Erskine Ave; dm $20-23) The best hostel in Lorne, set on a bushy hillside. If you ask nicely, the V/Line coach can stop 200m from the front gate.

Erskine River Caravan Park (☎ 5289 1382; 2 Great Ocean Rd; camp sites $20-25, cabins $80-100) A spiffing

site, right by the river. All five campsites in town are managed by the **Lorne Foreshore Committee** (www.lorneforeshore.asn.au). You'll need to book well in advance for a site at any of the parks during holiday time, when cabins can only be booked weekly.

MID-RANGE

Allenvale Cottages (☎ /fax 5289 1450; www.allenvale .com.au; 150 Allenvale Rd; d $100-200) A former timber mill and farm, aesthetically resurrected with self-contained cottages. There are sweeping lawns on one side, a wall of bush on the other, plus a bubbling brook, waterfalls and wildlife. This is an ideal place for bushwalking or just chilling out with a book. Children are welcome.

VICTORIA

Erskine on the Beach (☎ 5289 1209; www.er skineonthebeach.com; 1185 Mountjoy Pde; guesthouse s/d $70/115; resort d $190/320) This is a splendid 19th-century guesthouse and resort on the beachfront, with several hectares of gardens. The bedrooms in the guesthouse are pretty threadbare, however, and expect to add on 50% for a private bathroom. The resort accommodation is much fancier, but the main advantages of both are the wonderful facilities, including grass tennis courts, croquet lawn, an 18-hole putting green and table tennis.

Great Ocean Road Cottages & Backpackers (☎ 5289 1070; greatoceanroad_cotts@iprimus.com.au; 10 Erskine Ave; d $120-220; 🐾) If you want a bush setting, the cottages here are top banana. They're great looking and have well-designed, light interiors and balconies to maximise the view. For hostel options at this place, see the Budget section on p502.

Sandridge Motel (☎ 5289 2180; www.sandridge motel.com.au; 128 Mountjoy Pde; s $95, d $135-195; 🐾) Right in the thick of things, the colourful rooms have recently been done up; make sure you request a sea view.

TOP END

Grand Pacific Hotel (☎ 5289 1609; www.grandpacific .com.au; 268 Mountjoy Pde; d $125-250, apt from $160) This magnificent old hotel has been dramatically revamped by its new owner, a Melbourne architect. Décor is the cutting-edge of hip and there are uninterrupted seagull views from most rooms. The apartments are self-contained and have a one-week minimum stay.

Eating

Marks (☎ 5289 2787; 124 Mountjoy Pde; mains $18-25) Elegant, peaceful surroundings for the peckish, Marks has an innovative menu with lots of seafood specials. Try the blue Moroccan fishcakes or prawn risotto. More meaty fare includes kangaroo fillets.

Kafe Kaos (☎ 5289 2639; 52a Mountjoy Pde; dishes $5-10) A buzzy, popular place for a healthy breakfast or lunch. There's excellent wake-up coffee, including soyachino for non-dairy bods and, always a good sign, loose-leaf tea.

Reif's (☎ 5289 2366; 84 Mountjoy Pde; mains $12-22) Reif's is a sit in or out place with a pleasant, tiered terrace. It serves comfort food, including pasta and wicked puds, to a mainly local crowd.

Kosta's (☎ 5289 1883; 48 Mountjoy Pde; mains $19-27) This is a swish, white-tableclothed place (you'll need to book), but the food is delicious: edgy Med with a Greek influence. Finish up with the calorie-busting, homemade chocolate ice cream.

Lorne Pier Seafood Restaurant (☎ 5289 1119; Pier Head; mains $17-29) The emphasis is, not surprisingly, on catch-of-the-day-style seafood, which you can enjoy eating alfresco on a terrace over the sea.

Lorne Fisheries Co-op (☎ 5289 1453; Pier Head) The co-op sells its freshly landed fish next door to the seafood restaurant.

Drinking

Lorne Hotel (☎ 5289 1409; 176 Mountjoy Pde) Plenty of space to get jiggy in the downstairs bar, with bands most weekends, especially during the summer.

APOLLO BAY
☎ 03 / pop 1400

Less zippy than Lorne, Apollo Bay is primarily a fishing town, although the beaches are popular as well.

The **visitors centre** (☎ 5237 6529; www.great oceanroad.org; 100 Great Ocean Rd; ☼ 9am-5pm) is on the left as you arrive from Lorne. It includes a modest eco-centre with some interesting statistics and general bumph on the ecology of the region.

Sights & Activities

For folksy memorabilia, old photographs and artefacts, head for the **Old Cable Station Museum** (☎ 5237 7410; 6250 Great Ocean Rd; adult/child $2/0.20; ☼ 2-5pm Sat-Sun), 2km north of the centre. Be prepared: the curator loves to talk.

A 1km drive up Marriners Lookout Rd followed by a 500m walk takes you to **Marriner's Lookout**, which has panoramic views of the coast. There are seven popular waterfalls in the area. The visitors centre has a pamphlet on them, as well as information on local walks.

There are plenty of activities, including horse riding at the **Wild Dog Trails** (☎ 5237 6441; 225 Wild Dog Rd; 2hr/all day $50/85) in the bush and along the beaches. If you fancy a little high-flying, check out **12 Apostles Aerial Adventures** (☎ 5237 7370; 3 Telford St), which will fly you over the Otways ($55) or the Twelve Apostles ($140).

VICTORIA

Apollo Bay Seal Kayaking (☎ 0405-495 909; 2 McMinn Ct, Marengo; 2-hr trips $45) organises **kayaking** trips among seal colonies, and **Apollo Bay Fishing & Adventure Tours** (☎ 5237 7888; 16 Seymour Cres) offers half-day **fishing** trips (adult/child $70/50) and scenic **wildlife tours** (from $25 per hour).

Sleeping

Apollo Bay Real Estate (☎ 5237 6258; www.apollobay realestate.com.au; 93 Great Ocean Rd) and **CJ Keane & Co** (☎ 5237 6322; www.cjkeane.com.au; 63 Great Ocean Rd) book apartments (per night from $65) and houses (per week from $1500).

Surfside Backpackers (☎ 5237 7263; 7 Gambier St; dm/d $18/55, self-contained units $60-80; ☐) Across from the beach, this soothing, friendly place has lots of space, including two kitchens and two sitting rooms. The old-fashioned record player (and records) are a big hit. Advance accommodation, tours and activities can be booked. There are facilities for disabled guests.

Lighthouse Keepers Inn (☎ 5237 6278; 175 Great Ocean Rd; d $105-135; ☒) A cross between a genteel guesthouse and a modern motel, veering towards the former, this place enjoys a prime location, across from the beach. It has bright modern rooms; ask for a room with a view. •

Paradise (☎ 5237 6939; 715 Barham River Rd; d $70-120) The name's a tad over the top, but the setting is pretty dreamy if you don't mind being a 10-minute drive from the beach. The colourful gardens are framed by eucalyptus trees and a virgin hillside backdrop. Accommodation has a separate entrance and oozes luxury. Meals are available.

Ellura Cottage (☎ 5237 7436; www.elluraretreat.tour vic.com.au; 65 Telford Access; d $120-130) In a thicket of eucalyptus, this is a good spot for bushwalking and bird-watching. The owners are keen on both, and parrot feeding is a daily ritual. The cottages are pleasantly rustic, with wood panelling and polished floors.

Pisces Caravan Resort (☎ 5237 6749; www.great oceanroad.org/pisces; 113 Great Ocean Rd; sites $20-27, cabins $60-175) A lovely scenic setting 1.5km towards Lorne, although there is something mildly suburban about the carefully manicured landscaping and cheek-by-jowl accommodation. Facilities include a shared kitchen for campers and a games and TV room. There's also a bathroom equipped for disabled guests.

Eating

Bay Leaf Cafe (☎ 5237 6470; 131 Great Ocean Rd; mains $10-20) A chummy laid-back place for meals or coffee. The cuisine is a corking combo of Asian and Australian influences, and there are takeaway treats such as delicious sweet-potato bagels.

La Bimba (☎ 5237 6995; 125 Great Ocean Rd; mains $14-18) Grab one of the wicker seats in the bay window for the best sea views. Food here is fusion Mediterranean-Asian, with plenty of imaginative dishes to please a young, upmarket crowd.

Nautigals (☎ 5237 7939; nautigals@hotmail.com; Shop 1, 57 Great Ocean Rd; mains $5-12; ☐) This restaurant is hot – literally – with chilli-laced dishes, such as Mee Goreng and spicy wedges. Even the squid salad is given the red hot treatment. Brave curry fans can try the beef vindaloo.

Buffs Bistro (☎ 5237 6403; 51-53 Great Ocean Rd; mains $9-23) This is a friendly restaurant, decorated with famous Botero prints of a portly lady in the buff. There's a great range of cross-cultural cuisine and some interesting vegetarian options. Keep an eye out for the jazz nights, which attract a finger-clicking, fun crowd.

CAPE OTWAY & OTWAY NATIONAL PARK

From Apollo Bay, the road leaves the coast and winds through the Otway National Park, which boasts relatively untouched rainforests, fern gullies and huge forests of mountain ash.

A couple of unsealed roads lead off the highway and run through the park down to the coast. The first, about 6km southwest of Apollo Bay, leads to the **Elliot River picnic area** and **Shelly Beach**. Seventeen kilometres past Apollo Bay is **Maits Rest Rainforest Boardwalk**, a lovely 20-minute walk through a rainforest gully.

About 2km further on, Otway Lighthouse Rd leads 12km down to Cape Otway Light Station. Look out for koalas in the trees and for other motorists doing the same.

Sleeping

Cape Otway Log Cabins (☎ /fax 03-5237 9290; otway .cabins@bigpond.com; 760 Lighthouse Rd; cabins $145-155) These are upmarket hideaway cabins with wood fires, and lighthouse and ocean views. The new owners are constantly improving

VICTORIA

MARK DAFFEY

Do the dinky-di with a pie and dead horse (sauce) at a footy match at the **MCG** (p455)

JOHN BANAGAN

Stroll the popular **St Kilda pier** (p459)

GREG ELMS

Get high on culture at **Southbank** (p452)

Be dazzled by the fireworks at
Melbourne's **Moomba Festival** (p463)

DAWN DELANEY

SIMON FOALE

Impress the folks back home with the ultimate holiday snap of the **Twelve Apostles** (p505)

CHRIS MELLOR

Taste superb wines at the wineries dotted around **Rutherglen** (p528)

Take in stunning views across the vineyards of the **Yarra Valley** (p491)

JO

PATRICK HORTON

Grab your surfboard and check out the classic right-hander at **Bells Beach** (p500)

the place. This is a perfect spot for getting away from it all.

Bimbi Park (☎/fax 03-5237 9246; Mannagum Dr; dm $16-20, camp sites $15-22, caravan sites $30-55, cabins $60-85) Bimbi Park is signposted off Otway Lighthouse Rd about 3km before the lighthouse; facilities are in a remote and dramatic setting deep in the woodland. This is a great base for the Otways. Prices vary according to season. There are trail rides (1½ hours, $40) available here.

The **Lighthouse** (☎ 03-5237 9240, fax 5237 9245; Lighthouse Rd; guided tours adult/child $11/9; self-guided tours adult/child $5/4.50; ☺ 9am-5pm, later in summer) is well worth a visit.

There's also accommodation in the lightstation buildings. Blanket Bay Rd leads off Otway Lighthouse Rd across to Blanket Bay, where there are walking tracks and bush camping. You'll need to book during summer; phone **Parks Victoria** (☎ 13 19 63).

PORT CAMPBELL NATIONAL PARK

This is the most photographed stretch of the Great Ocean Road. Dramatic limestone cliffs tower above the ocean. Rock stacks, gorges, arches and blowholes combine to create a stunning organic landscape. The **Gibson Steps** lead down to Gibson Beach, but beware of being stranded by high tides or stormy seas. This beach is dangerous for swimming, as are others along this stretch of coast.

There's a **visitors centre** and car park here for the **Twelve Apostles**. These are rock stacks in the ocean, only seven of which can be seen from tourist viewing points. To view all 12 stacks, you must leave terra firma. **12 Apostles Helicopters** (☎ 0418-523 561, 03-5598 6161; www.12ah.com.au; Great Ocean Rd; trips per person $70; ☺ 9am-5pm) offers tours, as does **12 Apostles Aerial Adventures** (☎ 03-5237 7370; 3 Telford St; trips per person $140) in Apollo Bay (for more information see this entry on p503).

Loch Ard Gorge

This place is named after the wreck of the *Loch Ard*, which foundered off Mutton Bird Island in 1878 (see the boxed text 'The Shipwreck Coast').

West of Port Campbell are the **Arch** and **London Bridge**, which was once a rock platform linking a stack to the mainland. In 1990 it collapsed, stranding two astonished tourists who were later rescued by helicopter. On moonlit evenings this is a good spot to see penguins.

The **visitors centre** (☎ 1300 137 255, 03-5598 6089; portcampbellvisitor@corangamite.vic.gov.au; 26 Morris St; ☺ 9am-5pm) can book accommodation and trips, and Parks Victoria's information on the area is available here.

Sleeping

Port O'Call (☎ 03-5598 6206; poc@standard.net.au; 37 Lord St; d $70-120) The groovy owner has good taste; this is far homelier than the average motel, with a rustic feel and pretty garden. There are family and fancier units available, as well as a unit for handicapped visitors.

Port Campbell YHA Hostel (☎/fax 03-5598 6305; portcampbellyha@ansonic.com.au; 18 Tregea St; camp sites/dm $16/18, d $50-55, cabins $60-70; 🖳) A solid,

---

THE SHIPWRECK COAST

The Victorian coastline between Cape Otway and Port Fairy was a notoriously dangerous stretch of water in the days of sailing ships. Navigation was exceptionally difficult due to numerous barely hidden reefs and frequent heavy fog. More than 80 vessels came to grief on this 120km stretch in just 40 years.

The most famous wreck was that of the iron-hulled clipper *Loch Ard*, which foundered off Mutton Bird Island on the final night of its voyage from England in 1878. Of the 55 people on board, only two survived. Eva Carmichael clung to wreckage and was washed into the gorge, where she was rescued by apprentice officer Tom Pearce. Eva and Tom were both 18 years old. The press tried to create a romantic story but nothing actually happened. Eva soon returned to Ireland and they never saw each other again.

The *Falls of Halladale*, a Glasgow barque, foundered in 1908 en route from New York to Melbourne. There were no casualties, but it lay on the reef, fully rigged and with sails set, for a couple of months. Other notable wrecks were the *Newfield* in 1892 and *La Bella* in 1905.

Divers have investigated these wrecks; relics are on display in the Flagstaff Hill Maritime Village in Warrnambool (see its listing in the Warrnambool Sights & Activities section on p506).

VICTORIA

efficiently run hostel across from Campbell Creek. It offers cute cabins, OK dorms and a huge kitchen and dining area. The new managers will book advance YHA accommodation for you.

Port Campbell National Park Cabin and Camping Park (☎ 03-5598 6492; campinport@datafast.net.au; Morris St; camp sites $20, cabins $75-100) There's good-value, shady grass sites for camping here, plus beach and river frontages. Boat charter can be arranged.

Eating

Nico's Pizza & Pasta (☎ 03-5598 6130; 25 Lord St; mains $14-18) Earthy and inexpensive, this pizza and pasta joint, next to the surf shop, has unusual choices such as the Persian pizza with walnuts, feta cheese, pears and tomato topped with cumin, coriander, sesame seeds and herbs. Home-made breads here are exceptional, too; try the sun-dried tomato and cheese. YHA discounts are offered and there's wheelchair access.

Cray Pot Bistro (☎ 03-5598 6320; 40 Lord St; mains $14-18) Out the back of the Port Campbell Hotel. Despite the limited menu the meals here are good. If you're into catch of the day, go for the fresh crayfish – it's sublime.

Seafoam Cafe (☎ 03-5598 6166; 19 Lord St; dishes $8.50-15; 😿) Overlooking the water with an outside deck, the Seafoam is ideal for fussy families, with loads of menu choices, including fast-food-style favourites and more sophisticated fare.

SOUTHWEST

The Great Ocean Road ends 12km east of Warrnambool, where it meets the Princes Hwy, which continues into South Australia.

WARRNAMBOOL

☎ 03 / pop 26,800

The Princes Hwy approach to this former whaling and sealing station is flanked by a dreary strip of motels and commercial centres. Head towards the sea, it's much livelier. The **visitors centre** (☎ 1800 637 725, 5564 7837; www.warrnamboolinfo.com.au; Flagstaff Hill Maritime Village, Merri St; 😾 9am-5pm) can book accommodation.

Southern IT (☎ 5561 7280; 200 Timor St; 😾 9am-5pm Mon-Fri; 💻) offers Internet access.

Sights & Activities

Whale-watching is a major attraction between June and early October, when Southern Right Whales come to give birth and nurse their young off Logans Beach. There is a **whale-watching platform** (Logans Beach Rd) with interpretative panels, and the visitors centre has a pamphlet.

The main swimming beach is sheltered **Lady Bay**. **Logans Beach** has the best surf and there are good breaks at **Levy's Beach** and **Second Bay**.

Flagstaff Hill Maritime Village (☎ 5564 7841; gallery@warrnambool.vic.gov.au; Merri St; adult/child/family $14/5.50/34, laser show $20/13/60; 😾 9am-5pm, laser show 9 & 10.15pm) is modelled on an early port and has two restored ships. There's a fun sound and laser show where you'll experience the tragedy and drama of sailing the high seas without getting your feet wet; a must for kids.

The **Warrnambool Art Gallery** (☎ 5564 7832; 165 Timor St; admission $4; 😾 10am-5pm Mon-Fri, noon-5pm Sat & Sun) has an excellent Australian collection.

Live theatre and concerts can be enjoyed at **Warrnambool Performing Arts Centre** (☎ 5564 7904; 185 Timor St). Check the local paper to find out what's on.

The **Mahogany Walking Trail**, starting at the Thunder Point coastal reserve on the western edge of town, is a 22km **coastal walk** to Port Fairy.

Sleeping

Hotel Warrnambool (☎ 5562 2377; ozone@standard .net.au; cnr Koroit & Kepler Sts; s/d $40/95) A no-frills hotel with small, clean rooms and shared bathrooms. It's cheap and the restaurant downstairs is full of happily chomping locals. Breakfast is included. There's also a great bar (see Drinking; p508).

Warrnambool Beach Backpackers (☎ /fax 5562 4874; johnpearson@hotmail.com; 17 Stanley St; dm/d $20/60; 💻) This is one of the best backpacker places in Victoria; well equipped to the point of a giant telly with DVD and surround sound! The place is also friendly, clean and near the sea. The manager will book accommodation, tours and activities. Bike hire is free and there's a free pick-up service from the train or bus.

Raglan Motor Inn (☎ 5562 8511; penmax@bigpond .com; 37 Raglan Pde; s/d $60/80; 😿) Bit of a trek to the centre, but well priced, especially if

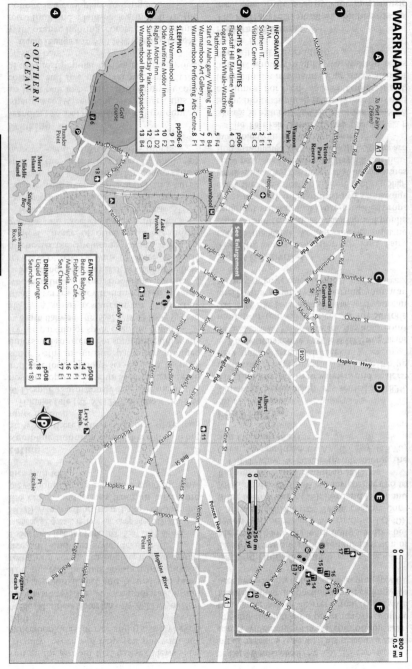

WARRNAMBOOL

VICTORIA

INFORMATION
ATM 1 F1
Southern IT 2 E1
Visitors Centre 3 C3

SIGHTS & ACTIVITIES p506
Flagstaff Hill Maritime Village,
Logans Beach Whale-Watching
Platform 4 C3
Start of Mahogany Walking Trail 5 F4
Warrnambool Art Gallery 6 F1
Warrnambool Performing Arts Centre .. 8 F1

SLEEPING pp506-8
Hotel Warrnambool 9 F1
Olde Maritime Motor Inn 10 F2
Raglan Motor Inn 11 D2
Surfside Holiday Park 12 C3
Warrnambool Beach Backpackers 13 B4

EATING p508
Beach Babylon 14 F1
Fishtales Cafe 15 F1
Malaysia 16 F1
Sea Change 17 E1

DRINKING p508
Liquid Lounge 18 F1
Seanchai .... (see 18)

SOUTHERN OCEAN

Merri Island
Middle Island
Stingray Bay
Breakwater Rock
Thunder Point
Golf Course

Lady Bay

Levy's Beach
Pt Ritchie
Logans Beach
Hopkins Point

0   800 m
0   0.5 mi

0   250 m
0   250 yd

you go for a room that has sea views. The friendly owner will help you out with advance bookings, advice and (possibly) even a lift in to town.

Olde Maritime Motor Inn (☎ 5562 2377; cnr Merri & Banyan Sts; d $95-140; 🔀) An upmarket motel with a colonial feel and heated spa pool. The adjacent bar has an open fire and the restaurant serves reasonable, if unimaginative, surf-and-turf-style tucker.

Surfside Holiday Park (☎ 5561 2611; alewis@war rnambool.vic.gov.au; Pertobe Rd; camp sites $19-28, cabins $60-95) Ace location near Lake Pertobe and the beach, and across from an adventure playground, so it's especially good for families with tots.

Eating

Rumbling tummies should head for Liebig St, where there's the best choice of restaurants in town.

Fishtales Cafe (☎ 5561 2957; 63 Liebig St; dishes $5-20) Despite a suspiciously extensive menu, the nosh is top-notch, with Med/Eastern/vegie and fast-food options served in a friendly space with an outside patio for summer diners and smokers. For something different, try the parsnip or spicy eggplant fritters.

Beach Babylon (☎ 5562 3714; 72 Liebig St; pasta $10-20) A smart restaurant for a dine-out treat, it serves fancy Italian food in a warm wooden dining room. Bookings essential.

Sea Change (☎ 5561 2823; 50 Kepler St) A better class of bakery, with 12 different kinds of cheesecake (including baked), it has an endless choice of other girth-expanding goodies and excellent coffee with a kick.

Malaysia (☎ 5562 2051; 69 Liebig St; mains $13-17; 🕙 dinner only) Reasonable Southeast Asian cuisine with plenty of noodle and curry choices. A good stuck-for-conversation spot, as the walls are covered by photos of famous – and not so famous – diners.

Drinking

Seanchai (☎ 5561 7900; 62 Liebig St) Pronounced 'shannakee' (Gaelic for storyteller), this is an Irish pub to be sure, with dimly lit cosy corners and live music at weekends. One of the most popular hangouts amid a noisy blast of bars.

Liquid Lounge (☎ 5561 1630; Level 1, 58 Liebig St) With orange lighting, comfy couch seating, retro funk and a laid-back atmosphere, the Lounge is a cool place to hang out.

Hotel Warrnambool (☎ 5562 2377; ozone@standard .net.au; cnr Koroit & Kepler Sts) This place is a treasure. A wide range of beers, comfortable seating and absolutely no poker machines allow the gentle art of conversation to survive. Have a look at the postmodernist ceiling. For accommodation details, see Sleeping (p506).

Getting There & Away

The train station is opposite the junction of Merri and Fairy Sts, with daily services between Melbourne and Warrnambool ($40). Connecting **V/Line** (☎ 13 61 96) coaches continue to Port Fairy ($5), Portland ($15) and Mt Gambier ($40). Weekday coaches go to Ballarat ($20) and Hamilton ($8).

On Friday, a coach travels along the Great Ocean Road to Apollo Bay ($5.70) and Geelong ($29).

PORT FAIRY

☎ 03 / pop 2600

This seaside township was settled in 1835. The first arrivals were whalers and sealers; to this day, Port Fairy still has a large fishing fleet and a relaxed, salty feel.

The **visitors centre** (☎ 5568 2682; www.moyne .vic.gov.au; Railway Pl; 🕙 9am-5pm) has an accommodation referral service. At the **Surfcafe** (☎ 5568 1585; Sackville St; 🕙 9am-5pm) you can check your emails while surfing your way through a large cappuccino.

Sights & Activities

The two **History Walks** through Port Fairy take in the white-washed cottages built by whalers and seamen, as well as grand public buildings and National Trust–classified properties (more than 50 of the town's buildings carry this classification). There is also a **Shipwreck Walk** along the beach that incorporates six wreck sites and the **Battery Hill** fortification established in the 1860s. Brochures are available from the visitors centre.

The **Port Fairy History Centre** (☎ 5568 2263; 30 Gipps St; adult/child $3/0.50; 🕙 2-5pm Wed, Sat & Sun) exhibits shipping relics, old photos and costumes. For birdwatchers, **Griffiths Island**, joined to the mainland by a narrow strip of land, is home to a colony of mutton birds (short-tailed shearwaters).

Festivals & Events

The **Port Fairy Folk Festival** (www.portfairyfolkfestival .com), one of the country's foremost music

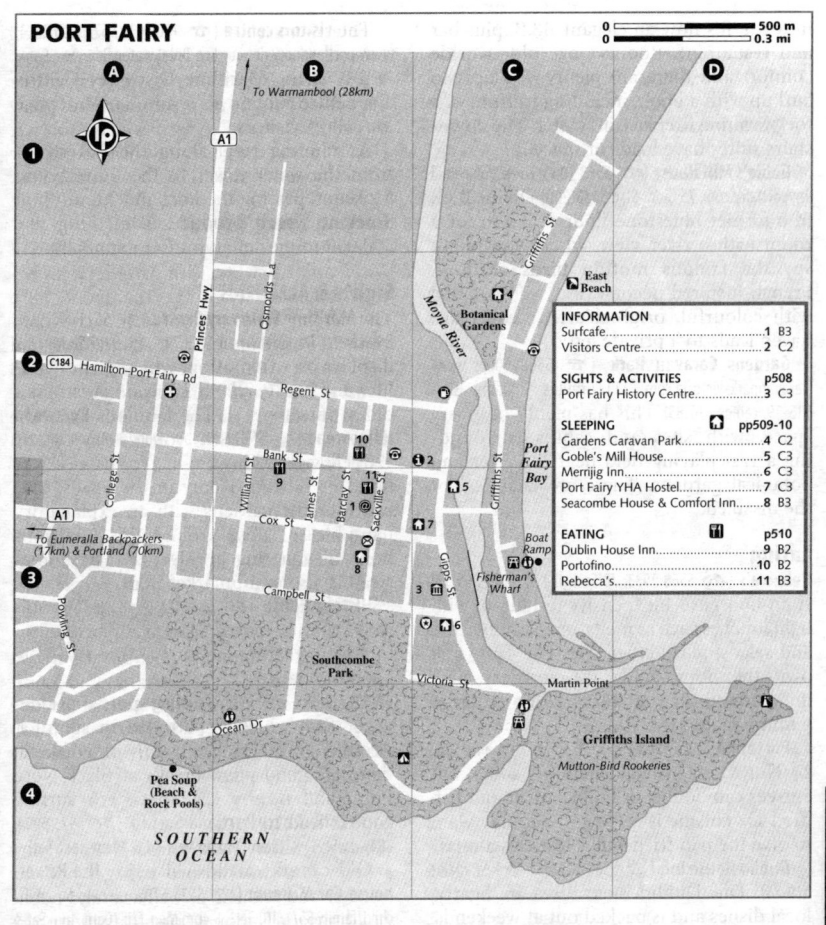

PORT FAIRY

festivals, is held over the Labour Day weekend (second Monday in March). Tickets are sold by ballot in October and November but there's plenty of free entertainment. Book accommodation well in advance.

Sleeping

Port Fairy YHA Hostel (☎ 5568 2468; portfairy@yha.vic.org.au; 8 Cox St; dm $18-20, s $35-38, d $50-55; ☐) Built in 1844, this is Victoria's oldest YHA and has an appropriate lived-in feel, with picnic tables in the gardens and a pool room. It offers a choice of bunk beds in the main house or more modern units out the back.

Eumeralla Backpackers (☎ 5568 4204; High St, Yambuck; dm $17) An excellent hostel in an old school building, run by a local Aboriginal trust, located off the beaten track, 17km west of Port Fairy on Princes Hwy. Canoes can be hired (per day $5) to paddle down the Eumeralla River to Lake Yambuk. Also good for bird-watching in the nearby wetlands. There are facilities for the disabled.

Seacombe House & Comfort Inn (☎ 5568 1082; www.seacombehouse.com.au; 22 Sackville St; hotel s/d $70/90, motel s/d $120/135, cottages from $175; ⊗) The Seacombe has plush motel units, some with spa, and nicely heritaged hotel rooms in the original 1847 inn. There are also National Trust–classified cottages that sleep up to four and have their own kitchen, lounge, spa and open fire.

Merrijig Inn (☎ 5568 2324; www.merrijiginn.com; 1 Campbell St; d/ste $120/180; ⊗) The oldest inn in town, it's now an elegant B&B, plus bar and restaurant. Rooms ooze olde-worlde comfort and there are plenty of places to curl up with a book, including in front of a toe-warming fireplace in winter. The downstairs suites have loads of space.

Goble's Mill House (☎ 5568 1060; www.goblesmill .myportfairy.com; 75 Gipps St; d $130-200) Divine B&B in a former bluestone flour mill. Go for a room with a river view, where you might spy the famous mutton birds at dusk. French-inspired décor works well coupled with colourful, original art. A courtyard haven leads to a private jetty.

Gardens Caravan Park (☎ 5568 1060; www .caravanparksvictoria.com; 111 Griffiths St; camp sites $15-19, cabins $70-85) This has plenty of grassy space, with sites and cabins surrounding a vast playing field near the river and botanical gardens. There are facilities for the disabled.

Eating

Rebecca's (☎ 5568 2533; 70 Sackville St; dishes $9-13) A no-nonsense, inexpensive restaurant with light lunches such as melts, open sandwiches and salads, plus heftier fare. The same folk own the home-made ice-creamery next door; round off your meal with a scoop of yummy mango.

Portofino (☎ 5568 2251; 26 Bank St; mains $22-27) Not as extensive a menu as some, but entrées can double as mains. Meat and fish mod-Oz cuisine is served – you may want to give the pan fried-bull's testicles a miss.

Dublin House Inn (☎ 5568 2022; 57 Bank St; mains $20-23) The Dublin specialises in hearty, local dishes and is packed out at weekends. The menu includes game, including pheasant, plus fillets of kangaroo guaranteed to put a spring in your step.

Getting There & Away

Daily coaches link Port Fairy and Warrnambool ($5), connecting with trains to/from Melbourne ($40). Daily coaches run to Portland ($10) and Mt Gambier ($35).

PORTLAND

☎ 03 / pop 9600

Portland is Victoria's oldest town. From the early 1800s it was a base for whaling and sealing. The first permanent settlers were the Henty family, arriving from Van Diemen's Land (Tasmania) in 1834.

The **visitors centre** (☎ 1800 035 567, 5523 2671; www.portlandnow.net.au; Lee Breakwater Rd; ☽ 9am-5pm) is at the Maritime Discovery Centre. The centre runs an accommodation service for call-in visitors.

A tramline runs along the waterfront from the water tower to the Powerhouse Museum, passing the Portland Aluminium Smelter, which produces something like 300,000 tonnes of aluminium annually.

Sights & Activities

The **Maritime Discovery Centre** (☎ 5521 0000; Lee Breakwater Rd; adult/child $8/3.30; ☽ 9am-5pm) has displays on exploration, whaling and wildlife, and the *Portland Lifeboat*, Australia's oldest intact vessel. The fabulous **Burswood Homestead** (☎ 5523 4686; burswood@ansonic.com.au; 15 Cape Nelson Rd; admission $3.30; ☽ 10am-dusk) was built for Edward Henty in the 1850s. You can tour the gardens with an explanatory pamphlet or nose around this luxurious home if you ring in advance. The homestead is also an upmarket B&B.

History House (☎ 5522 2266; off Cliff St; admission $1; ☽ 10am-noon & 1-4pm) is a place full of interesting stuff, including photos of the good old days.

There are some top **surfing** spots at Bridgewater Bay, which is patrolled in summer. Around Point Danger, south of Portland, there are good point breaks at Black Nose Point and nearby Crumpets. For surfing goods, head to **Portland Surf-In** (☎ 5523 5804; 88 Percy St; ☽ 10am-5.30pm Mon-Fri & 10am-noon Sat).

Old-car aficionados will enjoy the **Powerhouse Car Museum** (☎ 5523 5795; Glenelg St; adult/child/family $5/1/10; ☽ 1-4pm Mon-Fri; 10am-4pm Sat & Sun) with its collection of lovingly restored veteran, vintage and classic cars.

Sleeping

Mac's Hotel Bentinck (☎ 5523 2188, fax 5523 7011; 41 Bentinck St; s/d/ste $50/60/165; 🏊) Mac's is a grandiose 1850s hotel with double-storey verandas and seriously posh suites. There's cheaper motel accommodation at the back that lacks the luxury – and the air-con.

Portland Backpackers (☎ 0407-854 051; 5523 6390; bpackers@datafast.net.au; 14 Gawler St; dm $15; 🖳) A shabby yet friendly hostel in an old bluestone building, with chickens out the back. The owner can give surfing advice, and hires out bikes, surfboards and snorkelling gear.

Cape Nelson Lighthouse (☎ 5523 5100; www
.lightstation.com.au; Cape Nelson Rd; cottages from $110;
⌘) A rare treat of a place. These converted
lightkeepers' cottages have a salty, sophisticated charm and are perfectly located
for striding out on the Great Southwest
walk. The café/gallery has live jazz playing on occasions and sells sticky cakes and
other naughty nosh. Lighthouse tours are
available.

Sea View Lodge B&B (☎ 5526 7276; www.hotkey
.net.au/~seaviewlodge; 1636 Bridgewater Rd, Cape Bridgewater; s $90, d $110-130; ⌘) This B&B, 19km
from Portland, is very special. There's a
glassed-in sunroom and sitting room
with fireplace (to cover all seasons), plus
an extra-wide veranda for contemplating
the white sandy beach and sea. Rooms are
welcoming and light.

Centenary Caravan Park (☎/fax 5523 1487;
184 Bentinck St; sites/cabins from $17/70) The most
central caravan park in town, sitting right
on the riverfront. The owner is constantly
improving the place; the most recent addition is a playground.

Eating

Edward's Waterfront Cafe-Restaurant (☎ 5523
1032; 101 Bentinck St; mains $15-21) Portland's
swishest eatery has high-standard grub
and a dedicated local clientele. Edward's
has an extensive wine list and mains include pasta and seafood dishes, roast quail,
lamb curry and steaks, plus a diet-defying
cake selection.

Canton Palace (☎ 5523 3677; 9 Julia St; smorgasbord $15; ⏰ lunch Tue-Sat, dinner daily) There are
no surprises, but the Palace has reliably
inexpensive Chinese smorgasbords on Saturday and a cut-price lunch menu the rest
of the week.

Clare's Restaurant (☎ 5523 5355; 55 Bentinck St;
mains $8-15) Animated new restaurant on the
waterfront, with a sophisticated East and
West menu, including vegetarian options
like goat's cheese salad with pine nuts, and
stir-fries. The daily specials include home-
made soups. There's a leafy patio for summer days and smokers.

Getting There & Away

Daily **V/Line** (☎ 13 61 96) coaches run to
Port Fairy ($10), Warrnambool ($15) and
Mt Gambier ($25). Coaches depart from
Henty St.

PORTLAND TO SOUTH AUSTRALIA

From Portland, you can take the Princes
Hwy inland or drive along the slower,
more interesting Portland–Nelson road
(C192). There are turn-offs to beaches and
some great national parks, including **Discovery Bay Coastal Park**, **Mt Richmond National Park**
and **Lower Glenelg National Park**.

Great South-West Walk

This 250km walk between Portland and the
SA border follows the coast to Nelson and
then heads inland along the Glenelg River
to the border. It takes at least 10 days, but
there are shorter sections.

There are camp sites with fireplaces, toilets and fresh water. Take a fuel stove (firewood can be scarce) and carry water.

For more information, see Lonely Planet's
Walking in Australia, or buy *Short Walks
on and around the Great South-West Walk*
($3.50) from the Portland visitors centre.

Nelson

☎ 08

Nelson, a sleepy village at the mouth of
the mighty Glenelg River, is the main access point for the **Lower Glenelg National Park**.
From upstream Dartmoor, canoeists can
paddle 75km down the picturesque Glenelg
to Nelson. There are 11 riverside **camp sites**
for overnight stays.

The **visitors centre** (☎ 8738 4051; nelsonvic@
hotkey.net.au; Leake St; ⏰ 9am-5pm) issues camping permits (from $9.30 to $13) for the camp
sites in the national park.

Nelson Boat & Canoe Hire (☎ 8738 4048; Kellet
St; canoes & kayaks from $22/day, other boats from $28/hr;
⏰ 8.30am-5.30pm, later in summer) will transport
canoeists (for a fee) to various places on
the river.

The less energetic can take a cruise
from Nelson with **Nelson Endeavour River
Cruises** (☎ 8738 4191; Glenelg River; cruises adult/child
$20/10; ⏰ 1pm Tue-Thu, Sat & Sun, daily during school
holidays).

SLEEPING & EATING

Nelson Cottage B&B (☎ 8738 4161; cnr Kellett &
Sturt Sts; s/d $45/70) The new owner has re-
vamped the interior, which has made all
the difference at this cosy B&B across from
the river. She's also an alternative-health
therapist – handy if you're feeling under
the weather.

VICTORIA

Motel Black Wattle (☎ 8738 4008; www.motelblack wattle.com.au; Mt Gambier Rd; s/d $65/75; 🐾) While you have breakfast ($8) in the dining room, you can watch the galahs and other birds scoff theirs at the bird table outside. Be sure to order crayfish in season. The owners want to sell; let's all hope they don't as it's just dandy the way it is.

River-Vu Caravan Park (☎ 8738 4123; Kellet St; camp sites/cabins $18/55) Just the place for a spot of fishing, overlooking the Glenelg, this is a peaceful, leafy park near the centre of town.

Nelson Hotel (☎ 8738 4011; keg@dove.net.au; Kellet St; s/d $30/45, cottage d $70 with breakfast) Stay in tidy, functional rooms (shared bathroom), or the adjacent two-bedroom Keg's Cottage. The hotel does cheap bar meals and bistro-style grub, but can get noisy at weekends.

Princess Margaret Rose Cave

A pretty 12km drive from Nelson leads to **Princess Margaret Rose Cave** (☎ 8738 4171; Caves Rd, lwr Glenelg National Park; adult/child $7.50/4; ☾ tours low/high season 10am/9am). There are interesting displays at the entrance that explain the geology and history of the cave. Good **camp sites** ($12) and **cabins** ($45) are available.

THE WESTERN DISTRICT

This region is the third-largest volcanic plain in the world and has some of the best sheep and cattle country in Australia.

Hamilton

☎ 03 / pop 9100

Hamilton, the 'Wool Capital of the World', is the major town of the Western District. The town is a tad dour but there are a few things to see and do.

The **visitors centre** (☎ 1800 807 056; 5572 3746; www.sthgrampians.vic.gov.au; Lonsdale St; ☾ 9am-5pm) has an interesting free guide, *Volcanoes Discovery Trail*, for those interested in the extensive volcanic sites of the region.

SIGHTS & ACTIVITIES

The **Hamilton Art Gallery** (☎ 5573 0460; 107 Brown St; admission by donation; ☾ 10am-5pm Mon-Fri, 10am-noon & 2-5pm Sat, 2-5pm Sun) has an excellent permanent collection. On Coleraine Rd 2km west of the centre, the **Big Woolbales** (☎ 5571 2810; 230 Coleraine Rd; ☾ 9am-4.30pm) has wool-related displays.

Sir Reginald Ansett (founder of Ansett Airlines) founded his empire in Hamilton in

1931. The **Sir Reginald Ansett Transport Museum** (☎ 5571 2767; Ballarat Rd; adult/child $2/1; ☾ 10am-4pm) has a collection of airline memorabilia, including a 1936 Fokker aircraft similar to the one Ansett used on his first flight.

The lush and lovely **Botanical Gardens** (cnr Thompson & French Sts) is worth a stroll around. The trees here include a magnificent English oak which, with its 30m span, is one of the largest in the state.

SLEEPING & EATING

Commercial Hotel (☎ 5572 1078; 145 Thompson St; s/d $22/37) Dingy, threadbare rooms in a traditional old hotel, though the new owners have ambitious plans to upgrade the rooms (and prices). It's worth checking out for its central location and good, solid, bistro-style grub in the downstairs restaurant and bar.

Hamilton Lakeside Motel (☎ 5572 3757, fax 5572 4010; 24 Ballarat Rd; s/d $65/75; 🐾) Despite the lack of an aesthetic wow factor, units are good and cheap and have a kitchenette and two bedrooms. The motel is located within putting distance of a golf course, across from the lake.

Gilly's (☎ 5571 9111; 106 Gray St; mains $18-21) A restaurant that thinks it's a collectibles store, decorated with street signs and registration plates. It's a bustling place serving stylish dishes as well as grilled meats, pasta and seafood. Popular with ladies who lunch, and the briefcase brigade.

Mt Eccles National Park

Mt Eccles last erupted around 19,000 years ago. Its main features are Mt Eccles itself, the scenic lake, lava caves and a huge koala population.

There are camp sites and a **ranger's station** (☎ 03-5576 1338; ☾ 8.30am-4.30pm Mon-Fri & alternate weekends). **Camp sites** (from $10 per person) have toilets and showers.

THE WIMMERA

The Wimmera is an endless expanse of wheat fields and sheep properties bisected by the Western Hwy (A8), the main route between Melbourne and Adelaide.

The major attractions in the region are the Grampians National Park, Mt Arapiles State Park and the Little Desert National Park.

Getting There & Away

The Overland train between Melbourne and Adelaide runs through the Wimmera, stopping at Ararat, Horsham and Dimboola on Sunday, Monday, Thursday and Friday. **V/Line** (☎ 13 61 96) has train and coach services between Melbourne and the major towns in the Wimmera.

From Horsham, you can take a bus north to Mildura, west to Naracoorte or south to Hamilton.

GREAT WESTERN

Great Western is a tiny town nestled between Ararat and Stawell, and home to three wineries, which offer tours and tastings. **Seppelt** (☎ 03-5361 2238; www.seppelt.com .au; Moyston Rd, Great Western) produces the Great Western sparkling wine (once called champagne until French champagne-makers protested).

STAWELL

☎ 03 / pop 6150

Stawell is bypassed by the Western Hwy, which has a string of motels and petrol stations about 5km south of the town centre.

Alluvial gold was found near Stawell in 1853, but soon ran out. The discovery of rich quartz reefs in the Big Hill area led to the development of large-scale mining operations that lasted until the 1920s.

The **visitors centre** (☎ 1800 330 080, 5358 2314; www.ngshire.vic.gov.au; 50–52 Western Hwy; ☺ 9am-5pm) will book accommodation.

Sights

Stawell is famous for the **Stawell Gift**, a foot race run here every Easter Monday since 1878 and attracting up to 20,000 visitors. The **Stawell Gift Hall of Fame** (☎ 5358 1326; Main St; adult/child $3/1.50; ☺ 9am-noon Feb, 9am-3pm Mar-May, 9-11am rest of year) is opposite the Gift Hotel and houses memorabilia from the races. If you're interested in mining history, the **Oban & RSL Museum** (☎ 5358 1326; 3 Scallan St; adult/child $3/2; ☺ 10am-noon Tue-Fri) documents the period pretty thoroughly and also has a teashop to relax in with a cuppa.

Bunjil's Shelter, along a bone-rattling bumpy road 11km south of Stawell, signposted off the road to Pomonal, is one of the most significant Aboriginal rock-art sites in the state. Bunjil is the creator spirit of the Aboriginal people of this region.

Sleeping & Eating

Walmsley (☎ 5358 3164; jpcad@netconnect.com.au; 19-21 Seaby St; s $60-70 d $110-130) There's a museum of memorabilia in the main house of this Victorian-era B&B. The large and lacy rooms have bathrooms; exterior rooms cost much less – and there are no teddies on the bed – and you may prefer the privacy, including private terraces.

Stawell Park Caravan Park (☎ 5358 2709, fax 5358 2199; Western Hwy; tent/van sites $16/35, cabins $55-84; ☐) The quiet, secluded bush setting of this 87-acre park contains wild flowers, kangaroos and a creek. The new owners have lots of plans including backpackers' accommodation, a spa cabin and Internet access.

Diamond House Restaurant and Motel (☎ 5358 3366; ackland@connexus.net.au; 24 Seaby St; s/d $65/78; meals around $20; ☺ 6.30pm-late, closed Sunday; ✸) Hard to miss with its diamond-shaped stone and onyx exterior, Diamond House's rooms are wood-panelled and rustic. The restaurant is meat and seafood-orientated but vegetarian dishes can be ordered. Jim, the owner, collects Beatles memorabilia big-time.

Pleasant Creek Cafe (☎ 5358 2834; 54 Longfield St; dishes $5-8) The former old shire hall is a buzzy new restaurant. Its menu includes fat focaccias and baguettes with organic alternative-style fillings, plus squidgy cakes, sodas and fresh-fruit smoothies.

Getting There & Away

There are five daily weekday and three daily weekend services to/from Melbourne ($37), comprising a train between Melbourne and Ballarat with a coach connecting Ballarat and Stawell.

GRAMPIANS NATIONAL PARK

The Grampians are a major Victorian attraction with a rich diversity of flora and fauna, rock formations, Aboriginal rock art, bushwalking, climbing and plenty of other activities.

Orientation

The Grampians lie west of Ararat and stretch some 90km from Dunkeld in the south almost to Horsham in the north.

Halls Gap, the most central town to the Grampians, has a supermarket, restaurants and cafés, and a range of accommodation.

THE GRAMPIANS

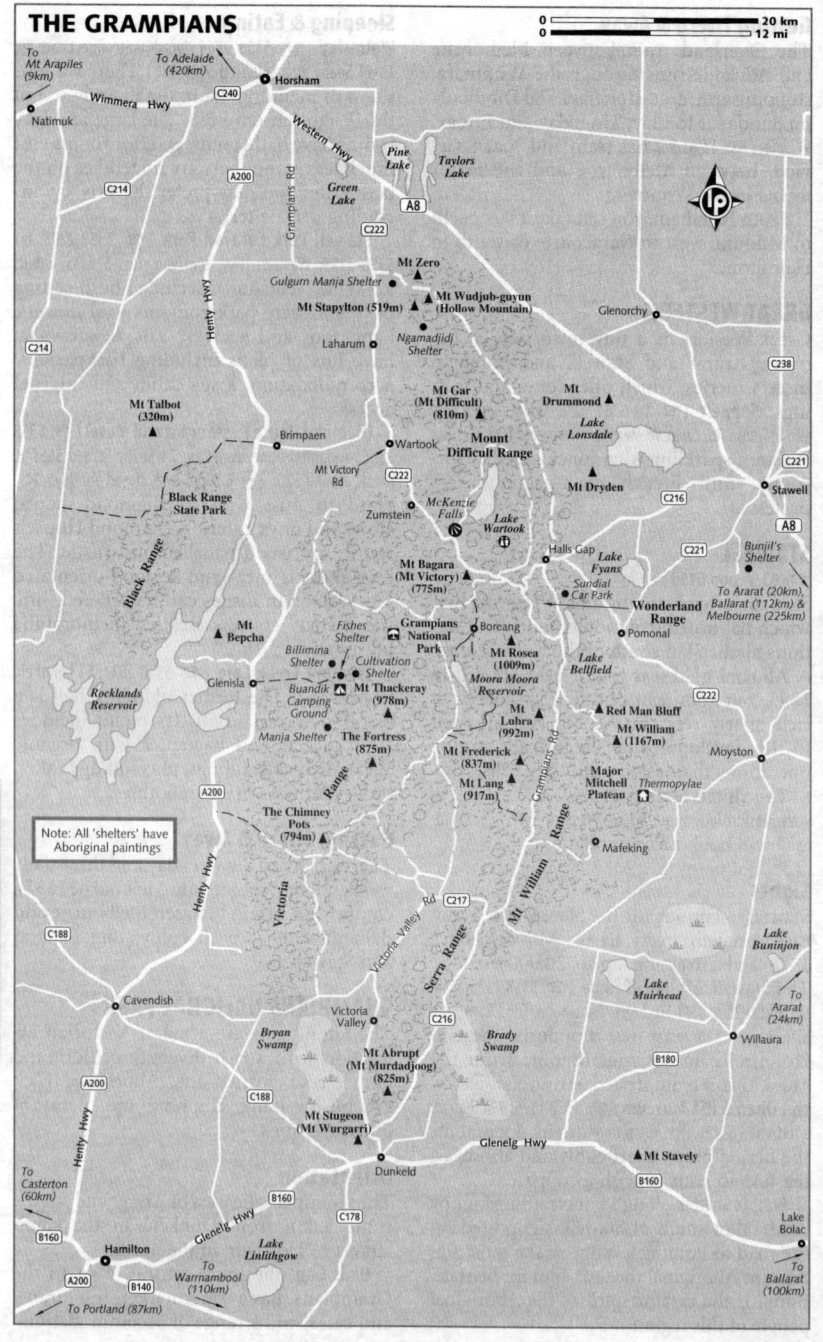

0 _____ 20 km
0 _____ 12 mi

To Mt Arapiles (9km)

To Adelaide (420km)

Horsham

Natimuk

Wimmera Hwy

C240

Western Hwy

Grampians Rd

A200

C214

C214

Pine Lake

Taylors Lake

Green Lake

A8

C222

Mt Zero

Gulgurn Manja Shelter

Mt Wudjub-guyun (Hollow Mountain)

Mt Stapylton (519m)

Glenorchy

C238

Laharum

Ngamadjidj Shelter

Henty Hwy

Mt Gar (Mt Difficult) (810m)

Mt Drummond

Mt Talbot (320m)

Brimpaen

Mount Difficult Range

Lake Lonsdale

C221

Stawell

Mt Victory Rd

C222

Wartook

Mt Dryden

C216

A8

Black Range State Park

Zumstein

McKenzie Falls

Lake Wartook

Bunjil's Shelter

To Ararat (20km), Ballarat (112km) & Melbourne (225km)

Black Range

Halls Gap

Lake Fyans

C21

Mt Bagara (Mt Victory) (775m)

Sundial Car Park

Wonderland Range

Fishes Shelter

Grampians National Park

Boreang

Mt Bepcha

Billimina Shelter

Cultivation Shelter

Mt Rosea (1009m)

Lake Bellfield

Pomonal

C222

Rocklands Reservoir

Glenisla

Buandik Camping Ground

Mt Thackeray (978m)

Moora Moora Reservoir

Red Man Bluff

Manja Shelter

Mt Lubra (992m)

Mt William (1167m)

Moyston

The Fortress (875m)

Mt Frederick (837m)

Major Mitchell Plateau

Thermopylae

A200

Mt Lang (917m)

Grampians Rd

Note: All 'shelters' have Aboriginal paintings

The Chimney Pots (794m)

Mafeking

Victoria Range

Mt William Range

C188

Henty Hwy

Serra Range

Victoria Valley Rd

C217

Lake Buninjon

Lake Muirhead

To Ararat (24km)

Cavendish

Bryan Swamp

Victoria Valley

C216

Brady Swamp

Willaura

B180

A200

Mt Abrupt (Mt Murdadjoog) (825m)

C188

Mt Stugeon (Mt Wurgarri)

Glenelg Hwy

Mt Stavely

Henty Hwy

Dunkeld

B160

To Casterton (60km)

B160

Glenelg Hwy

B178

C178

Lake Bolac

To Ballarat (100km)

Hamilton

A200

B140

Lake Linlithgow

To Warrnambool (110km)

To Portland (87km)

VICTORIA

Information

The **Grampians & Halls Gap Visitors Centre** (☎ 1800 065 599, 03-5356 4616; www.visitgrampians.com .au; Grampians Rd; ☼ 9am-5pm) will book accommodation and look after visitors' backpacks.

The excellent **Brambuk National Park & Cultural Centre** (☎ 03-5356 4381; www.parkweb.vic.gov .au; Grampians Rd; ☼ 9am-5pm) is 2.5km south of Halls Gap and combines the Victoria Parks office with the cultural centre. Come here to learn about the park, obtain advice on walks and camping and learn more about the area's fascinating Aboriginal history (see following for more information).

Sights

BRAMBUK CULTURAL CENTRE

Housed in a striking building shaped like a cockatoo (brambuk), the **Brambuk Cultural Centre** (☎ 03-5356 4452; brambuk@netconnect.com.au; Grampians Rd; ☼ 9am-5pm) is run by five Koori communities. There are very interesting displays, a bush tucker café (offering Internet access) and, during the holiday periods, Aboriginal music and dance. The **Gariwerd Dreaming Theatre** (adult/child $4.40/2.80) has a multimedia narration of traditional stories. A number of activities (including learning to throw a boomerang) and tours of rock art sites are run from here. See the Tours section for more information.

ABORIGINAL ROCK ART

There is a lot of rock art in the park, but not all is publicised or accessible. In the northern Grampians near Mt Stapylton, the main sites are **Gulgurn Manja Shelter** and **Ngamadjidj Shelter**. In the western Grampians, near the Buandik camping ground, the main sites are **Billimina Shelter** and **Manja Shelter**.

WONDERLAND RANGE

Close to Halls Gap, the Wonderland Range has some spectacular and accessible scenery. There are scenic drives and walks – from an easy half-hour stroll to Venus Baths, to a five-hour walk to the Pinnacles Lookout. Walking tracks start from Halls Gap, and the Wonderland and Sundial car parks.

WILDLIFE PARK & ZOO

This modest little **wildlife park** (☎ 03-5356 4668; Pomonal Rd; adult/child $8/5; ☼ 10am-5pm Wed-Mon), 3km southeast of Halls Gap, houses native and exotic animals.

MCKENZIE FALLS

There are two tracks from the Zumstein picnic area, northwest of Halls Gap, to the spectacular **McKenzie Falls**. The first track, taking two to three hours, follows the McKenzie River upstream via another set of falls. The second is a cop-out five- to 10-minute walk for those in a hurry – or just lazy.

Activities

The **Grampians Mountain Adventure Company** (☎ 0427-747 047; grampiansadventure.com.au) runs half-day introductory climbs for $60 to $70, led by accredited instructors, for those who fancy a taste of the vertical world.

Grampians Adventure Services (GAS; ☎ 03-5356 4556; www.grampians.org.au; Grampians Rd) offers rock-climbing, abseiling, canoeing, bike tours, bushwalking and caving. It also combines two or three of these activities into a day for $55 to $85.

Hanging Out (☎ 03-5356 4535; www.hanginout .com.au) is another multi-activity adventure company offering abseiling, bush walking and single- or multi-pitch climbing for $60/110 per half/full day.

Activities may be booked by phone, via the website or from the Grampians Central Booking Office in the Halls Gap Newsagency.

BUSHWALKING

There are more than 150km of tracks in the Grampians, ranging from half-hour strolls to overnight treks through difficult terrain. The rangers at the Victoria Parks office can provide maps and give good advice on choosing a walk.

Be sure to take a map and wear appropriate footwear; take a hat and sunscreen in summer and for longer walks carry water. Before you set off, always let someone know where you're going (preferably the rangers).

HORSE RIDING

Grampians Horse Riding Centre (☎ 03-5383 9255) gives you the opportunity to explore the forests and valleys by horseback. Rides cost $40 for 90 minutes.

JOY FLIGHTS

Stawell Aviation Services (☎ 03-5357 3234; Stawell Airport, Halls Gap Rd) offers 40-minute flights over the Grampians (3/5 adults $143/198).

VICTORIA

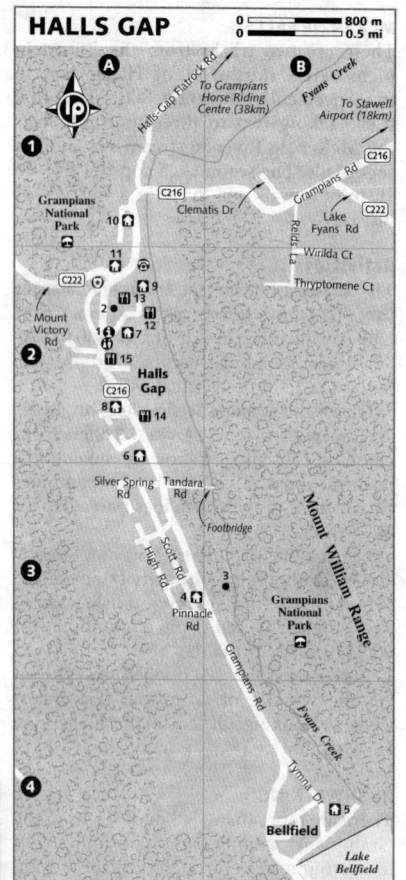

Tours

The **Grampians Central Booking Office** (☎ 03-5356 4654; 7353 Schmidt Rd, Brimpaen), in the Halls Gap Newsagency, books many tours.

The **Brambuk Cultural Centre** (☎ 03-5356 4452; Grampians Rd) runs tours to rock art sites departing from the centre most days at 10am. Tours cost $15 (4 people minimum) and need to be booked 24 hours in advance.

Sleeping

BUDGET

Grampians YHA Eco Hostel (☎ 03-5356 4544; grampians@yhavic.org.au; Grampians Rd; dm/s from $20/48; 💻) This 60-bed YHA is a real original. As the name suggests, there are several eco-friendly features, such as solar electricity and water conservation, plus a vegie patch and chicken run for fresh free-range eggs. Rooms are five-star hostel style and dorm rooms have either two or four beds.

Brambuk Backpackers (☎ 03-5356 4250; www.brambuk.com.au; Grampians Rd; dm/s/d $19/38/48; 💻) Brambuk is a light and airy hostel with a mellow friendly feel and mountain views. There's a large sitting room with outside terrace.

Tim's Place (☎ 03-5356 4288; www.timsplace.net; Grampians Rd; dm/s/d $22/40/50; 💻) Tim's Place is a tad scruffy, but gets good reviews from travellers. Several tour companies drop off here and there's free mountain bike use.

Halls Gap Lakeside Caravan Park (☎ 03-5356 4281; www.hallsgaplakeside.com.au; Tymna Dr; sites $17-23, basic cabins $50-63, deluxe cabins with spa $97-120) The park is one of several in the area and new facilities include some luxury cabins and a glassed-in dining area. This is a good spot for bird-watching; pick up a bag of seed at reception. The park also looks onto grassland where kangaroos habitually congregate at dusk.

Camping

Parks Victoria (☎ 13 19 63) has 13 camp sites with toilets and fireplaces, and most with at least limited drinking water. Permits ($11) cover one car and up to six people. You can self-register or pay at Brambuk National Park & Cultural Centre. Bush camping is permitted everywhere except in the Wonderland Range area, around Lake Wartook, and in marked parts of the Serra and Victoria Ranges and some other sites. Check at the centre for any other regulations that may be in force at the time.

MID-RANGE

Pinnacle Holiday Lodge (☎ 03-5356 4249; www.pin nacleholiday.com.au; Heath St; s/d $86/103; ☒) Pinnacle is a top-notch motel with large pleasant rooms with kitchenettes and second bedrooms. There's a heated indoor pool, tennis courts and a grassy lawn attracting kangaroos. You'll find local restaurants are a short hop around the corner.

Kingsway Holiday Flats (☎ 03-5356 4202, fax 5356 4625; Grampians Rd; s $65, d $75-85) This is one of the best deals for quality accommodation in town. The flats are simple and cheerful (some sleep up to five), with an outside barbecue area.

Kookaburra Lodge Motel (☎ 03-5356 4395, fax 5356 4490; 14 Heath St; d from $85; ☒) The best rooms at this cosy motel are at the back, with evening views of kangaroos. There's a pretty good restaurant here, as well.

TOP END

Manna House (☎ 03-5356 4679; 142 Grampians Rd; d $120; ☒) Manna House is a real family home surrounded by lofty manna gum trees. It's self-contained with large open-plan kitchen, separate entrance and private yard. The adjacent cheaper two-bed cabin could be the solution for those travelling with kids.

Eating

The Halls Gap **general store** (☺ 8am-8pm) has a café, takeaway and supermarket.

Flying Emu Cafe (☎ 03-5356 4400; shop 5, Stony Creek Stores, Grampians Rd; dishes $6-10; ☺ lunch only) The Emu serves a good range of gourmet snacks including the all-time favourite *eggs a la emu* with smoked salmon and hollandaise sauce.

Kookaburra Restaurant (☎ 03-5356 4222; Grampians Rd; mains $11-26) You'll need to book for dinner at Kookaburra. A house speciality is the venison, reared on the owner's property. Exclusive wines are available by the glass.

Halls Gap Tavern (☎ 03-5356 4416; Grampians Rd; mains $4-14) The best value in this modern colonial-style setting is a daily changing three-course meal for $10, with kids' meals available from $7. Alternatively, order from the menu with plenty of pasta choices. The desserts are pretty yummy as well.

Black Panther Café & Bar (☎ 03-5356 4511; 6 Stoney Creek Stores; mains $7.50-13) Black Panther's menu boasts an all day bumper breakfast

---

> ### WARNING: CAMPING UNDER TREES
>
> Don't camp under eucalyptus (or 'gum') trees, as river red gums, in particular, can drop limbs without warning, even in still conditions.

plus pizza, pasta, lunch specials, vegetarian lentils and the like. You can takeaway, or have meals delivered for a small charge within a reasonable distance. Be warned that BYO corkage is exorbitant here.

Getting There & Away

V/Line (☎ 13 61 96) has a coach service that does the run from Melbourne to Halls Gap daily ($46, 4 hours).

A daily coach runs between Halls Gap and Stawell ($8.70).

The road from Stawell to Halls Gap is flat, so it's an easy cycle of about 25km. It's a longer and hillier ride between Ararat and Halls Gap (via Moyston) but still fairly easy.

HORSHAM

☎ 03 / pop 13,250

First settled in 1841, Horsham is the main commercial centre of the Wimmera. There's little of interest here but it's a good base for nearby Little Desert National Park and Mt Arapiles State Park. For something kitsch, visit the Giant Koala at Dadswells Bridge.

The **visitors centre** (☎ 1800 633 218, 5382 1832; tourism@hrcc.vic.gov.au; 20 O'Callaghan's Pde; ☺ 9am-5pm; ☐) books accommodation.

Sights

Art lovers should visit the **Horsham Art Gallery** (☎ 5382 5575; 80 Wilson St; suggested $2 donation; ☺ 10am-5pm Tue-Fri, 1-4.30pm Sat & Sun), with its impressive collection of works by significant Australian artists.

The **Wool Factory** (☎ 5382 0333; 134 Golf Course Rd; admission $5; ☺ tours 10.15, 11am, 1.30 & 2.30pm) is a community project providing employment and skills for people with disabilities. It produces ultra fine wool and there's a walk-through sheep shed, café and shop.

Sleeping & Eating

Olde Horsham Motor Inn (☎ 5382 0033, fax 5382 4233; Western Hwy; s/d/f $69/77/119; ☒) Set on three acres with or without creek (depending

VICTORIA

on drought conditions), the Old Horsham Motel's old-fashioned but large rooms have pitched ceilings. It's well-located for tottering back from the excellent same name restaurant and bar next door.

Horsham House (☎ 5382 5053; www.horshamhouse .com.au; main house s/d $95/110; cottage s/d $99/130) Grand balconied house (1905) in the centre of town has a happy coupling of antiques and modern amenities – like a billiards table. The detached cottage has a spa, overlooks the rose garden and is popular with honeymooning couples.

Cafe Bagdad (☎ 5382 0068; 48 Wilson St; dishes $7-12) This café is an oasis of quirkiness, with imaginative food and great art work on the walls, in an otherwise straight-laced country town. Good for savouries and inexpensive dishes of the day.

Getting There & Away
The **Henty Highway Coach** (☎ 5382 4260) runs from Horsham to Mildura ($25) on Tuesday and Thursday.

MT ARAPILES STATE PARK
Mt Arapiles, 37km west of Horsham and 12km west of Natimuk, is probably Australia's best venue for rock-climbing, with more than 2000 climbs from basic to advanced. The park is also popular for walks. There are two short and steep walking tracks from Centenary Park to the top of Arapiles – or you can drive up.

TOTAL FIRE BAN

High temperatures and strong winds combine to give Victoria days of extreme fire danger in summer. To prevent bush fires there are stringently applied laws applying to camp fires and other activities involving flames. A camp fire can easily spread and wipe out huge tracts of forest and endanger lives.

On days of Total Fire Ban no camp fires of any type are allowed; you can be arrested and jailed for lighting one.

It is everybody's responsibility to know when fire restrictions have been declared. To help, Parks Victoria put up signs in camping areas, towns display warning flags and there are frequent radio messages and warnings in newspapers.

Climbing Instruction & Equipment
Several operators, including the **Climbing Company** (☎ 03-5387 1329; 117 Main St, Natimuk) and **Arapiles Climbing Guides** (☎ 03-5387 1284; www .wimmera.com.au/users/climbco) offer climbing and abseiling instruction for beginners. Group instruction costs from $45/60 per half/full day. Prices vary according to the size of the group.

Arapiles Mountain Shop (☎ 03-5387 1529; 67 Main St, Natimuk) sells and hires climbing equipment, but is open sporadically.

Sleeping & Eating
Sitting at the foot of Mt Arapiles, the **Pines** (☎ 03-5362 2111; Parks Vic, Horsham; $3) camp site in Centenary Park makes a good base for exploring the park.

Quamby Lodge (☎ 03-5387 1569; 71 Main St, Natimuk; s/d $25/55) Run by a delightful well-travelled couple, this lodge has been sympathetically designed with wheelchair access and amenities for the disabled. The pretty rambling garden is just the place to kick back and recharge the batteries before attempting those mountain peaks again. Breakfast included, reduced prices for longer stays.

Natimuk Lake Caravan Park (☎ 0419-516 370, 03-5387 1462, fax 5387 1467; Lake Rd; camp/van sites $9/30) This park is in a desolate sort of place beside the dried-up lake with its placard advertising watersports. It could all change if it rains, however. Check with the caretaker, Les, before taking the 4km or so drive here.

National Hotel (☎ 03-5387 1300; natipub@yahoo .com, 65 Main St, Natimuk; pub rooms/cabins $22/66, extra adult $11) The pub attracts earthy locals and serves reasonable counter meals for around $10.

Getting There & Away
Blands of Goroke (☎ 03-5386 1160) runs a daily (weekdays only) bus service between Horsham and Naracoorte, dropping people off at Mt Arapiles ($7).

DIMBOOLA
☎ 03 / pop 1500
This quaint one-horse town was made famous by Jack Hibbard's play, *Dimboola*, and the subsequent 1979 film of the same name directed by John Duigan. It provided the ideal setting for the story line which follows the interaction of various characters at a country wedding reception.

The town is just off the Western Hwy and has some fine old buildings.

The Little Desert National Park starts 4km south of town. **Pink Lake** is a colourful salt lake beside the Western Hwy about 9km northwest of Dimboola. **Ebenezer Aboriginal Mission Station** was established in Antwerp, 18km north of Dimboola, in 1859. It's signposted off the Dimboola–Jeparit road.

Sleeping

Victoria Hotel (☎ 5389 1630; 32 Wimmera St; s/d $30/45, d with bathroom $55) There are good renovated rooms in this lovely old (1924) pub; pity about the brewery signs messing up the façade.

Riverside Host Farm (☎ 5389 1550; Riverside Rd; d $66-77) This laid-back working farm on the banks of the Wimmera has cabins with bathroom and self-contained cabins. Serious DIY man Dennis can take you for a ride in his lovingly made covered wagon or for a tour on his boat (yes, he made that, too). This is a great spot for wildlife, birds and flowers. The farm grows lavender commercially; a pleasantly fragrant sideline.

Little Desert Log Cabins & Cottage (☎ 5389 1122; www.littledesertlogcabins.com.au; Horsehoebend Rd; d cabins from $70, 2-bedroom cottage $85) This is a good, quiet, out-of-town (4km) base from which to explore the Little Desert.

LITTLE DESERT NATIONAL PARK

This national park may not, initially, appear very desert-like as there's a rich diversity of plants and wildflowers. Two sealed roads between the Western and Wimmera Hwys pass through the park, or you can take the good gravel road from Dimboola.

The best-known resident here is the mallee fowl, which can be most easily seen in the aviary at the Little Desert Lodge.

There are several short walks in the eastern block. Longer walks leave from the camping ground south of Kiata, including a 12km trek south to the Salt Lake (carry water and notify rangers before you set out). **Oasis Desert Adventures** (☎ 0419-394 912; Horsehoebend Rd), 6km south of Dimboola, runs tailored tours. Little Desert Lodge also offers tours.

Sleeping

Little Desert Lodge (☎ 03-5391 5232; littledesert lodge@wimmera.com.au; camp sites/dm/s/d $12/20/55/ 75) This very special place, 14km south of

Nhill, is run by an extraordinary man. Whimpey Reichelt is passionately involved in conservation, particularly regarding the rare mallee fowl. Several emus strut around the property and there's an environmental study centre and mallee fowl aviary (entry $5.50). Four-wheel-drive tours of the park cost $35/70 for a half/full day and there's a special tour to a mallee fowl sanctuary for $28. The Lodge caters mainly for groups but takes individuals when there are vacancies. The rooms are well-equipped and spacious with good desert wildlife views (well, of the pet emus, anyway).

Parks Victoria has **camping grounds** (sites $11) at Horseshoe Bend and Ackle Bend, both on the Wimmera River south of Dimboola, and another about 10km south of Kiata. Sites have drinking water and toilets.

You can bush camp on overnight walks in the central and western blocks of the park, but speak to the rangers first at the **Parks Victoria office** (☎ 03-5389 1204; Wail Nursery Rd, south of Dimboola; ☺ 8am-4.30pm Mon-Fri).

THE MALLEE

This dry area includes the one genuinely empty part of the state – the semi-arid wilderness known as 'Sunset Country'. You don't have to visit central Australia to get a taste of the outback. The Mallee takes its name from the mallee scrub that once covered the area. A mallee is a hardy eucalypt with chunky roots and multiple slender trunks. Mallee gums are canny desert survivors – root systems over 1000 years old are not uncommon. 'Mallee scrub' may look desolate but is actually a rich ecosystem.

Getting There & Away

V/Line (☎ 13 61 96) runs coaches from Melbourne through the Mallee to Mildura ($63), via Donald ($43), nightly except Saturday. Alternatively, take a train to Bendigo and catch a coach from there.

The **Henty Highway Coach** (☎ 03-5382 4260, 5023 5658) runs from Mildura to Horsham ($56) on Monday, Wednesday and Friday.

BIG DESERT WILDERNESS PARK

This 113,500 hectare park is a desert wilderness with no roads, tracks, facilities or water. Walking and camping are permitted but only for the experienced and totally self-sufficient. In summer, temperatures are usually way too high for walking. Notify the rangers in **Wyperfeld National Park** (☎ 03-5395 7221; ⏱ 8.30am-4.30pm Mon-Fri) before going.

The area is mostly sand dunes, red sandstone ridges and mallee, but there's an abundance of flora and fauna, and some intriguing and unusual wildlife, such as Mitchell's hopping mouse.

A dry-weather road from Murrayville on the Mallee Hwy (B12) to Nhill separates this park from the Wyperfeld National Park. Parts of the road are very rough and may be impassable after rain.

There are basic free camping sites at Big Billy Bore, the Springs, Moonlight Tank and Broken Bucket Reserve, all on the eastern side.

MURRAY-SUNSET NATIONAL PARK

This park (663,000 hectares) includes the older **Pink Lakes State Park**. The lakes draw their colour from microscopic organisms that concentrate a pink pigment in their bodies.

The park is arid and mainly inaccessible. An unsealed road leads from **Linga** on the Mallee Hwy up to the Pink Lakes at the southern edge of the park, where there's a basic camping ground. Beyond this you must have a 4WD.

For more information about the park contact **Parks Victoria** (☎ 13 19 63), or rangers at the **Underbool office** (☎ 03-5094 6267; Mallee Hwy) or **Werrimull office** (☎ 03-5028 1218), north of the park.

MURRAY RIVER

The Murray River is Australia's most important inland waterway, and forms most of the border between Victoria and NSW. The Murray flows from the Great Dividing Range in north-eastern Victoria to Encounter Bay in South Australia, more than 2700km away, making it the third-longest navigable river in the world.

Before roads and railways crossed the land, the Murray River was an antipodean Mississippi, with paddle-steamers carrying

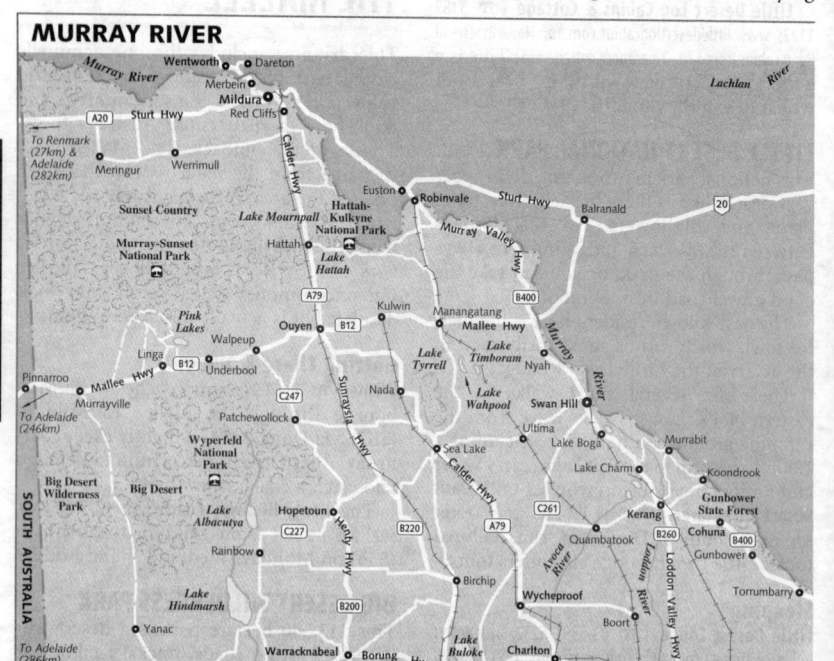

MURRAY RIVER

supplies to and carting wool from remote sheep stations and homesteads.

In the 1880s Canadian irrigation experts, the Chaffey brothers, established an irrigation settlement at Mildura, which attracted thousands of new settlers. It remains a good sized town.

Getting There & Away
BUS
McCafferty's/Greyhound (☎ 13 14 99, 13 20 30; www.mccaffertys.com.au) stops in Mildura daily on the Sydney to Adelaide run.

V/Line's Murraylink service connects towns along the Murray River between Mildura and Albury on weekdays. There's also a daily Speedlink service between Echuca and Albury (originating in Adelaide).

CAR & MOTORCYCLE
The main route along the Murray is the Murray Valley Hwy (B400), which starts near Mildura and follows the river all the way to Corryong.

While the highway links the towns, it rarely runs right beside the river. To experi-ence less tamed river country, get some good maps and follow the web of back roads on the northern bank. It'll add hours to your travel-ling time but exploration is never quick.

TRAIN
Daily **V/Line** (☎ 13 61 96) trains run between Melbourne and Swan Hill ($51, 4 hours), and there's a daily train/bus service be-tween Melbourne and Echuca ($32).

HATTAH-KULKYNE NATIONAL PARK
The beautiful and diverse Hattah-Kulkyne is 70km south of Mildura off the Calder Hwy. Vegetation ranges from sandy mallee country to fertile Murray riverside areas. The **Hattah Lakes** system fills when the Murray floods, supporting many species of birds.

The access road is from the small town of **Hattah** and about 5km into the park there's an information centre. There are tracks through the park, many are impassable after rain, and the old camel tracks are great for cycling. Tell the **rangers** (☎ 03-5029 3253; Hat-tah) where you're going and carry water, a compass and a map.

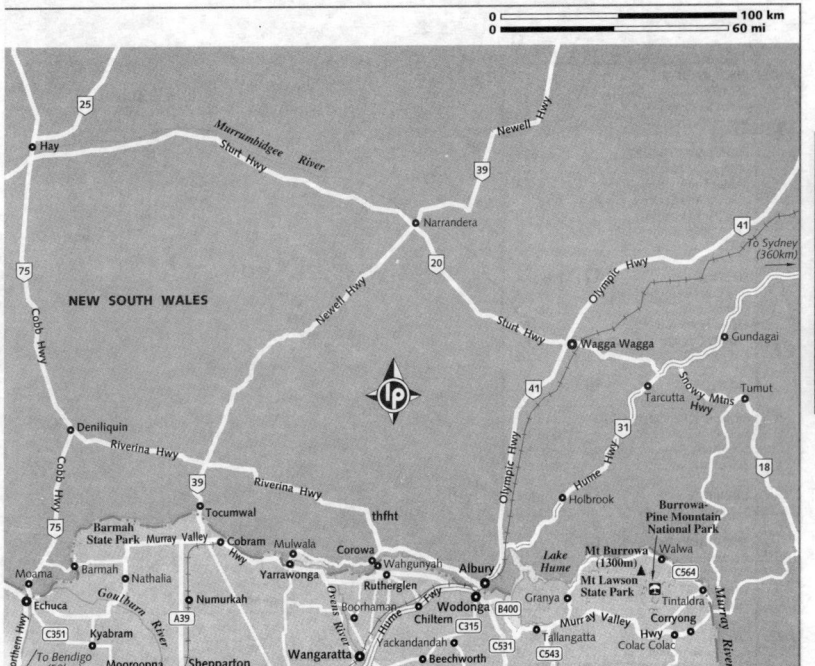

There are **camp sites** ($10) at Lake Hattah and Lake Mournpall, but limited water. Camping is free anywhere along the Murray River frontage, though resist camping under gum trees, as river red gums, in particular, can drop limbs without warning, even in still conditions.

MILDURA
☎ 03 / pop 28,060

After driving for hours through a dry and desolate landscape, you reach this thriving regional centre. Mildura, meaning 'red soil', is a true oasis town, watered by the mighty Murray River.

As well as being one of the richest agricultural areas in Australia, Mildura is a tourist town promoted as a place of endless blue skies and sunshine.

Information
The **visitors centre** (☎ 1300 550 858, 5188 8380; www.visitmildura.com.au; 180–190 Deakin Ave; ☒ 9am-5.30pm Mon-Fri, 9am-5pm Sat & Sun), located in the Alfred Deakin Centre, will book accommodation for you. They also have a leaflet, *The Chaffey Trail*, which guides you around local sights, including the paddle-steamer wharf, the Mildura weir and lock, Old Mildura Homestead, Mildara Wines and the Old Psyche Bend Pump Station. The theatrette shows two excellent short films on Mildura and the district. Also in the Alfred Deakin Centre is a café and aquatic

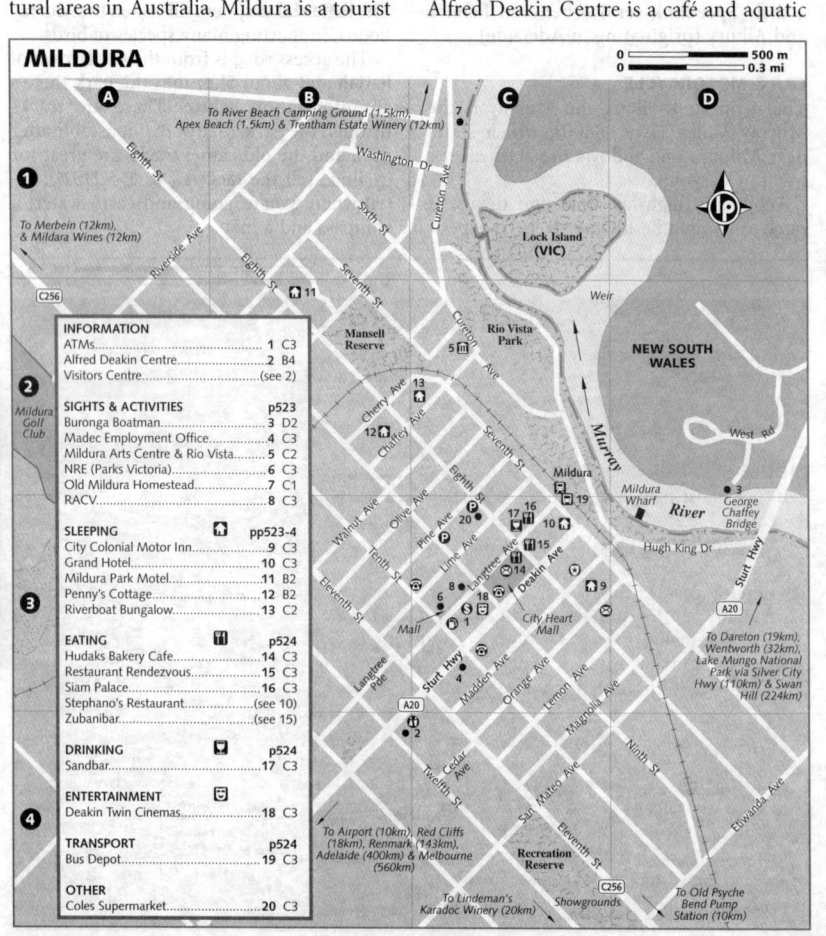

MILDURA

0 —————— 500 m
0 —————— 0.3 mi

To River Beach Camping Ground (1.5km),
Apex Beach (1.5km) & Trentham Estate Winery (12km)

Washington Dr

To Merbein (12km),
& Mildara Wines (12km)

Lock Island
(VIC)

Weir

INFORMATION	
ATMs	1 C3
Alfred Deakin Centre	2 B4
Visitors Centre	(see 2)

SIGHTS & ACTIVITIES	p523
Buronga Boatman	3 D2
Madec Employment Office	4 C3
Mildura Arts Centre & Rio Vista	5 C2
NRE (Parks Victoria)	6 C3
Old Mildura Homestead	7 C1
RACV	8 C3

SLEEPING	pp523-4
City Colonial Motor Inn	9 C3
Grand Hotel	10 C3
Mildura Park Motel	11 B2
Penny's Cottage	12 B2
Riverboat Bungalow	13 C2

EATING	p524
Hudaks Bakery Cafe	14 C3
Restaurant Rendezvous	15 C3
Siam Palace	16 C3
Stephano's Restaurant	(see 10)
Zubanibar	(see 15)

DRINKING	p524
Sandbar	17 C3

ENTERTAINMENT	
Deakin Twin Cinemas	18 C3

TRANSPORT	p524
Bus Depot	19 C3

OTHER	
Coles Supermarket	20 C3

Mildura
Golf
Club

Mansell
Reserve

Rio Vista
Park

NEW SOUTH
WALES

West Rd

Mildura

Mildura
Wharf

River

George
Chaffey
Bridge

Hugh King Dr

Stuart Hwy

City Heart
Mall

Mall

To Dareton (19km),
Wentworth (32km),
Lake Mungo National
Park via Silver City
Hwy (110km) & Swan
Hill (224km)

To Airport (10km), Red Cliffs
(18km), Renmark (143km),
Adelaide (400km) & Melbourne
(560km)

Recreation
Reserve

Showgrounds

To Lindeman's
Karadoc Winery (20km)

To Old Psyche
Bend Pump
Station (10km)

centre. The library next door to the centre provides Internet access.

FRUIT PICKING

Contact the employment agency **Madec** (☎ 5021 3359/2203, 5022 1797; cnr 10th St & Deakin Ave) for fruit-picking work. The main harvest season runs from about January to March and some casual work is available year round. The tourist office has a useful leaflet on fruit-picking work.

Sights & Activities

MILDURA ARTS CENTRE & RIO VISTA

This **complex** (☎ 5018 8322; 199 Cureton Ave; adult/child $4/2; ☯ 10am-5pm) at Rio Vista, the fabulously restored former home of WB Chaffey, combines an art gallery, theatre and museum.

WINERIES

The following wineries are open daily for tastings and sales, and have barbecue facilities.

Lindeman's Karadoc Winery (☎ 5051 3285; Karadoc; ☯ 10am-4.30pm) A huge complex 20km south of Mildura off the Calder Hwy. Café open 10am to 3pm Monday to Friday.

Mildara Wines (☎ 5025 2303; Merbein; ☯ 9am-5pm Mon-Fri, 10am-4pm Sat & Sun) On the Murray River 9km west of Mildura.

Trentham Estate Winery (☎ 5024 8888) Small winery in NSW, 12km from Mildura; the restaurant is open for lunch daily Tuesday to Sunday.

PADDLE-STEAMER CRUISES

Cruises depart from the Mildura Wharf at the end of Deakin Ave.

PS Melbourne (☎ 5023 2200) is the only original boat here still driven by steam. Two-hour cruises ($20/7.50 per adult/child) depart daily at 10.50am and 1.50pm.

The **PV Rothbury** (☎ 5023 2200) has two cruises on Thursday only. A winery cruise ($46/20 per adult/child, including lunch)

FRUIT FLY

An exclusion zone surrounding the Murray protects the fruit and vegetable crops from fruit fly and prohibits the carrying of fresh fruit or tomatoes into the zone. There are warning signs and disposal bins on the roads leading into the zone.

---

departs 10.30am and an evening dinner cruise ($45/20) departs at 7pm.

Paddle-steamer **Coonawarra** (☎ 1800 034 424; coonawarra@bigpond.com) has three- and five-day cruises starting from around $493.

BOAT HIRE

The **Buronga Boatman Boat Hire** (☎ 5023 5874), on the NSW side of the Murray River opposite Mildura Wharf, hires out kayaks, canoes and power boats.

Tours

Best known of several Aboriginal tour operations is **Harry Nanya Tours** (☎ 1800 630 864, 5027 2076), with a wide range of cultural tours, including a day trip ($75/37 per adult/child) to Mungo National Park, which is part of the Willandra Lakes system that contains the longest continual record of Aboriginal life in Australia, dating back some 45,000 years.

Jumbunna Walkabout Tours & Charter (☎ 0412-581 699) runs a similar tour, including barbecue lunch on Monday, Friday and Sunday ($60/29 per adult/child) departing from the visitors centre at 8am.

The **Broken Hill Express Coach** (☎ 5021 4424) goes from Mildura to Broken Hill ($50 one way) via Wentworth. You can book most tours at the visitors centre.

Sleeping

BUDGET

Mildura Park Motel (☎ 5023 0479, fax 5022 1651; 250 Eighth St; s/d $47/54; ☒) The Mildura Park is in a quiet residential area 1km or so west of Deakin Ave. It's a simple, standard motel and the welcoming management provides advice on the area.

Riverboat Bungalow (☎ 0418-147 363, 5021 5315; www.users.mildura.net.au/bungalow; 27 Chaffey Ave; dm per night/week $20/120; ▣) The Bungalow is in a nice old house and fairly close to most things. One-night stayers are welcome but rare. The Riverboat has a smaller property round the corner at 206 Eighth St (formerly called Zippy Koala) with the added perk of a small pool.

Riverbeach Camping Ground (☎ 5023 6879; apex@ ruralnet.net.au; Cureton Ave; camp/van sites $20/30, cabins $55-95) Blissfully located, right on the sandy river banks, Riverbeach has spick-and-span cabins and plenty of trees for shady sites. The fully-licensed café-bar is always a plus.

VICTORIA

MID-RANGE

City Colonial Motor Inn (☎ 5021 1800, fax 5023 4520; 24-30 Madden Ave; s/d $70/80; ❊) This solid efficiently-run motel with pool is one of a precious few within strolling distance of the restaurants and river. The rooms couple plush fitted-carpets with bare-brick walls; spa rooms and bridal suite available.

Grand Hotel (☎ 5023 0511; www.mildduragrandhotel .com; Seventh St; s/d from $77/110; ❊) The Grand is a palm-fronted Spanish mission-style building and is the swishest building in Mildura. Rooms have been given a slick new look; most have terraces overlooking the railtrack and river.

Acacia Houseboats (☎ 5022 1510; www.acacia boats.com.au; d $95, child $18) If you fancy an up-close river stay, this is one of several houseboats. You're on your own though – breakfast is provided for you to cook, let's hope they don't forget the milk.

There are several other houseboat companies in town. The visitors centre has a list.

TOP END

Penny's Cottage (☎ 5021 4043; www.pennyscottage .com.au; 34 Chaffey Ave; d from $130) This twee, self-contained cottage sits in a garden of lavender and roses. Rooms are small but cheerily painted in bright colours and decorated with a touch of class.

Eating

Zubanibar (☎ 5023 2336; 32 Langtree Ave; mains $8-15) This sympathetically designed eatery specialises in Greek flavours with heaping servings and a prevalence of paprika. Asian influences are here, too, in dishes like the tastily different five-spice quail and noodle salad.

Restaurant Rendezvous (☎ 5023 1571; 34 Langtree Ave; mains $18-21; ❊ dinner on Sat) There's serious history in this restaurant, which has been under the same owner since the 1950s. There's an old-fashioned opulent air with a menu influenced by French, Italian and modern Australian cuisine. Adjacent **Sunraysia Wine Centre** (☎ 5023 1571; 34 Langtree Ave) is a friendly laid-back place, run by the same owner.

Siam Palace (☎ 5023 7737; 35 Langtree Ave; mains $11-20) The Palace has absorbed a Japanese restaurant over the road so you can mix and match excellent Japanese, Chinese and Thai food. Avoid the house wine, it's boxed and better for pickling onions.

Stefano's Restaurant (☎ 5023 0511; Seventh St, entrance from Langtree Ave; banquet $80; ❊ dinner only) Bookings are essential for this award-winning restaurant in the cellars of the Grand Hotel. The chef, Stefano de Pieri, has become famous through his television series *A Gondola on the Murray*. You can buy the book, video and CD.

Hudaks Bakery Cafe (☎ 5023 1843; 139 Eighth St; lunch $4-7) Recently awarded the Oz Bakery of the Year award, this café has folk coming from as far as Melbourne to stock up their freezer with its orange and fruit loaf. Savoury treats include Mediterranean/Sicilian focaccias. Head upstairs to the terrace overlooking the mall for some people-watching.

Drinking

Sandbar (☎ 5021 2181; 43-45 Langtree St; snacks $7.50-12; ❊ noon-late Wed-Sat) This buzzy local watering-hole has a hip modern décor, beer garden and live entertainment.

Getting There & Away

AIR

Mildura airport is 10km west off the Sturt Hwy (A20). **Rex** (☎ 5023 5044; www.regional express.com.au) flies daily between Melbourne and Mildura ($120). **QantasLink** (☎ 13 13 13; www.qantas.com) also flies between Melbourne and Mildura ($125).

BUS

V/Line (☎ 13 61 96) has a nightly coach between Melbourne and Mildura (except Saturday), plus several daily train/coach services via Bendigo or Swan Hill ($63). V/Line also has a service connecting towns along the Murray River, including Swan Hill ($35), Echuca ($40) and Wodonga ($65).

CountryLink (☎ 5023 9065) bus lines operates a regular service to Sydney ($110). Book a week ahead for a 20% discount.

Long-distance coaches operate from near the train station on Seventh Ave.

SWAN HILL

☎ 03 / pop 9770

The hill which became Swan Hill was named by a weary Major Mitchell in 1836 after he was kept awake by swans in the nearby lagoon. Settled originally by sheep grazers, Swan Hill today is a major regional centre surrounded by irrigated farms producing grapes and other fruit.

The **visitors centre** (☎ 1800 625 373, 5032 3033; www.swanhillonline.com; 306 Campbell St; ☺ 9am-5pm) books riverboat cruises.

Sights & Activities

The **Swan Hill Pioneer Settlement** (☎ 5036 2410; www.pioneersettlement.com.au; Horseshoe Bend; adult/child $16/9; ☺ 9am-5pm) is a re-creation of a riverside port town and is essential visiting. The paddle-steamer PS *Pyap* makes short cruises along the Murray from here ($12/7 per adult/child) and at dusk there's a 45-minute **sound and light show** ($10/6).

The **MV Kookaburra** (☎ 5032 0003) has **lunch cruises** (adult/child $29/16). The **Tyntynder Homestead** (☎ 5037 6380; Murray Valley Hwy; adult/child $8.30/4; ☺ 10am-4pm school holidays, or by appointment), 16km northwest of the town, is a small museum of Aboriginal and pioneering relics.

Built in 1886, **Murray Downs Homestead** (☎ 02-5032 1225; Moulamein Hwy; adult/child $7.50/3.50; ☺ 9.30am-noon, closed Fri), 2km east of Swan Hill in NSW, has a private art collection and an authentic original look.

There are some excellent wineries in these parts including the **Buller's Caliope Winery** (☎ 5037 6305; Murray Valley Hwy; ☺ 9am-5pm Mon-Sat), 14km north of town on the Murray Valley Hwy, and **Best's St Andrews Vineyard** (☎ 5037 2154; Wilsons Rd; ☺ 10am-5pm Mon-Sat; tours 11am & 3pm Mon-Fri), 17km south of Swan Hill. The latter specialises in fortified wines and brandies.

Sleeping & Eating

Pioneer Station Motel (☎ 5032 2017, fax 5033 1387; 421 Campbell St; s/d $48/50) The Pioneer is one of the cheapest motels in these parts and is perfectly adequate. Although the rooms are small, they are gradually being reformed.

Burrabliss Farms (☎ 5037 2527; bliss@swanhill .net.au; 1556 Lakeside Dr; s/d $70/90, unit s/d $85/120) This gracious B&B is on the shores of Lake Boga's big puddle playground for watersports and pelicans. The rooms may be too floral and fussy for some, but the sitting room is super comfy and the newer separate unit is modern and bright. The owners run an ultrafine wool sheep farm if you fancy swotting up on your husbandry skills.

Sundowner Swan Hill Resort (☎ 5032 2726; www.sundownermotorinns.com.au; s/d $107/113; ☒) The rooms are nothing fancy but the range and quality of the facilities are mind-boggling. The exhaustive (and exhausting) list includes squash, tennis, mini-golf, inside/outside pools, a games room and even a trampoline, all in a Hollywood-style setting of lofty palms and tropical plants around the lagoon-shaped pool.

Allure (☎ 5032 4422; 247-249 Campbell St; dishes $7-13; ☺ dinner, lunch only Sun) No-nonsense healthy tucker with meat, fish and vegetarian options is the go here, plus a decadent Jamaican chocolate mousse. There's pavement seating on the quieter end of the main shopping street.

Tellers Cafe, Bar & Restaurant (☎ 5033 1383; 223 Campbell St; mains $8-16) Tellers is housed in a converted bank and has lots of dimly lit atmosphere at night, plus a bumper range of snacks and meals, including vegetarian options. The owner will also give backpackers a discount in return for an entertaining story (or two).

Getting There & Away

Trains and train/coach services run between Melbourne and Swan Hill ($51) via Bendigo. There are at least two daily coaches between Swan Hill and Mildura ($35), Echuca ($21) and Wodonga ($48).

GUNBOWER STATE FOREST

The forest, on 50km-odd-long Gunbower Island, stretches from Koondrook in the north to near Torrumbarry in the south. River red gum forests and swamps provide diverse habitats for the abundant bird and animal life.

Cohuna and Gunbower are the main access points, although there are tracks in from the highway; tracks on the island are impassable after rain. There are plenty of walks and many riverside campsites.

ECHUCA

☎ 03 / pop 10,950

Echuca, meaning 'the meeting of the waters', is where the Goulburn and Campaspe Rivers join the Murray.

The town was founded in 1853 by ex-convict Harry Hopwood, who established punt and ferry crossings over the Murray and Campaspe rivers. He built the Bridge Hotel in 1858 and watched his town grow into the busiest inland port in Australia. The wharf was once over a kilometre long and lined with shops and hotels.

VICTORIA

The **visitors centre** (☎ 1800 804 446, 5480 7555; www.echucamoama.com; 2 Heygarth St; ⏳ 9am-5pm) can book accommodation and sells V/Line tickets.

Coles supermarket on the corner of High and Darling Sts never closes. There's a laundrette near the American Hotel on Hare St.

Sights
HISTORIC PORT
The old-fashioned **Port of Echuca** (☎ 5482 4248; 52 Murray Esplanade; adult/child/family $11/7/30; ⏳ 9am-5pm) has a quasi-Disneyland appeal that all ages will enjoy.

A ticket combining the Port's attractions with a paddle-steamer cruise on the *Peven-sey, Alexander Arbuthnot* or *Adelaide* costs $22/12/54 per adult/child/family.

You can escape from the **Star Hotel** (45 Murray Esplanade), built in 1867, through an underground tunnel built to help drinkers avoid the police during the years when the pub was a 'sly grog shop'.

OTHER PORT AREA ATTRACTIONS
The **Red Gum Works** has woodturners and blacksmiths working river red gum wood. Nearby, the **Sharp's Magic Movie House & Penny Arcade** (☎ 5482 2361; Murray Esplanade; adult/child $13/9; ⏳ 9am-5pm) has a wonderful collection of penny-arcade machines and shows old movies. Try the mouth-watering home-made fudge here as well.

ECHUCA

0 ———— 800 m
0 ———— 0.5 mi

To Kingfisher Wetland Cruises (40km)

To Deniliquin (74km)

Moama

NEW SOUTH WALES

See Enlargement

Horseshoe Lagoon Park

Banyule Park State Forest

To Swan Hill (155km)

Echuca

0 ———— 200m
0 ———— 200yd

INFORMATION		Nomads Oasis Backpackers..............16 C3
Visitors Centre..............................1 D2		Steampacket Motor Inn....................17 A2
SIGHTS & ACTIVITIES	**pp526-7**	**EATING** 🍴 **p528**
Bridge Hotel....................................2 A1		Fiori..18 A2
Historical Society Museum................3 A1		Oscar W's at the Wharf..................19 A1
Murray Esplanade Cellars.................4 A2		Port Precinct Café...........................20 A1
Murray River		
Paddlesteamers.............................5 A1		**DRINKING**
National Holden Museum.................6 A1		Star Wine Bar Cafe......................(see 10)
Paddle-Steamer Wharf.....................7 A1		
Red Gum Works..............................8 A1		**ENTERTAINMENT** 🎬
Sharp's Magic Movie house & Penny		Cinema..21 C3
Arcade...9 A1		Paramount.....................................22 C3
Star Hotel.....................................10 A1		
Steven Brook Estate.......................11 A2		**OTHER**
World in Wax................................12 A1		Boat Ramp.....................................23 C1
		Coles Supermarket.........................24 C3
SLEEPING 🛏 **p527**		Echuca Boat & Canoe Hire...........(see 23)
Campaspe Lodge............................13 A2		MV Mary Ann Booking Office........25 A2
Echuca Gardens B&B......................14 D3		PS Emmylou Booking Office..........(see 9)
Echuca Gardens YHA...................(see 14)		PS Pride of the Murray Booking
High Street Motel...........................15 C2		Office..26 A1

875 ↓ Northern Hwy to Bendigo (91km) & Melbourne (203km)

Murray Valley Hwy B400

Industrial Estate

VICTORIA

World in Wax (☎ 5482 3630; 630 High St; adult/child $8.80/4.40; ⏱ 9am-5.30pm) immortalises a cast of 60 famous and gruesome people ranging from the British royal family to Paul Hogan.

You can take a 10-minute **tour** (adult/child/family $5/4/15) in a horse-drawn carriage daily in the Port precinct.

For tipplers, there are wine-tastings at **Murray Esplanade Cellars** (☎ 5482 6058; 2 Leslie St; ⏱ 9am-5pm) and the **Steven Brook Estate** (☎ 5480 1916; 620 High St).

MUSEUMS

Echuca's **Historical Society Museum** (☎ 5482 4225; 1-3 Dickson St; adult/child $2.50/1; ⏱ 11am-3pm) is in the old (1867) police station and includes interesting pictures from the riverboat era. Car buffs may prefer the **National Holden Museum** (☎ 5480 2033; 7-11 Warren St; adult/child $6/3; ⏱ 9am-5pm) which houses more than 40 restored Holden cars and associated automotive memorabilia.

Activities

A **paddle-steamer cruise** along the Murray is a real treat. **Murray River Paddlesteamers** (☎ 5480 2237; www.emmylou.com.au; 57 Murray Esplanade; ⏱ 9am-5pm) sells tickets for the **PS Emmylou** (adult/child $17/8 for 90 minutes) with overnight cruises available, and the **PS Pride of the Murray** (adult/child $13/6.50 per hr). **PS Adelaide** (☎ 5482 4248; 1-hr cruise adult/child $17.50/7.50) is the oldest wooden-hulled paddle-steamer still operating anywhere in the world; it occasionally has cruises. There's also **MV Mary Ann** (☎ 5480 2200; 624 High St), a cruising restaurant rather than a paddle-steamer.

Echuca Boat & Canoe Hire (☎ 5480 6208; www.echucaboatcanoehire.com) hires motor boats, kayaks and canoes from the Victoria Park boat ramp, about 700m north of the wharf. A four-hour paddle costs $65 for two, and longer hires are available.

For **horse riding**, contact **Billabong Trail Rides** (☎ 5483 5122), where a two-hour ride costs $50.

On a less energetic note, the spanking new **Paramount** (☎ 1900 931 166; 392 High St) has big screen movies and occasional live shows.

Sleeping

BUDGET

High Street Motel (☎/fax 5482 1013; 439 High St; s/d $55/66; ⏱) This motel has a lot going for it: it's closer to the port area than many of its considerably costlier neighbours. The word is out, however, so book ahead if you're here on a weekend. Rooms are unspectacular but comfy.

Nomads Oasis Backpackers (☎ 5480 7866; www.backpackersechuca.com; 410-424 High St; dm night/week $19/133) This is a purpose-built, large working hostel. Overnighters are welcome but rare. The owner can provide transport and find work in season.

Echuca Gardens YHA (☎ 0419 881 054, 5480 6522; www.echucagardens.com; 103 Mitchell St; dm $18-22; ⏱) This hostel is quiet and cosy with an intriguing warren of rooms and a pretty garden. The owner is a world traveller and pianist who, with a little arm-twisting, will perform for his guests. Bicycle hire costs $5 a day.

MID-RANGE

Steampacket Motor Inn (☎ 5482 3411, fax 5482 3408; 37 Murray Esplanade; s $80-100, d $95-130; ⏱) This refreshingly unfussy accommodation is in a National Trust classified building on the fringe of the old port. The friendly owner is also a whiz at bumper bacon and egg breakfasts. Children welcome.

Campaspe Lodge (☎ 5482 1087; 571 High St; www.echucahotel.com; d $100, family unit $150-180; ⏱) A surprising find at the back of the Echuca Hotel. The five doubles and two family units are modern and pleasant, and right on the banks of the tranquil Campaspe River. The location makes the place, including the handy proximity of bistro and beer garden.

Echuca Gardens B&B (☎ 0419-881 054, 5480 6522; www.echucagardens.com; 103 Mitchell St; d from $120) On the edge of Banyule State Forest near the river, this place is a 10-minute walk from the town centre. Each room has a bathroom and is individually decorated with an Australian theme in a quirky art-draped house that displays the creative talents of the owner.

TOP END

Murray House B&B (☎ 5482 4944; keephall@mcmedia.com.au; 55 Francis St; s/d $100/180) The Murray House is furnished in old-world-grandeur style with deep-pile carpets. This is the kind of place where a pre-dinner sherry is *de rigueur*. The rooms are pure luxury and there's a comfortable lounge-cum-library with piano.

Eating

Port Precinct Cafe (☎ 5480 2163; 591 High St; dishes $7-10; 🖥) The Port is an Internet café with painfully slow connection, but you can, at least, eat well while you wait. Food specialities here include fancy filled pancakes, tasty focaccias and, arguably the best caffeine hit in town. Dinner is not available.

Star Wine Bar & Cafe (☎ 5480 1181; 45 Murray Esplanade; dishes $6-12) Part of the Star Hotel, this café sells snacks and light meals during the day and dinner on Friday and Saturday. The bar has a nice moody atmosphere with interesting art work, and there's a leafy patio at the back. The food is typically cross-cultural with just enough eastern influence to spice things up.

Oscar W's at the Wharf (☎ 5482 5133; 101 Murray Esplanade; mains $12-26) Offering a whiff of charm and elegance, Oscar W's makes the heady claim of being the sole Australian restaurant overlooking the Murray. It seems unlikely but who cares, the food is excellent and not too pricey. Try the Murray Cod speciality.

Fiori (☎ 5482 6688; 554 High St; pasta $16-20) Come here for a better class of pizza and pasta. This is Echuca's smart Italian place and the food really is irresistible, particularly the *mama mia*–style desserts.

Getting There & Away

V/Line (☎ 13 61 96) runs daily between Melbourne and Echuca ($32), changing from train to coach at Bendigo ($8 from Echuca). V/Line coaches connect Echuca with Wodonga ($35), Swan Hill ($21) and Mildura ($40) four times a week. There's also a daily coach to Adelaide and Albury Wodonga, which takes you to destinations in southern NSW.

BARMAH STATE PARK

Located 9km north of the small town of **Barmah**, this park is a wetland area created by the flood plains of the Murray River. The plains are forested with old river red gums and the swamp beneath usually floods in winter, creating a breeding area for many bird species. It's the largest remaining redgum forest in Australia (and thus the world).

The **Dharnya Centre** (☎ 03-5869 3302; fax 5869 3249; Sandridge Rd; 🕙 10.30am-4pm), run by the Yorta Yorta people, is a visitors centre and a good little museum with displays on Aboriginal heritage and the park. Nearby evidence demonstrates more than 40,000 years of continuous occupation, but the Yorta Yorta people's Native Title claim for the area was rejected by the Federal Court in 1998.

Gondwana Canoe Hire (☎ 03-5869 3347), midway between Barmah and the Dharnya Centre, hires out canoes for $25 per hour.

Let someone else do the work and take a two-hour wetland cruise on the **Kingfisher** (☎ 03-5480 2237; adult/child $20/14)

Sleeping

You can camp anywhere in the park or at the Barmah Lakes camping area. There are also caravan parks and a hotel-motel in Barmah.

YARRAWONGA
☎ 03 / pop 4030

On the western edge of the large Lake Mulwala, Yarrawonga is known for its aquatic activities and as a retirement centre.

The **visitors centre** (☎ 1800 062 260, 5744 1989; www.yarrawongamulwala.com; Irvine Pde; 🕙 9am-5pm) books accommodation, tours and activities.

Two converted house boats, the **Lady Murray** (☎ 5744 2005) and the **Paradise Queen** (☎ 5744 1843), operate cruises along the lake and the Murray River, including the lunch cruise ($18/9 per adult/child, 1½ hours) which includes BBQ and a full bar; the afternoon cruise ($12/6 per adult/child); and the sunset dinner cruise ($35/17 per adult/child).

Ski Rides (☎ 0419-211 122) rents a huge array of watercraft and offers **water-skiing** ($50 per half hour), **parasailing** ($60 per flight) and other boat-towed thrills.

RUTHERGLEN
☎ 02 / pop 1850

Dating from gold-rush days, Rutherglen is a quaint town, and is also the centre of one of Victoria's major wine-growing districts.

The **visitors centre** (☎ 1800 622 871, 6032 9166; www.visitrutherglen.com.au; 57 Main St; 🕙 9am-5pm) operates an accommodation referral system.

Sights & Activities
WINERIES & BREWERIES

There are 20 wineries around Rutherglen. Most open daily for tastings and sales; several have restaurants (see Eating; p529). The *Rutherglen Touring Guide*, available at the visitors centre, gives all the details.

While wineries are 10-a-penny, small local breweries are like hens' teeth. The **Buffalo Brewery** (☎/fax 5726 9215) at the Boorhaman Hotel in Boorhaman, 26km southwest of Rutherglen, produces five beers. These are superb (especially the ginger ale) and regularly win awards.

So that you can imbibe and not drive, there are a few outfits that run tours. **Linga Longa Tours** (☎ 5726 8489) and **Rutherglen Bus and Tour Service** (☎ 6032 8774) will ferry you wherever you want to go. Alternatively, the **Poachers Paradise Express** (☎ 6032 9502) runs you around three wineries in a horse-drawn coach. For something different, **olive oil tasting** is offered 15km east of Rutherglen at **Gooramadda Olives** (☎ 02-6026 5658; River Rd, Gooramadda; 11am-5pm Fri-Mon).

Festivals & Events

The **Winery Walkabout Weekend**, held in June, involves plenty of eating and drinking. Other festivals include the **Tastes of Rutherglen** in March and the **Winemakers' Legends Weekend** in mid-November. The **Tour de Muscat**, a bike ride around the wineries, is held in early November. Accommodation in the area is likely to be tight during these festivals.

Sleeping

Star Hotel (☎ 6032 9625; 105 Main St; s/d $35/60) This hotel is clean, friendly and does good Chinese chow at night. The strip of motel rooms at the back are excellent value with continental breakfast included in the price.

Wine Village Motor Inn (☎ 6032 9900, fax 6032 8125; 217 Main St; s/d $76/88) Central to town, the Wine Village has comfy large brick-clad rooms, a pool and barbecue.

The **House at Mt Prior Vineyard** (☎ 6026 5256; www.houseatmountprior.com; Howlong Rd; d $120-170) One of Victoria's only B&Bs on a working vineyard, there are six rooms in this 1860s turreted mansion including the plush-red bordello room. The shared bathrooms are a downside, but breakfast is excellent and there's a fancy restaurant; book ahead.

The **Vineyards at Tuileries** (☎ 6032 9033; www.tuileriesrutherglen.com.au; 13-35 Drummond St; d from $165; 🐾) Rooms are decorated theme-style at this money-no-object boutique hotel, including African, Moroccan, continental and minimalist Zen. Verandas overlook the surrounding vineyard and olive groves. Could be a little soulless for some.

Rutherglen Caravan Park (☎ 6032 8577, fax 6032 8533; 72 Murray St; camp sites $14-18, cabins $55-110) This park is centrally located. The owner runs a wine tour.

Eating

Rendezvous Courtyard (☎ 6032 9114; 68 Main St; mains $15-19; dinner) The menu at this place is Italian-influenced with a vast pasta section, ideal for those with undecided taste buds. Lighter bites are available, including good-looking and imaginative salads.

Tuilieries (☎ 6032 9033; 13-35 Drummond St; mains $25) Bookings are advisable for dinner here and vegetarians are catered for. There's a less formal café open for breakfast and lunch, serving wraps, sandwiches and the like.

Beaumont's Cafe (☎ 6032 7428; 84 Main St; mains $8-13) This snazzy Mediterranean-looking restaurant has a menu to match, including a long list of tapas you can afford to fill up with at prices between $3 and $7.

Several wineries have cafés and restaurants, including:

All Saints (The Terrace; ☎ 6033 1922; All Saints Rd; mains $22-30; lunch & snacks daily, dinner Sat) The Terrace, set in a landscaped garden with pond, offers a good selection of gourmet meals and fine wines to lubricate the palate.

St Leonards (Lazy Grape; ☎ 6033 1004; St Leonards Rd; mains $12-17) The Lazy provides the ingredients and you barbecue them. There's live jazz on the first and third Sunday of every month. Try the handmade sparkling shiraz.

Cofield (Pickled Sisters; ☎ 6033 2377; Distillery Rd; mains $12-24; lunch Wed-Mon, dinner Fri & Sat) The sophisticated menu here includes tipsy wine-based dishes.

Getting There & Away

A **V/Line** (☎ 13 61 96) coach runs to Wangaratta ($5) and connects with the Melbourne train on Monday, Wednesday, Friday and Sunday. Four days a week, the Murray Link coach, operated by V/Line, links Rutherglen with Albury to the east and Mildura, via Echuca and Swan Hill, to the west.

CHILTERN

☎ 03 / pop 1040

Just off the Hume Fwy, tiny Chiltern is one of Victoria's most historic townships. Gold was discovered here in 1859 and mining continued until the early 1900s – not much has changed since then.

VICTORIA

There are a few places to see, such as the **Athenaeum Library & Museum**, now the historical society museum and the **Grapevine Hotel/Theatre** (formerly the Star). Just wandering around is interesting, especially if you're into antiques and collectibles. Not sure where the locals shop for bread and milk though…

There's a caravan park, a motel and a B&B or two.

WODONGA

☎ 02 / pop 27,730

The twin towns of Albury and Wodonga are separated by the Murray River, which acts as the Victoria-NSW border. They recently amalgamated as a single town, but what effect that will have on travellers remains to be seen.

The **visitors centre** (☎ 1800 800 743, 6041 3875, fax 6021 0322; Gateway Village, Lincoln Causeway; 🕑 9am-5pm), between Wodonga and the Murray, has information on both Victoria and NSW, and books accommodation.

Wodonga Caravan & Cabin Park (☎ /fax 6024 2598; 186 Melbourne Rd; tent/van sites from $21/43, cabins from $55) is the closest caravan park to the town centre and has a pool, barbecue and brand-new kiddie playground.

There is a better choice of places to stay across the river in Albury – for more information see p228.

Getting There & Away

There are daily V/line trains to/from Melbourne ($46).

WODONGA TO CORRYONG – THE UPPER MURRAY

The Murray Valley Hwy continues east of Wodonga skirting Lake Hume.

Boathaven Holiday Park (☎ 02-6020 6130, fax 6020 6066; www.boathaven.com.au; Boathaven Rd, Ebden; camp sites $22-25, cabins $69-155), on the edge of Lake Hume 12km east of Wodonga, is pure luxury with fabulous landscaping. It has a cool pool, playground, spa sports facilities and canoes for hire. It is also a good base for exploring Lake Hume.

Further east along the Murray Valley Hwy is new **Tallangatta**. The buildings were transported here from old Tallangatta, which disappeared when the valley was flooded to make the lake. Seven kilometres east of the town, there's a **lookout** from where you can see the streets and railway of

old Tallangatta – provided the lake is low. Otherwise there's an interpretative board and your imagination.

There's a turn-off to the town of **Granya**, 15km east of Tallangatta.

The small town of **Corryong** is the Victorian gateway to the NSW Snowy Mountains and Mt Kosciuszko National Park. **Jack Riley's Grave**, found in the cemetery at the top of Pioneer Ave, is engraved with the words: 'In memory of the Man from Snowy River, Jack Riley, buried here 16th July 1914'. The **Man from Snowy River Folk Museum** (☎ 02-6076 1114; 103 Hansen St; admission $4; 🕑 10am-noon & 2-4pm, closed Jun-Aug) isn't actually dedicated to the legend but is more of a local history museum. Still, it houses a fascinating collection of items and is a 'must see' museum.

GOLDFIELDS

The Goldfields region of central Victoria is a great area to explore, with quaint townships, impressive regional centres and pretty countryside. Explore the back roads and, if you have a few days, you could even hire a gypsy caravan. **Colonial Way** (☎ 02-5437 3054; www.colonialway.com.au; from $770/week) rents caravans pulled by Clydesdale horses.

There's still gold in 'them thar hills' and metal detectors and prospecting gear can be bought or hired in many towns.

The Goldfields Tourist Route takes in all the major gold-rush centres. A route map is available from most of the visitors centres along the way.

Central Victoria is also a major wine-producing area. The main regions are the Pyrenees Ranges near Avoca, the Heathcote region and around Bendigo.

The Goldfields Tourist Route takes in all the major gold-rush centres. A route map is available from most of the visitors centres along the way.

BALLARAT

☎ 03 / pop 73,000

The area was known to the Watha Warrung (Aboriginal people of the area) as 'Ballaarat' (resting place). European pastoralists arrived in 1837 and the discovery of gold at nearby Buninyong in 1851 saw thousands of diggers flood into the area. After alluvial goldfields were played out, deep shaft mines were sunk,

BALLARAT

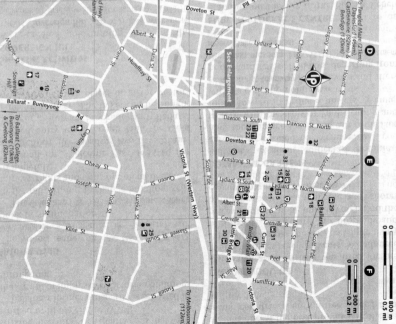

VICTORIA

INFORMATION
Hospital..................................	1 C2
Telephone..............................	2 E2
Visitors Centre.......................	3 E2

SIGHTS & ACTIVITIES p532
Adventure Playground...........	4 A1
Ballarat Fine Art Gallery........	5 E2
Ballarat Showgrounds...........	6 C1
Ballarat Wildlife Park............	7 F3
Eureka Stockade Centre.........	8 F3
Gold Museum........................	9 D4
Sovereign Hill Historical Park..	10 D4
The Gold Shop.......................	11 E2
Tram Musuem........................	12 A2

EATING p534
Chok Dee Thai Restaurant.....	20 F2
Da Vinci's..............................	21 E2
Gee Cees Cafe Bar.................	22 E2
L'Espresso.............................	23 D2
Tokyo Grill House..................	(see 20)
Views Bar & Café...................	24 C2

ENTERTAINMENT p534
Eureka Swimming Centre.......	25 F4
Her Majesty's Theatre............	26 E2
Irish Murphy's........................	27 E2
Regent Multiplex Cinema.......	28 E1

TRANSPORT pp534-5
Ballarat Coachlines...............	29 E1
Bus Terminal (Local).............	30 E1
Bus/Train Terminal................	31 F2

OTHER
Parks Victoria........................	32 E1
RACV....................................	33 E2

SLEEPING ☐ ppXXXX-XXX
Ballarat Goldfields Holiday Park.	13 F4
Craig's Royal Hotel................	14 E2
George Hotel.........................	15 E2
Nieder Wiesel.......................	16 C2
Sovereign Hill Lodge YHA......	17 D4
Tavana Lodge.......................	18 E1
The Bradvic..........................	19 C2

striking incredibly rich quartz reefs that were worked until the end of WWI.

Ballarat's former prosperity is reflected in the wealth of impressive Victorian buildings throughout.

Information

The **visitors centre** (☎ 1800 446 633, 5320 5672; www.ballarat.com; 39 Sturt St; ⏰ 9am-5pm) will book accommodation.

The **Gold Shop** (☎ 5333 4242; 8A Lydiard St North), in the old Mining Exchange building, sells miners' rights and rents out metal detectors to hopefuls.

A Ballarat 'Welcome Pass' ($34/16 per adult/child) gives visitors two days of un-limited entry to Sovereign Hill, the Gold Museum, Eureka Stockade and Ballarat Fine Art Gallery. The ticket can be bought from any of these places or at the visitors centre.

Sights & Activities

SOVEREIGN HILL

A re-created gold-mining town of the 1860s, **Sovereign Hill** (☎ 5331 1944; www.soverei gnhill.com.au; Bradshaw St; adult/child/family $27/13/70; ⏰ 10am-5pm) is an entertaining living his-tory museum, with actors dressed in period costumes. You can pan for gold and may find a speck or two. There are also two underground tours of re-created mines plus a gold pour, which transforms $50,000 of liquid gold into a 3kg bullion bar.

The nightly sound-and-light show 'Blood on the Southern Cross' is a simulation of the Eureka Stockade battle. There are two per-formances daily, Monday to Saturday, with start times dependent on the sunset. Show-only tickets are $32/25 per adult/child; dinner-and-show tickets costs $56/48. Bookings are essential (☎ 5333 5777).

GOLD MUSEUM

Over the road from Sovereign Hill, this excellent **museum** (☎ 5337 1107; Bradshaw St; admission included in Sovereign Hill ticket, separate admis-sion $6.30; ⏰ 9.30am-5.30pm) has imaginative displays, gold nuggets and coins. An audio-visual show tells the story of the Watha Wurrung (Aboriginal people of the area).

BALLARAT FINE ART GALLERY

The fine **art gallery** (☎ 5320 5858; 40 Lydiard St North; adult/child $4/1; ⏰ 10.30am-5pm) is the old-

est and one of the best provincial galleries in the country. There's a free guided tour at 2pm daily.

LAKE WENDOUREE

This large artificial lake was used for the 1956 Olympics rowing events. Wendouree Pde, which circles the lake, is where many of the city's particularly jaw-dropping and pricey houses can be found. You'll find the old timber boatsheds along the lake's shores equally charming, in their own way.

BOTANICAL GARDENS

Ballarat's excellent 40-hectare botanical gardens are beside Lake Wendouree. If you have the stomach for it, you can come face to face with the likes of Paul Keating and John Howard in Prime Ministers' Avenue, with its collection of bronze busts.

A tourist **tramway** runs on weekend after-noons and school holidays, departing from the **tram museum** (☎ 5334 1580; South Gardens Reserve, Lake Wendouree).

EUREKA STOCKADE CENTRE

Standing on the site of the Eureka Rebel-lion, the **Eureka Stockade Centre** (☎ 5333 1854; cnr Eureka & Rodier Sts; adult/child $9/5; ⏰ 9am-5pm) has multimedia galleries simulating the battle.

OTHER ATTRACTIONS

One of Australia's finest streetscapes of Victorian architecture is Ballarat's **Lydiard St**. Impressive buildings include Her Maj-esty's Theatre, the art gallery and Craig's Royal Hotel. A brochure is available from the visitors centre.

Good for families, the **Ballarat Wildlife Park** (☎ 5333 5933; cnr Fussell & York Sts; adult/child/family $14/8/41; ⏰ 9am-5.30pm) has native animals, reptiles and a few exotics. Guided tours are at 11am and there are several daily shows.

Who can resist a maze? The **Tangled Maze** (☎ 5345 2847; Midland Hwy; adult/child/family $6/5/22; ⏰ 10am-5.30pm), north of town, covers over an acre with plenty of twists and turns. There's also a mini golf course, tearoom and picnic areas.

Festivals & Events

Ballarat's 100-year-old **Begonia Festival** (which blooms in early March) attracts thousands of

GOLD FEVER

In May 1851 EH Hargraves discovered gold near Bathurst in NSW and sensational accounts of the find caused thousands of people to drop everything to try their luck.

News of the discovery reached Melbourne at the same time as the accounts of its influence on the people of New South Wales. Sydney had been virtually denuded of workers and the same misfortune soon threatened Melbourne.

A reward was offered to anyone who could find gold within 300km of Melbourne. Within a week, gold was discovered in the Yarra River but the find was soon eclipsed by a more significant discovery at Clunes. Prospectors headed to central Victoria, reversing the rush north across the Murray as fresh gold finds became an almost weekly occurrence in Victoria.

Gold was found in the Pyrenees, Warrandyte, Buninyong, and the Loddon and Avoca Rivers. Ballarat, in September 1851, produced the biggest discovery, followed by other significant finds at Bendigo, Mt Alexander, Beechworth, Walhalla, Omeo, and in the hills and creeks of the Great Dividing Range.

By the end of 1851 about 250,000 ounces of gold had been claimed. Farms and businesses lost their workforces and were often abandoned, as employers had no choice but to follow their workers to the goldfields. Hopeful miners came from England, Ireland, Europe, China and the failing goldfields of California – during 1852 about 1800 people arrived in Melbourne each week.

The government imposed a licence fee of 30 shillings a month for all prospectors. This entitled the miners to an eight-foot square claim in which to dig for gold and it provided the means to enforce improvised law. Any miner without a licence could be fined or imprisoned. Although this later caused serious unrest, it was successful in averting the lawlessness that had characterised the California rush.

The classic features accompanying gold fever were the backbreaking work, the unwholesome food, hard drinking and the primitive dwellings. Amazing wealth was the luck of some but the elusive dream of others; for every story of success, there were hundreds more of hardship, despair and death.

The gold rush had its share of rogues, including the notorious bushrangers, but it also had its heroes – the martyrs of the Eureka Stockade, a miners' rebellion that eventually forced political change in the colony (see the boxed text 'The Eureka Rebellion'; p535).

Above all, the gold rush ushered in a fantastic era of growth and material prosperity for Victoria, opening up vast areas of country previously unexplored by white people.

In the first 12 years of the rush, Victoria's population rose from 77,000 to 540,000. To cope with the moving population and the tonnes of gold and supplies, the development of roads and railways was accelerated.

The mining companies that followed the independent diggers invested heavily in the region over the next couple of decades. The huge shantytowns of tents, bark huts, raucous bars and police camps were eventually replaced by the timber and stone buildings which became the foundation of many of Victoria's provincial cities.

The gold towns reached the height of splendour in the 1880s. Gold gradually lost its importance but, by then, the gold towns had stable populations plus agriculture and other activities to maintain economic prosperity.

Gold also made Melbourne Australia's largest city and financial centre, a position it held for nearly half a century.

VICTORIA

visitors and accommodation can be hard to find at this time, so book in advance.

Sleeping
BUDGET
Tawana Lodge (☎ /fax 5331 3461; 128 Lydiard St North; s $33-44, d $58-70) With red the predominant colour in the OK furnished rooms, this is probably not the place to stay when it's 40°C outside. Have a look up the stairwell at the murals of reclining chaste young ladies.

Sovereign Hill Lodge YHA (☎ 5333 3409, fax 5333 5861; Magpie St; dm/s/d $21/30/60). This excellent and classy YHA is a good mid-priced hostel, though a bit heavy on the dark wood.

Single and double rooms with bathrooms are available. Book well in advance to avoid disappointment.

Ballarat Goldfields Holiday Park (☎ 5332 7888, fax 5332 4244; 108 Clayton St; camp sites $20-23, cabins $56-68; 🖳) This is the closest caravan park to Sovereign Hill and one of the best-equipped in these parts. There's a pool, games room and tennis courts, plus fancy three-bedroom villas for about double the cabin cost.

MID-RANGE

Bradvic (☎ 5334 4404; 5 Raglan St; s/d $100/130) This no-muddy-boots B&B is in-between the town centre and lake, although a bit of a hike to both. It features a quasi-French style interior with fitted carpets, queen-size brass beds, and a sitting room. Guests have use of the kitchen.

George Hotel (☎ 5333 4866; www.ballarat.com /george; 27 Lydiard St North; s/d $69/80) Rooms in this fine historic building have been blandly modernised, but are a good size and functional with bathrooms. There's a gaming room if you fancy a flutter.

THE AUTHOR'S CHOICE

Craig's Royal Hotel (☎ 5331 1377; www .craigsroyal.com, 10 Lydiard St South; d $56, d with bathroom $95-115, ste $150-300) The best of the grand old pubs, so named after it hosted visits by the Prince of Wales and the Duke of Edinburgh. This grand old Victorian building is a wonderful place to stay and, more importantly, because there are so many calibre rooms and suites, it comes remarkably cheap or fabulously expensive. Either way, the overall feel is old-fashioned opulence – despite the creaky floorboards. Choose from singles with washbasin and faded floral bedspreads to fabulously grand suites with sweeping city views.

TOP-END

Nieder Weisel (☎ 5331 8829; www.ballarat.com /niederweisel; 109 Webster St; d from $140) This palatial Victorian accommodation is difficult to describe without launching into serious superlative overdose. In short, this place is fabulous with vast rooms, incredible antiques and a wonderful classy yet comfortable feel. There are various packages available throughout the year.

Eating

L'Espresso (☎ 5333 1789; 417 Sturt St; dishes $10-24; 🕑 lunch daily, dinner Fri & Sat) Just the place to address your morning hangover, L'Espresso springs to life at breakfast. One wall is lined with jazz, blues and rock records. There's some interesting food and a buzzy duskier mood at dinner.

Gee Cees Cafe Bar (☎ 5331 6211; 427 Sturt St; mains $14-22) Gee Cees is a deservedly popular café with good food, including spicy stir-fries, wood-fired pizza and interesting, colourful salads. The interior is a little dinerlike – outside under the brollies is best.

Chok Dee Thai Restaurant (☎ 5331 7361; 113 Bridge Mall; mains $12-23) Chok Dee has a good vibe and wide-ranging Thai menu with all the right spices, like lemongrass and ginger.

Tokyo Grill House (☎ 5333 3945; 109-111 Bridge Mall; mains $17-24) Fresh, exquisite food is just as it should be at this appealing Japanese restaurant. There is also a range of set meals for the uninitiated.

Views Bar & Cafe (☎ 5331 4592; 22 Wendouree Pde; dishes $7.50-23) The buzzy atmosphere at this bistro-style restaurant by the lake attracts a hip young crowd, especially on live music nights. It serves sandwiches, pizza, smoothies and spiders,

Da Vinci's (☎ 5333 4114; 29 Sturt St; mains $13-24) Not just another bolognaise predictable, this one packs them in with its innovative sauces, man-size portions and, quite possibly, an Italian in the kitchen.

Entertainment

George Hotel (☎ 5333 4866; 27 Lydiard St North) The historic George is one of the better venues for bands from 9.30pm to 4am on Friday and Saturday nights.

Irish Murphy's (☎ 5331 4091; 36 Sturt St) This Guinness theme pub has bands from Thursday to Sunday night.

Her Majesty's Theatre (☎ 5333 5800; 17 Lydiard St South) Ballarat's posh venue hosts the performing arts.

Regent Multiplex Cinema (☎ 5331 1556; 49 Lydiard St) This is a super central cinema showing all the latest big-screen favourites.

Getting There & Around

V/Line (☎ 13 61 96) trains run frequently between Melbourne and Ballarat (1¾ hours, $17).

THE EUREKA REBELLION

Life on the goldfields was a great leveller, erasing social distinction as doctors, merchants, ex-convicts and labourers toiled side by side in the mud. But as the easily won gold began to run out, the diggers recognised the inequalities between themselves and the privileged few who held land and government.

The limited size of claims and the inconvenience of licence hunts (see the 'Gold Fever' boxed text; p533) coupled with police brutality, taxation without political representation and the realisation that they could not get good farming land, fired unrest that led to the Eureka Rebellion.

In September 1854, Governor Hotham ordered that the hated licence hunts be carried out twice a week. In the following October a miner was murdered near a Ballarat hotel after an argument with the owner, James Bentley.

When Bentley was found not guilty, by a magistrate who just happened to be his business associate, a group of miners rioted over the injustice and burned his hotel. Bentley was re-tried and found guilty, but the rioting miners were also jailed which fuelled their distrust of authority.

Creating the Ballarat Reform League, the diggers called for the abolition of licence fees, a miner's right to vote and increased opportunities to purchase land.

On 29 November, about 800 miners burnt their licences at a mass meeting and built a stockade at Eureka, led by Irishman Peter Lalor, where they prepared to fight for their rights.

On 3 December the government ordered troopers to attack the stockade. There were only 150 diggers within the makeshift barricades at the time and the fight lasted only 20 minutes, leaving 30 miners and five troopers dead.

Although the rebellion was short-lived, the miners were ultimately successful in their protest. They had won the sympathy of most Victorians and the government deemed it wise to acquit the leaders of the charge of high treason.

The licence fee was abolished. A miner's right, costing one pound a year, gave the right to search for gold and to fence in, cultivate and build a dwelling on a moderate-sized piece of land; and to vote. The rebel miner Peter Lalor actually became a member of parliament himself some years later.

V/Line also has daily services to Geelong ($12) and Mildura ($55) via St Arnaud and weekday services to Warrnambool ($20), Hamilton ($29), Maryborough ($8.70) and Bendigo ($21) via Daylesford ($12) and Castlemaine ($15). Coaches run to Ararat ($15) and Stawell ($18).

McCafferty's/Firefly/Greyhound (☎ 13 14 99, 13 20 30, 9670 7500; www.mccaffertys.com.au) buses stop at the train station on the Melbourne–Adelaide run.

The local bus line covers most of the town; timetables are available at the visitors centre.

For a cab, call **Ballarat Taxis** (☎ 13 10 08).

CLUNES

☎ 03 / pop 1100

Clunes, a charming little town 32km north of Ballarat, was the site of Victoria's first significant gold discovery in June 1851. There's little to see here, although it's worth stopping by for a tea-break, or to visit nearby **Mt Beckworth**, noted for its orchids and birdlife. You can also visit the old gold diggings of **Jerusalem** and **Ullina**.

If you've got time to kill, there's a small **museum** (☎ 5345 3592; 36 Fraser St; adult/child $2.50/0.50; ☺ 10am-4.30pm Sat, Sun & school holidays) in the town itself, with a collection of dusty pioneer-time relics.

Keebles of Clunes (☎ 5345 3200; www.ballarat.com/keebles.htm; 114 Bailey St; s/d $99/137, cottages $159) is a divine period-style guesthouse in a restored country pub. There are two self-contained cottages, plus rooms with bathrooms in the main building.

DAYLESFORD & HEPBURN SPRINGS

☎ 03 / pop 3420

The twin towns of Daylesford and Hepburn Springs are enjoying a revival as the 'spa centre of Victoria', a claim made as long ago as the 1870s.

As well as tourists, this area attracts hedonists, spirituality seekers and escapees from the city rat race. The population is an interesting blend of old-timers and alternative-lifestylers, and there's a thriving gay and lesbian scene. Winter is the busy time.

BUNINYONG by Michelle Coxall

☎ 03 / pop 2500

The historic gold-mining town of Buninyong is 10km south of Ballarat – follow the Midland Hwy out past Sovereign Hill. In addition to wonderful examples of colonial architecture and one of Victoria's oldest botanical gardens, there are a couple of fine-dining opportunities – **Cafe Pasha** (☎ 5341 2543) and **Tiggies** (☎ 5341 2999) – and a **pub** with bands on weekends. Other attractions are galleries, a great second-hand bookshop (☎ 5341 3080), walks, wineries, horse trail-riding and a mountain-view lookout with unsurpassed views over the region. Buninyong has several B&Bs with prices ranging from $100 to $150 per night, including **Brim Brim** (☎ 5341 2060). There are regular bus services that run between Ballarat and Buninyong; contact **Davis Motor Services** (☎ 5331 7777) for details.

The Daylesford **visitors centre** (☎ 5348 1339; visitorinfo@hepburn.vic.gov.au; 98 Vincent St; ⏱ 9am-5pm) is handily located next to the post office and an Internet café.

Sights & Activities

Swanky **Hepburn Spa Resort** (☎ 5348 2034; www .hepburnspa.com.au; Mineral Springs Reserve; ⏱ 10am-8pm Mon-Fri, 9am-10pm Sat & Sun) is a large and luxurious centre with heated spas, plunge pools, flotation tanks, beauty treatments, massages and saunas. It gets pretty packed on weekends and it's recommended to book in advance; prices are lower during the week.

Around the spa are several **mineral springs**, most pretty strong in flavour. There are some good **walking trails** and the visitors centre has maps and guides.

The **Convent Gallery** (☎ 5348 3211; Daly St; admission $3.50; ⏱ 10am-5pm) is a magnificent 19th-century convent converted into a craft-and-art gallery with café.

Boats and kayaks can be hired at **Lake Daylesford** and there's the even prettier **Jubilee Lake** about 3km southeast of town.

The **Historical Society Museum** (☎ 5348 3242; 100 Vincent St; adult/child $3/0.50; ⏱ 1.30-4.30pm Sat & Sun) is next to the visitors centre. The **Daylesford Sunday Market** is held on Sunday mornings at the train station.

For a whiff of Italia, stop by **Lavandula** (☎ 5476 4393; 350 Hepburn Newstead Rd; admission $3; ⏱ 10.30am-5.30pm Wed-Mon), a Swiss-Italian farm growing lavender, olives and grapes. You can buy all the associated products in the shop or try lavender scones (an acquired taste) in the restaurant.

Among the antique and collectibles shops are two good bookshops: **Avant Garden Bookshop & Gallery** (☎ 5348 1288; 46 Vincent St) and **Lake Daylesford Book Barn** (☎ 5348 3048; 1 Leggatt St).

Sleeping

There are several accommodation agencies in town, including **Daylesford Getaways** (☎ 5348 4422; www.dayget.com.au; 123 Vincent St) and **Daylesford Accommodation Booking Service** (☎ 5348 1448; www.dabs.spa-country.net.au; 94 Vincent St).

On Saturday and Sunday, and during holidays, many places stipulate a minimum two-night stay.

DAYLESFORD

Cedar Lodge (☎ 5348 3711; 3711 Hepburn Rd; s/d $65/75) Quiet, aside from the birdsong, the lodge backs on to a gully of eucalyptus trees in between Daylesford and Hepburn Springs and offers a cheap sleep in motel-style, child-friendly rooms. The friendly owner is a mine of information on the area and also provides complimentary muffins on the first night of a two-night stay.

Boomerang Holiday Ranch (☎/fax 5348 2525; Tipperary Springs Rd; dm $20/30/66) Boomerang is a horse-riding ranch and there are several accommodation packages linked to horse riding. The price varies according to whether you want breakfast or lunch included. A 'just test your bum' horse ride costs $25.

Kooringa Cottage (☎ 5348 1625; www.kooringa cottage.com.au; 3 Albert St; d $110-280; 🐾) A former miner's cottage has been magically transformed into one of the prettiest B&Bs in these parts. There's a choice of double suite or cottage accommodation, invitingly decorated with full-size tubs for that home-style soak after your spa visit.

Holyrood House (☎ 5348 4818; 51 Stanbridge St; d $150, cottage $360; 🐾) This wisteria-draped 19th-century manor overlooks a rambling garden. Holyrood Place is co-owned by an architect and a Malaysian chef which translates into a fabulous restoration job –

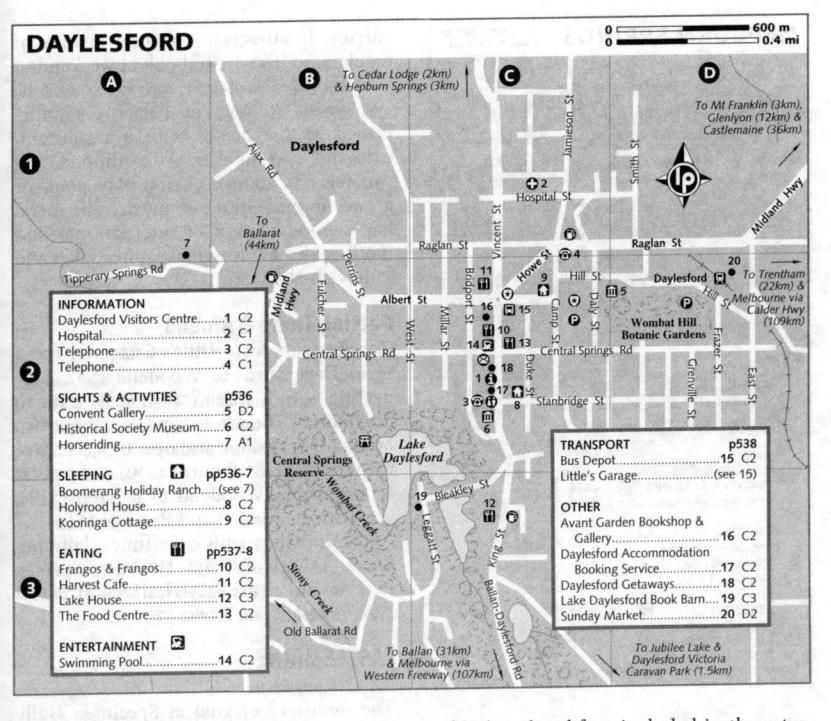

DAYLESFORD

INFORMATION
Daylesford Visitors Centre	1 C2
Hospital	2 C1
Telephone	3 C2
Telephone	4 C1

SIGHTS & ACTIVITIES (p536)
Convent Gallery	5 D2
Historical Society Museum	6 C2
Horseriding	7 A1

SLEEPING (pp536-7)
Boomerang Holiday Ranch	(see 7)
Holyrood House	8 C2
Kooringa Cottage	9 C2

EATING (pp537-8)
Frangos & Frangos	10 C2
Harvest Cafe	11 C2
Lake House	12 C3
The Food Centre	13 C2

ENTERTAINMENT
Swimming Pool	14 C2

TRANSPORT (p538)
Bus Depot	15 C2
Little's Garage	(see 15)

OTHER
Avant Garden Bookshop & Gallery	16 C2
Daylesford Accommodation Booking Service	17 C2
Daylesford Getaways	18 C2
Lake Daylesford Book Barn	19 C3
Sunday Market	20 D2

and equally superb Malaysian restaurant. Choose between a double in the main house or the detached cottage. Children are not catered to.

Daylesford Victoria Caravan Park (☎ 5348 3821; dayvicpark@bigpond.com; Ballan Rd; camp sites $15-17, cabins $46-85) A pleasant 1.5km stroll from the township, this park has leafy grounds and a kiddie-sized swimming pool. It's in beautiful landscaped grounds with giant redwoods, close to Daylesford Lake. There are BBQ facilities and a playground. Pets allowed.

HEPBURN SPRINGS

Wildwood YHA (☎ 5348 4435; beacham@tpgi.com.au; 42 Main Rd dm/d $20/32; 🗶). Wildwood is a better than average hostel with good facilities and the added treat of rooms with a view. Squeaky clean with the latest mod-cons, it can't be beat.

Mooltan Guesthouse (☎/fax 5348 3555; 129 Main Rd; s/d $55/85) The colourful and friendly guesthouse has enthusiastic staff and a peaceful leafy garden; the perfect haven for a lazy summer day. Prepare to feast on

a fabulous breakfast, included in the rates. Weekend packages are available and children are welcome.

Springs Retreat (☎ 5348 2202; www.thesprings .com.au; 124 Main Rd; d from $145) Patrons get a cultural kick from this overgrown 1930s mansion. Each room has been lovingly restored to Art Deco elegance, coupled with modern-day facilities, including various spa treatments and a steam room. There's a price-hike at weekends.

Eating
DAYLESFORD

Frangos & Frangos (☎ 5348 2363; 82 Vincent St; mains $9-26) Adventurous gourmets should try Frangos' delectable slow-simmered duck and finish off with a serving of their sweet sticky pudding. For afters, slip into the plush wine bar.

Harvest Cafe (☎ 5348 3994; 29 Albert St; mains $14-21) This is a funky Indian-run restaurant serving delicious vegetarian, fish and chicken dishes in hip cross-cultural surroundings. Great daily special choices include some eye-smarting spicy fare.

VICTORIA

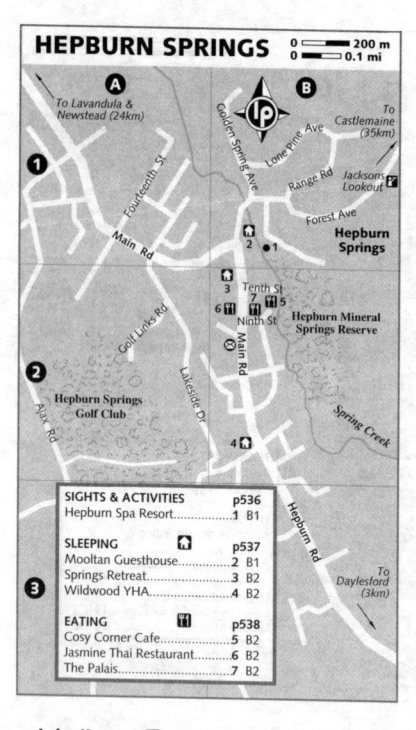

HEPBURN SPRINGS

To Lavandula & Newstead (24km)

To Castlemaine (35km)

Golden Spring Ave
Lone Pine Ave
Range Rd
Jacksons Lookout
Forest Ave
Fourteenth St
Main Rd
Tenth St
Ninth St
Golf Links Rd
Lakeside Dr
Alex Rd
Hepburn Springs Golf Club
Spring Creek
Hepburn Springs
Hepburn Mineral Springs Reserve
Hepburn Rd
To Daylesford (3km)

SIGHTS & ACTIVITIES	p536	
Hepburn Spa Resort	1	B1

SLEEPING	p537	
Mooltan Guesthouse	2	B1
Springs Retreat	3	B2
Wildwood YHA	4	B2

EATING	p538	
Cosy Corner Cafe	5	B2
Jasmine Thai Restaurant	6	B2
The Palais	7	B2

Lake House (☎ 5348 3329; King St; mains $25-30) Overlooking the lake, the Lake House is a serious dress-for-dinner restaurant with top-notch cuisine. This is recognised as being one of the best restaurants in the state, so arrive hungry, ready to fatten-up your credit card. Reservations are essential.

Food Centre (☎ 5348 1677; 71 Vincent St; dishes $7-16) This quick-bite eatery serves fat focaccia sandwiches, superior pasta, all-day breakfast and irresistible blueberry muffins. It does a roaring lunch trade; if you can't find a pew, then go for a takeaway.

HEPBURN SPRINGS

Cosy Corner Cafe (☎ 5348 3825; 3 Tenth St; mains $17-22; ✆ lunch daily, dinner Sat & Sun) is a fully licensed hole-in-the-wall restaurant with a great, moody atmosphere. The diverse menu caters for vegans, vegetarians and carnivores alike and includes Thai favourites such as Tom Yom soup.

Jasmine Thai Restaurant (☎ 5348 1163; 114 Main Rd; mains $13-24; ✆ dinner only) This friendly, inexpensive Thai restaurant offers all the standard Asian flavours, including tangy

curries. It attracts a constant stream of regulars, so it's wise to book at weekends.

Palais (☎ 5348 4849; 111 Main Rd; mains $16-18; ✆ 6pm-late Wed-Sun) The Palais is a refurbished 1920s theatre with a restaurant, café and cocktail bar. After dinner, you can relax in lounge chairs, play pool, or groove to modern dance music. The menu has a good variety of international and mod Oz dishes, as well as lighter salad and sandwich-style fare.

Getting There & Around

Coaches run from **Little's Garage** (45 Vincent St) in Daylesford, to Woodend ($5), connecting with a **V/Line** (☎ 13 61 96) train to Melbourne. The whole trip takes about two hours ($15). V/Line also operates a service for Woodend–Melbourne ($10) and regular services from Woodend to Ballarat ($12), Castlemaine ($5.70) and Bendigo ($11).

A return bus runs four times daily between Daylesford and Hepburn Springs ($2); or you can use **Bakers Taxi Service** (☎ 5348 3333) or **Haslett Taxi Service** (☎ 5348 1111).

CASTLEMAINE

☎ 03 / pop 6840

The discovery of gold at Specimen Gully in 1851 radically altered the pastoral landscape of the region around Castlemaine, as 30,000 diggers worked goldfields known collectively as the Mt Alexander Diggings. The town grew up around the government camp and soon became the marketplace for all the goldfields of central Victoria.

These days Castlemaine is a relaxed country town attracting an increasing number of arty and ex-city folk. Castlemaine hosts the **State Festival**, one of Victoria's leading arts events, in March/April in odd-numbered years.

The **visitors centre** (☎ 1800 171 888, 5470 6200; www.maldoncastlemaine.com; Mostyn St; ✆ 9am-5pm) is in the Castlemaine market building, along with a number of interesting displays on the development of the town.

Sights

Dating from 1861, **Buda** (☎ 5472 1032; cnr Hunter & Urquhart Sts; adult/child $7.50/3.50; ✆ noon-5pm Wed-Sun) was home to a Hungarian silversmith and his descendants for 120 years. The family's art and craft collections, and personal belongings are on display.

The impressive **Castlemaine Art Gallery & Historical Museum** (☎ 5472 2292; 14 Lyttleton St; admission $4; ☼ 10am-5pm Mon-Fri, noon-5pm Sat & Sun) has a collection of colonial and contemporary art; downstairs is a local history museum.

The imposing **Old Castlemaine Gaol** (☎ 5472 5311; cnr Bowden & Charles Sts; admission $5; ☼ 9am-5pm) is a daunting place to visit even though it's no longer a prison. You can wander around on a self-guided tour.

The **Bond Store** (☎ 5470 5989; 5-9 Elizabeth St; ☼ 9.30am-5.30pm), in a series of buildings, houses a maze of antiques and collectibles.

Les Simmons (☎ 5473 4387) provides excellent tours of **Herons Reef Gold Diggings** in nearby Fryerstown – once the world's richest alluvial gold diggings. Tours run from October to June by appointment only.

Australia's only **Dingo Farm** (☎ 5470 5711) is signposted off the Castlemaine–Chewton road. The farm has about 100 dingoes, Australia's original wild dog, to pat.

Sleeping

Old Castlemaine Gaol (☎ 5472 5311; cnr Bowden & Charles Sts; s/d $55/75) This has to be the most unusual B&B in Victoria. Guests now have to pay to stay in former cells, converted to very cramped bedrooms with tiny windows. The beds are comfier and locks are on the inside; otherwise, be warned, little else has changed. Breakfast is included.

Campbell St Motor Lodge (☎ 5472 3477, fax 5472 4957; 33 Campbell St; s/d $79/94) This solid no-surprises hotel has comfortable enough rooms in a somewhat austere National Trust–classified building near the centre.

Midland Private Hotel (☎ 5472 1085; www.midland hotel.cjb.net; 2-4 Templeton St; s/d $80/120). Sheltering travellers since 1879, the Midland is an interesting place to stay. It features a magnificent Art Deco entrance foyer and dining room, and a Victorian-era club-style lounge with two open fireplaces and a belvedere ceiling. Rooms are great value and breakfast is included; advance reservations are essential.

Clevedon Manor (☎ 5472 5212; 260 Barker St; s/d $75/110) Guests have a large wing and garden to themselves in this sumptuous Victorian manor house. Antiques, brass beds and a massive cooked breakfast help seal the (good value) deal.

Botanic Gardens Caravan Park (☎ 5472 1125; Walker St; camp sites $15, cabins $55) This park is ideally situated next to the gardens and public swimming pool. There is plenty of leafy shade and the cabins are particularly good value for money.

Eating

Saffs Cafe (☎ 5470 6722; 64 Mostyn St; mains $6-17) Saffs is a mellow place with a cool big city feel. There's lots of healthy vegie fare, salads and specials, plus marinated kangaroo fillets (and the like). Strong punchy coffee and breakfast is served until 4pm.

Tog's Place (☎ 5470 5090; 58 Lyttleton St; mains $6-11; ☼ lunch only Sun-Thu) Fashionable Tog's has painted brick walls and art for sale. There's curries, tofu-burgers and fancier dinner fare, but the sticky toffee pudding is too good to share. Bookings are advisable for dinner.

Meson Bar & Cafe (☎ 5470 6555; 16 Lyttleton St; dishes $5-12) Meson is a former funeral parlour, artfully revamped as a friendly restaurant serving Spanish-style *tapas*, as well as vegetarian, vegan and gluten-free foods.

Capones Pizzeria (☎ 5470 5705; 50 Hargraves St; pasta $10-14; ☼ dinner only) Capones serves 44 varieties of excellent pizza and average pastas against a backdrop of gangster memorabilia. There's a pretty garden and courtyard for al fresco dining.

Getting There & Away

Daily trains run between Melbourne and Castlemaine ($18) and continue on to Bendigo ($5) and Swan Hill ($32).

Daily coaches run to Daylesford ($5), Maldon ($3.50), Ballarat ($15, except Wednesday) and Geelong ($29).

MALDON
☎ 03 / pop 1230

The current population of Maldon is a tiny fraction of the 20,000 who once worked the goldfields. The town is a well-preserved relic of that era.

The **visitors centre** (☎ 5475 2569; www.maldon .org.au; 93 High St; ☼ 9am-5pm) is in the shire offices. Pick up the *Information Guide and Historic Town Walk* brochures.

The **historical museum** (☎ 5475 1633; adult/child $2/0.50; ☼ 1.30-4pm) is behind the visitors centre and has an interesting collection of local artefacts.

Carmen's Tunnel Goldmine (☎ 5475 2667; Parkin's Reef Rd; adult/child $4/2; ☼ 1.30-4pm Sat, Sun & holidays), excavated in the 1880s, is 2.7km south of town. Railway buffs will enjoy the **Victorian Goldfields Railway** (☎ 5475 1451; www.vgr.com.au; Hornsby St; adult/child $20/8; 🕙 Wed, Sun & Sat in school holidays), which has old-time **steam trains** running toward Castlemaine. **Porcupine Township** (☎ 5475 1000; cnr Bendigo & Allans Rd; adult/child $8/4; 🕙 10am-5pm), 2.5km out of town on the Bendigo road, is an interesting re-creation of a gold-mining village.

Foot-tapping folk-music fans will love the annual **Maldon Folk Festival** held in early November.

Sleeping

Aside from the following, there are plenty of self-contained cottages, many managed by **Heritage Cottages of Maldon** (☎ 5475 1094, fax 5475 1880; www.heritagecottages.com.au; 41 High St).

Central Service Centre (☎ 5475 2182; 1 Main St; s/d $30/60) In the unlikely setting of a former garage (the pumps are still out the front) is this excellent and inexpensive option. The MG room is the funkiest choice. There's a convenient laundrette right next door.

Maldon's Eaglehawk (☎ 5475 2750; www.eagle hawkmaldon,com; 35 Reff St; s/d $80/100; 🐾) Here the Federation-style architecture equals brass bedsteads, antiques, and prints of miserable-looking Victorians, but what bliss, the bathtubs. There's a delightful garden and secluded courtyard.

McArthur's Restaurant & B&B (☎ /fax 5475 2519; 43 Main St; d $90-100, cottage $130; 🐾) Behind the restaurant of the same name, McArthur's offers genteel accommodation in an original Victorian building.

Cornflower (☎ 5475 2015; 64 Main St; d from $100) There's a choice of accommodation here. The self-contained loft has a warm wooden interior and pleasant rooms. Or, if you're looking for something extra-special, the next door cottage is a fine choice – but only if you like the colour blue.

Eating

McArthur's (☎ 5475 2519; 43 Main St; mains $15-17; 🕙 closed Mon-Tue) This refreshingly un-heritaged Victorian house exudes loads of character, from water-stained wallpaper and plates on the walls to a choice of dining-rooms and a leafy outside terrace. Home-cooked–style meals are filling and range from toasted sandwiches to trout.

Alluvial (☎ 5475 1021; 24 High St; dishes $7-15) New face on the block and a good refuel-ling spot, Alluvial serves home-made soups, man-size burgers and other belly-filling favourites. The atmosphere is relaxed and friendly.

Grand Hotel (☎ 5475 2233; 26 High St; bar/restaurant meals $5/9) The Grand is popular with locals, as is the legendary rabbit and cheese pie. Other dining-room favourites include the char-grilled lamb baguette with chunky tomato relish.

Ruby's at Calder House (☎ 5475 2912; 44 High St; mains $21-23) Put on your best bib and tucker, and indulge. Set in an elegant Victorian dining room, this is creative country cuisine at its best, incorporating fine local produce. Reservations essential.

Getting There & Away

Castlemaine Bus Lines (☎ 5472 1455) runs a daily bus between Maldon and Castlemaine ($3.50), which connects with trains to and from Melbourne (2 hours total).

MARYBOROUGH

☎ 03 / pop 7500

In 1854, gold was discovered at White Hills and Four Mile Flat. A police camp at the diggings was named Maryborough and, at the height of the gold rush, the population was over 40,000. These days it's a fairly dull place, but has some fine buildings and a few sights.

The **visitors centre** (☎ 1800 356 511, 5460 4511; www.centralgoldfields.com.au; cnr Nolan & Ilma Sts; 🕙 9am-5pm) has a wide range of information on the area.

Built in 1892, **Maryborough Railway Station** was described by Mark Twain as 'a train station with a town attached'. It now houses a mammoth antique emporium, gallery and café. **Worsley Cottage** (☎ 5461 2800; 3 Palmerston St; 🕙 10am-noon Tue & Thu, 2-5pm Sun) is the historical society museum.

Have a fling at Maryborough's **Highland Gathering** held on New Year's Day since 1857.

Sleeping & Eating

Bull & Mouth Hotel (☎ 5461 1002, fax 5461 3676; 119 High St; s/d $40/50) The singles have shared bathrooms in this historic pub, while the doubles come with bathrooms. It also serves reliable down-home bistro food.

Golden Country Caratel (☎ 5461 7799, fax 5461 5166; 134 Park Rd; s/d $68/84; 🐾) The rooms are reasonably priced at this motel opposite a golf course. There are some enticing extras here, including volley ball, a playground, games room and solar heated pool. There's also a disabled unit.

Bella's Country House B&B (☎ 5461 5574; 39 Burns St; www.bellas.com.au; s/d $99/120) Bella's is the place if you need a slug of tranquillity. It's a handsome Victorian red-brick with white linen draped rooms, open fires and comfy lounges. You can stroll down the lavender path, admire the rose garden or just kick back in the arbour with a glass of wine and a book.

AVOCA & PYRENEES RANGES

Avoca is a small town and the centre of a rapidly expanding wine-growing region.

The **visitors centre** (☎ 03-5465 3767; High St; ☿ 9am-5pm) is by the post office. Pick up *A Guide to the Pyrenees* to explore local wineries.

Mt Avoca is the highest peak in the nearby Pyrenees Ranges, reaching 760m. There are walking tracks on the mountain, including the 18km-long **Pyrenees Trail**, which starts from the Waterfall Picnic Area 7km west of Avoca.

BENDIGO

☎ 03 / pop 68,700

When gold was discovered at Ravenswood in 1851, thousands of diggers converged on the fantastically rich Bendigo Diggings. The arrival of Chinese miners in 1854 had a lasting effect on Bendigo, which still has a rich Chinese heritage.

During the boom years between the 1860s and 1880s, mining companies poured money into the town, which resulted in the fine Victorian architecture that still graces Bendigo's streets today. By the 1860s, diggers were no longer tripping over surface nuggets and deep mining began; local legend has it that you can walk underground from one side of the town to the other. These days the town is a prosperous provincial centre.

Information

The **visitors centre** (☎ 1800 813 153, 5444 4445; www.bendigotourism.com; 51-57 Pall Mall; ☿ 9am-5pm) in the historic post office is also an interpretative centre. The staff books accommodation and activities, and you can purchase tram tickets here.

Sights

CHINESE JOSS HOUSE

The **Chinese Joss House** (☎ 5442 1685; Finn St; adult/child/family $3/1.10/6.60; ☿ 10am-5pm summer, 10am-4pm winter), in North Bendigo at the end of the tramline, is one of the few remaining practising joss houses (Chinese temples) in Victoria.

CENTRAL DEBORAH GOLD MINE

This 500m-deep **mine** (☎ 5443 8322; 76 Violet St; adult/child guided tour $17/10, self-guided tour $8/5.50; ☿ 9am-5pm) opened in the 1940s and was connected to two other Deborah shafts dating back to the early goldfield days. About 1000kg of gold was removed before it closed in 1954. The guided underground tour runs six times a day, starting at 10.10am, and takes an hour; booking is advisable. A combined ticket for the mine tour plus a ride on the 'talking tram' costs $26/15 per adult/child.

For even more of a thrill, the intrepid can take the two-hour adventure tour around the less accessible parts of the mine. You'll be equipped with boots, helmet and lamp to climb a few ladders. You get a turn with a mining drill and can keep any gold you find. Morning and afternoon tours cost $42 and the lunchtime tour (with lunch) costs $49.

TALKING TRAM & CAFÉ TRAM

That Bendigo still has a tramline is all thanks to the tenacity of its citizenry. The tram system was closed down in 1972, following closures in Ballarat and Geelong but a number of Bendigo residents took direct action. The wheels of the lead tram in the depot were welded to the rails and hundreds turned up to add their support. The rescued trams now run as a tourist feature.

The **talking tram** (adult/child $13/8) leaves on the hour from 10am to 3pm daily from Central Deborah Gold Mine, calling in five minutes later at Alexandra Fountain, then through the city centre to the **tramways museum** (admission free with tram ticket) and the Chinese Joss House, with a commentary along the way.

A **café tram** (☎ 5443 8322) trundles along for lunch ($30) on Sundays and dinner ($50) on Friday and Saturday nights. Bookings are essential.

VICTORIA

VICTORIA

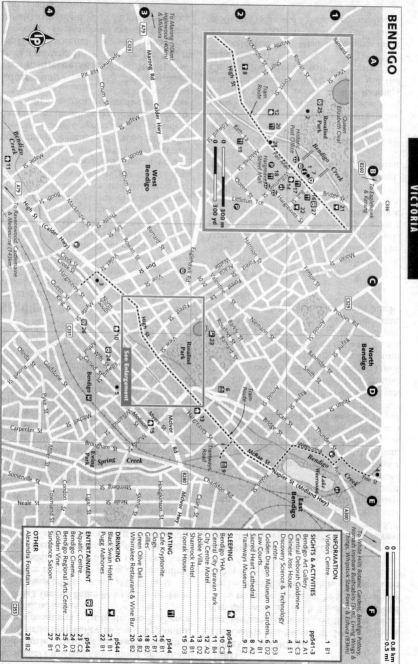

BENDIGO

BENDIGO ART GALLERY

One of Victoria's largest regional galleries, the **Bendigo Art Gallery** (☎ 5443 4991; 42 View St; admission by donation; ☺ 10am-5pm) has outstanding collections of Australian and 19th-century European art plus regular visiting overseas exhibitions.

SHAMROCK HOTEL

Built in 1897 on the corner of Pall Mall and Williamson St, this is a fine example of Italianate late-Victorian architecture. The story goes that floors were regularly washed down to collect gold dust brought in on miners' boots.

GOLDEN DRAGON MUSEUM & GARDENS

The excellent **Golden Dragon Museum** (☎ 5441 5044; Bridge St; adult/child $7/4; ☺ 9.30am-5pm) has two Chinese processional dragons, Old Loong and Sun Loong (the world's longest), which are centrepieces of the annual Easter Fair parade. Old Loong was paraded in Melbourne for the Federation celebrations in 1901 and the 100th anniversary in 2001. The museum traces the involvement of the Chinese community in the development of Bendigo. There are also Chinese gardens nearby. Entry is free with a museum ticket.

BENDIGO POTTERY & LIVING WINGS & THINGS

The oldest pottery works in Australia (1858), **Bendigo Pottery** (☎ 5448 4404; Midland Hwy; admission free; ☺ 9am-5pm) is at Epsom, 6km north of Bendigo. There's a café, sales gallery, historic kilns and you can watch potters at work or have a pottery lesson for $12.

Living Wings & Things (☎ 5448 3051; adult/child $7/4.50; ☺ 9am-5pm) is on the same site. It has lizards, pythons, butterflies, walk-through parrot enclosures, wallabies and dingoes.

DISCOVERY SCIENCE & TECHNOLOGY CENTRE

The family-friendly hands-on **Discovery Science & Technology Centre** (☎ 5444 4400; Railway Pl; adult/child/family $9/6/30; ☺ 10am-5pm) has the usual interactive exhibits. It's located across from the train station.

Festivals & Events

The **Easter Fair** attracts thousands of visitors with its carnival atmosphere and procession of Chinese dragons.

The November **Swap Meet** also attracts masses of enthusiasts in search of that elusive old motorcycle or car part.

Sleeping

BUDGET

Nomads Ironbark Bushcabins (☎ 5448 3344; www .bwc.com.au/ironbark; Watson St; cabin $18) Nomads is a horse-riding camp out in the bush. A two-day package of two nights accommodation with food and enough riding to make you sore costs $95. You can cool off by taking a ride in their zippy new waterslide; rides costs from $30 per hour. Breakfast is included in cabin rates.

Bendigo YHA (☎ 5443 7680; 33 Creek St South; dm $21; ⌨) This homey small hostel in a weatherboard cottage has all the usual facilities for a bargain-bucket price.

Central City Caravan Park (☎ 5443 6937; 362 High St, Golden Sq; dm $15, camp/van sites $18/37, cabins $65) One of about 10 caravan parks in and around Bendigo, this one includes a basic hostel section in prefab cabins with four bunks each and separate cooking and kitchen facilities. Central City is about 2km south of the centre – you can get to it by bus from Hargreaves St.

MID-RANGE

Shamrock Hotel (☎ 5443 0333; shamrock@origin.net .au; cnr Pall Mall & Williamson St; d $70-95, ste $145-180) Shamrock is a stunning Victorian building with stained glass, original paintings, fancy columns and a *Gone with the Wind*–style staircase. The cheaper rooms are on the small side.

City Centre Motel (☎ 5443 2077; fax 5443 2996; 26 Forest St; s/d $78/98; ⛆) The new owners of this motel are busy upgrading the swing-a-cat size rooms with shiny new furniture. Disabled facilities are available and there are cheaper rates during the week.

Jubilee Villa (☎ 5442 2920; 170 McCrae St; d $90-120) There's nothing spartan about these restored Victorian manor servants' quarters. There are fluffy quilts, English antiques and original fireplaces in the bedrooms (one has a spa). Cooked breakfast or a hamper is included.

TOP END

Toorak House (☎ 5442 9095; toorakhouse@hotmail.com; 135 Mollison St; d $140-145; ⛆) Gorgeous Toorak House dates from 1873 and has an extra-grand dining room, stylish comfortable

VICTORIA

suites and an atrium among the lavender bushes in the garden.

Eating

Gillies' (266 Hargreaves St) People come from far and wide for Gillies' fabled pies. Although you queue at a little window, there's nothing fast food about these pies with their melt-in-the-mouth pastry and unusual fillings. You can eat sitting outside in the mall.

Green Olive Deli (☎ 5442 2676; 11 Bath Lane; dishes $3.50-12) The Green Olive is one of those few places that you know is going to be outstanding the moment you open the door, smell the aroma of fresh coffee and eyeball the display of fresh pastas and focaccias.

Cafe Kryptonite (☎ 5443 9777; 92 Pall Mall; mains $6.50-18) Kryptonite is a café for every meal of the day, including coffee break time when you can indulge in the cheese cake specialty here. More substantial fare includes pizza, risotto, pasta and kangaroo. Take a look at the interesting art on the walls.

Clogs (☎ 5443 0077; 106 Pall Mall; mains $14-17) Gourmet pizzas and light meals are served to a dedicated local clientele at this stylish licensed restaurant/bar, with terrace seating opposite a leafy park.

Whirrakee Restaurant & Wine Bar (☎ 5441 5557; 17 View St; mains $13-20) Whirrakee offers fancy dining in a 100-year-old building. The modern-Australian cuisine includes everything from kangaroo kebabs to tempura and delicious melt-in-the-mouth gnocchi. Local wines are available by the glass.

Drinking

Pugg Mahones (☎ 5443 4916; 224 Hargreaves St) This Irish theme pub is a friendly place to chill out. There's Guinness and many beers on tap, a good pubby atmosphere and a beer garden.

Black Swan Hotel (☎ 5444 0944; 6-10 Howard Pl) Some 60 years ago this was the one and only licensed pub in town. It's since been artfully resurrected and is now the trendiest, with mobs at weekends.

Entertainment

Golden Vine (☎ 5443 6063; 135 King St) This is one of the best venues in town, with regular jam sessions and local and Melbourne bands playing everything from dance-friendly hits to the latest raw new sounds.

Sundance Saloon (☎ 5441 8222; 116 Pall Mall) Sundance is a 'howdy pardner' saloon with a Western theme – bare wood and basic. It has live bands.

Bendigo Regional Arts Centre (Capital Theatre; ☎ 5441 5344; 50 View St) This is the main venue for the performing arts.

Bendigo Cinema (☎ 5442 1666; 107 Queen St) is central.

Getting There & Around

At least four trains run between Bendigo and Melbourne daily ($25, 2 hours) via Castlemaine ($5) and Woodend ($11). Trains continue on to Swan Hill ($51).

Buses from Bendigo, departing outside the train station, include daily services to Castlemaine ($5), weekday services to Ballarat ($21) and Geelong ($33), and daily services to Echuca ($8) and Mildura via Swan Hill ($26).

Walkers Buslines (☎ 5443 9333) and **Christian's Buslines** (☎ 5447 2222) service the area. Timetables are available at the visitors centre.

For a taxi call **Bendigo Associated Taxis** (☎ 5443 0777).

THE HIGH COUNTRY

The High Country isn't particularly high – the highest point, Mt Bogong, only reaches 1986m – but it contains some stunningly beautiful and diverse country.

Although there are plenty of year-round activities in the High Country (check out the Activities section on p440), it is the ski resorts that have really put this area on the map for many people. Skiers and snow-boarders flock here from Melbourne and the outlying areas during the winter months, eager to indulge in a little adrenaline-fuelled snow sports. Others may prefer the year-round slothful delights of wine tasting while, during the summer, there are endless outdoor activities on offer, including horse riding, canoeing and abseiling.

Orientation & Information

Eildon and the gateway towns – Mansfield, Myrtleford, Harrietville and Bright – are in the northwestern foothills. Omeo is the High Country's southeastern gateway town.

The major visitors centres are at Mansfield, Beechworth, Mt Beauty and Bright.

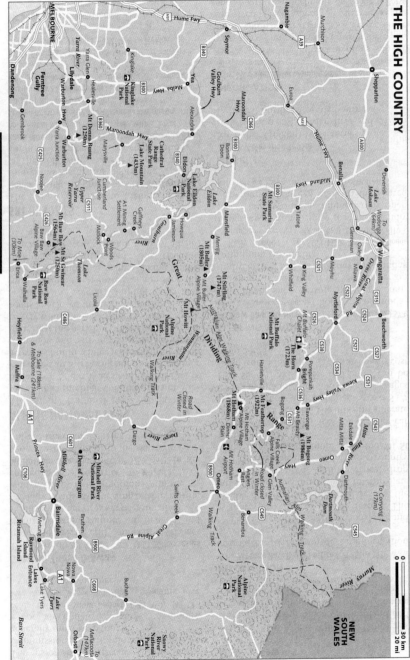

The major ski resorts have Alpine Resort Commission (ARC) information offices, generally open year-round.

For an update on snow conditions, refer to the **Snow Report** (☎ 1902 240 523; www.snowreport.vic.gov .au/). The 'sno-cams' give a view, even in summer.

Getting There & Away

There are direct **V/Line** (☎ 13 61 96) coaches from Melbourne and connecting services from the train stations at Benalla and Wangaratta. Services vary seasonally.

Many roads can be impassable during winter. Check road conditions with the recorded **information service** (☎ 1902 240 523) or **Mt Hotham access line** (☎ 03-5759 3531). In the snow season, roads into the ski resorts can only be travelled if chains are carried.

ALPINE NATIONAL PARK

The Alpine National Park (646,000 hectares) links the high country areas of Victoria, New South Wales and the ACT.

There's an increasing number of summer activities but in winter it's everything to do with snow and partying. Most ski resorts are in or near the park but otherwise the area is largely wilderness. Some of the many access roads are closed in the snow season.

There are several camping areas and bush camping is allowed in most of the park. The region has many walking tracks, including the Australian Alps Walking Track which wends 655km from Walhalla to Canberra.

SKI RESORTS

The closest snowfield to Melbourne is **Mt Donna Buang**, 95km east via Warburton, though it's mainly for sightseeing.

The following snowfields offer cross-country skiing but lack accommodation:

Lake Mountain (☎ 03-5963 3288) Ski region, 120km northeast of Melbourne via Marysville, with 37km of beginners, intermediate and advanced cross-country trails.

Mt Stirling (☎ 03-5777 0815) An excellent cross-country area a few kilometres northeast of Mt Buller Alpine Village, with over 60km of mostly advanced trails and a ski school.

Mt St Gwinear (☎ 03-5165 3204) Cross-country trails on this mountain, 171km from Melbourne via Moe, connect with Mt Baw Baw.

Mt Bogong Some tough downhill skiing routes around the summit of Mt Bogong.

Mt Baw Baw

☎ 03 / elevation 1564m

Mt Baw Baw Alpine Village (1480m) has stunning views of much of Gippsland and is a mere three-hour drive from Melbourne via the Princes Hwy (M1) and the C426.

INFORMATION

The **Mt Baw Baw Resort office** (☎ 5165 1136; www .mountbawbaw.com.au) provides an information service.

This is a good place for novice skiers and is more relaxed than the big resorts. The skiable downhill area is 25 hectares and the runs are 25% beginners, 64% intermediate and 11% advanced, with a vertical drop of 115m. It's also a base for cross-country trails, one of which connects to the Mt St Gwinear trails.

Snow season entry fees for the day car park cost $22 per car. The lifts only operate if there is snow and daily passes cost $47/24 per adult/child; lift-and-lesson packages cost $68/41. Skis, poles and boots can be hired from $28/18 per day; snowboards cost from $40/34.

SLEEPING & EATING

Mt Baw Baw Ski Hire (☎ 5165 1120, 1800 629 578; www.bawbawskihire.com.au) books accommodation. In the snow season, ski club accommodation is available from $30 per person midweek and $40 on Saturday and Sunday (minimum two nights).

Kelly's Lodge (☎ 5165 1129; lodge@kellyslodge .com.au; summer/snow season beds $50/70) Kelly's Lodge, apart from being a cosy and friendly place, is the only accommodation open year-round. You can cook in the shared kitchen or have meals in the **restaurant**.

Mt Buller

☎ 03 / elevation 1805m

Mt Buller (1600m) is Victoria's largest ski resort, 47km east of Mansfield and 237km (3 hours) northeast of Melbourne.

INFORMATION

The **Mt Buller Resort Management Board** (☎ 5777 6077; www.mtbuller.com.au; ❀ 8.30am-5pm in snow season, 10am-4pm rest of year) shares premises with the post office. During peak ski season there's an information booth at the Clock Tower. There are several places where you can rent ski and snowboard gear, including **Buller Sports Horse**

Hill (☎ 5777 6244), handily located at the bottom of the Horse Hill Chair Lift.

The skiable downhill area is 180 hectares and runs are divided into 25% beginner, 45% intermediate and 30% advanced, with a vertical drop of 400m. Cross-country trails link Mt Buller with Mt Stirling.

Snow season entry fees for the day car park are $20 per car. Lift tickets for a full day cost from $75 and include the use of up to 26 lifts and 400 hectares of varying terrain. Lift-and-lesson packages start at $110. The children's snow sports school offers various levels of skiing and snowboarding courses.

SLEEPING

There are over 7000 beds on the mountain. Rates vary according to season and the number per room. **Mt Buller Central Reservations** (☎ 1800 039 049) books accommodation in lodges from around $75 per person.

Avalanche Lodge (☎ 9873 5151; www.avalanche chalet.com.au; Delatite Lane; summer/snow season s/d $50/100, apartments $70/137). Appropriate for all-seasons, this alpine lodge, with open fire and pool table, offers a choice of rooms and apartments. Prices increase at weekends.

Mt Buller YHA Lodge (☎ /fax 5777 6181; The Avenue; midweek/weekend dm $55/100) Only open during the ski season so it pays to book well in advance. It's in a great location – you can ski right to the front door. Budget-priced packages available include accommodation, ski/snowboard hire, a lift ticket and transport from Melbourne.

Breathtaker All Suite Hotel/Spa Retreat (☎ 5777 6377; 8 Breathtaker Rd; www.breathtaker.com .au; d from $165) This boutique hotel has all the spa facilities, including the intriguing-sounding French Body Polish and Geisha Tub Experience. It's appropriately plush, and just 100m from the ski school and Bourke St. Extras include a kids' play area, business centre and in-room shopping.

EATING

There's a supermarket in the Moloney's building in the village centre. Various kiosks and takeaway places are open in the snow season.

Abom Bistro/Moosehead Bar (☎ 5777 7899; Summit Rd; mains $13-19) The calorie-stoking menu includes pizza, pasta and other hearty dishes. Good views over Bourke St

make this a top spot for checking out the designer ski-wear parade. The lower-level Moosehead Bar is a groovy après-ski venue with snazzy cocktails, bar snacks and occasional live music.

There are restaurants, bars and cafés at the **Mt Buller Chalet Hotel** (☎ 5777 6566) and the **Arlberg Hotel** (☎ 5777 6260). Both hotels are located on Summit Rd and are open all year.

GETTING THERE & AROUND

Mansfield-Mt Buller Buslines (☎ 5775 2606) has year-round daily buses up to Mt Buller ($20/35 one way/return). **Snowcaper** (☎ 1800 033 023, fax 5775 2719) and **APT** (☎ 1300 655 965, fax 9277 8477) run snow-season-only day trips from Melbourne for $69/49 and $110/54 per adult/child, respectively.

Snow-season parking is below the village and there's a 4WD taxi service; fares cost from $14 within the village and $22 return between the car parks and the village.

Ski hire and lift tickets are available at the base of the quad chairlift, so day visitors can take the chairlift straight into the skiing area. There is also a free bus shuttle between the day car park and the village.

Mt Hotham

☎ 03 / elevation 1868m

Mt Hotham is a good skiers' mountain with less emphasis on nightlife.

INFORMATION

Mt Hotham Alpine Resort Management (☎ 5759 3550; www.mthotham.com.au; village administration centre; ☽ 8am-5pm daily in snow season, Mon-Fri other times) administers the mountain. **Mt Hotham Reservation Centre** (☎ 5759 4444, 1800 354 555) publishes a list of events.

Mt Hotham's skiable downhill area is 245 hectares, with 27% beginner, 36% intermediate and 37% advanced runs and a vertical drop of 428m. There is night skiing at the Big D and over 35km of sheltered, scenic ski trails between Mt Hotham and Dinner Plain.

Off-piste skiing in steep and narrow valleys and cross-country skiing is good; ski touring on the Bogong High Plains over to Falls Creek is excellent. This is also the starting-point for trips across Razorback to beautiful Mt Feathertop. On the eastern side, below the village, trails run as far as Dinner Plain.

The snow-season entry fee is $25 per car. Lift tickets cost $78/41 per adult/child and lift-and-lesson packages cost $113/79.

SLEEPING

Snow-season accommodation is abundant but varies considerably during the rest of the year. Typically, summer accommodation costs $25 per person in dorms with shared kitchen and bathroom.

There are three accommodation booking agencies: **Mt Hotham Reservation Centre** (☎ 1800 354 555; www.hotham.net.au; Hotham Central) operates year-round; **Mt Hotham Accommodation Service** (☎ 1800 032 061, 5759 3636; hotham@netc.net.au; Lawlers Apartments) operates during snow season only; and **Mt Hotham Central Reservations** (☎ 1800 657 547, 5759 3522; www.mthotham-central res.com.au) can book local and off-mountain accommodation throughout the year.

Gravbrot Ski Club (☎ 5759 3533; Great Alpine Rd; d from $108) The price at this homely place includes all meals and pre-dinner nibbles.

Kalyna Ski Lodge (☎ 1800 633 611; www.kalyna .com.au; Hotham Central; d from $120) Near the Big D ski run, this is a good value lodge with loads of creature comforts including TV, video, table tennis, billiards and a reading room.

Arlberg (☎ 5986 8200; www.ski.com.au/arlberg .hotham; Great Alpine Rd; low/high snow season d $285/ 585) The Arlberg has a family bistro and you can save a few cents by paying an additional supplement ($32/26 per adult/child) to cover breakfast and dinner. There is also a heated indoor pool, sauna and spa, and supermarket.

Hotham High Chalets (☎ 1800 354 555, 5759 3522; Great Alpine Rd; summer/low/high snow season chalets $520/1380/3194) These apartments are as big as houses so ideal for large groups – they can sleep up to 13 people.

EATING

There's a small supermarket, several restaurants, and a few kiosks and takeaways.

General Store (☎ 5759 3523; Great Alpine Rd; dishes $11-16) Mount Hotham's only pub is predictably packed-out most of the time and is a friendly place to chill out (so to speak) after a day's skiing. The tasty pizzas and counter meals make it a low-cost place to stoke up. There's also a supermarket and post office here.

Zirky's (☎ 5759 3542; Great Alpine Rd; ☽ 8am-9.30pm snow season) This place incorporates a restaurant, coffee shop and bistro so there are many options available for a bite.

GETTING THERE & AROUND

Mt Hotham is 373km from Melbourne via the Great Alpine Rd. It can be reached from Melbourne via the Hume Fwy (M31) and Harrietville (4½ hours) or via the Princes Hwy and Omeo (5½ hours).

During the snow season, **Trekset** (☎ 1800 659 009, 9370 9055; www.mhothambus.com.au) runs a daily bus service between Melbourne and Mt Hotham ($115/75 return per adult/ child) stopping at Wangaratta, Myrtleford, Bright and Harrietville.

The Mt Hotham Airport also services Dinner Plain. **Southern Airlines** (☎ 13 13 13) flies throughout the week in the snow season from Melbourne (return from $252). **Eastern Australian Airlines** (☎ 13 13 13) flies weekends from Brisbane via Newcastle (return from $649) and from Sydney (return from $341) throughout the week.

The village is spread out and free shuttle minibuses frequently run along the ridge from 7am to 3am. Another shuttle service operates to Dinner Plain. If you want a day's skiing at Falls Creek, you can jump on the 'Helicopter Lift Link' for $89 return if you have a lift ticket. The six-minute flights are only possible on clear days.

Dinner Plain

Dinner Plain is a stylish village 11km east of the Mt Hotham ski resort. Whereas Hotham and Falls Creek are fairly soulless, with concrete egg carton style buildings, Dinner Plain blends happily into the landscape. In snow season it's a base for cross-country skiers, with more than 16km of world-class cross-country trails. There are also excellent trails around the village, some of which lead to Mt Hotham and Mt Loch. Dinner Plain has its own beginners' ski slope and toboggan run, complete with ski lift. It's about 12km from Mount Hotham: a short 20-minute drive away or visitors can use the convenient shuttle-bus service between the two resorts. See Getting There & Around (above) for details on getting to Dinner Plain. A shuttle bus runs to Mt Hotham.

SLEEPING & EATING

There are more than 200 chalets and lodges to choose from, and two accommodation agencies to help you with the dilemma; each deals with a separate number of properties. **Dinner Plain Central Reservations** (☎ 1800 670 019, 03-5159 6451; www.dinnerplain.com; Big Muster Dr) books accommodation from $130/205 for two people in summer/snow season. **Dinner Plain Accommodation** (☎ 03-5159 6696; info@accomm.dinnerplain.com.au; Big Muster Dr) can book accommodation from $100/140 for two people in summer/snow season.

Currawong Lodge (☎ 1800 635 589 snow season, 03-5159 6452 summer; www.currawonglodge.com.au; Big Muster Dr; summer/snow season d $120/160) The Lodge has rough timber lodges and chalets with bathrooms and multi-share rooms. It's a good choice for groups who, depending on how chummy they are, may well enjoy the 10-person spa.

Dinner Plain Hotel (☎ 03-5159 6462; dinnerplain hotel@start.com.au; Big Muster Dr; dishes $9-18) This is an excellent wake-up coffee place, especially if you can bag a comfy chair by the fire. The bistro here serves excellent pizzas, and delivers.

Mt Buffalo National Park

Mt Buffalo (1500m) is a very attractive ski resort, although not known for reliable snow. It's in an area (31,000 hectares) declared a national park in 1898. The main access road leads off the Great Alpine Rd at Porepunkah to just below the summit of the 1723m Horn. Apart from Mt Buffalo itself, the park is noted for its scenery of granite outcrops, streams and waterfalls, and an abundance of birdlife and walks.

INFORMATION

There are two skiing areas: Cresta Valley and Dingo Dell. Cresta has five lifts and the graded downhill runs cover 27 hectares with 45% beginner, 40% intermediate and 15% advanced runs, and a vertical drop of 157m. Cresta Valley is the starting point for many of the cross-country trails while Dingo Dell is perfect for beginner skiers.

The Bright **visitors centre** (☎ 1800 033 079, 03-5758 3490; www.fallscreek.com.au; bottom of Gully chair lift; ☼ 9am-6pm in snow season, 9am-5pm in summer) covers this region. Dingo Dell has a day visitor shelter with a kiosk.

The entry fee during the snow season is $12.50 per car ($9 at other times). Lift tickets cost $39/25 per adult/child, lift-and-lesson packages cost $69/49; you can get a private

one-hour lesson for $69, and toboggan hire costs $10. Mt Buffalo Chalet (for details see Sleeping & Eating; below) runs a ski school with an introductory course that guarantees you will be able to ski by the end of it, otherwise you get your money back!

Mt Buffalo is an experienced hang-glider's paradise and the walls of the Gorge provide really challenging rock climbs. **Lake Catani** is good for swimming and canoeing. **Adventure Guides Australia** (☎ 03-5728 1804; www.adventure guidesaustralia.com.au) has rock-climbing, caving, ski touring and other summer time activities for around $70 to $90 per half day.

SLEEPING & EATING

Mt Buffalo Wilderness Lodge (☎ 1800 037 038, 03-5755 1988; Mt Buffalo; mid-week/weekend d $140/212) The lodge has motel-style units or four-bed bunk rooms with shared bathrooms, plus a games room, indoor climbing wall, restaurant and ski hire. Breakfast and dinner are included in the rates.

Mt Buffalo Chalet (☎ 1800 037 038, 03-5755 1500; www.mtbuffalochalet.com.au; Mt Buffalo; summer/snow season d $148/268) The chalet is a huge guesthouse built in 1909 and retains a warm old-fashioned feel with simple bedrooms, large lounges and a games room with open fires. The chalet is open year-round; there's a three-night minimum stay.

Mt Buffalo Chalet Cafe (buffet lunches $29-39; dinner from $20) Open to the public, this place is so hip it's hard to get a seat – especially when booked out by chalet guests. Dinners are à la carte.

Sugar Maples (☎ 03-5756 2919; www.visitvictoria .com/sugarmaples; 133 Harris Lane, Porepunkah; s/d $90/ 120) This boutique B&B is set in the foothills of Mt Buffalo National Park on 11 acres with drop-dead gorgeous mountain views. There are over 100 Sugar Maple trees here, so time your visit when they are in brilliant scarlet bloom. There's an open fire, spa room and candlelit dining room. The breakfast option of banana pancakes and maple syrup sure makes a change from bacon and eggs.

Camping is allowed at Rocky Creek. Pick up the permit from the Parks Victoria ranger at the **Mt Buffalo entrance station** (☎ 5756 2328).

GETTING THERE & AROUND

There is no public transport to the plateau, though a **V/Line** (☎ 13 61 96) coach can drop you at Porepunkah, near the base of the mountain. A taxi to or from Bright costs about $55 (40 min). Transport from Wangaratta train station can be arranged for chalet and lodge guests.

Falls Creek

☎ 03 / elevation 1780m

Falls Creek is the most fashion-conscious of the resorts and combines great skiing with equally great après ski entertainment. It's a 4½ hour drive from Melbourne and gets packed with city folk at weekends during the snow season. There are some great hiking trails that start here, including the walk to Wallace's Hut, said to be the oldest cattleman's hut in the High Country.

INFORMATION

The **visitors centre** (☎ 1800 033 079, 5758 3490; www .fallscreek.com.au; bottom of Gully chair lift; 🕒 9am-6pm in snow season, 9am-5pm in summer) is the place to go for information about the whole region, including Mt Buffalo. The snow season entry fee is $23 per car. Full-day lift tickets cost $78/41 (per adult/child) and lift-and-lesson packages cost $113/77.

Skiing at Fall's Creek is spread over two main areas: the Village Bowl and Sun Valley. There are 19 lifts and the skiable downhill area covers 451 hectares, with 17% beginner, 60% intermediate and 23% advanced runs and a vertical drop of 267m. On Wednesday and Saturday there is night skiing in the Village Bowl.

Some of Australia's best cross-country skiing can be found here. A trail leads around Rocky Valley Pondage to some old cattlemen's huts and the more adventurous can tour to the summits of Nelse, Cope and Spion Kopje. Australia's major cross-country skiing event, the Kangaroo Hoppet, is held on the last Saturday in August. It's part of the Worldhoppet series of long-distance races.

SLEEPING

Accommodation may be booked via several agencies including **Falls Creek Central Reservations** (☎ 1800 033 079, 5758 3733; www.skifallscreek .com.au; Bogong High Plains Rd), **Mountain Multiservice** (☎ 1800 465 566, 5758 3499; www.mountainmultis ervice.com.au; Schuss St) and **Go Snow Go Falls Creek** (☎ 1800 253 545, 9873 5474; fallscreek.albury.net.au /~gosnow).

Alpha Lodge (☎ 5758 3488; www.alphaskilodge.co m.au; 5 Parallel St; summer/snow season d $88/150) This

is a great choice for larger groups. There's a huge kitchen with eight cooking stations, plus sauna and large lounge/TV area with panoramic views. The Alpha Lodge's four-bed bunk rooms cost slightly less.

Viking Lodge (☎ 5758 3247; www.vikinglodge .com.au; 13 Parallel St; summer/snow season d $100/180) Viking has good views and a good location, with full facilities including handy ski hire, a shop and even a ski-tuning service for the pros.

Summit Ridge (☎ 5758 3800; sumridge@fallscreek .albury.net.au; Schuss St; d $110) This place manages to be rustic and classy within a perfectly feng shui cradle of mountains. Rooms are nothing to write home about but comfy enough, and a bumper breakfast is included in the price. This place organises loads of special events, including wine-tasting on weekends.

EATING

The **supermarket** and **café** in the Snowland Centre at the bottom of Halley's Comet Chairlift are open year-round. In the snow season the usual **kiosks** and **snack bars** also open up.

Milch Cafe Wine Bar (☎ 5758 3770; 4 Schuss St; mains $12-18) A welcome treat, this place serves mainly Middle Eastern food and does a great mezze of dishes, including the hummus and falafel standards; always good for vegetarians.

Winterhaven (☎ 5758 3243; Falls Creek Rd; mains $15-25; 🕒 nightly in snow season, weekends in summer) Inside the Winterhaven apartment building, this is one of the better restaurants on the mountain. It serves modern Australian cuisine, has an excellent wine list and a heart-warming open fire.

GETTING THERE & AROUND

The only way to get to Falls Creek from Melbourne is with **Pyle's Coaches** (☎ 5754 4024; www.buslines.com.au/pyles) which runs snow season services from Albury to Mt Beauty ($36 one way) and Falls Creek ($63); and also from Melbourne (Spencer St) to Mt Beauty ($98) and Falls Creek ($115). There are reductions for children and students. Advance bookings are essential.

On the mountain, the **Over-Snow Taxi service** (☎ 5758 3285; $25 return) operates between the car parks and lodges from 8am to midnight (2am Friday night).

VICTORIA

If you want to ski Mt Hotham for the day, jump on the 'Helicopter Lift Link' (for details see Getting There & Around under Mt Hotham; p548).

EILDON

☎ 03 / pop 670

Eildon is a one-pub town with a few shops, and is a recreation base for Lake Eildon and the surrounding **Lake Eildon National Park**. It was built in the 1950s to house construction workers on the Eildon Dam.

You can make phone inquiries after hours at the **visitors centre** (☎ 5774 2909; www.tourism internet.com.au/eildon; Main St; ☷ 10am-2pm Sat-Mon, 10am-5pm Fri).

Activities

Lake Eildon has a shoreline of over 500km and is a favourite water-sports playground. You can charter a boat for a sightseeing trip from **Eildon Lake Charter** (☎ 0428 345 366) for $90 per hour.

If you'd prefer to stay on dry land, **Rubi-con Valley Horse Riding** (☎ 5773 2471; www.rubi conhorseriding.com) has introductory two-hour rides for $50 and overnight safaris from $280. Families should check out the **Fresh-water Discovery Centre** (☎ 5770 8052, Goulburn Valley Hwy, adult/child $5.50/2.75; ☷ 10am-4pm holi-days, 11am-4pm Fri-Mon at other times), 5km south-west of Eildon. This fish farm has short films on fish hatching, and aquarium tanks including a touch tank where children can feel the fish.

Sleeping & Eating

Lake Eildon Camping & Cabins (☎ 5772 1293) handles bookings for the many caravan parks and camp sites in Lake Eildon Na-tional Park.

Golden Trout Hotel & Motel (☎ 5774 2508, fax 5774 2429; 1 Riverside Dr; s $45-50, d $50-60; ☷) De-spite the lurid pink exterior, this motel is a good central choice with modern spacious accommodation. Ask for a room overlook-ing Goulburn River. The bistro is a plus for plain home cooking, and has a sundeck for sipping cocktails.

Robyn's Nest B&B (☎ 5774 2525; www.visitvictoria .com/robynsnest; d $100-140; ☷) This choice B&B has two classy rooms, one with spa bath, in a seriously romantic setting with views of the Eildon valley and a Mt Trobrek backdrop. In-room massage (shiatsu or aromatherapy)

is available for those who truly want to in-dulge. No children.

Eildon Caravan Park (☎ 5774 2105; Eildon Rd; camp sites $19, cabins $50-75) This park, situated on the lakeshore, is a cut above the aver-age with good value cabins and camp sites. There's volley-ball and tennis courts, play-grounds, barbecues and excellent fishing (or so they say).

Getting There & Away

V/Line (☎ 13 61 96) runs a daily bus service from Melbourne to Eildon ($21, 3½ hours).

MT BEAUTY

☎ 03 / pop 1630

Mt Beauty and nearby Tawonga South are the gateway to Falls Creek and the Bogong High Plains. There's a good choice of ac-commodation year-round, as well as snow-equipment hire.

The **visitors centre** (☎ 1800 808 277, 5754 1962; www.mtbeauty.com; Kiewa Valley Hwy; ☷ 9am-5pm) operates a booking service for accommoda-tion and activities. The centre also incorpo-rates the **Kiewa Valley Heritage Museum** which, while modest, gives some insight into the history of the area.

Activities

There are some wonderful walks in the Mt Beauty area. The pretty **Tree Fern Walk** (2km) graduates to the slightly longer **Peppermint Walk**; both start from Mountain Creek picnic and camping ground on Mountain Creek Rd.

If you prefer to be in the saddle, **Bo-gong Horseback Adventures** (☎ 5754 4849; www .bogonghorse.com.au) runs three-hour rides ($70) up to five-day rides over the Bogong High Plains ($275). **Ecotrek: Bogong Jack Adventures** (☎ 08-8383 7198; www.ecotrek.com.au) organises hiking, canoeing and cycling tours in the area.

Sleeping

Carver's Log Cabins (☎ 5754 4863; 16 Buckland St; cabins $120) Pleasantly situated with a rustic bare-boards charm, Carver's has lots of hik-ing scope on the doorstep. The cabins sleep six; there's a price hike and minimum stay at holiday time.

Meriki Motel (☎ /fax 5754 4145; meriki@netc.net.au; Lot 1 Tawonga Cres; s $50, d $65-88) If you are much more interested in a good kip than loads of atmosphere (at a price) then go for this motel; it's one of the cheapest in these parts and is clean, compact and even has a pool.

Dreamers (☎ 5754 1222; www.dreamers1.com; Kiewa Valley Hwy, Tawonga South; d $140-260) Dreamers is a place for romantic affairs, secret or otherwise. Take a look at the bathtubs and you'll understand why. The secluded chalets are dotted around a watery landscape demonstrating the owners' design flair.

Mount Beauty Holiday Centre (☎ 5754 4396; holidaycentre@netc.net.au; Kiewa Valley Hwy; tent sites/units/ cabins $18/66/56) This family-fun place on the riverbank is in two acres of native garden. Activities include mini golf, volleyball, tennis, river swimming and good fishing. The units and cabins are well-sized and modern, and there's a playground and spa.

Eating

Tuscany on Kiewa (☎ 5754 4804; 231 Kiewa Valley Hwy; mains $11-16). This small licensed restaurant serves mainly Italian food and is lots better than the fast-food alternative.

Roi's Diner Restaurant (☎ 5754 4495; 177 Kiewa Valley Hwy, Tawonga; mains $17-25) Roi's unassuming timber chalet on the highway is famed far and wide for its inventive, ever-changing menu of modern Italian cuisine. You won't go hungry – the starters are trucker size.

Getting There & Away

Pyle's Coaches (☎ 5754 4024; www.buslines.com.au /pyles) has snow season services from Albury to Mt Beauty ($36 return) and Falls Creek ($63), Melbourne (Spencer St) to Mt Beauty ($98) and Falls Creek ($115). Bookings are essential.

MANSFIELD
☎ 03 / pop 2670

Mansfield is a happening town with an historic high street, leafy avenues, good restaurants and plenty to do, including a race course if you fancy a flutter. Mansfield makes a handy base for Mt Buller with ski hire available and plenty of places to stay.

The graves of three police officers killed by 'armed criminals' (ie the Kelly gang – see the boxed text 'Kelly Country'; p557) in 1878 are in **Mansfield cemetery** at the end of Highett St.

The **visitors centre** (☎ 1800 039 049, 5775 7000; www.mansfield-mtbuller.com.au; Old Railway Station, Maroondah Hwy; ⏱ 9am-5pm) books accommo-

dation. **Mt Buller Central Reservations** (☎ 1800 039 049) shares the centre and books accommodation in the ski fields.

The **Mansfield Balloon Festival** takes place in April every year.

Activities

For a different way to travel the High Country, **High Country Camel Treks** (☎/fax 5775 1591; Rifle Butts Rd), 7km south of town, offers one-hour rides ($35/25 per adult/child), half-day treks and other options. The owners will pick up from town.

Several companies offer horse-riding activities through the High Country, including **Watson's Country Rides** (☎ 5777 3552; www.watsons trailrides.com.au), which charges $15 per hour, and **McCormack's Mountain Valley Trail Rides** (☎ 5775 2886; 12 Reynolds St) which offers short and long rides ranging from two hours ($50) to a week ($1610). **4WD Tours** (☎ 5777 3709; alpine4wdtours@hotmail.com; 1a Fielding Lane) offers day tours of the high country for ($85, including lunch) and overnight camping safaris (from $150).

Sleeping

Mansfield Backpackers' Inn & Travellers Lodge (☎ 5775 1800; travlodge@cnl.com.au; 112 High St; dm/d/ste $23/85/135) There's superior dorm accommodation in this restored heritage building. Motel rooms are large, with separate shower and toilet, and offer excellent value (price drops mid-week). There's a well-stocked kitchen and discount coupons for local restaurants if you prefer to eat out. Children are welcome.

Delatite Hotel (☎ 5775 2004, fax 5775 1824; 95 High St; d $30) If you can look beyond the dreary furnishings, this is a grand old hotel – a five-star equivalent in the gold-rush days. The rooms are a bit threadbare but the balconies are a plus; the bar and restaurant have a clubby feel and serve basic filling chow. Breakfast is included.

Arlberg Merrijig Resort (☎ 5777 5633, fax 5777 5780; cnr Omega St & Mt Buller Rd; d $75-95). Halfway between Mansfield and Mt Buller, this resort has lodges, a restaurant, pool, tennis courts and motel-style rooms, and also offers special spa packages.

Wappan Station (☎ 5778 7786; www.wappan station.com.au; Royal Town Rd; shearers' quarters d from $60, cottage d from $90) For those who want to live and breathe country living big-time;

this 10,000-acre scenic sheep and cattle station is just outside Mansfield on the banks of Lake Eildon. There are fairly basic shearers' quarters, plus self-contained cottages with fireplaces and outside barbecues.

Eating

Sweet Potato (☎ 5775 1955; 50 High St; mains $10-12) This is the place to eat in Mansfield. The prices are reasonable, the atmosphere friendly and the menu is a spicy cross-cultural mix of oriental flavours.

Bon Apetit (☎ 5775 2951; 39 High St; dishes $7-10; ☽ lunch only) Bon Apetit is an earthy and reliably inexpensive deli and café serving cakes, savouries and dishes of the day.

Mingo's Bar & Grill (☎ 5775 1766; 101 High St; mains $10-20) One of the fancier eateries in town, Mingo's has a mellow brick and wood interior, and a something-for-everyone menu of pasta, steaks, chicken and vegie dishes. There's a few surprises, like Spanish paella, and the chef *is* Spanish.

Country Brew (☎ 5775 2623; 28 High St; dishes $4-10) This informal place has plenty of filling fare for calorie-stoking skiers, including home-made soups, pies, vegie burgers and pasties.

Getting There & Away

V/Line (☎ 13 61 96) coaches run services between Melbourne and Mansfield ($32 return). **Mansfield-Mt Buller Bus Lines** (☎ 5775 2606) runs twice-daily between Mansfield and Mt Buller ($35 return).

HARRIETVILLE

☎ 03

Harrietville, 24km south of Bright, is a pretty little town nestled in the foothills of Mt Feathertop and offers cheaper off-mountain accommodation. During the ski season a bus shuttles between the town and Mt Hotham.

Sleeping & Eating

Harrietville Hotel/Motel (☎ 5759 2525, fax 5759 2766; Great Alpine Rd; s/d $30/60; meals $10-17) Standard motel rooms are available here and the pub serves bistro meals.

Shady Brook Cottages (☎ 5759 2741; www .shadybrook.com.au; Mountain View Walk; d from $130) Shady Brook is in a swallow-hard setting in 12 acres of secluded landscape and bush at the foot of Mt Hotham, bordered by

state forest on the Ovens river. There are two alpine-style cottages, both with spas and spacious verandas for contemplating the surroundings.

BRIGHT

☎ 03 / pop 2100

Bright has gained quite a bit of oomph with money flowing from passing ski tourists. Bright looks bright in all seasons, especially when the trees show their autumn colours. There are almost too many things to do: paragliding, abseiling, fishing, trail riding (on horses or motorbikes), scenic flights, microlight flights, gliding and anything else designed to produce a thrill.

The **Bright Autumn Festival**, held over a two-week period in April, features a prestigious art exhibition.

Bright is the gateway town to Mt Hotham (Great Alpine Rd, B500), Falls Creek (C531) and Mt Buffalo (C535).

The **visitors centre** (☎ 1800 500 117, 5755 2275; bright@dragnet.com.au; 119 Gavan St; ☽ 9am-5pm) will book accommodation, adventure activities and the like.

Sights & Activities

Most of the fun is outdoors, but there are a few places worth stepping inside for, such as the **Bright & District Historical Society Museum** (Railway Ave; adult/child $3/50; ☽ 2-4pm Sun Sep-May, also Tue & Thu during school holidays) in the old train station. There are plenty of walking trails and climbs to lookout points. The visitors centre sells a *Short Walks around Bright* brochure for $0.50.

Cyclepath Adventures (☎ 5752 1442) hires out a whole range of cross country, recreational and even tandem bikes from $24 a day.

Tandem Paragliding (☎ 5755 1753; www.alpine paragliding.com) offers introductory paragliding flights from $130 per hour. The **Eagle School of Hand-Gliding** (☎ 5750 1174; www.eagle school.com.au) offers microlight flights over Mt Buffalo gorge from $95 for 15 minutes. **Centenary Park**, beside the Ovens River, has some good picnic areas and swimming spots.

Sleeping

There's an abundance of accommodation in this small town.

Bright Central Motel and Lodge (☎ /fax 5755 1074; 2 Ireland St; dm $25, d $75) This friendly place is in a peaceful part of town with pleasant rustic-style dorm rooms and shared kitchen facilities. It also has motel-style doubles and pricier two-bedroom apartments.

Bright Hikers Backpackers' Hostel (☎ 5750 1244; www.brighthikers.com.au; 4 Ireland St; dm $19, d $40; 💻) Bright's attractive central hostel has a large community room and veranda overlooking the main street. The rooms are clean and compact and the owners can help arrange activities.

Coach House Inn (☎ 1800 813 992; www.alpine link.com.au/coachhouse; 100 Gavan St; s/d $66/88) This good central choice has plenty of grassy green space, basic accommodation and various dollar deals for long weekends and the like. The owners run a ski-hire outfit as well.

The **Odd Frog** (☎ 5755 2123; www.theoddfrog.com; 3 McFadyens Lane; d from $120) At the cutting edge of contemporary décor, thanks to architect/interior designer owners, Odd Frog's accommodation is eco-friendly and refreshingly un-fussy. Located on 10 acres of bushland connected to numerous walking and cycling trails, it's just a short walk to the town centre. For an extra $20 you can indulge in a gastronomic breakfast basket.

Eating
With savvy city-slickers passing through, Bright has developed a thriving dining scene.

Liquid Am-Bar (☎ 5755 2318; 8 Anderson St; mains $10-19) The Liquid has a wide-ranging menu including great pasta choices, yummy desserts and, for starters, tempting colourful cocktails.

Sasha's (☎ 5750 1711; 2D Anderson St; mains $15-35) The French owner of Sasha's has added a little *coq au vin* influence on the mainly Mediterranean-inspired cuisine. The wine list is predictably above average, with plenty of European and Australian choices.

Poplars (☎ 5755 1655; Star Rd; mains $18-22) Poplars' menu exudes a salivatory attention to detail. You should go for the dishes that feature local produce, such as venison, lamb, beef, veal and trout. The filling specials are fairly priced.

Cosy Kangaroo (☎ 5750 1838; 93-95 Gavan St; dishes $7-18) This café is just the place for rumbling tummies to head towards first thing in the morning. The lumberjack breakfast is superb, along with the pancakes and good strong coffee. The Cosy Kangaroo does parties for kids – possibly a time to avoid.

Getting There & Away
V/Line (☎ 13 61 96) operates a daily train/coach service via Wangaratta to Myrtleford, Porepunkah (for Mt Buffalo) and Bright ($46).

MYRTLEFORD
☎ 03 / pop 2520
Myrtleford is at the foot of Mt Buffalo and makes a handy overnight stop en route to the High Country. Nicotine users will notice the fields of tobacco in the region; it's the main crop here.

Sleeping
Railway Hotel/Motel (☎ 5752 1583, fax 5752 2134; 101 Standish St; s $35-50, d $60-77) This pub has been tastefully restored to ensure the bygone-era atmosphere lives on. The no-frills rooms are squeaky clean and comfortable enough to ensure a good night's kip.

Golden Leaf Motor Inn (☎ 5752 1566, fax 5751 1620; 186 Great Alpine Rd; s/d from $72/95) Golden Leaf offers large, well-furnished rooms in pleasant garden surrounds. There's a convenient adjacent restaurant, heated pool and spa, barbecue and bike hire.

BEECHWORTH
☎ 03 / pop 2800
Beechworth is a picturesque and historic town, rated by the National Trust as one of Victoria's two 'notable' towns. Dating from 1852, it developed into the main centre for the Ovens District goldfields.

The **visitors centre** (☎ 1300 366 321, ☎ /fax 5728 3233; www.beechworth.com; 103 Ford St; ⏰ 9am-5pm) books accommodation and activities, including the daily Beechworth **Legends Walking Tour** (adult/child $10/5) and **lantern tour** (adult/child $13/10) during the warmer months of the year.

Sights & Activities
Beechworth's historic and cultural precinct consists of many interesting old buildings including the **Burke Museum** (☎ 5728 1420; Loch St; adult/child/family $5.50/3/15; ⏰ 9am-3.30pm daily, 9am-4.30pm school holidays). This excellent museum has gold-rush relics and an arcade with 16 shopfronts preserved as they were over 140 years ago.

The **Beechworth Courthouse** (☎ 5728 2721; Ford St; adult/child/family $4/1.50/10; ⏰ 10am-4pm) is notable for Ned Kelly's first court appearance, where he was committed to trial for the murders of constables Scanlon and Lonigan in August 1880. You can send a telegram to anywhere in the world from the **Telegraph Station** (Ford St), the original morse-code office. Also, check out the **Powder Magazine** (Gorge St), an 1859 storage area for gunpowder. The *Echoes of History* video can be viewed at the 1858 **Town Hall** (Ford St) approximately half-hourly. The super-saver ticket covers the whole experience for $12.50/5.50/30 per adult/child/family.

Sleeping

Newtown Park Motel (☎ 5728 2244; 38 Bridge Rd; s/d $66/77;) You can save a few cents by staying five minutes out of town. This motel is more than adequate with large family-friendly rooms and lots of extra touches including an iron, hair dryer and a hip bath large enough for a de-stress soak.

Tanswells Commercial Hotel (☎ 5728 1480; fax 5728 1160; 30 Ford St; s/d $40/60) Tanswells is a Victorian period pub with good rooms and shared bathrooms, a card room and outside dining.

Rose Cottage (☎/fax 5728 1069; rose-cot@hotkey.net.au; 42 Camp St; s/d $99/130) Rose Cottage is an authentic Victorian period house. By nature, Victorians hated a vacuum and cluttered every space with paintings, sculptures, knick-knacks and furnishings but don't worry, there's no potty under the bed.

Bank (☎ 5728 2223; 86 Ford St; www.thebankrestaurant.com; s/d $120/160;) This swish B&B is in the original stables and coach house overlooking a pretty garden and private courtyard. There's a suitably grand restaurant here, in a former bank, with a wine cellar in the original gold vault basement.

Eating

Beechworth Bakery (☎ 5728 1132; 23-27 Camp St) Beechworth's gourmet bakery packs them in at breakfast and lunch. Popular pasties here include the Ned Kelly steak special. There are also lots of home-made breads, including cheese-and-bacon sticks, and fruit and nut; the only negative is the weak coffee.

Tanswells Commercial Hotel (☎ 5728 1480; 30 Ford St; mains $12-14) Tanswells innovative menu includes Thai green curry, rainbow trout and tofu with field mushrooms and a refreshing lack of chips. There's shady seating on the terrace.

Chinese Village (☎ 5728 1717; 11-15 Camp St; mains $9-16) Thankfully lacking the migraine-inducing décor of some Chinese restaurants, this one dishes up a few Australian favourites, as well as all the oriental standards. One of the most reasonable eateries in town.

Spring Creek Café (☎ 5728 2470; 78 Ford St; dishes $7-16) This small, cheery and bright restaurant has a floral-theme décor and varied menu with a Latin edge. There's a children's menu.

Beechworth Provender (☎ 5728 2650; 18 Camp St) This is just the place to stock up for that gourmet picnic, with a delectable choice of local wines, cheeses, chutneys, jams and fresh produce.

Getting There & Around

V/Line (☎ 13 61 96) has daily services between Melbourne and Beechworth ($40), changing from train to coach at Wangaratta. V/Line services run to Wodonga, to Bright and to Rutherglen.

Tickets for V/Line, CountryLink and McCafferty's/Greyhound can be booked at **Beechworth Animal World** (☎ 5728 1374; 34-36 Camp St), near the bus stop. Mountain bikes can be hired here for $6 per hour.

YACKANDANDAH
☎ 02 / pop 630

Classified by the National Trust, Yackandandah is an old, well-preserved gold-mining town. A part-time tourist town, many things only open part of the week.

The **visitors centre** (☎ 6027 1988; Athenaeum, High St) keeps such irregular hours that it's far better dealing with the Beechworth visitors centre.

The town has many fine buildings, including the 1850 **Bank of Victoria** (21 High St; admission $2; Sun afternoon, daily in school holidays), which is now a museum.

The **Kars Reef Goldmine Tour** (☎ 0438-271 875, 6027 1757; adult/child $11/5.50) takes you through a tunnel (dating from 1888) where you learn about gold mining. Phone ahead to book with a minimum party of four.

Sleeping & Eating

Star Hotel (☎ 6027 1493; fax 6027 0643; 30 High St; s/d $30/35) This wonderful old country pub has tastefully renovated rooms. Meals such as Scotch fillet with Milawa blue cheese are available for lunch and dinner.

Arcadia Cottage B&B (☎ 6027 1713; www.sky business.com/arcadiacottage; Mongan Lane; d from $115) Take a few candles along to this romantic B&B with its cosy wood fire, spa (for two) and birdsong in the garden. Any extra adults pay just $25 a night and children under five are free (your own, that is – not to take away).

Yackandandah Motor Inn (☎ 6027 1155; yackmotorinn@bigpond.com; 18 High St; s/d $69/91) This homely motel is near the shops; rates include a generous breakfast.

Serendipity B&B (☎ 6027 1881; 9 Windham St; d $50, cottage $90) There's a pretty B&B with separate suite in the house at Serendipity, but go for the cottage if you can, located at the bottom of a wonderfully untamed terraced garden with seamless field and flora views.

OMEO
☎ 03 / pop 260

Omeo is at the southern gateway to the High Country. Interesting old buildings here include the **log gaol** (1858) and the **courthouse** (1892) in the grounds of the **historical society museum** (Day Ave; adult/child $2/0.50; ☼ Sat & Sun). Also of interest are the **state school** (1860), several churches and the Post Office.

There's an unofficial visitors centre in the **German Cuckoo Clock Shop** (Day Ave).

Sleeping & Eating
Omeo Motel (☎ 5159 1297; Great Alpine Rd; s/d $55/66, spa rooms $95) Good standard budget to mid-range rooms are available here, and a light breakfast is included. There's a small café attached.

Omeo Caravan Park (☎ 5159 1351; Old Omeo Hwy; camp/van sites $11/26, cabins $47) This well-cared-for park is set in trees alongside the Livingstone River.

Gracie's Tea Rooms (☎ 5159 1428; 174 Day Ave; dishes $8-13) No one should pass by without tasting Gracie's vegetable bake in this excellent lunch place.

Getting There & Away
Omeo Bus Lines (☎ 5159 4231) runs between Omeo and Bairnsdale ($28 one way) from Monday to Friday.

ANGLERS REST
Along the Omeo Hwy, 29km north of Omeo, is Anglers Rest. This is not a singing and dancing kind of place; in fact, there's

no town here at all but it makes an excellent base for all kinds of activities.

Blue Duck Inn Hotel (☎ 03-5159 7220; Omeo Hwy; d from $65, extra person $20) Located beside the Cobungra River, one of Victoria's best trout rivers, it's popular with anglers, canoeists and bushwalkers. The owner can organise horse riding, fly fishing, rafting and kayaking trips.

GOULBURN VALLEY & HUME FREEWAY REGION

You can put your foot down on the Hume Fwy (M31) as it isn't particularly scenic, although there are a few attractions off the freeway.

West of the Hume is the Goulburn Valley, Victoria's fruit bowl. The valley's other main crop is wine and several wineries are worth a visit, notably the impressive Tahbilk and Mitchelton wineries near Nagambie.

East of the freeway are the foothills of the High Country.

GLENROWAN
☎ 03 / pop 350

Ned Kelly's bushranging exploits came to a bloody end here in 1880. The story of Ned and his gang has become an industry in this small town, with museums and a theatre dedicated to the local folk hero. It's interesting to muse on what peoples' reaction would be if he was alive today...

Sights
KELLYLAND
An over-the-top animated theatre, **Kellyland** (☎ 5766 2367; Gladstone St; adult/child $16/10; ☼ half-hourly 9.30am-4.30pm) tells the gory end of the Kelly story. It will either fascinate or amuse – either way it's well worth the steep admission. Read the promotional rhetoric out the front with statements such as '...most visitors to Glenrowan wouldn't know if the country shithouse fell on them!'

A couple of doors away is the **Ned Kelly Memorial Museum & Homestead** (☎ 5766 2448; 35 Gladstone St; adult/child $2.50/1; ☼ 9am-5.30pm) The museum contains a replica Kelly Homestead, which is more interesting than it sounds, with folksy old furniture, newspaper-lined walls and alarming-looking utensils and tools. The original, just out of town, is in ruins.

Dedicated to the eminently more worthy bushrangers is the **Glen Rowen Cobb & Co Museum** (☎ 5766 2409; 37 Gladstone St; adult/child $2/0.50; ☽ 9am-5.30pm).

Sleeping & Eating

Kelly Country Motel (☎ /fax 5766 2202; 44 Gladstone St; s/d $50/64) Right on the main street, this motel has compact cheery rooms. Breakfast and evening meals are provided at a minimal extra cost.

Glenrowan Caravan Park (☎ 5766 2288, fax 5766 2244; Warby Range Rd; camp/van sites $12/28, cabins $44-66) In a relaxed bushland setting a couple of kilometres north of town, this park is pretty basic, although the new owners have invested in two new cabins and have plans to keep improving the site.

Billy's Tea Rooms (next to Kellyland) Billy is the one with the long white beard dishing up Devonshire teas, pikelets and bread pudding topped with plenty of entertaining banter.

KELLY COUNTRY

The northeast of Victoria is 'Kelly Country', where Australia's most famous outlaw, Ned Kelly, had some of his more notorious brushes with the law. Kelly and his gang of bushrangers shot dead three police officers at Stringybark Creek in 1878 and robbed banks at Euroa and Jerilderie before their lives of crime ended in a siege at Glenrowan. Ned and members of his family were tried in Beechworth and Kelly was hanged at the Old Melbourne Gaol. His famous last words were 'Such is life'.

WANGARATTA
☎ 03 / pop 16,340

Wangaratta (commonly called 'Wang') is at the junction of the Ovens and King Rivers. Its name comes from two local Aboriginal words meaning 'resting place of the cormorants'. Wangaratta is the turn-off for the Great Alpine Rd leading to the High Country. There's not a whole lot to check out here – unless you're a jazz fan. The **Wangaratta Jazz Festival** is one of Australia's biggest and best jazz festivals held at the end of October, on the weekend before the Melbourne Cup.

The **visitors centre** (☎ 1800 801 065, 5721 5711; www.wangaratta.vic.gov.au; cnr Handley St & Tone Rd; ☽ 9am-5pm) has plenty of flyers and information on the town.

Sleeping

Billabong Motel & Guesthouse (☎ 5721 2353; 12 Chisholm St; s/d $30/45) The decoration of this Italian-run motel may be a bit stuffy for some, but the price is right and you can stroll into town. Guesthouse rooms share a bathroom, and there are also motel-style rooms.

Millers Cottage (☎ 5721 5755; www.millerscottage .com.au; Great Alpine Rd & Old Hume Hwy; s/d $54/66) Well-priced Miller's Cottage offers lots of extras (like hair-dryers!) and inexpensive evening meals. The rooms are on the small side, but how much space do you need once you get your head down?

Linger-a-While (☎ 5721 5808; Pinkerton Cres; d $95) This traditional and homey B&B has good-sized, plushly furnished bedrooms and filmstar size bathrooms, complete with clawfoot tubs. It overlooks parkland, so no alarm is needed when you've got the dawn chorus.

Painters Island Caravan Park (☎ 5721 3380; Pinkerton Cres; camp sites $14, cabins $66) This great spot, on the banks of the Ovens River, covers 25-acres of leafy grounds and has a playground, barbecue area and well-kitted-out camp kitchen.

Eating

Scribbler's Cafe (☎ 5721 3945; 66 Reid St; dishes $7-13) Scribbler's café-restaurant on the main drag has pavement seating and an innovative menu, including vegetarian and gluten-free options. Paper and pens are provided for budding Picassos, with the better efforts hung on the wall.

Vespa's (☎ 5722 4392; cnr Reid & Ovens Sts; mains $12-20) Scrubbed pine and spacious, this modern place has plenty of choices, ranging from well-stacked sandwiches to steaks and pastas. Satisfy your sweet tooth with a choice of gooey desserts.

Cafe Martini's (☎ 5721 9020; 87 Murphy St; mains $15-18) Located in the Bull's Head hotel, this good-sized restaurant does a roaring trade at lunch and dinner. The main draws are the wood-fired oven pizzas and other, mainly Italian, dishes which are reasonably priced and reliably good.

VICTORIA

Vine Hotel (☎ 5721 2605; Detour Rd; mains $18-23) This classic Victorian hotel has a cool and shady beer garden and bistro. The chef is a real pro and has won awards for his Asian-Mediterranean fusion cuisine. While you're here, check out the small history museum in the basement of the hotel.

Getting There & Away
Wangaratta train station is just west of the town centre in Norton St. Daily **V/Line** (☎ 13 61 96) trains between Melbourne and Wangaratta ($35) continue on to Albury ($12).

V/Line coaches run daily to Bright ($11) via Beechworth ($5.70) and Myrtleford ($7.10); the service to Rutherglen ($5) and Corowa ($5.70) runs from Sunday to Friday.

A bicycle and walking trail connects Wangaratta with Beechworth and Bright using disused railway lines. Eventually Wahgunyah (near Rutherglen), to the north, and Whitfield, to the south, will be added, giving 266km of linked trails.

SHEPPARTON
☎ 03 / pop 35,830
Shepparton is the regional centre of the Goulburn Valley. Fruit-picking work is the main attraction here; there are not too many attractions.

The **visitors centre** (☎ 1800 808 839, 5831 4400; www.shepparton.vic.gov.au; 534 Wyndham St; ☉ 9am-5pm) is at the southern end of the Victoria Park Lake and can book accommodation, tours and activities. **Spyderbyte Cafe** (☎ 5822 0688; 68 High St; ☉ 9am-5pm Mon-Fri; ☐) offers Internet access.

Fruit Picking
January to April is fruit-picking season but start looking for work in December. The **Harvest Office** (☎ 1300 720 126; 361 Wyndham St) arranges employment. Some orchards offer basic accommodation or camp sites, but for others you'll need to stay in town and use your own transport.

Sights
There are several wineries in the area around Shepparton and more are opening all the time. The closest is **Monochino Winery** (☎ 5864 6452; Berry's Rd; Katunga), 35km north at Katunga.

Smock-and-beret types will enjoy the **Shepparton Art Gallery** (☎ 5832 9861; 70 Welsford St;

☉ 10am-5pm Mon-Fri, 2-5pm Sat & Sun), with its permanent collection of Australian art and regular temporary exhibitions.

Sleeping
Hotel Australia (☎ 5821 4011, 5821 4052; aussie@shepparton.net.au; 73 Fryers St; s/d $33/55, weekly $132/220 per week) This hotel offers basic no-frills accommodation with shared bathrooms.

Victoria Hotel (☎ 5821 9955, fax 5831 1961; 272 Wyndham St; pub s/d $39/49; motel s/d $50/62; ☒) Victoria Hotel has adequate hotel rooms with shared bathrooms but the motel-style units are a better deal; for only slightly more bucks you can have en suites and air-con. There's a bistro and Irish pub here, too.

Belltower Motor Inn (☎ 5821 8755, fax 5831 3232; 587 Wyndham St; s/d $60/70; ☒) The Belltower has good rooms about 1km south of the town centre, opposite the lake. There's a disabled unit and a pool, playground and barbecue area.

Sherbourne Terrace Motel (☎ 5821 4977; shershep@cnl.com.au; 109 Wyndham St; s/d $93/159; ☒) Sherbourne's warm brick exterior makes a pleasing change from the concrete-block norm. Rooms are large with plenty of choices, including a VIP spa room, if money is no object. There is also a cocktail bar and bistro, and the location – a short stroll away from the shops – is good.

Victoria Lake Holiday Park (☎ /fax 5821 5431; www.viclakeholidaypark.com.au; Wyndham St; camp/van sites from $20/26, cabins from $59) This shady park is right beside the lake and the visitors centre. Sites and cabins on the waterfront cost slightly more, but are worth the hike. The luxury cabins have large balconies for soaking up the view.

Eating
Shepparton Family Restaurant (☎ 5821 3737; Shop 10, City Walk, 302 Wyndham St; dishes $10-13) This restaurant offers an all-you-can-eat Chinese and Australian smorgasbord. The food is nothing fantastic but it's filling.

Cafe On The Lake (☎ 5831 5464; Wyndham St; dishes $5-15) In one of the best locations in Shepparton, overlooking the lake, you can scoff cooked breakfasts and snacks, as well as lunch. The daily specials are the best bet.

Getting There & Away
The Shepparton train station is south of the town centre in Purcell St. There are daily

V/Line (☎ 13 61 96) trains and coaches to Melbourne ($28) and connecting buses run to Cobram ($8.70).

V/Line coaches also connect with Albury ($29), Benalla ($8.70) and Mildura ($48) daily, and Bendigo ($12) three times a week.

MURCHISON

Located 28km south of Shepparton, there's not a whole lot going on here, aside from a few handsome old buildings, a riverside picnic park and seasonal fruit picking work.

Murchison Backpackers Hostel (☎/fax 03-5826 2655; backpacker@origin.net.au; 17 Stephenson St; dm per night/week $19/135) This is a no-frills basic, but the rooms are clean. A do-it-yourself breakfast is included in the rate and the owner can organise work (no fee) and provide transport ($4). The Melbourne–Shepparton bus stops outside.

NAGAMBIE

A popular watersports venue, Nagambie is on the shores of **Lake Nagambie**, which was created by the construction of the Goulburn Weir back in 1887.

The **visitors centre** (☎ 1800 444 647, 03-5794 2647; www.nagambielakestourism.com.au; 145 High St; 9am-5pm) will book accommodation.

Two of the best-known wineries in Victoria are south of town. **Tahbilk** (☎ 03-5794 2555; www.tahbilk.com.au) is 6km southwest and the oldest continually operating winery in Victoria. **Mitchelton Winery** (☎ 03-5736 2222; www.mitchelton.com.au) is 14km southwest of town and has the added plus of a wine bar overlooking the river. A great way to visit them is to take a cruise with **Goulburn River Cruises** (☎ 03-5794 2877). Cruises run on Wednesday, and Friday to Sunday, from October to the end of April. The rest of the year there are cruises on Sunday. The town has motels and a caravan park.

GIPPSLAND

Gippsland forms the south-eastern corner of Australia and has some captivatingly wild and exciting scenery. The western part is divided into the Latrobe Valley, a coal-mining and electricity-generating centre, and South Gippsland, which includes the beautiful Wilsons Promontory National Park. East

Gippsland, backed by the wild forests of the Great Dividing Range, includes the Lakes District and the Wilderness Coast.

SOUTH GIPPSLAND

For a holiday with a difference, try a drive-yourself horse-drawn gypsy wagon tour through the Strzelecki Ranges. **Promway Horse Drawn Gypsy Wagons** (☎/fax 03-5184 1258; www.promway.com; Lanes Rd, Alberton West) hires out wagons for $177 per day, with a two day minimum. The wagons are more like caravans inside and sleep up to five. Promway provides all the gear but you bring your own food.

Korumburra

☎ 03 / pop 3040

The first sizeable town along the South Gippsland Hwy is Korumburra, on the edge of the Strzelecki Ranges.

INFORMATION

The **Prom Country Visitors Centre** (☎ 1800 630 704, 5655 2233; www.promcountrytourism.com.au; South Gippsland Hwy; 9am-5pm), in the east of the town, books accommodation and has good free maps of the area.

SIGHTS & ACTIVITIES

Next to the visitors centre is the **Coal Creek Heritage Village** (☎ 5655 1811; Princes Hwy; adult/child $9/5; 10am-4.30pm), a reasonably interesting re-creation of a 19th-century coal-mining town. The V/Line coach stops outside.

Korumburra is the headquarters for the **South Gippsland Railway** (☎ 1800 442 211) which runs between Nyora and Korumburra on Sundays and holidays.

GETTING THERE & AWAY

Daily **V/Line** (☎ 13 61 96) coaches from Melbourne run along the South Gippsland Hwy to Korumburra ($16), Leongatha ($18), Fish Creek ($23), Foster ($26) and Yarram ($31).

WILSONS PROMONTORY NATIONAL PARK

The 'Prom' is one of the most popular national parks in Australia. There's superb variety, including more than 130km of walking tracks, some wonderful beaches and abundant wildlife.

The day visit fee of $9 per car is included in the overnight charge if you're camping.

VICTORIA

VICTORIA

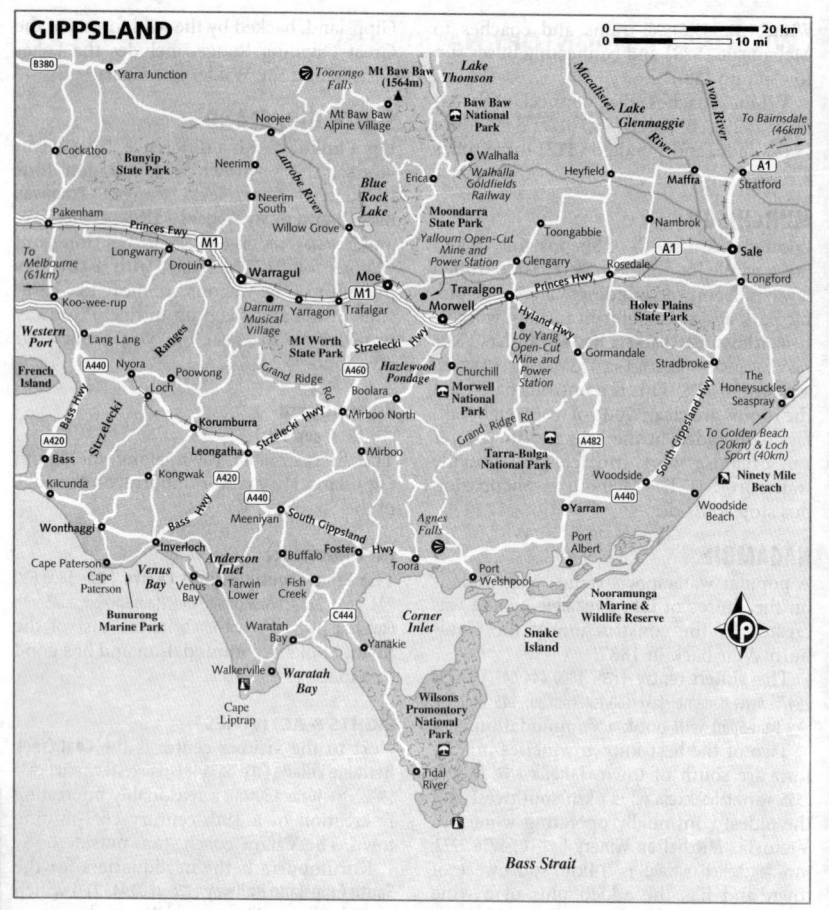

GIPPSLAND

The only access road leads to **Tidal River** on the western coast, which has a Parks Victoria office and education centre, a petrol station, general store, an open-air cinema (summer only), camp sites, cabins, lodges and facilities.

Information
The **Parks Victoria office** (☎ 1800 350 552, 03-5680 9516, fax 5680 9516; Tidal River; ☼ 8am-5pm) takes reservations for accommodation and issues permits for camping away from Tidal River.

Activities
BUSHWALKING
The park office has details of walks, from 15-minute strolls to overnight and longer

hikes. For serious exploration, buy a copy of *Discovering the Prom* ($15).

The northern area of the park is much less visited. Most walks in this 'Wilderness Zone' are overnight or longer and mainly for experienced bushwalkers. Drinking water can be a problem in summer. Fires are banned except in designated fireplaces in Tidal River (between May and October).

Tours
Taking a tour is one of the best ways of seeing the wildlife, such as wombats, close up as the guides will be familiar with their habitats.

Bunyip Bushwalking Tours (☎ 03-9531 0840; www.bunyiptours.com) has two-day bushwalking

WILSONS PROMONTORY NATIONAL PARK

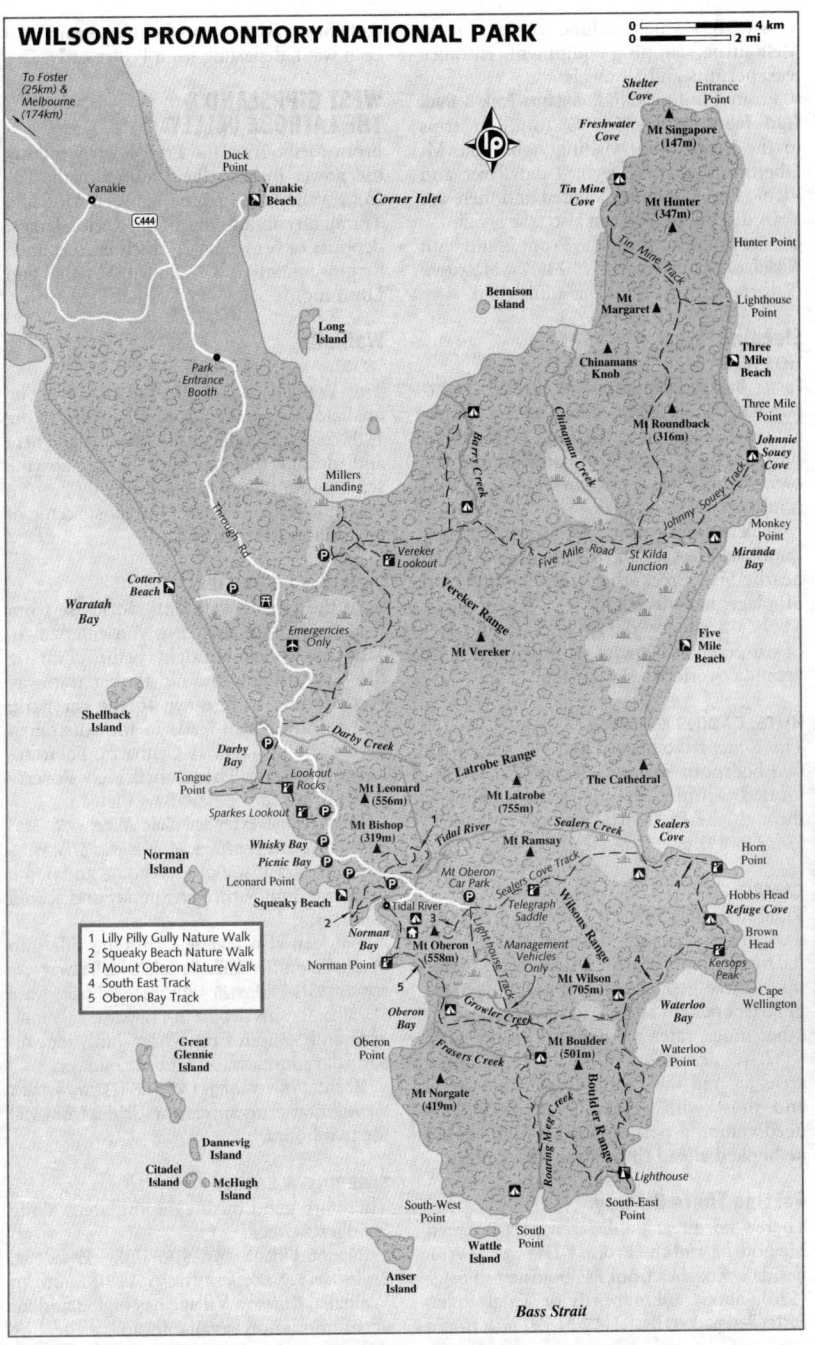

0 | 4 km
0 | 2 mi

To Foster (25km) & Melbourne (174km)

Yanakie

C444

Duck Point

Yanakie Beach

Corner Inlet

Shelter Cove

Entrance Point

Freshwater Cove

Mt Singapore (147m)

Tin Mine Cove

Mt Hunter (347m)

Hunter Point

Bennison Island

Mt Margaret

Lighthouse Point

Long Island

Three Mile Beach

Park Entrance Booth

Millers Landing

Barry Creek

Chinaman Creek

Chinamans Knob

Tin Mine Track

Three Mile Point

Mt Roundback (316m)

Johnnie Souey Cove

Vereker Lookout

Five Mile Road

St Kilda Junction

Johnny Souey Track

Monkey Point

Miranda Bay

Cotters Beach

Waratah Bay

Through Rd

Emergencies Only

Vereker Range

Mt Vereker

Five Mile Beach

Shellback Island

Darby Creek

Latrobe Range

The Cathedral

Darby Bay

Tongue Point

Lookout Rocks

Sparkes Lookout

Mt Leonard (556m)

Mt Latrobe (755m)

Sealers Creek

Sealers Cove

Horn Point

Whisky Bay

Mt Bishop (319m)

Tidal River

Mt Ramsay

Sealers Cove Track

Hobbs Head

Refuge Cove

Picnic Bay

Leonard Point

Mt Oberon Car Park

Telegraph Saddle

Wilsons Range

Brown Head

Norman Island

Squeaky Beach

Tidal River

Management Vehicles Only

Kersops Peak

Cape Wellington

Norman Bay

Mt Oberon (558m)

Mt Wilson (705m)

Waterloo Bay

Norman Point

1 Lilly Pilly Gully Nature Walk
2 Squeaky Beach Nature Walk
3 Mount Oberon Nature Walk
4 South East Track
5 Oberon Bay Track

Oberon Bay

Growler Creek

Mt Boulder (501m)

Waterloo Point

Great Glennie Island

Oberon Point

Frasers Creek

Roaring Meg Creek

Boulder Range

Dannevig Island

Citadel Island

McHugh Island

Mt Norgate (419m)

Lighthouse

South-West Point

South Point

South-East Point

Wattle Island

Anser Island

Bass Strait

VICTORIA

trips ($185) which include transport from Melbourne, camping equipment, entrance fees, permits and all meals.

From Phillip Island, **Amaroo Park & Duck Truck Tours** (☎ 03-5952 2548) runs day trips to the Prom ($85) visiting sights like Mt Oberon, Squeaky Beach, Tidal River and Picnic Bay. Lunch is included and there are YHA discounts. You can also take an all-day coastal cruise through the Prom island with **Wildlifecoast Cruises** (☎ 03-5952 3501; www.bayconne ctions.com.au) for $105/85 per adult/child.

Sleeping
HOSTELS
Foster Backpackers Hostel (☎ 03-5682 2614; 17 Pioneer St; dm/units $20/60) There are no hostels actually in the park; this one is in nearby Foster. The V/Line stops outside and the owner runs a bus service to Tidal River and rents out camping gear.

Appletrees Apartment (☎ 03-5683 2448; apple apart@hotmail.com; Falls Rd, Fish Creek; d from $110). In nearby Fish Creek, this 'couples only' kind of place has decadent four-poster beds. There's a cheery yellow kitchen and lots of sea-green and cream paintwork. A large veranda overlooks the garden.

HUTS, CABINS & UNITS
There are **self-contained huts** (4/6 beds $52/78), two-bedroom **cabins** ($136) and **units** ($98) located within the park and booked through the **Parks Victoria office** (☎ 1800 350 552, 03-5680 9516).

CAMPING
Tidal River has 500 camp sites and, in holiday periods, booking is essential.

During high season, sites cost $18 for up to three people and one car, plus $3.90 per extra person and $5.60 per extra car. At other times, rates are slightly cheaper.

There are another 11 bush camping areas around the Prom, 10 with pit toilets and most with water. Overnight hikers need camping permits ($5), which should be booked ahead through the park office.

Getting There & Away
There's no direct public transport between Melbourne and the Prom. **V/Line** (☎ 13 61 96) has daily coaches from Melbourne to Foster ($26), about 60km north of Tidal River. **Foster Backpackers Hostel** (☎ 03-5682 2614) runs a

daily bus service to and from the Prom ($15 each way), departing from Foster early.

WEST GIPPSLAND & THE LATROBE VALLEY
From Melbourne, the Princes Hwy follows the power lines to their source in the Latrobe Valley. The region between Moe and Traralgon contains one of the world's largest deposits of brown coal, which is consumed by power stations at Yallourn, Morwell and Loy Yang.

Walhalla
☎ 03
Tiny Walhalla, 46km north of Moe, was one of Victoria's great gold-mining towns in the 19th century. Today just 23 people live here and, despite the inevitable heritaging (the sepia photo salesman has evidently been in town), it remains one of the most scenic of Victoria's historic towns.

SIGHTS & ACTIVITIES
Take the circuit walk anti clockwise from the information shelter as you enter town. This passes the main sights before climbing the hill to follow the old timber tramway and heading back down to the car park. The tramway also leads to the Australian Alps Walking Track to Canberra. There are longer walks to Thomson Bridge, Poverty Point or on to the Baw Baw Plateau.

Long Tunnel Extended Gold Mine (☎ 5165 6259; off Walhalla-Beardmore Rd; adult/child $7/5) runs guided tours at 1.30pm weekdays and noon, 2pm and 3pm Saturday, Sunday and school holidays.

You can also take a 25-minute ride into Walhalla on the **Walhalla Goldfields Railway** (info line ☎ 9513 3969, 5126 4201; adult/child/family return $15/10/35). Trains depart at 11.30am, 12.30pm, 2pm and 3.30pm from Thomson Bridge on Saturday, Sunday and school holidays.

Mountain River Lodge (☎ 5165 3231; www.mount ainriverlodge.com) organises horse rides from $50 for two hours.

SLEEPING & EATING
There are good bush camping areas along Stringer's Creek.

Rawson Village (☎ 5165 3200; 1 Pinnacle Dr, Rawson; dm $20, lodge/motel rooms $68/91) South of Walhalla, Rawson Village has high-standard accommodation available for a healthy range of prices that (healthier still) include a cooked breakfast.

Wild Cherry Cottage (☎ 5165 6245; Church Hill Rd; d from $100) This choice B&B is perched high on a hillside at the southern end of town with camera-clicking valley views. There are two pink and pretty suites detached from the main house. Breakfast is a slap-up affair served on the veranda. Disabled facilities.

Star Hotel (☎ 5165 6262; www.starhotel.com.au; Main Rd; d from $140) The Star is a faithful replica of the original hotel's gold-era façade, coupled with sophisticated designer décor. There are twelve spacious suites with king-size beds and a choice of private cottage garden or veranda. The restaurant provides an interesting twist on international cuisine, with plenty of spicy sun-dried tomato choices.

> **WARNING**
>
> There are many mine shafts in the area so keep to the marked tracks.

Other Sights

Just off the Princes Hwy on the west side of Moe, the **Gippsland Heritage Park** (☎ 5127 3082; Lloyd St; adult/child/family $5/3/15; ✆ 9am-5pm) is a good re-creation of a 19th-century community. For the power-tripper in you, **Morwell** has the **PowerWorks Energy Technology Centre** (☎ 5135 3415; www.powerworks.com.au; Commercial Rd; display free, tours adult/child/family $10/4/22), which has displays on coal mining and power generation, and offers tours at 11am and 2pm.

Getting There & Away

Daily trains run between Melbourne and Sale via Morwell ($21) and Moe ($18).

THE LAKES DISTRICT

Gippsland's Lakes District is the largest inland waterway system in Australia. There are three main lakes which interconnect: Lake King, Lake Victoria and Lake Wellington. The 'lakes' are actually shallow lagoons, separated from the ocean by a narrow strip of sand dunes known as the Ninety Mile Beach.

Sale

☎ 03 / pop 12,850
Apart from some nicely restored old buildings, Sale has little to excite the traveller.

The town is connected by river to the Gippsland Lakes and, during the paddle-steamer era, was a busy port town.

The **visitors centre** (☎ /fax 5144 1108; toursale@i-o.net.au; 8 Foster St; ✆ 9am-5pm) is on the Princes Hwy on the Melbourne side of town.

Sale is the centre of the **Gippsland Wetlands** where lakes, waterways and billabongs harbour more than 130 species of water bird. Two kilometres south of Sale on the South Gippsland Hwy is the Sale Common Wildlife Refuge with a wetlands boardwalk.

Ninety Mile Beach

This pristine and seamless sandy beach is backed by dunes, swamplands and lagoons, stretching from Seaspray to Lakes Entrance. There are kangaroos and emus here so drive slowly, especially at night.

The beach is great for surf fishing and walking but can be dangerous for swimming, except where patrolled at Seaspray.

Camping is allowed at designated places between Seaspray and Golden Beach and there are general stores at Seaspray. **Seaspray Caravan Park** (☎ 03-5146 4364; Foreshore Rd; camp sites/cabins $17/48) is the only park near the beach.

Loch Sport, flanked by the lake on one side of the sand and the sea on the other, has a lot going for it. The general store rents out basic cabins from $40.

Extending into Lake Victoria is the **Lakes National Park**, which covers 2400 hectares of coastal bushland. The park can be reached by road via Loch Sport or by boat from Paynesville. The **Parks Victoria office** (☎ 03-5146 0278; ✆ 8.30-9.30am & 3-4pm) is located at the entrance to Loch Sport. There's camping at Emu Bight. Book sites ($12 for up to six people) through the park office.

Rotamah Island is only accessible by boat. **Rotamah Island Bird Observatory** (☎ /fax 03-5156 6398) has camping and accommodation in an old homestead. It sleeps up to 19 people in dorms and doubles (supply your own bedding) for $71 per person including meals and transport from the mainland. There are bird hides, observation points and study courses.

Mitchell River National Park

This park (12,200 hectares), about 40km northwest of Bairnsdale, has three camping areas, some beautiful green valleys and is perfect for hiking. Walking tracks include the two-day, 18km Mitchell River Walking Track. The **Den of Nargun** is a small cave which, according to Aboriginal legend, is haunted by a half-stone creature known as the Nargun.

Tarra-Bulga National Park

Tarra-Bulga (1.625 hectares), about 30km south of Traralgon, is one of the last remnants of original southern Gippsland forest and is well-worth a walkabout.

The Tarra Valley picnic ground is off Tarra Valley Rd, from where you can stroll through a rain forest gully to the **Cyathea Falls**. The main picnic area is in the northern section, on Grand Ridge Rd, where there's the **visitors centre** (☎ 03-5196 6166; ☷ 10am to 4pm Sat, Sun & holidays) and the 2km **Fern Gully Nature Walk**. Camping isn't allowed in the park.

Tarra-Bulga Guest House and Tea Rooms (☎ 03-5196 6141; www.users.bigpond.com/lcayzer; Grand Ridge Rd, Balook; s/d $50/65) is a welcoming, old-fashioned guesthouse near the park entrance. The small and comfy rooms share a bathroom. Dogs are allowed (on a leash) though children are not. Disabled facilities are available.

Bairnsdale

☎ 03 / pop 10,670

Bustling Bairnsdale is the major town of this district. The **visitors centre** (☎ 1800 637 060, 5152 3444, fax 5153 1563; 240 Main St; ☷ 9am-5pm) can book accommodation.

SIGHTS

The **Krowathunkoolong Keeping Place** (☎ 5152 1891; 37-53 Dalmahoy St; adult/child $3.50/2.50; ☷ 9am-5pm Mon-Fri) is a cultural centre with displays and information on the local Aboriginal people.

History buffs will enjoy the artefacts and memorabilia at the **Historical Museum** (☎ 5152 6363; MacArthur St; adult/child $3/1; ☷ 1-4pm Wed & Sun).

SLEEPING

Commercial Hotel (☎ 5152 3031; 124 Main St; dm/s/d $20/25/42) It's a bit threadbare around the edges but the Commercial is still good value. The friendly owner can help organise boat trips and other activities.

Riversleigh Hotel (☎ 5152 6966; riversleighnet-tech.com.au; 1 Nicholson St; d from $135; ☷) This comfortable classic hotel has rooms with

brass beds and bay windows overlooking pastoral farmland. A reading room and conservatory complete its gracious charm. Disabled facilities are available. Children welcome.

Mitchell Gardens Holiday Park (☎ 5152 4654; mitchell.gardens@net-tech.com.au; 2 Main St; camp sites $15, cabins $69-109) East of the centre and by the Mitchell River, the facilities at this holiday park are well kept and clean. The cabins have river views.

EATING

Arty Farty (☎ 5152 5556; 164 Main St; dishes $9-12) Black-and-white pictures adorn the walls at this hip eatery. Its healthy, hearty menu boasts brochettes, wedges, homemade soup and smoothies. Kiddie-size shakes available.

Tavern Bistro (☎ 5152 4030; 59 Main St; mains $13-17) Mains at this bistro are the typical chargrill/chicken/seafood selection but the $6 salad bar is fresher than most and nobody is counting when it comes to refilling your plate. A cheap children's menu, with free soft drink and ice-cream sundaes, makes this bistro a winner for families.

Commercial Hotel (☎ 5152 3031; 124 Main St; mains $14-20) Time-tested favourites are dished up in the friendly pubby atmosphere of this excellent bistro. Hungry folk should try the 425 gram steak.

Metung

☎ 03 / pop 520

The unhurried charm of this picture-postcard village on Bancroft Bay is contagious. Its shoreline is dotted with jetties and small wooden craft. Boat trips are, predictably, big news here:

Metung Cruisers (☎ 5156 2208; Metung Rd) Prices range from $900 to $1845 for a three-night minimum cruise.

Slipway (☎ 5156 2469; 50 Metung Rd) Runabout boats available for hire, taking up to eight people for $30/105 per hour/day.

Spray Cruises (☎ 04-2851 6055; www.metung.com /spraycruises; 50 Metung Rd) Daily cruise on a 14m-long ketch depart from the harbour at 11am.

SLEEPING & EATING

Metung Tourist Park (☎ 5156 2306, fax 5156 2186; cnr Stirling & Mairburn Rds; camp sites/cabins $17/65) This secluded park has shady trees, and is a reasonable place to stay. The welcoming owners can organise fishing trips.

Metung Hotel (☎ 5156 2206; www.metunghotel .com.au; Kirnai Ave; s/d $55/85) The pub takes prime position, with its large wooden terrace overlooking the bay. You're paying for the location, rather than the rooms which are bland and share a bathroom. If you're around at noon, they feed the pelicans. Breakfast is included in the rate and the **restaurant** has a varied menu with vegetarian options.

Meg's at Metung (☎ 5156 2330; 59 Metung Rd; 9am-9pm; dishes $6-15) Forget the fancy restaurants where you'll pay twice as much, this is the place for fish and chips. They also do an excellent seafood platter, pizzas, salads and breakfast.

Lakes Entrance
☎ 03 / pop 5500

In season, Lakes Entrance is a packed-out tourist town, as witnessed by the ugly strip of motels, caravan parks and shops lining the Esplanade. Its saving grace is the picturesque location on the gentle waters of Cunninghame Arm, backed by sand dunes and small fishing boats.

The **visitors centre** (☎ 1800 637 060, 5155 1966; www.lakesandwilderness.com.au; cnr Princes Hwy & Marine Pde; 9am-5pm) has plenty of information on the area. **Internet** access is available at **KB's Place** (357 The Esplanade; 10am-5pm).

ACTIVITIES

A footbridge crosses the Cunninghame Arm inlet from the east of town to the ocean and **Ninety Mile Beach**. From December to Easter, paddle boats, canoes and sailboats can be hired by the footbridge. Guided walks of the magnificent 90 hectare Gippsland forest are offered by the **Nature Sanctuary** (☎ 5156 5863; Toorloo Arm; adult/child $19/12). Night walks and family packages available.

Several outfits organise cruises. **Corque** (☎ 5155 1508), owned by the Wyanga Park, runs a dinner cruise (three courses and drinks, $60) and a Sunday brunch cruise $30/15). Most cruises include a visit to the winery. The **MB Rubeena** (☎ 5155 1283; Lake Tyers) runs two-hour cruises at 2pm on Tuesday, Thursday and Saturday ($22/14 per adult/child, including afternoon tea).

SLEEPING

Riviera Backpackers (☎ 5155 2444; riviera@net-tech .com.au; 5 Clarkes Rd; dm/d $18/38;) This YHA is in the east end of town. It's a good, clean

hostel with a large kitchen and pool table. Discounts for guests are available in restaurants and for tours. V/Line and other buses stop nearby on the Esplanade.

Lakeside Motel (☎ 5155 1811; 164 Marine Pde; low/high season d $45/100) Better looking than most motels on this holiday strip, Lakeside is clean and well-equipped. There's a children's playground, barbecue and private jetty for yachtie types. Note the price hike during holiday times.

Goat & Goose (☎ 5155 3079; www.babs.com.au /goatandgoose; 16 Gay St; d from $170) This wonderfully unusual multi-storey pole frame house has balconies at every turn to take advantage of Bass Strait views. A candlelit spa and breakfast banquet is included in the price. No children.

Eastern Beach Caravan Park (☎ 5155 1581; Eastern Beach; camp/van sites from $15/17) There's plenty of open space at this pleasant, clean and shady caravan park, unlike those in the inner city circuit of caravan parks. The owners are friendly and helpful, and the facilities are reasonable. Pets are allowed off season, and there's excellent fishing on the nearby beach.

EATING

Lakes Entrance Bakery (☎ 5155 2864; 537 The Esplanade) This is no ordinary bakery. The mouth-watering range of goodies includes vegetable fritatta, spinach and potato muffins, cheese and pumpkin loaf, and a blockbuster steak and curry pie. Try the apple and custard crumble for afters.

Miriams (☎ 5155 3999; 3 Bulber St; mains $12-16; dinner only) There are lake views from Miriams wood-and-brick interior. Fish is the specialty, including fresh Eden blue mussels and Tasmanian oysters, and there's a good salad and vegie choice.

Fisherman's Co-op (☎ 5155 1688; Bullock Island; 9am-5pm) You'll find the co-op on the right hand side of Princes Hwy when entering Lakes Entrance from the west. This is where the fishing boats unload their catch – fish, prawns and shellfish can be bought cheaply in the shop.

GETTING THERE & AWAY

Omeo Buslines (☎ 5159 4231) runs between Bairnsdale and Omeo ($28) on weekdays.

V/Line (☎ 13 61 96) trains/coaches pass through Bairnsdale ($40), Lakes Entrance,

Orbost ($54), Cann River, then out of the state into NSW and on to Canberra.

Wild-Life Tours (☎ 1300 650 288, 9747 1882; www.wildlifetours.com.au) runs tours from Melbourne to Sydney calling at Lakes Entrance, Buchan Caves and the Snowy Mountains National Park. Three stopovers are allowed and fares start at $169.

EAST GIPPSLAND & THE WILDERNESS COAST

This section of East Gippsland contains some of the most remote and spectacular national parks in the state. Much of the region was spared clearing for agriculture, and logging in these ancient forests is a hot issue.

Unexciting Orbost is the major town and gateway to the Snowy River and Errinundra National Parks, and the Wilderness Coast. There's a visitors centre at Orbost (p568) and Parks Victoria offices at Cann River and Mallacoota (see p569 for details).

Buchan

Buchan, known for its caves, is a tiny and beautiful town in the foothills of the Snowy Mountains.

SIGHTS & ACTIVITIES

The scenic **Caves Reserve** is just north of town. The Parks Victoria office sells tickets for caves tours ($11/6 per adult/child). Tours run at 11am, 1pm and 3pm from April to September; and 10am, 11.15am, 1pm, 2.15pm and 3.30pm at other times. Tours alternate between **Royal Cave** and **Fairy Cave**.

Snowy River Expeditions (☎ 03-5155 0220), at Karoonda Park (see below), runs one-, two- and four-day rafting trips ($120/240/550 respectively) on the Snowy during spring plus climbing, abseiling or caving trips (starting from $50 per day). Most trips require a minimum of six people.

SLEEPING & EATING

Buchan Motel (☎ 03-5155 9201; buchanmotel@datafast .net.au; s/d $53/64) On top of the hill behind the General Store, this motel is under new ownership and has been spruced up with welcome amenities like ceiling fans. The views are over pastoral farmland and the Buchan river, and it's more like a B&B than a motel. Dinner and breakfast are available in the cosy dining room.

Buchan Lodge Backpackers (☎ 03-5155 9421; buchanlodge@net-tech.com.au; Saleyard Rd; dm $20) There are good facilities here, including a fully-equipped kitchen, large dining room and barbecue. The lodge is surrounded by verandas and lawns. Breakfast is included; book ahead for high season.

Buchan Valley Log Cabins (☎ 03-5155 9494; Gelantipy Rd; s/d $55/75) These very pleasant cabins on hilly terrain with fine views are about 200m north of the main bridge into town. The cabins have large terraces. Facilities here include a campfire and playground; there's also a unit for the disabled. Children welcome.

Willow Cafe (☎ 03-5155 9387; Main Rd; meals & snacks $5.50-15) This earthy licensed café dishes up healthy meals from breakfast through to dinner. It also has live entertainment once a month.

Snowy River National Park

Dominated by gorges carved by the Snowy River, this is one of Victoria's most isolated and spectacular parks (95,000 hectares).

The main access roads are Gelantipy Rd from Buchan and Bonang Rd from Orbost, which are joined by McKillops Rd in the north, crossing the Snowy River at **McKillops Bridge**.

About 25km before the bridge on the Gelantipy Rd are **Little River Falls** and **Little River Gorge** lookouts. The latter, a half-a-kilometre-deep gorge, is one of the secrets of Victoria.

Either side of McKillops Bridge are camp sites, toilets and fireplaces, and access to sandy river beaches.

Bushwalking and canoeing are popular but be prepared as conditions can change suddenly. The classic canoe or raft trip down the Snowy River from McKillops Bridge to a finish point near Buchan takes at least four days.

For information, contact **Parks Victoria** (☎ 02-6458 1456; Bendoc) or the visitors centre in Orbost.

SLEEPING & EATING

Karoonda Park (☎ 03-5155 0220; karoonda@net-tech .com.au; Gelantipy Rd, Karoonda Park; dm/d $20/26; 💻) This cattle and sheep property and horse-riding ranch, 40km north of Buchan, also has YHA accommodation. Fully-catered packages are available and the owners may have work going.

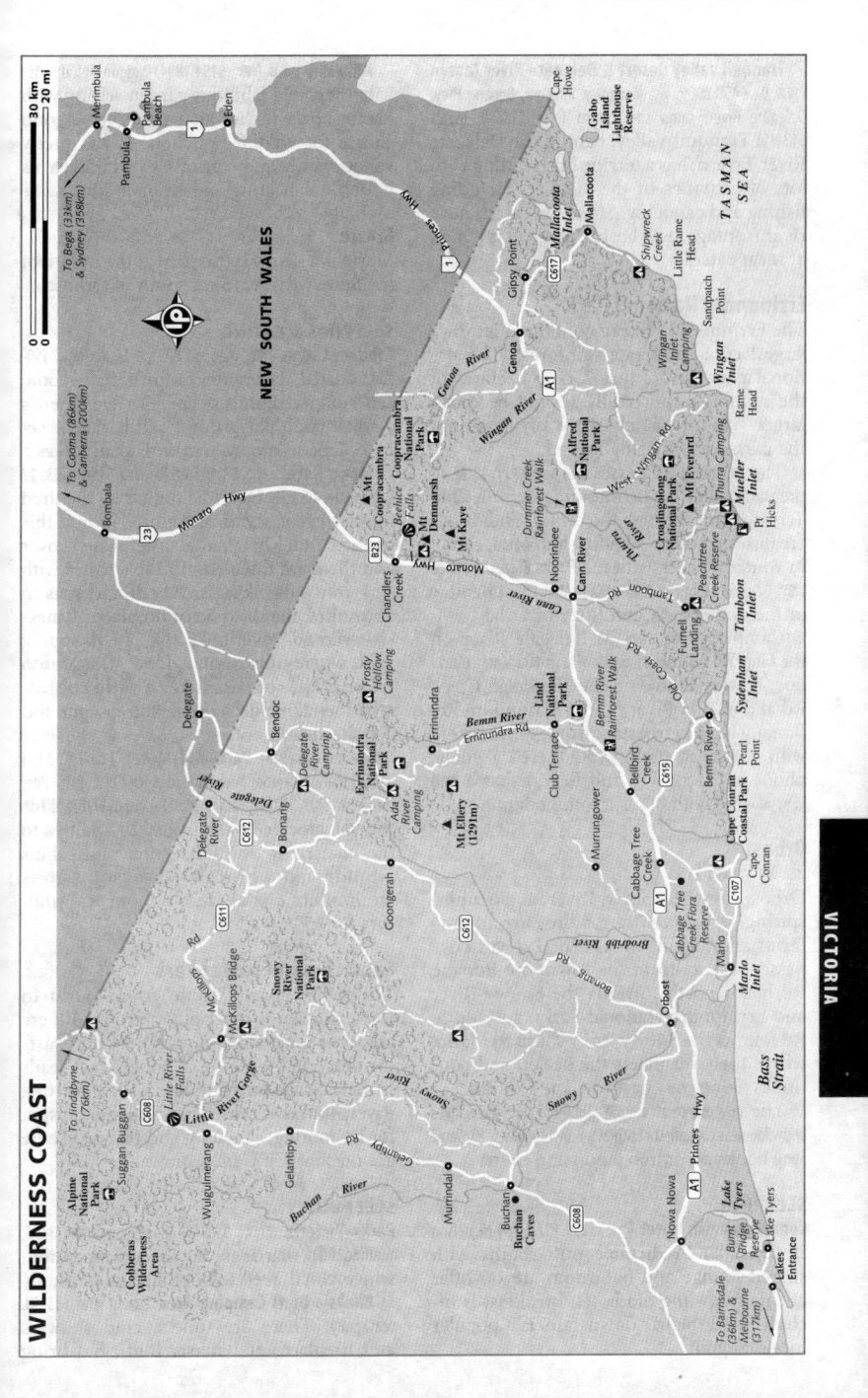

WILDERNESS COAST

NEW SOUTH WALES

VICTORIA

TASMAN SEA

Bass Strait

To Bega (33km) & Sydney (358km)

To Cooma (86km) & Canberra (200km)

To Jindabyne (76km)

To Bairnsdale (36km) & Melbourne (317km)

Merimbula
Pambula Beach
Pambula
Eden
Bombala
Delegate
Cape Howe
Cabo Island Lighthouse Reserve
Mallacoota Inlet
Mallacoota
Shipwreck Creek
Little Rame Head
Sandpatch Point
Gipsy Point
Genoa
Wingan Inlet Camping
Wingan Inlet
Rame Head
Genoa River
Wingan River
Alfred National Park
West Wingan Rd
Mt Everard
Thurra Camping
Croajingolong National Park
Mueller Inlet
Pt Hicks
Dummer Creek Rainforest Walk
Noorinbee
Cann River
Peachtree Creek Reserve
Tamboon Inlet
Coopracambra National Park
Beehive Falls
Mt Coopracambra
Mt Denmarsh
Mt Kaye
Chandlers Creek
Monaro Hwy
Cann River
Tamboon Rd
Furnell Landing
Sydenham Inlet
Old Coast Rd
Errinundra
Frosty Hollow Camping
Errinundra National Park
Bendoc
Delegate River Camping
Delegate River
Bonang
Ada River Camping
Mt Ellery (1291m)
Bemm River
Lind National Park
Bemm River Rainforest Walk
Club Terrace
Errinundra Rd
Bellbird Creek
Bemm River
Pearl Point
Murrungower
Cabbage Tree Creek
Cape Conran Coastal Park
Cape Conran
Goongerah
Snowy River National Park
McKillops Bridge
McKillops Rd
Little River Gorge
Little River Falls
Alpine National Park
Cobberas Wilderness Area
Suggan Buggan
Wulgulmerang
Gelantipy
Buchan River
Buchan
Buchan Caves
Murrindal
Snowy River
Broadbrib River
Cabbage Tree Creek Flora Reserve
Marlo
Marlo Inlet
Orbost
Bonang Rd
Nowa Nowa
Lake Tyers
Lake Tyers
Burnt Bridge Reserve
Lakes Entrance
Princes Hwy
Buchan Rd
Delegate
Monaro Hwy

30 km
20 mi

Tranquil Valley Resort & Delegate River Tavern
(☎ 02-6458 8009; www.countryhigh.com, Bonang Hwy, Delegate River; camp sites/cabins from $15/50; meals $13-15) Tranquil Valley, behind the Delegate River Tavern, has a terrific bush setting with lots of activities in the vicinity, including fishing and canoeing. Some log cabins have river frontage. The basic pub grub is aimed at meat eaters.

Errinundra National Park

The Errinundra Plateau contains Victoria's largest cool-temperate rainforest. The national park covers just 25,100 hectares of the rainforest, but really should be much larger – unfortunately many areas around the park are still being logged.

The Bonang Rd passes the western side of the park, while the Errinundra Rd, from Club Terrace, runs through the centre. Both roads are unsealed, steep, winding and often closed in winter – check with the **Parks Victoria office** (☎ 02-6458 1456; ☒ 8am-4.30pm Mon-Fri) at Bendoc or their offices at Cann River or Orbost.

Camping areas are at Delegate River on the Gap Rd connecting Bonang Rd with Bendoc, Frosty Hollow on the Hensleigh Creek Rd and at Ada River on the Errinundra Rd. Bonang has a petrol station and general store with a caravan park, while there's a public phone at Goongerah and Bendoc has a **pub** (☒ Mon-Sat) with basic accommodation.

Orbost
☎ 03 / pop 2100
Orbost, by the Snowy River, is an uninspiring service centre for the surrounding farms and logging areas. The Princes Hwy passes just south of the town, the Bonang Rd heads north towards the Snowy River and Errinundra National Parks, and Marlo Rd follows the Snowy River south to Marlo, where the river meets the ocean, and continues along the coast to Cape Conran.

The **visitors centre** (☎ 1800 637 060; www.lakes andwilderness.com.au; cnr Lochiel & Browning Sts; ☒ 9am-5pm) books accommodation and tours.

SLEEPING
Commonwealth Hotel (☎ 5154 1077; 159 Nicholson St; s/d $30/40) Predictable pub rooms with shared lounge and bathroom are on offer at this sprawling old hotel. Breakfast is included and the bar downstairs is a popular local hangout.

Killarney B&B (☎ 5154 1804; Duggans Rd; d $130) Killarney, in a fabulous garden setting with exotic birds including parrots, is a good choice for wildlife watchers. It has pretty valley views and various extras, such as underfloor heating and an open fire.

Marlo
Marlo is a sleepy settlement at the mouth of the Snowy River, 15km south of Orbost.

SLEEPING & EATING
Tabbara Lodge (☎ 03-5154 8231; 1 Marlo Rd; d $50-75) Located at the entry to town, these good, self-contained units sleep up to five. There's a small pool, playground and barbecue set in a pleasant grassy area with shady trees.

Marlo Hotel (☎ 03-5154 8201; fax 5154 8493; 17 Argyle Pde; d $110) Don't be put off by the tired looking exterior, the accommodation at this historic hotel has had a tasteful makeover and there are three comfortable suites with sink-into sofas, king-size beds and spas in two suites; the third has a fireplace. A massive veranda overlooks the jaw-dropping spot where the Snowy River flows into the sea. The restaurant has a varied bistro-style menu, including vegetable lasagne and T-bone steak.

Marlo Caravan Park and Motel (☎ 03-5154 8226; marlopark@net-tech.com.au; 10-12 Argyle Pde; camp/van sites $22/33, cabins/motel rooms $52/82) This centrally located park is just 200 metres to the boat ramp and jetty. Sites and cabins are tidy and well-maintained and tinnies (aluminium boats) are hired out with motors for $50/90 a half/full day.

Cape Conran Coastal Park
The 19km coastal route from Marlo to Cape Conran is especially pretty and there are some great beaches with the safest surfing beach in the region. A rough track leads from the cape to the mouth of the Yeerung River, 4km east, which is another good spot for swimming, canoeing and fishing. There are no shops at Cape Conran.

SLEEPING
Parks Victoria (☎ 03-5154 8438; fax 5154 8496; Yeerung Rd) manages the accommodation, which you'll need to book in high season.

Banksia Bluff Camping Area (camp sites $15-19, seasonally) There are toilets, cold showers and fireplaces at Banksia Bluff, but bring

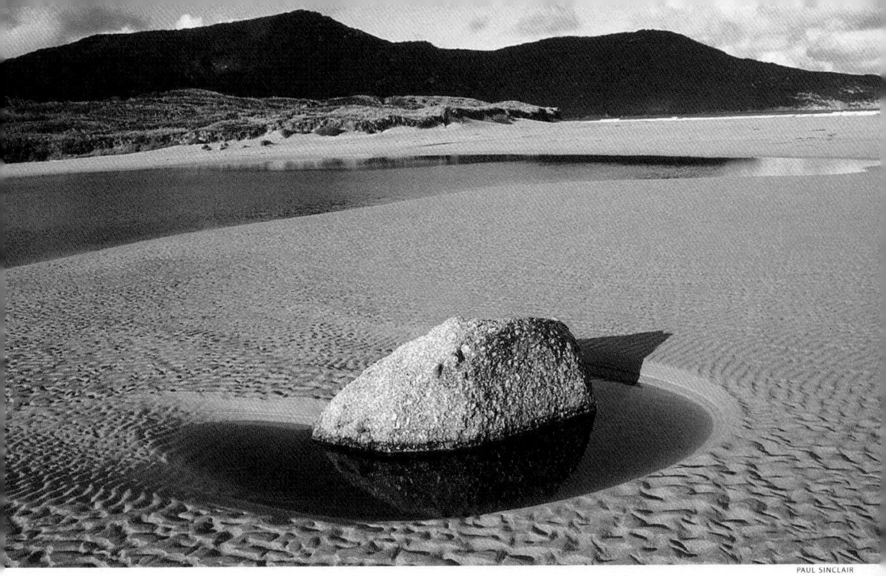

PAUL SINCLAIR

Explore the magnificent beaches along the edge of southern **Gippsland** (p559)

Grab the kids and head to Victoria's largest ski resort, **Mt Buller** (p546)

PHIL WEYMOUTH

KAREN TRIST

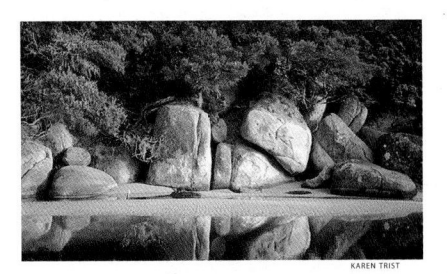

Wander along walking tracks through beautiful bushland in **Wilsons Promontory National Park** (p559)

JOHN BANAGAN

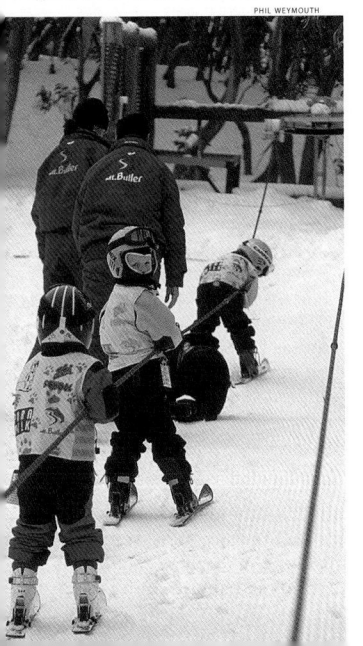

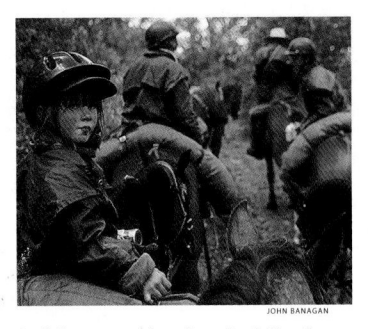

Saddle up and head to the hills of Victoria's **High Country** (p441)

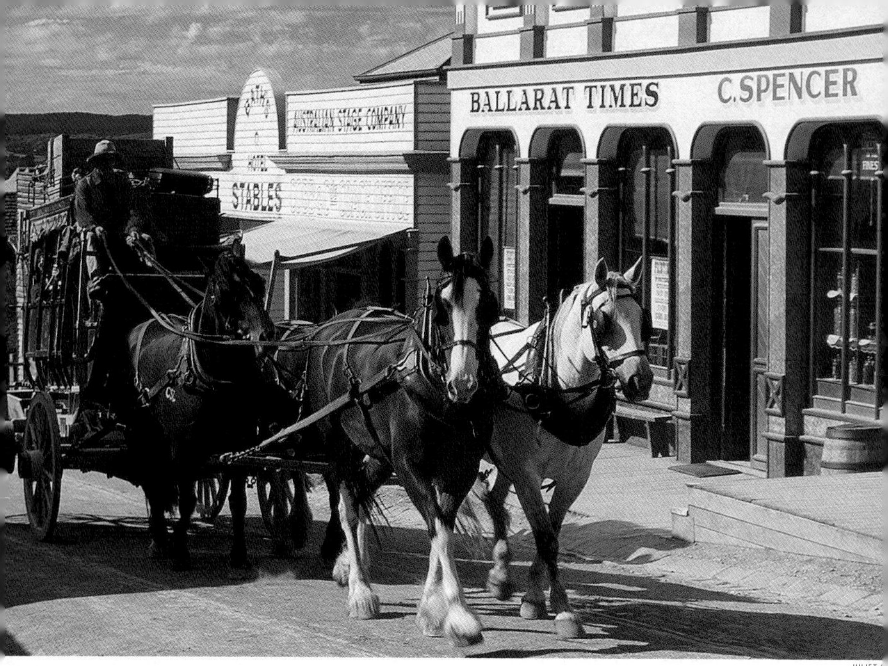

JULIET (

Re-visit bygone days at Ballarat's re-creation of an 1860s mining township, **Sovereign Hill** (p532)

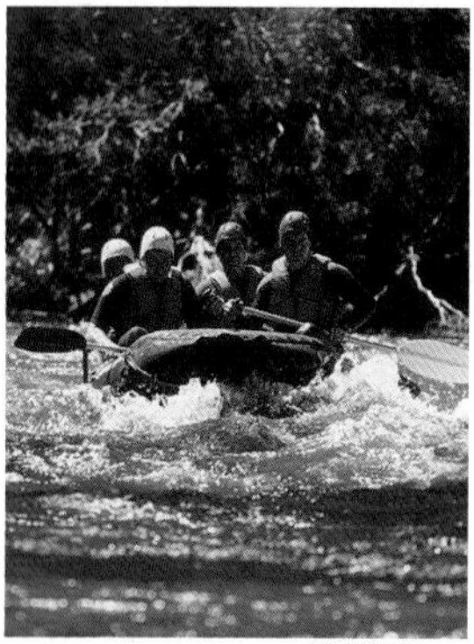

JON ARMSTRONG

Get doused in white water on a rafting trip down the mighty **Snowy River** (p566)

Kick back on a historic Murray River paddle-steamer at **Echuca** (p525)

CHRIS N

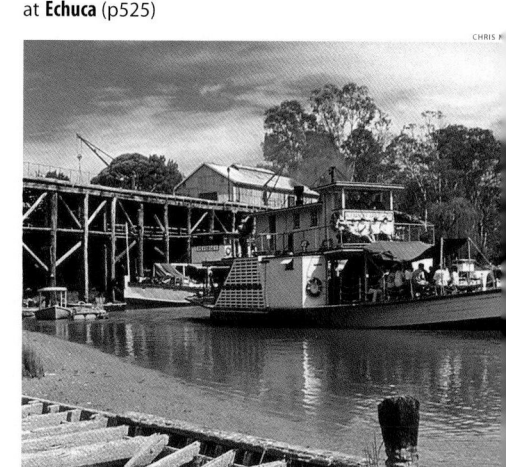

drinking water if you don't like the taste of bore water.

Cape Conran Cabins & Lodge (4–8-person cabins $78-118) These well-equipped, large cabins have an airy, beachcomber feel, and are just a short walk to the beach.

Cann River

Cann River is at the junction of the Princes and Monaro Hwys heading north into NSW. There are petrol stations, motels, a supermarket, a hotel and a caravan park here, as well as several places to grab a quick bite. Consult the **Parks Victoria office** (☎ 03-5158 6351) here about roads in the Croajingolong National Park and walking within the park.

Coopracambra National Park

Coopracambra (38,300 hectares) is remote and undeveloped. The original ecosystem is virtually intact, with many rare and endangered species living here. The landscape is rugged and spectacular, with deep gorges where the earliest fossil evidence of four-footed creatures was discovered. The only access is a 4WD track which runs from the Monaro Hwy to Genoa. Beehive Falls are 2km from the Monaro Hwy, 28km north of Cann River.

Coopracambra Cottage (☎ /fax 03-5158 8277; 2-/4-/6-person cabins $60/65/70) These beautifully furnished and eco-friendly cabins are 16km northwest of Genoa. The pastureland setting has emus, kangaroos, wombats, many birds and mountain views. The owners can take visitors on tours through the National Park.

Gipsy Point

Gipsy Point is a tiny settlement at the head of the Mallacoota Inlet.

Gipsy Point Lodge (☎ 1800 063 556, 03-5158 8205; www.gipsypoint.com; Mattson St; guest house/cottages from $95/135) These pleasant rooms are in beautiful surroundings overlooking the river or gardens. There is a well-recommended restaurant, a reading room and library. You can hire a motorboat from $65 a day.

Mallacoota

☎ 03 / pop 1040

Sleepy Mallacoota, which is surrounded by the Croajingolong National Park, becomes a crowded family holiday spot at Christmas and Easter.

The **Parks Victoria information centre** (☎ 5158 0219; 🕙 9.30am-noon & 1-3.30pm Mon-Fri) is opposite the main wharf. The informal **visitors centre** (www.mallacoota.com; 🕙 9am-5pm), in the green shed on the wharf, is run by volunteers and has information and a handy map on the 7km Mallacoota walking track.

ACTIVITIES

The 300km shoreline of Mallacoota Inlet is backed by national park. Pick up a copy of the informative *Stepping Stones, A Guide to Mallacoota* booklet.

A number of operators offer **cruises** and boat hire:

MV Loch Ard (☎ 5158 8291) Restored timber ferry runs different cruises on different days: the 2½-hour adventure cruise costs $22.

Buckland's Boat Hire (☎ 5158 0660; Lakeside Dr) Boat hire $25/100 per hour/day, canoes $15/50.

Mallacoota Hire Boats (☎ 5158 0704) Just left of the main wharf, rents paddle boats for $10 per half day, as well as kayaks and motor boats.

SLEEPING

Prices vary significantly with the seasons and at Christmas or Easter you'll need to book ahead.

Mallacoota Hotel Motel & Mallacoota Lodge YHA (☎ 5158 0455; inncoota@vicnet.net.au; 51-55 Maurice Ave; lodge dm/d $19/21, motel s/d $61/82; 🖳) It's nothing fancy but this place offers good value for this pack 'em in tourist town. The large motel rooms overlook an excellent pool and lawn. The YHA has good accommodation with a shared kitchen; book through the hotel-motel.

Silver Bream Motel (☎ 5158 0305; www .silverbream.com.au; 32-34 Maurice Ave; s/d from $60/70, flats from $320/week; 🖳) Silver Bream has pleasant rooms with the standard motel-style flowery fabrics and fitted carpets. The flats have good-sized kitchens and the gardens are lovely, with rose bushes and carefully manicured borders.

Adobe Mudbrick Flats (☎ 5158 0329; 17 Karbeethong Ave; d cabins from $120, flats from $280) At this creative and comfortable mud-brick village, the eco rule of not feeding the wildlife isn't followed, so expect a squawkfest of birds outside your door waiting to be fed. Here you can expect to see parrots, lorikeets, wild duck, wombats, possums and even the elusive lyrebird. The flats sleep four people.

VICTORIA

Blue Waters Holiday Cottages (☎ 5158 0261; www.bluewaters.com.au; 13-15 Karbeethong Ave; low/high season d from $190/330) The cottages have sweeping views over the lake. The new owners have been exquisitely reforming and decorating with a classy cool colour-scheme, adding new bathrooms and extended roofs to provide shade for the terraces. The prices quoted are for two nights minimum stay.

Mallacoota Foreshore Camp Park (☎ 5158 0300; Camping Reserve; camp/van sites $21/35) These sites extend right along the foreshore and have sublime views of the lake, with its resident population of black swans and pelicans.

EATING

Tide (☎ 5158 0100; cnr Maurice Ave & Allan Dr; mains $17-25) This candlelit-dinner kind of place has a large deck overlooking the inlet. Local oysters and abalone, when in season, are a catch-of-the-day specialty. There's a long list of slick-sounding cocktails and a regular live dinner show during peak-season.

Barnacles Seafood Bistro (☎ 5158 0455; 51-55 Maurice Ave; mains $16-19) Barnacles no-nonsense bistro in the Mallacoota Hotel serves mammoth portions of chips-with-everything cuisine. The atmosphere is diner-style but prices are reasonable if you are looking for a re-fuelling spot for the family.

Cafe 54 (☎ 5158 0646; 54 Maurice Ave; mains $9-20) This sunny little restaurant has a varied selection including vegetarian curries, T-bone steak, and tuna patties, plus a children's menu.

GETTING THERE & AWAY

Mallacoota is 23km off the Princes Hwy. Buses stop at Genoa, where some accommodation places and tour operators may pick you up by arrangement.

Croajingolong National Park

Croajingolong (87,500 hectares) is one of Australia's finest national parks. It stretches for about 100km from Bemm River to the NSW border and includes unspoiled beaches, inlets and forests. The 200m sand dunes at Thurra are the highest on the mainland.

Mallacoota Inlet is the largest and most accessible area. There's plentiful wildlife in the park, including huge goannas.

Walkers must be suitably equipped for long-distance walking, with sufficient maps and information on conditions. **Parks Victoria offices** (Cann River (☎ 03-5158 6351); Mallacoota (☎ 03-5158 0219) will give advice on the park and issue the necessary permits for camping overnight.

All access roads from the Princes Hwy, except Mallacoota Rd, are unsealed and can be very rough, so check road conditions with Parks Victoria.

The main camping areas are at Wingan Inlet, Shipwreck Creek, Thurra River, Peachtree Creek and Mueller Inlet. You may need to bring water so check with Parks Victoria. You'll also need to book during the main holiday seasons; camping fees cost up to $17 a site.

Point Hicks was the first part of Australia to be spotted by Captain Cook in 1770. Experience the windy and isolated ruggedness that the lightkeepers used to know, plus get a seagull's view when you climb to the top, of the remote but basic **Point Hicks Lighthouse** (☎ 03-5158 4268; www.pointhicks.bigpond.com; s/d cabin $80/100, lighthouse from $240; ☯ 10am-3pm). It sleeps up to eight and has a minimum two night stay. Bring all your own food.

GETTING THERE & AWAY

Daily **V/Line** (☎ 13 61 96) coaches run along the Princes Hwy from Bairnsdale into NSW. From Melbourne, take the train to Sale and connect with the bus there. Wild-Life Tours stop at Buchan (for details see Getting There & Away for the Lakes District; p565).

The Princes Hwy runs through the region and sealed roads lead from it to Mallacoota, Marlo, Cape Conran and Bemm River. The Monaro Hwy (B23) runs north from Cann River into NSW.

Most minor roads are unsealed and some are closed during the wetter winter months. Check road conditions with **Parks Victoria** (☎ 13 19 63; www.parks.vic.gov.au) and keep an eye out for logging trucks.

Tasmania

TASMANIA

Tasmania is Australia's only island state. Historically, this isolation made it an ideal location for penal settlements, and this isolation also later helped to preserve the state's rich colonial heritage and much of its wilderness (with some notable exceptions). Today Tasmania appeals to travellers with winning attractions such as a gracious capital in a magnificent setting, an appreciation of history, superb gourmet offerings, ecotourism and a wealth of outdoor pursuits, plus the chance to meet some of the friendliest folk in the country.

Compact in comparison to the mainland states and with a tiny population, Tasmania is a place designed for cruising the back roads at leisure and enjoying stunning scenery, like majestic Cradle Mountain or the white sand and crystal-clear waters of the east coast. Charming small settlements such as Stanley, presided over by an imposing rock formation, or Richmond, full of beautifully preserved sandstone buildings, are great places to savour meals of excellent local produce and the warmth and hospitality of old-fashioned accommodation. And for those occasions when you want to stretch your legs and breathe in some of the cleanest air in the world, Tasmania has postcard-perfect beaches, vast areas of untouched wilderness, more than 2000km of walking tracks and 19 national parks.

It's a pity so many travellers (both international and domestic) overlook Tasmania . Don't let the rough waters of Bass Strait act as a barrier – make your way to magical little Tassie and your efforts will be richly rewarded.

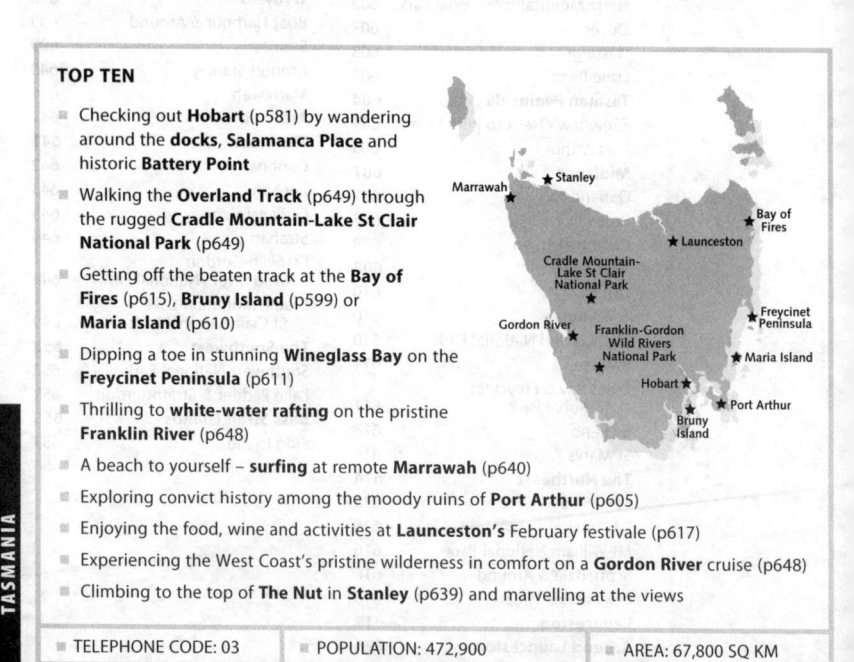

TOP TEN

- Checking out **Hobart** (p581) by wandering around the **docks**, **Salamanca Place** and historic **Battery Point**

- Walking the **Overland Track** (p649) through the rugged **Cradle Mountain-Lake St Clair National Park** (p649)

- Getting off the beaten track at the **Bay of Fires** (p615), **Bruny Island** (p599) or **Maria Island** (p610)

- Dipping a toe in stunning **Wineglass Bay** on the **Freycinet Peninsula** (p611)

- Thrilling to **white-water rafting** on the pristine **Franklin River** (p648)

- A beach to yourself – **surfing** at remote **Marrawah** (p640)

- Exploring convict history among the moody ruins of **Port Arthur** (p605)

- Enjoying the food, wine and activities at **Launceston's** February festivale (p617)

- Experiencing the West Coast's pristine wilderness in comfort on a **Gordon River** cruise (p648)

- Climbing to the top of **The Nut** in **Stanley** (p639) and marvelling at the views

▪ TELEPHONE CODE: 03	▪ POPULATION: 472,900	▪ AREA: 67,800 SQ KM

TASMANIA

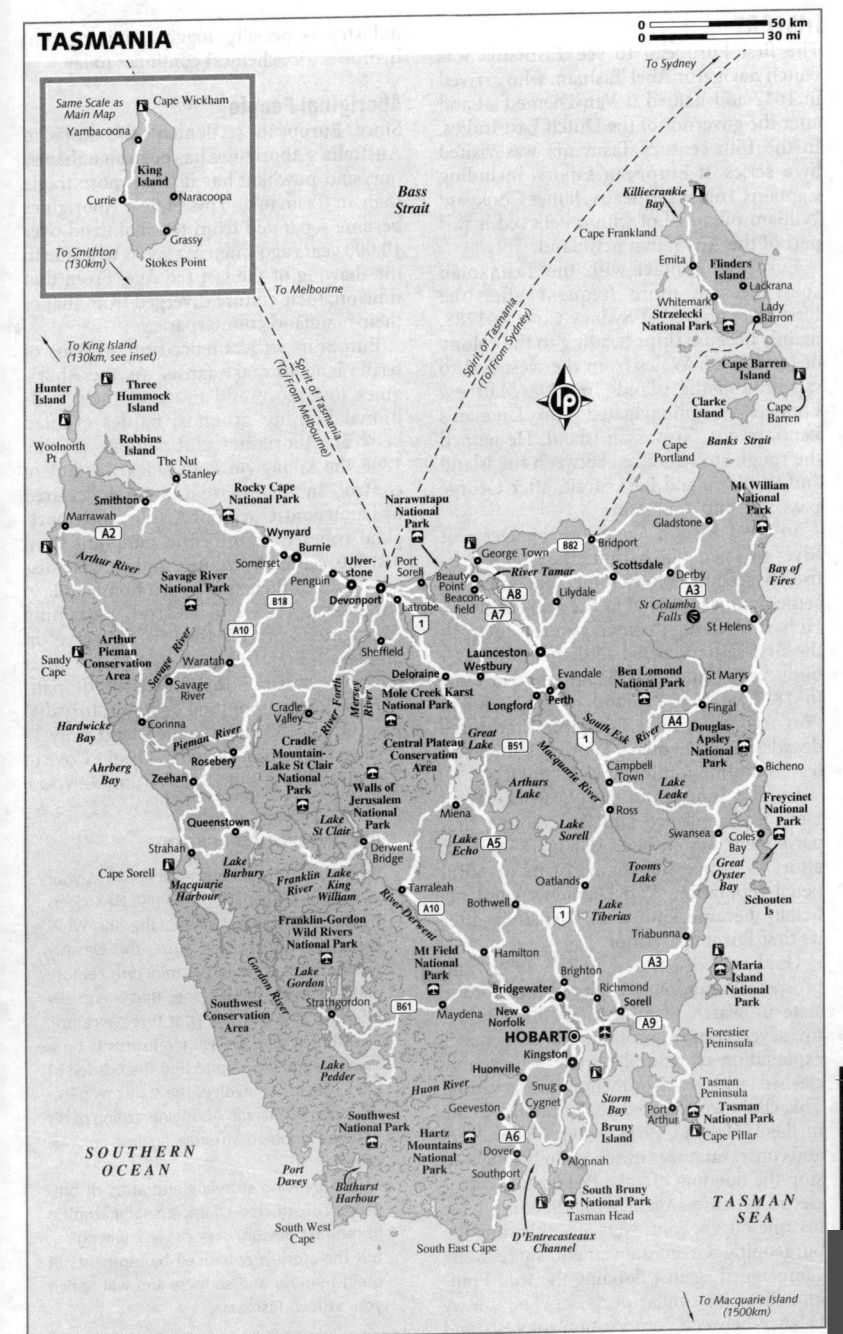

50 km
30 mi

To Sydney

Bass Strait

Same Scale as Main Map

Cape Wickham

Yambacoona

King Island

Currie ● ● Naracoopa

Grassy

Stokes Point

To Smithton (130km)

To Melbourne

Killiecrankie Bay

Cape Frankland

Emita

Flinders Island

Lackrana

Whitemark

Strzelecki National Park

Lady Barron

Spirit of Tasmania (To/From Sydney)

Cape Barren Island

Clarke Island

Cape Barren

To King Island (130km, see inset)

Spirit of Tasmania (To/From Melbourne)

Hunter Island

Three Hummock Island

Woolnorth Pt

Robbins Island

The Nut

Stanley

Smithton

Marrawah

Rocky Cape National Park

Wynyard

Somerset

Burnie

Penguin

Ulverstone

Devonport

Port Sorell

Narawntapu National Park

Beauty Point

Beaconsfield

George Town

River Tamar

Cape Portland

Banks Strait

Mt William National Park

Gladstone

Bridport

Scottsdale

Derby

Lilydale

St Columba Falls

Bay of Fires

St Helens

Latrobe

Arthur River

Savage River National Park

Savage River

Arthur Pieman Conservation Area

Sandy Cape

Waratah

Corinna

Pieman River

Rosebery

Ahrberg Bay

Zeehan

Hardwicke Bay

Queenstown

Strahan

Cape Sorell

Macquarie Harbour

Lake Burbury

Sheffield

Cradle Valley

River Forth

Mersey River

Cradle Mountain-Lake St Clair National Park

Deloraine

Mole Creek Karst National Park

Launceston

Westbury

Longford

Perth

Evandale

Ben Lomond National Park

St Marys

Fingal

Douglas-Apsley National Park

Bicheno

Central Plateau Conservation Area

Great Lake

Arthurs Lake

Walls of Jerusalem National Park

Lake St Clair

Miena

Lake Sorell

Campbell Town

Ross

Lake Leake

Swansea

Coles Bay

Freycinet National Park

Great Oyster Bay

Schouten Is

Lake Echo

Derwent Bridge

Tarraleah

Franklin River

Lake King William

Franklin-Gordon Wild Rivers National Park

Lake Gordon

River Derwent

Bothwell

Oatlands

Tooms Lake

Lake Tiberias

Lake Sorell

Gordon River

Strathgordon

Southwest Conservation Area

Lake Pedder

Mt Field National Park

Maydena

New Norfolk

Hamilton

Bridgewater

Brighton

Richmond

Sorell

Triabunna

Maria Island National Park

HOBART

Kingston

Huonville

Huon River

Geeveston

Snug

Cygnet

Storm Bay

Bruny Island

Port Arthur

Tasman Peninsula

Tasman National Park

Cape Pillar

Forestier Peninsula

Southwest National Park

Hartz Mountains National Park

Dover

Alonnah

SOUTHERN OCEAN

Port Davey

Bathurst Harbour

South West Cape

Southport

South East Cape

South Bruny National Park

Tasman Head

D'Entrecasteaux Channel

TASMAN SEA

To Macquarie Island (1500km)

TASM

HISTORY

The first European to see Tasmania was Dutch navigator Abel Tasman, who arrived in 1642 and named it Van Diemen's Land after the governor of the Dutch East Indies. In the 18th century Tasmania was visited by a series of European sailors, including Captains Tobias Furneaux, James Cook and William Bligh, all of whom believed it was part of the Australian mainland.

European contact with the Tasmanian coast became more frequent after the First Fleet arrived at Sydney Cove in 1788, mainly because ships heading to the colony of New South Wales from the west had to sail around the island. In 1798 Matthew Flinders circumnavigated Van Diemen's Land, proving it was an island. He named the rough stretch of sea between the island and the mainland Bass Strait, after George Bass, the ship's surgeon.

In 1803 Risdon Cove, on the Derwent River in Tasmania, became the site of Australia's second colony. One year later the settlement was moved to the present site of Hobart. Although convicts were sent with the first settlers, penal settlements weren't built until later: at Macquarie Harbour in 1822, at Maria Island in 1825 and at Port Arthur in 1830. For more than three decades, Van Diemen's Land was the most feared destination for British convicts.

In 1856 transportation to Van Diemen's Land was abolished and the colony's first parliament was elected. Also in 1856, in an effort to escape the stigma of its dreadful penal reputation, Van Diemen's Land officially became known as Tasmania, after its first European visitor.

Gold was discovered in the 1870s and prospectors randomly explored most of the state in search of mineral wealth, finding tin, silver, copper and lead. The subsequent exploitation of natural resources inevitably clashed with environmental preservation. This clash became a source of public debate in the 1960s and 1970s, when bushwalkers and conservationists unsuccessfully fought to stop the flooding of Lake Pedder for hydro-electric schemes. Again in the 1980s this issue became hugely controversial – this time the burgeoning Green movement successfully campaigned against flooding the wild Franklin River for similar purposes. The uneasy balance between conservation interests and industry (especially logging, mining and hydroelectric schemes) continues today.

Aboriginal People

Since European settlement the story of Australia's Aborigines has been an unhappy one, and nowhere has it been more tragic than in Tasmania. This state's Aborigines became separated from the mainland over 10,000 years ago when sea levels rose due to the thawing of the last Ice Age. From that time on, their culture diverged from that of their mainland counterparts.

European settlers fenced off sections of fertile land to make farms. As the Aborigines lost more and more of their traditional hunting grounds, battles erupted between Aborigines and settlers, and by 1806 the killing on both sides was out of control. In 1828 martial law was declared by Lieutenant-Governor Arthur, and Aboriginal tribes were forced at gunpoint from districts settled by whites, and so were dispossessed of their traditional homeland.

Between 1829 and 1834 all remaining Aborigines were resettled in a reserve on Flinders Island, to be 'civilised' and Christianised. Most of them died of despair, homesickness, poor food or respiratory disease. Of the 135 taken to the island, only 47 survived to be transferred to Oyster Cove in Tasmania's south in 1847. Within 32 years,

---

RECOMMENDED READING

If you fancy a bit of historical fiction in your holiday reading, pack *The English Passengers* by Matthew Kneale. Winner of the 2000 Whitbread Book of the Year prize, this cleverly written story is set in the mid-19th century and tells two parallel stories that eventually intersect. The first tale is of three eccentric Englishmen who set sail for Tasmania on a Manx smuggling ship to find the Garden of Eden; the other involves the tragic recollections of a Tasmanian Aborigine, telling of his people's doomed struggle against colonial powers.

The weaving storyline and array of brilliantly constructed characters (all narrating in the first person) may prove challenging, but the story is enhanced by moments of great humour and sadness and will enrich your visit to Tasmania.

the entire Aboriginal population at Oyster Cove had perished.

European sealers had been working in Bass Strait since 1798 and, although they occasionally raided tribes along the coast, their contact with Aboriginal people was mainly based on trade. Aboriginal women were also traded and many sealers settled on Bass Strait islands with these women and had families.

By 1847 an Aboriginal community, with a lifestyle based on both Aboriginal and European ways, had emerged on Flinders and other islands in the Furneaux group. Although the last full-blooded Tasmanian Aborigine died in the 19th century, the strength of this community helped save the race from total extinction. Today thousands of descendants of members of this community still live in Tasmania.

GEOGRAPHY & CLIMATE

Tasmania's population is concentrated mainly on the north and southeast coasts, where the undulating countryside is rich and fertile and the coasts and its bays are accessible and inviting. In winter the Midlands region looks very English, while the lakes country in the central highlands is serenely beautiful. By contrast, the southwest and west coasts are wild and remote. For much of the year large seas batter the west coast and rainfall is high. Inland, the rich forests and mountains of Tasmania's west and southwest form one of the world's last great wilderness areas, almost all of it a World Heritage–listed national park.

Tasmania has four distinct seasons, although storms can bring wintry conditions at any time of year. In summer the days are generally warm rather than hot, while the nights are mild. This is the most pleasant time of year, and conditions are usually good up until March, when temperatures drop. The rest of autumn is generally characterised by cool, sunny days and occasional frosty nights.

Winter is wet, cold and stormy, particularly in the west. Overcast days are common in the east, despite its lower rainfall. Snow lies on the higher peaks but is usually only deep enough for the state's two ski resorts to operate spasmodically.

Spring is windy and storms still sweep the island, but in between the sun shines and gradually warmth returns.

INFORMATION

The main tourism authority for the state is **Tourism Tasmania** (☎ 03-6230 8235, 1800 806 846; www.discovertasmania.com; GPO Box 399, Hobart 7001), which disseminates loads of information about Tasmania and has a comprehensive website.

A few useful websites on accommodation in Tasmania:

www.yha.com.au Outlines the YHA network in Tasmania.

www.tassiepubs.com.au A list of hotels offering pub accommodation.

www.caravantasmania.com Covers camping grounds and their facilities throughout the state.

www.innkeeper.com.au A large, Tasmania-wide accommodation group that includes hotels, motels, lodges and apartments.

www.tasmanianbedandbreakfast.com Details of many good B&Bs.

Tourist Offices & Publications

There are large, privately run visitors centres, often referred to as Tasmanian Travel & Information Centres (TTICs), in Hobart, Launceston, Devonport and Burnie, plus smaller visitors centres in other towns.

On the mainland, government-operated Tasmanian **travel centres** (www.tastravel.com.au); Sydney (☎ 1300 655 145; 60 Carrington St, Sydney); Melbourne (☎ 1300 655 145; 256 Collins St, Melbourne) provide information on just about everything to do with Tasmania, and you can book accommodation, tours and transport through them. Check the website for more information.

At visitors centres throughout the state you can pick up the invaluable free bimonthly newspaper *Tasmanian Travelways* (www.travelways.com.au). It contains comprehensive statewide listings of accommodation, activities, public transport and vehicle hire, and an indication of current costs. Visitors centres also stock the free magazine *This Week in Tasmania* (an odd name given that it's published monthly) and *Treasure Island*, a monthly newspaper. The *Tasmania Visitors Guide*, published twice a year, is also free. For comprehensive information about the entire state also see Lonely Planet's *Tasmania* guidebook.

There are a number of excellent road maps of Tasmania; the *Tasmanian Towns Street Atlas* is probably the best source of maps of individual towns and cities. These are available at Royal Automobile Club of Tasmania (RACT) offices, bookshops and

---

SEE TASMANIA

A recent initiative has seen the introduction of the **See Tasmania Smartvisit Card** (☎ 1300 661 711; www.seetasmaniacard.com), which might be of interest to short-term visitors. Purchase of the card allows free or discounted entry to some 60 attractions and activities around the state (including national parks, National Trust properties and big-ticket drawcards like the Port Arthur Historic Site, the Tahune Forest AirWalk and cruises on the Gordon River), plus a book and maps to help you plan your travels. The card is not cheap, however, and doesn't last long: it costs $130/70 per adult/child for three days, $190/120 for seven days, and $270/170 for 10 days, so you should intend to do a lot of sightseeing in a relatively short time to get your money's worth. It's worth noting that there's no card for families, and that the cards can only be used on consecutive days. Before purchasing, do some research to determine that it's a worthwhile investment for what you're planning to see and do on your trip. Cards can be purchased online, from many travel agents, at the larger visitors centres and from Thrifty car-rental outlets in Tasmania.

---

visitors centres around the state, and at the Tasmap counter at **Service Tasmania** (Map pp586-7; ☎ 1300 135 513; 134 Macquarie St, Hobart).

Useful Organisations

Parks & Wildlife Service (PWS; ☎ 1300 368 550; www.parks.tas.gov.au)

Royal Automobile Club of Tasmania (RACT; ☎ 13 27 22; www.ract.com.au) Provides roadside assistance in the event of car breakdown, plus a range of maps and directories of accommodation in the state.

NATIONAL PARKS

A greater percentage of land is national park or scenic reserve in Tasmania than in any other Australian state. In 1982 Tasmania's three largest national parks – Franklin-Gordon Wild Rivers, Cradle Mountain-Lake St Clair and Southwest – and much of the Central Plateau were placed on the Unesco World Heritage list. This listing acknowledged that these parks comprise one of the last great temperate wilderness areas left in the world. Today Tasmania has 19 national parks, comprising over 1.4 million hectares, or nearly 21% of the state's total land area.

An entry fee is charged for all of Tasmania's national parks; a pass is needed whether there is a collection booth or not. Passes are available at park entrances, from many tour operators, at some local stores and from Service Tasmania. A 24-hour pass to any number of parks costs $10 per car or $3.50 per person. The best value for most travellers is the two-month pass, which costs $33 per vehicle or $13.50 per person for bushwalkers, cyclists and motorcyclists, and provides entry into all parks.

An informative website is maintained by the **Parks and Wildlife Service** (PWS; ☎ 1300 368 550; www.parks.tas.gov.au; GPO Box 44, Hobart 7001). In the peak summer season (usually late December to mid-February) rangers run excellent free activities at the major national parks, including walks, talks and slide shows. These are a great way to learn about the parks and their flora and fauna. Information on the activity programme is available at park visitors centres.

ACTIVITIES

For good information on adventure tourism and various tour operators in Tasmania, visit the comprehensive website of **Networking Tasmanian Adventures** (www.tasmanianadventures.com.au), where activities are categorised as either 'wild' (eg scuba diving, white-water rafting, abseiling) or 'mild' (eg fishing, scenic flights, river cruises, horse riding). **Tourism Tasmania** (www.discovertasmania.com) also has extensive information (click on 'things to do & see').

Bushwalking

The best-known of Tasmania's many superb bushwalks is the **Overland Track** in the Cradle Mountain-Lake St Clair National Park (p649). Lonely Planet's *Walking in Australia* has a large section on some of Tasmania's best (longer) walks, and visitors should pick up a free copy of the excellent *60 Great Short Walks* brochure at visitors centres and PWS offices (you can also download it from the PWS website).

On long walks, it's important to remember that, in any season, a fine day can quickly deteriorate, so warm clothing, waterproof gear, a tent and a compass are vital. Tasmap produces an excellent series of maps available at visitors centres, **Service Tasmania** (☎ 1300 135 513; 134 Macquarie St, Hobart), the **Tasmanian Map Centre** (Map pp586-7; ☎ 03-6231 9043; 96 Elizabeth St, Hobart), outdoor-equipment shops, Wilderness Society shops and newsagencies throughout the state.

There are many excellent shops selling bush gear, and a few youth hostels hire out equipment and/or guide bushwalking tours.

Caving

Tasmania's caves are regarded as some of the most impressive in Australia. See the Hastings (p603), Mole Creek (p633) and Ulverstone sections (p635) for details.

Diving

On the east coast and around King and Flinders Islands there are some excellent scuba-diving opportunities. Equipment can be rented in Hobart, Launceston and towns on the north and east coasts; dive courses in Tasmania are considerably cheaper than those on the mainland.

Dive Tasmania (☎ 03-6265 2251; divetas@eaglehawkdive.com.au) is an industry organisation with information on a number of affiliated diving businesses. Otherwise, contact the following dive operators:

Aqua-Scuba Dive Services (☎ 03-6234 5678; www.aqua-scuba.com.au; 271 Elizabeth St, Hobart)

Bicheno Dive Centre (☎ 03-6375 1138; www.bichenodive.com.au; 2 Scuba Ct, Bicheno)

Eaglehawk Dive Centre (☎ 03-6250 3566; www.eaglehawkdive.com.au; 178 Pirates Bay Dr, Eaglehawk Neck)

See p653 and p655 for information on dive operators in the Bass Strait islands.

Fishing

Comprehensive information about fishing in Tasmania is online at www.fishonline.tas.gov.au. The sparsely populated Lake Country, on Tasmania's Central Plateau, is a region of glacial lakes, crystal-clear streams and world-class fishing. It's home to the state's best-known spots for both brown and rainbow trout.

A licence is required to fish in Tasmania's inland waters and there are bag, season and size limits on a number of fish (refer to the *Fishing Code* brochure that you receive when you purchase your licence). Licences cost $55 for the full season, $45 for 14 days, $27 for three days and $17 for one day. They're available from many fishing gear shops, post offices, petrol stations and visitors centres.

Rod fishing in salt water is allowed all year without a permit, although size restrictions and bag limits apply.

Rafting, Canoeing & Kayaking

Rafting, rowing and canoeing are all popular activities. The most challenging river to raft is the Franklin (p648). Tour operators also run rafting trips on the Picton, Huon, Weld and Leven Rivers. Ocean kayaking is another very popular activity on the east coast – see the Hobart (p588), Kettering (p599), Tasman Peninsula (p604) and Freycinet National Park (p612) sections.

Rock Climbing & Abseiling

Some excellent cliffs have been developed for climbing, particularly along the east coast, where the weather is usually best. The Organ Pipes on Mt Wellington (above Hobart), the Hazards at Coles Bay and cliffs on Mt Killiecrankie on Flinders Island provide excellent climbing on firm rock. The magnificent rock formations and coastal cliffs on the Tasman Peninsula are spectacular, but may be impossible to climb if the ocean swell is too big. A few companies offer abseiling and rock climbing in Launceston's Cataract Gorge.

If you want to climb or abseil with an experienced instructor, try one of these outfits:

Aardvark Adventures (☎ 0408-127 714; www.aardvarkadventures.com.au)

Freycinet Adventures (☎ 03-6257 0500; www.adventurestasmania.com; 2 Freycinet Dr, Coles Bay)

Summitsports (☎ 0418-362 210; summit@southcom.com.au; 444 Huon Rd, South Hobart)

Tasmanian Expeditions (☎ 03-6334 3477; www.tas-ex.com; 23 Earl St, Launceston)

Sailing

There are many good anchorages in the D'Entrecasteaux Channel, a wide, deep and beautiful place to sail.

Both the **Royal Yacht Club of Tasmania** (☎ 03-6223 4599; www.ryct.org.au; Marieville Esplanade, Sandy Bay) and the **Hobart Ports Corporation** (☎ 03-6235 1000; www.hpc.com.au; Macquarie Wharf) offer overnight and weekly berths. If you're an experienced sailor you can hire a yacht from **Yachting Holidays** (☎ 03-6224 3195; www .yachtingholidays.com.au), based in Hobart, with rates for a five-berth vessel from around $500 per day.

Skiing

Tasmania's ski fields are not as developed as those in New South Wales and Victoria, however there are two minor fields: Ben Lomond, 50km from Launceston, and Mt Mawson, in Mt Field National Park. Your best bet for downhill skiing is at Ben Lomond (p627).

Surfing

Tasmania has plenty of good surf beaches. Close to Hobart, the best spots are Clifton Beach and the surf beach en route to South Arm. The southern beaches of Bruny Island, particularly Cloudy Bay, are also good. The east coast from Bicheno north to St Helens has good surf when conditions are favourable. The best spot of all is Marrawah on the northwest coast.

Swimming

The north and east coasts have many sheltered white-sand beaches that offer excellent swimming. On the west coast there's some ferocious surf and the beaches are unpatrolled.

From Hobart it's best to head south to Kingston, Blackmans Bay or Seven Mile Beach.

TOURS

There's a sizable number of operators offering tours both to and within Tasmania. Many travel agents can help you arrange a package deal from the mainland that usually includes transport to Tasmania

(either by air or sea), car rental and accommodation. Contact **Tourism Tasmania** (☎ 03-6230 8235, 1800 806 846) or the travel centres in Sydney and Melbourne (see p575 for more information), **Qantas Holidays** (☎ 13 14 15; www.qantas.com.au) or **Tas Vacations** (☎ 1800 030 160; www.tasvacations.com.au) for ideas.

Once you're in Tasmania, there are operators who can guide you to the highlights (and some will take you off the beaten track), and many more who can offer a wilderness experience or activity-based tour. Most trips depart from Hobart, but some operators have tours out of Devonport and Launceston. Many businesses are listed in the relevant sections of this chapter. Some other suggestions:

Adventure Tours (☎ 1300 654 604; www.adventure tours.com.au) As well as the hop-on-hop-off bus network (see p580 for those details), this company offers three- to seven-day tours.

Bottom Bits Bus Tours (☎ 1800 777 103; www .bottombitsbus.com) Backpacker-friendly day trips from $80, or three-day tours ($285 to $315) taking in Cradle Mountain and the west coast, the east coast or the far south.

Craclair (☎ 03-6424 7833; www.southcom.com.au /~craclair/) Offers guided walks (day walks and longer) in national parks and wilderness areas, including Cradle Mountain, Frenchmans Cap and Walls of Jerusalem.

Island Cycle Tours (☎ 1300 880 334; www.islandcycle tours.com) Guided cycling trips from three to seven days, along the east coast, Tasman Peninsula or central wilderness area.

Island Escape Tours (☎ 1800 133 555; www.island escapetours.com) A Launceston-based company offering day trips as well as three- to seven-day tours and encouraging 'active participation', including walks in areas such as the Bay of Fires.

Tasmanian Expeditions (☎ 03-6334 3477; www .tas-ex.com) An excellent range of activity-based tours out of Hobart and Launceston, ranging in length from half

---

GOURMET TASMANIA

One of the highlights of travelling in Tasmania is sampling fine local produce, especially fresh seafood, luscious fruits, great dairy products and excellent cool-climate wines. If you intend expanding your waistline while touring Tassie, two recommended publications are *Eat Drink Tasmania* by Graeme Phillips (around $10 from some visitors centres and bookshops) and *Tasmania Wine & Food – Cellar Door & Farm Gate Guide*, a free brochure published by Tourism Tasmania and available at most visitors centres and online (www.discovertasmania.com – click on 'things to do & see', then 'wine & food'). Both publications have details of the best restaurants, cafés, wineries and farm stores around the state, classified by region, and the Tourism Tasmania brochure has details of wine and food events, plus a helpful chart detailing when particular foods are in season.

a day to 13 days and with a choice of bushwalking, river rafting, cycling and canoeing tours.

Tigerline Coaches (☎ 1300 653 633; www.tigerline .com.au) Less strenuous coach tours (day trips and short breaks) to major attractions in and around Hobart and Launceston.

Tiger Trails (☎ 03-6234 3931; www.tigertrails.green .net.au) Eco-tours – one-day and multiday – to pristine areas such as the Tarkine forest, Maria Island and along the South Coast Track, ranging in difficulty from easy to challenging.

Under Down Under (☎ 1800 064 726; www.under downunder.com.au) Offers nature-based, backpacker-friendly trips, with a pro-green leaning. There are tours from two to seven days, including a two-day tour into the Tarkine Wilderness. Evening meals and accommodation are not included in the tour costs, so you determine the total cost of the trip.

GETTING THERE & AWAY

There are stringent rules in place to protect the 'disease-free' status of the agriculture of this island state, and plants, fruit and vegetables cannot be brought into the state. Tourists must discard all items prior to their arrival (even if they're only travelling from mainland Australia).

Air

There are no direct flights between Tasmania and overseas destinations. The major airlines that have services between Tasmania and the Australian mainland:

Qantas (☎ 13 13 13; www.qantas.com.au)
Regional Express (Rex; ☎ 13 17 13; www .regionalexpress.com.au)
Virgin Blue (☎ 13 67 89; www.virginblue.com.au)

Qantas has regular direct flights to Hobart and Launceston from Melbourne and Sydney. One-way prices from Melbourne to Tasmania are in the $100 to $165 range, from Sydney to Tassie costs $190 to $250. Virgin Blue also has daily direct Melbourne–Hobart and Melbourne–Launceston flights (prices from $105 to $210). Qantas and Virgin Blue offer connecting flights from most other mainland capitals.

Qantas and Regional Express Airlines (Rex) fly direct from Melbourne to Devonport and Burnie; one-way prices range from $95 to $200.

See p654 and p656 for detailed information about flights to and from King and Flinders Islands.

Boat

Two high-speed **Spirit of Tasmania ferries** (☎ 13 20 10; www.spiritoftasmania.com.au) cruise nightly between Melbourne and Devonport on Tasmania's north coast, and three times a week between Sydney and Devonport. The vessels more closely resemble a floating hotel than a ferry, with restaurants, bars etc. The public areas of the ship and a handful of on-board cabins have been designed to cater for wheelchairs.

For details of a small weekly ferry service operating between Bridport and Flinders Island, see p656.

MELBOURNE–DEVONPORT

At 9pm nightly year-round, one ferry departs from Port Melbourne's Station Pier and the other departs from the terminal on the Esplanade in Devonport, with both arriving at their destinations across Bass Strait at around 7am the next morning. Additional daytime sailings are scheduled during the peak summer period (from late December to late January), and weekends from December to April. These daytime sailings depart at 9am, arriving at 6pm.

Fares depend on whether you're travelling in the peak (early December to late January), shoulder (late January to late April, and September to early December) or off-peak (late April to August) season. One-way adult fares to Melbourne cost $140/112/ 105 peak/shoulder/off-peak for airline-style seats on a night crossing, $212/193/184 for the cheapest berth (in a four-bed cabin). A bed in a twin-berth cabin costs $257/217/ 207. Passage on a day crossing (no cabins available) costs $145/115 peak/shoulder season. Children pay less (cots can be provided in cabins), and there are discounts on cabin berths for seniors and students. Linen is supplied in the cabins, and each cabin has a bathroom.

On both ferry routes the cost for accompanied vehicles depends on the size of the vehicle and the season. The fare for a standard car (5m or less in length) or a campervan is $55 in peak season, free for the rest of the year.

SYDNEY–DEVONPORT

One-way adult fares to Sydney cost $255/ 230 shoulder/off-peak for the cheapest berth (in hostel-style accommodation). A bed in a three- or four-bunk cabin costs $400 to $415 in the shoulder season and $360 to $372 off-peak. Twin and double cabins are also available. Dinner and brunch are included in Sydney–Devonport fares.

The Devonport–Sydney ferry departs Devonport at 3pm Monday, Thursday and Saturday, and arrives in Sydney at 11.30am the following day (20½ hours). In the opposite direction, ferries leave Sydney at 3pm Tuesday, Friday and Sunday, arriving in Devonport at 11.30am the following day.

GETTING AROUND

Tasmania is decentralised and its population small. Although public transport does exist between most larger towns and popular tourist destinations, many people wishing to visit more remote and interesting sights find transport schedules frustrating and prefer to hire a car.

Air

Both **Tasair** and **Par Avion** (☎ 03-6248 5390; www .paravion.com.au) offer air services to bushwalkers, flying between Hobart and remote Melaleuca in the southwest for around $150 one way.

Bicycle

Tasmania is a good size for exploring by bicycle and you can hire bikes in larger towns throughout the state. If you plan to cycle between Hobart and Launceston via either coast, count on it taking 10 to 14 days. For a full circuit of the island, you should allow 14 to 28 days. Get a copy of *Bicycling Tasmania* by Ian Terry and Rob Beedham to help plan your trip. If you're planning a circuit, consider following the Giro Tasmania, which is detailed on the website of **Bicycle Tasmania** (www.netspace.net.au/~dmurphy/giro.htm).

Bus

Tasmania has a reasonable bus network connecting major towns and centres, but weekend services are infrequent and this can be inconvenient for travellers with limited time. There are more buses in summer than in winter, but smaller towns are still not serviced terribly frequently.

The main bus lines are **Redline Coaches** (☎ 1300 360 000; www.tasredline.com.au) and **Tassie Link** (☎ 1300 300 520; www.tigerline.com.au), and between them they cover most of the state.

TassieLink's 'Spirit Shuttle' is designed to work with the Bass Strait ferry schedules; it provides an early-morning express service from Devonport to Launceston and Hobart, and an afternoon service in the opposite direction to meet evening boat departures.

To give some idea of the fares and travel times, a one-way trip between Devonport and Launceston is around $18 and takes 1½ hours; Hobart–Launceston costs $25 (2½ hours); Hobart–Queenstown is $50 (5 hours); and Launceston–Bicheno is $25 (2½ hours).

There are smaller transport operators that offer useful bus services on important tourist routes (eg between Bicheno and Coles Bay, or within the Cradle Mountain-Lake St Clair region); details of these are given in the relevant sections of the chapter.

TRAVEL PASSES

TassieLink has a 7-/10-/14-/21-day Explorer Pass that must be used within 10/15/20/30 days and costs $160/190/220/260. The pass is valid on all scheduled services for unlimited kilometres and can be bought from mainland Tasmanian travel centres, YHA and STA offices, most travel agents, or directly from TassieLink. If you intend to buy an Explorer Pass, ask for timetables in advance or check TassieLink's website and plan your itinerary carefully before making your purchase. This is the only way to ensure that you'll be able to get where you want to go within the life of the pass.

Adventure Tours Australia (☎ 1300 654 604; www.adventuretours.com.au) runs a useful hop-on/hop-off minibus service that covers most of the state, including out-of-the-way places like Cockle Creek in the south and Arthur River in the northwest. To use this guide-accompanied service you need to buy an Adventure Tours Pass ($395, valid for two months), available from travel agents and hostels. The pass allows you to start from Devonport, Hobart or Launceston (minibuses pick up from budget accommodation mainstays in each city at least four times a week) and travel in an anticlockwise direction around the state. You can get off as often and for as long as you like.

Car & Campervan

Although you can bring cars from the mainland to Tasmania, renting may be cheaper, particularly on short trips. Tasmania has many national and local car-rental agencies, and rates are considerably lower than on the mainland.

Tasmanian Travelways lists many of the rental options. Before you decide on a company, ask about any kilometre limitations and find out what the insurance covers – a number of Tasmania's natural attractions lie off unsealed roads, and many companies hike up the excess in the event of an accident on such roads. It's normal, however, for smaller rental companies to ask for a bond of around $300.

Large international firms such as Avis, Budget, Hertz and Thrifty have booking desks at airports and offices in major towns. They have standard rates for cars, from about $70 to $80 for high-season multiday hire of a small car. By booking in advance and choosing smaller cars, rates can be as low as $60 per day for one week's hire (outside the high season).

Savings can be made by going to the smaller operators but this must be weighed against the rental conditions and general condition of the vehicle – make sure you're familiar and confident with both before you sign. Small local firms rent older cars for as little as $30 a day, depending on the length of time and season. Prices then increase according to the model and age of the cars. With some companies you can collect your car from the airport or ferry terminal. Some operators:

Economy Car Rentals (☎ 03-6334 3299) In Launceston.

Lo-Cost Auto Rent (☎ 1800 647 060; www.locost autorent.com) In Hobart, Devonport and Launceston.

Rent-A-Bug (www.rentabug.com.au); Hobart (☎ 03-6231 0300); Devonport (☎ 03-6427 9034) Offering cheap Volkswagen Beetles, plus older-model vehicles, out of Hobart and Devonport.

Selective Car Rentals (☎ 03-6234 3311) In Hobart.

Tasmanian Travelways also has a listing of campervan rental companies. **Autorent-Hertz** (☎ 1800 030 500; www.autorent.com.au) has campervans for two people for around $640 a week from May to mid-September, rising to a hefty $1300 from Christmas to mid-January. Other companies offering campervan rental include **Tasmanian Campervan Hire** (☎ 1800 807 119; www.tascampervanhire.com.au) and **Cruisin' Tasmania** (☎ 1800 772 758; www.cruisin-tasmania.com.au).

WARNINGS FOR DRIVERS

There are a few road hazards to be aware of as you cruise around the state. Watch out for the wildlife and, if possible, avoid driving between dusk and dawn, as this is when marsupials are most active (you'll undoubtedly notice lots of roadkill on your travels). One-lane bridges on country roads, and log-trucks piled high and speeding around sharp corners, also demand caution. Finally, in cold weather be wary of 'black ice', an invisible layer of ice over the bitumen, especially on the shaded side of mountain passes.

Tasmanian Motorcycle Hire (☎ 03-6391 9139; www.tasmotorcyclehire.com.au; 17 Coachmans Rd, Evandale) has a range of motorcycles for rent from $105 per day (cheaper rates for longer rentals). Evandale is south of Launceston, not far from the airport.

Hitching

If you travel by thumb in Tasmania, wrap up in winter and keep a raincoat handy. A good number of the state's roads are still unsurfaced and the traffic can be very light, so although these roads often lead to interesting places, you normally have to give them a miss if you're hitching.

HOBART

☎ 03 / pop 128,048

Hobart is Australia's second-oldest city and its southernmost capital. Straddling the mouth of the Derwent River and backed by towering Mt Wellington, Hobart combines the liveliness of a youthful, modern city with a rich colonial heritage and a serene natural beauty. The attractive Georgian buildings, the busy harbour and the easygoing atmosphere make Hobart one of the most enjoyable and engaging of Australia's state capitals.

The first inhabitants of the area were the semi-nomadic Aboriginal Mouheneer tribe. The first European colony in Tasmania was founded in 1803 at Risdon Cove, but a year later it was decided that a site 10km below Risdon and on the opposite shore was a better place to settle. Hobart began as a village of tents and huts with a population of 262 (178 of whom were convicts).

Hobart Town, as it was known until 1881, was proclaimed a city in 1842. The deep-water harbour of the Derwent River estuary was important to its development; many merchants made their fortunes from the whaling trade, shipbuilding and the export of products such as merino wool and corn.

ORIENTATION

Being fairly small and simply laid out, Hobart is easy to navigate. The streets in the city centre, many of which are one way, are arranged in a grid around the Elizabeth St mall. The visitors centre and the main post office are on Elizabeth St, and the main shopping area extends west from the mall on Elizabeth St.

Salamanca Pl, a row of Georgian warehouses, is along the southern waterfront, and just south of this is Battery Point, Hobart's well-preserved early colonial district. If you follow the river south from Battery Point you'll come to Sandy Bay, the site of Hobart's university and the Wrest Point hotel/casino.

The northern side of the city centre is bounded by the recreation area known as the Domain (short for Queen's Domain), which includes the Botanical Gardens and the Derwent River. From here the Tasman Bridge crosses the river to the eastern suburbs and the airport.

Maps

The best maps of Hobart are the *Hobart Street Directory* and the Hobart maps in the *Tasmanian Towns Street Atlas*. You can usually purchase these and other good maps at larger newsagents and bookshops.

Other sources for maps in Hobart:

RACT (Map p583; ☎ 6232 6300, 13 27 22; www .ract .com.au; cnr Murray & Patrick Sts)

Service Tasmania (Map pp586-7; ☎ 1300 135 513; www.service.tas.gov.au; 134 Macquarie St)

Tasmanian Map Centre (Map pp586-7; ☎ 6231 9043; www.map-centre.com.au; 96 Elizabeth St)

Visitors centre (Map pp586-7; ☎ 6230 8233; tasbook ings@tasvisinfo.com.au; www.tasmaniasouth.com; cnr Davey & Elizabeth Sts; ☑ 8.30am-5.30pm Mon-Fri, 9am-5pm Sat, Sun & public holidays)

Disabled travellers can get a copy of the useful *Hobart CBD Mobility Map* at the visitors centre; it's a guide to the relevant facilities and access.

INFORMATION
Bookshops

Fullers (Map pp586-7; ☎ 6224 2488; www.fullers bookshop.com.au; 140 Collins St) A popular bookshop; has a good café upstairs.

Hobart Book Shop (Map pp586-7; ☎ 6223 1803; 22 Salamanca Sq) New and second-hand books.

Tasmanian Map Centre (Map pp586-7; ☎ 6231 9043; www.map-centre.com.au; 96 Elizabeth St) Specialises in maps and guidebooks.

HOBART IN...

Two Days

Start your day with breakfast at **Salamanca Place** (p584) and wander around the area's stores, galleries and cafés (and the market stalls, if you're here on Saturday), then venture up **Kellys Steps** (p588) to admire the village atmosphere and architecture of **Battery Point** (p584). In the afternoon make your way up **Mt Wellington** (p587) to take in the magnificent views and do some walking to work up an appetite. Return to town and enjoy a seafood dinner on the **waterfront** (p593) – splurge at Mures, or grab some fresh fish and chips from the floating barges. On the second day head out to the **Cadbury chocolate factory** (p586) for a chocky feast, followed by lunch at **Moorilla Estate** (p585). Make your way back to town and visit a central **museum** (p585) or two before taking a sunset **kayak tour** (p588) around the docks.

Four Days

Follow the two-day itinerary, then on the third day relax on a **river cruise** (p589) and/or at the **Botanical Gardens** (p587), or consider a tour of the **Cascade brewery** (p587). Dine at one of the excellent **restaurants in North Hobart** (p594). On day four, consider an easy **day trip** (p589) to a nearby area you hadn't planned to explore – Bruny Island, the Huon Valley, Richmond or Mt Field. Finish with either a **ghost tour** (p606) at the penitentiary or a **pub tour** (p589).

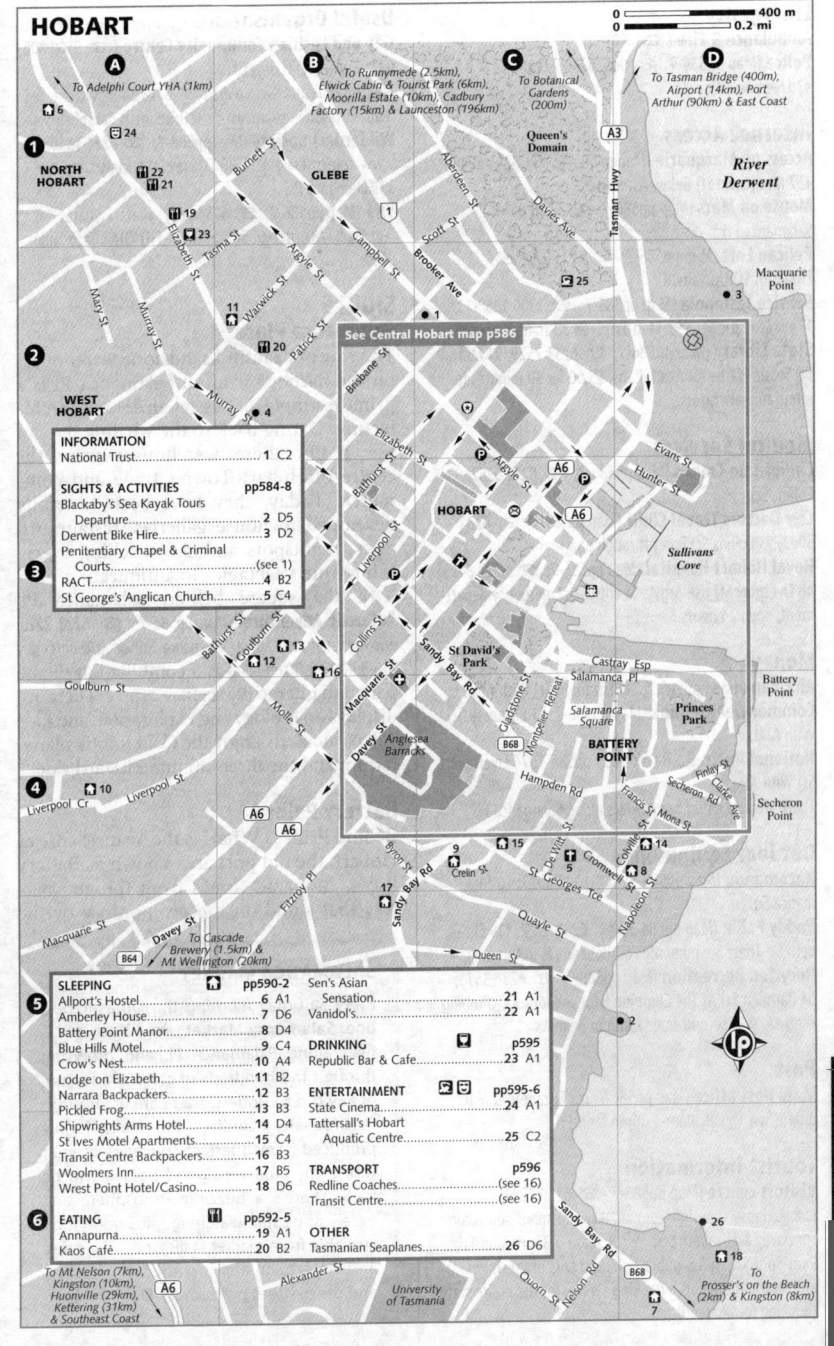

HOBART

| 0 | 400 m |
| 0 | 0.2 mi |

A To Adelphi Court YHA (1km)

B To Runnymede (2.5km), Elwick Cabin & Tourist Park (6km), Moorilla Estate (10km), Cadbury Factory (15km) & Launceston (196km)

C To Botanical Gardens (200m)

D To Tasman Bridge (400m), Airport (14km), Port Arthur (90km) & East Coast

1 NORTH HOBART

GLEBE

Queen's Domain

River Derwent

Macquarie Point

2 WEST HOBART

See Central Hobart map p586

HOBART

Sullivans Cove

3

St David's Park

Castray Esp
Salamanca Pl
Salamanca Square

Battery Point

BATTERY POINT

Princes Park

Anglesea Barracks

Hampden Rd

Secheron Point

4 Liverpool Cr

Macquarie St

Davey St
To Cascade Brewery (1.5km) & Mt Wellington (20km)

Queen St

5

To Mt Nelson (7km), Kingston (10km), Huonville (29km), Kettering (31km) & Southeast Coast

Alexander St

University of Tasmania

6

To Prosser's on the Beach (2km) & Kingston (8km)

INFORMATION
National Trust.....................1 C2

SIGHTS & ACTIVITIES pp584-8
Blackaby's Sea Kayak Tours
  Departure.......................2 D5
Derwent Bike Hire................3 D2
Penitentiary Chapel & Criminal
  Courts........................(see 1)
RACT.............................4 B2
St George's Anglican Church......5 C4

SLEEPING pp590-2
Allport's Hostel..................6 A1
Amberley House...................7 D6
Battery Point Manor..............8 D4
Blue Hills Motel.................9 C4
Crow's Nest.....................10 A4
Lodge on Elizabeth..............11 B2
Narrara Backpackers.............12 B3
Pickled Frog....................13 B3
Shipwrights Arms Hotel..........14 D4
St Ives Motel Apartments........15 C4
Transit Centre Backpackers......16 B3
Woolmers Inn....................17 B5
Wrest Point Hotel/Casino........18 D6

EATING pp592-5
Annapurna.......................19 A1
Kaos Café.......................20 B2

Sen's Asian
  Sensation......................21 A1
Vanidol's.......................22 A1

DRINKING p595
Republic Bar & Cafe.............23 A1

ENTERTAINMENT pp595-6
State Cinema....................24 A1
Tattersall's Hobart
  Aquatic Centre................25 C2

TRANSPORT p596
Redline Coaches...............(see 16)
Transit Centre................(see 16)

OTHER
Tasmanian Seaplanes.............26 D6

TASM

Emergency
Ambulance & Fire (☎ 000)
Police (Map pp586-7; ☎ 000, 6230 2111;
43 Liverpool St)

Internet Access
Access on Macquarie (Map pp586-7; ☎ 6231 6848;
157 Macquarie St) Below Astor Grill.
Mouse on Mars (Map pp586-7; ☎ 6224 0513; 27
Salamanca Pl)
Pelican Loft (Map pp586-7; ☎ 6234 2225; 35A
Elizabeth St) Upstairs.
Service Tasmania (Map pp586-7; ☎ 1300 135 513;
134 Macquarie St; ☽ Mon-Fri) Free 30-minute access.
State Library (Map pp586-7; ☎ 6233 7529; 91 Murray
St) Sessions free for Australians, $5.50 for 30 minutes for
international visitors.

Medical Services
Chemist on Collins (Map pp586-7; ☎ 6235 0257; 93
Collins St)
City Doctors Travel Clinic (Map pp586-7; ☎ 6231
3003; 93 Collins St) Enter through pharmacy.
Royal Hobart Hospital (Map pp586-7; ☎ 6222 8423;
48 Liverpool St) Use Argyle St entry for Emergency depart-
ment, open 24 hours.

Money
ANZ Bank (Map pp586-7; 40 Elizabeth St) With ATM.
Commonwealth Bank (Map pp586-7; 81 Elizabeth St)
With ATM.
National Australia Bank (Map pp586-7; 76 Liverpool
St) With ATM.
There are also a number of ATMs along Salamanca Pl.

Outdoor Equipment
Kathmandu (Map pp586-7; ☎ 6224 3027; 16 Salamanca Sq)
Paddy Pallin (Map pp586-7; ☎ 6231 0777; 119 Elizabeth St) There are numerous outdoor stores in this area.
Recycled Recreation (Map pp586-7; ☎ 6234 3575;
54 Bathurst St) At The Climbing Edge indoor rock-climbing
centre – sells second-hand outdoor gear.

Post
Main post office (Map pp586-7; cnr Elizabeth & Macquarie Sts; ☽ 8.30am-5.30pm Mon-Fri)

Tourist Information
Visitors centre (Map pp586-7; ☎ 6230 8233;
tasbookings@tasvisinfo.com.au; www.tasmaniasouth.com;
cnr Davey & Elizabeth Sts; ☽ 8.30am-5.30pm Mon-Fri,
9am-5pm Sat, Sun & public holidays) Lots of brochures
and information, plus a booking service for the entire state
(booking fee charged).

Useful Organisations
Gay and Lesbian Community Centre (☎ 0500 808
031; www.gaytas.org)
National Trust (Map p583; ☎ 6223 5200; www.tased
.edu.au/tasonline/nattrust/; cnr Brisbane & Campbell Sts)
Wilderness Society (Map pp586-7; ☎ 6224 1550;
www.wilderness.org.au; 130 Davey St) Society shop is at
33 Salamanca Pl.
YHA (Map pp586-7; ☎ 6234 9617; yhatas@yhatas.org
.au; 1st fl, 28 Criterion St; ☽ Mon-Fri) YHA's Tasmanian
office.

SIGHTS
Salamanca Place
The row of beautiful sandstone warehouses
on the harbour front at Salamanca Pl is a
prime example of Australian colonial architecture. Dating back to the whaling days of
the 1830s, these warehouses were the
centre of Hobart Town's trade and commerce. Today, they have been tastefully
developed to house galleries, restaurants,
cafés, nightspots and shops selling everything from vegetables to antiques.

In the square behind Salamanca Pl,
Antarctic Adventure (Map pp586-7; ☎ 6220 8220;
www.antarctic.com.au; 2 Salamanca Sq; adult/child/family
$16/8/40; ☽ 10am-5pm) is a combination theme
park and interactive science centre. There are
displays on ecology and exploration, and kids
will particularly enjoy the Cold Room, planetarium and the three-minute Blizzard ride.

Battery Point
Behind Princes Wharf is the historic core of
Hobart, the old port area known as Battery
Point. Its name comes from the gun bat-
tery that stood on the promontory by the

SALAMANCA MARKET

Every Saturday morning the fantastic outdoor **Salamanca Market** (☽ 8.30am-3pm) is
held along Salamanca Pl, and browsing
through the hundreds of stalls is a feature
of any trip to Hobart. There are great products for sale, including high-quality locally
produced items (perfect souvenirs of your
trip, with some very good bargains to be
had). There's a buzzing atmosphere and
excellent people-watching, plus good food
available from market stalls or nearby cafés,
and entertainment provided by buskers
and other street performers. Don't miss it!

THE AUTHOR'S CHOICE

Moorilla Estate (☎ 6277 9900; www.moorilla.com.au; 655 Main Rd, Berriedale; ⓨ 10am-5pm) can be found in the suburbs some 12km north of Hobart's centre on the banks of the Derwent River. It's a fascinating place with a number of reasons for visiting it: vineyard, restaurant, super-swish accommodation and a stunning museum.

The most unexpected attraction at the estate is the world-class **Moorilla Museum of Antiquities** (☎ 6277 9999; admission free; ⓨ 10am-4pm), which houses a beautifully presented collection. On display here are mosaics dating from the Roman Empire, an Egyptian mummy, sculptures and tribal art from Africa, gold jewellery and pre-Columbian figures from Central America, and a collection of coins dating from ancient Greek and Roman civilisations.

At the estate's vineyard you can taste and purchase some first-rate wines (including excellent pinot noir), and enjoy lunch at the **restaurant** (meals $12-25; ⓨ lunch only) overlooking the vines. Menu options range from light meals and snacks (eg sushi, warm chicken salad, soup of the day) to heartier dishes like steamed blue eye or char-grilled venison fillet. The antipasto platter is a good choice, and you can complement your meal with a sample of five house wines for only $8.

Finally, if you like this place so much you don't want to leave (that's understandable), rent one of the secluded, luxurious **vineyard chalets** (d from $220). These modern self-contained apartments (one- and two-bedroom) are superbly equipped, and winning features include private balconies, water views and even displays of antiquities from the museum's collection!

guardhouse (1818). During colonial times this area was a colourful maritime village.

Don't miss **Arthur Circus** (a circle of quaint cottages built around a village green) or **St George's Anglican Church**. To help with your exploration of the area, get the *Battery Point and Sullivan's Cove Trail of Discovery* ($2) pamphlet from the visitors centre.

Narryna Heritage Museum (Map pp586-7; ☎ 6234 2791; 103 Hampden Rd; adult/child/family $5/2/10; ⓨ 10.30am-5pm Tue-Fri, 2-5pm Sat, Sun & public holidays, closed Jul) is a fine Georgian sandstone mansion built in 1836, set in beautiful grounds and containing a treasure-trove of domestic colonial artefacts.

Historic Buildings

One of the things that makes Hobart exceptional among Australian cities is its wealth of remarkably well-preserved old buildings. There are more than 90 buildings classified by the National Trust and 60 of these, featuring some of Hobart's best Georgian architecture, are on Macquarie and Davey Sts. More information can be obtained from the National Trust.

Close to the city centre is **St David's Park**, with gravestones dating from the earliest days of the colony, while opposite is **Parliament House**, built in 1835. Hobart's prestigious **Theatre Royal** (Map pp586-7; 29 Campbell St) is the oldest theatre in Australia, established in 1837.

The fascinating **Penitentiary Chapel & Criminal Courts** (Map p583; ☎ 6231 0911; cnr Brisbane & Campbell Sts) can be explored via the excellent National Trust–run tours that take place at 10am, 11.30am, 1pm and 2.30pm daily. **Ghost tours** (☎ 0417-361 392; adult/child $8.80/5.50; ⓨ 8pm) are also held here nightly; bookings are essential.

Runnymede (☎ 6278 1269; 61 Bay Rd, New Town; adult/child $7.70/free; ⓨ 10am-4.30pm Mon-Fri, noon-4.30pm Sat & Sun), in the northern part of the city, is a gracious 1830s residence now managed by the National Trust.

Museums

The engrossing **Tasmanian Museum and Art Gallery** (Map pp586-7; ☎ 6211 4177; www.tmag.tas.gov.au; 40 Macquarie St; admission free; ⓨ 10am-5pm) incorporates Hobart's oldest existing building, the Commissariat Store (1808). The museum section features an Aboriginal display and relics from the state's colonial heritage, while the gallery has a collection of Tasmanian colonial art. Free guided tours take place at 2.30pm Wednesday to Sunday.

The **Maritime Museum of Tasmania** (Map pp586-7; ☎ 6234 1427; www.maritimetas.org; 16 Argyle St; adult/child/family $6/4/16; ⓨ 9am-5pm), in the historic Carnegie building, has an interesting salt-encrusted collection of photos, paintings, models and relics highlighting Tasmania's shipping past. Upstairs from

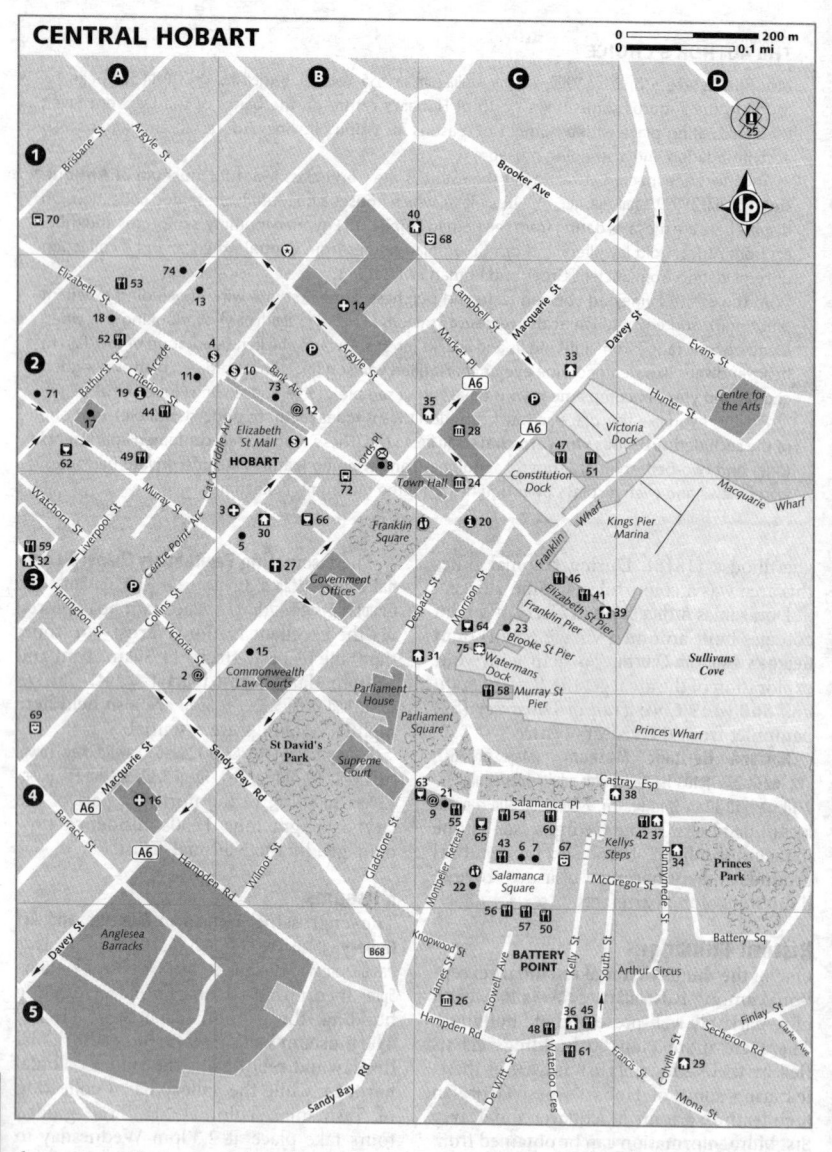

CENTRAL HOBART

the museum is the **Carnegie Gallery** (admission free; ❤ 10am-5pm), exhibiting Tasmanian art and photography.

Cadbury Chocolate Factory

This popular attraction is a must for sweettooths. The **Cadbury factory** (☎ 1800 627 367; Cadbury Rd, Claremont; tours adult/child/family \$13/6.50/ 32; bookings essential) offers guided tours weekdays except public holidays from 9am to 1.30pm (with additional tours on demand). Participants get to enjoy samples along the way, and can buy low-priced products at the completion of the tour. The factory is some 15km north of the city centre; many companies offer day trips and river cruises that incorporate this tour (p589), but you can also book directly with Cadbury and make your own way there.

Cascade Brewery

Australia's oldest brewery, **Cascade** (☎ 6221 8300; Cascade Rd; tours adult/child/family $15/6.50/32; 🕑 9.30am & 1pm Mon-Fri except public holidays; bookings essential) was established in its photogenic location on the southwestern edge of the city centre in 1832. It's still in use today, producing tasty beverages for nationwide consumption. Tours include free samples.

Natural Attractions

Just by the Tasman Bridge are the small but beguiling **Royal Tasmanian Botanical Gardens** (www.rtbg.tas.gov.au; admission free; 🕑 8am-6.30pm Oct-Mar, closing 5-5.30pm Apr-Sep). The gardens were established in 1818 and today boast the largest collection of mature conifers in the southern hemisphere. After wandering through the gardens, you can explore their world in more detail in the interactive **Botanical Discovery Centre** (☎ 6234 6299; Queens Domain; admission free; 🕑 10am-5pm Sep-Apr, to 4.30pm May-Aug).

Hobart is dominated by 1270m-high **Mt Wellington**, which has fine views and many walking tracks – the *Mt Wellington Walks* map ($4; available at the visitors centre) has

details. To get here, you can drive up winding roads, take a guided tour or travel on local bus No 48 or 49 from the Macquarie St side of Franklin Sq – the bus will take you to Fern Tree at the base of the mountain and from there it's an often stunning walk to the top (5 to 6 hours return, via the Springs and the Organ Pipes). **Mt Wellington Shuttle Bus Service** (☎ 0417-341 804; $25 return) departs from central Hobart three times daily; city pickups can be arranged, bookings are essential. See Cycling, under Activities (below), for information on bike trips down the mountain.

There are also wonderful views from **Mt Nelson**, a good alternative when Mt Wellington is in cloud.

ACTIVITIES
Cycling

If you fancy a ride beside the Derwent, hire a bicycle from **Derwent Bike Hire** (Map pp586-7; ☎ 6234 2143, 0419-344 278; Regatta Grounds; 🕑 daily Dec-Mar, Sat & Sun Sep-Nov & Apr-May), from $7/20 per hour/day (touring bikes also available from $100 per week). It can found by the Cenotaph in the Regatta Grounds.

Central **Mouse on Mars** (Map pp586-7; ☎ 6224 0513; 27 Salamanca Pl) also offers bikes for rent (from $13/80 per day/week).

A useful navigational tool is the *Hobart Bike Map* ($4), available from the visitors

TASMANIA

centre and containing details of the city's cycle paths and road cycling routes.

You can also participate in an organised ride from the top of Mt Wellington for around $45, including transport to the summit, bikes and safety equipment. Two local operators offer these tours: **Brake Out Cycling Tours** (☎ 6239 1080) and **Island Cycle Tours** (☎ 1300 880 334; www.islandcycletours.com).

Kayaking

Kayaking around the docks is popular, and **Blackaby's Sea Kayak Tours** (Map p583; ☎ 6267 1508) organises morning, afternoon or sunset paddles for around $45 per person (snacks included). The two-hour trips depart from Short Beach in Sandy Bay (turn off Sandy Bay Rd at Queen St).

WALKING TOUR

This walk starts at **Salamanca Place**, the tourist precinct of Hobart. While waterside activity has moved away from this once-bustling area, restoration work has preserved one of Hobart's best vistas. The sandstone Georgian warehouses were built from about 1835, replacing earlier wooden structures in what was called New Wharf. At street level, the majority of the warehouses are now speciality and craft shops, restaurants, cafés and bars.

WALKING TOUR

Distance: 2.8km
Duration: approximately 2½ hours

Moving east, a gap in the warehouses leads to **Kellys Steps** (1; 1839), which link the waterfront area with residential **Battery Point** (2). These stone stairs were built on private land owned by Captain James Kelly, by all accounts a larger-than-life character in early Hobart Town. You can take the steps to Kelly St, lined with small cottages (1850s), but continue your walk along Salamanca Pl past the old silo buildings, now luxury apartments.

At Runnymede St, either continue straight ahead to Princes Park or turn right and wander past **Lenna of Hobart** (3). Now an upmarket hotel, this splendid Italianate building (1880) was once a private residence. Continuing up Runnymede, you come to **Arthur Circus** (4),

a circle of quaint Georgian houses (some squeezed in by sacrificing plenty of living space) around a small village green.

Runnymede St ends at Hampden Rd, the main thoroughfare through Battery Point. Turn right for some window-shopping at the antique shops and peruse the restaurants to plan your evening meal. There are numerous interesting buildings for the period-architecture buff, but the highlight would have to be **Narryna** (5; 1836), now home to a heritage museum.

Just beyond Narryna, Hampden Rd meets busy Sandy Bay Rd; veer right and continue along Sandy Bay Rd to **St David's Park** (6). This was Hobart Town's original cemetery, which became an overgrown eyesore and was turned into a park in 1926. Across Salamanca Pl from St David's Park is **Parliament House** (7; 1835). Originally, this building was the Customs House for Hobart Town; it became Parliament House in 1856. Stroll through the manicured gardens of Parliament Sq, in front of Parliament House, to **Watermans Dock** (8). From here you can walk along the waterfront of **Sullivans Cove** (9).

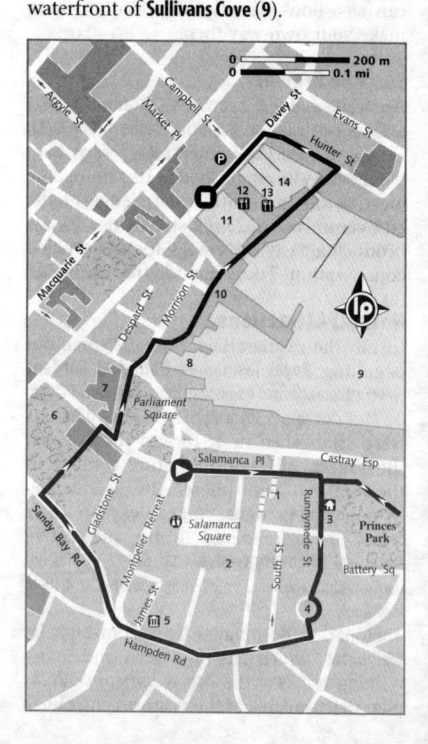

Just beyond Watermans Dock are the terminals for harbour ferries and cruises. The large **Elizabeth St Pier (10)** now houses upmarket accommodation and restaurants. Cross the drawbridge over the entrance to **Constitution Dock (11)**. This place really comes alive when yachties celebrate the finish of the famous Sydney to Hobart Yacht Race around New Year and also during the Royal Hobart Regatta in February. Moored along the northeastern side of the dock are several inexpensive **fish and chips barges (12)**, while behind them is **Mures Fish Centre (13)**, a gastronomic landmark, and **Victoria Dock (14)**, home to much of Hobart's fishing fleet.

From here it's a short walk back along the waterfront to Salamanca Pl or west to Elizabeth St and the mall.

HOBART FOR CHILDREN

There's no doubting Tasmania's status as a family-friendly holiday destination, but the historic buildings, museums and upmarket restaurants of the capital may not hold a child's interest for too long. Attractions worth seeking out to satisfy your child (and inner child) are the Cadbury chocolate factory and Antarctic Adventure.

The Salamanca Market has street performers to amuse all ages, and the docks area is great for wandering (the floating fish and chip stalls provide a budget way to keep a family well fed).

Activities in and around the capital should also appeal to kids – take a boat cruise, rent a bike and explore cycling paths, or do a kayaking tour (minimum age for Blackaby's kayak tours is 12 years).

The minute you head out of town the child-friendly options increase, with an abundance of animal parks, beaches, caves, nature walks and mazes to explore.

TOURS
Bus Tours
Day and half-day bus tours in and around Hobart are operated by **Tigerline Coaches** (☎ 1300 653 633; www.tigerline.com.au), which has free pick-up from many inner-city hotels and its kiosk at Pier One. Tours cost $30 to $115 per adult. Typical half-day tours include the Cadbury factory ($35), Richmond ($39), and Mt Wellington and City Sights ($34). Full-day tours include trips to Mt Field National Park and the Derwent

Valley ($110), Port Arthur ($60), the Huon Valley ($100) and Bruny Island ($115).

Gregory Omnibuses (☎ 6224 6169) offers double-decker sightseeing trips, including a trip visiting the Cascade brewery, Cadbury factory and Botanical Gardens for $70/31 per adult/child.

City Sights Under Lights (☎ 0418-576 489; www.citysights.com.au) operates a night-time coach excursion around Hobart. Tours begin at 8pm daily October to March, and 7pm daily April to September ($40/15 per adult/child); it does pick-ups from hotels.

Cruises
Several boat-cruise companies operate from the Franklin Pier, Brooke St Pier and Watermans Dock area, offering a variety of cruises in and around the harbour. The **Cruise Company** (☎ 6234 9294) has a popular 4½-hour Cadbury Cruise, which leaves from Brooke St Pier at 10am Monday to Friday ($38/19 per adult/child); the boat chugs to the Cadbury factory, where you disembark and tour the premises before returning to the city.

Sailings offered by **Roche O'May Cruises** (☎ 6223 1914) include a four-hour trip north, visiting the Cadbury factory and Moorilla Estate (11am weekdays, $50/27 per adult/child) as well as lunch ($30/15) and dinner ($40/20) cruises on the harbour.

Captain Fell's Historic Ferries (☎ 6223 6893) also offers good-value lunch (adult from $16) and dinner ($28) cruises, plus has sightseeing packages offering ferry and double-decker bus trips.

Guided Walks
Hobart Historic Tours conducts the informative two-hour **Hobart Historic Walk** (adult/child $19/free; ☺ 10am Sep-May, on request Jun-Aug) and also the fun two-hour **Hobart Historic Pub Tour** (adults $19, not appropriate for children; ☺ 5pm Sun-Thu, on request). All bookings and inquiries can be made at the visitors centre (p584), which is also the departure point for the tours.

The National Trust's 2½-hour **Battery Point Heritage Walk** (☎ 6223 7570; adult/child $10/2.50; ☺ 9.30am Sat) heads off once a week from the wishing well at Franklin Sq.

Scenic Flights
Scenic flights are offered by **Par Avion** (☎ 6248 5390; www.paravion.com.au) and **Tasair** (☎ 6248 5088; www.tasair.com.au); both companies fly from

Cambridge aerodrome, near Hobart airport some 15km from the city. Prices for 30-minute flights over Hobart cost around $75, and there are also options for longer flights over the southwest wilderness. Also offering a range of trips is **Tasmanian Seaplanes** (Map p583; ☎ 0419-147 755; www.tas-seaplane.com), based at a pontoon at Wrest Point.

FESTIVALS & EVENTS

FEBRUARY
Royal Hobart Regatta A major annual aquatic carnival, with boat races and other activities.
Australian Wooden Boat Festival (www.awoodboat fest.com) Held every two years (odd-numbered years) to coincide with the regatta, this features vessels from around Australia and celebrates Tasmania's boat-building heritage.

MARCH & APRIL
Ten Days on the Island (www.tendaysontheisland.org) Tasmania's major cultural festival, this biennial event (odd-numbered years) is a celebration of local and international 'island culture', with artists performing statewide. The festival incorporates the Tasmanian Readers & Writers Festival.

OCTOBER
Royal Hobart Show A large agricultural festival showcasing the state's primary industries, held annually in late October.

DECEMBER & JANUARY
Hobart Summer Festival (www.hobartcity.com.au/hsf) Hobart's premier festival, held from late December to mid-January. The docks are at their most festive for 10 days or so around the finish of the annual Sydney to Hobart Yacht Race and New Year. Highlights include a New Year's Eve party, and the Taste of Tasmania, a week-long food and wine extravaganza.

SLEEPING
The best areas of Hobart to stay in are the docks, Salamanca Pl and neighbouring Battery Point, though prices here are high and vacancy rates low. Accommodation in the affluent neighbouring suburb of Sandy Bay is also generally expensive (except for the somewhat dated motels). Sandy Bay Rd is long and winding, as is the suburb, so if you don't want to be too far from town, check distances from the city before making a booking.

The central business district and immediate surrounds is where you'll find most hostels and pubs offering rooms, plus a decent array of mid-range hotels. There's not a great deal of atmosphere to the area at night, but from most places it's only a 10-minute walk to the waterfront area and Salamanca Pl.

Away from the water on the other side of the city centre, but still reasonably close to town, are the adjoining suburbs of North Hobart and New Town. Here you'll find a couple of hostels, good B&Bs and moderately priced motels within walking distance of a cluster of lively restaurants and cafés.

If you're planning to visit in January and are particular about accommodation, you should book well ahead.

Budget
HOSTELS
Allport's Hostel (Map p583; ☎ 6231 5464; www.tassie .net.au/~allports/home_page.htm; 432 Elizabeth St, North Hobart; dm $17-20, s/d/f $35/50/70; **P** **Q**) Within walking distance of the restaurant strip of North Hobart is this bright and cheery hostel, in an impressive two-storey Italianate mansion. The atmosphere is relaxed and the facilities first-rate; they include two kitchens, a laundry and spacious common rooms.

Pickled Frog (Map p583; ☎ 6234 7977; www.the pickledfrog.com; 281 Liverpool St; dm $19-22, s/d $30/50; **Q**) This big red ramshackle hostel is well placed close to the transit centre and has a young, sociable vibe. Prices include continental breakfast, and there's an in-house café-bar and laid-back lounge for meeting fellow travellers. Extras include bike hire and good tour info.

Central City Backpackers (Map pp586-7; ☎ 6224 2404; www.centralbackpackers.com.au; 138 Collins St; dm $18-22, s/d $36/50) In the heart of the central business district, this rambling hostel has loads of communal space, OK rooms, friendly staff and extras such as baggage storage and bike hire.

Narrara Backpackers (Map p583; ☎ 6231 3191; nigelruddock@hotmail.com; 88 Goulburn St; dm/d $18/45; **Q**) This central, well-maintained backpackers has the appealing atmosphere of a large, friendly group house as well as very good facilities. It's run by an affable bloke with lots of regional knowledge and bushwalking advice.

Montgomery's Private Hotel & YHA Backpackers (Map pp586-7; ☎ 6231 2660; montys@southcom .com.au; 9 Argyle St; dm $20, s & d $65, d with bathroom $90; **Q**) Another well-placed option, this bright, modern hotel includes decent hostel rooms but cramped communal facilities. The private rooms with shared bathroom are overpriced but the en suite rooms are good value. Next door there's a pub with cheap meals and occasional live music and karaoke.

Adelphi Court YHA (☎ 6228 4829; adelphi@yhatas.org.au; 17 Stoke St, New Town; dm/s/d/f $22/50/60/65, d with bathroom $65; **P**) Hobart's other YHA hostel is the friendly, well-equipped Adelphi, offering rooms in a spruced-up 1950s-style block built around a courtyard. It's 2.5km from the city but reasonably close to the North Hobart restaurant strip. Breakfast is included with single and double room prices, or is $4.50 extra for those staying in dorms.

Transit Centre Backpackers (Map p583; ☎ 6231 2400; www.salamanca.com.au/backpackers; 199 Collins St; dm $18) This functional hostel is upstairs at the Redline bus station. It's small and the rooms are somewhat crowded, but it's a homely and relaxed place with helpful owners.

CAMPING & CABINS

With the closure of Hobart's most central caravan park at Sandy Bay, the nearest camping area to town is some 8km north of the centre, so it may be a better option to stay in one of the central city hostels. **Elwick Cabin & Tourist Park** (☎ 6272 7115; www.islandcabins.com.au; 19 Goodwood St, Glenorchy; camp/caravan sites $17/19 for 2 people, units & cabins $50-95) is served by an hourly bus into town and is well equipped, with a range of cabins.

Mid-Range

In this price-range your money will get you spruced-up rooms adjacent to or above well-located pubs (possibly quite noisy late in the week), decent B&Bs not too far from the centre, and motels that will be comfortable but possibly quite dated.

GUESTHOUSES & B&BS

Lodge on Elizabeth (Map p583; ☎ 6231 3830; www.thelodge.com.au; 249 Elizabeth St; s/d from $115/135; **P**) The Lodge is a highly recommended guesthouse in an elevated position in North Hobart, not far from the restaurant strip. Rooms in this grand Georgian manor are beautifully decorated, and extras include friendly owners and a hearty breakfast. In the pretty courtyard there's also a self-contained spa cottage ($180, two-night minimum).

Amberley House (Map p583; ☎ 6225 1005; www.babs.com.au/amberley; 391 Sandy Bay Rd; s $110-125, d $120-135; **P**) This elegant Victorian house, across the road from the casino, has well-equipped, period-style rooms and a smattering of antiques. The higher-priced rooms have views and/or spas. Breakfast isn't included in the price.

Crow's Nest (☎ 6234 9853; www.wwt.com.au/crowsnest; 2 Liverpool Cres; s/d from $70/90; **P**) Perched up in the hills of West Hobart, a brisk 15-minute walk from town, this B&B offers distant harbour views and two apartments, both with cooking facilities. Prices include breakfast provisions.

HOTELS & PUBS

Harringtons (Map pp586-7; ☎ 6234 9240; 102 Harrington St; d $70-120) After the shock of the ultra-bright colours in the reception area, you'll find the hotel rooms here are very well equipped but somewhat on the small side. Still, the price is good given continental breakfast is included and you're within walking distance of everywhere.

Astor Private Hotel (Map pp586-7; ☎ 6234 6611; www.astorprivatehotel.com.au; 157 Macquarie St; s/d/t $65/75/105) This central 1920s guesthouse has retained much of its character, full of stained-glass windows, great old furniture and family-run charm. Prices listed here are for rooms with shared bathrooms; at the time of research there were plans to add en suites to some rooms. Prices in the off-season (May to November) are $10 to $20 cheaper.

Customs House Hotel (Map pp586-7; ☎ 6234 6645; www.customshousehotel.com; 1 Murray St; s/d $75/95) At the time of research the finishing touches were being done on stylishly renovated rooms at this place by the docks. All rooms now have bathrooms. Downstairs is a great new restaurant and very popular bar.

Theatre Royal Hotel (Map pp586-7; ☎ 6234 6925; 31 Campbell St; d with bathroom $80, s/d without bathroom $45/60) Handily placed for theatregoers (right next door to the Theatre Royal), this gracious hotel has high-standard rooms (bathrooms have recently been added to some). Downstairs is a bright bar and dining room. Price includes continental breakfast.

Prince of Wales Hotel (Map pp586-7; ☎ 6223 6355; princeofwaleshotel@bigpond.com; 55 Hampden Rd, Battery Point; s/d from $75/85; **P**) Given this hotel's location in the heart of historic Battery Point, these rooms represent excellent value. Rates

TASMANIA

include light breakfast, and laundry facilities are free for guests. Hearty pub grub is served at the bistro.

Shipwrights Arms Hotel (Map p583; ☎ 6223 5551; shippies@southcom.com.au; 29 Trumpeter St, Battery Point; s/d $50/70) Also in Battery Point is this landmark 1834 yachties pub, known locally as Shippies. There are only four rooms here, with shared facilities, and they're OK but nothing special. The attraction is downstairs – the bar, restaurant and beer garden.

MOTELS & APARTMENTS

Avon Court Holiday Apartments (Map pp586-7; ☎ 6223 4837; www.batterypoint.net/avon/; 4 Colville St; s/d $90/120; P) If you overlook the dated interiors, these spacious, self-contained apartments in Battery Point represent excellent value for families and small groups. Larger apartments can sleep up to six.

There are two reasonable motels on Sandy Bay Rd, within walking distance of the city and docks. **Blue Hills Motel** (Map p583; ☎ 6223 1777; www.bestwestern.com.au/bluehills; 96a Sandy Bay Rd; d $110-120; P) is quite plain but offers comfortable motel rooms plus larger, self-contained apartments. Nearby **St Ives Motel Apartments** (Map p583; ☎ 6224 1044; www.stivesmotel.com.au; 67 St Georges Tce; d from $100; P) has respectable studio apartments with self-catering facilities.

Woolmers Inn (Map p583; ☎ 6223 7355; woolmersinn@bigpond.com.au; 123 Sandy Bay Rd; units from $100; P) Woolmers offers more attractive units than the motels listed above, but is slightly further from town. It's a large complex of modern studio and two-bedroom units, all with cooking facilities and bright décor.

Top End

As well as the typical big-city hotels, in this price range you'll find excellent historic guesthouses and cottages (especially in Battery Point), and also numerous modern apartments in great waterside spots or in the heart of Salamanca Pl.

Somerset on the Pier (Map pp586-7; ☎ 6220 6600; www.the-ascott.com; Elizabeth St Pier; apt from $200; P) In a brilliant location on Elizabeth St Pier and with excellent restaurants as its neighbours, this complex (formerly known as Oakford on the Pier) offers luxurious apartments and great views. All are self-contained and have modern décor; you'll

pay more for a spa and/or balcony. The same company also offers well-located, upmarket apartments at a second property, **Somerset on Salamanca** (Map pp586-7; ☎ 6220 6600; www.the-ascott.com; apt from $190; P); check-in is at Somerset on the Pier.

Lenna of Hobart (Map pp586-7; 6232 3900; www.lenna.com.au; 20 Runnymede St, Battery Point; d $170-250; P) This beautiful Italianate mansion is set in lovely grounds and is home to an elegant, fine-dining restaurant, Alexander's. The newer wing of the property is where you'll find the very comfortable, if slightly dated, hotel rooms. If you're after more contemporary surrounds, opposite Lenna and under the same management is **Salamanca Terraces** (Map pp586-7; ☎ 6232 3900; www.salamancaterraces.com.au; 93 Salamanca Pl; apt from $165; P), with upmarket self-contained apartments on offer.

Hotel Grand Chancellor (Map pp586-7; ☎ 6235 4535; www.hgchobart.com.au; 1 Davey St; r $280-310; P) You can't miss this waterfront monolith, offering international-standard indulgence. The lobby has shops, an atrium lounge and restaurants; there's also a gym and indoor pool. The well-equipped rooms have good views – you'll pay a little more for a harbour view. There are packages that bring the high rack-rates down considerably (as low as $150); see the website for details.

Wrest Point (Map p583; ☎ 6225 0112; www.wrestpoint.com.au; 410 Sandy Bay Rd, Sandy Bay; r $250-270; P) Located 3km south of the centre, this waterfront complex has luxurious hotel rooms in its tower, which is stuffed full of flashy diversions like a casino, restaurants, bars and shows. There's also a cheaper motel in the complex's grounds, with comfortable, functional rooms for around $130.

Battery Point Manor (Map p583; ☎ 6224 0888; www.batterypointmanor.com.au; 15 Cromwell St, Battery Point; d $125-195; P) Built in 1834, this guesthouse offers a wide range of inviting, well-equipped rooms, most with king-sized beds and great river views, and also a self-contained two-bedroom cottage. Prices include buffet-style breakfast.

EATING

Hobart's central business district has some great spots for brunch and lunch, but evening options are generally better closer to the water or historic precincts. The waterfront streets and docks are the collective epicentre of the city's restaurant scene, and quality seafood is on offer everywhere you look. Salamanca Pl is an excellent choice for cafés and restaurants, especially brunch-time during the Saturday market. For the most diverse selection of eateries, head to Elizabeth St in North Hobart, a cosmopolitan strip of pubs, cafés and restaurants. Pubs serve up dependable, if somewhat predictable, meals that usually represent good value.

City Centre
Map pp586–7

Criterion St Cafe (☎ 6234 5858; 10 Criterion St; lunch $6-12) Coffee-lovers, vegetarians and fans of quality café fare will be impressed by this light, bright and popular eatery. It serves breakfast from 7.30am, followed by an array of salads, pasta, sandwiches and tempting sweet treats,

Kafe Kara (☎ 6231 2332; 119 Liverpool St; lunch $8-18) Like the Criterion St Cafe, this local favourite offers early breakfasts and great all-day eating in its stylishly modern interior. Its speciality is tasty Italian-style fare (panini, pasta, risotto).

Nourish (☎ 6234 5674; 129 Elizabeth St; meals under $10) Marketing itself as a 'therapeutic food café', this new eating place is a godsend for people with food allergies and intolerances. The menu features tasty, well-prepared dishes (curries, salads, stir-fries, risotto) that are all gluten-free and largely dairy-free, too.

New Sydney Hotel (☎ 6234 4516; 87 Bathurst St; mains $9-18) This cosy watering hole is popular for cheap, filling counter meals and more options than just the usual pub grub offerings of steak, schnitzel and fish and chips (eg pasta with chicken and avocado, chicken Caesar salad).

Tandoor & Curry House (☎ 6234 6905; 101 Harrington St; mains $13-16) Serving some of the best curries in town, this friendly Indian restaurant has takeaway or eat-in service and menu favourites such as beef masala, rogan josh and chicken korma, plus good vegetarian dishes.

Waterfront
Map pp586–7

Fish Frenzy (☎ 6231 2134; Elizabeth St Pier; meals $8-12) Enjoy fish and chips (of course), spicy calamari salad or a fish burger, making your choice from a simple but appealing menu of fresh seafood. Dine outside by the water to fully appreciate this casual, affordable eatery.

Constitution Dock has a number of floating takeaway **seafood stalls** (you can't miss them), which are also a good option for an impromptu dockside picnic.

Mures (☎ 6231 2121; Victoria Dock) is a Hobart institution and well worth a visit. On the Lower Deck you'll find a fishmonger and an inexpensive, family-friendly food court (meals $6 to $12). **Mures Upper Deck** (mains $19-28) is a fancier restaurant with great harbour views and well-prepared seafood dishes, such as Tuscan blue eye (grilled blue eye and tiger prawns on roast pumpkin risotto), crayfish and upmarket versions of fish and chips. Also part of the Mures complex is the much praised **Orizuru Sushi Bar** (☎ 6231 1790; sushi $7-10, mains $15-27), which uses fresh seafood for delicate sushi creations and other popular Japanese dishes.

T-42° (☎ 6224 7742; Elizabeth St Pier; mains $15-22) A favourite among Hobart's fashionable crowd, especially on Friday and Saturday nights, is this cool waterfront bistro-wine bar. There are innovative, well-priced menu selections, a good wine list, and lounges and bar stools for a good night out.

Athena's on the Pier (☎ 6224 2200; Elizabeth St Pier; mains $18-25) Next door to T-42° is another good option, and here diners can choose from one of two menus. The 'Classically Greek' menu features authentic dishes like moussaka, lamb and seafood souvlaki, and 'Greek with a Twist' enables the chef to break with tradition and do his thing with fine Tasmanian produce (quail, salmon etc).

Sisco's on the Pier (☎ 6223 2059; Murray St Pier, upper level; mains $18-29) More Mediterranean influence – this time Spanish – can be found at this striking restaurant. Diners can enjoy great views alongside paella, a seafood platter or oven-roasted ocean trout, followed by a dessert of Catalan cream custard or caramel soufflé.

Sticky Fingers (☎ 6223 1077; Murray St Pier; snacks $3-6) Downstairs from Sisco's, Sticky Fingers is a fun place for a pit stop. This small café is full of sweet treats like sundaes, smoothies, cakes and loads of flavoured ice cream and gelati.

Salamanca
Map pp586–7

This historic area has something to please everyone: bright cafés excellent for people-watching over a coffee, upmarket restaurants, cosy pubs and bakeries for a quick

TASMANIA

snack. **Salamanca Bakehouse** (☎ 6224 6300; 5 Salamanca Sq) is good for late-night munchies. It's open 24 hours.

Retro Café (☎ 6223 3073; 31 Salamanca Pl; meals $5-13) A ritual for many locals is Saturday brunch along Salamanca Pl, among the market stalls, and this is a top spot to enjoy such a tradition. There are huge breakfasts on offer (how about sourdough bread with salmon, spinach, poached eggs and brie?), plus excellent coffee and hearty lunch fodder (focaccia, burgers, salads).

Popular Salamanca Sq is home to lots of cafés and outdoor tables, and standards are high. Have a browse and see what takes your fancy. At bright, retro-style **Machine Laundry Café** (☎ 6224 9922; 12 Salamanca Sq; meals $5-12) you can wash your dirty clothes while discreetly adding fresh juice, pasta or coffee stains to your clean ones (there's an on-site laundry). **Say Cheese** (☎ 6224 2888; 7 Salamanca Sq; meals $5-15) is a cheese deli-café serving breakfast, lunch and great platters of cheese (of course), seafood and antipasto – and even a kids' platter. The desserts are worth leaving room for. Stylish **Bar Celona** (☎ 6224 7557; 24 Salamanca Sq; meals $9-15) is a busy café/wine bar with lots of variety, including nachos, salads, burgers and pizzas, and it's a popular night-time spot for a beverage or three.

Ball & Chain Grill (☎ 6223 2655; 87 Salamanca Pl; mains $17-25) One for the carnivores (and best avoided by vegetarians), this informal place serves up some of the best steak in town, cooked on an authentic charcoal grill. The menu's not limited to steak – you can also have grilled game, chicken or seafood.

But Salamanca is not all chi-chi cafés and upmarket restaurants – there are some good bargains to be enjoyed, too. Bustling **Vietnamese Kitchen** (☎ 6223 2188; 61 Salamanca Pl) has quick service and cheap, tasty food: try two dishes with rice or noodles for only $7. Not far away, the **Parthenon Souvlaki Bar** (☎ 6223 4461; 51 Salamanca Pl) has souvlakis for around $5.

Battery Point   Map pp586–7

Jackman & McRoss (☎ 6223 3186; 57-59 Hampden Rd; snacks $3-7) This elegant bakery-café is deservedly popular for its wonderful array of fresh pies, tarts, baguettes and pastries, both sweet and savoury. Call in for an early-morning croissant and coffee, quiche for lunch and a pastry for afternoon tea.

Da Angelo Ristorante (☎ 6223 7011; 47 Hampden Rd; mains $11-19) Authentic Da Angelo specialises in Italian cuisine's best offerings. Choose from an impressively long menu of various homemade pastas, veal and chicken dishes, pizza with 20 different toppings, and calzone. It also offers takeaway.

Z's (☎ 6224 7124; 60 Hampden Rd; meals $12-25, tapas plates $7-10) Z's is an upbeat, spacious and trendy café-wine bar with an appealing courtyard. There are two menus – the à la carte menu has standard café-bistro fare, but the tapas list is much more interesting: graze on Moroccan lamb, fried haloumi cheese and mini frittatas.

There's decent food on offer at two of Battery Point's pubs. The **Shipwrights Arms Hotel** (☎ 6223 5551; 29 Trumpeter St; mains $15-25) has excellent seafood meals and a huge beer garden in which to enjoy them. The **Prince of Wales Hotel** (☎ 6223 6355; 55 Hampden Rd; meals $12-20) offers no-nonsense pub grub – its menu board proudly proclaims 'no yuppie food'!

North Hobart   Map p583

Elizabeth St in North Hobart has a reputation for good-value cuisine reflecting a range of nationalities. Try **Annapurna** (☎ 6236 9500; 305 Elizabeth St; mains $12-18) for a delicious variety of Indian dishes. Lunch specials here ($6 to $9) are great value. Busy **Vanidol's** (☎ 6234 9307; 353 Elizabeth St; mains $12-18) has an excellent mix of Thai, Indian and Indonesian dishes. **Sen's Asian Sensation**

THE AUTHOR'S CHOICE

Machine Laundry Café (☎ 6224 9922; 12 Salamanca Sq; meals $5-12) It may feel somewhat inappropriate to cart your dirty duds through Hobart's well-heeled Salamanca precinct, but if it means more time to linger at this combined café-laundrette you won't regret it. Load up one of the hi-tech washing machines then take a seat inside the bright, retro-style café, or at an outdoor table (perfect for people-watching). Order from the all-day breakfast menu (from homemade muesli to eggs and bacon) or opt for a lunch dish like spicy salad of Vietnamese chicken on rice noodles, or the parmesan and spinach pancakes served with a chunky tomato relish. Wash everything down with a fine coffee or fresh juice, transfer your laundry into a dryer and settle back in for more.

TASMANIA

(☎ 6236 9345; 345 Elizabeth St; dishes $8-18) is a large Chinese restaurant offering takeaways and cheap all-day yum cha.

Kaos Café (☎ 6231 5699; 237 Elizabeth St; meals $10-16) A few blocks south of the restaurants listed above, this cool café busies itself with a fine assortment of meat and vegie dishes, including upmarket burgers, salads and risotto. It serves until late (around 11.30pm most nights).

Sandy Bay

Prosser's on the Beach (☎ 6225 2276; Beach Rd, Long Point; lunch $13-22, dinner mains around $25) Often labelled 'best seafood restaurant in Tasmania' (a big claim!), Prosser's on the Beach serves upmarket seafood dishes in attractive but unpretentious premises overlooking the water. It's a taxi ride from town but worth the trip. Bookings recommended.

DRINKING

Salamanca Pl is home to some fine pubs and bars – lots of outdoor imbibing when the weather is warm, or cosy open fires and lounges in winter. See p589 for information on a guided pub tour, with lots of historical tales and drinking involved.

Knopwood's Retreat (Map pp586-7; ☎ 6223 5808; 39 Salamanca Pl) is a perennial Hobart favourite, usually hidden behind a solid mass of Friday-night drinkers loitering on the pavement section.

The requisite Irish pub is also down this way: the popular **Irish Murphy's** (Map pp586-7; ☎ 6223 1119; 21 Salamanca Pl) is a cosy place with low ceilings and small rooms.

If you are a yachtsman, you'll feel right at home amid the nautical artefacts of the **Shipwrights Arms Hotel** (Map p583; ☎ 6223 5551; 29 Trumpeter St) in Battery Point. Another favourite with boating folk is **Customs House Hotel** (Map pp586-7; ☎ 6234 6645; 1 Murray St), near the docks. **Republic Bar & Cafe** (Map p583; ☎ 6234 6954; www.republicbar.com; 299 Elizabeth St) is the pick of pubs in North Hobart, with good food, live music, a beer garden and a loyal following.

For those with a penchant for more upmarket wining and reclining, both **Bar Celona** (Map pp586-7; ☎ 6224 7557; 24 Salamanca Sq) and **T-42°** (Map pp586-7; ☎ 6224 7742; Elizabeth St Pier) are favourites; and **Cow** (Map pp586-7; ☎ 6231 1200; 112 Murray St) is another stylish option.

ENTERTAINMENT
Cinemas & Theatres

The **State Cinema** (Map p583; ☎ 6234 6318; 375 Elizabeth St, North Hobart) screens mainly independent local and international films. **Village Cinema** (Map pp586-7; ☎ 6234 7288; 181 Collins St) is a large inner-city complex showing mainstream releases.

The modern **Federation Concert Hall** (Map pp586-7; ☎ 6235 3633, 1800 001 190; 1 Davey St), welded to the Hotel Grand Chancellor, has the external aesthetics of a huge aluminium can and is home to the Tasmanian Symphony Orchestra (www.tso.com.au). The **Theatre Royal** (Map pp586-7; ☎ 6233 2299; www.theatreroyal.webcentral.com.au; 29 Campbell St), Australia's oldest theatre, stages a range of music, ballet, theatre and opera performances by local and touring companies. Tickets cost around $30 to $45.

Live Music

The *Mercury* newspaper lists most of Hobart's entertainment options in its Thursday insert, 'Pulse'. Also you should check out the online gig guide at www.nakeddwarf .com.au.

The best live music in Hobart is held every Friday year-round from 5.30pm to 7.30pm at Salamanca Arts Centre courtyard (off Salamanca Sq). Rektango play a cool combo of jazz-folk-gypsy music and their regular performances have become something of a Hobart institution. It's family-friendly with loads of atmosphere, and drinks are available (including sangria in summer, mulled wine in winter). Admission is by donation.

There's regular live music at most of the pubs listed under Drinking, above. Local bands play at Irish Murphy's from Wednesday to Saturday, with a traditional session on Sunday afternoons. **Republic Bar & Cafe** and the **New Sydney Hotel** (Map pp586-7; ☎ 6234 4516; 87 Bathurst St) have an eclectic range of live music every night of the week.

A great place for late-night drinks and a mixture of live music and DJs is **Round Midnight** (Map pp586-7; ☎ 6223 2491; upstairs, 39 Salamanca Pl), above Knopwood's Retreat. Sharing the premises is the popular bar/club **Syrup** (Map pp586-7; ☎ 6224 8249). The two venues are open Wednesday to Saturday nights. **Isobar** (Map pp586-7; ☎ 6231 6600; 11 Franklin Wharf) has a good bar downstairs and a club upstairs (more mainstream than Syrup).

TASMANIA

Like all decent jazz places, **Temple Place** (Map pp586-7; ☎ 6223 2883; 121 Macquarie St) is in a laneway and has a separate cigar lounge. Prior to the jazz (usually free, but not always), it does a good dinner trade.

GETTING THERE & AWAY
Air
For information on flights to/from Hobart, see p579. **Qantas** (Map pp586-7; ☎ 13 13 13; 77 Elizabeth Mall) has an office in the centre of town.

Bus
The main bus companies operating to/from Hobart are **Redline Coaches** (Map p583; ☎ 1300 360 000; www.tasredline.com.au), operating from the Transit Centre at 199 Collins St, and **TassieLink** (Map pp586-7; ☎ 1300 300 520; www.tassielink.com.au), operating from the new Hobart Bus Terminal at 64 Brisbane St.

For general information on local bus services around town see the Getting Around section (below).

Car
There are many car-rental firms in Hobart; most have representation at the airport. The large multinationals (eg Avis, Budget, Hertz, Thrifty) have desks inside the terminal; smaller local companies have representation in the car park area.

Some of the cheaper local firms, with daily rental rates starting around $30:
Lo-Cost Auto Rent (Map pp586-7; ☎ 1800 647 060; www.locostautorent.com; 105 Murray St)
Rent-A-Bug (Map pp586-7; ☎ 6231 0300; www.rentabug.com.au; 105 Murray St)
Selective Car Rentals (Map pp586-7; ☎ 6234 3311; 47 Bathurst St)

GETTING AROUND
To/From the Airport
The airport is 16km east of the centre. The **Airporter shuttle bus** (☎ 0419-382 240) operates a service between the city (via various places to stay) and the airport for $9/4.50 per adult/child.

A taxi between the airport and city centre should cost $30 to $35.

Bicycle
See Cycling (p587) for details of bike rental and details of where to go to find information on Hobart's cycling paths.

Boat
The **Wanderer** (☎ 6223 1914) ferry, operated by Roche O'May Cruises, has a service departing Brooke Street Pier daily at 10.30am, 11am, 1.30pm and 3pm, visiting the Botanical Gardens, Bellerive, Wrest Point hotel/casino and Battery Point. The trip is $15/7.50 return per adult/child and you can get on and off as many times as you like.

Bus
Metro (☎ 13 22 01; www.metrotas.com.au) operates the local bus network; there's an information desk inside the main post office on the corner of Elizabeth and Macquarie Sts. Most buses leave from this area of Elizabeth St, or from around the edges of nearby Franklin Sq. If you're planning to bus around Hobart it's worth buying Metro's timetable ($0.50). For $3.60 you can buy a daily pass that can be used after 9am Monday to Friday, and all day Saturday, Sunday and public holidays.

Taxi
Try **City Cabs** (☎ 13 10 08) or **Taxi Combined Services** (☎ 13 22 27). **Maxi Taxi** (☎ 6234 3573) has vehicles that accommodate disabled persons.

AROUND HOBART

Hobart is conveniently close to some great historic and scenic places. Reminders of Tasmania's convict history await at Richmond, and the natural highlights of Mt Field National Park are an easy day trip.

Getting There & Around
Metro-owned **Hobart Coaches** (☎ 13 22 01; www.metrotas.com.au) runs regular services to destinations around the capital such as Kingston, New Norfolk and Richmond; timetable and fare information is available from the Metro office inside Hobart's main post office.

The **Richmond Tourist Bus** (☎ 0408-341 804) runs a twice-daily service from Hobart (9.15am and 12.15pm) that gives you three hours to explore Richmond before returning. The cost is $25 return.

TassieLink (☎ 1300 300 520; www.tassielink.com.au) has a service from Hobart to the east coast that passes through Richmond ($5.20, 40 minutes) on weekdays (three times weekly in summer). It also has regular services to

Mt Field National Park from Hobart from November to April ($24, 1¾ hours).

Day trips to places near and around Hobart are offered by **Tigerline Coaches** (☎ 1300 653 633; www .tigerline.com.au).

RICHMOND

☎ 03 / pop 827

Richmond is just 24km northeast of Hobart and, with more than 50 buildings dating from the 19th century, is Tasmania's premier historic town. Straddling the Coal River on the old route between Hobart and Port Arthur, it was once a strategic military post and convict station. It's now a popular day trip from Hobart but is a good option for an overnight stay.

Information is available online at www .richmondvillage.com.

Sights & Activities

The much-photographed **Richmond Bridge** was constructed by convicts in 1823. The northern wing of the remarkably well preserved **Richmond Gaol** (☎ 6260 2127; 37 Bathurst St; adult/child/family $5.50/2.50/14; ☉ 9am-5pm) was built in 1825, five years before the settlement at Port Arthur.

There's also an interesting **Model Village** (☎ 6260 2502; laneway off Bridge St; adult/child/family $7.50/3.50/18; ☉ 9am-5pm), designed from original plans of Hobart Town as it was in the 1820s.

Other places of interest include: **St John's Church** (off Wellington St), the oldest Catholic church (1837) in Australia; **St Luke's Church of England** (Edwards St) built in 1834; the 1825 **courthouse** (Forth St); the 1817 **Bridge Inn** (Forth St); and the **Richmond Arms Hotel** (Bridge St) dating back to 1888.

Sleeping & Eating

Richmond Cabin & Tourist Park (☎ 6260 2192; 48 Middle Tea Tree Rd; camp/caravan sites $16/20 for 2 people, cabins from $55) This friendly park, a little out of town, has extensive facilities and the cheapest accommodation in Richmond in its neat, inexpensive cabins. Kids will be happy with the indoor heated pool and games room.

Mrs Currie's House (☎ 6260 2766; www.mrscurries house.com; 4 Franklin St; s/d $100/130) Enjoy a gourmet cooked breakfast or tea by the open fire at this warm and welcoming B&B. It's a lovely two-storey Georgian house dating from the 1850s, with pretty décor and antiques to match the era.

Millhouse on the Bridge (☎ 6260 2428; www .millhouse.com.au; 2 Wellington St; d $150-180) The 1850s mill by the historic bridge has been masterfully restored and transformed into a luxury guesthouse. The addition of a self-contained cottage in the grounds, combined with features like lovely gardens and superb décor, as well as friendly, helpful owners, have helped to make this one of the state's most appealing B&Bs.

Richmond Wine Centre (☎ 6260 2619; 27 Bridge St; meals $8-22) Don't be misled by the name – this place dedicates itself to fine Tasmanian food as well as wine. There's an extensive menu of local produce - deli-, café- and restaurant-style. Breakfast and lunch are served daily and dinner is served from Wednesday to Saturday.

As you'd expect in a historic town, there are a number of tearooms here – the pick is **Ma Foosies** (☎ 6260 2412; 46 Bridge St; meals $3-8), serving light lunches and Devonshire teas in pretty surrounds. The historic **Richmond Arms Hotel** (☎ 56260 2109; 42 Bridge St; meals $10-20) has a good menu selection (which includes a kids' menu) and better-than-average pub grub.

MT FIELD NATIONAL PARK

Mt Field, 80km northwest of Hobart, was declared a national park in 1916 and is well known for its spectacular mountain scenery, alpine moorland, dense rainforest, abundant wildlife and waterfalls. The park has a **visitors centre** (☎ 03-6288 1149; Lake Dobson Rd; ☉ 8.30am-5pm Dec-Apr, 9am-4pm Apr-Nov), which houses displays on the area, and a café.

To reach the magnificent 40m-high **Russell Falls**, take the easy 20-minute walk from behind the visitors centre. The path is suitable for prams and most wheelchair-users. There are also easy walks to Lady Barron and Horseshoe Falls, as well as much longer bushwalks, including the beautiful Tarn Shelf walk.

The abundance of wildlife that can be viewed here at dusk makes this a memorable place to stay overnight with children.

Sleeping & Eating

National Park Youth Hostel (☎ 03-6288 1369; Lake Dobson Hwy, 200m north of park turn-off; dm $17) This YHA hostel has little to recommend

TASMANIA

it except the location; the interior is dingy and rooms are crowded. At the time of writing, however, a new owner was about to take over, which may see some welcome changes.

The excellent **Land of the Giants Campground** (no bookings; camp/caravan sites $6/8.50 per adult) is a self-registration camping ground with good facilities just inside the park. Some 15km into the park are **Lake Dobson Cabins** (☎ 03-6288 1149; s & d $22, additional adult/child $11/5.50), three basic (no power) six-bunk cabins; visitors must take their own portable light and cooker. Book through the visitors centre.

Russell Falls Holiday Cottages (☎ 03-6288 1198; Lake Dobson Hwy; s/d $60/80, additional person $13) On the way to the park's entrance, off the highway, these self-contained cottages have dated furnishings but are roomy and extremely clean.

Well worth stopping at en route to Mt Field is the **Possum Café** (☎ 03-6288 1477; meals $8-13) at Westerway, about 8km east. This is a lovely little riverside café with a craft shop, outdoor seating, a resident platypus (sightings not guaranteed) and excellent lunches and snacks. It's closed Monday and Tuesday.

NEW NORFOLK
☎ 03 / pop 5011

Set in the lush Derwent Valley to the northwest of Hobart, New Norfolk is another interesting historical town. It was first settled in 1803 and became an important hop-growing centre, which is why the area is dotted with old oast houses used for drying hops. Also distinctive are the rows of tall poplars planted to protect crops from the wind.

Originally called Elizabeth Town, New Norfolk was renamed after the arrival of settlers (1807 onwards) from the abandoned Pacific Ocean colony on Norfolk Island.

The eye-catching old **Oast House** (☎ 6261 1322; Tynwald Park) is home to a hop museum, craft store and pancake café. **St Matthew's Anglican Church** (Bathurst St) is the oldest church in Tassie (built in 1823), while the **Bush Inn** (49 Montagu St) is among the oldest continuously licensed hotels in Australia (dating from 1815).

The black-and-white **Old Colony Inn** (☎ 6261 2731; 21 Montagu St; adult/child $2/free; ☼ 9am-5pm Nov-

Apr, 10am-4pm May-Oct) has a museum of colonial furnishings and artefacts, including a fascinating dolls house, and a tearoom serving homemade snacks.

You can take a 30-minute jet-boat ride with **Devil Jet** (☎ 6261 3460; www.deviljet.com.au; Esplanade; adult/child $50/25) on the Derwent River rapids. Free pick-up from Hobart can be arranged.

Sleeping & Eating
Bush Inn (☎ 6261 2256; 49 Montagu St; s/d $38/60) Plain but cheap rooms (shared bathroom) await you in this historic pub, as do hearty, meat-heavy meals ($12 to $16). There's a good view over gardens and the river from the dining rooms and outdoor deck.

Saints & Sinners (☎ 6261 1877; www.tassie.net.au /saintsandsinners; 93 High St; s/d from $90/120) Named for its central location among churches and hotels, this renovated mid-19th-century inn has comfortable rooms and guest lounge; prices include large cooked breakfast.

Tynwald (☎ 6261 2667; www.tynwaldtasmania.com; Tynwald St; d $145-180) This grand Victorian mansion overlooks the river by Oast House and has inviting, antique-furnished rooms. It's owned by two chefs and hence has a high-quality restaurant serving up local produce nightly (mains $23 to $25); bookings are advised.

KINGSTON
☎ 03 / pop 12,900

The town of Kingston, 11km south of Hobart, is home to the headquarters of the **Australian Antarctic Division** (☎ 6232 3209; www .antdiv.gov.au; Channel Hwy; admission free; ☼ 9am-5pm Mon-Fri except public holidays), which has a fine display on the exploration and ecology of the frozen continent.

Kingston Beach is a popular swimming and sailing spot, with attractive wooded cliffs at each end of a long arc of white sand. Behind the clubhouse at the southern end is the start of a short, pretty walk to the smaller, more secluded **Boronia Beach** and its deep rock pool. Further south by road are **Blackmans Bay**, which has a blowhole, and **Tinderbox Marine Reserve**, where you can go snorkelling along an underwater trail marked with submerged information plates.

The Kingston Beach area could be a relaxed base for travellers exploring Hobart and the southeast – it takes only 10 minutes to drive to the capital, and at the time of writing there was talk of a possible ferry service linking Kingston and the Hobart waterfront.

Kingston Beach Motel (☎ 6229 8969; 31 Osborne Esplanade; d $95), directly opposite Kingston Beach, has an old-style motel exterior but revamped rooms, and big plans for renovation and expansion (including the addition of cottages and a café). There are cheaper rates in the off-season or for longer stays. Next door, **Tranquilla** (☎ 6229 6282; 30 Osborne Esplanade; d $95, additional person $25) offers a roomy self-contained unit that can sleep up to four.

Citrus Moon Cafe (☎ 6229 2388; 23 Beach Rd; lunches under $10) is a bright, retro-style café with a predominantly vegetarian menu. Choose from salads, focaccia and bagels, or head straight for the ice cream.

SOUTHEAST COAST

South of Hobart are the scenic timber and fruit-growing areas of the Huon Peninsula, D'Entrecasteaux Channel and Port Esperance, as well as beautiful Bruny Island and the Hartz Mountains National Park. Once mainly an apple-growing region, the area has now diversified and produces a range of other fruits, Atlantic salmon and wines, as well as catering to the growing tourism industry.

Information about the region can be found online at www.huontrail.org.au and at www.farsouth.com.au.

Getting There & Around

The region south of Hobart has two distinct areas: the peninsula, which includes Kettering and Cygnet, and the coastal strip on which the Huon Hwy links Huonville to Cockle Creek. For details of the ferry service to Bruny Island, see p601.

Hobart Coaches (☎ 132201;www.metrotas.com.au) runs several buses on weekdays from Hobart to Kettering ($6.90). One bus runs each weekday from Hobart to Snug and inland across to Cygnet ($8.60).

TassieLink (☎ 1300 300 520; www.tigerline.com.au) has regular services from Hobart through Kingston ($3.30, 30 minutes), Huonville ($8.10, 1 hour), Geeveston ($12, 1½ hours) and on to Dover ($16, 2 hours).

From December to April on Monday, Wednesday and Friday, TassieLink runs buses along the Huon Hwy from Hobart through Huonville, Geeveston, Dover, Lune River and all the way to the end of the road at Cockle Creek ($52, 3½ hours). The service returns to Hobart from Cockle Creek on the same days.

KETTERING
☎ 03 / pop 310
The small port of Kettering, on a sheltered bay 34km south of Hobart, is the terminal for the Bruny Island car ferry. The **visitors centre** (☎ 6267 4494; kettering@tasvisinfo.com.au; 81 Ferry Rd; ☼ 9am-5pm) by the ferry terminal has information on accommodation and services on the island (including notes on walks and a self-guided driving tour).

At the marina, **Roaring 40's Ocean Kayaking** (☎ 6267 5000; www.roaring40skayaking.com.au) offers half-/full-day channel tours for $70/120, as well as gear rental, a huge range of overnight trips for different skill levels, and more challenging explorations of the southwest wilderness.

In a great setting with views over the scenic, boat-cluttered harbour, the **Oyster Cove Inn** (☎ 6267 4446; oyster.cove@tassie.net.au; Ferry Rd; s/d $45/75) has comfortable rooms with shared facilities. It also has an excellent **restaurant** (dinner mains $15-25) with an extensive menu and good local wine selections, and a more casual bar and outdoor deck.

Just north of town, **Herons Rise Vineyard** (☎ 6267 4339; www.heronsrise.com.au; Saddle Rd; d $120-130, additional adult/child $40/30) has two upmarket, self-contained cottages set in delightful gardens. Each bright, spacious unit has a log fire and breakfast provisions are supplied; dinner can be provided by prior arrangement.

Inside the visitors centre, **Mermaid Cafe** (meals $5-13) offers everything from toasted sandwiches and pies to salads and burgers.

BRUNY ISLAND
☎ 03 / pop 520
Bruny Island is almost two islands, joined by an isthmus where mutton birds and other waterfowl breed. It's a beautiful and sparsely populated retreat, renowned for varied wildlife, including fairy penguins.

The island was sighted by Abel Tasman in 1642 and later visited by Furneaux,

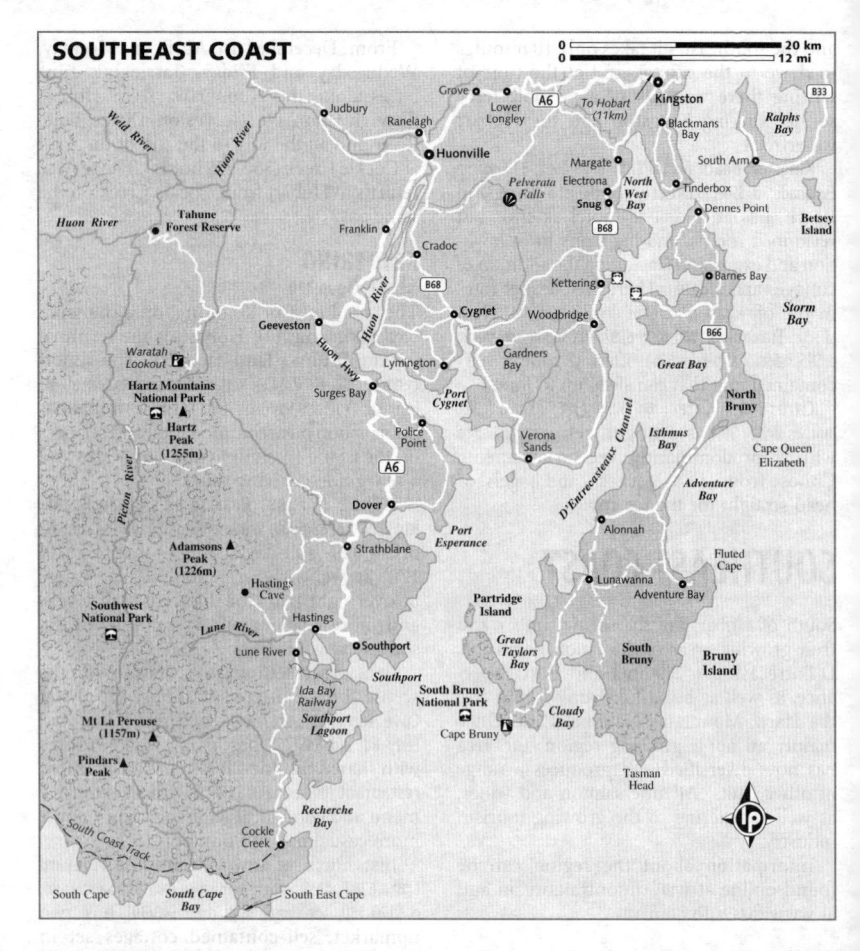

SOUTHEAST COAST

0 — 20 km
0 — 12 mi

Cook, Bligh and Cox between 1770 and 1790, but was named after Rear Admiral Bruni D'Entrecasteaux, who explored and surveyed the area in 1792. The Aboriginal people were initially friendly towards the Europeans, but relations deteriorated after the sealers and whalers arrived. The island itself changed little until the car ferry started in 1954.

Too many visitors try unsuccessfully to cram their experience of Bruny into a day or less. If you can, try to stay for a few days and really explore Bruny Island's superb coastal scenery, fine swimming and surf beaches, good fishing, and the walking tracks within the spectacular **South Bruny National Park**.

Tourism is important to the island's economy, though as yet there are no large resorts, just mostly self-contained cottages and guesthouses. Supplies are available at the well-stocked Adventure Bay Shop and there are also small shops at the other settlements. Managers often don't live next door to their rental cottages, so it's best to book (the visitors centre in Kettering can help). A car or bicycle is necessary for getting around.

The **Bligh Museum of Pacific Exploration** (☎ 6293 1117; Main Rd, Adventure Bay; adult/child/family $4/2/10; ⏰ 10am-3pm) details the local exploits of explorers such as Bligh, Cook and Furneaux. Also of interest is South Bruny's **lighthouse**, built in 1836. Visits are restricted

Wander at leisure through the well-preserved historic area of Hobart's **Battery Point** (p584)

RICHARD I'ANSON

JOHN HAY

Pick up a bargain at the **Salamanca Market** (p584)

Cross the drawbridge over the entrance to Hobart's **Constitution Dock** (p589)

JUDI WILLOUGHBY

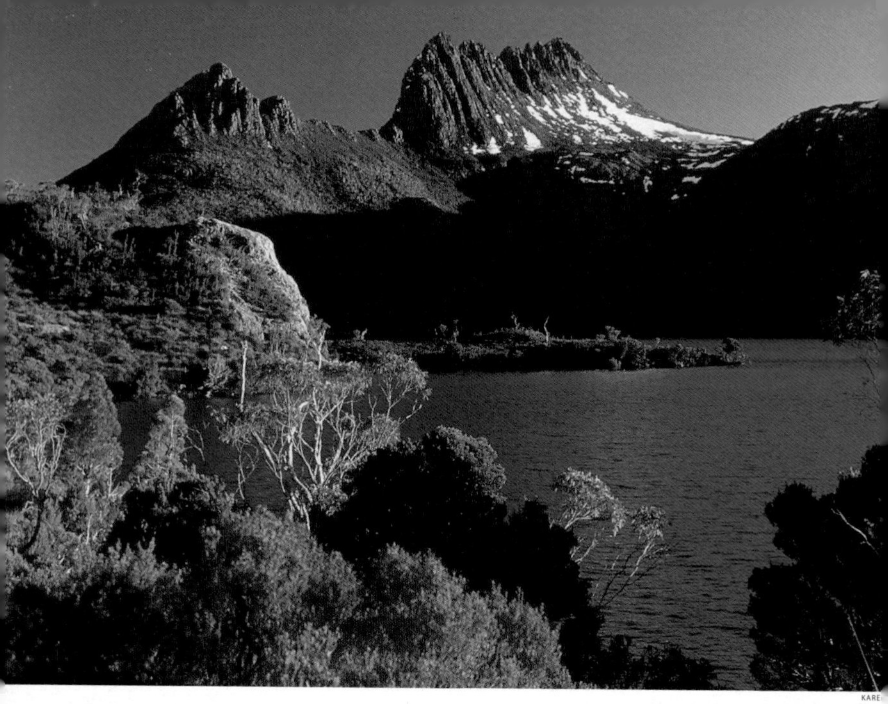

KARE

Bushwalk across Tasmania's incredibly beautiful and very rugged **Cradle Mountain-Lake St Clair National Park** (p649)

Seek out some excellent opportunities to fish, hike and surf around **Marrawah** (p640)

GARETH MCCORMACK

GRANT DIXON

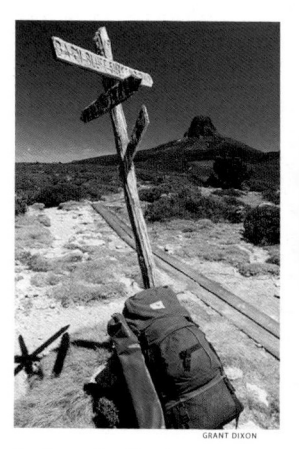

Look out for the signposts along the spectacular **Overland Track** (p649)

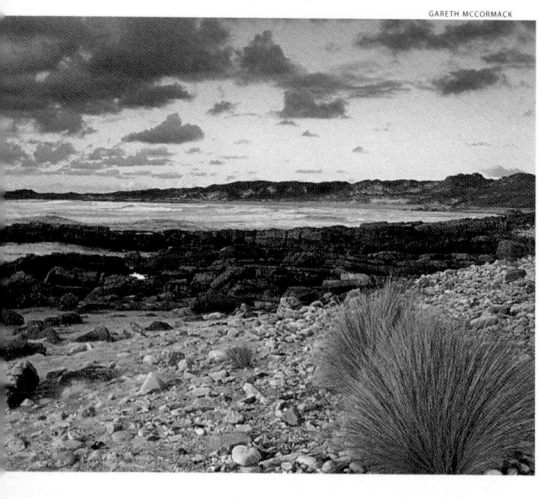

to the surrounding **reserve** (🕐 10am-4pm), with impressive panoramas.

From October to April, **Bruny Island Charters** (☎ 6293 1465; www.brunycharters.com) conducts highly recommended three-hour tours of the island's stunning southern coastline, taking in rookeries, seal colonies, bays, caves and towering sea cliffs. Trips leave the Adventure Bay jetty at 11am daily and it costs $70/30/200 per adult/ child/family; for $130/90 per adult/child the company offers a full-day tour from Hobart including transfers, the cruise and meals. Bookings are essential.

Sleeping & Eating
Adventure Bay is the main accommodation area, but there are places to stay throughout the island. Alonnah is the other main settlement.

There is no longer a hostel on the island – budget accommodation and good-value cabins can be found at the two caravan parks at Adventure Bay. **Captain James Cook Memorial Caravan Park** (☎ 6293 1128; Adventure Bay Rd; camp/caravan sites $12/15 for 2, on-site vans $32-40, cabins $80) has good facilities and a wonderful location opposite the beach. Fishing charters can be organised here. Further along the same road is **Adventure Bay Holiday Village Caravan Park** (☎ 6293 1270; adventurebay@tassie.net.au; camp/caravan sites $12/14 for 2, on-site vans $32, cabins $50-95), also in a great waterfront position.

Explorers' Cottages (☎ 6293 1271; www.bruny island.com; Lighthouse Rd; d $95, additional adult/child $12.50/8) In a secluded location south of Luna-wanna on the way to the lighthouse, these six cottages offer excellent self-contained accommodation. Each spacious unit can sleep six and has a lounge and kitchen, log fires, two bedrooms and an outdoor area.

Morella Island Retreats (☎ 6293 1131; www .morella-island.com.au; 46 Adventure Bay Rd; d $160-260) For something really special, book one of the unique secluded cottages at this fabulous complex a few kilometres north of Adventure Bay (they also have beachfront cottages down by The Neck). Cottages range from luxury retreats for couples (complete with garden bath and hammock for two) to family-sized holiday homes. All are self-contained, and the facilities, design and décor are superb. Prices are reduced for stays of more than one night.

There are free bush camping areas in the national park (park passes required). There's one at Jetty Beach, north of Cape Bruny Lighthouse, on a beautiful sheltered cove; others are at Cloudy Bay. You can also camp for free outside the national park on the beach at the southern end of The Neck.

The best place on the island for a meal is the **Hothouse Cafe** (Morella Island Retreats; meals $7-20). In a converted hothouse set in delightful gardens and with magnificent views of over the isthmus, you can order breakfast and tasty meals such as fish, curry, pasta, nachos and burgers, as well as fine coffee and wine. In Adventure Bay, beside the general store, is the **Penguin Tearoom** (☎ 6293 1352; Adventure Bay Rd; meals $6-12), an inviting old-style café serving light fare.

Getting There & Around
There are frequent daily **ferry services** (☎ 6272 3277). There's no charge for foot passengers; a car costs $21 return, $26 on public holidays and public holiday weekends; motorcycles cost $11 and bicycles $3. At least two buses operated by **Hobart Coaches** (☎ 13 22 01; www.metrotas.com.au) connect with the ferry at Kettering each weekday, but the ferry terminal on Bruny Island is a long way from anywhere and travellers will need their own transport.

For those without their own set of wheels, **Bruny Island Ventures** (☎ 6229 7465) offers a day trip from Hobart taking in the island's sights for $115/85 per adult/child, including transport and lunch.

CYGNET
☎ 03 / pop 800

Named 'Port de Cygne Noir' (Port of the Black Swan) by Rear Admiral D'Entre-casteaux after the numerous swans spotted on the bay, this small town is now known as Cygnet. The surrounding area has many orchards – fruit grown here includes apples, stone fruits and berries – and there is fruit-picking work for backpackers from November to March. The region also offers excellent fishing, bushwalking and good beaches with safe swimming conditions.

Sleeping & Eating
Huon Valley Backpackers (☎ 6295 1551; www.nom adsworld.com; 4 Sandhill Rd, Cradoc; camp sites $10 per person, dm/f $19/65, tw & d $45) Off the Channel Hwy

TASMANIA

5km north of town, this hostel has decent rooms, good facilities and a great view from the large communal area. It's especially busy and crowded here from November to May, when the friendly host helps backpackers find fruit-picking work.

Cygnet Guest House (☎ 6295 0080; 89 Mary St; s/d $85/95) This welcoming B&B has large, attractive rooms in a Heritage-listed building. Prices include cooked breakfast. Downstairs is the Old Bank Teashop, serving light meals such as soup, nachos and scones.

Hartzview Vineyard Homestead (☎ 6295 1623; www.hartzview.com.au; 70 Dillons Rd, Gardners Bay; d $145, additional person $33) An excellent three-bedroom house is available at this secluded vineyard, on the road between Woodbridge and Gardners Bay. The winery is open to the public, offering extensive tastings of wine and fruit liqueurs.

There are three pubs in Cygnet offering food and rooms, plus a good number of cafés. The top pick is **Red Velvet Lounge** (☎ 6295 0466; 87 Mary St; meals $8-12), a funky wholefood store and café with delicious food (sushi, Turkish pide with antipasto fillings, vegetable lasagne). It also offers takeaway wood-fired pizzas of an evening from Wednesday to Sunday.

HUONVILLE
☎ 03 / pop 1708
Named after Huon de Kermadec, second in command to D'Entrecasteaux, this small, busy town on the picturesque Huon River is another apple-growing centre. The valuable softwood, Huon pine, was first discovered here.

The **visitors centre** (☎ 6264 1838; hounville@ tasvis info.com.au; Esplanade; ☺ 9am-5pm) is by the river. Also here is the booking desk for **Huon River Jet Boats** (☎ 6264 1838; www.huonjet.com), which offers jet-boat rides ($50/32 per adult/child) and morning river cruises ($28/15).

At Grove, 6km to the northeast, is the **Huon Apple & Heritage Museum** (☎ 6266 4345; 2064 Main Rd; adult/child/family $5/2.20/14; ☺ 9am-5pm Sep-May, 10am-4pm Jun & Aug), which has displays on 500 types of apples. Not far away is **Dorans Jam Factory** (☎ 6266 4377; Pages Rd; ☺ 10am-4pm), where you can see jam being made, taste and purchase some, and also eat at JJ Cafe (the spiced apple butter is a taste sensation).

Two kilometres northwest of Huonville is **Matilda's of Ranelagh** (☎ 6264 3493; www.matildas ofranelagh.com.au; 44 Louisa St, Ranelagh; d $140-200), a luxurious, adults-only guesthouse with beautifully decorated rooms and the 'goldie gang' (a meet-and-greet team of five golden retrievers).

GEEVESTON
☎ 03 / pop 827
Geeveston is an important base for the timber industry and also the gateway to the Hartz Mountains National Park and the popular Tahune Forest AirWalk. The **Forest & Heritage Centre** (☎ 6297 1836; tasvisinfo.com.au; Church St; ☺ 9am-5pm) incorporates the visitors centre, comprehensive displays on all aspects of forestry and a gallery where local craftspeople have taken to wood with artistic fervour. To enter the forest room and gallery costs $5/3/15 per adult/child/family.

If you have your own transport, head 29km out of town to the **Tahune Forest Reserve**, where there are camping and picnic areas, plus a popular Huon pine walk on the banks of the Huon River. A much-publicised and very popular recent addition to the area is the **Tahune Forest AirWalk & visitors centre** (☎ 6297 0068; adult/child/family $9/6/26; ☺ 9am-5pm), a 620m-long elevated stroll between 25m and 45m above the ground, through the canopy of the forest where you can enjoy panoramic views. There is disabled access to the walk, and a good café at the visitors centre.

On the way back to Geeveston, take the Arve Loop Rd to see the **Big Tree**, indeed a very large *Eucalyptus regnans*.

Back in Geeveston, call in to **Ma Pippins** (☎ 6297 0099; Church St; lunch $5-15), a friendly, cosy café, for lunch or coffee and cake.

HARTZ MOUNTAINS NATIONAL PARK
This national park, classified as part of the World Heritage Area, is popular with weekend walkers and day-trippers as it's only 84km from Hobart. The park is renowned for its rugged mountains, glacial lakes, gorges, alpine moorlands and dense rainforest. The area is subject to rapid changes in weather, so even on a day walk take waterproof gear and warm clothing.

There are some great views from the **Waratah Lookout** (24km from Geeveston) –

look for the jagged peaks of the Snowy Range and the Devils Backbone. Other good walks include tracks to **Arve Falls** (20 minutes return), **Lake Osborne** (40 minutes return) and the more challenging **Hartz Pass** (3½ hours return).

DOVER
☎ 03 / pop 489

This picturesque fishing port, 21km south of Geeveston on the Huon Hwy, has some fine beaches and excellent bushwalks. In the 19th century the processing and exporting of Huon pine was Dover's major industry.

Dover is the region's main tourist base and has good accommodation options. If you have your own vehicle and are heading further south, it's a good idea to buy petrol and food supplies here.

Cruises in the area can be arranged on the historic **Olive May** (☎ 6298 1062), a 120-year-old, 42ft-long Huon pine vessel, at the office on Bayview Rd.

Sleeping & Eating
Far South Backpackers (☎ 6298 1922; www.farsouth wilderness.com.au; Narrows Rd, Strathblane; dm from $22) One of the finest hostels in Tasmania is signposted off the highway at Strathblane, a few kilometres south of Dover. It has a superb waterfront bush setting, quality accommodation including excellent kitchen and lounge, a strong environmental focus, plus bikes and kayaks for rent. In the low season it's often booked by groups, so it's worth calling ahead; pick-up can be arranged from the TassieLink bus stop in Strathblane.

Dover Beachside Tourist Park (☎ 6298 1301; www.dovercaravanpark.com.au; Kent Beach Rd; camp/ caravan sites $15/18 for 2, on-site vans/cabins $33/65) This well-maintained park has an excellent location opposite a sandy beach, friendly owners, plenty of greenery and good facilities.

Riseley Cottage (☎ 6298 1630; www.riseleycottage .com; 170 Narrows Rd, Strathblane; s/d $75/105) Not far from Far South Backpackers is this lovely guesthouse, with warm, hospitable owners and a great garden setting on a hill overlooking the water and bushland reserve. It's good value, with breakfast included in the price and three-course dinners by prior arrangement for only $35.

Driftwood Holiday Cottages (☎ 6298 1441; www .farsouth.com.au/driftwood; Bayview Rd; d $150-200, extra adult $40-50) Choose between modern, self-contained studio units or two large houses that accommodate four to eight guests at this central complex. All the accommodation has a veranda or outdoor area from which to enjoy the great bay views.

Dover Woodfired Pizza (☎ 6298 1905; Main Rd; meals $10-17; ☺ Wed-Sun) Easily the best eating option in town is this cosy pizza-pasta restaurant, offering traditional and gourmet wood-fired pizzas as well as filling pasta dishes.

HASTINGS
☎ 03 / pop 300

The **Hastings Cave & Thermal Springs** (☎ 6298 3209; Hastings Caves Rd; open 9am-5pm Mar-Apr & Sep-Dec, to 6pm Jan & Feb, 10am-4pm May-Aug), with a modern visitors centre and café, attract travellers to this once-thriving logging and wharf town, 21km south of Dover. The spectacular cave is situated in the lush vegetation of the Hastings Caves State Reserve, 10km inland from Hastings and well signposted from the Huon Hwy. Guided **cave tours** (adult/child/family $15/7.30/37 incl entry to pool) leave on the hour, the first an hour after the visitors centre opens and the last an hour before it closes.

Behind the visitors centre is a **thermal swimming pool** (adult/child/family $4.40/2.20/11), filled daily with warm water (28°C) from a thermal spring.

Two companies offer adventure-caving tours in the area, and no experience is necessary (equipment supplied; bookings essential). The **PWS** (☎ 6298 3209) runs tours of **King George V Cave** (3-/6-hr tour $76/149) and **Entrance Cave** ($55), which is also known as Mystery Creek Cave, and has a thriving glow-worm population. A wilder experience of Entrance Cave is offered by **Southern Wilderness Eco Adventure Tours** (☎ 6297 6368; $55; tours ☺ 1.15 & 6.15pm); its bus leaves from outside the Dover Hotel.

LUNE RIVER
A few kilometres southwest of Hastings is the tiny settlement of Lune River. From here you can take a scenic 7km, 1½-hour ride on the **Ida Bay Railway** (☎ 03-6223 5893; Main Rd; adult/child/family $20/10/50). There are trains to the lovely beach at Deep Hole Bay at 12.30pm and 2.30pm daily from late December to Easter, and every Sunday and Wednesday for the rest of year.

TASM

The most southerly drive you can make in Australia is along the 19km gravel road from Lune River to **Cockle Creek** and beautiful **Recherche Bay**. This is an area of spectacular mountain peaks and endless beaches, ideal for camping and bushwalking. It's also the start (or end) of the challenging **South Coast Track**, which, with the right preparation and a week or so to spare, will take you all the way to Port Davey in the southwest. See Lonely Planet's *Walking in Australia* for more detailed information.

TASMAN PENINSULA

The Arthur Hwy runs from Hobart through Sorell and Copping to Port Arthur, 100km away. The peninsula is famous for the convict ruins at Port Arthur and for its magnificent 300m-high cliffs, beautiful beaches and bays, and stunning bushwalks, much of which now constitutes the Tasman National Park.

The region's **visitors centre** (☎ 03-6251 2371; portarth@tasvisinfo.com.au; 10am-5.30pm Mon-Fri, 1-5pm Sat, noon-5pm Sun) is in the entrance building of the Port Arthur historic site. Information on the region is available online at www.portarthur-region.com.au.

Getting There & Around
TassieLink (☎ 1300 300 520; www.tigerline.com.au) connects Hobart and the Tasman Peninsula, but the timetable is geared more to students than to travellers. There's a weekday bus service between Hobart and Port Arthur ($20, 2¼ hours) during school terms, and two services three days a week in school holidays. Buses stop at all the main towns on the peninsula.

Those without their own transport might prefer to join a coach tour out of Hobart run by **Tigerline Coaches** (☎ 1300 653 633; www.tigerline.com.au); full-day tours cost from $60/38 per adult/child.

Once or twice a week, **Port Arthur Cruises** (☎ 03-6231 2655; www.portarthurcruises.com.au; adult/child $120/85) has a morning ferry service from Hobart to Port Arthur. The price includes transport (coach from Port Arthur back to Hobart) and entry to the historic site.

Activities
The following operators offer activities on the Tasman Peninsula:

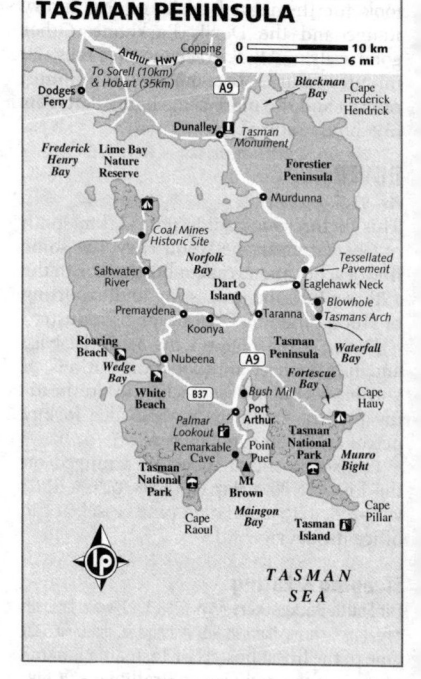

TASMAN PENINSULA

Blackaby's Sea Kayak Tours (☎ 03-6267 1508) One day tours of the historic site and surrounds for $185, plus multiday trips exploring the peninsula.
Eaglehawk Dive Centre (☎ 03-6250 3566; www.eaglehawkdive.com.au; 178 Pirates Bay Dr, Eaglehawk Neck) Underwater explorations, diving courses and equipment rental.
Hire it with Denis (☎ 03-6250 3103; hirewithdenis@hotmail.com; 6 Andersons Rd, Port Arthur) Rental of canoes, kayaks, bikes, tents and lots more.
Personalised Sea Charters (☎ 03-6250 3370; seachart@southcom.com.au; 322 Blowhole Rd, Eaglehawk Neck) Takes small groups on fishing and sight-seeing trips for around $100/500 per group per hour/day.

EAGLEHAWK NECK TO PORT ARTHUR
Near Eaglehawk Neck are the incredible coastal formations of the **Tessellated Pavement**, the **Blowhole**, **Devils Kitchen**, **Tasmans Arch** and **Waterfall Bay**. South of Port Arthur is **Remarkable Cave**.

There are some spectacular walks in the **Tasman National Park**, including Waterfall Bay (1 to 1½ hours return), Cape Raoul (1½ hours to the lookout, 5 hours return to the cape) and Cape Hauy (5 hours return).

Peninsula Tracks by Peter and Shirley Storey provides detailed notes and is available from the information centre.

You can visit the remains of the **penal outstations** at Eaglehawk Neck, Koonya, Premaydena and Saltwater River, and the restored ruins at the **Coal Mines Historic Site**. The *Convict Trail* booklet ($5.50), available from the visitors centre, covers the peninsula's key historic sites.

The **Tasmanian Devil Park** (☎ 03-6250 3230; Arthur Hwy, Taranna; adult/child/family $16/8/50; ☼ 9am-5pm) is a wildlife rescue centre with plenty of native birds and animals besides devils. There are scheduled animal feedings, plus shows featuring birds of prey.

The **Bush Mill** (☎ 03-6250 2221; www.bushmill.com.au; Arthur Hwy; adult/child/family $16/8/40; ☼ 9am-5pm daily, to 4pm Sun-Fri Jul-Aug), just to the north of Port Arthur, features a steam railway and pioneer settlement set in scenic bushland.

Sleeping

Eaglehawk Neck Backpackers (☎ 03-6250 3248; 94 Old Jetty Rd, Eaglehawk Neck; camp sites/dm $6/15) In a peaceful location down Old Jetty Rd to the west of the isthmus you'll find this small and friendly hostel. On offer is a small area for tents, simple rooms and bike rental for guests ($5).

Fortescue Bay Campground (☎ 03-6250 2433; Tasman National Park; camp sites $11) This remote and captivating area has very good facilities (including a small kiosk selling basic supplies) and is 12km off the highway on an unsealed road. National park entry fees apply in addition to camping fees; book ahead for the summer holiday period.

Lufra Hotel (☎ 03-6250 3262; Pirates Bay Dr, Eaglehawk Neck; s/d $66/80) There are great views from the water-facing rooms at this modernised hotel, perched above Tessellated Pavement. The rooms are pretty standard but comfortable and good value. Downstairs you'll find a public bar serving simple counter meals and a dining room with upmarket menu choices (mains $18 to $25).

Fox and Hounds Inn (☎ 03-6250 2217; www.foxtas.com; Arthur Hwy, Port Arthur; motel s/d $104/112, units $112, additional person $18) You can't miss this mock-Tudor complex, not far north of the historic site. Accommodation is in simple motel rooms or two-bedroom self-contained units, and the restaurant here serves good choices (dinner mains $14 to $27), from

Cajun chicken to rack of lamb, in a 'ye olde English' atmosphere.

Norfolk Bay Convict Station (☎ 03-6250 3487; www.convictstation.com; Arthur Hwy, Taranna; d $120) Overlooking Little Norfolk Bay, this historic 1838 building offers warm and cosy B&B. The knowledgeable hosts can help you decide what to explore in the area, or you can simply relax here and enjoy the great water views.

Osprey Lodge (☎ 03-6250 3629; www.view.com.au /osprey; 14 Osprey Rd, Eaglehawk Neck; d $180) Spoil yourself here in luxurious surrounds, not far from a peaceful beach. You can choose from a suite or self-contained unit, but you may find yourself spending a lot of time in the wonderful guest lounge, with its idyllic views. The price includes full gourmet breakfast and pre-dinner wine and cheese.

Eating

See Sleeping (earlier) for details of dining options at the Lufra Hotel in Eaglehawk Neck and the Fox and Hounds Inn. The **Officers' Mess** (☎ 03-6250 3635; 443 Pirates Bay Dr, Eaglehawk Neck; meals $5-12) offers light lunches and takeaways, and has a well-supplied store.

Eaglehawk Cafe (☎ 03-6250 3331; Arthur Hwy, Eaglehawk Neck; lunch under $12, dinner mains $19-25) Eclectic décor, a laid-back, social feel, and a menu of tempting dishes emphasising local produce are the attractions of this memorable café-gallery. Hours can be somewhat erratic so it's worth booking.

Mussel Boys (☎ 03-6250 3088; Arthur Hwy, Taranna; meals $7-20) As you would expect of a café-restaurant with such a name, the speciality here is mussels, oysters and other fresh seafood. Choose from chowder, fish and chips, prawn and scallop kebabs or salmon and scallop fettuccine. If you're just after a snack, they do toasted sandwiches and Devonshire teas, too. Dinner is served here on Thursday, Friday and Saturday nights.

PORT ARTHUR

☎ 03 / pop 170

In 1830 Governor Arthur chose the Tasman Peninsula as the place to confine prisoners who had committed further crimes in the colony. He called the peninsula a 'natural penitentiary' because it was connected to the mainland by a strip of land less than 100m wide, called Eaglehawk Neck. To deter escape, ferocious guard dogs were

TASM

chained in a line across the isthmus and a rumour circulated that the waters on either side were shark-infested.

Between 1830 and 1877, about 12,500 convicts served their sentences at Port Arthur. For some it was a living hell, but those who behaved often lived in better conditions than they had endured in England and Ireland.

The historic township of Port Arthur became the centre of a network of penal stations on the peninsula but was much more than just a prison town, with fine buildings and thriving industries built on convict labour, including shipbuilding, coal mining, shoemaking and brick and nail production.

Australia's first railway literally 'ran' the 7km between Norfolk Bay and Long Bay: convicts pushed the carriages along the tracks. A semaphore telegraph system allowed instant communication between Port Arthur, the penal outstations and Hobart. Convict farms provided fresh vegetables, a boys' prison was built at Point Puer to reform and educate juvenile convicts, and a church (today one of the most readily recognised tourist sights in Tasmania) was erected.

Port Arthur was reintroduced to tragedy in April 1996 when a gunman opened fire on visitors and staff, killing 35 people and injuring several others. The gunman was finally captured after burning down a local guesthouse and subsequently imprisoned. There is now a poignant memorial garden at the site.

The **Port Arthur Historic Site** (☎ 1800 659 101; www.portarthur.org.au; adult/child/family $22/10/50; tours and buildings 🕙 9am-5pm, grounds 🕙 8.30am-dusk) is among Tasmania's premier tourist attractions. The visitors centre includes an information counter, café, restaurant and gift shop. Downstairs is an excellent interpretation gallery, where you can follow the convicts' journey from England to Tasmania. For disabled visitors, some areas of the site require assisted access, and a courtesy buggy can be arranged; inquire at the visitors centre.

Guided tours of the site (included in the entry fee) are worthwhile and leave regularly from outside the visitors centre. You can visit all the restored buildings, including the Lunatic Asylum (now a museum and café) and the Model Prison.

The admission ticket, valid two consecutive days, also entitles you to a short harbour cruise circumnavigating (but not stopping at) the **Isle of the Dead**. Should you wish to visit this island on a 40-minute guided tour to see the remaining headstones and hear some of the stories, it costs an additional $6.60/5.50/20 per adult/child/family. Note that the cruises and Isle of the Dead tours don't operate in August.

Another extremely popular tour at the site is the 90-minute **ghost tour** (adult/child/family $14/8.60/37) by lamplight, which leaves from the visitors centre nightly at dusk and takes in a number of historic buildings, with guides telling of some rather spine-chilling occurrences.

Tasmanian Seaplanes (☎ 6250 1077; www.tas-seaplane.com) is based at the site and offers scenic seaplane flights starting at $80/40 per adult/child for 20 minutes.

Sleeping & Eating

Roseview Youth Hostel (☎ 6250 2311; roseview@southcom.com.au; Champ St; dm/d $19/45) With a great location at the edge of the Port Arthur site, this YHA hostel has OK facilities and crowded dorms but a rough-around-the-edges charm. To get here, continue 500m past the Port Arthur turn-off and turn left at the sign for the hostel into Safety Cove Rd.

Port Arthur Caravan & Cabin Park (☎ 6250 2340; www.portarthurcaravan-cabinpark.com.au; Garden Point; camp/caravan sites $16/18 for 2, dm $15, cabins $75-85) This large, attractive and well-equipped park is about 2km before Port Arthur and not far from a sheltered beach. You can pay entry fees to the Port Arthur site at reception and follow a track around the shoreline from here to the historic site.

Comfort Inn Port Arthur (☎ 6250 2101; www.portarthur-inn.com.au; 29 Safety Cove Rd; s/d $90/100) The rooms here are nothing special but the location, at the perimeter of the historic site, is excellent. There are also good dining options here. The **Convict Kitchen** (meals $12-16) serves up standard pub dishes such as schnitzel, roast and steak, and also has a kids' menu, while the **Commandant's Table** (mains $17-24) offers more formal dining and menu options to match (eg seared salmon fillet, oven-roasted lamb).

Sea Change Safety Cove (☎ 6250 2719; www.safetycove.com; 425 Safety Cove Rd; d $120-140) Whichever way you look from this recommended guesthouse there are fantastic views – of peninsular cliffs, the neighbouring beach or of bushland. It's 5km south of Port Arthur, just off the sandy sweep of Safety Cove Beach. There are a couple of B&B rooms, plus a large, homey self-contained unit that can sleep five.

At the historic site there are a few food options, including the Museum Coffee Shop in the Old Asylum and Port Café, a pricey place in the visitors centre serving café food and the usual takeaway suspects. **Felons** (☎ 6251 2310; mains $17-22), also in the visitors centre and with the catchy slogan 'dine with conviction', is a good choice before you head off on a ghost tour. It's an upmarket dinner spot serving carefully prepared meals with a seafood emphasis.

Back on the highway, almost opposite the turnoff to the historic site, is **Bites n' Berries** (☎ 6250 2227; Tasman Hwy; meals under $10; 🖳), serving a decent selection of salads and light meals such as nachos and focaccia, plus excellent desserts.

MIDLANDS

English trees and hedgerows give Tasmania's Midlands an English-countryside feel. The area's agricultural potential contributed to Tasmania's rapid settlement, and coach stations, garrison towns, stone villages and pastoral properties soon sprang up as convict gangs constructed the main road between Hobart and Launceston. Fine wool, beef cattle and timber milling put the Midlands on the map and these, along with tourism, are still the main industries.

The course of the Midland Hwy (called the Heritage Highway in many tourist publications) has changed slightly from its original route and many of the historic towns are now bypassed, but it's worth making a few detours to see them. The website www.heritagehighway.com.au has information on the towns along the route.

Getting There & Around
Redline Coaches (☎ 1300 360 000; www.tasredline .com.au) runs along the Midland Hwy several times daily and you can be dropped off at any of the main towns provided you're not travelling on an express service. The fare from Hobart to Launceston is $25, and

the journey takes around 2½ hours. Fares from Hobart/Launceston are: to Oatlands $14/18; to Ross $19/13; and to Campbell Town $21/11.

OATLANDS
☎ 03 / pop 585
Oatlands has the largest collection of Georgian architecture in regional Australia, with many buildings dating from the 1830s – in the main street alone there are 87 historic buildings. The helpful **visitors centre** (☎ 6254 1212; oatlands@tasvisinfo.com.au; 85 High St; 🕙 9am-5pm) is among the historic buildings of the main street.

Much of the sandstone for Oatlands' early buildings, including that used for the 1829 **courthouse** (Campbell St), came from the shores of **Lake Dulverton**, now a wildlife sanctuary. The nearby **Callington Mill** (☎ 6254 0039; Mill Lane; 🕙 9am-4pm) is undergoing a lengthy restoration – there's not a lot to do except for a vigorous climb of the 15m-high mill tower and a browse of the **doll collection** (admission $2) in the main house.

An unusual way to explore Oatlands is to go on one of Peter Fielding's **ghost tours** (☎ 6254 1135; 7 Gay St; adult/child $8/4; 🕙 8pm Apr-Sep, 9pm Oct-Apr). Peter also offers one-hour day tours ($5) on demand on Saturday and Sunday.

The town's two pubs, **Kentish Hotel** (☎ 6254 1119; 60 High St; s/d $30/50) and **Midlands Hotel** (☎ 6254 1103; 91 High St; s/d $35/45), offer just OK rooms and meals. The Kentish gets a better recommendation for its en suite rooms and better menu selections.

Much of the accommodation in Oatlands is of the more expensive colonial type, where 'convict-built' is ironically regarded as a mark of historical excellence. Attractive **Oatlands Lodge** (☎ 6254 1444; 92 High St; s/d $90/ 110) is one such convict-built building, now home to a B&B in pretty gardens. **Blossom's Georgian Tea Rooms** (☎ 6254 1516; 116 High St; meals $4-9) exudes old-fashioned warmth and is a good place for a cuppa and light meal (the homemade scones are great).

ROSS
☎ 03 / pop 266
This ex-garrison town, 120km from Hobart, is wrapped firmly in colonial charm and history. It was established in 1812 to protect travellers on the main north-south

road and was an important coach staging post. The **visitors centre** is in the **Tasmanian Wool Centre** (☎ 6381 5466; taswoolcentre@tassie.net .au; Church St; ☼ 9am-6pm, to 5pm in winter) and runs guided walks around Ross (minimum eight people; bookings essential).

The convict-built **Ross Bridge** (1836) is a well-photographed Ross landmark. Daniel Herbert, a convict stonemason, was granted a pardon for his detailed work on the 184 panels decorating the arches. In the heart of town are crossroads that can lead you in one of four directions: 'temptation' (represented by the Man-O-Ross Hotel), 'salvation' (the Catholic church), 'recreation' (the town hall) and 'damnation' (the old jail).

Historic buildings include: the 1832 **Scotch Thistle Inn** (Church St); the **old barracks** (Bridge St), now a private residence; the 1885 **Uniting Church** (Church St); **St John's Anglican Church** (Church St) built in 1868; and the **post office** (26 Church St) dating back to 1896.

The **Tasmanian Wool Centre** (☎ 6381 5466; Church St; admission by donation; ☼ 9am-6pm, to 5pm in winter) has a heritage museum, wool displays and a craft shop.

The **Ross Female Factory** (admission free; ☼ 9am-5pm) was one of only two female prisons in Tasmania during the convict period, and today only one building is still standing. There's little to see inside, but the descriptive signs and stories give a good idea of what life was like for these women. Walk to the site along the track near the Uniting Church, next to the visitors centre.

Sleeping & Eating

Ross Caravan Park & Cabins (☎ 6381 5224; Bridge St; camp/caravan sites $12/15 for 2 people, cabins $30-50) Next to Ross Bridge, this is a pleasant, well-maintained park, and the five cabins (sleep up to four; cooking facilities are provided; bathroom facilities are shared) are the best-value accommodation deal in town.

Man-O-Ross Hotel (☎ 6381 5445; Church St; s/d $60/80) This lovely old sandstone hotel has decent-standard rooms, but they're a bit pricey given that bathroom facilities are shared and breakfast isn't included. Good lunches and dinners ($14 to $20) are served in the dining room, which has a log fire in the cooler months, or outside in the leafy courtyard.

Ross Bakery Inn (☎ 6381 5246; www.rossbakery .com.au; Church St; s/d $85/115) You can wake up

to brekky fresh from a 100-year-old wood-fired oven if you stay in this friendly 1830s coaching house, attached to the excellent Ross Village Bakery. The rooms are cosy and well equipped and there's a guest lounge with open fire, but the bakery's menu is probably the top drawcard. Be sure to try one of its 'cannonballs' – dough filled with savoury treats – and to leave room for a sweet indulgence.

Somercotes (☎ 6381 5231; www.somercotes.com; off Mona Vale Rd; d $150) This superb historic estate, 4km south of Ross, was established in 1823 and offers accommodation in attractive outbuildings set in lovely gardens. The cottages have kitchens, TVs and log fires, and breakfast provisions are supplied.

CAMPBELL TOWN
☎ 03 / pop 755

Another former garrison settlement, Campbell Town is 12km north of Ross. It boasts many examples of early **colonial architecture**, including the 1836 convict-built **Red Bridge**, **St Luke's** Church of England (High St) dating from 1835, the 1840 **Campbell Town Inn** (100 High St) and the 1834 Georgian façade of **Foxhunters Return** (132 High St).

Stay among all the history at the **Grange** (☎ 6381 1686; www.thegrangecampbelltown.com.au; High St; s/d $100/135), a rather grand-looking guesthouse built in 1847 and set in lovely gardens. Easily the best choice in town to fill rumbling tummies is bustling **Zeps** (☎ 6381 1344; 92 High St; meals $8-25), serving brekky, panini, pizza and pasta throughout the day, with additional blackboard specials (eg porterhouse steak, grilled blue eye) of an evening.

EAST COAST

Tasmania's scenic east coast is known for its long sandy beaches, fine fishing and mild, sunny climate.

Exploration and settlement of the region, found to be most suitable for grazing, proceeded rapidly after the establishment of Hobart in 1803. Offshore fishing, and particularly whaling, also became important industries, as did tin mining and timber cutting. Many of the convicts who served out their terms in the area stayed on to help the settlers lay the foundations of the fishing, wool, beef and grain industries, still significant in the region today.

The region's best features are the major national parks of Maria Island and Freycinet. The spectacular scenery around Coles Bay shouldn't be missed, and Bicheno and Swansea make for pleasant seaside stays.

Getting There & Around
BICYCLE
Cycling along the east coast is one of the most enjoyable ways of seeing this part of Tasmania. Traffic is usually light and the hills are not too steep, particularly if you follow the coastal highway from Chain of Lagoons to Falmouth, both to the east of St Marys.

BUS
Redline Coaches (☎ 1300 360 000; www.tasredline .com.au) runs a weekday service between Launceston and Bicheno ($28, 2¾ hours) via Swansea ($22, 2 hours) along the Midland Hwy and inland linking roads. You can also catch a weekday service from Hobart and change at Campbell Town for the east coast services (there may be a considerable wait).

TassieLink (☎ 1300 300 520; www.tassielink.com.au) has a weekday service from Hobart to Swansea ($22, 2½ hours) via Richmond ($5.20, 40 minutes), Orford ($14, 1½ hours) and Triabunna ($15, 1¾ hours) – it operates only three times a week during school holiday periods. It also has a service from Hobart to Orford, Triabunna, Swansea and on to Bicheno ($26, 3 hours) and St Helens ($38, 3¾ hours) two to four times a week.

TassieLink also has a service between Launceston and Bicheno ($25, 2½ hours) via the A4 and St Marys ($18, 2 hours), running two to four times a week.

Broadby's (☎ 03-6376 3488), also operating as Suncoast, has services between St Marys and St Helens and other small towns in the northeast.

Neither Redline nor TassieLink services the Freycinet Peninsula. For this route you must rely on **Bicheno Coach Service** (☎ 03-6257 0293), which runs from Bicheno to Coles Bay (p613). This service connects with Redline and TassieLink services at the Coles Bay turn-off, but it's worth making a booking. The fare from Hobart to the Coles Bay turn-off is around $25, from Launceston it costs $27.

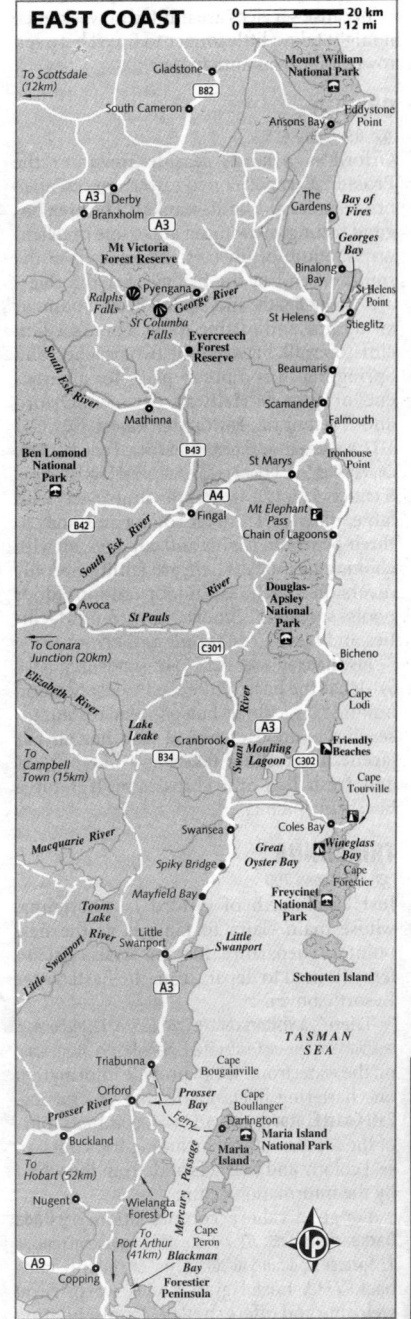

TASMANIA

Because services are limited at weekends, it might take a little longer to travel between towns than you anticipate.

ORFORD

☎ 03 / pop 485

Orford is a small seaside town on the Prosser River (named after an escaped prisoner caught on its banks). The area has good fishing, swimming and some excellent walks. South of town (signposted from the southern end of the bridge over the river) are **Shelly Beach** and **Spring Beach**, popular swimming and surfing spots. There's a 2km cliff-top walk between the two beaches, and Spring Beach is a pretty place for a barbecue or picnic. Halfway between Orford and Triabunna, **Eastcoaster Resort** (☎ 6257 1172; www.eastcoaster.com.au; Louisville Point Rd; camp/caravan sites $15/19 for 2 people, s/d motel $90/110, cabins & cottages $110-180) is a sprawling place with large, older-style motel rooms and one- to three-bedroom cabins and cottages, all with cooking facilities. There are family-friendly diversions such as indoor and outdoor pools, spa, tennis court, playground facilities and both a restaurant and tavern.

Just Hooked (☎ 6257 1549; Tasman Hwy; mains $11-18), at the back of the East Coast Seafood building, is a small but popular restaurant serving seafood dishes. It also has an adjacent store selling takeaways like burgers and fresh fish and chips – perfect for a beachside picnic.

TRIABUNNA

☎ 03 / pop 700

Just 8km north of Orford is Triabunna, whose main claim to fame is as the new point of departure for the Maria Island ferry (it used to depart from the Eastcoaster Resort; above).

There's a **visitors centre** (☎ 6257 4772; triabunna@tasvisinfo.com.au; cnr Charles St & Esplanade; ☽ 10am-4pm) on the waterfront. It can provide information on chartering boats for fishing or cruising. **East Coast Ecotours** (☎ 6257 3453) conducts tours of the local coastline, including trips out to a seal colony and Maria Island, from the wharf by the information centre.

For good-value accommodation, try **Udda Backpackers** (☎ 6257 3439; udda@southcom.com.au; 12 Spencer St; dm/d $16/36). This excellent, laid-back YHA hostel gives you a warm rural welcome and offers spotless rooms, inviting common areas and home-grown vegies for sale. Call ahead to arrange pick-up from the Triabunna bus stop.

MARIA ISLAND NATIONAL PARK

This secluded island features some magnificent scenery, including fossil-studded sandstone and limestone cliffs, sandy beaches, forests and fern gullies. Various brochures are available from the information centre in the old commissariat store (close to where the ferry docks are), including brochures for the Bishop & Clerk peaks walk, the Fossil Cliffs and tips for enjoying the island by bicycle.

Maria Island is very popular with birdwatchers, and also with hikers and mountain bikers. Forester kangaroos and Cape Barren geese are a common sight during the day. Visitors require a national park pass.

The marine life around the island is also diverse and plentiful, making for some spectacular snorkelling and diving – two of the best spots, both protected by a marine reserve that extends around the island's northwest coast, are at the ferry pier and further south at Painted Cliffs.

From 1825 to 1832, **Darlington** was Tasmania's second penal colony (the first was Sarah Island near Strahan). The remains of the penal village, including the **commissariat store** (1825), the **mill house** (1846) and the **coffee palace** (1888), are well preserved and easy to explore. There are no shops on the island so bring all your own supplies (and no, the 'coffee palace' doesn't serve coffee!).

The new, four-day **Maria Island Walk** (☎ 03-6227 8800; www.mariaislandwalk.com.au) is a guided walk of the island, with an emphasis on its nature and history. The price ($1450) includes transfers from Hobart to the island, all meals, and accommodation (in beachfront tent camps and an historic house in Darlington). There are two trips a week from January to April.

For independent visitors, there are **camp sites** on the island. The main camping area (☎ 03-6257 1420; adult/child/family $4.40/2.20/11) is by the creek to the east of Darlington; there are free sites further south at French's Farm and Encampment Cove (3 to 4 hours' walk from Darlington). The rooms in the **penitentiary** (☎ 03-6257 1420; dm $8.80, 6-bunk rooms $22) at Darlington have been converted into basic bunkhouses. Coin-operated hot showers are available. It's wise to book ahead as the bunk-rooms are popular with school groups.

The Maria Island **ferry** (☎ 0427-100 104) now leaves from the town jetty at Triabunna and runs two to four times daily. The return fare is $25/12 per adult/child; bicycles are carried for $2. It's worth calling ahead to confirm departure times.

SWANSEA
☎ 03 / pop 529

On the shores of Great Oyster Bay, with superb views across to Freycinet Peninsula, Swansea is a popular place for camping, boating, fishing and surfing.

Settled in the 1820s, Swansea has a number of interesting historic buildings, including the original 1860 **council chambers** (Noyes St), still in use, and the red-brick 1838 **Morris' General Store** (13 Franklin St), still trading. The community centre dates from the 1860s and houses a **museum of local history** (☎ 6257 8215; Franklin St; adult/child $3/1; ♡ 9am-5pm Mon-Sat).

At the **Swansea Bark Mill & East Coast Museum** (☎ 6257 8382; 96 Tasman Hwy; adult/child/family $5.50/3.30/14; ♡ 9am-5pm), a restored mill displays working models of equipment used in the processing of black-wattle bark, a basic ingredient used in the tanning of heavy leathers. The adjoining museum features displays of Swansea's early history, including superb old photographs. There's also a café, souvenir shop and some visitors information.

Sleeping & Eating

Swansea Holiday Park (☎ 6257 8177; www.swansea-holiday.com.au; Shaw St; camp/caravan sites $15/18 for 2 people, cabins $55-80) This neat, spruced-up park has a beachfront location signposted off the main road just north of town. On offer are camping sites right on the beach, budget cabins (with kitchen but no bathroom) and fully self-contained units, plus excellent amenities.

Swan Inn (☎ 6257 8899; 1 Franklin St; d $55) Budget beachfront motel units are available here, beside the old pub. You can also get decent pub fare for lunch and a more varied menu at dinnertime, with an emphasis on seafood.

Freycinet Waters (☎ 6257 8080; www.freycinetwaters.com.au; 16 Franklin St; s $100-115, d $110-130) Fresh and bright décor is a feature of this friendly B&B with a definite seaside ambience. Rooms are

well equipped and come with private deck for enjoying the water views.

Tubby & Padman (☎ 6257 8901; www.tubbyandpadman.com.au; 20 Franklin St; d $120-155, additional person $20) This interestingly named property (named for the original owners) has elegant heritage suites in a richly renovated 1840s cottage, or stylish and modern self-contained two-bedroom units set in gardens.

Kabuki by the Sea (☎ 6257 8588; www.kabukibythesea.com.au; Tasman Hwy; s/d $95/140) Now here's something you don't expect to find in eastern Tasmania! Some 12km south of Swansea is this unique complex, enjoying stupendous ocean views from its cliff-top location and offering excellent self-contained units 'with a touch of Japan', plus a restaurant serving simple, well-prepared Japanese or local dishes (or an interesting combination of the two, eg emu teriyaki). Mains are around $20, and there's a range of dinner and accommodation packages available.

Left Bank (☎ 6257 8896; cnr Main & Maria Sts; meals $6-14) Behind the bright red door is one of the east coast's best stops for great coffee and winning café fare in a cheery atmosphere. Choose from breakfast dishes, toasted panini, soup, antipasto, pasta and salads, plus a lemon tart worth travelling miles for!

Kate's Berry Farm (☎ 6257 8428; Addison St; meals $4-10) About 3km south of Swansea is another treat – a friendly farm with stunning views, a store selling fruity jams, sauces and divine ice cream, and a café serving light snacks like cheese platters, Devonshire teas and cakes.

COLES BAY & FREYCINET NATIONAL PARK
☎ 03 / pop 120

The small township of Coles Bay is dominated by the spectacular 300m-high pink granite outcrops called the **Hazards**. The town is the gateway to many white-sand beaches, secluded coves, rocky cliffs and excellent bushwalks in the Freycinet National Park. The park, incorporating Freycinet Peninsula, beautiful Schouten Island and the Friendly Beaches (on the east coast, north of Coles Bay), is noted for its coastal heaths, orchids and other wildflowers, and for its wildlife, including black cockatoos, yellow wattlebirds, honeyeaters and Bennett's wallabies.

This area is a walker's paradise, with walks such as a 27km circuit of the peninsula and many shorter tracks. The best known of these is to famously beautiful **Wineglass Bay**. The walk to the beach itself takes 2½ to three hours return, or you can just head to the Wineglass Bay Lookout for breathtaking views of white sand and crystal-clear water (1½ to 2 hours return, and some 600 steps each way).

Shorter walks include the 500m-long lighthouse boardwalk at **Cape Tourville**, which affords great coastal panoramas (including a less-strenuous glimpse of Wineglass Bay) and is suitable for some wheelchair-users and folks with prams.

On any long walk remember to sign in (and sign out) at the registration booth at the car park. A national parks pass is required.

Information

Park information is available from the helpful **visitors centre** (☎ 6256 7000; freycinet@dpiwe .tas.gov.au; ☻ 8am-5pm May-Oct, to 6pm Nov-Apr) at the park's entrance. In summer, inquire here about free ranger-led activities (eg walks, talks and slide shows).

Coles Bay Trading (☎ 6257 0109; 1 Garnet Ave; ☻ 7am-7pm) is the general store and post office. It has an ATM, and sells groceries and petrol. It also offers bicycle hire ($11/17 for a half-/full-day's rental).

The **Iluka Holiday Centre** (☎ 6257 0115; Coles Bay Esplanade) has its own store (with ATM) and bistro, and sells takeaway food and petrol.

You can hire tents, sleeping bags, fishing rods, canoes, boats and lots more at **Freycinet Rentals** (☎ 6257 0320; 5 Garnet Ave, Coles Bay).

See www.freycinetcolesbay.com for an excellent online guide to the area.

Activities

Aside from all the walks, the following companies offer you the chance to see Freycinet from a different angle:

Freycinet Adventures (☎ 6257 0500; www.adventur estasmania.com; cnr Coles Bay Esplanade & Freycinet Dr) You can participate in a range of great activities through this local company – rock climbing and abseiling (from $90), sea-kayaking (from $50), mountain-biking (from $50) and multiday walks and paddle trips.

Freycinet Air (☎ 6375 1694; www.freycinetair.com.au) Departing from Friendly Beaches airstrip, this company offers scenic flights over the park and great views of Wineglass Bay. Tours start at $82 for a 30-minute flight.

Freycinet Experience (☎ 1800 506 003, 6223 7565; www.freycinet.com.au) From October to April, this Hobart-based company offers four-day guided walks of the peninsula ($1475) with a degree of comfort and style. The price includes food, wine, accommodation and return transport from Hobart.

Freycinet Sea Charters (☎ 6257 0355) Cruises (from 2- to 6-hours' duration) leave daily from Coles Bay jetty to experience the scenery and wildlife of the peninsula and Schouten Island; prices start at around $60. Fishing charters are also available.

Sleeping & Eating

The scenery at the free **camp sites** of Wineglass Bay (one to 1½ hours walk from the car park), Hazards Beach (2 to 3 hours) and Cooks Beach (about 4½ hours) is well worth the walk. There's little reliable drinking water at any of these sites or elsewhere on the peninsula, so carry your own. Campfires are not permitted inside the park.

Richardsons Beach at the national park entrance is the main **camping ground** (☎ 6256 7000; fax 6256 7090; freycinet@dpiwe.tas.gov.au; camp/ caravan sites $5.50/6.60 per person). Facilities here include powered sites, toilets and water, however there are no showers. Camping at Richardsons Beach is extremely popular in summer and sites for the period from mid-December to mid-February are determined by a ballot drawn on 1 October (applications must be made by letter, fax or email before 30 September). During this peak period there is limited tent space available in the designated backpacker camping area (no vehicle access, no bookings taken; camping $5.50 per person), but this fills quickly. Outside of the ballot period, advance bookings are highly recommended for Richardsons Beach.

Iluka Holiday Centre (☎ 6257 0115, 1800 786 512; www.ilukaholidaycentre.com.au; Coles Bay Esplanade; camp/ caravan sites $12/20 for 2 people, on-site vans $60, cabins & units $75-110, additional adult/child $15/10) This large, busy park is well maintained and has good amenities, plus a shop, pub and bakery next door. There are good self-contained cabin options, but it's wise to book ahead. Also here is the popular **Iluka Backpackers** (☎ 6257 0115, 1800 786 512; dm/d $18.50/46), a YHA hostel that's light-on for character but is very clean and has a large kitchen.

Freycinet Rentals (☎ 6257 0320; 5 Garnet Ave, Coles Bay) manages a number of properties in and around Coles Bay – these are primarily self-contained holiday houses that can sleep up to six. Prices range from $110 to $140 for two, with additional guests costing $15 to $30; prices are lower in the off-season and for longer stays. Rates include linen, and the majority of properties have full kitchen, barbecue, laundry, TV and video.

Freycinet Lodge (☎ 6257 0101; www.freycinetlodge .com.au; d $190-325) Situated in the park at the southern end of Richardsons Beach, this lodge has 60 plush cabins with private balconies, some with self-catering facilities, several with disabled access. Activities and guided walks are organised for guests, and both the **Bay** (mains $19-30) licensed restaurant and the cheaper **Richardsons Bistro** (meals $7-20) here enjoy magnificent views.

Edge of the Bay (☎ 6257 0102; www.edgeofthebay .com.au; 2308 Main Rd; d $168-228) About 4km north of Coles Bay, this resort has stylish, modern suites with private deck, and secluded, well-equipped cottages that can sleep five; there's a minimum two-night stay. It offers free use of bikes and dinghies for guests, and there's a quality licensed restaurant, the **Edge** (mains $19-26), open daily for dinner.

Aside from the eateries at the two upmarket resorts, dining options in Coles Bay are limited but good. **Freycinet Cafe & Bakery** (☎ 6257 0272; Coles Bay Esplanade; meals $3-10, pizzas $10-22) offers all-day breakfast, sandwiches, cakes, freshly baked pies, and after 5pm, pizzas. Nearby is **Iluka Tavern** (☎ 6257 0115; Coles Bay Esplanade; meals $9-19), serving standard pub lunches and dinners daily, with a popular bar and occasional live music in summer. **Madge Malloys** (☎ 6257 0399; 7 Garnet Ave, Coles Bay; mains $18-25) has a good reputation for fresh seafood; it also prepares dishes such as eye fillet steak and duck confit.

Getting There & Around
Bicheno Coach Service (☎ 6257 0293; biccoa@vision .net.au) runs buses from Coles Bay to Bicheno, meeting east-coast TassieLink and Redline services at the Coles Bay turn-off. There are up to four services on weekdays and one on Saturday and Sunday. Some services only run if bookings exist and it's wise to book at least the night before. The bus will pick you up from your accommodation if requested. Buses depart in Bicheno from the Bicheno Takeaway (52 Burgess St); in Coles Bay they depart from the general store and run via Iluka Holiday Centre. The fare between Bicheno and Coles Bay is $7.50/14 one way/return; from the turn-off to Coles Bay the fare is $6.30/12.

It's more than 5km from Coles Bay to the national park walking-tracks car park and the buses will drop or pick up passengers at the car park if booked. There is also a morning shuttle bus service between Coles Bay and the walking-tracks car park on weekdays (Saturday and Sunday only if booked); the cost is $3/5 one way/return.

BICHENO
☎ 03 / pop 711

In the early 1800s, whalers and sealers used Bicheno's narrow harbour, called the Gulch, to shelter their boats. They also built lookouts in the hills to watch for passing whales. These days, fishing is still one of the town's major occupations. Bicheno has beautiful beaches and is a good spot to unwind.

Sights & Activities
An interesting 3km **foreshore walk**, from Redbill Point to the blowhole, continues south around the beach to Courland Bay. You can also walk up to **Whalers Lookout** for good views.

There's a **fairy penguin rookery** at the northern end of Redbill Beach. The best way to learn about the birds and avoid overly disturbing them is to take the one-hour **tour** (☎ 6375 1333; $16/8 adult/child) that leaves nightly at dusk from East Coast Surf on the main road; bookings are essential. You can also book **glass-bottom boat tours** (adult/child $15/8) here. There's also a dive operator in Bicheno – **Bicheno Dive Centre** (☎ 6375 1138; www.bichenodive.com.au; 2 Scuba Ct, Bicheno).

For something a little different, **Le Frog** (☎ 6375 1777) offers passenger rides on a three-wheeled trike (a cross between a motorcycle and convertible car) in and around town (with a French driver – hence the name). Prices start at $11 for a 10-minute cruise around Bicheno.

Seven kilometres north of town is the 32-hectare, family-friendly **East Coast Natureworld** (☎ 6375 1311; www.natureworld.com.au; Tasman Hwy; adult/child/family $13/6.60/35; ☼ 9am-5pm), which boasts a walk-through aviary, lots of native animals and a scenic lookout.

A few kilometres south of the animal park is the turn-off to **Douglas-Apsley National Park** (☎ 6257 0107). The park protects a large,

TASMANIA

undisturbed dry eucalypt forest and has a number of waterfalls and gorges; birds and animals are prolific here. There's rough road access to Apsley Gorge in the park's south, where there's a waterhole with excellent swimming.

Sleeping & Eating

Bicheno Hostel (☎ 6375 1651; bichenobackpackers@bigpond.com; 11 Morrison St; dm $17) With its well-designed bunks and young owners, this laid-back hostel is a very good choice for budget accommodation. There are plans for future renovations and expansion.

Bicheno East Coast Holiday Park (☎ 6375 1999; bichenoecholidaypark@bigpond.com; 4 Champ St; camp/caravan sites $15/18 for 2 people, cabins $65-85) This neat, well-maintained park has a central location, all the requisite amenities and a range of old and new cabins for rent.

Beachfront at Bicheno (☎ 6375 1111; beachfront_bicheno@bigpond.com; Tasman Hwy; d $105-125) Comfortable but generic motel units are available at this large, central complex. There are good on-site facilities, including swimming pool, pub and bistro plus a more upmarket restaurant, **Delmare's** (mains $14-19), offering Mediterranean fare such as pizza, pasta and salads.

Bicheno Gaol Cottages (☎ 6375 1430; www.bichenogaolcottages.com; cnr Burgess & James Sts; d $125-150) Impressive colonial accommodation is available here in lovely gardens. One cottage dates from 1845 and was once the jail, one was the old primary school and the third is converted stables. All cottages are self-contained, with breakfast provisions provided. **Mary Harvey's Kitchen** (mains $15-21), in the same pretty grounds as the Gaol Cottages, is a top choice for simple, good-quality meals – lots of seafood, and delectable fresh berry waffles to finish.

For something quick, simple and tasty, **Freycinet Café & Bakery** (☎ 6375 1972; 55 Burgess St) has pies, focaccia and other freshly baked treats, and **Cod Rock Café** (☎ 6375 1340; 45 Foster St) does fish and chips cooked to order. Both places offer pizzas of an evening.

Getting There & Away

The bus stop for TassieLink and Redline services to/from Hobart and Launceston is at the Four Square Store, Burgess St.

Bicheno Coach Service (☎ 6257 0293) has buses to/from Coles Bay ($7.50/14 one way/return)

that stop at the Bicheno Takeaway at 52 Burgess St; timetables are at the visitors centre.

ST MARYS
☎ 03 / pop 538
St Marys is a sleepy little town 10km inland from the coast, near the Mt Nicholas range. You can enjoy the peacefulness of the countryside, visit a number of waterfalls in the area and take walks in the state forest.

In a peaceful, get-away-from-it-all setting, **St Marys Seaview Farm** (☎ 6372 2341; www.seaviewfarm.com.au; Germantown Rd; dm $17.50, cabins s/d $33/55) offers simple, good-value accommodation on a working farm at the end of a dirt track, 8km from St Marys. It's surrounded by state forest and commands magnificent views of the coastline and mountains. There's a kitchen and lounge in the backpackers' cottage, and the cabins have bathrooms.

Crepe-fanciers have been known to go troppo over **Mount Elephant Pancake Barn** (☎ 6372 2263; Mt Elephant Pass; pancakes $8-17), well signposted off the highway north of Bicheno. It's a scenic drive to the café; once here, take your pick from a range of sweet and savoury pancakes.

THE NORTHEAST

It's remarkable that the northeast receives so little attention from visitors: it's seductively close to the Pipers River vineyards, yet it boasts some of Tasmania's most secluded, magnificent white-sand beaches. It encompasses the pretty seaside town of St Helens, the evocatively named Bay of Fires, Mt William National Park and St Columba Falls. A good online source of information is at www.tasnortheast.com.au.

Getting There & Around
Redline Coaches (☎ 1300 360 000; www.tasredline.com.au) runs buses from Launceston to Conara Junction near Campbell Town, then through Fingal and St Marys ($20, 2 hours) to St Helens ($25, 2¾ hours). It also runs a bus to Scottsdale ($12, 1¼ hours) and Derby ($19, 2½ hours).

Broadby's (☎ 03-6376 3488), also operating as Suncoast, runs a weekday return service from St Helens to St Marys (departing

7.30am, $5), and from St Helens to Derby (departing 10.15am, $7). Services depart from either the BP service station or the post office in St Helens – both are on Cecilia St. Phone ahead to confirm times.

TassieLink (☎ 1300 300 520; www.tassielink.com.au) has two services weekly between Hobart and St Helens via the east coast on Friday and Sunday ($38, 4 hours).

ST HELENS

☎ 03 / pop 1800

St Helens, sprawled around Georges Bay, is an old whaling town first settled in 1830. It is the largest town on the east coast. Its interesting and varied past is recorded in the **History Room** (☎ 6376 1744; 61 Cecilia St; adult/child $2/1; 🕑 9am-5pm Mon-Fri, 9am-noon Sat, 10am-2pm Sun), which shares its space and phone lines with the town's **visitors centre**. Next door is the library and **online access centre**.

St Helens is Tasmania's largest fishing port, with a big fleet based in the bay. Visitors can charter boats for game fishing or take a lazy cruise. **Ahoy! Boat Hire** (☎ 0418-140 436) is down on the waterfront, behind the Bayside Inn, and hires out kayaks, canoes, motor boats, sail boats and fishing tackle, plus a pontoon boat complete with barbecue for cruising in style ($35/200 per hour/day, takes six passengers).

Although the town's beaches are not that good for swimming, there are excellent scenic beaches at **Binalong Bay** (12km from St Helens), **Sloop Rock** (14km), **Stieglitz** (7km) and St Helens and Humbug Points. Out on St Helens Point are the spectacular **Peron Dunes**.

About 20km west of St Helens you'll encounter the turn-off to tiny **Pyengana**, worth a detour for a trio of attractions: a pub-in-a-paddock, excellent cheese factory and scenic **St Columba Falls**. At around 90m high, they're among the state's highest falls; there's a 20-minute return walk from the car park to their base.

Sleeping & Eating

St Helens Youth Hostel (☎ 6376 1661; 5 Cameron St; dm/d $17/38) The rooms at this simple, central YHA are nothing flash but the facilities (laundry, bike hire) are good. The hostel, in a converted house, is in a quiet spot but situated only a block from the centre of town.

St Helens Caravan Park (☎ 6376 1290; sthelens cp@hotmail.com; Penelope St; camp/caravan sites $17/22 for 2 people, on-site vans $30-45, cabins $40-90) This park has a pleasant bushland setting to the south of town and good, family-friendly amenities. Basic budget cabins are available, but you'll pay twice as much for the newer, better-equipped models.

Kellraine Units (☎ 6376 1169; 72 Tully St; d/tr $50/70, additional person $17) The best value in St Helens (and possibly in northern Tassie) is this unassuming collection of large, self-contained units. They're next to the highway about 800m northwest of the centre, and each roomy unit has full kitchen, laundry, video, living and dining areas (one has wheelchair access).

Bay of Fires Character Cottages (☎ 6376 8262; bayoffirescottages@bigpond.com; 64 Main Rd; Binalong Bay; d $130, additional adult/child $25/15) In a million-dollar location opposite stunning beaches some 11km from St Helens, these colourful cottages range in size but all have great facilities like private balconies and barbecues, full kitchens and laundry.

Wok Stop (☎ 6376 2665; 57a Cecilia St; meals $4-14) Drop in to this fresh, friendly eatery for your tomato or spinach dhal, satay chicken, lamb korma or one of the other delicious curries on offer. It's opposite the post office and you can eat in (there's outdoor seating) or take away.

Milk Bar Cafe (☎ 6376 2700; 57b Cecilia St; meals $6-12) Right next door to the Wok Stop, this bright, funky place serves up excellent café fare with flair. Choose from tasty brekky options, soup, burgers, salads, nachos and delish cakes.

BAY OF FIRES

From St Helens a minor road heads northeast to meet the coast at the start of the Bay of Fires and continues up as far as The Gardens. The northern end of the bay can be reached on the C843, the road to the settlement of Ansons Bay and Mt William National Park.

Early explorers named the bay after seeing Aboriginal fires along the shore. It's a series of sweeping beaches, rocky headlands, heath lands and lagoons, all part of a coastal reserve. The ocean beaches provide some good surfing and the lagoons safe swimming; it's not advisable to swim in the ocean, due to the many rips.

For those who like their wilderness experiences to involve some element of sophistication, **Bay of Fires Walk** (☎ 03-6331 2006; www.bayoffires.com.au) conducts a fully catered four-day walk ($1365) from Boulder Point south to Ansons Bay. Trips run from October to May, and accommodation includes two nights at the company's magnificent eco-friendly lodge.

There are some beautiful free **camping** spots along the bay, though usually without toilets or fresh water. Particularly recommended are the naturally sheltered beachfront sites at **Policemans Point**, reached via a turn-off just before Ansons Bay.

MT WILLIAM NATIONAL PARK

This little-known park consists of long sandy beaches, low ridges and coastal heath lands. The highest point, Mt William (one to 1½ hours return on foot from the car park), is only 216m high yet provides some fine views. The area was declared a national park in 1973 primarily in order to protect the Forester kangaroo. The activities here include bird-watching and wildlife-spotting, fishing, swimming, surfing and diving.

The impressive **Eddystone lighthouse**, at Eddystone Point, was built of granite blocks in the 1890s. A small picnic spot here overlooks a beach of red granite outcrops, while a short drive away, beside a lovely tannin-stained creek and yet another magnificent arc of white sand and aqua water, is the idyllic **camping ground** of Deep Creek.

Camping in the park is very basic, with only pit toilets, bore water and fireplaces – there's no power and you must bring your own drinking water and wood. Camping is also allowed at four areas at **Stumpys Bay** and **Musselroe Top Camp**.

You can enter Mt William National Park, which is well off the main roads, from the north or the south. The northern end is 17km from Gladstone, while the southern end is 58km from St Helens. Try to avoid driving here at night as that's when animals are most active.

SCOTTSDALE & AROUND

☎ 03 / pop 1904

Scottsdale, the major town in the northeast, services some of Tasmania's richest agricultural and forestry country. The **visitors centre** (☎ 6352 6520; scottsdale@tasvisinfo.com.au; 88 King St; ☉ 9am-5pm) is inside the Forest EcoCentre, an interestingly designed place built by Forestry Tasmania. There's also a café here.

The **Bridestowe Lavender Farm** (☎ 6352 8182; adult/child $4/free Dec & Jan, free Feb-Nov; ☉ 9am-5pm daily Nov-Apr, 10am-4pm Mon-Fri May, Sep & Oct) is near Nabowla, 21km west of Scottsdale. Guided tours are given during the spectacular flowering season over December and January. You can purchase numerous lavender products or sample lavender-flavoured fudge, muffins and ice cream.

Bridport, 21km northwest of Scottsdale, is a popular beach resort where there's plenty of accommodation. The Southern Shipping Company runs a passenger and car ferry from here to Flinders Island (p656) once a week.

Anabel's of Scottsdale (☎ 6352 3277; 46 King St; s/d $90/100) has a high-standard restaurant inside a lovely old Federation home, plus modern motel units behind the house, looking out on a beautiful garden setting. In Bridport, **Bridport Seaside Lodge Backpackers** (☎ 6356 1585; seasidelodge@bigpond.com.au; 47 Main St; dm $19, tw & d 50) is a relaxed YHA hostel-cum-beach-house, with tempting water views from the front porch.

PIPERS RIVER AREA

Travelling west from Bridport on the B82 brings you to the well-known and highly regarded **Pipers Brook** and **Pipers River** wine-producing regions, where there are several wineries with tastings available and cellar-door sales.

Established in 1974, **Pipers Brook** (☎ 03-6382 7527; www.pbv.com.au; 1216 Pipers Brook Rd; tastings $3; ☉ 10am-5pm) is the best-known vineyard in Tasmania and features an architecturally arresting winery, which also houses a **café** (lunch $10-20). The charge for tastings is refunded if you make a purchase – available here are Pipers Brook Vineyard and Ninth Island wines. Also at the estate, visit the new Jansz Wine Room, where you can taste this great range of 'methode Tasmanoise' sparkling wine.

Some 15km away, **Bay of Fires Wines** (☎ 03-6382 7622; 40 Baxters Rd, Pipers River; tastings free; ☉ 10am-5pm) has tastings plus a stylish **restaurant** (lunch $11-20) serving Tasmanian produce both indoors and in its outdoor, vine-covered eating area.

LAUNCESTON

☎ 03 / pop 68,443

Founded by Lieutenant-Colonel William Paterson in 1805, Launceston is Australia's third-oldest city and the commercial centre of northern Tasmania.

Launceston was the third attempt by the British to establish a permanent settlement on the Tamar River and was originally called Patersonia, after its founder. In 1907 the city was renamed in honour of Governor King, who was born in Launceston, England.

Launceston is still behind Hobart in the cosmopolitan stakes, although its appeal to tourists has grown in recent times, with plenty of social invigoration and the opening of new cafés, restaurants and museums. It's a pleasant place to spend a few days, and there are a number of attractions in the surrounding areas.

If you're planning a trip to Launceston in mid-February, coincide your visit with the major summer **Festivale** (www.festivale.com.au), but be sure to book your accommodation in advance. Festivale is a three-day, family-friendly event celebrating food, wine and the arts, staged in City Park.

ORIENTATION

The compact city centre is arranged in a grid pattern around the Brisbane St mall, between Charles and St John Sts. Two blocks north, in Cameron St, there's another public area in the centre of Civic Sq, home to two churches, the town hall, library and police. Waterfront development is happening down on the North Esk River, north of Royal Park, and there's plenty of greenery scattered throughout the town.

INFORMATION

The **visitors centre** (Map pp620–1; ☎ 1800 651 827, 6336 3133; info@gatewaytas.com.au; cnr Patterson & St John Sts; ☺ 9am-5pm Mon-Fri, 9am-3pm Sat, 9am-noon Sun & public holidays) dispenses lots of information on the town and surrounds, and makes bookings for tours accommodation and car rental.

For road maps and motoring information go to the **RACT** (Map pp620–1; ☎ 6335 5633; cnr George & York Sts), and for bushwalking maps and camping gear (sales or rental),

visit **Paddy Pallin** (Map pp620–1; ☎ 6331 4240; 110 George St) or **Allgoods** (Map pp620–1; ☎ 6331 3644; cnr York & St John Sts).

The main **post office** (Map pp620–1; 107 Brisbane St; ☺ 9am-5pm Mon-Fri, 9.30am-1pm Sat) is in the centre of town.

For Internet access, try **iCaf** (Map pp620–1; ☎ 6334 6815; 22 Quadrant Mall) or **Cyber King** (Map pp620–1; ☎ 6334 2802; 113 George St).

SIGHTS
Cataract Gorge

A 10-minute walk west of the city centre is the magnificent Cataract Gorge. Here, near-vertical cliffs line the banks of the South Esk River as it enters the Tamar. The area around the gorge is a wildlife reserve and one of Launceston's most popular tourist attractions.

Two walking tracks, one on either side of the gorge, lead from Kings Bridge up to First Basin, where there's a **swimming pool** (admission free; ☺ Nov-Mar), kiosks and an excellent restaurant. The walk takes about 30 minutes; the northern trail is the easier. The gorge is also worth visiting at night when it's lit up.

Both a suspension bridge and a **chairlift** (☎ 6331 5915; adult/child $6.50/4.50 one way, $8/5.50 return; ☺ 9am-4.30pm) cross the waters of the First Basin. A good walking track leads further up the gorge to Second Basin and Duck Reach (45 minutes each way).

Queen Victoria Museum & Art Gallery

This excellent museum (☎ 6323 3777; www.qvmag.tased.edu.au; adult/child $10/free; ☺ 10am-5pm) has two branches, one at Royal Park and the newest at the revamped Inveresk railyards (just across Victoria Bridge); the admission fee allows entry to both sites.

The **Royal Park site** (Map pp620-1) first opened in the late 19th century and displays the splendour of the period both inside and out. It has exhibitions on the island's Aboriginal inhabitants and Tasmanian fauna, an impressive joss house donated by descendants of Chinese settlers and a **planetarium** (adult/child $5/3; shows ☺ 3pm Tue-Sat). The **Inveresk site** (Map p618) houses a magnificent mixture that includes an art gallery, Aboriginal shell necklaces, stories of Tasmania's migration history and authentic railway workshops. Both sites have cafés.

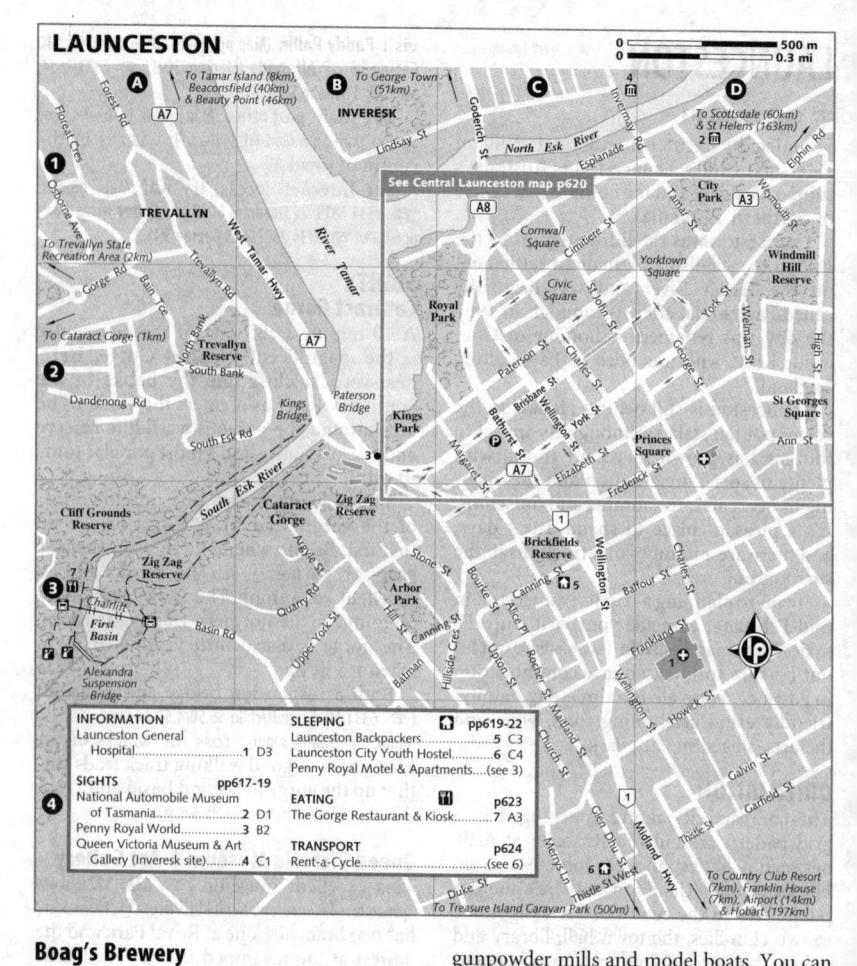

LAUNCESTON

0 ———————— 500 m
0 ———————— 0.3 mi

INFORMATION		SLEEPING	pp619-22
Launceston General		Launceston Backpackers.................5 C3	
Hospital..............................1 D3		Launceston City Youth Hostel........6 C4	
		Penny Royal Motel & Apartments....(see 3)	
SIGHTS	pp617-19		
National Automobile Museum		EATING	p623
of Tasmania.........................2 D1		The Gorge Restaurant & Kiosk..........7 A3	
Penny Royal World...................3 B2			
Queen Victoria Museum & Art		TRANSPORT	p624
Gallery (Inveresk site).........4 C1		Rent-a-Cycle...................................(see 6)	

Boag's Brewery

Boag's beer (the beer of choice for most northern Tasmanians – southerners are loyal to Cascade, brewed in Hobart) has been brewed at this site on William St since 1881. Tours (90 minutes) are operated from the irresistibly named **Boag's Centre for Beer Lovers** (Map pp620-1; ☎ 6332 6300; www.boags.com.au; 39 William St; adult/child $16/12; tours ⏱ 9, 11am Mon-Fri, also 2pm Fri), opposite the brewery. Bookings are essential.

Penny Royal World

The **Penny Royal complex** (Map p618; ☎ 6331 6699; 147 Paterson St; adult/child $20/9.50; ⏱ 9am-4.30pm) has historic exhibits including working 19th-century water mills and windmills,

gunpowder mills and model boats. You can take a ride on a barge or a restored city tram, or take a 45-minute cruise partway up the gorge on a paddle-steamer. Parts of the complex are interesting, but overall the complex struggles to justify the full admission price – you can, however, just pay to see single attractions.

Other Attractions

The **Design Centre of Tasmania** (Map pp620-1; ☎ 6331 5506; cnr Brisbane & Tamar Sts; ⏱ 9.30am-5.30pm), on the edge of City Park, is a retail outlet displaying high-quality work by Tasmanian craftspeople. The **Wood Design Collection** (www.twdc.org.au; adult/child $2.20/1.10) was recently incorporated into the centre.

TASMANIA

The **National Automobile Museum of Tasmania** (Map p618; ☎ 6334 8888; 86 Cimitiere St; adult/child/family $8.50/4.50/22; ☻ 9am-5pm Sep-May, 10am-4pm Jun-Aug) may confuse grammarians with its oxymoronic name but will definitely satisfy automotive enthusiasts. Its ground floor is devoted to classic cars and there's a loft replete with vintage motorcycles.

The **Old Umbrella Shop** (Map pp620-1; ☎ 6331 9248; 60 George St; admission free; ☻ 9am-5pm Mon-Fri, to noon Sat) was built from Tasmanian blackwood timber in the 1860s and has now been classified by the National Trust. It still houses a selection of old umbrellas but most of the shelf space is devoted to various National Trust and Tasmanian goods.

Well signposted some 8km south of the city, **Franklin House** (☎ 6344 7824; 413-419 Hobart Rd; adult/child $7.70/free; ☻ 9am-5pm Sep-May, to 4pm Jun & Aug) is one of Launceston's most attractive Georgian homes. Built in 1838, it is now beautifully restored and furnished by the National Trust.

Parks & Reserves

Launceston has some beautiful public squares, parks and reserves.

The 13-hectare **City Park** is a fine example of a Victorian garden and features an elegant fountain, a bandstand, a **monkey enclosure** (Map pp620-1) and a conservatory. **Princes Square**, between Charles and St John Sts, features a bronze fountain bought at the 1855 Paris Exhibition.

Other public parks and gardens include: **Royal Park**, near the junction of the North Esk and Tamar Rivers; **Punchbowl Reserve** in the city's southeast, with its magnificent rhododendron garden; the **Trevallyn State Recreation Area**, to the west of the Tamar River; and of course Cataract Gorge.

A 10-minute drive north of the city is **Tamar Island** (☎ 6327 3964; West Tamar Hwy; adult/child/family $2/1/5; ☻ 9am-dusk), where you'll find a 2km wheelchair-friendly boardwalk through a significant wetlands reserve, teeming with birdlife.

TOURS

Departing from the visitors centre on weekday mornings is a recommended one-hour guided **historic walk** (☎ 6331 3679; harris.m@bigpond.com; adult/child $15/11; tours ☻ 9.45am Mon-Fri) around the city centre. Bookings are preferred.

Of an evening, you can join an entertaining 90-minute **ghost tour** (☎ 0421-819 373; adult/family $20/45) around the city's back alleys and laneways. Tours depart from the **Royal Oak pub** (Map pp620-1; 14 Brisbane St) at 14 Brisbane St at dusk. Bookings are essential.

The **Coach Tram Tour Company** (☎ 6336 3133) offers three tours that depart from the visitors centre, which also handles bookings. A three-hour tour of the city's sights ($28/20 per adult/child) leaves daily at 10am (and also at 2pm January to April). There is also a half-day tour of the Tamar Valley ($50/39 per adult/child), and a four-hour evening tour of the countryside around Launceston ($55/48 per adult/child), which visits Evandale and Longford and includes dinner.

Tigerline (☎ 1300 653 633; www.tigerline.com.au) has bus tours around Launceston, the Tamar Valley and to Cradle Mountain year-round, starting with a 3½ hour tour of the gorge and city sights for $39/23 per adult/child. **Tiger Wilderness Tours** (☎ 6394 3212; www.tigerwilderness.com.au) also offers tours to the Tamar Valley, Cradle Mountain, Mole Creek and other surrounding destinations.

Based at Home Point in Royal Park, **Tamar River Cruises** (Map pp620-1; ☎ 6334 9900; www.tamar-river-cruises.com.au) offers catered river cruises from September to May. A four-hour cruise takes in the gorge and also travels north to Batman Bridge and costs $60/30/150 per adult/child/family, including lunch. From the same departure point, **Cataract Cruises** (☎ 6334 9900) operates good-value 50-minute cruises of the gorge for $10/6 per adult/child. Cruises operate every hour from 9.30am to 3.30pm.

SLEEPING
Budget

Metro Backpackers (Map pp620-1; ☎ 6334 4505; www.backpackersmetro.com.au; 16 Brisbane St; dm/d/f $20/50/90; 🖳) This is a first-rate YHA hostel with a clean, bright, modern interior and central location. It has excellent facilities, including an outdoor rooftop terrace and barbecue, laundry, bikes for rent and lots of tour information.

Launceston Backpackers (Map p618; ☎ 6334 2327; www.diveros.com.au/launcestonbackpackers; 103 Canning St; dm/s/d $17/38/40; 🖳) Another good budget choice is this large hostel, in a renovated Federation building opposite a park. The communal areas are big and bright and

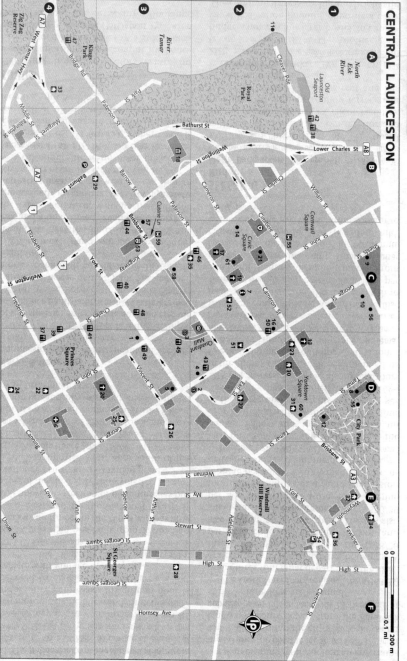

CENTRAL LAUNCESTON

the rooms plain but spacious. Facilities include laundry and plenty of travel info.

Launceston City Youth Hostel (Map pp618; ☎ 6344 9779; tasequiphire@email.com; 36 Thistle St; dm/s/f $15/20/40) Located 2km from the city centre, this rambling hostel building dates from the 1940s. It's a friendly, helpful place but the owner has old-fashioned policies (ie single-sex dorms and no unmarried couples sharing a double room!). The hostel provides an excellent service, hiring touring and mountain bikes, and bushwalking gear.

Irish Murphy's (Map pp620-1; ☎ 6331 4440; www .irishmurphys.com.au; 211 Brisbane St; dm/d $17/35) This is an excellent paddy's pub with good budget accommodation. It only sleeps 20 people so it's a small and friendly place, with good bunks, an appealing kitchen and common room and a lot going on in the bar and restaurant downstairs.

Treasure Island Caravan Park (☎ 6344 2600; 94 Glen Dhu St; camp/caravan sites $18/20 for 2 people, on-site vans $45, cabins $70-75) A few kilometres south of the city in a somewhat noisy location beside the highway, this green ground has all the requisite facilities, including good self-contained cabins.

Mid-Range
GUESTHOUSES & B&BS
Fiona's B&B (Map pp620-1; ☎ 6334 5965; 5/141a George St; s/d $80/100) Hospitable Fiona's offers immaculate modern rooms, some with great views over Launceston. It's in a prime location, just a short walk to the city centre.

Canning Cottages (Map pp620-1; ☎ 6331 4876; 28 Canning St; d $95, additional person $25) It's possible to rent one of two fully furnished two-bedroom colonial cottages here, both of which are cosy and equipped with lots of steep steps and narrow doorways. They can sleep up to four and have lounge and full kitchen, plus breakfast provisions.

Rose Lodge (Map pp620-1; ☎ 6334 0120; 270 Brisbane St; s/d $65/85) This friendly, older-style lodge has comfortable rooms in the western part of town, close to the gorge. The rooms nearest the street are prone to noise from the highway, so try for one at the rear of the house. Prices include cooked breakfast.

Airlie (Map pp620-1; ☎ 6334 2162; airlie.bed.b@big pond.com; 138 St John St; s & d $75-130) Airlie is a small and cosy B&B set in a warm Victorian terrace not far south of the centre. It has five rooms and good guest facilities; prices include continental breakfast.

PUBS, MOTELS & HOTELS
Star Bar Café & Hotel (Map pp620-1; ☎ 6331 6111; 113 Charles St; s/d $65/85) A stylish makeover has seen this old hotel transformed into a boutique-style guesthouse with smallish but modern, well-equipped rooms; downstairs is a fashionable brasserie and bar.

Great Northern Hotel (Map pp620-1; ☎ 6331 9999; nortlaun@ozemail.com; 3 Earl St; s/d $90/100) It's squat and fairly unappealing from the outside, but this hotel has above-average rooms, well appointed with hairdryers, irons and the like. It's surprisingly quiet inside.

TASMANIA

Batman Fawkner Inn (Map pp620-1; ☎ 6331 7222; 35 Cameron St; dm $20, s/d $45/85) Behind the eye-catching historic façade (1824) here is a rabbit-warren of plain, comfortable rooms with bathrooms. The rambling hotel has a central location, good atmosphere and plenty of history.

There are a handful of older-style motels along Brisbane St, overlooking City Park. They won't win any architectural awards but they are well situated and offer decent facilities – try for a front room with a park view. **Parklane Motel** (Map pp620-1; ☎ 6331 4233; www.parklane.trump.net.au, 9 Brisbane St; d $85, apt $105) offers motel rooms and self-contained apartments. The similarly priced **Sandors On The Park** (Map pp620-1; ☎ 6331 2055; sandors@tasparkside.com.au; 3 Brisbane St; d $80-105) offers standard, neat motel rooms and an on-site restaurant.

Colonial Motor Inn (Map pp620-1; ☎ 6331 6588; www.colonialinn.com.au; 31 Elizabeth St; d $100-145) Covered in ivy and once home to a posh school, this large and eye-catching inn has sumptuous colonial décor in its public areas (especially the restaurant and bar). The rooms, however, are plainly modern, although comfortable and well equipped.

Penny Royal Motel & Apartments (Map p618; ☎ 6331 6699; www.leisureinns.com.au; 147 Patterson St; d $134, additional person $30) This attractive complex includes Penny Royal World (the historic attraction) and offers high-standard accommodation in motel rooms or well-equipped apartments not far from the gorge. The apartments are the better choice, especially for larger groups (they can sleep up to eight). Standby rates are excellent value (from $85).

Top End

Waratah on York (Map pp620-1; ☎ 6331 2081; www .waratahonyork.com.au; 12 York St; d $165-220) Set in a lovely Victorian Italianate mansion built in 1862, this opulent and unashamedly old-fashioned B&B has great views over Launceston. It has elegant décor, friendly owners and immaculate rooms (some with spas). Prices include continental breakfast.

Launceston International Hotel (Map pp620-1; ☎ 6334 3434; www.dohertyhotels.com.au; 29 Cameron St; d $180) This large central hotel dominates the lower end of Cameron St and offers all the luxury you'd expect from a place with a fountain in its foyer. It has roomy,

well-equipped rooms and excellent guest services, and downstairs you'll find a bar, café and restaurant.

Country Club Resort (☎ 6335 5707; www.country clubresort.com.au; 10 Casino Rise, Prospect Vale; d from $250) There are so many distractions at this plush resort, a 15-minute drive south of the city, that you may not want to leave. Restaurants, café, bars, casino, swimming pool, golf course, gym, tennis courts, gardens etc. There are also regular package deals that significantly reduce the prices.

Hatherley House (Map pp620-1; ☎ 6334 7727; www.hatherleyhouse.com.au; 43 High St; d $200-250) Exuding style and good taste, this boutique hotel is a striking combination of antique and ultramodern inside a beautifully restored 1830s mansion set in delightful gardens. Great attention to detail has been paid in furnishing the nine suites, with individual décor, artworks, fireplaces and modern bathrooms (some with spa).

EATING
Cafés & Cheap Eats

For a quick bite in cheap and cheerful surrounds, **Morty's Food Hall** (Map pp620-1; cnr Brisbane & Wellington Sts), behind the cinema, has something to suit most tastebuds – shops selling fish and chips, Thai and Chinese dishes, kebabs, baked potatoes and ice creams.

Fresh (Map pp620-1; ☎ 6331 4299; 178 Charles St; meals $5-12) This funky, retro-style vegetarian café, opposite Princes Sq, lives up to its name with a tasty range of interesting light meals and good coffee. Try the potato rosti with spinach, feta and tomato salsa, or the pizza topped with mushrooms, feta and onion marmalade.

Sushi Shack (Map pp620-1; ☎ 6331 4455; 134 York St; sushi dishes $3.50-7.50) This place prepares fresh, mouth-watering sushi to eat in or take away, as well as classic Japanese mains such as tempura, yakisoba and teriyaki dishes for around $15. There's all-you-can-eat sushi ($18) every Wednesday and Thursday night.

Metz (Map pp620-1; ☎ 6331 7277; 119 St John St; meals $7-20) The Metz is a classic all-day café-bar that attracts a mixed crowd of locals who enjoy the casual setting and modern fare – from breakfast through to wood-fired pizzas, and cocktails of an evening.

Konditorei Cafe Manfred (Map pp620-1; ☎ 6334 2490; 106 George St; mains $10-16) A big decision – choose the downstairs café and delicious baked goods (gourmet breads, pastries, tarts), or upstairs for a long al fresco lunch of Mediterranean-influenced fare?

Pasta Resistance Too (Map pp620-1; ☎ 6334 3081; 23 Quadrant Mall; lunch $4.50-6) An excellent lunch spot, this tiny, no-frills place has a great range of freshly made pasta and sauces at piddling prices, which is why it's often packed.

Hotel Tasmania (Map pp620-1; ☎ 6331 7355; 191 Charles St; meals $5-13; ☯ from noon daily) The Saloon at Hotel Tasmania is not exactly flash, but the meals here are incredibly good value. Roast of the day is $5, and with burgers or lasagne for $7 to $8 and steak for $13, budget travellers can't go wrong.

Restaurants

Stillwater (Map pp620-1; ☎ 6331 4153; 2 Bridge Rd, in Ritchies Mill; lunch $10-20, dinner mains $20-30) Set in a stylishly renovated 1830s flour mill beside the Tamar is Stillwater, the recipient of many restaurant awards and one of Tasmania's finest eateries. By day it's a relaxed café churning out breakfast (smoked salmon bagels, home-made muesli) and lunch (roast pumpkin pizza, Thai lamb salad). Of an evening the restaurant struts its stuff, offering predominantly seafood and meat dishes using fresh local produce. Book ahead, as it's deservedly popular.

Fee & Me (Map pp620-1; ☎ 6331 3195; 190 Charles St; 3-/4-course dinner $55/65) Foodies should stay two nights in Launceston, if only to sample both Stillwater and Fee & Me, the city's other acclaimed restaurant. Set in the National Trust–registered Morton House, this elegant restaurant specialises in fine dining and an interesting menu structure – all dishes are small and most diners choose between three and five courses, depending on appetite. Book ahead.

Gorge Restaurant (Map p618; ☎ 6331 3330; Cliff Grounds; lunch $7-15, dinner mains $23-26) At Cataract Gorge's First Basin, this pretty restaurant has undoubtedly the best setting in Launceston. It offers light lunches (seafood chowder, salads, pasta) and dinners (fish, duck breast, rack of lamb) and attentive service. There's also a popular kiosk here serving drinks, ice creams, pies and other cheap snacks.

Down at the revitalised Old Launceston Seaport, waterfront development has seen the opening of busy new restaurant-bars, all offering al fresco dining. **JJ's Dockside** (Map pp620-1; ☎ 6331 0711; 27 Seaport Blvd; meals $10-25) has an extensive menu of light lunches, wood-fired pizzas, tapas dishes and more substantial mains (steak, veal, salmon). Nearby, the warehouse-like **Fish n' Chips** (Map pp620-1; ☎ 6331 1999; 30 Seaport Blvd; meals around $10-12) offers simple, affordable fish and chips, seafood salads and antipasto platters.

There are some inexpensive Asian choices scattered around town: **Hari's Curry** (Map pp620-1; ☎ 6331 6466; 150 York St; mains $10-15) has a budget selection of Indian dishes; **Star of Siam** (Map pp620-1; ☎ 6331 2786; cnr Charles & Paterson Sts; mains $12-18) has an extensive menu of Thai specialities; and **Vegiemania** (Map pp620-1; ☎ 6331 2535; 64 George St; mains $11-16) offers Singaporean/Asian vegetarian cuisine.

DRINKING & ENTERTAINMENT

There are a number of good pubs in Launceston, and many offer regular live music.

Hotel Tasmania (Map pp620-1; ☎ 6331 7355; 191 Charles St) If you can ignore the tacky Wild West décor, you'll find the Saloon Bar here isn't bad for a game of pool, a drink or a cheap meal. A mixture of bands and DJs entertain the locals from Wednesday to Saturday nights, and things often get pretty rowdy in the wee small hours.

Irish Murphy's (Map pp620-1; ☎ 6331 4440; 211 Brisbane St) Another themed pub, this excellent watering hole is stuffed full of Emerald Isle paraphernalia and has live music six days a week (not Tuesday), plus bar snacks, a good restaurant and a friendly feel.

Royal on George (Map pp620-1; ☎ 6331 2526; 90 George St) The Royal is a great refurbished pub dating from 1852, enhanced by the addition of the stylishly laid-back Gates Bar. The place spills over with live bands on Friday and Saturday nights, and occasional Sunday jazz. While you're here, grab a pavement table and a plate of the Royal's excellent food.

Lounge Bar (Map pp620-1; ☎ 6334 6622; 63 St John St) Inside a cavernous, atmospheric ex-bank building is one of the most recent additions to the city's nightlife. It's got a cool loungey interior, a vodka bar and snacks on offer, and it hosts regular live music.

GETTING THERE & AWAY
Air

See p579 for flight details. **Qantas** (Map pp620-1; ☎ 13 13 13; cnr Brisbane & Charles Sts) has an office in the centre of town.

Bus

The main bus companies operating out of Launceston are **Redline Coaches** (☎ 1300 360 000; www.tasredline.com.au) and **TassieLink** (☎ 1300 300 520; www.tassielink.com.au), and the new depot for their services is on Cornwall Sq (Map pp620–1) on the corner of St John and Cimitiere Sts).

Redline runs buses to Bicheno ($25, 2½ hours), Burnie ($24, 2¾ hours), Deloraine ($8.70, 1 hour), Devonport ($18, 1½ hours), George Town ($9.10, 45 minutes), Hobart ($25, 2½ hours), Stanley ($37, 4 hours), St Marys ($20, 2 hours), St Helens ($25, 2¾ hours) and Swansea ($22, 2 hours).

TassieLink has a regular city express service linking Launceston with Devonport ($17, 1¼ hours), tying in with the ferry schedules, and Hobart ($24, 2½ hours). It services the north and west from Launceston, including Sheffield ($22, 2 hours), Cradle Mountain ($55, 3 hours), Queenstown ($65, 6 hours) and, after a break in Queenstown, Strahan ($75, 8¾ hours). TassieLink also runs a twice-weekly service between Launceston and Bicheno ($25, 2½ hours) – service is increased to four times weekly in summer.

Tamar Valley Coaches (Map pp620–1; ☎ 6334 0828; 4 Cuisine Lane), off Brisbane St, operates bus services along the West Tamar Valley, stopping at Rosevears ($3.20), Beaconsfield ($6.40) and Beauty Point ($7.20).

Car

There are plenty of car-rental firms in Launceston. All the major firms (ie Budget, Hertz, Europcar, Avis) have desks at the airport, and most also have an office in town. Budget operators include **Economy Car Rentals** (Map pp620–1; ☎ 6334 3299; 27 William St), with prices starting at $31 per day (older cars, rentals of at least seven days), and **Lo-Cost Auto Rent** (Map pp620–1; ☎ 1800 647 060; www .locostautorent.com; 174 Brisbane St), which has a good selection of vehicles and starting rates from $30 to $45 daily for multiday hire.

GETTING AROUND
To/From the Airport

Launceston airport is about 15km south of the city. **Tasmanian Shuttle Bus Services** (☎ 0500 512 009) runs a door-to-door airport service for $10/5 per adult/child. A taxi to the city centre costs about $25.

Bicycle

Seaport Boat & Bike Hire (Map pp620–1; ☎ 6331 8999; hire@jmc.com.au; 26 Seaport Blvd) has bikes for rent (from $10/40 per hour/day), plus canoes ($10/50 per hour/day) and motor-boats ($35/155 per hour/day) for river exploration. Touring bikes are also available for longer-term hire.

Rent-A-Cycle (Map p618; ☎ 6344 9779; tasequip hire@email.com; 36 Thistle St), at the Launceston City Youth Hostel (see Sleeping; p621), has a good range of touring/mountain bikes from $10/15 a day, plus camping equipment for hire and lots of walking advice.

Bus

The local bus service is run by **Metro** (☎ 13 22 01; www.metrotas.com.au); the main departure points are on the two blocks of St John St between Paterson and York Sts. For $3.60 you can buy a daily pass that can be used after 9am Monday to Friday and all day Saturday, Sunday and public holidays. Most routes, however, don't operate in the evenings and Sunday services are limited.

AROUND LAUNCESTON

The Tamar River separates the east and west Tamar districts and links Launceston with its ocean port. Crossing the river near Deviot is Batman Bridge, the only bridge on the lower reaches of the Tamar. The river wends its way through some lovely orchards, pastures, forests and vineyards. The Tamar Valley and nearby Pipers River (p616) are among Tasmania's main wine-producing areas and the dry, premium wines created here have achieved widespread recognition.

European history in the region dates from 1798, when Bass and Flinders discovered the estuary; settlement commenced in 1804. Slowly the valley developed, despite resistance from the Aboriginal people, first as a port of call for sailors and sealers from the Bass Strait islands, and then as a sanctuary for some of the desperate characters who took to the bush during the convict days.

In the late 1870s, gold was discovered at Cabbage Tree Hill, now Beaconsfield, and the fortunes of the valley took a new turn. The region boomed and for a time this was the third-largest town in Tasmania, until the mines closed in 1914.

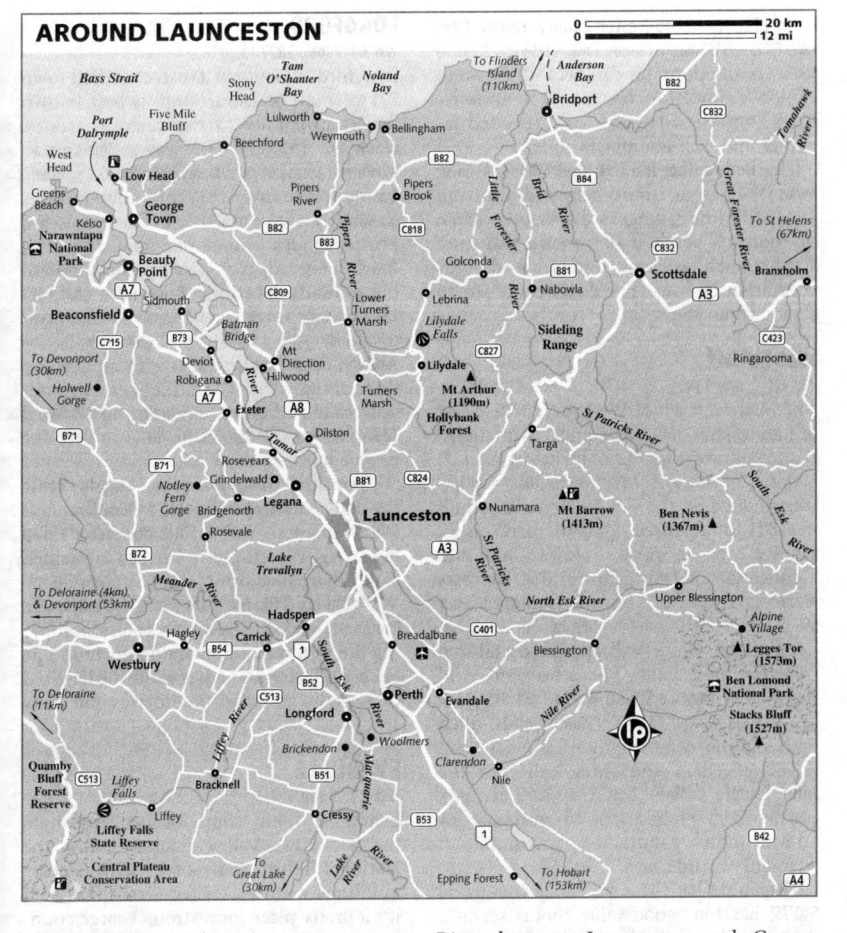

AROUND LAUNCESTON

Scattered around Launceston are a number of historic homesteads, such as the impressive Clarendon and Woolmers, and small towns littered with interesting 19th-century buildings.

Getting There & Around

On weekdays, **Tamar Valley Coaches** (☎ 03-6334 0828; 4 Cuisine Lane, Launceston) has at least two buses a day running up and down the West Tamar Valley, with stops at Rosevears ($3.20), Beaconsfield ($6.40) and Beauty Point ($7.20). At the time of writing a Saturday service was being trialled.

Redline Coaches (☎ 1300 360 000; www.tasredline.com.au) runs three buses Monday to Friday along the eastern side of the Tamar River between Launceston and George Town ($9.10, 45 minutes).

HADSPEN

☎ 03 / pop 1848

Hadspen, 12km southwest of Launceston, is home to some attractive 19th-century buildings, and just west of here is the National Trust–owned **Entally House** (☎ 6393 6201; off Old Bass Hwy; adult/child $7.70/free; ⏲ 9am-12.30pm & 1-5pm), one of Tasmania's best known historic homes. Built in 1819 and named after a Calcutta suburb, it's set in beautiful grounds and creates a vivid period picture of rural affluence. A few kilometres west of Hadspen is the photogenic, ivy-covered **Carrick Mill** (67 Bass Hwy), built in 1846 and now a casual restaurant.

TASMANIA

In Hadspen, **Launceston Cabin & Tourist Park** (☎ 6393 6391; Main St; camp/caravan sites $18/22, cabins $60-75) is an option for campers who wish to explore Launceston, being only 10 minutes' drive from the city. The park has good facilities and well-equipped cabins.

The **Red Feather Inn** (☎ 6393 6331; 42 Main St; mains $19-21) is an atmospheric old inn from 1844 with low ceilings and a rabbit-warren of rooms. There's a fine menu featuring staples such as steak and seafood, plus vegetarian options. The desserts are worth saving room for.

WESTBURY
☎ 03 / pop 1241

The historic town of Westbury, 32km west of Launceston, has a few quirky attractions. It's best known for its **White House** (☎ 6393 1171; King St; adult/child $7.70/free; ☾ 10am-4pm Tue-Sun), situated on the Village Green and built in 1841. It features colonial furnishings, vintage cars, an intricate doll's house and a collection of 19th-century toys. **Westbury Maze** (☎ 6393 1840; Bass Hwy; adult/child/family $5.50/4.50/20; ☾ 10am-5pm Sep-Jul) is a large hedge maze which will appeal to children (or your inner child), plus a tearoom. And the nearby **Pearn's Steam World** (☎ 6393 1414; Bass Hwy; adult/child $5/2; ☾ 9am-4pm) is filled with antique steam engines.

For excellent souvenirs, call into the **John Temple Gallery** (☎ 6393 1666; Bass Hwy; admission free; ☾ 10am-5pm) to purchase or admire John's panoramic photographs of Tasmania's wilderness.

Fitzpatricks Inn (☎ 6393 1153; 56 Bass Hwy; s/d $40/75) has four good-value rooms set in a pretty garden behind a large, white, porticoed building dating from 1833. Each room has a bathroom and tea- and coffee-making facilities. There are some lovely historic homes in the area providing self-contained accommodation, including **Egmont** (☎ 6393 1164; www.ontas.au/egmont; 429 Birralee Rd; d $88, additional adult/child $17/11), a four-bedroom rural retreat dating from 1838 that overlooks the Meander River, some 4km north of town.

Hobnobs (☎ 6393 2007; 47 William St; meals $6-18) is a cheery country café set in a renovated National Trust building. It has an appealing outdoor area and serves a variety of fresh, tasty meals (it's also open for dinner later in the week).

LONGFORD
☎ 03 / pop 2827

Longford, a National Trust–classified town 27km south of Launceston, is best known for its proximity to two historic estates. **Woolmers** (☎ 6391 2230; www.woolmers.com.au; Woolmers Lane; adult/child/family $17/4.50/40; ☾ 10am-4.30pm) was built in 1819 and now nurtures a two-hectare rose garden. The admission price includes a one-hour guided tour of the homestead, plus a self-guided tour of the grounds. Nearby is **Brickendon** (☎ 6391 1383; www.brickendon.com.au; Woolmers Lane; adult/child/family $8.50/3.50/25; ☾ 9.30am-5pm Tue-Sun Sep-Jun), dating from 1824, with an authentic farming village. Both these estates offer self-contained accommodation in restored colonial-era cottages from $145 to $165 for two people.

They don't make places like **Kingsley House** (☎ 6391 2318; Wellington St; d $100, additional adult/child $40/10) anymore, sadly. This character-filled lodge has cheerful, eclectic, self-contained suites that range from large to enormous.

JJ's Bakery & Old Mill Cafe (☎ 6391 2364; 52 Wellington St; lunch $10-17) is a busy eatery occupying the restored old Emerald flourmill. The bakery sells fresh goodies while the licensed café serves up wood-fired pizzas and daily specials.

EVANDALE
☎ 03 / pop 10357

Evandale, 19km south of Launceston in the South Esk Valley, is classified by the National Trust. Many of its 19th-century buildings are in excellent condition and it's a pretty place for a stroll. A large country **market** is held from 10am to 1pm every Sunday.

In keeping with its old-world atmosphere, Evandale hosts the **National Penny Farthing Championships** in February each year, and **Penny Farthing Cycle Tours** (☎ 6391 9101; www.pennyfarthingtours.com.au) offers regular tours of the town on these unique bikes (tours from $49).

Eleven kilometres south of Evandale is the National Trust property of **Tas** (☎ 6398 6220; off Nile Rd; adult/child $7.70/free; ☾ 10am-5pm, to 4pm Jun-Aug), a grand neoclassical mansion built in 1838 and surrounded by impressive parklands.

The **Tourism & History Centre** (☎ 6391 8128; evandale@tasvisinfo.com.au; 18 High St; ☾ 10am-3pm) is home to the **visitors centre**. It's on your left as you enter town (from the north) and has information on the many cottages in and around Evandale.

Clarendon Arms Hotel (☎ 6391 8181; 11 Russell St; s/d $35/65) is a classic country hotel. It has murals downstairs depicting the area's history, good-value meals, budget accommodation (shared facilities) and a leafy beer garden.

Grandma's House (☎ 6381 8088; www.grandmas house.com.au; 10 Rodgers Lane; d $130, additional person $30) is a two-storey, self-contained cottage set in pretty gardens, which can sleep up to seven.

Ingleside Bakery Café (☎ 6391 8682; 4 Russell St; meals $6-13) is a classy place churning out quality baked goods and light, café-style lunches of soups, gourmet sandwiches, pies and so on. The **Dalmeny** (☎ 6391 8988; 14 Russell St; mains $17-20) has a reputation for fine food in relaxed surrounds – it's open for lunch Wednesday to Sunday, and dinner Wednesday to Saturday. The evening pizza selection is impressive.

BEN LOMOND NATIONAL PARK

This 165-sq-km national park, 50km southeast of Launceston, includes the entire Ben Lomond Range and is best known for its skiing facilities. During the ski season (usually early July to late September), a kiosk, tavern, restaurant and hotel are open in the alpine village; lift tickets and equipment hire cost considerably less than they do on the mainland.

The scenery at Ben Lomond is magnificent, whatever the season, and the park is particularly noted for its wildflowers. It's a popular spot for sightseers and walkers as well as skiers, but accommodation is only available during the ski season, at **Creek Inn** (☎ 03-6390 6199; 1 High St, Alpine Village; dm $35, r & units $155).

During the ski season, there's a morning bus service from the Launceston visitors centre to the top of the mountain, returning in the late afternoon; inquire at the visitors centre. Outside the ski season, driving here is your only transport option. The route up to the alpine village from the mountain's base includes Jacob's Ladder, a very steep climb on an unsealed road with six hairpin bends – care should be taken, and snow chains are required in winter.

ROSEVEARS

☎ 03 / pop 160

Rosevears is a tiny, picturesque riverside settlement on a side road off the West Tamar Hwy, north of Launceston. It's definitely one for wine buffs, as it's home to three very good wineries.

Strathlynn (☎ 6330 2388; www.pbv.com.au; 95 Rosevears Dr; tastings $3; ☉ 10am-5pm) is an outlet for Pipers Brook Vineyard (p616) and has wine tastings and sales. Also here is an acclaimed restaurant open for lunch daily (mains around $25).

Not far away is the low-key **St Matthias** (☎ 6330 1700; www.moorilla.com.au; 113 Rosevears Dr; free tastings; ☉ 10am-5pm), the northern vineyard of Hobart's Moorilla Estate (see 'The Author's Choice' boxed text; p585). Here you can snack on cheese and antipasto platters as you sup. Back on the main road, you'll encounter the sizable hilltop headquarters of **Rosevears Estate** (☎ 6330 1800; www.rosevearsestate.com.au; Waldhorn Dr; tastings $2.50; ☉ 10am-5pm), where you can taste and purchase wine, enjoy sweeping views from the upmarket restaurant and also tour the winery ($5, daily at 11.30am; bookings advised).

The other attraction here is of the feathered variety: the **Waterbird Haven Trust** (☎ 6394 4087; Rosevears Dr; adult/child $4/2; ☉ 9am-dusk) is a nonprofit sanctuary for marine birds. And if you haven't overdone it on the vino and fine food, **Rosevears Waterfront Tavern** (☎ 6394 4074; 215 Rosevears Dr) has good meals and a scenic terrace that's a fine place to get acquainted with a beer.

BEAUTY POINT & AROUND

☎ 03 / pop 1176

Beauty Point is where you'll find the fascinating **Seahorse World** (☎ 6383 4111; www.sea horseworld.com.au; Wharf; adult/child/family $15/8/40; ☉ 9.30am-4.30pm), based around a seahorse farm where the tiny critters are grown to supply aquariums worldwide and, eventually it's hoped, the Chinese-medicine market. The facility incorporates an aquarium, displays on the local marine ecology, and a café with outstanding views over the Tamar. Admission includes an interesting one-hour tour of the farm (final tour 3.30pm).

Further north, at the mouth of the Tamar River, are the quiet holiday and fishing resorts of **Greens Beach** and **Kelso**, and south is the once-thriving but now somewhat

TASMANIA

subdued gold-mining town of Beacons-field, still dominated by the façades of its three original mine buildings. Two of these house the **Grubb Shaft Gold & Heritage Museum** (☎ 6383 1473; West St; adult/child/family $8/3/20; ☺ 9.30am-4.30pm Oct-Apr, 10am-4pm May-Sep), a good attraction for families with its hands-on interactive exhibits.

There's a decent selection of accommodation in Beauty Point. **Tamar Cove** (☎ 6383 4375; Main Rd; d from $60), on the way into town, is an old-style motel that's bene-fited from a facelift and the addition of a good restaurant, which has an inviting al fresco terrace. Rooms are comfortable, and there's also a pool.

GEORGE TOWN
☎ 03 / pop 4129

George Town, on the eastern shore of the Tamar River, close to the heads, is historic-ally significant as the site where Lieutenant Colonel Paterson landed in 1804 to estab-lish a beachhead against a feared French occupation, leading to the European settle-ment of northern Tasmania. The **visitors centre** (☎ 6382 1700; georgetown@tasvisinfo.com.au; Main Rd; ☺ 10am-4pm) is on the main road into town.

The **Grove** (☎ 6382 1336; 25 Cimitiere St; adult/child/family $5.50/2.20/15; ☺ 10am-5pm daily Oct-Apr, 10.30am-3pm Sat & Sun May-Sep) is an extensively restored Georgian bluestone residence built in 1835 and now classified by the National Trust. Lunch and light refreshments are available, served in the spirit of the past by staff in period costume.

Seal & Sea Adventure Tours (☎ 6382 3452, 0419-357 028; www.sealandsea.com) offers three- to four-hour cruises in a glass-bottom boat, taking in the seal colony at Tenth Island, for $121/66 per adult/child (less for groups of three or more). The owner will also help organise fishing or dive charters.

A pleasant excursion is to take the **Shuttlefish ferry** (☎ 6383 4479, 0412-485 611) to Beauty Point ($10 return). There are regular sailings from the pier at the end of Elizabeth St, but it's worth calling ahead to find out times.

George Town's excellent **YHA** (☎ 6383 3261; 4 Elizabeth St; dm/d $18/50, tent sites $10) is the best budget accommodation in town; there are also cabins and camping options available in Low Head (see following), plus there

are a few uninspiring but reasonable-value motels in George Town itself.

Your best option for both food and a bed is the **Pier Hotel Motel** (☎ 6382 1300; info@pierhotel.com.au; 5 Elizabeth St; pub room d $55, motels & villas $120-140). At the top of the price scale you'll get modern riverside lodgings in motel units or self-contained villas, or for considerably less you can choose pleas-ant pub-style rooms with shared facilities. The newly renovated dining room here has a stylish interior, outdoor seating and a modernised **pub menu** (meals $8-22).

Good-value **Nanna's Cottage** (☎ 6382 1336; thegrove@intas.net.au; 25 Cimitiere St; s/d $70/85, extra adult/child $20/10), within the gardens of the Grove, provides cosy B&B for up to three people in a self-contained cottage.

LOW HEAD
☎ 03 / pop 431

North of George Town is Low Head, which provides the navigation aids for ships to enter the Tamar. The **pilot station** (☎ 6382 1143; Low Head Rd; adult/child $5/3; ☺ 9am-8pm) is Australia's oldest (built in 1805) and houses an interesting **maritime museum**, cluttered with historical items and displays.

Penguins return to their burrows near the lighthouse daily at dusk and are best encountered via the tours run nightly by **Nocturnal Tours** (☎ 0418-361 860; adult/child $12/7). There's surf at **East Beach** on Bass Strait and safe swimming in the river.

The well-maintained **Low Head Beachfront Holiday Village** (☎ 6382 1000; 40 Gunns Pde; camp/caravan sites $15/18 for 2 people, cabins $60-75) has a great location on East Beach, plus good self-contained cabins and even camping sites with en suites for $20.

At the **Pilot Station** (☎ 6382 1143; Low Head Rd; s/d $70/90, additional adult/child $33/15) you can stay in three roomy, well-equipped cottages, perfect for large groups (they sleep up to eight people).

THE NORTH

Gently rolling hills and farmlands extend from the Tamar Valley north of Launceston and west to the Great Western Tiers. The best way to explore this area is to leave the highways and follow the quiet minor roads through small towns.

Getting There & Around

Redline Coaches (☎ 1300 360 000; www.tasred line.com.au) has several services daily from Launceston to Deloraine ($8.70, 1 hour) and on to Devonport ($18, 1½ hours), Ulverstone ($20, 2¼ hours) and Penguin ($21, 2½ hours), then on to Burnie ($24, 2¾ hours). Some of these services call at the ferry terminal in Devonport.

TassieLink (☎ 1300 300 520; www.tassielink.com.au) runs a daily express service designed to work in with the Bass Strait ferry schedules; it provides an early-morning service from Devonport to Launceston ($17, 1¼ hours) and Hobart ($41, about 4 hours), and an afternoon service in the opposite direction to meet evening boat departures. TassieLink also runs from both Launceston and Devonport to Cradle Mountain via Sheffield, and most of these services continue on to Queenstown and Strahan. See p641 for details.

From Monday to Friday, **Metro** (☎ 13 22 01; www.metrotas.com.au) has regular buses between Ulverstone and Burnie via Penguin.

DEVONPORT

☎ 03 / pop 21,575

Nestled behind the lighthouse-topped Mersey Bluff, Devonport is the terminal for the *Spirit of Tasmania*, vehicular ferries that run between Victoria and Tasmania and New South Wales and Tasmania.

The compact Bluff Lighthouse was built in 1889 to direct the colony's rapidly growing sea traffic and its light is visible up to 27km out to sea. Today, the port is still important and handles much of the export produce from northern Tasmania's rich agricultural areas.

Devonport's visitors are usually arriving or departing rather than staying, but the town is making a big effort to lift its profile and keep tourists here for a day or two.

Information

The busy **visitors centre** (☎ 6424 8176; ttic@ dcc.tas.gov.au; 92 Formby Rd; ☽ 7.30am-5pm or 9pm) is across the river from the ferry terminal. It's open to meet all ferry arrivals; the 9pm closure applies when there are day crossings of the ferry, which arrive at 6pm (daily late December to late January, weekends December to April), otherwise the visitors centre closes at 5pm.

For more information about Devonport and Tasmania in general, particularly on bushwalking and tours, head for the central **Backpacker's Barn** (☎ 6424 3628; www.tasweb.com.au/backpack; 10-12 Edward St; ☽ 9am-6pm Mon-Fri, 9am-noon Sat). It has an excellent bushwalking shop and extensive traveller services, including outdoor equipment hire, storage lockers and showers for travellers.

Internet access is available at the **online access centre** (☎ 6424 9413; 21 Oldaker St), adjacent to the library.

Sights & Activities

The **Tasmanian Aboriginal Culture Centre** (☎ 6424 8250; Bluff Rd; adult/child $3.30/2.20; ☽ 9am-5pm), on the road to the lighthouse, is known as 'Tiagarra' (the Tasmanian Aboriginal word for 'keep'). Established to preserve the art and culture of the Tasmanian Aborigines, it has a rare collection of more than 250 rock carvings, some of which can be seen by following the marked trail on Mersey Bluff.

The **Devonport Maritime Museum** (☎ 6424 7100; Gloucester Ave; adult/child $3/1; ☽ 10am-4.30pm Tue-Sun Oct-Mar, to 4pm Apr-Sep) is in the old harbourmaster's residence near the foreshore and has an interesting display of maritime paraphernalia, including old and new model ships.

The **Devonport Regional Gallery** (☎ 6424 8296; 45-47 Stewart St; admission free; ☽ 10am-5pm Mon-Sat, 2-5pm Sun) is housed in a converted church and has a collection of mainly 20th-century Tasmanian paintings, ceramics and glasswork.

A short distance from the YHA hostel is the National Trust–administered **Home Hill** (☎ 6424 8055; 77 Middle Rd; adult/child $7.70/free; ☽ 2-4pm Tue-Thu & Sat-Sun), former residence of Joseph and Dame Enid Lyons. Joseph Lyons is the only Australian to have been both the premier of his state and prime minister of Australia, and Dame Enid Lyons was the first woman to become a member of the House of Representatives.

The **Don River Railway** (☎ 6424 6335; Bass Hwy; adult/child/family $8/5/20; ☽ trips on the hour 10am-4pm) is 4km west of town on the highway. This popular attraction features a collection of steam locomotives and passenger carriages, and you can ride a vintage train (30-minute return) along the banks of the Don River.

Tours

Tasman Bush Tours (☎ 6423 2335; www.tasmanbush tours.com) is an outfit that operates from

Tasman House Backpackers (see Sleeping) and offers a wide range of tours, from day trips to Cradle Mountain, the Mole Creek caves or Stanley ($53 each) to three-day excursions through Walls of Jerusalem National Park ($490) or six days on the Overland Track ($980); longer trips are fully catered and equipment is supplied.

Sleeping

With ferry crossings now operating daily (and twice daily in high season), Devonport is a much busier place and accommodation can often be hard to come by if you haven't booked ahead. It's especially worth booking if you're travelling from late December to late January.

Inner City Backpackers (☎ 6424 1898; 34 Best St; dm/tw/d $15/30/50) The most central backpacker lodgings in Devonport are here, above Molly Malones Irish pub (see Eating; p631). There are comfortable no-frills rooms on offer (doubles with bathrooms), plus kitchen, lounge and laundry.

Tasman House Backpackers (☎ 6423 2335; www.tasmanhouse.com; 114 Tasman St; dm/tw/d $12/28/39; 🖳) This sprawling, ramshackle hostel has basic budget rooms in converted nurses quarters (doubles have bathrooms). Management is friendly and there are extensive facilities, including trekking tours departing from here (see Tours; p629). It's a 15-minute walk from town and can be accessed from both Tasman and Steele Sts, with the main car park area and entry off Steele St.

MacWright House (☎ 6424 5696; 115 Middle Rd; dm/s $13/19) This well-run YHA hostel, 3km southwest of town, has basic accommodation in a clean and humble old house. From the town centre, it's a 40-minute walk or a five-minute bus ride (No 40).

Abel Tasman Caravan Park (☎ 6427 8794; abel@tigerresortstas.com.au; 6 Wright St; camp/caravan sites $15/20 for 2 people, on-site vans $45, cabins $80) This busy park has friendly managers, decent

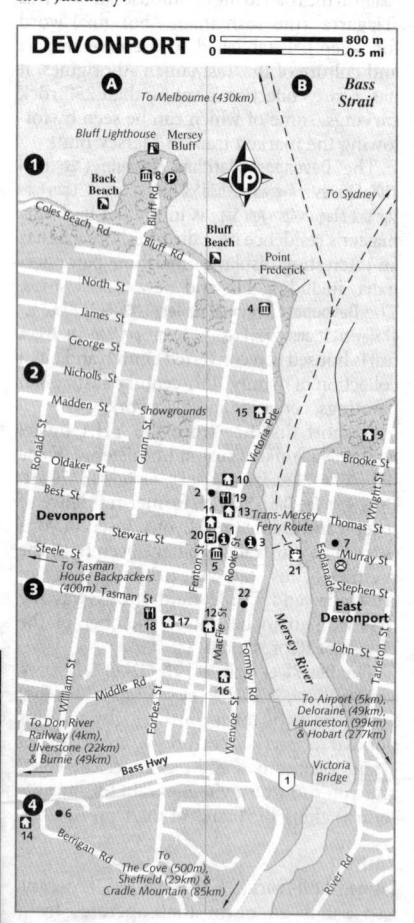

DEVONPORT

To Melbourne (430km)

Bass Strait

To Sydney

TASMANIA

A FOODIE'S TOUR FROM DEVONPORT TO DELORAINE

If you've just rolled off the ferry and are looking to start your tastebud-touring, make a beeline southeast along the Bass Hwy (follow the signs for Launceston). About 8km out of Devonport you'll come upon your first stop, the **House of Anvers** (☎ 6426 2958; Bass Hwy, Latrobe; ☯ 7am-5pm). This house of temptation produces delectable Belgian-style chocolates, and you can watch production, sample and buy. There's a café here and pretty gardens. Breakfast choices include Continental treats like croissants, *pain au chocolat* (of course) or even Rice Bubbles with chocolate milk!

Press on another 30km and you'll encounter **Ashgrove Farm Cheese** (☎ 6368 1105; Bass Hwy, Elizabeth Town; ☯ 9am-5.30pm), a cheese factory where you can learn a little of how cheese is made, plus sample and purchase some great produce (including deli fare for a picnic).

Eight kilometres south of Ashgrove is another worthwhile stop – **Christmas Hills Raspberry Farm** (☎ 6362 2186; off Bass Hwy, Elizabeth Town; ☯ 7.30am-5pm), with an inviting café serving light meals and an awesome array of drinks and desserts featuring (surprise!) raspberries. The desserts menu runs to two pages – just try to choose between the raspberry crepe, sundae, cheesecake, tart, pavlova, ice cream, sorbet, waffles…

From here it's about 6km to Deloraine, and if you feel like continuing this gastronomic *tour de force*, west of Deloraine towards Mole Creek you'll encounter some very good honey producers.

---

amenities and a good beachfront location at the northern tip of East Devonport. Its location (500m to the ferry terminal) means it's especially popular with people catching the early-morning ferry in summer.

River View Lodge (☎ 6424 7357; riverviewlodge@ microtech.com.au; 18 Victoria Pde; s/d with bathroom $65/85, without bathroom$50/60) On the river close to the centre of town, this homey 1877 guesthouse is deservedly popular for its friendliness, good-value rooms and peaceful location. Prices include cooked breakfast.

Gateway Inn (☎ 6424 4922; 16 Fenton St; s/d $100/ 110) Devonport's largest hotel has tidy but characterless rooms in the city centre, plus decent guest services and a café, restaurant and bar on site.

MacFie Manor (☎ 6424 1719; 44 MacFie St; d $95-110) With its Scottish theme and great attention to detail in the décor (antiques, stained glass etc), this inviting B&B in a two-storey Federation building is an excellent option. Next door and under the same management is **Heritage Hill** (s & d $120-130), two spacious and appealing self-contained apartments.

Birchmore (☎ 6423 1336; birch@southcom.com.au; 10 Oldaker St; s $100-110, d $110-120) This first-rate B&B is an oasis of elegance in the centre of town, with immaculate, spacious rooms and attentive owners. Breakfast (included in the price) is served in the conservatory.

Devonport Historic Cottages (☎ 6424 1560; d $140-150, additional person $36) manages two lovely old cottages in town that can sleep four or five. Both **Rosalie Cottage** (66 Wenvoe St)

and **Turton Cottage** (28 Turton St) have period furnishings, log fires, gardens, full kitchen and breakfast provisions. Extras include baltic-lined walls in Rosalie and a four-poster bed in Turton.

Eating

Molly Malones (☎ 6424 1898; 34 Best St; meals $9-20) It wouldn't be a fake Irish pub without the obligatory Guinness on tap, plus a menu of good-value pub standards (roast of the day for $10, bangers and mash, fish and chips). This cavernous pub is a decent choice for food (kids' menu available) and entertainment as the night wears on; there's often live music, especially later in the week.

Essence (☎ 6424 6431; 28 Forbes St; dinner mains $20-24) This strangely suburban-industrial neighbourhood isn't where you'd expect to find Devonport's best restaurant, but you'll be impressed by the menu of carefully prepared local produce: how about the lamb fillets wrapped in vine leaves on sautéed vegetables, or the Atlantic salmon on a warm rocket-and-potato salad? The service and wine list are also first rate. For a meal that's easier on the pocket but just as tasty, come for lunch.

Cove (☎ 6424 6200; 17 Devonport Rd; lunch $10-15, dinner mains $16-28) Just south of town off the road to Latrobe, this modern waterfront restaurant has a great range of interesting dishes (like ocean trout with wasabi mashed potatoes, or sweet potato gnocchi). There's lots of seafood, plus hearty meat and

TASMANIA

vegetarian options – savour the views and food from the outdoor deck.

Bakeries line Rooke St, and the street's northern end has a few interesting eateries, including **Indian Affair** (☎ 6423 5141; 153 Rooke St; mains $15-18), offering, as the name suggests, Indian cuisine. Its neighbours are **Rialto Gallery Restaurant** (☎ 6424 6793; 159 Rooke St; mains $12-18), serving Italian pasta and meat dishes, and **Mallee Grill** (☎ 6424 4477; 161 Rooke St; mains $12-25), definitely one for the carnivores, with a menu heavy on steaks.

Getting There & Away
AIR
For details of flights, see p579.

BOAT
See p579 for details on the *Spirit of Tasmania* ferry services between Melbourne and Devonport and Sydney and Devonport. The **ferry terminal** (☎ 13 20 10) is on the Esplanade, East Devonport. You can't miss the ferries, as they dominate the town when they're in port.

BUS
Redline Coaches (☎ 1300 360 000; www.tasredline .com.au; 9 Edward St) has its terminal opposite Backpacker's Barn. Buses also stop at the ferry terminal when the ferry is in town. Redline runs at least three services daily from Hobart to Launceston, then on to Devonport and Burnie, and return. On weekdays most services continue west to Smithton. The fare from Launceston to Devonport is around $18.

TassieLink (☎ 1300 300 520; www.tassielink.com.au) runs services to Sheffield, Gowrie Park, Cradle Mountain and the west coast, as well as a regular service connecting Devonport, Launceston and Hobart for incoming or outgoing ferry passengers. The arrival and departure point for TassieLink coaches is directly outside the visitors centre.

Maxwells (☎ 6492 1431) runs buses on demand to Cradle Mountain, Lake St Clair, the Walls of Jerusalem, Frenchmans Cap and other hiking destinations. You can arrange the pick-up/drop-off point when making a booking.

Outside the summer period, or if none of the scheduled services suit your needs, you can charter a minibus from Maxwells or the Backpacker's Barn.

CAR
Devonport has plenty of cheap car-rental firms, such as **Lo-Cost Auto Rent** (☎ 1800 802 724; www.locostauto.com.au; 57 Formby Rd) and **Rent-A-Bug** (☎ 6427 9034; www.rentabug.com.au; 5 Murray St), near the ferry terminal. Starting rates for old VW Beetles at both companies are $30 to $45 daily for multiday hire; prices then increase according to the model and age of the cars – see the websites for details.

Major companies have representatives at the airport and ferry terminal.

Getting Around
The airport is 5km east of town. An **airport shuttle** (☎ 6424 6333) operates on weekdays and the fare is $10.

Local buses, operated by **Merseylink** (☎ 1300 367 590; www.merseylink.com.au), run from Monday to Saturday – pick up a timetable at the visitors centre. Merseylink also runs a shuttle service between the hostels and the ferry terminal.

A small passenger ferry departs from a jetty in front of the visitors centre, docking on the eastern side of the river not far from the *Spirit of Tasmania* terminal. It runs on demand from Monday to Saturday ($2 each way).

DELORAINE
☎ 03 / pop 2032
Deloraine is Tasmania's largest inland town and, with its lovely riverside picnic area, superb setting at the foot of the Great Western Tiers, proximity to Cradle Mountain and good amenities, it's a great base from which to explore the surrounding area.

The **visitors centre** (☎ 6362 3471; gwtvc@tasvis info.com.au; 98 Emu Bay Rd; ☺ 9am-5pm), near the roundabout at the top of the main street, incorporates the **folk museum** and **Yarns: Artwork in Silk** (combined entry adult/child/family $7/2/15). 'Yarns' is a four-panel, hand-dyed silk depiction of life in the area, and the audio-visual display (shown every half-hour, 9.30am to 4pm daily) explaining its design and construction (involving some 300 locals) is worthwhile.

Many of the town's Georgian and Victorian buildings have been restored. Structures of interest include **St Mark's Anglican Church** (East Westbury Pl) built in 1859 and, 2km east of town, the 1853 **Bowerbank Mill** (4455 Meander Valley Hwy), now a gallery.

GRANT DIXON

Stay off the beaten track on wild, sparsely populated **Bruny Island** (p599)

Explore the fossil-studded sandstone and limestone cliffs of **Maria Island National Park** (p610)

ROB BLAKERS

LINDSAY BROWN

Visit the convict church at historic **Port Arthur** (p605)

Overleaf:
Head for the tranquil waters of Wineglass Bay and the pink-granite outcrops of the Hazards in **Freycinet National Park** (p611)

ROB BLAKERS

Sleeping & Eating

The visitors centre has information on country guesthouses and self-contained cottages in the area.

Highview Lodge YHA (☎ 6362 2996; bodach@ microtech.com.au; 8 Blake St; dm/d $18/40) Perched on a hillside, this small, homey place is a steep walk north of town but worth the hike for the magnificent views of the Great Western Tiers from the veranda. It's a well-equipped, older-style hostel.

Deloraine Hotel (☎ 6362 2022; Emu Bay Rd; s/d $40/60) Rooms at this grand old 1848 pub with a magnificent wrought-iron veranda are basic but clean and comfortable, and some have a bathrooms. Light breakfast is included in the price. It's a bit of a rabbit warren upstairs, but find your way downstairs to enjoy the cheap pub grub (meals from $6). The other pubs in town also offer budget-style rooms.

Highland Rose (☎ 6362 2634; highlandrose.bb@ bigpond.com, 47 West Church St; s/d $90/95) The name stems from the Scottish owner and the pretty garden, and this hospitable, home-style B&B has two simple, comfortable rooms; price includes a full cooked breakfast, served in the attractive sunroom.

Arcoona (☎ 6362 3443; www.arcoona.com; East Barrack St; s/d from $110/140) For a taste of rural luxury, bed down in one of the elegant rooms at this grand old hilltop home. Guests will love the king size beds, spas (in some rooms), cooked breakfasts, impressive billiards room and pretty gardens.

For hungry travellers, there are pubs, bakeries and takeaways lining the main street. **Deloraine Deli** (☎ 6362 2127; 36 Emu Bay Rd; meals $4-12) is an excellent choice for its café-style fare, including bagels, pies, quiche or a ploughman's lunch.

MOLE CREEK

☎ 03 / pop 213

About 25km west of Deloraine is tiny Mole Creek, and in its vicinity you'll find spectacular limestone caves, apiaries producing leatherwood honey, and an excellent wildlife park. Many of the area's features are now protected within the **Mole Creek Karst National Park**.

Marakoopa Cave, a wet cave 15km from Mole Creek, features two underground streams and a glow-worm display. **King Solomon Cave** is a dry cave with amazing calcite

crystals that reflect light; it has few steps in it, making it the better cave for the less energetic. In the high season, there are at least five tours in each cave daily between 10am and 4pm. A visit to one cave costs $8.80/4.40/22 per adult/child/family, or you can visit both for $14/6.60/33. Current tour times are prominently displayed on access roads, or ring the **PWS** (☎ 6363 5182). Wear warm clothes on the tours (temperatures inside average 9°C).

There are also some magnificent wild caves in the area. **Wild Cave Tours** (☎ 6367 8142; www.wildcavetours.com) offer half-/full-day tours for $75/150 and provide caving gear and guides. Above-ground exploration can be done with **Cradle Wilderness on the Edge** (☎ 6363 1173; www.tasadventures.com/cradlewilderness), offering half-/full-day 4WD tours along remote mountain tracks for $85/120.

The leatherwood tree only grows in the damp western part of Tasmania, so honey made from its flower is unique to this state. At **Stephens Tasmanian Honey** (☎ 6363 1170; Main Rd; ☒ 9am-4pm Mon-Fri), visitors can taste and purchase the sticky stuff.

Off the main road, a few kilometres east of the township, is the first-rate, family-friendly **Trowunna Wildlife Park** (☎ 6363 6162; adult/child $13/6; ☒ 9am-5pm Feb-Dec, 8am-8pm Jan). Here you can view local animals and birds in their natural environment, plus see hand-fed Tassie devils, pat a koala and hold a baby wombat.

Sleeping & Eating

Mole Creek Hotel (☎ 6363 1102; 90 Pioneer Dr; s/d $35/55) This classic small-town, main-street pub has good clean budget accommodation in the form of upstairs rooms with shared facilities; continental breakfast is included in the price. Downstairs is the Tiger Lair café-bar, dedicated to the Tasmanian tiger and serving up hearty portions of pub standards.

Mole Creek Guest House & Restaurant (☎ 6363 1399; sted.mcgh@tassie.net.au; 100 Pioneer Dr; s/d $90/112) Comfortable, heritage-style rooms are available at this friendly 19th-century guesthouse; price includes a full cooked breakfast. The restaurant serves good food from breakfast through to dinner (mains priced from $16 to $20).

Mole Creek Holiday Village (☎ 6363 6124; 1876 Mole Creek Rd; d $90, additional person $20) Just east of Trowunna, this 'village' provides a rustic retreat, with a collection of large, self-contained timber units, all enjoying mountain views from their verandas.

WALLS OF JERUSALEM NATIONAL PARK

This remote national park comprises a series of glacial valleys and lakes on top of the Central Plateau and is part of a World Heritage Area. The park is a favourite of experienced bushwalkers who prefer an isolated and spectacular hiking challenge. The most popular walk in the park is the full-day trek to the 'Walls' themselves (some 6 to 8 hours return); you can also camp in the park.

If you prefer a guided walk, see p578 for details of tour operators – Craclair and Tasmanian Expeditions both run walking trips in the national park.

The easiest access to the Walls is from Sheffield or Mole Creek. From Sheffield head south on the C137 until it meets the B12, just west of Mole Creek. From here (or from Mole Creek), take the B12 west, then the C138 south and finally the C171 (Mersey Forest Rd) to Lake Rowallan; follow this road south to the start of the track.

SHEFFIELD

☎ 03 / pop 982

Sheffield promotes itself as the 'town of murals', due to the fact that since 1986, 32 murals depicting the history of the area have been painted in and around the town, making it a fascinating place for a wander. There are a dozen more murals in the surrounding district. The **visitors centre** (☎ 6491 1036; sheffield @tasvisinfo.com.au; Pioneer Crescent; 9am-5pm Dec-Feb, 10am-4pm Mar-Nov), just off the main street, has maps with mural locations plus information on the area.

A great new attraction in town, and one that will delight kids (and grownups), is the **Tiger's Tale** (☎ 6492 2075; www.tigerstale.com.au; 38a Main St; theatre $5/3/13 adult/child/family; 9am-5pm). It's a unique animatronic theatre and robot display, the work of a local that took some four years to build. The main feature is an amazing 10-minute performance in which the Tasmanian tiger comes to life through computer-controlled robotics.

The scenery around Sheffield is another of its features, with **Mt Roland** (1231m) dominating the peaceful farmlands, thick forests and fish-filled rivers. Nearby is beautiful **Lake Barrington**, a major rowing venue. **Tasmazia** (☎ 6491 1934; 500 Staverton Rd;

A TIGER'S TALE

The story of the Tasmanian tiger (*Thylacinus cynocephalus* or thylacine), a striped carnivore once widespread in Tasmania, currently has two different endings.

Version one has it that thylacines were hunted to extinction by European settlers in the 19th and early 20th centuries, and that the last tiger died in miserable captivity in Hobart's Beaumaris Zoo in 1936. Those who put their faith in the thylacine's extinction point out that no living specimen has been conclusively discovered since then, regardless of hundreds of alleged 'sightings'.

Version two maintains that thylacines continue a furtive existence deep in the Tasmanian wilderness. Advocates of this theory refute that they live in a state of fanciful denial over the tiger's demise, curiously preferring to believe that the more unsubstantiated tiger encounters are reported, the more likelihood of there being a substantiated one.

The physical mystique of a large nocturnal hunter that carried its young in a pouch and had a large, powerful jaw, combined with the conveniently perpetuated enigma of its existence, has made the tiger prime corporate fodder – Tasmanian companies have plastered the animal's picture on everything from beer bottles to television network promos.

Meanwhile, scientists at Sydney's Australia Museum have begun scripting another possible ending to the tiger saga. Kicking off version three, biologists managed to scrape some high-quality DNA off a thylacine pup preserved in alcohol since 1866, and claim to have successfully replicated the DNA. Some scientists involved in the multimillion-dollar programme say they believe the first cloned thylacine pup could be born within a decade, although there are many obstacles. The project has drawn criticism from those who would rather see the money spent on helping currently endangered species, but the scientists seem intent on adding a new twist to the tiger's tale. Visit www.austmus.gov.au/thylacine for lots of information on the Tassie tiger and the cloning project.

adult/child $7/4; ⓨ 10am-5pm), at the wonderfully named Promised Land, near Lake Barrington, combines mazes, a model village, lavender farm and pancake parlour.

Sleeping & Eating

Sheffield Backpackers (☎ 6491 2611; www.sheffield backpackers.com.au; 82 Main St; dm/tw $18/40) Catch up on sleep at this excellent backpackers, with its well-designed bunks, good kitchen facilities, cosy communal area and trip-planning advice from the friendly owners.

Kentish Hills Retreat (☎ 6491 2484; www.kentish hills.com.au; 2 West Nook Rd; d $95-140) On the western edge of town, these modern motel units are attractive and extremely comfortable. The well-equipped units each feature a video and kitchenette; some units have spas, and all have access to an outdoor barbecue area.

Gowrie Park, 14km southwest of Sheffield, is at the foot of Mt Roland, making it an excellent base for walks up the mountain or for a rural retreat. The settlement here is home to a friendly, down-to-earth lodge, **Weindorfers** (☎ 6491 1385; www.weindorfers.com; dm $10, cabins $70, additional person $11), open from October to May. It's well known for its excellent restaurant serving simple, hearty country meals (priced from $10 to $23; dinner reservations recommended). It also has basic budget rooms and self-contained wooden cabins.

Back in Sheffield, central eating options include **Murray's Scottish Scone Shoppe** (☎ 6491 1077; 60 Main St), offering an old-fashioned tearoom experience, or the contrasting **Bossimi's Bakehouse & Café** (☎ 0409-336 740; 55 Main St), a bright modern café serving sandwiches, pies, salads and pasta.

ULVERSTONE & AROUND

☎ 03 / pop 9515

The coastal town of Ulverstone retains a relaxed, uncommercial atmosphere and has good surrounding attractions.

At Gunns Plains, 30km south of Ulverstone, there are entertaining guided tours (on the hour) of the spectacular **Gunns Plains Caves** (☎ 6429 1388; adult/child $10/5; ⓨ 10am-4pm). Also in Gunns Plains is **Wings Farm Park** (☎ 6429 1335; wfp@tassie.net.au; Winduss Rd; adult/child $10/5; ⓨ 10am-4pm), a low-key, family-oriented place where you can interact with farm and native animals, check out reptiles

or the animal nursery. There's also accommodation here (camping and cabins).

Sleeping & Eating

Ulverstone Caravan Park (☎ 6425 2624; 57 Water St; camp/caravan sites $14/16 for 2 people, cabins from $60) Near both the water and the town centre, this large park has plenty of greenery and sheltered camp sites, plus good amenities and a children's playground.

Waterfront Inn (☎ 6425 1599; Tasma Pde; s/d $60/65) Across the River Leven from the town centre, this friendly '70s-style motel has had a facelift and now offers good-value, well-equipped motel units in a peaceful setting (request a waterfront room). There's also an on-site restaurant with a surprisingly good menu.

Ocean View Guesthouse (☎ 6425 5401; 1-3 Victoria St; s $75-130, d $110-150) A friendly new owner manages this elegant, century-old building, only a few minutes' walk from both the beach and the town centre. The rates for the attractive heritage-style rooms include a cooked breakfast.

Pedro's the Restaurant (☎ 6425 5181; Wharf Rd; mains $21-25) Appealingly situated on the riverbank and with seating over the water, popular Pedro's specialises in upmarket fish and seafood dishes (including impressive platters) but there's something for most tastes. If your travel dollar is a little stretched, head next door to the takeaway section for some good-quality fish and chips.

PENGUIN

☎ 03 / pop 2910

The pretty seaside village of Penguin is worth a detour, and there are some good cafés here to tempt you. If you're driving from Ulverstone, take the old Bass Hwy (signposted 'Scenic Route') – as you approach Penguin the countryside takes on a gentrified feel as cottage gardens, a narrow-gauge railway track and the seaside squeeze themselves into the scene. In town, a large concrete penguin stands stolidly on the foreshore and smaller versions adorn items such as rubbish bins along the main street. An **historic train service** runs between Burnie, Penguin and Ulverstone on the second and fourth Sunday of each month, coinciding with Penguin's large **market** (ⓨ 9am-4pm), which features some 170 stalls.

If you like the relaxed feel of the town, treat yourself to a night at the **Madsen Guesthouse** (☎ 6437 2588; katpromo@bigpond.com; 64 Main St; d $110-150), a stylish new B&B in an old bank. The top rate will get you the large, elegantly furnished front room, complete with sea views; other rooms are just as lovely but don't enjoy the view. The price includes breakfast, and adjacent to the guesthouse is a café.

THE NORTHWEST

Tasmania's magnificent northwest coast is as rich in history as it is diverse in scenery. Its story goes back 40,000 years to a time when giant kangaroos and wombats inhabited the area. Aboriginal tribes once took shelter in the caves along the coast, leaving a legacy of rock carvings and middens.

Europeans quickly realised the potential of the region and settlers moved further and further west, building towns along the coast and inland on the many rivers. The area was soon transformed into a vital part of the young colony's developing economy.

The Nut at Stanley and the beautiful beach at Boat Harbour are highlights of this region.

Getting There & Around
AIR
The airport for the region is in Wynyard, and is known as both Wynyard and Burnie airport. See Air on p579 for further information on services to/from the region.

BUS
Redline Coaches (☎ 1300 360 000; www.tasredline.com.au) runs several buses daily from Hobart to Launceston ($25, 2½ hours), then from Launceston along the north coast to Devonport ($18, 1½ hours) and Burnie ($24, 2¾ hours).

From Burnie, you can catch another Redline service (weekdays only) to Wynyard ($3.60, 20 minutes), Stanley ($14, 1 hour) and Smithton ($14, 1½ hours).

From Monday to Friday, **Metro** (☎ 13 22 01; www.metrotas.com.au) local bus services run from Burnie to Wynyard (and also east to Penguin and Ulverstone, $3.20 each).

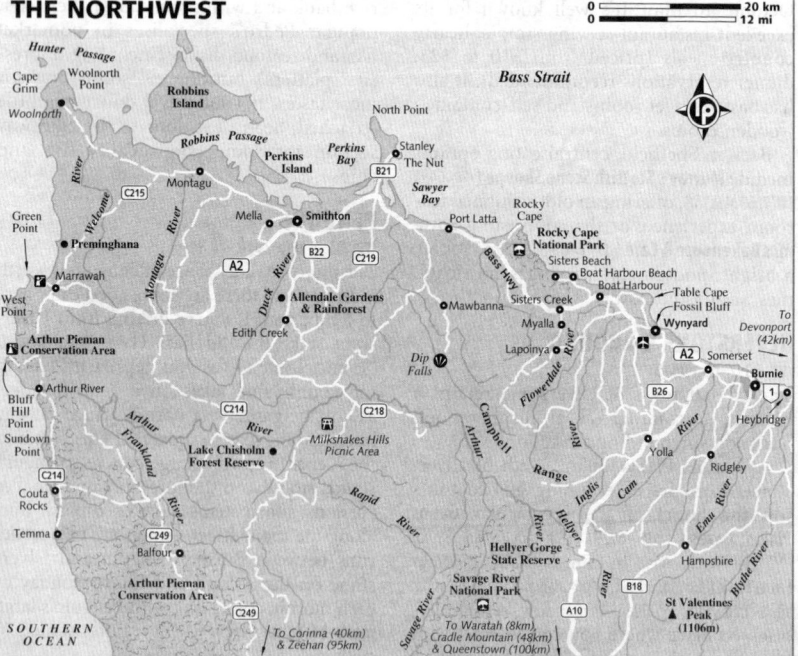

THE NORTHWEST

There are no public transport services to Marrawah or Arthur River.

CAR & MOTORCYCLE

The main route from the north to the west coast is the Murchison Hwy (A10) from Somerset (just west of Burnie) to Queenstown. The Western Explorer is the name given to an alternative inland route from Smithton to the west coast that incorporates a difficult section between Arthur River and Corinna. Although this road can be negotiated by vehicles without 4WD and is promoted as a tourist route, it's remote, mostly unsealed and can be potholed, so shouldn't be attempted in bad weather or at night (and, as one tourist brochure writes, 'don't tackle this in a pipsqueak city car'); see p641 for more details. At Corinna, there is a vehicular ferry across the Pieman River, from where you can continue on to Zeehan and the rest of the west coast.

The other important road in the area runs from the Murchison Hwy to Cradle Mountain. This is the link road (C132) that enables cars and buses to travel directly from Devonport to Queenstown, thereby avoiding the northwest coast altogether.

BURNIE

☎ 03 / pop 18,095

Burnie, Tasmania's fourth-largest town, sits on the shores of Emu Bay and is backed by rich farming land. Evidence of the town's heavy industry and cargo shipping port don't make a great first impression on visitors, but Burnie has been sprucing itself up and trying to develop a more appealing coastal atmosphere, and offers travellers a few decent attractions and good accommodation possibilities.

The town started growing mainly potatoes, until the discovery of tin at Mt Bischoff in Waratah. In 1878 the Van Diemen's Land Company opened a wooden tramway between the mine at Waratah and the port of Burnie, the humble beginning of the important Emu Bay Railway that linked the port to the rich silver fields of Zeehan and Rosebery in the 1900s.

The **visitors centre** (☎ 6434 6111; travel@burnie .net; www.burnie.net; Little Alexander St; ☑ 8.30am-5pm Mon-Fri, 9am-4pm Sat & Sun) is attached to the Pioneer Village Museum and is a good source of information on Tassie's northwest

region. Internet access is available at the **online access centre** (☎ 6431 9469; cnr Wilson & Spring Sts), opposite McDonald's.

Sights & Activities

The absorbing **Pioneer Village Museum** (☎ 6430 5746; Little Alexander St; adult/child $6/2.50; ☑ 8.30am-5pm Mon-Fri, 9am-4pm Sat & Sun), adjacent to the visitors centre, is an indoor re-creation of a historical street, complete with authentic blacksmith's shop, printer and boot shop. Not far away, the **Burnie Regional Art Gallery** (☎ 6431 5918; Wilmot St; admission free; ☑ 9am-5pm Mon-Fri, 1.30-4.30pm Sat, Sun) has both permanent and changing exhibitions.

In the visitors centre at the **Lactos cheese factory** (☎ 6431 2566; 145 Old Surrey Rd; admission free; ☑ 9am-5pm Mon-Fri, 10am-4pm Sat, Sun & public holidays), you can taste, and of course purchase, fine dairy produce. Good lunches are served here, including a ploughman's lunch ($9) or chicken and camembert pie ($3.30).

On the same road as Lactos is the **Creative Paper Mill** (☎ 6430 7717; www.creativepapermill.org; Old Surrey Rd; tours $8/5/20 adult/child/family; ☑ 9am-4pm Mon-Fri year-round, 10am-4pm Sat & Sun Nov-Apr; tours 11am & 1pm Mon-Fri), where paper is made by hand. There are paper products for sale and artworks on show; tours of the mill are conducted regularly.

There are a number of gardens, waterfalls and viewpoints in the Burnie area. **Fern Glade**, just 3km from the city centre, is a peaceful riverside spot offering picnic areas, walks and the chance to spot a platypus. There's also a boardwalk from Burnie's foreshore that leads to a **penguin observation centre** at the western end of West Beach.

Sleeping

The assortment of pubs around town are a good bet for budget-style accommodation, as well as standard (somewhat predictable) pub grub.

Treasure Island Caravan Park (☎ 6431 1925; ocean view@southcom.com.au; 253 Bass Hwy; camp/caravan sites $15/8 for 2 people, dorm beds $14, on-site vans/cabins $45/65) Located in Cooee, 4km west of Burnie's centre, this well-kept park is opposite the beach and also has an indoor pool. It offers the full gamut of accommodation, including two hostel rooms, and at the front of the property is the **Ocean View Motel** (☎ 6431 1925; s/d from $70/80) with neat, serviceable rooms, most with self-catering facilities.

Chancellor Inn (☎ 6431 4455; www.grandhotels international.com; 139 Wilson St; d $85-105) You can't miss this big yellow hotel, painted the same colour as the golden arches opposite. Inside are reasonable rooms (the higher price gets you a higher standard). Downstairs is the inviting Maginty's Irish Bar, and there should be a new restaurant here by the time you read this.

Apartments Down Town (☎ 6432 3219; www.ap artmentsdowntown.com.au; 52 Alexander St; s/d $100/130). These highly recommended Art Deco apartments are stylish, spacious and can sleep up to seven; each unit features individual décor, a living area, full kitchen (breakfast provisions provided) and laundry, and for $15 extra you can get a spa bath unit.

Glen Osborne House (☎ 6431 9866; 9 Aileen Crescent, off Mount St; s/d $95/130) Set in suburban hills in Burnie's south, this welcoming B&B offers large, attractive rooms in an elegantly furnished Victorian house set in impressive gardens.

Eating
Kinesis (☎ 6431 5963; 53 Mount St; lunch $5-10) Among the homely mishmash of furniture, some simple and wholesome food is served here, including fresh juices and smoothies, toasted focaccia, soup, salads and muffins.

Café Europa (☎ 6431 897; cnr Cattley & Wilson Sts; meals $5-12) In this bright and breezy corner café you'll find good-value Mediterranean fare (tapas dishes, moussaka, filled Turkish bread) served all day, fine coffee and a well-stocked bar.

La Porchetta (☎ 6432 2280; 25 Cattley St; mains $10-20) This big, bustling place can seat nearly 200 hungry folk and has a large range of Italian staples on offer, including well-priced pizza and pasta dishes plus unsurprising meat choices like scotch fillet and veal parmigiana.

Bocelli (☎ 6431 8441; 63 Mount St; lunch $8-10, dinner mains $15-21) Modern café-style fare is the order of the day here – lunch-time selections include pasta, risotto and toasted panini, and dinner choices include seafood curry, roast duck or ocean trout in lemon and olive oil.

WYNYARD
☎ 03 / pop 4635
Sheltered by the impressive Table Cape and Fossil Bluff, the agreeable small town of Wynyard sits on the seafront and the banks of the Inglis River. Although there's not much to see in the town, it's a good base from which to explore the attractions in the area.

There's a helpful **visitors centre** (☎ 6442 4143; wynyard@tasvisinfo.com.au; Goldie St; ☼ 9am-5pm Mon-Sat, 12.30-5pm Sun), which has lots of brochures on the surrounding region, including information on good scenic walks and drives.

Fossil Bluff is 3km from Wynyard, signposted from the roundabout on which the Wynyard Hotel sits – the route winds through several side-streets, so keep your eyes peeled for the signs. It's where the oldest marsupial fossil ever found in Australia was unearthed. The soft sandstone here features numerous shell fossils deposited when the level of Bass Strait was much higher.

Other attractions in the area include **Table Cape**, about 7km from Wynyard; it has unforgettable views. There's also a tulip farm (in bloom and open to the public from late September to mid-October) and a lighthouse (dating from 1888) on the cape.

Sleeping & Eating
Beach Retreat Tourist Park (☎ 6442 1998; 30 Old Bass Hwy; camp/caravan sites $13/16 for 2 people, s/d budget rooms $20/35, motels units & cabins $65-70) This well-situated park is on the beach and close to town. Friendly new owners have upgraded the facilities to a very high standard and there's accommodation to suit most people. The budget rooms are excellent value, and guests have access to a good kitchen and lounge. The spotless motel-style units and cabins are well equipped and brightly decorated.

Alexandria (☎ 6442 4411; alexandria@ozemail.com .au; 1 Table Cape Rd; s/d $120/150) By the Inglis River about 1.5km out of town, this B&B is in a well-groomed Federation-style home dating from 1905. Guests can enjoy the pool, barbecue area and impressive gardens, plus river views from the veranda.

Buckaneers (☎ 6442 4104; 4 Inglis St; restaurant meals $11-22) A number of restaurants, cafés and pubs line the main street, but the best choice for a good fishy feed is this inviting nautically themed place. Here you can buy fresh fish and seafood, order succulent fish and chips to takeaway or enjoy a more formal meal in the attached restaurant, with most seafood favourites featured on the menu.

BOAT HARBOUR & AROUND
☎ 03 / pop 400

Boat Harbour Beach, 14km west of Wynyard, is a beautiful bay with white sand and crystal-clear water. There is an ever-increasing number of places to stay in the tiny settlement here – as a sign of the times, the well-situated caravan park has closed and is set for redevelopment (possibly apartments). **Boat Harbour Beach Resort** (☎ 6445 1107; www .boatharbourbeachresort.com; Esplanade; s/d from $80/85), a revived and refurbished 1960s motel, has a good range of units – expect to pay more for the better suites. Facilities here include a restaurant, bar, indoor pool, spa and sauna. **Jolly Rogers** (☎ 6445 1710; Esplanade; lunch $8-15, dinner mains $16-25) is an inviting beachside eatery.

Nearby, bordering the coastal heath lands of the small **Rocky Cape National Park**, is **Sisters Beach**, an 8km expanse of bleached sand with safe swimming and good fishing. Redline Coaches service between Burnie and Smithton will drop you at the turn-off to Boat Harbour (3km) and Sisters Beach (8km) but your own transport is a better option.

STANLEY
☎ 03 / pop 463

Stanley is nestled at the foot of the extraordinary Circular Head (better known as The Nut) and has an undisturbed, peaceful air. In 1826 it became the headquarters of the London-based Van Diemen's Land Company, which was granted a charter to settle and cultivate Circular Head and the northwestern tip of Tasmania.

Today, Stanley is a charming fishing village with a range of accommodation and attractions; it's a lovely spot to unwind for a few days. Information is available at the **visitors centre** (☎ 6458 1330; stanley@tasvisinfo.com .au; 45 Main Rd; ☯ 10am-5pm Mon-Fri, noon-4pm Sat & Sun) on the road into town, or at the booking centre in the town hall; see Sleeping on p640 for details.

Sights
THE NUT

This striking 152m-high volcanic rock formation, thought to be 13 million years old, can be seen for miles around. It's a steep, 20-minute climb to the top, but the view is definitely worth it. For the less energetic, a **chairlift** (☎ 6458 1286; adult/child/family $8/6/20; ☯ 9.30am-5.30pm Oct-May, 10am-4pm Jun-Sep) also

operates, weather permitting. At the top you can take a leisurely stroll from one lookout to the next; at the base there's a pleasant café.

OTHER ATTRACTIONS
The old bluestone building on the seafront, designed by colonial architect John Lee Archer, was originally the 1844 **Van Diemen's Land Company Store** (Wharf Rd), and is now an interesting **gallery**. The company's headquarters were at gracious **Highfield** (☎ 6458 1100; Green Hills Rd; adult/family $6/14; ☯ 10am-4pm), 2km north of Stanley, which includes the elegant homestead, barns, stables, workers' cottages and a chapel. There are guided and self-guided tours, plus an evening tour by lamplight from January to March ($10/25 per adult/family; bookings essential).

Near the wharf is the mid-19th-century **Ford's Store**, a particularly fine old bluestone building that used to be a grain store (now a restaurant). Other buildings of historical interest include **Lyons Cottage** (☎ 6458 1145; 14 Alexander Tce; admission by donation; ☯ 10am-4pm Nov-Apr, 11am-3pm May-Sep), the birthplace of former prime minister Joseph Lyons, and **St James' Presbyterian Church** (Fletcher St), which was bought in England and transported to Stanley in 1885. By the church, the **Discovery Centre** (Church St; adult/child $3/50¢; ☯ 10am-4pm, closed Jun-Aug) is a one-room museum filled with old Circular Head photos and artefacts.

The **Seaquarium** (☎ 6458 2052; adult/child/family $7/4/20; ☯ 9.30am-4.30pm) is a kid-friendly but overpriced attraction at the wharf. Here you can view a variety of Tasmanian sea life in tanks, including commercial stocks of lobster and giant crab for the export market.

Tours
Stanley-based **Wilderness to West Coast Tours** (☎ 6458 2038; www.wildernesstasmania.com; Church St) offers local twilight tours to spot penguins and platypus ($35/15 per adult/child; bookings advised), plus highly regarded 4WD eco-tours into the northwestern wilderness. Passengers explore rugged coastline and isolated rainforest. Day tours cost around $195, including a gourmet lunch; a two-/three-day tour to remote Sandy Cape costs $500/700 (including transport, accommodation and meals) and runs from January to April. The company also arranges trout fishing tours, or 'tag along' 4WD trips (you follow the guide in your own 4WD vehicle).

TASMANIA

To view Australian fur seals, take a 75-minute cruise offered by **Stanley Seal Cruises** (☎ 6458 1312), departing daily from the wharf (weather permitting) and costing $35/17 per adult/child.

Sleeping

There's a helpful accommodation **booking centre** (☎ 1300 656 044; www.bookings.tassie.net.au; Church St; ✆ 8am-early evening) in the town hall.

Stanley Cabin & Tourist Park (☎ 6458 1266; www.stanleycabinpark.com.au; Wharf Rd; camp/caravan sites $16/18 for 2 people, on-site vans $40, cabins $50-75) This neat beachfront park is loaded with amenities and has well-serviced vans and self-contained cabins. It's also home to the town's small **YHA hostel** (dm $18, tw & d $40), a clean and comfy budget option.

Stanley Hotel (☎ 6458 1161; 19 Church St; dm/s/d $25/30/50, d with bathroom $70) The accommodation at this popular central pub has undergone a welcome renovation and has been well spruced up with a coat of very yellow paint! A few rooms have bathrooms, and some open onto the huge front balcony. Downstairs you can get good pub meals.

Dovecote Motel & Restaurant (☎ 6458 1300; www.dovecote.com.au; 58 Dovecote Rd; d $90-145) A little way out of town, this friendly place has an assortment of straightforward motel rooms and self-contained units, most with great views of The Nut and the town from their balconies (the cheapest rooms lack the view). The restaurant features local produce and has well-priced options (mains around $20).

There are oodles of B&Bs and self-contained cottages dotted in and around Stanley. They range in price from $100 to $165 a double in the summer, though you should bargain hard at other times. Some close in winter. Some recommendations:

Abbey's Cottages (☎ 1800 222 397; www.stanley tasmania.com; d $75-150) Offers a range of self-contained units and cottages in town, of varying sizes, standards and prices – check the website.

Hanlon House (☎ 6458 1149; www.tassie.net.au /hanlonhouse; 6 Marshall St; d $145-165) Upmarket B&B.

Eating

Hurseys Seafood (☎ 6458 1103; 2 Alexander Tce) is awash with tanks filled with live sea creatures, including crayfish, for the freshest of takeaways. The complex includes Kermies Café, serving quick meals and fish-and-chip takeaways, and upstairs is **Julie & Patrick's**

(☎ 6458 1103; mains $18-28), a more formal dinner restaurant where the menu is, naturally, heavy on the seafood (fancy reef and beef, abalone steaks or pasta marinara?).

Sealer's Cove (☎ 6458 1414; 2 Main Rd; meals $11-18) If you're not too keen on seafood, head along to this cheery BYO place, where you'll get an extensive selection of pizza, pasta and salad dishes, plus excellent desserts. Be adventurous and try the BBQ snag pizza (sausages, potato and onion) or the Malay chicken (chicken, bacon and mushroom on a satay base).

There are a couple of cafés and tearooms along the main street; try the quaint **Stranded Whale** (☎ 6458 1202; 6 Church St; meals $4-10) for its simple, home-cooked lunches and snacks (soup, sandwiches, scones etc).

AROUND STANLEY

Smithton, 22km from Stanley, serves one of Tasmania's largest forestry areas and is also the administrative centre for Circular Head. Twenty kilometres west of here is the site for Forestry Tasmania's new ecotourism venture, the Dismal Swamp Visitor Centre and Maze, under construction at the time of research. The site is set within a blackwood swamp forest, and will include a café, viewing platform, a slide and a forest maze. It's hoped this venture will replicate the success of another Forestry Tasmania initiative, the Tahune Forest AirWalk near Geeveston (p602) south of Hobart.

Allendale Gardens (☎ 03-6456 4216; Allendale Lane; adult/child $7.50/3.50; ✆ 9am-6pm daily Oct-Apr) is on the B22 road 12km south of Smithton towards Edith Creek. It has five hectares of beautiful bird-filled gardens and 26 hectares of old temperate rainforest to lose yourself in, plus a café serving Devonshire teas.

MARRAWAH
☎ 03 / pop 370

Marrawah is where the wild Indian Ocean occasionally throws up the remains of ships wrecked on the dangerous and rugged west coast. The area has experienced little disturbance from European development; many early signs of Tasmanian Aborigines remain and particular areas have been proclaimed reserves to protect the remaining rock carvings, middens and hut depressions. The main **Aboriginal sites** are at Preminghana, near Green Point, and West Point.

Marrawah consists of a tavern supplying daily counter meals (but not accommodation), a tearoom and a general store selling petrol and supplies. There's a free, basic **camping area** at beautiful Green Point, 2km from Marrawah. The rural **Glendonald Cottage** (☎ 6457 1191; www.redpa.tco.asn.au/glenking; 79 Arthur River Rd; s/d $60/85, additional person $20) is a comfortable self-contained cottage sleeping up to five; the owner also conducts environmental and wildlife tours in the area.

This region is good for fishing, canoeing, camping and bushwalking. Marrawah's main attraction, however, is its enormous surf – rounds of the state's surfing and windsurfing championships are held here each year.

ARTHUR RIVER

☎ 03 / pop 110

The quiet settlement of Arthur River, 14km south of Marrawah, is mainly a collection of holiday houses belonging to people who come here to fish. It's not serviced by public transport.

Apart from the excellent fishing, travellers also come to take a scenic cruise on the Arthur River. There are two operators: **Arthur River Cruises** (☎ 6457 1158; cruises adult/child $55/22) departs at 10am and returns at 3pm daily, cruising upriver to the confluence of the Arthur and Frankland Rivers, where passengers enjoy a barbecue and guided walk. **AR Reflections River Cruises** (☎ 6457 1288; 4 Gardiner St; cruises adult/child $55/22) also operates five-hour cruises on the Arthur, departing 10.15am daily. The price includes a rainforest walk and lunch back in the gardens at the kiosk. For those keen on self-exploration, **Arthur River Canoe & Boat Hire** (☎ 6457 1312), at the jetty, has canoes to rent from $8/40 per hour/day, or boats from $18/110.

From Arthur River you can drive 110km south to Corinna on the narrow, unsealed Western Explorer. This rough road passes through the wild and often spectacular **Arthur Pieman Protected Area**. Before heading off, get fuel in Marrawah as there's no petrol available until either Zeehan or Waratah; also get the latest on the road's condition from the **Arthur River PWS** (☎ 6457 1225).

There are several basic **camping grounds** in the area ($5 per site); self-register at the **PWS** (☎ 6457 1225) office. There are also a few decent accommodation options in Arthur River, but no eateries (there is only a kiosk with limited supplies, on Gardiner St).

Arthur River Holiday Units (☎ 6457 1288; 2 Gardiner St; s/d from $55/70) has comfortable, well-equipped riverside units. Further up the same road, **Sunset Holiday Villas** (☎ 6457 1197; 23 Gardiner St; s/d $60/79) offers two self-contained units that share a balcony and views of the beach (stunning at sunset).

THE WEST

Nature at its most awe-inspiring is the attraction of Tasmania's magnificent west coast. Formidable mountains, button-grass plains, ancient rivers, tranquil lakes, dense rainforests and a treacherous coast are all features of this beautiful region, some of which is now a World Heritage Area.

Many centuries before the arrival of Europeans, the west was home to many of the island's Aboriginal people, and plenty of archaeological evidence, some of it more than 20,000 years old, has been found of these original inhabitants.

Prior to 1932, when the road from Hobart to Queenstown was built, the only way into the area was by sea, through the dangerously narrow Hells Gates into Macquarie Harbour, near Strahan. Despite such near-inaccessibility, early European settlement brought explorers, convicts, soldiers, loggers, prospectors, railway gangs and fishermen, while the 20th century brought outdoor adventurers, naturalists and environmental crusaders.

It was over the wild rivers, beautiful lakes and tranquil valleys of Tasmania's southwest that battles between environmentalists and governments raged. The proposed damming of the Franklin and Lower Gordon Rivers caused the greatest and longest-running environmental debate in Australia's history in the 1980s and has subsequently led to the boom of ecotourism around Strahan.

See www.westcoasttourism.com.au for information on the region.

Getting There & Around

TassieLink (☎ 1300 300 520; www.tassielink.com.au) runs buses four to five times a week from Hobart to Lake St Clair ($38, 3 to 3½ hours), Queenstown ($48, 5 hours) and Strahan ($56, 6 to 9 hours, times vary depending on Queenstown stopover). There are return

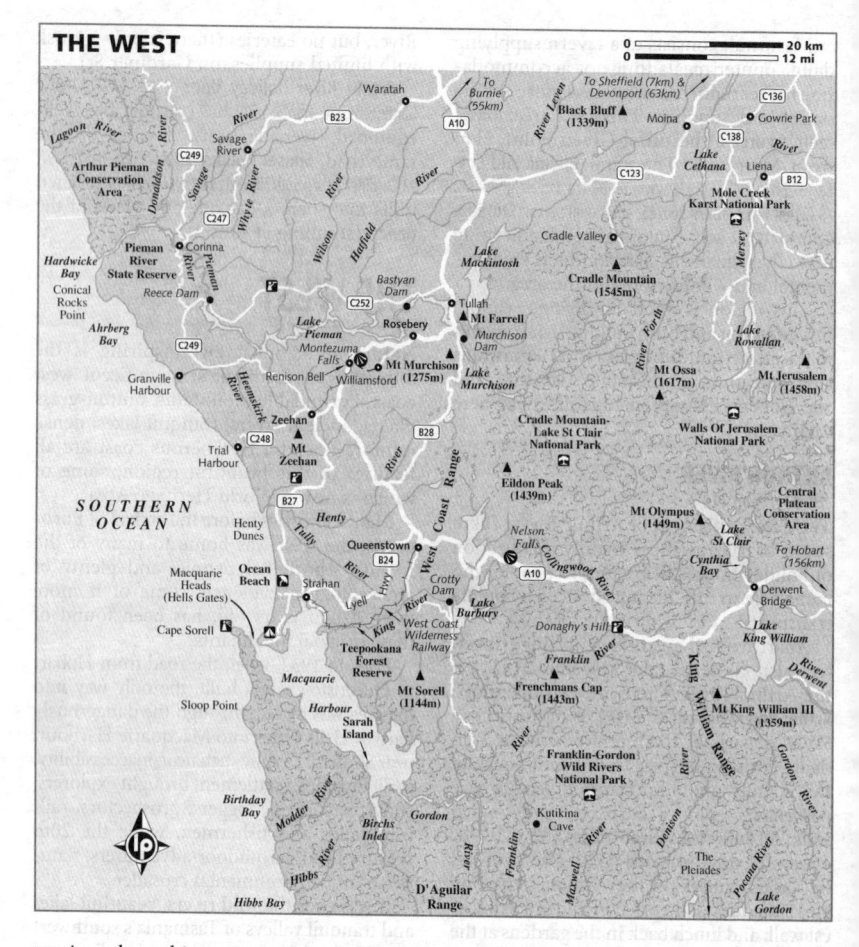

THE WEST

services along this route on the same days. TassieLink also has six services a week (daily except Sunday) from Launceston to Devonport ($17, 1¼ hours), Sheffield ($22, 2 hours), Cradle Mountain ($55, 3 hours), Zeehan ($55, 5½ to 6 hours), Queenstown ($65, 6 hours) and Strahan ($75, 8¾ hours), also with return services on the same days. In addition there is a twice-weekly TassieLink service linking Burnie and Strahan ($39, 4 to 4½ hours), running via Zeehan and Queenstown.

Redline Coaches (☎ 1300 360 000; www.tasredline .com.au) has a daily service between Cradle Mountain and Devonport, with connecting services from Launceston on weekdays only.

For information about alternative services for those walking the Overland Track see Getting There & Away on p651.

Drivers heading north along the coast should fill up at Zeehan or Waratah, as there's no fuel at either Savage River or Corinna, only at distant Marrawah. See p637 for details of this remote, largely unsealed road.

CORINNA
☎ 03

Tiny Corinna, on the northern bank of the Pieman River, was once a thriving gold-mining settlement, but nowadays people come for the serenity, scenery and the **Pieman River Cruises** (☎ 6446 1170). The four-hour cruises pass an impressive gorge and forests of eucalypts, ferns and Huon pines on the way to Pieman Heads. The cost is $40/20 per adult/child and cruises depart at 10.30am daily from November to May (by arrangement from June to October). Bookings are advised.

The only accommodation is at **Retreat Cabins** (☎ 6446 1170; d $70, additional person $12), which has large self-contained cabins sleeping up to six (bedding extra). There's also a small kiosk here, selling limited supplies.

The **Fatman ferry** (☎ 6446 1170) charges $11 to transport vehicles across the Pieman and runs on demand 9am to 5pm daily April to September and 9am to 7pm daily October to March.

ZEEHAN
☎ 03 / pop 892

In 1882 rich deposits of silver and lead were discovered in the tiny town of Zeehan; by the century's end it had become a booming mining centre known as Silver City, with a population of nearly 10,000. In its heyday Zeehan had 26 hotels; its Gaiety Theatre seated 1000 people. In 1908, however, the mines began to fail and the town declined. With the reopening and expansion of the Renison Tin Mine at nearby Renison Bell, Zeehan experienced a revival in the late 1960s, but it remains a small, quiet place, worth a stop for its museum.

Buildings that remain from the boom days include the once-famous **Grand Hotel** (encompassing the Gaiety Theatre), the **post office**, the **bank** (all on Main St) and **St Luke's Church** on Belstead St. The **Gaiety Theatre** is slowly being restored, and enthusiasts can tour it ($6.50/4.40 per adult/child) and hear some of its fascinating history – contact **Silver City Info/Tours** (☎ 0438-716 389; 129 Main St). The office is opposite the theatre and also acts as an information centre on the region.

For an excellent insight into the workings of a mine, visit the **West Coast Pioneers' Museum** (☎ 6471 6225; Main St; adult/child/family $6/3/15; ⏰ 8.30am-5pm Apr-Sep, to 6pm Oct-Mar), which also features an interesting mineral collection and a pictorial history of the west coast.

Trial Harbour, the original port for Zeehan, is a beautiful place for bush camping, while the sandy expanses of the **Henty Dunes**

should not be missed on the drive from Zeehan to Strahan.

Sleeping & Eating
Treasure Island Caravan Park (☎ 6471 6633; Hurst St; camp/caravan sites $16/18 for 2 people, on-site vans $35-45, cabins $50-70) In the northern part of town you'll find this simple, pleasant caravan park with OK cabins and camping sites set amongst plenty of greenery.

Hotel Cecil (☎ 6471 6221; Main St; s/d $45/65, units $95) This old pub has small and basic rooms (most with shared facilities), but at the time of writing there was talk of a possible refurbishment, which would see standards and prices rise. On an adjacent block are a few comfortable, self-contained miners cottages which can sleep up to four. Reasonably priced counter meals are available here daily.

Heemskirk Motor Hotel (☎ 1800 639 876; Main St; s/d from $80/90) A large complex at the eastern edge of town, the Heemskirk offers well-equipped and decent-sized motel units, plus a bar and bistro offering a decent selection of dishes.

There are pretty slim pickings for diners. The **coffee lounge** (Main St) inside the Pioneers' Museum is good for a light lunch, as is **Coffee Stop** (☎ 6471 6709; 110 Main St), although its hours are somewhat erratic. Of an evening, head to Hotel Cecil or the bistro at the Heemskirk.

QUEENSTOWN
☎ 03 / pop 2352

The final, winding descent into Queenstown from the Lyell Hwy is unforgettable. The deep, eroded gullies and seminaked, variegated hills testify to the destruction of the area by mining.

The discovery of alluvial gold in the Queen River valley in 1881 brought prospectors to the area. Two years later, mining began on the rich Mt Lyell deposits and for nearly a decade miners extracted a few ounces of gold a day, ignoring the mountain's rich copper reserves. In 1891, however, the Mt Lyell Mining Company began concentrating on copper, which soon became the most profitable mineral on the west coast.

After 20 years of mining, the previously rainforested hills around Queenstown had been stripped bare: three million tonnes of timber had been felled to feed the furnaces. By 1900, uncontrolled pollution from the copper smelters was killing any vegetation that hadn't already been cut down, and bushfires – fuelled by the sulphur-impregnated soils and dead stumps – raged through the hills every summer. The west's high rainfall then washed away all the topsoil, preventing revegetation for many years. However, the smelters closed in 1969 and in recent years patches of green have begun appearing on the slopes.

Today the town is beginning to occupy itself with tourism, and besides the wilderness railway it has something to offer those interested in social and industrial history. The meals and accommodation in Queenstown are cheaper than in Strahan, so if you're travelling on a tight budget and intend exploring more of the west than Strahan and the Gordon River, you might consider making Queenstown your base.

The Galley Museum (for details see below) is a good source of tourist information; and you can also check out the website www.queenstowntasmania.com.au

Sights & Activities

The biggest attraction is the **West Coast Wilderness Railway**, which runs between Queenstown and Strahan. The station is on Driffield St, opposite the Empire Hotel. For more information on the railway, see p645.

The **Galley Museum** (☎ 6471 1483; cnr Driffield & Sticht Sts; adult/child/family $4/2.50/10; 🕑 9.30am-6pm Mon-Fri & 12.30-6pm Sat & Sun Oct-Apr, 10am-5pm Mon-Fri & 12.30-5pm Sat & Sun May-Sep) started life as the Imperial Hotel in 1898. It now counts among its features an intriguing collection of old photographs with wonderfully idiosyncratic captions written by the photographer, Eric Thomas.

There are good views from **Spion Kopf Lookout** in the centre of town (follow Bowes St). You'll notice the football oval is cream-coloured instead of green: Queenstown's footy team is tough – it plays on gravel, not grass.

The mine can be viewed on excursions run by **Douggie's Tours** (☎ 0407-049 612; 2 Orr St, by Empire Hotel), which runs daily surface tours ($18/9.50 per adult/child, 1½ hours) as well as underground trips ($58/40, 2½ hours). The minimum age for tour participants is 12 years. Bookings are essential.

The geological wound of **Iron Blow**, the original but now abandoned open-cut mine, can be seen from a lookout off the Lyell Hwy.

Sleeping & Eating

Queenstown Cabin & Tourist Park (☎ 6471 1332; 17 Grafton St; camp/caravan sites $15/20 for 2 people, s/d $15/25, on-site vans/cabins $40/75) About 500m south of the town centre, this park covers most price brackets. It has a lodge with decent budget rooms, spotless vans and cabins, and good amenities.

Empire Hotel (☎ 6471 1699; empirehotel@tassie.net.au; 2 Orr St; d with bathroom $50, s/d without bathroom $25/40) The majestic, century-old Empire has basic but clean, good-value rooms in a prime location. It's also a good choice for a meal, serving a variety of hearty if unadventurous meals in its pleasant, open-fire-warmed dining room, or cheaper snacks at the bar.

Westcoaster Motor Inn (☎ 6471 1033; www.dohertyhotels.com.au; Batchelor St; d $99) There are a number of generic motels in town, but the well-maintained Westcoaster is probably the pick of them. It has comfortable, newly refurbished rooms and decent facilities, including a bar and restaurant on site.

Penghana (☎ 6471 2560; 32 The Esplanade; d $120-150) Built in 1898 for the first general manager of the Mt Lyell Mining Company, this upmarket B&B guesthouse stands grandly above the town amid a surprising number of trees (surprising, given that this is Queenstown). Guest facilities include a lounge with open fire, bar and billiard table.

There's not a great deal of choice for eating out. Takeaway stores line the main street, and the **Empire Hotel** (☎ 6471 1699; empirehotel@tassie.net.au; 2 Orr St) serves decent pub food. **Dottie's Coffee Shop** (Driffield St; meals $5-10), inside the train station, is the best choice for café fare, including focaccia, pies and scones.

STRAHAN

☎ 03 / pop 758

Strahan, 40km southwest of Queenstown on Macquarie Harbour, is the only sizeable town on the rugged west coast.

Treacherous seas, the lack of natural harbours and high rainfall discouraged early settlement of the region until Macquarie Harbour was discovered by sailors searching for the source of the Huon pine that frequently washed up on southern beaches.

WEST COAST WILDERNESS RAILWAY

Since December 2002, visitors to Tasmania's west coast have had a new option for exploring the pristine wilderness of the area – as passengers on the recently restored Abt Wilderness Railway, a 35km stretch of track between Queenstown and Strahan, passing through dense forest and crossing wild rivers and 40 restored bridges, with stops at a few historic stations en route.

The rack-and-pinion line was the reason why the company that mined Mt Lyell for so long was called the Mt Lyell Mining *and* Railway Company. For the mining to be profitable, a railway connecting Mt Lyell with the port of Teepookana on King River, and later with Strahan, was vital. Construction began in 1894 and by its completion had cost the mining company over half its capital investment and covered 35km of rugged terrain.

Opened in 1896 and extended to Strahan in 1899, the line ran along the Queen River and up the one-in-16 Abt section to Rinadeena, before heading down the one-in-20 Abt section through magnificent rainforest to the King River. Here it crossed a stunning, curved 400m-long bridge high above the water, before continuing on to Teepookana and Regatta Point.

The Abt system (named after its inventor) was used to cover terrain too steep for the standard haulage of large quantities of ore. In this arrangement, a third toothed rack rail is positioned between the two conventional rails, and locomotives are equipped with geared pinion wheels that lock into the rack rail, allowing trains to climb and descend gradients they'd otherwise be unable to negotiate fully loaded.

The railway eventually closed in 1963 and fell into disrepair. Today the entire track is magnificently restored and steam and diesel locomotives take passengers along its full length. The trains depart from Queenstown and Strahan at the same times (10am and 3pm daily); the entire journey takes a little over four hours and passengers can then take a later train or a bus back to their point of origin. Alternatively, travellers can ride to the track's half-way point at Dubbil Barril, change trains and return to the point of departure. Costs for riding the full length one way, or for a return journey to Dubbil Barril, are $65/28 per adult/child. The bus option costs $10/5, or to ride both ways on the railway costs $95/42.

Make inquiries or purchase tickets at either the **Queenstown Station** (☎ 03-6471 1700; Driffield St), in the centre of town, or the **Regatta Point Station** (☎ 03-6471 4300), on the waterfront 1.5km south of Strahan's centre.

In those days, the area was inaccessible by land and very difficult to reach by sea, and in 1821 these dubious assets prompted the establishment of a brutal penal settlement on **Sarah Island**, in the middle of the harbour. Its main function was to isolate the worst of the colony's convicts and to use their muscle to harvest the huge stands of Huon pine nearby. The convicts worked upriver 12 hours a day, often in leg irons, felling the pines and rafting them back to the island's saw-pits, where they were used to build ships and furniture.

In 1834, however, after the establishment of the 'escape-proof' penal settlement at Port Arthur, Sarah Island was abandoned. It appears in Marcus Clarke's graphic novel about convict life, *For the Term of His Natural Life*.

As the port for Queenstown, Strahan reached the peak of its prosperity with the west-coast mining boom and the comple-

tion of the Mt Lyell Mining Company's railway line in the late 1890s. Steamers operated regularly between Strahan and Hobart, and Launceston and Melbourne, carrying copper, gold, silver, lead, timber and passengers. But the closure of some of the mines and the opening of the Emu Bay Railway from Zeehan to Burnie led to Strahan's decline as a port.

Strahan's harbourside main street is undeniably attractive, but in a slightly artificial way. The town's true appeal lies in the natural and historical attractions around it rather than in the town itself, and as such it draws droves of visitors seeking a wilderness-in-comfort experience aboard a seaplane, Gordon River cruise or the wilderness railway.

Information

The architecturally innovative **visitors centre** (☎ 6471 7622; strahan@tasvisinfo.com.au; Esplanade; ☼ from 10am) offers Internet access and information on accommodation options, attractions and activities in the town. Its closing time varies, depending on the time of year (at 7pm in December, 9pm in January, 8pm in February and March, between 5pm and 6pm from April to November).

There's a **PWS office** (☎ 6471 7122; Old Customs House, Esplanade) close to the town centre. The same building also houses the post office and **online access centre**. There's an ATM by Banjo's on the main street.

Sights & Activities

Beyond the Huon pine reception desk at the visitors centre is **West Coast Reflections** (adult/child $2/free; ☽ from 10am), a creative and thought-provoking display on the history of the west, including a refreshingly blunt appraisal of environmental disappointments and achievements.

The visitors centre stages **The Ship That Never Was** (☎ 6471 7622; adult/child $12/2; ☽ 5.30pm year-round, also 8.30pm in Jan) daily in its amphitheatre. It's an entertaining pantomime-style show telling the story of the last ship built at Sarah Island, and the convicts who stole it and escaped. The show has something to please all age groups, including audience participation for the kids.

The walk to **Hogarth Falls** starts east of the town centre at Peoples Park; allow one-hour return. Other natural attractions include the impressive 33km-long **Ocean Beach**, 6km from town, where the sunsets have to be seen to be believed. In October the beach becomes a **mutton bird rookery** when the birds return from their winter migration. About 14km along the road from Strahan to Zeehan are the spectacular **Henty Dunes**, a series of 30m-high sand dunes. Ask at the Gordon River Cruises office about hiring sandboards and toboggans to ride these natural beauties.

Tours

See the boxed text 'West Coast Wilderness Railway' (p645) for information about this popular train journey between Strahan and Queenstown.

FOUR-WHEEL MOTORCYCLING

4 Wheelers (☎ 0419-508 175) offers an interesting way of exploring Henty Dunes, with guided tours of the area on four-wheel motorcycles. A 12km, 45-minute tour costs

$35, and you'll need your own transport to get to the dunes. Participants also need a full driving licence.

GORDON RIVER CRUISES

Both the following companies offer popular river cruises that include a rainforest walk at Heritage Landing, views of or passage through Hells Gates (the narrow entrance to Macquarie Harbour) and a land tour of Sarah Island. The major difference between the companies is that Gordon River Cruises has reserved seating, and World Heritage Cruises doesn't (it's more of a first-in-best-dressed arrangement).

World Heritage Cruises (☎ 6471 7174; www .worldheritagecruises.com.au; Esplanade) runs six- to 6½-hour cruises costing $60/25/150 per adult/child/family departing at 9am daily, and also at 2pm in the summer. There are half-day cruises offered from October to April (departing 9am, returning 1.30pm). This shorter tour costs $50/22/130, and note that it doesn't stop at Sarah Island. A good-value smorgasbord lunch is available on board ($9/6 per adult/child).

Gordon River Cruises (☎ 6471 4300; www.strahan village.com.au; Esplanade) has 5½-hour cruises from $55/28/149 per adult/child/family that depart at 8.30am daily, and also at 2.30pm over summer; it offers a buffet lunch on board for $13/7.50 per adult/child. Don't be sucked in to paying extra for 'better' seats – they're not worth it.

JET-BOAT RIDE

Wild Rivers Jet (☎ 6471 7174; www.wildriversjet.com .au; Esplanade) runs 50-minute jet-boat rides up the rainforest-lined gorges of the King River for $50/30/140 per adult/child/family.

SAILING

West Coast Yacht Charters (☎ 6471 7422; www .tasadventures.com/wcyc; Esplanade) offers overnight sightseeing cruises on the Gordon River on board the 60-foot steel ketch *Stormbreaker*. It's a more personal way to experience the river; the boat carries only 10 passengers. One night, including a visit to Sarah Island and all meals, costs $280/140 per adult/child. Two-day/two-night cruises cost $390/195 per adult/child. Also available are fishing trips ($40/20) and an evening crayfish cruise ($55/40) on Macquarie Harbour.

SCENIC FLIGHTS

Wilderness Air (☎ 6471 7280; wildair@tassie.net.au; Esplanade) offers excellent 80-minute seaplane flights ($140/80 per adult/child) departing regularly from Strahan harbour that fly up the Gordon River to Sir John Falls, where the plane lands so you can enjoy a rainforest walk, before flying back via the Franklin River valley and Frenchmans Cap. Minimum three people.

Seair Adventure Charters (☎ 6471 7718; www.seairac.com.au; Esplanade) has 60-minute helicopter flights for $140 (landing in the Teepookana Forest), and 45-/65-minute seaplane flights for $120/160. There are minimum numbers (two for the helicopter, three for the plane); children pay half price.

SEA-KAYAKING

Strahan Adventures (☎ 6471 7275; www.adventures tasmania.com; Esplanade) is an outfit that operates sea-kayaking trips, with tours from Risby Cove along the waterfront for $50, and twilight platypus-spotting trips on the Henty River for $80. Hardier trips to the Franklin or Gordon Rivers or to Sarah Island can also be arranged.

Sleeping

Although Strahan has a range of quality accommodation, places are often full in summer and it's wise to book ahead. There is a dearth of budget accommodation – most options in town are priced at the higher end of the mid-range scale (ie $120 and upwards), but outside the high season you should be able to negotiate reasonable stand-by discounts.

Strahan Youth Hostel (☎ 6471 7255; 43 Harvey St; dm/s/tw/d $20/24/45/50) This in-demand hostel, in a nice bush setting and with resident platypus, is a 10-minute walk from the centre and has plain but well-kept rooms. Larger groups or families should inquire about the self-contained cabin that sleeps four ($75 for two, $18 each additional person). At the time of research the hostel had been acquired by new owners, and while its long-term outlook is uncertain, it should continue to provide budget accommodation in the near future. Call ahead to book.

There's a basic **camping ground** (camp sites $5, book with on-site caretaker) at Macquarie Heads, 15km southwest of Strahan; follow the signs to Ocean Beach.

Strahan Caravan & Tourist Park (☎ 6471 7239; cnr Andrew & Innes Sts; camp/caravan sites $16/20 for 2 people, on-site vans/cabins $45/75) This well-maintained beachfront park is only a short distance from the heart of the village and offers popular, good-value accommodation, plus facilities like guest laundry and children's playground.

West Coast Yacht Charters (☎ 6471 7422; www.tasadventures.com/wcyc; Esplanade; bunks adult/child $30/10, d $70) An interesting and good-value option is to choose B&B (shared bathroom facilities) on a sailing boat moored at the wharf. Linen and light breakfast is included, but you usually check in at 8.30pm and disembark before 9am, when cruises start. The yacht is not moored every night (overnight cruises on Gordon River are available), so you'll need to book ahead.

Strahan Village (☎ 6471 4200, 1800 628 286; www.strahanvillage.com.au; r & units $100-230, additional person $30) Much of the accommodation in the centre of town is run by this conglomerate, which has its booking office (open daily) under the clock tower on the Esplanade. It has around 145 rooms on offer, including a group of terraces and cottages on the waterfront, built in various colonial styles (some with self-catering facilities, some with spas), and the Village Motor Inn, a refurbished motel high above the town with good harbour views. The lowest rates will get you a standard room at the motel, the highest a deluxe spa terrace in the town, but there are a number of options in between. Breakfast is not included in the price.

Sailors Rest (☎ 6471 7237; www.sailorsrest.com.au; 14-16 Harvey St; d $125, additional adult/child $28/20) A few blocks from the waterfront is this excellent complex of 10 spacious, self-contained cottages sleeping up to eight people. Choose from one-, two- or three-bedroom cottages and houses, all with winning extras like full kitchen and laundry, lounge area, CD player, video, and games and toys for the kids.

Risby Cove (☎ 6471 7572; www.risby.com.au; Esplanade; d $110-160 May-Sep, $145-190 Oct-Apr, additional adult/child $33/17) This eye-catching complex, 500m east of the centre, has accommodation in a large, modern house (sleeping seven, child-friendly) or in fine suites overlooking the marina, including two right on the water's edge. Sunsets here are wonderful, and there are bikes and dinghies for hire, plus a gallery and high-quality restaurant on site.

TASMANIA

Franklin Manor (☎ 6471 7311; www.franklinmanor .com.au; Esplanade; d $180-245) Not far from Risby Cove, this 1896 manor is an especially charming hideaway in lovely grounds. Visitors will appreciate the elegant rooms (the top rooms have king-sized beds, open fire and spa), underground wine cellar, cooked breakfasts and the superb on-site restaurant (see Eating later). There are also rustic cottages for larger parties (sleeping up to five), two with self-catering facilities.

Eating

Banjo's Bakehouse (☎ 6471 7794; Esplanade; pizzas $10-15) This popular central bakery does its best to cater to all: it serves cooked breakfasts from 6am, sandwiches, pies and pastries all day, and a choice of pizzas after 6pm.

Fish Café (☎ 6471 4386; Esplanade; meals $9-15) Fancy some fish? This bustling, informal eatery offers a variety of quick meals, from fresh fish and chips featuring catch of the day to salmon steak on couscous. It also does kids' serves and takeaways.

Hamer's Hotel (☎ 6471 7191; Esplanade; meals $13-22) One of the town's hotspots of an evening, the hotel serves up vegetarian options as well as wallaby sirloin, with lots of steak, seafood, curry and pasta choices in between. Its public bar is a good spot for a casual drink.

Risby Cove (☎ 6471 7572; Esplanade; lunch $8-15, dinner mains $17-26) The innovative, corrugated-iron-clad restaurant at Risby Cove serves breakfast, lunch and dinner in a great setting. There are salads, pasta and sandwiches on offer during the day, and fancier fare like game, salmon, eye fillet and lobster of an evening, plus a good selection of Tasmanian wines to choose from.

Franklin Manor (☎ 6471 7311; Esplanade; à la carte mains around $38) For sheer holiday indulgence, head to this fine restaurant for fabulous local produce carefully prepared by the Michelin-starred French chef. The *degustation* menus are exceptional value, with four/eight courses costing $65/95, and you can indulge further with selections from the acclaimed wine list. Bookings are essential.

Getting Around

Strahan Taxis (☎ 0417-516 071) offers services to surrounding attractions like Henty Dunes ($20), Ocean Beach ($10) and Macquarie Heads ($25). **Risby Cove** (☎ 6471 7572) has bikes for rent (around $10 per hour).

FRANKLIN-GORDON WILD RIVERS NATIONAL PARK

This World Heritage–listed park includes the catchment areas of the Franklin and Olga Rivers and part of the Gordon River, as well as the exceptional bushwalking and climbing region known as **Frenchmans Cap**. It has a number of unique plant species and the major Aboriginal archaeological site at **Kutikina Cave**.

Much of the park is impenetrable rainforest, but the Lyell Hwy traverses its northern end and there are a few short walks starting from the road. These include hikes to **Donaghys Hill** (40 minutes return), from where you can see the Franklin River and the magnificent white-quartzite dome of Frenchmans Cap, and a stroll to **Nelson Falls** (20 minutes return).

Rafting the Franklin

The Franklin is a wild river and rafting it can be sensational but hazardous. Whether you go with an independent group or a tour operator, you should contact the **Queenstown PWS office** (☎ 03-6471 2511) or **Lake St Clair visitors centre** (☎ 03-6289 1172) for the latest information on permits and regulations. You should also check out the detailed Franklin rafting notes on the **PWS website** (www.parks.tas.gov.au – then go to Outdoor Recreation, Boating & Rafting Notes).

All expeditions should register at the booth at the junction of the Lyell Hwy and the Collingwood River, 49km west of Derwent Bridge. Rafting the length of the river, starting at Collingwood River and ending at Sir John Falls, takes between eight and 14 days (it's also possible to do shorter trips on different sections of the river). From the exit point, you can be picked up by a **Wilderness Air** (☎ 03-6471 7280) seaplane or paddle 22km further downriver to be collected by a **Gordon River Cruises** (☎ 03-6471 4300; Esplanade) boat at Heritage Landing.

Tours run mainly from December to March. Tour companies with complete Franklin rafting packages:

Rafting Tasmania (☎ 03-6239 1080; www.view.com.au /raftingtas) Four-/seven-/10-day trips cost $1050/1380/1800.

Tasmanian Expeditions (☎ 03-6334 3477; www .tas-ex .com) Five-/nine-day trips cost $1250/1900. There's also the option of longer trips which combine rafting with hiking to Frenchmans Cap.

Tasmanian Wild River Adventures (☎ 0409-977 506; www.wildrivers.com.au) Five-/seven-/11-day trips cost $1300/1400/1900.

CRADLE MOUNTAIN-LAKE ST CLAIR NATIONAL PARK

Tasmania's best-known national park is the superb 1262-sq-km World Heritage Area of Cradle Mountain-Lake St Clair. Its spectacular mountain peaks, deep gorges, lakes and wild moorlands extend from the Great Western Tiers in the north to Derwent Bridge on the Lyell Hwy in the south. It's one of the areas affected most by glacial activity in Australia and includes Mt Ossa (1617m), Tasmania's highest peak, and Lake St Clair, Australia's deepest natural freshwater lake.

The preservation of this region as a national park is due in part to Gustav Weindorfer, an Austrian who fell in love with the area. In 1912 he built a chalet out of King Billy pine, called it Waldheim (German for 'Forest Home') and, from 1916, lived there permanently. Today, bushwalkers huts stand near his original chalet at the northern end of the park and the area is named Waldheim, after his chalet.

There are plenty of day walks in both the Cradle Valley and Cynthia Bay (Lake St Clair) regions, but it's the spectacular 80.5km walk between the two that has turned this park into a bushwalkers' mecca. The Overland Track is one of the finest bushwalks in the country and, in summer, up to 100 people a day set off on it. The track can be walked in either direction, but most people walk from north to south.

Sights & Activities

CRADLE VALLEY

At the northern park boundary is the **Cradle Mountain visitors centre** (☎ 03-6492 1110; cradlemt@dpiwe.tas.gov.au; Cradle Mountain Rd; ☑ 8am-5pm or 6pm), with informative displays on the area. It's staffed by helpful rangers who can advise on weather conditions, walking gear and bush safety. In summer, rangers run many excellent free activities (eg walks, talks and slide shows); inquire at the visitors centre.

For visitors in wheelchairs or with kiddies in prams, behind the centre is an easy but quite spectacular 500m circular **boardwalk** through the adjacent rainforest.

Whatever time of the year you visit, be prepared for cold, wet weather in the Cradle Valley area. On average it rains here on seven days out of 10, is cloudy eight days in 10, the sun shines all day only one day in 10 and it snows on 54 days each year!

LAKE ST CLAIR

Occupying a wing of the large building at the southern end of the walking trail is the **Lake St Clair visitors centre** (☎ 03-6289 1172; via Derwent Bridge; ☑ 8am-5pm or 6pm), with good advice and displays on the park. Register here to walk the Overland Track in the northerly direction. At the adjacent, separately run **Lakeside St Clair Wilderness Holidays** (☎ 03-6289 1137; www.view.com.au/lakeside), you can book a seat on a ferry (p652), organise a cruise on the lake or hire canoes and dinghies. This organisation also manages accommodation in the immediate area (p650).

THE OVERLAND TRACK

For prospective walkers, the visitors centre at Cradle Mountain has an Overland Track information kit (including map and track notes) that staff will send anywhere in the world for $23.

The best time to walk the Overland Track is during summer, when flowering plants are most prolific, although spring and autumn also have their attractions. You can walk the track in winter, but only if you're experienced.

Walkers sometimes start the track at Dove Lake, but the recommended route begins at Ronny Creek, about 5km from the visitors centre.

The trail is well marked its entire length and, at an easy pace, takes around five or six days to walk. There are many secondary paths leading up to mountains such as Mt Ossa or other natural features, so the length of time you actually take is really only limited by the amount of supplies you can carry. There are unattended huts along the track that you can use for overnight accommodation, but in summer they fill quickly so make sure you carry a tent. Campfires are banned so you must carry a fuel stove.

The most dangerous part of the walk is the exposed high plateau between Waldheim and Pelion Creek, near Mt Pelion West. The southwest wind that blows across here can be bitterly cold and sometimes strong enough to knock you off your feet.

If you're walking from Cradle Valley to Cynthia Bay, you have the option of radioing from Narcissus Hut on the northern end of Lake St Clair for a ferry to come and pick you up, saving a five- to six-hour walk, at a cost of $20 per person.

More detailed descriptions of the walk are given in Lonely Planet's *Tasmania* and *Walking in Australia* guides.

OTHER ACTIVITIES

Most travellers to Tasmania consider Cradle Mountain a must-see, so almost every tour operator in the state offers day trips or longer tours to the area (including guided walks along the Overland Track). See p578 for details of some tour operators.

For independent travellers, aside from all the walks, the ranger-led activity programme in summer and the activities organised by the large hotels, the following companies offer you the chance to see the national park and/or its surrounds from a different angle:

Cradle Mountain Huts (☎ 03-6331 2006; www.cradle huts.com.au) For walkers who want to enjoy a degree of luxury, this company offers a six-day guided walk of the Overland Track for $1800. The price includes private huts, soft beds, hot showers and cooked meals.

Hyland Adventure Tours (☎ 03-6492 1212; Cradle Mountain Rd) Offers tours of the highlands on four-wheel, all-terrain vehicles (1 hour $65, 2½ hours $100). No experience is necessary but a driving licence is essential.

Seair Adventure Charters (☎ 03-6492 1132; www .seairac.com.au; Cradle Mountain Rd) With its booking desk inside the Cradle Mountain Wilderness Cafe, this company offers scenic flights over the park and surrounding wilderness areas lasting 25/50/65 minutes for $95/135/160 (minimum three people).

Sleeping & Eating
CRADLE VALLEY

Cradle Mountain Tourist Park (☎ 03-6492 1395; www .cosycabins.com/cradle; Cradle Mountain Rd; camp & caravan sites $20-25 for 2 people, dorm beds $20-24, cabins & cottages $100-135, additional adult $15-20) Situated 2.5km from the national park entrance, this bushland complex has camping sites, a good YHA hostel with four-bed dorms, self-contained cabins and more upmarket cottages (with spa), plus excellent amenities. It pays to book in advance as this is the only place in the area offering budget accommodation and hence is in demand.

Waldheim Cabins (☎ 03-6492 1110; cradlemt@dp iwe.tas.gov.au; Waldheim; s & d $70, additional adult $25)

These basic four- to eight-bunk huts are found near Gustav Weindorfer's original hut some 5km into the national park. Each contains gas stoves, cooking utensils and wood or gas heaters, but no bedding. Bathroom facilities are shared. Check-in and bookings are handled by the Cradle Mountain visitors centre.

Cradle Mountain Highlander Cottages (☎ 03-6492 1116; www.cradlehighlander.com.au; Cradle Mountain Rd; d $105-175) The genuinely hospitable Highlanders has six rustic timber cottages in a beautiful setting. It's a friendly, family-run operation and each cottage is different, although all come equipped with kitchen (and continental breakfast provisions) and lounge area. The more luxurious have a wood-fired heater and a spa.

Cradle Mountain Lodge (☎ 03-6492 1303; www.cradle mountainlodge.com.au; Cradle Mountain Rd; d $230-360, additional person $60) This gloriously swish resort, right by the entrance to the park, is huge – nearly 100 generously appointed cabins surround the main lodge. There are three standards of cabin, in sizes to suit couples or families. Each has tea- and coffee-making facilities and fridge (no kitchens); prices include an extensive buffet breakfast. There are log fires in all cabins, and pricier suites have CD players and spa baths. You can undertake a plethora of activities (guided and self-guided) in the area, and the lodge has canoes and mountain bikes for hire.

As well as a lovely bar and library area, The Lodge is home to the **Highlander** (mains $19-27; reservations recommended), a fine-dining restaurant offering well-prepared dishes including local lamb, salmon, beef and even wallaby. The **Tavern Bar & Bistro** (meals $7-19) serves pub-style lunches and dinners in a more casual setting. Menu choices include soup, steak, fish and chips, pizza and burgers.

Lemonthyme Lodge (☎ 03-6492 1112; www.lemon thyme.com.au; Dolcoath Rd; lodge s/d $100/110, cabins $220-300) The turn-off to this peaceful, Ponderosa-style mountain retreat is on the way to Cradle Mountain from Devonport, near the crossroads at Moina. It's some 32km from the national park entry, 8km of which are on an unsealed road, so make sure you book before embarking. You can stay in comfortable rooms in the lodge (shared bathroom facilities), or in luxurious cabins, some with spa and most with rainforest outlook.

There's a reputable restaurant here, and lots of walking opportunities.

Aside from the hotel restaurants, **Cradle Mountain Wilderness Cafe** (☎ 03-6492 1018; Cradle Mountain Rd; lunch $5-10, dinner $13-17) is the only dining option. It's part of the Wilderness Village apartment complex but on the opposite side of the road from the accommodation, and it serves decent meals (lunch and dinner) and has an extensive takeaway section. The café also sells petrol and alcohol.

Self-caterers should stock up before heading to Cradle Valley; minimal supplies are sold at the café, the tourist park and Cradle Mountain Lodge.

CYNTHIA BAY & DERWENT BRIDGE

Lakeside St Clair Wilderness Holidays (☎ 03-6289 1137; www.view.com.au/lakeside; Cynthia Bay; camp/caravan sites $12/15 for 2 people, dorm beds $25, cabins $100-150, d $135-185, additional adult $35) This place has its office at Cynthia Bay by the visitors centre, adjacent to the shop and restaurant it manages. It also has a lakeside camping ground not far away (a groundsheet is recommended as there's little ground cover), plus basic two- to four-bunk dorm rooms, and high-quality self-contained cabins. The licensed restaurant has good lunch and dinner options, plus a range of takeaways.

Derwent Bridge Wilderness Hotel (☎ 03-6289 1144; Derwent Bridge; dorm beds $25; d $85-105) If you've got any sense, the moment you step off the Overland Track, you'll head here for a beer, a steak and some big talk about your big walk. The accommodation is nothing special (only the more expensive rooms have bathrooms) but the welcoming lounge bar has a high, timber-beamed ceiling, pool table and massive open fire. Meals are impressive – better than the usual pub offerings – with dinner mains costing $17 to $24.

Derwent Bridge Chalets (☎ 03-6289 1000; www.troutwalks.com.au; Derwent Bridge; d $115-200, additional adult $35) There are a half-dozen roomy self-contained cottages to choose from here, each with bush views from the back porch. The immaculate cottages can sleep up to eight and are very well equipped, with full kitchen, laundry and wood or gas heaters; some also have a spa. The cheaper option, and good for one-night stays, is one of the new studio units with kitchenette.

At the time of writing. Doherty Hotels was planning the construction of a new hotel inside the park, at beautiful Pumphouse Point. There has been some controversy surrounding this development, with opponents voicing concerns over whether a hotel should be built inside the national park boundaries rather than outside it (as has been the case with tourist development in the Cradle Valley).

Getting There & Away

TassieLink (☎ 1300 300 520; www.tassielink.com.au) has bus services from Launceston to Cradle Mountain (via Devonport) and from Hobart to Lake St Clair every day from November to April. There are three or four services weekly between Cradle Valley and Lake St Clair (via Queenstown). Services are less frequent outside these months. TassieLink also offers packages whereby it drops you off at one end of the Overland Track and picks you up at the other. There are myriad options depending on where you're coming from/going to, so call TassieLink for prices; the packages must be booked.

Redline Coaches (☎ 1300 360 000; www.tasredline.com.au) also offers a daily service between Cradle Mountain and Devonport ($28) and a weekday connecting service from Launceston.

Maxwells (☎ 03-6492 1431) runs services on demand from Devonport to Cradle Mountain ($40), Launceston to Cradle Mountain ($60), and from Hobart, Devonport or Launceston to Lake St Clair ($70), and Cradle Valley to Lake St Clair ($85). Prices quoted are per person for five or more passengers; for four or fewer passengers, there's a single collective price for the trip.

You might be able to find a more convenient or cheaper transport option by talking to staff at bushwalking shops or hostels.

Getting Around

In Cradle Valley, **Maxwells** (☎ 03-6492 1431) runs a shuttle bus between the tourist park, Cradle Mountain Lodge, the visitors centre, Waldheim and Dove Lake ($9 one way, bookings essential).

At the time of writing a second, summertime shuttle service was being trialled. Inquire at the visitors centre or your accommodation to see if it's officially up and running.

Maxwells (☎ 03-6289 1125) also runs a taxi bus on demand between Cynthia Bay and Derwent Bridge, a distance of around 5km ($7 one way).

A **ferry service** (☎ 03-6289 1137) does trips between Cynthia Bay and Narcissus Hut, at the northern end of Lake St Clair, for $20/25 (one way/return). It departs numerous times daily; expect to pay more if there are fewer than four people on board. Bookings are essential; if using this service at the end of your walk, you must radio the ferry operator on arrival at Narcissus Hut.

THE SOUTHWEST

SOUTHWEST NATIONAL PARK

There are few places left in the world as isolated and untouched as Tasmania's southwest wilderness, the state's largest national park. It's home to some of the world's last tracts of virgin temperate rainforest and these contribute much to the grandeur and extraordinary diversity of this ancient area.

The southwest is the habitat of the endemic Huon pine, which lives for more than 3000 years, and of the swamp gum, the world's tallest hardwood and tallest flowering plant. About 300 species of lichen, moss and fern, some rare and endangered, dapple the rainforest in many shades of green; glacial tarns are seamless silver mirrors on the jagged mountains; and in summer, the alpine meadows are picture-perfect with wildflowers and flowering shrubs. Through it all run the wild rivers, with rapids tearing through deep gorges and waterfalls plunging over cliffs.

The best-known walk in the park is the **South Coast Track**, between Port Davey and Cockle Creek, near Southeast Cape. This walk takes about 10 days and should only be tackled by experienced hikers, well prepared for the often vicious weather conditions. Light planes are used to airlift bushwalkers into the southwest and there is public transport access to/from Cockle Creek. Detailed notes are available in Lonely Planet's *Walking in Australia*.

A range of escorted wilderness adventures is possible in the area, involving flying, hiking, rafting, canoeing, mountaineering and camping. As a starting point for information, contact the **Mt Field PWS** (☎ 03-6288 1149). Mt Field is also the place to pick up your national parks pass.

Getting There & Around

A popular way to tackle the South Coast Track is to fly into remote Melaleuca and walk out. **Tasair** (☎ 1800 062 900; www .tasair.com.au) and **Par Avion** (☎ 03-6248 5390; www.paravion.com.au) offer air services to bushwalkers, flying between Hobart and Melaleuca for around $150 one way. The airlines also offer scenic flight packages and daytrips, which can include landings and bushwalks.

From November to April, **TassieLink** (☎ 1300 300 520; www.tassielink.com.au) runs three buses a week between Hobart and Scotts Peak ($59, 4 hours) via Mt Field, and between Hobart and the eastern end of the South Coast Track at Cockle Creek ($52, 3½ hours). There are no services to Strathgordon.

LAKE PEDDER & STRATHGORDON

☎ 03 / pop 70

At the northern edge of the southwest wilderness lies Lake Pedder, once a spectacularly beautiful natural lake considered the ecological jewel of the region. In 1972, however, it was flooded to become part of the Gordon River power development. Together with nearby Lake Gordon, Pedder now holds 27 times the volume of water that's in Sydney Harbour and is the largest inland freshwater catchment in Australia.

Built to service HEC employees, Strathgordon is the base from which to visit Lakes Pedder and Gordon. It's become a popular bushwalking, climbing, fishing and watersports destination. A **visitors centre** (☎ 6280 1134; Gordon River Rd; ☸ 10am-5pm Nov-Apr, 11am-3pm May-Oct) at the 140m-high **Gordon Dam**, 12km west of the township, provides information on the scheme. The views from the dam walls are quite spectacular.

Accommodation-wise, your only option in the township is the basic motel-style units of **Lake Pedder Motor Inn** (☎ 6280 1166; Gordon River Rd; r around $70). Note that hydro workers generally occupy most of the hotel, but a limited number of rooms are available to the public (book well ahead). The hotel offers standard hotel meals to the public daily. Fuel is also available in Strathgordon.

TASMANIA

There are two free camping grounds near the southern end of Lake Pedder. **Edgar Campground** has pit toilets, water, fine views of the area and usually a fisherman or two. A better place to camp is the nearby **Huon Campground,** with the same facilities as Edgar but hidden in tall forest near Scotts Peak Dam.

BASS STRAIT ISLANDS

Tasmania has two groups of islands, the Hunter and Furneaux Groups, at the western and eastern entrances of Bass Strait, respectively. Once the transient homes of sealers, sailors and prospectors, these islands, rich in wildlife and natural beauty, are today inhabited by rural communities and offer a peaceful retreat for those keen to get well off the beaten track.

Probably the best way to visit King or Flinders Islands is to buy a fly-drive package that includes accommodation. Make inquiries with the airlines listed here, or contact Tourism Tasmania or travel centres in Melbourne and Sydney (for contact details see p575).

KING ISLAND
☎ 03 / pop 1760

At the western end of Bass Strait in the Hunter Group, this small island has beautiful beaches and quiet lagoons. Discovered in 1798, King Island was soon known as a breeding ground for seals and sea elephants. Just as quickly, they were hunted close to extinction by brutal sealers and sailors known as the Straitsmen.

Over the years, the stormy seas of Bass Strait have claimed many ships and there are several wrecks around the island. The worst accident occurred in 1845 when the *Cataraqui*, an immigrant ship, went down with 399 people aboard.

The main township is Currie on the west coast, and other notable settlements are Naracoopa on the east coast and Grassy in the southeast. Currie has an ATM.

Pre-trip information can be obtained from **King Island Tourism** (☎ 1800 645 017; www.kingisland.org.au; PO Box 269, Currie 7256), or via its comprehensive website. For tourist information once you reach the island, visit the **Trend** (☎ 6462 1360; Main St, Currie; ⏰ 9am-6.30pm).

Sights & Activities
King Island's four **lighthouses** guard against its treacherous coasts. The 48m-high Cape Wickham lighthouse is the tallest in the southern hemisphere and is worth visiting for the view of the surrounding coast. The others are at Currie, Stokes Point and south of Naracoopa.

The **King Island Historical Museum** (☎ 6462 1512; 36 Lighthouse St, Currie; admission by donation; ⏰ 2-4pm mid-Sep–Jun), housed in what was once the lighthouse keeper's cottage, features many maritime and local-history displays.

King Island is probably best known for its dairy produce (especially heavenly, award-winning cheeses). **King Island Dairy** (☎ 6462 1348; www.kidairy.com.au; North Rd, Loorana; ⏰ 9am-4.30pm Mon-Fri, 12.30-4pm Sun), 8km north of Currie (just beyond the airport), has tastings and sales for *fromage* connoisseurs.

Crayfish and kelp are other valuable exports for the island. On Netherby Rd is the only **kelp-processing plant** in Australia; from the roadside you can see kelp drying on racks.

Swimming at deserted **beaches** or in freshwater lagoons, **scuba diving** among marine life and shipwrecks, **surfing** and **fishing** are all popular. If you're interested in a drier pastime, try **bushwalking**. There is abundant wildlife here, including a small colony of fairy penguins at Grassy.

Tours
King Island Coaches (☎ 6462 1138; www.kingislandgem .com.au; 95 Main St, Currie), based at the King Island Gem Motel, does various half-/full-day island explorations ($35/70), as well as an evening tour to view penguins ($35). You can also opt for a bird-watching or walking tour ($110, including dinner).

King Island Dive Charters (☎ 6461 1133; king .island.dive@bigfoot.com), based in Grassy, offers full-day dives ($150), including lunch and equipment hire, plus longer trips of up to seven days (around $1200, including equipment and accommodation).

Sleeping
Bass Caravan Park (☎ 6462 1260; www.kingislandgem .com.au; 100 Main St, Currie; on-site vans s/d $33/45, s & d cabins $95) Located a few kilometres from the beach, this park offers a handful of on-site caravans with bathrooms, plus two-bedroom cabins with full kitchen and bathroom. The

cabins are good value for groups or families – up to five people can stay for $125. All linen is provided, and continental breakfast provisions are supplied in the cabins.

Boomerang By the Sea (☎ 6462 1288; www.bythe sea.com.au; Golf Club Rd, Currie; s/d $100/120) Boomerang has decent, well-equipped motel rooms that all enjoy superb ocean views across the golf course. It's only a short stroll into town, and there's a high-quality restaurant on site (see Eating; below).

Baudins (☎ 6461 1110; baudins@kingisland.net.au; The Esplanade, Naracoopa; d $125-155, additional person $40) On the beachfront at Naracoopa, with views across Sea Elephant Bay, the attractive Baudins has one- and two-bedroom self-contained timber units. Extra guest facilities include the use of fishing rods and mountain bikes. The two-bedroom units have spas.

Contact King Island Tourism or see its website for details on more accommodation options, including self-contained houses for rent.

Eating
There are many good eating places in Currie, within walking distance of most accommodation here.

Nautilus Coffee Lounge (☎ 6462 1868; Edward St, Currie; meals $4-12) In a courtyard beside the roundabout, Nautilus serves Devonshire teas, fresh soup, burgers and other light meals.

King Island Bakery (☎ 6462 1337; 5 Main St, Currie; snacks $3-6) An excellent spot for picnic-fodder, this popular bakery sells lots of freshly baked goods, including raved-about gourmet pies with fillings like crayfish, camembert and asparagus, and King Island beef.

Boomerang By the Sea (☎ 6462 1288; Golf Club Rd; mains from $21) Recognised as one of the island's best eating options, this roomy restaurant has spectacular ocean views and serves up delicious, locally sourced produce nightly except Sunday.

Baudins (☎ 6461 1110; The Esplanade, Naracoopa; mains $20-25) On the eastern side of the island, Baudins serves beef, seafood and other well-prepared regional edibles in its à la carte restaurant on the bay.

Getting There & Away
Flying is the only way to get to the island. **Regional Express Airlines** (☎ 13 17 13; www.regional express.com.au) flies from Melbourne to King Island, as does **King Island Airlines** (☎ 95803777) – the latter flies to/from a small suburban airport (Moorabbin) in Melbourne's southeast. One-way flights cost around $200.

Tasair (☎ 1800 062 900; www.tasair.com.au) flies from Devonport and Burnie to King Island (around $165 one way); connecting flights from Hobart are available.

Getting Around
There is no public transport on the island and most roads are unsealed. Hire-car companies will meet you at the airport, but vehicles should be booked. **Howells Auto Rent** (☎ 6462 1282; Meech St, Currie) has cars from around $60 a day. The **Trend** (☎ 6462 1360; Main St, Currie) has bikes for rent.

FLINDERS ISLAND
☎ 03 / pop 925
Flinders Island is the largest of the 52 islands that comprise the Furneaux Group. First charted in 1798 by the British explorer Matthew Flinders, the Furneaux Group became a base for the Straitsmen, who slaughtered seals in their tens of thousands.

The most tragic part of Flinders Island's history, however, was its role in the virtual annihilation of Tasmania's Aboriginal people between 1829 and 1834. Of the 135 survivors who were forcibly removed from the Tasmanian mainland to Wybalenna (meaning 'Black Man's House') to be 'civilised and educated', only 47 survived to make the journey to Oyster Cove near Hobart in 1847.

The island's main industries are farming, fishing and seasonal mutton-birding. Its administrative centre is Whitemark, and Lady Barron in the south is the main fishing area and deep-water port. Petrol is available only at Whitemark and Lady Barron.

Pre-trip information can be obtained from **Flinders Island Area Marketing & Development Office** (☎ 1800 994 477; www.flindersislandon line.com.au; PO Box 103, Whitemark 7255), or by checking its comprehensive website. Another helpful site is www.focusonflinders.com.au. On the island, a good place for information is the **Gem Shop** (☎ 6359 2160; Patrick St, Whitemark; ☑ 8.45am-5pm), by the Interstate Hotel.

Sights & Activities
Today, all that remains of the unfortunate settlement at **Wybalenna** is the cemetery and the chapel, restored by the National Trust

and open to visitors. In 1999 the site was returned to the descendants of those who had lived there.

Nearby, the Furneaux Historical Research Association's **Emita Museum** (☎ 6359 2047; Fowlers Rd, Emita; $2; ⊙ 1-5pm Sat & Sun year-round, 1-5pm daily in summer) displays a variety of Aboriginal artefacts, as well as old sealing and shipwreck relics.

Bushwalking is popular and many visitors climb **Mt Strzelecki**. The walk starts about 12km south of Whitemark, is well signposted and takes three to five hours return. The island supports a wide variety of **wildlife**, including many bird species, the best-known being the protected Cape Barren goose and the mutton bird.

There are beautiful **beaches** around the island, and several **scuba diving** locations off the northern and western coasts. In many places you can enter these from the beach or shelving rocks. There are **shipwrecks** around the island, some clearly visible from shore.

Rock and beach **fishing** are popular all year. Fishing tackle and bait can be purchased from many stores, however you'll need your own rod.

A more unusual pastime is **fossicking** for 'diamonds' – actually fragments of topaz – on the beach and creek at Killiecrankie Bay.

Tours

Flinders Island Adventures (☎ 6359 4507; james luddington@bigpond.com; Avondale) offers half-/full-day 4WD tours ($55/100), evening cruises to view mutton birds ($28), cruises around the outer islands ($55), fishing and diving trips and other customised touring options.

Flinders Island Dive (☎ 6359 8429; flinders dive@yahoo.com; 22 Wireless Station Rd, Emita) offers full-day diving among the myriad rocks in the Furneaux Group for $140, as well as fishing trips, diving courses and equipment hire.

Sleeping

Flinders Island Cabin Park (☎ 6359 2188; fi_cabin park@yahoo.com; Bluff Rd; s & d units with bathroom $75, s/ d without bathroom $30/45) Just around the corner from the airport and 5km from Whitemark is this relaxed park, home to a number of good-value cabins. All have kitchen and TV, and linen is provided; a couple of the larger units have bathrooms. Guests can also rent cars here ($55 per day).

Interstate Hotel (☎ 6359 2114; interstatehotel@ trump.net.au; Patrick St, Whitemark; s/d with bathroom $60/90, without bathroom $35/55) In the centre of Whitemark, this large, family-run hotel was built in 1911 and has been renovated in heritage style. It's well located, within easy walking distance of shops and other facilities, and prices include cooked breakfast. Larger groups should inquire about the self-contained apartment that sleeps six ($100 for two people, $10 for each additional person).

Yaringa Holiday Cottages (☎ 6359 4522; Holloway St, Lady Barron; d $85, additional person $11) There are three modern, self-contained two-bedroom units available at Yaringa in Lady Barron. Each unit sleeps up to six and welcome extras include laundry facilities, balconies, gardens and a communal barbecue. There's a minimum stay of two nights.

Partridge Farm (☎ 6369 3554; Badger Corner; d $125-130, additional person $27) Just southwest of Lady Barron, this rustic retreat offers a choice of a B&B suite with spa, a self-contained unit for two or a three-bedroom house, all set in bushland and with meals provided by prior arrangement.

Eating

Whitemark is home to most of the island's eating options, however nearly all of them are closed Sunday. At **Flinders Island Bakery** (☎ 6359 2105; Lagoon Rd, Whitemark; snacks $2-5) you can buy an assortment of breads, pies and other baked treats. Nearby **Sweet Surprises** (☎ 6359 2138; 5 Lagoon Rd, Whitemark; meals $4-12) is a popular coffee shop serving a variety of light meals.

The **Interstate Hotel** (☎ 6359 2114; interstate hotel@trump.net.au; Patrick St, Whitemark) serves a range of moderately priced meals from Monday to Saturday in its dining room and public bar.

The **Flinders Island Sports Club** (☎ 6359 2220; meals $15-22), just south of the township of Whitemark (follow the Esplanade), has a cosy restaurant with a quality menu; bookings are essential. **Flinders Island Lodge** (☎ 6359 3521; Franklin Pde; meals $14-19) in Lady Barron is a good option for a meal if you're visiting the island's south.

For self-catering supplies, there's a **supermarket** (☎ 6359 2010; Patrick St) in Whitemark, and general stores in Lady Barron and Killiecrankie.

Getting There & Away

AIR

Island Airlines Tasmania (☎ 1800 645 875) operates daily services to Flinders Island from
Launceston, and three or four weekly
flights from Essendon (in Melbourne) via
Traralgon (in regional Victoria). Return
flights from Launceston cost around $280,
from Essendon cost $400. The airline's
package deals are a good option, eg $490
per person for three days and two nights
from Launceston, $610 from Essendon. Ac-
commodation (on a twin-share basis) and
car hire are included in these packages.

BOAT

The **Southern Shipping Company** (☎ 6356 1753;
s.ship.co@microtech.com.au) runs a small passenger and car ferry from Bridport on
the northeast coast of mainland Tasmania
to Lady Barron on Flinders Island once
a week (usually on a Monday); once a
month it continues on to Port Welshpool
in Victoria. The return fare from Bridport
to Flinders Island is around $80 (from $490
for a car and driver). Advance bookings are
essential.

Getting Around

There is no public transport on the island. Hire-car companies will meet you
at the airport and bookings are highly
recommended. A number of companies
in Whitemark offer cars for hire, including
Bowman-Lees (☎ 6359 2388; Patrick St), which
charges between $60 and $80 a day.

South Australia

CONTENTS

South Australia (SA) is a patchwork of magnificent landscapes. Miles of beautiful coastline and immense sandy beaches are a glorious contrast to the lush hills of the Mt Lofty Ranges and the vast reaches of the outback. Here you'll find the moonscapes of the opal fields, the salted horizons of Lake Eyre and the ancient red and purple of the majestic Flinders Ranges.

Kangaroo Island is a little beauty with turquoise seas, and is also one of the best places in Australia to watch wildlife. Spend a few tranquil days floating on a houseboat down the Murray River or explore the Peninsula's fraying hemlines, which provide some of the best surf breaks in the country.

A history crammed with migrant adventurers and refugees, and the hardships of developing a new and free colony has produced a resilient people who don't ask for much: a life filled with family and friends, weekends at the beach and simple sensual pleasures.

The mixture of nationalities is obvious in the fabulous bustle, colour and aromas of Adelaide's covered food market and in the vibrant alfresco café culture, which keep the city streets dancing night and day.

Sophisticated palates and a Mediterranean climate produce glorious food and luscious silken wines from renowned regions such as the Barossa Valley and the Coonawarra. Producing 70% of Australia's wine exports, SA's liquid gems are celebrated in numerous festivals, alongside the arts, sport and music.

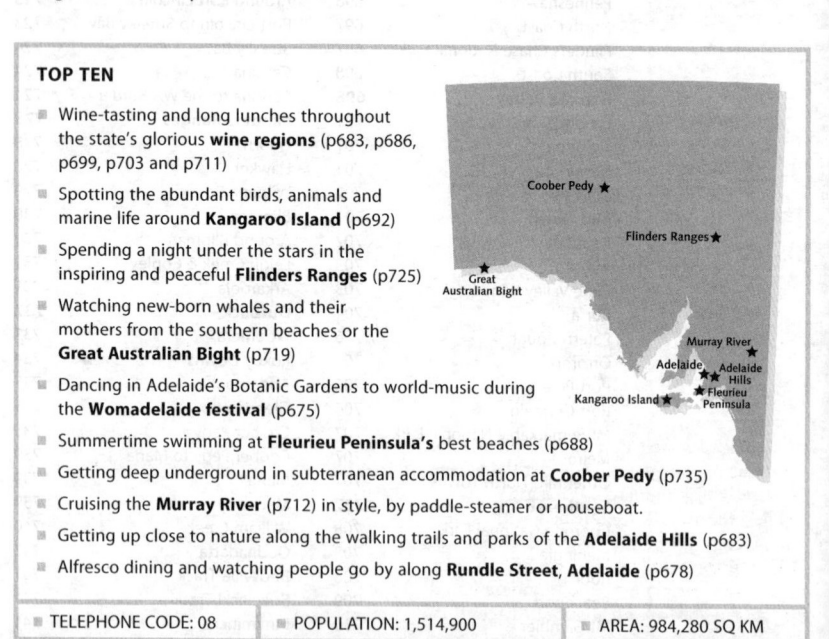

TOP TEN

- Wine-tasting and long lunches throughout the state's glorious **wine regions** (p683, p686, p699, p703 and p711)
- Spotting the abundant birds, animals and marine life around **Kangaroo Island** (p692)
- Spending a night under the stars in the inspiring and peaceful **Flinders Ranges** (p725)
- Watching new-born whales and their mothers from the southern beaches or the **Great Australian Bight** (p719)
- Dancing in Adelaide's Botanic Gardens to world-music during the **Womadelaide festival** (p675)
- Summertime swimming at **Fleurieu Peninsula's** best beaches (p688)
- Getting deep underground in subterranean accommodation at **Coober Pedy** (p735)
- Cruising the **Murray River** (p712) in style, by paddle-steamer or houseboat.
- Getting up close to nature along the walking trails and parks of the **Adelaide Hills** (p683)
- Alfresco dining and watching people go by along **Rundle Street, Adelaide** (p678)

| TELEPHONE CODE: 08 | POPULATION: 1,514,900 | AREA: 984,280 SQ KM |

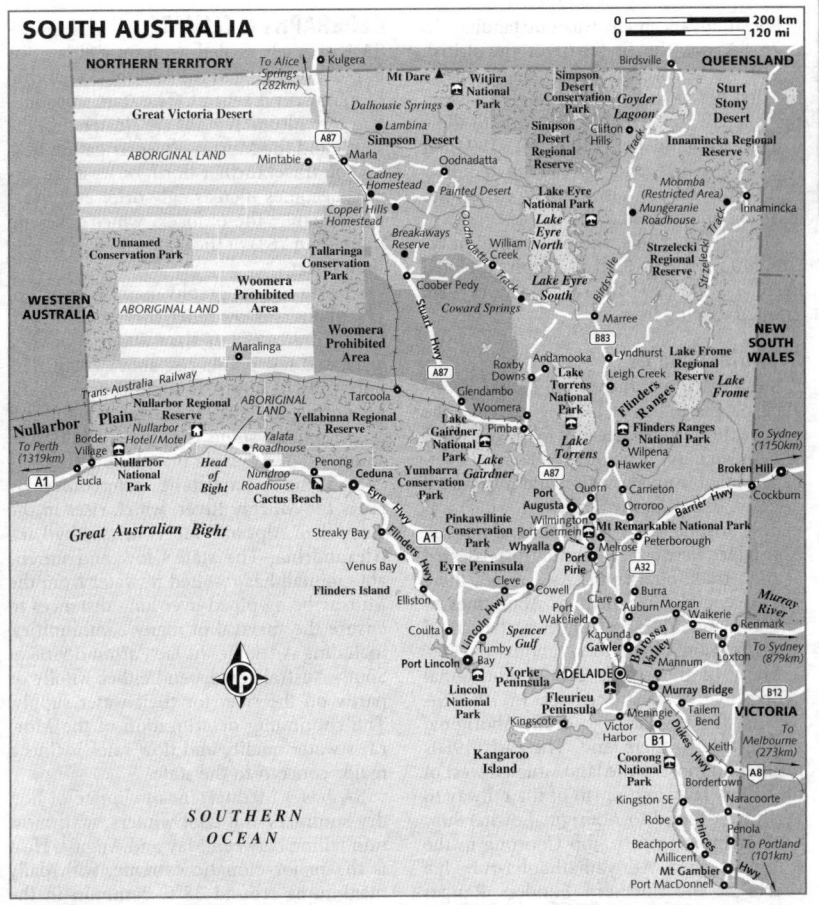

HISTORY

SA was declared a province and open for business on 28 December 1836, the day the first British settlers landed at Holdfast Bay. Colonel William Light chose a site about 10km inland for the state capital – and is still considered a hero for establishing Adelaide's simple street design and surrounding ring of green parklands. The first governor, Captain John Hindmarsh, named Adelaide after the wife of the then British monarch, William IV.

The colony was established with ambitious ideals. While the eastern states struggled with the problems of a convict society, SA's settlers were free. The founders based the colony on an idealistic 19th-century theory of systematic colonisation and social

engineering; land was sold at set prices by the British Government to help establish mainly skilled and young married couples. The ideal was that equal numbers of these men and women would be free from religious and political persecution to create a truly egalitarian new world.

At first, progress in the colony was slow and only British government funds saved it from bankruptcy. It was self-supporting by the mid-1840s and self-governing by 1856.

Local explorers successfully crossed the continent and SA won the contract to lay the Overland Telegraph from Port Augusta to Darwin – Australia would now be connected to the world by telegram (1872), and later, telephone.

SOUTH AUSTRALIA

Social advancement was outstanding. In 1876 SA was the first part of the British Empire to legalise trade unions and one of the first places in the world to give women the vote; it was the first in the world to allow women to stand for parliament (1894). It was also the first state in Australia to outlaw racial and gender discrimination, legalise abortion and decriminalise gay sex.

On top of all this, the first community-run hotel in the British Empire opened here, and the first Australian drivers were granted driving licenses.

Aboriginal People

It is estimated that there were 12,000 Aboriginal people in SA at the beginning of the 19th century. In the decades following white settlement, many were either killed by the settlers or died from starvation and introduced diseases. Except in the northwest, which was mainly unsuitable for pastoral development, Aborigines were usually forcibly dispossessed of their traditional lands. As a result, there was a general movement of Aborigines to missions and other centres where they could find safety and obtain food rations.

Many of the state's 21,000 Aboriginal people live in urban centres. In 1966 SA became the first state to grant Aboriginal people title to their land. The early 1980s resulted in most of the land situated west of the Stuart Hwy and north of the railway to Perth transferred to Aboriginal ownership.

Ngarrindjeri-run Camp Coorong in the southeast and Adnyamathanha-run Iga Warta in the northern Flinders Ranges offer cultural tours to give visitors a firsthand insight into traditional Aboriginal ways of life. In Adelaide, Tandanya is a major Aboriginal cultural centre while the Australian Aboriginal Cultures Gallery in Adelaide's South Australian Museum is the largest exhibition of its kind. Excellent indigenous guides from Tauondi Aboriginal Cultural Tours will take you around this exhibition and Adelaide's Botanic Gardens (p670).

The seminal *Survival in Our Own Land*, edited by Christobel Mattingley & Ken Hampton, is exhaustively researched and has beautifully written individual and historical accounts by Nungas (South Australian Aboriginal people). It is available from good bookshops in Adelaide.

GEOGRAPHY & CLIMATE

SA is sparsely settled, with over 80% of its population living in Adelaide and a handful of major rural centres. The state's productive agricultural regions are clustered in the south and the Murray River irrigation belt. As you travel further north or west the terrain becomes increasingly drier and more inhospitable; the outback, which takes up more than 75% of the state's area, is largely semidesert.

The state's topography mainly consists of vast plains and low relief. More than 80% of the land area is less than 300m above sea level, and few points rise above 700m. The only hills of any real significance are the Mt Lofty and Flinders Ranges, which form a continuous spine running 800km from southeast of Adelaide into the interior.

SA's most important watercourse by far is the Murray River, which rises in the Australian Alps and meets the sea by Lake Alexandrina. The state's low and unreliable rainfall has resulted in water from the Murray being piped over long distances to ensure the survival of many communities, including Adelaide. In fact, around 90% of South Australians depend either wholly or partly on the river for their water supply. The continuing deterioration of the Murray's water quality and flow rates is thus a major concern to the state.

SA has a Mediterranean climate of hot, dry summers and cool winters, with most rain falling between May and August. Heat is the major climatic extreme, with daily maximums around 38°C common in the outback from October to April.

SA is by far the driest Australian state. More than 80% of SA normally receives less than 250mm of rain annually.

INFORMATION

For comprehensive information about the entire state you could try Lonely Planet's *South Australia* guidebook; for other useful sources of information:

South Australian Tourism Commission Visitors Centre (SATC; Map pp668-9; ☎ 1300 655 276, 08-8303 2033; www.southaustralia.com; 18 King William St, Adelaide; ☼ 8.30am-5pm Mon-Fri, 9am-2pm Sat & Sun) The main SATC centre has a very good range of regional information, and advance bookings can be made here. The SATC also has outlets in most Australian capital cities, check its website for details.

State Library of SA (Map pp668-9; ☎ 1800 182 013, 08-8207 7250; www.slsa.sa.gov.au; North Tce, Adelaide; ⏰ 9.30am-8pm Mon-Wed & Fri, 9.30am-6pm Thu, noon-5pm Sat & Sun; 🖳) As well as a fascinating database on the state's settlers and explorers (including photographs), practical information is also available.

Service SA (Map pp668-9; ☎ 13 23 24, 08-8204 1900; www.info.sa.gov.au; 77 Grenfell St, Adelaide; ⏰ 9am-5pm Mon-Tue & Thu-Fri, 9.30am-5pm Wed; 🖳) This is a government resource centre with publications covering a vast range of topics – from museums, industries and legislation, to cycling and trekking routes.

Blaze (☎ 08-8211 9199; 213 Franklin St, Adelaide) Adelaide's free gay and lesbian newspaper is available at its office, **Imprints Booksellers** (Map pp668-9; Hindley St, Adelaide) and shops on Rundle St in the city. Also grab a copy of its **Adelaide Lesbian and Gay Business Directory** which has good listings of gay- and lesbian-friendly operators in the city.

Useful Organisations

Disability Information & Resource Centre (DIRC; Map pp668-9; ☎ 08-8223 7522, 8223 7579; www .dircsa.org.au; 195 Gilles St, Adelaide; ⏰ 9am-5pm Mon-Fri) Contact DIRC for information on accommodation, venues, tourist destinations and travel agencies that cater for people with disabilities.

Gay and Lesbian Counselling Service (GLCS; ☎ 1800 182 233, 08-8362 3223; ⏰ 2-5pm & 7-10pm Sat & Sun) Provides general information on social activities and gay-friendly service providers, along with counselling. A good website is www.gayadelaide.org.

Royal Automobile Association (RAA; Map pp668-9; ☎ 08-8202 4500; www.raa.net; 41 Hindmarsh Sq, Adel-

aide; ⏰ 8.30am-5pm Mon-Fri, 9am-noon Sat) This travel and motoring organisation also sells travel books and maps.

Traveller's Medical & Vaccination Centre (Map pp668-9; ☎ 08-8212 7522; 29 Gilbert Pl, Adelaide; ⏰ 9am-5pm Mon-Tue & Thu-Fri, 9am-7pm Wed, 9am-12.30pm Sat)

Womens Information Service (Map pp668-9; ☎ 08-8303 0590; www.wis.sa.gov.au; Station Arcade, 136 North Tce, Adelaide; ⏰ 8am-6pm Mon-Fri, 9am-5pm Sat; 🖳) Practical information and free Internet access are offered along with counselling services.

NATIONAL PARKS

SA has over 300 conservation reserves including national parks, recreation parks, wildlife reserves, waterways and regional reserves. In fact, around 22% of the state's land area is under some form of official conservation management; the largest areas are in the outback. Three of Australia's better-known national parks are in SA: Flinders Chase National Park, Kangaroo Island; Flinders Ranges National Park; and the Great Australian Bight Marine Park.

The day-to-day management of the state's conservation areas is handled by the National Parks and Wildlife SA (NPWSA), a division of the Department for Environment and Heritage.

The **Environment Shop** (Map pp668-9; ☎ 08-8204 1910; www.parks.sa.gov.au; 77 Grenfell St, Adelaide; ⏰ 9am-5pm Mon-Fri), a NPWSA outlet, can supply you with all the necessary parks information and passes. There is also a great range of maps, nature books and government publications

---

HEYSEN TRAIL

One of the world's great long-distance walks, the Heysen Trail, extends over 1200km from Cape Jervis at the tip of the Fleurieu Peninsula to Parachilna Gorge in the central Flinders Ranges. En route it travels along the Mt Lofty Ranges, through the Barossa Valley wine region and the old copper town of Burra, then heads into the Flinders Ranges. Here it scales Mt Remarkable and Mt Brown before continuing on to Wilpena Pound and beyond.

The trail was named in honour of Sir Hans Heysen (1877–1968), South Australia's best-known landscape artist. Sir Hans immigrated to Adelaide from Germany at the age of seven, and sold his first painting nine years later. Unlike many artists he became famous in his own lifetime, winning a number of prestigious awards. His favourite subjects were the Australian gum tree and the rural landscapes of the Mt Lofty and Flinders Ranges.

Overall, the Heysen Trail presents a remarkable challenge, but you can also follow short sections on day trips or longer. Due to fire restrictions, the trail is closed between December and April.

Good maps detailing each of the 15 sections are available from $4.50 to $6.50 from **Service SA** (Map pp668-9; ☎ 13 23 24, 08-8204 1900; www.info.sa.gov.au; 77 Grenfell St, Adelaide; ⏰ 9am-5pm Mon-Tue & Thu-Fri, 9.30am-5pm Wed) or the **Environment Shop** (Map pp668-9; ☎ 08-8204 1910; www.parks.sa.gov.au; 77 Grenfell St, Adelaide; ⏰ 9am-5pm Mon-Fri), as well as outdoor-gear shops on Rundle St in Adelaide.

covering environmental issues. The free guide *South Australia's National Parks* contains details on each park and their facilities, including disabled access, activities and local NPWSA offices.

Day Passes and Camping Permits are $7 (per vehicle). If appropriate buy the camping passes as they cover you for both eventualities – available at NPWSA outlets.

If you intend to visit a number of parks, you should inquire about the Four Week Holiday Parks Pass ($20 per vehicle). This covers the cost of entry (but not camping) at a number of the most popular parks, excluding the desert parks (p732).

ACTIVITIES
Bushwalking
Close to Adelaide there are many walks to suit all abilities in the Mt Lofty Ranges, including those at Belair National Park and Morialta Conservation Park.

Several bushwalking clubs in the Adelaide area organise weekend walks in the Mt Lofty and Flinders Ranges, and a number of Adelaide operators offer guided walks – ask at the outdoor shops on Rundle St.

In the Flinders Ranges there are excellent walks in the Mt Remarkable and Flinders Ranges National Parks, and further north in the Gammon Ranges National Park and adjoining Arkaroola-Mt Painter Wildlife Sanctuary.

Friends of the Heysen Trail (☎ 08-8212 6299; www.heysentrail.asn.au) welcome everyone to join its periodic excursions (between April and November) to different sections of the 1200km Heysen Trail. Covering every sort of vista imaginable, the trail winds north from Cape Jervis on the tip of the Fleurieu Peninsula to the central Flinders Ranges (p661).

Canoeing & Sailing
The Murray River and the Coorong (south of Murray Bridge) are popular for canoeing trips. Visitors can hire equipment and join trips organised by canoeing associations. There is good sailing all along Adelaide's shoreline in Gulf St Vincent, where there are a number of sailing clubs.

Yachting SA (☎ 08-8232 6032; www.sa.yachting .org.au; 73 Wakefield St, Adelaide) The state body website has great information including contacts for all SA's sailing clubs, courses and boating events.

Canoe South Australia (☎ 08-8240 3294; www .canoesa.asn.au; Aquatics Reserve, Old Port Rd, West Lakes) Another excellent website covering state clubs, equipment and events.

Diving
Any of the scuba-gear shops in Adelaide will be able to give pointers on places to dive close to the city. At Port Noarlunga (18km south of Adelaide) you can shore dive on the Marine Reserve or boat dive on the HA *Lum*, a sunken fishing boat.

You can snorkel at Snapper Point, but the Aldinga Reef is a better place for scuba diving. Second Valley (65km south of Adelaide) is a dive-training site and the water is generally clear, while 23km further on at Rapid Bay you can dive from the jetty and see abundant marine life.

HMAS *Hobart* was scuttled off Yankalilla Bay for divers, and the reefs, wrecks and drop-offs around nearby Kangaroo Island make it a very popular diving centre.

Other good areas include most jetties around the Yorke Peninsula and the reefs off Port Lincoln.

Rock Climbing
Rock spiders happy with cliffs between 10m to 15m high will enjoy the gorges in Morialta Conservation Park and Onkaparinga River Recreation Park. Both of these cater for beginners and advanced climbers and the locations are close to Adelaide.

Advanced lead climbers head for the Flinders Ranges. Moonarie on the southeastern side of Wilpena Pound has cliffs reaching 120m. Buckaringa Gorge close to Quorn and Hawker is another favourite for the more skilled climbers.

Paddy Pallin Adventure Equipment (☎ 08-8232 3155; www.paddypallin.com.au; 228 Rundle St, Adelaide) is a good place to start. Ask the climbing-mad staff about good spots, hire equipment, local climbing guidebooks and climbing courses.

Outdoor Adventure Skills (☎ 08-8227 1855; www .outdooradventure.com.au; 228 Rundle St, Adelaide) runs a number of climbing and abseiling courses on demand. Call before dropping in.

Swimming & Surfing
There are fantastic swimming beaches all along the SA coast.

The Adelaide suburbs of Seacliff, Somerton, Brighton, Glenelg, West Beach, Henley

Beach, Grange and Semaphore have safe, sandy and family-friendly beaches.

The immense Fleurieu Peninsula beaches are good for swimming and gentle surfing, while seminudist Maslin Beach is good for all-over tanning and scaring the seagulls.

Closer to Adelaide, and near Victor Harbor on the Fleurieu Peninsula, there's often good surf at Waitpinga Beach, Middleton and Port Elliot. The surf shops in Middleton and Port Elliot hire out boards and can recommend local surf schools. Goolwa beach is a paradise for beach layabouts. You have to get over to Pondalowie Bay on the Yorke Peninsula for the state's most reliable large waves. For the hardened surfers among us, there are good spots along the Eyre Peninsula between Port Lincoln and the Ceduna area; Cactus Beach, near Penong west of Ceduna, is world-famous for its surf.

Whale-Watching

This is a really special experience that can be enjoyed from the southern beaches or the Great Australian Bight. For details see the boxed text 'Southern Right Whales'.

TOURS

Most Adelaide-based tour companies run both day tours and short packages to destinations such as Kangaroo Island, the Coorong and the Murray river. Other operators specialise in longer trips to the Flinders Ranges, Eyre Peninsula and the Outback. Hostels will recommend backpacker-friendly tours, some even run their own.

Recommended coach tour operators are all based at Adelaide's central bus station. They include:

Premier Stateliner (☎ 08-8415 5555; www.premier stateliner.com.au; 111 Franklin St, Adelaide) The efficient and statewide transport service also offers good-value tours.

Adelaide Sightseeing (☎ 08-8231 4144; adssres@sealink.com.au; 101 Franklin St, Adelaide) Covers the standard destinations and is popular with tour groups.

Gray Line (☎ 1300 858 587; www.grayline.com; 101 Franklin St, Adelaide) Visits the Clare Valley and the Murray River paddle-wheelers.

Tourabout Adelaide Walking & Private Tours (☎ 08-8333 1111; www.touraboutadelaide.com.au) Offers private tours, bilingual guides and innovative themed tours around the state.

GETTING THERE & AROUND
Air

Adelaide airport is 7km, and a 20-minute drive, west of the city centre. A taxi costs around $17 between the airport and the city centre, and all the major hire-car agencies have desks at the airport.

Skylink (☎ 08-8332 0528; www.skylinkadelaide.com; adult/child one way $7/2.50; ☺ bookings 7am-10pm) does the airport–city run, covering international and domestic terminals, hourly between 6.30am and 9.45pm. The buses pick up from central hotels and a number of specific places in the city. If you're catching a flight on one of the smaller regional airlines, let the driver know, as the drop-off point is different.

Remember that most of the hostels will pick you up and drop you off if you're staying with them.

SOUTHERN RIGHT WHALES

Southern right whales are so called because they were once considered by whalers to be the right whales to hunt; they swam close to the coast and conveniently floated when killed. Additionally they surrendered large quantities of oil and fine whalebone.

Once roaming the seas in prolific numbers, unrestrained slaughter last century reduced this whale population from 100,000 to just a few hundred by 1935. Although considered an endangered species, they are fighting back and the population worldwide may be as high as 4000. From late June to September many southern rights migrate to the warmer waters along Australia's southern coast to breed, with around 100 whales born each year. These enchanting and majestic animals can be seen regularly from the southern coastal beaches (Goolwa through to Victor Harbor and Port Lincoln). Alternatively, it is possible to see more than 100 whales during their seasonal mating, calving and nursing from the dramatic cliffs at the Head of Bight (p725), around 79km west of the Yalata Roadhouse on the Nullarbor, where you can also buy the necessary permit ($8/6.50 per adult/child).

The South Australian Whale Centre (p689) operates a whale-spotting network and information centre. Call to report a sighting or to ask where any whales might be found.

Adelaide is connected by regular air services to all Australian capitals. Both Virgin Blue and Qantas have special deals advertised daily on their websites, and Virgin's Internet deals are especially good value. The rates quoted are one-way full economy fares.

Virgin Blue (☎ 13 67 89; www.virginblue.com.au) offers flights to a range of holiday towns and cities, including Melbourne ($209), Sydney ($259), Perth ($469) and Hobart ($369).

Qantas (☎ 13 13 13; www.qantas.com.au; 144 North Tce, Adelaide) covers cities including the busy Darwin route ($600), Melbourne ($324), Sydney ($423), Perth ($500) and Alice Springs ($484).

Regional Express (Rex; ☎ 13 17 13; www.regionalexpress.com.au) is the main regional operator with flights from Adelaide to Mt Gambier, Port Lincoln, Ceduna, Coober Pedy, Whyalla, Kingscote and Olympic Dam.

Airlines of South Australia (☎ 1800 018 234, 08-8234 3000; www.airlinesofsa.com.au) departs from Adelaide for Port Lincoln and for Port Augusta.

Emu Airways (☎ 08-8234 3711) flies between Kingscote on Kangaroo Island and Adelaide.

O'Connor Airlines (☎ 13 13 13, 08-8723 0666; www.oconnor-airlines.com.au) is a Qantas subsidiary, flying between Adelaide, Melbourne, Mildura, Mt Gambier and Whyalla.

Bus

Adelaide's **central bus station** (Map pp668-9; 101-111 Franklin St, Adelaide) contains terminals and ticket offices for all major interstate and statewide services. Left-luggage lockers are available and there's a taxi rank outside.

The **State Guide** (www.bussa.com.au) is a comprehensive timetable covering all the country bus services and their different operators.

Discounts are on offer from most operators for those holding backpacker associations/international student ID.

McCafferty's/Greyhound (☎ 13 14 99, 08-8212 5066; www.mccaffertys.com.au; ☯ 6am-8.30pm) has services between Adelaide and all major cities: Melbourne ($60, 11 hours), Sydney ($130, 25 hours), Alice Springs ($180, 21 hours) and Perth ($265, 35¼ hours).

V/Line (☎ 08-8231 7620; ☯ 7.30am-5pm Mon-Fri) runs daily services to Melbourne and Sydney; Melbourne via a bus to Bendigo with a connecting train to Melbourne ($60, 11½ hours), and Sydney via a bus to Albury and connecting train to Sydney ($150, 21 hours).

Firefly Express (☎ 08-8231 1488, 1300 730 740; ☯ 7am-8.30pm) runs to Melbourne every morning and evening at 7.30am and 8.30pm ($50, 11 hours) and from there on to Sydney (ex-Adelaide $100, 24 hours).

Premier Stateliner (☎ 08-8415 5555; ☯ 7am-9pm) is the largest statewide operator. Destinations from Adelaide include Ceduna ($85, 12 hours), McLaren Vale ($6.50, 1 hour), Moonta ($19, 2½ hours), Mt Gambier ($50, 6½ hours), Port Augusta ($36, 4 hours), Port Lincoln ($75, 8½ hours), Victor Harbor ($15, 2 hours) and Wilpena Pound ($65, 7 hours).

Car

If you want to hitch a ride (sharing petrol costs) or buy a second-hand car, check out the hostel notice boards. Hostels will also be able to tell you about recommended companies who do buy-back deals.

The Yellow Pages lists almost 100 vehicle rental companies including all the major national companies. You can expect to pay around $46 per day with the cheaper companies, such as those listed below:

Access Rent-a-Car (☎ 1800 812 580, 08-8212 5900; 121 Currie St, Adelaide)

Action Rent-a-Car (☎ 08-8352 7310; 280 Sir Donald Bradman Dr, Cowandilla)

Cut Price Car-&-Truck-Rentals (☎ 08-8443 7788; cnr Sir Donald Bradman Dr & South Rd, Mile End South)

Hawk-Rent-A-Car (☎ 1800 00 4295, 08-8371 3688; 415 Cross Rd, Edwardstown)

Rent-a-Bug (☎ 08-8443 8846; 91 Sir Donald Bradman Dr, Hilton)

Smile Rent-a-Car (☎ 08-8234 0655; 163-165 Richmond Rd, Richmond)

If you're travelling by car, it's worth noting that honey, plants, fruit and vegetables cannot be taken across the following Australian quarantine points. Travelling to Western Australia (WA) there's a checkpoint at Border Village, also at Ceduna for those heading east. There are checkpoints on the Victorian border on the Mallee Hwy at Pinnaroo and on the Sturt Hwy between Mildura and Renmark. There's another checkpoint at Oodla-Wirra, on the Barrier Hwy from Broken Hill.

Train

The interstate train terminal is at Railway Tce, Keswick, just southwest of the city

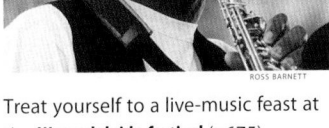

Try some luscious wines from the
Barossa Valley (p698)

JOHN HAY

Sit back and relax in the peaceful
Chambers Gorge (p730)

Treat yourself to a live-music feast at
the **Womadelaide festival** (p675)

ROSS BARNETT

CHRIS MELLOR

Find inspiration and tranquility in the picturesque landscape of the **Flinders Ranges** (p725)

RICHARD I'ANSON

MANFRED GOTT

Park yourself on the edge of the **Great Australian Bight** (p663)

Gaze into the gentle face of a young sea lion at **Seal Bay** (p698)

BOB CHARLTON

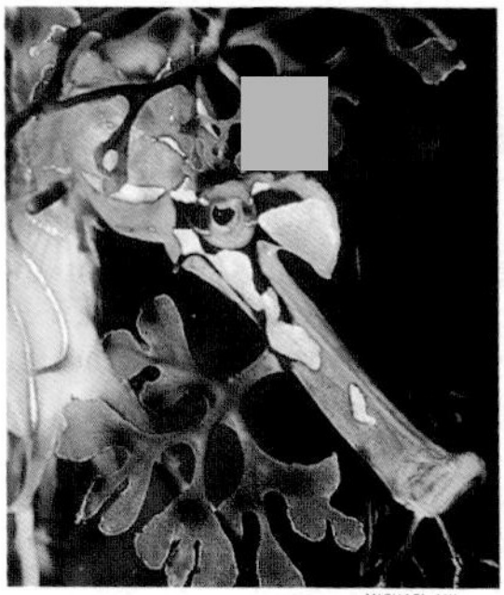

MICHAEL AW

Dive the waters off **Kangaroo Island** (p694) to see Leafy Sea Dragons

Feed the pelicans at the **Kangaroo Island Marine Centre** (p695)

CHR

centre, and **Skylink** (☎ 08-8332 0528; www.skylink adelaide.com; ✆ bookings 7am-10pm) will pick up prebooked passengers on its airport–city runs ($3.30/1.50 per adult/child).

Great Southern Railway (☎ 13 21 47, 08-8213 4444; www.trainways.com.au; ✆ 7.30am-8pm Mon-Fri, 8am-6pm Sat, 9am-5pm Sun) operate all train services in and out of SA. Backpackers are eligible for huge discounts (around 50%) and cheap six-month passes ($450) with specific ID.

The following trains depart from Adelaide regularly:

Overland To Melbourne (economy seat/twin-berth sleeper $60/150, 11 hours)

Indian Pacific To Sydney (economy seat/1st-class sleeper $223/450/570, 25 hours)

Indian Pacific To Perth (economy seat/twin-berth sleeper/1st-class sleeper $310/960/1190, 39 hours)

Ghan To Alice Springs (economy seat/twin-berth sleeper/ 1st-class sleeper $215/680/850, 19 hours)

Ghan To Darwin (economy seat/twin-berth sleeper/1st-class sleeper $440/1390/1740, 47 hours)

ADELAIDE

☎ 08 / pop 1,045,854

Leafy Adelaide is a cosmopolitan and cultural city bordered by the enchanted hills of the Mt Lofty Ranges and the long sandy beaches of the Gulf St Vincent.

The early European colonists built with stone, pride and plenty of style; the dignified city-centre buildings are encircled by green parklands, which host numerous galas celebrating a thriving arts community and a thoroughly hedonistic spirit.

The capital has a European feel, but the passion for sports is uniquely Australian. From motor racing to cricket, Australian Rules footy to water sports, weekends are enjoyed at the match or on the beach.

Adelaide's founder Colonel William Light and former premier (turned restaurateur) Don Dunstan are still applauded for their enlightened decisions, which shaped Adelaide into this civilised, social and peaceful place. The city's arts-mad community especially revere Dunstan, as wearing a pink safari suit in Parliament wasn't his only contribution to Adelaide's cultural life in the 1970s.

Much credit must go to the man for the riverside Festival Centre theatre complex.

Also the bi-annual Arts and youth-arts Coming Out festivals, as well as the relaxing of many social and censorship laws that encouraged free expression (and the creation of Australia's first nudist beach!).

Adelaide's beaches are bounteous, the streets are safe and lined with superb multi-ethnic restaurants, and magnificent wines flow at any excuse – isn't this known as quality of life?

ORIENTATION

The city centre is laid out on a grid and has several squares, with King William St as the main thoroughfare dissecting the city. Most cross streets change their name at King William St (because you mustn't cross the King!). Victoria Square is at the city's geographical centre and contains bus stops, a taxi rank and the Glenelg tram terminus. Franklin St runs off the square, containing Adelaide's central bus station and a taxi rank.

Rundle St is the social centre for all ages, with day- and night-time alfresco dining and drinking, bookshops, retro clothing and independent cinemas. Heading west the street becomes Rundle Mall, a colourful hive of activity containing most of the big shops and department stores. Across King William St, Rundle Mall turns into Hindley St where strip clubs rub shoulders with university buildings, specialist bookshops, bars and dance clubs.

The next street north of Hindley St is elegant North Tce. The dignified State Parliament buildings, casino and suburban train station are just to the west of King William St, and there's a string of magnificent public buildings, including the art gallery, museum, state library and the University of Adelaide, to the east.

Continue north and you're in the lush North Parklands, with the Festival Centre; King William Rd then crosses the Torrens River into North Adelaide.

There's a good shuttle bus service between the city, interstate train station at Keswick and Adelaide's airport.

Maps

The Royal Automobile Association (RAA), Hema and Westprint maps should cover your needs – available from the RAA and all bookshops.

ADELAIDE IN...

Two Days

Wake up over breakfast at **Zuma Caffé** (p679) in the vibrant covered market. Take a free loop bus around the city, stopping off at the excellent **Migration Museum** (p667) and then the **National Wine Centre** (p671) for some sniffing and supping. Walk along the **Torrens River** (p671) and visit **Cibo Ristorante** (p679) in North Adelaide for an Italian supper and **Rundle St** (p678) for an alfresco coffee and people watching.

Next morning stroll through the South Parklands taking in the **Veale Gardens** (p670) and the Japanese **Himeji Gardens** (p670), then take an Aboriginal guided walk of the leafy **Adelaide Botanic Garden** (p670) or enjoy Australian colours in the **Art Gallery of South Australia** (p667). Jump on a vintage tram to relax on the beach at **Glenelg** (p671), then enjoy a seafood dinner at **Sammy's on the Marina** (p679) or spicy Sri Lankan fare at **Papadums** (p679).

Four Days

Add a trip into the **Adelaide Hills** (p683) for a magnificent gourmet lunch at the historic **Petaluma's Bridgewater Mill** (p683) and a visit to the furry stars of the **Cleland Wildlife Park** (p683). Take in a night of live blues at the **Gov** (p681) or classics at the riverside **Festival Centre** (p680).

One Week

Include a day's wine tasting in the pretty **Barossa Valley** (p698), and a visit to the south coast's little penguins on **Granite Island** (p689) – keep a look out for whales, if it's the season. Enjoy some leisurely cricket or an evening footy match, and finally, don't forget to look at the stars!

INFORMATION

Most museums, attractions, shops and visitors centres open on weekends and public holidays (normally 10am to 4pm), except for Christmas Day.

Bookshops

Borders Books, Music & Café (Map pp668-9; ☎ 8223 3333; 97 Rundle Mall, City) A great store, with a vast collection of books, talking books, CDs, DVDs and videos.
Dymocks Booksellers (Map pp668-9; ☎ 8223 5380; 36 Rundle Mall, City) A chain store selling fiction, reference books and maps.
Imprints Booksellers (Map pp668-9; ☎ 8231 4454; 107 Hindley St, City) The booklover's bookshop – quality literature with a great selection of biographies.
Map Shop (Map pp668-9; ☎ 8231 2033; 6-10 Peel St, City; 🕐 open Mon-Fri, to noon Sat) On the corner of Hindley St, it has a comprehensive selection of maps.
Mary Martin's Bookshop (Map pp668-9; ☎ 8359 3525; 249 Rundle St, City) An Adelaide institution opening until late on Saturday and Sunday.

Emergency

Ambulance (☎ 000, 13 29 62)
Fire (☎ 000, 8204 3600)
Lifeline (☎ 13 11 14, 8202 5820) 24-hour counselling.
Police (☎ 000, assistance 13 14 44, 8463 7400; 60 Wakefield St, City)

RAA Emergency Roadside Assistance (☎ 13 11 11, 8202 4600)
Rape & Sexual Assault Service (☎ 8226 8787, 8226 8777; 55 King William Rd, North Adelaide)
Victim Support Service Inc (☎ 8231 5626)

Internet Access

Nearly all hostels have Internet access on the premises. Log on for free at the **State Library of SA** (see below) and at **Service SA** (Map pp668-9; ☎ 13 23 24, 8204 1900; 77 Grenfell St, City; 9am-5pm Mon-Fri). There are also other Internet providers around the city:
Cafe Boulevard (Map pp668-9; ☎ 8231 5734; 13 Hindley St, City)
Talking Cents (Map pp668-9; ☎ 8212 1266; 53 Hindley St, City)
The Zone Internet Café (☎ 8223 1947; 238 Rundle St, City; 🕐 9.30am-11pm)

Libraries

The **State Library of SA** (Map pp668-9; ☎ 8207 7242, Internet bookings 8207 7250; www.slsa.sa.gov.au; cnr North Tce & Kintore Ave, City; 🕐 9.30am-8pm Mon-Wed & Fri, 9.30am-6pm Thu, noon-5pm Sat & Sun; 🖳) contains a huge range of information including South Australiana, fabulous photographic and historical databases, international publications, historical treasures and free

Internet access. There are free library tours on Tuesday and the popular **White Gloves Treasures Tour** on the first Wednesday of every month ($14).

Media

The **Advertiser** (www.theadvertiser.com.au) is the state's happily parochial newspaper – with events listings and cinema programmes on Thursday and Saturday. Free sheets, including the *Adelaide Review*, *Rip it up* and *db*, cover alternative arts, theatre and music gigs.

Medical Services

Calvary Hospital (☎ 8239 9100; 89 Strangways Tce, North Adelaide)

St Andrew's Hospital (☎ 8408 2111; 350 South Tce, City)

Wakefield Hospital (☎ 8405 3333; 300 Wakefield St, City)

Women & Children's Hospital (☎ 8161 7000; 72 King William Rd, North Adelaide)

Money

There are plenty of banks and ATMs in the city centre. Adelaide's out-of-hours options for changing foreign currencies are restricted to the airport and the casino.

The following outlets will change money:

American Express (Amex; Map pp668-9; ☎ 1300 139 060; Shop 32, Rundle Mall, City; ✆ 9am-5pm Mon-Fri, 9am-noon Sat)

Thomas Cook (Map pp668-9; ☎ 8231 6977; Shop 4, Rundle Mall, City; ✆ 9am-5pm Mon-Fri, 10am-4pm Sat)

Post

The **main post office** (Map pp668-9; ☎ 13 13 18; 141 King William St, City; ✆ 8am-5.30pm Mon-Fri, 9am-12.30pm Sat) has a public fax service, as well as poste restante and philatelic sections.

Tourist Information

South Australian Tourism Commission Visitors Centre (SATC; Map pp668-9; ☎ 1300 655 276, 8303 2033; www.southaustralia.com; 18 King William St, City; ✆ 8.30am-5pm Mon-Fri, 9am-2pm Sat & Sun) City information and a booking service is available alongside a BASS ticket-selling outlet. There's also an information booth at the King William St end of Rundle Mall.

City of Adelaide Customer Centre (Map pp668-9; ☎ 8203 7203; www.adelaidecitycouncil.com; Adelaide Town Hall, 25 Pirie St; City; ✆ 8.30am-5.30pm Mon-Fri) Pick up information about city-based events and city-centre resources.

SIGHTS
Migration Museum

This fascinating and unmissable **museum** (Map pp668-9; ☎ 8207 7580; www.history.sa.gov.au; 82 Kintore Ave, City; admission by donation; ✆ 10am-5pm Mon-Fri, 1-5pm Sat & Sun) tells the stories of the migrants who came from all over the world to make SA their home. There's information on over a 100 nationalities in their database, along with poignant personal stories displayed to full effect.

Tandanya

Visit this excellent **indigenous cultural institute** (Map pp668-9; ☎ 8224 3200; 253 Grenfell St; adult/child $4/3; ✆ 10am-5pm) to learn about the people who were here first. Managed by Adelaide's Aboriginal community, it contains information on the local Kaurna people, as well as galleries, a café, and art and crafts. There's a free didgeridoo show (noon Monday to Friday) and a Torres Strait Islander dance (noon Saturday and Sunday).

South Australian Museum

This natural history **museum** (Map pp668-9; ☎ 8207 7368; www.samuseum.sa.gov.au; North Tce, City; ✆ 10am-5pm) has a fascinating exhibition on Antarctic explorer Sir Douglas Mawson (with expedition footage), and great tours of the Aboriginal Cultures Gallery (p674).

Old Adelaide Gaol

Decommissioned in 1988, the **Old Adelaide Gaol** (☎ 8231 4062; Gaol Rd, Thebarton; ✆ 11am-4pm Mon-Fri, 11am-3.30pm Sun) features a hanging tower. On weekdays there are self-guided tours with a commentary tape; guided tours are conducted on Sunday ($7/4.50 per adult/child).

Art Gallery of South Australia

This multifloored **gallery** (Map pp668-9; ☎ 8207 7000; www.artgallery.sa.gov.au; North Tce, City; ✆ 10am-5pm) has a superb collection of international and Australian art, from Rodin to Heysen. Enjoy the bookshop, café and free guided tours (11am and 2pm Monday to Friday, 11am and 3pm Saturday and Sunday).

Public Art & Other Galleries

Discover the city's **public art works** by walking around the city and along Hindley St (don't miss Rosina Street's *Carpark – Members Only*). Also see the walking tour (p672).

CENTRAL ADELAIDE

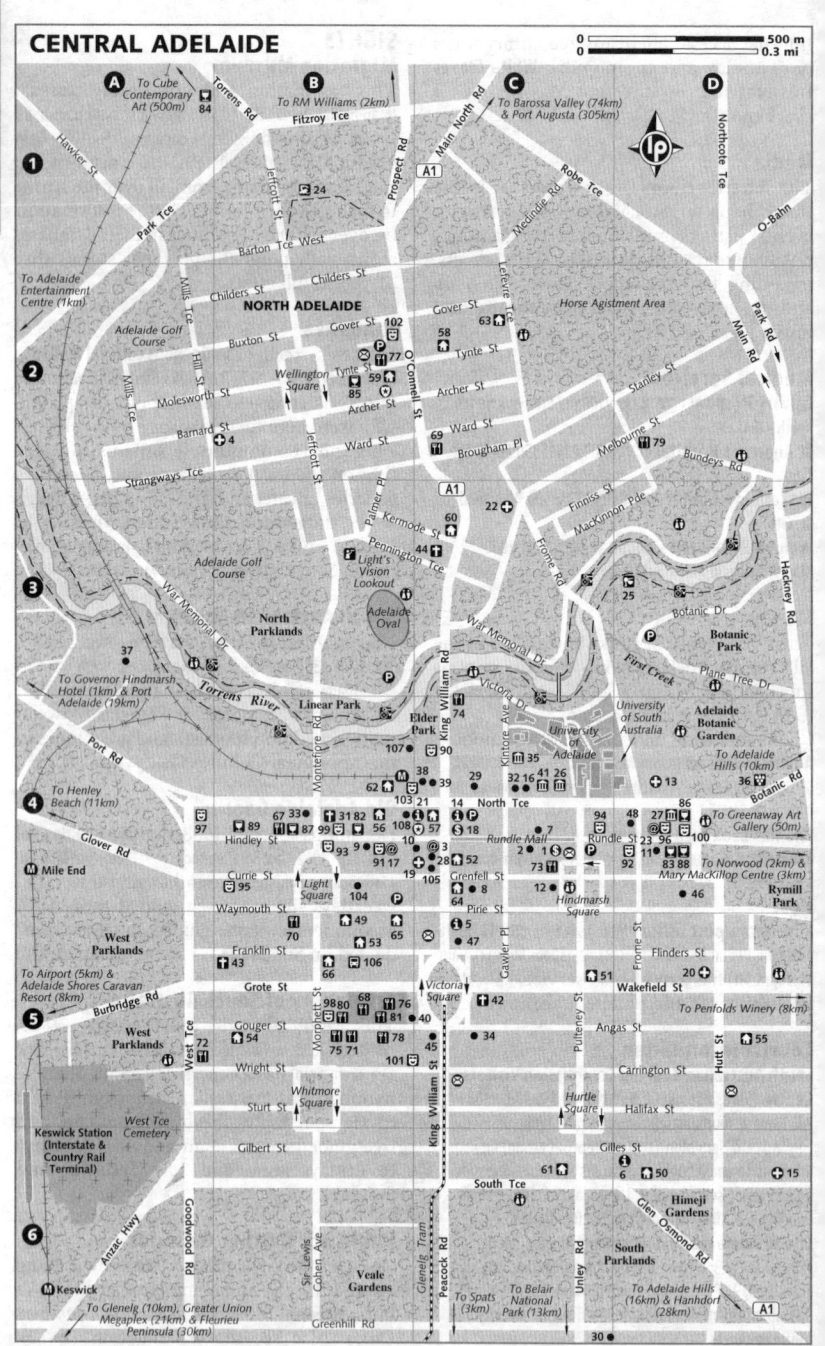

SOUTH AUSTRALIA

Contemporary works are exhibited for sale at the following studios:

Urban Cow Studio (Map pp668-9; ☎ 8232 6126; 11 Frome St, City; ☼ 10am-6pm Mon-Thu & Sat, 10am-9pm Fri, noon-5pm Sun)

Greenaway Art Gallery (Map pp668-9; ☎ 8362 6354; 39 Rundle St, Kent Town; ☼ 11am-6pm Tue-Sun)

Cube Contemporary Art (☎ 8346 7911; 91B Drayton St, Bowden; ☼ 11am-5pm Tue-Fri, 2-5pm Sat & Sun)

The **Bradman Collection** (☎ 8207 7271; cnr North Tce & Kintore Ave, City; adult/child $6/2; ☼ 9.30am-6pm Mon-Thu, 9.30am-8pm Fri, noon-5pm Sat & Sun), housed in the historic Institute Building (Map pp668-9), features personal items that belonged to cricketing legend Sir Donald Bradman. Group tours can be booked 24 hours ahead.

Jam Factory Contemporary Craft & Design (Map pp668-9; ☎ 8410 0727; 19 Morphett St, City; ☼ 9am-5.30pm Mon-Fri, 10am-5pm Sat & Sun) has three galleries displaying local artists' innovative and colourful work. Also browse around the studios, art spaces and glass-blowing room.

Grand City Buildings

Ayers Historic House (Map pp668-9; ☎ 8223 1234; 288 North Tce, City; admission $8; ☼ 10am-4pm Tue-Fri, 1-4pm Sat & Sun), built in 1845, was the elegant residence of Sir Henry Ayers, seven times SA's premier, and features period furnishings and costume displays.

Edmund Wright House (Map pp668-9; 59 King William St, City) was originally constructed in 1878 for the Bank of South Australia in an elaborate Renaissance style with intricate decoration. **Adelaide Town Hall** (Map pp668-9; ☎ 8203 7203; 128 King William St, City; ☼ 8.30am-5pm Mon-Fri), built between 1863 and 1866 in 16th-century Renaissance style, looks out onto King William St between Flinders and Pirie Sts. The faces of Queen Victoria and Prince Albert are carved into the façade. There are free tours on Monday (bookings essential). The **main post office** (Map pp668-9) building across the road is almost as impressive.

The façade of **Parliament House** (Map pp668-9; ☎ 8237 9100; North Tce, City; ☼ 2pm Mon-Thu Feb-May

& Aug-Dec) includes 10 marble Corinthian columns. Building commenced in 1883 but was not completed until 1939. Question time starts at around 2pm on sitting days, while on nonsitting days there are free guided tours (10am and 2pm Monday to Friday).

Holy Trinity Church (Map pp668-9; 87 North Tce; 🕑 9am-5pm Mon-Fri) was the state's first Anglican church (1838). Other early churches are the 1856 **St Francis Xavier Cathedral** (Map pp668-9; ☎ 8231 3551; Wakefield St; 🕑 daily) and the dramatic **St Peter's Cathedral** (Map pp668-9; ☎ 8267 4551; cnr King William Rd & Pennington Tce; 🕑 9.30am-4pm) in North Adelaide (1869–1904). Book for free guided tours of St Peter's (11am Wednesday and 3pm Sunday).

Victoria Sq contains a number of other important early buildings. The **Magistrate's Court** (Map pp668-9; ☎ 8214 0641; 1 Angas St, City; 🕑 9.30am-4.30pm Mon-Fri) is built around the original courthouse (1847–50). Built in 1839, the old **Treasury** (Map pp668-9; cnr King William & Flinders Sts, City) is now an upmarket hotel; the 1869 **Supreme Court** (Map pp668-9; 1 Gouger St, City) and 1912 **Sir Samuel Way Building** (Map pp668-9; Victoria Sq, City) house various courts.

Adelaide Botanic Garden & Other Parks

The Central Business District (CBD) and North Adelaide are completely surrounded by lush parkland. Walking and cycling paths run alongside the soothing Torrens River, which bisects the city.

Stroll through the leafy 20-hectare **Adelaide Botanic Garden** (Map pp668-9; ☎ 8222 9311; www .botanicgardens.sa.gov.au; North Tce; 🕑 7am-sunset Mon-Fri, 9am-sunset Sat & Sun) – there's all sorts of weird and wonderful plants and peaceful lakeside picnic spots. The stunning **Bicentennial Conservatory** (Map pp668-9; adult/child/family $3.30/1.70/8; 🕑 10am-5pm) re-creates a tropical rainforest environment. Free guided walks depart from the restaurant (10.30am Monday, Tuesday, Friday and Sunday; 90 minutes).

Rymill Park (Map pp668-9), in the East Parklands, has a boating lake, possums in the trees (they emerge at night) and a 600m-long jogging track. The South Parklands contain the **Veale Gardens** (Map pp668-9), with streams and flowerbeds, and the Japanese **Himeji Gardens** (Map pp668-9). To the west are a number of sports grounds, while the **North Parklands** (Map pp668-9) border the Torrens River and surround North Adelaide.

Adelaide Oval (Map pp668-9; ☎ 8300 3800; King William Rd, North Adelaide), the site of interstate and international cricket matches, is north of the Torrens River and is regarded as the most picturesque Test cricket ground in the world (p674).

CHAMPION OF THE POOR: A SAINT IN THE MAKING

Mother Mary MacKillop was beatified in 1995 and is now one step away from becoming Australia's first saint. To be canonised by the Catholic Church, you must help work two miracles. It's accepted that prayers to Mary helped cure a terminally ill woman in Melbourne but another miracle is yet to be sanctioned by the Vatican.

A fierce defender of equality, Mary MacKillop (1842–1909) was co-founder (with Father Julian Woods) of the Order of the Sisters of St Joseph of the Sacred Heart.

When Mary was 24 she and Woods started Australia's first free school at Penola (p711) in the southeast of South Australia (SA), where fees were paid only by those who could afford to pay. By the time she was 26, the 30 sisters of Mary's Order were running eight Josephite schools, an orphanage and a home for fallen women. Unfortunately, however, Mary's single-mindedness soon brought her into conflict with SA's Catholic religious hierarchy. In 1871 she was excommunicated, although she was reinstated five months later.

By the time of her death, Mary's Order had founded 117 schools and 11 charitable homes in Australia and New Zealand. Many of these institutions are still operating today, while around 1300 Josephite sisters continue the good work.

Mother Mary MacKillop lived in Adelaide for 16 years. She was excommunicated at **St Mary's Convent** (Map pp668-9; ☎ 8231 434; 253 Franklin St, City) and assisted **St Ignatius Church** (Queen St, Norwood) at Mass during this exile. **St Joseph's Convent** houses the **Mary MacKillop Centre** (☎ 8364 5311; cnr High & Phillips Sts, Kensington; admission $3; 🕑 10am-4pm Mon-Tue & Thu-Fri, 1.30-4pm Sun, closed Wed, Sat & public holidays), which holds historic photos, artefacts, and a leaflet describing eight significant pilgrimage sites.

Adelaide Suburbs
GLENELG

A cheerful and good old-fashioned seaside resort, Glenelg is where weekend crowds devour mountains of ice cream and a bustling alfresco café strip leads to a great swimming beach which is one of Adelaide's most popular. Locals mingle happily with tourists to stroll the promenade and to enjoy numerous galas and festivals.

The **visitors centre** (☎ 8294 5833; Glenelg foreshore; ☼ 9am-5pm Mon-Fri, 10am-3pm Sat & Sun) sits behind the Town Hall – ask about the myriad beachside events.

In the same premises, **Beach Hire** (☎ 8294 1477; ☼ sunny days Sep-Apr) rent out deck chairs, umbrellas, wave skis and body boards.

After surviving a ferocious shark attack, Rodney Fox became a local identity and spent years hunting great whites for film crews (including the feature film *Jaws*). The **Rodney Fox Shark Experience** (☎ 8376 3373; www.rodneyfox.com.au; grd fl, Glenelg Town Hall, Moseley Sq; adult/child $6.50/4.50; ☼ 10am-5pm) has great video shark footage, fossilised teeth and a full-scale model of a great white shark. If you'd like to reaffirm your mortality, ask about their pointer shark diving cruises!

On MacFarlane St, the **Old Gum Tree** marks the spot where the proclamation of SA was read in 1836. Governor Hindmarsh and the first colonists landed on the beach nearby.

Glenelg's past is depicted through an engaging exhibition at the **Bay Discovery Centre** (☎ 8179 9504; Moseley Sq; admission free; ☼ 10am-5pm) where settlers' personal accounts depict the vicious politics and hardships of the first European settlement. The local Kaurna Aboriginal people lost their land and their voice, and this is addressed along with other exhibits.

On the Patawalonga sits a full-size replica of **HMS Buffalo**, which carried the original free European settlers from England in 1836. An on-board restaurant displays original ship artefacts.

A vintage tram runs between Victoria Sq in the city centre and Moseley Sq in Glenelg, next to the beach (p682).

OTHER SUBURBS

North Adelaide (Bus No 222; King William St, North Adelaide) has a great alfresco Italian restaurant strip and some really nice old pubs. It's a pretty residential suburb, with old bluestone cottages and a fair bit of old money.

Norwood (Bus No 122-125; Grenfell & Currie Sts, Norwood), on the eastern side of town, has another popular residential café, pub and shopping street (The Parade), a market, and a great wine and food day in March.

Henley Beach (Bus No 130-137; Grenfell & Currie Sts, Henley Beach) is on the sea, and is much smaller and quieter than Glenelg. There is a central square edged with wine bars, restaurants and the best pub on the coast: the **Ramsgate Hotel** (☎ 8356 5411; 328 Seaview Rd, Henley Beach).

ACTIVITIES
Walking, Cycling & Swimming

The peaceful **Botanic Gardens** (Map pp668-9) have **free guided walks** (p670) and there are a number of free trail guides available from the city council and visitors centre, which cover the history of **North Adelaide** (Map pp668-9), Adelaide's **public art** and the wonderful riverside **Linear Park** (Map pp668-9) – a 40km sealed path which winds alongside the Torrens River through pretty parklands, from the Adelaide foothills right through to the sea.

Bike South (☎ 8343 2911), part of Transport SA (TSA), publishes an excellent set of free cycling maps detailing all the cycle paths and bicycle lanes throughout the city. Pick them up from TSA vehicle-licensing centres or bike shops.

Don't forget the wonderful adjoining city beaches – these beaches are perfect for long walks, safe swimming or just lying around people watching.

Wine-Tasting

The historic and multiaward-winning **Penfolds Magill Estate Winery** (☎ 8568 9408; 78 Penfolds Rd, Magill; ☼ 10am-5pm Mon-Fri, 11am-5pm Sat & Sun) sits on the city doorstep and has a gourmet restaurant and great city views.

Controversy has dogged the **National Wine Centre of Australia** (Map pp668-9; ☎ 8222 9222; www.wineaustralia.com.au; cnr Botanic & Hackney Rds; ☼ 10am-6pm) because of its location on the (development free) city parklands, appalling financial problems and questionable architecture. Make your own mind up about the building and take a self-guided tour with tastings of Australian wines ($8.50).

SOUTH AUSTRALIA

WALKING TOUR

North Tce is an elegant and broad boulevard lined with some of SA's finest public buildings. The earliest were constructed during the 1830s, but most are a legacy of the copper, wheat and wool booms that took place from the early 1840s through to around 1880.

WALKING TOUR

Distance: 4km
Duration: allow a full day with browsing

Starting from the grand old **Botanic Hotel** (**1**), head west along North Tce to the 1846 **Ayers Historic House** (**2**; p669), which is the elegant bluestone home of early premier Sir Henry Ayers.

Across the road, a small campus of the **University of South Australia** (**3**) is on the corner of leafy Frome Rd. Next door is the far more imposing façade of the **University of Adelaide** (**4**), founded in 1874 with a grant made from the profits of copper mining.

This was the first university in Australia to admit women to degree courses.

Continuing west along North Tce, you'll have no trouble filling a couple of hours at the **Art Gallery of South Australia** (**5**; p667). Next door the **South Australian Museum** (**6**; p667) has fine Aboriginal and natural history displays and a great little café.

Next door and on the corner of Kintore Ave is the **State Library of SA** (**7**; p666) and the 1836 **Institute Building** (**8**), the oldest building on North Tce, housing Sir Donald Bradman's cricketing memorabilia. Across Kintore Ave is the **National War Memorial** (**9**), but first divert down the avenue to the excellent **Migration Museum** (**10**; p667).

Back on North Tce and heading west from the war memorial, follow the stone wall surrounding the grounds of **Government House** (**11**; 1838–40) until you come to King William Rd. Right on the corner, and outside the wrought-iron gates of Government House, is the **South African War Memorial** (**12**) with its impressive statue. Turn right here and head north down King William Rd, past the **Adelaide Festival Centre** (**13**) and

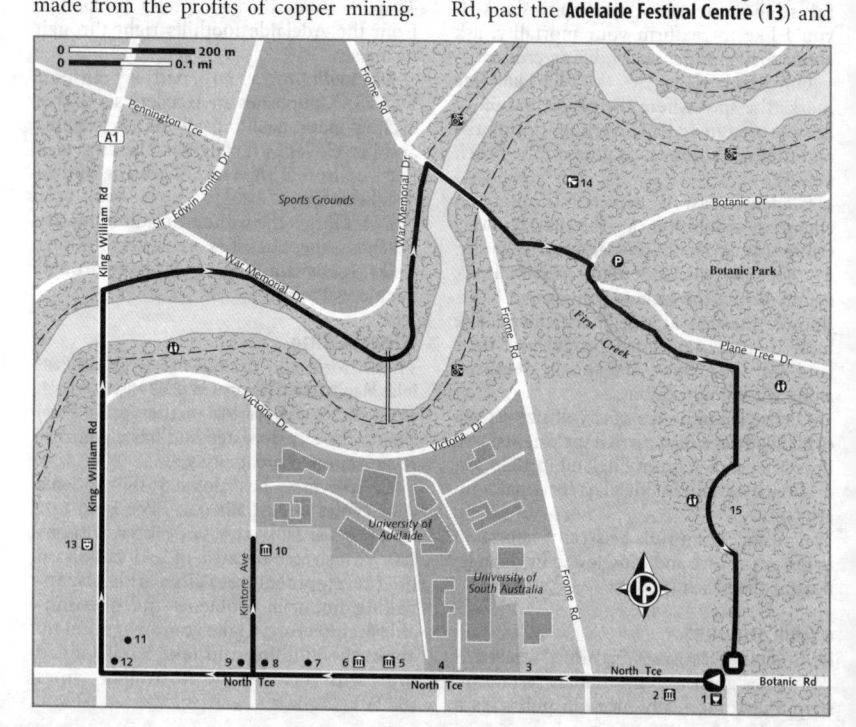

across the river, towards War Memorial Dr. Turn right and walk east along the riverside path. Pleasant walks meander through the parks and gardens that line both banks as far as Frome Rd. Here you cross the river to reach the entrance to the **Adelaide Zoo** (**14**; below).

When you've finished saluting the meerkats, walk south down Frome Rd and turn left off the road onto a footpath, following the fence of the zoo. You'll come to a forked road, take the right fork, Plane Tree Dr, and follow it to the gate of the **Adelaide Botanic Garden** (**15**; p670).

From here, a network of paths links speciality gardens, lakes, a tropical rainforest conservatory and a historic palm house (1877).

Head generally south following the signs to the main gate and you'll find yourself stepping out onto North Tce, directly opposite the Botanic Hotel where you began.

ADELAIDE FOR CHILDREN

A free monthly paper **Adelaide's Child** (www .adelaideschild.com.au) contains a comprehensive events calendar and adverts for child-minding/baby-sitting agencies. Pick this up from libraries and cafés. The **Advertiser** (www .theadvertiser.com.au) lists events on Thursday and Saturday. It's also worth buying a copy of *Adelaide for Kids; A Guide for Parents* by James Muecke ($22), which lists great walks and activities for youngsters and older kids (even those pretending to be adults). It's available from all bookshops.

It is always useful checking with the **State Library**, **South Australian Museum**, **Zoo**, **Botanic Gardens** and **Art Gallery of South Australia** about its school-holiday activities – some of these activities run more regularly than others.

The **Investigator Science & Technology Centre** (☎ 8410 1115; Wayville Showgrounds, Goodwood Rd, Goodwood; adult/child $8.50/5.50; ☼ 10am-5pm) is a real favourite, with live demonstrations at the weekends – don't miss *Slime* and *Lightning*.

Snowdome (☎ 8352 7977; 23 East Tce, Thebarton; adult/under 4 yr $11.50/6; ☼ 10am-4pm Mon-Tue, 10am-4pm & 7-10pm Wed, 10am-4pm & 7.30-11pm Fri, 12.30-4pm & 7.30-11pm Sat, 12.30-4pm Sun) has ice-skating, tobogganing, skiing and boarding (the latter two require a lesson). Evening dance-skating sessions are for wobblers of all ages.

Adelaide Aquatic Centre (Map pp668-9; ☎ 8344 4411; Jeffcott Rd, North Adelaide parklands; adult/child/family $5.50/3.80/13; ☼ 5am-10pm) has waterslides and great family deals. Don't miss the games and activities for kids during Splash-out from 6.30pm to 9pm every Friday and Saturday night throughout the year.

Take a cruise to the **Zoo** (below) on **Pop-Eye** (☎ 8295 4747; adult/child return $8/4.50; ☼ departs hourly 11am-3pm Mon-Fri, every 20 min 10.30am-4.30pm Sat & Sun), which departs from Elder Park in front of the Festival Centre.

The exhibits at the **Maritime Museum** (☎ 8207 6255; 126 Lipson St, Port Adelaide; adult/child $8.50/3.50; ☼ 10am-5pm) include ships' cabins (1840, 1910 and 1950), a lighthouse and a tugboat.

Australian Museum of Childhood (☎ 8240 5200; 95 Dale St, Port Adelaide; admission $3; ☼ 11am-4pm Sat & Sun) is a small, dusty folk museum that has toys dating from the early 20th century to the present, and you're allowed to play with most of them.

Wharf-side **Toytanic** (☎ 8241 2700; 21 Commercial Rd, Port Adelaide) sells vintage toys and collectables.

Adelaide Zoo (Map pp668-9; ☎ 8267 3255; Frome Rd; adult/child $15/9; ☼ 9.30am-5pm) has around 1500 exotic and native mammals, birds, reptiles and a children's zoo. The Southeast Asian rainforest exhibit is a major drawcard.

TOURS

There are a huge variety of tours covering Adelaide, the Adelaide Hills (see coach tours later in this section), Fleurieu Peninsula (p686) and Barossa Valley (p700).

When choosing one of the many wine tours check the number of wineries to be visited and ensure that you won't spend half of the day at tourist shops. Most hostels will recommend backpacker-friendly tours.

Tourabout Adelaide Walking & Private Tours (☎ 8333 1111; www.touraboutadelaide.com.au) brings to life Adelaide's founders, shakers, shapers and landmarks in these fabulous guided walks. Delightful snippets of scandal and fascinating historical context emerge throughout the following two-hour walks ($25); Adelaide's Cultural Heritage (Friday), West Tce Cemetery (first Sunday in the month) and West End Arts walks (Thursday). Bookings are essential for these tours; bilingual guides and private themed walks and tours are also available.

Temptation Sailing (☎ 0412-811 838; www .dolphinboat.com.au; Holdfast Shores Marina, Glenelg) offers a number of catamaran jaunts including a swim with dolphins ($98/88 per adult/child, 3½ hours), dolphin spotting ($48/38, 3½ hours), twilight cruises ($19/ 9.50, 1½ hours) and day sails ($19/9.50, 1½ hours).

Taundi Aboriginal Cultural Tours (☎ 8341 2777; 1 Lipson St, Port Adelaide) offers Aboriginal guided tours for three Adelaide landmarks: the plants and their uses in the Botanic Gardens (Wednesday to Friday and Sunday), dreaming stories in Cleland Wildlife Park (with bookings), and the very popular tour of the Aboriginal Cultures Gallery in the South Australian Museum. Bookings are essential (all three tours cost $10 to $15 and last around 45 minutes).

Adelaide's Top Food & Wine Tours (☎ 8231 4144; www.food-fun-wine.com.au) really gives an insight into South Australians' love for top-class food; there are dawn tours of the buzzing Central Market, stallholders introducing their varied produce and a cook's tour of Asia. The final option is not for those with timid appetites: a progressive luncheon in restaurants along the foodies' golden mile – Gouger St (from $40 to $100).

Adelaide Oval/Museum Tour (☎ 8300 3800; www .cricketsa.com.au; King William Rd, North Adelaide) is one for cricket fans who know that Sir Donald Bradman was the king of Australian cricket, but who may not know that British legend WG Grace played twice on this world-famous pitch – after it had been prepared by a flock of sheep (apocryphal) – and beat the Aussies both times (true). Tours depart from the south gate on War Memorial Dr ($10/5 per adult/child, 10am Monday to Friday, 2 hours).

Haigh's Chocolates Visitors Centre (Map pp668-9; ☎ 8372 7077; www.haighschocolates.com; 154 Greenhill Rd, Parkside) has tours for chocolate fanatics...You could just heighten your mood (and sugar levels) by buying this home-made delicacy in one of their shops in the city, or see how each melting morsel is lovingly made by a team of dedicated experts. Bookings are essential (admission free, 1pm and 2pm Monday to Saturday, 20 minutes).

Beyond the Barriers (☎ 8355 2954; www.beyond thebarriers.net; 332 Henley Beach Rd, Underdale) has a guide who is a former jockey and trainer and who introduces you to the sport of kings, horse racing. Meet trainers, jockeys, strappers and the four-legged beauties that make grown men weep. On Tuesday and Thursday horses are fast-worked for Saturday races ($110, Monday to Friday, 4½ hours).

Rolling On (☎/fax 8358 2401; http: members.ozemail .com.au/~rollingon/tours.htm) is an outfit that runs guided cycling tours to places such as the Barossa Valley (day tour $129) and further afield. The prices of the tours include bike hire, accommodation, most meals and entry fees.

Prime Mini Tours (☎ 8293 4900; www.primemini tours.com) runs a number of very good tours. The City & Brewery Tour combines a few goodies: the Rodney Fox Shark Experience, Haigh's Chocolates and the South Australian Brewing Company (minimum six people; $50; Tuesday, Wednesday and Thursday; 5½ hours).

Coach tours start at around $45 for Adelaide sights. Itineraries include Hahndorf and the Cleland Wildlife Park (both in the Adelaide Hills), the Barossa Valley and McLaren Vale, Victor Harbor, Murray River and the Coorong (the latter two incorporating cruises for around $90 to $140). Day trips to the southern Flinders Ranges and Kangaroo Island are very rushed and not recommended.

Try the following coach-trip operators, all based at Adelaide's **central bus station** (101-111 Franklin St, City):

Premier Stateliner (☎ 8415 5555; www.premierstate liner.com.au; 111 Franklin St, City)

Adelaide Sightseeing (☎ 8231 4144; www.adelaide sightseeing.com.au; 101 Franklin St, City)

Gray Line (☎ 1300 858 587; www.grayline.com; 101 Franklin St, City)

FESTIVALS & EVENTS

Adelaide has a well-earned reputation as the festival capital of Australia, and constant food and wine galas keep South Australians fat and happy. Meanwhile, any excuse to turn the city and parklands into a street party means that there is a continuous stream of truly fantastic international and local events.

The calibre of local and international performers is world-class, attracting audiences from around the world, particularly for the Glenelg Jazz Festival and the Adelaide Festival of the Arts.

At the Adelaide Fringe Festival, Aussie stand-up comedians are swamped by their European and American counterparts and other headline acts from the Edinburgh Fringe Festival.

A few of these festivals and events change dates from year to year, check listings with the SATC visitors centre (for contact details see Tourist Information; p667).

JANUARY
Jacob's Creek Tour Down Under One hundred of the world's best cyclists sweat their lycra to the limits over this week's six races and street parties. Stages 1 to 5 race through 55 of the state's towns with a grand finale in Adelaide.

MARCH
Adelaide Festival of Arts Held on even-numbered years for culture vultures; international and Australian dance, drama, opera and theatre performances that invigorate the mind.
Adelaide Fringe Second only to Edinburgh Fringe as the worlds largest independent arts festival; fabulous weird and wonderful acts impart comedy, acrobatics and the truly bizarre on a biennial basis.
Clipsall 500 Rev heads rejoice as Adelaide's streets become a four-day racing track for (Australian) Holden vs Ford racing cars. Cold beer and performances from leather-clad rockers such as Suzi Quatro top the fun!
Womadelaide Seven stages in the Botanic Gardens host over 400 musicians and performers from around the world, providing an unbelievable three days and nights of world music, arts and dance. One of the world's best live music events.
Santos Symphony Under the Stars The Adelaide Symphony Orchestra's free outdoor night concert, with the River Torrens as the backdrop, and a rousing finale of the 1812 Overture complete with cannons and fireworks – fabulous!

APRIL
Oakbank Easter Racing Carnival Picnics and flowery hats are in order for this country-town racing day.

JULY
Adelaide Festival of Ideas A great idea: get the glorious, the good and the innovative from around the world and put them together for a biennial talk-fest; from weapons inspectors to Franciscan friars, Muslim academics to judges and journos.

AUGUST
Royal Adelaide Show One of the oldest royal shows in the country, with major agricultural and horticultural exhibits and entertainment.

South Australian Living Artists Innovative exhibitions and displays across the city showcase the known and the up-and-coming.

SEPTEMBER
SA Water Bay to Birdwood Run A parade of hundreds of gleaming vintage cars and their proud owners.

OCTOBER
Sensational Adelaide Classic Adelaide Rally The old bones keep racing, and so do their cars!
Bartercard Glenelg Jazz Festival First-class New Orleans & Australian jazz bands stir up the soul and the beachside. While the energetic dance, lounging hedonists consume cheap gourmet food and wine.
Tasting Australia Internationally awarded chefs showcase their secrets, and gourmets get together (biennially) to eat, drink and talk about their passions – not for weight-watchers.
Adelaide Rose Festival A gentle celebration of the city's most popular flower.
Feast A great mix of events for the three-week-long lesbian and gay cultural festival; a big carnival opening-night party is followed by picnics, theatre performances, talks, walks and dances.

NOVEMBER
Mitsubishi Horse Trials One of the world's four Olympic-level events, held in the city-centre parklands.
Credit Union Christmas Pageant An Adelaide institution for over 70 years – floats, bands and marching troupes take over the city streets for the day; great family fun.

DECEMBER
Bay Sports Festivals The second-largest sports fest in Australia is held beachside in Glenelg and includes beach volleyball, an aquathon, surf carnival, hockey, a gridiron competition and a lot of lazy spectators.
Proclamation Day The day SA was put on the world map – 28 December – and another excuse to party.

SLEEPING

Adelaide is very easy to get around, and staying outside the compact CBD is a practical option. For example, attractive and peaceful North Adelaide is a five-minute bus ride or a 2km walk into town, while the city beach suburbs (Glenelg in particular) are a 30-minute bus or tram ride.

The best-value lodgings are often holiday apartments, most with modern amenities and good locations. Stays of a few days or more are often eligible for good reductions.

Book ahead for any beachside accommodation during December and January and expect prices to rise during all school holidays. Rates given here are off-peak.

Budget

A couple of city pubs have rooms. However, most hostels are only a short walk to the city centre, and much better value for your hard-won dollars! There are also some caravan parks both on the city coast and within 10km of the city centre – ask at the SATC visitors centre.

HOSTELS

Competition is fierce, and as a result all sorts of freebies (free tours, breakfasts, apple pie, and so forth) are offered to tempt you through the door, particularly in the winter off season. Those listed also have their own travel agencies or can book tours and car hire.

Most hostels offer a free pick-up/drop-off service from the airport, and bus and train stations. Several hostels are within easy walking distance of the bus station on Franklin St.

Adelaide Central YHA (Map pp668-9; ☎ 8414 3010; adlcentral@yhasa.org.au; 135 Waymouth St, City; s/d/f $20/60/90; ⊠ 🖳) Add $3.50 for non-YHA member rates. Simply the best, this spacious and gleaming hostel also has a central location. A large kitchen is well equipped and communal areas include TV viewing rooms. Security is excellent, with backpack lockers and a 24-hour reception. There's also good local information, an Internet café and bikes for hire ($10 per day).

East Park Lodge (Map pp668-9; ☎ 8223 1228; eastpark@dove.com.au; 341 Angas St, City; dm/s/d $19/39/50; ⊠ 🖳) This bluestone three-storey building was opened 90 years ago as a Salvation Army hostel for young country ladies. Now the refurbished and excellent facilities include a sauna, pool table, electric piano and small in-ground swimming pool. It enjoys the nicest location of any of Adelaide's hostels, with the up-market and leafy East Parklands just outside the door.

Glenelg Beach Resort (☎ 1800 066 422, 8376 0007; 7 Moseley St, Glenelg; dm/s/d $18/45/60; 🖳) Glenelg's only hostel sits five minutes from the beach, and even less to Jetty Rd's entertainment. The basement houses a lively bar/café, with karaoke for tuneless extroverts, Internet access and a tiny kitchen. The upstairs rooms are basic and stuffy but clean. Breakfast,

---

THE AUTHOR'S CHOICE

Adelaide Shores Caravan Resort (☎ 8356 7654; www.adelaideshores.com; 1 Military Rd, West Beach; camp sites/caravans $24/55, cabins $65-85; ⊠ 🖳) It's an age-old tradition for Adelaide families to spend summer holidays at this multiaward-winning and immaculate park, and understandably so – it's right on a great beach, has pristine accommodation and sits between the social suburbs of Glenelg (3.4km) and Henley Beach (3.5km). The park is packed with facilities and also offers brilliant value; the prices given are for two people ($14/10 extra per adult/child).

---

linen and lifts are provided, while a tour and seventh night are free.

Backpack Oz (Map pp668-9; ☎ 8223 3551; www.backpackoz.com.au; 144 Wakefield St, City; dm/s/d $20/45/50; 🖳) Not far from Rundle St, this family-run hostel has a friendly atmosphere, comfortable communal area (with bar) and a good kitchen. Couples can stay in the hostel's annexe over the road.

Blue Galah Backpackers Hostel (☎ 8231 9295; www.bluegalah.com.au; level 1, 62 King William St, City; dm $23; 🖳) This small hostel is right bang in the city centre. The comfy bunk beds are ex-Olympic issue and the central area has a large outdoor balcony, bar and excellent Internet set-up. The owners also provide good quality kitchen facilities and security.

Also recommended for the more casual fraternity, **Cannon St Backpackers** (☎ 1800 069 731, 8410 1218; www.cannonst.com.au; 110 Franklin St, City; dm/s/d $17/20/50; 🖳), despite being a bit tatty and cavernous, is clean and friendly, and has undercover parking and cheap meals. **Sunny's Backpackers Hostel** (☎ 1800 225 725, 8231 2430; sunnys@chariot.net.au; 139 Franklin St, City; dm/tw $21/52) is also popular, but note that people smoke in the dorms.

Mid-Range

HOLIDAY RENTAL APARTMENTS

Adelaide has many terrific holiday flats and serviced apartments; most are cheaper if you book for a week.

Quest on King William (Map pp668-9; ☎ 8217 5000; www.questapartments.com.au; 82 King William St, City; 2-person apt $130; ⊠) The city centre is on your doorstep, and these are immaculate and comfortable apartments from which to return after a hard day's sightseeing. Great en suite spas will tempt you to upgrade and negotiable rates make this a top-value choice.

Baybeachfront, Bayswaterfront & Bayview Apartments (Glenelg Letting Agency; ☎ 8294 9666; www.baybeachfront.com.au; 742 Anzac Hwy, Glenelg; 2-person apt $90-114) Three of the best, these bright, comfortable and modern apartment buildings are situated on the seafront, Adelphi Tce and central Glenelg. Two- or three-bedroom apartments rent from $595 a week, and there's a minimum three-night stay.

Directors Studios & Suites (Map pp668-9; ☎ 8213 2500; www.savillesuites.com.au; 259 Gouger St, City; d $88-112; 🗷) These very good-value apartments are popular with businessmen and are close to West Tce.

Also recommended are the attractive **Adelaide Park View Apartments** (Map pp668-9; ☎ 1800 882 774, 8223 0599; www.majestichotels.com.au; 274 South Tce, City; 2-person studios/4-person apt $115/125), and the older but convenient **Greenways Apartments** (Map pp668-9; ☎ 8267 5903; www.greenways.auz.net; 41-45 King William Rd, Adelaide; 2-person apt $92; 🗷).

MOTELS & HOTELS

Although there are motels all over Adelaide, there are also a few 'motel alleys' such as Glen Osmond Rd (which leads into the city from the southeast) and Anzac Hwy where it heads into central Glenelg.

Motels/hotels on the North, East, West and South Tces generally overlook the lovely city parklands and are a short walk into the city centre.

With extra adult or child rates around $12, rooms become a viable budget option for three or more people.

Patawalonga Motor Inn & Glenelg Conference Centre (☎ 8294 2122; www.patawalongahotel.com.au; Adelphi Tce, Glenelg; d with/without marina views $135/95; 🅿 🗷 🖳) This waterfront motel has spotless and comfortable rooms. The marina's bobbing boats and sea birds provide a picturesque backdrop for the short stroll to Glenelg's lively centre.

Princes Lodge Motel (Map pp668-9; ☎ 8267 5566; princeslodge@senet.com.au; 73 Lefevre Tce, North Adelaide; s/d/tr 60/70/80; 🗷) In a grand old house close to the restaurants of North Adelaide, this friendly but tatty lodgings has a great location: opposite a park with views over the hills, and still within walking distance of the city. Rates include breakfast.

Festival City Hotel/Motel (☎ 8212 7877; festival@ecite.net.au; 140 North Tce, City; s/d $90/110; 🗷) There's no on-site parking at this central and small motel opposite the casino. Ask about reduced rates at the nearby car park ($7.50 per day).

Also recommended are these very comfortable and convenient options:

Best Western Ensenada Inn (☎ 8294 5822; www.ensenada.com.au; 13 Colley Tce, Glenelg; d/tr $115/130; 🗷 🖳)

Holiday Inn Hotel (Map pp668-9; ☎ 8223 2744; http://adelaide.holiday-inn.com; 208 South Tce, City; d $80; 🗷)

Parkside Motel (Map pp668-9; ☎ 8408 6177; 215 South Tce, City; d $130; 🗷)

Top End

All of Adelaide's major hotels offer a variety of rates. Prices quoted here are the weekend rates (normally cheaper than weekday prices).

Hyatt Regency Adelaide (Map pp668-9; ☎ 8231 1234; www.hyatt.com; North Tce, City; d with/without river views $220/200; 🅿 🗷) With lovely views over the River Torrens and a location adjacent to the elegant Parliament buildings and city casino, this hotel has the prime spot in the city. Very good weekend deals offer two nights and a $100 meal voucher for $300.

Rendezvous Allegra Hotel (☎ 1800 358 358, 8115 8888; 55 Waymouth St, City; d from $155; 🅿 🗷) This new hotel is all class: the Rendezvous has understated luxury with modern elegant furnishings and bathrooms fit for spoiling yourself. The lap pool and spa are above street level with glass walls, which has created a relaxing environment and a great spot for people watching!

Ramada Plaza Pier Hotel & Suites (☎ 8350 6688; www.ramadainternational.com; 16 Holdfast Promenade, Glenelg; d $145) Absolute beachside and new luxurious hotel with upmarket rooms even equipped with Playstations.

The refurbished and idiosyncratic properties of the **North Adelaide Heritage Group** (☎ 8272 1355; www.adelaideheritage.com; d from $140; 🗷) include two fabulous heritage dwellings on Tynte St, North Adelaide, geared for luxurious and romantic weekends – and some wicked fantasies! They come equipped with all comforts and bubbling spas. Packages include gourmet continental breakfasts and complimentary treats ($220). See p678 for further details.

Fire Station Inn (Map pp668-9; 80 Tynte St, North Adelaide) This bluestone fire station (c 1866) was operating during Victorian times and now houses several apartments. Line up to book the Fire Engine Suite – outfitted with its own genuine red and shiny fire engine (you supply the bell, helmets and waterproofs!).

Friendly Meeting Chapel (Map pp668-9; 141 Tynte St, North Adelaide) Built around 1879, the romantic Victorian décor enhances this chapel's atmosphere of illicit love, and why not? You're just off O'Connell St, where a run of good restaurants, pubs and cafés will pull you back into the 21st century.

HOLIDAY RENTAL APARTMENTS

Embassy (8124 9900; www.pacifichotelscorporation .com.au; 96 North Tce, City; d $165; P) These modern and stylishly fitted apartments are also extremely comfortable and equipped with all mod cons. The spacious balconies are a fantastic addition, ensuring that rooms are light filled. The open glass walls in the lap pool and spa room increase the building's overall aura of uncluttered design.

EATING

All ages and incomes socialise over food in Adelaide, which is easy to do when eating out is so cheap and the standards are so high. There are reputedly 600 to 700 eating venues across the capital, more per head than any other Australian city. Be aware, a strict no smoking policy is enforced where food is served indoors.

Nearly all restaurants have good vegetarian choices, and there are huge variety of cuisines on offer.

City Centre
RUNDLE STREET

Rundle St hogs the limelight, with a vast array of lively alfresco Italian and Thai restaurants serving snacks, quick meals and coffee and cakes throughout the day and evening. This location is without a rival in the best-people-watching-as-you-sup competition, and is great fun on weekends.

Hotels on this street serving food include the **Austral** (8223 4660; 205 Rundle St) and the **Exeter** (8223 2623; 246 Rundle St).

AROUND THE CITY CENTRE

Caos Cafe Bar (Map pp668-9; 8231 8300, 188 Hindley St; lunch $9; 7.30am-8pm Mon-Fri, 11am-2.30pm Sat) This friendly licensed rendezvous is known for its all-day breakfasts.

Garage Bar & Dining (Map pp668-9; 8212 9577; 163 Waymouth St, Light Sq; lunch $16-20; 8am-3pm Mon-Fri, 11am-4pm Sun) Generous portions of modern Australian/Asian food are served at this favoured lunch and brunch venue. The bar is also great and takes off over the weekends (open till 8pm Monday and Tuesday, till late Wednesday to Sunday).

Hawkers Corner (Map pp668-9; 8231 6236; 141 West Tce; meals $6-12) The aromas coming from this long-established Asian food hall are wonderful. Try the Malaysian and Thai meals.

Jolleys Boathouse Restaurant (Map pp668-9; 8223 2891; Jolleys Lane, cnr King William Rd & Victoria Dr; mains $21-27; lunch daily, dinner Mon-Sat) Long-lunchers and business crowds enjoy the riverside setting and multiawarded modern Australian fare. Special three-course deals are offered Monday to Thursday ($35).

Jasmin Indian Restaurant (Map pp668-9; 8223 7837; 31 Hindmarsh Sq; mains $23-28; lunch Tue-Fri, dinner Tue-Sat) For over 20 years this mouthwatering North Indian cuisine has been garnering a full house and many awards. There's a good but pricey wine list, and fantastic service.

Lucia's Pizza & Spaghetti Bar (Map pp668-9; 8231 2303; 2 Western Mall, Central Market; meals $8) Renowned for the finest coffee in town, this is also Adelaide's oldest coffee shop. Breakfast and cheap tucker are served during market hours.

Spats (8272 6170; 108 King William Rd, Hyde Park; puddings $10; 6.30pm-2am) The ultrachic to the cardigan-brigade pack in to this night-time venue, for chatter and whipped cream with everything. Try its hot chocolate, wicked desserts and liqueur coffees.

GOUGER STREET   Map p668-9

There are over 11 different nationality restaurants in this one street, especially around **Chinatown** (by the Central Market). Many Asian eateries serve cheap lunches and yum-cha brunches (all you can eat for around $10).

Gauchos Argentinian Restaurant (8231 2299; 91 Gouger St; mains $25; lunch Mon-Fri, dinner Mon-Sun) For lovers of huge juicy steaks, this is the place for you!

Lime & Lemon (8231 8876; 89 Gouger St; mains from $10) This Thai restaurant has sizzling wok-based meals.

Paul's Restaurant (8231 9778; 79 Gouger St; mains $16.50) The fish and chips are famous around town.

T-Chow Chinese Restaurant (☎ 8410 1413; 68 Moonta St; mains $11-20) The authentic Chinese fare is very popular with foodies – especially for Chinese New Year celebrations.

Ying Chow Chinese Restaurant (☎ 8211 7998; 114 Gouger St; mains $10-18) Cheap and cheerful meals mean that this venue is generally always packed.

Zuma Caffé (☎ 8231 4410; 56 Gouger St; meals $8) Fight for a table to enjoy Zuma's excellent breakfasts (served 7am to 11.30am Monday to Friday, till 2pm on Saturday).

Other Areas

Choices flourish along The Parade in **Norwood**, Melbourne and O'Connell Sts in **North Adelaide**, and by the sea at **Henley Beach** and **Glenelg**.

Madame Wu's Noodle Bar (☎ 8431 7188; 195 The Parade, Norwood; meals $11-19; ⏲ lunch Wed-Fri, dinner daily) Customers return here for the succulent vegetarian red curry and spicy satay dishes. The yummy rich sauces are created in-house for this Thai cuisine with Chinese/Singaporean influences.

Caffé Buongiorno (☎ 8364 2944; 145 The Parade, Norwood; meals $10-20; ⏲ 9am-late) This café in central Norwood is known for its brusque staff, great coffee and tasty pizzas. This is a vibrant rendezvous for shoppers, local Italians and weekend brunchers.

Cibo Ristorante (Map pp668-9; ☎ 8267 2444; 8 O'Connell St, North Adelaide; mains $22-27) Just book a table, you won't regret a thing. This is one of the best Italian restaurants in town, with delicious garlicky dishes and a great wine list.

Manse (Map pp668-9; ☎ 8267 4636; 142 Tynte St, North Adelaide; mains $29-35; ⏲ lunch Fri, dinner Mon-Sat) One of Adelaide's oldest and finest restaurants serves modern European/Asian fare and great wines. A special vintage wine list will make your eyes (and wallet) open wide.

Store (Map pp668-9; ☎ 8361 6999; 157 Melbourne St, North Adelaide; meals $9; ⏲ 7am-11pm daily) This deli-cum-café is always busy. Popular all-day breakfasts include baguettes and bruschettas stuffed with marinated goodies and spicy sausages.

Sammy's on the Marina (☎ 8376 8211; 12 Holdfast Promenade, Glenelg; mains $25) Packed with sea-foodies enjoying seafood platters, this restaurant has sea views from the deck.

Glenelg Spices (☎ 8376 1388; 111 Jetty Rd, Glenelg; meals $10-17) Delightful spicy aromas and busy

chatter waft out onto the street from this very popular Malaysian/Thai restaurant (with good vegetarian options).

Papadums (☎ 8350 9199; 61 Tapleys Hill Rd, Glenelg; meals $4.50-10; ⏲ closed Mon) Try the absolutely delicious Sri-Lankan and Indian cooking at this little restaurant (and takeaway). Mouthwatering garlic and spices enhance the succulent sauces and fresh ingredients – don't miss out on this one!

Estia (☎ 8353 2875; 255 Seaview Rd, Henley Beach; mains $12-19; ⏲ lunch Fri-Sun, dinner Tue-Sun) Consistently excellent and tasty Greek/Australian cooking (with tasty vegetarian choices) and a seaside ambience mean that this is the place where you can while away an afternoon.

Grange Jetty Kiosk (☎ 8235 0822; cnr Jetty Rd & the Esplanade, Grange; mains $21; ⏲ closed Sun-Tue Jun-Aug) Another hidden jewel for seafood fans; the kiosk is right on the water's edge, serves great fish and seafood and is far from the madding crowd.

Sarah's (☎ 8341 2103; 85 Dale St, Port Adelaide; mains $14; ⏲ lunch Mon-Fri, dinner Wed-Fri & 1st Sat in month) Happy carnivores eat at this vegetarian restaurant along with their vegie cousins, simply because the French/Vietnamese food is so good.

DRINKING

Real ale drinkers will love the classy homegrown Coopers range of draft and bottled beers. Hotels also sell SA wines (are there any others?) by the glass and will not allow smoking indoors where food is served. These few venues hit the spot simply as good places to sup and enjoy the ambience.

Daniel O'Connell Hotel (Map pp668-9; ☎ 8267 4032; 165 Tynte St, North Adelaide) With the authentic feel of an old Irish pub you will find good beer, little wooden snugs and some great *craic* (Irish fun) – that's if you ignore the journos from the local TV station! A beautiful 150-year-old pepper tree embraces the beer garden and there's a nice little restaurant out back.

Belgian Beer Café (Map pp668-9; ☎ 8359 2233; 27-29 Ebenezer Pl, off Rundle St, City) This central bar has a European drinking-hall atmosphere, 26 imported Belgian super-brews and lots of noisy chatter: *Santé*!

Bombay Bicycle Club (Map pp668-9; ☎ 8269 4455; 29 Torrens Rd, Ovingham) Take the opportunity to become a member of the 100-beer club (it stocks 100 varieties of imported beer, you can guess the rest), and relish the Rudyard Kipling–inspired décor (and accompanying jungle soundtrack). This pub is truly the Raj of Kitsch!

Apothecary 1878 (Map pp668-9; ☎ 8212 9099; 118 Hindley St, City) Tucked-away niches in this wine bar create a lovely intimate atmosphere in which to enjoy your wine and eavesdrop on your neighbours.

Oyster Bar (☎ 8232 5422; 14 East Tce, City; half-a-dozen oysters $8.50) This groovy bar is full of slurping noises. On Tuesday oysters are half price, and the subsequent sound effects double in volume!

Townhall Wine Bar (☎ 8350 9555; upstairs Glenelg Town Hall; ☽ 5pm-late) The glass-walled venue is the perfect place from which to watch the sun set over the sea, with a chilled beer in your hand and your beloved by your side. DJs play Friday to Sunday.

Universal Wine Bar (Map pp668-9; ☎ 8232 5000; 285 Rundle St, City) This wine bar for the trendy folk has a great selection of wines by the glass, and some humdinger people-watching opportunities.

You'll find a few Uni student hangouts like the **Worldsend Hotel** (Map pp668-9; ☎ 8231 9137; 208 Hindley St, City) and a cluster of great little late-night bars at the western end of Hindley St. Try jazz and cocktails at the **Swingcat Club** (Map pp668-9; ☎ 8212 5557; 184 Hindley St, City), or the cool ambience of **Supermild Lounge Bar** (Map pp668-90; ☎ 8212 9699; 182 Hindley St, City) next door.

ENTERTAINMENT

Adelaide has always taken the Arts very seriously and has a phenomenal cultural life comparable with much larger cities.

Sophisticated and entertaining live theatre and musical concerts incorporate the state theatre and opera companies, a symphony orchestra, string quartet and numerous independent drama, dance and performance groups.

The state and other formal art galleries are supported by an active artists community that provides the main contributors to the witty and accessible public art found throughout the city streets.

For theatre and gallery listings check the free monthly **Adelaide Review** (www.adelaide review.com) and Thursday's and Saturday's **Advertiser** (www.theadvertiser.news.com.au).

Most music, theatre and sporting events are booked through **BASS** (☎ 13 12 46; www.bass .sa.com.au). BASS outlets can be found at the **visitors centre** (Map pp668-9; ☎ 1300 655 276, 8303 2033; www.southaustralia.com; 18 King William St, City), Adelaide Festival Centre (see below) and at the home of the **Adelaide Symphony Orchestra** (www.aso.com.au; 91 Hindley St, City).

The **Adelaide Festival Centre** (Map pp668-9; ☎ 8216 8600; King William Rd, City) architecture may not be inspiring, but the complex has a marvellous riverside setting. A variety of auditoriums and theatres house touring and local plays, festival events, concerts and musicals.

Casino

Housed in the grand old train station on North Tce, **Skycity Adelaide** (Map pp668-9; ☎ 8212 2811; North Tce, City; ☽ 10am-4am Sun-Thu, 10am-6am Fri & Sat) has a wide range of gambling facilities, two bars, two restaurants and a café. Smart casual dress is required (but clean jeans are OK).

Cinemas

Check the entertainment pages in the *Advertiser* for what's showing around town.

Moonlight Cinema (www.moonlight.com.au) Every summer old and new classics are played open-air in the Botanic Gardens – a brilliant setting, but bring the mozzie spray.

Greater Union Megaplex Marion (☎ 8296 7788; Westfield Marion, Oaklands Park; adult/child $13.70/9) There are 30 screens in the huge Westfield Marion shopping centre at Oaklands Park. Adults get tickets for child prices on Tuesday.

Nova & Palace East End Cinemas (Map pp668-9; ☎ 8232 3434; 251 & 274 Rundle St, City; adult/child/concession $13.50/8/9.50) The city centre venues for independent films; they show Australian, foreign-language, mainstream and art-house flicks. Concession prices are offered to bearers of ISC and YHA cards. Adults get tickets for concession prices on Tuesday.

Mercury Cinema (Lion Arts Centre; Map pp668-9; ☎ 8410 1934; www.mrc.org.au; 13 Morphett St, 3 Cinema Pl, City) Sharing space with festival programmes, such as The Fringe & Feast, this cinema runs shorts, foreign-language and domestic productions.

Gay & Lesbian Venues

Blaze (☎ 8211 9199; www.blazemedia.com.au) This free gay and lesbian publication also lists popular gay and lesbian venues on its website.

Mars Bar (Map pp668-9; ☎ 8231 9639; 120 Gouger St, City) This is a lively gay and lesbian dance club with drag shows on the weekend, and is very popular with all sorts, including La Minogue (when in town).

Queens Arms Hotel (Map pp668-9; ☎ 8211 8000; 88 Wright St, City) DJs play from 9pm on Friday, Saturday and Sunday at this lively gay- and lesbian-only hotel. Drag shows commence from 10pm on a Sunday night.

Edinburgh Castle Hotel (Map pp668-9; ☎ 8410 1211; 233 Currie St, City) This gay and lesbian venue has a dance floor, bistro and beer garden.

Church (Map pp668-9; ☎ 8223 4233; Synagogue Pl, Rundle St, City) A big rave club in the centre of the action, this place is enjoyed by all persuasions.

Live Music

Adelaide has an incredible lively music scene covering the gamut of tastes.

Lots of bars host regular live jazz while the **Adelaide Festival Centre** (Map pp668-9; ☎ 8216 8600; King William Rd, City) and **Adelaide Town Hall** (Map pp668-9) host most classical concerts. The Gig Guide in Thursday's **Advertiser** (www.theadvertiser.news.com.au) lists popular- and jazz-music gigs, while Saturday's pages advertise musical shows and classical concerts. **BASS** (☎ 13 12 46; www.bass.sa.com.au) ticket outlets also list the mainstream venue events.

The innovative **Adelaide Symphony Orchestra** (Map pp668-9; www.aso.com.au; 91 Hindley St, City) programme is obtainable from its café, Tempo, and the main visitors centre.

Pick up free music papers *Rip it Up* and *db* for alternative gigs and reviews at record shops, hotels, cafés and nightspots around town.

Governor Hindmarsh Hotel (The Gov; ☎ 8340 0744; www.thegov.com.au; 59 Port Rd, Hindmarsh) The Gov is the brilliant, and undisputed, top live-music venue in town. You'll find atmospheric bars with a mixed crowd of all ages (and flavours) who share a love of the good stuff. As well as the odd Irish fiddle band sitting around in the bar, a back venue hosts folk, jazz, blues, salsa, reggae and dance music. This is the place where the best international acts often play – big names wanting a more intimate venue.

Royal Oak Hotel (Map pp668-9; ☎ 8267 2488; 123 O'Connell St, North Adelaide) Another of the old

favourites that never lets you down, this is a great pub with a lively crowd. Monday is open mike night, Tuesday has regular bands, Friday is DJ night and on Sunday there is jazz on the menu.

On Rundle St the **Austral Hotel** (Map pp668-9; ☎ 8223 4660; 205 Rundle St, City) is popular for a beer from lunch-time through to the wee hours, with bands on Friday and Saturday nights and DJs every other night except Monday. Also brimming with life and music on Rundle St are the **Exeter Hotel** (Map pp668-9; ☎ 8223 2623; 246 Rundle St, City), the **Stag** (Map pp668-9; ☎ 8223 2934; 299 Rundle St, City) and, just around the corner, **PJ O'Brien's** (Map pp668-9; ☎ 8232 5111; 14 East Tce, City).

Bar on Gouger (☎ 8410 0042; 123 Gouger St, City) has Friday night lounge music and Saturday night jazz parties, while **Café Tapas** (Map pp668-9; ☎ 8211 7446; 147 Hindley St, City) has flamenco dancing and music that packs them in on Friday, Saturday and Sunday nights.

Nightclubs

Heaven Nightclub complex (Map pp668-9; ☎ 8216 5216; www.heaven.com.au; 7 West Tce, City; cover $8-10; 8pm-6am) This is the venue most clubbers head for, with its choice of different bars and music, including retro, rhythm and blues, house and dance.

Minke Bar (Map pp668-9; ☎ 8211 8088; 17-19 Crippen Pl, off Hindley St, City; cover $8-12) With the action on three different levels, this club has DJs mixing disco house and electroclash.

Sport

Sport is a huge part of the city's daily life, encompassing everything from lawn-bowls to international one-day cricket spectaculars. For matches, check the **Advertiser** (www.theadvertiser.news.com.au) and local television sports news.

Australian Football League (AFL) rules the city, with two local competitive teams: the **Adelaide Crows** and **Port Power** (☎ 8268 2088; Aami Stadium, Turner Dr, West Lakes). The **Redbacks** (☎ 8300 3800; Adelaide Oval, King William Rd, North Adelaide) are the state's cricket team, basketball has the looming and successful **Adelaide 36ers** (☎ 8444 6444; The Powerhouse, 44a Crittenden Rd, Findon) and the **Thunderbirds** (☎ 8238 0500; 155 Railway Tce, Mile End South) thrash their rivals in netball.

Adelaide hosts a number of world-class international events that take over the city streets and turn into big parties, including one-day cricket and tennis matches, golf and horse jumping (see Festivals & Events; p674).

SHOPPING

Rundle Mall in the city and Jetty Rd in Glenelg are good places for retro clothes, music, books and the Italian coffee that fuels this kind of browsing.

SA classics are led by **RM Williams** (☎ 8269 3752; 5 Percy St, Prospect), whose hand-made boots are a truly great buy (women/men from $220/250). First crafted for Aussie stockmen back in the early 1800s, these boots are hand-made from one piece of leather and can last for decades. Annual sales in June can halve the price.

Considered as Australia's finest chocolates, **Haigh's Chocolates** has outlets around Adelaide, such as 2 Rundle Mall in the city and 87b Jetty Rd, Glenelg (also see p674).

The ghoulish speciality at the **Goldsmithery** (☎ 8295 6188; cnr Sussex St & Jetty Rd, Glenelg; 9.30am-5pm Tue-Fri, 10am-1pm Sat) is recycling gold fillings! Broken cutlery and trinkets also inspire these creative jewellery-makers.

For local art try **Urban Cow Studio** (Map pp668-9; ☎ 8232 6126; 11 Frome St, City) who sell witty, clever and affordable artworks made by local artists. Also the **Jam Factory Contemporary Craft & Design** (Map pp668-9; ☎ 8211 9777; 44-60 Rundle

---

TOP MARKETS

Central Market (Map pp668-9; Gouger St; 7am-5.30pm Tue, 9am-5.30pm Thu, 7am-9pm Fri, 7am-3pm Sat) This is the largest undercover produce market in the country – but is much more than that (p674). The atmosphere and local produce is fantastic: breads, cheeses, olive oils, sauces and marinated olives, seafood and any fruit or veg you can think of. Find real bargains on Tuesday afternoon or just after lunch on Saturday, when unsold produce is disposed of at give-away prices.

Orange Lane Market (cnr Edward St & Orange Lane, Norwood; 10am-5pm Sat, Sun & public holidays) A small, uncommercialised indoor market, the emphasis here is on hand-made furniture, second-hand clothing, bric-a-brac and junk. Come here for a massage, a bowl of laksa or a tarot reading.

Mall, City), which sells handcrafted and colourful glassware (for its other city location, see p669).

GETTING AROUND
Bicycle
Linear Park Mountain Bike Hire (☎ 8223 6271; Elder Park; 9am-5pm) is situated just below the Festival Centre and adjacent to the Pop-Eye boat launch. Bicycle hire per day/week is $20/80 including helmets, locks and bike maps.

Glenelg Cycles (☎ 8294 4741; 754 Anzac Hwy, Glenelg; 9am-5pm Mon-Fri, 9am-4pm Sat & Sun) is run by a friendly crew with great deals for bike hire from $15/40 per day/week.

Public Transport
Adelaide has an integrated transport system covering all metropolitan buses and trains, as well as the Glenelg tram. The **Adelaide Metro Information Centre** (Map pp668-9; ☎ 8210 1000; www.adelaidemetro.com.au; cnr King William & Currie Sts, City; 8am-6pm Mon-Sat, 10.30am-5.30pm Sun) provides timetables and sells tickets.

The day-trip ticket allows unlimited travel on buses, trains and the tram ($6). Peak and off-peak tickets are valid for two hours from the commencement of the first journey. Travelling peak time (weekends or weekdays before 9am and after 3pm), tickets cost $3.20; off-peak (weekdays 9am to 3pm) costs $1.90. Tickets can be purchased on buses, trains and the Glenelg tram, or at staffed train stations.

The Bee Line and City Loop buses are free.

Bee Line (No 99B) runs in a loop from the Glenelg tram terminus at Victoria Sq, up King William St and around the corner past the train station to the City West campus of the University of South Australia.

City Loop (No 99C) runs around the margins of the CBD from the train station, passing the Central Market en route. It runs every 15 minutes on weekdays between 8am and 6pm (9pm Friday), 8am and 5pm Saturday, 10am and 5pm Sunday, and every 30 minutes on Saturday between 8.15am and 5.15pm.

Wandering Star Service operates for nightclubbers; it will pick you up from designated spots/nightclubs and deliver you to your front door – within most city suburbs ($7, between midnight and 3am Friday and Saturday).

Classic old **trams** rattle their way between Glenelg (Moseley Sq) and Victoria Sq in the city every 15 minutes from 6am to 11.50pm daily.

The **suburban train station** terminal is by the Casino on North Tce.

Taxi

There are licensed taxi ranks all over town, but you can also easily hail **Adelaide Independent Taxis** (☎ 13 22 11, for wheelchair users 1300 360 940) and **Suburban Taxis** (☎ 13 10 08).

ADELAIDE HILLS

Central to the Mt Lofty Ranges, the Adelaide Hills are a 30-minute drive from the city. Even in the driest summer months they offer cooler temperatures and lush woodland shade. Winding and narrow roads lead you through the leafy hills and farmed valleys to stunning views of the city and countryside. Many tucked-away working and gentrified villages sell orchard produce or have remnants from bygone eras to browse around.

However, the Hills' real stars are the numerous conservation, recreation and wildlife parks. They contain over 1000km of walking trails, catering for all energy levels, and enough furry fauna to melt the hardest of hearts.

It's worth hiring a car for a full day to encompass early morning views and breakfast at Mt Lofty Summit and a guided wildlife walk at sunset. Take a good map, as signage is appalling and it's easy to get lost.

Information

There are two visitors centres: **Mt Lofty Summit visitors centre** (☎ 08-8370 1054; mtloftysummit@saugov.sa.gov.au; Mt Lofty Summit; ⏱ 9am-5pm) and the **Adelaide Hills visitors centre** (☎ 1800 353 323, 08-8388 1185; maggie@adelaidehillsinfo.asn.au; 41 Main St, Hahndorf; ⏱ 9am-5pm Mon-Fri, 10am-4pm Sat & Sun).

Sights & Activities

WINERIES

The first exported Australian wine was a case of Adelaide Hills' hock, sent to Queen Victoria in 1845. There are around a dozen cellar doors including **Petaluma's Bridgewater Mill Winery & Restaurant** (☎ 08-8339 3422; bridgewatermill@petaluma.com.au; mains $33; ⏱ 10am-5pm, lunch

noon-2.30pm Thu-Sun), whose outstanding and award-winning wines are complemented by outstanding and award-winning food. The setting is a beautifully restored 200-year-old flour mill, complete with water wheel. Flagship wines include the Bridgewater Mill Sauvignon Blanc and Shiraz. Ignore this jewel at your gastronomic peril.

PARKS & GARDENS

From the Cleland Wildlife Park you can walk through the bush (2km) or drive up to **Mt Lofty Summit** (727m), which has a good restaurant and beautiful views over the city.

From here continue south for 1.5km to the stunning **Mt Lofty Botanical Gardens** (Map p684; ☎ 08-8370 8370; gates on Mawson Dr & Lampert Rd; parking $2.20; ⏱ 8.30am-4pm Mon-Fri, 10am-6pm Sat & Sun).

Belair National Park

This **park** (Map p684; ☎ 08-8278 5477; Upper Sturt Rd; admission per car $6.50; ⏱ 8am-5.30pm) has walking trails and picnic spots. Get here from Adelaide by bus (No 195 from King William St to stop 27) or take the train to Belair station on the edge of the park.

Wildlife Parks

Cleland Wildlife Park (Map p684; ☎ 08-8339 2444; www.environment.sa.gov.au/parks/cleland; Summit Rd, Cleland; adult/child $12/8; ⏱ 9.30am-5pm) is an excellent park with numerous species of Australian fauna including the rarely seen Tasmanian Devil and delightful snoring wombats. You can have your photo taken with a koala ($12, 2pm to 4pm). Dusk **wildlife and Aboriginal tours** (adult/child $20/12) run with minimum numbers only, so call ahead.

Public transport is limited; take bus No 163F from Grenfell St at 9.52am, 10.52am or 12.52pm and get off at Crafers for a connecting No 823 service to the wildlife park.

The founder of the **Warrawong Earth Sanctuary** (Map p684; ☎ 08-8370 9197; www.esl.com.au; Stock Rd, North Mylor; adult/child $23/17.50), John Wamsley, set up the first of the privately run Earth Sanctuaries to provide a safe place for endangered native wildlife and the shy platypus. Proposing the eradication of introduced predatory species, such as domestic pets (while gleefully wearing a cat-fur hat complete with tail), he was loathed by the cat-loving public. His departure was sad, but there are still great dawn and sunset guided walks (bookings

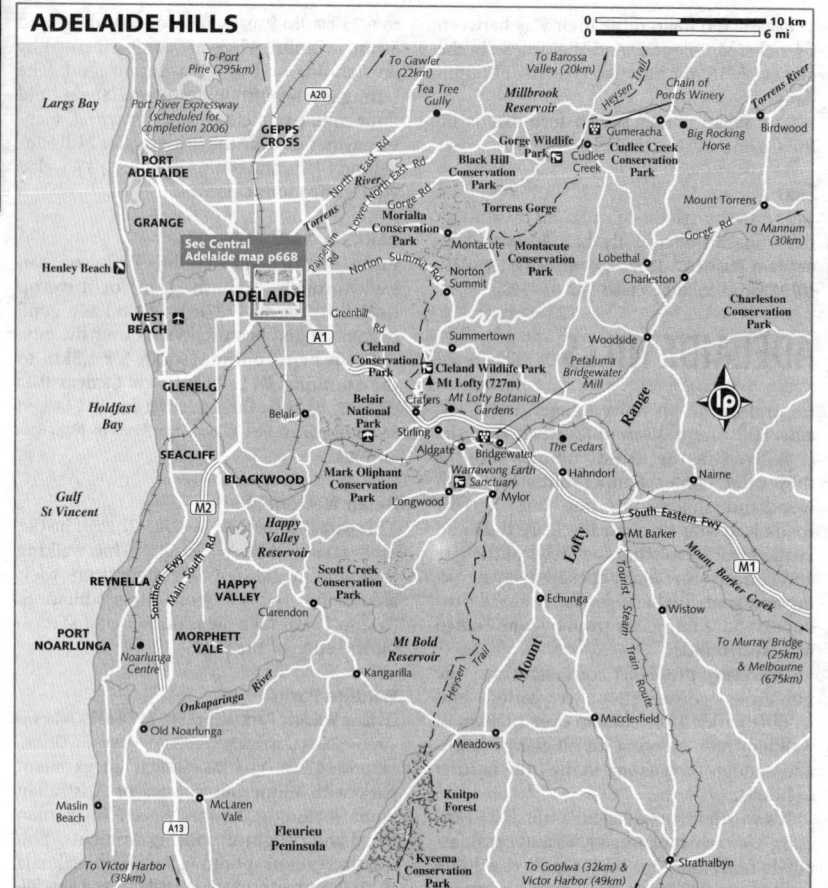

ADELAIDE HILLS

essential) and accommodation/walk/dinner packages in luxury tents for $120 a night. There is also a good licensed restaurant (with mains around $19).

To reach the sanctuary from Adelaide, turn off the freeway at Stirling and follow the signs from the Stirling roundabout. A taxi from Stirling is about $10.

Sleeping & Eating

Locals tend to make the Hills a day trip, and there is little budget accommodation. However, there are masses of good quality B&Bs geared towards couples, some around $100 but most $150 to $195 a night – ask at the Mt Lofty Summit or Adelaide Hills visitors centres. **Aldgate** and **Stirling** are two

of the nicest small residential communities with great family-friendly pubs and cafés all within strolling distance.

Warrawong Earth Sanctuary (Map above; ☎ 08-8370 9197; www.esl.com.au; Stock Rd, North Mylor) The park offers great night walk, dinner and overnight packages from $120. Its up-market tents have air-con and electric blankets, and are a great way to combine an overnight stay and a must-do wildlife-spotting walk.

Geoff & Hazels (☎ 08-8339 8360; www.geoffandhazels .com.au; 19 Kingsland Road, Aldgate; d $50; 🖳) Often booked out by families, this simple and peaceful place is only a two-minute walk to the old Aldgate Pump Hotel (which has great pub grub). Breakfast is inclusive, along with pick-ups and lifts to nearby attractions.

Mount Lofty Railway Station (☎ 08-8339 7400; www.mlrs.com.au; 2 Sturt Valley Road, Stirling; d/f from $85/105) Trains do actually whoosh through the station, which is central to Stirling. The rooms are simple and clean and sleep up to 18; perfect for groups and families.

The **YHA** has hostels at **Norton Summit**, **Mt Lofty** and **Mylor**. These basic lodges are all on the Heysen Trail (p661) and are $70 a night or $80 for nonmembers. Make bookings and collect keys at **Adelaide Central YHA** (Map pp668-9; ☎ 08-8414 3000; 135 Waymouth St, Adelaide).

Fuzzies Farm (☎ 08-8390 1111; fuzzyt@ozemail.com .au; Norton Summit; cabins per week $90) Learn practical skills in a friendly organic farm environment 15km east of Adelaide. The setting is great, as are its café and self-contained bushland cabins; the weekly rate for helpers includes meals and laundry. Stays of a one-week minimum are preferred, and bookings are essential.

Also recommended for extraordinary comforts and romantic luxury is the **Or-angerie B&B** (☎ 08-8339 5458; 4 Orley Ave, Stirling; www.orangerie.com.au; d $195) and, with private country grounds, the multiawarded **Adel-aide Hills Country Cottages B&Bs** (☎ 08-8388 4193; Oakwood Rd, Oakbank; d from $190).

Getting There & Around

Public transport to the Hills is very limited. There are a few buses, including some to Mt Lofty Summit and the Cleland Wildlife Park, but the best options are to hire a car or take an organised coach tour from Adelaide (p674).

Bus Nos 840 and 164F depart hourly for Hahndorf from Adelaide every day ($3.50, 70 minutes).

If you have a car, a good tour of the Hills loops from Adelaide to the northern Hills area, leaving the city via North Tce, Botanic Rd and then Payneham Rd and continuing on to Lower North East Rd. This scenic route takes you to Birdwood, from where you could continue north to the Barossa Valley, or head south at Birdwood and travel to Hahndorf, returning to Adelaide via the South Eastern Fwy.

For a smaller loop focussing on the region's beautiful national parks, you can turn into Magill Rd instead of Payneham Rd and onto Norton Summit Rd to check out **Morialta Conservation Park** (Map p684), which has walking trails, waterfalls and a rugged

gorge. Then continue south to **Cleland Wildlife Park** (Map p684), **Mt Lofty Summit**, the stunning **Mt Lofty Botanic Gardens** (Map p684) and **Belair National Park** (Map p684), before heading back to Adelaide via Crafers and the freeway.

ADELAIDE TO BIRDWOOD

Heading out from Adelaide on Lower North East Rd, turn right about 20km from the city at the noted **Chain of Ponds Winery** (Map p684) and right again at Gorge Rd to reach the west end of **Cudlee Creek** (Map p684). Here you'll find the **Gorge Wildlife Park** (Map p684; ☎ 08-8389 2206; Redden Dr, Cudlee Creek; adult/child $10/5; ◷ 8am-5pm), with koala cuddling.

An example of giant Aussie kitsch near **Gumeracha** (Map p684), is the very station-ary **Big Rocking Horse** (Map p684). About 6km further on at Birdwood is the **National Motor Museum** (Map p684; ☎ 08-8568 5006; Shannon St, Birdwood; adult/child $9/4; ◷ 9am-5pm) in the historic Birdwood Mill, with Australia's largest collection of vintage and classic cars and motorcycles.

HAHNDORF

☎ 08 / pop 1842

The oldest surviving German settlement in Australia, Hahndorf, 28km southeast of Adelaide, is a major tourist attraction. Settled in 1839 by Lutherans who left Prussia to escape religious persecution, the town took its name from the ship's captain, Hahn; *dorf* is German for village. It is a pretty little place with one main street. However, numerous tourism outlets overshadow any heritage charm.

Hahndorf Academy (☎ 8388 7250; 68 Main St; ◷ 10am-5pm Mon-Sat, noon-5pm Sun) was established in 1857 and houses an art gallery, craft shop and German museum – it has several original sketches by Sir Hans Heysen, a famous landscape artist who lived in Hahndorf for many years. For more information on the artist, see the boxed text 'Heysen Trail' (p661).

Tours through Sir Hans' studio and house, the **Cedars** (Map p684; ☎ 8388 7277; Heysen Rd), built 1878, about 2km northwest of Hahndorf, are conducted daily except Saturday, at 11am, 1pm and 3pm. You'll see over 300 of the artist's original works during tours ($8).

You can pick your own strawberries between November and May from the famous

Beerenberg Strawberry Farm (☎ 8388 7272; www
.beerenberg.com.au; Mount Barker Rd; ☒ 9am-5pm),
also renowned for yummy rose petal jam,
chutneys and sauces.

Sleeping & Eating

Hahndorf accommodation is mainly very
convenient, with a number of motels on
the main street.

Hahndorf Inn Motor Lodge (☎ 8388 1000; fax
8388 1092; 35a Main St; d $94; ☒) This central inn
offers all mod cons and is right bang in the
centre of town.

German Arms Hotel (☎ 8388 7013; 50 Main St;
mains $9-14) Dating from 1862, this pub is
always lively and gets packed on weekends.
The bratwurst and pies are popular.

Old Mill (☎ 8388 7888; 98 Main St; smorgasbord
lunch/dinner Mon-Fri $14/15, lunch or dinner Sat & Sun
$18) The all-you-can-eat smorgasbord here
is the best value-for-money feed in town.

FLEURIEU PENINSULA

South of Adelaide, the Fleurieu (*floo*-ree-o)
Peninsula is a mecca for vacationing and
day-tripping Adelaidians and for good reason: the coastline has fantastic vast beaches
that never feel crowded, while the adjacent
rolling hills of the lower Mt Lofty Ranges
create vivid and contrasting landscapes. The
Peninsula's residential and inland farming communities have maintained their
idiosyncratic character, with the inevitable
tourist-hustle kept to a few towns. Deep
Creek Conservation and Onkaparinga River
National Parks are equipped with beautiful
bouncing fauna, and boutique wineries are
dotted like little liquid gems throughout the
whole Peninsula.

The region was named after Napoleon's
naval minister and the man responsible for
financing explorer Nicholas Baudin's Australian expedition. In the early days, settlers on
the Peninsula ran a smuggling business, but
this was replaced by whaling in 1837 from
Encounter Bay. Protected baby whales and
their doting mothers can now be watched
capering off the southern beaches.

MCLAREN VALE WINE REGION

McLaren Vale (population 2313) is the
gateway for the surrounding wine region,
including the wineries around Reynella,

Willunga, Yankallila, Normanville and
Langhorne Creek. The area is particularly
well suited to red wines, but a trend towards
white-wine consumption in the 1970s
prompted growers to diversify.

The **McLaren Vale & Fleurieu visitors centre**
(☎ 08-8323 9944; www.visitorcentre.com.au; Main Rd,
McLaren Vale; ☒ 9am-5pm, Mon-Fri 10am-5pm Sat &
Sun) is at the northern end of McLaren Vale
and **McLaren Vale Video** (☎ 08-8323 850; 165 Main
Rd, McLaren Vale) has Internet access.

The **Sea & Vines Festival** in June is a great
weekend-long celebration of food, wine,
music and art.

Sights & Activities
WINERIES
There are over 50 wineries with cellar-door
sales in the area. Most open 10am to 5pm
daily, some have very good restaurants and
there are often informal food and wine days
at the larger estates.

In the same building as the visitors centre, **Stump Hill Café & Wine Bar** (☎ 08-8323 8999)
is run in cooperation with the McLaren Vale
Winemakers Association, offering tastings
from local wineries with no cellar door.

Tourism booklets list wineries and where
you can locate disabled facilities.

d'Arenberg (☎ 08-8323 8206; www.darenberg.com
.au; Osborn Rd, McLaren Vale) One of the better-
known McLaren Vale wineries, d'Arenberg
has produced consistently good wines since
1928. The excellent restaurant offers a superb panoramic view of the valley and is
surprisingly affordable.

Ingoldby & Andrew Garrett (☎ 08-8383 0005;
cellardoor@ingoldby.com.au; Ingoldby Rd, McLaren Vale) Ingoldby makes a cracking cabernet sauvignon
and shiraz, while Andrew Garrett's sparkling
reds appear at all good Sunday brunches.

Wirra Wirra (☎ 08-8323 8414; cellardoor@wirra.com
.au; off McMurtrie Rd, McLaren Vale) This friendly winery is best known for its wonderful Reserve
Shiraz, chocolate-enhancing stickies (dessert
wines), and their Scrubby Rise Viognier and
the Hand Picked Riesling, which are consistently delicious.

Tours
There are myriad regional and winery coach
tours that depart ex-Adelaide (p674). Ask at
the McLaren Vale & Fleurieu visitors centre
and try the wineries for details of local wine
tours – most only operate seasonally.

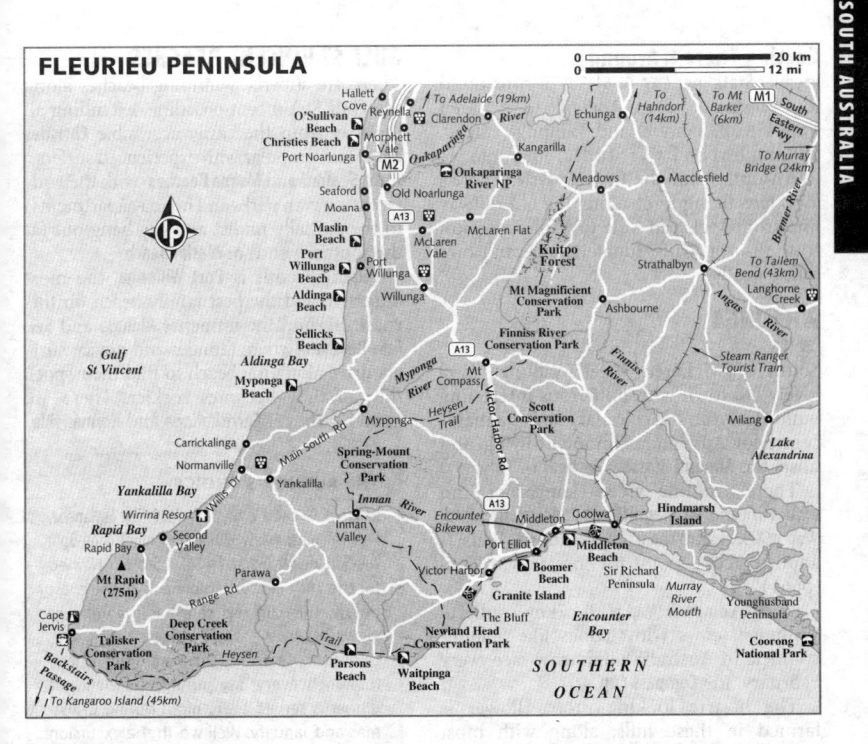

FLEURIEU PENINSULA

Lurch around the wineries on a camel with **Camel Winery Tours** (☎ 08-8383 0488; fax 8383 0666). Rates include lunch ($85).

Des's Minibus Tours (☎ 08-8234 8011; www.dess minibus.com.au) runs tailored tours of the McLaren Vale wine region, departing either from the visitors centre or Adelaide, with a minimum of six people ($85).

Sleeping & Eating

Most B&B accommodation is set in the middle of vineyards and offers luxury conditions perfect for spoiling yourself.

McLaren Vale Motel (☎ 08-8323 8265; www.mc larenvalemotel.com.au; cnr Main Rd & Caffrey St, McLaren Vale; s/d $80/95;) Right opposite the visitors centre, the motel is fairly close to the centre of town. Rooms and units are spacious and well equipped, if a bit stuffy.

McLaren Vale Lakeside Caravan Park (☎ 08-8323 9255; www.mclarenvale.net; Field St, McLaren Vale; 2-person camp sites/caravans/cabins $16/45/65) This well-kept caravan park has a pretty rural setting close to town complete with wandering water birds and information on winery labour.

Ashcroft Country Accommodation (☎ 08-8323 7700; www.ashcroftbnb.com.au; Johnston Rd, McLaren Vale; d & tw $180;) This truly comfortable (and award-winning) small B&B has friendly hosts and tremendous 360-degree views of the Vale. One room provides excellent disabled facilities and rates include cooked breakfasts.

Salopian Inn (☎ 08-8323 8769; salopian@bigpond .com; cnr Willunga & McMurtrie Rds, McLaren Vale; mains $27; lunch Thu-Tue, dinner Fri-Sat) An icon among food-lovers, this charming inn has a superb wine cellar to complement the mouth-watering seasonal menu, which features local produce. This place is not one for children and you'll need to book: it's small and extremely popular for long, long lunches.

Oscars Diner (☎ 08-8323 8707; 201 Main Rd, McLaren Vale; mains $8-27) The house speciality is a winner; good tasty pizza, green salad, and a glass of local vino.

Also recommended is the friendly **Southern Vales Bed & Breakfast** (☎ /fax 08-8323 8144; www.southernvales.net; 13 Chalk Hill Rd, McLaren Vale; s/d $100/115).

Getting There & Around

Premier Stateliner (☎ 08-8415 5555) runs up to four buses a day from Adelaide to McLaren Vale ($6.50, 1 hour) and Willunga ($6.50, 70 minutes) on its Victor Harbor route.

An option for the fit is to **cycle**. There's a cycle/walking track along the old railway line from McLaren Vale to Willunga, 6km to the south. Unfortunately you can't hire bikes locally.

WILLUNGA
☎ 08

South of McLaren Vale, Willunga is a lovely old town with numerous interesting buildings from the colonial era. It's a major centre for Australian almond growing, and hosts the **Almond Blossom Festival** in July.

There are fine views, kangaroos and walks in the **Mt Magnificent Conservation Park** (Map p687), 12km east of Willunga. This is another access point for the Heysen Trail (p661).

At **Mt Compass** (Map p687), 7km south of Willunga, cows with names like Splatter compete in Australia's only cow race every February: the **Compass Cup**.

The bizarre looking protea flower is farmed in these hills, along with most kinds of berries. Pick your own at the **Agon Berry Farm** (☎ 8556 8428; Main Rd, Mt Compass; ⏰ 9am-dusk Nov-Apr).

Another state special is **Fox Creek Wines** (☎ 8556 2403; www.foxcreekwines.com; Malpas Rd, Willunga). Ask anyone about the region's top shiraz, and one of those mentioned will be its Last Chance Reserve Shiraz, a classic.

Sleeping & Eating

Willunga Hotel (☎ 8556 2135; fax 8556 4379; 3-5 High St; s/d $30/60) This pub is good value if you just want a simple bed (with shared bathroom) and/or meal for the night. Lunches and dinner meals are $12 to $22.

An old wooden dance barn rocks here at the weekends; the legendary **Russell's** (☎ 8556 2571; 13 High St; mains $23; ⏰ dinner Fri & Sat) has one of the state's hottest chefs cooking fabulous wood-fired pizzas with much chutzpah – book weeks ahead to get in!

The **Willy Hill Café** (☎ 8556 2379; www.willyhill cafe.com.au; 27 High St; mains $10-20; ⏰ 8.30am-5pm) Housed in an old church, there are great vegetarian options served every day. It's also open for dinner on Friday nights.

GULF ST VINCENT BEACHES

There are superb swimming beaches along the Gulf St Vincent coastline, extending all the way from the easily accessible **Christies Beach** (also popular with experienced surfers), onto **Seaford** and **Moana Beaches** (with their adjacent caravan parks and holiday apartments) to the partially nudist and gay hang-out (at the southern end) of **Maslin Beach**.

Further south is **Port Willunga**, the most attractive and the best family beach on this coast. Beyond the immense **Aldinga** and **Sellicks Beaches** (where families and novice surfers drive along the beach to find their spot), the coastline becomes rockier. There are good beaches at **Carrickalinga** and **Normanville**.

THE AUTHOR'S CHOICE

Star of Greece (☎ 8557 7420; The Esplanade, Port Willunga; mains $20-30; ⏰ lunch noon-3pm Tue-Sun, dinner 6-9pm Fri & Sat Sep-Jul) Named for the 19th-century shipwreck on the coast below, this cliff-top café has magnificent views seaward – appropriate since it specialises in seafood. The restaurant opens for lunch every day during summer, and dinner is served every night during Christmas and January. Well worth the excursion from Adelaide.

Yankalilla, just in from the coast near Normanville, has gained fame thanks to the image of Jesus and the Virgin Mary that has mysteriously appeared on a wall of the **Anglican church** (132 Main St). Many local cynics will tell you that the vision is a mixture of rising damp and opportunism.

Scuttled off Yankalilla Bay in 2002, the destroyer **ex-HMAS Hobart** now entertains scuba divers as a wreck dive (obtain permits from the Marina St Vincent, ☎ 8598 3115).

Along the south coast near Cape Jervis (and the Kangaroo Island ferry terminal) is the **Deep Creek Conservation Park**, with walking tracks including the Heysen Trail, and bush camping areas.

VICTOR HARBOR
☎ 08 / pop 8968

The main town on the Peninsula, Victor Harbor is a hugely popular retirement and holiday town (83km south of Adelaide); the spot where SA schoolies come to let rip after final exams, and where whale-watchers and artists follow gentler pursuits.

A 10-minute drive gets you to the fabulous beaches of Middleton and Goolwa beloved of surfers and beach-layabouts of all ages. Or hire a bicycle – the 23km sealed Encounter Bikeway follows the truly beautiful coast between Victor Harbor's Bluff and Goolwa.

Overlooking Encounter Bay, close to where the explorers Flinders and Baudin had their historic meeting in 1802, Victor was founded as a sealing and whaling centre in 1837. Local businesses now hunt day-trippers for their dollars.

Information

The friendly **visitors centre** (☎ 8552 5738; www .tourismvictorharbor.com.au; The Causeway; ☒ 9am-5pm) is at the mainland end of the Granite Island causeway and has Internet access.

Sights & Activities

Children love the double-decker tram pulled by Clydesdale draught horses ($7 return) across the short causeway to tiny **Granite Island**, which also has a little penguin rookery.

Granite Island Gift Shop (☎ 8552 7555; fax 8552 8011; ☒ 9.30am-sunset) has a (wheelchair-friendly) one-hour guided **penguin walk** (adult/child $10/7), which observes these delightful creatures waddling home from fishing. The tours start at the shop's excellent interpretative centre at dusk, with a quick introduction from a hologram park ranger.

You can also watch sharks being fed through underwater windows at the **Below Decks Shark Aquarium** (adult/child $15/9; ☒ 11am-5pm), depending on visibility.

Between June and October you might be lucky enough to see a southern right whale swimming near the causeway. Victor Harbor is on the migratory path of these splendid animals and they can be observed from several points along the coast, including the Bluff at the southern end of the bay.

The **South Australian Whale Centre** (☎ 8552 5644; www.webmedia.com.au/whales; 2 Railway Tce; adult/child $5.50/3; ☒ 11am-4.30pm) monitors the movements of the whales, and has displays on the history of whaling and the physiology of the southern right whale.

Why not try parasailing over Encounter Bay? Contact **Odyssey Adventures** (☎ 8277 3233; fax 8277 3224; Granite Island Causeway; adult/group rate $75/65; ☒ 10am-4pm Nov-Apr).

Young children clamour to visit **Greenhills Adventure Park** (☎ 8552 5999; www.greenhills.com.au; Wagon Rd; adult/child $18/13; ☒ 10am-5pm).

Take portrait and landscape painting classes with the award-winning and affable Lorraine and Terry Lewitzka at the **Telegraph Station Art Centre** (☎ 8552 1865; cnr Coral St & Railway Tce; ☒ 10am-4pm Mon-Sat, 1-4pm Sun). There are also evocative oil landscapes and delicate watercolours for sale.

Sleeping

There's a fair choice, with B&Bs breeding along Encounter Bay. The town's hotels offer rooms that vary in quality, but all are central. The visitors centre has a booking service.

Anchorage at Victor Harbor (☎ 8552 5970; anchoragevh@ozemail.com.au; cnr Coral St & Flinders Pde; dm/s/d/ $25/40/65; ☒) This attractive seafront and heritage-listed hotel offers a variety of comfortable and clean rooms, and there's an in-house licensed restaurant (mains $14 to $26.) Book ahead for en suite rooms and dorm beds.

Hotel Victor (☎ 8552 1288; fax 8551 5150; Albert Pl; s/d $90/100; ☒) Despite the inevitable poker machines, this pleasant central hotel has relaxing rooms, a dining room and cheap bar meals ($11 to $17).

Victor Harbor Beachfront Caravan Park (☎ 8552 1111; 114 Victoria St; camp site/basic/cabins $22/55/65) This caravan park is well maintained, but is a bit of a walk from town, and sits on the grottier end of Victor's small beach.

Also recommended for those wanting a 'de luxe' stay in Victor, and a superb view of the bay, is the **Whalers Inn Resort** (☎ 8552 4400; www.whalers.com.au; The Bluff; d with/without balcony & sea views $160/95; ☒).

Eating

No 5 on Coral Cafe (☎ 8552 7344; 5 Coral St; lunches $6-10; ☒ 9am-5pm Thu-Tue) Retired Swiss chef Maestro and his wife bake the best little masterpieces in town; buttery savoury tartlets and succulent cakes. Indulge yourself!

Grosvenor Junction Hotel (☎ 8552 1011; 40 Ocean St; meals $10-12) The atmosphere here is nothing flash but you can get a decent feed and watch the miniature trains run around the top of the room.

Ben's Fish Cafe (☎ 8552 2573; 10 Ocean St; takeaway meals $7-11; ☒ 11am-8 or 10pm) This popular town centre takeaway offers fish and chips and burgers.

Cafe Bavaria (☎ 8552 7505; 11 Albert Pl; lunches $7; ✆ 9am-5pm, closed Mon off-season) Opposite the park, this popular café specialises in German pastries and cakes.

Getting There & Around

From June to November inclusive, **Steam Ranger** (☎ 8231 4366; adult/child $45/25) runs a tourist train on the last Sunday of the month from Mt Barker (in the Adelaide Hills) to Victor Harbor via Goolwa. It spends about three hours in town before making the return journey.

Every Sunday, and three times daily during school holidays, the steam **Cockle Train** (☎ 8552 2782; adult/child $22/12) travels the scenic Encounter Coast between Goolwa and Victor Harbor. Tickets can be purchased at the stations in Goolwa, Port Elliot and Victor Harbor.

Premier Stateliner (☎ 8415 5555) has up to five services daily on Monday to Friday from Adelaide, less on Saturday and Sunday ($15, 2 hours).

Kangaroo Island Sealink (☎ 13 13 01) offers day trips (with lunch) to Kangaroo Island from Victor ($175).

Victor Harbor Cycles & Skates (☎ 8552 1417; 73 Victoria St; ✆ 8am-6pm) hires mountain bikes for $8/20 per hour/day.

PORT ELLIOT

☎ 08 / pop 1527

Port Elliot, established in 1854 as the seaport for the Murray River trade, is on the picturesque **Horseshoe Bay**, which is a part of Encounter Bay. There's a safe and lovely swimming beach, whose turquoise waters are also enjoyed by dolphins, and a great cliff-top walk used by locals for seasonal whale-watching.

Nearby surf beaches include **Boomer Beach** on the western edge of town and **Middleton Beach**, the best surf beach in the area, to the east.

The **Southern Surf Shop** (☎ 8554 2376; 36 North Tce), a few doors west from the Royal Family Hotel, rents surfing gear and can provide information on surfing conditions, as can **Big Surf Australia** (☎ 8554 2399; Main Rd, Middleton; ✆ 9am-5.30pm) in Middleton. Novice and advanced surfers alike can learn with the recommended **Surf Academy** (☎ 8552 2541); lessons are $30 for 90 minutes (including all equipment).

Sleeping & Eating

The best accommodation in this coastal area are self-contained two-person or family-sized holiday apartments. Great for families and friends alike, choose the level of comfort you want from estate agent lists, and pay between $60 to $300 a night.

For Port Elliot and Middleton try **Dodd & Page** (☎ 8554 2029; doddandpage@bigpond.com; 51 The Strand).

Royal Family Hotel (☎ 8554 2219; rfhotel@ chariot.net.au; 32 North Tce; s/d $30/40; ✖) The rooms are clean and simple (with shared bathrooms) at this small and very popular family pub. Weekends are packed for its $9 Friday schnitzel nights and Sunday roasts and fish lunches.

Join the queues at the excellent **Port Elliot Bakery** across the road.

Port Elliot Caravan & Tourist Park (☎ 8554 2134; kate@portelliotcaravanpark.com.au; Middleton Rd; camp sites/cabins $16/55) Land developers must have gritted their teeth – this great park directly overlooks the beautiful Horseshoe Bay.

Arnella by the Sea (☎ 8554 3611; narnu@bigpond .com; 28 North Tce; dm $20) There are self-catering facilities and room options in this YHA-affiliated and (historic) former hotel.

Also recommended, **Seachange B&B** (☎ 8554 3243; www.citrus-seachange.com; 48 Goolwa Rd, Middleton; d/f $185/250; ✖) offers visitors informal opulence. Private dinners are available upon request.

Flying Fish Restaurant & Beachside Kiosk (☎ 8554 3504; No 1 The Foreshore, Horseshoe Bay; mains $26-30; ✆ noon-4.30pm Sun-Thu, noon-4.30pm & 6.30-9pm Fri-Sat) This restaurant overlooks the sea, and is a long-lunch institution in this part of the world. The fish is jumping-fresh, the wine list is excellent and the desserts are sumptuous. Its kiosk serves beachside oysters and good old fish and chips.

Getting There & Away

Premier Stateliner (☎ 8415 5555) has daily services between Adelaide and Port Elliot ($15, 2 hours).

GOOLWA

☎ 08 / pop 4345

A restful and unassuming place, Goolwa has the best beach on the southern coast. Water sports, fishing, skydiving and simple beach-pleasures are the preferred pastimes of locals and visitors alike. Whales (and dolphins) can be seen in season and artists revel in the glorious sunsets.

At the point where Australia's largest river, the Murray, enters the ocean, Goolwa initially grew with the developing trade along the river. In the 1880s a new railway line to Adelaide from Murray Bridge spelt the end for Goolwa as a port town. However, boat building is a continuing art, celebrated in the biennial **Wooden Boat Festival**.

Hindmarsh Island Bridge, with its unusual land- and sea-based animal murals, links the mainland to Hindmarsh Island. Disputes over the building of this bridge continued for years, dividing local opinion, Aboriginal communities and the state's academic and political powerhouses.

The **visitors centre** (☎ 8555 3488; www.visital exandrina.com; Goolwa Wharf; ⏱ 9am-5pm) has information on local interests like the **Goolwa Museum**, and includes the interactive **Signal Point River Murray Interpretive Centre** (admission $5.50) with child-friendly exhibits on the early history of life on the river.

Sights & Activities

For those who get twitchy sitting on a beach, you can hire a boat from Hindmarsh Island Marina or Clayton, body-boards from Goolwa beach kiosk in summer ($10), and surfboards in Port Elliot (p690).

Encounter Bikeway Trail maps are available from the visitors centre for the 23km (mainly) sealed Encounter Bikeway. Follow the stunning coastline from Goolwa (part cycle path, part public road) adjacent to the almost continuous beach to Victor Harbor's Bluff. Take your swimming things and make a day of it.

Goolwa Caravan Park (☎ 8555 2737; www.goo lwacaravanpark.com.au; Noble Ave) hires out bikes per hour/day $10/20, canoes per hour/day $10/35, and water-bikes per hour/day $11/35. This park has camp sites and cabins and is 3.5km from town, but close to the river.

Skydive Adelaide (☎ 8552 3234; www.skydive.org .au; Goolwa airfield) offers magnificent coastal views of Goolwa with skydiving. Tandem jumps from 8000ft are $300; a day's solo training and freefall jump are $450.

Goolwa & Spirit of the Coorong Cruises (☎ 8555 2203; www.coorongcruises.com.au; Goolwa Wharf) has the MV *Aroona* taking cruises on the lower Murray ($28), while the *Spirit of the Coorong* and *Wetlands Explorer* take longer trips into the Coorong ($70). Meals are extra and bookings essential.

Sleeping & Eating

The best accommodation for all-sized wallets is holiday rental properties. These will be fully equipped and vary in price, quality and location, but are excellent value. Four adults can rent a house for $200 to $350 per week. Beware, though, rents virtually double over school holidays.

All estate agents in town manage holiday properties; try **Weeks & Macklin** (☎ 8555 2233; www.wmgoolwa.com.au; 28 Cadell St) and the **Professionals** (☎ 8555 2122; www.professionalsgoolw a.com.au; 1 Cadell St).

PS Federal & Forester's Lodge (☎ 8362 6229; pgibberd@ozemail.com.au; 2-person $160) A retired paddle-steamer and church have been beautifully refurbished and offer peace and relaxation in their differing locations. Choose between the river surrounded by birdlife, or a more spiritual experience closer to Goolwa's pubs. Prices are for two nights.

Goolwa Central Motel (☎ 8555 1155; gentral@int ernode.on.net; 30 Cadell St; s/d $95/110; ✿) The best of the motel/hotels in town. Ignore the mock Irish décor in the bar and restaurant, it's central, clean and family-friendly.

PS Murray River Queen (☎ 8555 1733; Goolwa Wharf; dm/s/d $20/55/60) Now decommissioned, this diesel paddle ship is permanently moored at the town wharf. You can stay in its old crew quarters or in a room with private facilities. The rooms are tired so don't pay more for a higher deck.

Corio Hotel (☎ 8555 1136; Railway Tce; mains $17-25) The nicest pub in town, with a very amiable clientele and good-value meals.

Goolwa Central Health & Ali's Café (☎ 8555 1755; 34 Cadell St; meals $6-10) Don't be put off by the health label, it's really tasty food. Goolwa serves breakfast, lunch and many vegetarian options.

Hectors on the Wharf (☎ 8555 5885; Main Wharf; meals $7-21) Breakfasts and light lunches are served in this licensed café, which is right on the Wharf.

Getting There & Around

Premier Stateliner (☎ 8415 5555) runs several daily buses between Adelaide and Goolwa ($15, 2 hours).

See Getting There & Around under Victor Harbor (p690) for steam-train timetables.

KANGAROO ISLAND

☎ 08

Only 13km off SA's coast, Kangaroo Island (KI) is a serene and beautiful place with a small population mainly inhabiting the eastern towns. The coastline of towering rock and sheltered beaches is edged with turquoise seas, while acres of forest and bush cover the interior's red earth. However, the island's real treat is an abundance of glorious birds, animals and ocean-based creatures.

Many of the place names on the island are French – the first thorough survey of its coast was carried out in 1802 and 1803 by the French explorer Nicholas Baudin. Baudin's English counterpart Matthew Flinders named the island after his crew enjoyed a welcome feast of fresh kangaroo meat here. The first resident Europeans were a few sealers, whalers and escaped convicts.

Aboriginal people did not occupy Kangaroo Island at the time of European settlement; stone implements have been discovered, however, and these suggest human occupation more than 11,000 years ago.

This isolation from European diseases and (introduced) feral species greatly protected the island's native flora and fauna. This care of the natural ecosystem continues, with 30% of land now maintained as either conservation or national parks.

There are myriad tours operating from Adelaide and the towns on the island. However, don't discount a DIY trip. Although there's no public transport on Kangaroo Island, car hire is inexpensive and distances are not vast (you can drive the length of the island in two hours). There are also plenty of places to stay outside the main centres of Penneshaw, Kingscote and American River. This empowers you with the freedom to head for where the furry and feathered action really is to be found – down the southern coast and at the western end of the island.

Information

The **visitors centre** (☎ 8553 1185; www.tourkangaroo island.com.au; 9am-5pm Mon-Fri, 10am-4pm Sat & Sun) is just outside Penneshaw on the road to Kingscote. There's heaps of information here, including surfing, fishing and national parks pamphlets.

The main office of the **NPWSA** (☎ 8553 2381; 37 Dauncey St; 8.45am-5pm Mon-Fri) is in Kingscote.

Although covering national parks entry fees, the Island Parks Pass ($32) does not include camping fees, park cabin rentals and many of the park tours. For most short visits it's better value to buy individual park entry and tour tickets. Passes can be obtained from any of the island's seven NPWSA outlets and the visitors centre at Penneshaw. *Kangaroo Island on Foot* ($9.95), by Kangaroo Island park ranger Jody Gates, details some of the island's great nature trails (including their length, terrain and probable

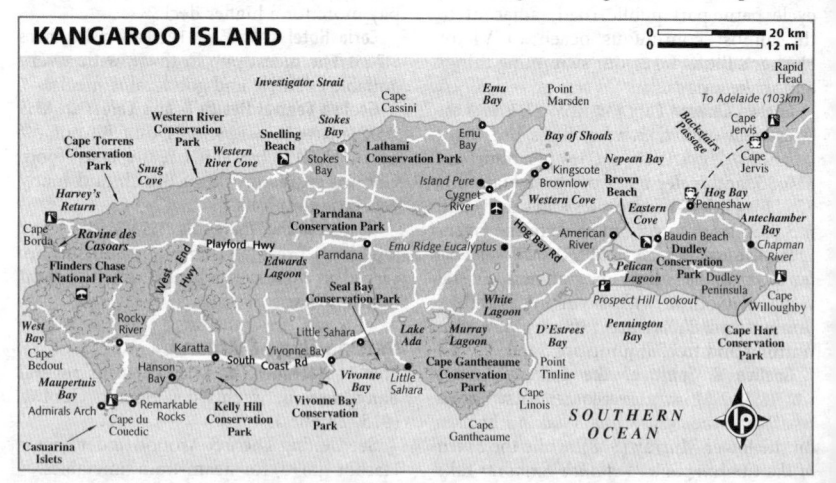

duration). It's available from the **Environment Shop** (77 Grenfell St) in Adelaide and the visitors centre in Penneshaw.

Fire restrictions are in force from 1 December to 30 April. Only gas fires may be lit in national parks, and on days of total fire ban, all fires are prohibited (including gas fires).

Tours

Competition is fierce for Kangaroo Island tours ex-Adelaide. Most two- and three-day tours and backpacker trips are inclusive of ferry fees, accommodation and meals.

If you're short on time, the following companies have day tours ex-Adelaide from around $160. It's also possible to book longer stays with these operators.

Kangaroo Island Sealink (☎ 13 13 01, 8202 8688; www.sealink.com.au; 440 King William St, Adelaide)

Penneshaw Youth Hostel (☎ 1800 686 620, 8553 1284; advhost@bigpond.com; 43 North Tce, Penneshaw)

KI Air & Sea Adventures (☎ 8231 1744; 101 Franklin St, Adelaide)

Kangaroo Island Ferry Connections (☎ 8553 1233; tours@ki-ferryconnections.com; 33 Middle Tce, Penneshaw)

Popular with all travellers are **Adventure Tours** (☎ 1300 654 604, 8309 2277; www.adventuretours .com.au), with two- and three-day tours ex-Adelaide (from $300). One option includes return flights ($390).

For budget travellers, **Daniel's Tours** (☎ 1800 454 454, 8559 7204; danielstours@bigpond.com) offers an all-inclusive two-day tour of the island that is good value ($300).

DAY & EVENING TOURS

Once you're on KI, every man and his dog will offer you a guided wildlife tour. However, you can't beat those run by the NPWSA. The rangers are passionate and knowledgeable about their varied broods. The nocturnal little penguin walk (held in both Kingscote and Penneshaw) and introduction to the endangered (but very relaxed) Australian sea-lion colony are both wonderful and should not be missed.

There's a number of other park tours; through the limestone caves at Kelly Hill Conservation Park (including adventure caving), and historic tours of the lighthouses at Cape Borda and Cape Willoughby. Ask for the parks pamphlet at the visitors centre in Penneshaw or at NPWSA offices.

There are numerous fishing charters, trail rides, yacht cruises, and 4WD and walking tours. These operate mainly from Penneshaw and Kingscote; inquire at the visitors centre for full details.

Kangaroo Island Sealink (☎ 13 13 01, 8553 1122; www.sealink.com.au; 7 North Tce, Penneshaw) run day tours from Penneshaw from $95.

Personalised 4WD tours are operated by **Adventure Charters of KI** (☎ 8553 9119; www.advent urecharters.com.au; Kingscote) and **Kangaroo Island Odyssey** (☎ 8553 0386; www.kiodysseys.com.au; 34 Addison St, Kingscote), both offering packages and day tours from $280. **Kangaroo Island Tourist Services** (☎ 8553 2657; islcourt@kin.net.au; Kingscote) offers bus charter and 4WD tours from $95 for a day trip.

Hire a quad bike to ride through 500 acres of ocean-side bush for views and a bit of fun during the day ($50) or at night when trail-riders can spot up to a 100 kangaroos ($60). Driving licences are required for larger vehicles. **KI Outdoor Action** (☎ /fax 8559 4296; South Coast Rd, Vivonne Bay) also hires out sea and river kayaks/surfboards for $25/35 per day.

DIVING TOURS

Kangaroo Island Diving Safaris (☎ /fax 8559 3225; www.kidivingsafaris.com; Telhawk Farm c/o Kingscote) have (totally inclusive) live-aboard diving trips from $695. These give you a chance to dive with fur seals and you're guaranteed to see leafy sea dragons. Boat-diving trips (two dives with equipment $255) also explore the northern coastal waters.

Operating from Penneshaw Youth Hostel, **Adventureland Diving** (☎ 1800 686 620, 8553 1284; advhost@bigpond.com; 43 North Tce, Penneshaw) has a three-day Professional Association of Diving Instructors (PADI) dive course ($310) including accommodation. For licensed divers, boat dives are $165 for two dives with equipment.

Sleeping

You won't go short of choices, whatever your budget. There are some fabulous private cabins around the coast in tucked-away bays that are great value for romancing couples or friends wanting to share expenses. Cabins start around $85 for two people, with extra adults $12 each. Off-season rates are negotiable. See tourism booklets and ask at the visitors centre in Penneshaw (p696).

WATCHING WILDLIFE ON KANGAROO ISLAND

Kangaroo Island's geographical isolation has mercifully kept it free from dingoes, rabbits and foxes. Thanks to this, native wildlife thrives in the island's pristine environment, and some threatened mainland species, such as the koala, platypus and ringtail possum, have been introduced to ensure their survival.

Kangaroos and Cape Barren geese are easily spotted at **Flinders Chase National Park** (Map p692). If you're lucky you may see a platypus here as well.

Koalas can usually be seen at **Hanson Bay Sanctuary**. You can spot sea lions at Seal Bay and you're almost guaranteed a sighting of New Zealand fur seals at **Admirals Arch**. Sea lions are pale and large, while seals are smaller, darker and more lively. Echidnas, Tamar wallabies, goannas and possums are found around the island.

Divers will see leafy sea dragons – a beautiful species of sea horse – particularly off the northern coastline. Dolphins sometimes come in to Pelican Lagoon at **American River**. Southern right and minke whales are often spotted during the whale-watching season (June to September) – ask at the visitors centre for whale-watching locations.

Birdlife includes little penguins and pelicans (for details on the island's marine centre, see p695), black cockatoos and black swans, as well as many other species.

Camping at Rocky River in Flinders Chase National Park costs $19.50 per site. Camping at Snake Lagoon, West Bay or Harveys Return costs $7.50 per site.

In addition to those at the main townships, small and mainly basic camping grounds are found around the island, including at Emu Bay, Stokes Bay, Vivonne Bay and Western River Cove.

The **NPWSA** (☎ 8559 7235; kiparksaccom@dehaa .sa.gov.au; cottages per person $41, linen $12.50) has 10 refurbished historic cottages for rent, but minimum charges apply. Book the lightkeepers' cottages in advance; they're very popular and are at Cape Willoughby, Cape Borda and Cape du Couedic.

Kangaroo Island Coastal Connections (www.ante chamberbay.on.net; PO Box 554, Penneshaw) These six properties are all individually owned and located at different points on the island. However, they operate special rental deals between them and all offer top-quality, self-contained properties with sea views.

Kangaroo Island Ferry Connections (☎ 1800 018 484, 8553 1233; www.ki-ferryconnections.com) This accommodation specialist in Penneshaw has a range of combined accommodation and car-hire packages. Staff can book self-contained properties around the island starting at $77 for a double (car hire extra).

Getting There & Away

The best option involves a bus trip to Cape Jervis and ferry across to the island, with a hire car booked for collection at the ferry terminus at Penneshaw. Flying is also an option (also with pre-arranged car hire).

Sealink's **bus service** (☎ 13 13 01) connects with ferry departures at Port Jervis. The one-way fare from Adelaide's central bus station is $17 ($8.50 off-peak, 2 hours) and bookings are essential. There are also connections from Goolwa and Victor Harbor ($13, 40 minutes).

AIR

Emu Airways (☎ 8234 3711; www.emuair.mtx.net) has daily Adelaide–Kingscote services ($121), as does **Rex** (☎ 13 17 13; www.regional express.com.au) with flights from $137.

FERRY

Departing from Cape Jervis, **Kangaroo Island Sealink** (☎ 13 13 01) operates two vehicular ferries that run all year, taking 50 minutes to Penneshaw. One-way fares are $32 for passengers, $6 for bicycles, $22 for motorcycles and $70 for cars or camper vans.

Getting Around

TO/FROM THE AIRPORT

There is a **shuttle bus** (☎ 8553 2390; $12) to Kingscote (14km), whilst the car rental companies will offer transfers if you book in advance.

TO/FROM THE FERRY LANDINGS

The **Sealink Shuttle** (☎ 13 13 01) on Kangaroo Island connects with the morning and evening ferries, with stops at American River

($8) and Kingscote ($11). Bookings for this service are essential.

BICYCLE
Hire bicycles from **Rent-A-Bike KI** (☎ 8553 2349; 1 Commercial St, Kingscote; ✆ 9am-5.30pm Mon-Fri) for $17 per day.

CAR & MOTORCYCLE
All the main roads on the island are sealed, although some of the rural roads are gravel and have loose surfaces. The distressingly high numbers of animal corpses that line roads are a testament to speeding idiots. Birds and animals feed from dusk to dawn so drive particularly carefully at these times.

Not all Adelaide car-rental companies will rent cars for Kangaroo Island trips, and with ferry prices it's cheaper to hire on the island – but do book ahead.

Wheels over Kangaroo Island (☎ 1800 750 850, 8553 3030; woki@ozemail.com.au; Kingscote airport) offers very good deals and will meet Penneshaw and Kingscote arrivals, as do **Budget** (☎ 8553 3133; www.budget.com.au; Kingscote airport). **Hertz** (☎ 1800 088 296, 8553 2390; hertz@kin.net.au; Kingscote airport) also has rentals available from Kingscote and the airport.

KINGSCOTE
☎ 08 / pop 1693
The main town on the island is 60km from Penneshaw, and 117km from Flinders Chase National Park. A quiet but nice little place, Kingscote's night life centres around the Ozone Hotel.

There's Internet access at the **library** (☎ 8553 2015; Dauncey St), adjacent to the post office, and at **Shop Six** (☎ 8553 3226; The Mall, Dauncey St).

Sights & Activities
The **tidal pool** about 500m south of the jetty is the best place in town to swim. However, most locals head out to the lovely **Emu Bay**, 18km away.

Hope Cottage Museum (☎ 8553 2656; Centenary Ave; admission $5; ✆ 1-4pm Feb-Dec, 10am-4pm Jan), built in 1858, is a good National Trust museum, with some interesting memorabilia including a eucalyptus-oil distillery and an old lighthouse.

Each evening at 7.30pm and 8.30pm (9pm and 9.40pm during daylight saving) rangers take visitors on a fabulous **Discovering Penguins**

Walk (adult/child $7.50/6). Arrive 30 minutes early at the Penguin Burrow at the Ozone Hotel and leave your camera flash behind.

KANGAROO ISLAND MARINE CENTRE
The **marine centre** (☎ 8553 3112; ayliffe@kin.net.au; Kingscote Wharf; adult/child $10/5; ✆ tours 7.30pm & 8.30pm, plus 1-5pm holidays & busy periods) includes a saltwater aquarium ($3), and a fairy penguin colony is included in nightly tours. Bookings are advised. **Pelican feeding** ($2) also takes place every evening at 5pm from the wharf. A number of these wonderful beaked battleships usually turn up for the free tucker, as does a Pacific gull or two.

CLIFFORD'S HONEY FARM
This **honey farm** (☎ 8553 8295; Elsegood Rd, btwn Moore & Barrett Rds; admission $3; ✆ 9am-5pm) is home to ligurian bees, which are the only strain allowed on the island, and which have a fascinating social structure. Observe their industry and savour the results; this renowned honey really is nectar from the gods and the honey ice cream is delicious.

EMU RIDGE EUCALYPTUS DISTILLERY
Most people find the working eucalyptus oil distillery at **Emu Ridge Eucalyptus** (☎ 8553 8228; Wilsons Rd; ✆ 9am-2pm), between Kingscote and American River, to be well worth a visit. It's the only enterprise of this type left in the state and there are continuous guided tours ($6) from September to April. Self-guided tours operate during the winter months ($4).

Sleeping & Eating
Outside of school holidays there are normally reductions on room rates, so do ask!

Kangaroo Island Central Backpackers Hostel (☎ 8553 2787; ki_backpackers@hotmail.com; 19 Murray St; dm/d $20/45) There are no outdoor facilities and little available information, but this small hostel is spotless, friendly and well maintained.

Queenscliffe Family Hotel (☎ 8553 2254; fax 8553 2291; 57 Dauncey St; s/d $70/80) This place has older rooms (one with a genuine four-poster bed) above a fairly rowdy pub.

Ozone Hotel (☎ 1800 083 133, 8553 2011; www.ozonehotel.com; Kingscote Tce; d & tw $110; ✆) You'll find a pool and spa, very nice rooms and definitely the best food in town; the fish and chips and steak dishes are top rate (meals $15 to $24). The restaurant/bar is packed on weekends and its bottle shop offers Kangaroo Island wine tastings.

Wisteria Motel (☎ 8553 2707; wisteria@kin.net.au; Cygnet Rd; d & tw $110; 🕱) Light and bright spacious rooms have great sea views, especially from the upper floor. There are older fittings in the rooms but a nice dining room and swimming pool.

Seaview Motel (☎ 8553 2030; www.seaview.net.au; Chapman Tce; hotel s/d $65/70, motel s/d $115/125; 🕱) Overlooking the sea and tidal pool, this friendly and clean motel/hotel (the motel rooms have been updated) is a short walk to the Ozone and town centre.

AMERICAN RIVER
☎ 08 / pop 250

Between Kingscote (37km) and Penneshaw (32km), this small settlement takes its name from the American sealers who built a boat here in 1804. The town is on a small peninsula and shelters an inner bay, named **Pelican Lagoon** by Flinders, which is now an aquatic reserve. **Fishing** is the main recreation, with boat charters readily available.

You can watch **pelican feeding** at 5pm daily down on the wharf.

Sleeping & Eating
Ulonga Lodge (☎ /fax 8553 7171; www.ulonga.com.au; The Esplanade; units/cottage $85/135; 🕱) The fabulous cottage (with sea views and a rowing skillet) and units have touches of the friendly South American hosts in their décor. Prices given are for two people, but with three or more adults this comfortable accommodation becomes affordable to all budgets. Meals also available.

Wanderer's Rest of Kangaroo Island (☎ 8553 7140; www.wanderersrest.com.au; Bayview Rd; $180/190; 🕱) Eight spacious rooms with bathrooms have superb sea views and share an intimate and pretty garden and solar-heated pool. There's also a 4WD for general use, and the dining room serves à la carte meals (mains around $23).

PENNESHAW
☎ 08 / pop 400

Looking across Backstairs Passage to the Fleurieu Peninsula, Penneshaw is a quiet resort town with a white sandy beach at **Hog Bay**. It's the arrival point for ferries from Cape Jervis, and dolphins can often be seen from the jetty.

There's no bank, but **Grimshaw's Corner Store & Cafe** (☎ 8553 1151; cnr Third St & North Tce; 🕑 8am-8pm summer, 8am-7pm rest of year) is a one-stop-shop or general store opposite the Penneshaw Hotel.

The **post office** (Nat Thomas St; 🕑 9am-5pm Mon-Fri, 9-11am Sat) acts as a bank agency. The island's main visitors centre is on the Kingscote Rd (see Information; p692)

Sights & Activities
In the evenings, rangers take visitors to view the wonderful and comic little penguins that nest along the shore near town – you'll generally see more penguins here than at Kingscote. Penguin tours ($7.50/6 per adult/child) depart from the **Penneshaw Penguin Centre** (☎ 8553 1103) on the foreshore near the ferry terminal, leaving at 7.30pm and 8.30pm (an hour later during daylight saving). Leave your camera flash behind.

Containing memorabilia on local history is the **Penneshaw Maritime & Folk Museum** (☎ 8553 1109; Howard Dr; admission $3; 🕑 3-5pm Wed-Sun Sep-May).

Pennington Bay has surf and the sheltered waters of **Chapman River** are quite popular for canoeing.

CAPE WILLOUGHBY LIGHTSTATION
The **lightstation** (☎ 8553 1191; Willoughby Rd; admission $7.50) first operated in 1852, and is now used as a weather station. There are interesting 45-minute tours from 10am to 3.15pm daily (until 2pm in winter, 4pm in summer and holiday periods).

Sleeping
The **visitors centre** (☎ 8553 1185; www.tourkangaroo island.com.au; 🕑 9am-5pm Mon-Fri, 10am-4pm Sat & Sun) issues camping permits for bush sites at Chapman River, Brown Beach and American River. Self-contained accommodation is plentiful and the best value around Penneshaw.

Penguin Walk YHA Hostel (☎ 8553 1233; www.ki -ferryconnections.com; 33 Middle Tce; dm/d $22/75; 🕱) This hostel is near the ferry terminal and is mainly booked by tour groups. The dorms and rooms are modern, pleasant and spacious, with their own bathroom and fridge. However, shared kitchen facilities are limited: one cooker, a microwave and a few pots – there's no space for food preparation.

Penneshaw Youth Hostel (☎ 8553 1072; adv host@bigpond.com; 43 North Tce; dm/tw/d $19/22/45) On our visit, we found this a cheerless hostel, with a grubby kitchen containing a meagre amount of filthy and broken kitchenware. There's a café on the premises. The owners run cheap tours from Adelaide (from $210), a diving school (see Diving Tours; p693) and can arrange car hire (although it may be cheaper to deal direct with the car-rental companies.)

Kangaroo Island Seafront Hotel (☎ 8553 1028; www.seafront.com.au; 49 North Tce; d & tw $120; 🏊) The rooms are bright and fresh, and contain all creature comforts. A central and pretty tropical garden encompasses a restful pool and spa while the bar stocks local wines and a restaurant serves tasty meals ($17 to $21).

NORTH COAST

There are several fine, sheltered beaches along the north coast. **Emu Bay** (18km from Kingscote) has a beautiful, long sweep of sand. It's a perfect getaway spot for a few days – an exclusive health resort on the hill (complete with garden gnomes) obviously agrees!

Other good beaches include **Stokes Bay** (hidden away through a limestone tunnel), **Snelling Beach** and **Western River Cove**.

Sleeping

There are a lot of holiday homes to rent, but bring food and provisions with you.

Owned and managed by the one family, **Emu Bay Holiday Homes** (☎ /fax 08-8553 5241; www.emubayholidays.com.au; Emu Bay) are perched on the hill overlooking the bay, while the **Wintersun Holiday House and Units** are situated down by the beach. All the accommodation is spotless, cheerful and really well maintained. Cabins will sleep from two to 10 people. Prices for two start at $65, beach-side units from $90. Great for families, couples and friends, weekly rates are cheaper.

Seascape on Emu Bay (☎ 08-8553 5199; www .seascape.ws; d $197) Set in five tranquil acres, the views down to the bay are as fabulous as this luxury B&B. It's all class, and one room has excellent disabled facilities. If you want to spoil yourself, this is the place to do it. Three-course dinners are available for $50 per person.

FLINDERS CHASE NATIONAL PARK

Occupying the western end of the island, Flinders Chase is one of SA's most significant national parks. There is plenty of mallee scrub, but also beautiful tall forests with amazing birdlife, koalas, echidnas, possums and platypuses (if you're lucky to see them); the kangaroos have become so fearless they'll brazenly badger you for food – the picnic area at the park's Rocky River HQ is fenced to protect visitors from these freeloaders.

The **NPWSA visitors centre** (☎ 08-8559 7235; fax 8559 7268; 🕑 9am-5pm) has touch-screen displays on local fauna and local Aboriginal history. Cabin bookings can be made here, and there's a souvenir shop and café.

Sights & Activities

On the northwestern corner of the island is the **Cape Borda lightstation** (☎ 08-8559 3257; Playford Hwy), built in 1858, which has 45-minute guided tours ($7) from 11am to 3pm daily (10am to 4pm in summer and school holidays). At nearby **Harvey's Return** are great views, a small, poignant cemetery on the cliff top and a **bush camping area**.

Just south of Cape Borda is the **Ravine des Casoars**, with one of the island's most pleasant walking trails (6.5km return). This lovely spot was named by Baudin after the dwarf emus he saw there (*casoars* means 'cassowaries'). The species became extinct soon after European settlement.

In the southeastern corner of the national park, **Cape du Couedic** is wild and remote, with towering cliffs. A picturesque lighthouse built in 1906 tops the cape; you can follow the path from the car park down to **Admirals Arch** – a large natural archway formed by pounding seas. New Zealand fur seals are usually seen here, including cows nursing their pups.

At Kirkpatrick Point, 2km east of Cape du Couedic, **Remarkable Rocks** is a cluster of large, weather-sculpted granite boulders on a huge dome swooping to the sea. Don't forget your camera and lots of film: you're bound to be inspired by their dramatic shapes.

Sleeping

In Flinders Chase you can camp at the Rocky River park headquarters and in other designated areas, with permits. There's also a choice of refurbished cabins. Watch out for the kangaroos, they occasionally rip their way into tents looking for food and can cause a lot of damage.

Western Kangaroo Island Caravan Park (☎ 08-8559 7201; beckwith@kin.on.net; South Coast Rd; 2-person camp sites/cabins $15/80; ✖) You're in the right place to see the birds and animals that make KI so famous, including wild koalas, at this well-facilitated park on the South Coast Rd just a few minutes drive east from Flinders Chase.

Flinders Chase Farm (☎ 08-8559 7223; chillers@kin.net.au; West End Hwy; dm/cabins $16/55) A five-minute drive from Flinders Chase, this very casual and simple place has dorms in wooden buildings, as well as tiny cabins. There's a good outdoor kitchen, a campfire area and tropical bathrooms. Kangaroos roam here at night.

Kangaroo Island Wilderness Resort (☎ 08-8559 7275; bliss@austdreaming.com.au; South Coast Rd; dm/d/motel $35/80/180; 🖳) Just outside the boundary of Flinders Chase park, this excellent accommodation caters for budget, mid-range and top-end travellers. A purpose-built lodge has modern, new and comfortable rooms with bathrooms and four-person dorms off a large central communal area, but sadly no kitchen. The up-market motel rooms are in a separate building. There's also a bar menu ($10 to $20), good restaurant, large-scale TV and Internet room, and takeaway shop.

SOUTH COAST

The south coast is rough and wave swept compared with the north. Horseshoe-shaped **Hanson Bay** is connected via a great bush trail that passes by lagoons (8 hours, 18km return) to **Kelly Hill Conservation Park** (☎ 08-8559 7231; South Coast Rd; ✖ 10am-4.30pm in summer, 10am-3.30pm rest of year). This park has a series of dry limestone caves discovered in the 1880s by a horse named Kelly that fell into them through a hole in the ground. There are adventure-caving tours ($24) with bookings, and daily tours of the caves every hour ($7.50/6 per adult/child).

Hanson Bay Cabins (☎ 08-8553 2603; www.esl.com.au/hansonbay.htm; d $125) overlook Hanson Bay and offer a quiet hideaway from the madding crowds.

Vivonne Bay

There is a long and beautiful beach with an adjacent camp site. There is also excellent fishing and surfing, but bathers should take great care: the undertows are fierce and you should stick close to the jetty or the river mouth. A general store is nearby on the main South Coast Rd.

Seal Bay Conservation Park

Located 60km southwest of Kingscote, **Seal Bay Conservation Park** (☎ 08-8559 4207; Seal Bay Rd; ✖ 9am-4.15pm, until 7pm in summer) has a large colony of Australian sea lions who enjoy the beach life and don't mind the close proximity of park rangers and their enchanted tour groups. Tours run every 45 minutes ($10.50/7.50 per adult/child).

Near Seal Bay and close to the South Coast Rd is **Little Sahara**, a series of enormous white-sand dunes.

BAROSSA VALLEY

The Barossa Valley is Australia's best-known wine-producing district, although its name is actually a misspelling of Barrosa in Spain. Crushing about 65,000 tonnes of grapes annually (around a quarter of the Australian vintage), this region is also known for producing many immensely quaffable red wines. International judges agree, announcing certain vintages of Penfolds Grange, and the Barossa Valley Estate's Black Pepper Shiraz as two of the best in the world. About 55km northeast of Adelaide, the Valley's 60 wineries all lie within easy reach of each other.

The rolling landscape is dotted with modest Lutheran churches and old cottages that date back to the original settlement of 1842. Fleeing religious persecution in Prussia and Silesia, these first settlers weren't actually wine makers, but came clutching vines that are the origin of today's full and silky red wines. Prior to WWI, place names in the Barossa probably sounded even more Germanic, but during the war many names were patriotically anglicised.

You have to get off the main road to begin to appreciate what the Barossa Valley has to offer. Take the scenic drive between Angaston and Tanunda, the palm-fringed road to Seppeltsfield and Marananga, or meander through the sleepy historic hamlet of Bethany. The Para Rd Trail is a cycling and walking path that follows the river to a number of cellar doors.

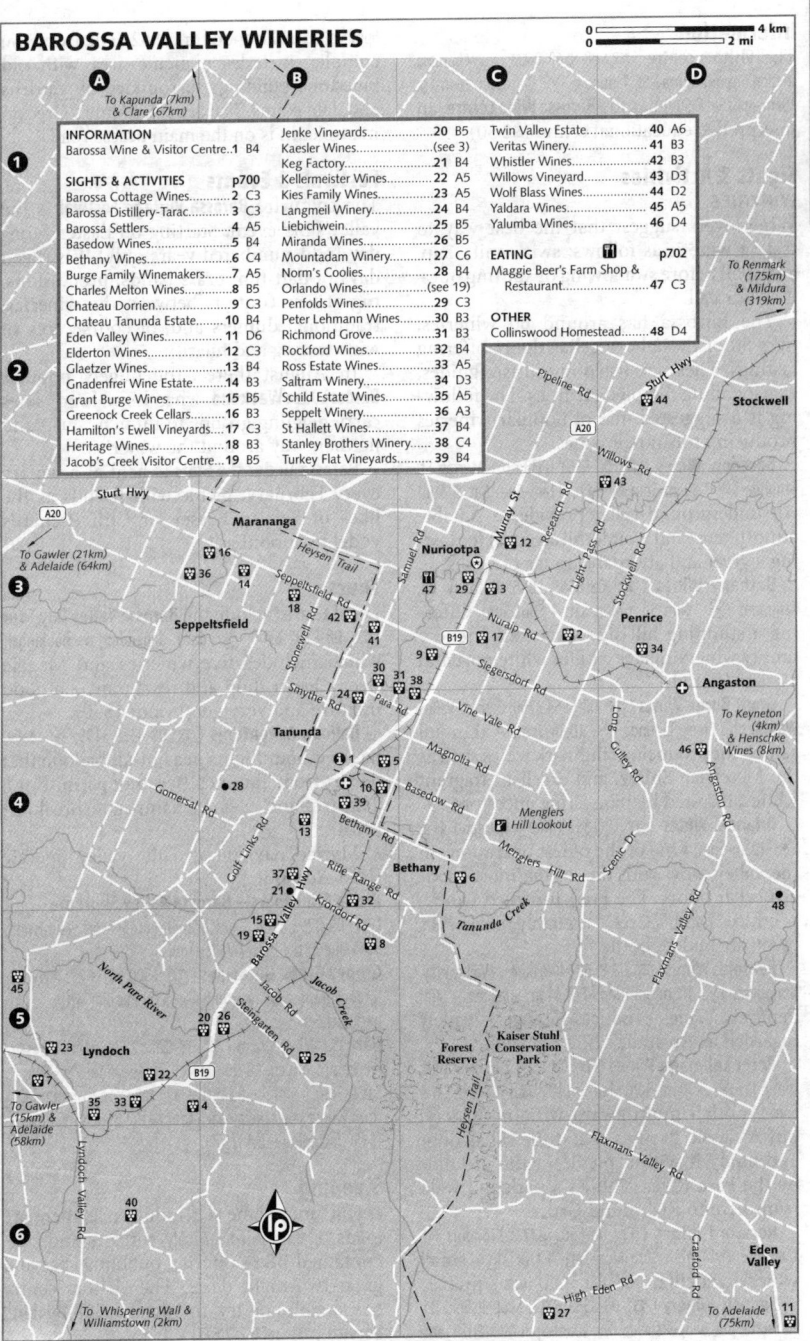

BAROSSA VALLEY WINERIES

0 — 4 km
0 — 2 mi

A   B   C   D

To Kapunda (7km)
& Clare (67km)

INFORMATION
Barossa Wine & Visitor Centre..1 B4

SIGHTS & ACTIVITIES p700
Barossa Cottage Wines............2 C3
Barossa Distillery-Tarac..........3 C3
Barossa Settlers....................4 A5
Basedow Wines......................5 B4
Bethany Wines......................6 C4
Burge Family Winemakers........7 A5
Charles Melton Wines.............8 B5
Chateau Dorrien...................9 C3
Chateau Tanunda Estate.........10 B4
Eden Valley Wines................11 D6
Elderton Wines....................12 C3
Glaetzer Wines....................13 B4
Gnadenfrei Wine Estate..........14 B3
Grant Burge Wines...............15 B5
Greenock Creek Cellars..........16 B3
Hamilton's Ewell Vineyards......17 C3
Heritage Wines...................18 B3
Jacob's Creek Visitor Centre....19 B5

Jenke Vineyards..................20 B5
Kaesler Wines..................(see 3)
Keg Factory.......................21 B4
Kellermeister Wines..............22 A5
Kies Family Wines................23 A5
Langmeil Winery.................24 B4
Liebichwein.......................25 B5
Miranda Wines....................26 B5
Mountadam Winery...............27 C6
Norm's Coolies...................28 B4
Orlando Wines.................(see 19)
Penfolds Wines...................29 C3
Peter Lehmann Wines............30 B3
Richmond Grove...................31 B3
Rockford Wines...................32 B4
Ross Estate Wines................33 A5
Saltram Winery...................34 D3
Schild Estate Wines..............35 A5
Seppelt Winery...................36 A3
St Hallett Wines..................37 B4
Stanley Brothers Winery..........38 C4
Turkey Flat Vineyards............39 B4

Twin Valley Estate...............40 A6
Veritas Winery...................41 B3
Whistler Wines...................42 B3
Willows Vineyard.................43 D3
Wolf Blass Wines.................44 D2
Yaldara Wines...................45 A5
Yalumba Wines...................46 D4

EATING p702
Maggie Beer's Farm Shop &
Restaurant......................47 C3

OTHER
Collinswood Homestead...........48 D4

To Renmark
(175km)
& Mildura
(319km)

Pipeline Rd   Sturt Hwy   Stockwell

A20   Willows Rd

Sturt Hwy

A20

Marananga   Hersen Trail   Samuel Rd   Nuriootpa   Murray St   Research Rd   Stockwell Rd

To Gawler (21km)
& Adelaide (64km)

Seppeltsfield Rd   Nuraip Rd   Penrice

Seppeltsfield   Stonewell Rd   Siegersdorf Rd   Angaston

Smythe Rd   Para Rd   Vine Vale Rd   To Keyneton
(4km)
& Henschke
Wines (8km)

Tanunda   Magnolia Rd   Long Gully Rd

Gomersal Rd   Golf Links Rd   Basedow Rd   Menglers
Hill Lookout   Scenic Dr

Bethany Rd   Menglers Hill Rd

Bethany   Flaxmans Valley Rd

Rifle Range Rd   Tanunda Creek

Krondorf Rd

North Para River   Jacob Rd   Jacob Creek

Steingarten Rd   Kaiser Stuhl
Conservation
Park   Flaxmans Valley Rd

Lyndoch   B19   Forest
Reserve   Hersen Trail

To Gawler
(15km) &
Adelaide
(58km)

Lyndoch Valley Rd

Flaxmans Valley Rd

Craeford Rd

Eden
Valley

To Whispering Wall &
Williamstown (2km)   High Eden Rd   To Adelaide
(75km)

Information

The **visitors centre** (☎ 08-8563 0600; www.barossa -region.org; 66 Murray St, Tanunda; ◷ 9am-5pm Mon-Fri, 10am-4pm Sat & Sun) has the **Barossa Wine Centre**, an interpretive educational centre ($2.50).

Sights & Activities
WINERIES

Wine-lovers suggest that the best way to taste a wine is as follows: swirl, sniff, sup, and swill before swallowing or spitting out – it's your call!

The Barossa has around 60 wineries, over 50 of these have cellar doors offering tastings. These are listed in tourism guides, also detailing disabled facilities. The following is a suggested mix of popular wineries producing top-notch wines.

Basedow Wines (☎ 08-8563 0333; 161 Murray St, Tanunda; ◷ 10am-5pm Mon-Fri, 11am-5pm Sat & Sun) An underground cellar provides a suitable atmosphere (and wonderful aromas) for tasting a great and affordable range of wines.

Bethany Wines (☎ 08-8563 2086; Bethany Rd, Tanunda; ◷ 10am-5pm Mon-Sat, 1-5pm Sun) Offering a stunning hill-side vista, this friendly family winery makes a killer white port and classic dry reds.

Grant Burge Wines (☎ 08-8563 3700; Barossa Valley Way, Jacob's Creek, Tanunda; ◷ 10am-5pm) A tranquil setting for producing landmark wines such as the Meschach Shiraz, and excellent fragrant whites, inspired by pioneering ancestors.

Orlando Wines (☎ 08-8521 3000; Rowland Flat; ◷ 10am-5pm) One of the oldest operations in the valley, now with one of the most modern cellar doors. The French-owned winery produces Jacob's Creek, arguably the world's favourite budget bottle.

Penfolds Wines (☎ 08-8568 9408; Barossa Valley Way, Nuriootpa; ◷ 10am-5pm Mon-Fri, 11am-5pm Sat & Sun) Penfolds Wines produces Grange – widely regarded as Australia's best red wine.

Peter Lehmann Wines (☎ 08-8563 2500; Para Rd, Tanunda; ◷ 9.30am-5pm Mon-Fri, 10.30am-4.30pm Sat & Sun) Another multi-award-winning winery; buy a classic Barossa red at the cellar door and enjoy it with a picnic in the grounds by the Para River. There's a parkland walk from here to Richmond Grove.

Rockford Wines (☎ 08-8563 2720; Krondorf Rd, Tanunda; ◷ 11am-5pm Mon-Sat) This is a small winery, widely noted for its black shiraz.

Seppelt Winery (☎ 08-8568 6217; Seppeltsfield Rd, via Nuriootpa, Seppeltsfield; ◷ 10am-5pm Mon-Fri, 11am-

5pm Sat & Sun) Founded in 1852. The extensive complex includes a picnic area with old bluestone buildings surrounded by gardens and date palms. The Seppelt family's Grecian mausoleum is on the main access road.

Festivals & Events

The colourful **Barossa Vintage Festival** is the valley's big event. Starting on Easter Monday (odd-numbered years only) it is seven days of daft fun: brass bands, processions, tug-of-war contests between the wineries, traditional dinners and, of course, lots of wine tasting and hilarity.

In August there's the hugely popular **Barossa Jazz Weekend**, when hired limousines carry giggling groups to munch, slurp and jig their way around the wineries.

Barossa Under the Stars is held at a winery every February; picnic with friends as the likes of Shirley Bassey or Cliff Richards yodel by moonlight.

Tours

Local tours include the **Barossa Valley Day Tour** (☎ 08-8262 6900; ◷ daily, depending on bookings), which includes five wineries and Maggie Beer's Farm shop and restaurant – a good mixture and very good value ($50).

Balloon Adventures (☎ 08-8389 3195; ◷ daily) has one-hour flights in a hot-air balloon that depart from Tanunda (weather permitting). The trip includes a champagne breakfast ($240).

Myriad day tours to the valley operate from Adelaide:

Prime Mini Tours – Barossa Valley Supreme (☎ 08-8293 4900; www.primeminitours.com; admission $65) One of the better Valley tours.

Groovy Grape Getaways (☎ 1800 66 11 77; www .groovygrape.com.au; admission $65) Popular with backpackers.

Barossa Wine Train (☎ 08-8212 7888; www.barossa winetrain.com.au; 18-20 Grenfell St, Adelaide; ◷ Thu, Sat & Sun) A vintage train that will take you to Tanunda, from where you take a coach tour of the Barossa Valley ($150 including lunch).

Sleeping

If you fancy some self-indulgence, there are loads of excellent luxury cottages and self-contained B&Bs offering bubbling spas and great two-night deals. The visitors centre has details, or try the **Barossa B&B Booking Service** (☎ 1800 227 677).

Getting There & Away

There are several routes from Adelaide, with the most direct being via Main North Rd through Elizabeth and Gawler. More picturesque routes go through the Torrens Gorge, then via either Williamstown or Birdwood. If you're coming from the east and want to tour the wineries before hitting Adelaide, the scenic route via Springton and Eden Valley to Angaston is the best bet.

Barossa Valley Coaches (☎ 08-8564 3022) has twice daily return services from Adelaide (once on Sunday) to Lyndoch ($11, 1½ hours), Tanunda ($13, 1½ hours), Nuriootpa ($14, 2 hours) and Angaston ($15, 2 hours).

Getting Around

The Barossa is good for cycling, with many interesting routes ranging from easy to challenging. Bicycles can be rented from the **Tanunda Caravan & Tourist Park** (www.tanundacarav antouristpark.com.au; per day $15) and the **Bunkhaus Travellers Hostel** (☎ 08-8562 2260; hire per day $11) in Nuriootpa. The Para Rd Trail runs past the Bunkhaus.

Barossa Valley Taxis (☎ 08-8563 3600) has a 24-hour service.

LYNDOCH

☎ 08 / pop 1251

Lyndoch is the first of the valley townships, reached en route from Adelaide (via Gawler). A quiet working township, there's not much here for visitors hell bent on wine tasting and exploration, but numerous wineries nearby offer creature comforts. About 7km southwest of Lyndoch, the Barossa Reservoir has the famous **Whispering Wall**, a concrete dam wall with amazing acoustics; normal conversations held at one end can be heard clearly at the other end, 150m away.

Southeast of Tanunda, **Bethany** was the first German settlement in the valley. There are still some old cottages that have been left standing around the Bethany reserve.

TANUNDA

☎ 08 / pop 3865

In the centre of the valley is Tanunda, the most Germanic of the towns. You can still see early cottages around **Goat Square** on John St – this was the site of the original *ziegenmarkt*, a meeting and market place laid out as the original centre of Tanunda in 1842.

Barossa Valley Historical Museum (☎ 8563 0507; 47 Murray St; admission $4; ☺ 11am-5pm Mon-Sat, 1-5pm Sun) has exhibits on the valley's early settlement and a crammed antique shop.

You can watch artisans making kegs and other wooden items at the **Keg Factory** (☎ 8563 3012; St Halletts Rd; ☺ 8am-4.30pm Mon-Sat, 10am-4.30pm Sun), 4km south of town.

About 3km from Tanunda, **Norm's Coolies** (☎ 8563 2198; off Gomersal Rd; adult/child $8/4) go through their paces at the Breezy Gully Farm. These trained sheepdogs put on a show that would shame any parade ground and are definitely worth seeing. Shows are at 2pm Monday, Wednesday and Saturday.

There are fine old Lutheran churches in all the valley towns but Tanunda has some of the most interesting, including the 1849 **Tabor Church** (79 Murray St) and 1868 **St John's Church** (Jane Pl), which has life-size wooden statues of Christ, Moses and the apostles Peter, Paul and John.

From Tanunda, turn off the main road and take the scenic drive through Bethany and via **Menglers Hill** to Angaston. It runs through beautiful, rural country featuring large gums; the view over the valley from Menglers Hill is superb as long as you ignore the dreadful sculptures in the foreground.

Sleeping & Eating

Most accommodation centres around Tanunda, and a pleasant caravan park has a kids' playground.

Tanunda Hotel (☎ 8563 2030; 51 Murray St; s/d $60/70) Rooms with privates bathrooms are more, but this is a good and comfortable family-run hotel in the centre of town. The pub grub is also popular.

Stonewell Cottages (☎ 8563 2019; www.stone wellcottages.com.au; Stonewell Rd; cottages $135-160; ☒) Award-winning waterfront vineyard retreats with spas, chocolate and ducks – what more do you need?

1918 Bistro & Grill (☎ 8563 0405; 94 Murray St; mains $19-26) A local institution, this is not one for vegetarians or those with picky appetites. Steamed-pudding lovers will rejoice.

NURIOOTPA

☎ 08 / pop 3865

At the northern end of the valley is the Barossa's commercial centre, Nuriootpa. There are several pleasant picnic areas along the Para River, as well as some nice river walks close to the town centre.

Sleeping & Eating

Barossa Bunkhaus Travellers Hostel (☎ 8562 2260; Barossa Valley Way; dm/cottage $17/50) Set among vineyards, 1km from town (look for the keg sign on the corner), this is a very pleasant and welcoming place with dorm beds and a self-contained cottage. There's a well-appointed kitchen and mountain bikes can be hired here.

Nurioopta Vine Inn & Vine Court (☎ 8562 2133; www.vineinn.com.au; 14 & 49 Murray St; d & tw $86; ✕) Both with pools and within walking distance of a couple of good wineries, these otherwise standard motels become *very* attractive!

Maggie Beer's Farm Shop & Restaurant (☎ 8562 4477; Pheasant Farm Rd; mains $16-20) Lucky you! Take the opportunity to sample mouth-watering and affordable lunches and picnics from the kitchens of celebrity-gourmet Maggie. She's famous for her pheasant dishes, but vegetarians still love her mushroom pâté.

ANGASTON
☎ 08 / pop 1933

On the eastern side of the valley, this town was named after George Fife Angas, one of the area's pioneers.

About 7km from town, magnificent **Collingrove Homestead** (☎ 8564 2061; Eden Valley, Angaston Rd; admission $8; ✆ 1-4.30pm Mon-Fri, 11am-4.30pm Sat & Sun) was built by Angas' son in 1856 and is now owned by the National Trust. Devonshire teas are served daily and formal banquets upon request.

Sleeping & Eating

Apart from B&Bs, there's little accommodation here. However, a classic restaurant and café make it worth a stop.

Angaston Hotel (☎ 8564 2428; 59 Murray St; s $30) This very basic hotel on the main street has small beds.

Vintners Bar Grill (☎ 8564 2488; Nurioopta Rd; mains $25) Lunch and dinner (using regional produce) are served with crisp white linen and a nice view of the lovely surrounding vineyards.

Seasons of the Valley Café & Gallery (☎ 8564 3688; 6-8 Washington St; lunch $11-17) Former restaurateurs have won a multitude of awards for this unpretentious café.

MID-NORTH

The area between Adelaide and Port Augusta is generally known as the Mid-North. It's a mixed bunch of landscapes and lifestyles, dominated by vast farms producing wheat and fine wool. The Clare Valley is lined with boutique wineries producing classic rieslings and shiraz, and there are a number of townships from the copper-mining era, such as Auburn, Burra, Kapunda and Mintaro, whose streetscapes have changed little over the past 100 years.

Two main routes from Adelaide run through the Mid-North. One runs to Gawler then on through Burra to Peterborough. From there you can head west to Port Augusta, northwest to the Flinders Ranges or continue along the Barrier Hwy to Broken Hill in New South Wales (NSW).

The second route heads through Port Wakefield and on to Port Augusta on the Spencer Gulf. You can then travel northeast to the Flinders Ranges, southwest to the Eyre Peninsula, north to Alice Springs or west towards the Nullarbor and WA.

Getting There & Away

Premier Stateliner (☎ 08-8415 5555) runs buses to Port Pirie ($28.50, 3 hours) and Port Germain ($36, 3½ hours) on Monday, Saturday and Sunday.

Yorke Peninsular Coaches (☎ 08-8823 2375) departs from Adelaide once a day (Sunday to Friday) to Auburn ($15, 2½ hours), Clare ($20, 3 hours) and Peterborough ($27.50, 5 hours). Buses for Orrorro ($30.50, 5½ hours) leave Monday, Wednesday and Friday and for Burra on Monday and Friday ($21, 3½ hours).

The **McCafferty's/Greyhound** (☎ 13 14 99; www.mccaffertys.com.au) Adelaide–Sydney service passes through Burra Monday to Saturday ($27, 2 hours). The Burra visitors centre (p704) is its agency.

KAPUNDA
☎ 08 / pop 2303

This is a welcoming and friendly little place, just outside the Barossa Valley and (80km) north of Adelaide. Superb **murals** of past heroes and (grinning) local personalities can be found outside the **post office** (Main St) and inside the Sir John Franklin Hotel.

Kapunda is modest about its heritage; a rich deposit of highest-grade copper was found here in 1842 and it became the first copper-mining town in Australia. By 1861 Kapunda was the colony's major commercial centre outside Adelaide. This was also the home to Sir Sidney Kidman (the famous Cattle King), whose properties covered 340,000 sq km of land and whose horse sales were reputed to be the largest in the world. Kidman apparently thought England would make a good horse paddock!

The **visitors centre** (☎ 8566 2902; kaptour@mail .kapunda.net; 7 Hill St; ☺ 9am-5pm Mon-Fri, 10am-1pm Sat, noon-3pm Sun) is centrally located.

In the big old Baptist church, **Kapunda Museum** (☎ 8566 2021; 11 Hill St; admission $5; ☺ 1-4pm daily summer, 1-4pm Sat & Sun winter) is one of the state's best folk museums. Entry to **Bagot's Fortune** (5 Hill St), in the old Herald printing office down the street, is included in the price. This mining interpretation centre has displays on the Cornish, Welsh, Irish and German pioneers and the different roles they played in the town's development.

Map Kernow (or 'Son of Cornwall' in old Cornish), an 8m-high bronze statue, stands at the Adelaide end of town as a tribute to pioneer miners.

Sleeping

Sir John Franklin Hotel (☎ 8566 3233; fax 8566 3873; 63 Main St; s/d $25/35) This amiable hotel has budget rooms, cheap bar meals and a great front bar. Check out the brilliant caricatures on the bar walls.

Kapunda Tourist & Leisure Park (☎ 8566 2094; fax 8566 2972; 3 Montefiore St; 2-person camp sites/cabins $13/60) The park has a good reputation and nice little cabins, but book ahead as the owners live off-site.

Peppertrees B&B (☎ 8566 2776; peptrees@big pond.com; 47 Clare Rd; s/d $80/95; ☒) You can't get much better than this: your own suite of beautifully decorated rooms in a classic Australian bluestone, set in pretty gardens. The rates also include champagne and a full breakfast. Booking is essential, and it is not for children.

AUBURN

☎ 08 / pop 334

This attractive and sleepy little township, 24km south of Clare, has some beautifully preserved old buildings, a timeless pub and

French restaurant. A free brochure – which is available from the post office – details a 3km walk to 26 historic sites. Auburn was the birthplace of CJ Dennis, one of Australia's best-known colonial poets.

Laugh not at the mock-castle roof of **Taylors Wines** (☎ 8849 2008; Taylors Rd; ☺ 9am-5pm Mon-Fri, 10am-4pm Sat & Sun), because this winery does produce wines fit for royalty. This is another SA favourite, selling gold-medal winners.

Sleeping & Eating

Rising Sun Hotel (☎ 8849 2015; rising@capri.net.au; Main North Rd; B&B s/d $49/82; ☒) This classic hotel has elegant rooms with private bathrooms and a choice of pub grub, à la carte or DIY dining (BBQ steak and salad $17.50).

Tatehams (☎ 8849 2030; tatehams@capri.net.au; Main North Rd; mains $26) This gourmet and award-winning restaurant/winery offers classic French cuisine, its own riesling, and delightful self-contained B&B cottages ($160 complete with discreetly placed condoms). The Swiss hosts offer divine meals and special three-course dinners.

Dennis Tea Rooms (☎ 8849 2262; St Vincent St; lunch $6) Memorabilia associated with CJ Dennis is on display here, and light lunches are served by willing volunteers.

CLARE VALLEY WINE REGION

An intimate and sociable atmosphere pervades the small family and boutique wineries distributed through the valley's heartland. The Clare Valley stretches from Auburn in the south to Jamestown in the north, but is concentrated around Clare (population 2815).

For casual work during March and April, contact the wineries directly.

The **visitors centre** (☎ 08-8842 2131; www.clare valley.com.au; 229 Main St; ☺ 9am-5pm Mon-Fri, 10am-4pm Sat & Sun) is in Clare.

Clare itself has a number of interesting buildings, including an impressive **Catholic church** (Victoria Rd). The first police station and courthouse date from 1850 and are preserved as the National Trust **Old Police Station Museum** (☎ 08-8842 2376; cnr Victoria & Neagles Rock Rds; admission $4; ☺ 10am-noon & 2-4pm Sat, Sun & school holidays).

You can walk or ride past some of the district's finest wineries on the **Riesling Trail**, which meanders through the valley from Auburn to Clare. Just be aware that it doesn't loop around to take you back to your starting point.

Sights & Activities
WINERIES
There are around 40 wineries in the valley.

Annie's Lane at Quelltaler (☎ 08-8843 0003; www.annieslanecom.au; Quelltaler Estate, Watervale; ☺ 8.30am-5pm Mon-Fri, 11am-4pm Sat) Its glorious flagship wines are Copper Trail Shiraz and Riesling. A welcoming cellar door includes a winery museum with lovely personal touches, such as the VE day closure notice from WWII.

Crabtree of Watervale (☎ 08-8843 0069, 8843 0144; North Tce, Watervale; ☺ 11am-5pm Mon-Sat) Its smooth fruity reds and distinctive Rose of Biscay (drink chilled) are all for sale at the same price – a bargain for the fabulous cabernet sauvignon.

Sevenhill Cellars (☎ 08-8843 4222; www.seven hillcellars.com.au; College Rd, Sevenhill; ☺ 9am-4.30pm Mon-Fri, 10am-4pm Sat) About 7km south of Clare, this was the valley's first winery, established in 1851 by Jesuit priests. It still produces communion wine, as well as a very good Verdelho. The marvellous St Aloysius Church adjoins the winery and dates from 1875.

Skillogalee (☎ 08-8843 4311; skilly@chariot.net.au; Trevarrick Rd, Sevenhill; mains $16-23; ☺ 10am-5pm) This delightfully named family winery is known for its top-range dry riesling, spicy shiraz and fabulous food. Indulge your sensual self with a long lunch on its shady veranda.

Festivals & Events
One of the Clare Valley's major events is the **Clare Valley Gourmet Weekend**, a festival of wine, food and music put on by local wineries over the long weekend in May (third weekend in the month). Another is the **Clare Valley Spring Garden Festival**, which features some of the valley's best private gardens and is held throughout November. The colourful **Romeria del Rocio Spanish Festival** takes place over four days in April.

Sleeping
There are numerous B&Bs throughout the valley; ask at the visitors centre. It's wise to book ahead at festival times as beds fill quickly. The caravan park is opposite the

local motorcycle club grounds and, quite astonishingly, charges for showers.

Taminga Hotel (☎ 08-8842 2808; fax 8842 2461; 302 Main St; s/d $22/44) This town pub has very basic rooms and a garden bar and grill.

Clare Central Motel (☎ 08-8842 2277; www.web logic.com.au/central; 325 Main North Rd; s/d $88/97; 🛈) Spacious and immaculate rooms also have refreshingly powerful showers. A complimentary continental breakfast and large salt-water swimming pool add to the extra touches that make this motel a class above the rest.

Clare Valley Cottages (☎ 08-8842 3131; fax 8842 4121; Warenda Rd; d $100; 🛈) These quiet and self-contained cottages come complete with spa baths and your very own garden gnome.

Bungaree Station (☎ 08-8842 2677; bungaree@ camtech.net.au; off Main North Rd; d & tw $66) Situated 12km north of Clare and established in 1841, this vast working station has nicely kitted cottages and is a popular venue for conferences. If you have your own swag you can sleep on a rather expensive piece of floor in the old shearers' quarters ($22).

Getting Around
Clare Valley Cycle Hire (☎ 08-8842 2782, 0418-802 077; 32 Victoria Rd; ☺ 8am-6pm) has rates for a half/full day ($17.50/23).

Clare Valley Taxis (☎ 0419-847 900; 261 Main North Rd; ☺ 8am-6pm Sun-Thu, 24hr Fri-Sat with bookings) can also drop you off or pick you up along the Riesling Trail.

BURRA
☎ 08 / pop 1106
This attractive little town is bursting at the seams with historic sites. Burra was a copper-mining centre from 1847 to 1877, with various British ethnic groups forming their own distinctive communities – the Cornish being the most numerous. The hardship of that era can especially be felt in the dugouts (underground rooms that miners excavated for themselves and their families).

The district Burra Burra takes its name from the Hindi word for 'great' by one account, and from the Aboriginal name of the creek by another.

Information
The helpful **visitors centre** (☎ 8892 2154; www .weblogic.com.au/burra; 2 Market Sq; ☺ 9am-5pm) can sell you the Burra Passport, which includes

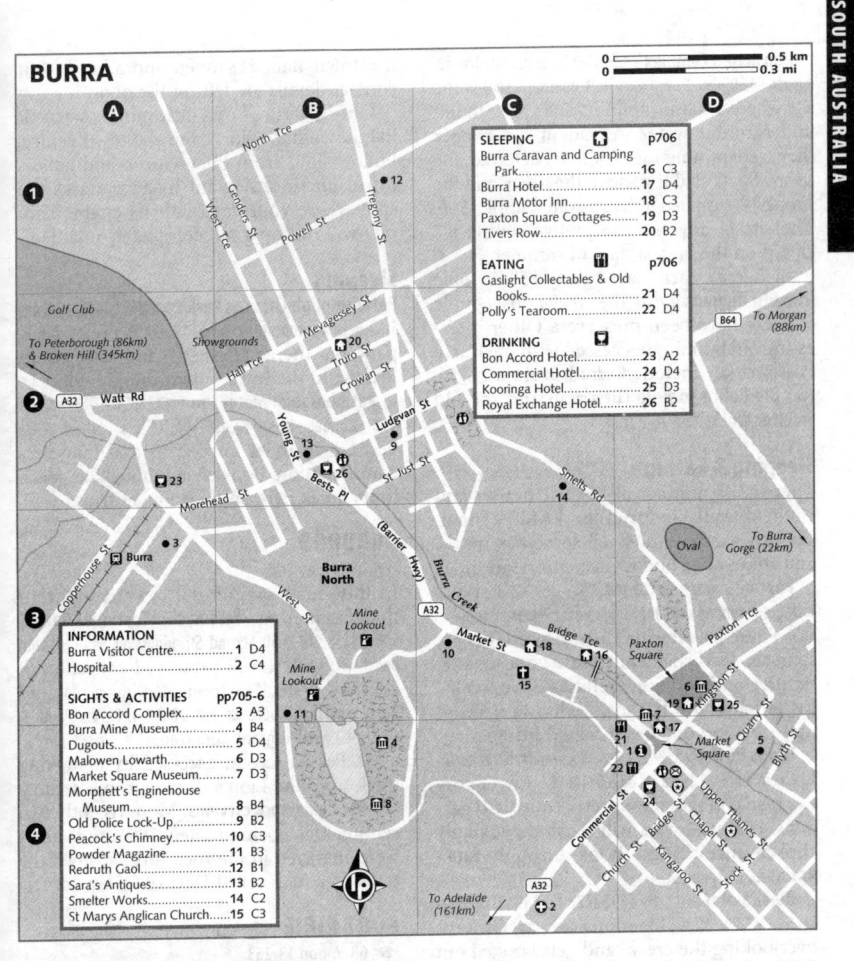

BURRA

0 ___ 0.5 km
0 ___ 0.3 mi

INFORMATION
Burra Visitor Centre..............**1** D4
Hospital..................................**2** C4

SIGHTS & ACTIVITIES pp705-6
Bon Accord Complex...............**3** A3
Burra Mine Museum................**4** B4
Dugouts.................................**5** D4
Malowen Lowarth...................**6** D3
Market Square Museum..........**7** D3
Morphett's Enginehouse
    Museum.............................**8** B4
Old Police Lock-Up.................**9** B2
Peacock's Chimney................**10** C3
Powder Magazine..................**11** B3
Redruth Gaol........................**12** B1
Sara's Antiques.....................**13** B2
Smelter Works......................**14** C2
St Marys Anglican Church......**15** C3

SLEEPING p706
Burra Caravan and Camping
    Park.................................**16** C3
Burra Hotel...........................**17** D4
Burra Motor Inn.....................**18** C3
Paxton Square Cottages........**19** D3
Tivers Row............................**20** B2

EATING p706
Gaslight Collectables & Old
    Books...............................**21** D4
Polly's Tearoom....................**22** D4

DRINKING
Bon Accord Hotel..................**23** A2
Commercial Hotel..................**24** D4
Kooringa Hotel......................**25** D3
Royal Exchange Hotel............**26** B2

the *Discovering Historic Burra* booklet (describing 49 sites on an 11km heritage trail), a key to the gates of the eight main sites on the trail (the others are unlocked) and entry into the town's four main museums. The passport costs $24 per person, or you can get an eight-site passport ($15). Two of the museums have free admission.

Sights & Activities

Burra has many substantial stone buildings, tiny Cornish cottages and numerous other reminders of the mining days. All the following attractions are included in the Burra Passport or have free admission.

Market Square Museum (Market Sq; 🕑 1-3pm Sat & Sun) has a shop, post office and a house set

up as they may have looked between 1880 and 1930.

The 33 attached cottages on **Paxton Square** were built for Cornish miners in the 1850s; some of these are available for accommodation (see p706). One of the cottages, **Malowen Lowarth** (☎ 8892 2577; Kingston St; 🕑 2-4pm Sat, 9.30-11.30am Sun), has furnishings and a garden in the 1850s style.

Morphett's Enginehouse Museum (☎ 8892 2244; off Market St; admission $3.50; 🕑 11am-1pm Mon, Wed & Fri) is a reconstructed three-storey Cornish enginehouse that once pumped water from the mine. The enginehouse is on the grounds of the original mine site, now converted into the open-air **Burra Mine Museum**. Information boards detail the history of the mine.

Bon Accord Complex (☎ 8892 2056; Railway Tce; admission $4.50; ⏰ 1-3pm Mon-Fri, 1-4pm Sat & Sun) is the site where a Scottish mining enterprise found underground water instead of the copper they were mining for. Not to be deterred, the canny Scots sold the site to the town, and the property supplied Burra's water until 1966. The site is now an interpretive centre; it's closed on the hottest days of summer.

In Burra's early days nearly 1500 people lived in **dugouts** along the creek and a couple of these have been preserved. Other interesting old buildings accessed with the Burra Passport key include **Redruth Gaol** (Tregony St), the **Old Police Lock-Up** (Tregony St) and the old **Smelter Works** (Smelts Rd).

Sleeping & Eating
There are a number of historic houses and cottages available for around $120 a night. The town's five hotels all serve bar meals, and some offer budget accommodation.

Paxton Square Cottages (☎ 8892 2622; paxton cottages@bigpond.com.au; Kingston St; 2-person cottages $65) These pristine and historic cottages are sparsely furnished, but with good-quality fixtures and cooking facilities. Good value for families and friends, each house sleeps up to six and one has disabled fittings.

Tivers Row (☎ 8892 2461; www.burraheritagecott ages.com.au; 8-18 Truro St; B&B $110) A row of cosy Cornish cottages have pretty courtyard gardens. History-lovers will relish the lovingly chosen furnishings. Book through **Sara's Antiques** (1 Young St).

Burra Motor Inn (☎ 8892 2777; fax 8892 2707; Market St; tw $88; ⌘) This motel has large rooms overlooking the creek, and gets booked out over weekends.

Polly's Tearoom (Shop 11, Commercial St; lunch $8.50; ⏰ 10am-3pm) Here you can sit among Victoriana and a large teddy-bear collection for cakes and light lunches.

Gaslight Collectables & Old Books (☎ 8892 3004; 20 Market Sq; ⏰ 10am-5pm) This delightful bookshop serves a range of great coffees, wicked cream teas and home-made cakes, while classical music helps soothe the soul.

PETERBOROUGH
☎ 08 / pop 1683
Peterborough is a dusty agricultural service town, very proud of its rail heritage. The **visitors centre and souvenir shop** (☎ 8651 2708; Main St) sits in an old railway carriage near

the town hall. It's open sporadically but contact details are left on the door.

One of nature's odd little quirks, **Magnetic Hill**, is around 10km from the town centre. Follow signs from the Orroroo and Jamestown junction. A giant magnet marks the spot where your car (with its engine shut off) will roll up a hill completely unaided!

Sleeping
Peterborough Caravan Park (☎ 8651 2545; 36 Grove St; 2-person camp sites/cabins $10/45) A pretty basic park, but there are grassy camp sites and it is close to the town's swimming pool.

Peterborough Motor Inn (☎ 8651 2078; fax 8651 2428; 25 Queen St; s/d $75/85; ⌘) This inn is your best bet in town for decent mid-range accommodation. Book ahead though, as coach tours break here on their longer trips.

ORROROO
☎ 08 / pop 504
In this small agricultural town, you'll find the fascinating **Yesteryear Costume Gallery** (☎ 8658 1032; 50 Second St; admission $4; ⏰ with bookings), with a well-preserved collection of period dresses. The town also has a restored **Early Settlers Cottage** (☎ 8658 1219; cnr Fouth & South Sts) and a **giant gum tree**.

At Pekina Creek, accessed by a walking track from the Lion's Picnic Grounds, there are **Aboriginal rock carvings**. More recently two sentimental poems (dated 1896 and 1901) were engraved in the rock further down the track by a man called David McDonald.

PORT PIRIE
☎ 08 / pop 13,263
Unless you've got a thing for huge lead- and zinc-smelting complexes, there's no reason to head here. Between that all-pervasive industry and the gigantic grain terminals dominating the town's horizon, any urges to explore will quickly pass.

If you're interested in the smelting industry, ask about tours at the helpful **visitors centre** (☎ 8633 0439; www.tourism.artspp.kangweb.com.au; 3 Mary Elie St; ⏰ 9am-5pm Mon-Fri, 9am-4pm Sat, 10am-3pm Sun), which shares space with the **Arts Centre**.

PORT GERMEIN
☎ 08 / pop 279
Port Germein is an understated but pleasant coastal town. It's on the map for sporting the longest wooden jetty in Australia, from

which dolphins are often seen frolicking. You'll understand why the jetty was built when the tide goes out: there is a 1283m-long walk across the beach to reach the sea!

You can head east from Port Germein to cut through the mountains via the beautiful **Germein Gorge** to Murray Town and north to Melrose.

Sleeping

Port Germein Caravan Park (☎ 8634 5266; The Esplanade; 2-person camp sites/cabins $15/42) This friendly park has few amenities and old caravans but is close to the jetty.

Casual Affair (☎ 8634 5242; 184 High St; dm $16) Harm and Tinky Folkers have created a gentle and tranquil lifestyle that you can share for a while. Their Japanese-inspired guestrooms, coffee shop and craft centre are in a restored and very attractive 140-year-old storehouse (complete with hand-crafted puppets and rugs). Meals are also available.

MT REMARKABLE NATIONAL PARK

This steep, rugged park covers 16,000 hectares and straddles the southern Flinders Ranges between Wilmington and the coast. There's a large, attractive bush camping area at Mambray Creek on the eastern side of the range. Obtain camping permits (admission per car including entry fee $16) from the self-registration booth at Mambray Creek.

From **Wilmington** (population 250), on the other (western) side of the park, you can access some nice bushwalks in the park, including the **Heysen Trail** (p661). One short walk is through colourful **Alligator Gorge** (admission per car $6.50), with walls that are only 2m apart in places.

Hancocks Lookout just north of the park and on the way to Horrocks Pass from Wilmington offers excellent views of Spencer Gulf. The 7km detour (one way) is well worth it.

MELROSE

☎ 08 / pop 200
This charming town, 265km north of Adelaide, was established in 1853 and has a beautiful setting at the foot of Mt Remarkable (956m). There are some interesting old buildings here, including the town's two pubs (both of which offer Internet access), police station and courthouse. The latter houses the **Melrose Courthouse Museum** (☎ 8666 2141; Stuart St; admission $4; ⏲ 2-5pm Thu-Tue).

Sleeping

Melrose Caravan Park (☎ 8666 2060; melrosecaravan park@rbe.net.au; Joe's Rd; camp sites/dm/caravans/cabins $14/16/40/65) Directly below Mt Remarkable, there are great bush sites and a well-appointed bunkhouse at this caravan park. Visitors centre inquiries are welcome 8am to 8pm daily.

Melrose Holiday Units (☎ 8666 2021; remark able@ozemail.com.au; Whitby St; 2-person units $80; ⚒) Self-contained and good value for families, these units also have disabled access.

Mt Remarkable Hotel/Motel (☎ 8666 2119; remarkable@ozemail.com.au; 18-20 Stuart St; d $60; 💻) This pub offers basic motel units, meals and a remarkable view of the mountain.

OTHER MID-NORTH TOWNS

Other towns include **Carrieton**, where a major rodeo is held towards the end of December each year. **Bruce**, **Hammond** and **Terowie** are old railheads, which have virtually faded away to ghost towns.

Heading south from Melrose you will come to tiny **Murray Town**, where there's a pub – and very little else. **Wirrabara** is on the **Heysen Trail** (p661).

SOUTHEAST

The Southeast, or Limestone Coast according to tourism authorities, is the country you will pass through if you travel between Adelaide and Melbourne (729km). The Dukes Hwy provides the most direct route, but if you take the coastal Princes Hwy it runs adjacent to the Coorong (an extensive coastal lagoon system) and some pretty little fishing and holiday towns.

These quiet communities delight in great swimming and surfing beaches and rock lobster (crayfish) on the menu between October and April. Don't miss the opportunity to slurp the superb *terra rossa* reds of the Coonawarra wine belt or to walk around the peaceful volcanic crater lakes at Mt Gambier.

Getting There & Away
AIR
Rex (☎ 13 17 13; www.regionalexpress.com.au) and **O'Connor Airlines** (☎ 08-8723 0666; www.oconnor -airlines.com.au) fly daily between Adelaide and Mt Gambier ($205).

BUS

Premier Stateliner (☎ 08-8415 5555) runs two routes between Adelaide and Mt Gambier ($50, 6½ hours).

You can either go along the coast Sunday to Friday via the Coorong and stopping at Meningie ($25 2 hours), Kingston SE ($38, 4 hours), Robe ($45, 4½ hours) and Beachport ($45, 5 hours), or inland daily via Bordertown ($37, 4 hours), Naracoorte ($45, 5 hours) and Penola ($50, 6 hours). It also runs services between Mt Gambier and Penola ($10, 30 minutes).

V/Line (☎ 1800 817 037) runs a daily service between Mt Gambier and Melbourne ($60, 6½ hours) – you take the bus from Mt Gambier to Ballarat or Warrnambool, where you hop on the train for Melbourne.

Green Triangle Coaches (☎ 1800 626 844, 08-8725 7413, 8723 0032; c/o The Old Jail, Mt Gambier) runs new connecting bus services between Mt Gambier and Apollo Bay ($60). A number of other pick-ups including Warrnambool ($40) are planned.

COORONG NATIONAL PARK

The Coorong is a narrow lagoon curving along the coast for 145km from Lake Alexandrina to near Kingston. A complex series of saltpans, it is separated from the sea by the huge sand dunes of the Younghusband Peninsula. Take the old and unsealed Coorong Rd south of Salt Creek to view the Coorong from the inside. There is also 4WD vehicle access through the southern dunes and onto the surf beach at 42 Mile Crossing and Tea Tree Crossing (possible in summer only).

This area is home to vast numbers of water birds. *Storm Boy,* a film about a young boy's friendship with a pelican, based on the novel of the same name by Colin Thiele, was shot on the Coorong. These wonderful birds are very evident at Jack Point and elsewhere in the park, as are ducks, waders and swans.

Sleeping

The park has plenty of bush **camp sites**, but you need a permit ($6.50 per car). These can be purchased from NPWSA outlets, the roadhouse at Salt Creek and the **NPWSA office** (☎ 08-8575 1200; 34 Main St; ☼ 9am-5pm Mon-Fri) in Meningie. General park and trail information can also be obtained here.

MENINGIE

☎ 08 / pop 897

On Lake Albert, a large arm of Lake Alexandrina, Meningie has been a popular windsurfing spot.

Coorong Nature Tours (☎ /fax 8574 0037; coorongnat@lm.net.au; Dadd Rd, Narrung) offers award-winning 4WD and bushwalking eco-tours of the area (day tours from $150), which can also be arranged ex-Adelaide.

Coorong Wilderness Lodge (☎ 8575 6001; off the Princes Hwy, about 25km south of Meningie) is at stunning Point Hack. This fish-shaped centre is owned by members of the Ngarrindjeri community, who offer guided bush-tucker walks and kayak tours (walking/kayak tours $7/17), as well as bush food like Coorong mullet, fresh damper and kangaroo meatballs. Lunch and dinner are around $13 with advance bookings only.

Sleeping

Camp Coorong (☎ 8575 1557; nlpa@lm.net.au; Princes Hwy; camp sites/dm/cabins $10/22/55; ☒) Simple modern cabins and dorms are great value, and there are also good laundry and kitchen facilities at this camp 10km south of Meningie. Run by the Ngarrindjeri Lands & Progress Association, for those who want to learn about Aboriginal history it's a great place to start. You need to book in advance and rates are cheaper for groups. Ask about linen hire, and bring your own food.

The **Cultural Museum** and cultural walks, (from $33 per hour), are run by an informed and passionate Ngarrindjeri curator and guide.

Lake Albert Caravan Park (☎ /fax 8575 141; lacp@lm.net.au; 25 Narrung Rd; camp sites/cabins $18/45) is right on the lake. This older park has shady sites and some disabled facilities.

ROBE

☎ 08 / pop 965

Wave to the wonderful giant **Larry the Big Lobster** in Kingston SE on your way to Robe, a charming holiday and fishing port.

Dating from 1846, and one of the state's first settlements, Robe's citizens made a fortune in the late 1850s when the Victorian government instituted a $10-per-head tax on Chinese gold miners. Many Chinese miners circumvented this by landing at Robe and walking hundreds of kilometres to the Victorian goldfields; 10,000 arrived in 1857 alone. The **Chinamen's Wells** along the route they took are a reminder of that time.

The **visitors centre** (☎ 8768 2465; www.robe.sa .gov.au; Mundy Tce; ☯ 9am-5pm Mon-Fri, 10am-4pm Sat & Sun) is in the public library and offers free Internet access.

There is a safe swimming beach opposite the town centre, and **Long Beach** (2km off town off the Kingston SE road) is good for windsurfing and boardsurfing.

Wilsons at Robe (☎ 8768 2459; Victoria St) offer wit and talent for sale in the guise of excellent art and craft works.

Sleeping
Robe is a hugely popular summer-holiday destination. There's plenty of accommodation, but as it is one of the best places to stay on the coast you'll be lucky to find any vacancies in peak periods. Most motel rooms are around $85 per night, but ask about self-contained units and up-market B&Bs (some in historic homes) at the visitors centre. Prices jump quite scarily during December and January.

BUDGET
Robe Hotel (☎ 8768 2077; fax 8768 2495; Mundy Tce; s/d $55/60) There are gloomy but good-value rooms in this geared-for-gambling hotel. However it's central to everything and really does overlook the sea.

Bushland Cabins (☎ 8768 2386; bushland@seol.net .au; Nora Creina Rd; camp sites $15, dm with/without bathroom $25/20) Around 1.5km out of town, these cabins are in a very peaceful setting with lots of wildlife.

MID-RANGE
Caledonian Inn (☎ 8768 2029; caled@seol.net.au; Victoria St; s/d/units $40/55/115) This delightful and historic place has two-storey units nestled between the hotel and adjacent beach. Room rates include continental breakfast. The hotel bar retains its Scottish heritage and has a great atmosphere. Bar meals service carnivores and seafood fans only ($19).

Robe Haven Motel (☎ 8768 2588; robehaven@big pond.com.au; cnr Smillie & Hagan Sts; s/d $70/85; ☒) Renovated accommodation at this small motel is surprisingly spacious and comfortable. Pricier rooms overlook the Boat Haven.

Eating
Wild Mulberry Café & Espresso Bar (☎ 8768 5276; 46 Victoria St; lunches $15) Breakfast, lunch and early dinner are served here, although freshly baked cakes, crepes and pastries are its fattening specialities.

Gallerie (☎ 8768 22560; cnr Victoria & Davenport Sts; mains $13-25) Home of Dawson Estate wines, this is a trendy and popular place with hair-tossing waiters. The pasta and seafood are fairly priced and it is cheaper to eat alfresco on the deck.

Locals buy their cooked seafood from **Robe Seafood & Takeaway** on Victoria St.

BEACHPORT
☎ 08 / pop 407
If you have a yen for peace and solitude, you'll love this quiet little seaside town with its stunning coastline of limestone cliffs edged with wild aquamarine seas.

Canunda National Park with its giant sand dunes lies 22km south of town. It features 4WD tracks, Boandik Aboriginal middens (traces of old camp sites), and pleasant walks. You can camp near Southend ($7 per vehicle).

The **visitors centre** (☎ 8735 8029; fax 8735 8309; Millicent Rd; ☯ 9am-5pm Mon-Fri, 11am-2pm Sat & Sun) is centrally placed.

Sights & Activities
The **Old Wool & Grain Store Museum** (☎ 8735 8313; 5 Railway Tce; admission $5; ☯ 10am-4pm Sun-Mon summer holidays) is in a National Trust building on the main street. It has relics of Beachport's whaling days and rooms furnished in 1870s style.

There's good board surfing, and windsurfing is popular at **Lake George**, 5km north of the township.

Also popular are walking trails in the **Beachport Conservation Park** (Railway Tce).

The hypersaline **Pool of Siloam** is a pretty lake among sand hills on the outskirts of town, and is perfect for young children, providing a safe and shallow swimming environment.

Sleeping & Eating
Beachport Motor Inn (☎ 8735 8070; beachportmotel@ bigpond.com; cnr Railway Tce & Lanky St; d/units $68/78; ☒) Within 300m of the town beach, this cheerful little motel also offers facilities for the disabled.

House of Siloam (☎ 8735 8388, 0427-358 388; roachpd@bigpond.com; 24 McCourt St; 4-/5-person units $80/90, 8-person house $120; ⊠) This modern and comfortable accommodation in the suburbs offers great value for families and friends. Disabled facilities exist in the smaller unit.

Bompa's (☎ 8735 8333; fax 8735 8101; 3 Railway Tce; dm/d $20/80) Beachport's only budget accommodation has TV but no kitchen facilities. Book ahead to beat the tour groups. Bompa's has a cosy bar and café (mains $9 to $21).

Southern Ocean Tourist Park (☎ 8735 8153; sotp@seol.net.au; Somerville St; camp sites/cabins $15/55) This great park sits sheltered behind a hill in the centre of town and has well-maintained grounds and facilities. The children's playground is a winner.

MT GAMBIER
☎ 08 / pop 22,751

The major town and commercial centre of the Southeast, Mt Gambier is 486km from Adelaide. Built on the slopes of the extinct volcano from which the town takes its name, it is a good friendly centre from which to explore the Crater Lakes or go cave diving under Mt Gambier itself. Harness racing and country music are big above-ground pursuits.

Information

The excellent **visitors centre** (☎ 8724 9750, 1800 087 187; theladynelson@mountgambier.sa.gov.au; Jubilee Hwy East; ☼ 9am-5pm) leaves information packs out overnight for late and weary travellers.

Allow time to look through the **discovery centre** (admission $9), which features a replica of the historic brig *Lady Nelson*, complete with sound effects and taped commentary. There's an audiovisual display that acknowledges the devastating impact of European settlement on local Aboriginal people.

Jontie's Cafe/Cave Internet Lounge (☎ 8723 9499; 15-17 Commercial St East) has Internet access and more. This multicoloured café (and art gallery) serves all-day breakfasts and delicious fruit and vegetable cocktails. A popular local rendezvous for all; lunch and dinner mains are around $18.

Sights & Activities

There are three volcanic craters, two with lakes. The beautiful **Blue Lake** is an almost implausible shade of sapphire during summer. Blue Lake is about 204m deep at its deepest point and has an encircling 3.6km scenic drive. The lakes are a popular recreation spot and have been developed with boardwalks (over Valley Lake), a wildlife park, picnic areas and cycle and walking trails.

Aquifer Tours (☎ /fax 8723 1199; cnr Bay Rd & John Watson Dr; adult/child $6/3) runs hourly tours that take you to the surface of the lake in a glass-panelled lift.

The floodlit sunken gardens in the **Umpherston Sinkhole** are pretty, but avoid the temptation to feed the flabby possums. Volunteers take tours on the hour most days ($6.50) down to the water table in the **Engelbrecht Cave**, a popular cave-diving spot (book at the visitors centre). Scuba divers can attain cave-diving qualifications (three-day courses) in Mt Gambier.

The **Gambier Dive Centre** (☎ 8723 4255; gambierdive@corprite.net; 60 Commercial St West, Mt Gambier) will organise three- and four-day cave-diving courses ($650) that cover both levels, including the necessary medical examination. To be eligible, scuba divers must have 12 months post-qualifying experience and a minimum of 15-hours bottom time (including two night and two 18m dives).

The surrounding region has some fine walks, including the path to the top of **Mt Schank**, an extinct volcano off the Mt Gambier road. The rugged coastline to the west of **Port Macdonnell** is worth a visit, while **Piccaninnie Ponds** is another popular cave-diving and snorkelling spot – for information contact the **Department for Environment and Heritage** (☎ 8735 1177).

Sleeping, Eating & Drinking

Mt Gambier has numerous mid-range motor inns, but many have tired and gloomy rooms, so check them out first. There are six caravan parks and some old hotels in the town's busy centre offering accommodation and meals.

Arkana Motor Inn (☎ 8725 5433; fax 8725 6080; 201 Commercial St East; s/d/units $75/80/120; ⊠) One of the best places around, this inn has bright and modern rooms and a heated pool and spa. Units offer great family deals ($12 per extra person), book ahead though.

Mid City Motel (☎ 1800 807 277, 8725 7277; fax 8724 9650; Helen St; d/4-person unit $87/120; ⊠) This is a small and quiet motel with comfortable and immaculate rooms.

Blue Lake Holiday Park (☎ 1800 676 028, 8725 9856; www.bluelakeholidaypark.com.au; Bay Rd; 2-person camp sites/cabins/units/bungalows $18/63/69/72) This park is adjacent to a golf course and walking and cycling trails, and it is also close to the Blue Lake. The bonus is great facilities for kids and for those with disabilities.

Old Jail (☎ 1800 626 844, 8723 0032; turnkey@ seol.net.au; Langlois Dr; dm/tw $20/25) This novelty stopover was an operating jail until 1995 and is not for claustrophobics – you sleep in original bare cells, slamming metal doors and all! However, the main house has a few beds and creature comforts. There's also a bar and rates include breakfast.

For bare-bones bar food and Guinness try **Flanagans** on Ferrers St or pub grub at the **Commercial Hotel** on Commercial St West.

Redfins (☎ 8725 0611; 2 Commercial St West; mains $22) Mt Gambiens love these seafood dinners, with Coffin Bay oysters a speciality.

COONAWARRA WINE REGION
Shout *terra rossa* with joy after tasting the peppery shiraz and silken cabernet sauvignons from the supreme and compact wine-producing area (25 sq km) of Coonawarra. Just north of Penola, over 23 cellar doors offer tastings and sales, most daily.

The **visitors centre** (☎ 8737 2855; penola@wattle range.sa.gov.au; 27 Arthur St, Penola; ☯ 9am-5pm Mon-Fri, 10am-5pm Sat, 9.30am-4pm Sun) is in Penola.

Penola
☎ 08 / pop 1222
Penola has won fame for its association with the Sisters of St Joseph of the Sacred Heart. This was the Order co-founded in 1867 by Mother Mary MacKillop (see the boxed text 'Champion of the Poor: A Saint in the Making'; p670). The **Mary MacKillop Interpretative Centre** (☎ 08-8737 2092; cnr Portland St & Petticoat Lane; admission $4.50; ☯ 10am-4pm) features the 1867 **Woods-MacKillop Schoolhouse**, which has information on the first school in Australia to welcome children from lower socioeconomic backgrounds, co-founded by MacKillop. The tiny historic **cottages** on Petticoat Lane are evocative and certainly worth a look.

Sights & Activities
WINERIES
Most of the region's wineries are signposted off the Riddoch Hwy. The following should not be missed and all, bar Padthaway's, have disabled access.

Padthaway Estate (☎ 8765 5039; Riddoch Hwy, Coonawarra; ☯ 10am-4pm) Stop to taste the rich

and sultry Padthaway reds, and then stay on for lunch or a sumptuous dinner and overnighter. This is a true gem, a beautiful old historic homestead set in private, lush gardens and surrounded by vineyards. Dinner is $55 and overnight packages start at $195.

Rymill (☎ 8736 5001; Riddoch Hwy, Coonawarra; ☯ 10am-5pm) Mellow merlot cabernets through to its popular shiraz and delicate sparkling chardonnay all taste well in this dramatic and modern cellar door.

Wynns Coonawarra Estate (☎ 8736 2225; Memorial Dr, Coonawarra; ☯ 10am-5pm) The founding winery in the Coonawarra, Wynn's cellar door is imbued with the scent of past great vintages. Renowned for its top quality and truly peppery shiraz, Wynn's also produce smooth and fruity reds, fragrant rieslings and fantastic golden chardonnays.

Zema Estate (☎ 8736 3219; Riddoch Hwy, Coonawarra; ☯ 9am-5pm) Trust SA taste buds, these reds are glorious examples of the region's rich shiraz and cabernet sauvignon.

Sleeping & Eating
Over 20 restored historic cottages in the Penola district offer accommodation, with prices starting at $100 for twin share. Penola also has a nice but older caravan park.

Coonawarra Motor Lodge (☎ 8737 2364; fax 8737 2543; 114 Church St; d/tr $100/120; ♿) This friendly and small motel is right on the winery strip, is very child friendly and has one room with disabled access. Stay downstairs to avoid the upstair's tragic décor.

Heyward's Royal Oak Hotel (☎ 8737 2322; fax 8737 2825; 31 Church St; s/tw/d $40/70/85; ♿) A busy and cosy hotel that is state heritage and National Trust listed. Locals pack in the bar to chomp schnitzels and seafood for around $13.

Chardonnay Lodge (☎ 8736 3309; www.chardon naylodge.com.au; Riddoch Hwy; d $125) A top-notch and highly recommended motel with lovely gardens.

Irises Café (☎ 8737 2967; 48 Church St; light meals $13) You will enjoy anything that is baked here! Choose from succulent home-made cakes, tasty pies or the juicy and pungent garlic bread.

NARACOORTE
☎ 08 / pop 4785
Settled in the 1840s, Naracoorte is one of the oldest towns in the state and one of the largest in the Southeast region.

The **visitors centre** (☎ 1800 244 421, 8762 1518; fax 8762 0745; Macdonnell St; ☺ 9am-4pm) is housed in an old flour mill.

The **Bool Lagoon Game Reserve** is usually home to 155 bird species, including 79 water birds, but a series of dry summers have left it pretty dry and moribund.

Naracoorte Caves National Park

About 12km southeast of Naracoorte, off the Penola road, is the only SA World Heritage–listed site. The fossil deposits and limestone cave formations here featured in the David Attenborough series *Life on Earth* (BBC). The signage is sporadic so take a good map.

The excellent **Wonambi Fossil Centre** (☎ 8762 2340; Hynam-Caves Rd; ☺ 9am-sunset summer, 9am-5pm rest of year) houses a re-creation of the rainforest environment that covered this area 200,000 years ago. The centre has life-size reconstructions of extinct animals which have been painstakingly put together. Some models grunt and move; children and adults alike will enjoy them.

Book here also for the cave tours through **Victoria Fossil Cave**, **Alexandra Cave**, **Blanche Cave** and **Wet Cave**. Wet Cave can be seen on a self-guided tour. For the others, ranger-guided tours run from 9.30am to 3.30pm.

BAT CAVE

Bats make a spectacular departure from this cave on summer evenings, and although it's not open to the public infrared TV cameras will allow you to see inside.

All the above activities, including the Bat Cave and Wonambi Fossil Centre, are priced on a sliding scale – one tour costs $11, two cost $19, and so on.

Adventure tours to undeveloped caves in the area (wear sneakers or trainers and old clothes) start at $26 for novices and $55 for a minimum of four advanced explorers.

Sleeping

William MacIntosh Motor Lodge (☎ 8762 1644; willnara@bigpond.com; Adelaide Rd, Naracoorte; d/tw $100/110; ☒) This lodge is on the right side of town, and has neat and pleasant rooms with a licensed restaurant on-site.

Naracoorte Holiday Park (☎ 8762 2128; www .naracoorteholidaypark.com.au; 81 Park Tce; 2-person camp sites/cabins/units $14/59/69) This immaculate park has spotless and modern accommo-

dation, a miniature train, mini-golf course and swimming lake.

Naracoorte Backpackers (☎ /fax 8762 3835, 0408-823 835; 4 Jones St; dm/dm per week $22/105) Nonworking travellers are not really welcome for more than a night as the manager acts as a casual labour contractor for local vineyards. The facilities are very shabby and barely adequate for more than a handful of backpackers. However, there is a friendly atmosphere and if you're looking for local work it is a central spot.

DUKES HIGHWAY

The last town on the SA side of the border with Victoria is **Bordertown** (population 2340). This town is the birthplace of former Labor prime minister Bob Hawke, and there's a bust of Bob outside the town hall. On the left as you enter from Victoria there is a wildlife park, with various species of Australian fauna, including rare white kangaroos dozing behind a wire fence.

MURRAY RIVER

Australia's greatest river starts in the Snowy Mountains, the Australian Alps, and for most of its length forms the boundary between NSW and Victoria. It meanders for 650km through SA, first heading west to Morgan and then turning south towards Lake Alexandrina.

En route, the river is tapped to provide domestic water for Adelaide as well as country towns as far away as Whyalla and Woomera. Between the Victorian border and Blanchetown, the usual vista of immense dry bush and farmlands is interrupted by a lush-green oasis of grapevines and citrus trees. This is where irrigation has turned previously unproductive land into an important agricultural region. This area is generally known as the Riverland.

North of the river, the Murray River National Park and Chowilla Regional Reserve form part of the renowned Unesco Bookmark Biosphere Reserve. These are major breeding grounds for the state's waterfowl and other birds.

The Murray has a fascinating history. Before the advent of railways, it was Australia's Mississippi, with paddle-steamers carrying trade from the interior down to the coast. Several of these shallow-draught vessels have been restored and you can relive the past on cruises of a few hours or several days. They include the huge sternwheeler PS *Murray River Princess,* which regularly makes its stately passage up and down the river from Mannum.

There are many places along the Murray where the road crosses the river by vehicle ferry. These are free and usually run 24 hours a day – phones are supplied to call the operator if the ferry is unattended.

Fruit-Picking

If you have a valid working visa and don't mind hard physical labour, the Riverland is the best region to find seasonal and harvest employment. There is generally work here year-round, although April is a slow month, so ring ahead to check on the current situation. It helps if you have your own transport as most farms are a long way from accommodation in the region.

The backpacker hostels at Berri, Kingston OM, Loxton and Murray Bridge all act as labour contractors. For seasonal information call the federal government's **Harvest Hotline** (☎ 1300 720 126), and private job agencies in Berri **Ozjobs** (☎ 08-8580 0709) and **Rivskills** (☎ 08-8582 2188).

Sights & Activities
HOUSEBOAT HIRE

South Australians love sailing serenely down the Murray, but in comfort. Try out the floating mansions that are laughingly called houseboats – they are extremely popular and great fun for families and friends alike.

Houseboats can be hired from Adelaide and in most riverside towns. Book well ahead, especially for the months from October to April. The **Houseboat Hirers Association** (☎ 08-8395 0999; www.houseboat-centre.com.au; 7 Gollop Cres, Redwood Park, Adelaide) can give advice and arrange a boat for you. Prices vary hugely, but in the high season you can expect to pay from around $180 per person per week depending on such factors as size of boat, number of people and duration of hire. Prices are usually considerably cheaper in winter.

KAYAKING & CANOEING

There's only one main equipment supplier in the region. Hire canoes, kayaks and other gear from **Riverland Leisure Canoe Tours**

(☎ 08-8588 2053; Thelma Rd, Barmera; canoe/kayak per day $25/15). It will deliver to all towns around the river (some reasonable mileage costs may apply) and offers guided canoe tours for an evening/half day/full day with meals for $15/25/50.

Getting There & Away

Premier Stateliner (☎ 08-8415 5555) has daily services from Adelaide to the Riverland; Waikerie ($28, 2½ hours), Kingston OM ($32, 3 hours), Berri ($35, 3½ hours) Loxton, Barmera and Renmark ($35, 4 hours).

Murray Bridge Passenger Service (☎ 08-8539 1142) runs from Adelaide to Mannum ($19.50, 2½ hours, 2pm Monday to Friday).

McCafferty's/Greyhound (13 14 99) runs daily through the Riverland en route to Sydney but you must cross a state border to travel with it; Renmark to Sydney ($100, 18 hours).

RENMARK
☎ 08 / pop 4470

The first major river town across from the NSW border is 254km from Adelaide. Renmark doesn't have the friendliness of nearby Loxton and Barmera, and social drinking can start early on the riverfront.

The **visitors centre** (☎ 8586 6704; tourist@riverland.net.au; 84 Murray Ave; ☼ 9am-5pm Mon-Fri, 9am-4pm Sat, 10am-4pm Sun) has a free **interpretive centre** and the recommissioned 1911 paddle-steamer **PS Industry** which cruises the first Sunday in every month.

Renmark River Cruises (☎ 8595 1862; fax 8595 1323; renriv@riverland.net.au), on the Main Wharf, offers cruises ($55/12 per adult/child) on the MV *Big River Rambler,* departing from the town wharf daily. It also conducts guided ecotours by dinghy ($45 per person, minimum two people).

Upstream from town, the huge **Chowilla Regional Reserve** (part of the sprawling Unesco Bookmark Biosphere Reserve) is great for bush camping, canoeing and bushwalking. Access is along the north bank from Renmark or along the south bank from Paringa. For details contact the **NPWSA office** (☎ 8595 2111; Vaughan Tce, Berri).

Sleeping

Renmark Hotel/Motel (☎ 8586 6755; www.renmarkhotel.com.au; Murray Ave; hotel s/d $55/65, motel s/d $76/80) The clean hotel rooms are good value in this huge hotel, which also serves meals.

Renmark Riverfront Caravan Park (☎ 8584 7862; renrivcarapk@riverland.net.au; Sturt Hwy; camp sites $7, 2-person cabins $55-60) This park appears geared for long-term workers but is not interested in working backpackers.

BERRI
☎ 08 / pop 4241
At one time a refuelling stop for wood-burning paddle-steamers, the town takes its name from the Aboriginal term *berri berri*, meaning 'big bend in the river'. It's an attractive but surprisingly low-key town (virtually closing down at night). This may be due to the mainly transient working population; Berri is the regional centre both for state government and agricultural casual labour agencies.

The **visitors centre** (☎ 8582 2188; bbtour@inter node.on.net; Vaughan Tce; 🕑 9am-5pm Mon-Fri, 10am-4pm Sat & Sun) is riverside.

Check out the excellent murals and totem poles on and around the base of Berri Bridge, created by local artists.

Sights & Activities
Willabalangaloo Reserve (☎ 8582 1804; Old Sturt Hwy; admission $4; 🕑 10am-4pm Thu-Mon, daily in school holidays) is a flora and fauna reserve with walking trails, a museum and a historic paddle-steamer.

Big Orange (☎ 8582 4255; Old Sturt Hwy; 🕑 8.30am-4pm Fri-Wed) is a tourist shop with a 360-degree painting of the Riverland.

Berri Estates (☎ 8582 0340; Old Sturt Hwy; 🕑 9am-5pm Mon-Fri, 10am-4pm Sat & Sun) at Glossop, 7km west of Berri, claims it is one of Australia's biggest wineries, although it certainly isn't one of the most alluring. It offers tastings and cellar-door sales.

Road access to the beautiful Katarapko Creek section of the **Murray River National Park** is through Berri or Winkie (near Glossop). This beautiful stretch of river is a great area for bush camping ($6.50), and for canoeing and bird-watching.

Sleeping & Eating
Berri Riverside Caravan Park (☎ 8582 3723; www .berricaravanpark.com.au; Riverview Dr; camp sites/dm/cabins $16/25/50) This award-winning and popular park is very well maintained and has a good camp kitchen.

Berri Backpackers (☎ 8582 3144; Sturt Hwy; dm/dm per week for workers $20/120; 🖳) On the

Barmera side of town, this hostel is beloved of hedonistic international travellers. Among other facilities on the huge grounds it has a swimming pool, sauna and tennis court, as well as bicycles and canoes for guests' use. There is even an elaborate tree house, a meditation hut and free Internet access. The atmosphere is great here and there's seasonal work in local orchards and vineyards.

Berri Resort Hotel (☎ 8582 1411; www.berriresort hotel.com; Riverview Dr; hotel s/d $55/70, motel s/d $110/120; 🕃) This hotel/motel has cornered the market for mid-range accommodation. The motel rooms are overpriced, but the large licensed restaurant serves very good bistro food to both locals and guests (meals $11 to $18).

LOXTON
☎ 08 / pop 3358
Loxton is a very appealing town, on the Murray River loop, and a great place from which to work, or to stay for a day or two (the accommodation for all budgets is first-rate). You can canoe from here across to the Katarapko Creek section of the Murray River National Park (a major breeding ground for waterfowl) or simply meander by the river.

The friendly **visitors centre** (☎ 8584 7919; loxtour@riverland.net.au; Bookpurnong Tce; 🕑 9am-5pm Mon-Fri, 9am-noon Sat, 1-4pm Sun) has national park information, Internet access and a welcome sense of fun. Ask for film listings for its **drive-in cinema**.

Sights & Activities
Katarapko Game Reserve is accessible by water only, and enthused about by bird-watchers and nature-lovers.

Canoes can be hired from Loxton Riverfront Caravan Park for $11 an hour or $55 a day (also see Kayaking & Canoeing; p713).

The town's major attraction is **Loxton Historical Village** (☎ 8584 7194; Scenic Dr; adult/child $7/3; 🕑 10am-4pm Mon-Fri, 10am-5pm Sat, Sun & school holidays), with over 30 fully furnished buildings from days gone by.

Find the **Tree of Knowledge** by the caravan park – it's marked with flood levels from previous years.

Simeon Wines Australian Vintage Winery (☎ 8584 7236; Bookpurnong Rd; 🕑 10am-5pm Mon-Sat) is a wine wholesaler offering tastings.

Sleeping & Eating

Loxton Riverfront Caravan Park (☎ /fax 8584 7862; loxtoncp@hotkey.net.au; Riverfront Rd; camp sites/cabins/ en suite cabins $13/40/55) At Habels Bend, 2km from town, this riverside park is spacious and very well kept. There are good cabins (prices are for two people).

Harvest Trail Lodge (☎ 8584 5646; lodge@dodo .com.au; 1 Kokoda Tce; dm/dm per week for workers $27/130; ⚡) The owner-managers have not skimped on a thing in outfitting this excellent hostel. Dorms are four-person (all with TV and fridge), there's good security, a great balcony BBQ communal area and fabulous showers. The staff will find you work, and transport to and from jobs is free.

Loxton Community Hotel/Motel (☎ 1800 656 686, 8584 7266; loxtonhotel@ozemail.com.au; East Tce; s/d $75/85; ⚡ 🖳) This is the best-value hotel seen in the region; top quality and immaculate rooms for very good rates. The hotel has a pool and serves meals ($10.50 to $18).

BARMERA
☎ 08 / pop 1946

Barmera was once on the overland stock route from NSW and sits on the shores of the serene **Lake Bonney**. This wide and attractive freshwater lake has small sandy beaches, and is popular for swimming and water sports. World land-speed record holder Donald Campbell attempted to break his water-speed record on this lake in 1964.

The ruins of **Napper's Old Accommodation House**, built in 1850 at the mouth of Chambers Creek, are a reminder of the old era, as is the **Overland Corner Hotel** (☎ 8588 7021; Old Coach Rd; ⚡ 11am-10pm Mon-Sat, 11am-8pm Sun), built in 1859 on the Morgan road, 19km northwest of town. It's still a pub serving bar food (meals $11 to $17), is owned by the National Trust and has a small museum and walking trails.

The **visitors centre** (☎ 8588 2289; fax 8588 2777; Barwell Ave; ⚡ 11am-late Thu-Sat, 11am-8pm Sun-Wed) is really a travel agent and booking service for coach companies.

Sights & Activities

Country music is a big deal here, with the **South Australian Country Music Awards** in June, and the **Country Music Hall of Fame** across from the visitors centre.

There's a nudist beach for goose-pimple addicts at **Pelican Point Nudist Resort** (☎ 8588 7366), bookings are essential.

You'll find a wildlife reserve at **Moorook** and another across the river from **Kingston-on-Murray** – the latter backs onto the Overland Corner Hotel. Both reserves have nature trails and are good spots for bird-watching and canoeing. For camping permits, contact the **NPWSA office** (☎ 8595 2111) in Berri.

BANROCK STATION

The **station** (☎ 8583 0299; fax 8583 0288; Sturt Hwy; ⚡ 10am-5pm), signposted off the highway at Kingston OM, is an eco-friendly winery. Its stylish wine-tasting centre and restaurant overlook a beautiful wetland. A 2.5km wetland walk to a bird-hide leaves from the centre, and is very popular with twitchers.

Sleeping

Lake Bonney Holiday Park (☎ 8588 2234; fax 8588 1974; Lakeside Dr; 2-person camp sites/cabins $15/55) The spacious lakeside park is fabulous for families. There are large areas for children to run around in, and small beaches for on-site swimming.

Barmera Backpackers (☎ 8588 3007; backpack@ riverland.net.au; 6 Bice St; dm/dm per week for workers $17/ 115; ⚡) This small and newish YHA is open to international (or card-holding) backpackers, mainly those who want to work. There's room for 25, and the manager also acts as a labour contractor. It's bright, friendly and clean, and in the centre of town.

Nomads on Murray (☎ 1800 665 166, 8583 0211; www.nomadsworld.com; Sturt Hwy; dm per week $100) This is an agency providing backpacking-labour for the citrus orchards. Dorms are very crowded, but the younger end of the backpacking market enjoys the casual atmosphere and seem to earn good money.

Barmera Lake Resort-Motel (☎ 8588 2555; lakeresort@riverland.net.au; Lakeside Dr; s/d $60/70; ⚡) Right on the lake and complete with a swimming pool, this motel is very good value, although 'resort' is stretching it a bit.

WAIKERIE
☎ 08 / pop 1770

A citrus-growing centre, the town takes its name from the Aboriginal word for 'anything that flies', after the teeming birdlife on nearby lagoons and river. The drought, however, has affected birds' breeding patterns.

The **visitors centre** (☎ 8541 2332; Sturt Hwy; ☺ 9.30am-5pm Mon-Fri, 10am-4pm Sat & Sun) is at the **Orange Tree** and sells fruit and souvenirs.

Notices advertising for casual workers are put up at Anglicare in the town and at the caravan park.

The sleepy old town of **Swan Reach** (population 255), 70km southwest of Waikerie, has picturesque river scenery but not many swans – there are lots of pelicans, however.

Bird-watchers will revel in the 180 bird species (including six endangered breeds) recorded at the **Gluepot Reserve** (☎ 8892 9600; gluepot@riverland.net.au; Gluepot Rd, off Lunn Rd; admission per vehicle $6, per campers vehicle $11; ☺ 8am-6pm). This huge 51,000 hectares of protected mallee scrub (64km north of Waikerie) was set up by Birds Australia, and is part of Unesco's Bookmark Biosphere Reserves.

Sleeping

Waikerie Hotel/Motel (☎ 8541 2999; www.waikerie hotel.com; 2 McCoy St; s/d/motel d $55/60/70; ☒) This motel, with clean and very good-value rooms, is right in the town centre. There's decent pub tucker in the front bar or bistro.

Waikerie Caravan Park (☎ /fax 8541 2651; 49 Peake Tce; 2-person camp sites/cabins $13/50) This park is down by the river on the west side of town; it's for casual workers and definitely not for the refined.

MORGAN
☎ 08 / pop 424

With the town's residents and visitors mainly living on houseboats, the two town pubs have become the centre of life. In its prime, this was one of Australia's busiest river ports, with wharves towering 12m high. A leaflet details a heritage walk that includes PS *Mayflower*, the state's oldest operating paddle-steamer.

Port of Morgan Museum (☎ 8540 2130; admission $3), down by the river, has exhibits on the paddle-steamer trade. It opens according to demand, so ask at the station master's residence next door.

Sleeping & Eating

Morgan Riverside Caravan Park (☎ /fax 8540 2207; morgancp@riverland.net.au; 2-person camp sites/cabins $15/45) This mundane park is down by the ferry landing, and rents out canoes for $9 per hour and kneeboards for $25 per day.

Commercial Hotel (☎ /fax 8540 2107; 13 Railway Tce; s/d $25/50) This pub is the more basic of the two in town, both in terms of its rooms and food, but it is cheap and friendly enough.

Terminus Hotel/Motel (☎ 8540 2006; borgi@big pond.com.au; Railway Tce; s/d/tr $50/55/70; ☒) Located across the road from the Commercial Hotel, the motel rooms at the Terminus are OK (and at the back of the car park). There are takeaways and bar meals ($7 to $11) available.

Mallyons on the Murray (☎ 8543 2263; Renmark-Morgan Rd; lunch $11; ☺ 10am-4pm Thu-Mon, closed Jul) About 20km from Morgan on the Renmark Rd, this licensed and BYO bush café and organic vegie outlet was originally an 1841 resthouse for cattle drovers on the overland run from NSW.

MANNUM
☎ 08 / pop 2195

This is the unofficial houseboat-hiring capital for the region, 84km east of Adelaide.

The *Mary Ann*, Australia's first riverboat, was built here in 1853 and made the first paddle-steamer trip up the Murray. There are many relics of the pioneering days, including the fully restored 1897 paddle-steamer PS *Marion* which is now a **floating museum** (admission $5), moored at the **visitors centre** (☎ 8569 1303; www.psmarion.com; 6 Randell St; ☺ 9am-5pm Mon-Fri, 10am-4pm Sat & Sun).

Purnong Rd Bird Sanctuary is a great spot to see water birds; it starts at the Mannum Caravan Park and you drive along it for several kilometres on the road to Purnong.

The huge open-range **Monarto Zoological Park** (☎ 8534 4100; Princes Hwy; adult/child/family $16/10/50; ☺ 10am-5pm), 11km west of Murray Bridge, has Australian and international creatures including herds of zebras and giraffes. The admission price includes a bus ride through the park (departing hourly between 10.30am and 3.30pm).

Activities
RIVER CRUISES

The grand paddle-steamer **Murray River Princess** does two-, three- and five-night cruises from Mannum. Very popular with partying groups from Adelaide, the prices include all meals. Bookings should be made well in advance with **Captain Cook Cruises** (☎ 1800 804 843, 8569 2511; www.captaincook.com.au; 96 Randell St; tw $400).

YORKE PENINSULA

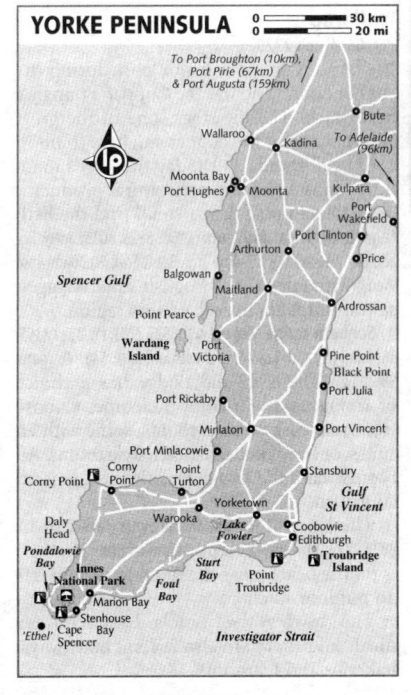

YORKE PENINSULA

With agriculture as its main industry, the peninsula is also a very low-key holiday region for Adelaidians. Beaches are tucked away behind farmlands and families gather at their holiday shacks to enjoy the solitude and fishing. Every October experienced surfers compete in the **Cutloose Ripcurl Yorke's Classic**, from celebrated points on the striking **Innes National Park** coastline. You might want to watch out for emus, kangaroos, ospreys and sea eagles in this unspoilt park, as well as passing southern right whales and dolphins.

The economy was originally based on the so-called Copper Triangle – Moonta (the mine), Wallaroo (the smelter) and Kadina (their service town), following a copper boom in the early 1860s. Many miners were from Cornwall in England, and the area still retains a Cornish flavour – notably in the Cornish pasty. A Cornish festival, **Kernewek Lowender**, is held here in alternate years during May (complete with wheelbarrow races). If you drink enough traditional beer you may see a *piskey* – a mischievous sprite believed to bring good fortune.

The boom peaked around the turn of the century, but in the early 1920s a slump in copper prices and rising labour costs closed all the peninsula's mines.

The regional **visitors centre** (☎ 1800 654 9921; www.coppercoast.sa.gov.au; 50 Moonta Rd, Kadina; ☼ 9am-5pm Mon-Fri, 10am-4pm Sat & Sun) is in Kadina.

Getting There & Around

Amazingly, there is no public transport to the end of the peninsula. Yorke Peninsula Coaches will take you as far as Warooka or Yorketown.

Premier Stateliner (☎ 08-8415 5555) operates a twice-daily bus Monday to Friday and once-daily bus Saturday and Sunday from Adelaide to Kadina, Wallaroo, Moonta, Port Hughes and Moonta Bay (all $19, 2 to 3 hours).

Yorke Peninsula Coaches (☎ 08-8823 2375) runs daily from Adelaide's central bus station to Yorketown. The route alternates between the east coast and down the centre of the peninsula. Destinations from Adelaide include Ardrossan ($23, 2 hours), Port Vin-

cent ($29, 3 hours), Yorketown, Edithburgh and Warooka (all $30, around 4 hours).

WEST COAST

The west coast, facing onto Spencer Gulf, has several quiet swimming beaches and the small Copper Triangle historic towns, which are all within a short drive of each other.

Kadina

☎ 08 / pop 3745

The town of Kadina has a number of historic sites. Get your tickets at the visitors centre for the nearby **Kadina Heritage Museum** (☎ 1800 654 991; Moonta Rd, Kadina; adult/child $8/2; ☼ 9am-5pm Mon-Fri, 10am-4pm Sat & Sun). The mining history includes the restored Matta House (1863), which illustrates the lifestyle of the mining folk, the Matta Matta mine, some old farming machinery and a blacksmith's shop.

There's also the **Banking & Currency Museum** (☎ 8821 2906; 3 Graves St; adult/child $4/1; ☼ 10am-4.30pm Sun-Thu, closed Jun) housed in an old bank; you can still buy and sell coins here.

Wallaroo

☎ 08 / pop 2720

Wallaroo was also a major port during the copper boom, and has the Copper Triangle's best beach. The big stack, one of the great chimneys from the copper smelters (built in 1861) still stands, but today the port's main function is exporting agricultural products.

In the old post office you'll find the **Heritage & Nautical Museum** (☎ 8823 3015; Jetty Rd; adult/child $4/2; ⏱ 2-4pm Thu, Sat & Sun, 10.30am-4pm Wed), with tales of the English square-rigged sailing ships that serviced this region.

Sonbern Lodge Motel (☎ 8823 2291; fax 8823 3355; 18 John Tce; s/d $28/45, s/d with en suite $45/60, motel $80; ✇) The 1912 old Lodge has a choice of rooms and a friendly welcome. Choose from refurbished hotel rooms, some with en suites, or from modern motel-style rooms. All rooms share the Lodge facilities and grassed courtyard.

The basic **Office Beach Caravan Park** (☎ /fax 8823 2722; 11 Jetty Rd; camp sites/cabins/units $16/45/55) is on the beach near the main jetty, and has an outdoor kitchen.

The town's five hotels have counter meals and there are also several takeaways, bakeries and tearooms.

Moonta

☎ 08 / pop 3084

In the late 19th century the copper mine at Moonta, 18km south of Wallaroo, was the richest mine in Australia.

Ask at the Yorke Peninsula visitors centre about the **Moonta Heritage Site** on the eastern outskirts of town.

At its peak, the town's grand old school had 1100 pupils on its rolls, but these days it's the excellent **Moonta Mines Museum** (☎ 8825 1891; Verran Tce; adult/child $3/1.50; ⏱ 1.30-4pm Wed, Fri, Sat & Sun). **Moonta Mines Sweet Shop** is across the road. On weekends a **tourist railway** (adult/child $3/1.50) runs from the museum to Kadina and Bute (50 minutes).

Nearby is an evocative and fully restored **Miner's Cottage** (☎ 8825 1891; off Verran Tce; adult/child $2/1; ⏱ 1.30-4pm Sat & Sun).

You can see a section of the underground workings at **Wheal Hughes mine** (☎ 8825 1891) on guided tours ($13), although this isn't one of the early mines. Book at the visitors centre.

Moonta Bay Patio Hotel (☎ 8825 2473; fax 8825 2566; 196 Bay Rd, Moonta Bay; s/d $70/80; ✇) This pleasant hotel sits right on the beach,

with tremendous views over Moonta Bay. Although it is 3km from town, there is a fully licensed restaurant and room service is also available.

Moonta Bay Caravan Park (☎ 8825 2406; www .adelaidecaravanpark.com.au/moontabay.html; Tossell St; camp sites/cabins/cabins with bathroom $19/65/70; ✇) This park sits on top of a cliff, but is only a 50m walk from the beach. The fabulous views, TV and kids' playground are there for all to enjoy.

Cornish Kitchen (☎ 8825 3030; 16 Ellen St; snacks $3) This takeaway sells Cornish pasties, sandwiches and casual lunches.

There are also cafés near the jetties in the adjoining seaside towns of Port Hughes and Moonta Bay.

EAST COAST

The east coast road from the top of Gulf St Vincent down to Stenhouse Bay near Cape Spencer is generally within 1km to 2km of the sea. En route, tracks and roads lead to sandy beaches and secluded coves.

There are many small coastal townships, usually with a caravan park, cabins or camping ground, including tranquil **Port Vincent**. Good off-season deals for couples, families and friends can be made at the central and friendly **Port Vincent Holiday Cabins** (☎ 08-8853 7411; abins@netyp.com.au; 12 Main St; d $85; ✇).

Further south, **Edithburgh** has a tidal swimming pool in a small cove; from the cliff tops you can look across to **Troubridge Island lighthouse** and **conservation park**. Tours on request (minimum of four people) are $35, and overnight stays ($70 per person, minimum two nights) with sole occupancy of the island are also available in the old **lighthouse keeper's cottage**. Migratory birds also stop to visit the island's permanent inhabitants, an enchanting fairy penguin colony.

The district's inland business and administrative centre **Yorketown** (population 750) is a friendly place and you may find accommodation here when the seaside resorts are full over summer.

INNES NATIONAL PARK

The southern tip of the peninsula, marked by Cape Spencer, is part of the **Innes National Park**. The park has spectacular coastal scenery as well as good fishing, reef diving and surfing. You'll go a long way to find quieter emus! There's a $7 entry fee per vehicle for day entry. **Stenhouse Bay** just outside the park, and **Pondalowie Bay** within the park are the principal settlements. Pondalowie Bay is the base for a large lobster-fishing fleet and also has a fine surf beach hosting regular surfing events – you can watch from the viewing platform. Beaches in the park are swimmable, but you should keep an eye on the swell and wind direction.

In the park is the wreck of the steel barque *Ethel*, a 711-tonne ship that ran aground in 1904. All that remains are the ribs of the hull rising forlornly from the sands – her anchor is mounted in a memorial on the cliff top above the beach. Just past the Cape Spencer turn-off, a sign on the right directs you to the ruins of the **Inneston Historic Site**. Inneston was a gypsum-mining community abandoned in 1930.

With a permit from $7 to $17 per car per night (depending on facilities), you can choose from 150 **camp sites**, or you can stay at one of the heritage-listed and renovated **lodges** at Inneston (within the park). These cottages sleep either four or 10 people and range from $65 to $85 per night with good weekly discounts. Book ahead at the **NPWSA** (☎ 08-8854 3200; fax 8854 3299; Stenhouse Bay Rd; 9am-4.30pm Mon-Fri, daily during school holidays).

EYRE PENINSULA

The wide, triangular Eyre Peninsula points south between Spencer Gulf and the Great Australian Bight.

Sections of the Eyre Peninsula coast are extremely popular summer-holiday and recreational-fishing spots, with sheltered bays and pleasant little port towns. Along the spectacular wild western side are important breeding grounds for the southern right whale, the Australian sea lion and the great white shark – the scariest scenes in the film *Jaws* were shot here.

The peninsula is also a major destination for surfers from around the world; there are lots of excellent breaks along the coast, including the famous Cactus Beach. However it's not for the faint-hearted. The ocean rips can be vicious and sharks are a constant threat; in 2000 two surfers were taken in two days off Cactus Beach and Elliston, and others have since perished. Ask the locals about safe swimming beaches.

Although the Eyre Hwy from Port Augusta to Ceduna is much quicker than the coast road (468km), it's a fairly dull drive. If you have the time, it's much more interesting to take the coast road via Port Lincoln (763km).

Eyre Peninsula is also a major agricultural region, while rich iron-ore deposits in the Middleback Ranges are processed and shipped from the busy port of Whyalla. The peninsula takes its name from Edward John Eyre, the hardy explorer who, in 1841, made the first overland crossing between Adelaide and Albany, WA.

Tours

Nullarbor Traveller (☎ 1800 816 858, 08-8364 0407; www.the-traveller.com.au) is an award-winning company running seven-/nine-day trips ex-Perth to Adelaide and ex-Adelaide to Perth. A new backpacker tour explores the Eyre Peninsula over five days, incorporating Streaky Bay and swimming with sea lions at Baird Bay ($650).

Getting There & Away
AIR
Airlines of South Australia (☎ 1800 018 234; www .airlinesofsa.com.au) flies daily from Adelaide to Port Lincoln ($170, 1 hour) and Port Augusta ($178, 1 hour).

Rex (☎ 13 17 13; www.regionalexpress.com.au) flies daily from Adelaide to Ceduna ($315, 1½ hours), Port Lincoln ($190, 1 hour) and Whyalla ($180, 45 minutes).

BUS
Premier Stateliner (☎ 08-8415 5555) has daily services from Adelaide to Port Augusta ($36, 4 hours), Whyalla ($45, 5 hours), Port Lincoln ($75, 8½ hours), Ceduna ($85, 12 hours) and Streaky Bay ($75, 10 hours).

TRAIN
For details of train and bus services in the region, see p721.

PORT AUGUSTA
☎ 08 / pop 13,194
Matthew Flinders was the first European to set foot in the area, but the town of Port Augusta was not established until 1854. Industries have come and gone since then, and the town has obviously suffered economically – it is a sad and tatty place despite

SOUTH AUSTRALIA

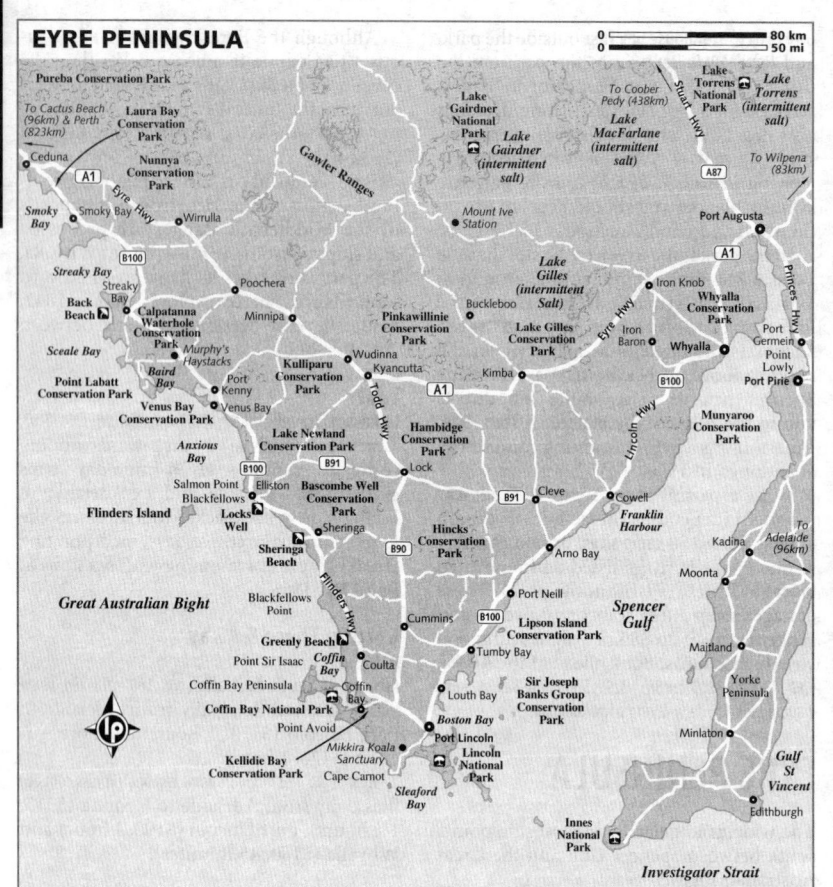

EYRE PENINSULA

being a major crossroads for travellers and the gateway to the outback.

From here, roads head west across the Nullarbor to WA, north to Alice Springs in the Northern Territory (NT), south to Adelaide and east to Broken Hill in NSW. With railway lines converging here, trains can be caught to Alice Springs and Darwin, the east and west coasts, Adelaide and Melbourne.

Information

The helpful and well-equipped **visitors centre** (☎ 8641 0793, 1800 633 060; www.portaugusta.sa.gov. au; 41 Flinders Tce; 🕑 9am-5.30pm Mon-Fri, 10am-4pm Sat & Sun) is a major information source for the Flinders Ranges and the SA outback.

The Eyre Peninsula is also well covered and there is Internet access.

The adjoining interpretative centre, the **Wadlata Outback Centre** (adult/child $9/5.50), is well worth a look. Numerous exhibits trace the histories of the Aboriginal and European people in the Flinders Ranges and outback. Nowadays remote outback education is conducted through satellite Internet access – a bit different from the old two-way radio in the kitchen. A demonstration shows how students use this ground-breaking technology.

Sights & Activities

Get a taste of how a phenomenal medical service operates: visit the **Royal Flying Doctor**

Service (☎ 8642 2044; 4 St Vincent St; admission by donation; 🕙 10am-3pm Mon-Fri).

Off the Stuart Hwy, **Australian Arid Lands Botanic Garden** (☎ 8641 1049; www.australian-arid lands-botanic-garden.org; 🕙 gardens 7am-sunset, visitors centre 9am-5pm Mon-Fri, 10am-4pm Sat & Sun) covers over 250 hectares on the northern edge of town. Tours ($6) operate at 11.30am Monday to Friday April to October and at 9.30am November to March.

Fountain Gallery (☎ 8642 4557; 43 Flinders Tce; 🕙 9am-4pm Mon-Fri) opens when there are exhibitions, as does **Curdnatta Art & Craft Gallery** (☎ 9641 0195; admission by donation; 105 Commercial Rd; 🕙 10am-4pm Mon-Fri) in Port Augusta's first train station.

Homestead Park Pioneer Museum (☎ 8642 2035; Elsie St; admission $2.50; 🕙 9am-4pm) features an original 1870s log-cabin homestead. The museum closes for an hour around lunch time.

On Saturday (returning Sunday) the **mail plane** flies to Boulia Queensland, making 26 stops along the way, including Innamincka and Birdsville. The return trip costs $660 and you'll need to book well in advance with **Airlines of South Australia** (☎ 1800 018 234, 8642 3100; augusta@airlinesofsa.com.au).

Sleeping & Eating
There are plenty of motels in Port Augusta, but little quality budget accommodation. Hotels are the best bet for meals.

Bluefox Lodge (☎ 8641 2960; www.bluefoxlodge .com; 8-10 Victoria Pde on National Hwy; dm $17) There are fairly cramped dorm rooms, but a cosy lounge, good kitchen and laundry at this friendly hostel. Pick-ups/drop-offs from the bus station are available until 10.30pm.

Hotel Flinders (☎ 8642 2544; fax 8641 0589; 39 Commercial Rd; s/d/tr $50/70/75) Tired rooms with bathrooms at this old hotel are worn and need a good airing.

Comfort Inn Augusta Westside (☎ 8642 2544; fax 8641 0589; 3 Loudon Rd; s/d $85/95; ⌘) One of life's enduring mysteries is why you need two toilet-roll holders in one bathroom. These motel rooms are uncomfortably stuffed with furniture designed to make you comfortable.

Pastoral Hotel Motel (☎ 8642 2818; fax 8641 0948; 17 Stirling Rd; motel s/d $80/90, hotel s/d $38/50; ⌘) There is a choice here: older budget rooms in the hotel, or clean and modern motel rooms in the car park.

Getting There & Away
AIR
Airlines of South Australia (☎ 1800 018 234, 8642 3100; augusta@airlinesofsa.com.au) has daily flights to Adelaide ($178).

BUS
The **bus station** for Premier Stateliner and McCafferty's/Greyhound is at 23 McKay St in the town centre. All the following are daily services unless specified.

Premier Stateliner (☎ 8642 5055) runs to Wilpena Pound on Wednesday, Friday and Sunday ($32, 2½ hours), Adelaide ($36, 4 hours), Port Lincoln ($50, 5 hours) and Ceduna ($70, 6½ hours).

McCafferty's/Greyhound (☎ 13 20 30; www.mc caffertys.com.au) travels to Coober Pedy ($70, 6 hours), Alice Springs ($170, 15½ hours) and Perth on Thursday only ($270, 30 hours).

TRAIN
The *Ghan* and *Indian Pacific* trains pass through Port Augusta, stopping at **Stirling Rd Station** (☎ 8642 6699). **Great Southern Railways** (☎ 13 21 47; www.trainways.com.au) offers excellent backpacker deals and discounts. These are some full-fare options departing from Port Augusta:

Adelaide (seat $38, 4 hours)
Alice Springs (seat/twin-share/1st-class sleepers $175/550/680, 16 hours)
Darwin (seat/twin-share/1st-class sleeper $410/1280/1600, 43 hours)
Perth (seat/twin-share/1st-class sleepers $280/850/1060, 33 hours)
Sydney (seat/twin-share/1st-class sleepers $270/590/740, 32 hours)

WHYALLA
☎ 08 / pop 21,271
An hour's drive from Port Augusta, Whyalla is a major steel-producing centre (with a deep-water port) that also supports oil and gas refineries. As the vast spread of towering chimneys, hideous port works and furnaces lurch into view, you'll be relieved to know that Whyalla is also a nuclear-free zone.

There is a surprisingly tiny central business district; the heart of the town is really a mall – the Westland Shopping Centre on Nicolson Ave.

The **visitors centre** (☎ 8645 7900; www.whyalla .sa.gov.au; Lincoln Hwy; 🕙 10am-4pm) is adjacent to the **Maritime Museum** (adult/child $6.60/3.30) featuring the 650-tonne, WWII corvette HMAS *Whyalla*. There are tours of the ship every hour from 11am to 3pm (included in the admission price).

Tours of the **Onesteel steel works** depart from the visitors centre at 9.30am Monday and Wednesday ($16). Long trousers, long-sleeved shirts and closed footwear are essential.

Thousands of **giant cuttlefish** used to flock here to spawn between May and August. Some protection has been given (from the decimating fishing industry) to this vastly important breeding ground. However, many say that it's not enough and that breeding cuttlefish are now greatly reduced in number. The dancing chameleons of the sea gather around Point Lowly and Black Point, where you can snorkel or dive to watch their graceful courtship. (For more information check out www.cuttlefishcapital.com.au.)

COWELL
☎ 08 / pop 792

Cowell is a pleasant little town near Australia's only large jade deposit – you can purchase a wide range of jade products from the Jade Motel at the northern end of town. Oysters are farmed locally – they're sold at several places for as little as $7 a dozen.

Cowell Jade Motel (☎ 8629 2002; fax 8629 2290; Lincoln Hwy; s/d/tr $67/77/133; 🞰) This classic old pub has a fine view of the town and harbour from its veranda.

COWELL TO PORT LINCOLN

The Lincoln Hwy keeps you close to the coast all the way to Port Lincoln. **Arno Bay** is a small beach resort with a pub and caravan park.

Further south is **Port Neill**, which is a pleasant little seaside town with a vintage-vehicle museum.

South again is **Tumby Bay**, with its long, curving white-sand beach, a National Trust **museum** (☎ 08-8688 2574; West Tce; admission $3; 🕑 2.30-4.30pm Fri & Sun), and a number of old buildings around the town. **Hales Mini Mart** (☎ 08-8688 2584; 1 Bratten Way; 🕑 7am-9pm) hires out boats.

PORT LINCOLN
☎ 08 / pop 12,664

The prosperous and bustling town of Port Lincoln, at the southern end of the Eyre Peninsula, is 662km from Adelaide. The first

settlers arrived in 1839 and the town has grown to become the tuna-fishing capital of Australia and a popular holiday spot, complete with marina and numerous sea-based activities.

Information

The consistently excellent **visitors centre** (☎ 8683 3544; www.visitportlincoln.net; 3 Adelaide Pl; 🕑 9am-5pm) also has national parks information and sells passes.

There are some good surfing and diving spots near the town. For information about the best areas, contact the **Port Lincoln Skin-Diving & Surfing Centre** (☎ 8682 4428; 1 King St), where licensed divers can hire scuba equipment (around $65 for a full set).

Sights & Activities

Celebrating the tuna industry, the **Tunarama Festival** is held over the Australia Day weekend in late January. There is keg rolling, slippery-pole climbing, a boat-building race, rodeo, stalls and bands, while the highlight of the festival is the tuna toss – the record distance for the toss is 37m for men and 17m for women.

Port Lincoln is well situated on Boston Bay. There are a number of historic buildings, including **Mill Cottage** (☎ 8682 4650; 20 Flinders Hwy; admission $4; 🕑 2-4.30pm Mon, Wed & Sat), built in 1866. The admission price includes a guided tour.

Various tours and activities can be booked through the visitors centre including **boat charters** and **yacht cruises** to off-shore islands and around Boston Bay, and **whale-watching** tours. Land-based tours include a day tour of the town and spectacular Whalers Way ($110) and a 4WD day-tour exploration of Coffin Bay Peninsula ($132).

Sleeping & Eating

There are a number of hotels, motels and holiday flats in and around town; the visitors centre has details on these and on the popular Kirton Point Caravan Park. There are plenty of restaurants in the city centre.

Grand Tasman Hotel (☎ 8682 2133; fran@grand tasmanhotel.com.au; 94 Tasman Tce; s/tw $50/75) The Grand Tasman is an upmarket pub with comfortable rooms on the foreshore. Local seafood is served in the bistro.

Blue Seas Motel (☎ 8682 3022; fax 8682 6932; 7 Gloucester Tce; s/d $65/75; 🞰) Great harbour views and a friendly atmosphere reinforce many recommendations for this motel.

AROUND PORT LINCOLN

Better known as Whalers Way, **Cape Carnot** is 32km south of Port Lincoln and features beautiful and rugged coastal scenery. It's privately owned but a 24-hour permit ($20 per car) enables you to visit and camp in this spectacular area. Buy the permit before you get out there. They're available from most petrol stations or the visitors centre in Port Lincoln.

These places also sell permits to **Mikkira Station and Koala Sanctuary** (☎ 08-8685 6020; on the road to Whalers Way; day permit/camping $12/17). This is the Eyre Peninsula's first sheep station and you can also visit its koala sanctuary. The owners of the station may give you a tour of the old homestead and property. There are camping areas and abundant birdlife including the attractive Port Lincoln parrots.

The beautiful beaches at **Sleaford Bay** are a 3km detour off the road to Whalers Way, but there's a strong rip so it's best not to swim.

Also south of Port Lincoln is **Lincoln National Park**, again with a magnificent coastline, including quiet coves with safe swimming and pounding surf beaches. Get a camping permit if you think you might want to stay – there's self-registration at the park entry ($7 per car). Most of the park's vehicle tracks are suitable for conventional vehicles but you will need a 4WD to visit tranquil **Memory Cove** – the visitors centre in Port Lincoln keeps the keys to the gate on this track for would-be happy campers ($19 per car).

PORT LINCOLN TO STREAKY BAY
Coffin Bay
☎ 08 / pop 453

Ominous-sounding Coffin Bay (it was named by Matthew Flinders to honour Sir Isaac Coffin) is a sheltered stretch of water with many quiet beaches and good fishing. The town of Coffin Bay is a popular holiday spot.

From here you can visit wild coastal scenery along the ocean side of Coffin Bay Peninsula, which is entirely taken up by **Coffin Bay National Park** ($7 per car). Access for conventional vehicles is limited within the park – you can get to scenic **Point Avoid** (a

good surf break) and **Yangie Bay** quite easily, but otherwise you need a 4WD.

Birdlife, including some unusual migratory species, is a feature of the **Kellidie Bay Conservation Park**, just outside Coffin Bay township.

Several places along the peninsula allow **bush camping** – generally with difficult access ($7 per car.) There are tonnes of holiday apartments covering all budgets.

Sheoak Holiday Homes (☎ 8686 4314; fax 8346 0485; 257-259 Esplanade; 2-6 persons $1125; 🐾) These upmarket seaside units are great value: modern and well equipped. Linen is $50 extra.

Mt Dutton Bay Woolshed Backpackers (☎ 8685 4031; www.duttonbay.com; 1 Woolshed Dr, Wangary; dm $20) This clean backpackers sits on the jetty; you'll need your own linen.

Coffin Bay Hotel (☎ 8685 4111; Sheppard Ave; d $75) This is the only pub in town, and it serves meals (around $18).

There are also a couple of **takeaways**.

Coffin Bay to Point Labatt

Just past **Coulta**, 40km north of Coffin Bay, there's good surfing at **Greenly Beach**. About 15km south of **Elliston** (a small resort and fishing town on peaceful Waterloo Bay), **Locks Well** is one of several good salmon-fishing spots along this wild coast. **Elliston** itself has holiday units/motel, two caravan parks, a pub, and a bakery which serves enormous cups of very good coffee.

Just north of Elliston, take the 7km detour to **Anxious Bay** and **Salmon Point** for some great ocean scenery – en route you will pass **Blackfellows**, which has some of the strongest waves on the west coast. From here you can see distant **Flinders Island**, where there's a sheep station and tourist accommodation.

At **Venus Bay** there are quiet beaches, plenty of pelicans and a small caravan park.

About 38km before Streaky Bay, the turn-off to **Point Labatt** takes you to one of the few permanent colonies of sea lions on the Australian mainland. You can view them from the cliff-top above the colony – take binoculars.

A few kilometres down the Point Labatt road are **Murphy's Haystacks**. This is the most impressive collection of inselbergs – these are curious granite outcrops (which are millions of years old) found at numerous places on the peninsula.

STREAKY BAY

☎ 08 / pop 1081

This attractive little town takes its name from the streaks of seaweed Flinders saw in the bay. The **visitors centre** (☎ 8626 1126; 15 Alfred Tce; 🕑 6.30am-9pm), in the Shell roadhouse/motel, has the cast of a 5.5m great white shark on display out the back, a replica of the biggest white pointer ever caught by rod and reel.

The National Trust **Streaky Bay Museum** (☎ 8626 1443; 42 Montgomerie Tce; admission by donation; 🕑 2-4pm Thu, 10am-noon & 2-5pm Fri) features a fully furnished pioneer hut.

Back Beach, 4km west of Streaky Bay, is good for surfing; there's some grand cliff scenery around the coast here.

There are lots of oyster farms out this way, as well as further along the coast at sleepy **Smoky Bay**. You can get fresh oysters from several outlets from as little as $8 a dozen.

Tours

Baird Bay Charters & Ocean Eco Tours (☎ 8626 5017; www.bairdbay.com; Lot 8, Government Rd, Baird Bay) have supervised swimming trips with dolphins and Australian sea lions in lovely Baird Bay, which are best taken between September and May ($70).

Sleeping & Eating

Streaky Bay Community Hotel (☎ 8626 1008; streakybayhotel@ozemail.com.au; 33-35 Alfred Tce; dm/s/d $25/60/75; ⛽) Right in the centre of town, this comfortable place serves good food, with pizzas on weekends ($16 to $19).

Foreshore Tourist Park (☎ 8626 1666; info@streakybayftpark.com.au; Wells St; 2-person camp sites/units $13/45) About 1km west of town, this park is thin on grass, but it's by a safe swimming beach. The adjoining kiosk does good takeaways.

The **Shell Roadhouse** (☎ 8626 1126; 15 Alfred Tce) has a self-contained unit (from $65).

CEDUNA

☎ 08 / pop 2588

Just past the junction of the Eyre and Flinders Hwys, Ceduna marks the end of the long, lonely drive across the Nullarbor Plain into WA. The town was established in 1896, although there had been a whaling station on St Peter Island, off nearby Cape Thevenard, back in 1850.

The **visitors centre** (☎ 1800 639 413, 8625 2780; www.ceduna.net; 58 Poynton St; 🕑 9am-5.30pm) is in Travelworld Ceduna, and onward coach tickets can be obtained here.

The National Trust's **Old Schoolhouse Museum** (2 Park Tce; 🕑 10am-noon Mon-Tue & Fri-Sat, 10am-noon & 2-4pm Wed-Thu) has pioneer exhibits as well as artefacts and newspaper clippings from the British atomic weapons programme at Maralinga.

There are many beaches and sheltered coves around Ceduna, with good surfing and fishing. **Laura Bay Conservation Park**, off the road to Smoky Bay 20km southwest of Ceduna, has mangroves and tidal flats that attract many species of sea birds and waders.

Sleeping & Eating

There are four caravan parks in Ceduna; ask about them at the visitors centre.

Highway One Motel (☎ 8625 2208; fax 8625 2866; 35 Eyre Hwy; s/d $70/75; ⛽) Renovated with comfortable facilities, and you are welcome to check in here day or night.

East West Motel (☎ 8625 2101; fax 8625 2829; 66-76 McKenzie St; s/d $75/80; ⛽) Also offering disabled access, this is one of the newer motels in the town.

Greenacres Backpackers (☎ 8625 3811; 12 Khulmann St; dm $17) Rates include breakfast at this small hostel.

Oyster Bar (☎ 8625 9086; Eyre Hwy; meals $8; 🕑 9.30am-6pm Mon-Sat, 1-6pm Sun) Head for the blue-and-white cabin by the big oyster at the information board. A serving of a dozen fresh oysters and a glass of wine is perfect fare – for finishing or beginning the long haul across the Nullarbor.

CEDUNA TO THE WA BORDER

It's 480km from Ceduna to the WA border and the only places with tourist facilities are at Penong (73km from Ceduna), Nundroo (151km), the Yalata Roadhouse (202km), the Nullarbor Hotel (294km) and the Border Village.

Wheat and sheep paddocks line the road to Nundroo, after which you're in attractive mallee until 50km beyond Yalata. Here the trees start to become sparser until petering out into a sea of shrubby bluebush 20km later. This is the true Nullarbor (derived from the Latin for 'no trees') and you travel through this surreal landscape for the next 40km or so.

Turn off the highway at **Penong** (population 200) and a 20km dirt road gets you to Point Sinclair and Cactus Beach.

Here you'll find **Cactus break**, one of Australia's most famous surfing breaks. Although Caves is the best break for experienced surfers, be warned that the locals don't take kindly to tourists dropping in. The area is private property but you can camp for $8; bring your own drinking water in summer.

Further west is **Head of Bight**, where southern right whales come in close to shore during their breeding season from June to October. Between 20 and 30 calves are born here each year, and you'll usually see several adult whales swimming close to the cliffs. There are excellent lookout points, like Twin Heads, but it's best if you have binoculars.

Head of Bight is on Aboriginal land – you can get entry permits ($8) and whale information from the **Yalata Roadhouse** and at the **White Well Ranger Station** on the way in to the viewing area. The signposted turn-off is 78km west of Yalata, and 14km east of the **Nullarbor Hotel/Motel** (Map p659).

You can also inspect **Murrawijinie Cave**, a large overhang behind the Nullarbor Hotel/Motel. There are several signposted coastal lookouts along the top of the 80m-high **Bunda Cliffs**.

Watch out for animals on the road if you're driving through here at night.

If you're heading west, dump all fruit, vegetables, cheese and plants as per quarantine regulations, and put your watch back 1½ hours or 2½ hours during daylight saving (from the last Sunday in October to the last Sunday in March).

Sleeping & Eating

There are basic caravan parks, budget and air-conditioned motel-style accommodation, restaurants and fuel sales at a number of places; you can also camp for free in roadside rest areas.

Penong Hotel (☎ /fax 08-8625 1050; Main St, Penong; s/d $33/45) This hotel on Penong's main street has very basic pub rooms (without fans), and serves evening meals.

Nundroo Hotel/Motel (☎ 08-8625 6120; fax 8625 6107; Eyre Hwy, Nundroo; dm/s/d/tr $18/70/85/120; ☒) There are also camp sites here ($13). If you're heading west, Nundroo has the last

mechanical repair service until Norseman, 1038km away.

Yalata Roadhouse (☎ 08-8625 6986; fax 8625 6987; ttj fisher@bigpond.com; Eyre Hwy, Yalata; d $65; ☺ 8am-8pm) Accommodation here is limited to two units (with linen) or the camping ground ($6), but you can get a meal at the restaurant.

Nullarbor Hotel/Motel (Map p659; ☎ 08-8625 6271; fax 8625 6261; Eyre Hwy, Nullarbor; camp sites $11, dm $19-32, s/d/tr $80/100/115; ☺ 7am-11pm) Both budget and motel rooms can be shared between a number of people. The hotel is licensed, offers meals and is close to the Head of Bight for whale watching. Also a service centre, it's 146km from the Yalata Roadhouse.

Border Village Motel (☎ 08-9039 3474; fax 9039 3473; Eyre Hwy, Border Village; camp sites/dm/s/d/f $11/25/80/90/85; ☒ ☐) This rebuilt motel has a variety of modern room and cabin options, all with air-con. It's licensed, serves meals, and has a swimming pool. The motel is on the WA–SA border, 186km west of the Nullarbor Hotel/Motel.

FLINDERS RANGES

The glowing red and purple folds of the majestic Flinders Ranges are the most spectacular sight in SA. Beloved of artists and bushwalkers alike, this ancient colossus rises from the northern end of the Spencer Gulf and runs 400km north into the arid outback. It's a superb area for wildlife and unique geological formations or for simply appreciating the outstanding beauty of the Australian bush. In the far north, the ranges are hemmed in by sand ridges and barren salt lakes.

As in many other dry regions of Australia, the vegetation here is surprisingly diverse and colourful. In the early spring, after good rains, the country is carpeted with wildflowers. In summer the days can be searingly hot but the nights usually cool down to a pleasant temperature. Winter and early spring are probably the best times to visit, although there are attractions at any time of the year.

In 1802, when Matthew Flinders landed near Port Augusta, several Aboriginal tribes lived in the region. You can visit some of their sites: the cave paintings at Yourambulla (near Hawker) and Arkaroo (near Wilpena); and the rock carvings at Sacred

SOUTH AUSTRALIA

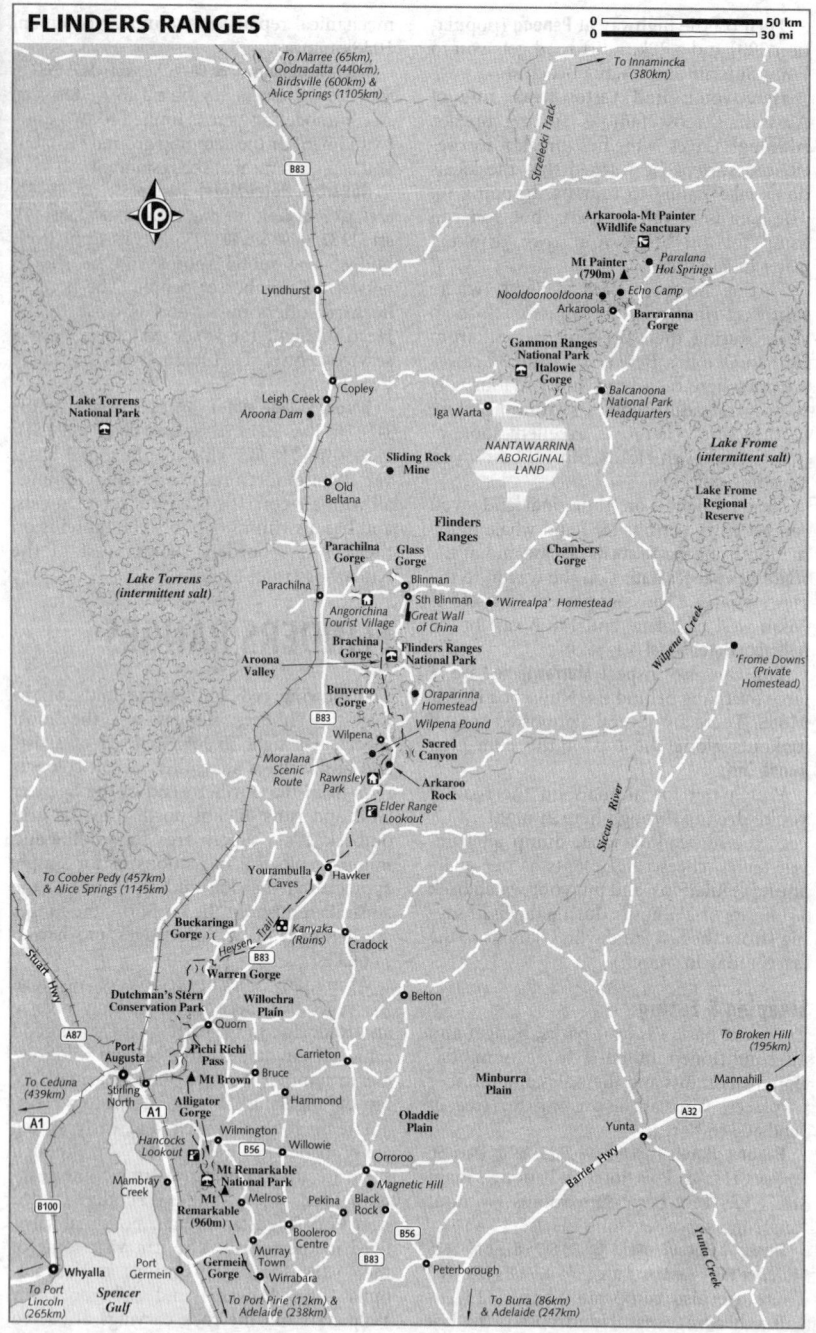

FLINDERS RANGES

0 —————————— 50 km
0 —————————— 30 mi

To Marree (65km),
Oodnadatta (440km),
Birdsville (600km) &
Alice Springs (1105km)

To Innamincka
(380km)

B83

Strzelecki Track

Arkaroola-Mt Painter
Wildlife Sanctuary

Mt Painter   Paralana
(790m)   Hot Springs

Nooldoonooldoona   Echo Camp
               Arkaroola
                         Barraranna
                         Gorge

Lyndhurst

Gammon Ranges
National Park
Italowie
Gorge

Copley   Iga Warta   Balcanoona
Leigh Creek   National Park
Aroona Dam   Headquarters

NANTAWARRINA
ABORIGINAL
LAND

Lake Torrens
National Park

Lake Frome
(intermittent salt)

Sliding Rock
Mine

Lake Frome
Regional
Reserve

Old
Beltana

Flinders
Ranges

Parachilna   Glass   Chambers
Gorge   Gorge   Gorge

Lake Torrens
(intermittent salt)

Parachilna   Blinman
                  Sth Blinman   'Wirrealpa' Homestead
Angorichina   Great Wall
Tourist Village of China

Brachina
Gorge   Flinders Ranges
             National Park

Aroona
Valley

                              'Frome Downs'
Wilpena Creek   (Private
                              Homestead)

Bunyeroo
Gorge   Oraparinna
              Homestead

B83   Wilpena Pound

Wilpena
         Sacred
Moralana Canyon
Scenic
Route   Rawnsley   Arkaroo
         Park   Rock

             Elder Range
             Lookout

Siccus River

To Coober Pedy (457km)
& Alice Springs (1145km)

Yourambulla   Hawker
Caves

Buckaringa   Kanyaka
Gorge   (Ruins)   Cradock

Heysen Trail

B83

Warren Gorge   Belton

Dutchman's Stern
Conservation Park

Willochra
Plain

To Broken Hill
(195km)

Port   Quorn
Augusta

A87   Pichi Richi   Carrieton
          Pass   Bruce
Stirling   Hammond   Mannahill
North

To Ceduna
(439km)

A1   Alligator
         Gorge   Willowie

Mambray
Creek

Whyalla

Spencer
Gulf

To Port
Lincoln
(265km)

Stuart Hwy

Minburra
Plain

Oladdie
Plain

Yunta   A32

Barrier Hwy

Mt Brown

Wilmington

B56

Hancocks
Lookout

Mt Remarkable
National Park

Mt
Remarkable
(960m)

Melrose

Orroroo

Magnetic Hill

Pekina   Black
           Rock

Boolooroo
Centre

Germein   Murray
Gorge   Town   Wirrabara

Port
Germein

Carrieton

B56

To Burra (86km)
& Adelaide (247km)

B100

To Port Pirie (12km) &
Adelaide (238km)

Peterborough

B83

A1

Yunta Creek

Canyon (near Wilpena) and remote Chambers Gorge.

Bushwalking is a major attraction of the area, but this is wild, rugged country and care should be taken before setting out. Wilpena Pound, the Arkaroola-Mt Painter Wildlife Sanctuary and Mt Remarkable National Park all have excellent walks, many of them along marked trails. The Heysen Trail (p661) ends in Parachilna Gorge, near Blinman, having come up through the Ranges.

Information

For good general and park trail information stop at the visitors centre in Port Augusta's **Wadlata Outback Centre** (☎ 1800 633 060, 08-8641 0793; www.portaugusta.sa.gov.au; 41 Flinders Tce, Port Augusta; ☼ 9am-5.30pm Mon-Fri, 10am-4pm Sat & Sun).

For national park inquiries (and passes) regarding the northern and central Flinders Ranges ask at the Wilpena Pound **visitors centre** (☎ 08-8648 0048; admin@wilpenapound.com.au; ☼ 8am-6pm daily), in the Flinders Ranges National Park headquarters.

For the southern Flinders (ie south of Quorn) contact the **NPWSA office** (☎ 08-8648 5300, for all desert parks inquiries 1800 816 078; www.parks.sa.gov.au; 9 McKay St, Port Augusta; ☼ 8.45am-5pm Mon-Fri) in Port Augusta.

You'll need a good map of the area as there are many back roads and a variety of road surfaces. According to local experts, Westprint puts out the most accurate touring map, Hema's is recommended and the RAA's map is also very good. Westprint and Hema's maps can be found at most map and book shops while RAA maps can be purchased from its own outlets.

Tours

You may prefer to take the **Premier Stateliner** coach from Adelaide (see Bus; following) and pick up tours departing from Port Augusta, Quorn, Hawker, Wilpena Pound, Iga Warta and Arkaroola. Local visitors centres and backpacker hostels will have details of these.

A number of operators offer different types of tours ex-Adelaide, check with visitors centres.

Specialised walking tours are led by professional guides from **Ecotrek & Bogong Jack Adventures** (☎ 08-8383 7198; www.ecotrek.com.au), with seven-day tours inclusive of meals, beds and wine (from $1230).

For those who prefer a more sedate coach trip, **Adelaide Sightseeing** (☎ 08-8231 4144; www.adelaidesightseeing.com.au; 101 Franklin St, Adelaide) has two-day coach tours, with one night at Wilpena Pound ($559 inclusive).

Sleeping

Motels, hotels, hostels and self-contained cottages (around $75 a night) can normally be found in the townships.

Old working (farming) stations have budget rooms (favoured by backpacker tours), and most hotels cater for both budget and mid-range travellers. Book ahead to beat the tour groups.

Visitors centres have comprehensive listings, or contact the **Flinders Ranges Accommodation Booking Service** (☎ 1800 777 880, 08-8648 4022; www.frabs.com.au).

Getting There & Away

BUS

Premier Stateliner (☎ 08-8415 5555) runs from Adelaide on Wednesday and Friday to Wilpena Pound ($65, 7 hours), Quorn ($50, 5 hours) and Hawker ($60, 6 hours). Return trips are on Thursday, Friday and Sunday.

CAR

There are good sealed roads all the way north to Wilpena Pound and Leigh Creek. The Marree road skirting the western edge of the Flinders Ranges is sealed to Lyndhurst.

Check with NPWSA offices for current information, as gravel roads can be closed by heavy rain. For recorded information on road conditions in the Flinders Ranges and the outback call ☎ 1300 361 033.

Getting Around

If you have a vehicle you can make a loop that takes you around an interesting section of the central part of the ranges. From Wilpena Pound continue north through the Flinders Ranges National Park past Oraparinna Homestead, then veer west through Brachina Gorge to the main Leigh Creek road.

Brachina Gorge has a self-guided **geology trail** with information signs en route – pick up a leaflet from the Wilpena visitors centre (p729). You can then either turn back to Hawker (directly or via the Moralana Scenic Route), or head north to Parachilna and take the scenic road east through Parachilna

Gorge and Blinman, before heading south back to Wilpena through the national park.

If you want to see the spectacular northern ranges head east from South Blinman to Wirrealpa Homestead, where you swing north via Chambers Gorge to meet the Frome Downs road south of Balcanoona. Continue up to Arkaroola, then head back to the sealed road through Gammon Ranges National Park via Italowie Gorge. You'll need a car with decent clearance to take this route.

QUORN

☎ 08 / pop 1005

The picturesque gateway to the Flinders is about 330km north of Adelaide and 40km northeast of Port Augusta. Quorn is the area's main service town, and is an agreeable place to stop, with a friendly community. It became an important railway town after the completion of the Great Northern Railway in 1878, and it still retains the atmosphere of its pioneering days.

The **visitors centre** (☎ 8648 6419; www.flinders rangescouncil.sa.gov.au/tourism; 3 Seventh St; ☻ 9am-5pm) is next to the council chambers.

The railway closed in 1957, but now a vintage tourist train – often pulled by a steam engine – follows the *Old Ghan* railway route through the scenic Pichi Richi Pass to Port Augusta and Woolshed. **Pichi Richi Railway** (☎ 8633 0380; www.prr.org.au; train station, Railway Tce) operates between April and November, return trips depart from Port Augusta ($58, Saturday) and Quorn ($32, public holidays). Train buffs should ask about tours of the **railway workshop** when the trains are running.

There are several good walks in Pichi Richi Pass out on the Port Augusta road, including the **Waukerie Creek Trail** and the **Heysen Trail** (p661). Closer to town are walks at **Dutchman's Stern** and **Devil's Peak**.

Tours

Some small operators offer 4WD trips, which go off road and really allow you to see the Flinders in their full glory.

Ozzie's Bush Track Tours (☎ 8648 6567; www .abouttozzietours.com; 22 Pool St) is run by a volunteer fire fighter who really understands the bush. He offers bush walks ($11), five-day tours to Arkaroola ($850 inclusive), and a popular half-day tour to nearby Dutchman

Stern Conservation Park ($65). Minimum numbers apply.

Wallaby Tracks Adventure Tours (☎ 8648 6655; www.headingbush.com/andulodge.html) runs recommended and good-value tours with interesting itineraries. These depart from Quorn and Port Augusta, and there are packages ex-Adelaide ($99 to $299).

Sleeping & Eating

Andu Lodge (☎ 8648 6655; www.headingbush.com /andulodge.html; 12 First St; dm/s/d $20/30/50) This is a very good YHA hostel in the old hospital, with spacious dorms, excellent facilities and a quiet, comfortable atmosphere. It also runs **Wallaby Tracks Adventure Tours**. Transfers to and from Port Augusta are $16, free if you take a tour. There's Internet access, and bed linen and breakfast are inclusive.

Transcontinental Hotel (☎ 8648 6076; fax 8648 6759; 15 Railway Tce; s/d $32/55; ✸) This genial family-run pub has a lively clientele, pleasant rooms and cheap bar food.

Flinders Ranges Motel (☎ 8648 6016; fax 8648 6279; 2 Railway Tce; s/d $70/80; ☻ 10am-5pm; ✸) A neat and tidy little motel, the staff keep strict office hours.

HAWKER

☎ 08 / pop 298

Hawker is 55km south of Wilpena Pound. This place is a popular pit stop for truckies and coach tours and is consequently a functional place.

Hawker's chatty and helpful **visitors centre** (☎ 8648 4014; www.hawkermotors.com.au; cnr Wilpena & Cradock Rds; ☻ 7.30am-6pm) has Internet access and wide-ranging information. The centre is based in Hawker Motors (at the Mobil service station).

Sights

About 10km south of Hawker are the impressive **Kanyaka ruins** (Map p726), all that's left of a sheep station founded in 1851. Close by, picturesque **Kanyaka Waterhole** is overlooked by the so-called **Death Rock**.

There are Aboriginal rock paintings 12km west of Hawker at **Yourambulla Caves** (Map p726), three rock shelters high up on the side of Yourambulla Peak; the first one is a 1km walk from the car park. **Jarvis Hill Lookout** is about 6km west of Hawker and affords good views over Hawker and north to Wilpena Pound.

The **Moralana Scenic Route** (Map p726) is a return-trip drive from Hawker, taking in the magnificent scenery along the Elder and Wilpena Pound ranges. It is 24km to the Moralana turn-off, then 28km along an unsealed road (take this road in the morning to avoid sun glare) that joins up with the sealed Hawker to Leigh Creek road. From here it's 46km back to Hawker.

Both the town's caravan parks offer 4WD tours.

Sleeping & Eating

Hawker Hotel/Motel (☎ 8648 4102; fax 8648 4151; 80 Elder Tce; s/d $35/55; ✷) The small hotel rooms are cheaper and a better bet than the smelly motel units beloved by truckies, who have made this hotel their own.

Flinders Ranges Caravan Park (☎ 8648 4266; jsitters@flinderscpk.com.au; 1 Leigh Creek Rd; 2-person camp sites/caravans/cabins $18/45/50; ✷) About 1km from town on the Leigh Creek road, this spacious and friendly place has a very good kitchen.

Outback Chapmanton Motor Inn (☎ 8648 4100; fax 8648 4109; 1 Wilpena Rd; s/d $75/90; ✷) Nice and clean units offer standard comforts and this is definitely the best accommodation in town.

Old Ghan Restaurant (☎ 8648 4176; Leigh Creek Rd; mains $7-17; ✷ 10.30am-late Wed-Sun) This attractive restaurant offers lunch specials for $8.50 and has a small art gallery.

WILPENA POUND

The large natural basin of Wilpena Pound is the best-known feature of the ranges and the main attraction in the 94,908-hectare **Flinders Ranges National Park** (Map p726). Covering about 80 sq km, it is generally accessible via the narrow gap through which Wilpena Creek exits the pound. On the outside, the external wall soars almost sheer for 500m; inside, the basin slopes away from the encircling ridge top.

There is plenty of wildlife in the park, particularly euros (hill kangaroos), red and grey kangaroos, and birds – everything from rosellas, galahs and budgerigars to emus and wedge-tailed eagles. You may even see endangered yellow-footed rock wallabies, whose numbers are increasing now that fox and rabbit populations are being controlled. **Brachina Gorge** (Map p726) is a good spot to see these beautiful animals.

Sacred Canyon (Map p726), with its many petroglyphs (rock carvings), is 20km east from the visitors centre on a rough road. To the north and still within the national park are striking scenic attractions, such as **Bunyeroo Gorge** (Map p726), **Brachina Gorge** (Map p726) and the **Aroona Valley**. There are several bush-camping areas, most accessible by 2WD. The 20km **Brachina Gorge Geological Trail** (you follow it in your car) features an outstanding geological sequence of exposed sedimentary rock.

The **visitors centre** (☎ 08-8648 0048; admin@wilpenapound.com.au; park entry/camping per car $7/11; ✷ 8am-6pm) is in Wilpena Resort, near the pound entrance. The centre also has plenty of tourist information on the district.

Activities
BUSHWALKING

Solo walks are not recommended. Also be sure that you are adequately equipped – particularly with drinking water, maps and sun protection. It's worth noting that searches are no longer initiated by rangers – so let someone know where you're headed and when you expect to return from your walk.

The park has a number of marked walking trails (sections that incorporate parts of the Heysen Trail are indicated by red markers) and these are listed in a free NPWSA leaflet. Topographical maps (scale 1:50,000) are available from the park's visitors centre.

Most of the walks start from the visitors centre, which is near the main camp site. They vary from short walks suitable for people with small children, to those only suitable for experienced and super-fit trekkers. One of the latter is **St Marys Peak** and **Tanderra Saddle**, from which you can enjoy the white glimmer of **Lake Torrens** off to the west, the beautiful Aroona Valley to the north, and the pound spread out below your feet.

For the rest of us mere mortals, a popular three-hour walk is **Ohlssen Bagg**, which will take you to the top of the mountain that sits on the rim above the resort. The views here are tremendous, as they are in spring from the **Arkaroo Rock** (Map p726) which is about 10km south of Wilpena off the Hawker road. It takes around 3km to walk from the car park to the rock shelter, where there are well-preserved Aboriginal paintings.

Wangara Hill lookout is a 7km return walk and **Cooinda** is the bush-camping area within the pound.

Tours

Ask for specific recommendations about **tag-along tour operators** (4WD self-drive) at the local visitors centre.

The most popular **scenic flights** from Wilpena Resort are the cheaper 20- and 30-minute flights covering Wilpena and immediate surrounds ($80 to $310).

The Wilpena Resort also runs **4WD day tours**, one trip taking the stunning Arkaroola Ridge-top track (from $110).

Sleeping & Eating

Groceries and last-minute camping requirements are available at the well-stocked store in the visitors centre.

Wilpena Pound Resort (☎ 08-8648 0004; www .wilpenapound.com.au; Wilpena Rd; dm/d $22/115; ※) This resort is just outside the pound, has all mod cons including a swimming pool, and nice but overpriced motel-style units. All rooms including dorms have air-con, but no kitchen facilities – a shame as the bar/bistro serves pretty lacklustre food.

The camping ground at the resort has two-person sites ($17), while bush camping within the national park costs $11 per car per night. You can pay all camping fees at the visitors centre.

Rawnsley Park (☎ 08-8648 0030; www.rawnsley park.com.au; Wilpena Rd; camp sites/caravans $18/45, cabins $60-95; ※ 🖵) Off the Hawker road, about 20km south of Wilpena and close to the pound's outer edge, this park is popular with backpacking tours. There are several good bushwalks from here, and you can also take two-hour horse trail-rides ($60), 4WD tours, or hire mountain bikes for an extortionate $50 per day. The licensed restaurant has pasta-style mains ($18 to $21) and opens 6.30pm to 8.30pm.

BLINMAN

☎ 08 / pop 16

A copper-mining centre from the 1860s to the 1890s, today Blinman is a quaint hamlet on the circular route around the Flinders Ranges National Park.

About 1km to the north of town is the historic **Blinman copper mine**, which has walking trails and interpretive signs.

Alpana Station (☎ 8648 4864; fax 8648 4661; Blinman-Wilpena Rd; cottage $200) Prices given for this cottage (on the station grounds) are for up to four people per night. However, visitors must stay for a minimum of two nights (linen is an extra $10 per head). Bare even by budget standards, there is a bonus: no dogs or guns are permitted! Situated 5km south of Blinman, there are 4WD tours and guided walks.

Blinman Hotel (☎ 8648 4867; blinman@senet.com .au; Mine Rd; s/d/tr $60/85/105; ※) This place has a real outback-pub flavour, and is a tad run-down. Who cares? There's a pool, the bar is a state legend and the dining room serves pizza (meals $9 to $16).

AROUND BLINMAN

Dramatic **Chambers Gorge** (Map p726), 64km to the northeast of Blinman towards Arkaroola, features a striking gallery of Aboriginal rock carvings. From Mt Chambers you can see over Lake Frome to the east and all along the Flinders Ranges from Mt Painter in the north to Wilpena Pound in the south.

An inspiring scenic drive links Blinman with Parachilna to the west, where there's the wonderful and renowned **Prairie Hotel**. This route takes you through **Parachilna Gorge** (Map p726) and past some lovely picnic and camping spots – the gorge marks the northern end of the **Heysen Trail** (p661).

North of Parachilna, on the Leigh Creek road, you turn east at the Beltana Roadhouse to get to historic **Old Beltana** (11km). This small settlement almost became a ghost town, but is now inhabited by artists and refugees from the rat race. There are boards with information on the town's heritage, or ask at the friendly **Beltana Roadhouse** (☎ 08-8675 2744; Main St, Beltana; ⏰ 8am-6pm).

Sleeping & Eating

Prairie Hotel (☎ 08-8648 4844; www.prairiehotel.com .au; Hawker-Leigh Creek Rd, Parachilna; camp sites/dm/d $13/21/130; ※ 🖵) Another state icon, this busy hotel at tiny Parachilna (population 5) is a real oasis of luxury in the harsh outback. Tastefully appointed rooms with private facilities and dorm rooms share a swimming pool, telephone and ATM. Famous for its local wildlife and menu – 'we came, we saw, we ate it' – the award-winning food is Australian bush tucker: camel, 'roo and emu dishes ($10 to $24).

FLINDERS RANGES DREAMING

The almost palpable 'spirit of place' of the Flinders Ranges has inspired a rich heritage of Aboriginal Dreaming stories. Many of these legends – some secret, but some related by Adnyamathanha elders – explain the creation of the landscape and the native birds and animals that inhabit it.

Arkaroola comes from Arkaroo, the name of a giant serpent ancestor. Suffering from a powerful thirst, Arkaroo drank Lake Frome dry, then carved out the sinuous Arkaroola Creek as he dragged his bloated body back into the ranges. He went underground to sleep it off, but all that salty water had given him a bellyache. The rumblings from his belly explain the 30 to 40 small earth tremors that occur in this area each year.

Another story relates that the walls of Wilpena Pound (Ikarra) are the bodies of two serpents (Akurra). They'd coiled up around an initiation ceremony, then created a whirlwind and devoured most of the participants.

In another story the bossy eagle Wildu, seeking revenge on his nephews who had tried to kill him, built a great fire. All the birds, which were originally white, were caught in the flames and emerged blackened and burnt. The magpies and willie wagtails were partially scorched, but the crows were entirely blackened and have remained so until this day.

Iga Warta is an Adnyamathanha centre offering Aboriginal cultural tours of the region. It's named after the Iga family who moved along a Dreaming path through the Flinders Ranges – their spirits are in the Iga trees of the area.

Angorichina Tourist Village and Store (☎ 08-8648 4842; www.angorichinavillage.com.au; Parachilna Gorge Rd; camp sites/s/d $9/21/60;) This dusty park in Parachilna Gorge boasts a magnificent setting, with steep hills all around. Shared cabins are fairly priced, if short on facilities. Be aware: dorms get booked out by backpacker tours. You can hire mountain bikes for a staggering $50 per day.

LEIGH CREEK & COPLEY

Leigh Creek (population 690) was developed in 1980 when the original settlement was demolished to make way for mining. The huge open-cut coal mine supplies Port Augusta power station. Landscaping has created a green suburban environment, reminiscent of Canberra in the desert. The old railway town of Copley (population 100), 5km north of Leigh Creek, is on the turn-off to Arkaroola.

About 60km from Leigh Creek, on the Arkaroola Rd, **Iga Warta** (Map p726; ☎ 08-8648 3737; www.igawarta.com; Arkaroola Rd, via Copley), run by members of the local Adnyamathanha Aboriginal community, offers a range of cultural tours that focus on the surrounding country and Aboriginal history (from $63). There are also bush tucker walks ($29) and campfire stories ($20). You can use the camp site ($15) with tents and swags for hire ($15).

From Leigh Creek you can also visit the scenic **Aroona Dam** (Map p726), 10km to the west, and **Gammon Ranges National Park** (Map p726), 100km to the east.

For information on Gammon Ranges National Park contact the local **NPWSA office** (☎ 08-8648 4829; Balcanoona) or the **NPWSA office** (☎ 08-8648 5300, for all desert parks inquiries 1800 816 078; www.parks.sa.gov.au; 9 McKay St, Port Augusta; 8.45am-5pm Mon-Fri).

Sleeping & Eating
Leigh Creek Tavern (☎ 08-8675 2025; www.leighcreektavern.com.au; s/tw/d $70/80/100;) This central inn offers cabins and motel rooms, a swimming pool and a good restaurant.

Copley Caravan Park (☎ /fax 08-8675 2288; www.copleycaravan.com.au; Railway Tce West; 2-person camp sites/cabins from $18/60;) This friendly park provides tourist information and has cabins with bathrooms ($80).

Sue Tulloch's Bush Bakery (☎ 08-8675 2683; Railway Tce; 8.30am-5pm Easter-Nov) This excellent bakery is Copley's main tourist attraction, specialising in quandong dishes (a native fruit).

ARKAROOLA
☎ 08

The 61,000-hectare **Arkaroola-Mt Painter Wildlife Sanctuary** (Map p726) sprawls across rugged and spectacular country near the northern end of the Flinders Ranges.

You can stay in the **Arkaroola Resort & Wilderness Sanctuary** (☎ 1800 676 042, 8648 4848;

www.arkaroola.on.net; Arkaroola Rd Camp; 2-person camp site/cabin/motel $15/30/65; [icon]), which offers good facilities, including a cosy bar/restaurant, small supermarket and service station. There are nice camp sites down along the creek.

There are several tours organised by the resort, including the highly recommended, half-day 4WD Ridgetop Tour ($71) through wild mountain scenery, passing close to magnificent **Mt Painter**. Another excellent tour ($30) allows you to view the heavens through a high-powered telescope at the sanctuary's **Astronomical Observatory**.

Dirt roads and tracks lead to **Paralana Hot Springs** (Map p726), rock pools at **Barraranna Gorge** and **Echo Camp**, and to water holes at **Arkaroola** and **Nooldoonooldoona**.

You can take a guided or tag-along tour, or do your own thing. Most places of interest are accessible to conventional vehicles, with some hiking involved.

OUTBACK

The area north of Eyre Peninsula and the Flinders Ranges stretches into the vast, empty red spaces of SA's outback. Although sparsely populated and often difficult to travel through, it is possible if you're properly prepared.

Note that fuel outlets, repair facilities and spare parts are often extremely limited, so be prepared in case of breakdown. Always travel with two spare tyres and enough water for several days; 5L per person per day in winter, 10L in summer.

The many brave (some foolhardy) explorers who mapped and equipped the state with communication systems managed to cross the 'big red' without air-conditioned vehicles! However, for us softies, it's not wise to stray far from the few main roads without a 4WD or camels.

Entry permits are required for large parts of the northwest (which are either Aboriginal land, desert parks or the Woomera Prohibited Area).

Information

The main visitors centre is in Port Augusta's **Wadlata Outback Centre** (☎ 08-8641 0793, 1800 633 060; www.portaugusta.sa.gov.au; 41 Flinders Tce, Port Augusta; ⊙ 9am-5.30pm Mon-Fri, 10am-4pm Sat & Sun).

For information on national parks and an update on the park permit system, contact the **NPWSA office** (☎ 08-8648 5300, desert parks inquiries 1800 816 078; www.parks.sa.gov.au; 9 McKay St, Port Augusta; ⊙ 8.45am-5pm Mon-Fri).

For information on the outback roads check with the state automobile associations or call the **Desert Parks Hotline** (☎ 1800 816 078).

Westprint does a good range of maps covering outback tracks. For more details on outback travel, see Lonely Planet's *Outback Australia*.

NATIONAL PARK PERMITS

To visit most of the outback's conservation areas you need a Desert Parks Pass, which costs $90 per vehicle. It's valid for a year and includes an excellent information book, detailed routes and area maps.

Desert Parks Passes are available from the following locations:

NPWSA regional offices (☎ 1800 816 078; www .parks.sa.gov.au)

Adelaide RAA (www.raa.net/); Environment Shop (Map pp668-9; ☎ 08-8204 1910; www.parks.sa.gov.au; 77 Grenfell St, Adelaide; ⊙ 9am-5pm Mon-Fri)

Alice Springs Shell Mt Gillen service station (☎ 08-8952 23476; Larapinta Dr, Alice Springs)

Birdsville Mobil service station and police station

Coober Pedy Underground Books (☎ 08-8672 5558; Post Office Hill Rd, Coober Pedy; ⊙ 8.30am-5pm Mon-Fri, 10am-4pm Sat)

Hawker Hawker Motors (☎ 08-8648 4014; Wilpena Rd, Hawker)

Innamincka Trading Post (☎ 08-8675 9900; fax 8675 9920)

Marree Outback Roadhouse (☎ 08-8675 9900; Railway Tce, North Marree)

Mt Dare Homestead (☎ 08-8670 7835; Witjira National Park)

Oodnadatta Pink Roadhouse (☎ 08-8670 7822; Main St, Oodnadatta; ⊙ 8am-5.30pm); Oodnadatta Hotel (☎ /fax 08-8670 7804; oodnadattahotel@bigpond.com; Main St, Oodnadatta)

Port Augusta Wadlata Outback Centre (☎ 1800 633 060, 08-8641 0793; www.portaugusta.sa.gov.au; 41 Flinders Tce, Port Augusta; ⊙ 9am-5.30pm Mon-Fri, 10am-4pm Sat & Sun)

William Creek William Creek Store & Campground (☎ 08-8670 7746; www.williamcreekcampground.com; Oodnadatta Track)

If you just want to visit Cooper Creek in the Innamincka Regional Reserve, Lake Eyre in the Lake Eyre National Park or Dalhousie

Springs in the Witjira National Park, you need only buy a day/night permit for $18 per vehicle. Camping permits are also available from Mt Dare Homestead, the Pink Roadhouse in Oodnadatta, William Creek Store & Campground, Marree Outback Roadhouse and the rangers at Innamincka and Dalhousie Springs.

Tours

There are a number of six- to 10-day tours ex-Adelaide and ex-Alice Springs that explore the outback. These take in the Flinders Ranges, Oodnadatta Track, Coober Pedy, Uluru and Kings Canyon (from $630 to $1000).

Operators include **Adventure Tours Australia** (☎ 1300 654 604, 08-8309 2299; www.adventuretours .com.au), and the backpacker tour groups **Wayward Bus** (☎ 1800 882 823, 08-8410 8833; www.waywardbus.com.au) and **Groovy Grape Getaways** (☎ 1800 661 177; www.groovygrape.com.au).

Getting There & Around

CAR

The Stuart Hwy is sealed all the way from Port Augusta to Darwin. The highway is a long, often boring drive and the temptation to get it over with quickly has resulted in many high-speed collisions between cars and cattle, sheep, kangaroos and wedge-tailed eagles. Take care, particularly at night time.

If you want to travel to NT by a more adventurous route, there's the **Oodnadatta Track**. This option takes you from Port Augusta through the Flinders Ranges to Leigh Creek, Lyndhurst, Marree and Oodnadatta before joining the Stuart Hwy at Marla, about 180km south of the NT border. For most of the way it runs close to the defunct *Old Ghan* train line.

The road is sealed as far as Lyndhurst, then you are on dirt (and often rough and dusty dirt, at that) all the way to Marla. There are several routes across to the Stuart Hwy: from Lake Eyre south via Roxby Downs to Pimba; from William Creek west to Coober Pedy; and from Oodnadatta either south to Coober Pedy or west to Cadney Homestead (a roadhouse on the Stuart Hwy). With a 4WD you can keep going up the old railway line from Oodnadatta to Alice Springs, visiting Witjira National Park and Old Andado Homestead on the way.

If you don't have your own vehicle it's also possible to catch a bus to Roxby Downs (p735) or Coober Pedy (p739) from Adelaide and hire a 4WD from there to explore Lake Eyre and the Oodnadatta Track.

Two other routes of interest to outback travellers are the legendary **Birdsville Track** (p741) and **Strzelecki Track** (p741). These days the tracks have been so much improved that it's usually quite feasible to travel them in any car that's in good condition and has reasonable ground clearance.

The SA outback includes much of the **Simpson Desert** and the harsh, rocky landscape of the **Sturt Stony Desert**. There are also huge salt lakes that fill with water every once in a long while. **Lake Eyre**, used by Donald Campbell for his attempt on the world's land-speed record in the 1960s, filled to capacity in 1974. Since then it has had water in it a number of times, including 1976, 1989, 1997 and 2000.

When soaking rain does fall on this usually dry land the effect can be amazing – flowers bloom and plants grow at a breakneck pace in order to complete their life cycles before the drought returns. There is even a species of water-holding frog that goes into suspended animation, remaining in the ground for years on end, only to pop up when the rains come again.

On a much more mundane level, roads can either be washed out or turned into gluelike mud. Venture into the wrong place after heavy rain and you may be stuck for days – or even weeks.

TRAIN

For information on the *Ghan*, see p806.

WOOMERA

☎ 08 / pop 602

Just off the Stuart Hwy, Woomera is a rather drab-looking government town with its roots in early British weapons testing and space rocket programmes. More recently it's been in the news as a proposed low-level nuclear waste dump and for a controversial detention centre (for further information, see the boxed text 'Secrets in the Desert'; p734).

Woomera Board Heritage Centre (☎ 8673 7042; Dewrang St; ☼ 9am-5pm), in the middle of town, has displays on Woomera's past and

SECRETS IN THE DESERT

The arid outback of South Australia (SA) can seem like the most inhospitable place in the world. Despite being the homeland of many different Aboriginal societies, the area is often viewed as the middle of nowhere. This, combined with the tiny population and unique environmental profile, means that SA's remotest regions have become centre stage for some major international dramas.

At Maralinga, near the Trans-Australia railway line, the British government detonated seven atomic bombs between 1952 and 1963 and conducted hundreds of other nuclear trials. The tests were carried out on the traditional lands of the Maralinga Tjarutja Aboriginal people, and although they were forcibly removed from the test site to places such as Yalata, many Aboriginal people were exposed to airborne radioactive fallout.

The 1985 Royal Commission into British Nuclear Tests in Australia brought about a cleanup that was completed in 2000; however, serious doubts were raised about its efficacy. In 2003 the land was due to be returned to the traditional Aboriginal owners.

Meanwhile, many of SA's desert regions have been put to use in the nuclear industry. The uranium-mining component of operations at Olympic Dam near Roxby Downs has long been controversial, while the US-owned Beverley Uranium Mine, opened in 2000 near the Flinders Ranges, has attracted criticism because of its *in-situ* leach extraction process. Environmentalists and traditional owners fear it will contaminate precious ground-water supplies. There are also plans to locate another uranium mine in the SA desert.

Woomera, 490km north of Adelaide, was used to launch top-secret experimental British rockets and conduct tests in an abortive European project to send a satellite into orbit during the 1950s and 1960s. The Woomera Prohibited Area occupies a vast stretch of land in the centre of the state and Woomera itself was closed to outsiders until 1982.

In 1971 the town's main business became servicing the mostly US personnel working at the Joint Defence Facility at Nurrungar, a short distance south. During the Cold War this facility was a pivotal component in US defence strategy and was reportedly on Russia's list of top 10 nuclear targets. More recently the spy station played a crucial role in monitoring Iraqi missile launches during the 1991 Gulf War, attracting strong protests from the Kokatha traditional owners and peace activists.

When the Nurrungar facility closed in October 1999, the town's population dropped dramatically and it became the uncomfortable host to the Woomera Detention Centre. Illegal immigrants and asylum seekers who entered Australia without a visa were locked up here while immigration authorities determined whether they were genuine refugees. Detainees were predominantly Middle Eastern and Southeast Asian refugees.

The lengthy application (and appeals) process helped create a tinderbox; riots, hunger strikes and attempts at escape into the surrounding desert played across Australia's TV screens. In 2003 the centre was downgraded to a backup facility.

Woomera has been pinning its hopes on a plan to use the rocket range for commercial satellite launches. However, the more likely resurgence will come from federal government plans to build a national dump for low-level radioactive waste in the region.

present roles and what may happen in the future. The given information is very sanitised. Outside is a collection of old military aircraft, rockets and missiles.

Eldo Hotel (☎ 8673 7867; woomeraeurest@bigpond.com; Kotara Cres; d/tw $65/75; ✷) This large hotel was originally built to house the space programme personnel. Facilities include a bar, pokies and bar food ($15 to $20).

Woomera Travellers' Village (☎ 8673 7800; fax 8673 7700; cnr Banool & Old Pimba Rds; 2-person camp sites/cabins/units $7/50/70; ✷) This place is a well-maintained and helpful park.

ROXBY DOWNS
☎ 08 / pop 3620

Roxby Downs is a modern, pleasantly landscaped town in sandy desert 92km from the Stuart Hwy via Woomera. There has to be a good reason for a town like Roxby to be in such a harsh area. In this case it's the nearby **Olympic Dam mine**, which produces uranium, copper, silver and gold from a huge mass of ore only discovered in 1975. Visit www.roxbydowns.com to find out more about the Roxby Downs and Olympic Dam communities.

Western Mining Corporation (WMC; ☎ 8671 8600; www.wmc.com) runs tours of the mine's **metallurgical plant** (surface only). Bookings are essential. The two-hour tour departs at 9am on Monday, Thursday and Saturday. A gold coin donation to the Royal Flying Doctor Service is requested.

Sleeping & Eating

Roxby Downs Myall Caravan Park (☎ 8671 1991; myallgr@bigpond.com; 56-94 Burgoyne St; camp sites/caravans/cabins $13/55/70; 🏊) This park has a swimming pool but charges for showers. Rates are for two people.

Roxby Downs Motor Inn (☎ 8671 0311; motor inn@roxbynet.com; 16 Richardson Pl; d & tw $110; 🏊) This is the up-market place in town – with a shady courtyard pool and spa, and a good restaurant (mains $12 to $22). Bookings are essential.

Getting There & Around

Rex (☎ 13 17 13; www.regionalexpress.com.au) flies daily to Olympic Dam from Adelaide ($315 one way, 1½ hours).

Premier Stateliner (☎ 8415 5555) runs buses daily from Adelaide except Saturdays ($80, 7 hours).

You can hire a **4WD** for around $130 to $155 per day to visit Lake Eyre and sights on the Oodnadatta Track. This is an excellent way to see this remote area if you don't have your own vehicle, but you'll need to book ahead. There are three car-hire companies with offices at Olympic Dam airport:

Hertz (☎ 8671 1865)
Avis (☎ 8671 0677; also 6 Charlton Rd)
Budget (☎ 8671 0767)

ANDAMOOKA

☎ 08 / pop 498

About 30km by sealed road from Roxby Downs, Andamooka is a rough-and-ready opal-mining town, known for its dark matrix opal. The contrast between this frontier town and leafy Roxby is breathtaking and even makes Coober Pedy look well planned and respectable.

For general information there's the **visitors centre** (☎ 8672 7007; andamookaopal@hotmail .com; Opal Creek Blvd) in the centre of town – it's at **Duke's Bottlehouse**, which, surprisingly enough, is built out of bottles. There's also a post office, motel and opal showroom as part of the complex.

GLENDAMBO

☎ 08 / pop 20

Glendambo, 113km north of Pimba and 252km south of Coober Pedy, is a service centre on the Stuart Hwy. It has a good pub, motel, two roadhouses and a caravan park. Fuel is available from 7am to midnight.

If you're heading north, remember that there are no refuelling stops between here and Coober Pedy, 259km away.

COOBER PEDY

☎ 08 / pop 2624

On the Stuart Hwy, 535km north of Port Augusta, charismatic Coober Pedy is the opal capital of Australia, if not the world. The lure of opal has brought people from all over the world to live here – about 45 nationalities are represented, making up about 60% of the population.

The name Coober Pedy is from an Aboriginal language and is said to mean 'white man's hole in the ground'. This aptly describes the place, as about half the population lives in dugouts to shelter from the extreme climate: daytime summer temperatures can soar to over 50°C and the winter nights are freezing cold. Apart from the dugouts, there are over 250,000 mine shafts in the area. Although these days the shafts are fenced off, it pays to walk carefully and keep your eyes open!

Coober Pedy is in an extremely inhospitable environment and the town's appearance reflects this: water is expensive and the rainfall scanty, so even in the middle of winter the town looks dried out and dusty. It's not as ramshackle as it used to be, but even so you could never describe it as attractive. In fact, the town looks a bit like the end of the world – which is probably why much of *Mad Max III* was filmed here.

If you stay here for any length of time, you'll soon be hearing outrageous stories of fortunes made and lost, shady international deals, vendettas, intrigues and crazy old timers. Every few years someone makes a million-dollar find, but opal mining is always a gamble – it's difficult to tell whether you're digging 1m away from a fortune and some miners spend decades hard at work and make very little for their efforts.

While Coober Pedy is a friendly enough place, the ready access to mine explosives, combined with fiery local politics, has led to some volatile periods. Since 1987 the police

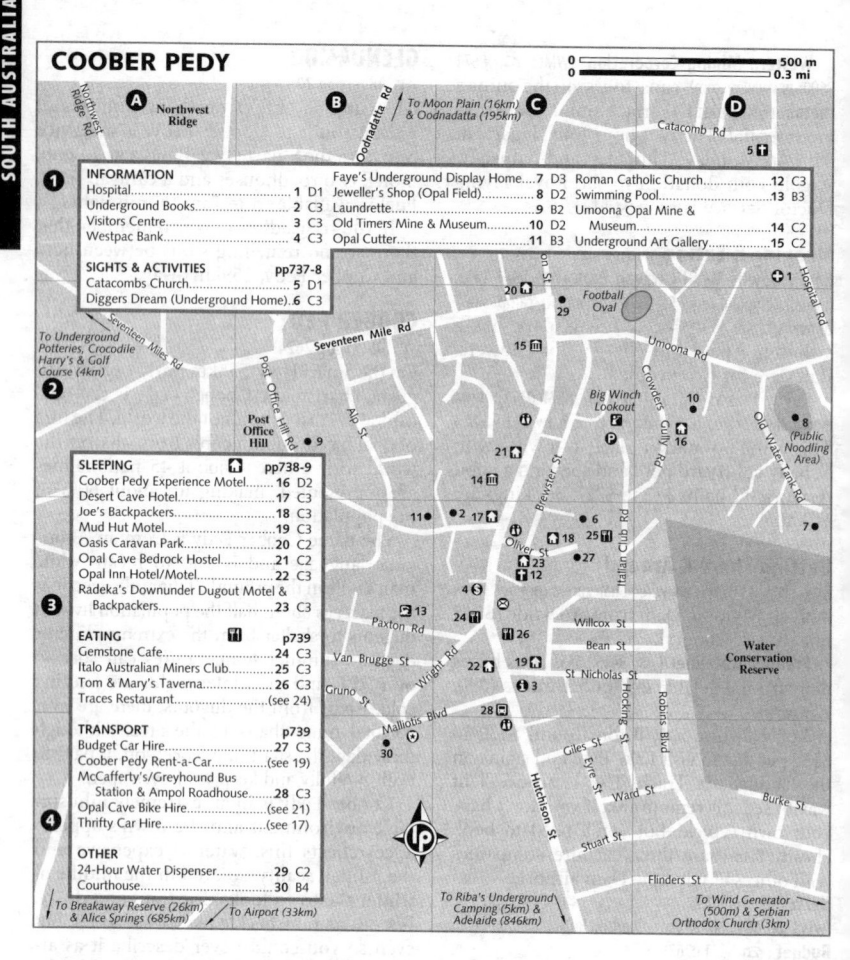

COOBER PEDY

INFORMATION		
Hospital	1	D1
Underground Books	2	C3
Visitors Centre	3	C3
Westpac Bank	4	C3

SIGHTS & ACTIVITIES		pp737-8
Catacombs Church	5	D1
Diggers Dream (Underground Home)	6	C3

Faye's Underground Display Home	7	D3
Jeweller's Shop (Opal Field)	8	D2
Laundrette	9	B2
Old Timers Mine & Museum	10	D2
Opal Cutter	11	B3

Roman Catholic Church	12	C3
Swimming Pool	13	B3
Umoona Opal Mine &		
Museum	14	C2
Underground Art Gallery	15	C2

SLEEPING		pp738-9
Coober Pedy Experience Motel	16	D2
Desert Cave Hotel	17	C3
Joe's Backpackers	18	C3
Mud Hut Motel	19	C3
Oasis Caravan Park	20	C2
Opal Cave Bedrock Hostel	21	C2
Opal Inn Hotel/Motel	22	C3
Radeka's Downunder Dugout Motel &		
Backpackers	23	C3

EATING		p739
Gemstone Cafe	24	C3
Italo Australian Miners Club	25	C3
Tom & Mary's Taverna	26	C3
Traces Restaurant	(see 24)	

TRANSPORT		p739
Budget Car Hire	27	C3
Coober Pedy Rent-a-Car	(see 19)	
McCafferty's/Greyhound Bus		
Station & Ampol Roadhouse	28	C3
Opal Cave Bike Hire	(see 21)	
Thrifty Car Hire	(see 17)	

OTHER		
24-Hour Water Dispenser	29	C2
Courthouse	30	B4

station has been bombed twice, the newspaper office and the courthouse once each, a local restaurant was demolished by a blast and hundreds of thousands of dollars worth of mining equipment has gone the same way. Retribution for night mining (stealing from another's mine) is a major reason for this explosive revenge, the other is the defecting (when vehicles are deemed not roadworthy) of battered mining trucks by the police – following one defecting two police cars were blown up! The council maintains, however, that the wild west days are long gone and no one has ever been hurt during these incidents. The town is pretty safe for travellers and is in fact one of the most popular travel destinations in the outback.

Bottled water is an expensive commodity here. For those headed into the outback, it's cheaper to refill water bottles at the coin-operated **24-hour water dispenser** (30L for $0.20) by the **Oasis Caravan Park** (☎ 8672 5169; Seventeen Mile Rd).

Information

The well-organised and obliging **visitors centre** (☎ 1800 637 076, 8672 5298; www.opalcapitalof theworld.com.au; Hutchison St; ☼ 9am-5pm Mon-Fri) is in the council offices, diagonally opposite the Ampol Roadhouse and bus station.

Otherwise **Underground Books** (☎ 8672 5558; Post Office Hill Rd; ☼ 8.30am-5pm Mon-Fri, 10am-4pm Sat) is very good for information on the local area and the outback in general.

Radeka's Downunder Dugout Motel & Backpackers (see Sleeping; p738) offers Internet access.

Sights & Activities
DUGOUT HOMES

Many of the early dugout homes were simply worked-out mines; now, however, they're usually cut specifically as residences. The average price for an underground home is $70,000 to $80,000 dollars. Open-for-viewing dugouts are normally occupied, so wipe your feet!

Faye's Underground Display Home (☎ 8672 5029; Jeweller Shop Rd; admission $4.50; ☉ 9am-5pm Mon-Sat) was hand-dug by three women in the 1960s. There's also **Diggers Dream** (☎ 8672 5442; Nayler Pl; admission $4; ☉ sunrise-sunset), which has a more contemporary décor.

OPAL MINING

The town of Coober Pedy survives on opals, which were first discovered by a teenage boy in 1915. Keen fossickers can have a go themselves, the safest area being the **Jeweller's Shop opal field** in the northeast corner of town – fossicking through the mullock, or waste dumps, is known as noodling.

There are literally hundreds of working mines around Coober Pedy but there are no big operators. When somebody makes a find, dozens of miners home in like bees around a honey pot. Looking at all the vacant ground between the various fields makes you wonder just how much opal is still down there!

OTHER ATTRACTIONS

Coober Pedy has a number of other attractions. The underground **Serbian Orthodox Church** and unique bare-earth **golf course** sum up this bizarre place and should be seen. The prominent **Big Winch Lookout** (☎ 8672 5264; Italian Club Rd; ☉ 9am-5pm Mon-Sat) provides views over the town.

There are numerous reputable – and some not so reputable – opal outlets in town; it's best to shop around and be wary of anyone offering discounts over 30% (this is a sign that the opal may be overpriced). An international guarantee provides some measure of security, as does dealing with members of the Coober Pedy Retail Business and Tourism Association. Remember too that different outlets sell the work of different jewellers, so keep looking until you find something to suit your taste. Some of the best buys are found at **Opal Cutter** (☎ 8672 3086; Post Office Hill Rd; ☉ 8.45am-6pm Mon-Sat, 10am-5pm Sun), which often has visiting jewellers working on the premises.

You can do self-guided tours of the **Old Timers Mine & Museum** (☎ 8672 5555; Crowders Gully Rd; admission $10; ☉ 9am-5pm), a really interesting early mine and underground home with opal still embedded in the rock.

The **Umoona Opal Mine & Museum** (☎ 8672 5288; Hutchison St; ☉ 8am-7pm) is right in the centre of town. It has a very good information centre, and offers tours ($11) including information on the local Aboriginal beliefs about the area and an excellent 18-minute documentary on opal and opal mining.

OPALS

Australia is the opal-producing centre of the world, and South Australia (SA) is where most of the country's opals come from. Opal is a kind of silica that contains 6% to 10% water. The colour is produced by white light being reflected and split by the regular arrangement of silica molecules.

Opals are cut in three different fashions: solids can be cut out of the rough into cabochons (domed-top stones); triplets consist of a layer of opal sandwiched between an opaque backing layer and a transparent cap; and doublets are simply an opal layer with an opaque backing. In Queensland, opals are often found embedded in rock; these are sometimes polished and left in the surrounding rock (boulder opals).

An opal's value is partly determined by its colour and clarity – the brighter and clearer the colour, the better. The type of opal is also an indicator of value: black and crystal opals are the most valuable, semiblack and semicrystal are in the middle and milk opal is the least valuable. The bigger the pattern, the better. Flaws (such as cracks) have a detrimental effect on value.

Shape is important – a high dome is better than a flat opal – as is size. As with the purchase of any sort of gemstone, don't expect to find great bargains unless you clearly understand what you are buying.

About 2km northwest of town, the friendly **Underground Potteries** (☎ 8672 5226; Rowe St; ✆ 8.30am-6pm) has some fine products – you can often have a yarn to the potters and watch them working.

About 3km further on is **Crocodile Harry's** (☎ 8672 5872; Seventeen Mile Rd; admission $2; ✆ 9am-6pm). This amazing decorated dugout home is the work of many artists who have stayed with Harry over the years. It featured in *Mad Max III, Ground Zero* and the miniseries *Stark*. Harry may be in his seventies but he's still an extremely lively character – a Latvian baron who emigrated to Australia after WWII who then spent 13 years in northern Queensland and the NT hunting crocodiles.

Tours

Several operators run tours that will take you into an opal mine, underground home and Serbian church, as well as various other places in and around town. The tour offered by **Radeka's Downunder Dugout Motel & Backpackers** (☎ 8672 5223; admission $30) is popular with backpackers, and includes fossicking for opal. So does **Stuart Ranger Tours** (☎ 8672 5179; admission $25), **Joe's Backpackers' Tour** (☎ 8672 5163; admission $28) and a more up-market tour offered by the **Desert Cave Hotel** (☎ 8672 5688; Hutchison St; admission $50).

Opal Quest Working Mine (☎ 8672 5288; admission $35) is the only one to enter a working mine and give hands-on mining experience. Minimum numbers apply.

Another good and popular tour is **Martin's Star Gazing** (☎ 8672 5223; admission $22) where you explore the heavens from the Moon Plain – an appropriate venue. Book at Radeka's (see Sleeping) for this one.

Desert Diversity Tours (☎ 8672 5226) offer day eco-tours to the Painted Desert ($135) and Lake Eyre ($140).

On Monday and Thursday you can travel with the **mail truck** (☎ 1800 069 911) along 600km of dirt roads as it does the return trip from Coober Pedy to Oodnadatta and William Creek. This is a great way to get off the beaten track and visit small, remote outback communities ($110). Book at **Underground Books** (☎ 8672 5558).

Sleeping

BUDGET

Riba's Underground Camping (☎ /fax 8672 5614; ribascamping@hotmail.com; William Creek Rd; above-ground/underground camp sites per person $6/9) This very friendly place is on the William Creek road, 5km from town. It offers cool underground facilities including a TV lounge, and showers are free. There's an interesting one-hour evening mine tour for $14, which includes the night's camping fee.

Radeka's Downunder Dugout Motel & Backpackers (☎ 8672 5223; www.radekadownunder.com.au; Oliver St; underground dm/tw $22/55, motel s/d $80/90; ✂ ▯) This motel offers the best standard in backpacker accommodation. There are bunks in open alcoves, but if you want privacy, its renovated twins and doubles are very pleasant. There are also comfortable motel units. Free linen and showers are included for all accommodation, and there's a very good kitchen, bar, restaurant and laundry. The owners offer free transfers from the airport and bus station if you book in advance.

Joe's Backpackers (☎ /fax 8672 5163; Brewster St; dm/d $18/55) Prices include linen and showers. This backpackers has apartment-style bedrooms and bunkhouses, each with their own facilities, sleeping up to 10. There are free airport transfers if you book in advance.

MID-RANGE

Mud Hut Motel (☎ 8672 3003; www.mudhutmotel.com.au; St Nicholas St; s/d/units $85/100/135; ✂ ▯) Above ground and made of rammed earth, this motel has pleasant modern rooms and all the mod cons you'd want including a laundry, restaurant and bar.

Coober Pedy Experience Motel (☎ 8672 5777; www.cooberpedyexperience.com.au; Crowders Gully Rd; dm/d $22/125) Although it is the largest motel in town, this underground residence is also very homely and has good facilities. Motel rooms have bathrooms and five-person dormitories are single-sex.

Opal Inn Hotel/Motel (☎ 8672 5054; www.opalinn.com.au; Hutchison St; pub s/d $40/45, budget s/d/tr $55/65/75, motel s/d $90/100; ✂ ▯) Central to the action, there are basic but clean pub rooms and motel-style accommodation here, all with air-con. The saloon bar serves counter meals and has pool tables, pokies and cable TV.

TOP END

Desert Cave Hotel (☎ 8672 5688; www.desertcave.com.au; Hutchison St; d/tr $175/195; ✂ ▯) This luxurious accommodation has rooms above and below ground. There's also an up-market restaurant, café, pool, spa and gymnasium. Additionally it offers disabled facilities and airport and train transfers.

Eating

The larger hotels and motels have restaurants and cafés and there are several takeaways and coffee lounges on the main street.

Italo Australian Miners Club (Italian Club; ☎ 8672 5101; Italian Club Rd; mains with salad bar $9) Only has meals on Thursday and Friday night (steak, schnitzels etc) but this local institution is a good place to go for a beer at other times.

Tom & Mary's Taverna (☎ 8672 5622; Hutchison St; meals $18) You can get a mean Greek salad here, or a platter that makes an economical meal for three or four people.

Traces Restaurant (☎ 8672 5147; Hutchison St; mains $16; ☼ 4pm-midnight) In the town centre, this popular Greek eatery has charcoal-grilled meals: gyros, steaks and kebabs. There are also large salads and specials ($11).

Gemstone Cafe (☎ 8672 3177; Hutchison St; lunch $5) This friendly café under Traces Restaurant is popular for breakfast and lunch.

Getting There & Away

Most motels and hostels will meet you at the airport if you ring ahead.

AIR

Rex (☎ 13 17 13; www.regionalexpress.com.au) has flights to and from Adelaide ($389, 2 hours, Sunday to Wednesday and Friday).

BUS

It's 413km from Coober Pedy to Kulgera (just across the border into NT) and from there it's another 275km to Alice Springs.

McCafferty's/Greyhound (☎ 13 14 99) departs daily from Adelaide to Coober Pedy ($105, 22½ hours) and from Alice Springs to Coober Pedy ($95, 8 hours).

Getting Around

CAR

Thrifty (☎ 8672 5688; reserve@desertcave.com.au) is based at the Desert Cave Hotel, **Budget** (☎ 8672 5333; cpdbudget@ozemail.com.au; Oliver St) can arrange one-way rentals, and **Coober Pedy Rent-a-Car** (☎ 8672 3003; res@mudhuthotel.com.au) is at the Mud Hut Motel.

The Opal Cave, part of the adjacent **Opal Cave Bedrock Hostel** (☎ 8672 5028; www.opalcave cooberpedy.com; Hutchison St, Coober Pedy) rents out mountain bikes for $12 a day.

COOBER PEDY TO MARLA
Breakaways Reserve

Breakaways Reserve is a stark but colourful area of mesa hills and scarps off the Stuart Hwy about 35km north of Coober Pedy. Here you'll find the white-and-yellow formation known as the **Castle**, which featured in the films *Mad Max III* and *The Adventures of Priscilla, Queen of the Desert*. Entry is subject to a permit ($4 per person), which you can get from the visitors centre or Underground Books (see Information; p736).

If you're heading for Oodnadatta, turning off the highway at Cadney Homestead, 151km north of Coober Pedy, gives you a shorter run on dirt roads than the routes via Marla or Coober Pedy. En route you pass through the aptly named and stunning **Painted Desert** (Map p659).

Cadney Homestead (Map p659; ☎ 08-8670 7994; www.cadneyhomestead.com.au; Stuart Hwy; camp sites/ cabins/s & d/tr $8/30/90/100; ⊠ 🖳) There are lawn sites, cabins with air-con ($5 for linen hire) or motel rooms with good three-person rates.

Copper Hills Homestead (Map p659; ☎ 08-8670 7995; Painted Desert Hwy; camp sites/cabins $6/30) About 32km east of Cadney Homestead, this is a great place to appreciate the desert's unique atmosphere while you camp by a peaceful billabong.

MARLA
☎ 08 / pop 150

In the mulga scrub, about 160km south of the NT border, Marla replaced Oodnadatta as the official regional centre when the *Ghan* railway line was re-routed in 1980. The rough-and-ready **Mintabie** opal field is on Aboriginal land, 35km west, and the recently opened **Lambina** opal field is 75km northeast. Fuel and provisions are available in Marla 24 hours a day.

Marla Travellers Rest Hotel/Motel (☎ 8670 7001; fax 8670 7021; marla@internode.on.net; Stuart Hwy; camp sites/dm/d $5/25/65; 🐾) There are spacious motel rooms and a pool. For meals, choose from a takeaway, à la carte or restaurant meals.

MARREE
☎ 08 / pop 80

Sleepy Marree was a major centre for the Afghan camel trains that serviced the outback from the 1870s into the 1930s. There are still a couple of date palms, an incongruously large pub, and relics of the *Old Ghan* train.

The township is at the southern end of the Birdsville and Oodnadatta tracks, and really fires up during the **Marree Australian Camel Cup**, held on the first Saturday in July.

You might want to ask at the café in the Oasis Caravan Park (see Sleeping; below) about scenic flights over **Lake Eyre** and **Marree Man**, the huge outline of an Aboriginal warrior that people unknown etched into the desert sands in 1998.

Around 60km west of Maree at **Alberrie Creek** is the **Mutonia Sculpture Park** (admission by donation) which is definitely worthy of some contemplation.

About 100km further on is the site of the **Curdimurka Outback Ball** (☎ 1800 254 000, 8358 6600), a rite of passage for young Aussies. Buses depart from Adelaide (in October on even-numbered years) to bring dressed-up party animals to frolic under the stars and shock the native fauna.

At **Coward Springs** (Map p659; ☎ 8675 8336; www .cowardsprings.com.au), about 150km west of Marree (70km south of William Creek), there's a beautiful natural warm-water spa and incongruous wetland in the desert, created by a bore sunk here in 1886. You can take a dip in the spa ($2) or camp in the basic camping ground ($7) – there are toilets and showers. Camel treks are also available in the cooler months ($185 per day).

Sleeping

Oasis Caravan Park (☎ 8675 8352; fax 8675 8399; Railway Tce; camp sites/cabins $13/40; 🗷) These self-contained and shaded cabins are in the town centre and can sleep three. The park also has a café and shop.

Marree Hotel (☎ 8675 8344; marreehotel@bigpond .com; Railway Tce South; s/d $50/70; 🗷) This rather grand hotel in the town centre has old-style pub rooms, a dining room and daily counter meals (around $17).

WILLIAM CREEK

☎ 08 / pop 12

Claims are made that this is Australia's smallest town. Consisting of a classic pub and store, it's about halfway between Oodnadatta and Marree.

William Creek Hotel (☎ 8670 7880; williamcreek@ ozemail.com.au; Oodnadatta Track; camp sites/dm/s/d $5/ 14/30/50) This weather-beaten hotel is a fair-dinkum outback pub, with more character than you'll find in a host of Adelaide hotels.

The pub has dusty camp sites and basic accommodation, and sells food, alcohol, fuel, tyres and meals.

William Creek Store & Campground (☎ 8670 7746; www.williamcreekcampground.com; Oodnadatta Track; camp sites/r $14/45; 🗷) Across the road from the pub, you will find good camping facilities and takeaway food.

OODNADATTA

☎ 08 / pop 200

It was in Oodnadatta, in 1912, that the Reverend John Flynn, founder of the Royal Flying Doctor Service (RFDS), established the Australian outback's first hospital, which is still operating.

One of the town's most distinctive features is the **Pink Roadhouse** (☎ 8670 7822; Main St; 🕑 8am-5.30pm), an excellent place for advice about track conditions (or call ☎ 1800 802 074) and attractions in any direction. The owners, Adam and Lynnie Plate, have spent a lot of time and effort putting road signs and kilometre pegs over a huge area in this district – even in the Simpson Desert you'll find signs erected by this dedicated pair.

The old train station has been converted into an interesting little **museum**. It is kept locked but you can pick up the key from the pub, store or roadhouse.

You can visit the **Oodnadatta Aboriginal School** (☎ 8670 7823; behind the Pink Roadhouse; 🕑 9am-3pm Mon-Fri), where the friendly staff will give you a free tour, but call first. You can also occasionally buy products made by the kids.

Oodnadatta Hospital (☎ 8670 7803; Main St; admission by donation; 🕑 9am-5pm Mon-Fri) was established by Reverend Flynn. A permanent staff of only two nurses covers the medical, veterinary and dentistry needs over 150,000 sq km of the outback, supported by the flying doctor in Port Augusta. Call before visiting.

Sleeping & Eating

Adam & Lynnie's Oodnadatta Caravan Park (☎ 8670 7822; pinkroadhouse@bigpond.com; Main St; camp sites/dm/ tw/cabins $15/12/50/80; 🗷) Self-contained cabin prices are for two, with extra people $10 per head. Takeaways and meals are also available at the Pink Roadhouse.

Oodnadatta Hotel (☎ /fax 8670 7804; oodnadatta hotel@bigpond.com; Main St; s/d/tr $40/65/75; 🗷) This lively and friendly pub has comfortable rooms and serves dinner.

BIRDSVILLE TRACK

Years ago cattle from the southwest of Queensland were walked down the Birdsville Track to Marree to be loaded onto trains. Motor transport took over from the drovers in the 1960s and now the cattle is trucked out in road trains. It's 520km between Marree and Birdsville, just across the border.

Although conventional vehicles can usually manage the track without difficulty, it's worth bearing in mind that traffic is anything but heavy – particularly in summer.

Petrol, diesel and minor mechanical repairs are available at **Mungerannie Roadhouse** (☎ 08-8675 8317; s/d $45/70; ☿ standard hrs 8am-8pm), about 205km from Marree (315km from Birdsville). It's also licensed and has camp sites, rooms and meals.

The track is more or less at the meeting point between the sand dunes of the Simpson Desert to the west and the desolate wastes of Sturt Stony Desert to the east. There are ruins of a couple of homesteads along the track and artesian bores gush out boiling-hot salty water at many places. At Clifton Hills, about 200km south of Birdsville, the track splits with the main route going around the eastern side of Goyder Lagoon.

Remember your water supplies, as even locals have got lost and perished from thirst.

STRZELECKI TRACK

These days, conventional vehicles can handle the Strzelecki Track. It starts at Lyndhurst, about 80km south of Marree, and runs 460km to the tiny outpost of Innamincka. The discovery of natural gas deposits near Moomba has brought a great deal of development and improvement to the track, although the amount of heavy transport means the surface is often rough.

The new Moomba-Strzelecki Track is better kept, but longer and less interesting than the old track, which follows Strzelecki Creek. Accommodation, provisions and fuel are available at Lyndhurst and Innamincka, but there's nothing in between. The mining town of Moomba, run by the Santos Corporation, is a closed town – travellers cannot buy fuel or supplies here.

INNAMINCKA

☎ 08 / pop 18

At the northern end of the Strzelecki Track, Innamincka is on Cooper Creek. The Burke

and Wills expedition of 1860–61 (the first expedition to cross Australia from the south to the north coast) came to its tragic end here. Nearby is the famous **Dig Tree**, as well as the memorials and markers where Burke and Wills died and where King, the sole survivor, was found. The Dig Tree is actually across the border in Queensland. The word 'dig' is no longer visible, but the expedition's camp number can still be made out.

Cooper Creek flows only after heavy soaking rains fall over central Queensland, but there are semipermanent water holes. The area had a large Aboriginal population prior to white settlement, and relics such as middens and grinding stones are common.

Westprint's *Innamincka-Coongie Lakes* map is a good source of information on the Innamincka area. For a moving account of the Burke and Wills expedition, read Alan Moorehead's *Cooper's Creek*, which can be purchased in most bookshops.

Mechanical repairs, tyres, fuel and provisions are available in town.

The old **Australian Inland Mission Hospital** now houses the **NPWSA ranger's office** (☎ 8675 9909; ☿ 8am-6pm), and also displays on the surrounding **Innamincka Regional Reserve**.

Sleeping & Eating

Innamincka Hotel (☎ 8675 9901; fax 8675 9961; s/d/tr $50/70/90; ✖) This hotel serves all meals – its Wednesday night Beef-and-Creek dinners and Sunday night roasts are good value.

Innamincka Trading Post (☎ 8675 9900; fax 8675 9920; s/d/tr $45/70/100; ✖) This place has three two-bedroom cabins. It also sells fuel and provisions.

Cooper Creek Homestay (☎ 8675 9591; fourmatthews@bigpond.com.au; s/d $55/75; ✖) About 400m from Cooper Creek, this friendly family offers rooms in a private home. All meals are available and yummy potato pancakes are included in a massive breakfast ($12.50).

You can camp in the open area in town (the common) for $6 per vehicle per night; there are pit toilets and a steel collection box at the entrance. For a donation to the Progress Association you can use the shower, toilet and laundry facilities (no washing machines here) outside the Trading Post.

There are also plenty of **bush camping spots** along Cooper Creek. See the ranger for a permit if you want to camp within the Innamincka Regional Reserve.

Northern Territory

CONTENTS

Few people who visit the Northern Territory (NT) leave untouched by the experience – it's that sort of place. While it's the most barren and least-populated area of Australia (only 1% of the nation's population living in nearly 20% of the country's area), this is where many people find the country's soul. It is in the Centre – the Red Heart – that the picture-book, untamed and sometimes surreal Australia exists.

The Territory is essentially two very different areas: the arid, red Centre and the monsoonal Top End, with the best-known attractions of these areas the iconic Uluru (Ayers Rock) and Kakadu National Park, respectively. But there are plenty of hidden treasures in this seemingly remote and harsh environment. There are meteorite craters, eerie canyons, lost valleys of palms, hot springs, raging waterfalls, quirky pubs and raucous outback festivals. Where else but Alice Springs would you find an annual boat regatta held on a dry riverbed?

Distance aside, getting around the Territory is straightforward – the Stuart Hwy travels its spine, connecting Alice Springs and the north coast. As you head up 'The Track' you'll notice the gradual contrast between the arid Centre and the tropical Top End. At the end of this 1500km drive is cosmopolitan Darwin. To its east, the wetlands and escarpments of Kakadu National Park are a treasure house of wildlife and Aboriginal rock paintings. Most of Arnhem Land belongs to traditional Aboriginal owners and is off limits to visitors, but there are many opportunities in the Territory to learn about Aboriginal culture.

TOP TEN

- Making a pilgrimage to the mesmerising desert monoliths, **Uluru** and **Kata Tjuta** (p817)
- Exploring the timeless landscape, stunning wetlands and rock-art at **Kakadu** (p773)
- Paddling a canoe along the spectacular **Nitmiluk National Park** (p787)
- Going the extra mile and hiking the **Larapinta** (p811) or **Jatbula Trails** (p788)
- Hooking a barramundi, the Top End's famous **game fish** (p748)
- Joining the locals to feast on tasty morsels and watch the sun go down at Darwin's **Mindil Beach Night Market** (p763)
- Gaping at the outrageously picturesque **Kings Canyon** (p815) in Watarrka National Park
- Making your own didgeridoo and learning to play it in **Katherine** (p783)
- Visiting traditional Aboriginal land and communities with a local guide in **Arnhem Land** (p782)
- Being part of the fun at the annual **Henley-on-Todd Regatta** (p801) in Alice Springs

Map locations: Mindil Beach Night Market, Kakadu, Arnhem Land, Top End, Katherine, Nitmiluk National Park/Jatbula Trail, Larapinta Trail, Henley-on-Todd Regatta, Kings Canyon, Kata Tjuta, Uluru

TELEPHONE CODE: 08	POPULATION: 200,000	AREA: 1,350,000 SQ KM

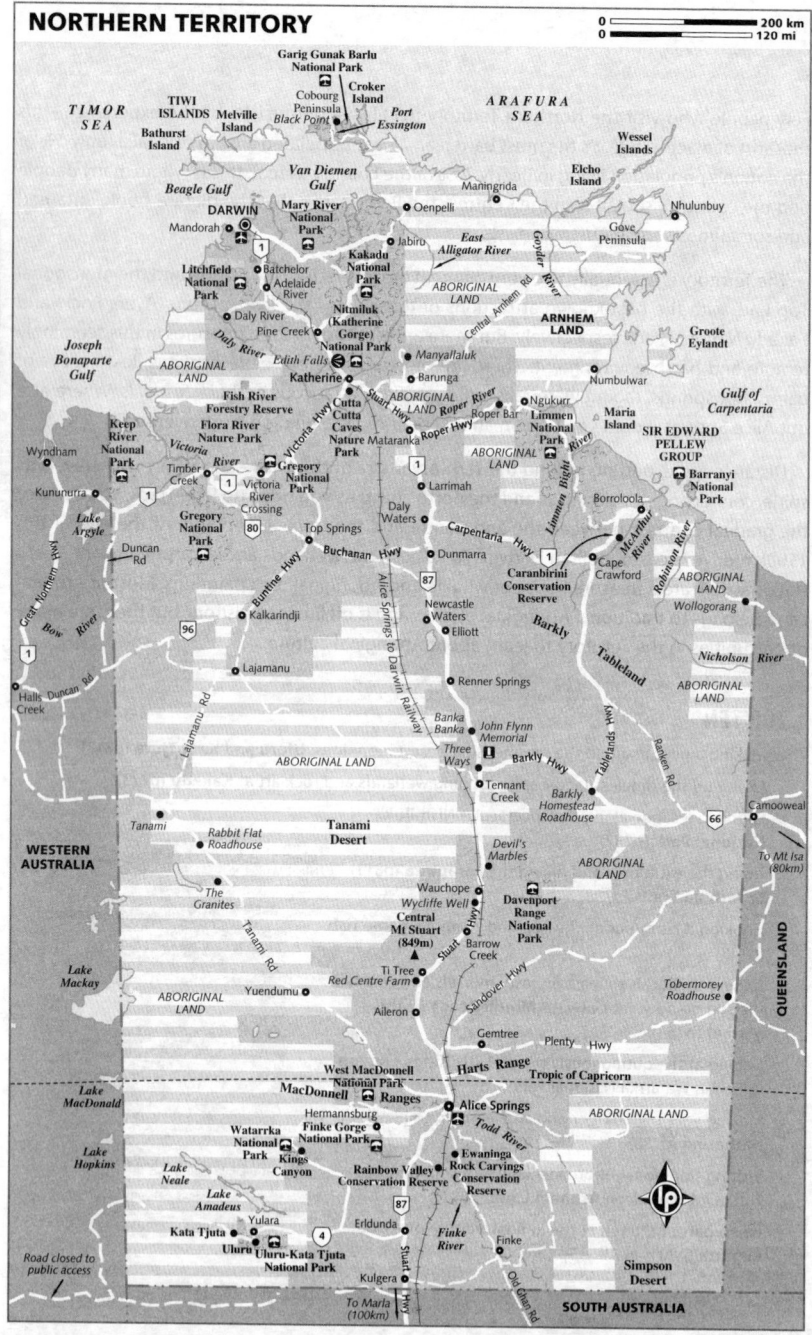

NORTHERN TERRITORY

0 — 200 km
0 — 120 mi

TIMOR SEA

TIWI ISLANDS

Garig Gunak Barlu National Park
Cobourg Peninsula
Croker Island
Black Point
Port Essington

ARAFURA SEA

Bathurst Island
Melville Island

Wessel Islands

Beagle Gulf

Van Diemen Gulf

Maningrida

Elcho Island

DARWIN
Mandorah

Mary River National Park
Oenpelli

Gove Peninsula

Nhulunbuy

Litchfield National Park
Batchelor
Adelaide River
Daly River
Pine Creek

Kakadu National Park
Jabiru

East Alligator River

Goyder River

Central Arnhem Rd

ARNHEM LAND

ABORIGINAL LAND

Groote Eylandt

Joseph Bonaparte Gulf

Nitmiluk (Katherine Gorge) National Park
Edith Falls

Manyallaluk

Numbulwar

Gulf of Carpentaria

ABORIGINAL LAND

Katherine
Barunga

Roper River
Ngukurr

Maria Island

SIR EDWARD PELLEW GROUP

Keep River National Park

Fish River Forestry Reserve
Flora River Nature Park
Cutta Cutta Caves Nature Park
Mataranka

ABORIGINAL LAND
Roper Hwy
Roper Bar

Limmen National Park

Barranyi National Park

Wyndham

Victoria River
Timber Creek

Gregory National Park
Victoria River Crossing

Larrimah

Limmen Bight River

Borroloola

McArthur River

Robinson River

Kununurra

Lake Argyle

Duncan Rd

Gregory National Park

Top Springs

Daly Waters

Carpentaria Hwy
Cape Crawford

Caranbirini Conservation Reserve

ABORIGINAL LAND

Wollogorang

Nicholson River

Great Northern Hwy

Bow River

Duncan Rd

Buchanan Hwy
Dunmarra

Barkly

Tableland

Ranken Rd

ABORIGINAL LAND

Halls Creek

Buntine Hwy

Kalkarindji

Newcastle Waters
Elliott

Camooweal

Lajamanu

Renner Springs

Tablelands Hwy

WESTERN AUSTRALIA

Tanami Rd

ABORIGINAL LAND

Banka Banka
John Flynn Memorial
Three Ways

Barkly Hwy

Tanami

Rabbit Flat Roadhouse

Tanami Desert

Tennant Creek

Barkly Homestead Roadhouse

ABORIGINAL LAND

To Mt Isa (80km)

The Granites

Devil's Marbles

Wauchope
Wycliffe Well

Davenport Range National Park

Tobermorey Roadhouse

Lake Mackay

Central Mt Stuart (849m)
Barrow Creek

Alice Springs to Darwin Railway

ABORIGINAL LAND

Ti Tree
Red Centre Farm

Yuendumu

Aileron

Sandover Hwy

QUEENSLAND

Lake MacDonald

Gemtree
Plenty Hwy

Harts Range

Tropic of Capricorn

West MacDonnell National Park
MacDonnell Ranges
Hermannsburg

Alice Springs
Todd River

ABORIGINAL LAND

Lake Hopkins

Watarrka National Park
Finke Gorge National Park
Kings Canyon

Ewaninga Rock Carvings Conservation Reserve

Lake Neale
Lake Amadeus

Rainbow Valley Conservation Reserve

Lake MacDonald

Yulara
Kata Tjuta
Uluru
Uluru-Kata Tjuta National Park

Erldunda

Finke River

Finke

Simpson Desert

Road closed to public access

Kulgera

Stuart Hwy
Old Ghan Rd

To Marla (100km)

SOUTH AUSTRALIA

HISTORY
Aboriginal People

Around 30% of the Territory's 200,000 people are Aboriginal.

The process of white settlement in the NT was slower but just as troubled and violent as elsewhere in Australia, with Aboriginal groups vainly resisting the takeover of their land. By the early 20th century, most Aboriginal people were confined to government reserves or Christian missions. Some took employment as stockmen or domestic servants on cattle stations (often in order to retain the connection to their land), while others lived on the edges of towns, taking on low-paid work, with alcohol abuse a common problem. Only a few were able to maintain much of their traditional way of life.

During the 1960s, Aboriginal people began to demand more rights. In 1963 the people of Yirrkala on the Gove Peninsula protested against plans for bauxite mining in the area. The Yirrkala people failed to stop the mining, but the way they presented their case – producing sacred objects and bark paintings that showed their right to the land under Aboriginal custom – was a milestone.

In 1976 the Aboriginal Land Rights (NT) Act was passed in Canberra. It handed over all reserves and mission lands in the Territory to the Aboriginal people and allowed Aboriginal groups to claim government land with which they had traditional ties – provided the land wasn't already leased, in a town or set aside for some other special purpose.

Today, Aboriginal people own about half of the land in the NT, including Kakadu and Uluru-Kata Tjuta National Parks, which are leased back to the federal government. Minerals on Aboriginal land are still government property – though the landowners' permission for exploration and mining is usually required and has to be paid for.

While non-Aboriginal Australia's awareness of the need for reconciliation with the

---

VINCENT LINGIARI & THE WAVE HILL STOCKMEN'S STRIKE OF 1966

Aboriginal stockmen played a large role in the early days of the pastoral industry in the Northern Territory (NT). Because they were paid such paltry wages, a pastoralist could afford to employ many of them, and run his station at a much lower cost. White stockmen received regular and relatively high wages, were given decent food and accommodation, and were able to return to the station homestead every week. By contrast Aboriginal stockmen received poor food and accommodation and would often spend months in the bush with the cattle.

In the 1960s, Vincent Lingiari was a stockman on the huge Wave Hill station. His concern over the way Aboriginal workers were treated led to an appeal to the North Australian Workers' Union (NAWU), which had already applied to the Federal Court for equal wages for Aboriginal workers. The Federal Court approved the granting of equal wages in March 1966, but it was not to take effect until December 1968. Lingiari asked the Wave Hill management directly for equal wages but was refused and, on 23 August 1966, the Aboriginal stockmen walked off the station and camped in nearby Wattie Creek. They were soon joined by others, and before long only stations that not only gave their Aboriginal workers good conditions but also respect were provided with workers by Lingiari and the other Gurindji elders.

The Wattie Creek camp gained a lot of local support, from both non-Aboriginal and Aboriginal people, and it soon developed into a sizable community with housing and a degree of organisation. Having gained the right to be paid equally, Lingiari and the Gurindji people felt, perhaps for the first time, that they had some say in the way they were able to live. This victory led to the hope that they could achieve something even more important – title to their own land. To this end Lingiari travelled widely in the eastern states campaigning for land rights and finally made some progress with the Whitlam government in Canberra. On 16 August 1975, Prime Minister Gough Whitlam attended a ceremony at Wattie Creek that resulted in the handing over of 3200 sq km of land, now known as Daguragu. He ceremonially poured sand into the cupped hands of Lingiari, signifying the giving back of their land.

Lingiari, awarded the Order of Australia Medal for service to the Aboriginal people, died at Daguragu in 1988.

Aboriginal community has increased in recent years, there are still huge gulfs between the cultures.

It's often difficult for short-term visitors to make meaningful contact with Aborigines as they generally prefer to be left to themselves. The impressions given by Aboriginal people on the streets in Alice Springs, Katherine and Darwin, where social problems and alcohol abuse among a few people can present an unpleasant picture, are not indicative of Aboriginal communities as a whole.

Tourism ventures to Aboriginal lands, some operated by the communities themselves, are gradually becoming more acceptable, as communities feel more inclined to share their culture. The benefits are twofold: financial gain, not only from conducting the tours but from selling arts and crafts direct to the public; and educating non-Aboriginal people about traditional culture and customs, helping to alleviate the problems caused by the ignorance and misunderstandings of the past.

GEOGRAPHY & CLIMATE

Although roughly 80% of the Territory is in the tropics – the Tropic of Capricorn cuts across just north of Alice Springs – only the northern 25%, known as the Top End, has anything resembling the popular idea of a tropical climate. The Top End is a distinct region of savannah woodlands and pockets of rainforest.

In the northeast, the Arnhem Land plateau rises abruptly from the plain and continues to the coast of the Gulf of Carpentaria. Much of the southern 75% of the Territory consists of desert or semi-arid plain.

The climate of the Top End is described in terms of the Dry and the Wet, with year-round maximum temperatures of 30°C to 34°C and minimums between 19°C and 26°C. Roughly, the Dry lasts from April to September, and the Wet from October to March, with the heaviest rain falling from January onwards.

In the Centre the temperatures are much more variable – plummeting below freezing on winter nights (June to August) and soaring over 40°C on summer days (November to March).

The most comfortable time to visit both the Centre and the Top End is June and July. The Centre is pleasant from April to June and you'll find fewer tourists around at this time. The Top End does have its good points during the Wet – everything is

---

ABORIGINAL FESTIVALS & EVENTS

There are many annual festivals worth attending. Although they are usually held on restricted Aboriginal land, permit requirements are generally waived for the festivals. Bear in mind that alcohol is banned in many communities.

Tiwi Grand Final

Held in early April on Bathurst Island, this sporting event is the culmination of a season of Australian rules football between Aboriginal communities from around the Top End. The Islanders are passionate followers of the game and the final is a major spectacle, with planeloads of people flying in from Darwin for the day. If you can afford the flight it's worth the trip. No permit is required (for this day only).

Merrepen Arts Festival

Nauiyu Nambiyu on the banks of the Daly River is the venue for the one-day Merrepen Arts Festival, held on the first weekend in June. Several Aboriginal communities from around the district, such as Wadeye, Nauiyu and Peppimenarti, display their arts and crafts. No permit is required.

Barunga Wugularr Sports & Cultural Festival

For four days including the Queen's Birthday long weekend in June, Barunga, 80km southeast of Katherine, becomes a gathering place for Aboriginal people from around 40 communities. There are displays of traditional arts and crafts, as well as dancing and athletics competitions. No

green, the barramundi fishing is at its best, there are spectacular electrical storms and relatively few tourists. However, the combination of heat and high humidity can be unbearable if you're not acclimatised, dirt roads are often impassable and some national parks and reserves are either totally or partially closed.

INFORMATION

The NT Tourism Commission (NTTC; www.nttc.com.au) doesn't operate any tourist offices as such, but works through travel agencies or through its comprehensive website.

For information on taking a driving holiday in the Territory, see www.ntexplore .com.au.

There are regional tourist offices in Darwin, Katherine, Tennant Creek and Alice Springs, as well as visitors centres at Kakadu and Uluru (Ayers Rock). For more information, see the appropriate sections in this chapter.

Permits

Permits are required to enter Aboriginal land. In some cases permits won't be necessary if you stay on recognised public roads that cross Aboriginal territory. However, as

soon as you leave the main road by more than 50m, even if you're 'only' going into an Aboriginal settlement for fuel and provisions, you may need a permit. If you're on an organised tour, the operator should take care of any permits – check before you book.

Three land councils deal with requests for permits; ask the permits officer of the appropriate council for an application form. The Central Land Council deals with all land south of a line drawn between Kununurra (Western Australia) and Mt Isa (Queensland), the Northern Land Council is responsible for land north of that line and the Tiwi Land Council deals with Bathurst and Melville Islands. Permits can take four to six weeks to be processed, although for Gunbalanya (Oenpelli) they are issued on the spot in Jabiru ($13.20).

Central Land Council (☎ 08-8951 6211; 33 Stuart Hwy, Alice Springs; postal address: PO Box 3321, Alice Springs, NT 0871)

Northern Land Council (www.nlc.org.au); Darwin (☎ 08-8920 5100; 9 Rowling St, Casuarina, NT 0810); Katherine (☎ 08-8972 2799; 5 Katherine Tce, Katherine NT 0850); Jabiru (☎ 08-8979 2410; Flinders St, Jabiru, NT 0886)

Tiwi Land Council (☎ 08-8981 4898; Unit 5/3 Bishop St, Stuart Park, NT 0820)

accommodation is provided so you'll need your own camping equipment, or to visit for the day from Katherine. No permit is required.

Alice Springs Beanie Festival
This arts and crafts festival, held during June and July, brings together communities from around central Australia and celebrates the work of indigenous artists. (The 'beanie' is a knitted woollen hat.)

Yuendumu Festival
In Yuendumu, 270km northwest of Alice Springs, Aboriginal people from the central and western desert region meet over the long weekend in early August. There's a mix of sporting and cultural events, both traditional and modern. You'll need to bring camping gear. No permit is required.

Oenpelli Open Day
Gunbalanya (Oenpelli), in Arnhem Land, across the East Alligator River not far from Jabiru, has an open day on the second Saturday in August. This event gives visitors a chance to buy local artefacts and watch the sports and dancing events. No permit is required.

Aboriginal & Torres Strait Islander Art Award
Each year (usually in September) an exhibition of works entered for this award is held at the Museum & Art Gallery of the Northern Territory in Darwin. It attracts entries from all over the country.

NATIONAL PARKS

The NT has some of Australia's wildest national parks. Both Kakadu and Uluru-Kata Tjuta have been listed on the World Heritage List.

Apart from the big-name stars, other parks in the Territory offer amazing diversity and are equally appealing. In the Top End, these include: Litchfield National Park, near Darwin, with its superb swimming holes and waterfalls, and 65km of hiking tracks; Mary River National Park with its many delights and numerous bird-watching opportunities; Nitmiluk (Katherine Gorge) National Park, with a series of rugged gorges and an awe-inspiring hiking track (five days) from the gorge to Edith Falls; Gregory National Park, which encompasses the Victoria River region; and the boutique-sized Keep River National Park, on the Western Australian (WA) border.

In central Australia, Watarrka National Park has the outrageously picturesque Kings Canyon as its centrepiece; and the West MacDonnell National Park, which encompasses some of the most spectacular gorge country in central Australia, offers excellent bushwalking opportunities, including the Larapinta Trail.

The Parks & Wildlife Commission (www.nt.gov.au /ipe/pwcnt) produces fact sheets on each park; these are available on its website or from tourist offices. See the relevant section for local Parks & Wildlife Commission offices.

ACTIVITIES
Bushwalking

To gain a true appreciation of the unique ecosystems that exist throughout the Territory, and to absorb its sights, smells and sounds, you'll need to venture out into the bush.

National Parks offer well-maintained tracks of varying lengths and degrees of difficulty with a wealth of attractions. For those looking for extended overnight hikes there's the Giles Track in Watarrka, the Jatbula Trail from Nitmiluk National Park to Edith Falls, the Larapinta Trail in the West MacDonnell Ranges near Alice Springs, or you can mark-up your own topographical maps for Litchfield and Kakadu National Parks (permits required).

Fishing

Many people come to the Top End specifically to fish, particularly for barramundi, a perch that often grows over 1m long and puts up a great fight. Landing the 'barra' is a challenge, but it's only half the fun; the other half is eating it. The taste of the flesh does depend to some extent on where the fish is caught; those caught in landlocked waterways can have a muddy flavour.

A host of commercial operators offer fishing trips for barramundi and other sporting fish throughout the Top End. Borroloola, Daly River and Mary River are the top spots, but tours are also run out of Darwin and Kakadu. See the relevant sections for further information.

The size limit on barramundi is 55cm (the length of a beer slab!) and the bag size for mud crabs is 13/14cm for males/females. For information contact the **Recreational Fishing Office** (☎ 08-8999 2372) in Darwin.

Fossicking

Fossicking is a popular pastime in the NT, although it is really only an option if you have a 4WD. Fossickers will find rewards such as agate, amethyst, garnet, jasper, zircon and, of course, gold. Good places to try include Gemtree and the Harts Range in central Australia, Pine Creek for gold and Brock's Creek (37km southwest of Adelaide River) for topaz, tourmaline, garnet and zircon.

You must first obtain a fossicking permit and permission must be obtained from the owner or leaseholder on freehold land and mineral leases. Contact the **Department of Business, Industry & Resource Development** (www.dme.nt.gov.au); Darwin (☎ 08-8999 5286); Alice Springs (☎ 08-8951 5658) for information on mining law, permits and the availability of geological maps, reports and fossicking guides.

Swimming

The cool waterfalls and waterholes and rejuvenating thermal pools hidden throughout the Territory are perfect spots to revitalise travel-weary batteries. Litchfield, in the Top End, and the West MacDonnell Ranges, in the Centre, are particularly rewarding.

Saltwater crocodiles inhabit both salt and fresh waters in the Top End (though there are quite a few safe, natural swimming holes). Before taking the plunge, use your head, read the signs and seek local advice. If in doubt, don't take a risk. Box jellyfish are out in force in the sea from October to May.

TOURS
A plethora of tours operate from both the Centre and Top End, offering a variety of options on any budget. See the various sections in this chapter for details, and stay open to word of mouth from other travellers.

From Darwin, make your way into Litchfield National Park with **Goanna Eco Tours** (☎ 1800 003 880, 08-8927 3880; www.goannaecotours .com.au), indulge in a one- or two-day tour to the Tiwi Islands through **Tiwi Tours** (☎ 1800 811 633; aussieadventure@attglobal.net) and organise your journey into Kakadu National Park with **Wilderness 4WD Adventures** (☎ 1800 808 288, 08-8941 2161; www.wildernessadventures.com.au), which runs great small-group tours into Kakadu and beyond, while **Billy Can Tours** (☎ 1800 813 484; www.billycan.com.au) offers bilingual staff. Inside Kakadu, supplement your own transport with **Kakadu Animal Tracks'** (☎ 08-8979 0145; www.animaltracks.com.au) wildlife safari and Aboriginal cultural tour, a cruise on the sublime Yellow Waters or discover the Arnhemland Escarpment country, rock art sites and aboriginal culture with **Magela Cultural & Heritage Tours** (☎ 08-8979 2422). Tours into Arnhem Land, originating in Kakadu, Darwin or Katherine, have spectacular experiences and few other travellers.

Nitmiluk Tours (☎ 1800 089 103) operates cruises through Katherine's spectacular gorge. From Katherine you can also take a didgeridoo-making tour with **Whoop Whoop** (☎ 08-8972 2941), or an Aboriginal cultural tour to Manyallaluk, with **Manyallaluk Cultural Tours** (☎ 1800 644 727).

From Alice Springs, **Emu Run** (☎ 08-8953 7057; www.emurun.com.au) tours to the East and West MacDonnell Ranges, and **Sahara Outback Tours** (☎ 08-8953 0881; www.saharatours.com.au) runs 4WD camping tours to some of the Centre's top sights.

Anangu's (☎ 08-8956 2123; www.anangutours.com .au) tours around Uluru guided by traditional owners give an insight into the land through Anangu eyes.

Tours on Aboriginal Land
One of the most rewarding aspects of travel in the NT is the opportunity to experience Aboriginal culture through tours and trips into Aboriginal land and communities with local guides. Tours into Arnhem Land are spectacular, though some are costly as the area is so remote.

Other places in the Top End with similar operations include Bathurst and Melville Islands, and the Litchfield and Katherine areas. In the Centre there are tours around Alice Springs and the MacDonnell Ranges area and at Uluru.

For more information on tours to Aboriginal land, see Tours under the relevant sections.

GETTING THERE & AWAY
There are direct international flights into Darwin from Brunei, East Timor, Indonesia and Malaysia.

See the Alice Springs, Darwin and Uluru sections in this chapter for interstate transport into the NT by air, bus, train and car. See also p985 for more information on getting around Australia.

Travellers will need to surrender all fruit and vegetables, nuts, honey and some other items at the NT/WA border.

GETTING AROUND
Air
Airnorth (☎ 1800 627 474; www.airnorth.com.au) connects Darwin and Alice Springs with most places in the Territory, including Borroloola, Gove, Katherine and Tennant Creek. **Qantas** (☎ 13 13 13; www.qantas.com.au) flies between Darwin, Alice Springs, Yulara and Gove. **Wimary** (☎ 08-8945 2755) flies to Bathurst Island and **Northern Air Charter** (☎ 08-8945 5444) services Darwin and Jabiru (in Kakadu).

For transport around Darwin see Getting Around (p766).

Bus
McCafferty's/Greyhound (☎ 13 20 30; www.mc caffertys.com.au) covers the main bus routes – including into Kakadu and to Uluru – fairly regularly. See Getting There & Away in the relevant sections in this chapter for more information.

Backpacker-type buses cover the vast distances while savouring the sights along the way. See the Darwin and Alice Springs sections for details.

Car & Motorcycle

When travelling off the beaten track, proceeding 'with care' is worth bearing in mind – all the usual precautions apply. Before heading away from sealed roads in the Territory check road conditions through the 24-hour **road information service** (☎ 1800 246 199), the **Automobile Association of the Northern Territory** (AANT; www.aant.com.au); Darwin (☎ 08-8953 1322); Alice Springs (☎ 08-8981 3837) and tourist offices.

Traffic may be fairly light and the roads dead straight, but watch out for the four great NT road hazards – speed (there are no speed limits on the open road), driver fatigue, road trains and animals (both native and domestic livestock).

Roadhouses offering fuel, food (sometimes dubious) and accommodation are spaced at regular intervals along the main highways. The price of fuel gets higher the farther from Darwin or Alice Springs you get, peaking in remote areas.

Train

The recently completed extension of the rail line to Darwin means that the famous *Ghan* train now stops in the Territory's capital, as well as Katherine and Alice Springs. See p806 for timetable and fare details.

DARWIN

☎ 08 / pop 71,350

The capital of northern Australia comes as a surprise to many people. Darwin is a lively, modern place with a youthful, easy-going lifestyle and a cosmopolitan atmosphere. It's still something of a frontier town, a long way from Australia's other major cities and closer to Jakarta than Canberra.

Darwin is a major stop for travellers and an obvious base for trips to Kakadu and other Top End natural attractions. It's a tropical oasis, too, with a pleasant harbourside location and plenty of nightlife. Wherever you're travelling to, there's a lot of distance to be covered and many people rest (and party) a bit in Darwin before leaving.

HISTORY

It took a long time to decide on Darwin as the site for the region's centre. Even after the city was established its growth was slow and troubled. Early attempts to settle the Top End were mainly due to British fears that the French or Dutch might get a foothold in Australia.

Between 1824 and 1829 Fort Dundas on Melville Island and Fort Wellington on the Cobourg Peninsula 200km northeast of Darwin, were settled and then abandoned. Fort Victoria, settled in 1838 on Cobourg's Port Essington harbour, survived a cyclone and an outbreak of malaria, but was abandoned in 1849.

In 1845 the German explorer Ludwig Leichhardt reached Port Essington overland from Brisbane, arousing prolonged interest in the Top End. The region came under the control of South Australia in 1863 and more ambitious development plans were made. Present-day Darwin was finally founded in 1869. The harbour had been discovered back in 1839 by John Lort Stokes aboard the *Beagle*, who named it Port Darwin after a former shipmate, the evolutionist Charles Darwin. At first the settlement was called Palmerston, soon becoming unofficially known as Port Darwin, and in 1911 its name was officially changed.

The growth of Darwin was accelerated by the discovery of gold at Pine Creek, about 200km south, in 1871, but it was WWII that put Darwin permanently on the map when the town became an important base for Allied action against the Japanese in the Pacific. The road heading south to the railhead at Alice Springs was surfaced, finally putting the city in direct contact with the rest of the country. Darwin was attacked 64 times during the war and at least 243 people lost their lives; it was the only place in Australia to suffer prolonged attack.

Today, Darwin has an important role as Australia's northern front door, and as a centre for administration and mining. The government and developers have long held dreams of Darwin becoming the main port connection between Australia and Asia. Perhaps the completion of the rail link between Alice Springs and Darwin will bring it that step closer.

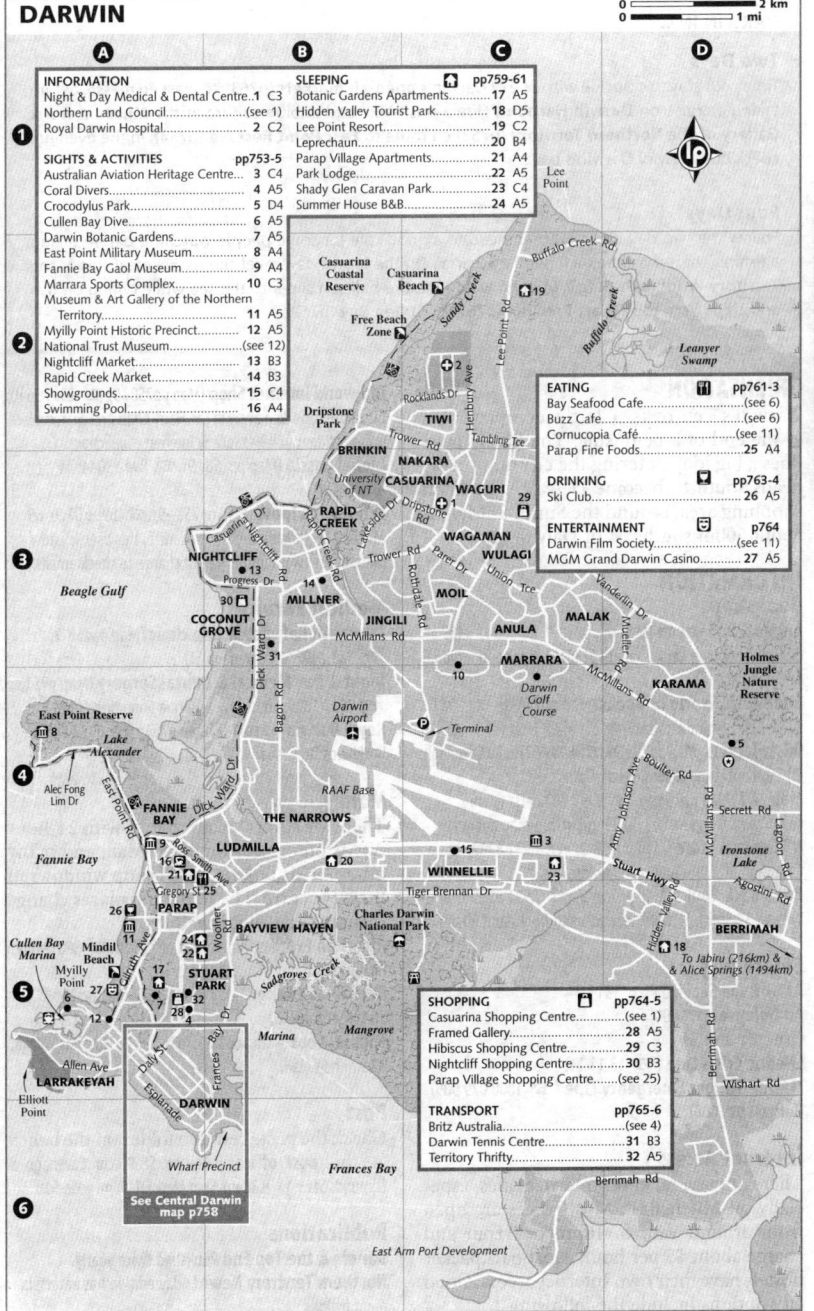

DARWIN

0 —————— 2 km
0 —————— 1 mi

INFORMATION
Night & Day Medical & Dental Centre..1 C3
Northern Land Council.....................(see 1)
Royal Darwin Hospital...........................2 C2

SIGHTS & ACTIVITIES   pp753-5
Australian Aviation Heritage Centre....3 C4
Coral Divers...4 A5
Crocodylus Park....................................5 D4
Cullen Bay Dive.....................................6 A5
Darwin Botanic Gardens........................7 A5
East Point Military Museum....................8 A4
Fannie Bay Gaol Museum.......................9 A4
Marrara Sports Complex.......................10 C3
Museum & Art Gallery of the Northern
   Territory...11 A5
Myilly Point Historic Precinct...............12 A5
National Trust Museum..................(see 12)
Nightcliff Market..................................13 B3
Rapid Creek Market.............................14 B3
Showgrounds.......................................15 C4
Swimming Pool.....................................16 A4

SLEEPING   pp759-61
Botanic Gardens Apartments................17 A5
Hidden Valley Tourist Park...................18 D5
Lee Point Resort..................................19 C2
Leprechaun...20 B4
Parap Village Apartments.....................21 A4
Park Lodge...22 A5
Shady Glen Caravan Park.....................23 C4
Summer House B&B..............................24 A5

EATING   pp761-3
Bay Seafood Cafe...........................(see 6)
Buzz Cafe.......................................(see 6)
Cornucopia Café...........................(see 11)
Parap Fine Foods.................................25 A4

DRINKING   pp763-4
Ski Club..26 A5

ENTERTAINMENT   p764
Darwin Film Society.....................(see 11)
MGM Grand Darwin Casino..................27 A5

SHOPPING   pp764-5
Casuarina Shopping Centre...............(see 1)
Framed Gallery....................................28 A5
Hibiscus Shopping Centre....................29 C3
Nightcliff Shopping Centre...................30 B3
Parap Village Shopping Centre......(see 25)

TRANSPORT   pp765-6
Britz Australia..................................(see 4)
Darwin Tennis Centre..........................31 B3
Territory Thrifty..................................32 A5

NORTHERN TERRITORY

See Central Darwin
map p758

To Jabiru (216km) &
& Alice Springs (1494km)

DARWIN IN...

Two Days

Time your stay to coincide with one of Darwin's **open-air markets** (p763), to feast en masse, before taking a cruise on **Darwin Harbour**. Hire a push-bike and imbibe culture at the **Museum & Art Gallery of the Northern Territory** (p753) en route to **East Point Reserve** (p754). In the evening, check out a few of Darwin's bars.

Four Days

Follow the two-day itinerary, then head to a good café for some people-watching before taking a fishing charter to hook a legendary 'barra'. On the fourth day, meet the native creatures at the **Territory Wildlife Park** (p770), then watch the fire-ball sun slip into the sea while dining on fish and chips from the **Wharf Precinct** (p762) or **Cullen Bay** (p762).

ORIENTATION

Darwin's centre is a fairly compact area at the end of a peninsula. The Stuart Hwy does a big loop entering the city and finally heads south to become Daly St. The main shopping area, around the Smith St Mall, is about 500m southeast of Daly St.

INFORMATION
Bookshops

Angus & Robertson (Map pppp758-9 ☎ 8941 3489; Galleria Shopping Centre, Smith St Mall) Maps and regional travel publications.

Bookworld/World of Books (Map pp758-9; ☎ 8981 5277; Centrepoint Arcade, Smith St Mall) New titles.

Dusty Jackets (Map pp758-9; ☎ 8981 6772; 30 Cavenagh St) Excellent range of second-hand books.

Maps NT (Map pp758-9; ☎ 8999 7032; 1st fl, cnr Cavenagh & Bennett Sts) Government-run map agency.

NT General Store (Map pp758-9; ☎ 8981 8242; 42 Cavenagh St) Maps and travel guides.

Read Back Books (Map pp758-9; ☎ 8981 8885; Star Village, 32 Smith St Mall) Second-hand books and CDs.

Emergency

AANT Road Service (☎ 13111)
Ambulance (☎ 000)
Fire (☎ 000)
Lifeline Crisis Line (☎ 13 11 14)
Marine Stinger Emergency Line (☎ 1800 079 909)
Police (☎ 000)

Internet Access

There are several good Internet cafés, especially on Mitchell St. Most places are open from around 9am to 10pm or 11pm and charge about $5 per hour. Most backpacker hostels have their own Internet access. Good city options include the following.

Didjworld Internet Shop (Map pp758–9; ☎ 8981 3510; 60 Smith St) Tucked away in the Harry Chan Arcade, this place sells no didgs but it has speedy Internet connections.

Global Gossip (Map pp758–9; ☎ 8942 3044; 44 Mitchell St)

Internet Outpost (Map pp758–9; ☎ 8981 0720; 69 Mitchell St) Outside the transit centre, this user-friendly place offers two minutes free of charge to check emails.

Medical Services

International vaccination clinic (Map pp758-9; ☎ 981 7492; 43 Cavenagh St)

Night & Day Medical & Dental Surgery (Map p751; ☎ 8927 1899; Shop 31, Casuarina Shopping Centre)

Royal Darwin Hospital (Map p751; ☎ 8922 8888; Rocklands Dr, Casuarina)

Money

There are several major banks with 24-hour ATMs on or near Smith St Mall, and many other ATMs poking out of shop windows in the city centre. The following places change cash and travellers cheques:

American Express (Amex; Map pp758-9; ☎ 8981 4699; 8 Knuckey St)

Bureau de Change (Map pp758-9; 69 Mitchell St & Smith St Mall)

Thomas Cook (Map pp758-9; ☎ 8981 6182; Star Village, 32 Smith St Mall)

Post

Check the poste restante folder on the bench at the **post office** (Map pp758-9; cnr Cavenagh & Edmunds Sts; ☼ 8.30am-5pm Mon-Fri, 9am-noon Sat) .

Publications

Darwin & the Top End Published twice yearly.
Northern Territory News Friday edition has entertainment listings.

The Top End Visitors' Guide Monthly guide to some of the city's attractions.

Tourist Information
The **visitors centre** (Map pp758-9; ☎ 8936 2499; www.tourismtopend.com.au; cnr Knuckey & Mitchell Sts; ☒ 9am-5.30pm Mon-Fri, 9am-3pm Sat, 10am-3pm Sun) run by Tourism Top End can book tours and accommodation throughout the Territory for service providers within its organisation. Top End national parks fact sheets are available and Kakadu park passes are sold here.

Travel Agencies
To book or confirm flights or bus travel, or book tours, there's no shortage of agencies in Darwin. Most backpacker hostels and many hotels have their own tour desks. The following can assist with onward travel:
Flight Centre (Map pp758-9; ☎ 8941 8002; 24 Cavenagh St)
STA Travel (Map pp758-9; ☎ 8941 2955; Galleria Shopping Centre, Smith St Mall)

SIGHTS
Myilly Point Historic Precinct
At the northwestern end of Smith St, in Burnett Place, is this small but important precinct of houses built in the 1930s. The buildings, known as Burnett houses, are elevated and feature asbestos-cement louvres and casement windows, so the ventilation could be regulated according to weather conditions. One of the buildings, Burnett House, is the site of the **National Trust museum** (Map p751; ☎ 8981 2848; admission free; ☒ 10am-3pm Mon-Fri). Indulging in the dainty high tea ($7.50) is a delightful way to spend a Sunday afternoon.

Aquascene
Half the stale bread in Darwin goes to a horde of milkfish, mullet and catfish – some 1.5m in length – that feed at **Aquascene** (Map pp758-9; ☎ 8981 7837; www.aquascene.com.au; 28 Doctors Gully Rd; adult/child $6/3.60), near the corner of Daly St and the Esplanade. It's a fascinating sight and children love it. Aquascene is open every day at high tide when the fish come in for feeding (they've been doing it for more than 40 years). Phone ahead for feeding times.

Darwin Botanic Gardens
The **botanic gardens** (Map p751; ☎ 8981 1958; Gardens Rd; admission free) northwest of the city centre were used to grow vegetables during the early days of Darwin's settlement, until Cyclone Tracy (for details see the boxed text 'Cyclone Tracy'; below) uprooted 75% of the plants. There's a noteworthy collection of tropical flora, a self-guided Aboriginal plant-use walk and a coastal section over the road, between Gilruth Ave and Fannie Bay.

It's an easy bicycle ride to the gardens from the city centre.

Museum & Art Gallery of the Northern Territory
Don't miss this superb **museum and art gallery** (Map p751; ☎ 8999 8201; Conacher St, Fannie Bay; admission free; ☒ 9am-5pm Mon-Fri, 10am-5pm Sat & Sun), about 4km from the city centre. It's bright, well presented and full of interesting displays. A highlight is the NT Aboriginal art collection with carvings and bark paintings from the Tiwi Islands and Arnhem Land.

CYCLONE TRACY

The statistics of this disaster are frightening. Cyclone Tracy built up over Christmas Eve 1974 and by midnight the winds began to reach their full fury. At 3.05am the airport's anemometer failed, just after it recorded a wind speed of 217km/h. It's thought the peak wind speeds were as high as 280km/h. In all, 66 people died. Of Darwin's 11,200 houses, 50% to 60% were destroyed either totally or beyond repair, and only 400 survived relatively intact.

Much criticism was levelled at the design and construction of Darwin's houses, but plenty of places at least a century old, and built as solidly as you could ask for, also toppled before the awesome winds. The new and rebuilt houses have been cyclone-proofed with strong steel reinforcements and roofs that are firmly pinned down.

Most people say that next time a cyclone is forecast, they'll jump straight into their cars and head down the Track – and come back afterwards to find out if their houses really were cyclone-proof! Those who stay will probably take advantage of the official cyclone shelter.

A fair amount of space is devoted to Cyclone Tracy, with photographs, newsreel and radio coverage from Christmas Day 1974. You can even step into a darkened room and hear a frightening recording from the night of the cyclone.

Pride of place among the stuffed birds and animals undoubtedly goes to 'Sweetheart' – a 5m, 780kg saltwater crocodile, who became quite a Top End personality after numerous encounters with fishing dinghies on the Finniss River south of Darwin. Apparently he had a taste for outboard motors. He died when captured in 1979.

The locally focused natural history section is set out into individual habitats; the gallery also features changing exhibitions.

The museum has a good bookshop, theatre and cafe. Bus Nos 4 and 6 travel close by, or you can get there on the Tour Tub (p757).

Fannie Bay Gaol Museum

This interesting **museum** (Map p751; ☎ 8999 8201; cnr East Point Rd & Ross Smith Ave; admission free; ☼ 10am-4.30pm) operated as Darwin's main jail from 1883 to 1979. You can wander around the old cells, see a gallows constructed for a hanging in 1952, and a minimum security section used at various times for juveniles, lepers and Vietnamese refugees.

East Point Reserve

This spit of land north of Fannie Bay is particularly good in the late afternoon when wallabies come out to feed, cool breezes drift in and you can watch the sunset across the bay. There are walking and cycling paths as well as a road to the tip of the point.

On the northern side of the point is a series of **wartime gun emplacements** and the small **Military Museum** (Map p751; ☎ 8981 9702; www.epmm.com.au; East Point Reserve; adult/child $10/5; ☼ 9.30am-5pm) devoted to Darwin's WWII activities.

Parliament House

Dominating the streetscape at the southeastern end of Mitchell St is the box-like **Parliament House** (Map pp758-9; tours ☎ 8946 1425; ☼ 9am-6pm Mon-Fri; tours 10am & noon Sat), dubbed 'the wedding cake', which evokes the grandeur of Southeast Asian architecture. It's

worth a wander around the cavernous interior. The building also houses the **Northern Territory Library**.

The nearby **Supreme Court building** contains some fine Aboriginal artworks.

Wharf Precinct   Map p758–9

The old **Stokes Hill Wharf**, below the cliffs at the southern end of the city centre, is worth exploring.

At the end of the jetty an old warehouse, known as the **Arcade**, houses a food centre that's great for an alfresco lunch or a cool drink on a balmy evening.

Back on the mainland, the precinct also features the old **oil-storage tunnels** (☎ 8985 6333; adult/child $4.50/3; ☼ 9am-5pm daily Apr-Sep, 10am-4pm Tue-Fri Oct-10 Dec & Feb-Mar), dug into the cliff face during WWII.

INDO-PACIFIC MARINE

This excellent **marine aquarium** (☎ 8981 1294; Stokes Hill Wharf; adult/child $16/6; ☼ 10am-6pm) gives you a close encounter with the organisms of Darwin Harbour. Each small tank is a complete ecosystem, with only the occasional extra fish introduced as food for some of the carnivores such as stonefish or angler fish. It sometimes has box jellyfish, as well as more attractive creatures like sea horses, clown fish and butterfly fish. The living coral reef display is especially impressive.

The **Coral Reef by Night** show, held at 7pm Wednesday, Friday and Sunday, includes a seafood dinner and costs $69.50; book in advance.

AUSTRALIAN PEARLING EXHIBITION

Housed in the same building as the aquarium, the **Pearling Exhibition** (☎ 8999 6573; adult/child/family $6.60/3.30/17; ☼ 10am-5pm) details the history of the local pearling industry. You can also experience life underwater inside a simulated diving helmet.

Australian Aviation Heritage Centre

Darwin's **aviation museum** (Map p751; ☎ 8947 2145; www.darwinsairwar.com.au; 557 Stuart Hwy, Winnellie; adult/child/family $11/6/28; ☼ 9am-5pm), about 10km from the city centre, is a large hanger crammed with aircraft and memorabilia. The mammoth American B52 bomber, one of only two displayed outside the USA, dwarfs the other aircraft, which include the wreck of a Japanese Zero fighter shot down in 1942.

Bus Nos 5 and 8 run along the Stuart Hwy.

Crocodylus Park

This **park** (Map p751; ☎ 8922 4500; McMillans Rd, Berrimah; adult/child/family $22/11/57; ⏰ 9am-5pm), a breeding complex, features hundreds of giant reptiles. Tours include a feeding demonstration and a chance to cuddle a baby croc (jaws firmly closed). A mini zoo on site houses lions and other big cats, spider monkeys, marmosets, tamarinds and large birds including ostriches and cassowaries. A comprehensive museum covers all things croc-related. Admission is a bit steep but it's worthwhile if you time your visit for one of the tours, at 10am, noon and 2pm.

You can get to the park by taking bus No 5 from Darwin or the **Crocodylus Shuttle** (☎ 8941 5358), which picks up from city hotels.

ACTIVITIES
Cycling

Darwin has a network of excellent bicycle tracks. The main track runs from the northern end of Cavenagh St to Fannie Bay, Coconut Grove, Nightcliff and Casuarina. At Fannie Bay a side track heads out to East Point Reserve.

For more information on bicycle hire see Bicycle & Scooter (p766).

Diving

Darwin Harbour offers some excellent diving, largely due to the wrecks from WWII and Cyclone Tracy, which are now encrusted with coral and support plentiful marine life. Wreck diving in the harbour is available throughout the year and equipment hire is available through both operators listed. Medical certificates are required to do the courses; equipment hire is included in the course price.

Cullen Bay Dive (Map p751; ☎ 8981 3049; www.divedarwin.com; 66 Marina Blvd, Cullen Bay) has double boat dives with tanks for $100; basic open-water PADI courses cost $500.

Coral Divers (Map p751; ☎ 8981 2686; 42 Stuart Hwy, Stuart Park) has single boat dives with tanks for $35, and open-water certification courses for $450.

Sailing

The **Winter School of Sailing** (☎ 0417-818 257) offers three-hour yachting tours at 9am, 1pm and 5pm daily, which include instruction in the basics of sailing, for $50. Longer sailing courses are also available.

You have to be a member to visit the **Darwin Sailing Club** (☎ 8981 1700; Atkins Dr) in Fannie Bay, but anyone residing more than 100km from Darwin can get temporary membership (free) on the spot. Although you can't charter boats here, you can meet local sailing enthusiasts at the restaurant and bar; there's a race programme from April to November.

Swimming

Darwin has plenty of beaches but swimming is out between October and May because of box jellyfish. Popular beaches outside the stinger season include Mindil and Vestey's on Fannie Bay, and Mandorah, across the bay from the town (see Around Darwin; p766).

A stretch of the 7km Casuarina Beach farther east is a nude beach. This is a good beach but at low tide it's a long walk to the water's edge. For stinger-free swimming, Lake Alexander, at East Point, is an easy cycle from the centre. It's a good spot for kids, or for a barbecue or picnic.

The main public **swimming pool** (Map p751; ☎ 8981 2662; Ross Smith Ave, Parap; adult/child $2.85/1.35) has a partly shaded 50m pool and a children's play pool.

WALKING TOUR

Despite its shaky beginnings and the destruction caused by WWII and Cyclone Tracy, Darwin still has a few historic buildings in the town centre. The National Trust produces an interesting booklet titled *A Walk through Historical Darwin*, available from the visitors centre.

Darwin's tropical climate doesn't lend itself to energetic exertions in the middle of the day, so the following walk is most pleasant early in the morning or late afternoon.

WALKING TOUR
Distance: 3.5km
Duration: 1 hour

Start in the very heart of the city at Smith St Mall. Near its southern end is the historic **Victoria Hotel** (**1**; 'The Vic'; p763), a popular pub and nightspot. Walking southeast along Smith St to the historic part of town you'll find the remains of the **Old Palmerston Town Hall** (**2**; 1883), which was virtually destroyed by Tracy, despite its solid Victorian construction. Opposite is the former mining exchange **Brown's Mart** (**3**; p764) built in 1885, which was also badly damaged, but now houses a theatre. On the other side of Civic Sq is **Christ Church Cathedral** (**4**; originally built in 1902). Only the porch, added in 1944, remained after the cyclone, and a contemporary cathedral has since been built around it. On the corner of Smith St and the Esplanade, the original **police station** and **courthouse** (**5**; 1884) were badly damaged, but have been restored and are now used as government offices.

Cross the Esplanade for **Survivors' Lookout** (**6**), which is perched at the top of the cliff and has views out over the harbour (somewhat obscured by trees). The lookout has some interesting interpretive displays, complete with WWII photos showing the history of the Japanese bombing missions over Darwin. Steps from here lead down to Kitchener Dr at the base of the cliff and to the **WWII oil-storage tunnels** (**7**; p754).

Back on the Esplanade, **Government House** (**8**), built in stages from 1870, was known as the Residency until 1911 and has been damaged by just about every cyclone to hit

Darwin. It is once again in fine condition. Outside is a memorial plaque commemorating the bombing of Darwin in 1942 and across the road is another **monument** (**9**) to the completion of the Overland Telegraph which linked a submarine cable from Java (Indonesia) with the telegraph line from Adelaide. This cable put Australia in instant communication with Britain for the first time.

Set back from the Esplanade is the modern **Parliament House** (**10**; p754). From here the Esplanade runs along the full length of the city centre. Turn off into the green expanse of **Bicentennial Park** (**11**) at Herbert St, where you'll pass the **Anzac Memorial** (**12**). From here you can walk all the way along the western edge of the gardens; there are views out over the bay, including a lookout at the northern end – a good spot for sunset viewing.

At the northern end of the park a footpath leads down to **Doctors Gully** (**13**). This is really only worthwhile when it is fish-feeding time at Aquascene (p753), as there is little else to see here, although a signboard has some historic detail and old photos. From the gully a **boardwalk** (**14**) leads up through a small patch of remnant vegetation, bringing you out on Daly St, where you can get back on the Esplanade and continue southeast to the city centre. At Knuckey St you'll come to two historic buildings: **Lyons Cottage** (**15**), the British-Australian Telegraph Residence and now a museum; and **Admiralty House** (**16**), an early Darwin residence raised on stilts and surrounded by tropical vegetation.

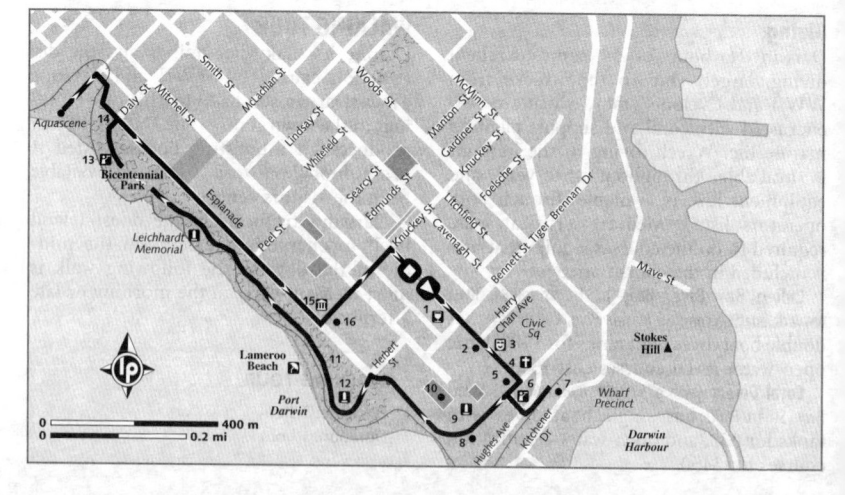

Turn left onto Knuckey St, then right on Smith St and you're back in the mall – and probably ready to pop into 'The Vic' for a cold drink!

DARWIN FOR CHILDREN

Darwin is a young city and as such is very child-friendly. You'll see many families enjoying the food and scene at the city's markets or loading up on fish and chips on the wharf (p754) – particularly when large cruise ships are about to set sail. Kids love getting among Darwin's attractions: feeding the fish at Aquascene (p753); interacting with the displays at the Museum & Art Gallery of the Northern Territory (p753); getting up close to all manner of wild animals at the Territory Wildlife Park (p770); and probably not straying too far from you at Crocodylus Park (p755). The Indo-Pacific Marine (p754) has a living reef and many fascinating creatures from Darwin Harbour.

TOURS

The visitors centre and most places to stay have a plethora of tour information for Darwin and the Top End; where possible, contact the operator directly.

Aboriginal Cultural Tours

A few Aboriginal culture tours depart from Darwin. Tours to remote communities that involve a chartered flight are naturally quite expensive.

Tiwi Tours (☎ 1800 811 633, 8924 1115; aussieadventure@attglobal.net) will fly you to Bathurst Island to experience some Tiwi culture (p768) on a one-/two-day tour for $298/564.

City Sights

Darwin Day Tours (☎ 8924 1124; www.darwinday tours.com) operates a half-day tour ($48/36 per adult/child) around the city, which takes in all the major attractions and can be linked with a harbour cruise.

The **Tour Tub** (☎ 8981 5233), an open-sided minibus, does a circuit of the city, calling at the major places of interest. You can hop on or off anywhere along its route; stops include Aquascene (only at fish-feeding times), the Wharf Precinct, MGM Grand Darwin casino, the Museum and Art Gallery, the Military Museum, Fannie Bay Gaol, Parap markets (Saturday only) and the botanic gardens. In the city centre it

leaves from Knuckey St, at the end of the Smith St Mall. There's a set fare ($25/15 per adult/child under 12 years) for the day; buses operate hourly from 9am to 4pm.

Harbour Cruises

You'll find plenty of cruise operators along the marina at Cullen Bay. Most cruises last two to three hours, depart daily and include nibbles and a glass of sparkling wine for around $45. Sunset cruises on the pearling lugger **Kim** (☎ 8942 3131) depart at 5.15pm. Sit back, relax and soak up the magnificent sunset aboard the 22m schooner **City of Darwin** (☎ 0417-855 829; www.darwincruises.com). Three-hour sunset cruises ($40) depart at 4.45pm; BYO drinks. The *Tumalaren* sunset cruise ($45) departs at 5pm, and also offers a barbecue lunch cruise ($55/33 per adult/child); contact **Darwin Cruises & Charters** (☎ 8942 3131; www.darwinharbourcruise.com.au) for details.

Spirit of Darwin (☎ 8981 3711) is a modern passenger boat that does two-hour sightseeing cruises ($31) at 1.40pm and 5.40pm daily from April to October.

Tours Farther Afield

Several operators do trips to the jumping crocodiles at Adelaide River and to the Territory Wildlife Park on the Cox Peninsula Rd. See Litchfield (p771) and Kakadu National Park (p780) for details of tours from Darwin.

Darwin Day Tours (☎ 8924 1124; www.darwinday tours.com) offers a variety of full- and half-day trips. The full-day Wildlife Spectacular Tour ($110/80 per adult/child) takes in the Territory Wildlife Park, Darwin Crocodile Farm, the Jumping Croc cruise and nearby Fogg Dam. A half-day trip to the Territory Wildlife Park is $48/36; there are also day trips to Litchfield National Park ($95/85), Kakadu ($150/125) and Katherine ($140/70).

NT Wilderness Expeditions (☎ 1300 656 071) runs an overnight Turtle Research Tour ($275) giving you the opportunity to carry out nest audits and collect data for turtle research programmes. Trips depart from Cullen Bay marina for the remote island camp on Monday, Wednesday, Friday and Saturday from April to October.

Aussie Overlanders (☎ 1300 880 118; www.aussie overlanders.com) runs three-day Kakadu camping safaris ($440) and combines visits to Kakadu,

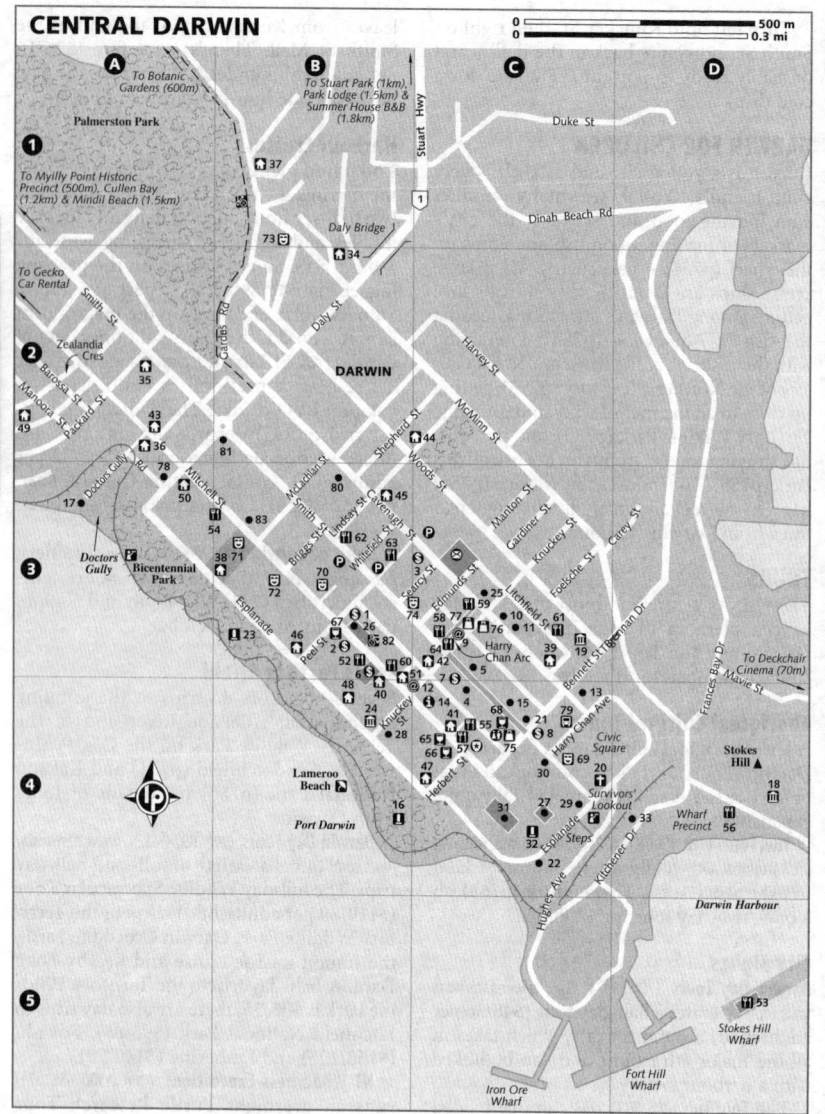

CENTRAL DARWIN

0 — 500 m
0 — 0.3 mi

To Botanic Gardens (600m)

Palmerston Park

To Stuart Park (1km), Park Lodge (1.5km) & Summer House B&B (1.8km)

Duke St

Stuart Hwy

To Myilly Point Historic Precinct (500m), Cullen Bay (1.2km) & Mindil Beach (1.5km)

Dinah Beach Rd

Daly Bridge

Daly St

DARWIN

Harvey St

McMinn St

Shepherd St

Woods St

Manton St

Gardiner St

Knuckey St

Foelsche St

Carey St

To Gecko Car Rental

Smith St

Zealandia Cres

Mitchell St

Briggs St

Lindsay St

Cavenagh St

Searcy St

Edmunds St

Litchfield St

Bennett St

Frances Bay Dr

Mavie St

To Deckchair Cinema (70m)

Doctors Gully

Bicentennial Park

Esplanade

McLachlan St

Smith St

Whitfield St

Harry Chan Arc

Knuckey St

Harbert St

Harry Chan Ave

Civic Square

Survivors' Lookout

Stokes Hill

Wharf Precinct

Lameroo Beach

Port Darwin

Esplanade Steps

Kitchener Dr

Hughes Ave

Darwin Harbour

Darwin Harbour

Stokes Hill Wharf

Iron Ore Wharf

Fort Hill Wharf

Daly River, Palumpa and Litchfield on a five-day camping safari, offering a wonderful opportunity to visit a remote Aboriginal community and camp out in the Aboriginal guide's beautiful country. Tours depart on Tuesday from June to November ($750).

Adventure Tours Australia (☎ 1300 654 604, 8309 2277; www.adventuretours.com.au) runs tours rang-ing from one to 10 days throughout the Territory. The camping tours use pre-set up sites.

FESTIVALS & EVENTS
Darwin is a colourful city with a rich cultural mix and plenty of reasons to celebrate (mostly in July and August).

Royal Darwin Show The agricultural show, on the fourth Friday-Saturday of July, features all the usual rides, demonstrations and competitions.

Darwin to Bali Yacht Race The city is abuzz in the days leading up to this hotly contested race in July.

Darwin Cup Carnival This racing carnival takes place in July and August; highlight is the running of the Darwin Cup.

Darwin Fringe Festival Local performing and visual arts held in July and August.

Beer Can Regatta An utterly insane festival in August, which features races for boats made entirely of beer cans, off Mindil Beach.

Darwin Rodeo Yee ha! The whips crack as international teams compete in numerous events; held in August.

Festival of Darwin A mainly outdoor arts and culture festival that highlights Darwin's unique cultural mix; held in August.

SLEEPING

For atmosphere, try Darwin's B&Bs and guesthouses; see the website www.bed-and -breakfast.au.com for complete listings. The rare places that lack a swimming pool in Darwin, or indeed the NT, will have a spa to cool off in. During the wet season, prices can plummet by 50% and you'll often receive the seventh night free at camping resorts, hostels and apartment complexes.

Budget

HOSTELS & LODGES

Darwin's backpacker hostels are clustered together on or near Mitchell St, a stone's throw from the transit centre.

Competition is keen and standards are pretty high, so it's worth asking about discounts, especially during the Wet or if you plan to stay a while. However, it gets busy in the peak season (May to September) so you should book ahead for the first night. The usual YHA/VIP and other discounts apply. Facilities normally include communal kitchen facilities, but most places turn the air-conditioning on only at night.

Park Lodge (Map p751; ☎ 8981 5692; 42 Coronation Dr, Stuart Park; s/d $45/55; ⚙) Not too far from the city centre, Park Lodge is friendly, clean and quiet. All rooms have a fridge and share the lodge's bathrooms, well-equipped kitchen, TV and sitting room, laundry and pool.

Cavenagh (Map pp758-9; ☎ 8941 6383; thecavenagh@ mail.com; 12 Cavenagh St; dm/s $23/60, d & tw per person $30;

❌ 🖥) The new kid on the block, part of the Nomad's chain, has comfortable, relatively spacious rooms with bathroom, TV and ample luggage storage areas. There's an enormous pool and café/bar downstairs plus a guest kitchen.

Darwin City YHA (Map pp758-9; ☎ 8981 3995; darwinyha@yhant.org.au; 69 Mitchell St; dm from $18, d $50, with bathroom $65, nonmembers extra $3.50; ❌ 🖥) In the centre of the action, this clean and popular hostel has a large open kitchen overlooking the pool. There are games and TV rooms and lockers.

Elke's Inner City Backpackers (Map pp758-9; ☎ 1800 808 365, 8981 8399; info@elkesbackpackers .com.au; 112 Mitchell St; dm/d $22/55; ❌ 🖥) The quiet gardens between Elke's two renovated houses are perfect for polishing off a novel and whittling away at the postcard list. There's a pool and spa, a fridge in each room, and a TV room.

Other recommendations:

Frogshollow Backpackers (Map pp758-9; ☎ 1800 068 686, 8941 2600; frogs@octa4.et.au; 27 Lindsay St; dm $21, d from $50; ❌ 🖥)

Chilli's Backpackers (Map pp758-9; ☎ 1800 351 313; www.chillis.com.au; 69a Mitchell St; dm/d $20/60; ❌ 🖥)

Banyan View Lodge (Map pp758-9; ☎ 8981 8644; fax 8981 6104; 119 Mitchell St; dm $18, s/d from $40/60; ❌)

CAMPING & CARAVAN PARKS

Hidden Valley Tourist Park (Map p751; ☎ 8947 1422; hvtp@topend.com.au; 25 Hidden Valley Rd; camp/caravan sites for 2 $18/20, d $36, units from $80; ❌ 🖥) The name says it all. Grassy surrounds and tropical plants give Hidden Valley the appeal of a hidden oasis. The units here are far superior to your average park cabins. The seventh night's camping is free of charge.

Shady Glen Caravan Park (Map p751; ☎ 8984 3330; contact@shadyglen.com.au; cnr Farrel Cres & Stuart Hwy; camp/caravan sites for 2 $21/24, cabins $75, with bathroom $95; ❌ 🖥) About 10km northeast of the city centre and just off the Stuart Hwy, Shady Glen is a lush, well-treed spot with immaculate facilities, a camp kitchen and friendly staff.

Leprechaun (Map p751; ☎ 8984 3400; www .geocities.com/leprechaunmotel/; 378 Stuart Hwy, Winellie; camp/caravan sites for 2 $20/22.50, s/d cabins $55/70; ❌) The Leprechaun's shady *green* grounds, close to town, have barbecues, a pleasant pool and a variety of accommodation options.

Lee Point Resort (Map p751; ☎ 8945 0535, fax 8945 0642; Lee Point Rd; camp/caravan sites $22/25, d cabins $70; ❌) This spacious park is 800m from the Lee Point beach and 15km north of the city. The facilities here are excellent and each powered site has a private bathroom.

Mid-Range

The resorts and tourist parks listed under Camping & Caravan Parks (earlier) offer comfortable motel-style units and self-contained cabins.

APARTMENTS

Botanic Gardens Apartments (Map p751; ☎ 8946 0300; botanic@octa4.net.au; 17 Geranium St, Stuart Park; d $140, 1-/2-/3-bedroom apt from $180/200/300; P ❌) Commanding prestigious views from the Botanic Gardens to Beagle Bay, each spacious apartment in this complex has a balcony, kitchen and laundry. There are two pools and the three-bedroom apartments sleep up to seven.

Parap Village Apartments (Map p751; ☎ 1800 620 913; pva@paspaley.com.au; 39 Parap Rd, Parap; 2-/3-bedroom apt from $185/240; ❌) Across the road from Parap Village and its thriving Saturday market, each comfortable self-contained apartment has a balcony and laundry. It offers two pools, a children's play area and discounts for stays over seven nights.

Alatai Holiday Apartments (Map pp758-9; ☎ 1800 628 833, 8981 5188; alatai@d130.aone.net.au; cnr McMinn & Finniss Sts; studio $135, 2-/3-bedroom apt $195/330; ❌) Alatai's modern, self-contained apartments at the northern edge of the city centre have their own washing facilities. The studios are quite compact; the apartments are roomier. Cheaper stand-by (walk-in) rates are available.

BED & BREAKFASTS

Summer House (Map p751; ☎ 8981 9992; shbb@ octa4.net.au; 3 Quarry Cres, Stuart Park; d $100, 2-bedroom apt $160; ❌) A breezy tropical ambience permeates throughout Summer House from its leafy garden to the spacious Oriental and Balinese-inspired rooms with private lounge, kitchen and bathroom facilities. The self-contained apartments sleep four. Breakfast $10.

Steeles (Map pp758-9; ☎ 8941 3636; rustynt@octa4 .net.au; 4 Zealandia Cres, Larrakeyah; s/d $95/125; ❌) Steeles' Spanish Mission-style B&B is

Be awestruck by the mesmerising desert monoliths of **Kata Tjuta (The Olgas)** (p820)

RICHARD I'A

Walk through an amazing field of **magnetic termite mounds** (p771)

MITCH REARDON

Overleaf:
Experience the timeless landscape of **Uluru (Ayers Rock)** (p819)

PAUL SINCLAIR

Nestle near the desert dunes, close to Uluru, at the village resort of **Yulara** (p821)

ALAIN E

perfectly positioned midway between the city centre, Cullen Bay and Mindil Beach. Swimming in the saltwater pool in the evening is a delight.

HOTELS & MOTELS

Barramundi Lodge (Map pp758-9; 8941 6466; www.barramundilodge.com.au; 4 Gardens Rd, The Gardens; s/d $45/80; P) Perched opposite the golf course, between the CBD, Botanic Gardens and Mindil Beach, this is a real find. Clean, spacious rooms have a TV and kitchenette, though the bathrooms are communal. There's a laundry, covered common area and a pool lounge area with a barbecue.

Value Inn (Map pp758-9; 8981 4733; www.valueinn.com.au; 50 Mitchell St; tr $80;) Relatively inexpensive rooms are available at this inner-city place opposite the transit centre. The cramped rooms come with a bathroom and sleep up to three people. They also have a fridge and TV.

Top End Hotel (Map pp758-9; 1800 626 151; cnr Mitchell & Daly Sts; s/d $100/105;) Handy for those who want to roll into bed after delving into the complex's nocturnal delights of five bars and nightclubs, each modern, standard motel room opens onto the pool and garden, and is surprisingly quiet.

Asti Motel (Map pp758-9; 1800 063 335, 8981 8200; asti@octa4.net.au; 7 Packard Pl; d from $95;) Asti's central location makes it handy to the city centre, botanic gardens, Mindil Beach and Cullen Bay. Studios sleep up to four people and have basic cooking facilities, or you can nick downstairs to Tim's Surf & Turf Restaurant (p763).

Mirambeena Tourist Resort (Map pp758-9; 1800 891 100, 8946 0111; 64 Cavenagh St; d $150, deluxe $205;) This gentle giant is surrounded by an attractive tropical garden in the city centre. It has comfortable rooms, a pool, spa and a good restaurant. The split-level town-houses sleep four.

Palms City Resort (Map pp758-9; 8982 9211; www.citypalms.com; 64 The Esplanade; motel d $140, villa d $150-200;) Palms' detached hexagonal villas huddle around the landscaped pool, overlooking Bicentennial Park on this compact site. Each has a lounge and outside decked area.

Top End

Most of Darwin's upmarket hotels are on the Esplanade, making best use of the prime

views across the bay. Rates given here are high season rack rates but you'll almost never pay this much. Most offer in-house movies and contain a collection of bars and restaurants.

Darwin Central Hotel (Map pp758-9; 8944 9000; www.darwincentral.com.au; cnr Smith & Knuckey Sts; d $220;) Right in the centre of town, this plush independent has a contemporary appeal and impeccable facilities. There's a guest laundry and the hotel's Waterhole Restaurant is popular with locals and travellers alike.

Carlton Hotel Darwin (Map pp758-9; 1800 891 119, 8980 0800; res@carlton-darwin.com.au; The Esplanade; d/ste $240/280; P) Adjacent to the Darwin Entertainment Centre, the Carlton has all the facilities you'd expect from a modern five-star hotel, including a fully equipped gym and inviting pool. The spacious rooms have harbour or city views.

Other options:

Saville (Map pp758-9; 1800 681 686, 8943 4333; www.savillesuites.com.au; 88 The Esplanade; d $240-260, 1-/2-bedroom apt from $260/370;) Stunning harbour views.

Novotel Atrium (Map pp758-9; 8941 0755; sales@novoteldarwin.com.au; 100 The Esplanade; d $220-250; 2-bedroom apt $320;)

Crowne Plaza Darwin (Map pp758-9; 1800 891 107, 8982 0000; 32 Mitchell St; d/ste from $155/210;)

EATING

You can feast your way around Darwin, starting with the fast and cheap nosh in the transit centre and bustling markets, before travelling through the exotic concoctions whipped up at top restaurants. The standard and variety tops anywhere else in the Territory, so enjoy it while you're here. There are plenty of options around Mitchell St and the city centre, or head down to the Wharf Precinct or Cullen Bay for water views.

Feeling peckish on a Sunday afternoon? Try high tea at **Burnett House** (Map p751; 8981 0165; 4 Burnett Pl; Myilly Point; high tea $7.50) with dainty sandwiches and delightful cakes.

Cafés

CITY CENTRE

Cheap eateries cluster in the transit centre arcade on Mitchell St. Most are hole-in-the-wall outlets, but there are sheltered tables and stools.

NORTHERN TERRITORY

THE AUTHOR'S CHOICE

Twilight on Lindsay (Map pp758-9; ☎ 8981 8631; 2 Lindsay St; lunch $6.50-13; dinner $17-24) Dine on delicious European-based cuisine with tropical ingredients at intimate tables in the pre–Cyclone Tracy house, or alfresco in the lush garden. Delightful, filling tapas is served with bread and salad (three/five items $7.50/13) from 11.30am to 6.30pm.

Mental Lentil (mains $5-7) serves wholesome vegetarian, including lentil burgers, vegetable curry, dhal, lassis and fruit smoothies.

Thai Noodlebox (mains $5.50-12) is a place that dishes up tasty noodle, stir-fry and curry dishes straight from the wok to you.

Relish (Map pp758-9; ☎ 8941 1900; cnr Air Raid Arcade & Cavenagh St; mains $5-6.50) Gusto, flavour, zest, delight – take your pick. This warm and rustic café serves tasty gourmet fare for breakfast and lunch, as well as juices, milkshakes, good coffee and chai.

Roma Bar (Map pp758-9; ☎ 8981 6729; 30 Cavenagh St; mains $4-10) You'll find many heads buried in newspapers or entered in discussion at this caffeine institution, reminiscent of an authentic Italian café. It's a good place to find out about local happenings and events in the arts.

Cafe Uno (Map pp758-9; ☎ 8940 2500; 69 Mitchell St; mains $13-23) Hearty Italian dishes are served between art-bedecked walls at the smooth Cafe Uno. There's a perfect people-watching terrace, decent coffee and decadent cakes; entrée sizes are filling.

Salvatore's (Map pp758-9; ☎ 8941 9823; cnr Knuckey & Smith Sts; mains $6-13) Salvatore's opens early to crank out aromatic coffee and serve delicious breakfast and lunch dishes.

WHARF PRECINCT

You could try dangling a line to hook some tucker or, failing that, duck into the food centre at the end of Stokes Hill Wharf.

Crustaceans (Map pp758-9; ☎ 8981 8658; Stokes Hill Wharf; mains $14-30) It's renowned for top-notch seafood and its prime position on the harbour. What more do you need to know?

The **Groovy Groper** (Map pp758-9), in a tram at the foot of the wharf, sells tantalising fresh fish burgers with chips ($8).

See also Indo-Pacific Marine (p754) for details on its Coral Reef by Night dinner and show.

CULLEN BAY & FANNIE BAY

The Cullen Bay marina, full of yachts, expensive apartments and trendy eateries, is where the beautiful people hang out.

Bay Seafood Cafe (Map p751; ☎ 8981 8789; 57 Marina Blvd, Cullen Bay; barra & chips $7.50) It may just be the best fish 'n' chips in Darwin. Team it with a crisp Greek salad and head to the beach for sunset.

Buzz Cafe (Map p751; ☎ 8941 1141; 48 Marina Blvd, Cullen Bay; mains $16-30) The decking here makes a stunning, sunny spot for afternoon drinks, though the seats are so comfy you'll soon be ordering a meal. The men's loos are a talking point (knock first, girls!).

Cornucopia Café (☎ 8981 1002; Conacher St, Fannie Bay; mains $8-22) Digest and ingest culture after a visit to the attached Museum & Art Gallery. Tasty, varied dishes are served under swishing fans on the veranda close to the sea.

Pubs

Pubs like **'The Vic'** (p763) and the **Blue Heeler Bar** (p754) dish up a limited choice of filling meals for around $5; budget travellers may even eat for free if you pick up a voucher from your hostel.

Rorke's Drift (Map pp758-9; ☎ 8941 7171; 46 Mitchell St; mains $6.60-16) There's something for everyone at Rorke's. Traditional pub grub is served with flair for breakfast, lunch and dinner. Choose your position in the shady beer garden, terrace or cavernous interior.

Lizards Outdoor Bar & Grill (Map pp758-9; ☎ 8981 6511; cnr Mitchell & Daly Sts; mains $9-21) Free and breezy, Lizards' open-air bar-restaurant, part of the Top End Hotel, has a great atmosphere during the Wet or Dry. It serves mostly grilled meats including 'roo', barramundi and crocodile.

Globetrotters Restaurant (Map pp758-9; ☎ 8981 5385; 97 Mitchell St; mains $5-8) Well, it is not really a pub but it's hard to beat the meal deals at Globetrotters for price – nachos, lasagne, fish and chips, steak and the like are dished up from 6.30pm to 9pm in front of large sport screens.

Restaurants

Nudel Bar (Map pp758-9; ☎ 8981 7078; 60 Smith St; mains $7.80-8.80) Popular for speedy noodles with

> **TO MARKET, TO MARKET**
>
> As the sun heads towards the horizon, half of Darwin descends on **Mindil Beach Night Market** (off Gilruth Ave, Mindil Beach; ☼ 5-10pm Thu May-Oct & 5-9pm Sun Jun-Sep, dry season only) with tables, chairs, rugs, grog and kids to settle under the coconut palms for sunset and decide which of the tantalising food-stall aromas has the greatest allure. Take your choice – there's Thai, Sri Lankan, Indian, Chinese, Malaysian, Brazilian, Greek, Portuguese and more, all at around $4 to $6 a serve. Top it off with fresh fruit salad, decadent cakes, luscious crepes or any type of jerky imaginable, before cruising past arts and crafts stalls bulging with hand-made jewellery, fabulous rainbow tie-dyed clothes, pummelling masseurs and wares from Indonesia and Thailand.
>
> Similar stalls can be found at the **Parap Village Market** (☼ Sat morning), **Nightcliff Market** (☼ Sun morning) and the **Palmerston Market** (☼ 5-10pm Fri, dry season only). **Rapid Creek Market** (☼ Sun morning) is reminiscent of an Asian marketplace, with exotic ingredients, a heady mixture of spices and the scent of jackfruit and durian to boot.

diners on the move, Nudel Bar dishes up tasty food with plenty of vegetarian options.

Rendezvous Cafe (Map pp758-9; ☎ 8981 9231; Star Village Arcade; mains $3.80-12) The laksa has gained legendary status at this institution for Thai and Malaysian cuisine, tucked away in a quiet arcade off Smith St Mall.

Go Sushi (Map pp758-9; ☎ 8941 1008; Shop 5, 28 Mitchell St; plates $3-5.50, sashimi $12) The sushi train continuously shunts by in this cheerful Japanese restaurant. Eat in or load up a tray and take away.

Tim's Surf 'n' Turf (Map pp758-9; ☎ 8981 9979; 8 Packard Pl; mains $8.50-21) Attached to the Asti Motel, Tim's has a big reputation for great steaks, seafood and generous servings. Don't expect gourmet fare but it's reasonable value for money.

Ten Litchfield (Map pp758-9; ☎ 8981 1024; 10 Litchfield St; lunch $8.50-21, dinner $22-28) Darwin's little secret, nestled in a back street of town, has got soul and a great vibe. Modern Australian is infused with lendings from Asia and the Middle East.

Hanuman (Map pp758-9; ☎ 8941 3500; 28 Mitchell St; mains $16-25) Darwin's proximity to Asia provides this award-winning restaurant with the ability to deliver authentic Thai and Indian dishes with an extra spark of innovation.

Self-Catering

Parap Fine Foods (Map p751; ☎ 8981 8597; 40 Parap Rd, Parap) This local foodie haunt is teeming with gourmet temptations, including organic and health foods.

There's a convenient **Woolworths** (Map pp758-9) supermarket between Smith and Cavenagh Sts, near Peel St. Brumby's bakery chain has an outlet here and at Parap Village.

DRINKING

Most of the popular pubs with travellers are on Mitchell St, all within a short walk or long stumble of each other. You'd be hard-pressed to find one without a large sports screen.

Rorke's Drift (Map pp758-9; ☎ 8941 7171; 46 Mitchell St) Rorke's décor features memorabilia of the Zulu War and even a scale model of the famous engagement at this English-style pub. The beer garden really gets jumping on weekends.

Shenannigans (Map pp758-9; ☎ 8981 2100; 69 Mitchell St) Step inside and you'll feel as though you've been transported far away to the temperate zone. This attractive Irish-style pub has Guinness and Kilkenny on tap and hearty stews to stick to your bones when you get peckish.

Top End Hotel (Map pp758-9; ☎ 8981 6511; cnr Mitchell & Daly Sts) This busy little entertainment enclave has three bars and clubs and a sports bar for those needing their fix of English Premier League football. **Hip.E Club** (☎ 8941 2400) is a psychedelic bar and dance club with a 'starving backpackers' night every Wednesday offering free admission, meal and pool, and cheap drinks. Pick up a pass from any hostel. **Lizards Bar** (☎ 8981 6511) has a great beer garden dominated by a huge stone horseshoe bar. It pulls in revellers of all ages and hosts live bands from Friday to Sunday.

Victoria Hotel ('The Vic'; Map pp758-9; ☎ 8981 4011; 27 Smith St) A lively backpacker crowd is drawn to this old haunt. It's a good place for a drink in the early evening; vie for a spot on the balcony overlooking the mall. Live bands play upstairs from Wednesday to Saturday and there are often different kinds of party themes.

More popular city watering holes:

Kitty O'Shea's (Map pp758-9; ☎ 8941 7947; Mitchell St) An Irish theme pub with a pleasant veranda and Guinness, Murphy's and Kilkenny on tap.

Blue Heeler Bar (Map pp758-9; ☎ 8941 7945; Mitchell St) A ramshackle bar with live music and cheap drink deals.

Pub Bar (Map pp758-9; ☎ 8982 0000; 32 Mitchell St) A relaxed and groovy little space with a funky mix of house and world music.

The **Ski Club** (☎ 8981 6630; Conacher St, Fannie Bay), on Vestey's Beach, is a sublime little spot for sundowners in the Dry. Indulge in a plate of mezzes along with your drinks at the Friday night Supper Club at **Ten Litchfield** (dry season only; p763).

ENTERTAINMENT

Darwin has some lively haunts, with bands at several venues and a selection of nightclubs. The venues in the CBD are close enough together that you can wander to find one you like. Other tastes are also catered for, with theatre, film, concerts and a casino.

You'll find up-to-date entertainment listings in the Friday edition of the *NT News*, or check the notice board at **Roma Bar** (Map pp758-9; ☎ 8981 6729; 30 Cavenagh St). **artsMARK** (www.darwinarts.com.au) lists events around town and is available at the tourist office.

Aboriginal Cultural Performances

Dancers of the Dreaming is an Aboriginal dance, story and cultural performance run by **NT Wilderness Expeditions** (☎ 1300 656 071) at the **Frontier Hotel Amphitheatre** (Map pp758-9; ☎ 1300 363 854; 3 Buffalo Ct). Shows start at 7pm on Monday, Wednesday and Saturday and cost $35/19 per adult/child.

Casino

MGM Grand Darwin (Map p751; ☎ 8943 8888; Gilruth Ave) Darwin's flashy casino on Mindil Beach has the full range of tools to entice you to blow your dough. There's a dress code but shorts are OK fellas, as long as you've packed a pair of long socks to go with them!

Cinemas

Deckchair Cinema (☎ 8981 0700; Mavie St) Recline in an old-fashioned beach deckchair and watch a movie under the stars at Darwin's fabulous open-air cinema. Bring mosquito

repellent and a cushion for extra comfort. The snack bar sells alcohol (no BYO).

Darwin Film Society (Map p751; ☎ 8981 0700; Conacher St, Fannie Bay) Offbeat and art-house films are regularly shown at the Museum & Art Gallery Theatrette.

Darwin City Cinema (Map p751; ☎ 8981 5999; 76 Mitchell St) The city's large cinema complex screens latest release blockbuster films.

Dance Venues

Keep an eye out for bills posted on notice boards and telegraph poles advertising dance and full-moon parties.

Discovery & Lost Arc (Map pp758-9; ☎ 8942 3300; 89 Mitchell St) Hey Dancing Queen, strut your stuff here! Discovery occasionally features big-name live acts as well as commercial dance music. Next door, the open-fronted Lost Arc bar is open nightly from 4pm with varying entertainment.

Throb (Map pp758-9; ☎ 8981 3358; 64 Smith St; cover charge; ☉ from 10pm Thu-Sun) Darwin's No 1 gay venue is open to all. It's a dance club and cocktail bar with drag shows on Saturday. Touring live acts occasionally play here.

Beachcombers (Map pp758-9; ☎ 8981 6511; Mitchell St) and the **Hip.E Club** (☎ 8941 2400), in the Top End Hotel enclave, are dance clubs which also host live bands.

Theatre

Brown's Mart (Map pp758-9; ☎ 8981 5522; Harry Chan Ave) Live theatre performances are held at this atmospheric, historic venue. An arty crowd congregates here for Bamboo Lounge on a Friday evening, which may include anything from a short film festival to touring bands. It's all-inclusive, hassle-free and has a bar.

Darwin Entertainment Centre (Map pp758-9; box office ☎ 8980 3333; www.darwinentcent.net.au; 93 Mitchell St) This large complex houses the Playhouse and Studio Theatres, and hosts events from fashion award nights to plays and major concerts.

SHOPPING

The city centre has a good range of outlets selling arts and crafts from the Top End, including bark paintings from western Arnhem Land, and carvings and screen printing by the Tiwi people of Bathurst and Melville Islands. Trawl Darwin's fabulous **markets** to find anything from jewellery and pottery to stock-whips and artworks.

(For more information see the boxed text 'To Market, To Market'; p763.)

Raintree Aboriginal Fine Arts (Map pp758-9; ☎ 8941 9933; 20 Knuckey St) This is a long-established shop that specialises in works from western Arnhem Land.

Framed (Map p751; ☎ 8981 2994; www.framed.com.au; 55 Stuart Hwy, Stuart Park) A fine range of contemporary art is featured at Framed gallery near the entrance to the botanic gardens.

Wadeye Arts & Crafts (Map pp758-9; ☎ 8981 9632; 31 Knuckey St) Owned by the Wadeye (Port Keats) community, this store stocks a good collection of art, crafts and didgeridoos.

Aboriginal Fine Arts (Map pp758-9; ☎ 8981 1315; 44 Mitchell St) The fine but pricey artwork adorning the walls of this gallery, above Red Rooster, are worth perusing – if just to appreciate the varying artistic styles.

Paspaley Pearls (Map pp758-9; ☎ 8982 5515; 19 Smith St Mall) This place reeks of culture, and sells top-quality locally harvested pearls.

Australian Crocodile Products (Map pp758-9; ☎ 8941 4470; Paspaley Pearls Building, 19 Smith St Mall) It seems there are many ways to skin a croc, and many more ways to wear them. Beautiful belts, wallets and the like are sold here.

GETTING THERE & AWAY
Air
International and interstate flights operate out of Darwin. Restricted fares on Qantas and Virgin Blue are around 50% less than the fully flexible fares listed here.

Qantas (☎ 13 13 13; www.qantas.com) has direct daily services to Adelaide ($600), Alice Springs ($380), Brisbane ($580), Cairns ($450), Melbourne ($620), Perth ($590) and Sydney ($630).

Virgin Blue (☎ 13 67 89; www.virginblue.com) flies daily to Melbourne ($600) and Sydney ($610) via Brisbane ($500).

Airnorth (☎ 8920 4001; www.airnorth.com.au) connects Darwin with Alice Springs, Broome, Cairns via Groote Eylandt, Gove, Katherine, Kununurra and Tennant Creek. Other, smaller routes are flown by local operators; ask your travel agent.

Bus
You can reach Darwin by bus on the Queensland route through Mt Isa to Three Ways; the Western Australian route from Broome and Kununurra; or straight up the Track from Alice Springs.

McCafferty's/Greyhound (☎ 13 20 30, 8941 0911; www.mccaffertys.com.au; transit centre, 69 Mitchell St; ◷ 8.30am-6pm) runs daily services via Katherine on all these routes. Examples of one-way fares from Darwin include: Alice Springs ($195, 21 hours), Brisbane ($375, 47 hours), Broome ($260, 27 hours), Katherine ($55, 4½ hours), Kununurra ($130, 9½ hours), Mt Isa ($240, 21 hours), Perth ($550, 60 hours) and Tennant Creek ($140, 13½ hours). Beware of services that schedule long waits for connections in Tennant Creek or Mt Isa.

Backpacker-type buses offer good alternative transport, as they stop at many sights along the way. **Desert Venturer** (☎ 1800 079 119; www.desertventurer.com.au) makes five-day trips between Darwin and Cairns ($470, food kitty $80) via the Atherton Tablelands, Cape Crawford and Katherine between March and November.

Car
PURCHASE
If you're planning to buy or sell a car for the next leg of your journey, check the noticeboards at backpacker hostels and Internet cafés, or head to the **Traveller's Car Market** (☎ 0418-600 830; ◷ 8am-4pm) behind the Mitchell St Nite Market.

RENTAL
Darwin has numerous budget car-rental operators, as well as all the major national and international companies:

Avis (☎ 8981 9922; 145 Stuart Hwy, Stuart Park)

Britz: Australia (Map p751; ☎ 8981 2081; 44 Stuart Hwy, Stuart Park)

Budget (Map pp758-9; ☎ 8981 9800; cnr Daly & Mitchell Sts)

Delta Europcar (Map pp758-9; ☎ 1800 881 541; 77 Cavenagh St)

Gecko (☎ 8981 2733; 146 Mitchell St)

Hertz (Map pp758-9; ☎ 8941 0944; cnr Smith & Daly Sts)

Nifty Rent-a-Car (Map pp758-9; ☎ 8941 7090; 86 Mitchell St)

Territory Thrifty Car Rental (Map p751; ☎ 8924 0000; 64 Stuart Hwy, Stuart Park)

Top End 4WD & Car Hire (☎ 8941 2922; 1 Westralia St, Stuart Park)

For driving around Darwin, small cars are cheap enough – Gecko has cars from $30 per day, while Nifty and Delta have them from $40 per day – but most companies offer only 100km free and charge about

27.5 cents per additional kilometre; outside of Darwin, 100km won't get you very far. Some companies will do a deal that will give you enough mileage to get to Kakadu and back with three or four days' rental (from around $85 per day). Bear in mind that if you book a rental car through a travel agency you may get those unlimited kilometres for no additional charge.

Territory Thrifty Car Rental is the biggest local operator and is reliable. You may be able to get some good deals for extended vehicle hire through this company, especially on one-way hire.

There are also plenty of 4WD vehicles available in Darwin, but you usually have to book ahead, and fees and deposits can be hefty. Expect to pay $160 to $230 per day for a decent vehicle such as a Toyota Landcruiser.

Hiring a campervan for a week or two of touring can be worthwhile when you consider that cooking facilities and accommodation are included. Britz: Australia has the largest range of 4WD campervans from around $115 per day (two-berth) or $165 (four-berth). There's an extra $40 per day to reduce the insurance excess to nil, otherwise you must pay a $5000 deposit. **Backpacker Campervans** (☎ 1800 670 232; www .backpackercampervans.com) has budget-priced three-berth campervans from $58 per day, plus $26 insurance cover.

Train
The weekly Darwin to Alice Springs, via Katherine, train service fares are $240/880/1100 one way for daynighter seats/sleeper cabins/1st class sleepers. Tickets can be booked through **Trainways** (☎ 13 21 47; www .gsr.com.au). Discounted fares are sometimes offered; bookings are recommended.

GETTING AROUND
To/From the Airport
Darwin's airport is 12km from the city centre. The **airport shuttle bus** (☎ 1800 358 945) will pick you up or drop you off almost anywhere in the city centre for $7.50/13 one way/return. Taxi fares between the airport and city centre are around $20.

Bicycle & Scooter
Darwin is a compact city with plenty of bike paths. **Darwin Scooter Hire** (Map pp758-9;

☎ 0418-892 885; Mitchell St Nite Market) rents scooters for $20/40 per two hours/days; two-seater scooters are also available.

Most of the backpacker hostels hire out bicycles; the usual charge is $5/16 per hour/day. **Kakadu Dreams** (Map pp758-9; ☎ 8941 0655; Mitchell St), opposite the transit centre, and the **Darwin Tennis Centre** (Map pp758-9; ☎ 0418-891 111; cnr Bagot & Old McMillans Rds) also rent bicycles.

Bus
Darwinbus (☎ 8924 7666; Harry Chan Ave) runs a comprehensive service from the small depot near the corner of Smith St.

Fares are on a zone system; one/six zone single trips cost $1.40/2.80, or you can buy unlimited all zone daily/weekly passes for $5/25. Bus No 4 (to Fannie Bay, Nightcliff, Rapid Creek and Casuarina) and No 6 (Fannie Bay, Parap and Stuart Park) are useful for getting to Mindil Beach, the museum and art gallery, Fannie Bay Gaol Museum and East Point. Bus Nos 5 and 8 travel along the Stuart Hwy past the airport to Berrimah.

The **Tour Tub** (☎ 8981 5233), an open-sided minibus, tours Darwin's sights throughout the day. You can hop on and off along the route (see City Sights; p757).

Taxi
As well as the regular taxi service, Darwin has two taxi bus services that will take you anywhere in the central area for a flat $2, and elsewhere, such as Fannie Bay and East Point, for a fixed fee. Phone **Arafura Shuttle** (☎ 8981 3300) or **Unique Minibus** (☎ 8928 1100).

AROUND DARWIN

MANDORAH
☎ 08
Mandorah is a popular beach resort on the tip of the Cox Peninsula, most easily reached by a 20-minute **Sea Cat** (☎ 8978 5015) boat ride across Darwin Harbour from Cullen Bay Marina. Ferries cross about 10 times daily; return fares are $16/8.50 per adult/child.

You can stay at **Mandorah Beach Hotel** (☎ 8978 5044; mandorahbeachhotel@bigpond.com; camp/caravan sites for 2 $6/15, doubles $85; 🐕 🖵), which has a large pool and also serves meals.

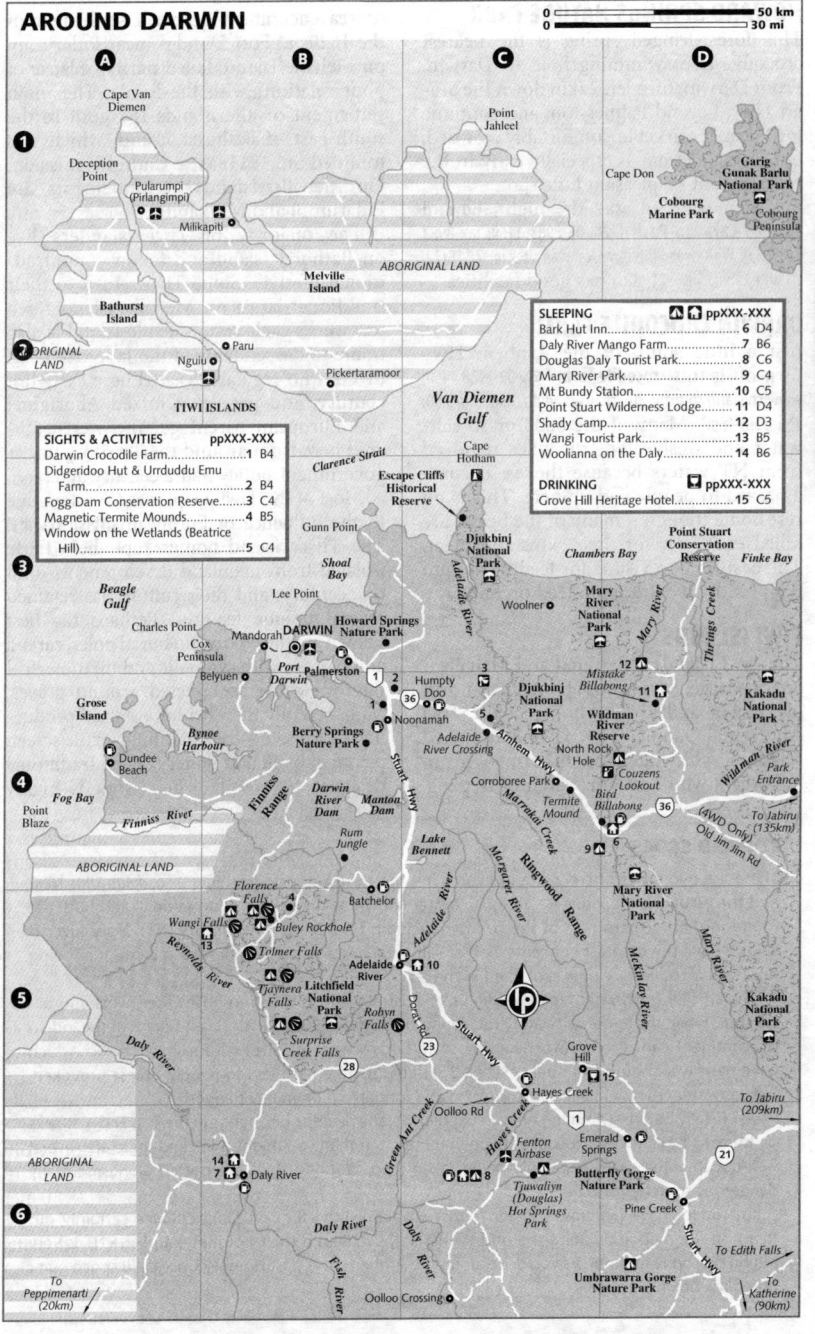

AROUND DARWIN

0 ——————— 50 km
0 ——————— 30 mi

SLEEPING 🔺 🏠 ppXXX–XXX
Bark Hut Inn...**6** D4
Daly River Mango Farm.................**7** B6
Douglas Daly Tourist Park.........**8** C6
Mary River Park..............................**9** C4
Mt Bundy Station.........................**10** C5
Point Stuart Wilderness Lodge...**11** D4
Shady Camp.....................................**12** D3
Wangi Tourist Park.......................**13** B5
Woolianna on the Daly...............**14** B6

DRINKING 🍺 ppXXX–XXX
Grove Hill Heritage Hotel...........**15** C5

SIGHTS & ACTIVITIES ppXXX–XXX
Darwin Crocodile Farm.................**1** B4
Didgeridoo Hut & Urrduddu Emu
Farm...**2** B4
Fogg Dam Conservation Reserve...**3** C4
Magnetic Termite Mounds............**4** B5
Window on the Wetlands (Beatrice
Hill)...**5** C4

HOWARD SPRINGS NATURE PARK

This forest-fringed spring is the nearest crocodile-free swimming hole to Darwin. From Darwin, turn left 24km down the Stuart Hwy, beyond Palmerston, and continue for 11km. It can get uncomfortably crowded, but on a quiet day – especially early in the morning – it's a pleasant little spot.

If you want to stay the night, **Howard Springs Caravan Park** (☎ 08-8983 1169; fax 8983 2487; 170 Whitewood Rd; camp/caravan sites for 2 $18/22, en suite cabins $80; 🔀 🖵) has good facilities.

DARWIN CROCODILE FARM

Just a little south of the Arnhem Hwy turn-off is this **crocodile farm** (☎ 08-8988 1450; www.crocfarm.com.au; Stuart Hwy; adult/child $10/5.50; ⏲ 9am-4pm). Many of the 8000 or so saltwater and freshwater crocodiles removed from NT waters because they've become a hazard to people end up here. This is no rest home though – many of the beasts are killed each year for their skins and meat. The best time to visit is for feeding at 2pm daily, with an extra noon feed on Sunday.

TIWI ISLANDS

The Tiwi Islands – Bathurst and Melville – are two large, flat islands about 80km north of Darwin and are the home of the Tiwi Aboriginal people. The Tiwi had mixed relations with Macassan fishermen (from Sulawesi), who came in search of trepang,

or sea cucumber. A British settlement in the 1820s at Fort Dundas, near Pularumpi on Melville Island, failed partly because of poor relations with the locals. The main settlement on the islands is Nguiu in the south-east of Bathurst Island, which was founded in 1911 as a Catholic mission. On Melville Island the settlements are Pularumpi and Milikapiti.

The majority of Tiwi Islanders live on Bathurst Island and follow a nontraditional lifestyle. Some Tiwi return to their traditional lands on Melville Island for a few weeks each year. Melville Island is also home to descendants of the Japanese pearl divers who regularly visited here early last century, and people of mixed Aboriginal and European parentage who were gathered here around the Territory under government policy half a century ago.

Most of the Tiwi people are Christian due to the influence of European missionaries. The Tiwi's island homes kept them fairly isolated from mainland developments until this century, and their culture has retained several unique features. Perhaps the best known are the *pukumani* burial poles, carved and painted with symbolic and mythological figures, which are erected around graves. More recently the Tiwi have started producing art for sale – bark painting, textile screen printing, batik and pottery, using traditional designs and motifs. Their work is highly

TOP-END CROCS

There are two types of crocodile in Australia – the freshwater or 'freshie' (Crocodylus johnstoni) and the estuarine crocodile (C. porosus), better known as the saltwater or 'saltie' – and both are found in the northern part of the country, including the Northern Territory (NT). Mary River is said to have the greatest concentration of saltwater crocs in the world. After a century of being hunted, crocodiles are now protected in the NT.

The smaller freshwater croc is endemic to Australia and is found in freshwater rivers and billabongs, while the larger saltwater croc, found throughout Southeast Asia and parts of the Indian subcontinent, can be found in or near almost any body of water, fresh or salt. Freshwater crocs, which have narrower snouts and rarely exceed 3m in length, are harmless to people unless provoked, but saltwater crocs, which can grow to 7m and longer, are definitely dangerous.

Ask locally before swimming or even paddling in any rivers or billabongs in the Top End – attacks on humans by saltwater crocodiles happen more often than you might think and there are several well-documented cases of people being taken here. Warning signs are posted alongside many dangerous stretches of water.

Crocodiles have become a major tourist attraction (the film Crocodile Dundee certainly put them on the map and eating the odd tourist helps maintain their notoriety) and the NT is very big on crocodile humour. As you drive along the Arnhem Hwy past Humpty Doo you'll spot a giant fibreglass boxing crocodile.

acclaimed – you can browse the showrooms and buy pieces directly from the artists for reasonable prices.

You need a permit to visit and the only realistic option is to take a tour. **Tiwi Tours** (☎ 1800 811 633, 08-8924 1115; aussieadventure@attglobal.net), a company which employs many Tiwi Islanders, is the main operator. Although interaction with the local Tiwi community tends to be limited to your guides, and the craft workshops and showrooms, the tours are fascinating and worthwhile. A one-day tour to Bathurst Island ($300) includes visits to the early Catholic mission buildings, morning tea with Tiwi women, swimming and a trip to a *pukumani* burial site. An overnight tour staying at a private bush camp ($570) allows you to see more, and get a better feel for the people and culture. Prices include the charter flight, permits, meals and, on the two-day tour, accommodation.

Australian Rules football is a passion among the Tiwi people and the **Tiwi grand final** in April is a huge event.

To arrange a =visit yourself, contact the **Tiwi Land Council** (☎ 08-8981 4898) in Darwin for a permit.

ARNHEM HIGHWAY

The Arnhem Hwy branches off towards Kakadu 33km southeast of Darwin. At the intersection is the **Didgeridoo Hut & Urrduddu Emu Farm** (☎ 08-8988 4457), where you can watch indigenous artists at work and take a tour of the workshops and emu farm.

About 10km farther along you come to a small town with an incredible name – Humpty Doo. Fronting the highway is the **Humpty Doo Hotel** (☎ 08-8988 1372), a good place to stop for a beer or a counter meal.

About 15km beyond Humpty Doo is the turn-off to **Fogg Dam Conservation Reserve**, frequented by a plethora of water birds. There are three short nature walks, including one along the dam wall to the pandanus lookout.

Window on the Wetlands Visitors Centre (☎ 08-8988 8188; wow.pwcnt@nt.gov.au; ◷ 7.30am-7.30pm) sits atop Beatrice Hill, by the Arnhem Hwy 3km past the Fogg Dam turn-off. It's the headquarters for the Mary River National Park (opposite), between Darwin and Kakadu. Interactive displays detail the wetland ecosystem, as well as local Aboriginal history and pastoral activity in the area.

There are also great views out over the Adelaide River floodplain.

Croc jumping cruises depart from the Adelaide River Crossing to gaze in awe at huge saltwater crocodiles which rise out of the water for bits of meat held on the end of poles. The whole thing is a bit of a circus, but it's an amazing sight. The **Adelaide River Queen** (☎ 08-8988 8144; adult/child $35/19) runs 1½-hour cruises at 9am, 11am, 1pm and 3pm May to August; and 9am, 11am and 2.30pm from September to April. About 2km past the Window on the Wetlands, along an unsealed road, **Jumping Croc** (☎ 08-8988 4547; adult/child $25/13) has one-hour tours at 9am, 11am, 1pm and 3pm all year (the 9am cruise includes breakfast, for you and the crocs).

An alternative route to Cooinda (in Kakadu) is via the unsealed Old Jim Jim Rd, 19km beyond the Bark Hut Inn. It's often impassable in the Wet, and you'll need to ensure your entry permit is current before taking this route. The entrance to Kakadu National Park is 19km farther along the highway.

Sleeping

There are a several places to stay between Window on the Wetlands and the entrance to Kakadu.

Mary River Park (☎ 08-8978 8877; www.maryriverpark.com.au; Arnhem Hwy; camp/caravan sites for 2 $16/20, dm $25, cabins from $75; ✵) This sprawling family-run bush retreat is a good alternative to staying right in Kakadu. As well as excellent value accommodation, there's a casual restaurant, pool, walking tracks and croc-spotting trips on the Mary River ($25). McCafferty's/Greyhound stops out front.

Bark Hut Inn (☎ 08-8978 8988; fax 8978 8932; camp/caravan sites for 2 $13.50/20; s/d $35/50; ✵) The rustic bar at this atmospheric roadhouse is adorned with boar and buffalo heads and an extensive bullet collection, though the meals are tender and tasty. Amenities are shared.

MARY RIVER NATIONAL PARK

Extending north and south of the Arnhem Hwy, **Mary River National Park** consists of a number of wetland areas, including Mary River Crossing, Wildman River, Shady Camp, Mary River Conservation Reserve, Stuart's Tree Historical Reserve and Swim Creek.

This area offers excellent fishing and wildlife-spotting opportunities, and because there is not much in the way of infrastructure, it is far less visited than nearby Kakadu.

Access to the northern part of the park is via Point Stuart Rd, an often rough dirt track (the first 8km is sealed) that heads north off the Arnhem Hwy 22km east of Annaburroo. North Rock Hole is 19km west of this road, and Shady Camp about 40km north of the highway. **Shady Camp Boat Hire** (☎ 08-8978 8937) has self-drive 3.7m boats for $60/105 per half/full day.

Sleeping

There are basic camp sites at Couzens Lookout and Shady Camp.

Point Stuart Wilderness Lodge (☎ 08-8978 8914; nttours@adventuretours.com.au; camp/caravan sites per person $7/10, dm/d $22/50; ☒) Part of an old cattle station, this camp, 1km off Point Stuart Rd, caters mainly to fishing parties and tour groups. There's a grassy camping area, swimming pool and good facilities; wallabies congregate on the lawns in the afternoon. Rooms with bathroom and aircon are available for $140. All meals are available from the restaurant/bar.

Mary River Houseboats (☎ 08-8978 8925; 6-/8-berth houseboats for 2 days $480/550, extra day $170/250) If you have a group, hiring a houseboat is a great way to see the Mary River at a leisurely pace. A $300 bond is required. The turn-off to the houseboat berth is 12km east of Corroboree Park, followed by 20km along an unsealed road to the Mary River.

ARNHEM HIGHWAY TO LITCHFIELD NATIONAL PARK
Territory Wildlife Park & Berry Springs Nature Park

The turn-off to Berry Springs is 48km down the Track from Darwin, then it's 10km to the **Territory Wildlife Park** (☎ 08-8988 7200; www.territorywildlifepark.com.au; Cox Peninsula Rd; adult/child/family $18/9/40; ☒ 8.30am-6pm, last admission 4pm). Set on 400 hectares of bushland, this excellent, open-air park features a wide variety of northern Australian birds, mammals, reptiles and fish, some of which are quite rare. The habitats are beautifully re-created, with wetlands and tropical rainforest environments.

A highlight is the walk-through aquarium, designed to replicate an entire Top End river system, and featuring a saltwater croc and

some enormous barramundi. There's also a reptile house, nocturnal house, aviaries and nature trails. You'll need half a day to see it all, especially if you want to see some of the regular ranger talks, including the birds of prey show (10am and 3pm).

To see everything, you can either walk around the 4km perimeter road, or hop on and off the little shuttle train that run every 15 to 20 minutes, stopping at all exhibits.

Close by is **Berry Springs Nature Park** (admission free; ☒ 8am-6.30pm). It's a great place for a swim and a picnic, with a thermal waterfall, spring-fed pools ringed with paperbarks and pandanus palms, and abundant birdlife. There's also a visitors centre and café. Please note: costly car break-ins have occurred in the Berry Springs car park, resulting in stolen cameras and backpacks.

Batchelor
☎ 08 / pop 730

The southern access road to Litchfield, which passes through this small town, 84km down the Track from Darwin, then another 14km west, once serviced the now-closed Rum Jungle uranium and copper mine. In recent years it has received a boost from the growing popularity of nearby Litchfield National Park – it's only about 18km from the park's eastern boundary. Signs throughout town mark the way to the vibrantly painted **Coomalie Cultural Centre** (☎ 8939 7404; cnr Awillia & Nurndina Sts; ☒ 10am-4pm Tue-Fri) which sells local and Territory art and craft.

Set in secluded tropical surrounds, the colourful **Jungle Drum Bungalows** (☎ 8976 0555; www.jungledrumbungalows.com.au; 10 Meneling Rd; s/d/tr bungalows $95/115/125; ☒) would be at home in Bali. There's a pool, and a restaurant serving home-made treats for breakfast and dinner.

Halfway between Batchelor and Litchfield, **Banyan Tree Caravan Park** (☎ 8976 0330; www.banyan-tree.info; Litchfield Park Rd; camp/caravan sites $16/16.50, dm $18, on-site vans per person $22, cabins $75; ☒) has shaded sites and a magnificent spreading banyan tree. The camp kitchen contains a barbecue, stove and fridge.

Mini-golf anyone? **Batchelor Caravillage** (☎ 8976 0166, 8976 0123; big4.batchelor.nt@bigpond .com; Rum Jungle Rd; camp/caravan sites for 2 $20/25, cabins $90; s/d $120/140; ☒) is a compact caravan park that has a few interesting additions along with a pool and flock of resident parrots. **Rum Jungle Motor Inn** is part of the resort and offers clean rooms in an uninspiring complex.

The **Batchelor General Store** (☎ 8976 0045) is well-stocked and has a takeaway counter.

LITCHFIELD NATIONAL PARK

Much of the Tabletop Range, a wide sandstone plateau mostly surrounded by cliffs, is encompassed within this park 115km south of Darwin. Four waterfalls, spilling into idyllic waterholes surrounded by patches of rainforest, drop off the edge of this plateau. It's a wonderful place to visit and a great spot to camp for a few days; avoid weekends in the Dry, though, as Litchfield is a very popular day-trip destination for locals. Though absent from the swimming holes mentioned here, saltwater crocodiles inhabit the Finniss and Reynolds Rivers.

The two routes to Litchfield National Park from the Stuart Hwy join up and loop through the park. The southern access road via Batchelor is sealed all the way, while the northern access route, off the Cox Peninsula Rd, is partly unsealed and may be impassable in the Wet.

About 17km after entering the park from Batchelor, there's a field of **magnetic termite mounds**, resembling a bush graveyard. The clever little termites build their narrow mounds in a narrow north-south orientation to catch the heat of the morning and afternoon sun. There's an information display and boardwalk on site.

About 6km farther is the turn-off to **Buley Rockhole** (2km) and **Florence Falls** (5km). Both are superb swimming holes in the dry season and have pleasant camp sites. There's a 3.2km walking track between the two places following Florence Creek.

About 18km beyond the turn-off to Florence Falls is the **Tolmer Falls** turn-off; the falls are a 450m walk off the road. The 1.5km-loop walking track here offers beautiful views of the area.

It's a farther 7km along the main road to the turn-off for the most popular attraction in Litchfield – **Wangi Falls** (*wong*-guy), 1.5km up a side road. The falls flow year round and fill a beautiful swimming hole (there's usually no swimming permitted during the Wet). There are also extensive picnic and camping areas.

Bush camping is also allowed at the pretty **Tjaynera (Sandy Creek) Falls**, in a rain-

---

> ### SCRUB TYPHUS
>
> Scrub typhus is spread by a tiny mite that lives in long grass and several cases have been associated with Litchfield National Park. The danger is small, but cover up your legs and feet if you are going to walk in this habitat (most visitors won't encounter the problem). If you fall ill after a visit to the park, advise your doctor that you have been to Litchfield.

forest valley in the south of the park (4WD access only). Several other 4WD tracks traverse the park, and there are plenty of bushwalking possibilities.

Tours

Plenty of companies offer trips to Litchfield from Darwin. Most day tours cost from about $80 to $100, and normally include a pick-up from your accommodation, guided tours of various sights, swimming, morning tea and lunch.

Goanna Eco Tours (☎ 1800 003 880, 08-8927 3880; www.goannaecotours.com.au) runs a one-day tour ($100) to Litchfield that includes a jumping-croc boat cruise on the *Adelaide River Queen*, lunch and rental of a swimming mask for swimming in the waterfall pools.

Track 'n' Trek (☎ 1800 355 766) runs two-day tours ($170), which include mountain biking.

Enquire at the kiosk next to the camping ground at Wangi Falls about cruises on the McKeddies Billabong, an extension of the Reynolds River.

Sleeping & Eating

There is good **camping** (adult/child $6.60/3.30) with toilets and fireplaces at Florence Falls, Buley Rockhole, Wangi Falls and Tjaynera (Sandy Creek) Falls. Fees are usually collected by the ranger. There's also camping at Surprise Creek, but no fees.

Wangi Tourist Park (☎ 08-8978 2185; wangi@down under.net.au; camp/caravan sites for 2 $15/20) This sparsely grassed park is on the Litchfield Park Rd just north of the Wangi Falls turn-off.

See Batchelor (p770) for information on caravan parks just outside the park.

The kiosk, next to the camping grounds at Wangi Falls, serves fast foods and refreshments until late in the afternoon.

ADELAIDE RIVER TO KATHERINE
Adelaide River
☎ 08 / pop 230

This sleepy settlement, 111km south of Darwin along the Stuart Hwy, has a few interesting sites which are worth a poke around. The well-kept **cemetery** has a sea of white crosses in honour of those who died in the 1942–43 Japanese air raids. This stretch of the highway is dotted with WWII airstrips.

Relax, fish or play bush golf at **Mt Bundy Station** (☎ 8976 7009, fax 8976 7113; mt.bundy@octa4.net.au; Haynes Rd; camp/caravan sites for 2 $16/18, tw $50, cottage $140, B&B d $150-180; 🔁), 3km from Adelaide River. The rooms are lush and if you book, the owners will pick you up from the highway where long-distance buses stop.

The **Adelaide River Inn** (☎ 8976 7047; fax 8976 7181; Memorial Tce; camp/caravan sites $10/15, d $65; 🔁) is the local pub, behind the roadhouse. It has comfortable rooms with bathrooms, a caravan park and serves mountainous bistro meals. Charlie, the water buffalo who shot to fame in Crocodile Dundee, looms large – stuffed atop the bar in the pub.

Old Stuart Highway

Just south of Adelaide River, a sealed section of the old Stuart Hwy (now called Dorat Rd) loops to the south before rejoining the main road 52km farther on. It's a scenic trip without the hustle of the main highway and leads to some pleasant spots, though access may be cut in the Wet.

The beautiful **Robyn Falls** are a short, rocky scramble 15km along this road. The falls, set in a monsoon-forested gorge, dwindle to a trickle in the Dry, but are spectacular in the Wet.

The turn-off to **Daly River** is 14km farther. To reach **Tjuwaliyn (Douglas) Hot Springs Park**, turn south onto Oolloo Rd and continue for about 35km. The springs are a farther 7km down a dirt track (usually OK for 2WD vehicles). The nature park includes a section of the Douglas River and several hot springs – a bit hot for a dip at 40°C to 60°C, but there's a good spot for bathing where the hot spring water mixes with the cool water from the Douglas River near the camp site river entrance. The **camping ground** (adult/child $4.50/1.50) has pit toilets, barbecues and drinking water.

Butterfly Gorge Nature Park is about 17km beyond Tjuwaliyn (Douglas) Hot Springs –

you'll need a 4WD to get there and even then the road is closed for much of the wet season. True to its name, butterflies sometimes swarm in the paper bark–lined gorge.

A farther 7.5km south along Oolloo Rd from the Tjuwaliyn turn-off is **Douglas Daly Tourist Park** (☎/fax 08-8978 2479; Oolloo Rd; camp/caravan sites for 2 $16/23, tw $36, cabins $110; meals $11-18; 🔁) The river frontage of this park is dotted with amazing swimming holes, including **the arches**, and numerous fishing spots. There's a small store with petrol bowsers; cooked meals are available at the bar.

Daly River
☎ 08 / pop 620

The big attraction at historic Daly River, 109km west of the Stuart Hwy, is the prospect of hooking a 'barra' in the river. But even if you're not into fishing, it can be a very pleasant spot to while away a few days. There are numerous fishing tour operators and boat hire (half/full day $100/160) is available at accommodation places.

Locally made arts and crafts are exhibited at **Merrepen Arts** (☎ 8978 2533; 🕑 8am-5pm Mon-Fri), the Naniyu Nambiyu Aboriginal community's exemplary gallery and resource centre. Visitors are welcome without a permit to the community, which is reached via a well-signed turn-off 6km before the Daly River crossing. The **Merrepen Arts Festival** (☎ 8980 3333), held on the first weekend of June, celebrates Aboriginal arts, crafts and music from the area.

The huge sandbar at the Daly River crossing is a popular, though dusty, camping spot. Note: the river is infested with saltwater crocodiles.

A magnificent grove of 90-year-old mango trees shades the camping ground at **Daly River Mango Farm** (☎ 1800 000 576, 8978 2464; www.mangofarm.com.au; camp/caravan sites for 2 $12/19, d $50, cabins $90, house $180; 🔁) on the Daly River, 7km from the crossing. There's a wide range of accommodation, including stone cabins, a well-equipped kitchen, pool and boat hire. Dinner is served from Wednesday to Sunday in the bar/bistro.

Woolianna on the Daly (☎ 8978 2478; Woolianna Rd; camp/caravan sites $11/15, unit per person $60) There's a beautiful, shady green lawn for camping at this place on the banks of the river. Take the sign-posted turn-off before town.

The **Daly River Roadside Inn** has a bar and restaurant, and there's a shop nearby.

Pine Creek
☎ 08 / pop 470

Pine Creek is a laid-back sort of place with some interesting historical attractions. It was the scene of a gold rush in the 1870s and some old timber and corrugated iron buildings survive from this time. The area is said to have the largest variety of bird species in the Territory. The Kakadu Hwy branches off the Stuart Hwy at Pine Creek, connecting it to Cooinda and Jabiru.

The old **train station** (1888) has a display on the Darwin to Pine Creek railway (1889–1970) and a lovingly restored steam engine. **Pine Creek Museum** (Railway Pde; adult/child $2.20/free; ☺ 10am-5pm) has mining memorabilia, a mineral collection, old telegraph equipment and bric-a-brac.

A visit to **Gun Alley Gold Mining** (☎ 8976 1221; ☺ 8.30am-3pm) will transport you back to the mining era. There's fully operational steam engine equipment and gold panning costs $6 a pop. Follow the signs through town.

SLEEPING & EATING
Pine Creek Diggers Rest Motel (☎ 8976 1442; fax 8976 1458; 32 Main Tce; s/d/quad cabins $75/85/95; ❄) There are immaculate self-contained cabins here that peer out of tranquil, tropical garden surrounds.

Pine Creek Hotel (☎ 8976 1288; 40 Moule St; d $100; mains $7-20; ❄) The standard motel rooms behind the pub are clean, with a fridge and TV. Room rates include breakfast and counter meals are available at the pub.

Lazy Lizard Tourist Park (☎ 8976 1224; camp/caravan sites $13/18; mains $12-18) Just off Main Tce, Lazy Lizard's open-fronted, colonial-style bar is supported by carved ironwood pillars and a variety of locals – honey ants, lizards, eagles… The camp sites here lack shade, but there's a pool to cool off in. The intriguing menu includes meals such as the 'glutton's delight'.

Mayse's Café (☎ 8976 1241; Moule St; mains $4-12, pizza $12-16) This welcoming spot, next to the pub, serves tasty home-made food. Incongruously, a life-sized model of James Dean slouches by the door and a 'Central Perk' T-shirt, signed by the cast of the TV series *Friends*, is encased in glass on the wall.

NORTH AUSTRALIAN RAILWAY

In the 1880s the South Australian government decided to build a railway line from Darwin (Palmerston) to Pine Creek. This was partly to improve the conditions on the Pine Creek goldfields, as the road south from Darwin was often washed out in the Wet, but was also partly spurred by the dream of a transcontinental railway line linking Adelaide and Darwin.

The line was built almost entirely by Chinese labourers and was eventually pushed south as far as Larrimah. It continued to operate until 1976, but was forced to close because the damage inflicted by Cyclone Tracy (p753) drained the Territory's financial resources.

The link between Alice Springs and Darwin has recently been completed. Services run via Katherine and Tennant Creek. See Train (p806) for timetable and fare details.

Around Pine Creek

A dirt road follows the old railway line east of the highway between Hayes and Pine Creeks. This is in fact the original 'north road', which was in use before the 'new road' (now the old Stuart Hwy) was built. It's pretty rough in parts, especially after rain, but if you have the time it's a worthwhile detour to see the 1930s **Grove Hill Hotel** (☎ 08-8978 2489). The pub, built entirely of corrugated iron to prevent it from being eaten by termites, is part-museum part-watering hole.

About 3km along the Stuart Hwy south of Pine Creek is the turn-off to the pretty **Umbrawarra Gorge Nature Park**, about 30km west along a dirt road (often impassable in the Wet). There's a camp site with pit toilets and fireplaces, and croc-free pools to swim in 1km from the car park.

KAKADU & ARNHEM LAND

KAKADU NATIONAL PARK

Kakadu National Park is a natural marvel encompassing a variety of habitats, a mass of wildlife and significant rock-art sites. It's possible to explore the main sights here in

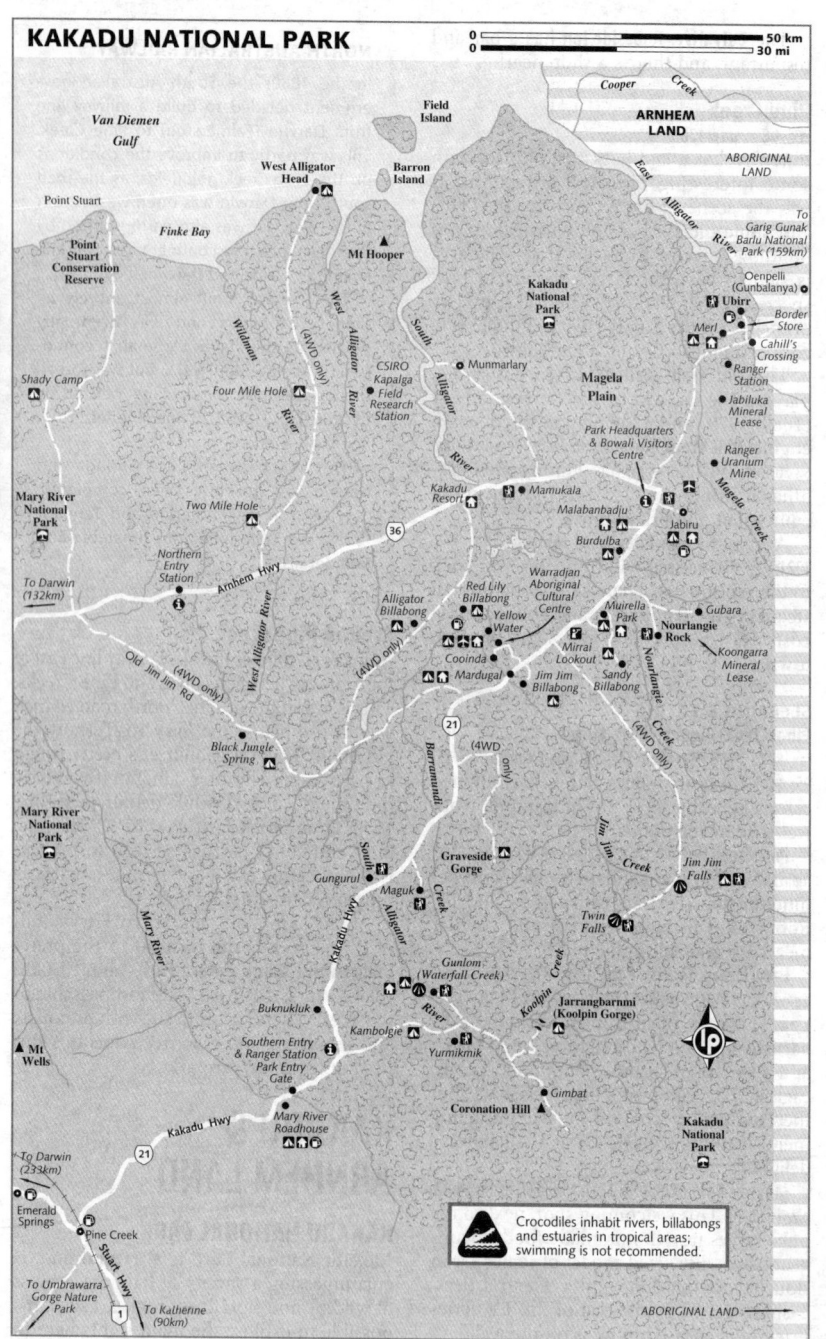

KAKADU NATIONAL PARK

0   50 km
0   30 mi

Cooper Creek

ARNHEM LAND

ABORIGINAL LAND

Van Diemen Gulf

West Alligator Head

Field Island

Barron Island

East Alligator River

To Garig Gunak Barlu National Park (159km)

Point Stuart

Finke Bay

▲ Mt Hooper

Kakadu National Park

Oenpelli (Gunbalanya)

Ubirr
Merl
Border Store
Cahill's Crossing
Ranger Station

Point Stuart Conservation Reserve

Magela Plain

Jabiluka Mineral Lease

Shady Camp

Wildman River

West Alligator River

South Alligator River

CSIRO Kapalga Field Research Station

● Munmarlary

Park Headquarters & Bowali Visitors Centre

Ranger Uranium Mine

Magela Creek

Four Mile Hole

Mary River National Park

Two Mile Hole

Northern Entry Station

Arnhem Hwy

(36)

Kakadu Resort

● Mamukala
Malabanbadju ▲
Burdulba ●

Jabiru

To Darwin (132km)

Old Jim Jim Rd (4WD only)

West Alligator River

(4WD only)

Alligator Billabong

Red Lily Billabong
Yellow Water

Warradjan Aboriginal Cultural Centre

Muirella Park

● Gubara

Nourlangie Rock

Cooinda
Mardugal

Mirrai Lookout
Jim Jim Billabong
Sandy Billabong

Koongarra Mineral Lease

Barramundi

Black Jungle Spring

(21)

(4WD only)

Nourlangie Creek

Mary River National Park

(4WD only)

Jim Jim Creek

Jim Jim Falls

Graveside Gorge

Gungurul

Maguk

South Alligator River

Creek

Koolpin Creek

Twin Falls

Mary River

Kakadu Hwy

Gunlom (Waterfall Creek)

Jarrangbarnmi (Koolpin Gorge)

▲ Mt Wells

Buknukluk

Kambolgie

Southern Entry & Ranger Station Park Entry Gate

Yurmikmik

● Gimbat

Coronation Hill ▲

Kakadu National Park

Mary River Roadhouse

(21)

Kakadu Hwy

To Darwin (233km)

Emerald Springs

Pine Creek

Stuart Hwy

(1)

To Umbrawarra Gorge Nature Park

To Katherine (90km)

Crocodiles inhabit rivers, billabongs and estuaries in tropical areas; swimming is not recommended.

ABORIGINAL LAND

two or three days, but the longer you stay, the more rewarding it becomes.

Kakadu stretches more than 200km south from the coast and 100km from east to west, with the main entrance 153km east of Darwin, along a bitumen road. It takes in a variety of superb landscapes, swarms with wildlife and has some of Australia's best Aboriginal rock art. It is World Heritage–listed for both its natural and cultural importance (a rare distinction).

The name Kakadu comes from Gagadju, a local Aboriginal language. Much of Kakadu is Aboriginal land, leased to the government for use as a national park. There are several Aboriginal settlements in the park and about one-third of the park rangers are Aboriginal people. Enclosed by the park, but not part of it, are a few tracts of land designated for other purposes – principally uranium mining.

Geography

The circuitous Arnhem Land escarpment, a dramatic 30m- to 200m-high sandstone cliff line, forms the natural boundary between Kakadu and Arnhem Land and winds some 500km through eastern and southeastern Kakadu.

Creeks cut across the rocky plateau and tumble off the escarpment as thundering waterfalls in the wet season. They then flow across the lowlands to swamp the vast flood plains of Kakadu, turning the north of the park into a kind of huge, vegetated lake. From west to east the rivers are: the Wildman, West Alligator, South Alligator and East Alligator. Such is the difference between dry and wet seasons that areas on river flood plains that are perfectly dry underfoot in September will be submerged in 3m of water a few months later. As the waters recede in the Dry, some loops of wet-season watercourses become cut off, but don't dry up. These are billabongs, which are often carpeted with water lilies and act as a magnet for water birds.

The coastal zone has long stretches of mangrove swamp, important for halting erosion and as a breeding ground for bird and marine life. The southern part of the park is dry lowlands with open grassland and eucalypts. Pockets of monsoon rainforest crop up here, as in most of the park's other landscapes.

JABILUKA MINE

In September 2002 the fate of the Jabiluka uranium mine was effectively decided when multinational mining company, Rio Tinto, stated that there would be no development of the project without the consent of the traditional landowners, the Mirrar people. As the Mirrar have staged a David and Goliath–style battle against the construction of the mine for many years, including launching a range of court cases, it is unlikely their position will change.

The efforts of the Gundjehmi Aboriginal Corporation, which represents the Mirrar people, were recognised by the awarding of the Goodman Prize, an international award for outstanding environmental activism, in 1999.

Uranium was discovered at Jabiluka in 1971, and an agreement to mine was negotiated with the Aboriginal people of the area. Mine development was delayed by the introduction of the 'Three Mines Policy' by the Federal Labor Government in 1984, and the proposal to mine did not get underway until the policy was scrapped by the Liberal-National Government when it was returned to power in 1996. However, by that time concern had grown that the Aboriginal elders had been coerced into signing the agreement.

Jabiluka mine was the scene of widespread protests and sit-in demonstrations during 1998, which resulted in massive numbers of arrests. A delegation from Unesco inspected the mine site and reported to the World Heritage Commission that the mine would endanger Kakadu's World Heritage listing. In response, an Independent Science Panel was set up to investigate the matter, and concluded that the World Heritage values of Kakadu would not be significantly impacted if the mine were to go ahead. However, the continuing level of controversy over the mine proposal, a depressed international uranium market, and an inability to form a new agreement with the traditional owners, has made the mining of Jabiluka less viable.

At the time this book went to print, there were calls for Rio Tinto to plug the decline tunnel into the deposit and to rehabilitate the disturbed area for incorporation into Kakadu National Park.

More than 80% of Kakadu is savannah woodland. It has over 1000 plant species, a number of which are still used by the local Aboriginal people for food, as well as for medicinal and other practical purposes.

Climate

The average maximum temperature in Kakadu is 34°C year-round. Broadly speaking, the Dry is from April/May to September/October and the Wet is from October/November to March/April; unsurprisingly, most of Kakadu's average rainfall of 130mm falls in the Wet.

The transition from Dry to Wet transforms Kakadu's landscape. As the wetlands and waterfalls grow, unsealed roads become impassable, cutting off some highlights such as Jim Jim Falls. The local Aboriginal people recognise six seasons in the annual cycle:

Gunumeleng This is the 'build-up' to the Wet, which starts in October. Humidity increases, the temperature rises to 35°C or more and mosquitoes, always plentiful near water, rise to near-plague proportions. By November the thunderstorms have started, billabongs are replenished and the waterbirds and fish disperse.

Gudjeuk The Wet proper continues through January, February and March, with violent thunderstorms and an abundance of plant and animal life thriving in the hot, moist conditions.

Banggereng In April, storms (known as 'knock 'em down' storms) flatten the spear grass, which during the course of the Wet has shot up to 2m in height.

Yekke The season of mists, when the air starts to dry out, extends from May to mid-June. The wetlands and waterfalls still have a lot of water and most of the tracks are open; and there aren't too many other visitors.

Wurrgeng and Gurrung The most comfortable time, weather-wise, is the late Dry, in July and August. This is when wildlife, especially birds, gather in large numbers around shrinking billabongs, but it's also when most tourists come to the park.

Wildlife

Kakadu has about 25 species of frogs, 51 freshwater fish species, 60 types of mammals, 120 types of reptile, 280 bird species (one-third of all those native to Australia) and at least 10,000 kinds of insects. There are frequent additions to the list and a few of the rarer species are unique to the park.

Most visitors see only a fraction of these creatures in a visit since many are shy, nocturnal or few in number. Take advantage of talks and walks led by park rangers –

mainly in the Dry – to get to know and see more of the wildlife. Cruises of East Alligator River and Yellow Water Billabong enable you to see the water life, including crocodiles.

BIRDS

Kakadu's abundant water birds, and their beautiful wetland setting, are a highlight of the park. This is one of the chief refuges in Australia for several species, among them the magpie goose, green pygmy goose and Burdekin duck. Other fine water birds include pelicans, darters and the jabiru, with its distinctive red legs and long, straight beak.

Herons, egrets, ibis and cormorants are common. The open woodlands harbour rainbow bee-eaters and kingfishers (of which there are six types in inland Kakadu) and the endangered bustard. Majestic white-breasted sea eagles are often seen near inland waterways, too, and wedge-tailed eagles, whistling kites and black kites are common. At night you might hear barking owls calling – they sound just like dogs. The raucous call of the spectacular red-tailed black cockatoo is considered by some to be the sound of Kakadu.

At **Mamukala**, 8km east of South Alligator on the Arnhem Hwy, is a wonderful observation building, as well as bird-watching hides and a 3km walking track.

FISH

You can't miss the silver barramundi, which creates a distinctive swirl near the water surface. It can grow to well over 1m in length and changes its sex from male to female at the age of five or six years.

MAMMALS

Several types of kangaroo and wallaby inhabit the park; the shy black wallaroo is unique to Kakadu and Arnhem Land. You might be lucky enough to see a sugar glider in wooded areas in the daytime. Kakadu is home to 26 bat species and is a key refuge for four endangered varieties. If you're driving at night, watch out for wildlife crossing the road – especially the destructive wild pig.

REPTILES

Both Twin Falls and Jim Jim Falls have resident freshwater crocodiles, which are considered harmless, while there are plenty of the dangerous saltwater variety throughout the park.

Kakadu's other reptiles include lizards, such as the frilled lizard, and five freshwater turtle species, of which the most common is the northern snake-necked turtle. Kakadu has many snakes, though most are nocturnal and rarely encountered. The striking Oenpelli python was first seen by non-Aboriginal people in 1976.

Rock Art

Kakadu is one of Australia's richest and most accessible repositories of rock art. There are over 5000 sites, which date from 20,000 years to 10 years ago. The vast majority of these sites are off-limits or inaccessible, but two of the finest collections are the galleries at Ubirr and Nourlangie.

The paintings have been classified into three roughly defined periods: Pre-estuarine, which is from the earliest paintings up to around 6000 years ago; Estuarine, which covers the period from 6000 to around 2000 years ago, when rising sea levels flooded valleys and brought the coast to its present level; and Freshwater, from 2000 years ago until the present day.

For the local Aboriginal people the rock-art sites are a major source of traditional knowledge, representing their historical archives, in place of a written form. Recent paintings, some executed in the 1980s, connect the local community with the artists. Older paintings are believed by many Aboriginal people to have been painted by spirit people, and depict stories that connect the people with creation legends and the development of Aboriginal law.

The majority of rock-art sites open to the public are relatively recent. There are often layers of styles painted over one another. This re-painting could only be done by a specific person who had knowledge of the story being depicted.

The conservation of the Kakadu rock-art sites is a major part of the park management task. As the paintings are all done with natural, water-soluble ochres, they are very susceptible to water damage. Drip-lines of clear silicon rubber have been made on the rocks above the paintings to divert the water flow. The most accessible sites receive up to 4000 visitors a *week*, which presents the problem of dust damage. Boardwalks

THE RAINBOW SERPENT

The story of the Rainbow Serpent is common in Aboriginal tradition across Australia, although the story varies from place to place.

In Kakadu the serpent is a woman, Kurangali, who painted her image on the rock wall at Ubirr while on a journey through this area. This journey forms a creation path which links the places she visited: Ubirr, Manngarre, East Alligator River and various places in Arnhem Land.

To the traditional owners of the park, Kurangali is the most powerful spirit. Although she spends most of her time resting in billabongs, if disturbed she can be very destructive, causing floods and earthquakes. One local story has it that she even eats people.

have been erected to keep the dust down and keep people a suitable distance from the paintings.

Orientation

The sealed Arnhem Hwy stretches 120km east from the Stuart Hwy to the Kakadu park entrance and another 107km to Jabiru. The Kakadu Hwy (also sealed) to Nourlangie, Cooinda and Pine Creek turns south off the Arnhem Hwy shortly before Jabiru.

Information

Bowali visitors centre (☎ 08-8938 1121; Kakadu Hwy; ☽ 8am-5pm) has beautifully presented walk-through displays which sweep you across the land, explaining Kakadu's ecology from both Aboriginal and non-Aboriginal perspectives. There's a 25-minute audio-visual presentation on Kakadu's changing seasons (screened hourly from 9am to 4pm), a theatre showing regular documentaries (from 8.30am to 3.30pm), and a café, gift shop and resource centre with a comprehensive selection of reference books. The centre is about 2.5km south of the Arnhem Hwy. It's a pleasant 2km walk to Bowali visitors centre from Jabiru, starting opposite the Crocodile Hotel.

Warradjan Aboriginal Cultural Centre (☎ 08-8975 0051; ☽ 9am-5.30pm Sep-Jun, 7.30am-6pm Jul-Aug), near Cooinda, gives a real insight into the culture of the park's traditional owners through creation stories and an introduction to the moiety system (internal tribal division) and skin names. The building's circular structure symbolises the way Aboriginal people sit in a circle when meeting and is also reminiscent of the *warradjan* (pig-nosed turtle), hence the name of the centre. There's a selection of videos to watch in the theatre, and a gallery. Warradjan is an easy (1km, 15 minutes) walk from the Cooinda resort.

Fuel is available at Kakadu Resort, Border Store (Ubirr), Jabiru and Cooinda. Jabiru also has a supermarket, post office and a Westpac bank. The **Northern Land Council office** (☎ 08-8979 2410) in Jabiru issues permits ($13.20) on the spot for the highly recommended trip to the Injalak Arts & Crafts Centre (p782) in Gunbalanya (Oenpelli), a 30-minute trip into Arnhem Land across the East Alligator River.

ENTRY FEES
The entry fee of $16.30 (children under 16 free) is paid at the park gates as you enter. This entitles you to stay in the park for seven days.

Ubirr
Ubirr is an outlying outcrop of the Arnhem escarpment, famous for its spectacular Aboriginal **rock-art site** (☼ 8.30am-sunset Apr-Nov, 2pm-sunset Dec-Mar). It lies 39km north of the Arnhem Hwy.

About 2km before Ubirr is a ranger station with an unstaffed visitors centre. From June to September, rangers give free guided tours of the rock art sites.

Shortly before Ubirr you pass the Border Store, behind which is a backpackers hostel and camping ground (see Sleeping; p780). Nearby, a couple of **walking tracks** skirt the East Alligator River, which forms the eastern boundary of the park here.

Guluyambi Cruises (☎ 1800 089 113; 1¾-hr tour adult/child $30/15) runs Aboriginal-guided cruises on the East Alligator River and offers a good chance to learn a little about Aboriginal culture and their relationship with the land. The tours depart from the upstream boat ramp at 9am, 11am, 1pm and 3pm from May to November. During the Wet, Guluyambi operates half-day tours including a boat transfer across the picturesque Magela Creek and a bus drive to Ubirr. It departs from Jabiru at

8am and noon daily and provides the only means by which visitors can get to Ubirr when the river is at its highest.

From Ubirr car park, an easily followed path takes you through the main galleries to the **Nardab Lookout**, with magnificent 360-degree views. Sunset here, over the wetlands with the Arnhem Land escarpment directly behind you, is stunning. There are paintings on numerous rocks along the path, but the highlight is the main gallery with a large array of well-preserved X-ray-style wallabies, possums, goannas, tortoises and fish, plus a couple of *balanda* (white men) with hands on hips, an intriguing Tasmanian tiger and *mimi* spirits. Also of major interest is the Rainbow Serpent painting and the picture of the Namarkan sisters, shown with string pulled taut between their hands. The Ubirr paintings are in many different styles. They were painted over a period spanning from 20,000 years ago to the 20th century.

All road access is sealed, although low-lying areas may be inundated during the wet season.

Jabiru
☎ 08 / pop 1780
The township, built to accommodate Ranger uranium mine workers, is the major service centre for Kakadu. It contains a bank, newsagent, medical centre, supermarket, bakery and service station. About 6km north is Jabiru airport and the Ranger uranium mine. There are minibus tours of the mine ($20) available twice daily through **Kakadu Parklink** (☎ 1800 089 113).

Nourlangie
The sight of this looming, mysterious, isolated outlier of the Arnhem Land escarpment makes it easy to understand why it has been important to Aboriginal people for so long. Its long red sandstone bulk, striped in places with orange, white and black, slopes up from surrounding woodland to fall away at one end in sheer, stepped cliffs. Below is Kakadu's best-known collection of rock art.

The name Nourlangie is a corruption of Nawulandja, an Aboriginal word that refers to an area bigger than the rock itself. The Aboriginal name of the rock is Burrunggui. You reach it at the end of a 12km sealed road that turns east off Kakadu Hwy, 21km south of Arnhem Hwy.

Other interesting spots nearby make it worth spending a whole day in this corner of Kakadu. The road is open from 8am to sunset daily.

From the main car park a circuit of about 2km takes you first to the **Anbangbang rock shelter**, which was used for 20,000 years as a refuge from heat, rain and frequent wet-season thunderstorms. From the gallery, a short walk takes you to a lookout with a view of the Arnhem Land escarpment and Lightning Dreaming (Namarrgon Djadjam), the home of Namarrgon. The 12km Barrk Sandstone Bushwalk follows the rock's base; track notes are available at the Bowali visitors centre.

Heading back towards the highway you can take turn-offs to three other places of interest. The first, on the left about 1km from the main car park, takes you to the lily-carpeted **Anbangbang billabong**. The second, also on the left, leads to a short walk up to **Nawulandja lookout** with good views back over Nourlangie Rock. The third turn-off, a dirt track on the right, takes you to the outstanding **Nanguluwur**, a little-visited rock-art gallery.

A farther 6km along this road, plus a 3km walk, you will come across **Gubara (Baroalba Springs)**, an area of shaded pools in monsoon forest.

Jim Jim & Twin Falls

These two spectacular waterfalls are along a 4WD dry-season track that turns south off the Kakadu Hwy between the Nourlangie and Cooinda turn-offs. It's about 57km to Jim Jim Falls (the last 1km on foot) and a farther 10km to Twin Falls, where the last few hundred metres are through the water up a snaking, forested gorge.

Jim Jim, a sheer 215m drop, is awesome after rain, but its waters can shrink to nothing by about June. Twin Falls flows year-round.

Note that the track to Jim Jim and Twin Falls is often still closed in late May and even into June. The only way to see them in the Wet is from the air.

Yellow Water & Cooinda

The turn-off to the Cooinda accommodation complex and the superb Yellow Water

wetlands is 47km down the Kakadu Hwy from its junction with the Arnhem Hwy. It's then 4.5km to the Warradjan Aboriginal Cultural Centre (p777), a farther 1km to the Yellow Water wetland turn-off, and about another 1km again to Cooinda.

The **boat trip** (☎ 08-8979 0111) on Yellow Water Billabong is one of the highlights of a visit to Kakadu. The dawn trip is the best as the birds are most active and the light is perfect. The mirror-image reflections as you glide through the melaleuca (paperbark) swamp on a still morning are sublime. Two-hour cruises cost $38/16.50 per adult/child and depart at 6.45am, 9am and 4.30pm. Shorter (1½ hours) cruises leave at 11.30am, 1.15pm and 2.45pm and cost $33/15. During the Wet all cruises are 1½ hours. Book your cruise the day before at Cooinda, especially for the early departure.

Yellow Water is also an excellent place to watch the sunset, particularly in the Dry, when the smoke from the many bushfires that burn in the Top End at this time of year turns the setting sun into a bright red fireball. Bring plenty of insect repellent as the mosquitoes are voracious.

Cooinda to Pine Creek

Just south of the Yellow Water and Cooinda turn-off, the Kakadu Hwy heads southwest out of the park on the Stuart Hwy to Pine Creek, 160km away. On the way there is a turn-off to the superb escarpment waterfall and plunge pool at **Gunlom (Waterfall Creek)**. It's 37km along a good dirt road.

Activities
BUSHWALKING

Kakadu is rewarding but tough bushwalking country. Many people will be satisfied with the marked tracks, which range from 1km to 12km in length. For the more adventurous there are infinite possibilities, especially in the drier southern and eastern sections of the park. Follow the lore of bushwalking – prepare well, tell people where you're going and don't walk alone. You'll need a permit from the Bowali visitors centre (p777) to camp outside established camp sites.

Darwin Bushwalking Club (☎ 08-8985 1484) welcomes visitors and may be able to help with information. It has walks most weekends, often in Kakadu.

Kakadu by Foot ($3.30) is a helpful guide to the marked walking tracks in Kakadu. It's published by Parks Australia and is on sale at the Bowali visitors centre.

Tours

All meals and entry fees are generally included in the tour price, and some operators offer discounts to VIP, YHA and Nomads members.

Wilderness 4WD Adventures (☎ 1800 808 288, 08-8941 2161; www.wildernessadventures.com.au) offers small group 4WD camping tours into Kakadu (3/5 days $430/670), and other extended and combined trips.

Billy Can Tours (☎ 1800 813 484, 08-8981 9813; www.billycan.com.au) is an upmarket operator which runs a variety of tours through Kakadu, some with German-speaking guides. Two-/three-day camping tours start at $330/740.

A few companies run 4WD trips to Jim Jim and Twin Falls from Cooinda and Jabiru, including lunch and paddling gear for around $115 to $130. These include **Kakadu Gorge & Waterfall Tours** (☎ 08-8979 0111; www.kakadu-touring.com.au), **Kakadu Park Connection** (☎/fax 08-8979 0388; kakaduconnection@hotmail.com), **Katch Kakadu** (☎ 08-8979 3315) and **Lord's Kakadu & Arnhem Land Safaris** (☎ 08-8979 2970; www.lords-safaris.com), which also runs trips into Arnhem Land (Oenpelli) for $165/130. Katch Kakadu also offers fishing trips (half-/full-day $126/220) on the South and East Alligator Rivers within Kakadu for the prime purpose of hooking that 'barra'.

Aboriginal-owned **Magela Cultural & Heritage Tours** (☎ 08-8979 2422; magela@austarnet.com.au; adult/child $175/100) has small-group 4WD tours from Jabiru, taking in Arnhem Land escarpment country and rock-art sites with an emphasis on Aboriginal culture. **Kakadu Animal Tracks** (☎ 08-8979 0145; www.animaltracks.com.au; adult/child $95/70) runs unique tours combining a wildlife safari and Aboriginal cultural tour on the buffalo farm. The seven-hour tours depart from Cooinda at 1.15pm.

Willis' Walkabouts (☎ 08-8985 2134; www.bushwalkingholidays.com.au) organises bushwalks of two days or more, guided by knowledgeable Top End walkers.

SCENIC FLIGHTS

The view of Kakadu from the air is spectacular. When the Jim Jim and Twin Falls access road is closed, the only way to see

the falls is by air. **Kakadu Air** (☎ 1800 089 113; kakair@kakair.com.au), at Jabiru, has half-/one-hour fixed-wing flights for $80/130. Both Kakadu Air and **North Australian Helicopters** (☎ 1800 898 977; www.northaustralianhelicopters.com.au) offer half-hour helicopter tours of the escarpment and Minkinj Valley for around $175, or you can go sky-high on a flight over Jim Jim and Twin Falls for $420.

Sleeping & Eating

Prices for accommodation in Kakadu can vary tremendously depending on the season – rates at resort accommodation given here plummet by as much as 50% during the Wet.

SOUTH ALLIGATOR

This is the first resort you'll pass if entering the park along the Arnhem Hwy.

Kakadu Resort (☎ 1800 818 845; kresort@aurora-resorts.com.au; Arnhem Hwy; camp sites per person $7.50, s/d $195; mains $17-26; **P** ⊠) A couple of kilometres west of the South Alligator River, this resort is set in sprawling manicured gardens with shady trees and plenty of birdlife. The rooms are comfortable, and there's a pool, tennis court, laundry and barbecue area. Meals are available at the restaurant, bar and café.

UBIRR

Kakadu Hostel (☎ 08-8979 2232; camp/caravan sites for 2 $16/25, dm $25; breakfast $5, mains $10-15; ⊠) Tucked in behind the Border Store, about 3km from Ubirr, is Kakadu's only true backpacker hostel. This simple but friendly place has rooms with two to 14 beds, a well-equipped kitchen, lounge room and swimming pool. Meals are usually available and the Border Store also has supplies. The hostel is open as long as the road remains open.

JABIRU

Jabiru has some good options.

Kakadu Lodge & Caravan Park (☎ 1800 811 154; www.aurora-resorts.com.au; Jabiru Dr; camp/caravan sites for 2 $20/25, dm $31, lodge rooms $121, cabins $199; breakfast $2.50-17, dinner $10-17.50; ⊠ ⊒) This impeccable resort has shady grassed sites and a landscaped swimming pool-bar-dining area. The comfortable cabins share facilities. There are coin-operated barbecues, a camp kitchen (no utensils) and laundry facilities. Book ahead.

Lakeview Park Bush Bungalows (☎ 08-8979 3144; 27 Lakeview Dr; rooms $61) The safari-style

CAMPING UNDER THE STARS IN KAKADU

Kakadu is the ideal environment for camping. Although you can pitch a tent on the manicured lawns of the Kakadu Resort (p780), Kakadu Lodge (p780) or Gagadju Lodge (below), the best way to appreciate nature here is to roll out a swag or set up your tent at one of the dozen or so designated bush camping areas. Most of these sites are free, but the national parks sites, which have fireplaces, flush toilets and running water, cost $5.40/free per adult/child. To camp away from a designated site, you need a permit from the Bowali visitors centre.

The three main national parks camp sites are: Merl, near the Border Store at Ubirr; Muirella Park, a few kilometres south of the Nourlangie turn-off and then 6km off the Kakadu Hwy; and Mardugal, just off the Kakadu Hwy 1.5km south of the Cooinda turn-off. Only the Mardugal site is open during the Wet.

About 20km into the park along the Arnhem Hwy, a turn-off to the north leads to camping areas at Two Mile Hole (8km) and Four Mile Hole (38km) on the Wildman River, which is popular for fishing. The track is not suitable for conventional vehicles except in the Dry, and then only as far as Two Mile Hole.

About 35km farther east along the highway, a turn-off to the south, again impassable to conventional vehicles in the Wet, leads to camping areas at Red Lily (35km) and Alligator Billabongs (39km), and on to the Old Jim Jim Rd (69km).

If you're camping in a swag you'll need a mosquito net – the mozzies can be voracious here.

fan-cooled rooms here sleep up to four people. The facilities are shared and guests have the use of a fridge, barbecues, and a laundry.

Gagadju Crocodile Hotel (☎ 1800 808 123; reservations@crocodileholidayinn.com.au; Flinders St; d $105-330; mains $18.50-29.50; 🌂) When viewed from the air, this hotel forms the shape of a 250m crocodile. The rooms (within the beast's gut) are comfortable, if a little tired. The upmarket Escarpment Restaurant serves inspiring buffet and à la carte meals, served with bush ingredients, and delectable desserts. Snacks are served in the Gingas Tavern, which has a pool table, and the art gallery in the foyer is worth a wander.

Jabiru has a shopping centre with several eating options, including the Jabiru Café and a bakery near the fire station.

COOINDA

The proximity of the Yellow Water wetlands and the early-morning boat cruises makes this a popular place to stay, so it can get mighty crowded at times.

Gagadju Lodge Cooinda (☎ 1800 500 401; reservations@kakadulodge.cooinda.com.au; Kakadu Hwy; camp/caravan sites for 2 $22/28, dm $30.50, d $150-270; 🌂) Plenty of trees shade the camping ground, though the facilities can be stretched at times. The lodge rooms are comfortable, but the budget accommodation resembles one-fifth of a shipping crate. There are barbecues and

a fly-wire protected kitchen amid the budget rooms. Fuel, basic supplies, insect repellant (you'll need it!) and film is sold at the shop.

Barra Bistro (breakfast $16.50-22.50, lunch & dinner $12.50-22.50) Generous, though average, cold or hot buffet meals are available at the bistro, and fast food nosh is sold near the bar. The pleasant, alfresco setting here can get lively at night.

Mimi Restaurant (mains $22.50-32.50) Modern Australian cuisine – including the requisite barra and roo – with native spices is served overlooking the swimming pool. Bookings are essential.

Getting There & Around

Ideally, take your own vehicle. In the Dry you can easily get to most sites in a conventional vehicle, excluding Jim Jim Falls which is also off-limits to many 4WD hire vehicles (check your policy). Sealed roads lead from the Kakadu Hwy to Nourlangie, the Muirella Park camping area and to Ubirr. Other roads are mostly dirt and blocked for varying periods during the Wet and early Dry.

Even if you don't have your own wheels, it's possible to explore Kakadu and its surrounds independently at your leisure and at a discount. Trying to get around on a bus pass alone will be frustrating, but you can see a lot by combining transport to Jabiru, Ubirr and Cooinda with a couple of tours, such as a trip to the big falls, the Yellow

Waters cruise and an Aboriginal cultural tour. Camping gear can be hired inexpensively in Darwin from **Gone Bush** (☎ 0413-757 000; gonebush@octa4.net.au) and **Into the Wild** (☎ 0407-786 637; intothewild@octa4.net.au), which will deliver to your accommodation. Stock up on food in Darwin – preferably items that will keep for a few days. If there are a few of you, rent a small car.

McCafferty's/Greyhound (☎ 13 20 30) has a daily return service between Darwin and Cooinda via Jabiru. Buses reach the Yellow Waters wetlands in time for the 1pm cruise and depart when the cruise finishes 1½ hours later. The bus leaves Darwin at 6.30am, Jabiru at 9.55am, and arrives at Cooinda at 12.10pm. It departs from Cooinda at 2.30pm, Jabiru at 4.20pm, and arrives in Darwin at 7pm. Tickets cost $45/80 one way/return.

Plenty of tours (p780) depart from Darwin for Kakadu – some combining Kakadu with Mary River, Litchfield, Katherine and Arnhem Land.

ARNHEM LAND

The entire eastern half of the Top End is the Arnhem Land Aboriginal Reserve, a vast and virtually undisturbed area with spectacular scenery, few people and some superb rock-art sites. Apart from Gunbalanya (Oenpelli), just across the East Alligator River in Kakadu, the remote Garig Gunak Barlu (formerly Gurig) National Park (on the Cobourg Peninsula at the northwest corner) and Gove (the peninsula at the northeast corner), Arnhem Land is virtually closed to independent travellers. Much of this is Yolngu country, brought to life in the film *Yolngu Boy* (2001).

TOURS

If you get the opportunity to head into the unique wonderland that is Arnhem Land – jump!

Umorrduk Safaris (☎ 08-8948 1306) transports guests in time and place to remote northwestern Arnhem Land on these trips. The highlight is a visit to the 20,000-year-old Umorrduk rock-art sites. There's a range of options, from one-day fly-in/fly-out tours from Darwin ($340) to extended tours.

Davidson's Arnhemland Safaris (☎ 08-8927 5240; www.arnhemland-safaris.com) has for years been taking people to its safari camp at Mt Borradaile, north of Gunbalanya (Oenpelli) in Arnhem

Land. Meals, guided tours, fishing and accommodation in the comfortable camp are included in the daily price of around $420; transfers from Darwin can be arranged.

Gove Diving & Fishing Charters (☎ 08-8987 3445; www.govefish.com.au) runs a plethora of fishing, diving and wilderness tours from the Gove Peninsula.

See also Magela Cultural & Heritage Tours and Lord's Kakadu & Arnhem Land Safaris (p780).

Gunbalanya (Oenpelli)
☎ 08

The drive into this Aboriginal community town, along a 17km dirt road from Kakadu, traverses the wildly spectacular East Alligator River flood plain (rivalling anything within Kakadu itself). The **Injalak Arts & Crafts Centre** (☎ 8979 0190; www.aboriginalart.org; Mon-Sat) here sells high-quality Aboriginal artefacts at very reasonable prices. Injalak is both a workplace and shopfront for artists and craftspeople who produce traditional paintings on bark and paper, didgeridoos, pandanus weavings and baskets, and screen-printed fabrics. All sales directly benefit the community and you can also be sure that you are buying authentic pieces. The **Northern Land Council** (☎ 8979 2410; Jabiru; 8am-4.30pm Mon-Fri) issues permits to visit Injalak ($13.20).

See the boxed text 'Aboriginal Festivals & Events' (p746) for details of the famous Gunbalanya (Oenpelli) open day in August.

Cobourg Peninsula

This remote wilderness includes **Cobourg Marine Park** and **Garig Gunak Barlu National Park**. Entry is by permit only.

The ruins of the early settlement known as Victoria can be visited on **Port Essington**, a superb 30km-long natural harbour on the northern side of the peninsula.

At Black Point (Algarlarlgarl) there's a **Ranger Station** (☎ 08-8979 0244) with a visitors centre and the **Gurig Store** (☎ 1800 000 871; 4-6pm Mon-Sat), which sells basic provisions, ice and camping gas. Credit cards and Eftpos are accepted.

PERMITS

The track to Cobourg passes through part of Arnhem Land and, as the Aboriginal owners here restrict the number of vehicles going through to 20 at any one time, you're advised to apply up to a year ahead for the necessary transit permit ($232 per vehicle, valid for seven days), which includes camping fees for the national park. Permits are only issued for travel between May and October and can be obtained from the **Parks & Wildlife Commission** (☎ 08-8999 4814; PO Box 496, Palmerston, NT 0831). If you book accommodation through a lodge (such as Cobourg Beach Huts) it will arrange a permit for you.

SLEEPING

There's a good, shady camping ground about 100m from the shore at Smith Point. Facilities include a shower, toilet, barbecues and limited bore water; generators are allowed in one area.

Cobourg Beach Huts (☎ 08-8979 0263; www .cobourg.gurig.com.au; huts $160) These secluded, self-contained huts sleep up to six people and have louvered window-walls and solar-heated showers.

GETTING THERE & AWAY

The quickest route is by air, though this will leave you without transport when you arrive.

The track to Cobourg starts at Gunbalanya (Oenpelli) and is accessible by 4WD vehicles only – it's closed in the Wet, usually opening early May. The 270km drive to Black Point from the East Alligator River takes four to six hours and must be completed in one day.

Straight after the Wet, the water level at Cahills Crossing can be high, and you can only drive across the ford about an hour either side of the low tide. Check the tide chart included with your permit, or at the Bowali visitors centre in Kakadu.

Eastern Arnhem Land

The Gove Peninsula has some fine beaches and fishing. **Nhulunbuy** (population 4000) is a remote community on the peninsula, built to service the **bauxite mining centre** (☎ 08-8987 5345) which runs free tours on Friday morning.

There are Aboriginal art and craft centres at Nhulunbuy and Yirrkala. **Nambara Arts & Crafts Aboriginal Gallery** (☎ 08-8987 2811) sells art and crafts from northeast Arnhem Land and often has artists in residence. **Buku Larrnggay Mulka Art Centre & Museum** (☎ 08-8987 1701; www.aboriginalart.com.au; museum admission $2), 20km south of Nhulunbuy, is a major

repository of bark painting, carved totems and other artefacts.

Groote Eylandt, a large island off the east Arnhem Land coast, is also Aboriginal land and has a large manganese mining operation. Alyangula (population 670) is the main settlement here.

PERMITS

Travelling overland through Arnhem Land from Katherine requires a permit (free); contact the **Northern Land Council** (☎ 08-8987 2602; Nhulunbuy). Permits are required to explore outside Nhulunbuy; there are three separate areas – contact the **East Arnhem Land Tourist Association** (☎ 08-8987 2255; www.ealta.org; Westall St, Nhulunbuy) for details.

GETTING THERE & AWAY

You don't need a permit to fly into Nhulunbuy. **Airnorth** (☎ 08-8920 4000; www.airnorth.com.au) flies from Darwin to Nhulunbuy ($300 one way) and from Cairns to Groote Eylandt ($450). In Nhulunbuy, you can hire bicycles and vehicles to explore the coastline and the local area (there are some fine beaches, but beware of crocodiles).

KATHERINE TO ALICE

The Stuart Hwy from Darwin to Alice Springs is known as 'the Track' and until WWII it really was just that – a dirt track connecting the Territory's two main towns, roughly following the Overland Telegraph Line. It is now sealed and punctuated with plaques at roadside stops.

The highway between Katherine and Alice Springs can be dull at times, but there are a few interesting diversions along the way, notably Mataranka's thermal pool, Daly Waters' pub, Tennant Creek's mining history and the much-photographed Devil's Marbles.

KATHERINE

☎ 08 / pop 6720

Apart from Tennant Creek, this is the only town of any size between Darwin and Alice Springs. It's a bustling place with a productive Aboriginal arts community – many of the didgeridoos and other artworks you'll find in Alice and Darwin come from around here. The town's population has grown rapidly in recent years, mainly

NORTHERN TERRITORY

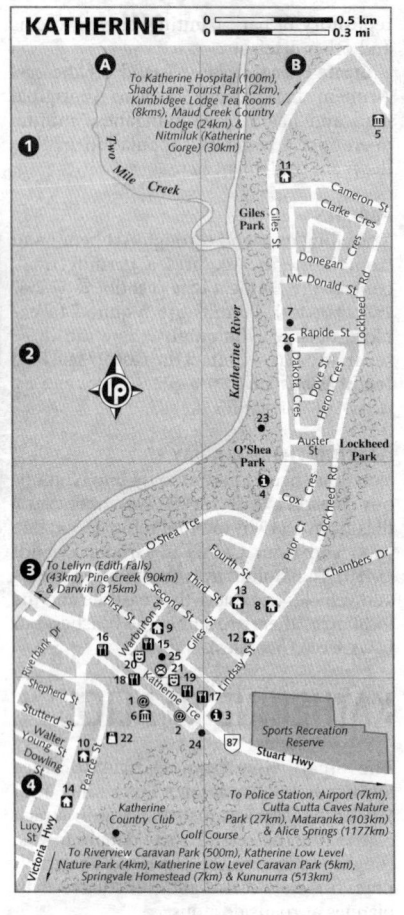

KATHERINE

INFORMATION
Didj Shop Internet Café	1	A4
Katherine Art Gallery	2	A4
Katherine Region Tourist Association	3	B4
Parks & Wildlife Commission	4	B3

SIGHTS & ACTIVITIES   p785
Katherine Museum	5	B1
Railway Precinct	6	A4
School of the Air	7	B2

SLEEPING   pp785-6
Beagle Motor Inn	8	B3
Coco's Didj Backpackers	9	A3
Jan's B&B	10	A4
Knotts Crossing Resort	11	B1
Kookaburra Lodge Backpackers	12	B3
Palm Court Backpackers	13	B3
Victoria Lodge	14	A4

EATING   p786
Cinema Café	15	A3
Katie's Bistro	(see 11)	
Mekhong Thai Café & Takeaway	16	A3
Nino's Pizza & Chicken Bar	17	A4
Starvin'	18	A4
Woolworths	19	A4

ENTERTAINMENT   p786
Crossways Hotel	20	A3
Katherine Cinema	(see 15)	
Katherine Hotel	21	A4
Rio's Nightclub	(see 20)	

SHOPPING   p786
Coco's Katherine Didjeridoos	(see 9)	
Mimi Aboriginal Art & Craft	22	A4

TRANSPORT   pp786-7
Europcar	(see 11)	
Hertz	23	B2
Thrifty	24	A4
Transit Centre	(see 24)	
Travel North	(see 24)	

OTHER
Bike Shop	25	A3
Whoop Whoop	26	B2

because of the establishment of the large Tindal air-force base just south of town.

Katherine has long been an important stopping point, as the river it's built on and named after is the first permanent running water north of Alice Springs. It's a mixed blessing really, because floods have caused plenty of damage and heartache over the years. The devastating flooding on Australia Day 1998 inundated the surrounding countryside and left a water line up to 2m high on buildings all over town.

Katherine has some historic buildings and is a good place to recharge and restock on the long drive north or south (or west, as the Victoria Hwy heads into WA from here). The main interest is the spectacular

Nitmiluk (Katherine Gorge) National Park, 30km to the northeast. It's a great place for camping, walking, swimming, canoeing, taking a cruise or simply floating along on an air mattress.

Orientation & Information

Katherine's main street, Katherine Tce, is the Stuart Hwy on its way through town. Giles St, the road to Nitmiluk National Park, branches off to the northeast in the middle of town.

At the southern end of town, the **Katherine Region Tourist Association** (☎ 8972 2650; www.krol.com.au; cnr Stuart Hwy & Lindsay St; ☯ 8.30am-5pm Mon-Fri, 10am-3pm Sat & Sun) stocks information on all areas of the NT and the Kimberley and Gulf regions. Park notes are available here or at the **Parks & Wildlife Commission** (☎ 8973 8770; 32 Giles St).

The major banks, with ATMs, line the main street, Katherine Tce.

Internet access is available at the **Didj Shop Internet Cafe** (☎ 8972 2485; www.didj.com.au; cnr Giles St & Railway Tce) and **Katherine Art Gallery** (☎ 8971 1051; 12 Katherine Tce).

In case of emergency, the **Katherine hospital** (☎ 8973 9211; Giles St) is about 2.5km north of the town, and the **police station** (☎ 8972 0111; Stuart Hwy) is southeast of town.

Sights & Activities

Katherine Low Level Nature Park is a great spot on the banks of the Katherine River, with a popular dry-season swimming hole, just off the Victoria Hwy 5km from town. A cycle-walking path links the nature park with town along the southern bank of the river. It passes Katherine's **thermal pools**. Floating in the clear, warm waters past pandanus palms to the rapids is a delight.

School of the Air (☎ 8972 1833; www.schools.nt.edu .au; Giles St; adult/child $5/2; ⏲ mid-Mar–mid-Dec) This is an opportunity to see how kids in the remote outback are taught. Guided tours, which usually include listening in on a live lesson, start at 9am, 10am, 11am, 1pm, 2pm from Monday to Friday.

Katherine Museum (☎ 8972 3945; Gorge Rd; adult/child $3.50/1; ⏲ 10am-4pm Mon-Fri & 10am-1pm Sat Mar-Oct, 2-5pm Sun year-round) The museum, in the old airport terminal building opposite Katherine Hospital, about 3km northeast of the town centre, has a good selection of old photos, including a display on the 1998 flood, and other pieces of interest. The Gypsy Moth biplane flown by Dr Clyde Fenton, the pioneering flying doctor, is housed here, along with a helicopter used for cattle mustering.

Springvale Homestead (☎ 8972 1355; Shadforth Rd; ⏲ 8am-5.30pm) Ernest Giles established Springvale, 8km southwest of town, in 1879 and it's claimed to be the oldest cattle station in the NT. You're welcome to wander around the homestead or take the daily tour at 3pm from May to October.

Katherine's **railway precinct** (Railway Tce; admission $2; ⏲ 1-3pm Mon-Fri May-Sep), owned by the National Trust, includes a display on railway history in the original station building (1926) and a dilapidated steam engine sitting on a section of the old north Australian rail line.

Tours

See the tourist office or **Travel North** (☎ 8971 9999; transit centre) for a full list of tour options in the Katherine area.

Gecko Canoeing (☎ 1300 555 542; www.geckocano eing.com.au) runs exhilarating extended canoe trips along remote stretches of the Katherine River. One-/three-day trips cost $155/ 580 including meals, transport and safety gear. The eight-day expedition combining a five-day hike along the awesome Jatbula Trail in Nitmiluk National Park with three days of canoeing costs $1360.

Whoop Whoop (☎ 8972 2941; Giles St) gets rave reviews from readers for its overnight didgeridoo-making tours ($220) which depart on Friday.

Sleeping
BUDGET

Hostels, camping grounds and caravan parks provide low-cost options in Katherine. YHA/VIP discounts are available at most hostels.

Kookaburra Lodge Backpackers (☎ 1800 808 211, 8971 0257; kookaburra@nt-tech.com.au; cnr Lindsay & Third Sts; dm/tw $18/50; 🖳) This popular hostel a few minutes' walk from the transit centre has a friendly relaxed atmosphere. There's a kitchen and bathroom in each converted motel-room dorm, an outdoor common area with TV, and bike and canoe hire.

Knotts Crossing Resort (☎ 1800 222 511, 8972 2511; www.knottscrossing.com.au; Cameron St; camp/caravan sites for 2 $20/22, cabins from $75, d $125-150; 🖳 🖳) This is a bit flash for any self-respecting camper, but it's well-located amid lush tropical gardens and has excellent facilities. All powered sites have bathroom facilities and there's a good pool, plus Katie's Bistro. Cabins with bathrooms are available from $90.

Katherine Low Level Caravan Park (☎ 8972 3962; lowlevel@austarnet.com.au; Shadforth Rd; camp/ caravan sites for 2 $19/22, cabins from $85; 🖳) Just across the river off the Victoria Hwy about 5km from town, this is a beautiful, grassy

THE AUTHOR'S CHOICE

Jan's B&B (☎ 8971 1005; jcomleybbaccom@ yahoo.com.au; 13 Pearce St; guesthouse s/d $50/85, B&B s/d $95/150; 🖳) This gem could well be the best accommodation in town. Rooms share bathroom facilities and guests are welcome to use the pool table, piano, lounge area, spa, pool and guesthouse kitchen. Jan also serves great evening meals ($23). Book ahead.

park with spotless amenities, a great pool and camp-kitchen facilities. Knock back sundowners under the massive fig tree in the outdoor bar area.

Other options:

Palm Court Backpackers (☎ 1800 089 103, 8972 2722; www.travelnorth.com.au; Giles St; dm/tw $18/45; 🟦) Motel-style rooms with a shared kitchen, pool and barbecue area.

Coco's Didj Backpackers (☎ 8971 2889; coco@ topend.com.au; 21 First St; camp sites $10, dm $16) An offbeat place; indigenous artists occasionally work here.

Victoria Lodge (☎ 1800 808 875; fax 8971 1738; 21 Victoria Hwy; dm/s/d $17/40/55; 🟦) A good-value budget lodge with clean facilities.

Riverview Caravan Park (☎ 8972 1011; fax 8971 0397; 440 Victoria Hwy; camp/caravan sites for 2 $17/21, s/d $20/30, cabins from $65, motel d $75-85; 🟦) Near Katherine's thermal pools.

Shady Lane Tourist Park (☎ 8971 0491; www.shady lanetouristpark.com.au; Gorge Rd; camp/caravan sites for 2 $19/22, cabins $45-90; 🟦) A quiet park towards Nitmiluk National Park.

Springvale Homestead (☎ 1800 089 103; www .travelnorth.com.au; Shadforth Rd; camp/caravan sites for 2 $15/18, s/d $45/55; 🟦) In a relaxing bush setting on the Katherine River about 8km from town.

MID-RANGE

Katherine's resorts and tourist parks offer comfortable motel units and cabins; see the Budget section, earlier, for details.

Beagle Motor Inn (☎ 8972 3998; fax 8972 3725; 2 Fourth St; s/d $70/80; 🟦) This no-frills place is in the centre of town and has a pool. Breakfast and dinner are available.

Maud Creek Country Lodge (☎ 8971 1814; julies@ nt-tech.com.au; d from $110; 🟦) Maud Creek is a peaceful rural retreat 6km from the gorge. There's a communal kitchen, guest lounge with TV, and bushwalking, bird-watching and river fishing.

Eating

Eating out in Katherine comes a distant third to Darwin and Alice Springs, but there's enough to keep you ticking over.

Cinema Café (17 First St; breakfast $2.50-11.50, mains $8.50-14) This pleasant spot in the cinema complex serves homemade specials and good breakfasts, lunches, cakes and coffee.

Kumbidgee Lodge Tea Rooms (☎ 8971 0699; Giles St; mains $7-16) Along the gorge road, 10km out of town, this is a tranquil spot to indulge in a hearty 'bush breakfast' ($10) or

Devonshire tea while catching up with the rest of the world in the papers.

Starvin' (☎ 8972 3633; 32 Katherine Tce; pizza $9.80-20, pasta $8-10.50) Café by day, BYO gourmet pizza parlour by night. Depending on how you time it, you could be feasting on focaccias, salads, pasta or pizza.

Nino's Pizza & Chicken Bar (☎ 8972 3700; Lindsay St) You guessed it – pizza and chicken make up the menu at this hole in the wall opposite the tourist office.

Mekhong Thai Cafe & Takeaway (☎ 8972 3170; cnr Katherine Tce & Murphy St; mains $7-15) Mekhong's extensive menu of tasty Thai dishes is in contrast to its sparse decorations. Vegetarians will rejoice here!

Katie's Bistro (☎ 8972 2511; Knotts Crossing Resort, cnr Giles & Cameron Sts; mains $16-24) Locally regarded as Katherine's best restaurant, Katie's serves good, fresh and well-prepared meals.

Woolworth's (Katherine Tce) This is the cheapest place for hundreds of kilometres around for you to stock up. It has a liquor shop and a bakery.

Entertainment

A block apart on the main street, **Katherine Hotel** (☎ 8972 1622) has occasional live bands and **Crossways Hotel** (☎ 8972 1022) has Rio's Nightclub. Both have pool tables. If you're after something less rowdy, **Katherine Cinema** (☎ 8971 2522; www.katherinecinemas.com.au; 20 First St) screens recent-release films daily.

Shopping

Mimi Aboriginal Art & Craft (☎ 8971 0036; 6 Pearce St) This Aboriginal-owned cooperative sells quality art and crafts from the Katherine region, Arnhem Land, and from the desert and Kimberley regions.

Coco's Katherine Didjeridoos (☎ 8971 2889; 21 First St) Didgeridoos are sold in a variety of keys (A to G) here.

Also worth a browse is **Katherine Art Gallery** (☎ 8971 1051; 12 Katherine Tce) and **Didj Shop Internet Cafe** (☎ 8972 2485; www.didj.com.au), which has a small collection of didjs and some high-quality art, as well as good coffee.

Getting There & Around

Katherine airport is 8km south of town, just off the Stuart Hwy. **Airnorth** (☎ 1800 627 474) flies to Katherine daily from Darwin ($200) and daily except Sunday from Alice Springs ($470) and Tennant Creek ($350).

BUYING A DIDGERIDOO

Didgeridoos are fast becoming one of the most popular forms of souvenir Aboriginal art among tourists. Not only are they artworks in themselves, but they are also an instrument and have important cultural significance.

Traditionally, didgeridoos were only used by Aborigines from the Top End of Australia. They were made from a single piece of eucalypt (often woollybutt) that was naturally hollowed out by termites only found in this part of Australia. Authentic didgeridoos are still made this way: reasonably straight, termite-hollowed pieces of wood are gathered in northern Australia, cleaned out, cut to the required length (which affects the key of the drone) and painted. Often the mouthpiece is moulded with beeswax. When shopping for a didg, take a look inside and run your finger around the inner edge – it should be rough and uneven, otherwise it has probably been bored out by a drill. Ask what type of wood was used and where it came from.

You can find didgeridoos for sale in many parts of Australia these days, but many of them are 'fakes', mass produced in factories for the tourist market and still outrageously overpriced. The best place to buy a genuine didgeridoo is in the NT. Expect to pay $200 to $350 (or more) for a reasonable-sized didg. Ask for a certificate of authenticity if it is claimed that it was made and decorated by an Aboriginal artist.

There are many didgeridoos on display in Alice, so it's worth a browse. However, if you're heading farther north, it's cheaper to buy them closer to the source. Katherine is the main regional centre for many Aboriginal artists making their traditional instrument. If you buy a didgeridoo, ask for a quick lesson – most vendors are more than happy to oblige.

All buses between Darwin and Alice Springs, Queensland or WA stop at Katherine's transit centre. Typical fares from Katherine include Alice Springs ($180, 15 hours), Darwin ($55, 4½ hours) and Kununurra ($75, 4½ hours).

There are a few car-rental outfits in town. **Thrifty** (☎ 1800 891 125) has a desk at the transit centre; **Hertz** (☎ 1800 891 112) is at Katherine River Lodge and **Europcar** (☎ 1800 811 541) is at Knott's Crossing Resort.

You can hire bikes at the **Bike Shop** (☎ 8972 1213; Shop 3/16 First St) for $18/33 per half/full day.

For taxis, call **Katherine Taxi** (☎ 8971 3399).

AROUND KATHERINE
Cutta Cutta Caves Nature Park
The karst (limestone) rock formations outside these tropical caves, 27km southeast of Katherine along the Stuart Hwy, are impressive. Orange horseshoe bats, a rare and endangered species, roost in the main cave, about 15m below the ground. The only way to see the caves is on a 45-minute **Guided Tour** (☎ 08-8972 1940; adult/child $12/6) at 9am, 10am, 11am, 1pm, 2pm, 3pm in the dry season.

Manyallaluk
The former 3000-sq-km Eva Valley cattle station **Manyallaluk** (☎ 1800 644 727, 08-8975 4727; camp/caravan sites for 2 $11/16.50) abuts the eastern edge of the Nitmiluk National Park. The land is owned by the Jawoyn Aboriginal people, some of whom now organise and lead highly regarded cultural tours.

You'll learn about traditional bush tucker and medicine, spear throwing and playing a didg on the one-day trip ($143/78.50 per adult/child), which includes transport to/from Katherine, lunch and tea. It runs from Monday to Friday from 15 March to 1 October (Monday, Wednesday and Friday only from 1 October to 15 December). If you have your own vehicle, you can camp at Manyallaluk and take the day tour from there ($110/66.50 per adult/child). The community store sells basic supplies and excellent crafts at competitive prices. No permits are needed to visit the community, but alcohol is prohibited.

NITMILUK (KATHERINE GORGE) NATIONAL PARK
Remote, beautiful Nitmiluk (Katherine Gorge) is 13 gorges, separated from each other by rapids and carved out by the Katherine River, which begins in Arnhem Land. The gorge walls aren't high, but they are rugged and sheer. Farther downstream the river becomes the Daly River before flowing into the Timor Sea at a point

80km southwest of Darwin. The difference in water levels between the Wet and Dry is staggering. During the dry season the gorge waters are calm, but from November to March they can become a raging torrent, so swimming and canoeing are restricted.

Swimming in the gorge is safe except when it's in flood. Usually the only crocodiles around are the freshwater variety and they're more often seen in the cooler months. The country surrounding the gorge is excellent for walking.

Information

The **Nitmiluk Centre** (☎ 08-8972 1253; ☽ 7am-7pm), at the gorge, has informative displays on the park's geology, wildlife, the traditional Jawoyn owners and European history. There's also a desk for the **Parks & Wildlife Commission** (☎ 08-8972 1886), which has information sheets on the marked walking tracks that meander through the picturesque country south of the gorge, descending to the river at various points. Some tracks pass Aboriginal rock paintings up to 7000 years old. You can register here between 7am and 3pm for overnight walks and camping permits ($3.30 per person per night), and 7am till noon for canoeing permits.

The **Katherine River Canoe Marathon**, organised by the Red Cross, takes place in June.

Leliyn (Edith Falls)

Also in Nitmiluk National Park, but reached via a turn-off from the Stuart Hwy about 43km north of Katherine and 20km down a sealed road, these pretty **falls** cascade through three pools. It's a beautiful spot for walking, swimming and camping.

Leliyn Camp Ground (☎ 08-8975 4869; camping per adult/child $6.60/3.30) This ranger-staffed site at the main pool has shady, grassed camping areas, toilets, showers and a laundry. The kiosk sells good-value breakfasts, snacks and basic supplies.

Activities
BUSHWALKING

There are fabulous marked bushwalking tracks in the park, ranging from 2km stretches to 20km overnight hikes. The **Jatbula Trail** is a 66km, five-day hike over the Arnhem Land escarpment from Nitmiluk National Park to Leliyn (Edith Falls). It's generally described as 'sensational', if not 'awesome'.

CANOEING

The ideal way to explore the gorges is to paddle a canoe through at your own pace. In the Dry you may have to carry your canoe over rocks to get from one gorge to the next, but if it gets too hot you can jump in for a swim. **Nitmiluk Tours** (☎ 1800 089 103, 08-8972 1253; boat ramp) hires out single/double canoes for a half-day ($30/45) or full day ($45/65), including the use of a waterproof drum for cameras and other gear, a map and life jacket. Three-day canoeing trips are also available ($390). The boat ramp is by the main car park, about 500m beyond the Nitmiluk Centre.

You can also be adventurous and take the canoes out overnight, but booking is essential as overnight permits are limited.

GORGE CRUISE

The other, much less energetic way to get out onto the water is on a cruise, also run by **Nitmiluk Tours** (☎ 1800 089 103, 08-8972 1253; boat ramp). The two-hour run goes to the second gorge and visits a rock-art gallery. It leaves at 9am, 11am, 1pm and 3pm daily and costs $40/15 per adult/child. The four-hour trip goes to the third gorge and includes a gorge swim and refreshments for $55/25, leaving at 9am, 11am and 1pm. Finally there's an eight-hour trip that takes you up to the fifth gorge, which involves walking about 5km and includes a barbecue lunch for $95. It departs at 9am daily from May to October. Bookings should be made a day ahead in peak season.

During the wet season, when the water level is high enough, power boat rides add an element of excitement.

Sleeping & Eating

Nitmiluk Caravan Park (☎ 08-8972 3150; fax 8971 0715; camp sites per adult/child $8.50/5, with power extra $4) Right next to the gorge entrance, this popular caravan park has plenty of grass and shade, showers, toilets and barbecues and a laundry. Wallabies and goannas are frequent visitors. You can book and pay at the visitors centre.

Nitmiluk Café (Nitmiluk Centre) Eat here for some of the best food in the Katherine region, including tasty yiros (similar to souvlaki or gyros) for $5.80, great lentil burgers ($7.50) and awesome salads ($11). Evening meals are served on the balcony with music to munch by nightly during the Dry and on Thursday and Friday at other times.

Getting There & Away

It's 30km by sealed road from Katherine to the Nitmiluk Centre and gorge.

Travel North (☎ 08-8972 1044) shuttles run from the transit centre in Katherine to the gorge every two hours from 8am to 4.15pm and make the return trip every two hours between 9am and 5pm. The one-way/return fare is $13/20; children travel at half-price.

KATHERINE TO WESTERN AUSTRALIA

The Victoria Hwy stretches 513km, linking Katherine to Kununurra in WA. It passes through beautiful sandstone scarps and as you approach the WA border you start to see the boab trees found in much of the northwest of Australia.

All fruit and vegetables must be left at the quarantine inspection post on the border. WA time is 1½ hours behind that of NT.

Flora River Nature Park

Limestone tufa outcrops form bars across the Flora River, which act as dams, creating small waterfalls in this interesting, scenic little park. The Parks & Wildlife Commission **camping ground** (sites per person $5) has an amenities block and there are boat and canoe ramps across the tufa. The Flora River is inhabited by crocs so there's no swimming.

The turn-off is 90km southwest of Katherine along the Victoria Hwy and a farther 45km north along a good dirt road.

Victoria River Crossing

The dramatic setting of Victoria River Crossing, where the highway crosses the Victoria River – snugly nestled between sandstone gorges and high cliffs – is superb. Much of this area forms the eastern section of the Gregory National Park. The settlement here basically consists of a roadhouse and the **Victoria River Wayside Inn** (☎ 08-8975 0744; camp/caravan sites $18/20, s/d $40/70, units $110). Boat cruises and fishing tours depart from here during the Dry.

Timber Creek

☎ 08 / pop 300

Timber Creek, 286km southwest of Katherine, is the only town between Katherine and Kununurra. It offers great opportunities to get out on the majestic Victoria River – whether fishing for barramundi from shore, taking a boat trip or hiring a tinny.

A **boab**, marked by early explorer AC Gregory, is at Gregory's Tree Historical Reserve, west of Timber Creek.

You can cruise down the river with Max's Tours, showcasing crocodiles (up close and personal), birds, fish and turtles. Four-hour tours ($55/25 per adult/child) depart at 8am daily during the Dry and can be booked at **Beverley's Booking Centre** (☎ /fax 8975 0850). Full-day fishing trips can also be booked here .

Northern Air Charter (☎ 8975 0628) flies over the Bungle Bungles in WA and many other sights, with a possible stop for Tim-Tams at Sara Henderson's 'Bullo Station,' made famous in her books. At $270 it's better value than flights originating in WA.

Timber Creek Gunumu Tourist Park (☎ /fax 8975 0722; camp/caravan sites for 2 $12/18, s/d $36/80, cabins from $70, motel d $90; ❄) Enormous trees shade the camping area bordered by a creek (unsafe for swimming); there are a couple of swimming pools. The pub serves standard bistro meals and snacks are available at the roadhouse.

Gregory National Park

This little-visited national park sits at the transitional zone between tropical and semi-arid regions. It covers 12,860 sq km, consisting of the eastern sector, also known as the Victoria River section, and the much larger Bullita section in the west, and offers good fishing, camping and bushwalking. The 90km 4WD **Bullita Stock Route** takes around eight hours, although it's better to break the journey at one of the three marked camp sites. Contact the **Parks & Wildlife Commission** (☎ 08-8975 0888) in Timber Creek before heading into the Bullita section.

Keep River National Park

Bordering WA just off the Victoria Hwy, this park is noted for its stunning sandstone formations and has some excellent **walking tracks** and rock-art sites. You can reach the main points in the park by conventional vehicle during the Dry. **Aboriginal art** can be seen near the car park at the end of the road.

There's a **rangers station** (☎ 08-9167 8827), 3km into the park from the main road, and there are basic **camp sites** (adult/child/family $3.30/1.65/7.70) with pit toilets at Gurranalng (15km into the park) and Jarrnarm (28km). Water is only available near the park entrance and Jarrnarm.

MATARANKA
☎ 08 / pop 500

The main attractions of Mataranka, 105km southeast of Katherine, include the nearby thermal pool and Elsey National Park.

Sights & Activities

The crystal-clear **thermal pool**, in a pocket of rainforest about 9.5km from town, is a great place to revitalise. Don't expect a secluded oasis though – the pool is reached via a boardwalk from the nearby Mataranka Homestead Resort and it can get mighty crowded.

About 200m away (follow the boardwalk from the resort) is the **Waterhouse River**, where you can walk along the banks or rent canoes for $10 per hour.

Outside the homestead entrance is a replica of the **Elsey Station Homestead**, which was made for the filming of *We of the Never Never*, set near Mataranka. It now houses interesting historical displays.

In Mataranka town, the **Museum of the Never Never** (adult/child $2.50/2; ✆ 8.30am-4.30pm Mon-Fri) has displays on the northern railway, WWII and local history. Nearby, the **Stockyard Gallery** (☎ 8975 4530) acts as a visitors centre and has a café and local arts and crafts.

Elsey National Park adjoins the thermal pool reserve and offers great camping, fishing and walking along the Waterhouse and Roper Rivers. It's also far less touristed than the thermal pools.

Bitter Springs is a tranquil thermal pool that falls within the park boundaries, and is accessed via Martin Rd from Mataranka town. The incredible blue colour of the 34°C water here is due to dissolved limestone particles.

About 7km south of the Roper junction is the turn-off to the **Elsey Cemetery**, with the graves of characters like 'the Fizzer' who came to life in the novel *We of the Never Never*.

The **Back to the Never Never Festival** is held in Mataranka in May and features art shows and a rodeo.

Sleeping & Eating

Mataranka Homestead Resort (☎ 1800 754 544, 8975 4544; www.travelnorth.com.au; Homestead Rd; camp/caravan sites for 2 $18/22, dm/s/d $17/80/95, cabins from $100; ✵) Just 100m or so from the hot springs, the homestead has a large camping ground with plenty of grass and shade, and excellent amenities. The rustic hostel has a small kitchen (borrow utensils at the shop) and the motel rooms have a fridge and bathroom. The shop sells basic groceries, snacks are available at the bar and there are pricey bistro meals or a pig-on-spit buffet ($14.50). Live country music warbles from the stage each evening during tourist season. Those who prefer a nature experience should try Jalmurark.

Old Elsey Roadside Inn (☎ 8975 4512; fax 8975 4323; Stuart Hwy; s/d $55/80; ✵) The graffiti-adorned old pub has a photogenic 'dunny' outside. The motel rooms, in a tin shed built in 1942, have bathrooms; bistro meals are available.

Jalmurark (John Hauser Dr; camp sites per adult/child $6/1) This tranquil camping ground at 12 Mile Yards on the Roper River, 12km from the Homestead Rd turn-off, has plenty of grass and shade. There's a kiosk, solar hot shower, toilets and barbecues.

Stockyard Gallery (☎ 8975 4530; Stuart Hwy; ✆ 8am-5pm daily) From the peaceful gardens, you can savour delicious home-made snacks, cakes, fresh mango smoothies and plunger coffee. The gallery is worth a browse and some tourist literature is available.

Getting There & Away

McCaffertys/Greyhound (☎ 13 20 30) buses stop in Mataranka en route to Katherine and Alice Springs. **Travel North** (☎ 1800 089 103; www.travelnorth.com.au) runs half-day tours ($80/60 per adult/child), including lunch, from Katherine.

BARKLY TABLELAND & GULF COUNTRY
Roper Highway

Not far south of Mataranka on the Stuart Hwy, the mostly sealed Roper Hwy strikes 175km eastwards to **Roper Bar**, on the Roper River. It's mainly visited by fishing enthusiasts and there's a store with a **camping area** (tent sites per person $7, d $65) and a few rooms. Roper Bar is an access point into southeastern Arnhem Land, or you can continue south to Borroloola through Limmen National Park (carry two spare tyres).

Carpentaria & Tablelands Highways

Just south of Daly Waters, the single-lane, sealed Carpentaria Hwy (Hwy 1) heads east to Borroloola, 378km away near the Gulf of Carpentaria and one of the top barramundi fishing spots in the Territory. After 267km the Carpentaria Hwy meets the sealed Tablelands Hwy at Cape Crawford, where you'll find the **Heartbreak Hotel** (☎ 08-8975 9928; fax 8975 9993; camp/caravan sites for 2 $10/15; s/tw $55/70). From here it's a desolate 374km south across the Barkly Tablelands to the Barkly Hwy and **Barkly Homestead Roadhouse** (☎ 08-8964 4549; fax 8964 4543; camp/caravan sites for 2 $12/21, s/d $75/90; mains $15-18; ☯ 6.30am-midnight). Both places have camping, motel-style rooms, restaurants and petrol. Although both highways are sealed, they're narrow and rough and may be cut off during the Wet.

Borroloola

☎ 08 / pop 770

Among fishers, Borroloola is something of a mecca, but unless you've come to catch a fish there's little here of interest to a traveller. Like a lot of the NT, the town has a colourful past, which is preserved in the interesting displays housed in the **old police station** (admission $2; ☯ 10am-5pm), built in 1886.

Offshore from Borroloola is **Barranyi National Park**, which is worth a visit if you can arrange it. The picturesque **Caranbirini Waterhole** and **Bukalara Rock Formations**, both right by the road, are 44km along the highway towards Cape Crawford. There's a one-hour walking track around the base of the eerie formations.

Cape Crawford Tourism (☎ 8975 9611; lost -city@bigpond.com) operates two-hour flights ($170) to the nearby Lost City sandstone formations. **Sea-Eagle Fishing Tours** (☎ 8975 8716) runs full-day fishing tours, including lunch.

SLEEPING & EATING

Borroloola Guest House (☎ 8975 8883; fax 8975 8877; cnr Robinson Rd & Broad St; dm/d $30/45, cabins $70, guesthouse d $70) This cosy spot has a breezy guesthouse, good common areas and a barbecue in the very relaxed garden. The

budget rooms share facilities, and the cabins are self-contained. Guesthouse doubles with a bathroom are $75.

McArthur River Caravan Park (☎ 8975 8734; camp/caravan sites for 2 $16/20; s/d cabins $80/90) Just down from the pub, this clean site has wood barbecues.

There's little to choose from in the way of eateries, but take-aways are available at the town's general stores, or try the **Borroloola Hotel** (☎ 8975 8766).

MATARANKA TO TENNANT CREEK

Larrimah

☎ 08 / pop 20

At one time the railway line from Darwin came as far as Birdum, 8km south of Larrimah, which is just a sleepy stop on the highway. There's an interesting **museum** (☎ 8975 9771; admission free; ☯ 7am-9pm) in the former telegraph repeater station opposite the Larrimah Hotel.

Shaded by trees, the **Larrimah Hotel & Caravan Park** (☎ 8975 9931; camp/caravan sites for 2 $6.60/11, s/f $25/50) is an outback pub with a rustic bar making a cool place for an afternoon drink. Takeaway and counter meals are available.

Fran's Homemade Devonshire Teahouse (☎ 8975 9945; Stuart Hwy; breakfast $11), in the old Larrimah police station, is a compulsory stop along the Track for lovers of pies ($4) and Devonshire tea ($6).

Daly Waters

About 3km off the highway and 160km south of Mataranka, Daly Waters was an important staging post in the early days of aviation – Amy Johnson landed here and it was used as a refuelling stop between Sydney and Singapore. The **Daly Waters Aerodrome** has an historical display in the old hangar, and John McDouall Stuart, on his explorations, carved an initial 'S' on a tree (now long dead but still standing and signposted) nearby.

These days Daly Waters is visited for its eccentric pub which, despite the remoteness, seems to be full most nights.

Daly Waters Pub (☎ 08-8975 9927; camp/caravan sites for 2 $10/15, s/d $35/50, cabins $95; mains $11-16; ☒) has an unusual array of mementos left by passing travellers – everything from bras to banknotes adorn the walls! It also lays claim to 'oldest pub in the Territory', as its liquor licence has been used since 1893. There's reasonable accommodation, and the fuel is substantially cheaper than on the highway. The camping area is grassy and shaded, the basic rooms are clean, and the 'flash' en suite cabins are comfortable. There's also a pool, tennis courts and a golf course.

Daly Waters to Three Ways

Heading south, the fascinating ghost town of **Newcastle Waters**, a few kilometres west of the highway, is worth a detour and leg-stretch; the road is often cut off in the Wet. South of the cattle town of Elliott, the land just gets drier and drier and the vegetation sparser and sparser. Farther south is **Renner Springs**, generally accepted as the dividing line between the seasonally wet Top End and the dry Centre.

Break up the trip along the highway at the historic **Banka Banka Station** (☎ 08-8964 4511; Stuart Hwy; camp sites per person $5), 100km north of Tennant Creek. There's a grassy camping area, spotless facilities, marked walking tracks (one leading to a tranquil waterhole) and a kiosk with basic supplies. In the evening, the station master holds a slide show covering all aspects of station life.

Three Ways

Three Ways, 537km north of Alice, is the junction of the Stuart and Barkly Hwys, from where you can head south to Alice (537km), north to Darwin (988km) or east to Mt Isa in Queensland (643km).

Threeways Roadhouse (☎ 08-8962 2744; Stuart Hwy; camp/caravan sites for 2 $16/20, d $60, cabins from $65; ☯ 6am-11pm; ✗) This roadhouse has the usual bar, restaurant and accommodation, but if you've made it this far Tennant Creek, only 26km away, has better accommodation options and cheaper fuel.

TENNANT CREEK
☎ 08 / pop 3290

Straddling the Stuart Hwy, Tennant Creek is the only town of any size between Katherine and Alice Springs. Many travellers spend a night here to break up the journey and see the town's few attractions, as well as the Devil's Marbles to the south.

To the Warumungu people, Tennant Creek is Jurnkurakurr, the intersection of a number of dreaming tracks.

There's a tale that Tennant Creek was first settled when a wagon carrying beer broke down here in the early 1930s and the drivers decided they might as well make themselves comfortable while they consumed the freight. The truth is somewhat more prosaic: the town was established as a result of the small gold rush around the same time. Tennant Creek was Australia's last gold-rush town. It is also unusual in that most of the gold deposits were not found in quartz, but in the jet-black ironstone.

Nobles Nob on Peko Rd, 16km east of the town, was the biggest open-cut gold mine in the country until mining ceased in 1985.

Information

The **visitors centre** (☎ 8962 3388; www.tennant creektourism.com.au; Peko Rd; ☯ 9am-5pm daily May-Sep, 9am-5pm Mon-Fri & 9am-noon Sat Oct-Apr) is inconveniently located at the Battery Hill Mining Centre 1.5km east of town, but the staff are very helpful.

Switch.com (☎ 8962 3124; 154 Paterson St; ☯ 8am-5pm Mon-Sat) has a few terminals for Internet access.

In case of emergency, contact the **police station** (☎ 8962 4444; Paterson St) or **Tennant Creek hospital** (☎ 8962 4399; Schmidt St).

Sights & Activities

Gold-bearing ore was originally crushed and treated at **Battery Hill Mining Centre** (☎ 8962 1281; Peko Rd; adult/child $13/6.50; ☯ 9am-5pm) next to the visitors centre, 1.5km east of town. The battery gets cranked up for visitors at 9.30pm and 5pm. An underground mine tour departs at 11am and 3.30pm daily for the same price as the battery, or combined admission costs $22/45 per adult/family. There's also a **museum**, detailing the history of the region, and a **Minerals Museum**.

The small **National Trust museum** (☎ 8962 2340; Schmidt St; ☯ 3-5pm May-Sep) has displays of local memorabilia and reconstructed mining scenes.

Have a picnic and plunge into the cooling water at **Mary Ann Dam**, about 5km north of town. About 7km north of here are the green-roofed stone buildings of the old **telegraph station**, even now looking as isolated and forlorn as they must have 100 years ago. This is one of only four of the original

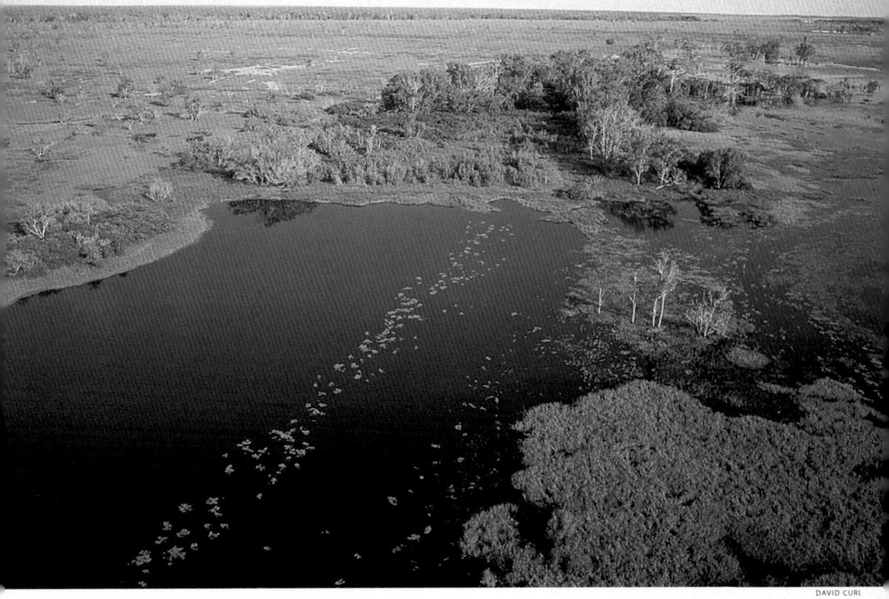
DAVID CURL

Expect to see floodplains like these during the wet season in **Kakadu National Park** (p773)

Seek a permit to camp at **Garig Gunak Barlu National Park** (p782)

RICHARD I'ANSON

JOHN BANAGAN

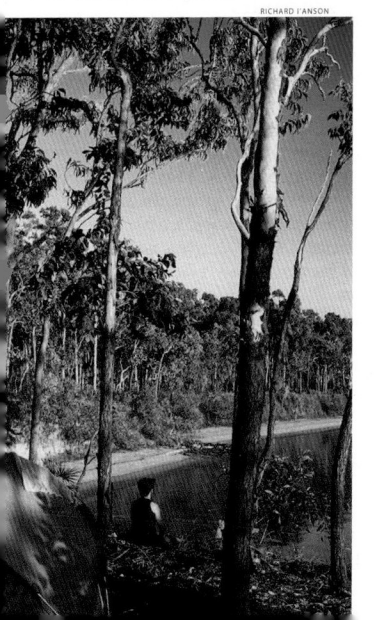

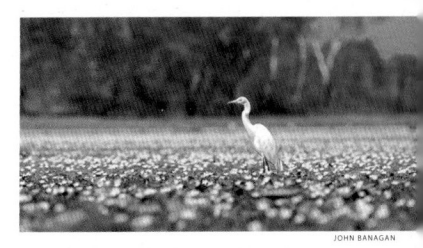

Watch abundant birdlife around **Mamukala** (p776)

DAVID CURL

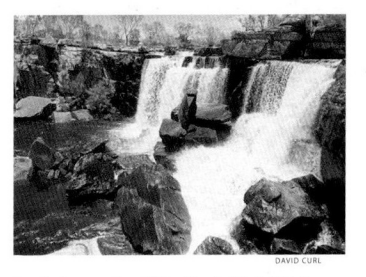

Feel the rush of **Jim Jim Falls** (p779)

JOHN BANAGAN

Explore the oasis of rare cabbage palms that thrive in **Palm Valley** (p814)

TONY WHEELER

Hike the remote and challenging
Larapinta Trail (p811)

JOHN HAY

See the gorgeous spring wildflowers
of the **West MacDonnell Ranges** (p810)

Paddle a canoe along the spectacular **Katherine Gorge** (p787)

JOHN BAN

12 stations remaining in the Territory (the others are at Barrow Creek, Alice Springs and Powell Creek). The station's telegraph functions ceased in 1935 when a new office opened.

Nyinkka Nyunyu (☎ 8962 2699; www.aboriginal experience.com.au; Paterson St) is an Aboriginal art and culture centre.

Anyinginyi Arts (☎ 8962 1713; 164 Paterson St) is a commercial gallery which mainly sells Aboriginal artwork from the Barkly Tablelands; prices rival those in Alice Springs. There are changing exhibits at the gallery on the corner of Irvine and Davidson Sts, and you may get to see artists at work.

The **Warrego Fossicking Area** is about 60km west of town along the Warrego Rd; a permit (free) must be obtained from the visitors centre at Battery Hill.

Tours
Kraut Downs Station (☎ 8962 2820) offers the chance to learn about bush tucker and medicine on a half-day tour ($28) – you can also try whip-cracking and wash down a witchetty grub (in season, of course) with billy tea and damper. The station owners will pick you up from your accommodation.

Devil's Marbles Tour (☎ 1300 666 070) runs – you guessed it – tours to the Devil's Marbles. The day tour ($60) out to these unusual rock formations includes lunch, while the sunset tour ($70) includes dinner.

Sleeping
BUDGET
Tourist's Rest Tennant Creek Hostel (☎ 8962 2719; info@touristrest.com.au; cnr Leichhardt & Windley Sts; camp sites per person $8, dm $17, d & tw $39; ⚡ 🖳) Very much a no-frills country backpackers, this compact hostel has clean rooms, kitchen, laundry and a shady barbecue and breakfast area.

Safari Backpackers YHA (☎ 8962 2207; safari@ swtch.com.au; 12 Davidson St; dm $16, d & tw $38; ⚡) Safari's nondescript but spotless block offers average accommodation in a big house, with shared facilities and a lounge.

Juno Horse Centre (☎ 8962 2783; fax 8962 2199; sites per person $6) The atmospheric camping ground on the station has a swimming pool made out of a squatter's tank. Inquire about the horseback cattle muster and track rides.

Outback Caravan Park (☎ 8962 2459; outback@ swtch.com.au; Peko Rd; camp/caravan sites $16/20, cabins

$50-75; ⚡) There's a good pool, plenty of shady lawn, lots of birds and a camp kitchen at this well-kept park, 1.5km east of the highway on the way to the visitors centre.

MID-RANGE
You'll find most of the motels along the Stuart Hwy. There are also comfortable self-contained cabins at caravan parks.

Desert Sands (☎ 8962 1346; fax 8962 1014; 780 Paterson St; s/d $65/70; ⚡) The clean, compact fully self-contained units at this complex south of town have washing facilities and offer excellent value.

Bluestone Motor Inn (☎ 8962 2617, fax 8962 2883; capefire@bigpond.com; Stuart Hwy; s $90-95, d $95-105, ⚡) Opposite Desert Sands, this is Tennant's top motel. The hexagonal 'lodge' rooms are spacious and much nicer than the standard rooms, and there's a laundry and an attached restaurant.

Eldorado Motor Inn (☎ 8962 2402; Paterson St; s/d $100/105; ⚡) On the highway at the northern edge of town, Eldorado has standard motel rooms with bathrooms, a swimming pool and an attached restaurant and bar.

Eating
Chompin' Charlies (☎ 8962 2388; 114 Paterson St; burgers from $6) Heavily fortified Chompin' Charlies is a popular night-time take-away place serving delicious burgers from beef to barramundi.

Top of the Town Cafe (☎ 8962 1311; 163 Paterson; mains $4-8) Just up from the transit centre, Top of the Town is the best breakfast option and serves sandwiches, takeaways, milkshakes and coffee throughout the day.

Margo Miles Steakhouse (☎ 8962 2227; Tennant Creek Hotel, 146 Paterson St; mains $14-20) At this local fave, in a homey and rustic colonial setting, you can wash down homemade pasta, juicy steaks or one of the vegetarian options. At **Jackson's Bar** (lunch & dinner $5-12), next door to Margo Miles, the bar can get lively but has a pleasant atmosphere and a beer garden.

Getting There & Away
All long-distance buses stop at the Paterson St Transit Centre. McCaffertys/Greyhound tickets are sold through **Ten Ant Tours** (☎ 8962 2358). Fares from Tennant Creek to Alice Springs/Darwin are $110/140.

If you're looking to rent a car to experience the mystery of the Devil's Marbles, contact **Territory Thrifty Car Rentals** (☎ 8962 2358; Ten Ant Tours, transit centre) or **Hertz** (☎ 1800 891 112; Outback Caravan Park).

Bike rental is available at **Bridgestone** (☎ 8962 2361; Paterson St) for $5/10 per half/full day.

TENNANT CREEK TO ALICE SPRINGS

The huge boulders in precarious piles straddling the Stuart Hwy about 105km south of Tennant Creek are the **Devil's Marbles**. Known as Karlukarlu to the local Warumungu Aboriginal people, several Dreaming trails cross the area and the rocks are believed to be the eggs of the Rainbow Serpent (for more information see the boxed text 'The Rainbow Serpent'; p777). According to scientists they are the granite remains of molten lava after millions of years of weathering and erosion. This area is particularly beautiful at sunset, when the boulders exude a rich glow. The **camping ground** (sites per adult/child $2.30/1.65) among the boulders has remarkably hard ground, pit toilets and fireplaces.

At Wauchope (*war*-kup), just south of the Devil's Marbles, is the **Wauchope Hotel** (☎ 08-8964 1963; Stuart Hwy; camp sites per person $6; meals $12-18). It rents out bicycles ($10 a day) to pedal the 10km back to see the Devil's Marbles and serves decent meals.

'Earthlings are welcome at Wycliffe Well', just 18km south of Wauchope, where a spate of UFO sightings have been claimed in recent years. **Wycliffe Well Roadhouse & Holiday Park** (☎ 08-8964 1966; www.wycliffe.com.au; camp/caravan sites for 2 $16/20, s/d from $28/34, cabins $85-90; meals $13-22) is festooned with alien critters, along with the Incredible Hulk and the Phantom, has excellent facilities, good-value meals and a range of imported beers at the bar.

Heading south, **Barrow Creek** is an old telegraph repeater station with one of the quirkier outback pub/roadhouses along the Track. The telegraph station was attacked by Kaytetye Aboriginal people in 1874 and the station master and linesman were killed – their graves are by the road. A great many Aboriginal people died in the inevitable reprisals. The walls of the **Barrow Creek Hotel** (☎ 08-8956 9753; Stuart Hwy; camping per person $5) are adorned with all manner of drawings, cartoons and banknotes.

The highway continues through **Ti Tree**, a good stop if you're in the market for a didgeridoo or some Aboriginal art. **Red Sand** (☎ 08-8956 9738; ☯ 7.30am-7pm), just west

of the highway, is an art gallery and café that primarily shows work from the Utopia homelands. Artists work here daily and prices for dot paintings and didgeridoos are some of the most competitive you'll find in the Territory.

About 12km south of Ti Tree is the **Red Centre Farm** (Shatto Mango; ☎ 08-8956 9828; ☯ 9am-7pm), which sells mango and grape products to go with virtually any meal.

About 70km north of Alice, the Plenty Hwy heads off to the east towards the **Harts Range**. The main reason to detour is to fossick in the **gemfields** about 78km east of the Stuart Hwy, which are well known for garnets and zircons. The best way is to join a tag-along tour ($50) from **Gemtree Caravan Park** (☎ 08-8956 9855; www.gemtree.com.au).

ALICE SPRINGS

☎ 08 / pop 24,640

In its brief 125-year history, the Alice, as it is usually known, has gone from a simple telegraph station on the Overland Telegraph Line (OTL) to a modern town and major supply centre for the region. The station was built near a permanent waterhole in the bed of the normally dry Todd River. The river was named after Charles Todd, superintendent of telegraphs back in Adelaide, and the waterhole was named after Alice, his wife.

A town, then named Stuart, was first established in 1888, a few kilometres south of the telegraph station, as a railhead for a

---

MPARNTWE

The Alice Springs area is known as Mparntwe to its traditional residents, the Arrernte Aboriginal people. The heart of the area is the junction of the Charles (Anthelke Ulpeye) and Todd (Lhere Mparntwe) Rivers, just north of Anzac Hill.

All the topographical features of the town were formed by the creative ancestral beings – the Yeperenye, Ntyarlke and Utnerrengatye caterpillars – as they crawled across the landscape from Emily Gap (Anthwerrke), in the MacDonnell Ranges southeast of town. Alice Springs' sizeable Aboriginal community retains strong links to the area.

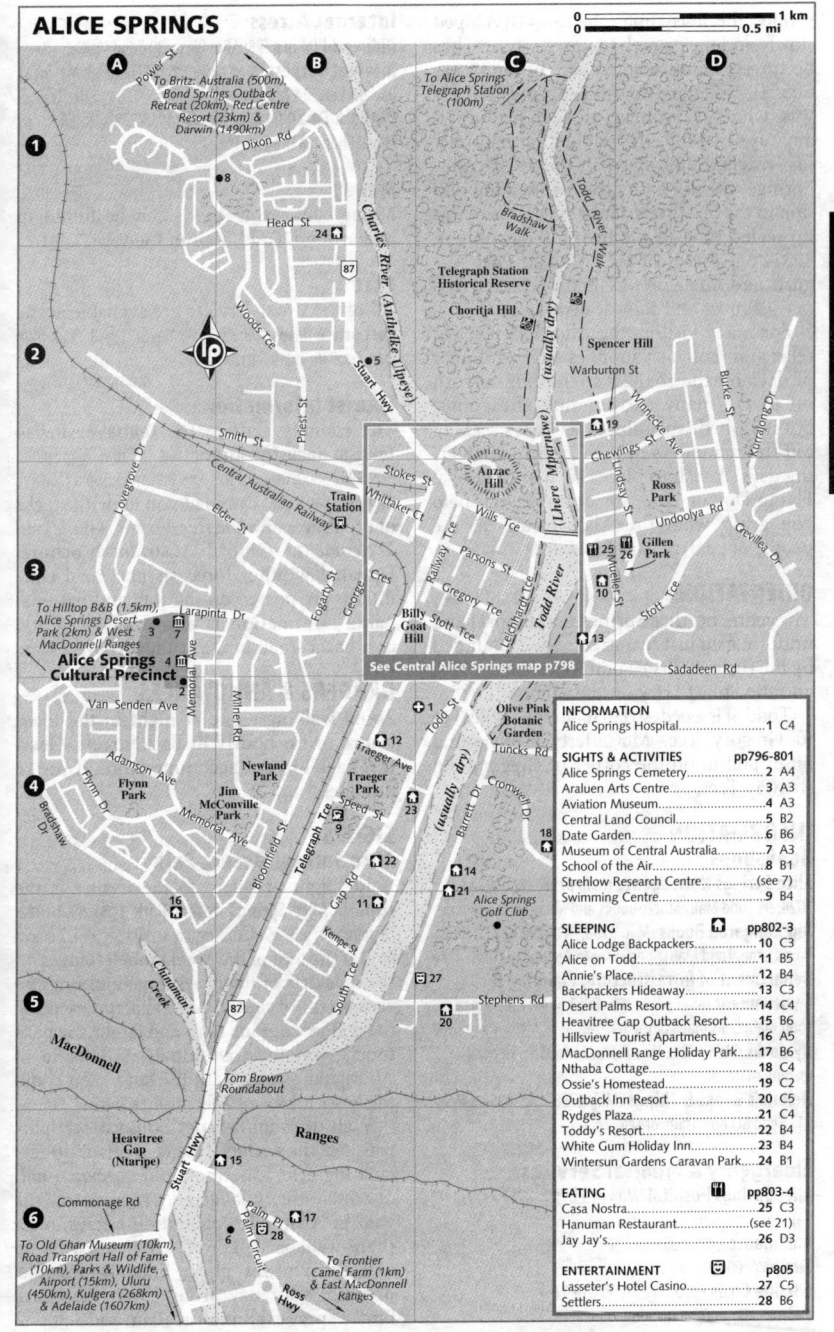

ALICE SPRINGS

0 ————— 1 km
0 ————— 0.5 mi

NORTHERN TERRITORY

To Britz: Australia (500m),
Bond Springs Outback
Retreat (20km), Red Centre
Resort (23km) &
Darwin (1490km)

Dixon Rd

Power St

Head St

24

Charles River (Anthelke Ulpeye)

To Alice Springs
Telegraph Station
(100m)

Bradshaw Walk

Todd River Walk

Telegraph Station
Historical Reserve

Choritja Hill

Spencer Hill

Warburton St

Winnecke Ave

Burke St

Kurralong Dr

Woods Tce

Stuart Hwy

5

Smith St

Priest St

Central Australian Railway

Elder St

Fogarty St

George Cres

87

Lovegrove Dr

Train
Station

Stokes St

Whittaker Ct

Anzac
Hill

Wills Tce

(Lhere Mparntwe)

Chewings St

Lindsay Ave

Ross
Park

Railway Tce

Parsons St

Gregory Tce

Leichhardt Tce

Stott Tce

25

10

26

Gillen
Park

Undoolya Rd

Grevillea Dr

To Hilltop B&B (1.5km),
Alice Springs Desert
Park (2km) & West
MacDonnell Ranges

Larapinta Dr

3

7

**Alice Springs
Cultural Precinct**

4

2

Memorial Ave

Todd River

(usually dry)

Billy
Goat Hill

13

Sadadeen Rd

See Central Alice Springs map p798

Van Senden Ave

Miller Rd

1

Olive Pink
Botanic
Garden

Tuncks Rd

Adamson Ave

Flynn
Park

Flynn Dr

Bradshaw Dr

Newland
Park

Jim
McConville
Park

Bloomfield St

Telegraph Tce

Memorial Ave

Traeger Ave

Traeger
Park

Speed St

12

23

9

Todd St

Barrett Dr

(usually dry)

Cromwell Dr

18

Cinnamon Creek

16

22

11

Gap Rd

Kempe St

14

21

Alice Springs
Golf Club

MacDonnell

87

Tom Brown
Roundabout

Heavitree
Gap
(Ntaripe)

Ranges

South Tce

27

20

Stephens Rd

Commonage Rd

To Old Ghan Museum (10km),
Road Transport Hall of Fame
(10km), Parks & Wildlife,
Airport (15km), Uluru
(450km), Kulgera (268km)
& Adelaide (1607km)

Stuart Hwy

15

17

Palm Pl

Palm Circuit

6

28

Ross Hwy

To Frontier
Camel Farm (1km)
& East MacDonnell
Ranges

INFORMATION
Alice Springs Hospital.....................1 C4

SIGHTS & ACTIVITIES   pp796-801
Alice Springs Cemetery...................2 A4
Araluen Arts Centre.........................3 A3
Aviation Museum.............................4 A3
Central Land Council.......................5 B2
Date Garden.....................................6 B6
Museum of Central Australia...........7 A3
School of the Air..............................8 B1
Strehlow Research Centre............(see 7)
Swimming Centre............................9 B4

SLEEPING   pp802-3
Alice Lodge Backpackers................10 C3
Alice on Todd.................................11 B5
Annie's Place..................................12 B4
Backpackers Hideaway...................13 C3
Desert Palms Resort.......................14 C4
Heavitree Gap Outback Resort......15 B6
Hillsview Tourist Apartments.........16 A5
MacDonnell Range Holiday Park....17 B6
Nthaba Cottage..............................18 C4
Ossie's Homestead.........................19 C2
Outback Inn Resort........................20 C5
Rydges Plaza..................................21 C4
Toddy's Resort...............................22 B4
White Gum Holiday Inn.................23 B4
Wintersun Gardens Caravan Park..24 B1

EATING   pp803-4
Casa Nostra....................................25 C3
Hanuman Restaurant..................(see 21)
Jay Jay's..26 D3

ENTERTAINMENT   p805
Lasseter's Hotel Casino..................27 C5
Settlers...28 B6

proposed railway line. The town developed slowly and the growth to its present size has been recent and rapid. When the name was officially changed to Alice Springs (which was what everyone had been calling it anyway) in 1933, the population had only just reached 200. Even in the 1950s Alice Springs was still a tiny town with a population in the hundreds. Until WWII there was no sealed road to the town; it was only in 1987 that the old road south to Port Augusta and Adelaide was finally replaced by a new, shorter and fully sealed highway.

For many visitors the Alice is a place to relax and replenish supplies after a number of days on the road. It's tempting to rush off to the many surrounding attractions, but it's worth spending a few days seeking out the reminders of the Centre's pioneering days. A visit to places such as the Royal Flying Doctor Base, for example, can help you grasp what the Alice means to the people of central Australia.

ORIENTATION

The centre of Alice Springs is a compact and uniform grid just five streets wide, bounded by the (usually dry) Todd River on one side and the Stuart Hwy on the other.

Todd St is a pedestrian mall from Wills Tce to Gregory Tce. McCafferty's/Greyhound buses pull in on the corner of Gregory and Railway Tces.

INFORMATION
Bookshops
Alice Springs Newsagency (Map p798; ☎ 8952 1024; 94 Todd Mall) Stocks books and Maps on the region.
Big Kangaroo Books (Map p798; ☎ 8953 2137; Reg Harris Lane, Todd Mall) Specialises in Australian titles.
Department of Infrastructure, Planning & Environment (Map p798; ☎ 8951 5344; Alice Plaza, Todd Mall) Sells maps of the NT.
Dymocks (Map p798; Alice Plaza, Todd Mall) General reading material.
Helene's Books & Things (Map p798; ☎ 8953 2465; 113 Todd St) Buy, trade or sell.

Emergency & Medical Services
Alice Springs Hospital (Map p795; ☎ 8951 7777; Gap Rd)
Ambulance (☎ 000)
Fire (☎ 000)
Lifeline Crisis Line (☎ 1800 019 116)
Police (☎ 000)

Internet Access
Didjworld (Map p798; Alice Plaza, 33 Todd Mall)
Internet Outpost (Map p798; ☎ 8952 8730; Melanka Backpackers, 94 Todd St)
Outback Email (Map p798; ☎ 8955 5288; Outback Travel Shop, 2a Gregory Tce)

Money
Major banks and ATMs can be found in and around Todd Mall in the town centre.

Post
All of the usual services are available at the **post office** (Map p798; 31-33 Hartley St; ☉ 8.15am-5pm Mon-Fri, 9am-noon Sat).

Tourist Information
The friendly staff in the **Central Australian Tourism Industry Association** (Catia; Map p798; ☎ 8952 5800; Gregory Tce; ☉ 8.30am-5.30pm Mon-Fri, 9am-4pm Sat & Sun) can load you up with stacks of brochures and the free *Visitors Guide and Welcome to Central Australia* brochure. Updated weather forecasts and road conditions are posted on the wall and national parks information is also available. Catia also has a small office at the airport.

DANGERS & ANNOYANCES
Avoid walking alone at night in the town centre or on poorly lit back streets. Get a taxi back to your accommodation if you're out late.

SIGHTS
Alice Springs Desert Park
A highlight of a trip to the Centre is the superb **Alice Springs Desert Park** (☎ 8951 8788; Larapinta Dr; adult $18, concession & child $9; ☉ 7.30am-6pm) at the foot of the MacDonnell Ranges on the outskirts of town. Arranged around the ecosystems of central Australia, representing the region's unique flora and fauna, the park touches on the traditional relationship of Aboriginal people with the land. You could easily spend four to five hours here.

Walk-through **aviaries** house desert parrots and the **nocturnal house** displays 20 fascinating arid-zone mammal species – half of which are endangered or extinct in the wild in Australia – including bilbies, mala (hare-wallabies), kowari (marsupial mice) and carnivorous ghost bats. If possible, organise your day around the impressive birds of prey exhibition at 10am and 3.30pm.

Ranger talks are held at various exhibits throughout the day.

Refreshments are available at the café and the gift shop hires out strollers.

It's an easy 2.5km cycle out to the park but if you don't have your own wheels, **Desert Park Transfers** (☎ 8952 4667) operates return trips including the park entrance fee for $30/20 per adult/concession.

Royal Flying Doctor Service Base

The **RFDS base** (Map p798; ☎ 8952 1129; www .flyingdoctor.net; Stuart Tce; adult/child $5.50/2.20; ☯ 9am-5pm Mon-Sat, 1-5pm Sun) still operates over-the-air routine medical clinics to isolated communities.

Entry is by a half-hour tour, which includes a video presentation and a look into an operational control room. There's also a museum with historical displays, an interactive cockpit and ancient medical gear. Tours begin every half-hour to 4pm.

The **café** (☯ 9am-4.45pm Mon-Sat) serves snacks, cakes and drinks in the courtyard or in cosy surrounds inside. The souvenir shop is a good place to pick up gifts; proceeds go towards the base's operational costs.

Alice Springs Reptile Centre

The **reptile centre** (Map p798; ☎ 8952 8900; 9 Stuart Tce; adult/child $7/4; ☯ 9am-5pm) has some of the most venomous snakes in the world, along with a collection of cute and cuddly creatures like thorny devils and various lizards to hand-feed. Oh, and pythons to play with, too. The centre is opposite the Flying Doctor Service.

School of the Air

The **School of the Air** (Map p795; ☎ 8952 8936; www.assoa.nt.edu.au; 80 Head St; adult/child $3.30/2.50; ☯ 8.30am-4.30pm Mon-Sat, 1.30-4.30pm Sun), about 3km north of the town centre, broadcasts lessons to children living on remote stations and is an education service unique to outback Australia. You can watch a live broadcast (depending on class schedules, usually 8am to 2pm Monday to Friday) during school terms and listen to recorded lessons at other times.

Telegraph Station Historical Reserve

Laying the Overland Telegraph Line across the dry harsh centre of Australia was no easy task, as you'll discover at the small museum at the old **Telegraph Station** (Map p795; ☎ 8952 3993, Heritage Dr; adult/child $6.50/3.50; ☯ 8am-5pm), 5km north of town. Built along the line in the early 1870s, the station was constructed of local stone and operated until 1932. It later served as a welfare home for Aboriginal children of mixed descent until 1963.

Guided tours operate between 9am and 4.30pm; there's also an informative self-guiding map which takes you through restored homestead buildings, a blacksmith shop and the telegraph station itself. The original **Alice Springs** ('Thereyurre' to the Arrernte Aboriginal people), a semipermanent waterhole in the Todd River, is just behind the station.

The station is part of a 450 hectare **historical reserve** (☯ 8am-9pm), with a grassy picnic area, free barbecues, tables and some shady gum trees. A number of walking tracks radiate from the reserve.

It's an easy 3.5km walk or ride to the station from town – just follow the path on the western side of the riverbed.

Anzac Hill

From the top of **Anzac Hill** you get a fine view over modern Alice Springs down to the MacDonnell Ranges – it's especially popular at sunset.

You can drive or walk the short sharp ascent to the top of Anzac Hill from the northern end of Hartley St (off Wills Tce). Aboriginal people call the hill Untyeyetweleye, which is the site of the Corkwood Dreaming, the *story* of a woman who lived alone on the hill. The Two Sisters ancestral beings (Arrweketye Therre) are also associated with the hill.

Alice Springs Cultural Precinct

Map p795

Connected by a walking path, the **Alice Springs Cultural Precinct** (☎ 8951 1120; www.nt.gov.au/dam; Larapinta Dr; precinct pass adult/child/family $8/5/20) combines several of the town's historical and cultural attractions in a neat block. Entry is at the **Araluen Arts Centre**, where you can buy a 'precinct pass' covering all the attractions; most are open from 10am to 5pm daily.

ARALUEN ARTS CENTRE

Beautiful stained-glass windows grace the foyer of the **centre** (☎ 8952 5022), which contains the **Albert Namatjira Gallery**,

NORTHERN TERRITORY

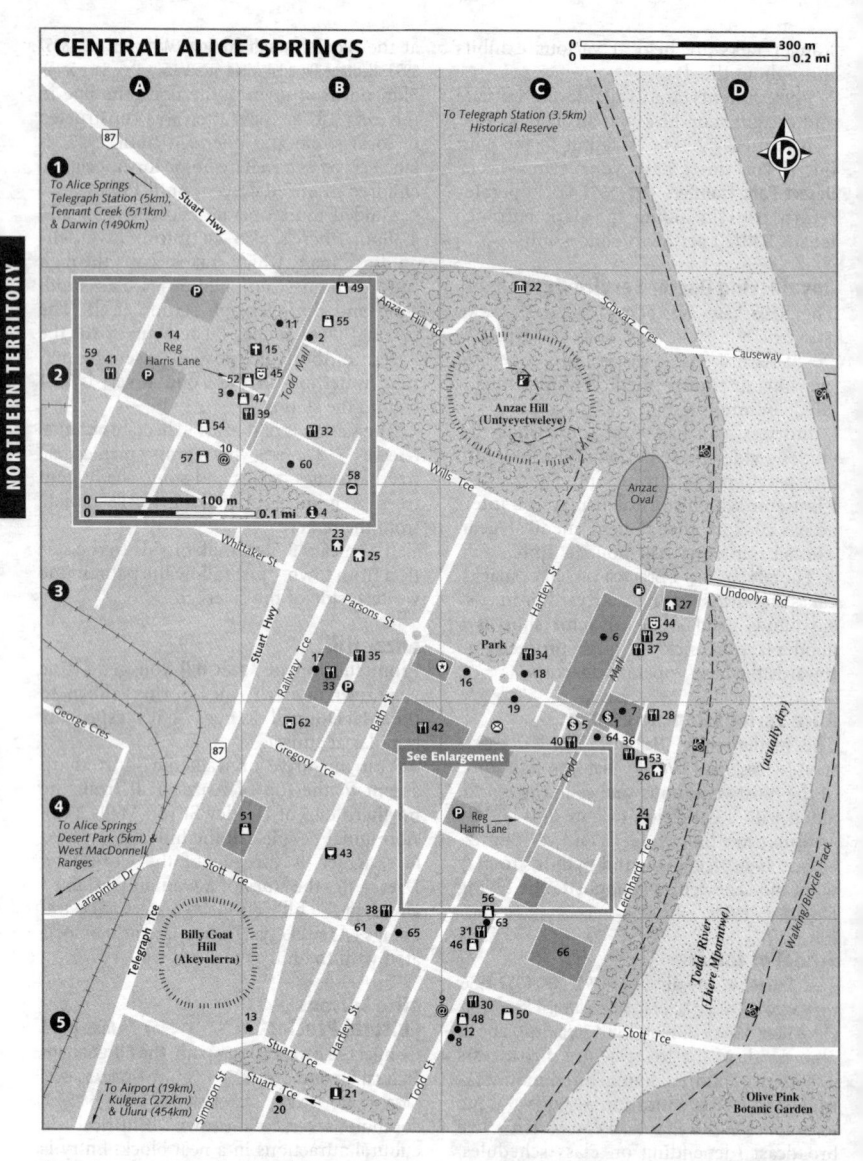

CENTRAL ALICE SPRINGS

0 ____ 300 m
0 ____ 0.2 mi

featuring paintings by Namatjira as well as his mentor Rex Battarbee and other artists from Hermannsburg school. Other galleries showcase art from the Central Desert region, contemporary art and include travelling exhibitions. A doorway leads through to the **sculpture garden**. A café here serves refreshments.

MUSEUM OF CENTRAL AUSTRALIA & STREHLOW RESEARCH CENTRE

Housed in a building partly constructed of a massive rammed-earth wall, the **museum** (☎ 8951 5532) has a fascinating collection with superb exhibits on natural history, including local megafauna fossils, meteorites and Aboriginal culture.

Upstairs in the same building, the **Strehlow Research Centre** (☎ 8951 8000) commemorates the work of Professor Strehlow among the Arrernte people of the district, particularly at the Hermannsburg Mission. (Professor Strehlow was born at the Mission to a German father, and lived with and studied the Arrernte people for many years.) It houses the most comprehensive collection of Aboriginal spirit items (known as *tjurunga*) in the country. These were entrusted to Strehlow for safekeeping by the Arrernte people years ago when they feared their traditional life was under threat. These items cannot be viewed by an uninitiated male or *any* female, and are kept in a vault in the centre. There is, however, a display detailing the works of Strehlow and the culture of the Arrernte people.

KOOKABURRA & AVIATION MUSEUM

Next you come to a small circular building housing the wreck of the **Kookaburra**, a tiny plane that crashed in the Tanami Desert in 1929 while searching for Charles Kingsford-Smith and his co-pilot Charles Ulm, who had gone down in their plane, *Southern Cross*. Keith Anderson and Bob Hitchcock perished in the desert, while Kingsford-Smith and Ulm were rescued. It's a fascinating story, explained here in detail.

The **Aviation Museum** is in the Connellan Hangar, Alice's original aerodrome. There are exhibits on pioneer aviation in the Territory and, of course, the famous Royal Flying Doctor Service (that's Flynn's old plane out the front).

ALICE SPRINGS CEMETERY

Adjacent to the aviation museum, this **cemetery** contains the graves of some prominent locals.

The most famous grave is that of **Albert Namatjira**; it's the sandstone one in the middle section to the left as you enter the cemetery. The headstone features a terracotta tile mural of three of Namatjira's Dreaming sites in the MacDonnell Ranges. The glazes forming the mural design were painted on by Namatjira's granddaughter, Elaine, while the rest was done by other members of the Hermannsburg Potters.

Other graves in the cemetery include that of Harold Lasseter, who perished in 1931 while trying to relocate the rich gold reef he supposedly found west of Uluru 20 years earlier, and that of the anthropologist Olive Pink, who spent many years working with the Aboriginal people of the central deserts. A number of the original Afghan cameleers are also buried here – in the newly palmed section.

NORTHERN TERRITORY

Olive Pink Botanic Garden

Just across the Todd River from the town centre, the **Olive Pink Botanic Garden** (Map p798; ☎ 8952 2154; www.opbg.com.au; Tuncks Rd; ☼ 10am-6pm) has a fine collection of native shrubs and trees found within a 500km radius of Alice Springs. Short walks in the reserve include the climb to the top of Annie Meyer Hill in the Sadadeen Range, from where there's a fine view over the town. The hill is known to the Arrernte people as Tharrarltneme and is a registered sacred site. Looking to the south, in the middle distance is a small ridge running east to west: this is Ntyarlkarle Tyaneme, one of the first sites created by the caterpillar ancestors (the name relates that this was where the caterpillars crossed the river). There's a visitors centre and the Garden Café, which serves drinks, ice cream, *real* coffee and scrumptious home-made cakes.

Date Garden

Dates are the deal at the **Date Garden** (Map p798; ☎ 8952 2977; Palm Circuit; ☼ 8am-5pm or 6pm) which is surrounded by aviaries and a roving managerie. Try the 'date'-vonshire tea or the glorious date ice cream.

Frontier Camel Farm

About 5km along Palm Circuit, south of Heavitree Gap, is the **Frontier Camel Farm** (☎ 8953 0444; www.cameltours.com.au; adult/child/family $6/3/12; ☼ 9am-5pm), where you can ride one of these strange 'ships of the desert'. Guided by their Afghani masters, camels were the main form of transport through the desert before the railways were built. The fascinating museum pays tribute to both the camels and their dedicated cameleers alike. See Activities (opposite) for details on camel rides, and also Eating (p804) if you'd like to take a camel to dinner or breakfast.

Old Ghan Museum & Road Transport Hall of Fame

At the MacDonnell siding, about 10km south of Alice Springs along the Stuart Hwy, a group of local railway enthusiasts have restored a collection of *Ghan* locomotives and carriages on a stretch of disused siding from the old narrow-gauge railway track. The **Old Ghan Museum** (☎ 8955 5047; www.maintraxnt.com.au; Norris Bell Ave; adult/child $5.50/3.50; ☼ 9am-5pm) has an interesting collection of railway memorabilia.

The **Road Transport Hall of Fame** (☎ 8952 7161; Norris Bell Ave; adult/child $6/4; ☼ 9am-5pm) is a motor vehicle buff's delight. The fine collection includes superbly restored vehicles, original road trains, vintage cars, and other transport memorabilia.

ACTIVITIES

Ballooning

Fancy quietly sailing through the desert skies at sunrise? Balloon flights cost from $180 for a 30-minute flight, including breakfast.

Local operators:

Ballooning Downunder (☎ 1800 801 601; www.ballooningdownunder.com.au)

Outback Ballooning (☎ 1800 809 790; www.outbackballooning.com.au)

Spinifex Ballooning (☎ 1800 677 893; www.balloonflights.com.au)

Bushwalking

If you really want to get to know this country, head for the bush. Several easy walks radiate from the Olive Pink Botanic Gardens and the Telegraph Station, which is the first stage of the Larapinta Trail.

Central Australian Bushwalkers (☎ 8953 1956; http://home.austarnet.com.au/longwalk), a group of local bushwalkers, schedule a wide variety of walks in the area; see the website.

Lone Dingo Adventures (☎ 8953 3866; 24 Parsons St) has ready-assembled packs of lightweight gear for hire for those keen to tackle part of the Larapinta Trail but who are lacking the equipment.

For information on guided Larapinta Trail walks, see p811.

Camel Riding

Camel treks are another central Australian attraction.

Frontier Camel Farm (☎ 8953 0444; www.cameltours.com.au) offers short rides ($10/6 per adult/child) and an atmospheric Todd River Ramble for an hour ($35/15).

Cycling

Alice is a flat town so grab a bicycle and be off with you – down the excellent track along the Todd River to the Telegraph Station, to the Alice Springs Desert Park, or along the designated track to Simpsons Gap. Carry plenty of water. See Getting Around (p807) for information on bike hire.

Steve's Mountain Bike Tours (☎ 8952 1542, 0417-863 800) guides trips through the Mac-Donnell Ranges (1/5 hours $30/85).

WALKING TOUR

You can do an easy town walk taking in most of the heritage buildings. Starting in Todd Mall, you'll find **Adelaide House** (Map p798; ☎ 8952 1856; Todd Mall; adult/child $3/2; ☽ 10am-4pm Mon-Fri, 10am-noon Sat), built in the early 1920s and now preserved as a memorial museum to John Flynn. Originally it was Alice Springs' first hospital. Flynn, who founded the flying doctor service, is also commemorated by the **John Flynn Memorial Church** (Map p798) next door.

Walk north and then west along Parsons St. On the left is the **Residency** (Map p798; cnr Hartley & Parsons Sts; admission free; ☽ 9am-5pm Mon-Fri, 10am-4pm Sat & Sun) dating from 1926–27. It was originally the home of the first governor of central Australia and has been re-furbished to reflect the period. The Queen and Prince Phillip stayed here during their 1964 visit.

Across the road is the Old Courthouse, which was in use until 1980 and now houses the **National Pioneer Women's Hall of Fame** (Map p798; ☎ 8952 9006; www.pioneerwomen.com.au; 27 Hartley St; adult/child $2.20/free; ☽ 10am-5pm Feb–mid-Dec), a thought-provoking tribute to pioneering women from all over Australia, with a special section on outback heroines.

Turn left onto Hartley St; just south of the car park is the **Hartley St School** (Map p798; ☎ 8952 4516; ☽ 10.30am-2.30pm Mon-Fri) and National Trust office. Historical displays here include a re-created early classroom that may spark memories for some.

Back on Parsons St, to the west, is the original **Stuart Town Gaol** (Map p798; Parsons St; adult/child $2.20/free; ☽ 10am-12.30pm Mon-Fri, 9.30am-noon Sat Mar-Nov), squeezed between the modern law courts and the police station. It was the town's main jail from 1909 to 1938; if you walk down the path behind the jail, a **mural** (Map p798) tells the history of policing in the Alice. Continuing along Parsons St, turn left at Railway Tce and you'll come to another giant **mural** (Map p798) on the back wall of the supermarket, which details the history of Alice Springs.

TOURS

The tourist office has details on all sorts of tours from Alice Springs.

Aboriginal Culture Tours

Aboriginal Art & Culture Centre (☎ 8952 3408; 86 Todd St), has a half-day Aboriginal desert-discovery tour ($85) leaving at 8.30am daily from its gallery.

Rod Steinert Tours (☎ 8558 8377; rstours@cobweb .com.au) operates a popular 'Dreamtime & Bushtucker Tour' ($80/40 per adult/child) which gives you a chance to meet some Warlpiri Aboriginal people and learn a little about their traditional life. As it caters for large groups, it can be impersonal. You can tag along on the same tour with your own vehicle for $60/30.

Tours Outside Alice Springs

There's at least one trip daily to the major attractions: Uluru-Kata Tjuta National Park (Ayers Rock and the Olgas), Kings Canyon, Palm Valley, the West and East MacDonnell Ranges, Simpsons Gap and Standley Chasm. See the respective sections for details of operators. Tours farther afield, such as Rainbow Valley and Chambers Pillar, operate less frequently. Most follow similar routes and you see much the same on them all, although the level of service and the degree of luxury will determine how much they cost.

FESTIVALS & EVENTS

Most of the local community gets involved in the Alice's many colourful activities.

Alice's Pioneer Park Racecourse is a surprisingly good track and through the cooler months there's a series of horse races. The **Alice Springs Cup** in May is the main event. Contact the **Alice Springs Turf Club** (☎ 8952 4977; www.alicespringsturfclub.org.au) for a programme.

The **Finke Desert Race** is a three-day event held on the Queen's Birthday weekend in June along the Old South Rd from Alice to Finke – about 218km of rough road. It attracts all sorts of rev heads and gives the town a carnival atmosphere.

The **Camel Cup**, a series of camel races, takes place in mid-July.

The town is full of bow-legged stockmen – swaggering around in their 10-gallon hats, cowboy shirts, moleskin jeans and RM Williams Cuban-heeled boots – in August for the **Alice Springs Rodeo**.

During late September, the **Henley-on-Todd Regatta** draws the biggest crowds of all.

Having a series of boat races on the Todd River would seem a challenge considering hardly any water ever flows along the river bed. In fact, they say that if you see the Todd River flow three times, you're a local! Nevertheless races are held for sailing boats, doubles, racing eights and every boat class you could think of. The boats are all bottomless, the crews' legs stick out and they simply run down the course.

See the boxed text 'Aboriginal Festivals & Events' (p746) for information on the annual **Beanie Festival**.

SLEEPING

Though seemingly remote, Alice has an abundance of accommodation, each with air-con and a swimming pool (or cool spa).

Budget
HOSTELS

Discounts (usually $1) apply at most hostels for YHA/VIP/Nomads members.

Pioneer YHA Hostel (Map p798; ☎ 8952 8855; alicepioneer@yhant.org.au; Parsons St; dm $22-26, d/tw $70/80; ﹟ ▯) The name is derived from the old Pioneer cinema, which this central hostel inhabits. It's spacious and friendly, with a guest kitchen and disabled access.

Toddy's Resort (Map p795; ☎ 1800 806 240, 8952 1322; toddys@saharatours.com.au; 41 Gap Rd; dm $14-18, tw & d $45, motel d $60; ﹟ ▯) Toddy's retains its relaxed friendliness despite its size. It has clean facilities, an open-air bar next to the pool and cheap, all-you-can-eat evening meals.

Annie's Place (Map p795; ☎ 1800 359 089, 8952 1545; anniesplace@octa4.net.au; 4 Traeger Ave; dm from $16, d $55; ﹟ ▯) Annie's converted motel rooms each have a bathroom and fridge. There are more utensils than you can juggle in the kitchen, and tasty meals at its café/bar.

Also recommended:

Backpackers Hideaway (Map p795; ☎ 8952 8686; 6 Khalick St; dm $16-20, d $45; ﹟) A quiet place in a big old house; bicycle hire costs $6/12 per half/full day.

Alice Lodge Backpackers (Map p795; ☎ 1800 351 925, 8953 1975; alice_lodge@hotmail.com; 4 Mueller St; dm $18, d $45; ﹟) Quiet and friendly.

Ossie's Homestead (Map p795; ☎ 1800 628 211; ossies@ossies.com.au; 18 Warburton St; dm $16-18, d $45; ﹟) Relaxed, with a pool table.

HOTELS

Todd Tavern (Map p798; ☎ 8952 1255; fax 8952 3830; 1 Todd Mall; d $50; ﹟) Being a pub, the Todd

Tavern might get a bit noisy on weekends, but is otherwise a reasonable choice.

CAMPING & CARAVAN PARKS

Most camping grounds are on the outskirts of Alice. The closest national park camp areas to Alice are at Trephina Gorge (60km to the east), Rainbow Valley (77km south) and Ellery Creek (87km west). See the MacDonnell Ranges sections for details.

Wintersun Gardens Caravan Park (Map p795; ☎ 8952 4080; Stuart Hwy; camp/caravan sites for 2 $18/21, cabins $50, 2-bedroom unit $100) There's a pleasant atmosphere and grassy shaded sites at this caravan park north of town.

MacDonnell Range Holiday Park (Map p795; ☎ 1800 808 373, 8952 6111; www.macrange.com.au; Palm Pl; camp/caravan sites for 2 $20/24, bunkhouse $55, cabins $80, with bath $90, villas from $100; ﹟ ▯) About 4km south of town, this holiday park is one of the best equipped in Alice Springs. As well as a mini-mart, TV and games room and camp kitchen, it holds entertainment nights in season (May to September). The cabins and villas accommodate six people.

Heavitree Gap Outback Resort (Map p795; ☎ 1800 896 119, 8950 4444; www.aurora-resorts.com.au; Palm Circuit; camp/caravan sites for 2 $18/20, bunkhouse $65, f $85, motel d $110; ﹟) Black-footed rock wallabies descend to feed at this gap in the range 3km south of town. It's a huge, friendly place with clean facilities and tree-lined sites. The bunk rooms have a bathroom and fridge, while the family rooms have kitchens. Meals are available at the pub and there's a supermarket on site.

Mid-Range

See the Camping & Caravan Parks section for comfortable motel units and cabins at resorts. Alice has a growing number of cosy, upmarket B&Bs – see the **Northern Territory Bed & Breakfast Council website** (www.bed-and-breakfast.au.com) for further listings.

APARTMENTS

Alice on Todd (Map p795; ☎ 8953 8033; fax 8952 9902; cnr Strehlow St & South Tce; studio $98, 1-/2-/3-bedroom apt from $110/140/165; ﹟ ▯) Peering over the banks of the Todd, these self-contained apartments can accommodate up to six people, and there's a barbecue area and games room. Stand-by and long-term rates are available.

Hillsview Tourist Apartments (Map 795; ☎ 0407-602 379, fax 8953 1921; 16 Bradshaw Dr; standard/deluxe apt from $92/100; ﹟) Well-positioned for monitoring the changing hues of the Mac-Donnell Ranges, each of the homely self-contained, two-bedroom apartments has a private courtyard.

BED & BREAKFASTS

Alice Springs Cottage (Map p798; ☎ 0414-854 590; alicesprings.cottage@octa4.net.au; 14 Railway Tce; s/d $100/120; ⊠) This quaint heritage-listed cottage (1929) has three rooms with shared facilities. It's right in town.

Nthaba Cottage (Map p795; ☎ 8952 9003; www.nthabacottage.com.au; 83 Cromwell Dr; s/d $125/150; ⊠) Near the golf course, this is a quaint spot with garden views from the rooms. The friendly owners will whip up a fruit platter and anything else you fancy for breakfast.

Hilltop (☎ 8955 0208; www.hilltopalicesprings.com; 9 Zeil St; s/d $130/150; ⊠) This place off Larapinta Dve, 5km from the town centre, maximises its impressive views of Mt Gillen. After a breakfast feast on the balcony, cycle out to Simpsons Gap or explore the Desert Park, 2km to the east. The comfortable rooms have private access and excellent beds.

MOTELS & RESORTS

Anything with a landscaped garden and a nice pool seems to be called a resort, but most have a range of accommodation and standard motel-style rooms.

Desert Palms Resort (Map p795; ☎ 1800 678 037, 8952 5977; despalms@saharatours.com.au; 74 Barrett Dr; d/tr/q villas $100/110/120; ⊠) With palms positioned for seclusion and cascades of bougainvillea pouring over balconies, this must be one of the most tranquil places in town. The bungalow-style villas have cathedral ceilings, tropical-style furnishings and a kitchenette. Forget the sightseeing – luxuriate in the island swimming pool.

Outback Inn Resort (Map p795; ☎ 1800 810 664; res@theoutbackinn.com; 46 Stephens Rd; d $140; ⊠ 🖵) At the foot of the ranges, opposite the casino, the Outback Inn has comfortable rooms with all the mod cons, a lovely pool area and a tennis court.

Desert Rose Inn (Map p798; ☎ 8952 1411; fax 8952 3232; 15 Railway Tce; d $60, with bathroom $95/105, ste $120; ⊠) Just a short walk from the town centre, this motel has a range of rooms (ask to see a few) and an inviting pool and courtyard area.

White Gum Holiday Inn (Map p795; ☎ 1800 896 131, 8952 5144; fax 8953 2092; 17 Gap Rd; d from $90; ⊠)

Though the rooms at this highway-motel-style place are a little tired, they're spacious and offer good value due to the kitchens.

Top End

Most of the top-end accommodation is east of the river and feature restaurants, bars, pools, bicycles and shuttle buses to town.

Bond Springs Outback Retreat (☎ 8952 9888; www.outbackretreat.com.au; d $220-264; ⊠) About 20km north of Alice, you can experience outback station life – in absolute luxury. The comfortable rooms are traditionally decorated; dinner ($44) is served around the pool and gourmet picnic baskets can be arranged. To get there, drive 10km north of Alice along the Stuart Hwy, turn right at the sign and continue a farther 6.5km.

Rydges Plaza (Map p795; ☎ 1800 675 212; reservations_alice@rydges.com; Barrett Dr; d $140-220, ste from $340; ⊠ 🖵) Across the river from town, Rydges has comfortable rooms and comes well equipped with a gym, sauna and tennis courts, and offers free golf. The excellent Hanuman restaurant serves Thai cuisine.

Aurora Alice Springs (Map p798; ☎ 1800 089 644; tti@aurora-resorts.com.au; Leichhardt Tce; d from $150; ⊠) The rooms have everything you're likely to need at this conveniently located hotel, between the Todd River and the mall. Ask to see a couple if possible, as some have a colder feel to them.

EATING

Alice has a reasonable range of eateries and most places have at least one vegetarian dish. If you've travelled from Melbourne or Sydney, you'll be astounded to find the prices here can top them.

Cafés

There are numerous places for a sandwich or light snack along Todd Mall and in the arcades running off it. Many have tables and chairs outside – ideal for breakfast on a sunny morning.

Café Mediterranean Bar Doppio (Map p798; ☎ 8952 6525; Fan Arcade; mains $6-11) Huge and wholesome tasty portions are served inside or in the shaded arcade at Bar Doppio's. There are cooked breakfasts, focaccias, curries, great coffee, fresh juices, and the walls and windows are a font of knowledge on the arty/alternative scene.

Sport Bistro (Map p798; ☎ 8953 0935; Todd Mall; focaccia $8.50-11.90, mains $15-25) 'The Sport' is as popular for a beer or coffee as it is for meals. Munch on a tasty pasta or nibble on tapas as you watch the world slowly pass by.

Red Dog and **Red Rock Café** (Map p798), almost side by side at the southern end of Todd Mall, serve early breakfasts, pastries, burgers and coffee.

Dining Tours

A few interesting possibilities involve taking a ride out of town.

Red Centre Dreaming (☎ 1800 089 616; Stuart Hwy; adult/child $85/50) At the Red Centre Resort, about 23km north of the town centre, a three-course dinner is combined with Aboriginal dancing, music and story-telling.

Take a Camel out to Breakfast or Dinner (☎ 8953 0444, Ross Hwy; adult/child breakfast $75/45, dinner $100/75) This popular tour combines a one-hour camel ride with a meal at the Frontier Camel Farm.

Pubs

Surprisingly, there are only a few spots in Alice Springs where you can buy pub-style meals.

Pub Caf (Map p798; ☎ 8952 1255; Todd Tavern, 1 Todd Mall; mains $6-16) The Pub Caf is a popular place for 'pub-grub' and puts on great Sunday evening roasts ($6.95). You can take your meals at barrel tables in the pub, or in the slightly more formal bistro. Ask about the Monday night movie-and-meal deal.

Bojangle's (Map p798; ☎ 8952 2873; 80 Todd St; mains $11-22, roast $13) A good range of hot meals are served in the bistro to the back of Bojangle's colonial-style bar.

Firkin & Hound (Map p798; ☎ 8953 3033; 21 Hartley St; mains $12-29) Nestled behind Alice Plaza is one of those curious English-theme pubs popular around Australia. The dining area is comfortable and the menu features staples such as bangers-and-mash and beef-and-Guinness pie.

Restaurants

Sultan's Kebab (Map p798; ☎ 8953 3322; cnr Hartley St & Gregory Tce; kebabs $6-8, mains $16) Delicious, fresh and filling Turkish food is on offer at this local haunt. Belly dancers shimmy around the tables on Friday and Saturday nights. You can eat in or take away.

Casa Nostra (Map p795; ☎ 8952 6749; cnr Undoolya Rd & Stuart Tce; meals $10-16) Across the river from the town centre, Casa Nostra is a long-standing, family-run pizza and pasta place. It's good value and you can BYO, which can make for a cheap night out.

Al Fresco (Map p798; ☎ 8953 4944; Todd Mall; pasta $14.50, mains $15-22) In the cinema complex at the northern end of the mall, Al Fresco serves up good pasta with plenty of sauces.

Jay Jay's (Map p795; ☎ 8952 3721; 20 Undoolya Rd; mains $11-19) With a low-slung terrace on a corner east of the river, Jay Jay's serves up a mix of Thai, Chinese and European-style dishes. Portions are large, drinks are cheap and children are well catered for; book ahead.

Oscar's (Map p798; ☎ 8953 0930; Todd Mall; mains $18-34) Oscar's Mediterranean cuisine is perfect for a light lunch or dinner splurge – paella perhaps? It's open for all meals, and coffee and cakes in between.

Overlanders Steakhouse (Map p798; ☎ 8952 2159; 72 Hartley St; mains $18-26) Overlanders is a local institution for steaks of all kind – emu, crocodile, kangaroo, camel… The 'Drover's Blowout' ($50) is a carnivore's delight!

Bluegrass Restaurant (Map p798; ☎ 8955 5188; cnr Stott Tce & Todd St; lunch $8-15, dinner $14-20) This groovy space, in the historic CWA (Country Women's Association) building, has a vibrant interior and a lovely garden setting. It's perfect for relaxed, intimate dining, and the inspired modern-Australian menu is full of gourmet delights.

Hanuman Restaurant (Map p795; ☎ 950 8000; Rydge's Plaza, Barrett Dve; mains $12-25) Hanuman is elegantly furnished to transport you on a journey along the spice route. Tantalising Thai dishes make for a perfect splurge.

Self-Catering

If you're stocking up for a trip into the wilds, you can experience the joys of several large supermarkets around the city centre. **Coles**, **Woolworths** and **Bi-Lo** (Map p795) are open daily.

Gourmet Bakehouse (Map p7798; ☎ 8953 0041; Coles Complex) has made-to-order sandwiches, cream cakes and sour dough bread, just off Gregory Tce.

It's worth the search for **Afghan Traders** (Map p798; ☎ 8955 5560), in a lane off Parsons St behind the ANZ bank. It stocks organic and health foods, as does **Health Country Store** (Map p798; ☎ 8952 0089; Parsons St).

DRINKING

Melanka's (Map p798; 94 Todd St) You can drink, you can dance, you may get to jelly-wrestle, and you'll get to witness a brawl most weekends. Melanka's gets packed to the rafters.

See also Live Music (below) for more information on venues around town.

ENTERTAINMENT

The gig guide in the entertainment section of the *Centralian Advocate* (published every Tuesday and Friday) lists what's on in and around town.

Alice Springs Cinemas (Map p798; ☎ 8952 4999; Todd Mall) Latest release movies screen between 10am and 9pm. Some hostels offer two-for-one movie ticket deals.

Araluen Arts Centre (Map p795; ☎ 8952 5022, bookings 8951 1122; Larapinta Dr) There's a hive of activity at the local arts centre which features theatre, music and dance. Art-house films are screened on Sunday evening; programmes are available from the arts centre or the visitors centre.

Lasseter's Hotel Casino (Map p795; ☎ 8950 7777; 93 Barrett Dve) Flashing lights and garish carpet could entice you to blow all of your travel funds. There's live music at the casino's Limerick Inn a few nights per week.

Live Music

Sean's Irish Bar (Map p798; ☎ 8952 1858; 51 Bath St) This rustic, partly open-air bar has karaoke on Thursday, live music from Friday to Sunday and a jam session at 4pm on Sunday.

Firkin & Hound (Map p798; ☎ 8953 3033; 21 Hartley St) There's a less-raucous atmosphere than at some other places at this English theme pub. Bands play from Wednesday to Sunday.

Bojangles (Map p798; ☎ 8952 2873; 80 Todd St) Wild West meets Aussie outback at this place, where shells from the complimentary peanuts carpet the floor by the end of the night. There's live music and entertainment most nights.

Sounds of Starlight Theatre (Map p798; ☎ 8953 0826; andrewlangford@ozemail.com.au; 40 Todd Mall; adult/concession $18.50/15.50) This is a unique musical performance evoking the spirit of the outback with a didgeridoo and various Latin American instruments. Performances are held at 7.30pm on Tuesday, Friday & Saturday between April and November.

Settlers (Map p795; ☎ 8953 4333; Palm Circuit; show $16) This restaurant stages performance of tall tales and bush songs four nights a week. The show starts at 8pm and the prices include meal and show.

SHOPPING

You can get most things you need in Alice. For general items, try **Kmart** (Map p798) between Bath St and Railway Tce. For camping and hiking gear, try **Alice Springs Disposals** (Map p798; ☎ 8952 5701; Reg Harris Lane) and **Lone Dingo Adventure** (Map p798; ☎ 8953 3866; 24 Parsons St). **Centre Canvas** (☎ 8952 2453; Smith St) sells quality locally made swags at reasonable prices.

The **craft market** (Todd Mall; ☒ 9am-1pm Sun) lines the mall with knick-knack stalls. There are some great home-made spring rolls and other snacks.

Leaping Lizards Gallery (Map p798; ☎ 8952 5552; Reg Harris Lane) has quality, locally produced crafts made from materials such as emu and kangaroo leather, Territory timbers and earth toned pottery for sale.

Alice is the centre for Aboriginal arts and crafts from all over central Australia and plenty of shops along Todd Mall sell them – including a forest of didgeridoos (an instrument not traditionally played in this part of the Territory). The choice is phenomenal but if you're heading north, save your didgeridoo purchase for later in the journey.

Plenty of art galleries and craft centres specialise in Aboriginal creations – if you have an interest in central Australian art or you're looking for a piece to buy, there are several places where you can buy direct from the artists, including **Papunya Tula Artists** (Map p798; ☎ 8952 4731; www.papunyatula.com.au; 78 Todd St), **Warumpi Arts** (Map p798; ☎ 8952 9066; 105 Gregory Tce), and **Jukurrpa Artists** (Map p798; ☎ 8953 1052; Stott Tce). The latter represents female artists.

The **Aboriginal Art & Culture Centre** (Map p798; ☎ 8952 3408; 86 Todd St), established by Southern Arrernte people, offers didgeridoo lessons ($11) and has cultural displays and a museum. The **Central Australian Aboriginal Media Association** (CAAMA; Map p798; ☎ 8952 9207; 101 Todd St) stocks Aboriginal books, CDs and cassettes, painted ceramics and various products with local Aboriginal designs.

Two good commercial outlets for Aboriginal art are **Gallery Gondwana** (Map p798; ☎ 8953 1577; 43 Todd Mall) and the **Original**

Aboriginal Dreamtime Gallery (Map p798; ☎ 8952 8861; 63 Todd Mall). **Mbantua Gallery** (Map p798; ☎ 8952 5571; 71 Gregory Tce) is also worth a wander, if just for a chance to see original works by Emily Kame Kngwarreye and other artists from the Utopia region. There are also some Hermannsburg pots.

GETTING THERE & AWAY
Air
Qantas (Map p798; ☎ 13 13 13; www.qantas.com.au; cnr Todd Mall & Parsons St) flies daily between Alice and Adelaide ($484 one way), Darwin ($380), Melbourne ($510), Perth ($510), Sydney ($510) and Yulara (Uluru; $320).
Virgin Blue (☎ 13 67 89; www.virginblue.com.au) flies from Alice Springs to Sydney daily ($460 one way). Restricted fares are around 50% less than the fully flexible fares listed here.

Bus
McCafferty's/Greyhound (Map p798; ☎ 8952 7888, 13 20 30; www.mccaffertys.com.au; cnr Gregory & Railway Tces) has daily services from Alice Springs to Adelaide ($180, 21 hours), Uluru ($75, 5½ hours), Cairns ($370, 36 hours) via Mt Isa ($210, 14 hours), Darwin ($195, 21 hours) and Katherine ($180, 15 hours).

Backpacker-type buses cover the distance while savouring the sights along the way. **Desert Venturer** (☎ 1800 079 119; www.desertventurer.com.au) makes three-day runs ($320, food kitty $55) between Cairns and the Alice thrice weekly. **Groovy Grape** (☎ 1800 661 177; www.groovygrape.com.au) has a two-day Alice to Adelaide run, via Coober Pedy ($145) and longer camping trips from Adelaide to Alice Springs.

Car & Motorcycle
Alice Springs is a long way from anywhere but the roads are sealed to the north and south. From Mt Isa, in Queensland, it's 1180km; Darwin to Alice Springs is 1476km (15 hours); and from Alice Springs to Yulara and Kings Canyon is 443km (4½ hours) and 331km (3½ hours) respectively.

These are outback roads, but you're not yet in the real, outer outback, where a breakdown can mean big trouble. Nevertheless, it's wise to have your vehicle well prepared since getting someone to come out if you break down is likely to be expensive. You won't get a signal on a mobile phone anywhere outside Alice or Yulara.

Carry drinking water and emergency food at all times, as even the Stuart Hwy can become impassable due to flooding, which could leave you stranded.

All major hire companies have offices in Alice Springs and most have 4WDs for hire; Avis, Budget, Hertz and Territory Thrifty also have counters at Alice Springs airport.

Rentals don't come cheap as most firms offer only 100km free a day (which won't get you anywhere). Among the local operators, **Outback Rentals** (Map p798; ☎ 8953 5333; www.outbackautorentals.com.au; 78 Todd St) has small cars for $54 a day with 100km free. There are also camping equipment kits.

Rental companies include:
Avis (Map p798; ☎ 8953 5533; 52 Hartley St)
Britz: Australia (☎ 8952 8814; cnr Stuart Hwy & Power St)
Budget (Map p798; ☎ 13 22 27, 8952 8899; Shop 6 Capricornia Centre, Gregory Tce)
Hertz (Map p798; ☎ 8952 2644; 76 Hartley St)
Territory Thrifty Car Rental (Map p798; ☎ 1800 891 125; cnr Stott Tce & Hartley St)

Train
A great way to reach Alice Springs is aboard the *Ghan*, which departs from Adelaide at 5.15pm on Sunday and Friday.

Tickets can be booked through **Trainways** (☎ 13 21 47; www.gsr.com.au). Discounted fares are sometimes offered, especially in the low season (February through June excluding Christmas). Bookings are recommended on this popular route.

Modes of travel are daynighter seat (no sleeper and no meals), sleeper cabin (a sleeper with shared facilities and no meals) and 1st-class sleeper (a self-contained sleeper with breakfast or lunch).

The *Ghan* is met in Adelaide by the *Indian Pacific*, which departs from Sydney at 2.55pm on Saturday and Wednesday, and the *Overland*, which departs from Melbourne at 10.10pm on Saturday and 9.10pm Thursday. One-way daynighter seat/sleeper cabin/1st-class sleeper fares from Adelaide are $215/680/850. You can also join the *Ghan* at Port Augusta in South Australia. From Alice Springs the departure for Adelaide is at 1pm on Tuesday and Friday, arriving at 7.40am the next day.

It's also possible to put your car on the *Ghan*, which gives you the luxury of transport when you arrive without the long drive

THE GHAN

The *Ghan* is one of Australia's great railway adventures. In the last 20-something years since the track was relaid, the trip has been made quicker and more comfortable. While weathered characters speak with fond nostalgia about the 'good old days of the *Ghan*', it's still a great trip into the heart of Australia on which you'll truly appreciate the remoteness of the area.

The *Ghan* saga started in 1877 when it was decided to build a railway line from Adelaide to Darwin. It eventually took over 50 years to reach Alice Springs, and the final 1500km to Darwin have only recently been completed, more than a century later. The basic problem was that a big mistake was made right at the start, a mistake that wasn't finally sorted out until 1980: the line was built in the wrong place.

The grand error was a result of concluding that because all the creek beds north of Marree were bone dry, and because nobody had seen rain, there wasn't going to be rain in the future. In fact, the initial stretch of line was laid right across a flood plain and when the rain came, even though it soon dried up, the line was simply washed away. In the century or so that the original *Ghan* line survived it was a regular occurrence for the tracks to be washed away.

The wrong route was only part of the *Ghan*'s problems. The foundations were flimsy, the sleepers were too light, the grading was too steep and it meandered hopelessly. It was hardly surprising that the top speed of the old *Ghan* was a flat-out 30km/h! Early rail travellers went from Adelaide to Marree on the broad-gauge line, changed there to narrow gauge as far as Oodnadatta, then had to make the final journey to Alice Springs by camel train. Afghani cameleers pioneered transport through the outback and it was from them that the *Ghan* took its name.

Finally, in 1929, the line was extended from Oodnadatta to Alice Springs. Though the *Ghan* was a great adventure, it simply didn't work. At the best of times it was chronically slow and uncomfortable as it bounced and bucked its way down the badly laid line. Worse, it was unreliable and expensive to run. And worst of all, a heavy rainfall could strand it at either end or even in the middle. Parachute drops of supplies to stranded train travellers became part of outback lore and on one occasion the *Ghan* rolled in 10 days late!

By the early 1970s the South Australian state railway system was taken over by the federal government and a new standard gauge line, laid from Tarcoola, northwest of Port Augusta on the transcontinental line, to Alice Springs was planned – to be laid where rain would not wash it out. In 1980 the line was completed ahead of time and on budget.

In 1982 the old *Ghan* made its last run and the old line was subsequently torn up. One of its last appearances was in the film *Mad Max III*. Whereas the old train took 140 passengers and, under ideal conditions, made the trip in 50 hours, the new train takes twice as many passengers and does it in about 20 hours. It's still the *Ghan*, but it's not the trip it once was.

from the south. The cost from Alice Springs to Adelaide is $470.

The weekly Alice Springs to Darwin service departs from Alice Springs at 4pm on Monday, arriving in Katherine at 8am and Darwin at 4pm on Tuesday, and costs $240/880/1100 one way.

The service from Darwin departs at 10am on Wednesday, departs Katherine at 5.45pm, and arrives in Alice Springs at 9am Thursday.

GETTING AROUND

Alice Springs is compact enough to get around to most parts on foot, and you can reach quite a few of the closer attractions by bicycle.

To/From the Airport

Alice Springs airport is 15km south of the town. It's about $26 by taxi.

An **airport shuttle** (☎ 8953 0310) meets flights and picks up and drops off passengers at city accommodation for $10/17 one way/return.

Bicycle

The town's flat landscape makes cycling out to the closer attractions, such as the Alice Springs Desert Park a breeze – particularly in winter when it's not too hot. Some accommodation places hire out bikes, or you can try **Bike Hire** (☎ 8952 2235), which offers half-/full-day rental for $12/20, including delivery and collection.

Bus

Alice Springs' public bus service, **Asbus** (☎ 8950 0500), departs from outside the Yeperenye shopping centre on Hartley St. Buses run about every 1½ hours from 7.45am to 6pm Monday to Friday, and from 9am to 12.45pm on Saturday. The fare for a short trip is $2.20. There are three routes of interest to travellers: No 1 has a daily detour to the cultural precinct; No 3 passes the School of the Air; and No 4 passes many southern hotels and caravan parks along Gap Rd and Palm Circuit. The tourist office has timetables.

The **Alice Wanderer bus** (☎ 1800 669 111) does a loop around 12 major sights – including out to the old Telegraph Station, School of the Air, the Old Ghan Museum and Road Transport Hall of Fame, and the cultural precinct. You can get on and off wherever you like; daily tickets cost $30. It runs every 70 minutes from 9am to 4pm from the southern end of Todd Mall and you can be picked up from your accommodation before the 9am departure.

Taxi

Taxis congregate near the corner of Todd St and Gregory Tce. To book one, call ☎ 13 10 08 or ☎ 8952 1877.

THE MACDONNELL RANGES

The MacDonnell Ranges, full of gorges, waterholes and walking tracks, stretch like a spine to the east and west of Alice Springs. The scenery in the ranges is superb. The many gorges, with spectacular sheer walls, cut through the rocky cliffs, harbouring rocky waterholes which nourish wildlife and spring wildflowers.

There are many places you can visit inside of a day, but if you've got time to linger, immerse yourself in the region's beauty by camping out or staying at a homestead. A plethora of walks range from sightseeing strolls to the challenge of the Larapinta Trail. There is no public transport to either the East or West MacDonnells, so without your own transport you'll have to take a tour. Some of the closer gorges are accessible by bicycle or on foot. By yourself, the

Centre's eerie emptiness and peace can touch you in a way that is impossible in a big group.

EAST MACDONNELL RANGES

The East MacDonnell Ranges stretch for 100km east of Alice Springs, intersected by a series of scenic gaps and gorges which see far fewer visitors than the West MacDonnell Ranges. The sealed Ross Hwy, just through the Heavitree Gap south of town, leads to most of the highlights. About 100km from Alice Springs, the dirt Arltunga Rd becomes the Arltunga Tourist Dr northwest of Arltunga and rejoins the Stuart Hwy 50km north of Alice Springs; this rougher section sometimes requires a 4WD. There are currently no facilities in the East MacDonnell Ranges, so take all provisions with you.

Emily & Jessie Gaps Nature Park

Both of these gaps are associated with the Eastern Arrernte Caterpillar Dreaming trail.

Emily Gap, 16km out of town, is a pleasant spot with rock art and a fairly deep waterhole in the narrow gorge. Known to the Arrernte as Anthwerrke, this is one of the most important Aboriginal sites in the Alice Springs area as it was from here that the caterpillar ancestral beings of Mparntwe (Alice Springs) originated (also see the boxed text 'Mparntwe'; p794). The gap is registered as a sacred site and there are some well-preserved paintings on the eastern wall. You may have to swim to get to them.

Jessie Gap, 8km farther, is an equally scenic and usually much quieter place. There is a walk (18km one way, 2 hours, unmarked) between the two gaps. Both of these sites have toilets.

Corroboree Rock Conservation Reserve

Past Jessie Gap you drive over eroded flats before entering a valley between red ridges. **Corroboree Rock**, 51km from Alice Springs, is one of many strangely shaped outcrops scattered over the valley floor. A small cave here was once used by Aboriginal people as a storehouse for sacred objects. Despite the name, it is doubtful if the rock was ever used as a corroboree area, due to the lack of water in the vicinity.

EAST MACDONNELL RANGES

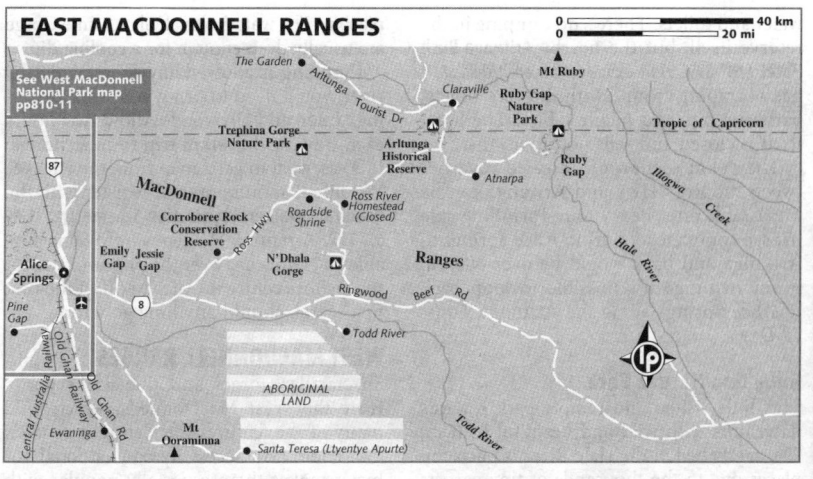

0 ——————— 40 km
0 ——————— 20 mi

See West MacDonnell National Park map pp810–11

The Garden
Arltunga Tourist Dr
Mt Ruby
Claraville
Ruby Gap Nature Park
Tropic of Capricorn
Trephina Gorge Nature Park
Arltunga Historical Reserve
Ruby Gap
87
MacDonnell
Corroboree Rock Conservation Reserve
Roadside Shrine
Ross River Homestead (Closed)
Atnarpa
Illogwa Creek
Hale River
Emily Gap
Jessie Gap
N'Dhala Gorge
Ranges
Alice Springs
Ross Hwy
Ringwood
Beef Rd
Pine Gap
8
Todd River
Old Ghan Railway
Central Australia Railway
Old Ghan Rd
ABORIGINAL LAND
Todd River
Ewaninga
Mt Ooraminna
Santa Teresa (Ltyentye Apurte)

Trephina Gorge Nature Park

About 60km from Alice Springs you cross the sandy bed of Benstead Creek and a lovely stand of red gums which continues for the 6km from the creek crossing to the Trephina Gorge turn-off. If you only have time for a couple of stops in the East MacDonnell Ranges, make Trephina Gorge Nature Park, 3km north of the Ross Hwy, one of these stops. The contrast between pale sand in dry river beds, red and purple tones of the valley walls, white tree trunks, eucalyptus-green foliage and blue sky is spectacular. The nature park offers some excellent walks, deep swimming holes, abundant wildlife and low-key camping areas. The main attractions here are the gorge itself, **Trephina Bluff** and **John Hayes Rockhole**.

Walks here range from short strolls to the **Ridgetop Walk** (10km one way, 5 hours, difficult), which traverses the ridges from Trephina Gorge to the delightful John Hayes Rockhole, offering splendid views and isolation. The 8km return along the road takes around 1½ hours.

There's a **ranger station** (☎ 08-8956 9765), and camp sites at Trephina Gorge, the Bluff and John Hayes Rockhole.

Roadside Shrine

Keep a look out for the fabulously adorned **roadside shrine**, complete with glistening motorcycle, on the south side of the Ross Hwy.

N'Dhala Gorge Nature Park

Shortly before reaching the Ross River Homestead, a former resort now closed, a strictly 4WD only track leads 10km south to N'Dhala Gorge. Around 5900 ancient Aboriginal rock carvings (petroglyphs) decorate a deep, narrow gorge, although they're not easy to spot. The small, exposed camping area has a toilet, but you need to bring your own water and firewood.

It's possible to turn off before the gorge and head to the Ringwood Homestead road, then west to rejoin the Ross Hwy 30km east of Alice Springs.

Arltunga Historical Reserve

☎ 08

At the eastern end of the MacDonnell Ranges, 110km northeast of Alice Springs, is the old gold-mining ghost town of **Arltunga**. Its history, from the discovery of alluvial (surface) gold in 1887 until mining activity petered out in 1912, is fascinating. **Old buildings**, a couple of **cemeteries** and the many deserted **mine sites** in this parched landscape give visitors an idea of what life was like for miners here. There are walking tracks (the Government Works area has the best collection of remnant drystone buildings) and old mines to explore (now hosting bat colonies), so make sure to bring a torch (flashlight).

The **visitors centre** (☎ 8956 9770; ⏰ 8am-8pm) has many old photographs and displays of the gold-extracting process. Maps of the reserve are available here, as are drinking water and toilets. There's no camping in the reserve itself, but the nearby **Arltunga Bush Hotel** (☎ 8956 9797; camp sites per adult/child $8/4) has a camping ground with showers, toilets, barbecue pits and picnic tables. The hotel itself is closed and sells no provisions.

The 40km section of unsealed road between the Ross Hwy and Arltunga can be impassable after heavy rain. Including side trips, a complete loop from Alice Springs to Arltunga and back would be over 300km. From Arltunga it's possible to loop back to Alice Springs along the Arltunga Tourist Dr.

Ruby Gap Nature Park

This little-visited and remote park rewards its visitors with wild and beautiful scenery. The sandy bed of the Hale River is purple in places due to the thousands of tiny garnets found here. The garnets were the cause of a 'ruby rush' to the area in the 19th century and a few miners did well out of it until the 'rubies' were discovered to be virtually worthless garnets. It's a remote, evocative place and is well worth the effort involved to reach it. The waterholes at Glen Annie Gorge are usually deep enough for a cooling dip.

Camping is allowed anywhere along the river; you'll need to bring your own drinking water and firewood. Allow two hours each way for the 44km trip from Arltunga. It is essential to get a map from the Parks & Wildlife Commission and register with the **Voluntary Walker Registration Scheme** (☎ 1300 650 730). A refundable deposit of $50 is payable by credit card over the phone or cash at the visitors centre in Alice to offset the cost of a search should anything go wrong.

WEST MACDONNELL RANGES

Spectacular gorges and fine walks punctuate the West MacDonnells, which hold many of the features the Centre is renown for. Their easy access by conventional vehicles makes them especially popular with day-trippers. Heading west from the Alice, Namatjira Dr turns northwest off Larapinta Dr 6km beyond Standley Chasm and is sealed all the way to Glen Helen, 132km from town. From the dirt road beyond, there is a turn-off south through Tylers

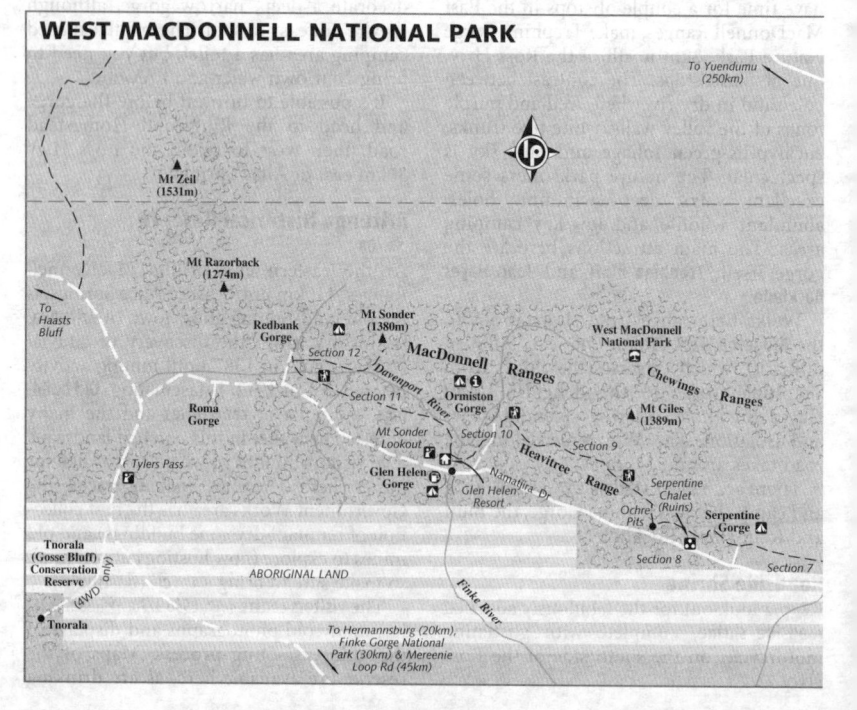

WEST MACDONNELL NATIONAL PARK

Pass to Tnorala (Gosse Bluff), which meets up with the Mereenie Loop Rd. Larapinta Dr continues southwest from Standley Chasm to Hermannsburg (sealed), then the Mereenie Loop Rd (a dirt road) loops all the way to Kings Canyon.

There are ranger stations at Simpsons Gap and Ormiston Gorge.

Activities
BUSHWALKING
The ranges provide ample opportunity for walking and many excellent tracks have been laid in the various parks and reserves.

Anyone attempting an overnight walk should register with the **Voluntary Walker Registration Scheme** (☎ 1300 650 730).

Larapinta Trail
The Larapinta Trail is a 12-stage, 220km track of varying degrees of difficulty along the backbone of the West MacDonnells, stretching from the Telegraph Station in Alice Springs to Mt Sonder, beyond Glen Helen Gorge. The following two-day to

two-week tracks take in a many of the attractions in the Western MacDonnells:

Section 1 Alice Springs Telegraph Station to Simpsons Gap (24km).

Section 2 Simpsons Gap to Jay Creek (23km).

Section 3 Jay Creek to Standley Chasm (15km).

Section 4 Standley Chasm to Birthday Water Hole (18km).

Section 5 Birthday Water Hole to Hugh Gorge (16km).

Section 6 Hugh Gorge to Ellery Creek (31km).

Section 7 Ellery Creek to Serpentine Gorge (14km).

Section 8 Serpentine Gorge to Ochre Pits (18km).

Section 9 Ochre Pits to Ormiston Gorge (27km).

Section 10 Ormiston Gorge to Glen Helen (12km).

Section 11 Glen Helen to Redbank Gorge (29km).

Section 12 Redbank Gorge to Mt Sonder (16km return).

Detailed track notes and maps ($1.10 per section) are available on the Parks & Wildlife Commission website (www.nt.gov.au/ipe/pwcnt) and at the visitors centre in Alice Springs. There's no public transport out to this area, but transfers can be arranged through **Glen Helen Gorge** (☎ 08-8956 7495; dave@glenhelen.com.au) to and from the Larapinta Trailheads for $100 per car load.

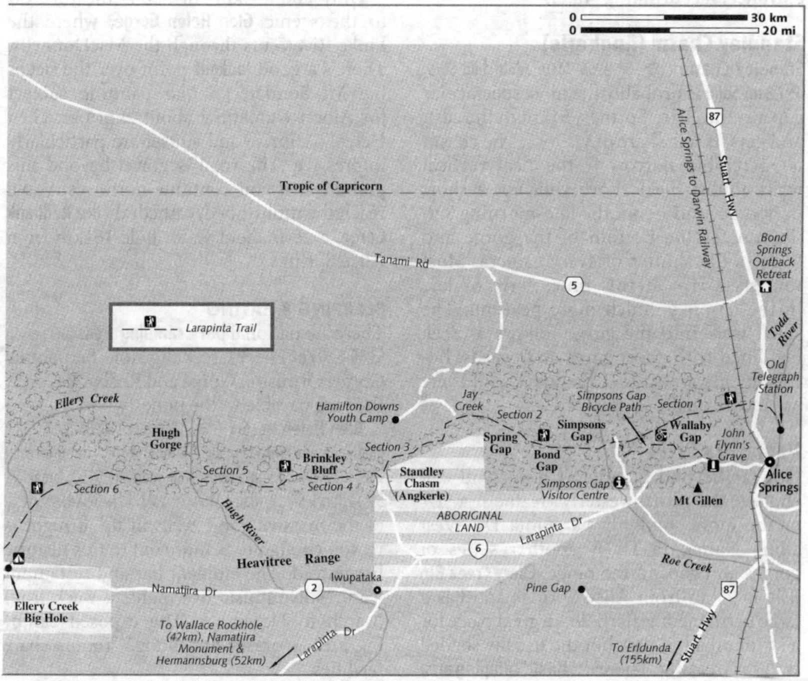

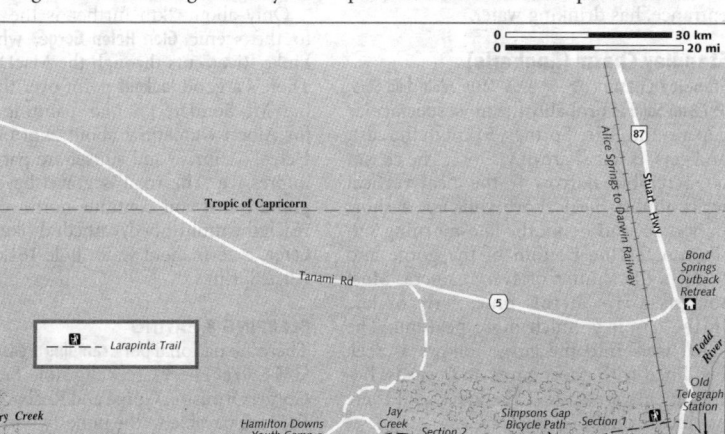

Trek Larapinta (☎ 08-8953 2933; www.treklarapinta .com.au) offers transport and catering for one-day walks ($132) and overnight walks ($198 for one night, $297 for two days/one night).

Simpsons Gap

Westbound from Alice Springs on Larapinta Dr you soon come to **John Flynn's Grave**. The flying doctor's final resting place is topped by a boulder donated by the Arrernte people. Opposite the car park is the start of the **cycling track** to Simpsons Gap, a pleasant three- to four-hour return ride.

By road, **Simpsons Gap** (☼ 8am-5pm) is 22km from Alice Springs and 9km off Larapinta Dr. The area makes a popular picnic spot and also has some good walks. The towering gap in the range is an awesome example of nature's power and patience. For a river to cut a path through solid rock is amazing, but for a river that rarely ever runs to cut such a path is positively mind-boggling – even if it did take 60 million years. There are often rock wallabies in the jumble of rocks on either side of the gap.

The visitors centre, 1km from the park entrance, has drinking water.

Standley Chasm (Angkerle)

Standley Chasm (☎ 08-8956 7440; adult/child $6/5; ☼ 8am-5pm) is probably the most spectacular gap around Alice Springs, 51km to the east, and gets its fair share of visitors. The chasm is incredibly narrow – the near-vertical walls almost meet above you. For a short period around noon, the late-morning sun illuminates the bottom of the gorge and triggers the shutter of every camera. Most tourists arrive at this time; early or late in the day it is much more peaceful. The short walk into the gorge follows a creek bed lined with ghost gums and cycads. Refreshments are sold at the kiosk and there are picnic facilities and toilets.

Namatjira Drive

Not far beyond Standley Chasm you can choose the northwesterly Namatjira Dr or the more southerly Larapinta Dr. West along Namatjira Dr is another series of gorges and gaps in the range. **Ellery Creek Big Hole** is 93km from Alice Springs and has a large permanent waterhole – a great place for a swim on a hot day, but the usually shaded water is freezing. There's a basic **camping area** (adult/child $3.30/1.65) close by with fees payable to an honesty box. **Serpentine Gorge**, a narrow gorge with a waterhole at the entrance (no swimming), is 13km farther.

The **Ochre Pits**, just off the road 11km west of Serpentine, were a source of paints for Aboriginal people. The various coloured ochres are weathered limestone – the colouring is actually iron oxide stains. The pits, lining a dry creek bed, make for a beautiful photo.

The large, rugged **Ormiston Gorge** is the most impressive in the West MacDonnells and well worth a couple of hours. There's a waterhole and the gorge curls around to the enclosed valley of **Ormiston Pound**. When the waterholes of the pound dry up, the fish burrow into the sand, going into a sort of suspended animation and reappearing after rain. There are some good short **walking tracks** around here, including the 30-minute **Ghost Gum Lookout** track, which climbs from the car park to a point looking down into the gorge, but it's worth allowing time to do the full circuit (7km, 2 to 3 hours). There's a **visitors centre** (☎ 08-8956 7799) and a good camping area.

Only about 2km further is the turn-off to the scenic **Glen Helen Gorge**, where the Finke River cuts through the MacDonnells. There's a good **lookout** point over the sleeping Mt Sonder, popular painting subject for Albert Namatjira, about 2km past Glen Helen – sunrise and sunset are particularly impressive. The road is gravel beyond this point, but if you continue northwest you'll reach the multi-hued, cathedral-like **Redbank Gorge**, a permanent water hole 161km from Alice Springs.

SLEEPING & EATING

There are national park **camping areas** (per person $3.30-6.60) at Ellery Creek Big Hole, Serpentine Gorge, Ormiston Gorge and Redbank Gorge. Fees are payable to the honesty box.

Glen Helen Resort (☎ 1800 896 110, 08-8956 7489; glenhelen@melanka.com.au; Namatjira Dr; camp/caravan sites $10/12, budget rooms $80, motel d $150; breakfast $5-11, lunch $4-12, mains $15-27; ☒) The idyllic view of the massive gorge walls lit up at night is reason enough to venture out to this historic homestead. The ambient bar and restaurant features live music five nights a week from March to December. The exposed camping area is grassy and budget rooms share facilities.

Tours

Emu Run (☎ 08-8953 7057; www.emurun.com.au) runs full-day trips from Alice Springs to the East and West MacDonnell Ranges (each $100, including lunch) among its comprehensive tours of the region. **Centre Highlights** (☎ 1800 659 574) offers small-group tours to the West MacDonnell Ranges ($95, including lunch) and others to Palm Valley and Hermannsburg ($105).

SOUTH OF ALICE

You can make some interesting diversions off the road south from Alice Springs. There are also attractions to the east of the Stuart

Hwy, but to visit most of these you will require a 4WD.

LARAPINTA DRIVE

The spectacular James Ranges form an east-west band south of the West MacDonnell Ranges. While not as well known as the MacDonnells, the ranges contain some of the Centre's best attractions: Hermanns-burg, Palm Valley and Kings Canyon.

Taking the alternative road to the south from Standley Chasm, Larapinta Dr crosses the Hugh River before reaching the **Wallace Rockhole** turn-off, 18km off the main road and 117km from Alice Springs.

The Arrernte Aboriginal community owns the **Wallace Rockhole Tourist Park** (☎ 08-8956 7993;

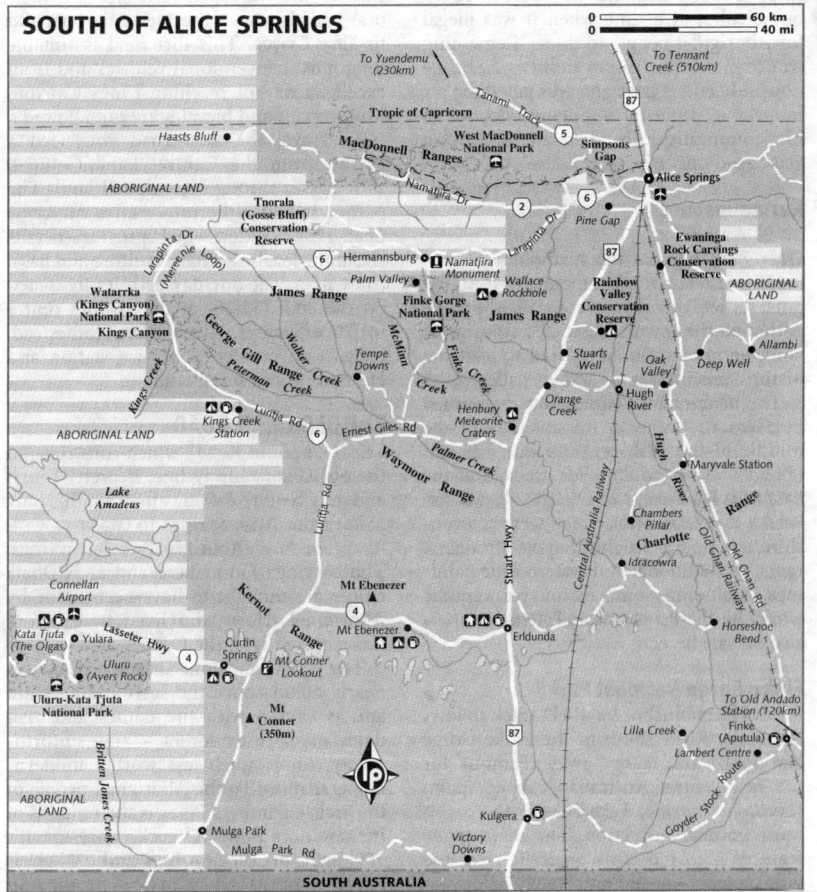

SOUTH OF ALICE SPRINGS

www.wallacerockholetours.com.au; camp/caravan sites $18/20, cabins from $85), which is a pleasant spot with good facilities. There are some excellent tours on offer here, including rock art and bush medicine ($9/5 per adult/child) and bush tucker ($30/20), and an arts and crafts outlet nearby.

Back on Larapinta Dr, shortly before Hermannsburg, is the **Namatjira Monument**. Albert Namatjira, the Aboriginal artist who made the stunning purple, blue and orange hues of this region famous in his water colours, lived at the Hermannsburg Lutheran Mission.

Namatjira supported many in his community with the income from his work. In 1957 Namatjira was the first Aboriginal person to be granted Australian citizenship. Due to this, he was permitted to buy alcohol at a time when it was illegal for Aboriginal people to do so. Remaining true to his kinship responsibilities, he broke non-indigenous laws and was jailed for six months in 1958 for supplying alcohol to his community. He died the following year, aged only 57.

Hermannsburg
☎ 08 / pop 460

Only 8km beyond the Namatjira Monument you reach the Hermannsburg Aboriginal settlement, 125km from Alice Springs. Although the town is restricted Aboriginal land, permits are not required to visit the historic precinct, store and art gallery.

The **Hermannsburg Mission** was established by German Lutheran missionaries in the middle of the 19th century. Entry tickets ($4.50/3.50 per adult/child) are sold at the **Kata-Anga Tea Rooms** (☎ 8956 7402; ✆ 9am-4pm Mar-Nov, 10am-4pm Dec-Feb), which serves Devonshire teas and a delightful apple strudel. A range of traditional and watercolour paintings, including some distinctive ceramic works by the **Hermannsburg Potters** group, is also on sale here.

Finke Gorge National Park

From Hermannsburg a 4WD track follows the Finke River south to the Finke Gorge National Park, 12km away. Famous for the rare central Australian cabbage palm (*Livistona mariae*), **Palm Valley** is the park's most popular attraction. The main gorge features high red cliffs, majestic river red gums, plenty of sand and stately palms.

A 4WD vehicle is essential to bump along the sandy Finke River bed and rocky access road.

There's some beautiful, short bushwalks here. The shady camping area has a serene setting opposite red sandstone ridges and has hot showers and flush toilets.

If you're up for some serious four-wheel driving, a rough track meanders through the picturesque Finke Gorge to the camping area at **Boggy Hole**, about 2½ hours from Hermannsburg. Lonely Planet's *Outback Australia* is a detailed guide suitable for such trips.

Mereenie Loop Road

From Hermannsburg you can continue west to the Areyonga turn-off (no visitors) and then take the Mereenie Loop Rd to **Kings Canyon**. This dirt road is suitable for robust conventional vehicles and is an excellent way of reaching Kings Canyon. Motorcycles and bicycles are not allowed.

To travel the loop road you need a permit from the Central Land Council, as it passes through Aboriginal land. The permit includes the informative *Mereenie Loop Pass* booklet, which provides details about the local Aboriginal culture and has a route map. The one-day permits are issued on the spot ($2.20) at the visitors centre in Alice Springs, Glen Helen Homestead, Kings Canyon Resort service station and Hermannsburg service station.

THE OLD GHAN ROAD

The 'Old South Road', which runs close to the old *Ghan* railway line, is pretty rough and may require a 4WD after rain. It's only 35km from Alice Springs to **Ewaninga**, with its prehistoric Aboriginal rock carvings. The carvings found here and at N'Dhala Gorge are thought to have been made by Aboriginal tribes who lived here before those currently in the Centre.

The eerie, sandstone **Chambers Pillar** rises nearly 60km above the surrounding plain and is carved with the names and visit dates of early explorers – and, unfortunately, some much less worthy modern-day graffitists. To the Aboriginal people of the area, Chambers Pillar is the remains of Itirkawara, a powerful gecko ancestor. It's 160km from Alice Springs and a 4WD is required for the last 44km from the turn-off at Maryvale Station. There's a basic camping area but you need to bring water and firewood.

Back on the main track south, you eventually arrive at **Finke (Aputula)**, a small Aboriginal community 230km from Alice Springs. When the old *Ghan* was running, Finke was a thriving little town; these days it seems to have drifted into a permanent torpor, except when the **Finke Desert Race** is staged (see Festivals & Events; p801). There's a basic community **store** (☎ 08-8956 0968; ⊙ 9-11.30am & 1.30-4.30pm Mon-Fri, 8.30-11.30am Sat), which is the outlet for the **Aputula Arts Centre** and also sells fuel.

From Finke you can turn west along the Goyder Stock Route to join the Stuart Hwy at Kulgera (150km), or east to Old Andado station on the edge of the Simpson Desert (120km). Just 21km west of Finke, and 12km north of the road along a signposted track, is the **Lambert Centre**. The point marks Australia's geographical centre and features a 5m-high replica of the flagpole found on top of Parliament House in Canberra.

RAINBOW VALLEY CONSERVATION RESERVE

This series of sandstone bluffs and cliffs, in shades ranging from cream to red, is one of the more extraordinary sights of central Australia, yet sees relatively few visitors. It attains real beauty at sunset. The park lies 22km off the Stuart Hwy along a 4WD track 75km south of Alice Springs. There's a basic camping ground with gas barbecues and pit toilets but you will need to bring water.

STUARTS WELL

Jump out of the car and onto a camel at Stuarts Well, 90km south of Alice Springs along the Stuart Hwy. At **Camel Outback Safaris** (☎ 08-8956 0925; www.camels-australia.com.au) you can take a short ride around the yard for $4, a 30-minute jaunt for $25 or a half/full day for $85/110. Extended safaris of two to five days through the gaps and gorges of the James Ranges cost $150/125 per adult/child per day.

Jim's Place (☎ 08-8956 0808; fax 8956 0809; camp/caravan sites for 2 $14/17, s/d cabins $70/85) is run by well-known outback identity Jim Cotterill, who along with his father opened up Kings Canyon to tourism.

ERNEST GILES ROAD

The Ernest Giles Rd heads off to the west of the Stuart Hwy about 140km south of Alice. This shorter but rougher route to Kings Canyon is often impassable after heavy rain and is not recommended for conventional vehicles. The section along the Luritja Rd to Kings Canyon is sealed.

Henbury Meteorite Craters

Eleven kilometres west of the Stuart Hwy, a dusty corrugated track leads 5km off Ernest Giles Rd to this cluster of 12 small craters. The largest of the craters is 180m wide and 15m deep.

There are no longer any fragments of the meteorites at the site, but the museum in Alice Springs has a small chunk that weighs 46.5kg.

There's a very basic, exposed camping area, which verges on unbearable when the flies are out in force.

WATARRKA (KINGS CANYON) NATIONAL PARK

Continuing west along Ernest Giles Rd, or detouring from the Lasseter Hwy, brings you to the Watarrka (Kings Canyon) National Park, which includes one of the most spectacular sights in central Australia – the sheer, 100m-high walls of **Kings Canyon**. It's well worth the diversion.

The short **Kings Creek Walk** follows the rocky creek bed to a raised platform with amphitheatre-like views of the towering canyon rim. Walkers are rewarded with awesome views on the **Kings Canyon Walk** (6km loop, 4 hours, strenuous) – think *Priscilla, Queen of the Desert*. After a steep climb, the walk skirts the canyon's rim overlooking sheer cliff faces, enters the **Garden of Eden**, with its tranquil pools and prehistoric cycads, and passes through a maze of giant eroded domes. Watch your step – the cliffs are unfenced and the wind can be strong. Carry plenty of water and a hat.

There's a **ranger station** (☎ 08-8956 7488) 22km east of the canyon.

The **Giles Track** (22km one way, overnight, easy) is a marked track that follows the ridge between the gorge and Kathleen Springs. You can register for the walk with the **Volunteer Walker Registration Scheme** (☎ 1300 650 730).

You can reach Kings Canyon, 230km southwest of Alice Springs, via the unsealed

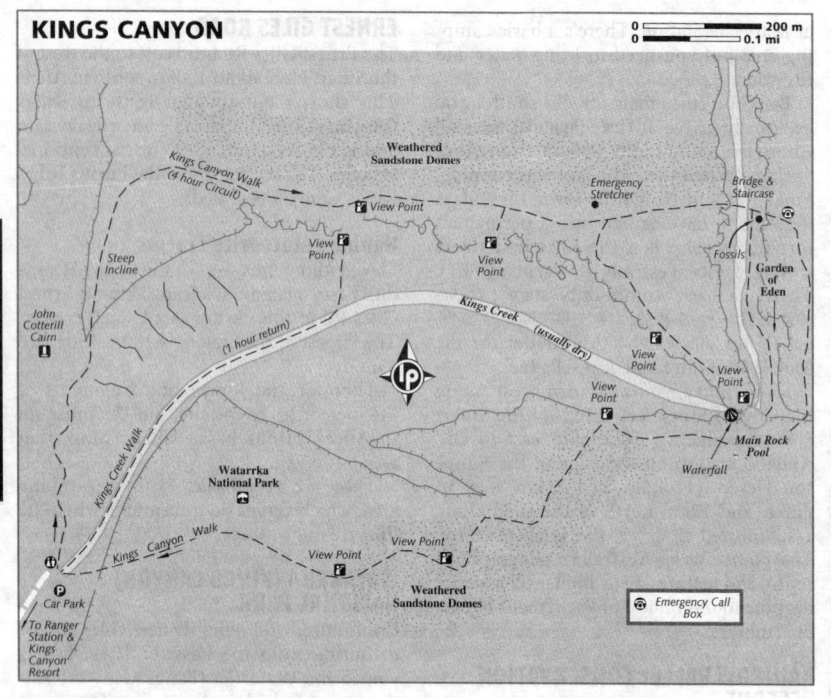

KINGS CANYON

0 — 200 m
0 — 0.1 mi

Weathered Sandstone Domes

Kings Canyon Walk (4 hour Circuit)

View Point

Emergency Stretcher

Bridge & Staircase

Steep Incline

View Point

View Point

Fossils

Garden of Eden

John Cotterill Cairn

Kings Creek (usually dry)

(1 hour return)

View Point

View Point

Kings Creek Walk

View Point

Main Rock Pool

Watarrka National Park

Waterfall

Kings Canyon Walk

View Point

View Point

Car Park

To Ranger Station & Kings Canyon Resort

Weathered Sandstone Domes

Emergency Call Box

Mereenie Loop Rd which joins Larapinta Dr west of Alice Springs. It's rough but usually passable with conventional vehicles when it's dry.

Tours

AAT-King's (☎ 1800 334 009) has daily guided walks of the canyon rim which depart from the Kings Canyon Resort at 7am (6.15am in summer) and cost $40/20 per adult/child.

Ranger Talks (tours 6.30pm Mon, Wed & Fri Apr-Oct) are held in the Kings Canyon Resort camping ground.

Helicopter flights are available from **Kings Canyon Resort** (☎ 08-8956 7873) and **Kings Creek Station** (☎ 08-8956 7474). Scenic flights over Kings Canyon start from $60.

For information on tours combining Kings Canyon and Uluru see p818.

Sleeping & Eating

Kings Canyon Resort (☎ 1800 089 622, 08-8956 7442; www.voyages.com.au; Luritja Rd; camp/caravan sites for 2 $28/32, dm $45, lodge rooms $170, d $100, motel d $330-420; ⊠ ▯) You'll pay top dollar for the well-maintained facilities at the resort,

6km west of the canyon. The grassy camping ground has plenty of shade, a laundry and barbecues. Four-bed dorm and lodge rooms share kitchen and bathroom facilities. There's a bar, café, restaurant, shop and fuel. The **Outback Barbecue** (mains $16-27) serves pizza, grills and some nonmeat options to the toe-tapping tunes of live Australiana, while **Carmichael's** (breakfast $16-22, buffet $45) serves swish breakfasts and an evening seafood buffet.

Kings Creek Station (☎ 08-8956 7474; www.kings creekstation.com.au; Luritja Rd; tent sites per adult/child $12/6, with power extra $2.65, cabins per adult/child $50/32) Located just outside the national park's eastern boundary, about 35km from the canyon, this friendly spot has pristine camp sites among the desert oaks and a pool. For evening entertainment, follow the whip cracking to the stock camp show with billy tea and damper ($25). Or, you can mosey on a camel. Cabin rates include breakfast; amenities are shared and there's also a kitchen/barbecue area. Fuel, ice and limited stores are available at the **shop** (⏰ 8am-7pm).

LASSETER HIGHWAY

The Lasseter Hwy connects the Stuart Hwy with Uluru-Kata Tjuta National Park, 244km to the west, from the turn-off at Erldunda. There are a couple of roadhouses along the way, plus a lookout for **Mt Conner** (350m), the large mesa (table-top mountain) that some eager souls mistake for Uluru. Local Aboriginal people know it as Artula, the home of the ice men.

Curtin Springs Station (☎ 08-8956 2906; camp sites free, s/d $35/45, with bathroom $70, showers $1; breakfast $4-11, lunch $7.50-11, dinner $16-22; 🕑 7am-9.30pm or later) is the last stop before Yulara, and if you're on a budget it's not a bad alternative to staying at the expensive Ayers Rock resort. There's a bar and restaurant, camel rides, and cattle station tours which take you out to Mt Conner.

ULURU-KATA TJUTA NATIONAL PARK

This entire area is of deep cultural significance to the owners, the Pitjantjatjara and Yankunytjatjara Aboriginal peoples (who refer to themselves as Anangu). To them the Ayers Rock area is known as Uluru and the Olgas as Kata Tjuta. The national park is leased to Environment Australia (the federal government's national parks body), who administer it in conjunction with the traditional owners.

It's easy to spend several days in the Uluru-Kata Tjuta area; there are plenty of walks and other activities, and the Rock never seems to look the same no matter how many times you see it. Unfortunately most group tours are very rushed and squeeze in a quick afternoon Rock climb, photos at sunset, a morning at the Olgas next day and then off – 24 hours in total if you're lucky. It's best experienced at your own pace, if you have the time.

Information

Uluru-Kata Tjuta National Park Cultural Centre

(☎ 08-8956 3138; 🕑 7am-5.30pm Apr-Oct, 7am-6pm Nov-Mar) is 1km before the Rock on the road from Yulara. You can easily spend an hour or three here to have a good look around the cultural centre before visiting Uluru itself. The two inspiring buildings represent

the ancestral figures of Kuniya and Liru and contained within them are two main display areas, both with multilingual information. The Tjukurpa display features Anangu art and *tjukurpa* (Aboriginal law, religion and custom), while the Nintiringkupai display focuses on the history and management of the national park.

The centre also houses the Aboriginal-owned **Maruku Art & Crafts** (☎ 08-8956 2558; 🕑 8.30am-5.30pm) and **Walkatjara Art Centre** (☎ 08-8956 2537; 🕑 9am-5.30pm). Here you can see artists from the Mututjulu community at work. Everything is created in the surrounding desert region and certificates of authenticity are issued with most artworks. It's a good place to buy souvenirs (carvings etc) since you're buying directly from the artists.

Ininti Souvenirs & Café (☎ 08-8956 2214; 🕑 7am-5.15pm) sells souvenirs and a good range of Aboriginal-interest books. The attached café serves breakfast, lunch, snacks and ice cream.

There's also a visitors centre in Yulara (see Orientation & Information; p821).

PARK ENTRY

The park itself is open from half an hour before sunrise to sunset daily. Three-day entry permits to the national park ($16.50/free per adult/child under 16) are available at the park entry station on the road from Yulara to Uluru and the Kata Tjuta turn-off.

Tours

AAT-KING'S

To allow for flexibility in your itinerary, one of the major operators, **AAT-King's** (☎ 1800 334 009) runs a range of daily coach tours. Generally it can work out cheaper to use the Uluru Express (see Getting Around; p824) or to hire a car between a group.

The 'Rock Pass' ($195/100 per adult/child) includes a guided base tour, sunset, climb, sunrise, Cultural Centre and the Olga Gorge walk. The pass is valid for three days and includes the park entry fee. The 'Rock Super Pass' ($270/135) also includes the Valley of the Winds walk and a barbecue.

All these activities are also available in various combinations on a one-off basis: base tour ($45/22), sunrise tour ($45/22), climb ($45/22), sunset ($34/16), sunrise and climb ($75/37), climb and base ($75/36), sunrise and base ($75/37), sunrise climb and base ($95/50). These prices do not include the park entry fee.

For Kata Tjuta viewing, the 'Explorer Pass' ($150/75) includes a base tour, Uluru sunrise and sunset, and the Valley of the Winds walk.

AAT-King's also has three-day tours from Alice Springs to Uluru, Kata Tjuta and Kings Canyon, starting at $610/510 depending on accommodation type.

ANANGU TOURS

Owned and operated by Anangu from the Mutitjulu community, **Anangu Tours** (☎ 08-8956 2123; www.anangutours.com.au) offers a range of tours led by an Anangu guide and gives an insight into the land through Anangu eyes.

The 4½-hour Aboriginal Uluru Tour ($110/75 per adult/child) starts with sunrise over Uluru and breakfast at the Cultural Centre, then takes in a base tour, Aboriginal culture and law, and demonstrations of bush skills and spear-throwing.

The Kuniya Sunset Tour ($85/60) leaves at 2.30pm (3.30pm between November and March) and includes a visit to Mutitjulu Waterhole and the Cultural Centre, finishing with sunset viewing.

Both trips can be combined over 24 hours with an Anangu Culture Pass ($175/120). Self-drive options are also available for $55/27. You can join an Aboriginal guide at 8.30am (7.30am November to February) for the morning walk or at 3.30pm (4.30pm) for the Kuniya Tour.

Anangu's tour desk is at the Tour & Information Centre, p821; bookings are essential.

DISCOVERY ECOTOURS

Discovery Ecotours (☎ 1800 803 174; bookings@eco tours.com.au) offers several possibilities, including a five-hour Uluru Walk around the base and breakfast for $105/80 per adult/child; Spirit of Uluru is a four-hour, vehicle-based tour around the base of the Rock for the same price. The Olgas and Dunes Tour includes the walk into Olga Gorge and the sunset at the Olgas for $80/60. It also does a tour to Mt Conner with dinner at the Curtin Springs Homestead ($210/160).

FROM ALICE SPRINGS

All-inclusive camping trips to Uluru by private operators start at $280/400 for two/three days, which includes Kings Canyon. If you're rushed for time there are two- or even one-day tours. Prices can vary with the season and demand, and sometimes there may be cheaper 'stand-by' fares available. Tours that include accommodation other than camping are generally much more expensive.

You should check out the company's vehicles, group size and types of meals etc before deciding. Companies popular with budget travellers include **Mulga's Adventures** (☎ 08-8952 1545; fax 8952 8280; www.mulgas.com.au), **Adventure Tours Australia** (☎ 08-8981 4255; www.adv enturetours.com.au) and **Sahara Outback Tours** (☎ 08-8953 0881; www.saharatours.com.au), which also runs recommended five-day 4WD camping trips.

If your time is limited, **Day Tours** (☎ 08-8953 4664) will race you to Uluru and back for $1200/150 per adult/child, including lunch and sunset viewing. It's a long day – the tour leaves at 6am and returns at 11.30pm.

MOTORCYCLE TOURS

If you like the wind in your hair (or face), then **Uluru Motorcycles** (☎ 08-8956 2019) can accommodate you with a variety of trips to the Rock and Kata Tjuta on the back of a Harley-Davidson. A trip to Uluru/Kata Tjuta at sunrise or otherwise is $145. Half-day rental of a Harley costs $365.

SCENIC FLIGHTS

While the enjoyment of those on the ground may be diminished by the constant buzz of light aircraft and helicopters overhead, for those actually up there it's an unforgettable experience. Bookings for these are essential – preferably a day in advance.

Ayers Rock Scenic Flights (☎ 08-8956 2345) charges $130 for a 30-minute flight over the Rock and Kata Tjuta, or $300 for a 120-minute flight, which includes Lake Amadeus and Kings Canyon.

Ayers Rock Helicopters (☎ 08-8956 2077) charges $85 for a 15-minute buzz over Uluru, or $130 including Kata Tjuta. **Professional Helicopter Services** (PHS; ☎ 08-8956 2003) charges $100 for the Uluru flight, and $195 for the 30-minute Uluru and Kata Tjuta flight. There are no child concessions on any helicopter flights, which make them an expensive proposition for families.

ULURU (AYERS ROCK)

Nothing in Australia is as readily identifiable as Uluru (Ayers Rock), the world's biggest monolith. Australia's favourite postcard image is 3.6km long and rises a towering 348m from the surrounding sandy scrubland (867m above sea level). It's believed that two-thirds of the Rock lies beneath the sand. If your first sight of the Rock is during the afternoon it appears as an ochre-brown colour, scored and pitted by dark shadows. As the sun sets, it illuminates the Rock in burnishing orange, then a series of deeper and darker reds before it fades into charcoal. A performance in reverse, with marginally fewer spectators, is given at dawn.

Activities

ULURU WALKS

There are walking tracks around Uluru, and guided walks delving into the plants, wildlife, geology and mythology of the area. All the walks are flat and are suitable for wheelchairs. Several areas of spiritual significance to Anangu are off-limits to visitors – these are marked with fences and signs. Photography of sacred sites is also forbidden.

The *Insight into Uluru* brochure ($1), available at the cultural centre, gives details on self-guided walks.

Base Walk   10km

You can spend three to four hours walking around the base of Uluru at a leisurely pace, looking at the caves and paintings along the

---

CLIMBING ULURU

For years, climbing Uluru has been the highlight of a trip to the Centre and many visitors consider it almost a rite of passage. For the Anangu, the path up the side of the Rock is part of the route taken by Mala men on their arrival at Uluru, and as such has great spiritual significance. The Anangu are the custodians of these lands and take responsibility for the safety of visitors. Any injuries or deaths that occur on the Rock (and they do occur) are a source of distress to them. For these reasons, the Anangu don't climb and they ask that you don't either.

If you compare climbing the Rock to, say, clambering over the altar in Notre Dame Cathedral or striding through a mosque during prayer, it's not hard to understand the Anangu perspective – it's a question of respect.

---

way (if you're pushed for time you can do it in two hours). As most people are too rushed (and too busy tackling the climb) to do this walk, you'll often find a bit of solitude.

Mala Walk   2km Return

This walk starts from the base of the climbing point and takes about one hour at an easy pace. Interpretive signs explain the *tjukurpa* of the Mala (hare-wallaby people), which is of great importance to the

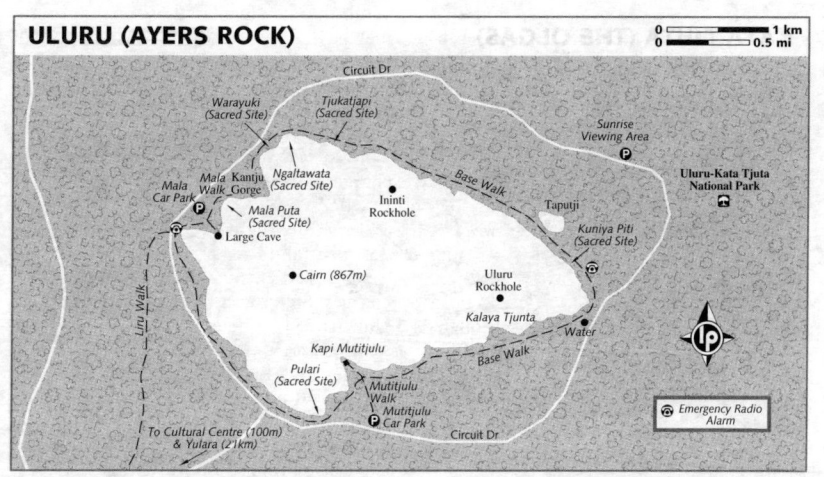

ULURU (AYERS ROCK)

0 — 1 km
0 — 0.5 mi

Circuit Dr

Warayuki (Sacred Site)
Tjukatjapi (Sacred Site)

Sunrise Viewing Area

Uluru-Kata Tjuta National Park

Mala Walk
Mala Car Park
Kantju Gorge
Ngaltawata (Sacred Site)

Base Walk

Taputji

Mala Puta (Sacred Site)
Large Cave

Ininti Rockhole

Kuniya Piti (Sacred Site)

Liru Walk

Cairn (867m)

Uluru Rockhole

Kalaya Tjunta

Water

Kapi Mutitjulu

Base Walk

Pulari (Sacred Site)
Mutitjulu Walk
Mutitjulu Car Park

Circuit Dr

To Cultural Centre (100m) & Yulara (21km)

Emergency Radio Alarm

Anangu. A ranger-guided walk (free) along this route departs at 10am daily (8am from October to April) from the car park. It's not necessary to book, just turn up and look for the ranger in the Mala car park.

Mutitjulu Walk   1km Return

Mutitjulu is a permanent waterhole a short walk from the car park on the southern side of Uluru. The *tjukurpa* tells of the clash between two ancestral snakes Kuniya and Liru. You'll learn more about the Kuniya *tjukurpa* and the food and medicinal plants found here with Anangu Tours (see Tours; p818).

The Climb

If you insist on climbing (see the boxed text 'Climbing Uluru'; p819), take note of the warnings. It's a demanding 1.6km climb that takes about two hours return to the memorial cairn, allowing for a good rest at the top, and there have been numerous deaths from falls and heart attacks. Be sun smart, take plenty of water and be prepared to turn around if it all gets too much. The first part of the walk is by far the steepest and most arduous, and there's a chain to hold on to. The climb is often closed due to strong winds, rain, mist, Anangu business, and from 8am on days forecast to reach 36°C or more.

KATA TJUTA (THE OLGAS)

Kata Tjuta (the Olgas), a bizarre collection of smaller, more rounded rocks, stands about 30km to the west of Uluru. Though less well known, the monoliths are equally impressive and many people find them more captivating. The tallest rock, **Mt Olga** (546m, 1066m above sea level) is about 200m higher than Uluru. Kata Tjuta, meaning 'many heads', is of great *tjukurpa* significance – climbing on the domed rocks themselves is definitely not on.

The main walking track here is the **Valley of the Winds**, a 7.4km loop track (2 to 4 hours) which winds through the gorges giving surreal views of the domes. It's not particularly arduous, but be prepared with water and sun protection. Starting this walk at first light may reward you with a track to yourself, enabling you to listen to the country and appreciate the sounds of the wind and bird calls carried up the valley. The short (2km return) signposted track into the pretty **Olga Gorge** (Tatintjawiya) is especially beautiful in the afternoon when sunlight floods the gorge.

There's a picnic and sunset-viewing area with toilet facilities just off the access road a few kilometres west of the base of Kata Tjuta. Like Uluru, the Olgas are at their glorious, blood-red best at sunset.

HEADING WEST

A lonely sign at the western end of the access road points out that there is a hell of a lot of nothing if you travel west – although, if suitably equipped, you can travel all the way to Kalgoorlie and on to Perth in WA. It's

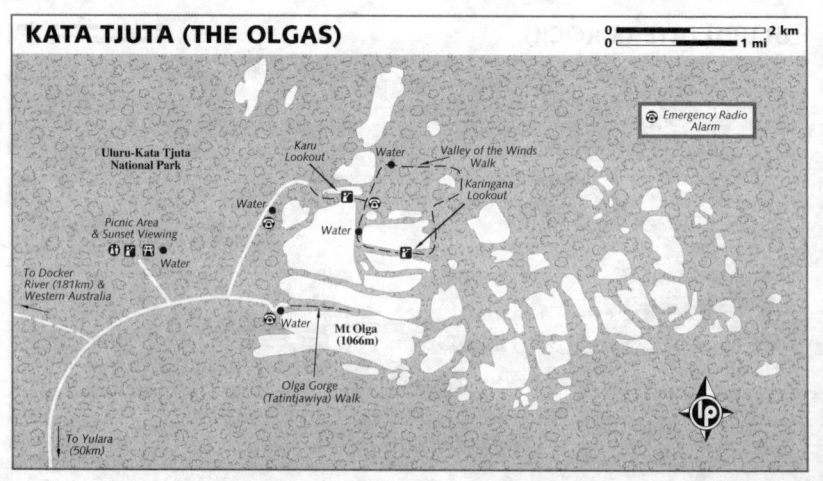

KATA TJUTA (THE OLGAS)

0   2 km
0   1 mi

Uluru-Kata Tjuta
National Park

Karu
Lookout

Water

Valley of the Winds
Walk

Emergency Radio
Alarm

Karingana
Lookout

Water

Picnic Area
& Sunset Viewing

Water

Water

To Docker
River (181km) &
Western Australia

Water

Mt Olga
(1066m)

Olga Gorge
(Tatintjawiya) Walk

To Yulara
(50km)

200km to Docker River, an Aboriginal settlement on the road west, and about 1500km to Kalgoorlie. You need a permit from the Central Lands Council for this trip – see the Great Central Road information (p993) for details. Lonely Planet's *Outback Australia* guide provides in-depth details.

YULARA (AYERS ROCK RESORT)

☎ 08 / pop 2530 (including Mutitjulu)

Yulara is the service village for the national park and has effectively turned one of the world's least hospitable regions into an easy and comfortable place to visit. Lying just outside the national park, 20km from Uluru and 53km from Kata Tjuta, the complex is administered by the Ayers Rock Corporation and makes an excellent – though expensive – base for exploring the area's renowned attractions. Opened in 1984, the village was designed to blend in with the local environment and is a low-rise affair nestled between the dunes. Yulara supplies the only accommodation, food outlets and other services available in the region; demand certainly keeps pace with supply and you'll have little

choice but to part with lots of money to stay in anything other than a tent here.

Orientation & Information

Yulara is built around a vaguely circular drive, Yulara Dr. Heading clockwise everything is on your left, starting with the Desert Gardens Hotel, visitors centre and Emu Walk Apartments, followed by the resort shopping centre, which is built around an outdoor eating area and contains most of the town's facilities (including a photo shop). Farther around the ring road is Sails in the Desert hotel, police station, medical centre and Royal Flying Doctor Service, camping ground, petrol station and Outback Pioneer Hotel & Lodge. *The Resort Guide* is a useful sheet available at the visitors centre and hotel desks.

The **visitors centre** (☎ 8957 7377; ☒ 8.30am-8pm daily) contains good displays on the geography, flora, fauna and history of the region. Information is also available at the cultural centre inside the park, near the Rock.

Most operators and car-hire firms have desks at the **Tour & Information Centre**

NORTHERN TERRITORY

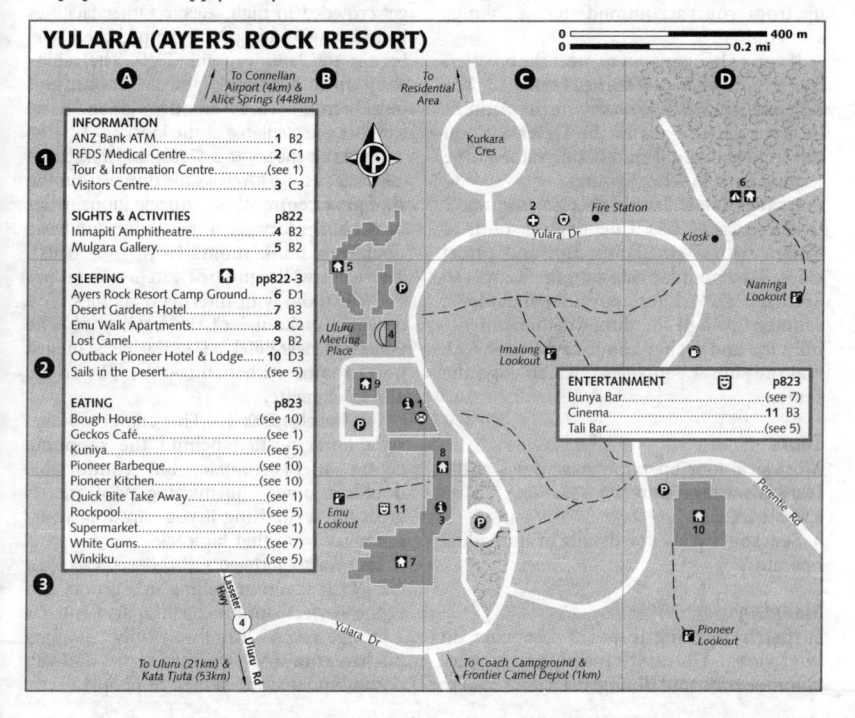

YULARA (AYERS ROCK RESORT)

0 ———————— 400 m
0 ———————— 0.2 mi

INFORMATION
ANZ Bank ATM..............................1 B2
RFDS Medical Centre.....................2 C1
Tour & Information Centre..........(see 1)
Visitors Centre..............................3 C3

SIGHTS & ACTIVITIES   p822
Inmapiti Amphitheatre....................4 B2
Mulgara Gallery..............................5 B2

SLEEPING   pp822-3
Ayers Rock Resort Camp Ground......6 D1
Desert Gardens Hotel.....................7 B3
Emu Walk Apartments....................8 C2
Lost Camel....................................9 B2
Outback Pioneer Hotel & Lodge....10 D3
Sails in the Desert......................(see 5)

EATING   p823
Bough House...............................(see 10)
Geckos Café................................(see 1)
Kuniya..(see 5)
Pioneer Barbeque.......................(see 10)
Pioneer Kitchen..........................(see 10)
Quick Bite Take Away..................(see 1)
Rockpool....................................(see 5)
Supermarket................................(see 1)
White Gums................................(see 7)
Winkiku......................................(see 5)

To Connellan
Airport (4km) &
Alice Springs (448km)

To Residential Area

Kurkara Cres

Fire Station

Yulara Dr

Kiosk

Naninga Lookout

Uluru Meeting Place

Imalung Lookout

ENTERTAINMENT   p823
Bunya Bar...................................(see 7)
Cinema.......................................11 B3
Tali Bar......................................(see 5)

Emu Lookout

Perentie Rd

Lasseter Hwy

Uluru Rd

Yulara Dr

To Uluru (21km) &
Kata Tjuta (53km)

To Coach Campground &
Frontier Camel Depot (1km)

Pioneer Lookout

(☎ 8957 7324; resort shopping centre; ☿ 7.30am-8.30pm). The central desk provides general information about the park and takes bookings for other tours.

The **post office** (☎ 8956 2288; ☿ 9.30am-6pm Mon-Fri, 10am-2pm Sat & Sun) is the bank agent for Commonwealth and Westpac banks; **ANZ** (☎ 8956 2070) has an ATM.

There are coin-operated Internet machines in the Tour & Information Centre and Outback Pioneer Hotel.

Sights & Activities

Take a stroll through **Mulgara Gallery** (Sails in the Desert) where quality hand-made Australian arts and crafts inspired by the landscape are displayed.

Each evening there's the **Night Sky Show** (☎ bookings 1800 803 174; adult/child $32/24), an informative look into Anangu and Greek astrological legends, with views of the startlingly clear outback night sky through telescopes and binoculars. Trips in English are at 8.30pm, with a further session at 7.30pm from June to August and 10.15pm from September to May. It includes a pick-up from your accommodation; bookings are required.

If you're hanging out to meet the beasties, check out **Predators of the Red Centre** (☎ 8956 2563; adult/child $22/15; ☿ noon), in the Amphitheatre next to Sails in the Desert. If you can hold on, you'll find better value at the Reptile Park in Alice Springs.

Frontier Camel Tours (☎ 8956 2444; arock@camel tours.com.au) has a depot just south of Yulara with a small museum and camel rides. Two popular rides are the 'Camel to Sunrise', a 2½-hour tour that includes a saunter through the dunes before sunrise, billy tea and a chat about camels for $90; and the sunset equivalent, which costs the same.

Tours

Most local tour operators have desks at the **Tour & Information Centre** (☎ 8956 2240; ☿ 8.30am-8.30pm) in Yulara.

See Tours p817 for details of individual operators.

Sleeping

If there's anything to put a dampener on your visit to Uluru, it's the high cost of accommodation and dining at Yulara – you're over a barrel so you'll just have to fork out the dough and grit your teeth.

Book all accommodation, including dorm beds, at the Outback Pioneer Lodge and tent or caravan sites at the camping ground, especially during school holidays. Bookings can be made through **central reservations** (☎ 1300 139 889; www.voyages.com.au) for accommodation other than that at the camping ground. The 'Red Centre Explore' rates offer substantial discounts if you're planning to stay for three nights; you can also save a reasonable amount through some Internet sites offering discount accommodation.

All buildings are air-conditioned in summer and heated in winter, and most have a swimming pool.

If you've got your own transport, Curtin Springs Station (p817) may tempt you with free camping and relatively inexpensive accommodation.

Ayers Rock Resort Camp Ground (☎ 8956 2055; campground@ayersrockresort.com.au; camp/caravan sites for 2 $25/30, cabins $150; ☒) Set among native gardens with well-kept patches of green grass and quite a bit of shade, the camping ground can get crowded in high season. Other facilities include a swimming pool, camp kitchen, barbecues and laundry (with TV!). The cabins sleep up to six people and get booked out quickly in the winter months. Gas and basic supplies are available at the kiosk.

Outback Pioneer (☎ 8957 7605; dm $32-40, budget rooms $185; ☒ ▢) Across the dunes from the shopping centre, the Outback Pioneer has hostel dormitory accommodation and basic double or bunk rooms (with four beds). There's a well-equipped kitchen, laundry, and TV room with Internet machines. You can also make use of the hotel pool. The **Outback Pioneer Hotel** (d $330-390) has standard hotel rooms with bathrooms, TV, fridge and kitchenette.

Lost Camel (d $300; ☒) This contemporary-style hotel nestled behind the shopping centre offers compact but comfortable double rooms. The inviting pool area is great for revitalising if you can drag yourself away from that big rock.

Emu Walk Apartments (1-/2-bedroom apt $360/450; ☒) If you're travelling in a group, this is the perfect option. Each apartment has a lounge room with TV, a fully equipped kitchen with a washer and dryer, and can accommodate four and eight people.

Sails in the Desert (d $470, spa $550, ste $820; 🈯) Along with the facilities you'd expect to find in a luxurious five-star hotel, each room has a balcony overlooking the landscaped pool area. There's a tennis court, several restaurants, a piano bar and an art gallery. The spa rooms have spas on private patios.

Eating

BUDGET

Quick Bite Take Away (resort shopping centre; 🕑 8am-8.30pm) You can pick up a range of quick fixes here, such as bacon and egg rolls ($6), burgers ($6.50) and barbecued chicken (half/whole $5/8.50).

Geckos Café (☎ 8956 2562; resort shopping centre; pizza $18-25, pasta & mains $19-26) The decent-size portions of wood-fired pizzas, pastas and other dishes are offset by the sometimes bland dishes. Yes, the coffee's good. The attached ice-cream parlour serves thick shakes and milkshakes as well as the obvious.

The well-stocked **supermarket** (resort shopping centre; 🕑 8.30am-9pm) has a salad bar and delicatessen and sells picnic portions, fresh fruit and vegetables, meat and camping supplies.

MID-RANGE

Pioneer Barbecue (Outback Pioneer Lodge; barbecue $15-23, salads $14) You can sizzle your choice of meat, fish, crocodile or veggie burger and help yourself to a range of salads in the shed-like BBQ Bar. Meals are accompanied by live Australiana music and the banter of lively crowds.

Also here is the **Pioneer Kitchen** (snacks $6.50-8.50), offering light meals and snacks, and the **Bough House** (☎ 8956 2170; breakfast buffet $19-23, dinner buffet $40), a family-style place overlooking the pool.

White Gums (☎ 8956 2100; Desert Gardens Hotel; mains $9-17, dinner buffet $45) For something a bit more intimate, this subtle candle-lit spot has good à la carte and buffet dining. You can choose any two/three courses for $50/55.

TOP END

The port of call for upmarket dining is the Sails in the Desert hotel – bookings are recommended for the following eateries.

Rockpool (lunch $10-23, 2-/3-course dinner $45/55) serves Thai and Indonesian influenced meals around the pool – the perfect spot on a balmy evening. **Winkiku** (breakfast $16-32,

> ### GROG
>
> Please be aware that alcohol (grog) is a problem among some of the local Mutitjulu Aboriginal people living near Uluru. It is a 'dry' community and, at the request of the Aboriginal leaders, the liquor outlet in Yulara has agreed not to sell alcohol to Aboriginal people. For this reason you may be approached at Yulara by Aboriginal people who want you to buy grog on their behalf. The community leaders appeal to you not to do so.

buffet $55) is far from cheap and cheerful, but certainly the most lively eatery in the hotel, it has an amazing array of buffet dishes with plenty of seafood. Yulara's most sophisticated restaurant, **Kuniya** (☎ 8956 2200; mains $32-50), serves inspired contemporary Australian cuisine, infused with native produce from around the country, in an intimate setting. Dress well.

Your shuttle awaits you for a 7km journey out of town to a unique desert experience – the **Sounds of Silence Dinner** (☎ 8957 7448; dinner & show $120). You'll watch the sun set on Uluru and Kata Tjuta while sipping champagne, listening to the didgeridoo and munching canapes. Dinner and stargazing ensue. The price may make you see stars, but what price the chance to see Jupiter's moons aligned or the rings around Saturn in the desert? Bookings essential.

Entertainment

The town's cinema screens films from Friday to Sunday; contact the visitors centre for details. There's also the Night Sky Show (see Sights & Activities; p822) and the Sound of Silence Dinner (see above).

You'll find the most thriving nightlife at the Outback Pioneer's BBQ Bar, which has pool tables and live music nightly. It's a good spot to meet fellow travellers, no dress standards apply and take-away alcohol can be bought here.

The **Bunya Bar** (Desert Gardens Hotel) has chess and games tables in a cigar lounge setting. At **Tali Bar** (Sails in the Desert) you can try cocktails inspired by the landscape, such as 'Valley of the Winds' and 'Desert Storm' while listening to the tinkling ivories. Dress up a bit for these places.

Getting There & Away

AIR

Connellan airport is about 5km north from Yulara. If you only have a short time in the Centre, it makes sense to fly directly to Uluru. Qantas has direct flights from Alice Springs ($320 one way), Cairns ($500), Perth ($600) and Sydney ($520). Flights from other capitals are routed through Alice Springs.

BUS

McCafferty's/Greyhound (☎ 13 14 99; www.mccaffertys.com.au) has daily services between Alice Springs and Uluru ($75, 5½ hours). Services between Adelaide and Uluru ($210) connect with the bus from Alice Springs at Erldunda. McCafferty's/Greyhound has a three-day Rock Pass from Alice Springs ($280). It includes transfers to Uluru and Kata Tjuta, a sunset tour and a guided tour of King's Canyon. It doesn't include the park entry fee or accommodation.

Australian Pacific Touring (☎ 1800 891 121) has a daily one-way transfer from Alice Springs to Uluru.

CAR & MOTORCYCLE

The road from the Alice to Yulara is sealed and there are regular food and petrol stops along the way. Yulara is 441km from Alice Springs, 241km west of Erldunda on the Stuart Hwy, and the whole journey takes about four to five hours.

If you don't have your own vehicle, renting a car in Alice Springs to go to Uluru and back can be expensive. You're looking at $60 to $100 a day for a car from the big

operators, and this only includes 100km a day, with each extra kilometre costing $0.28, but between four people it's cheaper than taking a bus there and back. See Car & Motorcycle (p806) for more information.

Getting Around

A free shuttle bus meets all flights and drops-off at all accommodation points around the resort.

The resort itself sprawls a bit, but it's not too large to get around on foot. A free **shuttle bus** runs between all accommodation points, the shopping centre and Frontier Camel Depot every 15 minutes from 10.30am to 6pm and 6.30pm to 12.30am daily.

Bike hire is available at the **Ayers Rock Resort Camp Ground** (☎ 8956 2055) for $30/40 per one/two days; a $200 deposit is required.

Uluru Express (☎ 8956 2152) falls somewhere between a shuttle bus service and an organised tour. It provides return transport from the resort to Uluru for $30/15 per adult/child (sunrise or sunset only $30/15). Morning shuttles to Kata Tjuta cost $45/25; afternoon shuttles include a stop at Uluru for sunset and cost $50/25.

Hiring a car gives you the flexibility to visit the Rock and the Olgas as often and whenever you want. **Hertz** (☎ 8956 2244) and **Avis** (☎ 8956 2266) have counters at the Tour & Information Centre in the resort shopping centre. **Territory Thrifty Car Rental** (☎ 8956 2030) is based at the Outback Pioneer Hotel – all three have desks at the airport. Hertz is the cheapest, with standby rates for small cars starting at about $50 a day with 100km.

Western Australia

CONTENTS

WESTERN AUSTRALIA

Visitors to Australia are often struck by its contrasting landscapes, immense size and sense of space. Nowhere are these qualities more apparent than in Western Australia (WA). Stretching from the foot of Southeast Asia to the Southern Ocean 2600km away, it is the continent's largest and most sparsely populated state. In the north you'll encounter rugged plains, dramatic gorges and waterfalls, isolated beaches and the most ancient rocks in the world. The south is a playground of snow-white beaches and turquoise waters, expanses of springtime wildflowers, and lush green karri forests that bristle with life and brush the sky. Cosmopolitan Perth and the vibrant southwest offer a rich gastronomic experience, with gourmet food and wines that rank with the best in the country. Inland is the rich, red arid interior, dotted with mysterious rock formations and eerie ghost towns – the Australia that many visitors come so far to see.

The west is packed with wonders – one of the most surprising is that it isn't overrun by visitors. Away from the most populated areas you can still wander along a beach for hours without seeing a footprint in the sand, be one of a handful of campers stargazing in a remote national park, or go bushwalking for days without seeing a soul.

Exploring WA thoroughly can be a challenge. Distances are vast, the terrain is often harsh and the elements can be forbidding. But the rewards are rich for those who make the effort.

TOP TEN

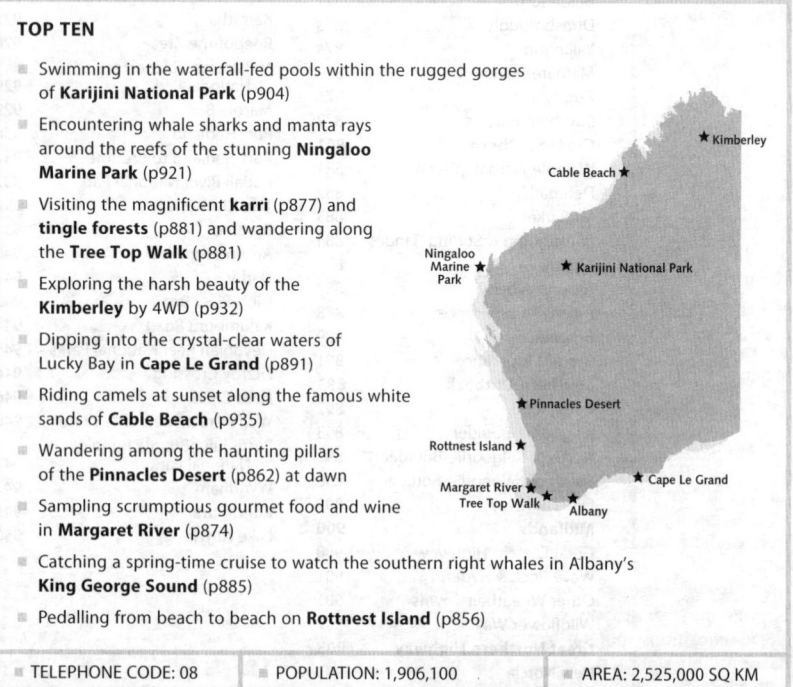

- Swimming in the waterfall-fed pools within the rugged gorges of **Karijini National Park** (p904)
- Encountering whale sharks and manta rays around the reefs of the stunning **Ningaloo Marine Park** (p921)
- Visiting the magnificent **karri** (p877) and **tingle forests** (p881) and wandering along the **Tree Top Walk** (p881)
- Exploring the harsh beauty of the **Kimberley** by 4WD (p932)
- Dipping into the crystal-clear waters of Lucky Bay in **Cape Le Grand** (p891)
- Riding camels at sunset along the famous white sands of **Cable Beach** (p935)
- Wandering among the haunting pillars of the **Pinnacles Desert** (p862) at dawn
- Sampling scrumptious gourmet food and wine in **Margaret River** (p874)
- Catching a spring-time cruise to watch the southern right whales in Albany's **King George Sound** (p885)
- Pedalling from beach to beach on **Rottnest Island** (p856)

★ Kimberley

Cable Beach ★

Ningaloo Marine ★ Park

★ Karijini National Park

★ Pinnacles Desert

Rottnest Island ★

Margaret River ★ ★ Tree Top Walk ★ Albany

★ Cape Le Grand

| TELEPHONE CODE: 08 | POPULATION: 1,906,100 | AREA: 2,525,000 SQ KM |

HISTORY

WA's proximity to the Indian Ocean trading routes led to early European contact with the Dutch. In 1616 Dirk Hartog was one of the first-known Europeans to land near the WA coast, and countryman Abel Tasman was the first to chart parts of the coastline in 1644.

William Dampier, an Englishman, comprehensively charted the coast in 1688 onboard the *Cygnet*, and in 1699 he returned to 'New Holland' to chart the coastline from the Houtman Abrolhos Islands, off the coast of Geraldton, as far north as Roebuck Bay, Broome.

Dampier's reports of a dry, barren land initially discouraged attempts at settlement, but French exploration in the late 18th century pushed the British to rethink the region. In 1826 Major Edmund Lockyer, some troops and a small party of convicts were sent from Sydney to establish a small military outpost at King George Sound (present-day Albany).

In 1829 the first British settlers arrived at the Swan River Settlement (later Perth). Because of its isolation, the region was seen as a natural prison, and in June 1850 the first group of convicts was transported to the new colony. For the next 18 years, convicts were used in the construction of public buildings and roads, and when settlers spread out into the southwest, many convicts went as their labour force.

WA's development as a British colony was painfully slow until the 1890s, when a series of gold rushes brought wealth and a renewed vigour to the state. With it came a strong sense of identity that was reinforced in the 1933 referendum for secession (Western Australians voted two to one in favour of leaving the Australian Commonwealth). Though their dream of breaking from the east coast didn't eventuate, a strong independent streak remains.

In the 1980s a group of high-flying entrepreneurs strutted across the business stage, epitomising Perth's nouveau riche, independent image, but by the early '90s political and corporate scandals had rocked the city and brought some high-profile bigwigs into bankruptcy court and prison. Today enormous mineral wealth forms the basis of the state's prosperity, which has created added challenges for negotiation over native title claims on land of interest to the mining companies and the Aboriginal people (for more information see the boxed text 'Aboriginal Australians'; p34).

ABORIGINAL PEOPLE

The state's archaeological record indicates that Aboriginal people lived as far south as present-day Perth at least 40,000 years ago. However, tragedy blights the more recent history of the Aboriginal people of WA, with tales of dispossession, incarceration and death. As elsewhere in Australia, the arrival of Europeans had disastrous consequences for the Aborigines. Pushed off their traditional lands, many who were not killed by the colonisers died of European diseases. Particularly hard hit were the Noongar people in the southwest.

After WWII many Aboriginal people banded together in protest against their appalling treatment on cattle stations, in the first public displays of political Aboriginal consciousness.

The 1992 *Mabo* ruling of the High Court on native title prompted the WA government to rush through its own Land Bill in December 1993 that protected mining and other landowners' interests. For more information on the *Mabo* decision, see the boxed text 'Aboriginal Australians' (p34). The state government of the time also unsuccessfully challenged the validity of the Commonwealth Native Title Act in the High Court. More than 120 native title claims have been made by Aboriginal people across the state – mainly on Crown land – with most currently going through mediation.

A history of dispossession and Western influences has bequeathed the state's Aboriginal population of 58,496 (14% of the nation's total) with more than its fair share of social problems. Aboriginal community leaders have called for greater autonomy in the use of the resources allocated to them.

GEOGRAPHY & CLIMATE

WA comprises one-third of the Australian land mass, and has a small fertile coastal strip in its southwest corner. Hills rise behind the coast, but are much smaller than those of the Great Dividing Range in the eastern states. Further north the landscape is dry and relatively barren. Fringing the central-west coast is the Great Sandy

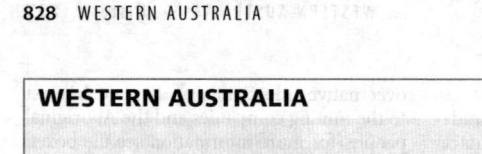

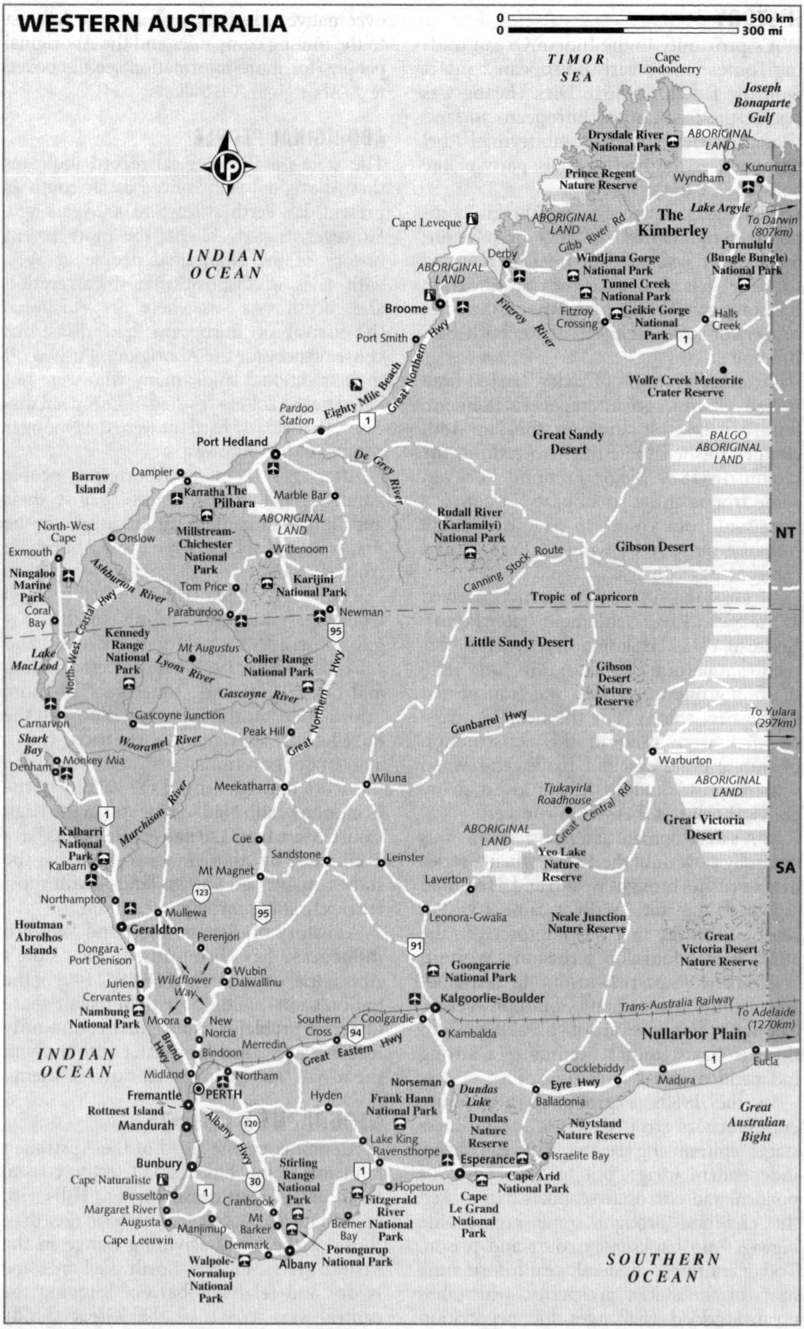
WESTERN AUSTRALIA
0 500 km
0 300 mi
TIMOR SEA
Cape Londonderry
Joseph Bonaparte Gulf
Drysdale River National Park
ABORIGINAL LAND
Kununurra
Wyndham
Prince Regent Nature Reserve
Lake Argyle
To Darwin (807km)
The Kimberley
Cape Leveque
ABORIGINAL LAND
Gibb River Rd
Derby
Windjana Gorge National Park
Purnululu (Bungle Bungle) National Park
INDIAN OCEAN
ABORIGINAL LAND
Tunnel Creek National Park
Broome
Fitzroy River
Fitzroy Crossing
Geikie Gorge National Park
Halls Creek
Port Smith
Great Northern Hwy
Eighty Mile Beach
Wolfe Creek Meteorite Crater Reserve
Pardoo Station
Port Hedland
Great Sandy Desert
BALGO ABORIGINAL LAND
De Grey River
Dampier
Barrow Island
Karratha
The Pilbara
Marble Bar
ABORIGINAL LAND
Rudall River (Karlamilyi) National Park
NT
North-West Cape
Onslow
Millstream-Chichester National Park
Wittenoom
Gibson Desert
Exmouth
Canning Stock Route
Ningaloo Marine Park
Ashburton River
Tom Price
Karijini National Park
Tropic of Capricorn
Coral Bay
Paraburdoo
Newman
North-West Coastal Hwy
Kennedy Range National Park
Mt Augustus
Little Sandy Desert
Lake MacLeod
Lyons River
Collier Range National Park
Gibson Desert Nature Reserve
Gascoyne River
Carnarvon
Gascoyne Junction
To Yulara (297km)
Gunbarrel Hwy
Shark Bay
Wooramel River
Peak Hill
Monkey Mia
Denham
Warburton
Meekatharra
Wiluna
Tjukayirla Roadhouse
ABORIGINAL LAND
Murchison River
Great Central Rd
Kalbarri National Park
Cue
ABORIGINAL LAND
Great Victoria Desert
Kalbarri
Sandstone
Leinster
Yeo Lake Nature Reserve
Mt Magnet
SA
Laverton
Northampton
Leonora-Gwalia
Mullewa
Neale Junction Nature Reserve
Houtman Abrolhos Islands
Geraldton
Perenjori
Great Victoria Desert Nature Reserve
Dongara-Port Denison
Wubin
Dalwallinu
Goongarrie National Park
Jurien
Wildflower Way
Cervantes
Kalgoorlie-Boulder
Trans-Australia Railway
Nambung National Park
Moora
New Norcia
Southern Cross
Coolgardie
To Adelaide (1270km)
Kambalda
Nullarbor Plain
Bindoon
Merredin
Brand Hwy
Great Eastern Hwy
INDIAN OCEAN
Eucla
Midland
Northam
Cocklebiddy
Norseman
Eyre Hwy
Madura
Fremantle
PERTH
Hyden
Dundas Lake
Balladonia
Rottnest Island
Frank Hann National Park
Mandurah
Albany Hwy
Great Australian Bight
Dundas Nature Reserve
Nuytsland Nature Reserve
Lake King
Ravensthorpe
Bunbury
Esperance
Israelite Bay
Stirling Range National Park
Cape Naturaliste
Cape Arid National Park
Hopetoun
Busselton
Cranbrook
Cape Le Grand National Park
Fitzgerald River National Park
Margaret River
Mt Barker
Augusta
Manjimup
Bremer Bay
Cape Leeuwin
Denmark
Porongurup National Park
Albany
Walpole-Nornalup National Park
SOUTHERN OCEAN

Desert, an inhospitable region running to the sea.

There are a couple of interesting variations, such as the Kimberley in the extreme north of the state – a wild and rugged area with a convoluted coastline and stunning inland gorges.

The Pilbara, in the northwest of the region, is magnificent ancient rock and gorge country from which the state derives vast mineral wealth. Away from the coast most of WA is simply a huge empty stretch of outback: the Nullarbor Plain in the south, the Great Sandy Desert in the north, and the Gibson and Great Victoria Deserts between.

The main climate zones are tropical (in the north), semiarid and arid (in the interior), and temperate (in the southwest). In general, rainfall decreases the further you get from the coast.

In the north the climate is characterised by the seasons known as the Dry and the Wet rather than winter and summer. Roughly, the Dry lasts from June to August and the Wet from December to February, with monsoonal rain falling from January onwards. As the monsoon develops there is thunderstorm activity, high humidity (the 'build-up'), followed by the occasional tropical cyclone. Although it makes many roads impassable, the rain is generally welcomed. Port Hedland sees a cyclone at least every two years.

Further south there is little rainfall during summer and the winds are generally hot, dry easterlies, though in the afternoon, coastal areas receive sea breezes such as the famed Fremantle Doctor.

INFORMATION

For general statewide information, try the excellent website of the **Western Australian Tourism Commission** (www.westernaustralia.net). Most country towns have their own visitors centre, but many are run by volunteers and get by on the smell of an oily rag – so don't expect miracles.

The **Royal Automobile Club of Western Australia** (RACWA; Map pp842-3; ☎ 08-9421 4444; www.rac.com.au; 228 Adelaide Tce, Perth) produces the excellent *Western Australia Experience Guide*, full of accommodation and touring information; its website has free basic maps to download (with distances, en-route facilities and road conditions).

For comprehensive information about the entire state, see also Lonely Planet's *Western Australia* guidebook.

Permits

You need a permit to enter or travel through Aboriginal land in WA. Permits are issued by the **Department of Indigenous Affairs** (☎ 08-9235 8000; www.dia.wa.gov.au; 197 St Georges Tce, Perth), and applications can be lodged on the Internet. For information on Aboriginal Culture Tours see p832.

NATIONAL PARKS

A visit to some of WA's national parks is a must, with most of the state's big-ticket natural attractions protected in these areas. Most parks are managed by the **Department of Conservation & Land Management** (CALM; ☎ 08-9334 0333; www.naturebase.net; Hackett Dr, Crawley, Perth), which has offices throughout the state. At the time of writing, 30 new national parks had been proposed, mostly as a means of protecting old-growth forests in the southwest. Names were still to be decided and even boundaries were fuzzy. Contact CALM for an update on these new protected areas.

Camping is allowed in designated areas of some parks (usually $12.50 per night for

YOUR TICKET TO NATURE

The national parks of Western Australia (WA) are some of the most spectacular in the country, and deserve a sizable chunk of your time in the west. Nature lovers can save some dosh with a Department of Conservation and Land Management (CALM) park pass: one of the most convenient is the Holiday Pass ($22.50), which gives unlimited entry for four weeks. If you need more time, the All Parks Annual Pass ($51) gives access for a year, while the Annual Local Park Pass ($17) gives 12 months' entry to one park. Passes are available from CALM and visitors centres around the state, as well as park entrances. Unfortunately, these passes do not cover entry to the Tree Top Walk or Monkey Mia Reserve. The unlucky folk who only have time for one or two parks should opt for the daily vehicle fee – $9 per car, per day ($3 for motorcycles and $3.40 for bus passengers).

two people). CALM produces informative brochures on the major national parks and nature reserves in the state, as well as reams of other literature and maps.

ACTIVITIES
Bird-Watching
WA is a bird-watcher's delight, with an enormous variety of species and two Birds Australia observatories – one in Eyre (p900) and the other in Broome (p940). Yalgorup National Park, south of Mandurah, is an important habitat for a wide variety of water birds, and is a magnet for local bird-watchers. The Kimberley is another twitchers' paradise, particularly in the Wet.

Bushwalking
Bushwalking clubs abound in Perth; you can get in touch with them through the umbrella organisation **Federation of Western Australia Bushwalking Clubs** (☎ 08-9362 1614; www.bushwalking.org.au/wapage.html).

The Stirling Range and Porongurup National Parks, both northeast of Albany, are prime bushwalking areas. There are also good walking tracks in coastal parks in the south and southwest, such as Walpole-Nornalup, Fitzgerald River, Cape Le Grand and Cape Arid. To the north the Kalbarri, Karijini and Purnululu National Parks provide an excellent, rugged walking environment.

There are interesting, varied walks through the hills around Perth, and for real enthusiasts there's the 964km Bibbulmun Track from Perth's outskirts to Albany; see the boxed text 'The Bibb Track' (below) for details. Information on this and many other tracks is available from CALM.

Bushwalking in much of the state's bushland is restricted because of the risk of spreading dieback, a nasty fungal disease that attacks the roots of plants and causes them to rot. Its spread can be prevented by observing 'no go' road signs and by cleaning soil from your boots before and after each walk.

Cycling
Rivalling the famous Bibb Track is the new **Munda Biddi Mountain Bike Trail** (www.munda biddi.org.au), which will eventually take off-road cyclists some 900km from Mundaring on Perth's outskirts through the beautiful scenic southwest to Albany on the south coast. The first stage (to Collie) has been completed, and you can pick up a map pack ($14.95) and more information from **CALM** (☎ 08-9334 0333).

Rottnest Island and Perth also offer excellent cycling conditions. For more tips, the **Bicycle Transportation Alliance** (☎ 08-9420 7210; www.multiline.com.au/~bta; 2 Delhi St, West Perth) produces a regular newsletter called *Cycling in the West*.

Crazy as it may seem, cyclists continue to make the long, arduous trip across the 1219km Nullarbor. This requires a tremendous amount of preparation and planning. Would you believe they do it just because it's there?

Diving
Divers have plenty of excellent possibilities in the west, particularly at Rottnest Island near Perth, the stunning reefs of the Ningaloo Marine Park and the artificial reefs created by sunken ships at Albany

---

THE BIBB TRACK

If you've got eight spare weeks up your sleeve, consider exploring the Bibbulmun Track, Western Australia's only true long-distance walking track that winds its way south from Kalamunda, near Perth, through virtually unbroken natural environment to Walpole and along the coast to Albany – a total of 964km. The first stages were officially opened in 1979, with the full track completed in 1998. Today bushwalkers trek through magnificent forest regions, passing by convenient snack stops at Dwellingup, Balingup, Pemberton, Northcliffe and Denmark along the way. Camp sites are spaced at regular intervals (there are 47), most with a three-sided shelter that sleeps eight to 12 people, plus a water tank and pit toilets.

Thousands of walkers use the Bibbulmun each year, though most are only on the track for two or three days. For more information, contact the nonprofit, community-run **Bibbulmun Track Foundation** (☎ 08-9481 0551; www.bibbulmuntrack.org.au), which can help with leaflets and advice, but also offers guided walks and a calendar of social events.

and Dunsborough. Older shipwrecks along the coast between Geraldton and Exmouth are also popular.

Fishing

With the longest coastline in the country, WA is a fisherman's paradise. Popular places to drop a line include Rottnest Island, Albany, Geraldton and the Houtman Abrolhos Islands, the Dampier Archipelago, Denham, Shark Bay, Northwest Cape, Broome and Kununurra.

Recreational fishing licences are required if you intend catching marron (freshwater crayfish) or rock lobsters, if you use a fishing net, or if you're freshwater angling in the southwest. They cost $20 to $35, or there's an annual licence covering all fishing activities for $70. Buy one from the **Department of Fisheries** (☎ 08-9482 7333; www.fish.wa.gov.au; SGIO Bldg, 168-170 St George's Tce, Perth), or from its regional offices.

Rock Climbing & Caving

WA's generally flat terrain does not great rock climbing make, but in the south, the sea cliffs of Wilyabrup, West Cape Howe and the Gap, and the huge cliffs of the Stirling and Porongurup Ranges attract plenty of daredevils. There are abseiling operations in the Murchison River gorges near Kalbarri and at Karijini National Park. The caves of the Margaret River region and the lesser-known 'holes' of Cape Range National Park offer plenty of opportunities for cavers.

Sailing, Canoeing & Kayaking

WA was once, briefly, the home of sailing's greatest prize, the America's Cup, and sailing is popular, especially on the sheltered Swan River.

Canoeing Western Australia (☎ 08-9285 8501; www.canoewa.asn.au) will provide information on the many good canoeing and kayaking rivers in the state.

Surfing

The state's surfing mecca is the southwest, particularly the beaches from Cape Naturaliste to Margaret River (see the boxed text 'Surfing WA'; p874). Another hotspot for your surf safari is the stretch from Geraldton to Kalbarri, particularly Jakes Corner (experienced surfers only). If you're stuck in the city, don't despair. Trigg

and Scarborough are nearby, and Rottnest Island is just a ferry trip away.

Windsurfers adore the windy conditions along Perth's city beaches and up in blustery Geraldton. Lancelin and Ledge Point are particularly popular for sailboarders and kitesurfers.

TOURS

If you don't feel like travelling solo or you crave hassle-free travels with everything organised for you, there are dozens of tours through WA to suit all tastes and budgets. A popular option is the jump-on, jump-off bus run by **Easyrider Backpacker Tours** (☎ 08-9226 0307; www.easyridertours.com.au; 144 William St). It's a fun, relaxed way to travel and a good way to meet people.

Options include a Southern Curl tour ($225), valid for three months, that departs two to five times a week from Perth and stops at Bunbury, Dunsborough, Margaret River, Augusta, Nannup, Pemberton, Walpole, Denmark and Albany. A longer southern option ($459) runs from December to March, and continues on to Wave Rock, Esperance, Kalgoorlie and York.

The Exmouth Exposure tour ($310) runs three days a week and will stop at all towns en route to Exmouth. The Broome trip ($559) leaves three days a week from April to November and once a week from December to March. The Over the Top tour ($949) runs two days a week from May to November, is valid for six months and goes all the way from Perth to Darwin.

The **Nullarbor Traveller** (☎ 1800 816 858; www.the-traveller.com.au) offers leisurely seven-day ($735) and nine-day ($945) minibus trips between Perth and Adelaide that take in camping, national parks and some great activities along the way, including stops at Wave Rock, Esperance, Eucla and SA's Streaky Bay.

Western Travel Bug (☎ 08-9204 4600, 1800 627 488; www.travelbug.com.au) is a southwest specialist, with day trips and tours from two to six days taking in Albany, Esperance and Wave Rock. There are separate day trips to the Pinnacles, Wave Rock and Margaret River, which cost $98/70 per adult/child each, while a four-day southwest tour is $495/400. Ask about YHA/VIP discounts.

With an enormous range of tours ranging from one-day Pinnacles trips ($125) to 24-day odysseys from Perth to Darwin ($3299), **Travelabout Outback Adventures** (☎ 08-9244 1200; www.travelabout.au.com) offers travellers the chance to go bush and see as many of the state's natural wonders as possible.

Finally, for something completely different, you can follow in the footsteps of the early explorers on one of **Dr Marion Hercock's Explorer Tours** (☎ 08-9361 0940; www.explorertours .com.au). Tours range from nine to 26 days, and whisk travellers off in 4WDs (no more than 10 people at a time) along the routes of 19th-century explorers, immersing them in the history of the time. Prices start at $1675 and include all meals, as well as guidance by experts in outback history, environment, flora and fauna.

Aboriginal Culture Tours

Tours that incorporate aspects of Aboriginal life and culture provide the best opportunity to make meaningful contact with Aboriginal people (for details of tours, see the relevant sections later in this chapter).

In the Kimberley, there are many operations run by local Aboriginal people. Operators include the Lombadina Aboriginal community and Middle Lagoon, both in the Dampier Peninsula, and Bungoolee Tours in Fitzroy Crossing.

The Purnululu Aboriginal Corporation and the Department of Conservation and Land Management (CALM) jointly manage the Purnululu (Bungle Bungle) National Park, one of the first attempts in Australia to balance the needs of local people with the demands of tourism. At Geikie Gorge, near Fitzroy Crossing, **Darngku Heritage Cruises** (☎ 08-9191 5552) offers a river cruise and cultural tour led by local Aboriginal people.

In the Pilbara region, Aborigines have worked closely with CALM in establishing an interpretive centre in the Karijini (Hamersley Range) National Park and an information centre in the Millstream Homestead that deals with the Yinjibarndi people's culture in Millstream-Chichester National Park.

GETTING THERE & AWAY

Qantas operates direct flights between Perth airport and Singapore, Tokyo, Denpasar (Bali), Jakarta, Hong Kong and Johannesburg. South African Airways flies direct between Perth and Johannesburg. Singapore Airlines, Malaysia Airlines, Thai Airways

and Garuda Indonesia all have direct flights from Perth to their home countries.

See Getting There & Away for Perth (p848), Broome (p933) and Kalgoorlie-Boulder (p897) for information on domestic transport into WA by air, bus and train.

GETTING AROUND

For information on getting around Perth, see p849.

Air

Qantas (☎ 13 13 13; www.qantas.com.au) has regular flights to Broome and Kalgoorlie. **Skywest** (☎ 1300 660 088; www.skywest.com.au) operates flights to many regional centres, including Albany, Esperance, Exmouth, Carnarvon and Kalgoorlie. Two- to 21-day advance-purchase tickets are cheaper, and students are eligible for discounts. **Northwest Regional Airlines** (☎ 1300 136 629; www.northwestregional.com .au) has daily flights to Broome, Fitzroy Crossing and Halls Creek, plus services to Karratha and Port Hedland (3 weekly).

Bus

McCafferty's/Greyhound (☎ 13 20 30) buses run from Perth along the coast to Darwin ($550, 60 hours), and from Perth to Adelaide ($265, 35¼ hours) via Kalgoorlie. Most people buy a kilometre pass (2000/5000/10,000km for $321/666/1231) or one of the set-route passes. Students and VIP/YHA cardholders are eligible for discounts. With kilometre passes, bear in mind that McCafferty's/Greyhound deducts double the kilometres for side trips off the main highway, such as to the Pinnacles, Kalbarri and Monkey Mia.

Perth Goldfields Express (☎ 1800 620 440; www.kalgoorlie.com/goldrush/express.asp) goes from Perth via Kalgoorlie to Laverton. **Integrity Coach Lines** (☎ 08-9226 1339; www.integritycoach lines.com.au) runs between Perth and Geraldton, Carnarvon, Coral Bay and Exmouth at least four times a week, and on to Broome twice a week. There's a 10% discount for YHA/VIP cardholders.

South West Coachlines (☎ 08-9324 2333) in the Transperth City Busport runs services from Perth to southwest towns such as Augusta, Bunbury, Busselton, Dunsborough, Nannup and Margaret River.

Transwa (☎ 1300 662 205; www.transwa.wa.gov.au) goes to Albany, Augusta, Esperance, Hyden, Kalgoorlie, Pemberton and York, and north to Geraldton, Kalbarri and Meekatharra. There's a 10% discount for concession card-holders, including YHA/VIP members.

Car

It's not surprising that many people end up hiring or buying a car to get around this monster of a state. Car travel offers a level of flexibility that is unmatched by other forms of transport. See p850 for information on car rental. Bear in mind that WA is not only enormous, it's also sparsely populated, so make safety preparations if you plan to travel any significant distance (for more information see Outback Travel; p993).

There are many spectacular, enticing areas of the state that don't have sealed roads, and a 4WD will come in handy. For instance, you'll need a 4WD to see any of the spectacular Kimberley, even in the Dry (you can hire one in Broome or Kununurra).

For up-to-date road information across the state, call ☎ 1800 013 314.

Train

WA's domestic rail network, operated by Transwa, is limited to services between Perth and Kalgoorlie (*Prospector*), Northam (*AvonLink*) and Bunbury (*Australind*); for details, see p849.

PERTH

☎ 08 / pop 1,380,000

Thousands of kilometres from the east-coast crowds, and set in the midst of stunning natural beauty, this vibrant, modern city perches on the pretty Swan River, which meanders down to the Indian Ocean. With its sunny disposition, first-rate ocean beaches, hillside hideaways and comfortable pace of life, it's not surprising the vast majority of West Australians choose to call the capital home. Despite its isolation, this friendly, easy-going city rivals its east-coast brethren for quality of life, with top-class food and wine, vibrant nightlife, a wealth of cultural events and more days of sunshine than any other capital city in the country.

HISTORY

The site of what is now Perth was occupied by groups of the Aboriginal Noongar tribe for thousands of years before the first

Europeans settled here. The Swan River Settlement was founded in 1829 and grew very slowly until 1850, when convicts were brought in to alleviate the labour shortage. Many of the city's fine buildings, such as Government House and the Perth Town Hall, were built with convict labour. Perth's development lagged behind that of the eastern cities until the discovery of gold in the 1890s increased the population fourfold in a decade and initiated a building boom. Unfortunately, many of these 19th-century buildings have been lost, replaced with towering glass and concrete. For remnants of the colonial days, see the Walking Tour (p838).

ORIENTATION

Perth's compact city centre sits on a sweeping bend of the Swan River, with waterfront to the south and east. Shoppers buzz through the Hay St and Murray St Malls and adjoining arcades, while the city's suits wheel and deal along St George's Tce, which is the centre of the Perth's business

PERTH IN...

Two Days
Catch the free Central Area Transit (CAT) bus to the major sights, including the **Perth Cultural Centre** (p837), the **Swan Bell Tower** (p837) and beautiful **Kings Park** (p837) with lush bushland and wonderful views. Grab dinner and drinks in one of Northbridge's many excellent restaurants or historic pubs. On your second day, head to popular **Fremantle** (p850) to visit the new **maritime museum** (p851) and spend a leisurely afternoon on the **cappuccino strip** (p855). Catch a train or ferry back to Perth for a meal in swish **Subiaco** (p846) or groovy **Leederville** (p846).

Four Days
Follow the two-day itinerary, then choose between a **winery cruise** (p840) on the Swan River, indulging in the region's best cheese and wine, or catch the ferry to **Rottnest Island** (p856) for a day of cycling around the virtually car-free island. On your final day, catch the bus to **Cottesloe** (p838) or **Scarborough** (p838) for a day of swimming and lazing in the sun.

WESTERN AUSTRALIA

GREATER PERTH

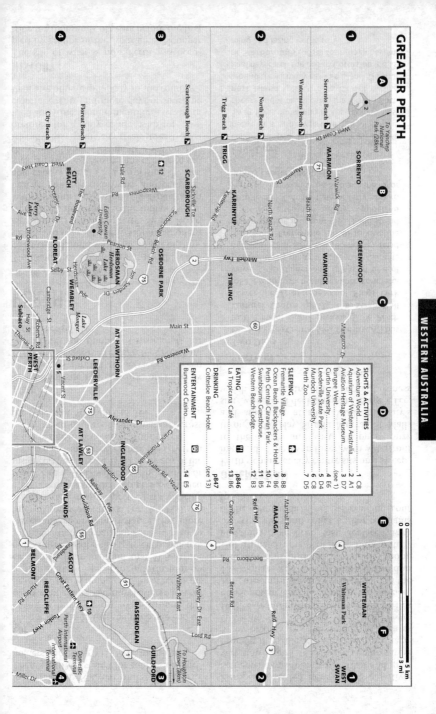

SIGHTS & ACTIVITIES	
Adventure World.......................	1 C8
Aquarium of Western Australia..	2 A1
Aviation Heritage Museum........	3 D7
Bungee West............................	(see 1)
Curtin University......................	4 E6
Leederville Skate Park..............	5 D4
Murdoch University...................	6 C8
Perth Zoo.................................	7 D5

SLEEPING	
Fremantle Village......................	8 B8
Ocean Beach Backpackers & Hotel..	9 B6
Perth Central Caravan Park.......	10 F4
Swanbourne Guesthouse...........	11 B5
Western Beach Lodge................	12 B3

EATING	p846
La Tropicana Café.....................	13 B6

DRINKING	p847
Cottesloe Beach Hotel..............	(see 13)

ENTERTAINMENT	
Burswood Casino......................	14 E5

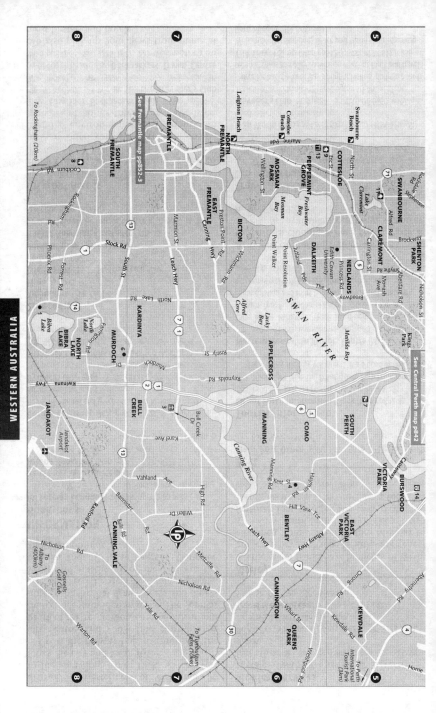

district. The western end of Perth slopes up to the sprawling Kings Park, which overlooks the city and Swan River.

Cross the railway line, just north of the city centre, and you'll find Northbridge, heart of the restaurant, entertainment and budget-accommodation scene. The popular inner suburbs that draw winers and diners are Subiaco, Leederville and Highgate. West and northwest of the city are the popular Indian Ocean beaches, Cottesloe and Scarborough.

INFORMATION
Bookshops

All Foreign Languages Bookshop (Map pp842-3; ☎ 9321 9275; 101 William St) Stocks a wide variety of travel books and language guides.

Arcane Bookshop (Map pp842-3; ☎ 9328 5073; 212 William St, Northbridge) Has an eclectic collection for an arty audience, and stocks the free gay and lesbian newspaper, *OutinPerth*.

Boffins Bookshop (Map pp842-3; ☎ 9321 5755; 806 Hay St) Technical and specialist books, including good Australiana and travel sections.

Dymocks (Map pp842-3; ☎ 9321 3969; Hay St Mall) You won't surface for hours in this sprawling chain store.

Elizabeth's Secondhand Bookshop (Map pp842-3; ☎ 9481 8848; 820 Hay St) Catalogued selection of second-hand books and magazines.

Emergency

Ambulance (☎ 000)
Fire (☎ 000)
Lifeline (☎ 13 11 14) Crisis counselling.
Police (☎ 000)
Police station (☎ 9222 1111)
RACWA Roadside Assistance (☎ 13 11 11)
Sexual Assault Resource Centre (☎ 9340 1828) Crisis line open 24 hours.

Internet Access

Cheap Internet rates are very easy to find along William St between Murray and Wellington Sts. You'll find that travel companies are often your best bet, with comfy, friendly environments, fast connection speeds and bonus travel tips and advice. Try **Easyrider Backpacker Tours** (Map pp834-5; ☎ 9226 0307; 144 William St), the **Traveller's Club** (Map pp842-3; ☎ 9226 0660; 499 Wellington St) or Northbridge's **Backpackers Travel Centre** (Map pp842-3; ☎ 9228 1877; 223 William St). You can also pick up your news from home at most hostels and hotels.

Medical Services

Lifecare – Dentist (Map pp842-3; ☎ 9221 2777; Forrest Chase; ☷ 8am-8pm) Directly opposite the train station.

Royal Perth Hospital (Map pp842-3; ☎ 9224 2244; Victoria Sq) Close to the city centre.

Travel Medicine Centre (Map pp842-3; ☎ 9321 7888; 5 Mill St; ☷ 8am-5.30pm Mon-Fri)

Money

All the major banks have branches in Perth, and currency-exchange facilities are generally open from 9.30am to 4pm Monday to Thursday (until 5pm Friday). There's also **American Express** (Amex; Map pp842-3; ☎ 1300 132 639; 109 St George's Tce) and **Thomas Cook** (Map pp842-3; ☎ 9321 7811; 760 Hay St).

Post

Main Post Office (GPO; ☎ 9326 5211; Forrest Pl; ☷ 8am-5.30pm Mon-Fri, 9am-12.30pm Sat)

Tourist Information

City of Perth Information Kiosk (Map pp842-3; ☎ 1300 361 351; cnr Forrest Pl & Murray St Mall; ☷ 10am-4pm Mon-Thu & Sat, 10am-8pm Fri, noon-4pm Sun) Staffed by friendly volunteers, it's a good option if the visitors centre is closed.

Western Australian Visitors Centre (Map pp842-3; ☎ 1300 361 351; www.westernaustralia.net; Albert Facey House, Forrest Pl; ☷ 8.30am-6pm Mon-Thu, 8.30am-7pm Fri, 8.30am-12.30pm Sat) Offers an accommodation and tours booking service, and multiple brochures on Perth and WA. Closes an hour earlier on weekdays in winter.

Also look out for the numerous free guides to Perth, including *What's On in Perth & Fremantle*, available from visitors centres, hostels and hotels.

Travel Agencies

Backpackers Travel Centre (Map pp842-3; ☎ 9228 1877; www.backpackerstravel.net.au; 223 William St, Northbridge) Budget travel and tours, and Internet access.

Map World (Map pp842-3; ☎ 9322 5733; 900 Hay St) Good selection of regional maps.

Traveller's Club (Map pp842-3; ☎ 9226 0660; www.travellersclub.com.au; 499 Wellington St) An excellent source for backpackers. Has a huge travellers' bulletin board, sells VIP cards and offers advice on discount tours and travel.

YHA Travel Shop (Map pp842-3; ☎ 9227 5122; 259 William St, Northbridge) Office and travel shop adjoining Northbridge's YHA Britannia.

SIGHTS

Perth's major attractions are all within easy reach of the city centre, and many have their own stops on the free Central Area Transit (CAT) bus service route (p849).

Perth Cultural Centre
Map pp842–3

Bounded by Roe, Francis, Beaufort and William Sts, just north of the Perth train station, the Perth Cultural Centre includes the state museum, gallery, library and the Perth Institute of Contemporary Arts.

Wander through the large **Western Australian Museum** (☎ 9427 2700; www.museum.wa.gov.au; James St Mall; admission gold coin donation; ☉ 9.30am-5pm) for an insight into the state's geology and early history (both Aboriginal and European). Highlights include a gallery of Aboriginal culture, a marine gallery and a large collection of meteorites. Don't forget to poke your head into Perth's Old Gaol (1856), which has fascinating displays of colonial Perth. Out in the courtyard, floating in its own preservative bath, is 'Megamouth', a large and extremely rare big-mouthed shark that is one of the ugliest creatures you're ever likely to see.

The **Art Gallery of Western Australia** (☎ 9492 6600; www.artgallery.wa.gov.au; 47 James St; admission free; ☉ 10am-5pm) is accessed from the footbridge directly behind the Perth train station. It has a fine permanent exhibition of European, Australian and Asia-Pacific art, including a rich display of Aboriginal art, and regular temporary exhibitions.

The **Perth Institute of Contemporary Arts** (PICA; ☎ 9227 6144; www.pica.org.au; 51 James St; ☉ 11am-8pm Tue-Sun) promotes the creation and presentation of new and experimental art. Ask about performances, which are regularly held in the Blue Room.

Kings Park
Map pp842–3

It's surprisingly easy to escape the city hubbub by wandering up to the tranquil hill-top **Kings Park and Botanic Garden** (☎ 9480 3659; Kings Park Rd, West Perth), with superb views of the sweeping Swan River and city. Set in the midst of 400 hectares of natural bushland, the garden boasts over 2500 WA plant species, with many of them in full flower during the October **wildflower festival**. Just 1.5km from the city centre, the park's peace and quiet is only occasionally broken by the raucous chorus of the local birdlife.

Next to the car park is a kiosk and **visitors centre** (☎ 9480 3659; ☉ 9.30am-4pm). Free guided walks by enthusiastic volunteers start opposite the war memorial at 10am and 2pm daily. Kings Park is a pleasant stroll up Mount St from the city, crossing the freeway overpass. Those who want to save their legs can catch the Red CAT bus service to the entrance or hop on the Perth Tram (p840).

Other Inner-City Attractions

The **Perth Mint** (Map pp842-3; ☎ 9421 7218; 300-310 Hay St; adult/child $7/3.50; ☉ 9am-4pm Mon-Fri, closes 1pm Sat & Sun) was originally opened in 1899 and still handles a tonne of gold every day – so security is tight! On the regular daily heritage tours, visitors can imagine what life was like in the heady goldfield days and watch molten gold being poured into gold bars. You can also mint your own coins, handle a solid gold bar and find out how much your weight would be worth in gold.

The distinctive green-glass **Swan Bell Tower** (Map pp842-3; Barrack St Jetty; adult/child $6/3; ☉ 10am-5pm), encased in copper sails, houses historic royal bells donated to Perth by the Academy of St-Martin-in-the-Fields, London. Visitors climb to the observation deck for river views, and can hear the bells ring from noon to 2pm daily.

Allan Green Plant Conservatory (Map pp842-3; The Esplanade; admission free; ☉ 10am-4pm, opens noon Sun), tucked away on the edge of parkland, houses a tropical and semitropical controlled-environment display.

South of the river across Narrows Bridge is one of Perth's landmarks: the finely restored, National Trust–classified **Old Mill** (☎ 9367 5788; Mill Point Rd, South Perth; adult/child $2/1; ☉ 10am-4pm Mon, Thu & Fri), which was built in 1835.

Perth Suburbs

Swan Valley **vineyards** are dotted along the river from Guildford to the Upper Swan, and many are open for tastings and cellar sales. A good place to start is **Houghton Wines** (☎ 9274 5100; Dale Rd, Middle Swan; ☉ 10am-5pm), which produced its first vintage in 1859.

Lake Monger, in Wembley, northwest of the city centre, is a hangout for local feathered friends, particularly the black swans, emblem of Perth.

Around 10km south of the city is the excellent **Aviation Heritage Museum** (Map pp834-5; ☎ 9311 4470; Bull Creek Dr, Bull Creek; adult/child $9/4; ☺ 10am-4pm), with a large collection of aviation memorabilia including a Spitfire and a Lancaster bomber.

ACTIVITIES

Bungee Jumping

Thrill-seekers can head south to **Bungee West** (Map pp834-5; ☎ 9417 2500; Progress Dr, Bibra Lake; $80; ☺ Wed-Mon, weather permitting), where they can leap from a 40m tower for the ultimate adrenaline rush. Bungee West is an easy 15km drive south of Perth down the Kwinana Fwy; take the Farrington Rd exit and follow the brown tourist signs to Adventure World, which is nearby. If you don't have your own wheels, it takes about an hour by bus, with one change. Catch Bus No 881 from the Wellington St bus station to the Carrington St/Rockingham Rd stop, walk 30m to the Carrington St/Forrest Rd stop and catch Bus No 510 to Progress Dr.

Cycling

Cycling is an excellent way to explore the city. Bicycle routes follow the Swan River all the way to Fremantle and along the Indian Ocean coast. The energetic can download city cycling maps from the website of the **Department for Planning and Infrastructure** (☎ 9216 8558; www.dpi.wa.gov.au/metro).

Need to rent some wheels? Try the **Cycle Centre** (Map pp842-3; ☎ 9325 1176; 282 Hay St; per day $18). If you feel like a tootle around the many tracks in Kings Park, bikes are available from **Koala Bike Hire** (☎ 9321 3061; Frazer Ave; per hr $5; ☺ 9am-4.30pm, closes 6pm Sat & Sun), on the western side of the main car park.

Swimming & Surfing

Perth locals swear they have the best city beaches in Australia, and with that clean white sand and warm aquamarine water, who can argue? Close to town, surf-free beaches on the Swan River include **Crawley**, **Peppermint Grove** and **Como**. As the summer temperature cranks up, the masses descend upon the patrolled surf beaches on the Indian Ocean coast. There's lovely **Cottesloe**, a safe-swimming beach popular with families; **Scarborough**, further north, with its wide, golden sands and permanent population of surfers and body-boarders;

and the comparatively quiet **City** and **Floreat** beaches in between. **Trigg Island** is another surf mecca, though it can be dangerous when rough. If you dare to bare, strip off and head to **Swanbourne**.

Catch any nonexpress Fremantle-bound train for Cottesloe and Swanbourne – in each case there's a bit of a walk to get to the beach itself. Alternatively, bus No 71 or 72 (destination Cottesloe) from the City Busport will get you to Cottesloe and Swanbourne. For Scarborough, take bus No 400 from the Wellington St bus station.

Whale-Watching

From September to December, humpback whales pass by Perth on their annual journey to Antarctic waters, offering visitors a once-in-a-lifetime encounter. **Mills Charters** (☎ 9246 5334; www.millscharters.com.au; adult/child $45/25) runs an informative three-hour whale-watching trip from Hillary's Boat Harbour. To get to Hillary's, take the train to Warwick and bus No 423 from there. Other whale-watching operators are **Rottnest Express** (☎ 9335 6406) and **Oceanic Cruises** (☎ 9325 1191), which both leave from Fremantle.

WALKING TOUR

The civic mothers and fathers haven't been kind to central Perth – charming old buildings have been bulldozed and replaced with giant concrete and glass towers. This tour, which commences at the Western Australian Visitors Centre on Forrest Pl, traces some remnants of the old Perth.

WALKING TOUR

Distance: 5.5km
Duration: 1½ hours

Pass the main post office, and duck down one of the arcades to the Hay St Mall. Turn left and look for the 1937 mock-Tudor **London Court** (1; p848) on your right. Wander down the cobblestone, souvenir-laden shopping court, with St George and the dragon at one end and jousting knights at the other.

Turn left at the end, follow St George's Tce to Barrack St, and head uphill to the historic **Perth Town Hall** (2), built by convicts in 1868–70. Backtrack to St George's Tce

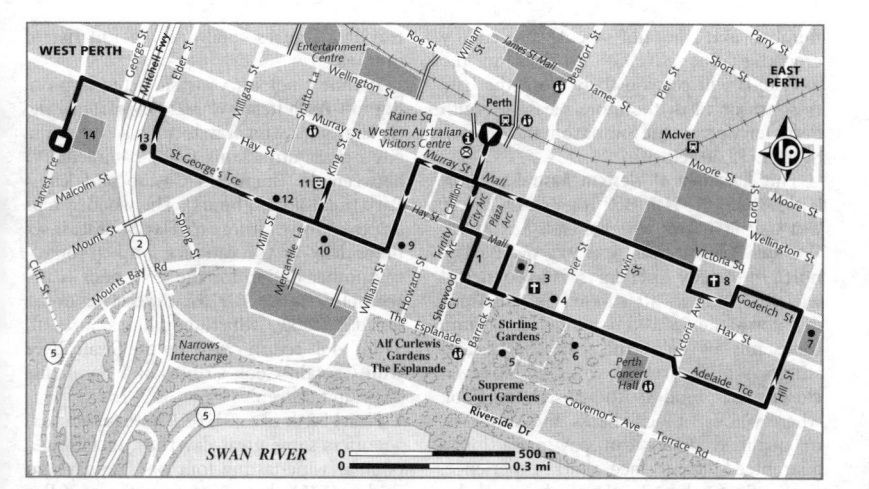

and turn left, passing the red-brick 1888 **St George's Cathedral** (**3**), constructed from local stone and jarrah. On the corner of Pier St is the 1859 **Deanery** (**4**), one of the few cottage-style houses that have survived from colonial days. Cross St George's Tce to get a closer look at the tranquil Stirling Gardens, which houses the Supreme Court and the 1836 Georgian-style **courthouse** (**5**), one of the oldest buildings in Perth. Further along St George's Tce is the Gothic-looking **Government House** (**6**), built 1859–64.

Follow St George's Tce to Hill St (at Victoria Ave, St George's Tce becomes Adelaide Tce). Turn left and head up to Hay St. On the right is the **Perth Mint** (**7**; p837). Continue up to Goderich St, head left to Victoria Square and you'll find the 1863 Gothic-style **St Mary's Cathedral** (**8**) and a grassy area popular with lunch-munching office workers. Follow Murray St, on the far side of the square, west to William St. Turn left into William St and return to St George's Tce. On the corner is the grand and once extravagant **Palace Hotel** (**9**), from 1895, now a banking chamber. Turn right into St George's Tce and head down to King St – on your left, at No 139, is the 1854 **Old Perth Boys' School** (**10**), which now houses Revely's Cafe.

At King St turn right and follow it to Hay St. On the corner is the restored Edwardian **His Majesty's Theatre** (**11**; 1904); there are free foyer tours of the 'Maj' between 10am and 4pm daily, and two-hour backstage 'Behind the Scenes' tours at 10.30am Thursday ($12,

book ahead on ☎ 9265 0900). Return to St George's Tce and turn right. Walk a short distance and note the beautiful brickwork of the **Cloisters** (**12**; 1858), originally a school, now part of a modern office development on your right. Towering glass structures line the road up to the distinctive **Barracks Archway** (**13**). It's all that remains of a barracks built in 1863 to house the pensioner guards of the British army – discharged soldiers who guarded convicts.

On the far side of the Mitchell Fwy is **Parliament House** (**14**). Tours of the parliament buildings can be arranged on weekdays through the parliamentary information officer (☎ 9222 7222) – you will of course get a more extensive tour when parliament is not in session. Take the Red CAT from Harvest Tce to return to the city centre.

PERTH FOR CHILDREN

There's plenty of great stuff to do in Perth that will keep the young 'uns happy. Cycling along the riverfront and ferry rides to Rottnest Island are popular boredom busters, as is the **Awesome Festival** (www.awesomearts.com) in November, a contemporary arts festival for children aged five to 16.

Perth Zoo (Map pp834–5; ☎ 9474 0444; www .perthzoo.wa.gov.au; 20 Labouchere Rd, South Perth; adult/child/family $14/7/37.50; 🕒 9am-5pm) is just a short ferry ride across the Swan River from the city. Visitors enjoy an up-close peek at many native animals, including wombats, wallabies and kangaroos, the adorable rare numbat and the not-so-cute-and-cuddly crocodile. Bus No 35 (No 108 on the weekend) will get you there from the City Busport, or catch the more pleasant South Perth ferry across the Swan from the Barrack St Jetty ($2.20 return).

The **Aquarium of Western Australia** (AQWA; Map pp834-5; ☎ 9447 7500; Hillary's Boat Harbour, West Coast Dr, Hillarys; adult/child/family $20/12.50/58; ☿ 10am-5pm year-round, closes 9pm Wed Dec-Apr), north of the city in Hillarys, is a wonderful way to spend an afternoon. As you wander down the 98m-long tunnel aquarium, thousands of colourful fish, sharks and stingrays glide around you. For an even closer look, head to the Discovery Pool, where you can touch sharks and stingrays, or qualified divers can pay extra for a guaranteed face-to-face shark experience. From September to December, whale-watching trips are also available from the aquarium. To get there from the Perth train station, take the Joondalup train to Warwick Station, then bus No 423 to Hillarys.

About 27km southeast of the city is **Tumbulgum Farm** (☎ 9525 5888; www.tumbulgumfarm .com.au; 1475 South Western Hwy, Mundijong; farm shows adult/child $13/6.50, Aboriginal culture displays $10/5; ☿ 9.30am-5pm), where you can get a taste for farm life and watch an aboriginal cultural show of music and dance.

Science nuts, young and old, will be amused for hours in the **Scitech Discovery Centre** (Map pp842-3; ☎ 9481 5789; www.scitech .org.au; cnr Railway Pde & Sutherland St, West Perth; adult/ child $12/8; ☿ 10am-5pm). From the Perth train station, catch the free train to City West on the Fremantle line.

Skateboarders can practise their skills at the graffiti-splattered **Leederville Skate Park** (Map pp834-5; ☎ 9328 3221; 60 Frame Ct, Leederville; child $2), with ramps for all sizes, plus a café and Internet. Skateboard hire is $5 and supervising adults get in for free. But a sign warns: queue here to hurt the head.

Older kids can get their thrills on the Powersurge and Rampage rides at **Adventure World** (Map pp834-5; ☎ 9417 9666; Progress Dr, Bibra Lake; adult/child $31.50/25; ☿ 10am-5pm Sep-Apr), a large amusement park 15km south of the city.

TOURS

There are countless tours on offer, so head to the visitors centre or one of the budget

traveller centres (p836) for a full list of options.

If time's not on your side, the hop-on, hop-off **Perth Tram** (☎ 9322 2006; adult/child $20/ 10) is a quick, fun way to tour some of the city's main attractions (with commentary) between the Burswood Casino and Kings Park (full tour 1½ hours). The wooden replica tram leaves from 565 Hay St at least six times daily, or you can pick it up en route.

Another option for the time-poor is the **Tourist Trifecta** (☎ 9322 2006; www.perthtram.com.au; adult/child $60/30), which combines a Perth Tram tour, return cruise up the Swan River with Captain Cook Cruises and Fremantle Tram in between.

Planet Perth (☎ 9225 6622; www.planettours.com .au) offers some great day trips, including a popular wine-tasting tour on Tuesday and Friday ($45) that visits four Swan Valley wineries and a boutique cheese factory. An after-dark trip into Caversham Wildlife Park on Monday ($45) features a big barbecue and plenty of animal interaction. You can also go bush on Monday and Thursday afternoon with horse-riding trips ($70). YHA/VIP members get a 5% discount.

Many companies offer day trips to the Pinnacles and Wave Rock, and extended trips (from two days) to the southwest. See p831 for more information.

Cruises

Several cruise companies run tours from Barrack St Jetty, including **Boat Torque** (☎ 9221 5844; www.boattorque.com.au), **Captain Cook Cruises** (☎ 9325 3341; www.captaincookcruises.com.au) and **Oceanic Cruises** (☎ 9325 1191; www.oceaniccrui ses.com.au). They offer lunch and dinner cruises on the Swan River, winery visits, and trips to Fremantle and Rottnest Island (p860).

Captain Cook Cruises offers a three-hour river cruise around Perth and Fremantle ($29/14 per adult/child), and a day cruise to the Swan Valley vineyards ($99/58). For wildlife enthusiasts, Oceanic Cruises offers the popular Carnac Island Luncheon Eco Cruise from October to April ($79/39 per adult/child), which includes a guided beach walk with a marine biologist, snorkelling and a buffet lunch.

FESTIVALS & EVENTS

Both the **Perth International Arts Festival** (www .perthfestival.com.au) and the **WA Fringe Festival**

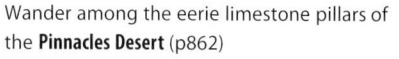

DIANA MAYFIELD

Swim in the glorious pools at the foot of **Fortescue Falls** (p904)

Wander among the eerie limestone pillars of
the **Pinnacles Desert** (p862)

CHRISTOPHER GROENHOUT

DIANA MAYFIELD

Walk across a carpet of wildflowers on **Wildflower Way** (p902)

Gaze in wonder at the spectacular tiers of **Mitchell Falls** (p944)

RICHARD I'ANSON

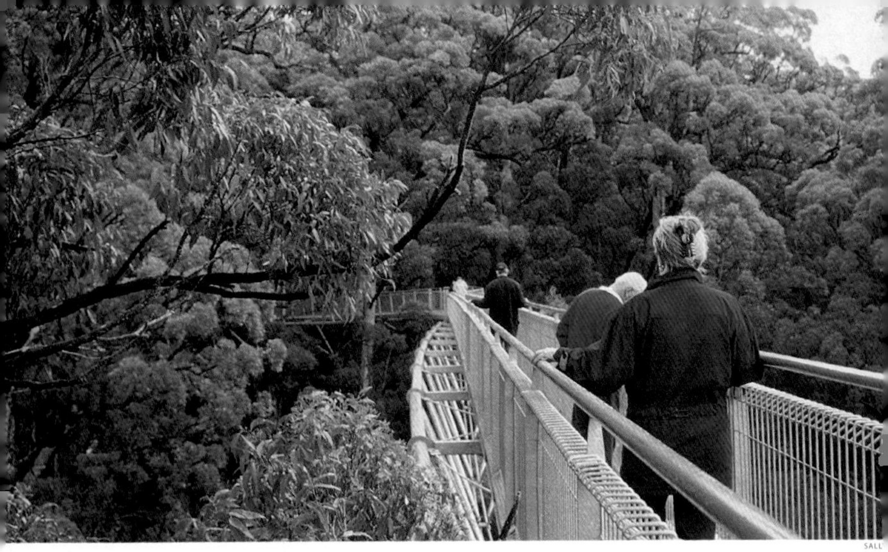

SALL

Wander along the Tree Top Walk in the **Valley of the Giants** (p881)

RICHARD I'ANSON

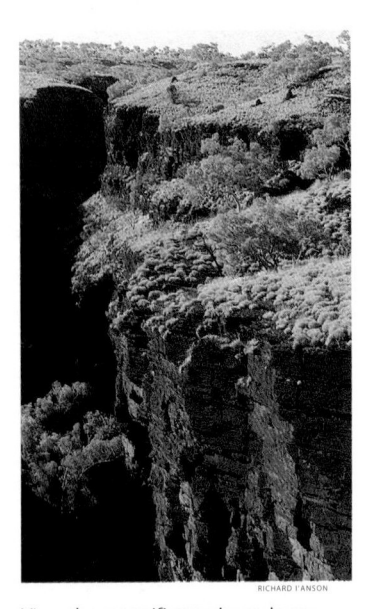

View the magnificent sheer drops of Karijini National Park's **Knox Gorge** (p904)

Drive through a splendid **karri forest** (p877)

NICOLA

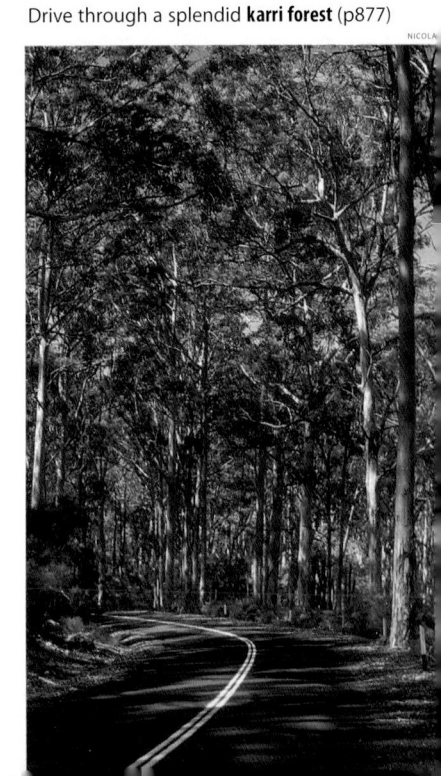

(www.adventureworld.net.au) offer packed programmes of music, drama, dance and films in January and February. For details on how to get there, see Bungee West (p830). For a taste of rural life, there's the **Perth Royal Show** (www.perthroyalshow.com.au) in late September, and for local contemporary arts and culture, check out **Artrage** (www.artrage.com.au) in October. Perth's **Gay Pride March** (www.pridewa.asn.au) is also held in October.

SLEEPING
Budget
HOSTELS

The budget traveller is well catered for in Perth, with possibly more backpacker hostels than the city needs. Competition is fierce and the choice often comes down to management, atmosphere and location. Needless to say, we can't list all hostels here; these are some of our favourites. Most hostels give a $1 discount for VIP, YHA or Nomads cards and offer significantly cheaper rates for longer stays. Internet access is usually available for $4 to $5 per hour. Be aware that in a bid to weed out 'undesirables', some hostels don't always give Australians the warmest welcome, demanding a passport or a driving licence to prove they are genuine travellers. All accommodation options have shared facilities unless otherwise stated.

City

Exclusive Backpackers (☎ 9221 9991; exclusiv@pielink .com; 158 Adelaide Tce; dm/s/d $15/35/50, d with bathroom $50-55) This charming hostel has won rave reviews from readers for its friendliness and warm, welcoming atmosphere. At the time of writing, new modern doubles with bathrooms were being built at the back.

Hay Street Backpackers (Map pp842-3; ☎ 9221 9880; 266-268 Hay St; dm/s/d $20/35/50, d with shower $60; 🛜 🖳 P) With excellent facilities (don't forget a dip in the pool) and comfortable rooms, this characterful house east of the city centre is a popular option. Cheaper weekly rates are available.

Grand Central Backpackers (Map pp842-3; ☎ 9421 1123; grandcentralbp@hotmail.com; 379 Wellington St; dm/s/d $18/36/50; 🖳) Pass the austere grey exterior into a bright, rambling former hotel with a low-key, cruisy vibe and a roomy Internet lounge. Cheaper weekly rates are available.

Northbridge

Underground Backpackers (Map pp842-3; ☎ 9228 3755; underground@electrolley.com.au; 268 Newcastle St; dm $19-22, tw & d $60; 🛜 🖳 P) Bright, breezy and brimming with facilities, this sprawling, social 170-bed hostel is an excellent place to meet people. Guests kick back in the bar, by the pool or in the cavernous TV room.

Spinner's Backpackers (Map pp842-3; ☎ 9328 9468; www.ic-net.com.au/~spinners; 342 Newcastle St; dm/d $17/45; 🛜 🖳 P) If you prefer smaller digs, try the friendly Spinner's (run by a former sheep-farming stand-up comic), with a comfortable lounge, good kitchen facilities, a laid-back atmosphere and a 50m stroll to La Bog (see Drinking; p846).

Governor Robinson's (Map pp842-3; ☎ 9328 3200; www.govrobinsons.com.au; 7 Robinson Ave; dm/d $20/55; 🛜 🖳) With only 15 rooms, peace and quiet is almost guaranteed at this beautifully renovated cottage with small dorms, welcoming staff and a home-away-from-home ambience.

Witch's Hat (☎ 9228 4228, 1800 818 358; www.witchs-hat.com; 148 Palmerston St; dm/d/tw $20/60/50; 🛜 🖳 P) This beautiful Federation-style building on Northbridge's outskirts boasts spacious, clean rooms, excellent facilities and a mellow atmosphere. Look for the distinctive turret at the front – it lights up like a beacon at night to guide you home from the pub!

Northbridge YHA (Map pp842-3; ☎ 9328 7794; northbridge@yhawa.com.au; 46 Francis St; dm from $18, d & tw from $55, nonmembers extra $3.50; 🖳) Right in the thick of the Northbridge action, this small former guesthouse is within stumbling distance of the area's finest pubs, and wins fans from the party crowd.

Britannia YHA (Map pp842-3; ☎ 9328 6121; britannia@yhawa.com.au; 253 William St; dm/s/d from $19/ 35/60, nonmembers extra $3.50; 🖳) Just minutes from the pub scene, this huge, efficiently run place attracts an older clientele with its low-key atmosphere, pleasant rooms and free breakfast and linen.

Cottesloe & Scarborough   Map pp834-5

Cottesloe, west of Perth, has a small, popular scrap of beach and a strip of beachfront cafés. Further north is Scarborough, with a long, white beach and better surf.

Ocean Beach Backpackers (☎ 9384 5111; www.obh.com.au/backpackers; cnr Marine Pde & Eric St, Cottesloe; dm/d/f $18/55/75; 🖳 P) Still in its

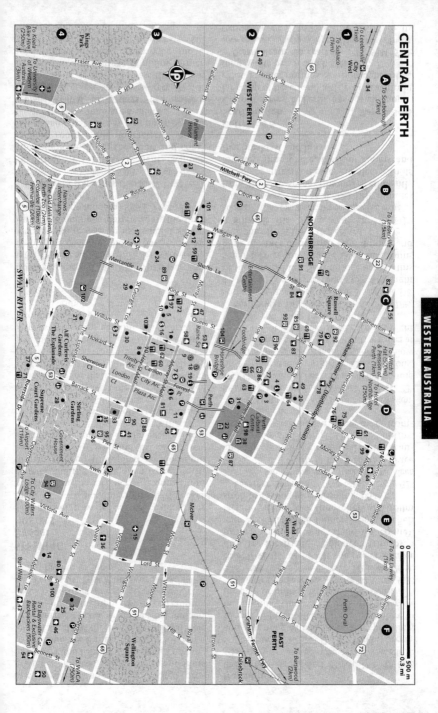

CENTRAL PERTH

WESTERN AUSTRALIA

0   500 m
0   0.3 mi

infancy, this bright beachside hostel behind the 'Obie' hotel has a friendly vibe and is already a favourite with beach-loving backpackers. Even the dorms have private bathrooms and fridge.

Western Beach Lodge (☎ 9245 1624; 6 Westborough St, Scarborough; dm/d $17/40, d with bathroom $50; 🖳 🅿) Just 500m from the beach, this small, clean converted house is tucked into a residential street at the back of Scarborough.

CAMPING
Most Perth caravan parks are in the suburbs, so having your own transport is always handy. Ask at the visitors centre for a full list of options.

Perth International Tourist Park (☎ 9453 6677; www.perthinternational.contact.com.au; 186 Hale Rd, Forrestfield; camp sites $24, cabins $90-105) Some 15km east of the city centre, this five-star park is one of Perth's best, and has a full complement of amenities, including a pool, disabled facilities and a children's playground.

Also recommended is **Perth Central Caravan Park** (Map pp834-5; ☎ 9277 1704; fax 9479 4434; 34 Central Ave, Ascot; camp sites $18, cabins $80-90), just 8km east of the city and pleasantly located close to the river.

Mid-Range
Perth has a good selection of convenient, modern mid-range hotels in the city centre. All options given include private bathrooms, unless stated otherwise.

GUESTHOUSES
Pension of Perth (☎ 9228 9049; www.pensionperth.com.au; 3 Throssell St; s $85-115, d & tw $120-155; 🖳 🅿) Guests enjoy plenty of pampering at this Federation-style B&B cottage, which is lovingly decorated with antiques and interesting collectables, and is across the road from pretty Hyde Park. Individual touches here include gourmet breakfasts, handmade chocolates, aromatherapy oils and purified water in the rooms.

WESTERN AUSTRALIA

Swanbourne Guesthouse (Map pp834-5; ☎ 9383 1981; www.swanbourne.ezcus.com; 5 Myera St, Swanbourne; s $75, d & tw $95) Set in well-tended gardens in a tranquil residential street just a few minutes' drive from the beach, the Swanbourne's three rooms are often snapped up, so book ahead.

CWA House (Map pp842-3; ☎ 9321 6081; fax 9321 6024; 1174 Hay St, West Perth; s $50, s/d with bathroom $70/80; ✷ Ⓟ) Run by the Country Women's Association, this quiet, old-fashioned non-smoking guesthouse on the fringes of town provides no-frills rooms and good disabled facilities.

HOTELS
City   **Map pp842-3**
Royal Hotel (☎ 9324 1510; wentpert@fc-hotels.com.au; 300 Wellington St; s/d $70/90; ✷) With all the grace of a bygone era, this grand old hotel has comfortable rooms and is in an excellent central location. There are cheaper rates for basic rooms with shared facilities (s/d $55/65).

Hotel Ibis (☎ 9322 2844; gm@htlibis.com.au; 334 Murray St; d $90; ✷ 💻) Couples will be hard-pressed to find better value than the Ibis. Though its rooms are unremarkable, all is forgiven when you see the excellent facilities, clean-as-a-whistle interior and prime central city position.

Sullivans Hotel (☎ 9321 8022; www.sullivans.com.au; 166 Mounts Bay Rd; d $110-130; ✷ 💻 Ⓟ) About 2km from the city centre near Kings Park, this friendly, family-run hotel offers comfy rooms, disabled facilities, a restaurant and pool to a mainly older clientele.

Emerald Hotel (☎ 9481 0866; www.emeraldhotel.com.au; 24 Mount St; d $125-145; ✷ 💻 Ⓟ) A dream position between the city and Kings Park, and perks such as a spa, sauna, fitness room and river views make this a tempting option for couples.

Wentworth Plaza (☎ 9481 1000; wentpert@fc hotels.com.au; 300 Murray St; s/d $95/120; ✷ Ⓟ) If you love English pubs, you can't get closer to the action than the Wentworth Plaza, squeezed between the Moon & Sixpence and Bobby Dazzler's.

Also recommended:

Perth City Hotel (☎ 9220 7000; www.perthcityhotel .com.au; 200 Hay St; tw & d $85, f $105; ✷ Ⓟ) Modern, comfortable rooms and disabled facilities.

Goodearth Hotel (☎ 9492 7777; www.goodearthhotel .com.au; 195 Adelaide Tce; d/f from $85/135; ✷ 💻 Ⓟ)

Wide range of rooms, some with balconies and views of the Swan River.

Criterion Hotel (☎ 9325 5155, 1800 245 155; www .criterion-hotel-perth.com.au; 560 Hay St; s/d with breakfast $110/140; ✷ Ⓟ) Restored Art Deco building in the centre.

Northbridge & Cottesloe
Hotel Northbridge (☎ 9328 5254; 210 Lake St; d $150; ✷ Ⓟ) Tucked into a quiet corner of Northbridge, this lovely heritage-listed hotel (built 1912) offers luxurious renovated spa rooms in the boutique section, as well as basic, clean budget rooms with shared facilities in the old section (s/d $40/50).

Ocean Beach Hotel (Map pp834-5; ☎ 9384 2555; www.obh.com.au; cnr Marine Pde & Eric St, Cottesloe; d/tw/ste $120/135/165; ✷ 💻 Ⓟ) If the Aussie beach holiday is what you crave, this spanking new boutique hotel is just a few paces from the ocean. Stylish contemporary rooms have all the mod cons, and deluxe suites impress with spas and water views.

MOTELS & HOLIDAY FLATS
Perth and the surrounding suburbs have an abundance of motels and holiday flats (see the useful *Western Australia Accommodation & Tours Listing*, available from the visitors centre). Most of the places listed here have cheaper weekly rates available.

Riverview on Mount Street (Map pp842-3; ☎ 9321 8963; www.riverview.au.com; 42 Mount St; studio/riverside apartments $85/95; ✷ 💻 Ⓟ) It's almost worth staying in one of the Riverview's pleasant, minimalist apartments to get first dibs on breakfast at the Mount St Foodstore (p845).

City Waters Lodge (☎ 9325 1566; www.citywaters .com.au; 118 Tce Rd; s/d $75/80; ✷ Ⓟ) Most motels are found on the outskirts of cities, but the appeal of City Waters is its convenient central location, fronting parkland and the Swan River. The simple units have amenities that include cooking facilities, bathroom and TV.

Adelphi Apartments Motel (Map pp842-3; ☎ 9322 4666; aba@iinet.net.au; 130a Mounts Bay Rd; s/d units from $60/70; ✷ Ⓟ) Around 2km from town, these unremarkable self-contained units are nonetheless good value for self-caterers seeking cheap rates and privacy. Vertigo-sufferers should give the top-floor units a wide berth.

Top End

Quest's West End Apartments (Map pp842-3; ☎ 9480 3888; www.questwa.com.au; cnr Murray & Milligan Sts; 1-/2-bedroom apt $180/230; ♻ ⬜) If you're craving home comforts and more room to move, Quests offers luxurious self-contained apartments with kitchen, laundry and lounge in the heart of the city.

Saville Park Suites (Map pp842-3; ☎ 9267 4888; www.savillesuites.com; 201 Hay St; 1-/2-bedroom ste from $170/200; ♻ Ⓟ) All suites have balconies (some with views of the Swan River) and access to an indoor heated swimming pool and gym at this luxurious boutique corporate hotel, east of the city centre.

THE AUTHOR'S CHOICE

Melbourne (Map pp842-3; ☎ 9320 3333; www.melbournehotel.com.au; cnr Hay & Milligan Sts; d from $240; ♻ ⬜ Ⓟ) Wander up the grand staircase at the Melbourne (built in 1897) and feel yourself transported to another time. Every inch of this gorgeous boutique hotel has been renovated in an old-style heritage design, from the luxurious rooms to the downstairs café, bar and restaurant. Don't forget to ask about discounts, as weekend rates and packages make a stay at this National Trust–listed hotel within more reasonable reach.

EATING
City
Map pp842-3

If you need a quick bite, try one of the popular food halls where you can fill up on international cuisine from as little as $6. Down an escalator from the Hay St Mall is the **Metro Food Hall** (cnr Hay & William Sts), and off the Hay St Mall is the slightly more up-market **Carillon Arcade Food Hall** (Carillon Arcade). Fast-food junkies can get their fill of burgers, hot chips and sundaes if they head for the grease strip on the east side of William St between Murray and Hay Sts.

Bobby Dazzler's (☎ 9481 1000; 300 Murray St; snacks $10-15, mains $18-25) Burgers, steak sangers and liberal lashings of sport and Australiana are on the menu at this popular corner bar-restaurant.

Moorings (☎ 9325 4574; Barrack St Jetty; mains $19-27) Bronzed Rottnest day-trippers can finish their day with barbecued kangaroo or pan-seared Tasmanian salmon on the open deck of this unpretentious waterfront restaurant, by the ferry.

café bocca (☎ 9226 4030; Shop 4, Shafto Lane; mains $16.50-26.50; ☺ Mon-Fri) Escape the city buzz and indulge in delicious Italian-style dishes and strong coffee in café bocca's quiet, leafy courtyard.

For tasty Japanese, choose between the modest **Hayashi** (☎ 9325 6009; 107 Pier St; mains $15-19) and the modern **Matsuri** (☎ 9322 7737; QV1 Bldg, 250 St George's Tce; mains $13-18), tucked underneath a city skyscraper.

No 44 King Street (☎ 9321 4476; 44 King St; mains $17-28) Foodies flock to this beautifully renovated restaurant and graze on an ever-changing menu of gourmet delights, including a selection of breads baked daily on the premises.

Mount St Foodstore (☎ 9485 1411; 42 Mount St; mains $9.50-18) If you're staying near Kings Park, an excellent choice for brekky or brunch is the Mount St Foodstore. Try the Asian congee chicken rice porridge with chillies, pancake roll and fried shallots ($14) for a rather unusual breakfast experience.

Northbridge
Map pp842-3

Every taste and budget is catered for in the Northbridge streets, particularly in the area bounded by William, Lake, Roe and Newcastle Sts.

Maya Masala (☎ 9328 5655; cnr Lake & Francis Sts; mains $12-16; ☺ closed Mon) If you like your Indian food with a kick, don't miss the authentic, spicy Southern Indian delights of Maya Masala. The huge selection of traditional desserts keeps locals coming back, though service can be slow.

Red Teapot (☎ 9228 1981; 413 William St; mains $7.80-14; ☺ closed Sun) This groovy, intimate newcomer has won accolades for its extensive menu of authentic Hong Kong–style dishes. Bookings are recommended.

Ignore the dowdy décor and indulge in tasty, good-value Vietnamese at **Han's Cafe** (☎ 9328 8122; 245 William St; mains $6.90-13) or **Viet Hoa** (☎ 9328 2127; cnr William St & Forbes Rd; mains $7-14).

Govinda's Restaurant (☎ 9227 1684; 200 William St; dishes $2-6; ☺ noon-2.30pm & 5-6pm Mon-Fri) For years, budget-conscious vegetarians have gravitated to this Hare Krishna kitchen to take advantage of the wholesome all-you-can-eat lunch ($6).

Thai Elephant (☎ 9227 5738; 323 William St; mains $8.90-15) This old Northbridge favourite is as reliable as ever, with pleasant surrounds and good-value Thai.

Grab a quick spring roll at the **Old Shanghai Markets Food Hall** (James St; ☺ closed Mon), at the back of the small Roe St in Chinatown. Self-caterers can stock up at **City Fresh Fruit Company** (393 William St), with healthy fruit and veg, or **Kakulas Bros** (14 William St; ☺ closed Sun), with a continental deli and a huge selection of European imported goods.

Leederville

The café scene is alive and thriving in groovy Oxford St, with wall-to-wall cool cafés, and tables and chairs spilling out onto the street. A long, languid lunch followed by a film at the local Luna is a tempting combination.

Giardini (☎ 9242 2602; 135 Oxford St; mains $17-28) Terracotta, cane and faux marble adorn this sprawling high-ceilinged restaurant, with an interesting fusion of Asian and Mediterranean influences on the menu.

Kailis Bros Fish Market & Cafe (☎ 9443 6300; 101 Oxford St; mains $22-28) This friendly eatery offers plenty of interesting seafood options, including tempura King George whiting ($27) and Malay king prawn curry ($28). Pay extra to hand-pick your fish from the adjoining fish market.

Banzai (☎ 9227 7990; 741 Newcastle St; mains $9.50-16) Directly opposite the Leederville Hotel, Banzai impresses its loyal fan base with a creative menu of Japanese dishes, including the delectable, Chinese-influenced Peking duck roll ($12.50).

See Drinking (p847) for a selection of Leederville's finest coffee houses.

Subiaco

Swish Subiaco is foodie heaven, with a string of up-market cafés and restaurants on Rokeby Rd.

Brew-Ha, The Ritual (☎ 9388 7272; Shop 3-4, 162 Rokeby Rd; snacks $2.60-6.50) Suits rub elbows with lycra-clad cyclists at this divine coffee shop tucked away from the main drag, with plush soft chairs, steaming bowls of latte and a mellow mood.

Food (☎ 6380 2000; 151 Rokeby Rd; mains $12-15) The food is something special at this intimate café-restaurant, which doubles as a specialist grocery. Potential picnickers can

indulge in hampers of gourmet produce in the warmer months ($40 to $60).

Subiaco Hotel (☎ 9381 3069; cnr Hay St & Rokeby Rd; mains $19-25) This lovingly restored historic hotel is rather glam these days, attracting a well-heeled crowd for lunch or dinner. The imaginative modern Australian menu won't disappoint.

Other Suburbs

La Tropicana Café (Map pp834-5; ☎ 9286 1111; 88 Marine Pde, Cottesloe; mains $12-19) Cottesloe beach bums find it hard to resist this colourful caff with big breakfasts and giant fruit painted on the walls. Grab a breezy window table if there's one available.

Another foodie enclave worth the trip is Beaufort St, Mt Lawley. Catch Bus No 67 or wander up from Northbridge.

Caffe Martino (☎ 9328 4400; 552 Beaufort St, Mt Lawley; mains $12-21) Friendly, efficient staff buzz between the tables of this popular family-friendly Italian restaurant that hums with good-natured noise and chatter. Huge, delicious helpings of pasta and pizza keep the hungry happy.

There's also the **Must Winebar** (☎ 9328 8255; 519 Beaufort St, Highgate; mains $15-30), indulging customers with quality French food and an extensive list of wine by the glass, or the fun, groovy two-level **Queens Tavern** (☎ 9328 7267; 520 Beaufort St, Highgate; mains $12-25) for above-average eats.

DRINKING

When the clock strikes beer o'clock every Sunday arvo, locals head to their favourite watering hole for the traditional 'Sunday session', a long afternoon of socialising and downing the amber liquid. Bursting with historic old pubs (many with live music on weekends), Northbridge is the perfect place to start a pub crawl.

Brass Monkey Bar & Brasserie (Map pp842-3; ☎ 9227 9596; 209 William St) You can sink boutique beers in the popular palm-filled beer garden, try the tapas in the funky adjoining Grapeskin Wine Bar & Cellar, or watch Northbridge go by from the upstairs brasserie balcony. For a belly laugh, there's live comedy on Wednesday nights.

Universal Bar (Map pp842-3; ☎ 9227 6771; 221 William St; ☺ 4pm-late) Also known as the House of Jazz & Blues, this open-fronted bar attracts a hip crowd with creative cocktails, delicious bar snacks and live music Monday to Saturday.

Mustang Bar (Map pp842-3; ☎ 9328 2350; 46 Lake St) With keg tables and moose heads on the wall, this American-style sports bar is a fun hangout to enjoy a few international beers and DJs, swing and rockabilly Friday to Monday nights.

Deen (Map pp842-3; ☎ 9227 9361; 84 Aberdeen St; ⏱ 5pm-1am Mon, 3pm-2am Fri, 5pm-2am Sat) No self-respecting backpacker should leave town without attending the Deen's Monday 'backpacker night'. Locals also flock here on weekends for live bands, DJs, funky pool tables and six separate bar zones with different moods and music.

La Bog (Map pp842-3; ☎ 9228 0900; 361 Newcastle St; ⏱ 8pm-6am Mon & Wed-Sat, closes late Tue & Sun) In Northbridge's backpacker heartland is this often jam-packed Irish pub, a popular stop for a big drink, long night of dancing or an early-morn nightcap.

Lovers of Brit-style décor and pub grub will feel right at home in the **Elephant & Wheelbarrow** (Map pp842-3; ☎ 9448 4433; 53 Lake St), with a pleasant street-front beer garden; and **Rosie O'Grady's** (Map pp842-3; ☎ 9328 1488; 205 James St), with Irish bands most nights.

Though quiet compared to Northbridge, the city still has some worthwhile places, including the **Moon & Sixpence** (Map pp842-3; ☎ 9481 1000; 300 Murray St), an English-style pub with overflowing outdoor tables; the waterfront **Lucky Shag** (Map pp842-3; ☎ 9221 0203; Barrack St Jetty), where frazzled city workers shake off the day's stresses; and the **Grosvenor Hotel** (Map pp842-3; ☎ 9325 3799; 339 Hay St), with live music belted out Wednesday to Sunday.

Of course, favourite traveller-haunts are often beachside. After a day of sun-lazing, few can fault the sunset view from Cottesloe's **Ocean Beach Hotel** (The Obie; Map pp834-5; ☎ 9384 5111; 1 Eric St) or the nearby **Cottesloe Beach Hotel** (Map pp834-5; ☎ 9383 1100; 104 Marine Pde).

In the 'burbs, popular venues for a Sunday session are the **Leederville Hotel** (☎ 9286 0150; 742 Newcastle St, Leederville), the **Subiaco Hotel** (☎ 9381 3069; cnr Rokeby Rd & Hay St, Subiaco) and Mt Lawley's **Queens Tavern** (☎ 9328 7267; 520 Beaufort St, Highgate).

For coffee in Leederville, head for **Cino to Go** (☎ 9242 4688; 136 Oxford St; snacks $5-10). Even the most discerning tastes will be satisfied at this coffee mecca that promises 'the greatest taste experience possible', and roasts and grinds its own daily. **Oxford 130** (130 Oxford St; snacks $5.50-8.30) will provide a more laid-back caffeine hit; it's a casual coffee stop that does a roaring trade in takeaways and attracts a hip, local crowd.

pulp Juice Bar (cnr William & Wellington Sts; snacks $3.95-5.95) Sore head? Need a pick-me-up? Choose from the 'morning glory' (hangover helper) or the 'active8' (immune booster) in this hole-in-the-wall juice factory, which also serves healthy snacks and organic coffee. Two popular branches of **Java Juice** (Murray & Hay Sts) also keep health fans happy.

ENTERTAINMENT

Northbridge, Leederville, Subiaco and Fremantle (p856) are the main places to go after dark. **Xpress** (www.xpressmag.com.au), the free weekly entertainment mag, produces a gig and clubbers' guide, available at music shops and on the Net. Check the *West Australian* for listings of theatre, cinema and nightclub events.

Cinemas

For quality art-house films, try **Cinema Paradiso** (Map pp842-3; ☎ 9227 1771; Galleria complex, 164 James St, Northbridge) or the **Astor** (☎ 9370 1777; 659 Beaufort St, Mt Lawley), on the corner of Beaufort and Walcott Sts.

Luna (☎ 9444 4056; www.lunapalace.com.au; 155 Oxford St, Leederville) Monday's discounted double feature is great value at the retro Luna. In the warmer months, the latest indie flicks feature in the outdoor courtyard cinema.

Mainstream films screen at **Hoyts**, **Greater Union** and **Village** city and suburban cinemas; budget night is Tuesday.

Sunset Cinema (☎ 1900 999 009; Kings Park) Grab a bottle of wine and some munchies, and watch your favourite flick in the open air on Tuesday to Sunday nights from December to March (gates open 6pm).

Camelot Outdoor Cinema (☎ 9370 1777; Memorial Hall, Lochee St, Mosman Park) Not far from Cottesloe, Camelot (December to April) offers wood-fired pizzas, a fully licensed bar and nightly movies under the stars.

Classical Music & Theatre

Regular classical concerts and recitals by local and international acts are usually performed at the **Perth Concert Hall** (Map pp842-3;

WESTERN AUSTRALIA

☎ 9231 9900; www.perthconcerthall.com.au; 5 St Georges Tce). You can usually catch the latest hit plays at the historic **His Majesty's Theatre** (Map pp842-3; ☎ 9265 0900; 825 Hay St), the modern **Playhouse Theatre** (Map pp842-3; ☎ 9325 3344, 3 Pier St) or the **Subiaco Theatre Centre** (Map pp842-3; ☎ 9382 3385; 180 Hamersley Rd, Subiaco). Session times and programmes appear daily in the *West Australian*, and you can book tickets for all four through **BOCS ticketing** (☎ 1800 193 300).

Gay & Lesbian Venues

For up-to-date venues, news and events, you could pick up your free copy of the fortnightly gay and lesbian newspaper *OutinPerth* (www.outinperth.com), or the magazine *Women out West* (www.womenoutwest.com .au) from the **Arcane Bookshop** (Map pp842-3; 212 William St, Northbridge).

At the time of writing, popular watering hole and drag-show venue, the **Court Hotel** (Map pp842-3; ☎ 9328 5292; 50 Beaufort St) was about to undergo a major revamp. Call ahead for developments. A mainly gay dance clientele hits **Connections** (Map pp842-3; ☎ 9328 1870; 81 James St) from Tuesday to Sunday.

Nightclubs

Many Northbridge clubs have free admission and cheap drinks during the week, but come Friday and Saturday night, the door bitches come out of the woodwork, the queues get longer and dress codes are more rigorously policed.

On the weekend, serious clubbers descend upon the **Rise** (Map pp842-3; ☎ 9328 7447; 139 James St), the **Pallas Hotel** (Map pp842-3; 44 Lake St) and the **Church** (Map pp842-3; ☎ 9328 1065; 69 Lake St).

Office Nightclub (Map pp842-3; ☎ 9228 0077; cnr Aberdeen & Parker Sts; ☼ 8pm-late Wed-Sat) Live bands and DJs alternate at this popular revamped club. Get there early to avoid the cover charge.

Paramount (Map pp842-3; ☎ 9228 1344; 163 Lake St) Live bands rock on the bottom level of this weekend club, while DJs keep the party going upstairs.

Metro City (Map pp842-3; ☎ 9228 0500; 146 Roe St) This enormous white colossus of a building is the original big city nightclub, band and dance party venue. Ring for upcoming events.

hip-e-club (Map pp842-3; ☎ 9227 8899; cnr Oxford & Newcastle Sts, Leederville; ☼ Tue-Sun) A back-

packer fave, this Leederville institution pumps out mainstream hits from the '70s, '80s and '90s. Tuesday's backpacker night is especially popular.

Sport

On winter weekends, obsessive Australian Football League (AFL) fans and curious onlookers descend upon Subiaco Oval to watch the Fremantle Dockers and West Coast Eagles tough it out against the other states. Sports fans can also watch the Perth Wildcats slam and dunk in the National Basketball League (NBL), or the Perth Glory weave and score in the National Soccer League. Check the *West Australian* for game details and venues.

In summer, allegiances quickly shift and the hoards head for the **WACA** (Western Australian Cricket Association ground; ☎ 9265 7222; Nelson Cres, East Perth) to catch the drama of one-day and test match cricket.

SHOPPING

Souvenirs for home can be found along the city's **London Court arcade**, while the Hay and Murray St Malls border the city's shopping heartland. Perth has some excellent outlets for Aboriginal arts and crafts, including the **Creative Native Gallery** (Map pp842-3; ☎ 9322 3398; www.creativenative.com.au; 32 King St), in swanky King St, and **Didges we doo** (Map pp842-3; ☎ 9228 1896; www.didgeswedoo.com.au; 223 William St, Northbridge), with an array of brightly painted didgeridoos.

Leederville's Oxford St has groovy boutiques and eclectic music and bookshops, while stylish Subiaco's Rokeby Rd and Hay St boast high-fashion, classy souvenirs and the **Subiaco Pavilion Markets** (cnr Roberts & Rokeby Rds, Subiaco; ☼ Thu-Sun). For a more unusual souvenir of your travels, try the weekend **Galleria Arts & Craft Market** (Perth Cultural Centre, James St; ☼ 9am-5pm Sat & Sun).

GETTING THERE & AWAY
Air

Qantas (Map pp842-3; ☎ 13 13 13; www.qantas.com.au; 55 William St) has direct, one-way economy flights to/from Adelaide ($500), Alice Springs ($510), Darwin ($590), Melbourne ($550), Sydney ($550) and Brisbane ($550). Within WA, Qantas also flies to Broome ($515) and Kalgoorlie ($274). **Virgin Blue** (☎ 13 67 89; www.virginblue.com.au) also offers flights from Perth to Adelaide ($469), Sydney ($600), Melbourne ($500) and Brisbane ($580). Of course, fares are changeable, so check both the Qantas and Virgin Blue websites for up-to-the-minute discounts and special deals.

Skywest (☎ 1300 660 088; www.skywest.com.au) flies to many regional centres, including Albany, Esperance, Exmouth, Carnarvon and Kalgoorlie.

Bus

McCafferty's/Greyhound (☎ 13 20 30, 13 14 99) operates daily bus services out of Perth from the Wellington St bus station, heading north to Darwin and east to Adelaide via Kalgoorlie. The **Nullarbor Traveller** (☎ 1800 816 858; www.the-traveller.com.au) runs leisurely minibus trips between Adelaide and Perth.

Transwa (☎ 1300 662 205; www.transwa.wa.gov.au) has bus services from the East Perth terminal to many regional destinations – as far as Esperance, Kalbarri and Kalgoorlie. **Integrity** (☎ 9226 1339) runs regular northbound buses as far as Broome from the Wellington St bus station. **South West Coachlines** (☎ 9324 2333) runs daily buses from the City Busport to/from Bunbury and Margaret River. **Perth Goldfields Express** (☎ 1800 620 440) has buses to/from Laverton via Kalgoorlie, while **Easyrider Backpacker Tours** (☎ 9226 0307) has jump-on, jump-off services in the southwest, and along the coastal route to Broome and on to Darwin.

Car

No matter which way you look at it and where you're coming from, driving to Perth from any other state is a bloody long way (around 4400km from Sydney). But if you've got your own wheels and companions to share the driving and the fuel costs, it's still probably the cheapest way of getting to Perth...and it's certainly the best way to see the country.

Train

The *Indian Pacific* travels twice weekly each way between Sydney and Perth via Kalgoorlie. One-way fares from Adelaide to Perth for an economy 'daynighter' seat/ economy sleeper/1st-class sleeper (including meals) are $310/960/1190, while fares from Sydney are $515/1250/1560. The *Indian Pacific* departs from East Perth train station at 10.55am Monday and Friday.

You can make rail connections in Adelaide for the *Overland* to Melbourne and for the *Ghan* to Alice Springs. Book your tickets through **Great Southern Railways** (☎ 13 21 47; www.gsr.com.au).

The *AvonLink* commuter service from Perth to Northam (via Midland and Toodyay) and the *Prospector* to Kalgoorlie arrive and depart from the East Perth terminal. The *Prospector* has at least one service in each direction daily, and the full trip takes eight hours. It leaves Perth around 7.15am Monday to Saturday and 2.10pm on Sunday. The 2½-hour *Australind* service to Bunbury departs from Perth train station at 9.30am and 5.55pm daily. Reservations can be made with **Transwa** (☎ 1300 662 205).

GETTING AROUND

Perth is easy to get around, with an efficient, fully integrated public transport system that is free in the city centre. **Transperth** (☎ 13 62 13; www.transperth.wa.gov.au) operates the city's public buses, trains and ferries, and has information offices in the Plaza Arcade (off the Hay St Mall), Perth train station, the City Busport on Mounts Bay Rd and at Wellington St bus station. These offices are open from 7.30am to 5.30pm Monday to Friday, but the Plaza Arcade office also opens from 8am to 5pm on Saturday, and the City Busport office from noon to 4pm on Sunday.

The free city transit zone involves Transperth buses and trains within the area bounded by Northbridge (Newcastle St) in the north, the river in the south, Kings Park in the west and the Causeway in the east. For more information on services, see the Bus entry under Public Transport in this section (p850).

To/From the Airport

The domestic and international terminals are about 11km and 15km from the city centre. **Swan Taxis** (☎ 13 13 88) can get you to the city from the terminals for around $22 and $28, respectively.

The privately run **Airport-City Shuttle Bus** (☎ 9479 4131) meets all incoming domestic and international flights, and provides transport to and from the city centre, hotels and hostels. It costs $8.80/11 to and from the domestic/international terminal. Call for more information on hotel and hostel pick-ups and timetables.

Alternatively, catch Transperth bus No 37 from the domestic airport to the City Busport for $3. It leaves the domestic terminal every half-hour or so from 5.30am to 11pm (less frequently on the weekend), and does the return trip from the City Busport every half-hour from 6.15am to 11.20pm.

Car & Motorcycle

RENTAL

Avis (Map pp842-3; ☎ 13 63 33), **Budget** (Map pp842-3; ☎ 13 27 27), **Hertz** (☎ 13 30 39) and **Thrifty** (☎ 1300 365 564) are all represented in Perth (including at the airport). Better deals are available from the smaller operators, but make sure you read the small print and know what your insurance covers you for. **Apex** (Map pp842-3; ☎ 9227 9091; 400 William St, Northbridge) and **Bayswater Car Rental** (☎ 9325 1000; 160 Adelaide Tce) offer cheaper rates.

Public Transport

BOAT

Transperth ferries (☎ 13 62 13) depart every half-hour on the hour from 7am to 7pm daily from the Barrack St Jetty to the zoo (one way, $1.30/0.50 per adult/child).

BUS

There are two excellent free CAT bus services in the city centre. The buses are state of the art and there are computer read-outs (and audio services) at the stops telling you when the next bus is due. Using the two CAT services, you can get to most sights in the inner city.

The Red CAT operates east–west from the WACA in East Perth to Outram St (next to Kings Park) and back; it runs every five minutes from 6.50am to 6.20pm on weekdays, and every 35 minutes from 10am on the weekend. The Blue CAT operates north–south from Barrack St Jetty to Northbridge; services run every seven minutes from 6.50am to 6.20pm Monday to Friday, and every 15 minutes from 10am on the weekend. Special Friday (6.50am to 6.20pm, every seven minutes; 6.20pm to 1am, every seven minutes), Saturday (8.30am to 1am, every 15 minutes) and Sunday (10am to 6.15pm, every 15 minutes) night services carry the party crowd from the city to Northbridge, running every 15 minutes to 1am.

On regular buses, a short ride of one zone is $2, two zones $3 and three zones $3.80.

Zone 1 covers the inner suburbs (including Subiaco and Claremont) and Zone 2 extends all the way west to Fremantle. Zone 3 extends to the outer suburbs, including Armadale. A MultiRider ticket gives 10 journeys for the price of nine, and a DayRider (available after 9am on weekdays) cost $7.50.

TRAIN

Transperth (☎ 13 62 13) also operates the Fastrak suburban train lines to Armadale, Fremantle, Midland and the northern suburb of Joondalup, from around 5.20am to midnight Monday to Friday, with reduced services on the weekend. Free train travel (in the free transit zone) is between the Claisebrook and City West train stations.

All local trains leave from the Perth train station on Wellington St. Your rail ticket can also be used on Transperth buses and ferries within its zone.

FREMANTLE

☎ 08 / pop 25,000

Fremantle ('Freo' to the locals) is virtually a suburb of Perth, but it retains its own identity with a laid-back charisma and a sense of history unmatched by its big brother upstream. Sitting at the mouth of the Swan River, the port is Fremantle's focus, from its flotilla of fishing boats and harbour-front restaurants to the impressive new maritime museum in the developing Victoria Quay precinct. Heritage buildings and historical sites help to capture a bygone era, but for many, Freo's appeal is in the more tangible pleasures it offers…letting your hair down at a lively Sunday session, spending a lazy afternoon sipping lattes on the famous 'cappuccino strip' or feeling the soothing Fremantle Doctor breeze through town on a scorching day.

HISTORY

Well before European settlement, the Noongar people used the area for ceremony and trade. In 1829 Charles Fremantle and the HMS *Challenger* arrived, but the new European settlement made little progress until it began taking in convicts in the 1850s. This cheap labour force constructed most of the town's earliest buildings, some of them among the oldest and most treasured in WA. As a port, Fremantle was ineffective until the Irish engineer CY O'Connor built an artificial harbour in the 1890s; it was later used as a submarine base during WWII and a dropping-off point for post-war migrant ships in the 1950s.

After Australia's 1983 America's Cup triumph, Fremantle went on a major spring-cleaning and development spree in anticipation of the influx of tourists four years later. Though the 1987 defence of the yachting trophy was unsuccessful, Fremantle has not been the same again, forever transformed from a sleepy port into a vibrant (and occasionally crowded) city.

INFORMATION

Chart & Map Shop (☎ 9335 8665; 14 Collie St) Excellent source of maps and travel books, with friendly, informative staff.

Fremantle Public Hospital (☎ 9431 3333; Alma St)

net.CHAT (Wesley Arcade, Market St; www.netchat.com .au; ☼ 8am-11pm Mon-Sat, 10am-10pm Sun) Has Internet access for $3 per hour.

Travel Lounge (☎ 9335 8776; www.thetravellounge .com.au; 16 Market St; ☼ 7am-11pm) Great place to plan your trip, check your email or just hang out.

Visitors Centre (☎ 9431 7878; fax 9431 7755; Town Hall, King's Sq; ☼ 9am-5pm Mon-Fri, 10am-3pm Sat, noon-3pm Sun)

WA Naturally (☎ 9430 8600; 47 Henry St) CALM's outdoor and nature information centre.

SIGHTS
Maritime Museums

The brand-new **Western Australian Maritime Museum** (☎ 9431 8334; www.mm.wa.gov.au; Victoria Quay; adult/child $10/3, with submarine tour $15/5; ☼ 9.30am-5pm), an imposing presence on the waterfront, is jam-packed with historic canoes, ferries and yachts (including America's Cup winner *Australia II*). Nonclaustrophobes can cosy up on the tour of the 90m-long submarine HMAS *Ovens*, which gives a taste of the difficult conditions submariners had to endure during WWII. These one-hour tours are popular, so book early.

Also worth a visit is the **Shipwreck Museum** (☎ 9431 8444; 1 Cliff St; admission by donation; ☼ 9.30am-5pm), housed in a beautiful historic building near the waterfront. Its interesting collection of shipwreck relics includes salvaged items from the famous *Batavia* wreck. Free tours are held at 10am and

3pm daily, and Aboriginal heritage walking tours ($10/5 per adult/child) leave from the front entrance at 11.30am Wednesday, Friday and Sunday.

Markets

If you're in town on the weekend, take a wander through the colourful covered **Fremantle Markets** (cnr South Tce & Henderson St; ☼ 9am-9pm Fri, 9am-5pm Sat, 10am-5pm Sun). Built in 1897, the National Trust–listed building attracts crowds seeking everything from souvenirs for the folks back home to arts and crafts and tonight's dinner ingredients. Late Sunday afternoon is the best time to buy discounted vegies.

You can shop for knick-knacks or grab a snack in the food court in the popular dockside **E Shed Markets** (E Shed, Victoria Quay; ☼ 9am-6pm Fri-Sun).

Fremantle History Museum & Arts Centre

The **arts centre** (☎ 9432 9555; www.fac.org.au; 1 Finnerty St; admission free; ☼ 10am-5pm) and **history museum** (☎ 9430 7966; www.museum.wa.gov.au; admission by donation; ☼ 10.30am-4.30pm Sun-Fri, 1-5pm Sat) share a former lunatic asylum constructed by convicts in the 1860s. The museum has a fine collection, including exhibits on Fremantle's Aboriginal history, the colonisation of WA and the Dutch East India Company ships that first 'discovered' the western coast of Australia. Art lovers shouldn't miss the adjoining arts centre, which has a changing programme of exhibitions.

Round House

On Arthur Head, at the western end of High St, is the **Round House** (admission by gold coin donation; ☼ 10.30am-3.30pm), the oldest public building in WA. Built in 1831, this 12-sided stone structure was originally the prison (in the days before convicts), and the site of the colony's first hanging. Later the building was used to hold Aboriginal prisoners before they were incarcerated on Rottnest Island. Before settlement, the site was a ceremonial meeting place for the Noongar people.

Old Fremantle Prison

The historic **prison** (☎ 9336 9200; www.fremantle prison.com; 1 The Tce; day tours adult/child $14.30/7.15, night tours $17.60/8.80; ☼ 10am-5pm) was one of the first building tasks of the convicts in

WESTERN AUSTRALIA

WESTERN AUSTRALIA

FREMANTLE

To Cottesloe (6km)

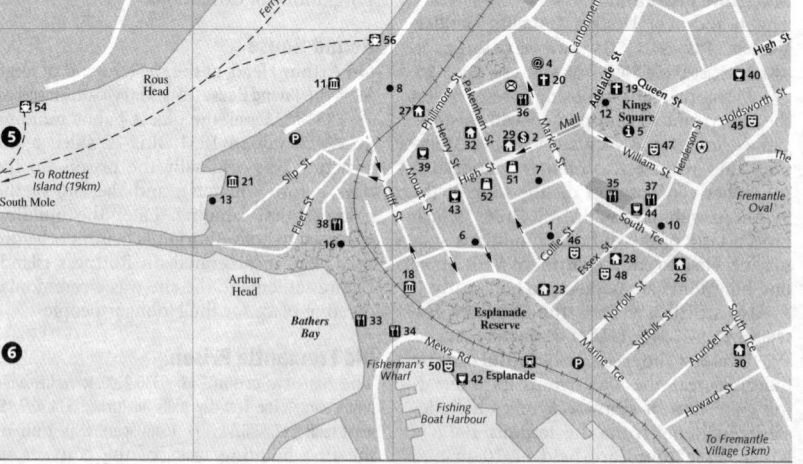

To Rottnest Island (19km)
South Mole

SWAN RIVER

Ferry to Rottnest Island

Fremantle Harbour

Rous Head

Arthur Head

Bathers Bay

Fisherman's Wharf

Fishing Boat Harbour

Esplanade Reserve

Kings Square

Fremantle Oval

To Fremantle Village (3km)

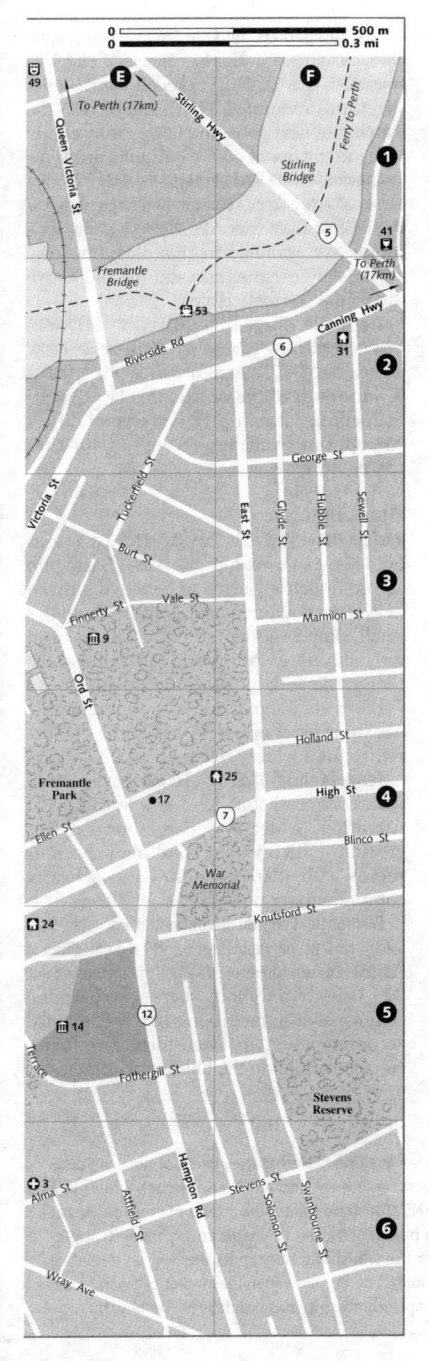

the 1850s, and operated as a maximum security prison until 1991. Tours of the main cell blocks are held every half-hour, with additional prison precinct tours every hour. For something different, try the eerie 1½-hour candlelight tours, held after 7pm on Wednesday and Friday.

Gold-Rush Landmarks

Fremantle boomed during the gold rush of the 1890s, and a visit to some of the buildings of this period hints at what Fremantle was like a century ago. They include **Samson House** (61 Ellen St; donation requested $3; 🕐 1-5pm Sun), a well-preserved 1888 colonial home, the 1882 **St John's Anglican Church** (cnr Adelaide & Queen Sts) near the visitors centre, and the nearby 1887 **Fremantle Town Hall** (Kings Sq). Also still standing is the **Proclamation Tree**, near the corner of Adelaide and Parry Sts, a Moreton Bay fig that was planted by Governor Robinson in 1890 to celebrate WA's new constitution.

Other Attractions

One of the new kids on the block is the **Fremantle Motor Museum** (☎ 9336 5222; www .fremantlemotormuseum.net; B Shed, Victoria Quay; adult/child $9/5; 🕐 9.30am-5pm), housed in a 1920s heritage building in the developing Victoria Quay precinct. Petrol-heads can easily spend a couple of hours wandering through this interesting collection of famous racing cars, beloved Australian icons (including the first Holden prototype), historic motorcycles and the earliest pioneers of the motor world.

Fremantle is a popular centre for artisans, and one of the best places to find them is at the imaginative **Bannister Street Workshops** (☎ 9336 2035; 8-12 Bannister St; 🕐 11am-5.30pm Tue-Sun).

TOURS

The **Fremantle Tram** (☎ 9339 8719; www.tramswest .com.au) does several daily 45-minute historical tours around Fremantle with commentary ($10/3/20 per adult/child/family). They depart from the town hall on the hour from 10am to 4pm daily. There's also the 1½-hour Top of the Port tour ($15/5/30) and the immensely popular Friday-night Ghostly Tour, which includes a fish and chips dinner, and a peek at all the spooky places in town, including little-known graveyards, the prison and Round House ($35/30 per adult/child; book ahead).

From September to June, the Fremantle-based **Capricorn Kayak Tours** (☎ 9433 3802; www.capricornkayak.com.au; $130) offers full-day kayaking trips around Penguin and Seal Islands, leaving from Fremantle at 8am. See p859 for details of other kayaking trips.

FESTIVALS & EVENTS

The 10-day **Festival of Fremantle** in November is the city's biggest annual event, featuring street parades, concerts, exhibitions and free performances. Freo's January **Sardine Festival** is fun for foodies, with gourmet yabbies, crocodile, seafood and sardines on offer. There's also the **Busker's Festival** in April, and the **Blessing of the Fleet** in October.

SLEEPING
Budget

Most budget places offer significantly cheaper weekly rates, so if you're planning to bunker down for a while, Freo could be the place for you.

Sundancer Backpackers (☎ 1800 061 144; www.sundancer-resort.com.au; 80 High St; dm $17-20, d with/without bathroom $70/50; ☐) Right in the centre of town, this excellent hostel is housed in a historic former hotel, with spacious rooms, high ceilings and funky murals on the walls. There's also an outdoor spa and cheap drinks in the residents' bar.

Old Firestation Backpackers (☎ 9430 5454; http://firestation.fdns.net; 18 Phillimore St; dm/d $17/45; ☐) With a social atmosphere, tight security and more free facilities than you can point a hose at, this busy former fire station is popular with the party crowd. Some rooms are pretty shabby, but freebies include Internet access (8am to 5pm), laundry, Playstations, pool tables, work advice and discounted curries (from $3.50).

YHA Backpackers Inn Freo (☎ 9431 7065; bpinn_freo@hotmail.com; 11 Pakenham St; dm/s/d $16/30/45, nonmembers extra $2; ☐) Tucked down a quiet street, this renovated YHA extends into the warehouse next door, and has a sunny courtyard and plenty of cosy communal areas.

Cheviot Marina Backpackers (☎ 9433 2055; cheviotmarina@hotmail.com; 4 Beach St; YHA/VIP members dm/s/d $15/28/40, nonmembers $16/30/45; ☐) Spacious rooms are available in this pleasant, low-key hostel near the train station and above the Flag & Whistle Hotel.

Fremantle Village (Map pp834-5; ☎ 9430 4866; www.fremantlevillage.com.au; Lot 1, Cockburn Rd; camp/caravan sites $19/23, 2-person chalets $85) About 3.5km south of the centre, this large, well-manicured caravan park has several different options available, though camp sites can be noisy.

Mid-Range

Norfolk Hotel (☎ 9335 5405; fax 9430 5908; 47 South Tce; s/d $45/65, s/d with bathroom $85/95) Basic pub accommodation seems to be a dying breed in ever-trendy Fremantle, but the Norfolk's small, simple rooms survive just paces from the main drag. Pub meals in the gorgeous beer garden are highly recommended.

B&Bs are popular and historic Fremantle has some great options – ask at the visitors centre for a wider selection.

Terrace Central B&B (☎ 9335 6600; portfremantle@bigpond.com; 83-85 South Tce; d & tw from $90; ☒) Attention to detail is paramount at this great little B&B with a handful of spacious rooms with shared facilities and a hearty complimentary breakfast.

Fremantle Colonial Accommodation (☎ 9430 6568; fremantle.col@westnet.net.au; 215 High St; B&B s/d $95/100, s/d with bathroom $120/125, cottages from $160; ☒) Guests can choose between charming colonial-style terrace rooms or self-contained accommodation in three former wardens' cottages adjoining the hill-top prison.

SANDGROPERS

Aussies love a nickname, and citizens of every state have one (whether they like it or not). In South Australia (SA) you'll rub shoulders with crow-eaters, in Queensland you'll knock back a beer in a bar full of banana-benders, in New South Wales (NSW) you'll sit among a crowd of cockroaches at the footy, and in Tasmania you'll trek alongside a bunch of (rather unimaginatively named) apple-eaters. But once you arrive in the West, you enter the world of sandgropers (named for a relative of the grasshopper that loves to burrow in sandy soils). The human variety has a diet of Swan Lager, enjoys sunbathing and the footy, eats in Freo's cappuccino strip and holidays at the beach.

Port Mill Bed & Breakfast (☎ 9433 3832; portmill@bigpond.com; 3/17 Essex St; s/d from $140/150) There's a touch of Tuscany about this lovely B&B, with limestone walls, terracotta tiles, and flower-filled window boxes and balconies overlooking a private courtyard.

Girton House (☎ 9335 3235; www.girton.com.au; 75 Ellen St; s/d $125/135) Built in 1890, this quaint two-level B&B overlooking extensive parkland is listed with the National Trust. With just two guest rooms and no children allowed, peace and quiet is virtually guaranteed.

Tradewinds Hotel (☎ 9339 8188; www.tradewinds hotel.com.au; 59 Canning Hwy; ste/f $155/185; 🕃) This pleasant rambling hotel has roomy suites and spa apartments tacked on to a lovely century-old pub. A resort-style pool brings welcome relief on sweltering summer days.

Top End
Esplanade Hotel (☎ 9432 4000; www.esplanadehotel fremantle.com.au; cnr Marine Tce & Essex St; d from $220; 🕃) At the time of writing, this enormous, ritzy four-star hotel was in the midst of expanding its empire of 259 luxury guest rooms and suites to 300. Ask about special deals and discounts.

EATING
Cappuccino Strip
Many an afternoon has been whiled away sipping beer or coffee and people-watching from pavement tables on the South Tce cappuccino strip.

Old Papa's (☎ 9335 4655; 17 South Tce; mains $7.90-18) There's a whole lot of table hopping going on in this local favourite, where everyone seems to know each other. Big breakfasts and delicious pizzas are served with a smile.

Gino's (☎ 9336 1464; 1 South Tce; mains $9-24) Gino's is in the thick of the action – and loving every minute of it. Young and old mingle, sipping coffee and munching on traditional Italian fare.

Dôme Café (☎ 9336 3040; 13 South Tce; mains $9-19) Serving delicious food in opulent surrounds, Dôme Café is ideal for wining and dining before catching afrobeats or salsa at Kulcha upstairs.

Mexican Kitchen (☎ 9335 1394; 19 South Tce; mains $15-26) Overflowing with cheese, frijoles and sour cream, these enormous dishes will keep you going all day. Grab a friend and share a tapas plate ($22) featuring the chef's favourite flavours.

Old Shanghai Food Market (4 Henderson St; mains $5-14) For a quick bite, this food hall offers delicious, good-value Asian and Italian food in large portions until 9pm most nights.

West End & Harbour
Scoffing fish and chips in one of the sprawling restaurants by the Fisherman's Wharf is a Freo tradition, but at weekend rush hour it can be a crowded affair.

Cicerello (☎ 9335 1911; 44 Mews Rd; mains $12-18) This big, old self-serve barn does a roaring trade filling families with fresh-off-the-boat seafood. Avoid if you have an aversion to queuing, children or crowds.

Cafe Il Porto (☎ 9335 6726; 47 Mews Rd; mains $16-25) Slightly removed from the waterfront feeding frenzy, this pleasant café has generous seafood and pasta dishes and a faux Tuscan feel.

Market Street Cafe (☎ 9430 4211; 21 Market St; mains $4-8) Stylish but unpretentious, this popular shoppers' pit stop offers excellent coffee, giant biscuits and light meals.

Roundhouse Restaurant & Tea Rooms (☎ 9431 7555; 9 Fleet St; mains $8-28) Far away from the South Tce scene, the Roundhouse is more about tradition than trendiness. Devonshire teas and old-fashioned desserts are a homy highlight.

Bengal Indian Curry House (☎ 9335 2400; 18 Phillimore St; mains $15.50-21; 🕒 6-9pm) Tucked underneath the Old Firestation Backpackers, this licensed eatery has tasty curries and a fun atmosphere. For takeaways, there's free Internet while you wait.

DRINKING
Sail & Anchor Hotel (☎ 9335 8433; 64 South Tce) Boutique beers rule in this heritage pub-brewery (circa 1884) with signs proudly warning that there are 'no beers of mass production'. Beer

---

THE AUTHOR'S CHOICE

Little Creatures Brewery (☎ 9430 5555; 40 Mews Rd) There's no better place on a Sunday afternoon than this groovy modern microbrewery on the waterfront. Perth day-trippers and travellers squeeze in among the beer vats, sampling the brews or choosing from an excellent local wine list.

boffins can sample six handcrafted beers on a brewery tour ($10).

Left Bank Bar & Cafe (☎ 9319 1315; 15 Riverside Rd) Near the East St jetty, the Lefty's popular riverside beer garden is just the place for a Sunday session or a pick-me-up latte the next morning.

La Bog Inn (☎ 9336 7751; 189 High St; ☺ 6pm-late Tue-Thu, 6pm-6am Fri & Sat, 8pm-midnight Sun) Like its Perth compadre, La Bog is *the* place for a big night out, kicking on to the wee hours. Tuesday and Thursday are backpacker nights, with free barbecue, live music and $5 jugs.

Two lovely historic hotels worth a pub-crawl stop are the **Orient Hotel** (☎ 9336 2455; 39 High St) and **His Majesty's Hotel** (☎ 9336 4681; cnr Phillimore & Mouat Sts).

ENTERTAINMENT

Luna SX (☎ 9430 5999; Essex St) screens the latest art-house and independents. For American blockbusters, try **Hoyts Millennium** (Collie St) or **Hoyts Queensgate** (6 William St).

Zanzibar (☎ 9433 3999; 42 Mews Rd; ☺ 6pm-late Thu, opens noon Fri-Sun) This multilevel night-club-bar attracts a young casual crowd with DJs and occasional lowbrow entertainment (mud wrestling and wet T-shirts anyone?).

Mojo's (☎ 9430 4010; 237 Queen Victoria St; ☺ 7pm-late Tue-Sun) Across the river in North Fremantle, this groovy bar is the most popular indie music venue in town.

Metropolis (☎ 9336 1880; 58 South Tce; ☺ 8pm-5am Fri, 9pm-6am Sat, 9pm-1am Sun) Young Metropolis regulars hang out on the balcony, schmooze in the upstairs bar or bust a move downstairs at this popular, often jam-packed club.

Kulcha (☎ 9336 4544; www.kulcha.com.au; 13 South Tce) There's almost always something interesting on at this eclectic world-music venue above Dôme Café. See the website for a recent calendar of events, which could include anything from classical guitar to belly dance to flamenco.

Fly by Night Musician's Club (☎ 9430 5976; www.flybynight.org; Parry St) Musicians breathe easy in this smoke-free, licensed venue that has an uncanny resemblance to an aircraft hangar. See the website for the latest programme.

SHOPPING

Aboriginal art and crafts are well represented along High St, with **Creative Native**

(☎ 9335 6795; 65 High St) and **Indigenart** (☎ 9335 2911; 82 High St). **Staircase Gallery** (☎ 9430 6447; 57 High St) is a worthwhile stop for lovers of fine art and woodcraft.

GETTING THERE & AROUND

The **Fremantle Airport Shuttle** (☎ 9335 1614) leaves for the airport eight times daily from 8.15am to 9.15pm, picking up passengers at their accommodation ($20 per person, bookings essential). It also runs shuttle services from the airport to Fremantle from 10am to 10.45pm. It costs $20 per person, $25 for two and $30 for a family of four.

The train between Perth and Fremantle runs every 10 minutes or so throughout the day ($2.90). Bus Nos 105, 106 and 111 from the City Busport in Perth go along St George's Tce to Fremantle via Canning Hwy. Bus Nos 103 and 104 depart from St George's Tce and head to Fremantle station via the north side of the river.

Oceanic Cruises (☎ 9325 1191) has daily ferries at 8.45am, 10am, noon and 2pm from Perth's Barrack St Jetty to Freo, and departs at 11am, 1pm, 3.15pm and 5.30pm for the return journey (one way $12/7 per adult/child, return $20/10).

Numerous one-way streets, ever-present parking meters and diligent inspectors make driving around town a frustrating experience. For sanity's sake, travel by foot or on the free CAT bus service, which takes in all the major sites on a continuous route every 10 minutes from 7.30am to 6pm on weekdays and 10am to 6pm on the weekend.

AROUND PERTH

ROTTNEST ISLAND
☎ 08 / pop 200

'Rotto', as it's known to the locals, is a sand island only 11km long and 4.5km wide, 19km off the coast from Fremantle. Superb white beaches fringe the isle, making up for its rather barren, eerie interior of salt lakes and scrub. Virtually car-free, Rottnest is a popular day-trip destination, with several high-speed ferries operating from Perth and Fremantle. Cyclists dominate here, with visitors of all ages and walks of life buzzing from beach to beach on two wheels. There are a handful of historic buildings in

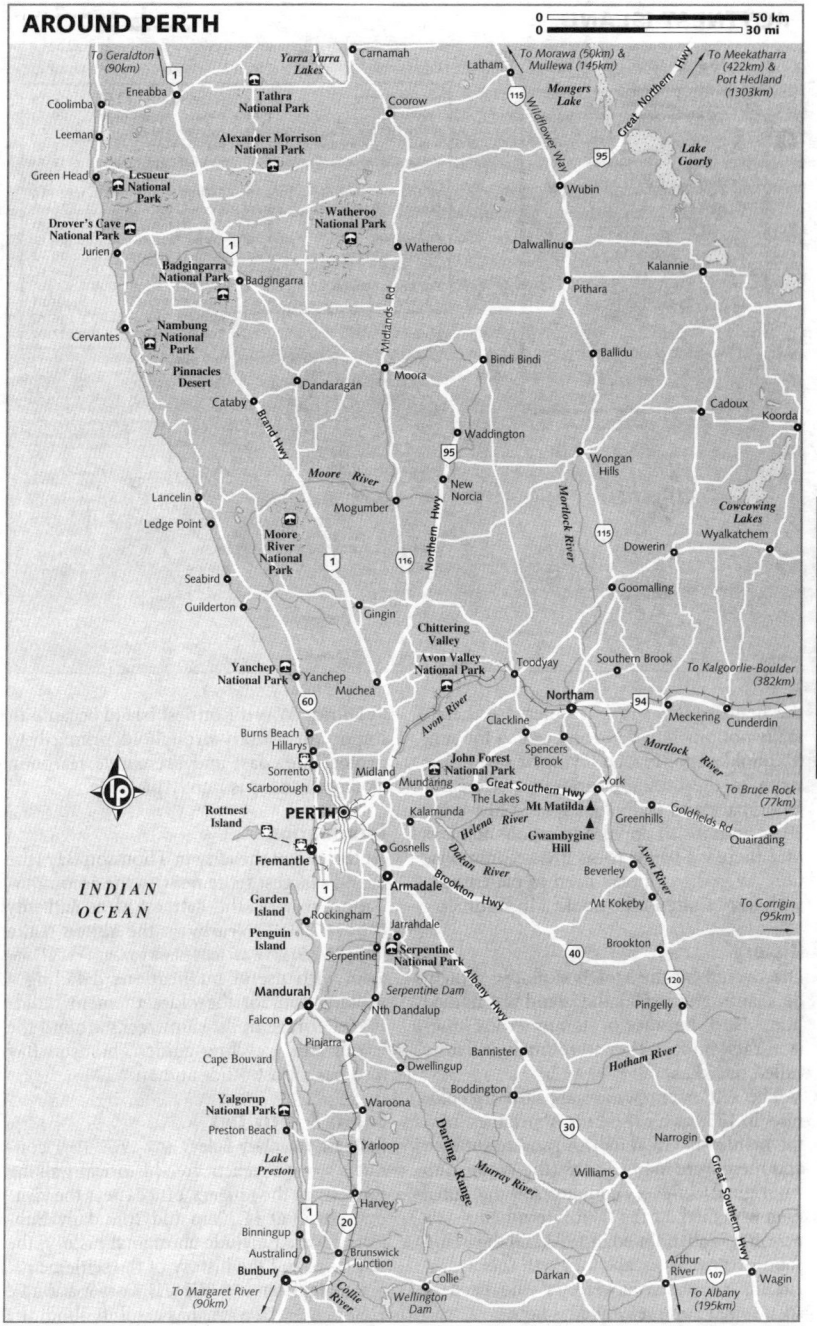

AROUND PERTH

0 _____ 50 km
0 _____ 30 mi

To Geraldton (90km)
Coolimba
Eneabba
Yarra Yarra Lakes
Carnamah
Latham
To Morawa (50km) & Mullewa (145km)
Great Northern Hwy
To Meekatharra (422km) & Port Hedland (1303km)
Tathra National Park
Coorow
Mongers Lake
Leeman
Alexander Morrison National Park
Wildflower Way
Lake Goorly
Green Head
Lesueur National Park
Drover's Cave National Park
Jurien
Watheroo National Park
Watheroo
Wubin
Dalwallinu
Badgingarra National Park
Badgingarra
Midlands Rd
Kalannie
Nambung National Park
Pithara
Cervantes
Pinnacles Desert
Bindi Bindi
Ballidu
Cadoux
Koorda
Cataby
Dandaragan
Moora
Brand Hwy
Moore River
Waddington
Wongan Hills
Cowcowing Lakes
Wyalkatchem
Lancelin
Mogumber
New Norcia
Mortlock River
Dowerin
Ledge Point
Moore River National Park
Northern Hwy
Goomalling
Seabird
Guilderton
Gingin
Chittering Valley
Avon Valley National Park
Toodyay
Southern Brook
To Kalgoorlie-Boulder (382km)
Yanchep National Park
Yanchep
Muchea
Avon River
Northam
Meckering
Cunderin
Mortlock River
Burns Beach
Hillarys
Sorrento
Scarborough
Midland
Mundaring
John Forest National Park
Clackline
Spencers Brook
York
To Bruce Rock (77km)
Rottnest Island
PERTH
The Lakes
Great Southern Hwy
Mt Matilda
Greenhills
Goldfields Rd
Quairading
Fremantle
Kalamunda
Helena River
Gwambygine Hill
Garden Island
Gosnells
Darkan River
Avon River
Penguin Island
Armadale
Rockingham
Brookton Hwy
Beverley
Mt Kokeby
To Corrigin (95km)
Jarrahdale
Serpentine
Serpentine National Park
Brookton
INDIAN OCEAN
Mandurah
Serpentine Dam
Albany Hwy
Pingelly
Falcon
Nth Dandalup
Bannister
Pinjarra
Cape Bouvard
Dwellingup
Hotham River
Boddington
Yalgorup National Park
Waroona
Narrogin
Preston Beach
Yarloop
Williams
Lake Preston
Darling Range
Murray River
Great Southern Hwy
Harvey
Binningup
Australind
Brunswick Junction
Bunbury
Collie
Darkan
Arthur River
Wagin
To Margaret River (90km)
Collie River
Wellington Dam
To Albany (195km)

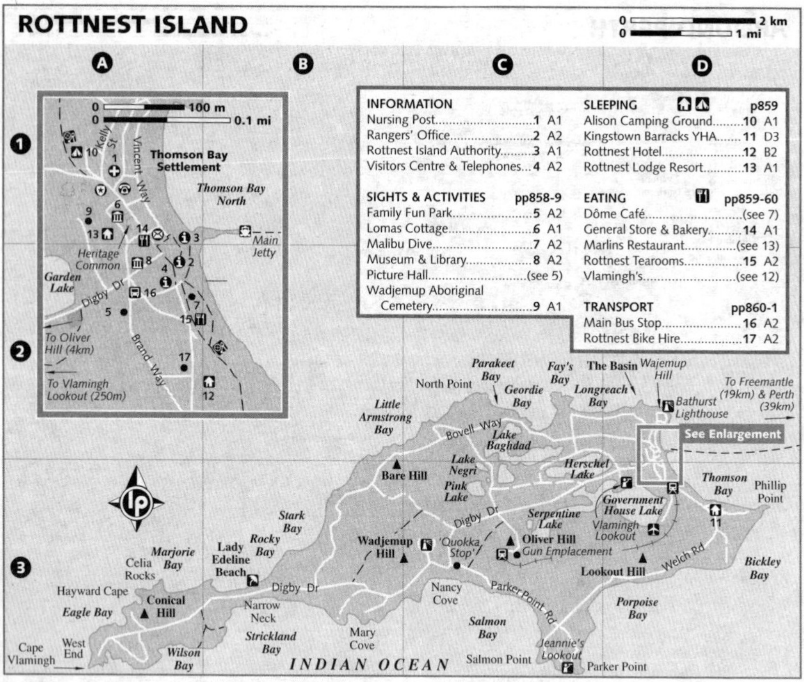
ROTTNEST ISLAND
0 2 km
0 1 mi
A B C D
1 2 3
0 100 m
0 0.1 mi
Thomson Bay Settlement
Thomson Bay North
Kelly St
Vincent Way
Heritage Common
Garden Lake
Digby Dr
Brand Way
Main Jetty
To Oliver Hill (4km)
To Vlamingh Lookout (250m)
INFORMATION
Nursing Post....1 A1
Rangers' Office....2 A2
Rottnest Island Authority....3 A1
Visitors Centre & Telephones....4 A2
SIGHTS & ACTIVITIES pp858-9
Family Fun Park....5 A2
Lomas Cottage....6 A1
Malibu Dive....7 A2
Museum & Library....8 A2
Picture Hall....(see 5)
Wadjemup Aboriginal Cemetery....9 A1
SLEEPING p859
Alison Camping Ground....10 A1
Kingstown Barracks YHA....11 D3
Rottnest Hotel....12 B2
Rottnest Lodge Resort....13 A1
EATING pp859-60
Dôme Café....(see 7)
General Store & Bakery....14 A1
Marlins Restaurant....(see 13)
Rottnest Tearooms....15 A2
Vlamingh's....(see 12)
TRANSPORT pp860-1
Main Bus Stop....16 A2
Rottnest Bike Hire....17 A2
Parakeet Bay
Fay's Bay
The Basin
Wajemup Hill
North Point
Geordie Bay
Longreach Bay
To Freemantle (19km) & Perth (39km)
Bathurst Lighthouse
Little Armstrong Bay
Bovell Way
Lake Baghdad
See Enlargement
Bare Hill
Lake Negri
Pink Lake
Herschel Lake
Thomson Bay
Phillip Point
Government House Lake
Serpentine Lake
Vlamingh Lookout
Stark Bay
Rocky Bay
Marjorie Bay
Lady Edeline Beach
Celia Rocks
Wadjemup Hill
'Quokka Stop'
Oliver Hill
Gun Emplacement
Lookout Hill
Welch Rd
Bickley Bay
Hayward Cape
Conical Hill
Eagle Bay
Digby Dr
Narrow Neck
Nancy Cove
Parker Point Rd
Porpoise Bay
Salmon Bay
Strickland Bay
Mary Cove
Cape Vlamingh
West End
Wilson Bay
INDIAN OCEAN
Salmon Point
Jeannie's Lookout
Parker Point

the main settlement, but otherwise there's really not much to do except laze in the sun, try quokka spotting, go diving or surfing, or swim in the crystal-clear waters. Its easygoing pace and lack of cars has a liberating effect, and it's so popular in school holidays that there's a ballot to secure accommodation. Even day-trippers need to plan ahead, with ferries often fully booked in summer.

History

Discovered by the Dutch explorer Willem de Vlamingh in 1696, the island was named 'Rats' Nest' because of its numerous king-size 'rats' (in fact, they were small wallabies called quokkas).

The settlement was established by colonists in 1838 as a prison for Aborigines from the mainland. Great hardships were suffered and there were many deaths (the Wadjemup Aboriginal Cemetery contains 360 aboriginal men who died during their internment). The prison was abandoned in 1903 and the island soon became an escape for Perth society, including successive governors who liked to spend their summer holidays here.

During WWII Rottnest Island became an important military stronghold, primarily to protect the coast and Fremantle Harbour. Today its focus is purely pleasure.

Information

At the end of the jetty in Thomson Bay (the island's largest settlement) is the accommodation service, the **Rottnest Island Authority** (☎ 9432 9111). Nearby is the **visitors centre** (☎ 9372 9752; www.rottnest.wa.gov.au; 🕑 8.15am-5pm), with useful publications detailing a walking tour of the old settlement buildings, heritage trails, shipwrecks around the island and a cycling guide. Thomson Bay also has a post office and an ATM.

Sights & Activities

Rottnest Voluntary Guides (☎ 9372 9757) conducts some excellent free historical walking tours from the rangers' office (near the visitors centre) at 11.30am and 2pm daily. Subjects covered include aboriginal history, the salt lakes and the history of the settlement.

The **museum** (☎ 9372 9753; Kitson St; adult/child $2.50/1.10; 🕑 11am-4pm) has exhibits about the island's sorry prison history, its wildlife and shipwrecks. Take the time to wander around the old convict-built buildings, including the prison **Quod** and **Lomas Cottage** (☾ 10.30am-12.30pm).

Of course, most visitors come for the **beaches**, with the best surf breaks at Strickland, Salmon and Stark Bays, and idyllic swimming beaches at the Basin, Longreach and Geordie Bays.

Rottnest's temperate waters, beautiful coral and shipwreck sights are an appealing combination for snorkellers and scuba divers. **Malibu Dive** (☎ 9292 5111; www.rottnestdiving.com.au; Thomson Bay) offers a range of snorkelling/diving day trips ($80/200) and scuba-diving courses (four-day open-water course $385). It also hires out snorkelling and fishing gear.

Vlamingh Lookout on View Hill has panoramic views of the island. Quokka-spotters will find the cute creatures around the low-lying salt lakes in the interior. You can also visit the guns and tunnels of the restored **Oliver Hill Gun Emplacement** (adult/child $15.50/7.70), west of Thomson Bay. It's linked by the Oliver Hill tourist railway line, and trains leave Thomson Bay four times daily.

The **Family Fun Park** (☎ 9292 5156; adult/child $8/5; ☾ 9am-7pm) has trampolines and an 18-hole mini golf course, while the nearby **Picture Hall** plays the latest movies several times a week.

Tours

Two-hour **coach tours** (adult/child $22/11) with commentary depart from the visitors centre daily.

From September to June, Fremantle-based **Capricorn Kayak Tours** (☎ 1800 625 688; www.capricorn kayak.com.au) takes visitors out on two-hour/half-day/full-day tours $50/80/130.

The **Rottnest Island Eco-Boat** (☎ 0419-863 602; http://ecoboat.com; adult/child full-day trips $135/125, cheaper off-peak rates; ☾ Oct-May) runs activity-packed day trips. A typical trip includes a visit to the Carnac Island sea lions, snorkelling, some light-tackle fishing and a barbecue lunch.

Sleeping

There's an interesting variety of accommodation options on the island, but beware of the summer frenzy when the place is chock-a-block with Perth holiday-makers. Prices given are high-season (you can expect significant reductions at other times).

Kingstown Barracks YHA (☎ 9372 9780; fax 9292 5141; dm/d $20/50; ☐) Backpackers occasionally share the old army barracks with school groups (ring ahead). Budget breakfasts, lunches and dinners are available in the adjoining dining room. Around 1.3km southeast of the ferry terminal, you can get here by foot, bike or shuttle bus.

Cabins, Bungalows & Villas (☎ 9432 9111; reservations@rottnest.wa.gov.au; 1st/2nd night 4-bed bungalows $75/35, 4-bed ocean-front villas from $180/95) There's a wide variety of self-contained accommodation on the island, with 250 cabins, bungalows, cottages and villas in Thomson Bay and around Geordie, Fays and Longreach Bays. Ask about off-peak and weekly rates, and book in advance, particularly in summer.

Rottnest Hotel (☎ 9292 5011; rottnesthotel@axismgt.com.au; Bedford Ave; s/d from $140/180) Once the governor's official summer residence, this historic hotel (1864) features pleasant rooms, an adjoining restaurant, bars and beer garden. It's worth paying extra for the bayside rooms with private beachfront courtyards (ask about mid-week specials).

Rottnest Lodge Resort (☎ 9292 5161; www.rott nestlodge.com.au; Kitson St; tw/d/f from $165/180/450; ☐) Choose from swish lakeside options, large family apartments or basic rooms in the former Quod (prison) at this luxurious resort; guests are welcome to use the resort-style pool, cocktail bar and restaurant.

Allison camping ground (☎ 9432 9111; Thomson Bay; camp sites per person $6) Affectionately known as Tentland, this shady camping ground has a laundry, ablution block and barbecues.

Eating

Thomson Bay's shopping centre has a well-stocked **general store** (☾ 8am-7pm) and a bakery famed for its fresh bread and pies.

Rottnest Tearooms (☎ 9292 5171; Thomson Bay; mains $9.50-26) This casual, licensed family-friendly place with fantastic bay views has a children's playground and serves burgers and gourmet sandwiches. Don't forget your novelty souvenir menu, which covers Rottnest news.

Dôme Café (☎ 9292 5026; Henderson Rd; mains $7.50-22) Next door to the Tearooms, a branch of the ever-reliable Dôme Café chain offers delicious food, a mellow atmosphere and idyllic views over the water.

Vlamingh's (☎ 9292 5011; Rottnest Hotel; mains $20-28) Based within the large Rottnest Hotel complex, this fully licensed restaurant offers fine dining all day and a lengthy à-la-carte menu. Fresh-off-the-boat oysters and mussels are specialities.

Also recommended for quality seafood is **Marlins Restaurant** (☎ 9292 5161; Rottnest Lodge Resort; mains $21-30), with pleasant poolside tables.

Getting There & Away

There are frequent ferries to Rottnest from Fremantle (30 minutes) and a handful of daily services from Perth (1½ hours). The following companies have similar prices – around $40/35/13 for adults/backpackers/children for a same-day return from Fremantle, and $55/50/18 from Perth, with $5 extra for an extended stay. You'll need a YHA or VIP card to get the backpacker rate.

BoatTorque (☎ 9430 5844; www.boattorque.com.au) runs at least nine daily ferries from Fremantle, departing from either Victoria Quay's C Shed or the Northport terminal. From Perth's Barrack St Jetty there are services at 8.45am, 9.45am and 2pm.

Oceanic Cruises (☎ 9430 5127) offers six daily ferries each way from Victoria Quay's B Shed, and an 8.15am service from the East St Jetty in Fremantle. From the Barrack St Jetty in Perth, ferries leave at 8.45am, 10am, noon and 2pm. If you're prepared to return to Fremantle on the 8pm ferry, you can save a few bucks with Oceanic's 'Sundowner' fare ($30/20 per adult/child).

Both companies offer several transport and accommodation packages.

Rottnest Air Taxi (☎ 1800 500 006) has a same-day return flight to Rotto (in four-/six-seater planes) from Perth's Jandakot Airport (from $60 per person if there are a few of you).

Getting Around

The number of cars is strictly limited, which makes cycling a real pleasure. The island is

---

CHRISTMAS & COCOS (KEELING) ISLANDS *by Virginia Jealous*

Christmas Island
☎ 08 / pop 1510

Christmas Island (CI), in Australia's remote Indian Ocean Territories, is 360km south of Jakarta, Indonesia, and 2300km northwest of Perth. A rugged limestone mountain, CI was settled in 1888 to mine phosphate and this is still the main economic activity. Its people are a mix of Chinese, Malays and European-Australians, a blend reflected in the island's food, languages, customs and religions. Several Singapore-style colonial buildings remain, as do traces from the three-year Japanese occupation in WWII.

The island had its 15 minutes of fame in August 2001 when the Norwegian container ship *Tampa*, with its cargo of rescued asylum seekers, was refused permission to land. For more information about the *Tampa* episode and Australia's policy towards refugees, see the boxed text 'Asylum Seekers & Mandatory Detention' (p58). Despite – or, possibly, because of – CI's remoteness from the mainland and the media, and the difficulty and expense of access to it, the island was subsequently excised from Australia's migration zone and designated a future holding-pen for asylum seekers. As such, asylum seekers held on Christmas Island do not have full access to legal challenges and reviews available on the mainland. Plans are underway for a permanent 'immigration reception and processing centre' (up to 1000 beds) to be completed by 2006, but rumour has it that on completion, given the nonarrival of boats and asylum seekers since *Tampa*, it's as likely to be used as a strategic military base instead. Along with a long-planned, much-delayed, and – in 2003 – barely started satellite launching facility, the island may be well on its way to full-scale entry onto the global political scene.

In spite of this flurry of activity, 63% of the island remains protected by Christmas Island National Park. There is tall rainforest on the plateau, and a series of limestone cliffs and terraces that attract endemic nesting seabirds, including the gorgeous golden bosun and rare Abbott's booby. Prior to *Tampa*, CI was – and remains – famous for a different sort of migratory activity, the spectacular annual movement in November/December of millions of red land crabs marching from the forest down to the coast to breed. They cover everything in sight on their migration routes, roads are closed, and playing a round of golf is particularly tricky. Marine life is also

just big enough to make a day's ride fine exercise. **Rottnest Bike Hire** (☎ 9292 5105; Thomson Bay; ☽ 8.30am-5pm) hires out bicycles for adults/children from $15/10 a day, including locks and helmets; a $25 deposit is required, and a breakdown service is available.

A free bus departs regularly from the main jetty in Thomson Bay between 8.15am and 9pm. It goes to Geordie Bay, Kingstown and the airport.

Bayseeker (adult/child all-day ticket $7/3.50) leaves Thomson Bay every half-hour from 8.40am to 4.40pm and does a circuit of the island, stopping at all the main bays and beaches.

NORTH OF PERTH

The coast north of Perth is windswept and barren, and although the sprawling sands look inviting, these beaches are much better for water sports than sun-worshipping. Popular with day-trippers is **Yanchep National Park**, 51km north, a pretty bushland park with plentiful wildlife, including a protected colony of koalas. Visitors can explore the limestone **Crystal Cave**, paddle boats on **Loch McNess** and wander down the **Yaberoo Budjara Aboriginal Heritage Trail**.

Lancelin
☎ 08 / pop 600

The wind sweeps up so dramatically from the Indian Ocean at Lancelin that it has made the once sleepy crayfishing town a mecca for windsurfers and kitesurfers in summer, particularly during January's three-day Ocean Classic (the popular Ledge Point to Lancelin race). In this resort town 130km north of Perth, it's not uncommon for European windsurfers to hang out for months, whooping it up in Lancelin's consistently windy conditions.

Head to the beach and watch the gun windsurfers do their stuff. If you're inspired, **Werner's Hot Spot** (☎ 9655 1553) offers lessons for newbies ($15 to $20) and hires out the latest boards and gear from a Kombi

dramatic, with bright corals and fish on the fringing reefs attracting snorkellers in the dry season (roughly April to November), when international yachties also drop anchor. Divers come throughout the year for the drop-off, wall and cave dives, and are especially drawn to the possibility of diving with seasonal whale sharks (roughly October to April). A sea swell can bring decent surf during the wet season (roughly December to March).

National Jet Systems (book through Qantas ☎ 13 13 13) flies a circle from Perth, usually via the Cocos (Keeling) Islands, two or three times a week ($1680 return; 5 to 7 hours, depending on route). There is also a return charter flight at least once a week from Jakarta ($650 return, 50 minutes), which must be booked directly with **CI Travel** (☎ 9164 7168; xch@citravel.com.au). Visa requirements are as for Australia, and Australians should bring their passports.

Visitor accommodation is in self-contained units, motel-style rooms or resort-style suites from $80 to $100 per room per night, or check out the cheaper combined flight and accommodation packages. Some budget rooms are expected to become available during 2003. Expect to pay around $5 to $10 for lunch and $20 for dinner in the several Chinese and European-Australian restaurants.

Christmas Island **visitors centre** (☎ 9164 8382; www.christmas.net.au) can coordinate accommodation, diving, fishing and car hire. Visit its excellent website for links to travel agents offering packages, other local businesses and detailed island information.

Cocos (Keeling) Islands
☎ 08 / pop 600

Some 900km further west are the Cocos (Keeling) Islands (CKI), the necklace of low-lying islands around a blue lagoon that inspired Charles Darwin's theory of coral atoll formation. Settled by John Clunies-Ross in 1826 (and briefly by a huge contingent of British forces during WWII), his family remained in control of the islands and their Malay workers until 1978, when CKI became part of Australia's Indian Ocean territories. Now, a population of about 500 Malays and 100 European-Australians live on the two settled islands. It's a *very* low-key place where people come to walk, snorkel, dive, fish, surf and relax. Check out the two island-information websites www.cocos-tourism.cc and www.cocos-solutions.com.

parked at the beach from October to March (phone at other times and the friendly Swiss will meet you). Thrill-seekers can learn kitesurfing for $70 per hour.

If you prefer to stay on dry land, the town is backed by enormous dunes that are ideal for **sand-boarding**. But be warned: it'll cost you 10 minutes of arduous climbing for a few seconds of thrills. This is also the home of the amazing 'Bigfoot' – a 32-seat American school bus on enormous monster-truck wheels that takes delighted (sometimes shrieking) travellers on a wild ride through the dunes daily; contact **Desert Storm Adventures** (☎ 9655 2550; www.desertstorm.com.au; adult/child $35/25).

SLEEPING & EATING

Lancelin Lodge YHA (☎ 9655 2020; www.lancelin lodge.com.au; 10 Hopkins St; dm $20, d/f from $50/60; 🖳) Friendly and well equipped, this purpose-built lodge has enthusiastic owners and small but comfy rooms. Catering to windsurfers and other sporty types, new additions include a pool and a volleyball court.

Windsurfer Beach Chalets (☎ 9655 1454; fax 9655 2454; 1 Hopkins St; d $95) A brand-new refit makes these compact self-contained two-bedroom chalets by the windsurfing beach an appealing option. Fantastic for families or groups of friends, each chalet can sleep six (extra people $15).

As close to the beach as you can get is the tidy, quiet **Lancelin Caravan Park** (☎ /fax 9655 1056; Hopkins St; 2-person camp/caravan sites $18/22, on-site caravans $22).

El Tropo (☎ 9655 1448; 119 Gingin Rd; mains $23-28) You'll find windsurfing Werner moonlighting at this fun, colourful seafood restaurant from Wednesday to Sunday nights. El Tropo serves up a range of modern Australian meals.

Crayside Restaurant & Café (☎ 9655 2828; Hopkins Rd; mains $4-15) For daytime filling fare, try this diner-style caff directly across from the caravan park, with an all-day brekky and delicious vegie burgers ($5).

Endeavour Tavern (☎ 9655 1052; 58 Gingin Rd) The views are priceless at this classic beach-front pub, with a beer garden, grassy area and excellent climbing tree for the kiddies. The only down side is the occasional pong that wafts over from the seafood company next door.

GETTING THERE & AWAY

Catch-a-bus (☎ 9655 2020; one way $25) is a shuttle service run by the YHA that offers drop-offs and pick-ups in Perth on Monday, Wednesday and Friday, more often at busy times.

A 4WD-only coast road continues up to Cervantes.

Pinnacles Desert

The small beach town of **Cervantes** (population 480), 257km north of Perth, is a busy cray-fishing port and the entry point for the eerie **Pinnacles Desert**. Part of the large coastal **Nambung National Park** (admission bus passenger/car $4/9), the Pinnacles are made up of thousands of peculiar limestone pillars resembling termite nests – some only a few centimetres high, others towering up to 5m – that jut out of the desert floor like so many soldiers. Dawn and dusk are the best times to visit, when crowds are low, the heat is bearable, and purple and orange hues provide a haunting note to the scene, as well as good photographic conditions. The park is also the scene of an impressive wildflower display from August to October.

The park is 13km from Cervantes and has a good gravel road that loops through the main concentrations of the Pinnacles. Nearby are two clean white-sand beaches (**Kangaroo Point** and **Hangover Bay**) for a cooling dip after your visit.

A string of towns runs north of Cervantes from Jurian Bay to Dongara – see p907 for details.

TOURS

Trips into the Pinnacles are offered by **Turquoise Coast Enviro Tours** (☎ 08-9652 7047; 59 Seville St, Cervantes; half-day Pinnacles tour $30, full-day regional tour $110). Hosted by a former national park ranger, these tours are fun and informative. The Pinnacles tours leave daily at 8am and 2½ hours before sunset, while the longer tour leaves at 8am, takes 10½ hours and also gives you a look at Lesueur National Park, Jurian Bay, Little Three Springs and Stockyard Tunnel Cave.

SLEEPING & EATING

All accommodation is found in Cervantes, where there's a tavern, takeaway shops, an ATM and a supermarket.

Pinnacles Caravan Park (☎ 08-9652 7060; fax 9652 7112; 35 Aragon St; camp/caravan sites $17/20, on-site vans/cabins $25/40) Right on the beach, this park is pleasant and shady, although you may need to book ahead for the limited number of cabins and vans.

Pinnacles Beach Backpackers (☎ 08-9652 7377, bookings ☎ 1800 245 232; www.wn.com.au /pbbackpackers; 91 Seville St; dm $20, s & d $55; 🖳) A clean and bright place close to the beach, it has friendly staff, a well-equipped kitchen, plenty of recreation space and tiny dorms.

Cervantes Holiday Homes (☎ /fax 08-9652 7115; cnr Malaga Ct & Valencia Rd; 1-/2-/3-bed units from $55/65/ 75) These good-value, stand-alone holiday units are classic holiday accommodation – simple, well worn and spacious with full kitchen, comfy lounges and TV. Prices increase by about $20 in high season.

Cervantes Pinnacles Motel (☎ 08-9652 7145; pinnacles@bigpond.com; 7 Aragon St; s, d & tw $105; 🏊) The best-appointed option in town, the rooms are small but comfortable and well cared for. The motel's Europa Anchor Restaurant serves fresh seafood from 6.30pm every night, but bookings are essential (last orders 8pm).

If it's cray season (November to June), the takeaway shop offers succulent lobster meals for $33. The other option is the **Ronsard Bay Tavern** (☎ 08-9652 7009; 1 Cadiz St; mains $11-21), which has a fair menu of counter meals, a big-screen TV and pool tables.

GETTING THERE & AWAY
McCafferty's/Greyhound (☎ 13 20 30) services to Perth ($28, 3¾ hours, 3 weekly) and Geraldton ($39, 2¾ hours, 3 weekly) leave from the Shell Roadhouse.

DARLING RANGE
The hills surrounding Perth are popular for picnics and bushwalks. Garden lovers gravitate to **Araluen Botanic Garden** (☎ 08-9496 1171; www.araluenbotanicpark.com.au; 362 Croydon Rd, Roleystone; adult/child $6/3; ☽ 9am-6pm) to the northeast, with terraced gardens full of colourful bulbs in spring. Directly east of the airport is the **Zig Zag Scenic Drive** through Gooseberry Hill National Park, and **Lake Leschenaultia**, a pleasant recreation area with canoe hire, barbecues and walks.

Mundaring
☎ 08 / pop 1900
Tranquil, pretty Mundaring is a real surprise – a haven for bushwalkers and nature lovers, but also a small but thriving arts centre with occasional big-ticket performances at the Mundaring Weir Hotel. Just 35km east of Perth, Mundaring's main claim to fame is its weir, which sits at the beginning of the Golden Pipeline and has pumped water to the goldfields for more than a century. The reservoir has an attractive bushland setting and a number of interesting walks.

Opposite the hotel is the **Mundaring Weir Gallery** (☎ 9295 0200; ☽ 11.30am-5pm Sat & Sun), which displays arts and crafts from 50 local artists and designers.

Excellent for bushwalking is the nearby **John Forrest National Park**, WA's first national park, with protected areas of jarrah and marri trees, and plenty of native animals.

CALM's **Hills Forest Discovery Centre** (☎ 9295 2244; www.naturebase.net; Mundaring Weir Rd) runs activity programmes year-round, including Encounter Animals trips, Indigenous Culture walks, and the Nightshift, a torchlight guided bushwalk. Camping is available at the centre.

In summer, the **Outdoor Kookaburra Cinema** (☎ 9295 6190; Allen Rd, Mundaring Weir; adult/child $10/7) runs the latest releases from Thursday to Sunday.

For 15 years the historic **Mundaring Weir Hotel** (☎ 9295 1106; www.mundaringweirhotel.com .au; Mundaring Weir Rd; weekday d $83; 🏊) has cultivated an impressive arts programme, hosting theatre, classical concerts and acts such as David Helfgott and Marianne Faithfull. Popular with Perth weekenders, the higher weekend rates (doubles from $160) include dinner for two.

If you want to go bush, the rustic **Djaril Mari YHA** (☎ 9295 1809; perthhillsyha@aol.com; Mundaring Weir Rd; dm/s/tw/f $19/33/44/59, nonmembers extra $3.50) has a peaceful, bushland setting near the reservoir. Staff can arrange pick-ups from Mundaring and meals if booked in advance.

Loose Box (☎ 9295 1787; www.loosebox.com; 6285 Great Eastern Hwy; 4-course dinners $80) remains a highlight of WA's thriving gastronomic scene, with a foyer-full of foodie accolades and dishes like works of art. Dinner and accommodation packages in luxury cottages are available.

To get to Mundaring by public transport, catch a Transperth train to Midland train station, and then bus No 320 out to Mundaring.

AVON VALLEY

A popular retreat for Perth weekenders, the lush Avon Valley, about 100km northeast of Perth, resembles England (in spring at least, when it's rich with wildflowers). The cooler months are the best time to visit, with the hills becoming parched and yellow in summer. The valley was first settled in 1830, only a year after Perth was founded, and there are many historic buildings to explore. New guesthouses and B&Bs seem to spring up in the valley each year, so check the local visitors centres for an up-to-date list.

GETTING THERE & AWAY

Transwa (☎ 1300 662 205) has regular buses to Toodyay ($11.70), Northam ($13.70, 1½ hours), York ($11.70, 2 hours) and Beverley ($15.55, 2½ hours). For the same fare, you can also get to Toodyay and Northam by train on the weekday *AvonLink* service or the daily *Prospector*. The best way to explore the valley, however, is in your own car.

Toodyay

☎ 08 / pop 800

With its numerous convict-constructed buildings in a charming riverside setting, Toodyay is a pleasant place to spend an afternoon. For a self-guided tour, grab the *Town Walk* brochure from the **visitors centre** (☎ 9574 2435; 7 Piesse St; 🕑 9am-5pm, opens 10am Sun), off Stirling Tce.

The **Old Newcastle Gaol Museum** (☎ 9574 5053; 17 Clinton St; adult/child $2/1; 🕑 10am-3pm) has some fascinating pioneering displays and tells the story of the renowned bushranger and escapologist Moondyne Joe. About 6km west of Toodyay is **Coorinja winery** (☎ 9574 2280; Toodyay Rd; 🕑 10am-5pm Mon-Sat), which dates from the 1870s.

The **Old Victoria Hotel/Motel** (☎ 9574 2206; fax 9574 4504; 116 Stirling Tce; s/d $30/60, motel units $75; ❄), known affectionately as the 'Vic', is a basic pub in the centre of town with simple renovated hotel rooms, and no-frills motel units (with bathrooms) at the back.

For campers, there's the riverside **Toodyay Caravan Park** (☎ 9574 2612; fax 9574 5010; Avon Banks, Railway Rd; camp/caravan sites $14/17, on-site caravans $39, chalets $65).

Cino's on the Terrace (☎ 9574 4888; 102 Stirling Tce; mains $11-20.50; 🕑 8am-10pm) is the best eating option in town, with alfresco dining and a range of tasty pizzas and salads.

The **Cola Café & Museum** (☎ 9574 4407; 122 Stirling Tce; mains $6-11) proudly (and bizarrely) displays 100 years of Coca-Cola memorabilia, and burgers are its speciality.

Other options along Stirling Tce are **Wendouree Tea Rooms** (☎ 9574 2246) and the **Toodyay Bakery** (☎ 9574 2617).

Avon Valley National Park

Downriver from Toodyay, this park is distinguished by its granite outcrops, diverse plant and birdlife, and transitional forests of jarrah and marri mixing with wandoo woodlands. There are **camp sites** (2 people $11) with basic facilities. The park is 30km from Toodyay and the entrance is 5km off the main road (park fees apply; see the boxed text 'Your Ticket to Nature'; p829).

Northam

☎ 08 / pop 7000

Though this large farming centre is now a stop on the railway line to Kalgoorlie, it was once the end of the line and the jumping-off point for miners trekking hundreds of kilometres to the goldfields. Today, the town is a hub for local farmers and the major town in the Avon Valley. Every year Northam is packed on the first weekend in August for the start of the gruelling 133km Avon Descent race for power boats and canoeists.

The friendly, modern **Avon Valley visitors centre** (☎ 9622 2100; 2 Grey St; 🕑 9am-5pm), overlooking the Avon River, has a fascinating free exhibition about Northam's post-war refugee camps.

A regional highlight is ballooning at dawn over the Avon Valley. Conditions are so good here that Steve Fossett chose Northam to launch his solo round-the-world ballooning effort in mid-2002. If you've got a head for heights, contact **Windward Balloon Adventures** (☎ 9621 2000; www.windwardballooning.com; weekdays/ weekends Mar-Nov $200/250). Prices include a one-hour flight, and after-flight breakfast and celebratory champagne.

Historical museums include the 1836 **Morby Cottage** (☎ 9622 2100; Old York Rd; adult/child $2/1; 🕑 10.30am-4pm Sun) and the National Trust–listed **old railway station** (☎ 9622 2100; Fitzgerald St; adult/child $2/0.50; 🕑 10am-4pm Sun). Look for the colony of **white swans** on the Avon River, the descendants of birds introduced in the early 1900s to remind British colonists of home.

SLEEPING & EATING

Colonial Tavern (☎ 9622 1074; colonialtavern@big
pond.com.au; 197 Duke St; s/d/f $45/60/75; ❷) Large,
comfy rooms are great value in this historic
1907 hotel with a large outdoor beer garden
and happy hour from 5pm to 6pm. The new
owner has big plans, so ask about new accommodation options.

Northam Caravan Park (☎ 9622 1620; 500 Great
Eastern Hwy; camp/caravan sites $9/17, on-site caravans
$39; ❷) If you're on a budget, this friendly
park is a good cheap alternative on the
fringes of town.

Shamrock Hotel (☎ 9622 1092; shamrockhotelnorth
am@bigpond.com; 112 Fitzgerald St; r from $110; ❷) The
up-market historic Shamrock offers lovingly
restored elegant rooms with bathrooms. Ask
about special discounts and packages, as
prices are often dramatically reduced (particularly from January to March).

Brackson House (☎ 9622 5262; brackson@avon.net
.au; 2 Old York Rd; s/d $100/105) This family-friendly
option has an adventure playground for the
kids and a spa and barbecue for the young
at heart. Rooms are spacious and there are
several comfortable recreational areas where
guests can kick back and relax.

Cafe Fium (☎ 9621 1062; 1 Grey St; mains $10-
12.50) Fium's lovely outdoor deck overlooking the river is the perfect place for a coffee
pick-me-up or a light meal while you pore
over brochures from the visitors centre
next door.

Central Cafe (☎ 9622 2702; 150 Fitzgerald St; breakfast $4-10) On the main drag, the convenient
Central Cafe opens at 7am most days and is
ideal for a quick, cheap breakfast.

York

☎ 08 / pop 3000

It's not surprising that the entire town of
York is classified by the National Trust,
with its picture-postcard main street and
countless historic buildings. Wander down
Avon Tce for excellent photo opportunities
at the Castle Hotel, the police station, gaol
and courthouse. Don't miss **St Patrick's Cathedral**, just off the main drag, or the nearby
Convent Gallery, now displaying furniture
and artwork.

One of the most impressive buildings in
town is the old town hall, which houses the
visitors centre (☎ 9641 1301; cnr Avon Tce & Joaquina
St; ❤ 9am-5pm). You can check your email at
Kookaburra Dream (☎ 9641 2936; 152 Avon Tce; per

hr $4) or **York IT & Communication** (89 Avon Tce;
per hr $8).

Learn how York's ancestors lived in the
horse-and-coach days at the 1850s **Residency
Museum** (☎ 9641 1751; Brook St; adult/child $3/1.50;
❤ 1-3pm Tue-Thu, noon-4pm Sat & Sun).

If you've ever toyed with the idea of jumping from a plane, the **Skydive Express** (☎ 9444
4199; www.skydive.com.au; tandem skydive $260) drop-
zone, five minutes from town, might be the
place to take that giant step. Pay an extra $99
to have your adventure videotaped for posterity. Facilities include café, bar, swimming
pool, sauna and free dorm accommodation
for jumpers.

The classy **Motor Museum** (☎ 9641 1288;
116 Avon Tce; adult/child $7.50/3.50; ❤ 9.30am-4pm)
houses an interesting collection of vintage,
classic and racing cars.

Housed in a disused timber mill, **Jah-Roc
Mill Gallery** (☎ 9641 2522; 7-13 Broome St) is the
largest regional gallery in the state, with fine
furniture and arts and crafts. The complex
includes an arts and crafts shop, a furniture
maker, wood turning, a blacksmith and a
café.

York loves a good festival, with as many
as a dozen major annual events. The bigger
ones are the **Jazz Festival** in September, the
Antique and Collectors fair in April, the **Festival
of the Car** in July and a **spring garden festival**.

SLEEPING & EATING

Kookaburra Dream (☎ 9641 2936; kookaburras@west
net.com.au; 152 Avon Tce; dm/s/f $22/29/85; 🖵) Small
and intimate, this brand new hostel on the
main street has a great vibe and a family
feel. Rates include a generous continental
breakfast with fresh fruit and eggs.

Mt Bakewell Caravan Park (☎ /fax 9641 1421;
Eighth Rd; camp/caravan sites $17/18, on-site caravans $40)
An adorable elderly couple run this tranquil
park in the shadow of Mt Bakewell, about
2km north of the town centre.

Castle Hotel (☎ 9641 1007; fax 9641 1564; 97 Avon
Tce; s/d $35/70, motel s/d with bathroom $70/100; ❷)
Rooms in this attractive historic hotel are
spacious and good value, with many opening onto the balcony. If you prefer privacy
and a complimentary breakfast, there are
motel units overlooking the swimming pool
at the back.

Langsford House (☎ 9641 1440; langsford@west
net.com.au; 18 Avon Tce; d from $150; ❷) Antique
four-poster beds and claw-foot baths help

transport guests to another time at this luxury five-star historic house, with gorgeous gardens and a solar-heated swimming pool and spa.

Imperial Inn (☎ 9641 1010; 83 Avon Tce; mains $15-18) Directly opposite the visitors centre, this grand old hotel offers standard pub grub, with fish and meat dishes, and the occasional Indian meal thrown in.

Yorky's Coffee Carriage (☎ 9641 1554; Glebe St; mains $6.70-15.50; ☺ opens 5pm Thu-Sun) Yorky's serves diner-style nosh from an old railway carriage by the Avon, and is a popular local hangout. If the kids need to burn some energy, there's a playground nearby.

Jule's Shoppe (☎ 9641 1832; 119 Avon Tce; snacks $3-10; ☺ closed Sun) Tummy rumbling but not ready for dinner? Try this cruisy caff with hearty sandwiches, filling kebabs and delicious pasties.

Beverley
☎ 08 / pop 790

Beverley is a tiny historic town on the Avon River, just south of York. Plane-spotters will enjoy a flying visit to its **aeronautical museum** (☎ 9646 1555; 139 Vincent St; adult $4; ☺ 9am-4pm); look for the Vampire jet mounted on the front lawn. Exhibits include a locally built 1930 biplane, *Silver Centenary*. The **visitors centre** is in the same building.

Thrill-seekers can take to the air with the **Beverley Soaring Society** (☎ 0407-385 361; www.beverley-soaring.org.au), which offers glider rides from Friday to Sunday at the nearby airfield.

The free **Avondale Discovery Farm** (☎ 9646 1004; Waterhatch Rd; ☺ 10am-4pm), 6km west of Beverley, is great for kids, with an adventure playground and animal nursery.

Overnighters will be content at the lovingly restored **Beverley Hotel** (☎ 9646 1190; fax 9646 1180; 137 Vincent St; s/d/f $25/50/66), with large, homy rooms and many quirky touches.

For a basic alternative, try the **Beverley Caravan Park** (☎ 9646 1200; fax 9646 1409; 136 Vincent St; 2-person caravan sites $11), behind the shire offices.

SOUTH OF PERTH

The coast south of Perth has a softer appearance than the often harsh landscape to the north, and is a popular beach-resort area for Perth residents, many of who have holiday homes here.

GETTING THERE & AWAY

Transperth city buses buzz back and forth between Perth and Rockingham many times a day. Catch bus No 920 or 126 from Fremantle ($5.50, 45 minutes), or bus No 866 from Perth's City Busport ($5.50, 1 hour). For Mandurah, catch bus No 107 from Perth ($7.80, 70 minutes). **South West Coachlines** (☎ 08-9324 2333) also does drop-offs at Mandurah ($13.80).

The *Australind* train service stops at Pinjarra ($10.90, 1¼ hours) twice daily. Unfortunately, there's no public transport to Dwellingup.

Rockingham
☎ 08 / pop 66,000

Rockingham is 47km south of Perth; it's a rather bland dormitory city and seaside resort which has sheltered and ocean beaches. Its main attraction is the Shoalwater Islands Marine Park offshore, a rich marine environment with submerged reefs, shipwrecks and a chain of limestone islands. Visitors flock to the islands to see wildlife up close, with colonies of Australian sea lions, penguins and sea birds, including silver gulls, fairy terns and crested terns. For information about the islands and activities in town, see the **visitors centre** (☎ 9592 3464; 43 Kent St; ☺ 9am-5pm, closes 4pm Sat & Sun).

Penguin & Seal Island Cruises (☎ 9528 2004; www.pengos.com.au; 153 Arcadia Dr, Shoalwater) runs a variety of wildlife-watching trips daily. The Penguin Experience ($13/9.50 per adult/child) includes a short ferry trip to Penguin Island, where you are free to explore, swim or snorkel, and visit the Penguin Experience Island Discovery Centre. There's also a 45-minute cruise of both islands ($29/20) and a snorkel cruise ($35/25).

Rockingham Dolphins (☎ 9591 1333; www.dolphins.com.au) takes small groups of people to swim with a group of wild bottlenose dolphins (daily September to March, $155). If you'd rather stay high and dry, there's a Dolphin Watch Tour, which allows you to watch dolphins play and feed from the comfort of the boat (daily September to May, $67/34 per adult/child). Tours depart from the jetty on Palm Beach; there's also a free shuttle bus from Perth.

Central budget accommodation with basic facilities is available at the **Palm Beach**

GETTING 'UP' TO SPEED

Once you've been in the southwest of the state for a day or two you start to wonder about the 'up' phenomenon. Yallingup, Manjimup, Nannup, Nornalup, Mullalyup, Boyanup, Gelorup… the ups are everywhere, but what does it all mean? Well, after following a few red herrings we finally stumbled across the answer. A friendly national parks officer from Nannup was somewhat of an 'up' expert and explained that it's the local Aboriginal term for 'place of'. So, for those linguists among you, Nannup is the 'Place of Parrots', Nornalup is the 'Place of the Tiger Snake' and Yallingup is, rather romantically, the 'Place of Love'.

Caravan Park (☎ 9527 1515; cnr Fisher & Lake Sts; caravan sites/cabins $20/55).

The **Anchorage** (☎ 9527 4214; http://anchorage .freeservers.com; 2 Smythe St; s/d $75/85), a block back from the beach, offers floral-themed B&B accommodation in a modern, two-storey building with peaceful gardens and guests' balcony.

Beachside Apartment Hotel (☎ 9529 3777; 58 Kent St; ste from $155; 💢) has an excellent beach-front position and some of the best suites and self-contained apartments in town.

Beachcombers (☎ 9527 7195; 43 Rockingham Rd; mains $11-20) is a casual foreshore eatery with hearty breakfasts and a library of trashy magazines for between-bites amusement.

For something different, there's **Zocalo Mexican Restaurant** (☎ 9592 1200; 45 Rockingham Rd; mains $8-18), with an authentic menu and fun atmosphere.

Mandurah

☎ 08 / pop 48,000

Just 74km south of Perth, waterfront Mandurah is a fisherman's paradise and an increasingly popular getaway for Perth weekenders. Mass development has trans-formed this once sleepy haven on the Mandurah Estuary into a town of big boats, palm trees, waterfront mansions and retirees living large on luxury estates.

The waterfront **visitors centre** (☎ 9550 3999; 75 Mandurah Tce) has transport schedules, maps and other information. For a tour among the grand canalside homes, take the **Mandurah City Tram** (adult/child $8/4) from the visitors centre at 10am, 11am and 2pm daily.

With regular dolphin sightings and prolific birdlife on the Peel Inlet and the narrow coastal salt lakes to the south, getting out on the water is a must. One-hour **estuary cruises** (adult/child $11/5.50) leave from the jetty near the visitors centre sev-eral times a day. If you want to go it alone,

you can hire a motorised dinghy from **Mandurah Boat Hire** (☎ 9535 5877).

SLEEPING & EATING

The visitors centre can give you a compre-hensive list of accommodation options, in-cluding several resorts and out-of-the-way B&Bs. Rates can vary according to season.

Yalgorup Eco Park (☎ 9582 1320; www.ecopark.com .au; 8 Henry Rd; Melros Beach; camp/caravan sites $17/20, budget cabins $55, luxury cabins from $120) Guests camp behind sand dunes overlooking a spectacular beach at this quality park, which has a range of accommodation, a tennis court, playground and swimming pool. It's a 15-minute drive south of town, across the Dawesville Channel on Melros Beach.

Foreshore Motel (☎ 9535 5577; foreshoremotel@ westnet.com.au; 2 Gibson St; s/d $80/90) Friendly staff, a convenient central location and swimming pool make this modest motel one of the best options in town.

Reading Room Book Cafe (☎ 9535 1633; 15 Mandurah Tce; mains $10-15) Try a bowl of Tim Winton's Wedgies ($6) or Jeffrey Archer's Nachos ($10) at this book-lovers' haven with comfy couches, shelves of books and a witty sense of humour.

Dôme Café (☎ 9581 1666; Mandurah Tce; mains $10.50-16.50) This breezy waterfront café is a popular spot to sip a latte, read the papers and graze on delicious light meals. Seafood lovers shouldn't miss the crab linguine ($16.50).

Cafe Pronto (☎ 9535 1004; cnr Pinjarra Rd & Mandurah Tce; mains $18-22) The all-day kitchen churns out tasty wood-fired pizzas to an apprecia-tive crowd, who sip beer on the outside deck and watch the world go by.

Miami Bakehouse (☎ 9534 2705; Falcon Grove Shop-ping Centre, Old Coast Rd, Falcon; pies $3-5.50) If you're heading south, schedule a stop at this award-winning bakehouse with 22 gourmet pies, including chilli beef, and crab and fetta.

WESTERN AUSTRALIA

Pinjarra

☎ 08 / pop 2000

It's hard to imagine that this unassuming town, 86km south of Perth on the banks of the Murray River, was once the scene of a bloody massacre. In 1834, five years after settling the area, colonists turned on a large group of the Bindjareb Noongar tribe in reprisal for a series of raids and the killing of a servant. You can learn more about this sorry tale and other historical events from the **visitors centre** (☎ 9531 1438; cnr George & Henry Sts; 🕒 8.30am-4.30pm Mon-Fri, 9am-4pm Sat, 9.30am-4pm Sun), housed in the historic Edenvale property.

Bellawood Parrots (☎ 9531 1457; Ravenswood Sanctuary, off Sutton St; adult/child $7.50/5; 🕒 10am-4pm Wed-Mon) displays 50 of Australia's 55 parrot species. Visitors can wander through a large aviary and handfeed the lorikeets, but beware: the experience can be a Hitchcockian nightmare, particularly during early morning feeds when birds are raucous and ravenous.

Nearby, visitors stroll through historic **Coopers Cottage**, with a mini history of colonial farmer Joseph Cooper and an arts and crafts shop; grab basic café fare at **Redcliffe Barn**.

One of the few places to stay in town is the rather nondescript but convenient **Pinjarra Motel** (☎ 9531 1811; fax 9531 1355; 131 South West Hwy; s/d from $60/75).

A more interesting alternative is **Fairbridge** (☎ 9531 1177; www.fairbridge.asn.au/accommodation; South West Hwy; 2-person cottages from $45), about 6km north of Pinjarra (you'll need your own transport). This former orphanage and farm school offers spartan accommodation in 25 heritage-listed English-style cottages in a mini village. With several cottages sleeping as many as 18 people, it can be overrun by school groups. Ring ahead.

Heritage Tearooms (☎ 9531 2273; 1 George St; mains $4-9) shares a building with the visitors centre, and offers light meals and the obligatory Devonshire tea.

Dwellingup

☎ 08

Destroyed by bushfire in 1961, the tiny timber town of Dwellingup, 24km from Pinjarra, is a modern-day jumping-off point for bushwalkers and canoeists drawn to its gorgeous jarrah forests and meandering Murray River. The friendly **visitors centre** (☎ 9538 1108; Marrinup St; 🕒 10am-3pm, closes 4pm Sat & Sun) has a small historical display and a popular *Bushwalking Trails* booklet ($2.50).

Lots of nature lovers gravitate to the unique rammed-earth **Forest Heritage Centre** (☎ 9538 1395; Acacia St; adult/child/family $5.50/2.20/11; 🕒 10am-5pm), which has an interpretive forest exhibition, woodwork gallery and tree-top walk. If you'd like to stay a while, basic accommodation is also available ($20/5.50 per adult/child).

Dwellingup Adventures (☎ 9538 1127) offers a series of canoeing adventures, including self-guided Murray River trips (two-person canoe half/full day $60/70) with pick-up. Overnight camping trips, and combined bushwalking and canoeing options are also popular.

Dwellingup is the terminus for the **Hotham Valley Tourist Railway** (☎ 9221 4444), which runs vintage steam train trips between May and October from Perth ($38/19 per adult/child) on Sunday, and Pinjarra ($28/14) on Sunday and Wednesday. Fun for families is the **Etmilyn Forest Tramway** (☎ 9538 1138; adult/child diesel locomotive $14/7, steam locomotive $18/9), with 1½-hour historic train trips from Dwellingup through virgin jarrah forests at 11am and 2pm from Tuesday to Thursday and weekends. The Etmilyn Diner lavishes a five-course meal on guests while choofing through the night forest on selected Friday and Saturday nights for $68. Schedules vary, so phone ahead.

Berryvale Lodge (☎ 9538 1239; www.berryvale lodge.com.au; off South West Hwy; s/d $60/90, r with bathroom $100), 1km west of town, is a 10-acre working berry farm with a menagerie of animals squeezed in among state forest. Homy attic-style rooms come with a scrumptious country breakfast, and three-course dinners ($25) can be arranged.

Mill House Cafe & Chocolate Co (☎ 9538 1122; McLarty St; mains $12-23; 🕒 10am-4pm Thu, 9am-late Fri & Sat, 9am-5pm Sun) has tasty wood-fired pizzas and a good wine list. Diners buzz around the glass cabinet of chocolates like bees.

Yalgorup National Park

Around 50km south of Mandurah is the beautiful Yalgorup National Park, a region of woodlands, tranquil lakes and coastal sand dunes. Bird lovers will be in their element, with enormous flocks of water birds, and amateur scientists can visit the peculiar thrombalites on the shores of Lake

Clifton, small rocklike structures built by micro-organisms that resemble the earliest forms of life.

SOUTHWEST

Lush green forests and spectacular coastline characterise the popular southwest, with two prominent capes and countless national parks, including the magnetic 'tall trees' region. This fertile area offers something for everyone, whether it's whale-watching from its jagged cliff tops, splashing around with wild bottlenose dolphins, hanging ten at world-class surfing beaches, tippling at Margaret River wineries or wandering through fields of springtime wildflowers. Particularly popular with Perth weekenders, you'll occasionally have to fight the crowds that flock to the area, particularly in the height of summer.

Getting There & Away

Transwa (☎ 1300 662 205) buses go daily from Perth to Bunbury ($21.70, 3 hours), Busselton ($25.60, 4¼ hours), Dunsborough ($27.60, 4½ hours), Yallingup ($28.50, 4¾ hours), Margaret River ($29.55, 5½ hours) and Augusta ($35.15, 6 hours).

There are also six buses a week from Perth to Pemberton ($36.85, 5½ or 8 hours); some go via Bunbury and Bridgetown ($31.50, 4½ hours) and some take the longer cape route

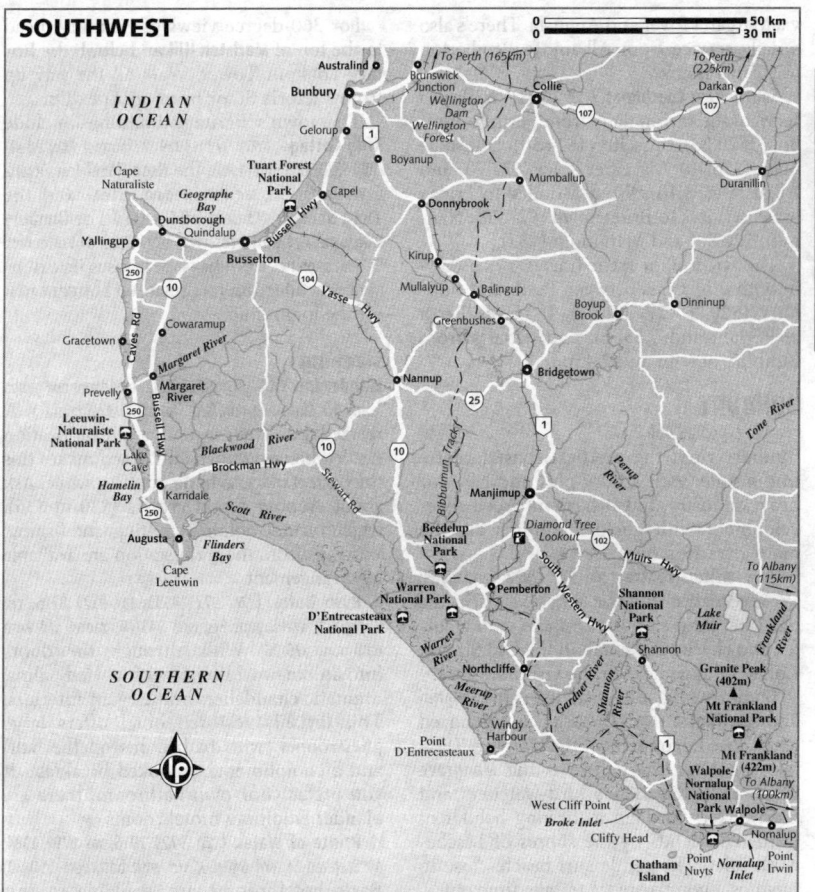

SOUTHWEST

CLOSE ENCOUNTERS OF THE DOLPHIN KIND

The highlight of a trip to Bunbury is seeing these wonderfully curious and fascinating creatures up close at the nonprofit **Dolphin Discovery Centre** (☎ 08-9791 3088; www.dolphindiscovery.com.au; adult/child $2/1) on Koombana Beach. Most days, wild bottlenose dolphins head to the shallows in front of the centre for some human interaction (less often in winter). The most likely time to see them is early morning, but there are no guarantees.

Visitors have access to the dolphin interaction zone, where they can wade into the water and watch the dolphins glide gracefully past. Simple rules of contact are explained by the volunteers: you can't touch the dolphins, but you are allowed to snorkel alongside them. The centre's museum and interpretive theatre will give you more background.

You're likely to see dolphins 'surfing' along in front of the boat on the excellent Dolphin Eco-Cruise ($27/20 per adult/child), run at 11am and 2pm daily. Alternatively, book a swim tour ($99, twice daily December to April), which has a marine biologist along for the ride. A maximum of 10 swimmers are ferried out to sea for a chance to get close to a pod of dolphins (wetsuits and instruction are provided). Cruises and swims are popular, so book ahead.

via Margaret River and Augusta. There's also a daily service from Albany to Pemberton ($24.50, 3 hours).

South West Coachlines (☎ 08-9324 2333) also services the region daily from Perth to Bunbury ($20.20), Busselton ($24.50), Dunsborough ($26.70), Margaret River ($27.70) and Augusta ($33.10). From Monday to Friday it has services to Bridgetown ($27.70), Nannup ($28.80) and Manjimup ($32).

The *Australind* train travels twice daily in both directions between Perth and Bunbury ($20.20, 2½ hours). It leaves Perth at 9.30am and 5.55pm, and departs from Bunbury at 6am and 2.45pm.

BUNBURY
☎ 08 / pop 28,000

Bunbury's not the prettiest coastal centre in the state, with a busy port and base for heavy industry, but it has embraced redevelopment with gusto. Dolphins are the main attraction here.

The **visitors centre** (☎ 9721 7922; Carmody Pl; ☉ 9am-5pm Mon-Sat, 9.30am-4.30pm Sun) is in the old 1904 train station. You can grab a coffee and check your email in the Old Station Coffee Lounge next to the visitors centre.

Bunbury's biggest attraction is the **Dolphin Discovery Centre** (☎ 9791 3088); see the boxed text 'Close Encounters of the Dolphin Kind' (above). Near the centre is the **Mangrove Boardwalk**, which leads bird-watchers and bushwalkers through a thriving habitat of feathered friends by the shores of Leschenault inlet. The gentle surf beach, close to town, is a popular place to take time out.

For 360-degree views of Bunbury, head to the top of **Marlston Hill** and climb the Rotary Lookout Tower. Walk all the way up from Victoria St, or head up Apex Dr.

The town's heritage buildings include **King Cottage** (☎ 9721 3929; 77 Forrest Ave; adult/child $3/0.50; ☉ 2-4pm), the **Rose Hotel** (cnr Victoria & Wellington Sts; see the Sleeping section) and the 1842 **St Mark's Church** (off Flynn St). The **Bunbury Regional Art Galleries** (☎ 9721 8226; 64 Wittenoom St; admission free; ☉ 10am-4pm) houses its extensive art collection in a restored convent just off the main drag.

Sleeping

Wander Inn YHA (☎ 9721 3242; wanderinnbp@yahoo .com; 16 Clifton St; dm/s/d from $20/32/50; ☐) A relaxed atmosphere and a great location nestled between town and beach makes this the perfect place to hang out for a while. Ask about evening sunset cruises ($30 to $35), which include dolphin spotting, and fishing. Pick-ups from the train station are available by arrangement.

Rose Hotel (☎ 9721 4533; fax 9721 8285; cnr Victoria & Wellington Sts; s/d $45/70, motel s/d with bathroom $75/90) Walk through the doors into an old-world hotel with potted palms, dramatic chandeliers and elegant interiors. This lavishly restored hotel offers large guestrooms (with bathrooms on the hall) and a complimentary cooked breakfast. If you prefer your own bathroom, there are blander adjoining motel rooms.

Prince of Wales (☎ 9721 2016; fax 9791 1984; 41 Stephen St; s/d $40/60, s/d with bathroom $50/70) Basic hotel rooms are available in this

WESTERN AUSTRALIA

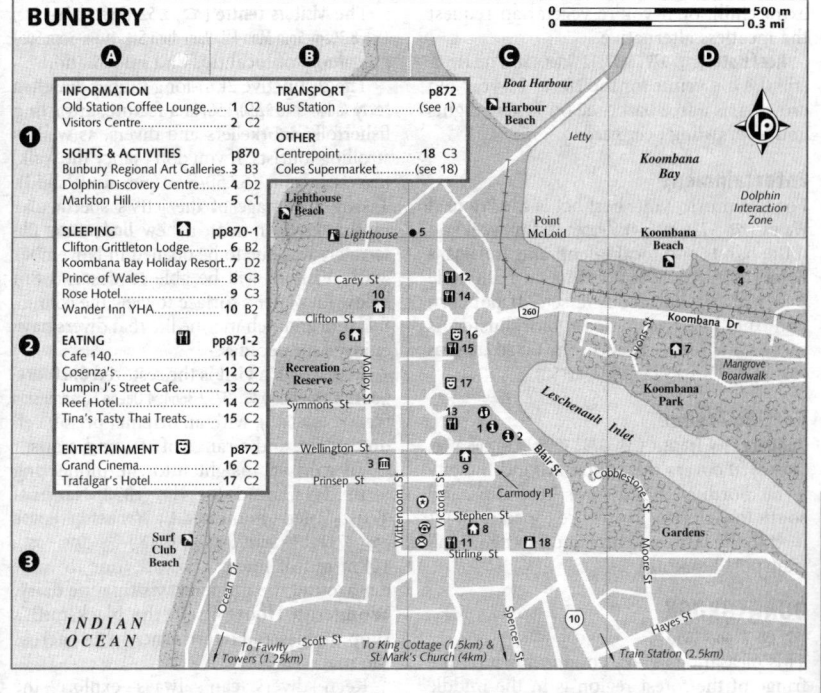

BUNBURY

0 ————— 500 m
0 ————— 0.3 mi

INFORMATION	
Old Station Coffee Lounge	1 C2
Visitors Centre	2 C2

SIGHTS & ACTIVITIES	pp870
Bunbury Regional Art Galleries	3 B3
Dolphin Discovery Centre	4 D2
Marlston Hill	5 C1

SLEEPING	pp870-1
Clifton Grittleton Lodge	6 B2
Koombana Bay Holiday Resort	7 D2
Prince of Wales	8 C3
Rose Hotel	9 C3
Wander Inn YHA	10 B2

EATING	pp871-2
Cafe 140	11 C3
Cosenza's	12 C2
Jumpin J's Street Cafe	13 C2
Reef Hotel	14 C2
Tina's Tasty Thai Treats	15 C2

ENTERTAINMENT	p872
Grand Cinema	16 C2
Trafalgar's Hotel	17 C2

TRANSPORT	p872
Bus Station	(see 1)

OTHER	
Centrepoint	18 C3
Coles Supermarket	(see 18)

central hotel that's well known for its live music (if you're staying here expect plenty of noise on the weekend).

Fawlty Towers (☎ 9721 2427; fawltyby@iinet.net.au; 205 Ocean Dr; s/d $65/75; ⊠) Don't let the name worry you. Friendly, attentive service, a beachfront position, spotless rooms and excellent facilities (including a solar-heated pool) make this motel a bargain.

Clifton Grittleton Lodge (☎ 9721 4300; www .theclifton.com.au; 2 Molloy St; d from $100, ste $240; ⊠) A range of elegant up-market options are available here, from standard motel rooms to the height of luxury in a suite in the Grittledon Lodge, a Victorian homestead built in 1885.

Koombana Bay Holiday Resort (☎ 9791 3900; www.kbhr.com.au; Koombana Dr; caravan sites $25, 2-person cabins/chalets $60/135; ⊠) A two-minute stroll from the Dolphin Discovery Centre, this manicured caravan park has a variety of accommodation options, including shady camp sites and waterfront three-bedroom chalets. There are also tennis and basketball courts and a swimming pool on-site.

Eating & Drinking

Bunbury's best restaurants and watering holes are conveniently huddled along Victoria St. In fact, the section from Wellington to Clifton Sts is known as the 'cappuccino strip', and there's as much variety here as in the Freo strip of the same name – here are just a few.

Cafe 140 (☎ 9721 2254; 140 Victoria St; mains $7-13) Late risers appreciate the relaxed vibe and all-day brekky at Cafe 140. Tasty salads, pastas, burgers and baguettes are available for light lunchers.

Cosenza's (☎ 9721 3866; 10 Victoria St; mains $5-32) Delicious hearty hotpots are a highlight at this popular seafood restaurant.

Jumpin' J's Street Cafe (☎ 9721 6075; 62 Victoria St; mains $11-30) Big and brash, Jumpin' J's has a simple kid-friendly menu of pastas, burgers and seafood.

Tina's Tasty Thai Treats (☎ 9791 1312; Grand Cinema Complex, Victoria St; mains $7-16; ⊠ closed Mon) Authentic northeastern Thai dishes are a nice departure from the usual café fare, and Tina's is happy to tweak the menu to suit your taste. If you can take the heat, ask for extra chilli, or if you're vegetarian request the meatless alternative.

Reef Hotel (☎ 9791 6677; 12 Victoria St) The Reef, still the top venue for the 18- to 25-year-old crowd, has a free barbecue on Friday nights and a sprawling beer garden.

Entertainment

For live music, your best bet is the **Prince of Wales** (☎ 9721 2016; 41 Stephen St) for weekend indie bands and local talent, and **Trafalgar's Hotel** (☎ 9721 2600; 36 Victoria St), an Irish-style pub with regular acoustic sets. If popcorn and the latest American blockbuster is more your scene, head to the **Grand Cinemas** (☎ 9791 4455; cnr Victoria & Clifton Sts).

Getting Around

Bunbury City Transit (☎ 9791 1955; Bicentennial Sq, Carmody Pl) covers the region around the city as far north as the town of Australind and south to Gelorup. The office (open daily) is next to the visitors centre and can handle all transport bookings.

DONNYBROOK
☎ 08 / pop 1650

This pleasant, low-key country town on the fringe of the forest region is in the middle of apple country and attracts plenty of summertime travellers seeking casual work. You can hit town for some apple-picking work from late October to June. The **visitors centre** (☎ 9731 1720; South West Hwy; ☉ 9am-5pm) is centrally located in the Old Railway Station on the South West Hwy.

Brook Lodge Backpackers (☎ 9731 1520; www .brooklodge.com.au; 3 Bridge St; dm/d $17/40; 🖳), on two acres, is a friendly place that fills with longer-term apple pickers in the warmer months. The hostel has an arrangement with Perth's Workstay Harvest Office and can help backpackers find work (though it's a good idea to book ahead as it can become very busy in peak season).

BUSSELTON
☎ 08 / pop 11,000

In summer, Australian holiday-makers flock to this family-friendly resort on the shores of Geographe Bay, with calm waters and white-sand beaches that stretch for many kilometres. Busselton is one of the fastest-developing towns in WA, with new estates hugging the beachfront in a long skinny line.

The **visitors centre** (☎ 9752 1288; 38 Peel Tce; ☉ 8.30am-5pm Mon-Fri, 9am-4pm Sat, 10am-3pm Sun) has plenty of local tips and information.

The distinctive 2km-long timber **Busselton Jetty** (adult/child $2.50/1.50) is a feature, attracting fisherfolk, snorkellers and divers, as well as strolling tourists. If you don't fancy the walk, there's a train ($7.50/5.50 per adult/child). Taking advantage of the jetty's spectacular marine environment, a new **Underwater Observatory** was due to be opened in November 2003. Visitors will be able to descend 8m below the water's surface to view the colourful coral and rich marine life that divers have enjoyed for decades.

Also worth a visit is the restored **Old Courthouse Complex** (☎ 9752 3664; 4 Queen St; admission free; ☉ 9am-5pm), with an original prison cell on display, and a range of arts and crafts.

To gain an insight into the pioneering farm days, head for the 1838 National Trust–listed homestead, **Wonnerup House** (☎ 9752 2039; adult/child $4.40/2.20; ☉ 10am-4pm), 10km out of town. Take the time to wander around the property, visiting the dairy, Wonnerup House itself, the blacksmith's shop, stables and one-teacher school across the road.

Keen divers can always explore the underwater world at Busselton Jetty and Dunsborough's Swan wreck with **Busselton Naturaliste Diving Academy** (☎ 9752 2096; www.natdive.com; 103 Queen St).

Sleeping & Eating

There's plenty of accommodation on offer in Busselton, including a string of holiday resorts and uninspiring (but cheap) motels along the Bussell Hwy. There are also several excellent guesthouses within walking distance of the jetty.

Observatory Guesthouse (☎ 9751 3336; www .observatory-guesthouse.com; 7 Brown St; s/d $80/90; 🐾) Opened in August 2002, this bright, cheerful guesthouse has all the comforts of home, including cooked brekky, breezy communal deck and beach-towel loans.

Jacaranda Guesthouse (☎ 9752 1246; jacaranda@ westnet.com.au; 30 West St; s/d $65/90) Simple and homy, Jacaranda boasts a heated guest spa in the garden and a hearty complimentary breakfast.

Goose (☎ 9754 7700; mains $13.50-19.50; ☉ 9am-late Tue-Sat) At the time of writing, the excellent Goose café-restaurant was plotting a

OLIVER STREWE

See the sandstone splendour of **Purnululu (Bungle Bungle) National Park** (p947)

Swim the waters of **Lake Argyle** (p950)

OLIVER STREWE

PETER PTSCHELINZEW

Explore by 4WD the harsh beauty of the **Kimberley** (p932)

Crawl inside the Kimberley's famous 1000-year-old bulging **Boab Prison Tree** (p941)

ANDREW MARSHALL & LEANNE WALKER

PETER PTSCHELIN

Catch a camel train along the famous white sand of **Cable Beach** (p935)

Sample scrumptious gourmet food and wine at **Margaret River** (p874)
SALLY WEBB

RICHARD I'ANSON

Pedal from beach to beach on **Rottnest Island** (p856)

MICHAE

Encounter the incredible underwater giant, the whale shark, at **Ningaloo Marine Park** (p921)

move to a prime waterfront spot near the jetty. Try the goose plate for a variety of gourmet flavours in the one dish ($19.50).

Equinox Cafe (☎ 9752 4641; Jetty end of Queen St; mains $13-19) On the beachfront, this laid-back local haunt overlooking the jetty serves tasty light meals and dinners.

Gelato Buonissimo (☎ 9751 1477; 13 Bussell Hwy; ⏰ 10am-9pm) Don't be put off by the garish yellow shopfront: inside is a delectable range of authentic Italian gelati.

DUNSBOROUGH
☎ 08 / pop 2500
Dunsborough is a tiny coastal town that sits on Cape Naturaliste, and is a great base for beaches and the nearby wineries. For accommodation and tour tips, see the **visitors centre** (☎ 9755 3299; Seymour Blvd; ⏰ 9am-5pm Mon-Fri, 9am-4pm Sat, 10am-4pm Sun), in the shopping centre.

Northwest of Dunsborough, Cape Naturaliste Rd leads to excellent beaches such as **Meelup**, **Eagle Bay** (also known locally as 'Ego Bay') and **Bunker Bay**, some fine coastal lookouts and the tip of **Cape Naturaliste**, which has a **lighthouse** (☎ 9755 3955; adult/child $6.50/2.50; ⏰ 9.30am-4.30pm) and a network of walking tracks.

From September to December you can marvel at humpback and southern right whales from the lookouts over Geographe Bay, or on three-hour cruises with **Naturaliste Charters** (☎ 9755 2276; www.whales-australia .com; adult/child $45/25). Scenic **Sugarloaf Rock** is the southernmost nesting colony of the rare red-tailed tropicbird.

The wreck of the Australian frigate HMAS *Swan*, sunk in Geographe Bay in 1997 specifically for **diving**, makes Dunsborough a mecca for divers. **Cape Dive** (☎ 9756 8778; 222 Naturaliste Tce) runs snorkelling trips ($50/40 with/without equipment) and diving ($160 for two dives with equipment provided).

Sleeping & Eating
Three Pines Resort YHA (☎ 9755 3107; dunsboroughyha @hotmail.com; 285 Geographe Bay Rd, Quindalup; dm $20, d & tw $50; 🖵) About 2km southeast of Dunsborough, this brightly painted, social YHA has a stunning beachfront location. Look for the three tall Norfolk pines in front.

Dunsborough Inn (☎ 9756 7277; dunnsinn@wn .com.au; 50 Dunn Bay Rd; dm/s/d/tr $22/32/55/70, d with bathroom $85; 🖵) Spotless and modern, this purpose-built budget inn has a large com-

munal kitchen, recreation room, disabled facilities plus several self-contained units. The friendly owners run a shuttle bus to nearby beaches for long-termers.

Dunsborough Lodge (☎ 9756 8866; fax 9756 8855; 13 Dunn Bay Rd; dm/d $20/65, d with bathroom $80) Spartan motel-style accommodation and backpacker rooms are available in this simple lodge close to town.

Dunsborough Rail Carriages & Farm Cottages (☎ 9755 3865; www.dunsborough.com; Commonage Rd; 2-person carriages/cottages from $100/130) For novelty value, these charming rail carriages set on 100 acres of bushland win hands down. If you need more space, ask for the roomier farm cottages.

artézen (☎ 9755 3325; 234 Naturaliste Tce; mains $8-16; ⏰ 7am-5pm Wed-Mon, plus dinner Fri & Sat) This hip espresso bar has a contemporary look, a café-style menu and delicious coffee.

My Thai (☎ 9755 3244; cnr Dunn Bay Rd & Naturaliste Tce; mains $14-24; ⏰ 6pm-late Wed-Sun) Sit out on the deck of this hot pink pad and enjoy warm chilli jam squid salad ($19) and a cruisy vibe.

Bay Cottage (☎ 9755 3554; 28 Dunn Bay Rd; mains $24-29; ⏰ 6.30pm-late Tue-Sat) Readers rave about this award-winning restaurant's innovative dishes, though vegetarians might despair of the meat-laden menu.

YALLINGUP
☎ 08 / pop 500
Beloved of surfers, Yallingup is a tiny settlement surrounded by spectacular coastline and fine beaches. Nearby is the **Ngilgi Cave** (see the boxed text 'Caving from Cape to Cape'; p875).

For something a little different, take a camel ride to the bush or beach with the camel whisperers at **Yallingup Camel Safaris** (☎ 9756 6070; Hemsley Rd; ⏰ 10am-5pm Wed-Sun Aug-May). Their devotion to their camel family is an attraction in itself. Nearby is the **Wicked Ale Brewery** (☎ 9755 2848; Hemsley Rd; ⏰ 10am-5pm Wed-Mon), where you can sample chilli beer, chocolate beer and bad frog citrus beer.

Caves House Hotel (☎ 9755 2131; www.caveshouse .com.au; Caves Rd; d $75-175) is a classic Art Deco lodge with ocean views and an English garden. Guests can choose standard rooms in the historic hotel or luxurious jacuzzi units in a separate house.

Caves Caravan Park (☎ 9755 2196; www.caves caravanpark.com; Yallingup Beach Rd; camp/caravan sites

SURFING WA

The beaches between Capes Leeuwin and Naturaliste offer powerful beach and reef breaks, both right- and left-handers. The wave at Margaret River ('Margaret's' to the locals) has been described by surfing legend Nat Young as 'epic', and by world surfing champ Mark Richards as 'one of the world's finest'.

The Margaret River Masters held in March attracts some of the world's best surfers and is worth being around for. The better locations include Rocky Point (short left-hander), the Farm and Bone Yards (right-handers), Three Bears (Papa, Mama and Baby, of course), Yallingup ('Yal's'; breaks left and right), Injidup Car Park and Injidup Point (right-hand tube on a heavy swell; left-hander), Guillotine/Gallows (right-hander), South Point (popular break), Left-Handers and Margaret River (with Southside, or 'Suicides').

Get a free copy of the *Down South Surfing Guide*, which indicates wave size, wind direction and swell size, from the Dunsborough and Busselton visitors centres. You can access daily surfing information on the Web at www.coastaldata.transport.wa.gov.au.

$16/22, on-site caravans/cabins/chalets $50/57/105) is an excellent park near Caves House, with luxurious cabins and good facilities. However, rates vary considerably at peak times.

Some of the finest restaurants in the region can be found in the vineyards, and **Flutes Cafe** (☎ 9755 6250; Brookland Valley, Caves Rd; Willyabrup; mains $16-35) is no exception. Guests nibble on delicious gourmet meals while dropping crumbs for the ducks on the lake below.

MARGARET RIVER
☎ 08 / pop 6000

Bronzed surfers and wine-quaffing city slickers rub shoulders in this buzzing tourist mecca that offers some of the best surfing in Australia and some of its most delicious wines. Wild coastal scenery, sophisticated restaurants, internationally acclaimed vineyards and a string of fascinating limestone caves attract big crowds, particularly over the Christmas and Easter holidays.

The **visitors centre** (☎ 9757 2911; cnr Bussell Hwy & Tunbridge Rd; ⊙ 9am-5pm) has lots of useful information and an impressive wine centre. For quick connection speeds and a comfy place to check your email, try **Cybercorner Cafe** (Willmott Ave; ⊙ 8am-8pm Mon-Sat, 1-5pm Sun).

Sights & Activities

One of the best ways to explore the region is to potter up and down Caves Rd (stretching from Yallingup to Augusta) and stop at any of the countless attractions along the way. Highlights include the arts and crafts galleries, **Ye Olde Lolly Shop**, the many fantastic vineyards, the **Sunflowers Animal Farm** and the **Bootleg Brewery**, an 'oasis of beer in a desert of wine'. Visitors also marvel at the limestone caves (see the boxed text 'Caving from Cape to Cape'; p875).

Everybody in Margaret River wants to surf – or so it seems. If you don't know how to, the **Surf Academy** (☎ 9757 3850; 2-hr lessons $35) will teach you. Otherwise, grab your board and head for popular surfing beaches, Margaret River Mouth, Gnarabup, Suicides and Redgate.

Eagles Heritage (☎ 9757 2960; Boodjidup Rd; adult/child $9/4.50; ⊙ 10am-5pm), 5km south of Margaret River, has a fascinating collection of raptors in a natural bush setting; there are flight displays at 11am and 1.30pm.

Tours

A trip to Margaret River wouldn't be complete without visiting some of its excellent wineries, and several tour companies act as guide and designated driver (book at the visitors centre). **Bushtucker Tours** (☎ 9757 9084; www.bushtuckertours.com) has a popular five-hour 4WD Great Wine Food Forest Adventure ($55) to five wineries with a gourmet lunch of wild foods including smoked emu. It also offers a four-hour cave canoe tour ($40/20 per adult/child), combining walking, canoeing, exploring a wilderness cave, and learning about Aboriginal culture and bush foods.

Milesaway Tours (☎ 1800 818 102; half-day tours $50) has a half-day minibus tour, and **Margaret River Tours** (☎ 0419-917 166; www.margaretrivertours.com; half-/full-day tours $50/85) offers half-day and full-day options.

Experienced and wannabe bushwalkers, canoeists, abseilers, cavers and rock climbers can try activities in the local area with **Outdoor Discoveries** (☎ 0407-084 945).

Sleeping

Margaret River Lodge & Backpackers (☎ 9757 9532; www.mrlodge.com.au; 220 Railway Tce; dm/s/d from $20/40/55, nonmembers extra $3.50; 🖳) About 1.5km southwest of town, this popular YHA has rammed-earth buildings and excellent facilities, including an organic vegie garden and a pool.

Inne Town Backpackers (☎ 9757 3698; innetown@bigpond.com; 93 Bussell Hwy; dm/d $19/50; 🖳) What this converted house lacks in slick facilities it makes up for in convenience and a friendly, social vibe. Almost opposite the visitors centre, it's stumbling distance from all the best restaurants and pubs in town.

Surf Point Lodge (☎ 9757 1777; www.surfpoint.com.au; Riedle Dr; dm $23, tw & d with/without bathroom $85/75; 🖳) If beaches are on your agenda, this clean modern lodge at Gnarabup Beach, 12km from Margaret River, is the obvious choice. It has a large communal

kitchen, several recreation areas and a courtesy bus to/from town.

Margaret River Hotel (☎ 9757 2655; www.margaretriverhotel.com.au; 139 Bussell Hwy; s/d $85/95) The refurbished rooms in this central, heritage-listed hotel are excellent value, with creature comforts such as bathroom, TV and minibar. A fun watering hole and restaurant beckon downstairs.

Cottages, B&Bs and farmstays abound; inquire at the visitors centre for a full list of recommendations.

Rosewood Cottage (☎ 9757 2845; www.westnet.com.au/rosewoodcottage; 54 Wallcliffe Rd; s/d from $90/100; 🐾) The flower-filled theme of Rosewood's gardens extends into the cottage with floral fabric throughout. The friendly owners have plenty of tips on the region, and preserve the peace with a child-free rule.

Old Bakehouse B&B (☎ 9755 5462; Bussell Hwy, Cowaramup; d $95) Foodies will be in their element at this charming historic B&B in Cowaramup (full of gourmet shops and farms, and known affectionately as Cow Town), 10km north of Margaret River. Picnic hampers ($35) and gourmet platters ($30) can be arranged.

WESTERN AUSTRALIA

CAVING FROM CAPE TO CAPE

Surf and plonk aside, the Margaret River region's biggest attraction is its string of beautiful limestone caves, with dramatic ceilings of stalactites and stalagmites. Dotted throughout the Leeuwin-Naturaliste Ridge between the capes, there are around 350 of them and several are open daily to the public.

The stunning **Ngilgi Cave** (Caves Rd, Yallingup; 🕙 9.30am-4.30pm, last entry 3.30pm) was discovered, or rather stumbled upon, in 1899 and has been a tourist attraction ever since. Tours go every half-hour; a guide will lead you down into the cave, and then you're free to wander and explore by yourself.

CaveWorks (☎ 9757 7411; Caves Rd; 🕙 9am-5pm), 25km south of Margaret River, is an interpretive centre with state-of-the-art computerised displays, a theatrette and enthusiastic staff. It's based at **Lake Cave**, which features a spectacular underground stream. There are guided daily tours for $15/6.50 per adult/child. Keen cavers can buy a Grand Tour Pass for Jewel, Lake and Mammoth Caves for $36/16.

Fossil remains have been found in both the **Mammoth Cave** (🕙 9am-4pm), 21km south of Margaret River, and **Jewel Cave** (🕙 9.30am-4pm), 8km north of Augusta.

For a more atmospheric underground experience, there's the unlit **Moondyne Cave** (🕙 2pm only), also 8km north of Augusta. Visitors are guided on a 1½-hour historic lantern tour (complete with hard hats) at 11am and 2pm daily ($20/10).

The other caves in the region are operated by the **Department of Conservation & Land Management** (CALM; ☎ 9757 7422), notably **Calgardup Cave** (🕙 9am-4.15pm) and **Giants Cave** (🕙 9.30am-3.30pm holidays only), 15km and 20km south of Margaret River, respectively (self-guided tours cost $10/5 per adult/child). Exploring Giants Cave is something of an adventure, with 20% on boardwalks and 80% negotiating ladders and scrambling over cave floors. Contact CALM for details, or look for signposts on Caves Rd.

Eating

Delicious food and wine are easy to find, particularly in the vineyards and along the Bussell Hwy in the town centre.

Urban Bean Cafe (☎ 9757 3480; 157 Bussell Hwy; mains $4.50-12) Locals and Perth weekenders flock to this gourmet caff to while away the hours over the papers, croissants and killer coffee.

Goodfella's Cafe (☎ 9757 3184; 97 Bussell Hwy; mains $12.50-19.50) Scrumptious gourmet pizzas are named after gangster flicks at this fun, friendly restaurant with an outdoor balcony (the Pulp Fiction is a vegetarian's dream). Tuesday night specials include pizza and a glass of beer or wine for $14.

Vat 107 (☎ 9758 8877; 107 Bussell Hwy; mains $16-29) This slick wine bar–restaurant serves gourmet dishes and divine wine to a well-heeled clientele.

Berry Farm (☎ 9757 5054; 222 Bessell Rd; mains $8.50-12; ☽ 10am-4.30pm) Cap off a spot of berry wine tasting with a visit to this excellent café 13km from town, with pretty gardens and light lunches.

Valley Cafe (☎ 9757 3225; cnr Carters & Caves Rds; mains $12.50-26.50; ☽ 7am-4pm & 6-10pm Wed-Sun) Set on a five-acre bush block out of town, the Valley Cafe is renowned for its creative food and for its flamboyant revues ($55), which feature drag shows and three-course dinners.

Sweet tooths will find tasty treats at **Simmo's Icecream** (Bussell Hwy) and the **Fudge Factory** (Bussell Hwy); and **Candy Cow** (cnr Bussell Hwy & Bottrill St, Cowaramup), 10 minutes' north of Margaret River.

Drinking

Wino's (☎ 9758 7155; 85 Bussell Hwy) Tipplers can choose a taste, glass or bottle of local vino at this groovy modern wine bar, which also offers a selection of beers and tasty tapas.

Settler's Tavern (☎ 9757 2398; 114 Bussell Hwy) For cheaper beer, a more laid-back scene and live bands on the weekend, try Settler's, in the middle of town.

AUGUSTA

☎ 08 / pop 2000

This low-key coastal town is 5km north of Cape Leeuwin, the most southwesterly point in Australia, and the spot where the Southern and Indian Oceans meet. Fisherfolk abound.

The **visitors centre** (☎ 9758 0166; 75 Blackwood Ave; ☽ 9am-5pm, closes 1pm Sat & Sun) is in the main street.

Whale-watching is popular at Cape Leeuwin between late May and September. **Naturaliste Charters** (☎ 9755 2276; www.whales-australia.com; adult/child $45/25) offers three-hour trips to see southern right and humpback whales, bottlenose dolphins and New Zealand fur seals daily from June to August. From September to June, **Miss Flinders** (☎ 9758 1944; adult/child $20/10; ☽ 10.30am Tue, Thu & Sat) sails up the Blackwood River, leaving from the Ellis St jetty. Times occasionally change, so ring ahead.

Another worthwhile side trip is the historic **lighthouse** (☎ 9758 1920; tours adult/child $6/3; ☽ 9am-4pm) that perches on Cape Leeuwin, and offers spectacular views of the rugged surrounding coastline. Not far away is the photogenic salt-encrusted **water wheel**.

The **Matthew Flinders memorial** on Leeuwin Rd commemorates Flinders' mapping of the Australian coastline, and offers wonderful lighthouse photo ops. **Augusta Historical Museum** (Blackwood Ave; adult/child $2/0.50; ☽ 10am-noon & 2-4pm Oct-Apr, 10am-noon May-Sep) has some interesting exhibits on whales and shipwrecks.

If you've got time and your own transport, pop in to fishing hot spot Hamelin Bay to watch the large stingrays patrol the shallows.

Sleeping & Eating

Baywatch Manor Resort (☎ 9758 1290; www.baywatchmanor.com.au; 88 Blackwood Ave; dm/s $20/50, d with/without bathroom from $70/55) This modern, purpose-built place has won the title of Australia's No 1 YHA for several years running, and is a quiet, low-key place to take time out.

Blackwood River Houseboats (☎ 9758 0181; blackwoodhouseboats@hotmail.com.au; Westbay; d from $120) For something different, spend a night at this houseboat moored at Westbay. More expensive weekend rates include the chance to cruise the surrounding waterways.

Doonbanks Caravan Park (☎ 9758 1517; doonbank@netserv.net.au; Blackwood Ave; camp/caravan sites $14/16, cabins with/without bathroom $70/60) This pretty waterfront caravan park is often busy, so book ahead.

Augusta Bakery (☎ 9758 1664; 121 Blackwood Ave; light meals $5.50-11) If you're fortunate enough to be here in January, the bakery serves tasty

pizzas every night ($6.50 to $22.50). At other times, it's pizza night on Fridays, but home-baked pies and breads are available daily.

Squirrels (☎ 9758 1858; 63 Blackwood Ave; light meals $9) The generous burgers will keep you going all day, and there's a good range of sandwiches and rolls on offer.

Colourpatch Cafe (☎ 9758 1295; 38 Alvany Tce; mains $9.50-22) 'The last eating house before the Antarctic' is a popular waterfront spot for breakfast, lunch or dinner.

SOUTHERN FORESTS

A visit to the magnificent towering jarrah, marri and karri trees of the southwest is a must for any traveller to WA. Though the timber industry remains a major player in this region, the state government's recent forest policies have scaled down native forest logging, brought an end to the controversial wood chipping of old-growth forests, and proposed several new national parks. Radical changes have come to the southwest, with former timber towns such as Nannup, Bridgetown, Pemberton, Manjimup and Northcliffe being forced to move into new industries and embrace new ways of thinking. This is all good news for travellers, with more national parks to explore, more protected pristine forest and a rapidly growing ecotourism industry.

CALM offices (Nannup ☎ 08-9756 1101; Warren Rd; Pemberton ☎ 08-9776 1207; Kennedy St) can help with information on new national parks, many of which didn't have names or boundaries at the time of writing.

Nannup

☎ 08 / pop 520

Nannup is a peaceful, picturesque town on the Blackwood River, set in the heart of forest and farmland. Its idyllic bush setting makes it a magnet for bushwalkers and folks looking for some good old-fashioned R&R.

The **visitors centre** (☎ 9756 1211; Brockman St; ☼ 9am-5pm) is in the old (1922) police station. Check your email at the **Telecentre** (Warren Rd).

Stroll up Warren Rd and browse through its many craft shops, furniture galleries and second-hand stores. Garden lovers can visit the pleasant, residential **Blythe Gardens** (Brockman St; gold coin donation; ☼ dawn-dusk), or picnic in the nearby **Arboretum**.

One of Australia's great canoe trips is the descent of the Blackwood River from the forest to the sea. **Blackwood Forest Canoeing** (☎ 9756 1252; River Rd; half-/full-day tours $25/35) will take you for paddles on the river.

SLEEPING & EATING

Black Cockatoo (☎ 9756 1035; 27 Grange Rd; dm $19, s/d from $30/45) A permaculture-conscious travellers' retreat with artistic accents and a mellow mood. Guests kip in a rustic room in the old loggers' cabin, the caravan plastered in aboriginal art, or a summertime teepee in the backyard.

Holberry House (☎ 9756 1276; www.holberryhouse .com; 14 Grange Rd; s $99, d $120-150) On five acres of gardens, offers floral-themed rooms with bathrooms in a reproduction English manor. Rates include continental breakfast.

Mulberry Tree (☎ 9756 3038; 62 Warren Rd; mains $22.50-26.50; ☼ closed Mon night) In a quaint country cottage surrounded by gardens, it's the best restaurant in town, with daily specials and a range of hearty dishes.

For snacks, light lunches and lots of vegie options, try the health-conscious **Good Food Shop** (☎ 9756 1351; 15 Warren Rd; mains $4-12).

Bridgetown

☎ 08 / pop 2100

In the midst of karri forests and apple orchards is this charming village on the Blackwood River. Bridgetown has interesting old buildings, including the mud-and-clay **Bridgedale House** (Hampton St; admission $3; ☼ 10am-2pm Sat & Sun), built by the area's first settler in 1862. There's a history display and a rather odd gallery of jigsaw puzzles in the **visitors centre** (☎ 9761 1740; Hampton St; ☼ 9am-5pm).

Interesting features of the Blackwood River valley are the burrawangs (grass trees) and large granite boulders. In **Boyup Brook**, 31km northeast of Bridgetown, there is a flora reserve and **Harvey Dickson's Country Music Centre** (☎ 9765 1125) with some 2000 titles. Nearby is **Norlup Pool** with glacial rock formations.

One of Bridgetown's major attractions is the **Blues at Bridgetown** festival, held in the second week of November each year. Phone ☎ 9761 1280 for a programme.

SLEEPING & EATING

Bridgetown Valley Lodge (☎ 9761 4144; cnr Phillips & Spencer Sts; tw/d $55/60) Built as a single men's

quarters for railway workers, the Valley Lodge provides small basic rooms and excellent communal facilities.

Nelson's of Bridgetown (☎ 9761 1641; www.nelsonsofbridgetown.com.au; 38 Hampton St; d $70-110) This lovely Federation-style hotel offers a range of accommodation from basic budget rooms to floral-themed deluxe options and executive spa units.

Ford House (☎ 9761 1816; www.wn.com.au/ford.house; Eedle Tce; s/d from $50/110) Details count at this award-winning historic B&B with a range of tasteful, individually designed rooms. Amateur chefs will adore the self-contained 'cooks' retreat' ($160) with a culinary theme and shelves full of cookbooks.

Cidery (☎ 9761 2204; 43 Gifford St; ⊙ 11am-4pm Wed-Sun, 7.30pm-late Fri & Sat) Take the time to do a tasting of alcoholic and nonalcoholic ciders, or grab a tasty light meal in the sprawling restaurant.

Manjimup & Around
☎ 08 / pop 4500

Manjimup, the agricultural centre of the southwest, once had a thriving timber and controversial wood-chipping industry and has suffered since the government's new logging policy was introduced. The **Timber Park Complex** (☎ 9771 1831; cnr Rose & Edwards Sts; ⊙ 9am-5pm) covers the history of the timber industry, including museums, old buildings and the visitors centre.

Though the town itself doesn't offer much of interest for travellers, some 22km down Graphite Rd to the west is **One-Tree Bridge**, the remains of a bridge constructed from a single karri log. The **Four Aces**, 1.5km from One-Tree Bridge, is a grove of superb karri trees believed to be over 300 years old. There are some lovely walking tracks around here, including the Bibbulmun Track; see the boxed text 'The Bibb Track' (p830) for details.

Time your visit to One-Tree Bridge at lunchtime, so you can pop into the **Graphiti Cafe** (☎ 9772 1283; Graphite Rd; mains $5-12; ⊙ 10am-5pm Wed-Sun), a groovy, architect-designed eatery in the middle of the bush. The small select menu of gourmet food won't disappoint.

Pemberton
☎ 08 / pop 800

Deep in the karri forests and surrounded by vineyards, pretty Pemberton is small enough to find wilderness just paces from town and big enough to offer a good choice of accommodation and restaurants. With the scaling down of logging operations in the region, wine making and nature-based tourism are fast taking over as growth industries.

The **visitors centre** (☎ 9776 1133; Brockman St; ⊙ 9am to 5pm) sells a Pemberton map ($3.95) and several touring maps and bushwalking books. It also incorporates a small **pioneer museum**, which has photos and antique equipment from the old logging days. To learn more about wildlife in the forests, ask about the **Karri Forest Discovery Centre** (admission by donation). Internet access is available at the **Telecentre**, next door. Buy national park passes from the visitors centre or the **CALM office** (☎ 9776 1207; Kennedy St).

SIGHTS & ACTIVITIES

The nerve-wracking 60m climb to the top of the **Gloucester Tree** is not for the faint-hearted, but rewards the brave with kudos from friends and views across to Windy Harbour. This former fire-lookout tree is in the Gloucester National Park, 3km from town. Tree-climbers can also hazard the **Dave Evans Bicentennial Tree** in the glorious **Warren National Park**, 12km to the south. If you prefer your feet firmly on the ground, it's still worth the trip to watch others make the climb and for the stunning karri-lined scenic drive.

The **Big Brook Dam**, 6km northeast, is a favourite local hangout, with a small swimming beach, an excellent 3.5km track circling the dam, and magnificent stands of karris.

For a different forest vantage point, catch a ride on the scenic **Pemberton Tramway** (☎ 9776 1322; www.pemtram.com.au; Pemberton Railway Station), which potters through lush marri and karri forests. Trams leave for Warren River ($18/9 per adult/child) at 10.45am and 2pm daily, and for Northcliffe ($48/24) at 10.15am on the third Saturday of each month. Steam trains run from Easter to November.

The **Fine Woodcraft Gallery** (☎ 9776 1399; Dickinson St; ⊙ 9am-5pm) has a large collection of beautifully handcrafted furniture in lush gardens.

It's knick-knack heaven in the shop at the **Lavender-Berry Farm** (☎ 9776 1661; Browns Rd), with lavender soap, oils, ornaments and hundreds of miniature lavender mice. Sample the berry, lavender or honey ice cream ($2.50).

TOURS

The **Pemberton Hiking & Canoeing Company** (☎ 9776 1559; half-/full-day trips $40/80) has eco tours that include a walk through old-growth forest and canoeing through Warren National Park.

Pemberton Discovery Tours (☎ 9776 0484; adult/child $60/40) whisks visitors off on half-day 4WD adventures, which stop at the spectacular Yeagarup Dunes, drive down remote beaches and include some munchies.

SLEEPING

Pemberton Backpackers YHA (☎ /fax 9776 1105; pembertonbackpackers@wn.com.au; 7 Brockman St; dm/s/d/f $19/33/55/65) You'll receive a warm welcome (and a foot spa if you've come off the Bibb Track) at this comfortable YHA in the town centre. Ask for a copy of the hostel's free day-walk maps. A self-contained cottage across the road is available for $70 a double, or $100 for five.

Pemberton Budget Cottages (☎ /fax 9776 1105; Stirling Rd; cottages from $65) Book these basic, rustic timber houses at the YHA. Set in a beautiful forest location 9km northwest of Pemberton, this basic good-value option is ideal for families, groups and nature lovers, though it's easier if you have your own transport.

Glenhaven B&B (☎ 9776 0028; glenhaven@wn.com.au; 25 Browns Rd; s/d with bathroom $65/90) Scottish hospitality is at its best at Glenhaven, where guests are greeted with afternoon tea and shortbread. Breakfasts are generous and there's a comfy country-cottage feel.

Marima Cottages (☎ /fax 9776 1211; Warren National Park, Old Vasse Rd; cottages from $145, with spa $175) With just four cottages on 100 acres

---

FANCY A TIPPLE?

Although the Western Australian wine industry accounts for only 3% of total Australian production, what it lacks in size, it makes up for in quality and variety. No visit to the Swan Valley (at Perth's doorstep), Margaret River, Pemberton or Mt Barker – the state's premium wine-producing regions – is complete without visiting a winery or two, sampling the wares, having a bite at one of many excellent vineyard restaurants and maybe even picking up a bargain.

The heart of the industry is Perth's Swan Valley, where vines were planted as early as the 1830s. Of the valley's 30-odd producers, veterans include **Houghton Wines** (☎ 08-9274 5100) and **Sandalford Wines** (☎ 08-9374 9300).

The Margaret River region is home to about 60 wine producers. Several companies offer tours (p874) and the visitors centre handles the bookings. The **Margaret River Regional Wine Centre** (☎ 08-9755 5501; 9 Bussell Hwy, Cowaramup) is run by wine buffs who can help you sample the region's delights. Wineries range from the big and flashy, such as **Leeuwin Estate** (☎ 08-9759 0000), **Howard Park Wines** (☎ 08-9755 9988) and **Voyager Estate** (☎ 08-9757 6354), to the small and quaint, such as **Woody Nook** (☎ 08-9755 7547) and **Ashbrook Estate** (☎ 08-9755 6262). Highlights include **Cape Mentelle** (☎ 08-9757 3266), **Evans & Tate** (☎ 08-9755 6244) and **Brookland Valley** (☎ 08-9755 6027), which has well-kept grounds, the excellent Flutes restaurant and a gallery. All wineries mentioned are open daily, usually until 4pm or 5pm.

Surrounded by spectacular karri forests, Pemberton's wineries are known for their top-notch chardonnay and pinot noir. **Gloucester Ridge** (☎ 08-9776 1035), with a delightful setting and award-winning restaurant, is on the edge of town, next to the Gloucester Tree, and **Salitage Wines** (☎ 08-9776 1771), on the Vasse Hwy a few kilometres east of Pemberton, has a free winery tour at 11am daily.

The Great Southern region is concentrated around the township of Mt Barker, and riesling and shiraz are its trademark varieties. **Plantagenet Wines** (☎ 08-9851 2150) is Mt Barker's most venerable producer, but **Goundrey** (☎ 08-9851 1777) is a huge modern complex that will steal some of the spotlight. It might prove more interesting to visit **Galafrey** (☎ 9851 2022) for the riesling, or **Pattersons** (☎ 08-9851 2063) for the excellent pinot noir and chardonnay. **Wignall's Wines** (☎ 08-9841 2848) is a convenient 10km drive from Albany, and one of several award-winning producers of pinot noir in the Great Southern region. Further west, Denmark boasts several premium producers, including **West Cape Howe Wines** (☎ 08-9848 2959) on the South Coast Hwy, the new kid on the block. The **Albany visitors centre** (☎ 08-9841 1088) can help with more information, including tours.

in the midst of karri-filled national park, Marima's appeal lies in its seclusion, and in the appearance of grazing kangaroos in the morning. The convenient Café Vasse, which is on the grounds, offers simple café fare from 10am to 4pm Wednesday to Sunday.

Pemberton Hotel (☎ 9776 1017; fax 9776 1600; 66 Brockman St; s/d/f $90/120/145) King-size beds and other comforts beckon in the stylish, architect-designed motel units adjoining the historic Pemberton Hotel.

If you really want to get away from it all, there are **camp sites** (2 people $10) in Warren National Park; contact **CALM** (☎ 9776 1207) for details.

EATING

In the midst of wine country, Pemberton has excellent eating options, including several vineyard restaurants; keep your eye out for local trout and marron (freshwater crayfish) on their menus.

Jan's Diner (☎ 9776 0011; Brockman St; mains $5-12) Hearty breakfasts are available at this casual diner on the main drag. Choose from the farmers', campers', hikers' or slimmers' breakfast.

Coffee Connection (☎ 9776 1159; Dickinson St; mains $8-10; ⏲ 10am-4pm) Don't leave town without indulging in coffee and a selection of chocolates and cakes at this tranquil café in bird-filled gardens on the town's fringes.

Café Mazz (☎ 9776 1017; 66 Brockman St; mains $16-28) Motel guests and locals partake of the tasty eclectic menu and good local wine list at Café Mazz. For less fancy fare, fill up on simple counter meals in the adjoining Pemberton hotel.

Gloucester Ridge Vineyard & Restaurant (☎ 9776 1035; Burma Rd; mains $20-30) Just around the corner from the Gloucester Tree, this picturesque vineyard is a tempting pit stop, with an award-winning chef and a seasonal menu of Mod Oz cuisine.

Shannon National Park

Some of the region's most magnificent karri country can be found in this 535-sq-km national park, 53km south of Manjimup. The 48km **Great Forest Trees Drive** leads you through the old-growth forest with the bonus of on-board commentary if you tune your radio in to 100 FM when

you see the signs. The full-colour *Great Forest Trees Drive* ($14.45) is a detailed map and drive guidebook that's available from CALM. As you would expect from a region renowned for its pristine forests, Shannon National Park offers some excellent bushwalking opportunities, including a section of the Bibbulmun Track; see the boxed text 'The Bibb Track' (p830) for details.

There is a fine **camping ground** (camp sites $13 for 2 people) on the spot where the original timber-milling village used to be. The ground also has huts equipped with potbelly stoves ($13) – all fees are on a self-registration basis.

Northcliffe

☎ 08 / pop 240

Northcliffe, 31km south of Pemberton, is a tiny town set in fertile farmland and forests, with excellent bushwalking and mountain-biking opportunities. The annual Karri Cup attracts mountain bikers from all over the state.

The **visitors centre** (☎ 9776 7203; Wheatley Coast Rd; ⏲ 9.30am-4pm Mon-Fri, 10am-2pm Sat & Sun) is next door to the **pioneer museum** (⏲ 10am-2pm, limited hr Jun-Aug). The nearby forest park offers opportunities for good walks through stands of grand karri, marri and jarrah trees.

Popular fishing destination **Windy Harbour**, 27km south of Northcliffe, has a sheltered beach on a stretch of wild coastline and a **camping ground** (☎ 9776 8398; camp sites $11 for 2 people) with basic camp sites. The cliffs of the fine **D'Entrecasteaux National Park** are accessible from here.

There are a few accommodation options in town, but several on the fringes get guests closer to nature.

Cheap and cheerful **Gilvonnie's Farmstay B&B** (☎ 9776 7022; Armstrong Rd; s/d $25/50) offers no-frills rooms in the family farmhouse. Guests are more than welcome to wander over the sprawling property and lend a hand in milking the cows.

Round Tu-It Holiday Park (☎ 9776 7276; roundtu -it@westnet.com.au; Muirillup Rd; dm $15, B&B s/d $45/65) is a haven for mountain bikers, nature lovers and orphaned baby 'roos, who are hand-reared by the owner. There are the usual camping options available, as well as B&B in the house and basic beds in a small dorm.

GREAT SOUTHERN

To the east of the southwestern capes and the karri forests is the vast Great Southern region of the state's south coast, stretching from Walpole-Nornalup in the west to Cape Arid, east of Esperance. The area is a nature lover's paradise, with spectacular (often empty) beaches and some of the best mountainous national parks in Australia, exemplified by the ecological 'islands' of the dramatic Stirling Range as well as by the ancient granite spires of the Porongurups.

Getting There & Away

Skywest (☎ 08-9334 2288) has daily flights from Perth to Albany ($204) and Esperance ($260).

Transwa (☎ 1300 662 205) offers a daily service from Perth to Albany (via Bunbury) that uses a combination of the *Australind* and road coach ($52.35). It passes through Walpole ($47.40) and Denmark ($50.05), and the journey takes about 8½ hours. Another daily bus service from Perth to Albany ($42.35, 6 hours) travels inland via Williams and stops in Mt Barker ($36.85, 5½ hours).

Transwa also has daily buses from Perth to Esperance ($63.45, 10 hours), two buses a week from Albany to Esperance ($46.50) and three buses a week between Esperance and Kalgoorlie ($40.40, 5 hours).

WALPOLE-NORNALUP AREA

The heavily forested **Walpole-Nornalup National Park** cradles Nornalup inlet and Walpole. Stunning beaches, rugged coastline and the famous Valley of the Giants are highlights, and scenic drives include Knoll Dr and Hilltop Rd (leading to the **Giant Tingle Tree**). Walpole is a tranquil pit stop around 14km from the Tree Top Walk and within cooee of the Bibbulmun Track, while tiny Nornalup is an even smaller outpost just minutes from the giants.

For more information, stop at the log cabin–style **visitors centre** (☎ 08-9840 1111; 🕑 9am-5pm, closes 4pm Sat & Sun) and **CALM** (☎ 08-9840 1027), both on the South Coast Hwy in Walpole.

WOW Wilderness Cruises (☎ 08-9840 1036; adult/child $25/12) runs entertaining and well-informed 2½-hour trips through the inlets and river systems at 10am daily.

Valley of the Giants

As you drive down the 6km Valley of the Giants Rd, almost brushing the magnificent Tolkienesque trees that crowd up to the bitumen, a sense of anticipation starts to build. For decades this valley has attracted nature lovers eager to see the giant tingle trees, but these days you can get a bird's-eye view from the impressive **Tree Top Walk** (☎ 08-9840 8263; adult/child/family $6/2.50/14; 🕑 8am-5.15pm Dec-Jan, 9am-4.15pm Feb-Nov). This 600m-long, wheelchair-accessible ramp structure leads visitors high up into the canopy 40m

WESTERN AUSTRALIA

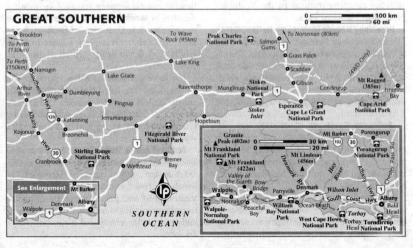

GREAT SOUTHERN

above the ground, offering stunning views and a few heart-in-the-mouth moments. Vertigo sufferers opt for the **Ancient Empire** (admission free), a 600m ground-level boardwalk through a grove of veteran tingles.

In summer, **CALM** (☎ 08-9840 1027; adult/child $12/5) runs regular guided Forest by Night tours, in which visitors can watch nocturnal creatures from the starlit canopy.

Sleeping & Eating

Walpole Backpackers (☎ 08-9840 1244; www.walpolebackpackers.com; Cnr Pier St & Park Ave; dm/d $20/50; 🖵) Guests quickly warm to this sprawling open-plan house and its casual, social atmosphere. Its chatty, friendly owners offer guided bushwalking and 4WD tours (from $20) to out-of-the-way spots in D'Entrecasteux National Park, and nearby Hush Hush Beach and Peaceful Bay.

Tingle All Over YHA (☎ /fax 08-9840 1041; Nockolds St; dm/s/d $19/33/50, nonmembers extra $3.50) Fronting the highway, Tingle All Over offers clean but small budget rooms, a giant courtyard chess set and a taxi service for those who are vehicularly challenged.

Rest Point Holiday Village (☎ 08-9840 1032; fax 9840 1302; Rest Point Rd; cabins from $55) Perfectly situated on the Walpole Inlet about 2km from town, this tranquil caravan park offers all a person with a bent for fishing could want, including accommodation at the water's edge and boats ($25/70 per hour/day) and canoes ($15/35) for hire.

See **CALM**'s Walpole office (☎ 08-9840 1027) for camping options in the Walpole-Nornalup National Park.

Nornalup Riverside Chalets (☎ /fax 08-9840 1107; 1164 South Coast Hwy; 2-person budget/luxury/spa chalets $65/90/100) Just 5km from Valley of the Giants Rd, this excellent option has riverside chalets that sleep eight. Hire-canoes are available for some easy-going exercise down the Frankland River ($20 per hour, $45/60 for a half/full day).

Wellington House (☎ 08-9840 1103; Station Rd; s/d $55/80, s/d with bathroom $65/95) Guests are greeted by the trilling of tiny wrens, biscuits and a hot cuppa at this good-value, homy B&B, tucked away in thick bushland in the Nornalup Valley.

Nornalup Tea House (☎ /fax 08-9840 1422; South Coast Hwy; mains $16-24; ☯ closed Tue) The region's best restaurant sits on the highway, serving tasty soups and sandwiches at lunchtime,

and delicious wines and modern Australian meals in the evening.

In Walpole, itself, grab a quick bite at the **Wooz & Suz Cafe** (☎ 08-9840 1214; 13 Nockolds St; mains $6-15) or find more substantial fare at the fully licensed **Top Deck Cafe** (☎ 08-9840 1344; 25 Nockolds St; mains $6-20).

DENMARK
☎ 08 / pop 2000

Vineyards, art galleries, orchards, alpaca farms...it seems that everyone with a slice of land and a dream of alternative living has headed for the hills around Denmark. This idyllic former timber town cultivates a laid-back village atmosphere and offers the magical combination of river, sea and forest at its doorstep. Fine beaches make Denmark a popular place to fish, surf or simply drop out for a while, while its proximity to the Tree Top Walk makes it an excellent base for travellers to the tingles.

The **visitors centre** (☎ 9848 2055; Strickland St; ☯ 9am-5pm) is in the RSL Memorial Hall, while the nearby **Telecentre** (Strickland St; ☯ 10am-4pm Mon-Fri) offers Internet access and has public toilets and a mothers' rest room behind.

Sights & Activities

Nearby hikes include the **Mokare Trail** (a 3km circuit along the Denmark River) and the **Wilson Inlet Trail** (6km, starting from the river mouth). William Bay National Park, 15km west of Denmark, has spectacular coastal scenery and safe-swimming beaches at **Madfish Bay** and **Green's Pool**. The massive rounded boulders of **Elephants Rocks** also attract many travellers. Closer to town you'll find **Ocean Beach**, which is popular with surfers.

If you've got your own transport, go for a burl along tree-lined **Mt Shadforth Rd**, with artists' galleries, potters' shops and luxury retreats, or **Scotsdale Rd**, lined with orchards, vineyards, berry farms and arts and crafts studios.

Pentland Alpaca Stud & Tourist Farm (☎ 9840 9262; cnr McLeod & Scotsdale Rds; adult/child $9/4.50; ☯ 10am-4pm), 20km west of Denmark, is worth the trip for animal lovers of all ages. Visitors feed and pet a menagerie of hand-reared animals, including alpacas, kangaroos, highland cattle, ferrets and a rambunctious donkey.

Tours

Little River Discovery Tours (☎ 9848 2604) offers 4WD day trips to the Valley of the Giants ($80/37 per adult/child) and to the isolated beaches of West Cape Howe National Park ($75/35). **Wild about Wilderness Tours** (☎ 9848 3502) runs guided bushwalks (from $28 per person) and a jam-packed two-day tour ($270) that includes meals, a boat cruise, canoeing up the Frankland River, a walk on the Bibb Track (see the boxed text 'The Bibb Track'; p830) and an aboriginal cultural experience with bush food.

Sleeping

Blue Wren Travellers' Rest (☎ 9848 3300; bluewren rest@yahoo.com.au; 17 Price St; dm/tw $19/50, d with bathroom $55; 🖳) Intimate and relaxed, this newish backpackers in the centre of town is an excellent place to hang out for a while. Facilities include disabled access, a kitchen, laundry, communal lounging areas and a friendly house dog. Free bikes are a bonus, and early birds can join the owner on a riverside bike ride most mornings.

Denmark Waterfront (☎ 9848 1147; www.den markwaterfront.com.au; 63 Inlet Dr; 3-bed lodge rooms $80, motel units/cottages $90/160) Located on the water's edge, this peaceful retreat offers a mixed bag of accommodation from luxury spa cottages to standard motel units and lodge rooms (all with bathroom).

Windrose B&B (☎ 9848 3502; www.westnet.com.au /windrose; 6 Harington Break; s/d/f $75/90/120) On the road to Ocean Beach around 5km from town, this new timber home near the foot of Mt Hallowell features individually themed guestrooms with bathrooms and complimentary breakfast. Guided bushwalks and tours are available.

Karma Chalets (☎ /fax 9848 1568; www.karmachalets .com.au; South Coast Hwy; chalets from $135) Excellent options for families or a group of friends, these hillside timber chalets boast verandas, barbecues, spas, attic bedrooms and spectacular valley views.

Rivermouth Caravan Park (☎ /fax 9848 1262; 1 Inlet Dr; camp/caravan sites $14/17, on-site caravans $36, cabins $45-65) An idyllic shady site 1km south of town makes this a tempting option for budget travellers.

Eating

Lushus (☎ 9848 1299; 18 Hollings Rd; mains $7-15) Bright, cheerful colours and a groovy at-mosphere set this quirky café apart, while its healthy options and herbal teas please the purists.

Figtree Cafe (☎ 9848 2051; 27 Strickland St; mains $7-14) Tucked into a garden-filled arcade with an outdoor deck, the Figtree is ideal for a coffee stop or light lunch.

Walker Street Pizzeria (☎ 9848 2479; cnr Walker & Strickland Sts; pizzas $9-19) Pizza lovers eat in or take away at this popular joint on the main drag.

Observatory (☎ 9848 2600; Mt Shadforth Rd; mains $11-33) Breathtaking views, divine cakes and sweet treats from the adjoining Toffee Factory make this up-market eatery 6km out of town irresistible.

Self-caterers can stock up at **Nookes Store** and the **Denmark Bakery** on Strickland St.

MT BARKER

☎ 08 / pop 1650

Sleepy Mt Barker, 50km north of Albany, is a gateway town to the nearby Porongurup and Stirling Range National Parks, and hub for the rapidly growing local wine industry. Big names include **Plantagenet Wines** (☎ 9851 2150; Albany Hwy) in the middle of town, and **Goundrey Wines** (☎ 9851 1777; Muirs Hwy), 10km west. For a list of vineyards and cellar-door opening times, see the **visitors centre** (☎ 9851 1163; Albany Hwy; ☉ 9am-5pm Mon-Fri, 9am-3pm Sat, 10am-3pm Sun).

Historical sites worth a visit are the picturesque 1873 **St Werburgh's Chapel** (☎ 9857 6041; St Werburgh's Rd) and the restored **Old Police Station Museum** (Albany Hwy; adult/child $5/free; ☉ 10am-4pm Sat, Sun & school holidays), which houses a collection of historical memorabilia. Enjoy panoramic views of the area from the **Mt Barker Lookout**, 5km south of town.

Aptly named, **Chill Out Backpackers** (☎ 9851 2798; 79 Hassell St; dm/s/d $20/25/40) is a fabulous big house that sleeps seven (plus the friendly neighbourhood 'backpacker cat') and feels more like a B&B (without the breakfast) than a hostel.

Rayanne Homestead (☎ 9851 1562; fax 9851 2440; Porongurup Rd; s/d with bathroom $60/80), on the town's fringes, offers small, modern rooms opening onto a sprawling wrap-around veranda. A basic complimentary breakfast is included.

Mount Barker Caravan Park (☎ 9851 1691; fax 9851 2691; Albany Hwy; camp/caravan sites $15/17, dm $20, cabins with/without bathroom $60/50) is a quiet,

spick-and-span park with friendly owners and comfortable cabins.

Mt Barker is a bit quiet on the foodie front, but the **Enchanted Tree Frog** (☎ 9851 1728; 34 Albany Hwy; mains $15-22) is a local favourite. Less fancy fare is on offer in the **Wing Hing Chinese Restaurant** (Albany Hwy) or the **BP Mt Barker Roadhouse** (Albany Hwy).

PORONGURUP & STIRLING RANGES

The region north of Albany is one of spectacular natural beauty with two rugged, mountainous national parks to explore. National park fees apply to vehicles entering both parks. For further information, contact Albany's **CALM office** (☎ 08-9842 4500; 120 Albany Hwy) or the rangers at **Porongurup National Park** (☎ 08-9853 1095) and **Stirling Range National Park** (☎ 08-9827 9230).

Porongurup National Park

With towering karri trees, 1100-million-year-old granite outcrops and excellent bush tracks, this panoramic park is a popular stomping ground for bushwalkers and naturalists. Trails include Castle Rock (2 hours), and the challenging Devil's Slide and Marmabup Rock walk (3 hours). There's a scenic 6km drive along the park's northern edge that starts at the ranger's residence.

Porongurup Shop & Tearooms (☎ 08-9853 1110; homebake@omninet.net.au; Porongurup Rd; dm/s/d $20/20/40) runs a family-friendly hostel. A children's playground and organic vegie patch out back completes the homy package. Pick-ups from Albany or Mt Barker are available (book ahead).

The higher-end rooms are pure indulgence at **Karribank Country Retreat** (☎ 08-9853 1022; www.karribank.com.au; Porongurup Rd; d $86-190), a lovingly restored historic estate in well-tended gardens. The adjoining Old Lodge Restaurant serves hearty brunch, lunch and dinner options.

Campers can pitch a tent at the clean, cosy **Porongurup Range Tourist Park** (☎/fax 08-9853 1057; Porongurup Rd; camp/caravan sites $16/18, cabins $60).

En route to Mt Barker, amid glorious farmland, you can (remarkably) indulge in *tom yum goong* (Thai prawn soup; $16) and jungle curry pork ($17) at **Maleeya's Thai Cafe** (☎ 08-9853 1123; 1376 Porongurup Rd; mains $13-21; ☽ 10.30am-9pm Thu-Sun, closed Jul-Aug).

Stirling Range National Park

Rising abruptly from the surrounding flat and sandy plains, the 96km-long Stirling Range is famous for its spectacular colour changes through blues, reds and purples and its spectacular wildflower season from late August to early December – the Queen of Sheba orchid and the Stirling Bells are especially magnificent in bloom. Most day-trippers try to squeeze in at least one half-day walk to Toolbrunup Peak (for views and a good climb), Bluff Knoll (at 1073m, the highest peak in the range) or Toll Peak (prolific wildflowers).

Stirling Range Retreat (☎ 08-9827 9229; www.stirlingrange.com.au; Chester Pass Rd; camp/caravan sites $18/22, dm $19, cabins $79-85, chalets $105-125) offers an array of accommodation in a tranquil setting on the northern boundary of the park. Ecotourism is the catch cry and TV is a no-no. The licensed Bluff Knoll café is opposite.

Lily (☎ 08-9827 9205; fax 9827 9206; Chester Pass Rd; d from $97), another 11km down the road, is a small slice of the Netherlands. Head towards the impossible-to-miss Dutch windmill to find a vineyard and some lovingly decorated country-style cottages. Visitors are welcome to pop in for a glass of wine or a meal at the new restaurant on the property.

ALBANY

☎ 08 / pop 29,900
Established shortly before Perth in 1826, Albany is the oldest European settlement in the state and the bustling commercial centre of the southern region. The area was occupied by Aboriginal people long before Europeans and there is much evidence of their earlier presence, especially around Oyster Harbour. Albany is blessed with pristine beaches, rugged coastline and the glorious King George Sound, now a mecca for divers. A thriving whaling port until the late 1970s, whales are still very much a part of the Albany experience, but thankfully these days they're shot by cameras instead of harpoons.

Information

The **visitors centre** (☎ 9841 1088, 1800 644 088; Proudlove Pde; ☽ 9am-5pm) in the old train station offers accommodation and tour tips. Internet access is available from the **Eco Tourist Centre** (☎ 9842 6886; cnr Stirling Tce & York St). The town has both **CALM** (☎ 9842

4500; Albany Hwy) and **RACWA** (Albany Hwy) offices. If you need a quick shower, the **Albany Rest Centre** (cnr Stirling Tce & York St) can accommodate; it also has toilets, disabled facilities and baby-changing rooms.

Sights
HISTORIC BUILDINGS

Albany has some fine colonial buildings, several with historical displays. Experience how prisoners and their gaolers lived in the 1852 **Old Gaol** (☎ 9841 1401; Lower Stirling Tce; adult/child $4/ 2.50; ☺ 10am-4.15pm). Admission includes entry to the 1832 wattle-and-daub **Patrick Taylor Cottage** (☎ 9841 6174; Duke St; ☺ 1-4.15pm), believed to be the oldest colonial dwelling in WA.

Albany Residency Museum (☎ 9841 4844; Residency Rd; admission gold coin donation; ☺ 10am-5pm), built in the 1850s, explores the social history of the region with seafaring subjects and Aboriginal artefacts. The excellent **Eclipse building**, across the car park, features a lighthouse optic among the displays rescued from Eclipse Island.

Alongside the museum is a full-scale replica of the **Brig Amity** (adult/child $3/1; ☺ 9am-5pm), which brought Albany's founders to the area in 1826.

Strawberry Hill Farm (☎ 9841 3735; 170 Middleton Rd; adult/child $3.30/$2.20; ☺ 10am-4pm) is a charming National Trust–listed property that showcases how the original owners used to live. For Devonshire tea or a hearty country snack, don't miss the traditional tearooms.

Other historic buildings include **St John's Anglican Church** (cnr York St & Peels Pl), the elegant home **Pyrmont** (110 Serpentine Rd), the **courthouse** (Stirling Tce West) and **Town Hall** (217 York St). A free walking tour brochure of Albany's colonial buildings is available from the visitors centre.

OTHER ATTRACTIONS

Water lovers gravitate to **Middleton Beach**, a popular swimming beach with wide stretches of sand, and family-friendly **Emu Point** 4km further east, a magical watery playground with enclosed swimming area and excellent fishing and boating.

The **Desert Mounted Corps Memorial** sits atop **Mt Clarence**, which you can climb along a track accessible from the end of Grey St East. Panoramic views are enjoyed from the lookout tower on **Mt Melville**; the signposted turn-off is off Serpentine Rd. There's also

a **whale-watching walk** from Marine Dr on Mt Adelaide to the harbour entrance (45 minutes return).

A relatively recent addition to the Albany skyline is the strangely popular and surprisingly beautiful **Albany Wind Farm**, with a row of modern white windmills on the cliff tops 12km from town.

The **Princess Royal Fortress** (Marine Dr; adult/child $4/2; ☺ 7.30am-5.30pm) on Mt Adelaide was built in 1893 as a strategic defence post, and today boasts restored buildings, gun emplacements and fine views.

The **Sandalwood Factory** (☎ 9841 7788; cnr Down Rd & Albany Hwy; ☺ 9am-5pm) produces sandalwood oil and perfumes, and offers free guided tours of the extraction plant.

Activities

After the 2001 scuttling of the warship **HMAS Perth** to create an artificial reef for divers, Albany's appeal as a top-class diving destination has grown, and there's plenty of competition for business among the companies in town. Offering a range of dive courses and guided dives to the wreck and reefs are the **Albany Scuba Diving Academy** (☎ 9842 3101; cnr Proudlove Pde & York St), **AlbanyDive.com** (☎ 9842 6886; www.albanydive.com; cnr York St & Stirling Tce) and **South Coast Diving Supplies** (☎ 9841 7176; www.divealbany.com.au; 84 Serpentine Rd).

If you're a little nervous about taking the plunge yourself, the semisubmersible underwater viewing vessel, the **Albany Reef Explorer** (☎ 0418-950 361), does several one-hour cruises daily ($24/15 per adult/child).

Tours

The whale-watching season is from July to October, when southern right whales are often spotted near the bays and coves of King George Sound. **Southern Ocean Charters** (☎ 0409-107 180) and **Silver Star Cruises** (☎ 0428-936 711; adult/child $45/30; ☺ 9.30am & 1pm) run 2½-hour whale-watching trips around King George Sound from the town jetty.

Kalgan Queen Scenic Cruises (☎ 9844 1949; adult/ child $36/20; ☺ 9am) leave from the Emu Point boat pens to cruise the Kalgan River and Oyster Harbour in search of wildlife. Half-day cruises feature a meal of damper and billy tea, and a comprehensive commentary.

Escape Tours (☎ 9844 1945; adult/child half-day tours $40/30, full-day tours $80/60) operates half-day

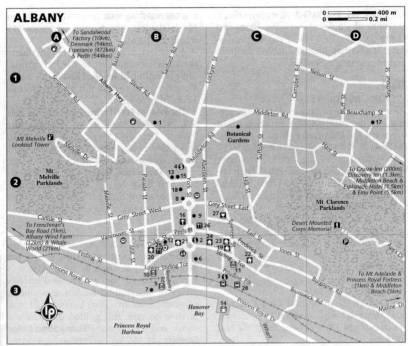

bus tours of historic Albany or the peninsula. Full-day tours head to the Tree Top Walk, West Cape Howe and the Porongurups, among other destinations.

You can tour around town or along scenic coastline on the back of a Harley Davidson with the **Albany Motorcycle Touring Co** (☎ 9841 8034; tours $5-30).

Sleeping
BUDGET
Blue Water Accommodation (☎ 9841 6599; www .bluewaterwa.com.au; 160 Stirling Tce; dm $17-22, s/d $28/ 50, s/d with bathroom $40/60; 🖳) This sprawling revamped hotel offers roomy communal areas, bright décor and a friendly vibe. Have a beer downstairs in the historic London Hotel, WA's first pub.

Bayview YHA (☎ 9842 3388; albany@yhawa.com.au; 49 Duke St; dm/d $18/50, nonmembers extra $3.50; 🖳) A great place to crash, this low-key, friendly YHA offers simple free breakfast, loans of body boards and snorkelling gear, and use of a cavernous TV room.

Albany Backpackers (☎ 9841 8848; www.albany backpackers.com.au; cnr Stirling Tce & Spencer St; dm/s $20/36, d & tw $55, nonmembers extra $3; 🖳) With loud, colourful wall murals, a range of theme nights, free evening coffee and cake, and a laid-back attitude, this is the place to meet people and party.

Albany has plenty of caravan parks in idyllic bush and beach locations. One of the best is the beachfront **Middleton Beach Holiday Park** (☎ 9841 3593, 1800 644 674; http: //members.iinet.net.au/~big4; Flinders Pde; camp/caravan sites $25/27, cabins from $80), which is located 3km from the town centre. Prices are reduced in low season.

MID-RANGE
Cruize-Inn (☎ 9842 9599; fax 9842 9588; 122 Middleton Rd; s/tw/d $33/55/60) Halfway to Middleton Beach, this big, breezy beachhouse sleeps 12 and has a friendly holiday atmosphere. Travellers kick back in the sprawling lounge or on the outer deck with stunning bay views.

Vancouver House (☎ 9842 1071; www.vancouver housebnb.com.au; 86 Stirling Tce; s/d $70/95, s/d with bathroom $85/120) Guests are spoilt rotten at this boutique B&B, with cooked breakfasts,

floral décor and more teddy bears than the proverbial picnic.

Devines Guesthouse (☎ 9841 8050; devinesbb@ bigpond.com; 20 Stirling Tce; s/d $45/70, with breakfast $55/85) The small, family-run Devines offers a home away from home, with clean, modest accommodation and breakfast in the family kitchen.

DiscoveryInn (☎ 98425535; www.discoveryinn.net.au; 9 Middleton Rd; s/d $45/75) If you'd like to have a morning dip, this charming 1920s house is just paces from Middleton Beach. A pretty cottage garden, covered outdoor courtyard and fully cooked breakfast complete the package.

Frederickstown Motel (☎ 9841 1600; www.albanyis .com.au/fredmtl; cnr Spencer & Frederick Sts; d from $90) There's nothing special about these standard motel rooms except their great location off Stirling Tce.

Esplanade Hotel (☎ 9842 1711; www.albanyesp lanade.com.au; cnr Adelaide Cres & Flinders Pde, Middle-

ton Beach; d from $170, self-contained apartments from $155) Overlooking swim-friendly Middleton Beach, this huge complex includes a bistro, restaurant and pub famous for its Sunday sessions.

Eating & Drinking

For a range of good quality eats, you could make a beeline for Stirling Tce, York St and Frederick St.

Naked Bean (☎ 9841 1815; 14 Peels Pl; mains $8-10; ⏳ closed Sun) Sophisticated city style and excellent freshly ground coffee keep the Naked Bean humming most mornings.

Al Fornetto's (☎ 9842 1060; 132 York St; mains $15-27) The crumbed stuffed mushrooms are a vegie highlight at this elegant Italian restaurant, with a tasty range of pastas, pizzas and meat dishes.

Dylan's on the Terrace (☎ 9841 8720; 82 Stirling Tce; meals $7-17; ⏳ 7am-late) Grab breakfast, a hamburger or pancakes at any time of day at this popular family-friendly place with lots of light meals.

Kooka's (☎ 9841 5889; 204 Stirling Tce; mains $22-28; ⏳ closed Sun & Mon) For a special night out, Kooka's is the gourmet's choice, with excellent country-style cuisine served in a beautiful restored house (c 1850).

Earl of Spencer Inn (☎ 9841 1322; cnr Earl & Spencer Sts; mains $12-28) Locals say you can't go past the inn's famous pie and pint ($13.95). This historic smoke-free tavern serves international beers on tap daily and live music on the weekend.

Legends Bar & Bistro (☎ 9842 1711; Esplanade Hotel, cnr Adelaide Cres & Flinders Pde, Middleton Beach) After a hard day's sunbathing it's only a brief stagger to this beachfront pub where you can grab an ale or a tasty counter meal.

Somewhat surprisingly, tiny Emu Point, 4km east of Middleton Beach, has some excellent options.

Gosuya-Ya (☎ 9844 1111; 1 Mermaid Ave; mains $13-23) Poised at the mouth of pretty Oyster Harbour is this popular Japanese restaurant with sushi, sashimi and other yummy treats.

Squid Shack (☎ 0417-170 857; Emu Point Boat Ramp; mains $6-15; ⏳ closed Fri) If fish and chips is more your style, head to this mobile van near the boat pens.

Getting Around

Love's (☎ 9841 1211) runs bus services around town on weekdays and Saturday morning.

WESTERN AUSTRALIA

Buses go along the Albany Hwy from Peel Place to the main roundabout, and to Middleton Beach, Emu Point and Bayonet Head. A short trip around town costs $1.90/0.80 per adult/child.

AROUND ALBANY
Whale World

Twenty-one kilometres from Albany, **Whale World** (☎ 08-9844 4021; www.whaleworld.org; adult/child/backpacker $13/5/10; Frenchman Bay; 🕑 9am-5pm, tours on the hour 10am-4pm) is based at Cheynes Beach Whaling Station (which closed operations in November 1978). Visitors can see the skeleton of the station's last victim, scramble over a rusting former whale-chaser outside, examine displays of harpoons and whaleboats, and view a gore-spattered film on whaling history (not for weak stomachs).

National Parks & Reserves

You can explore many different habitats in the excellent natural areas along the coast both west and east of Albany. **West Cape Howe National Park**, 30km west, is a favourite with naturalists, bushwalkers, rock climbers and anglers.

South of Albany, off Frenchman Bay Rd, is the **Torndirrup National Park**, with a stunning if treacherous stretch of coastline. Southern right whales can be seen from the cliffs during season. Don't take lightly the warning signs at the **Gap**, the **Natural Bridge** and the **Blowholes**; tragic accidents still occur thanks to carelessness and strong wind gusts. Other popular spots in the park are **Jimmy Newhill's Harbour** and **Salmon Holes** (popular with surfers, although these coves are quite dangerous).

East of Albany is **Two People's Bay**, a nature reserve with a good swimming beach, scenic coastline and a small colony of noisy scrub birds, a species once thought extinct.

Probably the best of the national parks, but the least visited, is **Waychinicup**, 65km east of Albany, which features its own population of noisy scrub birds and several other endangered animals.

ALBANY TO ESPERANCE

From Albany, the South Coast Hwy runs northeast along the coast before turning inland to skirt the Fitzgerald River National Park and ending in Esperance.

Fitzgerald River National Park

This 3300-sq-km park covers beautiful coastline, sand plains, the rugged Barren mountain range and deep, wide river valleys. The overnight wilderness bushwalking route from Fitzgerald Beach to Whalebone Beach is recommended, though there is no track and no water. Call the **ranger** (☎ 08-9835 5043) before you set out, and clean your shoes at each end of the walk to avoid the spread of dieback.

The park contains half the orchid species in WA (over 80 species, 70 of which occur nowhere else), 22 mammal species, 200 species of birds and 1700 species of plants. It is also the home of those floral marvels, the royal hakea (Hakea victoria) and Quaalup bell (Pimelia physodes).

Access to the park is from Bremer Bay (west) and Hopetoun (east) or from the South Coast Hwy along Devils Creek, Quiss and Hamersley Rds. Camping is allowed at numerous sites within the park. For more information, contact the Albany **CALM office** (☎ 08-9842 4500).

Ravensthorpe
☎ 08 / pop 350

Ravensthorpe is a small rural pit stop that started out as the centre of the Phillips River goldfield. Copper mining followed and modern nickel mines are rumoured to be in the pipeline, but the area is principally a farming centre these days. Tourist information and local crafts are available from the **Going Bush Information Stop** (☎ 9838 1277; Morgan St; 🕑 9am-4.30pm).

Befitting a town that is mainly an overnight stay en route to somewhere else, accommodation and services sit conveniently on the highway.

Ravensthorpe Caravan Park (☎ 9838 1050; fax 9838 1465; South Coast Hwy; camp/caravan sites $12/17, onsite caravans from $22, cabins from $36) offers camping and cabins in a bush setting, as well as beds in old miners' dorms ($13). Several cabins have limited disabled access.

If you need a drink and feed, consider taking a simple room in the **Palace Motor Hotel** (☎ 9838 1005; fax 9838 1200; 28 Morgans St; hotel s/d $22/38, motel s/d $50/70), which keeps guests sated in its downstairs bar and bistro.

The **Ravy Country Kitchen** (☎ 9838 1163; Morgan St; mains $6-12) sells tasty home-made pies and a selection of cakes.

Hopetoun

☎ 08 / pop 350

A worthwhile side trip is windswept Hopetoun, 50km south of Ravensthorpe, a pretty holiday town increasingly popular with retirees. It has fine beaches and bays, and is the eastern gateway to the Fitzgerald River National Park. The **visitors centre** (☎ 9838 3228; Cafe Barnacles Bldg, Veal St) has a small collection of brochures on the area. You can check your email at the **Telecentre** (☎ 9838 3062; Veal St).

The most appealing place to stay in the area is the **Hopetoun Motel & Chalet Village** (☎ 9838 3219; cnr Veal & Canning Sts; motel d/tw from $80/85, chalets $150), a rammed-earth complex nestled in a whisper-quiet bush setting with lovely native gardens.

Directly across from the beach, the ancient **Port Hotel** (☎ 9838 3053; fax 9838 3036; Veal St; dm/s/d $17/33/45) offers basic facilities in four freshly painted rooms and a 10-bed dorm.

Deck (☎ 9448 0200; cnr Veal & Clarke Sts; snacks $3-9), in the recently renovated historic post office building, is a spanking new eatery with scrumptious Italian ice cream and sundaes.

ESPERANCE

☎ 08 / pop 8650

Esperance, on the Bay of Isles, sits in the middle of some of Australia's most magnificent coastline. There are about 100 small islands in the Recherche Archipelago, home to colonies of fur seals, penguins and a variety of sea birds. A temperate climate, clear aquamarine waters and squeaky white beaches complete the idyllic picture. Esperance is 721km southeast of Perth and 200km south of Norseman.

Although the first settlers came to the area in 1863, it was during the 1890s gold rush that the town became established as a port. When the gold fever subsided, Esperance went into a state of suspended animation until after WWII. In the 1950s it was discovered that adding missing trace elements to the soil around Esperance increased its fertility – since then the town has rapidly grown into an agricultural centre.

Information

The **visitors centre** (☎ 9071 2330; Dempster St; ✆ 8.45am-5pm) can book tours to the islands and surrounding national parks, as well as onward transport.

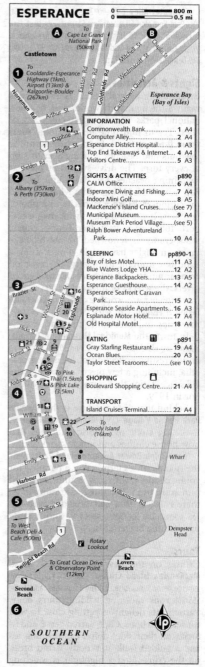

ESPERANCE

0 — 800 m
0 — 0.5 mi

INFORMATION	
Commonwealth Bank...............	**1** A4
Computer Alley........................	**2** A4
Esperance District Hospital........	**3** A3
Top End Takeaways & Internet....	**4** A4
Visitors Centre........................	**5** A3

SIGHTS & ACTIVITIES	p890
CALM Office............................	**6** A4
Esperance Diving and Fishing.......	**7** A4
Indoor Mini Golf......................	**8** A5
MacKenzie's Island Cruises.........	(see 7)
Municipal Museum....................	**9** A4
Museum Park Period Village.......	(see 5)
Ralph Bower Adventureland Park.	**10** A4

SLEEPING	pp890-1
Bay of Isles Motel....................	**11** A3
Blue Waters Lodge YHA.............	**12** A2
Esperance Backpackers..............	**13** A5
Esperance Guesthouse...............	**14** A2
Esperance Seafront Caravan Park.	**15** A2
Esperance Seaside Apartments....	**16** A3
Esplanade Motor Hotel..............	**17** A4
Old Hospital Motel...................	**18** A4

EATING	p891
Gray Starling Restaurant............	**19** A4
Ocean Blues............................	**20** A3
Taylor Street Tearooms.............	(see 10)

SHOPPING	
Boulevard Shopping Centre.......	**21** A4

TRANSPORT	
Island Cruises Terminal..............	**22** A4

WESTERN AUSTRALIA

Computer Alley (☎ 9072 1293; 69c Dempster St; ✹ 9am-5pm Mon-Fri, closes 4pm Sat) offers fast Internet access. If it's closed, you can check your email at **Top End Takeaways** (☎ 9071 2000; 119 Dempster St) until late.

Sights & Activities

Breathtaking natural beauty is Esperance's main attraction, with world-class beaches, national parks and the spectacular Bay of Isles. Try to find time for the 36km **Great Ocean Drive**, west of town, with stunning lookouts and beaches enticing you to stop at every turn. The drive sweeps by popular swimming beaches, **Blue Haven** and **Twilight Bay**, as well as striking white windmills and the curious **Pink Lake**, a favourite with photographers. If you don't have your own transport, tours are available (see Tours; below).

Esperance is renowned for its **fishing** – many an angler has caught dinner using a hand-line from the town jetty. There's good **diving** around the islands and, for experienced divers, the wrecks of the *Sanko Harvest* and the *Lapwing* are worth exploring. **Esperance Diving & Fishing** (☎ 9071 5111; 72 The Esplanade) runs trips and hires out equipment.

In town, the **Municipal Museum** (cnr Dempster & James Sts; adult/child $3/1; ✹ 1.30-4.30pm) displays an interesting collection of local memorabilia, including a few pieces of Skylab – the US space station that crashed on the Nullarbor in 1979.

Behind the visitors centre is the **Museum Park Period Village** (✹ 10am-4pm Mon-Fri, closes 1pm Sat), a circle of historic buildings that now house clothes and knick-knack shops.

The **Ralph Bower Adventureland Park**, near the island cruises terminal, is a paradise for young children, with playground, maze and miniature train. For those rare rainy days, there's **Indoor Mini Golf** (adult/child $6.60/4.40; ✹ opens 10am Sat, Sun & holidays), and a skate park for the bigger kids.

Tours

Cruises on the Bay of Isles are a must. **MacKenzie's Island Cruises** (☎ 9071 5757; www .emerge.net.au/~macruise; 71 The Esplanade; adult/child $55/20) runs morning wildlife tours daily. Participants delight in getting close to wild fur seals, sea lions, Cape Barren geese, and (if luck's on their side) dolphins. Morning tea and a guided walk at Woody Island break up the cruise, and a highlight is watching

sea eagles swoop down to pluck hand-fed fish from the sea. Full-day trips ($80/35) are available on Wednesday and Sunday.

Vacation Country Tours (☎ 9071 2227) runs daily trips around Esperance, including a town-and-coast tour for $31 and a Cape Le Grand tour for $50. More adventurous is **Aussie Bight Expeditions** (☎ 9071 7778; half-/full-day tours from $60/135), with 4WD safaris to secluded beaches and bays and to national parks.

Sleeping

BUDGET

Esperance Guesthouse (☎ 9071 3396; fax 9072 0298; 23 Daphne St; dm/d $20/45; ▣) Readers rave about this friendly, family-run house (previously known as Shoestring Stays), which features a big backyard, kitchen and TV room. Rates drop after the first night.

Esperance Backpackers (☎ 9071 4724; esperance backpackers@bigpond.com; 14 Emily St; dm/d from $18/45; ▣) In a quiet residential street, this homy hostel is another attractive option, with bonus half-day tours to national parks ($50), and fishing trips ($40).

Blue Waters Lodge YHA (☎ 9071 1040; yhaes perance@hotmail.com; 299 Goldfields Rd; dm/s/d/f from $18/30/45/70; ▣) Around 1.5km out of town, this sprawling, spartan lodge has spacious communal areas and lovely bay views from the balcony.

There are six caravan parks around Esperance, including **Esperance Seafront Caravan Park** (☎ 9071 1251; Goldfields Rd; camp/caravan sites $18/21, on-site caravans $55), which has an enviable beachfront position.

If you want to get away from it all, there's nowhere better than **Woody Island** (camp site per person $9, tent accommodation for 2 people $31), where you can BYO tent or rent a permanently erected tent with mattresses (see also mid-range accommodation for details on safari huts). Contact **MacKenzie's Island Cruises** (☎ 9071 5757) for details.

MID-RANGE

Old Hospital Motel (☎ 90713587; oldesp@emerge.net.au; William St; s/d/f $80/90/120) A crisp, clean look maintains the hospital theme at this appealing motel with country-style furnishings and friendly staff.

Esperance Seaside Apartments (☎ 9071 5313; www.esperanceseaside.com; 14-16 The Esplanade; 1-/ 2-bedroom apt from $130/150; ❄) Bright, breezy two-storey apartments offer luxury living

and home comforts, including barbecue on the balcony, a laundry, clothesline and kitchen.

Woody Island (Mackenzie's Island Cruises; ☎ 9071 5757; d from $70) Around 16km offshore from Esperance, tranquil Woody Island has a row of hillside safari huts with queen-size beds. Be prepared for 10pm lights out and 4am birdsong wake-up calls.

Bay of Isles Motel (☎ 9071 3999; www.bayofisles motel.com; 32 The Esplanade; s/d/f $85/105/130; 🌀) Excellent facilities and a fab bayside position make this one of the best motels in town.

Esperance Motor Hotel (☎ 9071 1555; fax 9071 1495; 14 Andrew St; s/d $55/65) If no-frills suits your taste and budget, try these simple motel rooms.

Eating
Taylor Street Tearooms (☎ 9071 4317; Taylor St; mains $11-23) This charming teahouse offers indulgent cakes ($5) and hearty big breakfasts ($15) on its sunswept deck by the water.

West Beach Deli & Cafe (☎ 9071 4622; 71 Phillips St; mains $4-22) Just off Twilight Beach Rd, this is the perfect pit stop to refuel after a day at the beach. Burgers on offer include lentil and surf 'n' turf (seafood and steak).

Pink Thai (☎ 9072 0000; Pink Lake Lodge, 85 Pink Lake Rd; mains $11-16; 🕒 from 5.30pm Thu-Sun) En route to Pink Lake, travellers stumble across this hot pink restaurant with surprisingly good Thai dishes. Start with the spicy fish cakes for a tasty chilli hit.

Ocean Blues (☎ 9071 7101; 19 The Esplanade; mains $10-21) Bright and cheerful, this family-friendly diner-style café serves burgers and focaccias, as well as more substantial fare.

Gray Starling Restaurant (☎ 9071 5880; 126 Dempster St; mains $18-30) For a quality dining experience, head to this beautiful renovated house off the Esplanade, with an eclectic menu for evening diners daily. Bookings are required.

AROUND ESPERANCE
If you've got any more than a day in this beautiful part of the world, don't miss a drive down to the magnificent **Cape Le Grand National Park**, extending from about 20km to 60km east of Esperance. The park boasts dramatic coastal scenery, excellent walking tracks and some of the best beaches in the state. Holiday-makers head here in summer

for good fishing, camping and swimming at **Lucky Bay** and **Le Grand Beach**. Day-trippers should try to squeeze in the steep (but worthwhile) climb to the top of **Frenchman's Peak** for breathtaking views.

Further east is the coastal **Cape Arid National Park** at the start of the Great Australian Bight, a rugged, isolated park with abundant flora and fauna, good bushwalking and beaches. Much of the park is only accessible by 4WD.

Other national parks in the area include **Stokes**, 92km west of Esperance, with an inlet, long beaches and rocky headlands, and **Peak Charles**, 130km north. For more information on all these parks, contact **CALM** (☎ 08-9071 3733; 92 Dempster St, Esperance).

If you are heading into national parks, take plenty of water as there is little or no fresh water in these isolated areas. Also, be wary of spreading dieback (clean your shoes before and after each hike). Entry fees apply to vehicles ($9).

There are limited-facility camp sites at **Cape Le Grand** (2 people $12.50) and **Cape Arid** (2 people $10); apply for permits at the park entrances. There are basic camp sites at **Stokes** (☎ 08-9076 8541; 2 people $10) and **Peak Charles** (☎ 08-9071 3733), which offers free camping.

SOUTHERN OUTBACK

The barren but beautiful semidesert and desert landscapes of the Southern Outback sprawl from the goldfields city of Kalgoorlie-Boulder across to SA and the Northern Territory (NT). Kalgoorlie-Boulder is its heartbeat, with a string of fascinating ghost towns to the north and the famous Nullarbor Plain to the east. For many travellers, this is the Australia that they've come to see – a remote, empty land of dramatic landscapes and thinly spread remnants of gold-rush history.

History
Fifty years after its establishment in 1829, the colony was still struggling, so the government in Perth was delighted when gold was discovered at Southern Cross in 1887. Gold put WA on the map and finally gave it the population to make it viable in its own right, rather than being just a distant offshoot of the east-coast colonies.

WESTERN AUSTRALIA

WESTERN AUSTRALIA

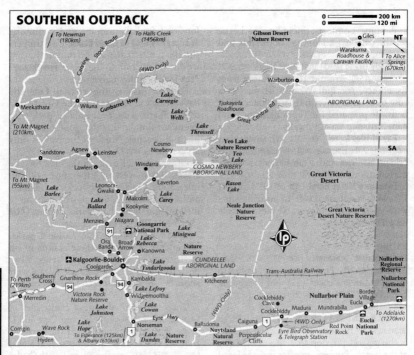

SOUTHERN OUTBACK

Major strikes were made in 1892 at Coolgardie and then a year later at Kalgoorlie. Some 50 towns had sprung up in the Eastern Goldfields by 1902, but within a decade most had been abandoned, and today Kalgoorlie-Boulder is the only large town remaining. Magnificent public buildings still stand in the ghost towns, and the region is a really fascinating place to explore.

Life on the early goldfields was hard. This region is extremely dry and the little rain that does fall quickly disappears into the porous soil. Many early gold-seekers, driven more by enthusiasm than common sense, died of thirst and disease while seeking the elusive metal. In 1903 the first precious drops of water made the 560km journey down the miraculous Golden Pipeline from the Perth outskirts, and the region's future was assured.

COOLGARDIE
☎ 08 / pop 1260

A popular, if sleepy, stopover for travellers on the Perth to Adelaide run, and also the turn-off for Kalgoorlie, Coolgardie is a shadow of its former self. Goldfields hysteria struck the town in 1892 and the population swelled to 15,000, but when it petered out, the town withered just as quickly.

The **visitors centre** (☎ 9026 6090; Warden's Ct, Bayley St; ☼ 9am-5pm) shares a magnificent historic building with the **Goldfields Museum** (adult/child $4/1.10; ☼ 9am-5pm), which showcases extensive mining memorabilia. History buffs will also enjoy the **Railway Station Museum** (☎ 9026 6388; 78 Woodward St; ☼ 9am-5pm) in the old train station.

One kilometre west of Coolgardie is the **town cemetery** (Great Eastern Hwy), which includes many old graves, such as that of explorer Ernest Giles (1835–97) and several Afghan camel drivers. It's said that one half of the population buried the other half due to unsanitary conditions and violence.

The most comfortable accommodation option in town is the **Coolgardie Motel** (☎ 9026 6080; hodgesbeverley@hotmail.com; 53 Bayley St; s/d with bathroom $60/75). Campers will be happy with tidy grounds and good facilities at the **Coolgardie Caravan Park** (☎ 9026 6238; fax 9026 6714; 99 Bayley St; camp/caravan sites $14/18, on-site caravans $40, 2-person chalets $60).

Hungry travellers can dig into that Aussie pub classic, surf 'n' turf (seafood and steak), at the **Denver City Hotel** (☎ 9026 6031; 73 Bayley St; mains $10-17).

McCafferty's/Greyhound (☎ 13 20 30) passes through Coolgardie on the Perth to Adelaide run ($265), with the Perth to Coolgardie segment costing $116. **Perth Goldfields Express** (☎ 1800 620 440) has a similar service to Perth, but is cheaper at $83. **Golden Lines** (☎ 9021 2655) runs on Monday to Friday from Kalgoorlie to Coolgardie ($5.30/2.10 per adult/child).

KALGOORLIE-BOULDER

☎ 08 / pop 30,500

Kalgoorlie ('Kal' to the locals) is a real surprise – a prosperous, humming metropolis in the middle of nowhere. In part it's modern, even urbane, but at heart it's still a frontier mining town with a taste for tatts, 'skimpies' (scantily clad bar staff), gambling, brothels and alcohol. These days, mining and pastoral development combine with a flourishing tourist trade to ensure its importance as an outback centre. With oppressively high summer temperatures, the winter months are the best time to visit, and travellers flock to the town in September to enjoy the surrounding wildflowers and the local horse races, making accommodation hard to find.

History

In 1893 long-time prospector Paddy Hannan set out from Coolgardie for another gold strike, but stopped at the site of Kal and stumbled across enough surface gold to spark another rush. Gold fever swept the nation, the region was flooded with eager hopefuls and a township quickly grew.

As it became increasingly hard to retrieve surface gold, the miners dug deeper, extracting the precious metal from the rocks by costly and complex processes. Kalgoorlie quickly prospered, and the town's magnificent public buildings constructed at the end of the 19th century are evidence of its fabulous wealth.

Despite its slow decline after WWI, Kalgoorlie is still the largest producer of gold in Australia, with giant mining conglomerates operating open-cut mines in the Golden Mile. Gone are the old headframes and corrugated iron shacks – instead, enormous homes on the approach to Kalgoorlie attest to the continuing profitability of modern mining.

Orientation

Although Kalgoorlie sprang up close to Paddy Hannan's original find, mining soon shifted a few kilometres away to the Golden Mile, a square mile that was one of the richest gold-mining areas for its size in the world; the satellite town of Boulder, 5km south, was developed to service it. The two towns amalgamated in 1989 into Kalgoorlie-Boulder city.

Kalgoorlie itself is a grid of broad, tree-lined streets. The main thoroughfare, Hannan St, is flanked by imposing buildings and is wide enough to turn a camel train – a necessity in early goldfield towns. You'll find most hotels, restaurants and offices on or close to Hannan St.

Information

CALM office (☎ 9021 2677; post office bldg, Hannan St)
Kalgoorlie Regional Hospital (☎ 9080 5888; Piccadilly St)
Netzone Internet Lounge (☎ 9091 4178; Shop 6, St Barbara's Sq; 🕙 10am-7pm, closes 5pm Sat & Sun) Excellent facilities and fast connection speeds.
RACWA office (☎ 9021 1511; cnr Porter & Hannan Sts)
Visitors Centre (☎ 9021 1966; 250 Hannan St; 🕙 8.30am-5pm, opens 9am Sat & Sun) Has a free map of Kal and excellent information on the area.

Sights
MINING HALL OF FAME

For a true insight into what Kal is all about, you can't beat a trip to the **Mining Hall of Fame** (☎ 9091 4074; www.mininghall.com; Eastern Bypass Rd; adult/child $20/10; 🕙 9am-4.30pm), 5km north of town. Visitors ride a lift-cage deep into the earth (not for claustrophobes or children under three) and are taken on a guided tour around the crosscuts of the mine. You can also learn about the hardships of the early prospectors, watch gold-pouring demonstrations and try your hand at panning for gold. Underground tours run at 10am, noon, 2pm and 3.20pm daily (remember to wear fully enclosed shoes).

MUSEUM OF THE GOLDFIELDS

The impressive Ivanhoe mine headframe at the northeastern end of Hannan St marks the entrance to this excellent **museum** (☎ 9021 8533; 17 Hannan St; admission by donation;

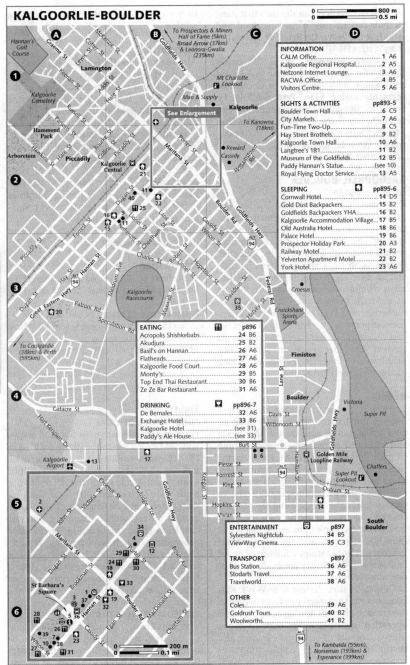

KALGOORLIE-BOULDER

0 ____ 800 m
0 ____ 0.5 mi

To Prospectors & Miners
Hall of Fame (5km),
Broad Arrow (37km)
& Leonora-Gwalia
(235km)

See Enlargement

To Kanowna
(18km)

Reward
Cassidy

To Coolgardie
(38km) & Perth
(595km)

Croesus

Cruickshank
Sports
Arena

Fimiston

Boulder

Victoria

Super Pit

Golden Mile
Loopline Railway

Super Pit
Lookout

Chaffers

South
Boulder

To Kambalda (55km),
Norseman (193km) &
Esperance (399km)

St Barbara's
Square

0 ____ 200 m
0 ____ 0.1 mi

INFORMATION
CALM Office...........................1 A6
Kalgoorlie Regional Hospital....2 A5
Netzone Internet Lounge..........3 A6
RACWA Office.........................4 B5
Visitors Centre........................5 A6

SIGHTS & ACTIVITIES pp893-5
Boulder Town Hall...................6 C5
City Markets............................7 A6
Fun-Time Two-Up....................8 C5
Hay Street Brothels..................9 B2
Kalgoorlie Town Hall..............10 A6
Langtree's 181........................11 B2
Museum of the Goldfields.......12 B5
Paddy Hannan's Statue.....(see 10)
Royal Flying Doctor Service....13 A5

SLEEPING pp895-6
Cornwall Hotel......................14 D5
Gold Dust Backpackers..........15 B2
Goldfields Backpackers YHA...16 B2
Kalgoorlie Accommodation Village...17 B2
Old Australia Hotel................18 B6
Palace Hotel.........................19 B6
Prospector Holiday Park.........20 A3
Railway Motel.......................21 B2
Yelverton Apartment Motel....22 B2
York Hotel............................23 A6

EATING p896
Acropolis Shishkebabs............24 B6
Akudjura..............................25 B2
Basil's on Hannan..................26 A6
Flatheads.............................27 A6
Kalgoorlie Food Court............28 A6
Monty's...............................29 B5
Top End Thai Restaurant........30 B6
Ze Ze Bar Restaurant.............31 A6

DRINKING pp896-7
De Bernales..........................32 A6
Exchange Hotel 33 B6
Kalgoorlie Hotel................(see 31)
Paddy's Ale House.............(see 33)

ENTERTAINMENT p897
Sylvesters Nightclub..............34 B5
ViewWay Cinema...................35 C3

TRANSPORT p897
Bus Station...........................36 A6
Stodarts Travel......................37 A6
Travelworld..........................38 A6

OTHER
Coles...................................39 A6
Goldrush Tours......................40 B2
Woolworths..........................41 B2

WESTERN AUSTRALIA

◷ 10am-4.30pm), which displays an underground vault full of gold watches, brooches and trinkets, a restored miner's cottage and plenty of mining memorabilia. Pick up a copy of the *One Hundred Women of the Eastern Goldfields* brochure ($2.50) for a less masculine perspective of the town's history, and if you've got a head for heights, take the lift to the top of the 31m-high headframe for views over the town.

OTHER ATTRACTIONS

A great way to tour the famous Golden Mile and learn about the goldfields is on the **Loopline Tourist Railway** (☎ 9093 3055; adult/child $9.90/5.50). The ramshackle 'Rattler' sets off from Boulder train station on its one-hour loop, complete with commentary, at 10am daily and 11.45am on Sunday.

To get a sense of the scale of mining operations in the area, head to the **Super Pit lookout** (Outram St; ◷ 6am-7pm), just off the Goldfields Hwy near Boulder, which has awesome views of an enormous open-cut mine. **Mt Charlotte Reservoir**, only 200m from the northern end of Hannan St, is another popular lookout.

If you want to see how an old-fashioned game of two-up is played, head to the **Fun-Time-Two-Up** (Sheffield's Bar & Grill, 140 Burt St, Boulder; ◷ 3pm Wed & Sun).

A block southwest of Hannan St is **Hay St**, one of Kal's more famous 'attractions'. This strip of brothels is where working women once beckoned passing men to their galvanised-iron doorways. They're no longer allowed to solicit on the street, but a blind eye has been turned to this activity for so long that it has become an accepted, historical part of the town. One of the brothels, the renovated **Langtree's 181** (☎ 9026 2181; 181 Hay St; admission $25; ◷ tours 11am, 3pm & 7pm), runs enlightening tours of the premises.

The **Royal Flying Doctor Service** (☎ 9093 7595; Kalgoorlie-Boulder airport; admission by donation; ◷ 11am-3pm Mon-Fri) offers guided tours on the hour (last tour 2pm).

There's an art gallery upstairs in the decorative Edwardian **town hall** (☎ 9021 9809; cnr Hannan & Wilson Sts; ◷ 8.30am-4.55pm Mon-Fri), while outside is a replica of a **statue of Paddy Hannan** holding a water bag. The original statue is in the foyer of the Mining Hall of Fame – safe from nocturnal graffiti artists.

You can get a bird's-eye view of the Golden Mile mining operations with **Goldfields Air Services** (☎ 9093 2116) and **AAA Charters** (☎ 9093 4115); flights cost from $50/25 per adult/child (minimum of two people).

Tours

Goldrush Tours (☎ 1800 620 440; 16 Lane St) is the main local operator with tours of Kal ($25/5 per adult/child) and Coolgardie ($55/10). Book through the visitors centre.

Aboriginal Bush Tours (☎ 9093 3745, 0407-387 602), which is run by Geoff Stokes, has informative trips covering bush tucker, tracking and Dreamtime stories. There are day trips ($200 for two people), twilight tours ($100 for two) and camping trips ($340 for two).

4WD Tours (☎ 0419-915 670; half-/full-day tours $120/165) takes visitors into the outback to fossick for gold and visit the ghost towns north of Kal. Full-day wildflower tours are also available from August to November for $130.

Festivals & Events

The **Kalgoorlie Racing Round** is the biggest outback horse-racing carnival in WA, drawing thousands of punters. It's held in early September, culminating with the 2300m Kalgoorlie Cup. The event coincides with the popular wildflower season, so getting a bed in town can be difficult.

If you're in town on the third Sunday of the month, wander down to Boulder's Burt St for **Boulder Market Day**.

Sleeping

BUDGET

There are two good hostels in the heart of the Hay St red-light district. Both have pools, do pick-ups from the bus or train stations on request and are occasionally full of Aussie workers.

Goldfields Backpackers YHA (☎ 9091 1482, 0412-110 001; backpackers@kalgoorlie.com; 166 Hay St; dm/s $18/28, d & tw $50, nonmembers $20/30/55; ▯ ▧) This small 40-bed corrugated-iron hostel is clean and well managed, with a social atmosphere. Long-termers who have managed to find work are housed in a former brothel next door.

Golddust Backpackers (☎ 9091 3737; www.kalgoorliebackpackers.com; 192 Hay St; dm/s $17/30, d & tw $40, nonmembers $18/35/45; ▧ ▯) Golddust has

a large kitchen, pool room and friendly atmosphere. Staff can help guests find work.

Kalgoorlie Accommodation Village (☎ 9039 4800, 1800 004 800; www.resortparks.com.au; 286 Burt St, Boulder; camp/caravan sites $19/22, chalets $85, spa units from $100) This award-winning park in Boulder offers a wide choice of accommodation, from basic camp sites to A-frame chalets and spa units.

Prospector Holiday Park (☎ 9021 2524; fax 9021 2960; Ochiltree St; camp/caravan sites from $20/22, cabins $65, cabins with bathroom $80-85; 🖳) Around 3km from the city centre, this child-friendly park has a pool, playground, grassed area for campers and a campers' kitchen.

MID-RANGE

In the heady gold-rush days, Kal had a pub on every corner, and several still offer comfy lodgings today. Be warned that weekend crowds in some pubs can be noisy.

York Hotel (☎ /fax 9021 2337; 259 Hannan St; s/d/tr $40/60/90) One of Kal's architectural gems, the York is also one of the best-value options in town, with a central location, simple, freshly painted rooms and a continental breakfast thrown in.

Palace Hotel (☎ 9021 2788; www.palacehotel.com.au; cnr Hannan & Maritana Sts; dm $18, s/d with bathroom $65/85, executive s/d $85/105; 🔀) A young Herbert Hoover (31st US president) was a regular at the Palace and donated the enormous antique mirror that still stands in the foyer. These days, the rambling historic hotel offers beds for all budgets, from simple backpacker rooms to plush executive options. All accommodation comes with a hot or continental breakfast.

Old Australia Hotel (☎ 9021 1320; www.theaustralia .com.au; cnr Hannan & Maritana Sts; s/d $75/95, d with bathroom $105; 🔀) Lavishly restored in the late 1990s, this former pub has been transformed into a beautiful boutique hotel. Though the rooms with bathrooms come with complimentary continental breakfast, the rooms without have direct access onto the timber veranda.

Cornwall Hotel (☎ 9093 2510; cornwallhotel@big pond.com; 25 Hopkins St, Boulder; s/d $40/60) A stone's throw from the Super Pit, this beautiful Aussie heritage hotel offers basic B&B in six simple rooms with shared facilities. Its restaurant meals are highly recommended.

Railway Motel (☎ 9088 0000; www.railwaymotel.com .au; 51 Forrest St; d weekend/weekday $100/120; 🔀)

There are plenty of uninspiring, ageing motels in town, but the Railway is a pleasant exception. Conveniently located opposite the train station, this newish motel features a pool, jacuzzi, restaurant, bar and buffet breakfast.

TOP END

Yelverton Apartment Motel (☎ 9022 8181; www .yelvertonmotel.com.au; 210 Egan St; s/d/tw from $130/145/165; 🔀) After a long, sweaty journey, there's nothing quite like putting your feet up in your own sprawling apartment, with bathroom, bedroom, kitchen and living room. Spoil yourself with a king-sized spa suite ($164).

Eating

Kalgoorlie's main drag has several reliable pubs that offer generous counter meals. If you're looking for something faster, try the **Kalgoorlie Food Court** (90 Brookman St), popular fish 'n' chippery **Flatheads** (28 Wilson St) or **Acropolis Shishkebabs** (86 Hannan St).

Basil's on Hannan (☎ 9021 7832; 268 Hannan St; breakfast $3.80-13.50) All-day breakfasts are a highlight at this cruisy caff with fast, friendly service and tasty create-your-own omelettes ($9.40).

Top End Thai Restaurant (☎ 9091 4027; 71 Hannan St; mains $15-19) Suffering from chilli withdrawal? Head to the top end of town for tasty curries and noodles.

Ze Ze Bar Restaurant (☎ 9021 3046; Kalgoorlie Hotel, cnr Hannan & Wilson Sts; mains $12-20) Locals rave about Ze Ze's gourmet pizzas, baked in a cavernous wood-fired oven and served on the upstairs balcony.

Monty's (☎ 9022 8288; cnr Hannan & Porter Sts; mains $14.50-29.50; 🕑 24hr) Open round the clock, this sprawling Italian-style restaurant is popular for late-night snacks and one last drink after the pubs close.

Akudjura (☎ 9091 3311; 418 Hannan St; mains $9.90-22) Daily soup, pie, tart and wok specials keep the menu interesting at this more up-market option, which has a friendly vibe and a good selection of wine available by the glass.

Drinking

Pubs feature heavily in the night scene, but the days of the rough-and-ready, frontier-type men-only bar rooms are waning in modern Kal. For a taste of the original

Kalgoorlie pub, try the **Federal Hotel** (1 Hannan St) and **Grand Hotel** (90 Hannan St).

Kalgoorlie Hotel (☎ 9021 3046; 319 Hannan St) Known locally as Judd's, this buzzing corner hotel has several jam-packed bars and features 'Tight Arse Tuesday', with free jukebox, free pool and discount drinks.

Paddy's Ale House (☎ 9021 2833; Exchange Hotel, 135 Hannan St) Sports TV, regular live music and a range of international beers keep this pub packed.

De Bernales (☎ 9021 4534; 193 Hannan St) If raucous pubs aren't your style, sip on a glass of wine at De Bernales, which has occasional live music in the evening.

The **Palace Hotel** (☎ 9021 2788; cnr Hannan & Maritana Sts) houses the recently renovated **Platform Bar** at the front, all designer corrugated iron and splashes of purple, and the **Tart 'n' Miner Scottish Bar** at the back, with obligatory tartan and bagpipes.

Entertainment

Missing the latest blockbusters? Then catch a movie at **ViewWay Cinemas** (☎ 9021 2199; cnr Davidson & Oswald Sts). In summer, there are outdoor screenings at the **Twilight Outdoor Cinema** (Hammond Park). Call ViewWay for details.

Sylvesters Nightclub (☎ 9021 1036; 52 Hannan St) is a dance oasis in a sea of pubs at the top end of town.

Getting There & Away

AIR
Skywest (☎ 1300 66 00 88) and **Qantas** (☎ 13 13 13) fly between Perth and Kal at least twice a day (full fare $274, but regular specials available). Qantas also offers flights to most major Australian capital cities. **Travelworld** (☎ 9021 2866; 314 Hannan St) and **Stodarts Travel** (☎ 9021 1855; 248 Hannan St) can help with bookings.

BUS
McCafferty's/Greyhound (☎ 13 20 30) buses stop in Kalgoorlie daily between Perth and Adelaide. **Perth Goldfields Express** (☎ 1800 620 440) has a service from Perth to Kal, continuing north to Menzies ($32 from Kal), Leonora ($43) and Laverton ($64) on Sunday, Wednesday and Friday. Services on Tuesday, Thursday and Saturday run between Perth and Kal only ($77).

Transwa (☎ 1300 662 205) runs a bus three times a week to/from Esperance (5 hours) –

twice via Kambalda and once via Coolgardie; it costs $21.70 to Norseman and $40.40 to Esperance. Buses stop outside the visitors centre on Hannan St.

TRAIN
The daily *Prospector* service from Perth takes around eight hours ($59.50). The *Indian Pacific* train also goes through Kal on Wednesday and Saturday (for Perth) and Monday and Friday (for Adelaide).

Getting Around

There's a regular bus service between Kal and Boulder, operated by **Golden Lines** (☎ 9021 2655) between 8am and 6pm Monday to Friday, and Saturday mornings ($1.90/ 0.80 per adult/child).

NORTH OF KALGOORLIE-BOULDER

Fascinating ghost towns and near-ghost towns dot the landscape in this remote region. The road north is surfaced from Kal all the way to Leonora-Gwalia (235km), Laverton (359km) and Leinster (361km). Off the main road, traffic is virtually nonexistent and rain can quickly close dirt roads.

Worth a side trip is **Kanowna**, 22km northeast of Kalgoorlie-Boulder along an unsealed road. In 1905 the town swarmed with miners, had 16 hotels and an hourly train service to Kal. Today, apart from an empty train station and the odd pile of rubble, not much remains. Once a thriving community of 15,000, **Broad Arrow** (37km north of Kalgoorlie-Boulder) now has just five locals and the **Broad Arrow Tavern** (☎ 08-9024 2058; ⏰ 11am-late), which serves cold beer and pub grub to appreciative travellers.

Menzies, 132km north of Kal, has several historical buildings worth a peek, including the train station with its 120m-long platform and the town hall, which was famously clockless for 100 years until a recent millennium celebration clock was installed.

A metropolis compared to surrounding towns, **Leonora** (population 3500) is a service centre for mining exploration and the pastoral industry. In the adjoining **Gwalia** is the Sons of Gwalia gold mine, managed by US-president-to-be Herbert Hoover at the end of the 19th century. The old mine office now houses the **Gwalia Historical Museum** (☎ 08-9037 7210; admission $2; ⏰ 10am-4pm), full of historical accounts of the town's heyday.

Don't miss the recently restored abandoned miners' camps and State Hotel.

South of Leonora-Gwalia, 25km off the main road to Laverton, is **Kookynie**, another interesting, once-flourishing mining town. For a true outback pub experience, stay in its **Grand Hotel** (☎ 08-9031 3010; Menzies-Kookynie Rd; s/d $45/80), built in 1901, which offers simple rooms with shared facilities. Continental/cooked breakfasts are available for $8/14.

From Leonora-Gwalia, you can turn northeast to **Laverton** (population 500), where the surfaced road ends. Described as the 'gateway to the desert', Laverton perches on the edge of the Great Victoria Desert. From here, it's 1710km to Alice Springs via the Great Central Rd (part of the Outback Hwy).

If you have your own wheels and want to go exploring, ask the Kalgoorlie visitors centre about the **Golden Quest Discovery Trail** (www.goldenquesttrail.com). This 965km drive takes travellers to 25 major sites of the region, and tells tales of the early prospectors and explorers who made their mark. Some 525km of the track is unsealed, so don't forget to ask about road conditions and safe travel tips.

Laverton to Giles

For those interested in an outback experience, the unsealed road from Laverton to Yulara (near Uluru), via Warburton, provides a rich landscape of red sand, spinifex, mulga and desert oaks. The road is well maintained and suitable for conventional vehicles, although a 4WD would give a much smoother ride.

Make sure you take precautions relevant to travel in such an isolated area – tell someone reliable of your travel plans and take adequate supplies of water, food, petrol and spare parts. Don't even consider travelling from November to March, when the heat is extreme, nor after heavy rain. Conditions should not be taken lightly. See Outback Travel (p993) for more information.

Petrol and supplies are available at Laverton, Warburton, Docker River and Yulara. Towards Warburton (about 315km from Laverton), **Tjukayirla Roadhouse** (☎ 08-9037 1108; Great Central Rd; camp sites $8, tw $30) has fuel and supplies, and offers basic accommodation. Meals are also possible if you book ahead.

As this road passes through Aboriginal land, transit permits are required from the **Central Land Council** (☎ 08-8951 6211) in Alice Springs for the NT end, and from the **Department of Indigenous Affairs** (☎ 08-9235 8000) in Perth for the WA end. Transit permits are free and can be arranged online (www.dia.wa.gov.au). Allow two to three weeks for your application to be processed. It's prohibited to leave the main road when travelling through Aboriginal lands.

SOUTH OF KALGOORLIE-BOULDER

Kambalda

☎ 08 / pop 1200

This major nickel-mining town 55km south of Kalgoorlie-Boulder has two town centres, Kambalda East and Kambalda West, about 4km apart. Don't miss the drive up to the **Red Hill Lookout** for sweeping views of **Lake Lefroy**, a popular spot for landsailers, which have been clocked skimming over the dry saltpans at 100km/h. Speed freaks should ask about landsailing at the **visitors centre** (☎ 9027 0192; Emu Rocks Rd, Kambalda West).

Norseman

☎ 08 / pop 600

For most travellers, quiet, pretty Norseman is a place to stop and recharge the batteries before or after the long sweaty trip across the Eyre Hwy (Nullarbor). From here, you can head south to Esperance or north to Kalgoorlie.

Facilities in town are set up for quick stopovers. Not far from the corrugated iron camels is the **visitors centre** (☎ 9039 1071; 68 Robert St; ☼ 9am-5pm), where you can pick up your 'I crossed the Nullarbor' sticker. At the back is a rest park with showers and barbecue facilities (open from 7am to 6pm). Check your email at the nearby **Telecentre** (Robert St; per hr $6).

Visitors can immerse themselves in the gold-rush days at the **Historical Collection** (☎ 9039 1593; Battery Rd; adult/child $2/1; ☼ 10am-1pm Mon, Wed, Thu & Sat) in the old School of Mines. A permit ($5.50) from the visitors centre allows you to try your hand at **gemstone fossicking** on a property about 12km north of town.

There are excellent views of the town and the surrounding salt lakes from the **Beacon Hill Lookout**, on the Old Mines Rd past the mountainous tailings dumps. For stunning

sunrise and sunset photo ops, amateur photographers should head for the dry, expansive **Lake Cowan**, north of town.

SLEEPING & EATING

Lodge 101 (☎ /fax 9039 1541; 101 Prinsep St; dm/s/d/f $17/28/50/70) A godsend to weary cross-Nullarbor cyclists, this homy, intimate hostel is run by a friendly English couple, and has comfy rooms and a barbecue area. Family photos, souvenirs and postcards complete the home-away-from-home ambience.

Norseman Hotel (☎ 9039 1023; fax 9039 1503; 90 Roberts St; s/d/tw/f $33/55/50/60; 🔀) A favourite with workers, the Norseman offers no-frills pub rooms in the centre of town with complimentary continental breakfast.

Great Western Motel (☎ 9039 1633; fax 9039 1692; Prinsep St; s/d $80/90; 🔀) Set in a quiet, bushland setting, this recently renovated motel with rammed-earth walls has a ski-lodge design and swimming pool.

Gateway Caravan Park (☎ /fax 9039 1500; 23 Prinsep St; camp/caravan sites $16/20, dm $15, cabins $55-60, cabins with bathroom $75) Excellent cabin accommodation in a quiet bushland spot makes this a great mid-range option. Campers are also well catered for, with clean facilities and a camp kitchen.

Travellers Inn Restaurant (☎ 9039 1633; Great Western Motel, Prinsep St; mains $19-25; 🕒 6-7.30pm) Convenient to both the caravan park and the motel, this pleasant restaurant offers the best meals in town, though you've got to be quick to catch the dinner hours.

The **Norseman Hotel** (☎ 9039 1023; 90 Roberts St; mains $12-18) also offers filling counter meals.

EYRE HIGHWAY

It's a little over 2700km between Perth and Adelaide – not much less than the distance from London to Moscow. The long, lonely Eyre Hwy crosses the southern edge of the vast **Nullarbor Plain** – Nullarbor is derived from the Latin for 'no trees' (a dog's worst nightmare!).

The highway takes its name from John Eyre, the explorer who, in 1841, was the first European to make the east–west crossing. Full of hardship and group conflict (his companion John Baxter was murdered), Eyre finally completed the five-month journey accompanied by his young Aboriginal guide Wylie.

In 1877 a telegraph line was laid across the Nullarbor, roughly outlining the route the first road would take. Later in the 19th century, miners en route to the goldfields followed this telegraph-line route across the empty plain. In 1896 the first bicycle crossing was made and in 1912 the first car was driven across.

In 1941 WWII inspired the building of a transcontinental highway, a rough-and-ready track that carried a handful of vehicles a day. By the '60s the traffic flow had increased to more than 30 vehicles a day, and in 1969 the WA government surfaced the road as far as the SA border. Finally, in 1976, the last stretch was surfaced and now the Nullarbor crossing is an easy, if long, drive.

The surfaced road runs close to the coast on the SA side, with the Nullarbor region ending dramatically at the cliffs of the Great Australian Bight. The Trans Australia Railway runs across the true Nullarbor Plain, while the highway is mainly to the south of the treeless area.

From Norseman it's 725km to the SA border, near Eucla, and a further 480km to Ceduna (meaning 'a place to sit down and rest' in the local Aboriginal language) in SA. From Ceduna, it's still another 793km to Adelaide via Port Augusta. It's a long way!

Crossing the Nullarbor

Although the Nullarbor is no longer the torture trail of old, it's wise to take some simple precautions. The longest distance between fuel stops is about 200km, so if you're foolish enough to run low on petrol midway, it can be a long trip to get more. Getting help for a mechanical breakdown can be expensive and time consuming, so make sure your vehicle is in good shape, you've got good tyres and at least a basic kit of simple spare parts. Carry some drinking water (an active adult needs 4L per day in hot weather) in case you do have to sit it out by the roadside on a hot summer's day. Be prepared for high fuel prices, which range from 15 to 30 cents a litre above city prices. If you plan to stay overnight at one of the Nullarbor roadhouses, book ahead to avoid disappointment.

Norseman to Eucla

The first settlement you reach from Norseman is **Balladonia**, 193km to the east. The

Balladonia Hotel Motel (☎ 08-9039 3453; Eyre Hwy; camp/caravan sites $12/19, dm $17, s/d with bathroom from $75/90) offers camping, backpacker beds and four-star rooms. It has a bar, café, shady playground, roadhouse facilities and scraps of the Skylab space station in its small interactive historical museum.

Between Balladonia and **Caiguna** is one of the longest stretches of straight road in the world –145km – known as the **90 Mile Straight**. If you need a break, you can get some shut-eye at the **John Eyre Motel** (☎ 08-9039 3459; Eyre Hwy; camp/caravan sites $12/18, s/d $55/70, s/d with bathroom $80/95; 🔀).

At **Cocklebiddy** are the stone ruins of an Aboriginal mission and the largest of the Nullarbor caves, **Cocklebiddy Cave**, some 10km northwest. With a 4WD, you can travel the 32km south to **Twilight Cove**, with its dramatic 75m-high limestone cliffs. There's accommodation, fuel and supplies available at the **Wedgetail Inn Cocklebiddy** (☎ 08-9039 3462; Eyre Hwy; camp/caravan sites $11/18, budget s/d/tr $55/70/85, motel s/d $80/95).

Birds Australia's **Eyre Bird Observatory** (☎ 08-9039 3450; eyrebirdobs@bigpond.com), housed in the former Eyre Telegraph Station, 50km south of Cocklebiddy on the Bight, is a haven for bird and nature lovers. Full board is $80/40 per adult/child (with reductions after the first night). Return transport from Cocklebiddy is available for overnight guests ($27.50 for day-trippers); otherwise, you'll need a 4WD with good clearance.

Madura, 83km east of Cocklebiddy, has a population of seven and is close to the Hampton Tablelands (just out of town is a scenic lookout). The one-stop shop for fuel, shower ($3), beer, meal or a bed is the **Madura Pass Oasis Inn** (☎ 08-9039 3464; Eyre Hwy; camp/caravan sites $12/18, budget s/d $60/70, motel s/d $80/100; 🔀).

In **Mundrabilla**, 116km to the east, is the friendly **Mundrabilla Motel Hotel** (☎ 08-9039 3465; Eyre Hwy; 2-person camp/caravan sites $10/15, motel s/d/f $70/85/105; 🔀).

Just before the SA border is **Eucla**, surrounded by stunning sand dunes and pristine beaches. Around 5km south of town are the photogenic ruins of an old **telegraph station** (1877), gradually being engulfed by the dunes. Camp sites and spacious rooms are available at the **Eucla Motor Hotel** (☎ 08-9039 3468; Eyre Hwy; camp/caravan sites $4/11, budget s/d $25/45, motel s/d $75/90; 🔀).

There are strict quarantine restrictions when crossing the border, so scoff or toss your fruit and vegetables before you get there; checkpoints are at Eucla and Ceduna.

Eucla to Ceduna
See p724 for details of the section of highway between the border and Ceduna.

MIDLANDS

This enormous rural region stretches from the base of the Pilbara down to the Wheatbelt towns some 300km or so south of the Great Eastern Hwy. Visitors head to the Midlands for its unusual, often dramatic rock formations – and particularly the iconic Wave Rock – its vast empty landscapes and its magnificent displays of spring wildflowers.

GREAT EASTERN HIGHWAY
The Golden Pipeline gave Kalgoorlie the valuable gift of water 100 years ago and has been its lifeline ever since. Today, the Great Eastern Hwy runs alongside the pipeline, stretching east from Perth's outskirts through barren but beautiful countryside, all the way to Kalgoorlie-Boulder. Several pretty country towns en route are convenient places to stop, stretch your legs and enjoy some historical sites.

Cunderdin, 64km east of Northam, has an excellent **museum** (Forrest St; adult/child $4/1.50; 🕑 10am-4pm), housed in a towering old pumping station, with an impressive collection of old farming equipment and historical artefacts.

Merredin
☎ 08 / pop 2900
The largest centre in the Wheatbelt and a convenient stopover, Merredin's main claim to fame is temporarily playing host to the world's longest road train – 45 trailers stretching over half a kilometre. Peak tourist season is August to October, when visitors hit the walking tracks in search of wildflowers.

A great source of information on the local area is the **visitors centre** (☎ 9041 1666; Barrack St; 🕑 9am-5pm Mon-Fri, 11am-1pm Sat, 11am-2pm Sun). The **Old Railway Station Museum** (Great Eastern Hwy; adult/child $3/1.50; 🕑 9am-noon & 1-3pm Mon-Fri, 10am-4pm Sat & Sun) houses a vintage 1897 locomotive

and old signal box, while the **Military Museum** (Barrack St; ☺ by appointment only) displays a diverse collection of war memorabilia.

A range of accommodation is available at the pleasant **Merredin Caravan Park** (☎ /fax 9041 1535; 2 Oats St; caravan sites $18, on-site caravans $40, cabins/villas $55/70). Otherwise, book in to the **Commercial Hotel** (☎ 9041 1052; fax 9041 1050; Barrack St; s/d $28/50) for rudimentary rooms and standard counter meals.

Southern Cross
☎ 08 / pop 2900
Further east, Southern Cross was the first gold-rush town on the WA goldfields, but its glory days flared and faded quickly. Packed with mining memorabilia and artefacts is the **Yilgarn History Museum** (Antares St; adult/child $2.50/0.50; ☺ 9.30am-noon & 1.30-4pm Mon-Sat, 1.30-4pm Sun), in the old courthouse. Summertime dips at the nearby **swimming pool** (Antares St; adult/child $2.50/1.50; ☺ 11am-6.30pm) help relieve the region's frequently unbearable heat.

For overnight stays, try the charmingly restored **Palace Hotel** (☎ 9049 1555; fax 9049 1509; Antares St; basic s $20, s/d $55/65, d with bathroom $75), with a children's playground and country-style comforts.

WAVE ROCK & HYDEN
☎ 08 / pop 190
The famous 15m-high Wave Rock, 4km from the tiny town of Hyden, is shaped like the perfect wave about to break, frozen in solid rock and streaked with colourful bands. It's an impressive sight, and many people do the 700km return day trip from Perth simply to stand under the rock and have their photo snapped for posterity. If you've got more time to explore, wander around other interesting rock formations such as the **Breakers**, **Hippo's Yawn** and the **Humps**. **Mulka's Cave**, 21km away, has intriguing Aboriginal rock paintings.

The **visitors centre** (☎ 9880 5182; ☺ 9am-5.30pm) is in the Wave Rock Wildflower Shoppe opposite the site. There's a small **museum** (☎ 9880 5022; admission $4; ☺ 8.30am-6pm) in the kiosk at the caravan park. There's a parking fee of $6 per car within the Wave Rock reserve.

Stargate Observatory (☎ 9880 7049; www.stargate observatory.com.au; East Hyden Bin Rd; adult/child $20/11; ☺ 8pm) is about 2km from the rock. The starry-eyed are treated to a slide show, a two-hour tour of the sky and supper. Ring ahead.

Hyden Hotel Motel (☎ 9880 5052; fax 9880 5041; 2 Lynch St; s/d/ste $90/110/160) has restaurants, gym and a solar-heated pool, which are a bonus at this comfortable motel with well-appointed rooms.

Wave Rock Caravan Park (☎ 9880 5022; wave rock@wn.com.au; Wave Rock Rd; camp/caravan sites $17/20, cabins $75, 2-bedroom cottages $120) is an inviting caravan park within a stone's throw of the rock, and offers camp sites and cabins in a natural bushland setting. Two-bedroom cottages are also available on the shores of Lake Magic, 1km north.

Transwa (☎ 1300 662 205) runs a bus from Perth to Hyden every Tuesday ($36.85, 5 hours), with the return service to Perth each Thursday.

OTHER WHEATBELT TOWNS
Most sizable Wheatbelt towns have a caravan park, a pub that serves counter meals, a motel, trio of wheat silos, a pervading ennui and little else.

There is a prominent granite rock formation, known as **Kokerbin** (Aboriginal for 'High Place'), 45km west of Bruce Rock. **Corrigin** has a **folk museum** (☎ 08-9063 2066; Brookton Hwy; ☺ 10am-4pm Sun, also by request) and a **miniature railway** (☎ 08-9063 2176; Campbell St; ☺ 10am-4pm Sun), but it's the **Dog Cemetery** (Brookton Hwy), 5km west, that delights visitors to the town. Here, elaborate headstones, crosses and epitaphs memorialise pets past such as Lassie, Shep, Dusty, Trigger and many more.

Narrogin (population 4500), 189km southeast of Perth, is an agricultural centre with a **courthouse museum** (☎ 08-9881 2064; Egerton St; ☺ 9.30am-4.30pm Mon-Fri, 9.30am-noon Sat). The **visitors centre** (☎ 08-9881 2064) is next door to the museum.

Some 26km north of Narrogin is the magnificent **Dryandra Woodland**, remnants of the open eucalypt woodlands that once covered most of the Wheatbelt. It supports many animal species, including numbats, and is excellent for bird-watching, bushwalking and, in season, wildflowers. About 45km northeast of Narrogin, in the town of Wickepin, is the **Albert Facey Homestead** (☎ 08-9888 1010; Wagin Rd; adult/child $2.50/1; ☺ 10am-4pm). This nicely maintained abode is well worth a visit, especially if you have read Facey's bestselling autobiography, *A Fortunate Life*.

The first thing you notice about **Wagin** (population 1350), 228km southeast of Perth, is its kitsch 15m-high fibreglass **ram**, a tribute to the surrounding merino industry and civic bad taste. Locals claim it's the biggest in the southern hemisphere (but the people of Goulburn, NSW, reckon they've got a bigger one, see p227). The visitors centre at the **Wagin Historical Village** (☎ 08-9861 1232; Showground Rd) will reveal more regional delights.

Near **Dumbleyung**, 40km east of Wagin, is the lake upon which Donald Campbell broke the world water-speed record (444.66km/h) in 1964; today it hosts a variety of birdlife.

Katanning, south of Wagin, has a large Muslim community (Christmas Islanders) and a mosque built in 1980. The old flour mill houses the **visitors centre** (☎ 08-9821 2634; Clive St; ✆ 10am-4pm Mon-Fri, closes noon Sat).

WILDFLOWER WAY

Between August and October, one of the best places to see WA's famous carpet of wildflowers is the area north of Perth, where three roads run roughly parallel towards Geraldton. Taking in a number of national parks and nature reserves, this area is notable for its varieties of everlasting daisy, kangaroo paws, foxgloves, wattles, featherflowers, banksias and the gorgeous low-lying wreath *Leschenaultia* (see also the boxed text 'Blooming Wildflowers'; below). There are multi day tours available, but these are really only for botany freaks – a better option is to include a look at the flowers as part of a trip north to Geraldton, Kalbarri or beyond.

There are three main routes north to Geraldton. Notable stops along the Brand Hwy between Midland and Dongara-Port Denison include **Moore River National Park**, **Badgingarra National Park**, **Coomalloo Nature Reserve** and the **Lesueur National Park**, although the latter requires a 4WD. Towns along the way include Cataby, Badgingarra and Eneabba. This road also connects you to the Pinnacles and several coastal towns, which have the area's best accommodation and a string of superb beaches – see Durian Bay to Dongara-Port Denison (p907) for details.

From Bindoon on the Great Northern Hwy, the Midland Road heads to Dongara-Port Denison, passing **Alexander Morrison National Park**, **Capamauro Nature Reserve** and **Depot Hill Reserve**, and the towns of Moora, Watheroo, Coorow and Mingenew. The **Yarra Yarra Lakes**, near Carnamah, are noted for their birdlife.

The stretch between Wubin, on the Great Northern Hwy, and Mullewa, east of Geraldton, has fewer formal wildflower areas, but there's plenty to see in the fields and along the verges as you drive. The surrounds of the tiny towns of **Tardun**, **Canna** and **Morawa** are the best places to look, and there are desolate gold-mining ghost towns near **Perenjori**.

Pick up a free copy of the *Wildflower Holiday Guide* from the **Western Australian Visitors Centre** (☎ 1300 361 351, 08-9483 1111; www.westernaustralia.net; Albert Facey House, Forrest Pl, Perth) for more-detailed information on driving tours and inland accommodation.

Getting There & Away

Transwa (☎ 1300 662 205; www.transwa.wa.gov.au) has three Perth–Geraldton bus services through

---

BLOOMING WILDFLOWERS

Western Australia (WA) is famed for its 8000 species of wildflower, which bloom in greatest number from August to October. Even some of the driest regions put on a colourful display after a little rainfall, and at any time of the year.

The southwest has over 3000 species, many of which are unique to this region. They're commonly known as everlastings because the petals stay attached after the flowers have died. You can find flowers almost everywhere in the state, but the jarrah forests in the southwest are particularly rich. The coastal national parks north of Perth, such as Fitzgerald River and Kalbarri, also have brilliant displays, as do the Stirling Ranges. Near Perth, the Badgingarra, Alexander Morrison, Yanchep and John Forrest National Parks are excellent choices. There's also a wildflower display in Kings Park, Perth. As you go further north, they tend to flower earlier in the season. Common flowering plants include various species of banksia, wattles, mountain bells, Sturt's desert peas, kangaroo paws and many orchids.

this area. The daily N1 service follows the Brand Hwy via Cataby ($19, 2¾ hours) and Dongara-Port Denison ($36, 5¾ hours). The N2 service runs four times weekly via Moora ($20, 3 hours), Coorow ($30, 3½ hours) and Mingenew ($38, 5 hours). The N3 goes via Wubin $30, 4 hours), Morawa ($40, 6 hours) and Mullewa ($50, 7½ hours). **McCafferty's/Greyhound** (☎ 13 20 30) and **Integrity** (☎ 08-9226 1339) also run regular services up the Brand Hwy.

GREAT NORTHERN HIGHWAY

Unless you're in a hurry, there are few reasons to take this road. Linking Perth and Port Hedland via a succession of small mining and agricultural towns, it's more direct than the coastal highway and is the designated route for long-haul road trains, so be prepared for gruesome road-kill. The highlight is the awesome gorge country of Karijini National Park (also accessible from the coast road), which is worth a couple of days' exploration – otherwise the country-side is fairly monotonous. The main centres along the road are New Norcia, Mt Magnet, Cue, Meekatharra and Newman, and accommodation gets more expensive the further north you are. Theft from cars can occur in the northern towns, so keep your belongings out of sight or in your room.

Getting There & Away

Qantas (☎ 13 13 00) links Perth with Newman every day, and plenty of air charter companies service the mining towns.

McCafferty's/Greyhound (☎ 13 20 30) heads up and down the Great Northern Hwy every Friday (northbound) and Saturday (south-bound) between Perth and Port Hedland ($206, 19½ hours), stopping at New Norcia ($40, 2½ hours), Mt Magnet ($120, 7¾ hours), Cue ($125, 8¾ hours), Meekatharra ($140, 10 hours), Newman ($185, 14½ hours) and Auski Tourist Village (for Karijini National Park; $165, 16½ hours). **Transwa** (☎ 1300 662 205; www.transwa.wa.gov.au) has northbound (Monday and Wednesday) and southbound (Tuesday and Thursday) services between Perth and Meekatharra, and charges similar prices.

NEW NORCIA
☎ 08 / pop 80

The small, meditative community of New Norcia is an historical oddity. Established by the Spanish Benedictine order in 1846 to proselytise among Aboriginal groups in the region, its work soon turned to raising orphans after European diseases ravaged the local communities. Today it remains a working monastery, and many of the town's remarkable buildings are registered by the National Estate. It also boasts a fine religious museum and people come from far and wide to try the monastery's renowned breads and olive oil.

New Norcia Museum & Art Gallery (☎ 9654 8056; Great Northern Hwy; adult/child $5/1; ⏱ 9.30am-5pm Aug-Oct, 10am-4.30pm Nov-Jul) is well worth a look, even if you're not into God. It details the town's fascinating history and its art collection includes minor works by Charles Blackman and Pro Hart, plus a cartoon fragment attributed to the circle of Raphael. It also runs daily **town tours** (adult/child $12/5.50; ⏱ 11am & 1.30pm) that take in the interior of chapels and other cloistered places.

New Norcia Hotel (☎ 9654 8034; fax 9654 8011; Great Northern Hwy; s/d $70/80) is set back from the highway and built along epic lines, with grand staircases, high ceilings and an enormous front veranda. The rooms are plain and clean, and the front bar is a friendly place to wet your whistle.

NEW NORCIA TO NEWMAN

More than 400km to the north is **Mt Magnet**, where gold was found in the late 19th century, and where mining remains the town's lifeblood. Some 11km north of town are the ruins of **Lennonville**, once a busy town. Some 80km to the north, the old gold-mining town of **Cue** is the route's architectural highlight, with several grand old buildings, while **Walga Rock**, 48km to the west, has a gallery of Aboriginal art (*walga* means 'ochre painting' in the local Warragi language). **Wilgie Mia**, 64km northwest of Cue via Glen Station, is the site of a 30,000-year-old Aboriginal red-ochre quarry.

Another 116km north of Cue, **Meekatharra** has little for the traveller, although there are some mining ghost towns nearby, such as **Peak Hill**. Further north, **Newman** is an incongruous piece of modern suburbia dropped intact into the middle of nowhere

by mining giant BHP during the 1970s. It's bland, but has all the facilities and is the place to stock up for further travels. Tours of the enormous open-cut **Mt Whaleback iron-ore mine** (☎ 08-9175 2888; adult/child $10/6.50; ☺ 8.30am Mon-Sat Nov-Apr; 8.30am, 10.30am & 1.30pm daily May-Oct; bookings essential) showcase colossal equipment and one seriously big hole.

Sleeping & Eating

Miners Rest (☎ 08-9963 4380; fax 9963 4390; Thurckle Cove, Mt Magnet; s/d $55/60; ☒) On the eastern edge of town, the units here are pretty basic, but there's air-con and the price is right. Head east down the Sandstone road and follow the signs. The town's three pubs on the highway offer counter meals.

Queen of the Murchison Hotel (☎ 08-9963 1625; fax 9963 1206; Great Northern Hwy, Cue; B&B s/d $70/90; ☒) The standout accommodation choice along the whole highway, this classic old pub has been converted to a spacious, unlicensed B&B with well-appointed rooms, pristine amenities and home-cooked evening meals ($22). There are also meals at the nearby **Murchison Club Hotel** (☎ 08-9963 1020; Great Northern Hwy, Cue; mains $10-21), including cook-your-own barbecue packs ($10).

Meekatharra's accommodation offers little value for money, and you're better off pushing on to Cue or Newman. The best rooms are at **Auski Inland Motel** (☎ 08-9981 1433; harstso@benet.net.au; Main St, Meekatharra; s & d $135; ☒), while the **Royal Mail Hotel** (☎ 08-9981 1148; fax 9980 1113; Main St, Meekatharra; mains $14-23) has an à-la-carte menu and a nice timber front bar.

Seasons Hotel Newman (☎ 08-9177 8666; www .seasonshotel.com.au; Newman Dr, Newman; budget s & tw $40 per person, motel s & d $135; ☒) has attractively furnished motel rooms around pleasant gardens and a small pool. The budget rooms service single working men and are basically a bed in a room. On the way into town, **Red Sands Tavern** (☎ 08-9177 8866; Newman Dr, Newman; mains $15-26) has generous counter meals plus pool tables and occasional live bands. There are several takeaway options in and around the shopping centre.

There are dusty caravan parks in **Mt Magnet** (☎ 08-9963 4198; Hepburn St), **Cue** (☎ 08-9963 1107; Great Northern Hwy) and **Meekatharra** (☎ 08-9981 1253; Great Northern Hwy) offering camp/caravan sites for around $16/20. Newman's **Dearlove's Caravan Park** (☎ 08-9175 2802; dearlovescp@benet .net.au; Cowra Dr; camp/caravan sites $15/19, budget s & d & tw per person $25) has better facilities, good prefab budget accommodation and some shady trees.

KARIJINI NATIONAL PARK

Almost 200km north of Newman, Karijini National Park is famous for its magnificent sheer gorges and beautiful swimming holes, as well as a carpet of wildflowers in early spring. It's also one of the few attractions in this part of the state that's best visited in the Wet – when the water's flowing, the water falls are more spectacular, the swimming holes are deeper (a perfect foil for the unrelenting sun) and there are generally fewer people around to detract from the beauty. The downsides are that flash floods occur after heavy rain, and you'll need to take care when walking along cliff faces and into gorges – there are unfenced sections along the cliff tops and the rocks can be very slippery near the water. Most of the attractions are in the park's north, off the 67km-long Banjima Dr – a rough and rocky dirt road that's hard on conventional vehicles. Entry is the $4/9 per bus passenger/car.

The excellent Karijini **visitors centre** (☎ 08-9189 8121; Banyjima Dr; ☺ 9am-4pm, 11am-3pm in the Wet), in the northeastern corner of the park, is run by the traditional owners of Karijini, the Banyjima. Pick up a copy of CALM's free *Karijini: Visitor Information/Walk Trail Guide* here.

Entering Banyjima Dr from the east, you soon reach the turn-off to **Dales Gorge**. A short sharp descent takes you to **Fortescue Falls** and the beautiful swimming hole of **Circular Pool**. There's a pleasant walk along the cliff top here.

Next is Kalimina Rd and a 30-minute walk into the depths of **Kalimina Gorge**, where there's a small shady pool. Another 11km along is Joffre Falls Rd that leads to **Knox Gorge**, passing a lookout over the spectacular Joffre Falls.

The final turn-off is Weano Rd, which takes you to the park's signature attraction – **Oxers Lookout**, from where there are extraordinary views of the junction of the Red, Weano, Joffre and Hancock Gorges. It's one of Australia's great sights. To get down into the gorges proper, take the steps down to Handrail Pool in Weano Gorge (stopping for a swim), or the more difficult

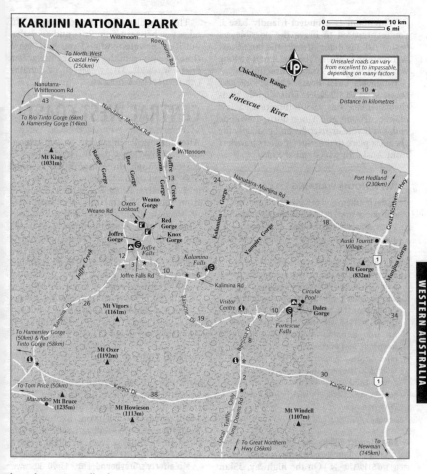

KARIJINI NATIONAL PARK

0 ————— 10 km
0 ————— 6 mi

Unsealed roads can vary from excellent to impassable, depending on many factors

★ 10 ★

Distance in kilometres

WESTERN AUSTRALIA

but dramatic walk down into stunning Hancock Gorge.

Other attractions include **Rio Tinto Gorge** and **Hamersley Gorge** off Nanutarra-Wittenoom Rd in the park's northwest, and **Wittenoom Gorge** in the far north (for details see the boxed text 'Wittenoom Warning'; p906). It's reached by an 11km sealed road that takes you past old asbestos mines, small gorges and pretty pools. Avoid the road if there's been rain, as there are several creek crossings to negotiate and flash flooding is a real possibility.

Tours

Given the park's remote location and unforgiving roads, it's well worth considering joining a tour, even if you have your own vehicle. Locally, **Design-a-Tour** (☎ 08-9841 7778; www.dat.com.au; adult/child $115/70) has good one-day tours of the gorges from Auski or Tom Price. **Lestok Tours** (☎ 08-9189 2032; lestok@norcom.net.au) has similar trips from Tom Price ($100/50 per adult/child), as well as a tour of the enormous Hamersley Iron mine ($15/7.50).

There are also longer trips from Karratha (p927) and Port Hedland (p930).

Sleeping & Eating

Within the park there are two basic **camping grounds** (☎ 08-9189 8157; sites $13) – there's an established one at Dales Gorge and a new one about 4km up Weano Rd.

Wittenoom is a budget-friendly base if you're prepared to brave the possible asbestos risk (as many are; see the boxed text 'Wittenoom Warning'; below), but it's a long way from the park's major attractions.

Wittenoom Guest House (☎ 08-9189 7060; Gregory St; dm/s/d $10/20/35). This slightly ramshackle place has 1950s furniture, a few plain bedrooms and a long dorm down one end, but it's clean, friendly and probably the cheapest place in the state. It offers transfers from Auski for $10 – call ahead.

WITTENOOM WARNING

At the northern end of Karijini National Park, the 'ghost' town of **Wittenoom** (population 25) is officially classified as 'abandoned' – and doesn't even appear on some maps – as a result of a series of deaths linked to the local blue asbestos mine. However, some hardy residents have refused to depart, and they offer accommodation, tours and counter-propaganda on the alleged dangers of the town. Although the mine closed in 1966, there is a potential health risk from airborne asbestos fibres in the township, and in the Wittenoom and Yampire Gorges. Avoid disturbing asbestos tailings in the area and keep your car windows closed on windy days. If you are concerned, seek medical advice before going to Wittenoom.

Auski Tourist Village (☎ 08-9176 6988; fax 9176 6973; Great Northern Hwy; camp/caravan sites $12/22, motel s/d $110/120; 🔀) On the highway, 35km north of the Karijini Dr turn-off, this is a convenient option. The McCafferty's/Greyhound bus stops here.

The mining town of Tom Price, 120km west of the Great Northern Hwy, also has some accommodation, including **Tom Price Hotel Motel** (☎ 1300 656 565; fax 08-9189 1164; motel s & d $120; 🔀), which has standard rooms and a reasonable restaurant.

Getting There & Away
Access to the park is via Karijini Dr, which leaves the Great Northern Hwy 226km south of Port Hedland and 162km northwest of Newman. **McCafferty's/Greyhound** (☎ 13 20 30) buses stop at the Auski Tourist Village, 35km north of the turn-off, on Saturday.

The unsealed Tom Price Railway Rd takes you between Tom Price and Karratha, but it's a private road and you must get a (free) permit from the visitors centre at **Tom Price** (☎ 08-9188 1112; 497 Sirus St) or **Karratha** (☎ 08-9144 4600; Karratha Rd).

CENTRAL WEST COAST

After leaving Perth's north coastal region, the North-West Coastal Hwy (Hwy 1) passes through three interesting regions. The Batavia Coast, including Geraldton and Kalbarri, is ablaze with wildflowers from July to November, evokes memories of precolonial shipwrecks and is chock-a-block full of heritage buildings. This area's also crayfish (rock lobster) fishing territory, and the coastal towns, with their attractive beaches, are popular with Perth families during school holidays. The Shark Bay World Heritage region, home of Monkey Mia, is the place to chase more diverse sea life such as dugongs and dolphins, while the Gascoyne takes in stretches east as far as Mt Augustus, the world's largest rock.

Getting There & Away
Qantas (☎ 13 13 00; www.qantas.com) links Perth with Carnarvon. **Skywest** (☎ 1300 660 088; www.skywest.com.au) has flights from Perth to Geraldton, and links to Denham (for Monkey Mia), Carnarvon, Exmouth and Karratha. A Perth–Kalbarri service is offered three times a week by **Great Western Airlines** (☎ 1800 883 066; www.gwairlines.com.au).

McCafferty's/Greyhound (☎ 13 20 30; www.mccaffertys.com.au) has daily north- and southbound buses between Perth and Dongara ($36, 5¾ hours), Geraldton ($39, 6¾ hours), Northampton ($50, 7½ hours), Overlander Roadhouse (for Denham and Monkey Mia, 10¾ hours) and Carnarvon ($110, 13 hours). Its Perth–Exmouth service also takes you into Kalbarri ($85, 11 hours, 3 weekly). **Integrity** (☎ 08-9226 1339; www.integrity coachlines.com.au) has five weekly services following the same route to and from Perth, although prices tend to be slightly lower. **Transwa** (☎ 1300 662 205; www.transwa.wa.gov.au) follows three routes to Geraldton – via the Brand Hwy, Mullewa and Mingenew. The latter two routes are good for the Wildflower Way (p902).

JURIAN BAY TO DONGARA-PORT DENISON

A newish road runs straight up the coast from Cervantes, passing through the small coastal towns of **Jurian Bay**, **Green Head** and **Leeman** on the way to Dongara-Port Denison. Apart from an unbroken run of magnificent white-sand beaches and great fishing, the main attractions are the **Lesueur National Park**, which is home to one of the most diverse and rich wildflower areas of WA (access is via a 4WD track off Cockleshell Gully Rd), and excellent tours to Australian sea-lion populations on offshore islands.

Jurian Sealion Charters (☎ 08-9652 1109; juriansealions@westnet.com.au; Jurian Marina; half-day tour including lunch adult/child $65/30) takes you snorkelling near the island colonies, and also offers whale-watching tours in season (same prices; September to December). At Green Head, **Sea Lion Charters** (☎ 08-9953 1012; tours $65/30) offers similar tours.

There are small, shady caravan parks near the beaches at **Jurian Bay** (☎ 08-9652 1595), **Green Head** (☎ 08-9953 1131) and **Leeman** (☎ 08-9953 1080).

DONGARA-PORT DENISON

☎ 08 / pop 3000

This laid-back historical town and port offers fine beaches and terrific fishing, as well as good accommodation. In the old post office, the Dongara **visitors centre** (☎ 9927 1404; www.lobstercapital.com.au; 9 Waldeck St; ☺ 9am-5pm Mon-Fri, 10am-2pm Sat & Sun) has information on the town's historical buildings (including the striking but dere- lict flour mill, built in 1894) and can book tours and accommodation. Next door, in the old police station, is the **Irwin District Museum** (admission free; ☺ 10am-3pm Mon-Fri), which has small historical displays in its cells. Challenge Bank on Moreton Tce has an ATM, while Internet access is available at **Dongara Telecentre** (☎ 9927 2111; 11 Moreton Tce; per hr $6; ☺ 9am-4pm Mon-Fri).

Just over the Irwin River is **Russ Cottage** (Pt Leander Dr; adult/child $2.50/0.50; ☺ 10am-noon Sun), built in 1870 and the birthplace of WA's first white baby. Further still is **Port Denison** with its marina full of crayfish boats and, to the north, the **mouth of the Irwin** – a great place for spotting pelicans and cormorants.

Sleeping

Priory Lodge Historic Inn (☎ /fax 9927 1090; priory@telstra.easymail.com.au; 11 St Dominics Rd; B&B s/d $45/70; ☒) Built on the Irwin River in 1881, the atmospheric priory started life as a hotel, before serving as a nunnery and girls school. It's now fully restored and boasts a cosy bar and restaurant, period furniture, deep verandas, landscaped grounds and a pool.

Dongara Denison Tourist Park (☎ /fax 9927 1210; touristpark@wn.com.au; 8 George St; camp/caravan sites $10/18, on-site vans from $33) A small private park with sites fronting the attractive South Beach, plus plenty of trees and grass, this is the best of the town's parks.

Dongara Backpackers YHA (☎ 9927 1581; dongara backpack@westnet.com.au; 32 Waldeck St; dm/s/d $17/25/45; ☐) This small, friendly hostel is in a colonial house on a quiet street and has additional (tiny) rooms in a 1906 train carriage, plus equipment hire, tours, a TV lounge and a kitchen.

Dongara Motor Hotel (☎ 9927 1023; 12 Moreton Tce; s & d $70; ☒) has reasonable rooms.

Eating

Coffee Tree (☎ 9927 1400; 8 Moreton Tce; light meals $6-15; ☺ 8am-5pm) In a small courtyard under the shade of a huge Moreton Bay fig, you can tuck into healthy brekkies, fresh juices, burgers, focaccia and kebabs.

Dongara Motor Hotel (☎ 9927 1023; 12 Moreton Tce; mains $12-20) Dongara's oldest pub (1867) is not that flash, but serves up a decent steak, plus well-priced cray in season.

Toko's Restaurant (☎ 9927 1497; 1 Moreton Tce; mains $16-25) A cosy little place with over- wrought décor, Toko's is open nightly and offers plenty of seafood plus European standards like duck l'orange; bookings are requested.

There are plenty of takeaways along Moreton Tce in Dongara and at the **Port Store** (52 Pt Leander Dr) in Port Denison, where there's also a bakery and deli.

Getting There & Around

McCafferty's/Greyhound (☎ 13 20 30) buses to Broome and Perth stop at the Shell road- house on Brand Hwy. **Transwa** (☎ 1300 6622 05; www.transwa.wa.gov.au) and **Integrity** (☎ 9226 1339) buses stop outside the visitors centre. **Dongara Backpackers YHA** (☎ 9927 1581) hires out bikes for $5 per day.

WESTERN AUSTRALIA

GREENOUGH

☎ 08 / pop 100

Just south of Geraldton, Greenough was once a busy little mining town, but today is notable for its host of National Trust buildings (mostly from the period 1860–90) and an insightful museum.

Greenough Hamlet **visitors centre** (☎ 9926 1084; Brand Hwy; ☿ 9am-5pm) has tourist information and 11 well-restored 19th-century **buildings** (adult/child $4.50/2.50; tours by arrangement). Across the road, the **Pioneer Museum** (☎ 9926 1058; Brand Hwy; adult/child $3/1; ☿ 10am-4pm daily) is a convincing recreation of an 1860s farmhouse, complete with cellar, butchery, two-hole dunny and creepy models of children in the bedroom.

Hampton Arms Inn (☎ 9926 1057; briant@wn.com.au; Company Rd; B&B d $75) is a classic, historic inn (1863); it's great for a beer, counter meal or overnight stay in an old-fashioned room with many original fittings. Attached is a bookshop that specialises in rare and out-of-print books.

Transwa (☎ 1300 662 205; www.transwa.wa.gov.au) services heading north and south stop at the Greenough turn-off on the Brand Hwy.

GERALDTON

☎ 08 / pop 23,400

Geraldton, the mid-west's major town and cray-fishing centre, has some good beaches, a fine museum and a good array of accommodation, eating and entertainment options. It's also the base for trips to the beautiful Houtman Abrolhos Islands, where more than 120 people were murdered by the despotic Jeronimus Cornelisz after the *Batavia* went down in 1629 (for details see the boxed text 'A Bloody Business'; p912).

Information

The useful Geraldton **visitors centre** (☎ 9921 3999; www.geraldtontourist.com.au; Chapman Rd; ☿ 9am-5pm) is in the Bill Sewell Complex, which is also home to a craft centre and hostel. Pick up a *Heritage Trail* leaflet if you want to explore the town's historic architecture.

The main post office is on Durlacher St and there are several banks and ATMs along the main drag, Marine Tce. Internet access is available at **Harvey World Travel** (☎ 9921 7377; Chapman Way Arcade; per hr $10; ☿ 8.30am-5.30pm Mon-Fri, 9am-1pm Sat) and **Go Health Lunch Bar** (☎ 9965 5200; 122 Marine Tce).

Sights

WESTERN AUSTRALIAN MUSEUM GERALDTON

WA's largest regional **museum** (☎ 9921 5080; www.museum.wa.gov.au; 1 Museum Pl; admission by donation; ☿ 10am-4pm) has a splendid new home and a good series of exhibits on the region's Aboriginal, pioneer, natural and economic history. Don't miss the Shipwreck Gallery, which details the gruesome story of the *Batavia* and includes a 50-minute video (hourly between 10.30am and 2.30pm). The museum also houses the **Marra Indigenous Art & Design shop** (☎ 9965 3440), which has artworks drawn from the Marra's vast traditional lands, which stretch as far as Meekatharra to the east.

ST FRANCIS XAVIER CATHEDRAL

This **cathedral** (Cathedral Ave; tours free; 10am Mon & 2pm Fri) is one of a number of buildings in the mid-west designed by Monsignor John Hawes, an unusual priest-cum-architect who left WA in 1939 to spend the rest of his life living as a hermit in the Caribbean (see the boxed text 'Monsignor John Hawes'; p909). Construction started in 1916, but the plans were so grandiose (for what was essentially a country town church) that it was not completed until 1938. External features include twin towers with arched openings, an enormous central dome and a cone-roofed tower. Inside there are Romanesque columns, huge arches beneath an octagonal dome and gaudily striped walls.

OTHER SIGHTS

Geraldton Regional Art Gallery (☎ 9964 7170; 24 Chapman Rd; admission free; ☿ 10am-5pm Tue-Sat, 1.30-4.30pm Sun & Mon), in the old town hall, has a reasonable permanent collection, including several works by Norman Lindsay, plus a rolling series of temporary exhibitions in a well-designed space.

The **Old Geraldton Gaol Craft Centre** (☎ 9921 1614; Bill Sewell Complex, Chapman Rd; admission free; ☿ 10am-4pm) has so-so crafts for sale, but more compelling are the tiny, grim cells that housed prisoners from 1858 all the way to 1986, plus historical documents detailing the appalling conditions the prisoners suffered.

At **Geraldton Fisherman's Co-op** (☎ 9921 7084; Geraldton Harbour; admission by donation; tours

MONSIGNOR JOHN HAWES

The architect-cum-priest Monsignor John Hawes has left a magnificent legacy of buildings in the midwest. He was born in Richmond, England, in 1876. He trained as an architect in London, then, following his ordination as an Anglican priest in 1903, worked in the London slums as a missionary. He then went to the Bahamas where he helped rebuild a number of churches.

Two years later, he converted to Catholicism and went to study in Rome. He came to Australia in 1915 at the invitation of the Bishop of Geraldton and worked as a country pastor in the Murchison goldfields. For the next 24 years he worked tirelessly as a parish priest at Mullewa and Greenough while designing 24 buildings – 16 of which were built.

His best works are the **Church of Our Lady of Mt Carmel** and the **Priest House** in Mullewa, the **Church of the Holy Cross** in Morawa, the **Church of St Joseph** in Perenjori and the beautiful, inspiring **St Francis Xavier Cathedral** in Geraldton.

Hawes left Australia in 1939 after witnessing the opening of his controversial Geraldton cathedral the previous year. His only regret at leaving Australia was that he couldn't take his fox terrier Dominie. He went to Cat Island in the Bahamas and lived as a hermit in a small stone building on a hilltop. He died in a Miami hospital in 1956 and his body was brought back to a tomb he had built for himself on Cat Island.

The *Monsignor Hawes Heritage Trail* pamphlet ($4.50) is available from the tourist office in Geraldton.

(🕑 9.30am Mon-Fri Nov-Jun) you get to see exactly how a live rock lobster gets from the ocean floor to a Hong Kong restaurant table. Nearby are a couple of places on Connell Rd where you can get a lobster fresh off the boat for around $20.

On a small hill overlooking the town is the **HMAS Sydney Memorial** (follow the signs from George St), commemorating the loss of 645 men and the ship after a skirmish with the German ship *Kormoran* in November 1941. There are good views of Geraldton from here.

Tours

Batavia Tours (☎ 9921 7760; $16; 🕑 9am Sat; 2 hr) City sights tour.

Wandering Albatross (☎ 9921 3999) Variety of tours, including cray pot pulls (adult/child $25/10; 2 hr) and fishing (adult/child $110/60; full day); book at the visitors centre.

Festivals & Events

Special events in Geraldton include the **Geraldton Windsurfing Classic** in January, the **Seajazz Festival** in March, **Batavia Celebrations** in June and the **Sunshine Festival** in October.

Sleeping

BUDGET

Foreshore Backpackers YHA (☎ 9921 3275; fax 9921 3233; 172 Marine Tce; dm/s/d $18/27/45; 🖥) A large, friendly and character-filled place, this

ageing hostel has high-ceilinged but small rooms (maximum of four beds). There's a pool, a good kitchen, TV lounge, Internet access, cool verandas with sea views, and tours to Greenough ($20) and Hutt River Province ($25); see also the boxed text 'Prince Leonard's Land'; p914.

Batavia Backpackers (☎ 9964 3001; fax 9964 3611; Bill Sewell Complex, Chapman Rd; dm/s/d $16/22/38; 🖥) Just behind the visitors centre, the relaxed Batavia has similar facilities to the YHA, although it does lack a little character.

Belair Gardens Tourist Park (☎ 9921 1997; Willcock Dr; camp/caravan sites $16/18, cabins from $60) Close to town on Point Moore by the old lighthouse, this park is across from an excellent sailboarding beach and has decent shade, a pool and a tennis court.

MID-RANGE & TOP END

Albrolhos Reef Lodge (☎ 9921 3811; www.modnet.com .au/~abrolhosreef; 126 Brand Hwy; budget/deluxe d $80/90; 🏊) On the fringe of town, Abrolhos' spacious units with kitchenettes and lounges offer excellent value. There's also a small pool and the enticing Tarcoola Beach is a short walk away.

Champion Bay B&B (☎ 9921 7624; www.westnet .com.au/championbay; 31 Snowdon St; s/d $60/80) A roomy family home atop a sharp hill, with sweeping views of the bay, this is a welcoming place with a friendly owner and tastefully decorated rooms.

WESTERN AUSTRALIA

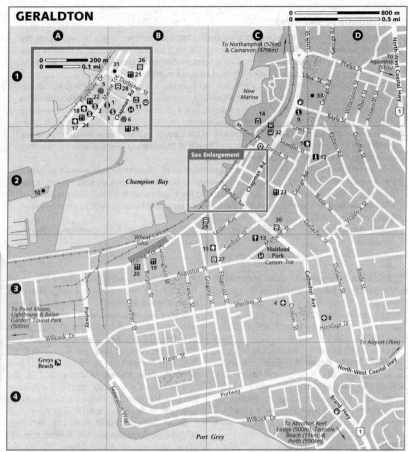

GERALDTON

To Northampton (52km) & Carnarvon (479km)

New Marina

Champion Bay

See Enlargement

Maitland Park

To Point Moore, Lighthouse & Belair Gardens Tourist Park (500m)

Greys Beach

To Airport (7km)

To Abrolhos Reef Lodge (500m), Tarcoola Beach (11km) & Perth (590km)

Port Grey

To Aquarena (1km)

North-West Coastal Hwy

Ocean Centre Hotel (☎ 9921 7777; fax 9964 1990; cnr Foreshore Dr & Cathedral Ave; d/ste with spa $95/150; ✖) A modern, spotless hotel in the centre of town with some rooms fronting Town Beach, plus a reasonable bar and restaurant.

Batavia Motor Inne (☎ 1800 014 628, 9921 3500; bat@wn.com.au; 54 Fitzgerald St; d $80, units from $90; ✖) A large and very central place, the Batavia has small and slightly weary rooms; the better ones have balconies overlooking the good-sized pool and spa. There's also a Scottish bar and restaurant.

Eating
Most restaurants and cafés are found along Marine Tce, while the major fast-food joints are scattered throughout town.

Go Health Lunch Bar (☎ 9965 5200; 122 Marine Tce; light meals $7-16; ☐) The only eatery in town with a touch of attitude, and the only place to go for drinkable coffee, it's lined with lounges and offers a fair selection of sandwiches, light lunches and fresh juices, plus one Internet terminal.

Sun City Food Hall (56 Durlacher St; mains $7-10; ☙ 11.30am-2pm & 6-9pm Wed-Mon) This food hall is a fine budget option, with roasts, fish and chips, and Middle Eastern, Chinese and Italian meals on offer.

Topolini's Cafe (☎ 9964 5866; 158 Marine Tce; pizzas $11-17, mains $21-28) A nice, breezy spot with plenty of outdoor tables, this licensed Italian eatery also offers dinner-movie deals for $25, and half-price pasta on Monday.

Skeetas Restaurant & Cafe (☎ 9964 1619; 101 Foreshore Dr; lunch $7-15, dinner $14-25) You'll always get a table at this laid-back, sprawling place across from the beach. Lunch is good value, while the more upmarket Mod Oz dinner menu concentrates on Euro-influenced steak and seafood.

Boatshed Restaurant (☎ 9921 5500; 357 Marine Tce; mains $19-30; ☽ dinner Tue-Sun) Arguably Geraldton's top seafood restaurant, the Boatshed has nautical décor and plenty of fishy goodness.

Geraldton Fish Market (☎ 9921 3755; 365 Marine Tce) If you have cooking facilities, this is place to go for seafood straight off the boat.

Geraldton also has plenty of supermarkets, including **Rules Supermarket** (Marine Tce) and **Woolworths** (Stirlings Centre, Chapman Rd. All the pubs in town havecounter meals available.

Entertainment

If you're into guitar rock, Geraldton has a surprisingly active live scene. **Breakers Tavern** (☎ 9921 8925; 41 Chapman Rd) attracts the under 30s and has bands Friday and Saturday night, while **Freemason's Hotel** (☎ 9964 3467; cnr Marine Tce & Durlacher St) also puts on bands and is equally popular, but generally has an older crowd. **Circuit Niteclub** (☎ 9921 1400; 60 Fitzgerald St) is the place to dance till the wee hours, once the pubs have closed.

Geraldton 4 Cinemas (☎ 9965 0568; cnr Marine Tce & Fitzgerald St; adult/child $13/8) has four screens showing the latest movie releases. For concerts, plays and comedy, head to **Queens Park Theatre** (☎ 9956 6662; www.midwestevents.com.au; cnr Catherdal Ave & Maitland St).

Getting There & Around

Skywest (☎ 1300 66 00 88) has flights to and from Perth daily, as well as regular flights to Carnarvon, Denham (for Monkey Mia), Exmouth and Karratha. **Great Western Airlines** (☎ 1800 883 066) flies to Kalbarri three times a week.

McCafferty's/Greyhound (☎ 13 20 30) buses run daily from the Bill Sewell Complex to Perth ($39, 6¾ hours), as well as Broome ($300, 26 hours) and all points in between. **Transwa** (☎ 1300 662 205; www.transwa.wa.gov.au) also goes daily to Perth and three times weekly to Kalbarri. **Integrity** (☎ 9226 1339) has five weekly services to Perth and points north. Both Transwa and Integrity buses stop at the old train station.

Geraldton Bus Service (☎ 9923 1100) operates eight routes to local suburbs (all-day ticket $2.50). **Bike Force** (☎ 9921 3279; 54 Marine Tce) hires out good bikes for $15/70 per day/week.

HOUTMAN ABROLHOS ISLANDS

Known locally as 'the Abrolhos', this archipelago is about 60km off the coast of Geraldton and takes in more than 100 coral islands. They are home to sea lion colonies and a host of sea birds, plus hefty golden orb spiders, carpet pythons and the small Tammar wallaby. However, much of the beauty of the Abrolhos lies beneath the water, where *Acropora* corals abound and (thanks to the warm Leeuwin Current) a rare and spectacular mix of tropical and temperate fish species thrives. The beautiful but treacherous reefs surrounding the islands have also claimed

many ships over the years, including the ill-fated *Batavia* – see the boxed text 'A Bloody Business' (below).

As the islands are protected and have no tourist facilities, it's not possible to stay on them overnight, although cray-fishing families have licences to set up camp from March to June – they live in groups of shacks on several of the islands.

You can visit from Geraldton by boat or air. Flights are faster, more fun and actually cheaper: **Geraldton Air Charters** (☎ 08-9923 3434) has scenic flights for $130, or day trips including lunch and snorkelling gear for $165; **Shine Aviation** (☎ 08-9923 3600) has similar tours. **Abrolhos Escape Charters** (☎ 0428-382 505) is among the boat operators that charge from $90 for a fishing and snorkelling day trip (dives extra).

NORTHAMPTON
☎ 08 / pop 780

Founded to exploit the lead and copper deposits discovered in 1848, Northampton is a National Trust–classified town with many historic buildings. It's worth a brief stop.

The **visitors centre** (☎ 9934 1488; ☼ 9am-4pm Mon-Fri, 9am-2pm Sat) is located in the old police station on Hampton Rd, the main highway, and has a free *Heritage Walk* pamphlet available. **Chiverton House** (☎ 9934 1215; Hampton Rd; admission $2; ☼ 10am-noon & 2-4pm Thu-Mon) is an early mining home that's been converted into a mildly interesting pioneer museum.

The **Northampton Caravan Park** (☎ 9934 1202; Hampton Rd; camp/caravan sites $10/15) has very basic facilities on offer; the better place to stay is the **Old Convent** (☎ 9934 1692; 61 Hampton Rd; dm/s/d $12/15/30), a lovely old stone building that was designed by Monsignor Hawes and then converted to a backpackers. Next door is the striking **St Mary's Church** (another Hawes building), a dignified and slender structure made from weathered red stone. The three pubs in town serve counter meals.

McCafferty's/Greyhound (☎ 13 20 30) stops at the **Miners Arms Hotel** (☎ 9934 1281; Hampton Rd) and **Integrity** (☎ 9226 1339) at the visitors centre. Both have regular services north and south.

A BLOODY BUSINESS

During the 17th century, the easiest way for ships of the Dutch East India Company to get to Batavia (Jakarta) in Java was to head due east from the Cape of Good Hope and then hoon up the WA coast to Indonesia. However, the many offshore reefs and island groups made this a risky business, and the whole area is littered with wrecks, including the ill-fated *Batavia*.

On 4 June 1629 the *Batavia* ran aground on the inhospitable Abrolhos Islands (*Abre Los Vos* means 'open your eyes'!) off the coast of modern-day Geraldton. The ship's commander, Francisco Pelsaert, took most of the officers and passengers to the mainland to search for water, leaving 268 people behind, including a sizeable body of soldiers. An undermerchant named Jeronimus Cornelisz, who had agitated against the commander during the voyage, saw his chance to act. Tricking the soldiers into relinquishing their arms, he banished them to a nearby island and instituted a reign of terror that resulted in the death of 125 men, women and children before Pelsaert returned three months later (having been forced to travel all the way to Batavia for help).

The first murders were carried out under the pretext of saving water supplies, but Cornelisz and his small band of followers became increasingly arbitrary and brutal, taking concubines and raping and murdering indiscriminately. Palsaert eventually returned with more soldiers, summarily executed Cornelisz, and dumped some of his men at Wittecarra Gully, just south of modern-day Kalbarri, making them the first white men on mainland Australia.

Another notable wreck was the *Zuytdorp*, which ran aground beneath the towering cliffs about 65km north of Kalbarri in 1712. Wine bottles, other relics and the remains of fires have been found on the cliff top, and the discovery of the extremely rare Ellis van Creveld syndrome (rife in Holland at the time the ship ran aground) in Aboriginal children suggests that *Zuytdorp* survivors lasted long enough to introduce the gene to Australia.

Relics from these shipwrecks, and others, can be seen in the Geraldton Museum (p908) and Shipwreck Museum in Fremantle (p851). The latter has a gallery devoted entirely to the *Batavia* that's well worth a look.

NORTHAMPTON TO KALBARRI

The coastal road is the more scenic option to get to Kalbarri, passing through the tiny coastal towns of **Horrocks** (23km west) and **Port Gregory** (47km northwest), and the superb coastal gorges in the southern reaches of **Kalbarri National Park** (p914). The caravan parks at **Port Gregory** (08-9935 1052) and **Horrocks** (08-9934 3039) both have camping grounds, on-site vans and cabins, and front onto quiet and attractive beaches.

KALBARRI

 08 / pop 2000

A laid-back and increasingly popular seaside resort, Kalbarri lies at the mouth of the Murchison River and attracts hordes of families and fishers during holiday periods. The town has plenty of accommodation options, an alluring coastline and the stunning gorges of the Kalbarri National Park.

The helpful Kalbarri **visitors centre** (1800 639 468, 9937 1104; ktb@wn.com.au; Grey St; 9am-5pm) books tours and accommodation. There are Internet facilities available at **Betty Russell's Book Exchange & Internet Cafe** (9937 2676; 42 Grey St) next to the post office, and **Kalbarri Cafe & Takeaways** (9937 1045) in the Kalbarri Shopping Centre. There are ATMs in the supermarket and Gilgai Tavern, and at the shopping centre. The **CALM office** (9937 1140; open 8am-5pm Mon-Fri), where you can ring rangers for Kalbarri National Park, is on Arjana-Kalbarri Rd.

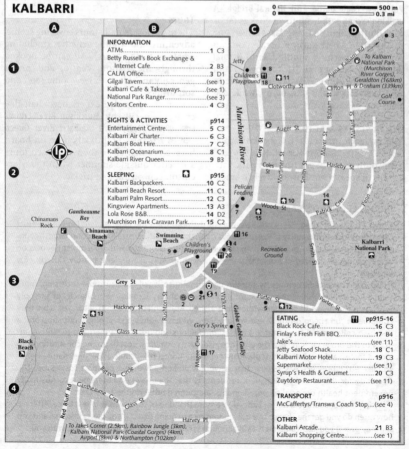

KALBARRI

INFORMATION	
ATMs	1 C3
Betty Russell's Book Exchange & Internet Cafe	2 B3
CALM Office	3 D1
Gilgai Tavern	(see 1)
Kalbarri Cafe & Takeaways	(see 1)
National Park Ranger	(see 3)
Visitors Centre	4 C3

SIGHTS & ACTIVITIES	p914
Entertainment Centre	5 C3
Kalbarri Air Charter	6 C3
Kalbarri Boat Hire	7 C2
Kalbarri Oceanarium	8 C1
Kalbarri River Queen	9 B3

SLEEPING	p915
Kalbarri Backpackers	10 C2
Kalbarri Beach Resort	11 C1
Kalbarri Palm Resort	12 C3
Kingsview Apartments	13 A3
Lola Rose B&B	14 D2
Murchison Park Caravan Park	15 C2

EATING	pp915-16
Black Rock Cafe	16 C3
Finlay's Fresh Fish BBQ	17 B4
Jake's	(see 11)
Jetty Seafood Shack	18 C1
Kalbarri Motor Hotel	19 C3
Supermarket	(see 1)
Syrup's Health & Gourmet	20 C3
Zuytdorp Restaurant	(see 11)

TRANSPORT	p916
McCaffertys/Transwa Coach Stop	(see 4)

OTHER	
Kalbarri Arcade	21 B3
Kalbarri Shopping Centre	(see 1)

WESTERN AUSTRALIA

Sights & Activities

KALBARRI NATIONAL PARK

This arid park boasts over 1000 sq km of bushland, scenic gorges on the Murchison River and rugged coastal cliffs. To get to the gorges from Kalbarri, head 11km east along Ajana–Kalbarri Rd to the turn-off, then follow the long stretches of dirt to the impressive gorges of the **Loop** (29km) and **Z-Bend** (25km). More accessible and just as attractive are two lookouts, **Hawk's Head** and **Ross Graham**. The turn-off to both is another 24km along Ajana–Kalbarri Rd. The park has a particularly fine display of **wildflowers** between July and November, including banksias, grevilleas and kangaroo paws.

South of town is a string of rugged cliff faces, including **Red Bluff**, **Rainbow Valley**, **Pot Alley**, **Eagle Gorge** and **Natural Bridge**. A **walking/cycling path** from town goes as far as Red Bluff (5.5km) passing **Jakes Corner**, one of the state's best surfing breaks, or you can take a morning shuttle bus to **Natural Bridge** and walk or cycle back to town. From August to November it may be possible to spot **humpback whales** passing by, while **dolphins** can be seen year-round.

OTHER SIGHTS & ACTIVITIES

Rainbow Jungle (☎ 08-9937 1248; Red Bluff Rd; adult/child $9/3.50; ☺ 9am-5pm Mon-Sat, 10am-5pm Sun), 4km south of town, is a fine bird park with dozens of species on show in lovely tropical gardens. It also breeds rare species, such as the endangered white-tailed cockatoo and the golden-shouldered parrot.

Kalbarri Oceanarium (☎ 08-9937 2027; Grey St; adult/child $6/4) is one for the kids, with half a dozen tanks and a touch pool. For water activities on the Murchison River, **Kalbarri Boat Hire** (☎ 9937 1245) is on the foreshore and hires out canoes and rowboats ($12 an hour), motorboats ($33) and basic sailboards ($15).

Entertainment Centre (☎ 08-9937 1105; Porter St) is one for the kiddies, with trampolines, electric cars, mini-golf and video games. It also hires out bikes (see Getting There & Around; p916).

Other activities include **abseiling** at Z-Bend, **fishing charters** and **camel safaris**; see the visitors centre (p913) for details.

Tours

There's a host of daily tours covering scenic, adventure and wildlife activities (including whale-watching tours). All can be booked through the visitors centre, and prices generally include park fees, some food and soft drinks.

For a leisurely experience, half-day cruises are run by **Murchison River Cruises** (☎ 08-9937 1393) and **Kalbarri River Queen** (☎ 08-9937 1104); both boats have on-board bars. Note that all of the river-based tours are better outside summer when the Murchison can shrink to a trickle.

PRINCE LEONARD'S LAND

Down a dusty, dirt road, 75km northwest of Northampton, lies the independent land of the **Hutt River Province Principality** (☎ /fax 9936 6035; www.huttriver.net). Australia's 'second largest country' was created on 21 April 1970 when farmer Len Casley, disgusted with government quotas on wheat production, seceded from the Commonwealth of Australia under a (hastily closed) legal loophole.

Despite concerted attempts by the WA government to legally overturn the secession, more than 30 years later HRH Prince Leonard and Princess Shirley remain the monarchs of the only principality in the world declared without bloodshed. Although they're both getting on a bit, they continue to run sheep on the 75-sq-km property, which features a post office, gift shop and a deadpan collection of flags, stamps, letters, medallions and other paraphernalia to lend legitimacy to the province. Similarly, the province also has its own flag, postal system, constitution and armed forces, although the latter plays a strictly ceremonial role. You can become naturalised if you like – the province has 13,000 citizens worldwide and a five-year passport costs $250. The downside for the 20 or so permanent residents is that they have no entitlement to Australian government health or social security benefits, although neither do they pay tax.

Visitors are encouraged, but call ahead to ensure that one of the royals is in residence. After all, how often do you get the chance of a guided tour by a genuine royal? It's all pretty informal and you can stay over if you like (camping is $10) although you'll need to bring your own food with you.

Also recommended:

Kalbarri Air Charter (☎ 08-9937 1130; Grey St) 20-minute flights over the Murchison River gorges (adult/child $45/30) and longer tours.

Kalbarri Adventure Tours (☎ 08-9937 1677; www.wn.com.au/kat) A popular all-day bushwalking and canoeing trip to the national park ($60/50).

Kalbarri Boat Hire (☎ 08-9937 1245) Four-hour canoe trip on the lower Murchison River that includes breakfast ($45/33).

Kalbarri Safari Tours (☎ 08-9937 1011; www.kalbarrisafaritours.com.au) Heads to the spectacular Z-Bend on a day trip ($55) or two-day camping safari ($135); can also take you to 280m-high dunes for sand boarding ($55).

Sleeping
BUDGET
Kalbarri is a popular resort and rooms can be tight during school holidays, when prices usually increase.

Kalbarri Backpackers (☎ 08-9937 1430; www.yha.com.au; cnr Woods & Mortimer Sts; dm/s/d $19/45/50; 🖳) The dorms are cramped with lots of beds, but there are great facilities here, including large common areas, a decent pool, free use of barbecues, bike hire ($10 per day) and huge number of tours. It's flat out in peak season.

Murchison Park Caravan Park (☎ 08-9937 1005; fax 9937 1415; cnr Woods & Grey Sts; camp/caravan sites $12/16, air-con cabins $55) The most central of Kalbarri's parks has just enough shade, gazebos overlooking the waterfront and a good camping kitchen. It also bottles its own water.

MID-RANGE & TOP-END
Lola Rose B&B (☎ 08-9937 2224; fax 08-9937 2324; 21 Patrick Cres; s & d $75, with bathroom $85; 🐕) The best mid-range deal in town, Lola Rose is friendly and spacious with a generous shared lounge and kitchen. There's even a measure of privacy as the managers live off-site.

Kingsview Apartments (☎ 08-9937 1274; cnr Stiles & Hackney Sts; d $180 🐕) Beautiful, modern and roomy, these apartments are decked out with luxurious touches, tasteful décor and kitchens worthy of a gourmet chef.

Kalbarri Palm Resort (☎ 08-9937 2333, 1800 819 029; www.bestwestern.com.au/kalbarri; 8 Porter St; 2-bedroom units $90, motel d $100, spa room d $140; 🐕) A large family-oriented place, it has two pools, tennis courts, an indoor cricket court and a restaurant. The units sleep five and are particularly good value.

Kalbarri Beach Resort (☎ 1800 096 002, 08-9937 1061; www.kalbarribeachresort.com.au; cnr Clotworthy & Grey Sts; 2-/3-bedroom self-contained units $140/160; 🐕) Across from the river, this is a huge place with a 25m pool, two spas, kids playgrounds and two restaurants. It's extremely popular during school holidays, so you'll need to book.

There are plenty of other holiday units and resort rooms that can be booked through the visitors centre.

Eating
Black Rock Cafe (☎ 08-9937 1062; 80 Grey St; breakfast $4-12, lunch mains $8-18, dinner mains $16-28) A casual place with plenty of outdoor seating overlooking the water, Black Rock is Kalbarri's best eatery with generous brekkies, gourmet sandwiches and pizzas at lunchtime, and a varied Mod Oz menu in the evening. The coffee is also good and the wine list is well priced, with all available by the glass.

Finlay's Fresh Fish BBQ (Magee Cres; mains $12-19; 🕭 dinner Tue-Sun) This ultra–laid-back and often raucous place is in a tree-shaded sand garden, and gives you Australiana in spades. Mismatched cutlery and crockery, BYO booze (and glass if you don't fancy a plastic tumbler) and large serves of seafood or steak makes for a great night, but get in early – you can't reserve a table.

Syrup's Health & Gourmet (☎ 08-9937 1995; 378 Grey St; light meals $5-9) A laid-back, neo-hippy cafe, Syrup's uses good, fresh ingredients in its juices, smoothies, salads, burgers and tortillas. There are also stocks of dried fruits and nuts, plus spirulina for a protein hit.

Jetty Seafood Shack (☎ 08-9937 1067; 1/108 Grey St; meals from $8) This basic takeaway opposite the jetty is known for the consistent quality of its fish and chips, and also has good-value combo packs with shellfish and salads ($14 to $26) – ideal for a picnic on the river.

Kalbarri Motor Hotel (☎ 9937 1000; 50 Grey St; mains $12-28) This popular pub has large seafood and steak bistro meals and a decent salad bar. There's loads of indoor and outdoor seating, and there's usually a band on Friday and Saturday nights.

Zuytdorp Restaurant (☎ 08-9937 2222; cnr Clotworthy & Grey Sts; mains $19-25) At Kalbarri Beach Resort, the marine theme here verges on the tacky, with sailcloth and marine lamps decorating the low-arched space. The food is well-prepared, but stock-standard à la

carte fare (rack of lamb, pork in bacon etc). Next door, **Jake's** (☎ 08-9937 2222; mains $6-11) offers low-end bistro fare for people on a tight budget.

There are takeaway options and a supermarket in the shopping centre.

Getting There & Around

The airport is 10km south of town. **Great Western Airlines** (☎ 1800 883 066; www.gwairlines.com.au) flies to Geraldton and Perth three times a week.

McCafferty's/Greyhound (☎ 13 20 30) buses stop at the visitors centre, heading for Perth ($85, 11 hours), Exmouth ($150, 10½ hours) and Broome ($260, 24½ hours). **Transwa** (☎ 1300 6622 05; www.transwa.wa.gov.au) has services to Perth on Monday, Wednesday and Friday, also leaving from the visitors centre. **Integrity** (☎ 08-9226 1339) has a shuttle service ($15, 1 hour) into town on Monday and Friday meeting its north- and southbound services at Ajana on the North-West Coastal Hwy (24 hours' notice required).

Bicycles can be rented from **Kalbarri Backpackers** (☎ 08-9937 1430; cnr Woods & Mortimer Sts) or the **Entertainment Centre** (☎ 08-9937 1105; Porter St) for $10 a day.

SHARK BAY AREA

This 130km detour off the highway takes you up the Peron Peninsula, which is surrounded by the captivating Shark Bay World Heritage & Marine Park with its spectacular beaches, important sea-grass beds, great fishing, ancient stromatolites and famously predictable dolphins of Monkey Mia. Among 16 endangered species in the area are dugongs (more than 10% of the world's population), loggerhead turtles, western barred bandicoots and banded hare wallabies (see also the boxed text 'Project Eden'; p918).

The first recorded landing on Australian soil by a European took place at Shark Bay in 1616 when Dutch explorer Dirk Hartog landed on the island that now bears his name, across the water from Shark Bay's main centre of Denham.

Overlander Roadhouse to Denham

Leaving the highway just past the Overlander Roadhouse, the first turn-off (about 27km along) takes you to **Hamelin Pool**, a marine reserve containing the world's best-known colony of **stromatolites**. These microbes are almost identical to organisms that existed 1900 million years ago and evolved into more complex life. They are extremely fragile, so there's a boardwalk that allows you to view them without causing further harm; it's best to visit at low tide when they're not completely submerged.

Information on the stromatolites forms part of the display in the nearby 1884 **Telegraph Station** (☎ 08-9942 5905; adult/child $6/3; ⏲ 8.30am-5.30pm), which served as a telephone exchange until 1977. Food and basic **camp/caravan sites** ($14/17) are also available.

Another 35km along is the turn-off to **Nanga Bay Holiday Resort** (☎ 08-9948 3992; nangabay@wn.com.au; camp/caravan sites $14/18, dm from $13, 2-bed cabins $50, motel/unit d $95/100; ☒), on a working sheep station, is a peaceful place with a broad range of accommodation and good facilities, including a pool, tennis courts, spa, shop, bar and restaurant. However, it's pretty isolated and caters mainly to families, fishing fans and grey nomads.

Just 5km away, the cockleshells at stunning **Shell Beach** are 10m deep in some places and in the past were used as building materials. The water is only knee-deep for at least 100m out, and the 'hypersalinity' of the whole bay is evident here – as you'll find out if you accidentally swallow some. There are superb cliff-top views at **Eagle Bluff**, halfway between Nanga and Denham.

Denham

☎ 08 / pop 1140

The most westerly town in Australia, Denham was established as a pearling port, but tourism is the main breadwinner today. A remarkably unspoilt little place, it is a convenient base for visiting Monkey Mia, 26km away.

Almost all visitor facilities are on Knight Tce, across from the pale-green waters of the bay. Staff at the privately run Shark Bay **visitors centre** (☎ 9948 1253; bayjet@wn.com.au; 71 Knight Tce; ⏲ 8am-5pm) are most friendly and can book tours (there's Internet access here). The **CALM office** (☎ 9948 1208; Knight Tce; ⏲ 9am-5pm) has plenty of information on the World Heritage area. There is a post office on Knight Tce and an ATM at Heritage Resort.

On the way into town, **Ocean Park** (☎ 9948 1765; www.oceanpark.com.au; Denham Hamelin Rd; adult/child $5/3; ⏲ noon-5pm) is a locally run aquaculture farm featuring an artificial lagoon

stocked with sharks, pink snapper, turtles and stingrays – they're fed every afternoon. An oceanarium and touch pool are under construction.

A couple of kilometres down the road to Monkey Mia is the shallow and picturesque **Little Lagoon**; you can walk there from the corner of Francis Rd and Stella Rowley Dr. The huge **wind turbines** west of Denham provide over half of the town's electricity.

TOURS
Shark Bay is spectacular from the air, and **Shark Bay Air Charter** (☎ 9948 1773; www.ozpal.com /sharkbayair; tours $45-250) has four tours of the region, including a full-day extravaganza that takes in Dirk Hartog Island, Zuytdorp Cliffs, Useless Loop and François Péron National Park.

Majestic Tours (☎/fax 9948 1627; www.ozpal.com /majestic) has full-day 4WD tours into François Péron National Park ($110), Hamelin Pool and Shell Beach ($110), and just Shell Beach ($60). **Shark Bay Coaches & Tours** (☎ 9948 1081) has similar day tours from $40.

A great option is to charter a boat for fishing or a cruise around the coast. Prices start at $90/150 for a half/full day and operators include **Sportfishing Safaris** (☎ 9948 1846) and the **Woomerangee** (☎ 9948 1185).

SLEEPING & EATING
There's accommodation for all budgets here.

Seaside Tourist Village (☎ 1300 133 733, 9948 1242; http://sharkbayfun.com; Knight Tce; camp/caravan sites $18/21, cabin d without/with bathroom $45/80) A large caravan park on the foreshore, it has good facilities, friendly staff and tidy aircon cabins overlooking the sea.

Bay Lodge (☎ 1800 812 780, 9948 1278; baylodge@wn .com.au; 95 Knight Tce; dm $19, d & tw $50, unit d from $110; 🖳) Across from the beach, this YHA hostel is very well set up. Three-room bungalows have their own kitchen and bathroom, there's a good pool and barbecue area, and a free daily bus to Monkey Mia.

Shark Bay Holiday Cottages (☎/fax 1800 681 777, 9948 1206; www.sharkbaycottages.com.au; 3-13 Knight Tce; 1-/2-/3-bedroom cottages $80/90/115) These cottages are nothing flash, but they're fully self-contained, which makes them good value. Boats can also be hired here.

Heritage Resort (☎ 9948 1133; www.heritage resort.net.au; cnr Knight Tce & Durlacher St; d from $120;

🅇 🖳) Denham's upmarket option offers very spacious rooms with king-size beds and balconies overlooking the beach, plus a decent pool. It discounts heavily when things are slow.

Heritage Resort Bistro (☎ 9948 1171; cnr Knight Tce & Durlacher St; mains $12-26, Fri night buffet $20, Sun night carvery $15) Within the Heritage Resort, this bar attracts a more upmarket crowd than the local pub.

Shark Bay Hotel (☎ 9948 1203; 43 Knight Tce; mains $15-21) This is a convivial place with a reasonable seafood and steak menu, plus pool tables and a jukebox.

Old Pearler Restaurant (☎ 9948 1373; Knight Tce; lunch $6-15, dinner mains $20-30) A cosy place built from Hamelin Pool shell blocks, it has good-value lunches, and a rather more-expensive seafood-based evening menu.

There are also supermarkets, a bakery and takeaways along Knight Tce.

GETTING THERE & AWAY
Skywest (☎ 1300 660 088) has flights from Geraldton and Carnarvon, linking to Perth, Exmouth and Karratha.

There are daily shuttle buses ($30, 1½ hours) from Denham and Monkey Mia that connect with the north- and southbound **McCafferty's/Greyhound** (☎ 13 20 30) services at the Overlander Roadhouse on the main highway. **Integrity** (☎ 9226 1339; www .integritycoachlines.com.au) offers similar services twice weekly.

Bay Lodge (☎ 9948 1278) also runs a daily shuttle bus to Monkey Mia ($16 return for nonguests) that leaves from the Shell service station on Knight Tce at 7.45am, returning from Monkey Mia at 4.30pm; bookings are essential.

François Péron National Park
About 4km from Denham on the Monkey Mia Rd is the turn-off to the wild **François Péron National Park** (admission per bus passenger/car $4/9), renowned for its untouched beaches, dramatic cliffs, salt lakes and rare marsupial species (see the boxed text 'Project Eden'; p918). There's a visitors centre at the old Peron Homestead, 6km from the main road, where a former artesian bore has been converted to a soothing 35°C hot tub. **Camp sites** ($8) with limited facilities are at Big Lagoon, Gregories, Bottle Bay, Capre Peron and Herald Bight.

PROJECT EDEN

Degraded by decades of poor farming practices and infested with feral foxes, cats, goats and rabbits, only 10 years ago Peron Peninsula was an ecological basket case – its sorry record including the loss of 12 out of 18 species of once-common ground mammals. Today, however, the area is the subject of Australia's largest and most ambitious ecosystem regeneration programme, Project Eden.

Established in 1995, the CALM project is attempting to eradicate the feral animals, re-establish populations of endemic species and develop techniques that can be applied to other degraded arid zones in Australia. The key has been the isolation of the peninsula from mainland Australia with an electric fence at the isthmus, preventing feral species from repopulating, and most of the foxes and cats have been destroyed through baits and traps (although cat populations persist).

A breeding centre in François Péron National Park has collected breeding pairs of rare marsupials from the offshore Dorre and Bernier islands, as well as zoos and rehabilitation centres across Australia, and is breeding bilbies, rufous-hare wallabies, banded-hare wallabies, western barred bandicoots and woylies for release into the wild.

Although woylie and malleefowl populations appear to be surviving, the jury is still out on the chances of more vulnerable species like bilbies and bandicoots, although there seems cause for optimism. Many locals have become involved with the project, and there are plans to upgrade the access road to François Péron National Park and set up night-viewing positions for visitors. If you're interested in the project, Denham's **CALM office** (☎ 08-9948 1208; Knight Tce; ☼ 9am-5pm) has plenty of information and knowledgeable rangers.

The sandy road to the homestead is generally suitable only for 4WD vehicles; check conditions with **CALM** (☎ 08-9948 1208; Knight Tce; ☼ 9am-5pm) in Denham. See Tours (p917) for 4WD operators that go into the park.

Monkey Mia

A pleasant beach resort 26km northeast of Denham, **Monkey Mia** (adult/child/family $6/3/12) has become world-famous for the bottlenose dolphins that turn up like clockwork every day. It's so popular these days that the morning feeding session can be a bit of a circus, but you will get a good look at these attractive creatures. Always observe the rules of behaviour outlined in your entry brochure; in particular don't touch the dolphins, as they can contract viruses from humans, and always follow the ranger's instructions. There is a swimming area next to the interaction zone. If a dolphin joins you, let it swim around you while you stay still – never chase or approach a dolphin, as it may cause it distress, particularly if it's accompanied by a calf.

The **Dolphin Information Centre** (☎ 08-9948 1366; ☼ 7.30am-4pm), near the beach viewing area, has lots of information on dolphins, including a 45-minute video and occasional evening talks by wildlife researchers.

TOURS

In truth, the wildlife tours through the shallow, crystal-clear waters are far more rewarding than the crowded 'dolphin interaction experience'.

Shotover (☎ 1800 241 481, 08-9948 1481; www.monkeymiawildsights.com.au), a former ocean-racing catamaran, offers a range of short wildlife cruises ($35 to $55) where you'll see dugongs, dolphins, turtles and, in summer, tiger sharks and sea snakes. There's also an underwater microphone to eavesdrop on the dolphins.

Aristocat II (☎ 08-9948 1446; www.monkey-mia.net) is a licensed, luxury catamaran with underwater windows and disabled access. It offers similar cruises to *Shotover*, as well as a full-day Cape Peron jaunt (from $120, on demand). The sunset cruise ($45) is a great way to unwind with a drink.

SLEEPING & EATING

Monkey Mia is not a town, but simply the resort and beachfront. It offers a good range of accommodation, which is reasonably priced considering it's the only show in town. The same cannot be said for the eateries, so if you're on a tight budget consider bringing your own food.

Monkey Mia Dolphin Resort (☎ 1800 653 611, 08-9948 1320; www.monkeymia.com.au; camp/caravan sites

$18/25, backpacker caravan beds $19, on-site vans from $39, canvas condos $85, cabins $90, motel r from $170) This is a bustling, compact resort and in peak season there's a definite lack of elbowroom. The top-end accommodation is not great value, but there are bargains to be had in the park homes and canvas condos, which each have one double and four bunk beds. Only the park homes have cooking facilities, so the campers kitchen can get incredibly busy.

Bough Shed Restaurant & Cocktail Bar (breakfast $5-13, lunch $8-18, dinner mains $28-33) A great setting overlooking the beach is spoilt by the poor-value meals, although the Mod Oz menu is interesting enough. The bar sells the resort's only booze (no takeaways). Nearby Peron Cafe has burgers and sandwiches ($6 to $11) and there's also a grocery shop.

GETTING THERE & AWAY
The only public transport to Monkey Mia from Denham is the Bay Lodge shuttle (see Getting There & Away; p917). It requires you to spend a full day here, but that's no hardship if you tie in a cruise or simply bring a towel and book for some serious lazing about.

CARNARVON
☎ 08 / pop 6900
At the mouth of the Gascoyne River, Carnarvon is a sleepy town with only a few minor attractions, although it's a useful stopover point between Denham and Exmouth, and has some fruit-picking work in season.

Carnarvon **visitors centre** (☎ 9941 1146; www.outbackcoast.com; Civic Centre, 11 Robinson St; ☼ 9am-5pm Mon-Fri, 9am-noon Sat) has information on the town and region. There's a post office on Camel Lane, a couple of ATMs on Robinson St and you can go online at **Gascoyne Photographics** (☎ 9941 3366; 24 Robinson St) or **Carnarvon Backpackers** (☎ 9941 1095; 97 Olivia Tce). **Wise Owl Book Exchange** (Babbage Island Rd) has a large selection of second-hand books.

Sights & Activities
You can catch a restored **steam train** (adult/child $5/2.50) from the end of the town footbridge to the **Historic Precinct**, and another along **One Mile Jetty**, where locals fish for mulloway; you can also walk the jetty's length ($2). Also in the precinct is the **Lighthouse Keeper's Cottage Museum** (admission by donation; ☼ 10am-4pm daily Apr-Nov, Sat & Sun Dec-

Mar) with a small collection of pioneer and railway artefacts.

Tours
Many of the local fruit plantations can be visited on day tours; the visitors centre has details. Also recommended:

Carnarvon Bus Charter (☎ 9941 8336) Half-day tours around town (adult/child $28/17, Monday to Friday) and an all-day tour incorporating Lake Macleod, Cape Cuvier, the Korean Star wreck and blowholes ($50/40, Wednesday).

Stockman Safaris (☎ 9941 2421; stockmansafariss@ wn.com.au) 4WD bush-experience tours to surrounding stations and the Kennedy Ranges. Prices range from $130 for one day to $600 for three days.

Sleeping
Gascoyne Hotel (☎ 9941 1412; 88 Olivia Tce; s/d/tw $65/80/85; ✲) The motel rooms at this attractive old pub are pretty good value, while the attached Good Paddock restaurant serves seafood and steak in a pleasant outdoor area.

Outcamp (☎ 9941 2421; 139 Olivia Tce; s/d $80/120; ✲) Right on the water, and a short walk to town, this spotless, welcoming B&B is run by the owners of Stockman Safaris, with tour discounts available for guests.

Carnarvon Backpackers (☎/fax 9941 1095; 97 Olivia Tce; dm around $20, tw $50; ✲ 🖳) A no-frills place that caters for long-term as well as short-stay travellers, it has good-sized common areas, local tours, Internet access and barbecues.

Carnarvon Tourist Centre Caravan Park (☎ 9941 1438; 108 Robinson St; camp/caravan sites $15/17, on-site van d $34-60, unit d $50-70; ✲) Well tended and close to town, the units here are clean and simple, but offer good value, and there's plenty of shade.

Eating
Old Post Office Cafe (☎ 9941 1800; 10 Robinson St; pizzas $15-23; ☼ 5-10pm Tue-Sat) Good pizza, a small selection of pasta dishes ($11) and fine gelati make this a great spot for a casual meal. It's both licensed and BYO, and the veranda tables fronting the main street are just the job on a steamy night.

Sails Restaurant (☎ 9941 1600; West St; mains $16-28) At the Hospitality Inn, Sails is reputedly the best of the motel restaurants. Its seafood-dominated menu has plenty of tropical fruit flourishes.

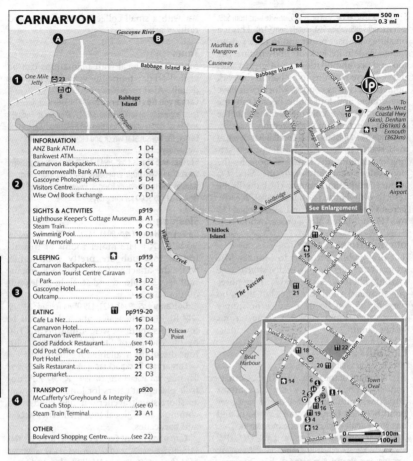

CARNARVON

0 ─────── 500 m
0 ─────── 0.3 mi

INFORMATION	
ANZ Bank ATM	1 D4
Bankwest ATM	2 D4
Carnarvon Backpackers	3 C4
Commonwealth Bank ATM	4 C4
Gascoyne Photographics	5 D4
Visitors Centre	6 D4
Wise Owl Book Exchange	7 D1

SIGHTS & ACTIVITIES	p919
Lighthouse Keeper's Cottage Museum	8 A1
Steam Train	9 C2
Swimming Pool	10 D1
War Memorial	11 D4

SLEEPING	p919
Carnarvon Backpackers	12 C4
Carnarvon Tourist Centre Caravan Park	13 D2
Gascoyne Hotel	14 C4
Outcamp	15 C3

EATING	pp919-20
Cafe La Nez	16 D4
Carnarvon Hotel	17 D2
Carnarvon Tavern	18 C3
Good Paddock Restaurant	(see 14)
Old Post Office Cafe	19 D4
Port Hotel	20 D4
Sails Restaurant	21 C3
Supermarket	22 D3

TRANSPORT	p920
McCafferty's/Greyhound & Integrity Coach Stop	(see 6)
Steam Train Terminal	23 A1

OTHER	
Boulevard Shopping Centre	(see 22)

Cafe La Nez (☎ 9941 1252; 16 Robinson St; light meals $6-9; ☽ breakfast & lunch Mon-Fri, dinner Fri) On the main drag, this is a good little café with outdoor seating, juices, focaccia, wraps and salads, plus coffee and cake.

All the pubs serve standard counter meals. **Carnarvon Tavern** (☎ 9941 1431; 8 Camel Lane), **Port Hotel** (☎ 9941 1704; Robinson St) and **Carnarvon Hotel** (☎ 9941 1181; 28 Olivia Tce) all have meals in the $10 to $20 range.

There's a supermarket and a couple of takeaways in the Boulevard shopping centre.

Getting There & Around

Skywest (☎ 1300 660 088) flies to Perth daily, and has less frequent flights to Denham

and Exmouth, with links to Geraldton and Karratha.

Daily **McCafferty's/Greyhound** (☎ 13 20 30) buses to Perth ($110, 13 hours) and Broome ($260, 20 hours), via Port Hedland ($140, 12 hours), stop at the visitors centre. **Integrity** (☎ 9226 1339; www.integritycoachlines.com.au) has two weekly services to Broome and four to Perth for similar rates.

GASCOYNE AREA

Good beaches south of Carnarvon include **Eundoo Creek** (turn-off 20km down the North-West Coastal Hwy), and **Bush Bay** and **New Beach** (turn-off 37km south of Carnarvon); all are accessed via reasonable dirt roads.

WESTERN AUSTRALIA

Heading north, it's a fair detour to the frenzied **blowholes**, 49km off the main highway, but they are worth a look, as is the desolate, windswept coastline. Keep a sharp eye on the ocean, as people have been killed by king waves here. Around 7km to the north, the **HMAS Sydney Memorial** commemorates the ship sunk here by the German raider *Kormoran* in 1941. Another couple of kilometres brings you to **Quobba Station** (☎ /fax 08-9941 2036; www.quobba.com.au; camp/caravan sites $16/18, fishing shack/chalet d from $38/80), an attractive ocean-front property with plenty of basic accommodation, a shop and legendary fishing.

Remote Gascoyne Junction, 177km east of Carnarvon on a good unsealed road, is in the gemstone-rich **Kennedy Range**. The classic old **Junction Hotel** (☎ 08-9943 0504; fax 9943 0564; s/d $25/60) has reasonable self-contained double rooms and a friendly front bar. From here, the adventurous can continue northeast another 300km to Mt Augustus (Burringurrah) National Park to see **Mt Augustus**, the biggest – but certainly not the most memorable – rock in the world. It has Aboriginal rock paintings and can be climbed in a day.

Mt Augustus Outback Tourist Resort (☎ 08-9943 0527; camp/caravan sites $18/22, motel d $70, units $165) is right at the base of Mt Augustus and has good facilities and a licensed restaurant. Around 50km to the west, the century-old **Cobra Station** (☎ 08-9943 0565; www.farmstaywa.com/north/cobra.htm; camp sites $12, s/d $55/70, unit s/d $70/95) offers limited supplies, fuel and meals (dinner and breakfast), plus sunset tours of the mountain.

CORAL COAST & PILBARA

The Coral Coast extends from Coral Bay to Onslow and takes in the magnificent Ningaloo Marine Park, arguably WA's greatest and most precious natural attraction. The world's largest west-coast reef, Ningaloo rivals the Great Barrier Reef in beauty and biodiversity, is far more accessible and doesn't get anything like the tourist numbers of its east-coast counterpart. Running alongside the reef on the North-West Cape, rugged Cape Range National Park

has several beautiful beaches and attractive gorges.

The Pilbara, composed of the world's oldest rocks, is an ancient, arid region with a glut of natural wonders. It stretches along the coast from Onslow to Port Hedland and inland beyond the superb Millstream-Chichester National Park. It takes in several rough-and-ready mining towns where tours of huge industrial complexes are heavily promoted – if you're into big machinery this is the place for you.

Getting There & Away

Skywest (☎ 1300 660 088) has daily flights from Perth to Exmouth (sometimes via Carnarvon) and on to Karratha.

McCafferty's/Greyhound (☎ 13 20 30) has three services a week from Perth to Exmouth ($180, 19¾ hours), via Coral Bay ($180, 18¼ hours). There are also daily services from Perth (with connecting shuttles into Exmouth) stopping at Karratha ($175, 22½ hours) and Port Hedland ($210, 25½ hours). Fares from Broome include Port Hedland ($90, 7½ hours), Karratha ($180, 11½ hours) and Exmouth turn-off ($250, 15½ hours). **Integrity** (☎ 08-9226 1339; www.integritycoachlines.com.au) also has two weekly services in each direction.

NINGALOO MARINE PARK

From Amherst Point in the southwest to Bundegi Reef in the northeast, stunning Ningaloo Reef stretches more than 250km along North-West Cape Peninsula and is protected within the boundaries of Ningaloo Marine Park. The reef is amazingly accessible, lying only 100m offshore from some parts of the peninsula, and is home to a staggering variety of marine life. Over 220 species of coral have been recorded in the waters, ranging from the slow-growing bommies to delicate branching varieties, and for eight or nine nights after the full moon in March there is a synchronised mass spawning of coral, with a soup of eggs and sperm being released into the water.

It's this coral that attracts the park's most popular visitor, the underwater giant *Rhiniodon typus*, otherwise known as the whale shark. Ningaloo is the only place in the world where these creatures reliably appear each year, making it a mecca for marine biologists and visitors alike. The largest fish

WESTERN AUSTRALIA

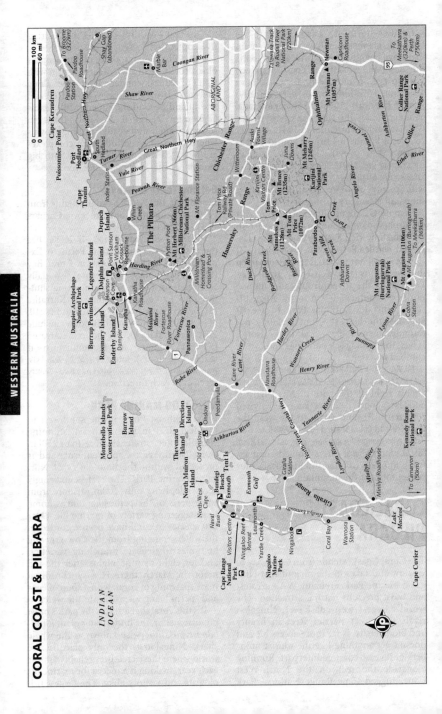

CORAL COAST & PILBARA

WESTERN AUSTRALIA

INDIAN OCEAN

in the world, it can weigh up to 21 tonnes, although most weigh between 13 and 15 tonnes, and reach up to 18m long, but this gentle giant is content to feed on plankton and small fish. There are also more than 500 species of fish, plus sharks, enormous manta rays, humpback whales, turtles and dugongs. Even if the whale sharks aren't about when you visit, there's always something fabulous to see here:

March–May Coral spawning.
March–June Whale sharks.
June–November Manta rays.
June/July and October/November Humpback whales.
November–March Turtle nesting and hatching.

The area's two centres are beautiful Coral Bay (the only settlement on the park's coastline) and the less beautiful Exmouth, a further 140km to the northeast on the continental side of the peninsula. If you only want to see the reef, there's little to be gained in venturing beyond Coral Bay – it's right on the water and has a more pleasant atmosphere than Exmouth. However, the western side of the peninsula beyond Exmouth has a string of superb beaches, many with small camping grounds right on the water. It helps to be independently mobile, but there is a bus service there (p927).

For more information on the park, contact **CALM** (☎ 08-99949 1676; 22 Nimitz St) in Exmouth, which has the excellent pamphlet *Parks of the Coral Coast*.

Whale Shark Tours

While there are all sorts of tours on offer, swimming with a whale shark is what most people are here for. Full-day whale shark tours cost around $320 and operate out of both Exmouth (up to eight boats) and Coral Bay (two boats). There's not much between them – Exmouth operators have shorter travel times and also adhere to a 'no sighting policy' (ie you can go on the next available trip if a whale shark isn't spotted), but Coral Bay operators have a higher encounter rate and you don't have to battle seven other boats and scores of people to reach a shark. All use spotter planes, and the price generally includes snorkelling gear, wetsuit, food and park fees. Outside the whale shark season, half-day manta ray tours are a pretty good substitute and cost around $115, including snorkelling gear, wetsuit and snacks. You

need to be a capable swimmer to get the most out of either experience.

Most operators also offer dive trips ($65 to $120) and courses (around $360 for PADI Open Water Certificates, plus medical), although conservation laws prevent you from diving with the whale sharks. Snorkelling equipment is available for around $8/15 per half/full day and it's possible to 'snuba' dive using an air hose for $40 per person.

Good dive spots include the **Labyrinth** and **Blizzard Ridge** in Lighthouse Bay, the **Navy Pier** near Bundegi Beach (one of Australia's top dive sites) and the **Muiron Islands**, 10km northeast of the cape. The last is a breeding sanctuary for green, loggerhead and hawksbill turtles.

Recommended dive operators:

Coral Bay Adventures (☎ 08-9942 5955; www.coral bayadventures.com.au; Coral Bay)

Exmouth Diving Centre (☎ 08-9949 1201; www .exmouthdiving.com.au; Exmouth)

Ningaloo Blue (☎ 1800 811 338, 08-9949 1119; www .ningalooblue.com.au; Exmouth)

Ningaloo Reef Dive (☎ 08-9942 5824; www.ningaloo reefdive.com; Coral Bay)

Three Islands Marine (☎ 08-9949 1994; www.whale sharkdive.com; Exmouth)

There are plenty of other water- and land-based tours available in the area; for details see Tours under Coral Bay (p927) and Exmouth (p925), and Cape Range National Park (p926).

CORAL BAY

☎ 08 / pop 120

At the southern end of Ningaloo Marine Park, this is a tiny, chilled-out resort on the edge of a picturesque bay with stunning beaches. Coral reefs lie just off the town beach, making it brilliant for snorkelling, swimming and sunbaking, and it's a good base for outer reef and wildlife-spotting trips.

Coral Bay's beauty and position has attracted the cold gaze of developers in the past few years, and a recent proposal to build a colossal marine, resort and residential complex at Point Maud attracted vociferous opposition from across the political spectrum. Just before this book went to press, WA Premier Dr Geoff Gallop rejected the proposal and said 'World Heritage', but flagged the future release of

WESTERN AUSTRALIA

a 'land use and tourism plan' for the whole area, so the fight may continue for a while yet (see www.save-ningaloo.org for details of the campaign).

There's no visitors centre in Coral Bay, but there are plenty of booking offices that can give you information. Coral Bay's two small shopping centres have supermarkets with Eftpos facilities, while Internet access is available at **Fins Cafe** (☎ 9942 5900) and **Club Ningaloo** (☎ 9948 5100).

The beach is the main focus of activity and there are many water-based activities on offer. You can hire snorkels ($13 per day), boogie boards ($6 per hour) and glass-bottomed canoes ($17 per hour) from the caravan on the beach.

For transport information see Getting There & Away (p921).

Tours

Glass Bottom Boats (☎ 9942 5885) and **Sub-Sea Explorer** (☎ 9942 5955) allow you to see beneath the waves without getting wet ($25/15 per adult/child, 1 hour); the latter also has a coral-viewing and snorkelling cruise ($35/18, 2 hours). **Coral Bay Adventures** (☎ 9942 5955) also offers scenic flights over Ningaloo Reef (from $50 for 30 minutes). **ATV Eco Tours** (☎ 9942 5873) and **Kim's Quad Treks** (☎ 9948 5190) have a range of self-drive quad bike tours around the bay, including snorkelling ($70) and sunset ($60) tours.

Sleeping & Eating

Despite the addition of a spiffing hostel, accommodation in Coral Bay remains pleasantly limited and you'll need to book ahead during school holidays.

Ningaloo Reef Resort (☎ 9942 5934; www.coralbay .org/resort.htm; dm $15, motel s/d $120/140, unit s/d $145/ 175, extra person $11; 🏊) Right on the beach, this place is that most rare of beasts – a decent resort. Laid-back, comfortable and well appointed, it has several levels of accommodation, including self-contained units, plus the town pub, bottle shop, swimming pool and great views.

Shades Restaurant (☎ 9942 5863; takeaways $7-12, dinner mains $17-28) At Ningaloo Reef Resort, Shades is licensed with takeaway food during the day and upmarket bistro meals for dinner (bookings essential).

Club Ningaloo (☎ 9948 5100; dm $18-23, d & tw $60-65, with bathroom $80-85; 🏊 🖥) This

excellent, purpose-built hostel opened in mid 2002 and boasts a great central pool, lockable cabinets in the dorms (four or 10 beds), a pool-side bar area, free movie nights and a well-equipped kitchen. You can pay a premium for air-con, which is worth it in high summer. The major bus lines stop here.

Peoples Park Caravan Village (☎ 9942 5933; camp/caravan sites $20/22; cabin d $100) This is a small, attractive park with lush lawns close to the beach. It's dearer than its older rival, **Bayview Holiday Village** (☎ 9385 7411) but far nicer.

Reef Cafe (☎ 9942 5882; Bayview Holiday Village; pizzas $8-19) opens nightly to dole out tasty pizzas, while **Fins Cafe** (☎ 9942 5900; mains $18-28; 🖥), in the shopping centre, opens early and has good-value brekkies and lunches to offset the up-market seafood menu at night. There's also plenty of shade and a decent cup of coffee.

A bakery and supermarket are in the shopping centre, but prices are high. If you're self-catering, stock up in Karratha, Carnarvon or Exmouth.

EXMOUTH
☎ 08 / pop 2500

Established in 1967 to serve the nearby naval communications base, Exmouth today is a creature of tourism and offers plenty of accommodation and tours, although there's little to do in town itself. The action is on the western side of the peninsula (p926).

Information

Exmouth **visitors centre** (☎ 1800 287 328, 9949 1176; www.exmouth-australia.com; Murat Rd; 🕙 8.30am-5pm) has plenty of information, including accommodation lists, while **CALM** (☎ 9949 1676; 22 Nimitz St; 🕙 8am-5pm Mon-Fri) can supply maps and guides to the national park. **Blue's Internet Café** (☎ 9949 1119; cnr Kennedy & Thew Sts; 🕙 9am-7pm) offers Internet access. The post office is on Maidstone Cres, as is the Challenge Bank ATM, while **D&A Hire Bookshop** (☎ 9949 1425; cnr Murat Rd & Pellew St; 🕙 10am-5pm Tue-Fri, 10am-1pm Sat & Sun) has a good selection of second-hand books.

Sights & Activities

There's not that much to do in Exmouth, but there are good beaches within cycling

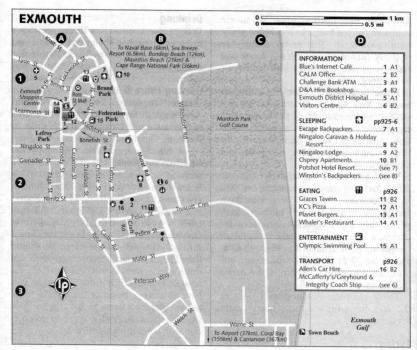

EXMOUTH

0 — 1 km
0 — 0.5 mi

INFORMATION	
Blue's Internet Café	1 A1
CALM Office	2 B2
Challenge Bank ATM	3 A1
D&A Hire Bookshop	4 B2
Exmouth District Hospital	5 A1
Visitors Centre	6 B2

SLEEPING 🛏	pp925-6
Excape Backpackers	7 A1
Ningaloo Caravan & Holiday Resort	8 B2
Ningaloo Lodge	9 A2
Osprey Apartments	10 B1
Potshot Hotel Resort	(see 7)
Winston's Backpackers	(see 8)

EATING 🍽	p926
Graces Tavern	11 B2
KC's Pizza	12 A1
Planet Burgers	13 A1
Whaler's Restaurant	14 A1

ENTERTAINMENT 🎭	
Olympic Swimming Pool	15 A1

TRANSPORT	p926
Allen's Car Hire	16 B2
McCafferty's/Greyhound and Integrity Coach Stop	(see 6)

WESTERN AUSTRALIA

or driving distance. **Town Beach** is OK, but **Bundegi Beach**, 12km north, is more attractive and has a licensed kiosk for sunset drinks, while clothing-optional **Mauritius Beach**, 21km from Exmouth near Vlamingh Head Lighthouse, is also popular.

Tours

Apart from Ningaloo Marine Park cruises and dives (p923), tours from Exmouth include gulf and gorge safaris and some other water-based options:

Capricorn Kayak Tours (☎ 1800 625 688, 9949 4431; www.capricornkayak.com.au) A range of coastal and camping tours between late March and November, including a sunset barbecue (adult/child $55/45), full day ($130/105) and overnight ($345/275) options.

Neil McLeod's Ningaloo Safari Tours (☎ 9949 1550; www.ningaloosafari.com) Well-regarded, full-day ($145/105 per adult/child) and half-day ($65/50) trips through Ningaloo Reef, Cape Range National Park and Vlamingh Head. Sunset turtle tour ($40/30) between November and March.

Ningaloo Coral Explorer (☎ 9949 1893) Two-hour coral-viewing and snorkelling tour at 2pm daily from Bundegi Beach (adult/child $35/16).

There are plenty of **fishing charters** and **whale watching tours** available, plus **camel treks, quad bike tours** and **surfing lessons**; see the visitors centre for details.

Sleeping

High-season (April to October) prices are quoted here; you can expect good discounts at other times.

Ningaloo Lodge (☎ 1800 880 949, 9949 4949; www.ningaloolodge.com.au; Lefroy St; d & tw $90; 🗷) With motel-style rooms, a huge communal kitchen, barbecue, TV room and pool, Ningaloo Lodge offers the best-value mid-range accommodation in town.

Osprey Apartments (☎ 9949 1200; www.pot shot resort.com; Murat Rd; 2-/3-bedroom units $175/195, d with spa $210, extra adult $12; 🗷) Operated by the Potshot Hostel Resort across the road, these luxury, self-contained apartments are Exmouth's best, with good-sized living spaces, private outdoor areas and modern kitchens. They sleep four or five adults and discounted weekly rates are available.

Sea Breeze Resort (☎ 13 17 79, 9949 1800; www.bestwestern.com.au; s/d $125/130; 🗷) Out at the

naval base, 6km north of town, Sea Breeze is in a converted barracks block, but you'd hardly know it. The motel rooms are stylishly furnished and there's a bar and restaurant, plus guests are able to use the base's pool.

Potshot Hotel Resort (☎ 9949 1200; www.potshot resort.com; Murat Rd; dm/s $19/50, d & tw $55, motel s/d $75/85, apt d from $140; ❂ ▣) This sprawling resort offers several levels of accommodation (including Excape Backpackers), plus two restaurants, four bars, two pools and a bottle shop.

Ningaloo Caravan & Holiday Resort (☎ 1800 652 665, 9949 2377; reception@exmouthresort.com; Murat Rd; camp/caravan sites $21/26, 1-/2-/3-bedroom chalets from $95/135/145; ❂) The best of the caravan parks, this shady resort has modern facilities, a café, dive shop, bike hire and an enormous pool. Attached is **Winston's Backpackers** (dm $19, d & tw $55; ▣) with reasonable four-bed dorms and the run of the park's facilities.

There are plenty of holiday homes in the area for rent; see the visitors centre for details.

Eating

Whaler's Restaurant (☎ 9949 2416; 5 Kennedy St; mains $14-25; ❂ lunch daily, dinner Tue-Sun) Also open for brekkie in summer, Whaler's is licensed and BYO, has a shady veranda and a Mod Oz menu that includes heaps of seafood.

Graces Tavern (☎ 9949 1000; Murat Rd; mains $19-26; ▣) A friendly place with a large dining room, a seafood-based bistro menu, jukeboxes, pool tables and Internet access, Graces gets very busy and also offers backpacker specials (around $10).

KC's Pizza (☎ 9949 1244; Exmouth shopping centre; pizzas $14-19; ❂ dinner Tue-Sun) A decent selection of pizza is available here, including tempting gourmet combinations. Delivery to your room is free.

Planet Burgers (Maidstone Cres; takeaways $7-10; ❂ dinner Wed-Sun in the high season) Offering standard burgers and kebabs from a van, this is a good budget option.

There's also a café, bakery and Chinese restaurant at Exmouth shopping centre, along with two supermarkets. There are two restaurants at **Potshot Hotel Resort** (☎ 9949 1200; Murat Rd; mains $16-24) and the very good **Sailfish Restaurant** (☎ 13 17 79, 9949 1800; mains $15-24) at Sea Breeze Resort.

Drinking

Potshot Hotel and Graces Tavern are town's main watering holes, and put on DJs and the occasional band. Sea Breeze Resort also has its own bar.

Getting There & Away

Exmouth airport is 37km south of town and there are daily **Skywest** (☎ 1300 660 088) flights to Karratha and Carnarvon, with links to Denham, Geraldton and Perth.

All buses stop at the visitors centre. **McCafferty's/Greyhound** (☎ 13 20 30) has three services a week from Perth ($180, 19¾ hours), via Kalbarri ($150, 10½ hours), Overlander (for Denham; $112, 8 hours) and Coral Bay ($165, 15½ hours). Alternatively, you can hop off the daily McCafferty's/Greyhound Perth–Darwin bus at the Giralia turn-off and pick up the Exmouth shuttle there ($60, 1¾ hours). From Exmouth there's three weekly services to Coral Bay ($65, 1¾ hours). Going north from Exmouth, you have to change buses at the Giralia turn-off. **Integrity Coach Lines** (☎ 9226 1339) has four weekly services to Perth and two to Broome, also with connecting shuttles.

Getting Around

The **Airport Shuttle Bus** (☎ 9949 1101; adult/child $17/11) meets all flights; reservations are required for a ride back to the airport.

There are several car-hire outfits in town, including **Allens** (☎ 9949 2403; Nimitz St), which charges from $35/55 per day for second-hand/new cars.

Excape Backpackers (☎ 9949 1200; Murat Rd) within the Potshot Hotel Resort offers free use of bikes, although those at **Ningaloo Caravan & Holiday Resort** (half/full day $5.50/9) are in better shape.

For transport options to the peninsula's west coast see Getting There & Away (p927).

CAPE RANGE NATIONAL PARK

This 510-sq-km park runs down the west coast of the peninsula and includes a variety of flora and fauna, rugged scenery, several gorges (the Shothole, Charles Knife and Yardie Creek) plus Owl's Roost Cave. The highlight, however, is the sensational swimming and snorkelling available off every beach (also see Sights & Activities; p924).

The modern and informative Milyering **visitors centre** (☎ 08-9949 2808; ⏰ 10am-4pm) houses a comprehensive display of the area's natural and cultural history, and has useful maps and publications.

From Tantabiddi at the northern end of the park, **Ningaloo Ecology Cruises** (☎ 08-9949 2255; www.ecology.com.au; adult child $35/10) has two-hour coral-viewing and snorkelling cruises; the price includes free transfers from Exmouth. In the park's far south, **Yardie Creek Tours** (☎ 08-9949 2659; adult/child $25/12) has good one-hour boat rides up this attractive, steep-sided gorge, where you'll see rare black-footed rock wallabies and lots of birdlife. It runs daily in school holidays and by appointment at other times.

One of the park's highlights is the **snorkel drift** at Turquoise Bay, 60km from Exmouth. Walk about 300m south of the beach side, then go about 30m to 50m into the water and allow the current to carry you across to the sand bar side of the bay while you admire the coral formations and fish below. Make sure you get out at the sand bar – and watch out for strong currents near the gap in the reef.

Those in 4WDs can continue south to Coral Bay via the coast (check at the visitors centre that Yardie Creek is passable).

There are several compact **camping grounds** ($10 per night for 2 people) along the coast within the park. Facilities and shade are usually minimal, but most have pit toilets; good options include Ned's Camp, Mesa Camp, Lakeside and Osprey Bay. You'll need to book during school holidays.

Ningaloo Reef Retreat (☎ 1800 999 941, 08-9942 1776; www.ningalooreefretreat.com; swag s $135, wilderness tents $195) is a real getaway; this wilderness experience in the dunes near the entrance to Mandu Mandu Gorge Rd allows you to camp out in swags under the stars or in a more civilized safari tent. Rates include all food (cook yourself), Exmouth transfers, park fees, guided nature walks and snorkelling – take a sleeping bag. The Ningaloo Reef bus stops here; see below.

Getting There & Away

For those without transport, the **Ningaloo Reef bus** (☎ 1800 999 941) is the best way to get to and from the park. It leaves Exmouth shopping centre at 8.50am (daily April to October; Monday, Tuesday, Friday and Saturday only November to March) returning from Ningaloo Reef Retreat at 2pm. En route it stops at **Vlaming Head Lighthouse** ($6), **Tantabiddi** ($10), **Milyering** ($20), **Turquoise Bay** ($22) and **Mandu Mandu Gorge** ($30, including lunch at the Reef Retreat). You can also take a turtle snorkel ($50) or kayak and snorkel ($80) at the resort.

KARRATHA
☎ 08 / pop 9500

The commercial centre of the Pilbara region, Karratha (Good Country) developed alongside the Hamersley Iron and Woodside LNG projects in the 1960s and '70s. There's little to do in town, but the Millstream-Chichester National Park is nearby and there are also tours to the spectacular Karijini National Park (p905). Karratha **visitors centre** (☎ 9144 4600; info@tourist.karratha.com; Karratha Rd; ⏰ 8.30am-5pm Mon-Fri, 9am-4pm Sat & Sun, shorter hours Dec-Mar) and the **CALM office** (☎ 9143 1488; 3 Anderson Rd; 8am-5pm Mon-Fri) have information on the local area. You can go online at the visitors centre or **Karratha Central Hotel** (☎ 9143 9888; cnr Warambie & Searipple Rds).

Plenty of indigenous artefacts remain here, such as middens, carvings, grindstones and etchings. Some of WA's most shameful massacres took place in this area. The 3.5km **Jaburara Heritage Trail** starts by the visitors centre, has many rock drawings and good views over town. Pick up a copy of the *Jaburara Heritage Trail* leaflet ($2) and ensure you have stout shoes and plenty of water.

Practically a suburb of Karratha, **Dampier** (population 2000), 20km west on King Bay, overlooks the 41 islands of the Dampier Archipelago – a fishing mecca. It's also a Hamersley Iron town and the region's main port facility. Just to the north, **Burrup Peninsula** has some 10,000 Aboriginal rock engravings depicting fish, turtles, kangaroos and a Tasmanian tiger. The best place to see them is near **Hearson's Cove**, a fine swimming beach.

Tours

Snappy Gum Safaris (☎ 9185 2141; www.snappygum.karratha.com) has well-regarded trips to Karijini National Park (2/3 days $290/390), plus a three-day tour through Karijini and Millstream-Chichester National Parks ($390). **Nor-West Explorer Tours** (☎ 9144 4600) offers a day tour to Millstream-Chichester ($100).

AUSTRALIA'S NUCLEAR ISLANDS

The Montebello Islands, a group of about 100 flat, limestone islands 200km southwest of Dampier, have the dubious distinction of being the site of Britain's first nuclear tests in Australia. It was here, in 1952, that a bomb was loaded on to HMS *Plym*, which was anchored in Main Bay off Trimouille Island at the time (the crater in the seafloor is still detectable by sonar). Two more tests were carried out on Alpha and Trimouille Islands in 1956.

While some endemic species, including the spinifexbird and the black-and-white wren, haven't been seen on the archipelago since the tests, Mother Nature has shown some resilience, and these days the islands are a conservation park with thriving land and marine fauna, more than 100 plant species, plenty of sea birds and good fishing. The radiation warning signs remain, along with commemorative plaques, but the islands are considered safe to visit. The best way is to charter a boat from Dampier (see Tours; p927).

There are plenty of industrial tours, including **Dampier Salt** (adult/child $25/12), **Dampier Port** (adult/child $5/3) and **Northwest Shelf Gas Venture** (admission free). Most run weekdays from April to November and by appointment at other times. All can be booked through the visitors centre, and you can also arrange a **fishing charter** (from $90) through the beautiful Dampier Archipelago or Montebello Islands.

Sleeping & Eating

Like most mining towns, there are no accommodation bargains in Karratha, even in the low season.

Mercure Inn (☎ 9185 1155; www.accorhotels.com.au; Searipple Rd; d $120; 🌊) Probably the best-value of Karratha's motels, this is central, has a large pool, in-house movies and **Hearson's Bistro** (mains $16-30), a good steak and seafood place that's popular with the locals.

Karratha Backpackers (☎ 9144 4904; www.kisser .net.au/backpackers; 110 Wellard Way; dm/s/d $20/36/50; 🌊) This is a very basic hostel, with tired rooms surrounding a small courtyard. The kitchen is good, however, and there's coin-operated air-con, a TV room and tours of the Burrup Peninsula and regional attractions.

Pilbara Holiday Park (☎ 1800 451 855, 9185 1855; www.fleetwoodparks.com.au/parks/pilbara.htm; Rosemary Rd; camp/caravan sites $20/23, on-site van d $50, unit d from $80; 🌊) This is the most central of the area's parks, and offers renovated shower blocks, grassed camp sites, a campers kitchen, TV room and café.

Barnacle Bob's (☎ 9183 1053; The Esplanade, Dampier; mains $9-18) Overlooking Dampier Harbour, Bob's has great sunset views to go along with a good list of seafood dishes.

Other restaurant options are limited. **Jasmine Restaurant** (☎ 9185 2725; Balmoral Rd; mains $12-19) has reasonable Thai and Chinese dishes, while there are a couple of cafés and a supermarket in Karratha shopping centre.

Getting There & Around

Qantas (☎ 13 13 13) has direct daily flights from Perth, while **Skywest** (☎ 1300 660 088) goes via Exmouth and has links to Carnarvon, Denham and Geraldton. **Northwest Regional Airlines** (☎ 1300 136 629) has flights to Port Hedland and Broome three times a week.

McCafferty's/Greyhound (☎ 13 20 30) has daily services to Perth and Broome from the Shell Service Station on Searipple Rd. **Integrity** (☎ 9226 1339) has two services a week to Perth and Broome from the visitors centre.

ROEBOURNE AREA

Around 40km east of Karratha, **Roebourne** (population 970) is the oldest town in the Pilbara (1866) and home to a large Aboriginal community. Once a grazing and copper-mining centre, it has some fine old buildings, including the **Old Gaol** (☎ 08-9182 1060; Queen St; 🕙 9am-5pm Mon-Fri, 9am-4pm Sat & Sun, shorter hours Nov-Apr), which is now the visitors centre and museum, **Holy Trinity Church** (1894) and **Victoria Hotel** – the last of five original pubs.

Just west of Roebourne, the Point Sampson–Roebourne Rd heads north to Cossack and Point Samson. **Cossack**, at the mouth of the Harding River, was the district's main port from the mid- to late-19th century, but was supplanted by Point Samson and then abandoned. Today, however, its stout stone buildings (1870 to 1898) and riverside location have given it a new lease on life. Attractions include the **Courthouse Museum** (adult/child $2/1; 🕙 9am-4pm), which celebrates the town's halcyon days, and

Cheeditha Aboriginal Gallery (☎ 08-9182 1060; ☺ 9am-4pm) in the old Galbraiths Store. Beyond town, the pioneer cemetery has a tiny Japanese section dating from the days when Cossack was WA's first major pearl-fishing town. **Cossack Adventure Cruises** (☎ 08-9182 1060) offers a cruise up the mangrove-lined Harding River and out to Jarman Island ($75).

Point Samson (population 250) also had its day in the sun as the area's main port, before Dampier shouldered it aside. Today it's an attractive seaside town that buzzes with 4WDs, boats and fishing fans. There's good **snorkelling** off the Point Samson and Honeymoon Cove beaches.

Sleeping & Eating

Point Samson Lodge Resort (☎ 08-9187 1052; www .pointsamson.com; 56 Samson Rd; motel/apt d $140/160; ☒) Pristine and welcoming place with well-appointed rooms in tropical grounds. Its restaurant, **Ta Ta's** (mains $22-35), has a seafood menu and generous brekkies ($7 to $15).

Cossack Backpackers (☎ 08-9182 1190; dm $17, family room $39) In the atmospheric old police barracks, this is the place to chill out for a few days' swimming and reading. The rooms are clean and pleasant, and you'll need to bring your own food as the nearby **Cossack Café** (☎ 08-9182 1550; light meals $5-9) opens for lunch only. If you're arriving by bus, call ahead for a pick-up from Roebourne.

Solveig Caravan Park (☎ 08-9187 1414; Samson Rd, Samson Point; camp/caravan sites $12/15) This pocket-sized shady park is conveniently close to both the water and the tavern. Bookings are essential in school holidays.

Also at Samson Point, **Moby's Kitchen** (☎ 08-9187 1435; mains $4-11) has excellent takeaway fish and chips, while upstairs the slightly more upmarket **Trawler's Tavern** (☎ 08-9187 1414; mains $15-30) has sweeping views of the bay from its veranda – perfect for a sunset session.

MILLSTREAM-CHICHESTER NATIONAL PARK

Around 150km south of Roebourne, this 2000-sq-km park is well worth the detour. The permanent waterholes of the Fortescue River are the attractions here, creating cool, lush oases in the midst of stony plateaus and basalt ranges.

Millstream **visitors centre** (☎ 08-9184 5144; ☺ 8am-4pm) was once the homestead of a pastoral station and now has good information on the park's history, ecosystems and on its traditional owners, the Yinjibarndi people.

In the park's north, the captivating **Python Pool** is linked to Mt Herbert by the **Chichester Range Camel Trail** (8km one way, 3 hours). Further south, **Chinderwarriner Pool** and **Crossing Pool** are the highlights, featuring shady palms and lilies. Other walks in the park include the **Murlunmunyjurna Trail** (5km, 1½ hours return) and the **Mt Herbert Track** (600m, 45 minutes return). Pick up a map from the visitors centre.

There are basic **camp sites** (☎ 08-9184 5144; per person $5) at Snake Creek, Crossing Pool and Deep Reach Pool, which have fireplaces and pit toilets. Regular tours of the park leave from Karratha (see Tours; p927).

MARBLE BAR

☎ 08 / pop 360

Reputed to be the hottest place in Australia, Marble Bar is 222km southeast of Port Hedland and the centre of a 377,000-sq-km shire that's larger than New Zealand. There isn't a whole lot to do here – west of town is **Chinaman Pool**, a nice swimming spot on the Coongan River. About 8km south of town, **Comet Gold Mine** (☎ 9176 1015; comet@norcom.net.au; ☺ 9am-4pm; tours 9 & 11.30am) no longer operates but has displays on mining and gemstones.

Ironclad Hotel (☎ 9176 1066; www.geocities.com /ironcladhotel; 15 Francis St; dm $20, donga s/d $70/80, motel s/d $90/100; mains $10-22) is a classic old pub that's the heart and soul of the town, and has pool tables, a beer garden and counter meals.

STAIRCASE TO THE MOON

If you're between Karratha and Derby two days after the full moon between March and October, don't miss the Staircase to the Moon. Named for the red-and-gold stairway effect caused when the reflections of the moon hit the rippling mud flats, it's a pretty cool experience. Broome has the biggest celebration of the monthly spectacle when Town Beach has a real carnival air with a lively evening market and food stalls. Visitors centres in the towns can tell you when the Staircase is next on show.

PORT HEDLAND

☎ 08 / pop 15,000

A quiet town attached to a massive industrial dock, Port Hedland has always enjoyed a position of regional importance. Established in 1864 as a pastoral centre, it became the base for a fleet of 150 pearling luggers in the 1870s, before gradually declining over successive decades. By 1946 the population had dwindled to a mere 150, but iron-ore mining operations revitalised the town and it now handles more export tonnage than any other Australian port.

The original settlement and port are built on a small island connected to the mainland by a 3km causeway. About 15km south of town, South Hedland is a modern residential centre with little for the traveller.

The helpful Port Hedland **visitors centre** (☎ 9173 1711; www.porthedlandtouristbureau.com; 13 Wedge St; ⊙ 8.30am-5pm Mon-Fri, 8.30am-4pm Sat, 10am-2pm Sun, shorter hours Nov-May) has Internet access.

Sights & Activities

Dalgety House Museum (☎ 9173 4300; cnr Wedge & Anderson Sts; admission $3; open 10am-3pm May-Oct, via Town Tour only Nov-Apr) has splendid displays and recorded dialogues that bring the town's Aboriginal and settler history to life, and its natural cooling system makes it a great place to escape Hedland's scorching sun.

You can survey the town and port from the 26m-high **observation tower** (adult/child $2/1) behind the visitors centre, where you have to pay and sign a waiver (you'll need enclosed shoes). Another good vantage point is **Marapikurrinya Park** at the end of Wedge St, where you can watch impossibly large tankers glide into dock during the day, or see BHP's Hot Briquetted Iron plant on Finucane Island light up like a fairy castle at night.

Pretty Pool, 7km east of the town centre, is a popular fishing and picnicking spot (beware of stonefish). Just to the north, Goode St is the best place to view Port Hedland's own **Staircase to the Moon** (see the boxed text 'Staircase to the Moon'; p929).

Between October and March **flatback turtles** nest on some of the nearby beaches, including Cooke Point, Cemetery and Pretty Pool. Ask at the visitors centre for the turtles' location, but be extremely careful not to spook them and keep your torch switched off.

In June, the **Blackrock Stakes** is run – a 122km race from the Whim Creek pub to Port Hedland contested by loons (or team of loons) pushing wheelbarrows weighed down with iron ore.

Tours

The visitors centre is the departure point for **BHP Billiton iron ore plant tours** (adult/child $13/5, ⊙ 9.30am Mon-Fri) and **Town Tours** ($13/5; ⊙ 11.30am Mon, Wed & Fri).

Big Blue Dive (☎ 9173 3202; Richardson St; www.bigbluedive.com.au) offers harbour cruises ($28/17 per adult/child, 1 hour), fishing trips (half/full day $95/145) and whale-watching tours ($75, 3 hours, July to October).

The Karijini tours offered by **Dingo's Oasis** (☎ 9173 1000; 59 Kingsmill St; www.dingotrek.com.au) have attracted rave reviews. All-inclusive three-day tours are $400 and leave twice a week. It also offers seven-day tours to remote Rudall River National Park ($700, monthly May to September); bookings are essential.

Sleeping

Bruno's Ocean Lodge (☎ 9173 2635; 7 Richardson St; motel d $65; ⊠) In town overlooking the water, Bruno's motel rooms are in good shape and represent the best mid-range value in town, although there's no outdoor area. You'll need to book ahead in season.

Harbour Lodge Backpackers (☎ 9173 4455; 11 Edgar St; dm $17, d & tw $40; ⊠ ⌨) Very close to town, this small and cosy place has a few rooms around a TV lounge, plus a shady front terrace, spa and sushi bar. Air-con is free in all the rooms.

Dingo's Oasis Backpackers (☎ 9173 1000; www.dingotrek.com.au; 59 Kingsmill St; dm $20, d & tw $50; ⌨) Right on the water, Dingo's has hammocks on the foreshore, a decent kitchen, TV lounge and Internet access.

Cooke Point Caravan Park (☎ 9173 1271; www.fleetwoodparks.com.au; cnr Athol & Taylor Sts; camp/caravan sites $20/24, budget s/d $28/50, motel d $90-115; ⊠) Overlooking Pretty Pool and the ocean, this neat-as-a-pin park has newish shower blocks and a pool, plus a good campers kitchen. Buses into town run every few hours (weekdays only).

Also recommended are **Mercure Inn Port Hedland** (☎ 9173 1511; www.mercure.com.au; cnr Lukis & McGregor Sts; d from $130; ⊠), which has a good position on the water and a restaurant, and

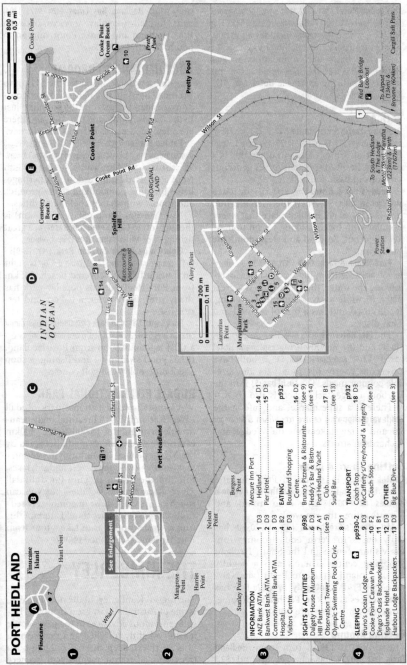

PORT HEDLAND

See Enlargement

WESTERN AUSTRALIA

INFORMATION
ANZ Bank ATM	**1**	D3
Bankwest Bank ATM	**2**	D3
Commonwealth Bank ATM	**3**	D3
Hospital	**4**	B2
Visitors Centre	**5**	D3

SIGHTS & ACTIVITIES   p930
Dalgety House Museum	**6**	D3
HBI Plant	**7**	A1
Observation Tower	(see 5)	
Olympic Swimming Pool & Civic Centre	**8**	D1

SLEEPING   pp930-2
Bruno's Ocean Lodge	**9**	D3
Cooke Point Caravan Park	**10**	F2
Dingo's Oasis Backpackers	**11**	B1
Esplanade Hotel	**12**	D3
Harbour Lodge Backpackers	**13**	D3
Mercure Inn Port Hedland	**14**	D1
Pier Hotel	**15**	D3

EATING   p932
Boulevard Shopping Centre	**16**	D2
Bruno's Pizzeria & Ristorante	(see 9)	
Heddy's Bar & Bistro	(see 14)	
Port Hedland Yacht Club	**17**	B1
Sushi Bar	(see 13)	

TRANSPORT   p932
Coach Stop	**18**	D3
McCafferty's/Greyhound & Integrity Coach Stop	(see 5)	

OTHER
Big Blue Dive	(see 3)	

the **Lodge Motel** (☎ 9172 2188; www.thelodgemotel
.com.au; Hawke Pl, South Hedland; motel/unit d $155/175;
[X] [□]), where the tariff includes all meals,
airport transfers and satellite TV.

There's basic accommodation at **Pier
Hotel** (☎ 9173 1488; The Esplanade; s/d $45/70) and
the neighbouring **Esplanade Hotel** (☎ 9173
1798; Anderson St; s/d $45/70).

Eating

Bruno's Pizzeria & Ristorante (☎ 9173 2047; 7 Richardson St; mains $10-18, pizzas $11-25; [⌚] from 5.30pm)
In front of Bruno's Ocean Lodge, this is a
pleasant, licensed spot that serves generous
portions of basic Italian fare.

Heddy's Bar & Bistro (☎ 9173 1511; cnr Lukis &
McGregor Sts; mains $17-29) At the Mercure Inn,
this is a huge, glitzy, tiled place that's very
popular with locals looking for an upmarket night out. Seafood and steak dominate
the menu.

Port Hedland Yacht Club (☎ 9173 3398; Sutherland St; mains $10-18) With a big garden over-
looking the water, the Yacht Club is a great
place to while away a summer's evening.
It's licensed and has a mix of seafood and
Thai dishes.

The **Pier Hotel** (☎ 9173 1488; The Esplanade; meals
$10-20) and the neighbouring **Esplanade Hotel**
(☎ 9173 1798; Anderson St; meals $10-20) both have
cavernous courtyards, long bars and sizeable counter meals. The **sushi bar** ($3-7) in the
Harbour Lodge Backpackers is also good.

There is a supermarket and café at the
Boulevard shopping centre (cnr Wilson & McGregor
Sts) and a few takeaways on Wedge and
Richardson streets.

Getting There & Away

Qantas (☎ 13 13 13) flies to Port Hedland
from Perth daily, while **Northwest Regional
Airlines** (☎ 1300 136 629) goes to Broome and
Karratha three times a week.

McCafferty's/Greyhound (☎ 13 20 30) has
daily buses to Perth and Broome from
the visitors centre and the South Hedland
shopping centre. There's also a slightly
quicker inland service to Perth (via Newman) on Friday. **Integrity** ☎ (9226 1339) has
two services a week to Perth and Broome,
from the same departure points.

Getting Around

The airport is 13km from town; **Hedland
Taxis** (☎ 91722 1010) charges around $22

one way. **Hedland Bus Lines** (☎ 9172 1394)
runs limited weekday services between
Port Hedland and Cooke Point, and on to
South Hedland ($3).

PORT HEDLAND TO BROOME

The highway stays inland for the 611km to
Broome, passing through fairly monotonous bushland. However, the coastline just
to the west is remote and unspoilt, and there
are a few good places to break the journey.

Pardoo Station (☎ 08-9176 4930; www.users.big
pond.com/pardoo.station; camp/caravan sites $16-19, May-
Sep only) is a working cattle station 133km
from Port Hedland, Pardoo has heritage-
listed buildings, a pool and shady grounds
and rooms with shared cooking facilities.

Not far from Pardoo Station (154km) is
the turn-off to **Cape Keraudren Reserve**, a great
fishing spot with **camp sites** ($5 per vehicle).

Eighty Mile Beach Caravan Park (☎ 08-9176
5941; camp/caravan sites $17/22, cabin d $70) is right
on a beautiful shell-covered beach, 245km
from Port Hedland; this popular park has
shady sites, fresh water, a bakery and terrific fishing.

Port Smith Caravan Park (☎ 08-9192 4983; camp/
caravan sites $15/22, cabin d $60, 6-bed units $130) is on
a tidal lagoon, 477km from Port Hedland.
It has good swimming and fishing, a shop
and a nine-hole bush golf course.

RUDALL RIVER NATIONAL PARK

WA's most isolated national park, Rudall
River (Karlamilyi) is a breathtakingly beautiful desert region of 15,000 sq km, 300km
east of Newman, which is still occupied by
the Martu people. It's unforgiving country
that features low-lying ranges and salt lakes,
split by the seasonal, gum-lined Rudall
River. There are no facilities, but you can
rough camp. Only those in completely self-
sufficient 4WD vehicles should attempt this
trip; an easier option is to take a tour from
Port Hedland (see Tours; p930).

THE KIMBERLEY

The rugged Kimberley, in the north of WA,
is one of Australia's last great frontiers. Despite enormous advances in the past decade
it's still a lightly travelled and remote area
of great rivers, deep chasms, bulging boab
trees and all-round magnificent scenery

WET OR DRY?

The climactic extremes of the Kimberley make for very different travel experiences, depending on the time of year you visit. The best, but the busiest, time to visit is between April and September (the Dry). There's little rain, the temperatures are low and all the roads are likely to be open. By October it's already getting hot as the build-up starts, and throughout the Wet (roughly November to March) temperatures of more than 40°C are common.

Probably the Wet's major drawback is the closure of the Gibb River Rd, which blocks exploration of the magnificent northern Kimberley. In addition, opening hours for visitors centres and attractions are reduced and tours run less frequently or not at all. Otherwise, the Wet is definitely not to be sneezed at. It's as hot as blazes, and humid to boot, but the locals are more relaxed, there's plenty of elbowroom and the lack of crowds makes accommodation prices plummet. And when the rains do arrive, you'll be glad you were here to see the spectacle – low, black clouds come at pace, dumping massive volumes of water in huge thunderstorms with awesome lightning displays. Rivers and creeks can rise rapidly and become impassable torrents within 15 minutes.

(plus deadly saltwater crocodiles in most of the river systems).

The Kimberley suffers from climatic extremes typical of the tropics – searing heat in the Dry followed by heavy rains in the Wet (which can close roads for weeks, particularly in the far north of the state). However, both the Wet and the Dry have their charms and the Kimberley's worth visiting at any time of the year. Pick up a copy of the useful and free *Kimberley Holiday Planner* from the Broome or Kununurra visitors centres (also see the boxed text 'Wet or Dry?'; above).

Tours

There are many multiday tours between Broome and Kununurra or Darwin that explore the Kimberley. The price usually includes all park fees, food and equipment. Itineraries, prices and departure dates can all vary, and you generally need to pay in advance, so it's worth checking out what will suit your own timing, interests and budgets.

Representative operators:

Flak Track Tours (☎ 08-8894 2228; www1.tpgi.com.au /users/flaktrak/index.html) A range of tours between Broome and Kununurra, including Mitchell Plateau and Gibb River Rd gorges ($1680, 7 days) and Purnululu National Park and Gibb River Rd gorges tour ($1920, 8 days).

Kimberley Adventure Tours (☎ 1800 083 368, 08-9191 2655; www.kimberleyadventures.com.au) Shuttles between Darwin and Broome, taking in Edith Falls, Lake Argyle, Purnululu National Park and the Gibb River Road ($1300, 9 days).

Other operators:

Kimberley Wild (☎ 08-9193 7778; www.kimberley wild.com.au)

Kimberley Wilderness Adventures (☎ 1800 804 005, 08-9192 5741; www.kimberleywilderness.com.au)

Travelabout Tours (☎ 1800 621 200, 08-9244 1200; www.travelabout.au.com)

More-specialised tours are also offered:

Alligator Airways (☎ 1800 632 533; www.alligatorair ways.com.au) Trips all over the Kimberley starting from Kununurra.

King Leopold Air (☎ 08-9193 7155; www.kingleopold air.com.au) Air tours of the western Kimberley including the Buccaneer Archipelago and Dampier Peninsula, with prices starting at $320 for a half day.

Willis's Walkabouts (☎ 08-8985 2134; www.bush walkingholidays.com.au) Offers bushwalking trips all over the Top End for about $125 per day.

Getting There & Away

Qantas (☎ 13 13 13; www.qantas.com.au) has daily flights from Broome to Perth and Darwin, while partner airline **Airnorth** (☎ 13 13 13) flies from Broome to Darwin (5 weekly) and Kununurra (3 weekly), as well as Kununurra to Darwin (5 weekly). **Northwest Regional Airlines** (☎ 1300 136 629; www.northwestregional.com.au) has daily flights to Broome, Fitzroy Crossing and Halls Creek, plus services to Karratha and Port Hedland (3 weekly). **Skippers Aviation** (☎ 08-9478 3989; www.skippers.com.au) flies between Broome and Derby (Monday to Saturday).

McCafferty's/Greyhound (☎ 13 20 30) stops at the Broome visitors centre on its daily Perth–Darwin service. From Darwin, destinations include Kununurra ($130, 9½ hours), Derby ($220, 23½ hours) and Broome ($260, 27 hours). From Broome, fares include Perth ($300, 32¾ hours), Port Hedland ($90, 7½ hours), Derby ($50, 2¾ hours) and

WESTERN AUSTRALIA

THE KIMBERLEY

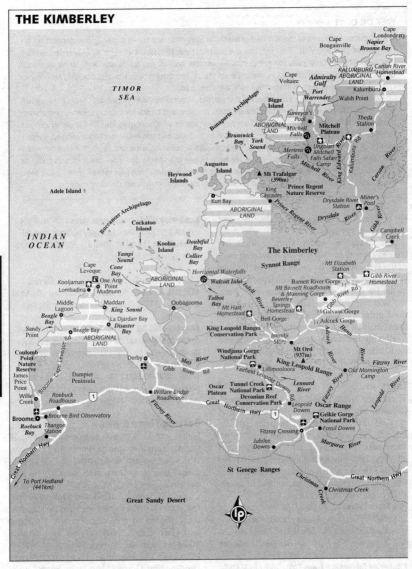

Kununurra ($175, 14¾ hours). **Integrity**
☎ 08-9226 1339; www.integritycoachlines.com.au) has
two services a week to Perth from Broome.

BROOME
☎ 08 / pop 14,000
Northern WA's largest and most attractive
town, Broome is an isolated oasis with wide,

sandy beaches and a relaxed cosmopolitan
atmosphere. It's also the gateway to the
superb wilderness, wildlife and indigenous
culture of the vast Kimberley region that
ranges to the north and northeast. Residents
may tell you that Broome has lost its charm,
but it remains an exciting and rewarding
place to visit, and is equally popular with

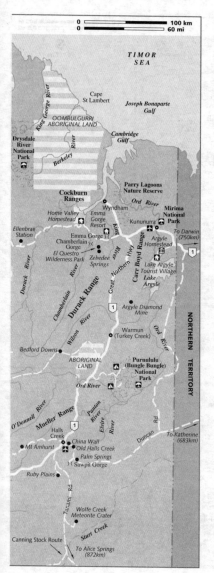

do much more advance planning to see the regional sights.

Established as pearling centre by Japanese entrepreneurs in the 1880s, Broome soon attracted communities of Chinese traders and Malay divers, with the latter joining many local Aboriginal people in the dangerous side of the business. Pearling peaked in the early 20th century, when the town's 400 luggers supplied 80% of the world's mother-of-pearl. Today only a handful of boats still operate, with pearl farms having largely replaced open-sea diving.

Orientation & Information

Broome's historical and commercial centre, known as Chinatown, is on the eastern coast of the Dampier Peninsula. Frederick St heads west from here towards Cable Beach, which runs the length of the western side of the peninsula. Most of Broome's accommodation, restaurants and sights are found around Chinatown and in the area south down to Town Beach.

The unflappable staff at Broome **visitors centre** (☎ 9192 2222; www.ebroome.com/tourism; cnr Great Northern Hwy & Bagot St; ☺ 8am-5pm Apr-Nov, 9am-5pm Mon-Fri & 9am-1pm Sat & Sun Dec-Mar) can help you with accommodation and tours. The post office is in Chinatown's Paspaley shopping centre, and there are ATMs nearby in Carnarvon St and Short St. Apart from the hostels, Internet access is available at **Chinatown Music Internet Café** (☎ 9192 1443; 20 Dampier Tce) and **Internet Outpost** (☎ 9193 6534; 16 Carnarvon St); both are open daily and charge around $7 per hour.

Woody's Book Exchange (☎ 9192 8999; Johnny Chi Lane) has a decent selection of used titles, while **Magabala Books** (☎ 9192 1991; www.maga bala.com; 2/28 Saville St; ☺ 9am-4pm Mon-Fri) publishes an rich selection of indigenous novels, poetry and biographies.

If you're going bush in a 4WD, **Kimberley Camping Hire** (☎ 9193 5354; 65 Frederick St) has a wide range of equipment, including portable fridges, and offers good weekly rates.

Sights & Activities
CABLE BEACH

About 4km west of town, **Cable Beach** is one of Australia's finest beaches and has azure waters and classic white sand as far as the eye can see. At the northern end (in the suburb of the same name), you can hire surfboards,

backpackers and wealthy weekenders from 'the Big Smoke'. In fact, at peak times the small town is so packed that it's a major feat just to cross the road. During the Wet, prices drop, tours often cease altogether and locals breathe a collective sigh of relief and get on with their lives. It's still worth visiting during this time, but you'll need to

WESTERN AUSTRALIA

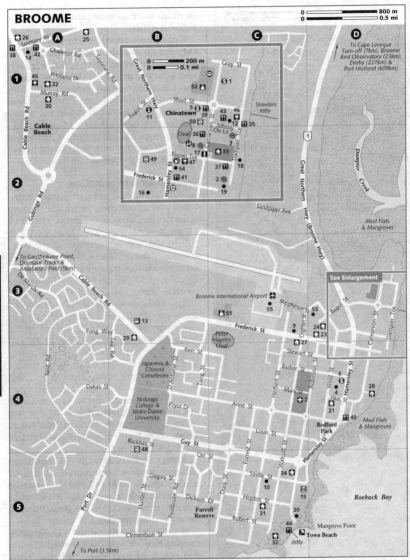

surf skis and other beach equipment from caravans in the dunes, and there's a popular nude-bathing beach to the north beyond the rocks. These days there are loads of resorts in the area, but they thankfully don't intrude on the beach's serenity.

Just back from the beach is **Broome Crocodile Park** (☎ 9192 1489; Cable Beach Rd; adult/child \$15/8;

⏱ 10am-5pm Mon-Fri, 2pm-5pm Sat & Sun Apr-Oct, 3.30-5.15pm daily Nov-Mar; tours 3.45pm daily), which features bellowing guides, cute hatchlings to fondle and some awesomely big crocs. Time your visit with the tour to get the most out of your experience.

The long sweep of Cable Beach ends at **Gantheaume Point**, 7km south of Broome.

The cliffs have been eroded into curious shapes and at very low tides 120 million-year-old **dinosaur tracks** are exposed (if the tide's in, there are casts on the cliff top). **Anastasia's Pool** is a rock pool built by the lighthouse keeper to soothe his wife's arthritis.

OTHER SIGHTS & ACTIVITIES

Chinatown refers to the old part of town, but there's scant evidence of this cultural group outside the street names – most of the simple wood-and-corrugated-iron buildings that line Carnarvon St and Dampier Tce now house restaurants, shops and galleries. The *Broome Heritage Trail* (get a pamphlet at the visitors centre) is a self-guided jaunt through the town's historic, architectural and cultural sights, and details some of the intense, and sometimes ugly, rivalry between the early settler groups.

These themes are expanded upon at **Broome Historical Society Museum** (☎ 9192 2075; Saville St; adult/child $5/1; ⌚ 10am-1pm Nov-May, 10am-4pm Mon-Fri & 10am-1pm Sat & Sun Jun-Oct) in the old customs house near Town Beach; it has a particularly fine collection of early photographs. Nearby, there's a **pioneer cemetery** at the end of Robinson St, while another **cemetery**, near Cable Beach Rd, has a large Japanese section, testifying to the dangers of pearl diving – in 1914 alone, 33 divers died of the bends.

At **Pearl Luggers** (☎ 9192 2059; 31 Dampier Tce; admission free; tours 11am & 2pm daily, adult/child $19/9),

two restored pearl boats and a storehouse of equipment and photographs provide a mildly interesting insight into Broome's pearling past.

The 1888 **courthouse** once housed the transmitting equipment for the old cable station (the cable ran to Banyuwangi on Java) and is the venue for a popular Saturday morning **market** with local craft and food stalls.

Tours

There are tours galore in and around Broome. The visitors centre has full details and makes bookings.

Astro Tours (☎ 9193 5362; $45) A close-up of the night sky.

Broome Day Tours (☎ 1800 801 068; adult/child $50/26) Half-day tours of Broome Peninsula.

Broome Sightseeing Tours (☎ 9192 5041; 3-day tour $20) Self-drive (you need your own transport) sightseeing kits with local music, tour information and discounts.

Mamabulanjin Tours (☎ 9192 2660; adult/child $55/29) Half-day indigenous perspective on Broome and its history.

Ships of the Desert (☎ 9192 6383) One of several operators providing sunset ($30) and full-day (from $75) camel tours of the area.

You can also take a hovercraft ride, fishing charter or art and craft tour; see the visitors centre for details. Tours of Dampier Peninsula (p941), the Kimberley (p933) and the Devonian Reef National Parks (p945) also operate out of Broome.

WESTERN AUSTRALIA

Festivals & Events

The people of Broome love nothing more than a good party and there are plenty of festivals. Exact dates vary from year to year – contact Broome visitors centre for more information and book accommodation well in advance. Highlights include the **Chinatown Street Party** (March), **Dragon Boat Classic** (April), **Fringe Festival** (June), **Shinju Matsuri** (Festival of the Pearl; August), **Stompem Ground** Aboriginal music festival (September/October) and **Mango Festival** (November).

Sleeping

Like all places up north, Broome's accommodation is very pricey, and rates go up even higher in the Dry when demand is strongest. If you're visiting in high season it's well worth booking well in advance, even for budget accommodation and camp sites. High-season prices are listed in this section.

BUDGET

With three great hostels, Broome's backpacker market offers the best value of all the accommodation levels.

Broome's Last Resort (☎ 1800 801 918, 9193 5000; www.yha.com.au; 2 Bagot St; dm $17-19, s & d & tw $55; ✖ 🖳) Under friendly management and close to the town centre, this fine old veranda-ed place has facilities including coin-operated air-con ($1 per four hours), a pool table, small kitchen, convivial and cheap bar, and a deep swimming pool.

Cable Beach Backpackers (☎ 1800 655 011, 9193 5511; www.cablebeachbackpackers.com; 12 Sanctuary Rd; dm $19, d & tw $65; ✖ 🖳) A long way from town, but close to the beach, this is an easy-going place with an excellent kitchen, standard dorms, nice grounds, roomy doubles in the original house and a free shuttle bus to town several times a day. It also has surfboards, bikes and scooters available for rent.

Kimberley Klub (☎ 9192 3233; 62 Frederick St; dm $18-20, d & tw $70; ✖ 🖳) This place has excellent facilities, plenty of greenery, large common areas, a tour desk and a bar overlooking the pool, but somehow manages to retain a detached, big-city feel. Air-con is $1 per three hours, and it's within walking distance of town.

Roebuck Bay Caravan Park (☎ 9192 1366; Walcott St; camp/caravan sites $18/22, on-site van d $50; ✖)

Right on the attractive Town Beach, about 25 minutes' walk from Chinatown, this has the best location of Broome's parks. The vans are great value, with air-con, gas stove and TV, and there's a good kitchen/barbecue area for campers.

MID-RANGE

Palm Grove Caravan Resort (☎ 1800 803 336, 9192 3336; www.palmgrove.com.au; cnr Cable Beach & Murray Rds; camp/caravan sites $24/27, studio d $110, cabins $145, extra adult $12; ✖) Across from Cable Beach, the studios and two-bedroom cabins here are modern and air-conditioned. They all have fully equipped kitchens, TV and front balcony, and some have spas. They represent excellent value, particularly outside of high season when good discounts are offered.

Broome Motel (☎ 1800 683 867, 9192 7775; www.broomemotel.com.au; 51-57 Frederick St; motel d $90, family apt $135; ✖) At these prices, it's pretty rude to charge for air-con ($1 per three hours), but this is one of Broome's most central motels. The small rooms here are in good nick and they are always in demand.

Ocean Lodge (☎ 1800 600 603, 9193 7700; www.oceanlodge.com.au; 1 Cable Beach Rd; motel d & tw $110, family rooms $130; ✖) Midway between Cable Beach and Chinatown, the rooms here are a little tired but comfortable enough and all come with a microwave in the kitchenette. Large shady lawns with barbecues and discounted weekly rates make this popular with families.

Roebuck Bay Hotel Motel (☎ 1800 098 824, 9192 1221; roey.accom@bigpond.com; 45 Dampier Tce; dm from $15, budget/standard/superior motel d $95/110/125; ✖) Smack in the middle of Chinatown, the Roey's rooms are in good shape and surround a large pool, although the budget rooms back onto the rowdy live band area. Proximity to the pub is the main attraction of its dorm rooms.

Broome Apartments Park Court (☎ 1800 801 225, 9193 5887; www.users.bigpond.com/parkcourt; Haas St; 1-/2-/3-bedroom units $95/120/185; ✖) These self-contained units have definitely seen better days, but they have all the facilities, are close to town and the price is very competitive (with cheaper weekly rates).

Also recommended:

Palms Resort (☎ 1800 094 848, 9192 1898; www.bestwestern.com.au/palmsresort; Hopton St; motel d $150, studio tr $175; ✖)

Tropicana Inn (☎ 1800 244 899, 9192 1204; www
.users.bigpond.com/parkcourt; cnr Saville & Robinson Sts;
s & d & t $130, family rooms $160; 🔀)

TOP END

Cable Beach Club (☎ 1800 199 099, 9192 0400; www
.cablebeachclub.com; Cable Beach Rd; d $290-460; 🔀)
This resort is enormous, beautifully designed, offers every service and amenity
you care to think of, and boasts killer views
of the beach. Even if you're not staying, it's
worth stopping in at the Sunset Bar for an
evening drink.

Also consider the following:

Mangrove Hotel (☎ 1800 094 818, 9192 1303; www
.mangrovehotel.com.au; Carnarvon St; d from $165; 🔀)
Recently renovated rooms and superb views of the eastern
coast.

Broome Beach Resort (☎ 1800 647 333, 9158 3300;
www.broomebeachresort.com; 4 Murray Rd, Cable Beach;
apt from $180; 🔀) Excellent self-contained apartments;
cricket fans can corner the manager – former test off-spinner,
Bruce Yardley.

Eating
CENTRAL BROOME

Broome has the only decent restaurant
scene between Perth and Darwin, so frus-
trated foodies should take full advantage.

noodlefish (☎ 9192 5529; cnr Frederick & Hamersley
Sts; mains $13-30) Broome's signature top-end
restaurant has gained national recognition
for its beautiful mix of Mediterranean and
Asian flavours, and deft handling of local
seafood. The lunchtime noodle bar allows you sample the fare for a reasonable
outlay.

THE AUTHOR'S CHOICE

2 Rice (☎ 9192 1395; 26 Dampier Tce; mains all
$19) Chilled-out, comfortable and licensed,
2 Rice has the best-value Asian food in
town, and Broome is one place in country WA where Asian food *doesn't* mean a
chop suey knocked up by a bloke called
Trevor. The menu includes Thai, Malay and
Japanese dishes deftly assembled from
authentic ingredients and topped with all
the right garnishes and condiments. There's
both takeaway and casual eat-in sections,
with plenty of mags strewn around. The
$10 lunchtime special (including bread and
condiments) is particularly good value.

Matso's Café & Brewery (☎ 9193 5811; 60 Hamersley St; mains $15-26) In a heritage-listed building
overlooking Roebuck Bay, Matso's offers all-
day dining, plus an upmarket Mod Oz menu
at night and its own range of boutique beers.
Reserve a table on the veranda.

Shady Lane Cafe (☎ 9192 2060; Johnny Chi Lane;
breakfast & light meals $4-12; 🕑 7.30am-3pm daily) A
perfect place to flee the sun, this tiny café
serves up healthy juices, tasty breakfasts,
focaccias, wraps, sandwiches and coffee.

Town Beach Cafe (☎ 9193 5585; Robinson St;
mains $9-18; 🕑 dinner Mon-Sat) Right on Town
Beach, this BYO café has plenty of outdoor
tables to enjoy both the seafood menu and
the cool breeze off the water. Arrive early
during the Dry to get a table.

Broome Pizza Bar (☎ 9192 1442; 2 Napier Tce; pizzas
$10-20) If you're hankering for pizza, there's a
good selection here and delivery is free.

Bloom's (☎ 9193 6366; 31 Carnarvon St; mains $13-20;
🕑 from 7am) and nearby **Henrys** (☎ 9192 3222;
cnr Carnarvon & Short Sts; mains $8-17; 🕑 from 7am) are
peas in a pod, both set in spacious old tim-
bered buildings and offering well-prepared
brekkies and light lunches, more substantial
dinners, rich cakes and good coffee. Bloom's
outdoor seating, tapas menu and vodka
granitas probably give it the edge.

There are supermarkets and bakeries
in the Paspaley and Boulevard shopping
centres.

CABLE BEACH

Old Zoo Cafe (☎ 9193 6200; 2 Challenor Rd; mains
$17-29) In the zoo's former feedhouse, this
small open-sided place has tasty brekkies,
fresh juices, enticing flavours in its Mod Oz
menu and a good wine list (all available by
the glass). The breezeways, shaded deck and
water feature help to keep the temperature
down during the Wet.

Cable Beach Sandbar & Grill (☎ 9193 5090; Cable
Beach Rd; mains $14-22) In a prime spot overlook-
ing the beach, this airy, licensed place prepares decent seafood and steak meals. Next
door, a takeaway kiosk has the deep-fryer
on during the day.

Drinking

Palms Café Bar (☎ 9192 1303; Carnarvon St), at the
Mangrove Hotel, and **Matso's Café & Brewery**
(☎ 9193 5811; 60 Hamersley St) both attract a mature, well-heeled crowd for cocktail-sipping
by the water.

Entertainment

Sun Pictures (☎ 9192 1077; 27 Carnarvon St; adult/child $12/7) is the world's oldest open-air cinema (1916) – settling back on a deck chair to watch the latest flick here is an absolute must. There are also two screens at the more modern **Sun Cinemas** (☎ 9192 1077; 3 Weld St; $13/8).

At Goolarri Media Enterprises, **GME GME Bar** (☎ 9192 1325; www.gme.com.au; 16 Blackman St) hosts the occasional film launch and band; call for a programme.

The **Roebuck Bay Hotel** (☎ 9192 1221; 45 Dampier Tce) puts on live music most nights. Along with **Diver's Tavern** (☎ 9193 6066; Cable Beach Rd), it's the place for a Sunday session.

When the pubs are shutting up shop, head for **Tokyo Joe's** (☎ 9193 7222; 52 Napier Tce) and the more upmarket **Nippon Inn** (☎ 9192 1941; Dampier Tce). Cover charges are around $6 and they pump till the early hours.

Shopping

Broome specialises in pearls and Aboriginal art, but you'll need room on your credit card if you want anything of quality.

Gecko Gallery (☎ 9192 8909; 9 Short St) has a broad range of local and regional Aboriginal art, as does **Short St Gallery** (☎ 9192 2658; 7 Short St) next door.

If you're after pearls, boutiques line Dampier Tce and Short St. For something more affordable, there are markets with local crafts and food outside the courthouse on Saturday morning, outside the museum on Sunday and at Town Beach during the Staircase to the Moon (see the boxed text 'Staircase to the Moon'; p929).

Getting There & Away

Broome is a regional hub with flights or links to all Australian capitals and major towns, as well as towns throughout the Kimberley. See Getting There & Away (p933) for details.

McCafferty's/Greyhound (☎ 13 20 30) stops at the visitors centre on its daily Perth–Darwin service. **Integrity** ☎ 9226 1339) has two services a week to Perth, leaving from **Terri's Travel** (☎ 9192 2992; 31 Carnarvon St), next to Bloom's.

Getting Around

The **Town Bus** (☎ 9193 6585; adult/child $2.70/1) links Chinatown with Cable Beach every hour (7.10am to 6.15pm), via most of Broome's places to stay. The day's first service extends to Gantheaume Point.

There are several international and local car-hire operators, most with airport offices. **Just Broome** (☎ 9192 6636) has cars from $33 a day (delivered to your door), but they're for local use only. Try also **Avis** (☎ 9193 5980; Coghlan St) or **Budget** (☎ 9193 5355; Broome Airport). If you're after a 4WD, check the daily kilometre allowance, as the charges can be ruinous.

Good mountain bikes are available for hire from **Broome Cycles** (☎ 9192 1871; 2 Hamersley St) for $18/70 per day/week. If you need a cab, contact **Chinatown Taxis** (☎ 1800 811 772).

AROUND BROOME
Broome Bird Observatory

On the mudflats of Roebuck Bay, 25km from Broome, this beautiful **observatory** (☎ 08-9193 5600; Crab Creek Rd; www.birdsaustralia.com.au; adult/child $5/free) is a vital staging post for hundreds of types of migratory species, including 49 wader species (nearly a quarter of the world's total species). An incredible 800,000 birds arrive in Broome each year. Excellent tours from the observatory/Broome cost $50/75, or you can do a one-hour introductory tour (from the observatory only; $12). There's also **accommodation** (camp/caravan sites $9/13, bunk s/d $28/35, d $50, self-contained chalets from $100). Access is via a good dirt road, although it may be closed in the Wet.

Dampier Peninsula

This beautiful peninsula, with its superb coastal scenery, great fishing and tiny Aboriginal communities, is readily accessible from Broome via the 200km-long dirt Cape Leveque Rd. Leaving the highway 9km east of Broome, this narrow 4WD track is as rough as bags, and can be impassable in the Wet, but this just adds to the attraction, as does the simple accommodation and lack of facilities – unless you're on a tour, you'll need to be completely self-sufficient.

Many people head straight for the 'resorts' of Middle Lagoon and Kooljaman, but most of the Aboriginal communities offer accommodation, plus cultural, fishing and mud-crabbing tours. The *Dampier Peninsula Travellers Guide* details the options – pick up a copy from the Broome visitors centre, where you can check on

the condition of the road and book your accommodation and tours.

The first turn-off (Manari Rd) takes you past **Willie Creek Pearl Farm** (☎ 08-9193 6000), which can be visited through a half-day bus tour from Broome ($60/30 per adult/child) or you can join the tour at the farm ($25/12). Another 40km north is **Coulomb Point Nature Reserve**, which protects unique pindan vegetation and the rare bilby.

Back on the main road, it's around 100km to Beagle Bay, chiefly notable for the extraordinary mother-of-pearl altar in the local **church** (☎ 08-9192 4913; admission $5 per person). There's a shop and fuel is available weekdays, but there's no accommodation.

THE AUTHOR'S CHOICE

Cape Leveque, at the tip of the peninsula, is a magnificent spot with wonderful beaches and stunning red cliffs. **Kooljaman** (☎ 08-9192 4970; www.kooljaman.com.au; camp sites $28, beach shelter d $40, unit d $90, safari tent d $190) is an unhurried, spacious place that gets very busy in season, but can be almost deserted off-season. Try to get a beach shelter (you'll need to book); they're open-air and as rough as bags, but you're right on the beach and each has its own barbecue – a steak, a coldie and a sunset, and all is well with the world. Other facilities include **Dinkas Restaurant** (mains $12-20; ☼ Apr-Oct only), mud-crabbing tours, dinghy hire, snorkelling (no crocs so far!) and a basic shop. The fishing at Hunter's Creek brings the punters in from far and wide, and you can also tour the local Aboriginal communities.

Next is **Middle Lagoon** (☎ 08-9192 4002; day entry per car $8; camp/caravan sites $26/32, beach shelter d $45, cabin d $120), a simple spot right on the beach run by a friendly local couple and boasting fantastic swimming, snorkelling and fishing.

Between Middle Lagoon and Cape Leveque are the turn-offs to **La Djardarr Bay** (☎ 08-9192 4896; camp sites $25; guided walks from $33), **Maddarr** (☎ 08-9192 6070; camp site $100, including guided walks; day pass $50), **Lombadina** (☎ 08-9192 4936; dm $44, unit d $143; guided walks $33-80, boat tours $145; fuel Mon-Fri) and **Mudnunn** (☎ 08-9192 4121; camp sites $28; mud-crabbing $55).

For these communities, everything needs to be booked in advance and permits may be required (available from Broome visitors centre). Some communities may encourage you to visit only on weekdays.

TOURS
Tour operators include **Kimberley Wild** (☎ 08-9193 7778; www.kimberleywild.com.au; $330) and **Over the Top Adventure Tours** (☎ 08-9192 5211; http://overthetoptours.com.au; $380), which both offer two-day 4WD adventure tours that include mud-crabbing and visits to Cape Leveque and Aboriginal communities (April to November only).

Golden Eagle Airlines (☎ 08-9191 1132; www.goldeneagleairlines.com) has a scenic flight from Derby ($250) that includes two hours at Kooljaman. You can also visit the peninsula's southern coast with **Discover the Kimberley Tours** (☎ 1800 636 802; $180), which takes you up to James Price Point by 4WD. Tours of Dampier Peninsula operate out of Broome.

DERBY
☎ 08 / pop 5000
The administrative centre for West Kimberley, the quiet town of Derby is a good base for trips to the spectacular gorges of the Devonian Reef national parks (p945) and the remote islands of the Buccaneer Archipelago; it's also the western entrance to the Gibb River Rd (p943). On a peninsula jutting into King Sound, 219km from Broome, Derby is surrounded by huge tidal mud flats, baked hard in the Dry and occasionally flooded by king tides.

Most shops and services are located in the town centre on Loch and Clarendon Sts. It's here you'll find **Derby visitors centre** (☎ 1800 621 426, 9191 1426; www.derbytourism.com.au; 2 Clarendon St; ☼ 8.30am-4.30pm Mon-Fri, 9am-4pm Sat & Sun, shorter hours Oct-Mar), the post office, an ATM and **Derby Telecentre** (☎ 9193 1272; Clarendon St; ☼ 9am-4pm Mon-Fri) where you can go online (there's also Internet access at the visitors centre).

Sights & Activities
The **Boab Prison Tree**, 7km south of town, is probably Derby's most famous attraction. With a girth of 14m and a hollow trunk it's said to be over 1000 years old. Prisoners were locked up here en route to the grim **Old Derby Gaol** (Loch St), next to the police station.

WESTERN AUSTRALIA

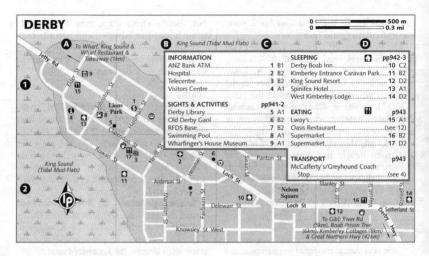

DERBY

0 ————— 500 m
0 ————— 0.3 mi

King Sound (Tidal Mud Flats)

To Wharf, King Sound &
Wharf Restaurant &
Takeaway (1km)

INFORMATION	
ANZ Bank ATM.................................1 B1	
Hospital...2 B2	
Telecentre..3 B2	
Visitors Centre.................................4 A1	

SIGHTS & ACTIVITIES	pp941-2
Derby Library...................................5 A1	
Old Derby Gaol................................6 A2	
RFDS Base.......................................7 B2	
Swimming Pool................................8 A1	
Wharfinger's House Museum............9 A1	

SLEEPING	pp942-3
Derby Boab Inn................................10 C2	
Kimberley Entrance Caravan Park.....11 B2	
King Sound Resort............................12 D2	
Spinifex Hotel..................................13 A1	
West Kimberley Lodge......................14 D2	

EATING	p943
Lwoy's...15 A1	
Oasis Restaurant..........................(see 12)	
Supermarket....................................16 B2	
Supermarket....................................17 D2	

TRANSPORT	p943
McCafferty's/Greyhound Coach	
Stop..(see 4)	

King Sound
(Tidal Mud Flats)

Panton St

Anderson St

Nelson
Square

Stanley St

Loch St

To Gibb River Rd
(5km), Boab Prison Tree
(6km), Kimberley Cottages (8km)
& Great Northern Hwy (42km)

Knowsley St West

Wharfinger's House Museum (cnr Loch & Elder Sts; ☺ by appointment) has historic displays on local shipping, aviation and communications (get the key from the visitors centre), while Derby's lofty **wharf**, revived by Western Metals in late 1997 to ship zinc and lead to Asia, is a good fishing spot and the best place to see the town's colossal tidal flow – generally about 11m difference between high and low. You can also visit the **Royal Flying Doctor Service** (RFDS; ☎ 9191 1211; Clarendon St; ☺ 9am, 11am & 2pm Mon-Fri) for a 'gold' coin donation. The **Boab Festival**, in the first two weeks of July, features concerts, sports (including mud footy) and street parades.

Derby's greatest attraction, however, is its access to the natural splendour of **King Sound** and the **Buccaneer Archipelago**, a combination of remote coastline and uninhabited islands that offer amazing walking, swimming, fishing, bird-watching and camping; see Tours, below, for details.

Tours
Kimberley Eco Charters (☎ 0417-998 535) offers a sunset cruise of King Sound ($70), plus half-day crabbing ($90) and full-day fishing ($125) trips. Sea safaris into the Buccaneer Archipelago, ranging from four to 21 days, are run by **Buccaneer Sea Safaris** (☎ 9191 1991; http://buccaneerseasafaris.com) and **One Tide Charters** (☎ 9193 1358; www.onetide.com). Prices start at around $1300 for four days, all inclusive, and you need to book and pay well in advance.

Golden Eagle Airlines (☎ 9191 1132; www.golden eagleairlines.com) has two-hour scenic flights over the archipelago for $160.

Sleeping
Accommodation here offers reasonable value compared with other Kimberley towns.

Derby Boab Inn (☎ 9191 1044; Loch St; budget s/d $65/70, deluxe s/d $80/100; ✹) The budget rooms here are small and basic, but fair value – the deluxe rooms are much better.

Kimberley Cottages (☎ 9191 1114; Windjana Rd; 2-/3-bedroom chalet d $125/140, extra adult $13; ✹) On a farm 8km from town off the Gibb River Rd, these comfortable, fully self-contained cottages are perfect for small groups.

Spinifex Hotel (☎ 9191 1233; Clarendon St; spini fexhotel@westnet.com.au; dm $20, budget s/d $50/55, motel s/d $60/75; ✹) Rooms at the Spinny are definitely not flash, but this central pub has Derby's only backpacker beds, and is the place to go for drinking, pool and the occasional band.

Kimberley Entrance Caravan Park (☎ 9193 1055; kecp@westenet.com.au; Rowan St; camp/caravan sites $18/24) New owners are incrementally upgrading this coastal park. Currently there's only tent and caravan accommodation, but units are planned over the next couple of years, along with upgraded amenity blocks and a campers kitchen.

Also recommended:
West Kimberley Lodge (☎ 9191 1031; Sutherland St; s/d $60/65, with bathroom $80/90; ✹) Small neat place on the eastern edge of town.

King Sound Resort (☎ 9193 1044; kingsoundresort@ wn.com.au; Loch St; motel s/d $110/130) Has a good pool and squash courts; the tariff's pretty steep for what you get.

Eating

Wharf Restaurant (☎ 9191 1195; mains $14-24) Right on the jetty, this BYO place is Derby's best, with lush tropical gardens and a good reputation for its seafood (including take-aways after 11am).

Otherwise your options are limited. Derby Boab Inn, the Spinnifex Hotel and King Sound Resort all have bistros, with the latter's **Oasis Restaurant** (☎ 9193 1044; Loch St; mains $11-20) the pick of the bunch, while **Lwoy's** (☎ 9191 1554; Loch St; mains $11-21) serves up predictable Chinese dishes. There's a couple of takeaways along Clarendon St, and supermarkets on Loch and Clarendon Sts.

Getting There & Away

Skippers Aviation (☎ 9478 3989) flies to Broome Monday to Saturday. Daily **McCafferty's/ Greyhound** (☎ 13 20 30) buses to Darwin and Perth stop at the visitors centre.

GIBB RIVER ROAD

The 664km dirt 'back road' from Derby to Wyndham/Kununurra is more direct than the highway by several hundred kilometres. However, it can be extremely rough after rain and is generally closed altogether during the Wet – it's definitely not recommended for conventional vehicles. Even if you plan to stay at stations along the way, you should carry several days' food and water in case you get stranded.

If you want just a taste of back-country adventure, consider the 'tourist loop' that takes you 125km along the Gibb River Rd from Derby to the Fairfield Leopold Downs Rd turn-off, and then another 124km past Winjana Gorge and Tunnel Creek (see Devonian Reef National Parks; p945) to the Great Northern Hwy, 43km west of Fitzroy Crossing.

Before you head off, grab a copy of the indispensable *Gibb River & Kalumburu Roads Travellers Guide* ($3) from any of the regional visitors centres. It has useful advice, plus accommodation (generally dinner, bed and breakfast – DBB), sights and tour information. Some tours also take in parts of this area; see Tours (p933) for more information.

INDIGENOUS MEDIA

For the average traveller, language and cultural barriers can make communication with Aboriginal people a complex business – outside of formal tours at least. If you're looking for an insight into the issues affecting the indigenous people in a particular town or region, community-produced radio and TV shows are a good first step. Many of the shows are broadcast in English and feature interviews, politics and comment you won't hear anywhere else, not to mention some great music. Regional broadcasters in the Kimberley include:

- Kununurra – Waringarri Radio (693 AM)
- Halls Creek – Radio Puranyangu Rangka Kerrem (98.1 FM)
- Fitzroy Crossing – Wangki Yupurnanu-purru Radio (936 AM)
- Broome – Radio Goolarri (99.7 FM) and Goolarri TV (GTV 35)

Mainstream networks with indigenous-produced programming include SBS TV (www.sbs.com.au), which shows ICAM (Indigenous Cultural Affairs Magazine), and ABC TV (www.abc.net.au), which runs Message Stick TV. Both broadcasters have indigenous content on their radio services; see their websites for details.

Derby to Mt Barnett Roadhouse

The Lennard River bridge is crossed at 120km and the Yamarra Gap in the King Leopold Range is at 145km. The 5km-long **Lennard River Gorge**, 8km off Gibb River Rd, has a waterfall and refreshing pool.

At 184km is the turn-off to the beautiful **Mt Hart Homestead** (☎ 08-9191 4645; www.mthart .com.au; DBB $150), 50km up a rough, 4WD road.

About 26km past the Mt Hart turn-off is **Bell Gorge**, 29km down a 4WD track. It's one of the region's finest, with a picturesque waterfall and you can camp nearby at **Silent Grove** (adult/child $9/2).

Old Mornington Camp (☎ 08-9191 7406; fax 9191 7037; camping/DBB $10/150), on the Fitzroy River, is 100km south of the 247km mark and has tours, a bar and canoe hire, while **Beverley Springs Homestead** (☎ 08-9191 4646; fax 9191 7192; camping/DBB $15/130) is a working

WESTERN AUSTRALIA

station in gorge country, 43km north off the 251km mark.

Horseshoe-shaped **Galvans Gorge** has a swimming hole less than 1km off the road at the 286km mark.

Mt Barnett Roadhouse (☎ /fax 08-9191 7007; camping $10; ☒ 7am-5pm, shorter hours Oct-Mar), at the 306km point, is owned by Kupingarri Aboriginal community and has fuel and a general store. **Manning Gorge** lies 7km along an easy dirt track and camping is by a lovely waterhole.

Mt Barnett to Wyndham– Kununurra Road

Barnett River Gorge is another good swimming spot, 5km off the 328km mark. Another 12km along is the turn-off to **Mt Elizabeth Station** (☎ /fax 08-9191 4644; camping/DBB $11/140), a working station 30km off the road.

At 406km you reach the Kalumburu turn-off (see Kalumburu Road; below). The road then continues through magnificent scenery; at 579km there are excellent views of the Cockburn Ranges to the north, the Cambridge Gulf and the Pentecost and Durack Rivers. About 2km further is **Home Valley Homestead** (☎ /fax 08-9161 4322; camping/DBB $9/120), and at 590km is **Pentecost River** crossing, which can be dodgy when the water is up.

At 614km, the million-acre **El Questro Wilderness Park** (☎ 08-9169 1777; www.elquestro.com.au; camping per person $13) is the best-known station in the Kimberley. Attractions include **El Questro Gorge**, **Zebedee Springs**, boat rides up **Chamberlain Gorge** and spectacular **Emma Gorge** (at 623km) where a 40-minute walk takes you to a pool with a high droplet waterfall. Accommodation is split between the **El Questro Homestead** (s/d with all meals from $850/1600) and **Emma Gorge Resort** (cabin d $135, 4-bed bungalow $200) – both have a restaurant and bar. Homestead/Emma Gorge entry fees are $13/5.50, although these are waived for guests and restaurant patrons.

At 630km you cross King River and at 647km you finally hit the bitumen road; Wyndham lies 48km to the northwest, Kununurra 52km east.

KALUMBURU ROAD

This dirt road traverses extremely rocky terrain in an isolated area. Distances are given from the junction of the Gibb River and Kalumburu Roads, 419km from the Derby

Hwy and 248km from the Wyndham– Kununurra Rd.

You need two permits to visit the Kalumburu community. The first is free, and available in advance online (www.dia.wa.gov.au) or from **Department of Indigenous Affairs offices** Perth (☎ 08-9235 8000); Broome (☎ 08-9192 2865); Derby (☎ 08-9191 2066); Kununurra (☎ 08-9168 2550). The second is issued by the **Kalumburu community** (☎ 08-9161 4300; kac10@bigpond.com; ☒ 8am-noon, 2-4pm Mon-Sat) in advance or on arrival. It costs $30 per car and is good for seven days.

Gibb River Road to Mitchell Plateau

After crossing the Gibb River at 3km and Plain Creek at 16km, **Drysdale River Station** (☎ 08-9161 4326; www.drysdaleriver.com.au; camp sites $9-12, d & tw $95) is the first fuel stop at 59km, and has supplies, meals and scenic flights (from $200). The homestead is 1km down a side road.

At 62km you can turn off to **Miners Pool** (adult/child $2/1; camping $5), also operated by Drysdale River Station. It's 3.5km to the river, and the last 200m is slow going.

The Mitchell Plateau turn-off is at 172km, from where it's 70km to the turn-off to the spectacular, multitiered **Mitchell Falls**. The falls are 16km downhill and you have to walk the final 3km; allow a full day for the walk. In the Dry the water falls from the centre of the terraces; in the Wet, however, they are vastly different – the muddied water stretches from escarpment to escarpment and thunders down submerged terraces. A scenic flight is a great way to see this spectacle. The road continues another 39km north to the coast.

There are several accommodation options in the area, including basic **camp sites** ($9) at King Edward River and Mitchell Plateau, and **Ungolan-Mitchell Falls Safari Camp** (☎ 1800 804 005; DBB $100), at the turn-off to the falls. See the *Gibb River & Kalumburu Roads Travellers Guide* for alternatives.

Mitchell Plateau Turn-Off to Kalumburu

From the Mitchell Plateau turn-off, the road heads northeast and crosses **Carson River** at 247km. Another 20km brings you to the **Kalumburu Aboriginal community** (☎ 08-9161 4333; camping $9, motel s/tw $45/70), about 5km from the mouth of the King Edward River and King Edward Gorge. The picturesque mission sits among giant mango trees and

coconut palms, and has a shop, food and **fuel** (🕑 7am-11am & 1.30pm-4pm Mon-Fri).

Drysdale River National Park

Very few people get into WA's northern-most national park, 100km south of Ka-lumburu. It's one of the most remote in Australia (there's no road access, but you can bushwalk) and is home to ancient Brad-shaw art figures and more recent Wandjina figures, plus waterfalls, gorges and many rare plants and animals. Visitors must register with **CALM** (☎ 08-9168 4200; Konkerberry Dr) at Ku-nunurra and get a permit from the **Kalumburu Aboriginal Corporation** (☎ 08-9161 4300).

DEVONIAN REEF NATIONAL PARKS

The West Kimberley has three national parks featuring beautiful gorges that were once part of a western coral 'great barrier reef' in the Devonian era, 350 million years ago. Windjana Gorge and Tunnel Creek National Parks are accessed via Fairfield Leopold Downs Rd (that links the Great Northern Hwy and Gibb River Rd), while Geikie Gorge National Park is just north of the town of Fitzroy Crossing.

The walls of **Windjana Gorge** soar 100m above the Lennard River, which rushes through in the Wet but becomes a series of pools in the Dry. You'll almost certainly see freshwater crocodiles sunning them-selves on sand banks or gliding through pools. Bring plenty of water, especially if you intend to make the 7km return walk from the **camping ground** (camp sites $18) to the end of the gorge.

Three kilometres from the river are the ruins of **Lillimooloora**, an early homestead and a police outpost that dates from 1893. It was here that Aboriginal tracker Jan-damarra shot Constable Richardson – see the boxed text 'Jandamarra' (below) for more details.

Tunnel Creek is a 750m-long passage, 3m to 15m wide, created by the creek cutting through a spur of the Napier Range. You can walk all the way along it in the Dry, but you'll need a torch and a change of shoes (preferably sandals); be prepared to wade through cold, knee-deep water in places. There are several Aboriginal paintings at either end. There's no camping here.

The magnificent **Geikie Gorge**, cut through the Devonian Reef by the Fitzroy River, is 18km north of Fitzroy Crossing on a sealed road; however, there are still creeks to be crossed and the park can be inaccessible in the Wet. The best way to see it is by boat (see Tours; below).

Tours

Tours of the gorges run from Broome, Derby and Fitzroy Crossing. **Australian Adventure Travel** (☎ 1800 621 625; $600) has a four-day camping tour from Broome that takes in all the gorges, plus Manning Gorge and Bells Falls along Gibb River Rd.

Tour operators to Windjana and Tunnel Creek include the following:
Broome Day Tours (☎ 1800 801 068; $180; 1 day) From Broome.
Bungoolee Tours (☎ 08-9191 5633; $115; 1 day) From Fitzroy Crossing. An Aboriginal company.

JANDAMARRA

Derby, Windjana Gorge, Tunnel Creek and Lillimooloora were the setting for the legendary exploits of the outlaw Aboriginal tracker Jandamarra, nicknamed Pigeon. As a teenager, Jandamarra, a member of the Bunuba tribe, was a highly skilled stockman working on the Lennard River Station. His skills eventually led him to become an armed tracker working with the local police to capture Aborigines who were spearing sheep.

In October 1894, Pigeon's tribal loyalty got the better of him – he shot a police colleague at Lil-limooloora, freed his captured tribesmen and escaped to lead a band of dissident Bunuba people who evaded search parties for almost three years. Despite being seriously wounded in a shootout at Windjana Gorge only a month after his escape, Pigeon survived and continued to taunt the settlers with raids and vanishing acts.

Pigeon killed another four men and in 1897 was finally trapped and killed near his Tunnel Creek hideout. For the full story, get a copy of the *Pigeon Heritage Trail* ($2.50) from the Derby or Broome visitors centres, or the fascinating *Jandamarra and the Bunuba Resistance* by Howard Pedersen and Banjo Woorunmurra.

Derby Bus Service (☎ 1800 621 426; $100; 1 day)
From Derby and Broome.
Kimberley Two-Tone Tours (☎ 1800 999 908;
kimberleyttt.com; $320; 2 days) From Broome.
Kimberley Wild (☎ 08-9193 7778; $195; 1 day) From
Broome.

Tours to Geikie Gorge are also on offer:
Broome Day Tours (☎ 1800 801 068; $190; 1 day)
CALM (adult/child $20/2.50; tours 8am & 3pm; 1 hr) From
Fitzroy Crossing; cruises year-round.
Darngku Heritage Cruises (☎ 08-9191 5552; half/
full day $50/100) Informative cruises on weekday mornings
between May and September.

FITZROY CROSSING
☎ 08 / pop 1500
A tiny settlement 392km east of Broome,
where the Great Northern Hwy crosses the
Fitzroy River, this is a convenient access
point for Geikie and Windjana Gorges and
is home to Gooniyandi, Bunuba, Walma-
jarri and Wangkajungka communities. The
old town site and pub are northeast of the
present town and the Fitzroy Crossing **visitors centre** (☎ 9191 5355; ☼ 9am-6pm, shorter hours
Nov-Apr) is on the highway.

Crossing Inn (☎ 9191 5080; crossinginn@bigpond
.com.au; Skuthorpe Rd; camp/caravan sites $11/17, motel
s/d $85/110; ☒), more or less a tin shed, is
the oldest pub in the Kimberley. It features
paintings by local students and is a lively
place to meet some locals. Newer motel
rooms are attached and have great verandas overlooking the river; there's also a
bistro (mains $12-22).

**Fitzroy River Lodge Motel Hotel & Caravan
Park** (☎ 9191 5141; Great Northern Hwy; camp/caravan
sites $20/23, safari tent d & tw $130, motel d $170; ☒).
Two kilometres east of town, this place
is way overpriced but has good camping
grounds, a swimming pool, bar and **bistro**
(mains $10-23).

Northwest Regional Airlines (☎ 1300 136 629)
has daily flights to Broome and Halls Creek.
McCafferty's/Greyhound (☎ 13 20 30) has daily
buses to Perth and Darwin that stop at the
visitors centre and Fitzroy River Lodge in
the middle of the night.

HALLS CREEK
☎ 08 / pop 1590
On the edge of the Great Sandy Desert, Halls
Creek is a small town with communities of
Kidja, Jaru and Gooniyandi people. Halls

Creek **visitors centre** (☎ 9168 6262; ☼ 8am-4pm;
shorter hours in the Wet) is on the Great Northern
Hwy.

There's nothing to do in town, but there
are tours and flights to the Wolfe Creek
Meteorite Crater (below) and Purnululu
(Bungle Bungle) National Park (p947),
while **China Wall**, 5km east and about 1.5km
off the road, is a small but picturesque sub-
vertical quartz vein. Off the gravel Duncan
Rd, southeast of town, are the swimming
holes of **Palm Springs** (45km) and **Sawpit
Gorge** (52km).

Sleeping & Eating
Halls Creek Caravan Park (☎ 1800 355 228, 9168
6169; lanus@bigpond.com.au; Roberta Ave; camp/caravan
sites $9/12, dongas $22, cabin d $55) It's nothing
much to look at, but this park is central,
has a pool, some shade and a shop.

Halls Creek Motel (☎ 9168 6001; hallscreekmotel@
westnet.com.au; 194 Great Northern Hwy; dongas $30-50,
motel s/d $85-110; ☒) This friendly place has
refurbished motel rooms, two types of
dongas (sharing facilities with two or 12
other rooms) and a fair licensed **restaurant**
(à la carte mains $12-20, buffet $12).

Kimberley Hotel Motel (☎ 9168 6101; Roberta
Ave; mains $16-31) has a French-influenced
menu, a decent wine list and a friendly
bar, as well as overpriced **rooms** (budget/motel
d $100/155).

Getting There & Away
Northwest Regional Airlines (☎ 1300 136 629)
has daily flights to Fitzroy Crossing and
Broome. **McCafferty's/Greyhound** (☎ 13 20 30)
buses running to Perth and Darwin stop at
the Poinciana Roadhouse.

WOLFE CREEK METEORITE CRATER
The 835m-wide and 50m-deep Wolfe Creek
meteorite crater is the second largest crater
in the world. To the local Jaru people, the
crater, called Kandimalal, marks the spot
where a huge snake emerged from the
ground.

The Wolfe Creek Crater turn-off is
16km west of Halls Creek, from where it's
137km south along the rough, rocky Tanami Track. A 4WD with food, water and
fuel supplies is definitely recommended.
Otherwise, **Oasis Air** (☎ 08-9168 6462; $110)
has a one-hour flight over the crater from
Halls Creek.

PURNULULU (BUNGLE BUNGLE) NATIONAL PARK

The 3000-sq-km Purnululu National Park contains the extraordinary Bungle Bungle Range, with its famous striped rock towers, and attracts huge numbers of visitors during the Dry. Amazingly, these formations were only 'discovered' during the 1980s (although the Kidja people were pretty familiar with them) and the park was created in 1987. The Bungle Bungles were added to the World Heritage list in 2003. The name *purnululu* means 'sandstone' in the local Kidja dialect and Bungle Bungle is thought to be a misspelling of 'bundle bundle', a common grass.

The distinctive rounded rock towers are made of sandstone and rough conglomerates, and their stripes reflect the amount of water the layers accept – the rock within the dark stripes is more permeable, allowing algae to flourish, while the less-permeable lighter layers are created by iron and manganese stains. However, the park is also noted for its Aboriginal art galleries, plus the beautiful pools hidden within the gorges and the rich wildlife they attract, including nailtail wallabies and over 130 bird species.

The park's main attractions all require some legwork to reach. **Echidna Chasm** in the north and **Cathedral Gorge** in the south are about an hour's walk from the car parks. The soaring **Piccaninny Gorge** is an 18km round trip that takes eight to 10 hours to walk; this makes for a good overnight trip. The restricted gorges in the northern part of the park can only be seen from the air.

The park is only open April to December. If you're driving, the turn-off from the highway is 53km south off Warmun. It's then 52km along a rough 4WD track to the Three Ways junction. From here it's 20 minutes north to **Kurrajong Camp** and 45 minutes south to **Walardi Camp**; both have fresh water and toilets, and camping costs $9 per person.

Tours

The Kununurra hostels offer 4WD **camping tours** (2/3 days $290/430) or, for something more swish, **East Kimberley Tours** (☎ 08-9168 2213; www .eastkimberleytours.com.au) has overnight fly-in tours with cabin accommodation for $740. Several operators also include Purnululu in multiday Kimberley tours – see p933 for details.

Both helicopters and light planes offer scenic flights, although the helicopters can get you much closer to the formations. **Heliwork WA** (☎ 08-9169 1300) charges $220/200 from Warmun/Purnululu for a 30-minute chopper flight. **Oasis Air** (☎ 08-9168 6462) has 80-minute plane flights from Halls Creek ($125).

WYNDHAM
☎ 08 / pop 1000

At the junction of five rivers, 60km north of the Great Northern Hwy, Wyndham's town centre is a few kilometres inland from its historic port. Although it has one of only two crocodile farms in WA, its tourism popularity has waned as Kununurra's has boomed, and these days it's a pretty quiet place. Call into **Kimberley Motors** (☎ 9161 1281; Great Northern Hwy; ☎ 6am-6pm) for tourist information.

This is real crocodile country (a 20m concrete croc greets you as you arrive in town) and **Wyndham Crocodile Farm** (☎ 9161 1124; Barytes Rd; adult/child $14/8; ☒ 8.30am-4pm in the Dry, 11am-2pm in the Wet) has some monstrous specimens, as well as a breeding programme and Komodo dragons (when they're not in Queensland on breeding missions). It's best to visit at feeding time (11am).

Five Rivers Lookout on Mt Bastion (with a view of the King, Pentecost, Durack, Forrest and Ord Rivers entering the Cambridge Gulf) is particularly good at sunrise and sunset, while **Warriu Dreamtime Park** (Koolama St) features enormous statues of a local family with their domestic animals – a striking sight. About 15km from Wyndham is **Parry Lagoons Nature Reserve**, a beautiful wetlands that teems with birds in the Wet, and the **Grotto**, a peaceful pool surrounded by lush vegetation in a small gorge.

Sleeping & Eating

Parry's Creek Farm (☎ 9161 1139; www.parrycreek farm.com.au; Parry Creek Rd; camp/caravan sites $16/20, s/ d $50/65, cabin d $180; meals $9-23; ☒) About 9km along a dirt track, 20km south of Wyndham, this former farm near Parry Lagoons is a bird-watcher's paradise. The tree-top-level cabins above the river are excellent, but there's accommodation at all levels, plus a reasonable restaurant (open

WESTERN AUSTRALIA

April to November only), a bar, free use of canoes, a good campers kitchen and a small pool.

Gulf Breeze Guest House (☎ /fax 9161 1401; 6 O'Donnell St; s/tw $30/50) This compact place at Wyndham Port is pretty basic, but has cool verandas, a kitchen, laundry and pool, and is across from the pub.

Three Mile Caravan Park (☎ 9161 1064; Baker St; camp/caravan sites $16/18; donga s $30) A great little place with an enormous boab, it has plenty of shade, a small campers kitchen and a tiny pool.

Wyndham Town Hotel (☎ 9161 1202; fax 9161 1190; O'Donnell St; standard/deluxe d $90/100; 🛱) A large bar, OK motel rooms and **counter meals** ($10-18) are available at this friendly pub.

Getting There & Away

The collapse of Ansett Airlines robbed Wyndham of its bus service with Kununurra. However, you can take a one-day tour from Kununurra with **Triangle Tours** (☎ 9168 1272; adult/child $165/90), or **Wyndham Coach Connection** (☎ 9161 1201) will take you there on a charter basis ($165 per busload).

KUNUNURRA
☎ 08 / pop 6000

Founded in 1960 as the centre for the Ord River irrigation scheme, Kununurra is a modern town in an attractive setting, flanked by the Lily Creek Lagoon and the diminutive Mirima National Park. Tourism has developed quickly in recent years thanks to the proximity of the Gibb River Rd, Lake Argyle and Purnululu National Park, although there isn't much to do it town itself.

There's 90 minutes' time difference between Kununurra and the Northern Territory, and strict quarantine restrictions apply in WA (don't bring fruit etc).

Information

The Kununurra **visitors centre** (☎ 9168 1177; www.eastkimberley.com; Coolibah Dr; ☻ 8.30am-5.30pm, shorter hours in the Wet) has lots of information and can book tours. You can go online at **Kununurra Telecentre** (☎ 9169 1868; Banksia St; ☻ 9am-4pm Mon-Fri) or **Farmers Market** (☎ 9168 2532; 1 Ebony St; ☻ 9am-5pm Mon-Fri, 9am-noon Sat). **CALM** (☎ 9168 0200) is on Konkerberry Dr.

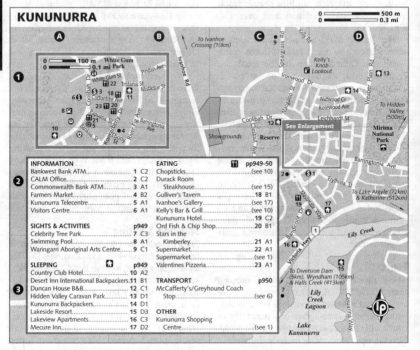

KUNUNURRA

0 — 500 m
0 — 0.3 mi

INFORMATION	
Bankwest Bank ATM	1 C2
CALM Office	2 C2
Commonwealth Bank ATM	3 A1
Farmers Market	4 B2
Kununurra Telecentre	5 A1
Visitors Centre	6 A1

SIGHTS & ACTIVITIES	p949
Celebrity Tree Park	7 C3
Swimming Pool	8 A1
Waringarri Aboriginal Arts Centre	9 C1

SLEEPING 🛏	p949
Country Club Hotel	10 A2
Desert Inn International Backpackers	11 B1
Duncan House B&B	12 C1
Hidden Valley Caravan Park	13 D1
Kununurra Backpackers	14 D1
Lakeside Resort	15 D3
Lakeview Apartments	16 C3
Mecure Inn	17 D2

EATING 🍴	pp949-50
Chopsticks	(see 10)
Durack Room Steakhouse	(see 15)
Gulliver's Tavern	18 B1
Ivanhoe's Gallery	(see 17)
Kelly's Bar & Grill	(see 10)
Kununurra Hotel	19 C2
Ord Fish & Chip Shop	20 B1
Stars in the Kimberley	21 A1
Supermarket	22 A1
Supermarket	(see 1)
Valentines Pizzeria	23 A1

TRANSPORT	p950
McCafferty's/Greyhound Coach Stop	(see 6)

OTHER	
Kununurra Shopping Centre	(see 1)

Sights & Activities
MIRIMA NATIONAL PARK
Only 2km from the town centre, **Mirima National Park** (admission per car $9) is a wonderful area of rugged sedimentary formations, steep gorges and great views, and is a good spot to while away half a day. While most of the park is made up of spinifex plains dotted with boab trees, the twisted sandstone gorges of **Hidden Valley** are the park's main attraction. Formed by uplift over the past 20 million years, they are home to agile wallabies, short-eared rock wallabies, dingoes, echidnas and snakes, while black kites and several types of finch are readily seen. There are two good walking tracks to check out – **Wuttuwutubin Trail** (500m return, 20 minutes), which takes you to a point overlooking Kununurra, and **Didbagirring Trail** (1km return, 1 hour), a steep, demanding scramble that rewards with even better views of town and the park. You can walk to both from the town centre in about 25 minutes.

OTHER SIGHTS & ACTIVITIES
Lily Creek Lagoon is a miniwetlands next to town with lots of birdlife; it's nice for an evening stroll and has a 'celebrity' tree park. Lake Kununurra, also called the **Diversion Dam**, has picnic spots and is popular with water-skiers and boating enthusiasts; there's good fishing below the Lower Dam.

There are good views from **Kelly's Knob**, a favourite sunset viewpoint on the town's northern fringe. During the Wet, distant thunderstorms are spectacular when viewed from the lookout, although it's sometimes struck by lightning.

The **Waringarri Aboriginal Arts Centre** (Speargrass Rd) is an Aboriginal community shop with arts and crafts for sale – you'll often find artists working here.

Tours
Popular, self-guided **canoe trips** ($145) on the Ord River, between Lake Argyle and Diversion Dam (55km), are offered by the hostels. Camping is at established river sites and all equipment is supplied. **Wild Adventure Tours** (☎ 0409-456 643) offers abseiling tours to Kelly's Knob ($60) and the Grotto ($110).

You can fly over Purnululu National Park ($190, 2 hours) with **Alligator Airways** (☎ 1800 632 533) or **Slingair** (☎ 1800 095 500; www.slingair.com.au). Both offer many other day and overnight regional tours, including flights over Lake Argyle.

Sleeping
There are good options in Kununurra, although prices rise steeply during the Dry.

Lakeview Apartments (☎ 9168 0000; lakeviewapartments@wn.com.au; 224 Victoria Hwy; 1-/2-/3-bedroom apt $155/180/250; 🐾) Across from the lagoon, this newish place is nothing to look at from the outside, but has Kununurra's best self-contained rooms with spacious living areas, good kitchens and weekly rates.

Lakeside Resort (☎ 1800 786 692, 9169 1092; www.lakeside.com.au; Casuarina Way; camp/caravan sites $18/22, cabin d $120, motel d & tw $155; 🐾) On the opposite shore of the lagoon, this three-acre place enjoys water frontage and a good mix of accommodation, and a restaurant.

Hidden Valley Caravan Park (☎ 9168 1790; www.hiddenvalleycp.com.au; Weaber Plains Rd; camp/caravan sites $20/22, cabin d $95, extra adult $10) Under the looming crags of Mirima National Park, this excellent little park is a bit out of the way, but the amenities are good, there's a large pool and the self-contained cabins are well priced.

Kununurra Backpackers (☎ 1800 641 998, 9169 1998; www.adventure.kimberley.net.au; 24 Nutwood Cres; dm/d $18/50; 🐾) and **Desert Inn International Backpackers** (☎ 1800 805 010, 9168 2702; www.yha.com.au; 257 Konkerberry Dr; dm $17-18, d & tw $45; 🐾) are both well set up for short- and long-term travellers, although they are busy in season. Each has a pool and good outdoor areas, and offer adventure tours throughout the Kimberley.

Also recommended are **Country Club Hotel** (☎ 9168 1024; 47 Coolibah Dr; motel/unit d $170/230), which has pleasant tropical gardens, and **Duncan House B&B** (☎ 9168 2436; johnsonk@bigpond.com; 167 Coolibah Dr; s/d $105/125; 🐾), a welcoming and stylish place with comfortable rooms with bathrooms and all the amenities.

Eating
Apart from one good café-restaurant, choices here are restricted to motel eateries, pub counter meals and a few takeaway places, but the quality is generally OK.

Stars in the Kimberley (☎ 9168 1122; 4 Papuana St; mains $18-29) Tuscan-inspired décor, well-spaced tables, prompt service, decent coffee and a good Mod Oz menu make this

the standout choice for lunch or dinner in Kununurra.

Ord Fish & Chip Shop (☎ 9169 1222; Konkerberry Dr; ☺ 4-8pm) The fish and chips here are top rate, especially the barramundi ($9).

Valentine's Pizzeria (☎ 9169 1167; Cottontree Ave; pizzas $12-20; ☺ 5pm-late) The pizza here is pretty good and can be eaten at a small booth or delivered to your room. There's also a Mexican menu (mains $8 to $18).

Chopsticks (☎ 9168 1024; 47 Coolibah Dr; mains $15-19) In the Country Club Hotel, the Chinese food here is good for a country Chinese place. Also in the complex is a steakhouse, **Kelly's Bar & Grill** (mains $18-30).

Kununurra Hotel (☎ 9168 1344; 8 Messmate Way) and **Gulliver's Tavern** (☎ 9168 1666; 196 Cottontree Ave) both have reasonable counter meals in the $13 to $23 range, plus convivial bars.

Ivanhoe's Gallery (☎ 9168 1455; cnr Victoria Hwy & Messmate Way; mains $18-30), at the Mercure Inn, looks over tropical gardens and has a popular seafood and steak menu.

Durack Room Steakhouse (☎ 1800 786 692, 9169 1092; www.lakeside.com.au; Casuarina Way; mains $19-26), at Lakeside Resort, reputedly has the best steaks in town.

There are two supermarkets in town (the one in the shopping centre is open 24 hours), plus a café and takeaway.

Getting There & Around

Qantas/Airlink (☎ 13 13 13) flies to Broome (3 weekly) and Darwin (5 weekly). **McCafferty's/Greyhound** (☎ 13 20 30) has daily buses to Darwin and Perth that stop at the visitors centre. Destinations include Halls Creek ($79, 4½ hours), Fitzroy Crossing ($130,

8 hours), Derby ($155, 11¾ hours) and Broome ($173, 14¾ hours).

LAKE ARGYLE

Created by the Ord River Dam, Lake Argyle is the second-biggest storage reservoir in Australia, holding somewhere between nine and 18 times as much water as Sydney Harbour, depending on who you ask. It was built to regulate the massive extremes of water between the Wet and the Dry and, for better or worse, has allowed mass agriculture to flourish in the region. The scenery is spectacular, with high, steep red ridges plunging into the lake's blue waters.

Seat of the noted pastoralist Durack family, the **Argyle Homestead** (admission $2; ☺ 8.30am-4.30pm Apr-Oct) was moved to its current location when its old site was flooded by the rising Argyle Dam. It has memorabilia from the good old days, as well as Aboriginal artefacts and a small cemetery.

Lake Argyle Cruises (☎ 08-9168 7361; www .lakeargyle.com) has morning/sunset/six-hour cruises for $38/48/108, plus $15 for Kununurra transfers. Bring swimming gear with you.

Triple J Tours (☎ 08-9168 2662; jjjtours@kimberley .net.au) has tours that include a visit to Argyle Homestead, a cruise on Lake Argyle and a boat trip back to Kununurra on the Ord River.

Lake Argyle Tourist Village (☎ 08-9168 7360; bigfish.in@bigpond.com.au; Parker Rd; camp/caravan sites $16/21, motel s/d $75/85), right by the lake, incorporates caravan park, motel, pub and bistro.

Directory

ACCOMMODATION

It's not difficult to get a good night's sleep in Australia, which offers everything from the tent-pegged confines of camping grounds and the communal space of hostels to gourmet breakfasts in guesthouses and at-your-fingertip resorts, plus the gamut of hotel and motel lodgings.

The listings in the accommodation sections of this guidebook are ordered from budget to mid-range to top-end options. We generally treat any place that charges up to $40 per single or $80 per double as budget accommodation. Mid-range facilities are usually in the range of $80 to $130 per double, while the top-end tag is applied

---

> **PRACTICALITIES**
>
> - Videos you buy or watch will be based on the PAL system.
>
> - Leaf through the daily Sydney Morning Herald, Melbourne's Age or the national Australian broadsheet.
>
> - Find tabloid titillation in the Daily Telegraph (Sydney), Herald Sun (Melbourne) and Courier Mail (Brisbane) papers.
>
> - Switch on the box to watch the ad-free ABC, the government-sponsored and multicultural SBS, or one of three commercial TV stations, namely Seven, Nine and Ten.
>
> - Plug your hairdryer into a three-pin adaptor (not the same as British three-pin adaptors) before plugging into the electricity supply (220–240V AC, 50Hz).

to places charging more than $130 per double. Of course, in more-expensive areas like metropolitan Sydney and Melbourne, 'budget' can mean paying up to $100 per double and 'mid-range' places can end up costing you in the vicinity of $160 for a double.

In most areas you'll find seasonal price variations. Over summer and at other peak times, particularly school and public holidays, prices are usually at their highest, whereas outside these times useful discounts and lower walk-in rates can be found. One exception is the Top End, where the wet season (summer) is the low season and prices can drop by as much as 50%.

The weekend escape is a notion that figures prominently in the Australian psyche, meaning accommodation from Friday night through Sunday can be in greater demand (and pricier) in major holiday areas. High-season prices are quoted in this guidebook unless otherwise indicated. For more information on Aussie climatic seasons, see p959, and for specific details on each state or territory see Geography & Climate in each destination chapter.

B&Bs

The local bed and breakfast (or guesthouse) birthrate is climbing rapidly. New places are opening all the time and the options include everything from restored miners' cottages, converted barns, rambling old houses, upmarket country manors and beachside bungalows to a simple bedroom in a family home. In areas that tend to attract weekenders – quaint historic towns, wine regions, accessible forest regions such as the Blue Mountains in New South Wales (NSW) and the Dandenongs in Victoria – B&Bs are often upmarket and will charge a fortune if you want to stay between Friday and Sunday in high season (assuming you could even get in). Tariffs are typically in the $70 to $150 (per double) bracket, but can be much higher.

Local tourist offices can usually give you a list of places. For some online information, try www.babs.com.au or www.innaustralia .com.au.

Camping & Caravan Parks

The cheapest accommodation lies outdoors, where the nightly cost of camping for two people is usually somewhere between $13 and $23, slightly more for a powered site. Whether you're packing a tent, driving a campervan or towing a caravan (house trailer in North American–speak), camping in the bush is a highlight of travelling in Australia. In places like the outback and northern Australia you often won't even need a tent, and nights spent around a camp fire under the stars are unforgettable. Stays at designated sites in national parks normally cost between $3 and $8 per person. When it comes to urban camping, remember that most city camping grounds are miles away from the centre of town.

Most caravan parks are good value, with almost all of them equipped with hot showers, flushing toilets and laundry facilities, and occasionally a pool. Many have old on-site caravans for rent, but these are largely being replaced by on-site cabins. Cabin sizes and facilities vary, but expect to pay $50 to $90 for two people in a cabin with a kitchenette. If you intend doing a lot of caravanning/camping, consider joining one of the major chains such as **Big 4** (www.big4.com.au), which offers discounts at member parks.

Hostels

Hostels are a highly social but low-cost fixture of the Australian accommodation scene. In some areas, travellers may find hostels are reinventing themselves as 'inns' or 'guesthouses', partly to broaden their appeal beyond backpackers.

HOSTEL ORGANISATIONS

There are 140 hostel franchisees of **VIP Backpacker Resorts** (☎ 07-3395 6111; www.back packers.com; 3/41 Steele Pl, Morningside, Qld 4170) in Australia and many more overseas. For $39 you'll receive a 12-month membership, entitling you to a $1 discount on accommodation and a 5% to 15% discount on other products such as air and bus transport, tours and activities. You can join online, at VIP hostels or at larger agencies dealing in backpacker travel.

Nomads Backpackers (☎ 1800 819 883, 08-8363 7633; www.nomadsworld.com; 43 The Parade, Kent Town, SA 5067) has around 46 franchisees in Australia alone. Membership ($29 for 12 months) likewise entitles you to numerous discounts. You can join at participating hostels, backpacker travel agencies, online, or via the Nomads head office.

INDEPENDENT HOSTELS

Australia has numerous independent hostels, with the fierce competition for the backpacker dollar prompting fairly high standards and plenty of enticements, such as free breakfasts, courtesy buses and discount meal vouchers. In the cities, some places are run-down hotels trying to fill empty rooms; the unrenovated ones are often gloomy and depressing. Others are converted motels where each four-to-six-bed unit has a fridge, TV and bathroom, but communal areas and cooking facilities may be lacking. There are also purpose-built hostels, often with the best facilities but these places are sometimes too big and impersonal – avoid 'we love to party' places if you're in an introspective mood. The best places tend to be the smaller, more intimate hostels where the owner is also the manager.

Independent backpacker establishments typically charge $19 to $26 for a dorm bed and $40 to $60 for a twin or double room (usually without bathroom), often with a small discount if you're a member of YHA,

VIP and sometimes Nomads (see the earlier Hostel Organisations section for details).

Some places will only admit overseas backpackers; this is mainly in city hostels that have had problems with locals sleeping over and bothering the backpackers. Hostels that discourage or ban Aussies say it's only a rowdy minority that makes trouble, and often these hostels will just ask for identification in order to deter potential troublemakers, but it certainly can be annoying, patronising and discriminatory for genuine people trying to travel in their own country. Also watch out for those hostels catering expressly to working backpackers, where wages and facilities are minimal but rent is high.

YHA HOSTELS

Australia has over 140 hostels as part of the Youth Hostels Association (YHA). The **YHA** (head office ☎ 02-9565 1699; www.yha.com.au; Level 11, 10 Mallett St, Camperdown, NSW 2050) is part of the **International Youth Hostel Federation** (IYHF; www.hihostels.com), also known as Hostelling International (HI), so if you're already a member of that organisation in your own country, your membership entitles you to YHA rates in the relevant Australian hostels. Nightly charges are between $10 and $30 for members; most hostels also take non-YHA members for an extra $3.50. Visitors to Australia should purchase a HI card preferably in their country of residence, but can also buy one at major local YHA hostels at a cost of $35 for 12 months; see the HI website for further details. Australian residents can become full YHA members for $55/85 for one/two years; join online, at a state office or any youth hostel.

YHA hostels provide basic accommodation, usually in small dormitories (bunk rooms), although many provide twin rooms and even doubles. They have 24-hour access, cooking facilities, a communal area with a TV, laundry facilities and, in larger hostels, travel offices. There's often a maximum-stay period (usually five to seven days). Bed linen is provided (sleeping bags are not allowed) in all hostels except those in wilderness areas, where you'll need your own sleeping sheet.

The annual *YHA Accommodation & Discounts Guide* booklet details all Australian hostels and any membership discount entitlements (transport, activities etc).

Hotels & Motels

Except for pubs (discussed below), the hotels that exist in cities or places visited by lots of tourists are generally of the business or luxury variety (insert the name of your favourite chain here) where you get a comfortable, anonymous and mod con–filled room in a multistorey block. These places tend to have a pool, restaurant/café, room service and various other facilities. We quote 'rack rates' (official advertised rates) throughout this book; often hotels/motels will offer regular discounts and special deals, too.

For comfortable mid-range accommodation that's available all over Australia, motels (or motor inns) are the places to stay in. Prices vary and there's rarely a cheaper rate for singles, so motels are better for couples or groups of three. Most motels are modern, low-rise and have similar facilities (tea- and coffee-making, fridge, TV, air-con, bathroom) but the price will indicate the standard. You'll mostly pay between $50 and $120 for a room.

Pubs

For the budget traveller, hotels in Australia are the ones that serve beer – commonly known as pubs (from the term 'public house'). In country towns, pubs are invariably found in the town centre. Many pubs were built during boom times, so they're often among the largest and most extravagant buildings in town. In tourist areas some of these pubs have been restored as heritage buildings, but generally the rooms remain small and old-fashioned, with a long amble down the hall to the bathroom. You can sometimes rent a single room at a country pub for not too much more than a hostel dorm, and you'll be in the social heart of the town to boot. But if you're a light sleeper, never (ever) book a room above the bar.

Standard pubs have singles/doubles with shared facilities starting from around $30/50, obviously more if you want a private bathroom. Few have a separate reception area – just ask in the bar if there are rooms available.

Rental Accommodation

The ubiquitous holiday flat resembles a motel unit but has a kitchen or cooking facilities. It can come with two or more bedrooms and is often rented on a weekly

basis – higher prices are often reserved for shorter stays. For a two-bedroom flat, you're looking at anywhere from $60 to $95 per night. The other alternative in major cities is to take out a serviced apartment.

If you're interested in a shared flat or house for a long-term stay, delve into the classified advertisements sections of the daily newspapers; Wednesday and Saturday are usually the best days. Notice boards in universities, hostels, bookshops and cafés are also good to check out.

Other Accommodation

Scattered throughout the country are lots of less-conventional accommodation possibilities and options.

A decent number of the country's farms offer a bed for a night. At some you sit back and watch other people raise a sweat, while others like to get you involved in day-to-day activities. At a couple of remote outback stations you can stay in homestead rooms or shearer's quarters and try activities such as horse riding. Check out the options on the website for **Australian Farmhost Holidays** (www.australiafarmhost.com); state tourist offices should also be able to tell you what's available.

Back in city limits, it's sometimes possible to stay in the hostels and halls of residence normally occupied by university students, though you'll need to time your stay to coincide with the longer uni holiday periods. Coober Pedy (SA), meanwhile, is famed for its underground dwellings, a couple of which have been turned into hostels and guesthouses. And wannabe sailors can investigate houseboat hire on easily navigable

watercourses such as the Murray River in SA and Victoria (for details on accommodation options visit www.murray-river.net/homepage.htm), or the Hawkesbury River in NSW; it can work out at reasonable rates if you have a big enough group.

ACTIVITIES

Although Australia provides plenty of excuses to sit back and do little more than roll your eyes across some fine landscape, that same landscape lends itself very well to any number of energetic pursuits, whether it's on the rocks, wilderness trails and mountains of dry land, or on the offshore swells and reefs. The following is just a general rundown of what's possible; for specifics, read the individual activities entries in each state and territory chapter.

Adrenalin-Charged Activities

Bungee jumping is quite big on either side of the country, with elastic entertainment on the Gold Coast (p301) and in Perth (p838).

Fantastic sites for **rock climbing** and **abseiling** include the Blue Mountains (p148) in NSW, Victoria's Mt Arapiles (p518) and at Mt Buffalo in Victoria's High Country (p549), the spectacular Hazards at Coles Bay (p611) on Tasmania's east coast, the Warrumbungle National Park (p204) in northwest NSW and Karijini National Park (p904) in Western Australia (WA). Local professionals can set you up with equipment and training. For online info on rock climbing in Australia, visit www.climbing.com.au.

Tandem **paragliding** flights are available anywhere there are good take-off and

---

PUBLIC LIABILITY

Huge increases in the cost of public liability insurance around Australia in the past few years have forced the closure or scaling back of numerous tours and organised outdoor activities like horse riding and rock climbing, and threatened the viability of many small businesses. Also at risk are volunteer-run community events that have been unable to get affordable insurance.

The exorbitant insurance costs faced by small businesses and volunteer organisations have been blamed on a vast range of issues: the relatively recent collapse of several major Australian insurance companies, insurance industry greed, some ridiculously high legal pay-outs awarded to people for minor incidents, a growing culture of litigation, low safety standards and ambulance-chasing lawyers seeking the biggest pay-out possible.

Federal, state and territory representatives have met several times to discuss the problem and at the time of writing appeared to have agreed on measures to reform negligence law. But these are yet to be fully implemented and, in the meantime, more businesses may go to the wall by the time you read this book.

landing points and thermal winds. A good place to learn is at Bright (p553) in the Victorian High Country; national paragliding championships are held annually in Manilla (p193) in NSW. **Sky-diving** and **parachuting** are also widely practised, with most clubs listed in the *Yellow Pages telephone book*.

Hot-air ballooning is much less adventurous but worth doing for sleepy dawn views. You can catch a flight in most capital cities, Alice Springs (p800), and the Hunter Valley (p161) and Barossa Valley (p700) wine regions.

Bird-Watching

Australia is a twitchers' haven, with a wide variety of habitats and birdlife, particularly water birds. **Birds Australia** (☎ 03-9882 2622; www .birdsaustralia.com.au; 415 Riversdale Rd, Hawthorn East, Vic 3123) runs feathered-friend observatories and nonprofit reserves in NSW, Victoria, NT, SA and WA.

Bushwalking

You can take fantastic trails through national parks around the country. Notable walks include the **Overland Track** (p649) and the **South Coast Track** (p652) in Tasmania; the **Australian Alps Walking Track** (p440) in Victoria's High Country; the **Thorsborne Trail** (p388) across Hinchinbrook Island in Queensland; the **Heysen Trail** (p661) in SA; the **Larapinta Trail** (p811) in the Centre; **Mt Kosciuszko** (p219) in NSW; and the **Bibbulmun Track** (p830) in WA.

Lonely Planet's *Walking in Australia* provides detailed information about bushwalking around the country.

Cycling

Those who cycle for fun have access to lots of great cycling routes and touring country for day, weekend or even multiweek trips, while very experienced pedallers can consider trips through the dry Centre or (if they've got a bit of spare time) a circumnavigation of the country. Most large cities have a recreational bike-path system and an abundance of bike-hire places. In most states there are helpful bicycle organisations that can provide maps, useful tips and advice; see Bicycle (p987) in the Transport chapter and individual state chapters for more details on cycling in Australia.

See Lonely Planet's *Cycling Australia* for other useful contacts and details of popular routes. More information and news

---

CONSIDERATIONS FOR RESPONSIBLE BUSHWALKING

Please consider the following when hiking, to help preserve the ecology and beauty of Australia.

▪ Do not urinate or defecate within 100m (320ft) of any water sources. Doing so can lead to the transmission of serious diseases and pollutes precious water supplies.

▪ Use biodegradable detergents and wash at least 50m (160ft) from any water sources.

▪ Avoid cutting wood for fires in popular bushwalking areas as this can cause rapid deforestation. Use a stove that runs on kerosene, methylated spirits or some other liquid fuel, rather than stoves powered by disposable butane gas canisters.

▪ Hillsides and mountain slopes are prone to erosion; it's important to stick to existing tracks.

---

on local pedal-power is available online at www.bicycles.net.au.

Diving & Snorkelling

There's excellent scuba diving (and many dive schools) along the **Great Barrier Reef** (p344). Open-water Professional Association of Diving Instructors' (PADI) courses (www.padi.com) typically cost $300 to $600 for three to five days, depending on how much time you actually spend on the reef. You'll need to procure a medical certificate (about $50) for all certified PADI courses.

In WA the **Ningaloo Reef** (p921) is every bit as interesting as the east-coast reefs, without the tourist numbers, and diving courses are available at **Coral Bay** (p923) and **Exmouth** (p924). In the southern waters around Melbourne, Adelaide, Perth, Tasmania and NSW you can dive around shipwrecks and with seals and dolphins; courses are generally cheaper in the south, too. And don't forget you can also just hire a mask, snorkel and fins for a few dollars.

Fishing

If you like to dangle your line, you've come to the right place. Barramundi fishing is

hugely popular across the Top End and ocean fishing is possible right around the country, from a pier, a beach, or on an organised deep-sea charter. There are many fine rivers and lakes where you can fish for trout, redfin and perch. There are particularly good fishing rivers and lakes in **Tasmania** (p577), and **Cooktown** (p427) in Far North Queensland also attracts a bit of attention.

The uninitiated may think the **Fishnet** website (www.fishnet.com.au) is devoted to stockings, but those keen on all aspects of Australian fishing know better.

Horse & Camel Riding

Exploring the bush by horseback has a peaceful edge over the ruckus of engine-powered transport. In Victoria you can go horse riding in the **High Country** (p544) and follow the spectacular routes of the Snowy Mountains cattle people. In northern Queensland you can ride horses through rainforests, along sand dunes and swim with them in the sea. There are also sundry riding opportunities in Australia's north and west.

Camel riding is an offbeat alternative, especially in central Australia and outback SA where there are camel farms. Originally

---

WHERE TO SURF IN AUSTRALIA   by Andrew Tudor

It was summer, 1915. Hawaiian waterman Duke Kahanamoku demonstrated the art of surfboard riding before a packed grandstand of Australians. He'd carved a board from local timbers before taking to the ocean at Freshwater, on Sydney's north shore. Today, the scene is rip and gouge, as compared to Australian surfing's humble beginnings. Aussies flock to the coast in record numbers searching out the next new swell. But given Australia's vast coastline and relatively small population, there are still days when you, like the Duke, could be the only one out.

Australia boasts several world champions and many world-class breaks. For more information, news, surf cams and photos, look up www.coastalwatch.com, or for daily reports call **The Surf & Snow Line** (☎ 1900 911 525).

New South Wales

Name practically any coastal town in New South Wales (NSW) and there will be good surf nearby.

Sydney's beaches (surf report: www.realsurf.com) are well known for their good surf (p106). Manly, Dee Why, Narrabeen and Avalon are the most popular northern beaches. To the east of Sydney check out the areas around Bondi, and to the south there's good surf around Cronulla.

On the far north coast of the state are Byron Bay (p180), Lennox Head (p179) and Angourie Headland (p178), while on the mid-north coast are Coffs Harbour (p174) and Nambucca Heads (p173). On the lower north coast are the beaches off Newcastle (p153). Down on the south coast, you could try the beaches off Wollongong (p210), Jervis Bay (p216), Ulladulla (p216), Merimbula and Pambula (p218).

Queensland

Surfers Paradise, south of Brisbane, is not what the name suggests. The Gold Coast (p302), however, can be world-class – Burleigh Heads (surf report and photos: www.burleighcam.com.au) and Kirra Point are the better-known breaks, with hollow rights on a solid ground swell. Also check out Coolangatta's Greenmount Point and Duranbah on the southern side of the Point Danger headland.

Just north of Surfers Paradise, North Stradbroke Island (p296) usually has some very powerful beach breaks.

North of Brisbane is the Sunshine Coast, which has a variety of breaks at Caloundra (p310) and Maroochydore (p311).

When it works, Noosa National Park (p313) has a good right-hander but does draw large crowds. Double Island Point (p322), north of Noosa, near Rainbow Beach, is worth getting to, but you'll need a 4WD.

brought in from the Middle East to be used as transport in Australia's harsh desert environment, camels now run wild all over the interior. A sunset camel ride on Cable Beach is *de rigueur* in **Broome** (p935), while at **Stuart's Well** (p815), south of Alice Springs, you can take camel rides lasting from a five-minute stroll to a five-day desert expedition.

Skiing & Snowboarding

Australia has an enthusiastic skiing industry, with snowfields straddling the NSW-Victoria border. The season is relatively short, how-ever, running from about mid-June to early September, and snowfalls can be unpredict-able. The top places to ski are **Thredbo** (p224) and **Perisher** (p224) in NSW's Snowy Moun-tains, and **Falls Creek** (p550) and **Mt Hotham** (p547) in Victoria's High Country. Equip-ment can be hired at the snowfields.

The website for **Skiing Australia** (www.skiing australia.org.au) has links to major resorts and race clubs.

Surfing

World-class waves can be ridden all around the whole of the country, from Queensland's

---

South Australia

Cactus Beach (p719), west of Ceduna on remote Point Sinclair, is SA's best-known surf spot and is also renowned worldwide for one of Australia's best remote waves. Keep an eye out for white pointers (Great White sharks) though. Other places to check are the Eyre and southern Yorke Pe-ninsulas (p662), while closer to Adelaide (surf cam and reports: www.southcam.com.au) and near Victor Harbor there are good waves on the west and south side of the Fleurieu Peninsula (p686).

Tasmania

Despite the cold water, Tasmania has some fine surfing. The best places on the exposed west coast are around Marrawah (p640) and there are many quality spots along the east coast. Check north and south of St Helens, around Eaglehawk Neck (p604) on the Tasman Peninsula and Shelly Beach (p610) near Orford. Bruny Island (p599) also has some surfable waves, and closer to Hobart try Cremorne Point and Clifton Beach (p578).

Victoria

Bells Beach has become synonymous with surfing in Australia and does have a classic right-hander if the swell is up. There are many other excellent breaks throughout the state.

Phillip Island, the Mornington Peninsula and the southwest coast are all within a two-hour drive from Melbourne. On Phillip Island (p495) check Woolamai, Surfies Point, Smiths Beach and Cat Bay. The best places on Mornington Peninsula are Point Leo, Flinders, Gunnamatta, Rye and Portsea.

On the southwest coast you can try Barwon Heads (p491), Torquay, Bells Beach (p500) and numerous spots along the Great Ocean Road. There is also the big and powerful shipwreck coast near Port Campbell (p505), which only experienced surfers should attempt. In Gippsland try Lakes Entrance (p565) and Wilsons Promontory (p559).

For a surf report and photos of Victorian surf spots, check out www.surfshop.com.au.

Western Australia

WA's best-known surfing spot is probably Margaret River (p874) and the surf here can be huge. The beaches and points north and south of Margaret River also offer excellent surf. Scarborough beach (p838), north of Perth has beginners surf and Rottnest Island (p856) has some good breaks, too.

Farther north, Geraldton (p908), Kalbarri (p913) and Carnarvon (p919) are also well worth checking out. However, you may need a 4WD on the coast road north of Carnarvon, and only experienced surfers should attempt these waves.

For details on great surf spots in WA check out the surf report online at www.srosurf.com.

Andrew Tudor is a Lonely Planet employee and an avid surfer.

Gold Coast (p302), the beaches in Sydney (p88) and Victoria's Bells Beach (p500) to Marrawah (p640) in Tasmania, SA's Cactus Beach (p719) and Margaret River (p874) in WA – you could basically spend your whole trip shuttling your board from one break to another.

(More) Water Sports

Most major beach resorts will rent out windsurfing gear and there are outfits on the east coast offering parasailing (behind a speedboat) and jet-boating. The places with the most activities on offer are usually those with the most visitors, such as Airlie Beach (p366), Cairns (p400) and the Gold Coast (p301) in Queensland.

Sailing is a popular activity around the islands of the Great Barrier Reef (see the boxed text 'Sailing the Whitsunday Islands'; p372) and all along the east coast, where you can take lessons or just pitch in and help crew a yacht. The best places for information are the local sailing clubs.

There are a couple of good white-water rafting trips available in Australia, with the best of these being enjoyed on the upper Murray River (p220) in southern NSW, the Nymboida River (p176) in northern NSW, the Tully River (p389) in north Queensland and the Franklin River (p648) in Tasmania. Canoeing and kayaking can be enjoyed on rivers at locales like Katherine Gorge (p788) in the NT, Barrington Tops National Park (p167) in NSW, the Coorong (p708) in SA and Blackwood River (p877) in the southern region of WA.

Whale- & Dolphin-Watching

Migrating southern right and humpback whales pass close to Australia's southern coast on their way between the Antarctic and warmer waters, and whale-watching cruises allow you to get close to these magnificent creatures. The best spots are Eden (p219) in southern NSW, the mid-north coast of NSW, Warrnambool (p506) in Victoria, and Albany (p884) on the southwest cape of WA. Whale-watching seasons are roughly May to October on the west coast and in southwestern Victoria, and September to November on the east coast.

Dolphins can be seen year-round at many places on the east coast, such as Jervis Bay (p216), Port Stephens (p165) and Byron Bay (p181) (which are all in NSW); off WA at places like Bunbury (for more information see the boxed text 'Close Encounters of the Dolphin Kind'; p870), Rockingham (p866), Esperance (p889) and Monkey Mia (p918); and off the coast of Victoria at Sorrento (p493) and at Gippsland (p559).

BUSINESS HOURS

Business hours may vary a little from state to state but most shops and businesses close at 5pm Monday to Friday, and at either noon or 5pm on Saturday. Sunday trading is becoming increasingly common but it is currently limited to the major cities and, to a lesser extent, regional Victoria. In most towns there are usually one or two late shopping nights each week, normally Thursday and/or Friday, when the doors will stay open until around 9pm. Most supermarkets are generally open until at least 8pm and are sometimes open 24 hours. You'll also find milk bars (general stores) and convenience stores often open until late.

Banks are normally open from 9.30am to 4pm Monday to Thursday and until 5pm on Friday. Some large city branches are open from 8am to 6pm weekdays, and a few are also open from 8am to 9pm on Friday. Post offices are open from 9am to 5pm Monday to Friday, but you can also buy stamps on Saturday morning at post office agencies (operated from newsagencies) and from Australia Post shops in all the major cities.

Restaurants across the country typically open at noon for lunch and between 6pm and 7pm for dinner; most dinner bookings are made for 7.30pm or 8pm. Restaurants are typically open until at least 9pm but tend to serve food until later in the evening on Friday and Saturday. That said, the main restaurant strips in large cities keep longer hours throughout the week. Cafés tend to be all-day affairs that either close around 5pm or continue their business into the night. Pubs usually serve food from noon to 2pm and from 6pm to 8pm. Pubs and bars often open for drinking at lunchtime and continue well into the evening, particularly from Thursday to Saturday.

You should keep in mind that nearly all attractions across Australia are closed on Christmas Day.

CHILDREN
Practicalities

All cities and most major towns have centrally located public rooms where mothers (and sometimes fathers) can go to nurse their baby or change its nappy; check with the local tourist office or city council for details. While many Australians have a relaxed attitude about breast-feeding or nappy changing in public, others frown on it.

Most motels and the better-equipped caravan parks have playgrounds and swimming pools, and can supply cots and baby baths – motels may also have in-house children's videos and child-minding services. Top-end hotels and many (but not all) mid-range hotels are well versed in the needs of guests who have children. B&Bs, on the other hand, often market themselves as sanctuaries from all things child-related. Some cafés and restaurants make it difficult to dine with small children, lacking a specialised children's menu, but many other do have kids' meals, or will provide small serves from the main menu. Some also supply high chairs.

If you want to leave Junior behind for a few hours, some of Australia's numerous licensed child-care agencies have places set aside for casual care. To find them, check under 'Baby Sitters' and 'Child Care Centres' in the *Yellow Pages* telephone book, or phone the local council for a list. Licensed centres are subject to government regulation and usually adhere to high standards; to be on the safe side, avoid unlicensed ones.

Child concessions (and family rates) often apply for such things as accommodation, tours, admission fees, and air, bus and train transport, with some discounts as high as 50% of the adult rate. However, the definition of 'child' can vary from under 12 to under 18 years. Accommodation concessions generally apply to children under 12 years sharing the same room as adults. On the major airlines, infants travel free provided they don't occupy a seat – child fares usually apply between the ages of two and 11 years.

Medical services and facilities in Australia are of a high standard, and items such as baby food formula and disposable nappies are widely available in urban centres.

Major hire-car companies will supply and fit booster seats for you, for which you'll be charged around $16 for up to three days' use, with an additional daily fee for longer periods.

Lonely Planet's *Travel with Children* contains plenty of useful information.

Sights & Activities

There's no shortage of active, interesting or amusing things for children to focus on in Australia. Every town or city has at least some parkland, or you could head into the countryside for wide open spaces, bushland, rainforests or beaches. Not all of Australia's museums will hold the interest of kids, but there are still plenty of historical, natural or science-based exhibits to get them thinking – these range from zoos and aquariums to pioneer villages and interactive technology centres. And as for entertainment, if the theme parks of the Gold Coast are not on your itinerary, there will always be a cinema within reach. For more ideas on how to keep kids occupied, see Childish Delights (p23). See also the children-specific information detailed in each state/territory capital city section.

CLIMATE

Australia's size means there's a lot of climatic variation, but without severe extremes. The southern third of the country has cold (though generally not freezing) winters (June through August). Tasmania and the alpine country in Victoria and New South Wales get particularly chilly. Summers (December to February) are pleasant and warm, sometimes quite hot. Spring (September to November) and autumn (March through May) are transition months, much the same as in Europe and North America.

As you head north the climate changes dramatically, but seasonal variations become fewer until, in the far north around Darwin and Cairns, you're in the monsoon belt where there are just two seasons: hot and wet, and hot and dry. The centre of the continent is arid – hot and dry during the day, but often bitterly cold at night.

See When to Go (p13) for more information on Australia's seasons.

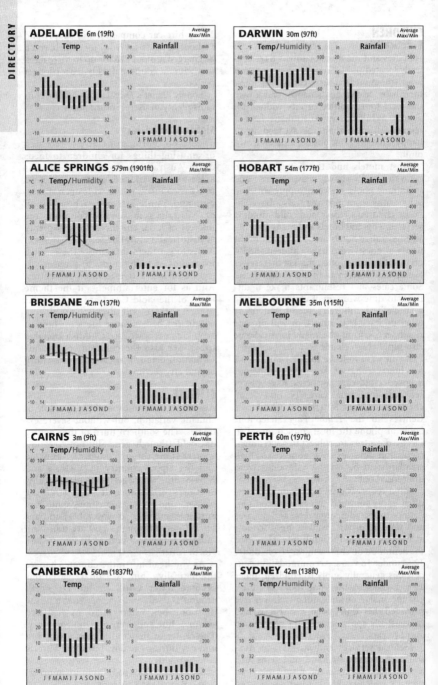

CUSTOMS & QUARANTINE

For comprehensive information on customs regulations, contact the **Australian Customs Service** (☎ 1300 363 263, 02-6275 6666; www.customs .gov.au).

When entering Australia you can bring most articles in free of duty provided that customs is satisfied they are for personal use and that you'll be taking them with you when you leave. There's a duty-free quota per person of 1125mL of alcohol, 250 cigarettes and dutiable goods up to the value of A$400.

There are duty-free stores at international airports and in their associated cities. Treat them with healthy suspicion: 'duty-free' is one of the world's most overworked catchphrases and it's often just an excuse to sell things at prices you can easily beat with a little shopping around. Alcohol and cigarettes are certainly cheaper duty free, though, as they are heavily taxed in Australia.

When it comes to prohibited goods, there are a few things you should be particularly conscientious about. The first is drugs, which customs authorities are adept at sniffing out – unless you want to make a first-hand investigation of conditions in Australian jails, don't bring illegal drugs in with you. And note that all medicines must be declared.

The second is all food, plant material and animal products. You will be asked to declare on arrival all goods of animal, or plant origin (wooden spoons, straw hats, the lot) and show them to a quarantine officer. The authorities are naturally keen to protect Australia's unique environment and important agricultural industries by preventing weeds, pests or diseases getting into the country – Australia has so far managed to escape many of the pests and diseases prevalent elsewhere in the world. Food is also prohibited, particularly meat, cheese, fruit, vegetables and flowers, plus there are restrictions on taking fruit and vegetables between states; for more details see the boxed text 'Interstate Quarantine' (p1000). And if you lug in a souvenir, such as a drum with animal hide for a skin, or a wooden article (though these items are not strictly prohibited they are strictly subject to inspection) that shows signs of insect damage, it won't get through. Some items may require treatment to make them safe before they are allowed in.

Weapons and firearms are either prohibited or require a permit and safety testing. Other restricted goods include products made from protected wildlife species (such as animal skins, coral or ivory), unapproved telecommunications devices and live animals.

It's worth mentioning that Australia takes quarantine very seriously. All luggage is screened or X-rayed – if you fail to declare quarantine items on arrival and are caught, you risk an on-the-spot fine of A$220, or prosecution which may result in fines over $A60,000, as well as up to 10 years imprisonment. For more information on quarantine regulations contact the **Australian Quarantine and Inspection Service** (AQIS; www.aqis.gov.au). See also the boxed text 'Crikey – Quarantine Matters' (opposite).

DANGERS & ANNOYANCES
Animal Hazards

Judging by Australia's remarkable profusion of dangerous creatures, Mother Nature must have been really pissed off when she concocted the local wildlife. Apart from the presence of poisonous snakes and spiders, the country has also had its share of shark and crocodile attacks and, to top it off, is home to the world's deadliest creature, the box jellyfish (see following). Travellers don't need to be in a constant state of alarm, however – you're unlikely to see many of these creatures in the wild, much less be attacked by one.

Hospitals have antivenin on hand for all common snake and spider bites, but it helps to know what it was that bit you.

CRIKEY – QUARANTINE MATTERS!
by Steve Irwin (Crocodile Hunter)

Lucky for us, our remoteness and quarantine keeps pests and diseases out of Australia. But if you're not careful, they can sneak in, hiding in things brought in from overseas. That's why you must declare all food, plant and animal material and have it checked by Quarantine. If you don't, and you're caught – and you will be – you could be whacked with a whopping big fine. So if you travel to Australia, remember: quarantine matters. Don't muck with it!

BOX JELLYFISH

There have been numerous fatal encounters between swimmers and these large jellyfish on the northern coast. Also known as the sea wasp or 'stinger', their venomous tentacles can grow up to 3m long. You can be stung during any month, but the worst time is from November to the end of April when you should stay out of the water unless you're wearing protective clothing such as a 'stinger suit', available from swimwear and sporting shops in the stinger zone. The box jellyfish also has a tiny, lethal relative called an Irukandji, though to date only one north-coast death has been attributed to it.

For information on treating box jellyfish stings, see p1020.

CROCODILES

Up north, saltwater crocodiles ('salties') are a real danger. As well as living around the coast they are found in estuaries, creeks and rivers, sometimes a long way inland. Observe safety signs or ask locals whether an inviting waterhole or river is croc-free before plunging in – these precautions have been fatally ignored in the past.

INSECTS

For four to six months of the year you'll have to cope with those two banes of the Australian outdoors: the fly and the mosquito ('mozzie'). Flies aren't too bad in the cities but they start getting out of hand in the outback, and the further into the outback you go, the more numerous and persistent they seem to be. In central Australia the flies emerge with the warmer spring weather (late August), particularly if there has been good winter rain, and last until the next frosts kill them off. Flies also tend to be bad in various coastal areas. The humble fly net, which fits on a hat, is very effective, but don't expect to land a contract to strut the fashion catwalks of Milan by wearing one. Widely available repellents such as Aerogard and Rid may also help to deter the little bastards, but don't count on it.

Mozzies are a problem in summer, especially near wetlands in tropical areas, and some species are carriers of viral infections; see p1018. Try to keep your arms and legs covered as soon as the sun goes down and make liberal use of insect repellent. For details of what ticks can get up to, see p1018.

SNAKES

There are many venomous snakes in the Australian bush, the most common being the brown and tiger snakes, but few are aggressive – unless you're interfering with one, or have the misfortune to stand on one, it's extremely unlikely that you'll be bitten. The golden rule if you see a snake is to do a Beatles and *let it be*.

For information on treating snake bites, see p1020.

SPIDERS

The deadly funnel-web spider is found in NSW (including Sydney) and its bite is treated in the same way as a snake bite. Another eight-legged critter to stay away from is the black one with a distinctive red stripe on its body, called (strangely) the redback spider; for bites, apply ice and seek medical attention. The white tail is a long, thin black spider with, you guessed it, a white tail, and has a fierce bite that can lead to local inflammation and ulceration. The disturbingly large huntsman spider, which often enters homes, is harmless, though seeing one for the first time can affect your blood pressure.

Bushfires & Blizzards

As has been dramatically illustrated in recent times, bushfires are a regular occurrence in Australia. Don't be the mug who starts one. In hot, dry and windy weather, be extremely careful with any naked flame – cigarette butts thrown out of car windows have started many a fire. On a total fire ban day it's forbidden even to use a camping stove in the open. Locals will not be amused if they catch you breaking this particular law; they'll happily dob you in, and the penalties are severe.

Bushwalkers should seek local advice before setting out. When a total fire ban is in place, delay your trip until the weather improves. If you're out in the bush and you see smoke, even a long way away, take it seriously – bushfires move very quickly and change direction with the wind. Go to the nearest open space, downhill if possible. A forested ridge, on the other hand, is the most dangerous place to be.

BETWEEN THE FLAGS

On any popular ocean beach in Australia during summer you'll probably find a pair of poles stuck in the sand about 200m apart, each with a red-and-yellow flag on them. They signify that the area of the beach between the flags is patrolled by surf lifeguards. It also means that the area outside the flags may not be safe for swimming because of undertows and currents. If you swim between the flags help should arrive quickly if you get into trouble; raise your arm (and yell!) if you need help. Outside the flags and on unpatrolled beaches you are, more or less, on your own.

Australia has a strong tradition of surf life-saving, with regular carnivals in which super-fit athletes compete in a series of events such as swimming, surf kayaking and running. The most well-known competition is the Iron Man series. There are surf life-saving clubs all along the east coast and in Victoria, and most of the lifeguards are volunteer members.

More bushwalkers actually die of cold than in bushfires. Even in summer, temperatures can drop below freezing at night in the mountains and the weather can change very quickly. Blizzards in the mountains of Tasmania, Victoria and NSW can occur at almost any time of the year, even January. Exposure in even moderately cool temperatures can sometimes result in hypothermia – for more information on hypothermia and how to minimise its risk, see p1019.

Crime

Australia is a relatively safe place to visit but you should still take reasonable precautions. Don't leave hotel rooms or cars unlocked, and don't leave your valuables unattended or visible through a car window. Sydney, the Gold Coast, Cairns and Byron Bay all get a dishonourable mention when it comes to theft, so keep an extra-militant eye on your belongings or it'll all end in tears.

Many pubs in Sydney and other major cities have begun posting warnings about drugged drinks, after several reported cases of women accepting a drink from a stranger only to later fall unconscious and be sexually assaulted. Women are being advised to refuse drinks offered by strangers in bars and to drink bottled alcohol rather than from a glass.

On the Road

Australian drivers are generally a courteous bunch, but risks can be posed by rural petrol heads, inner-city speedsters and particularly drink drivers. Potential dangers on the open road include animals, such as kangaroos, which can leap out in front of your vehicle (mainly at dusk); fatigue, caused by travelling long distances without the necessary breaks; and excessive speed. Driving on dirt roads can also be tricky if you're not used to them. For more information on these and other potential dangers see Road Conditions (p998) and Road Hazards (p998).

Swimming

Popular beaches are patrolled by surf lifesavers and patrolled areas are marked off by flags (for details see the boxed text 'Between the Flags'). Even so, surf beaches can be dangerous places to swim if you aren't used to the conditions. Undertows (or 'rips') are the main problem. If you find yourself being carried out by a rip, the important thing to do is just keep afloat; don't panic or try to swim against the rip, which will exhaust you. In most cases the current stops within a couple of hundred metres of the shore and you can then swim parallel to the shore for a short way to get out of the rip and make your way back to land.

A number of people are also paralysed every year by diving into waves in shallow water and hitting a sand bar; check the depth of the water before you leap.

DISABLED TRAVELLERS

Disability awareness in Australia is pretty high and getting higher. Legislation requires that new accommodation meets accessibility standards, and discrimination by tourism operators is illegal. Many of Australia's key attractions provide access for those with limited mobility and a number of sites have also begun addressing the needs of visitors with visual or aural impairments; contact attractions in advance to confirm the facilities. Tour operators with accessible vehicles operate from most capital cities.

AUSTRALIA FOR THE TRAVELLER WITH A DISABILITY

Information

Reliable information is the key ingredient for travellers with a disability and the best source is the **National Information Communication and Awareness Network** (Nican; ☎ /TTY 02-6285 3713, TTY 1800 806 769; www.nican.com.au; 4/2 Phipps Cl, Deakin, ACT 2600). It's an Australia-wide directory providing information on access issues, accessible accommodation, sporting and recreational activities, transport and specialist tour operators.

The website of the **Australian Tourist Commission** (www.australia.com) publishes detailed, downloadable information for people with disabilities, including travel and transport tips and contact addresses of organisations in each state. For more on the commission, see under Tourist Information (p976).

Another source of quality information is the **Disability Information & Resource Centre** (DIRC; ☎ 08-8223 7522; www.dircsa.org.au) in South Australia (SA).

The publication *Easy Access Australia* (www.easyaccessaustralia.com.au) is available from various bookstores and provides details on easily accessible transport, accommodation and attraction options.

A comprehensive website covering over 13,000 public toilets nationwide lists every one that has disability access. For more information, visit www.toiletmap.gov.au.

Air

Accepted only by Qantas, the **Carers Concession Card**, (☎ 13 13 13, TTY 1800 652 660; www.qantas .com.au), entitles a disabled person and the carer travelling with them to a 50% discount on full economy fares; call Nican (see earlier for details) for eligibility and an application form. All of Australia's major airports have dedicated parking spaces, wheelchair access to terminals, accessible toilets and skychairs to convey passengers onto planes via airbridges.

Car Hire

Avis and Hertz offer hire cars with hand controls at no extra charge for pick-up at capital cities and the major airports, but advance notice is required.

The international wheelchair symbol (blue on a white background) for parking in allocated bays is recognised. Maps of central business districts showing accessible routes, toilets etc are available from major city councils, some regional councils and at visitors centres.

Taxi

Most taxi companies in major cities and towns have modified vehicles that will take wheelchairs.

Train

In NSW, CountryLink's XPT trains have at least one carriage (usually the buffet car) with a seat removed for a wheelchair and an accessible toilet. Queensland Rails' *Tilt Train* from Brisbane to Cairns has a wheelchair-accessible carriage.

Melbourne's suburban rail network is accessible and V/Line's country trains and stations are equipped with ramps. Some rural services employ hoist-equipped accessible coaches. Twenty-four hours advance booking is required; **V/Line Disability Services** (☎ 03-9619 2300) is at Spencer St station. **The Travellers' Aid Society** (☎ 03-9670 2873), also at Spencer St train station, provides a meet-and-greet service (arrange this in advance).

DISCOUNT CARDS

The **International Student Travel Confederation** (ISTC; www.istc.org) is an international collective of specialist student travel organisations. It's also the body behind the internationally recognised International Student Identity Card (ISIC), only issued to full-time students aged 12 years and over, and gives the bearer discounts on accommodation, transport and admission to various attractions. The ISTC also produces the International Youth Travel Card (IYTC or Go25), which is issued

to people who are between 12 and 26 years of age and not fulltime students, and gives equivalent benefits to the ISIC. A similar ISTC brainchild is the International Teacher Identity Card (ITIC), available to teaching professionals. All three cards are chiefly available from student travel companies.

Senior travellers and travellers with disabilities who reside in Australia are eligible for concession cards; most states and territories issue their own version and these can be used Australia-wide. Senior and disabled travellers who live overseas will generally find that the cards issued by their respective countries are not 'officially' recognised in Australia, but that most places (though not all) will still acknowledge such a card and grant a concession where one applies.

Travellers over 60 years of age (both Australian residents and visitors) will simply need to present current age-proving identification to be eligible for discounts of up to 70% off regular air fares.

EMBASSIES & CONSULATES
Australian Embassies & Consulates
The website of the **Department of Foreign Affairs & Trade** (www.dfat.gov.au) provides a full listing of all Australian diplomatic missions overseas. They include:

Canada Ottawa (☎ 613-236 0841; www.ahc-ottawa .org; Suite 710, 50 O'Connor St, Ottawa, Ontario K1P 6L2) Also in Vancouver and Toronto.

France Paris (☎ 01-40 59 33 00; www.austgov.fr; 4 Rue Jean Rey, 75724 Cedex 15, Paris)

Germany Berlin (☎ 030-880 0880; www.australian -embassy.de; Friedrichstrasse 200, 10117 Berlin) Also in Frankfurt.

Indonesia Jakarta (☎ 021-2550 5555; www.austembjak .or.id; Jalan HR Rasuna Said Kav C15-16, Kuningan, Jakarta Selatan 12940) Also in Medan (Sumatra) and Denpasar (Bali).

Ireland Dublin (☎ 01-664 5300; www.australianemb assy.ie; 2nd fl, Fitzwilton House, Wilton Terrace, Dublin 2)

Japan Tokyo (☎ 03-5232 4111; www.australia.or.jp; 2-1-14 Mita, Minato-Ku, Tokyo 108-8361) Also in Osaka, Nagoya and Fukuoka City.

Netherlands The Hague (☎ 070-310 82 00; www .australian-embassy.nl; Carnegielaan 4, The Hague 2517 KH)

New Zealand Wellington (☎ 04-473 6411; www .australia.org.nz; 72-78 Hobson St, Thorndon, Wellington); Auckland (☎ 09-921 8800; Level 7, Price Waterhouse Coopers Bldg, 186-194 Quay St, Auckland)

Singapore Singapore (☎ 6836 4100; www.singapore .embassy.gov.au; 25 Napier Rd, Singapore 258507)

Thailand Bangkok (☎ 0 2287 2680; www.austembassy .or.th; 37 South Sathorn Rd, Bangkok 10120) Also in Chiang Mai.

UK London (☎ 020-7379 4334; www.australia.org.uk; Australia House, The Strand, London WC2B 4LA) Also in Edinburgh and Manchester.

USA Washington DC (☎ 202-797 3000; www.austemb .org; 1601 Massachusetts Ave NW, Washington DC 20036) Also in Los Angeles, New York and other major cities.

Embassies & Consulates in Australia
The principal diplomatic representations to Australia are in Canberra. There are also representatives in other major cities, particularly from countries with a strong connection with Australia such as the USA, the UK or New Zealand; or in cities with important connections, such as Darwin, which has an Indonesian consulate.

Addresses of major offices include the following. Look in the *Yellow Pages* phone directories of the capital cities for a more complete listing.

Canada Canberra (Map p251; ☎ 02-6270 4000; www .dfait-maeci.gc.ca/australia; Commonwealth Ave, Canberra, ACT 2600); Sydney (Map pp94-6; ☎ 02-9364 3000; Level 5/111 Harrington St, Sydney, NSW 2000)

France Canberra (Map p251; ☎ 02-6216 0100; www .ambafrance-au.org; 6 Perth Ave, Yarralumla, ACT 2600); Sydney (Map pp94-6; ☎ 02-9261 5779; www.consul france-sydney.org; Level 26, St Martins Tower, 31 Market St, Sydney, NSW 2000)

Germany Canberra (Map p251; ☎ 02-6270 1911; www.germanembassy.org.au; 119 Empire Cct, Yarralumla, ACT 2600); Sydney (Map pp90-1; ☎ 02-9328 7733; 13 Trelawney St, Woollahra, NSW 2025); Melbourne (☎ 03-9864 6888; 480 Punt Rd, South Yarra, Vic 3141)

Indonesia Canberra (Map p251; ☎ 02-6250 8600; www.kbri-canberra.org.au; 8 Darwin Ave, Yarralumla, ACT 2600); Darwin (☎ 08-8941 0048; 20 Harry Chan Ave, Darwin, NT 0801); Sydney (☎ 02-9344 9933; 236-238 Maroubra Rd, Maroubra, NSW 2035)

Ireland Canberra (Map p251; ☎ 02-6273 3022; irish emb@cyberone.com.au; 20 Arkana St, Yarralumla, ACT 2600); Sydney (Map pp94-6; ☎ 02-9231 6999; Level 30, 400 George St, Sydney, NSW 2000)

Japan Canberra (Map p251; ☎ 02-6273 3244; www .japan.org.au; 112 Empire Cct, Yarralumla, ACT 2600); Sydney (Map pp94-6; ☎ 02-9231 3455; Level 34, Colonial Centre, 52 Martin Pl, Sydney, NSW 2000)

Netherlands Canberra (Map p251; ☎ 02-6220 9400; www.netherlands.org.au; 120 Empire Cct, Yarralumla, ACT 2600); Sydney (Map pp90-10; ☎ 02-9387 6644; Level 23, Plaza Tower II, 500 Oxford St, Bondi Junction, NSW 2022)

DIRECTORY

New Zealand Canberra (Map p251; ☎ 02-6270 4211; nzhccba@austarmetro.com.au; Commonwealth Ave, Canberra, ACT 2600); Sydney (Map pp94-6; ☎ 02-8256 2000; nzcgsydney@bigpond.com; Level 10, 55 Hunter St, Sydney, NSW 2000)

Singapore Canberra (Map p251; ☎ 02-6273 3944; 17 Forster Cres, Yarralumla, ACT 2600)

Thailand Canberra (Map p251; ☎ 02-6273 1149; 111 Empire Cct, Yarralumla, ACT 2600); Sydney (Map pp94-6; ☎ 02-9241 2542; http://thaisydney.idx.com.au; Level 8, 131 Macquarie St, Sydney, NSW 2000)

UK Canberra (Map p251; ☎ 02-6270 6666; www.uk.emb .gov.au; Commonwealth Ave, Yarralumla, ACT 2600); Sydney (Map pp94-6; ☎ 02-9247 7521; 16th fl, 1 Macquarie Pl, Sydney Cove, NSW 2000); Melbourne (Map pp450-1; ☎ 03-9652 1600; 17th fl, 90 Collins St, Melbourne, Vic 3000)

USA Canberra (Map p251; ☎ 02-6214 5600; http://us embassy-australia.state.gov/embassy; 21 Moonah Pl, Yarralumla, ACT 2600); Sydney (Map pp94-6; ☎ 02-9373 9200; Level 59, 19-29 Martin Pl, Sydney, NSW 2000); Melbourne (Map p457; ☎ 03-9526 5900; 553 St Kilda Rd, Melbourne, Vic 3004)

It's important to realise what your own embassy – the embassy of the country of which you are a citizen – can and can't do to help you if you get into trouble. Generally speaking, it won't be much help in emergencies if the trouble you're in is even remotely your own fault. Remember that while in Australia you are bound by Australian laws. Your embassy will not be sympathetic if you end up in jail after committing a crime locally, even if such actions are legal in your own country.

In genuine emergencies you might get some assistance, but only if other channels have been exhausted. For example, if you need to get home urgently, a free ticket is exceedingly unlikely – the embassy would expect you to have insurance. If you have all your money and documents stolen, it might assist with getting a new passport, but a loan for onward travel is out of the question.

FESTIVALS & EVENTS

Some of the most enjoyable Australian festivals are also the most typically Australian – like the surf life-saving competitions on beaches all around the country during summer; or outback race meetings, which draw together isolated communities. There are also some big city-based street festivals, sporting events and arts festivals that show-case comedy, music and dance, and some important commemorative get-togethers.

Details of festivals and events that are grounded in a single place – be it a city, town, valley or reserve – are provided throughout the state and territory chapters of this book. But the following events are pursued throughout a particular region, state or even around the country.

JANUARY
Big Day Out (www.bigdayout.com) This huge open-air music concert tours Sydney, Melbourne, Adelaide, Perth and the Gold Coast, stopping over for one day in each city. It attracts big-name international acts and dozens of attention-seeking local bands and DJs.

MARCH & APRIL (AROUND EASTER)
Ten Days on the Island (www.tendaysontheisland.org) This major Tasmanian cultural festival was inaugurated in 2001. It's a biennial celebration that brings together local and international performers in venues around the state.
Targa Tasmania (www.targa.org.au) This is a six-day rally for exotic cars that runs around the entire state, appropriating 2000km of roads as it goes.

MAY
Sorry Day (www.journeyofhealing.com) On 26 May each year, the anniversary of the tabling in 1997 of the *Bringing Them Home* report, concerned Australians acknowledge the continuing pain and suffering of Indigenous people affected by Australia's one-time child-removal practices and policies. Events are held in most cities countrywide.

JULY
Naidoc Week (www.atsic.gov.au) Communities across Australia celebrate the National Aboriginal and Islander Day of Celebration (inaugurated in 1957), from the annual Melbourne Naidoc Ball to local street festivals.

DECEMBER & JANUARY
Sydney to Hobart Yacht Race (http://rolexsydney hobart.com) Sydney Harbour is a fantastic sight as hundreds of boats farewell the competitors in the gruelling Sydney to Hobart Yacht Race.

FOOD

Australia is not renowned for having a unique cuisine, but many people are surprised by the range and wealth of food available in the country's restaurants, markets, delicatessens (delis) and cafés – especially in the major cities – but often in far less populated surrounds as well. The fine dining to be had in Australia is in large part due

to the abundance of reasonably priced fresh produce, including seafood. Also, many people from different cultures have made their home here, bringing with them a huge range of ethnic cuisines that are now part of the country's culinary repertoire.

Vegetarian eateries and vegetarian selections in nonvegie places (including menu choices for vegans and coeliac-sufferers) are becoming more common in large cities and are forging a stronger presence in the smaller towns visited by tourists, though rural Australia – as exemplified by pub grub – mostly continues its stolid dedication to meat. Those who enjoy a pre- or post-digestive puff will need to go outside, as smoking has been made illegal in most enclosed public places in all Australian states and territories, including indoor cafés, restaurants and (sometimes only at mealtime) pub dining areas.

When it comes to cities, the eating recommendations provided in this book are often broken down into the main food-infatuated areas or suburbs. The innovative food offered in top-quality Australian eateries doesn't necessarily cost a fortune. Best value are the modern cafés, where you can get a good meal in casual surroundings for under $20. A full cooked breakfast at a café costs around $10. Some inner-city pubs offer upmarket restaurant-style fare, but most pubs serve standard (often large-portion) bistro meals, usually in the $10 to $19 range, and these are served in the dining room or lounge bar. Bar (or counter) meals, which are eaten in the public bar, usually cost between $6 and $10. For general open hours consider that breakfast is normally served between 6am and 11am, lunch starts around noon till about 3pm and dinner usually starts after 6pm.

It's customary to tip in restaurants and upmarket cafés if the service warrants it – a gratuity of between 5% to 10% of the bill is the norm.

See also the Food & Drink chapter (p71) for more details on Australian specialities and 'Modern Australian' cuisine.

GAY & LESBIAN TRAVELLERS

Australia is a popular destination for gay and lesbian travellers, with the so-called 'pink tourism' appeal of Sydney especially big thanks largely to the city's annual, high-profile and spectacular Sydney Gay & Les-

bian Mardi Gras. Throughout the country, but particularly on the east coast, there are tour operators, travel agents, resorts and other accommodation places that are either exclusively gay and lesbian or make a point of welcoming gays – just one example of exclusivity is **Turtle Cove** (p403), near Cairns.

Certain areas are the focus of the gay and lesbian communities, among them **Cairns** (p396) and **Noosa** (p312) in Queensland; Oxford St and King's Cross in **Sydney** (p85); the **Blue Mountains** (p143), **Hunter Valley** (p159) and south coast in NSW; the **Melbourne** (p443) suburbs of Prahran, St Kilda and Collingwood; **Daylesford** and **Hepburn Springs** (p535) in Victoria; and the WA capital **Perth** (p833).

In terms of major gay and lesbian events, there's the aforementioned **Sydney Gay & Lesbian Mardi Gras** (www.mardigras.org.au) in February and March, Melbourne's **Midsumma Festival** (www.midsumma.org.au) from mid-January to mid-February, and Adelaide's **Feast** (www.feast.org.au) in November. Sydney also hosted the 6th international Gay Games in November 2002, further enhancing its reputation as the San Francisco of the southern hemisphere. See also the boxed texts 'Gay & Lesbian Sydney' (p110), 'Hello there Gorgeous! Out in Queer Melbourne' (p478) and 'Gay & Lesbian Brisbane' (p282).

In general Australians are open-minded about homosexuality, but the further into the country you get, the more likely you are to run into overt homophobia. Having said that, you will find active gay communities in places like Alice Springs and Darwin. Even Tasmania, once a bastion of sexual conservatism, now actively encourages gay and lesbian tourism. Homosexual acts are legal in all states but the age of consent between males varies – in the Australian Capital Territory (ACT), Victoria, NSW and WA it's 16 years, in SA and Tasmania it's 17, and in NT and Queensland it's 18.

For more on Australian attitudes to homosexuality, see p61.

Publications & Contacts

All major cities have gay newspapers, which are available from gay and lesbian venues and from newsagents in popular gay and lesbian residential areas. Gay lifestyle magazines include *DNA*, *Lesbians on the Loose*, *Women Out West* and the bi-monthly *Blue*.

Perth has the free monthly *Shout* and Adelaide has the fortnightly *Blaze*.

The website of **Gay and Lesbian Tourism Australia** (GALTA; www.galta.com.au) is a good place to look for general information, though you need to become a member to receive the full benefits. Other helpful websites include **Gay Australia** (www.gayaustralia.com.au) and the Sydney-based **Pinkboard** (www.pinkboard.com.au). Gay telephone counselling services (you'll find them in most capital cities) are often a useful source of general information.

Tour Operators

Tour operators that cater exclusively or partly for gay and lesbian travellers include:

Beyond the Blue Sydney (☎ 02-8399 0070; 685-687 South Dowling St, Surrey Hills, NSW 2010)

Boyz Brick Road Sydney (☎ 02-9380 4115; 102 Oxford St, Darlinghurst, NSW 2010); Cairns (☎ 07-4031 5011; City Arcade, Suite 21, Grafton St, Cairns QLD 4870)

Parkside Travel Adelaide (☎ 08-8274 1222; 70 Glen Osmond Rd, Parkside, SA 5063)

Rainbow Tours Melbourne (☎ 03-9397 0023; www .rainbowtours.com.au; Suite 3, 24 Albert Rd, South Melbourne, Vic 3205)

Tearaway Travel Melbourne (☎ 03-9510 6644; 52 Porter St, Prahran, Vic 3181)

HOLIDAYS
Public Holidays

The following is a list of the main national and state public holidays (* indicates holidays are only observed locally). As the timing can vary from state to state, check locally for precise dates.

NATIONAL
New Year's Day 1 January
Australia Day 26 January
Easter (Good Friday to Easter Monday inclusive) March/April
Anzac Day 25 April
Queen's Birthday (except WA) 2nd Monday in June
Queen's Birthday (WA) Last Monday in September
Christmas Day 25 December
Boxing Day 26 December

AUSTRALIAN CAPITAL TERRITORY
Canberra Day March*
Bank Holiday 1st Monday in August
Labour Day 1st Monday in October

NEW SOUTH WALES
Bank Holiday 1st Monday in August
Labour Day 1st Monday in October

NORTHERN TERRITORY
May Day 1st Monday in May
Show Day (Alice Springs) 1st Friday in July*; (Tennant Creek) 2nd Friday in July*; (Katherine) 3rd Friday in July*; (Darwin) 4th Friday in July*
Picnic Day 1st Monday in August

QUEENSLAND
Labour Day 1st Monday in May
RNA Show Day (Brisbane) August*

SOUTH AUSTRALIA
Adelaide Cup Day 3rd Monday in May*
Labour Day 1st Monday in October
Proclamation Day Last Tuesday in December

TASMANIA
Regatta Day 14 February
Launceston Cup Day February*
Eight Hours Day 1st Monday in March
Bank Holiday Tuesday following Easter Monday
King Island Show March*
Launceston Show Day October*
Hobart Show Day October*
Recreation Day (northern Tasmania only) 1st Monday in November*

VICTORIA
Labour Day 2nd Monday in March
Melbourne Cup Day 1st Tuesday in November*

WESTERN AUSTRALIA
Labour Day 1st Monday in March
Foundation Day 1st Monday in June

School Holidays

The Christmas holiday season, from mid-December to late January, is part of the summer school holidays – it's the time you are most likely to find transport and accommodation booked out, and long, restless queues at tourist attractions. There are three shorter school holiday periods during the year, but they vary by a week or two from state to state. They fall roughly from early to mid-April, late June to mid-July, and late September to early October.

INSURANCE

Don't underestimate the importance of a good travel-insurance policy that covers theft, loss and medical problems – nothing is guaranteed to ruin your holiday plans quicker than an accident or having that brand new digital camera stolen. Most

policies offer lower and higher medical-expense options; the higher ones are chiefly for countries that have extremely high medical costs, such as the USA. There is a wide variety of policies available, so compare the small print.

Some policies specifically exclude designated 'dangerous activities' such as scuba diving, parasailing, bungee jumping, motorcycling, skiing and even bushwalking. If you plan on doing any of these things, make sure the policy you choose fully covers you for your activity of choice.

You may prefer a policy that pays doctors or hospitals direct rather than you having to pay on the spot and claim later. If you have to claim later make sure you keep all documentation. Some policies ask you to call back (reverse charges or collect) to a centre in your home country where an immediate assessment of your problem is made. Check that the policy covers ambulances and emergency medical evacuations by air.

See also Predeparture (p1017) in the Health chapter. For information on insurance matters relating to cars that are bought or rented, see p993.

INTERNET ACCESS

Email and Internet addicts will find it fairly easy to get connected throughout Australia.

Cybercafés

Cybercafés are usually not as futuristic as their name implies, and connection speeds and prices vary from one to the next, but they all offer straightforward access to the Internet. Most public libraries also have Internet access, but generally there are a limited number of terminals and these are provided for research needs, not for travellers to check their emails – so head for a cybercafé first. You'll find Internet cafés in cities, sizeable towns and pretty much anywhere else that travellers congregate. The cost ranges from under $5 an hour in the cut-throat King's Cross places in Sydney to $10 an hour in more-remote locations. The average is about $6 an hour, usually with a minimum of 10 minutes access. Most youth hostels and backpacker places can hook you up, as can many hotels and caravan parks. In remote areas of WA, SA and NSW, telecentres provide Internet access, while

Tasmania has set up access centres in numerous local libraries and schools.

Free Web-based email services include **ekno** (www.ekno.lonelyplanet.com), **Yahoo** (www.yahoo.com), **MSN Hotmail** (www.hotmail.com) and **Excite** (www.excite.com).

Hooking Up

If you've brought your palmtop or notebook computer and want to get connected to a local ISP (Internet Service Provider), there are plenty of options, though some ISPs limit their dial-up areas to major cities or particular regions. Whatever enticements a particular ISP offers, make sure it has local dial-up numbers for the places where you intend to use it – the last thing you want is to be making timed STD calls every time you connect to the Internet. If you're based in a large city there's no problem. Telstra (BigPond) uses a nationwide dial-up number at local call rates. Some major ISPs:

America Online (AOL; ☎ 1800 265 265; www.aol.com.au) Also has log-in numbers in all capitals and many provincial cities.

Australia On Line (☎ 1300 650 661; www.ozonline.com.au)

CompuServe (www.compuserve.com.au) Users who want to access the service locally can check the website or phone CompuServe Pacific (☎ 1300 555 520) to get the local log-in numbers.

iPrimus (☎ 1300 850 000; www.iprimus.com.au)

OzEmail (☎ 13 28 84; http://au.ozemail.yahoo.com)

Telstra BigPond (☎ 13 12 82; www.bigpond.com)

Australia uses RJ-45 telephone plugs and Telstra EXI-160 four-pin plugs, but neither are universal – electronics shops such as Tandy and Dick Smith should be able to help. You'll also need a plug adaptor, and a universal AC adaptor will enable you to plug in without frying the innards of your machine. Most mid-range accommodation and all top-end hotels will have sockets but you'll be hit with expensive call charges. In most cheaper places you'll probably find that phones are hardwired into the wall.

Keep in mind that your PC-card modem may not work in Australia. The safest option is to buy a reputable 'global' modem before you leave home or buy a local PC-card modem once you get to Australia.

For a list of useful Australia-savvy websites, see p16.

LEGAL MATTERS

Most travellers will have no contact with the Australian police or any other part of the legal system. Those that do are likely to experience it while driving. There is a significant police presence on the country's roads, with the power to stop your car and ask to see your licence (you're required to carry it), check your vehicle for road-worthiness, and also to insist that you take a breath test for alcohol – needless to say, drink driving offences are taken very seriously here.

First offenders caught with small amounts of illegal drugs are likely to receive a fine rather than go to jail, but nonetheless the recording of a conviction against you may affect your visa status. Speaking of which, if you remain in Australia beyond the life of your visa, you will officially be an 'overstayer' and could face detention and expulsion, and then be prevented from returning to Australia for up to three years. It's extremely unlikely that overstaying your visa will actually land you in one of Australia's immigration detention centres; see the boxed text 'Asylum Seekers & Mandatory Detention' (p58) for the sad story of the men, women and children who do end up behind razor wire for not following Australian immigration procedures.

If you are arrested, it's your right to telephone a friend, relative or lawyer before any formal questioning begins. Legal Aid is available only in serious cases and only to the truly needy (for links to Legal Aid offices see www.nla.aust.net.au). However, many solicitors do not charge for an initial consultation.

COMING OF AGE

For the record:

- You can drive when you're 17.

- The legal age for voting in Australia is 18.

- The homosexual age of consent varies from state to state; see p967.

- The legal drinking age is 18.

MAPS

Good-quality road and topographical maps are plentiful in Australia. The various state motoring organisations are a dependable source of road maps, while local tourist offices usually supply free maps, though the quality varies.

Lonely Planet publishes handy fold-out city maps of Melbourne and Sydney. Commercially available city street guides, such as those produced by Ausway (publishers of *Melway* and *Sydway*), Gregorys and UBD are useful for in-depth urban navigation, but they're expensive, bulky and only worth getting if you intend to do a lot of city driving.

If you plan on bushwalking or taking part in other outdoor activities for which large-scale maps are an essential item, browse the topographic sheets published by **Geoscience Australia** (☎ 1800 800 173, 02-6201 4201; www.ga.gov.au; Scrivener Bldg, Dunlop Crt, Fern Hill Park, Bruce, ACT 2617), which is part of the Department of Industry, Tourism and Resources. You'll find that many of the more popular sheets are usually available over the counter at shops that sell specialist bushwalking gear and outdoor equipment.

MONEY
ATMs, Eftpos & Bank Accounts

The ANZ, Commonwealth, National and Westpac bank branches (and branches of affiliated banks) are found all over Australia, and many have 24-hour automated teller machines (ATMs) attached to them. But don't expect to find ATMs *everywhere* (you certainly shouldn't count on finding them off the beaten track or in very small towns). Most ATMs accept cards issued by other banks, and are linked to international networks.

Eftpos (Electronic Funds Transfer at Point Of Sale) is a convenient service that many Australian businesses have embraced. It means you can use your bank card (credit or debit) to pay direct for services or purchases, and often withdraw cash as well. Eftpos is available practically everywhere these days, even in outback roadhouses where it's a long way between banks. Just like an ATM, you need to know your Personal Identification Number (PIN) to use it.

OPENING A BANK ACCOUNT

If you're planning to stay in Australia a while – on a working-holiday visa for instance – it makes sense to open up a local bank account with one of the many

banks trading in the country. This is easy enough for overseas visitors provided you do it within six weeks of arrival. You simply present your passport and provide the bank with a postal address and they'll open the account and send you an ATM card.

After six weeks it's much more complicated. A points system operates and you need to score a minimum of 100 points before you can have the privilege of letting the bank take your money. Passports or birth certificates are worth 70 points; an international driving licence with photo earns you 40 points; and minor IDs, such as credit cards, get you 25 points – it's like a perverse game show. You must have at least one ID with a photograph. Once the account is open, you should be able to have money transferred across from your home account (for a fee, of course).

If you don't have an Australian Tax File Number (TFN), interest earned from your funds will be taxed at a rate of up to 47%. See p979 for tax-related information.

Credit Cards
Perhaps the best way to carry most of your money is in the form of a plastic card, especially if that's the way you do it at home. Australia is well and truly a card-carrying society – it's becoming unusual to line up at a supermarket checkout, petrol station or department store in cities and see someone actually paying with cash these days. Credit cards such as Visa and MasterCard are widely accepted for everything from a hostel bed or a restaurant meal to an adventure tour, and a credit card is pretty much essential (in lieu of a large deposit) if you want to hire a car. They can also be used to get cash advances over the counter at banks and from many ATMs, depending on the card, but be aware that these incur immediate interest. Charge cards such as Diners Club and American Express (Amex) are not as widely accepted.

Apart from losing them, the obvious danger with credit cards is maxing out your limit and going home to a steaming pile of debt and interest charges. A safer option is a debit card with which you can draw money directly from your home bank account using ATMs, banks or Eftpos machines around the country. Any card connected to the international banking network – Cirrus,

Maestro, Plus and Eurocard – should work, provided you know your PIN. Fees for using your card at a foreign bank or ATM vary depending on your home bank; ask before your leave.

The most flexible option is to carry both a credit and a debit card.

Currency
Australia's currency is the Australian dollar, made up of 100 cents. There are 5c, 10c, 20c, 50c, $1 and $2 coins, and $5, $10, $20, $50 and $100 notes. Although the smallest coin in circulation is 5c, prices are often still marked in single cents and then rounded to the nearest 5c when you come to pay.

There are no notable restrictions on importing or exporting travellers cheques. Cash amounts equal to or in excess of the equivalent of A$10,000 (in any currency) must be declared on arrival or departure.

In this book, unless otherwise stated, all prices given in dollars refer to Australian dollars. For an idea of the money required to travel Down Under, see p14.

Exchange Rates
The Australian dollar tends to act a little insecure around the US dollar and can fluctuate markedly. In recent years it has generally been quite weak (the currency nose-dived below US$0.50 for the first time in early 2001), but has lately regained some of its strength. In better times it stays around US$0.65. See the Quick Reference on the inside front cover for a list of exchange rates.

Exchanging Money
Changing foreign currency or travellers cheques is usually no problem at banks throughout Australia or at licensed money-changers such as Thomas Cook or Amex in the major cities.

Taxes & Refunds
The Goods and Services Tax (GST), introduced by the federal government in 2000 amid much controversy, is a flat 10% tax on all goods and services – accommodation, eating out, transport, electrical and other goods, books, furniture, clothing and so on. There are, however, some exceptions, such as basic foods (milk, bread, fruits and vegetables etc). By law the tax is included

in the quoted or shelf prices, so all prices in this book are GST-inclusive. International air and sea travel to/from Australia is GST-free, as is domestic air travel when purchased outside Australia by nonresidents.

If you purchase new or second-hand goods with a total minimum value of $300 from any one supplier no more than 30 days before you leave Australia, you are entitled under the Tourist Refund Scheme (TRS) to a refund of any GST paid. The scheme only applies to goods you take with you as hand luggage or wear onto the plane or ship. Also note that the refund is valid for goods bought from more than one supplier, but only if at least $300 is spent in each. For more details, contact the **Australian Customs Service** (☎ 1300 363 263, 02-6275 6666; www.customs.gov.au).

Travellers Cheques

If your stay is short, then travellers cheques are safe and generally enjoy a better exchange rate than foreign cash in Australia. Also, if they are stolen (or you lose them), they can readily be replaced. There is, however, a fee for buying travellers cheques (usually 1% of the total amount) and there may be fees or commissions when you exchange them.

Amex, Thomas Cook and other well-known international brands of travellers cheques are easily exchanged. You need to present your passport for identification when cashing them.

Fees per transaction for changing foreign-currency travellers cheques vary from bank to bank. Of the 'big four' banks, ANZ charges $7; Commonwealth Bank charges a minimum of $8 or 1% of the total dollar amount; Westpac (also called Bank of Melbourne in Victoria and Challenge Bank in WA) charges $8; and the National Australia Bank charges their account holders $15 and non-customers an extortionate $30. Clearly you're better off using an Amex or Thomas Cook exchange bureau, who are commission-free if you use their cheques. The private moneychangers found in the big cities are sometimes commission-free, but shop around for the best rates.

Buying travellers cheques in Australian dollars is an option worth looking at. These can be exchanged immediately at banks without being converted from a foreign currency or incurring commissions, fees and exchange-rate fluctuations.

PHOTOGRAPHY & VIDEO

Print film is relatively inexpensive in Australia and can be purchased almost anywhere, including supermarkets and petrol stations – a roll of Kodak 36/100 ISO costs about $7.50 and you can have it processed the same day for as low as $8 (less for overnight processing). For slide film you'll usually need to go to a camera shop, though city chemists (pharmacies) often stock it. A roll of 36-exposure Kodachrome 64 or Fujichrome 100 slide film costs $25 to $30 with developing included, or $11 to $15 for film only. E6 processing costs about $18 a roll.

There are plenty of camera shops in all big cities and the standard of camera service and film processing is usually high. Many places offer one-hour developing of print film.

In the outback you have to allow for the exceptional intensity of the light, with the best results obtained early in the morning and late in the afternoon. As the sun gets higher, colours appear washed out. You must also allow for the intensity of reflected light when taking shots on the Great Barrier Reef or at other coastal locations. Especially in the summer, allow for temperature extremes and do your best to keep film as cool as possible, particularly after exposure. Other film and camera hazards are dust in the outback and humidity in the Far North tropical regions.

Please note: photography of indigenous sacred sites is forbidden.

Lonely Planet's *Travel Photography: A Guide to Taking Better Pictures* by respected photographer Richard I'Anson offers a comprehensive guide to technical and creative travel photography.

POST
Letters

Australia's postal services are efficient and reasonably cheap. It costs 50c to send a standard letter or postcard within the country. **Australia Post** (www.auspost.com.au) has divided international destinations into two regions: Asia-Pacific and Rest of the World; airmail letters up to 50g cost $1.10/1.65, respectively. The cost of a postcard (up to 20g) is $1 and an aerogram to any country is 85c.

Parcels

There are five international parcel zones. You can send parcels by seamail to the

USA/Canada (Zone 4) and to Europe and South Africa (Zone 5) only; it's cheap but they can take forever. A 1/1.5/2kg parcel costs $15/21/27 to both zones. Each 500g over 2kg costs $3 extra with a maximum of 20kg. Economy airmail rates are $18/26/34 to Zone 4 and $20/29/38 to Zone 5. To all other destinations, including New Zealand (Zone NZ), airmail is the only option. A 1/1.5/2kg parcel sent by 'economy air' to New Zealand costs $12/17/22, while to Asia-Pacific nations (Zones 1, 2 and 3) the cost is $15/21/27.

Sending & Receiving Mail

All post offices will hold mail for visitors, and some city GPOs (main or general post offices) have very busy poste restante sections. You need to provide some form of identification (such as a passport) to collect mail. You can also have mail sent to you at city Amex offices if you have an Amex card or travellers cheques.

See p958 for post office open times.

SHOPPING

Australians appear to be fond of spending their money (and pushing their credit facilities to the limit), a fact evidenced by the huge variety of local- and international-brand shops, and the feverish crowds that gather at every clearance sale. Big cities can satisfy most consumer appetites with everything from high-fashion boutiques to second-hand emporiums, while many smaller places tend towards speciality retail, be it homegrown produce, antiques or arts and crafts.

Markets are a good place to go shopping and most cities have at least one permanent bazaar, such as Hobart's **Salamanca Market** (p584). Melbourne and Sydney have a couple – try the **Queen Victoria Market** (p451) in Melbourne or the **Paddington Bazaar** (p134) in Sydney. The alternative markets around **Nimbin** (p187) on the NSW north coast are also well worth poking around.

You may be able to get a refund on the tax you pay on goods; see p971.

Aboriginal Art & Artefacts

One of the most evocative reminders of your trip is an Aboriginal artwork or artefact. By buying authentic items you are supporting Aboriginal culture and helping to ensure that traditional and contemporary expertise and designs continue to be of economic and cultural benefit for Aboriginal individuals and communities. Unfortunately, much of the so-called Aboriginal art sold as souvenirs is ripped-off, consisting of appropriated designs illegally taken from Aboriginal people; or it's just plain fake, usually made overseas by underpaid workers.

The best place to buy artefacts is either directly from the communities that have art-and-craft centres or from galleries and outlets that are owned, operated or supported by Aboriginal communities. There are also many reputable galleries that have long supported the Aboriginal arts industry, usually members of the Australian Commercial Galleries Association (ACGA) and that will offer certificates of authentication with their goods.

If you're interested in buying a painting, possibly in part for its investment potential, then it's best to purchase the work from a community art centre, Aboriginal-owned gallery or reputable non-Aboriginal-owned gallery. Regardless of its individual aesthetic worth, a painting purchased without a certificate of authenticity from either a reputable gallery or community art centre will probably be hard to resell at a later time, even if the painting is attributed to a well-known artist.

Didgeridoos are in high demand, but you need to decide whether you want a decorative piece or an authentic and functional musical instrument. The didgeridoos on the market are not always made by Aboriginal people, which means that at a nonsupportive souvenir shop in Darwin or Cairns you could pay anything from $200 to $400 or more for something that looks pretty but is really little more than a painted bit of wood. From a community outlet such as **Manyallaluk** (p787) in the NT, however, you could expect to pay $100 to $200 for a functional, authentic didgeridoo that has been painted with ochre paints/natural pigments.

Australiana

Overseas visitors looking for gifts for all the friends, aunts and uncles, nieces and nephews, and other sundry bods back home will stumble across plenty of inexpensive souvenirs in their travels. The cheapest, usually produced en masse and with little to distinguish them, are known collectively by the euphemism 'Australiana' – they are

supposedly representative of Australia and its culture, but in reality are just lowest-common-denominator trinkets. Speaking of authenticity, far too many of these supposedly Australian items are actually made in Asia, so if you're going to buy any, at least check the label to see where it was manufactured.

Genuine Australian offerings include the seeds of many native plants that are on sale everywhere – try growing kangaroo paws (see the boxed text 'Blooming Wildflowers' on p902 for more information on Australia's unique wildflowers) back home (if your own country will allow them in). You could also consider a bottle of fine Australian wine, honey (leatherwood honey is one of many powerful local varieties), macadamia nuts (native to Queensland) or Bundaberg Rum, with its unusual sweet flavour.

Clothing

Modern Australian fashion collections that are in demand include Collette Dinnigan, Claude Maus, Ty & Melita, Morrissey, Sass & Bide, Tsubi and Akira Isogawa. For a rustic look, try wrapping yourself in a waterproof Drizabone coat, an Akubra hat, moleskin pants and Blundstone boots – RM Williams is a well-known bush-clothing brand.

Surf-wear labels such as Rip Curl, Quicksilver, Mambo and Billabong make good buys. You can pick up printed T-shirts, colourful boardshorts and the latest beach and street fashion from surf and sports shops all over the country, especially on the east coast. Rip Curl and Quicksilver were both born in Torquay, Victoria, in the 1960s and are now internationally renowned surf brands, marketing wetsuits, boards and surf wear.

Opals & Gemstones

The opal, Australia's national gemstone, is a popular souvenir, as is the jewellery made with it. It's a beautiful stone but buy wisely and shop around, as quality and prices vary widely from place to place. **Coober Pedy** (p735) in SA and **Lightning Ridge** (p205) and **White Cliffs** (p235) in NSW are opal-mining towns where you can buy the stones or perhaps fossick for your own.

On **Cape York** (p430) and the **Torres Strait Islands** (p434) look out for South Sea pearls, while in **Broome** (p934) in WA, cultured pearls are produced and sold in many local shops.

Australia is a mineral-rich country and semiprecious gemstones such as topaz, garnets, sapphires, rubies, zircon and others can sometimes be found lying around in piles of dirt at various locations. The gemfields around Anakie, Sapphire and Rubyvale in Queensland's **Capricorn Hinterland** (p346) are a good place to shop for jewellery and gemstones, and there are sites around rural and outback Australia where you can pay a few dollars and fossick for your own stones. You can also head to **Flinders Island** (p654), where Killiecrankie 'diamonds' (actually topaz) are the stone of choice.

SOLO TRAVELLERS

People travelling alone in Australia face the unpredictability that is an inherent part of making contact with entire communities of strangers: sometimes you'll be completely ignored as if you didn't exist, and other times you'll be greeted with such enthusiasm it's as if you've been spontaneously adopted. Suffice to say that the latter moments will likely become highlights of your trip.

Solo travellers are a common sight throughout the country and there is certainly no stigma attached to lone visitors. But in some places there can be an expectation that the visitor should engage in some way with the locals, particularly in rural pubs where keeping to yourself can prove harder than it sounds. Women travelling on their own should exercise caution when in less-populated areas, and will find that guys can get annoyingly attentive in drinking establishments (with mining town pubs arguably the nadir); see also Women Travellers (p977).

TELEPHONE

There are a number of providers offering various services. The two main players are the mostly government-owned **Telstra** (www.telstra.com.au) and the fully private **Optus** (www.optus.com.au). Both are also major players in the mobile (cell) market, along with **Vodafone** (www.vodafone.com.au) – other mobile operators include **AAPT** (www.aapt.com.au) and **Orange** (www.orange.net.au).

Domestic & International Calls
INFORMATION & TOLL-FREE CALLS

Numbers starting with ☎ 190 are usually recorded information services, charged at anything from 35c to $5 or more per minute

(more from mobiles and payphones). To make a reverse-charge (collect) call from any public or private phone, just dial ☎ 1800-REVERSE (738 3773), or ☎ 12 550.

Toll-free numbers (prefix ☎ 1800) can be called free of charge from anywhere in the country, though they may not be accessible from certain areas or from mobile phones. Calls to numbers beginning with ☎ 13 or ☎ 1300 are charged at the rate of a local call – the numbers can usually be dialled Australia-wide, but may be applicable only to a specific state or STD district. Telephone numbers beginning with either ☎ 1800, ☎ 13 or ☎ 1300 cannot be dialled from outside Australia.

INTERNATIONAL CALLS

Most payphones allow ISD (International Subscriber Dialling) calls, the cost and international dialling code of which will vary depending on which provider you're using. International calls from Australia are very cheap and subject to specials that reduce the rates even more, so it's worth shopping around – look in the *Yellow Pages* for a list of providers.

The **Country Direct service** (☎ 1800 801 800) connects callers in Australia with operators in nearly 60 countries to make reverse-charge (collect) or credit-card calls.

When calling overseas you need to dial the international access code from Australia (☎ 0011 or ☎ 0018), the country code and the area code (without the initial 0). So for a London number you'd dial ☎ 0011-44-171, then the number. Also, certain operators will have you dial a special code to access their service.

Following is a list of some country codes:

Country	International Country Code
France	☎ 33
Germany	☎ 49
Japan	☎ 81
Netherlands	☎ 31
New Zealand	☎ 64
UK	☎ 44
USA & Canada	☎ 1

If dialling Australia from overseas, the country code is ☎ 61 and you need to drop the 0 (zero) in the state/territory area codes.

LOCAL CALLS

Calls from private phones cost 15c to 25c while local calls from public phones cost 40c; both involve unlimited talk time. Calls to mobile phones attract higher rates and are timed. Blue phones or gold phones that you sometimes find in hotel lobbies or other businesses usually cost a minimum of 50c for a local call.

LONG DISTANCE CALLS & AREA CODES

For long-distance calls, Australia uses four STD (Subscriber Trunk Dialling) area codes. STD calls can be made from virtually any public phone and are cheaper during off-peak hours, generally between 7pm and 7am. Long-distance calls (ie to more than about 50km away) within these areas are charged at long-distance rates, even though they have the same area code. Broadly, the main area codes are:

State/Territory	Area Code
ACT	☎ 02
NSW	☎ 02
NT	☎ 08
QLD	☎ 07
SA	☎ 08
TAS	☎ 03
VIC	☎ 03
WA	☎ 08

Area code boundaries don't necessarily coincide with state borders – NSW, for example, uses each of the four neighbouring codes.

Mobile (Cell) Phones

Local numbers with the prefixes ☎ 04xx or ☎ 04xxx belong to mobile phones. Australia's two mobile networks – digital GSM and digital CDMA – service more than 90% of the population but leave vast tracts of the country uncovered. The east coast, southeast and southwest get good reception, but elsewhere (apart from major towns) it's haphazard or nonexistent.

Australia's digital network is compatible with GSM 900 and 1800 (used in Europe), but generally not with the systems used in the USA or Japan. It's easy and cheap enough to get connected short-term, though, as the main service providers (Telstra, Optus and Vodafone) all have prepaid mobile systems. Just buy a starter kit, which may include a phone or, if you have your own phone,

a SIM card (around $15) and a prepaid charge card. The calls tend to be a bit more expensive than with standard contracts, but there are no connection fees or line-rental charges and you can buy the recharge cards at convenience stores and newsagents. Don't forget to shop around between the three carriers as their products differ.

Phonecards

A wide range of phonecards is available, which can be bought at newsagents and post offices for a fixed dollar value (usually $10, $20, $30 etc) and can be used with any public or private phone by dialling a toll-free access number and then the PIN number on the card. Once again, it's well worth shopping around, as call rates vary from company to company. Some public phones also accept credit cards.

The **ekno** (www.ekno.lonelyplanet.com) global communication service provides low-cost international calls – for local calls you're usually better off with a local phonecard. ekno also offers free messaging services, email, travel information and an online travel vault, where you can securely store details of all your important documents. You can join online, where you'll find the local-access numbers for the 24-hour customer-service centre. Once you've joined, always check the ekno website for the latest access numbers for each country and updates on new features. The current dial-in numbers for Australia are: Sydney ☎ 02-8208 3000, Melbourne ☎ 03-9909 0888 and elsewhere (toll-free) ☎ 1800 114 478.

TIME

Australia is divided into three time zones: the Western Standard Time zone (GMT/UTC plus eight hours) covers WA; Central Standard Time (plus 9½ hours) covers the NT and SA; and Eastern Standard Time (plus 10 hours) covers Tasmania, Victoria, NSW, the ACT and Queensland. There are minor exceptions – for instance, Broken Hill (NSW) is on Central time.

So when it's noon in WA, it's 1.30pm in the NT and SA, and 2pm in the rest of the country. When it's noon in Sydney, the time in London is 3am (April to October) or 1am (November to March). For more on international timing, see the map of world time zones (p1023) at the back of the book.

'Daylight saving' – for which clocks are put forward an hour – operates in most states during the warmer months (October to March). However, things can get pretty confusing, with WA, the NT and Queensland staying on standard time, while in Tasmania daylight saving starts a month earlier than in SA, Victoria, the ACT and NSW.

TOURIST INFORMATION

Australia's highly self-conscious tourism infrastructure means that when you go looking for information, you can easily end up being buried neck-deep in brochures, booklets, maps and leaflets, or get utterly swamped with detail during an online surf.

Local Tourist Offices

Within Australia, tourist information is disseminated by various regional and local offices. In this book, the main state and territory tourism authorities are listed in the introductory Information section of each destination chapter. Almost every major town in Australia seems to maintain a tourist office of some type and in many cases they are very good, with friendly staff (often volunteers) providing local information not readily available from the state offices. If you're going to book accommodation or tours from local offices, bear in mind that they often only promote businesses that are paying members of the local tourist association. Details of local tourism offices are given in the relevant city and town sections throughout this book.

Tourist Offices Abroad

The **Australian Tourist Commission** (ATC; ☎ 1300 361 650, 02-9360 1111; www.australia.com; Level 4, 80 William St, Woolloomooloo, NSW 2011) is the government body charged with improving foreign tourist relations. A good place to start some pre-trip research is the commission's website, which has information in nine languages (including French, German, Japanese and Spanish).

ATC agents can supply various publications on Australia, including a number of handy fact sheets on topics such as camping, fishing, skiing, disabled travel and national parks, plus provide a handy map for a small fee. This literature is only distributed overseas, but local travellers can download and print the information from the ATC website.

Some countries with ATC offices:

Germany (☎ 069-2740 0622; Neue Mainzer Strasse 22, Frankfurt D 60311)

Japan (☎ 03-5214 0720; Australian Business Centre, New Otani Garden Court Bldg 28F, 4-1 Kioi-cho Chiyoda-ku, Tokyo 102-0094)

New Zealand (☎ 09-915 2826; Level 3, 125 The Strand, Parnell, Auckland)

Singapore (☎ 65-255 4555; 26-05 United Sq, 101 Thomson Rd, Singapore 307591)

Thailand (☎ 0 2670 0640; Unit 1614, 16th fl, Empire Tower, 195 Sth Sathorn Rd, Yannawa, Sathorn, Bangkok 10120)

UK (☎ 020-8780 2229; Gemini House, 10-18 Putney Hill, London SW15 6AA)

USA (☎ 310-229 4870; Suite 1920, 2049 Century Park East, Los Angeles, CA 90067)

VISAS

All visitors to Australia need a visa – only New Zealand nationals are exempt, and even they receive a 'special category' visa on arrival. Visa application forms are available from Australian diplomatic missions overseas, travel agents or the website of the **Department of Immigration & Multicultural & Indigenous Affairs** (☎ 13 18 81; www.immi.gov.au). There are several types of visa.

Electronic Travel Authority (ETA)

Many visitors can get an ETA through any International Air Transport Association (IATA)–registered travel agent or overseas airline. They make the application direct when you buy a ticket and issue the ETA, which replaces the usual visa stamped in your passport – it's common practice for travel agents to charge a fee for issuing an ETA, in the vicinity of US$15. This system is available to passport holders of some 33 countries, including the UK, the USA and Canada, most European and Scandinavian countries, Malaysia, Singapore, Japan and Korea.

You can also make an online ETA application at www.eta.immi.gov.au, where no fees apply.

Tourist Visas

Short-term tourist visas have largely been replaced by the free Electronic Travel Authority (ETA; see earlier). However, if you are from a country not covered by the ETA, or you want to stay longer than three months, you'll need to apply for a visa. Standard visas (which cost A$65) allow one (in some cases multiple) entry, stays of up to three months, and are valid for use within 12 months of issue. A long-stay tourist visa (also A$65) can allow a visit of up to a year.

Visa Extensions

Visitors are allowed a maximum stay of 12 months, including extensions. Visa extensions are made through the Department of Immigration & Multicultural & Indigenous Affairs and it's best to apply at least two or three weeks before your visa expires. The application fee is $160 – it's nonrefundable, even if your application is rejected.

Working Holiday Maker (WHM) Visas

Young, single visitors from Canada, Cyprus, Denmark, Finland, Germany, Hong Kong, Ireland, Japan, Korea, Malta, the Netherlands, Norway, Sweden and the UK are eligible for a WHM visa, which allows you to visit for up to 12 months and gain casual employment. 'Young' is defined as between 18 and 30 years of age.

The emphasis of this visa is on casual and not full-time employment, so you're only supposed to work for any one employer for a maximum of three months. This visa can only be applied for in Australian diplomatic missions abroad (citizens of Cyprus, Germany, Hong Kong, Japan, Korea and Malta must apply in their home country) and you can't change from a tourist visa to a WHM visa once you're in Australia. You can also apply for this visa online (www.immi.gov.au/e_visa/visit.htm).

You can apply for this visa up to a year in advance, which is worthwhile as there's a limit on the number issued each year. Conditions include having a return air ticket or sufficient funds for a return or onward fare, and an application fee of A$160 is charged.

For details of what sort of employment is available and where, see p979.

WOMEN TRAVELLERS

Australia is generally a safe place for women travellers, although the usual sensible precautions apply. It's best to avoid walking alone late at night in any of the major cities and towns. And if you're out on the town, always keep enough money aside for a taxi back to your accommodation. The same applies to outback and

rural towns where there are often a lot of unlit, semideserted streets between you and your temporary home. When the pubs and bars close and there are inebriated people roaming around, it's not a great time to be out and about. Lone women should also be wary of staying in basic pub accommodation unless it looks safe and well managed.

Sexual harassment is an ongoing problem, be it via an aggressive cosmopolitan male or a rural bloke living a less-than-enlightened pro-forma bush existence. Stereotypically, the further you get from 'civilisation' (ie the big cities), the less enlightened your average Aussie male is probably going to be about women's issues. Having said that, many women travellers say that they have met the friendliest, most down-to-earth blokes in outback pubs and remote roadhouse stops. And cities still have to put up with their unfortunate share of 'ocker' males who regard a bit of sexual harassment as a right, and chauvinism as a desirable trait.

Lone female hitchers are tempting fate – hitching with a male companion is safer.

See p963 for a warning on drugged drinks, and the boxed text 'Sailing the Whitsunday Islands' (p372) includes some cautionary words on crewing private boats.

WORK

If you come to Australia on a tourist visa then you're not allowed to work for pay – working for approved volunteer organisations (for details see p980) in exchange for board is OK. If you're caught breaching your visa conditions you can be expelled from the country and placed on a banned list for up to three years.

Equipped with a Working Holiday Maker visa (WHM; see p977), you can begin to sniff out the possibilities for temporary employment. Casual work can often be found in the peak season at the major tourist centres. Places like Alice Springs in the Centre, Cairns and various resort towns along the Queensland coast, as well as the ski fields of Victoria and NSW, are all good prospects when the country is in holiday mode.

Many travellers have found work cleaning or attending the reception desk at backpacker hostels, which usually means free accommodation – a number of hostels, however, are now employing their own locally based staff.

Seasonal fruit-picking (harvesting) relies on casual labour and there is something to be picked, pruned or farmed somewhere in Australia all year round. It's hard work that involves early-morning starts, and you're usually paid by how much you pick (per bin, bucket or whatever) – expect to earn $50 to $60 a day to start with, more when you get quicker at it. Some work, such as pruning or sorting, is paid by the hour at around $12. If you're looking for fruit-picking work, the **Harvest Hotline** (☎ 1300 720 126) run by Employment National (see Information; below) can connect you through to the relevant regions.

Other prospects for casual employment include factory work and labouring, bar work, waiting on tables, domestic chores at outback roadhouses, nanny work, working as a station hand (jackaroo/jillaroo) and collecting for charities. People with computer or secretarial skills should have little difficulty finding work temping in the major cities (registering with an agency is your best bet), and agency work is often available for qualified nurses and teachers.

Though there are certainly many possibilities for picking up short-term work in Australia, finding something suitable will not always be easy, regardless of how straightforward it may look from afar on work-touting websites. Be prepared to hunt around for worthwhile opportunities, and to make your own well-being the priority if you find yourself coping with unsatisfactory conditions.

Information

The Internet is a good place to research work opportunities. **Employment National** (☎ 13 34 44; www.employmentnational.com.au) is a country-wide recruiting company. It has a large database that lists jobs in various fields (skilled and unskilled) and specialises in harvest and agricultural positions.

Australian Job Search (www.jobsearch.gov.au) is a Commonwealth government agency with plenty of jobs on offer, including a 'Harvest Trail' for backpackers to follow around the country. At the time of research, there were over 6000 jobs listed on the website for Sydney alone.

Monster (www.monster.com.au) is an Internet-based employment agency that has links to a

number of big Sydney recruitment agencies. A good website for travellers with general information on working in Australia is www.workoz.com.

Backpacker accommodation, magazines and newspapers are good sources of information for local work opportunities. *Workabout Australia* by Barry Brebner gives a state-by-state breakdown of seasonal work opportunities; you can check online at (www.workaboutaustralia.com.au).

Casual Employment Seasons

The table below lists the main times and regions where casual employment, mainly fruit-picking, is a possibility:

New South Wales

Job	Time	Region(s)
Tomatoes	Jan–Mar	Forbes
Grapes	Feb–Mar	Griffith, Hunter Valley
Apples	Feb–Apr	Orange, Batlow, Gundagai
Asparagus	Oct–Dec	Jugiong (northeast of Gundagai)
Cotton	Oct–Jan	Narrabri
Bananas	Nov–Jan	North Coast
Cherries	Nov–Jan	Orange, Batlow, Young
Apples	Dec–Jan	Forbes
Citrus	Dec–Mar	Griffith

Northern Territory

Job	Time	Region(s)
Tourism	May–Sep	Darwin, Alice Springs, Katherine
Mangoes	Oct–Nov	Darwin, Katherine

Queensland

Job	Time	Region(s)
Grapes	Jan–Apr	Stanthorpe
Apples	Feb–Mar	Warwick
Tourism	Apr–Oct	Cairns
Fishing trawlers	May–Aug	Cairns
Vegies	May–Nov	Bowen
Asparagus	Aug–Dec	Warwick
Tomatoes	Oct–Dec	Bundaberg
Mangoes	Dec–Jan	Atherton, Mareeba
Bananas	year-round	Tully, Innisfail

South Australia

Job	Time	Region(s)
Tomatoes	Jan–Feb	Riverland
Grapes	Feb–Apr	Riverland, Barossa, Clare
Peaches	Feb–Jun	Riverland
Apples/pears	Feb–Jul	Adelaide Hills
Citrus	May–Dec	Berri, Riverland
Pruning	Aug–Dec	Adelaide Hills
Apricots	Dec	Riverland

Tasmania

Job	Time	Region(s)
Strawberries/ raspberries	Jan–Apr	Huonville
Apples/pears	Mar–Apr	Huon/Tamar Valleys
Grapes	Mar–Apr	Tamar Valley
Cherries	Dec–Jan	Huonsville

Victoria

Job	Time	Region(s)
Tomatoes	Jan–Mar	Shepparton, Echuca
Grapes/oranges	Jan–Mar	Mildura
Peaches/pears	Feb–Apr	Shepparton
Apples	Mar–May	Bendigo
Ski fields	June–Oct	Wangaratta/Alps
Strawberries	Oct–Dec	Echuca, Dandenongs
Cherries	Nov–Dec	Dandenongs

Western Australia

Job	Time	Region(s)
Grapes	Feb–Mar	Albany, Margaret River, Mt Barker, Manjimup
Apples/pears	Feb–Apr	Donnybrook, Manjimup
Prawn trawlers	Mar–June	Carnarvon
Bananas	Apr–Dec	Kununurra
Vegies	May–Nov	Kununurra, Carnarvon
Tourism	May–Dec	Kununurra
Flowers	Sept–Nov	Midlands
Lobsters	Nov–May	Esperance
Bananas	year-round	Carnarvon

Paying Tax

Even with a TFN (Tax File Number), non-residents (including anyone with a WHM visa) pay a considerably higher rate of tax than Australian residents, especially those on a low income. For a start, there's no tax-free threshold – you pay tax on every dollar you earn, starting at 29% on an annual income of up to $20,000 ($384 per week), then 30% up to $50,000, 42% from $50,000 to $60,000, and 47% above $60,000.

If you have had tax deducted as you earn, it's unlikely you'll be entitled to much of a tax refund when you leave Australia. However, if you have had tax deducted at 47% because you did not submit a TFN, you will be entitled to a partial refund of the tax paid. To get the refund you must lodge a tax return with the ATO (Australian Taxation Office).

Before you can lodge a tax return, however, you must have a TFN. As well, the tax return must include a Group Certificate (an official summary of your earnings and tax payments) provided by your employer, who must be given written advice at least 14 days in advance that you want the certificate on your last day at work – otherwise you may have to wait until the end of the financial year (30 June).

Superannuation
As part of the government's compulsory superannuation scheme, if you're earning more than $450 per calendar month your employer must make contributions on your behalf to a retirement or superannuation (super) fund. These contributions are at the rate of 9% of your wage, and the money must remain in the fund until you reach 'preservation age' (no embalming fluid is involved), which is currently 55 years.

Current legislation does not allow for the early release of superannuation funds. You can find out the latest from the **Australian Taxation Office** (ATO; ☎ 13 28 61; www.ato.gov.au); also check with the super fund with which your contributions have been lodged.

Tax File Number
If you have a WHM visa, it's important that you apply for a TFN. Without it, tax will be deducted from any wages you receive at the maximum rate (around 47%). You can apply for a TFN online at the website of the **Australian Taxation Office** (ATO; ☎ 13 28 61; www.ato.gov.au). A TFN takes about four weeks to issue.

Volunteer Work
AUSTRALIAN VOLUNTEERS INTERNATIONAL
Mainly involved in recruiting Australians to work overseas, **AVI** (www.ozvol.org.au; Darwin ☎ 08-8941 9743) also places skilled volunteers into Aboriginal communities in northern and central Australia. Most of the placements are paid contracts for a minimum of a year and you will need a work visa. There are, however, occasional short-term placements, especially in the medical or accounting fields, and short-term unskilled jobs, usually helping out at community-run road houses.

CONSERVATION VOLUNTEERS AUSTRALIA
The nonprofit **Conservation Volunteers Australia** (☎ 1800 032 501, 03-5333 1483; www.atcv.com.au; 13-15 Lydiard St Nth, Ballarat, Vic 3350) organises practical conservation projects for volunteers (including overseas visitors) such as tree planting, walking-track construction and flora and fauna surveys. It's an excellent way to get involved with conservation-minded people and visit some interesting areas of the country.

Most projects are either for a weekend or a week and all food, transport and accommodation is supplied in return for a small contribution to help cover costs ($25 per day). Most overseas travellers who take part join a Conservation Experience package of either four/six weeks ($790/1175), both of which comprise several different projects – additional weeks can be added for $192 per each seven-day block.

WWOOF
Willing Workers on Organic Farms (Wwoof; ☎ 03-5155 0218; www.wwoof.com.au) is well established in Australia. The idea is that you do a few hours work each day on a farm or cottage business in return for bed and board, often in a family home. Some places have a minimum stay of a couple of days but many will take you for just a night.

There are about 1600 Wwoof associates in Australia, mostly in Victoria, NSW and Queensland. As the name states, the farms are supposed to be organic (including permaculture and biodynamic growing), but that isn't always so. Some places aren't even farms – you might help out at a pottery or do the books at a seed wholesaler. Whether participants in the scheme have a farm or just a vegie patch, most are concerned to some extent with alternative lifestyles.

To join, send $50/60 for singles/couples to Wwoof, Mt Murrindal Co-op, W Tree, Victoria 3885, or alternatively join through the website. Wwoof will send you a membership number and a booklet that lists participating places all over Australia.

Transport

CONTENTS

GETTING THERE & AWAY

They don't call Australia the land 'down under' for nothing. It's a long way from just about everywhere, and getting here usually means a long-haul flight. That 'over the horizon' feeling doesn't stop once you're here either – the distances between key cities (much less opposing coastlines) can be vast, requiring a minimum of an hour or two of air time but up to several days of highway cruising or dirt-road jostling to traverse.

ENTERING THE COUNTRY

Disembarkation in Australia is generally a straightforward affair, with only the usual customs declarations (p961) and the fight to be first to the luggage carousel to endure. If you're flying in with Qantas, Air New Zealand, British Airways, Cathay Pacific, Japan Airlines or Singapore Airlines, ask the carrier about the 'Express' passenger card, which will speed your way through customs.

Recent global instability, thanks (or rather, no thanks) to terrorism and war-fever have resulted in conspicuously increased security in Australian airports, both in domestic and international terminals, and you may find that customs procedures are now more time-consuming.

Passport

There are no restrictions when it comes to citizens of foreign countries entering Australia. If you have a visa (p977), you should be fine.

AIR

There are lots of competing airlines and a wide variety of air fares to choose from if you're flying in from Asia, Europe or North America, but you'll still pay a lot for a flight. Because of Australia's size and diverse climate, any time of year can prove busy for inbound tourists – if you plan to fly at a particularly popular time of year (Christmas is notoriously difficult for Sydney and Melbourne) or on a particularly popular route (such as Hong Kong, Bangkok or

Singapore to Sydney or Melbourne), make your arrangements well ahead.

Airports & Airlines

Australia has a number of international gateways, with Sydney and Melbourne being the busiest. The full list of international airports follows:

Adelaide (code ADL; ☎ 08-8308 9211)

Brisbane (code BNE; ☎ 07-3406 3190; www.brisbane airport.com.au)

Cairns (code CNS; ☎ 07-4052 9703; www.cairnsport .com.au/airport)

Darwin (code DRW; ☎ 08-8945 1120; www.ntapl.com.au)

Melbourne Tullamarine (code MEL; ☎ 03-9297 1600; www.melair.com.au)

Perth (code PER; ☎ 08-9478 8888; www.perthairport .net.au)

Sydney Kingsford Smith (code SYD; ☎ 02-9667 9111; www.sydneyairport.com.au)

Australia's own overseas carrier is Qantas, which is regarded as one of the world's safest airlines and flies chiefly to runways across Europe, North America, Asia and the Pacific. A subsidiary of Qantas, Australian Airlines, flies between the prime east-coast destination of Cairns and Japan, Hong Kong, Singapore and Taiwan, and at the time of writing was gearing up to fly nonstop between Bali and both Sydney and Melbourne.

Airlines that visit Australia include the following (note all phone numbers mentioned here are for dialling from within Australia):

Air Canada (☎ 1300 655 757, 02-9286 8900; www .aircanada.ca; airline code AC; hub Pearson International Airport, Toronto)

Air New Zealand (☎ 13 24 76, 03-9613 4850; www .airnz.com.au; airline code NZ; hub Auckland International Airport)

Air Paradise International (☎ 03-9341 8000; www.airparadise.co.id; airline code AD; hub Ngurah Rai, Denpasar)

Australian Airlines (☎ 1300 799 798; http://australian airlines.com.au; airline code AO; hub Kingsford-Smith Airport, Sydney)

British Airways (☎ 1300 767 177, 02-9258 3200; www.britishairways.com.au; airline code BA; hub Heathrow Airport, London)

Cathay Pacific (☎ 13 17 47, 02-9667 3816; www.cathay pacific.com.au; airline code CX; hub Hong Kong International Airport)

Emirates (☎ 1300 303 777, 02-9290 9776; www .emirates.com; airline code EK; hub Dubai International Airport)

Freedom Air (☎ 1800 122 000; www.freedomair.com; airline code SJ; hub Auckland International Airport)

Garuda Indonesia (☎ 1300 365 330, 02-9334 9900; www.garuda-indonesia.com; airline code GA; hub Soekarno-Hatta International Airport, Jakarta)

Gulf Air (☎ 13 12 23, 02-9244 2199; www.gulfairco .com; airline code GF; hub Abu Dhabi International Airport)

Japan Airlines (☎ 02-9272 1100; www.jal.com; airline code JL; hub Narita Airport, Tokyo)

KLM (☎ 1300 303 747, 02-9231 6333; www.klm.com; airline code KL; hub Schiphol Airport, Amsterdam)

Lufthansa (☎ 1300 655 727; www.lufthansa.com; airline code LH; hub Frankfurt Airport)

Malaysia Airlines (☎ 13 26 27, 02-9364 3500; www .malaysiaairlines.com.au; airline code MH; hub Kuala Lumpur International Airport)

Qantas (☎ 13 13 13; www.qantas.com.au; airline code QF; hub Kingsford-Smith Airport, Sydney)

Royal Brunei Airlines (☎ 08-8941 0966; www.brunei air.com; airline code BI; hub Bandar Seri Begawan Airport)

Singapore Airlines (☎ 13 10 11, 02-9350 0100; www.singaporeair.com.au; airline code SQ; hub Changi International Airport)

South African Airways (☎ 1800 099 281, 08-9216 2200; www.flysaa.com; airline code SA; hub Johannesburg International Airport)

ECONOMY-CLASS SYNDROME

Deep vein thrombosis (DVT) is a relatively rare but potentially serious condition that may develop when flying. DVT is the formation of a blood clot, usually in the legs, caused by sitting in cramped conditions for an extended period. It can be fatal if the clot moves to the lungs.

The term 'Economy-Class Syndrome' is a bit of a misnomer since it can happen in any class, and indeed any situation. Awareness of the link between DVT and flying economy class heightened a few years ago when a passenger died at Heathrow airport after a long-haul flight. Many passengers have since come forward to say they experienced blood clotting during or after flying.

You can't really avoid the flight to Australia, but you *can* get up and walk around during the flight, factor in stopovers rather than taking a direct flight, and see your doctor prior to flying if you feel you may be at risk. The elderly and overweight are most at risk of DVT complications.

Thai Airways International (☎ 1300 651 960, 02-9251 1922; www.thaiairways.com.au; airline code TG; hub Bangkok International Airport)

United Airlines (☎ 13 17 77, 02-9292 4111; www.unitedairlines.com.au; airline code UA; hub Los Angeles International Airport)

Tickets

Be sure you research the options carefully to make sure you get the best deal. The Internet is an increasingly useful resource for checking airline prices.

Automated online ticket sales work well if you're doing a simple one-way or return trip on specified dates, but are no substitute for a travel agent with the lowdown on special deals, strategies for avoiding stopovers and other useful advice.

Paying by credit card offers some protection if you unwittingly end up dealing with a rogue fly-by-night agency in your search for the cheapest fare, as most card issuers provide refunds if you can prove you didn't get what you paid for. Alternatively, buy a ticket from a bonded agent, such as one covered by the **Air Travel Organiser's Licence** (ATOL; www.atol.org.uk) scheme in the UK. If you have doubts about the service provider, at the very least call the airline and confirm that your booking has been made.

For online bookings, start with the following websites:

Airbrokers (www.airbrokers.com) This US company specialises in cheap tickets. To fly LA–Hong Kong–Singapore–Sydney–Auckland–Fiji/Tahiti–LA will cost around US$1700.

Cheap Flights (www.cheapflight.com) Very informative site with specials, airline information and flight searches from the USA and other regions.

Cheapest Flights (www.cheapestflights.co.uk) Cheap worldwide flights from the UK; get in early for the bargains.

Expedia (www.expedia.msn.com) Microsoft's travel site; mainly US-related.

Flight Centre International (www.flightcentre.com) Respected operator handling direct flights, with sites for Australia, New Zealand, the UK, the USA and Canada.

Flights.com (www.tiss.com) Truly international site for flight-only tickets; cheap fares and an easy-to-search database.

STA (www.statravel.com) Prominent in international student travel but you don't necessarily have to be a student; site linked to worldwide STA sites.

Travel Online (www.travelonline.co.nz) Good place to check worldwide flights from New Zealand.

Travel.com (www.travel.com.au) Good Australian site; look up fares and flights into and out of the country.

Travelocity (www.travelocity.com) US site that allows you to search fares (in US$) to/from practically anywhere.

Roundtheworld.com (www.roundtheworldflights.com) This excellent site allows you to build your own trips from the UK with up to six stops. A four-stop trip including Asia, Australia and the USA costs from £800.

INTERCONTINENTAL (RTW) TICKETS

If you are flying to Australia from the other side of the world, round-the-world (RTW) tickets can be real bargains. They're generally put together by the two biggest airline alliances, **Star Alliance** (www.staralliance.com) and **Oneworld** (www.oneworldalliance.com), giving you a limited period (usually a year) in which to circumnavigate the globe. You can go anywhere the carrying airlines go, as long as you stay within the set mileage or number of stops and don't backtrack.

An alternative type of RTW ticket is one put together by a travel agent. These are usually more expensive than airline RTW fares but allow you to devise your own itinerary.

RTW tickets start around UK£800 from the UK or around US$1800 from the USA.

CIRCLE PACIFIC TICKETS

A Circle Pacific ticket is similar to a RTW ticket but covers a more limited region, using a combination of airlines to connect Australia, New Zealand, North America and Asia with stopover options in the Pacific Islands. As with RTW tickets, there are restrictions and limits as to how many stopovers you can take.

From Asia

Most Asian countries offer fairly competitive air fare deals, with Bangkok, Singapore and Hong Kong being the best places to shop around for discount tickets.

Flights between Hong Kong and Australia are notoriously heavily booked. Flights to/from Bangkok and Singapore are often part of the longer Europe-to-Australia route so they are also sometimes full. The motto of the story is to plan your preferred itinerary well in advance.

DEPARTURE TAX

There is a A$38 departure tax when leaving Australia. This is included in the price of airline tickets.

TRANSPORT

Typical one-way fares to Sydney are US$350 from Singapore, US$340 from Penang or Kuala Lumpur, and US$330 from Bangkok. From Tokyo, fares start at US$650.

From east-coast Australia, return fares to Singapore and Kuala Lumpur range from A$750 to A$1600; to Bangkok from A$900 to $1600; and to Hong Kong from A$950 to A$1900, depending on the airline and when you're travelling.

You can get cheap short-hop flights between Darwin and Indonesia, a route serviced by Garuda Indonesia and Qantas. Royal Brunei Airlines flies between Darwin and Bandar Seri Begawan, while Malaysia Airlines flies from Kuala Lumpur.

Early in 2003, the new Air Paradise International airline began operating regular flights between Denpasar in Bali and both Perth and Melbourne – launch fares from Australia were a low A$740 return. At the time of writing, the airline was hoping to extend its services to Sydney.

Hong Kong's travel market can be unpredictable, but excellent bargains are sometimes available. Some local agents:

Phoenix Services (☎ 2722 7378)

STA Travel Bangkok (☎ 02-236 0262; www.statravel .co.th); Singapore (☎ 65-6737 7188; www.statravel.com .sg) Tokyo (☎ 03-5391-3205; www.statravel.co.jp).

From Canada

The air routes from Canada are similar to those from mainland USA, with most Toronto and Vancouver flights stopping in one US city such as Los Angeles or Honolulu before heading on to Australia. Air Canada flies from Vancouver to Sydney via Honolulu and from Toronto to Melbourne via Honolulu.

Canadian discount air ticket sellers are known as consolidators (although you won't see a sign on the door saying 'Consolidator') and their air fares tend to be about 10% higher than those sold in the USA. **Travel Cuts** (☎ 800-667-2887; www.travelcuts.com) is Canada's national student travel agency and has offices in all major cities.

Fares out of Vancouver to Sydney or Melbourne cost from C$1650/2100 in the low/ high season via the US west coast. From Toronto, fares go from around C$1800/2200.

In the low season, fares from Australia start at around A$1700 return from Sydney to Vancouver. In the high season, fares start at around A$1850.

From Continental Europe

From the major destinations in Europe, most flights travel via one of the Asian capitals. Some flights are also routed through London before arriving in Australia via Singapore, Bangkok, Hong Kong or Kuala Lumpur.

Fares from Paris in the low/high season cost from €1000/1200. Some agents in Paris:

Nouvelles Frontières (☎ 08 25 00 08 25; www .nouvelles-frontieres.fr) Also has branches outside of Paris.

OTU Voyages (☎ 01 40 29 12 12; www.otu.fr) Student/ youth oriented, with offices in many cities.

Usit Connect Voyages (☎ 01 43 29 69 50; www .usitconnections.fr) Student/youth specialists, with offices in many cities.

Voyageurs du Monde (☎ 01 42 86 16 00; www.vdm .com/vdm) Has branches throughout France.

A good option in the Dutch travel industry is **Holland International** (☎ 070-307 6307; www.hollandinternational.nl). From Amsterdam, return fares start at around €1500.

In Germany, good travel agencies include the Berlin branch of **STA Travel** (☎ 030-311 0950; www.statravel.de). Fares start at around €900/1000 in the low/high season.

From New Zealand

Air New Zealand and Qantas operate a network of flights linking Auckland, Wellington and Christchurch in New Zealand with most major Australian gateway cities. Good deals are also available through Asian airlines such as Thai Airways International and US carriers like United Airlines. A newcomer to the trans-Tasman route is Emirates, which is also offering some reasonable fares. Virgin Blue has also been angling for some airspace between Australia and New Zealand, which, if granted, should result in some very cheap fares as competition between all the aforementioned airlines heats up even more.

Fares from New Zealand to Sydney on any one of the major airlines cost around NZ$350/700 one way/return. There's not a great deal of difference in price between seasons, as this is a popular route all year.

Other trans-Tasman options:

Flight Centre (☎ 0800 243 544; www.flightcentre.co .nz) Has a large central office in Auckland and many branches throughout the country.

Freedom Air (☎ 0800 600 500; www.freedomair.com) An Air New Zealand subsidiary that operates direct flights and offers excellent rates year-round.

STA Travel (☎ 09-309 0458; www.statravel.co.nz) Has offices in various cities.

From the UK & Ireland

There are two routes from the UK: the western route via the USA and the Pacific, and the eastern route via the Middle East and Asia; flights are usually cheaper and more frequent on the latter. Some of the best deals around are with Emirates, Gulf Air, Malaysia Airlines, Japan Airlines and Thai Airways International. Unless there are special deals on offer, British Airways, Singapore Airlines and Qantas generally have higher fares but may offer a more direct route.

Discount air travel is big business in London. Advertisements for many travel agencies appear in the travel pages of the weekend broadsheet newspapers, in *Time Out*, the *Evening Standard* and in the free magazine *TNT*.

A popular agent in the UK is the ubiquitous **STA Travel** (☎ 0870-160 0599; www.sta travel.co.uk).

Typical direct fares from London to Sydney are UK£400/650 one-way/return during the low season (March to June). In September and mid-December fares go up by as much as 30%, while the rest of the year they're somewhere in-between. High-season fares start at around UK£450/750 one way/return.

From Australia you can expect to pay around A$900/1650 one-way/return in the low season to London and other European capitals (with stops in Asia on the way) and A$1100/2050 in the high season.

From the USA

Airlines directly connecting Australia across the Pacific with Los Angeles or San Francisco include Qantas, Air New Zealand and United Airlines. There are also numerous airlines offering flights via Asia, with stopover possibilities including Tokyo, Kuala Lumpur, Bangkok, Hong Kong and Singapore; and via the Pacific with stopover possibilities like Nadi (Fiji), Rarotonga (Cook Islands), Tahiti (French Polynesia) and Auckland (NZ).

As in Canada, discount travel agents in the USA are known as consolidators. San Francisco is the ticket consolidator capital of America, although some good deals can be found in Los Angeles, New York and other big cities.

Council Travel (☎ 800-2268 6245; www.council travel.com), America's largest student travel organisation, has been acquired by **STA Travel** (☎ 800-777 0112; www.statravel.com), but its offices and website will continue to operate under their current name.

Typically you can get a return ticket to Australia from the west coast for US$1300/1700 in the low/high season, or from the east coast for US$1600/1900.

Return low/high-season fares from Australia to the US west coast cost around A$1750/1850; to New York A$1800/1950.

SEA

It's possible (though by no means easy or safe) to make your way to/from countries such as New Zealand, Papua New Guinea and Indonesia by hitching rides or crewing on yachts – usually you have to at least contribute something towards food. Try asking around at harbours, marinas, and yacht and sailing clubs. Good places on the Australian east coast include Coffs Harbour, Great Keppel Island, Airlie Beach and the Whitsundays, and Cairns – basically anywhere boats call. Darwin could yield Indonesia-bound possibilities. A lot of boats move north to escape the winter, so April is a good time to look for a berth in the Sydney area.

There are no passenger liners operating to/from Australia and finding a berth on a cargo ship is difficult – that's if you actually wanted to spend months at sea aboard an enormous metal can.

GETTING AROUND

AIR

Australia is so vast and there's so much to see that unless your time is unlimited, you might have to take to the skies at some stage.

All domestic flights are nonsmoking.

Airlines in Australia

The Australian airline industry experienced large-scale upheaval a few years ago when the country's second-largest carrier, Ansett, went suddenly and dramatically out of business. Today Qantas is the chief domestic airline, while the highly competitive newcomer Virgin Blue also flies all over Australia.

Australia also has numerous smaller operators flying regional routes. In many

places, such as remote outback destinations or islands, these are the only viable transport option. Many of these airlines operate as subsidiaries of Qantas. Australian regional airlines include:

Airnorth (☎ 08-8920 4000; www.airnorth.com.au) Flies across northern Australia, taking in destinations like Darwin, Alice Springs, Katherine, Cairns and Broome; also flies across the Timor Sea to Dili (East Timor).

Alliance Airlines (☎ 1300 130 092; www.allianceair lines.com.au) Touches down in Townsville, Brisbane, Norfolk Island and Sydney.

Australian Airlines (☎ 1300 799 798; www.australian airlines.com.au) This Qantas subsidiary flies exclusively between Cairns and both the Gold Coast and Sydney.

Macair (☎ 13 13 13, 07-4729 9444; www.macair.com.au) Commercially partnered with Qantas, this Townsville-based airline flies throughout western and northern Queensland.

Northwest Regional Airlines (☎ 1300 136 629, 08-9192 1369; www.northwestregional.com.au) Flies from Broome to Karratha, Port Hedland, Fitzroy Crossing, Halls Creek and Exmouth.

O'Connor (☎ 13 13 13, 08-8723 0666; www.oconnor -airlines.com.au) Another Qantas partner, flying between Melbourne, Adelaide, Mildura, Mount Gambier and Whyalla.

Qantas (☎ 13 13 13; www.qantas.com.au) Qantas is the chief domestic airline.

QantasLink (☎ 13 13 13; www.qantas.com.au) Flying under this Qantas subsidiary brand across Australia is a collective of regional airlines that includes Eastern Australia Airlines, Airconnex and Sunstate Airlines.

Regional Express (Rex; ☎ 13 17 13, 02-6393 5550; www.regionalexpress.com.au) Flies to Sydney, Melbourne, Adelaide, Canberra, Devonport, as well as 12 other destinations in New South Wales, Victoria, South Australia and Tasmania.

Skywest (☎ 1300 66 00 88; www.skywest.com.au) Flies from Perth to many regional centres, including Albany, Esperance, Exmouth, Carnarvon and Kalgoorlie.

Virgin Blue (☎ 13 67 89; www.virginblue.com.au) Highly competitive, Virgin Blue flies all over Australia – Virgin fares are cheaper if booked online ($10/20 less per one-way/return ticket).

Air Passes

With discounting being the norm these days, air passes are not great value. Qantas' **Boomerang Pass** (☎ 13 13 13) can only be purchased overseas and involves buying coupons for either short-haul flights (eg Hobart to Melbourne) at $260 one way, or

AUSTRALIAN AIR ROUTES

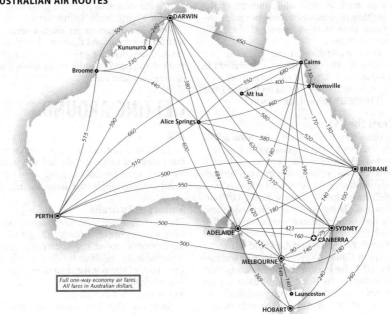

Full one-way economy air fares.
All fares in Australian dollars.

multizone sectors (including New Zealand and the Pacific) for $330. You must purchase a minimum of two coupons before you arrive in Australia, and once here you can buy up to eight more.

Regional Express (Rex) has a **Rex Backpacker** (☎ 13 17 13) scheme, where international visitors (Australian residents aren't eligible) pay $500 for one month's worth of unlimited travel on the airline – standby fares only.

BICYCLE

Australia has much to offer cyclists, from leisurely bike paths winding through most major cities (Canberra has one of the most extensive networks) to thousands of kilometres of good country roads where you can wear out your chainwheels. Mountainous is not an adjective that applies to this country; instead, there's lots of flat countryside and gently rolling hills.

Bicycle helmets are compulsory in all states and territories, as are white front lights and red rear lights for riding at night.

There are countless touring options. Try a tasty circuit of South Australian wineries, lengthy meanders along the Murray or Murrumbidgee Rivers, a month's exploration of Tasmania, or spin your wheels on the growing network of rail trails built beside disused railway lines. Mountain bikers love Australia's forestry tracks and high country: try the Australian Alps between Canberra and Melbourne, the hills around Cairns and the Flinders Ranges in SA.

If bringing your own bike, check with your airline for costs and the degree of dismantling and packing required. Within Australia, bus companies require you to dismantle your bike and some don't guarantee that it will travel on the same bus as you. On trains, supervise the loading, if possible tie your bike upright, and check for possible restrictions: most intercity trains will only carry two to three boxed bikes per service.

Eastern Australia was settled on the principle of not having more than a day's horse ride between pubs, so it's possible to plan even ultralong routes and still get a shower at the end of each day. Most riders carry camping equipment but, on the east coast at least, it's feasible to travel from town to town staying in hostels, hotels or caravan parks.

You can get by with standard road maps but, as you'll probably want to avoid both the highways and the low-grade unsealed roads, the government series is best. The 1:250,000 scale is the most suitable, though you'll need a lot of maps if you're going far. The next scale up, 1:1,000,000, is adequate and is widely available in speciality map shops.

Carry plenty of water to avoid becoming dehydrated. Cycling in the summer heat can be made more endurable by wearing a helmet with a peak (or a cap under your helmet), using plenty of sunscreen, not cycling in the middle of the day, and drinking lots of water (not soft drinks). It can get very cold in the mountains, so pack appropriate clothing. In the south, beware the blistering hot northerlies that can make a north-bound cyclist's life hell in summer. The southeast trade winds begin to blow in April, when you can have (theoretically at least) tail winds all the way to Darwin.

Outback travel needs to be properly planned, with the availability of drinking water the main concern – those isolated water sources (bores, tanks, creeks and the like) shown on your map may be dry or undrinkable, so you can't depend entirely on them. Also make sure you've got the necessary spare parts and bike-repair knowledge. Check with locals if you're heading into remote areas, and let someone know where you're headed before setting off.

Hire

The rates charged by most outfits for renting road or mountain bikes (not including the discounted fees offered by budget accommodation places to their guests) are anywhere between $8 to $12 per hour and $18 to $40 per day. Security deposits can range from $50 to $200, depending on the rental period.

Information

The national cycling body is the **Bicycle Federation of Australia** (☎ 02-6249 6761; www.bfa .asn.au). Each state and territory (except the Northern Territory; NT) has a touring organisation that can also help with cycling information and put you in touch with touring clubs.

Australian Capital Territory Pedal Power ACT (☎ 02-6248 7995; www.pedalpower.org.au)

NSW Bicycle New South Wales (☎ 02-9283 5200; www .bicyclensw.org.au)

Queensland Bicycle Queensland (☎ 07-3844 1144; www .biq.org.au)

SA Bicycle SA (☎ 08-8232 2644; www.bikesa.asn.au)

Tasmania Bicycle Tasmania (☎ 03-6229 3811; www.netspace.net.au/~dmurphy/bt.htm)

Victoria Bicycle Victoria (☎ 03-8636 8888; www.bv .com.au)

WA Bicycle Transportation Alliance (☎ 08-9420 7210; www .multiline.com.au/~bta/)

For even more information, see Lonely Planet's *Cycling Australia*.

Purchase

If you arrive in Australia without a set of wheels and want to buy a new road cycle or mountain bike that won't leave a trail of worn-out or busted metal parts once it leaves the city limits, your starting point (and we mean your absolute bottom-level starting point) is $400 to $500. To set yourself up with a new bike, plus all the requisite on-the-road equipment such as panniers, helmet etc, your starting point becomes $1500 to $2000. Second-hand bikes are worth checking out in the cities, as are the post-Christmas sales and mid-year stocktakes, when newish cycles can be heavily discounted.

Your best bet for re-selling your bike is via the **Trading Post** (☎ 1300 138 016; www .tradingpost.com.au), which is distributed in newspaper form in urban centres around Australia, and which also has a busy online trading site.

BOAT

There's a hell of a lot of water around Australia but unless you're fortunate enough to hook up with a yacht, it's not a feasible way of getting around. The only regular passenger services of note are run by **TT-Line** (☎ 13 20 10; www.spiritoftasmania.com.au), which dispatches three high-speed, vehicle-carrying ferries – *Spirit of Tasmania I, II & III* – across Bass Strait between Sydney, Melbourne and Devonport. See p579 for more details.

BUS

Australia's extensive bus network is a relatively cheap and reliable way to get around, though it can be a tedious form of transport at times and requires planning if you intend to do more than straightforward city-to-city trips. Most buses are equipped with air-con, toilets and videos, and all are smoke-free zones. The smallest towns eschew formal bus terminals for a single drop-off/pick-up point, usually outside a post office, newsagent or shop.

It may look like there are two national bus networks, **McCafferty's** (☎ 13 14 99; www.mc caffertys.com.au) and **Greyhound Pioneer** (☎ 13 20 30; www.greyhound.com.au), but McCafferty's took over Greyhound a few years ago and consequently the tickets, terminals and passes of both companies are interchangeable. Despite this, both brand names continue to be used, which is why we refer to 'McCafferty's/ Greyhound' throughout this guidebook. Fares purchased online are roughly 5% cheaper than over-the-counter tickets.

Smaller regional operators running key routes or covering a lot of ground are listed following:

Firefly Express (☎ 1300 730 740, 02-9211 6556; www .fireflyexpress.com.au) Runs between Sydney, Melbourne and Adelaide.

Integrity Coach Lines (☎ 08-9226 1339; www .integritycoachlines.com.au) Heads north from Perth up to Exmouth and Broome.

Premier Motor Service (☎ 13 34 10; www.premier ms.com.au) Runs along the east coast between Cairns and Melbourne.

Premier Stateliner (☎ 08-8415 5555; www.premier stateliner.com.au) Services towns around SA.

Redline Coaches (☎ 1300 360 000; www.tasredline .com.au) Services Tasmania's northern and eastern coasts.

TassieLink (☎ 1300 300 520; www.tassielink.com.au) Crisscrosses Tasmania, with extra summer links to bushwalking locales.

Transwa (☎ 1300 662 205; www.transwa.wa.gov.au) Hauls itself around the southern half of Western Australia (WA).

V/Line (☎ 13 61 96; www.vline.vic.gov.au) Runs to most major towns and cities in Victoria.

Bus Passes

The following McCafferty's and Greyhound passes can be used on either bus service. There's a 10% discount for members of YHA, VIP, Nomads and other approved organisations, as well as card-carrying seniors/pensioners.

AUSSIE EXPLORER PASS

This popular pass gives you from one to 12 months to cover a set route – there are 24 in all and the validity period depends on distance. You haven't got the go-anywhere flexibility of the Kilometre Pass (you can't backtrack), but if you can find a route that suits you it generally works out cheaper.

The Aussie Highlights pass allows you to loop around the eastern half of Australia from Sydney, taking in Melbourne, Adelaide, Coober Pedy, Alice Springs, Darwin, Cairns, Townsville, the Whitsundays, Brisbane and Surfers Paradise for $1330, including tours of Uluru-Kata Tjuta and Kakadu National Parks. Or there are one-way passes, such as the Aussie Reef & Rock, which goes from Sydney to Alice Springs (and Uluru) via Cairns and Darwin (and Kakadu) for $1080; the Top End Explorer, which takes in Cairns to Darwin (and Kakadu) for $450; and the Western Explorer from Perth to Darwin ($660).

AUSSIE KILOMETRE PASS

This is the simplest pass and gives you a specified amount of travel, starting at 2000km ($321) and going up in increments of 1000km to a maximum of 20,000km

($2190). The pass is valid for 12 months and you can travel where and in what direction you like, and stop as many times as you like. For example, a 2000km pass will get you from Cairns to Brisbane, 4000km ($530) from Cairns to Melbourne, and 12,000km ($1400) will cover a loop from Sydney to Melbourne, Adelaide, central Australia, Darwin, Cairns and back to Sydney. On the west coast you'll need 3000km to get from Perth to Broome and 5000km from Perth to Darwin.

Phone at least a day ahead to reserve a seat if you're using this pass and bear in mind that side-trips or tours off the main route (eg to Kakadu, Uluru or Shark Bay) may be calculated at double the actual kilometre distance.

Backpacker Buses

While the companies offering transport options for budget travellers in various parts

PRINCIPAL BUS ROUTES & RAILWAYS

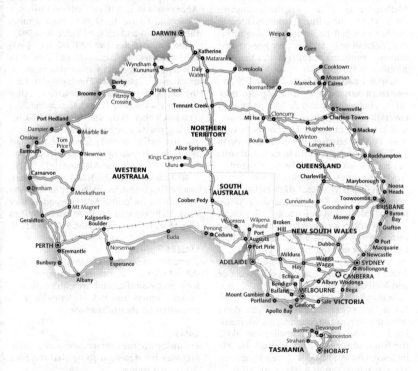

of Australia are pretty much organised-tour operators, they do also get you from A to B (sometimes with hop-on, hop-off services) and so can be a cost-effective alternative to the big bus companies. The buses are usually smaller, you'll meet lots of other travellers, and the drivers sometimes double as tour guides; conversely, some travellers find the tour-group mentality and inherent limitations don't suit them. Discounts for card-carrying students and members of hostel organisations are regularly available.

Adventure Tours Australia (☎ 1300 654 604; www .adventuretours.com.au) This company runs a hop-on, hop-off minibus service around Tasmania, taking in key tourist destinations and some out-of-the-way places like Cockle Creek. The Adventure Tours Pass ($395) allows two months' travel in an anticlockwise direction around the state, starting from either Devonport, Launceston or Hobart.

Autopia Tours (☎ 1800 000 507, 03-9326 5536; www.autopiatours.com.au) Autopia runs three-day trips along the Great Ocean Road from Melbourne to Adelaide via the Grampians for $150, not including accommodation or meals (both can be arranged). The three-day Melbourne to Sydney tour goes via the Snowy Mountains, Canberra and the Blue Mountains ($180).

Easyrider Backpacker Tours (☎ 08-9226 0307; www.easyridertours.com.au) A true hop-on, hop-off bus, but you can also do trips as tours. It covers the west coast from Albany to Broome, with trips out of Perth. The Southern Curl goes Perth–Margaret River–Albany–Perth ($225); Perth to Exmouth costs $310, while Exmouth to Broome (April to November only) costs $250 one way.

Groovy Grape (☎ 1800 661 177, 08-8371 4000; www .groovygrape.com.au) This SA-based operator, formerly dedicated to Barossa Valley tours, now also offers a seven-day Adelaide–Alice camping trip for an all-inclusive $750, a two-day Boomerang return (with a night in Coober Pedy) for $145, and a three-day Great Ocean Road trip between Adelaide and Melbourne for $285.

Heading Bush 4WD Adventures (☎ 1800 639 933, 08-8356 5501; www.headingbush.com) If you don't mind pitching in and roughing it a bit, Heading Bush does a 10-day, small-group 4WD trip from Adelaide to Alice Springs. The all-inclusive cost is $1200, or there's an express two-day return run to Adelaide for $110.

Nullarbor Traveller (☎ 1800 816 858, 08-8364 0407; www.the-traveller.com.au) This small company runs relaxed minibus trips across the Nullarbor – there's a nine-day Adelaide–Perth trip ($945) via the southern forests, while the seven-day return journey ($735) goes straight through Kalgoorlie. Prices include accommodation (camping and hostels), entry fees and most meals.

Oz Experience (☎ 1300 300 028, 02-8356 1766; www.ozexperience.com) This is one of those hop-on hop-off services you'll either love or hate. Many travellers complain they can't get a seat on the bus of their choice and are left on stand-by lists for days, or summarise it as a party bus for younger travellers, while others rave about it as a highly social experience. The country's biggest backpacker bus network, it covers central and eastern Australia (Northern Territory Adventure Tours takes over in that territory). Travel is one-directional and passes are valid for six months with unlimited stops. A Sydney–Darwin pass via Melbourne, Adelaide and Alice Springs is $1030; Sydney–Cairns is $390; and Cairns to Darwin right around the east coast and up the Centre is $1380.

The Wayward Bus (☎ 1800 882 823, 08-8410 8833; www.waywardbus.com.au) Most trips with this reputable company allow you to get on or off where you like. The eight-day Face the Outback run travels Adelaide to Alice Springs via Wilpena Pound, the Oodnadatta Track, Coober Pedy and Uluru ($820 including meals, camping and hostel charges, and national park entry fees). Classic Coast is a 3½-day trip along the Great Ocean Road between Adelaide and Melbourne ($310).

Wild-Life Tours (☎ 03-9534 8868; www.wildlifetours .com.au) This company offers various trips ex-Melbourne, including Adelaide and Sydney runs. Melbourne to Adelaide can be done in two, three or four days (cost $150 to $210).

Classes

There are no separate classes on buses, and the vehicles of the different companies all look pretty similar and are equipped with air-con, toilets and videos. Smoking isn't permitted on Australian buses.

Costs

Following are the average, non-discounted, one-way bus fares on some well-travelled Australian routes.

Adelaide–Darwin adult/child/concession $352/279/297
Adelaide–Melbourne adult/child/concession $60/50/55
Adelaide–Perth adult/child/concession $265/215/240
Brisbane–Cairns adult/child/concession $185/155/175
Canberra–Melbourne adult/child/concession $60/50/55
Canberra–Sydney adult/child/concession $35/30/30
Sydney–Melbourne adult/child/concession $65/55/60
Sydney–Brisbane adult/child/concession $90/75/85

Reservations
Over summer, school holidays and public holidays, you should book well ahead on the more popular routes, including intercity and east-coast services. At other times you should have few problems getting on to your preferred service. But if your long-term travel plans rely on catching a particular bus, book at least a day or two ahead just to be safe.

You should make a reservation at least a day in advance if you're using a McCafferty's/Greyhound pass.

CAR & MOTORCYCLE
Australia is a vast, mostly sparsely populated country where public transport is often neither comprehensive nor convenient, and sometimes nonexistent. Anyone whose experience of Australia is limited to travelling the east coast might hotly dispute this, but on the whole it's true. Many travellers find that the best way to see the place is to buy a car, and it's certainly the only way to get to those interesting out-of-the-way places without taking a tour.

Motorcycles are another popular way of getting around. The climate is good for bikes for much of the year, and the many small trails from the road into the bush lead to perfect spots to spend the night. Bringing your own motorcycle into Australia will entail an expensive shipping exercise, valid registration in the country of origin and a *Carnet De Passages en Douanes*. This is an internationally recognised customs document that allows the holder to import their vehicle without paying customs duty or taxes. To get one, apply to a motoring organisation/association in your home country. You'll also need a rider's licence and a helmet. A fuel range of 350km will cover fuel stops up the Centre and on Hwy 1 around the continent. The long, open roads are really made for large-capacity machines above 750cc, which Australians prefer once they outgrow their 250cc learner restrictions.

Automobile Associations
The national **Australian Automobile Association** (www.aaa.asn.au) is the umbrella organisation for the various state associations and maintains links with similar bodies throughout the world. Day-to-day operations are handled by the state bodies, which provide emergency breakdown services, literature, excellent touring maps and detailed guides to accommodation and camping grounds.

The state organisations have reciprocal arrangements with other states in Australia and with similar organisations overseas. So if you're a member of the NRMA in NSW, for example, you can use the RACV facilities in Victoria. Similarly, if you're a member of the AAA in the USA, or the RAC or AA in the UK, you can use any of the Australian state organisations' facilities. Bring proof of membership with you.

Association details for each state follow:
NSW & ACT National Roads and Motorists Association (NRMA; ☎ 13 11 22; www.nrma.com.au)
NT Automobile Association of the Northern Territory (AANT; ☎ 08-8981 3837; www.aant.com.au)
Queensland Royal Automobile Club of Queensland (RACQ; ☎ 13 19 05; www.racq.com.au)
SA Royal Automobile Association of South Australia (RAA; ☎ 08-8202 4600; www.raa.net)
Tasmania Royal Automobile Club of Tasmania (RACT; ☎ 13 27 22; www.ract.com.au)
Victoria Royal Automobile Club of Victoria (RACV; ☎ 13 19 55; www.racv.com.au)
WA Royal Automobile Club of Western Australia (RACWA; ☎ 13 17 03; www.rac.com.au)

Driving Licence
You can generally use your own country's driving licence in Australia, as long as it's in English (if it's not, you'll need a certified translation) and carries your photograph for identification. Confusingly, some states prefer that you have an **International Driving Permit** (IDP), which must be supported by your home licence. It's easy enough to get an IDP – just go to your home country's automobile association and they issue it on the spot. The permits are valid for 12 months.

Fuel & Spare Parts
Fuel (super, diesel and unleaded) is available from service stations sporting the well-known international brand names. LPG (gas) is not always stocked at more remote roadhouses; if you're on gas it's safer to have

dual-fuel capacity. Prices vary from place to place and from price war to price war – wars such as the one in Iraq are also a major influence on prices – but basically fuel is heavily taxed and continues to hike up, much to the shock and disgust of local motorists. Unleaded petrol (used in most new cars) is now hovering around $0.90 to $1 a litre even in the cities. Once out into the country, prices soar – in outback NT and Queensland it was as high as $1.40 a litre at the time of writing. Distances between fill-ups can be long in the outback but there are only a handful of tracks where you'll require a long-range fuel tank. On main roads there'll be a small town or roadhouse roughly every 150km to 200km.

The further you get from the cities, the better it is to be in a Holden or a Ford – if you're in an older vehicle that's likely to require a replacement part, life is much simpler if it's a make for which spare parts are more readily available. VW Kombi vans may be the quintessential backpackers' wheels, but they're notoriously bad for breaking down and difficult to find parts for, and so are a poor choice for remote Australia.

Hire

Competition between car-rental companies in Australia is pretty fierce, so rates tend to be variable and lots of special deals come and go. The main thing to remember when assessing your options is distance – if you want to travel far, you need unlimited kilometres.

As well as the big firms, there are a vast number of local firms, or firms with outlets in a limited number of locations. These are almost always cheaper than the big operators – sometimes half the price – but cheap car hire can often come with serious restrictions.

Big firms sometimes offer one-way rentals – pick up a car in Adelaide and leave it in Sydney, for example – but there are a variety of limitations, including a substantial drop-off fee. Ask plenty of questions about this before deciding on one company over another. One-way rentals into or out of the NT or WA may be subject to a hefty repositioning fee; however, there have previously been good deals for taking a car or campervan (with Britz) from Broome back to Perth.

Major companies offer a choice: either unlimited kilometres, or 100km or so a day free plus so many cents per kilometre over this.

Daily rates in cities or on the east coast are typically about $55 to $60 a day for a small car (Holden Barina, Ford Festiva, Hyundai Excel), about $65 to $80 a day for a medium car (Mitsubishi Magna, Toyota Camry, Nissan Pulsar), or $85 to $100 a day for a big car (Holden Commodore, Ford Falcon), all including insurance. You must be at least 21 years old to hire from most firms – if you're under 25 you may only be able to hire a small car or have to pay a surcharge. It's cheaper if you rent for a week or more and there are often low-season and weekend discounts. Credit cards are the usual payment method.

Major companies all have offices or agents in most cities and towns.

Avis (☎ 13 63 33; www.avis.com.au)
Budget (☎ 1300 362 848; www.budget.com.au)
Delta Europcar (☎ 1800 030 118; www.deltaeuropcar .com.au)
Hertz (☎ 13 30 39; www.hertz.com.au)
Thrifty (☎ 13 61 39; www.thrifty.com.au)

If you want short-term car hire, smaller local companies are generally the cheapest and are pretty reliable. You can usually get a small car with limited kilometres from $45 a day. **Apex** (☎ 07-3260 7609; www.apexrentacar.com.au) is a good-value company with offices in mainland capital cities and Cairns.

For a less orthodox form of car rental, namely an organised car-pooling scheme where travellers prepared to pay for lifts and drivers looking for cash-paying passengers are brought together, check out **Ezi-Ride** (☎ 07-5559 5938; www.ezi-ride.com).

4WD & CAMPERVAN HIRE

Renting a 4WD enables you to get right off the beaten track and out to some of the natural wonders that most travellers miss. Something small like a Suzuki Vitara or Toyota Rav4 costs $85 to $100 per day. For a Toyota Landcruiser you'll spend at least $150, which should include insurance and some free kilometres (typically 100km to 200km per day, sometimes unlimited).

Check the insurance conditions carefully, especially the excess, as they can be onerous – in the NT $5000 is typical, although this can often be reduced to around $1000 (or even to nil) on payment of an additional daily charge (around $50). Even for a 4WD, the insurance offered by most companies does not cover damage caused

when travelling 'off-road', which basically means anything that is not a maintained bitumen or dirt road.

Hertz, Budget and Avis have 4WD rentals, with one-way rentals possible between the eastern states and the NT. **Territory Thrifty Car Rental** (☎ 1800 891 125, 08-8924 0000) rents 4WDs from Darwin and Alice Springs.

Britz Rentals (☎ 1800 331 454, 03-8379 8890; www.britz.com) hires fully equipped 4WDs fitted out as campervans, which are commonplace on northern Australian roads. The high-season costs start from around $120 (two-berth) or $215 (four-berth) per day for a minimum hire of five days (with unlimited kilometres), but the price climbs from there; to reduce the insurance excess from $5000 to zero costs an extra $50 per day. Britz has offices in all the mainland capitals except Canberra, as well as in Alice Springs, Broome and Cairns, so one-way rentals are also possible.

Many other places rent campervans, especially in Tasmania and the Top End where they're very popular. Check out **Backpacker Campervans** (☎ 1800 670 232, 02-9667 0402; www.backpackercampervans.com).

Insurance

In Australia, third-party personal injury insurance is always included in the vehicle registration cost. This ensures that every registered vehicle carries at least minimum insurance. You'd be wise to extend that minimum to at least third-party property insurance as well – minor collisions with other vehicles can be amazingly expensive.

When it comes to hire cars, know exactly what your liability is in the event of an accident. Rather than risk paying out thousands of dollars if you do have an accident, you can take out your own comprehensive insurance on the car, or (the usual option) pay an additional daily amount to the rental company for an 'insurance excess reduction' policy. This brings the amount of excess you must pay in the event of an accident down from between $2000 and $5000 to a few hundred dollars.

Be aware that if you're travelling on dirt roads you will not be covered by insurance unless you have a 4WD – in other words, if you have an accident you'll be liable for all the costs involved. Also, most companies' insurance won't cover the cost of damage to glass (including the windscreen) or tyres. Always read the small print.

Outback Travel

You can drive all the way around Australia on Hwy 1 and through the Centre from Adelaide to Darwin without leaving sealed roads. However, if you really want to see outback Australia, there are plenty of routes that bring new meaning into the phrase 'off the beaten track'.

While you may not need 4WD or fancy expedition equipment to tackle most of these roads, you do need to be carefully prepared for the loneliness and lack of facilities. Vehicles should be in good condition and have reasonable ground clearance. Always carry a tow rope so that some passing good Samaritan can pull your broken-down car to the next garage.

When travelling to very remote areas, such as the central deserts, it's advisable to carry a high-frequency (HF) radio transceiver equipped to pick up the relevant Royal Flying Doctor Service bases. A satellite

---

OUTBACK ROAD SHOW

On many outback highways you'll see thundering road trains – huge trucks (a prime mover plus two or three trailers) up to 50m long. These things don't move over for anyone and it's like something out of a *Mad Max* movie to have one bearing down on you at 120km/h. When you see a road train approaching on a narrow bitumen road, slow down and pull over – if it has to put its wheels off the road to pass you, the resulting shower of stones will almost certainly smash your windscreen. When trying to overtake one make sure you have plenty of room to complete the manoeuvre – allow about a kilometre. Road trains throw up a lot of dust on dirt roads, so if you see one coming it's best to pull over and stop until it's gone past.

And while you're on outback roads, don't forget the standard bush wave to oncoming drivers – it's simply a matter of lifting the index finger off the steering wheel to acknowledge your fellow motorist.

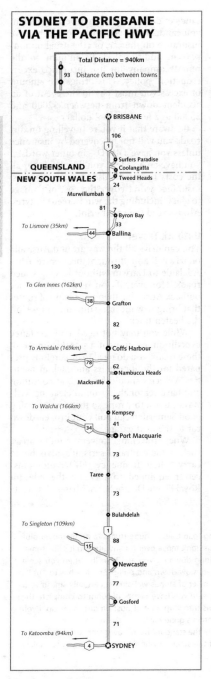

SYDNEY TO BRISBANE VIA THE PACIFIC HWY

Total Distance = 940km

93 Distance (km) between towns

- BRISBANE
- 106
- 1
- **QUEENSLAND**
- **NEW SOUTH WALES**
- Surfers Paradise
- Coolangatta
- Tweed Heads
- Murwillumbah
- 24
- 81
- 7
- Byron Bay
- 33
- To Lismore (35km) — 44 — Ballina
- 130
- To Glen Innes (162km) — 38 — Grafton
- 82
- To Armidale (169km) — Coffs Harbour
- 78
- 62
- Nambucca Heads
- Macksville
- 56
- To Walcha (166km) — Kempsey
- 34
- 41
- Port Macquarie
- 73
- Taree
- 73
- Bulahdelah
- To Singleton (109km) — 1
- 15
- 88
- Newcastle
- 77
- Gosford
- 71
- To Katoomba (94km) — 4 — SYDNEY

phone and Global Positioning System (GPS) finder can also be handy. Of course, all this equipment comes at a cost, but travellers have perished in the Australian desert after breaking down.

Always carry plenty of water. In warm weather allow 5L per person per day and an extra amount for the radiator, carried in several containers.

It's wise not to attempt the tougher routes during the hottest part of the year (October to April inclusive) – apart from the risk of heat exhaustion, simple mishaps can easily lead to tragedy at this time. Conversely, there's no point going anywhere on dirt roads in the outback if there has been recent flooding. Get local advice before heading off into the middle of nowhere. For more information regarding Australia's climate see p959.

If you do run into trouble in the back of beyond, don't wander off – stay with your car. It's easier to spot a car than a human being from the air, and you wouldn't be able to carry a heavy load of water very far anyway. South Australian police suggest that you carry two spare tyres (for added safety) and, if stranded, try to set fire to one of them (let the air out first) – the pall of smoke will be seen for miles.

Of course, before you set out, let family, friends or your car-hire company know where you're going and when you intend to be back. For the full story on safe outback travel, including exhaustive firsthand detail of the tracks summarised below, get hold of Lonely Planet's *Outback Australia*.

OUTBACK TRACKS

- **Birdsville Track** Running 517km from Marree in SA to Birdsville just across the border of Queensland, this old droving trail is one of the best-known outback routes in Australia. These days it is generally feasible to travel it in any well-prepared, conventional vehicle.

- **Canning Stock Route** This old 1700km-long cattle-droving trail runs southwest from Halls Creek to Wiluna in WA. The route crosses the Great Sandy Desert and Gibson Desert and, since the track is entirely unmaintained, this is a route to be taken very seriously. Like the Simpson Desert crossing, you should only travel in a well-equipped 4WD party. Nobody does this trip in summer.

- **Gibb River Road** This 'short cut' between Derby and Kununurra runs through the heart of the spectacular Kimberley in northern WA – it's 710km, compared with about 920km via Hwy 1. The going is much slower but the surroundings are so beautiful you'll probably find yourself lingering anyway. Although badly corrugated in places, it can usually be negotiated without too much difficulty by conventional vehicles in the dry season (May to November); it's impassable in the wet season.

- **Great Central Road** This route runs west from Uluru to Laverton in WA, from where you can drive down to Kalgoorlie and on to Perth. There are plans to seal this road so that you'll be able to drive on a sealed highway all the way from Alice Springs across to Perth. Of course, then it won't be an outback 'track' any more. In the meantime the road is well maintained and is normally OK for conventional vehicles, but it's pretty remote. It passes through Aboriginal land for which travel permits must be obtained in advance – see Permits (NT; p747) and (WA; p829) for details. It's almost 1500km from Yulara to Kalgoorlie. For 300km, near the Giles Meteorological Station, this road and the Gunbarrel Hwy run on the same route. Taking the old Gunbarrel (to the north of Warburton) to Wiluna in WA is a much rougher trip requiring a 4WD.

- **Oodnadatta Track** Running mainly parallel to the old Ghan railway line through Alice Springs, this track is comprehensively bypassed by the sealed Stuart Hwy to the west. It's 429km from Marree to Oodnadatta, then another 216km to the Stuart Hwy at Marla. So long as there's no rain, any well-prepared conventional vehicle should be able to manage this fascinating route.

- **Peninsula Development Road** This road up to the tip of Cape York has a number of river crossings, such as the Jardine, that can only be made in the dry season. Only those in 4WD vehicles should consider the journey to Cape York, via any route. The shortest route from Cairns is 1000km, but a worthwhile alternative route is Cooktown to Musgrave via Lakefield National Park, which then meets up with the main route.

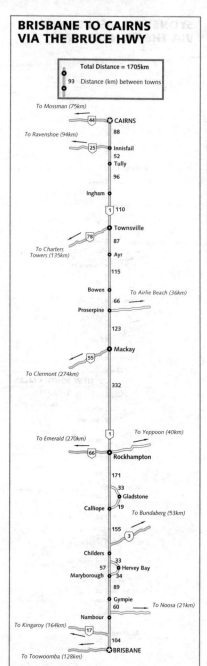

BRISBANE TO CAIRNS VIA THE BRUCE HWY

Total Distance = 1705km
93 Distance (km) between towns

To Mossman (75km)

44 — CAIRNS
88
To Ravenshoe (94km)
25 — Innisfail
52
Tully
96
Ingham
1 110
Townsville
78 87
To Charters Towers (135km)
Ayr
115
Bowen — To Airlie Beach (36km)
66
Proserpine
123
Mackay
55
To Clermont (274km)
332
1 — To Yeppoon (40km)
To Emerald (270km)
66 — Rockhampton
171
33
Gladstone
Calliope 19
To Bundaberg (53km)
155
3
Childers
33
57 — Hervey Bay
Maryborough 34
89
Gympie — To Noosa (21km)
60
Nambour
To Kingaroy (164km)
17
104
BRISBANE
To Toowoomba (128km)

TRANSPORT

TRANSPORT

SYDNEY TO MELBOURNE VIA THE PRINCES HWY

Total Distance = 1041km

93 Distance (km) between towns

🞊 SYDNEY

93

[1]

Wollongong

28

Kiama

47

Nowra

68

To Canberra (144km) Ulladulla

48

[52] Batemans Bay

69

Narooma

To Cooma (101km)

77

[18]

Bega

35

Merimbula

Pambula

19

Eden

57 **NEW SOUTH WALES**

VICTORIA

To Bombala (85km) Genoa

47 To Mallacoota (23km)

[B23]

Cann River

To Bemm River (23km)

75

To Marlo (15km) & Cape Conran (34km)

Orbost

59

Lakes Entrance

36 To Metung (10km)

[8500] Bairnsdale

To Omeo (120km)

69

[A1]

Sale

To Yarram (72km)

[A440]

49

[C482] To Yarram (60km)

Traralgon

31

[B460]

Moe

28

To Leongatha (56km)

Warragul

72

Dandenong

34

🞊 MELBOURNE

Plenty & Sandover Hwys These remote routes run east from the Stuart Hwy north of Alice Springs to Boulia or Mt Isa in Queensland. They're normally suitable for conventional vehicles, though are often rough.

Simpson Desert Crossing the Simpson Desert from the Stuart Hwy to Birdsville is becoming increasingly popular, but this route is still a real test of driver and vehicle. A 4WD is definitely required and you should be in a party of at least three vehicles equipped with HF radios.

Strzelecki Track This track covers much the same territory as the Birdsville Track, starting south of Marree at Lyndhurst and going to Innamincka, 460km northeast and close to the Queensland border. It was at Innamincka that the hapless explorers Burke and Wills died. This route has been much improved due to work on the Moomba gas fields.

Tanami Track Turning off the Stuart Hwy just north of Alice Springs, this route goes northwest across the Tanami Desert to Halls Creek in WA. The road has been extensively improved in recent years and conventional vehicles are normally OK, although there are sandy stretches on the Western Australian side and it's very corrugated if it hasn't been graded for a while. Be warned that the Rabbit Flat roadhouse in the middle of the desert is only open from Friday to Monday, so if you don't have long-range fuel tanks, plan your trip accordingly. Get advice on road conditions in Alice Springs.

Purchase

If you're planning a stay of several months that involves lots of driving, buying a second-hand car will be much cheaper than renting. You should be able to pick up a 1982 to 1984 XE Ford Falcon station wagon (a very popular model with backpackers) in good condition from $1500 to $2500. The XF Falcon (1985 to 1986) is also popular and costs around $3000 to $3500. Japanese cars of a similar size and age are more expensive, but old Mitsubishi Sigmas and Nissan Bluebirds are usually cheap and reliable. If there are only two of you, a panel van with a mattress in the back is a good option – it's cheaper than a campervan and more comfortable to sleep in than a station wagon.

You'll probably get any car cheaper by buying privately through the newspaper than through a car dealer. Buying through a dealer does have the advantage of some sort of guarantee, but this is not much use if you're buying a car in Sydney for a trip to Perth.

Sydney, Perth and Darwin are particularly good places to buy cars from backpackers who have finished their trip. These vehicles will have done plenty of kilometres but they often come complete with camping gear, Eskies, water containers, tools, road maps and old Lonely Planet guides. The large car markets in Sydney, Melbourne, Perth and Darwin are worth investigating too. See Buying/Selling a Car in the Sydney (p135) and Darwin (p765) sections for the situation at these popular starting/finishing points.

When it comes to buying or selling a car, every state has its own regulations, particularly in regard to registration (rego). In Victoria, for example, a car has to have a compulsory safety check (Certificate of Roadworthiness) before it can be registered in the new owner's name. In NSW and the NT, safety checks are compulsory every year when you come to renew the registration. Stamp duty has to be paid when you buy a car and, as this is based on the purchase price, it's not unknown for buyer and seller to agree privately to understate the price.

Note that it's much easier to sell a car in the same state that it's registered in, otherwise you (or the buyer) must re-register it in the new state, and that's a hassle. Vehicles with interstate plates are particularly hard to get rid of in WA.

If you don't have your own motorcycle but do have a little bit of time up your sleeve, getting mobile on two wheels in Australia is quite feasible. The beginning of winter (June) is a good time to start looking. Australian newspapers and the local bike-related press have classified advertisement sections; $3500 should get you something that will take you around the country, provided you know a bit about bikes. The main drawback is that you'll have to try to sell it again afterwards.

ROAD DISTANCES (KM)

MAINLAND AUSTRALIA

	Adelaide	Albany	Alice Springs	Birdsville	Brisbane	Broome	Cairns	Canberra	Cape York	Darwin	Kalgoorlie	Melbourne	Perth	Sydney	Townsville
Albany	2649														
Alice Springs	1512	3573													
Birdsville	1183	3244	1176												
Brisbane	1942	4178	1849	1573											
Broome	4043	2865	2571	3564	5065										
Cairns	3079	5601	2396	1919	1636	4111									
Canberra	1372	4021	2725	2038	1287	5296	2923								
Cape York	4444	6566	3361	2884	2601	5076	965	3888							
Darwin	3006	5067	1494	2273	3774	1844	2820	3948	3785						
Kalgoorlie	2168	885	3092	2763	3697	3052	5234	3540	6199	4896					
Melbourne	728	3377	2240	1911	1860	4811	3496	637	4461	3734	2896				
Perth	2624	411	3548	3219	4153	2454	6565	3996	7530	4298	598	3352			
Sydney	1597	4246	3109	2007	998	5208	2634	289	3599	3917	3765	862	3869		
Townsville	3237	5374	2055	1578	1295	3770	341	2582	1306	2479	4893	3155	5349	2293	
Uluru	1559	3620	441	1617	2290	3012	2837	2931	3802	1935	3139	2287	3595	2804	2496

TASMANIA

	Bicheno	Cradle Mountain	Devonport	Hobart	Launceston
Cradle Mountain	383				
Devonport	283	100			
Hobart	186	296	334		
Launceston	178	205	105	209	
Queenstown	443	69	168	257	273

These are the shortest distances by road; other routes may be considerably longer.
For distances by coach, check the companies' leaflets.

BUY-BACK DEALS

One way of getting around the hassles of buying and selling a vehicle privately is to enter into a buy-back arrangement with a car or motorcycle dealer. However, dealers may find ways of knocking down the price when you return the vehicle (even if it was agreed to in writing), often by pointing out expensive repairs that allegedly will be required to gain the dreaded roadworthiness certificate needed to transfer the registration.

A company that specialises in buy-back arrangements on cars and campervans is **Travellers Auto Barn** (☎ 02-9360 1500; www.travellers -autobarn.com.au), which has offices in Sydney, Melbourne, Brisbane and Cairns, and offers a range of vehicles. The buy-back arrangement is guaranteed in writing before you depart and the basic deal is 50% of the purchase price if you have the vehicle for eight weeks, 40% for up to six months, or 30% for up to 12 months.

Another option, for cars and motorcycles, is **Car Connection** (☎ 03-5473 4469; www.car connection.com.au). Rather than requiring you to outlay the full amount and then sell it back, you post a bond that is actually less than the value of the vehicle (a credit-card imprint is fine) and only pay a fixed 'user fee' for any period up to six months. A Ford Falcon station wagon or Yamaha XT600 trail bike will set you back $2150 for any period up to six months; a diesel Toyota Landcruiser, suitable for serious outback exploration, costs around $4950; a campervan costs $6050. Information and bookings are also handled by the company's Germany-based agent, **Travel Action GmbH** (☎ 0276-47824).

Buy-back arrangements are also possible with large motorcycle dealers in major cities. They're usually keen to do business, and basic negotiating skills allied with a wad of cash (say, $8000) should secure an excellent second-hand road bike with a written guarantee that they'll buy it back in good condition minus around $2000. **Better Bikes** (☎ 02-9718 6668; www.betterbikes.com.au; 605 Canterbury Rd, Belmore) is a Sydney dealer that offers buy-back deals.

Road Conditions

Australia has few multilane highways, although there are stretches of divided road (four or six lanes) in some particularly busy areas, including the Princes Hwy from Murray Bridge to Adelaide, most of the Pacific Hwy from Sydney to Brisbane, and the Hume and Calder Hwys in Victoria. Elsewhere the major roads are sealed two-laners.

You don't have to get far off the beaten track to find dirt roads. In fact, anybody who sets out to see the country in reasonable detail should expect some dirt-road travelling. And if you seriously want to explore the more remote Australia, you'd better plan on having a 4WD and a winch. A few basic spare parts, such as fan belts and radiator hoses, are worth carrying if you're travelling in places where traffic is light and garages are few and far between.

Motorcyclists should beware of dehydration in the dry, hot air – carry at least 5L of water on remote roads in central Australia and drink plenty of it, even if you don't feel thirsty. If riding in Tasmania (a top motorcycling destination) or southern and eastern Victoria, you should be prepared for rotten weather in winter and rain at any time of year. It's worth carrying some spares and tools even if you don't know how to use them, because someone else often does. Carry a workshop manual for your bike and spare elastic (octopus) straps for securing your gear.

Road Hazards

The 'road-kill' that you unfortunately see a lot of in the outback and alongside roads in many other parts of the country (Tasmania being a prime example) is mostly the result of cars and trucks hitting animals during the night. Many Australians avoid travelling altogether once the sun drops because of the risks posed by animals on the roads.

Kangaroos are common hazards on country roads, as are cows and sheep in the unfenced outback – hitting an animal of this size can make a real mess of your car. Kangaroos are most active around dawn and dusk. They often travel in groups, so if you see one hopping across the road in front of you, slow right down, as its friends may be just behind it.

If you're travelling at night and a large animal appears in front of you, hit the brakes, dip your lights (so you don't continue to dazzle and confuse it) and only swerve if it's safe to do so – numerous travellers have been killed in accidents caused by swerving to miss animals.

A not-so-obvious hazard is driver fatigue. Driving long distances (particularly in hot weather) can be so tiring that you might fall asleep at the wheel – it's not uncommon and the consequences can be unthinkable. So on a long haul, stop and rest every two hours or so – do some exercise, change drivers or have a coffee.

Road Rules

Driving in Australia holds few real surprises, other than the odd animal caught in your headlights. Australians drive on the left-hand side of the road and all cars are right-hand drive. An important road rule is 'give way to the right' – if an intersection is unmarked (unusual), you must give way to vehicles entering the intersection from your right.

The general speed limit in built-up areas is 60km/h, although this has been reduced to 50km/h on residential streets in most states – keep an eye out for signs. Near schools, the limit is 40km/h in the morning and afternoon. On the open highway it's usually 100km/h or 110km/h – in the NT there's no speed limit outside built-up areas, except along the Lasseter Hwy to Uluru where the limit is 110km/h. The police have speed radar guns and cameras and are fond of using them in strategically concealed locations.

Oncoming drivers who flash their lights at you may be giving you a friendly warning of a speed camera ahead – or they may be telling you that your headlights are not on. Whatever, it's polite to wave back if someone does this. Try not to get caught doing it yourself, since it's illegal.

All new cars in Australia have seat belts back and front and it's the law to wear yours – you're likely to get a fine if you don't. Small children must be belted into an approved safety seat.

Drink-driving is a real problem, especially in country areas. Serious attempts to reduce the resulting road toll are ongoing and random breath-tests are not uncommon in built-up areas. If you're caught with a blood-alcohol level of more than 0.05% be prepared for a hefty fine and the loss of your licence. In Victoria you must be *under* 0.05%.

PARKING

One of the big problems with driving around big cities like Sydney and Melbourne (or popular tourist towns like Byron Bay) is finding somewhere to park. Even if you do find a spot there's likely to be a time restriction, meter (or ticket machine) or both. It's one of the great rorts in Australia that by overstaying your welcome (even by five minutes) in a space that may cost only a few dollars to park in, local councils are prepared to fine you anywhere from $50 to $120. Also note that if you park in a 'clearway' your car will be towed away or clamped – look for signs. In the cities there are large multistorey car parks where you can park all day for between $10 and $25.

Many towns in NSW have a peculiar form of reverse-angle parking, a recipe for disaster if ever there was one. If in doubt, park your car in the same direction and at the same angle as other cars.

HITCHING

Hitching is never entirely safe in any country in the world, and we don't recommend it. Travellers who decide to hitch should understand that they are taking a small but potentially serious risk. People who do choose to hitch will be safer if they travel in pairs and let someone know where they are planning to go.

In Australia, the hitching signal can be a thumbs up, but a downward-pointed finger is more widely understood.

TRAIN

Rail travel in Australia is something you do because you really want to – not because it's cheaper or more convenient, and certainly not because it's fast. That said, trains are more comfortable than buses, and on some of Australia's long-distance train journeys the romance of the rails is alive and kicking. The *Indian Pacific* across the Nullarbor Plain and the *Ghan* from Adelaide to Darwin are two of Australia's great rail journeys.

Rail services within each state are run by that state's rail body, either government or private – see the introductory transport section of the relevant state or territory chapter for details.

The three major interstate services in Australia are operated by **Great Southern Railways** (☎ 13 21 47, 08-8213 4592; www.gsr.com .au), namely the *Indian Pacific* between Sydney and Perth; the *Overland* between

TRANSPORT

TRANSPORT

INTERSTATE QUARANTINE

When travelling in Australia, whether by land or air, you'll come across signs (mainly in airports, interstate train stations and at state borders) warning of the possible dangers of carrying fruit, plants and vegetables (which may be infected with a disease or pest) from one area to another. Certain pests and diseases – such as fruit fly, cucurbit thrips, grape phylloxera and potato cyst nematodes, to name a few – are prevalent in some areas but not in others, and so for obvious reasons authorities would like to limit them spreading.

There are quarantine inspection posts on some state borders and occasionally elsewhere. While quarantine control often relies on honesty, many posts are staffed and the officers are entitled to search your car for undeclared items. Generally they'll confiscate all fresh fruit and vegetables, so it's best to leave shopping for these items until the first town past the inspection point.

Melbourne and Adelaide; and the *Ghan*, which originally ran from Adelaide to Alice Springs and at the time of writing was being extended all the way through to Darwin.

The **Great South Pacific Express** (☎ 1800 000 395, 07-3247 6595; www.gspe.com), Australia's answer to the *Orient-Express*, is the last word in luxury train travel. This five-star hotel on rails travels weekly from Sydney to Cairns and Kuranda. The fares, in plain old Pullman car, start at $4700 per person for Sydney–Cairns (six nights), or $3320 for Brisbane–Cairns (two nights). One-night trips from Sydney to Canberra and back have also been offered. Don't forget your diamonds and dinner suit.

Costs

Some standard one-way train fares:
Adelaide–Darwin adult/child/concession in a travel seat $440/200/220, from $1390/840/840 in a cabin
Adelaide–Melbourne adult/child/concession in a travel seat $60/35/45, from $150/90/90 in a cabin
Adelaide–Perth adult/child/concession in a travel seat $310/140/160, from $960/580/580 in a cabin
Brisbane–Cairns $187 per adult (economy seat)
Canberra–Melbourne $58 per adult (economy seat); involves a bus ride from Canberra to Wodonga, then a train to Melbourne
Canberra–Sydney $50 per adult (economy seat)
Sydney–Melbourne $110 per adult (economy seat)
Sydney–Brisbane $110 per adult (economy seat)
Sydney–Perth adult/child/concession in a travel seat $520/240/260, from $1250/810/810 in a cabin

Reservations

As the railway booking system is computerised, any station (other than those on metropolitan lines) can make a booking for any journey throughout the country. For reservations telephone ☎ 13 22 32 during office hours; this will connect you to the nearest main-line station.

Discounted tickets work on a first-come/first-served quota basis, so it can help to book in advance.

Train Passes

The **Great Southern Railways Pass** (☎ 13 22 32), which is only available to passport-equipped non-Australian residents, allows unlimited travel on the rail network for a period of six months. The pass costs a meagre $590/450 per adult/concession (meagre considering the amount of ground you could cover over the life of the pass), but note that you'll be travelling in a 'Daynighter' reclining seat and not a cabin. You need to pre-book all seats at least 24 hours in advance.

CountryLink (☎ 13 22 32; www.countrylink.nsw .gov.au) is a rail and coach operation that visits destinations in NSW, the ACT, Queensland and Victoria, and offers two types of pass to foreign nationals with valid passports. The **East Coast Discovery Pass** (☎ 13 22 32) allows one-way economy travel between Melbourne and Cairns (in either direction) with unlimited stopovers, and is valid for six months – the full trip costs $375, while Brisbane to Cairns is $205 and Sydney to Cairns is $295. The **Backtracker Rail Pass** (☎ 13 22 32) allows travel on the entire CountryLink network and comes in four versions: a 14-day/1-/3-/6-month pass costing $165/200/220/330 respectively.